RUSSIAN ALPHABET AND CONCISE PRONUNCIATION GUIDE

The Russian (or Cyrillic) alphabet consists of 33 letters: 21 consonant letters, 10 vowel letters, and 2 signs of separation that give information on the pronunciation of a preceding consonant.

Note: The pronunciation of several of the vowel letters changes when that vowel is unstressed. The values given in this guide are for stressed vowels only. (See next page for the pronunciation of unstressed vowels.)

Letter	Russian Name	Closest Equivalent Sound in English
1 А а	а	calm, father
2 Б б	бэ	bit, rob
3 В в	вэ	vest, love
4 Г г	гэ	get, bag
5 Д д	дэ	day, bad
6 Е е	е	yes, yet
7 Ё ё	ё	yo-yo
8 Ж ж	жэ	measure, azure
9 З з	зэ	zero, size
10 И и	и	machine
11 Й й	и крáткое	boy, noise
12 К к	ка	kind, back
13 Л л	эль	lead, wool
14 М м	эм	man, am
15 Н н	эн	no, can
16 О о	о	hot, box
17 П п	пэ	pin, top
18 Р р	эр	Slightly to moderately trilled **r** (no English equivalent; similar to Spanish arriba!)
19 С с	эс	say, less
20 Т т	тэ	top, pot
21 У у	у	fool, ooze
22 Ф ф	эф	fine, off
23 Х х	ха	as in German Ba**ch**, or Scottish lo**ch**
24 Ц ц	цэ	hats, its
25 Ч ч	чэ	church, whi**ch**
26 Ш ш	ша	sharp, mash
27 Щ щ	ща	Slightly longer than letter **ш**; similar to ha**sh**ish.
28 Ъ ъ	твёрдый знак	(not pronounced)
29 Ы ы	ы	(approximately) bit, hit, still
30 Ь ь	мя́гкий знак	(not pronounced)
31 Э э	э оборóтное	let, set
32 Ю ю	ю	you, yule
33 Я я	я	yarn, yard

W9-BPK-913

Stress and Pronunciation of Vowels

Russian words, even very long ones, have only *one* stress per word. Stress (or accent) in Russian is free (or mobile). It is not fixed on the same syllable in the various inflected forms of an individual word. There are recurring patterns of stress within noun and verb paradigms, but there are many variations, exceptions, and subpatterns. Unlike Italian, Spanish, or Polish which have reasonably regular stress patterns, Russian stress must be memorized for each word.

Pronunciation of Unstressed Vowels

Of the ten vowel letters shown in the preceding pronunciation guide (а е ё и о у ы э ю я), three (е о я) are pronounced rather differently when they are in an unstressed syllable. In a syllable preceding an accented syllable, unstressed **о** is pronounced like the **u** in **but** (/ʌ/in the English pronunciation guide). In other unstressed syllables **о** is pronounced like the **e** in **mother** (/ə/ in the English pronunciation guide). For example: хорошо́—/khərʌ'ʃɔ/.

In unstressed syllables (with the exception of certain grammatical endings), **е** and **я** are pronounced close to a short **i** (/ɪ/ in the pronunciation guide). For example: тепе́рь—/tɪp'ɛr/; прямо́й—/prɪ'mɔi/.

In this dictionary each word is given in its basic form with the correct stress mark for that form: nouns, pronouns, and adjectives are given in the nominative singular, and verbs are given in the infinitive. In the few cases where a word is listed in two differently stressed forms, the first form is the preferred or more commonly encountered form.

Except in a few compound words, the letter **ё** is always stressed. Ё also has an orthographical peculiarity. Russian printing conventions omit the dieresis (double dots over the **e**), and therefore **ё** (printed simply **e**) and regular **e** appear identical. Ё appears in print only in textbooks of Russian, or in those cases where it could be confused with **e**. While **ё** is numbered among the 33 letters of Russian, dictionaries do not treat **ё** as a separate letter of the alphabet and do not separate it out in the alphabetization. In this dictionary, although interalphabetized with **e**, **ё** is always identified as **ё**.

RUSSIAN INFLECTION

Russian is an inflected language. It has three genders (masculine, feminine, and neuter), two numbers (singular and plural) and six cases (nominative, accusative, genitive, dative, instrumental, and prepositional). The case endings establish the syntactic role of various words in a sentence.

English words have lost their inflectional endings. Therefore, in English, word order determines the subject and object of the action. Since Russian is richly inflected, word order is less important and therefore more flexible than in English.

This brief space does not permit a full description of the full set of rules of pronunciation and syntax that are part of the workings of Russian. We recommend that the user of this dictionary consult one of the new reference grammars of Russian for a full treatment of each topic.

INFLECTION OF NOUNS

Nouns marked FILL in this dictionary belong to the large group of nouns that have a fill vowel in part of their declension. In these nouns, the vowel in the final syllable disappears in some or all of the oblique cases (accusative, genitive, dative, instrumental, and prepositional). The FILL vowel **o** appears, for example, in **замо́к** "door lock"; genitive замка́, dative замку́. An example of a noun with the FILL vowel **e** is **оте́ц** "father", thus: отца́, отцу́. **Знато́к** "connoisseur" or **игро́к** "player" do *not* have a FILL vowel, and so we can expect знатока́, знатоку́, etc. (or игрока́, игроку́, etc.) in the oblique cases.

INFLECTION OF VERBS

Russian has only two verb conjugations and a small set (ten) of anomalous verbs. There are, however, 23 variations of the first conjugation, and three variations of the second conjugation. Stress constitutes an additional set of patterns and subpatterns which co-occur with the various subsets of the two conjugations.

One subset (of the first conjugation) is specially marked in this dictionary: the OVA verbs. OVA verbs have a present tense suffix (or "theme") that departs significantly from the infinitive. This verb ending is extremely productive in Russian and is used frequently for verbs borrowed into Russian from foreign languages. An example of an OVA verb is сове́товать "to advise": сове́тую, сове́туешь, сове́тует in the present, but сове́товал, сове́товала in the past.

ЗАМЕЧАНИЯ ПО ФОНЕТИКЕ АНГЛИЙСКОГО ЯЗЫКА

Правописание английских букв часто не соответствует их произношению, один и тот же звук может быть выражен различным сочетанием букв, и в то же время одна и та же буква может выражать различные звуки. Правописание не может быть точным указателем произношнения. Полезно знать несколько общих замечаний по фонетике английского языка.

Гласные

В английском языке на одну букву **a** существует три разных произношения:

Длинное **a** /ɑ/ произносится подобно русскому **а** (**сам**), но длиннее—car, alms.

Смешанное **a** /æ/ произносится как **а** и **э** одновременно—rat, can.

Короткое, глухое **a** /ʌ/: подобно русскому неударное **а** и **о** (**да, хорошо**)—but, some.

Длинный звук **e** /ei/—двугласный (дифтонг), который звучит как **е** и **й** вместе—may (=мей).

Длинное полуоткрытое **o** /ou/—дифтонг, который начинается как **о** и заканчивается как **у**—no (=ноу).

Длинное открытое **o** /ɔ/ произносится как **а** и **о** одновременно—all, or. Если этот звук короткий, то он звучит ближе к **а** /ɒ/—not, hot, god.

Длинный открытый звук /зг/ в таких словах как—fir, girl, learn произносится как немецкий ö, или как русское ё но он более глухой и подавленный.

Буква **e** в конце слова, как правило, не произносится.

Согласные

b, d, g всегда остаются звучными, даже в конце слова—bib, dead, gag.

j /dʒ/ произносится как **д** и **ж** вместе (**джем**)—Jew. Часто этот звук пишется через **g**—gin.

r перед гласными произносится кончиком языка, но не раскатисто (**рж**авчина)—rid, proud.

s между двумя гласными всегда звучит как **з**—rose, в других случаях звучит как **с**.

th—при этом звуке кончик языка находится между зубами. Это особенный английский звук, не соответствующий ни одному русскому звуку. Он может быть беззвучным /θ/, как—thick, или звучным /ð/, как—them.

w—при этом звуке надо вытянуть губы для буквы **у**, но резко произнести **в**.

h—близкий русскому **х**, но очень легкий, почти неслышный звук-выдох.

Concise Pronunciation Guide for English Vowels and Consonants
Краткое описание произношений английских гласных и согласных

Phonetic Symbol Фонетический символ	Example Английский пример	Closest Equivalent in Russian Приблизительное соответствие в русском языке

English Vowels
Английские гласные

/æ/	bat, hat	(no equivalent) (нет соответствия)
/ɑ/	father, calm	палка, папа, мать
/ɒ/	pot, knot	(no equivalent) (нет соответствия)
/ɛ/	bet	эра, эхо, поэт
/i/	beat	пить, или, рис
/ɪ/	bit	(нет прямого соответствия; краткое, очень открытое и)
/ɔ/	talk, bought	(нет соответствия; краткое, очень открытое о)
/u/	food, rule, do	ну, кухня
/ʊ/	put, book	ну-ну, кнут (краткое у)
/ɜ/	burn, fir	(no equivalent) (нет соответствия)
/ə/	mother	хорошо (безударный слабый звук)
/ʌ/	but, nut	хорошо (подобно на русское неударное о и а, но английский звук почти всегда под ударением)

English Diphthongs
Английские двугласные (дифтонги)

/ei/	bait, take	музей, змей
/ou/	boat, hope, no	шоу-бизнес
/ai/	pie, by, bite	рай, чай
/au/	out, now	фрау
/ɔi/	oil, boy, toy	мой, слой, домой

In all diphthongs stress falls on the first vowel sound.
Ударение в двугласных падает на первый элемент.

English Consonants
Английские согласные

/p/	page, stop	папа, стоп
/b/	back, rub	банк, брат
/t/	ten, bit	так, театр, тот
/d/	do, bed	дом, дача
/k/	keep, make	как, крик
/g/	give, beg	год, глаз
/f/	fit, puff	фильм, граф
/v/	voice, live	ваш, вечер

/θ/	thin, path	(no equivalent) (нет соответствия)
/ð/	that, other	(no equivalent) (нет соответствия)
/s/	see, miss	сила, нос
/z/	zeal, those	завод, зуб
/ʃ/	shoe, push	шум, ваш
/ʒ/	vision, measure	жена, жить
/h/	hat, help	(нет соответствия, звук-выдох)
/tʃ/	chest, church	час, врач
/dʒ/	just, judge, gin	джаз, джинсы
/m/	my, him	мой, нам
/n/	now, on	нос, сон
/ŋ/	going, long	(нет соответствия, задненебное **н**)
/l/	low, all	лук, класс, мол
/r/	rip, butter	(нет соответствия; нераскатистое слабое **р**)
/w/	with, away	(нет прямого соответствия)
/y/	yes, yet	**и**езуит, **Й**емен

Abbreviations Used in This Dictionary

abbr.	abbreviation
acc.	accusative case
adj.	adjective
adv.	adverb
aero.	aeronautics
agric.	agriculture
anat.	anatomy
approx.	approximately
arch.	archaic
archit.	architecture
astr.	astronomy, astrology
athl.	athletics
attrib.	attributive
biol.	biology
bot.	botany
cap.	capital letter
chem.	chemistry
coll.	collective
colloq.	colloquial
comm.	commerce
comp.	comparative degree of adjective
comput.	computers
conj.	conjunction
cul.	culinary
dat.	dative case
decl. f.	declined with feminine endings
derog.	derogatory
det.	determinate verb of motion
dial.	dialectal
dim.	diminutive
dir.	direction
eccl.	ecclesiastic
econ.	economics
elec.	electricity
f.	feminine
fig.	figurative
fut.	future tense
gen.	genitive case
geog.	geography
geol.	geology
geom.	geometry
gram.	grammar
hist.	historical
impers.	impersonal
impf.	imperfective verb
indecl.	indeclinable
indet.	indeterminate verb of motion
infin.	infinitive
instr.	instrumental case
interj.	interjection
leg.	law
ling.	linguistics
lit.	literature
loc.	location

m.	masculine
mar.	marine
math.	mathematics
mech.	mechanical
med.	medicine
metal.	metallurgy
mil.	military
mus.	music
myth.	mythology
n.	noun
naut.	nautical
neg.	negative
neut.	neuter
nom.	nominative case
num.	numeral
obs.	obsolete
ord.	ordinal
ornith.	ornithology
pej.	pejorative
pers. pron.	personal pronoun
pf.	perfective verb
phon.	phonetics; phonology
photog.	photography
phys.	physics
physiol.	physiology
pl.	plural
poet.	poetic
polit.	politics
poss.	possessive
pre-rev.	pre-revolutionary (pre-1917)
pred.	predicate
prep.	prepositional case; preposition
pres.	present tense
pron.	pronoun
psychol.	psychology
refl.	reflexive verb
relig.	religion
sing.	singular
s.t.	something
superl.	superlative
surg.	surgery
swim.	swimming
tech.	technical
theat.	theater
trig.	trigonometry
typog.	typography
usu.	usually
v.	verb
v.i.	intransitive verb
v.t.	transitive verb
vulg.	vulgar
zool.	zoology
FILL	fill vowel in nominative case
OVA	"ova" pattern of conjugation

Russian-English
Dictionary

А

а *conj.* but; and. — **а то** otherwise, else, or. — **а
именно** namely, that is.
абажу́р *m.* lampshade.
абба́т *m.* abbot.
аббревиату́ра *f.* abbreviation; acronym.
аббревиа́ция *f.* acronym.
абза́ц *m.* paragraph.
абисси́нец *m. f.* **абисси́нка** Abyssinian.
абисси́нский *adj.* Abyssinian.
абитурие́нт *m.* applicant to a university.
абонеме́нт *m.* subscription.
абоне́нт *m.* subscriber.
абориге́н *m.* aborigine.
або́рт *m.* abortion.
абракада́бра *f.* abracadabra.
Абра́мцево *neut.* Abramtsevo.
абрико́с *m.* apricot.
абсе́нт *m.* absinthe.
абсолю́т *m.* (*philos.*) the absolute.
абсолюти́зм *m.* absolutism.
абсолюти́ст *m.* absolutist.
абсолюти́стский *adj.* absolutist.
абсолю́тно *adv.* absolutely.
абсолю́тный *adj.* absolute.
абсорби́ровать OVA *impf. and pf.* to absorb.
абсо́рбция *f.* absorption.
абстра́ктный *adj.* abstract.
абстракциони́зм *m.* abstract art.
абстра́кция *f.* abstraction.
абсу́рд *m.* absurdity.
абсу́рдный *adj.* absurd.
абсце́сс *m.* abscess.
аванга́рд *m.* advance guard; avant-garde.
ава́нс *m.* advance.
ава́нсом *adv.* in advance.
авансце́на *f.* proscenium.
авантю́ра *f.* adventure.
авантюри́ст *m. f.* **--ка** adventurer.
авантю́рный *adj.* risky.
авари́йность *f.* accident rate.
авари́йный *adj.* salvage.
ава́рия *f.* wreck, crash.
ава́ры *pl.* Avars (*Turkic tribe of 6th to 9th centuries*).
а́вгуст *m.* August. **—овский** *adj.* (*attrib.*) August.
авеню́ *neut. indecl.* avenue.
авиазаво́д *m.* aircraft plant.
авиакомпа́ния *f.* **1.** airline. **2.** aviation company.
авиаконстру́ктор *m.* aircraft designer.
авиакосми́ческий *adj.* (*attrib.*) aerospace.
авиамоде́ль *f.* model airplane.
авиано́сец *m.* aircraft carrier.
авиапо́чта *f.* (*abbr. of* **авиацио́нная по́чта** *f.*) air
mail.
авиатра́сса *f.* air route.
авиацио́нный *adj.* (*attrib.*) aviation.
авиа́ция *f.* **1.** aviation. **2.** (*colloq.*) aircraft.
Авиньо́н *m.* Avignon.
авока́до *neut. indecl.* avocado.
аво́сь *adv.* perhaps. — **на аво́сь** on the chance
(that).

аво́ська *f.* (*colloq.*) string bag.
авра́л *m.* **1.** (*mar.*) work involving all hands. **2.**
(*colloq.*) rush job.
австрали́ец FILL *m. f.* **австрали́йка** Australian.
Австра́лия *f.* Australia.
австри́ец FILL *m. f.* **австри́йка** Austrian.
А́встрия *f.* Austria.
автоба́за *f.* motor transport depot.
автобиогра́фия *f.* autobiography.
авто́бус *m.* bus.
авто́граф *m.* autograph.
автодро́м *m.* speedway.
автозаво́д *m.* automobile factory.
автока́р *m.* self-propelled cart.
автокра́т *m.* autocrat.
автѐл *m.* motor oil.
автомагистра́ль *f.* superhighway.
автома́т *m.* **1.** automatic machine. **2.** public telephone. **3.** vending machine. **4.** (*of persons*) automaton.
автоматиза́ция *f.* automation.
автома́тика *f.* automation.
автомати́чески *adv.* automatically.
автомати́ческий *adj.* automatic.
автома́тчик *m.* submachine gunner.
автомаши́на *f.* motor vehicle.
автомобили́ст *m.* motorist.
автомоби́ль *m.* automobile.
автоно́мный *adj.* autonomous.
автопортре́т *m.* self-portrait.
а́втор *m.* author.
авторефера́т *m.* abstract (*written by the author*).
авторита́рный *adj.* authoritarian.
авторите́т *m.* authority. **—ный** *adj.* authoritative.
а́вторский *adj.* author's. — **а́вторское пра́во** *neut.*
copyright.
а́вторство *neut.* authorship.
авторучка *f.* pen, fountain pen.
автостра́да *f.* expressway.
автотра́нспорт *m.* motor transport.
ага́ *interj.* aha!
агглютинати́вный *adj.* agglutinative.
аге́нт *m.* agent. **—ство** *neut.* agency.
агенту́ра *f.* intelligence agency.
агита́тор *m.* agitator; propagandist.
агита́ция *f.* agitation; propaganda.
агити́ровать OVA *impf. pf.* **с- 1.** to disseminate
propaganda. **2.** to agitate.
аги́тка *f.* (*colloq.*) piece of art propaganda.
агитпу́нкт *m.* propaganda center.
а́гнец FILL *m.* (*obs.*) lamb.
аго́ния *f.* agony.
агра́рный *adj.* agrarian.
агрега́т *m.* unit. — **силово́й агрега́т** power unit.
агре́ссия *f.* aggression.
агроно́м *m.* agronomist. **—и́ческий** *adj.* agricultural. **—ия** *f.* agriculture.
ад *m.* hell; Hades.
ада́мово я́блоко *neut.* Adam's apple.
адапта́ция *f.* adaptation.

адвока́т *m.* **1.** lawyer, attorney for the defense. **2.** advocate.

адвокату́ра *f.* the practice of law.

А́ддис-Абе́ба *m.* Addis Ababa.

адеква́тный *adj.* **1.** adequate. **2.** identical.

аде́пт *m.* adherent; disciple.

администра́тор *m.* manager.

администра́ция *f.* administration.

адмира́л *m.* admiral.

адмиралте́йство *neut.* admiralty.

адренали́н *m.* adrenalin.

а́дрес *m.* address. **—а́нт** *m.* sender. **—а́т** *m.* addressee. **—ный** *adj.* address.

адресова́ть OVA *impf.* and *pf.* to address (*mail*).

Адриати́ческое мо́ре *neut.* Adriatic Sea.

а́дский *adj.* **1.** hellish, of hell. **2.** fiendish, diabolical.

адсо́рбция *f.* adsorption.

адъюта́нт *m.* aide-de-camp.

ажиота́ж *m.* **1.** price fixing. **2.** (*colloq.*) commotion, hullabaloo.

ажу́р *m.* (*obs.*) open-work.

ажу́рный *adj.* **1.** finely made. **2.** delicate. **3.** open-work.

аза́рт *m.* **1.** excitement. **2.** passion.

аза́ртный *adj.* ardent; reckless; passionate.

а́збука *f.* alphabet.

а́збучный *adj.* (*attrib.*) alphabet.

Азербайджа́н *m.* Azerbaijan.

азербайджа́нец FILL *m.* *f.* **азербайджа́нка** Azerbaijanian.

азиа́т *m.* *f.* **азиа́тка** Asian.

азиа́тский *adj.* Asiatic.

а́зимут *m.* azimuth.

А́зия *f.* Asia.

азо́т *m.* nitrogen.

а́ист *m.* stork.

ай *interj.* oh!

айва́ *f.* quince.

айда́ *interj.* (*colloq.*) go!; let's go!

А́йдахо *m.* Idaho.

Айо́ва *m.* Iowa.

акаде́мик *m.* academician.

академи́ческий *adj.* academic.

акаде́мия *f.* academy.

а́канье *neut.* akanie (*pronunciation of unstressed o as a*).

ака́ция *f.* acacia.

аквала́нг *m.* aqualung.

аквамари́н *m.* aquamarine.

акваре́ль *f.* water color.

аква́риум *m.* aquarium.

аквато́рия *f.* area of water (*on the globe*).

акклиматиза́ция *f.* acclimatization.

аккомпанеме́нт *m.* accompaniment.

аккомпаниа́тор *m.* accompanist.

аккомпани́ровать OVA *impf.* and *pf.* to accompany.

акко́рд *m.* chord.

аккордео́н *m.* accordion.

акко́рдный *adj.* by the piece. **— акко́рдная рабо́та** *f.* piecework.

аккредити́в *m.* letter of credit.

аккумуля́тор *m.* battery.

аккура́тно *adv.* **1.** punctually. **2.** neatly. **3.** efficiently.

аккура́тность *f.* meticulousness.

аккура́тный *adj.* **1.** regular. **2.** accurate. **3.** punctual.

акроба́т *m.* acrobat.

акрости́х *m.* acrostic.

акселера́тор *m.* accelerator.

аксельба́нт *m.* aiguillette.

аксессуа́р *m.* accessory.

аксио́ма *f.* axiom.

акт *m.* act; deed.

актёр *m.* actor.

актёрство *neut.* affected behavior.

акти́в *m.* **1.** (financial) assets. **2.** active membership.

активи́ст *m.* *f.* **--ка** political *or* social activist.

акти́вно *adv.* actively.

акти́вность *f.* involvement.

акти́вный *adj.* active; energetic.

акти́ния *f.* sea anemone.

а́ктовый зал *m.* assembly hall.

актри́са *f.* actress.

актуа́льность *f.* timeliness; relevance.

актуа́льный *adj.* **1.** actual. **2.** urgent. **3.** topical.

аку́ла *f.* shark.

акупункту́ра *f.* acupuncture.

аку́стика *f.* acoustics.

акуше́р *m.* **—ка** obstetrician; midwife.

акуше́рство *neut.* obstetrics; midwifery.

акце́нт *m.* accent.

акци́з *m.* excise; excise tax.

акционе́р *m.* shareholder.

а́кция *f.* share; action.

Алаба́ма *f.* Alabama.

алба́нец FILL *m.* *f.* **алба́нка** Albanian.

Алба́ния *f.* Albania.

алба́нский *adj.* Albanian.

а́лгебра *f.* algebra. **—и́ческий** *adj.* algebraic.

алгори́тм *m.* algorithm.

алеба́рда *f.* halberd.

алеба́стр *m.* alabaster.

александри́т *m.* alexandrite.

але́ть *impf.* *pf.* **за-** **1.** to turn scarlet; to turn red. **2.** to blush. **3.** to glow red.

Але́утские острова́ *pl.* Aleutian Islands.

Алжи́р *m.* Algiers.

а́либи *m.* *indecl.* (*leg.*) alibi.

алиме́нты *pl.* alimony.

алкало́ид *m.* alkaloid.

алка́ть *impf.* *pres.* **а́лчу, а́лчешь** **1.** to hunger for. **2.** to crave.

алка́ш *m.* (*pej.*) drunkard; alcoholic.

алкоголи́зм *m.* alcoholism.

алкого́лик *m.* *f.* **алкоголи́чка** alcoholic.

алкого́ль *m.* alcohol.

Алла́х *m.* Allah.

аллего́рия *f.* allegory.

алле́гро *neut.* allegro.

аллерги́я *f.* allergy.

алле́я *f.* avenue; path.

аллига́тор *m.* alligator.

аллилу́йя *interj.* halleluia.

аллитера́ция *f.* alliteration.

алло́ *interj.* hello.

аллопа́тия *f.* allopathy.

аллю́вий *m.* alluvium.

аллю́р *m.* gait (*of horse*).

алма́з *m.* diamond.
Алма́ты *m. indecl.* Almaty (*formerly: Alma Ata*).
ало́э *neut. indecl.* (*plant*) aloe.
Алта́й *m.* (*mountain range*) Altay.
алта́рь *m.* altar.
алты́н *m.* altyn (*old coin worth three copecks*).
алфави́т *m.* alphabet. —**ный** *adj.* alphabetical.
алхи́мик *m.* alchemist.
алхи́мия *f.* alchemy.
а́лчный *adj.* greedy.
а́лый *adj.* scarlet.
алыча́ *f.* cherry plum.
альбатро́с *m.* albatross.
альбо́м *m.* album.
Альбуке́рке *m. indecl.* Albuquerque.
альбуми́н *m.* albumin.
альвео́ла *f.* alveolus.
альмана́х *m.* literary miscellany.
альпи́йский *adj.* Alpine.
альпини́зм *m.* mountain climbing.
А́льпы *pl.* Alps.
альт *m.* **1.** alto (*part* or *voice*). **2.** viola.
альтернати́ва *f.* alternative.
альто́вый *adj.* alto.
альтруи́зм *m.* altruism.
а́льфа *f.* alpha.
алья́нс *m.* alliance.
алюми́ний *m.* aluminum.
аляпова́тый *adj.* **1.** crude. **2.** tasteless. **3.** crudely constructed.
Аля́ска *f.* Alaska.
амазо́нка *f.* (*myth.*) Amazon.
Амазо́нка *f.* (*river*) Amazon.
амальга́ма *f.* amalgam.
амальгама́ция *f.* (*chem.*) amalgamation.
амара́нт *m.* amaranth.
амари́ллис *m.* amaryllis.
амба́р *m.* barn; silo.
амбицио́зный *adj.* ambitious.
амби́ция *f.* arrogance; conceit.
а́мбра *f.* ambergris.
амбразу́ра *f.* loophole.
амбро́зия *f.* **1.** ambrosia. **2.** ragweed.
амбулато́рия *f.* dispensary; outpatient clinic.
амбулато́рный *adj.* (*attrib.*) dispensary.
амёба *f.* ameba.
Аме́рика *f.* America.
америка́нец FILL *m. f.* **америка́нка** American.
америка́нский *adj.* American.
амети́ст *m.* amethyst.
аминокислота́ *f.* amino acid.
ами́нь *particle* and *interj.* amen.
аммиа́к *m.* ammonia.
аммиа́чный *adj.* ammonia.
аммо́ний *m.* ammonium.
амни́стия *f.* amnesty.
амора́льный *adj.* amoral; immoral.
амортиза́тор *m.* shock absorber.
амортизацио́нный *adj.* shock-absorbing.
амортиза́ция *f.* amortization.
амо́рфный *adj.* amorphous.
ампе́р *m.* ampere.
амплиту́да *f.* amplitude.
амплуа́ *neut. indecl.* (*theater*) a kind of role.
а́мпула *f.* ampule.
ампута́ция *f.* amputation.

ампути́ровать OVA *impf.* and *pf.* to amputate.
Амстерда́м *m.* Amsterdam.
Амударья́ *f.* (*river*) Amu Darya (*also: Oxus*).
амуле́т *m.* amulet; charm.
Аму́р *m.* (*river*) Amur.
аму́р *m.* **1.** Cupid. **2.** (*colloq.*) love; amorousness.
амфи́бия *f.* amphibian.
амфитеа́тр *m.* amphitheater.
Амье́н *m.* Amiens.
анабапти́зм *m.* Anabaptism.
анагра́мма *f.* anagram.
Ана́дырский зали́в *m.* Anadyr Gulf.
Ана́дырь *m.* Anadyr.
анако́нда *f.* anaconda.
ана́лиз *m.* analysis.
анализи́ровать OVA *impf. pf.* **про—** to analyze.
анали́тик *m.* analyst.
аналоги́чный *adj.* analogous.
анало́гия *f.* analogy.
анало́й *m.* (*church*) lectern.
ана́льный *adj.* anal.
анана́с *m.* pineapple.
ана́пест *m.* anapest.
анархи́зм *m.* anarchism.
анархи́ст *m.* anarchist.
анархи́стский *also* **анархи́ческий** *adj.* anarchist.
анархи́чный *adj.* anarchic; chaotic.
ана́рхия *f.* anarchy.
ана́том *m.* anatomist.
анатоми́ровать OVA *impf.* and *pf.* to anatomize.
анато́мия *f.* anatomy.
ана́фема *f.* anathema.
анахрони́зм *m.* anachronism.
анахрони́ческий *adj.* anachronistic.
анаэро́б *m.* anaerobe.
анга́р *m.* **1.** hangar. **2.** shed.
Ангара́ *f.* (*river*) Angara.
а́нгел *m.* angel.
анги́на *f.* tonsillitis.
англи́йский *adj.* English. — **англи́йская була́вка** safety pin.
англика́нский *adj.* Anglican.
англици́зм *m.* Anglicism.
англича́нин *m.* Englishman.
англича́нка *f.* Englishwoman.
А́нглия *f.* England.
англофи́л *m.* Anglophile.
Анго́ла *f.* Angola.
Андалу́зия *f.* (*province*) Andalusia.
анда́нте *adv.* andante.
Андо́рра *f.* Andorra.
анекдо́т *m.* **1.** anecdote. **2.** joke. **3.** amusing incident; funny thing.
анекдоти́ческий *adj.* anecdotal.
анеми́я *f.* anemia.
анемо́н *m.* anemone.
анеро́ид *m.* aneroid barometer.
анестезио́лог *m.* anesthesiologist.
анестези́рующий *adj.* anesthetic.
анестези́я *f.* anesthesia.
анили́н *m.* aniline.
аними́зм *m.* animism.
ани́с *m.* anise.
ани́совка *f.* anisette.
ани́совый *adj.* anise.
анке́та *f.* (*printed*) form; questionnaire.

анке́тный *adj.* (*attrib.*) survey, questionnaire.
анкла́в *m.* enclave.
анна́лы *pl.* annals.
анне́ксия *f.* annexation.
аннота́ция *f.* synopsis.
аннули́рование *neut.* cancellation.
аннули́ровать OVA *impf.* and *pf.* to annul; to cancel.
ано́д *m.* anode.
анома́лия *f.* anomaly.
анони́м *m.* anonymous author.
анони́мный *adj.* anonymous.
ано́нс *m.* **1.** announcement. **2.** notice (*of a performance*).
анорма́льный *adj.* abnormal.
анса́мбль *m.* ensemble.
антагони́зм *m.* antagonism.
антагони́ст *m.* antagonist.
антагонисти́ческий *adj.* antagonistic.
Анта́рктика *f.* Antarctica.
анте́нна *f.* antenna.
антиамерикани́зм *m.* anti-Americanism.
антибио́тик *m.* antibiotic.
антивещество́ *neut.* antimatter.
антивое́нный *adj.* antiwar.
антиге́н *m.* antigen.
антидемократи́ческий *adj.* undemocratic.
антиква́р *m.* antique dealer.
антикоммунисти́ческий *adj.* anticommunist.
антикоммуни́зм *m.* anticommunism.
антило́па *f.* antelope.
антиобще́ственный *adj.* antisocial.
антипарти́йный *adj.* anti-party.
антипати́чный *adj.* antipathetic.
антипа́тия *f.* aversion; antipathy.
антирелигио́зный *adj.* antireligious.
антисанита́рный *adj.* insanitary.
антисеми́т *m.* anti-Semite.
антисемити́зм *m.* anti-Semitism.
антисеми́тский *adj.* anti-Semitic.
антисе́птика *f.* antiseptics.
антисове́тский *adj.* anti-Soviet.
антите́за *f.* antithesis.
антите́зис *m.* (*logic*) antithesis.
антите́ло *neut.* antibody.
антитети́ческий *adj.* antithetical.
антитокси́н *m.* antitoxin.
антифри́з *m.* antifreeze.
анти́христ *m.* Antichrist.
анти́чный *adj.* **1.** antique. **2.** ancient.
антоло́гия *f.* anthology.
анто́ним *m.* antonym.
анто́новка *f.* antonovka (*kind of winter apple*).
антра́кт *m.* intermission.
антраци́т *m.* anthracite.
антреко́т *m.* entrecote; rib steak.
антрепренёр *m.* impresario.
антресо́ли *pl.* **1.** mezzanine. **2.** attic.
антропо́ид *m.* anthropoid.
антропо́лог *m.* anthropologist.
ант死рологи́ческий *adj.* anthropological.
антрополо́гия *f.* anthropology.
антропоморфи́зм *m.* anthropomorphism.
анфа́с *adv.* full-face.
анфила́да *f.* suite of rooms.
анча́р *m.* (*tree*) upas.

анчо́ус *m.* anchovy.
аншла́г *m.* **1.** notice. **2.** (*theater*) full house.
ао́рта *f.* aorta.
апартаме́нт *m.* usu. pl. luxurious living quarters.
апарте́йд *m.* apartheid.
апати́чный *adj.* apathetic.
апа́тия *f.* apathy.
апелли́ровать OVA *impf.* and *pf.* to appeal.
апелляцио́нный *adj.* (*leg.*) of appeal.
апелля́ция *f.* appeal.
апельси́н *m.* orange.
аплоди́ровать OVA *impf.* to applaud.
аплодисме́нты *pl.* applause.
апло́мб *m.* self-assurance.
апоге́й *m.* (*astr.*) apogee.
апока́липсис *m.* apocalypse.
апо́криф *m.* an apocryphal work.
апокрифи́ческий *adj.* apocryphal.
аполити́чный *adj.* apolitical.
апологе́т *m.* apologist.
апологе́тика *f.* apologetics.
аполо́гия *f.* apologia.
апоплекси́ческий *adj.* apoplectic.
апопле́ксия *f.* apoplexy; apoplectic stroke.
апо́стол *m.* apostle.
апостро́ф *m.* apostrophe.
апофео́з *m.* apotheosis.
аппара́т *m.* apparatus.
аппарату́ра *f.* apparatus; equipment.
аппара́тчик *m.* **1.** party functionary. **2.** machine operator. **3.** maintenance man.
аппе́ндикс *m.* (*anat.*) appendix.
апперце́пция *f.* (*psychol.*) apperception.
аппети́т *m.* appetite.
аппети́тный *adj.* appetizing.
аппликату́ра *f.* (*mus.*) fingering.
апплика́ция *f.* appliqué work.
апре́ль *m.* April. —**ский** *adj.* (*attrib.*) April.
априо́ри *adv.* a priori.
апроба́ция *f.* approbation.
апси́да *f.* (*archit.*) apse; apsis.
апте́ка *f.* pharmacy, drug store.
апте́карь *m.* druggist.
апте́чка *f.* medicine chest.
апте́чный *adj.* of or for drugs.
ар *m.* are (*100 square meters*).
а́ра *f.* macaw.
ара́б *m.* f. **ара́бка** Arab.
арабе́ска *f.* arabesque.
ара́бский *also* **араби́йский** *adj.* Arabian, Arabic.
Ара́гви *f.* (*river*) Aragvi.
Ара́льск *m.* Aralsk.
аранжиро́вка *f.* (*mus.*) arrangement.
ара́пник *m.* hunting whip.
ара́ра *f.* macaw.
ара́хис *m.* **1.** peanut. **2.** peanut plant.
арби́тр *m.* arbitrator.
арбитра́ж *m.* arbitration.
арбу́з *m.* watermelon.
арго́ *neut. indecl.* **1.** argot. **2.** jargon. **3.** slang.
арго́н *m.* argon.
аргуме́нт *m.* argument.
аргумента́ция *f.* argumentation.
аре́на *f.* **1.** arena, ring. **2.** scene (*of action*).
аре́нда *f.* lease.
аренда́тор *m.* tenant; leaseholder.

аре́ндный *adj.* rental.
аре́ндовать OVA *impf. and pf.* to rent (from).
аре́ст *m.* 1. arrest. 2. custody. 3. attachment.
ареста́нт *m.* person under arrest.
аресто́ванный DAA *m.* 1. person arrested. 2. prisoner.
аресто́вывать OVA *impf. pf.* **арестова́ть** to arrest.
Аризо́на *f.* Arizona.
аристокра́т *m.* aristocrat.
арифме́тика *f.* arithmetic.
арифмети́ческий *adj.* arithmetical.
арифмо́метр *m.* automatic calculating machine.
а́рия *f.* aria.
а́рка *f.* arch.
арка́да *f.* (*archit.*) arcade.
арка́н *m.* lasso.
Арка́нзас *m.* Arkansas.
А́рктика *f.* the Arctic.
аркти́ческий *adj.* arctic.
арлеки́н *m.* harlequin.
Арль *m.* Arles.
арма́да *f.* armade.
армату́ра *f.* 1. fixtures; fittings. 2. armature. 3. steel framework.
арме́ец FILL *m.* army man.
арме́йский *adj.* (*attrib.*) army.
Арме́ния *f.* Armenia.
а́рмия *f.* army.
армяни́н *m. f.* **армя́нка** Armenian.
армя́нский *adj.* Armenian.
арома́т *m.* aroma, fragrance.
а́рочный *adj.* arched.
арпе́джио *neut. indecl.* arpeggio.
арсена́л *m.* armory.
аре́ст *m.* 1. arrest. 2. custody. 3. attachment.
арта́читься *impf.* (*colloq.*) to balk.
артезиа́нский коло́дец *m.* artesian well.
арте́ль *f.* cooperative.
артериа́льный *adj.* arterial.
артериосклеро́з *m.* arteriosclerosis.
арте́рия *f.* (*anat.*) artery.
арти́кль *m.* (*gram.*) article.
артикуля́ция *f.* articulation.
артилле́рия *f.* artillery.
арти́ст *m.* artist; actor. **—и́ческий** *adj.* artistic.
артисти́чность *f.* artistic talent.
артишо́к *m.* artichoke.
артри́т *m.* arthritis.
а́рфа *f.* harp.
арха́изм *m.* archaism.
арха́ичный *adj.* archaic.
арха́нгел *m.* archangel.
Арха́нгельск *m.* Arkhangelsk.
археоло́гия *f.* archeology.
архи́в *m.* archive.
архива́риус *m.* archivist.
архи́вный *adj.* (*attrib.*) archive.
архидья́кон *m.* archdeacon.
архиепи́скоп *m.* archbishop.
архиере́й *m.* (*eccl.*) member of higher orders of clergy (*e.g.* bishop; archbishop; metropolitan).
архимандри́т *m.* (*eccl.*) archimandrite.
архипела́г *m.* archipelago.
архите́ктор *m.* architect.
архитекту́ра *f.* architecture.

арши́н *m.* arshin (*old unit of length, ca. 28 inches*).
арьерга́рд *m.* rear guard.
ас *m.* ace (*pilot*).
асбе́ст *m.* asbestos.
асе́птика *f.* asepsis.
асимметри́чный *adj.* asymmetric.
асимметри́я *f.* asymmetry.
аске́т *m.* ascetic.
аскети́зм *m.* asceticism.
аскети́ческий *adj.* ascetic.
аскорби́новая кислота́ *f.* ascorbic acid.
аспе́кт *m.* viewpoint; perspective.
а́спид[1] *m.* (*obs.*) slate.
а́спид[2] *m.* asp; viper.
а́спидный *adj.* slate.
аспира́нт *m. f.* **—ка** postgraduate student. **—у́ра** *f.* postgraduate studies *or* research.
аспири́н *m.* aspirin.
ассамбле́я *f.* assembly.
ассениза́ция *f.* sewage disposal.
ассигнова́ние *neut.* allocation.
ассигнова́ть OVA *impf. and pf.* to assign, to allocate.
ассимиля́ция *f.* assimilation.
ассисте́нт *m. f.* **—ка** assistant.
ассона́нс *m.* assonance.
ассортиме́нт *m.* assortment; selection.
ассоциа́ция *f.* association.
ассоции́ровать OVA *impf. and pf.* 1. to associate. 2. to make an association between.
астеро́ид *m.* asteroid.
астигмати́зм *m.* astigmatism.
а́стма *f.* asthma.
а́стра *f.* aster.
астроло́гия *f.* astrology.
астроля́бия *f.* astrolabe.
астронавига́ция *f.* celestial navigation.
астроно́м *m.* astronomer. **—ия** *f.* astronomy.
астрофи́зика *f.* astrophysics.
асфа́льт *m.* asphalt.
асфа́льтовый *adj.* asphalt.
асфи́ксия *f.* asphyxia; asphyxiation.
атави́зм *m.* atavism.
ата́ка *f.* attack.
атакова́ть OVA *impf. and pf.* to attack.
атакси́я *f.* ataxis.
атама́н *m.* ataman (*Cossack chieftain*).
атеи́ст *m. f.* **—ка** atheist.
ателье́ *neut. indecl.* studio.
атипи́ческий *adj.* atypical.
атланти́ческий *adj.* Atlantic.
а́тлас *m.* atlas.
атла́с *m.* satin.
атла́сный *adj.* satin.
атле́т *m.* athlete. **—ика** *f.* athletics.
атлети́ческий *adj.* athletic.
атмосфе́ра *f.* atmosphere.
атмосфе́рный *adj.* atmospheric.
ато́лл *m.* atoll.
а́том *m.* atom.
а́томный *adj.* atomic.
атона́льность *f.* atonality.
атона́льный *adj.* atonal.
атрибу́т *m.* characteristic.
атропи́н *m.* atropine.

атрофия *f.* atrophy.

атташе́ *m. indecl.* attaché.

аттеста́т *m.* **1.** certificate. **2.** endorsement.

аттеста́ция *f.* written recommendation.

аттестова́ть OVA *impf.* and *pf.* **1.** to certify; to endorse. **2.** to recommend.

аттракцио́ны *pl.* amusements; attractions (*in a park*).

ату́ *interj.:* **ату́ его́!** Sic 'em!

ау́ *interj.* hello!; hello there!

аудие́нция *f.* formal interview.

аудито́рия *f.* **1.** auditorium. **2.** audience.

ау́кать *impf. pf.* **ау́кнуть** to shout "hello" to one another.

аукцио́н *m.* auction.

ау́л *m.* aul (*village in the Caucasus*).

аутенти́чный *adj.* authentic.

аутса́йдер *m.* outsider.

афа́зия *f.* aphasia.

афга́нец FILL *m. f.* **афга́нка** Afghan.

Афганиста́н *m.* Afghanistan.

афе́ра *f.* fraud; swindle.

Афи́ны *pl.* Athens.

афи́ша *f.* placard, poster.

Афо́н *m.* Mount Athos.

афори́зм *m.* aphorism.

афористи́чный *adj.* aphoristic.

А́фрика *f.* Africa.

африка́нец *m. f.* **африка́нка** African.

афро́нт *m.* (*obs.*) affront.

аффе́кт *m.* **1.** fit. **2.** paroxysm (*of rage*).

аффекта́ция *f.* affectation.

аффекти́рованный *adj.* affected.

ах *interj.* ah!; oh!

а́хать *impf. pf.* **а́хнуть** to exclaim; to gasp.

ахине́я *f.* (*colloq.*) nonsense.

ахтерште́вень FILL *m.* sternpost.

ахти́ *interj.* oh!; alas!

ацетиле́н *m.* acetylene.

ацето́н *m.* acetone.

аэра́рий *m.* aerarium; terrace for sunbathing.

аэра́ция *f.* aeration.

аэровокза́л *m.* air terminal.

аэродина́мика *f.* aerodynamics.

аэродинами́ческий *adj.* aerodynamic.

аэродро́м *m.* aerodrome.

аэрозо́ль *m.* aerosol.

аэрона́вт *m.* balloonist.

аэропла́н *m.* (*obs.*) airplane.

аэропо́рт *m.* airport.

аэросни́мок FILL *m.* aerial photograph.

аэроста́т *m.* balloon.

аятолла́ *m.* (*decl. f.*) ayatollah.

Б

б *see* бы.
ба *interj.* (*obs.*) well!
ба́ба¹ *f.* (*colloq.*) woman. — сне́жная ба́ба *f.* snow woman.
ба́ба² *f.* (*tech.*) ram.
ба́ба³ *f.* (*pastry*) baba.
ба́бка *f.* (*colloq.*) old woman; grandmother.
ба́бник *m.* (*colloq.*) ladies' man.
ба́бочка¹ *f.* butterfly. — ночна́я ба́бочка *f.* moth.
ба́бочка² *f.* (*colloq.*) bow tie.
ба́бушка *f.* grandmother.
ба́бье ле́то *neut.* Indian summer.
бага́ж *m.* luggage; baggage.
бага́жник *m.* **1.** trunk (*of automobile*). **2.** luggage carrier; rack.
бага́жный *adj.* (*attrib.*) baggage.
Багда́д *m.* Baghdad.
баго́р *m.* hook; boat hook.
багро́вый *adj.* crimson.
багря́нец FILL *m.* crimson.
бадминто́н *m* badminton.
бадья́ *f.* **1.** pail. **2.** bucket.
ба́за *f.* base; basis.
база́льт *m.* basalt.
база́р *m.* market, bazaar.
база́рный *adj.* (*attrib.*) market.
Ба́зель *m.* Basel.
бази́лик *m.* basil.
бази́лика *f.* basilica.
бази́ровать OVA *impf. and pf.* **1.** to base; to found. **2.** to ground.
ба́зис *m.* basis; base.
ба́зисный *adj.* base.
бай-бай *interj.* rock-a-bye.
байба́к *m.* a species of marmot, bobac.
байда́рка *f.* canoe; kayak.
ба́йка *f.* flannel; baize.
Байка́л *m.* (*lake*) Baikal.
бак *m.* tank, cistern; boiler.
бакала́вр *m.* bachelor.
бакале́йный *adj.* grocery.
бакале́йщик *m.* grocer.
бакале́я *f.* (*colloq.*) groceries.
бакели́т *m.* bakelite.
ба́кен *m.* buoy.
бакенба́рды *pl.* whiskers.
ба́ки *pl.* whiskers.
баккара́ *f.* baccarat.
баклажа́н *m.* eggplant.
бакла́н *m.* (*bird*) cormorant.
бактериа́льный *adj.* bacterial.
бактериоло́гия *f* bacteriology.
бакте́рия *f.* bacterium.
Баку́ *m. indecl.* Baku.
бал *m.* ball, dance.
балага́н *m.* **1.** booth; show. **2.** (*fig.*) farce.
балага́нный *adj.* farcical.
балагу́р *m.* (*colloq.*) joker, jester.
балагу́рить *impf.* to joke, to jest.
балагу́рство *neut.* witty talk.
балала́ечник *m.* balalaika player.

баламу́тить *impf. pf.* вз- to confuse; to trouble; to disturb.
бала́нс *m.* balance.
баланси́р *m.* balancing pole.
бала́нсовый *adj.* balance.
балбе́с *m.* (*colloq.*) nitwit; boob; jerk.
балда́ *m. and f.* (*decl. f.*) (*colloq.*) blockhead.
балдахи́н *m.* canopy.
Балеа́рские острова́ *pl.* Balearic Islands.
балери́на *f.* ballerina.
бале́т *m.* ballet.
балетме́йстер *m.* ballet master.
бале́тный *adj.* (*attrib.*) ballet.
балетома́н *m. f.* —ка ballet lover.
ба́лка *f.* beam, girder.
балко́н *m.* balcony.
балл *m.* **1.** mark (*in school*). **2.** point (*in sports*).
балла́да *f.* **1.** ballad. **2.** (*mus.*) ballade.
балла́ст *m.* ballast.
балли́стика *f.* ballistics.
балло́н *m.* **1.** cylinder. **2.** rubber tire.
баллоти́ровать OVA *impf.* to vote by ballot —ся to be a candidate, to run for an office.
баллоти́ровка *f.* **1.** balloting, voting. **2.** ballot, poll.
ба́ловать OVA *impf.* to pamper; to spoil. —ся (*colloq.*) to play pranks; to frolic.
ба́ловень *m.* pet; favorite.
баловни́к *m.* (*colloq.*) naughty child.
баловство́ *neut.* **1.** pampering, spoiling. **2.** mischievousness.
Балти́йское мо́ре *neut.* Baltic Sea.
бальза́м *m.* balsam.
бальзами́ровщик *m.* embalmer.
балюстра́да *f.* balustrade.
баля́сник *m.* baluster.
баля́сы точи́ть *impf.* (*colloq.*) to joke; to talk nonsense.
бамбу́к *m.* bamboo. —овый *adj.* bamboo.
ба́мия *f.* okra; gumbo.
ба́мпер *m.* bumper.
бана́льность *f.* banality.
бана́льный *adj.* banal, trite.
бана́н *m.* banana.
Бангко́к *m.* Bangkok.
ба́нда *f.* gang.
банда́ж *m.* **1.** bandage. **2.** truss, belt.
бандеро́ль *f.* wrapper; small package.
ба́нджо *neut. indecl.* banjo.
банди́т *m.* thug, bandit.
банк *m.* bank.
ба́нка¹ *f.* jar, pot.
ба́нка² *f.* bank, shoal.
банке́т *m.* banquet.
банки́р *m.* banker.
банкно́т *m. also* банкно́та *f.* banknote.
ба́нковский *also* ба́нковый *adj.* (*attrib.*) bank.
банкомёт *m.* **1.** banker (*at cards*). **2.** croupier.
банкро́т *m.* bankrupt. —ство *neut.* bankruptcy.
ба́нный *adj.* (*attrib.*) bath.
бант *m.* bow.

ба́нщик *m.* bathhouse attendant.
ба́ня *f.* **1.** bath; bathhouse. **2.** (*fig.*) hothouse.
баоба́б *m.* baobab.
бапти́ст *m.f.* **—ка** Baptist.
баптисте́рий *m.* baptistery.
бапти́стский *adj.* Baptist.
бар *m.* bar.
бараба́н *m.* drum.
бараба́нить *impf.* to drum.
бараба́нный *adj.* (*attrib.*) drum.
бараба́нщик *m. f.* **бараба́нщица** drummer.
барабу́лька *f.* red mullet.
бара́к *m.* temporary wooden barrack; hut.
бара́н *m.* ram. **—ина** *f.* mutton.
бара́ний *adj.* sheep's, sheep.
бара́нка *f.* bagel.
барахло́ *neut.* **1.** junk; trash. **2.** old clothes; old things.
бара́хтаться *impf.* to flounder; to roll; to wallow.
бара́чный *adj.* (*attrib.*) barrack.
бара́шек *m.* lamb; lambskin.
бара́шки *pl.* **1.** fleecy clouds. **2.** (*naut.*) white-caps.
бара́шковый *adj.* lambskin.
барбитура́т *m.* barbiturate.
барбо́с *m.* watchdog.
барви́нок FILL *m.* periwinkle.
бард *m.* bard.
барелье́ф *m.* bas-relief.
ба́ржа *f.* barge.
ба́рий *m.* barium.
ба́рин *m.* gentleman; nobleman.
бари́т *m.* barite; heavy spar.
барито́н *m.* baritone.
баритона́льный *adj.* (*attrib.*) baritone.
барк *m.* (*sailing vessel*) bark.
ба́рка *f.* barge.
баркаро́ла *f.* barcarole.
барка́с *m.* **1.** launch. **2.** longboat.
Барнау́л *m.* Barnaul.
баро́кко *neut.* baroque.
баро́метр *m.* barometer.
баро́н *m.* baron.
бароне́сса *f.* baroness.
бароне́т *m.* baronet.
баро́нство *neut.* barony.
баро́чный *adj.* baroque.
ба́рочный *adj.* (*attrib.*) barge.
ба́ррель *m.* (*measure*) barrel.
баррика́да *f.* barricade.
барс *m.* snow leopard.
Барсело́на *f.* Barcelona.
ба́рский *adj.* **1.** gentleman's. **2.** supercilious.
ба́рственный *adj.* lordly.
ба́рство *neut.* gentry.
барсу́к *m.* badger.
барха́н *m.* sand dune.
ба́рхат *m.* velvet. **—истый** *adj.* velvety. **—ный** *adj.* velvet.
ба́рхатка *f.* velvet ribbon.
ба́рхатцы *pl.* (*French* or *African*) marigold.
ба́рыня *f.* wife of **ба́рин**; lady, mistress; noblewoman.
бары́ш *m.* profit, gain. **—ник** *m.* profiteer. **—ничество** *neut.* profiteering.
ба́рышня *f.* young lady; miss.

барье́р *m.* barrier; hurdle.
бас *m.* (*mus.*) bass.
баси́стый *adj.* (*colloq.*) deep, low (*in sound*); bass.
баскетбо́л *m.* basketball.
баснопи́сец *m.* fabulist.
баснословный *adj.* **1.** legendary. **2.** (*fig.*) incredible.
ба́сня *f.* fable.
басо́вый *adj.* (*mus.*) bass.
бассе́йн *m.* **1.** pond; pool. **2.** basin.
ба́ста *interj.* enough.
бастио́н *m.* bastion.
бастова́ть OVA *impf.* to strike; to go on strike.
басту́ющий *adj.* striking. — *m.* striker.
батали́ст *m.* painter of battle scenes.
бата́лия *f.* (*obs.*) battle.
баталь́он *m.* battalion.
батаре́йка *f.* (*elec.*) battery.
батаре́йный *adj.* (*attrib.*) battery.
батаре́я *f.* (*mil.*) battery; radiator.
бата́т *m.* sweet potato; yam.
ба́тенька *m.* (*decl. f.*) (*obs.*) (*familiar form of address*) my friend; old boy.
бати́ст *m.* batiste, cambric.
бато́н *m.* **1.** long loaf of bread. **2.** stick of candy.
батра́к *m. f.* **батра́чка** farm hand, farm laborer.
батра́чить *impf.* to work as a farm laborer.
баттерфля́й *m.* (*swim.*) butterfly stroke.
бату́т *m.* trampoline.
ба́тюшка *m.* (*decl. f.*) **1.** father. **2.** (*colloq.*) old fellow!; my dear boy!
бау́л *m.* (*luggage*) trunk.
бах *interj.* bang!
бахва́л *m.* (*colloq.*) braggart.
бахва́литься *impf.* (*colloq.*) to brag.
бахва́льство *neut.* (*colloq.*) bragging.
бахрома́ *f.* fringe.
бахча́ *f.* melon field.
бац *interj.* bang!; crack!
баци́лла *f.* bacillus.
ба́шенка *f.* turret.
ба́шенный *adj.* (*attrib.*) tower.
башка́ *f.* (*colloq.*) head; noggin; pate.
башки́р *m. f.* **—ка** Bashkir.
башкови́тый *adj.* (*colloq.*) brainy.
башлы́к *m.* hood.
башма́к *m.* shoe.
башма́чник *m. f.* **башма́чница** shoemaker.
ба́шня *f.* tower.
ба́ян *m.* **1.** accordion. **2.** bard.
бде́ние *neut.* vigil.
бди́тельный *adj.* vigilant.
бег *m.* **1.** race. **2.** run, running.
бега́ *pl.* races. **— быть в бега́х** *impf.* (*colloq.*) to be on the run.
бе́гать *impf. indet. det.* **бежа́ть** to run, to run about; to hurry.
бегемо́т *m.* hippopotamus.
бегле́ц *m. f.* **бегля́нка** fugitive.
бе́гло *adv.* **1.** fluently. **2.** hastily; in a cursory manner.
бе́глый *adj.* **1.** fluent. **2.** cursory. **3.** fugitive.
бегово́й *adj.* (*attrib.*) **1.** running. **2.** race; racing.
бего́м *adv.* on the double.
бего́ния *f.* begonia.

беготня́ *f.* (*colloq.*) running about; scurrying about.

бе́гство *neut.* flight; escape.

бегу́н *m.* (*tech.*) runner.

беда́ *f.* misfortune, trouble.

бедла́м *m.* bedlam.

бедне́ть *impf.* to become poor.

бе́дно *adv.* in poverty; shabbily.

бе́дность *f.* poverty.

беднота́ *f.* (*coll.*) the poor.

бе́дный *adj.* poor.

бедня́га *m.* (*decl. f.*) *f.* **бедня́жка** (*colloq.*) poor thing, poor creature.

бедня́к *m.* poor man.

бедо́вый *adj.* (*colloq.*) daring.

бедоку́р *m.* mischief-maker.

бе́дренный *adj.* hip.

бедро́ *neut.* **1.** thigh. **2.** hip.

бе́дственный *adj.* disastrous; calamitous.

бе́дствие *neut.* calamity; disaster.

бе́дствовать OVA *impf.* to live in poverty.

беж *adj. indecl.* beige.

бежа́ть *impf. det. indet.* **бе́гать** *pf.* **побежа́ть** to run; to escape; to flee.

бе́жевый *adj.* beige.

бе́женец FILL *m. f.* **бе́женка** refugee.

без (**бе́зо**) *prep.* (*with gen.*) without.

безала́берный *adj.* disorderly.

безалкого́льный *adj.* nonalcoholic.

безапелляцио́нный *adj.* peremptory; categorical.

безбе́дный *adj.* comfortable, well-to-do.

безбиле́тный *adj.* without a ticket.

безбо́жие *neut.* godlessness, atheism.

безбо́жник *m. f.* **безбо́жница** atheist.

безбо́жный *adj.* godless, atheistic.

безболе́зненный *adj.* painless.

безбоя́зненный *adj.* fearless.

безбра́чие *neut.* celibacy.

безбре́жный *adj.* boundless.

безве́стный *adj.* obscure.

безве́тренный *adj.* **1.** windless. **2.** calm; still.

безве́трие *neut.* absence of wind.

безви́нный *adj.* innocent, guiltless.

безвку́сие *neut.* lack of taste; tastelessness.

безвку́сный *adj.* tasteless.

безвла́стие *neut.* anarchy.

безво́дный *adj.* waterless; arid.

безвозвра́тный *adj.* irrevocable.

безвозду́шный *adj.* airless.

безвозме́здный *adj.* gratuitous.

безво́лие *neut.* weakness of will.

безволо́сый *adj.* hairless.

безво́льный *adj.* weak-willed.

безвре́дный *adj.* harmless, innocuous.

безвре́менный *adj.* untimely; premature.

безвы́ездно *adv.* **1.** uninterruptedly. **2.** without a break.

безвы́ездный *adj.* permanent (*of residence*).

безвы́ходный *adj.* hopeless; desperate.

безгла́зый *adj.* without eyes.

безгла́сный *adj.* soundless; mute.

безголо́вый *adj.* **1.** headless. **2.** (*fig.*) brainless.

безголо́сый *adj.* voiceless.

безгра́мотный *adj.* **1.** ungrammatical. **2.** illiterate.

безграни́чный *adj.* infinite, boundless.

безгре́шный *adj.* sinless.

безда́рность *f.* lack of talent.

безда́рный *adj.* untalented.

безде́йственный *adj.* inactive; idle.

безде́йствие *neut.* inaction, inertia, inertness.

безде́йствовать OVA *impf.* to be inactive, inert, idle.

безде́лица *f.* (*colloq.*) trifle.

безделу́шка *f.* trinket; knickknack.

безде́лье *neut.* idleness.

безде́льник *m. f.* **безде́льница** idler, loafer.

безде́льничать *impf.* to loaf.

безде́нежный *adj.* impecunious.

безде́нежье *neut.* lack of money.

безде́тный *adj.* childless.

безде́ятельный *adj.* inactive, inert.

бе́здна *f.* abyss, chasm.

бездоказа́тельный *adj.* unsubstantiated; unsupported.

бездо́мный *adj.* homeless.

бездо́нный *adj.* bottomless.

бездоро́жье *neut.* bad roads; time of year when roads are bad.

безду́мный *adj.* thoughtless; unthinking.

безду́мье *neut.* inability to think clearly; daze.

безду́шие *neut.* heartlessness; callousness.

безду́шный *adj.* callous; heartless.

бездыха́нный *adj.* lifeless.

безжа́лостный *adj.* pitiless, merciless.

безжи́зненный *adj.* **1.** lifeless. **2.** lackluster.

беззабо́тный *adj.* carefree, unconcerned.

беззаве́тный *adj.* selfless.

беззако́ние *neut.* lawlessness.

беззако́нность *f.* lawlessness.

беззасте́нчивый *adj.* **1.** shameless. **2.** impudent.

беззащи́тный *adj.* defenseless, unprotected.

беззвёздный *adj.* starless.

беззву́чный *adj.* soundless, noiseless.

безземе́льный *adj.* landless.

беззло́бие *neut.* good nature.

беззло́бный *adj.* good-natured.

беззу́бый *adj.* toothless.

безле́сный *adj.* treeless.

безле́сье *neut.* absence of forests.

безли́кий *adj.* faceless.

безли́чно *adv.* impersonally.

безли́чный *adj.* **1.** lacking individuality or personality. **2.** (*gram.*) impersonal.

безлю́дный *adj.* **1.** uninhabited. **2.** (*of streets*) deserted.

безлю́дье *neut.* absence of people.

безме́н *m.* steelyard.

безме́рный *adj.* immeasurable; boundless.

безмо́зглый *adj.* (*colloq.*) witless, brainless.

безмо́лвие *neut.* silence.

безмо́лвный *adj.* speechless, silent, mute.

безмяте́жный *adj.* serene, tranquil.

безнадёжный *adj.* hopeless.

безнадзо́рный *adj.* neglected, unsupervised.

безнака́занно *adv.* with impunity.

безнали́чный *adj.* (*of transaction*) performed without cash.

безнача́лие *neut.* anarchy.

безно́гий *adj.* legless; with only one leg.

безнра́вственный *adj.* immoral; dissolute.

безоби́дный *adj.* inoffensive; harmless.

безо́блачный *adj.* cloudless; serene.

безобра́зие *neut.* ugliness; deformity.
безобра́зник *m.* (*colloq.*) rowdy.
безобра́зный *adj.* **1.** ugly; deformed. **2.** formless. **3.** disgraceful, outrageous.
безо́бразный *adj.* **1.** shapeless. **2.** unadorned. **3.** vague.
безогля́дный *adj.* headlong.
безоговоро́чный *adj.* unconditional.
безопа́сно *adv.* safely.
безопа́сность *f.* safety.
безопа́сный *adj.* safe.
безору́жный *adj.* unarmed.
безостано́вочный *adj.* ceaseless, unceasing; non-stop.
безотве́тный *adj.* **1.** unrequited. **2.** unresponsive. **3.** meek.
безотве́тственный *adj.* irresponsible.
безотка́зный *adj.* (*colloq.*) smooth; steady.
безотка́тный *adj.* recoilless.
безотлага́тельный *adj.* urgent.
безотлу́чный *adj.* **1.** ever-present. **2.** continual.
безотноси́тельно *adv.* without regard to; irrespective of.
безотчётный *adj.* instinctive.
безоши́бочный *adj.* **1.** unerring, faultless. **2.** correct.
безрабо́тица *f.* unemployment.
безрабо́тный *adj.* unemployed.
безра́достный *adj.* joyless.
безразде́льный *adj.* undivided.
безразли́чие *neut.* **1.** indifference. **2.** nonchalance.
безразли́чно *adv.* indifferently. — **мне безразли́чно** it makes no difference to me.
безразли́чный *adj.* **1.** indifferent. **2.** nonchalant.
безразме́рный *adj.* stretch, one-size-fits-all.
безрассу́дный *adj.* **1.** thoughtless, foolhardy. **2.** rash, reckless.
безрассу́дство *neut.* recklessness.
безрезульта́тный *adj.* **1.** futile, ineffectual. **2.** unsuccessful, vain.
безро́гий *adj.* hornless.
безро́дный *adj.* without kith or kin.
безро́потность *f.* **1.** resignation. **2.** meekness.
безро́потный *adj.* resigned; uncomplaining.
безрука́вка *f.* sleeveless jacket.
безрука́вный *adj.* sleeveless.
безру́кий *adj.* lacking one *or* both arms; lacking one *or* both hands; clumsy.
безуда́рный *adj.* (*gram.*) unaccented, unstressed.
безу́держный *adj.* unrestrained; uncontrollable.
безукори́зненно *adv.* flawlessly.
безукори́зненный *adj.* irreproachable, unimpeachable.
безу́мец FILL *m.* fool, idiot; madman.
безу́мие *neut.* folly; madness.
безу́мно *adv.* madly; terribly. — **безу́мно за́нят** terribly busy.
безу́мный *adj.* **1.** senseless, foolish. **2.** reckless. **3.** mad.
безумо́лчный *adj.* (*of noise*) incessant.
безу́мство *neut.* madness.
безупре́чный *adj.* irreproachable, blameless.
безусло́вно *adv.* certainly; absolutely.
безусло́вный *adj.* unconditional, absolute.
безуспе́шный *adj.* unsuccessful.
безу́сый *adj.* without a mustache.
безуте́шный *adj.* inconsolable.

безуча́стный *adj.* apathetic, indifferent.
безъя́дерный *adj.* nuclear-free.
безыде́йность *f.* lack of proper ideology.
безыде́йный *adj.* lacking proper ideology.
безымя́нный *adj.* nameless, anonymous.
безынициати́вный *adj.* unenterprising.
безыску́сственный *adj.* ingenuous.
безысхо́дный *adj.* **1.** hopeless. **2.** endless.
бейсбо́л *m.* baseball.
бека́р *m.* (*mus.*) natural sign; natural.
бека́с *m.* snipe.
беко́н *m.* bacon.
Белгра́д *m.* Belgrad.
белена́ *f.* henbane.
белёный *adj.* bleached.
беле́сый *adj.* whitish; off-white.
беле́ть *impf.* *pf.* **по-** *v.i.* to become white, to whiten.
белиберда́ *f.* (*colloq.*) nonsense; rubbish.
белизна́ *f.* whiteness.
бели́ла *f.* whiting; ceruse (*cosmetics*).
бели́ть *impf.* to whiten, to bleach.
бе́лка *f.* squirrel.
беллетри́ст *m.* fiction writer, novelist. —**ика** *f.* belles-lettres; fiction.
белобры́сый *adj.* towheaded.
белова́тый *adj.* whitish; off-white.
белови́к *m.* clean copy.
белово́й *adj.* (*of manuscript, copy*) clean; final.
белогварде́ец FILL *m.* White Guard.
белоголо́вый *adj.* fair-haired.
бело́к FILL *m.* white of an egg.
белокро́вие *neut.* leukemia.
белоку́рый *adj.* blond, fair, fair-haired.
белоли́цый *adj.* white-faced.
белору́с *m. f.* —**ка** Belarussian.
Белору́сь *also* **Белору́ссия** *f.* Belarus (*also:* Byelorussia).
белору́чка *m.* and *f.* (*decl. f.*) one .who does not wish to soil his hands; one who despises manual labor.
белосне́жный *adj.* snow-white.
белоте́лый *adj.* fair-skinned, white-skinned.
белошве́йка *f.* seamstress.
белу́га *f.* beluga; white sturgeon.
Бе́лфаст *m.* Belfast.
бе́лый *adj.* white. — **бе́лые стихи́** *pl.* blank verse.
бельги́ец FILL *m. f.* **бельги́йка** Belgian.
бельги́йский *adj.* Belgian.
Бе́льгия *f.* Belgium.
бельё *neut.* linen.
бельево́й *adj.* linen.
бельме́с *m.*: **ни бельме́са** (*colloq.*) (*to know*) nothing.
бельмо́ *neut.* walleye.
бельэта́ж *m.* **1.** first floor. **2.** (*theat.*) dress circle.
беля́к *m.* white hare.
бемо́ль *m.* (*mus.*) flat.
бенга́лец FILL *m. f.* **бенга́лка** Bengali.
бенефи́с *m.* (*theat.*) benefit performance.
бензи́н *m.* benzine; gasoline.
бензоба́к *m.* gas tank.
бензоколо́нка *f.* gasoline pump.
бензо́л *m.* benzene; benzol.
бенуа́р *m.* (*theat.*) boxes (*at orchestra level*).
бе́рег *m.* shore; coast.

береговой *adj.* coast; coastal; (*attrib.*) shore.
— береговая линия *f.* coastline.
Берег Слоновой Кости *m.* Ivory Coast.
бередить *impf. pf.* раз- (*colloq.*) to irritate; to reopen (*a wound*).
бережливый *adj.* thrifty, economical.
бережный *adj.* careful; considerate.
берёза *f.* birch.
Березина *f.* (*river*) Berezina.
березняк *m.* birch forest.
берёзовый *adj.* birch.
беременеть *impf. pf.* за- to become pregnant, to be pregnant.
беременная *adj.* pregnant.
беременность *f.* pregnancy.
береста *f.* birch bark.
берет *m.* beret.
беречь *impf.* 1. to take care of. 2. to spare. 3. to protect. —ся to be careful; to beware; to be on one's guard.
берилл *m.* beryl.
бериллий *m.* beryllium.
Берингов пролив *m.* Bering Strait.
беркут *m.* golden eagle.
Берлин *m.* Berlin.
берлога *f.* den, lair.
берцовый *adj.* (*attrib.*) shin.
бес *m.* demon.
беседа *f.* conversation, talk, chat.
беседка *f.* gazebo.
беседовать OVA *impf.* to talk.
бесить *impf. pf.* вз- to enrage; to infuriate.
бесклассовый *adj.* classless.
бескозырка *f.* peakless cap.
бескомпромиссный *adj.* uncompromising.
бесконечно *adv.* endlessly.
бесконечность *f.* infinity.
бесконечный *adj.* endless, infinite; eternal.
бесконтрольный *adj.* unsupervised; uncontrolled.
бескорыстный *adj.* disinterested; unselfish.
бескровие *neut.* bloodlessness, anemia.
бескровный *adj.* 1. bloodless, anemic. 2. pallid.
бескрылый *adj.* wingless.
бескультурье *neut.* (*colloq.*) lack of culture.
бесноватый *adj.* raging, raving, frenzied.
бесноваться OVA *impf.* to rage, to rave.
бесовский *adj.* devilish; diabolical.
беспалый *adj.* 1. having no fingers. 2. having no toes.
беспамятный *adj.* forgetful.
беспамятство *neut.* unconsciousness.
беспардонный *adj.* (*colloq.*) unceremonious, impudent, insolent.
беспартийный *adj.* non-party; without a party.
беспатентный *adj.* unlicensed.
бесперебойный *adj.* regular; uninterrupted.
беспересадочный билет *m.* through-ticket.
бесперспективный *adj.* hopeless; without prospects.
беспечный *adj.* careless; unconcerned, care-free.
бесписьменный *adj.* unwritten; with no written language.
беспланный *adj.* unplanned; without a plan.
бесплатный *adj.* free of charge, complimentary.
бесплацкартный *adj.* 1. (*of passenger car on a*

train) unreserved. 2. (*of ticket*) without seat reservation.
бесплодие *neut.* sterility, barrenness.
бесплодность *f.* futility.
бесплодный *adj.* 1. sterile, barren. 2. fruitless. 3. vain.
бесплотный *adj.* incorporeal.
бесповоротный *adj.* irrevocable.
бесподобный *adj.* (*colloq.*) matchless, incomparable.
беспозвоночный *adj.* invertebrate.
беспокоить *impf.* 1. to perturb, to trouble. 2. to disturb, to bother. —ся to worry; to be anxious or uneasy. — не беспокойтесь! Don't worry!
беспокойный *adj.* uneasy, troubled, perturbed.
беспокойство *neut.* 1. worry; anxiety; concern. 2. trouble; bother.
бесполезно *adv.* uselessly.
бесполезный *adj.* useless.
бесполый *adj.* sexless, asexual.
беспомощный *adj.* helpless.
беспорочный *adj.* irreproachable; faultless.
беспорядок FILL *m.* disorder.
беспорядочный *adj.* disorderly.
беспосадочный перелёт *m.* non-stop flight.
беспочвенный *adj.* groundless.
беспошлинный *adj.* duty-free.
беспощадный *adj.* merciless, ruthless.
бесправие *neut.* 1. lawlessness. 2. illegality.
бесправный *adj.* without any rights.
беспредельный *adj.* boundless, infinite.
беспредметный *adj.* pointless, aimless, purposeless.
беспрекословный *adj.* unquestioning.
беспрепятственный *adj.* unimpeded; unhampered.
беспрерывный *adj.* incessant.
беспрестанный *adj.* continuous, incessant.
беспрецедентный *adj.* unprecedented.
бесприбыльный *adj.* unprofitable.
бесприданница *f.* girl without dowry.
беспризорник *m. f.* беспризорница waif; homeless child.
беспризорничать *impf.* to live on the streets.
беспризорный *adj.* neglected; homeless.
беспримерный *adj.* 1. unexampled. 2. unparalleled.
беспринципный *adj.* unprincipled, unscrupulous.
беспристрастный *adj.* impartial, unbiased.
беспричинный *adj.* groundless.
бесприютный *adj.* homeless.
беспробудный *adj.* deep; heavy (*of sleep or state of intoxication*).
беспроволочный *adj.* wireless.
беспроигрышный *adj.* safe; risk-free.
беспросветный *adj.* 1. lightless), dark; black. 2. (*fig.*) cheerless, gloomy.
беспроцентный *adj.* bearing no interest.
беспутный *adj.* dissolute.
бессвязный *adj.* incoherent.
бессемейный *adj.* without a family.
бессемянный *adj.* seedless.
бессердечие *neut.* heartlessness; callousness.
бессердечный *adj.* heartless; callous.
бессилие *neut.* 1. impotence. 2. debility. 3. weakness.
бессильный *adj.* 1. impotent. 2. feeble, weak.

бессистéмный *adj.* unsystematic.
бесслáвие *neut.* ignominy.
бесслáвный *adj.* infamous, ignominious.
бесслéдно *adv.* without a trace.
бессловéсный *adj.* meek.
бессмéнный *adj.* continuous, constant, permanent; uninterrupted.
бессмéртие *neut.* immortality.
бессмéртный *adj.* immortal.
бессмы́сленно *adv.* senselessly.
бессмы́сленный *adj.* senseless, foolish.
бессмы́слица *f.* (*colloq.*) foolishness; nonsense.
бессóвестный *adj.* unscrupulous, dishonest.
бессодержáтельный *adj.* **1.** empty. **2.** insipid, vapid.
бессознáтельный *adj.* unconscious.
бессóнница *f.* insomnia, sleeplessness.
бессóнный *adj.* sleepless.
бесспóрный *adj.* indisputable, unquestionable.
бессрóчный *adj.* indefinite; having no time limit.
бесстрáстный *adj.* impassive.
бесстрáшный *adj.* fearless, intrepid.
бессты́дник *m. f.* **бессты́дница** (*colloq.*) shameless person.
бессты́дный *adj.* shameless.
бессчётный *adj.* innumerable; countless.
бестáктность *f.* tactlessness.
бестáктный *adj.* tactless.
бесталáнный *adj.* untalented; luckless.
бестелéсный *adj.* incorporeal.
бéстия *m. and f.* (*decl. f.*) knave; rogue.
бестолкóвый *adj.* **1.** stupid; slow-witted. **2.** disconnected; incoherent. **3.** confused.
бестсéллер *m.* bestseller.
бесфóрменный *adj.* shapeless, amorphous.
бесхарáктерный *adj.* spineless, weak-willed.
бесхи́тростный *adj.* artless; ingenuous.
бесхóзный *adj.* (*colloq.*) ownerless.
бесхозя́йный *adj.* without an owner.
бесхозя́йственный *adj.* **1.** inefficient. **2.** wasteful. **3.** incompetent.
бесхребéтный *adj.* weak-willed.
бесцвéтный *adj.* colorless, drab.
бесцéльный *adj.* aimless.
бесцéнный *adj.* priceless.
бесцéнок *m.*: **за бесцéнок** for next to nothing.
бесцеремóнный *adj.* unceremonious.
бесчеловéчный *adj.* inhuman; brutal.
бесчéстить *impf.* to disgrace.
бесчéстный *adj.* dishonorable.
бесчи́нство *neut.* outrage.
бесчи́сленный *adj.* innumerable, numberless.
бесчýвственный *adj.* insensible; insensitive; unconscious.
бесчýвствие *neut.* insensibility; insensitivity; unconsciousness.
бесшабáшный *adj.* reckless.
бесшýмный *adj.* noiseless.
бетóн *m.* concrete.
бетóнный *adj.* concrete.
бефстрóганов *m.* beef stroganoff.
бечевá *f.* towrope; towline.
бечёвка *f.* string; twine.
бечеви́к *m.* towpath.
бéшенство *neut.* **1.** hydrophobia, rabies. **2.** fury, rage.

бéшеный *adj.* **1.** rabid, mad. **2.** furious, frenzied.
библéйский *adj.* Biblical.
библиогрáфия *f.* bibliography.
библиотéка *f.* library.
библиотéкарь *m.* librarian.
библиотéчный *adj.* (*attrib.*) library.
Би́блия *f.* Bible.
бивáк *also* **бивуáк** *m.* bivouac.
би́вень FILL *m.* tusk.
бигуди́ *pl.* hair curlers.
бидóн *m.* large can.
биéние *neut.* beating, throbbing, pulsation.
би́знес *m.* business.
бизóн *m.* bison.
билéт *m.* ticket.
билетёр *m.* usher.
билéтный *adj.* (*attrib*) ticket.
би́ло *neut.* **1.** beater. **2.** striking part (*in mechanisms*). **3.** gong.
билья́рд *m.* billiards.
бинáрный *adj.* binary.
бинóкль *m.* binoculars.
бинт *m.* bandage.
бинтовáть OVA *impf.* to bandage.
биогрáфия *f.* biography.
биолóгия *f.* biology.
биопси́я *f.* biopsy.
биофи́зика *f.* biophysics.
биохи́мия *f.* biochemistry.
биплáн *m.* biplane.
би́ржа *f.* exchange.
биржеви́к *m.* trader in stocks.
биржевóй *adj.* (*attrib*) stock; stock market.
би́рка *f.* **1.** name tag. **2.** label; tag; marker. **3.** tally (*notched stick*).
Би́рма *f.* Burma.
бирмáнец FILL *m. f.* **бирмáнка** Burmese.
бирюзá *f.* turquoise.
бирюзóвый *adj.* turquoise.
бирю́к *m.* lone wolf.
бирю́льки *pl.* jackstraws.
би́сер *m.* beads.
би́серина *f.* bead.
би́серный *adj.* beaded.
биси́ровать OVA *impf. and pf.* **1.** to repeat. **2.** to play encores.
бискви́т *m.* sponge cake.
би́тва *f.* battle.
биткóм набúт packed; filled to capacity.
битóк FILL *m.* **1.** mallet; club. **2.** beef cutlet, rissole.
битýм *m.* bitumen.
би́тый *adj.* **1.** beaten; whipped. **2.** broken.
бить *impf.* **1.** to beat, to hit. **2.** to kill. **3.** to break.
битьё *neut.* beating; smashing.
бифштéкс *m.* steak; beefsteak.
би́цепс *m.* biceps.
бич *m.* whip, lash.
бичевáние *neut.* flagellation.
бичевáть *impf.* **1.** to whip, to lash, to flagellate. **2.** to castigate.
Бишкéк *m.* Bishkek (*formerly: Frunze*).
бишь *particle* (*colloq., used when one forgets something*): **как бишь егó зовýт?** What was his name again?

бла́го *neut.* blessing, boon.
Благове́щение *neut.* Annunciation.
благови́дный *adj.* seemly.
благоволе́ние *neut.* goodwill; kindness.
благовоспи́танный *adj.* **1.** well-bred. **2.** polite, courteous, civil.
благогове́йный *adj.* reverent; reverential.
благогове́ние *neut.* reverence; awe; veneration.
благодаре́ние *neut.* thanksgiving.
благодари́ть *impf.* to thank.
благода́рность *f.* gratitude; thanks. — **не сто́ит благода́рности** Don't mention it.
благода́рный *adj.* grateful, thankful; gratifying.
благодаря́ *prep.* (*with dat.*) thanks to; owing to.
благода́тный *adj.* **1.** bringing joy. **2.** fertile; abundant. **3.** beneficial.
благода́ть *f.* **1.** abundance. **2.** grace. **3.** blessing.
благоде́нствие *neut.* (*obs.*) prosperity.
благоде́тель *m. f.* —**ница** benefactor.
благоде́тельный *adj.* beneficial.
благодея́ние *neut.* good deed.
благоду́шный *adj.* **1.** complacent; placid. **2.** good-natured; good-humored.
благожела́тельный *adj.* kindly, kind; benevolent; kindly disposed.
благозву́чие *neut.* euphony.
благозву́чный *adj.* harmonious; euphonious; melodious.
благо́й *adj.* good, useful.
благоле́пие *neut.* splendor, grandeur.
благонадёжный *adj.* trustworthy.
благообра́зный *adj.* good-looking; handsome.
благополу́чие *neut.* welfare; well-being.
благоприпя́тствовать OVA *impf.* (*with dat.*) to favor; to be advantageous to.
благоприя́тный *adj.* favorable; propitious; auspicious.
благоразу́мие *neut.* sense, wisdom, prudence.
благоразу́мный *adj.* **1.** sensible, reasonable. **2.** judicious, wise, prudent.
благоро́дный *adj.* noble.
благоро́дство *neut.* nobility.
благоскло́нный *adj.* favorable.
благослове́ние *neut.* blessing(s).
благословля́ть *impf. pf.* **благослови́ть** to bless, to give one's blessings.
благосостоя́ние *neut.* welfare; well-being.
бла́гостный *adj.* **1.** serene. **2.** lovely.
благотвори́тель *m. f.* —**ница** philanthropist.
благотвори́тельность *f.* philanthropy, charity.
благоустро́енный *adj.* **1.** equipped with all modern conveniences. **2.** well-designed.
благоустро́йство *neut.* welfare; providing of public amenities.
благоуха́ние *neut.* fragrance; aroma.
благоуха́ть *impf.* to smell sweet; to be fragrant.
благочести́е *neut.* piety.
блаже́нный *adj.* **1.** blessed. **2.** blissful. **3.** eccentric.
блаже́нство *neut.* bliss, felicity, beatitude.
блажь *f.* (*colloq.*) fancy; whim.
бланк *m.* blank; form.
бланширова́ть OVA *impf.* (*tech.*) to blanch.
блат *m.* **1.** thieves' jargon. **2.** pull; connections.
блатно́й *adj.* thieves'.
бледне́ть *impf.* to pale, to turn pale.
бле́дность *f.* pallor.

бле́дный *adj.* pale, pallid; colorless.
блёклый *adj.* faded.
блёкнуть *impf. pf.* **по- 1.** to fade. **2.** to wither.
блеск *m.* brilliance, luster.
блесна́ *f.* spoon bait.
блесну́ть *pf.* to flash.
блесте́ть *impf.* **1.** to shine, to glitter. **2.** to sparkle.
блёстки *pl.* **1.** spangles; sequins. **2.** flashes (*of wit*).
блестя́щий *adj.* brilliant.
блеф *m.* bluff.
блея́ние *m.* bleating.
бле́ять *impf.* to bleat.
ближа́йший *adj.* **1.** nearest. **2.** next, immediate.
бли́же *adv.* nearer, closer; more intimate.
бли́жний *adj.* neighboring. — *m.* neighbor, fellow.
близ *prep.* (*with gen.*) near, close to.
бли́зиться *impf.* to approach, to draw near.
бли́зкий *adj.* **1.** near; imminent. **2.** like, similar; intimate.
бли́зко *adv.* near, close.
близлежа́щий *adv.* neighboring, nearby.
близне́ц *m.* twin.
близору́кий *adj.* **1.** near-sighted. **2.** (*fig.*) short-sighted.
близору́кость *f.* nearsightedness, myopia.
бли́зость *f.* **1.** nearness. **2.** proximity; propinquity.
блик *m.* patch of light.
блин *m.* pancake.
блинда́ж *m.* (*mil.*) bunker; dugout.
бли́нчик *m.* small pancake.
блиста́тельный *adj.* brilliant, resplendent; splendid.
блиста́ть *impf.* **1.** to shine. **2.** to be conspicuous.
блиц *m.* flash bulb.
блок *m.* (*tech.*) pulley.
блока́да *f.* blockade.
блоки́ровать OVA *impf. and pf.* to blockade.
блокно́т *m.* notebook; writing pad.
блонди́н *m.* blond. —**ка** *f.* blond(e).
блоха́ *f.* flea.
блёшки *pl.* tiddlywinks.
блуд *m.* lechery. —**ли́вый** *adj.* lascivious.
блуди́ть *impf.* to lecher, to fornicate.
блу́дный сын *m.* prodigal son.
блужда́ть *impf.* to roam, to wander.
блу́за *also* **блу́зка** *f.* blouse.
блю́до *neut.* dish; course.
блю́дце *neut.* saucer.
блюз *m.* (*mus.*) blues.
блюсти́ *impf.* **1.** to maintain, to observe. **2.** to guard, to protect.
блюсти́тель *m. f.* —**ница** observer.
бля́ха *f.* **1.** badge. **2.** name plate.
боа́ *m.* boa constrictor.
боб *m.* bean.
бобёр *m.* beaver.
бобо́вый *adj.* (*attrib.*) bean, leguminous.
бобр *m.* beaver.
бо́брик *m.* (*cloth*) castor.
бобро́вый *adj.* (*attrib.*) beaver.
бобсле́й *m.* bobsled.
Бове́ *m.* Beauvais.
Бог *m.* God.
богаде́льня *f.* almshouse; poorhouse.

богате́ть *impf.* to grow rich.
бога́то *adv.* richly.
бога́тство *neut.* wealth; riches.
бога́тый *adj.* rich; wealthy.
богаты́рь *m.* bogatyr (*hero in Russian folklore*); (*fig.*) hero; Hercules.
бога́ч *m.* rich man.
бога́че *adj. comp. of* бога́тый.
боге́ма *f.* **1.** (*fig.*) Bohemia. **2.** (*colloq.*) Bohemian way of life.
Боге́мия *f.* (*geog.*) Bohemia.
боги́ня *f.* goddess.
богобоя́зненный *adj.* god-fearing.
Богома́терь *f.* Mother of God; the Virgin Mary.
богомо́л *m.* praying mantis.
богомо́лец FILL *m.* *f.* богомо́лка **1.** devout person. **2.** pilgrim.
Богоро́дица *f.* Mother of God; the Virgin Mary.
богосло́в *m.* theologian.
богосло́вие *neut.* theology.
богосло́вский *adj.* theological.
богослуже́ние *neut.* religious service.
боготвори́ть *impf.* to worship; to idolize.
богоху́льство *neut.* blasphemy.
Богоявле́ние *neut.* Epiphany.
бода́ть *impf.* to butt.
Бо́дензее *m.* (*lake*) Lake Constance; Bodensee.
бодли́вый *adj.* (*of animal*) that butts a lot.
бо́дрость *f.* **1.** energy; vigor. **2.** cheerfulness.
бо́дрый *adj.* **1.** brisk. **2.** cheerful.
бодря́щий *adj.* invigorating.
боеви́к *m.* (*colloq.*) action movie.
боеви́тость *f.* fighting spirit.
боево́й *adj.* (*attrib.*) **1.** battle; combat. **2.** militant. **3.** urgent.
боеголо́вка *f.* warhead.
боегото́вность *f.* combat readiness.
боеприпа́сы *pl.* ammunition.
боеспосо́бность *f.* (*mil.*) fighting efficiency.
бое́ц FILL *m.* fighter, warrior.
бо́же *interj.* *vocative case of* Бог God!
боже́ственный *adj.* divine.
божество́ *neut.* deity; idol.
божи́ться *impf. pf.* по- to swear.
божо́к FILL *m.* idol.
бой *m.* battle, combat.
бо́йкий *adj.* **1.** brisk; lively; animated. **2.** clever. **3.** glib.
бойко́т *m.* boycott.
бойни́ца *f.* embrasure.
бо́йня *f.* slaughterhouse.
бок *m.* side. — бок о́ бок side by side, shoulder to shoulder. — с бо́ку на́ бок from side to side.
бока́л *m.* glass; wineglass; goblet.
боково́й *adj.* lateral; side.
бо́ком *adv.* sideways.
бокс *m.* boxing.
боксёр *m.* boxer.
бокси́ровать OVA *impf.* to box.
бокси́т *m.* bauxite.
болва́н *m.* **1.** (*colloq.*) blockhead, dummy. **2.** (*cards*) dummy.
Болга́рия *f.* Bulgaria.
бо́лее *adv.* more. — бо́лее и́ли ме́нее more or less. — тем бо́лее, что the more so, since.

боле́зненно *adv.* **1.** painfully. **2.** hard, with difficulty.
боле́зненность *f.* sickliness.
боле́зненный *adj.* **1.** ailing, sickly. **2.** morbid.
боле́знь *f.* illness, disease, ailment.
боле́знь Альцге́ймера *f.* Alzheimer's disease.
боле́льщик *m.* *f.* боле́льщица (*sports*) fan.
бо́лен *adj.* short form for больно́й.
боле́ть[1] *impf. pres.* боле́ю, боле́ешь to be ill.
боле́ть[2] *impf. pres.* боли́т, боля́т to ache, to hurt.
болеутоля́ющий *adj.* analgesic, pain-relieving.
Боли́вия *f.* Bolivia.
болиголо́в *m.* (*bot.*) hemlock (*poisonous*).
боли́д *m.* fireball, meteor.
боло́нка *f.* Maltese dog.
Боло́нья *f.* Bologna.
боло́тистый *adj.* swampy, marshy.
боло́то *neut.* swamp, marsh, bog.
болта́нка *f.* (*colloq.*) air turbulence.
болта́ть[1] *impf.* (*colloq.*) to talk, to chatter.
болта́ть[2] *impf.* to stir; to shake.
болта́ться *impf.* **1.** to dangle, to swing. **2.** (*colloq.*) to hang around, to loaf.
болтли́вый *adj.* talkative, garrulous.
болтовня́ *f.* chatter, gossip.
болтоло́гия *f.* (*colloq.*) doubletalk, babble.
болту́н *m.* *f.* болту́нья chatterbox.
болту́нья *f.* scrambled eggs.
боль *f.* pain, ache.
больни́ца *f.* hospital.
бо́льно *adv.* **1.** painfully. **2.** badly. — *impers.* it is painful.
больно́й *adj.* sick, ill, diseased. — *m.* *f.* больна́я patient, sick person.
бо́льше *adj.* bigger, larger, greater. — *adv.* more.
большеви́к *m.* *f.* большеви́чка Bolshevik.
большеви́стский *adj.* (*attrib.*) Bolshevik.
большеголо́в *m.* (*fish*) orange roughy.
бо́льший *adj.* (*comp. of* большо́й *and* вели́кий.) larger; greater.
большинство́ *neut.* majority.
большо́й *adj.* big, large, great. — большо́й па́лец *m.* thumb; large toe. — Большо́е (вам) спаси́бо! Thank you very much!
большу́щий *adj.* (*colloq.*) huge.
боля́чка *f.* (*colloq.*) sore, scab.
бо́мба *f.* **1.** bomb. **2.** (*colloq.*) three-quarter liter bottle of wine.
бомбарди́р *m.* bombardier.
бомбардирова́ть OVA *impf.* to bomb, to bombard.
бомбардиро́вка *f.* bombing.
бомбардиро́вщик *m.* bomber.
бомбёжка *f.* (*colloq.*) bombing.
Бомбе́й *m.* Mumbai (*formerly: Bombay*).
бомби́ть *impf.* (*colloq.*) to bomb.
бомбомета́ние *neut.* bombing.
бомбоубе́жище *neut.* air-raid shelter, bomb shelter.
бомж *m.* (*abbr. of* без определённого ме́ста жи́тельства) vagrant; bum; drifter.
бо́ндарь *m.* cooper.
бо́нза *m.* (*decl.*) (*colloq.*) bigwig, superior (*person*).
Бонн *m.* Bonn.
бор[1] *m.* coniferous forest.
бор[2] *m.* boron.

бордéль *m.* (*colloq.*) brothel, bordello.
Бордó *m.* Bordeaux.
бордó *neut.* (*wine*) claret.
бордю́р *m.* (*on cloth*) trimming, border.
борéц FILL *m.* **1.** fighter. **2.** wrestler.
борзáя *f.* borzoi; Russian greyhound.
бóрзый *adj.* (*obs.* or *poet.*) fleet, swift.
Борисоглéбск *m.* Borisoglebsk.
бормашúна *f.* drill (*used by dentist*).
бормотáние *neut.* rumbling; muttering.
бормотáть *impf.* to mutter, to mumble.
бормоту́ха *f.* (*colloq.*) any cheap and strong wine of low quality.
бóрная кислотá *f.* boric acid.
бóров *m.* **1.** gelded hog. **2.** (*tech.*) chimney flue.
бородá *f.* beard.
бородáвка *f.* wart.
бородáвочник *m.* wart hog.
бородáтый *adj.* bearded.
бородáч *m.* **1.** (*bird*) bearded vulture. **2.** (*colloq.*) bearded man.
бороздá *f.* **1.** furrow. **2.** (*anat.*) fissure.
бороздúть *impf.* **1.** to furrow. **2.** to wrinkle.
боронá *f.* harrow.
борóться *impf.* to fight, to struggle, to contend.
борт *m.* **1.** side (*of a ship*). — за бортóм (*past.*) overboard. **2.** breast (*of a coat*). **3.** (*billiards*) cushion.
бортмехáник *m.* flight engineer.
бортовóй *adj.* on-board.
бортпроводнúк *m.* steward.
бортпроводнúца *f.* stewardess.
борщ *m.* borscht.
борьбá *f.* **1.** struggle, fight. **2.** wrestling.
босикóм *adv.* barefoot.
Бóсния *f.* Bosnia.
босóй *adj.* **1.** barefoot. **2.** (*of feet*) bare.
босонóгий *adj.* barefoot.
босонóжки *pl.* sandals, mules.
босс *m.* boss, political boss.
бося́к *m.* tramp, hobo, vagabond.
бот *m.* boat.
ботáник *m.* botanist.
ботáника *f.* botany.
ботанúческий *adj.* botanical.
ботвá *f.* leafy tops of vegetables.
ботвúнья *f.* cold soup made of fish, cooked vegetables, and kvass.
ботéль *m.* boatel, ship used as a hotel.
бóтик[1] *m.* small boat.
бóтик[2] *m.* high rubber overshoe.
ботúнки *pl.* boots.
ботфóрты *pl.* (*obs.*) jack-boots.
бóцман *m.* boatswain.
бочáр *m.* cooper.
бóчка *f.* barrel, cask.
бочкóм *adv.* sideways.
бочóнок FILL *m.* keg, small barrel.
боязлúвый *adj.* timid, fearful.
боя́зно *adj.* (*pred.*) (*with dat.*) afraid.
боя́знь *f.* dread, fear.
боя́рин *m.* boyar.
боя́рский *adj.* (*attrib.*) boyar, boyars'.
боя́рышник *m.* (*bot.*) hawthorn.
боя́ться *impf.* (*with gen.*) to fear, to be afraid (of).
бра *neut. indecl.* sconce; lamp or candle bracket.

бравáда *f.* bravado.
бравúровать OVA *impf.* **1.** to brave, to defy. **2.** to flaunt.
брáво *interj.* bravo!
брав́урный *adj.* (*of music*) stirring, rousing.
брáвый *adj.* dashing, gallant.
брáга *f.* home-brew, home-brewed beer.
брáжник *m.* (*obs.*) reveller, carouser.
Брáйль *m.* (*alphabet*) Braille.
брак[1] *m.* marriage.
брак[2] *m.* **1.** defect, flaw. **2.** defective merchandise.
бракóванный *adj.* **1.** rejected. **2.** defective.
браковáть OVA *impf. pf.* **за-** to reject as defective.
бракóвщик *m.* quality control inspector.
бракодéл *m.* sloppy worker, slipshod worker.
браконьéр *m.* poacher.
браконьéрство *neut.* poaching.
бракоразвóдный *adj.* (*attrib.*) divorce.
бракосочетáние *neut.* marriage; nuptials.
брамúн *m.* Brahman.
брáмсель *m.* topsail.
брандспóйт *m.* nozzle of a fire hose.
бранúть *impf.* to scold, to reprove, to rebuke.
брáнный *adj.* abusive; scolding.
бранчлúвый *adj.* quarrelsome.
брань *f.* profanity, swearing.
браслéт *m.* bracelet.
брасс *m.* breast stroke.
братáние *neut.* fraternization.
братáться *impf.* to fraternize.
брáтец FILL *m.* **1.** *dim. of* **брат. 2.** old fellow, old man.
Братислáва *f.* Bratislava.
братúшка *m.* (*decl. f.*) *dim. of* **брат**.
брáтия *f.* fraternity, brotherhood.
братоубúйство *neut.* fratricide.
Братск *m.* Bratsk.
брáтский *adj.* brotherly, fraternal.
брáтство *neut.* fraternity, brotherhood.
брать *impf. pf.* **взять 1.** to take. **2.** to seize. **3.** to buy, to get. **4.** to charge (*a price*). **5.** to clear (*a hurdle*).
брáться *impf. pf.* **взя́ться 1.** to take hold of, to grasp. **2.** (за *with acc.*) to begin, to take up. **3.** (*with infin.*) to undertake.
брахмáн *m.* Brahman.
брáчный *adj.* matrimonial, marital, conjugal.
брáшпиль *m.* windlass; capstan.
бревéнчатый *adj.* made of logs.
бревнó *neut.* log.
бред *m.* delirium, ravings.
брéдень FILL *m.* dragnet.
брéдить *impf.* to be delirious or mad; to rave.
брéдни *pl.* **1.** ravings; nonsense. **2.** delirium.
бредовóй *also* бредóвый *adj.* delirious, nonsensical.
брéзгать *impf. pf.* **по- 1.** to be squeamish. **2.** to have an aversion to.
брезглúвый *adj.* squeamish; fastidious.
брезéнт *m.* tarpaulin.
брéзжить *impf.* **1.** to glimmer, to gleam faintly. **2.** to dawn.
брейк-дáнс *m.* break dancing.
брелóк *m.* **1.** charm (*on a bracelet*). **2.** key ring.

бре́мя *neut.* burden, load.

бре́нный *adj.* (*obs.*) perishable; transitory.

бренча́ть *impf.* to jingle, to clink; to strum (*on an instrument*).

брести́ *impf.* to shuffle along, to amble; to stroll pensively.

Брета́нь *f.* (*province*) Bretagne.

брете́лька *f.* strap, shoulder strap.

бреха́ть *impf. pf.* брехну́ть (*colloq.*) **1.** to yelp, to bark. **2.** to tell lies.

бреху́н *m. f.* —ья́ (*colloq.*) liar.

брешь *f.* breach; gap.

бре́ющий полёт *m.* low-altitude flight.

брига́да *f.* **1.** brigade. **2.** team, crew.

бридж *m.* (*cards*) bridge.

бри́джи *pl.* breeches.

бриз *m.* breeze.

брике́т *m.* briquette.

бриллиа́нт *m.* diamond. —овый *adj.* diamond (*attrib.*).

Брита́нская Колу́мбия *f.* British Columbia.

бри́тва *f.* razor.

бри́твенный *adj.* shaving.

бритоголо́вый (подро́сток) *adj.* skinhead, neofascist youth.

бри́тый *adj.* shaved; clean-shaven.

брить *impf. v.t.* to shave.

бритьё *neut.* shaving.

бри́чка *f.* (*obs.*) light carriage.

бровь *f.* eyebrow, brow.

брод *m.* ford.

броди́льный *adj.* fermenting, fermentative.

броди́ть *impf.* **1.** to wander, to roam, to rove. **2.** to ferment.

бродя́га *m. f.* бродя́жка tramp, vagrant, hobo.

бродя́жничать *impf.* **1.** to live on the streets. **2.** to roam.

бродя́жничество *neut.* **1.** vagrancy. **2.** wandering.

бродя́чий *adj.* vagrant; itinerant.

броже́ние *neut.* **1.** fermentation; ferment. **2.** discontent.

бро́кколи *pl. indecl.* broccoli.

бром *m.* bromine.

бронеавтомоби́ль *m.* armored car.

бронебо́йный *adj.* armor-piercing.

броневи́к *m.* armored car.

бронево́й *adj.* armored.

бронено́сец FILL *m.* **1.** battleship. **2.** armadillo.

бронепо́езд *m.* armored train.

бронета́нковый *adj.* armored.

бронетранспортёр *m.* armored personnel carrier.

бро́нза *f.* bronze.

бро́нзовый *adj.* made of bronze; bronze.

брониро́ванный *adj.* armored.

брони́ровать OVA *impf. and pf.* to reserve.

бронтоза́вр *m.* brontosaurus.

бро́нхи *pl.* bronchi.

бронхи́т *m.* bronchitis.

бро́ня *f.* reservation (*advance booking*).

броня́ *f.* armor, armor plating.

броса́ть *impf. pf.* бро́сить to throw, to hurl, to fling. —ся **1.** to throw oneself. **2.** to rush.

бросо́к FILL *m.* throw, heave.

бро́шенный *adj.* **1.** thrown, hurled. **2.** abandoned, deserted.

брошь *f.* brooch.

брошю́ра *f.* booklet, brochure, pamphlet.

брус *m.* beam. — бру́сья *pl.* (*sports*) bars; parallel bars.

брусни́ка *f.* cowberries.

брусо́к FILL *m.* **1.** bar; ingot. **2.** whetstone.

бру́ствер *m.* parapet; breastwork.

брусча́тка *f.* paving stones.

бру́тто *adv., adj. indecl.* gross.

брыжи́ *pl.* (*obs.*) frilled collar.

бры́згать *impf. pf.* бры́знуть **1.** to splash. **2.** to spatter, to sprinkle.

бры́зги *pl.* **1.** spray. **2.** splash. **3.** sparks.

брыка́ть *impf. pf.* брыкну́ть to kick.

бры́нза *f.* brynza (*sheep's milk cheese*).

брюзга́ *m. and f.* (*decl. f.*) grouch.

брюзгли́вый *adj.* peevish, grumbling.

брюзжа́ть *impf.* to grumble.

брю́ква *f.* rutabaga.

брю́ки *pl.* trousers, pants; breeches.

брюне́т *m. f.* —ка brunette.

Брюссе́ль *m.* Brussels.

брю́хо *neut.* abdomen, belly.

брюши́на *f.* peritoneum.

брюшко́ *neut.* potbelly; paunch.

брюшно́й *adj.* abdominal.

бря́кать *impf. pf.* бря́кнуть **1.** to clatter; to clang; to rattle. **2.** to let fall with a bang. **3.** (*colloq.*) to blurt out.

Бря́нск *m.* Bryansk.

бря́цать *impf.* **1.** to rattle; to clang; to clank. **2.** to jingle; to jangle.

бубенцы́ *pl.* little bells; sleigh bells.

бу́блик *m.* bagel; bublik (*thick, ring-shaped bread roll*).

бубни́ть *impf. pf.* про- to mumble; to mutter.

бубно́вый *adj.* (*cards*) of diamonds.

бу́бны *pl.* (*cards*) diamonds.

буго́р FILL *m.* **1.** knoll; mound. **2.** lump; bump.

бугоро́к FILL *m. dim. of* буго́р.

буго́рчатый *adj.* covered with lumps.

бугри́стый *adj.* bumpy.

Будапе́шт *m.* Budapest.

будди́зм *m.* Buddhism.

бу́дет *3rd person sing. of* быть. — Бу́дет тебе́! *interj.* That will do!; enough!

буди́льник *m.* alarm clock.

буди́ть *impf.* **1.** to wake, to awaken. **2.** to arouse, to provoke.

бу́дка *f.* **1.** box, booth, stall. **2.** cabin. — соба́чья бу́дка dog-house.

бу́дни *pl.* weekdays. —чный *adj.* everyday, humdrum, prosaic. — бу́дничный день weekday.

бу́дний день *m.* weekday.

будора́жить *impf. pf.* вз- (*colloq.*) to rouse; to excite; to stir up.

бу́дто *conj., particle* as if, as though.

будуа́р *m.* boudoir.

бу́дучи *verbal adverb of* быть being.

бу́дущее *neut.* future.

бу́дущий *adj.* future.

бу́дущность *f.* future.

будь *imperative of* быть.

буже́нина *f.* boiled, salted pork.

бузина́ *f.* elder (*shrub*).

буй *m.* buoy.

бу́йвол *m.* buffalo.

бу́йный *adj.* **1.** violent. **2.** lush, thick.
бу́йство *neut.* uproar.
бу́йствовать OVA *impf.* to behave violently.
бук *m.* beech.
бу́ка *f.* (*colloq.*) bogy.
бука́шка *f.* bug; insect.
бу́ква *f.* letter (*of the alphabet*).
буква́льный *adj.* literal.
буква́рь *m.* primer.
буквое́д *m.* pedant.
буке́т *m.* bouquet.
букини́ст *m.* secondhand bookseller.
букле́т *m.* booklet.
букме́кер *m.* bookmaker.
бу́ковый *adj.* (*attrib.*) beech.
букси́р *m.* tug, tugboat.
букси́ровать OVA *impf.* to tow.
букси́ровка *f.* towing.
буксова́ть OVA *impf.* (*of wheels*) to spin around (*without effect*).
булава́ *f.* (*weapon*) mace.
була́вка *f.* pin.
бу́лка *f.* roll, bun.
бу́лочка *f.* small bun; small roll.
бу́лочная *f.* bakery.
бу́лочник *m. f.* **бу́лочница** baker.
булты́х *interj.* (*colloq.*) splash!; plop!
булы́жник *m.* cobble, cobblestone.
бульва́р *m.* boulevard, avenue.
бульва́рный *adj.* boulevard.
бульдо́г *m.* bulldog.
бульдо́зер *m.* bulldozer.
бу́льканье *neut.* gurgling.
бу́лькать *impf.* to gurgle.
бульо́н *m.* broth.
бум *m.* boom.
бума́га *f.* paper.
бума́жка *f.* piece of paper.
бума́жник *m.* wallet, pocketbook.
бума́жный *adj.* (*attrib.*) paper.
бумера́нг *m.* boomerang.
бу́нкер *m.* bunker.
бунт *m.* riot, mutiny, revolt.
бунта́рский *adj.* rebellious.
бунта́рь *m. f.* **бунта́рка** (*obs.*) rebel.
бунтова́ть OVA *impf.* to rebel, to revolt.
бунтовщи́к *m. f.* **бунтовщи́ца** rebel, insurgent, mutineer, rioter.
бур¹ *m.* auger; drill.
бур² *m.* Boer.
бура́ *f.* borax.
бура́в *m.* auger; gimlet.
бура́вить *impf.* (*tech.*) to drill, to perforate.
бура́вчик *m.* auger; gimlet.
бура́к *m.* (*colloq.*) beet.
бура́н *m.* snowstorm.
бургоми́стр *m.* burgomaster.
бурда́ *f.* (*colloq.*) slop.
бурдю́к *m.* wineskin.
буреве́стник *m.* (*bird*) petrel; stormy petrel.
буело́м *m.* fallen trees; storm-damaged trees.
буре́ние *neut.* boring, drilling.
буре́ть *impf. pf.* **по-** to turn brown; to become brown.
буржуа́ *m. and f. indecl.* bourgeois.
буржуази́я *f.* bourgeoisie.

буржуа́зный *adj.* bourgeois.
бури́льный *adj.* drilling.
бури́ть *impf.* to bore; to drill.
бу́ркать *impf. pf.* **бу́ркнуть** to mutter; to growl.
бурла́к *m.* bargeman.
бурле́ск *m.* burlesque.
бурли́вый *adj.* turbulent.
бурли́ть *impf.* to seethe.
бу́рный *adj.* **1.** stormy. **2.** impetuous. **3.** violent.
бурово́й *adj.* drilling.
бурунду́к *m.* chipmunk.
бурча́ть *impf. pf.* **про-** **1.** to mutter; to mumble. **2.** (*of stomach*) to rumble; to growl.
бу́рый *adj.* brown.
бурья́н *m.* tall weeds.
бу́ря *f.* storm, tempest, gale.
буря́т *m. f.* **—ка** Buryat.
Буря́тия *f.* Buryatia.
бу́сина *f.* bead.
буссо́ль *f.* surveyor's compass.
бу́сы *pl.* beads.
бута́н *m.* butane.
бутафо́рия *f.* (*theat.*) stage props; flats.
бути́л *m.* butyl.
бутиле́н *m.* butylene.
буто́н *m.* bud.
бутонье́рка *f.* boutonniere.
буту́з *m.* (*colloq.*) roly-poly child.
буты́лка *f.* bottle.
буты́лочный *adj.* (*attrib.*) bottle; bottled.
буты́ль *f.* large bottle.
буфе́т *m.* **1.** sideboard, buffet. **2.** canteen, refreshment bar.
буфе́тчик *m. f.* **буфе́тчица** **1.** person who works at a counter. **2.** barman; bartender.
буффо́н *m.* buffoon.
буха́нка *f.* loaf of bread.
Бухара́ *f.* Bukhoro (*formerly: Bukhara*).
Бухаре́ст *m.* Bucharest.
бу́хать *impf.* (*colloq.*) to bang; to slam.
бухга́лтер *m.* bookkeeper, accountant.
бухгалте́рия *f.* **1.** accounting; bookkeeping. **2.** accounting department.
бу́хнуть *impf. pf.* **раз-** to swell; to swell up.
бу́хта *f.* **1.** (*geog.*) bay. **2.** (*rope*) coil.
бу́хточка *f.* inlet; cove.
бушева́ть *impf.* **1.** to rage, to storm. **2.** to create an uproar.
бушла́т *m.* pea jacket.
бушпри́т *m.* bowsprit.
буя́н *m.* roughneck; ruffian.
буя́нить *impf.* to run wild; to run amuck.
бы *particle used with verbs to form the subjunctive or conditional mood.*
быва́ло *particle* (*colloq.*) would often.
быва́лый *adj.* **1.** former; bygone. **2.** worldly-wise; experienced.
быва́ть *impf.* **1.** to be from time to time. **2.** to frequent. **3.** to happen. **4.** to be held, to take place.
бы́вший *adj.* **1.** former, one-time. **2.** late.
Бы́дгощ *m.* Bydgoszcz.
бык *m.* **1.** bull, ox. **2.** abutment, pier.
были́на *f.* bylina (*Russian traditional heroic epic*).
были́нка *f.* blade of grass.
бы́ло *particle* (*without stress*) **1.** *expresses sudden*

end to an action that has just begun **он поéхал было, но заболéл** He was on the point of going, but fell ill. **2.** expresses cancelling an action that one is about to begin, often with a change of mind **он отпрáвился было с нáми, но вернýлся** He would have started out with us, but he turned back. **3. чуть бы́ло не** very nearly; practically; almost.

былóе neut. the past.

былóй adj. former, bygone, past.

быль f. fact; true story.

быльё neut. (obs.) weeds.

бы́стро adv. quickly; rapidly; fast.

быстронóгий adj. swift-footed, fleet-footed.

быстрораствори́мый adj. dissolving quickly; (of coffee, etc.) instant.

быстротá f. quickness, rapidity, speed.

быстрохóдный adj. high-speed.

бы́стрый adj. quick, rapid, swift.

быт m. (no plural) **1.** way of life; life. **2.** daily life.

бытиé neut. being, existence.

бытовáть OVA impf. **1.** to exist. **2.** to occur; to be current.

бытовóй adj. social.

быть impf. to be.

бычáчий also **бы́чий** adj. (attrib.) ox; bovine.

бычóк FILL m. young ox, young bull.

бювáр m. letter case.

бюджéт m. budget.

бюллетéнь m. bulletin, report. — **избирáтельный бюллетéнь** ballot.

бю́ргер m. burgher.

бюрó neut. indecl. office.

бюрокрáт m. bureaucrat.

бюрократи́зм m. bureaucracy.

бюрокрáтия f. bureaucracy.

бюст m. bust.

бюстгáльтер m. brassiere.

бязь f. heavy cloth.

В

в *also* **во** *prep.* **1.** (*with acc.*) (*dir.*) in, into, to. **2.** (*with prep.*) (*loc.*) in, at.

ва-ба́нк *adv.:* **идти́ ва-ба́нк** *imp.* to go for broke.

ва́га *f.* **1.** weighing machine. **2.** lever. **3.** crowbar.

ваго́н *m.* **1.** carriage; coach. **2.** car.

ваго́нный *adj.* (*attrib.*) wagon; car.

вагоновожа́тый *m.* motorman (*on a streetcar*).

важне́йший *adj.* paramount; most important.

ва́жничать *impf.* to put on airs.

ва́жно *adv.* with an air of importance; grandly.

ва́жность *f.* importance; significance.

ва́жный *adj.* important; significant.

ва́за *f.* **1.** vase. **2.** bowl.

вазели́н *m.* Vaseline.

вазо́н *m.* flowerpot.

Вайо́минг *m.* Wyoming.

вака́нсия *f.* vacancy.

ва́кса *f.* shoe polish.

вакуо́ль *f.* vacuole.

ва́куум *m.* vacuum.

вакци́на *f.* vaccine.

вакцини́ровать OVA *impf.* to vaccinate.

вал *m.* **1.** (*naut.*) billow, roller. **2.** bank, rampart.

вале́жник *m.* windfallen tree branches.

валёк *m.* roller.

ва́ленок FILL *m.* felt boot.

вале́нтность *f.* valence.

валерья́на *also* **валериа́на** *f.* valerian.

вале́т *m.* (*cards*) jack.

ва́лик *m.* roller.

вали́ть *impf. pf.* **по-** to overturn, to knock down, to fell.

ва́лка *f.* chopping down (*of trees*).

ва́лкий *adj.* unsteady; wobbly.

валово́й *adj.* gross.

валто́рна *f.* French horn.

валу́н *m.* boulder.

ва́льдшнеп *m.* woodcock.

вальс *m.* waltz.

вальси́ровать OVA *impf.* to waltz.

вальцева́ть OVA *impf.* to roll (*metal*); to mill (*metal*).

вальцо́вка *f.* rolling.

Вальядоли́д *m.* Valladolid.

валю́та *f.* currency.

валю́тный *adj.* currency.

валя́льщик *m.* fuller.

ва́ляный *adj.* made of felt.

валя́ть *impf.* **1.** *impf. only* to drag. **2.** *pf.* **по-** to drag along. **3.** to roll (*in breadcrumbs*). — **валя́ть дурака́** to play the fool.

валя́ться *impf.* **1.** *pf.* **по-** to roll; to wallow. **2.** *impf. only* to lie scattered about. **3.** to lounge around; to lie around.

вам *pron., dat. pl. of* **вы.**

ва́ми *pron., instr. pl. of* **вы.**

вампи́р *m.* vampire.

вана́дий *m.* vanadium.

вани́ль *f.* vanilla. **—ный** *adj.* (*attrib.*) vanilla.

ва́нна *f.* **1.** bath. **2.** bathtub.

ва́нная *also* **ва́нная ко́мната** *f.* bathroom.

ва́нька-вста́нька *m.* (*decl. f.*) self-righting doll.

вар *m.* pitch; cobbler's wax.

Вара́ждин *m.* Varadin.

вара́н *m.* monitor lizard.

ва́рвар *m. f.* **—ка** barbarian. **—ский** *adj.* barbaric.

варе́жка *f.* mitten.

варене́ц FILL *m.* fermented boiled milk.

варе́ние *neut.* boiling.

варе́ник *m.* curd *or* fruit dumpling.

варёный *adj.* boiled.

варе́нье *neut.* jam.

вариа́нт *m.* version; alternative.

вариа́ция *f.* variation.

варико́зный *adj.* varicose.

вари́ть *impf. pf.* **с-** **1.** to boil; to cook. **2.** to brew.

ва́рка *f.* boiling.

Варша́ва *f.* Warsaw (*Polish: Warszawa*).

варьете́ *neut. indecl.* variety show.

варьи́ровать OVA *impf.* to vary; to modify.

варя́г *m.* Varangian.

вас *pron., gen., acc., prep. of* **вы.**

василёк FILL *m.* cornflower.

васса́л *m.* vassal.

ва́та *f.* cotton.

вата́га *f.* (*colloq.*) gang; band; crowd.

ватерли́ния *f.* waterline.

Ватерло́о *m.* Waterloo.

ватерпа́с *m.* spirit level.

ватерпо́ло *neut. indecl.* water polo.

ва́тин *m.* batting.

ва́тник *m.* quilted jacket.

ва́тный *adj.* quilted; wadded.

ватру́шка *f.* jam *or* cheese pastry.

ватт *m.* watt.

ва́фля *f.* waffle.

ва́хта *f.* (*naut.*) watch.

ва́хтенный *adj.* (*naut.*) (*attrib.*) watch.

вахтёр *m.* watchman; janitor.

ваш *pron.* your; yours.

Вашингто́н *m.* Washington.

вая́ние *neut.* (*obs.*) sculpture.

вая́ть *impf. pf.* **из-** to sculpture.

вбега́ть *impf. pf.* **вбежа́ть** to rush in, to run in.

вбива́ть *impf. pf.* **вбить** *v.t.* to drive in.

вбира́ть *impf. pf.* **вобра́ть** **1.** to absorb. **2.** to take in.

вблизи́ *prep.* (*with gen.*) near; not far from.

вбок *adv.* to one side; to the side.

вброд *adv.:* **переходи́ть вброд** to ford.

введе́ние *neut.* introduction; preface.

ввезти́ *pf. of* **ввози́ть.**

вверга́ть *impf.* to plunge; to throw (*into despair*).

вверх *adv.* up, upwards. — **вверх дном** upside down.

вверху́ *adv.* above; overhead.

вверя́ть *impf. pf.* **вве́рить** to entrust.

ввиду́ *prep.* (*with gen.*) in view of.

вви́нчивать *impf. pf.* **ввинти́ть** to screw (in).

ввод *m.* bringing into; putting into.

вводи́ть *impf. pf.* **ввести́** **1.** to introduce. **2.** to lead in *or* into. **3.** to bring in *or* into.

вво́дный *adj.* introductory.

ввоз *m.* importation; imports.

ввози́ть *impf. pf.* ввезти́ to import.

вво́лю *adv.* (*colloq.*) to one's heart's content.

ввысь *adv.* upwards; high into the air.

вглубь *adv.* deep in *or* into.

вгля́дываться *impf. pf.* вгляде́ться **1.** to peer at *or* into. **2.** to observe closely.

вгоня́ть *impf. pf.* вогна́ть *v.t.* to drive in.

вдава́ться *impf. pf.* вда́ться to jut out.

вдалеке́ *adv.* in the far distance; far off.

вдали́ *adv.* in the distance.

вдаль *adv.* far; into the far distance.

вдво́е *adv.* doubly, double; twice. — вдво́е бо́льше twice as much.

вдвоём *adv.* two together.

вдвойне́ *adv.* doubly, double.

вдева́ть *impf. pf.* вдеть *v.t.* **1.** to put into. **2.** to pass through.

вдёргивать *impf. pf.* вдёрнуть to draw something through; to thread (*a needle*).

вде́сятеро *adv.* ten times; tenfold.

вдесятеро́м *adv.* ten together.

вдоба́вок *adv.* (*colloq.*) in addition; on top of everything else.

вдова́ *f.* widow.

вдове́ц FILL *m.* widower.

вдо́воль *adv.* enough, plenty.

вдовство́ *neut.* widowhood.

вдо́вый *adj.* widowed.

вдого́нку *adv.* in pursuit of; after.

вдоль *prep.* (*with gen.*) along. — вдоль и поперёк **1.** far and wide. **2.** thoroughly.

вдо́сталь *adv.* (*colloq.*) in abundance.

вдох *m.* (a single) breath.

вдохнове́ние *neut.* inspiration.

вдохнови́тель *m. f.* —ница inspiration; inspiring person.

вдохновля́ть *impf. pf.* вдохнови́ть to inspire. —ся to become (*or* feel) inspired.

вдохну́ть *pf. of* вдыха́ть.

вдре́безги *adv.* to pieces, into smithereens.

вдруг *adv.* suddenly, all of a sudden.

вду́мчивый *adj.* thoughtful.

вдыха́ние *neut.* inhalation.

вдыха́тельный *adj.* **1.** (*attrib.*) intake. **2.** respiratory.

вдыха́ть *impf. pf.* вдохну́ть to inhale.

вегетариа́нец FILL *m. f.* вегетариа́нка vegetarian.

вегета́ция *f.* vegetation process.

ве́дать *impf.* **1.** (*with instr.*) to be in charge of. **2.** (*obs.*) to know.

ве́дение *neut.* authority; competence.

веде́ние *neut.* conduct; direction; management.

ве́домо *neut.*: без их ве́дома without their knowledge or consent.

ве́домость *f.* **1.** list; register. **2.** record.

ве́домственный *adj.* departmental.

ве́домство *neut.* department.

ведро́ *neut.* bucket, pail.

веду́щий *adj.* **1.** leading. **2.** chief.

ведь *particle* but; indeed, well.

ве́дьма *f.* witch.

ве́ер *m.* fan.

веерообра́зный *adj.* fan-shaped.

ве́жливый *adj.* polite, courteous.

везде́ *adv.* everywhere.

вездесу́щий *adj.* ubiquitous; omnipresent.

вездехо́д *m.* cross-country vehicle; four-wheel drive.

везе́ние *neut.* (*colloq.*) luck.

везти́ *impf. det. of* вози́ть.

Везу́вий *m.* (*volcano*) Vesuvius.

век *m.* **1.** century; age. **2.** (*colloq.*) lifetime. —ово́й *adj.* century-old, age-old.

ве́ко *neut.* eyelid.

ве́ксель *m.* promissory note.

ве́ктор *m.* vector.

веле́невый *adj.* (*paper*) vellum.

веле́ние *neut.* command.

веле́ть *impf. and pf.* **1.** to order. **2.** to tell.

велика́н *m.* giant.

вели́кий *adj.* great.

Великобрита́ния *f.* Great Britain.

великоду́шный *adj.* magnanimous, generous.

великоле́пие *neut.* magnificence.

великоле́пно *adv.* magnificently.

великоле́пный *adj.* magnificent; splendid; glorious.

великопо́стный *adj.* Lenten.

Вели́ко Ты́рново *neut.* Turnovo (the Great).

велича́вый *adj.* majestic; stately.

велича́йший *adj.* greatest; supreme.

вели́чественный *adj.* majestic; grand; sublime.

вели́чество *neut.* majesty.

вели́чие *neut.* greatness; grandeur.

величина́ *f.* **1.** size. **2.** (*math.*) quantity; magnitude.

велого́нщик *m.* (*abbr. of* велосипе́дный го́нщик) cyclist, bicycle racer.

велодро́м *m.* velodrome.

велосипе́д *m.* bicycle.

велоспо́рт *m.* (*abbr. of* велосипе́дный спорт) cycling.

вельве́т *m.* velveteen.

вельмо́жа *m.* (*decl. f.*) **1.** (*arch.*) aristocrat. **2.** grandee.

велю́р *m.* velour.

веля́рный *adj.* velar.

Ве́на *f.* Vienna.

ве́на *f.* (*anat.*) vein.

венге́рский *adj.* Hungarian.

венгр *m. f.* венге́рка Hungarian.

Ве́нгрия *f.* Hungary.

венери́ческий *adj.* venereal.

Венесуэ́ла *f.* Venezuela.

венесуэ́лец FILL *m. f.* венесуэ́лка Venezuelan.

вене́ц FILL *m.* **1.** crown. **2.** wreath.

Вене́ция *f.* Venice.

вене́чный *adj.* coronary.

ве́ник *m.* twig broom; besom.

вено́зный *adj.* venous.

ве́нский *adj.* Viennese.

вентили́ровать OVA *impf. pf.* про- to ventilate.

ве́нтиль *m.* valve.

вентиля́тор *m.* fan.

вентиля́ция *f.* ventilation.

венча́льный *adj.* (*attrib.*) wedding.

венча́ние *neut.* **1.** wedding *or* marriage ceremony. **2.** coronation.

венча́ть *impf. pf.* по- **1.** to crown. **2.** to marry.

ве́нчик *m.* corolla.

вепрь *m.* wild boar.

ве́ра *f.* faith, belief; trust.
вера́нда *f.* veranda.
ве́рба *f.* pussy willow.
вербе́на *f.* verbena.
верблю́д *m.* camel.
верблю́жий *adj.* (*attrib.*) camel; camel's-hair.
ве́рбный *adj.* (*attrib.*) pussy willow.
вербова́ть OVA *impf. pf.* за- to recruit, to enlist.
вербо́вка *f.* recruitment.
ве́рбовый *adj.* (*attrib.*) pussy-willow.
верди́кт *m.* verdict.
верёвка *f.* **1.** cord, rope. **2.** string.
верёвочный *adj.* (*attrib.*) rope.
верени́ца *f.* line; row.
ве́реск *m.* heather.
веретено́ *neut.* spindle.
верещ́а́ть *impf. pres.* -щу́, -щи́шь to chirp.
верзи́ла *m.* and *f.* (*decl. f.*) tall, lanky person.
вери́ги *pl.* chains; fetters (*worn by ascetics*).
вери́тельные гра́моты *pl.* credentials of a diplomat.
ве́рить *impf. pf.* по- **1.** (*with dat.*) to believe. **2.** (**в** *with acc.*) to believe (in); to trust.
вермише́ль *f.* vermicelli.
Вермо́нт *m.* Vermont.
ве́рмут *m.* vermouth.
верне́е *adj. comp. of* ве́рный. — *particle* rather; or to be more precise.
верниса́ж *m.* (*art*) **1.** private viewing. **2.** opening day (*of an art exhibit*).
ве́рно *adv.* correctly; right; faithfully. — *impers.* it is true.
ве́рность *f.* **1.** correctness, truth. **2.** faithfulness, fidelity.
верну́ть *pf. v.t.* **1.** to return, to give back. **2.** to recover; to compel. —ся *v.i.* to return, to come back.
ве́рный *adj.* **1.** correct, right. **2.** true; faithful.
ве́рование *neut.* belief.
ве́ровать OVA *impf.* (**в** *with acc.*) to believe in.
вероиспове́дание *neut.* faith; denomination; religion.
вероло́мный *adj.* perfidious, treacherous.
вероло́мство *neut.* perfidy, treachery.
вероуче́ние *neut.* dogma.
вероя́тно *adv.* probably.
вероя́тность *f.* probability.
вероя́тный *adj.* probable, likely.
Верса́ль *m.* Versailles.
ве́рсия *f.* version.
верста́ *f.* old Russian unit of distance equal to approx. one kilometer.
верста́к *m.* **1.** carpenter's bench. **2.** locksmith's bench.
верста́ть *impf.* to make into pages.
вёрстка *f.* (*typog.*) **1.** page proofs. **2.** page makeup.
верстово́й столб *m.* milepost.
верте́п *m.* cave; den (*of thieves*).
верте́ть *impf.* to twirl, to turn, to twist.
верте́ться *impf. pres.* верчу́сь, ве́ртишься **1.** to turn, to spin, to rotate. **2.** to fidget. **3.** (*colloq.*) to hang around.
вертика́ль *f.* vertical line.
вертика́льный *adj.* vertical.
вёрткий *adj.* (*colloq.*) agile; nimble.
вертлю́г *m.* swivel.

вертля́вый *adj.* (*colloq.*) fidgety.
вертолёт *m.* helicopter.
верту́шка *f.* (*colloq.*) **1.** any revolving device. **2.** flighty woman.
ве́рующий *adj.* believer.
верфь *f.* shipyard; dockyard.
верх *m.* top, summit; height.
ве́рхний *adj.* **1.** upper; top. **2.** outer (*clothing*).
верхова́я езда́ *f.* horseback riding.
верхо́вный *adj.* **1.** supreme. **2.** sovereign.
верхово́д *m.* (*colloq.*) boss.
верхо́вье *neut.* upper reaches (*of a river*).
ве́рхом *adv.* along the top.
верхо́м *adv.* (*on*) horseback.
верху́шка *f.* **1.** top; summit; apex. **2.** (*colloq.*) the bosses; the elite.
ве́рша *f.* creel.
верши́на *f.* **1.** summit, peak; acme. **2.** (*math.*) apex, vertex.
верши́ть *impf.* **1.** to decide. **2.** (*with instr.*) to direct; to control.
вершо́к FILL *m.* old Russian measurement of approx. 75 inches.
вес *m.* **1.** weight. **2.** (*fig.*) influence.
весь *adj.* вся *f.*, всё *neut.*, все *pl.* all; the whole.
весели́ть *impf. pf.* раз- to cheer; to amuse. —ся to enjoy oneself, to have fun, to have a good time.
ве́село *adv.* happily; merrily.
весёлость *f.* gaiety; merriment.
весёлый *adj.* **1.** merry, gay. **2.** cheerful, jovial.
весе́лье *neut.* merriment, merry-making.
весельча́к *m.* (*colloq.*) jolly fellow.
веселя́щий газ *m.* laughing gas.
весе́нний *adj.* (*attrib.*) spring.
ве́сить *impf.* to weigh.
ве́ский *adj.* **1.** weighty; significant. **2.** convincing, persuasive.
весло́ *neut.* oar, paddle.
весна́ *f.* spring.
весно́й *also* весно́ю *adv.* in the spring.
весну́шка *f.* freckle.
весну́шчатый *adj.* (*colloq.*) freckled.
весо́мый *adj.* **1.** having weight. **2.** weighty.
вести́ *impf. det. of* води́ть. — вести́ себя́ to behave.
вестибю́ль *m.* lobby.
вести́сь *impf.* (*colloq.*) **1.** to be under way. **2.** to progress.
ве́стник *m.* **1.** herald, messenger. **2.** (*in title of a publication*) bulletin.
вестово́й *m.* orderly.
ве́сточка *f. dim. of* весть.
весть *f.* news, word.
весы́ *pl.* scale, scales.
весьма́ *adv.* very; extraordinarily; highly.
ветви́стый *adj.* with many branches.
ветвь *f.* branch, bough.
ве́тер *m.* FILL **1.** wind. **2.** breeze.
ветера́н *m.* veteran.
ветерина́р *m.* veterinarian.
ветеро́к FILL *m.* light breeze.
ве́тка *f.* branch, twig.
ветла́ *f.* white willow.
ве́то *neut. indecl.* veto.
ве́точка *f.* twig, spring, shoot.
ве́тошь *f.* tatters; rags.

ве́треник *m.* (*colloq.*) scatterbrain; frivolous person.

ве́треница *f.* flighty woman.

ве́трено *adv.* frivolously. — *adj.* (*pred.*) windy.

ве́треный *adj.* **1.** windy. **2.** frivolous, flighty.

ветрово́й *adj.* (*attrib.*) wind.

ветря́нка *f.* chicken pox.

ветряно́й *adj.* (*attrib.*) wind. — **ветряна́я ме́льница** *f.* windmill.

ве́тхий *adj.* decrepit; dilapidated. — **Ве́тхий Заве́т** *m.* the Old Testament.

ве́тхость *f.* disrepair; dilapidation.

ветчина́ *f.* ham.

ветша́ть *impf. pf.* **об-** to deteriorate; to become dilapidated.

ве́ха *f.* boundary mark; landmark.

ве́че *neut.* veche (*democratic assembly in medieval Russian cities*).

ве́чер *m.* **1.** evening. **2.** (*evening*) party.

вечери́нка *f.* (evening) party.

вече́рний *adj.* (*attrib.*) evening.

вече́рня *f.* vespers.

ве́чером *adv.* in the evening. — **вчера́ ве́чером** yesterday evening. — **за́втра ве́чером** tomorrow evening. — **сего́дня ве́чером** this evening.

ве́чно *adv.* **1.** eternally. **2.** (*colloq.*) constantly.

вечнозелёный *adj.* evergreen.

ве́чность *f.* eternity.

ве́чный *adj.* eternal, everlasting.

ве́шалка *f.* **1.** hanger. **2.** clothes rack.

ве́шать *impf. pf.* **пове́сить** *v.t.* **1.** to hang. **2.** to hang up. —**ся** to hang oneself.

веща́ние *neut.* broadcasting.

веща́ть *impf.* **1.** to preach. **2.** to broadcast. **3.** (*obs.*) to prophesy.

вещево́й *adj.* (*attrib.*) clothing.

веще́ственность *f.* materiality.

веще́ственный *adj.* material.

вещество́ *neut.* matter, substance.

ве́щий *adj.* (*obs.*) **1.** wise. **2.** prophetic.

вещи́ца *f.* **1.** *dim. of* **вещь. 2.** little thing; trifle; bagatelle.

вещь *f.* thing; object; work.

ве́ялка *f.* winnowing machine.

ве́яние *neut.* **1.** winnowing. **2.** tendency.

ве́ять *impf.* **1.** to winnow. **2.** to blow. **3.** to wave, to flutter.

вжива́ться *impf.* to get used to.

вживля́ть *impf.* (*med.*) to implant.

взад и вперёд up and down, back and forth.

взаи́мный *adj.* mutual, reciprocal.

взаимовы́годный *adj.* mutually beneficial.

взаимоде́йствие *neut.* interaction, reciprocal action.

взаимоде́йствовать OVA *impf.* **1.** to interact. **2.** to cooperate.

взаимозави́симый *adj.* interdependent.

взаимозаменя́емый *adj.* interchangeable.

взаимоотноше́ние *neut.* interrelation(ship).

взаимопо́мощь *f.* mutual aid.

взаимопонима́ние *neut.* mutual understanding.

взаимосвя́занный *adj.* interconnected.

взаймы́ *adv.*: **брать взаймы́** to borrow. — **дава́ть взаймы́** to lend.

взаме́н *prep.* (*with gen.*) in exchange for.

взаперти́ *adv.* under lock; locked up.

вза́пуски *adv.* (*colloq.*) racing one another.

взбаламу́тить *pf. of* **баламу́тить.**

взба́лмошный *adj.* (*colloq.*) eccentric; erratic.

взба́лтывать *impf.* to shake up.

взбега́ть *impf.* to run up.

взбелени́ться *impf.* to fly into a rage.

взбеси́ть *pf.* to enrage.

взбива́ть *impf.* to whip up.

взбира́ться *impf.* to climb up.

взби́тый *adj.* beaten; whipped (*e.g. cream*).

взбреда́ть *impf.* (*colloq.*) to mount with difficulty.

взбунтова́ться OVA *pf.* to revolt, to mutiny.

взбу́чка *f.* (*colloq.*) beating; thrashing.

взва́ливать *impf. pf.* **взвали́ть** (**на** *with acc.*) **1.** to load onto. **2.** to place (the blame) on. **3.** to load work on someone.

взве́шивать *impf. pf.* **взве́сить** to weigh oneself.

взвива́ть *impf.* to blow up; to swirl.

взви́зг *m.* (*colloq.*) yelp; screech.

взви́згивать *impf. pf.* **взви́гнуть 1.** (*of a dog*) to yelp. **2.** to scream; to cry out.

взви́нчивать *impf.* (*colloq.*) to excite; to arouse.

взво́д *m.* **1.** platoon. **2.** cocking notch (*of guns*).

взводи́ть *impf.* to lead up.

взво́дный *adj.* (*attrib.*) platoon.

взволно́ванный *adj.* agitated; anxious.

взволнова́ть OVA *pf. of* **волнова́ть.**

взгляд *m.* glance, look; opinion, view.

взгля́дывать *impf. pf.* **взгляну́ть** (**на** *with acc.*) to glance at, look at.

взго́рье *neut.* hill.

взгромозжда́ть *impf. pf.* **взгромозди́ть** (**на** *with acc.*) (*colloq.*) to pile onto; to load onto.

вздёргивать *impf.* (*colloq.*) to raise; to jerk up.

вздёрнутый нос *m.* snub nose.

вздо́рный *adj.* **1.** absurd, preposterous. **2.** cantankerous; quarrelsome.

вздох *m.* sigh.

вздохну́ть *pf. of* **вздыха́ть.**

вздра́гивать *impf. pf.* **вздро́гнуть 1.** to shudder. **2.** to wince.

вздремну́ть *pf.* to nap.

вздӯмать *pf.* **1.** to conceive. **2.** to take it into one's head.

взду́тие *neut.* swelling.

взду́тый *adj.* **1.** inflated. **2.** swollen.

вздыха́ть *impf. pf.* **вздохну́ть 1.** to sigh. **2.** to long (for).

взима́ть *impf.* to collect; to levy.

взира́ть *impf.* (*obs.*) to look; to gaze.

взла́мывать *impf. pf.* **взлома́ть** to break into.

взлёт *m.* take-off.

взлета́ть *impf. pf.* **взлете́ть 1.** to fly up. **2.** to take off.

взлётный *adj.* (*attrib.*) take-off.

взлом *m.* break-in.

взлома́ть *pf. of* **взла́мывать.**

взло́мщик *m. f.* **взло́мщица** burglar.

взлохма́ченный *adj.* disheveled.

взмах *m.* **1.** stroke. **2.** movement. **3.** wave.

взма́хивать *impf. pf.* **взмахну́ть 1.** to flap. **2.** to wave.

взмо́рье *neut.* seashore, beach.

взмы́ленный *adj.* (*of horse*) foaming.

взнос *m.* payment, fee.

взойти́ *pf. of* **всходи́ть.**

взор *m.* look; gaze.

взра́щивать *impf. pf.* взрасти́ть **1.** to grow; to cultivate. **2.** to raise; to bring up.

взро́слый *m. and adj.* adult.

взрыв *m.* explosion.

взрыва́тель *m.* fuse.

взрыва́ть *impf. pf.* взорва́ть *v.t.* **1.** to blow up. **2.** to infuriate.

взрывно́й *adj. (attrib.)* blasting.

взрывча́тка *f. (colloq.)* explosive substance.

взры́вчатый *adj.* explosive.

взъеро́шенный *adj.* disheveled.

взыва́ть *impf.* **1.** to appeal. **2.** to call.

взыска́ние *neut.* penalty.

взыска́тельный *adj.* demanding; exacting.

взы́скивать *impf. pf.* взыска́ть to exact.

взя́тие *neut.* seizure, capture.

взя́тка *f.* bribe; graft.

взя́точничество *neut.* bribery.

взя́ть(ся) *pf. of* бра́ть(ся).

виаду́к *m.* viaduct.

вибра́тор *m.* vibrator.

вибра́ция *f.* vibration.

виве́рра *f.* civet; civet-cat.

вигва́м *m.* wigwam.

виго́нь *m.* vicuna.

вид *m.* **1.** appearance, look. **2.** shape, form, view. **3.** sight. **4.** *(gram.)* aspect.

ви́данный *adj.:* ви́данное ли э́то де́ло? *(colloq.)* did you ever see such a thing?

вида́ть *impf. pf.* по- *(colloq.)* to see.

ви́дение *neut.* vision, sight.

виде́ние *neut.* vision, apparition.

видеоза́пись *f.* video tape.

ви́деть *impf. pf.* у- to see.

ви́димо *adv.* apparently, evidently.

ви́димость *f.* **1.** visibility. **2.** appearance. — по всей ви́димости from all appearances.

ви́димый *adj.* visible.

ви́дно *adj. (pred.)* obvious *or* clear.

ви́дный *adj.* **1.** visible. **2.** prominent, eminent.

видово́й *adj.* aspectual.

видоизмене́ние *neut.* **1.** alteration; modification. **2.** variety.

видоиска́тель *m. (photog.)* view finder.

ви́за *f.* visa.

визави́ *adv.* face to face.

визг *m.* squeal; yelp.

визгли́вый *adj.* shrill.

визи́р *m. (photog.)* view finder.

визи́рь *m.* vizier.

визи́тка *f.* business card.

визи́тный *adj.* of *or* for visiting. — визи́тная ка́рточка *m.* business card.

ви́ка *f.* vetch; tares *(plant of pea family)*.

вика́рий *m.* vicar.

ви́кинг *m.* Viking.

вико́нт *m.* viscount.

виктори́на *f.* (television) quiz show; game show.

ви́лка *f.* **1.** fork. **2.** electric plug.

ви́лла *f.* villa.

ви́ллис *m.* jeep.

вило́к FILL *m. (colloq.)* head of cabbage.

ви́лы *pl.* pitchfork.

Ви́льнюс *m.* Vilnius.

виля́ть *impf.* **1.** to wag. **2.** to zigzag. **3.** to equivocate.

вина́ *f.* **1.** guilt. **2.** fault.

винегре́т *m.* beet and potato salad.

вини́л *m.* vinyl.

вини́тельный *adj. (gram.)* accusative.

вини́ть *impf. pf.* об- to blame.

Ви́нница *f.* Vinnytsya *(Russian: Vinnitsa).*

виннока́менный *adj.* tartaric.

ви́нный *adj. (attrib.)* wine.

вино́ *neut.* wine.

винова́т *interj.* I'm sorry! Excuse me!

винова́тый *adj.* guilty.

вино́вник *m.* culprit.

вино́вность *f.* guilt.

вино́вный *adj.* guilty.

виногра́д *m.* grapes. —ник *m.* vineyard.

виногра́дный *adj. (attrib.)* grape.

виноде́л *m.* winegrower.

вино́вный *m.* distiller.

винт *m.* screw.

ви́нтик *m. dim. of* винт.

винто́вка *f.* rifle.

винтово́й *adj.* spiral.

винто́вочный *adj. (attrib.)* rifle.

винто́вщик *m.* rifleman.

винтообра́зный *adj.* spiral.

винье́тка *f.* vignette.

вио́ла *f.* viola.

виолончели́ст *m. f.* —ка cellist.

виолонче́ль *f.* cello.

вира́ж *m.* **1.** turn; curve *(in road).* **2.** *(photog.)* toning agent.

Вирги́ния *f.* Virginia.

виртуо́з *m.* virtuoso.

виртуо́зно *adv.* masterfully.

виртуо́зность *f.* virtuosity.

виртуо́зный *adj.* masterful.

вируле́нтность *f.* virulence.

вируле́нтный *adj.* virulent.

ви́рус *m.* virus.

ви́рши *pl.* doggerel; bad verse.

висе́ть *impf. pf.* пови́снуть *v.i.* to hang, to be suspended.

ви́ски *m. indecl.* whiskey.

виско́за *f.* viscose.

Виско́нсин *m.* Wisconsin.

Ви́сла *f. (river)* Vistula.

вислоу́хий *adj.* lop-eared.

ви́смут *m.* bismuth.

висо́к FILL *m.* temple *(of the head).*

високо́сный год *m.* leap year.

вист *m.* whist.

вису́лька *f. (colloq.)* pendant.

вися́чий *adj.* hanging; suspended.

витами́н *m.* vitamin.

вита́ть *impf.* to hang (over); to hover (over).

Ви́тебск *m.* Vitsyebsk *(Russian: Vitebsk).*

витиева́тый *adj.* ornate.

вито́й *adj.* twisted.

вито́к FILL *m.* **1.** turn; coil; loop. **2.** strand.

витра́ж *m.* stained-glass window.

витри́на *f.* display window.

Ви́ттенберг *m.* Wittenberg.

вить *impf. pf.* с- **1.** to weave. **2.** to twist. ви́ться *v.i.* **3.** to curl. **4.** to wind.

ви́тязь *m.* warrior; hero *(in folk poetry).*

вихо́р FILL *m.* tuft (of hair).
вихрь *m.* whirlwind.
вишнёвка *f.* cherry brandy.
вишнёвый *adj.* (*attrib.*) cherry.
ви́шня *f.* cherry; cherry tree.
вка́лывать *impf. pf.* вколо́ть (в *with acc.*) to stick in(to).
вка́пывать *impf. pf.* вкопа́ть (в *with acc.*) to implant; to set in the ground.
вка́тывать *impf. pf.* вкати́ть *v.t.* to roll in, to wheel in.
вклад *m.* **1.** investment. **2.** deposit. **3.** contribution.
вкла́дка *f.* supplement; insert (*in a publication*).
вкладно́й *adj.* (*attrib.*) deposit; deposited.
— вкладно́й лист *m.* inserted page.
вкла́дчик *m.* depositor.
вкла́дывание *neut.* inserting.
вкла́дывать *impf. pf.* вложи́ть to put in; to invest.
вкле́ивать *impf. pf.* вкле́ить to paste in.
вкле́йка *f.* inset.
включа́ть *impf. pf.* включи́ть **1.** to include. **2.** to embrace. **3.** to switch on.
включа́я *prep.* (*with acc.*) including.
включе́ние *neut.* **1.** inclusion. **2.** insertion.
включи́тельно *adv.* inclusively.
вконе́ц *adv.* (*colloq.*) utterly; completely.
вкореня́ться *impf. pf.* вкорени́ться to take root.
вкось *adv.* aslant.
вкра́дчивый *adj.* insinuating.
вкра́пить *pf.* to sprinkle into.
вкра́тце *adv.* in brief, in short; briefly.
вкругову́ю *adv.* in a circle.
вкруту́ю *adv.:* яйцо́ вкруту́ю *neut.* hard-boiled egg.
вку́пе *adv.* (*obs.*) together.
вкус *m.* taste. —ный *adj.*
вку́сно *adv.* tasty; delicious; well.
вку́сный *adj.* tasty; delicious; good.
вкусово́й *adj.* gustatory.
вла́га *f.* moisture, dampness.
влага́лище *neut.* vagina.
владе́лец FILL *m. f.* владе́лица owner, proprietor.
владе́ние *neut.* **1.** property. **2.** possession, ownership.
владе́ть *impf. pf.* за- **1.** to own, to possess. **2.** to control.
Владивосто́к *m.* Vladivostok.
Влади́мир *m.* Vladimir.
влады́ка *m.* (*obs.*) ruler; sovereign.
вла́жность *f.* humidity; moisture.
вла́жный *adj.* **1.** humid. **2.** moist, damp.
вла́ствовать OVA *impf.* (над *with instr.*) to dominate, to rule (over).
властели́н *m.* **1.** master. **2.** absolute ruler.
власти́тель *m.* (*obs.*) ruler.
вла́стный *adj.* **1.** commanding, dominating. **2.** imperious.
властолюби́вый *adj.* power-hungry; power-seeking.
власть *f.* power.
вле́во *adv.* to the left.
влеза́ть *impf. pf.* влезть to get in, to climb in, to crawl in.
влета́ть *impf. pf.* влете́ть to fly in or into.
влече́ние *neut.* inclination; bent.

влечь *impf.* to draw; to attract.
влива́ть *impf. pf.* влить *v.t.* to pour in or into.
влия́ние *neut.* influence.
влия́тельный *adj.* influential.
влия́ть *impf. pf.* по- to influence; to have influence (on, over).
вложе́ние *neut.* **1.** enclosure. **2.** investment.
вложи́ть *pf. of* вкла́дывать.
Влта́ва *f.* Moldau River (*Czech: Vltava*).
влюблённый *adj.* in love.
влюбля́ться *impf. pf.* влюби́ться to fall in love.
влю́бчивый *adj.* amorous.
вменя́емый *adj.* responsible; competent; of sound mind.
вменя́ть *impf. pf.* вмени́ть to impute.
вме́сте *adv.* together.
вмести́лище *neut.* receptacle; container.
вмести́мость *f.* capacity.
вмести́тельный *adj.* spacious; capacious.
вмести́ть *pf. of* вмеща́ть.
вме́сто *prep.* (*with gen.*) instead of, in place of.
вмеша́тельство *neut.* **1.** interference. **2.** intervention.
вме́шиваться *impf. pf.* вмеша́ться **1.** to interfere. **2.** to meddle; to intervene.
вмеща́ть *impf. pf.* вмести́ть **1.** to contain, to hold. **2.** to accommodate.
вмиг *adv.* in an instant or moment.
вмя́тина *f.* dent.
внаём *also* внаймы́ *adv.:* брать внаём (внаймы́) to hire, to rent. — отдава́ть внаём (внаймы́) to let, to hire out.
внаки́дку *adv.* over one's shoulders.
внакла́де *adv.* (*colloq.*): оста́ться внакла́де *pf.* to end up losing.
внача́ле *adv.* at first, in the beginning.
вне *prep.* (*with gen.*) **1.** outside, out of. **2.** beyond. — вне себя́ beside oneself.
внебра́чный *adj.* **1.** extramarital. **2.** (*child*) illegitimate.
внедре́ние *neut.* **1.** inculcation. **2.** indoctrination. **3.** adoption.
внедря́ть *impf. pf.* внедри́ть to inculcate.
внеза́пно *adv.* suddenly.
внеза́пный *adj.* **1.** sudden. **2.** unexpected.
внеочередно́й *adj.* **1.** out of turn. **2.** (*of a meeting*) special; extraordinary.
внести́ *pf. of* вноси́ть.
вне́шне *adv.* on the surface; externally; outward.
вне́шний *adj.* external, outward.
вне́шность *f.* **1.** exterior. **2.** external appearance.
вниз *adv.* (*dir.*) down, downwards.
внизу́ *adv.* (*loc.*) below; downstairs.
вника́ть *impf. pf.* вни́кнуть **1.** to delve into. **2.** to try to understand.
внима́ние *neut.* attention.
внима́тельно *adv.* **1.** attentively. **2.** with consideration.
внима́тельность *f.* attentiveness.
внима́тельный *adj.* attentive.
вничью́ *adv.* in or to a draw.
вновь *adv.* again, anew, once again.
вноси́ть *impf. pf.* внести́ *v.t.* **1.** to carry in, to bring in. **2.** to enter; to insert.
внук *m.* grandson; grandchild.
вну́тренний *adj.* inner, inside, internal.
вну́тренности *pl.* (*anat.*) internal organs.

внутренность f. interior.
внутри adv. in, inside. — prep. (with gen.) within, inside.
внутривенный adj. intravenous.
внутрь adv. in, inside. — prep. (with gen.) in, into; inside.
внучатый племянник m. grandnephew.
внучка f. granddaughter.
внушать impf. pf. внушить 1. to suggest. 2. to impress. 3. to inspire.
внушение neut. suggestion.
внушительный adj. imposing; impressive.
внятный adj. 1. distinct. 2. audible.
во see в.
вовек adv. forever.
вовлекать impf. pf. вовлечь v.t. 1. to involve. 2. to draw in.
вовлечение neut. involvement.
вовне adv. outside.
вовремя adv. in time.
вовсе adv. (colloq.) quite. — вовсе нет not at all.
вовсю adv. (colloq.) to the utmost extent.
во-вторых adv. in the second place; secondly.
вогнать pf. of вгонять.
вогнутый adj. concave.
вода f. water.
водворение neut. settlement.
водворять impf. pf. водворить 1. to settle, to install. 2. to establish.
водевиль m. vaudeville.
водитель m. f. —ница driver.
водительский adj. (attrib.) driver's, driver. — водительские права pl. driver's licence.
водительство neut. (obs.) leadership.
водить impf. indet. det. вести v.t. 1. to conduct, to lead. 2. to drive. 3. to carry on.
водиться impf. 1. (of animals) to be found (in a certain area). 2. (с with instr.) to associate with. 3. to be noticed or observed.
водка f. vodka.
воднолыжный спорт m. water skiing.
водный adj. (attrib.) water.
водобоязнь f. hydrophobia.
водовместилище neut. water reservoir.
водоворот m. whirlpool, eddy.
водоём m. reservoir.
водоизмещение neut. (water) displacement.
водокачка f. pumping station.
водолаз m. diver.
Водолей m. Aquarius.
водолечебный adj. hydropathic.
водолечение neut. hydropathy.
водомер m. water meter.
водонапорная башня f. water tower.
водонепроницаемый adj waterproof; watertight.
водонос m. water carrier.
водопад m. waterfall.
водоплавающая птица f. waterfowl.
водопой m. watering place.
водопровод m. water pipe.
водопроводный adj. related to plumbing.
водопроводчик m. plumber.
водоразборный кран m. hydrant.
водораздел m. watershed.
водород m. hydrogen.

водородный adj. hydrogen. — водородная бомба f. hydrogen bomb.
водоросль f. (bot.) 1. water plant. 2. seaweed.
водосвинка f. capybara.
водослив m. spillway.
водоснабжение neut. water supply.
водосток m. water drain; gutter.
водосточный жёлоб m. gutter.
водохранилище neut. reservoir; tank.
водочный adj. (attrib.) vodka.
водружать impf. pf. водрузить to hoist, to erect.
водянистый adj. watery.
водянка f. dropsy.
водяной adj. (attrib.) water, aquatic.
воевать impf. 1. to wage war. 2. to quarrel, to war with.
воевода m. (hist.) military governor.
воедино adv. together.
военачальник m. commander.
военно-воздушные силы pl. air force.
военно-морской флот m. navy.
военнообязанный m. person subject to the draft.
военнопленный m. prisoner of war.
военнослужащий m. serviceman.
военный adj. military, martial.
военщина f. (derog.) the military; militarists.
вожак m. 1. leader. 2. guide.
вожатый m. 1. guide. 2. driver.
вожделение neut. 1. lust; desire. 2. craving.
вождение neut. driving; steering.
вождь m. leader.
вожжи pl. reins.
воз m. cart; cartful.
возбудимый adj. excitable.
возбудитель m. agent; stimulus.
возбуждать impf. pf. возбудить to excite, to arouse, to stimulate.
возбуждающий adj. rousing; stirring.
возбуждение neut. excitement; stimulation.
возбуждённый adj. excited.
возведение neut. 1. erection. 2. (math.) raising to (n-th) power.
возвещать impf. pf. возвестить to announce; to proclaim.
возврат m. 1. return. 2. reimbursement, repayment.
возвратный adj. 1. (attrib.) return. 2. (gram.) reflexive.
возвращать impf. pf. возвратить 1. to return, to give back. 2. to repay. —ся impf. pf. возвратиться, вернуться 3. v.i. to return. 4. to recur, to revert.
возвращение neut. 1. return (e.g. returning home). 2. return; giving back. 3. repayment.
возвышать impf. pf. возвысить to raise.
возвышение neut. rise; elevation.
возвышенность f. 1. height, heights. 2. loftiness.
возвышенный adj. 1. high, lofty. 2. elevated; exalted.
возглавлять impf. pf. возглавить to be at the head (of); to head.
возглас m. exclamation; ejaculation.
возглашать impf. pf. возгласить to proclaim.
возгонка f. (chem.) sublimation.
возгораемый adj. flammable.
воздавать impf. pf. воздать 1. to repay with. 2. to render.

воздвига́ть *impf. pf.* воздвигну́ть to erect.

возде́йствие *neut.* influence.

возде́йствовать OVA *impf.* **1.** to influence. **2.** to affect.

воздержа́вшийся *m.* abstainer.

воздержа́ние *neut.* abstention; abstinence; temperance.

возде́ржанность *f.* moderation; temperance.

возде́рживаться *impf. pf.* воздержа́ться to refrain from; to abstain from.

во́здух *m.* air.

воздушнодеса́нтный *adj.* (*mil.*) airborne.

возду́шный *adj.* air; aerial.

воззва́ние *neut.* appeal.

воззре́ние *neut.* view, opinion.

вози́ть *impf. ind. det.* везти́ **1.** to carry, to convey. **2.** to cart. **3.** to drive.

вози́ться *impf.* (*colloq.*) (c *with instr.*) to fiddle around with; to putter.

возлага́ть *impf. pf.* возложи́ть *v.t.* **1.** to lay, to place, to rest. **2.** to entrust.

во́зле *adv., prep.* (*with gen.*) by, near, beside.

возлия́ние *neut.* libation.

возлю́бленный *adj.* beloved. *m. f.* возлю́бленная sweetheart.

возме́здие *neut.* **1.** requital. **2.** retribution.

возмеща́ть *impf. pf.* возмести́ть **1.** to compensate; to repay. **2.** to make up for.

возмеще́ние *neut.* reimbursement; compensation.

возмо́жно *pred.* it is possible.

возмо́жность *f.* possibility, opportunity.

возмо́жный *adj.* possible.

возмужа́лый *adj.* grown-up man.

возмути́тельно *adv.* outrageously.

возмути́тельный *adj.* **1.** scandalous. **2.** outrageous.

возмуща́ть *impf. pf.* возмути́ть to arouse indignation.

возмуще́ние *neut.* indignation.

возмущённый *adj.* indignant; outraged.

вознагражда́ть *impf. pf.* вознагради́ть to reward; to recompense.

вознагражде́ние *neut.* reward; remuneration; compensation.

возненави́деть *pf. pres.* -жу, -дишь to come to hate.

Вознесе́ние *neut.* (*relig.*) the Ascension (Day).

возника́ть *impf. pf.* возни́кнуть to arise; to originate.

возникнове́ние *neut.* rise; origin.

возни́ца *m. and f.* (*decl. f.*) coachman.

возня́ *f.* bustle; noise, racket.

возобновле́ние *neut.* **1.** renewal. **2.** resumption.

возобновля́ть *impf. pf.* возобнови́ть **1.** to renew. **2.** to resume.

возража́ть *impf. pf.* возрази́ть to object.

возраже́ние *neut.* objection.

во́зраст *m.* age.

возраста́ние *neut.* increase.

возраста́ть *impf. pf.* возрасти́ **1.** to grow. **2.** to increase. **3.** to rise.

возрастно́й *adj.* (*attrib.*) age.

возрожда́ть *impf. pf.* возроди́ть to revive; to regenerate.

возрожде́ние *neut.* revival; regeneration. — эпо́ха Возрожде́ния *f.* Renaissance.

во́зчик *m.* carter.

во́ин *m.* warrior.

во́инский *adj.* military.

во́инственный *adj.* warlike; martial; militant.

во́инствующий *adj.* militant.

во́истину *adv.* (*arch.*) verily.

вой *m.* **1.** howl. **2.** wail; whine.

во́йлок *m.* felt.

война́ *f.* war.

войска́ *pl.* forces, troops.

во́йско *neut.* army.

войсково́й *adj.* (*attrib.*) army; troop.

войти́ *pf. of* входи́ть.

вокали́ст *m. f.* —ка vocal performer; voice teacher.

вока́льный *adj.* vocal.

вокза́л *m.* railroad station; railroad terminal. — авто́бусный вокза́л *m.* bus station; bus terminal. — речно́й вокза́л *m.* riverboat station; riverboat landing *or* terminal. — морско́й вокза́л *m.* maritime station; maritime terminal.

вокру́г *adv., prep.* (*with gen.*) round, around; about.

вол *m.* ox.

вола́н *m.* **1.** flounce (*on woman's skirt*). **2.** shuttlecock (*in badminton*).

Волгогра́д *m.* Volgograd (*formerly: Tsaritsyn, Stalingrad*).

волды́рь *m.* blister.

волево́й *adj.* strong-willed.

волейбо́л *m.* volleyball.

во́лей-нево́лей *adv.* willy-nilly.

волк *m.* wolf.

волкода́в *m.* wolfhound.

волна́ *f.* wave; breaker.

волне́ние *neut.* **1.** agitation. **2.** alarm.

волни́стый *adj.* wavy; corrugated.

волнова́ть OVA *impf. pf.* вз- **1.** to agitate. **2.** to alarm. **3.** to disturb.

волнова́ться OVA *impf.* to worry; to be upset.

волноло́м *m.* breakwater.

волнообра́зный *adj.* undulating.

волноре́з *m.* breakwater.

волну́ющий *adj.* **1.** stirring; exciting. **2.** troubling; upsetting.

воло́вий *adj.* (*attrib.*) ox.

во́лок *m.* portage; place of portage.

волоки́та *f.* red tape.

волокни́стый *adj.* fibrous.

волокно́ *neut.* fiber; filament.

Волокола́мск *m.* Volokolamsk.

волонтёр *m.* volunteer.

во́лос *m.* hair.

волоса́тый *adj.* hairy.

волосо́к FILL *m.* **1.** *dim. of* во́лос. **2.** filament; hairspring (*of watch*).

во́лость *f.* (*obs.*) administrative district.

волосяно́й *adj.* (*attrib.*) hair.

волочи́ть *impf. v.t.* **1.** to drag. **2.** to trail.

волхв *m.* magician; sorcerer. — Три волхва́ Three Wise Men; the Magi.

Во́лхов *m.* Volkhov River.

волча́нка *f.* (*skin disease*) lupus.

во́лчий *adj.* (*attrib.*) wolf, wolf's.

волчо́к FILL *m.* (*toy*) top.

волчо́нок FILL *m.* wolf cub.

волше́бник *m. f.* волше́бница magician.

волшебный *adj.* magical.
волшебство *neut.* magic.
волынка *f.* **1.** bagpipes. **2.** (*colloq.*) delay; procrastination.
Волыня *f.* Volynya.
вольер *m.* enclosure (*for birds* or *animals*).
вольно *adv.* **1.** freely. **2.** (*mil.*) at ease!
вольнодумец FILL *m.* (*obs.*) freethinker.
вольнолюбивый *adj.* freedom-loving.
вольнонаёмный *adj.* civilian; non-military.
вольнослушатель *m.* (*obs.*) non-matriculated student.
вольность *f.* **1.** freedom; liberty. **2.** undue familiarity.
вольный *adj.* free.
вольт *m.* volt. —аж *m.* voltage.
вольтметр *m.* voltmeter.
вольфрам *m.* tungsten.
воля *f.* **1.** will. **2.** liberty, freedom.
вон *adv.* out; there.
вонь *f.* stench.
вонзать *impf. pf.* вонзить *v.t.* to plunge, to thrust. —ся *v.i.* to pierce.
вонючий *adj.* stinking; foul.
вонючка *f.* skunk.
вонять *impf.* to stink
воображаемый *adj.* imaginary.
воображать *impf. pf.* вообразить to imagine.
воображение *neut.* imagination.
вообразимый *adj.* imaginable.
вообще *adv.* in general, generally.
воодушевление *neut.* enthusiasm.
воодушевлять *impf. pf.* воодушевить to inspire, to make enthusiastic.
вооружать *impf. pf.* вооружить *v.t.* to arm.
вооружение *neut.* arms; armament.
вооружённый *adj.* armed. — вооружённые силы *pl.* armed forces.
воочию *adv.* with one's own eyes.
во-первых **1.** *adv.* in the first place. **2.** first of all; firstly.
вопить *impf.* **1.** to howl. **2.** to wail.
вопиющий *adj.* crying, flagrant, scandalous.
воплощать *impf. pf.* воплотить to embody, to personify; to incarnate.
воплощение *neut.* embodiment.
вопль *m.* cry, wail.
вопреки *prep.* (*with dat.*) in spite of, despite.
вопрос *m.* **1.** question. **2.** issue.
вопросительный *adj.* **1.** questioning. **2.** (*gram.*) interrogative. — вопросительный знак *m.* question mark.
вопросник *m.* questionnaire.
вор *m.* thief.
ворвань *f.* blubber.
ворваться *pf. of* врываться.
воришка *m.* and *f.* (*decl. f.*) petty thief.
ворковать OVA *impf.* to coo.
воркотня *f.* (*colloq.*) griping; grumbling.
воробей *m.* sparrow.
воробьиный *adj.* sparrow's.
ворованный *adj.* stolen.
вороватый *adj.* furtive.
воровать OVA *impf.* to steal.
воровской *adj.* thieves'.
воровство *neut.* thievery; stealing.

ворожба *f.* (*obs.*) fortune telling.
ворожить *impf. pf.* по- to tell fortunes.
ворон *m.* raven.
ворона *f.* crow.
Воронеж *m.* Voronezh.
вороний *adj.* crow's.
воронить *impf.* to burnish.
воронка *f.* **1.** funnel. **2.** bomb crater.
вороной *adj.* (*of horse*) black.
ворот *m.* **1.** collar. **2.** windlass. —ник *also* —ничок *m.* collar.
ворота *pl.* gate; gates.
воротила *m.* and *f.* (*decl. f.*) (*colloq.*) bigwig.
ворох *m.* pile, heap.
ворочать *impf.* **1.** to move; to shift. **2.** (*with instr.*) to boss; to manipulate.
ворочаться *impf. v.i.* to turn, to toss.
Ворошиловград *m.* Voroshilovgrad.
ворс *m.* nap; pile.
ворсинка *f.* fiber; hair.
ворчанье *neut.* growling; grumbling.
ворчать *impf.* **1.** to growl, to snarl. **2.** to grumble.
ворчливый *adj.* grumbling; grumpy.
ворчун *m. f.* —ья griper; grumbler.
восемнадцатый *adj.* eighteenth.
восемнадцать *num.* eighteen.
восемь *num.* eight.
восемьдесят *num.* eighty.
восемьсот *num.* eight hundred.
восемью *adv.* eight times.
воск *m.* wax.
воскликнуть *pf. of* восклицать.
восклицание *neut.* exclamation.
восклицательный *adj.* exclamatory; exclamation.
восклицать *impf. pf.* воскликнуть to exclaim.
восковой *adj.* (*attrib.*) wax; waxy.
воскресать *impf. pf.* воскреснуть **1.** to rise again. **2.** to rise from the dead. **3.** to revive.
воскресение *neut.* resurrection; revival.
воскресенье *neut.* Sunday.
воскресный *adj.* (*attrib.*) Sunday.
воскресение *neut.* resurrection; revival.
воспаление *neut.* inflammation. — воспаление лёгких pneumonia.
воспалённый *adj.* inflamed.
воспалительный *adj.* inflammatory, inflammation.
воспевать *impf. pf.* воспеть to glorify, to celebrate.
воспитание *neut.* education, training, rearing.
воспитанник *m. f.* воспитанница pupil.
воспитанность *f.* good breeding.
воспитанный *adj.* well-bred.
воспитатель *m. f.* —ница teacher, tutor.
воспитательный *adj.* educational.
воспитывать *impf. pf.* воспитать **1.** to rear, to bring up. **2.** to teach, to educate.
воспламенение *neut.* **1.** ignition. **2.** combustion.
воспламенять *impf. pf.* воспламенить **1.** to inflame, to fire up.
воспользоваться OVA *pf.* (*with instr.*) **1.** to make use of; to use. **2.** to take advantage of.
воспоминание *neut.* recollection; reminiscence.
воспрещать *impf. pf.* воспретить to forbid, to prohibit.
воспрещение *neut.* prohibition.

восприёмник *m.* godfather. — восприёмница *f.* godmother.

восприймчивость *f.* **1.** receptivity. **2.** susceptibility.

восприймчивый *adj.* susceptible.

воспринимáть *impf. pf.* воспринять **1.** to perceive. **2.** to assimilate.

восприятие *neut.* perception.

воспроизведёние *neut.* reproduction.

воспроизводительный *adj.* reproductive.

воспроизводить *impf. pf.* воспроизвести **1.** to reproduce. **2.** to reprint.

воспротивиться *pf.* **1.** to oppose. **2.** to resist.

воспрянуть дýхом *pf.* to cheer up.

воссоединёние *neut.* reunification.

воссоздавáть *impf. pf.* воссоздáть **1.** to re-create. **2.** to reconstruct; to reconstitute.

восставáть *impf. pf.* восстáть (прóтив *with dat.*) **1.** to rise. **2.** to revolt; to rebel (against).

восстанáвливать *impf. pf.* восстановить to restore, to reestablish; to rehabilitate.

восстáние *neut.* revolt, insurrection, uprising.

восстановлёние *neut.* restoration, reconstruction, rehabilitation.

востóк *m.* east.

востоковéд *m.* Orientalist.

востóрг *m.* rapture; enthusiasm.

восторгáть *impf.* **1.** to entrance, to enrapture. **2.** to delight.

востóрженность *f.* ecstacy; delight.

востóрженный *adj.* rapturous; ecstatic.

востóчный *adj.* east, easterly, eastern; oriental.

вострéбование *neut.* claim, claiming. — до вострéбования general delivery; poste restante.

вострéбовать OVA *pf.* to claim.

восхвалёние *neut.* praise, praising; praises.

восхвалять *impf. pf.* восхвалить **1.** to praise, to laud. **2.** to eulogize.

восхитительный *adj.* delightful, charming; exquisite.

восхищáть *impf. pf.* восхитить to charm, to delight. —ся (*with instr.*) to admire; to be delighted (with); to be charmed (by).

восхищёние *neut.* admiration; delight.

восхóд *m.* rise, rising.

восходящий *adj.* rising.

восхождёние *neut.* ascent.

восшéствие *neut.* (*obs.*) ascent.

восьмáя *f.* eighth.

восьмёрка *f.* (*cards*) eight.

вóсьмеро *coll. num.* eight.

восьмигрáнник *m.* octahedron.

восьмидесятый *adj.* eightieth.

восьмилéтний *adj.* eight-year-old.

восьмисóтый *adj.* eight hundredth.

восьмиугóльный *adj.* octagonal.

восьмóй *adj.* eighth.

восьмýшка *f.* eighth of a pound.

вот *particle* there; there is.

вот-вóт *adv.* (*colloq.*) just; on the point of; just about to.

воткнýть *pf. of* втыкáть.

вóтум *m.* vote.

вóтчина *f.* **1.** home territory. **2.** ancestral lands.

вошь *f.* louse.

вощáнка *f.* wax paper.

вощёный *adj.* waxed.

воюющий *adj.* warring, belligerent.

воякá *m. and f.* (*decl. f.*) (*colloq.*) (*ironic*) warrior.

впадáть *impf. pf.* впасть (в *with acc.*) to fall in or into.

впадёние *neut.* confluence.

впáдина *f.* **1.** hollow. **2.** cavity.

впáлый *adj.* hollow; caved in.

впасть *pf. of* впадáть.

впервые *adv.* the first time; first.

впаревáлку *adv.*: ходить впаревáлку *impf.* to waddle.

вперёд *adv.* forward; in the future, henceforth.

впереди *adv.* in front, before, ahead.

вперемéжку *adv.* alternately.

вперемéшку *adv.* pell-mell.

впечатлéние *neut.* impression.

впечатлительный *adj.* impressionable.

впечатляющий *adj.* impressive.

впивáть *impf. pf.* впить to absorb.

вписывать *impf. pf.* вписáть **1.** to inscribe. **2.** to register, to enter in writing.

впитывать *impf. pf.* впитáть **1.** to absorb. **2.** to imbibe.

впихивать *impf. pf.* впихнýть **1.** to stuff in or into; to cram in or into. **2.** to shove in or into.

вплавь *adv.* by swimming.

вплотнýю *adv.* close, closely.

вплоть *adv.* close to the end. — вплоть до (*with gen.*) right up to.

вполгóлоса *adv.* in a low voice; in an undertone.

вползáть *impf. pf.* вползти to crawl in, to creep in.

вполнé *adv.* **1.** entirely, completely, fully. **2.** quite.

вполоборóта *adv.* half-turned.

впопáд *adv.* (*colloq.*) to the point.

впопыхáх *adv.* hastily, in a hurry.

впорхнýть *pf.* to fly in.

впослéдствии *adv.* **1.** later, afterwards. **2.** consequently.

впотьмáх *adv.* in the dark.

впрáвду *adv.* (*colloq.*) really.

впрáве *adv.* having a right.

вправлять *impf. pf.* впрáвить *v.t.* (*surg.*) to set.

впрáво *adv.* to the right of.

впредь *adv.* **1.** henceforth. **2.** in the future.

вприкýску *adv.*: пить чай вприкýску *impf.* to drink tea eating lumps of sugar at the same time.

вприпрыжку *adv.*: бежáть вприпрыжку to skip along.

вприсядку *adv.* in a squatting position (*while dancing*).

впрóголодь *adv.* half-starving.

впрок *adv.* **1.** for future use. **2.** (*with* идти) to one's advantage.

впросáк *adv.*: попáсть впросáк *impf.* to commit a gaffe.

впросóнках *adv.* (*colloq.*) while half-asleep.

впрóчем *adv.* however; nevertheless.

впрыгивать *impf. pf.* впрыгнуть (в *with acc.*) to jump in; (на *with acc.*) to jump on.

впрыскивание *neut.* injection.

впрыскивать *impf. pf.* впрыснуть to inject.

впрямýю *adv.* (*colloq.*) directly.

впрямь *adv.* (*colloq.*) really; indeed.

впуск *m.* **1.** admission. **2.** admittance. **3.** intake.

впускáть *impf. pf.* впустить *v.t.* to admit.

впустýю *adv.* in vain; to no purpose.

впу́тывать *impf. pf.* впу́тать **1.** to involve. **2.** to entangle. **—ся** to meddle, to interfere; to become involved.

впя́теро *adv.* five times.

впятеро́м *adv.* five together.

враг *m.* enemy, foe.

вражда́ *f.* enmity, hostility.

вражде́бный *adj.* hostile.

высыпа́ть *impf. pf.* вы́сыпать **1.** to pour out. **2.** *impers. (of rash, etc.)* to break out.

вразби́вку *adv.* at random.

вразбро́д *adv. (colloq.)* **1.** separately. **2.** in disunity.

вразбро́с *adv. (colloq.)* scattered around; lying about.

вразва́лку *adv.*: ходи́ть вразва́лку *(colloq.)* to waddle.

вразре́з *adv.* contrary; contrary to.

вразуми́тельный *adj.* intelligible, clear.

вра́ки *pl. (colloq.)* lies.

враль *m. (colloq.)* liar.

Вра́нгеля: о́стров Вра́нгеля *m.* Wrangel Island.

враньё *neut.* **1.** lying. **2.** lies.

врасплóх *adv.* by surprise, unawares.

врассыпну́ю *adv.* in all directions; every which way.

враста́жку *adv. (colloq.)* stretched out.

врата́рь *m.* goal keeper, goalie.

врать *impf. pf.* совра́ть to lie, to tell lies.

врач *m.* physician, doctor. **—éбный** *adj.* medical.

враща́тельный *adj.* rotary.

враща́ть *impf. v.t.* to revolve, to rotate, to turn. **—ся** *v.i.* **1.** to revolve, to rotate, to turn. **2.** to mingle, to associate with.

враще́ние *neut.* rotation.

вред *m.* harm; hurt; injury.

вреди́тель *m.* **1.** pest; vermin. **2.** wrecker, saboteur. **—ство** *neut.* sabotage.

вреди́ть *impf. pf.* по- **1.** to harm, to injure, to hurt. **2.** to damage.

вре́дно *adv.* in a harmful manner.

вре́дный *adj.* **1.** harmful, injurious. **2.** unhealthful.

вредонóсный *adj.* harmful.

времена́ми *adv.* at times, from time to time.

вре́менно *adv.* temporarily.

временнóй *adj.* time; temporal.

вре́менный *adj.* **1.** temporary. **2.** provisional.

вре́мя *neut. pl.* времена́ **1.** time. **2.** *(gram.)* tense. **— вре́мя гóда** season.

времяисчисле́ние *neut.* calendar.

време́нка *f.* **1.** temporary construction. **2.** *(colloq.)* small stove.

времяпрепровожде́ние *neut.* pastime.

врóвень *adv.* even (with); on a level (with).

врóде *prep. (with gen.)* like; not unlike.

врождённый *adj.* innate, inborn.

врозь *adv.* apart; separately.

Врóцлав *m.* Wrocław *(also: Breslau).*

врукопа́шную *adv.* hand-to-hand combat.

врун *m. f.* **—ья** liar, fibber.

вруча́ть *impf. pf.* вручи́ть **1.** to present, to award. **2.** to deliver.

вруче́ние *neut.* **1.** presentation. **2.** delivery.

вручну́ю *adv.* by hand; manually.

врыва́ть *impf. pf.* врыть (в *with acc.*) **1.** to implant. **2.** to set into the ground.

врыва́ться[1] *impf. pf.* ворва́ться (в *with acc.*) to burst in or into.

врыва́ться[2] *impf. pf.* врьться (в *with acc.*) to dig in; to be dug in.

вряд ли *particle* hardly; it is unlikely.

вса́дник *m. f.* вса́дница rider; horseman.

вса́сывание *neut.* **1.** suction. **2.** absorption.

вса́сывать *impf. pf.* всосáть to absorb.

все *adj., see* весь. — *pron.* everyone, all.

всё *adj., see* весь. — *pron.* all, everything. — *adv.* always; still, yet.

всеве́дение *neut.* omniscience.

всеве́дущий *adj.* omniscient.

всевозмóжный *adj.* all possible.

всегда́ *adv.* always.

всегда́шний *adj. (colloq.)* customary; regular.

всегó *pron., gen. of* весь. — *adv.* in all; only.

всезна́йка *m.* and *f. (decl. f.) (colloq.)* know-it-all.

вселе́ние *neut.* moving in *(into a new house).*

вселе́нная *f.* **1.** universe. **2.** world.

вселе́нский *adj.* universal; ecumenical.

вселя́ть *impf. pf.* всели́ть **1.** to install. **2.** to establish. **3.** to instill.

всеме́рный *adj.* **1.** utmost. **2.** all possible.

всеми́рная паути́на *f.* World Wide Web *(abbr.* WWW).

всеми́рный *adj.* universal.

всемогу́щий *adj.* all-powerful; omnipotent.

всенарóдный *adj.* nationwide.

всенóщная *f.* vespers.

всеóбщий *adj.* general, universal.

всеобъе́млющий *adj.* comprehensive; all-embracing.

всеору́жие *neut.*: во всеору́жии *adv.* fully armed.

всепобежда́ющий *adj.* all-conquering.

всероссийский *adj.* All-Russian.

всерьёз *adv.* seriously; in earnest.

всесою́зный *adj.* All-Soviet.

всесторóнний *adj.* comprehensive, thorough.

всё-таки *adv.* nevertheless; still, however.

всеуслы́шание *neut.*: во всеуслы́шание *adv.* for everyone to hear.

всеце́ло *adv.* entirely, completely, wholly.

всея́дный *adj.* omnivorous.

вска́кивать *impf. pf.* вскочи́ть (на *with acc.*, в *with acc.*) to jump on or into; to jump or leap up.

вска́пывать *impf. pf.* вскопа́ть to dig.

вскара́бкиваться *impf. pf.* вскара́бкаться (на *with acc.*) to climb onto; to clamber up.

вска́чь *adv.* at a gallop.

вски́дывать *impf. pf.* вски́нуть **1.** to throw up. **2.** (на *with acc.*) to toss onto.

вскипа́ть *impf. pf.* вскипе́ть *v.i.* **1.** to boil, to begin to boil. **2.** to become enraged.

вскипяти́ть *pf. of* кипяти́ть.

всклокóченный *adj. (colloq.)* disheveled.

всколыхну́ть *pf.* to stir up; to agitate.

вскользь *adv.* casually, in passing.

вскóре *adv.* shortly or soon after.

вскочи́ть *pf. of* вска́кивать.

вскри́кивать *impf. pf.* вскри́кнуть to scream, to shriek.

вскрыва́ть *impf. pf.* вскрыть **1.** to open, to unseal. **2.** to disclose, to reveal. **3.** to dissect, to lance.

вскры́тие *neut.* **1.** opening, unsealing. **2.** revelation, disclosure; dissection,

всласть *adv.* (*colloq.*) to one's heart's content.

вслед *adv.* after; behind; following.

вследствие *prep.* (*with gen.*) owing to, on account of.

вслепую *adv.* (*colloq.*) **1.** blindly. **2.** blindfolded.

вслух *adv.* out loud.

всматриваться *impf. pf.* **всмотреться 1.** to peer into. **2.** to scrutinize.

всмятку *adv.*: **яйцо всмятку** soft-boiled egg.

всосать *pf. of* **всасывать**.

вспарывать *impf. pf.* **вспороть** (*colloq.*) to cut open; to rip open.

вспашка *f.* plowing.

всплеск *m.* splash; splashing.

вспоминать *impf. pf.* **вспомнить** to remember; to recollect; to recall.

вспомнить *pf. of* **вспоминать**.

вспомогательный *adj.* auxiliary.

вспорхнуть *pf.* to take wing; to flutter up.

вспотеть *pf. of* **потеть**.

вспрыскивание *neut.* sprinkling.

вспухать *impf. pf.* **вспухнуть** to swell up.

вспыхивать *impf. pf.* **вспыхнуть 1.** to blaze up. **2.** (*of war or panic*) to break out. **3.** to blush.

вспышка *f.* **1.** flash. **2.** outbreak. **3.** outburst.

вспять *adv.* (*obs.*) back; in the opposite direction.

вставание *neut.* standing up; rising.

вставать *impf. pres.* **встаю, встаёшь** *pf.* **встать 1.** to stand up; to get up. **2.** (*of the sun*) to rise. **3.** to arise; to come up.

вставка *f.* **1.** mounting; setting. **2.** insert, insertion. **3.** inset.

вставлять *impf. pf.* **вставить 1.** to put in; to insert. **2.** to interject; to interpose.

вставной *adj.* inserted.

вставной зуб *m.* false tooth.

встарь *adv.* in the old days.

встревоженный *adj.* alarmed.

встревожить *pf. of* **тревожить**.

встрёпанный *adj.* (*colloq.*) disheveled.

встреча *f.* **1.** meeting. **2.** welcome. **3.** (*sports*) match; contest.

встречать *impf. pf.* **встретить** to meet, to encounter; to greet.

встречный 1. *adj.* approaching; oncoming. **2.** counter.

встряска *f.* shaking; shock.

встряхивать *impf. pf.* **встряхнуть** to shake out; to shake up.

вступать *impf. pf.* **вступить** (**в** *with acc.*) to enter; to join; to enter into *or* upon.

вступительный *adj.* introductory; entrance; opening.

вступление *neut.* entry; prelude, preamble, introduction.

всуе *adj.* (*obs.*) in vain.

всухомятку *adv.* (*colloq.*) dry (*about food eaten without a beverage*).

всухую *adv.* (*colloq.*) without grease.

всучивать *impf. pf.* **всучить** (*colloq.*) to palm off (*on someone*).

всхлипывать *impf. pf.* **всхлипнуть** to sniffle; to sob.

всходить *impf. pf.* **взойти** (**на** *with acc.*) to mount, to ascend, to rise.

всходы *pl.* shoots; sprouts.

всхрапывать *impf.* to snore.

всюду *adv.* everywhere.

вся *adj.*, *see* **весь**.

всякий *adj.* any; every. — *pron.* anyone; everyone.

всякое *neut.* anything.

всячески *adv.* (*colloq.*) in every possible way *or* manner.

всячина *f.* (*colloq.*): **всякая всячина** all sorts of things.

втайне *adv.* secretly, in secret.

втирание *neut.* **1.** rubbing in. **2.** liniment.

втирать *impf. pf.* **втереть** to rub in *or* into.

втихомолку *adv.* secretly, stealthily.

вторгаться *impf. pf.* **вторгнуться** (**в** *with acc.*) **1.** to invade. **2.** to trespass; to intrude on *or* upon.

вторжение *neut.* invasion; intrusion.

вторично *adv.* for the second time.

вторичный *adj.* **1.** second. **2.** secondary.

вторник *m.* Tuesday.

вторничный *adj.* (*attrib.*) Tuesday.

второгодник *m. f.* **второгодница** student left back in school.

второе *neut.* main course; entrée.

Второзаконие *neut.* Deuteronomy.

второй *f.* **1.** *ord.* second. **2.** the latter.

второклассник *m. f.* **второклассница** pupil in the second grade.

второкурсник *m. f.* **второкурсница** student in the second year; sophomore.

второпях *adv.* hurriedly; hastily.

второразрядный *adj.* second-rate.

второсортный *adj.* second-rate.

второстепенный *adj.* **1.** secondary, minor. **2.** grade B.

в-третьих *adv.* thirdly; third; in third place.

втридорога *adv.* (*colloq.*) triple the price; three times as much.

втрое *adv.* thrice; three times as much.

втроём *adv.* three together.

втройне *adv.* triple; three times as much.

втулка *f.* **1.** (*mech.*) bushing. **2.** plug; stopper.

втуне *adv.* (*obs.*) in vain; for nothing.

втыкать *impf. pf.* **воткнуть** (**в** *with acc.*) to run, to drive, to stick, to thrust in *or* into.

втягивать *impf. pf.* **втянуть 1.** to draw into. **2.** to pull in *or* into.

вуаль *f.* veil.

вуз *m.* (*abbr. of* **высшее учебное заведение** *neut.*) institution of higher education.

вузовец FILL *m.* (*colloq.*) college student.

вулкан *m.* volcano.

вулканизация *f.* vulcanization.

вулканизировать OVA *impf. and pf.* to vulcanize.

вулканический *adj.* volcano; volcanic.

вульгаризм *m.* vulgarism.

вульгарный *adj.* vulgar.

вундеркинд *m.* child prodigy.

вурдалак *m.* vampire; werewolf.

вход *m.* entrance, entry, admittance.

входить *impf. pf.* **войти** to enter, to go *or* come in.

входной *m. and adj.* entrance; admission.

входящий *adj.* incoming.

вхождение *neut.* entering; joining.

вхожий *adj.* (*colloq.*) having entrance.

вхолостую *adv.*: **работать вхолостую** (*motor*) to idle.

вчера́ *adv.* yesterday.

вчера́шний *adj.* yesterday's; of yesterday.

вчерне́ *adv.* in the rough.

вче́тверо *adv.* **1.** four times; quadruple. **2.** in four parts.

вчетверо́м *adv.* four together.

в-четвёртых *adv.* in fourth place.

вшивно́й *adj.* sewn in.

вши́вый *adj.* **1.** infested with lice. **2.** (*colloq.*) meager; miserable.

вширь *adv.* in breadth.

въе́дливый *adj.* (*colloq.*) meticulous.

въезд *m.* entry, entrance (*by conveyance*).

въезжа́ть *impf. pf.* въе́хать (в *with acc.*). **1.** to enter. **2.** to drive in *or* into.

вы *pron. pl.* you.

выбега́ть *impf. pf.* вы́бежать to run out *or* out of.

выбира́ть *impf. pf.* вы́брать **1.** to choose. **2.** to elect.

выбира́ться *impf.* **1.** to be chosen. **2.** (из *with gen.*) to get out of.

вы́бор *m.* choice, selection.

Вы́борг *m.* Vyborg.

вы́борка *f.* **1.** choice; selection. **2.** sample; sampling. — *pl.* вы́борки excerpts.

вы́борность *f.* election; electibility.

вы́борный *adj.* elective; electible.

вы́борочный *adj.* selective.

вы́борщик *m. f.* вы́борщица elector; voter.

вы́боры *pl.* election(s).

выбра́сывание *neut.* throwing out; ejection.

выбра́сывать *impf. pf.* вы́бросить to throw out

вы́брать *pf. of* выбира́ть.

выбыва́ть *impf.* to leave; to depart.

выва́ливать *impf* (*colloq.*) to throw out; to dump out.

выве́дывать *impf.* (*colloq.*) to worm out; to ferret out.

вы́везти *pf. of* вывози́ть.

вы́верка *f.* adjustment.

вы́вернуть *pf. of* вывора́чивать.

вы́верт *m.* (*colloq.*) turn; twist.

вывёртывать *impf. pf.* вы́вернуть **1.** to unscrew. **2.** to turn inside out.

вы́веска *f.* sign, signboard.

вы́вести *pf. of* выводи́ть.

выве́тривание *neut.* **1.** ventilation. **2.** erosion.

выве́шивать *impf. pf.* вы́весить to hang out.

вы́вих *m.* dislocation.

вы́вихнуть *pf.* to dislocate, to sprain.

вы́вод *m.* **1.** conclusion, inference. **2.** withdrawal, removal.

выводи́ть *impf. pf.* вы́вести **1.** to withdraw, to remove. **2.** to exterminate. **3.** to conclude, to infer.

выводи́ться *impf. pf.* вы́вестись **1.** to disappear. **2.** to become extinct. **3.** to hatch; be hatched.

выводно́й *adj.* **1.** discharge. **2.** (*anat.*) excretory.

вы́воз *m.* export.

вывози́ть *impf. pf.* вы́везти **1.** to remove. **2.** to export.

вы́возка *f.* (*colloq.*) carting out.

выпора́чивать *impf. pf.* вы́вернуть to unscrew.

вы́гиб *m.* curve; bend.

выгиба́ть *impf. pf.* вы́гнуть to bend; to curve.

вы́гладить *pf. of* гла́дить.

выгля́дывать *impf. pf.* вы́глянуть to look out, to peep out.

вы́гнать *pf. of* выгоня́ть.

вы́гнутый *adj.* curved; bent.

вы́гнуть *pf. of* выгиба́ть.

вы́говор *m.* **1.** reprimand. **2.** pronunciation.

вы́года *f.* **1.** gain, profit. **2.** advantage.

вы́годно *adv.* **1.** favorably. **2.** at a profit.

вы́годный *adj.* **1.** profitable. **2.** advantageous.

вы́гон *m.* pasture.

выгоня́ть *impf. pf.* вы́гнать **1.** to drive out. **2.** to turn out.

выграви́ровать OVA *pf. of* грави́ровать.

выгребна́я я́ма *f.* cesspool.

выгружа́ть *impf. pf.* вы́грузить to unload.

вы́грузка *f.* unloading.

выдава́ть *impf. pf.* вы́дать **1.** to distribute, to give out. **2.** to betray.

вы́дача *f.* **1.** distribution. **2.** extradition.

выдаю́щийся *adj.* **1.** outstanding. **2.** eminent, distinguished.

выдвига́ть *impf. pf.* вы́двинуть to pull out.

выдвиже́ние *neut.* **1.** moving forward; advancement. **2.** nomination. **3.** promotion.

выдвижно́й *adj.* sliding.

выделе́ние *neut.* **1.** apportionment; allotment. **2.** secretion; excretion; discharge.

выдели́тельный *adj.* secretory; excretory.

вы́делка *f.* manufacture.

выде́лывать *impf. pf.* вы́делать to manufacture, to make.

выделя́ть *impf. pf.* вы́делить **1.** to single out. **2.** to choose. **3.** to detach. **4.** to secrete.

выделя́ться *impf.* **1.** to stand out. **2.** to exude. **3.** to take one's share (*of a legacy*).

вы́держанность *f.* endurance, firmness, steadfastness.

вы́держанный *adj.* **1.** self-possessed. **2.** (*cheese, wine*) aged; mellowed.

выде́рживать *impf. pf.* вы́держать **1.** to bear, to endure. **2.** to sustain. **3.** to control *or* contain oneself.

вы́держка *f.* **1.** endurance; self control. **2.** extract. **3.** (*photog.*) exposure.

вы́дох *m.* exhalation.

вы́дра *f.* otter.

вы́драть *pf.* to thrash, to flog.

вы́думанный *adj.* fictitious.

вы́думка *f.* **1.** invention. **2.** fib, made-up story.

вы́думщик *m. f.* вы́думщица (*colloq.*) person who easily invents *or* fabricates something.

выду́мывать *impf. pf* вы́думать to invent, to make up, to conceive.

выдыха́ние *neut.* exhalation.

выдыха́ть *impf. pf.* вы́дохнуть to exhale; to breathe out.

вы́езд *m.* departure.

выездно́й *adj.* (*horse*) for riding.

выезжа́ть *impf. pf.* вы́ехать to leave, to depart.

вы́емка *f.* depression, hollow.

выжива́ние *neut.* survival.

выжива́ть *impf. pf.* вы́жить to survive.

выжига́ние *neut.* burning out.

выжига́ть *impf. pf.* вы́жечь to burn down.

выжида́ние *neut.* waiting.

выжида́тельный *adj.* waiting.

выжима́ть *impf. pf.* вы́жать to wring out, to squeeze out.

вы́звать *pf. of* вызыва́ть.

выздора́вливать *impf. pf.* вы́здороветь to recover, to get well.

выздоровле́ние *neut.* convalescence, recovery.

вы́зов *m.* **1.** summons; call. **2.** challenge.

вызыва́ть *impf. pf.* вы́звать **1.** to call, to summon. **2.** to challenge. **3.** to evoke. **4.** to cause.

вызыва́ющий *adj.* **1.** defiant. **2.** challenging.

вы́игрывать *impf. pf.* вы́играть **1.** to win. **2.** to gain.

вы́игрыш *m.* winnings, prize.

вы́игрышный *adj.* **1.** winning (*e.g. ticket*). **2.** advantageous.

вы́йти *pf. of* выходи́ть.

выкара́бкиваться *impf. pf.* вы́карабкаться (*colloq.*) **1.** to extricate oneself. **2.** to pull through (*an illness, etc.*).

выка́чивать *impf. pf.* вы́качать to pump; to pump out.

вы́кидыш *m.* abortion; miscarriage.

выкла́дывать *impf. pf.* вы́ложить **1.** to lay out, to spread out. **2.** to cover with.

выключа́тель *m.* switch.

выключа́ть *impf. pf.* вы́ключить **1.** to turn off, to shut off. **2.** to switch off.

выко́вывать *impf. pf.* вы́ковать to forge (*metal*).

выкра́ивать *impf. pf.* вы́кроить to cut out.

вы́крик *m.* shout; yell; cry.

вы́кройка *f.* pattern.

выкрута́сы *pl.* (*colloq.*) **1.** flourishes (*in handwriting*). **2.** twists and turns.

выкру́чивать *impf. pf.* вы́крутить **1.** to twist. **2.** to make by twisting.

вы́куп *m.* **1.** redemption. **2.** ransom.

выкупа́ть *impf. pf.* вы́купить **1.** to redeem. **2.** to ransom.

вы́купать *pf. of* купа́ть.

вы́ку́ривать *impf. pf.* вы́курить to smoke; to smoke out.

выла́вливать *impf. pf.* вы́ловить to fish out.

вы́лазка *f.* **1.** (*mil.*) sortie. **2.** outing; excursion.

вылеза́ть *impf. pf.* вы́лезть **1.** to climb out. **2.** to come out, to get out. **3.** to emerge.

вы́лепить *pf. of* лепи́ть.

вы́лет *m.* **1.** flight. **2.** takeoff (*of an airplane*).

вылета́ть *impf. pf.* вы́лететь **1.** to fly out. **2.** to take off. **3.** to dash out.

вылечивать *impf. pf.* вы́лечить to cure.

вылива́ть *impf. pf.* вы́лить to pour out.

вы́литый оте́ц *m.* (*colloq.*) the very image of one's father.

вы́ложить *pf. of* выкла́дывать.

вылупля́ться *impf. pf.* вы́лупиться to hatch.

выма́нивать *impf. pf.* вы́манить (*colloq.*) **1.** (из with gen.) to lure out of. **2.** (у with gen.) to cheat out of. **3.** (у with gen.) to coax out of.

выма́щивать *impf. pf.* вы́мостить to pave.

вы́мести *pf. of* мести́.

вымё́тывать *impf. pf.* вы́метать to throw out.

вымира́ние *neut.* dying out; extinction.

вымира́ть *impf. pf.* вы́мереть **1.** to die out. **2.** to become extinct.

вымога́тель *m. f.* —ница extortionist.

вымога́тельство *neut.* extortion.

вымога́ть *impf.* to extort; to wring (out).

вы́мпел *m.* pennant.

вы́мысел *m.* **1.** fabrication, fiction. **2.** lie.

вы́мышленный *adj.* imaginary; fictitious.

вы́мя *neut.* udder.

вына́шивать *impf. pf.* вы́носить **1.** to be pregnant with. **2.** to hatch plans. **3.** (*colloq.*) to wear out.

вынима́ть *impf. pf.* вы́нуть to take out.

вы́нос *m.* carrying out. — вы́нос те́ла funeral procession. — на вы́нос (*of food*) to take out.

выноси́ть *impf. pf.* вы́нести **1.** to carry *or* take *or* bring out. **2.** to carry away. **3.** to pass *or* pronounce (*a decision*). **4.** to endure.

выно́сливость *f.* endurance.

выно́сливый *adj.* hardy; capable of extreme endurance.

вы́нужденный *adj.* forced; constrained.

вы́нуть *pf. of* вынима́ть.

вы́пад *m.* **1.** attack. **2.** thrust.

выпада́ть *impf. pf.* вы́пасть **1.** to fall out, to drop out. **2.** to come out. **3.** (*of snow, etc.*) to fall.

выпаде́ние *neut.* falling; falling out.

выпека́ть *impf. pf.* вы́печь to bake.

вы́печка *f.* baking.

выпива́ть *impf. pf.* вы́пить **1.** to drink (up). **2.** to drain.

вы́пивка *f.* (*colloq.*) **1.** binge; (*drinking*) spree. **2.** drinks.

вы́писка *f.* certificate.

выпи́сывать *impf. pf.* вы́писать **1.** to write out. **2.** to copy. **3.** to order. **4.** to discharge.

вы́пить *pf. of* выпива́ть.

вы́плавка *f.* **1.** smelting. **2.** smelted metal.

вы́плата *f.* payment.

выпла́чивать *impf. pf.* вы́платить to pay, to pay out, to pay off.

выплё́вывать *impf. pf.* вы́плюнуть to spit out.

выплё́скивать *impf. pf.* вы́плеснуть to splash out.

выпола́скивать *impf. pf.* вы́полоскать to rinse out.

выполне́ние *neut.* **1.** execution. **2.** fulfillment.

выполни́мый *adj.* feasible.

выполня́ть *impf. pf.* вы́полнить **1.** to execute, to carry out. **2.** to fulfill.

вы́порхнуть *pf.* **1.** to fly out; to flit out. **2.** (*colloq.*) to dash out.

вы́правка *f.* bearing; carriage.

выправля́ть *impf. pf.* вы́править **1.** to straighten. **2.** to straighten out; to rectify. **3.** to correct (*e.g., a manuscript*).

выпрова́живать *impf. pf.* вы́проводить (*colloq.*) to send on one's way.

вы́пуклость *f.* bulge; protuberance.

вы́пуклый *adj.* **1.** bulging. **2.** prominent. **3.** convex.

вы́пуск *m.* **1.** issue, edition. **2.** output.

выпуска́ть *impf. pf.* вы́пустить **1.** to release, to let out. **2.** to issue. **3.** to publish. **4.** to omit.

выпускни́к *m. f.* выпускни́ца **1.** senior (*in college*). **2.** university graduate.

выпускно́й *adj.* (*attrib.*) **1.** (*mech.*) exhaust. **2.** graduation.

выпь *f.* (*bird*) bittern.

выраба́тывать *impf. pf.* вы́работать **1.** to manufacture, to produce. **2.** to work out. **3.** to earn.

вы́работка *f.* output, produce.

выра́внивание *neut.* **1.** smoothing. **2.** leveling. **3.** alignment.

выража́ть *impf. pf.* вы́разить to express.

выраже́ние *neut.* expression.

вы́раженный *adj.* pronounced; marked.

вырази́тельный *adj.* expressive.

вы́разить *pf. of* выража́ть.

выраста́ть *impf. pf.* **вы́расти 1.** to grow; to grow up. **2.** to grow out of.

выра́щивать *impf. pf.* **вы́растить 1.** to bring up, to rear. **2.** to grow.

вы́рез *m.* cut; cut-out section.

выреза́ть *impf. pf.* **вы́резать 1.** to cut out, to carve out. **2.** to engrave.

вы́резка *f.* **1.** cutting out. **2.** tenderloin; fillet (*of beef*).

вырезно́й *adj.* carved.

вырисо́вывать *impf. pf.* **вы́рисовать** to draw in great detail; to draw carefully.

вы́родок FILL *m.* (*colloq.*) outcast.

вырожда́ться *impf. pf.* **вы́родиться** to degenerate.

вырожде́ние *neut.* degeneration.

вы́рубка *f.* cutting down; chopping down.

вы́ругать *pf. of* руга́ть.

выруча́ть *impf. pf.* **вы́ручить 1.** to rescue. **2.** to help someone out. **3.** to make (*money or a profit*).

вы́ручка *f.* **1.** (*colloq.*) rescue. **2.** proceeds; receipts; takings.

вырыва́ть[1] *impf. pf.* **вы́рвать** to pull out, to tear out.

вырыва́ть[2] *impf. pf.* **вы́рыть** to dig up, to dig out.

вы́садка *f.* **1.** debarkation. **2.** transplanting. **3.** (*mil.*) landing.

выселе́ние *neut.* eviction.

выселя́ть *impf. pf.* **вы́селить** to evict.

вы́ситься *impf.* to tower; to loom; to rise.

вы́сказать *pres.* -скажу́, -ска́жешь *pf. of* выска́зывать.

выска́зывание *neut.* **1.** opinion, saying. **2.** declaration.

выска́зывать *impf. pf.* **вы́сказать 1.** to express. **2.** to declare. —**ся** to express oneself, to speak out.

вы́скочка *m. and f.* (*decl. f.*) (*colloq.*) upstart.

вы́слать *pf. of* высыла́ть.

вы́слуга *f.*: **за вы́слугу лет** by virtue of long service.

выслу́шивать *impf. pf.* **вы́слушать 1.** to hear, to hear out. **2.** to listen. **3.** (*med.*) to ausculate.

вы́сморкаться *pf. of* сморка́ться.

высо́вывать *impf. pf.* **вы́сунуть** to stick out.

высо́кий *adj.* **1.** high. **2.** tall.

высоко́ *adv.* high, high up.

высокока́чественный *adj.* high-quality.

высокоме́рие *neut.* arrogance; haughtiness.

высокоме́рный *adj.* haughty.

высокоопла́чиваемый *adj.* high-paid.

высокопа́рный *adj.* high-flown; bombastic.

высокопоста́вленный *adj.* high-ranking.

высокора́звитый *adj.* highly developed.

высота́ *f.* height; altitude.

высо́тный *adj.* **1.** (*of a building*) very tall. **2.** (*of an airplane*) high-altitude.

высотоме́р *m.* altimeter.

вы́сохнуть *pf. of* высыха́ть.

высоча́йший 1. *superl. of* высо́кий. **2.** royal; imperial.

высоче́нный *adj.* (*colloq.*) very tall; very high.

Высо́чество *neut.* Highness (*royal title*).

вы́ставка *f.* exhibition.

выставля́ть *impf. pf.* **вы́ставить 1.** to exhibit. **2.** to expose.

вы́ставочный *adj.* (*attrib.*) exhibition.

вы́стрел *m.* shot.

вы́ступ *m.* **1.** projection. **2.** ledge.

выступа́ть *impf. pf.* **вы́ступить 1.** to appear, to come out. **2.** to come forward.

выступле́ние *neut.* appearance.

вы́сушить *pf. of* суши́ть.

вы́сший *adj.* **1.** higher. **2.** superior.

высыла́ть *impf. pf.* **вы́слать** to send out, to forward; to dispatch.

вы́сылка *f.* **1.** sending; dispatch. **2.** deportation.

высыпа́ться[1] *impf. pf.* **вы́сыпаться** *v.i.* to spill out.

высыпа́ться[2] *imp. pf.* **вы́спаться** to have a good night's sleep.

высыха́ть *impf. pf.* **вы́сохнуть 1.** to dry out. **2.** to wither.

высь *f.* height.

выта́скивать *impf. pf.* **вы́тащить** to drag out; to pull out.

вы́тачка *f.* tuck (*on a garment*).

вытека́ть *impf. pf.* **вы́течь** to flow out, to leak out.

вы́тертый *adj.* (*colloq.*) threadbare.

вытесне́ние *neut.* exclusion; ouster.

вытира́ть *impf. pf.* **вы́тереть 1.** to dry. **2.** to wipe.

вытрезви́тель *m.* sobering-up station.

выть *impf.* to howl.

вытьё *neut.* (*colloq.*) howling; wailing.

вытя́гивать *impf. pf.* **вы́тянуть** to stretch (out).

вытяже́ние *neut.* stretching.

вы́тяжка *f.* **1.** drawing out. **2.** (*chem.*) extract.

вытяжно́й *adj.* (*attrib.*) exhaust.

вы́тянутый *adj.* outstretched.

вы́учка *f.* **1.** training. **2.** skill; level of training.

вы́хлоп *m.* (*mech.*) exhaust.

вы́ход *m.* **1.** egress; exit, outlet. **2.** issue.

вы́ходец FILL *m.* person originally from a different nation *or* social class.

выходи́ть *impf. pf.* **вы́йти 1.** to go out. **2.** to look out on.

вы́ходка *f.* trick; prank.

выходно́й день *m.* day off.

вы́холенный *adj.* well-groomed; neat; trim.

вы́хухоль *m.* desman (*European muskrat*).

вы́цветший *adj.* faded.

вычёркивание *neut.* deleting.

вычёркивать *impf. pf.* **вы́черкнуть** to cross off; to cross out; to delete.

вы́честь *pf. of* вычита́ть.

вы́чет *m.* deduction.

вычисле́ние *neut.* **1.** computation. **2.** calculation.

вычисли́тель 1. calculator; computer. **2.** computer specialist.

вычисли́тельный *adj.* (*attrib.*) **1.** computing. **2.** computer. — **вычисли́тельная маши́на** *f.* computer.

вычисля́ть *impf. pf.* **вы́числить** to calculate.

вычита́емое *neut.* subtrahend.

вычита́ние *neut.* (*math.*) subtraction.

вычита́ть *impf. pf.* **вы́честь** to deduct; to subtract.

вычища́ть *impf. pf.* **вы́чистить** to clean; to brush; to polish.

вы́чурный *adj.* fancy; elaborate.

вы́ше *adv.* higher.

вышеприведённый *adj.* cited above.

вышеска́занный *adj.* said above; said before; aforesaid.

вышеука́занный *adj.* above-named, above-mentioned.

вышеупомя́нутый *adj.* above-mentioned.

вышиба́ла *m. and f.* (*decl. f.*) (*colloq.*) bouncer.

вышиба́ть *impf. pf.* вы́шибить **1.** to kick out. **2.** to throw out.

вышива́ние *neut.* embroidery.

вышива́ть *impf. pf.* вы́шить to embroider.

вы́шивка *f.* embroidery.

вышина́ *f.* height.

вы́шитый *m.* embroidered.

вы́шка *f.* tower.

выштукату́ривать *impf. pf.* вы́штукатурить to stucco; to plaster.

выявле́ние *neut.* **1.** revelation. **2.** discovery.

выявля́ть *impf. pf.* вы́явить to reveal.

выясне́ние *neut.* clarification.

выясня́ть *impf. pf.* вы́яснить to elucidate.

Вьетна́м *m.* Vietnam.

вьетна́мец FILL *m. f.* вьетна́мка Vietnamese.

вьюга *f.* snowstorm, blizzard.

вьюк *m.* pack; load.

вьюно́к FILL *m.* bindweed; convulvulus.

вьюро́к FILL *m.* **1.** brambling. **2.** finch.

вьюшка *f.* damper.

вьющийся *adj.* **1.** (*of hair*) curly. **2.** (*of plant*) climbing.

вьючное живо́тное *neut.* beast of burden.

вяз *m.* elm, elm tree.

вяза́льный *adj.* (*attrib.*) knitting.

вяза́ние *neut.* **1.** knitting. **2.** crocheting.

вя́заный *adj.* knitted.

вяза́ть *impf. pf.* с- **1.** to tie, to bind. **2.** to knit.

вя́зка *f.* **1.** binding; tying. **2.** (*colloq.*) bundle. **3.** knitting.

вя́зкий *adj.* **1.** viscous. **2.** swampy, marshy.

вя́знуть *impf. pf.* за- *or* у- to get stuck.

Вя́зьма *f.* Vyazma.

вя́леный *adj.* dried; cured by drying.

вя́лый *adj.* **1.** flabby. **2.** sluggish.

вя́нуть *impf. pf.* за- **1.** to wither, to fade. **2.** to droop.

Вя́тка *f.* (*river*) Vyatka.

вя́щий *adj.* (*obs.*) greater.

Га́ага *f.* The Hague.
габари́т *m.* dimensions; size.
Гава́йи *pl.* Hawaii.
Гава́на *f.* Havana.
га́вань *f.* **1.** harbor. **2.** haven.
Гавр *m.* Le Havre.
га́га *f.* eider.
гага́ра *f.* (*bird*) loon.
гага́рка *f.* (*bird*) auk.
гад *m.* **1.** reptile. **2.** (*colloq.*) rat, louse.
гада́лка *f.* fortuneteller.
гада́ние *neut.* **1.** fortunetelling. **2.** guessing; guesswork.
гада́тельный *adj.* **1.** conjectural; problematical. **2.** hypothetical.
гада́ть *impf. pf.* **по- 1.** to tell fortunes. **2.** to surmise, to conjecture.
га́дкий *adj.* repulsive, vile, horrid.
гадли́вый *adj.* of revulsion, of disgust.
га́дость *f.* **1.** filth. **2.** dirty trick.
гадю́ка *f.* viper; adder.
га́ечный ключ *m.* wrench.
газ *m.* **1.** gas. **2.** gauze, gossamer.
газе́ль *f.* gazelle.
газе́тный *adj.* (*attrib.*) newspaper.
газе́тчик *m. f.* **газе́тчица 1.** news vendor. **2.** (*colloq.*) journalist.
газиро́ванный *adj.* carbonated.
газоме́р *m.* gas meter.
газо́н *m.* lawn. — **газонокоси́лка** *f.* lawn mower.
газообра́зный *adj.* gaseous.
газопрово́д *m.* gas pipeline.
ГАЙ *f. indecl.* (*abbr. of* **Госуда́рственная автомоби́льная инспе́кция** *f.*) traffic police.
га́йка *f.* (*mech.*) nut.
Гаи́ти *m.* Haiti.
гала́ктика *f.* galaxy.
галантере́я *f.* haberdashery; dry goods.
гала́нтный *adj.* gallant.
галдёж *m.* (*colloq.*) uproar, hubbub.
галере́я *f.* gallery.
галёрка *f.* (*colloq.*) gallery (*in a theater*).
галиматья́ *f.* (*colloq.*) rubbish, nonsense.
галифе́ *pl. indecl.* riding breeches.
Гали́ция *f.* (*province*) Galicia.
га́лка *f.* (*bird*) jackdaw.
га́ллий *m.* gallium.
галлици́зм *m.* gallicism.
галло́н *m.* gallon.
галлюцина́ция *f.* hallucination.
галоге́н *m.* halogen.
гало́п *m.* **1.** gallop. **2.** (*dance*) galop.
га́лочка *f.* (*colloq.*) check, mark.
гало́ши *pl.* galoshes, rubbers.
га́лстук *m.* tie, necktie.
галу́шки *pl.* dumplings.
гальвани́ческий *adj.* galvanic.
га́лька *f.* pebble.
гам *m.* (*colloq.*) racket; commotion.
гама́к *m.* hammock.
гама́ши *pl.* leggings.

гамби́т *m.* gambit.
Га́мбург *m.* Hamburg.
га́мма *f.* **1.** (*mus.*) scale. **2.** (*fig.*) gamut.
гангре́на *f.* gangrene.
га́нгстер *m.* gangster.
гандбо́л *m.* handball.
гандика́п *m.* (*sports*) handicap.
ганте́ль *f.* dumbbell.
гара́ж *m.* garage.
гаранти́ровать OVA *impf. and pf.* to guarantee; to vouch.
гара́нтия *f.* guarantee.
гарде́ния *f.* gardenia.
гардеро́б *m.* wardrobe.
гардеро́бщик *m. f.* **гардеро́бщица** cloakroom attendant.
гарди́на *f.* window curtain.
гарево́й *adj.* (*attrib.*) cinder.
гаре́м *m.* harem.
га́ркать *impf. pf.* **га́ркнуть** (*colloq.*) to bark, to shout.
гармонизи́ровать OVA *impf.* to harmonize.
гармо́ника *f.* accordion — **губна́я гармо́ника** *f.* harmonica, mouth organ.
гармони́ст *m.* accordionist.
гармони́ческий *also* **гармони́чный** *adj.* harmonic; harmonious.
гармо́ния *f.* harmony; concord.
гармо́нь *f.* accordion.
гарнизо́н *m.* garrison.
гарни́р *m.* garnish.
гарниту́р *m.* **1.** set. **2.** (*furniture*) suite.
Гаро́нна *f.* (*river*) Garonne.
гарпу́н *m.* harpoon.
га́рус *m.* worsted.
гарцева́ть OVA *impf.* to prance.
га́ршнеп *m.* (*bird*) jacksnipe.
гарь *f.* material that is burning; cinders.
гаси́ть *impf. pf.* **по-** to extinguish.
га́снуть *impf. pf.* **у- 1.** to go out, to stop burning. **2.** to decline.
гастри́т *m.* gastritis.
гастри́ческий *adj.* gastric.
гастролёр *m.* guest performer.
гастро́ли *pl.* tour.
гастроно́м *m.* epicure; gourmet.
гастроно́мия *f.* gastronomy.
гать *f.* log road (*in marshy area*).
га́убица *f.* howitzer.
гауптва́хта *f.* (*mil.*) guardhouse.
гаше́ние *neut.* extinction; extinguishing.
гашёный *adj.* **1.** (*of a stamp*) used; cancelled. **2.** (*of lime*) slaked.
гашётка *f.* trigger.
гаши́ш *m.* hashish.
гвалт *m.* din, hubbub.
гварде́ец FILL *m.* guardsman.
гва́рдия *f.* guard.
Гватема́ла *f.* Guatemala.
гвоздь *m.* small nail; tack.
гвозди́ка *f.* **1.** carnation. **2.** clove.

гвоздичный *adj.* (*attrib.*) clove.

гвоздь *m.* nail.

Гданьск *m.* Gdańsk (*also: Danzig*).

где *adv.* where. — где-либо, где-нибудь, где-то somewhere; anywhere.

Гебридские острова *pl.* Hebrides.

гегемония *f.* hegemony.

гедонизм *m.* hedonism.

гей *interj.* (*arch.*) hey!

Гейдельберг *m.* Heidelberg.

гейзер *m.* geyser.

гейша *f.* geisha.

гектар *m.* hectare.

гелий *m.* helium.

гелиограф *m.* heliograph.

гелиотроп *m.* heliotrope.

гемоглобин *m.* hemoglobin.

геморрой *m.* hemorrhoids.

гемофилия *f.* hemophilia.

ген *m.* gene.

генеалогия *f.* genealogy.

генезис *m.* genesis.

генерал *m.* general. — генерал-лейтенант *m.* lieutenant general. — генерал-майор *m.* major general. — генерал-полковник *m.* colonel general (*equivalent to U.S. lieutenant general*).

генералиссимус *m.* generalissimo.

генералитет *m.* the generals.

генеральный *adj.* general.

генетика *f.* genetics.

гениальность *f.* genius.

гениальный *adj.* exceptionally gifted, talented.

гений *m.* genius.

геноцид *m.* genocide.

Генуя *f.* Genoa.

географ *m.* geographer.

география *f.* geography.

геодезия *f.* geodesy.

геолог *m.* geologist.

геология *f.* geology.

геометрия *f.* geometry.

геополитика *f.* geopolitics.

георгин *m. also* георгина *f.* (*flower*) dahlia.

геотермальный *adj.* geothermal.

геофизика *f.* geophysics.

геоцентрический *adj.* geocentric.

гепард *m.* cheetah.

гепатит *m.* hepatitis.

геральдика *f.* heraldry.

герань *f.* geranium.

герб *m.* coat of arms.

гербарий *m.* herbarium.

гербицид *m.* herbicide; weed-killer.

гербовый *adj.* bearing the coat of arms.

гериатрия *f.* geriatrics.

германец FILL *m. f.* германка Teuton.

германий *m.* germanium.

Германия *f.* Germany.

германский *adj.* German.

гермафродит *m.* hermaphrodite.

герметически *adv.* hermetically.

герметический *adj.* airtight, pressurized.

героизм *m.* heroism.

героин *m.* heroin.

героиня *f.* heroine.

героический *adj.* heroic; epic.

герой *m.* hero. —ство *neut.* heroism.

герольд *m.* (*hist.*) herald.

геронтология *f.* gerontology.

герундий *m.* gerund.

герц *m.* (*elec.*) cycle per second.

Герцеговина *f.* Herzegovina.

герцог *m.* duke. — герцогиня *f.* duchess.

герцогство *neut.* dukedom.

гетман *m.* Ukrainian Cossack chief; hetman.

гетры *pl.* gaiters; spats.

Гёттинген *m.* Göttingen.

гетто *neut. indecl.* ghetto.

гиацинт *m.* hyacinth.

гиббон *m.* gibbon.

гибель *f.* **1.** death. **2.** annihilation; destruction. —ный *adj.* destructive, ruinous.

гибискус *m.* hibiscus.

гибкий *adj.* **1.** flexible. **2.** subtle. **3.** pliable, pliant.

гиблый *adj.* (*colloq.*) worthless, hopeless.

гибнуть *impf. pf.* по- to perish, to lose one's life.

Гибралтарский пролив *m.* Strait of Gibraltar.

гибрид *m.* hybrid.

гигант *m.* giant. —ский *adj.* gigantic.

гигиена *f.* hygiene.

гидра *f.* hydra.

гидравлика *f.* hydraulics.

гидрант *m.* hydrant.

гидрат *m.* hydrate.

гидродинамика *f.* hydrodynamics.

гидролиз *m.* hydrolysis.

гидрология *f.* hydrology.

гидролокатор *m.* (*device*) sonar.

гидролокация *f.* (*method*) sonar.

гидросамолёт *m.* seaplane.

гидроэлектростанция *f.* hydroelectric station.

гиена *f.* hyena.

гикать *impf. pf.* гикнуть (*colloq.*) to whoop.

гильдия *f.* (*hist.*) guild.

гильза *f.* **1.** cartridge case; shell. **2.** cigarette wrapper.

гильотина *f.* guillotine.

Гималаи *pl.* Himalayas.

гимн *m.* anthem.

гимназист *m. f.* —ка secondary school student.

гимназия *f.* **1.** secondary school. **2.** gymnasium.

гимнастёрка *f.* soldier's blouse.

гимнастика *f.* gymnastics.

гимнастический *adj.* gymnastic.

гинекология *f.* gynecology.

гинея *f.* guinea.

гипербола *f.* **1.** hyperbola. **2.** hyperbole.

гипертония *f.* hypertension.

гипноз *m.* hypnosis.

гипнотизировать OVA *impf. pf.* за- to hypnotize.

гипнотизм *m.* hypnotism.

гипотеза *f.* hypothesis.

гипотенуза *f.* hypotenuse.

гипотетический *adj.* hypothetical.

гипофиз *also* гипофиз *m.* pituitary gland.

гиппопотам *m.* hippopotamus.

гипс *m.* **1.** gypsum. **2.** plaster. — гипсовый *adj.* plaster.

гипюровый *adj.* (*attrib.*) lace.

гиревик *m.* weightlifter.

гирлянда *f.* garland.

ги́ря f. **1.** dumbbell. **2.** weight (of a clock).
гистоло́гия f. histology.
гита́ра f. guitar.
глава́ f. **1.** chapter (of a book). **2.** head, chief.
глава́рь m. leader; ringleader.
главе́нство neut. supremacy.
главнокома́ндующий m. commander in chief.
гла́вный adj. main, chief, principal. — **гла́вным о́бразом** mainly.
глаго́л m. (gram.) verb.
глаго́лица f. Glagolitic alphabet.
глаго́льный adj. verbal.
гладиа́тор m. gladiator.
гла́ди́льный adj. (attrib.) ironing.
гладио́лус m. gladiolus.
гла́дить impf. pf. **вы́гладить, погла́дить 1.** to iron, to press. **2.** to stroke, to pat.
гла́дкий adj. smooth, even, sleek.
гладкоство́льный adj. smoothbore.
гла́дкость f. smoothness.
гладь f. **1.** smooth surface. **2.** satin stitch.
гла́женье neut. ironing, pressing.
глаз m. eye. — **в глаза́** to one's face. — **за глаза́** behind one's back.
глазе́ть impf. to stare; to gape at; to gawk.
глазиро́ванный adj. **1.** glazed. **2.** iced.
глазни́к m. (colloq.) eye doctor.
глазни́ца f. eye socket.
глазно́й adj. optic(al), (attrib.) eye.
глазо́к[1] m. dim. of **глаз**.
глазо́к[2] m. (colloq.) peephole.
глазоме́р m. ability to measure with the naked eye.
глазу́нья f. fried eggs.
глазу́рь f. glaze (on pottery); icing.
гла́нды pl. tonsils.
глас m. (arch.) voice.
гласи́ть impf. (of written material) to read; to say.
гла́сность f. **1.** honesty; openness. **2.** publicity.
гла́сный adj. vowel.
глауко́ма f. glaucoma.
глаша́тай m. herald; messenger.
гле́тчер m. glacier.
Гли́вице pl. Gliwice.
гликоге́н m. glycogen.
гли́на f. clay.
гли́нистый adj. clayey, loamy.
глиноби́тный adj. (attrib.) clay; adobe.
гли́няный adj. (attrib.) clay; earthenware.
гли́ссер m. hydroplane.
глист m. intestinal worm.
глицери́н m. glycerine.
глицери́новый adj. (attrib.) glycerine.
глици́ния f. (flower) wisteria.
глоба́льный adj. global.
гло́бус m. **1.** globe. **2.** sphere.
глода́ть impf. pres. **гложу́, гло́жешь** to gnaw.
гло́сса f. gloss (commentary).
глосса́рий m. glossary.
глота́ние neut. swallowing.
глота́ть impf. to swallow, gulp.
гло́тка f. throat; gullet. — **во всю гло́тку** (colloq.) at the top of one's voice.
глото́к FILL m. swallow, sip, mouthful.
гло́хнуть impf. pf. **о-** to grow deaf.
глу́бже adj. comp. of **глубо́кий**.

глубина́ f. **1.** depth, depths. **2.** heart, interior. **3.** substance.
глуби́нный adj. **1.** (attrib.) deep-water. **2.** remote.
глубо́кий adj. deep; profound. — **глубо́кая о́сень** late fall.
глубоко́ adv. deeply; profoundly.
глубоково́дный adj. deep-water.
глубокомы́сленный adj. profound.
глубокоуважа́емый adj. (used in salutation of a letter) dear.
глубь f. depth; depths.
глуми́ться impf. pf. **по-** (над with instr.) to mock, to jeer.
глумле́ние neut. mockery.
глумли́вый adj. derisive; mocking.
глупе́ц FILL m. dolt, blockhead.
глу́по adv. foolishly; stupidly.
глупова́тый adj. doltish, stupid.
глу́пость f. stupidity; dullness.
глу́пый adj. stupid; dull.
глупы́ш m. f. **—ка** (colloq.) silly person.
глуха́рь m. **1.** wood grouse. **2.** (colloq.) deaf person.
глуха́я завя́зка f. (colloq.) cold turkey (withdrawal from use of alcohol).
глухо́ adv. **1.** softly. **2.** vaguely. **3.** thickly.
глухо́й adj. deaf.
глухома́нь f. (colloq.) remote, out-of-the-way place.
глухонемо́й adj. deaf-mute. — m. deaf-mute.
глухота́ f. deafness.
глуши́тель m. **1.** silencer. **2.** muffler.
глушь f. wilds, wilderness; out-of-the-way place.
глы́ба f. **1.** block of ice or stone. **2.** clod of earth.
глюко́за f. glucose.
гляде́ть impf. pf. **по-** (на with acc.) to look at, to stare at.
гля́нец m. gloss; lustre.
гля́нцевый adj. glossy; lustrous.
гнать impf. **1.** to drive. **2.** to pursue. **3.** to persecute.
гнев m. anger. — **гне́вный** adj. angry.
гне́вить impf. pf. **про-** (obs.) to anger.
гнедо́й adj. (of a horse) bay.
гнезди́ться impf. **1.** to nest. **2.** to nestle.
гнездо́ neut. **1.** nest. **2.** (tech.) socket. **3.** family (of languages).
гнести́ impf. pres. **гнету́, гнетёшь** to oppress, to weigh upon.
гнёт m. oppression.
гнету́щий adj. oppressive.
гни́да f. nit.
гние́ние neut. **1.** decay, rotting. **2.** corruption.
гнило́й adj. rotten, decayed.
гни́лостный adj. putrid.
гни́лость f. rottenness.
гниль f. something decayed or rotten.
гнить impf. pf. **с-** to rot, to decay.
гное́ние neut. festering.
гнои́ть impf. pf. **с- 1.** to leave to rot. **2.** to cause to rot.
гной m. pus. — **гно́йный** adj. purulent, festering.
гно́йник m. abscess.
гно́йничо́к FILL m. pustule.
гном m. gnome.
гнус m. bloodsucking insects.

гнуса́вить *impf.* to speak with nasal resonance.

гнуса́вый *adj.* (*of a person's voice*) nasal, with nasal resonance.

гну́сность *f.* heinousness; heinous act.

гну́сный *adj.* **1.** infamous. **2.** villainous.

гнуть *impf. pf.* со- *v.t.* to bend.

гнуша́ться *impf. pf.* по- to disdain, to have an aversion to.

гобеле́н *m.* tapestry.

гобо́й *m.* oboe.

гове́ть *impf.* to prepare for Holy Communion (*by fasting*).

го́вор *m.* **1.** sound of voices. **2.** accent; manner of speaking.

говори́ть *impf.* **1.** *pf.* сказа́ть to say, to tell. **2.** *pf.* поговори́ть to talk.

говорли́вый *adj.* talkative, loquacious.

говору́н *m. f.* —ья (*colloq.*) talker, chatterbox.

говя́дина *f.* beef.

говя́жий *adj.* (*attrib.*) beef.

го́голь *m.* (*bird*) goldeneye duck.

го́гот *m.* cackle (*of a goose*).

гогота́ние *neut.* cackling (*of geese*).

гогота́ть *impf. pres.* гогочу́, гого́чешь (*of geese*) to cackle.

год *m.* year. —а́ми *adv.* for years and years, for years on end.

годи́ться *impf.* to be fit *or* suited for.

годи́чный *adj.* **1.** a year's; lasting a year. **2.** annual.

го́дность *f.* suitability.

го́дный *adj.* fit; suitable.

годова́лый *adj.* (*attrib.*) year-old.

годово́й *adj.* annual, yearly.

годовщи́на *f.* anniversary.

гол *m.* (*sports*) goal.

голени́ще *neut.* boot top.

го́лень *f.* shin.

голла́ндец FILL *m. f.* голла́ндка Dutchman.

Голла́ндия *f.* Holland.

голла́ндский *adj.* Dutch.

Голливу́д *m.* Hollywood.

голова́ *f.* head.

голова́стик *m.* tadpole.

голове́шка *f.* smoldering piece of wood.

голо́вка *f.* **1.** *dim. of* голова́. **2.** head (*of a pin*).

головна́я боль *f.* headache.

головно́й *adj.* (*attrib.*) head; leading.

головня́[1] *f.* charred log.

головня́[2] *f.* (*plant disease*) blight, rust, smut.

головокруже́ние *neut.* dizziness.

головоло́мка *f.* (*colloq.*) puzzle.

головомо́йка *f.* (*colloq.*) scolding; reprimand.

головоре́з *m.* (*colloq.*) bandit; desperado.

голо́вушка *f.* (*colloq.*) *dim. of* голова́.

го́лод *m.* **1.** hunger. **2.** starvation. —о́вка *f.* hunger strike.

голода́ние *neut.* starvation.

голода́ть *impf.* to starve.

голода́ющий *adj.* starving.

голо́дный *adj.* hungry.

гололе́дица *f.* **1.** icy conditions. **2.** icy surface.

го́лос *m.* **1.** voice. **2.** vote. — в оди́н го́лос unanimously.

голоси́стый *adj.* with a loud voice.

голосло́вный *adj.* unfounded; unsubstantiated.

голосова́ние *neut.* voting.

голосова́ть *pf.* про- OVA *impf.* to vote.

голосово́й *adj.* (*attrib.*) voice; vocal.

голубе́ть *impf. pf.* по- to turn blue, to become blue.

голубе́ц FILL *m.* stuffed cabbage.

голубизна́ *f.* light blue color.

голуби́ный *adj.* (*attrib.*) pigeon.

голу́бка *f.* **1.** female pigeon. **2.** (*in direct address*) dear, darling.

голубова́тый *adj.* bluish.

голубо́й *adj.* **1.** light blue; pale blue; sky-blue. **2.** (*colloq.*) homosexual.

голубо́к FILL *m. dim. of* го́лубь.

голу́бчик *m.* (*endearing address*) my dear.

го́лубь *m.* pigeon, dove.

голубя́тня *f.* dovecote; pigeon house.

го́лый *adj.* naked, bare.

голы́ш *m.* **1.** (*colloq.*) naked child. **2.** pebble.

голышо́м *adv.* (*colloq.*) stark naked; in the nude.

голь *f.* (*obs.*) the poor.

гольф *m.* golf.

голья́н *m.* minnow.

Го́мель *m.* Homyel (*Russian: Gomel*).

гомеопа́тия *f.* homeopathy.

гомоге́нный *adj.* homogenous.

го́мон *m.* (*colloq.*) hubbub.

гомосексуали́ст *m.* homosexual.

гонг *m.* gong.

Гондура́с *m.* Honduras.

гоне́ние *neut.* persecution.

гоне́ц FILL *m.* messenger.

гони́тель *m. f.* —ница persecutor.

го́нка *f.* haste, hurry.

го́нки *pl.* **1.** races. **2.** regatta.

Гонко́нг *m.* Hong Kong.

гоноко́кк *m.* gonococcus.

Гонолу́лу *m.* Honolulu.

го́нор *m.* arrogance; conceit.

гонора́р *m.* fee.

гоноре́я *f.* gonorrhea.

го́ночный *adj.* (*attrib.*) racing.

гонт *m.* shingles (*for roofing*).

гонча́р *m.* potter.

гонча́рное иску́сство *neut.* ceramics.

го́нчая *f.* hound.

го́нщик *m.* racer.

гоня́ть *impf.* **1.** to drive. **2.** to send.

гопа́к *m.* hopak (*Ukrainian dance*).

гора́ *f.* **1.** mountain. **2.** heap, pile.

гора́зд *adj.* (*colloq.*) (на *with acc.* or в *with prep.*) good at.

гора́здо *adv.* much, far.

горб *m.* hump, hunch.

горба́тый *adj.* hunchbacked; humpbacked.

горби́на *f.* bump; rise.

горбу́н *m. f.* —ья hunchback; humpback.

горбу́шка *f.* end crust.

горделивый *adj.* proud.

горде́ц FILL *m. f.* горды́чка arrogant person.

горди́ться *impf.* (*with instr.*) to be proud (of).

го́рдо *adv.* proudly.

го́рдость *f.* pride.

го́рдый *adj.* proud.

го́ре *neut.* **1.** grief. **2.** misfortune.

горева́ть *impf.* to grieve.

горе́лка *f.* burner.
горе́лки *pl.* (*game of*) tag; (*game of*) catch.
горемы́ка *m.* and *f.* (*decl. f.*) (*colloq.*) unlucky creature; hapless person.
горе́ние *neut.* burning; combustion.
го́рестный *adj.* sad.
го́ресть *f.* **1.** sorrow; grief. **2.** го́рести *pl.* misfortunes.
горе́ть *impf.* to burn, blaze.
го́рец FILL *m. f.* **горя́нка** mountaineer.
гореча́вка *f.* gentian.
го́речь *f.* bitterness; bitter taste.
горже́т *m.* fur neckpiece.
горизо́нт *m.* horizon.
горизонта́ль *f.* horizontal line. —**ный** *adj.* horizontal.
гори́лла *f.* gorilla.
гори́стый *adj.* mountainous.
горихво́стка *f.* (*bird*) redstart.
го́рка *f.* **1.** hill; hillock. **2.** (*glass*) cabinet. **3.** sliding board.
горла́нить *impf.* (*colloq.*) to bellow.
го́рлица *f.* turtledove.
го́рло *neut.* throat.— дыха́тельное го́рло *neut.* windpipe.
горлово́й *adj.* **1.** (*attrib.*) throat. **2.** guttural.
гормо́н *m.* hormone.
горн[1] *m.* furnace, forge.
горн[2] *m.* bugle.
горни́ло *neut.* crucible.
горни́ст *m.* bugler.
го́рничная *f.* maid, chambermaid.
горноста́й *m.* ermine.
го́рный *adj.* (*attrib.*) **1.** mountain. **2.** mountainous. **3.** mining. **4.** mineral.
горня́к *m.* miner.
го́род *m.* city; town. —**ско́й** *adj.* city, municipal, urban, metropolitan.
городки́ *pl.* game similar to skittles.
городо́к *m.* small town.
го́род-побрати́м *m.* sister city.
горожа́нин *m. f.* **горожа́нка** metropolitan.
горо́х *m.* (*coll.*) peas.
горо́ховый *adj.* (*attrib.*) pea.
горо́шек *m.* **1.** *dim. of* горо́х. **2.** polka dots.
горо́шина *f.* pea.
горсове́т *m.* (*abbr. of* городско́й сове́т) City Council.
го́рсточка *f.* handful.
горсть *f.* handful.
горта́нный *adj.* guttural.
горта́нь *f.* larynx.
горте́нзия *f.* hydrangea.
горчи́ца *f.* mustard.
горшо́к FILL *m.* pot.
го́рькая *f.* (*colloq.*) vodka.
го́рький *adj.* bitter.
го́рько *adv.* bitterly.
горю́чее *neut.* fuel.
горю́чий *adj.* combustible.
горя́чий *adj.* **1.** hot, warm. **2.** passionate, ardent, fervent.
горячи́ть *impf. pf.* **раз-** to excite; to anger.
горя́чка *f.* fever.
горя́чность *f.* ardor, fervor.

горячо́ *adv.* **1.** hotly; heatedly. **2.** fervently; ardently.
госдепарта́мент *m.* (*abbr. of* госуда́рственный департа́мент) State Department.
госпитализа́ция *f.* hospitalization.
го́спиталь *m.* military hospital. — **госпита́льный** *adj.* (*attrib.*) hospital.
го́споди *interj.* Good Lord!; Good heavens!
господи́н *m.* gentleman; Mr.
госпо́дство *neut.* supremacy, domination, reign.
госпо́дствовать OVA *impf.* **1.** to reign. **2.** to dominate; to predominate.
госпо́дствующий *adj.* ruling; prevailing.
Госпо́дь *m.* Lord; God.
госпожа́ *f.* Mrs.
гостеприи́мный *adj.* hospitable.
гостеприи́мство *neut.* hospitality.
гости́ная *f.* living room.
гости́ница *f.* hotel; inn.
гости́ть *impf.* (у *with gen.*) to be a guest in someone's home.
гость *m.* guest; visitor.
госуда́рственный *adj.* **1.** (*attrib.*) state; government. **2.** national.
госуда́рство *neut.* state, nation, country.
госуда́рь *m.* sovereign.
го́тика *f* Gothic architecture.
готи́ческий *adj.* Gothic.
Го́тланд *m.* (*island*) Gotland.
гото́вить *impf. pf.* **при-** *v.t.* to prepare.
гото́вность *f.* readiness; preparedness.
гото́вый *adj.* ready; prepared.
гофри́ровать OVA *impf.* **1.** to corrugate. **2.** to emboss.
граб *m.* (*tree*) hornbeam.
грабёж *m.* plunder; robbery.
граби́тель *m. f.* —**ница** burglar; plunderer.
граби́тельский *adj.* predatory.
гра́бить *impf. pf.* **о-** to rob; to sack, to pillage, to plunder.
гра́бли *pl.* rake.
гравёр *m.* engraver; etcher.
гра́вий *m.* gravel.
гравирова́льный *adj.* (*attrib.*) engraving.
грави́ровать OVA *impf. pf.* **вы-** to engrave.
гравиро́вка *f.* engraving.
гравита́ция *f.* gravitation.
гравю́ра *f.* engraving, print.
град *m.* hail.
града́ция *f.* gradation.
градие́нт *m.* (*phys.*) gradient.
гра́дина *f.* hailstone.
гради́рня *f.* **1.** salt pan. **2.** water cooling tower.
гра́дом *adv.* profusely.
градострои́тельство *neut.* town planning; urban development.
градуи́рованный *adj.* graded.
гра́дус *m.* degree. —**ник** *m.* thermometer.
граждани́н *m. f.* **гражда́нка** *pl.* **гра́ждане** citizen.
гражда́нский *adj.* civil; civilian.
гражда́нство *neut.* citizenship.
грамза́пись *f.* recording.
грамм *m.* gram.
грамма́тика *f.* grammar.
граммати́ческий *adj.* grammatical.
граммофо́н *m.* phonograph.

гра́мота *f.* **1.** reading and writing. **2.** deed, charter. **3.** document.

гра́мотно *adv.* **1.** grammatically. **2.** competently.

гра́мотность *f.* **1.** literacy. **2.** grammatical correctness. **3.** competency.

гра́мотный *adj.* literate.

грампласти́нка *f.* phonograph record.

Грана́да *f.* Granada.

грана́т *m.* **1.** pomegranate. **2.** garnet.

грана́та *f.* grenade.

грана́товый *adj.* **1.** (*attrib.*) pomegranate. **2.** garnet.

гранатомёт *m.* grenade launcher.

грандио́зный *adj.* grandiose; tremendous.

Гранд-Каньо́н *m.* Grand Canyon.

гранёный *adj.* (*of glass, gems, etc.*) cut.

грани́т *m.* granite. **—ный** *adj.* (*attrib.*) granite.

грани́ть *impf.* to cut (*glass, gems, etc.*).

грани́ца *f.* boundary; border, frontier. **— за грани́цей** (*loc.*) abroad. **— за грани́цу** (*dir.*) abroad.

грани́чить *impf.* (**с** *with instr.*) to border (*on* or *upon*).

гра́нка *f.* (*galley*) proof.

грануля́ция *f.* granulation.

грань *f.* **1.** boundary. **2.** verge, brink. **3.** surface, side.

граф *m.* count.

графа́ *f.* column (*of a page*).

гра́фик¹ *m.* **1.** graph, chart. **2.** schedule.

гра́фик² *m.* graphic artist.

гра́фика *f.* graphic arts.

графи́н *m.* carafe; decanter.

графи́ня *f.* countess.

графи́т *m.* graphite.

графи́ческий *adj.* graphic.

графлёный *adj.* (*of paper*) ruled.

гра́фство *neut.* county.

грацио́зный *adj.* graceful.

гра́ция *f.* grace.

грач *m.* (*bird*) rook.

гребёнка *f.* comb.

гре́бень *m.* **1.** comb. **2.** comb; crest (*of a bird*). **3.** crest (*of a wave* or *mountain*). **4.** ridge (*of a roof*).

гребе́ц FILL *m.* oarsman.

гребешо́к *m.* **1.** *dim. of* **гре́бень** **2.** scallop.

гре́бля *f.* rowing.

гребно́й *adj.* (*attrib.*) rowing. **— гребна́я ло́дка** *f.* rowboat.

грёза *f.* daydream.

гре́зить *impf.* to dream, to daydream.

гре́йдер *m.* grader.

грейпфру́т *m.* grapefruit.

грек *m. f.* **греча́нка** Greek.

гре́лка *f.* hot-water bottle.

греме́ть *impf.* to thunder.

грему́чий *adj.* thundering; thunderous.— **грему́чая змея́** *f.* rattlesnake.

гренадёр *m.* grenadier.

гренки́ *pl.* croutons.

грести́ *impf.* **1.** to row, to pull. **2.** to rake.

греть *impf.* to warm; to give off warmth.

грех *m.* sin.

Гре́ция *f.* Greece.

гре́цкий оре́х *m.* walnut.

гре́ческий *adj.* Greek.

гречи́ха *f.* buckwheat.

гре́чневый *adj.* buckwheat.

греши́ть *impf. pf.* **со-** to sin.

гре́шник *m. f.* **гре́шница** sinner.

грешно́ *adv.* (*pred.*) it's a sin (to).

гре́шный *adj.* sinful.

грешо́к FILL *m.* sin, peccadillo.

гриб *m.* mushroom.

грибко́вый *adj.* (*attrib.*) fungus, fungal.

грибно́й *adj.* (*attrib.*) mushroom.

грибо́к FILL *m.* fungus.

гри́ва *f.* mane.

гри́зли *m. indecl.* grizzly bear.

грим *m.* stage make-up.

грима́са *f.* grimace.

грима́сничать *impf.* to grimace.

гримёр *m.* makeup artist.

грипп *m.* flu, influenza; grippe.

гриф¹ *m.* **1.** vulture. **2.** griffin.

гриф² *m.* (*mus.*) finger board.

гриф³ *m.* rubber stamp.

гри́фель *m.* slate pencil.

грифо́н *m.* griffin.

гроб *m.* coffin. **—ни́ца** *f.* tomb.

гробово́й *adj.* **1.** (*attrib.*) coffin. **2.** deathly.

гробовщи́к *m.* coffin maker.

грог *m.* grog.

Гро́дно *neut.* Hrodna (*Russian: Grodno*).

гроза́ *f.* storm, thunderstorm.

гроздь *f.* cluster; bunch.

грози́ть *impf. pf.* **при-** to threaten.

гро́зный *adj.* **1.** threatening, menacing. **2.** terrible.

грозово́й *adj.* (*attrib.*) storm; stormy.

гром *m.* thunder.

грома́да *f.* mass; heap.

грома́дный *adj.* vast; huge.

громи́ть *impf. pf.* **раз-** **1.** to smash, to destroy. **2.** to rout.

гро́мкий *adj.* **1.** loud. **2.** famous, celebrated.

громкоговори́тель *m.* loudspeaker.

гро́мкость *f.* loudness; volume.

громово́й *adj.* (*attrib.*) thunder; thunderous.

громогла́сный *adj.* loud; loud-voiced.

громозди́ть *impf. pf.* **на-** to pile up.

громо́здкий *adj.* unwieldy; cumbersome.

громоотво́д *m.* lightning rod.

громыха́ние *neut.* (*colloq.*) rumble; rumbling.

громыха́ть *impf.* (*colloq.*) to rumble; to clatter.

гроссбу́х *m.* ledger.

гроссме́йстер *m.* (*chess*) grandmaster.

грот *m.* **1.** grotto. **2.** mainsail.

гроте́ск *m.* (*art*) grotesque style.

гро́хать *impf. pf.* **гро́хнуть** (*colloq.*) **1.** to bang down. **2.** to come crashing down.

гро́хот *m.* **1.** crash. **2.** rattle; rumble.

грохота́ть *impf. pf.* **про-** **1.** to rumble; to crash. **2.** to rattle.

грош *m.* **1.** half a kopeck. **2.** penny.

грошо́вый *adj.* (*colloq.*) cheap (*in quality*).

грубе́ть *impf. pf.* **о-** to become coarse, rude.

груби́ть *impf. pf.* **на-** (*with dat.*) to be rude (to).

грубия́н *m. f.* **—ка** rude person; boor.

гру́бо *adv.* **1.** roughly. **2.** crudely. **3.** rudely.

гру́бость *f.* **1.** rudeness. **2.** crudity. **3.** rude remark.

гру́бый *adj.* rude; coarse; rough.
гру́да *f.* heap, pile.
груди́на *f.* breastbone; sternum.
груди́нка *f.* brisket.
груди́ца *f.* mastitis.
грудно́й *adj.* (*attrib.*) **1.** chest. **2.** (*of an infant*) suckling.
грудобрюшна́я прегра́да *f.* diaphragm.
грудь *f.* **1.** breast. **2.** bosom; chest.
гружёный *adj.* loaded.
груз *m.* **1.** load. **2.** cargo, freight. **3.** burden, weight.
грузи́ло *neut.* (*fishing*) sinker.
грузи́н *m. f.* —ка Georgian.
Гру́зия *f.* Georgia (*country in Caucasus*).
грузови́к *m.* truck.
грузово́й *adj.* (*attrib.*) freight, cargo.
грузоотправи́тель *m.* shipper.
грузоподъёмный *adj.* (*attrib.*) loading (*of crane*).
гру́зчик *m.* stevedore, longshoreman.
грунт *m.* **1.** soil. **2.** ground, base.
грунтова́я доро́га *f.* dirt road.
гру́ппа *f.* group.
группирова́ть *impf. pf.* **с-** *v.t.* to group; to gather.
группиро́вка *f.* group; grouping.
группово́й *adj.* (*attrib.*) group.
грусти́ть *impf.* to be sad *or* melancholy.
гру́стно *adv.* sadly.
гру́стный *adj.* melancholy; sad, sorrowful.
грусть *f.* melancholy, sadness.
гру́ша *f.* pear; pear tree.
гру́шевый *adj.* (*attrib.*) pear.
гры́жа *f.* (*med.*) rupture, hernia.
грызня́ *f.* (*colloq.*) fight; squabble.
грызть *impf.* **1.** to gnaw. **2.** to nibble. — грызться *v.i.* (*of dogs*) to fight; to quarrel.
грызу́н *m.* rodent.
гряда́ *f.* **1.** (*of soil*) bed. **2.** (*of clouds*) bank.
гря́дка *f.* bed (*for flowers, vegetables*).
гряду́щий *adj.* coming; future.
грязево́й *adj.* (*attrib.*) mud.
грязни́ть *impf. pf.* **за-** to soil, to sully; to dirty.
гря́зно *adv.* sloppily.
грязну́ля *m. and f.* (*decl. f.*) slob.
гря́зный *adj.* dirty; filthy.
грязь *f.* dirt; filth.
гря́нуть *pf.* **1.** to sound, to ring out. **2.** to erupt, to break out.
гуа́шь *f.* gouache.
губа́¹ *f.* lip.
губа́² *f.* (*geog.*) inlet.
губа́стый *adj.* (*colloq.*) thick-lipped.
губерна́тор *m.* governor.
губе́рния *f.* province.
губи́тельный *adj.* **1.** disastrous. **2.** destructive; fatal.

губи́ть *impf. pf.* **по- 1.** to destroy. **2.** to ruin.
гу́бка *f.* sponge.
губна́я пома́да *f.* lipstick.
гу́бчатый *adj.* spongy.
гуверна́нтка *f.* governess.
гуде́ние *neut.* buzzing; hum.
гуде́ть *impf.* **1.** to buzz. **2.** to hoot, to honk. **3.** to drone.
гудо́к FILL *m.* whistle; horn.
гудро́н *m.* tar.
гул *m.* rumble; hum; din.
ГУЛа́г *m.* (*abbr. of* Гла́вное управле́ние лагере́й *neut.*) gulag (*Soviet concentration camp*).
гу́лкий *adj.* hollow.
гуля́ка *m. and f.* (*decl. f.*) playboy.
гуля́нье *neut.* **1.** walking; promenade. **2.** public outdoor festivity.
гуля́ть *impf.* to walk, to take a walk.
гуля́ш *m.* goulash.
ГУМ *m.* (*abbr. of* Госуда́рственный универса́льный магази́н *m.*) State Department Store (*on Red Square, Moscow*).
гумани́зм *m.* humanism.
гуманита́рный *adj.* humanitarian, humanistic.
гума́нность *f.* humaneness, humanity.
гума́нный *adj.* humane; humanitarian.
гуммиара́бик *m.* gum arabic.
гумно́ *neut.* threshing floor.
гу́мус *m.* humus.
гурма́н *m. f.* —ка gourmet.
Гуро́н о́зеро *neut.* Lake Huron.
гурт *m.* herd; flock.
гурто́м *adv.* (*colloq.*) **1.** in bulk; wholesale. **2.** as one group.
гурьба́ *f.* (*colloq.*) crowd; throng.
гуса́к *m.* gander.
гуса́р *m.* hussar.
гу́сеница *f.* **1.** caterpillar. **2.** Caterpillar tractor.
гу́сеничный *adj.* (*attrib.*) caterpillar.
гусёнок FILL *m.* gosling.
гуси́ный *adj.* (*attrib.*) goose.
гу́сли *pl.* (*mus.*) old Russian stringed instrument; gusli.
густе́ть *impf. v.i.* to thicken.
гу́сто *adv.* **1.** densely. **2.** (*colloq.*) in abundance.
густо́й *adj.* thick; dense.
густонаселённый *adj.* densely populated.
густота́ *f.* thickness; denseness.
гусы́ня *f.* female goose.
гусь *m.* goose.
гусько́м *adv.* (in) single file.
гуся́тина *f.* goose (*prepared as food*).
гутали́н *m.* shoe polish.
гу́ща *f.* **1.** grounds, lees. **2.** thickness; thicket.
гу́ще *adj.* thicker, denser. — *adv.* more thickly *or* densely.

Д

да *adv.* yes. — *conj.* and; but.
давáй **1.** *particle* let's. **2.** go ahead! go!
давáть *impf. pf.* дать to give. — давáть знать to let know.
давúльный *adj.* for pressing.
давúльня *f.* wine press.
давúть *impf.* **1.** to press down on. **2.** to squeeze. **3.** to pinch; to be tight. **4.** to crush.
давúться *impf. pf.* по- **1.** to be pressed. **2.** to choke.
дáвка *f.* crowding together; crush.
давлéние *neut.* pressure.
дáвний *adj.* **1.** old, ancient. **2.** bygone. — с дáвних пор long, for a long time.
давнúшний *adj.* (*colloq.*) old; olden.
давнó *adv.* long ago; for a long time. — давнó прошéдший *adj.* remote (*of time*).
дáвность *f.* **1.** remoteness. **2.** antiquity.
давным-давнó *adv.* long, long ago.
дáже *adv.* even.
Дакáр *m.* Dakar.
дáлее *adv.* further.
далёкий *adj.* distant, remote.
далекó *adv.* far. — далекó не far from being.
Дáллас *m.* Dallas.
дальнéйший *adj.* further.
дальновúдный *adj.* foresighted.
дальнозóркий *adj.* farsighted.
дáльний *adj.* **1.** far-off; distant. **2.** long (*trip; distance*) — Дáльний Востóк *m.* the Far East.
дáльность *f.* distance; range.
дальтонúзм *m.* color blindness. — дальтóник *m. f.* дальтóничка (*colloq.*) color-blind person.
дáльше *adv.* **1.** *comp. of* далекó. **2.** then, next. **3.** further on. — *interj.* continue!
дáма *f.* **1.** lady. **2.** (*cards*) queen.
дамáн *m.* hyrax.
Дамáск *m.* Damascus.
дáмба *f.* dike.
дáмка *f.* (*checkers*) king.
дáмский *adj.* lady's, ladies'.
Дáния *f.* Denmark.
дáнник *m.* one who pays tribute.
дáнные *pl.* data, facts.
дáнный *adj.* **1.** given. **2.** present.
дань *f.* **1.** tribute. **2.** contribution.
дар *m.* gift; donation.
дарёный *adj.* (*colloq.*) received as a present.
дарúтель *m. f.* —ница donor.
дарúть *impf. pf.* по- **1.** to give, to donate. **2.** to favor.
дармоéд *m. f.* —ка (*colloq.*) sponger, parasite.
даровáние *neut.* gift; talent.
даровúтый *adj.* talented, gifted.
даровóй *adj.* (*colloq.*) free, gratuitous.
дáром *adv.* **1.** free of charge. **2.** (*colloq.*) for next to nothing. **3.** in vain; to no purpose.
дáта *f.* date.
дáтельный *adj.* (*gram.*) dative.
дáтский *adj.* Danish.
датчáнин *m. f.* датчáнка Dane.
дáтчик *m.* sensor.

дать *pf. of* давáть.
дáча *f.* **1.** summer cottage, country house. **2.** portion. **3.** act of testifying or giving. — на дáче in the country.
дáчник *m. f.* дáчница summer visitor in the country.
дáчный *adj.* suburban; cottage.
два *num.* two.
двадцатилéтие *neut.* twentieth anniversary.
двадцатилéтний *adj.* twenty-year-old.
двадцáтый *adj.* twentieth.
двáдцать *num.* twenty.
двáжды *adv.* twice.
двенадцатипéрстная кишкá *f.* duodenum.
двенáдцатый *adj.* twelfth.
двенáдцать *num.* twelve.
двéрка *f. dim. of* дверь.
двернóй *adj.* (*attrib.*) door.
дверь *f.* door.
двéсти *num.* two hundred.
двúгатель *m.* motor, engine. —ный *adj.* motive, impellent.
двúгать *impf. pf.* двúнуть **1.** to move. **2.** to move (*a part of one's body*) **3.** *impf. only* to drive, to propel. **4.** to promote; to further.
движéние *neut.* **1.** motion, movement. **2.** traffic.
движúмость *f.* (*law*) personal property; movable property.
движúмый *adj.* movable.
движущий *adj.* motive; driving.
двóе *num.* (*coll.*) two.
двоебрáчие *neut.* bigamy.
двоевлáстие *neut.* diarchy.
двоежéнец FILL *m.* bigamist.
двоетóчие *neut.* colon (*punctuation mark*).
двоúть *impf.* to divide in two. — ся to divide *or* be divided in two. — *impers.* у меня двоúтся в глазáх I see double.
двóйка *f.* **1.** two. **2.** (*cards*) deuce.
двойнúк *m.* double; counterpart.
двойнóй *adj.* double, twofold.
двóйня *f.* twins.
двóйственность *f.* duality; ambivalence.
двóйственный *adj.* **1.** dual. **2.** bipartite. **3.** ambivalent. **4.** two-faced.
двор *m.* court, yard.
дворéц FILL *m.* palace.
дворéцкий *m.* butler.
двóрник *m.* caretaker.
двóрницкая DAA *f.* caretaker's house.
дворня́га *m. and f.* (*decl. f.*) (*colloq.*) mongrel.
дворóвый *adj.* (*attrib.*) yard.
дворцóвый *adj.* (*attrib.*) palace.
дворянúн *m. f.* дворя́нка nobleman; noble.
двою́родная сестрá *f.* first cousin.
двою́родный брат *m.* first cousin.
двоя́кий *adj.* double; dual.
двоя́ко *adv.* in two ways.
двубóртный *adj.* double-breasted.
двуглáвый *adj.* two-headed.
двуглáсный *adj.* (*attrib.*) diphthong.
двугрáнный *adj.* dihedral.

двугри́венный *m.* twenty-kopeck piece.
двузна́чный *adj.* two-digit.
двуко́лка *f.* two-wheeled cart.
двукра́тный *adj.* double, twofold.
двули́кий *adj.* two-faced; double-dealing.
двули́чие *neut.* duplicity.
двули́чный *adj.* two-faced; double-dealing.
двуно́гий *adj.* two-legged.
двуо́кись *f.* dioxide.
двупо́лый *adj.* bisexual.
двуру́шник *m. f.* двуру́шница double-dealer.
двуска́тная кры́ша *f.* gable roof.
двусло́жный *adj.* two-syllable.
двусмы́сленность *f.* ambiguity.
двусмы́сленный *adj.* 1. ambiguous; equivocal. 2. suggestive, indecent.
двуспа́льный *adj.* (*of bed*) double.
двуство́лка *f.* double-barreled gun.
двуство́рчатый *adj.* 1. (*of doors*) folding. 2. bivalve.
двусторо́нний *adj.* 1. double-sided. 2. two-way. 3. bilateral.
двууглеки́слый *adj.* (*chem.*) bicarbonate (of).
двухвале́нтный *adj.* bivalent.
двухгоди́чный *adj.* (*attrib.*) two-year.
двухдне́вный *adj.* (*attrib.*) two-day.
двухколёсный *adj.* two-wheeled.
двухко́мнатный *adj.* (*attrib.*) two-room.
двухле́тний *adj.* two-year-old.
двухме́стный *adj.* for two; accomodating two persons.
двухме́сячник *m.* bimonthly (*of publication*).
двухме́сячный *adj.* two-month-old.
двухмото́рный *adj.* (*attrib.*) twin-engine.
двухнеде́льный *adj.* two-week-old.
двухобъёмный ку́зов *m.* hatchback (*automobile*).
двухпала́тный *adj.* bicameral.
двухпарти́йный *adj.* two-party.
двухсотле́тие *neut.* bicentennial.
двухсо́тый *adj.* two-hundredth.
двухфо́кусный *adj.* bifocal.
двухчасово́й *adj.* (*attrib.*) two-hour.
двухэта́жный *adj.* two-story.
двучле́н *m.* binomial.
двуязы́чие *neut.* bilingualism.
двуя́йцевые близнецы́ *pl.* fraternal twins.
деба́ты *pl.* debate; discussion.
дебе́лый *adj.* (*colloq.*) plump; buxom.
деби́л *m.* (*slang*) idiot; moron; nut(case), screwball, deranged person.
дебо́ш *m.* brawl; fracas; row.
де́бри *pl.* 1. jungle. 2. the wilds. 3. backwoods. 4. labyrinth.
дебю́т *m.* debut.
дебюта́нт *m. f.* —ка person making his or her debut.
де́ва *f.* 1. (*obs.*) maid; maiden. 2. (*cap.*) the Virgin.
дева́ть *impf. pf.* деть (*colloq.*) to put; to do with.
де́верь *m.* brother-in-law (*husband's brother*).
деви́з *m.* motto.
деви́ца *f.* 1. girl. 2. unmarried woman.
деви́чество *neut.* girlhood.
деви́чий *adj.* girlish, maidenly.
де́вка *f.* (*colloq.*) girl, wench.
де́вочка *f.* girl, little girl.

де́вственник *m. f.* де́вственница virgin.
де́вственный *adj.* virgin.
де́вушка *f.* young girl.
девчо́нка *f.* (*colloq.*) girl.
девяно́сто *num.* ninety.
девяно́стый *adj.* ninetieth.
девя́тая *adj.* ninth.
девятеро *coll.* nine.
девятиле́тний *adj.* nine-year-old.
девятисо́тый *adj.* nine hundredth.
девя́тка *f.* 1. the numeral nine. 2. an item numbered nine. 3. (*cards*) nine.
девятна́дцатый *adj.* nineteenth.
девятна́дцать *num.* nineteen.
девя́тый *adj.* ninth.
де́вять *num.* nine. —со́т *num.* nine hundred. —со́тый *adj.* nine hundredth.
де́вятью *adv.* nine times.
дегаза́ция *f.* decontamination.
дегази́ровать *impf. and pf.* OVA to decontaminate.
дегенера́т *m. f.* —ка degenerate.
дегенера́ция *f.* degeneration.
дёготь *m.* tar.
деграда́ция *f.* degeneration.
дегради́ровать OVA *impf.* to degenerate.
дегтя́рный *adj.* tar.
дегуста́тор *m.* taster.
дед *m.* 1. grandfather. 2. old man. 3. *pl.* де́ды forefathers.
дед-моро́з *m.* Santa Claus.
де́дов *adj.* grandfather's.
де́довский *adj.* grandfather's.
деду́кция *f.* (*logic*) deduction.
де́душка *m.* (*decl. f.*) grandpa, granddad.
дееприча́стие *neut.* gerund, verbal adverb.
дееспосо́бный *adj.* 1. effective. 2. able to function. 3. (*law*) competent.
дежу́рить *impf.* to be on duty.
дежу́рный *adj.* on duty. — *m.* person on duty.
дежу́рство *neut.* duty.
дезерти́р *m.* deserter. —ство *neut.* desertion.
дезерти́ровать OVA *impf. and pf.* to desert.
дезинфе́кция *f.* disinfection.
дезинфици́ровать OVA *impf. and pf.* to disinfect.
дезинформа́ция *f.* disinformation.
дезинформи́ровать OVA *impf.* to give wrong information; to misinform.
дезодора́нт *m.* deodorant.
дезоргани́зация *f.* disorganization.
дезорганизова́ть OVA *impf.* to disorganize.
дезориенти́ровать OVA *impf.* to disorient.
деи́зм *m.* deism.
де́йственный *adj.* effective, efficacious.
де́йствие *neut.* 1. activity, action. 2. operation; conduct.
действи́тельно *adv.* really; truly; actually; indeed.
действи́тельность *f.* 1. reality. 2. validity.
действи́тельный *adj.* 1. real, actual. 2. valid. 3. (*gram.*) active.
де́йствовать OVA *impf. pf.* по- 1. to be active. 2. to operate, to work. 3. to function. 4. to have an effect on *or* upon.
де́йствующий *adj.* 1. active, operating, functioning, working. 2. in force. — де́йствующие ли́ца *pl.* cast of characters.

дейте́рий *m.* deuterium.

де́ка *f.* (*mus.*) sounding board.

декабри́ст *m.* (*hist.*) Decembrist.

дека́брь *m.* December. —ский *adj.* (*attrib.*) December.

дека́да *f.* decade.

декаде́нство *neut.* decadence.

дека́дный *adj.* (*attrib.*) ten-day.

дека́н *m.* dean (*at a university*).

дисквалифика́ция *f.* disqualification.

дисквалифици́роваться OVA *impf.* to be disqualified; to disqualify oneself.

деклама́тор *m.* reciter.

деклама́ция *f.* recitation.

деклами́ровать OVA *impf. pf.* про- to recite; to declaim.

деклара́ция *f.* declaration.

декольте́ *neut. indecl.* decolletage.

декорати́вный *adj.* decorative.

декора́тор *m.* decorator.

декора́ция *f.* **1.** (*theat.*) scenery. **2.** window dressing.

деко́рум *m.* decorum.

декре́т *m.* decree, edict.

декре́тный *adj.* (*attrib.*) decree.

декстро́за *f.* dextrose.

Де́лавэр *m.* Delaware.

де́ланный *adj.* **1.** artificial. **2.** feigned; affected.

де́лать *impf. pf.* с- to make; to do. —ся **1.** to become. **2.** to get. **3.** to grow. **4.** to happen, to occur.

делега́т *m. f.* —ка delegate.

делега́ция *f.* delegation.

делеги́ровать OVA *impf. and pf.* to delegate.

деле́ние *neut.* **1.** division. **2.** degree.

деле́ц *m.* shrewd businessman.

Де́ли *m. indecl.* Delhi.

деликате́с *m.* (*item of food*) delicacy.

деликáтный *adj.* delicate; tactful.

дели́мое *neut.* (*math.*) dividend.

дели́мый *adj.* divisible.

дели́тель *m.* (*math.*) divisor.

дели́ть *impf.* **1.** *pf.* раз- to divide; to dismember; to share. **2.** *pf.* по- to divide.

дели́ться *impf.* **1.** *pf.* раз- to divide, to be divided; (на *with acc.*) to be divisible (by). **2.** *pf.* по- to share, to give; to transmit, to communicate, to impart.

де́ло *neut.* **1.** affair, business, matter. **2.** cause. **3.** deed, act. **4.** дела́ (*pl.*) things, affairs. — име́ть де́ло с (*with instr.*) to deal with. — в са́мом де́ле as a matter of fact. — на са́мом де́ле actually; in fact. — не в э́том де́ло that is not the point.

делови́тый *adj.* businesslike.

делово́й *adj.* (*attrib.*) business.

делопроизво́дство *neut.* office work.

де́льный *adj.* efficient, effective.

де́льта *f.* delta.

дельтови́дный *adj.* deltoid.

дельфи́н *m.* dolphin.

Де́льфы *pl.* Delphi.

демаго́г *m.* demagogue.

демарка́ционный *adj.* of demarcation.

демарка́ция *f.* demarcation.

дема́рш *m.* démarche.

демилитариза́ция *f.* demilitarization.

демилитаризова́ть OVA *impf.* to demilitarize.

демисезо́нный *adj.* worn in the spring *or* fall.

демобилиза́ция *f.* demobilization.

демобилизова́ть OVA *impf.* to demobilize.

демогра́фия *f.* demography.

демокра́т *m.* democrat.

демократиза́ция *f.* democracy.

демократизи́ровать OVA *impf. and pf.* to democratize.

демократи́ческий *adj.* democratic.

демокра́тия *f.* democracy.

де́мон *m.* demon. —и́ческий *adj.* demoniac(al).

демонстра́нт *m.* demonstrator.

демонстрати́вно *adv.* in an emphatic manner; for everyone to see.

демонстрати́вный *adj.* pointed, emphatic.

демонстра́тор *m.* demonstrator.

демонстрацио́нный *adj.* used for demonstrations.

демонстра́ция *f.* demonstration.

демонстри́ровать OVA *impf. and pf.* to demonstrate.

демонта́ж *m.* dismantling.

демонти́ровать OVA *impf.* to dismantle.

демо́рализа́ция *f.* demoralization.

деморализова́ть OVA *impf.* demoralize.

де́мпинг *m.* (*econ.*) dumping.

денатура́т *m.* denatured alcohol.

денатури́ровать OVA *impf.* to denature (*alcohol*).

дендра́рий *m.* dendrarium.

дендри́т *m.* dendrite.

де́нежный *adj.* (*attrib.*) money, monetary, pecuniary; moneyed.

денёк *m. dim. of* день.

де́нно и но́щно *adv.* day and night.

денонси́ровать OVA *impf.* to repudiate; to renounce.

денти́н *m.* dentine.

день *m.* day. — на дня́х (*past*) the other day; (*future*) in a day or two, one of these days.

де́ньги *pl.* money.

департа́мент *m.* governmental department.

депе́ша *f.* dispatch.

депо́ *neut. indecl.* (*railroad*) repair shop.

депони́ровать OVA *impf. and pf.* to deposit.

депре́ссия *f.* depression.

депута́т *m.* deputy.

депута́ция *f.* deputation.

де́рби *m. indecl.* derby.

де́рбник *m.* (*bird*) merlin.

дёргать *impf. pf.* дёрнуть to pull, to tug, to jerk.

дерга́ч *m.* (*bird*) corn crake.

дереве́нский *adj.* rural; rustic.

деревéнщина *m. and f.* (*decl. f.*) (*colloq.*) country bumpkin.

дере́вня *f.* **1.** village. **2.** the country.

де́рево *neut.* **1.** tree. **2.** wood.

деревообде́лочник *m.* woodworker.

деревýшка *f.* small village; hamlet.

де́ревце *also* деревцо́ *neut.* sapling.

деревяни́стый *adj.* woody.

деревя́нный *adj.* wooden.

деревя́шка *f.* piece of wood.

держа́ва *f.* **1.** state. **2.** power.

держа́тель *m.* holder.

держа́ть *impf.* to hold; to keep. — держа́ть пари́ to bet.

держа́ться *impf.* **1.** to hold (on); to adhere; to be held. **2.** to restrain oneself. **3.** to behave.

дерза́ние *neut.* daring.

дерза́ть *impf.* *pf.* дерзну́ть to dare.

дерзи́ть *impf.* *pf.* на- (*colloq.*) to be rude to; to be insolent to.

де́рзкий *adj.* **1.** impertinent, impudent. **2.** audacious.

де́рзость *f.* **1.** impudence, insolence. **2.** audacity.

дерива́т *m.* derivative.

дерматоло́гия *f.* dermatology.

дёрн *m.* turf, sod.

дёрнуть *pf.* *of* дёргать.

дерю́га *f.* sackcloth; burlap.

деса́нт *m.* landing (*of troops*). — ный *adj.* (*attrib.*) landing; parachute.

десе́рт *m.* dessert.

де́скать *particle* (*colloq.*) They say; He/she says.

Десна́ *f.* (*river*) Desna.

десна́ *f.* (*anat.*) gum.

десни́ца *f.* (*poet.*) hand; right hand.

деспоти́ческий *adj.* despotic.

деся́тая *f.* tenth.

де́сятеро *coll.* ten.

десятибо́рье *neut.* decathlon.

десятигра́нник *m.* decahedron.

десятидне́вный *adj.* (*attrib.*) ten-day.

десятикра́тный *adj.* tenfold.

десятиле́тие *neut.* **1.** tenth anniversary. **2.** decade.

десятиле́тка *f.* ten-year secondary school.

десятиле́тний *adj.* ten-year-old.

десяти́на *f.* **1.** tithe. **2.** measure of approx. 2.7 acres.

десятирублёвка *f.* (*colloq.*) ten-rouble note.

десятиуго́льник *m.* decagon.

десяти́чный *adj.* decimal.

деся́тка *f.* **1.** the numeral ten. **2.** an item numbered ten. **3.** (*cards*) ten. **4.** (*colloq.*) a ten-ruble note.

деся́ток FILL *m.* **1.** ten. **2.** деся́тки *pl.* tens; scores; dozens.

деся́тый *adj.* tenth.

де́сять *num.* ten.

де́сятью *adv.* ten times.

детализа́ция *f.* working out in detail.

детализи́ровать OVA *impf.* to work out in detail.

дета́ль *f.* detail. — ный *adj.* detailed; minute.

дета́льно *adv.* in detail.

детвора́ *f.* (*colloq.*) children; kids.

детдо́м *m.* (*abbr. of* де́тский дом) orphanage.

детекти́в *m.* **1.** detective. **2.** detective story.

детекто́р *m.* detector.

детёныш *m.* **1.** young one. **2.** calf, cub. **3.** детёныши *pl.* (*coll.*) the young.

детермини́зм *m.* determinism.

де́ти *pl.* children; (*colloq.*) kids.

дети́шки *m.* (*colloq.*) children; kids.

дети́ще *neut.* (*obs.*) child; offspring.

детона́тор *m.* detonator.

детона́ция *f.* detonation.

детони́ровать OVA *impf.* to detonate.

деторо́дный *adj.* (*attrib.*) genital.

деторожде́ние *neut.* **1.** childbearing. **2.** procreation.

детоуби́йство *neut.* infanticide.

детса́д *m.* (*abbr. of* де́тский са́д) kindergarten.

де́тская *f.* nursery.

де́тский *adj.* childish; children's, child's.

де́тство *neut.* childhood.

деть *pf.* *pres.* де́ну, де́нешь *impf.* дева́ть (*colloq.*) to put; to do with.

де-фа́кто *adv.* de facto.

дефекти́вный *adj.* defective.

дефи́с *m.* hyphen.

дефици́т *m.* deficit.

дефици́тный *adj.* **1.** (*of merchandise*) scarce; in short supply. **2.** unprofitable.

деформа́ция *f.* deformation.

деформи́ровать OVA *impf.* to change the shape of.

децентрализа́ция *f.* decentralization.

децентрализова́ть OVA *impf.* to decentralize.

дециба́л *m.* decibel.

децигра́мм *m.* decigram.

децили́тр *m.* deciliter.

дециме́тр *m.* decimeter.

дешеве́ть *impf.* *pf.* по- to become cheaper, to cheapen.

дешеви́зна *f.* cheapness.

дешёвка *f.* (*colloq.*) low-price of merchandise.

деше́вле *adj.* *comp.* *of* дешёвый.

дёшево *adv.* cheap, cheaply.

дешёвый *adj.* cheap.

дешифри́ровать *also* дешифрова́ть OVA *impf.* and *pf.* to decipher.

дешифро́вка *f.* deciphering.

де-ю́ре *adv.* de jure.

дея́ние *neut.* deed; act.

де́ятель *m.* *f.* —ница **1.** worker. **2.** activist.

де́ятельность *f.* **1.** activities; activity. **2.** action; functioning.

де́ятельный *adj.* active.

джаз *m.* jazz.

Джака́рта *f.* Jakarta.

Джамбу́л *m.* Zhambyl (*Russian: Dzhambul*).

джем *m.* jam.

дже́мпер *m.* pullover; jersey.

джентльме́нский *adj.* gentlemanly.

джи́га *f.* (*dance*) jig.

джиги́т *m.* Caucasian horseman.

джин[1] *m.* gin.

джин[2] *m.* genie.

джи́нсы *pl.* jeans.

джип *m.* jeep.

джи́у-джи́тсу *neut.* *indecl.* jujitsu.

джо́ггинг *m.* jogging.

джо́кер *m.* joker.

джо́нка *f.* (*boat*) junk.

Джо́рджия *f.* Georgia (*U.S. state*).

джо́уль *m.* joule.

джу́нгли *pl.* jungle.

джут *m.* jute.

дзюдо́ *neut.* *indecl.* judo.

диабе́т *m.* diabetes.

диа́гноз *m.* diagnosis.

диагно́ст *m.* diagnostician.

диагности́ровать OVA *impf.* and *pf.* to diagnose.

диагона́ль *f.* diagonal.

диагра́мма *f.* diagram.

диаде́ма *f.* diadem.

диакрити́ческий *adj.* diacritical.

диале́кт *m.* dialect. —ика *f.* dialectics. —и́ческий *adj.* dialectical.

диале́ктный *adj.* dialectal.

диало́г *m.* dialogue.

диа́метр *m.* diameter.

диаметра́льно *adv.* diametrically.

диапазо́н *m.* **1.** range; scope. **2.** (*mus.*) range. **3.** (*radio*) band.

диапозити́в *m.* (*photog.*) slide; transparency.

диатерми́я *f.* diathermy.

диатони́ческий *adj.* diatonic.

диафра́гма *f.* (*anat.*) diaphragm.

дива́н *m.* sofa.

диверса́нт *m.* saboteur.

диверсио́нный *adj.* (*mil.*) diversionary.

диверсифика́ция *f.* diversification.

диве́рсия *f.* (*mil.*) diversion.

дивиде́нд *m.* dividend.

дивизио́н *m.* artillery battalion.

дивизио́нный *adj.* (*mil.*) (*attrib.*) division.

диви́зия *f.* (*mil.*) division.

диви́ться *impf.* (*colloq.*) to marvel, to be astonished.

ди́вный *adj.* wonderful, marvelous.

ди́во *neut.* wonder, marvel.

дида́ктика *f.* didactics.

дие́з *m.* (*mus.*) sharp.

дие́та *f.* diet.

диетвра́ч *m.* dietitian.

диете́тика *f.* dietetics.

диети́ческий *adj.* dietary.

Дижо́н *m.* Dijon.

диза́йн *m.* (*industrial*) design.

ди́зель *m.* diesel engine.

дизентери́я *f.* dysentery.

дика́рь *m. f.* дика́рка savage.

ди́кий *adj.* **1.** wild, savage. **2.** queer. **3.** preposterous, outrageous.

ди́ко *adv.* wildly.

дикобра́з *m.* porcupine.

дико́вина *f.* (*colloq.*) novelty; wonder; strange thing.

дико́винный *adj.* (*colloq.*) strange; bizarre.

дикорасту́щий *adj.* growing wild.

ди́кость *f.* savagery, savageness.

дикта́нт *m.* (classroom) dictation.

дикта́т *m.* imposed settlement *or* decision.

дикта́тор *m.* dictator.

диктату́ра *f.* dictatorship.

диктова́ть OVA *impf. pf.* **про-** to dictate.

дикто́вка *f.* dictation.

ди́ктор *m.* (radio) announcer.

диктофо́н *m.* dictaphone.

ди́кция *f.* diction, articulation, enunciation.

диле́мма *f.* dilemma.

дилета́нт *m. f.* —ка dilettante; amateur.

дилета́нтство *neut.* dilettantism.

дилижа́нс *m.* stagecoach.

димину́эндо *adv.* diminuendo.

динами́зм *m.* dynamism.

дина́мика *f.* dynamics.

динами́т *m.* dynamite.

динами́ческий *also* динами́чный *adj.* dynamic; of dynamics.

дина́мо *neut. indecl.* dynamo.

динамо́метр *m.* dynamometer.

династи́ческий *adj.* dynastic.

дина́стия *f.* dynasty.

диноза́вр *m.* dinosaur.

дио́д *m.* diode.

дипло́м *m.* diploma.

диплома́т *m.* diplomat.

дипломати́ческий *adj.* diplomatic.

дипломати́чный *adj.* diplomatic; tactful.

диплома́тия *f.* diplomacy.

дипломи́рованный *adj.* with a college degree.

дипло́мный *adj.* pertaining to a (university) degree.

директи́ва *f.* **1.** directive. **2.** instructions, directions.

дире́ктор *m. f.* директри́са director.

директора́т *m.* board of directors.

дире́кторский *adj.* director's.

дире́кция *f.* **1.** top management. **2.** director's office.

дирижа́бль *m.* dirigible.

дирижёр *m.* (*mus.*) conductor.

дирижи́ровать OVA *impf.* (*mus.*) to conduct.

дисгармони́ровать OVA *impf.* to clash (with).

дисгармо́ния *f.* disharmony.

диск *m.* discus. —обо́л *m.* discus thrower.

диска́нт *m.* (*mus.*) treble.

дисквалифика́ция *f.* disqualification.

дисквалифици́ровать OVA *impf. and pf.* disqualify.

ди́сковый *adj.* disk-shaped.

дискредити́ровать OVA *impf. and pf.* to discredit.

дискримина́ция *f.* discrimination.

дискримини́ровать OVA *impf. and pf.* to discriminate.

дискуссио́нный *adj.* (*attrib.*) discussion.

диску́ссия *f.* discussion.

дискути́ровать OVA *impf.* to discuss.

дислока́ция *f.* disposition (*troops*).

дислоци́ровать OVA *impf. and pf.* to deploy (*troops*).

диспансе́р *m.* dispensary.

диспепси́я *f.* dyspepsia.

диспе́рсия *f.* (*phys.*) dyspersion.

диспе́тчер *m.* **1.** traffic manager. **2.** air traffic controller.

диспе́тчерская *adj.* DAA control tower.

диспропо́рция *f.* disproportion.

ди́спут *m.* dispute; debate.

диссерта́ция *f.* dissertation; thesis.

диссона́нс *m.* dissonance; disharmony.

дистанцио́нный *adj.* remote; controlled from a distance.

диста́нция *f.* distance.

дистилли́ровать OVA *impf. and pf.* to distill.

дистилля́ция *f.* distillation.

дистрофи́я *f.* dystrophy.

дисципли́на *f.* discipline.

дисциплина́рный *adj.* disciplinary.

дисциплини́ровать OVA *impf. and pf.* to discipline.

дитя́ *neut.* child.

дифира́мб *m.* (*obs.*) praise.

дифтери́я *f. also* дифтери́т *m.* diphtheria.

дифто́нг *m.* diphthong.

диффама́ция *f.* defamation.

дифференциа́л *m.* differential.

дифференциа́ция *f.* differentiation.
дифференци́ровать OVA *impf.* and *pf.* to differentiate.
диффу́зия *f.* (*phys.*) diffusion.
дича́ть *impf. pf.* **о- 1.** to become wild. **2.** to become unsociable.
дичь *f.* game; wildfowl.
длина́ *f.* length. — **в длину́** lengthwise.
длинново́лновый *adj.* (*attrib.*) long-wave.
длинново́лосый *adj.* long-haired.
длинноно́гий *adj.* long-legged.
длинно́ты *pl.* drawn-out lengthy passages.
дли́нный *adj.* long.
дли́тельный *adj.* long, prolonged; protracted.
дли́ться *impf. pf.* **про-** to last; to continue.
для *prep.* (*with gen.*) for; to.
днева́льный DAA *m.* (*mil.*) man on duty.
днева́ть *impf. pres.* **дню́ю, дню́ешь** to spend the day.
дневни́к *m.* diary; journal.
дневно́й *adj.* day; daily. — **ла́мпа дневно́го све́та** *m.* fluorescent light.
дневно́й спекта́кль *m.* matinee performance.
днём *adv.* in the daytime; by day.
Днепр *m.* (*river*) Dnieper.
Днепродзержи́нск *m.* Dniprodzerzhynsk (*Russian: Dneprodzerzhinsk*).
Днепропетро́вск *m.* Dnipropetrovsk (*Russian: Dnepropetrovsk*).
дни́ще *neut.* bottom (*of a container* or *barrel*).
дно *neut.* bottom. — **вверх дном** upside down. — **до дна** *interj.* bottoms up!
до *prep.* (*with gen.*) to; until; up to; as far as; about; before.
доба́вка *f.* (*colloq.*) addition; (*food*) helping.
добавле́ние *neut.* **1.** addition. **2.** appendix.
добавля́ть *impf. pf.* **доба́вить** to add.
доба́вочный *adj.* **1.** additional; extra. **2.** (*of telephone*) (*attrib.*) extension.
добела́ *adv.* **1.** until something is spotlessly clean. **2.** to white heat.
добива́ть *impf. pf.* **доби́ть** to finish off; to kill. **—ся 1.** to obtain; to attain; to achieve. **2.** to secure. **3.** *imperf. only* to strive for.
добира́ться *impf. pf.* **добра́ться** (**до** *with gen.*) to reach, to get to.
доби́ть *pres.* **добью́, добьёшь** *pf. of* **добива́ть**.
до́блестный *adj.* valiant; valorous.
до́блесть *f.* valor.
добре́ть *impf. pf.* **по-** to become gentle; to become kinder.
добро́ *neut.* **1.** good, benefit. **2.** property, possessions.
доброво́лец FILL *m.* volunteer.
доброво́льный *adj.* voluntary.
доброво́льческий *adj.* (*attrib.*) volunteer.
доброде́тель *f.* virtue.
доброде́тельный *adj.* virtuous.
доброду́шие *neut.* good nature.
доброжела́тель *m. f.* **—ница** well-wisher.
доброка́чественный *adj.* of high quality.
добро́м *adv.* (*colloq.*) of one's own free will.
Добро́ пожа́ловать *interj.* Welcome!
добросерде́чный *adj.* good-hearted; kindhearted.
добросо́вестность *f.* conscientiousness; integrity.
добросо́вестный *adj.* conscientious.
доброта́ *f.* goodness; kindness.

добро́тный *adj.* of high quality.
до́брый *adj.* good; kind.
добря́к *m. f.* **добря́чка** (*colloq.*) good-natured person.
добыва́ть *impf. pf.* **добы́ть 1.** to get, to obtain; to procure. **2.** to extract; to mine.
добы́ча *f.* **1.** obtainment; procurement. **2.** extraction. **3.** loot; plunder.
довезти́ *pf. of* **довози́ть**.
дове́ренность *f.* power of attorney.
дове́ренный *adj.* authorized; possessing power of attorney. — *m.* proxy; agent.
дове́рие *neut.* trust; confidence.
дове́рить *pf. of* **доверя́ть**.
до́верху *adv.* to the top; to the brim.
дове́рчивый *adj.* trustful, trusting; credulous.
доверша́ть *impf. pf.* **доверши́ть 1.** to complete. **2.** to conclude.
доверше́ние *neut.* completion.
доверя́ть *impf. pf.* **дове́рить 1.** to entrust. **2.** to trust.
дове́сок FILL *m.* makeweight.
до́вод *m.* reason; argument. — **до́воды за и про́тив** the pros and cons.
доводи́ть *impf. pf.* **довести́** to bring to; to drive to.
доводи́ться *impf. pres.* **довожу́сь, дово́дишься** *pf.* **довести́сь 1.** *impers.* (*with dat.* and *infin.*) to happen to; to have occasion to. **2.** (*with dat.* and *instr.*) (*colloq.*) to be related to someone as (*with degree of relationship*).
довое́нный *adj.* (*attrib.*) prewar.
дово́льно *adv.* rather; fairly; sufficiently; quite.
дово́льный *adj.* content; contented; satisfied.
дово́льствие *neut.* (*mil.*) allowance.
дово́льство *neut.* contentment.
дог *m.* Great Dane.
дога́дка *f.* guess; conjecture.
дога́дливый *adj.* bright; keen; quick-witted.
дога́дываться *impf. pf.* **догада́ться 1.** to guess, to surmise; to conjecture. **2.** to suspect.
догна́ть *pf. of* **догоня́ть**.
догова́риваться *impf. pf.* **договори́ться 1.** to arrange *or* settle something. **2.** to agree to something. **3.** to talk at some length.
догово́р *m.* **1.** agreement; contract. **2.** pact, treaty.
договорённость *f.* understanding, arrangement.
догово́рный *adj.* contractual.
догола́ *adv.* (*with verbs of undressing*) naked; to the skin.
догоня́ть *impf. pf.* **догна́ть 1.** to overtake. **2.** to catch up with *or* to.
доду́мываться *impf. pf.* **доду́маться** to think of; to hit upon an idea.
доезжа́ть *impf. pf.* **дое́хать** to reach; to arrive (at).
дое́ние *neut.* milking.
дож *m.* doge.
дожда́ться *pf. conjugated like* **ждать 1.** to wait (*as long as necessary*). **2.** to wait (*until something happens*).
дождева́льный *adj.* (*attrib.*) sprinkling; sprinkler.
дождева́ние *neut.* sprinkling (*of crops, etc.*).
дождеви́к *m.* (*colloq.*) raincoat.
дождево́й *adj.* (*attrib.*) pluvial; rain.
до́ждик *m.* light rain; rain shower.
дождли́вый *adj.* rainy.

дождь *m.* rain. — **дождь идёт** it's raining. — **на дождé** in the rain.

доживáть *impf. pf.* **дожúть 1.** to live; to live to see. **2.** to live out (one's days).

дóза *f.* dose.

дозапрáвка *f.* refueling.

дозвóленный *adj.* permitted; permissible.

дозволя́ть *impf. pf.* **дозвóлить** to permit, to allow.

дозвуковóй *adj.* subsonic.

дозирóвка *f.* dosage.

дознáние *neut.* (*leg.*) inquest; inquiry.

дозóр *m.* patrol.

дóильный *adj.* used for milking.

доисторúческий *adj.* prehistoric.

доúть *impf. pf.* **по-** to milk.

дóйка *f.* milking.

дойтú *pf. of* **доходúть.**

док *m.* dock.

доказáтельный *adj.* conclusive; demonstrative.

доказáтельство *neut.* proof; evidence.

доказýемый *adj.* demonstrable.

докáзывать *impf. pf.* **доказáть** to prove.

дóкер *m.* dock worker; longshoreman.

доклáд *m.* lecture; (conference) paper; report.

докладнóй *adj.* report.

доклáдчик *m. f.* **доклáдчица** speaker; lecturer; person delivering a report.

доклáдывать *impf. pf.* **доложúть 1.** to report, to make a report. **2.** to announce (a visitor).

докóле *adv.* (*obs.*) **1.** how long? **2.** as long as.

докраснá *adv.* until something is red; red-hot.

дóктор *m.* doctor.

доктрúна *f.* doctrine.

докумéнт *m.* document.

документáльный *adj.* documentary.

документúровать *OVA impf. and pf.* to document.

докучáть *impf.* (*with dat.*) to bother; to pester.

докýчливый *adj.* bothersome; annoying.

долбúть *impf. pf.* **про- 1.** to hollow out. **2.** (*colloq.*) to memorize; to learn by rote.

долг *m.* **1.** debt. **2.** duty.

дóлгий *adj.* long.

дóлго *adv.* long; for a long time.

долговéчный *adj.* long-lasting; long-lived.

долговóй *adj.* of *or* for a debt.

долговрéменный *adj.* of long duration.

долговя́зый *adj.* (*colloq.*) gangling; lanky.

долгождáнный *adj.* long-awaited.

долгоигрáющий *adj.* long-playing.

долголéтний *adj.* of many years.

долгонóсик *m.* weevil.

долгосрóчный *adj.* long-term.

долготá *f.* **1.** length. **2.** (*geog.*) longitude.

дóлее *adv.* longer.

дóлжен *adj. f.* **—жнá;** *neut.* **—жнó;** *pl.* **—жны́ 1.** must; to have to. **2.** should; ought to. **3.** to be supposed to. **4.** to owe.

должнúк *m. f.* **должнúца** *DAA* debtor.

дóлжное *neut. DAA* one's due.

должностнóй *adj.* official.

дóлжность *f.* position; post.

дóлжный *adj.* due; proper.

долúна *f.* valley.

дóллар *m.* dollar.

доложúть *pf. of* **доклáдывать.**

долóй *adv.* away with!; down with!

долотó *neut.* chisel.

дóлька *f.* **1.** lobule. **2.** section (*of a citrus fruit*).

дóльше *adv.* longer.

дóля *f.* **1.** portion; share. **2.** fate; lot.

дом *m.* house; home.

дóма *adv.* at home.

домáшние *pl.* members of one's family.

домáшний *adj.* domestic; home.

дóмик *m.* small house; cottage.

доминиóн *m.* dominion.

доминúровать *OVA impf.* (**над** *with instr.*) to (pre)dominate (over).

доминúрующий *adj.* dominant.

доминó *neut. indecl.* (*game*) dominoes.

домúшко *neut.* tiny house.

домкрáт *m.* jack (*for lifting*).

дóмна *f.* blast furnace.

домовúтый *adj.* thrifty; good at homemaking.

домовладéлец *FILL m. f.* **домовладéлица** homeowner.

домовóдство *neut.* housekeeping.

домовóй *m. DAA* elf; goblin.

домóвый *adj.* (*attrib.*) house.

домогáтельство *neut.* **1.** solicitation; importunity. **2.** demand; bid.

доморóщенный *adj.* homebred.

домосéд *m. f.* **—ка** homebody.

домоткáный *adj.* homespun.

домоуправлéние *neut.* building management.

домохозя́йка *f.* housewife.

домочáдцы *pl.* (*obs.*) household.

дóмра *f.* domra (*stringed instrument similar to a mandolin*).

домработница *f.* maid; housemaid.

дóмысел *FILL m.* conjecture; guess.

донагá *adv.* (*colloq.*) (*with verbs of undressing*) to the skin.

донáшивать *impf. pf.* **доносúть** to wear out.

донéльзя *adv.* (*colloq.*) completely; utterly.

донесéние *neut.* report; dispatch; message.

Донéц *m.* Donets.

дóнизу *adv.* to the bottom.

донкихóтский *adj.* quixotic.

дóнор *m.* blood donor.

донóс *m.* denunciation; accusation.

доносúть[1] *impf. pf.* **донестú 1.** to denounce; to inform (against). **2.** to report.

доносúть[2] *pf. of* **донáшивать.**

доносúться *impf. pf.* **донестúсь** to reach; to be heard.

донóсчик *m .f.* **донóсчица** informer; stool pigeon.

доны́не *adv.* (*poet.*) to this day.

доплáта *f.* additional payment; surcharge.

доплáчивать *impf. pf.* **доплатúть 1.** to make an additional payment. **2.** to pay in full.

доподлинный *adj.* (*colloq.*) true; authentic.

допоздná *adv.* till late at night.

дополнá *adv.* (*colloq.*) to the brim.

дополнéние *neut.* **1.** supplement; addition. **2.** (*gram.*) object.

дополнúтельно *adv.* in addition.

дополнúтельный *adj.* supplementary; additional.

дополня́ть *impf. pf.* **дополнить** to supplement; to add.

допотóпный *adj.* antediluvian.

допра́шивать *impf. pf.* допроси́ть to examine, to question; to cross-examine.

допро́с *m.* examination; interrogation, cross-examination.

до́пуск *m.* **1.** admissions. **2.** (*mech.*) tolerance.

допуска́ть *impf. pf.* допусти́ть **1.** to admit. **2.** to permit, to allow. **3.** to assume.

допусти́мый *adj.* permissible.

допусти́ть *pf. of* допуска́ть. — допу́стим let us assume.

допуще́ние *neut.* **1.** admission. **2.** assumption.

допьяна́ *adv.* (*colloq.*) till one is totally drunk.

дореволюцио́нный *adj.* prerevolutionary.

доро́га *f.* **1.** road; way. **2.** journey.

до́рого *adv.* **1.** expensive; expensively. **2.** dear; dearly.

дороговизна́ *f.* dearness; expensiveness.

дорого́й *adj.* **1.** dear; darling. **2.** dear; expensive.

дорогосто́ящий *adj.* high-priced; costly.

доро́дный *adj.* portly; corpulent.

дорожа́ть *impf. pf.* вз- *or* по- to go up in price.

доро́же *adj. comp. of* дорого́й.

дорожи́ть *impf.* (*with instr.*) **1.** to value. **2.** to care for; to treasure.

доро́жка *f.* **1.** path; lane; (athl.) track. **2.** (*small carpet*) runner.

доро́жный *adj.* (*attrib.*) road; travel.

доро́жный компью́тер *m.* laptop computer.

дортуа́р *m.* (*obs.*) dormitory.

доса́да *f.* **1.** nuisance; annoyance. **2.** disappointment.

доса́дный *adj.* **1.** annoying. **2.** regrettable.

доса́довать OVA *impf.* (на *with acc.*) to be annoyed with.

досажда́ть *impf. pf.* досади́ть to annoy; to vex.

досе́ле *adv.* (*obs.*) up to now.

доска́ *f.* **1.** board; plank. **2.** blackboard. — от доски́ до доски́ from cover to cover.

доскона́льный *adj.* thorough.

досло́вный *adj.* literal; word for word.

досмо́тр *m.* examination; inspection.

доспе́хи *pl.* armor.

досро́чно *adv.* ahead of schedule.

досро́чный *adj.* ahead of schedule.

достава́ть *impf. pf.* доста́ть **1.** to get; to obtain; to procure. **2.** (до *with gen.*) to reach; to touch.

доста́вка *f.* delivery.

доставля́ть *impf. pf.* доста́вить **1.** to deliver. **2.** to furnish; to supply. **3.** to give; to cause.

доста́ток FILL *m.* sufficiency.

доста́точно *adv.* enough; sufficiently.

доста́точность *f.* sufficiency.

доста́точный *adj.* sufficient.

доста́ть *pf. of* достава́ть.

достига́ть *impf. pf.* дости́чь, дости́гнуть (*with gen.*) **1.** to achieve; to attain. **2.** to reach.

достиже́ние *neut.* achievement; attainment.

достижи́мый *adj.* attainable.

достове́рно *adv.* for certain; for sure.

достове́рность *f.* authenticity.

достове́рный *adj.* trustworthy; reliable.

досто́инство *neut.* **1.** merit; virtue. **2.** dignity.

досто́йно *adv.* **1.** in a fitting manner. **2.** with dignity.

досто́йный *adj.* **1.** worthy; deserving. **2.** fitting; suitable.

достопа́мятный *adj.* memorable.

достопримеча́тельность *f.* object *or* place of interest; sight.

достопримеча́тельный *adj.* notable; remarkable; of special interest.

достоя́ние *neut.* property; holdings.

до́ступ *m.* **1.** access. **2.** approach.

досту́пный *adj.* accessible.

досу́г *m.* leisure.

досу́жий *adj.* (*colloq.*) idle.

до́суха *adv.* until completely dry.

до́сыта *adv.* to the point of satiation; to one's heart's content.

досье́ *neut. indecl.* dossier.

досю́да *adv.* (*colloq.*) to here; up to here; as far as this.

досяга́емость *f.* reach; (*mil.*) range.

дот *m.* (*abbr. of* долговре́менная огнева́я то́чка) pillbox.

дота́ция *f.* subsidy; grant.

дотемна́ *adv.* until dark; until nightfall.

дотла́ *adv.* to the ground.

дото́ле *adv.* (*obs.*) hitherto.

дото́шный *adj.* (*colloq.*) meticulous.

дофи́н *m.* dauphin.

доха́ *f.* fur coat (*with fur on both sides*).

до́хлый *adj.* **1.** (*of animals*) dead. **2.** (*colloq.*) sickly.

дохля́тина *f.* (*colloq.*) carrion.

до́хнуть[1] *impf. pf.* по- (*of animals*) to die.

дохну́ть[2] *pf.* to breathe.

дохо́д *m.* income; return.

доходи́ть *impf. pf.* дойти́ (до *with gen.*) to reach.

дохо́дный *adj.* profitable; remunerative.

дохо́дчивый *adj.* easy to understand; lucid.

доце́нт *m.* **1.** docent. **2.** university lecturer.

доче́рний *adj.* daughter's.

до́чиста *adv.* clean; until something is spotless.

до́чка *f. dim. of* дочь *f.*

дочь *f.* daughter.

дошко́льный *adj.* preschool.

до́шлый *adj.* (*colloq.*) clever; shrewd.

доща́тый *adj.* made of boards *or* planks.

доще́чка *f.* small board.

доя́рка *f.* milkmaid.

Дра́ва *f.* (*river*) Drava.

дра́га *f.* dredge.

драгоце́нность *f.* **1.** jewel; precious stone. **2.** драгоце́нности *pl.* valuables.

драгоце́нный *adj.* precious.

драгу́н *m.* dragoon.

драже́ *neut. indecl.* drops (*candy*).

дразни́ть *impf.* to tease.

дра́ить *impf.* to scrub; to swab.

дра́ка *f.* fight.

драко́н *m.* dragon.

дра́ма *f.* drama. —ти́ческий *also* —ти́чный *adj.* dramatic. —ту́рг *m.* playwright.

драматизи́ровать OVA *impf. and pf.* to dramatize.

драмати́зм *m.* dramatic effect.

драматурги́я *f.* dramaturgy.

драндуле́т *m.* (*colloq.*) jalopy, heap, clunker, wreck.

дра́нка *f.* **1.** lath. **2.** shingle.

дра́ный *adj.* torn; ragged.

драп *m.* heavy woolen cloth.

драпирова́ть OVA *impf.* to drape.

драпиро́вка *f.* drapery.
драпиро́вщик *m.* upholsterer.
дра́повый *adj.* made of heavy woolen cloth.
драть *impf. pf.* **вы́-, со-** **1.** to tear. **2.** to flay; to flog. **—ся** *impf. pf.* **по-** to fight.
драчу́н *m.* (*colloq.*) brawler.
дребеде́нь *f.* (*colloq.*) **1.** nonsense. **2.** junk.
дребезжа́ние *neut.* rattle.
дребезжа́ть *impf.* **1.** to rattle. **2.** to jingle.
древеси́на *f.* wood; timber.
древе́сница *f.* tree frog.
древе́сный *adj.* (*attrib.*) wood.
дре́вко *neut.* **1.** pole; staff; flagstaff. **2.** (*spear*) shaft.
древнеангли́йский *adj.* Old English.
древнегре́ческий *adj.* Ancient Greek.
древнееве́рейский *adj.* Hebrew.
древнеру́сский *adj.* Old Russian.
дре́вний *adj.* ancient.
дре́вность *f.* antiquity.
дрези́на *f.* (*railroad*) handcar.
дрейф *m.* (*ocean*) drift.
дрейфова́ть OVA *impf.* to drift.
дрель *f.* drill (*tool*).
дрема́ть *impf.* to doze; to nap.
дремо́та *f.* drowsiness.
дремо́тный *adj.* drowsy.
дрему́чий *adj.* dense, thick (*of a forest*).
дрена́ж *m.* drainage.
дрени́ровать OVA *impf. and pf.* to drain.
дрессиро́ванный *adj.* (*animal*) trained.
дрессирова́ть *impf. pf.* **вы́дрессировать** to train (*animals*); to school.
дрессиро́вщик *m.* (*animal*) trainer.
Дри́на *f.* (*river*) Drina.
дроби́лка *f.* crusher; crushing machine.
дроби́льный *adj.* crushing.
дроби́на *f.* pellet.
дроби́ть *impf. pf.* **раз-** **1.** to divide *or* split up. **2.** to crush. **3.** to splinter.
дробле́ние *neut.* crushing, grinding.
дроблёный *adj.* crushed.
дро́бный *adj.* **1.** fragmented; separate. **2.** (*math.*) fractional. **3.** (*of sounds*) rhythmic.
дробови́к *m.* shotgun.
дробь *f.* **1.** shot; pellets. **2.** drumming. **3.** (*math.*) fraction.
дрова́ *pl.* firewood.
дро́вни *pl.* sledge.
дровосе́к *m.* (*obs.*) woodcutter.
дровяно́й *adj.* (*attrib.*) wood.
дро́ги *pl.* hearse.
дро́гнуть *pf.* **1.** to quiver; to shake. **2.** to flinch.
дрожа́ние *neut.* trembling; shivering.
дрожа́ть *impf.* to shiver; to tremble.
дро́жжи *pl.* yeast.
дро́жки *pl.* open carriage; droshky.
дрожь *f.* **1.** tremor, quaver. **2.** trembling, quivering.
дрозд *m.* thrush. **— чёрный дрозд** blackbird.
дрок *m.* (*bot.*) furze.
дро́ссель *m.* throttle; choke.
дро́тик *m.* javelin.
дрофа́ *f.* (*bird*) bustard.
друг *m.* friend. **— друг дру́га** one another.
други́е *pl.* others; the rest.

друго́й *adj.* other; another; next.
дру́жба *f.* amity, friendship.
дружелю́бный *adj.* friendly; amicable.
дру́жеский *adj.* friendly.
дру́жественный *adj.* friendly; amicable.
дружи́на *f.* **1.** military retinue of a medieval prince. **2.** militia unit.
дружи́ть *impf.* to be friends with.
дру́жно *adv.* amicably.
дру́жный *adj.* amicable, friendly; unanimous.
дружо́к FILL *m.* (*colloq.*) friend; pal.
дры́гать *impf.* to jerk, twitch; to kick (one's feet).
дря́блый *adj.* flabby; flaccid.
дря́зги *pl.* (*colloq.*) squabbles; petty quarrels.
дрянно́й *adj.* worthless; bad; trashy.
дрянь *f.* rubbish; trash.
дря́хлый *adj.* **1.** decrepit. **2.** senile.
дуали́зм *m.* dualism.
дуб *m.* oak.
дуби́льный *adj.* tanning.
дуби́льня *f.* tannery.
дуби́на *f.* club; bludgeon; truncheon.
дуби́ть *impf. pf.* **вы́-** to tan (leather).
дубле́ние *neut.* tanning.
дублёнка *f.* (*colloq.*) sheepskin coat.
дублёный *adj.* tanned.
дублёр *m.* **1.** (*theat.*) understudy. **2.** (*cinema*) person who dubs in a part.
дубле́т *m.* duplicate.
дублика́т *m.* duplicate.
Ду́блин *m.* Dublin.
дубли́рование *neut.* **1.** duplication. **2.** dubbing.
дубня́к *m.* oak forest.
дубова́тый *adj.* (*colloq.*) clumsy; coarse.
дубо́вый *adj.* oak.
дубо́к *m.* young oak.
дубоно́с *m.* (*bird*) grosbeak.
дубра́ва *f.* oak forest.
Дубро́вник *m.* Dubrovnik.
Дувр *m.* Dover.
дуга́ *f.* **1.** arc. **2.** shaft bow.
дугообра́зный *adj.* arched.
ду́дка *f.* fife.
ду́дник *m.* (*bot.*) angelica.
ду́жка *f.* hoop.
ду́ло *neut.* muzzle (*of gun*).
ду́ма *f.* **1.** meditation; thought. **2.** Duma.
ду́мать *impf. pf.* **по-** to think. **— (**with inf.*) to intend.
ду́мка *f.* (*colloq.*) small pillow.
Дуна́й *m.* Danube.
дунове́ние *neut.* puff (*of air*); breath (*of wind*).
ду́пель *m.* (*bird*) double snipe.
дупле́т *m.* (*billiards*) bank shot.
дупли́стый *adj.* (*of a tree*) hollow.
дупло́ *neut.* **1.** hollow (*in a tree*). **2.** cavity.
ду́ра *f.* ду́ра́к fool.
дурале́й *m.* (*colloq.*) fool; jerk.
дура́цкий *adj.* (*colloq.*) fool's; ridiculous.
дура́чество *neut.* (*colloq.*) prank.
дурачо́к FILL *m.* (*colloq.*) little fool.
дура́шливый *adj.* (*colloq.*) silly.
ду́рень FILL *m.* (*colloq.*) idiot; dope.
дурма́н *m.* **1.** thorn apple; jimsonweed. **2.** narcotic; drug.
дурма́нить *impf. pf.* **о-** to stupefy; to intoxicate.

ду́рно *adv.* badly. — мне ду́рно I feel faint.
дурно́й *adj.* **1.** foul; bad. **2.** evil. **3.** ugly.
дурнота́ *f.* (*feeling of*) faintness.
дурну́шка *f.* (*colloq.*) plain girl.
дуршла́г *m.* colander.
дурь *f.* (*colloq.*) folly; foolishness.
ду́тый *adj.* **1.** hollow. **2.** exaggerated; inflated.
дуть *impf.* to blow.
дутьё *neut.* blowing.
ду́ться *impf. pres.* ду́юсь, ду́ешься (*colloq.*) to pout; to sulk.
дух *m.* **1.** spirit; heart; courage. **2.** ghost.
духи́ *pl.* perfume.
духове́нство *neut.* clergy.
духо́вка *f.* oven.
духовни́к *m.* confessor.
духо́вный *adj.* **1.** spiritual. **2.** ecclesiastical.
духово́й инструме́нт *m.* wind instrument.
духово́й орке́стр *m.* (*mus.*) brass band.
духота́ *f.* **1.** stuffiness, closeness. **2.** stuffy heat.
душ *m.* shower; shower bath.
душа́ *f.* soul.
Душанбе́ *m.* Dushanbe.
душева́я *f.* shower; shower bath.
душевнобольно́й *adj.* mentally ill. — *m.* insane person; mental case.
душе́вный *adj.* **1.** sincere; cordial; heartfelt. **2.** mental.
душево́й *adj.* (*attrib.*) **1.** per capita. **2.** shower.
душегу́б *m.* (*colloq.*) killer, murderer.
душегу́бка *f.* **1.** mobile gas chamber. **2.** dugout; canoe.
ду́шенька *f.* (*colloq.*) dear, darling, sweetheart.
душеприка́зчик *m.* (*obs.*) executor (*of a will*).
душераздира́ющий *adj.* heart-rending; harrowing.
ду́шечка *f.* (*used in address*) dear; darling.
души́стый *adj.* fragrant; scented.
души́ть¹ *impf. pf.* за- **1.** to strangle; to stifle, to smother. **2.** to oppress, to repress, to suppress.
души́ть *impf. pf.* на- to perfume, to scent.²
ду́шка *m.* and *f.* (*decl. f.*) (*colloq.*) dear person; lovely person.
ду́шно *adj.* (*pred.*) stuffy. — здесь ду́шно it is stuffy here.
ду́шный *adj.* close; stuffy.

душо́к FILL *m.* (*colloq.*) smell of something beginning to decompose.
дуэ́ль *f.* duel.
дуэ́нья *f.* (*obs.*) chaperone.
Дуэ́ро *neut.* (*river*) Douro.
дуэ́т *m.* duet.
ды́ба *f.* rack (*instrument of torture*).
ды́бом *adv.* (*of hair*) on end.
дыбы́ *adv.*: станови́ться на дыбы́ *impf.* (*of horses*) to rear.
ды́лда *m.* and *f.* (*decl. f.*) (*colloq.*) tall, ungainly person.
дым *m.* smoke.
дыми́ть *impf. pf.* на- to fill with smoke. —ся *v.i.* to smoke; to give off smoke *or* steam.
ды́мка *f.* haze.
ды́мный *adj.* smoky.
дымово́й *adj.* (*attrib.*) smoke.
дымо́к FILL *m.* thin smoke.
дымохо́д *m.* flue; stovepipe.
ды́мчатый *adj.* smoky; smoke-colored.
ды́нный *adj.* (*attrib.*) melon.
ды́ня *f.* melon; muskmelon.
дыра́ *also* ды́рка *f.* hole.
дыроко́л *m.* hole punch.
дыря́вый *adj.* full of holes.
дыха́ние *neut.* respiration; breathing.
дыха́тельный *adj.* respiratory.
дыша́ть *impf.* to breathe, respire.
ды́шло *neut.* pole; beam; shaft (*on a carriage*).
дья́вол *m.* devil. —ьский *adj.* devilish; diabolical; horrible.
дья́кон *m.* deacon.
дю́жий *adj.* (*colloq.*) sturdy; hefty; robust.
дю́жина *f.* dozen.
дю́жинный *adj.* ordinary; run-of-the-mill.
дюйм *m.* inch.
дю́на *f.* dune.
дюралюми́ний *m.* duralumin.
Дю́ссельдорф *m.* Düsseldorf.
дя́гиль *m.* (*bot.*) angelica.
дя́денька *m.* (*decl. f.*) (*colloq.*) uncle.
дя́дя *m.* (*decl. f.*) uncle.
дя́тел *m.* woodpecker.

E

Ева́нгелие *neut.* Gospel.
евангели́ст *m.* Evangelist.
евге́ника *f.* eugenics.
е́внух *m.* eunuch.
Евпато́рия *f.* Yevpatoriya.
евре́й *m. f.* —ка Jew; Hebrew. —ский *adj.* Jewish; Hebrew.
Евро́па *f.* Europe.
европе́ец FILL *m. f.* **европе́йка** European.
европеизи́ровать *impf. and pf.* to Europeanize.
европе́йский *adj.* European.
евста́хиева труба́ eustachian tube.
Евхари́стия *f.* Eucharist.
е́герь *m.* professional hunter.
Еги́пет *m.* Egypt.
еги́петский *adj.* Egyptian.
египтоло́гия *f.* Egyptology.
египтя́нин *m. f.* **египтя́нка** Egyptian.
его́ *pron. gen. and acc. of* **он, оно́.**
егоза́ *m. and f. (decl. f.) (colloq.)* fidgety person.
егозли́вый *adj. (colloq.)* fidgety.
еда́ *f.* **1.** food. **2.** meal.
едва́ *adv.* hardly. — **едва́ не** nearly; almost.
едине́ние *neut.* unity.
едини́ца *f.* unit; the numeral one.
едини́чный *adj.* single; isolated.
единобо́жие *neut.* monotheism.
единобо́рство *neut.* single combat.
единобра́чие *neut.* monogamy.
единове́рец FILL *m.* coreligionist.
единове́рный *adj.* of the same religion.
единовла́стие *neut.* absolute rule.
единовре́менно *adv.* once; all at once.
единовре́менный *adj.* one-time.
единогла́сие *neut.* unanimity.
единогла́сный *adj.* unanimous.
единоду́шие *neut.* unanimity.
единоду́шный *adj.* unanimous.
единокро́вный *adj.* having the same father.
единоли́чный *adj.* individual.
единомы́слие *neut.* like-mindedness.
единомы́шленник *m.* like-minded person.
единообра́зие *neut.* uniformity.
единоро́г *m.* unicorn.
единоутро́бный *adj.* having the same mother.
еди́нственно *adv.* only; solely.
еди́нственный *adj.* sole, only.
еди́нство *neut.* unity.
еди́ный *adj.* united; common.
е́дкий *adj.* caustic.
е́дкость *f.* **1.** corrosiveness. **2.** cutting remark.
едо́к FILL *m.* mouth to feed; eater.
её *pron. gen. and acc. of* **она́.**
ёж *m.* hedgehog.
ежеви́ка *f. (coll.)* blackberries.
ежего́дник *m.* yearbook; annual.
ежего́дный *adj.* annual.
ежедне́вный *adj.* daily.
е́жели *conj. (obs.) (colloq.)* if.
ежеме́сячник *m.* monthly.
ежемину́тный *adj.* continual, incessant.

еженеде́льник *m.* weekly.
еженеде́льный *adj.* weekly.
ежено́щный *adj.* nightly.
ежеча́сный *adj.* hourly.
ёжиться *impf. pf.* **съ- 1.** to huddle up. **2.** to hesitate; to waver.
езда́ *f.* ride; drive; driving, traveling.
е́здить *impf. indet. det.* **е́хать** *pf.* **пое́хать** to ride; to drive, to go *(by vehicle)*; to travel, to journey.
ездово́й *adj.* for riding.
ездо́к FILL *m.* **1.** rider; horseman. **2.** cyclist.
е́зженый *adj. (colloq.) (road)* well-trodden.
ей *pron. dat. and instr. of* **она́.**
ей-бо́гу *interj. (colloq.)* really; really and truly.
Ейск *m.* Yeysk.
Екатеринбу́рг *m.* Yekaterinburg.
ёкать *impf. pf.* **ёкнуть** *(of a heart)* to skip a beat.
е́ле *adv.* scarcely.
еле́й *m.* **1.** holy oil; unction. **2.** balm; solace.
еле́йный *adj.* unctuous.
ёлка *f.* **1.** fir tree; spruce. **2.** Christmas tree.
ель *f.* spruce. —**ник** *m.* spruce grove.
ёмкий *adj.* capacious.
ёмкость *f.* capacity, capaciousness.
ему́ *pron. dat. of* **он, оно́.**
ено́т *m.* raccoon. — **овый** *adj. (attrib.)* raccoon.
епа́рхия *f.* diocese.
епи́скоп *m.* bishop. —**а́льный** *adj.* Episcopalian. —**ский** *adj.* episcopal. —**ство** *neut.* episcopate.
ерала́ш *m. (colloq.)* muddle; confusion; jumble.
Ерева́н *m.* Yerevan.
е́ресь *f.* heresy.
ерети́к *m. f.* **ерети́чка** heretic.
ёрзать *impf. (colloq.)* to fidget.
ермо́лка *f.* skullcap.
еро́шить *impf. pf.* **взъ-** to muss; to tousle.
ерунда́ *f.* nonsense; rubbish.
ерунди́ть *impf. (colloq.)* to talk nonsense.
ерунди́вый *adj. (colloq.)* **1.** nonsensical. **2.** petty.
ёрш *m.* **1.** *(fish)* ruff. **2.** brush; lampbrush.
есау́л *m.* Cossack captain.
е́сли *conj.* if. — **е́сли бы не** were it not for.
есте́ственник *m.* naturalist; natural scientist.
есте́ственно *adv.* **1.** naturally. **2.** of course.
есте́ственный *adj.* natural.
естество́ *neut.* nature; essence.
естествозна́ние *neut.* natural sciences.
естествоиспыта́тель *m.* naturalist.
есть[1] *impf. pf.* **съ- 1.** to eat (away). **2.** to smart.
есть[2] *3rd person sing. pres. of* **быть** there is, there are. —*interj. (mil.)* aye-aye.
ефре́йтор *m. (mil.) (approx. rank of)* lance corporal *or* private first class.
е́хать *impf. det. of* **е́здить.**
ехи́дна *f.* **1.** spiny anteater. **2.** vicious person. **3.** viper, snake.
ехи́дный *adj. (colloq.)* malicious; venomous.
ехи́дство *neut.* malice; spite; venom.
ещё *adv.* still, yet; more; as far back as.
е́ю *pron. instr. of* **она́.**

Ж

ж *see* же.
жа́ба¹ *f.* toad.
жа́ба² *f.* (*obs.*) angina.
жа́бры *pl.* gills.
жа́воронок FILL *m.* lark.
жа́дничать *impf.* (*colloq.*) to be greedy.
жа́дно *adv.* **1.** greedily. **2.** eagerly; avidly.
жа́дность *f.* greed; stinginess.
жа́дный *adj.* greedy; avid, covetous.
жа́жда *f.* thirst.
жа́ждать *impf.* to thirst; to crave.
жаке́т *m.* jacket (*for a woman or child*).
жале́ть *impf. pf.* по- to be *or* feel sorry; to regret.
жа́лить *impf. pf.* у- to sting; to bite.
жа́лкий *adj.* pitiful; pitiable; miserable.
жа́лко *adv.* pitifully. — как жа́лко! what a pity!
жа́ло *neut.* (*zool.*) sting; stinger.
жа́лоба *f.* complaint.
жа́лобный *adj.* plaintive; sorrowful; mournful.
жа́лобщик *m. f.* жа́лобщица person registering a complaint.
жа́лованье *neut.* salary; wages.
жа́ловать OVA *impf. pf.* по- **1.** to grant; to bestow; to confer. **2.** to favor, to be gracious. **3.** to visit. —ся to complain.
жа́лостливый *adj.* pitiful; compassionate.
жа́лость *f.* pity.
жаль *impers. pred.* it's a pity. — мне его́ жаль I feel sorry for him.
жалюзи́ *pl. indecl.* Venetian blinds.
жанда́рм *m.* gendarme.
жанр *m.* genre.
жар *m.* **1.** heat; ardor. **2.** fever.
жара́ *f.* heat.
жарго́н *m.* jargon, slang.
жа́реный *adj.* fried; grilled; broiled.
жа́риться *impf. pf.* из- *v.i.* **1.** to fry; to roast. **2.** to broil; to grill. **3.** (*colloq.*) to sun, to bask.
жа́ркий *adj.* **1.** hot, torrid. **2.** ardent.
жа́рко *adv.* hotly, hot.
жарко́е *neut.* meat dish; roast.
жаро́вня *f.* brazier.
жар-пти́ца *f.* firebird.
жа́рче *adj. comp.* of жа́ркий *and* жа́рко.
жасми́н *m.* jasmine. —ный *adj.* jasmine.
жа́тва *f.* harvest, reaping; harvest time.
жа́твенный *adj.* harvesting.
жа́тка *f.* harvester; reaper.
жать¹ *impf. pres.* жму, жмёшь *pf.* с-, по- to press, to squeeze; to pinch.
жать² *impf. pres.* жну, жнёшь *pf.* с- to reap.
жбан *m.* jug.
жва́чка *f.* **1.** cud. **2.** chewing gum.
жва́чные *pl.* ruminants.
жгут *m.* **1.** twisted braid. **2.** tourniquet.
жгу́чий *adj.* burning.
ждать *impf. pf.* подо- to wait, to await, to expect.
же *also* ж *conj.* (*expresses contrast*) but. — *particle* **1.** (*used for emphasis*) что же ты де́лаешь? What are you doing? **2.** (*expresses sameness or identity*) так же in the same way.
жева́ние *neut.* mastication.

жёваный *adj.* **1.** chewed. **2.** crumpled.
жева́тельный *adj.* (for) chewing.
жева́ть *impf.* to chew, to masticate; to ruminate.
жезл *m.* **1.** rod. **2.** baton; staff.
жела́ние *neut.* wish, desire.
жела́нный *adj.* **1.** desired. **2.** welcome.
жела́тельно *adv.* (*pred.*) desirable.
жела́тельный *adj.* desirable.
желати́н *m.* gelatin. —овый *adj.* gelatinous.
жела́ть *impf. pf.* по- to wish, to desire.
жела́ющие *pl.* those who wish.
желва́к *m.* lump; tumor; swelling.
желе́ *neut. indecl.* jelly.
железа́ *f.* gland.
желе́зистый¹ *adj.* glandular.
желе́зистый² *adj.* ferriferous.
желе́зка *f.* **1.** (*colloq.*) piece of iron; iron bar. **2.** (*obs.*) railway.
желе́зка *f.* glandule.
желе́зная доро́га *f.* railway; railroad.
железнодоро́жный *adj.* railway; railroad.
желе́зный *adj.* iron; ferrous.
железня́к *m.* iron ore.
желе́зо *neut.* iron.
железобето́н *m.* reinforced concrete.
жёлоб *m.* chute.
желобо́к FILL *m.* groove.
желте́ть *impf. pf.* по- *v.i.* to become yellow.
желтизна́ *f.* **1.** yellowness. **2.** yellow color. **3.** sallow complexion.
желтова́тый *adj.* yellowish; sallow.
желто́к FILL *m.* yolk (*of an egg*).
желторо́тый *adj.* **1.** yellow-beaked. **2.** (*colloq.*) immature; inexperienced.
желтофио́ль *f.* wallflower.
желту́ха *f.* (*med.*) jaundice.
жёлтый *adj.* yellow.
желудёвый *adj.* acorn.
желу́док FILL *m.* stomach.
желу́дочек FILL *m.* ventricle.
желу́дочный *adj.* stomach; gastric.
жёлудь *m.* acorn.
жёлчность *f.* biliousness.
жёлчный *adj.* bilious; bitter.
жёлчь *f.* **1.** bile; gall. **2.** bitterness.
жема́ниться *impf.* (*colloq.*) to put on airs.
жема́нный *adj.* affected; unnatural.
жёмчуг *m.* (*colloq.*) pearls.
жемчу́жина *f.* (*single*) pearl.
жемчу́жница *f.* pearl oyster.
жена́ *f.* wife.
жена́тый *adj.* (на *with prep.*) (*of a man*) married (to).
Жене́ва *f.* Geneva.
жени́ть *impf. and pf.* to marry, to wed. —ся (на *with prep.*) (*of a man*) to marry, to get married (to).
жени́тьба *f.* marriage.
жени́х *m.* fiancé; bridegroom.
женолю́б *m.* womanizer.
женолюби́вый *adj.* with a fondness for women.

женолю́бие *neut.* fondness for women.
женонави́стник *m.* misogynist.
женоподо́бный *adj.* effeminate.
же́нский *adj.* female; feminine; womanly.
же́нственность *f.* femininity.
же́нщина *f.* woman.
женьше́нь *m.* ginseng.
жердь *f.* rod, pole; long stick.
жеребёнок FILL *m.* foal.
жеребе́ц FILL *m.* stallion.
жереби́ться *impf. pf.* **о-** to foal.
жеребьёвка *f.* casting of lots.
жерло́ *neut.* **1.** mouth (*of a volcano*). **2.** muzzle (*of a gun*).
жёрнов *m.* millstone.
же́ртва *f.* **1.** sacrifice. **2.** victim; casualty.
же́ртвенник *m.* altar.
же́ртвенный *adj.* **1.** sacrificial. **2.** selfless.
же́ртвовать OVA *impf. pf.* **по- 1.** to donate, to endow. **2.** to sacrifice.
жертвоприноше́ние *neut.* sacrifice; (*burnt*) offering.
жест *m.* gesture.
жестикули́ровать OVA *impf.* to gesticulate.
жестикуля́ция *f.* gesticulation.
жёсткий hard; strong; firm; rigid.
жёстко *adv.* **1.** harshly. **2.** decisively. **3.** abruptly.
жёсткость *f.* **1.** hardness; toughness. **2.** rigidity.
жесто́кий *adj.* **1.** cruel. **2.** fierce. **3.** harsh.
жесто́ко *adv.* cruelly; harshly; severely.
жестокосе́рдие *neut.* hardheartedness; callousness.
жесто́кость *f.* **1.** cruelty. **2.** atrocity. **3.** severity.
жёстче *adj. comp. of* **жёсткий.**
жесть *f.* tin.
жестя́нка *f.* tin can.
жестяно́й *adj.* tin.
жестя́нщик *m.* tinsmith.
жето́н *m.* **1.** token. **2.** medal. **3.** badge.
жечь *impf. pf.* **с-** to burn; to sting.
Же́шув *m.* Rzeszów.
жже́ние *neut.* burning sensation.
жжёнка *f.* hot punch.
жжёный *adj.* burned, burnt.
живе́й! *interj.* Hurry!; Speed it up!
живе́ц FILL *m.* small fish used for bait.
живи́тельный *adj.* vivifying; bracing.
жи́вность *f.* (*colloq.*) living things.
жи́во *adv.* **1.** lively, animatedly. **2.** quickly. **3.** vividly, graphically.
живодёр *m. f.* **—ка** (*colloq.*) hustler.
живо́й *adj.* living; live; alive.
жи́вокость *f.* (*bot.*) delphinium; larkspur.
живопи́сец FILL *m.* painter.
живопи́сный *adj.* picturesque.
жи́вопись *f.* (*art*) painting.
живородя́щий *adj.* viviparous.
жи́вость *f.* liveliness, animation.
живо́т *m.* stomach; belly.
животво́рный *adj.* life-giving.
живо́тик *m.* (*colloq.*) tummy.
животново́дство *neut.* livestock breeding; animal husbandry.
живо́тное *neut.* animal; beast.
живо́тный *adj.* **1.** animal. **2.** organic; bestial, brute.
животрепе́щущий *adj.* timely; vital.

живу́честь *f.* **1.** viability. **2.** tenaciousness.
живу́чий *adj.* viable; tenacious of life.
жи́вчик *m.* (*colloq.*) lively person.
живьём *adv.* (*colloq.*) alive.
жи́дкий *adj.* **1.** liquid. **2.** thin; watery.
жидкова́тый *adj.* watery.
жи́дкость *f.* liquid; fluid.
жи́жа *f.* swill; liquid; wash.
жи́же *adj. comp. of* **жи́дкий.**
жи́зненно *adv.* **1.** true to life. **2.** vitally.
жи́зненность *f.* vitality.
жи́зненный *adj.* lifelike; vital.
жизнеописа́ние *neut.* biography.
жизнера́достный *adj.* cheerful, joyous; enjoying life.
жизнеспосо́бный *adj.* viable.
жизнь *f.* life.
жиклёр *m.* (*carburetor*) jet; nozzle.
жи́ла *f.* **1.** vein. **2.** sinew.
жи́л-был once upon a time there was *or* lived.
жиле́т *m. f.* **—ка** vest, waistcoat.
жиле́тный *adj.* (*attrib.*) vest.
жиле́ц FILL *m. f.* **жили́ца** tenant; lodger.
жи́листый *adj.* sinewy; stringy; wiry.
жили́ще *m.* dwelling; abode; living quarters.
жи́лка *f.* **1.** (*bot.*) fiber. **2.** vein, nerve.
жило́й *adj.* **1.** dwelling. **2.** habitable.
жилпло́щадь *f.* floorspace.
жильё *neut.* **1.** dwelling; domicile. **2.** habitation. **3.** accommodation.
жим *m.* (*weightlifting*) press.
жи́молость *f.* honeysuckle.
жир *m.* fat.
жира́ф *m.* giraffe.
жире́ть *impf. pf.* **раз-** to become *or* grow fat.
жи́рно *adv.* with a lot of fat.
жи́рный *adj.* **1.** fat; plump. **2.** rich. **3.** greasy. **4.** boldface.
жи́ро *neut. indecl.* endorsement (*on a check*).
жирови́к *m.* fatty tumor.
жирово́й *adj.* fatty; adipose.
жите́йский *adj.* worldly; mundane.
жи́тель *m. f.* **—ница** inhabitant; resident.
жи́тельство *neut.* residence. **—вид на жи́тельство** residence permit.
жи́тница *f.* granary.
жи́то *neut.* **1.** rye, barley, wheat. **2.** grain in general.
Жито́мир *m.* Zhitomir.
жить *impf.* to live. **—как живёте?** (*colloq.*) how are things?
житьё *neut.* life; existence.
жлоб *m.* **1.** penny pincher. **2.** rude person. **3.** jerk.
жмот *m.* (*colloq.*) cheapskate; miser; tightwad; penny pincher.
жму́рить *impf. pf.* **за-.** — **жму́рить глаза́** to squint.
жму́рки *pl.* blindman's buff.
жне́йка *f.* (*machine*) harvester; reaper.
жнец *m. f.* **жни́ца** (*person*) reaper.
жни́во *also* **жнивьё** *neut.* stubble.
жоке́й *m.* jockey.
жонглёр *m.* juggler.
жонгли́ровать OVA *impf.* to juggle.
жонки́ль *m.* jonquil.

жра́ть *impf. pres.* **жру, жрёшь** *pf.* **со-** **1.** (*of animals*) to eat. **2.** (*vulg.*) to gobble; to guzzle.
жре́бий *m.* **1.** lot. **2.** fate, destiny.
жрец *m.* pagan priest.
жри́ца *f.* pagan priestess.
жужжа́ние *neut.* hum; buzz.
жужжа́ть *impf.* to hum; to buzz; to drone.
жуи́р *m.* playboy.
жук *m.* beetle.
жу́лик *m.* crook; cheat; swindler.
жу́льничать *impf.* (*colloq.*) to cheat.
жу́льнический *adj.* (*colloq.*) crooked.
жу́льничество *neut.* (*colloq.*) cheating.
жу́пел *m.* bugbear; bugaboo.
жура́вль *m.* (*bird*) crane.
жури́ть *impf.* (*colloq.*) to rebuke, to scold.
журна́л *m.* **1.** magazine, periodical, journal. **2.** register; diary.
журнали́ст *m.* *f.* **—ка** journalist.

журнали́стика *f.* journalism.
журнали́стский *adj.* journalistic.
журна́льный *adj.* magazine.
жу́рфак *m.* (*abbr. of* **факульте́т журнали́стики** *m.*) department of journalism.
журча́ние *neut.* babble; babbling (*of a brook* or *stream*).
журча́ть *impf.* (*of water*) to gurgle; to babble; to murmur.
жу́ткий *adj.* dreadful; horrible; terrible.
жу́тко *adv.* **1.** frighteningly. **2.** (*colloq.*) terribly.
жу́ткость *f.* dread; horror; terror.
жуть *f.* (*colloq.*) horror.
жу́хлый *adj.* **1.** dried up; withered. **2.** (*of colors*) faded.
жу́хнуть *impf. past* **жух** *or* **жу́хнул, жу́хла** **1.** to wither; to dry up. **2.** (*of colors*) to fade.
жучо́к *m. dim. of* **жук.**
жюри́ *neut. indecl.* **1.** judges (*competition*). **2.** jury. **3.** (*obs.*) umpires.

3

за *prep.* (*with acc.*) (*dir.*) behind; beyond; across, over; out of; for, by. — (*with instr.*) (*loc.*) behind, beyond; after.

зааплоди́ровать OVA *pf.* to begin to applaud.

заатланти́ческий *adj.* transatlantic.

заба́ва *f.* amusement.

забавля́ть *impf.* to amuse; entertain.

заба́вник *m.* (*colloq.*) funny person.

заба́вно *adv.* in an amusing way.

заба́вный *adj.* amusing.

забастова́ть OVA *pf. of* бастова́ть.

забасто́вка *f.* strike.

забасто́вщик *m. f.* забасто́вщица striker.

забве́ние *neut.* oblivion.

забе́г *m.* (*athl.*) heat; round; race.

забега́ловка *f.* (*colloq.*) snack bar; fast food place.

забели́ть *pf.* **1.** to whiten; to paint white. **2.** (*colloq.*) to add milk *or* cream to (*e.g., coffee*).

забере́менеть *pf. of* бере́менеть.

забива́ть *impf. pf.* заби́ть **1.** to drive *or* hammer in. **2.** to stop *or* block up.

забинтова́ть OVA *pf. of* бинтова́ть.

забира́ть *impf. pf.* забра́ть to take.

заби́тый *adj.* cowed; downtrodden.

забия́ка *m.* and *f.* (*decl. f.*) (*colloq.*) roughneck; bully.

заблаговре́менно *adv.* **1.** in good time. **2.** in advance.

заблесте́ть *pf.* (*conjugated like* блесте́ть) to begin to sparkle; to begin to shine.

заблуди́ться *pf.* to lose one's way.

заблу́дший *adj.* **1.** lost; stray. **2.** gone astray.

заблужда́ться *impf.* to be mistaken; to err.

заблужде́ние *neut.* error.

забода́ть *pf.* to gore.

заболева́емость *f.* incidence; prevalence; number of cases (*of a sickness*).

заболева́ние *neut.* illness; disease.

заболева́ть *impf. pf.* заболе́ть to become ill.

за́болонь *f.* (*bot.*) alburnum; sapwood.

забо́р *m.* fence.

забо́ристый *adj.* (*colloq.*) strong; pungent.

забо́рный *adj.* **1.** (*attrib.*) fence. **2.** coarse; vulgar.

забо́та *f.* care; concern; trouble.

забо́титься *impf. pf.* по- (о *with prep.*) to be concerned about; to take care of.

забо́тливый *adj.* careful, thoughtful; concerned.

забра́ло *neut.* visor (*of a helmet*). — с откры́тым забра́лом openly; frankly.

забра́ть *pf. of* забира́ть.

заброни́ровать OVA *pf. of* брони́ровать.

забро́с *m.* (*colloq.*) neglect.

забро́шенный *adj.* neglected; deserted, abandoned.

забыва́ть *impf. pf.* забы́ть to forget.

забы́вчивый *adj.* forgetful; absent-minded.

забы́тый *adj.* forgotten.

забы́ть *pres.* забу́ду, забу́дешь *pf. of* забыва́ть.

забытьё *neut.* **1.** drowsiness. **2.** semiconsciousness. **3.** (*state of*) distraction.

зава́л *m.* **1.** accumulation (*e.g., of snow*); pile. **2.** barrier; obstruction.

зава́ливать *impf. pf.* завали́ть to fill up; to encumber; to overload.

за́валь *f.* unsold merchandise; unsaleable goods.

зава́ривать *impf. pf.* завари́ть to brew.

заварно́й *adj.* boiled.

заведе́ние *neut.* institution; establishment.

заве́дование *neut.* management.

заве́довать OVA *impf.* (*with instr.*) to manage; to head.

заве́домо *adv.* **1.** obviously. **2.** knowingly; wittingly.

заве́домый *adj.* notorious.

заве́дующий DAA *m.* manager, director.

завербова́ть OVA *pf. of* вербова́ть.

завере́ние *neut.* assurance.

заве́ренный *adj.* certified. — заве́ренная ко́пия *f.* certified copy.

завёртывать *impf. pf.* заверну́ть **1.** to wrap, to wrap up. **2.** to turn. **3.** to roll up.

заверша́ть *impf. pf.* заверши́ть to complete, conclude.

заверша́ющий *adj.* concluding; closing.

заверше́ние *neut.* completion.

заверя́ть *impf. pf.* заве́рить **1.** to assure. **2.** to certify.

заве́са *f.* curtain; screen.

завести́ *pf. of* заводи́ть.

заве́т *m.* precept; legacy, behest. — Ве́тхий Заве́т Old Testament. — Но́вый Заве́т New Testament.

заве́тный *adj.* cherished; intimate (*desire*); secret; hidden.

заве́шивать *impf. pf.* заве́сить **1.** to cover; to curtain off. **2.** to hang with.

завеща́ние *neut.* will; testament.

завеща́тель *m.* testator.

завеща́ть *impf.* and *pf.* to bequeath.

завзя́тый *adj.* **1.** inveterate; confirmed. **2.** avid, ardent.

завива́ть *impf. pf.* зави́ть to wave, to curl; (*colloq.*) perm.

зави́вка *f.* curling; wave.

зави́дно *adj.* (*pred., impers. with dat.*) to feel envious.

зави́дный *adj.* enviable.

зави́довать OVA *impf. pf.* по- (*with dat.*) to envy; to be jealous of.

завиду́щий *adj.* (*colloq.*) covetous; envious.

завизжа́ть *pf. of* визжа́ть.

зави́нчивать *impf. pf.* за- to tighten (*a screw, nut*).

зави́сеть *impf.* (от *with gen.*) to depend on *or* upon.

зави́симость *f.* dependence. — в зави́симости от (*with gen.*) depending on.

зави́симый *adj.* dependent.

зави́стливый *adj.* envious.

зави́стник *m.* envious person.

за́висть *f.* envy.

завито́й *adj.* (hair) curled; waved.

завито́к *m.* lock; ringlet; flourish (*in handwriting*).

завиту́шка *f.* (*colloq.*) ringlet; lock.

зави́ть *pf. of* завива́ть.

завко́м *m.* (*abbr. of* заводско́й комите́т) factory committee.

завладева́ть *impf. pf.* **завладе́ть** (*with instr.*) to take possession of; to seize; to conquer; to capture.

завладе́ть *pf. of* **владе́ть, завладева́ть.**

завлека́тельный *adj.* enticing; alluring.

завлека́ть *impf. pf.* **завле́чь** to entice; to lure.

заво́д *m.* factory; plant; works; mill.

заводи́ть *impf. pf.* **завести́ 1.** to bring; to take *or* lead to. **2.** to acquire. **3.** to establish. **4.** to introduce. **5.** to wind (*a mechanism, e.g., a watch*).

заводно́й *adj.* **1.** operated by winding. **2.** used for winding.

заводско́й *adj.* factory.

заво́дчик *m.* factory owner.

за́водь *f.* inlet; creek.

завоева́ние *neut.* conquest.

завоева́тель *m.* conqueror.

завоёвывать *impf. pf.* **завоева́ть 1.** to conquer. **2.** to win.

заво́з *m.* delivery.

завози́ть *impf. pf.* **завезти́ 1.** to deliver; to drop off. **2.** to take far away. **3.** to bring.

заволáкивать *impf. pf.* **заволо́чь** to cloud; to obscure.

заволнова́ться *OVA pf.* to become agitated.

заворáживать *impf. pf.* **заворожи́ть 1.** to bewitch. **2.** to captivate.

заворáчивать *impf. pf.* **заверну́ть** *also* **завороти́ть 1.** to turn. **2.** to turn around. **3.** to turn *or* roll up (*a sleeve, etc.*). **4.** to wrap (up).

заворожённый *adj.* spellbound; bewitched.

заворо́т *m.* **1.** sharp turn. **2.** bend (*in road; in river*).

завсегда́тай *m.* habitué.

за́втра *adv.* tomorrow.

за́втрак *m.* breakfast.

за́втракать *impf. pf.* **по-** to (eat) breakfast.

за́втрашний *adj.* tomorrow's.

завуали́ровать *OVA pf.* to veil, to conceal.

за́вуч *m.* (*colloq.*) (*abbr. of* **заве́дующий уче́бной ча́стью** *m.*) director of studies.

завхо́з *m.* (*abbr. of* **заве́дующий хозя́йством** *m.*) supply manager.

завыва́ть *impf.* to howl; to wail.

завя́зка *f.* **1.** string. **2.** lace. **3.** (*lit.*) beginning; opening of a plot.

завя́зывать *impf. pf.* **завяза́ть** to bind; to fasten; to tie.

за́вязь *f.* (*bot.*) ovary.

завя́нуть *pf. of* **вя́нуть.**

зага́дка *f.* riddle; enigma, mystery.

зага́дочный *adj.* enigmatic; mysterious.

зага́дывать *impf. pf.* **загада́ть 1.** to ask a riddle. **2.** to think of, to think ahead; to tell fortunes.

зага́р *m.* sunburn; tan.

загаси́ть *pf.* to put out; to extinguish.

загво́здка *f.* (*colloq.*) hitch; catch; snag; problem.

заги́б *m.* **1.** bend. **2.** (*colloq.*) exaggeration.

загиба́ть *impf. pf.* **загну́ть 1.** to bend. **2.** to turn up *or* down. — **загиба́ть уголо́к страни́цы** to earmark.

загипнотизи́ровать *OVA pf. of* **гипнотизи́ровать.**

загла́вие *neut.* title, heading.

загла́вная бу́ква capital letter.

загла́живать *impf. pf.* **загла́дить 1.** to press; to iron. **2.** to make amends for.

заглáзно *adv.* (*colloq.*) behind one's back.

заглáзный *adj.* (*colloq.*) done behind one's back.

заглóхнуть *pf. of* **глóхнуть.**

заглуша́ть *impf. pf.* **заглуши́ть 1.** to muffle; to drown out. **2.** to deaden; to alleviate (*pain, etc.*). **3.** to suppress, to stifle.

загляде́нье *neut.* (*colloq.*) lovely sight.

загля́дывать *impf. pf.* **загляну́ть 1.** to look *or* peep into. **2.** (*colloq.*) to drop in.

за́гнанный *adj.* **1.** exhausted (*from being chased*). **2.** downtrodden.

загна́ть *pf. of* **загоня́ть.**

загнива́ть *impf. pf.* **загни́ть** to rot; to decay.

загова́ривать *impf. pf.* **заговори́ть 1.** to start a conversation with. **2.** to wear someone out with talk.

за́говор *m.* conspiracy; plot.

загово́рщик *m.* plotter; conspirator.

за́годя *adv.* (*colloq.*) in advance; ahead of time.

заголо́вок FILL *m.* **1.** title, heading. **2.** headline.

заго́н *m.* enclosure; cattle pen.

загоня́ть *impf. pf.* **загна́ть 1.** to drive in, into, *or* under. **2.** to exhaust.

загора́живать *impf. pf.* **загороди́ть 1.** to enclose; to fence in. **2.** to bar; to block.

загора́ть *impf. v.i. pf.* **загоре́ть 1.** to sunburn, to tan. **2.** to bask in the sun. **—ся 3.** to catch fire. **4.** to light up. **5.** to break out.

загоре́лый *adj.* sunburned; tanned.

загоро́дка *f.* (*colloq.*) fence; enclosure.

за́городный *adj.* **1.** out-of-town. **2.** country; rural.

загота́вливать *impf. pf.* **загото́вить** to prepare; to lay in store.

загото́вка *f.* **1.** (*state*) procurement, purchase. **2.** stockpiling; stocking up.

загото́влять *impf. pf.* **загото́вить 1.** to prepare in advance. **2.** to store up.

загради́тель *m.* minelayer.

загради́тельный *adj.* (*mil.*) covering; protecting.

загражда́ть *impf. pf.* **загради́ть** to block.

загражде́ние *neut.* obstacle; obstruction; barrier.

заграни́ца *f.* (*colloq.*) foreign countries.

заграни́чный *adj.* foreign.

За́греб *m.* Zagreb.

загреба́ть *impf. pf.* **загрести́** to rake up; to gather in.

загреме́ть *pf.* **1.** to begin to sound, to clang, to thunder. **2.** to resound. **3.** to rattle.

загри́вок FILL *m.* withers; nape (*of the neck*).

загро́бный *adj.* beyond the grave; after death.

загромозжда́ть *impf. pf.* **загромозди́ть** to encumber; to jam, to block.

загрубе́лый *adj.* calloused.

загрубе́ть *pf.* to become calloused; to become rough.

загружа́ть *impf. pf.* **загрузи́ть 1.** to load (*a vessel*). **2.** to give a full load of work to someone.

загру́зка *f.* **1.** loading. **2.** capacity; workload.

загрыза́ть *impf. pf.* **загры́зть 1.** to bite to death; to tear to pieces. **2.** to nag.

загрязне́ние *neut.* **1.** soiling. **2.** contamination; pollution.

загрязня́ть *impf. pf.* **загрязни́ть** to soil, to dirty; to pollute.

загс *m.* (*abbr. of* за́пись а́ктов гражда́нского состоя́ния *f.*) civilian registry office.

загуби́ть *pf.* **1.** to ruin. **2.** to squander.

зад *m.* back; hind part; buttocks; hind quarters.

задава́ть *impf. pf.* **зада́ть** to set; to pose; to assign.

зада́ние *neut.* task.

Задар *m.* Zadar.

зада́ривать *impf. pf.* **задари́ть** to lavish gifts upon.

зада́ток FILL *m.* deposit; advance.

зада́ча *f.* problem; task.

зада́чник *m.* book of (mathematical) problems.

задвига́ть *impf. pf.* **задви́нуть 1.** to push under; to slide behind. **2.** to slide shut.

задви́жка *f.* bolt; door bolt.

задвижно́й *adj.* sliding.

задво́рки *pl.* yard; area behind a house.

задева́ть *impf. pf.* **заде́ть 1.** to brush against. **2.** (**за** *with acc.*) to snag on something. **3.** to touch (*emotionally*); to offend.

задёргать *pf.* **1.** to tug at. **2.** to wear out by tugging on reins **3.** to harass.

задёргивать *impf. pf.* **задёрнуть** to draw *or* close a curtain.

задеревене́лый *adj.* (*colloq.*) stiff, numb.

задеревене́ть *pf.* to become numb *or* stiff.

задержа́ние *neut.* **1.** detention; arrest. **2.** retention.

заде́рживать *impf. pf.* **задержа́ть 1.** to detain, to delay. **2.** to arrest. **3.** to retard.

заде́ржка *f.* delay.

заде́ть *pres.* заде́ну, заде́нешь *pf. of* задева́ть.

задира́ *m. and f.* (*decl. f.*) (*colloq.*) bully; roughneck.

задира́ть *impf. pf.* **задра́ть 1.** to turn up; to pull up; to lift up. **2.** to pick on.

задненёбный *adj.* velar.

заднепрохо́дный *adj.* anal.

за́дний *adj.* back; hind; rear. — за́дний план *m.* background. — за́дний ход *m.* reverse gear.

за́дник *m.* **1.** back of a shoe. **2.** (*theat.*) backdrop.

задо́к *m.* back (*of vehicle or furniture*).

задо́лго *adv.* long before.

задолжа́ть *pf.* (*with dat.*) to be in debt.

задо́лженность *f.* **1.** indebtedness. **2.** liabilities.

за́дом *adv.* **1.** backwards. **2.** (**к** *with dat.*) with one's back to.

задо́р *m.* fervor; enthusiasm.

задо́ринка *f.*: без сучка́, без задо́ринки without a hitch.

задо́рный *adj.* **1.** ardent; passionate. **2.** lively.

задра́ивать *impf. pf.* **задра́ить** to batten down; to dog down (*a hatch*).

задра́ть *pf. of* задира́ть *or* драть.

заду́мчивость *f.* pensiveness.

заду́мчивый *adj.* pensive; thoughtful.

заду́мывать *impf. pf.* **заду́мать 1.** to conceive; to plan. **2.** to intend. **3.** to decide on. **—ся** to become pensive; to become thoughtful; to meditate.

задуше́вный *adj.* sincere; intimate; innermost.

задуши́ть *pf. of* души́ть.

заеда́ть *impf. pf.* **зае́сть 1.** to chew to death. **2.** to chase away the taste of something. **3.** to torment; to oppress. **4.** to jam.

зае́зд *m.* **1.** visit. **2.** horserace.

заезжа́ть *impf. pf.* **зае́хать 1.** to stop in at; to drop in on. **2.** (**за** *with instr.*) to pick someone up.

зае́зженный *adj.* (*colloq.*) hackneyed, trite.

зае́зжий *adj.* visiting; touring. — *m.* person passing through.

заём *m.* loan.

заёмщик *m.* borrower.

зажа́ть *pf. of* зажима́ть.

заже́чь *pf. of* зажига́ть.

зажива́ть *impf. pf.* **зажи́ть** to heal (up).

за́живо *adv.* alive (*in deadly situations*).

зажига́лка *f.* cigarette lighter.

зажига́ние *neut.* lighting; act of lighting.

зажига́тельный *adj.* incendiary.

зажига́ть *impf. pf.* **заже́чь** to set fire (to); to light.

зажи́м *m.* clamp.

зажима́ть *impf. pf.* **зажа́ть** to squeeze; to clutch, to grip; to suppress, to keep down.

зажи́точный *adj.* prosperous.

здра́вный тост *m.* toast to someone's health.

заземле́ние *neut.* (*elec.*) ground connection.

зазимова́ть OVA *pf.* to spend the winter.

зазна́йство *neut.* (*colloq.*) conceit.

зазно́ба *f.* (*colloq.*) sweetheart; ladylove.

зазо́р *m.* (*mech.*) clearance.

зазо́рный *adj.* (*colloq.*) shameful.

зазре́ние *neut.*: без зазре́ния со́вести without compunction.

зазу́бренный[1] *adj.* jagged; notched; serrated.

зазу́бренный[2] *adj.* (*colloq.*) memorized; by rote.

зазу́брина *f.* notch.

зазыва́ть *impf. pf.* **зазва́ть** (*colloq.*) to invite repeatedly; to urge to come.

заи́грывание *neut.* flirting. — заи́грывания *pl.* advances.

заи́грывать *impf. pf.* **заигра́ть 1.** to wear out (*cards*) by playing. **2.** (*colloq.*) to play up to someone; to flirt.

заи́ка *m. and f.* (*decl. f.*) stutterer.

заика́ние *neut.* stuttering; stutter.

заика́ться *impf. pf.* **заикну́ться 1.** to stutter; to stammer. **2.** (*colloq.*) (**о** *with prep.*) to mention.

заимода́вец FILL *m.* (*obs.*) moneylender.

заи́мствование *neut.* borrowing.

заи́мствовать OVA *impf. pf.* **позаи́мствовать 1.** to adopt. **2.** to borrow.

заиндеве́ть *pf. of* индеве́ть.

заинтересо́ванность *f.* interest.

заинтересо́ванный *adj.* interested (in); concerned.

заинтересова́ть *pf.* to interest. **—ся** (*with instr.*) to take interest in; to become interested in.

заинтригова́ть *pf. of* интригова́ть.

заи́скивать *impf.* **1.** to court. **2.** (**перед** *with instr.*) to ingratiate oneself; to make up to.

зайти́ *pf. of* заходи́ть.

за́йчик *m. dim. of* за́яц.

закабаля́ть *impf. pf.* **закабали́ть** to enslave.

закавка́зский *adj.* Transcaucasian.

закады́чный друг (*colloq.*) bosom friend.

зака́з *m.* order.

заказно́й *adj.* **2.** made to order *or* measure. **3.** registered. — заказно́е письмо́ *neut.* registered letter.

зака́зчик *m.* customer.

зака́зывать *impf. pf.* **заказа́ть** to order.

зака́л *m.* tempering; hardening; toughness.

закалённый *adj.* tempered; hardened.

зака́лка *f.* hardening; tempering; (*fig.*) toughness.

зака́лывать *impf. pf.* **заколо́ть 1.** to stab to death. **2.** to kill, to slaughter.

закаля́ть *impf. pf.* **закали́ть** to temper; to strengthen.

зака́нчивать *impf. pf.* **зако́нчить** to finish, to complete; to conclude.

зака́пать *pf.* **1.** to spot; to stain. **2.** to begin to drip.

зака́пывать *impf. pf.* **закопа́ть** to bury.

зака́т *m.* **1.** sunset. **2.** (*fig.*) decline.

зака́тывать¹ *impf. pf.* **заката́ть 1.** to roll in. **2.** to roll up one's sleeves.

зака́тывать² *impf. pf.* **закати́ть 1.** to roll; to wheel (behind, into, under). **2.** (*colloq.*) to make (a scene).

закача́ть *pf.* **1.** to rock to sleep. **2.** *impers.* to feel nauseous.

заква́ска *f.* **1.** ferment; leaven. **2.** mold.

закипа́ть *impf. pf.* **закипе́ть 1.** to simmer; to begin to boil. **2.** to seethe with.

закиса́ть *impf. pf.* **заки́снуть 1.** to turn sour. **2.** to become listless.

за́кись *f* protoxide. — **за́кись желе́за** ferrous oxide.

закла́д *m.* **1.** pledge. **2.** pawn, pawning.

закла́дка *f.* **1.** bookmark. **2.** laying.

закладна́я *f.* mortgage.

закла́дчик *m.* (*obs.*) pawnbroker.

закла́дывать *impf. pf.* **заложи́ть 1.** to place, to put, to lay. **2.** to install. **3.** to pawn.

заклёвывать *impf. pf.* **заклева́ть** to peck to death; to nag, to harass.

закле́ивать *impf. pf.* **закле́ить** to glue, to seal.

заклейми́ть *pf. of* **клейми́ть.**

закле́пка *f.* rivet.

заклина́ние *neut.* **1.** entreaty. **2.** incantation.

заклина́тель *m.* conjurer. — **заклина́тель змей** snake charmer.

заклина́ть *impf.* to conjure; to invoke; to entreat.

заключа́ть *impf. pf.* **заключи́ть 1.** to conclude; to infer. **2.** to close, to wind up. **3.** to confine; to imprison.

заключе́ние *neut.* **1.** conclusion. **2.** inference. **3.** detention, imprisonment.

заключённый *adj.* **1.** concluded. **2.** confined, detained. — *m.* prisoner; convict.

заключи́тельный *adj.* **1.** closing, final. **2.** conclusive.

закля́тие *neut.* (*obs.*) **1.** oath; pledge. **2.** incantation.

закля́тый *adj.* sworn.

зако́вывать *impf. pf.* **закова́ть** to chain; to shackle.

заколдо́ванный *adj.* enchanted; bewitched; charmed. — **заколдо́ванный круг** *m.* vicious circle.

зако́лка *f.* hairpin.

заколо́ть *pf. of* **зака́лывать.**

зако́нник *m.* (*colloq.*) expert in law.

законнорождённый *adj.* (*child*) legitimate.

зако́нность *f.* legitimacy; legality.

зако́нный *adj.* **1.** legal; lawful. **2.** legitimate.

законове́д *m.* jurist; specialist in the law. —**ение** *neut.* jurisprudence.

законода́тель *m.* **1.** lawmaker; legislator. **2.** arbiter.

законода́тельный *adj.* legislative.

закономе́рный *adj.* regular; natural.

законоположе́ние *neut.* statute.

законопослу́шный *adj.* law-abiding.

законопрое́кт *m.* (*legislative*) bill.

зако́нченность *f.* completeness.

зако́нченный *adj.* **1.** complete; finished. **2.** (*of an artist*) accomplished.

зако́нчить *pf. of* **зака́нчивать.**

закопа́ть *pf. of* **зака́пывать.**

закопте́лый *adj.* sooty.

закорене́лый *adj.* inveterate; deep-rooted.

зако́рки *pl.*: **на зако́рках** *adv.* piggyback.

закорю́чка *f.* (*colloq.*) **1.** hook. **2.** ploy; trick. **3.** snag; hitch.

закосне́лый *adj.* inveterate; ingrained.

закостене́лый *adj.* **1.** numb, numbed. **2.** stiff.

закостене́ть *pf.* to become numb; to become stiff.

закоу́лок *m.* **1.** side street, back street. **2.** nook.

закочене́лый *adj.* frozen stiff; numb.

закра́дываться *impf. pf.* **закра́сться** to steal in *or* into.

закра́шивать *impf. pf.* **закра́сить** to paint over; to cover over.

закрепи́тель *m.* (*photog.*) fixing agent.

закрепле́ние *neut.* fastening.

закрепля́ть *impf. pf.* **закрепи́ть** to fasten; to secure; to attach.

закрепоща́ть *impf. pf.* **закрепости́ть** to enslave.

закрепоще́ние *neut.* enslavement.

закрича́ть *pf.* **1.** to shout. **2.** to begin to shout *or* yell.

закро́йщик *m.* cutter of cloth.

за́кром *m.* grain bin.

закругле́ние *neut.* **1.** curve. **2.** curving; rounding.

закружи́ть *pf. pres.* **закружу́, закру́жишь,** *or* **кружи́шь. 1.** to begin to whirl; to begin to swirl. **2.** to begin to spin. **ся** to begin to spin; to be dizzy.

закру́чивать *impf. pf.* **закрути́ть** to twist, to twirl.

закрыва́ть *impf. pf.* **закры́ть 1.** to shut, to close. **2.** to shut off. **3.** to cover. **4.** to shut down.

закры́лок FILL *m.* flap (*on aircraft wing*).

закры́тие *neut.* **1.** closing. **2.** close; end.

закры́тый *adj.* **1.** closed, shut. **2.** secret.

закули́сный *adj.* **1.** backstage. **2.** hidden, secret. **3.** occurring behind the scenes.

закупа́ть *impf. pf.* **закупи́ть** to buy up.

заку́пка *f.* purchase.

заку́порка *f.* **1.** stopping up; plugging up. **2.** *med.* thrombosis; embolism.

заку́почный *adj.* (*attrib.*) purchasing; purchase.

заку́пщик *m.* (*wholesale*) buyer.

закури́ть *pf.* **1.** to begin to smoke. **2.** to light a cigarette *or* pipe.

заку́ска *f.* snack; hors d'oeuvres.

заку́сочная *f.* snack bar.

заку́сывать *impf. pf.* **закуси́ть** to have a snack.

заку́тывать *impf. pf.* **заку́тать** to wrap in; to bundle in. **—ся** (*with instr. or* **в** *with acc.*) to bundle oneself in.

зал *m.* hall; room.

залата́ть *pf. of* **лата́ть.**

залега́ть *impf. pf.* **зале́чь 1.** to lie down (*for a long time*). **2.** to lie low.

заледене́лый *adj.* icy; frozen; covered with ice.

залежа́лый *adj.* stale; (*of merchandise*) unsold.

залёживаться *impf. pf.* залежа́ться **1.** to lie around unsold. **2.** to become stale.

за́лежный *adj.* (*land*) long fallow.

за́лежь *f.* deposit; stale goods.

залеза́ть *impf. pf.* зале́зть **1.** to climb into *or* onto. **2.** to climb under.

залепля́ть *impf. pf.* залепи́ть **1.** to seal up. **2.** to cover; to plaster.

залета́ть *impf. pf.* залете́ть **1.** to fly into. **2.** to stop briefly in. **3.** to fly over.

залётный *adj.* stray.

зали́в *m.* (*geog.*) bay.

залива́ть *impf. pf.* зали́ть to flood; to inundate.

заливно́е *neut.* aspic.

заливно́й *adj.* **1.** flood. **2.** jellied.

залихва́тский *adj.* devil-may-care.

зало́г *m.* **1.** pawn; pledge; security. **2.** (*gram.*) voice.

зало́говый *adj.* (*attrib.*) pawn; (*attrib.*) mortgage.

залогода́тель *m.* person who pawns *or* mortgages s.t.

залогодержа́тель *m.* pawnbroker.

заложи́ть *pf. of* закла́дывать.

зало́жник *m.* hostage.

залп *m.* volley.

за́лпом *adv.* **1.** in one volley. **2.** (*colloq.*) in one gulp.

За́льцбург *m.* Salzburg.

зама́зка *f.* putty.

зама́лчивать *impf. pf.* замолча́ть to hush up; to be *or* keep silent about.

зама́нивание *neut.* enticement.

зама́нивать *impf. pf.* замани́ть to tempt; to lure.

зама́нчивый *adj.* tempting.

замара́ть *pf. of* мара́ть.

замара́шка *f.* (*colloq.*) untidy girl.

замаскиро́ванный *adj.* masked; camouflaged.

замаскиро́вывать *impf. pf.* замаскирова́ть **1.** to mask, to disguise. **2.** to conceal, to hide. **3.** to camouflage.

зама́хиваться *impf. pf.* замахну́ться to threaten with; to brandish; to wave around.

зама́шки *pl.* (*colloq.*) ways; manner.

зама́щивать *impf. pf.* замости́ть to pave.

За́мбия *f.* Zambia.

замедле́ние *neut.* deceleration; slowing down.

заме́дленный *adj.* slowed-down.

замедля́ть *impf. pf.* заме́длить *v.t.* to slow down; to delay.

заме́на *f.* substitution; replacement; substitute.

замени́мый *adj.* replaceable.

замени́тель *m.* substitute.

заменя́ть *impf. pf.* замени́ть (*with instr.*) to substitute; to replace.

замерза́ние *neut.* freezing.

замерза́ть *impf. pf.* замёрзнуть *v.i.* to freeze; (*of person*) to be freezing; to freeze to death.

за́мертво *adv.* unconscious; in a faint.

замести́тель *m.* substitute; assistant; deputy.

замести́ть *pf. of* замеща́ть.

замета́ть *impf. pf.* замести́ **1.** to sweep into. **2.** (*of snow*) to cover.

заме́тка *f.* **1.** note; notice. **2.** mark.

заме́тно *adv.* noticeably; visibly.

заме́тный *adj.* **1.** noticeable; visible. **2.** marked; outstanding.

замеча́ние *neut.* **1.** remark; observation. **2.** rebuke.

замеча́тельно *adv.* remarkably; marvelously.

замеча́тельный *adj.* remarkable.

замеча́ть *impf. pf.* заме́тить to note; to observe; to notice; to remark.

замеша́тельство *neut.* confusion; disorder.

заме́шивать[1] *impf. pf.* замеша́ть (в *with acc.*) to mix up in; to implicate in.

заме́шивать[2] *impf. pf.* замеси́ть to knead.

замеща́ть *impf. pf.* замести́ть to replace; to substitute for.

замеще́ние *neut.* replacement; substitution.

зами́нка *f.* (*colloq.*) **1.** delay; hitch. **2.** hesitation (*in speech*).

замира́ть *impf. pf.* замере́ть **1.** to stand motionless. **2.** (*of sound*) to die down. **3.** (*of heart*) to sink.

за́мкнутый *adj.* **1.** closed; (*of person*) reserved. **2.** secluded.

замкну́ть *pf. of* замыка́ть.

замоги́льный *adj.* **1.** (*obs.*) occuring after death. **2.** (*colloq.*) (*voice*) sepulchral.

за́мок FILL *m.* castle.

замо́к FILL *m.* lock; padlock. — под замко́м under lock and key.

замолка́ть *impf. pf.* замо́лкнуть *v.i.* to become silent; (*of conversation*) to cease.

замолча́ть *impf. pf. pres.* -чу́, -чи́шь **1.** to fall silent; to stop talking. **2.** *pf. of* зама́лчивать.

замора́живание *neut.* freezing.

замора́живать *impf. pf.* заморо́зить *v.t.* to freeze.

замори́ть *impf. pf. of* мори́ть. **2.** to starve. **3.** to satisfy one's hunger.

заморо́женный *adj.* frozen.

за́морозки *pl.* light frost.

замо́рский *adj.* (*obs.*) from overseas; foreign.

замо́рыш *m.* (*colloq.*) starveling.

замо́чный *adj.* of a lock. — замо́чная сква́жина *f.* keyhole.

замполи́т *m.* (*abbr. of* замести́тель команди́ра по полити́ческой ча́сти *m.*) deputy chief for political indoctrination.

за́муж *adv.*: вы́йти за́муж (за *with acc.*) (*of a woman*) to marry.

за́мужем *adv.* (за *with instr.*) (*of a woman*) married (to).

заму́жество *neut.* (*of a woman*) marriage.

заму́жняя *adj.* (*of a woman*) married.

заму́чить *pf.* **1.** to torture; to torment. **2.** to wear out.

за́мша *f.* suede; chamois.

за́мшевый *adj.* suede.

замше́лый *adj.* moss-grown.

замыка́ние *neut.*: коро́ткое замыка́ние (*elec.*) short circuit.

замыка́ть *impf. pf.* замкну́ть *v.t.* to lock; to close.

за́мысел *m.* **1.** plan, conception. **2.** intention.

замvillслова́тый *adj.* **1.** ingenious. **2.** abstruse. **3.** elaborate; fancy.

замышля́ть *impf. pf.* замы́слить to conceive; to plan.

замя́ть *pf.* (*colloq.*) to stifle; to hush up.

за́навес *m.* curtain.

занаве́ска *f.* window curtain.

зана́шивать *impf. pf.* заноси́ть to wear out.

занесе́ние *neut.* entering; recording.

занести́ *pf. of* **заноси́ть**.

Занзиба́р *m.* Zanzibar.

занима́тельный *adj.* entertaining; diverting; engaging.

занима́ть *impf. pf.* **заня́ть 1.** to occupy. **2.** to borrow. **—ся 3.** (*with instr.*) to be occupied (with). **4.** (*with instr.*) to be engaged (in). **5.** to study.

за́ново *adv.* over again, anew.

зано́за *f.* splinter.

зано́зистый *adj.* (*colloq.*) rough; jagged.

зано́с *m.* **1.** drift. **2.** skidding.

заноси́ть[1] *impf. pf.* **занести́ 1.** to bring, to carry. **2.** to drop something off. **3.** to enter (*on a list*).

заноси́ть[2] *pf. of* **зана́шивать**.

зано́счивый *adj.* arrogant.

зано́шенный *adj.* worn; threadbare.

заня́тие *neut.* occupation. — **заня́тия** *pl.* studies.

заня́тный *adj.* (*colloq.*) engaging, amusing, entertaining.

занято́й *adj.* busy; occupied.

за́нятость *f.* **1.** being busy. **2.** (*econ.*) employment.

за́нятый *adj. short form* за́нят, занята́, за́нято **1.** busy. **2.** occupied.

заня́ть(ся) *pf. of* **занима́ть(ся)**.

заодно́ *adv.* in unison, in concert.

заокеа́нский *adj.* transoceanic; located across the ocean.

заострённый *adj.* pointed; sharp; acute.

заостря́ть *impf. pf.* **заостри́ть 1.** to sharpen. **2.** (*fig.*) to stress, to emphasize.

зао́чник *m.* student taking correspondence courses.

зао́чно *adv.* in absentia.

зао́чный *adj.* **1.** in absentia. **2.** by correspondence. — **зао́чные ку́рсы** *pl.* correspondence courses.

за́пад *m.* west; the West. **—ный** *adj.* west, western.

запада́ть *impf. pf.* **запа́сть 1.** to become hollow, to become sunken. **2.** to fall into; to fall behind s.t. **3.** to become ingrained (*in memory*).

За́падная Вирги́ния *f.* West Virginia.

За́падная Двина́ *f.* (*river*) Western Dvina.

западня́ *f.* trap, snare; pitfall.

запа́здывание *neut.* tardiness.

запа́здывать *impf. pf.* **запозда́ть** to be late.

запа́ивать *impf. pf.* **запая́ть** to solder.

запа́йка *f.* soldering.

запа́л[1] *m.* ignition; fuse.

запа́л[2] *m.* (*animal disease*) heaves.

запа́льная свеча́ *f.* spark plug.

запа́льчивый *adj.* quick-tempered; explosive.

запанибра́та *adv.* (*colloq.*) on equal terms; as equals.

запа́с *m.* supply, stock; reserve.

запаса́ть *impf. pf.* **запасти́** to store, to stock. **—ся** (*with instr.*) to stock up on.

запа́сливый *adj.* provident.

запа́сник *m.* (*mil.*) (*colloq.*) reservist.

запасно́й *also* **запа́сный** spare, reserve; (for an) emergency.

за́пах *m.* smell, odor; scent.

запева́ла *m. and f.* (*decl. f.*) **1.** leading singer in a choir. **2.** leader; initiator.

запева́ть *impf. pf.* **запе́ть** *pres.* **запою́, запоёшь** to be the first to sing; to lead the singing.

запека́нка *f.* **1.** baked dish. **2.** spiced brandy.

запина́ться *impf. pf.* **запну́ться 1.** to stumble on. **2.** to stumble (*in speech*).

запи́нка *f.* stumbling (*in speech*).

запира́тельство *neut.* denial, disavowal.

запира́ть *impf. pf.* **запере́ть** to lock; to bolt.

запи́ска *f.* note, memorandum. — **запи́ски** *pl.* **1.** notes; papers. **2.** memoirs. **3.** transactions.

записно́й *adj.* intended for notes. — **записна́я кни́жка** *f.* notebook.

запи́сывание *neut.* recording; writing down.

запи́сывать *impf. pf.* **записа́ть** to note, to jot down, to write down.

за́пись *f.* **1.** entry, notation. **2.** recording (*e.g., on tape*).

запи́хивать *impf. pf.* **запиха́ть** *or* **запихну́ть** (*colloq.*) to stuff into; to cram into.

запла́канный *adj.* tearful; tear-stained.

запла́та *f.* patch.

заплати́ть *pf. of* **плати́ть**.

заплёсневелый *adj.* mildewed; moldy.

заплечье *neut.* (*colloq.*) shoulder blade.

заплы́в *m.* (*swim.*) heat, lap.

запове́дник *m.* (*nature*) reserve; preserve.

запове́дный *adj.* forbidden; (*of memories, etc.*) secret.

за́поведь *f.* (*relig.*) commandment.

запо́ем *adv.* (*colloq.*) nonstop; avidly.

запозда́лый *adj.* late, tardy; belated, delayed.

запозда́ние *neut.* tardiness; lateness.

запозда́ть *pf. of* **запа́здывать**.

запо́й *m.* **1.** drinking bout. **2.** addiction to alcohol.

заполня́ть *impf. pf.* **запо́лнить 1.** to fill (up). **2.** to fill out (*a form, etc.*).

запомина́ть *impf. pf.* **запо́мнить 1.** to remember. **2.** to memorize.

запо́нка *f.* cuff link.

запо́р *m.* **1.** bolt, lock. **2.** constipation.

Запоро́жье *neut.* Zaporozhe.

запотева́ть *impf. pf.* **запоте́ть** to become misted.

запоте́лый *adj.* steamed up.

запоте́ть *pf. of* **запотева́ть**, **потеть**.

заправи́ла *m. and f.* (*decl. f.*) (*colloq.*) bigwig.

запра́вка *f.* **1.** seasoning (*food*). **2.** refueling (*automobile*).

заправля́ть *impf. pf.* **запра́вить 1.** to tuck in, to tuck under. **2.** to season (*food*). **3.** to put fuel into.

запра́вочный *adj.* (*attrib.*) refueling. — **запра́вочная ста́нция** *f.* gas station.

запра́вский *adj.* (*colloq.*) real; regular.

запра́шивать *impf. pf.* **запроси́ть 1.** to inquire about. **2.** to question someone. **3.** to charge a high price.

запре́т *m.* prohibition.

запрети́тельный *adj.* prohibitive.

запре́тный *adj.* forbidden.

запреща́ть *impf. pf.* **запрети́ть** to prohibit; to forbid.

запреще́ние *neut.* prohibition; ban.

запроекти́ровать OVA *pf. of* **проекти́ровать**.

запро́с 1. *m.* inquiry; demand. **2. запро́сы** *pl.* requirements; interests.

за́просто *adv.* (*colloq.*) informally, without ceremony.

запру́да *f.* dam.

запру́живать *impf. pf.* запруди́ть to dam up; to block; to jam.

запряга́ть *impf. pf.* запря́чь to harness.

запря́жка *f.* harnessing.

запу́гивание *neut.* intimidation.

запу́гивать *impf. pf.* запуга́ть to intimidate.

за́пуск *m.* **1.** launching. **2.** starting.

запуска́ть[1] *impf. pf.* запусти́ть to launch; (*of motor*) to start. — запуска́ть зме́я to fly a kite.

запуска́ть[2] *impf. pf.* запусти́ть to neglect.

запусте́лый *adj.* desolate; neglected.

запусте́ние *neut.* **1.** neglect. **2.** desolation.

запу́танный *adj.* **1.** tangled; confused. **2.** intricate.

запу́тывать *impf. pf.* запу́тать **1.** to tangle. **2.** to muddle. **3.** (*colloq.*) to confuse.

запу́щенный *adj.* neglected.

запыха́ться *impf. and pf.* to pant; to be out of breath.

запя́стье *neut.* **1.** wrist. **2.** (*obs.*) bracelet.

запята́я *f.* comma.

зараба́тывать *impf. pf.* зарабо́тать to earn.

за́работная пла́та *f.* salary; wages; pay.

за́работок FILL *m.* earnings.

заража́ть *impf. pf.* зарази́ть to infect; to contaminate. —ся to become infected with.

зараже́ние *neut.* infection.

зара́з *adv.* (*colloq.*) all at once; in one sitting.

зара́за *f.* contagion; infection; pest.

зарази́тельный *also* зара́зный *adj.* infectious; contagious.

зарази́ть(ся) *pf. of* заража́ть(ся).

зара́нее *adv.* beforehand.

зарапортова́ться OVA *pf.* (*colloq.*) to run off at the mouth.

зараста́ть *impf. pf.* зарасти́ **1.** (*with instr.*) to be overgrown with. **2.** to heal.

зарде́ться *pf.* to blush; to flush.

за́рево *neut.* glow.

зарегистри́ровать OVA *pf. of* регистри́ровать.

заре́з *m.:* до заре́зу *adv.* desperately, urgently.

заре́зать *pf. v.t.* **1.** to slaughter, to butcher. **2.** to cut someone's throat.

заре́каться *impf. pf.* заре́чься (*colloq.*) to renounce.

зарекомендова́ть себя́ OVA *pf.* to prove to be.

заре́чный *adj.* on the other side of the river.

заре́чье *neut.* area on the other side of the river.

заржа́веть *pf.* to become rusty.

заржа́вленный *adj.* rusty.

зарисо́вка *f.* **1.** sketch. **2.** sketching.

зарни́ца *f.* summer lightning.

заро́дыш *m.* embryo.

заро́дышевый *adj.* embryonic.

зарожда́ть *impf. pf.* зароди́ть to conceive; to engender. —ся **1.** to be born. **2.** to be conceived *or* engendered.

зарожде́ние *neut.* conception.

заро́к *m.* vow, pledge; solemn promise.

за́росль *f. usu. pl.* growth; undergrowth.

зарпла́та *f.* (*abbr. of* за́работная пла́та) wages.

заруба́ть *impf. pf.* заруби́ть **1.** to slash to death. **2.** to make a notch in.

зарубе́жный *adj.* foreign; beyond a country's border.

зару́бка *f.* notch, incision.

зарыва́ть *impf. pf.* зары́ть to bury.

заря́ *f.* light; glow; dawn.— у́тренняя заря́ dawn, daybreak. — вече́рняя заря́ dusk, twilight.

заря́д *m.* **1.** charge (*of powder; of electricity*). **2.** warhead. **3.** cartridge.

заря́дка *f.* **1.** charging (*of a battery*). **2.** loading (*of a gun*). **3.** exercise(s); calisthenics.

заряжа́ние *neut.* loading (*gun*); charging (*battery*).

заряжа́ть *impf. pf.* заряди́ть **1.** to charge (a battery). **2.** to load (a gun).

заря́нка *f.* robin.

заса́да *f.* ambush.

заса́ливать *impf. pf.* заса́лить to get grease on.

заса́харенный *adj.* candied.

за́светло *adv.* before nightfall.

засвиде́тельствовать OVA *pf. of* свиде́тельствовать.

засе́в *m.* sowing, seeding.

засева́ть *impf. pf.* засе́ять to sow; to seed.

заседа́ние *neut.* meeting, conference.

заседа́тель *m.* representative.

засе́ка *f.* barricade of felled trees.

засека́ть[1] *impf. pf.* засе́чь **1.** to notch. **2.** to plot on a map.

засека́ть[2] *impf. pf.* засе́чь to flog to death.

засекре́ченный *adj.* **1.** secret. **2.** (*of documents*) classified.

заселе́ние *neut.* **1.** settlement (*of an area*). **2.** occupancy (*of a building*).

засе́чка *f.* notch.

заси́живаться *impf. pf.* засиде́ться **1.** to sit for a long time. **2.** to remain for a long time.

заси́лье *neut.* dominance.

заскору́злый *adj.* hardened; calloused.

засло́н *m.* barrier; screen.

засло́нка *f.* **1.** oven door. **2.** damper.

заслоня́ть *impf. pf.* заслони́ть to screen, to hide, to shield.

заслу́га *f.* merit. —заслу́ги *pl.* achievements.

заслу́женно *adv.* deservedly.

заслу́женный *adj.* **1.** deserved. **2.** distinguished. **3.** (*in title*) Honored.

заслу́живать *impf. pf.* заслужи́ть (*with gen.*) to earn, to merit, to deserve.

заслы́шать *pf. pres.* -шу, -шишь to catch the sound of.

засма́триваться *impf. pf.* засмотре́ться (на *with acc.*) **1.** to be lost in contemplation of s.t. **2.** to stare at.

засмея́ть *pf.* to ridicule, to scoff at. —ся to laugh, to begin to laugh.

засне́женный *adj.* snow-covered.

засну́ть *pf. of* засыпа́ть.

засня́ть *pf.* (*conjugated like* снять) to film; to photograph; to shoot.

засо́в *m.* bolt; bar.

засо́вывать *impf. pf.* засу́нуть to stick; to thrust.

засо́л *m.* salting; pickling.

засоре́ние *neut.* clogging up.

засоря́ть *impf. pf.* засори́ть **1.** to litter. **2.** to clog up. **3.** to clutter up.

засо́хнуть *pf. of* засыха́ть.

засо́хший *adj.* dry, withered.

за́спанный *adj.* sleepy.

заста́ва *f.* gate, gates.

застава́ть *impf. pf.* заста́ть to find in *or* at home.

заставля́ть[1] *impf. pf.* заста́вить to compel, to force.

заставля́ть[2] *impf. pf.* заста́ть to fill, to cram; to obstruct.

заста́иваться *impf. pf.* застоя́ться **1.** to stand too long. **2.** to become stale; to stagnate.

застаре́лый *adj.* inveterate; chronic.

застёгивать *impf. pf.* застегну́ть to button (up); to buckle, to clasp.

застёжка *f.* fastening; buckle, clasp.

засте́нок FILL *m.* torture chamber.

засте́нчивость *f.* shyness, bashfulness.

засте́нчивый *adj.* shy, bashful; timid.

застила́ть *impf. pf.* застла́ть **1.** to cover. **2.** to cloud; to obscure.

засто́й *m.* stagnation, stagnancy.

засто́лье *neut.* **1.** meal. **2.** feast.

засто́льный *adj.* happening at the table.

застрахова́ть *pf. of* страхова́ть.

застрева́ть *impf. pf.* застря́ть to get stuck; to stick.

застрели́ть *pf.* to shoot. —ся to shoot oneself.

застре́льщик *m.* initiator; leader.

застро́йка *f.* development; building up.

застря́ть *pf. pres.* застря́ну, застря́нешь *pf. of* застрева́ть.

засту́живать *impf. pf.* застуди́ть to chill, to cool.

за́ступ *m.* spade.

заступа́ться *impf. pf.* заступи́ться (за *with acc.*) to intercede (for); to stand up (for).

засту́пник *m.* intercessor; defender.

застыва́ть *impf. pf.* засты́ть, засты́нуть to congeal, to set; to thicken, to harden.

за́суха *f.* drought.

засу́чивать *impf. pf.* засучи́ть to roll (up).

засу́шливый *adj.* arid; area of drought.

засыпа́ть[1] *impf. pf.* засну́ть to fall asleep.

засыпа́ть[2] *impf. pf.* засы́пать **1.** to fill (up). **2.** to cover, to bury. **3.** to strew.

засыха́ть *impf. pf.* засо́хнуть to dry up, to wither.

затаённый *adj.* **1.** secret. **2.** restrained, repressed.

зата́ить *pf.* to hold, to restrain.

зата́пливать *impf. pf.* затопи́ть to light *or* make a fire.

зата́птывать *impf. pf.* затопта́ть **1.** to trample down. **2.** to press into the ground.

зата́сканный *adj.* (*colloq.*) **1.** worn out. **2.** hackneyed, trite.

зата́чивать *impf. pf.* заточи́ть to sharpen.

затверде́лый *adj.* hardened.

затверде́ние *neut.* hardening.

затво́р *m.* **1.** lock; bolt. **2.** shutter (*of camera*).

затво́рник *m.* recluse; hermit.

затворя́ть *impf. pf.* затвори́ть to close, to shut.

затева́ть *impf. pf.* зате́ять **1.** to start; to venture; to launch. **2.** to make up one's mind to.

зате́йливый *adj.* **1.** elaborate. **2.** intricate. **3.** clever.

зате́йник *m.* **1.** jokester. **2.** entertainer. **3.** organizer (of entertainment).

затека́ть *impf. pf.* зате́чь (в *with acc.*) **1.** to leak into. **2.** to swell up. **3.** to become numb.

зате́м *adv.* then; thereupon; subsequently.

затемне́ние *neut.* **1.** darkening. **2.** blackout.

за́темно *adv.* (*colloq.*) before dawn.

затемня́ть *impf. pf.* затемни́ть to darken; to obscure.

зате́рянный *adj.* lost; forgotten.

затеря́ть *pf.* (*colloq.*) to mislay; to lose.

зате́я *f.* venture, undertaking; amusement.

затира́ть *impf. pf.* затере́ть **1.** to rub out. **2.** to trap in. **3.** to hold s.t. fast.

затиха́ть *impf. pf.* зати́хнуть to subside; to abate.

зати́шье *neut.* calm, lull.

заткну́ть *pf. of* затыка́ть.

затмева́ть *impf. pf.* затми́ть **1.** to obscure. **2.** to overshadow; to outshine.

затме́ние *neut.* eclipse.

зато́ *conj.* in return; for this; but then.

зато́н *m.* creek; inlet.

затону́ть *pf. v.i.* to sink.

затопи́ть[1] *pf. of* зата́пливать.

затопи́ть[2] *pf. of* затопля́ть.

затопле́ние *neut.* flooding.

затопля́ть *impf. pf.* затопи́ть to flood; to inundate; to submerge.

зато́р *m.* jam (*of people; automobiles; etc.*)

заточе́ние *neut.* incarceration; imprisonment.

затра́гивать *impf. pf.* затро́нуть to affect; to touch; to graze.

затра́та *f.* expenditure, expense.

затре́бовать OVA *pf.* to request; to order; to ask for.

затре́щина *f.* (*colloq.*) box on the ears.

затрудне́ние *neut.* difficulty.

затруднённый *adj.* difficult.

затрудни́тельный *adj.* difficult; embarassing.

затрудня́ть *impf. pf.* затрудни́ть to render difficult; to hamper; to impede.

затума́нивать *impf. pf.* затума́нить to cloud; to obscure.

за́тхлый *adj.* musty.

затыка́ть *impf. pf.* заткну́ть to stop up; to cork up.

заты́лок FILL *m.* back of the head; occiput.

заты́лочный *adj.* cervical.

заты́чка *f.* (*colloq.*) stopper; plug.

затя́гивать *impf. pf.* затяну́ть **1.** to tighten. **2.** to cover. **3.** to delay.

затя́жка *f.* **1.** delay, dragging out. **2.** puff; drag (*on a cigarette*).

затяжно́й *adj.* protracted; lengthy.

зау́мный *adj.* arcane; esoteric.

зауны́вный *adj.* plaintive; mournful.

заупоко́йный *adj.* for the repose of the dead.

заура́дный *adj.* **1.** average, mediocre. **2.** ordinary.

заусе́ница *f.* **1.** burr (*on metal*). **2.** hangnail.

зау́треня *f.* morning prayers; matins.

зау́ченный *adj.* studied; affected.

зау́чивать *impf. pf.* заучи́ть to memorize; to learn by heart.

зауша́тельский *adj.* abusive; offensive; insulting.

зауша́тельство *neut.* abuse; offense.

захва́т *m.* seizure, capture.

захва́тнический *adj.* (*war*) of conquest; (*policy*) expansionist.

захва́тчик *m.* invader.

захва́тывать *impf. pf.* захвати́ть **1.** to seize; to capture. **2.** to take along. **3.** to thrill; to engross.

захва́тывающий *adj.* gripping; thrilling; exciting.

захлёбываться *impf. pf.* захлебну́ться (*with str.*) to choke (with).

захлёстывать *impf. pf.* захлестну́ть **1.** (*of rope, etc.*) to wind around. **2.** to overwhelm. **3.** to overflow.

захло́пывать *impf. pf.* захло́пнуть *v.t.* to slam.

заходи́ть *impf. pf.* зайти́ 1. to set. 2. to call on; to drop in. 3. to go behind.

захо́д со́лнца *m.* sunset.

захолу́стный *adj.* out-of-the-way; remote.

захолу́стье *neut.* out-of-the-way place.

захорони́ть *pf. pres.* —роню́, —ро́нишь to bury.

захоте́ть(ся) *pf. of* хоте́ть(ся).

захуда́лый *adj.* 1. insignificant. 2. impoverished.

заце́пка *f.* (*colloq.*) 1. peg; hook. 2. connections; influence.

зацепля́ть *impf. pf.* зацепи́ть 1. to hook. 2. to snag on. 3. to engage.

зачаро́ванный *adj.* 1. bewitched. 2. enchanted. 3. spellbound.

зачасту́ю *adv.* often, frequently.

зача́тие *neut.* (*physiol.*) conception.

зача́ток FILL *m.* 1. embryo. 2. sprout. 3. source. 4. rudiment.

зача́точный *adj.* rudimentary.

зача́ть *pf. pres.* —чну́, —чнёшь *past f.* зачала́ to conceive (a child).

заче́м *adv.* why, for what reason.

заче́м-то *adv.* for some reason *or* purpose or other.

зачёркивать *impf. pf.* зачеркну́ть to cross out; to strike out.

заче́рпывать *impf. pf.* зачерпну́ть to ladle; to scoop up.

зачерстве́лый *adj.* 1. hard; stale. 2. callous.

зачёсывать *impf. pf.* зачеса́ть to comb hair to the side *or* back.

зачёт *m.* test, examination.

зачётный *adj.* (*attrib.*) test; (*attrib.*) record.

зачина́тель *m.* pioneer; initiator.

зачи́нивать *impf. pf.* зачини́ть to mend; to repair.

зачи́нщик *m.* instigator.

зачисле́ние *neut.* enrollment, enlistment.

зачисля́ть *impf. pf.* зачи́слить *v.t.* 1. to include. 2. to enlist, to enroll.

зашага́ть *pf.* to set out.

зашива́ть *impf. pf.* заши́ть to sew up; to mend.

защёлка *f.* catch; latch.

защёлкивать *impf. pf.* защёлкнуть to snap (closed).

защемля́ть *impf. pf.* защеми́ть 1. to squeeze. 2. to crush. 3. (*colloq.*) to jam; to catch.

защи́та *f.* defense; protection.

защити́тельный *adj.* defending.

защи́тник *m.* 1. defender, protector. 2. defense attorney.

защи́тный *adj.* protective.

защища́ть *impf. pf.* защити́ть to defend; to protect.

зая́вка *f.* 1. claim. 2. requisition; order. 3. application.

заявле́ние *neut.* 1. declaration, statement. 2. application.

заявля́ть *impf. pf.* заяви́ть to declare, to announce; to report.

зая́длый *adj.* (*colloq.*) inveterate, avid.

за́яц FILL *m.* 1. hare. 2. (*colloq.*) stowaway; person without ticket (for transport).

за́ячий *adj.* hare.

зва́ние *neut.* rank, title.

зва́ный ве́чер *m.* party by invitation.

зва́тельный паде́ж vocative case.

зва́ть *impf. pf.* по- to call, to call upon; to invite.

— как вас зову́т? what is your name? —ся *impf.* to be called.

звезда́ *f.* star.

звёздный *adj.* starry.

звездочёт *m.* (*obs.*) astrologer.

звёздочка *f.* 1. asterisk. 2. little star.

звене́ть *impf. v.i.* to ring; to jangle, to clank.

Звени́город *m.* Zvenigorod.

звено́ *neut.* 1. link. 2. team, group.

зверёк *m.* small animal.

зверёныш *also* зверёнок FILL *m.* (*colloq.*) cub.

звери́нец FILL *m.* menagerie.

звери́ный *adj.* 1. (*attrib.*) animal. 2. savage; brutal.

зверобо́й[1] *m.* hunter.

зверобо́й[2] *m.* (*bot.*) St.-John's-wort.

звероло́в *m.* trapper.

зве́рский *adj.* bestial, brutal.

зве́рство *neut.* 1. bestiality; brutality. 2. зве́рства *pl.* atrocities.

зве́рствовать OVA *impf.* to behave brutally; to commit atrocities.

зверь *m.* wild animal; beast; brute.

звон *m.* ringing; peal.

звона́рь *m.* bell ringer.

звони́ть *impf. pf.* по- to ring; to phone. — звони́ть по телефо́ну to telephone.

зво́нкий *adj.* 1. ringing. 2. clear. 3. (*phon.*) voiced.

зво́нница *f.* bell tower; belfry.

звоно́к FILL *m.* bell; phone call. — звоно́к по телефо́ну telephone call.

звук *m.* sound. —оизоляцио́нный *adj.* soundproof. —оподража́ние *neut.* onomatopoeia.

звуково́й *adj.* (*attrib.*) sound.

звукоза́пись *f.* sound recording.

звуконепроница́емый *adj.* soundproof.

звукоопера́тор *m.* sound technician.

звукоусиле́ние *neut.* amplification.

звуча́ние *neut.* sound.

звуча́ть *impf. pf.* про- to sound; to resound, to be heard.

зву́чный *adj.* resounding, sonorous.

звя́канье *neut.* jingling; jangling; tinkling.

звя́кать *impf. pf.* звя́кнуть to tinkle; to jingle.

зги *neut.:* ни зги не ви́дно it is pitch dark.

зда́ние *neut.* building, edifice.

здесь *adv.* here.

зде́шний *adj.* local, pertaining to this place.

здоро́ваться *impf. pf.* по- (с *with instr.*) to greet, to exchange greetings.

здорове́нный *adj.* (*colloq.*) healthy, hale; robust, strapping.

здо́рово *adv.* well, excellently; very. –*interj.* wonderful; well done; excellent.

здоро́вый *adj.* healthy.

здоро́вье *neut.* health.

здорову́к *m.* (*colloq.*) healthy, robust person.

здра́вница *f.* sanatorium; health resort.

здра́во *adv.* reasonably, soundly, sensibly.

здравомы́слящий *adj.* of sound judgment; sensible.

здравоохране́ние *neut.* public health.

здра́вствовать OVA *impf.* to be well; to prosper, to thrive.

здра́вствуй(те) (*interj.*) how do you do; good morning; good afternoon; good evening; hello.

здра́вый *adj.* sensible.
зе́бра *f.* zebra.
зе́бу *m. indecl.* zebu.
зев *m.* pharynx.
зева́ка *m.* and *f.* (*decl. f.*) gawker; idle onlooker.
зева́ть *impf. pf.* **зевну́ть** to yawn.
зево́к *m.* yawn.
зево́та *f.* yawning.
зек *m.* (*abbr. of* заключённый) prisoner; convict.
зелене́ть *impf. pf.* **по-** to turn *or* become green.
зеленова́тый *adj.* greenish.
Зеленого́рск *m.* Zelenogorsk.
зеленщи́к *m.* greengrocer.
зелёный *adj.* green.
зе́лень *f.* verdure; greens, vegetables.
зе́лье *neut.* potion.
земе́льный *adj.* earth, ground, land.
землеве́дение *neut.* physical geography.
землевладе́лец FILL *m. f.* **землевладе́лица** landowner.
земледе́лец FILL *m.* farmer, agriculturist.
земледе́лие *neut.* agriculture.
землеко́п *m.* digger.
землеме́р *m.* surveyor; geodesist.
землеро́йка *f.* shrew.
землеро́йный *adj.* (*attrib.*) excavation.
землетрясе́ние *neut.* earthquake.
земли́стый *adj.* **1.** earthy. **2.** sallow.
земля́ *f.* earth, soil; (*cap.*) the earth.
земля́к *m. f.* **земля́чка** compatriot.
земляни́ка *f.* wild strawberries.
земля́нка *f.* mud hut; dugout.
земляно́й *adj.* earth; earthen.
земново́дный *adj.* amphibious.
земно́й *adj.* terrestrial; earthly.
зе́мский *adj.* (*hist.*) people's.
зе́мство *neut.* (*hist.*) zemstvo (*elected local assembly*).
зени́т *m.* zenith.
зени́тка *f.* (*colloq.*) antiaircraft gun.
зени́тный *adj.* **1.** (*attrib.*) zenith. **2.** (*mil.*) antiaircraft.
зени́ца *f.* (*obs.*) pupil (*of the eye*).
зе́ркало *neut.* mirror, looking glass.
зерка́льный *adj.* mirror; mirror-like; reflecting.
зерка́льце *neut.* small mirror.
зерни́стый *adj.* grainy; granular.
зерно́ *neut.* **1.** grain. **2.** seed, bean. **3.** kernel.
зерново́й *adj.* (*attrib.*) grain; cereal.
зернохрани́лище *neut.* granary.
зёрнышко *neut.* grain, granule.
зефи́р *m.* marshmallow.
Зи́бенгебирге *neut.* (*region*) Siebengebirge.
зигза́г *m.* zigzag.
зима́ *f.* winter.
зи́мний *adj.* winter, wintry.
зимова́ть OVA *impf. pf.* **про-, от-** to winter; to pass *or* spend the winter.
зимо́вка *f.* **1.** spending the winter. **2.** winter quarters.
зимо́вье *neut.* winter camp; winter habitat.
зимо́й *adv.* in (the) winter.
зиморо́док *m.* kingfisher; halcyon.
зимосто́йкий *adj.* winter-hardy.
зипу́н *m.* homespun coat.
зия́ние *neut.* (*ling.*) hiatus.

злак *m.* cereal.
зла́ковый *adj.* (*attrib.*) cereal.
зла́то *neut.* (*poet.*) gold.
зле́йший *adj.* worst; most bitter.
злить *impf. pf.* **разо-** to anger; to irritate.
зло *neut.* evil; harm; malice; anger.
зло́ба *f.* spite; malice.
зло́бный *adj.* malicious; spiteful.
злободне́вный *adj.* actual, topical, timely.
зло́бствовать OVA *impf.* (**на** *with acc.*) to bear malice, to bear a grudge.
злове́щий *adj.* sinister; ominous.
злово́нный *adj.* stinking, fetid.
зловре́дный *adj.* harmful, noxious.
злоде́й *m.* villain, scoundrel.
злоде́йский *adj.* **1.** vicious. **2.** insidious.
злоде́йство *neut.* villainy.
злодея́ние *neut.* crime; evil act.
злой *adj.* wicked, evil; malicious, vicious; bad tempered.
злока́чественный *adj.* (*med.*) malignant.
злоключе́ние *neut.* misadventure.
злонаме́ренный *adj.* malicious; ill-intentioned.
злопа́мятный *adj.* unforgiving; rancorous.
злополу́чный *adj.* ill-fated; hapless.
злопыха́тель *m.* malicious critic.
злора́дный *adj.* gloating.
злора́дство *neut.* malicious pleasure, gloating.
злора́дствовать OVA *impf.* to gloat.
злосло́вие *neut.* malicious gossip.
злосло́вить *impf.* to say malicious things.
зло́стный *adj.* **1.** malicious. **2.** (*of an offender*) habitual.
зло́сть *f.* **1.** malice. **2.** rage, fury.
зло́тый DAA *m.* złoty (*monetary unit of Poland*).
злоупотребле́ние *neut.* (*with instr.*) abuse; misuse.
злоупотребля́ть *impf. pf.* **злоупотреби́ть** (*with instr.*) to abuse.
злю́ка *m.* and *f.* (*decl. f.*) (*colloq.*) grouch; ill-tempered person.
змееви́дный *adj.* serpentine; sinuous.
змеи́ный *adj.* snake; snake's.
змеи́ться (*impf.*) to snake; to wind.
змей *m.* **1.** serpent, dragon. **2.** kite.
змея́ *f.* snake; serpent.
знак *m.* **1.** sign, token, symbol, mark. **2.** omen; signal.
знако́мить *impf. pf.* **по-** to acquaint; to introduce. **—ся** (**с** *with instr.*) to make the acquaintance of; to meet; to get to know.
знако́мство *neut.* acquaintance.
знако́мый *adj.* familiar; (**с** *with instr.*) acquainted with. **—** *m.* acquaintance, friend.
знамена́тель *m.* denominator.
знамена́тельный *adj.* **1.** memorable; momentous. **2.** significant.
знаме́ние *neut.* sign.
знамени́тость *f.* celebrity; fame.
знамени́тый *adj.* celebrated; famous.
знаменова́ть OVA *impf. pf.* **о-** to signify; to mark.
знамено́сец FILL *m.* standard bearer.
зна́мя *neut.* (*pl.* **знамёна**) banner; colors; standard.
зна́ние *neut.* knowledge; erudition.
зна́тный *adj.* distinguished, notable.
знато́к *m.* authority, expert, conoisseur.

знать[1] *impf.* **1.** to know; to be aware of. **2.** to be acquainted with. **3.** have a knowledge of. **—ся** (*colloq.*) (**с** *with instr.*) to know, to be acquainted with, to associate with.

знать[2] *f.* nobility; aristocracy.

зна́харь *m. f.* **зна́харка** person practicing folk medicine; witch doctor.

зна́чащий *adj.* significant; meaningful.

значе́ние *neut.* meaning; significance.

зна́чимость *f.* significance.

зна́чимый *adj.* significant.

зна́чит *particle* (*colloq.*) so; well then.

значи́тельно *adv.* significantly; considerably.

значи́тельность *f.* significance; importance.

значи́тельный *adj.* considerable; sizable, substantial.

зна́чить *impf.* to mean, to signify.

значо́к FILL *m.* mark; badge; (small) pin.

зна́ющий *adj.* learned, well-informed.

знобить *impf. impers.*: **меня́ знобит** I feel feverish or shivery.

зной *m.* intense heat.

зно́йный *adj.* burning hot; sultry.

зоб *m.* **1.** crop (*of bird*). **2.** (*med.*) goiter.

зо́бный *adj.*: **зо́бная железа́** *f.* thymus gland.

зов *m.* call; summons.

зодиа́к *m.* zodiac.

зо́дчество *neut.* architecture.

зо́дчий *m.* architect.

зола́ *f.* (*sg. only*) ashes.

золо́вка *f.* sister-in-law (*husband's sister*).

золота́рник *m.* goldenrod.

золоти́стый *adj.* golden.

золоти́ть *impf. pf.* **по-** to gild.

зо́лото *neut.* gold.

золотоиска́тель *m.* prospector for gold.

золото́й *adj.* gold; golden.

золотоно́сный *adj.* containing gold, gold-bearing.

золоту́ха *f.* (*med.*) scrofula.

золоче́ние *neut.* gilding.

золочёный *adj.* gilded; gilt.

Зо́лушка *f.* Cinderella.

зо́на *f.* zone.

зона́льный *adj.* (*attrib.*) zone.

зонд *m.* **1.** probing device. **2.** weather balloon.

зонди́ровать OVA *impf.* **1.** to probe. **2.** to sound out.

зонт *also* **зо́нтик** *m.* umbrella.

зоо́лог *m.* zoologist. **—и́ческий** *adj.* zoological.

зооло́гия *f.* zoology.

зоопа́рк *m.* zoo.

зо́ркий *adj.* eagle-eyed; perspicacious; vigilant.

зра́зы *pl.* meat cutlets stuffed with rice.

зрачо́к FILL *m.* pupil (*of the eye*).

зре́лище *neut.* **1.** spectacle, sight. **2.** performance. **3.** attraction.

зре́лость *f.* ripeness; maturity.

зре́лый *adj.* ripe; mature.

зре́ние *neut.* sight, eyesight; vision. **— то́чка зре́ния** *f.* point of view.

зреть[1] *impf. pf.* **созре́ть** *v.i.* to ripen.

зреть[2] *impf. pf.* **узре́ть** to behold.

зри́тель *m. f.* **—ница** spectator. **—ный** *adj.* visual, optical.

зря *adv.* for nothing; in vain; to no purpose.

зря́чий *adj.* sighted; able to see.

зуб *m.* tooth.

зуба́стый *adj.* (*colloq.*) toothy; with large teeth.

зубе́ц *m.* tooth; cog.

зуби́ло *neut.* chisel; cutting tool.

зубно́й *adj.* (*attrib.*) tooth; dental. **— зубно́й врач** *m.* dentist. **— зубна́я па́ста** *f.* tooth paste.

зубоврачёбный *adj.* dental; dentistry.

зубо́к FILL *m.* (*colloq.*) *dim. of* зуб.

зубоска́л *m.* (*colloq.*) joker, jester.

зубочи́стка *f.* toothpick.

зубр *m.* (European) bison.

зубрёжка *f.* (*colloq.*) cramming.

зубри́ла *m. and f.* (*decl. f.*) (*colloq.*) crammer.

зубцо́вка *f.* perforation (*on stamps*).

зубцо́вый *adj.* perforated.

зубча́тый *adj.* **1.** jagged, indented. **2.** toothed. **3.** cogged.

зуд *m.* itch.

зуде́ть *impf.* (*colloq.*) to itch.

зуёк FILL *m.* plover.

зу́ммер *m.* buzzer.

зы́биться *impf.* (*obs.*) **1.** to surge. **2.** to swell.

зы́бкий *adj.* unstable, unsteady.

зыбу́чий *adj.* (*sand*) shifting.

зыбь *f.* rippling; ripple (*on water*).

зы́чный *adj.* stentorian; loud, resounding.

зюйд *m.* (*naut.*) south.

зя́бкий *adj.* (*colloq.*) chilly; sensitive to cold.

зя́блик *m.* chaffinch.

зя́бнуть *impf. v.i.* to shiver; to freeze; to suffer from cold.

зябь *f.* land plowed in autumn for spring sowing.

зять *m.* son-in-law; brother-in-law (*sister's husband*).

И Й

и *conj.* and. — и... и... both... and...

и́бис *m.* ibis.

Ѝбиса *f.* (*island*) Ibiza.

и́бо *conj.* for.

и́ва *f.* willow. — плаку́чая и́ва weeping willow.

Ива́ново *neut.* Ivanovo.

ива́новский *adj.*: во всю ива́новскую at the top of one's lungs.

ивня́к *m.* willow bed.

и́вовый *adj.* (*attrib.*) willow.

и́волга *f.* oriole.

иври́т *m.* (*modern*) Hebrew.

игла́ *f.* needle.

и́глистый *adj.* covered with needles *or* quills.

иглови́дный *adj.* needle-shaped.

иглотерапи́я *f.* acupuncture.

игнори́ровать OVA *impf. and pf.* to ignore, to disregard.

и́го *neut.* yoke.

иго́лка *f.* needle.

иго́лочный *adj.* (*attrib.*) needle.

иго́льник *m.* needle cushion; needle case.

иго́льный *adj.* (*attrib.*) needle; of a needle.

иго́рный *adj.* (*attrib.*) gambling.

игра́ *f.* 1. game. 2. play; acting. 3. performance.

игра́-аттракцио́н *m.* video game.

игра́льный *adj.* (*attrib.*) playing. — игра́льные ко́сти *pl.* dice.

игра́ть *impf. pf.* сыгра́ть 1. to play. 2. to act.

игра́ючи *adv.* (*colloq.*) effortlessly; like child's play.

и́грек *m.* the letter y.

игри́вый *adj.* playful.

игри́стый *adj.* (*of wine* and *champagne*) sparkling.

игрово́й *adj.* 1. (*attrib.*) acting. 2. playing. 3. full of action.

игро́к *m.* player; gambler.

игру́шечка *f. dim. of* игру́шка.

игру́шечный *adj.* (*attrib.*) toy; miniature.

игру́шка *f.* toy.

игуа́на *f.* iguana.

игу́мен *m.* abbot; head of a Russian monastery. — игу́менья *f.* abbess.

идеа́л *m.* ideal. —исти́ческий *adj.* idealistic. —ьный *adj.* ideal.

идеализи́ровать OVA *impf. and pf.* to idealize.

идеали́зм *m.* idealism.

иде́йный *adj.* 1. ideological. 2. lofty.

идентифици́ровать OVA *impf. and pf.* to identify.

иденти́чность *f.* identity.

иденти́чный *adj.* identical.

идеогра́мма *f.* ideogram.

идео́лог *m.* ideologist. —и́ческий *adj.* ideological.

иде́я *f.* idea, notion, concept.

иди́ллия *f.* idyll.

идио́ма *f.* idiom. —ти́ческий *adj.* idiomatic.

идио́т *m.* idiot. —и́зм *m.* imbecility. —ский *adj.* idiotic.

и́диш *m.* Yiddish.

и́дол *m.* idol.

идолопокло́нник *m. f.* идолопокло́нница idolater.

идолопокло́нничество *neut.* idolatry.

и др. (*abbr. of* и други́е) et al.; and others.

идти́ *impf. det. indet.* ходи́ть *pf.* пойти́ 1. to go. 2. to come; to proceed. 3. *pf. only* to start, to leave (*on a trip*).

иезуи́т *m.* Jesuit.

Ие́на *f.* Jena.

иѐна *f.* yen (*Japanese currency*).

иера́рхия *f.* hierarchy.

иеро́глиф *m.* hieroglyph.

иждиве́нец FILL *m. f.* иждиве́нка dependant.

иждиве́ние *neut.* support; maintenance. — на иждиве́нии (*with gen.*) at the expense of.

из *also* изо *prep.* (*with gen.*) from, out, out of; made of; consisting of.

изба́ *f.* cottage, hut, hovel.

избави́тель *m.* redeemer, savior.

избавле́ние *neut.* deliverance; rescue.

избавля́ть *impf. pf.* изба́вить (от *with gen.*) to save, to rescue; to deliver. —ся (от *with gen.*) to get rid of.

избало́ванный *adj.* spoiled.

избало́вывать *impf. pf.* избалова́ть to spoil; to pamper.

избега́ть *impf. pf.* избежа́ть, избе́гнуть (*with gen.*) to avoid; to evade; to shun.

избежа́ние *neut.*: во избежа́ние (*with gen.*) in order to avoid.

избива́ть *impf. pf.* изби́ть 1. to beat. 2. to slaughter, to massacre. 3. to assault.

избие́ние *neut.* 1. slaughter, massacre. 2. (*leg.*) assault and battery.

избира́тель *m.* voter; elector.

избира́тельный *adj.* (*attrib.*) electoral; selective; election; ballot. — избира́тельная у́рна *f.* ballot box.

избира́ть *impf. pf.* избра́ть 1. to elect. 2. to choose.

изби́тый *adj.* 1. beaten up. 2. familiar (*road, way*). 3. well-trodden.

изби́ть *pf. of* избива́ть.

избра́ние *neut.* election.

избра́нник *m. f.* избра́нница the elected one; the chosen one.

и́збранный *adj.* elected; selected.

избра́ть *pf. of* избира́ть.

избу́шка *f.* log cabin; hut.

избы́ток FILL *m.* surplus.

избы́точный *adj.* surplus.

изва́ние *neut.* piece of sculpture.

изва́ять *pf. of* вая́ть.

изве́дывать *impf. pf.* изве́дать to experience.

и́зверг *m.* monster; fiend.

изверга́ть *impf. pf.* изве́ргнуть *v.t.* 1. to disgorge, to eject. 2. —ся to erupt.

изверже́ние *neut.* 1. eruption. 2. discharge, ejection. 3. excretion.

изве́рженный *adj.* igneous.

изве́риться *pf.* (в *with prep.*) to lose faith in.

извести́ *pf. of* изводи́ть.

изве́стие *neut.* 1. piece of news. 2. изве́стия *pl.* information.

известить *pf. of* **извещать.**

извёстка *f.* (*colloq.*) lime.

известко́вый *adj.* lime.

изве́стно *impers.* it is known.

изве́стность *f.* fame, reputation.

изве́стный *adj.* famous, well-known.

известня́к *m.* limestone.

и́звесть *f.* lime.

изве́чный *adj.* ancient; age-old.

извеща́ть *impf. pf.* **извести́ть** to inform, to notify.

извеще́ние *neut.* notification; notice.

изви́в *m.* curve (*in road*); bend (*in river*).

извива́ться *impf.* **1.** to coil. **2.** to wriggle; to twist; to wind. **3.** to cringe.

изви́лина *f.* curve (*in a road*), bend (*in a river*).

изви́листый *adj.* sinuous, tortuous; winding.

извине́ние *neut.* **1.** apology. **2.** excuse.

извини́тельный *adj.* **1.** pardonable, excusable. **2.** apologetic.

извиня́ть *impf. pf.* **извини́ть** to excuse, to pardon.

извиня́ющийся *adj.* apologetic.

извлека́ть *impf. pf.* **извле́чь** to extract; to elicit; to derive.

извлече́ние *neut.* extraction, extract; excerpt.

извне́ *adv.* from without.

изво́д *m.* recension.

изводи́ть *impf. pf.* **извести́** **1.** to expend, to spend. **2.** to exterminate. **3.** to exhaust.

изво́зчик *m.* coachman; driver.

извора́чиваться *impf. pf.* **изверну́ться** to twist and turn; to be evasive.

изворо́т *m. usu. pl.* twist.

изворо́тливый *adj.* resourceful; evasive.

извраща́ть *impf. pf.* **изврати́ть** **1.** to pervert. **2.** to misconstrue, to distort.

извраще́ние *neut.* **1.** perversion. **2.** distortion, misconstruing.

изга́живать *impf. pf.* **изга́дить** (*colloq.*) to spoil, to befoul.

изги́б *m.* curve; bend.

изгна́ние *neut.* banishment; exile.

изгна́нник *m. f.* **изгна́нница** exile.

изго́й *m.* outcast.

изголо́вье *neut.* head of a bed.

изголода́ться *pf.* **1.** to be starving. **2.** (**по** *with dat.*) to yearn for.

изгоня́ть *impf. pf.* **изгна́ть** to banish.

и́згородь *f.* fence.

изгота́вливать *impf. pf.* **изгото́вить** to make, to manufacture.

изгото́вка *f.*: **на изгото́вку** (*of a gun*) at the ready.

изготовле́ние *neut.* manufacture.

изготовля́ть *impf. pf.* **изгото́вить** to make; to manufacture.

издава́ть *impf. pf.* **изда́ть** to publish; to give off.

и́здавна *adv.* for a very long time.

издалека́ *also* **и́здали** *adv.* from afar *or* far away.

изда́ние *neut.* publication; edition, issue.

изда́тель *m.* publisher.

изда́ть *pf. of* **издава́ть.**

издева́тельский *adj.* mocking; derisive.

издева́тельство *neut.* mockery; harassment.

издева́ться *impf.* (**над** *with instr.*) to mock; to taunt.

изде́лие *neut.* product; manufactured article.

изде́рживать *impf. pf.* **издержа́ть** to spend; to expend.

изде́ржки *pl.* costs; expenses.

издо́льщик *m.* sharecropper.

издре́вле *adv.* from time immemorial.

издыха́ть *impf. pf.* **издо́хнуть** (*of animals or derog. of people*) to die.

изжива́ть *impf. pf.* **изжи́ть** to eliminate; to get rid of.

изжо́га *f.* heartburn.

и́з-за *prep.* (*with gen.*) **1.** from behind. **2.** because of.

излага́ть *impf. pf.* **изложи́ть** to state, to set forth; to expound.

изла́мывать *impf. pf.* **излома́ть** to shatter; to smash.

излече́ние *neut.* **1.** recovery; cure. **2.** medical treatment.

изле́чивать *impf. pf.* **излечи́ть** (*med.*) to cure. **—ся** (**от** *with gen.*) to be cured (of).

излечи́мый *adj.* curable.

излива́ть *impf. pf.* **изли́ть** to pour out; to give vent to.

изли́шек *m.* surplus; excess.

изли́шество *neut.* excess; immoderation; overabundance.

изли́шне *adv.* excessively.

изли́шний *adj.* superfluous; unnecessary; excessive.

излия́ние *neut.* outpouring.

изложе́ние *neut.* account; statement.

изложи́ть *pf. of* **излага́ть.**

изло́м *m.* fracture; break.

изло́манный *adj.* **1.** fractured; broken. **2.** crooked.

излуча́ть *impf.* to radiate.

излуче́ние *neut.* radiation; emanation.

излу́чина *f.* bend; curve.

излю́бленный *adj.* favorite.

изме́на *f.* **1.** treason; treachery. **2.** infidelity.

измене́ние *neut.* change, alteration.

изме́нник *m. f.* **изме́нница** traitor.

изме́нчивый *adj.* changeable; fickle.

изменя́ть[1] *impf. pf.* **измени́ть** *v.t.* to change, to alter. **—ся** *v.i.* to change.

изменя́ть[2] *impf. pf.* **измени́ть** (*with dat.*) to be unfaithful.

измере́ние *neut.* measurement, measuring.

измери́мый *adj.* measurable.

измери́тель *m.* gauge; indicator.

измеря́ть *impf. pf.* **изме́рить** to measure; to gauge.

измождённый *adj.* emaciated; haggard.

измо́р *m.*: **взять измо́ром** to starve into submission.

и́зморозь *f.* hoarfrost, rime.

и́зморось *f.* drizzle.

изму́ченный *adj.* exhausted; worn out.

изму́чивать *impf. pf.* **изму́чить** **1.** to torture. **2.** to tire, to exhaust.

измыва́ться *impf.* to make fun of.

измышле́ние *neut.* falsehood; invention; fabrication.

измя́тый *adj.* **1.** haggard. **2.** battered. **3.** crumpled.

измя́ть *pf. pres.* **изомну́, изомнёшь** to rumple, to crumple.

изна́нка *f.* reverse side; wrong side.

изнаси́лование *neut.* rape; violation.

изнаси́ловать OVA *pf. of* **наси́ловать.**

изнача́льный *adj.* primordial.

изна́шивание *neut.* wearing out (*of clothes, shoes, etc.*).

изна́шивать *impf. pf.* **износи́ть** *v.t.* to wear out (*clothes, etc.*). **—ся** to be worn out.

изне́женный *adj.* soft; spoiled.

изнемога́ть *impf. pf.* **изнемо́чь** to be exhausted.

изнеможе́ние *neut.* extreme exhaustion.

изнеможённый *adj.* completely exhausted.

изно́с *m.* wear; wearing out.

изно́шенный *adj.* worn out; shabby.

изнуре́ние *neut.* physical exhaustion.

изнури́тельный *adj.* **1.** exhausting. **2.** enervating. **3.** debilitating.

изнуря́ть *impf. pf.* **изнури́ть** to exhaust.

изнутри́ *adv.* from within.

изныва́ть *impf. pf.* **изны́ть** to languish.

изо *prep., see* из.

изоби́лие *neut.* abundance.

изоби́льный *adj.* abundant.

изоблича́ть *impf. pf.* **изобличи́ть** **1.** to expose. **2.** to give away; to reveal.

изобличе́ние *neut.* exposure; unmasking.

изобличи́тель *m.* exposer.

изобличи́тельный *adj.* incriminating.

изобража́ть *impf. pf.* **изобрази́ть** to portray; to represent.

изображе́ние *neut.* **1.** image; picture. **2.** depiction. **3.** portrait; representation.

изобрази́тельный *adj.* figurative; pictorial. **— изобрази́тельные иску́сства** *pl.* fine arts.

изобрета́тель *m.* inventor. **—ный** *adj.* inventive.

изобрета́ть *impf. pf.* **изобрести́** to invent; to devise.

изобре́тение *neut.* invention.

изо́гнутый *adj.* bent; curved.

изолга́ться *pf.* (*conjugated like* лгать) to become an inveterate liar.

изоли́ровать OVA *impf. and pf.* to isolate; to insulate.

изоля́тор *m.* **1.** isolation ward. **2.** insulator.

изоляциони́зм *m.* isolationism.

изоляциони́ст *m.* isolationist.

изоляциони́стский *adj.* isolationist.

изоляцио́нный *adj.* **1.** (*attrib.*) isolation. **2.** insulation.

изоля́ция *f.* isolation; quarantine; insulation.

изоме́р *m.* isomer.

изо́рванный *adj.* tattered; torn.

изорва́ть *pf.* to rend; to tear.

изото́п *m.* isotope.

изощре́ние *neut.* refinement; sharpening.

изощрённый *adj.* keen; acute.

изощря́ть *impf. pf.* **изощри́ть** to sharpen (*one's faculties*). 2. to refine (*one's taste*).

из-под *prep.* (*with gen.*) from under.

изразе́ц FILL *m.* glazed tile.

изразцо́вый *adj.* (*attrib.*) tile; tiled.

Изра́иль *m.* Israel.

израильтя́нин *m. f.* **израильтя́нка** Israeli.

израни́ть *pf.* to wound severely; to cover with wounds.

израсхо́довать OVA *pf. of* расхо́довать.

и́зредка *adv.* rarely; now and then; from time to time.

изре́занный *adj.* cut up; sliced up.

изрека́ть *impf. pf.* **изре́чь** (*obs.*) to say *or* speak solemnly; to utter.

изрече́ние *neut.* dictum; saying.

изрисова́ть OVA *pf.* to cover with drawings.

изруби́ть *pf.* **1.** to hack to pieces; to chop up. **2.** to massacre.

изрыва́ть *impf. pf.* **изры́ть** to dig up; to dig all over.

изрыга́ть *impf. pf.* **изрыгну́ть** **1.** to belch up. **2.** belch forth.

изры́тый *adj.* **1.** bumpy; uneven. **2.** dug up.

изря́дно *adv.* rather, fairly; pretty well.

изря́дный *adj.* (*colloq.*) a goodly; quite a.

изуве́р *m.* **1.** fiend; monster. **2.** fanatic, bigot.

изуве́рство *neut.* fanaticism.

изуве́чивать *impf. pf.* **изуве́чить** to maim.

изукра́шивать *impf. pf.* **изукра́сить** to decorate lavishly.

изуми́тельно *adv.* amazingly; astoundingly.

изуми́тельный *adj.* amazing, wonderful.

изумле́ние *neut.* amazement, wonder.

изумля́ть *impf. pf.* **изуми́ть** to amaze.

изумру́д *m.* emerald. **—ный** *adj.* emerald.

изуро́дованный *adj.* disfigured.

изуро́довать OVA *pf. of* уро́довать.

изуча́ть *impf. pf.* **изучи́ть** **1.** to study. **2.** to learn; to master.

изуче́ние *neut.* studying; study.

изъе́здить *pf.* **1.** to travel all over. **2.** to wear out (*a road by traveling*).

изъяви́тельное наклоне́ние *neut.* (*gram.*) indicative mood.

изъявле́ние *neut.* declaration; expression.

изъя́н *m.* defect; flaw.

изъя́тие *neut.* **1.** withdrawal, removal. **2.** exception.

изыма́ть *impf. pf.* **изъя́ть** to withdraw, to remove.

изыска́ние *neut.* seeking. **— изыска́ния** *pl.* **1.** research. **2.** prospecting (*for minerals*).

изы́сканность *f.* refinement.

изы́сканный *adj.* exquisite; refined.

изыска́тель *m.* prospector.

изю́бр *m.* type of red deer; Altai wapiti.

изю́м *m.* (*sg. only*) raisins.

изю́мина *f.* raisin.

изю́минка *f.* **1.** raisin. **2.** spirit, sparkle (*in a person*).

изя́щество *neut.* refinement; elegance.

изя́щно *adv.* elegantly.

изя́щный *adj.* refined; elegant. **— изя́щные иску́сства** *pl.* fine arts.

ика́ть *impf. pf.* **икну́ть** to hiccup.

ико́на *f.* icon.

иконобо́рец FILL *m.* iconoclast.

иконопи́сец FILL *m.* icon painter.

иконоста́с *m.* iconostasis.

икота *f.* hiccups.

икра́[1] **1.** roe. **2.** caviar.

икра́[2] *f. usu.* **и́кры** *pl.* calf (of a leg).

икромета́ние *neut.* spawning.

икс *m.* the letter x.

ил *m.* silt.

и́ли *also* иль *conj.* or. **— и́ли... и́ли...** either... or...

и́листый *adj.* silty; muddy.

Иллино́йс *m.* Illinois.

иллюзиони́ст *m.* magician.

иллю́зия *f.* illusion.

иллюзо́рный *adj.* illusory.

иллюмина́тор *m.* porthole.
иллюмина́ция *f.* illumination.
иллюминова́ть OVA *impf.* to decorate with lights.
иллюстра́тор *m.* illustrator.
иллюстра́ция *f.* illustration.
иллюстри́ровать OVA *impf. and pf.* to illustrate.
Иль-де-Франс *m.* (*province*) Île-de-France.
ильм *m.* elm.
Йльмень *m.* (*lake*) Ilmen.
им *pron. instr. of* **он, оно́** *dat. of* **они́.**
имби́рь *m.* ginger.
име́ние *neut.* estate.
имени́нник *m. f.* **имени́нница** person celebrating his/her name day.
имени́нный *adj.* pertaining to one's name day.
имени́ны *pl.* name day.
имени́тельный *adj.* (*gram.*) nominative.
имени́тый *adj.* eminent; distinguished.
и́менно *particle* precisely; namely; that is.
именно́й *adj.* nominal; inscribed.
имено́ванное число́ *neut.* (*math.*) concrete number.
именова́ть OVA *impf. pf.* **на-** to name.
име́ть *impf.* to have. — **име́ть в виду́ 1.** to mean. **2.** to bear in mind. — **име́ть ме́сто** to take place, to occur.
име́ться *impf. impers.* **1.** to be available. **2.** to be.
име́ющийся *adj.* available.
и́ми *pron. instr. of* **они́.**
имита́тор *m.* imitator; mimic.
имита́ция *f.* imitation; mimicry.
имити́ровать OVA *impf.* to imitate.
иммигра́нт *m. f.* **—ка** immigrant.
иммиграцио́нный *adj.* (*attrib.*) immigration.
иммигра́ция *f.* immigration.
иммигри́ровать OVA *impf. and pf.* to immigrate.
иммуниза́ция *f.* immunization.
иммунизи́ровать OVA *impf.* to immunize.
иммуните́т *m.* immunity.
императи́вный *adj.* imperative; peremptory.
импера́тор *m.* emperor. **—ский** *adj.* imperial.
императри́ца *f.* empress.
империали́зм *m.* imperialism.
импе́рия *f.* empire.
импи́чмент *m.* impeachment.
импоза́нтный *adj.* imposing.
импони́ровать OVA *impf.* (*with dat.*) to impress; to strike.
и́мпорт *m.* import; importation.
импортёр *m.* importer.
импорти́ровать OVA *impf. and pf.* to import.
и́мпортный *adj.* imported.
импоте́нтный *adj.* (*med.*) impotent.
импоте́нция *f.* (*med.*) impotence.
импресса́рио *m. indecl.* impresario.
импрессиони́зм *m.* impressionism.
импровиза́тор *m.* improviser.
импровиза́ция *f.* improvisation.
импровизи́рованный *adj.* improvised; impromptu.
импровизи́ровать OVA *impf. pf.* **сымпровизи́ровать** to improvise.
и́мпульс *m.* impulse.
иму́щественный *adj.* (*attrib.*) property.
иму́щество *neut.* property; belongings.
иму́щий *adj.* propertied.

и́мя *neut.* (*pl.* **имена́**) name; first name; reputation. — **от и́мени** (*with gen.*) on behalf of.
и́мя прилага́тельное *neut.* (*gram.*) adjective.
и́мя со́бственное *neut.* (*gram.*) proper noun.
и́мя существи́тельное *neut.* (*gram.*) noun; substantive.
и́мя числи́тельное *neut.* (*gram.*) numeral.
инакомы́слие *neut.* dissidence; dissent.
инакомы́слящий *adj. and m.* dissident.
ина́че *adv.* differently; otherwise.
инвали́д *m. f.* **— ка** invalid; disabled person.
инвали́дный *adj.* invalid; invalid's.
инвентариза́ция *f.* taking of inventory.
инвентаризи́ровать OVA *impf. and pf.* to take inventory.
инвента́рный *adj.* (*attrib.*) inventory.
инвента́рь *m.* inventory.
инве́рсия *f.* inversion.
инвести́рованный *adj.* invested.
инвести́ровать OVA *impf. pf.* **про-** to invest.
инвести́ция *f.* investment.
инве́стор *m.* investor.
ингаля́тор *m.* (*med.*) inhaler.
ингредие́нт *m.* ingredient.
индеве́ть *impf. pf.* **за-** to become covered with frost.
инде́ец FILL *m. f.* **индиа́нка** (*American*) Indian.
инде́йка *f.* turkey.
инде́йский *adj.* (*American*) Indian.
и́ндекс *m.* index.
Индиа́на *f.* Indiana.
индиа́нка *f.* **1.** (*American*) Indian woman. **2.** woman from India.
индиви́д *m.* individual.
индивидуали́зм *m.* individualism.
индивидуали́ст *m.* individualism.
индивидуа́льный *adj.* individual.
индиви́дуум *m.* individual.
инди́го *neut. indecl.* indigo.
инди́ец FILL *m. f.* **индиа́нка** Indian (*Asian*).
и́ндий *m.* indium.
инди́йский *adj.* Indian.
Инди́йский океа́н *m.* Indian Ocean.
индика́тор *m.* indicator.
индифере́нтный *adj.* indifferent.
Йндия *f.* India.
индоевропе́йский *adj.* Indo-European.
Индоне́зия *f.* Indonesia.
индоссаме́нт *m.* (*econ.*) endorsement.
индуи́зм *m.* Hinduism.
индукти́вный *adj.* inductive.
инду́ктор *m.* inductor.
индукцио́нный *adj.* (*attrib.*) induction.
инду́кция *f.* induction.
инду́с *m. f.* **—ка** Hindu. **—ский** *adj.* Hindu.
Индуста́н *m.* Hindustan.
индустриализа́ция *f.* industrialization.
индустриализи́ровать OVA *impf. and pf.* to industrialize.
индустриа́льный *adj.* industrial.
инду́стрия *also* **индустри́я** *f.* industry.
индю́к *m.* turkey cock. — **индю́шка** *f.* turkey hen; (*colloq.*) turkey.
и́ней *m.* hoarfrost; rime.
ине́ртный *adj.* inert; sluggish.

инéрция *f.* inertia.
инженéр *m.* engineer.
инжúр *m.* fig; fig tree.
инициáлы *pl.* initials.
инициатúва *f.* initiative.
инициáтор *m.* initiator.
инквизúтор *m.* inquisitor.
инкóгнито *neut. indecl.* and *adv.* incognito.
инкорпорáция *f.* incorporation.
инкорпорúровать OVA *impf.* and *pf* incorporate.
инкриминúровать OVA *impf.* and *pf.* (*with dat.*) to accuse; to charge.
инкрустáция *f.* inlay; inlaid work.
инкрустúровать OVA *impf.* and *pf.* to inlay; to encrust.
инкубáтор *m.* incubator.
инкубáция *f.* incubation.
иногдá *adv.* sometimes.
иногорóдний *adj.* from another city.
инозéмец FILL *m. f.* инозéмка (*obs.*) foreigner.
инозéмный *adj.* foreign.
инóй *adj.* another, other; different.
úнок *m.* monk.
инорóдный *adj.* foreign.
иносказáние *neut.* allegory.
инострáнец FILL *m. f.* инострáнка foreigner.
инострáнный *adj.* foreign.
инохóдец FILL *m.* pacer (*horse*).
úноходь *f.* amble; pace.
иноязы́чный *adj.* foreign; belonging to another language.
инсектицúд *m.* insecticide.
инсинуáция *f.* insinuation.
инспектúровать OVA *impf.* to inspect.
инспéктор *m.* inspector.
инспéкция *f.* inspection.
инспирúровать OVA *impf.* and *pf.* to influence; to inspire.
инстáнция *f.* **1.** (*law*) instance. **2.** level of command; echelon.
инстúнкт *m.* instinct.
инстинктúвный *adj.* instinctive.
институ́т *m.* institute; institution.
инструктáж *m.* instructing; instructions.
инструктúвный *adj.* instructive.
инструктúрование *neut.* instructing.
инструктúровать OVA *impf.* and *pf.* to instruct.
инстру́ктор *m.* instructor.
инстру́кция *f.* instructions; directions.
инструмéнт *m.* instrument; tool.
инструменталúст *m.* instrumentalist.
инструментáльный *adj.* instrumental.
инструментáльщик *m.* toolmaker.
инструментáрий *m.* tools; instruments.
инструментовáть OVA *impf.* and *pf.* to orchestrate.
инструментóвка *f.* orchestration.
инсулúн *m.* insulin.
инсу́льт *m.* (*med.*) stroke.
инсценúровать OVA *impf.* and *pf.* **1.** to stage. **2.** to dramatize.
инсценирóвка *f.* **1.** staging. **2.** dramatization.
интегрáл *m.* (*math.*) integral.
интегрáльный *adj.* integral; integrated.
интегрáция *f.* integration.
интегрúровать OVA *impf.* and *pf.* to integrate.

интеллéкт *m.* intellect.
интеллектуáльный *adj.* intellectual.
интеллигéнт *m. f.* —ка intellectual. —ный *adj.* educated, cultured.
интеллигéнция *f.* intelligentsia.
интендáнт *m.* quartermaster.
интенсúвность *f.* intensity.
интенсúвный *adj.* intense.
интенсифицúровать OVA *impf.* and *pf.* to intensify.
интервáл *m.* interval.
интервéнция *f.* intervention.
интервью́ *neut. indecl.* interview.
интервьюúровать OVA *impf.* and *pf.* to interview.
интерéс *m.* interest. —ный *adj.* **1.** interesting. **2.** attractive.
интерéсно *adv.* interestingly.
интересовáть *impf.* to interest. —ся (*with instr.*) to be interested in.
интерлю́дия *f.* interlude.
интермéццо *neut. indecl.* intermezzo.
интéрн *m.* intern.
интернáт *m.* boarding school; dormitory. — шкóла-интернáт boarding school.
интернационалúзм *m.* internationalism.
интернациональный *adj.* international.
интернúрование *neut.* internment.
интернúровать OVA *impf.* and *pf.* to intern.
интерполúровать OVA *impf.* and *pf.* to interpolate.
интерполя́ция *f.* interpolation.
интерпретáтор *m.* interpreter.
интерпретáция *f.* interpretation.
интерпретúровать OVA *impf.* to interpret.
интерсéть *f.* Internet.
интерьéр *m.* interior (*of building*).
интúмный *adj.* intimate.
интонáция *f.* intonation.
интрúга *f.* intrigue.
интригáн *m. f.* —ка schemer.
интриговáть OVA *impf. pf.* за- **1.** to plot, to scheme. **2.** to intrigue.
интроду́кция *f.* (*mus.*) introduction.
интроспéкция *f.* introspection.
интуитúвный *adj.* intuitive.
интуúция *f.* intuition.
инфáркт *m.* heart attack.
инфéкция *f.* infection, contagion.
инфинитúв *m.* infinitive.
инфля́ция *f.* inflation.
информáтор *m.* informant.
информáция *f.* information.
информбюрó *neut. indecl.* (*abbr. of* информациóнное бюрó *neut.*) information bureau.
информúровать OVA *impf. pf.* про- to inform.
инфракрáсный *adj.* infrared.
инцидéнт *m.* incident.
инъéкция *f.* injection.
иóн *m.* ion. —ный *adj.* ionic.
ионизáция *f.* ionization.
ионизúровать OVA *impf.* and *pf.* to ionize.
ионúйский *adj.* Ionic, Ionian.
иóнный *adj.* ionic; ion.
ионосфéра *f.* ionosphere.
Иордáния *f.* Jordan.
ипомéя *f.* morning-glory.

ипотéка *f.* mortgage.
ипохóндрия *f.* hypochondria.
ипподрóм *m.* racetrack.
и пр. (*abbr. of* и прóчее) and so forth.
иприт *m.* mustard gas.
Ирáк *m.* Iraq.
ирáкец FILL *m.* Iraqi.
Ирáн *m.* Iran.
ирáнец FILL *m. f.* ирáнка Iranian.
ири́дий *m.* iridium.
и́рис *m.* (*bot.*) iris.
ири́с *m.* toffee; taffy.
Иркýтск *m.* Irkutsk.
ирлáндец FILL *m. f.* ирлáндка an Irish person.
Ирлáндия *f.* Ireland.
иронизи́ровать OVA *impf.* (над *with instr.*) to be ironic.
ирони́ческий *adj.* ironic(al).
ирóния *f.* irony.
иррадиáция *f.* irradiation.
иррационáльный *adj.* irrational.
ирригáция *f.* irrigation.
иск *m.* legal action, suit.
искажáть *impf. pf.* исказйть to distort; to misrepresent.
искажéние *neut.* distortion.
искалéчить *pf. of* калéчить.
искáние *neut.* search; quest.
искáтель *m.* seeker.
искáть *impf.* to search (for), to seek; to look (for).
исключáть *impf. pf.* исключи́ть to exclude; to except; to rule out.
исключáя *prep.* (*with gen.*) except, excepting.
исключéние *neut.* 1. exception, exclusion. 2. expulsion.
исключи́тельно *adv.* 1. exclusively; solely. 2. exceptionally.
исключи́тельность *f.* exceptional nature.
исключи́тельный *adj.* 1. exceptional. 2. exclusive.
исковéркать *pf. of* ковéркать.
искóмый *adj.* 1. sought after. 2. searched for.
исконú *adv.* (*obs.*) from time immemorial.
искóнный *adj.* primordial; indigenous.
ископáемое DAA *n.* 1. fossil. 2. mineral.
ископáемый *adj.* fossil, fossilized.
искоренéние *neut.* eradication.
искореня́ть *impf. pf.* искорени́ть to eradicate.
и́скоса *adv.* askance.
и́скра *f.* spark; glimmer.
и́скренний *adj.* sincere.
искривлéние *neut.* 1. bend, curve. 2. distortion.
искривля́ть *impf. pf.* искриви́ть 1. to bend, to crook. 2. to distort.
искри́стый *adj.* sparkling.
искромётный *adj.* sparkling; dazzling; flashing.
искупáть *impf. pf.* искупи́ть 1. to atone for. 2. to make amends for.
искупи́тельный *adj.* expiatory.
искуплéние *neut.* (*with gen.*) atonement (for); expiation (of).
и́скус *m.* trial, test; ordeal.
искуси́тель *m.* tempter.
искýсник *m.* (*colloq.*) master craftsman.
искýсный *adj.* skillful.
искýсственный *adj.* artificial; unnatural.
искýсство *neut.* 1. art. 2. skill, proficiency.

искусствовéд *m.* art critic.
искýсственный интеллéкт *m.* (*abbr.* ИИ) artificial intelligence (*abbr.* A.I.).
искушáть *impf. pf.* искуси́ть to tempt; to seduce.
искушéние *neut.* temptation; seduction.
искушённый *adj.* knowledgeable; experienced.
ислáм *m.* Islam.
isláндец FILL *m. f.* islándka Icelander.
Islándия *f.* Iceland.
испáнец FILL *m. f.* испáнка Spaniard.
Испáния *f.* Spain.
испáнский *adj.* Spanish.
испарéние *neut.* evaporation.
испари́на *f.* perspiration.
испари́тель *m.* vaporizer.
испаря́ть *impf. pf.* испари́ть *v.t.* to evaporate. —ся *v.i.* to evaporate; (*colloq.*) to disappear.
испáчкать *pf. of* пáчкать.
испестря́ть *impf. pf.* испестри́ть to make colorful; to color.
испéчь *pf. of* печь.
испещря́ть *impf. pf.* испещри́ть 1. to spot (*with color*). 2. to mark all over with.
испи́сывать *impf. pf.* исписáть 1. to cover with writing. 2. to use up (*paper, pencil*).
испитóй *adj.* (*colloq.*) drawn; gaunt.
исповедáльня *f.* confessional.
исповéдание *neut.* 1. religious belief. 2. profession of a religion.
исповéдник *m.* confessor.
исповéдовать *impf. and pf. v.t.* to confess. —ся *v.i.* to confess.
и́споведь *f.* confession.
и́сподволь *adv.* slowly; gradually.
исподлóбья *adv.*: смотрéть исподлóбья to glower at.
исподтишкá *adv.* stealthily; on the sly.
испокóн векóв since time immemorial.
исполи́н *m.* giant.
исполкóм *m.* (*abbr. of* исполни́тельный комитéт *m.*) executive committee.
исполнéние *neut.* 1. execution, fulfillment. 2. performance.
испóлненный *adj.* (*with gen.*) full of.
исполни́мый *adj.* feasible.
исполни́тель *m.* executor; performer.
исполни́тельный *adj.* 1. executive. 2. efficient.
исполня́ть *impf. pf.* испóлнить to fulfill, to carry out; to execute.
испóльзование *neut.* use; utilization.
испóльзовать OVA *impf. and pf.* 1. to utilize. 2. to take advantage of. 3. to exploit.
испóртить *pf. of* пóртить.
испóрченный *adj.* 1. spoiled. 2. tainted. 3. depraved; perverted.
исправи́мый *adj.* 1. repairable. 2. remediable.
исправи́тельный *adj.* remedial; corrective.
исправлéние *neut.* correction; correcting.
исправля́ть *impf. pf.* испрáвить 1. to correct. 2. to repair, to mend. 3. to reform.
испрáвность *f.* 1. good condition. 2. good working order.
испрáвный *adj.* in good condition; in working order; meticulous.
испражнéние *neut.* 1. defecation, evacuation (of the bowels). 2. испражнéния *pl.* feces.
испражня́ться *impf. pf.* испражни́ться to defecate.

испро́бовать OVA *pf.* **1.** to try out. **2.** to test. **3.** to experience.

испу́г *m.* fright, scare. **—анный** *adj.* frightened; startled.

испуга́ть *pf. of* пуга́ть.

испуска́ние *neut.* emission.

испуска́ть *impf. pf.* **испусти́ть** to emit; to utter.

испыта́ние *neut.* **1.** trial, probation. **2.** test, examination.

испы́танный *adj.* **1.** tested, tried. **2.** experienced.

испыта́тель *m.* tester.

испыта́тельный *adj.* test; testing; trial.

испыту́ющий *adj.* penetrating; searching.

испы́тывать *impf. pf.* **испыта́ть 1.** to try, to test. **2.** to experience.

иссека́ть *impf. pf.* **иссе́чь 1.** to carve. **2.** to slash in many places.

иссле́дование *neut.* **1.** investigation; research. **2.** analysis. **3.** exploration.

иссле́дователь *m.* **1.** researcher. **2.** explorer.

иссле́довательский *adj.* (*attrib.*) research.

иссле́довать OVA *impf.* and *pf.* **1.** to investigate. **2.** to explore. **3.** to examine. **4.** to do research.

и́сстари *adv.* since ancient times; from *or* of old.

исступле́ние *neut.* frenzy.

исступлённый *adj.* frenzied.

иссуша́ть *impf. pf.* **иссуши́ть 1.** to dry completely. **2.** to exhaust someone.

иссыха́ть *impf. pf.* **иссо́хнуть 1.** to dry up. **2.** to shrivel; to wither.

иссяка́ть *impf. pf.* **исся́кнуть 1.** to dry up. **2.** to run dry. **3.** to be used up.

иста́пливать *impf. pf.* **истопи́ть 1.** to heat up (*a stove*). **2.** (*colloq.*) to use up (*firewood*).

иста́птывать *impf. pf.* **истопта́ть 1.** to trample down. **2.** to wear out (*shoes*). **3.** to track up (*a clean floor*).

истека́ть *impf. pf.* **исте́чь 1.** to flow out. **2.** to expire; to elapse.

исте́кший *adj.*: **за исте́кший год** during the past year.

истёрзанный *adj.* **1.** slashed to pieces. **2.** tormented. **3.** bedraggled.

истерза́ть *pf.* **1.** to tear to pieces. **2.** to torment.

исте́рик *m.* hysterical person.

исте́рика *f.* hysterics.

истери́ческий *adj.* hysterical.

исте́ричка *f.* (*colloq.*) hysterical woman.

истери́чный *adj.* hysterical.

истери́я *f.* hysteria.

истёртый *adj.* **1.** worn down; worn out. **2.** trite.

исте́ц FILL *m.* plaintiff.

истече́ние *neut.* **1.** expiration. **2.** outflow.

исте́чь *pf. of* истека́ть.

и́стина *f.* truth.

и́стинный *adj.* veritable, true.

истира́ние *neut.* abrasion; wear.

истира́ть *impf. pf.* **истере́ть 1.** to grate. **2.** to use up (*by rubbing*); to wear out.

истлева́ть *impf. pf.* **истле́ть** to rot; to decay.

и́стовый *adj.* **1.** proper; sedate. **2.** real. **3.** assiduous; vigorous.

исто́к *m.* source. **—исто́ки** *pl.* headwaters; origin.

истолкова́ние *neut.* interpretation.

истолкова́тель *m.* expounder; commentator.

исто́ма *f.* languor; lassitude.

истомля́ть *impf. pf.* **истоми́ть** to tire; to exhaust; to fatigue.

истопни́к *m.* stoker; boilerman.

исторга́ть *impf. pf.* **исто́ргнуть 1.** to wrest (from). **2.** to throw out; to expel. **3.** to evoke. **4.** to extract.

исто́ргнуть *past* исто́рг *or* исто́ргнул, исто́ргла, *pf. of* исторга́ть.

истори́зм *m.* historical method.

исто́рик *m.* historian.

историогра́фия *f.* historiography.

истори́ческий *adj.* historical.

исто́рия *f.* **1.** history. **2.** event. **3.** story.

истоскова́ться OVA *pf.* (**по-** *with dat.*) to miss very much; to yearn for.

источа́ть *impf.* **1.** to give off; to emit. **2.** to shed (*tears*).

исто́чник *m.* source, spring.

исто́шный *adj.* (*colloq.*) heart-rending; blood-curdling.

истоща́ть *impf. pf.* **истощи́ть 1.** to exhaust, to drain. **2.** to wear out.

истоще́ние *neut.* **1.** exhaustion. **2.** emaciation.

истра́тить *pf. of* тра́тить.

истреби́тель *m.* **1.** destroyer. **2.** (*aircraft*) fighter.

истреби́тельный *adj.* destructive.

истребле́ние *neut.* extermination.

истребля́ть *impf. pf.* **истреби́ть** to destroy; to annihilate, to exterminate.

И́стрия *f.* (*peninsula*) Istria.

истука́н *m.* idol.

истфа́к *m.* (*abbr. of* истори́ческий факульте́т *m.*) department of history.

и́стый *adj.* true; real.

истяза́ние *neut.* torture.

истяза́ть *impf.* to torture.

исхо́д *m.* **1.** outcome, result. **2.** end.

исходи́ть[1] *impf.* (из *or* от *with gen.*) to issue (from); to proceed (from); to emanate (from).

исходи́ть[2] *impf. pf.* **изойти́** (*with instr.*) to be consumed (by).

исхо́дный *adj.* starting; initial.

исходя́щий *adj.* (*letters, documents*) outgoing.

исхуда́лый *adj.* gaunt; haggard; emaciated.

исхуда́ть *pf.* to become emaciated.

исцели́тель *m.* healer.

исцеля́ть *impf. pf.* **исцели́ть** to heal; to cure.

исча́дие *neut.* (*obs.*) child; offspring.

исча́хнуть *pf. past* исча́х, исча́хла to waste away.

исчеза́ть *impf. pf.* **исче́знуть** to disappear, to vanish.

исчезнове́ние *neut.* disappearance.

исче́рпывать *impf. pf.* **исче́рпать** to exhaust.

исче́рпывающий *adj.* exhaustive; comprehensive.

исче́рчивать *impf. pf.* **исчерти́ть** to cover with lines.

исчисле́ние *neut.* **1.** calculation. **2.** (*math.*) calculus.

исчисля́ть *impf. pf.* **исчи́слить** to calculate; to estimate. **—ся** (**в** *with prep.*) amount to.

ита́к *conj.* thus; so.

и так да́лее and so forth.

Ита́лия *f.* Italy.

италья́нец FILL *m. f.* италья́нка Italian.

италья́нский *adj.* Italian.

и т. д. (*abbr. of* и так да́лее) and so forth.

ито́г *m.* **1.** sum, total; result. **2.** score.

итого́ *adv.* in all, altogether.
ито́говый *adj.* **1.** total. **2.** concluding.
и тому́ подо́бное and the like.
и т. п. (*abbr. of* **и тому́ подо́бное**) and the like.
итте́рбий *m.* ytterbium.
и́ттрий *m.* yttrium.
иудаи́зм *m. also* **иуде́йство** *neut.* Judaism.
иуде́й *m. f.* —**ка** Jew; Israelite. —**ский** *adj.* Judaic.
их *pron. gen., acc. of* **они́**. — *poss. adj.* their, theirs.
ихневмо́н *m.* ichneumon.
ихтиоло́гия *f.* ichthyology.
иша́к *m.* donkey.
ишь particle. look!; see!: oh!.

ище́йка *f.* bloodhound; police dog.
июль *m.* July. —**ский** *adj.* (*attrib.*) July.
ию́нь *m.* June. —**ский** *adj.* (*attrib.*) June.
Йе́ллоустон *m.* Yellowstone.
Йе́мен *m.* Yemen.
йог *m.* yogi. —**йо́га** *f.* yoga.
йо́гурт *m.* yogurt.
йод *m.* iodine.
йо́дистый *adj.* containing iodine.
йо́дный *adj.* (*attrib.*) iodine.
йон *see* **ио́н.**
Йорк *m.* York.
йо́та *f.* iota.
Йо́шкар-Ола́ *f.* Yoshkar Ola.

К

к *also* ко *prep.* (*with dat.*) to, towards; by; for, of, to.

каба́к *m.* **1.** tavern. **2.** (*colloq.*) pigsty.

кабала́ *f.* **1.** bondage. **2.** (*hist.*) debt-slavery.

каба́льный *adj.* serving to enslave.

каба́н *m.* **1.** wild boar. **2.** hog.

кабарга́ *f.* musk deer.

кабаре́ *neut. indecl.* cabaret.

кабачо́к[1] FILL *m.* (*vegetable*) squash.

кабачо́к[2] FILL *m. dim. of* каба́к cheap restaurant.

ка́бель *m.* cable.

ка́бельное телеви́дение *neut.* cable television.

каби́на *f.* **1.** booth. **2.** cockpit; cabin.

кабине́т *m.* **1.** study. **2.** conference room. **3.** (*polit.*) cabinet.

кабине́тный роя́ль *m.* baby grand piano.

каби́нка *f. dim. of* каби́на.

каблу́к *m.* heel (*of a shoe*).

каблучо́к FILL *m. dim. of* каблу́к.

кабриоле́т *m.* cabriolet.

Кабу́л *m* Kabul.

ка́бы *conj.* (*colloq.*) **1.** if. **2.** if only.

кавале́р *m.* **1.** (*colloq.*) admirer. **2.** dancing partner.

кавалери́йский *adj.* (*attrib.*) cavalry.

кавале́рия *f.* cavalry.

кавалька́да *f.* cavalcade.

кавардак *m.* (*colloq.*) mess; disorder.

ка́верза *f.* (*colloq.*) **1.** intrigue. **2.** mean trick.

ка́верзный *adj.* (*colloq.*) intricate; tricky.

каве́рна *f.* (*med.*) cavity.

Кавка́з *m.* (*mountains*) Caucasus.

кавка́зец FILL *m. f.* кавка́зка Caucasian.

кавы́чки *pl.* quotation marks.

кагебе́шник *also* кагеби́ст *m.* (*colloq.*) KGB policeman (*secret police agent*).

каде́тский *adj.* cadet.

Кади́кс *m.* Cadiz.

кади́ло *neut.* censer.

ка́дка *f.* tub.

ка́дмий *m.* cadmium.

кадр *m.* (*movies*) **1.** frame. **2.** shot; scene.

кадри́ль *f.* quadrille.

ка́дровый *adj.* (*of a worker*) trained; skilled.

ка́дры *pl.* **1.** personnel. **2.** cadres.

кады́к *m.* Adam's apple.

каёмка *f.* edging; border.

каждодне́вный *adj.* everyday.

ка́ждый *adj.* each, every. — *pron.* everyone, each one.

ка́жется *impers. impf.* it seems.

ка́жущийся *adj.* seeming; imaginary.

каза́к *m. f.* каза́чка Cossack.

Каза́нь *f.* Kazan.

каза́рка *f.* brant goose.

каза́рма *f.* barracks.

каза́ться *impf. pf.* по- to seem, to appear; to strike as.

каза́х *m. f.* каза́шка Kazakh.

Казахста́н *m.* Kazakhstan.

каза́цкий *adj.* (*attrib.*) Cossack.

каза́чество *neut.* the Cossacks.

каза́чий *adj.* (*attrib.*) Cossack.

казачо́к FILL *m.* **1.** Ukrainian dance. **2.** page; boy servant.

Казбе́к *m.* (*mountain*) Kazbek.

казеи́н *m.* casein.

казема́т *m.* casemate.

казённый *adj.* **1.** fiscal; State. **2.** formal; bureaucratic.

казино́ *neut.* (*indecl.*) casino.

казна́ *f.* (*obs.*) **1.** the State. **2.** treasury. **3.** money.

казначе́й *m.* **1.** treasurer. **2.** paymaster.

казни́ть *impf. and pf.* to execute; to put to death.

казнокра́д *m.* misappropriator of public funds.

казнь *f.* **1.** punishment, penalty. **2.** execution; death penalty.

казуи́стика *f.* casuistry.

ка́зус *m.* complex legal case.

ка́зусный *adj.* complex; complicated.

Каи́р *m.* Cairo.

ка́йзер *m.* Kaiser.

Кайзерсла́утерн *m.* Kaiserslautern.

кайло́ *neut.* pick; hack.

кайма́ *f.* border; edging.

кайф *m.* euphoria (*state of pleasure*).

как *adv.* how. —*conj.* as; like.

какаду́ *m.* (*indecl.*) cockatoo.

кака́о *neut. indecl.* cocoa; cacao.

ка́к-либо *also* ка́к-нибудь *adv.* somehow; any which way.

как-ника́к *adv.* (*colloq.*) still; after all.

каково́ *adv.* (*colloq.*) how. — каково́ ей жить! how does she manage?

каково́й *rel. pron.* (*obs.*) which.

како́й *pron.* which?; what?; what kind of; what a...!

како́й-либо *also* како́й-нибудь *adj.* some, some kind of.

како́й-то *adj.* **1.** some. **2.** some kind of.

какофо́ния *f.* cacophony.

ка́к-то *adv.* somehow.

ка́ктус *m.* cactus.

кал *m.* excrement.

каламбу́р *m.* pun.

кала́н *m.* sea otter.

каланча́ *f.* watch tower; fire tower.

кала́ч *m.* kalach (*a loaf of white wheat bread*).

кала́чик *m. dim. of* кала́ч.

Ка́лгари *m.* Calgary.

калейдоско́п *m.* kaleidoscope.

кале́ка *m. and f.* (*decl. f.*) a handicapped person.

календа́рь *m.* calendar.

кале́ние *neut.* incandescence.

калёный *adj.* red-hot.

кале́чить *impf. pf.* ис- to mutilate; to cripple, to maim.

кали́бр *m.* **1.** caliber. **2.** gauge.

калиброва́ние *neut.* calibration.

калиброва́ть OVA *impf.* calibrate.

ка́лий *m.* potassium.

кали́льный *adj.* used for heating metals.

кали́на f. viburnum; guelder rose; snowball bush.
кали́тка f. gate.
кали́ть impf. to make s.t. red hot; to roast.
кали́ф m. caliph.
калифо́рний m. californium.
Калифо́рния f. California.
каллигра́фия f. calligraphy.
кало́рия f. calorie.
кало́ши also **гало́ши** pl. galoshes; rubbers.
калу́жница f. marsh marigold.
ка́лька f. tracing paper.
кальки́ровать OVA impf. pf. **с-** to trace.
калькули́ровать OVA impf. pf. **с-** to calculate.
калькуля́тор m. calculator.
Кальку́тта f. Calcutta.
кальма́р m. squid.
кальсо́ны pl. men's long underpants.
ка́льцевый adj. (attrib.) calcium.
ка́льций m. calcium.
кама́ринская DAA f. Russian folk dance.
камбала́ f. flounder; plaice.
ка́мбий m. cambium.
Камбо́джа f. Kampuchea (formerly Cambodia).
ка́мбуз m. **1.** ship's galley. **2.** ship's boiler.
камво́льный adj. worsted.
каме́дь f. gum.
камелёк FILL m. small fireplace.
каме́лия f. camelia.
камене́ть impf. pf. **о-** to turn to stone; to petrify; to harden.
Ка́менец-Подо́льский m. Kamyanets Podilskyy (Russian: Kamenets-Podolskiy).
камени́стый adj. stony; rocky.
Каменного́рск m. Kamennogorsk.
каменноуго́льный adj. coal.
ка́менный adj. stone; stony. — **ка́менный век** the Stone Age.
ка́менный у́голь m. coal.
каменоло́мня f. quarry.
ка́менщик m. **1.** bricklayer. **2.** mason.
ка́мень FILL m. stone, rock.
ка́мера f. **1.** chamber; cell. **2.** inner tube. **3.** film camera.
камерге́р m. chamberlain.
камерди́нер m. valet.
камери́стка f. lady's maid.
ка́мерный adj. (mus.) chamber.
камерто́н m. tuning fork.
ка́мешек FILL m. small stone; pebble.
каме́я f. cameo.
ками́н m. fireplace.
ками́нный adj. (attrib.) fireplace.
камнедроби́лка f. stone crusher.
камнело́мка f. saxifrage.
камнере́з m. stonecutter.
камо́рка f. closet; tiny room.
кампа́ния f. campaign.
камуфли́ровать OVA impf. and pf. to camouflage.
камуфля́ж m. camouflage.
ка́мушек FILL m. little stone; pebble.
ка́мфара f. camphor.
Камча́тка f. (peninsula) Kamchatka.
камы́ш m. reed; rush; cane.
Кан m. Caen (Normandy).
кана́ва f. ditch.
кана́дец FILL m. f. **кана́дка** Canadian.

кана́дский adj. Canadian.
кана́л m. **1.** canal; channel. **2.** duct. **—иза́ция** f. sewerage.
канаре́ечный adj. (attrib.) canary.
канаре́йка f. canary.
Кана́рские острова́ pl. Canary Islands.
кана́т m. cable; rope.
канатохо́дец FILL m. tightrope walker.
канва́ f. **1.** canvas. **2.** background.
Кандага́р m. Kandahar.
кандалы́ pl. irons; shackles.
канделя́бр m. candelabrum.
кандида́т m. f. **—ка** candidate; nominee. **—ский** adj. candidate's.
кандидату́ра f. candidacy.
Ка́нзас m. Kansas.
кани́кулы pl. vacation.
каните́ль f. **1.** gold thread; silver thread. **2.** (colloq.) long drawn-out proceedings.
канифо́ль f. rosin.
канка́н m. cancan.
Ка́нны pl. Cannes (Riviera).
канниба́л m. cannibal.
каннибали́зм m. cannibalism.
канниба́льский adj. cannibalistic.
канниба́льство neut. cannibalism.
кано́ист m. f. **—ка** canoeist.
кано́н m. canon.
канона́да f. cannonade.
каноне́рка f. gunboat.
канонизи́ровать OVA impf. and pf. to canonize.
кано́ник m. canon (clergyman).
канони́ческий adj. canonical.
кано́э neut. indecl. canoe.
кант m. edging; piping.
каталу́па f. cantaloupe.
канта́та f. cantata.
ка́нтик m. small edging.
кантова́ть OVA impf. pf. **о-** **1.** to mount (a picture). **2.** impf. only to turn over; to invert.
канто́н m. canton.
кантона́льный adj. cantonal.
ка́нтор m. cantor.
ка́нтри neut. indecl. country and western (music).
кану́н m. eve.
канцеляри́ст m. clerk.
канцеля́рия f. office.
канцеля́рский adj. **1.** bureaucratic. **2.** (attrib.) office.
канцеля́рщина f. bureacracy; red tape.
канцероге́н m. carcinogen.
канцероге́нный adj. carcinogenic.
ка́нцлер m. chancellor.
каньо́н m. canyon.
каню́к m. buzzard.
каоли́н m. kaolin.
ка́панье neut. dripping, drip.
ка́пать impf. pf. **ка́пнуть** to drip, to dribble; to spill.
капе́лла f. choir; chapel.
капелла́н m. chaplain.
ка́пелька f. droplet.
ка́пельку adv. (colloq.) a little; a tiny bit.
капельме́йстер m. conductor (of a band).
ка́пельница f. (medicine) dropper.
ка́персы pl. capers (condiment).

капилля́р *m.* capillary. —ный *adj.* capillary.
капита́л *m.* capital (*money*). —и́зм *m.* capitalism.
капитализа́ция *f.* capitalization.
капитализи́ровать OVA *impf.* and *pf.* to capitalize.
капитали́ст *m.* capitalist.
капиталисти́ческий *adj.* capitalist.
капиталовложе́ние *neut.* capital investment.
капита́льный *adj.* (*econ.*) capital; major.
капита́н *m.* captain.
капита́нский *adj.* captain's.
капитлиза́ция *f.* capitalization.
капитули́ровать OVA *impf.* and *pf.* to capitulate.
капитуля́ция *f.* capitulation, surrender.
ка́пище *neut.* pagan temple.
капка́н *m.* trap.
каплу́н *m.* capon.
ка́пля *f.* drop.
ка́пор *m.* bonnet; hood.
капо́т[1] *m.* woman's housecoat.
капо́т[2] *m.* (*mech.*) hood.
капра́л *m.* corporal.
Ка́при *m.* (*island*) Capri.
капри́з *m.* whim; caprice.
капри́зничать *impf. pf.* по- to behave capriciously.
капри́зный *adj.* capricious.
капро́н *m.* kapron (*type of nylon*).
капро́новый *adj.* ((*attrib.*)) kapron (*type of nylon*).
ка́псула *f.* 1. capsule. 2. space capsule.
ка́псюль *f.* primer; percussion cap.
капу́ста *f.* cabbage. — цветна́я капу́ста cauliflower.
капу́стница *f.* cabbage butterfly.
капу́стный *adj.* (*attrib.*) cabbage.
капу́т *adv.* (*colloq.*) done for.
капуци́н *m.* Capuchin.
капюшо́н *m.* hood.
ка́ра *f.* retribution; punishment.
караби́н *m.* carbine.
карава́й *m.* (round) loaf of bread.
карава́н *m.* caravan; convoy.
караве́лла *f.* caravel.
Караганда́ *f.* Qaraghandy (*formerly: Karaganda*).
карага́ч *m.* elm.
кара́емый *adj.* punishable.
Каракалпа́кстан *f.* Karakalpakstan.
карака́тица *f.* cuttlefish.
кара́ковый *adj.* (*of a horse*) dark bay.
кара́кули *pl.* scribble; scrawl.
Кара́куль *m.* Karakul.
кара́куль *m.* astrakhan; karacul.
караку́льский *adj.* karacul (*Persian lamb*).
каракульча́ *f.* broadtail; astrakhan (*fur*).
Караку́мы *pl.* (*desert*) Kara Kum.
карамбо́ль *m.* (*billiards*) carom shot.
караме́ль *f.* caramel.
караме́лька *f.* (*colloq.*) a caramel.
караме́льный *adj.* caramel.
каранда́ш *m.* pencil. —ный *adj.* (*attrib.*) pencil.
каранти́н *m.* quarantine.
кара́сь *m.* (*fish*) crucian; European carp.
кара́т *m.* carat.
Карата́у *m.* Karatau.
кара́тельный *adj.* punitive.
кара́ть *impf. pf.* по- to punish; to chastise; to penalize.

карау́л *m.* watch; guard. — крича́ть карау́л *impf.* to scream for help.
карау́лить *impf.* to stand watch or guard.
карау́льный *adj.* (*attrib.*) guard; sentry.
карау́льня *f.* guardhouse.
карау́льщик *m.* (*colloq.*) watchman.
кара́чки *pl.* (*colloq.*): на кара́чках on one's hands and knees.
карби́д *m.* carbide.
карбо́лка *f.* (*colloq.*) carbolic acid.
карбо́ловый *adj.* carbolic.
карбона́т *m.* carbonate.
карбонизи́ровать OVA *impf.* and *pf.* to carbonize.
карбору́нд *m.* carborundum.
карбу́нкул *m.* carbuncle.
карбюра́тор *m.* carburetor.
карга́ *f.* (*colloq.*) hag; crone.
Карго́поль *m.* Kargopol.
кардина́л *m.* cardinal (*bird*). cardinal (*prelate*).
кардина́льный *adj.* cardinal; fundamental.
кардиогра́мма *f.* cardiogram.
кардио́граф *m.* cardiograph.
кардиоло́гия *f.* cardiology.
каре́л *m. f.* —ка Karelian. —ьский *adj.* Karelian.
Каре́лия *f.* Karelia.
каре́та *f.* carriage, coach.
каре́тка *f.* carriage (*typewriter*).
каре́тный *adj.* of or for a coach.
кариати́да *f.* caryatid.
ка́риес *m.* caries.
ка́рий *adj.* (*of eyes*) brown.
карикату́ра *f.* caricature.
карикату́рный *adj.* like a caricature; grotesque.
Кари́нтия *f.* (*province*) Carinthia.
карио́зный *adj.* carious.
ка́рканье *neut.* caw; cawing.
карка́с *m.* frame; framework.
карка́сный *adj.* (*attrib.*) frame.
ка́ркать *impf. pf.* ка́ркнуть (*of a bird*) to caw.
ка́рлик *m. f.* ка́рлица dwarf. —овый *adj.* dwarfish; miniature.
Ка́рловы-Ва́ры *pl.* Karlovy Vary.
карма́н *m.* pocket.
карма́нник *m.* pickpocket.
карми́н *m.* carmine. —ный *adj.* carmine.
карнава́л *m.* carnival.
карни́з *m.* cornice.
карп *m.* carp.
Карпа́тские го́ры *also* Карпа́ты *pl.* Carpathian Mountains.
Ка́рское мо́ре *neut.* Kara Sea.
ка́рта *f.* 1. map. 2. playing card.
карта́вить *impf.* to distort the sounds "r" and "l" in one's speech.
карта́вость *f.* burr; distorted pronunciation of the sounds "r" and "l".
Картахе́на *f.* Cartagena.
картёжник *m.* (*colloq.*) inveterate cardplayer.
картёжный *adj.* (*attrib.*) pertaining to card playing.
карте́чь *f.* buckshot.
карти́на *f.* 1. picture; painting; canvas. 2. (*theat.*) scene.
карти́нка *f. dim. of* карти́на *f.*
карти́нный *adj.* (*attrib.*) 1. picturesque. 2. picture.
карто́граф *m.* cartographer.

картографи́ровать OVA *impf.* to map; to draw a map.
картографи́ческий *adj.* cartographic.
картогра́фия *f.* cartography.
карто́н *m.* cardboard. **—ка** *f.* cardboard box.
картона́ж *m.* article made of cardboard.
картона́жный *adj.* cardboard.
карто́нный *adj.* cardboard.
картоте́ка *f.* card index; card file.
картоте́чный *adj.* of *or* for a card file.
картофели́на *f.* (*colloq.*) a potato.
карто́фель *m.* (*sg. only*) potatoes. **—ный** *adj.* (*attrib.*) potato.
карто́фельное пюре́ *neut.* mashed potatoes.
ка́рточка *f.* **1.** photograph, snapshot. **2.** (file) card; rationing card.
ка́рточный *adj.* (*attrib.*) card.
карто́шка *f.* (*colloq.*) potato, potatoes.
карту́з *m.* peaked cap.
карусе́ль *f.* carousel, merry-go-round.
ка́рцер *m.* prison cell.
карцино́ге́н *m.* carcinogen.
карье́р¹ *m.* full gallop. **— с ме́ста в карье́р** *adv.* at once, right away.
карье́р² *m.* quarry.
карье́ра *f.* career.
карьери́ст *m.* careerist.
Касабла́нка *f.* Casablanca.
каса́ние *neut.* contact; touch.
каса́тельная DAA *f.* (*geom.*) tangent.
каса́тельно *prep.* (*with gen.*) concerning.
каса́тельство *neut.* relation; connection.
каса́тик *m.* (*flower*) iris.
каса́тка *f.* barn swallow.
каса́ться *impf. pf.* **косну́ться** (*with gen.*) **1.** to touch, to touch upon. **2.** to concern. **— что каса́ется** (*with gen.*) as for.
каса́ющийся *prep.* (*with gen.*) pertinent to, concerning.
ка́ска *f.* helmet.
каска́д *m.* cascade.
Каспи́йское мо́ре *neut.* Caspian Sea.
ка́сса *f.* **1.** box-office. **2.** cash register; cash box. **3.** cashier's desk.
касса́ция *f.* (*leg.*) appeal.
кассе́та *f.* cassette.
касси́р *m. f.* **—ша** cashier; teller.
касси́ровать OVA *impf. and pf.* (*leg.*) to annul.
ка́ссовый *adj.* (*attrib.*) cash.
ка́ста *f.* caste.
кастанье́ты *pl.* castanets.
кастеля́нша *f.* linen-keeper (*in a hotel or hospital*).
кастет *m.* brass knuckles.
Касти́лия *f.* (*province*) Castile.
ка́стовый *adj.* (*attrib.*) caste.
касто́р *m.* castor (*heavy woolen cloth*).
касто́рка *f.* (*colloq.*) castor oil.
касто́ровое ма́сло *neut.* castor oil.
касто́ровый *adj.* castor.
кастра́т *m.* eunuch; castrated boy *or* man.
кастри́ровать OVA *impf. and pf.* to castrate.
кастрю́ля *f.* saucepan; pot.
катакли́зм *m.* cataclysm.
катако́мбы *pl.* catacombs.
катале́псия *f.* catalepsy.

ката́лиз *m.* catalysis.
катализа́тор *m.* catalyst.
каталити́ческий *adj.* catalytic.
катало́г *m.* catalogue.
каталогиза́тор *m.* cataloguer.
каталогизи́ровать OVA *impf. and pf.* to catalogue.
катало́жный *adj.* (*attrib.*) catalogue.
Катало́ния *f.* (*province*) Catalonia.
ката́ние *neut.* **1.** drive, driving. **2.** rolling.
ката́нье *neut.*: **не мытьём, так ката́ньем** by hook or by crook.
катапу́льта *f.* catapult.
ката́р *m.* catarrh.
катара́кт *m.* cataract (*waterfall*).
катара́кта *f.* cataract (*of eyes*).
катастро́фа *f.* **1.** catastrophe. **2.** accident.
ката́ть *impf. indet. pf.* **по- 1.** to drive, to take for a drive. **2.** to roll, to wheel, to trundle. **3.** to mangle (*clothing*). **—ся** *impf.* **4.** to take a drive. **5.** to roll.
катафа́лк *m.* hearse.
категори́чески *adv.* categorically.
категори́чный *adj.* categorical.
катего́рия *f.* category.
ка́тер *m.* cutter; launch; boat.
кате́тер *m.* catheter.
катехи́зис *m.* catechism.
кати́ть *impf. pf.* **по- 1.** to roll; to wheel. **2.** (*colloq.*) (*of a vehicle*) to roll along. **—ся** to roll; to flow; to slide down.
Катманду́ *m.* Kathmandu.
Като́вице *pl.* Katowice.
като́д *m.* cathode.
като́к FILL *m.* **1.** skating rink. **2.** roller. **3.** rolling press.
като́лик *m. f.* **католи́чка** Catholic.
католици́зм *m.* Catholicism.
католи́ческий *adj.* Catholic.
ка́торга *f.* hard labor.
ка́торжник *m.* convict.
ка́торжный *adj.* pertaining to penal servitude.
кату́шка *f.* **1.** spool. **2.** reel; bobbin. **3.** roll (*of film*).
катю́ша *f.* rocket launcher.
Ка́унас *m.* Kaunas.
каусти́ческий *adj.* caustic.
каучу́к *m.* rubber.
кафе́ *neut. indecl.* cafe.
ка́федра *f.* **1.** chair, rostrum. **2.** department, faculty.
кафедра́льный собо́р *m.* cathedral.
ка́фель *m.* tile.
кафете́рий *m.* cafeteria.
кафта́н *m.* caftan.
кача́лка *f.* rocking chair, rocker.
кача́ние *neut.* rocking; swinging.
кача́ть *impf. pf.* **качну́ть** *v.t.* **1.** to rock, to swing. **2.** to shake. **—ся** *v.i.* to swing; to rock; to stagger.
каче́ли *pl.* (child's) swing.
ка́чественный *adj.* qualitative; of high quality.
ка́чество *neut.* quality.
ка́чка *f.* **1.** rolling (*of a ship*). **2.** pitching; tossing.
качу́рка *f.* (*bird*) petrel.
ка́ша *f.* porridge; gruel. **— ма́нная ка́ша** farina.

кашалóт *m.* cachalot; sperm whale.
кáшель FILL *m.* cough.
кашемúр *m.* cashmere.
кашемúровый *adj.* cashmere.
Кашúра *f.* Kashira.
кáшица *f.* thin gruel.
кáшка *f.* pap.
кáшлять *impf. pf.* кáшлянуть to cough.
кашнé *neut. indecl.* muffler, scarf.
каштáн *m.* chestnut.
каштáновый *adj.* chestnut (colored).
каюта *f.* cabin; stateroom.
кáющийся *adj.* contrite; repentant.
кая́к *m.* kayak.
кая́ться *impf. pres.* кáюсь, кáешься *pf.* по- **1.** to repent; to be sorry. **2.** to confess.
квадрáнт *m.* quadrant.
квадрáт *m.* square. —ный *adj.* square.
квадрáтный кóрень *m.* square root.
квадратýра *f.* squaring.
квадриллиóн *m.* quadrillion.
квазáр *m.* quasar.
квáканье *neut.* croaking.
квáкать *impf. pf.* квáкнуть to croak.
квáкер *m.* Quaker. —ский *adj.* Quaker.
кваква *f.* tree frog.
квалификáция *f.* qualification.
квалифицúрованный *adj.* skilled.
квалифицúровать OVA *impf. and pf.* to qualify; to categorize.
квант *m.* (*phys.*) quantum.
квáрта *f.* **1.** quart. **2.** (*mus.*) fourth.
квартáл *m.* quarter; city block.
квартéт *m.* (*mus.*) quartet.
квартúра *f.* apartment; quarters.
квартирáнт *m.* —ка tenant.
квартирмéйстер *m.* quartermaster.
квартúрный *adj.* housing; apartment.
квартировáть OVA *impf.* to lodge; (*mil.*) to be quartered.
квартиронанимáтель *m. f.* —ница tenant.
квартплáта *f.* (*abbr. of* квартúрная плáта *f.*) rent.
кварц *m.* quartz.
квáрцевый *adj.* quartz.
кварцúт *m.* quartzite.
квас *m.* kvass.
квáсить *impf. v.t.* to pickle.
кваснóй *adj.* (*attrib.*) kvass.
квасцы́ *pl.* alum.
квáшеный *adj.* pickled; fermented. — квáшеная капýста sauerkraut.
квашня́ *f.* kneading trough.
Квебéк *m.* Quebec.
квéрху *adv.* upward(s), up.
квинтéт *m.* quintet.
квинтэссéнция *f.* quintessence.
квитáнция *f.* acknowledgement; receipt.
квúты *adj.* (*colloq.*) all even. — мы с вáми квúты we are quits.
квóрум *m.* quorum.
квóта *f.* quota.
квохтáнье *neut.* clucking.
квохтáть *impf. pres.* квóхчеть to cluck.
КГБ *m.* (*abbr. of* Комитéт госудáрственной безопáсности *m.*) Committee for State Security; the KGB.

кегельбáн *m.* bowling alley.
кегль *m.* (*typog.*) point.
кéгля *f.* bowling pin.
кедр *m.* cedar. —óвый *adj.* cedar.
кéды *pl.* sneakers.
Кейптáун *m.* Cape Town.
кекс *m.* biscuit; raisin cake.
келéйный *adj.* in secret; in private.
Кёльн *m.* Cologne.
кéльнер *m.* waiter.
кельт *n.* Celt. —ский *adj.* Celtic.
кéлья *f.* cell (*in monastery*).
кем *pron. instr. of* кто.
Кéмбридж *m.* Cambridge.
кéмпинг *m.* campsite.
кенгурý *m. indecl.* kangaroo.
Кéния *f.* Kenya.
кент *m.* (*slang*) **1.** swinger. **2.** well-dressed, self-confident person.
кентáвр *m.* centaur.
Кентýкки *m.* Kentucky.
кéпка *f.* cap.
керáмика *f.* ceramics.
керогáз *m.* kerosene stove.
керосúн *m.* kerosene.
керосúнка *f.* kerosene stove.
керосúновый *adj.* kerosene.
Керчь *f.* Kerch.
кéсарево сечéние *neut.* Cesarean section.
кессóн *m.* caisson; coffer dam.
кессóнный *adj.* caisson.
кéта *f.* Siberian salmon.
кетгýт *m.* catgut.
кéтовая икрá *f.* red caviar.
кефáль *f.* gray mullet.
кефúр *m.* kefir (*a yogurt-like drink*).
кибернéтика *f.* cybernetics.
киберпространство *neut.* cyberspace.
кибúтка *f.* **1.** covered wagon. **2.** nomad's tent.
кивáть *impf. pf.* кивнýть (*with instr.* or на *with acc.*) to nod; to motion (to).
кúви *f. indecl.* kiwi.
кивóк FILL *m.* nod.
кидáть *impf. pf.* кúнуть to throw, to cast, to fling. —ся to throw oneself.
Кúев *m.* Kiev.
Кижú *pl.* (*island*) Kizhi.
кизúл *m.* dogwood; cornel.
кий *m.* billiard cue.
кикúмора *f.* (*folklore*) female hobgoblin.
Киклáды *pl.* (*islands*) Cyclades.
килó *neut. indecl.* (*colloq.*) (*abbr. of* килогрáмм *m.*) kilogram.
киловáтт *m.* kilowatt.
киловáтт-чáс *m.* kilowatt-hour.
килогéрц *m.* kilocycle.
килогрáмм *m.* kilogram.
киломéтр *m.* kilometer.
килотóнна *f.* kiloton.
Киль *m.* Kiel.
киль *m.* keel.
кильвáтер *m.* (*naut.*) wake.
кúлька *f.* sprat.
кимонó *neut. indecl.* kimono.
кинематогрáфия *f.* cinematography.
кинескóп *m.* kinescope.

кинéтика *f.* kinetics.

кинети́ческий *adj.* kinetic.

Ки́нешма *f.* Kineshma.

кинжáл *m.* dagger.

кино́ *neut. indecl.* motion picture; movie house.

киноактёр *m.* movie actor.

киноактри́са *f.* movie actress.

киноарти́ст *m.* movie actor. —ка *f.* movie actress.

ки́новарь *f.* cinnabar; vermilion.

киножурнáл *m.* (*movies*) short subject.

кинозвездá *f.* (*colloq.*) movie star.

кинокáмера *f.* movie camera.

кинокарти́на *f.* film; movie; picture.

кинокри́тик *m.* film critic.

кинолéнта *f.* (reel of) film.

киномехáник *m.* projectionist.

киноператор *m.* cameraman.

киноплёнка *f.* movie film.

кинорежиссёр *m.* film director.

киносту́дия *f.* movie studio.

кинотеáтр *m.* cinema; movie theater.

киноустано́вка *f.* movie projector.

кинофестивáль *f.* film festival.

кинофи́льм *m.* film; movie.

кинохро́ника *f.* newsreel.

ки́нуть *pf. of* кидáть.

Киншáса *f.* Kinshasa.

кио́ск *m.* 1. booth, kiosk. 2. newsstand.

кио́т *m.* icon case.

ки́па *f.* 1. pile; stack. 2. (*measure*) pack; bale.

кипари́с *m.* cypress. —ный *or* —овый (*attrib.*) cypress.

кипéние *neut.* boiling.

кипéть *impf.* to boil; to seethe.

Кипр *m.* Cyprus.

кипу́чий *adj.* boiling; seething.

кипяти́льник *m.* heating coil.

кипяти́ть *impf. pf.* вскипяти́ть *v.t.* to boil. —ся *v.i.* to boil.

кипято́к FILL *m.* boiling water.

кипячéние *neut.* boiling.

кипячёный *adj.* boiled.

кирáса *f.* cuirass.

кирги́з *m. f.* —ка Kyrgyz.

Кирги́зстáн *m.* Kyrgyzstan.

кири́ллица *f.* Cyrillic alphabet.

ки́рка *f.* Protestant church.

киркá *f.* pickax; pick (*tool*).

Ки́ров *m.* Kirov.

кирпи́ч *m.* brick.

кирпи́чный *adj.* (*attrib.*) brick.

Киру́на *f.* Kiruna.

ки́са *f.* (*colloq.*) pussy cat; puss.

кисéт *m.* pouch, tobacco pouch.

кисéя *f.* muslin.

ки́ска *f.* pussy cat; puss.

кисли́ца *f.* wood sorrel.

кисловáтый *adj.* sourish.

кислоро́д *m.* oxygen.

кисло-слáдкий *adj.* sweet-and-sour.

кислотá *f.* 1. sourness; acidity. 2. (*chem.*) acid.

кисло́тность *f.* acidity.

ки́слый *adj.* sour.

ки́снуть *impf. pf.* про- 1. to turn sour. 2. (*of a person*) to vegetate; to stagnate.

кистá *f.* cyst.

кистéнь *m.* bludgeon; flail.

ки́сточка *f.* paintbrush; tassel.

кисть[1] *f.* 1. cluster; bunch. 2. paintbrush.

кисть[2] *f.* hand.

кит *m.* whale.

китáец FILL *m. f.* китая́нка Chinese.

Китáй *m.* China.

китáйский *adj.* Chinese.

ки́тель *m.* tunic.

китобо́ец FILL *m.* whaling ship.

китобо́й *m.* 1. whaler. 2. whaling ship. —ный *adj.* (*attrib.*) whaling.

кичи́ться *impf.* 1. to boast. 2. to brag about.

кичли́вый *adj.* arrogant; conceited.

кишéть *impf. pres.* киши́т (*with instr.*) to swarm (with).

кишéчник *m.* intestines; bowels.

кишéчный *adj.* intestinal.

кишкá *f.* intestine.

кишмя́ кишéть *adv.*: кишмя́ кишéть *impf.* to swarm.

клавеси́н *m.* harpsichord.

клавиату́ра *f.* keyboard.

клавико́рды *pl.* clavichord.

клáвиша *f.* (*piano, etc.*) key.

Клáгенфурт *m.* Klagenfurt.

клад *m.* (buried) treasure.

клáдбище *neut.* cemetery.

клáдезь *m.* (*obs.*) fountain; well.

клáдка *f.* laying (*masonry*).

кладовáя *f.* pantry; larder; storeroom.

кладо́вка *f.* (*colloq.*) small pantry.

кладовщи́к *m.* storekeeper.

кладь *f.* load. — ручнáя кладь *f.* hand luggage.

Клáйпеда *f.* Klaipèda (*formerly:* Memel).

клáка *f.* claque.

клакёр *m.* claqueur.

клан *m.* clan.

клáняться *impf. pf.* поклони́ться 1. to bow, to greet. 2. to extend one's regards.

клáпан *m.* valve; flap.

кларнéт *m.* clarinet. —и́ст *m.* clarinetist.

класс *m.* class; classroom.

клáссик *m.* classic.

клáссика *f.* the classics.

классификáция *f.* classification.

классифици́ровать OVA *impf. and pf.* to classify.

классици́зм *m.* classicism.

класси́ческий *adj.* classic(al).

клáссный *adj.* (*attrib.*) class; classroom.

клáссовый *adj.* (*social*) class.

клáссы *pl.* (*children's game*) hopscotch.

класть *impf. pf.* положи́ть 1. to put; to place; to lay. 2. to put down, to place down.

клаустрофо́бия *f.* claustrophobia.

клевáть *impf. pf.* клю́нуть to peck; to bite (*of fish*).

клéвер *m.* clover. —ный *adj.* (*attrib.*) clover.

клеветá *f.* slander.

клеветáть *impf. pf.* на- (на *with acc.*) to slander.

клеветни́к *m. f.* клеветни́ца slanderer.

клеветни́ческий *adj.* slanderous, libelous.

клево́к FILL *m.* peck.

клеврéт *m.* follower; supporter.

клеёнка *f.* oilcloth.

клéить *impf. pf.* с- to glue; to paste. —ся to stick.

клеймо́ *neut.* stamp; mark; brand.

клейми́ть *impf. pf.* за- to stamp; to mark; to brand.

кле́йстер *m.* paste.

клёкот *m.* (*of birds*) screech; scream.

клён *m.* maple.

клено́вый *adj.* maple.

клепа́льщик *m.* riveter.

клепа́ть *impf.* to rivet.

клёпка *f.* riveting.

клептома́н *m. f.* —ка kleptomaniac.

клептома́ния *f.* kleptomania.

клерк *m.* clerk.

клёст *m.* (*bird*) crossbill.

кле́тка[1] *f.* **1.** cage, coop. **2.** check, square. — в кле́тку (*design*) checked.

кле́тка[2] *f.* (*biol.*) cell.

кле́точка *f. dim. of* кле́тка.

кле́точный *adj.* cell; cellular.

клету́шка *f.* (*colloq.*) tiny room.

клетча́тка *f.* cellulose.

кле́тчатый *adj* (*design*) checked.

клешня́ *f.* claw (*of crustaceans*); nipper.

клещ *m.* tick; mite.

кле́щи *pl.* pincers; nippers; tongs.

кли́вер *m.* (*naut.*) jib.

клие́нт *m. f.* —ка client, customer.

клиенту́ра *f.* clientele.

кли́зма *f.* enema.

клик *m.* call; honk (*of geese*).

кли́ка *f.* clique, faction.

кли́кать *impf. pf.* кли́кнуть to call; (*of geese*) to honk.

кли́макс *also* климакте́рий *m.* menopause.

кли́мат *m.* climate. —и́ческий *adj.* climatic.

клин *m.* wedge.

кли́ника *f.* clinic.

клини́ческий *adj.* clinical.

клинови́дный *adj.* wedge-shaped.

клино́к FILL *m.* blade (*of knife, etc.*).

клинообра́зный *adj.* wedge-shaped.

кли́нопись *f.* cuneiform.

кли́пер *m.* (*naut.*) clipper.

клипс *m.* (*clip-on*) earring.

кли́ринг *m.* (*comm.*) clearing.

кли́рос *m.* choir (*part of church*).

кли́тор *m.* clitoris.

клич *m.* call; appeal.

кли́чка *f.* nickname.

клише́ *neut. indecl.* cliche.

клоа́ка *f.* sewer; cesspool.

клок *m.* **1.** shred. **2.** tuft of hair. **3.** wisp (*of hay*).

клокота́ть *impf. pres.* клокочу́, клоко́чешь to bubble; to seethe.

клони́ть *impf.* **1.** to bend; to incline. **2.** (*of sleep*) to overcome.

клоп *m.* bedbug.

кло́ун *m.* clown.

кло́унский *adj.* clown; clownish.

клохта́нье *neut.* clucking.

клохта́ть *impf. pres.* кло́хчеть to cluck.

клочо́к FILL *m.* scrap; shred; wisp.

клуб[1] *m.* club.

клуб[2] *m.* cloud; puff.

клу́бень *m.* tuber.

клуби́ть *impf.* to swirl; to blow into the air. —ся to swirl; (*of smoke*) to curl.

клубнево́й *adj.* tuberous.

клубни́ка *f.* strawberry.

клу́бный *adj.* (*attrib.*) club.

клубо́к FILL *m.* ball.

Клуж-Напо́ка *f.* Cluj-Napoca (*German Klausenburg*).

клу́мба *f.* flower bed.

клык *m.* fang; tusk.

клюв *m.* beak; bill.

клюка́ *f.* walking stick.

клю́ква *f.* cranberry.

клю́нуть *pf. of* клева́ть.

ключ[1] *m.* **1.** key. **2.** (*mus.*) clef; key. — га́ечный ключ wrench.

ключ[2] *m.* spring; source.

ключево́й *adj.* **1.** key (*attrib.*). **2.** key; vital.

клю́чик *m. dim. of* ключ.

ключи́ца *f.* collarbone; clavicle.

клю́шка *f.* **1.** golf club. **2.** hockey stick.

кля́кса *f.* inkblot; smudge.

кля́нчить *impf.* (*colloq.*) to pester; to beg.

кляп *m.* gag.

кля́сть *impf. v.t.* to curse. —ся *v.i.* to swear.

кля́тва *f.* oath.

кля́твенный *adj.* solemn; sworn.

клятвопреступле́ние *neut.* perjury.

клятвопресту́пник *m.* perjurer.

кля́уза *f.* petty complaint; petty lie.

кля́ча *f.* nag; old horse.

кни́га *f.* book.

кни́га жа́лоб *f.* book of complaints.

книголю́б *m.* bibliophile.

кни́жка *f.:* сберега́тельная кни́жка *f.* bankbook; passbook. — че́ковая кни́жка *f.* checkbook.

кни́жник *m.* bibliophile.

кни́жный *adj.* (*attrib.*) book.

кни́зу *adv.* down, downwards.

кни́ксен *m.* curtsy.

кно́пка *f.* **1.** button. **2.** snap fastener. **3.** thumbtack.

кнут *m.* whip.

кнутови́ще *neut.* whip handle.

княги́ня *f.* princess (*wife of a prince*).

кня́жеский *adj.* prince's; princely.

кня́жество *neut.* principality.

княжи́ть *impf.* to reign (*as a prince*).

княжна́ *f.* princess (*daughter of a prince*).

князь *m.* prince. — вели́кий князь *m.* grand prince; grand duke.

ко *see* к.

коагуля́нт *m.* coagulant.

коагуля́ция *f.* coagulation.

коалицио́нный *adj.* (*attrib*) coalition.

коали́ция *f.* coalition.

ко́бальт *m.* cobalt.

ко́бальтовый *adj.* cobalt.

Ко́бе *m.* Kobe.

кобе́ль *m.* male dog.

ко́бра *f.* cobra.

кобура́ *f.* holster.

кобы́ла *f.* mare.

кобы́лка *f.* filly.

ко́ваный *adj.* forged.

кова́рный *adj.* perfidious; treacherous.

кова́ть OVA *impf.* **1.** to forge. **2.** to shoe.

ковбо́й *m.* cowboy.

ковбо́йка *f.* (*colloq.*) **1.** cowboy shirt. **2.** cowboy hat.

ковбо́йский *adj.* (*attrib.*) cowboy; cowboy's.

ковёр *m.* carpet; rug.

кове́ркать *impf. pf.* **ис- 1.** to break; to mangle; to wreck. **2.** to distort; to warp. **3.** to mispronounce.

ко́вка *f.* forging.

ко́вкий *adj.* malleable.

ко́вкость *f.* malleability.

коври́га *f.* large round loaf of bread.

коври́жка *f.* gingerbread; honey cake.

кита́йский *adj.* Chinese.

ко́врик *m.* **1.** small rug. **2.** mat.

ковро́вый *adj.* (*attrib.*) carpet.

ковче́г *m.* ark. — **Но́ев ковче́г** *m.* Noah's ark.

ковш *m.* scoop; dipper.

ковы́ль *m.* feather grass.

ковыля́ть *impf.* **1.** to hobble. **2.** (*of a child*) to toddle.

ковыря́ть *impf.* **1.** to dig up (*earth*). **2.** to pick (*one's teeth*).

когда́ *adv., conj.* when.

когда́-либо *also* **когда́-нибудь** *adv.* sometime, someday; ever.

когда́-то *adv.* once, at one time; sometime.

кого́ *pron. gen., acc. of* **кто.**

ко́готь *m.* claw, talon.

когти́стый *adj.* with sharp claws.

когти́ть *impf.* to claw.

код *m.* code; postal code.

кодеи́н *m.* codeine.

ко́декс *m.* code.

коди́ровать OVA *impf. and pf.* to encode.

кодифика́ция *f.* codification.

кодифици́ровать OVA *impf. and pf.* to codify.

ко́довый *adj.* (*attrib.*) code.

ко́е-где *adv.* here and there.

ко́е-ка́к *adv.* **1.** any old way; carelessly. **2.** with great difficulty.

ко́е-како́й *adj.* some.

ко́е-когда́ *adv.* now and then.

ко́е-кто *pron.* someone, somebody.

ко́е-куда́ *adv.* somewhere.

ко́е-что *pron.* something.

ко́жа *f.* skin; leather.

ко́жаный *adj.* leather.

кожевенный *adj.* leather; tanning.

коже́вник *m.* currier; tanner.

кожими́т *m.* (*abbr. of* **имита́ция ко́жи** *f.*) imitation leather; leatherette.

ко́жица *f.* skin; peel.

ко́жный *adj.* (*attrib.*) skin.

кожура́ *f.* rind; peel.

кожу́х *m.* **1.** sheepskin coat. **2.** casing; housing.

коза́ *f. m.* **козёл** goat.

козеро́г *m.* **1.** ibex; mountain goat. **2.** (*cap.*) Capricorn.

ко́зий *adj.* goat, goat's.

козлёнок FILL *m.* kid, young goat.

ко́злик *m. dim. of* **козёл.**

козли́ный *adj.* goat, goat's.

козло́вый *adj.* (*attrib.*) goatskin.

ко́злы *pl.* **1.** coachman's seat. **2.** sawhorse; trestle.

козля́тина *f.* goat meat.

ко́зни *pl.* machinations; intrigues.

козодо́й *m.* (*bird*) goatsucker.

ко́зочка *f. dim. of* **коза́.**

козырёк *m.* peak; visor.

козырно́й *adj.* (*attrib.*) trump.

ко́зырь *m.* trump.

козыря́ть¹ *impf. pf.* **козырну́ть 1.** to play a trump. **2.** to flaunt.

козыря́ть² *impf. pf.* **козырну́ть** to salute.

козя́вка *f.* (*colloq.*) insect; bug.

Ко́имбра *f.* Coimbra.

кой *adj.*: **ни в ко́ем слу́чае** no way; under no circumstances.

ко́йка *f.* cot, bunk; berth.

койо́т *m.* coyote.

кок *m.* cook (*on a ship*).

кокаи́н *m.* cocaine.

кока́рда *f.* cockade.

коке́тка *f.* coquette.

коке́тливый *adj.* coquettish; flirtatious.

коке́тство *neut.* coquetry; flirting.

кокк *m.* coccus.

ко́клюш *m.* whooping cough.

ко́кон *m.* cocoon.

коко́с *m.* coconut.

коко́совый *adj.* (*attrib.*) coconut.

коко́тка *f.* kept woman.

коко́шник *m.* old Russian woman's headdress.

кокс *m.* coke.

ко́ксовый *adj.* (*attrib.*) coke.

коксу́ющийся *adj.* coking (*coal*).

кокте́йль *m.* cocktail. — **моло́чный кокте́йль** *m.* milkshake.

кол *m.* stake; picket.

ко́лба *f.* retort; flask.

колбаса́ *f.* sausage.

колба́сник *m.* sausage maker.

колба́сный *adj.* (*attrib.*) sausage.

колго́тки *pl.* pantyhose.

колдо́бина *f.* (*colloq.*) rut; pothole.

колдова́ть OVA *impf.* to practice witchcraft.

колдовство́ *neut.* witchcraft.

колду́н *m.* sorcerer; wizard.

колду́нья *f.* sorceress.

колеба́ние *neut.* **1.** swaying. **2.** oscillation; vacillation. **3.** fluctuation.

колеба́ться *impf. pf.* **по- 1.** to oscillate; to fluctuate. **2.** to hesitate.

коле́нка *f.* (*colloq.*) knee.

коленко́р *m.* (*textile*) buckram.

коле́нный *adj.* (*attrib.*) knee.

коле́но *neut.* **1.** knee. **2.** bend (*in river, etc.*). **3.** (*Bibl.*) tribe.

коле́нчатый *adj.* elbow-shaped; cranked. — **коле́нчатый вал** *m.* crankshaft.

коле́сико *neut. dim. of* **колесо́.**

колесни́ца *f.* chariot.

колёсный *adj.* (*attrib.*) wheel.

колесо́ *neut.* wheel.

колесова́ть OVA *impf. and pf.* to break on the wheel.

коле́чко *neut. dim. of* **кольцо́.**

колея́ *f.* rut; track.

ко́ли *conj.* (*obs.*) if.
коли́бри *m.* or *f. indecl.* hummingbird.
ко́лики *pl.* colic.
коли́т *m.* colitis.
коли́чественный *adj.* quantitative.
коли́чество *neut.* quantity; amount.
ко́лкий *adj.* **1.** prickly. **2.** caustic; sharp; biting.
ко́лкость *f.* **1.** mordancy. **2.** caustic remark.
коллаборациони́ст *m.* collaborator.
колле́га *m.* and *f.* (*decl. f.*) colleague.
коллегиа́льный *adj.* collective; joint.
колле́гия *f.* **1.** board. **2.** collegium; college. **3.** panel.
колле́дж *m.* college.
коллекти́в *m.* collective body. —ный *adj.* collective.
коллективиза́ция *f.* collectivization.
коллективизи́ровать OVA *impf.* and *pf.* to collectivize.
коллективи́зм *m.* collectivism.
коллекционе́р *m.* collector. —ский *adj.* collector's.
коллекциони́ровать OVA *impf.* to collect.
колле́кция *f.* collection.
ко́лли *m.* and *f. indecl.* collie.
колло́дий *m.* collodion.
колло́ид *m.* colloid.
колло́идный *adj.* colloidal.
колло́квиум *m.* **1.** oral examination. **2.** colloquium.
колобро́дить *impf. pres.* —жу, —дишь (*colloq.*) **1.** to drift; to wander. **2.** to carouse.
коловоро́т *m.* drill brace.
коло́да[1] *f.* (*wood*) log.
коло́да[2] *f.* (*cards*) deck, pack.
коло́дезный *adj.* (*attrib.*) well.
коло́дец FILL *m.* well.
коло́дка *f.* **1.** shoetree. **2.** shoe last. **3.** shoe (*for a brake*).
коло́к FILL *m.* peg (*of mus. instrument*).
ко́локол *m.* bell.
колоко́льный *adj.* of bells.
колоко́льня *f.* belfry.
колоко́льчик *m.* small bell.
Коло́мбо *m.* Colombo.
Коло́мна *f.* Kolomna.
колониали́зм *m.* colonialism.
колониа́льный *adj.* colonial.
колониза́тор *m.* colonialist; colonizer.
колониза́ция *f.* colonization.
колонизи́ровать *also* колонизова́ть OVA *impf.* and *pf.* to colonize.
колони́ст *m. f.* —ка colonist; settler.
коло́ния *f.* colony.
коло́нка *f.* **1.** *dim. of* коло́нна. **2.** hot-water heater. **3.** column (*of print; figures*). — бензи́новая коло́нка *f.* gas pump.
коло́нна *f.* column.
колонна́да *f.* colonnade.
коло́нный *adj.* columned
колонти́тул *m.* running head.
Колора́до *m.* Colorado.
колорату́ра *f.* coloratura.
колорату́рный *adj.* coloratura.
колори́т *m.* coloring; color.
колори́тный *adj.* colorful.
ко́лос *m.* ear (*of corn*).

колосовы́е *pl.* cereals.
коло́сс *m.* colossus.
колосса́льный *adj.* colossal; tremendous.
колоти́ть *impf. pres.* колочу́, коло́тишь *pf.* по- to strike; to bang.
колоту́шка *f.* **1.** mallet. **2.** watchman's stick.
коло́ть *impf.* **1.** to prick, to thrust. **2.** to stab. **3.** to chop. **4.** to slaughter.
колпа́к *m.* **1.** pointed cap. **2.** cone-shaped cover. **3.** cowl.
колпачо́к FILL *m. dim. of* колпа́к.
ко́лпица *f.* (*bird*) spoonbill.
Колу́мб *m.* (Christopher) Columbus.
Колу́мбия *f.* Colombia.
Колу́мбус *m.* Columbus.
колу́н *m.* heavy axe.
колхо́з *m.* (*abbr. of* коллекти́вное хозя́йство *neut.*) collective farm.
колхо́зник *m. f.* колхо́зница collective farmer.
колча́н *m.* quiver.
колчеда́н *m.* pyrites.
колчено́гий *adj.* with one leg shorter than the other.
колыбе́ль *f.* cradle.
колыбе́льная пе́сня *f.* lullaby.
Колыма́ *f.* (*river*) Kolyma.
колыма́га *f.* (*colloq.*) jalopy, heap, clunker, wreck.
колыха́ние *neut.* swaying.
колыха́ть *impf. pf.* колыхну́ть to sway.
ко́лышек FILL *m.* peg.
кольдкре́м *m.* cold cream.
колье́ *neut. indecl.* necklace.
кольра́би *f.* kohlrabi.
Ко́льский полуо́стров *m.* Kola Peninsula.
кольцева́я доро́га *f.* beltway.
кольцево́й *adj.* **1.** circular. **2.** (*attrib.*) ring.
кольцо́ *neut.* ring.
ко́льчатый *adj.* made of rings; ring-shaped.
кольчу́га *f.* mail; chain mail.
колю́чая про́волока *f.* barbed wire.
колю́чий *adj.* prickly, thorny.
колю́чка *f.* thorn; barb.
ко́люшка *f.* stickleback.
ко́лющий *adj.* stabbing.
коля́дка *f.* Christmas carol.
коля́ска *f.* carriage.
ком[1] *m.* lump; ball; clod.
ком[2] *pron. prep. of* кто.
ко́ма *f.* coma.
кома́нда *f.* **1.** command. **2.** (*athl.*) team.
команди́р *m.* commander.
командирова́ть OVA *impf.* and *pf.* to send on a business trip.
командиро́вка *f.* **1.** assignment; mission. **2.** business trip.
командиро́вочный *adj.* related to a business trip. — командиро́вочные *pl.* travel allowance.
кома́ндный *adj.* (*attrib.*) **1.** command. **2.** team.
кома́ндование *neut.* command; headquarters.
кома́ндовать OVA *impf. pf.* с- to order, to command; to be in command.
кома́ндующий DAA *m.* commander.
кома́р *m.* mosquito; gnat.
Кома́рно *neut.* Komarno.
кома́то́зный *adj.* comatose.

комбайн *m.* **1.** (*harvesting machine*) combine. **2.** food processor.

комбинат *m.* **1.** combine. **2.** center (*e.g. service center*).

комбинация *f.* combination.

комбинезон *m.* overalls.

комбинировать OVA *impf. pf.* **с-** to combine.

комедийный *adj.* (*attrib.*) comedy.

комедия *f.* comedy.

комендант *m.* **1.** commandant. **2.** building superintendent.

комендантский час *m.* curfew.

комендатура *f.* commandant's headquarters.

комета *f.* comet.

комизм *m.* comedy; humor.

комик *m.* comedian.

комикс *m. usu. pl.* comic book; cartoons.

комиссар *f.* commissar.

комиссионные DAA *pl.* commission; fee.

комиссионный *adj.* (*attrib.*) commission.

комиссия *f.* commission; committee.

комитет *m.* committee.

комический *also* **комичный** *adj.* comic(al).

комкать *impf. pf.* **с-** **1.** to crumple. **2.** (*colloq.*) to make a mess of.

комковатый *adj.* uneven; bumpy.

комментарий *m.* commentary.

комментатор *m.* commentator.

комментировать OVA *impf. and pf.* **1.** to annotate. **2.** to comment on.

коммерсант *m.* merchant.

коммерция *f.* commerce.

коммерческий *adj.* commercial.

коммивояжёр *m.* traveling salesman.

коммуна *f.* commune.

коммуналка *f.* (*colloq.*) communal apartment.

коммунальный *adj.* **1.** municipal; public. **2.** communal.

коммунизм *m.* communism.

коммуникабельный *adj.* communicative; easy to talk to.

коммуникационный *adj.* of communication.

коммуникация *f.* communications.

коммунист *m. f.* **—ка** communist. **—ический** *adj.* communist.

коммутатор *m.* switchboard.

коммюнике *neut.* communique.

комната *f.* room.

комнатный *adj.* room.

комод *m.* chest of drawers.

комок FILL *m.* lump; ball.

комолый *adj.* hornless.

компактный *adj.* compact; solid.

компактный диск *m.* compact disc (*abbr.* C.D.).

компанейский *adj.* (*colloq.*) outgoing; sociable.

компания *f.* company.

компаньон *m.* (male) companion.

компаньонка *f.* (female) companion.

компартия *f.* (*abbr. of* **коммунистическая партия** *f.*) Communist Party.

компас *m.* compass. **—ный** *adj.* (*attrib.*) compass.

компендиум *m.* compendium.

компенсационный *adj.* compensatory.

компенсация *f.* compensation.

компенсировать OVA *impf. and pf.* to compensate.

компетентный *adj.* **1.** competent; qualified. **2.** having jurisdiction.

компетенция *f.* jurisdiction.

компилировать OVA *impf. pf.* **с-** to compile.

компиляция *f.* compilation.

комплекс 1. *m.* complex. **2.** system. **3.** series.
— **комплекс неполноценности** *m.* inferiority complex.

комплект *m.* **1.** complete set. **2.** full staff.

комплектный *adj.* (*set*) complete.

комплектовать OVA *impf. pf.* **с-, у-** to complete a set.

комплекция *f.* build; frame; figure.

комплимент *m.* compliment.

композитор *m.* composer.

композиция *f.* composition.

компонент *m.* component.

компоновать OVA *impf. pf.* **с-** **1.** to put together. **2.** to arrange; to group.

компоновка *f.* layout; arrangement.

компост *m.* compost.

компостер *m.* punch (*for punching tickets or cards*).

компостировать OVA *impf. pf.* **про-** to punch a ticket.

компот *m.* stewed fruit; compote.

компресс *m.* compress.

компрессор *m.* compressor.

компрометировать OVA *impf. pf.* **с-** to compromise.

компромисс *m.* compromise.

компромиссный *adj.* (*attrib.*) compromise.

Компьень *m.* Compiègne.

компьютер *m.* computer.

компьютеризация *n.* computerization.

комсомол *m.* (*abbr. of* **Коммунистический Союз Молодёжи** *m.*) Komsomol. **—ец** *m. f.* **—ка** a member of the Komsomol.

комсомольский *adj.* (*attrib.*) Komsomol.

кому *pron. dat. of* **кто.**

комфорт *m.* comfort. — **с полным комфортом** with all amenities.

комфортабельный *adj.* comfortable.

конвейер *m.* conveyor.

конвейерный *adj.* conveyer.

конвенция *f.* convention.

конверт *m.* envelope.

конвертер *m.* converter.

конвертировать OVA *impf. and pf.* to convert.

конвертируемый *adj.* convertible. **—конвертируемая валюта** *f.* convertible currency.

конвой *m.* escort. — *adj.* armed guard.

конвоировать OVA *impf.* (*mil.*) to escort.

конвой *m.* armed escort. **—под конвоем** *adv.* under guard.

конвойный *adj.* (*attrib.*) escort.

конвульсивный *adj.* convulsive.

конвульсия *f.* convulsion.

конгломерат *m.* conglomerate; conglomeration.

Конго *m.* Congo.

конгресс *m.* congress.

конгрессмен *m.* congressman.

конгруэнтный *adj.* (*math.*) congruent.

конгруэнция *f.* (*math.*) congruence.

конденсатор *m.* (*chem., phys.*) condenser.

конденсационный *adj.* obtained by condensation.

конденсация *f.* (*chem., phys.*) condensation.

конденси́ровать OVA *impf.* and *pf.* to condense.

конди́тер *m.* pastry chef.

конди́терская *f.* pastry shop; confectionery shop.

конди́терский *adj.* (*attrib.*) pastry.

кондиционе́р *m.* air conditioner.

кондициони́рование *neut.* conditioning.

кондициони́ровать OVA *impf.* and *pf.* to condition.

кондоми́ниум *m.* condominium.

Кондопо́га *f.* Kondopoga.

ко́ндор *m.* condor.

кондотье́р *m.* soldier of fortune.

конду́ктор *m.* conductor (*on a train* or *bus*).

конево́дство *neut.* horse breeding.

конёк[1] FILL *m.* *usu.* *pl.* коньки́ skate.

конёк[2] FILL *m.* 1. *dim.* of конь. 2. one's chief interest; hobby horse.

коне́ц FILL *m.* end. — в конце́ концо́в *adv.* in the end.

коне́чно *adv.* of course.

коне́чность *f.* extremity (*of body*).

коне́чный *adj.* final; terminal.

кони́на *f.* horsemeat.

кони́ческий *adj.* conical.

ко́нка *f.* horsecar.

конкла́в *m.* (*relig.*) conclave.

Ко́нкорд *m.* Concord.

конкорда́т *m.* concordat.

конкретизи́ровать *impf.* and *pf.* to make specific.

конкре́тный *adj.* concrete.

конкуре́нт *m.* —ка competitor.

конкури́ровать OVA *impf.* (c *with instr.*) to compete.

ко́нкурс *m.* competition; contest.

Конне́ктику́т *m.* Connecticut.

ко́нник *m.* cavalryman.

ко́нница *f.* cavalry.

коннозаво́дство *neut.* horse breeding.

ко́нный *adj.* (*attrib.*) horse.

конова́л *m.* horse doctor.

ко́новязь *f.* hitching post.

конокра́д *m.* horse thief. —ство *f.* horse stealing.

конопа́тить *impf.* *pf.* за- to caulk.

конопля́ *f.* hemp.

конопля́нка *f.* (*bird*) linnet.

конопля́ный *adj.* (*attrib.*) hemp.

коносаме́нт *m.* bill of lading.

консе́нсус *m.* consensus.

консерва́нт *m.* preservative.

консервати́вный *adj.* conservative.

консервати́зм *m.* conservatism.

консерва́тор *m.* conservative.

консервато́рия *f.* conservatory.

консерва́ция *f.* preservation; temporary closing (of enterprise).

консерви́ровать OVA *impf.* *pf.* за- to preserve.

консе́рвный *adj.* canning.

консе́рвный нож *m.* can opener.

консе́рвы *pl.* canned food.

конси́лиум *m.* consultation (*between doctors*).

консисте́нция *f.* consistency; texture.

ко́нский *adj.* (*attrib.*) horse.

консолида́ция *f.* consolidation.

консо́ль *f.* 1. pedestal; stand. 2. console (*bracket*).

консо́льный мост *m.* cantilever bridge.

консона́нс *m.* consonance.

консо́рциум *m.* consortium.

конспе́кт *m.* synopsis; summary; abstract.

конспекти́вный *adj.* brief; concise.

конспекти́ровать OVA *impf.* *pf.* про-, за- to make an abstract of.

конспирати́вный *adj.* secret.

конспира́тор *m.* conspirator; schemer.

конспира́ция *f.* conspiracy; secrecy.

конста́нта *f.* (*phys.*, *math.*) constant.

Константи́новка *f.* Konstantinovka.

Конста́нца *f.* Constanţa.

констата́ция *f.* certification; establishment.

констати́ровать OVA *impf.* and *pf.* 1. to ascertain. 2. to state.

консте́бль *m.* constable.

конституцио́нный *adj.* constitutional.

конститу́ция *f.* constitution.

констру́и́ровать OVA *impf.* *pf.* с- 1. to construct. 2. to design. 3. to form.

конструкти́вный *adj.* 1. structural. 2. constructive.

констру́ктор *m.* designer.

констру́кторский *adj.* (*attrib.*) design.

констру́кция *f.* construction; structure; design.

ко́нсул *m.* consul. —ьство *neut.* consulate.

консульта́нт *m.* consultant.

консультати́вный *adj.* consultative.

консульта́ция *f.* consultation.

консульти́ровать OVA *impf.* *pf.* про- to advise; (c *with instr.*) to consult (with).

конта́кт *m.* contact.

конта́ктный *adj.* (*attrib.*) contact.

конте́йнер *m.* container.

конте́йнерное су́дно *neut.* container ship.

конте́йнерный *adj.* (*attrib.*) container.

конте́кст *m.* context.

континге́нт *m.* 1. contingent. 2. quota.

контине́нт *m.* continent; mainland.

континента́льный *adj.* continental.

конто́ра *f.* office.

конто́рка *f.* high old-fashioned desk.

конто́рский *adj.* (*attrib.*) office.

ко́нтра *m.* and *f.* (*decl.* *f.*) rebel; counterrevolutionary.

контраба́нда *f.* smuggling; smuggled goods.

контрабанди́ст *m.* smuggler.

контраба́ндный *adj.* contraband.

контраба́с *m.* bass viol; contrabass; double bass.

контраге́нт *m.* contractor.

контр-адмира́л *m.* rear admiral.

контра́кт *m.* contract; agreement.

контрактова́ть OVA *impf.* *pf.* за- to contract.

контра́льто *neut.* *indecl.* contralto (*voice*).

контра́льтовый *adj.* contralto.

контрама́рка *f.* complimentary ticket.

контрапу́нкт *m.* (*mus.*) counterpoint.

контрапункти́ческий *adj.* contrapuntal.

контра́ст *m.* contrasting.

контрасти́ровать OVA *impf.* to contrast.

контра́стный *adj.* contrasting.

контрата́ка *f.* counterattack.

контратакова́ть OVA *impf.* and *pf.* to counterattack.

контрафаго́т *m.* contrabassoon; double bassoon.

контрибу́ция *f.* contribution; indemnity.

контрме́ра *f.* countermeasure.

контрнаступле́ние *neut.* counteroffensive.

контролёр *m.* controller; ticket collector (*on bus, etc.*).

контроли́ровать OVA *impf. pf.* про- to control.

контро́ль *m.* **1.** control. **2.** supervision; inspection.

контро́льный *adj.* (*attrib.*) control; check.

контрпредложе́ние *neut.* counteroffer.

контрразве́дка *f.* counterintelligence.

контрразве́дчик *m.* counterintelligence agent.

контрреволюционе́р *m.* counterrevolutionary.

контрреволюцио́нный *adj.* counterrevolutionary.

контрреволю́ция *f.* counterrevolution.

контруда́р *m.* counterblow.

контрфо́рс *m.* buttress.

конту́зить *impf.* to contuse.

конту́зия *f.* contusion.

ко́нтур *m.* contour.

ко́нтурный *adj.* (*attrib.*) contour.

конура́ *f.* kennel.

ко́нус *m.* (*geom.*) cone.

конусообра́зный *adj.* cone-shaped.

конфедерати́вный *adj.* confederate.

конфедера́ция *f.* confederation; confederacy.

конферансье́ *m. indecl.* master of ceremonies.

конфере́нц-за́л *m.* conference hall.

конфере́нция *f.* conference.

конфе́та *also* конфе́тка *f.* piece of candy.

конфе́тный *adj.* (*attrib.*) candy.

конфетти́ *neut. indecl.* confetti.

конфигура́ция *f.* configuration.

конфиденциа́льно *adv.* confidentially.

конфиденциа́льный *adj.* confidential.

конфирма́ция *f.* (*relig.*) confirmation.

конфирмова́ть OVA *impf. and pf.* (*relig.*) to confirm.

конфиска́ция *f.* confiscation.

конфискова́ть *impf. and pf.* to confiscate.

конфли́кт *m.* conflict.

конфо́рка *f.* stove burner.

конформи́зм *m.* conformism.

конфронта́ция *f.* confrontation.

конфу́з *m.* embarrassment.

конфу́зить *impf. pf.* с- to disconcert, to confuse.

конфу́зливый *adj.* shy; bashful.

конфу́зный *adj.* (*colloq.*) awkward; embarrassing.

концентра́т *m.* concentrate.

концентрацио́нный ла́герь *m.* concentration camp.

концентра́ция *f.* concentration.

концентри́ровать OVA *impf. pf.* с- to concentrate; to mass. —ся *v.i.* to concentrate (on).

концентри́ческий *adj.* concentric.

конце́пция *f.* conception.

конце́рн *m.* business concern.

конце́рт *m.* concert; recital.

концерта́нт *m. f.* —ка a concert performer.

концерти́но *neut. indecl.* concertina.

концерти́ровать OVA *impf.* to give concerts.

концертме́йстер *m.* concertmaster.

конце́ртный *adj.* (*attrib.*) concert.

концессионе́р *m.* concessionaire.

конце́ссия *f.* (*comm.*) concession.

концла́герь *m.* (*abbr. of* концентрацио́нный ла́герь *m.*) concentration camp.

конча́ть *impf. pf.* ко́нчить **1.** to finish; to end; to complete. **2.** (*with inf.*) to stop, to cease.

ко́нченый *adj.* (*colloq.*) hopeless.

ко́нчик *m.* tip; end.

кончи́на *f.* death, demise.

конъюнктиви́т *m.* conjunctivitis.

конъюнкту́ра *f.* **1.** situation; state of affairs. **2.** state of the market.

конъюнкту́рный *adj.* momentary; of the moment.

конь *m.* **1.** horse, steed. **2.** (*chess*) knight.

коньки́ *pl.* skates.

конькобе́жец FILL *m.* skater.

конькобе́жный *adj.* skating.

конья́к *m.* cognac.

ко́нюх *m.* groom; stable hand.

коню́шня *f.* stable.

коопера́тив *m.* cooperative.

коопера́тивный *adj.* cooperative.

коопера́ция *f.* cooperation.

коопери́ровать OVA *impf. and pf.* to organize into a cooperative. —ся to cooperate; to be organized into a cooperative.

координа́ты *pl.* one's location; whereabouts.

координа́ция *f.* coordination.

координи́ровать OVA *impf. and pf.* to coordinate.

копа́ние *neut.* digging.

копа́тель *m.* (*obs.*) digger.

копа́ть *impf.* **1.** *pf.* копну́ть to dig. **2.** *pf.* вы́- to dig; to dig out; to dig up.

копе́ечка *f. dim. of* копе́йка.

копе́ечный *adj.* worth one kopeck.

копе́йка *f.* kopeck.

Копенга́ген *m.* Copenhagen.

Ко́пер *m.* Koper.

копёр FILL *m.* pile driver.

ко́пи *pl.* mines, pits.

копи́лка *f.* piggy bank.

копи́рка *f.* (*colloq.*) carbon paper.

копирова́льный *adj.* (*attrib.*) copying.

копирова́ние *neut.* copying.

копи́ровать OVA *impf. pf.* с- to copy; to imitate; to mimic.

копиро́вка *f.* copying.

копиро́вщик *m.* (*person*) copier; copyist.

копи́ть *impf. pf.* с- to accumulate, to save; to store up.

ко́пия *f.* copy.

копна́ *f.* **1.** haycock. **2.** shock (of hair).

ко́поть *f.* soot, lampblack.

копоши́ться *impf.* **1.** to swarm around; to swim around. **2.** (*colloq.*) to putter around.

ко́пра *f.* copra.

копте́ть *impf. pres.* копчу́, копти́шь **1.** to smoke; to emit smoke. **2.** (*colloq.*) to vegetate.

копти́лка *f.* wick lamp.

копти́льня *f.* smokehouse.

копти́ть *impf. pres.* копчу́, копти́шь **1.** *pf.* за- to smoke (*ham; fish; glass*). **2.** *pf.* на- (*of a lamp or candle*) to emit smoke.

копчёная ры́ба *f.* smoked fish.

копче́ние *neut.* smoking.

копчёности *pl.* smoked products.

ко́пчик *m.* coccyx.

копы́тный *adj.* (*attrib.*) hoof.

копы́то *neut.* hoof.

копьё *neut.* javelin, spear.

кора́ *f.* **1.** bark. **2.** crust.

корабе́льный *adj.* (*attrib.*) ship; ship's.

кораблевождéние *neut.* navigation.
кораблекрушéние *neut.* shipwreck.
кораблестроéние *neut.* shipbuilding.
кораблестройтель *m.* shipbuilder.
корáблик *m. dim. of* **корáбль**.
корáбль *m.* ship.
корáлл *m.* coral.
корáлловый *adj.* coral.
Корáн *m.* the Koran.
корвéт *m.* corvette.
кордебалéт *m.* corps de ballet.
Кордóва *f.* Córdoba.
кордóн *m.* cordon.
корéец FILL *m. f.* **корéйнка** Korean.
корéйка *f.* brisket (*pork* or *veal*).
корéйский *adj.* Korean.
коренáстый *adj.* stocky; heavyset.
коренннк *m.* shaft horse; wheel horse.
коренннóй *adj.* **1.** radical. **2.** native, indigenous.
кóрень *m.* root.
корéнья *pl.* root vegetables.
кóреш *m.* (*colloq.*) pal; buddy.
корешóк FILL *m.* **1.** *dim. of* **кóрень**. **2.** counterfoil; stub. **3.** spine (*of a book*).
Корéя *f.* Korea.
кóржик *m.* cookie.
корзйна *f.* basket.
корзйнка *f. dim. of* **корзйна**.
кориáндр *m.* coriander.
кориáндровый *adj.* (*attrib.*) coriander.
коридóр *m.* corridor.
коридóрный *adj.* (*attrib.*) corridor; hall.
корйнка *f.* currants.
Корйнф *m.* Corinth.
корифéй *m.* luminary; leading light.
корйца *f.* cinnamon.
корйчневый *adj.* brown.
кóрка *f.* crust; rind.
корм *m.* fodder.
кормá *f.* (*naut.*) stern.
кормёжка *f.* (*colloq.*) feeding.
кормйлец FILL *m.* **1.** breadwinner. **2.** benefactor.
кормйлица *f.* **1.** wet nurse. **2.** female breadwinner.
кормйло *neut.* (*arch.*) helm.
кормйть *impf. pf.* **на-**, **по-** to feed; to suckle.
кормлéние *neut.* feeding; suckling.
кормовóй¹ *adj.* (*attrib.*) (*naut.*) stern.
кормовóй² *adj.* (*attrib.*) fodder; forage.
кормýшка *f.* feeding trough.
кóрмчий *m.* helmsman.
корневйще *neut.* rhizome.
корневóй *adj.* (*attrib.*) root.
корнéт *m.* cornet.
корнишóн *m.* gherkin.
кóроб *m.* basket.
коробéйник *m.* peddler.
корóбить *impf. pf.* **по-**, **с-** **1.** to warp. **2.** to grate on; to irk. **—ся** *v.i.* to warp.
корóбка *f.* box.
корóбление *neut.* warping.
корóбок FILL *m.* small box.
корóбочка *f.* **1.** small box. **2.** (*bot.*) boll.
корóва *f.* cow.
корóвий *adj.* cow; cow's.

корóвка *f. dim. of* **корóва**. — **бóжья корóвка** *f.* ladybug.
корóвник *m.* cowshed.
королéва *f.* queen.
королéвский *adj.* royal.
королéвство *neut.* kingdom.
королёк *m.* **1.** (*bird*) kinglet. **2.** blood orange.
корóль *m.* king.
коромьісло *neut.* **1.** yoke for carrying buckets. **2.** (*tech.*) rocker arm; rocking shaft.
корóна *f.* crown.
коронáция *f.* coronation.
корóнка *f.* (*dental*) crown.
корóнный *adj.* (*attrib.*) crown.
короновáть OVA *impf. and pf.* to crown.
корóста *f.* sores; pustules.
коростéль *m.* (*bird*) corn crake.
корóтенький *adj.* (*colloq.*) short.
корóткий *adj.* short.
кóротко *adv.* **1.** short. **2.** briefly.
коротковóлновый *adj.* short-wave.
корóткость *f.* shortness.
коротьíш *m. f.* **—ка** (*colloq.*) runt; shrimp.
корóче *adj. comp. of* **корóткий**.
корпоратйвный *adj.* corporate, corporative.
корпорáция *f.* corporation.
кóрпус *m.* torso; trunk; body; corps; large building (*part of complex*); (*athl.*) length.
корректйв *m.* correction; change.
корректйвный *adj.* remedial.
корректирóвщик *m.* (*mil.*) spotter.
коррéктность *m.* proper behavior.
коррéктный *adj.* correct; proper (*person* or *behavior*).
коррéктор *m.* proofreader.
корректýра *f.* proofs; proof sheet.
корреспондéнт *m. f.* **—ка** correspondent.
корреспондéнтский *adj.* correspondent's.
корреспондéнция *f.* correspondence.
коррóзия *f.* corrosion.
коррýпция *f.* corruption.
корсáж *m.* bodice; corsage.
корсáр *m.* corsair.
корсéт *m.* corset.
корт *m.* tennis court.
кортизóн *m.* cortisone.
кóртик *m.* dagger.
кóрточки *pl.*: **сидéть на кóрточках** *impf.* to squat.
корýнд *m.* corundum.
Корф *m.* Korf.
корчевáть *impf.* to uproot.
кóрчи *pl.* (*colloq.*) convulsions; cramps.
кóрчить *impf. pf.* **с-** **1.** *impers.* to writhe. **2.** (*with* **из себя** *and acc.*) to pose as.
корчмá *f.* tavern; inn.
кóршун *m.* (*bird*) kite.
корьíстный *adj.* mercenary.
корыстолюбйвый *adj.* mercenary.
корыстолюбие *neut.* self-interest.
корьíсть *f.* self-interest.
корьíто *neut.* trough.
корь *f.* measles.
корюшка *f.* (*fish*) smelt.
корявый *adj.* **1.** twisted; gnarled. **2.** clumsy. **3.** pockmarked.
косá¹ *f.* scythe.

коса́² *f.* plait.
коса́рь¹ *m.* person who cuts hay *or* mows grass.
коса́рь² *m.* chopping knife.
коса́тка *f.* killer whale.
ко́свенно *adv.* obliquely; indirectly.
ко́свенный *adj.* indirect; oblique.
косе́ц FILL *m.* one who mows grass, cuts hay, etc.
коси́лка *f.* mower.
ко́синус *m.* (*math.*) cosine.
коси́ть¹ *impf. pf.* с- to mow.
коси́ть² *impf. pf.* по-, с- to twist; to squint; to distort.
коси́чка *f.* pigtail.
косма́тый *adj.* shaggy.
косме́тика *f.* cosmetics; make-up.
космети́ческий *adj.* cosmetic.
космети́чка *f.* (*colloq.*) make-up bag.
косми́ческий *adj.* (*attrib.*) space; cosmic.
космого́ния *f.* cosmogony.
космодро́м *m.* space center.
космоло́гия *f.* cosmology.
космона́вт *m. f.* —ка cosmonaut; astronaut.
космополи́т *m. f.* —ка cosmopolitan.
космополити́зм *m. f.* —ка cosmopolitanism.
космополити́ческий *adj.* cosmopolitan.
ко́смос *m.* (outer) space; the cosmos.
ко́смы *pl.* (*colloq.*) disheveled locks of hair.
ко́сность *f.* stagnation, stagnancy; inertness.
косноязы́чный *adj.* tongue-tied.
косну́ться *pf. of* каса́ться.
ко́сный *adj.* stagnant; inert.
ко́со *adv.* obliquely; aslant.
кособо́кий *adj.* lopsided; crooked.
косоворо́тка *f.* man's blouse (*with the collar fastening at the side*).
косогла́зие *neut.* being cross-eyed; strabismus.
косогла́зый *adj.* cross-eyed.
косого́р *m.* 1. slope. 2. hillside.
косо́й *adj.* 1. slanting, oblique. 2. squinting. 3. (*of person*) cross-eyed.
косола́пый *adj.* pigeon-toed.
Ко́ста-Ри́ка *f.* Costa Rica.
костёл *m.* (*Roman Catholic*) church.
костене́ть *impf. pf.* о- 1. to become numb. 2. (*of a corpse*) to stiffen; to ossify.
костёр *m.* bonfire.
кости́стый *adj.* bony; full of bones.
костля́вый *adj.* bony; skinny.
ко́стный *adj.* (*attrib.*) bone.
костое́да *f.* (*med.*) caries; bone decay.
ко́сточка *f.* 1. *dim. of* кость. 2. pit *or* stone (*of fruit*). 3. bone (*of corset*).
Кострома́ *f.* Kostroma.
косты́ль *m.* crutch.
кость *f.* bone. — игра́льные ко́сти dice. — слоно́вая кость ivory.
костю́м *m.* 1. costume. 2. dress, suit.
костюме́р *m. f.* —ша costume designer.
костюмиро́ванный *adj.* costumed.
костю́мный *adj.* of a suit.
костя́к *m.* skeleton.
костяно́й *adj.* (made of) bone.
кости́шка *f.* (*colloq.*) button; bead.
косу́ля *f.* roe deer.
косы́нка *f.* kerchief; scarf.

косьба́ *f.* mowing.
коси́к¹ *m.* doorpost.
коси́к² *m.* flock (of birds); school (of fish).
кот *m.* tomcat.
кота́нгенс *m.* (*math.*) contangent.
котёл *m.* boiler.
котело́к FILL *m.* kettle, pot.
коте́льная DAA *f.* boiler room.
котёнок FILL *m.* kitten.
ко́тик¹ *m. dim. of* кот.
ко́тик² *m.* 1. seal. 2. sealskin.
котильо́н *m.* cotillion.
коти́ровать OVA *impf.* and *pf.* (*finance*) to quote.
котиро́вка *f.* (*finance*) quotation.
коти́ться *impf. pf.* о- to have kittens.
котле́та *f.* cutlet; chop.
котлова́н *m.* foundation pit; excavation.
котлови́на *f.* hollow; basin.
кото́мка *f.* knapsack.
кото́рый *pron.* which.
Ко́ттбус *m.* Cottbus.
котте́дж *m.* cottage.
ко́фе *m. indecl.* coffee.
кофева́рка *f.* coffee maker.
кофеи́н *m.* caffeine.
кофе́йник *m.* coffeepot.
кофе́йница *f.* coffee mill.
кофе́йный *adj.* (*attrib.*) coffee.
ко́фта *f.* woman's jacket.
ко́фточка *f.* blouse.
коча́н *m.* head of cabbage.
Ко́чани *pl.* Kočani.
кочева́ть *impf.* to wander; to lead a nomadic life.
коче́вник *m. f.* коче́вница nomad.
кочево́й *adj.* nomad's; nomadic.
коче́вье *neut.* nomads' camp.
кочега́р *m.* stoker; fireman.
кочене́ть *impf. pf.* о- *or* за- to become numb.
кочерга́ *f.* poker.
кочеры́жка *f.* cabbage stump.
ко́чка *f.* hummock.
коша́чий *adj.* feline.
кошелёк *m.* purse; wallet.
коше́лка *f.* (*colloq.*) basket.
кошени́ль *f.* cochineal.
коше́рный *adj.* kosher.
ко́шечка *f.* pussy cat.
Ко́шице *pl.* Košice.
ко́шка *f.* cat.
кошма́р *m.* nightmare.
кошма́рный *adj.* nightmarish.
Коще́й *m.* (*folklore*) a bony old man who knows the secrets of eternal life.
кощу́нственный *adj.* sacrilegious; blasphemous.
кощу́нство *neut.* sacrilege; blasphemy.
кощу́нствовать OVA *impf.* to blaspheme.
коэффицие́нт *m.* coefficient; ratio.
краб *m.* crab.
кра́бовый *adj.* (*attrib.*) crab.
кра́ги *pl.* leggings.
кра́деное DAA *neut.* stolen goods.
кра́деный *adj.* stolen.
краеве́дение *neut.* study of history and lore of a region.
краево́й *adj.* regional.
краеуго́льный ка́мень *m.* cornerstone.

кра́ешек *m.* (*colloq.*) edge.
кра́жа *f.* theft.
край *m.* **1.** border, brim, edge. **2.** land, country.
кра́йне *adv.* extremely.
кра́йний *adj.* **1.** extreme. **2.** last. **3.** (*of a surprise*) complete; utter. — по кра́йней ме́ре at least.
кра́йность *f.* extreme; extreme situation.
Кра́йстчерч *m.* Christchurch.
Кра́ков *m.* Kraków (*also: Cracow*).
кран¹ *m.* faucet. — водоразбо́рный кран hydrant.
кран² *m.* crane.
крап *m.* specks; spots.
кра́пать *impf. pres.* кра́плет *or* кра́пает (*of rain*) to drizzle.
крапи́ва *f.* nettle.
крапи́вник *m.* wren.
крапи́вница *f.* hives; nettle rash.
кра́пинка *f.* spot; speck; dot.
кра́пчатый *adj.* spotted.
краса́ *f.* beauty.
краса́вец FILL *m.* handsome man.
краса́вица *f.* beautiful woman, beauty.
краси́во *adv.* beautifully.
краси́вый *adj.* beautiful.
краси́льный DAA *m.* dyer.
краси́льня *f.* dye works.
краси́льщик *m. f.* краси́льщица dyer.
краси́тель *m.* dye.
кра́сить *impf. pf.* по- to color; to dye; to paint.
кра́ска *f.* color; paint; dye.
кра́сная строка́ *f.* new paragraph.
красне́ть *impf. pf.* по- to flush, to redden; to blush.
краснобай *m.* windbag.
краснова́тый *adj.* reddish.
Красново́дск *m.* Krasnovodsk.
красногварде́ец FILL *m.* Red Guard.
красногварде́йский *adj.* (*attrib.*) Red Guard.
Краснода́р *m.* Krasnodar.
кра́сное де́рево *neut.* mahogany.
Краснозаво́дск *m.* Krasnozavodsk.
краснознамённый *adj.* decorated with the Order of the Red Banner (*USSR*).
красноко́жий *adj.* red-skinned.
краснолесье *neut.* pine forest.
красноли́цый *adj.* ruddy-faced.
красноречи́вый *adj.* eloquent.
красноре́чие *neut.* eloquence.
краснота́ *f.* redness; ruddiness.
краснота́л *m.* red willow.
Красноя́рск *m.* Krasnoyarsk.
красну́ха *f.* German measles.
кра́сный *adj.* red.
красота́ *f.* beauty.
красо́тка *f.* (*colloq.*) pretty girl.
кра́сочный *adj.* **1.** colorful. **2.** (*attrib.*) paint.
красть *impf. pf.* у- to steal.
кра́сящий *adj.* (*attrib.*) dye; dyeing.
крат *m.*: во́ сто крат *adv.* a hundredfold.
кра́тер *m.* crater.
кра́ткий *adj.* brief; short.
кра́тко *adv.* briefly.
кратковре́менный *adj.* of short duration; transitory.
краткосро́чный *adj.* short-term.
кра́ткость *f.* brevity.

кра́тное DAA *neut.* (*math.*) multiple.
кратча́йший *adj.* shortest.
крах *m.* crash, bankruptcy; failure.
крахма́л *m.* starch.
крахма́лить *impf. pf.* на- to starch.
крахма́льный *adj.* starched.
кра́чка *f.* tern.
кра́ше *adj.* (*colloq.*) more beautiful.
кра́шение *neut.* dyeing.
кра́шеный *adj.* painted, dyed, colored.
краю́ха *f.* (*colloq.*) hunk of bread.
креве́тка *f.* shrimp.
креди́т *m.* credit. —оспосо́бный *adj.* solvent.
креди́тная ка́рточка *f.* credit card.
креди́тный *adj.* (*attrib.*) credit.
кредитова́ть *impf. and pf.* to extend credit.
кредито́р *m.* creditor.
кре́до *neut. indecl.* credo.
кре́йсер *m.* cruiser.
кре́йсерский *adj.* (*attrib.*) cruiser; cruising.
крейси́ровать *impf.* to cruise.
крем *m.* cream.
кремато́рий *m.* crematorium.
крема́ция *f.* cremation.
Кре́менец *m.* Kremenets.
Кременчу́г *m.* Kremenchuk.
креме́нь *m.* flint.
креми́ровать OVA *impf. and pf.* to cremate.
кремлёвский *adj.* (*attrib.*) Kremlin; of the Kremlin.
Кремль *m.* **1.** the Kremlin. **2.** (*l.c.*) a fortress in old Russian cities.
кремнёвый *adj.* (*attrib.*) flint; made of flint.
кремнезём *m.* silica.
кре́мниевый *adj.* silicic.
кре́мний *adj.* silicon.
кремни́стый *adj.* siliceous.
кре́мовый *adj.* (*attrib.*) cream.
крен *m.* (*naut.*) list, heel.
кре́ндель *m.* pretzel.
крени́ть *impf. pf.* на- to tip; to tilt.
креозо́т *m.* creosote.
креп *m.* crêpe.
крепи́тельный *adj.* invigorating; tonic.
крепи́ть *impf.* **1.** to strengthen; to reinforce. **2.** to constipate.
кре́пкий *adj.* **1.** strong; firm, sturdy. **2.** robust.
кре́пко *adv.* firmly; tightly; sturdily.
крепле́ние *neut.* strengthening; fastening.
кре́пнуть *impf. pf.* о-, *past* креп *or* кре́пнул to grow stronger.
крепостни́чество *neut.* serfdom.
крепостно́й *adj.* **1.** (*attrib.*) serf. **2.** of a fortress.
кре́пость *f.* **1.** fortress. **2.** strength.
кре́пче *adj. comp. of* кре́пкий.
крепы́ш *m.* (*colloq.*) robust man.
кре́сло *neut.* armchair.
кресс *m.* cress.
крест *m.* cross.
кресте́ц FILL *m.* **1.** (*anat.*) sacrum. **2.** rump (*of an animal*).
кре́стик *m. dim. of* крест.
крести́льный *adj.* baptismal.
крести́ны *pl.* christening.
крести́ть *impf.* **1.** *pf.* пере- to make the sign of the cross over. **2.** *pf.* о- to baptize, to christen.

крест-на́крест *adv.* crisscross; crosswise.

кре́стная *f.* godmother.

кре́стник *m.* godson.

кре́стница *f.* goddaughter.

кре́стное знаме́ние *neut.* the sign of the cross.

кре́стный оте́ц > *m.* godfather.

кре́стная мать *f.* godmother.

кре́стный сын *m.* godson.

кре́стная дочь *f.* goddaughter.

крестови́на *f.* crosspiece.

кресто́вый похо́д *m.* crusade.

крестоно́сец FILL *m.* crusader.

крестообра́зно *adv.* crosswise.

крестообра́зный *adj.* cruciform.

крестья́нин *m. f.* крестья́нка peasant.

крестья́нский *adj.* (*attrib.*) peasant.

крестья́нство *neut.* peasantry.

кретини́зм *m.* cretinism.

крето́н *m.* cretonne.

крето́нный *also* крето́новый *adj.* cretonne.

кре́чет *m.* gyrfalcon.

креще́ндо *adv.* crescendo.

креще́ние *neut.* **1.** christening; baptism. **2.** Epiphany.

креще́ный *adj.* baptized.

крива́я *f.* (*math.*) curve.

кривизна́ *f.* **1.** crookedness. **2.** curvature.

кривля́ка *m.* and *f.* (*decl. f.*) affected person; oaf.

кри́во *adv.* askew; awry.

кривобо́кий *adj.* lopsided.

криво́й *adj.* **1.** crooked. **2.** curved.

Криво́й Рог *m.* Kryvyy Rih (*Russian: Krivoy Rog*).

криволине́йный *adj.* curvilinear.

кривоно́гий *adj.* bandy-legged; bowlegged.

кривото́лки *pl.* false rumors.

кривоши́п *m.* (*mech.*) crank.

кри́зис *m.* (*attrib.*) crisis.

кри́зисный *adj.* crisis.

крик *m.* shout, cry.

крике́т *m.* (*sports*) cricket.

крикли́вый *adj.* **1.** loud; noisy. **2.** loud; flashy.

крику́н *m. f.* —ья (*colloq.*) noisy person.

кримина́л *m.* (*colloq.*) a crime.

криминали́ст *m.* criminal lawyer.

криминали́стика *f.* criminal law.

криминалисти́ческий *adj.* related to criminal law.

кримина́льный *adj.* criminal.

кримино́лог *m.* criminologist.

криминоло́гия *f.* criminology.

кри́нка *f.* milk jar.

кринолин *m.* hoop skirt.

криптогра́мма *f.* cryptogram.

криптографи́ческий *adj.* cryptographic.

криптогра́фия *f.* cryptography.

крипто́н *m.* krypton.

криста́лл *m.* crystal.

кристаллиза́ция *f.* crystallization.

кристаллизова́ть OVA *impf.* and *pf.* to crystallize.

кристаллизова́ться OVA *impf.* and *pf.* to crystallize.

кристалли́ческий *adj.* crystalline.

криста́льный *adj.* crystal-clear.

Крит *m.* (*island*) Crete.

крите́рий *m.* criterion.

кри́тик *m.* critic.

кри́тика *f.* criticism.

критика́н *m. f.* —ка faultfinder.

критика́нство *neut.* faultfinding.

критикова́ть OVA *impf.* to criticize.

крити́ческий *adj.* critical.

крича́ть *impf. pf.* кри́кнуть to shout, to yell.

крича́щий *adj.* loud; flashy.

кров *m.* roof; shelter; house.

крова́вый *adj.* bloody; murderous.

крова́тка *f. dim. of* крова́ть.

крова́ть *f.* bed.

кро́вельный *adj.* (*attrib.*) roofing.

кро́вельщик *m.* roofer.

кровено́сный *adj.* of the circulatory system.

крови́нка *f.* (*colloq.*) drop of blood.

кро́вля *f.* roof; roofing.

кро́вно *adv.* **1.** by blood. **2.** grievously.

кро́вный *adj.* (*attrib.*) blood.

кровожа́дный *adj.* bloodthirsty.

кровоизлия́ние *neut.* hemorrhage.

кровообраще́ние *neut.* blood circulation.

кровооостана́вливающий *adj.* styptic; hemostatic.

кровопи́йца *m.* and *f.* (*decl. f.*) bloodsucker.

кровоподтёк *m.* bruise.

кровопроли́тие *neut.* bloodshed.

кровопуска́ние *neut.* bloodletting.

кровосмеше́ние *neut.* incest.

кровосо́с *m.* vampire bat.

кровотече́ние *neut.* bleeding.

кровоточи́вость *f.* bleeding.

кровоточи́ть *impf.* to bleed.

кровь *f.* blood.

кровяно́й *adj.* (*attrib.*) blood.

кровяно́й ша́рик *m.* blood corpuscle.

кро́ить *impf. pf.* с- to cut, to cut out.

кро́йка *f.* cutting.

кроке́т *m.* croquet.

крокоди́л *m.* crocodile.

крокоди́ловый *adj.* (*attrib.*) crocodile; made of crocodile skin.

крокоди́ловы слёзы *pl.* crocodile tears.

кро́кус *m.* crocus.

кро́лик *m.* rabbit.

кро́личий *adj.* (*attrib.*) rabbit.

кроль *m.* (*swim.*) crawl.

кро́ме *prep.* (*with gen.*) except; besides, in addition to.

кроме́шный *adj.*: ад кроме́шный *m.* sheer hell.

кро́мка *f.* selvage.

кронци́ркуль *m.* calipers.

кро́ншнеп *m.* (*bird*) curlew.

Кроншта́дт *m.* Kronshtadt.

кронштейн *m.* (*tech.*) corbel; holder; bracket.

кропи́ть *impf.* **1.** (*of rain*) to drizzle; to fall lightly. **2.** to sprinkle.

кропотли́вый *adj.* laborious; painstaking.

кросс *m.* cross-country race.

кроссво́рд *m.* crossword puzzle.

кроссо́вка *f. usu. pl.* sneaker.

крот *m.* mole; moleskin.

кро́ткий *adj.* gentle; meek.

кро́товый *adj.* (*attrib.*) mole; moleskin.

кро́тость *neut.* gentleness; meekness.

кро́ха *f.* crumb.

кроха́ль *m.* (*bird*) merganser.

кро́хотный *adj.* (*colloq.*) tiny.

кро́шечный *adj.* (*colloq.*) tiny.

кроши́ть *impf. pf.* **ис-, рас-** *v.t.* to crumble. **—ся** *v.i.* to crumble.

кро́шка *f.* crumb.

круг *m.* circle.

кру́гленький *adj.* round.

кругле́ть *impf. pf.* **о-** to become round.

круглоли́цый *adj.* round-faced.

круглосу́точный *adj.* round the clock.

кру́глый *adj.* round. — кру́глые су́тки *pl.* round the clock; day and night.

круговой *adj.* circular.

круговоро́т *m.* **1.** rotation. **2.** flow (*of events, etc.*).

кругозо́р *m.* **1.** range of vision. **2.** range of interests; one's outlook.

круго́м *adv.* **1.** all around. **2.** entirely.

круглообра́зный *adj.* circular.

кругосве́тный *adj.* round-the-world.

кружевно́й *adj.* (*attrib.*) lace.

кру́жево *neut.* lace.

круже́ние *neut.* **1.** twisting; spinning. **2.** torsion.

кружи́ть *impf. v.t.* to turn, to spin, to whirl. *–v.i.* to circle; to wander. **—ся** to spin; to circle.

кру́жка *f.* **1.** mug; tankard. **2.** box for alms.

кружной *adj.* (*colloq.*) roundabout.

кружо́к FILL *m.* **1.** disk. **2.** circle, club.

круи́з *m.* cruise.

круп *m.* croup.

крупа́ *f.* groats.

крупи́нка *f.* grain.

крупи́ца *f.* **1.** grain. **2.** fragment.

кру́пно *adv.* into large pieces.

крупноинформа́тная электро́нная табли́ца *f.* (*abbr.* **КЭТ**) spreadsheet.

крупномасшта́бный *adj.* large-scale.

кру́пный *adj.* big, large; large-scale.

крупча́тый *adj.* coarse; grainy.

крупье́ *m. indecl.* croupier.

крупяно́й *adj.* (*attrib.*) groats.

крутизна́ *f.* steepness.

крути́ть *impf. v.t.* to turn, to roll; to whirl.

кру́то *adv.* **1.** steeply. **2.** tightly. **3.** sharply.

круто́е яйцо́ *neut.* hard-boiled egg.

круто́й *adj.* **1.** steep. **2.** stern.

кру́тость *f.* steepness.

кру́ча *f.* steep slope.

кру́че *adj. comp. of* круто́й.

кручи́на *f.* (*poet.*) grief; sorrow.

круше́ние *neut.* **1.** accident, wreck. **2.** downfall, ruin.

круши́на *f.* buckthorn.

круши́ть *impf.* to destroy; to shatter.

крыжо́вник *m.* **1.** gooseberries. **2.** gooseberry bush.

крыла́тое су́дно *neut.* hydrofoil.

крыла́тые слова́ *pl.* popular saying.

крыла́тый *adj.* winged.

крыле́чко *neut. dim. of* крыльцо́.

крыло́ *neut.* **1.** wing. **2.** blade; vane.

кры́лышко *neut. dim. of* крыло́.

крыльцо́ *neut.* porch.

Крым *m.* Crimea.

кры́нка *f.* milk jug.

кры́са *f.* rat.

крысоло́вка *f.* rattrap.

кры́тый *adj.* sheltered; covered.

крыть *impf. pf.* **по-** to cover. **—ся** *impf. –v.i.* to lie beneath; to be concealed.

кры́ша *f.* roof.

кры́шка *f.* cover; lid.

крюк *m.* hook.

крючкова́тый *adj.* hooked.

крючкотво́рство *neut.* (*obs.*) chicanery.

крючо́к FILL *m.* **1.** hook. **2.** hitch; catch. **3.** curlicue.

крюшо́н *m.* wine punch.

кря́ду *adv.* (*colloq.*) in a row.

кряж *m.* **1.** mountain ridge. **2.** stump (*of wood*).

кря́жистый *adj.* **1.** thick. **2.** stocky; thickset.

кря́канье *neut.* quacking.

кря́кать *impf. pf.* **кря́кнуть 1.** to quack. **2.** to grunt.

кря́ква *f.* wild duck; mallard.

кряхте́ть *impf. pres.* **-хчу́, -хти́шь** to groan.

ксено́н *m.* xenon.

ксерокопи́ровать OVA *impf. pf.* **от-** to photocopy.

ксероко́пия *f.* photocopy.

ксе́рокс *m.* photocopier.

ксилогра́фия *f.* wood engraving.

ксилофо́н *m.* xylophone.

кста́ти *adv.* by the way; apropos.

кто *pron.* who, whom, anyone.

кто́-либо *also* кто́-нибудь *pron.* somebody, someone; anybody, anyone.

кто́-то *pron.* somebody.

Куа́ла-Лумпу́р *m.* Kuala Lumpur.

куб *m.* **1.** (*geom.*) cube. **2.** boiler, still.

Ку́ба *f.* Cuba.

Куба́нь *f.* Kuban.

ку́барем *adv.* (*colloq.*): кати́ться ку́барем *impf.* to roll head over heels.

куба́рь *m.* peg top.

кубату́ра *f.* cubic capacity.

куби́зм *m.* (*art*) cubism.

куби́нец FILL *m. f.* **куби́нка** Cuban.

куби́ческий *adj.* cubic.

ку́бовый *adj.* indigo.

ку́бок FILL *m.* **1.** goblet. **2.** (*sport*) trophy.

кубоме́тр *m.* cubic meter.

ку́брик *m.* crew's quarters.

кубы́шка *f.* money box.

кува́лда *f.* sledgehammer.

Куве́йт *m.* Kuwait.

кувши́н *m.* pitcher; jug.

кувши́нка *f.* water lily.

кувырка́ться *impf. pf.* **кувыркну́ться** to turn somersaults; to tumble.

кувырко́м *adv.* (*colloq.*) topsy-turvy; head over heels.

куда́ *adv.* where, whither.

куда́-либо *adv.* somewhere; anywhere.

куда́-нибудь *adv.* somewhere; anywhere.

куда́-то *adv.* somewhere.

куда́хтать *impf. pres.* **-хчу, -хчешь** to cackle.

куде́ль *f.* tow (*fiber*).

куде́сник *m.* magician; sorcerer.

ку́дри *pl.* curls.

кудря́вый *adj.* curly, curly-headed.

кудря́шки *pl.* ringlets of hair.

кузе́н *m.* (male) cousin.

кузи́на *f.* (female) cousin.

кузне́ц FILL *m.* blacksmith.

кузне́чик *m.* grasshopper.
кузне́чный *adj.* blacksmith's.
ку́зница *f.* blacksmith's shop; forge.
ку́зов *m.* **1.** body (*of a car*). **2.** basket.
кукаре́канье *neut.* crowing (*of rooster*).
кукаре́кать *impf.* to crow.
ку́киш *m.* (*colloq.*) fig (*gesture of contempt or derision*).
ку́кла *f.* doll; puppet.
кукова́ть OVA *impf.* to cuckoo.
ку́колка *f.* **1.** *dim. of* ку́кла. **2.** (*zool.*) chrysalis.
ку́коль *m.* (*weed*) cockle.
ку́кольный *adj.* (*attrib.*) doll.
кукуру́за *f.* maize, corn. — возду́шная кукуру́за popcorn.
куку́шка *f.* cuckoo.
кула́к¹ *m.* fist.
кула́к² *m.* kulak.
кула́цкий *adj.* (*attrib.*) kulak; kulak's.
кула́чество *neut.* the kulaks.
кула́чки *pl.*: дра́ться на кула́чках *impf.* to engage in fisticuffs.
кулачко́вый вал *m.* camshaft.
кула́чный *adj.* (*attrib.*) fist.
кулачо́к FILL *m.* **1.** *dim. of* кула́к. **2.** (*mech.*) cam.
кулебя́ка *f.* pie containing cabbage, fish, *or* meat.
ку́ли *m. indecl.* coolie.
кули́к *m.* snipe.
кулинари́я *f.* cookery; cooking.
кулина́рный *adj.* culinary.
кули́сы *pl.* (*theat.*) wings. — за кули́сами behind the scenes.
кули́ч *m.* kulich (*Easter cake*).
кули́чки *pl.*: у чёрта на кули́чках in the middle of nowhere.
куло́н *m.* **1.** pendant. **2.** coulomb (*unit of electricity*).
кулуа́рный *adj.* unofficial; (*fig.*) secretive.
кулуа́ры *pl.* corridors.
куль *m.* sack.
кульминацио́нный *adj.* climactic.
кульмина́ция *f.* culmination.
культ *m.* cult.
культиви́ровать *impf.* to cultivate.
культу́ра *f.* **1.** culture. **2.** (*agric.*) crop.
культу́рность *f.* level of culture; high level of culture.
культу́рный *adj.* **1.** cultural. **2.** cultured. **3.** refined.
культя́ *f.* stump (*of amputated limb*).
кум *m.* godfather of one's child.
кума́ *f.* godmother of one's child.
куманúка *f.* (*shrub*) bramble.
кума́ч *m.* red calico.
кумúр *m.* idol.
кумовство́ *neut.* (*colloq.*) nepotism.
кумуляти́вный *adj.* cumulative.
ку́мушка *f. dim. of* кума́.
кумы́к *m.* Kumyk (*people inhabiting the Caucasus*).
кумы́с *m.* kumiss (*fermented mare's milk*).
кунжу́т *m.* sesame.
кунúца *f.* marten.
ку́па *f.* group, clump (*of bushes or trees*).
купа́льник *adj.* bathing suit.

купа́льный *adj.* (*attrib.*) bathing.
купа́льня *f.* bathhouse.
купа́льщик *m. f.* купа́льщица bather.
купа́ние *neut.* bathing.
купа́ть *impf. pf.* вы́- *v.t.* to bathe.
купе́ *neut. indecl.* train compartment.
купе́ль *f.* baptismal font.
купе́ц FILL *m.* merchant.
купи́ть *pf. of* покупа́ть.
купле́т *m.* verse; stanza.
ку́пля *f.* purchase.
ку́пол *m.* dome.
купо́н *m.* coupon.
купоро́с *m.* vitriol.
купчи́ха *f.* woman merchant; merchant's wife.
купю́ра *f.* **1.** cut *or* deletion in work of literature *or* music. **2.** denomination (*paper money*).
курага́ *f.* dried apricots.
кура́житься *impf.* to swagger; to boast; to lord it over.
кура́нты *pl.* chimes.
Курга́н *m.* Kurgan.
курга́н *m.* kurgan; burial mound.
ку́рево *neut.* (*colloq.*) something to smoke.
куре́ние *neut.* smoking.
курúльница *f.* incense burner; censer.
курúльня *f.* place where narcotics are smoked.
курúльщик *m. f.* курúльщица smoker.
курúный *adj.* (*attrib.*) chicken; chicken's.
курúтельный *adj.* (*attrib.*) smoking.
курúть *impf.* to smoke.
ку́рица *f.* hen, chicken.
ку́рия *f.* curia.
куркýма *f.* turmeric.
курно́сый нос *m.* pug-nose; snub-nose.
коровóдство *neut.* poultry breeding.
куро́к *m.* cock; hammer (*gun*).
куропа́тка *f.* partridge.
куро́рт *m.* health resort.
куро́ртник *m. f.* куро́ртница (*colloq.*) person staying at a resort.
куро́ртный *adj.* (*attrib.*) resort.
курослéп *m.* buttercup.
ку́рочка *f.* **1.** pullet. **2.** crake.
курс *m.* **1.** course. **2.** rate of exchange.
курса́нт *m.* cadet.
курси́в *m.* italics.
курси́вный *adj.* italic.
курси́ровать OVA *impf.* to travel back and forth.
Курск *m.* Kursk.
курсово́й *adj.* (*attrib.*) course; term.
куртиза́нка *f.* courtesan.
ку́ртка *f.* man's jacket.
курча́вый *adj.* curly; curly-headed.
ку́ры *pl. of* ку́рица.
курьёз *m.* funny thing.
курьéр *m.* messenger.
курьéрский пóезд *m.* express train.
куря́тина *f.* (*colloq.*) chicken meat.
куря́тник *m.* chicken coop; henhouse.
куря́щий DAA *m.* smoker.
куса́ть *impf. pf.* укуси́ть *v.t.* to sting, to bite.
куса́чки *pl.* **1.** pliers. **2.** wire cutter.
кусково́й *adj.* (*attrib.*) lump.
кусо́к FILL *m.* **1.** piece. **2.** lump.
кусо́чек *m. dim. of* кусо́к.

куст *m.* bush, shrub.
куста́рник *m.* bushes; shrubs; shrubbery.
куста́рный *adj.* handicraft.
куста́рь *m.* handicraftsman.
Кута́иси *m.* Kutaisi.
ку́тать *impf. pf.* за- to wrap; to bundle.
кутёж *m.* drinking bout; spree; binge.
кутерьма́ *f.* (*colloq.*) commotion; stir.
кути́ла *m.* (*decl. f.*) (*colloq.*) hard drinker; reveler.
кути́ть *impf.* to carouse.
куту́зка *f.* (*obs., colloq.*) jail.
куха́рка *f.* cook.
ку́хня *f.* 1. kitchen. 2. cuisine.
ку́хонный *adj.* (*attrib.*) kitchen.

ку́цый *adj.* 1. short-tailed. 2. (*of clothes*) short; skimpy.
ку́ча *f.* heap; pile.
кучево́й *adj.* (*clouds*) cumulous.
ку́чер *m.* coachman.
ку́чка *f. dim. of* ку́ча.
куш *m.* large sum of money.
куша́к *m.* sash.
ку́шанье *neut.* 1. food. 2. dish. 3. eating.
ку́шать *impf. pf.* по- to eat.
куше́тка *f.* couch.
Кызы́л-Орда́ *f.* Kyzyl Orda.
кыш *interj.* shoo!
кюве́т *m.* ditch (*at side of road*).
кю́рий *m.* curium.
Кюстенди́л *m.* Kyustendil.

Л

лабири́нт *m.* labyrinth; maze.
лабора́нт *m. f.* —ка laboratory assistant.
лаборато́рия *f.* laboratory.
лаборато́рный *adj.* (*attrib.*) laboratory.
ла́ва *f.* lava.
лава́нда *f.* lavender.
лава́ндовый *adj.* (*attrib.*) lavender.
лави́на *f.* avalanche.
лави́ровать OVA *impf.* to maneuver.
ла́вка[1] *f.* bench.
ла́вка[2] *f.* shop.
ла́вочка[1] *f.* small bench.
ла́вочка[2] *f.* small store.
ла́вочник *m. f.* ла́вочница shopkeeper.
лавр *m.* laurel.
ла́вра *f.* monastery.
лавро́вый *adj.* (*attrib.*) laurel. — лавро́вый лист
  bay leaf.
ла́герный *adj.* (*attrib.*) camp.
ла́герь *m.* camp.
лагу́на *f.* lagoon.
лад *m.* **1.** harmony; concord. **2.** manner, way.
ла́дан *m.* incense.
ла́дить *impf.* (**с** *with instr.*) to get along with; to
  be on good terms with.
ла́дно *adv.* well; all right.
ла́дный *adj.* (*colloq.*) graceful.
Ла́дожское о́зеро *neut.* Lake Ladoga.
ладо́нь *f.* palm.
ладо́ши *pl.*: **бить в ладо́ши** *impf.* to clap one's
  hands.
ладья́ *f.* (*chess*) rook; castle.
лаз *m.* manhole.
ла́занье *neut.* climbing.
лазаре́т *m.* hospital; infirmary.
лазе́йка *f.* **1.** small opening. **2.** loophole.
ла́зер *m.* laser.
ла́зерно-цифрово́й прои́грыватель *m.* CD (compact
  disk) player.
ла́зерный *adj.* (*attrib.*) laser.
ла́зить *impf. indet. of* **лезть**.
лазу́рный *adj.* azure.
лазу́рь *f.* azure.
лазу́тчик *m.* (*obs.*) scout; spy.
лай *m.* barking.
ла́йка[1] *f.* (*dog*) husky.
ла́йка[2] *f.* kidskin.
лайм *m.* lime (*fruit and tree*).
ла́йнер *m.* ocean liner. — возду́шный ла́йнер airliner.
лак *m.* varnish.
лака́ть *impf. pf.* вы- to lap (up).
лаке́й *m.* **1.** footman. **2.** lackey.
лаке́йский *adj.* of a footman.
лакиро́ванный *adj.* lacquered; varnished.
лакирова́ть OVA *impf. pf.* от- to varnish.
лакиро́вка *f.* lacquering; varnishing.
ла́кмусовый *adj.* (*attrib.*) litmus.
ла́ковый *adj.* lacquered.
ла́комиться *impf. pf.* по- (*with instr.*) to feast on.

ла́комка *m.and f.* (*decl. f.*) (*colloq.*) person with a
  sweet tooth.
ла́комство *neut.* **1.** delicacy. **2.** ла́комства *pl.*
  sweets.
ла́комый **1.** *adj.* tasty; dainty; luscious. **2.** fond of.
лакони́зм *m.* brevity; terseness.
лакони́ческий *adj.* laconic.
лакони́чность *f.* terseness; brevity.
лакони́чный *adj.* laconic.
лакри́ца *f.* licorice.
лакри́чный *adj.* licorice.
лакта́ция *f.* lactation.
лакто́за *f.* lactose.
лакфио́ль *f.* wallflower.
ла́ма[1] *f.* llama.
ла́ма[2] *m.* lama.
ламаи́зм *m.* Lamaism.
ламаи́стский *adj.* Lamaistic.
ламанти́н *m.* manatee.
Ла-Ма́нш проли́в *m.* English Channel.
ла́мпа *f.* lamp.
лампа́да *f.* icon lamp.
лампа́с *m.* stripe (*on side of trousers*).
ла́мповый *adj.* (*attrib.*) lamp.
ла́мпочка *f.* light bulb.
ланге́т *m.* sliced steak.
лангу́ст *m.* spiny lobster.
ландша́фт *m.* landscape.
ла́ндыш *m.* lily of the valley.
ланоли́н *m.* lanolin.
ланта́н *m.* lanthanum.
ланце́т *m.* lancet.
лань *f.* doe; fallow deer.
Лао́с *m.* Laos.
ла́па *f.* paw.
ла́пка *f.* paw.
ла́поть *m.* shoe made of bark.
Ла́ппеэранта *f.* Lappeenranta.
лапта́ *f.* lapta (*a ball game*).
ла́птоп *m.* laptop computer.
лапша́ *f.* noodles; noodle soup.
лапше́вник *m.* noodle pudding.
ла́рго *neut.* (*indecl.*) (*mus.*) largo.
ларёк FILL *m.* stall.
ларе́ц FILL *m.* small box.
ларинги́т *m.* laryngitis.
ла́рчик *m.* small box.
ларь *m.* bin.
ла́ска[1] *f.* caress, endearment; kindness, goodness.
ла́ска[2] *f.* weasel.
ласка́тельный *adj.* tender; caressing; affectionate.
ласка́ть *impf.* to caress, to pet.
ла́сковый *adj.* affectionate, tender.
лассо́ *neut. indecl.* lasso.
ласт *m.* flipper (*of a seal or walrus*).
ла́стик *m.* eraser.
ла́сточка *f.* (*bird*) swallow.
ла́сточкин *adj.* swallow; swallow's.
лата́ть *impf. pf.* за- to patch (up).
латви́ец FILL *m. f.* латви́йка Latvian.
латви́йский *adj.* Latvian.

Ла́твия *f.* Latvia.
ла́текс *m.* latex.
лате́нтный *adj.* latent.
лати́нский *adj.* Latin.
лату́к *m.* lettuce.
лату́нный *adj.* brass.
лату́нь *f.* brass.
ла́ты *pl.* armor.
латы́нь *f.* Latin.
латы́ш *m. f.* латы́шка Latvian.
лауреа́т *m.* laureate.
лафе́т *m.* gun carriage.
Ла́хти *m.* Lahti.
ла́цкан *m.* lapel.
лачу́га *f.* hovel; shanty.
ла́ять *impf.* to bark.
лганьё *neut.* lying.
лгать *impf. pf.* со-, на- to lie, to tell a lie.
лгун *m. f.* лгу́нья liar.
лебеди́ный *adj.* (*attrib.*) swan, of swans.
— лебеди́ная пе́сня *f.* swan song.
лебёдка[1] *f.* female swan.
лебёдка[2] *f.* (*mech.*) winch.
ле́бедь *m.* swan.
лебези́ть *impf.* (пе́ред *with instr.*) to be obsequious to.
лебя́жий *adj.* swan, swan's.
лев FILL *m.* lion.
левиафа́н *m.* leviathan.
левко́й *m* gillyflower.
левре́тка *f.* Italian greyhound.
левша́ *m. and f.* (*decl. f.*) left-handed person; (*colloq.*) southpaw.
ле́вый *adj.* left.
легализа́ция *f.* legalization.
легализи́ровать OVA *impf. and pf.* to legalize.
легализова́ть OVA *impf. and pf.* to legalize.
лега́льность *f.* legality.
лега́льный *adj.* legal.
лега́то *neut. indecl.* (*mus.*) legato.
леге́нда *f.* legend.
легенда́рный *adj.* legendary.
легио́н *m.* legion.
легионе́р *m.* legionnaire.
лёгкий *adj.* 1. light; easy. 2. slight.
легко́ *adv.* 1. easily. 2. lightly.
легкоатле́т *m. f.* —ка track-and-field athlete.
легкоатлети́ческий *adj.* track-and-field.
легкове́рие *neut.* gullibility; credulity.
легкове́рный *adj.* credulous.
легкове́с *m.* (*sports*) lightweight.
легкове́сный *adj.* lightweight.
легково́й автомоби́ль passenger car.
лёгкое *neut.* lung.
легкомы́сленный *adj.* flippant, frivolous.
легкомы́слие *neut.* frivolity.
лёгкость *f.* lightness.
лёгочный *adj.* (*attrib.*) lung; pulmonary.
ле́гче *adj. comp. of* лёгкий. 1. easier. 2. lighter.
лёд FILL *m.* ice.
ледене́ть *impf. pf.* за-, о- to freeze; to become numb.
ледене́ц FILL *m.* piece of hard candy.
ледени́ть *impf. pf.* о- to freeze; to cause to freeze.
ле́дник *m.* 1. icehouse. 2. icebox.
ледни́к *m.* glacier.

леднико́вый *adj.* glacial.
Ледови́тый океа́н *m.* Arctic Ocean.
ледо́вый *adj.* (*attrib.*) ice.
ледоко́л *m.* icebreaker (*ship*).
ледохо́д *m.* drifting of ice.
леды́шка *f.* (*colloq.*) piece of ice.
ледяно́й *adj.* icy.
лёжа *adv.* in a lying position; reclining.
лежа́лый *adj.* old; stale.
лежа́нка *f.* stove bench; sleeping ledge on a Russian chimney stove.
лежа́ть *impf. v.i.* 1. to lie. 2. to be (situated).
лежа́чий *adj.* lying, recumbent.
ле́жбище *neut.* animal breeding ground.
лежебо́ка *m. and f.* (*decl. f.*) (*colloq.*) loafer.
лежмя́ лежа́ть *impf.* to lie prostrate.
ле́звие *neut.* blade; edge.
лезть *impf. pf.* по-, за- to climb, to clamber; (в *with acc.*) to get in or into.
лейбори́ст *m.* Labourite.
лейбори́стский *adj.* Labour.
ле́йка *f.* 1. watering can. 2. funnel.
лейкеми́я *f.* leukemia.
лейкоци́т *m.* leukocyte.
Ле́йпциг *m.* Leipzig.
лейтена́нт *m.* lieutenant.
лейтмоти́в *m.* leitmotif.
лека́ло *neut.* 1. French curve. 2. template, gauge.
лека́рственный *adj.* medicinal.
лека́рство *neut.* medicine; drug.
ле́карь *m.* (*obs.*) doctor.
ле́ксика *f.* vocabulary; lexicon.
лексико́граф *m.* lexicographer.
лексикографи́ческий *adj.* lexicographical.
лексикогра́фия *f.* lexicography.
лексико́н *m.* lexicon.
лекси́ческий *adj.* lexical.
ле́ктор *m.* lecturer.
лекцио́нный *adj.* (*attrib.*) lecture.
ле́кция *f.* lecture.
леле́ять *impf. pres.* леле́ю, леле́ешь 1. to coddle; to pamper. 2. to cherish (*a dream, hope*).
Ле-Ма́н *m.* Le Mans.
ле́мех *m.* plowshare.
ле́мминг *m.* lemming.
лему́р *m.* lemur.
лён FILL *m.* flax.
Ле́на *f.* (*river*) Lena.
лени́вец FILL *m.* 1. lazy person. 2. (*zool.*) sloth.
лени́вый *adj.* lazy.
Ленингра́д *m.* St. Petersburg (*formerly: Leningrad*).
лени́нец FILL *m.* Leninist.
ленини́зм *m.* Leninism.
ле́нинский *adj.* Leninist.
лени́ться *impf. pf.* по- to be lazy.
ле́ность *f.* laziness.
ле́нта *f.* ribbon, tape; band.
ле́нто *neut. indecl.* (*mus.*) lento.
лентопротя́жный механи́зм *m.* (*abbr.* ЛПМ) tape drive (*electronics*).
ле́нточный *adj.* (*attrib.*) tape; band.
лентя́й *m. f.* —ка lazy person.
лентя́йничать *impf.* (*colloq.*) to loaf.
ленца́ *f.* (*colloq.*) lazy streak.
ленч *m.* lunch.

лень *f.* laziness.
леопа́рд *m.* leopard.
леопа́рдовый *adj.* (*attrib.*) leopard; leopard's.
лепесто́к FILL *m.* petal.
ле́пет *m.* babble; prattle.
лепета́ние *neut.* babble; prattle.
лепета́ть *impf. pf.* про- to babble; to prattle.
лепёшка *f.* **1.** flat cake. **2.** (*medicine*) tablet; lozenge.
лепи́ть *impf.* **1.** *pf.* вы́лепить to model, to fashion, to shape. **2.** *pf.* слепи́ть to build, to make.
ле́пта *f.* mite; small contribution.
лес *m.* forest, wood; timber.
леса́ *pl.* scaffold(ing).
лесби́йский *adj.* lesbian.
лесбия́нка *f.* lesbian.
ле́сенка *f.* small ladder.
леси́стый *adj.* wooded.
ле́ска *f.* fishing line.
лесни́к *m.* forester; forest ranger.
лесни́чество *neut.* forest district.
лесни́чий DAA *m.* forester.
лесно́й *adj.* (*attrib.*) forest.
лесово́д *m.* specialist in forestry.
лесово́дство *neut.* forestry.
лесозаво́д *m.* lumber mill.
лесоматериа́л *m. usu. pl.* timber; lumber.
лесопи́лка *f.* sawmill.
лесопи́льный *adj.* sawing; sawmill.
лесору́б *m.* lumberjack; woodcutter.
ле́стница *f.* staircase, stairs; ladder.
ле́стничный *adj.* (*attrib.*) stair.
ле́стно *adv.* flattering.
ле́стный *adj.* flattering.
лесть *f.* flattery.
лёт *m.* flight. — на лету́ in flight.
лета́ *pl.* years; age.
летарги́ческий *adj.* lethargic.
летарги́я *f.* lethargy.
лета́тельный *adj.* (*attrib.*) flying.
лета́ть *impf. indet. det.* лете́ть *pf.* полете́ть to fly; to flutter.
лета́ющая таре́лка *f.* flying saucer.
ле́тний *adj.* (*attrib.*) summer.
лётный *adj.* (*attrib.*) flying.
ле́то *neut.* summer.
летоисчисле́ние *neut.* chronology.
ле́том *adv.* in (the) summer.
летопи́сец FILL *m.* chronicler.
ле́топись *f.* chronicle; annal.
летосчисле́ние *neut.* method of numbering the years.
лету́н *m. f.* —ья (*colloq.*) flier.
лету́честь *f.* volatility.
лету́чий *adj.* flying. — лету́чая мышь (*zool.*) bat.
лету́чка *f.* **1.** leaflet. **2.** quick *or* emergency meeting. **3.** mobile unit.
лётчик *m. f.* лётчица flier, pilot.
летя́га *f.* flying squirrel.
лече́бный *adj.* curative; medicinal.
лече́ние *neut.* treatment; cure.
лечи́ть *impf.* to treat; to cure.
лечь *pf. of* ложи́ться.
ле́ший DAA *m.* wood goblin.
лещ *m.* (*fish*) bream.
лещи́на *f.* hazel.

лженау́ка *f.* pseudoscience.
лженау́чный *adj.* pseudoscientific.
лжесвиде́тель *m.* false witness; perjurer.
лжесвиде́тельство *neut.* false evidence; perjury.
лжесвиде́тельствовать OVA *impf.* to commit perjury.
лжец *m.* liar.
лжи́вость *f.* falsity.
лжи́вый *adj.* false; lying.
ли *conj.* whether; if.
либера́л *m. f.* —ка liberal.
либерали́зм *m.* liberalism.
либера́льничать *impf.* (*colloq.*) to be too tolerant.
либера́льный *adj.* liberal.
ли́бо *conj.* or. — ли́бо... ли́бо... either... or....
либретти́ст *m.* librettist.
либре́тто *neut.* (*indecl.*) libretto.
Лива́н *m.* Lebanon.
ли́вень *m.* downpour.
ли́вер *m.* giblets.
ли́верная колбаса́ *adj.* liverwurst.
Ливерпу́ль *m.* Liverpool.
Ли́вия *f.* Libya.
ливмя́ *adv.* (*colloq.*): ливмя́ лить *impf.* to rain cats and dogs.
ливре́йный *adj.* (*attrib.*) livery.
ливре́я *f.* livery.
ли́га *f.* league.
лигату́ра *f.* ligature.
лигни́т *m.* lignite.
ли́дер *m.* leader.
ли́дерство *neut.* leadership.
лиди́ровать OVA *impf.* to be in the lead.
Лиепа́я *f.* Liepāja (*formerly: Libau*).
лиза́ние *neut.* licking.
лиза́ть *impf. pf.* лизну́ть to lick.
лизоблю́д *m.* (*colloq.*) bootlicker.
ликвида́ция *f.* liquidation.
ликвиди́ровать OVA *impf. and pf.* to liquidate.
ликви́дность *f.* (*finance*) liquidity.
ликви́дный *adj.* (*finance*) liquid.
ликёр *m.* cordial.
ликова́ние *neut.* rejoicing; exultation.
лику́ющий *adj.* jubilant; exultant.
ли́лия *f.* lily.
Лиллеха́ммер *m.* Lillehammer.
Лилль *m.* Lille.
лилове́ть *impf.* to become purple.
лило́вый *adj.* violet; purple.
Ли́ма *f.* Lima.
лима́н *m.* estuary.
Ли́мерик *m.* Limerick.
лими́т *m.* limit; quota.
лимити́ровать OVA *impf. and pf.* to limit.
Лимо́ж *m.* Limoges.
лимо́н *m.* lemon.
лимона́д *m.* **1.** lemonade. **2.** carbonated fruit drink.
лимо́нный *adj.* lemon; citric.
лимузи́н *m.* limousine.
ли́мфа *f.* lymph.
лимфати́ческий *adj.* lymph; lymphatic.
лингви́ст *m.* linguist.
лингви́стика *f.* linguistics.
лине́йка *f.* ruler; line; line-up.
лине́йный *adj.* linear.

ли́нза *f.* lens.
ли́ния *f.* line.
линова́нный *adj.* lined; ruled.
линова́ть OVA *impf.* *pf.* на- to draw lines on; to rule.
лино́леум *m.* linoleum.
линоти́п *m.* linotype.
Линц *m.* Linz.
линчева́ть *impf.* and *pf.* to lynch.
ли́нька *f.* molting.
линю́чий *adj.* (*colloq.*) (*fabric*) that bleeds easily.
линя́лый *adj.* (*colloq.*) faded.
линя́ть *impf.* **1.** *pf.* по- to fade; (*of colors*) to run **2.** *pf.* вы́- (*of animals*) to shed hair.
Лио́н *m.* Lyon.
ли́па *f.* linden tree; lime tree.
ли́пкий *adj.* sticky.
ли́пнуть *impf.* *past* лип *or* ли́пнул, ли́пла (к *with dat.*) to stick to.
ли́повый *adj.* **1.** (*attrib.*) linden; basswood. **2.** (*colloq.*) fake.
липу́чий *adj.* sticky.
липу́чка *f.* (*colloq.*) sticky paper.
ли́ра *f.* lyre.
лири́зм *m.* lyricism.
ли́рика *f.* lyrics; lyric poetry.
лири́ческий *adj.* lyric(al).
лиса́ *also* лиси́ца *f.* fox.
лиси́чка *f.* chanterelle (*an edible mushroom*).
Лиссабо́н *m.* Lisbon.
лист[1] *m.* *pl.* ли́стья leaf.
лист[2] *m.* *pl.* листы́ sheet (*of paper, etc.*).
листа́ть *impf.* to leaf through.
листва́ *f.* foliage.
ли́ственница *f.* larch.
ли́ственный *adj.* leafy.
листо́вка *f.* leaflet.
листово́й *adj.* (*attrib.*) sheet.
листо́к FILL *m.* **1.** leaf. **2.** sheet of paper.
листопа́д *m.* falling of leaves.
лита́ния *f.* litany.
Литва́ *f.* Lithuania.
лите́йный *adj.* founding; casting.
литера́тор *m.* literary person.
литерату́ра *f.* literature.
литерату́рный *adj.* literature.
ли́терный *adj.* **1.** marked with a letter. **2.** (*of a seat*) reserved.
ли́тий *m.* lithium.
лито́вец FILL *m.* *f.* лито́вка Lithuanian.
лито́вский *adj.* Lithuanian.
литограф *m.* lithograph.
литографи́ровать OVA *impf.* to lithograph.
лито́й *adj.* (*of metals*) cast.
литори́на *f.* (*mollusk*) periwinkle.
литосфе́ра *f.* lithosphere.
литр *m.* liter.
литро́вый *adj.* (*attrib.*) one-liter.
литурги́ческий *adj.* liturgical.
литурги́я *f.* liturgy.
лить[1] *impf.* to pour; to spill; to flow.
лить[2] *impf.* to cast; to form.
литьё *neut.* **1.** founding; casting; molding. **2.** castings.
лиф *m.* bodice.
лифт *m.* elevator.

лифтёр *m.* *f.* —ша elevator operator.
ли́фчик *m.* brassiere.
лиха́ч *m.* **1.** (*obs.*) coachman. **2.** daredevil; reckless driver.
лиха́чество *neut.* recklessness.
лихва́ *f.* interest (*on a loan*).
ли́хо *neut.* misfortune; evil.
лихо́й *adj.* evil.
лихора́дить *impf.* to have a fever.
лихора́дка *f.* fever.
лихора́дочный *adj.* feverish.
Лихтенште́йн *m.* Liechtenstein.
лицева́я сторона́ *f.* **1.** right side. **2.** front; facade.
лицезре́ть *impf.* to behold.
лице́й *m.* lycée.
лицеме́р *m.* *f.* —ка hypocrite.
лицеме́рие *neut.* hypocrisy.
лицеме́рить *impf.* to be hypocritical.
лицеме́рный *adj.* hypocritical.
лице́нзия *f.* license.
лицо́ *neut.* **1.** face. **2.** person; personage. **3.** right side. **4.** (*gram.*) person. — лицо́м к лицу́ face to face.
ли́чико *neut.* *dim. of* лицо́.
личи́на *f.* mask.
личи́нка *f.* **1.** larva. **2.** maggot.
ли́чно *adv.* **1.** in person. **2.** personally.
ли́чность *f.* personality.
ли́чный *adj.* personal, individual, private.
ли́чный соста́в *m.* personnel.
лиша́й[1] *m.* lichen.
лиша́й[2] *m.* (*med.*) herpes.
лиша́ть *impf.* *pf.* лиши́ть (*with gen.*) to deprive of. — лиши́ть себя́ жи́зни *pf.* to commit suicide.
лише́ние *neut.* **1.** deprivation. **2.** лише́ния *pl.* privations, hardship.
лишённый *adj.* (*with gen.*) lacking; without; devoid of.
ли́шнее DAA *neut.* extras.
ли́шний *adj.* surplus; superfluous.
лишь *adv.* only. — *conj.* лишь бы if only. — лишь то́лько as soon as.
лоб *m.* forehead.
ло́бби *neut.* *indecl.* lobby.
лобби́зм *m.* lobbyism.
лобби́ст *m.* lobbyist.
лобза́ть *impf.* (*obs.*) to kiss.
ло́бзик *m.* fret saw.
ло́бный *adj.* frontal; front.
лобово́й *adj.* frontal; front.
лоботря́с *m.* (*colloq.*) loafer; lazybones.
лобыза́ть *impf.* (*obs.*) to kiss.
лов *m.* catch (*of fish*).
ловела́с *m.* ladies' man.
лове́ц FILL *m.* **1.** hunter. **2.** fisherman.
лови́ть *impf.* *pf.* пойма́ть to catch; to entrap, to trap.
ло́вкий *adj.* adroit, dexterous.
ло́вко *adv.* adroitly; nimbly.
ло́вкость *f.* adroitness, dexterity.
ло́вля *f.* catching; trapping (*of animals*).
лову́шка *f.* snare, trap.
ло́вчий *adj.* (*attrib.*) hunting.
лог *m.* ravine.
логари́фм *m.* logarithm.
логарифми́ческий *adj.* logarithmic.

ло́гик *m.* logician.
ло́гика *f.* logic.
логи́чески *adv.* logically.
логи́ческий *also* логи́чный *adj.* logical.
ло́гично *adv.* logically.
логи́чность *f.* logic.
ло́говище *neut.* lair, den.
логопе́д *m.* speech therapist.
логопе́дия *f.* speech therapy.
Лодзь *f.* Łódź.
ло́дка *f.* boat.
ло́дочник *m.* boatman.
ло́дочный *adj.* (*attrib.*) boat, boating.
лоды́жка *f.* ankle.
ло́дырничать *impf.* (*colloq.*) to loaf.
ло́дырь *m.* loafer; idler.
ло́жа *f.* (*theat.*) box.
ложби́на *f.* **1.** dale, glen. **2.** narrow gully.
ло́же *neut.* **1.** (*obs.*) bed. **2.** riverbed.
ло́жечка *f. dim. of* ло́жка.
ложи́ться *impf. pf.* лечь to lie down. —ложи́ться
(лечь) спать to go to bed *or* sleep.
ло́жка *f.* spoon.
ло́жно *adv.* falsely; wrongly; incorrectly.
ло́жность *f.* falsity.
ло́жный *adj.* false.
ложь *f.* lie; falsehood.
лоза́ *f.* **1.** vine. **2.** twig (*e.g. willow*).
Лоза́нна *f.* Lausanne.
лозня́к *m.* willow bush.
ло́зунг *m.* slogan.
локализа́ция *f.* localization.
локализова́ть OVA *impf. and pf.* to localize.
локализова́ться OVA *pf.* to become *or* be local-
ized.
лока́льный *adj.* local.
лока́тор *m.* locator; radar.
лока́ут *m.* lockout.
локомоти́в *m.* locomotive.
ло́кон *m.* curl, lock.
ло́коть FILL *m.* elbow.
локтево́й *adj.* (*attrib.*) elbow.
лом[1] *m.* crowbar.
лом[2] *m.* (*coll.*) scrap.
лома́ка *m. and f.* (*decl. f.*) (*colloq.*) affected person.
ло́маный *adj.* broken.
лома́ть *impf. pf.* с-, по- *v.t.* to break.
ломба́рд *m.* pawnshop.
ломба́рдный *adj.* related to a pawnshop.
ло́мберный стол *adj. m.* card table.
ломи́ться *impf.* **1.** to break, to snap. **2.** (от *with
gen.*) to be loaded with.
ло́мка *f.* breaking.
ло́мкий *adj.* brittle; fragile.
ло́мкость *f.* fragility.
ломови́к *m.* (*colloq.*) carter.
ломово́й *adj.* (*attrib.*) dray.
ломоно́с *m.* clematis.
ломо́та *f.* dull ache.
ломо́ть *m.* hunk; chunk; big piece.
ло́мтик *m.* slice.
Ло́ндон *m.* London.
ло́но *neut.* (*poet.*) bosom; lap.
ло́пасть *f.* blade; vane.
лопа́та *f.* spade, shovel.

лопа́тка[1] *f.* **1.** small shovel; trowel. **2.** blade.
лопа́тка[2] *f.* shoulder blade.
ло́пать *impf. pf.* с- (*colloq.*) to devour, to gobble
up.
ло́паться *impf. pf.* ло́пнуть **1.** to snap, to break,
to burst. **2.** (*of patience*) to be at an end.
лопота́ть *impf.* to mutter, to mumble.
лопоу́хий *adj.* (*colloq.*) lop-eared.
лопу́х *m.* burdock.
лорд *m.* lord.
лорне́т *m.* lorgnette.
Лос-А́нджелес *m.* Los Angeles.
лоси́на *f.* **1.** elk meat. **2.** elk skin. — лоси́ны *pl.*
buckskin breeches.
лоси́ный *adj.* (*attrib.*) elk, elk's.
лоск *m.* luster, gloss.
лоску́т *m.* scrap of cloth; shred.
лоску́тный *adj.* patchwork.
лососёвый *adj.* (*attrib.*) salmon.
лососи́на *f.* (*cul.*) salmon.
ло́сось *m.* salmon.
лось *m.* elk.
лосьо́н *m.* face lotion.
Лотари́нгия *f.* Lorraine.
лотере́йный *adj.* (*attrib.*) lottery.
лотере́я *f.* lottery.
лото́ *neut. indecl.* lotto; bingo.
лото́к FILL *m.* **1.** tray, stand (*of street hawker*). **2.**
chute.
ло́тос *m.* lotus.
лото́чник *m. f.* лото́чница street vendor.
Лофоте́нские острова́ *pl.* Lofoten Islands.
лоха́нь *f.* washtub.
лохма́тый *adj.* shaggy; tousled.
лохмо́тья *pl.* rags.
ло́цман *m.* **1.** harbor pilot. **2.** pilot fish.
лошади́ный *adj.* (*attrib.*) horse.
лоша́дка *f. dim. of* ло́шадь.
ло́шадь *f.* horse.
лощёный *adj.* glossy.
лощи́на *f.* dale; glen.
лощи́ть *impf. pf.* на- to buff, to polish.
лоя́льность *f.* loyalty.
лоя́льный *adj.* loyal.
Луа́ра *f.* (*river*) Loire.
луб *m.* bast.
лубо́к FILL *m.* **1.** bast strip. **2.** splint. **3.** woodcut.
лубяно́й *adj.* (*attrib.*) bast.
луг *m.* meadow.
Луга́но *neut.* Lugano.
лугови́на *f.* (*colloq.*) small meadow.
лугово́й *adj.* (*attrib.*) meadow.
луди́льщик *m.* tinsmith.
луди́ть *impf. pf.* по- to tin; to plate with tin.
лу́жа *f.* puddle.
лужа́йка *f.* **1.** lawn. **2.** clearing (*in a forest*).
лужёный *adj.* tin-plated.
лу́жица *f. dim. of* лу́жа.
лужо́к FILL *m. dim. of* луг.
Луизиа́на *f.* Louisiana.
лук[1] *m.* onion, onions.
лук[2] *m.* bow.
лука́ *f.* **1.** bend (*in a river*). **2.** pommel (*on a saddle*).
лука́вить *impf.* to be cunning *or* sly.
лука́вство *neut.* slyness, cunning.

лука́вый *adj.* sly, cunning.
лу́ковица *f.* **1.** an onion. **2.** (*bot.*) bulb. **3.** onion dome (*of a Russian church*).
лу́ковичный *adj.* bulbous.
лу́ковый *adj.* (*attrib.*) onion.
лу́к-поре́й *m.* scallion; leek.
луна́ *f.* moon.
луна́-па́рк *m.* amusement park.
луна́-ры́ба *f.* sunfish.
лунати́зм *m.* sleepwalking.
луна́тик *m. f.* лунати́чка sleepwalker.
лу́нка *f.* **1.** small hole. **2.** alveolus.
лу́нный *adj.* lunar, moon.
лунь *m.* (*bird*) harrier.
лу́па *f.* magnifying glass.
лупи́ть¹ *impf. pf.* об- to peel, to pare.
лупи́ть² *impf. pf.* от- (*colloq.*) to thrash; to flog.
луфа́рь *m.* bluefish.
луч *m.* ray, beam.
лучево́й *adj.* (*attrib.*) **1.** radial. **2.** radiation.
лучеза́рный *adj.* radiant; resplendent.
лучеиспуска́ние *neut.* radiation.
лучи́на *f.* thin stick; sliver.
лучи́стый *adj.* radiant.
лучи́ться *impf.* **1.** to sparkle; to shine. **2.** (*with instr.*) to radiate.
лучко́вая пила́ *f.* whipsaw.
лу́чше *adv.* better.
лу́чшее *neut.* something better. — оставля́ть жела́ть лу́чшего to leave much to be desired.
лу́чший *adj.* better.
лущи́ть *impf. pf.* об- to husk; to shell.
лы́жа *f. usu. pl.* **1.** ski. **2.** snowshoe.
лы́жник *m. f.* лы́жница skier.
лы́жный *adj.* (*attrib.*) ski; skiing.
лы́ко *neut.* bast.
лы́ковый *adj.* made of bast.
лысе́ть *impf. pf.* об-, по- to grow bald.
лы́сина *f.* baldness, bald spot.
лы́суха *f.* coot.
лы́сый *adj.* bald.
львёнок FILL *m.* lion cub.
льви́ный *adj.* lion's. — льви́ная до́ля the lion's share.
льви́ца *f.* lioness.
Льво́в *m.* Lviv (*Russian: Lvov*).
льго́та *f.* privilege.
льго́тный *adj.* **1.** privileged. **2.** favorable. **3.** (*of ticket, etc.*) reduced.
льди́на *f.* ice floe.
Льеж *m.* Liège.
льнуть *impf. pf.* при- (к *with dat.*) **1.** to cling to; to stick to. **2.** to have a weakness for.
льняно́й *adj.* flaxen; linen.
льстец *m.* flatterer.
льсти́вый *adj.* flattering.
льстить *impf. pf.* по- to flatter.
любвеоби́льный *adj.* full of love.
любе́зничать *impf.* (*colloq.*) (с *with instr.*) to say nice things to.
любе́зность *f.* courtesy; kindness.
любе́зный *adj.* **1.** courteous, kind, amiable. **2.** obliging, polite.
Лю́бек *m.* Lübeck.

люби́мец FILL *m. f.* люби́мица favorite, pet.
люби́мчик *m.* (*colloq.*) favorite.
люби́мый DAA *m.* beloved; favorite; pet.
люби́тель *m. f.* люби́тельница **1.** lover. **2.** amateur. —ский *adj.* amateur.
люби́ть *impf.* **1.** to love. **2.** to like.
Лю́блин *m.* Lublin.
Любля́на *f.* Ljubljana.
лю́бо *pred.* (*colloq.*) it's a pleasure to.
любова́ться *impf. pf.* по- (*with instr.* or на *with acc.*) to admire.
любо́вник *m.* lover.
любо́вница *f.* lover; mistress.
любо́вный *adj.* love, loving.
любо́вь *f.* love.
любозна́тельный *adj.* inquisitive; curious.
любо́й *adj.* any. — DAA *m.* anyone; either (*of two*).
любопы́тно *adv.* curiously.
любопы́тный *adj.* curious.
любопы́тство *neut.* curiosity.
любопы́тствовать OVA *impf. pf.* по- to be curious.
лю́бящий *adj.* affectionate; loving.
люд *m.* (*colloq.*) people.
лю́ди *pl.* people.
людно́й *adj.* crowded; populous.
людое́д *m.* cannibal.
людое́дский *adj.* cannibalistic.
людое́дство *neut.* cannibalism.
людска́я DAA *f.* servants' quarters.
людско́й *adj.* human.
люк *m.* hatch; trap door; manhole.
люкс *adj. indecl.* de luxe.
Люксембу́рг *m.* Luxembourg.
лю́лька *f.* cradle.
люмба́го *neut. indecl.* lumbago.
люмина́л *m.* phenobarbital.
люминесце́нтный *adj.* luminescent.
люминесце́нция *f.* luminescence.
лю́стра *f.* chandelier.
лютера́нин *m. f.* лютера́нка Lutheran.
лютера́нский *adj.* Lutheran.
лютера́нство *neut.* Lutheranism.
люте́ций *m.* lutetium.
лю́тик *m.* buttercup.
лю́тня *f.* lute.
лю́тость *f.* ferocity.
лю́тый *adj.* severe; fierce.
Люце́рн *m.* Lucerne (*also: Luzern*).
люце́рна *f.* alfalfa.
ля *f.* (*mus.*) la; A.
ляга́ть *impf. pf.* лягну́ть *v.t.* to kick.
лягу́шечий *adj.* frog, frog's.
лягу́шка *f.* frog.
ля́жка *f.* **1.** thigh. **2.** haunch.
лязг *m.* clang; clank.
ля́згать *impf. pf.* лязгну́ть **1.** to clang; to clank. **2.** (*with instr.*) to rattle.
ля́мка *f.* shoulder strap.
ля́пис *m.* silver nitrate.
ля́пис-лазу́рь *f.* lapis-lazuli.
ля́пнуть *pf.* to blurt out.
ля́псус *m.* blunder.

M

м *abbr. of* **метр.**
Ма́астрихт *m.* Maastricht.
мавзоле́й *m.* mausoleum.
маг *m.* wizard; magician.
магази́н *m.* store, shop.
магази́нная кра́жа *f.* shoplifting.
магази́нный *adj.* (*attrib.*) store; shop.
магара́джа *f.* maharajah.
Магелла́нов проли́в *m.* Strait of Magellan.
маги́стр *m.* holder of a master's degree.
магистра́ль *f.* **1.** (water, etc.) main. **2.** highway.
магистра́льный *adj.* main; arterial.
магистра́т *m.* city council.
магистрату́ра *f.* magistracy.
маги́ческий *adj.* magic.
ма́гия *f.* magic.
магна́т *m.* magnate; tycoon.
магне́зия *f.* magnesia.
магнети́зм *m.* magnetism.
магнети́т *m.* magnetite.
магнети́ческий *adj.* magnetic.
магне́то *neut. indecl.* magneto.
ма́гниевый *adj.* (*attrib.*) magnesium.
ма́гний *m.* magnesium.
магни́т *m.* magnet. **—ный** *adj.* magnetic.
магни́тить *impf.* to magnetize.
магнитофо́н *m.* tape recorder.
магнитофо́нный *adj.* of a tape recorder.
магно́лия *f.* magnolia.
магомета́нин *m. f.* **магомета́нка** Mohammedan.
магомета́нский *adj.* Mohammedan.
магомета́нство *neut.* Mohammedanism.
Мадагаска́р *m.* Madagascar.
мада́м *f. indecl.* madam.
мадемуазе́ль *f. indecl.* mademoiselle.
маде́ра *f.* Madeira wine.
мадо́нна *f.* madonna.
Мадра́с *m.* Madras.
мадрига́л *m.* madrigal.
Мадри́д *m.* Madrid.
маёвка *f.* **1.** (*pre-rev. Russia*) illegal May-day socialist meeting. **2.** spring picnic.
мажо́р *m.* (*mus.*) major key.
мажордо́м *m.* majordomo.
мажо́рный *adj.* (*mus.*) major.
ма́зать *impf.* **1.** to oil, to grease, to lubricate. **2.** to smear; to daub.
мазня́ *f.* (*colloq.*) poor painting.
мазо́к FILL *m.* **1.** stroke; dab (*in painting*). **2.** (*med.*) smear.
мазохи́зм *m.* masochism.
мазохи́ст *m. f.* **—ка** masochist.
мазохи́стский *adj.* masochistic.
мазу́рка *f.* mazurka.
мазу́т *m.* fuel oil.
мазь *f.* ointment; grease.
маи́с *m.* maize.
май *neut.* May. **—ский** *adj.* (*attrib.*) May.
ма́йка *f.* T-shirt.
майоне́з *m.* mayonnaise.
майо́р *m.* major.

майора́н *m.* marjoram.
майо́рский *adj.* major's.
мак *m.* poppy; poppy seed.
мака́ка *f.* macaque.
макаро́ны *pl.* macaroni.
мака́ть *impf. pf.* **макну́ть** to dip in *or* into.
македо́нец FILL *m. f.* **македо́нка** Macedonian.
Македо́ния *f.* Macedonia.
макиавелле́вский *adj.* Machiavellian.
макинто́ш *m.* mackintosh.
ма́клер *m.* broker.
ма́клерский *adj.* of a broker.
ма́клерство *neut.* brokerage.
ма́ковка *f.* **1.** poppy head. **2.** (*colloq.*) crown of head. **3.** (*colloq.*) dome; cupola (*of a church*).
ма́ковый *adj.* (*attrib.*) poppy; poppyseed.
макре́ль *f.* mackerel.
макроко́см *m.* macrocosm.
максима́льно *adv.* to the maximum.
максима́льный *adj.* maximum.
ма́ксимум *m.* maximum.
макулату́ра *f.* **1.** paper for recycling. **2.** pulp fiction.
маку́шка *f.* **1.** crown of the head. **2.** top.
Мала́ви *m.* Malawi.
мала́га *f.* Malaga wine.
Мала́йзия *f.* Malaysia
мала́йский *adj.* Malayan.
малахи́т *m.* malachite.
малахи́товый *adj.* malachite.
Ма́лая А́зия *f.* Asia Minor.
малева́ть *impf. pf.* **на-** (*colloq.*) to paint
мале́йший *adj.* smallest, least, slightest.
малёк *m.* newly-hatched fish.
ма́ленький *adj.* small, little; diminutive. — *neut.* baby, the young one.
мале́нько *adv.* (*colloq.*) a bit; somewhat.
мале́ц FILL *m.* (*colloq.*) lad.
Мали́ FILL *m.* Mali.
мали́на *f.* raspberry; raspberries.
мали́новка *f.* **1.** robin. **2.** raspberry brandy.
мали́новый *adj.* **1.** (*attrib.*) raspberry. **2.** crimson.
ма́ло *adv.* little; a little.
малова́жный *adj.* of little importance.
малова́то *adv.* (*colloq.*) on the small side; not quite enough.
малове́р *m.* skeptic.
малове́рность *f.* unlikelihood.
малове́роятный *adj.* improbable; unlikely.
маловодный *adj.* arid.
маловодье *neut.* shortage of water.
малогабари́тный *adj.* small-size; compact.
малогра́мотный *adj.* semiliterate.
малодосту́пный *adj.* inaccessible.
малоду́шие *neut.* cowardice.
малоду́шный *adj.* fainthearted.
малозаме́тный *adj.* **1.** barely noticeable. **2.** ordinary.
малознако́мый *adj.* unfamiliar.
малоизве́стный *adj.* little-known.
малоиму́щий *adj.* poor.

малоинтере́сный *adj.* of little interest.
малокро́вие *neut.* anemia.
малокро́вный *adj.* anemic.
малоле́тний *adj.* underage; juvenile.
малоле́тство *neut.* (*colloq.*) childhood.
малолитра́жный *adj.* fuel-efficient.
малолю́дный *adj.* sparsely populated.
мало-ма́льски *adv.* (*colloq.*) the slightest bit.
маломо́щный *adj.* not powerful, with little power.
малонаселённый *adj.* sparsely populated.
ма́ло-пома́лу *adv.* little by little; gradually.
малопоня́тный *adj.* hard to understand.
малоприбыльный *adj.* bringing little profit; of little profit.
малора́звитый *adj.* undeveloped; underdeveloped.
малоро́слый *adj.* undersized.
малосве́дущий *adj.* poorly informed.
малосеме́йный *adj.* with a small family.
малоси́льный *adj.* not strong.
малосодержа́тельный *adj.* lacking substance.
малосо́льный *adj.* lightly salted; kept in brine for a short time only (*vegetables*).
ма́лость *f.* **1.** trifle. **2.** tiny bit.
малотира́жный *adj.* **1.** having a small circulation. **2.** of limited printing.
малоупотреби́тельность *f.* limited use.
малоупотреби́тельный *adj.* little used.
малоце́нный *adj.* of little value.
малочи́сленность *f.* small number.
малочи́сленный *adj.* not numerous.
ма́лый *adj.* small, little.
малы́ш *m.* small child.
ма́льва *f.* mallow.
Мальо́рка *f.* (*island*) Mallorca.
мальто́за *f.* maltose.
ма́льчик *m.* boy, lad.
мальчи́шеский *adj.* boyish; childish.
мальчи́шество *neut.* childish behavior.
мальчи́шка *f.* (*colloq.*) little boy.
мальчуга́н *m.* (*colloq.*) little boy.
малю́сенький *adj.* (*colloq.*) tiny; minuscule.
малю́тка *m.* and *f.* (*decl. f.*) little one.
маля́р *m.* house painter.
маляри́йный *adj.* malarial.
маляри́я *f.* malaria.
маля́рный *adj.* (*attrib.*) painting; paint.
ма́ма *f.* mother, mama.
мамалы́га *f.* polenta; hominy.
мама́ша *f.* (*colloq.*) mom.
ма́менька *f.* (*obs.*) mom.
ма́менькин *adj.* (*colloq.*) mother's; mama's.
ма́мин *adj.* mother's.
ма́монт *m.* mammoth.
ма́мочка *f.* mother dear.
мана́тки *pl.* (*colloq.*) things; belongings.
ма́нго *neut. indecl.* mango.
мандари́н[1] *m.* tangerine; mandarin.
мандари́н[2] *m.* mandarin (*Chinese official*).
манда́т *m.* mandate.
манда́тный *adj.* (*attrib.*) mandate; mandated.
мандоли́на *f.* mandolin.
мандраго́ра *f.* mandrake.
мандри́л *m.* mandrill.
манёвр *m.* maneuver.
манёвренность *f.* (*mil.*) mobility.
манёвренный *adj.* (*mil.*) mobile.

маневри́ровать OVA *impf. pf.* с- to maneuver.
мане́ж *m.* **1.** riding school. **2.** circus area; ring.
манеке́н *m.* mannequin; dummy.
манеке́нщик *m. f.* манеке́нщица fashion model.
мане́р *m.* (*colloq.*) manner; way.
мане́ра *f.* manner.
мане́рность *f.* affectation.
мане́рный *adj.* mannered; affected.
манже́та *f.* cuff.
маниака́льно-депресси́вный *adj.* manic-depressive.
маниака́льный *adj.* maniacal; manic.
маникю́р *m.* manicure.
маникю́рный *adj.* (*attrib.*) manicure.
маникю́рша *f.* manicurist.
манио́ка *f.* manioc.
манипули́ровать OVA *impf.* to manipulate.
манипуля́тор *m.* manipulator.
манипуля́ция *f.* manipulation.
Манито́ба *f.* Manitoba.
мани́ть *impf. pf.* по- **1.** to beckon; to wave to. **2.** to lure, to attract, to entice.
манифе́ст *m.* manifesto. —а́ция *f.* demonstration.
мани́шка *f.* shirt front; dickey.
ма́ния *f.* mania.
ма́нна *f.* manna.
ма́нная ка́ша *f.* cereal made from farina.
мано́метр *m.* manometer; pressure gauge.
манометри́ческий *adj.* manometric.
манса́рда *f.* attic; garret.
манса́рдный *adj.* of a garret.
манти́лья *f.* mantilla.
ма́нтия *f.* mantle; cloak; robe.
манто́ *f. indecl.* woman's fur coat.
мануфакту́ра *f.* (*hist.*) manufacturing.
мануфакту́рный *adj.* (*attrib.*) manufacturing.
Манхэ́ттэн *m.* Manhattan.
Манче́стер *m.* Manchester.
маньчжу́р *m. f.* -ка Manchurian.
маньчжу́рский *adj.* Manchurian.
манья́к *m.* maniac.
маня́щий *adj.* alluring; enticing.
марабу́ *m. indecl.* marabou.
мара́зм *m.* marasmus.
мара́л *m.* Siberian red deer; maral.
мара́нье *neut.* (*colloq.*) soiling.
мараски́н *m.* maraschino.
мара́ть *impf.* **1.** *pf.* за- to soil; to stain; to sully. **2.** *pf.* на- to daub; to scribble.
марафо́н *m.* marathon.
ма́рганец FILL *m.* manganese.
ма́рганцевый *adj.* (*attrib.*) manganese.
маргари́н *m.* margarine.
маргари́тка *f.* daisy.
маргина́лии *pl.* marginalia.
ма́рево *neut.* **1.** mirage. **2.** haze.
мари́ец FILL *m. f.* мари́йка Mari.
марина́д *m.* marinade.
марини́ст *m.* painter of seascapes.
марино́ванный *adj.* marinated; pickled.
маринова́ть OVA *impf. pf.* за- to marinate, to pickle.
марионе́тка *f.* puppet; marionette.
марионе́точный *adj.* (*attrib.*) puppet.
марихуа́на *f.* marijuana.
ма́рка *f.* **1.** postage stamp. **2.** brand, grade, model. **3.** trademark.

марки́з *m.* marquis.

марки́за[1] *f.* marquise; marchioness.

марки́за[2] *f.* **1.** sun awning. **2.** marquee.

ма́ркий *adj.* that soils easily.

маркирова́ть OVA *impf.* and *pf.* to mark.

маркси́зм *m.* Marxism.

маркси́ст *m. f.* —ка Marxist.

маркси́стский *adj.* Marxist.

ма́рлевый *adj.* (*attrib.*) gauze.

ма́рля *f.* gauze.

Ма́рна *f.* (*river*) Marne.

мароде́р *m.* marauder.

мароде́рский *adj.* marauding.

мароде́рство *neut.* marauding.

мароде́рствовать OVA *impf.* to maraud.

Маро́кко *m.* Marocco.

ма́рочные ви́на *pl.* vintage wines; fine wines.

Марс *m.* Mars.

ма́рсель *m.* topsail.

Марсе́ль *m.* Marseille.

марсиа́нин *m.* Martian.

марсиа́нский *adj.* Martian.

март *m.* March. — ма́ртовский *adj.* (*attrib.*) March.

марте́н *m.* open-hearth furnace.

марте́новский *adj.* (*attrib.*) open-hearth.

марты́шка *f.* marmoset.

марципа́н *m.* marzipan.

марш *m.* march.

ма́ршал *m.* marshal.

ма́ршальский *adj.* marshal's.

марширова́ть OVA *impf.* to march.

марширо́вка *f.* marching.

марширо́вочный *adj.* (*attrib.*) marching.

маршру́т *m.* itinerary; route.

Мары́ *m.* Mary (*formerly: Merv*).

ма́ска *f.* mask.

маскара́д *m.* masquerade.

маскара́дный *adj.* (*attrib.*) masquerade.

маскирова́ть OVA *impf. pf.* за- to mask, disguise; to camouflage.

маскиро́вка *f.* masking; concealing; camouflage.

маскиро́вочный *adj.* (*attrib.*) camouflage.

Ма́сленица *f.* Shrovetide; carnival.

масле́нка *f.* **1.** butter dish. **2.** oil can.

*масле́нок *m.* Boletus lutens (*edible mushroom*).

ма́сленый *adj.* oily; greasy.

масли́на *f.* olive; olive tree.

ма́слить *impf. pf.* на-, по- to butter; to grease.

масли́чный *adj.* oil-bearing.

масли́чный *adj.* (*attrib.*) olive.

ма́сло *neut.* **1.** butter. **2.** oil.

маслобо́йка *f.* churn.

маслобо́йня *f.* creamery.

маслоде́лие *neut.* butter making.

маслоде́льный *adj.* butter-making.

маслозаво́д *m.* creamery.

масляни́стый *adj.* oily.

ма́сляный *adj.* (*attrib.*) oil; grease.

масо́н *m.* Mason.

масо́нский *adj.* Masonic.

масо́нство *neut.* Masonry.

ма́сса *f.* mass; pulp; (*with gen.*) a lot of. — ма́ссы *pl.* masses.

масса́ж *m.* massage.

массажи́ст *m.* masseur.

массажи́стка *f.* masseuse.

Массачу́сетс *m.* Massachusetts.

масси́в *m.* mountain range.

масси́вный *adj.* massive.

масси́ровать OVA *impf.* and *pf.* to massage, to rub.

массо́вка *f.* (*colloq.*) (*theat., film*) crowd scene.

ма́ссовый *adj.* mass; of the masses.

ма́стер *m.* **1.** foreman. **2.** expert.

мастери́ть *impf. pf.* с- **1.** to fashion. **2.** to build; to put together.

мастерска́я *f.* workshop; studio.

ма́стерски *adv.* masterfully; like an expert.

мастерско́й *adj.* masterly.

мастерство́ *neut.* skill, mastery; craftmanship.

масти́ка *f.* **1.** mastic. **2.** floor polish.

масти́ковый *adj.* mastic.

масти́т *m.* mastitis.

масти́тый *adj.* venerable.

мастодо́нт *m.* mastodon.

масть *f.* **1.** (*of animal*) color, shade. **2.** (*cards*) suit.

масшта́б *m.* scale.

мат[1] *m.* (*chess*) checkmate, mate.

мат[2] *m.* obscene language.

матема́тик *m.* mathematician. —а *f.* mathematics.

математи́ческий *adj.* mathematical.

материа́л *m.* material.

материали́зм *m.* materialism.

материализова́ть OVA *impf.* and *pf.* to realize; to give shape to.

материали́ст *m. f.* —ка materialist.

материалисти́ческий *adj.* materialistic.

материа́льно *adv.* materially; financially.

материа́льный *adj.* material; financial.

матери́к *m.* mainland; continent.

материко́вый *adj.* continental.

матери́нский *adj.* maternal.

матери́нство *neut.* motherhood.

мате́рия *f.* **1.** matter. **2.** subject.

ма́терный *adj.* (*colloq.*) obscene.

мате́рчатый *adj.* (*attrib.*) cloth; made of cloth.

матёрый *adj.* **1.** (*animal*) full-grown; old. **2.** inveterate.

ма́тка *f.* **1.** uterus; womb. **2.** (*of animals*) female, dam, queen.

ма́товый *adj.* mat; dull.

ма́точный *adj.* uterine.

матра́с *also* матра́ц *m.* mattress.

матра́сный *adj.* (*attrib.*) mattress.

матрёшка *f.* set of nesting wooden dolls.

матриарха́льный *adj.* matriarchal.

матриарха́т *m.* matriarchy.

матримониа́льный *adj.* (*obs.*) matrimonial.

ма́трица *f.* matrix.

матро́на *f.* matron.

матро́с *m.* sailor, seaman.

матро́ска *f.* sailor's jacket.

матро́сский *adj.* (*attrib.*) sailor; sailor's.

ма́тушка *f.* (*obs.*) mother.

матч *m.* (*athl.*) match.

мать *f.* mother.

ма́узер *m.* Mauser.

мах *m.* stroke.

махао́н *m.* swallowtail (butterfly).

маха́ть *impf. pf.* махну́ть (*with instr.*) to wave.

маши́на *f.* (*colloq.*) large cumbersome object.
махина́ция *f.* machination.
махови́к *m.* flywheel.
махово́е колесо́ *neut.* flywheel.
махо́рка *f.* a kind of inferior tobacco.
махро́вый *adj.* (*attrib.*) **1.** terry cloth. **2.** blatant. **3.** fanatical.
маца́ *f.* matzo.
ма́чеха *f.* stepmother.
ма́чта *f.* mast.
маши́на *f.* **1.** engine. **2.** machine. **3.** car.
машина́льный *adj.* mechanical; automatic.
машиниза́ция *f.* mechanization.
машинизи́ровать OVA *impf. and pf.* to mechanize.
машини́ст *m.* **1.** machinist. **2.** engineer.
машини́стка *f.* typist.
маши́нка *f.* **1.** typewriter. **2.** sewing machine.
маши́нный *adj.* (*attrib.*) machine.
машинопи́сный *adj.* typewritten.
машинопись *f.* typing.
машинострое́ние *neut.* machine building.
машинострои́тельный *adj.* machine-building.
мае́стро *m. indecl.* maestro.
мая́к *m.* lighthouse.
ма́ятник *m.* pendulum.
ма́яться *impf.* (*colloq.*) **1.** to toil. **2.** to suffer.
мая́чить *impf.* to loom in the distance.
мгла *f.* mist, haze; gloom.
мгли́стый *adj.* misty, hazy.
мгнове́ние *neut.* instant; moment.
мгнове́нно *adv.* instantly.
мгнове́нный *adj.* instantaneous; momentary.
ме́бель *f.* furniture.
ме́бельный *adj.* (*attrib.*) furniture.
ме́бельщик *m.* furniture maker.
меблиро́ванный *adj.* furnished.
меблирова́ть OVA *impf. and pf.* to furnish.
меблиро́вка *f.* furnishings, furniture; furnishing.
мегафо́н *m.* megaphone.
меге́ра *f.* shrew; termagant; virago.
мёд *m.* honey.
медали́ст *m. f.* —ка medalist; medal winner.
меда́ль *f.* medal.
медальо́н *m.* medallion.
медбра́т *m.* male nurse.
медве́дица *f.* female bear. — Больша́я Медве́дица *f.* Big Dipper; Ursa Major.
медве́дь *m.* bear.
медве́жий *adj.* bear, bear's.
медвежо́нок *m.* bear cub.
Медвежьего́рск *m.* Medvezhyegorsk.
медвя́ный *adj.* smelling of honey.
медиа́на *f.* median.
ме́дик *m.* doctor; health provider; medical student.
медикаме́нты *pl.* medicines.
ме́диум *m.* medium; spiritualist.
медици́на *f.* medicine.
медици́нский *adj.* medical.
ме́дленно *adv.* slowly.
ме́дленный *adj.* slow.
медли́тельность *f.* slowness; sluggishness.
медли́тельный *adj.* slow; sluggish.
ме́длить *impf.* to linger; to delay.
ме́дник *m.* coppersmith.
ме́дный *adj.* copper.

медо́вый *adj.* (*attrib.*) honey.
медоно́сный *adj.* producing honey.
медосмо́тр *m.* (*abbr. of* медици́нский осмо́тр) physical examination.
медпу́нкт *m.* first-aid station.
медсестра́ *f.* female nurse.
меду́за *f.* jellyfish; medusa.
медь *f.* copper. — жёлтая медь brass.
медя́к *m.* (*colloq.*) copper coin.
медя́нка *f.* **1.** grass snake. **2.** (*chem.*) verdigris.
меж *prep.* (*with instr.*) between.
межа́ *f.* boundary.
междоме́тие *neut.* (*gram.*) interjection.
междоусо́бие *neut. also* междоусо́бица *f.* civil strife; internecine strife.
междоусо́бный *adj.* internecine.
ме́жду *prep.* (*with instr.*) between; among, amongst. — ме́жду тем meanwhile. — ме́жду тем как while. — ме́жду про́чим by the way, incidentally.
междугоро́дный *adj.* (*phone call*) long-distance.
междунаро́дный *adj.* international.
междуца́рствие *neut.* interregnum.
межева́ние *neut.* surveying.
межева́ть OVA *impf.* to survey; to mark boundaries.
межево́й *adj.* (*attrib.*) boundary.
межзвёздный *adj.* interstellar.
межконтинента́льный *adj.* intercontinental.
межпланётный *adj.* interplanetary.
межсезо́нье *neut.* off-season.
мезозо́йский *adj.* Mesozoic.
мезо́н *m.* meson.
мезони́н *m.* **1.** attic (*story*). **2.** mezzanine. **3.** (*archit.*) mansard.
Ме́ксика *f.* (*country*) Mexico.
мексика́нец FILL *m. f.* мексика́нка Mexican.
мел *m.* chalk.
меланхо́лик *m. f.* меланхоли́чка melancholic person.
меланхоли́ческий *also* меланхоли́чный *adj.* melancholic.
меланхо́лия *f.* melancholy.
меле́ть *impf. pf.* об- to become shallow.
мелиора́ция *f.* land reclamation.
ме́лкий *adj.* **1.** small; fine. **2.** shallow. **3.** petty, minor.
мелкобуржуа́зный *adj.* petit-bourgeois; of lower middle class.
мелково́дный *adj.* shallow.
мелково́дье *neut.* shallow water.
мелкота́ *f.* (*colloq.*) small fry.
мелово́й *adj.* chalk; chalky.
мело́дика *f.* melodics.
мелоди́чность *f.* melodiousness.
мелоди́чный *adj.* melodious.
мело́дия *f.* melody.
мелодра́ма *f.* melodrama.
мелодрамати́ческий *adj.* melodramatic.
мело́к FILL *m.* piece of chalk.
мелома́н *m.* music lover.
ме́лочность *f.* pettiness.
ме́лочный *adj.* petty; small-minded.
ме́лочь *f.* **1.** trifle; trivia. **2.** (*money*) change.
мель *f.* shoal; (*sand*) bank. — сесть на мель *pf.* to run aground.

Ме́льбурн *m.* Melbourne.
мелька́ть *impf. pf.* мелькну́ть 1. to be glimpsed for an instant; to flash by. 2. (*of stars*) to glimmer.
ме́льком *adv.* in passing; cursorily.
ме́льник *m.* miller.
ме́льница *f.* mill.
мельча́ть *impf. pf.* из- 1. to become smaller. 2. to become shallow.
мелюзга́ *f.* (*colloq.*) small fry.
мембра́на *f.* diaphragm (*in an earphone, etc.*)
мемора́ндум *m.* memorandum.
мемориа́льный *adj.* memorial.
ме́на *f.* exchange, barter.
ме́нее *comp. adv.* less. — тем не ме́нее *adv.* nonetheless.
менестре́ль *m.* minstrel.
менинги́т *m.* meningitis.
меново́й *adj.* of exchange.
менструа́льный *adj.* menstrual.
менструа́ция *f.* menstruation.
менструи́ровать OVA *impf.* to menstruate.
менто́л *m.* menthol.
менто́ловый *adj.* (*attrib.*) menthol.
ме́нтор *m.* (*obs.*) mentor.
менуэ́т *m.* minuet.
ме́ньше *adv.* smaller; less.
меньшеви́к *m. f.* меньшеви́чка Menshevik.
меньшеви́стский *adj.* Menshevik.
ме́ньший *adj.* lesser, smaller.
меньшинство́ *neut.* minority.
меню́ *neut. indecl.* menu.
меня́ *pron. gen., acc. of* я.
меня́ла *m. and f.* (*decl. f.*) moneychanger.
меня́ть *impf. pf.* по- to change; to exchange (for). —ся to change; to exchange.
ме́ра *f.* measure.
ме́ргель *m.* (*geol.*) marl.
мере́нга *f.* meringue.
мере́щиться *impf. pf.* по- (*with dat.*) (*colloq.*) to seem to.
мерза́вец FILL *m. f.* мерза́вка vile person.
ме́рзкий *adj.* vile.
мерзлота́ *f.* frozen earth.
мёрзлый *adj.* frozen.
мёрзнуть *impf. pf.* за- to freeze.
ме́рзость *f.* abomination; vile thing.
меридиа́н *m.* meridian.
мери́ло *neut.* criterion; standard.
мерино́с *m.* merino sheep.
мерино́совый *adj.* merino.
ме́рить *impf. pf.* по- to measure; to try on.
ме́рка *f.* measure; yardstick.
меркантили́зм *m.* mercantilism.
ме́ркнуть *impf. pf.* по- to grow dark or dim.
мерлу́шка *f.* lambskin.
ме́рный *adj.* measured; measuring.
мероприя́тие *neut.* 1. measure; step. 2. social event.
мертвенный *adj.* deathly; ghastly.
мертве́ть *impf. pf.* по-, о- to grow numb or stiff.
мертве́ц *m.* corpse.
мертве́цкая *f.* (*colloq.*) morgue; mortuary.
мертве́цки пьян *adj.* dead drunk.
мертвечи́на *f.* carrion.
мертви́ть *impf.* to kill, to destroy.

Мёртвое мо́ре *neut.* the Dead Sea.
мертворождённый *adj.* stillborn.
мёртвый *adj.* dead. — *m.* dead person.
мерца́ние *neut.* glimmer; flickering.
мерца́ть *impf.* to shimmer; to glimmer.
меси́ть *impf. pf.* вы́месить to knead.
ме́сса *f.* (*relig.*) Mass.
мессиа́нский *adj.* Messianic.
Месси́я *m.* Messiah.
месте́чко *neut.* 1. *dim. of* ме́сто. 2. small town.
мести́ *impf. pf.* вы́мести to sweep.
местко́м *m.* (*abbr. of* ме́стный комите́т) local committee.
ме́стность *f.* area; locality.
ме́стный *adj.* local.
ме́сто *neut.* 1. place. 2. room. 3. seat. 4. job. —жи́тельство *neut.* place of residence.
местоиме́ние *neut.* pronoun.
местоиме́нный *adj.* pronominal.
местонахожде́ние *neut.* location.
местоположе́ние *neut.* site; location.
местопребыва́ние *neut.* residence; habitat.
месть *f.* vengeance; revenge.
ме́сяц *m.* 1. month. 2. moon.
ме́сячник *m.* month (*devoted to something*).
ме́сячный *adj.* monthly.
ме́та *f.* mark.
мета́лл *m.* metal.
металли́ст[1] *m.* metalworker.
металли́ст[2] *m.* heavy metallist (*music performer or fan*).
металли́ческий *adj.* metal; metallic.
металли́ческий рок *m.* (*mus.*) heavy metal rock.
металло́ид *m.* metalloid.
металлоло́м *m.* scrap metal.
металлоно́сный *adj.* metalliferous.
металлоплави́льный *adj.* (*attrib.*) smelting.
металлурги́ческий *adj.* metallurgic.
металлурги́я *f.* metallurgy.
метаморфо́за *f.* metamorphosis.
мета́н *m.* methane.
мета́ние *neut.* throwing.
метаста́з *m.* metastasis.
мета́тель *m. f.* —ница thrower, hurler.
мета́тельный *adj.* intended to be thrown or launched.
мета́ть[1] *impf. pf.* метну́ть to throw, to cast, to fling.
мета́ть[2] *impf. pf.* с- to baste.
мета́ть икру́ to spawn.
мета́ться *impf. pres.* мечу́сь, ме́чешься 1. to rush around. 2. to toss about (*in one's sleep*).
метафи́зик *m.* metaphysician.
метафи́зика *f.* metaphysics.
метафизи́ческий *adj.* metaphysical.
мета́фора *f.* metaphor.
метафори́ческий *adj.* metaphorical.
мете́лица *f.* snowstorm.
мете́лка *f.* whisk broom.
мете́ль *f.* snowstorm.
метео́р *m.* meteor.
метеори́зм *m.* (*med.*) flatulence.
метеори́т *m.* meteorite.
метео́рный *adj.* (*attrib.*) meteor; meteoric.
метеоро́лог *m.* meteorologist.
метеорологи́ческий *adj.* meteorological.

метеороло́гия *f.* meteorology.
метеоспу́тник *m.* weather satellite.
метиза́ция *f.* crossbreeding.
мети́л *m.* methyl.
метиле́н *m.* methylene.
мети́ловый *adj.* (*attrib.*) methyl.
мети́с *m.* **1.** mongrel; half-breed. **2.** mestizo.
ме́тить[1] *impf. pf.* по-, на- to mark, to stamp.
ме́тить[2] *impf. pf.* на- (в *with acc.*) to aim at; to aspire to.
ме́тка *f.* mark.
ме́ткий *adj.* well-aimed; accurate.
ме́ткость *f.* accuracy.
метла́ *f.* broom.
метну́ть *pf. of* мета́ть[1].
ме́тод *m.* method.
методи́зм *m.* Methodism.
мето́дика *f.* methods.
методи́ст *m. f.* —ка Methodist.
методи́стский *adj.* Methodist.
методи́ческий *adj.* methodical; systematic.
методологи́ческий *adj.* methodological.
методоло́гия *f.* methodology.
метр *m.* meter.
метра́ж *m.* **1.** length in meters. **2.** area (*in square meters*). **3.** (*of movies*) footage.
метрдоте́ль *m.* maître d'hôtel.
ме́трика *f.* birth certificate.
метри́ческий *adj.* metric.
метро́ *neut. indecl.* subway, metro.
метроно́м *m.* metronome.
метрополите́н *m.* metro; subway.
метропо́лия *f.* mother country or center (*of an empire*).
мех *m. pl.* меха́ fur.
механиза́тор *m.* specialist in mechanization.
механиза́ция *f.* mechanization.
механизи́ровать OVA *impf. and pf.* to mechanize.
механи́зм *m.* mechanism.
меха́ник *m.* mechanic.
меха́ника *f.* mechanics.
механи́ческий *adj.* mechanical.
мехи́ *pl.* bellows.
Ме́хико *m. indecl.* Mexico City.
мехово́й *adj.* fur.
меховщи́к *m.* furrier.
мецена́т *m.* patron of the arts; Maecenas.
ме́ццо-сопра́но *neut. indecl.* mezzo-soprano.
меч *m.* sword.
мечено́сец FILL *m.* **1.** Teutonic knight. **2.** swordbearer.
ме́ченый *adj.* marked.
мече́ть *f.* mosque.
меч-ры́ба *f.* swordfish.
мечта́ *f.* dream.
мечта́ние *neut.* reverie; daydreaming.
мечта́тель *m. f.* —ница dreamer; daydreamer.
мечта́тельность *adj.* reverie.
мечта́тельный *adj.* given to dreaming.
мечта́ть *impf.* to dream.
меша́лка *f.* mixer.
мешани́на *f.* mishmash; hodgepodge.
меша́ть[1] *impf. pf.* по- (*with dat.*) **1.** to disturb. **2.** to hinder, to hamper. **3.** to interfere.
меша́ть[2] *impf. pf.* по-, с- to stir; to blend.

ме́шкать *impf.* (*colloq.*) to dawdle; to dally; to tarry.
мешкова́тый *adj.* **1.** awkward; clumsy. **2.** (*of clothing*) baggy.
мешкови́на *f.* sackcloth.
ме́шкотный *adj.* (*colloq.*) sluggish.
мешо́к FILL *m.* bag; sack.
мешо́чек *m.* **1.** *dim. of* мешо́к. **2.** sac. — яйцо́ в мешо́чек *neut.* medium-boiled egg.
Мешхе́д *m.* Mashhad.
мещани́н *m. f.* меща́нка **1.** petit-bourgeois person. **2.** narrow-minded person.
меща́нский *adj.* petit-bourgeois.
меща́нство *neut.* **1.** petite bourgeoisie. **2.** narrow-mindedness.
мзда́ *f.* (*obs.*) payment.
миа́змы *pl.* miasma.
миг *m.* instant.
мига́лка *f.* (*colloq.*) **1.** blinking light. **2.** wick lamp.
мига́ние *neut.* winking; blinking.
мига́ть *impf. pf.* мигну́ть to blink; to wink; to twinkle.
ми́гом *adv.* (*colloq.*) in a flash; in an instant.
мигра́ция *f.* migration.
мигре́нь *f.* migraine.
мигри́ровать OVA *impf.* to migrate.
ми́дия *f.* mussel.
мизансце́на *f.* (*theat.*) staging.
мизантро́п *m. f.* —ка misanthrope.
мизантропи́ческий *adj.* misanthropic.
мизантро́пия *f.* misanthropy.
мизе́рный *adj.* **1.** scanty; wretched. **2.** meager; paltry.
мизи́нец FILL *m.* little finger.
Ми́конос *m.* (*island*) Mikonos.
микро́б *m.* microbe; germ.
микробио́лог *m.* microbiologist.
микробиоло́гия *f.* microbiology.
микроко́см *m.* microcosm.
микроме́тр *m.* micrometer.
микро́н *m.* micron.
микроорганизм *m.* microorganism.
микроско́п *m.* microscope.
микроскопи́ческий *adj.* microscopical.
микросхе́ма *f.* microcircuit.
микрофи́льм *m.* microfilm.
микрофо́н *m.* microphone.
миксту́ра *f.* **1.** mixture. **2.** (liquid) medicine.
Мила́н *m.* Milan.
ми́лая *f.* darling; sweetheart; dear one.
ми́ленький *adj.* (*colloq.*) dear; sweet.
милитариза́ция *f.* militarization.
милитари́зм *m.* militarism.
милитаризова́ть OVA *impf. and pf.* to militarize.
милитари́ст *m.* militarist.
милитари́стский *adj.* (*attrib.*) militarist.
милице́йский *adj.* police.
милиционе́р *m.* policeman.
мили́ция *f.* **1.** the police. **2.** militia.
миллиа́рд *m.* billion.
миллиарде́р *m.* multimillionaire.
миллиа́рдный *adj.* billionth.
миллиме́тр *m.* millimeter.
миллио́н *m.* million. —ный *adj.* millionth.
миллионе́р *m.* millionaire.

ми́ло *adv.* nicely.
ми́ловать *impf. pf.* **по-** (*obs.*) to pardon.
милови́дный *adj.* comely.
милосе́рдие *neut.* mercy; charity.
милосе́рдный *adj.* merciful; charitable.
ми́лостивый *adj.* gracious.
ми́лостыня *f.* alms.
ми́лость *f.* favor, kindness; mercy.
ми́лый *adj.* pleasant; nice; dear.
ми́ля *f.* mile.
мим *m.* mime.
ми́мика *f.* facial expressions.
мимикри́я *f.* (*biol.*) mimicry.
мими́ст *m. f.* **—ка** mimic.
мими́ческий *adj.* mimic.
ми́мо *adv., prep.* (*with gen.*) past, by.
мимо́за *f.* mimosa.
мимолётный *adj.* fleeting, passing.
мимохо́дом *adv.* in passing; by the way.
ми́на[1] *f.* countenance, facial expression.
ми́на[2] *f.* (*mil.*) mine.
минаре́т *m.* minaret.
миндалеви́дный *adj.* almond-shaped.
минда́лина *f.* tonsil.
минда́ль *m.* almond tree; (*colloq.*) almonds.
минда́льный *adj.* (*attrib.*) almond.
минёр *m.* specialist in mine-laying.
минера́л *m.* mineral.
минерало́г *m.* mineralogist.
минералоги́ческий *adj.* mineralogical.
минерало́гия *f.* mineralogy.
минера́льный *adj.* mineral.
миниатю́ра *f.* miniature.
миниатю́рный *adj.* miniature, tiny.
минима́льный *adj.* minimum.
ми́нимум *m.* minimum. *–adv.* at least; a minimum of.
мини́ровать OVA *impf.* and *pf.* (*mil.*) to lay mines; to mine.
министе́рский *adj.* ministerial.
министе́рство *neut.* ministry, department.
мини́стр *m.* minister.
Миннесо́та *f.* Minnesota.
ми́нный *adj.* (*attrib.*) mine.
минова́ть OVA *impf.* and *pf.* **1.** to pass (by). **2.** to avoid. — **чему́ быть, того́ не минова́ть** whatever will be, will be; it's inevitable.
мино́га *f.* lamprey.
миноиска́тель *m.* mine detector.
миноме́т *m.* (*mil.*) mortar.
миноме́тный *adj.* (*attrib.*) mortar.
миноно́сец FILL *m.* torpedo boat. — **эска́дренный миноно́сец** *m.* destroyer.
мино́р *m.* (*mus.*) minor.
мино́рный *adj.* (*mus.*) minor.
Минск *m.* Minsk.
мину́вший *adj.* past.
ми́нус *m.* **1.** minus. **2.** defect.
мину́та *f.* minute; moment, instant.
мину́тка *f. dim. of* **мину́та**.
мину́тный *adj.* (*attrib.*) minute; momentary.
мину́точка *f. dim. of* **мину́тка**.
мину́ть *pf.* to pass; (*impers., with dat.*) to turn (a certain age).
мир[1] *m.* peace.
мир[2] *m.* world.

мира́ж *m.* mirage.
Ми́ргород *m.* Myrhorod (*Russian: Mirgorod*).
мириа́ды *pl.* myriads.
мири́ть *impf. pf.* **по-, при-** to reconcile. **—ся** (**с** *with instr.*) to be reconciled with.
ми́рно *adv.* peacefully.
ми́рный *adj.* peace; peaceful.
мирова́я *f.* (*colloq.*) amicable agreement.
мирова́я паути́на *f.* World Wide Web (*abbr.* WWW).
мировоззре́ние *neut.* world view; world outlook.
мирово́й *adj.* (*attrib.*) world. — **Втора́я мирова́я война́** *f.* World War II.
миролюби́вый *adj.* peace-loving; peaceful.
миролю́бие *neut.* peaceful character.
миропома́зание *neut.* anointing.
миротво́рец FILL *m.* peacemaker.
ми́рра *f.* myrrh.
мирско́й *adj.* secular; worldly.
мирт *m.* myrtle.
ми́ртовый *adj.* myrtle.
миря́нин *m. f.* **миря́нка** (*obs.*) layperson.
ми́ска *f.* bowl; tureen.
мисс *f. indecl.* Miss; miss.
миссионе́р *m. f.* **—ка** missionary.
миссионе́рский *adj.* missionary.
миссионе́рство *neut.* missionary work.
ми́ссис *f. indecl.* Mrs.
Миссиси́пи *f.* Mississippi.
ми́ссия *f.* mission.
Миссу́ри *f.* Missouri.
ми́стер *m.* Mr.; mister.
ми́стик *m.* mystic.
ми́стика *f.* mysticism.
мистифика́ция *f.* hoax; practical joke.
мистици́зм *m.* mysticism.
мисти́ческий *adj.* mystical.
ми́тинг *m.* rally; mass meeting.
митка́левый *adj.* calico.
митка́ль *m.* calico.
мито́з *m.* mitosis.
ми́тра *f.* (*eccl.*) miter.
митрополи́т *m.* (*Orthodox*) metropolitan.
миф *m.* myth.
мифи́ческий *adj.* mythical.
мифологи́ческий *adj.* mythological.
мифоло́гия *f.* mythology.
Мичига́н *m.* Michigan.
ми́чман *m.* (*naval*) warrant officer; midshipman.
мише́нь *f.* target. — **я́блоко мише́ни** *neut.* bull's-eye.
ми́шка *f.* teddy bear.
мишура́ *f.* **1.** tinsel. **2.** show; ostentation.
мишу́рный *adj.* (*attrib.*) tinsel.
младе́нец FILL *m.* infant.
младе́нческий *adj.* infantile.
младе́нчество *neut.* infancy.
младо́й *adj.* (*obs.*) young.
мла́дше *adv.* younger.
мла́дший *adj.* younger; junior.
млекопита́ющее *neut.* mammal.
мле́ть *impf.* **1.** (**от** *with gen.*) to be overcome (*with an emotion*). **2.** to become numb.
Мле́чный Путь *m.* the Milky Way.
мне *pron. dat., prep. of* **я**.
мнемо́ника *f.* mnemonics.

мнемони́ческий *adj.* mnemonic.

мне́ние *neut.* opinion.

мни́мый *adj.* imaginary.

мни́тельный *adj.* **1.** hypochondriac. **2.** mistrustful; suspicious.

мно́гие *adj.*, *pron.* many.

мно́го *adv.* much. — *adj.* (*with gen.*) a lot of.

многобо́жие *neut.* polytheism.

многобра́чие *neut.* polygamy.

многобра́чный *adj.* polygamous.

многова́то *adv.* (*colloq.*) a bit much.

многогра́нный *adj.* many-sided; multifaceted; polyhedral.

мно́гое *neut.* much; a large amount.

многожёнец FILL *m.* polygamist.

многожёнство *neut.* polygamy.

многозначи́тельный *adj.* **1.** significant. **2.** (*of a glance* or *smile*) knowing.

многокра́сочный *adj.* multicolored.

многокра́тно *adv.* repeatedly.

многокра́тный *adj.* **1.** repeated, frequent. **2.** (*gram.*) frequentative.

многоле́тний *adj.* **1.** of many years. **2.** (*bot.*) perennial. **3.** long-lasting.

многолю́дный *adj.* **1.** crowded. **2.** populous.

многомиллио́нный *adj.* of many millions.

многонациона́льный *adj.* multinational.

многоно́жка *f.* millipede; centipede.

многообеща́ющий *adj.* **1.** promising. **2.** significant. **3.** up-and-coming.

многообра́зие *neut.* variety; diversity.

многообра́зный *adj.* diverse; varied.

многоречи́вый *adj.* long-winded; verbose.

многосеме́йный *adj.* with a large family.

многосло́вие *neut.* verbosity.

многосло́вный *adj.* verbose.

многосло́жный *adj.* polysyllabic.

многосторо́нний *adj.* **1.** versatile. **2.** multilateral.

многосторо́нность *f.* versatility.

многострада́льный *adj.* long-suffering.

многоступе́нчатый *adj.* multistage.

многотира́жка *f.* (*colloq.*) company newspaper.

многотира́жный *adj.* (*of publication*) with a large circulation.

многото́мный *adj.* multivolume.

многото́чие *neut.* omission points; suspension points (...).

многоуважа́емый *adj.* (*in written greetings*) dear.

многоуго́льник *m.* polygon.

многоуго́льный *adj.* polygonal.

многоцве́тный *adj.* multicolored.

многочи́сленность *f.* large number.

многочи́сленный *adj.* multiple, numerous.

многочле́н *m.* polynomial.

многочле́нный *adj.* polynomial.

многоэта́жный *adj.* multistoried.

многоязы́чный *adj.* multilingual; polyglot.

мно́жественность *f.* multiplicity.

мно́жественный *adj.* plural. — **мно́жественное число́** *neut.* (*gram.*) the plural.

мно́жество *neut.* multitude.

мно́жимое *neut.* multiplicand.

мно́житель *m.* multiplier, factor.

мно́жить *impf.* **1.** *pf.* **по-** to multiply. **2.** *pf.* **у-** to increase.

мной *also* **мно́ю** *pron.*, *instr. of* **я**.

мобилизацио́нный *adj.* (*attrib.*) mobilization.

мобилиза́ция *f.* mobilization.

мобилизова́ть *impf. and pf.* to mobilize.

моби́льность *f.* mobility.

моби́льный *adj.* mobile.

моги́ла *f.* grave.

Моги́лёв *m.* Mahilyow (*Russian: Mogilyov*).

моги́льный *adj.* (*attrib.*) grave; burial.

моги́льщик *m.* gravedigger.

могу́чий *adj.* powerful; mighty.

могу́щественный *adj.* mighty; powerful.

могу́щество *neut.* power; might.

мо́да *f.* fashion.

мода́льный *adj.* modal.

модели́ровать OVA *impf. and pf.* **1.** to model; to fashion. **2.** to design clothes.

моде́ль *f.* model.

модельє́р *m.* fashion designer.

моде́льный *adj.* (*attrib.*) model; pattern.

моде́льщик *m. f.* **моде́льщица** modeler.

мо́дем *m.* modem.

моде́рн *m.* modernist style.

модерниза́ция *f.* modernization.

модернизи́ровать OVA *impf. and pf.* to modernize.

модерни́зм *m.* modernism.

модерни́ст *m.* modernist.

модерни́стский *adj.* modernist.

моди́стка *f.* milliner.

модифика́ция *f.* modification.

модифици́ровать OVA *impf. and pf.* to modify.

мо́дник *m. f.* **мо́дница** (*colloq.*) fashion plate.

мо́дно *adv.* fashionably; stylishly.

мо́дный *adj.* fashionable.

модули́ровать OVA *impf.* to modulate.

мо́дуль *m.* module; modulus.

модуля́тор *m.* modulator.

модуля́ция *f.* modulation.

моёвка *f.* kittiwake.

Можа́йск *m.* Mozhaysk.

мо́жет быть *adv.* perhaps, maybe.

можжеве́ловый *adj.* (*attrib.*) juniper.

можжеве́льник *m.* juniper.

мо́жно *impers.* it is possible; one may, one can.

моза́ика *f.* mosaic.

моза́ичный *adj.* mosaic; inlaid.

Мозамби́к *m.* Mozambique.

мозг *m.* **1.** brain. **2.** marrow. —**овóй** *adj.* cerebral.

мозгови́тый *adj.* (*colloq.*) brainy.

мозжечо́к FILL *m.* cerebellum.

мозо́листый *adj.* calloused.

мозо́ль *f.* callus; corn.

мозо́льный *adj.* for treatment of corns.

мой *poss. adj.* my; mine.

мо́йка *f.* washing; washer.

мо́йщик *m. f.* **мо́йщица** (*person*) washer.

мока́си́н *m.* moccasin.

мо́кко *neut.* mocha.

мо́кнуть *impf.* to become wet; to soak.

мокри́ца *f.* wood louse.

мокрова́тый *adj.* damp; moist.

мокро́та *f.* phlegm.

мокрота́ *f.* humidity.

мо́крый *adj.* wet.

мол *m.* **1.** pier. **2.** breakwater, jetty.

молва́ *f.* rumor.

молдава́нин *m. f.* молдава́нка Moldavian.
молдава́нский *also* молда́вский Moldavian.
Молда́вия *also* Молдо́ва *f.* Moldavia.
моле́бен *m.* short church service.
моле́кула *f.* molecule.
молекуля́рный *adj.* molecular.
моле́льня *f.* prayer house.
моле́ние *neut.* 1. prayer service. 2. supplication.
молески́н *m.* moleskin.
молески́новый *adj.* moleskin.
молибде́н *m.* molybdenum.
молибде́новый *adj.* molybdic.
моли́тва *f.* prayer.
моли́твенник *m.* prayer book.
моли́твенный *adj. (attrib.)* prayer.
моли́ть *impf.* to entreat, to implore, to beseech.
  —ся (о *with prep.*) to pray (for); (на *with acc.*) to
  adore, to idolize.
моллю́ск *m.* mollusk.
молниено́сный *adj.* lightning-fast.
молниеотво́д *m.* lightning rod.
мо́лния *f.* 1. lightning. 2. zipper.
молодёжный *adj. (attrib.)* youth.
молодёжь *f.* youth; the young.
моло́денький *adj. (colloq.)* young.
молоде́ц FILL *m.* good boy; fine lad. –*interj.* well
  done!
молоде́цкий *adj.* bold; dashing.
молоде́чество *neut.* bravado.
молодня́к *m.* young animals.
молодожёны *pl.* newlyweds.
молодо́й *adj.* young.
мо́лодость *f.* youth.
молодцева́тый *adj.* dashing.
молодчик *m. (colloq.)* thug; punk.
молодчи́на *m. and f. (decl. f.) (colloq.)* good boy;
  good girl.
молоды́е *pl.* young couple.
моложа́вый *adj.* youthful; young-looking.
моло́же *adj., compr. of* молодо́й.
моло́ка *f. also* моло́ки *pl.* milt; soft roe.
молоко́ *neut.* milk.
молокосо́с *m. (colloq.)* neophyte; greenhorn.
мо́лот *m.* (large) hammer.
молоти́лка *f. (machine)* thresher.
молоти́льщик *m. f.* молоти́льщица *(person)*
  thresher.
молоти́ть *impf.* to thresh; to thrash.
молото́к FILL *m.* hammer.
мо́лот-ры́ба *f.* hammerhead.
мо́лотый *adj.* ground.
моло́ть *impf. pf.* с- to grind; to mill.
молотьба́ *f.* threshing.
моло́чная *f.* dairy; creamery.
моло́чник *m.* 1. milk pitcher. 2. milkman.
моло́чница¹ *f.* dairymaid.
моло́чница² *f. (disease)* thrush.
моло́чный *adj. (attrib.)* 1. milk. 2. dairy. 3. lactic.
мо́лча *adv.* silently, in silence.
молчали́вость *f.* reticent character; taciturnity.
молчали́вый *adj.* 1. taciturn. 2. tacit.
молча́ние *neut.* silence.
молча́ть *impf.* to be *or* keep silent.
моль *f.* clothes moth.
мольба́ *f.* entreaty, plea.
мольбе́рт *m.* easel.

моля́щийся *m.* worshiper.
моме́нт *m.* moment; factor.
момента́льно *adv.* immediately; instantly.
момента́льный *adj.* instantaneous.
Мона́ко *neut. indecl.* Monaco.
мона́рх *m.* monarch.
монархи́зм *m.* monarchism.
монархи́ст *m. f.* —ка monarchist.
монархи́ческий *adj.* monarchist; monarchical.
мона́рхия *f.* monarchy.
монасты́рский *adj.* of a monastery; of a nunnery.
монасты́рь *m.* monastery; cloister, nunnery, convent.
мона́х *m.* monk.
мона́хиня *f.* nun.
мона́шенка *f. (colloq.)* nun.
мона́шеский *adj.* monastic.
мона́шество *neut.* monkhood.
Монбла́н *m. (mountain)* Mont Blanc.
монго́л *m. f.* —ка Mongolian.
Монго́лия *f.* Mongolia.
моне́та *f.* coin.
моне́тный *adj.* monetary.
мони́зм *m.* monism.
монисти́ческий *adj.* monistic.
мони́сто *neut.* necklace *(of coins or beads)*.
монога́мия *f.* monogamy.
моногра́мма *f.* monogram.
монографи́ческий *adj.* monographic.
моно́кль *m.* monocle.
моноли́т *m.* monolith.
моноли́тность *f.* monolithic nature.
моноли́тный *adj.* monolithic.
моноло́г *m.* monologue.
мононуклео́з *m.* mononucleosis.
монопла́н *m.* monoplane.
монополиза́ция *f.* monopolization.
монополизи́ровать OVA *impf. and pf.* to monopolize.
монополи́ст *m.* monopolist.
монополисти́ческий *adj.* monopolistic.
монопо́лия *f.* monopoly.
монопо́льный *adj. (attrib.)* monopoly.
монотеи́зм *m.* monotheism.
монотеисти́ческий *adj.* monotheistic.
моноти́п *m.* monotype.
моното́нность *f.* monotony.
моното́нный *adj.* monotonous.
монохромати́ческий *adj.* monochromatic.
монсеньо́р *m.* Monsignor.
монта́ж *m.* 1. installing *(of machinery)*. 2. editing
  (of film or novel). 3. montage.
Монта́на *f.* Montana.
монтёр *m.* electrician.
монти́ровать OVA *impf. pf.* с- 1. to assemble. 2.
  to mount.
монуме́нт *m.* monument.
монумента́льный *adj.* monumental.
мопе́д *m.* moped.
мопс *m. (dog)* pug.
мор *m.* pestilence; plague.
Мора́ва *f. (river)* Morava.
морализи́ровать OVA *impf.* to moralize.
морали́ст *m. f.* —ка moralist.
мора́ль *f.* moral; morals.
мора́льно *adv.* morally.

мора́льный *adj.* moral.

морато́рий *m.* moratorium.

морг *m.* morgue.

морганати́ческий *adj.* morganatic.

морга́ть *impf. pf.* **моргну́ть** to wink; to blink.

мо́рда *f.* muzzle.

мордви́н *m. f.* —ка Mordvin.

мо́ре *neut.* sea.

Мо́ре Ла́птевых *neut.* Laptev Sea.

море́на *f.* moraine.

морёный *adj.* stained.

морепла́вание *neut.* navigation.

морепла́ватель *m. f.* —ница navigator.

морехо́д *m.* navigator.

морехо́дный *adj.* navigational; nautical.

морж *m.* walrus.

мори́лка *f.* stain (*for wood*).

мори́ть *impf. pf.* **по-** to exterminate.

морко́вный *adj.* (*attrib.*) carrot.

морко́вь *f.* a carrot; carrots.

мормо́н *m.* Mormon.

мормо́нский *adj.* Mormon.

моро́женое *neut.* ice cream.

моро́женщик *m. f.* **моро́женщица** ice-cream vendor.

моро́женый *adj.* frozen.

моро́з *m.* frost.

моро́зец FILL *m.* (*colloq.*) slight frost.

морози́лка *f.* freezer; freezing compartment (*in refrigerator*).

моро́зить *impf.* to freeze; to be freezing

моро́зный *adj.* frosty.

морозосто́йкий *adj.* frost-resistant.

мороси́ть *impf. usu. impers.* to drizzle.

моро́чить *impf. pf.* **об-** (*colloq.*) **1.** to trick; to fool. **2.** to mislead.

моро́шка *f.* cloudberries.

морс *m.* fruit drink.

морско́й *adj.* sea; maritime, nautical; marine.

морфе́ма *f.* (*ling.*) morpheme.

мо́рфий *m.* morphine.

морфологи́ческий *adj.* morphological

морфоло́гия *f.* (*ling.*) morphology.

морщи́на *f.* wrinkle.

мо́рщить *impf. pf.* **на-, с-** to wrinkle.

моря́к *m.* seaman, sailor.

Москва́ *f.* Moscow.

москви́ч *m. f.* —ка Muscovite.

моски́т *m.* sand fly.

моско́вский *adj.* (*attrib.*) Moscow, Muscovite.

мост *m.* bridge.

мо́стик *m.* small bridge.

мости́ть *impf. pf.* **вы-** to pave.

мостки́ *pl.* **1.** planked walkway. **2.** wooden platform. **3.** footbridge.

мостова́я *f.* pavement.

мостово́й *adj.* (*attrib.*) bridge.

мосье́ *m. indecl.* monsieur.

мо́ська *f.* (*colloq.*) (*dog*) pug.

мот *m.* (*colloq.*) spendthrift.

мота́льный *adj.* (*mech.*) winding.

мота́ть *impf. pf.* **на-** **1.** to wind. **2.** (*colloq.*) to shake one's head.

моти́в *m.* **1.** motive, reason. **2.** (*mus.; lit.*) motif.

мотиви́ровать OVA *impf.* and *pf.* to explain; to justify.

мотиви́ровка *f.* motivation; justification.

мотобо́л *m.* soccer played on motorcycles.

мотовство́ *neut.* prodigality.

мотого́нки *pl.* motorcycle races.

мото́к FILL *m.* **1.** skein (*of yarn*). **2.** hank (*of thread*).

мотопехо́та *f.* motorized infantry.

мотопила́ *f.* power saw.

мото́р *m.* motor, engine.

моторизо́ванный *adj.* motorized.

мото́рный *adj.* (*attrib.*) motor.

моторо́ллер *m.* motor scooter.

мотоци́кл *also* **мотоцикле́т** *m.,* **мотоцикле́тка** *f.* motorcycle.

моты́га *f.* hoe.

мотылёк *m.* butterfly; moth.

мох *m.* moss.

мохе́р *m.* mohair.

мохе́ровый *adj.* mohair.

мохна́тый *adj.* hairy; shaggy.

моча́ *f.* urine.

моча́лка *f.* bath sponge; loofa.

моча́ло *neut.* bast.

мочеви́на *f.* urea.

мочево́й *adj.* uric; urinary.

мочего́нный *adj.* diuretic.

мочеиспуска́ние *neut.* urination.

мочеиспуска́тельный *adj.* urinary.

мочёный *adj.* (*of food*) soaked.

мочи́ть *impf. pf.* **на-, за-** to soak; to wet. —**ся** *impf. pf.* **по-** to urinate.

мо́чка уха *f.* ear lobe.

мочь[1] *impf. pf.* **с-** to be able to.

мочь[2] *f.* power, might. — **что есть мо́чи** with all one's might.

моше́нник *m. f.* **моше́нница** swindler.

моше́нничать *impf. pf.* **с-** to swindle.

моше́ннический *adj.* fraudulent.

мо́шка *f.* midge; gnat.

мошо́нка *f.* scrotum.

моще́ние *neut.* paving.

мощёный *adj.* paved.

мо́щи *pl.* relics (*of a saint*).

мо́щность *f.* **1.** power. **2.** capacity; output.

мо́щный *adj.* powerful.

мощь *f.* power, might.

мо́ющий *adj.* cleansing.

мрак *m.* gloom; darkness, blackness.

мракобе́сие *neut.* obscurantism.

мра́мор *m.* marble.

мра́морный *adj.* marble.

мра́чность *f.* dreariness; gloom.

мра́чный *adj.* gloomy; dark, dreary.

мсти́тель *m. f.* —ница avenger.

мсти́тельность *f.* vindictiveness.

мсти́тельный *adj.* vindictive.

мстить *impf. pf.* **ото-** to revenge oneself; to avenge.

муа́р *m.* moiré.

муа́ровый *adj.* moiré.

мудрёный *adj.* (*colloq.*) hard to understand; complicated.

мудре́ц *m.* wise man; sage.

мудри́ть *impf.* (*colloq.*) **1.** to try to be clever. **2.** to complicate matters unnecessarily.

му́дрость *f.* wisdom.

мудрствовать OVA *impf.* (*colloq.*) to philosophize.

мудрый *adj.* wise, sage.

муж *m.* husband.

мужеподобный *adj.* man-like.

мужественно *adv.* courageously; bravely.

мужественность *f.* manliness, masculinity.

мужественный *adj.* courageous, manly.

мужество *neut.* courage.

мужик *m.* muzhik; (*pre-rev.*) peasant.

мужской *adj.* masculine, male.

мужчина *m.* (*decl. f.*) man; male.

муза *f.* muse.

музей *m.* museum.

музейный *adj.* (*attrib.*) museum.

музыка *f.* music.

музыкальный *adj.* music; musical.

музыкант *m.* musician.

музыковед *m.* musicologist.

музыковедение *neut.* musicology.

мука *f.* suffering, torment.

мука *f.* flour; meal.

мукомольный *adj.* (*attrib.*) flour-milling.

мул *m.* mule.

мулат *m. f.* —ка mulatto.

мулла *m.* (*decl. f.*) mullah.

мультимиллионер *m.* multimillionaire.

мультипликация *f.* multiplication.

мультфильм *m.* animated cartoon.

мульча *f.* mulch.

Мумбай *m.* Mumbai (*formerly: Bombay*).

мумия *f.* mummy.

мундир *m.* uniform.

мундштук *m.* cigarette *or* cigar holder; mouthpiece.

муниципалитет *m.* municipality.

муниципальный *adj.* municipal.

мура *f.* (*colloq.*) nonsense.

муравей FILL *m.* ant.

муравейник *m.* anthill.

муравьед *m.* anteater.

муравьиный *adj.* ant; ant's.

мурашки бегают по спине it gives (me) the creeps.

мурена *f.* (*eel*) moray.

мурлыканье *neut.* purring.

мурлыкать *impf.* to purr.

Мурманск *m.* Murmansk.

мускат *m.* **1.** nutmeg. **2.** (*grape*) muscat. **3.** (*wine*) wine.

мускатник *m.* (*tree*) nutmeg.

мускатный *adj.* nutmeg.

мускул *m.* muscle. —истый *adj.* muscular.

мускулатура *f.* muscles.

мускульный *adj.* (*attrib.*) muscle; muscular.

мускус *m.* musk.

мускусный *adj.* (*attrib.*) musk.

муслин *m.* muslin.

муслиновый *adj.* muslin.

мусор *m.* rubbish, trash.

мусорный *adj.* (*attrib.*) garbage; waste.

мусоропровод *m.* garbage chute.

мусоросжигательная печь *f.* incinerator.

мусорщик *m.* garbage collector.

мусс *m.* mousse.

муссировать OVA *impf.* **1.** to spread (*rumors*). **2.** to fan (*fears*).

муссон *m.* monsoon.

мустанг *m.* mustang.

мусульманин *m. f.* мусульманка Muslim.

мусульманский *adj.* Muslim.

мусульманство *neut.* Islam.

мутация *f.* mutation.

мутить *impf.* **1.** *pf.* за- to make muddy *or* cloudy (*water*). **2.** *pf.* по- to dull *or* cloud (*the senses*).

мутнеть *impf. pf.* по- to become cloudy; to become muddy.

мутность *f.* turbidity.

мутный *adj.* turbid; cloudy; muddy; dull.

мутовка *f.* churning *or* whipping stick.

муть *f.* **1.** lees; sediment. **2.** murk. **3.** haze; mist.

муфта *f.* muff.

муфтий *m.* mufti (*interpreter of Muslim law*).

муха *f.* fly.

мухоловка *f.* **1.** flycatcher; flytrap. **2.** (*bird*) flycatcher. **3.** (*bot.*) Venus's flytrap.

мухомор *m.* fly agaric (*poisonous mushroom*).

мучение *neut.* torture.

мученик *m. f.* мученица martyr.

мученический *adj.* martyr's.

мученичество *neut.* martyrdom.

мучитель *m. f.* —ница tormentor, torturer. —ный *adj.* agonizing.

мучительно *adv.* painfully.

мучить *impf.* **1.** to torture. **2.** to harass, to torment, to worry.

мучнистый *adj.* farinaceous.

мучной *adj.* (*attrib.*) flour.

мушкет *m.* musket.

мушкетёр *m.* musketeer.

муштровать *impf. pf.* вы- to drill.

муштровка *f.* drilling.

муэдзин *m.* muezzin.

мчаться *impf. pres.* мчусь, мчишься *pf.* по- **1.** to rush. **2.** to race along; to speed along.

мшистый *adj.* mossy.

мщение *neut.* vengeance.

мы *pron.* we.

мылить *impf. pf.* на- to soap, to lather.

мылкий *adj.* lathery.

мыло *neut.* soap.

мыловарение *neut.* soap making.

мыловаренный завод *m.* soap works.

мыльница *f.* soap dish.

мыльный *adj.* soapy.

мыльнянка *f.* soapwort.

мыс *m.* (*geog.*) cape.

мысленно *adv.* mentally; in one's mind.

мысленный *adj.* mental.

мыслимый *adj.* conceivable.

мыслить *impf.* to think; to reason.

мысль *f.* thought, idea.

мыслящий *adj.* thinking.

мытарство *neut.* ordeal; hardship; tribulation.

мыть *impf. pf.* по- *v.t.* to wash. —ся to wash oneself.

мытьё *neut.* washing.

мычание *neut.* mooing.

мычать *impf.* to low, to moo.

мышеловка *f.* mousetrap.

мышечный *adj.* (*attrib.*) muscle; muscular.

мыши́ный *adj.* (*attrib.*) mouse.

мы́шка¹ *f. dim. of* мышь

мы́шка² *f.*: под мы́шкой (*loc.*) *and* под мы́шку (*dir.*) under one's arm.

мышле́ние *also* мы́шление *neut.* thinking; mentality.

мышо́нок FILL *m.* baby mouse.

мы́шца *f.* muscle.

мышь *f.* mouse. — лету́чая мышь *f.* bat.

мышья́к *m.* arsenic.

мышья́ко́вый *adj.* arsenic.

Мьянма́р *m.* Myanmar (*formerly: Burma*).

Мэн *m.* Maine.

Мэн *m.* о́стров, Man, Isle of.

мэр *m.* mayor.

Мэ́риленд *m.* Maryland.

мэ́рия *f.* city hall.

мю́зикл *m.* musical.

мю́зик-хо́лл *m.* music hall.

Мю́нстер *m.* Münster.

Мю́нхен *m.* Munich.

мя́гкий *adj.* soft; mild, gentle.

мя́гко *adv.* softly; gently. — мя́гко говоря́ putting it mildly.

мягкосерде́чие *neut.* tenderheartedness.

мягкосерде́чность *f.* tenderheartedness

мягкосерде́чный *adj.* tenderhearted.

мя́гкость *f.* softness; gentleness, mildness.

мягкоте́лый *adj.* (*fig.*) spineless.

мя́гче *adj., comp. of* мя́гкий.

мяки́на *f.* chaff.

мя́киш *m.* the inside *or* soft part (*of bread*).

мя́кнуть *impf. pf.* раз-, *past* мяк, мя́кла to become soft; to become mushy.

мя́коть *f.* **1.** fleshy part. **2.** pulp (*of fruit*).

мя́млить *impf.* **1.** *pf.* про- (*colloq.*) to mumble. **2.** *impf. only* to procrastinate.

мя́мля *f.* (*colloq.*) wishy-washy person.

мяси́стый *adj.* fleshy.

мясна́я *f.* meat market.

мясни́к *m.* butcher.

мясно́е *neut.* meat dish.

мясно́й *adj.* (*attrib.*) meat; meaty.

мя́со *neut.* meat; flesh.

мясору́бка *f.* meat grinder.

мя́та *f.* (*bot.*) mint.

мяте́ж *m.* **1.** mutiny. **2.** rebellion, revolt.

мяте́жник *m.* rebel; insurgent.

мяте́жный *adj.* rebellious.

мя́тный *adj.* **1.** (*attrib.*) mint. **2.** peppermint; mint-flavored.

мя́тый *adj.* crushed; crumpled.

мять *impf. pf.* по-, из- to crumple, to rumple; to crush.

мяу́канье *neut.* meowing.

мяу́кать *impf.* to meow.

мяч *m.* ball.

мя́чик *m. dim. of* мяч.

на[1] *prep.* (*with acc.*) on, onto, upon; to; till; for; (*with prep.*) during; in, at; on.

на[2] *particle* (*colloq.*) here! — **вот тебе и на!** look at that! see what happened!

набавля́ть *impf.* *pf.* **наба́вить** to add on; to increase.

набалда́шник *m.* handle (*of walking stick*).

наба́т *m.* alarm; tocsin.

наба́тный *adj.* (*attrib.*) alarm.

набе́г *m.* raid.

набе́дренная повя́зка *f.* loincloth.

набекре́нь *adv.* (*colloq.*) at an angle; to one side.

на́бело *adv.* clean; without corrections *or* erasures.

на́бережная *f.* embankment.

набива́ть *impf.* *pf.* **наби́ть** to stuff (with); to fill (with).

наби́вка *f.* stuffing, filling.

набивно́й *adj.* (*of textiles*) printed.

наби́вщик *m.* *f.* **наби́вщица** (*person*) stuffer.

набира́ть *impf.* *pf.* **набра́ть 1.** to gather, to collect. **2.** to recruit.

наби́тый *adj.* stuffed; crammed; jammed in.

наблюда́тель *m.* *f.* **-ница** observer. **—ный** *adj.* observant.

наблюда́тельность *f.* powers of observation.

наблюда́ть *impf.* to observe.

наблюде́ние *neut.* **1.** observation. **2.** surveillance; supervision.

на́божность *f.* piety.

на́божный *adj.* pious, devout.

на́бок *adv.* to one side.

наболе́вший *adj.* painful; sore (*subject, topic*).

набо́р *m.* **1.** recruitment. **2.** set; collection. **3.** (*typog.*) typesetting; composition.

набо́рный *adj.* (*attrib.*) typesetting; composition.

набо́рщик *m.* *f.* **набо́рщица** compositor, typesetter.

набра́ть *pf.* *of* **набира́ть.**

набро́сок FILL *m.* sketch; outline.

набуха́ть *impf.* *pf.* **набу́хнуть** to swell.

нава́га *f.* navaga (*small fish of codfish family*).

наважде́ние *neut.* hallucination; delusion.

нава́лом *adv.* (*colloq.*) in a pile; in a heap.

нава́ристый *adj.* (*of soup*) rich; concentrated; with large fat content.

наварно́й *adj.* welded.

наведе́ние *neut.* **1.** aiming (*a weapon*). **2.** application (*of polish*). **3.** guidance (*of missiles*).

навек *also* **наве́ки** *adv.* forever.

наве́рно *adv.* probably.

наверняка́ *adv.* (*colloq.*) for sure, for certain.

навёрстывать *impf.* *pf.* **наверста́ть** to make up (for).

навёртывать *impf.* *pf.* **наверну́ть** (**в** *with acc.*) **1.** to wind onto; to wind around. **2.** to screw onto.

наве́рх *adv.* (*dir.*) **1.** up, upwards. **2.** upstairs.

наверху́ *adv.* (*loc.*) **1.** upstairs. **2.** above.

наве́с *m.* **1.** awning. **2.** cover.

навеселе́ *adv.* (*colloq.*) tipsy.

навесно́й *adj.* hanging.

наве́т *m.* (*obs.*) slander; calumny.

наве́тренный *adj.* windward.

наве́чно *adv.* forever; for eternity.

навеща́ть *impf.* *pf.* **навести́ть** to visit, to call on.

на́взничь *adv.* on one's back.

навзры́д *adv.*: **пла́кать навзры́д** to sob uncontrollably.

навига́тор *m.* navigator.

навигацио́нный *adj.* navigational.

навига́ция *f.* navigation.

нависа́ть *impf.* *pf.* **нави́снуть** (**над** *with instr.*) to hang over; to overhang.

нави́сший *adj.* overhanging.

навлека́ть *impf.* *pf.* **навле́чь** (**на** *with acc.*) to bring on; to incur.

наводи́ть *impf.* *pf.* **навести́** (**на** *with acc.*) **1.** to direct (at). **2.** to cover, to coat.

наво́дка *f.* aiming (*weapon*).

наводне́ние *neut.* flood.

наводня́ть *impf.* *pf.* **наводни́ть** to flood, to inundate.

наво́дчик *m.* (*mil.*) one who aims a weapon.

наводя́щий вопро́с *m.* leading question.

наво́з *m.* manure.

наво́зник *m.* dung beetle.

наво́зный *adj.* (*attrib.*) manure; dung.

на́волочка *f.* pillowcase.

навря́д ли *particle* (*colloq.*) hardly.

навсегда́ *adv.* for ever. — **раз (и) навсегда́** once and for all.

навстре́чу *adv.* from the opposite direction. — *prep.* (*with dat.*) towards; to meet.

навы́ворот *adv.* (*colloq.*) **1.** inside out. **2.** upside down.

на́вык *m.* skill; knack; habit.

навы́кате *adv.*: **глаза́ навы́кате** *pl.* bulging eyes.

навы́лет *adv.* (*of a bullet* or *wound*) going (*right*) through.

навы́нос *adv.* (*food*) to go.

навы́тяжку *adv.*: **стоя́ть навы́тяжку** *impf.* to stand at attention.

навя́зчивый *adj.* obtrusive.

навя́зывать *impf.* *pf.* **навяза́ть 1.** (**на** *with acc.*) to tie (to); to fasten. **2.** (*with dat.*) to force *or* thrust (on).

нага́йка *f.* whip.

нага́н *m.* revolver.

нага́р *m.* snuff (*of a candle*).

нагиба́ть *impf.* *pf.* **нагну́ть** to bend. **—ся** to bend over; to stoop.

нагишо́м *adv.* (*colloq.*) stark naked.

нагла́зник *m.* **1.** blinder; blinker. **2.** eyeshade.

нагле́ть *impf.* *pf.* **об-** to become insolent.

нагле́ц *m.* insolent person; impudent person.

на́глость *f.* **1.** insolence; impudence. **2.** effrontery.

на́глухо *adv.* tightly.

на́глый *adj.* impudent; insolent.

нагля́дно *adv.* graphically.

нагля́дность *f.* clarity.

нагля́дный *adj.* **1.** visual. **2.** obvious, clear. **3.** graphic.

нагнета́тель *m.* supercharger.

нагнета́ть *impf.* *pf.* **нагнести́** to force; to pump.

нагное́ние *neut.* festering, suppuration.

наговаривать *impf. pf.* наговорить (на *with acc.*) to calumniate, to slander.

наговор *m.* calumny; slander.

нагой *adj.* nude; bare.

наголо *adv.*: стричь наголо *impf.* to cut off all of someone's hair.

нагоняй *m.* (*colloq.*) scolding.

нагонять *impf. pf.* нагнать to overtake.

нагорный *adj.* (*attrib.*) mountain. — Нагорная проповедь *f.* Sermon on the Mount.

нагорье *neut.* upland.

нагота *f.* nakedness; nudity.

наготове *adv.* in readiness.

награда *f.* reward; decoration.

наградной *adj.* (*attrib.*) reward.

награждать *impf. pf.* наградить to reward; to decorate.

награждение *neut.* 1. rewarding. 2. awarding. 3. reward.

награждённый *m.* award recipient.

нагрев *m.* heating.

нагревание *neut.* heating.

нагреватель *m.* heater.

нагревать *impf. pf.* нагреть to warm (up); to heat.

нагромождать *impf. pf.* нагромоздить to pile up.

нагромождение *neut.* piling up.

нагрубить *pf. of* грубить.

нагрудник *m.* bib.

нагрудный *adj.* (*attrib.*) breast.

нагружать *impf. pf.* нагрузить to load.

нагрузка *f.* load; workload.

нагрянуть *pf.* to arrive unexpectedly.

над (надо) *prep.* (*with instr.*) over, above.

надбавка *f.* increment, increase.

надвигающийся *adj.* approaching, imminent.

надводный *adj.* (*attrib.*) surface.

надвое *adv.* in two; in half.

надворный *adj.* located outside.

надгортанник *m.* epiglottis.

надгробие *neut.* 1. tombstone. 2. epitaph.

надгробный памятник *or* камень *m.* tombstone.

надевание *neut.* putting on; donning.

надевать *impf. pf.* надеть to put on, to don.

надежда *f.* hope.

надёжность *f.* reliability; dependability.

надёжный *adj.* dependable; reliable; safe.

надел *m.* allotment.

наделать *pf.* 1. to make a quantity (*of something*). 2. to cause (*trouble*); to make (*mistakes*).

наделение *neut.* allotment.

надеть *pf. of* надевать.

надеяться *impf.* (на *with acc.*) 1. to hope for. 2. to rely on.

надземный *adj.* above-ground; overhead.

надзиратель *m. f.* —ница supervisor; overseer.

надзирательский *adj.* supervisory.

надзор *m.* surveillance.

надлежать *pres.* надлежит *impers.* to be required.

надлежащий *adj.* proper, suitable, fit.

надлом *m.* fracture, break.

надломленный *adj.* broken; cracked; shattered.

надменный *adj.* haughty, arrogant.

надо¹ *prep., see* над.

надо² *impers.* it is necessary.

надобно *adv.* (*obs.*) *see* надо.

надобность *f.* need; necessity.

надобный *adj.* (*obs.*) needed.

надоеда *m. and f.* (*decl. f.*) (*colloq.*) pest; nuisance.

надоедала *m. and f.* (*decl. f.*) (*colloq.*) pest; nuisance.

надоедать *impf. pf.* надоесть 1. to plague, to bother, to annoy. 2. *impers.* to be tired of.

надоедливый *adj.* boring, tiresome.

надой *m.* yield of milk.

надолго *adv.* for a long time.

надомник *m. f.* надомница homeworker.

надпись *f.* inscription.

надпочечник *m.* adrenal gland.

надпочечный *adj.* adrenal.

надрать *pf.* conjugated like драть tear off (*a quantity of something*).

надрез *m.* incision, cut.

надругательство *neut.* an outrage.

надрыв *m.* 1. slight tear. 2. strain; great effort. 3. emotional outburst.

надрывать *impf. pf.* надорвать to overtax, to strain.

надрывный *adj.* heartrending; hysterical.

надсмотр *m.* supervision; surveillance.

надсмотрщик *m. f.* надсмотрщица supervisor.

надставка *f.* 1. lengthening. 2. extra piece.

надстройка *f.* 1. building onto. 2. superstructure.

надстрочный знак *m.* superscript; diacritical mark.

надтреснутый *adj.* cracked.

надувание *neut.* blowing up.

надувать *impf. pf.* надуть 1. to inflate. 2. (*colloq.*) to cheat; to dupe.

надувной *adj.* inflatable.

надуманный *adj.* 1. artificial. 2. farfetched. 3. forced.

надутый *adj.* 1. inflated. 2. swollen. 3. (*colloq.*) haughty; pompous.

надушить *pf. of* душить.

надымить *pf. of* дымить.

наедаться *impf. pf.* наесться to eat one's fill.

наедине *adv.* in private, privately.

наезд *m.* quick visit; raid, incursion.

наездник *m. f.* наездница rider (*on horse*).

наезжать *impf. pf.* наехать 1. (на *with acc.*) to run into, to collide with. 2. *impf. only* to visit from time to time.

наезженный *adj.* (*of a road*) worn; well-traveled.

наём *m.* hire; hiring; renting.

наёмник *m.* mercenary (*soldier*).

наёмный *adj.* 1. hired. 2. mercenary.

нажать *pf. of* нажимать.

наждак *m.* emery.

наждачная бумага *f.* sandpaper.

наждачный *adj.* emery.

нажива *f.* 1. making money; gain; profit. 2. bait.

наживать *impf. pf.* нажить to acquire; to gain.

наживка *f.* bait.

нажим *m.* pressure.

нажимать *impf. pf.* нажать to press; to push.

назавтра *adv.* the next day.

назад *adv.* back, backwards. — тому назад ago.

название *neut.* name; title.

назвать *pf. of* называть.

наземный *adj.* (*attrib.*) 1. ground. 2. surface.

наземь *adv.* (*colloq.*) to the ground.

назида́ние *neut.* edification.

назида́тельный *adj.* edifying.

назло́ *adv.* for spite; out of spite. — как назло́ as ill luck would have it. — *prep.* (*with dat.*) to spite someone.

назнача́ть *impf. pf.* назна́чить 1. to appoint, to nominate. 2. to prescribe.

назначе́ние *neut.* 1. appointment, nomination. 2. prescription. 3. purpose.

назо́йливый *adj.* importunate; intrusive.

назрева́ть *impf. pf.* назре́ть 1. to ripen. 2. to mature.

назре́вший *adj.* (*of question*) urgent.

назубо́к *adv.* (*colloq.*): знать назубо́к *impf.* to know thoroughly.

называ́емый *adj.*: так называ́емый the so-called.

называ́ть *impf. pf.* назва́ть to name; to call.

наибо́лее *adv.* the most.

наибо́льший *adj.* the largest; the greatest.

наи́вный *adj.* naive.

наивы́сший *adj.* the highest; the greatest.

наи́гранный *adj.* affected; pretended.

наизна́нку *adv.* inside out.

наизу́сть *adv.* by heart.

наилу́чший *adj.* the best.

наиме́нее *adv.* the least.

наименова́ние *neut.* name; title.

наименова́ть OVA *pf. of* именова́ть.

наискосо́к *adv.* (*colloq.*) at an angle.

на́искось *adv.* aslant; obliquely.

наи́тие *neut.* inspiration; intuition.

наиху́дший *adj.* the worst.

найдёныш *m.* foundling.

найми́т *m.* hireling.

Найро́би *m.* Nairobi.

найти́(сь) *pf. of* находи́ть(ся).

нака́з *m.* order, instruction.

наказа́ние *neut.* punishment, penalty.

наказу́емый *adj.* (*leg.*) punishable.

нака́зывать *impf. pf.* наказа́ть to punish; to penalize.

нака́л *m.* 1. incandescence; white heat. 2. fever pitch.

накалённый *adj.* burning hot.

нака́ливание *neut.*: ла́мпа нака́ливания *f.* incandescent lamp.

нака́ливать *impf. pf.* накали́ть to make red hot; to inflame.

накану́не *adv.* the day *or* evening before. — *prep.* (*with gen.*) on the eve (of).

нака́чивать *impf. pf.* накача́ть 1. to pump. 2. to inflate; to pump up.

наки́дка *f.* 1. (*colloq.*) extra charge. 2. pillow cover. 3. cloak; mantle.

наки́дывать *impf. pf.* наки́нуть to throw on *or* over; to slip on.

накипа́ть *impf. pf.* накипе́ть 1. (*of passions*) to smoulder. 2. to form a scum.

на́кипь *f.* scum.

накла́дка *f.* 1. hairpiece. 2. protective pad *or* plate.

накладна́я *f.* invoice; waybill.

накладно́й *adj.* 1. superimposed. 2. false (*beard, hair*); paste-on.

накла́дывать *impf. pf.* наложи́ть to impose; to lay *or* place on.

накле́йка *f.* label.

накло́н *m.* inclination; slope.

наклоне́ние *neut.* 1. inclination. 2. (*gram.*) mood.

накло́нность *f.* inclination; leaning; tendency.

накло́нный *adj.* slanting; sloping.

наклоня́ть *impf. pf.* наклони́ть *v.t.* to bend; to incline.

накова́льня *f.* anvil.

нако́жный *adj.* (*attrib.*) skin; on the skin.

наколе́нник *m.* kneepad.

наконе́ц *adv.* finally, at last.

наконе́чник *m.* tip.

накопле́ние *neut.* accumulation.

накопля́ть *impf. pf.* накопи́ть *v.t.* to accumulate.

накорми́ть *pf. of* корми́ть.

накоротке́ *adv.* (*colloq.*) (с *with instr.*) on friendly terms (with).

накрахма́лить *pf. of* крахма́лить.

на́крепко *adv.* firmly.

на́крест *adv.* crosswise.

накрыва́ть *impf. pf.* накры́ть 1. to cover (with). 2. to set a table.

налага́ть *impf. pf.* наложи́ть to impose.

нала́дчик *m.* adjuster.

нала́живание *neut.* adjustment.

нала́живать *impf. pf.* нала́дить to adjust; to repair.

налга́ть *pf.* conjugated like лгать (на *with acc.*) 1. to tell lies about. 2. to slander.

нале́во *adv.* to the left; on the left.

налегке́ *adv.* with little baggage.

налёт *m.* 1. (air) raid. 2. thin coating.

налётчик *m. f.* налётчица robber; assailant.

налива́ть *impf. pf.* нали́ть to pour; to spill; to fill.

нали́вка *f.* fruit liqueur.

наливно́й *adj.* liquid; (*of fruit*) fully ripe.

нали́м *m.* (*fish*) burbot; eelpout.

налицо́ *adv.* present; on hand.

нали́чие *neut.* presence.

нали́чность *f.* cash on hand.

нали́чные *pl.* cash.

нали́чный *adj.* present; available.

наловчи́ться *pf.* (*colloq.*) to become proficient at.

нало́г *m.* tax.

нало́говый *adj.* (*attrib.*) tax.

налогообложе́ние *neut.* taxation.

налогоплате́льщик *m. f.* —пла́тельщица taxpayer.

наложе́ние *neut.* 1. imposition of a fine. 2. application (*of a bandage* or *makeup*).

нало́женным платежо́м *adv.* cash on delivery (*abbr.* C.O.D.).

наложи́ть *pf. of* накла́дывать, налага́ть.

на́лысо *adv.*: брить на́лысо *impf.* to shave someone's head.

нам *pron. dat. of* мы.

намара́ть *pf. of* мара́ть.

намёк *m.* hint; allusion.

намека́ть *impf. pf.* намекну́ть (на *with acc.*) to hint (at); to allude (to).

намерева́ться *impf.* to intend; to mean.

наме́рен *adj.* (*pred.*) intending.

наме́рение *neut.* intention.

наме́ренно *adv.* intentionally.

наме́ренный *adj.* intentional; deliberate.

на́мертво *adv.* (*colloq.*) firmly; fast.

наме́стник *m.* 1. deputy. 2. provincial governor.

намётка *f.* **1.** outline; rough draft. **2.** basting. **3.** basting thread.

намеча́ть *impf. pf.* наме́тить **1.** to plan, to contemplate. **2.** to mark. **3.** to map out.

на́ми *pron. instr. of* мы.

намно́го *adv.* greatly; much.

намо́рдник *m.* muzzle.

намо́рщить *pf. of* мо́рщить.

намы́лить *pf. of* мы́лить.

нанесе́ние *neut.* **1.** inflicting. **2.** tracing; plotting. **3.** applying.

нани́зывать *impf. pf.* наниза́ть to string; to thread.

нанима́тель *m. f.* —ница **1.** employer. **2.** tenant.

нанима́ть *impf. pf.* наня́ть to rent; to hire; to engage.

на́ново *adv.* (*colloq.*) anew; all over again.

нано́с *m.* (*geol.*) alluvium; drift.

наноси́ть *impf. pf.* нанести́ **1.** to bring, to deposit. **2.** to inflict, to cause.

нано́сный *adj.* (*fig.*) external; superficial.

наоборо́т *adv.* on the contrary; vice versa.

наобу́м *adv.* at random.

наотма́шь *adv.* with full force.

наотре́з *adv.* flatly; pointblank.

напада́ть *impf. pf.* напа́сть (на *with acc.*) to attack.

напада́ющий *m.* (*sports*) forward (*offensive player*).

нападе́ние *neut.* attack, assault.

напа́лм *m.* napalm.

напа́лмовый *adj.* napalm.

напа́рник *m.* (*colloq.*) partner; buddy.

напа́сть[1] *pf. of* напада́ть.

напа́сть[2] *f.* misfortune.

напе́в *m.* tune, air.

напе́вный *adj.* melodious.

наперебо́й *adv.* (*colloq.*) **1.** interrupting one another. **2.** trying to outdo one another.

напереве́с *adv.* (*of a weapon*) **1.** aimed; at the ready. **2.** pointed forward.

наперего́нки *adv.* (*colloq.*) racing one another.

наперёд *adv.* (*colloq.*) in advance.

напереко́р *prep.* (*with dat.*) contrary to; in defiance of.

наперере́з *prep.* (*with dat.*) so as to intercept; so as to head off.

наперерыв *adv.* **1.** interrupting one another. **2.** trying to outdo one another.

наперечёт *adv.* (*colloq.*) **1.** inside out; like a book. **2.** few and far between.

напе́рсник *m. f.* наперсница (*obs.*) confidant(e).

напе́рсный крест *m.* pectoral cross.

напёрсток FILL *m.* thimble.

наперстя́нка *f.* foxglove; digitalis.

напи́люк FILL *m.* (*colloq.*) file.

напи́льник *m.* file.

написа́ние *neut.* **1.** writing. **2.** spelling.

написа́ть *pf. of* писа́ть.

напи́ток FILL *m.* beverage, drink.

напи́ться *impf.* **1.** to drink one's fill. **2.** to get drunk.

наплавно́й мост *m.* floating bridge.

напластова́ние *neut.* (*geol.*) bedding; stratification.

наплева́тельский *adj.* (*colloq.*) couldn't-care-less.

наплева́ть *impf. pres.* наплюю́, наплюёшь (на *with acc.*) **1.** to spit on. **2.** (*colloq.*) not to give a damn about.

напли́в *m.* **1.** influx (*of people, etc.*). **2.** canker; excrescence (*on trees*).

напова́л *adv.*: уби́ть напова́л to kill on the spot.

наподо́бие *prep.* (*with gen.*) resembling; like.

напо́йть *pf. of* пои́ть.

напока́з *adv.* for show.

наполне́ние *neut.* filling.

наполня́ть *impf. pf.* напо́лнить *v.t.* to fill.

наполови́ну *adv.* half; in half; by half.

напомина́ние *neut.* **1.** reminder; reminding. **2.** notice.

напомина́ть *impf. pf.* напо́мнить (*with dat.*) to remind.

напо́р *m.* pressure.

напо́ристый *adj.* aggressive; assertive.

напо́рный *adj.* (*attrib.*) pressure.

напосле́док *adv.* at last; in the end.

направле́ние *neut.* direction.

напра́вленность *f.* **1.** direction. **2.** orientation.

напра́вленный *adj.* **1.** (*radio*) directional. **2.** purposeful; directed.

направля́ть *impf. pf.* напра́вить to direct; to send, to refer. —ся (к *with dat.*, в *with acc.*) to head (towards or for).

напра́во *adv.* to the right; on the right.

напра́слина *f.* (*colloq.*) false charge.

напра́сно *adv.* in vain; to no purpose.

напра́сный *adj.* vain; futile.

напра́шиваться *impf. pf.* напроси́ться **1.** (на *with acc.*) to invite oneself to. **2.** to be suggested.

наприме́р *adv.* for example.

напрока́т *adv.* for hire.

напролёт *adv.* (*colloq.*) long; straight through; through.

напроло́м *adv.* straight ahead (*disregarding obstacles*).

напропалу́ю *adv.* (*colloq.*) headlong.

напро́тив *adv.* **1.** opposite; on the contrary. **2.** across the street. — *prep.* (*with gen.*) opposite.

на́прочь *adv.* (*colloq.*) completely.

напряже́ние *neut.* **1.** strain, effort. **2.** tension. **3.** (*elec.*) voltage.

напряжённость *f.* tension.

напряжённый *adj.* **1.** strained. **2.** tense.

напрями́к *adv.* (*colloq.*) straight.

напуга́ть *pf.* to frighten; to scare.

напу́дрить *pf. of* пу́дрить.

напу́льсник *m.* wristband.

напускно́й *adj.* **1.** affected; put on. **2.** assumed.

напу́тственный *adj.* parting; farewell.

напу́тствие *neut.* parting words.

напы́щенность *f.* pomposity.

напы́щенный *adj.* pompous; inflated.

напя́ливать *impf. pf.* напя́лить **1.** to stretch on(to). **2.** to struggle into (*a tight item of clothing*).

наравне́ *adv.* (с *with instr.*) on the same level; equally (with).

нараспа́шку *adv.* unfastened; unbuttoned.

нараспе́в *adv.* in a singsong voice; in a drawl.

нараста́ние *neut.* expansion; increase.

нараста́ть *impf. pf.* нарасти́ to grow; to increase.

нарасхва́т *adv.* (*colloq.*) in great demand.

нара́щивание *neut.* buildup; increase.

нара́щивать *impf. pf.* нарасти́ть **1.** to increase; to augment. **2.** to grow. **3.** to lengthen.

На́рва *f.* Narva.

нарва́ть[1] *pf.* to gather; to pluck.
нарва́ть[2] *pf. of* **нарыва́ть**.
На́рвик *m.* Narvik.
нард *m.* nard.
наре́зка *f.* **1.** cutting. **2.** thread (*of screw*).
нарека́ние *neut.* reprimand; censure.
нарека́ть *impf. pf.* **наре́чь** (*obs.*) to name; to give a name to.
наре́чие *neut.* adverb.
наре́чный *adj.* adverbial.
нарза́н *m.* Narzan (*a mineral water*).
нарисова́ть OVA *pf. of* **рисова́ть**.
нарица́тельный *adj.* nominal. — **и́мя нарица́тельное** *neut.* (*gram.*) common noun.
наркобизнес *m.* drug business.
нарко́з *m.* anesthesia.
наркома́н *m. f.* **—ка** drug addict.
наркома́ния *f.* drug addiction.
наркотизи́ровать OVA *impf.* and *pf.* to anesthetize.
нарко́тик *m.* narcotic; drug.
наркоти́ческий *adj.* narcotic.
наро́д *m.* nation; people. **—ность** *f.* nationality. **—ный** *adj.* national; people's.
наро́дник *m.* (*hist.*) Populist.
наро́днический *adj.* Populist.
наро́дничество *neut.* Populism.
народонаселе́ние *neut.* population.
нарожда́ться *impf. pf.* **народи́ться** to arise; to come into being.
наро́ст *m.* growth; tumor.
наро́чито *adv.* intentionally; deliberately.
нарочи́тый *adj.* deliberate.
наро́чно *adv.* on purpose, purposely.
на́рты *pl.* dog sled; reindeer sled.
нару́жно *adv.* outwardly; externally.
нару́жность *f.* exterior, appearance.
нару́жный *adj.* external.
нару́жу *adv.* out, outside; outward.
нарука́вник *m.* sleeve cover.
нарука́вный *adj.* worn on the sleeve.
нару́чник *m. usu. pl.* handcuff.
нару́чный *adj.* worn on the arm.
наруша́ть *impf. pf.* **нару́шить** to violate; to disrupt.
наруше́ние *neut.* violation, breach.
наруши́тель *m. f.* **—ница** violator.
на́ры *pl.* plank bed.
нары́в *m.* abscess; boil.
нарыва́ть *impf. pf.* **нарва́ть** to get infected.
наря́д[1] *m.* order, warrant.
наря́д[2] *m.* attire, apparel. **—ный** *adj.* smart, well-dressed; elegant.
наряду́ **1.** *adv.* (**с** *with instr.*) side by side (*with*). **2.** on a par with.
наряжа́ть[1] *impf. pf.* **наряди́ть** to dress up.
наряжа́ть[2] *impf. pf.* **наряди́ть** to detail; to assign.
нас *pron. gen., acc. of* **мы.**
наса́дка *f.* **1.** putting on. **2.** attachment (*for a tool*). **3.** bait.
насажда́ть *impf. pf.* **насади́ть** to implant; to instill.
насажде́ние *neut.* planting.
насе́дка *f.* brood hen.
насеко́мое *neut.* insect.
населе́ние *neut.* population.

населённость *f.* population density.
населённый *adj.* populated.
населя́ть *impf. pf.* **насели́ть** to settle, to populate; to inhabit.
насе́ст *m.* perch; roost.
насе́чка *f.* **1.** groove; notch. **2.** inlay.
наси́лие *neut.* violence; force.
наси́ловать OVA *impf. pf.* **из-** to violate; to rape; to force.
наси́лу *adv.* (*colloq.*) with great difficulty; barely.
наси́льник *m.* **1.** tyrant, oppressor. **2.** rapist.
наси́льно *adv.* by force.
наси́льственный *adj.* forcible; violent.
насквозь *adv.* through; through and through; throughout.
наско́к *m.* (*colloq.*) attack.
наско́лько *adv.* as far as; so far as.
на́скоро *adv.* (*colloq.*) in a hurry; hastily.
наслажда́ться *impf. pf.* **наслади́ться** (*with instr.*) to enjoy; to take pleasure in.
наслажде́ние *neut.* delight; enjoyment; pleasure.
насле́дие *neut.* legacy.
насле́дник *m.* heir.
насле́дница *f.* heiress.
насле́дование *neut.* inheritance.
насле́дственность *f.* heredity.
насле́дственный *adj.* hereditary.
насле́дство *neut.* inheritance.
наслое́ние *neut.* **1.** layer. **2.** stratification.
насма́рку *adv.*: **идти** *or* **пойти́ насма́рку** to go down the drain; to come to nothing.
на́смерть *adv.* **1.** to death. **2.** to the death. **3.** to an extreme degree.
насме́шка *f.* mockery; mocking.
насме́шливый *adj.* mocking.
насме́шник *m. f.* **насме́шница** (*colloq.*) mocker.
на́сморк *m.* head cold.
насори́ть *pf. of* **сори́ть**.
насо́с *m.* pump.
насо́сный *adj.* (*attrib.*) pump; pumping.
на́спех *adv.* hastily; in a hurry.
наст *m.* thin crust of ice on snow.
настава́ть *impf. pf.* **наста́ть** (*of a season* or *of a time*) to come.
настави́тельный *adj.* didactic.
наставле́ние *neut.* **1.** admonition, exhortation. **2.** instruction, directions.
наста́вник *m.* teacher; mentor; tutor.
наста́ивать *impf. pf.* **настоя́ть** (**на** *with prep.*) to insist; to persist (in).
на́стежь *adv.* wide open.
насте́нный *adj.* (*attrib.*) wall.
насти́л *m.* flooring.
насти́лка *f.* (*colloq.*) flooring.
насто́й *m.* extract.
насто́йка *f.* **1.** fruit brandy. **2.** tincture.
насто́йчивость *f.* persistence.
насто́йчивый *adj.* persistent.
насто́лько *adv.* so. — **насто́лько... наско́лько...** as (much)... as...
насто́льный *adj.* (*attrib.*) table; desk.
настора́живать *impf. pf.* **насторожи́ть** to put on one's guard. **—ся** to prick up one's ears.
насторожё *adv.* on one's guard; on the alert.
насторо́женный *adj.* watchful; wary.
настоя́ние *neut.* insistence.

настоятель *m.* **1.** abbot; prior. **2.** senior priest.
настоятельница *f.* mother superior.
настоятельно *adv.* urgently.
настоятельность *f.* persistence.
настоятельный *adj.* urgent, pressing.
настоять *pf. of* **настаивать.**
настоящее *neut.* the present.
настоящий *adj.* **1.** present. **2.** genuine, real.
настраивать *impf. pf.* **настроить 1.** to tune (*a musical instrument; a radio*). **2.** to adjust. **3.** to put someone in a certain mood.
настрого *adv.* strictly.
настроение *neut.* **1.** mood. **2.** humor.
настроенность *f.* attitude; mood.
настройка *f.* tuning.
настройщик *m.* tuner.
настряпать *pf.* to cook up (*a quantity of food*).
наступательный *adj.* (*mil.*) offensive.
наступление *neut.* **1.** approach, coming. **2.** (*mil.*) offensive.
настурция *f.* nasturtium.
насупить брови *pf.* to frown.
насухо *adv.* dry.
насушить *pf.* to dry (*a quantity of something*).
насущный *adj.* **1.** urgent. **2.** vital.
насчёт *adv.; prep.* (*with gen.*) regarding.
насчитывать *impf. pf.* **насчитать** to count; to number.
насылать *impf. pf.* **наслать** (*of the gods*) to inflict.
насыпать *impf. pf.* **насыпать 1.** to sprinkle, to spread. **2.** to pour. **3.** to fill (*a sack*).
насыпь *f.* embankment.
насыщать *impf. pf.* **насытить** to satiate; to saturate.
насыщение *neut.* satiation; saturation.
наталкиваться *impf. pf.* **натолкнуться** (**на** *with acc.*) to come across; to encounter.
нате *particle* (*colloq.*) here you are!; there you are!
натекать *impf. pf.* **натечь** (*of water*) to accumulate.
нательный *adj.* (*item of clothing*) worn close to the body.
натирать *impf. pf.* **натереть 1.** to rub. **2.** to irritate. **3.** to polish.
натиск *m.* charge; onslaught.
натощак *adv.* on an empty stomach.
натр *m.*: **едкий натр** *m.* caustic soda.
натриевый *adj.* (*attrib.*) sodium.
натрий *m.* sodium.
натрое *neut. adv.* into three parts.
натуга *f.* (*colloq.*) exertion; strain.
натуго *adv.* (*colloq.*) tightly.
натужно *adv.* (*colloq.*) strenuously.
натужный *adj.* (*colloq.*) strenuous.
натура *f.* nature; character; kind. — **с натуры** from real life.
натурализация *f.* naturalization.
натурализм *m.* naturalism.
натурализовать *OVA impf and pf.* to naturalize; to grant citizenship (to).
натурализоваться *OVA impf. and pf.* to get naturalized.
натуралист *m.* naturalist.
натуралистический *adj.* naturalistic.
натуральный *adj.* natural.
натурой *adv.* in kind.
натурщик *m.* (*artist's*) model.

натурщица *f.* (*artist's*) female model.
натыкать *pf.* (*colloq.*) to stick in (*a quantity of something*).
натюрморт *m.* still life.
натягивать *impf. pf.* **натянуть** to stretch, to strain; to draw *or* pull on *or* over.
натяжение *neut.* pull; tension.
натяжка *f.* stretching.
натянутость *f.* strain; tension.
натянутый *adj.* **1.** strained. **2.** forced; unnatural.
наугад *adv.* **1.** at random. **2.** by guesswork.
наудачу *adv.* at random.
наука *f.* science.
научить(ся) *pf. of* **учить(ся).**
научно *adv.* scientifically.
научный *adj.* scientific.
наушник *m. usu pl.* **1.** earphone. **2.** earflap.
наушничество *adj.* talebearing; informing.
наущение *neut.* (*obs.*) instigation.
нафталин *m.* naphthalene.
нафтол *m.* naphthol.
нахал *m. f.* —**ка** insolent person.
нахальный *adj.* impudent.
нахальство *neut.* impertinence; insolence.
Нахичевань *m.* Naxçivan (*Russian; Nakhichevan*)
нахлебник *m.* **1.** parasite. **2.** (*obs.*) boarder; paying guest.
нахлобучивать *impf. pf.* **нахлобучить** (*colloq.*) to pull down (a hat) over one's ears.
нахлобучка *f.* scolding; bawling out.
нахлынуть *pf.* **1.** to stream; to gush; to flow. **2.** (*of people*) to throng; to rush.
нахмуренный *adj.* frowning.
нахмуриться *pf. of* **хмуриться.**
находить *impf. pf.* **найти 1.** to find, to discover. **2.** (**на** *with acc.*) to come across *or* upon.
находиться *impf. pf.* **найтись 1.** to turn up, to be found. **2.** to be, to be situated *or* located.
Находка *f.* Nakhodka.
находка *f.* find.
находчивый *adj.* **1.** resourceful. **2.** inventive.
нахождение *neut.* finding.
наценка *f.* price increase; markup.
нацизм *m.* Nazism.
национализация *f.* nationalization.
национализировать *OVA impf. and pf.* to nationalize.
национализм *m.* nationalism.
националист *m. f.* —**ка** nationalist.
националистический *adj.* nationalist.
национальность *f.* nationality.
национальный *adj.* national.
нацист *m. f.* —**ка** Nazi.
нация *f.* nation.
начало *neut.* beginning; source. — **начала** *pl.* principles.
начальник *m. f.* **начальница** boss; head; chief; superior.
начальный *adj.* elementary; beginning; initial.
начальственный *adj.* domineering; bossy.
начальство *neut.* **1.** the authorities. **2.** command; direction.
начальствование *neut.* command.
начальствовать *OVA impf.* (*obs.*) to command.
начатки *pl.* rudiments.

нача́ть *pf. of* **начина́ть** *pres.* **начну́, начнёшь** to begin; to start.

начеку́ *adv.* on the alert; on one's guard.

на́черно *adv.* roughly; in the rough.

начерта́ние *neut.* tracing; outline.

начерта́тельная геоме́трия *f.* descriptive geometry.

начёс *m.* nap (*of cloth*).

начётчик *m. f.* **начётчица** pedant.

начина́ние *neut.* project; undertaking.

начина́тельный *adj.* (*gram.*) inceptive.

начина́ть *impf. pf.* **нача́ть** *v.t.* to begin, to start, to commence. **—ся** *v.i.* to begin.

начина́ющий *m.* beginner.

начина́я *prep.* (**с** *with gen.*) beginning with.

начи́нка *f.* filling; stuffing.

на́чисто *adv.* clean.

начистоту́ *adv.* frankly; straight.

начи́танность *f.* erudition.

начи́танный *adj.* well-read.

начита́ть *pf.* (*colloq.*) to read (*a quantity of something*).

наш *poss. adj.* our, ours.

нашаты́рный спирт *m.* liquid ammonia.

нашаты́рь *m.* ammonium chloride.

наше́ствие *neut.* invasion.

наши́вка *f.* (*mil.*) chevron; stripe.

нашивно́й *adj.* sewn-on.

нашуме́вший *adj.* sensational.

наяву́ *adv.* while awake.

на́яда *f.* naiad.

не *particle* not.

неаккура́тность *f.* sloppiness.

неаккура́тный *adj.* sloppy; messy.

Неа́поль *m.* Naples.

неаппети́тный *adj.* unappetizing.

небезопа́сный *adj.* unsafe.

небезоснова́тельный *adj.* not without foundation.

небезразли́чный *adj.* interested; concerned; not indifferent.

небезызве́стный *adj.* rather well known.

небезынтере́сный *adj.* rather interesting.

небелёный *adj.* unbleached.

небе́сный *adj.* celestial; heavenly.

неблагови́дный *adj.* improper; unseemly.

неблагода́рность *f.* ingratitude.

неблагода́рный *adj.* ungrateful.

неблагожела́тельность *f.* unfriendliness.

неблагожела́тельный *adj.* unfriendly.

неблагозву́чие *neut.* disharmony.

неблагозву́чный *adj.* discordant.

неблагонадёжность *f.* unreliability.

неблагонадёжный *adj.* unreliable.

неблагополу́чие *neut.* trouble(s).

неблагополу́чно *adv.* in an unfortunate way.

неблагополу́чный *adj.* troubled; unfortunate.

неблагопристо́йность *f.* indecency; impropriety.

неблагопристо́йный *adj.* indecent; improper.

неблагоприя́тный *adj.* unfavorable.

неблагоразу́мие *neut.* imprudence.

неблагоразу́мный *adj.* imprudent.

неблагоро́дный *adj.* ignoble.

неблагоскло́нно *adv.* unfavorably.

неблагоскло́нность *f.* unfavorable attitude.

неблагоскло́нный *adj.* ill-disposed.

неблагоустро́енный *adj.* lacking conveniences (*house* or *apartment*).

неблестя́щий *adj.* mediocre; undistinguished.

нёбный *adj.* palatal.

не́бо *neut.* sky; heaven.

нёбо *neut.* palate.

небога́тый *adj.* not rich.

небоеспосо́бный *adj.* unfit for military action.

небольшо́й *adj.* **1.** small; not large. **2.** (*of distance* or *time*) short.

небосво́д *m.* firmament.

небоскло́н *m.* horizon (*more precisely: sky immediately above the horizon*).

небоскрёб *m.* skyscraper.

небо́сь *particle* (*colloq.*) in all probability.

Небра́ска *f.* Nebraska.

небре́жно *adv.* carelessly.

небре́жность *f.* carelessness.

небре́жный *adj.* careless; negligent.

небри́тый *adj.* unshaven.

небыва́лый *adj.* unprecedented.

небыли́ца *f.* fable; tall story.

небытие́ *neut.* nonexistence.

небью́щийся *adj.* unbreakable.

Нева́да *f.* Nevada.

нева́жный *adj.* **1.** unimportant. **2.** not very good; poor. **3.** indifferent.

недалеке́ *adv.* not far away.

невдомёк *adj.* (*pred.*) (*colloq.*) having no idea.

неве́дение *neut.* ignorance.

неве́домо *adv.* (*colloq.*) God (only) knows; there is no way of knowing.

неве́домый *adj.* unknown.

неве́жа *m. and f.* (*decl. f.*) boor; lout.

неве́жда *m. and f.* (*decl. f.*) ignoramus.

неве́жественный *adj.* ignorant.

неве́жество *neut.* ignorance.

неве́жливость *f.* impoliteness.

неве́жливый *adj.* rude.

невезе́ние *neut.* bad luck.

невезу́чий *adj.* (*colloq.*) unlucky.

невели́кий *adj.* (*colloq.*) not large.

неве́рие *neut.* **1.** disbelief. **2.** lack of faith.

неве́рно *adv.* **1.** incorrectly. **2.** unsteady; uncertain.

неве́рность *f.* **1.** incorrectness. **2.** disloyalty; infidelity.

неве́рный *adj.* **1.** incorrect. **2.** unfaithful; disloyal.

невероя́тно *adv.* unbelievably; incredibly.

невероя́тность *f.* unbelievability.

невероя́тный *adj.* incredible.

неве́рующий *adj.* nonbelieving. — *m.* nonbeliever.

невесёлый *adj.* sad; blue.

невесо́мость *f.* weightlessness.

невесо́мый *adj.* weightless.

неве́ста *f.* bride; fiancée.

неве́стка *f.* daughter-in-law; sister-in-law (*brother's wife*).

неве́сть *adv.* (*colloq.*) God (only) knows; heaven knows.

невеще́ственный *adj.* immaterial.

невзго́да *f.* misfortune; adversity.

невзнача́й *adv.* (*colloq.*) accidentally; by chance.

невзно́с *m.* nonpayment of dues.

невзыска́тельный *adj.* undemanding.

не́видаль *f.* (*colloq.*) wonder; something marvelous.

неви́данный *adj.* unprecedented.

невиди́мка *m.* and *f.* (*decl. f.*) invisible man *or* creature.
невиди́мый *adj.* invisible.
неви́дный *adj.* **1.** invisible. **2.** insignificant. **3.** (*colloq.*) unattractive.
невидящий *adj.* unseeing; blind.
неви́нность *f.* innocence; virginity.
неви́нный *adj.* innocent; naive.
невино́вность *f.* innocence.
невино́вный *adj.* innocent; not guilty.
невку́сный *adj.* tasteless.
невменя́емый *adj.* (*leg.*) not responsible for one's actions.
невмеша́тельство *neut.* noninterference; nonintervention.
невмоготу́ *adv.* (*colloq.*) unbearable; unendurable.
невнима́ние *neut.* inattention.
невнима́тельность *f.* lack of consideration.
невнима́тельный *adj.* inattentive.
невнуши́тельный *adj.* unimpressive.
невня́тный *adj.* indistinct; imperceptible; barely audible.
невозвра́тный *adj.* irrevocable.
невозвраще́нец FILL *m. f.* **невозвраще́нка** defector.
невозде́ланный *adj.* uncultivated.
невоздержа́ние *neut.* intemperance.
невоздержанность *f.* intemperance.
невозде́ржанный *adj.* immoderate; intemperate.
невозде́ржный *adj.* intemperate.
невозмо́жно *adv.* (*pred.*) impossible.
невозмо́жное *neut.* the impossible.
невозмо́жность *f.* impossibility.
невозмо́жный *adj.* impossible.
невозмути́мость *f.* imperturbability.
невозмути́мый *adj.* **1.** imperturbable. **2.** (*of calm or quiet*) undisturbed.
невознагради́мый *adj.* irreparable.
нево́льник *m. f.* **нево́льница** slave.
нево́льничество *neut.* slavery.
нево́льничий *adj.* (*attrib.*) slave; slave's.
нево́льно *adv.* **1.** unintentionally. **2.** instinctively.
нево́льный *adj.* involuntary.
нево́ля *f.* **1.** slavery. **2.** captivity. **3.** (*colloq.*) necessity.
невообрази́мый *adj.* inconceivable.
невооружённый *adj.* unarmed.
невоспе́тый *adj.* unsung.
невоспи́танность *f.* lack of upbringing.
невоспи́танный *adj.* ill-mannered.
невоспламеня́емый *adj.* incombustible.
невосполни́мый *adj.* irreparable.
невосприи́мчивый *adj.* **1.** immune. **2.** slow to learn; slow to perceive.
невостре́бованный *adj.* unclaimed.
невою́ющий *adj.* nonbelligerent.
невпопа́д *adv.* (*colloq.*) not to the point.
невразуми́тельный *adj.* unintelligible.
невралги́ческий *adj.* neuralgic.
невралги́я *f.* neuralgia.
неврастени́я *f.* nervous breakdown; neurasthenia.
невреди́мый *adj.* unharmed; safe.
невре́дный *adj.* harmless.
неври́т *m.* neuritis.
невро́з *m.* neurosis.
невро́лог *m.* neurologist.
неврологи́ческий *adj.* neurological.

невроло́гия *f.* neurology.
невропато́лог *m.* neuropathologist.
невроти́ческий *adj.* neurotic.
Невшате́ль *m.* Neufchâtel.
невы́года *f.* disadvantage.
невы́годно *adv.* not to one's advantage.
невы́годность *f.* unprofitableness; disadvantage.
невы́годный *adj.* **1.** unprofitable. **2.** unfavorable. **3.** unattractive.
невы́держанность *f.* lack of self-control.
невы́держанный *adj.* lacking self-control.
невы́лазный *adj.* (*colloq.*) impassable.
невыноси́мо *adv.* unbearably; intolerably.
невыноси́мый *adj.* unbearable; intolerable.
невыполне́ние *neut.* nonfulfillment.
невы́полненный *adj.* unfulfilled.
невыполни́мость *f.* impracticability.
невыполни́мый *adj.* impracticable.
невырази́мые *pl.* (*jocular*) unmentionables.
невырази́мый *adj.* inexpressible.
невырази́тельность *f.* lack of expression.
невырази́тельный *adj.* inexpressive.
невы́сказанный *adj.* unspoken.
невысо́кий *adj.* low.
невы́ход *m.* failure to appear.
не́га *f.* **1.** comfort; contentment. **2.** bliss. **3.** ease.
негати́в *m.* (*photog.*) negative.
негати́вный *adj.* negative.
негашёный *adj.* (*stamps*) uncanceled.
не́где *adv.* (*with infin.*) nowhere.
неги́бкий *adj.* inflexible.
неги́бкость *f.* inflexibility.
негла́сный *adj.* secret.
неглубо́кий *adj.* shallow.
неглу́пый *adj.* rather intelligent.
негну́щийся *adj.* stiff.
него́дник *m. f.* **него́дница** brat.
него́дность *f.* uselessness.
него́дный *adj.* unfit.
негодова́ние *neut.* indignation.
негодова́ть OVA *impf.* to be indignant.
негоду́ющий *adj.* indignant.
него́дяй *m. f.* **—ка** scoundrel; lowlife.
негостеприи́мный *adj.* inhospitable.
него́то́вый *adj.* unready.
негр *m.* black person. **—итя́нка** *f.* black woman.
негра́мотность *f.* illiteracy.
негра́мотный *adj.* illiterate.
негритя́нский *adj.* (*person*) black.
негро́идный *adj.* Negroid.
негро́мкий *adj.* not loud.
негро́мко *adv.* in a low voice.
неда́вний *adj.* recent.
неда́вно *adv.* recently; not long ago.
недалеко́ *also* **недалёко** *adv.* not far.
недальнови́дность *f.* shortsightedness.
недальнови́дный *adj.* shortsighted.
неда́ром *adv.* not without reason; not in vain.
недви́жимость *f.* real estate.
недви́жимый *adj.* motionless.
недви́жимый *adj.* immovable.
недвусмы́сленно *adv.* unequivocally.
недвусмы́сленный *adj.* unambiguous.
недееспосо́бность *f.* inability to function.
недееспосо́бный *adj.* unable to function.
недействи́тельный *adj.* invalid; ineffective.

неделика́тность f. indelicacy; tactlessness.
неделика́тный adj. indelicate; tactless.
недели́мость f. indivisibility.
недели́мый adj. indivisible.
неде́льный adj. weekly.
неде́ля f. week.
недержа́ние neut. (med.) incontinence; irretention of urine.
недёшево adv. not cheap.
недисциплини́рованность f. lack of discipline.
недисциплини́рованный adj. undisciplined.
недо́брое neut. trouble.
недоброжела́тельный adj. unfriendly.
недоброжела́тельство neut. ill will.
недоброка́чественность f. poor quality.
недоброка́чественный adj. poor-quality.
недобросо́вестность f. negligence; lack of conscientiousness.
недобросо́вестный adj. unscrupulous.
недо́брый adj. 1. malicious; mean. 2. bad; evil.
недове́рие neut. distrust; mistrust.
недове́рчивость f. distrust.
недове́рчивый adj. distrustful.
недово́льный adj. discontented.
недово́льство neut. discontent; displeasure.
недовыполне́ние neut. failure to fulfill completely.
недога́дливый adj. slow to grasp things; dense.
недоговорённость f. failure to tell all.
недоде́ланный adj. unfinished.
недоде́лка f. (colloq.) defect.
недоде́ржка f. (photog.) underexposure.
недоеда́ние neut. malnutrition.
недозво́ленный adj. unlawful.
недозре́лый adj. not completely ripe.
недои́мка f. 1. arrears. 2. back rent; back taxes.
недои́мщик m. person in arrears.
недока́занный adj. unproved.
недоказу́емый adj. unprovable.
недолга́ f.: вот и вся недолга́ (colloq.) and that's all there is to it!
недо́лгий adj. short; brief.
недо́лго adv. not long.
недолгове́чный adj. short-lived.
недомога́ние neut. indisposition.
недомо́лвка f. innuendo.
недомы́слие neut. thoughtlessness.
недонесе́ние neut. failure to report a crime.
недоно́сок FILL m. prematurely born child.
недоно́шенный adj. born prematurely.
недооце́нивать impf. pf. **недооцени́ть** to underestimate.
недооце́нка f. underestimation.
недопечённый adj. half-baked.
недопроизво́дство neut. underproduction.
недопусти́мый adj. inadmissible.
недора́звитый adj. underdeveloped.
недоразуме́ние neut. misunderstanding.
недо́рого adv. inexpensively.
недорого́й adj. inexpensive.
недоро́д m. poor harvest.
недо́росль m. young ignoramus; young oaf.
недоро́сток FILL m. (colloq.) runt; shrimp.
недосмо́тр m. oversight.
недоспе́лый adj. not completely ripe.
недостава́ть impf. pf. **недоста́ть** impers. (with

gen.) 1. to be lacking; to be insufficient. 2. impf. only to be missing.
недоста́ток FILL m. lack; shortage.
недоста́точно adv. insufficiently; not enough.
недоста́точность f. insufficiency.
недоста́точный adj. insufficient.
недоста́ча f. (colloq.) shortage.
недостижи́мый adj. unattainable.
недостове́рный adj. of doubtful authenticity.
недосто́йный adj. 1. unworthy. 2. dishonorable. 3. undignified.
недостро́енный adj. (building) unfinished.
недосту́пность f. inaccessibility.
недосту́пный adj. inaccessible.
недосу́г m. (used impers. with dat.) (colloq.) lacking time.
недосчи́тываться impf. pf. **недосчита́ться** (with subject in gen.) to be short; to be missing.
недосыпа́ние neut. lack of sleep.
недосяга́емый adj. unattainable.
недотёпа m. and f. (decl. f.) (colloq.) clod.
недотро́га m. and f. (decl. f.) (colloq.) touchy person.
недоу́здок FILL m. halter (for a horse).
недоумева́ющий adj. bewildered; puzzled.
недоуме́ние neut. bewilderment.
недоу́чка m. and f. (decl. f.) (colloq.) person with little education.
недочёт m. deficit; shortcoming.
не́дра pl. 1. bowels of the earth. 2. (fig.) depths; heart.
недремлющий adj. watchful; vigilant.
не́друг m. enemy; foe.
недружелю́бие neut. unfriendliness.
недружелю́бный adj. unfriendly.
неду́г m. ailment.
неду́рно adv. rather well.
недурно́й adj. not bad.
недю́жинный adj. unusual; outstanding; uncommon; exceptional..
неесте́ственный adj. unnatural; affected.
нежда́нный adj. unexpected.
нежела́ние neut. reluctance; unwillingness.
нежела́тельный adj. undesirable.
нежена́тый adj. (of a man) unmarried.
не́женка m. and f. (decl. f.) (colloq.) sissy.
неживо́й adj. lifeless; dead.
нежи́зненный adj. unrealistic.
нежило́й adj. (house) vacant.
не́жить impf. to pamper; to coddle.
не́жно adv. tenderly.
не́жность f. tenderness.
не́жный adj. tender; affectionate; loving.
незабве́нный adj. unforgettable.
незаброни́рованный adj. unreserved.
незабу́дка f. forget-me-not.
незабыва́емый adj. unforgettable.
незавершённый adj. unfinished.
незави́дный adj. unenviable.
незави́симо adv. independently.
незави́симость f. independence.
незави́симый adj. independent.
незада́ча f. (colloq.) bad luck.
незада́чливый adj. (colloq.) luckless.
незадо́лго adv. (до with gen.) not long before.
незаинтересо́ванный adj. disinterested.

незако́нно *adv.* illegally.
незаконноро́ждённый *adj.* (*of a child*) illegitimate.
незако́нность *f.* illegality.
незако́нный *adj.* illegal; illegitimate; illicit.
незако́нченный *adj.* unfinished.
незамедли́тельный *adj.* immediate.
незамени́мый *adj.* irreplaceable.
незаме́тный *adj.* imperceptible.
незаме́ченный *adj.* unnoticed.
незаму́жняя *adj.* (*of a woman*) unmarried.
незамыслова́тый *adj.* (*colloq.*) simple; unimaginative.
неза́нятый *adj.* unoccupied.
незапа́мятный *adj.* immemorial.
неза́пертый *adj.* unlocked.
незапя́тнанный *adj.* unblemished.
незара́зный *adj.* noncontagious.
незаря́женный *adj.* (*of weapon*) unloaded.
незаселённый *adj.* unsettled.
незаслу́женный *adj.* undeserved.
незате́йливый *adj.* simple; unpretentious.
незауря́дный *adj.* outstanding.
не́зачем *adv.* (*with infin.*) (*colloq.*) there is no need to.
незащищённый *adj.* unprotected.
незва́ный *adj.* uninvited.
незде́шний *adj.* not of this place.
нездоро́вый *adj.* unhealthy.
нездоро́вье *neut.* ill health.
неземно́й *adj.* unearthly.
незло́й *adj.* good-natured.
незлопа́мятный *adj.* forgiving.
незнако́мец FILL *m. f.* **незнако́мка** stranger.
незнако́мство *neut.* unfamiliarity.
незнако́мый *adj.* unknown.
незна́ние *neut.* ignorance.
незна́чащий *adj.* insignificant.
незначи́тельность *f.* insignificance.
незначи́тельный *adj.* insignificant.
незре́лость *f.* immaturity.
незре́лый *adj.* immature; unripe.
незы́блемый *adj.* **1.** solid; firm. **2.** unshakable; unwavering.
неизбе́жно *adv.* inevitably.
неизбе́жность *f.* inevitability.
неизбе́жный *adj.* inevitable.
неизве́данный *adj.* unexplored.
неизве́стно *adj.* (*pred.*) unknown; not known.
неизве́стное *neut.* (*math.*) unknown.
неизве́стный *adj.* unknown.
неизглади́мый *adj.* indelible.
неи́зданный *adj.* unpublished.
неизлечи́мый *adj.* incurable.
неизме́нно *adv.* invariably.
неизме́нный *adj.* unchanging; invariable.
неизменя́емый *adj.* unalterable.
неизмери́мо *adv.* immeasurably; infinitely.
неизмери́мый *adj.* immeasurable.
неизъясни́мый *adj.* unexplainable.
неиме́ние *neut.*: **за неиме́нием** (*with gen.*) due to the lack of.
неимове́рный *adj.* **1.** incredible; unbelievable. **2.** fantastic.
неиму́щий *adj.* poor; indigent.
неинтеллиге́нтный *adj.* not cultured; unsophisticated.

неинтере́сный *adj.* uninteresting.
неискорени́мый *adj.* ineradicable.
неи́скренний *adj.* insincere; false.
неи́скренность *f.* insincerity.
неискушённый *adj.* unexperienced.
неисполне́ние *neut.* failure to carry out.
неисполни́мость *f.* impracticability.
неисполни́мый *adj.* impossible to carry out; impracticable.
неиспо́льзованный *adj.* unused.
неиспо́рченный *adj.* unspoiled.
неисправи́мый *adj.* incorrigible.
неиспра́вность *f.* failure; malfunctioning.
неиспра́вный *adj.* out of order; defective.
неиспы́танный *adj.* untested; untried.
неиссле́дованный *adj.* unexplored.
неи́стовство *neut.* rage; fury.
неи́стовствовать OVA *impf.* to rage.
неи́стовый *adj.* **1.** furious; violent. **2.** frenzied.
неистощи́мый *adj.* inexhaustible.
неисцели́мый *adj.* incurable.
неисчерпа́емый *adj.* inexhaustible.
неисчисли́мый *adj.* incalculable; countless.
нейло́н *m.* nylon.
нейло́новый *adj.* nylon.
нейро́н *m.* neuron.
нейрохиру́рг *m.* neurosurgeon.
нейрохирурги́я *f.* neurosurgery.
нейтрализа́ция *f.* neutralization.
нейтрализова́ть OVA *impf. and pf.* to neutralize.
нейтралите́т *m.* neutrality.
нейтра́льный *adj.* neutral.
нейтро́н *m.* neutron.
нейтро́нный *adj.* (*attrib.*) neutron.
неказѝстый *adj.* (*colloq.*) **1.** ugly; homely. **2.** unseemly; unattractive.
неквалифици́рованный *adj.* unskilled.
не́кий *pron.* a certain.
не́когда[1] *adv.* once; formerly.
не́когда[2] *adv.* (*pred.*) there is no time.
неколеби́мый *adj.* unshakable; steadfast.
некомпете́нтный *adj.* incompetent; unqualified.
неконституцио́нный *adj.* unconstitutional.
некороно́ванный *adj.* uncrowned.
некорре́ктный *adj.* indecorous; improper.
не́который *pron.* some. — **не́которые** *pl.* some people.
некраси́вый *adj.* ugly; unattractive.
некра́шеный *adj.* unpainted.
некре́пкий *adj.* **1.** not firm; flimsy. **2.** not strong; diluted.
некрити́ческий *adj.* uncritical.
некро́з *m.* necrosis.
некроло́г *m.* obituary.
некста́ти *adv.* **1.** inopportunely. **2.** not to the point.
некта́р *m.* nectar.
не́кто *pron.* someone; a certain.
не́куда *adv.* (*with infin.*) nowhere.
некульту́рность *f.* lack of culture.
некульту́рный *adj.* uncultured; uncivilized.
некуря́щий *adj.* nonsmoking. — *m.* nonsmoker.
нела́дно *adv.* badly. — *adj.* (*pred.*) wrong.
нела́дное *neut.* something wrong.
нела́дный *adj.* (*colloq.*) wrong.
нелакиро́ванный *adj.* not lacquered; unvarnished.

нела́сковый *adj.* unfriendly; cold.
нелега́льно *adv.* illegally.
нелега́льность *f.* illegality.
нелега́льный *adj.* illegal.
нелёгкий *adj.* not easy; difficult.
нелегко́ *adv.* not easily.
неле́пый *adj.* absurd; nonsensical.
неле́стный *adj.* unflattering.
нелётный *adj.* unsuitable for flying.
нели́шне *adj.* (*pred.*) worthwile.
нели́шний *adj.* useful; necessary.
нело́вкий *adj.* awkward.
нело́вко *adv.* awkward(ly).
нело́вкость *f.* awkwardness.
нелоги́чный *adj.* illogical.
нелоя́льность *f.* disloyalty.
нелоя́льный *adj.* disloyal.
нельзя́ *adv.* (*pred.*) one must not; it's prohibited.
нелюбе́зный *adj.* ungracious.
нелюби́мый *adj.* unloved.
нелюбо́вь *f.* (к *with dat.*) dislike (for).
нелюди́м *m. f.* —ка unsociable person.
нелюди́мость *f.* unsociability.
нелюди́мый *adj.* unsociable.
нема́ло *adv.* **1.** (*with gen.*) quite a bit of. **2.** (*with verbs*) quite; quite a lot.
немаловажный *adj.* of no small importance.
нема́лый *adj.* rather large.
Нёман *m.* (*river*) Nyoman (*German: Memel, Russian: Neman*).
немеблиро́ванный *adj.* unfurnished.
неме́дленно *adv.* immediately.
неме́для *adv.* immediately.
неме́ркнущий *adj.* never fading.
не́мец FILL *m. f.* не́мка German.
неме́цкий *adj.* German.
неми́лостивый *adj.* (*obs.*) ungracious.
неми́лость *f.* disgrace.
немину́емо *adv.* inevitably; unavoidably.
немину́емый *adj.* unavoidable; inevitable.
немно́гие *pron. pl.* few; not many.
немно́гим *adv.* (*used with comp. adjectives*) a little.
немно́го *adv.* a little, not much.
немно́гое *neut.* little.
немногосло́вный *adj.* of few words; laconic.
немногочи́сленный *adj.* not numerous.
немно́жко *adv.* (*colloq.*) **1.** a little. **2.** little; not much. **3.** a little; rather.
немо́й *adj.* dumb; mute.
немолодо́й *adj.* not young.
немота́ *f.* muteness.
не́мочь *f.* (*colloq.*) sickness.
немощёный *adj.* unpaved.
не́мощный *adj.* feeble.
не́мощь *f.* debility.
немудрено́ *adv.* no wonder.
немудрёный *adj.* (*colloq.*) simple; plain.
нему́дрый *adj.* not very smart.
немы́слимый *adj.* unthinkable.
ненаблюда́тельный *adj.* unobservant.
ненави́деть *impf.* to hate; to abhor.
ненави́стник *m. f.* ненави́стница hostile person.
ненави́стничество *neut.* hostile attitude.
ненави́стный *adj.* hated; hateful.
не́нависть *f.* hatred.

ненагля́дный *m.* beloved.
ненадёжность *f.* unreliability.
ненадёжный *adj.* unreliable.
ненадобность *f.* lack of need.
ненадо́лго *adv.* for a short time.
нена́званный *adj.* unnamed.
ненаказу́емый *adj.* not punishable by law.
ненаме́ренно *adv.* unintentionally.
ненаме́ренный *adj.* unintentional.
ненападе́ние *neut.* nonaggression.
ненаро́ком *adv.* (*colloq.*) by chance.
нена́стный *adj.* (*of weather*) foul; inclement.
нена́стье *neut.* foul weather.
ненасы́тный *adj.* insatiable.
ненасы́щенный *adj.* unsaturated.
ненатура́льный *adj.* unnatural; artificial.
ненау́чный *adj.* unscientific.
не́нец FILL *m. f.* не́нка Nenets.
ненорма́льно *adv.* abnormally.
ненорма́льность *f.* abnormality.
ненорма́льный *adj.* abnormal.
нену́жность *f.* uselessness.
нену́жный *adj.* unnecessary.
необду́манный *adj.* hasty; rash.
необескура́женный *adj.* not discouraged.
необеспе́ченный *adj.* without means.
необеспоко́енный *adj.* undisturbed.
необита́емый *adj.* uninhabited.
необозри́мый *adj.* vast; boundless.
необосно́ванный *adj.* groundless, without foundation.
необрабо́танный *adj.* uncultivated; unfinished.
необразо́ванность *f.* lack of education.
необразо́ванный *adj.* uneducated.
необрати́мый *adj.* irreversible.
необу́зданный *adj.* unrestrained.
необу́ченный *adj.* untrained.
необходи́мо *adj.* (*pred.*) necessary; essential.
необходи́мое *neut.* necessities.
необходи́мость *f.* necessity; need.
необходи́мый *adj.* necessary; urgent; essential.
необщи́тельность *f.* unsociability.
необщи́тельный *adj.* unsociable.
необъекти́вность *f.* lack of objectivity.
необъекти́вный *adj.* not objective; biased.
необъя́вленный *adj.* undeclared; not announced.
необъясни́мый *adj.* inexplicable.
необъя́тный *adj.* boundless.
необыкнове́нно *adv.* unusually; uncommonly.
необыкнове́нный *adj.* unusual; uncommon.
необыча́йность *f.* extraordinary nature.
необыча́йный *adj.* extraordinary; exceptional.
необы́чный *adj.* unusual.
необяза́тельный *adj.* optional; not obligatory.
неограни́ченный *adj.* unlimited.
неодина́ковый *adj.* dissimilar.
неоднокра́тно *adv.* time and again; repeatedly.
неоднокра́тный *adj.* repeated.
неодноро́дность *f.* heterogeneity.
неодноро́дный *adj.* heterogeneous.
неодобре́ние *neut.* disapproval.
неодобри́тельно *adv.* in disapproval.
неодобри́тельный *adj.* disapproving.
неодоли́мый *adj.* irresistible.
неодушевлённый *adj.* inanimate.
неожи́данно *adv.* unexpectedly.

неожи́данность f. suddenness.
неожи́данный adj. unexpected.
неокласси́цизм m. neoclassicism.
неокласси́ческий adj. neoclassical.
неоконча́тельный adj. not final.
неоко́нченный adj. unfinished.
неолити́ческий adj. neolithic.
неологи́зм m. neologism.
нео́н m. neon.
нео́новый adj. neon.
неопа́сный adj. not dangerous.
неопера́бельный adj. (med.) inoperable.
неопери́вшийся adj. unfledged.
неопису́емый adj. indescribable.
неопла́тный adj. that cannot be repaid.
неопла́ченный adj. unpaid.
неопо́знанный adj. unidentified.
неопра́вданный adj. unjustified.
неопределённо adv. vaguely.
неопределённость f. vagueness.
неопределённый adj. indefinite; vague.
неопредели́мый adj. indefinable.
неопровержи́мо adv. conclusively.
неопровержи́мый adj. irrefutable; conclusive.
неопря́тность f. untidiness.
неопря́тный adj. sloppy; untidy.
неопублико́ванный adj. unpublished.
нео́пытность f. inexperience.
нео́пытный adj. inexperienced.
неорганизо́ванность f. disorganization.
неорганизо́ванный adj. disorganized.
неоргани́ческий adj. inorganic.
неосведомлённость f. lack of information.
неосведомлённый adj. uninformed.
неосвещённый adj. unlit.
неослабева́ющий adj. unremitting.
неосла́бный adj. unremitting.
неосмотри́тельность f. imprudence; carelessness.
неосмотри́тельный adj. imprudent; careless.
неоснова́тельный adj. unfounded.
неоспори́мый adj. indisputable.
неосторо́жно adv. carelessly.
неосторо́жность f. carelessness.
неосторо́жный adj. careless.
неосуществи́мость f. impracticability.
неосуществи́мый adj. impracticable.
неося́заемый adj. intangible.
неотврати́мость f. inevitability.
неотврати́мый adj. inevitable.
неотвя́зчивый adj. nagging; annoying.
неотдели́мость f. inseparability.
неотдели́мый adj. inseparable.
неотёсанный adj. (colloq.) uncouth.
неотзы́вчивый adj. unresponsive.
не́откуда adv. (with infin.) there is nowhere.
неотло́жка f. (colloq.) ambulance service.
неотло́жность f. urgency.
неотло́жный adj. urgent.
неотлу́чно adv. constantly.
неотлу́чный adj. ever-present.
неотполиро́ванный adj. unpolished.
неорази́мость f. irresistibility.
неотрази́мый adj. irresistible.
неотсту́пность f. relentlessness; persistence.
неотсту́пный adj. relentless; persistent.
неотчётливость f. indistinctness.

неотчётливый adj. indistinct.
неотшлифо́ванный adj. unpolished.
неотъе́млемый adj. inalienable.
неофи́т m. neophyte.
неофициа́льный adj. unofficial.
неохо́та f. reluctance.
неохо́тно adv. reluctantly.
неохо́тный adj. reluctant.
неоцени́мый adj. invaluable.
неочи́щенный adj. unrefined; crude.
неощути́мый adj. imperceptible.
Непа́л m. Nepal.
непа́рный adj. odd.
непарти́йный adj. non-party.
непереводи́мый adj. untranslatable.
непередава́емый adj. indescribable.
непереноси́мый adj. unbearable.
непереходный adj. intransitive.
неперспекти́вный adj. unpromising.
непеча́тный adj. unprintable (obscene).
непи́саный adj. unwritten.
непла́тёж m. nonpayment.
неплатёжеспосо́бность f. insolvency.
неплатёжеспосо́бный adj. insolvent.
неплате́льщик m. f. —**тельщица** person who has
    not paid; defaulter.
неплодоро́дность f. infertility.
неплодоро́дный adj. infertile.
непло́тно adv. not densely; not tightly.
непло́тный adj. not dense; thin.
непло́хо adv. not badly; rather well.
неплохо́й adj. not a bad.
непобеди́мость f. invincibility.
непобеди́мый adj. invincible.
непови́нный adj. innocent.
неповинове́ние neut. disobedience.
непово́ротливость f. clumsiness.
непово́ротливый adj. clumsy.
неповтори́мый adj. inimitable; unique.
непого́да f. bad weather.
непого́жий adj. (colloq.) (weather) dreary.
непогреши́мость f. infallibility.
непогреши́мый adj. infallible.
неподалёку adv. **1.** not far away. **2.** not far
    (from).
неподатливый adj. unyielding; intractable.
неподви́жно adv. motionless(ly).
неподви́жность f. immobility.
неподви́жный adj. immobile.
неподгото́вленный adj. unprepared.
неподде́льный adj. genuine.
неподку́пность f. incorruptibility.
неподку́пный adj. incorruptible.
неподоба́ющий adj. improper; unseemly.
неподража́емый adj. inimitable.
неподтверждённый adj. unconfirmed.
неподходя́щий adj. unsuitable.
неподчине́ние neut. insubordination.
непозволи́тельный adj. impermissible.
непоколеби́мость f. steadfastness.
непоколеби́мый adj. unshakable; steadfast.
непоко́рность f. recalcitrance.
непоко́рный adj. recalcitrant; unruly.
непокры́тый adj. uncovered.
непола́дки pl. (colloq.) defects; bugs.
неполнопра́вный adj. not enjoying full rights.

неполнота́ f. incompleteness.
неполноце́нность f. inferiority.
неполноце́нный adj. inferior.
непо́лный adj. not full; incomplete.
непоме́рный adj. excessive.
непонима́ние neut. lack of understanding.
непоня́тливый adj. dense; dull.
непоня́тно adv. incomprehensibly.
непоня́тность f. incomprehensibility.
непоня́тный adj. incomprehensible.
непопада́ние neut. miss (in shooting).
непоправи́мый adj. irreparable.
непопуля́рность f. unpopularity.
непопуля́рный adj. unpopular.
непоро́чность f. chastity; purity; innocence.
непоро́чный adj. innocent; chaste.
непо́ртящийся adj. nonperishable.
непоря́док FILL m. disorder.
непоря́дочный adj. dishonorable.
непосвящённый adj. uninitiated.
непосе́да m. and f. (decl. f.) (colloq.) fidgety person.
непосе́дливость f. restlessness.
непосе́дливый adj. fidgety; restless.
непосеще́ние neut. failure to attend.
непоси́льный adj. backbreaking.
непосле́довательность f. inconsistency.
непосле́довательный adj. inconsistent..
непослуша́ние neut. disobedience.
непослу́шный adj. disobedient.
непосре́дственно adv. immediately.
непосре́дственность f. spontaneity.
непосре́дственный adj. direct.
непостижи́мость f. incomprehensibility.
непостижи́мый adj. incomprehensible.
непостоя́нный adj. inconstant; changeable.
непостоя́нство neut. inconstancy.
непоти́зм m. nepotism.
непотопля́емый adj. unsinkable.
непотре́бный adj. (obs.) indecent; obscene.
непохо́жий adj. (на with acc.) unlike.
непоча́тый adj. untouched; unused.
непочте́ние neut. disrespect.
непочти́тельность f. disrespect.
непочти́тельный adj. disrespectful.
непра́вда f. untruth.
неправдоподо́бие neut. improbability.
неправдоподо́бный adj. 1. improbable; unlikely. 2. implausible.
непра́вильно adv. incorrectly. –adj. (pred.) incorrect.
непра́вильность f. fallacy.
непра́вильный adj. incorrect; wrong.
неправомо́чность f. (leg.) incompetence.
неправомо́чный adj. not legally qualified.
неправота́ f. error.
непра́вый adj. mistaken; wrong.
непракти́чность f. impracticality.
непракти́чный adj. impractical.
непревзойдённый adj. unsurpassed; unexcelled.
непредви́денный adj. unforeseen.
непреднаме́ренный adj. unintentional.
непредприи́мчивый adj. unenterprising.
непредска́зуемый adj. unpredictable.
непредубеждённый adj. unbiased.
непреду́мышленный adj. unpremeditated.

непредусмотри́тельность f. improvidence; lack of foresight.
непредусмотри́тельный adj. improvident; lacking foresight.
непрекло́нность f. inflexibility.
непрекло́нный adj. inflexible.
непрело́жный adj. immutable.
непреме́нно adv. without fail.
непреме́нный adj. indispensable.
непреобори́мый adj. irresistible.
непреодоли́мый adj. insurmountable.
непререка́емый adj. unquestionable.
непреры́вно adv. continuously.
непреры́вность f. continuity.
непреры́вный adj. continuous.
непреста́нно adv. incessantly; continuously.
непреста́нный adj. incessant; continual.
неприве́тливость f. unfriendliness.
неприве́тливый adj. unfriendly; uninviting.
непривлека́тельный adj. unattractive.
непривы́чка f. not being used to something.
непривы́чно adv. unusually. — adj. (pred.) unaccustomed to.
непривы́чный adj. 1. strange; unfamiliar. 2. unaccustomed to.
непригля́дный adj. unsightly; unattractive.
неприго́дность f. uselessness.
неприго́дный adj. unfit; useless; unusable.
неприе́млемость f. unacceptability.
неприе́млемый adj. unacceptable.
непризна́ние neut. nonrecognition.
непри́знанный adj. unrecognized.
неприкаса́емые pl. untouchables (in India).
неприка́янный adj. (colloq.) aimless.
неприкоснове́нность f. inviolability.
неприкоснове́нный adj. inviolable.
неприкра́шенный adj. plain; unadorned.
неприкреплённый adj. unattached.
неприкры́тый adj. 1. slightly open; ajar. 2. (of person) uncovered; naked.
неприли́чие neut. indecency.
неприли́чно adv. indecently; improperly.
неприли́чный adj. indecent.
неприме́тный adj. 1. ordinary; not noteworthy. 2. imperceptible.
непримеча́тельный adj. undistinguished; ordinary.
непримири́мость f. irreconcilability.
непримири́мый adj. irreconcilable.
непринуждённость f. ease; abandon.
непринуждённый adj. natural; unconstrained; spontaneous.
неприсоедине́ние neut. nonalignment.
неприсоедини́вшийся adj. nonaligned.
неприспосо́бленность f. maladjustment.
неприспосо́бленный adj. maladjusted.
непристо́йность f. obscenity.
непристо́йный adj. obscene.
непристу́пный adj. inaccessible.
непритво́рный adj. unfeigned; genuine.
непритяза́тельный adj. unassuming; unpretentious.
неприхотли́вый adj. 1. unpretentious; modest. 2. simple; plain.
неприча́стность f. noninvolvement.
неприча́стный adj. (к with dat.) not involved (in).
неприя́знь f. hostility; enmity.

неприя́тель *m. f.* —**ница** enemy.
неприя́тельский *adj.* (*attrib.*) enemy.
неприя́тно *adj.* (*pred.*) unpleasant.
неприя́тность *f.* unpleasantness; nuisance, annoyance, trouble.
неприя́тный *adj.* unpleasant.
непробива́емый *adj.* impenetrable.
непробу́дный *adj.* (*of sleep*) deep.
непрове́ренный *adj.* unverified.
непроводни́к *m.* (*phys.*) nonconductor.
непрогля́дный *adj.* pitch-dark.
непродолжи́тельность *f.* shortness.
непродолжи́тельный *adj.* short; of short duration.
непродукти́вность *f.* lack of productivity.
непродукти́вный *adj.* unproductive.
непроду́манный *adj.* not thought out.
непрое́зжий *adj.* impassable.
непрозра́чность *f.* opacity; opaqueness.
непрозра́чный *adj.* opaque.
непроизводи́тельность *f.* lack of productivity.
непроизводи́тельный *adj.* unproductive.
непроизво́льный *adj.* involuntary.
непроизноси́мый *adj.* unpronounceable.
непрола́зный *adj.* (*colloq.*) impassable.
непромока́емый *adj.* waterproof; impermeable.
непроница́емость *f.* impenetrability.
непроница́емый *adj.* impenetrable.
непропорциона́льно *adv.* disproportionately.
непропорциона́льность *f.* disproportion.
непропорциона́льный *adj.* disproportionate.
непросвещённый *adj.* unenlightened.
непрости́тельный *adj.* unpardonable; unforgivable.
непроходи́мость *f.* impassability.
непроходи́мый *adj.* impassable; impenetrable.
непро́чность *f.* flimsiness.
непро́чный *adj.* not durable.
непро́шеный *adj.* uninvited.
непрямо́й *adj.* indirect.
непту́ний *m.* neptunium.
непутёвый *adj.* (*colloq.*) shiftless; good-for-nothing.
непью́щий *adj.* not drinking. — *m.* nondrinker.
неработоспосо́бный *adj.* disabled; incapacitated.
нерабо́чий *adj.* nonworking.
нера́венство *neut.* inequality.
неравноду́шный *adj.* (**к** *with dat.*) not indifferent (to).
неравноме́рно *adv.* unevenly.
неравноме́рность *f.* unevenness.
неравноме́рный *adj.* uneven; irregular.
неравнопра́вие *neut.* lack of equal rights.
неравнопра́вный *adj.* not having equal rights.
нера́вный *adj.* unequal.
нераде́ние *neut.* (*obs.*) lackadaisical attitude.
неради́вость *f.* lackadaisical attitude.
неради́вый *adj.* lackadaisical.
неразбери́ха *f.* (*colloq.*) disorder; confusion; chaos.
неразбо́рчивость *f.* illegibility.
неразбо́рчивый *adj.* **1.** (*of handwriting*) illegible.
2. undiscriminating.
неразве́данный *adj.* unexplored.
нера́звитость *f.* backwardness.
нера́звитый *adj.* undeveloped.
неразга́данный *adj.* unsolved.
неразгово́рчивость *f.* uncommunicativeness.
неразгово́рчивый *adj.* uncommunicative.

нераздели́мый *adj.* indivisible.
неразлу́чность *f.* inseparability.
неразлу́чный *adj.* inseparable.
неразре́занный *adj.* uncut.
неразрешённый *adj.* **1.** unsolved, not solved. **2.** forbidden, prohibited.
неразреши́мый *adj.* insoluble.
неразруши́мый *adj.* indestructible.
неразры́вный *adj.* indestructible; indissoluble.
неразу́мность *f.* irrationality.
неразу́мный *adj.* unwise; unreasonable.
нераска́янный *adj.* (*obs.*) impenitent.
нерасположе́ние *neut.* (**к** *with dat.*) dislike of *or* for.
нераспоряди́тельный *adj.* lacking administrative ability.
нераспростране́ние *neut.* nonproliferation.
нерасска́занный *adj.* untold.
нерассуди́тельность *f.* lack of common sense.
нерассуди́тельный *adj.* lacking common sense.
нераствори́мый *adj.* insoluble.
нерасторжи́мый *adj.* indissoluble.
нерасторо́пный *adj.* sluggish; inert.
нерастро́ганный *adj.* unmoved.
нерасчётливость *f.* improvidence.
нерасчётливый *adj.* **1.** wasteful; extravagant. **2.** improvident.
нерациона́льный *adj.* inefficient.
нерв *m.* nerve. —**ный** *adj.* nervous.
нерви́ческий *adj.* (*obs.*) nervous.
нервни́чать *impf.* to be nervous.
не́рвность *f.* nervousness.
нервно́зность *f.* nervousness.
нервно́зный *adj.* nervous; high-strung.
нереа́льный *adj.* unreal; unrealistic.
нерегуля́рность *f.* irregularity.
нерегуля́рный *adj.* irregular.
нере́дкий *adj.* not infrequent; quite common.
нере́дко *adv.* often.
нерента́бельный *adj.* unprofitable.
нерести́лище *neut.* spawning ground.
нерешённый *adj.* unresolved.
нереши́мость *f.* indecision.
нереши́тельность *f.* indecisiveness.
нереши́тельный *adj.* undecisive; irresolute.
нержаве́ющий *adj.* rust-resistant.
неритми́чный *adj.* irregular.
Нерль *f.* (*river*) Nerl.
неро́бкий *adj.* not timid.
неро́вно *adv.* unevenly.
неро́вность *f.* unevenness.
неро́вный *adj.* uneven.
неро́вня *m.* and *f.* (*decl. f.*) (*colloq.*) person not the equal of another.
не́рпа *f.* ringed seal.
нерукотво́рный *adj.* (*relig.*) not made by human hands.
неру́сский *adj.* non-Russian.
неруши́мость *f.* inviolability.
неруши́мый *adj.* inviolable; indissoluble.
неря́ха *m.* and *f.* (*decl. f.*) slob; slovenly person.
неря́шество *neut.* sloppiness.
неря́шливость *f.* sloppiness.
неря́шливый *adj.* **1.** sloppy; slovenly; untidy. **2.** careless.
несбы́точный *adj.* unrealizable.

несваре́ние желу́дка *neut.* indigestion.
несве́дущий *adj.* ignorant.
несве́жий *adj.* stale.
несвоевре́менно *adv.* at an inopportune time.
несвоевре́менный *adj.* ill-timed.
несвя́зность *f.* incoherence.
несвя́зный *adj.* incoherent.
несгиба́емый *adj.* unbending.
несгово́рчивый *adj.* intractable; uncooperative.
несгора́емый *adj.* incombustible; fireproof.
несде́ржанный *adj.* **1.** broken; unkept. **2.** unrestrained.
несекре́тный *adj.* not secret.
несерьёзный *adj.* not serious.
несессе́р *m.* toilet case.
несимметри́чность *f.* asymmetry.
несимметри́чный *adj.* asymmetrical.
несказа́нный *adj.* indescribable.
нескла́дный *adj.* **1.** awkward; ungainly. **2.** discordant. **3.** incoherent. **4.** absurd.
несклоня́емый *adj.* (*gram.*) indeclinable.
не́сколько *adj.* several, a few. — *adv.* somewhat.
несконча́емый *adj.* endless.
нескро́мность *f.* immodesty.
нескро́мный *adj.* immodest.
нескрыва́емый *adj.* unconcealed.
несло́жный *adj.* simple.
неслы́ханный *adj.* unheard-of; unprecedented.
неслы́шный *adj.* inaudible.
несме́лый *adj.* timid.
несменя́емость *f.* constant presence; tenure.
несменя́емый *adj.* ever-present.
несме́тный *adj.* **1.** countless. **2.** incalculable.
несмолка́емый *adj.* (*of sound*) incessant.
несмотря́ на *prep.* (*with acc.*) in spite of.
несмыва́емые черни́ла *pl.* indelible ink.
несмышлёный *adj.* (*colloq.*) dense; dull.
несно́сный *adj.* unbearable; unendurable.
несоблюде́ние *neut.* failure to observe.
несовершенноле́тие *neut.* minority (*being under legal age*).
несовершенноле́тний *adj.* underage. — *m.* minor.
несоверше́нный *adj.* **1.** imperfect. **2.** (*gram.*) imperfective.
несоверше́нство *neut.* lack of perfection.
несовмести́мость *f.* incompatibility.
несовмести́мый *adj.* incompatible.
несогла́сие *neut.* disagreement; discord.
несогла́сный *adj.* disagreeing.
несогласо́ванность *f.* lack of coordination.
несогласо́ванный *adj.* uncoordinated.
несозна́тельный *adj.* unconscious.
несоизмери́мость *f.* incommensurability.
несоизмери́мый *adj.* incommensurable.
несокращённый *adj.* unabridged.
несокруши́мый *adj.* indestructible.
несо́лоно хлеба́вши (*colloq.*) getting nothing for one's trouble.
несомне́нно *adv.* undoubtedly; doubtlessly.
несомне́нный *adj.* undoubted.
несообрази́тельный *adj.* dense; dull.
несообра́зность *f.* incongruity.
несообра́зный *adj.* incongruous.
несоотве́тствие *neut.* discrepancy; disparity.
несоразме́рно *adv.* (с *with instr.*) disproportionately (to).

несоразме́рность *f.* disproportion.
несоразме́рный *adj.* disproportionate.
несостоя́тельность *f.* insolvency.
несостоя́тельный *adj.* of modest means.
несочу́вствующий *adj.* unsympathetic.
неспе́лый *adj.* unripe.
неспе́шный *adj.* unhurried.
неспоко́йно *adv.* anxiously.
неспорти́вный *adj.* unsportsmanlike.
неспосо́бность *f.* inability.
неспосо́бный *adj.* incapable.
несправедли́во *adv.* unjustly; unfairly.
несправедли́вость *f.* injustice; unfairness.
несправедли́вый *adj.* unjust, unfair.
неспровоци́рованный *adj.* unprovoked.
непроста́ *adv.* (*colloq.*) for a definite reason; not by chance.
несравне́нно *adv.* incomparably.
несравне́нный *adj.* incomparable.
несравни́мый *adj.* incomparable.
нестерпи́мый *adj.* unbearable; unendurable.
нестесня́емый *adj.* uninhibited.
нести́[1] *impf. pf.* по- to carry; to bear.
нести́[2] *impf. pf.* с- to lay (eggs).
нести́сь[1] *impf.* **1.** to race (by *or* along); to rush. **2.** to be heard. **3.** to float.
нести́сь[2] *impf. pf.* с- to lay eggs.
несто́йкий *adj.* **1.** unstable. **2.** (*of an odor*) slight; weak.
несто́ящий *adj.* (*colloq.*) worthless.
нестроево́й *adj.* unfit for building purposes.
нестро́йный *adj.* ungainly.
несть *pred.* (*obs.*) there is no...
несудохо́дный *adj.* unnavigable.
несура́зный *adj.* **1.** absurd; ridiculous. **2.** awkward.
несусве́тный *adj.* (*colloq.*) **1.** utter; absolute. **2.** not of this world.
несу́шка *f.* hen that lays eggs.
несхо́дный *adj.* different.
несхо́дство *neut.* difference; disparity.
несчастли́вец FILL *m. f.* несчастли́вица (*colloq.*) unlucky person.
несчастли́вый *adj.* **1.** unhappy. **2.** unlucky; unfortunate.
несча́стный *adj.* unhappy; unfortunate; unlucky. — несча́стный слу́чай *m.* accident.
несча́стье *neut.* misfortune; disaster. — к несча́стью *adv.* unfortunately.
несчётный *adj.* innumerable.
несъедо́бный *adj.* inedible.
нет *particle* no; not. — ещё нет not yet.
нетакти́чный *adj.* tactless.
нетала́нтливый *adj.* untalented.
нетвёрдо *adv.* not firmly.
нетвёрдый *adj.* not hard.
нетерпели́во *adv.* impatiently.
нетерпели́вость *f.* impatience.
нетерпели́вый *adj.* impatient.
нетерпе́ние *neut.* impatience. — ждать с нетерпе́нием to look forward to.
нетерпи́мость *f.* intolerance.
нетерпи́мый *adj.* **1.** intolerable. **2.** intolerant.
нетипи́чный *adj.* not typical.
нетле́нный *adj.* (*obs.*) imperishable.
нетопы́рь *m.* large bat.

неторопли́вый *adj.* leisurely; unhurried.
нето́чность *f.* inaccuracy.
нето́чный *adj.* inexact; inaccurate.
нетре́бовательный *adj.* undemanding.
нетре́звый *adj.* intoxicated; drunk.
нетро́нутый *adj.* untouched.
нетру́дный *adj.* not difficult.
нетрудово́й *adj.* unearned.
нетрудоспосо́бность *f.* incapacity; disability.
нетрудоспосо́бный *adj.* disabled; incapacitated.
не́тто *adj. indecl.* and *adv.* net.
не́ту *particle (colloq.)*, *see* нет.
неубеди́тельный *adj.* unconvincing.
неу́бранный *adj.* not cleaned; not straightened; not put away.
неуваже́ние *neut.* disrespect.
неуважи́тельный *adj.* inadequate; disrespectful.
неуве́ренность *f.* uncertainty; lack of confidence.
неуве́ренный *adj.* uncertain.
неувяда́емый *adj.* never fading.
неувяда́ющий *adj.* never fading.
неугаси́мый *adj.* unquenchable.
неуго́дный *adj.* disagreeable.
неуда́ча *f.* failure.
неуда́чливый *adj.* unlucky.
неуда́чник *m.* f неуда́чница unlucky person.
неуда́чно *adv.* unsuccessfully.
неуда́чный *adj.* unsuccessful.
неудержи́мый *adj.* irrepressible; uncontrollable.
неудиви́тельно *adv.* not surprisingly.
неудиви́тельный *adj.* not surprising.
неудо́бно *adv.* uncomfortably.
неудо́бный *adj.* uncomfortable; inconvenient.
неудобовари́мый *adj.* indigestible.
неудобопроизноси́мый *adj.* difficult to pronounce.
неудобочита́емый *adj.* difficult to read.
неудо́бство *neut.* inconvenience.
неудовлетворе́ние *neut.* dissatisfaction.
неудовлетворённость *f.* dissatisfaction.
неудовлетворённый *adj.* dissatisfied.
неудовлетвори́тельно *adv.* unsatisfactorily.
неудовлетвори́тельный *adj.* unsatisfactory.
неудово́льствие *neut.* displeasure.
неужо́ли *particle* indeed?; really?
неужи́вчивый *adj.* hard to get along with.
неузнава́емость *f.*: до неузнава́емости beyond recognition.
неузнава́емый *adj.* unrecognizable.
неука́занный *adj.* unspecified.
неукло́нный *adj.* 1. (*of growth*) steady. 2. unwavering; steadfast.
неукло́же *adv.* awkwardly; clumsily.
неукло́жесть *f.* awkwardness.
неукло́жий *adj.* awkward; clumsy.
неукосни́тельно *adv.* unfailingly.
неукосни́тельный *adj.* unfailing; absolute.
неулови́мость *f.* elusiveness.
неулови́мый *adj.* elusive.
неуме́лый *adj.* clumsy; inept.
неуме́ние *neut.* inability.
неуме́ренность *f.* immoderation.
неуме́стность *f.* impropriety.
неуме́стный *adj.* 1. inappropriate; out of place. 2. irrelevant.
неу́мный *adj.* unintelligent.
неумоли́мый *adj.* implacable.

неумолка́емый *also* неумо́лчный *adj.* (*of sound*) incessant.
неумы́шленный *adj.* unintentional.
неупла́та *f.* nonpayment.
неупла́ченный *adj.* unpaid; outstanding.
неупотребля́емый *adj.* not in use.
неуравнове́шенность *f.* instability.
неуравнове́шенный *adj.* unbalanced; unstable.
неурегули́рованный *adj.* unsettled.
неурожа́й *m.* poor harvest.
неурожа́йный год *m.* year of poor harvest.
неуро́чный *adj.* untimely.
неуря́дица *f.* (*colloq.*) 1. disorder; confusion. 2. squabbling.
неуси́дчивый *adj.* restless.
неуспева́емость *f.* poor progress (*among students*).
неуспева́ющий *adj.* (*of student*) poor; not making progress.
неуспе́х *m.* failure.
неуспе́шный *adj.* unsuccessful.
неуста́нный *adj.* untiring.
неусто́йка *f.* (*leg.*) forfeit.
неусто́йчивость *f.* instability.
неусто́йчивый *adj.* 1. unsteady; shaky; unstable. 2. fluctuating; variable.
неустрани́мый *adj.* irremovable.
неустраши́мость *f.* fearlessness.
неустраши́мый *adj.* fearless.
неустро́енность *f.* unsettled state.
неустро́енный *adj.* unsettled.
неустро́йство *neut.* disorder.
неуступчивость *f.* obstinacy; unwillingness to compromise.
неусту́пчивый *adj.* uncompromising.
неусы́пный *adj.* 1. untiring; tireless. 2. unflagging.
неутеши́тельный *adj.* unencouraging.
неуте́шный *adj.* inconsolable.
неутоли́мый *adj.* unquenchable; unsatiable.
неутоми́мость *f.* indefatigability.
неутоми́мый *adj.* indefatigable.
не́уч *m.* (*colloq.*) ignoramus.
неучти́вость *adj.* discourtesy.
неучти́вый *adj.* discourteous.
неую́тно *adv.* uncomfortably.
неую́тный *adj.* uncomfortable.
неязви́мость *f.* invulnerability.
неязви́мый *adj.* invulnerable.
нефри́т *m.* nephritis.
нефтеналивно́й *adj.* carrying oil.
нефтено́сный *adj.* containing oil.
нефтеперего́нный заво́д *m.* oil refinery.
нефтепрово́д *m.* oil pipeline.
нефтехими́ческий *adj.* petrochemical.
нефтехрани́лище *neut.* oil storage tank.
нефть *f.* petroleum; oil.
нефтяно́й *adj.* (*attrib.*) oil; petroleum.
нехара́ктерный *adj.* not typical.
нехва́тка *f.* (*colloq.*) shortage.
нехи́трый *adj.* ingenuous; without guile.
неходово́й *adj.* 1. not in working order. 2. (*of goods*) not selling well.
нехоро́ший *adj.* bad. — нехоро́ш собо́й *adj.* (*pred.*) ugly; unattractive.
нехорошо́ *adv.* bad, badly; unwell.
не́хотя *adv.* unwillingly.
нецензу́рный *adj.* unprintable; obscene.

нецеремонный *adj.* unceremonious.
нецивилизованный *adj.* uncivilized.
нечаянно *adv.* unintentionally; accidentally.
нечаянный *adj.* unexpected; chance; accidental.
нечего *pron.* (*with infin.*) it is no good; there is no need (to). — нечего делать there is nothing one can do.
нечеловеческий *adj.* inhuman.
нечёсаный *adj.* unkempt.
нечестивый *adj.* (*obs.*) wicked; unholy.
нечестно *adv.* dishonestly.
нечестность *f.* dishonesty.
нечестный *adj.* dishonest.
нечет *m.* (*colloq.*) odd number.
нечёткий *adj.* 1. unclear; illegible. 2. careless.
нечётный *adj.* (*of a number*) odd.
нечистокровный *adj.* of mixed blood; not pure-bred.
нечистоплотный *adj.* dirty; sloppy.
нечистота *f.* uncleanliness.
нечистый *adj.* 1. unclean; impure. 2. (*fig.*) shady.
нечисть *f.* (*colloq.*) 1. evil spirits. 2. scum; vermin.
нечленораздельный *adj.* inarticulate; unintelligible.
нечто *pron.* something.
нечувствительность *f.* insensitivity.
нечувствительный *adj.* insensitive.
нечуткий *adj.* insensitive.
нечуткость *f.* insensitivity.
нешуточный *adj.* not to be taken lightly.
нещадно *adv.* mercilessly.
нещадный *adj.* unmerciful; merciless.
неэкономный *adj.* uneconomical.
неэтилированный *adj.* (*of gasoline*) unleaded.
неэтичный *adj.* unethical.
неэффективность *f.* inefficiency.
неэффективный *adj.* 1. inefficient. 2. ineffective.
неявка *f.* 1. absence; nonattendance. 2. failure to appear.
неяркий *adj.* dim; faint.
неясно *adv.* dimly; faintly; unclear.
неясность *f.* lack of clarity.
неясный *adj.* vague; unclear.
неясыть *f.* tawny owl.
ни *particle* not a; (*in combination with adverbs*) -ever. — ни... ни... neither... nor... — ни один not one.
нива *f.* field; cornfield.
нивелир *m.* (*instrument*) level.
нивелировать OVA *impf.* and *pf.* to level.
нивелировка *f.* leveling.
нивяник *m.* oxeye daisy.
нигде *adv.* nowhere.
Нигерия *f.* Nigeria.
нигилизм *m.* nihilism.
нигилист *m. f.* —ка nihilist.
нигилистический *adj.* nihilist.
нидерландец FILL *m. f.* нидерландка a Dutch person.
Нидерланды *pl.* the Netherlands.
ниже *adv.* lower; below, beneath, under.
нижеподписавшийся *m.* the undersigned.
нижеследующий *adj.* the following.
нижестоящий *adj.* (*in an organization*) lower-level.
нижний *adj.* lower.

Нижний Новгород *m.* Nizhniy Novgorod.
низ *m.* bottom.
низать *impf. pres.* нижу, нижешь *pf.* на- to string; to thread.
низвергать *impf. pf.* низвергнуть to overthrow.
низвержение *neut.* overthrow.
низина *f.* low-lying area; hollow.
низкий *adj.* low; base, mean.
низко *adv.* low.
низкооплачиваемый *adj.* low-paid.
низкопоклонник *m.* sycophant.
низкопоклонство *neut.* servility.
низкопробный *adj.* (*of precious metals*) low-grade.
низкорослый *adj.* undersized.
низкосортный *adj.* low-quality.
низлагать *impf. pf.* низложить to overthrow; to bring down.
низложение *neut.* overthrow.
низменность 1. *f.* lowland. 2. baseness.
низовой *adj.* 1. low; close to the ground. 2. located downstream. 3. at the local level; grass-roots.
низовье *neut.* (*river*) lower reaches.
низом *adv.* along the lower road; along the bottom.
низость *f.* lowness; baseness.
никак *adv.* in no way, by no means.
никакой *adj.* not any; no... whatever.
Никарагуа *f.* Nicaragua.
никелевый *adj.* nickel.
никелировать OVA *impf.* and *pf.* to plate with nickel.
никелировка *f.* nickel-plating.
никель *m.* nickel.
никем *pron. instr. of* никто.
никнуть *impf. pf.* по- to droop.
никогда *adv.* never.
никого *pron. gen., acc. of* никто.
никой *adj.:* ни в коем случае under no circumstances; no way.
Николаев *m.* Nikolaev.
никому *pron. dat. of* никто.
никотин *m.* nicotine.
никотиновый *adj.* (*attrib.*) nicotine.
никто *pron.* nobody, no one.
никуда *adv.* (*dir.*) nowhere.
никудышный *adj.* (*colloq.*) 1. good-for-nothing. 2. useless; worthless.
никчёмность *f.* (*colloq.*) uselessness.
никчёмный *adj.* (*colloq.*) 1. good-for-nothing. 2. useless; worthless.
Ним *m.* Nîmes.
нимало *adv.* not in the least.
нимб *m.* nimbus.
нимфа *f.* nymph.
нимфомания *f.* nymphomania.
нимфоманка *f.* nymphomaniac.
ниобий *m.* niobium.
ниодимий *m.* neodymium.
ниоткуда *adv.* from nowhere.
нипочём *adv.* (*colloq.*) 1. (*with dat.*) it is nothing (*for someone to do s.t.*). 2. for nothing; dirt-cheap. 3. under no circumstances.
ниппель *m.* nipple (*threaded pipe*).
нирвана *f.* nirvana.
нисколько *adv.* not in the least.

ниспроверже́ние *neut.* overthrow.
нисходя́щий *adj.* descending.
ни́тка *f.* thread.
ни́точка *f. dim. of* ни́тка.
ни́точный *adj.* of thread.
нитра́т *m.* nitrate.
нитра́тный *adj.* (*attrib.*) nitrate.
нитри́т *m.* nitrite.
нитроглицери́н *m.* nitroglycerine.
нить *f.* 1. thread. 2. filament. 3. suture.
нитяно́й *adj.* made of thread.
ниц *adv.* face downwards.
Ни́цца *f.* Nice.
ничего́ *pron.* nothing.
ничегонеде́лание *neut.* (*colloq.*) idleness.
ниче́й *pron.* nobody's, no one's.
ниче́йный *adj.* 1. (*sports* and *games*) tied. 2. (*colloq.*) no man's.
ниче́м *pron. instr. of* ничто́.
ничему́ *pron. dat. of* ничто́.
ничко́м *adv.* face downwards; prone.
ничто́ *pron.* nothing.
ничто́жество *neut.* nonentity.
ничто́жность 1. *m.* insignificance. 2. nonentity.
ничто́жный *adj.* 1. insignificant; paltry. 2. worthless.
ничу́ть *adv.* (*colloq.*) not in the least.
ничья́ *f.* (*sports*) draw, drawn game.
Ниш *m.* Niš.
ни́ша *f.* niche; recess.
ни́щенка *f.* (*colloq.*) beggarwoman.
ни́щенский *adj.* beggarly.
ни́щенство *neut.* poverty; destitution.
ни́щенствовать OVA *impf.* to go begging.
нищета́ *f.* poverty.
ни́щий *adj.* indigent; poor. — *m.* beggar.
НЛО *m.* (*abbr. of* неопо́знанный лета́ющий объе́кт) U.F.O. (*abbr. of* unidentified flying object).
но *conj.* but.
нобе́лий *m.* nobelium.
нова́тор *m.* innovator.
нова́торский *adj.* innovative.
нова́торство *neut.* innovation.
Но́вая Гвине́я *f.* New Guinea.
Но́вая Зела́ндия *f.* New Zealand.
Но́вая Земля́ *f.* (*island*) Novaya Zemlya.
Но́вая Шотла́ндия *f.* Nova Scotia.
Но́вгород *m.* Novgorod.
Но́вгород-Се́верский *m.* Novgorod Severskiy.
нове́йший *adj.* newest, latest.
нове́лла *f.* novella; short story.
новелли́ст *m.* short story writer.
но́венький *m.* (*colloq.*) newcomer.
новизна́ *f.* novelty.
нови́нка *f.* something new.
новичо́к FILL *m.* novice.
новобра́нец FILL *m.* recruit.
новобра́чные *pl.* newlyweds.
нововведе́ние *neut.* innovation.
нового́дний *adj.* New Year's.
новогре́ческий *adj.* modern Greek.
новозаве́тный *adj.* (*attrib.*) New Testament.
новоиспечённый *adj.* (*colloq.*) newly made.
новокаи́н *m.* novocaine.
новокаи́новый *adj.* novocaine.
новолу́ние *neut.* new moon.

новомо́дный *adj.* in the latest style.
новообразова́ние *neut.* new formation.
новообращённый *adj.* newly converted. — *m.* neophyte.
новоприбы́вший *adj.* newly arrived. — *m.* newcomer.
новорождённый *adj.* newborn.
Новоросси́йск *m.* Novorossiysk.
новосёл *m.* new settler.
новосе́лье *neut.* housewarming.
но́вость *f.* 1. news. 2. novelty.
но́вшество *neut.* innovation; novelty.
но́вый *adj.* new. — с Но́вым Го́дом Happy New Year!
Но́вый Орлеа́н *m.* New Orleans.
новь *f.* virgin soil.
нога́ *f.* foot; leg.
ноготки́ *pl.* marigold.
но́готь FILL *m.* fingernail; toenail.
нож *m.* knife.
ножево́й *adj.* (*attrib.*) knife.
но́жик *m.* small knife.
но́жка *f.* (*of furniture*) leg; stem.
но́жницы *pl.* scissors.
ножно́й *adj.* (*attrib.*) foot.
но́жны *pl.* scabbard; sheath.
ножо́вка *f.* handsaw; hacksaw.
ноздрева́тый *adj.* porous.
ноздря́ *f.* nostril.
нока́ут *m.* knockout.
нокаути́ровать OVA *impf.* and *pf.* (*boxing*) to knock out.
нокда́ун *m.* knockdown.
ноктю́рн *m.* nocturne.
нолево́й *adj.* zero.
ноль *m.* zero; nil; nought.
номенклату́ра *f.* 1. nomenclature. 2. (*colloq.*) top-level administrative positions.
но́мер *m.* number; hotel room; size.
номерно́й знак *m.* license plate.
номеро́к FILL *m.* ticket; receipt.
номина́льный *adj.* nominal.
нора́ *f.* hole; lair, den, burrow.
Норве́гия *f.* Norway.
норве́жец FILL *m. f.* норве́жка Norwegian.
норве́жский *adj.* Norwegian.
норд *m.* (*naut.*) north.
норд-ве́ст *m.* (*naut.*) northwest.
норд-о́ст *m.* (*naut.*) northeast.
Нори́льск *m.* Norilsk.
но́рка[1] *dim. of* нора́.
но́рка[2] *f.* mink.
но́рковый *adj.* (*attrib.*) mink.
но́рма *f.* norm, standard; rate.
нормализа́ция *f.* normalization.
нормализова́ть OVA *impf.* and *pf.* to normalize.
норма́ль *f.* (*math.*) normal.
норма́льно *adv.* normally. –*adj.* (*pred.*) (*colloq.*) all right; O.K.
норма́льность *f.* normality.
норма́льный *adj.* normal.
Норма́ндия *f.* (*province*) Normandy.
Норма́ндские острова́ *pl.* Channel Islands.
норма́нн *m.* Norseman.
нормати́в *m.* norm.
нормати́вный *adj.* normative.

нормирова́ние *neut.* standardization.
нормирова́ть OVA *impf.* and *pf.* to standardize.
но́ров *m.* (*colloq.*) character; temperament.
норови́стый *adj.* (*colloq.*) (*of a horse*) restive.
порови́ть *impf.* (*colloq.*) to try; to strive.
нос *m.* nose.
носа́тый *adj.* (*colloq.*) big-nosed.
но́сик *m.* 1. *dim. of* нос. 2. spout (*on a teapot*).
носи́лки *pl.* stretcher.
носи́льщик *m.* porter.
носи́тель *m. f.* —ница bearer.
носи́ть *impf. indet. det.* нести́ 1. to carry, to bear. 2. to wear. —ся 3. to rush about. 4. to be carried *or* worn. 5. (с *with instr.*) to fuss over.
но́ска[1] *f.* 1. carrying. 2. wearing.
но́ска[2] *f.* laying (eggs).
но́ский[1] *adj.* giving long wear; durable.
но́ский[2] *adj.* producing many eggs (*of hens*).
носово́й плато́к *m.* handkerchief.
носо́к FILL *m.* sock.
носоро́г *m.* rhinoceros.
ностальги́ческий *adj.* nostalgic.
ностальги́я *f.* nostalgia.
носу́ха *f.* coati.
но́та *f.* (*mus.*) note. — но́ты *pl.* sheet music.
нотариа́льный *adj.* (*attrib.*) notary.
нота́риус *m.* notary; notary public.
нота́ция *f.* 1. notation. 2. reprimand.
но́тка *f.* faint note; hint; trace.
но́тный *adj.* (*attrib.*) music.
ночева́ть *impf. pf.* пере- to spend the night.
ночёвка *f.* (*colloq.*) spending the night.
ночле́г *m.* lodging for the night.
ночле́жка *f.* (*colloq.*) flophouse.
ночле́жный дом *m.* flophouse.
ночна́я ба́бочка *f.* moth.
ночни́к *m.* night light.
ночно́й *adj.* (*attrib.*) night.
ночь *f.* night.
но́чью *adv.* at night.
но́ша *f.* 1. load. 2. burden.
ноше́ние *neut.* 1. carrying; bearing. 2. wearing.
но́щно *adv.*: де́нно и но́щно *adv.* (*colloq.*) day and night.
но́ющий *adj.* gnawing; nagging.
ноя́брь *m.* November. —ский *adj.* November.
нрав *m.* disposition; temper.
нра́виться *impf. pf.* по- (*with dat.*) to please.
нравоуче́ние *neut.* 1. moralizing. 2. (*lit.*) the moral (*of a story*).
нравоучи́тельный *adj.* moralistic; moralizing.
нра́вственно *adv.* morally.
нра́вственность *f.* morality, morals.
нра́вственный *adj.* moral.
нра́вы *pl.* customs; ways; way of life.

ну *interj.* well.
нуга́ *f.* nougat.
ну́дный *adj.* tedious; tiresome; boring.
нужда́ *f.* need.
нужда́ться *impf.* (в *with prep.*) to need; to be in need (of).
нужда́ющийся *adj.* indigent; needy.
ну́жно *adv.* (*pred.*) it is necessary; one must; one should.
ну́жный *adj.* necessary.
ну́-ка *interj.* (*colloq.*) 1. well?; well then? 2. come!; come on!
нулево́й *adj.* (*attrib.*) zero.
нуль *m.* nought; zero.
нумера́тор *m.* numbering machine.
нумера́ция *f.* numeration; numbering.
нумеро́ванный *adj.* numbered.
нумерова́ть *impf. pf* про-, за- to number.
нумизма́т *m.* numismatist.
нумизма́тика *f.* numismatics.
нумизмати́ческий *adj.* numismatic.
ну́нций *m.* nuncio.
ну́трия *f.* 1. coypu. 2. (*fur of coypu*) nutria.
нутро́ *neut.* (*colloq.*) innards; insides.
ны́не *adv.* now, at present.
ны́нешний *adj.* (*colloq.*) present.
ны́нче *adv.* (*colloq.*) now; nowadays.
ныро́к FILL *m.* dive.
ныря́льщик *m.* diver.
ныря́ть *impf. pf.* нырну́ть to dive.
ны́тик *m.* (*colloq.*) whiner.
ныть *impf. pres.* но́ю, но́ешь 1. to ache. 2. to whine.
нытьё *neut.* whining; complaining.
Нью-Гэ́мпшир *m.* New Hampshire.
Нью-Дже́рси *m.* New Jersey.
Нью-Йо́рк *m.* New York.
Нью-Ме́ксико *m.* New Mexico.
Ньюфа́ундленд *m.* Newfoundland.
н.э. (*abbr. of* на́шей э́ры) A.D.
нэп *m.* (*abbr. of* но́вая экономи́ческая поли́тика) N.E.P., New Economic Policy (1921-27).
нюа́нс *m.* nuance.
ню́ни *pl.*: распуска́ть ню́ни *impf.* (*colloq.*) to whine; to cry.
ню́ня *m.* and *f.* (*decl. f.*) (*colloq.*) crybaby.
Ню́рнберг *m.* Nürnberg.
нюх *m.* sense of smell.
ню́хательный *adj.* for smelling.
ню́хать *impf. pf.* по- to smell; to sniff.
ня́нчить *impf.* to nurse.
ня́нька *f.* (*colloq.*) nurse.
ня́ня *f.* nurse, nursemaid.

O

о *also* об, óбо *prep.* **1.** (*with prep.*) of, about. **2.** (*with acc.*) against.

оáзис *m.* oasis.

óба *m. and neut.*, *f.* óбе *num.* both.

обалдéлый *adj.* (*colloq.*) dazed.

обалдéть *pf.* (*colloq.*) to go crazy; to lose one's mind.

обанкрóтиться *pf.* to go bankrupt.

обаáние *neut.* attraction; charm.

обаáтельный *adj.* charming; fascinating.

обвáл *m.* fall, collapse, landslide.

обвáливаться *impf. pf.* обвалúться to fall; to collapse.

обвáривать *impf. pf.* обварúть **1.** to scald. **2.** to pour boiling water over.

обвéтренный *adj.* **1.** weather-beaten. **2.** (*of lips or hands*) chapped.

обветшáлый *adj.* decrepit; decayed.

обвинéние *neut.* accusation.

обвинúтель *m.* prosecutor.

обвинúтельный *adj.* accusatory.

обвинúть *pf. of* обвинять.

обвиняемый *m.* defendant; accused person.

обвинять *impf. pf.* обвинúть (в *with prep.*) to accuse (of).

обвúслый *adj.* sagging, drooping.

обводúть *impf. pf.* обвестú **1.** to lead around. **2.** to enclose; to surround. **3.** to circle.

обворожúтельный *adj.* enchanting; charming.

обвязывать *impf. pf.* обвязáть to tie around (*e.g. a kerchief around one's head*).

обгонять *impf. pf.* обогнáть **1.** to pass (*on the road*). **2.** to surpass; to excel.

обгорáть *impf. pf.* обгорéть to get a (bad) sunburn.

обгорéлый *adj.* charred; burned.

обдавáть *impf. pf.* обдáть **1.** to splash (*with water or mud*). **2.** *impers.* to be filled with.

обдéлывать *impf. pf.* обдéлать **1.** to finish; to dress. **2.** to arrange; to manage; to handle.

обделять *impf. pf.* обделúть to cheat (someone) out of his rightful share.

обдирáть *impf. pf.* ободрáть **1.** to skin; to flay. **2.** (*colloq.*) to rob, to fleece.

обдýманный *adj.* carefully thought out.

обдýмывать *impf. pf.* обдýмать to consider carefully.

óбе *see* óба.

обéд *m.* **1.** dinner. **2.** midday meal.

обéдать *impf. pf.* по- to dine; to have dinner; to have lunch.

обéденный *adj.* (*attrib.*) dinner; lunch.

обеднéвший *adj.* impoverished.

обеднéние *neut.* impoverishment.

обеднéть *pf.* to become *or* grow poor.

обéдня *f.* (*relig.*) Mass.

обезбóливание *neut.* anesthetization.

обезбóливающий *adj.* anesthetic. — обезбóливающее *neut.* analgesic, painkiller.

обезглáвливание *neut.* decapitation.

обезглáвливать *impf. pf.* обезглáвить to behead; to decapitate.

обездóленный *adj.* destitute; indigent.

обеззарáживание *neut.* decontamination; disinfection.

обезлéсение *neut.* deforestation.

обезобрáживание *neut.* disfigurement.

обезопáсить *pf.* to guarantee *or* secure against.

обезорýживать *impf. pf.* обезорýжить to disarm.

обезьяна *f.* monkey; ape.

обезьяний *adj.* (*attrib.*) monkey, ape.

обезьяноподóбный *adj.* apelike.

обезьяночеловéк *m.* ape-man.

обелúск *m.* obelisk.

оберегáть *impf. pf* оберéчь to guard against; to protect.

обёртка *f.* **1.** wrapper; wrapping. **2.** book cover.

обертóн *m.* (*mus.*) overtone.

обёрточная бумáга *f* wrapping paper.

обёртывание *neut.* (*med.*) pack.

обескурáженность *f.* (*colloq.*) discouragement.

обескурáживать *impf. pf.* обескурáжить **1.** to dishearten. **2.** to discourage.

обеспéчение *neut.* providing; supplying.

обеспéченность *f.* financial security.

обеспéченный *adj.* well-to-do.

обеспéчивать *impf. pf.* обеспéчить **1.** to ensure. **2.** to supply with. **3.** to provide for.

обеспокóить *pf.* to worry; to disturb.

обессúлеть *pf.* to grow *or* become weak.

обессúливать *impf. pf.* обессúлить to weaken.

обесцвéчивание *neut.* discoloration.

обесцéнение *neut.* depreciation.

обéт *m.* **1.** promise. **2.** vow; pledge.

обетовáнная земля *f.* the Promised Land.

обещáние *neut.* promise.

обещáть *impf. and pf.* to promise.

обжáлование *neut.* (*leg.*) appeal.

обжигáть *impf. pf.* обжéчь **1.** to burn. **2.** to bake (*e.g. pottery, bricks*).

обжóра *m. and f.* (*decl. f.*) (*colloq.*) glutton.

обжóрливый *adj.* (*colloq.*) gluttonous.

обжóрство *neut.* gluttony.

обзóр *m.* survey.

обивáть *impf. pf.* обúть **1.** to cover. **2.** to pad; to upholster.

обúвка *f.* upholstering; upholstery.

обúда *f.* offense.

обúдно *adj.* (*pred.*) unfortunate; disturbing.

обúдный *adj.* offensive.

обúдчивость *f.* touchiness.

обúдчивый *adj.* touchy; susceptible; sensitive.

обúдчик *m. f.* обúдчица offender.

обижáть *impf. pf.* обúдеть to offend.

обúженный *adj.* **1.** offended. **2.** resentful.

обúлие *neut.* abundance.

обúльно *adv.* abundantly.

обúльный *adj.* abundant, plentiful.

обиняк *m.*: говорúть обиняками *impf.* to beat around the bush.

обитáемый *adj.* inhabited.

обитáтель *m. f.* —ница inhabitant.

обитáть *impf.* to inhabit.

обитель *f.* cloister.

обитый *adj.* upholstered.

обить *pf. of* обивать.

обиход *m.* **1.** daily life. **2.** everyday use.

обиходный *adj.* everyday.

обкатывать *impf. pf.* обкатать **1.** to make smooth (*by rolling*). **2.** to wear smooth. **3.** to break in (*a new motor* or *a car*).

обкладывать *impf. pf.* обложить **1.** to surround. **2.** to face (*with stone*).

обком *m.* regional committee.

обкрадывать *impf. pf.* обокрасть to rob.

облава *f.* **1.** hunt. **2.** police raid *or* roundup.

облагать *impf. pf.* обложить to assess; to tax.

обладание *neut.* possession.

обладатель *m. f.* —ница possessor.

обладать *impf.* (*with instr.*) to possess, to own.

облако *neut.* cloud.

областной *adj.* regional.

область *f.* region; district; province.

облатка *f.* (*eccles.*) host.

облачко *neut. dim. of* облако.

облачность *f.* cloudiness.

облачный *adj.* cloudy.

облегать *impf. pf.* облечь **1.** to envelop. **2.** (*of clothes*) to fit tightly.

облегчать *impf. pf.* облегчить **1.** to lighten. **2.** to relieve. **3.** to facilitate.

облегчение *neut.* relief.

облегчённо *adv.* with relief.

облегчённый *adj.* of relief.

обледенелый *adj.* covered with ice.

обледенение *neut.* icing up.

обледенеть *pf.* to become coated with ice.

облезлый *adj.* **1.** shabby, bare. **2.** with the paint wearing off.

обливание *neut.* dousing with water.

обливать *impf. pf.* облить **1.** to pour water over. **2.** to cover (*with tears, etc.*). **3.** to soil (*by spilling something*).

облигация *f.* (*finance*) bond.

облик *m.* **1.** appearance; look. **2.** character.

облицовка *f.* facing; revetment.

обличать *impf. pf.* обличить to expose; to reveal.

обличение *neut.* exposure.

обличитель *m. f.* —ница exposer.

обличительный *adj.* exposing.

обличье *neut.* (*colloq.*) look; appearance.

обложение *neut.* taxation; levying.

обложить *pf.* to face; to cover.

обложка *f.* cover.

обложной дождь *m.* (*colloq.*) steady downpour.

облокачиваться *impf. pf.* облокотиться (о *or* на with acc.) to lean one's elbows against *or* on.

обломовщина *f.* lethargy; sluggishness (*after* Обломов, *hero of Goncharov's novel*).

обломок FILL *m.* fragment.

облупить *pf. of* лупить.

облучение *neut.* irradiation; radiation treatment.

облучок FILL *m.* coachman's seat.

облыселый *adj.* bald.

обман *m.* fraud; deception.

обманка *f.*: роговая обманка *f.* hornblende.

обманный *adj.* fraudulent; deceitful.

обманчивый *adj.* **1.** deceptive. **2.** illusory.

обманщик *m. f.* обманщица liar; faker; cheat.

обманывать *impf. pf.* обмануть to deceive; to cheat.

обмен *m.* exchange.

обменный *adj.* (*attrib.*) exchange.

обмер *m.* **1.** measurement. **2.** false measure.

обминать *impf. pf.* обмять to press down; to trample down.

обмолвка *f.* slip of the tongue.

обморожение *also* обмораживание *neut.* frostbite.

обмороженный *adj.* frostbitten.

обморок *m.* faint; fainting spell.

обмотки *pl.* puttees.

обмундирование *neut.* uniform.

обмундировать OVA *pf.* to outfit (*with a uniform*).

обмундировка *f.* uniform.

обмылок FILL *m.* (*colloq.*) remaining piece of a soap bar.

обмякать *impf. pf.* обмякнуть (*colloq.*) **1.** to become soft. **2.** to become flabby.

обнадёживать *impf. pf.* обнадёжить **1.** to reassure. **2.** to give hope to.

обнажать *impf. pf.* обнажить to bare; to uncover; to reveal.

обнажённый *adj.* naked; nude.

обнародование *neut.* promulgation.

обнародовать OVA *pf.* **1.** to promulgate. **2.** to publish.

обнаружение *also* обнаружение *neut.* discovery.

обнаруживать *impf. pf.* обнаружить to discover; to reveal.

обнимать *impf. pf.* обнять to embrace.

обнимка *f.* (*colloq.*): в обнимку in each other's embrace.

обнищалый *adj.* impoverished; destitute.

обнищание *neut.* impoverishment; destitution.

обнищать *pf.* to become impoverished.

обнова *f.* (*colloq.*) new outfit.

обновка *f.* (*colloq.*) new article of clothing.

обновление *neut.* renovation.

обновлять *impf. pf.* обновить to renovate; to renew.

обноски *pl.* (*colloq.*) old clothes.

обнять *pf. of* обнимать.

обо *see* о.

обобщать *impf. pf.* обобщить to generalize.

обобщение *neut.* **1.** generalization. **2.** summarizing.

обобществление *neut.* socialization; collectivization.

обобществлять *impf. pf.* обобществить to socialize; to collectivize.

обобщить *pf. of* обобщать.

обогащать *impf. pf.* обогатить to enrich.

обогащение *neut.* enrichment.

обоготворение *neut.* deification.

обогревание *neut.* heating.

обогреватель *m.* heater.

обогревать *impf. pf.* обогреть to warm, to heat.

обод *m.* rim (*of a wheel*).

ободок FILL *m.* rim; ring.

ободочная кишка *f.* (*anat.*) colon.

ободранный *adj.* (*colloq.*) ragged; tattered; torn.

ободрение *neut.* encouragement.

ободрительный *adj.* encouraging; reassuring.

ободрять *impf. pf.* ободрить to encourage.

обожание *neut.* adoration.

обожа́тель *m. f.* **—ница** admirer.
обожа́ть *impf.* to admire; to worship.
обожествле́ние *neut.* deification.
обожествля́ть *impf. pf.* обожестви́ть to deify.
обо́з *m.* column *or* line (*of vehicles*).
обознача́ть *impf. pf.* обозна́чить **1.** to mean. **2.** to designate; to mark.
обозначе́ние *neut.* designation.
обозрева́тель *m.* columnist; author of a review.
обозре́ние *neut.* review; survey.
обозри́мый *adj.* visible.
обо́и *pl.* wallpaper.
обо́йма *f.* cartridge clip.
обо́йный *adj.* (*attrib.*) wallpaper.
обойти́(сь) *pf. of* обходи́ть(ся).
обо́йщик *m.* upholsterer.
о́бок *adv., prep.* (*with gen.*) (*colloq.*) alongside.
оболо́чка *f.* **1.** shell (*of fruit* or *seed*). **2.** membrane.
обо́лтус *m.* (*colloq.*) blockhead; dolt.
обольсти́тельный *adj.* seductive.
обольща́ть *impf. pf.* обольсти́ть to seduce. **—ся** to delude oneself.
обольще́ние *neut.* seduction.
обомле́ть *pf.* (*colloq.*) **1.** to be stunned. **2.** to freeze (*in shock*).
обомше́лый *adj.* moss-grown.
обоня́ние *neut.* sense of smell.
обоня́тельный *adj.* olfactory.
оборва́нец FILL *m. f.* оборва́нка (*colloq.*) vagabond.
обо́рванный *adj.* torn; ragged.
оборва́ть(ся) *pf. of* обрыва́ть(ся).
обо́рвыш *m.* (*colloq.*) ragamuffin.
обо́рка *f.* ruffle; flounce; frill.
оборо́на *f.* defense.
оборони́тельный *adj.* defensive.
оборо́нный *adj.* (*attrib.*) defense.
обороня́ть *impf. pf.* обарони́ть to defend.
оборо́т *m.* revolution; turn.
оборо́тень FILL *m.* werewolf.
оборо́тливый *adj.* (*colloq.*) resourceful.
оборо́тный *adj.* **1.** (*finance*) circulating; working. **2.** (*side*) reverse; obverse.
обору́дование *neut.* equipment.
обору́довать OVA *impf. and pf.* to equip.
обоснова́ние *neut.* basis.
обосно́ванность *f.* validity.
обосно́ванный *adj.* well-founded; sound.
обосно́вывать *impf. pf.* обоснова́ть to base; to ground. **—ся** to settle down.
обособле́ние *neut.* isolation.
обосо́бленный *adj.* **1.** solitary. **2.** isolated.
обостре́ние *neut.* **1.** intensification. **2.** aggravation.
обостре́нный *adj.* (*facial features*) prominent; (*of relations*) tense.
обостря́ть *impf. pf.* обостри́ть **1.** to sharpen. **2.** to aggravate; to strain.
обо́чина *f.* **1.** curb. **2.** side *or* shoulder (*of road*).
обою́дно *adv.* mutually.
обою́дность *f.* mutuality.
обою́дный *adj.* mutual.
обоюдоо́стрый *adj.* double-edged
обрабо́тка *f.* **1.** treatment; processing. **2.** cultivation, tillage.
обра́довать OVA *pf. of* ра́довать.

о́браз[1] *m.* **1.** form, image. **2.** mode; manner; way.
о́браз[2] *m. pl.* образа́ icon.
образе́ц FILL *m.* example; model; specimen.
о́бразность *f.* vividness.
о́бразный *adj.* vivid; graphic; colorful.
образова́ние *neut.* **1.** education. **2.** formation.
образо́ванный *adj.* educated.
образо́вывать *impf. pf.* образова́ть **1.** to form, to make, to shape. **2.** to organize.
образцо́вый *adj.* model.
обра́зчик *m.* specimen; sample; pattern.
обрамля́ть *impf. pf.* обра́мить to frame.
обрати́мость *f.* reversibility.
обрати́мый *adj.* **1.** convertible. **2.** reversible.
обра́тно *adv.* **1.** back, backwards. **2.** conversely, inversely.
обра́тное *neut.* the reverse; the opposite.
обра́тный *adj.* **1.** reverse; opposite. **2.** return; round-trip.
обраща́ть *impf. pf.* обрати́ть to turn; to direct. **—ся 1.** (к *with dat.*) to appeal to; to address. **2.** (в *with acc.*) to turn into.
обраще́ние *neut.* **1.** appeal; address. **2.** (с *with instr.*) treatment. **3.** circulation.
обре́з *m.* **1.** edge. **2.** sawed-off rifle.
обре́зание *neut.* circumcision.
обреза́ние *neut.* trimming; cutting.
обреза́ть *impf. pf.* обреза́ть to cut (off), to clip, to pare.
обре́зок FILL *m. usu. pl.* scrap (*of paper; of meat*).
обрека́ть *impf. pf.* обре́чь (на *with acc.*) to doom (to).
обремени́тельный *adj.* burdensome.
обременя́ть *impf. pf.* обремени́ть to burden.
обречённость *f.* impending doom.
обречённый *adj.* doomed.
обрисо́вывать *impf. pf.* обрисова́ть **1.** to draw a line around. **2.** to highlight.
обро́к *m.* quitrent.
обруба́ть *impf. pf.* обруби́ть to chop off.
обру́бок FILL *m.* stump.
обрусе́ть *pf.* to become Russified *or* Russianized.
обруча́льный *adj.* (*attrib.*) engagement.
обруче́ние *neut.* engagement; betrothal.
обры́в *m.* precipice.
обрыва́ть *impf. pf.* оборва́ть *v.t.* to tear off; to break; to snap. **—ся** *v.i.* to break (off); to snap.
обры́вистый *adj.* steep; precipitous.
обры́вок FILL *m.* scrap; fragment.
обры́згивать *impf. pf.* обры́згать **1.** to bespatter; to splash. **2.** to sprinkle.
обрю́зглый *adj.* flabby.
обрю́зглый *adj.* flabby.
обря́д *m.* rite, ritual, ceremony. **—ный** *also* **—овый** *adj.* ritual.
обсле́дование *neut.* inspection; examination.
обсле́дователь *m.* inspector.
обсле́довать OVA *impf. and pf.* to inspect; to investigate.
обслу́живание *neut.* service.
обслу́живать *impf. pf.* обслужи́ть to attend; to serve; to service.
обставля́ть *impf. pf.* обста́вить **1.** to surround with; to encircle. **2.** to furnish (*a home*). **3.** to arrange.

обстановка *f.* **1.** furniture. **2.** (*theat.*) set. **3.** situation.
обстоятельный *adj.* detailed; thorough.
обстоятельственный *adj.* (*gram.*) adverbial.
обстоятельство[1] *neut.* circumstance.
обстоятельство[2] *neut.* (*gram.*) adverbial modifier.
обстоять *impf.* **1.** to be. **2.** (*of matters*) to stand.
обстрел *m.* shelling; firing; fire; bombardment.
обстрелянный *adj.* battle-hardened.
обструкционизм *m.* obstructionism.
обструкционист *m.* obstructionist.
обструкционный *adj.* obstructionist.
обструкция *f.* obstruction.
обступать *impf. pf.* обступить to surround.
обсуждать *impf. pf.* обсудить to discuss.
обсуждение *neut.* discussion.
обсушивать *impf. pf.* обсушить to dry; to dry off; to dry out.
обсчитываться *impf. pf.* обсчитаться to miscount; to make an error in counting.
обтекаемый *adj.* streamlined.
обтёсывать *impf. pf.* обтесать **1.** to trim. **2.** (*colloq.*) to teach (somebody) good manners.
обтирание *neut.* rubdown.
обтрёпанный *adj.* **1.** tattered; frayed. **2.** dressed shabbily.
обтяжка *f.* covering; cover.
обувать *impf. pf.* обуть to shoe. —ся to put on one's shoes.
обувной *adj.* (*attrib.*) shoe.
обувь *f.* footwear.
обугливать *impf. pf.* обуглить to char.
обуза *f.* **1.** burden. **2.** chore.
обуздание *neut.* restraint.
обуздывать *impf. pf.* обуздать to bridle; to restrain.
обуревать *impf.* to seize; to grip.
обусловливать *impf. pf.* обусловить **1.** to stipulate; to condition. **2.** to cause.
обуть *pf. of* обувать.
обух *m.* butt; butt end.
обучать *impf. pf.* обучить to instruct; to teach. —ся (*with dat.*) to learn.
обучение *neut.* (*with gen.*) teaching; training (*of people*); (*with dat.*) instruction (in).
обхват *m.* circumference; girth.
обход *m.* **1.** going around. **2.** detour. **3.** rounds.
обходительность *f.* politeness.
обходительный *adj.* polite; courteous.
обходить *impf. pf.* обойти **1.** to go *or* pass around; to make the rounds. **2.** to avoid.
обходиться *impf. pf.* обойтись **1.** (с *with instr.*) to treat. **2.** (*colloq.*) to cost. **3.** to manage; to get along.
обходной *adj.* roundabout.
обходчик *m.* inspector.
обхождение *neut.* **1.** behaviour; attitude. **2.** treatment.
обшарпанный *adj.* (*colloq.*) **1.** run-down. **2.** dilapidated.
обшивка *f.* **1.** trimming; bordering. **2.** planking; plating.
обширность *f.* extent; magnitude.
обширный *adj.* vast, extensive; spacious.
обшлаг *m.* cuff.
общаться *impf.* (с *with instr.*) to associate (with).

общедоступный *adj.* generally accessible *or* available.
общежитие *neut.* **1.** dormitory; hostel. **2.** society, community.
общеизвестный *adj.* generally known.
общенародный *adj.* national; of all the people.
общение *neut.* intercourse; personal contact.
общеобразовательный *adj.* (*school* or *subject*) general; not specialized.
общепринятый *adj.* in general use; conventional.
общественник *m. f.* общественница public figure.
общественность *f.* the public.
общественный *adj.* public; social.
общество *neut.* society; company.
общий *adj.* common; general.
община *f.* community; commune.
общинный *adj.* communal.
общительность *f.* sociability.
общительный *adj.* sociable; outgoing.
общность *f.* commonality.
объедение *neut.* overeating.
объединение *neut.* unification.
объединённый *adj.* **1.** united. **2.** joint. — Организация Объединённых Наций *f.* United Nations.
объединять *impf. pf.* объединить to unite.
объёдки *pl.* (*colloq.*) leftovers; scraps.
объезд *m.* **1.** traveling around. **2.** detour.
объездка *f.* breaking in (*of horse*).
объездчик *m.* warden; ranger.
объект *m.* object.
объектив *m.* lens.
объективно *adv.* objectively.
объективность *f.* objectivity.
объективный *adj.* objective.
объективный *adj.* (*gram.*) objective.
объём *m.* **1.** extent; scope. **2.** volume.
объёмистый *adj.* (*colloq.*) large; bulky.
объёмный *adj.* **1.** by volume; volumetric. **2.** three-dimensional.
объявление *neut.* declaration; announcement
объявлять *impf. pf.* объявить to declare; to announce.
объяснение *neut.* explanation.
объяснимый *adj.* explainable; explicable.
объяснительный *adj.* explanatory.
объяснять *impf. pf.* объяснить to explain.
объятие *neut.* embrace.
обыватель *m. f.* —ница **1.** (*obs.*) resident; inhabitant. **2.** philistine.
обывательский *adj.* narrow; narrow-minded.
обыденный *adj.* ordinary; commonplace; everyday.
обыкновение *neut.* habit.
обыкновенно *adv.* usually; as a rule.
обыкновенный *adj.* usual; ordinary; plain, simple.
обыск *m.* search (*of a person* or *of a house*).
обыскивать *impf. pf.* обыскать *v.t.* to search.
обычай *m.* custom.
обычно *adv.* usually; generally.
обычный *adj.* usual; ordinary, commonplace.
Обь *f.* (*river*) Ob.
обязанность *f.* duty.
обязанный *adj.* obliged (to); required (to).
обязательно *adv.* without fail.
обязательный *adj.* obligatory.
обязательство *neut.* obligation; commitment;

обя́зывать *impf. pf.* обяза́ть **1.** to oblige; to obligate. **2.** to bind.

ова́л *m.* oval.

ова́льный *adj.* oval.

ова́ция *f.* ovation.

овева́ть *impf. pf.* ове́ять **1.** (*of wind*) to blow upon. **2.** to infuse; to pervade.

овёс FILL *m.* oats.

ове́чий *adj.* (*attrib.*) sheep.

ове́чка *f. dim. of* овца́.

ОВИР *m.* (*abbr. of* отде́л виз и регистра́ции) visa and registration department; OVIR.

овладева́ть *impf. pf.* овладе́ть (*with instr.*) to seize; to take possession of.

овладе́ние *neut.* **1.** capture. **2.** mastery (*e.g. of a foreign language*).

о́вод *m.* gadfly.

о́вощи *pl.* vegetables.

овощно́й *adj.* (*attrib.*) vegetable.

овра́г *m.* ravine.

О́вруч *m.* Ovruch.

овся́нка *f.* oatmeal.

овся́ный *adj.* (*attrib.*) oat.

овуля́ция *f.* ovulation.

овца́ *f.* **1.** sheep. **2.** ewe.

овцебы́к *m.* musk ox.

овцево́д *m.* sheep farmer.

овцево́дство *neut.* sheep raising.

овцево́дческий *adj.* related to the raising of sheep.

овча́рка *f.* sheepdog. — неме́цкая овча́рка German shepherd.

овча́рня *f.* sheepfold.

овчи́на *f.* sheepskin.

овчи́нный *adj.* sheepskin.

Ога́йо *m.* Ohio.

ога́рок FILL *m.* candle end.

Ога́ста *f.* Augusta.

оглавле́ние *neut.* contents; table of contents.

огла́ска *f.* publicity.

оглаша́ть *impf. pf.* огласи́ть to make public; to announce.

огло́бля *f.* shaft (*attaching horse to cart*).

огло́хнуть *pf. of* гло́хнуть.

оглуша́ть *impf. pf.* оглуши́ть to deafen; to stun.

оглуши́тельный *adj.* deafening.

огля́дка *f.* (*obs.*) looking back.

огля́дываться *impf. pf.* огляде́ться *or* огляну́ться **1.** to look around. **2.** to look back.

огнево́й *adj.* (*attrib.*) fire.

огнемёт *m.* flame thrower.

О́гненная Земля́ *f.* Tierra del Fuego.

о́гненный *adj.* fiery.

огнеопа́сный *adj.* flammable.

огнесто́йкий *adj.* fireproof.

огнестре́льное ору́жие *neut.* firearms.

огнетуши́тель *m.* fire extinguisher.

огнеупо́рный *adj.* heat-resistant.

огово́р *m.* slander.

огово́рка *f.* **1.** reservation; stipulation. **2.** slip of the tongue.

оголённый *adj.* naked; nude; bare.

оголте́лый *adj.* (*colloq.*) mad; rabid.

огонёк FILL *m.* **1.** light; point of light. **2.** zest; pep; vigor; verve.

ого́нь FILL *m.* **1.** fire. **2.** light.

огоро́д *m.* vegetable garden.

огоро́дник *m. f.* огоро́дница vegetable gardener.

огоро́дничество *neut.* vegetable gardening.

огоро́дный *adj.* (*attrib.*) (vegetable) garden.

огорче́ние *neut.* distress; grief.

огорчи́тельный *adj.* distressing.

огра́бить *pf. of* гра́бить.

ограбле́ние *neut.* robbery.

огра́да *f.* **1.** fence. **2.** wall (*around property*).

огражда́ть *impf. pf.* огради́ть to guard against; to protect against.

огражде́ние *neut.* **1.** fence; fencing. **2.** protection. **3.** barrier.

ограниче́ние *neut.* limitation; restriction.

ограни́ченный *adj.* limited.

ограни́чивать *impf. pf.* ограни́чить to limit; to restrict.

ограничи́тельный *adj.* restrictive.

огре́х *m.* (*colloq.*) shortcoming; fault.

огро́мный *adj.* enormous.

огрубе́лый *adj.* rough; coarse.

огрубе́ть *pf. of* грубе́ть.

огры́зок FILL *m.* bit; end; stub.

огу́лом *adv.* (*colloq.*) indiscriminately.

огу́льно *adv.* **1.** unfairly. **2.** indiscriminately.

огу́льный *adj.* sweeping; indiscriminate.

огуре́ц FILL *m.* cucumber.

огуре́чный *adj.* (*attrib.*) cucumber.

о́да *f.* ode.

ода́лживать *impf. pf.* одолжи́ть to lend.

одарённость *f.* gifts; giftedness.

одарённый *adj.* gifted.

одева́ть *impf. pf.* оде́ть *v.t.* **1.** to dress, to clothe. **2.** to cover. —ся to get dressed.

оде́жда *f.* clothes.

одеколо́н *m.* eau de Cologne.

одёр FILL *m.* old horse.

одёргивать *impf. pf.* одёрнуть **1.** to pull down. **2.** to silence; to restrain.

одеревене́лый *adj.* stiff; numb.

одержи́мость *f.* obsession; preoccupation.

одержи́мый *adj.* (*with instr.*) obsessed by.

Оде́сса *f.* Odessa.

одея́ло *neut.* blanket.

оде́яние *neut.* (*obs.*) attire.

оди́н *m. f.* одна́, *neut.* одно́ *num.* one. –*adj.* a; a certain; alone.

одина́ково *adv.* **1.** identically. **2.** equally.

одина́ковый *adj.* identical.

одина́рный *adj.* single.

оди́ннадцатый *adj.* eleventh.

оди́ннадцать *num.* eleven.

одино́кий *adj.* lonely; solitary.

одино́ко *adv.* alone; lonely.

одино́чество *neut.* solitude; loneliness.

одино́чка *m.* and *f.* (*decl. f.*) lone person.

одио́зный *adj.* odious.

одиссе́я *f.* odyssey.

одича́лый *adj.* wild.

одна́ *see* оди́н.

одна́жды *adv.* once.

одна́ко *conj.* however; nevertheless; yet.

одно́ *see* оди́н.

однобо́кий *adj.* lopsided.

однобо́ртный *adj.* single-breasted.

одновре́менно *also* одновреме́нно *adv.* simultaneously; at the same time.

одновре́менность *f.* simultaneity.

одновре́менный *adj.* simultaneous.

одногла́зый *adj.* one-eyed.

одногоди́чный *adj.* (*attrib.*) one-year.

одного́док FILL *m. f.* одного́дка (*colloq.*) age mate; contemporary.

однозву́чный *adj.* monotonous.

однозна́чный *adj.* synonymous; unambiguous.

одноимённый *adj.* of the same name.

одношка́шник *m.* (*colloq.*) fellow student.

однокла́ссник *m. f.* однокла́ссница classmate.

однокле́точный *adj.* one-celled.

одноколе́йный *adj.* (*attrib.*) single-track.

одноко́лка *f.* gig.

однокомнатный *adj.* (*attrib.*) one-room.

однокра́тный *adj.* (*gram.*) semelfactive.

одноку́рсник *m. f.* одноку́рсница (*college students*) classmate.

одноле́тний *adj.* (*attrib.*) one-year.

одноле́ток FILL *m.* (*colloq.*) age mate; contemporary.

одноме́стный *adj.* (*attrib.*) single-seat.

одноно́гий *adj.* one-legged.

однообра́зный *adj.* monotonous.

однопала́тный *adj.* unicameral.

однопо́лый *adj.* unisexual.

одноре́льсовый *adj.* (*attrib.*) single-rail.

одноро́дность *f.* homogeneity.

одноро́дный *adj.* homogeneous; similar; uniform.

однору́кий *adj.* one-armed.

односельча́нин *m. f.* односельча́нка person from the same village.

односло́жный *adj.* monosyllabic.

односпа́льный *adj.* (*of a bed*) single.

односторо́нний *adj.* one-sided.

одноти́пный *adj.* of the same type.

одното́мный *adj.* (*attrib.*) one-volume.

однотонный *adj.* 1. monotone. 2. single-colored.

однофами́лец FILL *m. f.* однофами́лица person with the same last name.

одноцве́тный *adj.* (*attrib.*) one-color.

одноэта́жный *adj.* (*attrib.*) one-story.

одобре́ние *neut.* approval.

одобри́тельно *adv.* approvingly.

одобри́тельный *adj.* approving.

одобря́ть *impf. pf.* одо́брить to approve (of).

одолева́ть *impf. pf.* одоле́ть 1. to overcome. 2. to master.

одолже́ние *neut.* favor.

одома́шнивание *neut.* domestication.

одо́метр *m.* odometer.

одонтоло́гия *f.* odontology.

О́дра *f.* (*river*) Oder River.

одряхле́вший *adj.* decrepit; enfeebled.

одува́нчик *m.* dandelion.

одуре́лый *adj.* 1. stupid. 2. dazed.

одуре́ние *neut.* (*colloq.*) stupor.

одурма́нить *pf. of* дурма́нить.

о́дурь *f.* (*colloq.*) trance; stupor.

одутлова́тый *adj.* puffy.

одушевле́ние *neut.* animation.

одушевлённый *adj.* animated.

одушевля́ть *impf. pf.* одушеви́ть to animate.

оды́шка *f.* shortness of breath.

ожереби́ться *pf. of* жереби́ться.

ожере́лье *neut.* necklace.

ожесточа́ть *impf. pf.* ожесточи́ть to harden; to embitter.

ожесточе́ние *neut.* bitterness.

ожесточённый *adj.* embittered; fierce.

ожива́ть *impf. pf.* ожи́ть to come to life.

оживле́ние *neut.* 1. revival; resuscitation. 2. animation.

оживлённо *adv.* with great animation.

оживлённый *adj.* animated; lively.

оживля́ться *impf. pf.* оживи́ться to become lively or animated.

ожида́ние *neut.* expectation.

ожида́ть *impf.* (*with gen.*) 1. to expect; to await. 2. to look forward to. 3. to look forward to.

ожире́ние *neut.* obesity.

ожи́ть *pf. of* ожива́ть.

ожо́г *m.* burn.

озабо́ченность *f.* concern; anxiety.

озабо́ченный *adj.* preoccupied.

озагла́вливать *impf. pf.* озагла́вить to entitle.

озада́ченность *f.* perplexity; bafflement.

озада́ченный *adj.* puzzled; baffled; perplexed.

озвере́лый *adj.* crazed.

озвере́ние *neut.* ferocity; brutality.

оздорови́тельный *adj.* sanitary; (*attrib.*) health.

оздоровле́ние *neut.* making healthier.

озелене́ние *neut.* planting of trees.

озеленя́ть *impf. pf.* озелени́ть to plant trees and bushes.

о́земь *adv.* (*colloq.*) to the ground.

озёрный *adj.* of a lake.

о́зеро *neut.* lake.

ози́мый *adj.* (*of crops*) winter.

о́зимь *f.* winter crops.

озлобле́ние *neut.* bitterness; animosity.

ознакомле́ние *neut.* acquainting; familiarizing.

ознакомля́ться *impf. pf.* ознако́миться (с *with instr.*) to become acquainted (with).

ознаменова́ние *neut.:* в ознаменова́ние (*with gen.*) in honor of.

ознаменова́ть *pf.* to mark; to commemorate.

означа́ть *impf.* to mean; to signify.

озно́б *m.* chill; shivering.

озокери́т *m.* ozocerite.

озо́н *m.* (*attrib.*) ozone.

озо́новый *adj.* ozone.

озорнича́ть *impf.* to make mischief.

озорно́й *adj.* mischievous.

озорство́ *neut.* mischief.

ой *interj.* oh!; o!

Ока́ *f.* (*river*) Oka.

оказа́ние *neut.* rendering; providing.

ока́зия *f.* opportunity.

ока́зывать *impf. pf.* оказа́ть to render; to show. —ся (*with instr.*) to prove to be; to turn out to be.

окаймля́ть *impf. pf.* окайми́ть to border; to edge.

ока́лина *f.* dross.

окамене́лость *f.* fossil.

окамене́лый *adj.* petrified.

окамене́ть *pf. of* камене́ть.

ока́нчивать *impf. pf.* око́нчить *v.t.* to finish; to end.

о́канье *neut.* okanie (*pronunciation of unstressed* o *as* o).

окари́на *f.* ocarina.

ока́янный *adj.* damned, cursed.
океа́н *m.* ocean.
Океа́ния *f.* Oceania.
океано́граф *m.* oceanographer.
океанографи́ческий *adj.* oceanographic.
океаногра́фия *f.* oceanography.
океа́нский *adj.* (*attrib.*) ocean; oceanic.
о́кисел FILL *m.* oxide.
окисле́ние *neut.* oxidation.
о́кись *f.* oxide.
оккульти́зм *m.* occultism.
окку́льтный *adj.* occult.
оккупа́нт *m.* invader.
оккупацио́нный *adj.* of occupation.
оккупа́ция *f.* military occupation.
оккупи́ровать OVA *impf. and pf.* to occupy.
окла́д *m.* salary; wages.
Оклахо́ма *f.* Oklahoma.
о́клик *m.* **1.** call. **2.** challenge (*part of challenge and password*).
окно́ *neut.* window.
о́ко *neut.* (*arch.*) eye.
око́вы *pl.* shackles.
околе́сица *f.* (*colloq.*) nonsense.
око́лица *f.* **1.** outskirts of a village. **2.** fence (*around a village*)
околи́чности *pl.* (*obs.*) circumlocution.
о́коло *prep.* (*with gen.*) by, near, around; about, nearly, approximately.
околопло́дник *m.* pericarp.
околосерде́чный су́мка *f.* pericardium.
около́ток FILL *m.* (*obs.*) district; neighborhood.
околощитови́дный железа́ *f.* parathyroid gland.
око́лыш *m.* hatband.
око́льный *adj.* circuitous; roundabout.
оконе́чность *f.* extremity (*island* or *continent*).
око́нное стекло́ *neut.* windowpane.
оконча́ние *neut.* termination; end; ending; graduation.
оконча́тельно *adv.* **1.** definitively. **2.** completely; utterly.
оконча́тельность *f.* finality.
оконча́тельный *adj.* final; definitive.
око́нчить *pf. of* ока́нчивать.
око́п *m.* trench.
око́пный *adj.* (*attrib.*) trench.
о́корок *m.* **1.** ham. **2.** leg (*of veal* or *mutton*).
окостене́лый *adj.* **1.** ossified. **2.** numb; stiff.
окостене́ние *neut.* ossification.
окочене́лый *adj.* numb (*from the cold*).
окочене́ние *neut.* rigidity.
око́шко *neut. dim. of* окно́.
окра́ина *f.* outskirts.
окра́инный *adj.* outlying.
окра́ска *f.* **1.** painting; dyeing. **2.** color.
окре́пнуть *pf.* to recover one's strength; to become stronger.
окрести́ть *pf. of* крести́ть.
окре́стность *f.* environs; environment.
окре́стный *adj.* neighboring.
о́крик *m.* shout; cry.
окрова́вленный *adj.* bloodstained.
окропля́ть *impf. pf.* окропи́ть to sprinkle; to besprinkle.
окро́шка *f.* okroshka (*cold kvass soup with vegetables and meat* or *fish*).

о́круг *m.* district.
окру́га *f.* (*colloq.*) neighborhood.
окру́глый *adj.* round; rounded.
окружа́ть *impf. pf.* окружи́ть to surround.
окружа́ющий *adj.* surrounding.
окруже́ние *neut.* encirclement; entourage.
окружно́й *adj.* (*attrib.*) district.
окру́жность *f.* circumference; circle.
О́ксфорд *m.* Oxford.
окта́ва *f.* octave.
окта́н *m.* octane.
окте́т *m.* octet.
октя́брь *m.* October. —ский *adj.* (*attrib.*) October.
окули́ст *m.* oculist.
окуля́р *m.* eyepiece.
окуна́ть *impf. pf.* окуну́ть (в *with acc.*) to dip something (*into a liquid*).
о́кунь *m.* (*fish*) perch.
оку́ривание *neut.* fumigation.
оку́рок FILL *m.* cigarette butt.
ола́дья *f.* fritter; pancake.
олеа́ндр *m.* oleander.
олеа́ндровый *adj.* (*attrib.*) oleander.
оледене́лый *adj.* frozen.
оленебы́к *m.* (*antelope*) eland.
оленево́д *m.* reindeer breeder.
оленево́дство *neut.* reindeer breeding.
оленево́дческий *adj.* (*attrib.*) reindeer-breeding.
Оленего́рск *m.* Olenegorsk.
оле́ний *adj.* (*attrib.*) deer.
олени́на *f.* venison.
олену́ха *f.* doe (*female deer*).
оле́нь *m.* deer.
оли́ва *f.* **1.** olive. **2.** olive tree.
оли́вковый *adj.* (*attrib.*) olive.
олига́рх *m.* oligarch.
олигархи́ческий *adj.* oligarchic.
олига́рхия *f.* oligarchy.
Оли́мп *m.* (*mountain*) Olympus.
олимпиа́да *f.* Olympiad; Olympics.
олимпи́йский *adj.* Olympic.
оли́фа *f.* drying oil.
олицетворе́ние *neut.* personification.
олицетворя́ть *impf. pf.* олицетвори́ть to personify.
о́лово *neut.* tin.
оловя́нный *adj.* tin.
о́лух *m.* (*colloq.*) dolt; oaf.
о́луша *f.* (*bird*) gannet.
ольха́ *f.* alder.
оля́пка *f.* dipper; water ouzel.
ом *m.* ohm.
ома́р *m.* lobster.
оме́га *f.* omega.
оме́ла *f.* mistletoe.
омерзе́ние *neut.* loathing.
омерзи́тельный *adj.* loathsome.
омертве́лый *adj.* (*tissues, cells*) dead.
омёт *m.* stack of straw.
омле́т *m.* omelet.
о́мнибус *m.* (*obs.*) horse-drawn coach for public transportation.
омове́ние *neut.* ablution.
омоложе́ние *neut.* rejuvenation.
омо́ним *m.* homonym.
Омск *m.* Omsk.

óмут *m.* **1.** deep place in river *or* lake. **2.** whirl-pool. **3.** maelstrom.

он *pron.* he.

она́ *pron.* she.

она́гр *m.* onager.

онани́зм *m.* masturbation.

онани́ровать OVA *impf.* to masturbate.

онда́тра *f.* muskrat.

Онéжское óзеро *neut.* Lake Onega.

онемéлый *adj.* numb; stiff.

онемéние *neut* numbness.

онемéть *pf.* to be dumbfounded; to become numb.

онéр *m.:* **со всéми онéрами** (*colloq.*) with all honors.

они́ *pron.* they.

óникс *m.* onyx.

óниксовый *adj.* onyx.

óно *see* óный.

оно́ *pron.* it.

Онта́рио *neut.* Ontario.

онтологи́ческий *adj.* onotological.

онтоло́гия *f.* ontology.

ону́ча *f.* piece of cloth worn instead of a sock.

óный *adj.* (*obs.*) that. — **во врéмя óно** long ago.

опа́здывать *impf. pf.* опозда́ть to be late.

опа́ивать *impf. pf.* опои́ть **1.** to make someone drunk. **2.** to give (an animal) too much to drink.

опа́л *m.* opal.

опа́ла *f.* disgrace.

опа́ловый *adj.* opal.

опа́льный *adj.* in disgrace; in disfavor.

опа́ра *f.* leavened dough.

опаса́ться *impf.* (*with gen.*) to fear; to avoid.

опасéние *neut.* fear, apprehension.

опа́ска *f.* (*colloq.*) caution.

опа́сливый *adj.* cautious.

опа́сно *adv.* dangerously.

опа́сность *f.* danger.

опа́сный *adj.* dangerous.

опаха́ло *neut.* large fan.

опéка *f.* **1.** guardianship. **2.** trusteeship.

опекáемый *m.* ward.

опеку́н *m. f.* **—ша** guardian.

опеку́нский *adj.* (*attrib.*) guardian; guardian's.

опеку́нство *neut.* guardianship.

óпера *f.* opera.

операти́вный *adj.* operative; surgical.

опера́тор *m.* operator.

операцио́нная *f.* operating room.

операцио́нный *adj.* (*med.*) operating.

опера́ция *f.* operation.

оперéние *neut.* plumage.

оперённый *adj.* feathered.

оперéточный *adj.* of operetta.

оперéтта *f.* operetta.

оперéться *pf. of* опира́ться.

опери́ровать OVA *impf. and pf.* to operate.

óперный *adj.* operatic, opera.

опеча́ленный *adj.* sad; sorrowful.

опеча́тка *f.* misprint.

опéшить *pf.* (*colloq.*) to be taken aback.

óпий *m.* opium.

óпийный *adj.* (*attrib.*) opium.

опи́лки *pl.* sawdust.

опира́ться *impf. pf.* оперéться to lean on; to be based on *or* upon.

описа́ние *neut.* description.

описа́тельный *adj.* descriptive.

опи́ска *f.* slip of the pen.

опи́сывать *impf. pf.* описа́ть to describe.

óпись *f.* list; inventory.

óпиум *m.* opium.

óпиумный *adj.* (*attrib.*) opium.

опла́кивать *impf. pf.* опла́кать to mourn.

опла́та *f.* payment.

опла́чиваемый *adj.* paid.

опла́чивать *impf. pf.* оплати́ть to remunerate; to pay.

оплодотворéние *neut.* fecundation, fertilization.

оплодотворя́ть *impf. pf.* оплодотвори́ть to fecun-date; to impregnate; to fertilize.

опло́т *m.* bastion; bulwark.

опло́шность *f.* blunder; mistake.

оповещéние *neut.* notification.

опóек FILL *m.* (*gen.* опóйка) calfskin.

опозда́ние *neut.* tardiness; lateness.

опозда́ть *pf. of* опа́здывать.

опознава́тельный *adj.* identifying; identification.

опозна́ние *neut.* identification.

опо́йковый *adj.* (*attrib.*) calfskin.

óползень FILL *m.* mudslide; landslide.

ополчéнец FILL *m.* militiaman.

ополчéние *neut.* militia.

опóмниться *pf.* to come to one's senses.

опóр *m.:* **во весь опóр** at full speed.

опóра *f.* support.

опóрный *adj.* supporting.

опорóс *m.* farrow.

опóссум *m.* opossum.

опохмеля́ться *impf. pf.* опохмели́ться (*colloq.*) to take a drink in order to relieve a hangover.

опошля́ть *impf. pf.* опо́шлить **1.** to vulgarize. **2.** to debase.

оппозицио́нный *adj.* (*attrib.*) opposition.

оппози́ция *f.* (*polit.*) opposition.

оппонéнт *m. f.* **—ка** opponent (*in a debate*).

оппони́ровать OVA *impf.* to oppose (*in a debate*).

оппортуни́зм *m.* opportunism.

оппортуни́ст *m. f.* **—ка** opportunist.

оппортунисти́ческий *adj.* opportunist.

опра́ва *f.* setting; mounting.

оправда́ние *neut.* **1.** justification. **2.** excuse.

оправда́тельный пригово́р *m.* verdict of "not guilty."

опра́вдывать *impf. pf.* оправда́ть to justify; to ac-quit; to vindicate.

опра́вка *f.* **1.** mandrel; chuck. **2.** riveting drift. **3.** mounting; setting.

определéние *neut.* **1.** definition. **2.** (*gram.*) attrib-ute.

определённо *adv.* definitely.

определённый *adj.* definite; certain.

определи́мый *adj.* definable.

определи́тель *m.* determining factor.

определя́ть *impf. pf.* определи́ть to define; to de-termine.

опреснéние *neut.* desalinization.

опри́чнина *f.* oprichnina (*administrative elite estab-lished by Ivan IV*).

опроверга́ть *impf. pf.* опрове́ргнуть to refute.

опровержéние *neut.* refutation.

опроки́дывать *impf. pf.* опроки́нуть **1.** to overturn; to upset. **2.** to knock over; to topple; to tip over.

опромётчивый *adj.* rash; imprudent.

о́прометью *adv.* headlong.

опро́с *m.* inquest; interrogation; poll.

опро́сный *adj.* (*attrib.*) questionnaire; interrogatory.

опря́тно *adv.* tidily; neatly.

опря́тность *f.* tidiness; neatness.

опря́тный *adj.* neat; tidy.

о́птика *f.* optics.

оптима́льный *adj.* optimal.

оптими́зм *m.* optimism.

оптими́ст *m. f.* —ка optimist.

оптимисти́ческий *adj.* optimistic.

о́птимум *m.* optimum.

опти́ческий *adj.* optic(al).

опто́вый *adj.* wholesale.

опубликова́ние *neut.* publication; promulgation.

опубликова́ть *pf. of* публикова́ть.

опу́нция *f.* prickly pear.

о́пус *m.* opus.

опуска́ть *impf. pf.* **опусти́ть 1.** to lower; to pull down. **2.** to omit.

опусте́лый *adj.* deserted.

опусте́ть *pf. of* пусте́ть.

опустоша́ть *impf. pf.* **опустоши́ть** to devastate.

опустоше́ние *neut.* devastation.

опустоши́тельный *adj.* devastating.

опуха́ть *impf. pf.* **опу́хнуть** to swell.

опу́хлый *adj.* (*colloq.*) swollen.

о́пухоль *f.* swelling; tumor.

опу́шка *f.* **1.** edge of the forest. **2.** (*fur*) trimming.

опуще́ние *neut.* omission.

о́пыт *m.* experiment; experience.

о́пытный *adj.* **1.** experienced. **2.** experimental.

опьяне́лый *adj.* (*colloq.*) intoxicated.

опьяне́ние *neut.* intoxication.

опьяне́ть *pf. of* пьяне́ть.

опя́ть *adv.* again.

ора́ва *f.* (*colloq.*) **1.** mob; crowd. **2.** horde; throng.

ора́кул *m.* oracle.

орангута́нг *m.* orangutan.

ора́нжевый *adj.* orange.

оранжере́йный *adj.* (*attrib.*) hothouse.

оранжере́я *f.* hothouse; greenhouse.

Ора́ниенбург *m.* Oranienburg.

ора́тор *m.* orator; speaker.

орато́рия *f.* oratorio.

ора́торский *adj.* oratorical.

ора́торствовать OVA *impf.* (*colloq.*) to orate; to perorate.

ора́ть *impf. pres.* **ору́, орёшь** to yell; to scream.

орби́та *f.* orbit.

орбита́льный *adj.* orbital.

орга́зм *m.* orgasm.

о́рган *m.* organ.

орга́н *m.* (*mus.*) organ.

организа́тор *m.* organizer.

организа́торский *adj.* organizational.

организацио́нный *adj.* of organization.

организа́ция *f.* organization.

органи́зм *m.* organism.

организо́ванно *adv.* in an organized manner.

организо́ванность *f.* good organization.

организо́ванный *adj.* organized; well-organized.

организова́ть OVA *impf. and pf.* to organize.

органи́ст *m. f.* —ка organist.

органи́ческий *adj.* organic.

орга́нный *adj.* (*mus.*) (*attrib.*) organ.

о́ргия *f.* orgy.

орда́ *f.* horde.

о́рден[1] *m.* order, decoration.

о́рден[2] *m.* order (*relig. society*).

орденоно́сец FILL *m.* holder of an order.

ордина́рец FILL *m.* (*mil.*) orderly.

ордина́рный *adj.* ordinary.

ордина́та *f.* (*geom.*) ordinate.

Óрегон *m.* Oregon.

Орёл FILL *m.* Oryol.

орёл FILL *m.* eagle. — **орёл и́ли ре́шка** heads or tails.

Оренбу́рг *m.* Orenburg.

орео́л *m.* **1.** halo; aureole. **2.** aura.

оре́х *m.* nut.

оре́ховый *adj.* (*attrib.*) nut; walnut.

оре́шек *m. dim. of* оре́х. — **бу́ковый оре́шек** *m.* beechnut.

оре́шник *m.* hazel tree.

оригина́л *m.* **1.** original. **2.** (*colloq.*) unique character.

оригина́льность *f.* originality.

оригина́льный *adj.* original.

ориента́льный *adj.* oriental.

ориента́ция *f.* orientation.

ориенти́р *m.* reference point; landmark.

ориенти́ровать OVA *impf. and pf.* to orient.

ориентиро́вка *f.* orientation.

ориентиро́вочный *adj.* (*attrib.*) reference.

орке́стр *m.* orchestra.

оркестрова́ть OVA *impf. and pf.* to orchestrate.

оркестро́вка *f.* orchestration.

оркестро́вый *adj.* orchestral.

орла́н *m.* sea eagle; bald eagle.

орлёнок FILL *m.* eaglet.

орли́ный *adj.* (*attrib.*) eagle.

орна́мент *m.* ornament.

орнито́лог *m.* ornithologist.

орнитологи́ческий *adj.* ornithological.

орнитоло́гия *f.* ornithology.

оробе́лый *adj.* frightened; timid.

ороси́тельный *adj.* (*attrib.*) irrigation.

ороше́ние *neut.* irrigation.

ортодокса́льный *adj.* orthodox.

ортодо́ксия *f.* orthodoxy.

ортодо́нтия *f.* orthodontics.

ортопе́д *m.* orthopedist.

ортопеди́ческий *adj.* orthopedic.

ортопе́дия *f.* orthopedics.

ору́дие *neut.* instrument; tool; implement.

оруди́йный *adj.* (*mil.*) (*attrib.*) weapon; gun.

ору́довать OVA *impf.* (*colloq.*) to handle; to wield (*a tool*).

оруже́йник *m.* gunsmith.

оруже́йный *adj.* (*attrib.*) gun; arms.

ору́жие *neut.* weapon.

орфогра́фия *f.* orthography.

орхиде́я *f.* orchid.

Óрхус *m.* Aarhus.

Óрша *f.* Orsha.

оса́ *f.* wasp.

оса́да *f.* siege.

осáдка *f.* **1.** settling; sinking (*of soil, etc.*). **2.** draft (*of a ship*).

осáдный *adj.* (*attrib.*) siege.

осáдок FILL *m.* sediment.

осáдочный *adj.* sedimentary.

осáнистый *adj.* stately; imposing.

осáнка *f.* bearing; carriage.

осáнна *f.* hosanna.

освáивать *impf. pf.* освóить to master, to assimilate. —ся (с *with instr.*) to make oneself familiar with.

осведомитель *m. f.* —ница informant; informer.

осведомительный *adj.* (*attrib.*) information.

осведомлéние *neut.* notification; information.

осведомлённость *f.* knowledgeability.

осведомлённый *adj.* informed; knowledgeable.

осведомлять *impf. pf.* осведомить (о *with prep.*) to inform (of).

освежáющий *adj.* refreshing.

освежéние *neut.* refreshment.

освежительный *adj.* refreshing.

Освéнцим *m.* Auschwitz (*Polish: Oświęcim*).

осветительный *adj.* (*attrib.*) lighting; illuminating.

освещáть *impf. pf.* осветить to illuminate, to elucidate.

освещéние *neut.* light, lighting.

освещённость *f.* luminosity.

освидéтельствовать OVA *pf. of* свидéтельствовать to examine; to inspect.

освободитель *m. f.* —ница liberator, emancipator.

освободительный *adj.* (*attrib.*) liberation.

освобождáть *impf. pf.* освободить **1.** to free; to liberate. **2.** to deliver. **3.** to exempt.

освобождéние *neut.* **1.** liberation; deliverance. **2.** exemption.

освоéние *neut.* mastering.

освóить(ся) *pf. of* освáивать(ся).

освящáть *impf. pf.* освятить **1.** to sanctify. **2.** to consecrate. **3.** to bless.

освящéние *neut.* sanctification; consecration.

освящённый *adj.* sanctified; honored.

осевóй *adj.* axial.

оседáть *impf. pf.* осéсть *v.i.* to settle (down).

осéдлость *f.* settled (*way of*) life. — чертá осéдлости the Jewish Pale of Settlement.

осéдлый *adj.* settled.

осёл FILL *m.* donkey; ass.

оселóк FILL *m.* whetstone.

осеменéние *neut.* insemination.

осéнний *adj.* (*attrib.*) autumn, autumnal.

óсень *f.* autumn, fall.

óсенью *adv.* in the fall; in the autumn.

осенять *impf. pf.* осенить **1.** to shade. **2.** (*of a thought* or *an idea*) to strike.

осéсть *pf. of* оседáть.

осётр *m.* sturgeon.

осéчка *f.* misfire.

осиливать *impf. pf.* осилить **1.** to overpower; to overcome. **2.** to manage; to handle. **3.** to master (*a subject*).

осина *f.* aspen.

осиновый *adj.* (*attrib.*) aspen.

осиный *adj.* (*attrib.*) wasp; wasp's.

осиплый *adj.* husky; hoarse.

осипнуть *pf. past* осип, осипла to become hoarse.

осиротéлый *adj.* (*attrib.*) orphan; orphaned.

осиротéть *pf.* **1.** to become an orphan. **2.** to be deserted *or* abandoned.

оскáлить зýбы *pf.* to show one's teeth; to bare one's teeth.

осквернéние *neut.* desecration.

осквернять *impf. pf.* осквернить to defile; to profane.

оскóлок FILL *m.* splinter.

оскóлочный *adj.* (*mil.*) fragmentation.

оскóмина *f.* soreness of the mouth; bitter taste (*in the mouth*).

оскоплять *impf. pf.* оскопить to castrate.

оскорбительный *adj.* insulting; offensive.

оскорблéние *neut.* insult; offense.

оскорблять *impf. pf.* оскорбить to insult; to offend.

ослабевáть *impf. pf.* ослабéть to grow feeble *or* weak.

ослабéлый *adj.* (*colloq.*) weakened.

ослабéть *pf. of* ослабевáть, слабéть.

ослаблéние *neut.* weakening.

ослепительный *adj.* blinding; dazzling.

ослеплéние *neut.* blinding.

ослеплять *pf. of* ослепить to blind.

ослéпнуть *pf. of* слéпнуть to become *or* go blind.

óслик *m.* small donkey; burro.

ослиный *adj.* (*attrib.*) donkey; donkey's.

ослица *f.* female donkey.

Óсло *m.* (*indecl.*) Oslo.

осложнéние *neut.* complication.

осложнять *impf. pf.* осложнить to complicate.

ослушáние *neut.* disobedience.

ослышаться *pf.* to mishear.

ослышка *f.* mishearing; mistake of hearing.

осмáтривать *impf. pf.* осмотрéть **1.** to examine; to survey. **2.** to scan. —ся to look about *or* around; to get one's bearings.

осмéивать *impf. pf.* осмеять to ridicule.

осмéливаться *impf. pf.* осмéлиться to dare.

осмеяние *neut.* mockery; ridicule.

óсмий *m.* osmium.

óсмос *m.* osmosis.

осмóтр *m.* examination, inspection; checkup.

осмотрéть(ся) *pf. of* осмáтривать(ся).

осмотрительный *adj.* circumspect; wary.

осмотрщик *m.* inspector.

осмыслéние *neut.* comprehension.

осмысленный *adj.* sensible; intelligent.

оснáстка *f.* **1.** (*naut.*) rig *or* rigging. **2.** fitting out.

оснащéние *adj.* equipment.

оснóва *f.* **1.** base; basis. **2.** оснóвы *pl.* fundamentals. **3.** (*gram.*) stem. **4.** (*textiles*) warp.

основáние *neut.* **1.** founding. **2.** foundation, basis.

основáтель *m. f.* —ница founder.

основáтельно *adv.* soundly; thoroughly.

основáтельность *f.* soundness; thoroughness.

основáтельный **1.** *adj.* well-founded. **2.** solid; stable. **3.** dependable. **4.** thorough.

основáть OVA *pf. of* оснóвывать.

основнóй *adj.* fundamental, basic; principal; cardinal.

основополагáющий *adj.* fundamental.

основополóжник *m.* founder.

оснóвывать *impf. pf.* основáть to found; (на *with prep.*) to base (on).

осóба *f.* person.

осо́бенно *adv.* especially; particularly.

осо́бенность *f.* peculiarity; feature. — в осо́бенности especially, in particular.

осо́бенный *adj.* especial; particular.

особня́к *m.* private residence; mansion.

осо́бо *adv.* separately; apart.

осо́бый *adj.* 1. special; particular. 2. separate.

о́собь *f.* 1. individual. 2. specimen.

осознава́ть *impf. pf.* осозна́ть to realize.

осозна́ние *neut.* realization; awareness.

осо́ка *f.* sedge.

осоко́рь *m.* black poplar.

осолове́лый *adj.* (*colloq.*) bleary-eyed.

о́спа *f.* smallpox.

о́спенный *adj.* (*attrib.*) smallpox.

о́спина *f.* pockmark.

оспоприва́ние *neut.* smallpox vaccination.

оспори́мый *adj.* questionable; debatable.

ост *m.* (*naut.*) east.

остава́ться *impf. pf.* оста́ться 1. to remain; to stay. 2. to be left over. — оста́ться в живы́х *pf.* to survive.

оставля́ть *impf. pf.* оста́вить 1. to leave; to abandon. 2. to retain; to keep. 3. to give up.

остально́е *neut.* the rest.

остально́й *adj.* the rest, the remaining.

остальны́е *pl.* the others; the rest.

остана́вливать *impf. pf.* останови́ть *v.t.* to stop, bring to a stop. —ся *v.i.* to stop; to stay (for the night).

оста́нки *pl.* (human) remains.

остано́вка *f.* 1. stop, halt. 2. interruption. 3. station, stop.

оста́ток FILL *m.* 1. rest. 2. (*math.*) remainder; remnant. — оста́тки *pl.* remains.

оста́точный *adj.* remaining; residual.

оста́ться *pf. of* остава́ться.

остео́лог *m.* osteologist.

остеоло́гия *f.* osteology.

остервене́лый *adj.* frenzied.

остервене́ние *neut.* frenzy.

остервене́ть *pf.* to become enraged.

острега́ть *impf. pf.* остере́чь (от *with gen.*) to warn. —ся (*with gen.*) to beware (of).

остолбене́лый *adj.* (*colloq.*) stupefied.

остолбене́ние *neut.* stupefaction; stupor.

остоло́п *m.* (*colloq.*) bonehead; blockhead.

осторо́жно *adv.* carefully; cautiously. –*interj.* be careful!; watch out!

осторо́жность *f.* care; caution.

осторо́жный *adj.* careful; cautious, wary.

Остра́ва *f.* Ostrava.

остраки́зм *m.* ostracism.

остра́стка *f.* (*colloq.*) warning.

острига́ть *impf. pf.* остри́чь to cut; to crop, to shear.

острие́ *neut.* point; edge.

остри́чься *pf. of* стри́чься.

о́стро *adv.* sharply; acutely.

о́стров *m.* island, isle.

острови́тянин *m. f.* острови́тянка islander.

острово́й *adj.* (*attrib.*) island; insular.

острово́к FILL *m.* small island.

остро́г *m.* 1. (*obs.*) jail. 2. stockaded town. 3. stockade.

острога́ *f.* fish-spear; harpoon.

острогла́зый *adj.* (*colloq.*) sharp-eyed.

острогу́бцы *pl.* cutting pliers.

остр"коне́чный *adj.* pointed.

остроли́ст *m.* holly.

остро́та *f.* witticism; a clever remark.

острота́ *f.* sharpness; acuteness; keenness.

остроу́мие *neut.* wit.

остроу́мно *adv.* wittily; cleverly.

остроу́мный *adj.* witty; clever.

о́стрый *adj.* sharp; acute; keen.

остря́к *m. f.* остря́чка witty person.

оступа́ться *impf. pf.* оступи́ться to stumble.

остыва́ть *impf. pf.* осты́ть *v.i.* to cool off.

осужда́ть *impf. pf.* осуди́ть to blame; to condemn; to convict.

осужде́ние *neut.* blame; censure; condemnation; conviction.

осуждённый *m.* convict.

осуше́ние *neut.* drainage.

осуши́тельный *adj.* (*attrib.*) drainage.

осуществи́мость *f.* feasibility.

осуществи́мый *adj.* feasible; practicable.

осуществле́ние *neut.* realization; implementation; fulfillment.

осуществля́ть *impf. pf.* осуществи́ть 1. to realize; to carry out. 2. to accomplish. —ся to come true.

осцилло́граф *m.* oscillograph.

осциллоско́п *m.* oscilloscope.

осцилля́тор *m.* oscillator.

ось *f.* 1. axis. 2. (*tech.*) axle.

осьмино́г *m.* octopus.

осяза́емый *adj.* tangible.

осяза́ние *neut.* touch.

осяза́тельный *adj.* tactile.

осяза́ть *impf.* to feel.

от *also* ото *prep.* (*with gen.*) from, away from.

ота́ра *f.* flock (*of sheep*).

отбивна́я котле́та *f.* chop; cutlet.

отбира́ть *impf. pf.* отобра́ть 1. to take away. 2. to select.

о́тблеск *m.* reflection.

отбо́й *m.* 1. repulse; repelling. 2. retreat; the all-clear signal.

отбо́йный молото́к *m.* mechanical pick.

отбо́р *m.* selection, choice.

отбо́рный *adj.* 1. select; choice. 2. (*colloq.*) (*of swearwords*) choice.

отбо́рочный *adj.* (*attrib.*) selection.

отбра́сывать *impf. pf.* отбро́сить 1. to throw away *or* off. 2. to repulse. 3. to reject; to discard.

отбро́сы *pl.* garbage; waste.

отбыва́ть *impf. pf.* отбы́ть 1. to depart; to leave. 2. to serve out (*time*).

отбы́тие *neut.* departure.

отва́га *f.* courage; bravery.

отва́жно *adv.* bravely; courageously.

отва́жный *adj.* brave; courageous.

отва́л *m.* 1. casting off (*of a ship*). 2. dump; heap.

отва́р *m.* decoction.

отва́рный *adj.* boiled.

отве́дывать *impf. pf.* отве́дать (*colloq.*) 1. to try; to taste. 2. to experience.

отвезти́ *pf. of* отвози́ть.

отверга́ть *impf. pf.* отве́ргнуть to reject.

отвердева́ть *impf. pf.* **отверде́ть** to harden; to solidify.

отверде́лый *adj.* hardened.

отве́рженный *adj.* outcast. — *m.* outcast.

отве́рстие *neut.* opening; slot.

отвёртка *f.* screwdriver.

отве́с *m.* **1.** precipice; steep cliff. **2.** plumb.

отве́сный *adj.* sheer; vertical.

отвести́ *pf. of* **отводи́ть**.

отве́т *m.* reply, answer.

ответвле́ние *neut.* offshoot; branch; branching.

отве́тить *pf. of* **отвеча́ть**.

отве́тный *adj.* (*attrib.*) return; retaliatory.

отве́тственность *f.* responsibility.

отве́тственный *adj.* responsible.

отве́тственный реда́ктор *m.* editor-in-chief.

отве́тчик *m. f.* **отве́тчица** (*leg.*) defendant.

отвеча́ть *impf. pf.* **отве́тить** (**на** *with acc.*) to answer; (**за** *with acc.*) to be responsible for.

отви́нчивать *impf. pf.* **отвинти́ть** to unscrew.

отвиса́ть *impf. pf.* **отви́снуть** to hang down; to droop; to sag.

отви́слый *adj.* loose-hanging; flaccid.

отвлека́ть *impf. pf.* **отвле́чь** *v.t.* **1.** to distract; to divert. **2.** to abstract.

отвлече́ние *neut.* abstraction; distraction.

отвлечённо *adv.* in the abstract manner.

отвлечённый *adj.* abstract.

отводи́ть *impf. pf.* **отвести́ 1.** to lead *or* draw aside. **2.** to ward off.

отво́дный *adj.* (*attrib.*) **1.** drain. **2.** drainage.

отвози́ть *impf. pf.* **отвезти́** to take *or* drive away; to take *or* drive back.

отвора́чивать *impf. pf.* **отверну́ть 1.** to turn aside; to turn away. **2.** to turn down. **3.** to turn; to make a turn.

оборо́т *m.* **1.** lapel. **2.** cuff.

отворя́ть *impf. pf.* **отвори́ть** *v.t.* to open.

отврати́тельный *adj.* disgusting; repulsive.

отвраща́ть *impf. pf.* **отврати́ть** to avert; to repulse.

отвраще́ние *neut.* aversion; disgust.

отвыка́ть *impf. pf.* **отвы́кнуть** to get out of a habit.

отвя́зывать *impf. pf.* **отвяза́ть** *v.t.* to untie.

отга́дка *f.* answer *or* solution (*to a riddle*).

отга́дчик *m. f.* **отга́дчица** (*colloq.*) guesser.

отга́дывать *impf. pf.* **отгада́ть** to guess.

отглаго́льный *adj.* (*gram.*) verbal.

отгова́ривать *impf. pf.* **отговори́ть** (**от** *with gen.*) to dissuade.

отгово́рка *f.* excuse; pretext.

отголо́сок *m.* **1.** echo. **2.** faint sound.

отгора́живать *impf. pf.* **отгороди́ть 1.** to fence off. **2.** to isolate.

отдава́ть *impf. pf.* **отда́ть 1.** to return, to give back. **2.** to devote.

отдале́ние *neut.* distance; removal.

отдалённый *adj.* remote; distant.

отдаля́ть *impf. pf.* **отдали́ть** to remove. —**ся** (**от** *with gen.*) to move away from.

отда́ть *pf. of* **отдава́ть**.

отда́ча *f.* return; payment; output.

отде́л *m.* section; department. —**е́ние** *neut.* **1.** separation. **2.** compartment, section. **3.** department, branch. —**и́мый** *adj.* separable. —**ьный** *adj.* separate.

отде́лка *f.* **1.** furnishing. **2.** trim; trimming.

отде́лывать *impf. pf.* **отде́лать** to decorate; to finish, to trim.

отде́льно *adv.* **1.** separately. **2.** individually.

отде́льность *f.*: **в отде́льности** *adv.* individually; separately.

отдели́ть *impf. pf.* **отдели́ть** *v.t.* to separate, to detach.

отду́шина *f.* vent; air-vent.

о́тдых *m.* rest.

отдыха́ть *impf. pf.* **отдохну́ть** to rest; to take a rest

отдыша́ться *pf. pres.* **отдышу́сь, отды́шишься** to catch one's breath.

отёк *m.* (*med.*) edema.

оте́ль *m.* hotel.

оте́ц FILL *m.* father.

оте́ческий *adj.* paternal.

оте́чественный *adj.* **1.** native; home. **2.** national; civil.

оте́чество *neut.* fatherland.

отжи́вший *adj.* having lived out one's life.

о́тзвук *m.* echo; repercussion.

о́тзыв *m.* **1.** reference, opinion. **2.** response, comment; review.

отзы́в *m.* recall (*of an ambassador*).

отзыва́ться *impf. pf.* **отозва́ться 1.** (**на** *with acc.*) to answer, to reply. **2.** (**о** *with prep.*) to speak of.

отзы́вчивый *adj.* sympathetic; responsive.

отка́з *m.* refusal; rejection.

отка́зывать *impf. pf.* **отказа́ть** to refuse; to deny. —**ся 1.** to decline. **2.** to renounce.

отка́рмливать *impf. pf.* **откорми́ть** to fatten up.

отка́т *m.* recoil (*of an artillery piece*).

откидно́й *adj.* folding; collapsible.

откла́дывать *impf. pf.* **отложи́ть 1.** to lay *or* put aside. **2.** to suspend; to postpone.

о́тклик *m.* response; echo.

отклоне́ние *neut.* **1.** deflection. **2.** digression. **3.** rejection.

отклоня́ть *impf. pf.* **отклони́ть 1.** to deflect. **2.** to decline.

откозыря́ть *pf.* (*with dat.*) (*colloq.*) to salute.

отко́с *m.* side (*of a hill*); slope.

открове́ние *neut.* revelation.

открове́нно *adv.* frankly.

открове́нность *f.* candor; sincerity.

открове́нный *adj.* frank, outspoken, candid.

открыва́тель *m.* discoverer.

открыва́ть *impf. pf.* **откры́ть 1.** to open. **2.** to reveal, to disclose. **3.** to unveil.

откры́тие *neut.* **1.** discovery. **2.** unveiling.

откры́тка *f.* postcard.

откры́то *adv.* openly.

откры́тый *adj.* open.

отку́да *adv.* from where, whence.

отку́да-нибудь *adv.* from somewhere or other.

отку́да-то *adv.* from somewhere.

отку́поривать *impf. pf.* **отку́порить** to uncork; to open.

отку́сывать *impf. pf.* **откуси́ть** to bite off.

отлёт *m.* takeoff.

отли́в *m.* low tide.

отли́вка *f.* casting; founding.

отлича́ть *impf. pf.* **отличи́ть** to distinguish. —**ся** (**от** *with gen.*) **1.** to be different. **2.** to distinguish oneself.

отли́чие *neut.* difference.
отличи́тельный *adj.* distinctive.
отли́чник *m. f.* отли́чница outstanding student; outstanding worker.
отли́чно *adv.* excellently; very well.
отли́чный *adj.* **1.** different (from). **2.** excellent.
отло́гий *adj.* not steep; gently sloping.
отложе́ние *neut.* (*geol.*) sediment.
отложи́ть *pf. of* откла́дывать.
отложно́й *adj.* (*of collar*) turndown.
отлупи́ть *pf. of* лупи́ть.
отлуче́ние *neut.* separation. — отлуче́ние от це́ркви excommunication.
отлу́чка *f.* absence.
отлы́нивать *impf.* (от *with gen.*) (*colloq.*) to shirk.
о́тмель *f.* shoal; sandbank; sand bar.
отме́на *f.* abolition; cancellation.
отме́нный *adj.* excellent.
отменя́ть *impf. pf.* отмени́ть to cancel; to abolish; to abrogate.
отме́стка *f.* (*colloq.*): в отме́стку *adv.* in revenge.
отме́тка *f.* **1.** note. **2.** (*school*) mark, grade.
отмеча́ть *impf. pf.* отме́тить **1.** to mark; to note. **2.** to celebrate.
отмира́ть *impf. pf.* отмере́ть **1.** to die. **2.** to die off; to die out.
отморо́жение *neut.* frostbite.
отмы́чка *f.* **1.** master key; skeleton key. **2.** lockpick.
отне́киваться *impf.* (*colloq.*) to decline; to refuse.
отнести́(сь) *pf. of* относи́ть(ся).
отнима́ть *impf. pf.* отня́ть **1.** to take off *or* away. **2.** to amputate.
относи́тельно *adv.* relatively. –*prep.* (*with gen.*) concerning.
относи́тельность *f.* relativity. — тео́рия относи́тельности *f.* theory of relativity.
относи́тельный *adj.* relative.
относи́ть *impf. pf.* отнести́ to carry away, to remove. —ся (к *with dat.*) **1.** to treat, to regard. **2.** to concern.
отноше́ние *neut.* **1.** attitude. **2.** treatment. — отноше́ния *pl.* relations.
отны́не *adv.* from this moment on; from here on.
отню́дь *adv.* (*with* не) by no means; not in the least.
отня́тие *neut.* taking away; seizure.
отня́ть *pf. of* отнима́ть.
отображе́ние *neut.* representation; reflection.
отобра́ть *pf. of* отбира́ть.
отовсю́ду *adv.* from everywhere.
отодвига́ть *impf. pf.* отодви́нуть **1.** to move aside; to move away. **2.** (*colloq.*) to postpone.
отож(д)ествля́ть *impf. pf.* отож(д)естви́ть to equate.
отозва́ть(ся) *pf. of* отзыва́ть(ся).
отойти́ *pf. of* отходи́ть.
отомсти́ть *pf. of* мстить.
отопи́тельный *adj.* (*attrib.*) heating.
отопле́ние *neut.* heating; heat.
оторва́ть *pf. of* отрыва́ть.
оторопе́лый *adj.* (*colloq.*) dazed; dumbfounded.
о́торопь *f.* (*colloq.*) confusion; fright.
оторо́чка *f.* trimming; edging.
отосла́ть *pf. of* отсыла́ть.
отоща́лый *adj.* (*colloq.*) emaciated.
отпева́ние *neut.* (*relig.*) funeral service.

отпе́тый *adj.* (*colloq.*) incorrigible.
отпеча́ток FILL *m.* imprint.
отпива́ть *impf. pf.* отпи́ть to take a sip of.
отпира́тельство *neut.* persistent denial.
отпи́ска *f.* noncommittal written answer.
отпи́хивать *impf. pf.* отпихну́ть (*colloq.*) to push away; to push aside.
отпла́та *f.* repayment.
отплыва́ть *impf. pf.* отплы́ть **1.** to swim away. **2.** (*of a ship*) to depart; to sail.
отплы́тие *neut.* sailing; departure.
о́тповедь *f.* reproof; rebuke.
отпо́р *m.* rebuff.
отправи́тель *m. f.* —ница sender.
отпра́вка *f.* (*colloq.*) dispatch.
отправле́ние *neut.* **1.** sending; dispatch. **2.** departure. **3.** performance; discharge.
отправля́ть *impf. pf.* отпра́вить **1.** to send, to dispatch. **2.** to forward. —ся to set out, to depart, to leave.
отправно́й *adj.* (*attrib.*) dispatch.
отпра́здновать OVA *pf. of* пра́здновать.
о́трыск *m.* **1.** (*of a plant*) shoot; offshoot. **2.** (*obs.*) offspring.
отпря́нуть *pf.* to recoil; to jump back.
о́тпуск *m.* leave; vacation.
отпуска́ть *impf. pf.* отпусти́ть **1.** to release, to free. **2.** to slacken.
отпускни́к *m.* person on leave.
отпускно́й *adj.* (*attrib.*) vacation.
отпуще́ние *neut.* remission (of sins).
отра́ва *f.* poison.
отравле́ние *neut.* poisoning.
отравля́ть *impf. pf.* отра́вить **1.** to poison. **2.** to spoil.
отра́да *f.* **1.** joy; delight. **2.** comfort.
отра́дный *adj.* gratifying; comforting; pleasing.
отража́тель *m.* reflector.
отража́ть *impf. pf.* отрази́ть **1.** to reflect. **2.** to repulse.
отраже́ние *neut.* reflection.
отраслево́й *adj.* of a particular branch *or* field.
о́трасль *f.* branch.
отре́бье *neut.* rabble.
отре́з *m.* length of material.
отреза́ть *impf. pf.* отре́зать to cut off.
отрезно́й *adj.* detachable.
отре́зок FILL *m.* segment; section.
отрека́ться *impf. pf.* отре́чься (от *with gen.*) to renounce; to repudiate.
отрекомендова́ть OVA *pf.* to recommend.
отре́пье *neut.*, *often pl.* (*colloq.*) tatters; rags.
отрече́ние *neut.* renunciation. — отрече́ние от престо́ла abdication.
отрешённый *adj.* **1.** aloof; isolated. **2.** (*of a look*) blank.
отрица́ние *neut.* **1.** negation. **2.** denial.
отрица́тельно *adv.* negatively.
отрица́тельный *adj.* negative.
отрица́ть *impf.* to deny; to refute.
отро́г *m.* spur (*of a mountain range*).
о́троду *adv.* (*with* не) (*colloq.*) never in one's life.
о́трочество *neut.* adolescence.
о́труби *pl.* bran.
отры́в *m.* **1.** tearing off. **2.** alienation. **3.** hiatus; break.

отрыва́ть *impf. pf.* **оторва́ть** *v.t.* to tear off *or* away.

отры́вистый *adj.* **1.** (*of speech*) disjointed; uneven. **2.** (*of sounds*) jerky; abrupt; curt.

отрывно́й *adj.* that can be torn off.

отры́вок FILL *m.* fragment.

отры́вочный *adj.* fragmentary.

отры́жка *f.* belch.

отря́д *m.* detachment.

отсве́т *m.* reflection.

отсебя́тина *f.* (*colloq.*) words of one's own put into another's mouth.

отсе́в *m.* sifting out.

отсе́к *m.* **1.** compartment. **2.** space module.

отсека́ть *impf. pf.* **отсе́чь** to cut off; to chop off.

отсече́ние *neut.* chopping off.

отска́бливать *impf. pf.* **отскобли́ть** to scrape off.

отсло́йка *f.* detachment.

отсове́товать OVA *pf.* (*with dat. and infin.*) to dissuade from; to talk someone out of.

отсро́чивать *impf. pf.* **отсро́чить** to postpone.

отсро́чка *f.* postponement.

отстава́ние *neut.* lag.

отстава́ть *impf. pf.* **отста́ть 1.** to fall behind. **2.** to be backward *or* slow.

отста́вка *f.* resignation; retirement.

отставно́й *adj.* retired.

отста́ивать *impf. pf.* **отстоя́ть 1.** to uphold (*a principle*). **2.** to assert (*one's rights*). **3.** to defend.

отста́лость *f.* backwardness.

отста́лый *adj.* backward.

отста́ть *pf. of* **отстава́ть.**

отстоя́ть¹ *pf. pres.* —**стою́,** —**стои́шь 1.** *pf. of* **отста́ивать. 2.** to stand through (*an event*).

отстоя́ть² *impf. pres.* —**стою́,** —**стои́шь 1.** to be. **2.** to be a (certain) distance from.

отстране́ние *neut.* dismissal; removal.

о́тступ *m.* indentation (*in printing*); indention.

отступа́ть *impf. pf.* **отступи́ть 1.** to retreat, to fall back. **2.** to deviate.

отступле́ние *neut.* **1.** retreat. **2.** deviation.

отсту́пник *m. f.* **отсту́пница** apostate.

отступно́е *neut.* compensation; idemnity.

отступя́ *adv.* a distance away.

отсу́тствие *neut.* absence.

отсу́тствовать OVA *impf.* to be absent.

отсу́тствующий *adj.* absent. — *m.* absentee.

отсчёт *m.* **1.** marking off; counting out. **2.** reading (*on an instrument*).

отсыла́ть *impf. pf.* **отосла́ть** to send away; to send.

отсы́лка *f.* **1.** dispatch; sending. **2.** reference.

отсыре́лый *adj.* soggy; damp.

отсыха́ть *impf. pf.* **отсо́хнуть** to wither.

отсю́да *adv.* from here, hence.

Отта́ва *f.* Ottawa.

отте́нок FILL *m.* **1.** shade; hue. **2.** nuance.

о́ттепель *f.* thaw.

оттира́ть *impf. pf.* **оттере́ть 1.** to rub out; to rub off. **2.** to rub one's hands.

о́ттиск *m.* impression; reprint.

оттого́ *adv.* that is why; which is why.

оттома́нка *f.* ottoman.

оттопы́ренный *adj.* prominent; protruding.

отту́да *adv.* from there.

оття́жка *f.* (*colloq.*) (deliberate) delay.

отупе́лый *adj.* (*colloq.*) dazed.

отупе́ние *neut.* daze; torpor; stupor.

отхо́д *m.* **1.** departure. **2.** deviation.

отходи́ть *impf. pf.* **отойти́** to depart, to leave.

отходна́я *f.* prayer said for a dying person.

отхо́дчивый *adj.* quickly forgiving.

отхо́жее ме́сто *neut.* latrine; outhouse.

отцеуби́йство *neut.* patricide.

отцо́вский *adj.* paternal.

отча́ливать *impf. pf.* **отча́лить** (*of a boat*) to cast off.

отча́сти *adv.* partly, in part.

отча́яние *neut.* despair.

отча́янно *adv.* desperately.

отча́янный *adj.* **1.** desperate; despairing. **2.** reckless.

отчего́ *adv.* why, for what reason.

отчего́-нибудь *adv.* for some reason or other.

отчего́-то *adv.* for some unknown reason.

отчека́нить *pf. of* **чека́нить.**

о́тчество *neut.* patronymic.

отчёт *m.* **1.** account. **2.** report.

отчётливый *adj.* distinct; clear.

отчётность *f.* accounting.

отчётный *adj.* related to a report.

отчи́зна *f.* (*obs.*) fatherland.

о́тчим *m.* stepfather.

отчисле́ние *neut.* deduction.

отчисля́ть *impf. pf.* **отчи́слить 1.** to deduct. **2.** to dismiss.

отчужде́ние *neut.* alienation; estrangement.

отчуждённость *f.* estrangement; aloofness.

отше́льник *m. f.* **отше́льница** hermit; recluse.

отше́льнический *adj.* like that of a hermit.

отше́льничество *neut.* solitary life; hermit's life.

отши́б *m.*: **на отши́бе 1.** at a distance. **2.** (**от** *with gen.*) aloof from; apart from.

отщепе́нец FILL *m. f.* **отщепе́нка** renegade.

отъе́зд *m.* departure.

отъезжа́ть *impf. pf.* **отъе́хать** to depart; to drive off.

отъя́вленный *adj.* unmitigated; arrant.

оты́скивать *impf. pf.* **отыска́ть 1.** to find. **2.** *impf. only* to search for.

офице́р *m.* officer.

офице́рский *adj.* (*attrib.*) officer; officer's.

офице́рство *neut.* the officers.

официа́льно *adv.* officially.

официа́льный *adj.* official.

официа́нт *m.* waiter.

официа́нтка *f.* waitress.

официо́з *m.* semiofficial publication.

официо́зный *adj.* semiofficial.

оформи́тель *m. f.* —**ница 1.** designer. **2.** stage designer.

оформле́ние *neut.* **1.** mounting. **2.** registration; legalization. **3.** processing (*of documents*). **4.** design.

офо́рт *m.* etching.

офсе́т *m.* offset.

офсе́тный *adj.* (*attrib.*) offset.

офтальмо́лог *m.* ophthalmologist.

офтальмоло́гия *f.* ophthalmology.

ох *interj.* oh!; ah!

о́ханье *neut.* moaning; groaning.

оха́пка *f.* armful.

охарактеризова́ть OVA *pf.* to characterize; to describe.

о́хать *impf. pf.* о́хнуть to moan; to groan.

охва́т *m.* **1.** scope. **2.** inclusion.

охва́тывать *impf. pf.* охвати́ть **1.** to embrace, to include. **2.** to seize, to overcome.

охлажде́ние *neut.* cooling.

охмеле́ть *pf.* (*colloq.*) to become intoxicated.

охо́та[1] *f.* hunt, hunting.

охо́та[2] *f.* wish; desire.

охо́титься *impf.* to hunt.

охо́тник[1] *m.* hunter.

охо́тник[2] *m. f.* охо́тница amateur, lover.

охо́тничий *adj.* (*attrib.*) hunting.

охо́тно *adv.* willingly, gladly.

Охо́тское мо́ре *neut.* Sea of Okhotsk.

о́хра *f.* ocher.

охра́на *f.* guard; guarding.

охране́ние *neut.* safeguarding; protection.

охра́нка *f.* (*obs.*) (*colloq.*) (pre-rev.) secret police.

охра́нный *adj.* safe-conduct. — охра́нная гра́мота *f.* safe-conduct pass.

охраня́ть *impf. pf.* охрани́ть to guard; to protect.

О́хридское о́зеро Lake Ohrid.

охри́плый *adj.* (*colloq.*) hoarse.

охри́пнуть *pf.* to become hoarse.

охри́пший *adj.* hoarse.

оцело́т *m.* ocelot.

оце́нивать *impf. pf.* оцени́ть to evaluate; to estimate; to value.

оце́нка *f.* estimate, appraisal, appraisement.

оце́нщик *m. f.* оце́нщица appraiser.

оцепене́лый *adj.* dazed; stunned.

оцепене́ние *neut.* stupor; torpor.

оцепля́ть *impf. pf.* оцепи́ть to surround; to seal off.

оча́г *m.* **1.** hearth. **2.** breeding ground; center.

очарова́ние *neut.* charm; enchantment.

очаро́ванный *adj.* **1.** spellbound. **2.** charmed.

очарова́тельный *adj.* charming; fascinating.

очаро́вывать *impf. pf.* очарова́ть to charm; to fascinate.

очеви́дец FILL *m. f.* очеви́дица eyewitness.

очеви́дно *adv.* obviously.

очеви́дный *adj.* obvious.

о́чень *adv.* very; very much.

очередно́й *adj.* next, next in turn; usual.

очерёдность *f.* **1.** sequence. **2.** prescribed order.

о́чередь *f.* **1.** turn. **2.** line. **3.** order.

о́черк *m.* sketch; outline.

очерстве́лый *adj.* callous; hardened.

очерта́ние *neut.* outline.

оче́рчивать *impf. pf.* очерти́ть to outline.

очёски *pl.* combings.

очини́ть *pf. of* чини́ть.

очисти́тельный *adj.* cleansing.

очи́стка *f.* cleaning.

очище́ние *neut.* **1.** cleansing. **2.** purification. **3.** clearing.

очки́ *pl.* eyeglasses, spectacles.

очко́ *neut.* (*in games*) point.

очко́вая змея́ *f.* cobra.

очко́вый *adj.* (*sports*) based on points scored.

очну́ться *pf.* **1.** to come to; to regain consciousness. **2.** to awaken.

о́чное обуче́ние *neut.* classroom instruction (*vs. correspondence courses*).

очути́ться *pf. pres.* очу́тишься (*1st pers. sg. not used*) to find oneself (*in a certain place*); to end up (*in a certain place*).

ошеломи́тельный *adj.* stunning; staggering.

ошиба́ться *impf. pf.* ошиби́ться to make a mistake; to err.

оши́бка *f.* error, mistake.

оши́бочно *adv.* by mistake.

оши́бочный *adj.* erroneous; mistaken.

ошпа́ривать *impf. pf.* ошпа́рить (*colloq.*) to scald.

оштрафова́ть OVA *pf. of* штрафова́ть.

о́щупь *f.* touch.

о́щупью *adv.* by groping one's way.

ощути́мый *adj.* perceptible; tangible.

ощути́тельный *adj.* perceptible; tangible.

ощуща́ть *impf. pf.* ощути́ть to feel; to sense.

ощуще́ние *neut.* feeling; sensation.

П

па́ва *f.* peahen.
павиа́н *m.* baboon.
павильо́н *m.* pavilion.
павли́н *m.* peacock.
павли́ний *adj.* (*attrib.*) peacock.
Па́вловск *m.* Pavlovsk.
Павлода́р *m.* Pavlodar.
па́водок FILL *m.* high water; flood.
па́вший *adj.* fallen.
пагина́ция *f.* pagination.
па́года *f.* pagoda.
па́губный *adj.* pernicious; disastrous.
па́даль *f.* carrion.
па́дать *impf. pf.* упа́сть, пасть to fall.
па́дающий *adj.* falling.
паде́ж *m.* (*gram.*) case.
падёж *m.* murrain, cattle plague.
паде́жный *adj.* (*gram.*) (*attrib.*) case.
паде́ние *neut.* fall; downfall.
па́дкий *adj.* susceptible to.
па́дуб *m.* holly.
Па́дуя *f.* Padova (*also: Padua*).
па́дчерица *f.* stepdaughter.
па́дший *adj.* fallen.
паёк FILL *m.* ration.
паж *m.* page; attendant.
паз *m.* **1.** crack; crevice. **2.** slot; groove. **3.** mortise.
па́зуха *f.* **1.** bosom. **2.** (*anat.*) sinus. **3.** (*bot.*) axil.
па́инька *m.* and *f.* (*decl. f.*) (*colloq.*) good child.
пай *m.* share.
па́йка *f.* soldering.
па́йщик *m. f.* па́йщица shareholder.
паке́т *m.* **1.** packet; package. **2.** paper bag.
пакетбо́т *m.* (*steamship*) packet.
Пакиста́н *m.* Pakistan.
пакиста́нец FILL *m. f.* пакиста́нка Pakistani.
па́кля *f.* tow; oakum.
пакова́ть OVA *impf. pf.* за-, у- to pack.
па́костный *adj.* (*colloq.*) vile; foul; nasty.
па́кость *f.* **1.** dirty trick. **2.** filth. **3.** obscenity; dirty word.
пакт *m.* pact.
пала́та[1] *f.* hospital ward; (*ob.*) mansion.
пала́та[2] *f.* (*of a legislature*) house; chamber; bureau.
палатализа́ция *f.* palatalization.
палатализова́ть OVA *impf. and pf.* (*phon.*) to palatalize.
палата́льный *adj.* (*phon.*) palatal.
пала́тка *f.* **1.** tent. **2.** booth; stall.
пала́точный *adj.* (*attrib.*) tent.
пала́ч *m.* executioner; hangman.
пала́ш *m.* broadsword.
палёный *adj.* singed; scorched.
палеоазиа́тский *adj.* Paleo-Asiatic.
палео́граф *m.* paleographer.
палеографи́ческий *adj.* paleographic.
палеогра́фия *f.* paleography.
палеозо́йский *adj.* paleozoic.

палеолити́ческий *adj.* paleolithic.
палеонтологи́ческий *adj.* paleontological.
палеонтоло́гия *f.* paleontology.
Пале́рмо *m.* Palermo.
па́лец FILL *m.* finger; toe.
палиса́д *m.* palisade.
палиса́дник *m.* small garden.
палиса́ндр *m.* rosewood; palisander.
палиса́ндровый *adj.* (*attrib.*) rosewood.
пали́тра *f.* palette.
пали́ть *impf.* **1.** *pf.* о- to singe. **2.** *pf.* с- to burn; to scorch.
па́лка *f.* stick; cane.
палла́дий *m.* palladium.
паллиати́в *m.* palliative.
паллиати́вный *adj.* palliative.
пало́мник *m. f.* пало́мница pilgrim.
пало́мнический *adj.* (*attrib.*) pilgrim; pilgrim's.
пало́мничество *neut.* pilgrimage.
па́лочка *f.* **1.** small stick. **2.** drumstick. **3.** baton; wand. **4.** bacillus. — па́лочки *pl.* chopsticks.
па́лочный *adj.* using a stick.
па́лтус *m.* halibut.
па́луба *f.* (*naut.*) deck.
па́лубный *adj.* (*attrib.*) deck.
пальба́ *f.* (*colloq.*) firing.
Па́льма *f.* Palma.
па́льма *f.* palm.
па́льмовый *adj.* (*attrib.*) palm.
пальто́ *neut. indecl.* coat, overcoat.
па́льчик *m. dim. of* па́лец.
паля́щий *adj.* burning; scorching.
Пами́р *m.* (*mountain range*) Pamirs.
пампа́сы *pl.* pampas.
памфле́т *m.* (*polit.*) pamphlet.
памфлети́ст *m.* pamphleteer.
па́мятка *f.* reminder.
па́мятливость *f.* (*colloq.*) retentive memory.
па́мятливый *adj.* (*colloq.*) having a retentive memory.
па́мятник *m.* monument.
па́мятный *adj.* memorable; commemorative.
па́мятуя *gerund* (о *with prep.*) recalling; remembering.
па́мять *f.* memory.
Пана́ма *f.* Panama.
пана́ма *f.* Panama hat.
панаце́я *f.* panacea.
па́нда *f.* panda.
пандеми́я *f.* pandemic.
панеги́рик *m.* panegyric; eulogy.
панегири́ст *m.* panegyrist.
пане́ль *f.* **1.** paneling. **2.** sidewalk; pavement.
панибра́тский *adj.* (*colloq.*) familiar; overly familiar.
панибра́тство *neut.* (*colloq.*) undue familiarity.
па́ника *f.* panic.
паникёр *m. f.* —ша alarmist.
панихи́да *f.* funeral service, requiem.
пани́ческий *adj.* panic-stricken.
панора́ма *f.* panorama.

панора́мный adj. panoramic.
пансио́н m. boarding house.
пансиона́т m. **1.** resort hotel. **2.** boarding school.
пансионе́р m. f. —ка boarder.
панталóны pl. **1.** (obs.) pants; trousers. **2.** (women's) drawers.
панталы́к m. (colloq.): сбить с панталы́ку pf. to confuse.
пантеи́зм m. pantheism.
пантеи́ст m. pantheist.
пантеисти́ческий adj. pantheistic.
пантео́н m. pantheon.
панте́ра f. **1.** panther. **2.** leopard.
пантоми́ма f. pantomime.
панхромати́ческий adj. panchromatic.
па́нцирь m. **1.** coat of mail; armor. **2.** shell (of a turtle).
па́па[1] m. (decl. f.) papa, daddy.
па́па[2] m. (decl. f.) Pope.
папа́ха f. tall fur hat.
папа́ша m. (decl. f.) (colloq.) daddy.
па́перть f. church portico.
папильóтка f. (hair) curler.
папирóса f. cigarette.
папирóсница f. cigarette case.
папирóсный adj. (attrib.) cigarette.
папи́рус m. papyrus.
па́пка f. file; folder.
па́поротник m. fern.
па́прика f. paprika.
па́пский adj. papal.
па́пство neut. papacy.
па́пула f. papule.
папье́-маше́ neut. indecl. papier-mâché.
пар m. **1.** steam. **2.** exhalation.
па́ра f. pair, couple.
пара́бола f. parabola.
параболи́ческий adj. parabolic.
Парагва́й m. Paraguay.
пара́граф m. paragraph.
пара́д m. parade; review.
паради́гма f. paradigm.
пара́дное neut. front door.
пара́дный adj. (attrib.) parade; gala.
парадóкс m. paradox.
парадокса́льный adj. paradoxical.
парази́т m. parasite. — парази́тка f. (fig.) (of female) parasite.
паразити́зм m. parasitism.
паразити́ческий also парази́тный adj. parasitic.
парализова́ть impf. and pf. to paralyze.
парали́тик m. f. парали́чка paralytic.
паралити́ческий adj. paralytic.
парали́ч m. paralysis.
парали́чный adj. paralytic.
паралла́кс m. parallax.
параллелепи́пед m. parallelepiped.
параллели́зм m. parallelism.
параллелогра́мм m. parallelogram.
паралле́ль f. parallel.
паралле́льный adj. parallel.
паранои́ческий adj. paranoid.
паранóйя f. paranoia.
парапе́т m. parapet.
параплеги́я f. paraplegia.
парати́ф m. paratyphoid.

парафи́н m. paraffin.
парафи́новый adj. (attrib.) paraffin.
парафи́ровать OVA impf. and pf. to initial (a treaty or a document).
парашю́т m. parachute.
парашюти́зм m. (sport) parachute jumping.
парашюти́ст m. f. —ка parachutist.
парашю́тный adj. (attrib.) parachute.
паращитови́дная железа́ f. parathyroid gland.
па́реный adj. steamed.
па́рень m. lad, young lad; fellow.
пари́ m. indecl. bet, wager.
Пари́ж m. Paris.
парижа́нин m. f. парижа́нка Parisian.
пари́к m. wig.
парикма́хер m. **1.** barber. **2.** hair dresser; hair stylist.
парикма́херская f. barbershop; beauty shop, hairdresser's.
пари́льня f. steam room.
пари́ровать OVA impf. and pf. **1.** to parry; to ward off. **2.** to counter.
парите́т m. parity.
парите́тный adj. equal.
па́рить impf. **1.** to steam. **2.** to stew. **3.** (impers.) to be sultry.
пари́ть impf. to soar; to glide.
па́рия m. and f. (decl. f.) pariah; outcast.
парк[1] m. park.
парк[2] m. (of vehicles) depot; fleet.
па́рка f. parka.
парке́т m. parquet.
парке́тный adj. parquet.
парла́мент m. parliament.
парламентари́зм m. parliamentarianism.
парламента́рий m. member of parliament.
парламента́рный adj. parliamentary.
парламентёр m. bearer of a flag of truce.
парла́ментский adj. parliamentary.
парни́к m. hothouse; greenhouse.
парнико́вый adj. (attrib.) hotbed; hothouse.
парни́шка m. (decl. f.) (colloq.) lad; boy.
парно́й adj. **1.** (of milk) fresh from the cow. **2.** (of meat) freshly slaughtered. **3.** (colloq.) steamy; sultry.
па́рный adj. paired; paired off.
парово́з m. locomotive, engine.
парово́зный adj. (attrib.) locomotive.
пароди́ровать OVA impf. and pf. to parody.
паро́дист m. parodist.
паро́дия f. parody.
парокси́зм m. paroxysm.
паро́ль m. password.
паро́м m. **1.** ferry. **2.** raft.
паро́мный adj. (attrib.) ferry.
паро́мщик m. ferryman.
парообра́зный adj. vaporous.
парообразова́ние neut. vaporization.
парохо́д m. steamship; steamer.
парохо́дный adj. (attrib.) steamship.
парохо́дство neut. steamship line.
па́рочка f. (colloq.) pair; couple.
па́рта f. school desk.
партбиле́т m. Party membership card.
партеногене́з m. parthenogenesis.
парте́р m. (theat.) orchestra.

парти́ец FILL *m. f.* парти́йка (*colloq.*) member of the Communist Party.
партиза́н *m. f.* —ка guerrilla.
партиза́нский *adj.* (*attrib.*) guerrilla.
парти́йность *f.* **1.** membership in the Communist Party. **2.** spirit *or* principle of the Communist Party.
парти́йный *adj.* (Communist) Party.
партиту́ра *f.* (*mus.*) score.
па́ртия *f.* **1.** party. **2.** game, match.
партнёр *m. f.* —ша partner.
парто́рг *m.* (*abbr. of* парти́йный организа́тор *m.*) Party organizer.
па́рус *m.* sail. —ный *adj.* (*attrib.*) **1.** sail. **2.** yacht.
паруси́на *f.* canvas; sailcloth.
паруси́новый *adj.* canvas.
па́русник *m.* **1.** sailboat; sailing vessel. **2.** sailfish. **3.** swallowtail butterfly.
парфюме́р *m.* perfumer.
парфюме́рия *f.* perfumes.
парфюме́рный *adj.* (*attrib.*) perfume.
парча́ *f.* brocade.
парчо́вый *adj.* brocade; brocaded.
парша́ *f.* mange.
парши́вый *adj.* **1.** mangy. **2.** (*colloq.*) lousy; rotten; nasty.
пас *m.* pass (*in cards* or *in sports*).
па́сека *f.* apiary; bee garden.
па́сечник *m.* beekeeper.
па́сквиль *m.* piece of writing that is libelous or slanderous; pasquinade; lampoon.
паску́дный *adj.* (*colloq.*) vile; foul.
паслён *m.* nightshade.
па́смурный *adj.* **1.** cloudy; gloomy; dull. **2.** sullen.
пасова́ть OVA *impf. pf.* с- **1.** (*cards*) to pass. **2.** to retreat (in the face of). **3.** *impf. only* (*sports*) to pass (*the ball*).
па́спорт *m.* passport.
па́спортный *adj.* (*attrib.*) passport.
пасса́ж *m.* arcade.
пассажи́р *m. f.* —ка passenger.
пассажи́рский *adj.* (*attrib.*) passenger.
пасса́т *m.* trade wind.
пасси́в *m.* (*financial*) liabilities.
пасси́вность *f.* passivity.
пасси́вный *adj.* passive.
па́ссия *f.* (*obs.*) passion; flame.
па́ста *f.* paste. — зубна́я па́ста *f.* toothpaste.
па́стбище *neut.* pasture.
па́ства *f.* (*relig.*) parishoners; flock; congregation.
пасте́ль *f.* pastel.
пасте́льный *adj.* pastel.
пастериза́ция *f.* pasteurization.
пастеризова́ть OVA *impf. and pf.* to pasteurize.
пастерна́к *m.* parsnip.
пасти́ *impf. pres.* пасу́, пасёшь; *past* пас, пасла́ **1.** to tend (*flocks*). **2.** to graze; to herd. —сь *v.i.* to graze.
па́стор *m.* pastor; minister.
пастора́ль *f.* pastoral.
пастора́льный *adj.* pastoral.
пасту́х *m. f.* пасту́шка shepherd.
пасту́шеский *adj.* shepherd's.
пасту́ший *adj.* shepherd's.
пастушо́к FILL *m.* **1.** young shepherd. **2.** swain. **3.** rail (*bird*).

па́стырь *m.* (*poet.*) shepherd; pastor.
пасть[1] *f.* (*of animal*) mouth, jaws.
пасть[2] *pf. of* па́дать **1.** to fall. **2.** to fall to action.
пастьба́ *f.* pasturage.
Па́сха *f.* Easter.
па́сынок FILL *m.* stepson.
пасья́нс *m.* (*cards*) solitaire.
пат *m.* (*chess*) stalemate.
пате́нт *m.* patent.
пате́нтный *adj.* (*attrib.*) patent.
патенто́ванный *adj.* (*attrib.*) patent; patented.
патентова́ть OVA *impf. pf.* за- to patent.
патети́ческий *adj.* passionate; impassioned.
патефо́нная пласти́нка *f.* (*obs.*) phonograph record.
па́тио *neut. indecl.* patio.
па́тлы *pl.* (*slang*) locks of hair (*often disheveled*).
па́тока *f.* molasses; treacle.
патологи́ческий *adj.* pathological.
патоло́гия *f.* pathology.
па́точный *adj.* made of molasses.
патриа́рх *m.* patriarch.
патриарха́льный *adj.* patriarchal.
патриарха́т *m.* patriarchy.
патриа́ршество *neut.* patriarchate.
патрио́т *m. f.* —ка patriot.
патриоти́зм *m.* patriotism.
патриоти́ческий *adj.* patriotic.
патри́ций *m.* patrician.
патро́н[1] *m.* patron; boss.
патро́н[2] *m.* **1.** cartridge. **2.** (*mech.*) chuck (*of drill* or *lathe*). **3.** socket (*for lightbulb*).
патро́н[3] *m. also* патро́нка *f.* tailor's pattern.
патро́нник *m.* chamber (*of gun*).
патро́нный *adj.* (*attrib.*) cartridge.
патронта́ш *m.* ammunition belt.
патрули́ровать OVA *impf.* to patrol.
патру́ль *m.* patrol.
патру́льный *adj.* (*attrib.*) patrol.
па́уза *f.* pause.
пау́к *m.* spider.
паути́на *f.* spider web.
па́фос *m.* fervor; zeal.
пах *m.* groin.
па́харь *m.* plowman.
па́хнуть *impf. v.i.* to smell.
пахну́ть *pf. impers.* to blow in.
па́хота *f.* **1.** plowing. **2.** plowed land.
па́хотный *adj.* arable.
па́хта *f.* buttermilk.
па́хтать *impf.* to churn.
паху́честь *f.* strong smell.
паху́чий *adj.* strong-smelling.
пацие́нт *m. f.* —ка patient.
пацифи́зм *m.* pacifism.
пацифи́ст *m. f.* —ка pacifist.
пацифи́стский *adj.* pacifist.
па́чка *f.* **1.** pack; bundle. **2.** batch. **3.** tutu.
па́чкать *impf. pf.* за-, ис- to soil.
пачкотня́ *f.* (*colloq.*) poorly painted picture.
пачку́н *m. f.* —ья (*colloq.*) slovenly person.
паша́ *m.* (*decl. f.*) pasha.
па́шня *f.* plowed land.
паште́т *m.* pâté.
па́юсная икра́ *f.* pressed caviar.
пая́льник *m.* soldering iron.

па́льный *adj.* (*attrib.*) soldering.
па́льщик *m. f.* па́льщица solderer.
па́ние *neut.* soldering.
па́сничать *impf.* (*colloq.*) to clown around.
па́ть *impf.* to solder.
па́яц *m.* clown.
певе́ц FILL *m. f.* певи́ца singer.
певу́н *m. f.* —ья (*colloq.*) person who likes to sing.
певу́честь *f.* melodiousness.
певу́чий *adj.* melodious.
пега́нка *f.* (*bird*) sheldrake; shelduck.
пе́гий *adj.* piebald.
педаго́г *m.* pedagogue; teacher.
педаго́гика *f.* pedagogy.
педагоги́ческий *adj.* pedagogical.
педа́ль *f.* pedal.
педа́нт *m. f.* —ка pedant.
педанти́зм *m.* pedantry.
педанти́чный *adj.* pedantic.
педера́стия *f.* male homosexuality.
педиа́тр *m.* pediatrician.
педиатри́ческий *adj.* pediatric.
педиатри́я *f.* pediatrics.
педикю́р *m.* pedicure, chiropody.
педикю́рша *f.* (*female*) chiropodist.
пейза́ж *m.* **1.** landscape. **2.** landscape painting.
пейзажи́ст *m. f.* —ка landscape painter.
пейза́жный *adj.* (*attrib.*) landscape.
пека́н *m.* pecan.
пе́кари *m. indecl.* peccary.
пека́рный *adj.* (*attrib.*) baking.
пека́рня *f.* bakery.
пе́карский *adj.* baker's.
пе́карь *m.* baker.
пеклева́нный *adj.* (*of flour*) fine; finely ground.
пелена́ *f.* cover; veil.
пелена́ть *impf. pf.* с- *or* за- to diaper; to swaddle.
пеленга́тор *m.* direction finder.
пеленгова́ть OVA *impf. pf.* за- to take a bearing on.
пелёнка *f.* diaper.
пелери́на *f.* cape.
пелика́н *m.* pelican.
пелла́гра *f.* pellagra (*a deficiency disease*).
пельме́ни *pl.* pelmeni (*meat dumplings*).
пе́мза *f.* pumice.
пе́на *f.* **1.** foam. **2.** lather.
пена́л *m.* pencil case.
пенёк FILL *m.* stump (*of tree*).
Пе́нза *f.* Penza.
пе́ние *neut.* singing.
пе́нистый *adj.* foamy.
пеницилли́н *m.* penicillin.
пе́нка *f.* skin (*forming on milk*). — морска́я пе́нка *f.* meerschaum.
пе́нковый *adj.* meerschaum.
пе́нни *m. indecl.* penny.
пе́нный *adj.* foamy.
пенопла́ст *m.* foam plastic.
пенс *m.* penny (*in Great Britain*).
Пенсильва́ния *f.* Pennsylvania.
пенсионе́р *m. f.* —ка pensioner.
пенсио́нный *adj.* (*attrib.*) pension.
пе́нсия *f.* pension.
пенсне́ *neut. indecl.* pince-nez.

пень FILL *m.* stump.
пенька́ *f.* hemp.
пенью́ар *m.* peignoir.
пе́ня *f.* penalty.
пеня́ть *impf. pf.* по- to blame; to reproach.
пе́пел FILL *m.* ashes.
пепели́ще *neut.* site of a fire.
пе́пельница *f.* ashtray.
пе́пельный *adj.* ash-colored.
пепси́н *m.* pepsin.
пепто́н *m.* peptone.
перве́йший *adj.* (*colloq.*) primary.
пе́рвенец FILL *m.* first-born.
пе́рвенство *neut.* **1.** superiority. **2.** championship.
пе́рвенствовать OVA *impf.* to come in first.
перви́чный *adj.* **1.** primary. **2.** initial.
первобы́тный *adj.* primitive.
пе́рвое *neut.* **1.** the first thing. **2.** first course.
первозда́нный *adj.* primeval; primordial.
первоисто́чник *m.* original source.
первокла́ссный *adj.* first-class.
первоку́рсник *m. f.* первоку́рсница freshman.
первома́йский *adj.* (*attrib.*) May-Day.
первонача́льный *adj.* primary; elementary.
первообра́з *m.* prototype.
первоочередно́й *adj.* primary.
перворазря́дный *adj.* first-rate.
перворо́дный *adj.* first-born.
перворо́дство *neut.* primogeniture.
первосвяще́нник *m.* high priest.
первосо́ртный *adj.* of the best quality; first-class.
первостепе́нный *adj.* paramount.
первоцве́т *m.* primrose.
пе́рвый *adj.* first.
перга́мент *m.* parchment.
перебази́ровать OVA *pf.* to relocate.
перебега́ть *impf. pf.* перебежа́ть (через *with acc.*) to run across, to cross.
перебе́жка *f.* **1.** run; rush. **2.** defection. **3.** (*sports*) running.
перебе́жчик *m. f.* перебе́жчица defector.
перебинтова́ть OVA *pf.* to rebandage.
перебира́ть *impf. pf.* перебра́ть **1.** to sort out. **2.** to go through. **3.** to run one's fingers over. **4.** (*printing*) to reset.
перебо́й *m.* **1.** interruption. **2.** irregularity.
перебо́рка *f.* **1.** sorting out. **2.** partition. **3.** bulkhead (*on a ship*).
перебра́нка *f.* (*colloq.*) hassle; squabble.
перебро́ска *f.* transfer.
перева́л *m.* mountain pass.
перева́ривать *impf. pf.* перевари́ть **1.** to recook. **2.** to overcook. **3.** to digest. **4.** (*colloq.*) to stomach something; to put up with something.
перевёртывание *neut.* inversion.
перевёртывать *impf. pf.* переверну́ть to turn over; to overturn.
переве́с *m.* preponderance, predominance.
перево́д *m.* **1.** transfer, transference. **2.** translation. —чик *m. f.* —чица translator, interpreter.
переводи́ть *impf. pf.* перевести́ **1.** to transfer. **2.** to translate.
переводно́й *adj.* of a money order.
перево́дческий *adj.* of translating; of a translator.
перево́з *m.* transportation.

перевози́ть *impf. pf.* **перевезти́** to transport (across).

перево́зка *f.* transportation.

перево́зочные сре́дства *pl.* means of conveyance.

перево́зчик *m.* ferryman.

перевооруже́ние *neut.* rearmament.

перевоплоще́ние *neut.* reincarnation.

переворо́т *m.* revolution; upheaval.

перевоспита́ние *neut.* re-education.

перевыполне́ние *neut.* overfulfillment.

перевя́зка *f.* bandage, dressing.

перевя́зочный *adj.* for the dressing of wounds.

перевя́зывать *impf. pf.* **перевяза́ть** 1. to tie, to tie up. 2. to bandage, to dress.

пе́ревязь *f.* sling.

переги́б *m.* (*fig.*) excess; extreme.

перегласо́вка *f.* (*phon.*) mutation.

перегля́дываться *impf. pf.* **перегляну́ться** to exchange glances.

перегно́й *m.* humus.

переговоры *pl.* 1. negotiations. 2. talks.

перего́н *m.* 1. driving. 2. space between two railroad stations.

перего́нка *f.* distillation.

перего́нный *adj.* for distilling.

перегоро́дка *f.* partition.

перегре́в *m.* overheating.

перегружа́ть *impf. pf.* **перегрузи́ть** 1. to load from one place to another. 2. to overburden; to overload.

перегру́зка *f.* 1. transfer of cargo. 2. overloading.

перегру́зочный *adj.* (*attrib.*) transfer.

перегруппиро́вка *f.* regrouping.

перегрыза́ть *impf. pf.* **перегры́зть** to bite through.

пе́ред *also* **пе́редо** *prep.* (*with instr.*) before; in front of.

перёд *m.* front.

передава́ть *impf. pf.* **переда́ть** 1. to pass, to hand. 2. to transmit. 3. to broadcast. 4. to communicate, to tell.

переда́тчик *m.* transmitter.

переда́ча *f.* 1. transmission. 2. transfer. 3. broadcast.

передвиже́ние *neut.* movement; transportation.

передвижно́й *adj.* 1. movable. 2. mobile; traveling.

переде́л *m.* redistribution.

переде́лка *f.* alteration.

передёргивать *impf. pf.* **передёрнуть** 1. to pull; to jerk on; to tug on. 2. (*colloq.*) to cheat (*with cards* or *with facts*). 3. *impers.* to wince.

переде́ржка *f.* (*photog.*) overexposure.

пере́дний *adj.* front.

пере́дник *m.* apron.

пере́дняя *f.* vestibule; entry hall.

передови́ца *f. also* **передова́я статья́** *f.* editorial, leading article.

передово́й *adj.* 1. advanced. 2. front.

передо́к FILL *m.* front (*of vehicle*).

передо́хнуть *pf. past* **передо́х, передо́хла** to die off (*usually of animals*).

передохну́ть *pf.* 1. to take a breath. 2. (*colloq.*) to take a breather; to take a short rest.

передря́га *f.* (*colloq.*) scrape; row.

переду́мывать *impf. pf.* **переду́мать** to change one's mind.

переды́шка *f.* respite; rest.

перее́зд *m.* 1. passage. 2. crossing. 3. move, moving.

переезжа́ть *impf. pf.* **перее́хать** 1. to cross, to cross over. 2. to move.

пережива́ние *neut.* experience. — **пережива́ния** *pl.* tribulations.

пережива́ть *pf.* **пережи́ть** 1. to experience, to live through. 2. to endure.

пережи́тое *neut.* past experiences.

пережи́ток FILL *m.* 1. vestige, remnant. 2. survival.

перезво́н *m.* ringing of bells.

перезимова́ть OVA *pf.* to winter; to spend the winter.

перезре́лый *adj.* overripe.

переизбра́ние *neut.* reelection.

переиздава́ть *impf. pf.* **переизда́ть** to republish; to reissue.

переизда́ние *neut.* republication.

переименова́ть OVA *pf.* to rename.

переймчивый *adj.* (*colloq.*) imitative.

перейти́ *pf. of* **переходи́ть**.

перека́т[1] *m. usu.* **перека́ты** *pl.* clap (*of thunder*); crack (*of shots*).

перека́т[2] *m.* shoal; sandbank.

переквалифика́ция *f.* retraining.

переквалифици́ровать *impf. and pf.* to retrain.

пе́рекись *f.* peroxide.

перекла́дина *f.* 1. crossbar; crossbeam. 2. (*sports*) horizontal bar.

перекла́дывать *impf. pf.* **переложи́ть** 1. to lay *or* place in a different place. 2. to transfer. 3. (*with instr.*) to interlay. 4. to shift.

перекли́чка *f.* roll call.

переключа́тель *m.* switch (*e.g. light switch*).

переключе́ние *neut.* switch; switching over.

перекошенный *adj.* twisted out of shape.

перекрёсток FILL *m.* crossing, crossroad.

переку́р *m.* (*colloq.*) smoke break.

переле́сок FILL *m.* coppice; copse.

перелёт *m.* 1. flight. 2. (*of birds*) migration.

перелета́ть *impf. pf.* **перелете́ть** to fly over *or* across.

перелётный *adj.* (*of bird*) migratory.

перели́в *m.* 1. flowing. 2. **перели́вы** *pl.* play of colors.

перелива́ние *neut.* 1. pouring (*from one container into another*). 2. transfusion.

перели́вчатый *adj.* (*of colors*) iridescent.

перели́стывать *impf. pf.* **перелиста́ть** to leaf through.

перелицева́ть *pf. of* **перелицо́вывать**.

перелицо́вывать *impf.* to alter by turning inside out.

переложе́ние *neut.* (*mus.*) arrangement; transposition.

переложи́ть *pf. of* **перекла́дывать**.

перело́м *m.* 1. fracture. 2. crisis.

перело́мный *adj.* crucial; critical.

перемежа́ющийся *adj.* intermittent.

переме́на *f.* 1. change. 2. recess, interval.

перемени́ть *pf.* to change.

переме́нный *adj.* variable; alternating.

перемеще́ние *neut.* shift; movement.

перемещённые ли́ца *pl.* displaced persons.

переми́рие *neut.* truce; armistice.

перемы́чка *f.* crosspiece.

перенапряже́ние *neut.* overexertion.
перенаселе́ние *neut.* overpopulation.
перенаселённость *f.* overpopulation.
перенаселённый *adj.* overpopulated.
перенесе́ние *neut.* moving; transferring.
перенима́ть *impf. pf.* переня́ть **1.** to adopt. **2.** to imitate.
перено́с *m.* moving; transferring.
переноси́ть *impf. pf.* перенести́ **1.** to transfer. **2.** to carry over. **3.** to endure.
перено́сица *f.* bridge of the nose.
переночева́ть *pf. of* ночева́ть.
переоборудование *neut.* re-equipping.
переоце́нка *f.* **1.** reappraisal. **2.** overestimation.
перепада́ть *impf. pf.* перепа́сть **1.** (*of rain or snow*) to fall intermittently. **2.** (*with dat.*) (*colloq.*) to come one's way.
перепа́лка *f.* (*colloq.*) exchange of gunfire.
перепе́в *m.* repetition; rehash.
пе́репел *m.* quail.
перепёлка *f.* female quail.
перепеля́тник *m.* sparrow hawk.
перепеча́тка *f.* reprinting; reprint.
перепи́ска *f.* correspondence.
перепи́счик *m. f.* перепи́счица copier; copyist.
перепи́сываться *impf.* (с *with instr.*) to correspond with.
пе́репись *f.* census.
перепла́та *f.* (*colloq.*) overpayment.
переплёт *m.* **1.** binding (*of a book*); bookcover. **2.** window sash. **3.** caning (*of a chair*). **4.** (*colloq.*) mess; scrape; trouble.
переплете́ние *neut.* interlacing; interweaving.
переплётная *f.* bindery.
переплётный *adj.* (*attrib.*) bookbinding.
переплётчик *m. f.* переплётчица bookbinder.
переполо́х *m.* **1.** panic. **2.** turmoil; confusion; commotion.
перепо́нка *f.* **1.** membrane. **2.** (*zool.*) web.
перепо́нчатый *adj.* (*zool.*) webbed.
перепра́ва *f.* crossing (*of a river*).
перепре́лый *adj.* rotten.
перепроизво́дство *neut.* overproduction.
перепу́г *m.* (*colloq.*) fright.
перепуга́ть *pf.* to frighten; to terrify.
перепу́тье *neut.* crossroads.
перерабо́тка *f.* **1.** processing. **2.** refining. **3.** reworking; revision. **4.** overtime work.
перераспределе́ние *neut.* redistribution.
перераста́ние *neut.* outgrowing.
перерожде́ние *neut.* regeneration.
переро́сток FILL *m.* youngster who is slow to develop.
переры́в *m.* recess; break.
переса́дка *f.* **1.** change (*of bus, plane etc.*). **2.** transplantation.
переса́живать *impf. pf.* пересади́ть **1.** to transplant. **2.** to move somebody to another seat.
переса́живаться *impf. pf.* пересе́сть **1.** to move to another seat. **2.** to change (*trains, planes etc.*).
переселе́нец FILL *m. f.* переселе́нка migrant.
переселе́ние *neut.* migration.
пересече́ние *neut.* crossing; intersection.
пересечённый *adj.* (*of terrain*) rough, broken.
переска́з *m.* retelling.
пересме́шник *m.* mockingbird.

пересмо́тр *m.* **1.** review. **2.** revision. **3.** reconsideration.
пересо́л *m.* excess of salt.
переспа́ть *pf. conjugated like* спать (*colloq.*) **1.** to oversleep. **2.** to spend the night. **3.** (*euphemism*) to sleep with.
переспе́лый *adj.* overripe.
переставать *impf. pf.* переста́ть to stop, to cease.
перестано́вка *f.* **1.** rearrangement. **2.** (*math.*) permutation.
перестра́ивать *impf. pf.* перестро́ить **1.** to rebuild. **2.** to reorganize.
перестрахо́вка *f.* reinsurance.
перестрахо́вщик *m. f.* перестрахо́вщица (*colloq.*) person who takes extra precautions.
перестре́лка *f.* exchange of gunfire.
перестро́йка *f.* **1.** rebuilding. **2.** reorganization.
пересу́д *m. usu.* пересу́ды *pl.* (*colloq.*) gossip.
пересчёт *m.* recount; recounting.
пересыла́ть *impf. pf.* пересла́ть **1.** to send. **2.** to forward by mail. **3.** to remit.
пересы́лка *f.* sending; forwarding.
перетасо́вка *f.* reshuffle; shuffling.
переу́лок FILL *m.* side street; lane, alley.
переустро́йство *neut.* reconstruction.
переутомле́ние *neut.* **1.** overwork. **2.** overtiredness; exhaustion; fatigue.
переучёт *m.* inventory; stock-taking.
перефразиро́вка *f.* paraphrase.
перехва́т *m.* (*colloq.*) interception.
перехва́тчик *m.* **1.** person who intercepts something. **2.** interceptor (*military aircraft*).
перехо́д *m.* crossing; passage.
переходи́ть *impf. pf.* перейти́ **1.** to cross. **2.** (в *with acc.*) to turn into.
перехо́дный *adj.* **1.** transitional. **2.** (*gram.*) transitive.
переходя́щий *adj.* transitory.
пе́рец FILL *m.* pepper.
пе́речень FILL *m.* list, listing.
перечёркивать *impf. pf.* перечеркну́ть to cross out.
перечисле́ние *neut.* enumeration.
переч́ить *impf.* (*with dat.*) (*colloq.*) to contradict.
пе́речница *f.* pepper shaker, peppermill.
пе́речный *adj.* (*attrib.*) pepper.
переше́ек FILL *m.* isthmus.
переэкзамено́вка *f.* repeat examination (*for those who have failed*).
периге́й *m.* perigee.
периге́лий *m.* perihelion.
пери́ла *pl.* banister; railing.
пери́метр *m.* perimeter.
пери́на *f.* feather bed.
пери́од *m.* period.
перио́дика *f.* periodicals.
периоди́чески *adv.* periodically.
периоди́ческий *also* периоди́чный *adj.* periodic.
перипети́я *f. usu.* перипети́и *pl.* vicissitudes.
периско́п *m.* periscope.
периста́льтика *f.* peristalsis.
перистальти́ческий *adj.* peristaltic.
перисти́ль *m.* peristyle.
пери́стый *adj.* feathered.
перитони́т *m.* peritonitis.
перифери́йный *adj.* provincial.
перифери́ческий *adj.* peripheral.

перифери́я *f.* periphery.
перифра́за *f.* periphrasis.
пёрка *f.* drill bit.
перка́ль *m.* or *f.* (*textiles*) percale.
перл *m.* (*obs.*) pearl.
перламу́тр *m.* mother-of-pearl.
перламу́тровый *adj.* (*attrib.*) mother-of-pearl.
пе́рлинь *m.* hawser.
перло́вая крупа́ *f.* pearl barley.
перлюстра́ция *f.* secret opening of mail.
пермане́нт *m.* permanent wave.
пермане́нтный *adj.* permanent.
Пермь *f.* Perm.
перна́тый *adj.* feathered.
перо́[1] *neut.* feather, plume.
перо́[2] *neut.* pen.
перочи́нный но́жик *m.* penknife.
перпендикуля́р *m.* perpendicular.
перпендикуля́рный *adj.* perpendicular.
перро́н *m.* platform (*in a railroad station*).
перс *m. f.* **—ия́нка** Persian.
пе́рсик *m.* peach.
пе́рсиковый *adj.* (*attrib.*) peach.
персо́на *f.* person.
персона́ж *m.* personage; character.
персона́л *m.* personnel.
персона́льный *adj.* personal.
персона́льный код *m.* personal identification number (*abbr.* P.I.N.).
персона́льный компьютер *m.* personal computer. (*abbr.* P.C.).
перспекти́ва *adj.* perspective.
перспекти́вный *adj.* **1.** perspective. **2.** having good prospects; promising.
перст *m.* (*obs.*) finger.
пе́рстень FILL *m.* ring set with a stone.
пертурба́ция *f.* (*astr.*, *fig.*) perturbation.
Перу́ *m.* Peru.
Перу́джа *f.* Perugia.
перфе́кт *m.* (*gram.*) perfect.
перфока́рта *f.* punch card.
перфора́тор *m.* perforator.
перфора́ция *f.* perforation.
перфори́ровать OVA *impf.* and *pf.* to perforate.
перхо́та *f.* (*colloq.*) desire to cough; tickling sensation in the throat.
пе́рхоть *f.* dandruff.
перцо́вка *f.* pepper brandy.
перцо́вый *adj.* (*attrib.*) pepper.
перча́тка *f.* glove.
перши́ть *impf.* (*impers.*) (*colloq.*) to have a tickling feeling in one's throat.
пёрышко *neut. dim. of* **перо́.**
пёс FILL *m.* dog.
пе́сенка *f. dim. of* **пе́сня.**
пе́сенник[1] *m.* songwriter.
пе́сенник[2] *m.* songbook.
песе́та *f.* peseta (*monetary unit of Spain*).
песе́ц FILL *m.* polar fox.
песка́рь FILL *m.* gudgeon.
песнопе́ние *neut.* religious song; hymn; chant.
пе́сня *f.* song.
пе́со *neut. indecl.* peso (*monetary unit of several Latin American countries*).
песо́к FILL *m.* sand.
песо́чник *m.* sandpiper.

песо́чница *f.* sandbox.
песо́чный *adj.* (*attrib.*) sand.
пессими́ст *m. f.* **—ка** pessimist.
пессимисти́ческий *adj.* pessimistic.
пест *m.* pestle.
пе́стик *m. dim. of* **пест.**
пе́стовать OVA *impf. pf.* **вы-** **1.** (*obs.*) to nurse; to nurture. **2.** to cherish; to foster.
пестрота́ *f.* diversity of colors.
пёстрый *adj.* **1.** multicolored. **2.** mixed; motley; diverse. **3.** heterogenious.
песча́ник *m.* sandstone.
песча́нка *f.* **1.** gerbil. **2.** sanderling.
песча́ный *adj.* (*attrib.*) sand.
песча́ный вездехо́д *m.* beach buggy, dune buggy.
песчи́нка *f.* grain of sand.
пета́рда *f.* **1.** petard. **2.** firecracker.
пе́телька *f. dim. of* **пе́тля.**
петли́ца *f.* **1.** buttonhole. **2.** colored stripe *or* patch (*on a uniform*).
пе́тля *f.* loop; noose.
Петрозаво́дск *m.* Petrozavodsk.
Петропа́вловск *m.* Petropavl (*Russian: Petropavlovsk*).
петру́шка *f.* parsley.
пету́ния *f.* petunia.
пету́х *m.* rooster.
пету́ший *adj.* (*attrib.*) rooster; rooster's.
петуши́ный *adj.* (*attrib.*) rooster; rooster's.
петушо́к FILL *m.* cockerel.
петь *impf.* **1.** to sing. **2.** to crow.
пехо́та *f.* infantry. — **морска́я пехо́та** *f.* the marines.
пехоти́нец FILL *m.* infantryman.
пехо́тный *adj.* infantry.
печа́лить *impf. pf.* **о-** *v.t.* to grieve.
печа́ль *f.* sorrow, grief. **—ный** *adj.* sad.
печа́льно *adv.* sadly.
печа́тание *neut.* printing.
печа́тать *impf. pf.* **на-** **1.** to print. **2.** to type.
печа́тка *f.* signet.
печа́тник *m.* printer.
печа́тный *adj.* (*attrib.*) printing; printed.
печа́ть *f.* **1.** seal. **2.** press; print, printing.
пече́ние *neut.* baking.
печёнка *f.* liver (*as food*).
печёночник *m.* liverwort.
печёночница *f.* hepatica.
печёный *adj.* baked.
пе́чень *f.* (*anat.*) liver.
пече́нье *neut.* pastry; cookies.
пе́чка *f.* stove.
печно́й *adj.* (*attrib.*) stove.
печу́рка *f.* small stove.
печь[1] *f.* **1.** stove; oven. **2.** furnace.
печь[2] *impf. pf.* **ис-** to bake.
пешехо́д *m.* pedestrian.
пе́ший *adj.* traveling on foot.
пе́шка *f.* (*chess*) pawn.
пешко́м *adv.* on foot.
пеще́ра *f.* cave.
пеще́рный *adj.* (*attrib.*) cave.
пиани́но *neut. indecl.* upright piano.
пиани́ссимо *adv.* and *neut. indecl.* (*mus.*) pianissimo.
пиани́ст *m. f.* **—ка** pianist.

пиа́но *adv.* (*mus.*) piano; soft.

пиано́ла *f.* player piano.

пиа́стр *m.* piaster (*monetary unit of several Middle Eastern countries*).

пивна́я *f.* tavern; pub; bar.

пивно́й *adj.* (*attrib.*) beer.

пи́во *neut.* beer.

пивова́р *m.* brewer.

пивоваре́ние *neut.* brewing.

пивова́ренный *adj.* (*attrib.*) brewing.

пи́галица *f.* lapwing; pewit.

пигме́й *m.* pygmy.

пигме́нт *m.* pigment.

пигмента́ция *f.* pigmentation.

пиджа́к *m.* man's suit jacket; coat.

пижа́ма *f.* pajamas.

пижо́н *m.* (*slang*) fop; dandy.

Пи́за *f.* Pisa.

пик *m.* **1.** peak (*of a mountain*). **2.** peak (*of work or of traffic*). — час пик *m.* rush hour.

пи́ка *f.* lance, pike.

пика́нтность *f.* piquancy.

пика́нтный *adj.* **1.** spicy. **2.** pungent.

пика́п *m.* pickup truck.

пике́ *neut. indecl.* piqué.

пике́йный *adj.* piqué.

пике́т *m.* picket line.

пикети́ровать OVA *impf.* to picket.

пике́тчик *m. f.* пике́тчица picket (*person who pickets*).

пи́ки *pl.* (*cards*) spades.

пики́рование *neut.* (*aero.*) dive; diving.

пики́ровать OVA *impf. and pf.* (*of an airplane*) to go into a dive.

пики́роваться OVA *impf.* to bicker; to squabble.

пики́ровка *f.* bickering; squabbling.

пики́ровщик *m.* dive bomber.

пики́рующий бомбарди́ровщик *m.* dive bomber.

пи́кколо *neut. indecl.* piccolo.

пикни́к *m.* picnic.

пи́кнуть *pf.* (*colloq.*) **1.** to let out a squeak. **2.** to make a sound (of protest).

пи́ковый *adj.* **1.** (*cards*) of spades. **2.** awkward.

пиктогра́мма *f.* pictograph.

пи́кули *pl.* pickles.

пи́кша *f.* haddock.

пила́ *f.* saw.

пила́в *m.* pilaf.

пила́-ры́ба *f.* sawfish.

пилёный *adj.* sawed.

пили́грим *m. f.* —ка pilgrim.

пили́ть *impf.* **1.** to saw. **2.** (*fig.*) to nag.

пи́лка *f.* sawing.

пило́н *m.* pylon.

пило́т *m.* pilot.

пилота́ж *m.* piloting; flying.

пилоти́ровать OVA *impf.* to pilot.

пило́тка *f.* (*colloq.*) (*mil.*) overseas cap.

пи́льщик *m.* sawyer; woodcutter.

пилю́ля *f.* pill.

пиля́стра *f.* pilaster.

пина́ть *impf. pf.* пнуть (*colloq.*) to kick.

пингви́н *m.* penguin.

пинг-по́нг *m.* ping-pong.

пи́ния *f.* stone pine.

пино́к FILL *m.* (*colloq.*) kick.

пи́нта *f.* pint.

пинце́т *m.* tweezers.

пио́н *m.* peony.

пионе́р *m. f.* —ка pioneer.

пиоре́я *f.* pyorrhea.

пипе́тка *f.* eye dropper.

пир *m.* banquet; feast.

пирами́да *f.* pyramid.

пирами́дальный *adj.* pyramidal.

пира́т *m.* pirate.

пира́тский *adj.* (*attrib.*) pirate.

пира́тство *neut.* piracy.

Пирене́и *pl.* (*mountains*) Pyrenees.

пири́т *m.* pyrite.

пирова́ть OVA *impf.* to feast.

пиро́г *m.* pie.

пиро́жное *neut.* pastry.

пирожо́к FILL *m.* small pie; patty.

пирома́ния *f.* pyromania.

пироте́хника *f.* pyrotechnics.

пирс *m.* pier.

пиру́шка *f.* (*colloq.*) lively party.

пируэ́т *m.* pirouette.

пи́ршество *neut.* (*obs.*) sumptuous feast.

писа́ка *m. and f.* (*decl. f.*) poor writer.

писа́ние *neut.* writing. — Свяще́нное Писа́ние *neut.* Holy Scripture.

пи́саный *adj.* handwritten.

пи́сарь *m.* clerk.

писа́тель *m. f.* —ница writer.

писа́тельский *adj.* (*attrib.*) writer; writer's.

писа́тельство *neut.* (*colloq.*) writing.

писа́ть *impf. pf.* на- to write; to paint. — писа́ть кра́сками to paint.

писе́ц FILL *m.* scribe.

писк *m.* peep; cheep.

пискли́вый *adj.* squeaky.

писсуа́р *m.* urinal.

пистоле́т *m.* pistol.

пистоле́тный *adj.* (*attrib.*) pistol.

писто́н *m.* **1.** percussion cap. **2.** (*mus.*) piston.

пису́лька *f.* (*colloq.*) note; short letter.

писчебума́жный *adj.* (*attrib.*) stationery.

пи́счий *adj.* (*attrib.*) writing.

письмена́ *pl.* characters; letters.

пи́сьменно *adv.* in writing.

пи́сьменность *f.* **1.** written language. **2.** system of writing. **3.** literature. **4.** literary texts.

пи́сьменный *adj.* (*attrib.*) writing.

письмо́ *neut.* letter.

письмоно́сец FILL *m.* (*obs.*) mailman.

пита́ние *neut.* feeding.

пита́тельный *adj.* nourishing.

пита́ть *impf.* to feed; to nourish.

пито́мец FILL *m. f.* пито́мица **1.** pupil. **2.** ward. **3.** graduate; alumnus.

пито́мник *m.* **1.** plant nursery. **2.** farm (*for raising animals*).

пито́н *m.* python.

пить *impf. pf.* вы- to drink. —пить до дна to drink to the bottom of one's glass.

питьё *neut.* drink; drinking.

питьево́й *adj.* (*attrib.*) drinking.

пифаго́ров *adj.* Pythagorean.

пиха́ть *impf. pf.* пи́хнуть (*colloq.*) **1.** to push; to shove. **2.** to shove into; to cram into.

пи́хта *f.* fir.

пиццика́то *adv. and neut. indecl.* (*mus.*) pizzicato.

пичу́жка *f.* (*colloq.*) small bird.

пи́шущая маши́нка *f.* typewriter.

пи́ща *f.* food.

пища́ль *f.* arquebus; harquebus.

пища́ть *impf. pres.* пищу́, пищи́шь *pf.* пи́скнуть to peep; to cheep.

пищваре́ние *neut.* digestion.

пищу́ха *f.* **1.** (*animal*) pika. **2.** (*bird*) creeper.

пия́вка *f.* leech.

пла́вание *neut.* **1.** swimming. **2.** navigation.

пла́вать *impf. indet. det.* плыть **1.** to swim. **2.** to float. **3.** to sail.

пла́вень FILL *m.* flux (*in soldering*).

плавико́вая кислота́ *f.* hydrofluoric acid.

пла́вить *impf.* to melt; to smelt.

пла́вки *pl.* swimming trunks.

плавни́к[1] *m.* fin (*of a fish*).

плавни́к[2] *m.* driftwood.

пла́вный *adj.* **1.** fluent. **2.** smooth.

плаву́нчик *m.* (*bird*) phalarope.

плаву́честь *f.* buoyancy.

плагиа́т *m.* plagiarism.

плака́т *m.* poster, placard.

пла́кать *impf.* to cry; to weep.

пла́кса *m. and f.* (*decl. f.*) (*colloq.*) crybaby.

плаку́чий *adj.* **1.** (*obs.*) whining. **2.** (*of trees*) weeping. — плаку́чая и́ва *f.* weeping willow.

пла́мя *neut. pl.* пла́мени flame; blaze.

план *m.* plan. — уче́бный план *m.* curriculum.

пла́нер *m.* (*aero.*) glider.

плане́та *f.* planet.

планиме́трия *f.* plane geometry.

плани́ровать[1] OVA *impf. pf.* за- to plan.

плани́ровать[2] *impf. pf.* с- (*aero.*) to glide.

планирова́ть *impf. pf.* рас- to lay out.

пла́новый *adj.* planned.

планше́т *m.* map case.

планши́р *m.* gunwale.

пласт *m.* layer; stratum. — лежа́ть пласто́м to be flat on one's back.

пласти́нка *f.* **1.** phonograph record. **2.** metal plate. **3.** photographic plate.

пла́стырь *m.* plaster (*applied to a wound*).

пла́та *f.* payment; fee; fare.

плата́н *m.* plane tree.

платёж *m.* payment.

пла́тина *f.* platinum.

плати́ть *impf. pf.* за- to pay.

пла́тный *adj.* **1.** paying. **2.** paid. **3.** requiring payment.

плато́к FILL *m.* shawl. — носово́й плато́к *m.* handkerchief.

пла́тье *neut.* **1.** dress. **2.** (*coll.*) clothes, clothing.

Пла́уен *m.* Plauen.

пла́ха *f.* **1.** block; log. **2.** execution block.

плац *m.* parade ground.

плацда́рм *m.* **1.** beachhead. **2.** springboard.

плацка́рта *f.* reserved seat coupon (*for train*).

плач *m.* weeping.

плашмя́ *adv.* flat.

плащ *m.* cloak; raincoat.

плева́ *f.* membrane; film.

плева́ть *impf. pf.* плю́нуть to spit.

пле́вел *m.* **1.** darnel. **2.** weed.

плево́к FILL *m.* spit; spittle; sputum.

плед *m.* rug; plaid.

плектр *m.* plectrum.

пле́мя *neut. pl.* племена́ tribe.

племя́нник *m.* nephew.

племя́нница *f.* niece.

плен *m.* captivity.

плена́рный *adj.* plenary.

плени́тельный *adj.* captivating; enchanting.

плёнка *f.* **1.** film. **2.** tape.

пле́нник *m. f.* пле́нница prisoner; captive.

плени́ть *impf. pf.* плени́ть to fascinate; to captivate.

пле́сень *f.* mold.

плеск *m.* splash.

плеска́ть *impf. pf.* плесну́ть to splash.

плете́ние *neut.* **1.** weaving. **2.** wickerwork.

плете́нь FILL *m.* wattle fence.

плётка *f.* lash.

плеть *f.* lash.

плечо́ *neut.* shoulder.

плешь *f.* bald spot.

плея́да *f.* brilliant group of people. — Плея́ды *pl.* Pleiades.

пли́нтус *m.* plinth.

плита́ *f.* **1.** plate, slab. **2.** stove; cooker.

пли́тка *f.* **1.** thin slab; tile. **2.** bar (of choclate). **3.** small stove.

плитня́к *m.* flagstone.

плов *m.* pilaf.

пловец FILL *m. f.* пловчи́ха swimmer.

плод *m.* **1.** fruit. **2.** fetus.

плодови́тый *adj.* fruitful; prolific.

плодоно́сный *adj.* fruit-bearing.

плодоро́дный *adj.* fertile.

плодотво́рный *adj.* fruitful.

пло́мба *f.* (*dental*) filling.

пломби́р *m.* ice cream topped with fruit.

пло́ский *adj.* flat.

плоскогу́бцы *pl.* pliers.

плоскосто́пие *neut.* flatfoot; fallen arches.

пло́скость *f.* flatness; platitude.

плот *m.* raft.

плотва́ *f.* (*fish*) roach.

плоти́на *f.* dam.

пло́тник *m.* carpenter.

пло́тно *adv.* **1.** tightly. **2.** densely.

пло́тность *f.* density.

пло́тный *adj.* dense.

плотоя́дный *adj.* carnivorous.

плоть *f.* flesh.

пло́хо *adv.* badly.

плохо́й *adj.* bad; inferior.

плоша́ть *impf. pf.* о- (*usually used negatively*) (*colloq.*) to make a mistake.

площа́дка *f.* **1.** ground; site. **2.** (*sports*) court. **3.** landing (*of a staircase*).

пло́щадь *f.* **1.** area. **2.** square.

плуг *m.* plow.

плут *m. f.* плуто́вка cheat, swindler.

плу́тни *pl.* (*colloq.*) tricks.

плыть *impf. det. of* пла́вать.

Пльзень *f.* Pilsen (*Czech: Plzeň*).

плюга́вый *adj.* (*colloq.*) **1.** ugly; miserable-looking. **2.** trivial.

плю́нуть *pf. of* плева́ть.

плюс *m.* plus; advantage.
плюшка *f.* bun.
плющ *m.* ivy.
пляж *m.* beach.
плясать *impf. pf.* c- to dance.
пляска *f.* dance.
По *f. indecl.* (*river*) Po.
по *prep.* **1.** (*with dat.*) on, along; according to; over. **2.** (*with acc.*) to, up to; (*with time expressions*) through. **3.** (*with prep.*) upon; after.
по-английски *adv.* in English.
побаиваться *impf.* (*colloq.*) to be somewhat fearful.
побаливать *impf.* (*colloq.*) to ache now and then.
побег¹ *m.* escape.
побег² *m.* (*bot.*) sprout; shoot.
победа *f.* victory.
победитель *m. f.* —ница victor; winner.
побежать *pf. of* бежать.
побеждать *impf. pf.* победить to conquer; to be victorious.
побелеть *pf. of* белеть.
побережье *neut.* shore, coast.
побледнеть *pf.* to turn pale.
поблизости *adv.* nearby.
побои *pl.* beating.
побоище *neut.* massacre; slaughter.
побольше *adj.* a little larger. — *adv.* a little more.
побочный *adj.* **1.** accessory. **2.** secondary; collateral.
по-братски *adv.* fraternally; in a brotherly fashion.
побудка *f.* reveille.
побуждать *impf. pf.* побудить **1.** to impel. **2.** to induce. **3.** to prompt.
побывать *pf.* **1.** to visit (*a place*). **2.** to visit (*a person*).
побыть *pf.* to stay some time; to spend some time.
повадка *f.* habit; mannerism. — повадки *pl.* manner; ways.
повалить *pf. of* валить.
повальный *adj.* **1.** general, mass. **2.** epidemic.
повар *m. f.* повариха cook.
поваренный *adj.* culinary.
по-вашему *adv.* in your opinion; (according to) your way.
поведать *pf.* **1.** to announce. **2.** to reveal; to disclose.
поведение *neut.* behavior; conduct.
повезти *pf. of* везти.
повеление *neut.* command.
повелитель *m. f.* —ница **1.** sovereign; ruler. **2.** (*colloq.*) lord; master.
повелительный *adj.* **1.** imperative, authoritative. **2.** (*gram.*) imperative.
повенчать *pf. of* венчать.
поверенный *m.* **1.** attorney. **2.** confidant.
поверить *pf. of* верить.
поверка *f.* **1.** checkup; verification. **2.** roll call.
повернуть *pf. of* поворачивать.
поверх *prep.* (*with gen.*) above, over. —ностный *adj.* superficial. —ность *f.* surface.
поверять *impf. pf.* поверить to believe; to confide; to verify, to check.
повеса *m.* (*decl. f.*) playboy.
повесить(ся) *pf. of* вешать(ся).
повествование *neut.* narration; narrative.

повести *pf. of* вести.
повестка *f.* **1.** notice. **2.** summons.
повесть *f.* story; tale; narrrative.
по-видимому *adv.* apparently.
повидло *neut.* jam.
повинность *f.* duty.
повиноваться OVA *impf.* and *pf.* (*with dat.*) to obey.
повиновение *neut.* obedience.
повлиять *pf. of* влиять.
повод¹ *m.* occasion, reason.
повод² *m.* bridle, rein.
поводок FILL *m.* leash.
повозка *f.* wagon.
повойник *m.* povoynik (*kerchief worn on the head by married peasant women*).
поворачивать *impf. pf.* повернуть to turn; to change.
поворот *m.* **1.** turn. **2.** turning point; change.
поворотливый *adj.* **1.** nimble; agile. **2.** maneuverable.
поворотный *adj.* **1.** turning. **2.** rotary; (*attrib.*) swivel. **3.** decisive.
повредить *pf. of* вредить, повреждать.
повреждать *impf. pf.* повредить **1.** to damage. **2.** to harm, to hurt.
повседневный *adj.* daily, everyday.
повстанец FILL *m.* rebel; insurgent.
повсюду *adv.* everywhere.
повторение *neut.* repetition.
повторительный *adj.* repeated, recapitulative.
повторять *impf. pf.* повторить to repeat.
повышать *impf. pf.* повысить to raise, to increase.
повязка *f.* bandage.
погадать *pf. of* гадать.
поганить *impf.* (*colloq.*) **1.** to soil; to get dirty. **2.** to defile.
поганка *f.* **1.** toadstool. **2.** (*bird*) grebe.
поганый *adj.* **1.** (*of food*) inedible. **2.** (*colloq.*) foul; vile.
погасить *pf. of* гасить.
погибать *impf. pf.* погибнуть to perish.
погибший *adj.* fallen, perished; lost.
погладить *pf. of* гладить.
поглощать *impf. pf.* поглотить to absorb; to swallow up.
поглощение *neut.* absorption.
поглумиться *pf. of* глумиться.
поглядеть *pf. of* глядеть.
поговорка *f.* proverb; saying.
погода *f.* weather.
погодить *pf.* (*colloq.*) to wait a while. — немного погодя *adv.* a little while later.
поголовный *adj.* general; total. — поголовно *adv.* to a man.
погон *m.* (*mil.*) shoulder strap.
погост *m.* village cemetery.
пограничный *adj.* (*attrib.*) border, frontier.
погреб *m.* cellar.
погребальный *adj.* (*attrib.*) funeral.
погребение *neut.* burial, internment.
погром *m.* pogrom; massacre.
погружать *impf. pf.* погрузить to immerse.
погрузка *f.* loading.
погубить *pf. of* губить.

под *also* подо *prep.* (*with acc.*) under; towards. (*with instr.*) under; near, by.
подавáть *impf. pf.* подáть 1. to give. 2. to serve.
подавúться *pf. of* давúться.
подáвленный *adj.* depressed; despirited.
подавлять *impf. pf.* подавúть to press down; to suppress.
подавляющий *adj.* 1. overwhelming. 2. depressing. — подавляющее большинствó *neut.* overwhelming majority.
подáгра *f.* gout.
подарúть *pf. of* дарúть.
подáрок FILL *m.* gift.
подáтливый *adj.* 1. pliable. 2. malleable. 3. amenable.
подáть *pf. of* подавáть.
подаяние *neut.* (*obs.*) alms.
подбегáть *impf. pf.* подбежáть to run up to.
подбóр *m.* selection.
подбóрка *f.* 1. selection. 2. selection of related articles in a newspaper.
подбородóк FILL *m.* chin.
подвáл *m.* basement, cellar.
подвергáть *impf. pf.* подвéргнуть (*with dat.*) 1. to subject (to). 2. to expose (to).
подвéрженный *adj.* (*with dat.*) 1. subject to; liable to. 2. susceptible to.
подвеснóй *adj.* 1. hanging. 2. suspended. — подвеснóй мотóр *m.* outboard motor.
подвестú *pf. of* подводúть.
подвéтренный *adj.* leeward.
пóдвиг *m.* feat; exploit.
подвúд *m.* subspecies.
подвúжник *m. f.* подвúжница 1. religious ascetic. 2. champion of.
подвижнóй *adj.* mobile.
подвúжный *adj.* agile; lively.
подвóда *f.* wagon; cart.
подводúть *impf. pf.* подвестú to lead up to.
подвóдный *adj.* (*attrib.*) submarine.
подвóх *m.* (*colloq.*) dirty trick.
подвыпивший *adj.* (*colloq.*) tipsy; slightly drunk.
подвязка *f.* 1. garter. 2. suspender.
подгорéлый *adj.* slightly burnt.
подготовúтельный *adj.* preparatory.
подготóвка *f.* preparation.
подготовлять *impf. pf.* подготóвить *v.t.* to prepare.
подгрýдок FILL *m.* dewlap (*fold of loose skin hanging from throat*).
подгрýппа *f.* subgroup.
поддавáться *impf. pf.* поддáться (*with dat.*) to yield (to).
поддáкивать *impf. pf.* поддáкнуть (*with dat.*) (*colloq.*) to say yes to; to agree with.
пóдданный *m.* subject.
пóдданство *neut.* citizenship.
поддёвка *f.* man's long tight-fitting coat.
поддéлка *f.* counterfeit; forgery.
поддéлывать *impf. pf.* поддéлать to counterfeit; to forge.
поддéрживать *impf. pf.* поддержáть to support.
поддéржка *f.* support.
поддувáло *neut.* ash pit (*of a furnace*).
подéйствовать OVA *pf. of* дéйствовать.
поделúть(ся) *pf. of* делúть(ся).
подёнка *f.* mayfly.

подёнщик *m. f.* подёнщица dayworker; day laborer.
подéржанный *adj.* used, second-hand.
подешевéть *pf. of* дешевéть.
поджелýдочная железá *f.* pancreas.
поджигáть *impf. pf.* поджéчь to set fire (to).
поджимáть *impf. pf.* поджáть 1. to purse (one's lips). 2. to draw up (one's legs).
поджóг *m.* arson.
подзаголóвок FILL *m.* subtitle.
подзéмный *adj.* underground.
подкúдыш *m.* foundling; abandoned child.
подклáдка *f.* lining.
подклáдывать *impf. pf.* подложúть 1. to line (with). 2. to lay under.
подкóва *f.* horseshoe.
подкóжный *adj.* hypodermic.
подкóп *m.* 1. undermining. 2. underground passage. — подкóпы *pl.* intrigues; machinations; underhand plotting.
подкóс *m.* strut; cross brace.
подкрáдываться *impf. pf.* подкрáсться to steal up (to).
пóдкуп *m.* bribery.
подкупáть *impf. pf.* подкупúть to bribe.
пóдле *prep.* (*with gen.*) near, by; beside, alongside of.
подлежáть *impf. pres.* -жý, -жúшь (*with dat.*) to be subject to; to be liable to.
подлежáщее *neut.* (*gram.*) subject.
подлéсок FILL *m.* underbrush; undergrowth.
подлéц *m.* scoundrel.
подлúвка *f.* gravy; sauce.
подлúза *m. and f.* (*decl. f.*) (*colloq.*) bootlicker; toady.
пóдлинник *m.* original.
пóдлинный *adj.* original.
подлóг *m.* forgery.
подлóдка *f.* (*colloq.*) submarine.
подлóжный *adj. pf. of* подклáдывать.
пóдлость *f.* 1. meanness; baseness. 2. dirty trick.
пóдлый *adj.* mean, base.
подмéна *f.* substitution.
подменять *impf. pf.* подменúть *v.t.* to substitute (for).
подметáть *impf. pf.* подместú to sweep.
подмётка *f.* sole (*of a shoe*).
подмосквный *adj.* located near Moscow.
подмóстки *pl.* 1. scaffold. 2. the stage.
подмышка *f.* armpit.
поднимáть *impf. pf.* поднять to lift, to raise. —ся 1. to rise. 2. to climb (up).
поднóжие *neut.* pedestal.
поднóжка *f.* running board.
поднóс *m.* tray.
подносúть *impf. pf.* поднестú 1. to bring. 2. to present.
поднять(ся) *pf. of* поднимáть(ся).
подóбие *neut.* (*with gen.*) likeness; similarity.
подóбно *adv.* similarly. –*prep.* (*with dat.*) like, similar to.
подóбный *adj.* similar. — и тому́ подóбное and the like. — ничегó подóбного nothing of the sort.
подобострáстие *neut.* obsequiousness; servility.
подогревáть *impf. pf.* подогрéть *v.t.* to warm up.
пододеяльник *m.* blanket cover.
подождáть *pf. of* ждать.

подозревать *impf.* (в *with prep.*) to suspect.
подозрение *neut.* suspicion.
подозрительный *adj.* suspicious.
подойть *pf. of* дойть.
подойти *pf. of* подходить.
подоконник *m.* window sill.
подол *m.* lap (*of a skirt*).
Подольск *m.* Podolsk.
подонки *pl.* **1.** residue. **2.** dregs.
подопечный *adj.* under the care of a guardian.
подоплёка *f.* underlying cause *or* reason.
подопытный *adj.* experimental.
подорвать *pf. of* подрывать.
подорожать *pf.* to become more expensive.
подорожник *m.* **1.** (*weed*) plantain. **2.** (*colloq.*) food taken on a journey.
подоснова *f.* real cause; underlying reason.
подоходный налог *m.* income tax.
подошва *f.* **1.** sole (*of a shoe*). **2.** foot (*of a mountain*).
подпасок FILL *m.* shepherd boy.
подпевать *impf.* **1.** to sing along with. **2.** (*colloq.*) to echo; to parrot.
подписка *f.* subscription.
подписывать *impf. pf.* подписать to sign. —ся *v.i.* to sign; (на *with acc.*) to subscribe (to).
подпись *f.* signature.
подполковник *m.* lieutenant colonel.
подполье *neut.* **1.** cellar. **2.** underground.
подпорка *f.* prop.
подражание *neut.* imitation.
подражать *impf.* (*with dat.*) to imitate.
подразумевать *impf.* to imply.
подраться *pf. of* драться.
подробность *f.* detail.
подробный *adj.* detailed.
подруга *f.* **1.** (*female*) friend. **2.** girlfriend.
по-дружески *adv.* friendly.
подручный *adj.* **1.** handy; on hand. **2.** at hand. **3.** makeshift. **4.** assistant. — *m.* assistant.
подрывать *impf. pf.* подорвать to sap; to undermine.
подряд *adv.* one after another.
подрядчик *m.* contractor.
подряжать *impf. pf.* подрядить to hire.
подсвечник *m.* candlestick.
подсказывать *impf. pf.* подсказать to prompt.
подслащивать *impf. pf.* подсластить to sweeten.
подслушивать *impf.* **1.** to eavesdrop. **2.** *pf.* подслушать to overhear.
подснежник *m.* (*flower*) snowdrop.
подсобный *adj.* **1.** auxiliary; accessory. **2.** subsidiary. **3.** additional.
подсознание *neut.* the subconscious.
подсолнечник *m.* sunflower.
подспудный *adj.* hidden; secret.
подставка *f.* support; stand.
подставной *adj.* **1.** false; substitute. **2.** placed under *or* near.
подстерегать *impf. pf.* подстеречь to lie in wait for.
подстрочник *m.* word-for-word translation.
подступ *m.* approach.
подсудимый *m.* accused; defendant.
подсчёт *m.* **1.** count; counting. **2.** calculations.

подтверждать *impf. pf.* подтвердить to confirm; to acknowledge.
подтёк *m.* **1.** streak. **2.** bruise.
подтекст *m.* underlying theme; subtext.
подтрунивать *impf. pf.* подтрунить (над *with instr.*) to poke fun at.
подтяжки *pl.* suspenders.
подтянутый *adj.* smart; neat; fresh.
подумать *pf. of* думать to think, to think a little *or* for a while.
подушка *f.* pillow; cushion.
подхалим *m. f.* —ка sycophant; toady.
подход *m.* approach.
подходить *impf. pf.* подойти to approach.
подходящий *adj.* suitable.
подчас *adv.* sometimes; at times.
подчёркивать *impf. pf.* подчеркнуть to underline; to emphasize.
подчинение *neut.* submission; subordination.
подчинённый *adj. and m.* subordinate.
подчинять *impf. pf.* подчинить to subordinate. —ся (*with dat.*) to submit to.
подшипник *m.* (*mech.*) bearing. — шариковый подшипник *m.* ball bearing.
подъезд *m.* **1.** driveway; entrance. **2.** approach.
подъезжать *impf. pf.* подъехать to drive up to.
подъём *m.* **1.** ascent. **2.** lifting, hoisting. **3.** slope, rise.
подытоживать *impf. pf.* подытожить **1.** to add up; to total. **2.** to sum up.
поединок FILL *m.* duel.
поезд *m.* train.
поездка *f.* trip, journey, excursion.
поехать *pf. of* ехать.
пожалеть *pf. of* жалеть.
пожаловаться *pf. of* жаловаться.
пожалуйста *particle* **1.** please. **2.** certainly!, by all means! **3.** don't mention it.
пожар *m.* fire.
пожатие руки *neut.* handshake.
пожелать *pf. of* желать.
пожелтеть *pf. of* желтеть.
пожертвовать OVA *pf. of* жертвовать.
поживать *impf.* to get along, to get on. — как вы поживаете? how are you?
пожилой *adj.* elderly.
поза *f.* pose.
позаботиться *pf. of* заботиться.
позавидовать OVA *pf. of* завидовать.
позавтракать *pf. of* завтракать.
позавчера *adv.* the day before yesterday.
позади *adv., prep.* (*with gen.*) behind.
позаимствовать OVA *pf. of* заимствовать.
позвать *pf. of* звать.
позволение *neut.* permission.
позволять *impf. pf.* позволить to allow; to permit.
позвонить *pf. of* звонить.
позвонок FILL *m.* vertebra.
позвоночник *m.* spine.
поздний *adj.* late.
поздороваться *pf. of* здороваться.
поздравлять *impf. pf.* поздравить to congratulate.
позеленеть *pf. of* зеленеть.
позже *adv.* later, later on.
познавать *impf. pf.* познать to become acquainted (with).

познако́мить(ся) *pf. of* знако́мить(ся).
По́знань *f.* Poznań
позо́р *m.* disgrace; shame.
пои́стине *adv.* indeed; in truth.
пои́ть *impf. pf.* на- **1.** to give someone a drink. **2.** (*of animals*) to water.
пойма́ть *pf. of* лови́ть.
пойти́ *pf. of* идти́.
пока́ *conj.* while; (*with* не) until. — *adv.* for the present.
пока́з *m.* demonstration; show.
показа́ние *neut.* **1.** testimony, evidence. **2.** deposition.
показа́тель *m.* index.
показа́ться *pf. of* каза́ться.
пока́зывать *impf. pf.* показа́ть to show.
покара́ть *pf. of* кара́ть.
покая́ние *neut.* **1.** confession. **2.** repentance.
пока́яться *pf.* **1.** to confess. **2.** to repent.
покида́ть *impf. pf.* поки́нуть to leave; to abandon.
поки́нутый *adj.* abandoned.
покло́н *m.* **1.** bow. **2.** compliments, best regards.
поклоне́ние *neut.* worship.
поклони́ться *pf. of* кла́няться.
покло́нник *m. f.* покло́нница admirer, worshipper.
поко́й¹ *m.* rest.
поко́й² *m.* room, ward.
поко́йник *m. f.* поко́йница deceased.
поколе́ние *neut.* generation.
поко́нчить *pf.* (с *with instr.*) to finish (*with*).
покоре́ние *neut.* subjugation.
поко́рный *adj.* submissive; obedient.
покоря́ть *impf. pf.* покори́ть to subdue; to subjugate. —ся **1.** to submit. **2.** to give in, to yield.
покра́сить *pf. of* кра́сить.
покрасне́ть *pf. of* красне́ть.
покро́в *m.* cover; shroud.
покрови́тель *m. f.* —ница patron; protector.
покрыва́ть *impf. pf.* покры́ть to cover.
покры́шка *f.* cover, covering.
покупа́тель *m. f.* —ница buyer; customer.
покупа́ть *impf. pf.* купи́ть to buy.
поку́пка *f.* purchase.
поку́шать *pf. of* ку́шать.
покуше́ние *neut.* assasination attempt.
пол¹ *m.* floor.
пол² *m.* gender, sex.
пола́ *f.* **1.** skirt. **2.** flap.
полага́ть *impf.* to think, to suppose; to believe. —ся (на *with acc.*) to rely (on).
полго́да *adv.* half a year.
по́лдень FILL *m.* noon.
по́ле *neut.* field. — поля́ margin; brim (*of hat*).
поле́зный *adj.* useful.
поле́зть *pf. of* лезть to start to climb.
полете́ть *pf. of* лете́ть to take off.
по́лзать *impf. indet. det.* ползти́ to creep, to crawl.
полирова́ть OVA *impf. pf.* от- to polish.
поли́тика *f.* politics.
полити́ческий *adj.* political.
поли́ция *f.* police.
полк *m.* regiment.
по́лка *f.* shelf.
полнокро́вный *adj.* full-blooded.
полнолу́ние *neut.* full moon.

полномо́чный *adj.* plenipotentiary.
по́лностью *adv.* completely; in full.
по́лночь *f.* midnight.
по́лный *adj.* full.
по́ло *neut. indecl.* polo.
полови́на *f.* half.
половой¹ *adj.* (*attrib.*) floor.
половой² *adj.* sexual.
положе́ние *neut.* **1.** position, location, situation. **2.** condition.
положи́тельный *adj.* affirmative,
положи́ть *pf. of* класть.
полоса́ *f.* **1.** strip. **2.** region, zone.
полоска́ть *impf.* **1.** to rinse. **2.** to gargle.
по́лость *f.* (*anat.*) cavity.
полоте́нце *neut.* towel.
полотно́ *neut.* linen.
полотня́ный *adj.* linen.
По́лоцк *m.* Polatsk (*Russian: Polotsk*).
Полта́ва *f.* Poltava.
полтора́ *num.* one and a half. —ста *num.* one hundred and fifty.
полу́денный *adj.* (*attrib.*) midday, noon.
полукру́г *m.* semicircle.
полуме́сяц *m.* half moon.
полуо́стров *m.* peninsula.
получа́ть *impf. pf.* получи́ть to receive. —ся to result; to turn out to be.
полуша́рие *neut.* hemisphere.
полчаса́ *pl.* half-hour.
по́льза *f.* use; benefit.
по́льзоваться *impf. pf.* вос- (*with instr.*) **1.** to make use of. **2.** to profit by. **3.** *impf. only* to enjoy.
по́льский *adj.* Polish.
польсти́ть *pf. of* льсти́ть.
По́льша *f.* Poland.
полюби́ть *pf.* to become fond of; to take a liking to.
полюбо́вный *adj.* amicable.
по́люс *m.* (*geog.*) pole.
поля́к *m. f.* по́лька Pole.
поля́рный *adj.* polar.
Поля́рный круг *m.* the Arctic Circle.
поменя́ть *pf. of* меня́ть.
поме́ркнуть *pf. of* ме́ркнуть.
помёт¹ *m.* dung.
помёт² *m.* litter; brood.
поме́тка *f.* mark; note.
поме́шанный *adj.* crazy, insane, mad.
помеша́ть *pf. of* меша́ть to stir a little *or* for a while. —ся to go mad; to become insane.
помеща́ть *impf. pf.* помести́ть **1.** to place. **2.** to invest. **3.** to accomodate, to lodge.
помеще́ние *neut.* **1.** location. **2.** investment. **3.** lodging.
помидо́р *m.* tomato.
поми́мо *prep.* (*with gen.*) besides.
помина́ть *impf. pf.* помяну́ть to remember; to mention; to make mention (of).
помири́ть(ся) *pf. of* мири́ть(ся).
по́мнить *impf.* to remember; to recall.
помно́жить *pf. of* мно́жить.
помога́ть *impf. pf.* помо́чь (*with dat.*) to help.
по-мо́ему *adv.* in my opinion; to my mind.
помо́щник *m. f.* помо́щница assistant, helper.

по́мощь *f.* help; assistance.
по́мысел *m.* thought; design.
помы́ть *pf. of* мыть.
помяну́ть *pf. of* помина́ть.
помя́ть *pf. of* мять.
понеде́льник *m.* Monday.
понеде́льный *adj.* weekly.
понести́(сь) *pf. of* нести́(сь).
понижа́ть *impf. pf.* пони́зить **1.** to lower. **2.** to reduce.
понима́ние *neut.* understanding.
понима́ть *impf. pf.* поня́ть to understand; to comprehend.
поноси́ть *pf. of* носи́ть to carry *or* wear for a while.
понра́виться *pf. of* нра́виться.
поню́хать *pf. of* ню́хать.
поня́тие *neut.* idea; notion; conception.
поня́тный *adj.* clear, intelligible, understandable.
поня́ть *pf. of* понима́ть.
пообе́дать *pf. of* обе́дать.
поперёк *adv.* crosswise. *–prep.* (*with gen.*) across.
— вдоль и поперёк *adv.* **1.** far and wide. **2.** thoroughly.
поплы́ть *pf. of* плыть.
попола́м *adv.* in half.
пополу́дни *adv.* in the afternoon.
попра́вка *f.* **1.** correction. **2.** recovery.
поправля́ть *impf. pf.* попра́вить to repair, to mend; to correct. —ся to get well, to recover; to improve.
по-пре́жнему *adv.* as before, as usual.
попрёк *m.* reproach.
по́прище *neut.* field; walk of life.
попро́бовать OVA *pf. of* про́бовать.
попроси́ть *pf. of* проси́ть.
по́просту *adj.* simply; without ceremony.
попуга́й *m.* parrot.
популя́рный *adj.* popular.
попу́тно *adv.* **1.** in passing. **2.** on one's way. **3.** incidentally.
попу́тчик *m. f.* попу́тчица fellow traveler.
попыта́ться *pf. of* пыта́ться.
попы́тка *f.* attempt.
попя́титься *pf. of* пя́титься.
пора́ *f.* time. — (*impers.*) it is time. — с тех пор *adv.* since then.
порабо́тать *pf. of* рабо́тать.
порабоща́ть *impf. pf.* поработи́ть to enslave.
поража́ть *impf. pf.* порази́ть **1.** to strike. **2.** to amaze. **3.** to defeat.
порази́тельный *adj.* striking.
по́ристый *adj.* porous.
порица́ть *impf.* to blame; to censure.
поро́г *m.* **1.** threshold. **2.** *usu. pl.* rapids.
поро́да *f.* **1.** breed. **2.** (*geol.*) rock.
поро́дистый *adj.* pedigreed.
по́рознь *adv.* separately.
поро́к *m.* **1.** vice. **2.** defect.
по́рох *m.* powder.
поро́чный *adj.* vicious; depraved.
порошо́к FILL *m.* powder.
порт *m.* port; harbor.
по́ртить *impf. pf.* ис- *v.t.* **1.** to spoil, to damage. **2.** to corrupt.
портни́ха *f.* (female) dressmaker.

портно́й *m.* tailor.
Порт-о-Пре́нс *m.* Port au Prince.
портре́т *m.* portrait.
Португа́лия *f.* Portugal.
портфе́ль *m.* briefcase.
по-ру́сски *adv.* (in) Russian.
поруча́ть *impf. pf.* поручи́ть (*with dat.*) to commission; to charge (with).
поруче́ние *neut.* commission; message.
поручи́ть *pf. of* поруча́ть.
поручи́ться *pf. of* руча́ться.
по́рция *f.* portion.
поры́в *m.* gust. —истый *adj.* **1.** gusty. **2.** impetuous.
поря́дковое числи́тельное *neut.* (*gram.*) ordinal numeral.
поря́док FILL *m.* order; sequence.
поря́дочный *adj.* decent, honest.
посади́ть *pf.* **1.** to plant. **2.** to imprison.
по-сво́ему *adv.* in one's own way.
посвяща́ть *impf. pf.* посвяти́ть (*with dat.*) to devote; to dedicate (to).
посети́тель *m. f.* —ница visitor, guest.
посеща́ть *impf. pf.* посети́ть **1.** to visit. **2.** to attend.
посе́ять *pf. of* се́ять.
поскака́ть *pf. of* скака́ть.
поско́льку *conj.* so far as; since.
посла́ние *neut.* message.
посла́нник *m.* minister.
посла́ть *pf. of* посыла́ть.
по́сле *adv.* later, afterwards. *–prep.* (*with gen.*) after.
после́дний *adj.* last; latter; the latest.
после́довательный *adj.* successive; consecutive.
после́довать OVA *pf. of* сле́довать.
после́дствие *neut.* consequence.
после́дующий *adj.* following, next.
послеза́втра *adv.* the day after tomorrow.
послесло́вие *neut.* epilogue.
посло́вица *f.* proverb.
послужи́ть *pf. of* **2.** служи́ть.
послу́шать(ся) *pf. of* слу́шать(ся).
посме́ртный *adj.* posthumous.
посмотре́ть *pf. of* смотре́ть.
посо́бие *neut.* **1.** text, textbook. **2.** grant, allowance. **3.** aid.
посоли́ть *pf. of* соли́ть.
посо́льство *neut.* embassy.
поспеши́ть *pf. of* спеши́ть.
поспе́шный *adj.* **1.** prompt, hurried, hasty. **2.** rash.
поспо́рить *pf. of* спо́рить.
посреди́ *adv.* in the middle. *–prep.* (*with gen.*) in the middle of.
посре́дник *m. f.* посре́дница mediator.
посре́дничество *neut.* mediation.
посре́дственность *f.* mediocrity.
посре́дством *prep.* (*with instr.*) by means of.
поста́вить *pf. of* поставля́ть, ста́вить.
поставля́ть *impf. pf.* поста́вить to supply.
постано́вка *f.* (*theat.*) production, staging.
постановле́ние *neut.* decision; decree.
постановля́ть *impf. pf.* постанови́ть to decide; to decree.
постара́ться *pf. of* стара́ться.

посте́ль *f.* bed.
постепéнный *adj.* gradual.
постига́ть *impf. pf.* пости́гнуть, пости́чь 1. to comprehend, to perceive. 2. to befall; to strike. 3. to overtake.
постиже́ние *neut.* comprehension, understanding.
постижи́мый *adj.* comprehensible, understandable.
посто́льку *conj.* insofar as.
посторони́ться *pf. of* сторони́ться.
посторо́нний *adj.* strange, foreign. — *m.* outsider.
постоя́нный *adj.* constant, permanent.
пострада́ть *pf. of* страда́ть.
построе́ние *neut.* construction.
постро́ить *pf. of* стро́ить.
поступа́тельный *adj.* progressive.
поступа́ть *impf. pf.* поступи́ть 1. to act. 2. (с *with instr.*) to treat, to deal with. 3. (на, в *with acc.*) to enter, to join.
посту́пок FILL *m.* action, deed.
по́ступь *f.* step; tread.
посу́да *f.* dishes; ware; utensils.
посыла́ть *impf. pf.* посла́ть to send.
посяга́ть *impf. pf.* посягну́ть (на *with acc.*) to encroach on *or* upon.
пот *m.* sweat, perspiration.
потемне́ть *pf. of* темне́ть.
потепле́ть *pf. of* тепле́ть.
поте́ря *f.* 1. loss. 2. waste.
потеря́ть(ся) *pf. of* теря́ть(ся).
поте́ть *impf.* 1. *pf.* вс- to sweat, to perspire. 2. *pf.* за- *v.i.* to steam up.
поте́шить *pf. of* те́шить.
пото́к *m.* stream, torrent; flow, flood.
потоло́к FILL *m.* ceiling.
потолсте́ть *pf. of* толсте́ть.
пото́м *adv.* afterwards; then. —ок *m.* descendant; offspring. —ство *neut.* posterity.
потому́ *adv.* for this reason. — потому́ что *conj.* because; for.
пото́п *m.* flood, deluge.
поторопи́ть(ся) *pf. of* торопи́ть(ся).
потребля́ть *impf. pf.* потреби́ть to consume; to use.
потре́бный *adj.* necessary; required.
потре́бовать OVA *pf. of* тре́бовать.
потряса́ть *impf. pf.* потрясти́ to astound, to shock.
потрясе́ние *neut.* shock.
Потсда́м *m.* Potsdam.
потуши́ть *pf. of* туши́ть.
потяну́ть(ся) *pf. of* тяну́ть(ся).
похвала́ *f.* praise.
похвали́ть(ся) *pf. of* хвали́ть(ся).
похваля́ться *impf.* (with *instr.*) (*colloq.*) to boast of, to brag.
похища́ть *impf. pf.* похи́тить 1. to kidnap. 2. to steal. 3. to hijack.
походи́ть *impf.* (на *with acc.*) to resemble, to look like.
похо́жий *adj.* (на *with acc.*) similar, resembling.
похорони́ть *pf. of* хорони́ть.
по́хороны *pl.* burial, funeral.
по́хоть *f.* lust.
похуде́ть *pf. of* худе́ть.
поцелова́ть OVA *pf. of* целова́ть.
поцелу́й *m.* kiss.
по́чва *f.* soil.

почём *adv.* how much is?
почему́ *adv.* why.
почему́-либо *adv.* for some reason or other.
по́черк *m.* handwriting.
почёт *m.* honor. —ный *adj.* honorary, honorable.
почини́ть *pf. of* чини́ть.
по́чта *f.* mail. —льо́н *m.* postman.
почта́мт *m.* post office.
почте́ние *neut.* respect.
почти́ *adv.* almost, nearly.
почти́тельный *adj.* respectful.
почто́вый *adj.* (*attrib*) mail.
пошёл вон *interj.* get out!
по́шлина *f.* duty; customs.
по́шлый *adj.* vulgar.
поща́да *f.* mercy.
пощади́ть *pf. of* щади́ть.
поэ́зия *f.* poetry.
поэ́ма *f.* poem.
поэ́т *m.* poet. —и́ческий *adj.* poetic(al).
поэ́тому *adv.* therefore; for this reason.
появле́ние *neut.* appearance.
появля́ться *impf. pf.* появи́ться to appear; to emerge.
по́яс *m.* 1. belt. 2. zone.
поясни́тельный *adj.* explanatory.
прабабка *also* прабабушка *f.* great-grandmother.
пра́вда *f.* truth.
правдоподо́бный *adj.* plausible; likely.
пра́ведный *adj.* 1. righteous. 2. just.
пра́вило *neut.* rule.
пра́вильно *adv.* 1. correctly. 2. regularly. 3. properly.
пра́вильный *adj.* right, correct.
прави́тель *m. f.* —ница ruler.
прави́тельственный *adj.* government(al).
пра́вить *impf.* (with *instr.*) to govern, to rule.
пра́вка *f.* 1. reading; correcting. 2. setting (*of metal tools*).
правле́ние *neut.* 1. government; rule. 2. management.
пра́внук *m.* great-grandson.
пра́во *neut.* right; law.
правоме́рный *adj.* legitimate.
правомо́чный *adj.* (*leg.*) competent.
правонаруши́тель *m. f.* —ница lawbreaker; offender.
правописа́ние *neut.* spelling, orthography.
правосла́вие *neut.* Orthodoxy; the Orthodox faith.
правосла́вный *adj.* orthodox.
правосу́дие *neut.* justice.
пра́вый *adj.* 1. (*direction*) right. 2. correct, just.
пра́вящий *adj.* ruling.
Пра́га *f.* Prague.
пра́дед *m.* great-grandfather.
пра́здник *m.* holiday.
пра́здничный *adj.* (*attrib.*) holiday.
пра́здно *adv.* idly.
пра́здновать OVA *impf. pf.* от- to celebrate.
пра́здный *adj.* idle.
пра́ктика *f.* practice.
пра́ктикум *m.* practical training; practical work.
практи́чески *adv.* 1. practically; in a practical manner. 2. for all practical purposes.
практи́ческий *also* практи́чный *adj.* practical.

пра́порщик *m.* (*mil.*) **1.** warrant officer. **2.** (*in czarist army*) ensign.

прапраба́бка *also* прапраба́бушка *f.* great-great-grandmother.

прапра́внук *m.* great-great-grandson.

прапра́внучка *f.* great-great-granddaughter.

прапра́дед *m.* great-great-grandfather.

прах *m.* **1.** (*poet.*) dust. **2.** earthly remains.

пра́чечная *f.* laundry.

пра́чка *f.* laundress.

пребыва́ние *neut.* **1.** one's stay. **2.** tenure (*in office*).

пребыва́ть *impf. pf.* пребы́ть to stay, to sojourn.

превали́ровать OVA *impf.* **1.** to predominate. **2.** (над *with instr.*) to dominate.

превозмога́ть *impf. pf.* превозмо́чь to overcome.

превосходи́тельство *neut.* (*title*) Excellency.

превосходи́ть *impf. pf.* превзойти́ to surpass.

превосхо́дный *adj.* excellent.

превра́тный *adj.* **1.** wrong; incorrect. **2.** (*of luck*) capricious; fickle.

превраща́ть *impf. pf.* преврати́ть (в *with acc.*) to transform (into).

превыша́ть *impf. pf.* превы́сить to exceed.

прегра́да *f.* bar; obstacle.

прегражда́ть *impf. pf.* прегради́ть to bar; to block.

предава́ть *impf. pf.* преда́ть to betray.

пре́данный *adj.* devoted.

преда́тель *m. f.* —ница traitor. —ство *neut.* treason; betrayal.

предвари́тельный *adj* preliminary.

предве́стие *neut.* omen; portent.

предвеща́ть *impf.* to portend; to augur; to presage. — предвеща́ть хоро́шее to bode well.

предви́дение *neut.* **1.** foresight. **2.** prediction. **3.** anticipation.

предвкуше́ние *neut.* **1.** foretaste. **2.** anticipation.

предводи́тель *m. f.* —ница leader.

предвосхище́ние *neut.* anticipation.

предго́рье *neut.* foothill.

преддве́рие *neut.* threshold.

преде́л *m.* limit; boundary. —ьный *adj.* limiting; extreme.

преде́льно *adv.* to the extreme; utterly.

предзнаменова́ние *neut.* omen; portent; augury.

предисло́вие *neut.* preface.

предлага́ть *impf. pf.* предложи́ть **1.** to present, to offer. **2.** to suggest. **3.** to propose.

предло́г[1] *m.* (*gram.*) preposition.

предло́г[2] *m.* pretext.

предложе́ние[1] *neut.* **1.** offer, suggestion. **2.** motion, proposal.

предложе́ние[2] *neut.* (*gram.*) sentence, clause.

предло́жный *adj.* (*gram.*) prepositional.

предме́стье *neut.* suburb.

предме́т *m.* object, subject.

предназнача́ть *impf. pf.* предназна́чить to intend, to destine, to earmark.

предназначе́ние *neut.* destination; predestination.

преднаме́ренный *adj.* **1.** premeditated; deliberate. **2.** intentional.

предначерта́ть *pf.* to predetermine; to foreordain.

пре́док FILL *m.* ancestor.

предопределе́ние *neut.* predetermination.

предопределя́ть *impf. pf.* предопредели́ть to predetermine; to foreordain.

предоставля́ть *impf. pf.* предоста́вить **1.** to grant; to give. **2.** to leave (*to someone to do something*).

предостерега́ть *impf. pf.* предостере́чь (от *with gen.*) to warn against.

предостереже́ние *neut.* warning.

предосторо́жность *f.* caution; precaution.

предосуди́тельный *adj.* **1.** blameworthy. **2.** reprehensible.

предохране́ние *neut.* protection.

предохрани́тельный *adj.* **1.** precautionary. **2.** (*attrib.*) safety.

предпи́сывать *impf. pf.* предписа́ть to order, to direct; to prescribe.

предполага́емый *adj.* **1.** supposed; presumed. **2.** planned.

предполага́ть *impf. pf.* предположи́ть **1.** to assume. **2.** to intend, to propose.

предположе́ние *neut.* **1.** supposition, assumption. **2.** plan.

предположи́тельно *adv.* **1.** hypothetically. **2.** presumably; supposedly.

предпосле́дний *adj.* next to last.

предпосы́лка *f.* **1.** precondition; prerequisite. **2.** premise.

предпочита́ть *impf. pf.* предпоче́сть to prefer.

предпочте́ние *neut.* preference.

предпочти́тельный *adj.* **1.** preferable; preferred. **2.** preferential.

предприи́мчивый *adj.* enterprising.

предпринима́тель *m.* **1.** entrepreneur. **2.** owner (*of a firm*).

предпринима́ть *impf. pf.* предприня́ть to undertake.

предприя́тие *neut.* **1.** undertaking; enterprise. **2.** venture.

предрасполога́ть *impf. pf.* предрасположи́ть to predispose toward.

предрасполо́женный *adj.* (к *with dat.*) predisposed to.

предрассу́док FILL *m.* prejudice.

предрека́ть *impf. pf.* предре́чь **1.** to predict. **2.** to portend.

председа́тель *m. f.* —ница chairperson.

предсказа́ние *neut.* prediction.

предска́зуемый *adj.* predictable.

предска́зывать *impf. pf.* предсказа́ть to foretell; to predict; to forecast.

предсме́ртный *adj.* **1.** occurring just before death. **2.** (*attrib.*) death.

представа́ть *impf. pf.* предста́ть to appear (before).

представи́тель *m. f.* —ница **1.** representative. **2.** spokesperson.

представи́тельный *adj.* **1.** representative. **2.** imposing.

представле́ние *neut.* **1.** performance. **2.** presentation. **3.** idea; notion.

представля́ть *impf. pf.* предста́вить **1.** to present, to introduce. **2.** *impf. only* to represent. —ся **3.** to occur, to present itself. **4.** to introduce oneself.

предста́тельная железа́ *f.* prostate gland.

предстоя́щий *adj.* **1.** impending. **2.** forthcoming.

предте́ча *m.* and *f.* (*decl. f.*) (*arch.*) forerunner; precursor. — Иоа́нн Предте́ча *m.* John the Baptist.

предубежде́ние *neut.* prejudice.

предупреди́тельный *adj.* preventive; precautionary.

предупрежда́ть *impf. pf.* предупреди́ть **1.** to notify. **2.** to warn; to prevent. **3.** to let know beforehand.

предусма́тривать *impf. pf.* предусмотре́ть to foresee.

предчу́вствие *neut.* presentiment.

предчу́вствовать OVA *impf.* to have a presentiment *or* foreboding.

предше́ственник *m. f.* предше́ственница predecessor.

предше́ствовать OVA *impf.* (*with dat.*) to precede.

предше́ствующий *adj.* preceding; previous.

предъявля́ть *impf. pf.* предъяви́ть **1.** to present. **2.** to show. **3.** to produce.

предыду́щий *adj.* previous.

прее́мник *m. f.* прее́мница successor.

прее́мственный *adj.* successive.

пре́жде *adv.* formerly, before. –*prep.* (*with gen.*) before.

преждевре́менный *adj.* **1.** premature. **2.** untimely.

пре́жний *adj.* previous; former.

презервати́в *m.* condom.

презира́ть *impf. pf.* презре́ть **1.** *impf. only* to despise; to scorn. **2.** to disregard.

презри́тельный *adj.* contemptuous, scornful.

преиму́щественный *adj.* principal.

преиму́щество *neut.* advantage.

преиспо́дняя *f.* hell; the underworld.

преисполня́ть *impf. pf.* преиспо́лнить **1.** to fill. **2.** to imbue.

прейскура́нт *m.* price list; catalogue.

преклоне́ние *neut.* (пе́ред *with instr.*) worship (of); reverence (for).

прекло́нный *adj.* old; advanced in age.

прекосло́вить *impf.* (*with dat.*) to contradict.

прекра́сный *adj.* beautiful; fine; excellent.

прекраща́ть *impf. pf.* прекрати́ть **1.** to break off; to cut short. **2.** to stop, to cease, to put an end (to).

прекраще́ние *neut.* cessation.

преле́стный *adj.* charming; lovely; delightful.

пре́лесть *f.* charm.

преломле́ние *neut.* refraction.

преломля́ть *impf. pf.* преломи́ть to refract.

пре́лый *adj.* rotten.

прелюбодея́ние *neut.* adultery.

пре́мия *f.* **1.** prize. **2.** premium. **3.** bonus.

прему́дрый *adj.* **1.** (*obs.*) very wise. **2.** arcane; abstruse.

премье́ра *f.* (*theat.*) first night, première.

пренебрега́ть *impf. pf.* пренебре́чь (*with instr.*) to neglect; to disregard.

пренебреже́ние *neut.* neglect; disregard.

пре́ния *pl.* debate.

преоблада́ть *impf.* to predominate, to prevail.

преоблада́ющий *adj.* predominant; prevailing.

преображе́ние *neut.* **1.** transformation. **2.** (*cap.*) (*relig.*) the Transfiguration.

преобразова́ние *neut.* transformation. — преобразова́ния *pl.* reforms.

преодолева́ть *impf. pf.* преодоле́ть **1.** to overcome. **2.** to surmount (*e.g. difficulties*).

преодоли́мый *adj.* surmountable.

препина́ние *neut.*: знак препина́ния *m.* punctuation mark.

препира́ться *impf.* to squabble.

преподава́тель *m. f.* —ница teacher.

преподава́ть *impf.* to teach, to instruct.

преподо́бный *adj.* (*title*) Reverend.

препо́на *f.* (*obs.*) impediment; obstacle.

препя́тствие *neut.* obstacle.

препя́тствовать OVA *impf. pf.* вос- (*with dat.*) to hinder; to impede.

пререка́ние *neut.* squabble; argument.

пре́рия *f.* prairie.

прерыва́ть *impf. pf.* прерва́ть to interrupt; to break off.

преры́вистый *adj.* intermittent; irregular.

пресека́ть *impf. pf.* пресе́чь **1.** to put a stop to. **2.** to cut short.

пресле́довать OVA *impf.* to persecute; to pursue, to haunt.

пресловутый *adj.* notorious; famous.

пресмыка́ться *impf.* (пе́ред *with instr.*) to grovel (before).

пресмыка́ющееся *neut.* reptile.

пре́сная вода́ *f.* fresh water.

пресс *m.* press; punch (*machine*).

пре́сса *f.* the press.

пресс-конфере́нция *f.* press-conference.

пресс-папье́ *neut. indecl.* **1.** paperweight. **2.** blotter.

престаре́лый *adj.* aged. — дом (для) престаре́лых *m.* old age home; senior citizens' home.

престо́л *m.* throne.

преступа́ть *impf. pf.* преступи́ть (*obs.*) **1.** to transgress. **2.** to trespass.

преступле́ние *neut.* crime; offense.

престу́пник *m. f.* престу́пница criminal.

пресыще́ние *neut.* satiety; satiation.

претендова́ть OVA *impf.* (на *with acc.*) **1.** to lay claim to. **2.** to aspire to.

претенцио́зный *adj.* pretentious.

претерпева́ть *impf. pf.* претерпе́ть **1.** to endure; to suffer. **2.** to undergo (*changes*).

прети́ть *impf.* (*with dat.*) to sicken; to disgust.

Прето́рия *f.* Pretoria.

преть *impf. pf.* со- to rot.

преувели́чивать *impf. pf.* преувели́чить to exaggerate.

преуменьша́ть *impf. pf.* преуме́ньшить to underestimate.

пре́фикс *m.* prefix.

при *prep.* (*with prep.*) **1.** by, at, near. **2.** in the presence of. **3.** in the time of, during. **4.** attached to.

прибавля́ть *impf. pf.* приба́вить to increase; to add.

прибалти́йский *adj.* Baltic.

приба́утка *f.* humorous saying.

прибе́жище *neut.* refuge.

приближа́ться *impf. pf.* прибли́зиться (к *with dat.*) to approach; to draw near.

приблизи́тельный *adj.* approximate.

прибо́й *m.* surf; breakers.

прибо́р *m.* **1.** apparatus. **2.** instrument, implement.

прибо́рная доска́ *f.* instrument panel.

прибыва́ть *impf. pf.* прибы́ть **1.** to arrive. **2.** to increase.

при́быль *f.* **1.** profit. **2.** increase. **3.** (*colloq.*) gain; benefit.

прибы́тие *neut.* arrival.

прива́л *m.* **1.** rest; halt. **2.** resting place.

привере́дливый *adj.* (*colloq.*) choosy; picky; fussy.

приве́рженец FILL *m.* supporter; adherent.

приве́т *m.* greeting(s).

приве́тственный *adj.* (*attrib.*) welcome; welcoming.

приве́тствовать OVA *impf. pf.* **по-** to welcome; to greet.

приви́вка *f.* inoculation.

привиде́ние *neut.* ghost; phantom; apparition.

при́вкус *m.* **1.** touch; tinge. **2.** aftertaste. **3.** taste; flavor.

привлека́ть *impf. pf.* **привле́чь** to attract.

приво́д[1] *m.* taking into custody; arrest.

приво́д[2] *m.* (*mech.*) drive; driving gear.

приводни́ться *impf. pf.* **приводни́ться** to land on water.

привози́ть *impf. pf.* **привезти́** to bring (*by vehicle*).

приво́лье *neut.* **1.** free space. **2.** freedom to move around.

привра́тник *m. f.* **привра́тница** doorkeeper; gatekeeper.

привыка́ть *impf. pf.* **привы́кнуть** (**к** *with dat.*) to become accustomed *or* used to.

привы́чка *f.* habit.

привы́чный *adj.* **1.** usual; customary. **2.** (**к** *with dat.*) (*colloq.*) accustomed to; used to.

привя́занный *adj.* attached.

привя́зывать *impf. pf.* **привяза́ть** **1.** (**к** *with dat.*) to tie to; to attach to. **2.** (*with* **к себе́**) to win over.

приглаша́ть *impf. pf.* **пригласи́ть** to invite.

приглаше́ние *neut.* invitation.

приглуша́ть *impf. pf.* **приглуши́ть** to muffle; to deaden.

пригляну́ться *pf.* (*with dat.*) (*colloq.*) to catch the fancy of.

пригова́ривать *impf. pf.* **приговори́ть** to sentence; to condemn.

пригово́р *m.* sentence.

приго́дный *adj.* (**к** *with dat.* or **для** *with gen.*) suitable for; fit for.

пригоре́лый *adj.* burnt.

при́городный *adj.* suburban.

приго́рок FILL *m.* knoll; hillock.

приготови́тельный *adj.* preparatory.

пригото́вить *pf. of* **гото́вить, приготовля́ть.**

приготовля́ть *impf. pf.* **пригото́вить** *v.t.* to prepare.

пригрози́ть *pf. of* **грози́ть.**

придава́ть *impf. pf.* **прида́ть** **1.** to give; to impart. **2.** to attach significance to. **3.** (*mil.*) to assign (to a military unit).

прида́вливать *impf. pf.* **придави́ть** **1.** to press (down). **2.** to weigh down.

прида́ное *neut.* dowry.

прида́ток FILL *m.* **1.** appendage. **2.** adjunct.

прида́точный *adj.* **1.** additional, accessory. **2.** (*gram.*) subordinate.

прида́ча *f.* **1.** giving; imparting. **2.** attaching. **3.** (*mil.*) assigning. **4.** addition.

приде́рживать *impf. pf.* **придержа́ть** to hold *or* stick to.

придира́ться *impf. pf.* **придра́ться** (**к** *with dat.*) **1.** to find fault with. **2.** to carp at.

приди́рка *f.* quibble; cavil.

придоро́жный *adj.* roadside.

приду́мывать *impf. pf.* **приду́мать** to think up; to invent.

прие́зд *m.* arrival.

приезжа́ть *impf. pf.* **прие́хать** to arrive (*by vehicle*).

прие́зжий *adj.* **1.** newly arrived. **2.** touring; visiting. — *m.* newcomer.

приём *m.* **1.** reception. **2.** (*med.*) dose. **3.** method, way. — *f.* reception room.

приёмлемый *adj.* acceptable.

приёмник *m.* (*radio*) receiver.

прижива́льщик *m. f.* **прижива́лка** parasite; sponger; hanger-on.

прижива́ться *impf. pf.* **прижи́ться** to become acclimated.

прижи́зненный *adj.* happening in one's lifetime.

прижима́ть *impf. pf.* **прижа́ть** (**к** *with dat.*) to press (against).

призва́ние *neut.* vocation, calling.

приземи́стый *adj.* stocky; heavyset; squat.

приземля́ть *impf. pf.* **приземли́ть** to land (*a plane*).

призёр *m.* prizewinner.

признава́ть *impf. pf.* **призна́ть** to acknowledge, recognize. **—ся** (**в** *with prep.*) to confess, to admit.

при́знак *m.* sign.

призна́ние *neut.* **1.** acknowledgement. **2.** recognition. **3.** confession.

призна́тельный *adj.* appreciative; grateful.

призна́ть(ся) *pf. of* **признава́ть(ся).**

при́зрак *m.* ghost; specter; phantom; apparition.

при́зрачный *adj.* unreal; illusory.

призы́в *m.* **1.** appeal, call. **2.** slogan.

призыва́ть *impf. pf.* **призва́ть** to call (for); to call upon; (*mil.*) to call up.

призывно́й *adj.* (*attrib.*) (*mil.*) draft.

при́иск *m.* mine (*for minerals*).

прийти́(сь) *pf. of* **приходи́ть(ся).**

прика́з *m.* order, command. **—а́ние** *neut.* order, instruction.

прика́зчик *m.* (*obs.*) **1.** salesman. **2.** steward; bailiff.

прика́зывать *impf. pf.* **приказа́ть** to order; to command.

прикаса́ться *impf. pf.* **прикосну́ться** (**к** *with dat.*) to touch.

прикла́д[1] *m.* rifle butt; butt-stock.

прикла́д[2] *m.* (*sewing*) trimmings; findings.

прикладно́й *adj.* applied.

прикла́дывать *impf. pf.* **приложи́ть** (**к** *with dat.*) **1.** to add. **2.** to enclose. **3.** to apply.

прикле́ивать *impf. pf.* **прикле́ить** to stock *or* paste to.

приключе́ние *neut.* adventure.

приключи́ться *pf.* (*colloq.*) to happen, to occur.

прико́л *m.:* **на прико́ле** (*naut.*) **1.** moored. **2.** laid up; idle.

прикоснове́ние *neut.* touch, contact.

прикрепля́ть *impf. pf.* **прикрепи́ть** (**к** *with dat.*) to fasten; to attach (to).

прикрыва́ть *impf. pf.* **прикры́ть** to cover; to close.

прилага́тельное *neut. also* **и́мя прилага́тельное** *adjective.*

прилага́ть *impf. pf.* **приложи́ть** to attach; to apply.

прила́живать *impf. pf.* **прила́дить** to fit; to adjust.

приласка́ть *pf.* **1.** to pet. **2.** to caress. **3.** to be nice to.

прилега́ть *impf.* (**к** *with dat.*) **1.** to be located adjacent to. **2.** (*of clothes*) to fit; to fit snugly.

прилега́ющий *adj.* adjoining, adjacent.

приле́жный *adj.* diligent.

прилепля́ть *impf. pf.* **прилепи́ть** (**к** *with dat.*) to stick to; to affix to.

прилета́ть *impf. pf.* **прилете́ть** to arrive (*by air*).

прили́в *m.* high tide.

прилипа́ние *neut.* adhesion; sticking to.

прили́чие *neut.* decency; decorum.

прили́чно *adv.* **1.** properly; decently. **2.** (*colloq.*) quite well; quite a lot of.

прили́чный *adj.* decent.

приложе́ние *neut.* **1.** supplement. **2.** enclosure.

приложи́ть *pf. of* **прикла́дывать, прилага́ть.**

прима́нка *f.* **1.** bait; lure. **2.** attraction.

прима́с *m.* (*eccl.*) primate.

примене́ние *neut.* application.

примени́мый *adj.* applicable.

примени́тельно *adv.* (**к** *with dat.*) in conformity with; with reference to.

применя́ть *impf. pf.* **примени́ть 1.** to apply, adapt. **2.** to employ, use.

приме́р *m.* example. **—ный** *adj.* exemplary.

приме́рно *adv.* **1.** approximately. **2.** in an exemplary manner. **3.** (*colloq.*) for example.

примеря́ть *impf. pf.* **приме́рить** to try on; to fit.

при́месь *f.* admixture; tinge; dash.

приме́та *f.* sign, token, mark.

приме́тный *adj.* **1.** noticeable. **2.** conspicuous.

примеча́ние *neut.* note, footnote; comment.

примеча́тельный *adj.* notable, remarkable.

примина́ть *impf. pf.* **примя́ть 1.** to crush. **2.** to flatten; to trample down.

примире́ние *neut.* reconciliation.

примири́тельный *adj.* reconciliatory.

примиря́ть *impf. pf.* **примири́ть** to reconcile; to conciliate.

примо́рье *neut.* littoral; seaside.

при́мула *f.* primrose.

принадлежа́ть *impf.* (*with dat.*) to belong to.

принадле́жность *f.* belonging; affiliation. — **принадле́жности** *pl.* accessories.

принижа́ть *impf. pf.* **прини́зить 1.** to humiliate. **2.** to belittle.

приниже́ние *neut.* **1.** humiliation. **2.** disparagement.

принима́ть *impf. pf.* **приня́ть** to receive; to accept; to assume; to adopt.

приноси́ть *impf. pf.* **принести́ 1.** to bring. **2.** to yield.

приноше́ние *neut.* offering; gift.

принуди́тельный *adj.* compulsory.

принужда́ть *impf. pf.* **прину́дить** to compel, to force.

принужде́ние *neut.* compulsion.

принуждённый *adj.* **1.** forced; constrained. **2.** unnatural.

при́нцип *m.* principle. — **в при́нципе** in principle.

принципиа́льно *adv.* in essence, in principle.

приня́тие *neut.* **1.** adoption. **2.** reception. **3.** acceptance.

при́нятый *adj.* accepted.

приня́ть *pf. of* **принима́ть.**

приобрета́ть *impf. pf.* **приобрести́** to acquire; to gain.

приорите́т *m.* **1.** priority. **2.** being first.

приостано́вка *f.* halt; suspension.

приостановле́ние *neut.* halt; suspension.

припа́док FILL *m.* attack; fit.

припа́рка *f.* fomentation; poultice.

припа́сы *pl.* supplies, stores.

припе́в (*mus.*) refrain.

припёк *m.* the full heat from the sun.

припи́ска *f.* postscript. — **припи́ски** *pl.* falsification of figures.

припи́сывать *impf. pf.* **приписа́ть 1.** to add (*in a written text*). **2.** to attribute.

припла́та *f.* surcharge; extra charge.

припло́д *m.* **1.** litter. **2.** offspring.

приподнима́ть *impf. pf.* **приподня́ть** to raise slightly.

припо́днятый *adj.* **1.** exultant; elated. **2.** (*of language* or *style*) elevated.

припо́й *m.* solder.

припомина́ть *impf. pf.* **припо́мнить** to remember, to recollect.

припра́ва *f.* **1.** seasoning; flavoring. **2.** dressing. **3.** condiment.

При́пять *f.* (*river*) Pripet.

прираще́ние *neut.* increase; increment.

приро́да *f.* nature.

приро́дный *adj.* natural; inborn, innate.

приро́ст *m.* increase.

прируча́ть *impf. pf.* **приручи́ть** to domesticate; to tame.

приса́дка *f.* additive.

приса́живаться *impf. pf.* **присе́сть** to sit down; to take a seat.

присва́ивать *impf. pf.* **присво́ить** to appropriate.

приседа́ние *neut.* **1.** squatting. **2.** crouch.

приседа́ть *impf. pf.* **присе́сть** to squat.

при́сказка *f.* **1.** introduction; prelude. **2.** saying.

приско́рбие *neut.* (*obs.*) sorrow; regret.

присла́ть *pf. of* **присыла́ть.**

прислу́га *f.* **1.** (*mil.*) team; crew. **2.** *m. and f.* (*decl. f.*) (*obs.*) servant. **3.** (*obs.*) servants.

присмо́тр *m.* supervision.

присни́ться *pf. of* **сни́ться.**

присоединя́ть *impf. pf.* **присоедини́ть** *v.t.* **1.** to join, to add. **2.** to annex.

приспе́шник *m. f.* **приспе́шница** henchman.

приспособле́ние *neut.* **1.** adaptation. **2.** accomodation. **3.** device.

приспособля́ть *impf. pf.* **приспосо́бить 1.** to adapt. **2.** to accomodate.

при́став *m.* (*pre-rev.*) police officer. — **суде́бный при́став** *m.* (*pre-rev.*) bailiff.

пристава́ть *impf. pf.* **приста́ть 1.** to stick *or* adhere (to) **2.** to come alongside. **3.** to pester, to nag, to bother.

приста́вка *f.* (*gram.*) prefix.

приставля́ть *impf. pf.* **приста́вить** (**к** *with dat.*) to put *or* set against; to lean against.

приста́льный *adj.* (*of look*) fixed.

при́стань *f.* pier, dock, wharf.

приста́ть *pf. of* **пристава́ть.**

пристойный *adj.* proper; decorous.

пристрастие *neut.* (к *with dat.*) **1.** bent; predilection. **2.** bias.

пристрастность *f.* partiality.

пристрелка *f.* **1.** adjusting the sights on a weapon. **2.** zeroing in (*on a target*).

пристройка *f.* annex; extension.

приструнивать *impf. pf.* приструнить (*colloq.*) to crack down on.

приступ *m.* **1.** assault. **2.** attack, fit.

приступать *impf. pf.* приступить (к *with dat.*) to begin, to start; to proceed (to).

присутствие *neut.* presence.

присутствовать OVA *impf.* to be present, to attend.

присущий *adj.* (*with dat.*) inherent in.

присылать *impf. pf.* прислать to send.

присяга *f.* oath.

присягать *impf. pf.* присягнуть to swear; to take an oath.

притворный *adj.* affected, feigned; sham.

притворяться *impf. pf.* притвориться *v.i.* **1.** to be shut, to be closed. **2.** (*with instr.*) to feign.

притеснять *impf. pf.* притеснить to oppress.

приток *m.* tributary.

притом *conj.* besides.

притон *m.* den (*e.g. gambling den*).

приторный *adj.* sugary; saccharine.

притча *f.* parable. — что это за притча! (*colloq.*) what a strange thing!

притягательный *adj.* attractive.

притягивать *impf. pf.* притянуть to attract.

притяжательный *adj.* (*gram.*) possessive.

притяжение *neut.* attraction.

притязательный *adj.* pretentious.

приурочивать *impf. pf.* приурочить (к *with dat.*) to time to coincide with.

прихватывать *impf. pf.* прихватить (*colloq.*) **1.** to grip. **2.** to tie up. **3.** to take along. **4.** (*of frost*) to damage.

прихлебатель *m. f.* —ница (*colloq.*) parasite; sponger; hanger-on.

прихлёбывать *impf. pf.* прихлебнуть (*colloq.*) to sip.

прихлынуть *pf.* to rush; to surge.

приход *m.* **1.** arrival. **2.** receipts.

приходить *impf. pf.* прийти to come, to arrive.

приходиться *impf. pf.* прийтись **1.** to fit. **2.** to land on; to fall on. **3.** to fall (*on a certain date*). **4.** *impers.* (*with dat.* and *infin.*) to have to.

приходо-расходный *adj.* (*attrib.*) receipts and disbursements.

прихожанин *m. f.* прихожанка parishioner.

прихожая *f.* hall; entryway; vestibule.

прихотливый *adj.* capricious, whimsical.

прихоть *f.* caprice, whim.

прицел *m.* sight (*on a gun*).

прицеп *m.* trailer.

прицеплять *impf. pf.* прицепить (к *with dat.*) **1.** to hook (on). **2.** to couple; to join.

причал *m.* **1.** berth (*at a dock*). **2.** mooring. **3.** mooring line.

причаливать *impf. pf.* причалить **1.** to moor. **2.** (к *with dat.*) to tie up at.

причастие *neut.* participle.

Причастие *neut.* (*relig.*) the Eucharist.

причастный *adj.* **1.** participating. **2.** involved in *or* with.

причём *conj.* **1.** in which connection. **2.** moreover; and. **3.** at that.

причёска *f.* coiffure.

причёсывать *impf. pf.* причесать to comb; to dress (*hair*).

причина *f.* cause; reason.

причинять *impf. pf.* причинить to cause.

причитание *neut.* lamentation.

причуда *f.* whim; caprice.

причудливый *adj.* **1.** odd; queer; quaint. **2.** (*colloq.*) whimsical; capricious.

пришелец FILL *m. f.* пришелица newcomer.

пришибленный *adj.* crushed.

пришивать *impf. pf.* пришить to sew on.

прищемлять *impf. pf.* прищемить to catch (*e.g. one's finger in a door*).

прищуривать *impf. pf.* прищурить to squint.

приют *m.* asylum, shelter, refuge. — детский приют *m.* orphanage.

приятель *m. f.* —ница friend. —ский *adj.* friendly.

приятно *adv.* pleasantly. –*adj.* (*pred.*) pleasant.

приятный *adj.* pleasant.

про *prep.* (*with acc.*) about; for.

проанализировать OVA *pf. of* анализировать.

проба *f.* trial, test. **2.** sample.

пробег *m.* run.

пробегать *pf.* to run around (*for a certain length of time*).

пробегать *impf. pf.* пробежать to run past.

пробел *m.* gap; flaw.

пробивать *impf. pf.* пробить to make *or* punch a hole in.

пробиваться *impf. pf.* пробиться **1.** to force one's way to *or* through. **2.** to seep through.

пробивной *adj.* (*colloq.*) aggressive; pushy.

пробираться *impf. pf.* пробраться to make one's way through.

пробирка *f.* test tube.

пробка *f.* cork; stopper.

проблема *f.* problem.

проблеск *m.* **1.** gleam. **2.** flash. **3.** glimmer (*of hope*).

пробовать OVA *impf. pf.* по- **1.** to attempt, to try. **2.** to taste.

пробой *m.* hasp.

пробор *m.* part, parting (*in one's hair*).

пробуждать *impf. pf.* пробудить to wake up; to awaken; to arouse.

пробыть *pf.* to stay, to remain (*for a certain time*).

провал *m.* **1.** collapse. **2.** failure, flop.

проваливаться *impf. pf.* провалиться **1.** to fail. **2.** to fall through.

Прованс *m.* (*province*) Provence.

проведывать *impf. pf.* проведать **1.** to find out; to learn. **2.** to pay a visit to someone.

провезти *pf. of* провозить.

провентилировать OVA *pf. of* вентилировать.

проверка *f.* **1.** check, examination. **2.** control.

проверять *impf. pf.* проверить to check; to verify.

провести *pf. of* проводить.

проветривать *impf. pf.* проветрить to air, to ventilate.

провидение *neut.* foresight.

провидение *neut.* (*relig.*) Providence.

провизия *f.* provisions.

прови́зор *m.* pharmacist.

про́вод *m.* wire.

проводи́ть[1] *pf. of* провожа́ть.

проводи́ть[2] *impf. pf.* **провести́ 1.** to lead. **2.** to build. **3.** to conduct, to carry out.

прово́дка *f.* **1.** installation. **2.** wiring.

проводни́к[1] *m. f.* **проводни́ца 1.** guide. **2.** conductor (*on train*).

проводни́к[2] *m.* (*phys. and fig.*) conductor.

про́воды *pl.* send-off; seeing someone off.

провожа́тый *m.* guide.

провожа́ть *impf. pf.* **проводи́ть** to accompany; to see off.

прово́з *m.* transport.

провозглаша́ть *impf. pf.* **провозгласи́ть** to announce; to proclaim.

провози́ть *impf. pf.* **провезти́** to transport; to convey.

про́волока *f.* wire. — **колю́чая про́волока** *f.* barbed wire.

проволо́чка *f.* (*colloq.*) delay.

прово́рный *adj.* quick, agile, adroit.

провоци́ровать OVA *impf. and pf.* to provoke.

прога́лина *f.* glade.

проги́б *m.* sagging; sag.

прогля́дывать[1] *impf. pf.* **прогляну́ть** to appear, to be visible *or* perceptible.

прогля́дывать[2] *impf. pf.* **прогляде́ть** to look through; to skim.

прогневи́ть *pf. of* гневи́ть.

проголода́ть *pf.* to endure hunger (*for a certain time*).

проголосова́ть *pf. of* голосова́ть.

прогоня́ть *impf. pf.* **прогна́ть** to drive away *or* off.

прого́рклый *adj.* rank, rancid.

програ́мма *f.* **1.** program; schedule. **2.** syllabus.

прогресси́ровать OVA *impf.* to progress, to advance.

прогрохота́ть *pf. of* грохота́ть.

прогу́ливаться *impf.* to take a walk *or* stroll.

прогу́лка *f.* walk, stroll.

продава́ть *impf. pf.* **прода́ть** to sell.

продаве́ц FILL *m.* salesman.

продавщи́ца *f.* saleswoman.

прода́жа *f.* sale; selling.

прода́жный *adj.* **1.** for sale. **2.** corrupt, mercenary.

продвига́ться *impf. pf.* **продви́нуться** to advance.

продвиже́ние *neut.* advancement, progress.

продви́нутый *adj.* advanced.

продеклами́ровать OVA *pf. of* декламировать.

проде́лка *f.* trick.

продиктова́ть OVA *pf. of* диктова́ть.

продлева́ть *impf. pf.* **продли́ть** to prolong.

продли́ть *pf. of* продлева́ть.

продово́льствие *neut.* food; foodstuffs.

продолгова́тый *adj.* oblong.

продолжа́ть *impf. pf.* **продо́лжить** *v.t.* to continue.

продолже́ние *neut.* continuation.

продолжи́тельность *f.* duration.

продолжи́тельный *adj.* of long duration.

продо́льный *adj.* longitudinal.

проду́кт *m.* product. — **проду́кты** *pl.* groceries; products.

продукти́вность *f.* productivity; efficiency.

продукто́вый магази́н *m.* grocery store.

проду́кция *f.* production; output.

проду́мывать *impf. pf.* **проду́мать** to think over *or* through.

проеда́ть *impf. pf.* **прое́сть** to eat away; to corrode.

прое́зд *m.* passage; trip; thoroughfare.

проездно́й биле́т *m.* ticket.

проезжа́ть *impf. pf.* **прое́хать** to pass; to go by *or* past (*by vehicle*).

прое́зжий *m.* person traveling through (*a certain place*).

проекти́ровать OVA *impf. pf.* **за- 1.** to project. **2.** to plan, to design.

прое́ктор *m.* projector.

проём *m.* opening (*for a door or window*).

прое́сть *pf. of* проеда́ть.

прое́хать *pf. of* проезжа́ть.

прожа́ренный *adj.* (*of meat*) well-done.

прожёктор *m.* searchlight.

прожива́ние *neut.* **1.** residing. **2.** squandering.

прожива́ть *impf. pf.* **прожи́ть 1.** to live through. **2.** *impf. only* to live, to reside.

прожига́ть *impf. pf.* **прожёчь** to burn through.

прожи́лка *f.* vein; streak.

прожо́рливый *adj.* voracious.

про́за *f.* prose.

проза́ический *adj.* prosaic.

про́звище *neut.* nickname.

прозвуча́ть *pf. of* звуча́ть.

прозимова́ть OVA *pf. of* зимова́ть.

прозо́рливый *adj.* sagacious; perspicacious.

прозра́чный *adj.* transparent.

прозыва́ть *impf. pf.* **прозва́ть** to nickname.

прозяба́ть *impf.* to vegetate.

прои́грывать *impf. pf.* **проигра́ть** to lose.

про́игрыш *m.* loss.

произведе́ние *neut.* work; product.

производи́тель *m.* producer.

производи́ть *impf. pf.* **произвести́** to produce.

произво́дный *adj.* derivative.

произво́дственный *adj.* industrial.

произво́дство *neut.* production; manufacture.

произво́л *m.* **1.** arbitrary rule; despotism. **2.** arbitrariness.

произво́льный *adj.* arbitrary.

произнесе́ние *neut.* **1.** pronouncing (*of a sentence*). **2.** giving (*of a speech*).

произноси́ть *impf. pf.* **произнести́** to pronounce.

произноше́ние *neut.* pronunciation.

про́иски *pl.* intrigues; plotting.

происходи́ть *impf. pf.* **произойти́ 1.** to happen. **2.** to descend (from), to originate.

происхожде́ние *neut.* origin.

происше́ствие *neut.* event; occurrence.

пройдо́ха *m. and f.* (*decl. f.*) (*colloq.*) scoundrel; rascal.

про́йма *f.* armhole.

пройти́ *pf. of* проходи́ть.

прок *m.* (*colloq.*) good; use. — **како́й в э́том прок?** what's the good of it?

прока́за[1] *f.* leprosy.

прока́за[2] *f.* mischief.

прока́лывать *impf. pf.* **проколо́ть** to pierce.

прока́т *m.* hire.

прока́тка *f.* rolling (*of metal*).

прока́шливаться *impf. pf.* **прока́шляться** to clear one's throat.

прокла́дка *f.* **1.** laying; building; construction. **2.** (*tech.*) washer; gasket. **3.** padding; packing.

прокла́дывать *impf. pf.* **проложи́ть 1.** to build, to construct. **2.** to lay. **3.** to interlay.

проклама́ция *f.* leaflet.

проклами́ровать OVA *impf. and pf.* to proclaim.

проклина́ть *impf. pf.* **прокля́сть** to damn; to curse.

прокля́тие *neut.* curse; damnation.

прокля́тый *adj.* cursed; damned.

проко́л *m.* puncture.

проколо́ть *pf. of* **прока́лывать.**

проконсульти́ровать OVA *pf. of* **консульти́ровать.**

прокорректи́ровать OVA *pf. of* **корректи́ровать.**

проко́с *m.* swath.

прокуро́р *m.* prosecutor.

прокути́ть *pf.* to squander.

про́лежень FILL *m.* bedsore.

пролёт *m.* **1.** flight. **2.** bridge span.

пролета́рий *m. f.* **пролета́рка** proletarian.

пролётка *f.* open carriage.

проли́в *m.* (*geog.*) strait.

пролива́ть *impf. pf.* **проли́ть** to spill; to shed.

проло́м *m.* break; fracture.

прома́тывать *impf. pf.* **промота́ть** (*colloq.*) to squander; to dissipate.

про́мах *m.* miss; blunder.

прома́чивать *impf. pf.* **промочи́ть** to drench.

промедле́ние *neut.* delay.

проме́жность *f.* crotch.

промежу́ток FILL *m.* interval; space.

промежу́точный *adj.* intermediate.

проме́нивать *impf. pf.* **променя́ть** to exchange; to barter.

промо́зглый *adj.* dank; damp.

промока́тельная бума́га *f.* blotter.

промока́ть[1] *impf. pf.* **промо́кнуть** to get wet; to be drenched.

промока́ть[2] *impf. pf.* **промокну́ть** to blot.

промолча́ть *pf.* to keep silent.

промота́ть *pf. of* **прома́тывать.**

промча́ться *pf.* to rush past; to fly by.

промыва́ть *impf. pf.* **промы́ть** *v.t.* to wash.

про́мысел FILL *m.* **1.** trade; business. **2.** hunting; catching. — **про́мыслы** *pl.* fields; mines.

про́мысл *m.* (*relig.*) Providence.

промы́шленник *m.* industrialist; manufacturer.

промы́шленность *f.* industry.

пронза́ть *impf. pf.* **пронзи́ть 1.** to pierce. **2.** to run through.

пронзи́тельный *adj.* piercing.

прони́зывать *impf. pf.* **прониза́ть** to penetrate.

проника́ть *impf. pf.* **прони́кнуть** to penetrate.

проникнове́ние *neut.* penetration.

прони́кнутый *adj.* (*with instr.*) imbued *or* inspired with.

пронича́емый *adj.* permeable.

проница́тельный *adj.* perspicacious; acute.

проны́ра *m. and f.* (*decl. f.*) (*colloq.*) **1.** string-puller. **2.** pushy person.

пропаганди́ровать OVA *impf. pf.* to propagandize.

пропада́ть *impf. pf.* **пропа́сть** to disappear; to be missing *or* lost.

пропа́жа *f.* loss.

пропа́лывать *impf. pf.* **прополо́ть** to weed.

пропа́сть *pf. of* **пропада́ть.**

про́пасть *f.* chasm; abyss.

пропи́ска *f.* **1.** residence permit. **2.** registration.

описна́я бу́ква *f.* capital letter.

пропи́сывать *impf. pf.* **прописа́ть 1.** to prescribe. **2.** to register.

пропита́ние *neut.* subsistence.

пропи́тывать *impf. pf.* **пропита́ть** to saturate.

пропове́дник *m. f.* **пропове́дница 1.** preacher. **2.** exponent; proponent; advocate.

пропове́довать OVA *impf.* to preach.

про́поведь *f.* sermon.

пропо́рция *f.* proportion.

про́пуск *m.* **1.** absence. **2.** omission. **3.** pass, permit.

пропуска́ть *impf. pf.* **пропусти́ть 1.** to let pass, to admit. **2.** to omit, to leave out. **3.** to miss.

прора́б *m.* construction superintendent (*abbr. of* **производи́тель рабо́т** *m.*).

прораста́ть *impf. pf.* **прорасти́** to germinate; to sprout.

прорва́ть(ся) *pf. of* **прорыва́ть(ся).**

проре́з *m.* cut.

прореза́ть *impf. pf.* **прореза́ть** to cut through.

про́резь *f.* slit; opening; cut.

проре́ха *f.* **1.** tear. **2.** deficiency. **3.** shortcoming.

прорица́ние *neut.* soothsaying; prophecy.

прорица́ть *impf.* to prophesy.

проро́к *m. f.* **проро́чица** prophet.

проро́чество *neut.* prophecy.

про́рубь *f.* hole in the ice.

проры́в *m.* break-through; breach; gap.

прорыва́ть[1] *impf. pf.* **прорва́ть** to break through. —**ся 1.** to burst open, to tear. **2.** to break.

прорыва́ть[2] *impf. pf.* **проры́ть** to dig through *or* across.

проса́ливать[1] *impf. pf.* **проса́лить** to grease.

проса́ливать[2] *impf. pf.* **просоли́ть** to salt.

проса́чиваться *impf. pf.* **просочи́ться 1.** to seep. **2.** to penetrate. **3.** to leak out.

просве́рливать *impf. pf.* **просверли́ть 1.** to bore a hole. **2.** to drill through.

просве́т *m.* **1.** shaft of light. **2.** (*archit.*) slit; aperture; opening.

просвети́тельный *adj.* instructive.

просветле́ние *neut.* brightening; (*fig.*) lucidity.

просве́чивание *neut.* x-raying; radioscopy.

просве́чивать *impf. pf.* **просвети́ть** to x-ray.

просвеща́ть *impf. pf.* **просвети́ть** to enlighten.

просвеще́ние *neut.* enlightenment; education.

просвира́ *f.* (*Orth. Church*) host; communion bread.

просви́рник *also* **просвирня́к** *m.* marsh mallow.

просе́ивать *impf. pf.* **просе́ять** to sift.

просе́ка *f.* cleared path in the forest.

просёлок FILL *m.* country road; secondary road.

про́синь *m.* bluish tint.

проси́тель *m. f.* **—ница** applicant, petitioner.

проси́ть *impf. pf.* **по- 1.** to ask; to request. **2.** to beg. **3.** to invite.

просия́ть *pf.* to clear up; to brighten; to light up (with).

проскрипе́ть *pf. of* **скрипе́ть.**

проскурня́к *m.* marsh mallow.

просла́вить *pf. of* **прославля́ть.**

прославле́ние *neut.* glorification.

прославля́ть *impf. pf.* **просла́вить** to glorify; to make famous; to bring fame to.

прослёживать *impf. pf.* проследи́ть 1. to trace, to track. 2. to monitor.

просло́йка *f.* 1. layer. 2. social stratum.

просма́тривать *impf. pf.* просмотрёть to look through; to miss, to overlook.

просмо́тр *m.* 1. examination. 2. review.

просну́ться *pf. of* просыпа́ться.

про́со *neut.* millet.

просоли́ть *pf. of* проса́ливать.

проспа́ть *pf. of* просыпа́ть.

просро́ченный *adj.* overdue.

просро́чивать *impf. pf.* просро́чить to exceed a time limit.

просро́чка *f.* 1. delinquency (*in paying a bill*). 2. expiration.

проста́к *m.* simpleton.

простёртый *adj.* 1. outstretched (*hand or arm*). 2. stretched out on the floor.

простира́ть[1] *impf. pf.* простерёть to reach out; to extend. —ся *v.i.* to stretch; to range.

простира́ть[2] *pf. of* прости́рывать to wash (out).

прости́тельный *adj.* pardonable, excusable.

проститу́тка *f.* prostitute.

прости́ть(ся) *pf. of* проща́ть(ся).

про́сто *adv.* simply. —ва́тый *adj.* (*colloq.*) simple, simpleminded. —ду́шие *neut.* artlessness. —рёчие *neut.* popular speech. —сердёчный *adj.* simple-hearted.

просто́й[1] *adj.* 1. simple; easy. 2. plain, ordinary, common.

просто́й[2] *m.* downtime; idle time.

простоква́ша *f.* thick sour milk; clabber.

просто́р *m.* 1. spaciousness. 2. scope.

просто́рный *adj.* spacious; roomy.

простота́ *f.* simplicity.

простофи́ля *m. and f.* (*decl. f.*) (*colloq.*) nincompoop.

простра́нный *adj.* extensive; vast.

простра́нство *neut.* space.

простра́ция *f.* prostration.

прострёл *m.* lumbago.

просту́да *f.* cold; chill.

простужа́ться *impf. pf.* простуди́ться to catch a cold.

просту́пок FILL *m.* fault; misdemeanor.

простыня́ *f.* bedsheet.

просущёствова́ть OVA *pf.* 1. to exist; to subsist. 2. to endure.

просчёт *m.* 1. error (*in counting*). 2. miscalculation.

просчи́тываться *impf. pf.* просчита́ться to miscalculate.

просыпа́ть[1] *impf. pf.* проспа́ть to oversleep.

просыпа́ть[2] *impf. pf.* просы́пать *v.t.* to spill. —ся *v.i.* to spill.

просыпа́ться *impf. pf.* просну́ться to wake up, to awake.

про́сьба *f.* request.

прота́лина *f.* patch of earth where snow has thawed.

прота́пливать *impf. pf.* протопи́ть 1. to heat sufficiently. 2. *impf. only* to heat slightly; to warm slightly.

протёз *m.* prosthetic device; artificial limb.

протека́ть *impf. pf.* протёчь 1. to leak. 2. to go by.

протерёть *pf. of* протира́ть.

протестова́ть *impf.* to protest.

про́тив *prep.* (*with gen.*) against; opposite.

про́тивень FILL *m.* baking sheet; roasting pan.

проти́виться *impf. pf.* вос- 1. to oppose. 2. to object to. 3. to resist.

проти́вник *m. f.* проти́вница opponent.

проти́вно *adv.* 1. repulsively. 2. in a disgusting way. — *adj.* (*pred.*) offensive; disgusting.

проти́вный *adj.* 1. opposite, contrary. 2. disgusting.

противовёс *m.* counterbalance.

противодёйствовать OVA *impf.* 1. to oppose. 2. to counteract.

противозако́нный *adj.* illegal.

противозача́точный *adj.* contraceptive.

противолежа́щий *adj.* 1. opposite; facing. 2. (*of an angle*) alternate.

противополо́жное *neut.* the opposite.

противополо́жный *adj.* contrary; opposite.

противопоставля́ть *impf. pf.* противопоста́вить (*with dat.*) 1. to oppose to. 2. to contrast with.

противорёчить *impf.* (*with dat.*) to contradict.

противостоя́ть *impf.* 1. to resist. 2. to withstand.

противоя́дие *neut.* antidote.

протира́ть *impf. pf.* протерёть 1. to wear out *or* through. 2. to dry, to wipe dry.

прото́к *m.* 1. channel. 2. (*anat.*) duct.

протоко́л *m.* minutes; record.

протопи́ть *pf. of* прота́пливать.

проторённый *adj.* (*of a road or path*) beaten; well-trodden.

прото́чный *adj.* flowing; running.

протра́ва *f.* mordant.

протыка́ть *impf. pf.* проткну́ть to pierce.

протя́гивать *impf. pf.* протяну́ть to stretch; to stretch out; to reach out.

протяжёние *neut.* extent; stretch.

протяжённый *adj.* extensive, lengthy.

протя́жный *adj.* 1. drawn out. 2. drawling.

протяну́ть *pf. of* протя́гивать.

профа́н *m.* ignoramus.

профани́ровать OVA *impf. and pf.* to profane.

профессиона́л *m.* professional. —ьный *adj.* professional.

профёссия *f.* profession.

профёссор *m.* professor.

профессу́ра *f.* 1. professorship. 2. professors.

про́филь *m.* 1. profile. 2. type.

профо́рг *m.* union leader.

профсою́з *m.* trade union.

прохво́ст *m.* (*colloq.*) scoundrel.

прохла́да *f.* coolness.

прохла́дно *adv.* cooly. — *adj.* (*pred.*) 1. cool. 2. chilly.

прохла́дный *adj.* cool, chilly, fresh.

прохлажда́ться *impf. pf.* прохлади́ться (*colloq.*) to refresh oneself; to cool off.

прохо́д *m.* passage.

проходи́мость *f.* 1. (*of roads*) passability. 2. permeability. 3. (*of a vehicle*) cross-country ability.

проходи́ть *impf. pf.* пройти́ 1. to pass; to elapse. 2. to come to an end. 3. to cover, to study.

прохо́жий *m.* passer-by.

процвета́ть *impf.* to prosper.

процёнт *m.* 1. percentage; percent. 2. interest.

процёсс *m.* 1. process. 2. lawsuit, case, trial.

прочёсть *pf. of* чита́ть.

про́чий *adj.* other. — и про́чее and so on; etc. — ме́жду про́чим by the way.
прочита́ть *pf.* **1.** *pf. of* чита́ть to read. **2.** to spend time reading.
про́чно *adv.* securely; solidly; firmly.
про́чный *adj.* firm, solid; lasting.
прочу́вствовать OVA *pf.* to feel deeply *or* acutely.
прочь *adv.* away; off.
проше́дшее *neut.* the past.
проше́дший *adj.* past.
проше́ние *neut.* petition.
проши́вка *f.* lace trim.
про́шлое *neut.* the past.
про́шлый *adj.* past; last.
прошмы́гивать *impf. pf.* прошмыгну́ть to sneak into; to slip (*into or* past).
проща́й(те) *interj.* good-bye!
проща́льный *adj.* (*attrib.*) farewell, parting.
проща́ние *neut.* farewell, parting.
проща́ть *impf. pf.* прости́ть to forgive; to excuse. —ся **1.** to take leave. **2.** to say good-bye.
про́ще *adj., adv.* simpler, easier.
проще́ние *neut.* forgiveness; pardon.
проявитель (*photog.*) developer.
проявле́ние *neut.* display; manifestation.
проявля́ть *impf. pf.* прояви́ть to display, show; to manifest.
проясня́ть *impf. pf.* проясни́ть to make clear. —ся **1.** to clear up. **2.** to brighten up. **3.** to become clear.
пруд *m.* pond.
пружи́на *f.* spring.
пруса́к *m.* (*colloq.*) cockroach.
пру́сский *adj.* Prussian.
Прут *m.* (*river*) Prut.
прут *m.* twig; rod.
пры́гать *impf. pf.* пры́гнуть to jump; to leap; to hop.
прыжо́к FILL *m.* jump, leap. — прыжо́к в во́ду dive.
пры́ткий *adj.* (*colloq.*) quick.
прыщ *also* пры́щик *m.* pimple.
пряде́ние *neut.* spinning.
пряди́льный *adj.* (*attrib.*) spinning.
пря́дь *f.* lock (*of hair*).
пря́жа *f.* thread, yarn.
пря́жка *f.* buckle, clasp.
пря́лка *f.* **1.** distaff. **2.** spinning wheel.
пряма́я речь *f.* direct discourse.
пря́мо *adv.* **1.** straight. **2.** frankly. —ду́шный *adj.* frank; straightforward.
прямо́й *adj.* **1.** straight; direct. **2.** frank. — прямо́й у́гол *m.* (*math*) right angle.
прямо́й шрифт *m.* (*typog.*) Roman type.
прямолине́йный *adj.* **1.** straightforward. **2.** rectilinear.
прямота́ *f.* uprightness.
прямоуго́льник *m.* rectangle.
пря́ник *m.* spice cake; gingerbread.
пря́ность *f.* spice.
пря́тать *impf. pf.* с- to hide; to conceal.
пря́тки *pl.* hide-and-seek.
пря́ха *f.* spinner (*woman*).
псало́м FILL *m.* psalm.
Псалты́рь *m.* or *f.* Psalter.
пса́рня *f.* kennel.

псевдони́м *m.* pseudonym.
псих *m.* (*colloq.*) lunatic; nut; mental case.
психиа́тр *m.* psychiatrist.
пси́хика *f.* psyche.
психи́ческий *adj.* mental; psychic(al).
психоана́лиз *m.* psychoanalysis.
психо́з *m.* psychosis.
психо́лог *m.* psychologist.
психоневро́з *m.* psychoneurosis.
психопа́т *m. f.* —ка psychopath.
психотерапи́я *f.* psychotherapy.
Псков *m.* Pskov.
пта́шка *f.* (*colloq.*) little bird; birdie.
птене́ц FILL *m.* baby bird; fledgling.
пти́ца *f.* bird.
пти́чий *adj.* **1.** (*attrib.*) bird. **2.** bird-like.
пу́блика *f.* the public; audience.
публикова́ть OVA *impf. pf.* о- to publish.
публи́чный *adj.* public.
пу́гало *neut.* scarecrow.
пуга́ть *impf. pf.* ис-, пугну́ть to frighten; to scare.
пугли́вый *adj.* timid; fearful.
пу́говица *f.* button.
пуд *m.* pood (*old unit of weight of approx. 36 pounds*).
пу́дель *m.* poodle.
пу́дра *f.* powder.
пу́дреница *f.* lady's compact.
пу́дрить *impf. pf.* на- to powder.
пу́зо *neut.* (*colloq.*) belly; paunch.
пузырёк FILL *m.* **1.** bubble. **2.** small bottle.
пузы́рь *m.* **1.** bubble; blister. **2.** bladder.
пук *m.* **1.** bundle; bunch. **2.** tuft. **3.** wisp.
пулемёт *m.* machine gun.
пуло́вер *m.* pullover.
пульс *m.* pulse.
пульси́ровать OVA *impf.* to pulsate; to throb.
пульт *m.* **1.** console; control panel. **2.** music stand.
пу́ля *f.* bullet.
пункт *m.* **1.** point. **2.** station; post.
пункти́р *m.* dotted line.
пунктуа́льный *adj.* punctual.
пунктуа́ция *f.* (*gram.*) punctuation.
пунцо́вый *adj.* crimson.
пуп *m.* (*colloq.*) navel; bellybutton.
пупа́вка *f.* camomile.
пупови́на *f.* umbilical cord.
пупо́к FILL *m.* navel.
пурга́ *f.* blizzard; snowstorm.
пу́рпур *m.* purple.
пурпу́рный *adj.* purple.
пуск *m.* **1.** setting in motion; starting (up). **2.** launching.
пуска́ть *impf. pf.* пусти́ть **1.** to set free. **2.** to let in, to admit. **3.** to permit. **4.** to put into circulation.
пустельга́ *f.* kestrel.
пусте́ть *impf. pf.* о- to become empty *or* deserted.
пустова́ть OVA *impf.* to be empty.
пустозво́н *m.* (*colloq.*) windbag.
пусто́й *adj.* **1.** empty, hollow. **2.** uninhabited; vacant.
пустоме́ля *m. and f.* (*decl. f.*) (*colloq.*) windbag.
пустота́ *f.* emptiness; vacuum.
пу́стошь *f.* uncultivated plot of land.

пусты́нник *m. f.* пусты́нница hermit.
пусты́нный *adj.* (*attrib.*) desert; uninhabited.
пусты́ня *f.* desert.
пусты́рь *m.* neglected plot of land; abandoned lot.
пусть *particle* let. — пусть он идёт let him go.
пустя́к *m.* trifle.
пу́таница *f.* confusion.
пу́таный *adj.* 1. tangled. 2. rambling; confused. 3. mixed up.
пу́тать *impf.* to confuse; to mix up.
путёвка *f.* 1. (travel) voucher. 2. permit; pass. 3. place in a tourist group.
путеводи́тель *m.* guidebook.
путе́ец FILL *m.* railway engineer.
путём *prep.* (*with gen.*) by way of; by means of.
путеше́ственник *m. f.* путеше́ственница traveler.
путеше́ствие *neut.* voyage, trip, journey.
путеше́ствовать OVA *impf.* to travel.
Пути́вль *f.* Putyvel (*Russian: Putivl*).
пу́тник *m. f.* пу́тница (*obs.*) traveler.
пу́тный *adj.* (*colloq.*) 1. sensible. 2. worthwhile.
пу́ты *pl.* fetters; shackles.
путь *m.* 1. road; way; journey. 2. means, way.
пуф *m.* hassock; padded stool.
пух *m.* down.
пу́хлый *adj.* chubby, plump.
пу́хнуть *impf. pf.* вс-, о- *v.i.* to swell.
пухо́вка *f.* powder puff.
пучи́на *f.* abyss; the deep.
пучо́к FILL *m.* 1. bunch. 2. tuft, wisp.
пуши́нка *f.* 1. fluff. 2. flake.
пуши́стый *adj.* fluffy; downy.
пу́шка *f.* 1. cannon. 2. gun.
Пу́шкино *neut.* Pushkino.
пушно́й *adj.* fur-bearing.
пушо́к FILL *m.* fluff; fuzz.
пу́ща *f.* primeval forest.
Пуэ́рто-Ри́ко *m.* Puerto Rico.
Пхенья́н *m.* Pyŏngyang.
пчела́ *f.* bee.
пчелово́дство *neut.* bee-keeping.
пшени́ца *f.* wheat.
пшено́ *neut.* millet.
пыж *m.* wad (*in loading a pistol*).
пы́жик *m.* baby reindeer.
пы́житься *impf. pf.* на- (*colloq.*) 1. to make every effort. 2. to be all puffed up.
пыл *m.* ardor, passion.
пыла́ть *impf.* 1. to flame; to blaze. 2. to glow. 3. (*with instr.*) to burn (*with love* or *rage*).
пылесо́с *m.* vacuum cleaner.

пыли́ть *impf.* 1. *pf.* на- to raise (a cloud of) dust. 2. *pf.* за- to get dust on.
пы́лкий *adj.* ardent; passionate.
пыль *f.* dust.
пы́льный *adj.* dusty.
пыльца́ *f.* pollen.
пыта́ть *impf.* to torture.
пыта́ться *impf. pf.* по- to attempt, to try, to endeavor.
пы́тка *f.* 1. torture. 2. sheer hell; agony.
пытли́вый *adj.* inquisitive.
пыхте́ние *neut.* puffing; panting.
пы́шка *f.* 1. bun; doughnut. 2. (*colloq.*) chubby child; plump woman.
пы́шность *f.* splendor; magnificence.
пы́шный *adj.* magnificent; luxuriant.
пье́са *f.* 1. (*theat.*) play. 2. (*mus.*) piece.
пьяне́ть *impf. pf.* о- to become drunk.
пьяни́ть *impf. pf.* о- to make drunk; to intoxicate.
пья́ница *m.* and *f.* (*decl. f.*) drunk, drunkard.
пья́ный *adj.* drunk(en).
пядь *f.* span.
пя́лить глаза́ *impf.* (на *with acc.*) to stare at.
пясть *f.* metacarpus.
пята́ *f.* (*anat.*) heel.
пятёрка *f.* (*num., cards*) five; five-ruble note.
пя́теро *num. coll.* five.
пятибо́рье *neut.* pentathlon.
пятидесятиле́тие *neut.* 1. fiftieth anniversary; fiftieth birthday. 2. fifty-year period.
Пятидеся́тница *f.* Pentecost.
пятидеся́тый *adj.* fiftieth.
Пятикни́жие *neut.* the Pentateuch.
пятиле́тие *neut.* 1. fifth anniversary; fifth birthday. 2. five-year period.
пятиле́тка *f.* five-year plan.
пя́титься *impf. pf.* по- to back up; to step back.
пятиуго́льник *m.* pentagon.
пя́тка *f.* (*anat.*) heel.
пятна́дцатый *adj.* fifteenth.
пятна́дцать *num.* fifteen.
пятна́ть *impf. pf.* за- 1. to spot; to stain. 2. to tarnish; to sully.
пятна́шки *pl.* tag (*children's game*).
пятни́стый *adj.* spotty, spotted.
пя́тница *f.* Friday.
пятно́ *neut.* stain, spot.
пя́тый *adj.* fifth.
пять *num.* five.
пятьдеся́т *num.* fifty.
пятьсо́т *num.* five hundred.

Р

раб *m.* slave.
рабовладе́лец FILL *m.* *f.* **рабовладе́лица** slaveowner.
раболе́пие *neut.* servility.
раболе́пный *adj.* servile.
рабо́та *f.* work.
рабо́тать *impf. pf.* **по-** to work.
рабо́тник *m. f.* **рабо́тница** worker.
работода́тель *m.* employer.
работоспосо́бный *adj.* **1.** able-bodied. **2.** hardworking.
работя́га *m.* and *f.* (*decl. f.*) hard worker.
рабо́чий *m.* worker.
ра́бство *neut.* slavery.
равви́н *m.* rabbi.
ра́венство *neut.* equality.
равни́на *f.* plain.
равно́ *adv.* equally.
равнобе́дренный *adj.* (*math.*) isosceles.
равнове́сие *neut.* equilibrium; balance.
равноде́нствие *neut.* equinox.
равноду́шный *adj.* indifferent.
равноме́рный *adj.* **1.** even. **2.** uniform.
равнопра́вие *neut.* equality; equal rights.
равноуго́льный *adj.* equiangular.
равноце́нный *adj.* **1.** equal in price. **2.** equal in value.
ра́вный *adj.* equal.
равня́ть *impf.* to equalize. **—ся 1.** (с *with instr.*) to compete. **2.** (*math.*) to be equal to.
рад *adj.* (*pred.*) glad; pleased.
ра́ди *prep.* (*with gen.*) for the sake of.
радиа́ция *f.* radiation.
ра́дий *m.* radium.
ра́дио *neut.* indecl. radio. **—веща́ние** *neut.* broadcasting. **—переда́тчик** *m.* radio transmitter. **—приёмник** *m.* radio receiver; tuner.
радиома́як *m.* radio beacon.
ра́диус *m.* radius.
ра́довать OVA *impf. pf.* **об-** to gladden.
ра́достный *adj.* joyous; joyful.
ра́дость *f.* joy.
ра́дуга *f.* rainbow.
ра́дужный *adj.* **1.** iridescent. **2.** bright; rosy. **3.** (*of spirits* or *hopes*) high.
раду́шный *adj.* cordial.
раз *m.* time; one time. **—** *conj.* (*colloq.*) since.
разбавля́ть *impf. pf.* **разба́вить** to dilute.
разба́лтывать *impf. pf.* **разболта́ть** (*colloq.*) **1.** to shake up; to stir up. **2.** to knock loose. **3.** to reveal (a secret).
разбе́г *m.* running start.
разбега́ться *impf. pf.* **разбежа́ться** *v.i.* to scatter, to run away.
разбива́ть *impf. pf.* **разби́ть** *v.t.* **1.** to break; to fracture. **2.** to defeat. **3.** to divide, to split.
разби́вка *f.* **1.** laying out; spacing out (*e.g., of a printed page*). **2.** dividing up (*e.g., of property*).
разбира́тельство *neut.* investigation.
разбира́ть *impf. pf.* **разобра́ть 1.** to strip, to dismantle, to take apart. **2.** to investigate. **3.** to analyze.

разбира́ться *impf.* (в *with prep.*) to understand; to have an understanding of.
разби́тый *adj.* broken.
разбогате́ть *pf.* to get or become rich.
разбо́й *m.* robbery.
разбо́р *m.* sorting out; analysis. **—чивый** *adj.* **1.** legible. **2.** fastidious.
разбо́рный *adj.* collapsible (*e.g., furniture*).
разбра́сывать *impf. pf.* **разброса́ть** to scatter.
разбро́д *m.* **1.** confusion; disorder. **2.** discord.
разбро́санный *adj.* scattered; dispersed.
разбуди́ть *pf.* to wake.
разва́л *m.* breakdown; chaos, disorder.
разва́ливаться *impf. pf.* **развали́ться** to collapse; to fall into pieces.
разва́лины *pl.* ruins.
ра́зве *particle* really?
разведе́ние *neut.* **1.** breeding. **2.** cultivation.
разведённый *adj.* divorced.
разве́дка *f.* reconnaisance; intelligence.
разве́дчик *m. f.* **разве́дчица** scout; intelligence officer.
развёрнутый *adj.* **1.** (*mil.*) deployed; extended. **2.** full-scale; comprehensive. **3.** detailed.
развёртка *f.* reamer; broach bit.
развёртывать *impf. pf.* **разверну́ть 1.** to unfold, to open. **2.** to spread out.
рассели́ть(ся) *pf. of* **весели́ть(ся)**.
разве́систый *adj.* (*of tree branches*) spreading.
разве́ска *f.* weighing.
развести́(сь) *pf. of* **разводи́ть(ся)**.
разветвле́ние *neut.* **1.** forking; branching; ramification. **2.** fork (*in a road*).
развива́ть *impf. pf.* **разви́ть** *v.t.* to develop.
разви́лина *f.* fork; bifurcation.
разви́лка *f.* fork (*in a road*).
разви́тие *neut.* development.
развито́й *adj.* **1.** mature. **2.** highly developed.
развлека́ть *impf. pf.* **развле́чь** to amuse.
развлече́ние *neut.* amusement.
разво́д *m.* divorce.
разводи́ть *impf. pf.* **развести́** *v.t.* **1.** to conduct. **2.** to pull apart. **3.** to dilute. **4.** to divorce. **5.** to breed; to rear.
разводи́ться *impf. v.i.* **1.** (с *with instr.*) to divorce, to be divorced. **2.** to breed; to multiply.
разводно́й мост *m.* drawbridge.
разво́ды *pl.* **1.** design; pattern. **2.** streaks.
разво́з *m.* transport; delivery.
развози́ть *impf. pf.* **развезти́ 1.** to deliver; to transport. **2.** *impers.* (*colloq.*) to become impassable.
разволнова́ться *pf.* to become very worried.
развора́чивать *impf.* **1.** *pf.* **разверну́ть** to turn (*a car*) around. **2.** *pf.* **развороти́ть** to make havoc of; to break up; to smash up.
разворо́т *m.* **1.** turn. **2.** U-turn. **3.** development. **4.** centerfold; double page.
развра́т *m.* depravity.
развраща́ть *impf. pf.* **разврати́ть** to corrupt; to deprave.

развя́зка *f.* **1.** outcome; result. **2.** climax; dénouement.

развя́зный *adj.* overly forward; (excessively) familiar.

развя́зывать *impf.* *pf.* **развяза́ть** to untie; to unleash.

разга́дка *f.* **1.** solving; solution. **2.** unraveling.

разга́дывать *impf.* *pf.* **разгада́ть** to solve; to guess.

разга́р *m.* climax.

разглаго́льствовать OVA *impf.* (*colloq.*) to speak at length; to expatiate; to hold forth.

разглаша́ть *impf.* *pf.* **разгласи́ть** to divulge.

разгляде́ть *pf.* *pres.* **—жу́,** **—ди́шь** to discern; to make out.

разгля́дывать *impf.* to examine closely.

разгова́ривать *impf.* to speak, to talk, to converse.

разгово́р *m.* conversation.

разгово́рник *m.* phrase book.

разгово́рный *adj.* **1.** conversational. **2.** colloquial.

разгово́рчивый *adj.* talkative; loquacious.

разго́н *m.* **1.** dispersal. **2.** momentum.

разгоня́ть *impf.* *pf.* **разогна́ть** *v.t.* to disperse.

разгорячи́ть *pf.* *of* **горячи́ть.**

разграбле́ние *neut.* plunder; pillage; looting.

разграни́чивать *impf.* *pf.* **разграни́чить** to demarcate; to delimit.

разгро́м *m.* defeat, rout; devastation.

разгроми́ть *pf.* *of* **громи́ть.**

разгружа́ть *impf.* *pf.* **разгрузи́ть** to unload.

разгру́зка *f.* unloading.

разгрыза́ть *impf.* *pf.* **разгры́зть** **1.** to bite in two. **2.** to crack (*with one's teeth*).

разгу́л *m.* **1.** carousing. **2.** wave (*e.g., of violence*).

раздава́ть *impf.* *pf.* **разда́ть** to distribute. **—ся** to resound; to be heard; to ring out.

раздави́ть *pf.* **1.** to crush. **2.** to smash.

разда́точный *adj.* (*attrib.*) distribution; distributing.

разда́ча *f.* distribution.

раздвижно́й *adj.* **1.** expandable; extensible (*e.g., table*). **2.** sliding (*e.g., door* or *curtain*).

раздвое́ние *neut.* split; division.

раздева́лка *f.* (*colloq.*) coatroom; checkroom.

раздева́льня *f.* **1.** coatroom; checkroom. **2.** locker room; dressing room.

раздева́ть *impf.* *pf.* **разде́ть** *v.t.* to undress.

разде́л *m.* **1.** division. **2.** section. **—е́ние** *neut.* division. **—ьный** *adj.* separate.

раздели́ть *pf.* *of* **дели́ть, разделя́ть. —ся** *pf. of* **дели́ться.**

разделя́ть *impf.* *pf.* **раздели́ть** **1.** to separate. **2.** to divide.

раздира́ющий *adj.* heartbreaking; heart-rending.

раздо́лье *neut.* **1.** expanse. **2.** freedom; liberty.

раздо́р *m.* discord.

раздража́ть *impf.* *pf.* **раздражи́ть** to irritate.

раздраже́ние *neut.* irritation.

раздражи́тельный *adj.* irritable.

раздразни́ть *pf.* **1.** to tease; to provoke. **2.** to whet (*one's appetite*).

раздробля́ть *impf.* *pf.* **раздроби́ть** to fragment; to smash to pieces.

раздува́ть *impf.* *pf.* **разду́ть** **1.** to fan, to rouse. **2.** (*colloq.*) to exaggerate.

разду́мать *pf.* to change one's mind.

разду́мывать *impf.* to deliberate; to think; to ponder.

разду́мье *neut.* meditation.

разду́тый *adj.* (*colloq.*) **1.** swollen. **2.** inflated. **3.** excessive. **4.** exaggerated; overblown.

разева́ть *impf.* *pf.* **рази́нуть** (*colloq.*) to open one's mouth wide.

разжа́лование *neut.* demotion.

разжига́ть *impf.* *pf.* **разже́чь** to kindle.

разжима́ть *impf.* *pf.* **разжа́ть** **1.** to unclench; to release. **2.** to relax (*one's grip*).

разжире́ть *pf.* *of* **жире́ть.**

рази́тельный *adj.* striking.

рази́ть[1] *impf.* **1.** to strike. **2.** to defeat; to crush.

рази́ть[2] *impf.* impers. (*with instr.*) (*colloq.*) to stink of; to reek of (*e.g., of garlic* or *of vodka*).

разлага́ть *impf.* *pf.* **разложи́ть** *v.t.* **1.** to break down. **2.** to demoralize. **—ся** *v.i.* to decompose, to decay.

разла́д *m.* discord.

разлени́ться *pf.* (*colloq.*) to become lazy.

разли́в *m.* **1.** flood. **2.** overflow.

разлива́ние *neut.* pouring.

разлива́ть *impf.* *pf.* **разли́ть** to spill; to pour out.

разливно́й *adj.* (*of beer*) draft; on tap.

различа́ть *impf.* *pf.* **различи́ть** to distinguish. **—ся** *impf.* only to differ.

разли́чие *neut.* difference; distinction.

различи́тельный *adj.* distinctive.

разли́чный *adj.* different; diverse; various.

разложе́ние *neut.* **1.** decomposition, decay. **2.** corruption, demoralization.

разложи́ть(ся) *pf.* *of* **разлага́ть(ся).**

разло́м *m.* **1.** breaking up. **2.** break.

разлу́ка *f.* **1.** separation. **2.** parting.

разлуча́ть *impf.* *pf.* **разлучи́ть** to separate.

разлюби́ть *pf.* to fall out of love; to cease to love.

разма́тывать *impf.* *pf.* **размота́ть** to unwind.

разма́х *m.* sweep; scope, range.

разма́хивать *impf.* *pf.* **размахну́ть** (*with instr.*) **1.** to brandish. **2.** to swing. **3.** to gesticulate.

разма́чивать *impf.* *pf.* **размочи́ть** to soak; to steep.

размаши́стый *adj.* (*colloq.*) **1.** (*of an expanse*) broad. **2.** (*of a motion*) sweeping. **3.** (*of handwriting*) sprawling; expansive.

разме́н *m.* exchange.

разме́нивать *impf.* *pf.* **разменя́ть** to change (money).

разме́р *m.* **1.** dimension, size. **2.** (*prosody*) meter. **3.** (*mus.*) measure.

разме́ренный *adj.* measured.

размеря́ть *impf.* *pf.* **разме́рить** to measure (off).

размета́ть *impf.* *pf.* **размести́** **1.** to sweep (clean). **2.** to sweep away. **3.** to sweep up.

разме́тка *f.* marking; mark.

разме́тчик *m.* marker.

разме́шивать *impf.* *pf.* **размеша́ть** to stir.

размеща́ть *impf.* *pf.* **размести́ть** **1.** to place. **2.** to accommodate, to quarter.

размина́ть *impf.* *pf.* **размя́ть** **1.** to mash; to knead. **2.** (*colloq.*) to stretch one's legs.

размина́ться *f.* (*colloq.*) warm-up; limbering up.

размножа́ть *impf.* *pf.* **размно́жить** to multiply.

размноже́ние *neut.* reproduction; propagation.

размо́л *m.* grinding; milling.

размо́лвка *f.* spat; tiff; disagreement.

размота́ть *pf. of* **разма́тывать**.

размы́в *m.* erosion; washing away.

размыка́ть *impf. pf.* **разомкну́ть 1.** to open. **2.** to break a circuit.

размышле́ние *neut.* reflection.

размышля́ть *impf. pf.* **размы́слить** to reflect; to ponder.

разнаря́дка *f.* order; voucher.

разнести́ *pf. of* **разноси́ть**.

ра́зниться *impf.* to differ.

ра́зница *f.* difference.

разнобо́й *m.* inconsistency; lack of coordination.

разнови́дность *f.* variety.

разногла́сие *neut.* **1.** variance, difference. **2.** disagreement.

разноголо́сый *adj.* discordant.

ра́зное *neut.* **1.** miscellaneous. **2.** various things.

разнообра́зие *neut.* variety, diversity.

разнообра́зный *adj.* diverse; varied.

разноречи́вый *adj.* conflicting; contradictory.

разноро́дный *adj.* heterogeneous.

разно́с *m.* **1.** carrying; delivery. **2.** (*colloq.*) sharp reproach. **3.** (*colloq.*) blowing up.

разноси́ть *impf. pf.* **разнести́ 1.** to carry. **2.** to deliver. **3.** to spread.

разносторо́нний *adj.* many-sided; versatile.

разно́счик *m. f.* **разно́счица 1.** delivery man. **2.** peddler; hawker.

разноцве́тный *adj.* of different colors.

распу́зданный *adj.* **1.** unruly; rowdy. **2.** (*of a horse*) unbridled.

ра́зный *adj.* different; diverse; various.

разоблача́ть *impf. pf.* **разоблачи́ть** to expose; to unmask.

разобра́ть *pf. of* **разбира́ть**.

ра́зовый *adj.* valid for one time; for one-time use only.

разогна́ть *pf. of* **разгоня́ть**.

разогрева́ть *impf. pf.* **разогре́ть** to warm up.

разодра́ться *pf.* (*colloq.*) **1.** to tear; to rip. **2.** to have a big fight.

разозли́ть *pf.* to anger; to enrage.

разойти́сь *pf. of* **расходи́ться**.

ра́зом *adv.* (*colloq.*) **1.** at the same time. **2.** at once; instantly. **3.** with one stroke.

разорва́ть(ся) *pf. of* **разрыва́ть(ся)**.

разоре́ние *neut.* **1.** destruction; devastation. **2.** ruin.

разори́тельный *adj.* devastating; ruinous.

разоружа́ть *impf. pf.* **разоружи́ть** *v.t.* to disarm.

разоруже́ние *neut.* disarmament.

разоря́ть *impf. pf.* **разори́ть** to ruin; to destroy.

разочаро́ванный *adj.* disappointed; disenchanted.

разочаро́вывать *impf. pf.* **разочарова́ть** to disillusion; to disappoint.

разраба́тывать *impf. pf.* **разрабо́тать 1.** to work out. **2.** to elaborate. **3.** to cultivate. **4.** (*mining*) to exploit.

разрабо́тка *f.* **1.** development. **2.** mining. **3.** cultivation; working (*of land*).

разре́з *m.* **1.** cut. **2.** section.

разреза́ть *impf. pf.* **разре́зать 1.** to cut; to slit. **2.** to section. **3.** to carve.

разреша́ть *impf. pf.* **разреши́ть 1.** to permit, to allow. **2.** to solve.

разреше́ние *neut.* **1.** permission. **2.** solution.

разрисова́ть OVA *pf.* to cover with drawings.

разро́зненный *adj.* odd; (*of set*) incomplete.

разруба́ть *impf. pf.* **разруби́ть 1.** to chop up. **2.** to cut up.

разру́ха *f.* ruin, devastation.

разруша́ть *impf. pf.* **разру́шить** to destroy; to raze; to demolish.

разруше́ние *neut.* destruction.

разруши́тельный *adj.* destructive.

разры́в *m.* break, rupture; bursting.

разрыва́ть[1] *impf. pf.* **разры́ть** to dig up.

разрыва́ть[2] *impf. pf.* **разорва́ть** *v.t.* to tear; to rend.

разрыва́ться *impf. pf.* **разорва́ться** *v.i.* to break; to burst; to explode.

разрывно́й *adj.* explosive.

разря́д[1] *m.* category.

разря́д[2] *m.* discharge (*of electricity, of a weapon, etc.*).

разря́дка *f.* **1.** détente; lessening (*of tension*). **2.** unloading (*of a gun*); using or running down (*of a battery*). **3.** (*typog.*) spacing.

разряжа́ть[1] *impf. pf.* **разряди́ть 1.** to lessen *or* relax (tension). **2.** to unload (*a gun*); to use *or* run down (*a battery*).

разряжа́ть[2] *impf. pf.* **разряди́ть** (*colloq.*) to dress up; to put on fine clothes.

разува́ть *impf. pf.* **разу́ть** to take off (someone's) shoes. — **разува́ться** to take off (one's own) shoes.

разузнава́ть *impf. pf.* **разузна́ть 1.** *impf. only* to try to find out. **2.** to find out.

ра́зум *m.* reason; mind; intellect.

разуме́ется *impers.* of course; it goes without saying.

разу́мный *adj.* intelligent; reasonable.

разъеда́ть *impf. pf.* **разъе́сть** to eat away; to corrode.

разъединя́ть *impf. pf.* **разъедини́ть** to disjoin; to disconnect.

разъездно́й *adj.* **1.** traveling. **2.** for traveling.

разъезжа́ть *impf.* to travel.

разъясне́ние *neut.* explanation; clarification.

разъясня́ть *impf. pf.* **разъясни́ть** to explain; to clarify.

разы́скивать *impf. pf.* **разыска́ть** to search for.

рай *m.* paradise.

райко́м *m.* district committee.

райо́н *m.* region; district.

рак[1] *m.* crayfish.

рак[2] *m.* (*med.*) cancer.

ра́ка *f.* shrine (*of a saint*).

раке́та *f.* **1.** rocket. **2.** missile.

раке́тка *f.* (*athl.*) tennis racket.

ра́ковина *f.* **1.** shell. **2.** sink. **3.** bandstand.

ра́курс *m.* **1.** (*art*) foreshortening. **2.** perspective.

раку́шка *f.* shell; seashell.

ра́ма *f.* frame.

Ра́менское *neut.* Ramenskoe.

ра́мпа *f.* footlights.

ра́на *f.* wound.

ранг *m.* rank.

рангоу́т *m.* (*naut.*) masts and spars.

Рангу́н *m.* Rangoon.

ра́нее *adv.* earlier; sooner.

ра́неный *adj.* wounded; injured. — *m.* wounded person; casualty.

ра́нец FILL *m.* **1.** knapsack. **2.** pack. **3.** satchel.

ра́нить *impf.* and *pf.* to wound.
ра́нний *adj.* early.
ра́но *adv.* early. — *adj.* (*pred.*) early.
рант *m.* welt (*of a shoe or boot*).
ра́ньше *adv.* earlier.
рапи́ра *f.* (*fencing*) foil, rapier.
ра́порт *m.* report.
рапс *m.* (*plant*) rape.
ра́са *f.* race.
раска́иваться *impf. pf.* **раска́яться** to be sorry; to repent
раскалённый *adj.* red-hot; scorching.
раска́лывать *impf. pf.* **расколо́ть 1.** to split; to cleave. **2.** to divide.
раска́т *m.* peal.
раска́тистый *adj.* **1.** resounding. **2.** rolling; booming.
раска́шляться *pf.* to have a coughing fit.
раска́яние *neut.* remorse; repentance.
расквартирова́ть OVA *impf.* to quarter; to billet.
раскла́дка *f.* **1.** laying out; spreading. **2.** apportioning. **3.** making (*of a fire; of a bed*).
раскладу́шка *f.* (*colloq.*) cot.
расклейка *f.* posting; hanging up.
раско́ванный *adj.* uninhibited; unconstrained.
расковывать *impf. pf.* **расковать 1.** to unshoe (*a horse*). **2.** to unchain; to unshackle.
раско́л *m.* split; schism.
раско́льник *m. f.* **раско́льница 1.** religious dissenter; schismatic. **2.** splitter.
раско́пки *pl.* excavations.
раскоря́ка *m.* and *f.* (*decl. f.*) (*colloq.*) bowlegged person.
раско́сый *adj.* (*of a person's eyes*) slanting.
раскоше́ливаться *impf. pf.* **раскоше́литься** (*colloq.*) to loosen one's purse strings; to fork out; to shell out.
раскра́ска *f.* coloring; coloration.
раскрасне́ться *pf.* to flush; to become flushed.
раскра́шивать *impf. pf.* **раскра́сить** to color; to paint.
раскрепоща́ть *impf. pf.* **раскрепости́ть** to set free; to liberate.
раскритикова́ть *pf.* to criticize severely.
раскрыва́ть *impf. pf.* **раскры́ть** to uncover; to open; to disclose.
раскры́тие *neut.* **1.** opening. **2.** exposure. **3.** disclosure; revelation.
раскупа́ть *impf. pf.* **раскупи́ть** to buy up.
раскупо́ривать *impf. pf.* **раскупо́рить** to uncork; to open.
ра́совый *adj.* racial.
распа́д *m.* disintegration; collapse.
распада́ться *impf. pf.* **распа́сться 1.** to disintegrate; to break up. **2.** to dissolve.
распако́вывать OVA *impf. pf.* **распакова́ть** to unpack.
распа́хивать[1] *impf. pf.* **распаха́ть** to plow up.
распа́хивать[2] *impf. pf.* **распахну́ть 1.** to open wide. **2.** to throw open.
распашо́нка *f.* baby's undershirt.
распеча́тка *f.* printout.
распеча́тывать *impf. pf.* **распеча́тать** to unseal; to open.
распина́ть *impf. pf.* **распя́ть** to crucify.
расписа́ние *neut.* schedule; timetable.
распи́ска *f.* receipt.

распи́сывать *impf. pf.* **расписа́ть 1.** to paint; to decorate. **2.** (*colloq.*) to register someone's marriage.
распи́хивать *impf. pf.* **распиха́ть** (*colloq.*) **1.** to push aside. **2.** to force one's way through. **3.** to shove; to stuff.
распла́вленный *adj.* molten.
распла́каться *pf.* to burst into tears.
распла́стывать *impf. pf.* **распласта́ть 1.** to slice into layers. **2.** to spread flat; to spread out.
распла́та *f.* **1.** payment. **2.** atonement.
распла́чиваться *impf. pf.* **расплати́ться** to pay off; to settle an account.
расплета́ть *impf. pf.* **расплести́** to untwist; to unbraid.
расплы́вчатый *adj.* **1.** indistinct; diffuse. **2.** vague; dim.
распознава́ть *impf. pf.* **распозна́ть** to recognize; to discern.
располага́ть *impf. pf.* **расположи́ть 1.** to dispose (of). **2.** to arrange, to situate. **—ся** to settle. **3.** to settle down.
располага́ющий *adj.* pleasing; attractive.
расположе́ние *neut.* **1.** disposition; inclination. **2.** arrangement. **3.** location.
расположенный *adj.* **1.** located; situated. **2.** (к with *dat.*) fond of. **3.** (к with *dat.*) disposed toward. **4.** (*with infin.*) in the mood for.
распоро́ть *pf.* **1.** to rip (up). **2.** to undo.
распоряди́тель *m. f.* **—ница** manager; superintendant.
распоряди́тельный *adj.* efficient; businesslike.
распоря́док FILL *m.* **1.** order. **2.** routine.
распоряжа́ться *impf. pf.* **распоряди́ться 1.** to order; to be in command. **2.** to manage.
распоряже́ние *neut.* order; instruction.
распра́ва *f.* **1.** reprisal. **2.** violent revenge.
расправля́ть *impf. pf.* **распра́вить 1.** to smooth out. **2.** to straighten. **3.** to spread (*one's wings*).
распределе́ние *neut.* distribution.
распредели́тель *m.* **1.** (*person*) distributor; retailer. **2.** (*mech.*) distributor.
распределя́ть *impf. pf.* **распредели́ть** to distribute.
распрода́жа *f.* clearance sale.
распростране́ние *neut.* **1.** spreading. **2.** expansion; extension. **3.** dissemination. **4.** distribution.
распространённый *adj.* prevalent; widespread; widely distributed.
распространя́ть *impf. pf.* **распространи́ть** to spread; to disseminate.
ра́спря *f.* **1.** discord. **2.** strife.
распуска́ние *neut.* blossoming, blooming.
распуска́ть *impf. pf.* **распусти́ть 1.** to dismiss, to disband. **2.** to let out; to unfurl.
распуска́ться *impf. pf.* **распусти́ться 1.** to open; to come undone. **2.** (*colloq.*) to become flabby. **3.** (*colloq.*) to let oneself go. **4.** (*colloq.*) to get out of hand.
распу́тица *f.* time (*during spring and autumn*) of impassable roads.
распу́тник *m. f.* **распу́тница** profligate; libertine.
распу́тный *adj.* dissolute.
распу́тывать *impf. pf.* **распу́тать** to disentangle.
распу́тье *neut.* crossroads.
распуха́ть *impf. pf.* **распу́хнуть** to swell (up).
распу́щенность *f.* **1.** lack of discipline. **2.** dissoluteness; dissipation.

распу́щенный *adj.* dissolute.
распыли́тель *m.* sprayer; atomizer.
распя́тие *neut.* **1.** crucifixion. **2.** crucifix.
распя́ть *pf. of* **распина́ть**.
расса́да *f.* seedlings.
расса́дник *m.* **1.** plant nursery. **2.** center (*for learning*). **3.** breeding ground (*of crime*).
рассве́т *m.* dawn, daybreak.
рассе́ивать *impf. pf.* **рассе́ять** *v.t.* to disperse; to dispel.
рассека́ть *impf. pf.* **рассе́чь 1.** to split (in two). **2.** to gash; to slash. **3.** to cut in two; to cleave.
рассе́лина *f.* cleft; fissure.
рассели́ть *impf. pf.* **рассели́ть** *v.t.* to settle.
рассерди́ть *pf.* to anger.
рассе́янный *adj.* scattered; absent-minded.
расска́з *m.* story; tale; narrative.
расска́зчик *m. f.* **расска́зчица** narrator; storyteller.
расска́зывать *impf. pf.* **рассказа́ть** to narrate; to tell.
расслабле́ние *neut.* weakness; debility.
рассла́бленный *adj.* **1.** weak; debilitated. **2.** (*of walking*) unsure; unsteady.
рассле́довать OVA *impf. and pf.* to investigate; to inquire into.
рассло́ение *neut.* stratification.
рассма́тривать *impf. pf.* **рассмотре́ть 1.** to regard, to consider. **2.** to examine, to scrutinize.
рассмея́ться *pf.* to burst out laughing.
рассмотре́ние *neut.* examination; consideration.
рассо́л *m.* brine.
рассо́льник *m.* rassolnik (*meat* or *fish soup with pickled cucumbers*).
расспра́шивать *impf. pf.* **расспроси́ть** to question; to make inquiries (about).
расспро́сы *pl.* questions; questioning.
рассро́чка *f.* installment.
расстава́ться *impf. pf.* **расста́ться** *v.t.* to part; to separate.
расставля́ть *impf. pf.* **расста́вить 1.** to place, to arrange. **2.** to post. **3.** to move apart.
расстано́вка *f.* **1.** placement; arrangement. **2.** intermittent pauses.
расстёгивать *impf. pf.* **расстегну́ть** to undo; to unbutton; to unhook.
расстоя́ние *neut.* distance.
расстра́ивать *impf. pf.* **расстро́ить 1.** to disturb. **2.** to put out of tune. **3.** to upset.
расстре́л *m.* execution by a firing squad.
расстри́га *m.* (*decl. f.*) unfrocked priest *or* monk.
расстрига́ть *impf. pf.* **расстри́чь** to unfrock; to defrock.
расстро́енный *adj.* upset; out of tune.
расстро́йство *neut.* disorder.
рассуди́тельный *adj.* reasonable; sensible.
рассу́док FILL *m.* reason; common sense.
рассужда́ть *impf.* to discuss; to reason.
рассужде́ние *neut.* reasoning. — **рассужде́ния** *pl.* remarks; comments; objections; arguments.
рассу́чивать *impf. pf.* **рассучи́ть 1.** to untwist. **2.** to roll down (one's sleeves).
рассчи́танный *adj.* **1.** intentional; calculated. **2.** (**на** *with acc.*) intended for; meant for.
рассчи́тывать *impf. pf.* **рассчита́ть** to calculate, to reckon; to intend.
рассы́лка *f.* sending out; mailing out.

рассыпа́ть *impf. pf.* **рассы́пать** to spill; to strew; to scatter.
рассы́пчатый *adj.* **1.** friable. **2.** crumbly.
рассыха́ться *impf. pf.* **рассо́хнуться** to crack (*as a result of drying*).
раста́пливать *impf. pf.* **растопи́ть 1.** to light (*a stove*). **2.** to melt.
раста́ять *pf. of* **та́ять**.
раство́р *m.* solution.
растворе́ние *neut.* dissolution; solution.
раствори́мый *adj.* soluble.
растворя́ть[1] *impf. pf.* **раствори́ть** *v.t.* to dissolve.
растворя́ть[2] *impf. pf.* **раствори́ть** to open.
растворя́ющий *adj.* solvent.
расте́ние *neut.* plant.
растерза́ть *pf.* **1.** to tear to pieces. **2.** to torment.
расте́рянный *adj.* confused; dismayed.
растеря́ть *pf.* to lose.
расти́ *impf. v.i.* to grow; to increase.
растира́ние *neut.* **1.** grinding. **2.** rubbing; massaging.
расти́ть *impf. pf.* **вы́растить 1.** to raise; to grow. **2.** to rear, to bring up. **3.** to cultivate.
растле́ние *neut.* **1.** rape (*of a minor*). **2.** decay. **3.** decadence.
растле́нный *adj.* **1.** decadent. **2.** corrupt.
растолко́вывать *impf. pf.* **растолкова́ть** to explain.
растоло́чь *pf.* **1.** to grind. **2.** to pound.
расто́пка *f.* **1.** lighting (*of a stove*). **2.** (*colloq.*) kindling wood.
растопы́ривать *impf. pf.* **растопы́рить** (*colloq.*) to spread apart.
расторга́ть *impf. pf.* **расто́ргнуть 1.** to dissolve. **2.** to cancel, to annul.
расторже́ние *neut.* dissolution; cancellation.
расторо́пный *adj.* efficient; quick, prompt.
расточа́ть *impf. pf.* **расточи́ть 1.** to waste; to dissipate. **2.** to lavish.
расточи́тельный *adj.* extravagant; wasteful.
растра́та *f.* waste; embezzlement.
растра́тить *pf.* to squander; to embezzle.
растра́тчик *m. f.* **растра́тчица** embezzler.
растрёпа *m. and f.* (*decl. f.*) (*colloq.*) slob; slovenly person.
растрёпанный *adj.* tattered; tousled.
растро́гать *pf.* to move; to touch.
растру́б *m.* **1.** funnel-shaped opening. **2.** bell; bell mouth (*of instrument, etc.*).
растя́гивать *impf. pf.* **растяну́ть** to stretch; to prolong.
растяже́ние *neut.* stretching; tension.
растя́жка *f.* stretching.
растя́нутый *adj.* **1.** stretched out. **2.** long-winded; loquacious.
растя́па *m. and f.* (*decl. f.*) (*colloq.*) dullard; dolt; dope.
расфасо́вка *f.* packaging.
расхва́ливать *impf. pf.* **расхвали́ть** to extol; to rave about.
расхити́тель *m. f.* **—ница** embezzler.
расхища́ть *impf. pf.* **расхи́тить** to plunder.
расхище́ние *neut.* embezzlement; theft; misappropriation.
расхля́банный *adj.* (*colloq.*) **1.** wobbly. **2.** lax; slack.

расхо́д *m.* expenditure.
расходи́ться *impf. pf.* разойти́сь 1. to break up; to disperse. 2. to diverge.
расхо́дование *neut.* 1. spending. 2. expenditure.
расхо́довать OVA *impf. pf.* из- to spend.
расхожде́ние *neut.* divergence.
расхола́живать *impf. pf.* расхолоди́ть to dim the enthusiasm of someone.
расхоте́ть *pf.* (*conjugated like* хоте́ть) to lose all desire for; to want no longer.
расхохота́ться *pf.* to burst into laughter.
расцве́т *m.* blossoming; flowering.
расцвета́ть *impf. pf.* расцвести́ to blossom out; to flourish.
расцве́тка *f.* color scheme; color combination.
расцелова́ть OVA *pf.* 1. to kiss ardently. 2. to smother with kisses.
расце́нивать *impf. pf.* расцени́ть 1. to estimate; to value. 2. to consider.
расце́нка *f.* evaluation; valuation.
расчёсывать *pf.* расчеса́ть to comb (out).
расчёт *m.* calculation.
расчётливый *adj.* thrifty; economical; prudent.
расчи́стка *f.* clearing (*of land or of roads*).
расчленя́ть *impf. pf.* расчлени́ть to dismember.
расша́ркиваться *impf. pf.* расша́ркаться 1. (*obs.*) to bow, scraping one's feet. 2. (*colloq.*) to bow and scrape.
расша́танный *adj.* 1. wobbly. 2. rickety. 3. in bad health. 4. (*of one's nerves*) shattered.
расшиба́ть *impf. pf.* расшиби́ть (*colloq.*) to hurt; to bruise.
расшива́ть *impf. pf.* расши́ть to embroider.
расшире́ние *neut.* widening.
расширя́ть *impf. pf.* расши́рить to widen; to enlarge; to extend.
расшифро́вывать *impf. pf.* расшифрова́ть OVA to decipher.
расшнуро́вывать *impf. pf.* расшнурова́ть OVA to untie (*shoes*); to unlace.
расще́лина *f.* cleft; fissure; crevice.
расщепле́ние *neut.* 1. splitting. 2. splintering.
ратифика́ция *f.* ratification.
ра́товать OVA *impf.* 1. (*obs.*) to fight; to battle. 2. (за *with acc.*) to fight for. 3. (про́тив *with gen.*) to fight against.
ра́туша *f.* city hall; town hall.
рать *f.* (*arch.*) 1. host; army. 2. war; battle.
рахáт-луку́м *m.* Turkish delight.
рахи́т *m.* rickets.
рационализи́ровать OVA *impf. and pf.* to rationalize.
рациона́льный *adj.* rational.
ра́ция *f.* walkie-talkie.
ра́шпер *m.* gridiron; grill.
ра́шпиль *m.* rasp.
рвану́ть 1. *impf.* to tug; to jerk. 2. (*colloq.*) to dash; to dart. 3. (*colloq.*) to lurch forward.
рва́ный *adj.* 1. torn. 2. full of holes. 3. uneven; jagged.
рвать *impf. v.t.* 1. to tear; to rend. 2. to pick, to pluck; to pull out *or* off.
рве́ние *neut.* 1. zeal. 2. ardor.
рво́та *f.* vomiting.
рво́тный *adj.* emetic.
рдест *m.* pondweed.
рдеть *impf.* 1. to glow red. 2. to loom red.

реабилити́ровать OVA *impf. and pf.* to rehabilitate.
реаги́ровать OVA *impf.* to react; to respond.
реакти́вный *adj.* 1. reactive. 2. (*attrib.*) jet. 3. jet propelled.
реакцио́нный *adj.* reactionary.
реа́льность *f.* reality.
ребёнок FILL *m.* child; baby.
ребо́рда *f.* flange (*of a wheel*).
ребро́ *neut.* 1. rib. 2. edge.
ребя́та *pl.* children; boys.
ребяти́шки *pl.* (*colloq.*) children; kids.
ребя́ческий *adj.* 1. of a child; child's. 2. childish.
ребя́чество *neut.* childishness.
рёв *m.* 1. roar, bellow. 2. weep, howl.
реве́нь *m.* rhubarb.
ревера́нс *m.* curtsy.
реви́зия *f.* 1. inspection. 2. revision.
ревизо́р *m.* inspector.
ревмати́зм *m.* rheumatism.
ревни́вый *adj.* jealous.
ревни́тель *m. f.* —ница (*obs.*) 1. adherent of. 2. enthusiastic supporter.
ревнова́ть OVA *impf.* to be jealous.
ре́вностный *adj.* zealous; ardent.
ре́вность *f.* jealousy.
револьве́р *m.* revolver.
революционе́р *m. f.* —ка revolutionary.
револю́ция *f.* revolution.
ре́гби *neut. indecl.* rugby.
регио́н *m.* region.
реги́стр *m.* register; list.
регистра́тор *m.* registrar; registering clerk.
регистри́ровать OVA *impf. pf.* за- to register.
регла́мент *m.* 1. (*obs.*) rules; regulations. 2. agenda. 3. speaker's allotted time.
регули́ровать OVA *impf.* to regulate.
регуля́рный *adj.* regular.
регуля́тор *m.* regulator.
редакти́ровать OVA *impf. pf.* от- to edit.
реда́ктор *m.* editor.
реда́кция *f.* 1. editing. 2. editorial offices.
реде́ть *impf. pf.* по- to thin out.
реди́с *m.* radish; radishes.
реди́ска *f.* radish.
ре́дкий *adj.* rare.
ре́дко *adv.* rarely, seldom.
ре́дкость *f.* 1. rarity. 2. a rarity. 3. sparseness; thinness.
ре́дька *f.* radish.
рее́стр *m.* 1. register. 2. list; log.
ре́же *adj. comp. of* ре́дкий. — *adv. comp. of* ре́дко.
режи́м *m.* regime.
режиссёр *m.* director; producer.
реза́к *m.* large knife; cutter.
ре́зальщик *m.* (*person*) cutter.
ре́занный *adj.* 1. cut. 2. sliced.
ре́зать *impf.* to cut; to carve.
резви́ться *impf.* to frolic; to romp.
ре́звый *adj.* playful, frisky.
резеда́ *f.* (*plant*) mignonette.
резе́рв *m.* reserve.
резе́ц FILL *m.* 1. cutter; cutting tool. 2. (*tooth*) incisor.
рези́на *f.* rubber.
рези́нка *f.* 1. elastic. 2. eraser; gum.

рези́новый adj. rubber.
ре́зкий adj. harsh; biting, sharp.
ре́зкость f. **1.** sharpness; harshness. **2.** sharpness; clarity. **3.** ре́зкости pl. harsh words.
резня́ f. slaughter.
резолю́ция f. resolution.
резона́нс m. **1.** resonance. **2.** response; reaction to.
резони́ровать OVA impf. to resound.
результа́т m. result.
резь f. sharp pain.
резьба́ f. carving.
Рейкья́вик m. Reykjavík.
Ре́ймс m. Reims.
рейс m. trip, voyage.
рейсши́на f. T square.
рейту́зы pl. **1.** riding breeches. **2.** knit pants.
река́ f. river.
реквизи́ровать OVA impf. and pf. to requisition.
реквизи́т m. (theat.) stage props; properties.
рекла́ма f. advertisement; publicity.
реклами́ровать OVA impf. and pf. to advertise; to publicize.
рекоменда́тельный adj. (attrib.) recommendation; introduction.
рекомендова́ть impf. and pf. also pf. по- to recommend. —**ся** to be recommended; to be advisable.
реконстру́кция f. reconstruction.
реко́рд m. record.
ре́ктор m. rector (of a university).
религио́зный adj. religious.
рели́гия f. religion.
рели́кт m. **1.** relic. **2.** ancient artifact.
релье́ф m. relief (in art or topography).
рельс m. rail.
рема́рка f. **1.** note. **2.** (theat.) stage direction.
ремёнь FILL m. strap; belt.
реме́сленник m. f. **реме́сленница** artisan; handicraftsman.
реме́сленный adj. (attrib.) craft; vocational.
ремесло́ neut. **1.** trade. **2.** handicraft.
ремешо́к FILL m. small strap.
ремо́нт m. repair; overhaul.
ремонти́ровать impf. pf. от- to repair; to overhaul.
Ренн m. Rennes.
ре́нта f. rent.
рента́бельный adj. profitable; paying.
рентге́н m. **1.** X-rays. **2.** X-ray machine.
реорганизова́ть impf. and pf. to reorganize.
ре́па f. turnip.
репе́йник m. **1.** burdock (coarse weed). **2.** bur.
репе́р m. **1.** reference point. **2.** bench mark.
репети́тор m. **1.** tutor. **2.** coach.
репети́ция f. rehearsal.
ре́плика f. **1.** retort; rejoinder. **2.** (theat.) cue.
репо́лов m. (bird) linnet.
репорта́ж m. **1.** reporting. **2.** news report.
репортёр m. reporter.
репре́ссия f. repression.
репроду́ктор m. loudspeaker.
репута́ция f. reputation.
ресни́ца f. eyelash.
респекта́бельный adj. respectable.
респу́блика f. republic.
рессо́ра f. spring.

реставри́ровать OVA impf. and pf. to restore.
рестора́н m. restaurant.
ресу́рсы pl. resources.
рети́вый adj. zealous.
ретирова́ться OVA impf. and pf. to retire; to withdraw.
ретуши́рование neut. retouching.
рефера́т m. **1.** essay, paper. **2.** lecture. **3.** synopsis.
рефере́нт m. **1.** reviewer. **2.** adviser; consultant.
рефо́рма f. reform.
рефре́н m. refrain.
рехну́ться pf. (colloq.) to go crazy; to go mad.
рецензе́нт m. reviewer; critic.
реце́нзия f. **1.** review. **2.** criticism.
реце́пт m. **1.** prescription. **2.** recipe.
рециди́в m. **1.** recurrence. **2.** (of an illness) relapse. **3.** (leg.) second offense.
речево́й adj. (attrib.) speech.
рече́ние neut. expression; locution.
ре́чка f. small river; rivulet.
речно́й adj. (attrib.) river; fluvial.
речь f. speech.
реша́ть impf. pf. **реши́ть** **1.** to decide. **2.** to solve.
реша́ющий adj. decisive.
реше́ние neut. **1.** decision. **2.** solution.
решётка f. grating; lattice.
решето́ neut. sieve.
реши́мость f. resolution; determination.
реши́тельный adj. decisive; resolute.
ре́шка f.: **орёл и́ли ре́шка?** heads or tails.
ре́ять impf. pres. **ре́ю, ре́ешь** **1.** to soar. **2.** to hover. **3.** to flutter.
ржа f. rust. —**вый** adj. rusty.
ржаве́ть impf. to rust.
ржа́вчина f. rust.
ржа́нка f. plover.
ржано́й adj. (attrib.) rye.
ржать impf. to neigh.
Ри́га f. Riga.
ри́га f. threshing barn.
ри́за f. **1.** (eccl.) chasuble. **2.** riza (metal plating on an icon). **3.** (obs.) raiment; garments.
ри́зница f. sacristy; vestry.
Рим m. Rome.
ри́млянин m. f. **ри́млянка** Roman.
ри́мский adj. Roman.
ри́нуться pf. **1.** to dash; to rush to. **2.** (в with acc.) to plunge into (e.g., a task).
Ри́о-Гра́нде m. (river) Rio Grande.
Ри́о-де-Жане́йро m. Rio de Janeiro.
рис m. rice.
риск m. risk.
риско́ванный adj. **1.** risky. **2.** risqué.
рискова́ть OVA impf. pf. **рискну́ть** to risk.
рисова́ние neut. drawing.
рисова́ть impf. pf. на- to draw; to depict.
рису́нок m. drawing.
ритм m. rhythm.
ритми́ческий also **ритми́чный** adj. rhythmic; rhythmical.
рито́рика f. rhetoric.
риф m. (geog.) reef.
рифлёный adj. **1.** corrugated. **2.** fluted; channelled. **3.** grooved.
ри́фма f. rhyme.

рици́новое ма́сло *neut.* castor oil.
ро́ба *f.* overalls.
робе́ть *impf.* to be timid; to be shy.
ро́бкий *adj.* timid; shy.
ро́бот *m.* robot.
ров *m.* ditch.
рове́сник *m. f.* рове́сница agemate.
Ро́вно *neut.* Rivne (*Russian: Rovno*).
ро́вно *adv.* **1.** equally; evenly. **2.** exactly.
ро́вный *adj.* **1.** flat; even. **2.** equal.
ровня́ть *impf. pf.* с- to even; to make level.
рог *m.* horn, antler. **—а́тый** *adj.* horned.
рога́тка *f.* **1.** bar; barrier. **2.** obstacle. **3.** slingshot.
рога́ч *m.* **1.** stag; hart. **2.** stag beetle.
рогови́ца *f.* cornea.
рого́жа *f.* matting.
рого́з *m.* cattail.
род *m.* **1.** kin; family; stock. **2.** sort; kind. **3.** (*gram.*) gender.
Род-А́йленд *m.* Rhode Island.
роди́льный *adj.* (*attrib.*) **1.** maternity. **2.** puerperal (*e.g., fever*).
ро́дина *f.* motherland; fatherland; homeland; native land.
роди́нка *f.* mole (*on skin*); birthmark.
роди́тели *pl.* parents.
роди́тельный *adj.* (*gram.*) genitive.
роди́тельский *adj.* parental.
роди́ться *pf. of* рожда́ться.
родни́к *m.* spring.
родни́ть *impf. pf.* с- *or* по- to unite; to bring together.
родно́й *adj.* own; native.
родня́ *f.* (*coll.*) relatives.
родово́й *adj.* ancestral.
ро́дом *adv.* by birth.
родонача́льник *m.* progenitor; father, forefather.
Ро́дос *m.* (*island*) Rhodes.
родосло́вный *adj.* genealogical.
ро́дственник *m. f.* ро́дственница relative, relation.
ро́дственный *adj.* kindred, related.
родство́ *neut.* relationship; kinship.
ро́ды *pl.* childbirth.
рое́ние *neut.* swarming.
ро́жа¹ *f.* (*skin disease*) erysipelas.
ро́жа² *f.* (*colloq.*) mug; puss; ugly face.
рожа́ть *impf. pf.* роди́ть to give birth; to have a child.
рожда́емость *f.* birth rate.
рожда́ть *impf. pf.* роди́ть to give birth (to). **—ся** to be born.
рожде́ние *neut.* birth.
Рождество́ *neut.* Christmas.
рожо́к FILL *m.* **1.** small horn. **2.** (*mus.*) horn. **3.** ear trumpet. **4.** feeding bottle. **5.** shoehorn.
рожь *f.* rye.
ро́за *f.* rose.
ро́звальни *pl.* low wide sled.
ро́зга *f.* rod (*for whipping*).
розмари́н *m.* rosemary.
ро́зничный *adj.* retail.
рознь *f.* difference; dissention.
розове́ть *impf.* to turn pink.
ро́зовый *adj.* pink; rose-colored.

ро́зыгрыш *m.* **1.** drawing (*in a lottery*). **2.** (*sport*) playoffs (*in a tie for the cup*). **3.** drawn game.
ро́зыск *m.* **1.** search. **2.** investigation.
рой *m.* swarm.
рок *m.* fate.
рокирова́ть OVA *impf. and pf.* (*chess*) to castle.
роково́й *adj.* fatal.
ро́кот *m.* roar; rumble.
рокота́ть *impf.* to rumble; to resound.
ро́лик *m.* **1.** roller; caster. **2.** reel (*for movie film*). **— ро́лики** *pl.* roller skates.
ро́ликовая доска́ *f.* skateboard.
роль *f.* role, part.
ром *m.* rum.
рома́н *m.* novel.
рома́нс *m.* (*mus.*) romance.
рома́нский *adj.* **1.** Romance (*e.g., languages*). **2.** Romanesque.
рома́нтика *f.* **1.** romanticism. **2.** romance; romantic appeal.
романти́ческий *adj.* romantic.
рома́шка *f.* camomile.
Ро́на *f.* (*river*) Rhône.
роня́ть *impf. pf.* урони́ть to drop; to shed.
ро́пот *m.* murmur; grumble.
ропта́ть *impf.* to murmur.
роса́ *f.* dew.
роси́нка *f.* dewdrop.
роско́шный *adj.* luxurious.
ро́скошь *f.* luxury.
росома́ха *f.* wolverine.
ро́спись *f.* **1.** painting; mural. **2.** (*obs.*) list; inventory.
росси́йский *adj.* Russian.
Росси́я *f.* Russia.
рост *m.* **1.** growth; increase; rise. **2.** height; stature.
ро́стбиф *m.* roast beef.
Росто́в *m.* Rostov.
ростовщи́к *m. f.* росто́вщица **1.** money lender. **2.** usurer.
Ро́сток *m.* Rostock.
росто́к FILL *m.* sprout; shoot.
рося́нка *f.* sundew (*small bog-plant*).
рот FILL *m.* mouth.
ро́та *f.* (*mil.*) company.
ротово́й *adj.* oral; of the mouth.
ротозе́й *m. f.* **—ка** **1.** gaper; gawker. **2.** onlooker. **3.** dimwit.
Ро́ттердам *m.* Rotterdam.
ро́ща *f.* grove.
роя́ль *m.* (*grand*) piano.
РСФСР *f.* (*abbr. of* Росси́йская Сове́тская Федерати́вная Социалисти́ческая Респу́блика) RSFSR.
ртуть *f.* mercury.
Руа́н *m.* Rouen.
руба́ха *f.* shirt.
руба́шка *f.* shirt; chemise.
рубе́ж *m.* boundary, border. **— за рубежо́м** abroad.
рубе́ц¹ FILL *m.* **1.** scar; welt. **2.** hem.
рубе́ц² FILL *m.* **1.** paunch (*of an animal*). **2.** tripe.
руби́н *m.* ruby.
руби́ть *impf.* to fell; to chop; to hack.
ру́бище *neut.* rags; tatters.
ру́бка¹ *f.* felling (*of wood*); chopping.

рýбка² *f.* (*naut.*) deckhouse.
рýбленный *adj.* **1.** chopped. **2.** made of logs.
рубль *m.* ruble.
рýбрика *f.* heading.
рýбчатый *adj.* ribbed.
рýбчик *m.* **1.** *dim. of* рубéц. **2.** ridge (*on material*).
рýгань *f.* verbal abuse; swearing.
ругáтельство *neut.* swearword; expletive.
ругáть *impf. pf.* **вы́-** to scold; to swear at; to curse out.
рудá *f.* ore.
руднúк *m.* mine; pit.
Рýдные гóры *pl.* Ore Mountains.
ружéйник *m.* gunsmith.
ружьё *neut.* gun; arms.
руúны *pl.* ruins.
рукá *f.* **1.** hand **2.** arm. — **пóд руку** arm in arm.
рукáв *m.* sleeve.
рукавúца *f.* mitten.
руководúть *impf.* (*with instr.*) to manage; to lead. **—ся** to follow; to be guided (by).
руковóдство *neut.* guidance, leadership.
руковóдствоваться *impf.* to follow; to be guided (*by*).
руководя́щий *adj.* **1.** leading; guiding. **2.** senior. **3.** supervisory.
рукодéлие *neut.* needlework.
рукомóйник *m.* washstand.
рукопáшный бой *m.* hand-to-hand fighting.
рýкопись *f.* manuscript.
рукоплескáть *impf.* to applaud, to clap.
рукопожáтие *neut.* handshake.
рукоя́тка *f.* **1.** handle. **2.** hilt.
рулевóй *adj.* (*attrib.*) steering.
рулéт *m.* meatloaf *or* potato loaf.
рулéтка *f.* **1.** tape measure. **2.** roulette.
рулóн *m.* roll; bolt (*of cloth*).
руль *m.* **1.** rudder; helm. **2.** steering wheel.
румы́н *m. f.* **-ка** Romanian.
Румы́ния *f.* Romania.
румя́на *pl.* rouge.
румя́нец FILL *m.* **1.** high color (*in one's face*). **2.** flush; blush. **3.** redness in one's cheeks.
румя́нить *impf.* to apply rouge.
румя́ный *adj.* rosy, rubicund.
рунó *neut.* fleece. — **золотóе рунó** *neut.* the Golden Fleece.
рýпор *m.* **1.** megaphone. **2.** mouthpiece.
русáк *m.* hare.
русáлка *f.* mermaid.
русúст *m.* specialist in Russian philology.
русифицúровать OVA *impf. and pf.* to Russify; to Russianize.
рýсло *neut.* channel; riverbed.
рýсский *m. f.* **рýсская** Russian. — *adj.* Russian.
русскоязы́чный *adj.* (*attrib.*) Russian-language.
рýсый *adj.* light brown.
рутúна *f.* routine.
рýхлядь *f.* (*colloq.*) junk.

рýхнуть *pf.* to crash; to tumble; to collapse.
ручáтельство *neut.* guarantee.
ручéй *m.* brook; stream.
рýчка *f.* handle; knob.
ручнóй *adj.* **1.** (*attrib.*) hand; manual. **2.** portable.
рýшить *impf.* to tear down. **—ся** *impf.* to collapse.
ры́ба *f.* fish.
рыбáк *m. f.* **рыбáчка** fisherman.
ры́бий *adj.* (*attrib.*) fish.
Ры́бинск *m.* Rybinsk.
ры́бка *f. dim. of* ры́ба. — **золотáя ры́бка** *f.* goldfish.
рывóк FILL *m.* **1.** jerk. **2.** (*sport*) spurt; dash; burst.
рыгáть *impf. pf.* **рыгнýть** to belch.
рыдáть *impf.* to sob.
ры́жий *adj.* red; red-haired; ginger.
ры́жик *m.* (*mushroom*) saffron milk-cap.
рык *m.* roar.
рыкáть *impf. pf.* **рыкнýть** to roar.
ры́ло *neut.* snout.
ры́нда *f.* ship's bell.
ры́нок FILL *m.* marketplace.
рыса́к *m.* trotter.
ры́скать *impf. pres.* **ры́щу, ры́щешь 1.** to prowl. **2.** (*colloq.*) to roam; to wander around.
рысца́ *f.* slow trot; jog trot.
рысь¹ *f.* lynx.
рысь² *f. trot.* — **ры́сью** *adv.* at a trot.
ры́твина *f.* rut; pothole.
рыть *impf.* to dig; to burrow.
ры́ться *impf. pf.* **по- 1.** to dig (*in the sand, etc.*). **2.** to search; to rummage through; to ransack.
рыхлéть *impf.* **1.** to become soft. **2.** to become friable.
рыхлúть *impf. pf.* **вз- 1.** to loosen. **2.** to make friable. **3.** to turn up (*e.g., soil*).
ры́хлый *adj.* loose; crumbly; friable.
ры́царство *neut.* knighthood; chivalry.
ры́царь *m.* knight.
рыча́г *m.* lever.
рыча́ть *impf.* to growl; to snarl.
ря́ный *adj.* zealous.
рюкза́к *m.* knapsack; backpack.
рю́мка *f.* liqueur glass.
ряби́на¹ *f.* **1.** mountain ash; rowantree. **2.** rowanberries.
ряби́на² *f.* pockmark.
ряби́ть *impf.* to ripple.
рябóй *adj.* pitted, pocked, pock-marked.
рябь *f.* ripples.
ря́вкать *impf. pf.* **ря́вкнуть** (*colloq.*) to roar; to bellow.
ряд *m.* **1.** row. **2.** line. **3.** series, number. **—овóй** *adj.* ordinary, common. — *m.* (*mil.*) private.
ря́дом *adv.* side by side. — **ря́дом с** (*with instr.*) next (to).
Ряза́нь *f.* Ryazan.
ря́са *f.* cassock.
ря́ска *f.* duckweed.

C

с *also* со *prep.* **1.** (*with instr.*) with; and. **2.** (*with gen.*) from; since; off; down from. **3.** (*with acc.*) about.

сáбельный *adj.* (*attrib.*) saber.

сáбля *f.* saber.

сабота́ж *m.* sabotage.

сабота́жник *m. f.* сабота́жница saboteur.

саботи́ровать *impf. and pf.* to sabotage.

сáван *m.* **1.** shroud. **2.** blanket; cover.

сава́нна *f.* savanna.

савра́сый *adj.* (*of horses*) light brown with black mane and tail.

сáга *f.* saga.

сагити́роавть *pf. of* агити́ровать.

сад *m.* garden. — де́тский сад *m.* kindergarten.

сади́зм *m.* sadism.

сáдик *m. dim. of* сад.

сади́ст *m. f.* —ка sadist.

сади́стский *adj.* sadistic.

сади́ть *impf.* to plant.

сади́ться *impf. pf.* сесть **1.** to sit down. **2.** to board (*a plane, a train etc.*).

сáднить *impf.* **1.** to scratch. **2.** to smart; to sting; to burn.

садо́вник *m. f.* садо́вница gardener.

садово́д *m.* horticulturist; gardener.

садо́вый *adj.* (*attrib.*) garden.

садо́к FILL *m.* **1.** fish tank. **2.** pen; coop.

сáжа *f.* soot.

сажа́лка *f.* (*machine*) planter.

сажа́ть *impf. pf.* посади́ть to plant; to seat.

сáженец FILL *m.* seedling.

сажéнь *f.* Russian measure of length of 2.13 meters.

саза́н *m.* (*fish*) carp.

сайга́ *f.* saiga (*variety of antelope*).

Сайго́н *m.* Saigon.

сáйка *f.* roll of bread.

Сáйма *f.* (*lake*) Saimaa.

сакрамента́льный *adj.* (*attrib.*) ritual.

саксау́л *m.* saxaul (*tree of Central Asia*).

саксофо́н *m.* saxophone.

сала́зки *pl.* small sled.

салама́ндра *f.* salamander.

Салама́нка *f.* Salamanca.

сала́т *m.* lettuce, salad.

сала́тник *m.* salad bowl.

сала́тный *adj.* (*attrib.*) lettuce; salad.

сáлить *impf.* to grease.

сáлки *pl.* game of tag.

сáло *neut.* fat; suet.

сало́н *m.* salon.

сало́н-ваго́н *m.* parlor car.

Сало́ники *m.* Salonica (*also: Thessaloníki*).

салфéтка *f.* napkin.

Сальвадо́р *m.* El Salvador.

сáльдо *neut. indecl.* (*bookkeeping*) balance.

сáльность *f.* profanity; obscenity.

сáльный *adj.* **1.** greasy. **2.** (*attrib.*) tallow. **3.** salacious.

сáльто *also* сáльто-морта́ле *neut. indecl.* somersault.

салю́т *m.* salute.

салютова́ть OVA *impf. and pf.* to salute.

саля́ми *f. indecl.* salami.

сам *pron.* сама́ *f.*, само́ *neut.*, сáми *pl.* oneself. — сам по себе́: per se; in and of itself.

сама́н *m.* adobe.

Самáра *f.* Samara.

самáрий *m.* samarium.

Самарка́нд *m.* Samarqand.

самéц FILL *m.* male.

самизда́т *m.* underground publication of manuscripts in the USSR.

сáмка *f.* female.

само- *prefix* self-.

Само́а *f.* Samoa.

самоана́лиз *m.* self-analysis; introspection.

самобы́тный *adj.* original; distinctive.

самова́р *m.* samovar.

самовла́стие *neut.* (*obs.*) one-man rule.

самовла́стный *adj.* despotic.

самовлюблённый *adj.* conceited.

самовнушéние *neut.* autosuggestion.

самовозгора́ние *neut.* spontaneous combustion.

самово́лие *neut.* high-handedness; arbitrariness.

самово́льно *adv.* without permission.

самово́льный *adj.* self-willed; unauthorized.

самовоспламенéние *neut.* spontaneous combustion.

самого́н *m.* homemade vodka.

самодви́жущийся *adj.* self-propelled.

самодéльный *adj.* homemade.

самодержáвие *neut.* autocracy.

самодержáвный *adj.* autocratic.

самодéржец FILL *m. f.* самодéржица autocrat.

самодéятельность *f.* individual initiative.

самодéятельный *adj.* **1.** independent. **2.** amateur.

самодисципли́на *f.* self-discipline.

самодовлéющий *adj.* self-contained; independent.

самодово́льный *adj.* self-satisfied; self-complacent; smug.

самодово́льство *neut.* self-satisfaction; smugness.

самоду́р *m. f.* —ка high-handed person.

самоду́рство *neut.* high-handedness.

самозарождéние *neut.* spontaneous generation.

самозащи́та *f.* self-defense.

самозвáнец FILL *m. f.* самозвáнка pretender; impostor.

самозвáнный *adj.* self-styled.

самокáт *m.* scooter.

самокрити́ческий *adj.* self-critical.

самолёт *m.* airplane.

самоли́чно *adv.* (*colloq.*) personally.

самолюби́вый *adj.* proud; self-esteeming.

самолю́бие *neut.* pride; self-respect.

самомнéние *neut.* conceit; self-importance.

самонаблюдéние *neut.* introspection.

самонадéянность *f.* self-assurance; presumption.

самонадéянный *adj.* self-assured; presumptuous.

самоназвáние *neut.* self-designation.

самооблада́ние *neut.* self-control; composure.
самообма́н *m.* self-deception.
самооборо́на *f.* self-defense.
самообслу́живание *neut.* self-service.
самоопределе́ние *neut.* self-determination.
самоотве́рженность *f.* selflessness.
самоотве́рженный *adj.* selfless.
самоотрече́ние *neut.* self-denial.
самоочеви́дный *adj.* self-evident.
самопи́сец FILL *m.* recorder.
самопи́ска *f.* (*colloq.*) (*obs.*) fountain pen.
самопоже́ртвование *neut.* self-sacrifice.
самопроизво́льно *adv.* spontaneously.
самопроизво́льность *f.* spontaneity.
самопу́ск *m.* self-starter.
саморо́дный *adj.* (of *minerals*) native.
саморо́док FILL *m.* **1.** nugget. **2.** person with extraordinary natural talent.
самоса́д *m.* (*colloq.*) home-grown tobacco.
самосва́л *m.* dump truck.
самосожже́ние *neut.* self-immolation.
самосозна́ние *neut.* consciousness.
самосохране́ние *neut.* self-preservation.
самостоя́тельность *f.* independence.
самостоя́тельный *adj.* independent.
самостре́л *m.* self-inflicted wound (*to evade military service*).
самосу́д *m.* lynching.
самотёк *m.* unplanned course of affairs; drift.
самотёком *adv.* spontaneously; of its own momentum.
самоуби́йственный *adj.* suicidal.
самоуби́йство *neut.* suicide.
самоуби́йца *m.* and *f.* (*decl. f.*) person who has committed suicide.
самоуваже́ние *neut.* self-respect.
самоуве́ренность *f.* self-confidence.
самоуве́ренный *adj.* self confident; self assured.
самоуничтоже́ние *neut.* self-destruction.
самоуправле́ние *neut.* self-government.
самоуправля́ющийся *adj.* self-governing.
самоупра́вный *adj.* arbitrary.
самоупра́вство *neut.* arbitrariness.
самоучи́тель *m.* self-study guide.
самоу́чка *m.* and *f.* (*decl. f.*) (*colloq.*) self-taught person.
самохва́льство *neut.* (*colloq.*) boasting.
самохо́дка *f.* (*colloq.*) self-propelled gun.
самохо́дный *adj.* self-propelled.
самоцве́т *m.* semiprecious stone.
самоцве́тный *adj.* semiprecious.
самоце́ль *f.* end in itself.
самочи́нный *adj.* **1.** arbitrary. **2.** unauthorized.
самура́й *m.* samurai.
самши́т *m.* box tree.
са́мый *pron.*, *adj.* the very; most. — тот же са́мый the very same.
сан *m.* rank; title.
санато́рий *m.* sanitorium.
сангвини́ческий *adj.* sanguine.
санда́л *m.* sandalwood.
санда́лия *f.* sandal.
санда́ловый *adj.* sandalwood.
са́ни *pl.* sleigh.
санита́р *m.* hospital attendant *or* orderly.
санитари́я *f.* sanitation.

санита́рный *adj.* **1.** sanitary. **2.** (*mil.*) medical. — санита́рный день *m.* day for cleaning.
са́нки *pl.* sled.
Санкт-Петербу́рг *m.* St. Petersburg.
санкциони́ровать *impf.* and *pf.* to sanction.
са́нкция *f.* sanction.
са́нный *adj.* (*attrib.*) sled; sleigh.
санови́тый *adj.* high-ranking.
сано́вник *m.* dignitary; high official.
сано́вный *adj.* **1.** high-ranking. **2.** dignified. **3.** stately.
Сан-Сальвадо́р *m.* San Salvador.
сантигра́мм *m.* centigramm.
санти́м *m.* centime.
сантиме́тр *m.* centimeter.
Сантья́го *m.* Santiago.
Сан-Франци́ско *m.* San Francisco.
сап[1] *m.* (*vet.*) glanders.
сап[2] *m.* stertorous breathing.
сапёр *m.* (*mil.*) sapper.
сапо́г *m.* boot.
сапо́жник *m.* shoemaker.
сапо́жный *adj.* (*attrib.*) shoe.
Са́пporo *m.* Sapporo.
сапса́н *m.* peregrine falcon.
сапфи́р *m.* sapphire.
сапфи́рный *also* сапфи́ровый *adj.* sapphire.
Сараго́са *f.* Zaragoza.
сара́й *m.* shed; barn.
саранча́ *f.* locust.
Сара́тов *m.* Saratov.
сарафа́н *m.* sarafan (*peasant woman's dress*).
сарде́лька *f.* small sausage.
сарди́на *also* сарди́нка *f.* sardine.
сардони́ческий *adj.* sardonic.
Са́рема *f.* (*island*) Saaremaa.
са́ржа *f.* serge.
са́ржевый *adj.* serge.
сарка́зм *m.* sarcasm.
саркасти́чески *adv.* sarcastically.
саркасти́ческий *adj.* sarcastic.
саркофа́г *m.* sarcophagus.
сары́ч *m.* buzzard.
Саска́чеван *m.* Saskatchewan.
Сатана́ *f.* Satan.
сатани́нский *adj.* satanic.
сати́р *m.* satyr.
сати́ра *f.* satire. — сати́рик *m.* **1.** comedian. **2.** satirist.
сатири́ческий *adj.* satirical.
сатра́п *m.* satrap.
сатра́пия *f.* satrapy.
Сау́довская Ара́вия *f.* Saudi Arabia.
сафло́р *m.* safflower.
сафья́н *m.* morocco leather.
сафья́нный *also* сафья́новый *adj.* morocco.
Сахали́н *m.* (*island*) Sakhalin.
са́хар *m.* sugar.
сахари́н *m.* saccharin.
сахари́стый *adj.* containing sugar; rich in sugar.
са́харница *f.* sugar bowl.
са́харный *adj.* (*attrib.*) sugar; sugary.
сахаро́за *f.* sucrose.
сачо́к FILL *m.* net on a long handle.
сба́вка *f.* (*colloq.*) reduction.

сбавля́ть *impf. pf.* сба́вить to reduce (*a price; speed*).

сбаланси́рованный *adj.* balanced.

сбаланси́ровать OVA *pf.* to regain one's balance.

сберега́тельный *adj.* (*attrib.*) savings.

сберега́ть *impf. pf.* сбере́чь to save; to preserve.

сберка́сса *f.* savings bank.

сберкни́жка *f.* bankbook.

сби́вчивый *adj.* 1. confusing. 2. inconsistent. 3. muddled.

сближа́ть *impf. pf.* сбли́зить to draw *or* bring together. —ся 1. to approach. 2. to draw near.

сближе́ние *neut.* rapprochement.

сбо́ку *adv.* from one side; on one side.

сбор *m.* 1. collection. 2. gathering. 3. dues; duty.

сбо́рище *neut.* (*colloq.*) gathering; crowd.

сбо́рка *f.* 1. putting together; assembly; erection. 2. gather (*in a dress*).

сбо́рная *also* сбо́рная кома́нда *f.* combined team.

сбо́рник *m.* collection; anthology.

сбо́рный *adj.* (*attrib.*) gathering; meeting.

сбо́рочный *adj.* (*attrib.*) assembly.

сбо́рщик *m. f.* сбо́рщица 1. collector (*of taxes*). 2. assembler. 3. picker; gatherer (*of cotton*).

сбра́сывать *impf. pf.* сбро́сить 1. to throw off; to throw down. 2. to overthrow. 3. to shed. 4. (*cards*) to discard.

сброд *m.* (*colloq.*) riffraff; rabble.

сбро́сить *pf. of* сбра́сывать.

сбру́я *f.* harness.

сбыт *m.* sale.

сва́дебный *adj.* (*attrib.*) wedding.

сва́дьба *f.* wedding.

сва́йный *adj.* built on piles.

сва́лка *f.* 1. dump; dumping ground. 2. (*colloq.*) scuffle; fight.

сва́ривать *impf. pf.* свари́ть to weld together.

свари́ть *pf. of* вари́ть, сва́ривать.

сва́рка *f.* welding.

сварли́вый *adj.* cantankerous; quarrelsome.

сварно́й *adj.* welded.

сва́рочный *adj.* (*attrib.*) welding.

сва́рщик *m.* welder.

сва́стика *f.* swastika.

сват *m.* 1. matchmaker. 2. son-in-law's father; daughter-in-law's father.

сватовство́ *neut.* matchmaking.

сва́тья *f.* mother of one's son-in-law *or* daughter-in-law.

сва́ха *f.* matchmaker.

сва́я *f.* pile (*wooden pole*).

сведе́ние *neut.* 1. reduction. 2. (*med.*) cramp; contraction.

све́дения *pl.* 1. information. 2. intelligence; knowledge.

све́дущий *adj.* knowledgeable; well-versed.

свежева́ть *impf. pf.* о- to skin; to dress (*an animal*).

све́жесть *f.* freshness.

све́жий *adj.* fresh.

свекла́ *f.* beet.

свекло́ви́ца *f.* sugar beet.

свекло́ви́чный *adj.* (*attrib.*) beet.

свеклоса́харный *adj.* (*attrib.*) beet-sugar.

свеко́льник *m.* 1. beet soup. 2. beet tops *or* leaves.

свеко́льный *adj.* (*attrib.*) beet.

све́кор FILL *m.* father-in-law (*husband's father*).

свекро́вь *f.* mother-in-law (*husband's mother*).

сверже́ние *neut.* overthrow; dethronement.

сверка́ние *neut.* sparkle.

сверка́ть *impf. pf.* сверкну́ть to sparkle; to twinkle.

сверли́льный *adj.* (*attrib.*) boring; drilling.

сверли́ть *impf.* 1. *pf.* про- to drill; to bore through. 2. (*of a thought*) to weigh on one's mind.

сверло́ *neut.* (*tool*) drill, borer.

сверля́щий *adj.* (*of pain*) gnawing.

све́рстник *m. f.* све́рстница person of one's own age; peer; contemporary.

свёрток FILL *m.* 1. package; parcel; bundle. 2. roll (*of paper*).

свёртывание *neut.* 1. rolling up. 2. coagulation.

сверх *prep.* (*with gen.*) beyond; above; over. — сверх того́ moreover.

сверхдержа́ва *f.* superpower.

сверхзвуково́й *adj.* supersonic.

сверхпла́новый *adj.* in excess of the plan.

сверхпри́быль *f.* excess profits.

сверхсро́чный *adj.* additional; extra.

све́рху *adv.* from above, from the top.

сверхуро́чно *adv.* overtime.

сверхуро́чные *pl.* overtime (*working hours*).

сверхуро́чный *adj.* (*attrib.*) overtime.

сверхчелове́к *m.* superman.

сверхчелове́ческий *adj.* superhuman.

сверхчувстви́тельный *adj.* supersensitive.

сверхшта́тный *adj.* supernumerary.

сверхъесте́ственный *adj.* supernatural.

сверчо́к FILL *m.* (*insect*) cricket.

свести́ *pf. of* своди́ть.

свет[1] *m.* light.

свет[2] *m.* 1. world. 2. society.

света́ть *impf. impers.* to dawn.

свети́ло *neut.* luminary.

свети́льник *m.* (oil) lamp.

свети́ть *impf.* to shine; to give off light.

светле́ть *impf. pf.* по- *or* про- to become bright; to brighten up.

светло- *prefix* (*of colors*) light.

светло́ *adj.* (*pred.*) light.

све́тлость *f.* 1. brightness. 2. (*cap.*) (*with* Ва́ша, Его́, Её, *etc.*) lordship; grace.

све́тлый *adj.* 1. bright. 2. light. 3. (*of liquids, glass*) clear.

светля́к *m.* lightning bug; firefly.

светлячо́к FILL *m.*, *see* светля́к.

светонепроница́емый *adj.* lightproof.

светопреставле́ние *neut.* the end of the world.

светофо́р *m.* traffic light.

свето́ч *m.* (*obs.*) torch.

светочувстви́тельный *adj.* (*photog.*) sensitive to light.

све́тский *adj.* 1. fashionable; (*attrib.*) society. 2. refined. 3. secular; lay.

светя́щийся *adj.* luminous; luminescent.

свеча́ *also* све́чка *f.* 1. candle. 2. suppository.

свече́ние *neut.* luminescence.

свечно́й *adj.* (*attrib.*) candle.

свива́льник *m.* swaddling clothes.

свида́ние *neut.* appointment; meeting; date. — до свида́ния! goodbye!

свидетель *m. f.* **—ница** witness.

свидетельство *neut.* **1.** testimony; evidence. **2.** license; certificate.

свидетельствовать *impf.* **1.** *pf.* **за-** to witness; to testify. **2.** *pf.* **о-** to examine, to inspect.

свинарник *m.* pigpen; pigsty.

свинец FILL *m.* (*metal*) lead.

свинина *f.* pork.

свинка *f.* mumps.

свиной *adj.* (*attrib.*) pig; pig's.

свиноматка *f.* sow.

свинопас *m.* swineherd.

свинский *adj.* (*colloq.*) swinish.

свинство *neut.* (*colloq.*) squalor; filth.

свинцовый *adj.* (*metal*) (*attrib.*) lead.

свинья *f.* pig.

свирель *f.* (*musical instrument*) pipe; reed pipe.

свирепость *f.* ferocity.

свирепствовать OVA *impf.* to rage; to wreak havoc.

свирепый *adj.* fierce, ferocious.

свиристель *m.* (*bird*) waxwing.

Свирь *f.* (*river*) Svir.

свист *m.* (*sound*) whistle.

свистать *also* **свистеть** *impf.* **1.** to whistle. **2.** (*of birds*) to sing.

свисток FILL *m.* whistle.

свистопляска *f.* (*colloq.*) pandemonium; chaos; bedlam.

свистулька *f.* (*colloq.*) whistle.

свистун *m. f.* **—ья** (*colloq.*) whistler.

свистящий *adj. and m.* sibilant.

свита *f.* suite; retinue.

свитер *m.* sweater.

свиток FILL *m.* **1.** roll. **2.** scroll.

свиться *pf.* to roll up into a ball (*of snakes, etc.*).

свихнуть *pf.* (*colloq.*) to dislocate. **—ся** (*colloq.*) **1.** to go nuts; to go crazy. **2.** to go astray.

свищ *m.* (*med.*) fistula.

свиязь *f.* (*duck*) widgeon.

свобода *f.* freedom; liberty.

свободно *adv.* **1.** freely. **2.** loosely. **3.** fluently. **4.** easily.

свободный *adj.* **1.** free; vacant. **2.** loose; spare.

свободолюбивый *adj.* freedom-loving.

свободолюбие *neut.* love of freedom.

свободомыслие *neut.* free thought.

свободомыслящий *adj.* free thinking.

свод *m.* **1.** arch, vault. **2.** code.

сводить *impf. pf.* **свести 1.** to bring together. **2.** to remove (*a stain, etc.*).

сводка *f.* summary. — **сводка погоды** *f.* weather report.

сводник *m.* pimp; procurer.

сводничество *neut.* procuring.

сводный *adj.* (*attrib.*) summary. — **сводный брат** *m.* step-brother.

сводчатый *adj.* vaulted; arched.

своеволие *neut.* arbitrariness.

своевольный *adj.* headstrong; strong-willed.

своевременно *adv.* in time.

своевременность *f.* timeliness.

своевременный *adj.* timely; opportune.

своекорыстие *neut.* self-interest.

своекорыстный *adj.* self-seeking.

своенравие *neut.* arbitrariness; capriciousness.

своенравный *adj.* arbitrary; capricious.

своеобразно *adv.* in a peculiar manner.

своеобразный *adj.* **1.** original. **2.** distinctive.

свой *adj.* one's own.

свойственник *m. f.* **свойственница** in-law; relation by marriage.

свойственный *adj.* (*with dat.*) characteristic.

свойство *neut.* property; characteristic.

свойство *neut.* relationship by marriage.

сволочь *f.* (*colloq.*) **1.** (*term of abuse*) swine; bastard. **2.** riffraff; rabble.

свора *f.* **1.** pack (*of dogs or wolves*). **2.** gang. **3.** leash.

свояк *m.* brother-in-law (*wife's sister's husband*).

своячениица *f.* sister-in-law (*wife's sister*).

свысока *adv.* with disdain.

свыше *adv.* from above. — *prep.* (*with gen.*) **1.** more than. **2.** beyond.

связанный *adj.* **1.** related. **2.** connected. **3.** (*chem.*) combined; bound.

связать *pf. of* **вязать, связывать**.

связка *f.* **1.** bunch; bundle. **2.** ligament; link.

связки *pl.*: **голосовые связки** *pl.* vocal cords.

связной *adj.* (*attrib.*) liaison.

связность *f.* coherence.

связный *adj.* connected; coherent.

связующий *adj.* connecting.

связывать *impf. pf.* **связать** to tie, to bind, to connect.

связь *f.* tie; bond; connection.

Святейшество *neut.* (*title*) Holiness.

святилище *neut.* sanctuary; holy place.

Святки *pl.* yuletide.

свято *adv.* as if sacred.

святой *adj.* holy, sacred.

святость *f.* holiness; sanctity.

святотатственный *adj.* sacrilegious.

святотатство *neut.* sacrilege.

святотатствовать OVA *impf.* to commit sacrilege.

святочный *adj.* (*attrib.*) Christmas.

святоша *m. and f.* (*decl. f.*) sanctimonious person.

святыня *f.* sacred object *or* place.

священник *m.* priest; clergyman.

священнический *adj.* priestly.

священный *adj.* sacred.

священство *neut.* priesthood.

сгиб *m.* bend.

сгибать *impf. pf.* **согнуть** *v.t.* to bend; to curve.

сглазить *pf.* **1.** to jinx. **2.** to give someone the evil eye.

сгнить *pf. of* **гнить**.

сговариваться *impf. pf.* **сговориться** to arrange (to do something); to come to an agreement.

сговор *m.* conspiracy; collusion.

сговорчивый *adj.* amenable.

сгорание *neut.* combustion.

сгорать *impf. pf.* **сгореть** to burn down; to burn; to be consumed.

сгорбленный *adj.* hunched; stooped.

сгоряча *adv.* in a fit of temper; in the heat of the moment.

сгребать *impf. pf.* **сгрести 1.** to rake. **2.** to sweep; to sweep off.

сгруппировать *pf. of* **группировать**.

сгусток FILL *m.* **1.** bundle. **2.** clot. — **сгусток крови** blood clot.

сгуща́ть *impf. pf.* **сгусти́ть** **1.** to thicken. **2.** to condense. **3.** (*of blood*) to clot.

сгуще́ние *neut.* thickening; clotting.

сгущённый *adj.* condensed; (*of milk*) evaporated.

сдава́ть *impf. pf.* **сдать** **1.** to pass *or* hand in. **2.** to surrender, to yield. **3.** (*cards*) to deal. **4.** to rent; to lease.

сда́вливать *impf. pf.* **сдави́ть** **1.** to squeeze. **2.** to constrict.

сда́точный *adj.* (*attrib.*) delivery.

сда́ча *f.* **1.** surrender. **2.** (*cards*) deal. **3.** (*money*) change.

сдвиг *m.* **1.** change; shift. **2.** change for the better. **3.** step forward.

сде́лать(ся) *pf. of* де́лать(ся).

сде́лка *f.* deal; transaction.

сде́льный *adj.* by the piece.

сде́льщик *m. f.* **сде́льщица** pieceworker.

сде́льщина *f.* piecework.

сде́ржанность *f.* restraint; reserve.

сде́ржанный *adj.* **1.** reserved. **2.** restrained.

сде́рживать *impf. pf.* **сдержа́ть** **1.** to restrain, to hold in, to keep back. **2.** to keep, to fulfill.

сдо́ба *f.* **1.** shortening. **2.** sweet rolls; sticky buns.

сдо́бный *adj.* (*of pastry*) rich.

сдо́хнуть *pf. past* **сдох, сдо́хла** (*of animals*) to die.

сду́ру *adv.* (*colloq.*) foolishly; stupidly.

сё *demonstrative pron.* this (*used only in idiomatic expressions.*) — **то и сё; то да сё** this and that.

сеа́нс *m.* **1.** session. **2.** performance; showing. **3.** sitting.

себе́ *pron., dat. and prep. of* себя́. *See* себя́.

себесто́имость *f.* cost, price.

себя́ *refl. pron.* oneself.

сев *m.* sowing.

Сева́н *m.* (*lake*) Sevan.

Севасто́поль *m.* Sevastopol.

се́вер *m.* north. —**ный** *adj.* North, northern. —**янин** *m. f.* —**янка** northerner.

Се́верная Дако́та *f.* North Dakota.

Се́верная Двина́ *f.* (*river*) Northern Dvina.

Се́верная Земля́ *f.* (*islands*) Severnaya Zemlya.

Се́верная Кароли́на *f.* North Carolina.

Се́верное мо́ре *neut.* North Sea.

Се́верный Ледови́тый океа́н *m.* Arctic Ocean.

Се́верный тро́пик *m.* Tropic of Cancer.

се́веро-восто́к *m.* northeast.

се́веро-восто́чный *adj.* northeastern.

се́веро-за́пад *m.* northwest.

се́веро-за́падный *adj.* northwestern.

Севи́лья *f.* Seville.

севооборо́т *m.* crop rotation.

севрю́га *f.* stellate sturgeon.

сегме́нт *m.* (*math.*) segment.

сего́дня *adv.* today.

сего́дняшний *adj.* today's.

сегрега́ция *f.* segregation.

седа́лище *neut.* (*obs.*) seat.

седа́лищный *adj.* sciatic.

седе́льник *m.* saddler.

седе́льный *adj.* (*attrib.*) saddle.

седе́ть *impf. pf.* **по-** to turn gray.

седи́ль *f.* cedilla.

седина́ *f.* gray hair.

седло́ *neut.* saddle.

седлови́на *f.* depression.

седоволо́сый *adj.* gray-haired; white-haired.

седо́й *adj.* (*of hair*) grey.

седо́к *m.* **1.** rider; horseman. **2.** passenger (*in a carriage*).

седьмо́й *adj.* seventh.

сеза́м *m.* sesame.

сеза́мовый *adj.* sesame.

сезо́н *m.* season.

сезо́нный *adj.* seasonal.

сей *pron.* **сия́** *f.*, **сие́** *neut.*, **сии́** *pl.* (*obs.*) this.

сейсми́ческий *adj.* seismic.

сейсмо́граф *m.* seismograph.

сейсмо́лог *m.* seismologist.

сейсмологи́ческий *adj.* seismological.

сейсмоло́гия *f.* seismology.

сейф *m.* safe.

сейча́с *adv.* now; at once.

се́канс *m.* (*trig.*) secant.

сека́ч *m.* (*tool*) chopper.

секве́стр *m.* sequestration.

секвестрова́ть OVA *impf. and pf.* to sequester.

секи́ра *f.* poleaxe.

секре́т *m.* secret.

секретариа́т *m.* secretariat.

секрета́рский *adj.* secretarial.

секрета́рствовать OVA *impf.* to serve as a secretary.

секрета́рь *m. f.* **секрета́рша** secretary.

секрете́р *m.* desk.

секре́тно *adv.* secretly. — **соверше́нно секре́тно** *adv.* top secret.

секре́тность *f.* secrecy.

секре́тный *adj.* secret.

секре́ция *f.* secretion.

секс *m.* sex.

се́кста *f.* (*mus.*) sixth.

секста́нт *m.* sextant.

сексте́т *m.* sextet.

сексуа́льность *f.* sexuality.

сексуа́льный *adj.* sexual.

се́кта *f.* sect.

секта́нт *m. f.* —**ка** sectarian.

секта́нтский *adj.* sectarian.

секта́нтство *neut.* sectarianism.

се́ктор *m.* sector.

секуляриза́ция *f.* secularization.

секуляризи́ровать OVA *impf. and pf.* to secularize.

секу́нда *f.* second.

секунда́нт *m.* second (*in a duel*).

секу́ндный *adj.* (*time*) (lasting a) second.

секундоме́р *m.* stopwatch.

секу́щая *f.* (*geom.*) secant.

секцио́нный *adj.* sectional.

се́кция *f.* section.

селёдка *f.* herring.

селёдочный *adj.* (*attrib.*) herring.

селезёнка *f.* spleen.

селезёночный *adj.* splenetic.

се́лезень FILL *m.* drake; male duck.

селе́кция *f.* selection.

селе́н *m.* selenium.

селе́ние *neut.* village; settlement.

селени́т *m.* selenite.

сели́тра *f.* saltpeter; niter.

сели́тряный *adj.* (*attrib.*) saltpeter.
село́ *neut.* village.
сельдере́й *m.* celery.
сельдере́йный *adj.* (*attrib.*) celery.
сельдь *f.* herring.
се́льский *adj.* **1.** rural. **2.** (*attrib.*) village.
— **се́льское хозя́йство** *neut.* agriculture.
сельскохозя́йственный *adj.* agricultural.
сельсове́т *m.* (*abbr.* of **се́льский сове́т**) village council.
сема́нтика *f.* semantics.
семанти́ческий *adj.* semantic.
семафо́р *m.* semaphore.
сёмга *f.* salmon.
семе́йный *adj.* domestic; family.
семе́йственность *adj.* attachment to one's family.
семе́йственный *adj.* attached to one's family.
семе́йство *neut.* family.
семени́ть *impf.* to mince (*manner of walking*).
семенни́к *m.* **1.** seed plant. **2.** testicle.
семенно́й *adj.* (*attrib.*) seed; seminal.
семёрка *f.* **1.** seven; the numeral seven. **2.** (*cards*) the seven. **3.** group of seven persons. **4.** (*colloq.*) anything numbered seven.
се́меро *num.* (*coll.*) seven.
семе́стр *m.* semester.
се́мечко *neut.* **1.** *dim.* of **се́мя. 2. се́мечки** *pl.* sunflower seeds.
семидесятиле́тие *neut.* **1.** seventieth birthday. **2.** seventieth anniversary. **3.** seventy-year period.
семидесятиле́тний *adj.* (*attrib.*) seventy-year.
семидеся́тый *adj.* seventieth.
семидне́вный *adj.* seven-day.
семикра́тный *adj.* sevenfold.
семиле́тие *f.* **1.** seventh birthday. **2.** seventh anniversary. **3.** seven-year period.
семиле́тка *f.* **1.** Seven-Year Plan. **2.** seven-year school.
семиле́тний *adj.* (*attrib.*) seven-year.
семина́р *m.* seminar.
семинари́ст *m.* seminary student.
семина́рия *f.* seminary.
Семипала́тинск *m.* Semipalatinsk.
семисо́тый *adj.* seven-hundredth.
семиуго́льник *m.* heptagon.
семиуго́льный *adj.* heptagonal.
семичасово́й *adj.* (*attrib.*) seven-hour.
семна́дцатый *adj.* seventeenth.
семь *num.* seven.
се́мьдесят *num.* seventy.
семьсо́т *num.* seven hundred.
се́мью *adv.* seven times.
семьяни́н *m.* family man.
се́мя *neut. pl.* **семена́** seed; semen.
семья́ *f.* family.
семядо́ля *f.* cotyledon.
семяизлия́ние *neut.* ejaculation.
семяпо́чка *f.* (*bot.*) ovule.
Се́на *f.* (*river*) Seine.
сена́т *m.* senate.
сена́тор *m.* senator.
сена́торский *adj.* senatorial; senator's.
сена́тский *adj.* (*attrib.*) senate.
сенберна́р *m.* (*dog*) Saint Bernard.
Сен-Дени́ *m.* Saint Denis.
Сенега́л *m.* Senegal.

се́ни *pl.* vestibule; entrance hall.
сенно́й *adj.* (*attrib.*) hay.
се́но *neut.* hay.
сенова́л *m.* hayloft.
сеноко́с *m.* haymaking.
сенокоси́лка *f.* mowing machine (*for hay*).
сенсацио́нный *adj.* sensational.
сенса́ция *f.* sensation.
сенсо́рный *adj.* sensory.
сентенцио́зный *adj.* sententious.
сенте́нция *f.* maxim; saying; adage.
сентимента́льность *f.* sentimentality.
сентимента́льный *adj.* sentimental.
сентя́брь *m.* September.
сентя́брьский *adj.* (*attrib.*) September.
сень *f.* (*obs.*) cover; canopy.
сепарати́зм *m.* separatism.
сепарати́ст *m.* separatist.
сепарати́стский *adj.* separatist.
сепара́тный *adj.* (*polit.*) separate.
сепара́тор *m.* separator.
се́пия *f.* sepia.
се́псис *m.* sepsis.
се́птима *f.* (*mus.*) seventh.
септи́ческий *adj.* septic.
се́ра *f.* sulphur.
сера́ль *m.* seraglio.
серафи́м *m.* seraph.
серб *m. f.* **се́рбка** Serb.
серва́нт *m.* sideboard.
серви́з *m.* set (*of dishes*).
сервирова́ть OVA *impf. and pf.* to set (*a table*).
сервиро́вка *f.* setting (*of table*).
Се́ргиев Поса́д *m.* Sergiev Posad (*formerly: Zagorsk*).
серде́чник *m. f.* **серде́чница** (*colloq.*) person with a heart ailment.
серде́чно *adv.* cordially; warmly.
серде́чно-сосу́дистый *adj.* cardiovascular.
серде́чность *f.* cordiality; warmth.
серде́чный *adj.* **1.** (*attrib.*) heart. **2.** tender, cordial.
серди́то *adv.* angrily.
серди́тый *adj.* angry.
серди́ть *impf. pf.* **рас-** to anger.
сердобо́льный *adj.* tender-hearted.
се́рдце *neut.* heart.
сердцебие́ние *neut.* heartbeat; palpitation.
сердцеви́дка *f.* (*mollusk*) cockle.
сердцеви́дный *adj.* heart-shaped.
сердцеви́на *f.* core.
сердцее́д *m.* (*colloq.*) lady-killer.
серебри́стый *adj.* silvery.
серебро́ *neut.* silver.
серебря́ник *m.* silversmith.
сере́бряный *adj.* silver.
середи́на *f.* middle.
середи́нный *adj.* middle.
серёдка *f.* (*colloq.*) middle; center.
серёжка *f.* earring.
серена́да *f.* serenade.
сержа́нт *m.* sergeant.
сержа́нтский *adj.* sergeant's.
сери́йный *adj.* (*attrib.*) mass (production); mass-produced.
се́рия *f.* series.

сермя́га *f.* coarse, heavy cloth.
се́рна *f.* chamois.
серни́стый *adj.* containing sulfur; sulfurous.
сернобы́к *m.* oryx (*African antelope*).
сернокислый *adj.* sulfate (of).
Серо́в *m.* Serov.
серова́тый *adj.* greyish.
сероводоро́д *m.* hydrogen sulfide.
сероло́гия *f.* serology.
серп *m.* sickle.
серпанти́п *m.* streamer; paper streamer.
Се́рпухов *m.* Serpukhov.
сертифика́т *m.* certificate.
се́рый *adj.* grey.
серьга́ *f.* earring.
серьёзность *f.* seriousness.
серьёзный *adj.* serious; earnest.
се́ссия *f.* session.
сестра́ *f.* sister. — медици́нская сестра́ *f.* nurse.
сестрёнка *f.* little sister.
се́стрин *adj.* (*obs.*) one's sister's.
Сестроре́цк *m.* Sestroretsk.
сесть *pf. of* сади́ться.
сет *m.* (*tennis*) set.
се́тка *f.* 1. net. 2. netting; grid. 3. (*math.*) system.
се́тование *neut.* complaining.
се́товать *impf.* (**на** *with acc.*) to complain.
се́ттер *m.* setter.
Се́тубал *m.* Setubal.
сетча́тка *f.* retina.
сетча́тый *adj.* 1. netted; (*attrib.*) network. 2. reticular.
сеть *f.* 1. net. 2. system.
Сеу́л *m.* Seoul.
сече́ние *neut.* section.
се́чка *f.* fine-cut straw.
сечь *impf. pf.* вы́- to flog, to whip.
се́ялка *f.* seeding machine.
се́янец FILL *m.* seedling.
се́ятель *m.* sower.
се́ять *impf. pf.* по- to sow.
сжа́литься *pf.* (**над** *with instr.*) to take pity on *or* upon.
сжа́тие *neut.* 1. pressure, pressing. 2. compression. 3. grip.
сжа́тость *f.* conciseness.
сжа́тый *adj.* 1. concise. 2. (*of fists*) clenched. 3. (*of air*) compressed.
сжа́ть[1] *pf. of* сжима́ть.
сжа́ть[2] *pf. of* жать.
сжечь *pf. of* жечь.
сжижа́ть *impf. pf.* сжиди́ть to liquefy.
сжиже́ние *neut.* liquefaction.
сжи́женный *adj.* liquefied.
сжима́ть *impf. pf.* сжать 1. to press, to squeeze. 2. to condense.
сза́ди *adv.* from behind. — *prep.* (*with gen.*) behind.
си *neut. indecl.* (*mus.*) si; ti; B.
сибари́т *m. f.* —ка sybarite.
сибари́тский *adj.* sybaritic.
сиби́рка *f.* anthrax.
сиби́рский *adj.* Siberian.
Сиби́рь *f.* Siberia.
сибиря́к *m. f.* сибиря́чка Siberian.

си́вка *m.* and *f.* (*decl. f.*) gray horse.
сиву́ха *f.* raw vodka.
си́вый *adj.* (*of horses* or *of hair*) gray.
сиг *m.* whitefish.
сига́ра *f.* cigar.
сигаре́та *f.* cigarette.
сигаре́тный *adj.* (*attrib.*) cigarette.
сига́рный *adj.* (*attrib.*) cigar.
сигна́л *m.* signal.
сигнализа́тор *m.* signaling device.
сигнализа́ция *f.* alarm system.
сигнализи́ровать OVA *impf.* and *pf.* to signal.
сигна́льный *adj.* (*attrib.*) signal.
сигна́льщик *m.* signalman; flagman.
сигнату́ра *f.* label (*on a medicine bottle*).
сиде́лка *f.* nurse.
сиде́ние *neut.* sitting.
си́день *m.* (*obs.*) stay-at-home.
сиде́нье *neut.* seat.
сиде́ть *impf.* to sit, to be seated, to be.
Сидне́й *m.* Sydney.
сидр *m.* cider.
си́дровый *adj.* (*attrib.*) cider.
сидя́чий *adj.* 1. sitting. 2. sedentary.
Сие́на *f.* Siena.
сие́на *f.* sienna.
сиза́ль *m.* sisal.
си́зый *adj.* blue-gray.
сикомо́р *m.* sycamore.
си́ла *f.* strength; power; force.
сила́ч *m. f.* —ка strong person.
силика́т *m.* silicate.
силико́н *m.* silicone.
силлоги́зм *m.* syllogism.
силлогисти́ческий *adj.* syllogistic.
силлоги́ческий *adj.* syllogistic.
силово́й *adj.* (*attrib.*) power.
сило́к FILL *m.* snare.
сило́мер *m.* dynamometer.
си́лос *m.* silo.
си́лосный *adj.* (*attrib.*) silage.
силуэ́т *m.* silhouette.
си́льно *adv.* 1. strongly; powerfully. 2. very much.
си́льный *adj.* strong.
сильф *m.* sylph.
сильфи́да *f.* sylphid.
симбио́з *m.* symbiosis.
си́мвол *m.* symbol.
символизи́ровать OVA *impf.* to symbolize.
симво́ли́зм *m.* symbolism.
симво́лика *f.* symbolism; symbols.
символи́ческий *also* символи́чный *adj.* symbolic.
симметри́ческий *also* симметри́чный *adj.* symmetrical.
симпатизи́ровать OVA *impf.* to like; to be fond of.
симпати́ческий *adj.* sympathetic.
симпати́чный *adj.* likable; nice.
симпа́тия *f.* (**к** *with dat.*) liking for.
симпо́зиум *m.* symposium.
симпто́м *m.* symptom.
симптомати́ческий *adj.* (*med.*) symptomatic.
симптомати́чный *adj.* symptomatic; significant.
симули́ровать OVA *impf.* and *pf.* to simulate; to feign.
симуля́нт *m. f.* —ка simulator.

симуляция *f.* simulation.
Симферополь *m.* Simferopol.
симфонический *adj.* (*attrib.*) symphony; symphonic.
симфония *f.* symphony.
синагога *f.* synagogue.
Сингапур *m.* Singapore.
синдикат *m.* syndicate.
синдром *m.* syndrome.
синева *f.* **1.** blue color. **2.** blue expanse.
синеватый *adj.* bluish.
синеглазый *adj.* blue-eyed.
синекура *f.* sinecure.
синель *f.* chenille.
синий *adj.* dark blue.
синильный *adj.* prussic.
синица *f.* titmouse.
синкопа *f.* (*mus.*) syncopation.
синкопировать OVA *impf.* and *pf.* (*mus.*) to syncopate.
синод *m.* synod.
синодальный *adj.* synodal.
синоним *m.* synonym.
синонимический *also* **синонимичный** *adj.* synonymous.
синоптик *m.* weather forecaster.
синоптика *f.* weather forecasting.
синоптический *adj.* related to weather forecasting.
синтаксис *m.* syntax.
синтаксический *adj.* syntactical.
синтез *m.* synthesis.
синтезировать OVA *impf.* and *pf.* to synthesize.
синтетический *adj.* synthetic.
синтоизм *m.* Shinto; Shintoism.
синус *m.* **1.** (*math.*) sine. **2.** (*anat.*) sinus.
синусит *m.* sinusitis.
синхронизация *f.* synchronization.
синхронизировать OVA *impf.* and *pf.* to synchronize.
синхронический *adj.* synchronic.
синхронный *adj.* synchronous.
синь *f.* blue color.
синька *f.* blueing.
синюшность *f.* cyanosis.
синяк *m.* bruise.
сионизм *m.* Zionism.
сионист *m. f.* **—ка** Zionist.
сионистский *adj.* Zionist.
сип *m.* griffon vulture.
сиплый *adj.* hoarse.
сипнуть *impf. pf.* **о-** *past* **сип** *or* **сипнул, сипла** to become hoarse.
сипуха *f.* barn owl.
Сиракузы *pl.* Siracusa (*also: Syracuse*).
сирена *f.* siren.
сирень *f.* lilac.
сириец FILL *m. f.* **сирийка** Syrian.
Сирия *f.* Syria.
сирокко *m. indecl.* sirocco.
сироп *m.* syrup.
сирота *m.* and *f.* (*decl. f.*) orphan.
сиротливый *adj.* lonely.
сиротский *adj.* (*attrib.*) orphan.
сиротство *neut.* orphanhood.
система *f.* system.

систематизировать OVA *impf.* and *pf.* to systematize.
систематически *adv.* systematically.
систематический *adj.* systematic.
систола *f.* systole.
систолический *adj.* systolic.
ситец FILL *m.* **1.** cotton print. **2.** calico print. **3.** chintz.
ситечко *neut.* filter; strainer.
Ситка *m.* Sitka.
ситник *m.* (*colloq.*) bread made of sifted flour.
сито *neut.* sieve.
ситуация *f.* situation.
ситцевый *adj.* made of printed cotton.
сифилис *m.* syphilis.
сифилитик *m. f.* **сифилитичка** (*colloq.*) syphilitic.
сифилитический *adj.* syphilitic.
сифон *m.* siphon.
Сицилия *f.* (*island*) Sicily.
сияние *neut.* glow; radiance.
сиять *impf.* to shine; to beam.
скабрёзность *f.* indecent expression.
скабрёзный *adj.* indecent.
сказ *m.* tale; epic tale.
сказание *neut.* **1.** tale; lay. **2.** legend.
сказанное DAA *neut.* that which has been said.
сказать *pf. of* **говорить.**
сказитель *m. f.* **—ница** teller of folk tales.
сказка *f.* fairy tale; tale, story.
сказочник *m. f.* **сказочница** storyteller.
сказочный *adj.* **1.** (*attrib.*) fairy-tale. **2.** fabulous; fantastic.
сказуемое *neut.* (*gram.*) predicate.
сказываться *impf. pf.* **сказаться** (*obs.*) **1.** to be told. **2.** (**в** *with prep.*) to be evident in. **3.** (**на** *with prep.*) to have an effect on.
скакалка *f.* jump rope.
скакать *impf. pf.* **по-** **1.** to skip, to jump. **2.** to gallop.
скаковой *adj.* (*attrib.*) racing.
скакун *m.* fast horse; racer.
скала *f.* rock.
Скалистые горы *pl.* Rocky Mountains.
скалистый *adj.* rocky.
скалить *impf. pf.* **скалить зубы** **1.** to bare one's teeth. **2.** to smile; to grin.
скалка *f.* rolling pin.
скалывать *impf. pf.* **сколоть** **1.** to split *or* chop off. **2.** to pin (together).
скальп *m.* scalp (*taken from the head of an enemy*).
скальпель *m.* scalpel.
скамеечка *f.* small bench.
скамейка *f.* bench.
скамья *f.* bench.
скандал *m.* scandal.
скандализировать OVA *impf.* and *pf.* to scandalize.
скандалист *m. f.* **—ка** trouble-maker.
скандалить *impf. pf.* **на-** to brawl; to start a row.
скандальный *adj.* **1.** scandalous. **2.** rowdy; boisterous.
скандий *m.* scandium.
скандировать OVA *impf.* and *pf.* **1.** to scan (*verse*). **2.** (*of a crowd*) to chant. **3.** to stress individual syllables *or* words.

скарабе́й *m.* scarab.

скарб *m.* (*colloq.*) household belongings.

ска́редный *adj.* (*colloq.*) miserly; stingy.

скарлати́на *f.* scarlet fever.

скарлати́нный *adj.* (*colloq.*) of scarlet fever.

скат *m.* slope; ramp.

ска́терть *f.* tablecloth.

ска́тывать *impf. pf.* **скати́ть** to roll *or* slide down.

ска́ут *m.* boy scout.

скафа́ндр *m.* protective suit (*of astronauts or of divers*).

ска́чки *pl.* the races.

скачкообра́зный *adj.* uneven; spasmodic.

скачо́к FILL *m.* jump; leap.

сква́жина *f.* chink; slit.

сквайр *m.* squire.

сквалы́га *m.* and *f.* (*decl. f.*) (*colloq.*) cheapskate; miser.

сквалы́жник *m.* cheapskate; skinflint.

сква́ттер *m.* squatter.

сквер *m.* public garden.

скве́рно *adv.* badly; bad.

скверносло́в *m. f.* —ка foul-mouthed person.

кверносло́вие *neut.* foul language.

скве́рный *adj.* nasty.

сквозно́й *adj.* (*hole* or *wound*) going all the way through.

сквозня́к *m.* draft.

сквозь *prep.* (*with acc.*) through.

скворе́ц FILL *m.* starling.

скворе́чник *m.* bird house (*for starlings*).

скворе́чня *f.* bird house (*for starlings*).

скеле́т *m.* skeleton.

скеле́тный *adj.* skeletal.

ске́птик *m.* skeptic.

скептици́зм *m.* skepticism.

скепти́ческий *adj.* skeptical.

ске́рцо *neut. indecl.* scherzo.

скетч *m.* sketch; skit.

ски́дка *f.* deduction; reduction.

ски́петр *m.* scepter.

скипида́р *m.* turpentine.

скипида́рный *adj.* (*attrib.*) turpentine.

скирд *m.* haystack.

скита́лец FILL *m. f.* **скита́лица** wanderer.

склад[1] *m.* storehouse.

склад[2] *m.* mold; mode; coherence.

скла́дка *f.* fold, crease, pleat.

скла́дно *adv.* smoothly.

складно́й *adj.* folding; collapsible.

скла́дный *adj.* (*colloq.*) **1.** well-built; well-proportioned. **2.** (*of speech*) smooth; coherent.

скла́дчатый *adj.* pleated.

скла́дывать *impf. pf.* **сложи́ть 1.** to fold (up). **2.** to compose. **3.** to pack up.

скла́дываться *impf. pf.* **сложи́ться 1.** to take shape; to form. **2.** to fold. **3.** to develop.

скле́ивающая ле́нта *f.* scotch tape.

скле́ить *pf. of* кле́ить.

склеп *m.* crypt; burial vault.

склеро́з *m.* sclerosis.

склероти́ческий *adj.* sclerotic.

скло́ка *f.* squabble; row.

склоне́ние *neut.* **1.** inclination. **2.** disposing; inclining. **3.** (*gram.*) declension. **4.** (*astr.*) declination.

скло́нность *f.* (к *with dat.*) inclination; tendency.

скло́нный *adj.* (к *with dat.* or *infin.*) **1.** inclined to; prone to; given to. **2.** disposed toward.

склоня́емый *adj.* (*gram.*) declinable.

склоня́ть[1] *impf. pf.* **склони́ть 1.** to incline; to bend. **2.** to bow to. **3.** to win over to; to persuade.

склоня́ть[2] *impf. pf.* **про-** (*gram.*) to decline.

склоня́ться *impf. pf.* **склони́ться 1.** to bend; to bend over. **2.** to yield to.

скло́чный *adj.* (*colloq.*) argumentative.

скля́нка *f.* vial; small bottle.

скоба́ *f.* **1.** bracket. **2.** staple.

ско́бка *f.* bracket, parenthesis.

скобли́ть *impf.* to scrape.

скобяно́й *adj.* (*attrib.*) hardware.

ско́ванность *f.* awkwardness; constraint.

ско́ванный *adj.* awkward; constrained.

сковорода́ *f.* frying pan.

Сковородино́ *neut.* Skovorodino.

сковоро́дка *f.* (*colloq.*) frying pan.

ско́вывать *impf. pf.* **скова́ть** to forge (together).

скола́чивать *impf. pf.* **сколоти́ть 1.** to nail together. **2.** (*colloq.*) to knock together; to build. **3.** (*colloq.*) to form; to put together.

сколо́ть *pf. of* ска́лывать.

сколь *adv.* (*obs.*) how.

скольже́ние *neut.* sliding; slippage.

скользи́ть *impf. pf.* **скользну́ть** to slip; to slide.

ско́льзкий *adj.* slippery.

ско́льзко *adj.* (*pred.*) slippery.

скользя́щий *adj.* sliding.

ско́лько *adv.* how much *or* many.

ско́лько-нибу́дь *adv.* any.

скоморо́х *m.* (*colloq.*) buffoon; clown.

скоморо́шество *neut.* (*colloq.*) buffoonery.

скомпромети́ровать OVA *pf. of* компромети́ровать.

сконфу́женный *adj.* confused; flustered.

сконфу́зить *pf. of* конфу́зить.

сконча́ться *pf.* to pass away; to die.

скопа́ *f.* osprey.

скопе́ц FILL *m.* **1.** eunuch. **2.** member of the skoptsy religious sect.

скопидо́м *m. f.* —ка (*colloq.*) cheapskate; miser.

ско́пище *neut.* crowd; mob.

скопле́ние *neut.* accumulation.

ско́пом *adv.* (*colloq.*) in a group; in a crowd.

ско́рбно *adv.* sorrowfully.

ско́рбный *adj.* sorrowful, sad.

скорбь *f.* sorrow; grief.

скорлупа́ *f.* shell.

скорня́жный *adj.* (*attrib.*) fur.

скорня́к *m.* furrier.

ско́ро *adv.* **1.** quickly. **2.** soon.

скорогово́рка *f.* **1.** tongue twister. **2.** rapid speech.

скоропали́тельный *adj.* (*colloq.*) hasty.

ско́ропись *f.* cursive handwriting (*of old manuscripts*).

скоропдъёмность *f.* (*aero.*) rate of climb.

скоропо́ртящийся *adj.* perishable.

скоропости́жный *adj.* (*of death*) sudden.

скороспе́лый *adj.* early-ripening.

скоростни́к *m.* high-speed worker.

скоростно́й *adj.* of speed; speed.

скорострéльный *adj.* (*gun*) rapid-firing.
скóрость *f.* **1.** speed; velocity. **2.** (*of a motor*) gear.
скоросшивáтель *m.* binder (*for papers*).
скоротéчный *adj.* transitory; short-lived.
скорохóд *m.* (*colloq.*) fast runner.
скорпиóн *m.* scorpion.
скóрый *adj.* quick, fast.
скос *m.* **1.** slant; slope. **2.** bevel; miter.
скосúть *pf. of* косúть.
скот *m.* (*coll.*) cattle; livestock.
скотúна *f.* **1.** (*colloq.*) cattle. **2.** (*fig.*) animal.
скóтник *m. f.* скóтница person who tends cattle.
скóтный *adj.* (*attrib.*) cattle.
скотобóйня *f.* slaughterhouse.
скотовóдство *neut.* cattle raising; cattle breeding.
скотовóдческий *adj.* (*attrib.*) cattle-breeding.
скотолóжство *neut.* bestiality.
скотопригóнный *adj.*: скотопригóнный двор *m.* stockyard.
скóтский *adj.* (*attrib.*) cattle; livestock.
скóтство *neut.* animal-like existence.
скрáдывать *impf.* to conceal.
скребнúца *f.* currycomb; horse comb.
скребóк FILL *m.* scraper.
скрéжет *m.* **1.** grinding; grating. **2.** gnashing (*of teeth*).
скрéпа *f.* clamp; brace.
скрéпка *f.* paper clip.
скреплять *impf. pf.* скрепúть **1.** to fasten together. **2.** to strengthen.
скрещéние *neut.* crossing; intersection.
скрéщивание *neut.* crossing; crossbreeding.
скривúть *pf.* to bend; to distort.
скрип *m.* squeak.
скрипáч *m. f.* —ка violinist.
скрипéть *impf. pf.* про- to squeak.
скрипúчный *adj.* (*attrib.*) violin.
скрипка *f.* violin.
скройть *pf. of* кройть.
скрóмник *m. f.* скрóмница modest person.
скрóмничать *impf.* to be excessively modest.
скрóмно *adv.* modestly.
скрóмность *f.* modesty.
скрóмный *adj.* modest.
скрупулёзный *adj.* scrupulous; meticulous.
скрýчивать *impf. pf.* скрутúть **1.** to twist. **2.** to tie up. **3.** to roll (*a cigarette*).
скрывáть *impf. pf.* скрыть to hide; to conceal.
скрытие *neut.* hiding; concealment.
скрытность *f.* secretiveness.
скрытный *adj.* reserved; secretive.
скрючиваться *impf.* to hunch up.
скряга *m. and f.* (*decl. f.*) miser; cheapskate.
скудéть *impf. pf.* о- to become depleted.
скýдность *also* скýдость *f.* scarcity; paucity.
скýдный *adj.* scanty; sparse.
скýка *f.* boredom; tedium.
скулá *f.* cheekbone.
скулáстый *adj.* with high cheekbones.
скулúть *impf.* to whine; to whimper.
скýльптор *m.* sculptor.
скульптýра *f.* sculpture.
скульптýрный *adj.* sculptural.
скýмбрия *f.* mackerel.
скунс *m.* skunk.

скýнсовый *adj.* (*attrib.*) skunk.
скупердяй *m. f.* —ка (*colloq.*) cheapskate; skinflint.
скупéц FILL *m.* miser.
скупóй *adj.* stingy.
скýпщик *m. f.* скýпщица buyer (*of items for resale*).
скуфья *f.* skullcap.
скучáть *impf.* to be bored.
скучáющий *adj.* bored.
скýченность *f.* congestion; overcrowding.
скýченный *adj.* congested; overcrowded.
скýчно *adv.* boring; in a boring manner.
скýчный *adj.* boring; tedious.
слабéть *impf. pf.* о- to weaken, to grow weak.
слабинá *f.* weak spot.
слабúтельное *neut.* laxative, purgative.
слабúтельный *adj.* cathartic.
слáбо *adv.* weakly; faintly.
слабовóлие *neut.* weakness of will.
слабовóльный *adj.* weak-willed.
слаборáзвитый *adj.* (*of countries*) underdeveloped.
слабосúлие *neut.* weakness.
слабосúльный *adj.* weak; feeble.
слáбость *f.* weakness.
слабоýмие *neut.* feeble-mindedness.
слабоýмный *adj.* feeble-minded.
слáбый *adj.* weak.
слáва *f.* **1.** fame. **2.** glory.
славúст *m.* Slavist; Slavicist.
славúстика *f.* Slavic studies.
слáвить *impf. pf.* о- to glorify.
слáвка *f.* warbler.
слáвно *adv.* wonderfully. — *adj.* (*pred.*) (*colloq.*) nice; wonderful.
слáвный *adj.* glorious; famous.
славослóвие *neut.* glorification.
славянин *m. f.* славянка Slav.
славянофúл *m.* Slavophile.
Славянск *m.* Slovyansk.
славянский *adj.* Slavic; Slavonic.
слагáемое *neut.* element; component.
слагáть *impf. pf.* сложúть to compose. — сложúть с себя to give up; to decline.
слагáться *impf.* (из *with gen.*) to be composed of; to consist of.
слáдкий *adj.* sweet.
слáдко *adv.* sweetly; sweet.
слáдкое DAA *neut.* **1.** sweets. **2.** dessert.
сладкоéжка *m. and f.* (*decl. f.*) (*colloq.*) person with a sweet tooth.
сладкозвýчный *adj.* sweet-sounding.
сладкорéчивый *adj.* smooth-spoken.
слáдостный *adj.* sweet.
сладострáстный *adj.* voluptuous; sensual.
слáдость *f.* sweetness.
слáженность *f.* harmony.
слáлом *m.* slalom.
слáнец FILL *m.* **1.** slate. **2.** shale.
слáнцевый *adj.* (*attrib.*) slate; shale.
Слáнцы *pl.* Slantsy.
сластёна *m. and f.* (*decl. f.*) (*colloq.*) person with a sweet tooth.
слáсти *pl.* sweets.
сластолюбúвый *adj.* sensual.
слащáвый *adj.* sugary; honeyed.

слева *adv.* from the left; on the left.

слегка *adv.* somewhat; a little.

след *m.* **1.** trace. **2.** track. **3.** sign.

следить *impf.* (за *with instr.*) to watch; to spy on *or* upon; to follow, to shadow.

следование *neut.* **1.** following. **2.** travel; movement.

следователь *m.* investigator.

следовательно *adv.* consequently; therefore.

следовать OVA *impf. pf.* по- (за *with instr.*) **1.** to follow; to come next. **2.** *impers.* ought, should; to be owed.

следом *adv.* immediately afterwards; immediately behind.

следопыт *m.* hunter (*who tracks down animals*).

следственный *adj.* investigatory.

следствие *neut.* consequence.

следуемый *adj.* due.

следующее *neut.* the following.

следующий *adj.* next; following.

слежение *neut.* (*aerospace*) monitoring; tracking; following.

слежка *f.* surveillance.

слеза *f.* tear.

слезать *impf. pf.* слезть to get down *or* off.

слезинка *f.* tear; teardrop.

слезливый *adj.* easily moved to tears.

слёзный *adj.* (*attrib.*) tear; tearful.

слезоточивый *adj.* (*of one's eyes*) teary.

слепень FILL *m.* horsefly.

слепец FILL *m.* blind man.

слепить *pf. of* лепить.

слепнуть *impf. pf.* о- to become blind.

слепо *adv.* blindly.

слепой *adj.* blind. — *m.* blind man.

слепок FILL *m.* cast; mold.

слепота *f.* blindness.

слепыш *m.* mole rat.

слесарный *adj.* (*attrib.*) metalworking.

слесарь *m.* plumber.

слива *f.* plum.

сливать *impf. pf.* слить to pour out *or* off.

сливки *pl.* cream.

сливовый *adj.* (*attrib.*) plum.

сливочник *m.* creamer; cream pot.

сливочный *adj.* (*attrib.*) cream; creamy.

сливянка *f.* plum brandy.

слизень *m.* (*gastropod*) slug.

слизистый *adj.* **1.** slimy. **2.** mucous.

слизняк *m.* slug (*gastropod*).

слизь *f.* **1.** mucus. **2.** slime. **3.** mucilage.

слинялый *adj.* (*colloq.*) faded.

слипаться *impf. pf.* слипнуться **1.** to stick together. **2.** *impf. only* (*of eyes*) to be heavy with sleep; to be sleepy.

слитно *adv.* **1.** together. **2.** (*spelled*) as one word.

слитный *adj.* conjunct; continuous.

слиток FILL *m.* **1.** ingot; bar. **2.** слитки *pl.* bullion.

слить *pf. of* сливать.

сличать *impf. pf.* сличить to collate; to compare and check.

слишком *adv.* too.

слияние *neut.* **1.** confluence; junction. **2.** blending, merging.

слобода *f.* (*hist.*) sloboda (*settlement inhabited by tradesmen*).

Словакия *f.* Slovakia.

словарный *adj.* (*attrib.*) dictionary.

словарь *m.* **1.** dictionary. **2.** glossary, vocabulary.

Словения *f.* Slovenia.

словесник *m. f.* словесница teacher of Russian language and literature.

словесность *f.* **1.** literature. **2.** philology.

словесный *adj.* verbal, oral.

словечко *neut. dim. of* слово.

словник *m.* glossary; word list.

слово *conj.* **1.** as if; as though. **2.** like.

слово *neut.* word. — слово в слово word for word.

словом *adv.* in short.

словоохотливый *adj.* talkative; loquacious.

словосочетание *neut.* combination of words. — устойчивое словосочетание *neut.* set expression; set phrase.

слог¹ *m.* syllable.

слог² *m.* style.

слоговой *adj.* syllabic.

слоёный *adj.* (*attrib.*) puff; flaky.

сложение *neut.* composition; build; constitution.

сложённый *adj.* formed, built.

сложить *pf. of* складывать and слагать.

сложно *adv.* in a complicated way.

сложноподчинённое предложение *neut.* complex sentence.

сложносочинённое предложение *neut.* compound sentence.

сложность *f.* complexity.

сложный *adj.* **1.** complex, complicated. **2.** compound.

слоистый *adj.* **1.** stratified. **2.** laminated.

слой *m.* layer.

слойка *f.* (*pastry*) puff.

слом *m.* tearing down; demolition.

сломать *pf. of* ломать.

слон *m.* elephant.

слонёнок FILL *m.* baby elephant; young elephant.

слониха *f.* female elephant.

слоновость *f.* elephantiasis.

слоновый *adj.* (*attrib.*) elephant.

слоняться *impf.* to loiter; to drift around.

слуга *m.* (*decl. f.*) servant.

служанка *f.* servant; maid.

служащий *adj.* serving. — *m.* employee.

служба *f.* **1.** service. **2.** work.

служебный *adj.* **1.** (*attrib.*) service; office. **2.** auxiliary.

служение *neut.* service; serving.

служитель *m. f.* —ница (*obs.*) servant.

служить *impf. pf.* по- to serve.

слух *m.* hearing; rumor.

слуховой *adj.* (*attrib.*) hearing; auditory.

случай *m.* **1.** case. **2.** occasion, chance. **3.** event, incident.

случайно *adv.* by chance; accidentally.

случайность *f.* accidental nature; accident.

случайный *adj.* **1.** chance; accidental; random. **2.** incidental.

случать *impf. pf.* случить to couple, to pair.

случаться *impf. pf.* случиться to happen, to occur.

слу́шание *neut.* listening; hearing.
слу́шатель *m. f.* **—ница** listener.
слу́шать *impf.* **1.** *pf.* **по-** to listen, to hear. **2.** *pf.* про- to attend (*a lecture, etc.*).
слу́шаться *impf. pf.* **по- 1.** to obey. **2.** to heed advice. **3.** (*leg.*) (*of a case*) to be heard.
слыть *impf. pf.* **про-** (*with instr.*) **1.** to be reputed to be. **2.** to have a reputation for.
слыха́ть *impf.* to hear about *or* of.
слы́шать *impf. pf.* **у-** to hear; to hear of.
слы́шимость *f.* audibility.
слы́шимый *adj.* audible.
слы́шно *adv.* audibly. — *adj.* (*pred.*) **1.** audible. **2.** heard.
слы́шный *adj.* audible.
слюда́ *f.* mica.
слюдяно́й *adj.* (*attrib.*) mica.
слюна́ *f.* saliva.
слю́ни *pl.* (*colloq.*) saliva.
слюни́ть *impf. pf.* **по-** to moisten with saliva.
слю́нки *pl.* (*colloq.*) saliva.
слю́нный *adj.* salivary.
слюня́вый *adj.* (*colloq.*) driveling.
сля́коть *f.* slush.
сма́зка *f.* **1.** grease; greasing. **2.** lubrication.
смазли́вый *adj.* (*colloq.*) good-looking; pretty.
сма́зочный *adj.* (*attrib.*) lubrication.
сма́зчик *m.* grease monkey.
сма́зывание *neut.* greasing; oiling.
сма́зывать *impf. pf.* **сма́зать 1.** to oil; to grease. **2.** to paint; to swab. **3.** to wipe off.
смак *m.* (*colloq.*) relish; gusto.
смакова́ть OVA *impf.* (*colloq.*) to savor; to relish.
сма́тывать *impf. pf.* смота́ть **1.** to wind (in). **2.** (с *with gen.*) to wind off; to unwind from.
сма́хивать *impf. pf.* смахну́ть **1.** to brush off; to brush away. **2.** (на *with acc.*) (*colloq.*) to look like; to resemble.
сма́чивать *impf. pf.* смочи́ть to moisten.
сма́чно *adv.* (*colloq.*) with relish.
сма́чный *adj.* (*colloq.*) tasty.
сме́жность *f.* contiguity.
сме́жный *adj.* **1.** adjacent; adjoining. **2.** allied. **3.** related.
смека́листый *adj.* (*colloq.*) clever; sharp.
смека́лка *f.* (*colloq.*) shrewdness.
смека́ть *impf. pf.* смекну́ть (*colloq.*) to get the point; to come to understand.
сме́ло *adv.* **1.** boldly. **2.** (*colloq.*) safely.
сме́лость *f.* audacity; boldness.
сме́лый *adj.* bold; daring.
смельча́к *m.* daredevil.
сме́на *f.* **1.** changing; replacement. **2.** shift (*at work*). **3.** alternation (*of seasons*).
сме́нный *adj.* (*attrib.*) shift.
сменя́емый *adj.* removeable.
сменя́ть *impf. pf.* смени́ть **1.** to change. **2.** to replace. **3.** to relieve; to remove.
смерка́ться *impf. pf.* сме́ркнуться *impers.* to get dark.
смерте́льно *adv.* mortally; fatally.
смерте́льный *adj.* **1.** deadly; mortal; fatal. **2.** (*of insult*) grievous. **3.** (*of boredom*) utter.
сме́ртник *m. f.* сме́ртница prisoner condemned to death.
сме́ртность *f.* mortality; death rate.

сме́ртный *adj.* **1.** (*attrib.*) death. **2.** mortal. — *m.* mortal.
смертоно́сный *adj.* lethal; fatal.
смерть *f.* death.
смерч *m.* **1.** tornado. **2.** waterspout. **3.** whirlwind; sandstorm.
смеси́тель *m.* mixer; blender.
смесь *f.* mixture; blend.
сме́та *f.* estimate.
смета́на *f.* sour cream.
сме́тка *f.* (*colloq.*) quick wit; savvy.
сметли́вый *adj.* bright; quick-witted.
сме́тный *adj.* estimated.
сметь *impf. pf.* **по-** to dare.
смех *m.* laughter; laugh.
сме́шанный *adj.* **1.** mixed. **2.** hybrid. **3.** compound.
смеше́ние *neut.* mixture; blend.
сме́шивание *neut.* mixing.
сме́шивать *impf. pf.* смеша́ть *v.t.* **1.** to mix, to blend. **2.** to confuse.
смеши́ть *impf. pf.* насмеши́ть to cause to laugh.
смешли́вый *adj.* given to laughter.
смешно́ *adv.* in a funny way.
смешно́й *adj.* funny; ludicrous; ridiculous.
смешо́к FILL *m.* (*colloq.*) chuckle.
смеща́ть *impf. pf.* смести́ть *impf.* **1.** to displace. **2.** to remove (*from office*).
смеще́ние *neut.* removal; displacement.
смея́ться *impf.* **1.** to chuckle, to laugh. **2.** (над *with instr.*) to laugh at.
смире́ние *neut.* humility.
смире́нно *adv.* humbly.
смире́нность *f.* humility.
смире́нный *adj.* humble; meek.
смири́тельная руба́шка *f.* strait jacket.
сми́рно *adv.* quietly. — *interj.* (*mil.*) attention!
сми́рный *adj.* **1.** quiet. **2.** mild.
смиря́ть *impf. pf.* смири́ть to restrain; to subdue.
смо́ква *f.* fig.
смо́кинг *m.* tuxedo; (formal) dinner jacket.
смоко́вница *f.* fig tree.
смола́ *f.* **1.** resin. **2.** tar.
Смоле́нск *m.* Smolensk.
смолёный *adj.* tarred.
смоли́стый *adj.* resinous.
смолка́ть *impf. pf.* смо́лкнуть to become *or* grow silent.
смо́лоду *adv.* **1.** from one's youth. **2.** in one's youth.
смоло́ть *pf. of* моло́ть.
смоль *f.:* чёрный как смоль jet-black.
смоляно́й *adj.* (*attrib.*) resin.
смонти́ровать OVA *pf. of* монти́ровать.
сморка́ться *impf. pf.* вы- to blow one's nose.
сморо́дина *f.* (*coll.*) currants.
сморо́динный *adj.* (*attrib.*) currant.
сморчо́к FILL *m.* (*mushroom*) morel.
смо́рщенный *adj.* wrinkled.
смо́рщить *pf. of* мо́рщить.
смотр *m.* review.
смотре́ть *impf. pf.* **по- 1.** to look (at); to examine. **2.** to look through.
смотри́тель *m. f.* **—ница** guard; watchman.
смотрово́й *adj.* (*attrib.*) observation.
смочи́ть *pf. of* сма́чивать.

смочь *pf. of* **мочь.**

смошённичать *pf. of* **мошённичать.**

смрад *m.* stench.

смрáдный *adj.* stinking.

смýглый *adj.* dark-skinned.

смýта *f.* (*obs.*) civil strife.

смýтный *adj.* vague; dim; troubled.

смутьян *m. f.* —ка (*colloq.*) agitator.

смущáть *impf. pf.* **смутить 1.** to confuse. **2.** to embarrass; to trouble.

смущéние *neut.* **1.** confusion. **2.** embarrassment.

смывáть *impf. pf.* **смыть** to wash away; to wash off.

смысл *m.* sense, meaning; purport.

смысловóй *adj.* semantic.

смычка *f.* **1.** joining; linking; coupling. **2.** unifying.

смычкóвый *adj.* (*of mus. instruments*) played with a bow.

смычóк FILL *m.* (*mus.*) bow.

смышлёный *adj.* (*colloq.*) clever; bright.

смягчáть *impf. pf.* **смягчить** *v.t.* **1.** to soften; to mollify. **2.** to ease. **3.** (*phon.*) to palatalize.

смягчéние *neut.* **1.** softening. **2.** mitigation.

смятéние *neut.* **1.** confusion. **2.** panic.

смятéнный *adj.* (*obs.*) troubled.

смять *pf.* to rumple, to crush, to crumple.

снабжáть *impf. pf.* **снабдить** to supply, to provide, to furnish.

снабжéние *neut.* supply; provision.

снáйпер *m.* sniper.

снарýжи *adv.* from the outside.

снаряд *m.* **1.** shell; missile. **2.** device; apparatus.

снарядный *adj.* (*attrib.*) shell; ammunition.

снаряжáть *impf. pf.* **снарядить 1.** to equip; to outfit. **2.** (*colloq.*) to send; to dispatch.

снаряжéние *neut.* equipping; equipment.

снасть *f.* tackle.

сначáла *adv.* **1.** at first; first. **2.** all over again.

снáшивать *impf. pf.* **сносить** to wear out (*clothes*).

снег *m.* snow.

снегирь *m.* bullfinch.

снеговóй *adj.* (*attrib.*) snow.

снегоочистúтель *m.* snowplow.

снегопáд *m.* snowfall.

снегостýп *m.* snowshoe.

снегохóд *m.* snowmobile.

снегýрочка *f.* snow maiden.

снедáть *impf.* to gnaw; to torment.

снедь *f.* (*obs.*) food.

снежинка *f.* snowflake.

снéжный *adj.* (*attrib.*) snow, snowy.

снежóк FILL *m.* **1.** light snow. **2.** snowball.

снести[1] *pf. of* **нести.** —ся *pf. of* **нестись.**

снести[2] *pf. of* **сносить.**

снижáть *impf. pf.* **снизить** to lower; to reduce; to decrease.

снижéние *neut.* lowering; reduction.

снизойти *pf. of* **снисходить.**

снизу *adv.* from below, from the bottom.

снимáть *impf. pf.* **снять 1.** to take away *or* off. **2.** to take down. **3.** to photograph.

снимок FILL *m.* photograph.

снисходúтельность *f.* condescension.

снисходúтельный *adj.* **1.** condescending. **2.** lenient.

снисходúть *impf. pf.* **снизойти** to condescend.

снисхождéние *neut.* condescension.

снúться *impf. pf.* **при-** (*with dat.*) to appear in one's dreams. — мне снúлось I had a dream.

сноб *m.* snob.

снобúзм *m.* snobbery.

снóва *adv.* anew; again.

сновáть OVA *impf.* to scamper about.

сновидéние *neut.* dream.

сногсшибáтельный *adj.* (*colloq.*) stunning; mind-boggling.

сноп *m.* **1.** sheaf. **2.** shaft (*of light*).

снорóвка *f.* skill; knack.

снос *m.* **1.** tearing down; demolition. **2.** wear; wearing something out. **3.** (*of planes* or *ships*) drift.

снóси *pl.*: **быть на сносях** *impf.* to be about to give birth.

сносить[1] *impf. pf.* **снести 1.** to take down; to demolish. **2.** to bear; to endure. **3.** to bring together.

сносить[2] *pf. of* **снáшивать.**

снóска *f.* footnote.

снóсно *adv.* **1.** tolerably well. **2.** so-so.

снóсный *adj.* tolerable.

снотвóрный *adj.* soporific.

снохá *f.* daughter-in-law.

сношéния *pl.* intercourse, dealings.

снятие *neut.* removal.

снятóе молокó *neut.* skim milk.

снять *pf. of* **снимáть.**

со *prep., see* **с.**

соáвтор *m.* coauthor.

соáвторство *neut.* coauthorship.

собáка *f.* dog.

собáчий *adj.* canine, dog's.

собáчка[1] *f.* **1.** trigger. **2.** pawl (*of ratchet*). **3.** catch; trip.

собáчка[2] *f.* little dog; doggie.

собáчник *m. f.* **собáчница** (*colloq.*) dog lover.

собесéдник *m. f.* **собесéдница** person with whom one is speaking.

собесéдование *neut.* conversation; discussion.

собирáние *neut.* **1.** gathering; collecting. **2.** collection.

собирáтель *m. f.* —ница collector.

собирáтельный *adj.* (*gram.*) collective.

собирáтельство *neut.* collecting (*as a hobby*).

собирáть *impf. pf.* **собрáть** to gather; to collect.

собирáться *impf.* (*with infin.*) to intend (to).

соблаговолúть *pf.* (*obs.*) to deign to.

соблáзн *m.* temptation.

соблазнúтель *m. f.* —ница tempter; seducer.

соблазнúтельный *adj.* seductive; tempting.

соблазнять *impf. pf.* **соблазнúть** to entice; to tempt; to seduce.

соблюдáть *impf. pf.* **соблюсти** to observe.

соблюдéние *neut.* **1.** observance. **2.** maintenance.

собóй *also* **собóю** *pron., instr. of* **себя.**

соболéзнование *neut.* condolences; sympathy.

соболéзновать OVA *impf.* (*with dat.*) to commiserate with.

собóлий *also* **соболúный** *adj.* (*attrib.*) sable.

сóболь *m.* sable.

собóр *m.* cathedral.

собóрный *adj.* (*attrib.*) cathedral.

соборова́ние *neut.* extreme unction.
собо́ю *pron.*, *see* собо́й.
собра́ние *neut.* **1.** meeting, gathering. **2.** collection.
со́бранный *adj.* **1.** tensed up; intense. **2.** erect; straight. **3.** (*of a person*) precise; accurate.
собра́т *m.* colleague.
собра́ть *pf. of* собира́ть.
со́бственник *m. f.* со́бственница owner.
со́бственнический *adj.* proprietary; possessive.
со́бственно *adv.* actually; in fact. — со́бственно говоря́ strictly speaking.
собственнору́чно *adv.* with one's own hands.
собственнору́чный *adj.* handwritten.
со́бственность *f.* property.
со́бственный *adj.* own; personal.
собуты́льник *m. f.* собуты́льница (*colloq.*) drinking companion; drinking buddy.
собы́тие *neut.* event.
сова́ *f.* owl.
сова́ть OVA *impf. pres.* сую́, суёшь *pf.* су́нуть to stick; to slip; to thrust.
сове́рен *m.* (*British coin*) sovereign.
соверша́ть *impf. pf.* соверши́ть **1.** to accomplish. **2.** to perform. **3.** to commit.
соверше́ние *neut.* **1.** accomplishment, fulfillment. **2.** perpetration.
соверше́нно *adv.* completely; absolutely.
совершенноле́тний *adj.* of age.
соверше́нный *adj.* **1.** complete; absolute; perfect. **2.** (*gram.*) perfective.
соверше́нство *neut.* perfection.
соверше́нствование *neut.* perfectability.
соверше́нствовать *impf. pf.* у- to perfect.
соверши́ть *pf. of* соверша́ть.
со́вестить *impf.* (*obs.*) (*colloq.*) to shame; to chide.
со́вестливый *adj.* conscientious.
со́вестно *adj.* (*pred., with dat.*) ashamed.
со́весть *f.* conscience.
сове́т *m.* **1.** soviet. **2.** council. **3.** advice; counsel. —ский *adj.* Soviet.
сове́тник *m. f.* сове́тница advisor (*official position*).
сове́товать OVA *impf. pf.* по- to advise. —ся (с *with instr.*) to consult.
совето́лог *m.* specialist in Soviet studies.
сове́тчик *m. f.* сове́тчица someone who gives advice.
совеща́ние *neut.* conference.
совеща́тельный *adj.* consultative; deliberative.
совеща́ться *impf.* to deliberate.
сови́ный *adj.* of an owl.
совладе́лец FILL *m. f.* совладе́лица joint owner.
совладе́ние *neut.* joint ownership.
совмести́мость *f.* compatibility.
совмести́мый *adj.* compatible.
совмести́тельство *neut.* the holding of more than one job.
совме́стно *adv.* together; jointly.
совме́стное предприя́тие *neut.* (*abbr.* СП) joint venture.
совме́стный *adj.* common; joint; combined.
совмеща́ть *impf. pf.* совмести́ть to combine.
сово́к FILL *m.* scoop.
совокупле́ние *neut.* copulation.
совоку́пно *adv.* jointly.

совоку́пность *f.* aggregate; totality.
совоку́пный *adj.* aggregate, combined, total.
совпада́ть *impf. pf.* совпа́сть to coincide.
совпаде́ние *neut.* coincidence.
соврати́тель *m. f.* —ница seducer; corrupter.
совра́ть *pf. of* врать.
совраща́ть *impf. pf.* соврати́ть to pervert; to seduce.
совраще́ние *neut.* seduction; corruption.
совреме́нник *m. f.* совреме́нница contemporary.
совреме́нность *f.* the present time; modernity.
совреме́нный *adj.* contemporary; modern.
совсе́м *adv.* completely; quite.
совхо́з *m.* state farm.
согла́сие *neut.* agreement; consent.
согла́сно *adv.* in accord *or* agreement. — *prep.* (с *with instr.*) in accordance (with).
согла́сный[1] *adj.* agreeable.
согла́сный[2] *m.* consonant.
согласова́ние *neut.* agreement, concordance.
согласо́ванность *f.* coordination.
согласо́ванный *adj.* coordinated.
согласова́ться OVA *impf.* and *pf.* (с *with instr.*) **1.** to be in conformance with. **2.** (*gram.*) to agree (with).
согласо́вывать OVA *impf. pf.* согласова́ть to coordinate.
соглаша́тель *adj.* compromiser; appeaser.
соглаша́тельский *adj.* of appeasement.
соглаша́тельство *adj.* appeasement.
соглаша́ться *impf. pf.* согласи́ться to agree.
соглаше́ние *neut.* **1.** understanding; consent. **2.** agreement.
со́гнутый *adj.* **1.** bent. **2.** stooped; bent over.
согну́ть *pf. of* гнуть, сгиба́ть.
согрева́ние *neut.* warming; heating.
согрева́ть *impf. pf.* согре́ть to warm (up); to heat (up).
со́да *f.* soda.
соде́йствие *neut.* help; assistance.
соде́йствовать OVA *impf. pf.* по- (*with dat.*) to assist.
содержа́ние *neut.* **1.** support; upkeep; maintenance. **2.** content; contents. **3.** matter; substance. **4.** table of contents.
содержа́нка *f.* kept woman.
содержа́тель *m. f.* —ница (*obs.*) owner; operator.
содержа́тельность *f.* wealth of information.
содержа́ть *impf.* **1.** to contain. **2.** to maintain, to keep; to support.
содержи́мое *neut.* contents.
со́довый *adj.* (*attrib.*) soda.
Содо́м *m.* Sodom.
содо́м *m.* (*colloq.*) commotion; uproar.
содрога́ние *neut.* shudder.
содрога́ться *impf. pf.* содрогну́ться to shudder.
содру́жество *neut.* **1.** concord. **2.** community; commonwealth.
со́евый *adj.* (*attrib.*) soybean.
соедине́ние *neut.* linking; combination; junction.
Соединённые Шта́ты *pl.* United States.
соединённый *adj.* united.
соедини́тельный *adj.* connecting.
соедини́ть *impf. pf.* соедини́ть *v.t.* **1.** to join, to unite. **2.** to connect.
сожале́ние *neut.* regret.

сожале́ть *impf.* (о *with prep.*) to regret; to be sorry (for).

сожже́ние *neut.* cremation; burning.

сожи́тель *m. f.* —**ница 1.** roommate. **2.** (*colloq.*) lover.

сожи́тельство *neut.* cohabitation.

сожи́тельствовать OVA *impf.* to live together.

созва́ниваться *impf. pf.* **созвони́ться 1.** to get in touch by phone. **2.** to call on the phone.

созва́ть *pf. of* **созыва́ть**.

созве́здие *neut.* constellation.

созву́чие *neut.* accord.

созву́чный *adj.* **1.** (*of sounds*) harmonious. **2.** in keeping with.

создава́ть *impf. pf.* **созда́ть** to create.

созда́ние *neut.* creation.

созда́тель *m. f.* —**ница** creator; originator.

созерца́ние *neut.* contemplation.

созерца́тельный *adj.* contemplative.

созерца́ть *impf.* to contemplate.

созида́ние *neut.* creation.

созида́тель *m. f.* —**ница** creator.

созида́ть *impf.* to create.

сознава́ть *impf. pf.* **созна́ть** to be conscious of; to realize; to recognize.

созна́ние *neut.* **1.** consciousness. **2.** confession; acknowledgement.

созна́тельно *adv.* consciously; deliberately.

созна́тельность *f.* consciousness.

созна́тельный *adj.* conscious; deliberate.

созрева́ние *neut.* ripening.

созрева́ть *impf. pf.* **созре́ть** to ripen.

созы́в *m.* calling (together); convening.

созыва́ть *impf. pf.* **созва́ть** to convoke; to summon.

соизмери́мый *adj.* commensurable.

соиска́ние *neut.* competition (*for a prize or an advanced degree*).

соиска́тель *m. f.* —**ница** competitor.

со́йка *f.* (*bird*) jay.

сойти́(сь) *pf. of* **сходи́ть(ся)**.

сок *m.* juice; sap.

сока́мерник *m. f.* **сока́мерница** cellmate.

соковыжима́лка *f.* juice extractor.

со́кол *m.* falcon.

соко́линый *adj.* falcon's.

сокраща́ть *impf. pf.* **сократи́ть** to shorten; to abbreviate.

сокраще́ние *neut.* reduction; abbreviation; shortening.

сокращённо *adv.* for short.

сокрове́нный *adj.* concealed, secret; innermost.

сокро́вище *neut.* treasure.

сокро́вищница *f.* treasure house.

сокруша́ть *impf. pf.* **сокруши́ть** to destroy; to distress.

сокруше́ние *neut.* destruction.

сокруше́нно *adv.* sorrowfully.

сокруши́тельный *adj.* crushing; shattering.

сокры́тый *adj.* (*obs.*) concealed; secret.

солга́ть *pf. of* **лгать**.

солда́т *m.* soldier.

солда́тик *m.* toy soldier.

солда́тка *f.* soldier's wife.

солда́тский *adj.* soldier's.

солева́ренный заво́д *m.* saltworks.

солева́рня *f.* saltworks.

солево́й *adj.* saline.

соле́ние *neut.* salting; pickling.

солено́ид *m.* solenoid.

солёность *f.* saltiness.

солёный *adj.* salty, salt; pickled; salted.

соле́нье *neut.* pickled foods.

солеци́зм *m.* solecism.

солидаризи́роваться OVA *impf. and pf.* to express one's solidarity with.

солида́рность *f.* solidarity.

солида́рный *adj.* united; in agreement with.

соли́дно *adv.* seriously; sizeably.

соли́дный *adj.* solid; reliable.

соли́ст *m. f.* —**ка** soloist.

солите́р *m.* (*gem*) solitaire.

солитёр *m.* tapeworm.

соли́ть *impf. pf.* **за-, по-** to salt; to pickle.

со́лка *f.* salting; pickling.

со́лнечно *adv.* (*pred.*) sunny.

Солнечного́рск *m.* Solnechnogorsk.

со́лнечный *adj.* solar, sun; sunny.

со́лнце *neut.* sun.

солнцезащи́тный *adj.* protecting from the sun.

солнцепёк *m.* the full blaze of the sun.

солнцестоя́ние *neut.* solstice.

со́ло *neut. indecl.* solo.

солове́й FILL *m.* nightingale.

Солове́цкие острова́ *pl.* Solovetskie Islands.

соловьи́ный *adj.* nightingale's.

со́лод *m.* malt.

соло́дка *f.* licorice.

соло́довый *adj.* (*attrib.*) malt.

соло́ма *f.* straw.

соло́менный *adj.* made of straw; straw-colored.

соло́минка *f.* a straw.

солоне́ц FILL *m.* dark alkaline soil.

солони́на *f.* corned beef.

соло́нка *f.* salt shaker.

солонова́тый *adj.* brackish.

солонча́к *m.* salt marsh; saline soil.

соль *f.* salt.

со́льный *adj.* solo.

сольфе́джио *neut. indecl.* solfeggio.

соля́нка *f.* thick soup with vegetables and fish *or* meat.

соляно́й *adj.* saline.

соля́ный *adj.* hydrochloric.

соля́рий *m.* solarium.

сом *m.* sheatfish.

сомати́ческий *adj.* somatic.

со́мкнутый *adj.* (*of ranks or military formation*) close.

Со́мма *f.* (*river*) Somme.

сомнева́ться *impf.* to doubt, to have doubts.

сомне́ние *neut.* doubt.

сомни́тельно *adv.* (*pred.*) doubtful.

сомни́тельный *adj.* doubtful, dubious.

сомно́житель *m.* (*math.*) factor.

сон *m.* **1.** sleep. **2.** dream.

Со́на *f.* (*river*) Saône.

сона́та *f.* sonata.

соне́т *m.* sonnet.

сонли́вость *f.* sleepiness; drowsiness.

сонли́вый *adj.* sleepy; drowsy.

сонм *m.* **1.** assembly. **2.** throng; swarm. **3.** multitude.

со́нный *adj.* sleepy; drowsy.

со́ня *f.* dormouse. — *m.* and *f.* (*decl. f.*) (*colloq.*) sleepyhead.

соображать *impf. pf.* сообрази́ть **1.** to think out; to ponder. **2.** to grasp, to understand.

соображе́ние *neut.* consideration.

сообрази́тельность *f.* cleverness; quickness of wit.

сообрази́тельный *adj.* clever; quick-witted.

сообра́зно *prep.* (*with dat.* or **с** *with instr.*) in accordance with.

сообра́зность *f.* conformity.

сообра́зный *adj.* (**с** *with instr.*) consistent (with).

сообразова́ть OVA *impf.* and *pf.* (**с** *with instr.*) to make conform.

сообразова́ться OVA *impf.* and *pf.* (**с** *with instr.*) to conform to; to take account of.

сообща́ *adv.* together.

сообща́ть *impf. pf.* сообщи́ть to announce; to inform; to communicate.

сообще́ние *neut.* **1.** report; message. **2.** communication. **3.** communications.

сообщество *neut.* association; company (*of people*).

сообщник *m. f.* сообщница accomplice.

сооруже́ние *neut.* **1.** erection; construction. **2.** structure; building. **3.** (*mil.*) installation; works.

соотве́тственно *adv.* accordingly.

соотве́тственный *adj.* corresponding.

соотве́тствие *neut.* accordance; conformity.

соотве́тствовать OVA *impf.* (*with dat.*) to correspond (to).

соотве́тствующий *adj.* **1.** corresponding. **2.** suitable; appropriate.

соотéчественник *m. f.* соотéчественница compatriot.

соотноси́тельный *adj.* correlative.

соотноше́ние *neut.* correlation.

сопе́рник *m. f.* сопе́рница rival; competitor.

сопе́рничать *impf.* (**с** *with instr.*) to compete (with).

сопе́рничество *neut.* rivalry.

сопе́ть *impf. prcs.* соплю́, сопи́шь to sniffle; to wheeze.

со́пка *f.* **1.** knoll; mound; hill. **2.** volcano (*in Kamchatka*).

со́пли *pl.* (*vulg.*) snot.

сопли́вый *adj.* (*colloq.*) having a stuffed nose; (*character*) snotty.

сопло́ *neut.* nozzle.

сопоставле́ние *neut.* comparison.

сопоставля́ть *impf. pf.* сопоста́вить to compare.

сопра́нный *also* сопра́новый *adj.* soprano.

сопра́но *neut. indecl.* soprano.

сопреде́льный *adj.* **1.** neighboring; adjacent. **2.** contiguous.

сопредседа́тель *m.* co-chairman.

соприкаса́ться *impf. pf.* соприкосну́ться **1.** to touch on; to border on. **2.** to be adjacent; to be contiguous. **3.** (*with instr.*) to touch; to bump.

соприкоснове́ние *neut.* contact.

сопроводи́тельный *adj.* accompanying.

сопровожда́ть *impf. pf.* сопроводи́ть to accompany.

сопровожде́ние *neut.* accompaniment; escort.

сопротивле́ние *neut.* resistance.

сопротивля́емость *f.* ability to resist.

сопротивля́ться *impf.* (*with dat.*) to resist.

сопряжённый *adj.* (**с** *with instr.*) entailing; involving.

сопу́тствовать OVA *impf.* to accompany.

сопу́тствующий *adj.* attendant; concomitant.

сор *m.* garbage; litter.

соразме́рность *f.* balance; proportion.

соразме́рный *adj.* **1.** commensurate; proportionate. **2.** well-proportioned.

сора́тник *m. f.* сора́тница comrade in arms.

сорване́ц FILL *m.* (*colloq.*) **1.** brat. **2.** (*of a child*) terror.

сорва́ть(ся) *pf. of* срыва́ть(ся).

сорвиголова́ *m.* and *f.* (*decl. f.*) (*colloq.*) daredevil.

со́рго *neut. indecl.* sorghum.

соревнова́ние *neut.* **1.** competition. **2.** (*sports*) contest.

соревнова́ться OVA *impf.* to compete.

сори́нка *f.* speck of dust.

сори́ть *impf. pf.* на- to litter; (*fig.*) to waste (*money, etc.*).

со́рная трава́ *f.* weeds.

сорня́к *m.* weed.

со́рок *num.* forty. —ово́й *adj.* fortieth.

соро́ка *f.* magpie.

сорокале́тие *neut.* forty years; forty-year anniversary.

сорокале́тний *adj.* (*attrib.*) forty-year.

сороконо́жка *f.* centipede.

сорокопу́т *m.* shrike.

соро́чка *f.* **1.** shirt; blouse. **2.** nightgown. **3.** back or reverse side (*of playing card*).

сорт *m.* **1.** sort, kind. **2.** quality.

сортирова́ть OVA *impf. pf.* рас- to sort.

сортиро́вка *f.* sorting; arrangement.

сортиро́вочный *adj.* (*attrib.*) sorting.

сортиро́вщик *m. f.* сортиро́вщица sorter.

сортово́й *adj.* high-quality.

соса́ние *neut.* sucking.

соса́тельный *adj.* (*attrib.*) sucking.

соса́ть *impf.* to suck.

сосе́д *m. f.* —ка neighbor. —ний *adj.* neighboring. —ский *adj.* neighborly. —ство *neut.* neighborhood, proximity.

соси́ска *f.* sausage.

со́ска *f.* **1.** nipple (*of nursing bottle*). **2.** pacifier.

сослага́тельный *adj.* (*gram.*) subjunctive.

сосла́ть *pf. of* ссыла́ть.

сосло́вие *neut.* estate; class.

сосло́вный *adj.* (*attrib.*) class.

сослужи́вец FILL *m. f.* сослужи́вица colleague; fellow worker.

сосна́ *f.* pine; pine tree.

Сосно́вец FILL *m.* Sosnowiec.

сосно́вый *adj.* (*attrib.*) pine.

сосня́к *m.* pine forest.

сосо́к FILL *m.* nipple; teat.

сосредото́чение *neut.* (act of) concentration.

сосредото́ченность *f.* (degree of) concentration.

сосредото́ченный *adj.* **1.** concentrated. **2.** lost in concentration. **3.** rapt; intent.

сосредото́чивать *impf. pf.* сосредото́чить to concentrate.

соста́в *m.* **1.** composition; structure. **2.** staff. —и́тель *m. f.* —ница compiler; author.

составле́ние *neut.* compilation.

составля́ть *impf. pf.* соста́вить **1.** to compose; to put together. **2.** to draw up.

составно́й *adj.* **1.** composite. **2.** component.

соста́риться *pf. of* ста́риться.

состоя́ние *neut.* **1.** condition. **2.** state.

состоя́тельность *f.* affluence; soundness.

состоя́тельный *adj.* **1.** wealthy; well-to-do. **2.** solvent. **3.** sound (*of an argument*).

состоя́ть *impf.* **1.** to be. **2.** (из *with gen.*) to consist (of). —ся to take place.

страда́ние *neut.* compassion.

сострада́тельный *adj.* compassionate.

состяза́ние *neut.* contest; competition.

состяза́тельный *adj.* competitive.

сосу́д *m.* vessel.

сосу́дистый *adj.* vascular.

сосу́лька *f.* icicle.

сосу́н *m.* suckling.

сосуно́к FILL *m.* suckling.

сосуществова́ние *neut.* coexistence.

сосуществова́ть OVA *impf.* to coexist.

сот *num., gen. pl. of* сто.

со́тая *f.* hundredth; hundredth part.

сотворе́ние *neut.* creation.

сотвори́ть *pf. of* твори́ть to create. —ся *pf. of* твори́ться.

со́тенный *adj.* (*attrib.*) hundred-ruble.

соте́рн *m.* sauterne.

со́тня *f.* (*coll.*) hundred.

сотова́рищ *m.* colleague; associate.

со́товый *adj.* of a honeycomb; (*telephone*) cellular.

сотру́дник *m. f.* сотру́дница **1.** colleague; associate. **2.** collaborator. — нау́чный сотру́дник *m.* research assistant.

сотру́дничать *impf.* to collaborate.

сотру́дничество *adj.* cooperation.

сотрясе́ние *neut.* **1.** vibration; shaking. **2.** impact.

со́ты *pl.* honeycomb.

со́тый *adj.* hundredth.

со́ус *m.* sauce.

со́усник *m.* gravy boat.

соуча́ствовать OVA *impf.* to participate.

соуча́стие *neut.* complicity.

соуча́стник *m. f.* соуча́стница accomplice.

соучени́к *m. f.* соучени́ца classmate.

софа́ *f.* sofa.

софи́зм *m.* sophism.

софи́ст *m.* sophist.

софи́стика *f.* sophistry.

софисти́ческий *adj.* sophistic.

Софи́я *f.* Sofia.

соха́ *f.* (wooden) plow.

со́хнуть *impf. pf.* вы́- to dry.

сохране́ние *neut.* preservation; conservation.

сохра́нность *f.* safety; state of preservation.

сохра́нный *adj.* safe; unharmed.

сохраня́ть *impf. pf.* сохрани́ть to preserve; to maintain; to keep.

соцве́тие *neut.* (*bot.*) raceme.

социализа́ция *f.* socialization.

социализи́ровать OVA *impf. and pf.* to socialize.

социали́ст *m. f.* —ка socialist.

социалисти́ческий *adj.* socialist; socialistic.

социа́льный *adj.* social.

социо́лог *m.* sociologist.

социологи́ческий *adj.* sociological.

социоло́гия *f.* sociology.

Соче́льник *m.* **1.** Christmas Eve. **2.** Eve of the Epiphany.

сочета́ние *neut.* combination.

сочета́ть *impf. and pf.* to combine.

сочине́ние *neut.* **1.** work. **2.** composition.

сочини́тель *m. f.* —ница **1.** (*colloq.*) liar; storyteller. **2.** (*arch.*) writer; composer.

сочини́тельный *adj.* (*gram.*) coordinate.

сочиня́ть *impf. pf.* сочини́ть to write; to compose; to invent.

сочи́ть *impf.* to exude. —ся to ooze; to trickle.

со́чность *adj.* juiciness.

со́чный *adj.* juicy.

сочу́вственно *adv.* sympathetically.

сочу́вственный *adj.* sympathetic.

сочу́вствие *neut.* sympathy.

сочу́вствовать OVA *impf.* to sympathize.

со́шка *f.* **1.** prop. **2.** gun support.

сошни́к *m.* plowshare.

сою́з[1] *m.* union; alliance. —ник *m. f.* —ница ally. —ный *adj.* allied.

сою́з[2] *m.* (*gram.*) conjunction.

со́я *f.* soy.

спаге́тти *neut. indecl.* spaghetti.

спад *m.* **1.** decline. **2.** recession; slump. **3.** receding (*of water*).

спада́ть *impf. pf.* спасть to fall down.

спазм *m.* *also* спа́зма *f.* spasm.

спазмати́ческий *adj.* spasmodic.

спа́ивать *impf. pf.* спая́ть **1.** to solder together; to weld. **2.** to unite.

спа́йка *f.* soldering.

спали́ть *pf. of* пали́ть.

спа́льный *adj.* for sleeping on *or* in.

спа́льня *f.* bedroom.

спание́ль *m.* spaniel.

спанье́ *neut.* (*colloq.*) sleeping.

спа́ренный *adj.* dual; twin.

спа́ржа *f.* asparagus.

спа́ржевый *adj.* (*attrib.*) asparagus.

спа́ривание *neut.* **1.** mating. **2.** pairing off (*to work together*).

Спа́рта *f.* Sparta.

спартакиа́да *f.* Spartacist Games.

спарта́нский *adj.* Spartan.

спа́рывать *impf. pf.* споро́ть **1.** to remove. **2.** to unstitch.

спаса́ние *neut.* saving, rescuing.

спаса́тель *m. f.* —ница **1.** rescue worker. **2.** lifeguard.

спаса́тельный *adj.* (*attrib.*) rescue.

спаса́ть *impf. pf.* спасти́ to save; to rescue.

спасе́ние *neut.* rescue.

спаси́бо *particle* thanks; thank you.

спаси́тель *m. f.* —ница rescuer. — Спаси́тель the Savior.

спаси́тельный *adj.* that which saves.

спасти́ *pf. of* спаса́ть.

спасти́ческий *adj.* spastic.

спасть *pf. of* спада́ть.

спать *impf.* to sleep; to be asleep.

спа́янность *f.* cohesion.

спа́янный *adj.* united; cohesive; close-knit.

спе́вка *f.* choir practice.

спекта́кль *m.* performance.

спектр *m.* spectrum.
спектра́льный *adj.* spectral.
спектроско́п *m.* spectroscope.
спектроскопи́ческий *adj.* spectroscopic.
спекули́ровать OVA *impf.* to speculate (*in a business*).
спекуля́нт *m. f.* —ка **1.** speculator. **2.** exploiter; profiteer.
спекуляти́вный *adj.* **1.** speculative. **2.** (*of prices*) artificially high.
спекуля́ция *f.* speculation.
спе́лый *adj.* ripe.
сперва́ *adv.* at first.
спе́реди *adv.* at *or* from the front.
спере́ть *pf. pres.* сопру́, сопрёшь, *past* спёр, спёрла (*colloq.*) to steal; to filch; to swipe.
спе́рма *f.* sperm.
спёртый *adj.* (*colloq.*) close; stuffy.
спеси́вый *adj.* haughty.
спесь *f.* haughtiness; conceit.
спеть *impf. pres.* спе́ю, спе́ешь *pf.* по- to ripen; to become ripe.
спех *m.* (*colloq.*) hurry.
специализа́ция *f.* specialization.
специализи́ровать OVA *impf.* and *pf.* to specialize.
специали́ст *m. f.* —ка specialist.
специа́льно *adv.* especially (for).
специа́льность *f.* **1.** specialty. **2.** field of specialization; (*university*) major. **3.** profession.
специа́льный *adj.* special.
специ́фика *f.* characteristic.
специфика́ция *f* specification.
специфи́ческий *adj.* specific.
спе́ция *f.* spice.
спецоде́жда *f.* working clothes; overalls, coveralls; boiler suit.
спеши́ть *impf. pf.* по- **1.** to hurry **2.** (*of a watch*) to be fast.
спе́шка *f.* rush.
спе́шно *adv.* in a hurry; in haste.
спе́шность *f.* haste.
спе́шный *adj.* **1.** urgent. **2.** hasty.
спива́ться *impf. pf.* спи́ться to become an alcoholic.
спидо́метр *m.* speedometer.
спи́кер *m.* speaker (*of the House of Commons or the House of Representatives*).
спина́ *f.* (*anat.*) back.
спи́нка *f.* **1.** *dim.* of спина́. **2.** back (*of a chair or of a piece of clothing*).
спинно́й *adj.* spinal; dorsal.
спинномозгово́й *adj.* of the spinal cord.
спира́льный *adj.* spiral.
спирити́зм *m.* spiritualism; communication with spirits.
спирити́ческий *adj.* spiritualistic.
спиритуали́зм *m.* spiritualism; spiritual movement in religion *or* philosophy.
спиритуали́ст *m.* spiritualist.
спирт *m.* alcohol.
спиртно́е DAA *neut.* alcohol.
спиртно́й *adj.* containing alcohol.
спирто́вка *f.* spirit lamp.
спиртово́й *adj.* (*attrib.*) spirit; alcohol.
спи́сок FILL *m.* list.

спи́сывать *impf. pf.* списа́ть **1.** to copy. **2.** to crib; to write off.
спито́й *adj.* (*colloq.*) (*of tea or coffee*) weak.
спи́ца *f.* **1.** knitting needle. **2.** spoke.
спич *m.* (short) speech.
спи́чечница *f.* (*obs.*) matchbox.
спи́чечный *adj.* (*attrib.*) match.
спи́чка *f.* match.
сплав *m.* **1.** alloy; fusion. **2.** floating (*of timber*).
сплавно́й *adj.* floating (*of timber*).
сплете́ние *neut.* **1.** junction. **2.** (*anat.*) plexus.
спле́тник *m. f.* спле́тница (*person*) gossip.
сплетни́чать *impf. pf.* на- to gossip.
спле́тня *f.* gossip.
сплеча́ *adv.* in haste; without thought.
Сплит *m.* Split.
сплохова́ть OVA *pf.* (*colloq.*) to make a blunder.
сплоче́ние *neut.* uniting; rallying.
сплочённость *f.* unity; solidarity.
сплочённый *adj.* united.
сплошно́й *adj.* continuous, unbroken.
сплошь *adv.* entirely.
сплю́снутый *adj.* flat; flattened.
сплю́щенный *adj.* flat; flattened.
сплю́щивать *impf. pf.* сплю́щить to flatten.
сподви́жник *m. f.* сподви́жница associate.
сподру́чный *adj.* (*colloq.*) convenient; handy.
спозара́нку *adv.* (*colloq.*) early in the morning.
споко́йно *adv.* calmly; peacefully.
споко́йной но́чи *interj.* good night!
споко́йный *adj.* quiet; calm.
споко́йствие *neut.* **1.** tranquility. **2.** quiet; calm. **3.** public order. **4.** composure.
споласкивать *impf.* (*colloq.*) to rinse out.
сполна́ *adv.* completely; in full.
спо́лох *m.* flash of lightning. — спо́лохи *pl.* northern lights.
спонта́нный *adj.* spontaneous.
спор *m.* argument.
спо́ра *f.* spore.
спора́ди́ческий *adj.* sporadic.
Спора́ды *pl.* (*islands*) Sporades.
спо́рить *impf. pf.* по- to argue.
спо́рный *adj.* **1.** controversial. **2.** debatable; disputed. **3.** moot. **4.** unsettled.
спорт *m.* sport.
спорти́вный *adj.* (*attrib.*) sports.
спортсме́н *m. f.* —ка athlete; sportsman.
спортсме́нский *adj.* sportsmanlike.
спорхну́ть *pf.* to flutter off; to flit away.
спо́рщик *m. f.* спо́рщица person who likes to argue.
спо́рый *adj.* (*colloq.*) smooth.
спорынья́ *f.* ergot.
спо́соб *m.* way; method.
спосо́бность *f.* ability; capacity.
спосо́бный *adj.* able; clever; capable.
спосо́бствовать OVA *impf.* **1.** to further; to promote. **2.** to be conducive (to).
спотыка́ться *impf. pf.* споткну́ться to stumble; to trip.
спра́ва *adv.* to the right; from the right.
справедли́во *adv.* fairly; justly.
справедли́вость *f.* justice.
справедли́вый *adj.* just; fair.

спра́вка *f.* **1.** information. **2.** certificate.
— спра́вки *pl.* reference.
справля́ть *impf. pf.* спра́вить to celebrate.
справля́ться[1] *impf. pf.* спра́виться (о *with prep.*) to ask (about).
справля́ться[2] *impf. pf.* спра́виться (с *with instr.*) to cope with, to manage.
спра́вочник *m.* reference book.
спра́вочный *adj.* (*attrib.*) reference; information.
спра́шивать *impf. pf.* спроси́ть to ask.
спринт *m.* sprint.
спри́нтер *m.* sprinter.
спринцева́ть OVA *impf.* to use a syringe.
спринцо́вка *f.* syringe.
спрова́живать *impf. pf.* спрова́дить (*colloq.*) to send on one's way; to escort out.
спрос *m.* demand.
спросо́нок *adv.* (*colloq.*) half-awake.
спроста́ *adv.* on the spur of the moment.
спрут *m.* octopus.
спряже́ние *neut.* (*gram.*) conjugation.
спря́тать *pf. of* пря́тать.
спуд *m.*: под спу́дом **1.** hidden; under wraps. **2.** (kept) tucked away. **3.** without use *or* application.
спуск *m.* **1.** descent; slope. **2.** landing.
спуска́ть *impf. pf.* спусти́ть to let down; to lower.
спускно́й *also* спусково́й *adj.* (*attrib.*) drain.
спустя́ *prep.* (*with acc.*) after.
спу́танный *adj.* **1.** tangled. **2.** muddled; confused.
спу́тник *m.* **1.** *f.* спу́тница companion; fellow traveler. **2.** (*astr.*) satellite.
спья́на *also* спья́ну *adv.* (*colloq.*) while drunk.
спя́тить *pf.* (*colloq.*) to go nuts; to go crazy.
спя́чка *f.* hibernation.
срабо́танность *f.* harmony in work.
сравне́ние *neut.* comparison.
сра́внивать[1] *impf. pf.* сравни́ть to compare.
сра́внивать[2] *impf. pf.* сравня́ть to level out; to make even.
сравни́мый *adj.* comparable.
сравни́тельно *adv.* comparatively.
сравни́тельный *adj.* comparative.
сравня́ться *pf.* to compete with.
сража́ть *impf. pf.* срази́ть **1.** to strike. **2.** to overwhelm. —ся to fight, to battle; to engage in a fight.
сраже́ние *neut.* battle.
сра́зу *adv.* at once.
срам *m.* (*colloq.*) shame.
срамни́к *m. f.* срамни́ца (*colloq.*) shameless person.
срамно́й *adj.* (*colloq.*) shameful.
сраста́ние *neut.* knitting *or* growing together (*of bones*).
сраще́ние *neut.* **1.** joining together. **2.** growing together.
сра́щивание *neut.* setting (*of a bone*).
сре́бреник *m.* **1.** piece of silver. **2.** silver coin.
среда́[1] *f.* Wednesday.
среда́[2] *f.* environment, surroundings.
среди́ *also* средь *prep.* (*with gen.*) among; amidst.
Средизе́мное мо́ре *neut.* Mediterranean Sea.
среди́нный *adj.* middle.
сре́дне *adv.* (*colloq.*) fair; so-so.
средне- *prefix* Central; Middle.
средневеко́вый *adj.* medieval.

средневеко́вье *neut.* the Middle Ages.
сре́днее DAA *neut.* average; the average.
сре́дний *adj.* **1.** average. **2.** middle.
средото́чие *neut.* focus.
сре́дство *neut.* means; remedy — сре́дства *pl.* means; funds.
средь *prep., see* среди́.
срез *m.* **1.** slice; cut. **2.** section.
среза́ть *impf. pf.* сре́зать to cut off.
сровня́ть *pf. of* сра́внивать.
сродни́ *adv.* (*with dat.*) (*colloq.*) **1.** related to. **2.** akin to.
сро́дный *adj.* related.
сродство́ *neut.* affinity.
сро́ду *adv.* (*colloq.*) always; since one was born.
срок *m.* **1.** date. **2.** term; period.
сро́чно *adv.* **1.** urgently. **2.** immediately.
сро́чность *f.* urgency.
сро́чный *adj.* urgent; pressing.
сруб *m.* **1.** felling of timber. **2.** framework.
сруба́ть *impf. pf.* сруби́ть to cut down; to fell.
срыв *m.* collapse; failure.
срыва́ть[1] *impf. pf.* сорва́ть **1.** to tear off. **2.** to pick.
срыва́ть[2] *impf. pf.* срыть to level to the ground, to raze.
срыва́ться *impf. pf.* сорва́ться, *v.i.* **1.** to break off. **2.** to become loose.
сря́ду *adv.* (*colloq.*) in a row.
сса́дина *f.* scratch; abrasion.
ссо́ра *f.* quarrel.
ссо́риться *impf. pf.* по- to quarrel.
СССР *m.* (*abbr. of* Сою́з Сове́тских Социалисти́ческих Респу́блик) USSR.
ссу́да *f.* loan.
ссыла́ть *impf. pf.* сосла́ть to exile.
ссы́лка[1] *f.* exile.
ссы́лка[2] *f.* (cross) reference.
ссы́лочный *adj.* (*attrib.*) reference.
ссы́льный *adj.* in exile. — *m.* exile.
ссыха́ться *impf. pf.* ссо́хнуться **1.** to shrink. **2.** to become warped. **3.** to become caked.
стабилиза́тор *m.* stabilizer.
стабилиза́ция *f.* stabilization.
стабилизи́ровать OVA *impf. and pf.* to stabilize.
стаби́льность *f.* stability.
стаби́льный *adj.* stable.
ста́вень FILL *m.* shutter.
ста́вить *impf. pf.* по- **1.** to put. **2.** to stage.
ста́вка *f.* **1.** rate. **2.** (*cards*) stake.
ста́вленник *m. f.* ста́вленница protégé.
ста́вня *f.* shutter.
Ста́врополь *m.* Stavropol.
стадиа́льный *also* стади́йный *adj.* occurring in stages.
стадио́н *m.* stadium.
ста́дия *f.* stage.
ста́дный *adj.* (*of animals*) living in herds.
ста́до *neut.* herd, flock.
стаж *m.* length of service.
стажёр *m. f.* —ка trainee.
стажиро́вка *f.* practical training; on-the-job training.
ста́ивать *impf. pf.* ста́ять to melt.
ста́йка *f. dim. of* ста́я.
стака́н *m.* glass.

стакка́то *neut. indecl.* staccato.

ста́ксель *m.* staysail.

сталагми́т *m.* stalagmite.

сталакти́т *m.* stalactite.

сталева́р *m.* steelworker.

сталелите́йный *adj.* related to the making of steel.

сталелите́йщик *m.* steelwoorker.

сталеплави́льный *adj.* pertaining to the melting of steel.

ста́лкивать *impf. pf.* столкну́ть to push off *or* down. —ся (с *with instr.*) to collide.

сталь *f.* steel. —но́й *adj.* steel.

Стамбу́л *m.* Istanbul.

стаме́ска *f.* chisel.

стан¹ *m.* **1.** build. **2.** figure.

стан² *m.* mill (*e.g., rolling mill*).

стан³ *m.* camp.

станда́рт *m.* standard.

стандартиза́ция *f.* standardization.

стандартизи́ровать OVA *impf. and pf.* to standardize.

стандартизова́ть OVA *impf. and pf.* to standardize.

станда́ртный *adj.* standard.

станио́ль *m.* tin foil.

стани́ца¹ *f.* large Cossack village.

стани́ца² *f.* flock (*of birds*).

станко́вый *adj.* (*attrib.*) machine.

станови́ться *impf. pf.* стать (*with instr.*) to become.

становле́ние *neut.* formation.

станово́й *adj.* (*attrib.*) district.

стано́к FILL *m.* **1.** machine tool. **2.** gun mount.

стано́чник *m.* machine operator.

станс *m.* stanza.

станцио́нный *adj.* (*attrib.*) station.

ста́нция *f.* **1.** station. **2.** base; mount.

стара́ние *neut.* endeavor, effort.

стара́тельно *adv.* diligently.

стара́тельность *f.* diligence.

стара́тельный *adj.* diligent; assiduous.

стара́ться *impf. pf.* по- to endeavor; to try.

Ста́рая Ру́сса *f.* Staraya Russa.

старе́ние *neut.* aging.

старе́ть *impf. pf.* по- **1.** to grow old; to age. **2.** *impf. only* to become obsolete.

ста́рец FILL *m.* old man.

стари́к *m.* old man.

старина́ *f.* **1.** ancient times. **2.** old ways; old customs. **3.** relic of the past.

стари́нка *f.:* по стари́нке *adv.* the old way.

стари́нный *adj.* ancient; old.

ста́риться *impf. pf.* со- to become *or* grow old.

старичо́к FILL *m.* little old man.

старове́р *m. f.* —ка Old Believer.

старода́вний *adj.* ancient.

старожи́л *m. f.* —ка long-time resident.

старозаве́тный *adj.* old-fashioned.

старомо́дный *adj.* old-fashioned.

старообра́зный *adj.* old-looking.

старообря́дец FILL *m. f.* старообря́дка Old Believer.

ста́роста *m.* **1.** village elder. **2.** monitor (*in school*).

ста́рость *f.* old age.

старт *m.* (*sports*) start.

ста́ртер *m.* (*mech. and sports*) starter.

стартова́ть OVA *impf. and pf.* **1.** (*of a plane*) to take off. **2.** (*sports*) to start.

ста́ртовый *adj.* **1.** (*sports*) starting. **2.** launching.

стару́ха *f.* old woman.

стару́шка *f.* old woman.

ста́рческий *adj.* senile.

ста́рше *adv.comp. of* ста́рый.

старшекла́ссник *m. f.* старшекла́ссница senior high-school student.

старшеку́рсник *m. f.* старшеку́рсница senior (*in college*).

ста́рший *adj.* older; oldest; eldest; senior.

старшина́ *f.* **1.** master sergeant. **2.** (*naval*) petty officer.

старшинство́ *neut.* seniority.

ста́рый *adj.* old.

старьё *neut.* (*colloq.*) old things; junk.

старьёвщик *m. f.* старьёвщица old-clothes dealer.

стасова́ть *pf. of* тасова́ть.

ста́тика *f.* statics.

стати́ст *m. f.* —ка **1.** (*theat.*) extra. **2.** supernumerary; extra person.

стати́стик *m.* statistician.

стати́стика *f.* statistics.

стати́ческий *adj.* (*phys., elec.*) static.

стати́чный *adj.* static (*not in motion*).

ста́тный *adj.* stately.

ста́тус *m.* status.

ста́тус-кво́ *m. indecl.* status quo.

стату́т *m.* statute.

статуэ́тка *f.* statuette; figurine.

ста́туя *f.* statue.

стать¹ *pf. of* стано́виться. — (*with infin.*) to begin, to commence.

стать² *m.* figure; build. — с како́й ста́ти? why?; what for?

ста́ться *pf. pres.* ста́нется (с *with instr.*) (*colloq.*) to happen to; to become of.

статья́ *f.* article.

стаха́новец FILL *m. f.* стаха́новка Stakhanovite (*good worker*).

стаха́новский *adj.* (*attrib.*) Stakhanovite (*good worker's*).

стациона́р *m.* permanent establishment.

стациона́рный *adj.* permanent.

ста́чечник *m. f.* ста́чечница striker.

ста́чечный *adj.* (*attrib.*) strike.

ста́чка *f.* strike.

ста́я *f.* flock; pack.

ствол *m.* **1.** trunk (*of tree*). **2.** barrel (*of gun*).

ство́рка *f.* **1.** leaf; fold (*of door, mirror, window, etc.*). **2.** valve (*of mollusk*).

ство́рчатый *adj.* folding.

стеари́н *m.* stearin.

сте́бель FILL *m.* stem, stalk.

стёганка *f.* (*colloq.*) quilted jacket.

стёганый *adj.* quilted.

стега́ть¹ *impf.* to quilt.

стега́ть² *impf. pf.* стегну́ть to whip.

стежо́к FILL *m.* stitch.

стезя́ *f.* (*obs.*) way; road; path.

стека́ть *impf. pf.* стечь to flow down.

стекло́ *neut.* glass.

стекловолокно́ *m.* fiberglass.

стеклоду́в *m.* glass blower.

стеклоочисти́тель *m.* windshield wiper.
стекля́нный *adj.* glass.
стекля́рус *m.* bugles (*tube-shaped glass beads*).
стеко́льный *adj.* (*attrib.*) glass.
стеко́льщик *m. f.* стеко́льщица glazier.
стелла́ж *m.* **1.** shelves. **2.** rack.
сте́лька *f.* insole; inner sole.
стена́ *f.* wall.
стенгазе́та *f.* wall newspaper.
стенд *m.* stand.
сте́ндовая стрельба́ *f.* trap-shooting.
сте́нка *f.* **1.** *dim. of* стена́. **2.** (*anat.*) wall. **3.** side (*of a container*).
стенно́й *adj.* (*attrib.*) wall.
стеноби́тный *adj.* for wall-battering.
стеногра́мма *f.* transcript (*of lecture, etc.*)
стено́граф *m.* stenographer.
стенографи́ровать OVA *impf. pf.* за- to write down in shorthand.
стенографи́ст *m. f.* —ка stenographer.
стенографи́ческий *adj.* stenographic; shorthand.
стеногра́фия *f.* stenography; shorthand.
стенокарди́я *f.* angina pectoris.
сте́нопись *f.* mural painting.
сте́ньга *f.* topmast.
Степанаке́рт *m.* Stepanakert.
степе́нный *adj.* sedate, staid.
сте́пень *f.* degree; extent.
степно́й *adj.* (*attrib.*) steppe.
степь *f.* steppe.
стервя́тник *m.* Egyptian vulture.
стереоме́трия *f.* solid geometry.
стереоско́п *m.* stereoscope.
стереоскопи́ческий *adj.* stereoscopic.
стереоскопи́я *f.* stereoscopy.
стереоти́п *m.* stereotype.
стереотипи́ровать OVA *impf. and pf.* (*printing*) to stereotype.
стереоти́пный *adj.* stereotyped.
стереофони́ческий *adj.* stereophonic.
стере́ть *pf. of* стира́ть.
стере́чь *impf.* to watch, to guard.
сте́ржень FILL *m.* **1.** rod; dowel; bar. **2.** pivot. **3.** heart; core.
стержнево́й *adj.* (*of an issue*) key; pivotal.
стерилиза́тор *m.* sterilizer.
стерилиза́ция *f.* sterilization.
стерилизова́ть OVA *impf. and pf.* to sterilize.
стери́льность *f.* sterility.
стери́льный *adj.* sterile.
сте́рлинг *m.* sterling.
сте́рлинговый *adj.* (*attrib.*) sterling.
сте́рлядь *f.* (*fish*) sterlet.
стерня́ *f.* harvested field; stubble field.
стеро́ид *m.* steroid.
стёртый *adj.* **1.** worn smooth. **2.** trite. **3.** worn; effaced.
стесне́ние *neut.* constraint.
стеснённый *adj.* **1.** crowded together; packed. **2.** inhibited. **3.** labored (*of breathing*). **4.** squeezed for (*money*).
стесни́тельность *f.* shyness; diffidence.
стесни́тельный *adj.* **1.** shy, diffident. **2.** restrictive.
стесня́ться **1.** *impf. pf.* по- to be shy. **2.** *impf. only* to feel awkward.
стети́т *m.* steatite.

стетоско́п *m.* stethoscope.
стече́ние *neut.* confluence.
стечь *pf. of* стека́ть.
стиле́т *m.* stiletto.
стилиза́ция *f.* stylization.
стилизова́ть OVA *impf. and pf.* to stylize.
стили́ст *m. f.* —ка stylist.
стили́стика *f.* stylistics.
стилисти́ческий *adj.* stylistic.
стиль *m.* style.
стиля́га *m. and f.* (*decl. f.*) young person in extravagant clothes.
сти́мул *m.* stimulus; incentive.
стимули́рование *neut.* stimulation.
стимули́ровать OVA *impf. and pf.* to stimulate.
стипе́ндия *f.* grant; scholarship.
стира́льный *adj.* (*attrib.*) washing.
стира́ть *impf. pf.* вы- to wash.
сти́рка *f.* washing, laundry.
стиро́л *m.* styrene.
стих *m.* verse. — стихи poetry; poems.
стиха́рь *m.* surplice.
стихи́йность *f.* spontaneity.
стихи́йный *adj.* **1.** elemental. **2.** spontaneous.
стихи́я *f.* element.
стихоплёт *m.* (*colloq.*) rhymer.
стихосложе́ние *neut.* versification.
стихотворе́ние *neut.* poem; short poem.
стихотво́рный *adj.* **1.** poetical. **2.** in verse form.
стишо́к FILL *m. dim. of* стих.
стлать *impf. pres.* стелю́, сте́лешь *pf.* по- **1.** to make a bed. **2.** to lay (*a tablecloth*).
сто *num.* hundred.
стог *m.* haystack.
стогра́дусный *adj.* centigrade.
сто́ик *m.* stoic.
сто́имость *f.* **1.** cost. **2.** value.
сто́ить *impf.* **1.** to cost. **2.** (*with gen.*) to be worth.
стоици́зм *m.* stoicism.
сто́ически *adv.* stoically.
сто́ический *adj.* stoical.
сто́йка *f.* counter.
сто́йкий *adj.* firm; stable.
сто́йко *adv.* **1.** firmly. **2.** stoically.
сто́йкость *f.* durability; hardiness.
сто́йло *neut.* stall.
сто́ймя *adv.* upright.
сток *m.* gutter.
Стокго́льм *m.* Stockholm.
сто́кер *m.* (*machine*) stoker.
стокра́т *adv.* (*obs.*) a hundred times.
стокра́тный *adj.* hundredfold.
стол *m.* **1.** table. **2.** desk. **3.** board; meals.
столб *m.* pillar, post.
столбе́ц FILL column (*of newspaper, etc.*).
сто́лбик *m.* small column.
столбня́к *m.* tetanus.
столе́тие *neut.* **1.** century. **2.** centenary.
столе́тний *adj.* (*attrib.*) hundred-year.
столе́тник *m.* aloe.
сто́лик *m.* small table.
столи́ца *f.* **1.** (*city*) capital. **2.** metropolis.
столи́чный го́род *m.* capital city.
столкнове́ние *neut.* collision, clash.
столкну́ть(ся) *pf. of* ста́лкивать(ся).

столова́ться OVA *impf.* to board; to take meals.
столо́вая DAA *f.* dining room.
столо́вый *adj.* (*attrib.*) table; dining.
столо́чь *pf.* to grind, to pound.
столпотворе́ние *neut.*: вавило́нское столпотворе́ние *neut.* chaos.
сто́лько *adv.* so much; so many. — сто́лько... ско́лько... as many as; as much as.
столя́р *m.* cabinetmaker; joiner.
столя́рный *adj.* joiner's.
стомато́лог *m.* stomatologist; dentist.
стоматоло́гия *f.* stomatology; dentistry.
стон *m.* groan; moan.
стона́ть *impf.* to moan, to groan.
стоп *interj.* stop!
стопа́[1] *f.* foot, step.
стопа́[2] *f.* **1.** ream. **2.** pile; heap.
сто́пка[1] *f.* pile; heap.
сто́пка[2] *f.* small glass (*for vodka*).
сто́пор *m.* (*mech.*) stop; catch.
сто́порить *impf. pf.* за- to stop (*a machine or an engine*).
сто́порный *adj.* (*mech.*) locking; arresting.
стоп-сигна́л *m.* stoplight; brake light.
сторгова́ться OVA *pf.* to agree on a price (*after bargaining*).
стори́цей *adv.* many times over.
сто́рож *m.* watchman; guard.
сторожево́й *adj.* (*attrib.*) watch; sentry.
сторожи́ть *impf.* to guard, to watch.
сторо́жка *f.* cabin; lodge (*of warden, watchman, etc.*)
сторона́ *f.* **1.** side. **2.** aspect. **3.** direction.
сторони́ться *impf. pf.* по- **1.** to stand aside. **2.** *impf. only* (*with gen.*) to avoid, to shun.
сторо́нний *adj.* (*obs.*) outside; detached.
сторо́нник *m. f.* сторо́нница supporter, advocate.
сторубле́вка *f.* (*colloq.*) hundred-ruble note.
стоскова́ться OVA *pf.* (по *with dat.*) to miss; to long for.
сто́чный *adj.* (*attrib.*) drainage.
стошни́ть *impf. impers.* to vomit; to throw up.
сто́я *adv.* standing up; on one's feet.
сто́йк *m.* upright post.
стоя́нка *f.* stand (*for taxis, etc.*); parking lot; parking place.
стоя́ть *impf.* **1.** to stand. **2.** to be. **3.** to be situated.
стоя́чий *adj.* standing; (*of water*) stagnant.
сто́ящий *adj.* (*colloq.*) worthwhile.
страда́ *f.* hard work at harvest time.
страда́лец FILL *m. f.* страда́лица sufferer.
страда́льческий *adj.* of suffering.
страда́ние *neut.* suffering.
страда́тельный *adj.* (*gram.*) passive.
страда́ть *impf. pf.* по- to suffer.
стра́дный *adj.* (*of time*) busy; hectic.
стра́ж *m.* (*obs.*) guard; guardian.
стра́жа *f.* (*obs.*) guard; watch.
страна́ *f.* country.
страни́ца *f.* page.
стра́нник *m. f.* стра́нница wanderer.
стра́нно *adv.* strangely.
стра́нность *f.* strangeness.
стра́нный *adj.* strange.
страноведе́ние *neut.* area studies.

стра́нствие *neut.* traveling; wandering.
стра́нствование *neut.* traveling; wandering.
стра́нствовать OVA *impf.* to wander.
стра́стно *adv.* **1.** passionately. **2.** ardently.
страстно́й *adj.* of Holy Week. — Страстно́й Четве́рг *m.* Holy Thursday. — Страстна́я Пя́тница *f.* Good Friday.
стра́стность *f.* passion; ardor.
стра́стный *adj.* passionate.
страсть *f.* passion.
стратаге́ма *f.* stratagem.
страте́г *m.* strategist.
стратеги́ческий *adj.* strategic.
страте́гия *f.* strategy.
стратифика́ция *f.* stratification.
стратосфе́ра *f.* stratosphere.
стра́ус *m.* ostrich.
стра́усовый *adj.* (*attrib.*) ostrich.
страх *m.* fear.
страхова́ние *neut.* insurance.
страхова́ть OVA *impf. pf.* за- to insure.
страхо́вка *f.* insurance.
страхово́й *adj.* (*attrib.*) insurance.
страхо́вщик *m.* insurer.
страши́лище *neut.* (*colloq.*) fright; terrible sight.
страши́ть *impf.* to frighten.
стра́шно *adv.* terribly; awfully.
стра́шный *adj.* terrible; awful.
стре́жень FILL *m.* (*obs.*) channel *or* main stream (*of river*).
стрекоза́ *f.* dragon fly.
стре́кот *m.* chirping.
стрекота́ние *neut.* chirping.
стрекота́ть *impf. pres.* стрекочу́, стреко́чешь to chirp.
стрела́ *f.* arrow.
стреле́ц FILL *m.* **1.** member of military corps in 16th and 17th centuries. **2.** — Стреле́ц Sagittarius.
стре́лка *f.* arrow, pointer, hand. — по часово́й стре́лке clockwise. — про́тив часово́й стре́лки counterclockwise.
стрелко́вый *adj.* (*attrib.*) rifle; shooting.
стрелови́дный *adj.* arrow-shaped.
стрело́к FILL *m.* **1.** marksman. **2.** gunner.
стре́лочник *m. f.* стре́лочница railroad switchman.
стрельба́ *f.* shooting.
стре́льбище *neut.* firing range.
стре́льчатый *adj.* arched.
стре́ляный *adj.* having been under fire.
стремгла́в *adv.* headlong.
стреми́тельно *adv.* rapidly.
стреми́тельный *adj.* swift; impetuous.
стреми́ться *impf.* (к *with dat.*) to aspire.
стремле́ние *neut.* aspiration.
стремни́на *f.* rapids (*on a river*).
стре́мя *neut.* stirrup.
стремя́нка *f.* stepladder.
стре́пет *m.* (*bird*) little bustard.
стрептоко́кк *m.* streptococcus.
стрептомици́н *m.* streptomycin.
стресс *m.* (*emotional*) stress.
стреха́ *f.* eaves.
стригу́щий лиша́й *m.* ringworm.
стриж *m.* (*bird*) swift.
стри́женый *adj.* (*of hair*) closely cropped.

стри́жка *f.* haircut.

стрипти́з *m.* striptease.

стрихни́н *m.* strychnine.

стри́чься *impf. pf.* **о-, об-** to have one's hair cut; to get a haircut.

стробоско́п *m.* stroboscope.

строга́льный *adj.* (*of tool*) planing.

строга́льщик *m.* planer.

строга́ть *impf. pf.* **вы́-** to plane (*wood*).

стро́гий *adj.* strict.

стро́го *adv.* strictly.

стро́гость *f.* strictness.

строево́й *adj.* (*mil.*) (*attrib.*) drill.

строе́ние *neut.* structure; building.

стро́итель *m.* builder.

стро́ительный *adj.* (*attrib.*) building; construction.

стро́ительство *neut.* **1.** building; construction. **2.** construction project. **3.** building site. **4.** organization; structuring.

стро́ить *impf. pf.* **по-** to build, to construct.

строй *m.* system; order.

стро́йка *f.* building; construction.

стро́йный *adj.* **1.** slender; graceful. **2.** (*of columns*) regular. **3.** harmonious. **4.** logical; coherent.

строка́ *f.* line of text.

стро́нций *m.* strontium.

стропи́ло *neut.* rafter.

стропти́вый *adj.* obstinate; contrary.

строфа́ *f.* stanza.

стро́чка¹ *f. same as* **строка́**.

стро́чка² *f.* stitch.

стро́чная бу́ква *f.* lower case letter.

стро́чный *adj.* (*letter*) small; lower-case.

струг¹ *m.* (*tool*) plane.

струг² *m.* (*obs.*) wooden boat.

стру́жки *pl.* **1.** shavings; filings. **2.** excelsior; packing material.

стру́йка *f.* **1.** stream; trickle. **2.** wisp (*of smoke*).

стру́йный *adj.* (*attrib.*) jet.

структу́ра *f.* structure.

структу́рный *adj.* structural.

струна́ *f.* string.

стру́нка *f.*: **вы́тянуться в стру́нку** *pf.* to stand at attention.

стру́нный *adj.* **1.** (*attrib.*) string. **2.** stringed. — **стру́нный кварте́т** *m.* string quartet.

стручко́вый *adj.* leguminous.

стручо́к FILL *m.* pod.

струя́ *f.* **1.** stream, jet. **2.** current.

стря́пать *impf. pf.* **со-** to cook.

стряпня́ *f.* (*colloq.*) cooking.

студе́нт *m. f.* **—ка** student.

студе́нческий *adj.* (*attrib.*) student; student's.

студе́нчество *neut.* (*coll.*) students; student body.

студёный *adj.* (*colloq.*) very cold; freezing.

сту́день *m.* aspic.

студи́ть *impf. pf.* **о-** to cool.

сту́дия *f.* studio.

сту́жа *f.* (*colloq.*) severe cold.

стук *m.* **1.** knock, tap. **2.** thump.

стука́ч *m.* (*colloq.*) stool pigeon; informer.

стул *m.* chair.

сту́льчик *m. dim. of* **стул**.

сту́па *f.* (*bowl*) mortar.

ступа́ть *impf. pf.* **ступи́ть** to step.

ступе́нчатый *adj.* stepped; graded.

ступе́нь *f.* step; stage.

ступе́нька *f.* step (*on a staircase*).

ступи́ца *f.* hub (*of a wheel*).

сту́пка *f.* (*bowl*) mortar.

ступня́ *f.* foot.

сту́пор *m.* stupor.

стуча́ть *impf. pres.* **стучу́, стучи́шь** *pf.* **по- 1.** to knock. **2.** (*of one's heart*) to throb; (*of one's teeth*) to chatter.

стушева́ться *pf.* to become flustered.

стыд *m.* shame.

стыди́ться *impf. pf.* **по-** (*with gen.*) to be ashamed (of).

стыдли́вость *f.* bashfulness; modesty.

стыдли́вый *adj.* modest; bashful; shy.

сты́дно *adj.* (*pred.*) it is a shame. — **сты́дно!** shame on you!

сты́дный *adj.* shameful.

стык *m.* **1.** joint. **2.** junction.

стыкова́ться OVA *pf.* (*of space vehicles*) to dock.

стыко́вка *m.* docking (*of spaceships*).

сты́нуть *also* **стыть** *impf. pf.* **о-** *v.i.* to cool off.

стю́ард *m.* steward (*on a ship* or *airplane*).

стюарде́сса *f.* stewardess.

стяг *m.* banner; standard.

стя́гивать *impf. pf.* **стяну́ть 1.** to tighten. **2.** to tie up. **3.** to gather.

стяжа́тель *m. f.* **—ница** money-grubber.

стяжа́тельство *neut.* making money.

суахи́ли *m. indecl.* Swahili.

субаре́нда *f.* sublease.

суббо́та *f.* Saturday.

суббо́тний *adj.* (*attrib.*) Saturday; Sabbath.

суббо́тник *m.* voluntary unpaid work (*originally performed on Saturday*).

субконтине́нт *m.* subcontinent.

сублима́т *m.* sublimate.

сублима́ция *f.* sublimation.

сублими́ровать OVA *impf. and pf.* (*chem.*) to sublimate.

субордина́ция *f.* deference to rank.

субподря́д *m.* subcontract.

субподря́дчик *m.* subcontractor.

субсиди́ровать OVA *impf. and pf.* to subsidize.

субси́дия *f.* subsidy.

субста́нция *f.* substance.

субстра́т *m.* substratum.

субти́льный *adj.* frail; fragile.

субти́тр *m.* (*movies*) subtitle.

субтро́пики *pl.* subtropics.

субтропи́ческий *adj.* subtropical.

субъе́кт *m.* **1.** subject. **2.** (*colloq.*) fellow; character.

субъективи́зм *m.* subjectivism.

субъекти́вность *f.* subjectivity.

субъекти́вный *adj.* subjective.

Сува́лки *pl.* Suwałki.

сува́льда *f.* tumbler (*of a lock*).

сувени́р *m.* souvenir.

сувере́н *m.* sovereign.

суверените́т *m.* sovereignty.

суверенный *adj.* sovereign.

сугли́нистый *adj.* loamy.

сугли́нок FILL *m.* loam.

сугро́б *m.* snowdrift.

сугу́бо *adv.* especially; particularly; exclusively.

сугу́бый *adj.* special, especial; particular.

суд *m.* court. —**ебный** *adj.* (*attrib.*) court; legal. —**имость** *f.* previous convictions.

суда́к *m.* pike perch.

Суда́н *m.* Sudan.

суда́рыня *f.* (*obs.*) madam.

су́дарь *m.* (*obs.*) sir.

суда́чить *impf.* to gossip.

суде́йский *adj.* judge's.

суди́лище *neut.* (unfair) trial.

суди́ть *impf.* **1.** to try, to judge. **2.** to umpire, to referee.

су́дно *neut.* ship, vessel.

су́дный *adj.* judicial; judgment.

судове́рфь *f.* shipyard.

судовладе́лец FILL *m.* shipowner.

судово́й *adj.* (*attrib.*) ship; ship's.

судо́к FILL *m.* **1.** gravy boat. **2.** cruet stand. — судки́ set of pots with covers for transporting food.

судомо́йка *m.* and *f.* (*decl. f.*) dishwasher.

судомо́йня *f.* scullery.

судопроизво́дство *neut.* legal proceedings.

су́дорога *f.* cramp.

су́дорожный *adj.* convulsive.

судостро́ение *neut.* shipbuilding.

судостро́итель *m.* shipbuilder.

судостро́ительный *adj.* (*attrib.*) shipbuilding.

судоустро́йство *neut.* judicial system.

судохо́дность *f.* navigability.

судохо́дный *adj.* navigable.

судохо́дство *neut.* shipping; navigation.

судьба́ *f.* fate, destiny.

судья́ *m.* **1.** judge. **2.** (*sports*) umpire.

суеве́рие *neut.* superstition.

суеве́рный *adj.* superstitious.

суета́ *f.* fuss.

суетли́вый *adj.* **1.** restless. **2.** bustling.

сужде́ние *neut.* judgment.

сужде́но *participle* (*pred.*) fated; destined.

суже́ние *neut.* narrowing; contraction.

Су́здаль *m.* Suzdal.

сук *m.* bough.

су́ка *f.* bitch.

сукно́ *neut.* cloth.

суко́нка *f.* **1.** cloth. **2.** rag.

суко́нный *adj.* **1.** (*attrib.*) cloth. **2.** (*of language*) dull; vapid.

сулема́ *f.* **1.** mercuric chloride. **2.** corrosive sublimate.

сули́ть *impf. pf.* **по-** **1.** to promise. **2.** *impf. only* to portend.

султа́н[1] *m.* sultan.

султа́н[2] *m.* plume.

султана́т *m.* sultanate.

султа́нка *f.* red mullet.

сульфаниламидный *adj.* sulfa.

сульфа́т *m.* sulfate.

сульфи́д *m.* sulfide.

сума́ *f.* (*obs.*) bag.

сумасбро́д *m. f.* —**ка** nut; screwball.

сумасбро́дный *adj.* wild; extravagant.

сумасбро́дство *neut.* erratic behavior.

сумасше́дший *adj.* mad. — *m.* madman, lunatic.

сумасше́ствие *neut.* madness.

сумато́ха *f.* commotion; tumult.

сумато́шный *also* сумато́шливый *adj.* (*colloq.*) hectic; tumultuous; bustling.

сума́х *m.* sumac.

сумбу́р *m.* confusion.

сумбу́рный *adj.* confused.

су́меречный *adj.* (*attrib.*) twilight.

су́мерки *pl.* twilight.

суме́ть *pf.* (*with infin.*) to succeed (in), to be able (to).

су́мка *f.* bag; handbag.

су́мма *f.* sum.

сумма́рный *adj.* total.

сумми́ровать OVA *impf.* and *pf.* to sum up.

су́мочка *f.* purse; handbag; pocketbook.

су́мрак *m.* dusk, twilight.

су́мрачный *adj.* gloomy.

Су́мы *pl.* Sumy.

суми́тица *f.* (*colloq.*) **1.** commotion; bustle. **2.** confusion; turmoil.

сунду́к *m.* trunk; chest.

суп *m.* soup.

суперма́ркет *m.* supermarket.

суперобло́жка *f.* dust jacket.

суперта́нкер *m.* supertanker.

су́песь *f.* loam.

су́пить *impf.* (*colloq.*) to knit one's brows.

су́пник *m. also* су́пница *f.* soup tureen.

супово́й *adj.* (*attrib.*) soup.

супру́г *m. f.* супру́га spouse.

супру́жеский *adj.* marital; spousal.

супру́жество *neut.* matrimony.

сургу́ч *m.* sealing wax.

сургу́чный *adj.* of sealing wax.

сурди́нка *f.* (*mus.*) mute.

суре́пица *f.* (*plant*) rape. — суре́пное ма́сло rapeseed oil.

суре́пный *adj.* (*attrib.*) rapeseed.

су́рик *m.* red lead.

суро́во *adv.* severely; sternly.

суро́вость *f.* severity; harshness.

суро́вый *adj.* severe; stern.

суро́к FILL *m.* marmot.

суррога́т *m.* substitute.

суррога́тный *adj.* substitute; ersatz.

сурьма́ *f.* antimony.

суса́льное зо́лото *neut.* gold leaf.

су́слик *m.* a kind of ground squirrel; gopher.

су́сло *neut.* mash.

суста́в *m.* (*anat.*) joint.

суставно́й *adj.* of the joints.

сутенёр *m.* gigolo.

су́тки *pl.* **1.** (*period of*) twenty-four hours. **2.** day.

су́толока *f.* bustle; commotion.

су́точно *pl.* per diem.

су́точный *adj.* a day's; daily.

суту́лый *adj.* round-shouldered; stooped.

суть *f.* essence; main *or* principal point.

суфле́ *neut. indecl.* soufflé.

суфлёр *m.* (*theat.*) prompter.

суфли́ровать *impf.* to prompt.

суфражи́стка *f.* suffragette.

су́ффикс *m.* suffix.

суха́рь *m.* zwieback; rusk.

суха́я *f.* (*colloq.*) (*sports*) shutout.

су́хо *adv.* dryly; coldly. — *adj.* (*pred.*) dry.

суховей *m.* hot dry wind.

сухожи́лие *neut.* tendon.
сухо́й *adj.* dry.
сухопа́рый *adj.* (*colloq.*) lean; skinny.
сухопу́тный *adj.* (*attrib.*) land; ground.
су́хость *f.* dryness.
сухоща́вый *adj.* (*colloq.*) lean; skinny.
Суху́ми *m.* Sokhumi.
сучёный *adj.* twisted.
сучи́ть *impf.* **1.** to twist. **2.** to spin.
сучкова́тый *adj.* knotty; gnarled.
сучо́к *m.* twig.
су́ша *f.* land; dry land.
суше́ние *neut.* drying.
сушёный *adj.* dried.
суши́лка *f.* **1.** dryer. **2.** drying room.
суши́льный *adj.* (*attrib.*) drying.
суши́льня *f.* drying room.
суши́ть *impf. pf.* **вы-** to dry (out).
су́шка¹ *f.* drying.
су́шка² *f.* small, round, bagel-shaped cracker.
сушь *f.* (*colloq.*) **1.** dry place. **2.** dry land. **3.** dry spell.
суще́ственно *adv.* substiantially; essentially.
суще́ственный *adj.* essential.
существи́тельное *also* **и́мя существи́тельное** *neut.* noun.
существо́ *neut.* being; creature; essence.
существова́ние *neut.* existence.
существова́ть OVA *impf.* to exist.
су́щий *adj.* existing; real.
су́щность *f.* essence.
сфабрикова́ть OVA *pf.* to forge.
сфе́ра *f.* sphere.
сфери́ческий *adj.* spherical.
сферо́ид *m.* spheroid.
сфероида́льный *adj.* spheroidal.
сфинкс *m.* sphinx.
сформули́ровать *pf. of* **формули́ровать**.
сфотографи́ровать *pf. of* **фотографи́ровать**.
схвати́ть *pf. of* **схва́тывать, хвата́ть.** **—ся** *pf. of* **хвата́ться.**
схва́тка *f.* fight; skirmish. — **схва́тки** cramps.
схва́тывать *impf. pf.* **схвати́ть** to grab; to seize.
схе́ма *f.* scheme.
схемати́ческий *adj.* schematic.
схи́зма *f.* schism.
схизмати́ческий *adj.* schismatic.
схлы́нуть *pf.* **1.** (*of water*) to surge back; to sweep back. **2.** (*of emotions*) to subside.
сход *m.* **1.** descent; slope. **2.** (*obs.*) meeting; assembly.
сходи́ть¹ *impf. pf.* **сойти́ 1.** to go down. **2.** to get off; to leave. **3.** to come off.
сходи́ть² *pf.* to make a quick round trip.
сходи́ться *impf. pf.* **сойти́сь 1.** to become intimate. **2.** to agree. **3.** to meet.
схо́дка *f.* meeting.
схо́дни *pl.* gangway; gangplank.
схо́дный *adj.* similar.
схо́дство *neut.* resemblance; similarity.
схо́жесть *f.* (*colloq.*) similarity; resemblance.
схорони́ть *pf. of* **хорони́ть**.
сца́пать *pf.* (*colloq.*) to grab hold of.
сце́живать *impf. pf.* **сцеди́ть** to strain off.
сце́на *f.* (*theat.*) **1.** stage. **2.** scene.
сцена́рий *m.* scenario; script.

сценари́ст *m. f.* **—ка** script writer.
сцени́ческий *adj.* (*attrib.*) stage; scenic.
сцени́чный *adj.* suitable for the stage.
сцепле́ние *neut.* **1.** coupling. **2.** cohesion.
сцепно́й *adj.* (*attrib.*) coupling.
счастли́вец FILL *m. f.* **счастли́вица** lucky person.
счастли́во *adv.* **1.** happily. **2.** luckily. — *interj.* good luck!; all the best!
счастли́вчик *m.* lucky person.
счастли́вый *adj.* happy; fortunate.
сча́стье *neut.* happiness; luck.
счесть *pf. of* **счита́ть**.
счёт *m.* **1.** calculation. **2.** account. **3.** bill; check. **4.** (*athl.*) score.
счётный *adj.* (*attrib.*) **1.** counting; calculating. **2.** accounts; accounting.
счетово́д *m.* bookkeeper.
счетово́дный *adj.* (*attrib.*) bookkeeping; accounting.
счетово́дство *neut.* bookkeeping; accounting.
счётчик *m.* **1.** meter. **2.** *f.* **счётчица** (*person*) counter.
счёты *pl.* abacus.
счисле́ние *neut.* (*math.*) numbering.
счи́таные *adj.* only a few.
счита́ть *impf.* **1.** *pf.* **счесть** (*with instr.*) to consider. **2.** *pf.* **со-** to count.
счи́тывание *neut.* (*comput.*) reading; read out.
США *pl.* (*abbr. of* **Соединённые Шта́ты Аме́рики**) USA.
сшиба́ть *impf. pf.* **сшиби́ть** (*colloq.*) **1.** to knock off. **2.** to knock down.
сшива́ть *impf. pf.* **сшить** to sew (together).
сшить *pf. of* **сшива́ть, шить**.
съеда́ть *impf. pf.* **съесть** to eat.
съедо́бный *adj.* edible.
съёживаться *impf. pf.* **съёжиться 1.** to shrivel; to shrink. **2.** to huddle up. **3.** to become haggard.
съезд *m.* congress, convention.
съезжа́ться *impf. pf.* **съе́хаться** to assemble.
съёмка *f.* **1.** survey. **2.** filming, photographing.
съёмный *adj.* removable.
съёмочный *adj.* (*film*) shooting.
съёмщик *m. f.* **съёмщица** tenant; renter.
съестно́е *neut.* provisions; food supplies.
съесть *pf. of* **съеда́ть**.
съе́хаться *pf. of* **съезжа́ться**.
сы́воротка *f.* **1.** whey. **2.** (*med.*) serum.
сы́гранность *f.* coordination; teamwork.
сыгра́ть *pf. of* **игра́ть**.
сы́змала *adv.* (*colloq.*) since childhood.
сы́знова *adv.* (*colloq.*) all over again.
Сыктывка́р *m.* Syktyvkar.
сын *m.* son.
сыни́шка *m. dim. of* **сын**.
сыно́вний *adj.* filial.
сыно́к FILL *m.* (*colloq.*) son.
сы́пать *impf.* to strew; to pour.
сыпно́й тиф *m.* typhus.
сыпня́к *m.* (*colloq.*) typhus.
сыпу́чий *adj.* crumbly; loose.
сыпь *f.* **1.** skin eruption. **2.** rash.
сыр *m.* cheese.
Сырдарья́ *f.* (*river*) Syr Darya.
сыре́ц FILL *m.* product in its raw state.
сы́рник *m.* cheese pancake.

сы́рный *adj.* cheesy.
сыроваре́ние *neut.* cheese making.
сыро́й *adj.* **1.** damp. **2.** raw; uncooked.
сыромя́тный *adj.* rawhide.
сы́ромять *f.* rawhide.
сы́рость *f.* dampness.
сырьё *neut.* raw material.
сыск *m.* (*pre-rev.*) criminal investigation.
сыскна́я поли́ция (*obs.*) criminal investigation department.
сы́тно *adv.* heartily.
сы́тный *adj.* **1.** nourishing. **2.** substantial; satiating.
сы́тость *f.* satiety.
сы́тый *adj.* satiated.
сыч *m.* little owl.
сычу́г *m.* **1.** rennet bag. **2.** fourth stomach of a ruminant animal.
сычу́жина *f.* rennin.

сычу́жный *adj.* (*attrib.*) rennet.
сы́щик *m. f.* **сы́щица** detective.
сэр *m.* sir.
сюда́ *adv.* (*dir.*) here, to this place.
сюже́т *m.* subject matter; plot.
сюже́тный *adj.* of a plot.
сюзере́н *m.* suzerain.
сюзерените́т *m.* suzerainty.
сюзере́нный *adj.* (*attrib.*) suzerain.
сюрпри́з *m.* surprise.
сюрпри́зный *adj.* (*attrib.*) surprise.
сюрреали́зм *m.* surrealism.
сюрреали́ст *m.* surrealist.
сюрреалисти́ческий *adj.* surrealistic.
сюрту́к *m.* frock coat.
сюсю́канье *neut.* (*colloq.*) baby talk.
сюсю́кать *impf.* (*colloq.*) to lisp.
сяк *adv.*: **и так и сяк** this way and that (way).
сям *adv.*: **там и сям** here and there.

T

та *pron.*, *see* тот.
таба́к *m.* tobacco.
табаке́рка *f.* snuffbox.
табаково́д *m.* tobacco grower.
табаково́дство *neut.* tobacco growing.
табаково́дческий *adj.* tobacco-growing.
таба́чный *adj.* (*attrib.*) tobacco.
та́бель *m.* **1.** table; chart. **2.** sign-out board.
та́бельный *adj.* shown on a table.
та́бельщик *m. f.* та́бельщица timekeeper.
табле́тка *f.* tablet.
табли́ца *f.* **1.** table. **2.** list.
табли́чка *f.* tablet.
табли́чный *adj.* tabular.
табло́ *neut. indecl.* **1.** scoreboard. **2.** electronic indicator panel.
табльдо́т *m.* table d'hôte.
та́бор *m.* gypsy band.
табу́ *neut. indecl.* taboo.
табуля́тор *m.* tabulator.
табу́н *m.* herd; flock.
табу́нщик *m.* herdsman.
табуре́т *m.* stool.
табуре́тка *f.* stool.
та́волга *f.* (*bird*) meadowsweet.
таврёный *adj.* branded.
таври́ть *impf.* to brand (*cattle*).
тавро́ *neut.* brand (*on cattle*).
тавтологи́ческий *adj.* tautological.
тавтоло́гия *f.* tautology.
тага́н *m.* trivet.
таджи́к *m. f.* таджи́чка Tajik.
Таджикиста́н *m.* Tajikistan.
таёжный *adj.* of the taiga; in the taiga.
таз[1] *m.* wash basin.
таз[2] *m.* pelvis.
та́зовый *adj.* pelvic.
Таила́нд *m.* Thailand.
таи́нственность *f.* mystery.
таи́нственный *adj.* mysterious.
та́инство *neut.* (*obs.*) secret, mystery.
Таи́ти *m.* Tahiti.
таи́ть *impf. v.t.* to conceal, to hide.
Тайва́нь *m.* Taiwan.
тайга́ *f.* (*geog.*) taiga.
тайко́м *adv.* secretly.
Та́йланд *m.* Thailand.
тайм *m.* period (*of a game*).
та́йна *f.* **1.** mystery.
Та́йная Вече́ря *f.* the Last Supper.
тайни́к *m.* hiding place.
та́йно *adv.* secretly; in secret.
та́йнопись *f.* secret writing.
та́йный *adj.* secret.
тайфу́н *m.* typhoon.
Тайше́т *m.* Tayshet.
так *adv.* **1.** so, thus. **2.** like this, like that. — *particle* then. — так как *conj.* since.
такела́ж *m.* (*naut.*) rigging (*of a ship*).
та́кже *adv.* also, too.

тако́в *indef. pron.* **1.** such. **2.** like that; the same; alike.
таково́й *indef. pron.* such; the same. — как таково́й as such.
тако́й *pron., adj.* such. — что э́то тако́е? what is this?
тако́й-то *adj.* so-and-so; such and such.
та́кса[1] *f.* dachshund.
та́кса[2] *f.* tariff, price.
такси́ *neut. indecl.* taxi; cab.
таксо́метр *m.* taximeter.
таксономи́ческий *adj.* taxonomic.
таксоно́мия *f.* taxonomy.
такт[1] *m.* tact.
такт[2] *m.* (*mus.*) time; measure.
та́к-таки *particle* (*colloq.*) still, anyway.
та́ктик *m.* tactician.
та́ктика *f.* tactics.
такти́ческий *adj.* tactical.
такти́чно *adv.* tactfully.
такти́чность *f.* tactfulness; tact.
такти́чный *adj.* tactful.
тала́нт *m.* talent; gift.
тала́нтливый *adj.* talented.
талисма́н *m.* talisman.
та́лия *f.* waist.
та́ллий *m.* thallium.
Та́ллинн *m.* Tallinn.
талму́д *m.* Talmud.
талмуди́зм *m.* talmudism; dogmatism.
талмуди́ст *m.* Talmudic scholar.
талмуди́стский *adj.* talmudic; dogmatic.
талмуди́ческий *adj.* Talmudic.
тало́н *m.* coupon.
та́лый *adj.* melting; melted.
тальк *m.* talc.
та́льковый *adj.* (*attrib.*) talc; talcum.
там *adv.* there.
тамада́ *m.* master of ceremonies; toastmaster (*at a banquet*).
тама́ринд *m.* tamarind.
тама́риск *m.* tamarisk.
Тамбо́в *m.* Tambov.
та́мбур[1] *m.* **1.** vestibule. **2.** platform (*of a railroad car*).
та́мбур[2] *m.* chain stitch.
тамбури́н *m.* tambourine.
та́мбурный шов *m.* chain stitch.
тамо́женник *m.* customs official.
тамо́женный *adj.* (*attrib.*) customs.
тамо́жня *f.* customs; custom house.
та́мошний *adj.* (*colloq.*) of that place; local.
Та́мпере *m.* Tampere.
тампо́н *m.* tampon.
тамта́м *m.* tom-tom.
тана́гра *m.* tanager.
та́нгенс *m.* (*trig.*) tangent.
тангенциа́льный *adj.* tangential.
та́нго *neut. indecl.* tango.
танде́м *m.* tandem.
та́нец FILL *m.* dance.

Танза́ния f. Tanzania.
тани́н m. tannin.
тани́нный adj. tannic.
танк¹ m. (mil.) tank.
танк² m. tank; cistern.
та́нкер m. tanker.
танке́тка f. (mil.) light tank.
танки́ст m. member of a tank crew.
та́нковый adj. (mil.) tank.
танцева́льный adj. (attrib.) dance.
танцева́ть OVA impf. to dance.
танцо́вщик m. f. танцо́вщица ballet dancer.
танцо́р m. dancer.
тапёр m. f. —ша hired pianist.
тапио́ка f. tapioca.
тапи́р m. tapir.
та́почки pl. 1. slippers. 2. sneakers.
та́ра f. 1. (shipping) container. 2. packing material. 3. (com.) tare.
тараба́нить impf. (colloq.) to chatter.
тараба́рщина f. (colloq.) gibberish.
тарака́н m. cockroach.
тара́н m. 1. battering ram. 2. (mech.) ram.
таранта́с m. tarantass (large carriage).
тара́нтул m. tarantula.
тара́нь f. (fish) roach.
тарара́м m. (colloq.) uproar; hubbub.
тарата́йка f. two-wheeled carriage.
тарато́рить impf. (colloq.) to chatter; to jabber.
тарахте́ть impf. pres. тарахчу́, тарахти́шь (colloq.) 1. to clatter. 2. to chatter.
тара́щить impf. pf. вы- (colloq.): тара́щить глаза́ to stare; to gape.
таре́лка f. plate.
таре́лочка f. dim. of таре́лка.
тари́ф m. tariff; rate.
тари́фный adj. (attrib.) tariff.
та́ры-ба́ры pl. indecl. (colloq.) chatter.
таска́ть impf. indet. det. тащи́ть to drag; to pull.
тасова́ть impf. pf. с- to shuffle (cards).
тата́рин m. f. тата́рка Tatar.
тата́рский adj. Tatar.
Татарста́н m. Tatarstan.
татуи́ровать OVA impf. and pf. to tattoo.
татуиро́вка f. tatooing; tattoo.
тафта́ f. taffeta.
тафтяно́й adj. taffeta.
тахо́метр m. tachometer.
тахта́ f. ottoman; divan.
тача́нка f. high open cart. 2. machine-gun cart.
тача́ть impf. pf. вы-, с- to stitch.
та́чка f. wheelbarrow.
Ташке́нт m. Toshkent.
тащи́ть impf. pf. по- 1. to pull; to draw; to tow. 2. to drag; to lug. 3. pf. вы- to pull out. 4. pf. с- (colloq.) to swipe; to pilfer.
та́яние neut. melting.
та́ять impf. pf. рас- v.i. to thaw; to melt.
Тбили́си m. Tbilisi (also: Tiflis).
тварь f. creature.
твердёть impf. pf. за- v.i. to harden.
тверди́ть impf. to reiterate; to say over and over again.
твёрдо adv. firmly; firm.
твердока́менный adj. callous; insensitive.
твердоло́бый adj. thickheaded.

твёрдость f. hardness; firmness.
твёрдый adj. hard, solid; firm.
тверды́ня f. 1. stronghold. 2. bulwark.
Тверь f. Tver (formerly: Kalinin).
твид m. tweed.
твой pron., see твой.
твой pron. твоя́ f., твоё neut., твои́ pl. your, yours.
творе́ние neut. creation.
творе́ц FILL m. creator; maker.
твори́тельный adj. (gram.) instrumental.
твори́ть impf. pf. со- to create.
твори́ться impf. (colloq.) to take place.
творо́г m. 1. cottage cheese. 2. curds.
творо́жник m. cottage-cheese pancake.
тво́рческий adj. creative.
тво́рчество neut. 1. creation, (creative) works. 2. creative activity.
те pron., see тот.
т.е. (abbr. of то есть) i.e.; that is.
теа́тр m. theater.
театра́л m. f. —ка theatergoer; playgoer.
театра́льность f. theatrics.
театра́льный adj. (attrib.) theater; theatrical.
тебе́ pron. dat. of ты.
Тебри́з m. Tabriz.
тевто́н m. Teuton.
тевто́нский adj. Teutonic.
Тегера́н m. Tehran.
теза́урус m. thesaurus.
те́зис m. thesis.
тёзка m. and f. (decl. f.) namesake.
тейзм m. theism.
тейст m. theist.
теисти́ческий adj. theistic.
текст m. 1. text. 2. (mus.) libretto; lyrics.
тексти́льный adj. textile.
тексти́льщик m. f. тексти́льщица textile worker.
те́кстовая обрабо́тка f. (comput.) word processing.
текстово́й adj. textual.
текстово́й реда́ктор m. (comput.) text editor.
теку́честь f. 1. fluctuation. 2. fluidity. 3. turnover (of employees).
теку́чий adj. fluid; fluctuating.
теку́щий adj. 1. flowing. 2. current, present.
телеви́дение neut. television.
телеви́дение высо́кой чёткости neut. (abbr. ТВЧ) High Definition T.V.
телевизио́нный adj. (attrib.) television.
телеви́зор m. television set.
теле́га f. cart.
телегра́мма f. telegram.
телегра́ф m. telegraph.
телеграфи́ровать OVA impf. and pf. to wire, to telegraph.
телеграфи́ст m. f. —ка telegraph operator.
телегра́фия f. telegraphy.
телегра́фный adj. (attrib.) telegraph.
теле́жка f. light cart; luggage cart.
телезри́тель m. f. —ница television viewer.
телека́мера f. television camera.
телеме́тр m. telemeter.
телеметри́я f. telemetry.
телёнок FILL m. pl. теля́та calf.
телеобъекти́в m. telephoto lens.

телеологи́ческий *adj.* teleological.
телеоло́гия *f.* teleology.
телепати́ческий *adj.* telepathic.
телепа́тия *f.* telepathy.
телепереда́ча *f.* **1.** television transmission. **2.** television broadcast.
телеско́п *m.* telescope.
телескопи́ческий *adj.* telescopic.
телеско́пный *adj.* (*attrib.*) telescope.
теле́сный *adj.* corporeal.
телесту́дия *f.* television studio.
телета́йп *m.* teletype.
телефо́н *m.* telephone.
телефони́ровать OVA *impf. and pf.* to telephone.
телефони́ст *m. f.* —ка telephone operator.
телефони́я *f.* telephony.
телефо́нный *adj.* (*attrib.*) telephone.
телёц FILL *m.* **1.** (*obs.*) calf. **2.** (*cap.*) (*astr.*) Taurus.
тёлка *f.* heifer.
теллу́р *m.* tellurium.
те́ло *neut.* body.
телогре́йка *f.* padded jacket.
телодвиже́ние *neut.* body movement.
телосложе́ние *neut.* build; frame.
телохрани́тель *m.* bodyguard.
те́льный *adj.* (*colloq.*) worn next to the body.
те́льце *neut.* **1.** little body. **2.** corpuscle.
теля́тина *f.* veal.
теля́чий *adj.* (*attrib.*) calf; calf's.
тем *pron. instr. of* тот. — *conj.* (so much) the. — тем не ме́нее nevertheless.
те́ма *f.* subject, topic; theme.
тема́тика *f.* subject matter.
темати́ческий *adj.* thematic.
тембр *m.* timbre.
те́мень *f.* (*colloq.*) darkness.
Темирта́у *m.* Temirtau.
темне́ть *impf. pf.* по- to become *or* grow dark.
темни́ть **1.** *impf.* to make darker; to darken. **2.** (*colloq.*) to hide, to conceal.
темни́ца *f.* (*obs.*) prison; dungeon; jail.
темно́ *adj.* (*pred.*) dark.
тёмно- *prefix* (*of colors*) dark.
темноволо́сый *adj.* dark-haired.
темноко́жий *adj.* dark-skinned.
темнота́ *f.* **1.** darkness, dark. **2.** (*fig.*) ignorance. **3.** obscurity.
тёмный *adj.* **1.** dark. **2.** obscure. **3.** ignorant.
темп *m.* **1.** rate. **2.** pace; tempo.
те́мпера *f.* tempera.
темпера́ментный *adj.* **1.** temperamental. **2.** spirited; lively.
температу́ра *f.* temperature.
температу́рный *adj.* (*attrib.*) temperature.
темь *f.* (*colloq.*) darkness.
те́мя *neut.* top *or* crown of the head.
тенденцио́зность *f.* tendentiousness.
тенденцио́зный *adj.* **1.** tendentious. **2.** biased.
тенде́нция *f.* tendency.
те́ндер *m.* (*railroad*) tender.
теневой́ *adj.* shady.
тенёта *pl.* net; snare.
тени́стый *adj.* shady.
Теннесси́ *m.* Tennessee.
те́ннис *m.* tennis.

тенниси́ст *m. f.* —ка tennis player.
те́нниска *f.* (*colloq.*) sport shirt.
те́ннисный *adj.* (*attrib.*) tennis.
те́нор *m.* tenor.
теноро́вый *adj.* (*attrib.*) tenor.
тент *m.* awning.
тень *f.* shade; shadow.
теократи́ческий *adj.* theocratic.
теокра́тия *f.* theocracy.
теологи́ческий *adj.* theological.
теоло́гия *f.* theology.
теоре́ма *f.* theorem.
теоретизи́ровать OVA *impf.* to theorize.
теоре́тик *m.* theoretician.
теорети́чески *adv.* theoretically.
теорети́ческий *adj.* theoretical.
тео́рия *f.* theory.
теосо́ф *m.* theosophist.
теософи́ческий *adj.* theosophical.
теосо́фия *f.* theosophy.
теосо́фский *adj.* theosophical.
тепе́решний *adj.* present-day.
тепе́рь *adv.* now.
тепле́ть *impf. pf.* по- to grow warm.
тепли́ца *f.* hothouse.
тепли́чный *adj.* hothouse.
тепло́ *neut.* warmth; heat. — *adv.* warmly. — *adj.* (*pred.*) warm. —во́й *adj.* thermal.
теплова́тый *adj.* tepid.
теплово́з *m.* diesel locomotive.
теплокро́вный *adj.* warm-blooded.
тепломе́р *m.* calorimeter.
теплопрово́дный *adj.* heat-conducting.
теплосто́йкий *adj.* heat-resistant.
теплота́ *f.* warmth, heat.
теплохо́д *m.* motor ship; motor vessel.
теплу́шка *f.* (*colloq.*) heated freight car (*for the transport of people*).
тёплый *adj.* warm.
тепль́нь *f.* (*colloq.*) warm weather.
терапевти́ческий *adj.* therapeutic.
терапи́я *f.* internal medicine.
те́рбий *m.* terbium.
тереби́ть *impf.* **1.** to pull at; to tug at. **2.** (*colloq.*) to pester; to nag.
те́рем *m.* (*hist.*) tower-chamber for women.
тере́ть *impf.* **1.** to rub. **2.** to grate.
Тере́шка *f.* (*river*) Tereshka.
терза́ние *neut.* torment; torture; agony; anguish.
терза́ть *impf.* to tear apart; to torment.
тёрка *f.* grater.
Терме́з *m.* Termiz.
те́рмин *m.* term.
термина́л *m.* computer terminal.
терминоло́гия *f.* terminology.
терми́т *m.* termite.
терми́ческий *adj.* thermal.
термодина́мика *f.* thermodynamics.
термодинами́ческий *adj.* thermodynamic.
термодина́ника *f.* thermodynamics.
термо́метр *m.* thermometer.
термопа́ра *f.* thermocouple.
те́рмос *m.* thermos (bottle).
термоста́т *m.* thermostat.
термоя́дерный *adj.* thermonuclear.
тёрн *m.* **1.** blackthorn. **2.** sloe; sloes.

тернистый *adj.* thorny.
терновник *m.* blackthorn.
Тернополь *m.* Ternopil.
терпеливо *adv.* patiently.
терпеливость *f.* patience.
терпеливый *adj.* patient.
терпение *neut.* patience.
терпеть *impf.* **1.** to endure, to suffer. **2.** to have patience. **3.** to tolerate. —ся *impers.* (*used negatively with dat.*) to be unable to wait. — мне не терпится пойти туда I can't wait to go there.
терпимо *adv.* with tolerance.
терпимость *f.* tolerance.
терпимый *adj.* tolerant; tolerable.
терпкий *adj.* tart.
терракота *f.* terra cotta.
терракотовый *adj.* terra-cotta.
терраса *f.* terrace.
террасный *adj.* terraced.
территориальный *adj.* territorial.
территория *f.* territory.
террор *m.* terror.
терроризировать OVA *impf. and pf.* to terrorize.
терроризм *m.* terrorism.
террорист *m. f.* —ка terrorist.
террористический *adj.* (*attrib.*) terrorist.
тёртый *adj.* **1.** grated. **2.** (*colloq.*) experienced.
терция *f.* (*mus.*) third.
терьер *m.* terrier.
терять *impf. pf.* по- **1.** to lose. **2.** to waste. —ся to be *or* get lost; to be at a loss.
тёс *m.* boards; planks.
тесак *m.* cutlass.
тесание *neut.* cutting; hewing.
тёсаный *adj.* cut; hewn.
тесать *impf. pres.* тешу, тешешь to cut; to hew.
тесёмка *f.* braid.
тесина *f.* board; plank.
тёска *f.* cutting; hewing.
тесло *neut.* adz.
теснина *f.* **1.** ravine; gorge. **2.** defile.
тесно *adv.* **1.** close together. **2.** closely.
теснота *f.* **1.** tightness. **2.** crowdedness.
тесный *adj.* **1.** tight; close. **2.** crowded.
тесовый *adj.* (*attrib.*) board; plank.
тесто *neut.* dough.
тесть *m.* father-in-law (*wife's father.*)
тесьма *f.* braid.
тётенька *f.* (*colloq.*) aunt; aunty.
тетерев *m.* black grouse; blackcock.
тетеревятник *m.* goshawk.
тетеря *f.* **1.** (*dial.*) black grouse. **2.** (*colloq.*) chap; fellow.
тетива *f.* bowstring.
тётка *f.* aunt.
тетрадный *adj.* (*attrib.*) notebook.
тетрадь *f.* notebook.
тётушка *f. dim. of* тётя.
тётя *f.* aunt.
тефтели *pl.* meatballs.
Техас *m.* Texas.
технеций *m.* technetium.
техник *m.* technician.
техника *f.* technology; technique.
техникум *m.* technical school.
технически *adv.* technically.

технический *adj.* technical.
технолог *m.* technologist.
технологический *adj.* **1.** technological. **2.** (*attrib.*) production.
технология *f.* technology.
течение *neut.* **1.** flow. **2.** course. — в течение *prep.* (*with gen.*) during.
течка *f.* heat (*in animals*).
течь¹ *f.* leak.
течь² *impf.* **1.** to flow. **2.** to leak.
тешить *impf. pf.* по- to amuse.
тёща *f.* mother-in-law (*wife's mother.*)
тиара *f.* tiara.
тибетский *adj.* Tibetan.
Тибр *m.* (*river*) Tiber.
тигель FILL *m.* crucible.
тигр *m.* tiger.
тигрёнок FILL *m.* tiger cub.
тигрица *f.* tigress.
тигровый *adj.* (*attrib.*) tiger; tiger's.
тик *m.* tic.
тиканье *neut.* ticking (*of a clock*).
тикать *impf.* (*of a clock*) to tick.
тиккер *m.* ticker.
тиковый *adj.* teak.
Тимишоара *f.* Timişoara.
тимофеевка *f.* (*plant*) timothy, timothy grass.
тимпан *m.* (*mus.*) timpani.
тимьян *m.* thyme.
тина *f.* slime.
тинистый *adj.* slimy.
тинктура *f.* tincture.
тип *m.* type.
типаж *m.* model; prototype.
типический *adj.* typical.
типично *adv.* typically.
типичный *adj.* typical.
типовой *adj.* model; standard.
типография *f.* printing house; printer.
типографский *adj.* typographical.
типун *m.* (*bird disease*) pip.
тир *m.* shooting range; shooting gallery.
тирада *f.* tirade.
тираж *m.* **1.** printing (*of books*). **2.** circulation.
тиран *m. f.* —ка tyrant.
Тирана *f.* Tirana.
тиранить *impf.* to tyrannize.
тиранический *adj.* tyrannical.
тирания *f.* tyranny.
тиранство *neut.* tyranny.
тиранствовать OVA *impf.* (*colloq.*) to be a tyrant.
Тирасполь *m.* Tiraspol.
тире *neut. indecl.* (*typog.*) dash.
тис *m.* yew.
тискать *impf. pf.* тиснуть (*colloq.*) to squeeze.
тиски *pl.* (*mech.*) vise.
тиснение *neut.* stamping; embossing.
тиснёный *adj.* embossed; stamped.
титан *m.* titan.
титанический *adj.* titanic.
титр *m.* (*movies*) subtitle.
титул *m.* title.
титулованный *adj.* titled.
титуловать OVA *impf. and pf.* to give a title.
титульный *adj.* (*typog.*) (*attrib.*) title.
тиф *m.* typhus; typhoid.

тифо́зный *adj.* typhoid; typhus.
тифя́к *m.* mattress.
Ти́хвин *m.* Tikhvin.
ти́хий *adj.* **1.** quiet; still. **2.** gentle, soft.
Ти́хий океа́н *also* **Вели́кий океа́н** *m.* Pacific Ocean.
ти́хо *adv.* **1.** quietly. **2.** softly. — *adj.* (*pred.*) quiet.
тихомо́лком *adv.* (*colloq.*) quietly.
тихо́нько *adv.* (*colloq.*) quietly; softly.
тихо́ня *m. and f.* (*decl. f.*) timid person.
ти́ше *interj.* quietly!
тишина́ *f.* quiet; stillness.
тишь *f.* quiet; stillness.
тка́ный *adj.* woven.
ткань *f.* **1.** cloth. **2.** fabric.
тканьё *neut.* weaving.
ткать *impf. pf.* **со-** to weave.
тка́цкий *adj.* (*attrib.*) weaving.
ткач *m. f.* **—и́ха** weaver.
ткнуть *pf. of* **ты́кать.**
тле́ние *neut.* **1.** smoldering. **2.** decay; decaying.
тле́нный *adj.* mortal.
тлень *m.* seal.
тлетво́рный *adj.* **1.** noxious; pernicious. **2.** putrid.
тлеть *impf.* **1.** to smolder. **2.** to rot, to decay.
тля *f.* plant louse.
тмин *m.* caraway.
то *pron., see* **тот.** — *conj.* then. — **то есть** that is. — **а не то** *conj.* or else; otherwise.
тобо́й *also* **тобо́ю** *pron. instr. of* **ты.**
Тобо́льск *m.* Tobolsk.
това́р *m.* goods; commodity.
това́рищ *m.* comrade; friend, buddy.
това́рищеский *adj.* friendly; comradely.
това́рищество *neut.* comradeship; fellowship.
товарообме́н *m.* barter.
товарооборо́т *m.* turnover of goods.
то́га *f.* toga.
тогда́ *adv.* then. — **тогда́ как** *conj.* while.
тогда́шний *adj.* (*colloq.*) pertaining to that time.
того́ *adj. gen. of* **тот.**
тожде́ственность *f.* identity.
тожде́ственный *adj.* identical.
то́ждество *neut.* identity.
то́же *adv.* also, too, as well.
той *adj., f. gen., dat., prep.,* and *instr. of* **тот.**
ток *m.* (*also elec.*) current.
тока́рный *adj.* (*attrib.*) lathe.
то́карь *m.* turner; lathe operator.
То́кио *m.* Tokyo.
Токма́к *m.* Tokmak.
токова́ние *neut.* mating call.
токова́ть OVA *impf.* (*of birds*) to utter a mating call.
токсеми́я *f.* toxemia.
токсико́лог *m.* toxicologist.
токсилоги́ческий *adj.* toxicological.
токсиколо́гия *f.* toxicology.
токси́н *m.* toxin.
токси́ческий *adj.* toxic.
тол *m.* TNT; tolite.
Толе́до *m.* Toledo.
толи́ка *f.* (*with gen.*) (*colloq.*) small amount of.
толк *m.* sense.
толка́ние *neut.* pushing.
толка́ть *impf. pf.* **толкну́ть** to push.

толка́ч *m.* (*colloq.*) **1.** fixer; expediter; go-getter. **2.** pusher.
толкова́ние *neut.* **1.** interpretation. **2.** commentary.
толкова́тель *m.* interpreter; commentator.
толкова́ть OVA *impf.* to interpret.
толко́вый *adj.* **1.** intelligent. **2.** explanatory. **3.** intelligible.
то́лком *adv.* (*colloq.*) **1.** clearly; plainly. **2.** properly. **3.** in earnest.
толкотня́ *f.* (*colloq.*) crush (*of people*).
толку́чий ры́нок *m.* (*colloq.*) flea market.
толку́чка *f.* (*colloq.*) flea market.
толокно́ *neut.* oatmeal.
толо́чь *impf. pf.* **ис-, рас-** to pound; to crush.
толпа́ *f.* crowd.
толпи́ться *impf.* to crowd.
толсте́ть *impf. pf.* **по-** to grow fat *or* stout.
толстогу́бый *adj.* thick-lipped.
толстоко́жий *adj.* thick-skinned.
толстосу́м *m.* rich man; moneybags.
толсту́ха *f.* (*colloq.*) plump wóman.
то́лстый *adj.* fat, stout.
толстя́к *m.* (*colloq.*) fat man.
толуо́л *m.* (*chem.*) toluene.
толчёный *adj.* ground.
толчея́ *f.* (*colloq.*) crowd; crush of people.
толчо́к FILL *m.* push; shove.
то́лща *f.* thick layer; thick mass.
толщина́ *f.* thickness; corpulence; stoutness.
толь *m.* tarred roofing paper.
то́лько *adv.* only.
том[1] *adj. prep. of* **тот.**
том[2] *m.* (*book*) volume.
томага́вк *m.* tomahawk.
тома́т *m.* tomato.
тома́тный *adj.* (*attrib.*) tomato.
то́мик *m. dim. of* **том.**
томи́тельный *adj.* **1.** tiring. **2.** tedious. **3.** oppressive.
томи́ть *impf.* **1.** to weary, to tire. **2.** to wear out. **—ся** (**по** *with dat.*) to pine *or* languish (for).
томле́ние *neut.* suffering; languor.
то́мность *f.* languor.
то́мный *adj.* languid.
Томск *m.* Tomsk.
тому́ *adj. dat. of* **тот.** — **тому́ наза́д** ago.
тон *m.* tone.
тона́льность *f.* (*mus.*) key.
тона́льный *adj.* tonal.
то́ненький *adj.* (*colloq.*) thin.
тонзу́ра *f.* tonsure.
тонизи́ровать OVA *impf. and pf.* **1.** to tone up. **2.** to refresh.
тони́ческий *adj.* tonic.
то́нкий *adj.* thin; fine; slim, slender.
то́нко *adv.* thinly.
тонкоко́жий *adj.* thin-skinned.
то́нкость *f.* **1.** thinness, slimness. **2.** delicacy. **3.** subtlety.
то́нна *f.* ton.
тонна́ж *m.* tonnage.
тонне́ль *also* **тунне́ль** *m.* tunnel.
то́нус *m.* (*physiol.*) tone.
тону́ть *impf. pf.* **у-** *v.i.* **1.** to drown. **2.** to sink.
то́ный *adj.* exact, precise, accurate.

топа́з *m.* topaz.
топа́зовый *adj.* topaz.
то́пать *impf. pf.* то́пнуть to stamp one's feet.
топи́ть[1] *impf.* **1.** to heat. **2.** to melt.
топи́ть[2] *impf. pf.* y- *v.t.* to drown, to sink.
то́пка *f.* **1.** stoking. **2.** heating. **3.** furnace. **4.** melting.
то́пкий *adj.* swampy.
топлёный *adj.* melted.
то́пливо *neut.* fuel.
то́пнуть *pf. of* то́пать.
топо́граф *m.* topographer.
топографи́ческий *adj.* topographical.
топогра́фия *f.* topography.
то́полевый *adj.* (*attrib.*) poplar.
тополо́гия *f.* topology.
то́поль *m.* poplar.
топо́р *m.* ax.
топо́рик *m.* hatchet.
топо́рище *neut.* ax handle.
топо́рный *adj.* (*attrib.*) ax; (*of an article*) crudely made.
топо́рщить *impf.* to make (*hair, etc.*) stand on end.
то́пот *m.* **1.** tramping; stamping. **2.** clatter.
топта́ние *neut.* trampling.
топта́ть *impf.* to trample.
топча́к *m.* treadmill.
топь *f.* marsh; swamp; bog.
то́ра *f.* Torah.
то́рба *f.* feedbag.
торг *m.* trade; bargaining.
То́ргау *m.* Torgau.
торга́ш *m.* hawker; peddler.
торги́ *pl.* auction.
торгова́ть OVA *impf.* to trade; to deal. —ся to bargain.
торго́вец FILL *m. f.* торго́вка merchant, dealer, tradesman.
торго́вля *f.* trade; commerce.
торго́вый *adj.* (*attrib.*) trade; commercial.
тореадо́р *m.* toreador.
торе́ц FILL *m.* **1.** butt end; face (*of beam, etc.*). **2.** wooden paving block.
торже́ственность *f.* solemnity.
торже́ственный *adj.* solemn.
торжество́ *neut.* celebration; triumph.
торжествова́ть OVA *impf.* to triumph.
торжеству́ющий *adj.* triumphant.
то́ри *m. indecl.* Tory.
то́рий *m.* thorium.
торма́шки *pl.:* вверх торма́шками (*colloq.*) **1.** head over heels. **2.** topsy-turvy.
торможе́ние *neut.* braking.
то́рмоз *m.* brake.
тормози́ть *impf. pf.* за- **1.** to apply brakes. **2.** to hinder, to hamper.
тормозно́й *adj.* (*attrib.*) brake.
тормоши́ть *impf.* **1.** to tug at. **2.** to pester; to bother.
то́рный *adj.* (*of a road*) smooth; even; worn down.
торова́тый *adj.* (*obs.*) generous.
Торо́нто *m.* Toronto.
торопи́ть *impf. pf.* по- *v.t.* to hurry, to hasten.
торопли́во *adv.* hastily.

торопли́вость *f.* haste, hurry.
торопли́вый *adj.* hasty.
торо́с *m.* ice hummock.
торпе́да *f.* torpedo.
торпеди́ровать OVA *impf. and pf.* to torpedo.
торпе́дный *adj.* (*attrib.*) torpedo.
торс *m.* torso.
торт *m.* cake.
торф *m.* peat.
торфяно́й *adj.* peat.
торча́ть *impf.* to protrude.
торчко́м *adv.* (*colloq.*) on end; erect; upright.
торше́р *m.* floor lamp.
тоска́ *f.* **1.** melancholy, pangs; anguish. **2.** boredom. **3.** yearning, longing; nostalgia.
Тоска́на *f.* (*province*) Tuscany.
тоскли́вый *adj.* dull; dreary.
тоскова́ть OVA *impf.* to be melancholy, to long for.
тост *m.* toast.
то́стер *m.* toaster.
тот *pron., adj.* та *f.,* то *neut.,* те *pl.* that; the other.
тотализа́тор *m.* totalizator.
тоталитари́зм *m.* totalitarianism.
тоталита́рный *adj.* totalitarian.
тота́льный *adj.* total.
тоте́м *m.* totem.
то́-то *particle* (*colloq.*) **1.** that is why; that is how. **2.** that's just the point.
то́тчас *adv.* immediately.
точе́ние *neut.* sharpening.
точёный *adj.* sharpened.
точи́лка *f.* **1.** sharpener. **2.** pencil sharpener.
точи́ло *neut.* grindstone; whetstone.
точи́льный *adj.* (*attrib.*) sharpening.
точи́ть *impf. pf.* на- to sharpen; to grind.
то́чка *f.* point; dot; period.
то́чно *adv.* exactly. — *conj.* as if, as though.
то́чность *f.* **1.** exactness. **2.** accuracy. **3.** punctuality.
то́чный *adj.* exact; precise; accurate.
точь-в-то́чь *adv.* (*colloq.*) exactly.
тошни́ть *impf., impers.* to feel nauseous.
то́шно *adv.* (*pred.*) nauseating; sickening.
тошнота́ *f.* nausea.
тошнотво́рный *adj.* nauseating; sickening.
то́шный *adj.* nauseating; tiresome.
то́щий *adj.* **1.** meager. **2.** emaciated.
тпру *interj.* whoa!
трава́ *f.* grass.
трави́нка *f.* blade of grass.
трави́ть *impf.* **1.** to exterminate. **2.** to hunt. **3.** to poison. **4.** to persecute. **5.** to etch.
травле́ние *neut.* etching.
тра́вля *f.* hunt; hunting.
тра́вма *f.* trauma; injury.
травмати́ческий *adj.* traumatic.
травматоло́гия *f.* traumatology.
травми́ровать OVA *impf. and pf.* to damage; to injure.
травоя́дный *adj.* herbivorous.
травяни́стый *adj.* herbaceous.
травяно́й *adj.* (*attrib.*) grass; grassy.
траге́дия *f.* tragedy.
траги́зм *m.* tragic element.

тра́гик *m.* tragedian.
трагикоме́дия *f.* tragicomedy.
трагикоми́ческий *adj.* tragicomic(al).
траги́чески *adv.* tragically.
траги́ческий *adj.* tragic.
траги́чно *adv.* tragically.
траги́чность *f.* tragedy; tragic nature.
траги́чный *adj.* tragic.
традицио́нный *adj.* traditional.
тради́ция *f.* tradition.
траекто́рия *f.* trajectory.
тракт *m.* canal; tract.
тракта́т *m.* treatise.
тракти́р *m.* inn; tavern.
тракти́рщик *m. f.* **тракти́рщица** (*obs.*) innkeeper.
трактова́ть OVA *impf.* **1.** to interpret. **2.** (*o with prep.*) to discuss (*a subject*).
тракто́вка *f.* treatment; interpretation.
тра́ктор *m.* tractor.
тра́кторный *adj.* (*attrib.*) tractor.
трал *m.* trawl.
тра́лить *impf.* to trawl.
тра́льщик *m.* **1.** trawler. **2.** minesweeper.
трамбова́ть OVA *impf. pf.* **у-** to beat down.
трамва́й *m.* trolley; streetcar; tram.
трамва́йный *adj.* (*attrib.*) streetcar.
трампли́н *m.* springboard.
транжи́р *m. f.* **—ка** (*colloq.*) spendthrift.
транжи́рить *impf. pf.* **рас-** to squander.
транзи́стор *m.* transistor.
транзи́т *m.* transit.
транзи́тный *adj.* (*attrib.*) transit.
транс *m.* trance.
трансатланти́ческий *adj.* transatlantic.
Трансильва́ния *f.* (*region*) Transylvania.
трансконтинента́льный *adj.* transcontinental.
транскри́пция *f.* transcription.
трансли́ровать OVA *impf. and pf.* to broadcast.
транслитери́ровать OVA *impf. and pf.* to transliterate.
трансляцио́нный *adj.* (*attrib.*) transmission; broadcast.
трансми́ссия *f.* transmission.
трансокеа́нский *adj.* transoceanic.
транспара́нт *m.* **1.** banner; streamer. **2.** black lined paper (*placed under unlined paper*).
транспони́ровать OVA *impf. and pf.* (*mus.*) to transpose.
транспониро́вка *f.* (*mus.*) transposition.
тра́нспорт *m.* transport; transportation.
тра́нспорт *m.* (*accounting*) carrying forward.
транспорта́бельный *adj.* transportable.
транспортёр *m.* conveyor.
транспорти́р *m.* protractor.
транспорти́ровать OVA *impf. and pf.* to transport.
транспортиро́вка *f.* transporting.
тра́нспортник *m.* transport worker.
тра́нспортный *adj.* (*attrib.*) transport.
транссиби́рский *adj.* trans-Siberian.
трансформа́тор *m.* (*elec.*) transformer.
трансформа́ция *f.* transformation.
трансформи́ровать OVA *impf. and pf.* to transform.
трансцендента́льный *adj.* transcendental.
трансценде́нтный *adj.* transcendent; transcendental.

транше́йный *adj.* (*attrib.*) trench.
транше́я *f.* trench.
трап *m.* **1.** ship's ladder. **2.** boarding ramp.
тра́пеза *f.* food; meal (*in monastery*).
тра́пезная *f.* refectory (*in monastery*).
тра́пезный *adj.* (*attrib.*) meal; dining.
трапе́ция *f.* **1.** (*geom.*) trapezoid. **2.** trapeze.
тра́сса *f.* route; highway.
трасса́нт *m.* (*comm.*) drawer.
трасси́ровать OVA *impf. and pf.* to trace (*on a map*).
трасси́рующий *adj.* tracer.
тра́та *f.* **1.** expense; expenditure. **2.** waste.
тра́тить *impf. pf.* **ис-, по- 1.** to spend. **2.** to waste.
тра́улер *m.* trawler.
тра́ур *m.* mourning.
тра́урница *f.* (*butterfly*) mourning cloak.
тра́урный *adj.* (*attrib.*) mourning.
трафаре́т *m.* **1.** stencil. **2.** stereotype.
трафаре́тный *adj.* stenciled.
трах *interj.* bang!
трахе́йный *adj.* tracheal.
трахе́я *f.* trachea.
тра́хнуть *pf.* **1.** to shoot. **2.** (*of a sound* or *a shot*) to ring out. **3.** to bang; to smash; to hit.
трахо́ма *f.* trachoma.
тре́ба *f.* religious rite performed by demand (*marriage, funeral, etc.*).
тре́бование *neut.* **1.** demand. **2.** requisition; order.
— **тре́бования** *pl.* requirements.
тре́бовательный *adj.* demanding, exacting.
тре́бовать OVA *impf. pf.* **по-** to demand; to require.
требуха́ *f.* entrails.
трево́га *f.* alarm.
трево́жить *impf.* **1.** *pf.* **по-** to disturb. **2.** *pf.* **вс-** to worry, to trouble.
трево́жный *adj.* anxious.
треволне́ние *neut.* (*colloq.*) worry; agitation.
тре́звенник *m. f.* **тре́звенница** (*colloq.*) teetotaler.
трезве́ть *impf. pf.* **о-** to sober up.
трезво́н *m.* **1.** ring or peal (of bells). **2.** (*colloq.*) gossip; rumors. **3.** (*colloq.*) row; ruckus.
тре́звость *f.* sobriety.
трезву́чие *neut.* (*mus.*) triad.
тре́звый *adj.* sober.
трезу́бец FILL *m.* trident.
трек *m.* track, racetrack.
тре́ковый *adj.* (*attrib.*) track.
трель *f.* trill; warble.
трелья́ж *m.* trellis.
тре́моло *neut. indecl.* tremolo.
тре́нер *m.* (*sports*) coach.
тре́нзель *m.* snaffle.
тре́ние *neut.* friction.
трениро́ванный *adj.* trained.
тренирова́ть OVA *impf. pf.* **на-** *v.t.* to train.
трениро́вка *f.* **1.** training. **2.** workout.
трениро́вочный *adj.* (*attrib.*) training.
трено́га *f.* tripod.
трено́гий *adj.* three-legged.
трено́жник *m.* tripod.
трепа́к *m.* trepak (*folk dance*).
трепа́лка *f.* scutch; swingle.
трепа́ло *neut.* scutch; swingle.
трёпаный *adj.* (*colloq.*) tattered; ragged.

трепа́ть *impf. pres.* **треплю́, тре́плешь** *pf.* **по- 1.** to dishevel; to tousle. **2.** to fray; to wear out. **3.** (*colloq.*) to chatter; to babble.
тре́пет *m.* quiver, quivering.
трепета́ние *neut.* quivering; trembling.
трепета́ть *impf.* to quiver, to tremble.
тре́петно *adv.* with a quiver.
тре́петный *adj.* **1.** quivering; flickering. **2.** trembling. **3.** fearful.
трёпка *f.* (*colloq.*) beating; trashing.
треск *m.* crackle, crack.
треска́ *f.* cod.
треско́вый *adj.* (*attrib.*) cod; codfish.
трескотня́ *f.* (*colloq.*) rattle.
треску́чий моро́з *m.* (*colloq.*) bitter cold.
тре́снуть *pf.* **1.** to crack. **2.** to burst.
трест *m.* (*econ.*) trust.
трете́йский *adj.* of arbitration. — **трете́йский суд** *m.* court of arbitration.
тре́тий *adj.* third.
трети́ровать OVA *impf.* to slight; to snub.
трети́чный *adj.* tertiary.
треть *f.* a third.
тре́тье *neut.* third course; dessert.
третьесо́ртный *adj.* third-rate.
третьестепе́нный *adj.* insignificant.
треуго́лка *f.* cocked hat.
треуго́льник *m.* triangle.
треуго́льный *adj.* triangular.
трефно́е *neut.* non-kosher food.
трефно́й *adj.* (*of food*) non-kosher.
трефо́вый *adj.* (*cards*) of clubs.
тре́фы *pl.* (*cards*) clubs.
трёхвале́нтный *adj.* trivalent.
трёхгла́вый *adj.* three-headed.
трёхгоди́чный *adj.* (*attrib.*) three-year.
трёхгодова́лый *adj.* three-year-old.
трёхгра́ник *m.* trihedron.
трёхгра́нный *adj.* trihedral.
трёхдне́вный *adj.* (*attrib.*) three-day.
трёхколёсный *adj.* three-wheeled.
трёхко́мнатный *adj.* three-room.
трёхле́тие *neut.* third anniversary.
трёхле́тний *adj.* (*attrib.*) three-year.
трёхме́рный *adj.* three-dimensional.
трёхме́сячный *adj.* (*attrib.*) three-month.
трёхнеде́льный *adj.* (*attrib.*) three-week.
трёхсло́жный *adj.* three-syllable.
трёхсотле́тие *neut.* three-hundredth anniversary; tercentenary.
трёхсотле́тний *adj.* (*attrib.*) three-hundred-year.
трёхсо́тый *adj.* three hundredth.
трёхсторо́нний *adj.* three-sided.
трёхцве́тный *adj.* three-colored; tricolored.
трёхчасово́й *adj.* (*attrib.*) three-hour.
трёхчле́н *m.* trinomial.
трёхчле́нный *adj.* trinomial.
трёхэта́жный *adj.* three-story.
треща́ние *neut.* cracking; crackling.
треща́ть *impf.* **1.** to crack, to crackle. **2.** to chirp, to chatter.
тре́щина *f.* **1.** crack; split. **2.** cleft; fissure.
трещо́тка *f.* **1.** rattle. **2.** ratchet drill. **3.** *m.* and *f.* (*decl. f.*) (*colloq.*) chatterbox.
три *num.* three.
триа́да *f.* triad.

триангуля́ция *f.* triangulation.
триа́совый *adj.* Triassic.
трибу́н *m.* tribune.
трибу́на *f.* rostrum; grandstand.
трибуна́л *m.* tribunal.
тривиа́льность *f.* banality.
тривиа́льный *adj.* trite; banal.
тригонометри́ческий *adj.* trigonometrical.
тригономе́трия *f.* trigonometry.
три́девять *num.* (*colloq.*): **за три́девять земе́ль** at the other end of the world.
тридцатиле́тний *adj.* (*attrib.*) thirty-year.
тридца́тый *adj.* thirtieth.
три́дцать *num.* thirty.
Трие́ст *m.* Trieste.
три́жды *adv.* thrice.
тризм *m.* lockjaw.
трико́ *neut. indecl.* tricot.
трикота́ж *m.* **1.** knitted fabric. **2.** knitted wear.
трикота́жный *adj.* knitted.
триктра́к *m.* backgammon.
трили́стник *m.* trefoil; shamrock.
триллио́н *m.* quadrillion (*U.S.*); trillion (*British*).
трило́гия *f.* trilogy.
триме́стр *m.* trimester.
трина́дцатый *adj.* thirteenth.
трина́дцать *num.* thirteen.
Тринида́д *m.* Trinidad.
тринитротолуо́л *m.* trinitrotoluene.
три́о *neut. indecl.* trio.
трио́д *m.* triode.
трио́ль *f.* (*mus.*) triplet.
три́ппер *m.* gonorrhea.
три́птих *m.* triptych.
три́ста *num.* three hundred.
три́тий *m.* tritium.
трито́н *m.* newt.
триумви́р *m.* triumvir.
триумвира́т *m.* triumvirate.
триу́мф *m.* triumph.
триумфа́льный *adj.* triumphal.
трихи́на *f.* trichina.
трихинеллёз *m.* trichinosis.
тро́гательность *f.* poignancy.
тро́гательный *adj.* touching.
тро́гать *impf. pf.* **тро́нуть** to touch; to move (*emotionally*).
тро́е *num.* (*coll.*) three.
троекра́тный *adj.* three-time.
Тро́ица *f.* Trinity. — **тро́ица** (*colloq.*) trio.
Тро́ицын День *m.* Whitsunday.
тро́йка *f.* **1.** the numeral three. **2.** troika. **3.** (*school mark*) three (*signifying "satisfactory"*). **4.** (*cards*) three.
тройно́й *adj.* triple.
тро́йня *f.* triplets.
тро́йственный *adj.* triple.
тролле́йбус *m.* trolley bus.
тролле́йбусный *adj.* of a trolley bus.
тролль *m.* (*folklore*) troll.
тромб *m.* blood clot. — **тромбо́з** *m.* thrombosis.
тромбо́н *m.* trombone. —**и́ст** *m.* trombonist.
трон *m.* throne.
тро́нный *adj.* (*attrib.*) throne.
тро́нутый *adj.* touched; moved (*emotionally*).
тро́нуть *pf.* of **тро́гать**.

троп *m.* trope.
тропá *f.* path.
трóпики *pl.* tropics.
тропи́нка *f.* path; track.
тропи́ческий *adj.* tropical.
тропосфéра *f.* troposphere.
трос *m.* rope; cable.
тростни́к *m.* reed.
тростникóвый *adj.* (*attrib.*) reed; rush.
трóсточка *f.* cane.
трость *f.* cane.
тротуáр *m.* pavement; sidewalk.
трофéй *m.* trophy.
трофéйный *adj.* looted.
трохеи́ческий *adj.* trochaic.
трохéй *m.* trochee.
трою́родный брат *m. f.* трою́родная сестрá second cousin.
троя́кий *adj.* triple; threefold.
троя́нский *adj.* Trojan.
трубá *f.* **1.** pipe. **2.** chimney, smokestack. **3.** (*mus.*) trumpet.
трубадýр *m.* troubadour.
трубáч *m.* trumpeter; trumpet player.
труби́ть *impf. pf.* про- **1.** (в *with acc.*) to blow (*a trumpet*). **2.** to sound (*a signal*). **3.** (*colloq.*) to crow about.
трýбка *f.* **1.** tube; pipe. **2.** (telephone) receiver. **3.** pipe (*for smoking*).
трубкозýб *m.* aardvark.
трýбный *adj.* (*attrib.*) pipe; trumpet.
трубопровóд *m.* pipe; pipeline; conduit.
трубочи́ст *m.* chimney sweep.
трýбочный *adj.* (*attrib.*) pipe.
трýбчатый *adj.* tubular.
труд *m.* **1.** labor, work. **2.** trouble, difficulty.
труди́ться *impf.* to work, to toil.
трýдно *adv.* with difficulty.
трýдность *f.* difficulty.
трýдный *adj.* difficult.
трудовóй *adj.* (*attrib.*) labor.
трудодéнь FILL *m.* workday (*unit of payment on collective farms*).
трудоёмкий *adj.* labor-intensive.
трудолюби́вый *adj.* industrious, hard-working.
трудолю́бие *neut.* industriousness.
трудоспосóбность *f.* ability to work.
трудоспосóбный *adj.* able to work; able-bodied.
трудоустрóйство *neut.* job placement.
трудя́щийся *m.* worker.
трýженик *m. f.* трýженица worker; toiler.
труни́ть *impf.* (над *with instr.*) (*colloq.*) to make fun of; to mock.
труп *m.* corpse.
трýпный *adj.* of a corpse.
трýппа *f.* troupe, company.
трус *m. f.* —и́ха coward.
трýсики *pl.* shorts; panties.
трýсить *impf. pf.* с- to be a coward; to get cold feet.
трусли́вый *adj.* cowardly.
трýсость *f.* cowardice.
трусцá *f.* (*colloq.*) jogging.
трусы́ *pl.* **1.** shorts. **2.** underpants; undershorts.
трут *m.* tinder.
трýтень FILL *m.* drone.

трухá *f.* **1.** dust (*of rotted wood, etc.*). **2.** bits (*of hay or straw*). **3.** (*colloq.*) trash.
трухля́вый *adj.* rotten.
трущóба *f.* **1.** thicket. **2.** out-of-the-way place. **3.** slum.
трын-травá *pred.* (*with dat.*) (*colloq.*) all the same.
трюи́зм *m.* truism.
трюк *m.* trick; stunt.
трю́ковый *adj.* (*attrib.*) trick.
трюм *m.* hold of a ship.
трюмó *neut. indecl.* **1.** cheval glass; pier glass. **2.** (*archit.*) pier.
трю́фель *m.* truffle.
тряпи́чник *m. f.* тряпи́чница ragman.
тряпи́чный *adj.* (*attrib.*) rag.
тря́пка *f.* rag. — тря́пки *pl.* (*colloq.*) clothes.
тряпьё *neut.* rags.
тряси́на *f.* quagmire.
тря́ска *f.* shaking.
тря́ский *adj.* **1.** (*of a vehicle*) shaky. **2.** (*of a road*) bumpy.
трясогýзка *f.* (*bird*) wagtail.
трясти́ *impf. pf.* тряхнýть **1.** to shake. **2.** to shake out. **3.** *impers.* to be shaking.
трясти́сь *impf. v.i.* to shake, to tremble.
тсс *interj.* hush!
тсýга *f.* (*tree*) hemlock.
ту *adj., f. acc. of* тот.
тýба *f.* tuba.
туберкулёз *m.* tuberculosis.
туберкулёзный *adj.* tubercular.
туберóза *f.* tuberose.
Тувá *f.* Tuva.
туви́нец FILL *m. f.* туви́нка Tuvinian.
тýго *adv.* **1.** tightly, fast. **2.** (*colloq.*) with difficulty.
тугодýм *m. f.* —ка dimwit.
тугóй *adj.* tight.
тугоýхий *adj.* hard of hearing.
тудá *adv.* there, to that place.
тудá-сюдá *adv.* (*colloq.*) **1.** here and there. **2.** all right. **3.** so-so; passable.
тужи́ть *impf.* (*colloq.*) to grieve.
тýжиться *impf.* (*colloq.*) to exert oneself.
тужýрка *f.* man's double-breasted jacket.
туз *m.* (*cards*) ace.
тузéмный *adj.* native.
тукáн *m.* toucan.
Тýла *f.* Tula.
тýлий *m.* thulium.
тýловище *neut.* trunk; torso.
Тулýза *f.* Toulouse.
тулýп *m.* sheepskin coat.
тумáк *m.* (*colloq.*) wallop; clout.
тумáн *m.* fog, mist. —ный *adj.* foggy, misty.
тумáнность *f.* fogginess; (*astr.*) nebula.
тýмба *f.* **1.** curbside post. **2.** stand; pedestal. **3.** advertisement kiosk.
тýмбочка *f.* night table.
тунг *m.* tung tree.
тýнговый *adj.* (*attrib.*) tung.
Тунгýска *f.* (*river*) Tunguska.
тýндра *f.* tundra.
тýндровый *adj.* (*attrib.*) tundra.
тунéц FILL *m.* tuna.

туне́ядец FILL *m. f.* туне́ядка parasite; sponger.
туне́ядство *neut.* parasitism.
туни́ка *f.* tunic (*worn in ancient times*).
Туни́с *m.* Tunis.
тунне́ль *m.* tunnel.
тупе́ть *impf.* **1.** to become dull. **2.** to become blunt.
ту́пик *m.* (*bird*) puffin.
тупи́к *m.* **1.** blind alley. **2.** deadlock.
тупи́ца *m.* and *f.* (*decl. f.*) (*colloq.*) dimwit.
тупоголо́вый *adj.* (*colloq.*) thickheaded.
тупо́й *adj.* dull; blunt.
ту́пость *f.* dullness; obtuseness.
тупоу́мный *adj.* dimwitted.
Тур *m.* Tours.
тур¹ *m.* **1.** round (*of a tournament* or *negotiations*). **2.** turn (*in dancing*). **3.** stage; phase.
тур² *f.* aurochs.
тура́ *f.* (*chess*) castle; rook.
турба́за *f.* tourist center.
турби́на *f.* turbine.
турби́нный *adj.* (*attrib.*) turbine.
турбовинтово́й *adj.* (*attrib.*) turboprop.
турбореакти́вный *adj.* (*attrib.*) turbojet.
туре́цкий *adj.* Turkish.
тури́зм *m.* tourism.
тури́ст *m. f.* —ка tourist.
турести́ческий *adj.* (*attrib.*) tourist.
тури́стский *adj.* (*attrib.*) tourist.
туркме́н *m. f.* —ка Turkmen.
Туркмениста́н *m.* Turkmenistan.
турмали́н *m.* tourmaline.
турне́ *neut. indecl.* tour.
тури́к *m.* (*sports*) horizontal bar.
турнике́т *m.* turnstile.
турни́р *m.* tournament, contest.
ту́рок FILL *m. f.* турча́нка Turk.
турухта́н *m.* (*bird*) ruff.
Ту́рция *f.* Turkey.
ту́скло *adv.* dimly.
ту́склость *f.* dimness.
ту́склый *adj.* dim; dull.
тут *adv.* here.
ту́товая я́года *f.* mulberry.
ту́товник *m.* mulberry tree.
ту́товый *adj.* (*attrib.*) mulberry.
ту́фелька *f.* small shoe.
ту́фля *f.* slipper, shoe.
туфта́ *f.* (*slang*) **1.** baloney. **2.** padding; chiseling. **3.** inflated results.
ту́хлый *adj.* rotten.
тухля́тина *f.* (*colloq.*) food that has spoiled.
ту́хнуть¹ *impf. past* тух *or* ту́хнул, ту́хла *pf.* по- (*of s.t. burning*) to go out.
ту́хнуть² *impf. past* тух *or* ту́хнул, ту́хла *pf.* про- to spoil; to become rotten.
ту́ча *f.* **1.** cloud; storm cloud. **2.** (*fig.*) swarm.
ту́чный *adj.* **1.** obese, fat. **2.** (*of soil*) fertile.
туш *m.* (*mus.*) flourish.
ту́ша *f.* carcass.
туше́ *neut. indecl.* touch (*when playing a musical instrument*).
тушева́ть OVA *impf. pf.* за- **1.** to add shading to. **2.** to tone down.
тушёвка *f.* shading.
туше́ние *neut.* extinguishing.

тушёный *adj.* stewed.
туши́ть¹ *impf. pf.* по- to extinguish.
туши́ть² *impf. pf.* с- to stew.
тушка́нчик *m.* jerboa.
тушь *f.* India ink.
тща́тельно *adv.* carefully; thoroughly.
тща́тельность *f.* care.
тща́тельный *adj.* careful.
тщеду́шие *neut.* frailty.
тщеду́шный *adj.* frail.
тщесла́вие *neut.* vanity.
тщесла́вный *adj.* vain.
тще́тно *adv.* in vain.
тще́тность *f.* futility.
тще́тный *adj.* vain; futile.
тщи́ться *impf.* (*with infin.*) to take pains to; to try to.
ты *pers. pron. 2nd pers. sg.* you.
ты́кать¹ *impf. pf.* ткнуть to poke.
ты́кать² *impf.* (*colloq.*) to address someone with ты.
ты́ква *f.* pumpkin.
ты́квенный *adj.* (*attrib.*) pumpkin.
тыл *m.* rear.
тылово́й *adj.* rear.
ты́льный *adj.* rear.
тын *m.* paling; palisade; stockade.
ты́сяча *f.* a thousand.
тысячекра́тный *adj.* thousandfold.
тысячеле́тие *neut.* **1.** millenium. **2.** thousandth anniversary.
тысячеле́тний *adj.* (*attrib.*) thousand-year.
ты́сячная *f.* a thousandth.
ты́сячный *adj.* thousandth.
тычи́нка *f.* stamen.
тычо́к FILL *m.* (*colloq.*) poke; jab.
тьма *f.* dark, darkness.
тьфу *interj.* pah!, phooey!
тюбете́йка *f.* tyubeteyka (*embroidered skullcap worn in Central Asia*).
тю́бик *m.* tube (*for toothpaste, glue, etc.*)
тю́бинг *m.* tubing; piping.
тюк *m.* **1.** bale; package. **2.** bundle.
тю́кать *impf.* to bang.
тю́левый *adj.* tulle.
тюле́невый *also* тюле́ний *adj.* (*attrib.*) seal.
тюль *m.* tulle.
тюльпа́н *m.* tulip.
тюльпа́нный *adj.* (*attrib.*) tulip.
Тюме́нь *m.* Tyumen.
тюрба́н *m.* turban.
тюрбо́ *neut. indecl.* turbot; halibut.
тюре́мный *adj.* (*attrib.*) prison.
тюре́мщик *m. f.* тюре́мщица jailer.
тю́ркский *adj.* Turkic.
тюрьма́ *f.* prison.
тюфя́к *m.* straw mattress.
тя́вкать *impf. pf.* тя́вкнуть to yap; to yelp.
тя́га *f.* **1.** thrust (*of engine*); pulling power. **2.** draft (*of chimney*). **3.** traction. — дать тя́гу *impf.* (*colloq.*) to take to one's heels.
тяга́ч *m.* tractor (*for hauling trailers*).
тягло́ *neut.* (*hist.*) tax.
тя́гловый¹ *adj.* (*of animals*) draft.
тя́гловый² *adj.* (*hist.*) taxed.
тя́глый *adj.* (*of animals*) draft.

тя́говый *adj.* tractive.

тя́гостный *adj.* **1.** burdensome. **2.** painful; distressing.

тя́гость *f.* burden.

тягота́ *m.* burden.

тяготе́ние *neut.* **1.** gravitation. **2.** attraction; inclination.

тяготе́ть *impf.* (**к** *with dat.*) to gravitate (towards).

тяготи́ть *impf.* to be a burden.

тягу́честь *f.* **1.** stretchability; ductility. **2.** viscosity.

тягу́чий *adj.* **1.** stretchable; ductile. **2.** viscous. **3.** (*fig.*) slow; leisurely. **4.** (*fig.*) dull; boring.

тя́жба *f.* (*obs.*) lawsuit.

тяжело́ *adv.* **1.** heavily. **2.** gravely; seriously. — *adj.* (*pred.*) hard; difficult; wretched; painful.

тяжелоатле́т *m.* weightlifter.

тяжелове́с *m.* (*sports*) heavyweight.

тяжелове́сный *adj.* ponderous.

тяжёлый *adj.* **1.** heavy. **2.** severe. **3.** hard, difficult.

тя́жесть *f.* **1.** weight; gravity. **2.** heaviness.

тя́жкий *adj.* **1.** heavy. **2.** grave, serious.

тяну́ть *impf. pf.* **по-** to pull, to draw, to tow. —**ся 1.** to stretch (out). **2.** to drag on. **3.** to last.

тяну́чка *f.* taffy.

тя́пка *f.* chopper; chopping knife.

тя́тя *m.* (*obs.*) (*colloq.*) dad; pop.

у

у *prep.* (*with gen.*) **1.** at, by. **2.** with, at. **3.** from, of. **4.** in. **5.** (*possession*): **у меня** I have, **у тебя** you have, *etc.*

убавля́ть *impf. pf.* **уба́вить** *v.t.* to reduce.

убаю́кивать *impf. pf.* **убаю́кать** to lull (to sleep).

убега́ть *impf. pf.* **убежа́ть** to run away; to flee.

убеди́тельно *adv.* convincingly.

убеди́тельность *f.* persuasiveness.

убеди́тельный *adj.* convincing, persuasive.

убежда́ть *impf. pf.* **убеди́ть** (**в** *with prep.*) to convince (of); to persuade.

убежде́ние *neut.* **1.** conviction. **2.** persuasion.

убежде́нно *adv.* with conviction.

убежде́нность *f.* conviction; certainty.

убежде́нный *adj.* **1.** convinced. **2.** confirmed.

убе́жище *neut.* refuge; sanctuary; asylum.

убива́ть *impf. pf.* **уби́ть** to kill, to murder.

уби́йственный *adj.* deadly; murderous.

уби́йство *neut.* murder.

уби́йца *m.* and *f.* (*decl. f.*) murderer.

убира́ть *impf. pf.* **убра́ть** **1.** to remove. **2.** to put away. **3.** to harvest. **4.** to clean *or* tidy up. **5.** to decorate.

уби́тый *adj.* **1.** murdered. **2.** killed. **3.** crushed (*in spirit*).

уби́ть *pf. of* **убива́ть**.

ублю́док FILL *m.* (*colloq.*) cur; mongrel.

убо́гий *adj.* wretched; squalid.

убо́гость *f.* utter poverty; squalor.

убо́жество *neut.* poverty.

убо́й *m.* slaughter.

убо́йный *adj.* (*of animals*) to be slaughtered.

убо́р *m.* (*obs.*) attire.

убо́ристый *adj.* (*of writing*) close.

убо́рка *f.* **1.** harvest, harvesting. **2.** cleaning.

убо́рная *f.* **1.** bathroom; lavatory; toilet. **2.** (*theat.*) dressing room.

убо́рочный *adj.* (*attrib.*) harvesting.

убо́рщик *m.* janitor.

убо́рщица *f.* cleaning woman.

убра́нство *neut.* furnishings.

убра́ть *pf. of* **убира́ть**.

убыва́ть *impf. pf.* **убы́ть** *v.i.* to decrease.

у́быль *f.* decrease, diminution.

убы́ток FILL *m.* loss.

убы́точный *adj.* losing, unprofitable.

убы́ть *pf. of* **убыва́ть**.

уважа́емый *adj.* respected, esteemed.

уважа́ть *impf.* to respect, to esteem.

уваже́ние *neut.* respect.

уважи́тельный *adj.* **1.** respectful; deferential. **2.** legitimate.

у́валень FILL *m.* (*colloq.*) lout.

уведомле́ние *neut.* notification; information.

уведомля́ть *impf. pf.* **уве́домить** to notify; to inform.

увезти́ *pf. of* **увози́ть**.

увекове́чивать *impf. pf.* **увекове́чить** to immortalize; to perpetuate.

увеличе́ние *neut.* increase.

увели́чивать *impf. pf.* **увели́чить** *v.t.* to increase, to enlarge.

увеличи́тель *m.* (*photog.*) enlarger.

увеличи́тельный *adj.* magnifying.

увере́ние *neut.* assurance.

уве́ренность *f.* **1.** confidence. **2.** assurance.

уве́ренный *adj.* **1.** assured, certain. **2.** confident.

уверну́ться *pf.* (**от** *with gen.*) to dodge; to evade.

уве́ровать OVA *pf.* (**в** *with acc.*) to come to believe in.

уве́ртка *f.* (*colloq.*) subterfuge; dodge.

уве́ртливый *adj.* evasive; shifty.

увертю́ра *f.* overture.

уверя́ть *impf. pf.* **уве́рить** **1.** to assure. **2.** to convince.

увеселе́ние *neut.* entertainment.

увесели́тельный *adj.* (*attrib.*) amusement.

увеселя́ть *impf.* to amuse.

уве́систый *adj.* weighty; heavy.

увести́ *pf. of* **уводи́ть**.

уве́чить *impf.* to mutilate; to cripple.

уве́чье *neut.* mutilation.

увеща́ние *neut.* exhortation; admonition.

увещева́ть *also* **увеща́ть** *impf.* to admonish.

увида́ть *pf.* (*colloq.*) to see. —**ся** *v.i.* to meet; to get together.

уви́деть **1.** *pf. of* **ви́деть**. **2.** to catch sight of.

увлажне́ние *neut.* moistening.

увлажня́ть *impf. pf.* **увлажни́ть** to moisten.

увлека́тельный *adj.* fascinating; captivating.

увлека́ть *impf. pf.* **увле́чь** **1.** to fascinate, to captivate. **2.** to carry away *or* off.

увлека́ющийся *adj.* easily carried away.

увлече́ние *neut.* **1.** animation. **2.** (*with instr.*) passion (for).

увлечённый *adj.* enthusiastic.

увлечённость *m.* enthusiasm.

уво́д *m.* **1.** evacuation; withdrawal. **2.** theft.

уводи́ть *impf. pf.* **увести́** to take away; to steal.

уво́з *m.* abduction.

увози́ть *impf. pf.* **увезти́** **1.** to take *or* carry away (*by vehicle*). **2.** to kidnap.

увольне́ние *neut.* **1.** discharge; firing (*from work*). **2.** dismissal.

увольни́тельный *adj.*: **увольни́тельная запи́ска** *f.* written leave of absence.

увольня́ть *impf. pf.* **уво́лить** **1.** to discharge; to fire (*from work*); to dismiss. **2.** (**от** *with gen.*) to spare from.

увы́ *interj.* alas!

увяда́ть *impf. pf.* **увя́нуть** **1.** to fade. **2.** to wither; to droop.

увя́дший *adj.* withered; faded.

увя́зка *f.* **1.** tying up. **2.** tying together; coordination.

увя́зывать *impf. pf.* **увяза́ть** **1.** to tie *or* pack up. **2.** to coordinate.

уга́дчик *m. f.* **уга́дчица** (*colloq.*) guesser.

уга́дывать *impf. pf.* **угада́ть** to guess.

уга́р *m.* **1.** carbon-monoxide fumes. **2.** carbon-monoxide poisoning. **3.** (*fig.*) ecstasy; intoxication.

уга́рный *adj.* (*attrib.*) carbon-monoxide.

угаса́ние *neut.* fading; waning.

угаса́ть *impf.* *pf.* уга́снуть to fade, to die away.

углево́д *m.* carbohydrate.

углеводоро́д *m.* hydrocarbon.

углекислота́ *f.* carbonic acid.

углеки́слый *adj.* carbonate (of).

углеко́п *m.* (*obs.*) coal miner.

углепромы́шленность *f.* coal industry.

углеро́д *m.* carbon.

углеро́дистый *adj.* carbon.

У́глич *m.* Uglich.

углова́тый *adj.* angular; awkward.

углово́й *adj.* 1. (*attrib.*) corner. 2. angular.

углубле́ние *neut.* 1. deepening. 2. hollow.

углублённый *adj.* sunken.

углубля́ть *pf.* углуби́ть *v.t.* to deepen. —ся 1. to become deeper. 2. (*fig.*) to become absorbed (in). 3. to delve (in).

угнета́тель *m. f.* —ница oppressor.

угнета́ть *impf.* 1. to oppress. 2. to depress.

угнете́ние *neut.* 1. oppression. 2. dejection; depression.

угнетённый *adj.* oppressed.

угова́ривать *impf.* *pf.* уговори́ть to persuade.

угово́р *m.* 1. persuasion. 2. (*colloq.*) agreement.

уго́да *f.*: в уго́ду (*with dat.*) to please.

угоди́ть *pf.* *of* угожда́ть.

уго́дливый *adj.* obsequious; officious.

уго́дник *m. f.* уго́дница (*colloq.*) sycophant.

уго́дничество *neut.* obsequiousness; servility.

уго́дно *pred.* (*with dat.*): как вам уго́дно as you please.

уго́дный *adj.* (*with dat.*) pleasing to.

уго́дье *neut.* area of economic significance *or* use.

угожда́ть *impf.* *pf.* угоди́ть to please.

у́гол FILL *m.* 1. corner. 2. angle.

уголёк FILL *m.* small piece of coal.

уголо́вник *m. f.* уголо́вница criminal.

уголо́вный *adj.* criminal; penal.

уголо́вщина *f.* (*colloq.*) criminal acts.

уголо́к FILL *m.* corner, nook.

у́голь FILL *m.* coal.

у́гольник *m.* 1. drawing triangle. 2. try square.

у́гольный *adj.* (*attrib.*) coal.

у́гольный *adj.* (*colloq.*) (*attrib.*) corner.

у́гольщик *m. f.* у́гольщица coal miner.

угомони́ть *pf.* (*colloq.*) to calm; to calm down.

уго́н *m.* driving away.

угоня́ть *impf.* *pf.* угна́ть 1. to drive away. 2. to hijack (*a vehicle* or *aircraft*). 3. (*colloq.*) to steal (*cattle*).

угора́здить *pf.* (*with infin., usually impers.*) to urge; to make.

угоре́лый *adj.* (*colloq.*) crazy; mad.

у́горь[1] FILL *m.* blackhead.

у́горь[2] FILL *m.* eel.

угоща́ть *impf.* *pf.* угости́ть to entertain, to treat.

угоще́ние *neut.* 1. entertaining. 2. food; refreshments.

угрожа́ть *impf.* to threaten.

угрожа́ющий *adj.* threatening.

угро́за *f.* threat; menace.

угрызе́ния со́вести *pl.* pangs of conscience.

угрю́мость *f.* sullenness.

угрю́мый *adj.* 1. sullen. 2. morose.

уда́в *m.* boa; boa constrictor.

удава́ться *impf.* *pf.* уда́ться 1. to work *or* turn out successfully. 2. *impers.* (*with dat.* and *infin.*) to succeed.

удави́ть *pf.* to strangle.

удавле́ние *neut.* strangulation.

удале́ние *neut.* withdrawal; removal.

удалённый *adj.* remote.

удалённость *f.* remoteness.

удале́ц FILL *m.* daring person.

удало́й *also* уда́лый *adj.* bold; daring; dashing.

у́даль *f.* boldness; bravado.

удальство́ *neut.* (*colloq.*) boldness; bravado.

удаля́ть *impf.* *pf.* удали́ть to remove; to extract.

уда́р *m.* 1. blow. 2. (*med.*) stroke.

ударе́ние *neut.* 1. stress; accent. 2. (*gram.*) accent mark. 3. (*fig.*) emphasis.

уда́рник[1] *m. f.* уда́рница shock worker.

уда́рник[2] *m.* firing pin.

уда́рник[3] *m.* drummer.

уда́рный *adj.* 1. (*attrib.*) shock. 2. accelerated. 3. percussive, percussion. 4. accented.

ударя́ть *impf.* *pf.* уда́рить to strike; to hit.

уда́ться *pf.* *of* удава́ться.

уда́ча *f.* success.

уда́чливый *adj.* lucky.

уда́чник *m. f.* уда́чница lucky person.

уда́чно *adv.* successfully.

уда́чный *adj.* successful.

удва́ивать *impf.* *pf.* удво́ить *v.t.* to double; to re-double.

удвое́ние *neut.* doubling.

уде́л *m.* lot, destiny.

уде́льный *adj.* specific.

уделя́ть *impf.* *pf.* удели́ть to spare; to give.

у́держ *m.*: без у́держу without restraint.

удержа́ние *neut.* 1. deduction. 2. retention, keeping.

уде́рживать *impf.* *pf.* удержа́ть to restrain; to retain; to hold (back). —ся 1. to refrain (from). 2. to hold one's ground.

удешевля́ть *impf.* *pf.* удешеви́ть to cheapen; to reduce the price of.

удиви́тельно *adv.* 1. surprisingly. 2. extremely. 3. marvelously. — *adj.* (*pred.*) surprising.

удиви́тельный *adj.* 1. surprising. 2. wonderful. 3. marvelous.

удивле́ние *neut.* surprise.

удивлённо *adv.* in surprise.

удивлённый *adj.* surprised.

удивля́ть *impf.* *pf.* удиви́ть to astonish; to amaze; to surprise.

удила́ *pl.* bit.

уди́лище *neut.* fishing rod.

уди́льщик *m. f.* уди́льщица angler.

удира́ть *impf.* *pf.* удра́ть (*colloq.*) to run away.

уди́ть *impf.* *pres.* ужу́, у́дишь to fish for.

удлине́ние *neut.* lengthening.

удлинённый *adj.* oblong; elongated.

удлини́тель *m.* extension cord.

удлини́тельный *adj.* (*attrib.*) extension.

удлиня́ть *impf.* *pf.* удлини́ть to lengthen.

удо́бно *adv.* comfortably. — *adj.* (*pred.*) 1. (*with dat.*) comfortable. 2. (*with dat.*) convenient. 3. all right.

удо́бный *adj.* comfortable; convenient.

удобо- *prefix* easy to.

удобовари́мость *f.* digestibility.

удобовари́мый *adj.* digestible.

удобоисполни́мый *adj.* easy to perform.

удобочита́емый *adj.* easy to read.

удобре́ние *neut.* fertilization.

удо́бство *neut.* comfort.

удовлетворе́ние *neut.* satisfaction.

удовлетворённость *f.* satisfaction.

удовлетворённый *adj.* contented; satisfied.

удовлетвори́тельно *adv.* **1.** satisfactorily. **2.** (*school grade*) "satisfactory."

удовлетвори́тельный *adj.* satisfactory.

удовлетворя́ть *impf. pf.* удовлетвори́ть to satisfy.

удово́льствие *neut.* pleasure.

удо́й *m.* **1.** milking. **2.** yield of milk.

удо́йный *adj.* (*of dairy animal*) giving much milk.

удостовере́ние *neut.* certificate.

удостоверя́ть *impf. pf.* удостове́рить **1.** to certify. **2.** to attest.

у́дочка *f.* fishing rod.

удра́ть *pf. of* удира́ть.

удруча́ть *impf. pf.* удручи́ть to depress.

удручённый *adj.* depressed; despondent.

удуша́ть *impf. pf.* удуши́ть **1.** to smother; to suffocate. **2.** to stifle.

удуше́ние *neut.* suffocation.

уду́шливый *adj.* suffocating.

уду́шье *neut.* difficulty in breathing.

уедине́ние *neut.* solitude.

уединённый *adj.* solitary.

уе́зд *m.* district. —ный *adj.* (*attrib.*) district.

уезжа́ть *impf. pf.* уе́хать to leave; to depart.

уж¹ *adv., see* уже́. — *particle* really.

уж² *m.* grass snake.

ужа́лить *pf. of* жа́лить.

у́жас *m.* horror; terror.

ужаса́ть *impf. pf.* ужасну́ть to terrify; to horrify; to awe.

ужа́сно *adv.* terribly; awfully.

ужа́сный *adj.* horrible; terrible.

У́жгород *m.* Uzhhorod.

у́же *adj., comp. of* у́зкий.

уже́ *adv.* already.

уже́ние *neut.* fishing; angling.

ужива́ться *impf. pf.* ужи́ться (с *with instr.*) to get along with.

ужи́вчивый *adj.* easygoing.

ужи́мка *f.* grimace.

у́жин *m.* supper.

у́жинать *impf. pf.* по- to have supper.

узаконе́ние *neut.* legalization.

узаконя́ть *impf. pf.* узако́нить to legalize.

узбе́к *m. f.* узбе́чка Uzbek.

узда́ *f.* bridle.

узде́чка *f.* bridle.

у́зел FILL *m.* **1.** knot. **2.** junction; hub.

узело́к FILL *m.* small knot.

у́зенький *adj.* (*colloq.*) narrow.

у́зкий *adj.* narrow.

у́зко *adv.* tightly.

узкоколе́йный *adj.* (*of a railroad*) narrow-gauge.

узколо́бый *adj.* narrow-minded.

узлова́тый *adj.* knotted; full of knots.

узлово́й *adj.* (*attrib.*) junction.

узнава́ние *neut.* recognition.

узнава́ть *impf. pf.* узна́ть **1.** to learn; to find out. **2.** to recognize.

у́зник *m. f.* у́зница prisoner.

узо́р *m.* pattern; design.

узо́рчатый *adj.* having a design.

у́зость *f.* narrowness.

узре́ть *pf. of* зреть.

узурпа́тор *m.* usurper.

узурпа́ция *f.* usurpation.

у́зы *pl.* bonds; ties.

у́йма *f.* (*colloq.*) (*with gen.*) heaps of; a lot of.

уйти́ *pf. of* уходи́ть.

ука́з *m.* edict.

указа́ние *neut.* indicating; indication. — указа́ния *pl.* directions; instructions.

ука́занный *adj.* indicated.

указа́тель *m.* **1.** pointer; indicator. **2.** directory. **3.** index.

указа́тельный *adj.* demonstrative; serving to indicate.

ука́зка *f.* pointer.

ука́зчик *m. f.* ука́зчица (*colloq.*) one who gives orders.

ука́зывать *impf. pf.* указа́ть **1.** to indicate. **2.** to show; to point to *or* out.

ука́тывать *impf. pf.* уката́ть to roll.

ука́чивать *impf. pf.* укача́ть to rock to sleep.

укла́д *m.* **1.** mode. **2.** system.

укла́дка *f.* **1.** laying. **2.** stacking; piling. **3.** arranging.

укла́дчик *m. f.* укла́дчица packer.

укла́дывать *impf. pf.* уложи́ть **1.** to lay. **2.** to pack. **3.** to put to bed. —ся to pack up.

укло́н *m.* **1.** slope. **2.** deviation.

уклоне́ние *neut.* **1.** deviation. **2.** evasion.

укло́нчивость *f.* evasiveness.

укло́нчивый *adj.* evasive.

уклоня́ться *impf. pf.* уклони́ться (от *with gen.*) to deviate; to evade.

уклю́чина *f.* oarlock.

уко́л *m.* prick, pricking.

укомплектова́ние *neut.* **1.** manning; staffing. **2.** bringing up to strength.

уко́р *m.* reproach.

укора́чивать *impf. pf.* укороти́ть to shorten.

укорени́вшийся *adj.* ingrained.

укореня́ться *impf. pf.* укорени́ться to take root; to become enrooted.

укори́зненный *adj.* reproachful.

укороти́ть *pf. of* укора́чивать.

укоря́ть *impf. pf.* укори́ть (в *with prep.*) to reproach (for).

укра́дкой *adv.* stealthily.

Украи́на *f.* Ukraine.

украи́нец FILL *m. f.* украи́нка Ukrainian.

укра́сть *pf. of* красть.

украша́ть *impf. pf.* укра́сить to adorn, to decorate.

украше́ние *neut.* decoration.

укрепле́ние *neut.* strengthening.

укрепля́ть *impf. pf.* укрепи́ть to strengthen, to fortify.

укро́мный *adj.* secluded.

укро́п *m.* dill.

укроти́тель *m. f.* —ница tamer.

укроща́ть *impf. pf.* укроти́ть to tame; to subdue.

укроще́ние *neut.* taming.

укрупне́ние *neut.* enlargement.

укрыва́тельство *neut.* concealment (*of a crime*).

укрыва́ть *impf. pf.* укры́ть to cover; to conceal; to harbor.

укры́тие *neut.* shelter; cover.

у́ксус *m.* vinegar.

уксуснокисслый *adj.* acetate (of).

у́ксусный *adj.* (*attrib.*) vinegar; acetic.

уку́с *m.* bite.

укуси́ть *pf. of* куса́ть.

уку́тывать *impf. pf.* уку́тать (в *with acc.*) to wrap (in).

ула́живать *impf. pf.* ула́дить to arrange; to settle.

Ула́н-Ба́тор *m.* Ulaanbaatar (*also: Ulan Bator*).

Ула́н-Удэ́ *m.* Ulan Ude.

у́лей FILL *m.* beehive.

улета́ть *impf. pf.* улете́ть to fly away *or* off.

ули́ка *f.* piece of evidence.

ули́тка *f.* snail.

ули́точная по́чта *f.* (*colloq.*) snail mail.

у́лица *f.* street.

уло́в *m.* catch (*quantity caught*).

улови́мый *adj.* audible; perceptible.

улови́ть *pf. of* ула́вливать.

уло́вка *f.* trick; trap; ruse.

уложе́ние *neut.* (*hist.*) law code.

уложи́ть(ся) *pf. of* укла́дывать(ся).

улучша́ть *impf. pf.* улу́чшить to improve; to better; to ameliorate.

улучше́ние *neut.* improvement.

улыба́ться *impf. pf.* улыбну́ться to smile.

улы́бка *f.* smile.

улы́бчивый *adj.* smiling.

ультима́тум *m.* ultimatum.

ультра- *prefix* ultra-.

ультразвуково́й *adj.* ultrasonic.

ультрамари́н *m.* ultramarine.

ультрамари́новый *adj.* ultramarine.

ультрасовреме́нный *adj.* ultramodern.

ультрафиоле́товый *adj.* ultraviolet.

ум *m.* mind; intellect.

умале́ние *neut.* belittling.

умалишённый *adj.* mentally deranged.

ума́лчивать *impf. pf.* умолча́ть to pass over in silence.

умаля́ть *impf. pf.* умали́ть to belittle; to disparage.

у́мбра *f.* umber.

У́мбрия *f.* (*province*) Umbria.

уме́лец FILL *m. f.* уме́лица skilled craftsman.

уме́лый *adj.* skillful.

уме́ние *neut.* skill.

уменьша́емое *neut.* (*math.*) minuend.

уменьша́ть *impf. pf.* уме́ньшить *v.t.* to decrease, to diminish.

уменьше́ние *neut.* reduction.

уменьши́тельный *adj.* (*gram.*) diminutive.

уме́ренность *f.* moderation.

умере́ть *pf. of* умира́ть.

уме́рший *adj., m.* the deceased.

умерщвле́ние *neut.* killing.

умерщвлённый *adj.* dead; killed.

умерщвля́ть *impf. pf.* умертви́ть to kill.

умеря́ть *impf. pf.* уме́рить to moderate.

уме́стно *adv.* appropriately; apt. — *adj.* (*pred.*) appropriate.

уме́стность *neut.* relevance; pertinence.

уме́стный *adj.* 1. proper. 2. to the point.

уме́ть *impf.* to know, to know how to.

умиле́ние *neut.* 1. tenderness. 2. deep feeling; deep emotion.

умили́тельный *adj.* touching; moving.

уми́льный *adj.* touching; affecting.

умиля́ть *impf. pf.* умили́ть to move; to touch.

умира́ние *neut.* dying.

умира́ть *impf. pf.* умере́ть to die.

умира́ющий *adj.* dying.

умиротворе́ние *neut.* pacification.

умля́ут *m.* umlaut.

умне́ть *impf. pf* по- to grow wiser.

у́мник *m.* (*colloq.*) smart aleck.

у́мница *m.* and *f.* (*decl. f.*) (*colloq.*) clever person.

у́мничать *impf.* (*colloq.*) 1. to show off one's intelligence. 2. to try to be clever.

умножа́ть *impf. pf.* умно́жить *v.t.* 1. to increase. 2. (*math.*) to multiply.

умноже́ние *neut.* multiplication.

у́мный *adj.* clever, intelligent.

умозаключа́ть *impf.* to conclude.

умозаключе́ние *neut.* conclusion; deduction.

умозре́ние *neut.* speculation.

умозри́тельный *adj.* speculative.

умоисступле́ние *neut.* frenzy.

у́молк *m.*: без у́молку endlessly; incessantly.

умолка́ть *impf. pf.* умо́лкнуть to become silent, to lapse into silence.

умолча́ние *neut.* failure to mention.

умолча́ть *pf. of* ума́лчивать.

умоля́ть *impf.* to entreat; to implore.

умонастрое́ние *neut.* frame of mind.

умопомеша́тельство *neut.* mental derangement.

умопомраче́ние *neut.* stupor; daze; trance.

умо́ра *f.* (*colloq.*) a scream; a hoot; a riot.

умори́тельный *adj.* (*colloq.*) hilarious.

умори́ть *pf.* 1. to kill. 2. to exhaust.

у́мственно *adv.* mentally.

у́мственный *adj.* mental, intellectual.

у́мствовать OVA *impf.* (*colloq.*) to philosophize, to reason.

умыва́льник *m.* washstand.

умыва́льный *adj.* (*attrib.*) wash; washing.

умыва́ние *neut.* washing.

умыва́ть *impf. pf.* умы́ть *v.t.* to wash.

у́мысел *m.* design; intent; intention.

умы́шленно *adv.* deliberately; intentionally.

умы́шленный *adj.* designed; intentional, deliberate.

умышля́ть *impf. pf.* умы́слить to design, to plan out.

умягча́ть *impf. pf.* умягчи́ть to soften.

унести́ *pf. of* уноси́ть.

униа́т *m.* Uniat.

униа́тский *adj.* Uniat.

универма́г *m.* (*abbr. of* универса́льный магази́н) department store.

универса́льность *f.* universality.

универса́льный *adj.* 1. universal. 2. veratile. 3. all-purpose.

университе́т *m.* university.

университе́тский *adj.* (*attrib.*) university.

унижа́ть *impf. pf.* уни́зить 1. to humble; to humiliate. 2. to abase; to belittle.

униже́ние *neut.* 1. humiliation. 2. abasement.

уни́женный *adj.* 1. humiliated. 2. abject.

унизи́тельный *adj.* humiliating; degrading.

уника́льный *adj.* unique.

у́никум *m.* unique person *or* object.

унима́ть *impf. pf.* **уня́ть 1.** to calm; to pacify. **2.** to suppress. **3.** to stop.

унисо́н *m.* unison.

унита́з *m.* toilet.

унифика́ция *f.* standardization.

унифици́ровать OVA *impf. and pf.* to standardize.

уничтожа́ть *impf. pf.* **уничто́жить 1.** to destroy; to annihilate. **2.** to eliminate; to abolish.

уничтожа́ющий *adj.* (*fig.*) scathing; devastating.

уничтоже́ние *neut.* **1.** destruction, annihilation. **2.** abolition.

у́ния *f.* union (*especially of churches*).

уноси́ть *impf. pf.* **унести́** to take *or* carry away; to carry off.

у́нтер-офице́р *m.* noncommissioned officer.

у́нция *f.* ounce.

уныва́ть *impf.* to lose heart; to be dejected.

уны́лый *adj.* dejected; dismal; cheerless.

уны́ние *neut.* despondency; dejection.

уня́ть *pf. of* **унима́ть.**

упа́док FILL *m.* decline; decay. — **упа́док сил** loss of strength.

упа́дочнический *adj.* decadent.

упа́дочничество *neut.* decadence.

упа́дочный *adj.* **1.** decadent. **2.** depressive.

упако́вка *f.* **1.** packing. **2.** packing material.

упако́вочный *adj.* (*attrib.*) packing.

упако́вщик *m. f.* **упако́вщица** packer.

упако́вывать *impf. pf.* **упакова́ть** to pack, to pack up.

упа́сть *pf. of* **па́дать** to fall.

упива́ться *impf. pf.* **упи́ться 1.** (*colloq.*) to get drunk. **2.** (*with instr.*) to revel in; to be intoxicated by.

упира́ться *impf. pf.* **упере́ться** *impf.* to rest *or* lean against; to rest on.

упи́танный *adj.* well-fed; plump.

упла́та *f.* payment.

упла́чивать *impf. pf.* **уплати́ть** to pay.

уплотне́ние *neut.* packing down; compression.

уплотни́тель *m.* seal.

уплотня́ть *impf. pf.* **уплотни́ть** to pack down; to compress.

уподобле́ние *neut.* likening.

упое́ние *neut.* ecstasy; rapture.

упои́тельный *adj.* entrancing; ravishing.

упоко́й *m.:* **за упоко́й** (*with gen.*) for the repose of.

уполномо́ченный *m.* representative; authorized agent.

уполномо́чивать *impf. pf.* **уполномо́чить** to authorize, to empower.

уполномо́чие *neut.:* **по уполномо́чию** (*with gen.*) by authority of.

упомина́ть *impf. pf.* **упомяну́ть** to mention; to refer to.

упо́мнить *pf.* (*colloq.*) to remember.

упо́р *m.* **1.** support. **2.** prop.

упо́рный *adj.* stubborn; persistent.

упо́рство *neut.* persistence; perseverance.

упо́рствовать OVA *impf.* **1.** to persist. **2.** to be stubborn *or* obstinate.

упоря́доченный *adj.* **1.** orderly; efficient. **2.** well-organized.

употреби́тельный *adj.* in common use.

употребле́ние *neut.* use.

употребля́ть *impf. pf.* **употреби́ть** to use; to apply.

упра́ва *f.* **1.** (*pre-rev.*) council; board. **2.** (*colloq.*) justice.

управле́ние *neut.* management, government.

управле́нческий *adj.* administrative.

управля́емый *adj.* guided. — **управля́емый снаря́д** *m.* guided missile.

управля́ть *impf.* (*with instr.*) to manage, to govern.

управля́ющий *adj.* (*attrib.*) managing, governing. — *m.* manager.

упражне́ние *neut.* exercise.

упражня́ться *impf.* to practice.

упраздне́ние *neut.* abolition.

упраздня́ть *impf. pf.* **упраздни́ть** to abolish.

упра́шивать *impf. pf.* **упроси́ть** to prevail upon; to persuade.

упрежда́ющий *adj.* preemptive.

упрёк *m.* reproach; rebuke.

упрека́ть *impf. pf.* **упрекну́ть** to reproach.

упроси́ть *pf. of* **упра́шивать.**

упро́чение *neut.* consolidation.

упро́чивать *impf. pf.* **упро́чить** *v.t.* to strengthen; to consolidate.

упроща́ть *pf.* **упрости́ть** to simplify.

упроще́ние *neut.* simplification.

упрощённый *adj.* simplified.

упроще́нческий *adj.* oversimplified.

упроще́нчество *neut.* oversimplification.

упру́гий *adj.* elastic; resilient.

упру́гость *f.* elasticity.

упря́жка *f.* **1.** team (*of horses, etc.*). **2.** harness.

упряжно́й *adj.* (*attrib.*) harness.

у́пряжь *f.* harness.

упря́мство *neut.* stubbornness; obstinacy.

упря́мый *adj.* stubborn; obstinate.

упуска́ть *impf. pf.* **упусти́ть 1.** to miss; to let go by. **2.** to let go.

упуще́ние *neut.* omission.

упы́рь *m.* vampire.

ура́ *interj.* hurrah!

уравне́ние *neut.* **1.** equalization. **2.** (*math.*) equation.

ура́внивать¹ *impf. pf.* **уровня́ть** to make even; to level.

ура́внивать² *impf. pf.* **уравня́ть** to equalize.

уравни́тельный *adj.* equalizing.

уравнове́шенность *f.* even temper.

уравнове́шенный *adj.* **1.** balanced; steady. **2.** even-tempered.

урага́н *m.* hurricane.

Ура́льск *m.* Uralsk.

Ура́н *m.* Uranus.

ура́н *m.* uranium.

ура́новый *adj.* uranium.

урегули́рование *neut.* settlement.

урезо́нивать *impf. pf.* **урезо́нить** (*colloq.*) **1.** to bring to reason. **2.** *impf. only* to try to reason with.

уреза́ть *impf. pf.* **уре́зать** to cut off; to shorten.

уреми́ческий *adj.* uremic.

уреми́я *f.* uremia.

уре́тра *f.* urethra.

ури́на *f.* urine.

у́рна *f.* urn.
у́ровень *m.* **1.** level. **2.** standard.
уровня́ть *pf. of* **ура́внивать.**
уро́д *m.* **1.** freak. **2.** monster, monstrosity.
уро́дливость *adj.* ugliness.
уро́дливый *adj.* **1.** ugly; hideous. **2.** distorted. **3.** deformed; misshapen.
уро́довать OVA *impf. pf.* **из-** to disfigure, to deform; to mutilate.
уро́дский *adj.* (*colloq.*) ugly.
уро́дство *neut.* **1.** deformity. **2.** ugliness. **3.** abnormality.
урожа́й *m.* harvest; yield. **—ный** *adj.* fruitful; productive.
урожа́йность *f.* productivity; yield.
урождённая *adj.* born, née.
уроже́нец FILL *m. f.* **уроже́нка** native.
уро́к *m.* lesson.
уро́лог *m.* urologist.
урологи́ческий *adj.* urological.
уроло́гия *f.* urology.
уро́н *m.* damage; losses.
урони́ть *pf. of* **роня́ть.**
уро́чище *neut.* natural boundary.
уро́чный *adj.* (*obs.*) fixed; set.
Уругва́й *m.* Uruguay.
урча́ние *neut.* rumbling.
урча́ть *impf. pres.* **урчу́, урчи́шь** to rumble.
уры́вками *adv.* (*colloq.*) in snatches.
урю́к *m.* dried apricots.
ус *m.* mustache.
уса́дка *f.* shrinkage.
уса́дьба *f.* **1.** country estate; country seat. **2.** farmstead.
уса́живать *impf. pf.* **усади́ть** *v.t.* to seat. **—ся** to take a seat.
уса́тый *adj.* mustached; (*of animal*) whiskered.
уса́ч *m.* (*colloq.*) man with a (big) mustache.
усва́ивать *impf. pf.* **усво́ить** to master, to learn; to assimilate.
усвое́ние *neut.* **1.** mastering, learning. **2.** adoption.
усе́рдие *neut.* zeal.
усе́рдный *adj.* zealous; diligent.
усе́рдствовать OVA *impf.* to show great zeal.
уси́дчивость *f.* assiduousness.
уси́дчивый *adj.* assiduous; persevering.
у́сик *m.* **1.** small mustache. **2.** feeler (*of an insect*). **3.** tendril (*of a plant*).
усиле́ние *neut.* **1.** reinforcement. **2.** intensification; amplification.
уси́ленно *adv.* **1.** with great force; with great effort. **2.** diligently; in earnest.
уси́ленный *adj.* **1.** increased; extra. **2.** intense. **3.** earnest; urgent; persistent (*of requests*).
уси́ливать *impf. pf.* **уси́лить** **1.** to strengthen. **2.** to intensify; to amplify.
уси́лие *neut.* effort.
усили́тель *m.* amplifier; booster.
ускольза́ть *impf. pf.* **ускользну́ть** to slip away *or* off; to steal away.
ускоре́ние *neut.* acceleration.
ускори́тель *m.* accelerator.
ускоря́ть *impf. pf.* **уско́рить** **1.** to hasten, to quicken. **2.** to accelerate.
усла́да *f.* (*obs.*) pleasure, delight.
услажда́ть *impf. pf.* **услади́ть** (*obs.*) to delight.

усло́вие *neut.* condition.
усло́вленный *adj.* agreed; agreed upon.
усло́вливаться *impf. pf.* **усло́виться** **1.** to arrange. **2.** to agree (on).
усло́вно *adv.* conditionally; tentatively.
усло́вность *f.* convention.
усло́вный *adj.* conditional.
усложне́ние *neut.* complication.
усложня́ть *impf. pf.* **усложни́ть** to complicate.
услу́га *f.* service; favor.
услу́живать *impf. pf.* **услужи́ть** to render a service; to serve.
услу́жливый *adj.* helpful; obliging.
услы́шать *pf. of* **слы́шать.**
усмеха́ться *impf. pf.* **усмехну́ться** to smile (ironically); to grin.
усме́шка *f.* (ironical) smile.
усмире́ние *neut.* suppression.
усмиря́ть *impf. pf.* **усмири́ть** **1.** to pacify. **2.** to suppress.
усмотре́ние *neut.* discretion; judgment.
усну́ть *pf.* to fall asleep.
усовершенствование *neut.* improvement.
усовершенствовать OVA *pf. of* **совершенствовать.**
усоно́гий рак *m.* barnacle.
усо́пший *adj.* (*obs.*) deceased.
успева́емость *f.* progress (*in one's studies*).
успева́ть *impf. pf.* **успе́ть** to manage (to); to have time (to); to succeed (in).
успе́ние *neut.* death. **— Успе́ние** Assumption; Dormition.
успе́х *m.* success. **— успе́хи** *pl.* progress.
успе́шно *adv.* successfully.
успе́шность *f.* success.
успе́шный *adj.* successful.
успока́ивать *impf. pf.* **успоко́ить** to calm; to quiet; to soothe; to assuage.
успокое́ние *neut.* **1.** calming; soothing. **2.** peace of mind.
успокои́тельный *adj.* **1.** calming; soothing. **2.** reassuring.
Уссу́ри *f.* (*river*) Ussuri.
уста́в *m.* regulations; statute.
уста́вать *impf. pf.* **уста́ть** to get tired.
уставля́ть *impf. pf.* **уста́вить** (*colloq.*) **1.** to place; to arrange. **2.** to cover with. **3.** to point; to aim.
уста́вный *adj.* regulation.
уста́лость *f.* fatigue.
уста́лый *adj.* fatigued, weary, tired.
у́сталь *f.* (*obs.*): **без у́стали** tirelessly.
устана́вливать *impf. pf.* **установи́ть** **1.** to place; to mount. **2.** to establish.
устано́вка *f.* **1.** installation; establishment. **2.** mounting. **3.** setting.
установле́ние *neut.* establishment.
устаре́лый *adj.* outdated; obsolete.
уста́ть *pf. of* **устава́ть.**
устила́ть *impf. pf.* **устла́ть** to cover; to overlay.
у́стный *adj.* oral; verbal.
усто́й *m.* **1.** foundation. **2.** abutment (*of a bridge*). **— усто́и** *pl.* basis; foundation.
усто́йчивость *f.* stability.
усто́йчивый *adj.* steady; firm; stable.
устоя́ть *pf.* to keep one's balance.
устра́ивать *impf. pf.* **устро́ить** **1.** to arrange; to organize; to establish. **2.** to make, to create (*trouble, a scandal, etc.*).

устране́ние *neut.* removal; elimination.

устраня́ть *impf. pf.* устрани́ть to remove; to eliminate.

устраша́ть *impf. pf.* устраши́ть to frighten, to scare.

устраши́ть *pf. of* устраша́ть.

устремле́ние *neut.* aspiration.

устремля́ть *impf. pf.* устреми́ть **1.** to direct. **2.** to fix (*one's gaze, etc.*).

у́стрица *f.* oyster.

у́стричный *adj.* (*attrib.*) oyster.

устро́итель *m. f.* —ница organizer.

устро́ить *pf. of* устра́ивать.

устро́йство *neut.* **1.** arrangement. **2.** organization. **3.** structure.

усту́п *m.* **1.** ledge. **2.** projection.

уступа́ть *impf. pf.* уступи́ть to yield; to cede.

уступи́тельный *adj.* (*gram.*) concessive.

усту́пка *f.* concession.

усту́пчивый *adj.* **1.** yielding. **2.** pliant, tractable.

у́стье *neut.* **1.** estuary, mouth. **2.** orifice.

усугуби́ть *pf. of* усугубля́ть.

усугубля́ть *impf. pf.* усугуби́ть **1.** to increase; to intensify. **2.** to make (even) worse.

усы́ *pl.* **1.** mustache. **2.** whiskers (*of an animal*).

усыновле́ние *neut.* adoption (*of a child*).

усыновля́ть *impf. pf.* усынови́ть to adopt (*a child*).

усыпа́льница *f.* crypt; burial vault.

усыпа́ть *impf. pf.* усы́пать **1.** to strew. **2.** to stud (*e.g., the sky with stars*).

усыпи́тельный *adj.* soporific.

усыпля́ть *impf. pf.* усыпи́ть **1.** to lull *or* put to sleep. **2.** (*of animals*) to put to death.

усыпля́ющий *adj.* soporific.

усыха́ть *impf. pf.* усо́хнуть **1.** to wither. **2.** to dry up; to dry out.

ута́ивать *impf. pf.* утаи́ть **1.** to conceal; to withhold. **2.** to hide. **3.** to steal.

ута́йка *f.* (*colloq.*): без ута́йки without concealing anything.

у́тварь *f.* utensils.

утверди́тельный *adj.* affirmative.

утвержда́ть *impf. pf.* утверди́ть **1.** to confirm. **2.** to maintain, to assert, to contend. **3.** to approve.

утвержде́ние *neut.* **1.** assertion; claim. **2.** confirmation; approval.

утека́ть *impf. pf.* уте́чь to leak; to flow off.

утёнок FILL *m.* duckling.

утере́ть *pf. of* утира́ть.

уте́ря *f.* loss (*of documents*).

утеря́ть *pf.* to lose; to mislay.

утёс *m.* rock; cliff; crag.

утёсистый *adj.* rocky.

уте́ха *f.* **1.** joy; delight; pleasure. **2.** comfort; consolation.

уте́чка *f.* **1.** loss; leakage. **2.** drain.

утеша́ть *impf. pf.* уте́шить to comfort; to console.

утеше́ние *neut.* consolation; comfort.

утеши́тель *m. f.* —ница comforter.

утеши́тельный *adj.* comforting.

утилиза́ция *f.* utilization.

утилизи́ровать OVA *impf. and pf.* to utilize.

утилитари́зм *m.* utilitarianism.

утилита́рный *adj.* utilitarian.

ути́ль *m.* (*coll.*) scrap.

утильсырьё *neut.* scrap.

утира́ть *impf. pf.* утере́ть to wipe; to dry.

утиха́ть *impf. pf.* ути́хнуть **1.** to cease; to abate. **2.** to become calm.

у́тка *f.* duck.

уткну́ть *pf.* **1.** to plant firmly. **2.** to bury; to hide.

утконо́с *m.* duck-billed platypus.

у́тлый *adj.* **1.** rickety. **2.** wretched.

уто́к FILL *m.* (*of textiles*) woof; weft.

утоле́ние *neut.* quenching; appeasing (*thirst or hunger*).

утолще́ние *neut.* thickening; bulge.

утоля́ть *impf. pf.* утоли́ть to quench; to appease.

утоми́тельный *adj.* tiresome; tiring; exhausting.

утомле́ние *neut.* fatigue.

утомлённый *adj.* tired.

утомля́ть *impf. pf.* утоми́ть *v.t.* to tire; to weary; to fatigue; to exhaust.

утонча́ть *impf. pf.* утончи́ть **1.** to thin (out). **2.** to refine.

утончённость *f.* refinement.

утончённый *adj.* refined; cultivated.

утопа́ть *impf. pf.* утону́ть **1.** to drown. **2.** *impf. only* (в *with prep.*) to be rolling (*in money*); to be bathed (*in light*).

утопа́ющий *m.* drowning person.

утопи́зм *m.* utopianism.

утопи́ть *pf. of* топи́ть.

утопи́ческий *adj.* utopian.

уто́пия *f.* utopia.

утопле́ние *neut.* drowning.

уто́пленник *m. f.* уто́пленница drowned person.

у́точка *f. dim. of* у́тка.

уточне́ние *neut.* making something more precise.

уточня́ть *impf. pf.* уточни́ть **1.** to clarify; to amplify. **2.** to render more precise *or* accurate.

утра́та *f.* loss.

у́тренний *adj.* (*attrib.*) morning.

у́тренник *m.* **1.** morning performance. **2.** early-morning frost.

у́треня *f.* matins; morning prayer.

У́трехт *m.* Utrecht.

утри́рование *neut.* exaggeration.

утри́ровать OVA *impf. and pf.* to exaggerate.

утриро́вка *f.* exaggeration.

у́тро *neut.* morning. — по утра́м in the morning(s). — у́тром in the morning.

утро́ба *f.* womb.

утро́бный *adj.* uterine.

утрое́ние *neut.* trebling, tripling.

утружда́ть *impf. pf.* утруди́ть to trouble.

утю́г *m.* (*appliance*) iron.

утю́жить *impf.* to iron, to press.

утю́жка *f.* ironing; pressing.

Уфа́ *f.* Ufa.

уфи́мец FILL *m. f.* уфи́мка resident of Ufa.

уха́ *f.* fish soup.

уха́бистый *adj.* bumpy.

ухажёр *m.* (*colloq.*) suitor; admirer.

уха́живание *neut.* looking after.

уха́живать *impf.* (за *with instr.*) **1.** to care for; to tend. **2.** to court.

у́харский *adj.* (*colloq.*) dashing.

у́харство *neut.* (*colloq.*) bravado.

у́харь *m.* **1.** lad. **2.** dashing fellow; gay blade.

у́хать *impf. pf.* у́хнуть (*colloq.*) **1.** to cry out. **2.** (*of an owl*) to hoot. **3.** to ring out; to resound.

ухва́т *m.* **1.** oven fork. **2.** (*tech.*) clip.

ухва́тка *f.* (*colloq.*) manner; way.

ухва́тывать *impf. pf.* ухвати́ть to catch, to grasp.

ухитря́ться *impf. pf.* ухитри́ться to contrive.

ухищре́ние *neut.* contrivance; device.

ухищря́ться *impf.* to contrive; to scheme.

ухмы́лка *f.* (*colloq.*) grin; smirk.

ухмыля́ться *impf. pf.* ухмыльну́ться (*colloq.*) to grin; to smirk.

у́хо *neut.* (*pl.* у́ши) ear.

ухо́д *neut.* departure.

уходи́ть *impf. pf.* уйти́ to leave; to go away. — уходи́ть в себя́ to withdraw into oneself.

Ухта́ *f.* Ukhta.

ухудша́ть *impf. pf.* уху́дшить to worsen, to make worse.

ухудше́ние *neut.* worsening; deterioration.

уцеле́ть *pf.* to survive.

уцепи́ть *pf.* (*colloq.*) to grab.

уча́ствовать OVA *impf.* (**в** *with prep.*) to participate.

уча́стие *neut.* **1.** participation. **2.** share.

участко́вый *adj.* (*attrib.*) district.

уча́стливый *adj.* sympathetic, compassionate.

уча́стник *m. f.* уча́стница participant.

уча́сток FILL lot, plot, strip; parcel (*of land*).

у́часть *f.* lot, fate.

уча́щийся *m.* student.

учёба *f.* **1.** studies; learning. **2.** training; drill.

уче́бник *m.* textbook, manual.

уче́бный *adj.* educational, school.

уче́ние *neut.* learning, studies.

учени́к *m. f.* учени́ца pupil.

учени́ческий *adj.* pupil's.

учени́чество *neut.* time spent as a student.

учёность *f.* learning; erudition.

учёный *adj.* learned, erudite. — *m.* scholar, scientist.

уче́сть *pf. of* учи́тывать.

учёт *m.* **1.** stock-taking. **2.** registration.

учётный *adj.* (*attrib.*) **1.** record. **2.** registration. **3.** (*sales*) discount.

учи́лище *neut.* vocational school; college.

учиня́ть *impf. pf.* учини́ть **1.** to conduct (*an interrogation*). **2.** to carry out (*reprisals*). — учиня́ть сканда́л to make a scene; to raise a scandal.

учи́тель *m. f.* **-ница** teacher.

учи́тельская *f.* teachers' room.

учи́тельский *adj.* teacher's.

учи́тельство *neut.* teaching.

учи́тельствовать OVA *impf.* to be a teacher.

учи́тывать *impf. pf.* уче́сть to take into account; to allow for.

учи́ть *impf. pf.* вы- **1.** to learn; **2.** *pf. also* на- to teach.

учи́ться *impf.* **1.** *pf.* вы-, на- to learn. **2.** *impf. only* to study.

учреди́тель *m. f.* **—ница** founder.

учреди́тельный *adj.* constituent. — учреди́тельное собра́ние *neut.* constituent assembly.

учрежда́ть *impf. pf.* учреди́ть to found; to establish.

учрежде́ние *neut.* **1.** institution. **2.** establishment. **3.** (*social*) institution.

учти́вость *f.* politeness; courtesy.

учти́вый *adj.* polite; courteous.

учу́ять *pf. pres.* учу́ю, учу́ешь (*colloq.*) to smell; to sense.

уша́нка *f.* (*colloq.*) cap with earflaps.

уша́стый *adj.* (*colloq.*) with big ears.

уша́т *m.* tub (*carried on a pole slung through handles*).

у́ши *pl. of* у́хо.

уши́б *m.* injury.

ушиба́ться *impf. pf.* ушиби́ться to hurt oneself.

уши́бленный *adj.* injured.

у́шко *neut. dim. of* у́хо.

ушко́ *neut.* eye (*of needle*).

ушни́к *m.* (*colloq.*) ear specialist.

ушно́й *adj.* aural; (*attrib.*) ear.

уще́лье *neut.* ravine, gorge.

ущемле́ние *neut.* **1.** catching; jamming. **2.** abridgement. **3.** (*med.*) strangulation.

ущемля́ть *impf. pf.* ущеми́ть **1.** to jam; to catch. **2.** to restrict (*someone's freedom*). **3.** to oppress. **4.** to aggrieve. **5.** to wound (*someone's pride*).

уще́рб *m.* **1.** damage, loss. **2.** detriment.

уще́рбный *adj.* **1.** (*of the moon*) waning. **2.** on the decline.

ущипну́ть *pf.* to pinch.

Уэ́льс *f.* Wales.

ую́т *m.* comfort.

ую́тный *adj.* cosy; comfortable.

уязви́мость *f.* vulnerability.

уязви́мый *adj.* vulnerable.

уясня́ть *impf. pf.* уясни́ть **1.** to understand; to make out. **2.** to size up.

Ф

фа́брика f. factory.
фабрика́нт m. manufacturer.
фабрика́т m. product.
фабрика́ция f. manufacture; fabrication.
фабрикова́ть OVA impf. pf. c- to produce, to manufacture.
фабри́чный adj. (attrib.) factory.
фа́була f. plot (of a story).
фаво́р m. favor.
фавори́т m. f. —ка favorite.
фавори́зм m. favoritism.
фаго́т m. bassoon.
фаготи́ст m. bassoonist.
фагоци́т m. phagocyte.
фа́за f. phase.
фаза́н m. pheasant.
фа́зис m. phase.
фа́кел m. torch.
фа́кельный adj. (attrib.) torch.
фа́кельщик m. f. фа́кельщица torchbearer.
факс m. fax.
факси́миле neut. indecl. facsimile.
факт m. fact.
факти́чески adv. in fact; practically; virtually.
факти́ческий adj. 1. actual. 2. factual. 3. real.
фа́ктор m. factor.
факто́рия f. trading post.
факту́ра¹ f. bill; invoice.
факту́ра² f. 1. texture. 2. style (in art or literature).
факультати́вный adj. optional.
факульте́т m. faculty, department (of a university).
фал m. halyard.
фа́лда f. coattail.
фалли́ческий adj. phallic.
фа́ллос m. phallus.
фальсифика́тор m. falsifier.
фальсифика́ция f. falsification.
фальсифици́ровать OVA impf. and pf. to falsify.
фальце́т m. falsetto.
фальши́вить impf. pf. c- 1. to be insincere. 2. to sing off key.
фальши́вка f. (colloq.) forged document.
фальши́во adv. falsely; off key.
фальшивомоне́тчик m. f. —моне́тчица counterfeiter.
фальши́вый adj. false.
фальшь f. falsity, falseness.
фами́лия f. surname.
фами́льный adj. (attrib.) family.
фамилья́рный adj. unceremonious; familiar.
фанабе́рия f. (obs.) arrogance.
фанати́зм m. fanaticism.
фана́тик m. f. фана́тичка fanatic.
фанати́ческий also фанати́чный adj. fanatical.
фане́ра f. 1. veneer. 2. plywood.
фане́рный adj. (attrib.) plywood.
фантазёр m. f. —ка visionary; dreamer.
фантази́ровать OVA impf. 1. to dream; to indulge in fantasies. 2. pf. c- to dream up. 3. to improvise.
фанта́зия f. 1. fantasy. 2. fancy; imagination.
фантасмаго́рия f. phantasmagoria.
фанта́ст m. f. —ка 1. visionary. 2. writer or artist depicting the fantastic.
фанта́стика f. fantasy. — нау́чная фанта́стика f. science fiction.
фантасти́ческий also фантасти́чный adj. fantastic.
фанто́м m. phantom.
фанфа́ра f. fanfare.
фа́ра f. headlight.
фарва́тер m. channel; waterway.
Фаренге́йт m. Fahrenheit.
фарисе́й m. f. —ка pharisee.
фарисе́йский adj. pharisaic.
фармако́лог m. pharmacologist.
фармакологи́ческий adj. pharmacological.
фармаколо́гия f. pharmacology.
фармакопе́я f. pharmacopeia.
фармаце́вт m. pharmacist.
фармаце́втика f. pharmaceutics.
фармацевти́ческий adj. pharmaceutical.
фармаци́я (obs.) f. pharmaceutics.
фарс m. farce.
фа́рсовый adj. farcical.
фа́ртинг m. farthing.
фа́ртук m. apron.
фарфо́р m. porcelain; china.
фарфо́ровый adj. (attrib.) porcelain.
фарш m. stuffing; minced meat.
фарширо́ванный adj. stuffed.
фарширова́ть OVA impf. pf. за- to stuff.
фас m. front (of one's face).
фаса́д m. facade.
фасе́т m. also фасе́тка f. facet (of gem).
фасова́ть OVA impf. pf. рас- to package food.
фасо́вка f. packaging.
фасо́вочный adj. (attrib.) packaging.
фасо́вщик m. f. фасо́вщица packer.
фасо́левый adj. (attrib.) (kidney) bean.
фасо́ль f. (kidney) beans; (kidney) bean.
фасо́н m. fashion, mode, style.
фасо́нистый adj. (colloq.) fashionable.
фасо́нный adj. shaped.
фат m. (obs.) fop.
фата́ f. bridal veil.
фатали́ст m. f. —ка fatalist.
фаталисти́ческий adj. fatalistic.
фата́льный adj. fatal; of resignation.
фатова́тый adj. foppish.
фатовство́ neut. foppery.
фа́уна f. fauna.
фаши́ст m. f. —ка fascist.
фаши́стский adj. fascist.
фаэто́н m. phaeton.
фая́нс m. glazed earthenware; faience.
фая́нсовый adj. (attrib.) faience.
февра́ль m. February. —ский adj. (attrib.) February.
федерали́зм m. federalism.

федералист *m.* federalist.
федера́льный *adj.* federal.
федерати́вный *adj.* federative.
федера́ция *f.* federation.
фееричес́кий *adj.* (*fig.*) magical; fabulous.
фее́рия *f.* (*fig.*) enchanting spectacle.
фейерве́рк *m.* fireworks.
фельдма́ршал *m.* field marshal.
фе́льдшер *m.* medical assistant.
фельето́н *m.* satirical *or* humorous article.
фельстоши́ст *m* *f* —ка writer of satirical articles.
фельето́нный *adj.* satirical.
фемини́зм *m.* feminism.
фемини́ст *m.* *f.* —ка feminist.
феминисти́ческий *also* феминистский *adj.* feminist.
фен *m.* hair dryer.
фенобарбита́л *adj.* phenobarbitral.
фено́л *m.* phenol.
фено́мен *m.* phenomenon.
феномена́льный *adj.* phenomenal.
фе́нхель *m.* fennel.
фео́д *m.* fief; feud.
феодали́зм *m.* feudalism.
феода́льный *adj.* feudal.
Феодо́сия *f.* Feodosiya.
Фергана́ *f.* Farghona.
фе́рзевый *adj.* (*chess*) queen's.
ферзь *f.* (*chess*) queen.
фе́рма[1] *f.* farm.
фе́рма[2] *f.* girder; truss.
ферме́нт *m.* ferment.
фе́рмер *m.* farmer. —ство *neut.* farming.
фе́рмерский *adj.* farmer's.
фе́рмий *m.* fermium.
фермуа́р *m.* (*obs.*) necklace.
ферроти́пия *f.* ferrotype.
фе́ска *f.* fez.
фестива́ль *m.* festival.
фестива́льный *adj.* (*attrib.*) festival.
фесто́нный *also* фесто́нчатый *adj.* scalloped.
фети́ш *m.* fetish.
фетишизи́ровать OVA *impf.* to make a fetish of.
фетр *m.* felt.
фе́тровый *adj.* felt.
фехтова́льный *adj.* (*attrib.*) fencing.
фехтова́льщик *m.* *f.* фехтова́льщица fencer.
фехтова́ние *neut.* fencing.
фехтова́ть OVA *impf.* to fence.
фешене́бельный *adj.* fashionable; high class.
фе́я *f.* fairy.
фи *interj.* фи!; pshaw!
фиа́кр *m.* fiacre; hired carriage.
фиа́лка *f.* (*bot.*) violet.
фиа́ско *neut.* *indecl.* fiasco; failure.
фи́бра *f.*: все́ми фи́брами души́ with every fiber of one's soul.
фибро́зный *adj.* (*attrib.*) fiber; fibrous.
Фи́вы *pl.* Thebes.
фи́га *f.* fig.
фи́говый *adj.* (*attrib.*) fig.
фигу́ра *f.* 1. figure. 2. (*cards*) face card. 3. (*chess*) piece.
фигура́льный *adj.* figurative; metaphorical.
фигури́ровать OVA *impf.* to figure *or* appear (as).
фигури́ст *m.* *f.* —ка figure skater.
фигу́рка *f.* *dim. of* фигу́ра.

фигу́рный *adj.* (*attrib.*) figure.
Фи́джи *m.* Fiji.
фи́зик *m.* physicist.
фи́зика *f.* physics.
физио́лог *m.* physiologist.
физиологи́ческий *adj.* physiological.
физиоло́гия *f.* physiology.
физионо́мия *f.* 1. face. 2. physiognomy. 3. facial expression.
физиотерапе́вт *m.* physical therapist.
физиотерапи́я *f.* physical therapy.
физи́чески *adv.* physically.
физи́ческий *adj.* physical.
физкульту́ра *f.* (*abbr. of* физи́ческая культу́ра) physical training; physical education.
физкульту́рник *m.* *f.* физкульту́рница athlete, gymnast.
физкульту́рный *adj.* athletic.
фикса́ж *m.* (*photog.*) fixing agent.
фикти́вный *adj.* fictitious.
фи́кус *m.* fig tree.
фи́кция *f.* fiction.
филантро́п *m.* *f.* —ка philanthropist.
филантропи́ческий *adj.* philanthropic.
филантро́пия *f.* philanthropy.
филатели́ст *m.* *f.* —ка philatelist.
филателисти́ческий *adj.* philatelic.
филате́лия *adj.* philately.
филе́ *neut.* *indecl.* filet; sirloin.
филёнка *f.* panel.
филёночный *also* филёнчатый *adj.* paneled.
филёр *m.* detective.
филиа́л *m.* branch.
филиа́льный *adj.* (*attrib.*) branch.
филигра́нный *adj.* filigree.
филигра́нь *f.* filigree.
фи́лин *m.* eagle owl.
фили́ппика *f.* philippic.
филоде́ндрон *m.* philodendron.
фило́лог *m.* philologist.
филологи́ческий *adj.* philological.
филоло́гия *f.* philology.
филосо́ф *m.* philosopher.
филосо́фия *f.* philosophy.
филосо́фский *adj.* philosophical.
филосо́фствовать OVA *impf.* to philosophize.
филфа́к *m.* (*abbr. of* филологи́ческий факульте́т) department of language and literature.
фильм *m.* film; movie.
фильмоте́ка *f.* film library.
фильм у́жасов *m.* horror film, horror show.
фи́льтр *m.* filter.
фильтра́ция *f.* filtration.
фильтрова́льный *adj.* (*attrib.*) filter.
фильтрова́ть OVA *impf.* *pf.* от-, про- *impf.* to filter.
фимиа́м *m.* incense.
фина́л *m.* finale.
финали́ст *m.* finalist.
фина́льный *adj.* final.
финанси́ровать OVA *impf.* and *pf.* to finance.
финанси́ст *m.* financier.
фина́нсовый *adj.* financial.
фина́нсы *pl.* finances.
фи́ник *m.* (*fruit*) date.
фи́никовый *adj.* (*attrib.*) date.

финифть *f.* (*obs.*) enamel.

финиш *m.* **1.** finish (*of a race*). **2.** finish line.

финишировать OVA *impf.* and *pf.* (*sports*) to finish.

финишная *f.* home stretch (*in racing*).

финка[1] *f.* (*colloq.*) knife.

финка[2] *f.*, *see* **финн**.

Финляндия *f.* Finland.

финн *m. f.* **финка** Finn.

финно-угорский *adj.* Finno-Ugric.

финский *adj.* Finnish.

финт *m.* (*sports*) feint.

финтить *impf. pres.* **-чу́, -ти́шь** (*colloq.*) to be tricky; to use deception.

финтифлюшка *f.* (*colloq.*) knickknack.

фиолетовый *adj.* violet.

фиорд *m.* fjord.

фирма *f.* firm, company.

фирменный *adj.* (*attrib.*) company; brand name; house. — **фирменное блюдо** specialty of the house.

фисгармония *f.* harmonium.

фискал *m. f.* **—ка** (*colloq.*) tattler.

фискалить *impf.* (*colloq.*) to tattle.

фискальный *adj.* (*attrib.*) tax.

фисташка *f.* pistachio.

фисташковый *adj.* pistachio.

фистула *f.* (*med.*) fistula.

фитиль *m.* wick.

фишка *f.* chip (*used in games*).

флаг *m.* flag, banner.

флагман *m.* **1.** flag officer. **2.** flagship. **3.** leader.

флагманский корабль *m.* flagship.

флагшток *m.* flagpole.

флажный *adj.* (*attrib.*) flag.

флажок FILL *m.* small flag.

флакон *m.* bottle.

фламинго *m. indecl.* flamingo.

фланг *m.* (*mil.*) flank.

фланговый *adj.* flanking.

фланелевый *adj.* flannel.

фланель *f.* flannel.

фланец FILL *m.* flange.

фланировать OVA *impf.* (*obs.*) to stroll.

фланкировать OVA *impf.* and *pf.* (*mil.*) to flank.

флегма *f.* phlegm; apathy.

флегматик *m.* phlegmatic person.

флегматический *also* **флегматичный** *adj.* phlegmatic.

флейта *f.* flute.

флейтист *m. f.* **—ка** flutist.

флексия *f.* (*gram.*) inflection.

флективный *adj.* inflected.

флёр *m.* crepe.

флигель *m.* wing.

флирт *m.* flirting.

флиртовать OVA *impf.* to flirt.

флокс *m.* phlox.

фломастер *m.* soft-tip pen; marker.

флора *f.* flora.

Флоренция *f.* Florence.

Флорида *f.* Florida.

флорин *m.* florin.

флот *m.* fleet. — **военно-морской флот** *m.* navy. — **воздушный флот** *m.* air force.

флотилия *f.* flotilla.

флотский *adj.* naval.

флоэма *f.* phloem.

флюгарка *f.* **1.** weather vane. **2.** ship's emblem.

флюгер *m.* weather vane.

флюоресценция *f.* fluorescence.

флюоресцировать OVA *impf.* to fluoresce.

флюс[1] *m.* (*metal.*) flux.

флюс[2] *m.* gumboil.

фляга *also* **фляжка** *f.* flask.

фобия *f.* phobia.

фойе *neut. indecl.* foyer.

фок *m.* foresail.

фок-мачта *f.* foremast.

фокстерьер *m.* fox terrier.

фокстрот *m.* foxtrot.

фокус *m.* **1.** focus. **2.** trick, whim, freak.

фокусировать OVA *impf.* and *pf.* to focus.

фокусничать *impf.* (*colloq.*) to play tricks.

фокусный *adj.* focal.

фокус-покус *m.* (*colloq.*) hocus-pocus.

фол *m.* (*sports*) foul.

фолио *m. indecl.* folio.

фолликул *m.* follicle.

фольга *f.* foil.

фольклор *m.* folklore.

фольклорист *m.* specialist in folklore.

фон *m.* background.

фонарик *m. dim. of* **фонарь**.

фонарный *adj.* (*attrib.*) lamp; lantern.

фонарщик *m.* (*obs.*) lamplighter.

фонарь *m.* **1.** lantern, lamp. **2.** street lamp. **3.** flashlight.

фонд *m.* fund.

фондовый *adj.* (*attrib.*) stock. — **фондовая биржа** *f.* stock exchange.

фонема *f.* phoneme.

фонематический *adj.* phonemic.

фонетика *f.* phonetics.

фонетический *adj.* phonetic.

фонология *f.* phonology.

фонотека *f.* record library.

фонтан *m.* fountain.

фонтанировать OVA *impf.* to gush forth.

Фонтенбло *m.* Fontainebleau.

фора *f.* (*sports*) head start; advantage.

форейтор *m.* postilion.

форель *f.* trout.

форзац *m.* flyleaf (*of a book*).

форма *f.* **1.** form, shape. **2.** mold. **3.** uniform.

формалист *m. f.* **—ка** formalist.

формалистический *adj.* formalistic.

формальдегид *m.* formaldehyde.

формальность *f.* formality.

формальный *adj.* formal.

формат *m.* size; format.

формация *f.* **1.** formation. **2.** structure.

форменный *adj.* (*attrib.*) uniform.

формировать OVA *impf. pf.* **с-** to form, to mold.

формовать OVA *impf. pf.* **с-** to shape; to mold.

формула *f.* formula.

формулировать OVA *impf.* and *pf.*, *pf. also* **с-** to formulate.

формулировка *f.* **1.** formulation. **2.** formula.

форсированный *adj.* forced; accelerated.

форсировать OVA *impf.* and *pf.* to force.

форсунка *f.* sprayer; injector.

форт *m.* fort.

фо́рте *adv.* (*mus.*) forte.

фо́ртель *m.* (*colloq.*) trick; stunt.

фортепья́нный *adj.* (*attrib.*) piano.

фортепья́но *neut. indecl.* piano.

форти́ссимо *adv.* fortissimo.

фортификацио́нный *adj.* (*attrib.*) fortification.

фортифика́ция *f.* fortification.

фо́рточка *f.* small hinged pane for ventilation in a window.

форту́на *f.* fortune

фо́рум *m.* forum.

форштёвень FILL *m.* (*naut.*) stern.

фосге́н *m.* phosgene.

фосфа́т *m.* phosphate.

фосфа́тный *also* фосфа́товый *adj.* (*attrib.*) phosphate.

фо́сфор *m.* phosphorus.

фосфоресце́нция *f.* phosphorescence.

фосфоресци́рующий *adj.* phosphorescent.

фо́сфорный *adj.* phosphoric.

фо́то *neut. indecl.* photo.

фотоаппара́т *m.* camera.

фотогени́чный *adj.* photogenic.

фотогравю́ра *f.* photogravure.

фото́граф *m.* photographer.

фотографи́ровать OVA *impf. pf.* с- to photograph.

фотографи́ческий *adj.* photographical.

фотогра́фия *f.* photograph.

фотока́рточка *f.* (*colloq.*) photograph.

фотоко́пия *f.* photocopy.

фотолюби́тель *m. f.* —ница amateur photographer.

фото́метр *m.* photometer.

фото́н *m.* photon.

фотоси́нтез *m.* photosynthesis.

фотосни́мок FILL *m.* snapshot; photograph.

фотоста́т *m.* photostat machine.

фотосфе́ра *f.* photosphere.

фотоэлектри́ческий *adj.* photoelectric.

фотоэлеме́нт *m.* photocell.

фрагме́нт *m.* fragment.

фрагмента́рный *adj.* fragmentary.

фра́за *f.* phrase.

фразеологи́ческий *adj.* phraseological.

фрак *m.* tails; tail coat.

Фра́кия *f.* (*province*) Thrace.

фракцио́нный *adj.* factional.

фра́кция *f.* political faction; group.

фраму́га *f.* transom.

франки́ровать OVA *impf. and pf.* to put postage on.

франкмасо́н *m.* freemason.

франкмасо́нство *neut.* freemasonry.

Фра́нкфурт *m.* Frankfurt.

франт *m.* dandy.

франти́ть *impf.* (*colloq.*) to dress like a dandy.

Фра́нция *f.* France.

францу́з *m. f.* францу́женка a French person.

францу́зский *adj.* French.

фрахт *m.* freight.

фрахтова́ть OVA *impf. pf.* за- to charter.

фрега́т *m.* frigate.

фре́за *f.* milling cutter.

фре́зерный *adj.* (*attrib.*) milling.

фрезерова́ние *neut.* milling.

фрезерова́ть OVA *impf. and pf.* to cut (*metal*); to mill (*metal*).

фре́йлина *f.* lady in waiting.

френоло́гия *f.* phrenology.

френч *m.* military jacket.

фре́ска *f.* fresco.

фре́сковый *adj.* (*attrib.*) fresco.

фриво́льный *adj.* ribald.

фриз *m.* frieze.

Фри́зские острова́ *pl.* Frisian Islands.

фрикаде́лька *f.* ball of minced meat *or* fish.

фрикасе́ *neut. indecl.* fricassee.

фрикати́вный *adj.* fricative.

фронт *m.* front.

фронта́льный *adj.* frontal.

фронтиспи́с *m.* frontispiece.

фронтови́к *m.* front-line soldier.

фронтово́й *adj.* (*attrib.*) front; front-line.

фронто́н *m.* pediment; gable.

фрукт *m.* piece of fruit.

фрукто́вый *adj.* (*attrib.*) fruit. — фрукто́вый сад *adj.* orchard.

фрустра́ция *f.* frustration.

фтор *m.* fluorine.

фтори́д *m.* fluoride.

фто́ристый *adj.* fluoride (of).

фу *interj.* 1. (*expressing contempt, revulsion*) ugh! 2. (*expressing relief or fatigue*) whew!

фу́га *f.* (*mus.*) fugue.

фуга́с *m.* land mine.

фуга́ска *f.* (*colloq.*) land mine.

фуга́сный *adj.* (*attrib.*) land mine; high-explosive.

фуже́р *m.* tall wine glass.

фу́кать *impf.* to snort.

фукси́н *m.* magenta; fuchsin.

фунда́мент *m.* foundation; groundwork. —а́льный *adj.* fundamental; solid; thorough; basic.

фунду́к *m.* filbert.

функциона́льный *adj.* functional.

функциони́ровать OVA *impf.* to function.

фунт *m.* pound (*unit of weight; unit of money*).

фу́нтик *m.* cone-shaped paper bag.

фу́ра *f.* van; wagon.

фура́ж *m.* forage, fodder.

фура́жка *f.* peak-cap; service cap.

фура́жный *adj.* (*attrib.*) forage; fodder.

фурго́н *m.* van.

фу́рия *f.* 1. fury. 2. (*colloq.*) shrew; termagant.

фуру́нкул *m.* (*med.*) boil.

фут *m.* (*measurement*) foot.

футбо́л *m.* soccer. —и́ст *m. f.* —ка soccer player.

футбо́лка *f.* T-shirt.

футбо́льный *adj.* (*attrib.*) soccer.

футля́р *m.* case.

фу́товый *adj.* one foot in length.

футуристи́ческий *adj.* futurist.

фуфа́йка *f.* jersey.

фы́ркание *neut.* snorting.

фы́ркать *impf. pf.* фы́ркнуть 1. to snort. 2. (*colloq.*) to sneer at.

фюзеля́ж *m.* fuselage.

X

ха́ки *neut. indecl.* khaki.
хала́т *m.* **1.** bathrobe. **2.** smock.
хала́тность *f.* indifference; negligence.
хала́тный *adj.* negligent.
хали́ф *m.* caliph.
халифа́т *m.* caliphate.
халту́ра *f.* hack work.
халту́рщик *m. f.* халту́рщица hack worker.
халцедо́н *m.* chalcedony.
хам *m.* **1.** boor. **2.** *f.* ха́мка crude person. —ский *adj.* crude, vulgar.
хамелео́н *m.* chameleon.
Ха́ммерфест *m.* Hammerfest.
ха́мство *neut.* (*colloq.*) boorishness.
хан *m.* khan.
хандра́ *f.* depression; melancholy.
ханжа́ *m. and f.* (*decl. f.*) hypocrite.
ха́нжеский *adj.* sanctimonious; hypocritical.
ха́нжество *neut.* sanctimony.
Хано́й *m.* Hanoi.
ха́нство *neut.* khanate.
ха́ос *m.* chaos.
хаоти́ческий *also* хаоти́чный *adj.* chaotic.
хаоти́чность *f.* chaotic nature.
хараки́ри *neut. indecl.* hara-kiri.
хара́ктер *m.* character; nature.
характеризова́ть OVA *impf. and pf.* to characterize.
характери́стика *f.* **1.** character reference. **2.** characterization.
хара́ктерно *adv.* in one's own distinctive way.
хара́ктерный *adj.* **1.** characteristic. **2.** typical. **3.** distinctive.
ха́рза *f.* yellow-throated marten.
ха́ркать *impf. pf.* ха́ркнуть to spit, to expectorate.
Ха́рлем *m.* Haarlem.
Ха́ррисберг *m.* Harrisburg.
ха́ртия *f.* charter.
харче́вня *f.* (*obs.*) cheap eatery.
харчи́ *pl.* (*colloq.*) grub; food.
харчо́ *neut. indecl.* mutton soup.
Ха́рьков *m.* Kharkiv.
ха́ря *f.* (*colloq.*) mug; puss; face.
ха́та *f.* hut.
хвала́ *f.* praise.
хвале́бный *adj.* laudatory.
хвалёный *adj.* famous; greatly praised.
хвали́ть *impf. pf.* по- to praise. —ся to boast.
хвастли́вость *f.* boastfulness.
хвастли́вый *adj.* boastful.
хвастовство́ *neut.* boasting, bragging.
хвасту́н *m. f.* —ья braggart.
хвата́ть[1] *impf. pf.* схвати́ть to grab, to grasp. —ся *impf.* **1.** to grip. **2.** to grasp (at).
хвата́ть[2] *impf. pf.* хвати́ть *impers.* (*with gen.*) to suffice.
хва́тка *f.* **1.** grasp; grip. **2.** skill.
хво́йный *adj.* coniferous.
хвора́ть *impf.* (*colloq.*) to be ill.
хво́рост *m.* **1.** brushwood. **2.** pastry straws.
хворости́на *f.* stick; rod.

хво́рый *adj.* (*colloq.*) ailing.
хворь *f.* (*colloq.*) ailment.
хвост *m.* tail.
хвоста́тый *adj.* with a tail.
хво́стик *m.* small tail.
хвостово́й *adj.* (*attrib.*) tail.
хво́щ *m.* (*plant*) horsetail.
хвоя́ *f.* **1.** pine needles. **2.** pine branches.
Хе́льсингёр *m.* Helsingør.
Хе́льсинки *m.* Helsinki.
Хе́мниц *m.* Chemnitz.
Херсо́н *m.* Kherson.
херуви́м *m.* cherub.
херуви́мский *adj.* cherubic.
хиба́ра *f.* hovel; shanty.
хи́жина *f.* hut, cabin.
хи́лый *adj.* feeble, sickly.
химе́ра *f.* chimera.
химери́ческий *adj.* chimerical.
Хи́мзее *m.* (*lake*) Chiemsee.
хи́мик *m.* chemist. —а́лии *pl.* chemicals.
химиотерапи́я *f.* chemotherapy.
хими́ческий *adj.* chemical.
хи́мия *f.* chemistry.
химчи́стка *f.* **1.** dry cleaning. **2.** dry cleaner's.
хини́н *m.* quinine.
хи́нный *adj.* (*attrib.*) quinine.
хире́ть *impf. pf.* за- **1.** to decline (*in health*). **2.** to wither.
хирома́нт *m.* palm reader.
хирома́нтия *f.* palmistry.
хиру́рг *m.* surgeon. —и́ческий *adj.* surgical. —и́я *f.* surgery.
хитре́ц *m.* cunning person.
хитреца́ *also* хитри́нка *f.* (*colloq.*) shrewdness; cunning.
хитри́ть *impf. pf.* с- **1.** to use cunning. **2.** to try to outwit.
хи́тро *adv.* slyly.
хитросплете́ние *neut., usu. pl.* intricacies.
хи́трость *f.* cunning; guile.
хитроу́мие *neut.* cleverness.
хитроу́мный *adj.* clever; ingenious.
хи́трый *adj.* cunning.
хихи́канье *neut.* giggling.
хихи́кать *impf.* to giggle; to titter.
хище́ние *neut.* theft; embezzlement.
хи́щник *m.* beast *or* bird of prey.
хи́щнический *adj.* predatory; rapacious.
хи́щничество *neut.* preying on others.
хи́щный *adj.* predatory; rapacious.
хладнокро́вие *neut.* coolness; composure; sangfroid.
хладнокро́вно *adv.* calmly; in cold blood.
хладнокро́вный *adj.* composed, cool; cold-blooded.
хлам *m.* garbage; trash; rubbish.
хлеб *m.* bread; corn, grain.
хлеба́ть *impf. pf.* хлебну́ть to gulp down.
хле́бец FILL *m.* small loaf of bread.
хле́бница *f.* breadbasket.

хле́бный *adj.* (*attrib.*) **1.** bread. **2.** grain. **3.** profitable.

хлебопёк *m.* baker.

хлеборо́б *m.* farmer.

хлебосо́льный *adj.* hospitable.

хлебосо́льство *neut.* hospitality.

хлеб-со́ль *m.* or *f.* **1.** bread and salt (*symbol of hospitality*). **2.** hospitality.

хлев *m.* barn.

хлеста́ть *impf. pres.* хлещу́, хле́щешь *pf.* хлестну́ть **1.** to whip, to lash. **2.** (*of rain*) to come down in torrents.

хлёсткий *adj.* **1.** (*of wind*) biting; sharp. **2.** scathing; lashing.

хли́пкий *adj.* (*colloq.*) rickety.

хлоп *interj.* bang!

хло́панье *neut.* banging; slamming.

хло́пать *impf. pf.* хло́пнуть to bang, to slam.

хло́пец FILL *m.* lad; youth; boy.

хлопково́д *m.* cotton grower.

хлопково́дство *neut.* cotton growing.

хлопково́дческий *adj.* cotton-growing.

хло́пковый *adj.* cotton.

хлопкоочисти́тельный маши́на *f.* cotton gin.

хло́пок FILL *m.* cotton.

хлопо́к FILL *m.* **1.** bang; pop. **2.** slap; pat (*on the back*).

хлопота́ть *impf. pf.* по- **1.** *impf. only* to bustle around. **2.** to seek; to try to get.

хлопотли́вый *adj.* busy; bustling.

хло́потный *adj.* (*colloq.*) difficult; troublesome.

хлопотня́ *f.* (*colloq.*) bustling about.

хлопоту́н *m. f.* —ья (*colloq.*) hustler; busybody.

хло́поты *pl.* **1.** cares; worries. **2.** efforts. **3.** chores.

хлопу́шка *f.* fly swatter.

хлопча́тник *m.* cotton plant.

хлопчатобума́жный *adj.* cotton.

хло́пья *pl.* flakes (*of snow; of corn*).

хлор *m.* chlorine.

хлори́д *m.* chloride.

хлори́рование *neut.* chlorination.

хлори́ровать OVA *impf. and pf.* to chlorinate.

хло́ристый *adj.* chlorous.

хло́рный *adj.* chloric.

хлорофи́лл *m.* chlorophyll.

хлорофо́рм *m.* chloroform.

хлороформи́ровать OVA *impf. and pf.* to chloroform.

хлы́нуть *pf.* **1.** to gush; to pour. **2.** (*of rain*) to come down in torrents.

хлыст *m.* **1.** whip. **2.** khlyst (*flagellant*).

хлыщ *m.* (*colloq.*) fop, dandy.

хлю́пать *impf.* to splash.

хлю́пкий *adj.* (*colloq.*) soggy.

хля́бь *f.* (*colloq.*) mud.

хмелёк FILL *m.:* под хмелько́м *adj.* tipsy; high.

хмеле́ть *impf.* to become intoxicated *or* tipsy.

хмель[1] *m.* hops.

хмель[2] *m.* drunkenness, intoxication. —ное *neut.* intoxicating beverage. —но́й *adj.* intoxicating.

хму́риться *impf. pf.* на- to frown.

хму́рый *adj.* gloomy.

хна *f.* henna.

хны́кать *impf.* (*colloq.*) to whimper.

хо́бби *neut. indecl.* hobby.

хо́бот *m.* trunk, proboscis.

ход *m.* **1.** motion, speed. **2.** course, turn; move, stroke; lead.

хода́тайство *neut.* **1.** intercession. **2.** petition; solicitation.

хода́тайствовать OVA *impf. pf.* по- (о *with prep.*) to petition for.

ходи́ть *impf. indet. det.* идти́ to go; to walk; (*of transport*) to run.

хо́дкий *adj.* **1.** current. **2.** marketable.

ходово́й *adj.* **1.** operational, working. **2.** (*attrib.*) performance. **3.** fast-selling; in demand.

ходо́к FILL *m.* walker.

ходу́ли *pl.* stilts.

ходу́лочник *m.* (*bird*) stilt.

ходу́льный *adj.* stilted.

ходу́н *m.:* ходи́ть ходуно́м *impf.* to shake violently.

ходунки́ *pl.* (*device*) walker.

ходьба́ *f.* walking.

ходя́чий *adj.* walking; ambulatory.

хожде́ние *neut.* **1.** walking; going. **2.** circulation. **3.** currency.

хозрасчёт *m.* undertaking on a self-supporting basis.

хозя́ин *m.* **1.** master. **2.** owner, proprietor. **3.** host.

хозя́йка *f.* **1.** mistress. **2.** proprietress. **3.** hostess.

хозя́йничать *impf.* to keep house; to be in charge.

хозя́йский *adj.* master's; proprietary.

хозя́йственник *m.* administrator.

хозя́йственность *f.* efficiency.

хозя́йственный **1.** *adj.* economic. **2.** (*attrib.*) household. **3.** economical.

хозя́йство *neut.* **1.** economy. **2.** household.

хозя́йствование *neut.* managing.

хозя́йствовать OVA *impf.* to manage.

хозя́йчик *m.* (*colloq.*) small proprietor.

Хокка́йдо *m.* Hokkaido.

хокке́й *m.* hockey.

хокке́йный *adj.* (*attrib.*) hockey.

хо́леный *adj.* well-groomed.

холе́ра *f.* cholera.

холе́рик *m.* high-strung person.

холери́ческий *adj.* choleric.

холе́рный *adj.* (*attrib.*) cholera.

холестери́н *m.* cholesterol.

хо́лить *impf.* to take care of.

хо́лка *f.* withers.

холл *m.* **1.** meeting hall. **2.** lobby.

холм *m.* hill. —и́стый *adj.* hilly.

хо́лмик *m.* small hill.

хо́лод *m.* cold.

холоде́ц FILL *m.* (*colloq.*) aspic (*of meat or fish*).

холоди́льник *m.* icebox; refrigerator.

холоди́льный *adj.* (*attrib.*) refrigeration.

холо́дненький *adj.* (*colloq.*) chilly.

хо́лодно *adv.* coldly. — *adj.* (*pred.*) cold.

холоднова́тый *adj.* rather cold.

холоднокро́вный *adj.* (*zool.*) cold-blooded.

хо́лодность *f.* coldness.

холо́дный *adj.* cold.

холодо́к FILL *m.* (*colloq.*) coolness; chill.

холо́п *m. f.* —ка (*hist.*) serf.

холо́пский *adj.* serf's.

холо́пство *neut.* serfdom.

холо́пствовать OVA *impf.* to be servile.
холости́ть *impf. pf.* вы́- to castrate; to geld (*an animal*).
холосто́й[1] *adj.* unmarried.
холосто́й[2] *adj.* 1. idle. 2. blank.
холостя́к *m.* bachelor.
холостя́цкий *adj.* (*colloq.*) (*attrib.*) bachelor.
холоще́ние *neut.* castration.
холощёный *adj.* castrated; (*of an animal*) gelded.
холст *m.* canvas; linen.
холсти́на *f.* sackcloth.
холсти́нка *f.* piece of cloth.
холщо́вый *adj.* linen.
хо́ля *f.*: жить в хо́ле *impf.* to be lovingly cared for.
хому́т *m.* horse's collar.
хомя́к *m.* hamster.
хор *m.* chorus, choir.
хора́л *m.* chorale.
хорва́т *m. f.* —ка Croat.
Хорва́тия *f.* Croatia.
хо́рда *f.* (*math.*) chord.
Хорéзм *m.* Khorezm.
хорéй *m.* trochee. — хорéйческий *adj.* trochaic.
хорёк FILL *m.* polecat; ferret.
хореóграф *m.* choreographer.
хореографи́ческий *adj.* choreographic.
хореогра́фия *f.* choreography.
хорéя *f.* chorea.
хори́ст *m. f.* —ка member of a choir.
хормéйстер *m.* choirmaster.
хорово́д *m.* round dance (*folk dance*).
хорово́й *adj.* choral.
хорони́ть *impf. pf.* по-, с- to bury, to inter.
хоро́шенький *adj.* pretty.
хоро́шенько *adv.* (*colloq.*) properly; thoroughly.
хоро́ший *adj.* good.
хорошо́ *adv.* well. — *adj.* (*pred.*) all right; good.
хо́ры *pl.* gallery; balcony
хорь *m.* fitch; ferret.
хорько́вый *adj.* (*attrib.*) fitch.
хотéть *impf. pf.* за- to want, to wish, to have a desire.
хотéться *impf. impers.* (*with dat.*) 1. to want, to wish. 2. to feel like (*doing*). — мне хо́чется есть (спать) I want to eat (sleep); I'm hungry (sleepy).
хоть *conj.* although; at least. — хоть бы if only.
хотя́ *conj.* although. — хотя́ бы even though; even if; if only.
хохла́тый *adj.* crested.
хохла́ч *m.* hooded seal.
хо́хлиться *impf. pf.* на- (*of a bird*) to ruffle its feathers.
хохо́л *m.* 1. crest (*of a bird*). 2. topknot.
хохоло́к FILL *m. dim. of.* хохо́л.
хо́хот *m.* loud laughter.
хохота́ть *impf.* to roar with laughter.
хохоту́н *m. f.* —ья (*colloq.*) merry fellow.
Хо-Ши-Мин-Си́ти *m.* Ho Chi Minh City (*formerly: Saigon*).
хра́бро *adv.* bravely.
хра́брость *f.* bravery.
хра́брый *adj.* brave, courageous.
храм *m.* temple; church.
хранéние *neut.* keeping, storing, storage.

храни́лище *neut.* 1. storage. 2. warehouse.
храни́тель *m. f.* —ница custodian, keeper.
храни́ть *impf.* to keep, to store.
храп *m.* snoring.
храпéть *impf.* to snore.
храпови́к *m.* ratchet.
храпово́й *adj.* (*attrib.*) ratchet.
храпу́н *m. f.* —ья (*colloq.*) snorer.
хребéт FILL *m.* 1. (*anat.*) spine. 2. mountain range.
хрен *m.* horseradish.
хрестома́тия *f.* reader; selections of literature.
хризантéма *f.* chrysanthemum.
хрип *m.* wheeze. —лый *adj.* hoarse. —отá *f.* hoarseness.
хри́пло *adv.* hoarsely.
христиа́нин *m. f.* христиа́нка Christian.
Христиа́нство *neut.* Christianity.
Христóс *m.* (*gen.* Христа́) Christ.
хром *m.* chromium.
хромати́ческий *adj.* chromatic.
хрома́ть *impf.* to limp.
хроми́рование *neut.* chrome plating.
хроми́ровать OVA *impf.* and *pf.* to plate with chrome.
хро́мистый *adj.* (*attrib.*) chrome.
хроми́т *m.* chromite.
хро́мовый *adj.* (*attrib.*) chrome.
хромо́й *adj.* lame — *m.* lame person.
хромоно́гий *adj.* lame.
хромосо́ма *f.* chromosome.
хромотá *f.* lameness.
хро́ник *m.* (*colloq.*) chronically ill person.
хро́ника *f.* chronicle.
хроника́льный *adj.* (*attrib.*) chronicle.
хрони́ческий *adj.* chronic.
хронологи́ческий *adj.* chronological.
хрономéтр *m.* chronometer.
хронометра́ж *m.* time (and motion) study.
хронометражи́ст *m.* time-study man.
хронометри́ровать OVA *impf.* and *pf.* to time; to clock.
хрономéтрист *m.* timer.
хру́пкий *adj.* fragile; frail; delicate.
хру́пкость *f.* fragility.
хруст *m.* crackle, to crunch.
хруста́лик *m.* (*colloq.*) item made of crystal.
хруста́ль *f.* crystal.
хруста́льный *adj.* crystal.
хруста́н *m.* dotterel.
хрустéть *impf. pf.* хру́стнуть to crackle, to crunch.
хрущ *m.* may bug; cockchafer.
хрю́канье *neut.* grunting.
хрю́кать *impf. pf.* хрю́кнуть to grunt.
хряк *m.* male hog.
хрящ[1] *m.* (*anat.*) cartilage.
хрящ[2] *m.* gravel.
хрящева́тый *adj.* cartilaginous.
хрящево́й *adj.* (*attrib.*) cartilage.
худéть *impf. pf.* по- to get thin; to lose weight.
ху́до[1] *neut.* (*colloq.*) harm, evil.
ху́до[2] *adv.* bad, badly. — *adj.* (*pred.*) (*with dat.*) (to feel) unwell.
худобá *f.* thinness.
худо́жественность *f.* artistry; artistic value.

худо́жественный *adj.* **1.** (*attrib.*) art. **2.** artistic. — худо́жественная литерату́ра *f.* belles-lettres.

худо́жество *neut.* art.

худо́жник *m. f.* худо́жница artist; painter.

худо́й *adj.* **1.** lean; meager. **2.** evil, bad.

худоща́вый *adj.* skinny; lean; thin.

ху́дшее *neut.* the worse.

ху́дший *adj.* worst.

ху́же *adv.* worse.

хула́ *f.* verbal abuse; hostile criticism.

хулига́н *m. f.* —ка ruffian, hooligan.

хулига́нить *impf.* to behave like a hoodlum.

хулига́нский *adj.* like a hoodlum.

хулига́нство *neut.* disorderly conduct.

хули́тель *m. f.* —ница detractor.

хули́ть *impf.* to disparage.

ху́нта *f.* junta.

хурма́ *f.* persimmon.

ху́тор *m.* farmstead.

хуторско́й *adj.* (*attrib.*) farm.

хэ́кер *m.* (*slang*) hacker.

Ц

ца́пля *f.* heron.
цара́пать *impf. v.t.* to scratch.
цара́пина *f.* scratch.
царе́вич *m.* czarevich.
царе́вна *f.* czarevna.
цареуби́йство *neut.* regicide.
цари́зм *m.* czarism.
цари́ть *impf.* to reign.
цари́ца *f.* czarina.
ца́рский *adj.* the czar's; of the czar.
ца́рственный *adj.* majestic; regal.
ца́рствование *neut.* reign.
царь *m.* czar.
Царьгра́д *m.* Tsarigrad (*older name for Istanbul*).
цвести́ *impf.* to bloom, to flower, to blossom.
цвет[1] *m.* color.
цвет[2] *m.* **1.** flower. **2.** blossom.
цвете́ние *neut.* blooming; blossoming.
цвети́стый *adj.* colorful.
цветко́вый *adj.* (*of plants*) flowering.
цветна́я капу́ста *f.* cauliflower.
цветни́к *m.* flower bed.
цветно́й *adj.* colored.
цветово́дство *neut.* floriculture.
цветово́й *adj.* (*attrib.*) color.
цвето́к *m.* (*pl.* цветы́) **1.** flower. **2.** blossom.
цветоло́же *neut.* (*bot.*) receptacle.
цветоно́жка *f.* (*bot.*) pedicel.
цвето́чек FILL *m. dim. of* цвето́к.
цвето́чница *f.* flower girl.
цвето́чный *adj.* (*attrib.*) flower.
цвету́щий *adj.* **1.** flowering. **2.** flourishing.
цеди́ть *impf.* to strain; to filter.
це́дра *f.* dried orange *or* lemon peel.
Це́зарь *m.* Caesar.
це́зий *m.* cesium.
цейтно́т *m.* (*chess*) time difficulty.
целе́бный *adj.* medicinal, curative.
целево́й *adj.* with a particular purpose.
целесообра́зный *adj.* expedient, practical.
целеустремлённый *adj.* purposeful.
целико́м *adv.* entirely, completely.
целина́ *f.* virgin soil.
цели́нный *adj.* (*of land*) virgin.
цели́тельный *adj.* healing.
це́лить *impf.* to aim.
целлофа́н *m.* cellophane.
целлофа́новый *adj.* cellophane.
целлуло́ид *m.* celluloid.
целлуло́идный *adj.* celluloid.
целлюло́за *f.* cellulose.
целлюло́зный *adj.* cellulose.
целова́ть OVA *impf. pf.* по- *v.t.* to kiss.
це́лое *neut.* whole.
целому́дрие *neut.* chastity.
це́лостность *f.* wholeness; unity.
це́лостный *adj.* integral.
це́лость *f.* **1.** safety. **2.** unity. — в це́лости intact.
це́лый *adj.* whole.
цель *f.* aim, purpose, intention.
це́льность *f.* unity; (*territorial*) integrity.

це́льный *adj.* **1.** whole. **2.** single; unified. **3.** complete; finished.
Це́льсий *m.* Celsius; centigrade. — **10 гра́дусов по Це́льсию** ten degrees Celsius/centigrade.
цеме́нт *m.* cement.
цементи́ровать OVA *impf. and pf.* to cement.
цеме́нтный *adj.* cement.
цена́ price; cost.
ценз *m.* requirement.
це́нзор *m.* censor.
цензу́ра *f.* censorship.
цензу́рный *adj.* (*attrib.*) censorship.
цени́тель *m. f.* —ница judge; connoisseur.
цени́ть *impf.* to value; to estimate.
це́нник *m.* price list.
це́нность *f.* value.
це́нный *adj.* valuable.
цент *m.* cent.
це́нтнер *m.* centner (100 kilograms).
центр *m.* center.
централиза́ция *f.* centralization.
централи́зм *m.* centralism.
централизо́ванный *adj.* centralized.
централизова́ть OVA *impf. and pf.* to centralize.
центра́льный *adj.* central.
центробе́жный *adj.* centrifugal.
центрово́й *adj.* (*attrib.*) center; central.
центростреми́тельный *adj.* centripetal.
цеп *m.* flail.
цепене́ть *impf. pf.* о- to become rigid; to become numb.
це́пкий *adj.* **1.** prehensile. **2.** tenacious. **3.** perceptive.
це́пкость *f.* tenacity.
цепля́ться *impf.* (за *with acc.*) to cling to.
цепно́й *adj.* (*attrib.*) chain. — **цепна́я реа́кция** chain reaction.
цепо́чка *f.* small chain.
цепь *f.* chain.
церебра́льный *adj.* cerebral. — **церебра́льный парали́ч** cerebral palsy.
церемониа́л *m.* ritual; ceremonial.
церемониа́льный *adj.* ceremonial.
церемо́ниться *impf. pf.* по- (*colloq.*) to stand on ceremony.
церемо́ния *f.* ceremony.
церемо́нный *adj.* ceremonious.
це́рий *m.* cerium.
церковнославя́нский *adj.* Church Slavonic.
церко́вный *adj.* (*attrib.*) church.
це́рковь *f.* church.
цесаре́вич *m.* (*hist.*) crown prince.
цеса́рка *f.* guinea hen.
цех *m.* **1.** factory shop. **2.** guild.
цехово́й *adj.* (*attrib.*) shop.
цеце́ *m. indecl.:* му́ха цеце́ tsetse (*Glossina morsitans*).
циа́н *m.* cyanogen.
циани́д *m.* cyanide.
циани́стый *adj.* cyanic.
циа́новый *adj.* cyanic.

цианóз *m.* cyanosis.
цивилизáция *f.* civilization.
цивилизóванный *adj.* civilized.
цивилизовáть OVA *impf.* and *pf.* to civilize.
цивильный *adj.* (*obs.*) civilian.
цигáрка *f.* (*colloq.*) hand-rolled cigarette.
цигéйка *f.* wool of the tsigai sheep.
цикáда *f.* cicada.
цикл *m.* cycle.
цикламéн *m.* cyclamen.
цикли́ческий *also* цикли́чный *adj.* cyclical.
циклóн *m.* cyclone.
циклони́ческий *adj.* cyclonic.
циклотрóн *m.* cyclotron.
цикóрий chickory.
цикóрный *adj.* (*attrib.*) chicory.
цику́та *f.* (*tree*) water hemlock.
цили́ндр *m.* cylinder. —и́ческий *adj.* cylindrical.
цимбáлы *pl.* dulcimer.
цини́зм *m.* cynicism.
ци́ник *m.* cynic.
цини́ческий *adj.* cynical.
цини́чность *m.* cynicism.
цинк *m.* zinc. —овый *adj.* (*attrib.*) zinc.
ци́нния *f.* zinnia.
цинóвка *f.* mat.
цирк *m.* circus.
циркáч *m. f.* —ка (*colloq.*) circus performer.
цирковóй *adj.* (*attrib.*) circus.
циркóн *m.* zircon.
циркóний *m.* zirconium.
циркули́ровать OVA *impf.* to circulate.
ци́ркуль *m.* pair of compasses; dividers.
циркуля́р *m.* circular. —ный *adj.* pertaining to a circular.
циркуля́ция *f.* circulation.
циррóз *m.* cirrhosis.

цирю́льник *m.* (*obs.*) barber.
цирю́льня *f.* (*obs.*) barbershop.
цистéрна *f.* **1.** cistern. **2.** tank car.
цитадéль *f.* citadel.
цитáта *f.* quotation.
цити́рование *neut.* quoting.
цити́ровать OVA *impf. pf.* про- to quote.
цитологи́ческий *adj.* cytological.
цитолóгия *f.* cytology.
ци́тра *f.* zither.
цитрáт *m.* citrate.
ци́трус *m.* citrus.
ци́трусовые *pl.* citrus plants.
ци́трусовый *adj.* citrus.
циферблáт *m.* dial; face (*of a clock*).
ци́фра *f.* number; figure.
цифровóй *adj.* numerical. — цифровóй прои́грыватель *m.* compact disk *or* CD player.
цóкать *impf. pf.* цóкнуть to clatter, to clank.
цóколь *m.* socle.
цóкот *m.* clatter.
ЦРУ *neut.* (*abbr. of* Центрáльное развéдывательное управлéние) C.I.A. (*abbr. of* Central Intelligence Agency).
цуг *m.* team of horses (*harnessed in tandem* or *in pairs*).
цу́гом *adv.* in tandem.
цукáт *m.* candied fruit.
цыгáн *m.* —ка *f.* Romany (*formerly: Gypsy*).
цыгáнский *adj.* Romany (*formerly: Gypsy*).
цы́кать *impf. pf.* цы́кнуть to silence; to hush.
цынгá *f.* scurvy.
цы́пки *pl.* (*colloq.*) red spots (*on the hands, etc.*).
цыплёнок FILL *m.* chick.
цы́почки *pl.*: на цы́почках on tiptoe.
Цю́рих *m.* Zürich.

Ч

чабан *m.* shepherd.
чабёр FILL *m.* (*plant*) savory.
чабрец *m.* thyme.
чавкать *impf.* **1.** to munch. **2.** to tramp.
Чад *m.* Chad.
чад *m.* fumes.
чадить *impf. pf.* на- to smoke; to give off fumes.
чадный *adj.* **1.** smoky. **2.** dazed. **3.** deadening.
чадо *neut.* (*arch.*) child; offspring.
чадра *f.* veil (*worn by Moslem women*).
чаевые *pl.* tip; gratuity.
чаепитие *neut.* drinking of tea.
чайка *f.* tea leaf.
чай *m.* tea.
чайка *f.* seagull.
чайная *f.* tea room.
чайная ложка *f.* teaspoon.
чайник *m.* teapot.
чайница *f.* tea caddy
чайный *adj.* (*attrib.*) tea.
чал *m.* mooring line.
чалить *impf.* to moor (*a ship*).
чалка *f.* mooring line.
чалма *f.* turban.
чалый *adj.* roan.
чан *m.* tub, vat.
чара *f.* (*obs.*) goblet.
чарка *f.* (*obs.*) cup.
Чарлстон *m.* Charleston.
чаровать OVA *impf.* to charm, to bewitch.
чаровница *f.* charming woman.
чародей *m.* magician, sorcerer.
чародейка *f.* sorceress.
чародейство *neut.* sorcery.
чарующий *adj.* charming; enchanting.
чары *pl.* **1.** charm; charms. **2.** magic charm.
час *m.* hour; o'clock. — который час? what time is it?
часовня *f.* chapel.
часовой *adj.* **1.** hour-long. **2.** (*attrib.*) clock; watch; time. — *m.* sentry.
часовщик *m.* watchmaker.
частенько *adv.* (*colloq.*) fairly often.
частица *f.* (*gram.*) particle.
частично *adv.* partly; partially.
частичный *adj.* partial.
частник *m. f.* частница (*colloq.*) private trader.
частное *neut.* **1.** the particular. **2.** (*math.*) quotient.
частный *adj.* private; particular.
часто *adv.* frequently.
частокол *m.* fence; paling; palisade.
частота *f.* frequency.
частотный *adj.* (*attrib.*) frequency.
частушка *f.* ditty; jingle.
частый *adj.* frequent.
часть *f.* part.
частью *adv.* partly; in part.
часы *pl.* clock, watch.
чахлый *adj.* **1.** sickly. **2.** withered.

чахнуть *impf. pf.* за- **1.** to wither. **2.** to become weak. **3.** to fade away.
чахотка *f.* (*med.*) consumption.
чаша *f.* **1.** large bowl. **2.** drinking bowl.
чашелистик *m.* sepal.
чашечка *f.* small cup.
чашка *f.* cup.
чаща *f.* thicket; dense forest.
чаще *adv.* more frequently *or* often.
чащоба *f.* (*colloq.*) dense forest.
чаяние *neut.* expectation; hope.
чаять *impf.* (*obs.*) to expect; to hope.
чваниться *impf.* to boast.
чванливый *adj.* conceited; pretentious.
чванный *adj.* conceited; arrogant.
чванство *neut.* arrogance.
чебурек *m.* mutton pie (*Caucasian dish*).
чего *pron. gen. of* что.
чей *indef. pron.* whose.
чей-либо *indef. pron.* someone's; anyone's.
чей-нибудь *indef. pron.* somebody's; anybody's.
чей-то *indef. pron.* somebody's.
чек *m.* check.
чека *f.* pin; cotter pin.
чекан *m.* stamp; die; punch.
чеканить *impf. pf.* от- to coin, to mint.
чеканка *f.* **1.** minting of coins. **2.** embossed design.
чеканный *adj.* **1.** embossed; engraved. **2.** crisp; precise.
чековый *adj.* (*attrib.*) check; checking.
челеста *f.* celesta.
чёлка *f.* bangs of hair; forelock.
челн *m.* canoe.
челнок *m.* shuttle.
челночный *adj.* (*attrib.*) shuttle.
челночный корабль *m.* space shuttle.
человек *m.* **1.** man. **2.** person, human being.
человеконенавистник *m. f.* —ненавистница misanthrope.
человеконенавистнический *adj.* misanthropic.
человеконенавистничество *neut.* misanthropy.
человекообразный *adj.* anthropomorphous; manlike.
человекоподобный *adj.* manlike; anthropoid.
человеко-час *m.* man-hour.
человеческий *adj.* human; humane.
человечество *neut.* humanity.
человечность *f.* humaneness.
человечный *adj.* humane.
челюстной *adj.* (*attrib.*) jaw.
челюсть *f.* jaw.
Челябинск *m.* Chelyabinsk.
челядь *f.* (*coll.*) servants.
чем *pron. instr. of* что — *conj.* than.
чём *pron. prep. of* что.
чемерица *f.* hellebore.
чемодан *m.* suitcase; valise.
чемоданчик *m.* small suitcase.
чемпион *m. f.* —ка champion.
чемпионат *m.* championship.

чемпио́нский *adj.* (*attrib.*) championship.
чемпио́нство *neut.* championship.
чему́ *pron. dat. of* **что.**
Ченна́й *m.* Chennai (*formerly: Madras*).
чепе́ц FILL *m.* woman's cap.
чепуха́ *f.* (*colloq.*) nonsense.
че́пчик *m.* **1.** *dim. of* **чепе́ц. 2.** baby's bonnet.
червеобра́зный *adj.* vermiform.
че́рви *pl.* (*cards*) hearts.
черви́вый *adj.* worm-eaten.
черво́нец FILL *m.* **1.** ten ruble banknote circulated from 1922 to 1947. **2.** chervonets (*gold coin*).
черво́нный¹ *adj.* (*cards*) of hearts.
черво́нный² *adj.* red; scarlet.
че́рвы *pl.* (*cards*) hearts.
червь *also* **червя́к** *m.* worm.
червя́чная шестерня́ *f.* worm gear.
червячо́к FILL *m.* small worm. — **замори́ть червячка́** to have a bite to eat.
черда́к *m.* attic; garret.
черда́чный *adj.* (*attrib.*) attic.
черёд *m.* (*colloq.*) (*one's*) turn.
череда́¹ *f.* **1.** file; column. **2.** chain; sequence.
череда́² *f.* bur marigold.
чередова́ние *neut.* alternation.
чередова́ть OVA *impf. v.t.* to alternate.
чередова́ться OVA *impf. v.i.* to alternate.
че́рез *also* **чрез** *prep.* (*with acc.*) across, over; through; (*time*) in; after. — **че́рез день** every other day.
черёмуха *f.* bird cherry.
черено́к FILL *m.* **1.** handle. **2.** graft; cutting.
че́реп *m.* skull.
черепа́ха *f.* tortoise, turtle.
черепа́ховый *adj.* (*attrib.*) turtle.
черепа́ший *adj.* (*attrib.*) turtle; turtle's.
черепи́ца *f.* tile.
черепи́чный *adj.* (*attrib.*) tile; tiled.
черепна́я коро́бка *f.* cranium.
черепо́к FILL *m.* shard of pottery.
черессе́дельник *m.* saddle girth.
чересчу́р *adv.* too; exceedingly.
чере́шневый *adj.* (*attrib.*) cherry.
чере́шня *f.* cherry; cherry tree.
чере́шок FILL *m.* **1.** petiole. **2.** handle. **3.** graft; cutting.
Черка́ссы *pl.* Cherkasy.
черке́с *m. f.* **черке́шенка** Circassian.
черне́ть *impf.* to become *or* turn black.
Черни́гов *m.* Chernihiv (*Russian: Chernigov*).
черни́ка *f.* blueberries; whortleberries; huckleberries.
черни́ла *pl.* ink.
черни́льница *f.* inkstand.
черни́ть *impf.* **1.** to blacken. **2.** to slander.
черни́чный *adj.* (*attrib.*) blueberry.
чёрно-бе́лый *adj.* black and white.
чёрно-бу́рый *adj.* dark brown.
Черно́быль *m.* Chernobyl.
чернови́к *m.* draft; rough copy.
черново́й *adj.* (*of document*) rough; preliminary.
черного́рец FILL *m. f.* **черного́рка** Montenegrin.
чернозём *m.* rich black topsoil.
черноко́жий *adj.* dark-skinned; black.
черномазый *adj.* dark; swarthy.
чернорабо́чий *m.* unskilled worker.

черносли́в *m.* (*coll.*) prunes.
чернота́ *f.* blackness.
чёрный *adj.* black.
чернь *f.* riffraff; rabble.
черпа́лка *f.* (*colloq.*) scoop.
черстве́ть *impf.* to become stale.
чёрствый *adj.* stale.
чёрт *m.* devil.
черта́ *f.* **1.** trait, characteristic. **2.** line.
чертёж *m.* sketch; draft.
чертёжник *m. f.* **чертёжница** draftsman.
чертёжный *adj.* (*attrib.*) drawing.
чертёнок FILL *m.* (*colloq.*) little devil.
черти́ть *impf. pf.* **на-** to draw.
чёртова дю́жина *f.* baker's dozen.
чёртово колесо́ *neut.* Ferris wheel.
черто́вски *adv.* (*colloq.*) awfully; rather.
черто́вский *adj.* devilish; (*colloq.*) damnable.
чертовщи́на *pl.* devils.
черто́г *m.* (*arch.*) **1.** chamber. **2.** mansion. **3.** hall.
чертополо́х *m.* thistle.
чёрточка *f.* line; hyphen.
черче́ние *neut.* drawing.
чеса́лка *f.* combing machine.
чеса́льный *adj.* (*attrib.*) combing; carding.
чеса́ние *neut.* combing; carding.
чеса́ть *impf. pf.* **по-** to scratch; to comb; to card. **—ся** to scratch oneself.
Че́ске-Будеёвице *pl.* Budějovice (*German: Budweis*).
чесно́к *m.* garlic.
чесно́чный *adj.* (*attrib.*) garlic.
чесо́тка *f.* mange.
че́ствование *neut.* honoring.
че́ствовать OVA *impf.* **1.** to celebrate. **2.** to honor.
че́стно *adv.* honestly. — **че́стно говоря́** in all honesty.
честно́й *adj.* (*obs.*) honored.
че́стность *f.* honesty.
че́стный *adj.* honest; fair.
честолю́бец FILL *m.* ambitious person.
честолюби́вый *adj.* ambitious.
честолю́бие *neut.* ambition.
честь *f.* honor.
чёт *m.* (*colloq.*) even number.
чета́ *f.* pair; couple; married couple.
четве́рг *m.* Thursday.
четверёньки *pl.:* **на четвере́ньках** on all fours.
четвёрка *f.* four; foursome.
четверно́й *adj.* fourfold; quadruple.
четверня́ *f.* team of four horses.
че́тверо *num.* (*coll.*) four.
четвероно́гий *adj.* four-legged.
четвероно́гое *neut.* quadruped.
четверости́шие *neut.* quatrain.
четверта́к *m.* (*obs.*) twenty-five kopecks.
четверти́на *f.* twenty-five-ruble note.
четвертно́й *adj.* (*of a grade*) for a school quarter.
четвертова́ние *neut.* execution by quartering.
четвертова́ть OVA *impf. and pf.* to execute by quartering.
четвёртый *adj.* fourth.
че́тверть *f.* quarter; fourth.
четвертьфина́л *m.* quarterfinal.

четвертьфина́льный *adj.* quarterfinal.

чётки *pl.* rosary (*string of beads*).

чёткий *adj.* clear; legible.

чётко *adv.* clearly; distinctly.

чёткость *f.* **1.** precision. **2.** efficiency. **3.** clarity.

чётный *adj.* (*of a number*) even.

четы́ре *num.* four. **—ста** *num.* four hundred.

четы́режды *adv.* four times.

четырёхгоди́чный *adj.* (*attrib.*) four-year.

четырёхголо́сный *adj.* (*mus.*) four-part.

четырёхгра́нник *m.* tetrahedron.

четырёхгра́нный *adj.* tetrahedral.

четырёхдне́вный *adj.* (*attrib.*) four-day.

четырёхкла́ссный *adj.* (*of schools* and *courses*) four-year.

четырёхколёсный *adj.* four-wheeled.

четырёхкра́тный *adj.* fourfold; quadruple.

четырёхле́тие *neut.* fourth anniversary.

четырёхме́сячный *adj.* (*attrib.*) four-month.

четырёхнеде́льный *adj.* (*attrib.*) four-week.

четырёхсотле́тие *neut.* four-hundredth anniversary.

четырёхсотле́тний *adj.* (*attrib.*) four-hundred-year.

четырёхсо́тный *adj.* four-hundredth.

четырёхсто́пный *adj.* tetrameter.

четырёхсторо́нний *adj.* four-sided.

четырёхуго́льник *m.* quadrangle.

четырёхуго́льный *adj.* quadrangular.

четырёхэта́жный *adj.* four-story.

четы́рнадцатый *adj.* fourteenth.

четы́рнадцать *num.* fourteen.

чех *m. f.* **че́шка** Czech.

чехарда́ *f.* leapfrog.

Че́хия *f.* Czech Lands.

чехо́л FILL *m.* (slip) cover; case.

чечеви́ца *f.* lentil.

чече́нец FILL *m. f.* **чече́нка** Chechen.

чечётка *f.* tap dance.

Че́чня́ *f.* Chechnya.

Че́шская Респу́блика *f.* Czech Republic.

че́шский *adj.* Czech.

чешу́йчатый *adj.* scaly.

чешуя́ *f.* scales (*of a fish, snake*).

чи́бис *m.* pewit; lapwing.

чиж *m.* (*bird*) siskin.

Чика́го *m.* Chicago.

Чимке́нт *m.* Shymkent.

чин *m.* grade; rank.

чина́р *m. also* **чина́ра** *f.* Oriental plane tree.

чини́ть[1] *impf. pf.* **по-** to repair.

чини́ть[2] *impf. pf.* **о-** to sharpen.

чини́ться *impf.* (*obs.*) to stand on ceremony.

чи́нный *adj.* decorous; proper; orderly.

чино́вник *m.* official; bureaucrat.

чино́внический *adj.* official's; official.

чино́вничество *neut.* **1.** officials. **2.** bureaucracy.

чино́вничий *adj.* official's; official.

чино́вный *adj.* (*obs.*) high-ranking.

чи́псы *pl.* potato chips.

чири́канье *neut.* chirping; twittering.

чири́кать *impf.* to chirp; to twitter.

чи́ркать *impf. pf.* **чи́ркнуть** **1.** to rub something against. **2.** to strike a match.

чиро́к FILL *m.* teal.

чи́сленно *adv.* numerically.

чи́сленность *f.* number, quantity.

чи́сленный *adj.* numerical.

числи́тель *m.* (*math.*) numerator.

числи́тельное *also* **и́мя числи́тельное** *neut.* numeral.

число́ *neut.* **1.** number; quantity. **2.** date. **3.** (*gram.*) number.

числово́й *adj.* numerical.

чи́стик *m.* (*bird*) guillemot.

чисти́лище *neut.* purgatory.

чи́стильщик *m. f.* **чи́стильщица** cleaner.

чи́стить *impf.* **1.** to clean. **2.** to brush. **3.** to peel.

чи́стка *f.* **1.** cleaning. **2.** purge, purging.

чи́сто *adv.* **1.** neatly; cleanly. **2.** purely.

чистово́й *adj.* (*of a document*) final, clean.

чистога́н *m.* (*colloq.*) cash; ready money.

чистокро́вный *adj.* thoroughbred.

чистописа́ние *neut.* penmanship.

чистопло́тный *adj.* tidy; neat; clean.

чистопоро́дный *adj.* thoroughbred.

чистосерде́чие *neut.* open-heartedness.

чистосерде́чный *adj.* frank, sincere.

чистота́ *f.* **1.** cleanliness. **2.** purity, innocence.

чи́стый *adj.* clean.

Чита́ *f.* Chita.

чита́лка *f.* (*colloq.*) reading room.

чита́льный зал *m.* reading room.

чита́льня *f.* reading room.

чита́тель *m. f.* **—ница** reader.

чита́тельский *adj.* reader's; readers'.

чита́ть *impf. pf.* **про-** to read. — **чита́ть ле́кцию** to deliver a lecture.

чих *m.* (*colloq.*) sneeze.

чиха́нье *neut.* sneezing.

чиха́ть *impf. pf.* **чихну́ть** to sneeze.

чи́ще *adv. comp. of* **чи́стый**.

член *m.* **1.** member. **2.** (*gram.*) article.

члены-корреспонде́нт *m.* associate member (*of an academy*).

членовреди́тельство *neut.* (deliberate) mutilation.

членоразде́льный *adj.* articulate.

чле́нский *adj.* (*attrib.*) membership.

чле́нство *neut.* membership.

чмо́кать *impf. pf.* **чмо́кнуть** to smack one's lips.

чо́каться *impf. pf.* **чо́кнуться** to clink glasses (*in a toast*).

чо́порный *adj.* prim; stiff.

чрева́тый *adj.* (*with instr.*) fraught with.

чре́во *neut.* (*obs.*) stomach; womb.

чревовеща́ние *neut.* ventriloquism.

чревовеща́тель *m. f.* **—ница** ventriloquist.

чреда́ *f.* (*obs.*) turn.

чрезвыча́йно *adv.* extremely.

чрезвыча́йный *adj.* extraordinary.

чрезме́рно *adv.* excessively.

чрезме́рный *adj.* excessive; exceeding.

чте́ние *neut.* reading.

чтец *m. f.* **чти́ца** reader; reciter.

чти́во *neut.* (*colloq.*) (piece of) literary trash.

чтить *impf.* to honor; to respect.

что *pron.* what. — *conj.* that.

что́бы *conj.* in order to or that.

что́-либо *pron.* something; anything.

что́-нибудь *indef. pron.* something; anything.

что́-то *indef. pron.* something.

чуб *m.* forelock.

чуба́рый *adj.* (*of a horse's coat*) dappled.

чува́ш *m. f.* —ка Chuvash.

Чува́шия *f.* Chuvashia.

чу́вственный *adj.* sensual.

чувстви́тельность *f.* sensitivity.

чувстви́тельный *adj.* sensitive; sentimental.

чу́вство *neut.* sense; feeling.

чу́вствовать OVA *impf. pf.* по- to sense; to feel.

чугу́н *m.* cast iron.

чугунолите́йный *adj.* (*attrib.*) iron.

чуда́к *m. f.* чуда́чка (*person*) crank, eccentric.

чудакова́тый *adj.* odd; queer.

чуда́чество *neut.* quirk; peculiarity.

чудеса́ *pl. of* чу́до.

чуде́сно *adv.* **1.** wonderfully. **2.** marvelously. **3.** miraculously.

чуде́сный *adj.* wonderful, miraculous.

чу́диться *impf. pf.* по- *impers.* to seem.

чу́дище *neut.* (*obs.*) monster.

чудно́ *adv.* (*colloq.*) strangely; oddly.

чу́дно *adv.* **1.** wonderfully. **2.** marvelously. — *interj.* wonderful!

чудно́й odd; strange.

чу́дный *adj.* **1.** wonderful. **2.** marvelous. **3.** beautiful.

чу́до *neut.* wonder.

чудо́вище *neut.* monster.

чудо́вищность *f.* monstrosity.

чудо́вищный *adj.* monstrous.

чудоде́й *m.* (*colloq.*) miracle worker.

чудоде́йственный *adj.* wonder-working.

чудотво́рец FILL *m.* miracle worker.

Чудотво́рец FILL *m.* (icon of) St. Nikolay the Miracle worker.

чудотво́рный *adj.* wonder-working.

Чу́дское о́зеро *neut.* Lake Peipus.

чужа́к *m. f.* чужа́чка (*colloq.*) stranger.

чужби́на *f.* foreign land.

чужда́ться *impf.* (*with gen.*) **1.** to keep away from. **2.** to keep aloof; to avoid.

чу́ждый *adj.* alien.

чужезе́мец FILL *m. f.* чужезе́мка foreigner.

чужезе́мный *adj.* (*obs.*) foreign.

чужестра́нец FILL *m. f.* чужестра́нка foreigner.

чужестра́нный *adj.* (*obs.*) foreign.

чужо́й *adj.* **1.** strange. **2.** someone else's.

Чуко́тское мо́ре *neut.* Chukchi Sea.

чула́н *m.* storeroom; pantry.

чуло́к FILL *m.* stocking; hose.

чуло́чный *adj.* (*attrib.*) stocking; hose.

чума́ *f.* plague.

чума́зый *adj.* (*colloq.*) dirty.

чумно́й *adj.* (*attrib.*) plague.

чурба́н *m.* **1.** block of wood. **2.** (*fig.*) blockhead.

чу́рка *f.* block (*of wood*).

чу́ткий *adj.* **1.** sensitive. **2.** delicate, considerate.

чу́тко *adv.* closely.

чу́ткость *f.* **1.** sensitivity. **2.** consideration.

чу́точку *adv.* (*colloq.*) a little bit; a bit.

чуть *adv.* **1.** slightly. **2.** hardly. — чуть ли не almost.

чутьё *neut.* **1.** scent. **2.** intuition.

чуть-чу́ть *adv.* a tiny bit.

чу́чело *neut.* scarecrow.

чу́шка *f.* (*colloq.*) baby pig.

чушь *f.* (*colloq.*) nonsense; rubbish.

чу́ять *impf. pf.* по- to feel.

чьё *pron., see* чей.

чьи *pron., see* чей.

чья *pron., see* чей.

Ш

ша *interj.* (*slang*) stop it! shut up! enough!

шáбаш *m.* sabbath.

шабáшить *impf. pf.* по- (*colloq.*) to knock off work.

шáбер *m.* scraper.

шаблóн *m.* stencil; pattern; mold.

шаблóнный *adj.* (*fig.*) stereotyped; trite.

шаг *m.* step.

шагáть *impf. pf.* шагнýть to step; to pace; to stride.

шáгом *adv.* at a walk. — шáгом марш! forward march!

шáйба *f.* 1. (*sports*) puck. 2. (*tool*) washer.

шáйка *f.* gang, band.

шакáл *m.* jackal.

шалáнда *f.* (*naut.*) scow.

шалáш *m.* hut.

шалé *neut. indecl.* chalet.

шалúть *impf.* to misbehave; to be naughty.

шаловлúвость *f.* playfulness.

шаловлúвый *adj.* playful.

шалопáй *m.* (*colloq.*) idler; playboy.

шáлость *f.* trick; prank.

шалóт *m.* shallot.

шалýн *m. f.* —ья mischievous child.

шалфéй *m.* (*plant*) sage.

шáлый *adj.* (*colloq.*) crazy; mad.

шаль *f.* shawl.

шальнóй *adj.* 1. crazy; nuts. 2. (*of a bullet*) stray.

шамáн *m.* shaman.

шамáнство *neut.* shamanism.

шампáнское *neut.* champagne.

Шампáнь *f.* (*province*) Champagne.

шампýнь *m.* shampoo.

шанкр *m.* chancre.

шанс *m.* chance.

шансонéтка *f.* light comic song.

шантáж *m.* blackmail.

шантажúровать OVA *impf.* to blackmail.

шантажúст *m. f.* —ка blackmailer.

Шанхáй *m.* Shanghai.

шáпка *f.* cap.

шáпочка *f. dim. of* шáпка. — Крáсная шáпочка Little Red Riding Hood.

шáпочник *m. f.* шáпочница hatter.

шáпочный *adj.* (*attrib.*) hat.

шар *m.* ball; sphere. — воздýшный шар *m.* balloon.

шарабáн *m.* (*carriage*) gig.

шарáда *f.* charade.

шарж *m.* cartoon; caricature.

шаржúровать OVA *impf.* to caricature.

шáрик *m.* 1. marble; small ball. 2. globule.

шáриковый *adj.* ball-shaped.

шарикоподшúпник *m.* ball bearing.

шáрить *impf.* to fumble around; to rummage.

шáрканье *neut.* shuffling (*of feet*).

шáркать *impf.* to shuffle one's feet.

шарлатáн *m.* charlatan. —ство *neut.* quackery; charlatanism.

шарлатáнский *adj.* fraudulent.

шармáнка *f.* barrel organ.

шармáнщик *m.* organ grinder.

шарнúр *m.* hinge; joint.

шаровáры *pl.* wide loose trousers.

шаровúдный *adj.* spherical.

шаровóй *adj.* spherical.

шарообрáзный *adj.* spherical.

Шартр *m.* Chartres.

шарф *m.* scarf.

шассú *neut. indecl.* 1. chassis. 2. (*aero.*) landing gear.

шатáние *neut.* 1. swaying. 2. wavering. 3. wandering.

шатáть *impf.* 1. to sway; to rock. 2. to shake. —ся 3. to be(come) loose. 4. to stagger, to reel.

шатéн *m. f.* —ка person with brown hair.

шатёр FILL *m.* large tent.

шáткий *adj* unsteady; precarious.

шатýн *m.* connecting rod.

шáфер *m.* best man (*at wedding*).

шафрáн *m.* saffron.

шафрáнный *adj.* (*attrib.*) saffron.

шах *m.* (*chess*) check. — шах и мат (*chess*) checkmate.

шахматúст *m. f.* —ка chess player.

шáхматный *adj.* (*attrib.*) chess.

шáхматы *pl.* chess.

шáхта *f.* 1. mine. 2. pit.

шахтёр *m. f.* —ка miner.

шахтёрский *adj.* miner's.

шáхтный *adj.* (*attrib.*) mine.

шáшечница *f.* checkerboard.

шáшечный *adj.* (*attrib.*) checkers.

шáшки *pl.* (*game*) checkers.

шашлык *m.* shashlik; kebab.

шáшни *pl.* (*colloq.*) pranks; tricks.

швáбра *f.* mop.

шваль *f.* 1. junk; trash. 2. rabble; riffraff.

швартóв *m.* mooring line. — швартóвы *pl.* mooring.

швартовáть OVA *impf. pf.* при-, о- to moor (*a ship*).

Швáрцвальд *m.* Schwarzwald; Black Forest.

швед *m. f.* —ка Swede.

швéдский *adj.* Swedish.

швéйник *m. f.* швéйница sewer; garment worker.

швéйный *adj.* (*attrib.*) sewing.

швейцáр *m.* porter; doorman.

швейцáрец FILL *m. f.* швейцáрка Swiss.

Швейцáрия *f.* Switzerland.

Швéция *f.* Sweden.

швея *f.* seamstress.

швырóк *m.* 1. firewood; logs. 2. toss.

швыряние *neut.* tossing; hurling.

швырять *impf. pf.* швырнýть to toss; to fling; to hurl.

шевелúть *impf. pf.* по- to move; to stir.

шевелюра *f.* (head of) hair.

шевиóт *m.* cheviot.

шевиóтовый *adj.* (*attrib.*) cheviot.

шеврó *neut. indecl.* kidskin.

шевро́вый *adj.* kidskin; kid.
шевро́н *m.* (*mil.*) chevron.
шеде́вр *m.* masterpiece.
шезло́нг *m.* chaise longue.
ше́йка *m.* **1.** *dim. of* ше́я. **2.** neck; narrow part.
ше́йный *adj.* (*attrib.*) neck.
шейх *m.* sheik.
ше́лест *m.* rustle, rustling.
шелесте́ть *impf.* to rustle.
шёлк *m.* silk.
шелкови́нка *f.* (piece of) silk thread.
шелкови́стый *adj.* silky.
шелкови́ца *f.* mulberry.
шелкови́чный *adj.* (*attrib.*) mulberry.
шелково́дство *neut.* sericulture.
шёлковый *adj.* silk.
шелкопря́д *m.* silkworm.
шелла́к *m.* shellac.
шелохну́ть *pf.* to move slightly.
шелуди́вый *adj.* (*colloq.*) mangy.
шелуха́ *f.* peel; husk; hull.
шелуши́ть *impf.* to shell, to husk.
ше́льма *m. and f.* (*decl. f.*) (*colloq.*) rascal; scoundrel.
шельмова́ть OVA *impf. pf.* **о-** to cheat; to swindle.
шемя́кин суд *m.* unjust trial.
шепеля́вить *impf.* to lisp.
шепеля́вость *f.* lisp.
шепеля́вый *adj.* lisping.
шёпот *m.* whisper. — шёпотом *adv.* in a whisper.
шептала́ *f.* dried peaches; dried apricots.
шепта́ние *neut.* whispering.
шепта́ть *impf. pf.* шепну́ть to whisper.
шепту́н *m. f.* **—ья** (*colloq.*) whisperer.
шере́нга *f.* rank.
шери́ф *m.* sheriff.
шерохова́тость *f.* roughness.
шерохова́тый *adj.* rough; rugged.
шерсти́нка *f.* strand of wool.
шерсти́стый *adj.* woolly.
шерсть *f.* **1.** hair (*of animals*). **2.** wool.
шерстяно́й *adj.* woolen.
шерша́вый *adj.* rough.
ше́ршень FILL *m.* hornet.
шест *m.* pole.
шеста́я *f.* sixth.
ше́ствие *neut.* procession; train.
ше́ствовать OVA *impf.* to parade; to march.
шестёрка *f.* the numeral six.
шестерня́ *f.* wheel gear; cogwheel; pinion.
ше́стеро *coll. num.* six.
шестидеся́тый *adj.* sixtieth.
шестидне́вный *adj.* (*attrib.*) six-day.
шестикра́тный *adj.* (*attrib.*) sixfold.
шестиме́сячный *adj.* (*attrib.*) six-month.
шестисо́тый *adj.* six-hundredth.
шестиуго́льник *m.* hexagon.
шестиуго́льный *adj.* hexagonal.
шестна́дцатый *adj.* sixteenth.
шестна́дцать *num.* sixteen.
шесто́й *adj.* sixth.
шесто́к FILL *m.* **1.** hearth of a Russian stove. **2.** roost.
шесть *num.* six. —деся́т *num.* sixty. —со́т *num.* six hundred.

ше́стью *adv.* six times.
шеф *m.* **1.** chief. **2.** chef. —ство *neut.* patronage.
шеф-по́вар *m.* chef.
ше́фствовать OVA *impf.* to sponsor.
ше́я *f.* neck.
ши́бкий *adj.* (*colloq.*) fast.
ши́бко *adv.* (*colloq.*) fast.
ши́ворот *m.*: за ши́ворот by the scruff of the neck.
— ши́ворот-навы́ворот topsy-turvy.
шизофре́ник *m. f.* шизофрени́чка schizophrenic.
шизофрени́ческий *adj.* schizophrenic.
шизофрени́я *f.* schizophrenia.
шик *m.* chic; stylishness.
шика́рный *adj.* chic, smart.
ши́кать *impf. pf.* ши́кнуть (*colloq.*) (на *with acc.*) **1.** to say hush to. **2.** to shoo someone away.
ши́ллинг *m.* shilling.
ши́ло *neut.* awl.
шилоклю́вка *f.* (*bird*) avocet.
шилохво́ст *m.* (*duck*) pintail.
шимпанзе́ *m. indecl.* chimpanzee.
ши́на *f.* **1.** tire. **2.** (*med.*) splint.
шине́ль *f.* overcoat.
шинка́рь *m. f.* шинка́рка (*obs.*) tavern keeper.
шинкова́ть OVA *impf.* to chop; to shred (*vegetables*).
ши́нный *adj.* (*attrib.*) tire.
шино́к *m.* (*obs.*) tavern.
шинши́лла *f.* chinchilla.
шиньо́н *m.* chignon.
шип *m.* thorn.
шипе́ние *neut.* **1.** hissing. **2.** splitting. **3.** sizzling.
шипе́ть *impf.* to hiss.
шипо́вник *m.* wild rose.
шипу́чее *neut.* sparkling beverage.
шипу́честь *f.* effervescence.
шипу́чий *adj.* sparkling.
шипу́чка *f.* (*colloq.*) sparkling beverage.
шипя́щий *adj.* **1.** hissing. **2.** (*phon.*) sibilant.
ши́ре *adj. comp. of* широ́кий.
ширина́ *f.* width; breadth.
шири́нка *f.* (*colloq.*) fly (*on trousers*).
ши́рить *impf.* **1.** to widen. **2.** to expand.
ши́рма *f.* **1.** screen. **2.** cover.
широ́кий *adj.* wide.
широко́ *adv.* widely.
широковеща́ние *neut.* broadcasting.
широковеща́тельный *adj.* (*attrib.*) broadcasting.
ширококоле́йный *adj.* (*of railroad*) wide-gauge.
широкопле́чий *adj.* broad-shouldered.
широкоуго́льный *adj.* wide-angle.
широта́ *f.* **1.** width. **2.** breadth. **3.** (*geog.*) latitude.
ширпотре́б *m.* (*colloq.*) consumer goods in mass consumption.
ширь *f.* expanse.
шить *impf. pf.* **с-** sew.
шитьё *neut.* **1.** sewing. **2.** embroidering; embroidery.
ши́фер *m.* slate.
ши́ферный *adj.* (*attrib.*) slate.
шифо́н *m.* chiffon.
шифо́новый *adj.* chiffon.
шифонье́р *m.* chiffonier.
шифр *m.* cipher.
шифрова́льщик *m. f.* шифрова́льщица cipher clerk.

шифро́ванный *adj.* coded.
шифрова́ть OVA *impf. pf.* за- to encode; to encipher.
шифро́вка *f.* enciphering; encoding.
шиш *m.* (*colloq.*) **1.** nothing. **2.** (*fig.*) insulting gesture.
ши́шка *f.* **1.** (*bot.*) cone. **2.** bump, lump.
шишкова́тый *adj.* knobby.
шишкови́дный *adj.* cone-shaped.
шкала́ *f.* scale.
шка́лик *m.* old Russian unit of liquid measure equal to about one-eighth of a pint.
шка́нцы *pl.* quarterdeck.
шкату́лка *f.* **1.** box, case. **2.** casket.
шкаф *m.* **1.** cupboard. **2.** wardrobe.
шка́фик *also* шка́фчик *m.* small closet.
шквал *m.* squall.
шква́листый *adj.* gusty.
шква́рки *pl.* cracklings.
шкво́рень FILL *m.* pivot; kingpin; kingbolt.
шкив *m.* pulley.
шки́пер *m.* skipper; captain.
шко́ла *f.* school; schoolhouse.
шко́льник *m.* schoolboy.
шко́льница *f.* schoolgirl.
шко́льнический *adj.* schoolboy(ish).
шко́льничество *neut.* schoolboyish behavior.
шко́льный *adj.* (*attrib.*) school.
шку́ра *f.* **1.** skin. **2.** hide.
шку́рка *f.* sandpaper.
шку́рник *m. f.* шку́рница (*colloq.*) self-seeker.
шку́рный *adj.* selfish.
шлагба́ум *m.* barrier; gate.
шлак *m.* slag.
шланг *m.* hose.
шлейф *m.* train of a dress.
шлем *m.* helmet.
шлёпанцы *pl.* (*colloq.*) bedroom slippers.
шлёпать *impf. pf.* шлёпнуть **1.** to smack. **2.** to shuffle, to tramp. **3.** to make a noise with.
шлёпка *f.* (*colloq.*) spanking.
шлифова́льный *adj.* (*attrib.*) polishing.
шлифова́льщик *m. f.* шлифова́льщица polisher.
шлифова́ть OVA *impf. pf.* от- **1.** to grind. **2.** to polish.
шлифо́вка *f.* polishing.
шлюз *m.* **1.** lock (*in a canal*). **2.** sluice.
шлюп *m.* sloop.
шлю́пка *f.* boat.
шлю́ха *f.* (*slang*) slut; tart.
шля́па *f.* hat.
шля́пка *f.* **1.** *dim. of* шля́па. **2.** cap of a mushroom. **3.** head (*of a nail*).
шля́пник *m. f.* шля́пница hatter.
шля́пный *adj.* (*attrib.*) hat.
шля́ться *impf.* **1.** to wander around. **2.** to gallivant.
шмель *m.* bumblebee.
шмы́гать *impf. pf.* шмыгну́ть (*colloq.*) **1.** to scurry, to scamper. **2.** to scrape one's feet.
шнитт-лу́к *m.* chive.
шни́цель *m.* schnitzel.
шнур *m.* string; cord.
шнурова́ть OVA *impf. pf.* за-, про- **1.** to string. **2.** to lace, to lace up.
шнуро́вка *f.* lacing.

шнуро́к FILL *m.* lace; shoelace.
шныря́ть *impf.* (*colloq.*) **1.** to scurry, to scamper. **2.** to prowl around.
шов *m.* seam.
шовини́зm *m.* chauvinism.
шовини́ст *m. f.* —ка chauvinist.
шовинисти́ческий *adj.* chauvinist.
шок *m.* (*med.*) shock.
шоки́ровать OVA *impf.* to shock.
шокола́д *m.* chocolate.
шокола́дный *adj.* chocolate.
шо́мпол *m.* ramrod.
шо́рник *m.* saddler; harness-maker.
шо́рный *adj.* (*attrib.*) saddle; harness.
шо́рох *m.* rustle.
шо́рты *pl.* shorts.
шо́ры *pl.* blinkers; blinders.
шоссе́ *neut. indecl.* highway.
шоссе́йный *adj.* (*attrib.*) road; highway.
шосси́ровать OVA *impf. and pf.* to make into a highway.
шотла́ндец FILL *m. f.* шотла́ндка Scot, Scotsman.
Шотла́ндия *f.* Scotland.
шотла́ндский *adj.* Scotch, Scottish.
шофёр *m.* chauffeur, driver.
шофёрский *adj.* driver's.
шпа́га *f.* sword, épée.
шпага́т *m.* **1.** string; cord. **2.** (*gymnastics*) a split.
шпа́жный *adj.* (*attrib.*) sword.
шпаклева́ть OVA *impf. pf.* за- to seal up; to putty.
шпаклёвка *f.* **1.** putty. **2.** puttying; sealing up.
шпа́ла *f.* railroad tie.
шпале́ра *f.* **1.** trellis. **2.** rows; columns. **3.** row of trees.
шпа́нка *f.* Spanish fly.
шпа́нский *adj.* (*obs.*) Spanish.
шпарга́лка *f.* crib notes (*concealed, for cheating*).
шпат *m.* spar.
шпа́тель *m.* spatula.
шпенёк *m.* peg; prong.
шпигова́ть OVA *impf. pf.* на- to lard.
шпик *m.* small cube of lard.
шпиль *m.* **1.** steeple; spire. **2.** capstan.
шпи́лька *f.* **1.** hairpin. **2.** tack. **3.** brad, stud.
шпина́т *m.* spinach.
шпина́тный *adj.* (*attrib.*) spinach.
шпингале́т *m.* catch; latch; bolt.
шпио́н *m. f.* —ка spy. —а́ж *m.* espionage.
шпио́нить *impf.* to spy.
шпио́нский *adj.* (*attrib.*) spy.
шпио́нство *neut.* spying.
шпиц *m.* (*dog*) spitz.
Шпи́цберген *m.* Spitzbergen.
шпон *m.* slug; printing lead.
шпо́нка *f.* (*mech.*) dowel; key.
шпо́ра *f.* spur.
шпо́рник *m.* larkspur; delphinium.
шприц *m.* syringe.
шпу́лька *f.* spool, bobbin.
шпунт *m.* groove.
шрам *m.* scar.
шрапне́ль *f.* shrapnel.
шрапне́льный *adj.* (*attrib.*) shrapnel.

Шри-Ла́нка *f.* Sri Lanka
шрифт *m.* **1.** print. **2.** type.
штаб *m.* staff; headquarters.
шта́бель *m.* pile; stack.
штаб-кварти́ра *f.* headquarters.
штабно́й *adj.* (*mil.*) (*attrib.*) staff.
штаке́тник *m.* fence; picket fencing.
штамп *m.* **1.** stamp. **2.** (*fig.*) cliché.
штампова́льный *adj.* (*mech.*) (*attrib.*) punching.
штампо́ванный *adj.* pressed; shaped.
штампова́ть OVA *impf. pf.* от- **1.** to stamp. **2.** to punch; to press. **3.** (*fig.*) to grind out.
штампо́вка *f.* stamping.
штампо́вочный *adj.* (*mech.*) (*attrib.*) punching.
шта́нга *f.* (*athl.*) bar; barbell.
штанги́ст *m. f.* —ка weightlifter.
штанда́рт *m.* (*obs.*) standard; banner.
штани́на *f.* (*colloq.*) pants leg.
штани́шки *pl.* (*colloq.*) short pants.
штаны́ *pl.* pants; trousers.
штат¹ *m.* (*admin. unit*) state.
штат² *m.* staff; personnel.
штати́в *m.* stand; base; tripod.
шта́тный *adj.* staff; permanent.
шта́тский *adj.* civil; civilian.
штéвень FILL *m.* stempost *or* sternpost (*of a ship*).
штемпелева́ть OVA *impf. pf.* за- to stamp; to postmark.
штéмпель *m.* rubber stamp.
штéмпельный *adj.* (*attrib.*) stamp.
штéпсель *m.* **1.** electric plug. **2.** electric socket.
штéпсельный *adj.* (*attrib.*) electric plug *or* outlet.
штибле́ты *pl.* boots; shoes.
штилево́й *adj.* (*naut.*) calm.
Шти́рия *f.* (*province*) Styria.
штиль *m.* (*naut.*) calm.
штифт *m.* dowel; pin; peg.
шток *m.* rod.
штокро́за *f.* hollyhock.
штопальный *adj.* (*attrib.*) darning.
што́пать *impf. pf.* за- to darn.
што́пка *f.* darning; darning wool.
што́пор *m.* corkscrew.
што́ра *f.* window shade; window blind.
шторм *m.* storm.
штормова́ть OVA *impf.* to weather a storm.
штормово́й *adj.* (*attrib.*) storm.
штоф *m.* damask.
што́фный *adj.* damask.
штраф *m.* fine; penalty.
штрафно́й *adj.* (*attrib.*) penalty.
штрафова́ть OVA *impf. pf.* о- to fine.
штрейкбре́хер *m.* strikebreaker.
штри́пка *f.* strap for fastening trousers.
штрих *m.* **1.** stroke (*in drawing*). **2.** trait; feature.
штрихова́ть OVA *impf. pf.* за- to shade; to hatch.
штрихо́вка *f.* shading *or* hatching in drawing.
штуди́ровать OVA *impf. pf.* про- to study.

шту́ка *f.* **1.** piece. **2.** thing.
штука́рь *m.* joker; trickster.
штукату́р *m.* plasterer.
штукату́рить *impf. pf.* от-, о- to plaster.
штукату́рка *f.* **1.** plaster. **2.** plastering.
штукату́рный *adj.* (*attrib.*) plaster.
штурва́л *m.* steering wheel; helm (*of a ship*).
штурва́льный *adj.* (*attrib.*) steering.
штурм *m.* storm; assault.
шту́рман *m.* navigator.
штурмова́ть OVA *impf.* to storm; to assault.
штурмови́к *m.* low-flying attack aircraft.
штурмово́й *adj.* (*attrib.*) assault.
шту́цер *m.* carbine.
шту́чка *f. dim. of* шту́ка.
шту́чный *adj.* by the piece.
штык *m.* bayonet.
штыково́й *adj.* (*attrib.*) bayonet.
штырь *m.* dowel; pin.
шу́ба *f.* fur coat.
шубе́йка *f.* (*colloq.*) short fur coat.
шуга́ *f.* drift ice.
шу́лер *m.* cardsharp; cheat.
шу́лерский *adj.* (*cards*) cheating; dishonest.
шу́лерство *neut.* cheating; foul play.
шум *m.* noise.
Шума́ва *f.* Bohemian Forest, Böhmerwald (*Czech: Šumava*).
шуме́ть *impf.* to make a noise, to be noisy.
шуми́ха *f.* (*colloq.*) fuss; uproar.
шумли́вый *adj.* noisy.
шу́мно *adv.* noisily.
шу́мный *adj.* **1.** noisy; loud. **2.** tumultuous.
шумови́к *m.* (*theat.*) sound-effects man.
шумо́вка *f.* straining spoon; skimmer.
шумово́й *adj.* (*attrib.*) sound.
шумо́к FILL *m.* (*colloq.*) slight noise.
шу́рин *m.* brother-in-law (*wife's brother*).
шуру́п *m.* screw.
шурша́ние *neut.* rustling.
шурша́ть *impf.* to rustle.
шу́стрый *adj.* (*colloq.*) sharp; bright; smart.
шут *m. f.* шути́ха jester.
шути́ть *impf. pf.* по- to joke, to jest.
шути́ха *f.* (*firework*) rocket.
шу́тка *f.* joke; jest.
шутли́вый *adj.* playful.
шутни́к *m. f.* шутни́ца joker; jokester.
шутовско́й *adj.* (*attrib.*) jester.
шутовство́ *neut.* buffoonery.
шу́точный *adj.* **1.** comical. **2.** facetious.
шутя́ *adv.* in jest; for fun.
шушу́каться *impf.* (*colloq.*) to whisper.
шхе́ры *pl.* (*geog.*) skerries (*rocky coastal islets*).
шху́на *f.* schooner.
шш *interj.* shh!

Щ

щаве́ль *m.* sorrel.

щади́ть *impf. pf.* по- to spare; to have mercy on.

ще́бень FILL *m.* crushed stone (*as road surface*).

щебета́ть *impf.* to chirp.

щего́л FILL *m.* goldfinch.

щёголь *m.* fop; dandy.

щего́льско́й *adj.* **1.** handsome; elegant. **2.** dashing.

щего́льство́ *neut.* foppery; dandyism.

щеголя́ть *impf. pf.* щегольну́ть **1.** *impf. only* to wear fancy clothes. **2.** (*colloq.*) to show off; to flaunt.

ще́дро *adv.* generously.

ще́дрый *adj.* generous.

щека́ *f.* cheek.

щеко́лда *f.* door latch.

щекота́ние *neut.* tickling.

щекота́ть *impf. pf.* по- to tickle.

щеко́тка *f.* tickling.

щекотли́вость *f.* ticklishness.

щекотли́вый *adj.* ticklish; delicate.

щеко́тно *adj.* (*pred.*) tickling.

щеко́тный *adj.* tickling.

щели́стый *adj.* (*colloq.*) full of cracks.

щёлк *m.* (*colloq.*) snap; click.

щёлка *f.* crack; slit.

щёлканье *neut.* snapping; clicking.

щёлкать *impf. pf.* щёлкнуть **1.** to click. **2.** to smack. **3.** to crack.

щелкопёр *m.* (*obs.*) (*der.*) hack writer.

щёлок *m.* lye.

щелочно́й *adj.* alkaline.

щёлочность *neut.* alkalinity.

щёлочь *f.* alkali.

щелчо́к FILL *m.* **1.** flick of the fingers. **2.** (*colloq.*) insult; slight; snub.

щель *f.* crack, chink. — голосова́я щель (*anat.*) glottis.

щеми́ть *impf.* **1.** to constrict. **2.** to ache. **3.** (*fig.*) to weigh on.

щемя́щий *adj.* **1.** aching; nagging. **2.** painful.

щено́к FILL *m.* pup, puppy.

щепа́ *f.* **1.** chip of wood. **2.** kindling.

щепа́ть *impf. pres.* щеплю́, ще́плешь **1.** to chip wood. **2.** to chop.

щепети́льный *adj.* fussy; scrupulous.

ще́пка *f.* chip.

щепо́тка *f.* pinch.

щепо́ть *also* ще́поть *f.* **1.** a pinch (*e.g., of salt*). **2.** three fingers held together.

щерба́тый *adj.* chipped.

щерби́на *f.* **1.** gap; hole (*between teeth*). **2.** chip. **3.** pockmark.

щети́на *f.* bristle.

щети́нистый *adj.* bristly.

щётка *f.* brush.

щёточный *adj.* (*attrib.*) brush.

Ще́цин *m.* Szczecin (*German: Stettin*).

щёчный *adj.* (*attrib.*) cheek.

щи *pl.* cabbage soup.

щи́колотка *f.* ankle.

щипа́ть *impf. pf.* щипну́ть **1.** to pinch. **2.** *impf. only* to nibble.

щипко́вые инструме́нты *pl.* instruments played by plucking.

щипко́м *adv.* pizzicato.

щипо́к FILL *m.* pinch; tweak; nip.

щипцы́ *pl.* tongs; pincers.

щи́пчики *pl.* tweezers.

щит *m.* shield.

щитови́дный *adj.* thyroid.

щито́к FILL *m. dim. of* щит.

щитомо́рдник *m.* (*snake*) copperhead.

щу́ка *f.* (*fish*) pike.

щуп *m.* probe.

щу́пальце *neut.* tentacle; feeler.

щу́пать *impf. pf.* по- to feel.

щу́плый *adj.* (*colloq.*) puny, frail, thin.

щу́рить *impf. pf.* со-: щу́рить глаза́ to squint.

щу́чий *adj.* pike's.

Э

эбе́новый *adj.* ebony.
эбони́т *m.* ebonite.
эвакуацио́нный *adj.* (*attrib.*) evacuation.
эвакуа́ция *f.* evacuation.
эвакуи́ровать OVA *impf. and pf.* to evacuate.
эвкали́пт *m.* eucalyptus.
эвкали́птовый *adj* (*attrib.*) eucalyptus.
ЭВМ *f.* (*abbr. of* электро́нная вычисли́тельная маши́на *f.*) computer.
эволюциони́ровать OVA *impf. and pf.* to evolve.
эволюцио́нный *adj.* evolutional; evolutionary.
эволю́ция *f.* evolution.
э́врика *interj.* eureka!
эвфеми́зм *m.* euphemism.
эвфемисти́ческий *adj.* euphemistic.
эгалита́рный *adj.* egalitarian.
Эге́йское мо́ре *neut.* Aegean Sea.
эги́да *f.* aegis.
эго́изм *m.* egoism.
эго́ист *m. f.* —ка egoist.
эгоисти́ческий *also* эгоисти́чный *adj.* egoistic; selfish.
эготи́зм *m.* egotism.
эдельве́йс *m.* edelweiss.
Эде́м *m.* Eden.
Э́динбург *m.* Edinburgh.
эй *interj.* hey!
эйнште́йний *m.* einsteinium.
эйфори́я *f.* euphoria.
Эквадо́р *m.* Ecuador.
эква́тор *m.* equator. —иа́льный *adj.* equatorial.
эквивале́нтность *f.* equivalence.
эквивале́нтный *adj.* equivalent.
эквилибри́ст *m. f.* —ка tightrope walker.
эквилибри́стика *f.* balancing act.
экзальта́ция *f.* exaltation.
экзальти́рованный *adj.* in a state of exaltation.
экза́мен *m.* examination.
экзамена́тор *m.* examiner.
экзаменацио́нный *adj.* (*attrib.*) examination.
экзаменова́ть OVA *impf. pf.* про- to examine. —ся to take an examination; to be examined.
экзеку́ция *f.* (*obs.*) **1.** whipping; flogging. **2.** execution.
экземпля́р *m.* copy; specimen.
экзистенциали́зм *m.* existentialism.
экзистенциали́ст *m.* existentialist.
экзистенциа́льный *adj.* existentialist.
экзо́тика *f.* exotic things.
экзоти́ческий *adj.* exotic.
эквиво́к *m.*, *usu. pl.* ambiguity.
э́кий *adj.* (*colloq.*) what a...!
экипа́ж *m.* carriage.
экипирова́ть OVA *impf. and pf.* to equip.
экипиро́вка *f.* equipping.
эклекти́зм *m.* eclecticism.
экле́ктик *m.* eclectic.
эклекти́ческий *also* экле́кти́чный *adj.* eclectic.
экле́р *m.* éclair.
экли́птика *f.* (*astr.*) ecliptic.
эко́лог *m.* ecologist.

э漏экологи́ческий *adj.* ecological.
эколо́гия *f.* ecology.
эконо́м *m. f.* —ка (*obs.*) housekeeper.
эконо́мика *f.* economics.
экономи́ст *m.* economist.
эконо́мить *impf. pf.* с- to economize.
экономи́ческий *adj.* economic.
экономи́чный *adj.* economical.
эконо́мия *f.* economy.
эконо́мный *adj.* economical.
экра́н *m.* screen.
экраниза́ция *f.* filming.
экранизи́ровать OVA *impf. and pf.* to make into a movie.
экскава́тор *m.* steam shovel.
э́кскурс *m.* digression.
экскурса́нт *m. f.* —ка person on an excursion.
экскурсио́нный *adj.* (*attrib.*) excursion.
экску́рсия *f.* excursion.
экскурсово́д *m.* tour guide; excursion leader.
эксли́брис *m.* bookplate.
экспанси́вный *adj.* expansive.
экспансиони́зм *m.* expansionism.
экспансиони́ст *m.* expansionist.
экспансиони́стский *adj.* expansionist.
экспа́нсия *f.* expansion.
экспатриа́нт *m. f.* —ка expatriate.
экспатриа́ция *f.* expatriation.
экспатрии́ровать OVA *impf. and pf.* to expatriate.
экспедицио́нный *adj.* expeditionary.
экспеди́ция *f.* expedition.
эксперимéнт *m.* experiment. —а́льный *adj.* experimental.
эксперименти́рование *neut.* experimentation.
эксперименти́ровать OVA *impf.* to experiment.
экспе́рт *m.* expert.
эксперти́за *f.* examination by experts.
экспе́ртный *adj.* expert.
эксплуата́тор *m.* exploiter.
эксплуата́торский *adj.* (*attrib.*) exploiter.
эксплуатацио́нный *adj.* operating.
эксплуата́ция *f.* exploitation.
эксплуати́ровать OVA *impf.* to exploit.
экспози́ция *f.* layout; display; exposition.
экспона́т *m.* exhibit.
экспоне́нт *m.* **1.** exhibitor. **2.** (*math.*) exponent; index.
экспоно́метр *m.* (*photog.*) light meter.
э́кспорт *m.* export; exports.
экспортёр *m.* exporter.
экспорти́ровать OVA *impf. and pf.* to export.
э́кспортный *adj.* (*attrib.*) export.
экспре́сс *m.* express.
экспресси́вный *adj.* expressive.
экспре́ссия *f.* expressiveness.
экспро́мт *m.* **1.** impromptu. **2.** improvisation. **3.** extemporization.
экспро́мтом *adv.* impromtu.
экспроприа́ция *f.* expropriation.
экспроприи́ровать OVA *impf. and pf.* to expropriate.

экста́з *m.* ecstasy.
экстати́ческий *adj.* ecstatic.
экстéрн *m.*: сдать экза́мен экстéрном *pf.* to take examinations without attending classes.
экстерриториа́льный *adj.* extraterritorial.
экстравага́нтный *adj.* eccentric; bizarre.
экстраги́ровать OVA *impf.* and *pf.* to extract.
экстра́кт *m.* extract.
экстра́кция *f.* extraction.
экстраордина́рный *adj.* extraordinary.
экстраполи́ровать OVA *impf.* and *pf.* to extrapolate.
экстраполя́ция *f.* extrapolation.
экстрасенсóрное воздéйствие *neut.* E.S.P. (*abbr. of* extra-sensory perception).
экстреми́зм *m.* extremism.
экстреми́ст *m.* extremist.
экстреми́стский *adj.* extremist.
эксцéнтрик *m.* **1.** clown. **2.** eccentric person. **3.** (*mech.*) cam.
эксцентри́ческий *adj.* eccentric.
эксцентри́чность *f.* eccentricity.
эксцентри́чный *adj.* eccentric.
эксцéсс *m.* usu. *pl.* excesses.
эктопла́зма *f.* ectoplasm.
Э́ланд *m.* (*island*) Öland.
эласти́чность *f.* elasticity.
эласти́чный *adj.* elastic.
элева́тор *m.* **1.** grain elevator. **2.** hoist; lift.
элега́нтность *f.* elegance.
элега́нтный *adj.* elegant.
элеги́ческий *also* элеги́чный *adj.* elegiac.
элéгия *f.* elegy.
электризова́ть OVA *impf. pf.* на- to electrify.
элéктрик *m.* electrician.
электрифика́ция *f.* electrification.
электрифици́ровать OVA *impf.* and *pf.* to provide with electric power.
электри́ческий *adj.* electric.
электри́чество *neut.* electricity.
электри́чка *f.* suburban electric train.
электро- *prefix* electrical.
электровóз *m.* electric locomotive.
электрóд *m.* electrode.
электродви́гатель *m.* electric motor.
электрока́р *m.* electric vehicle.
электрокардиогра́мма *f.* electrocardiogram.
электрокардиóграф *m.* electrocardiograph.
электрóлиз *m.* electrolysis.
электроли́ния *f.* electric power line.
электроли́т *m.* electrolyte.
электромагнети́зм *m.* electromagnetism.
электромагни́т *m.* electromagnet.
электромагни́тный *adj.* electromagnetic.
электромонтёр *m.* electrician.
электрóн *m.* electron.
электрóника *f.* electronics.
электрóнная пóчта *f.* electronic mail.
электрóнная табли́ца *f.* spreadsheet.
электрóнный *adj.* electronic.
электропита́ние *neut.* power supply.
электроста́нция *f.* power station.
электроста́тика *f.* electrostatics.
электростати́ческий *adj.* electrostatic.
электротéхник *m.* electrical engineer.
электротéхника *f.* electrical engineering.

электротехни́ческий *adj.* electrical engineering.
электроэнéргия *f.* electrical energy.
элемéнт *m.* element. —а́рный *adj.* elementary.
элерóн *m.* aileron.
эли́та *f.* elite.
эллипсóид *m.* ellipsoid.
эллипти́ческий *adj.* elliptical.
эль *m.* ale.
Э́льба¹ *f.* (*island*) Elba.
Э́льба² *f.* (*river*) Elbe.
Эльбру́с *m.* (*mountain*) Elbrus.
Эль-Па́со *m.* El Paso.
эльф *m.* elf.
эма́левый *adj.* (*attrib.*) enamel.
эмали́рованный *adj.* enameled.
эмалирова́ть OVA *impf.* to enamel.
эма́ль *f.* enamel.
эмана́ция *f.* emanation.
эмансипа́тор *m.* emancipator.
эмансипа́ция *f.* emancipation.
эмансипи́ровать OVA *impf.* and *pf.* to emancipate.
эмба́рго *neut. indecl.* embargo.
эмблéма *f.* emblem.
эмблемати́ческий *adj.* emblematic.
эмболи́я *f.* embolism.
эмбриóлог *m.* embryologist.
эмбриолóгия *f.* embryology.
эмбриóн *m.* embryo.
эмбриона́льный *adj.* embryonic.
эмигра́нт *m. f.* —ка emigrant; émigré.
эмигра́нтский *adj.* (*attrib.*) émigré.
эмигра́ция *f.* emigration.
эмигри́ровать OVA *impf.* and *pf.* to emigrate.
эми́р *m.* emir.
эмира́т *m.* emirate.
эмисса́р *m.* emissary.
эмоциона́льный *adj.* emotional.
эмóция *f.* emotion.
эмпири́зм *m.* empiricism.
эмпи́рик *m.* empiricist.
эмпири́ческий *adj.* empirical.
э́му *m. indecl.* emu.
эму́льсия *f.* emulsion.
эмфизéма *f.* emphysema.
эндеми́ческий *adj.* endemic.
эндокри́нный *adj.* endocrine.
эндокринолóгия *f.* endocrinology.
э́ндшпиль *m.* (*chess*) end game.
энергéтика *f.* energy.
энергети́ческий *adj.* (*attrib.*) energy.
энерги́чно *adv.* energetically.
энерги́чный *adj.* energetic.
энéргия *f.* energy.
э́нный *adj.* a certain; an unspecified.
э́нский *adj.* X (*used to designate something unidentified*).
энтери́т *m.* enteritis.
энтомóлог *m.* entomologist.
энтомологи́ческий *adj.* entomological.
энтомолóгия *f.* entomology.
энтузиа́зм *m.* enthusiasm.
энтузиасти́ческий *adj.* enthusiastic.
энцефали́т *m.* encephalitis.
энци́клика *f.* encyclical.
энциклопеди́ст *m. f.* —ка encyclopedist.
энциклопеди́ческий *adj.* encyclopedic.

энциклопéдия *f.* encyclopedia.
эпигóн *m.* imitator; copier.
эпигрáмма *f.* epigram.
эпиграммати́ческий *adj.* epigrammatic.
эпи́граф *m.* epigraph.
эпидеми́ческий *adj.* epidemic.
эпидéмия *f.* epidemic.
эпидéрмис *m.* epidermis.
эпизóд *m.* episode.
эпизоди́ческий *adj.* episodic.
э́пик *m.* epic poet.
эпикурéец FILL *m.* epicurean.
эпикурéйский *adj.* epicurean.
эпилéпсия *f.* epilepsy.
эпилéптик *m.* epileptic.
эпилепти́ческий *adj.* epileptic.
эпи́стола *f.* epistle.
эпистоля́рный *adj.* epistolary.
эпитáфия *f.* epitaph.
эпителиáльный *adj.* epithelial.
эпитéлий *m.* epithelium.
эпицéнтр *m.* epicenter.
эпи́ческий *adj.* epic.
эполéта *m.* epaulet.
эпопéя *f.* epic work.
эпóха *f.* epoch.
эпохáльный *adj.* epochal.
э́ра *f.* era.
э́рбий *m.* erbium.
эрг *m.* erg.
эрéкция *f.* (*physiol.*) erection.
эрóзия *f.* erosion.
эроти́зм *m.* eroticism.
эрóтика *f.* **1.** erotic literature. **2.** sensuality.
эруди́рованный *adj.* erudite.
эруди́т *m.* erudite person.
эруди́ция *f.* erudition.
эрцгéрцог *m.* archduke.
эрцгерцоги́ня *f.* archduchess.
эрцгéрцогство *neut.* archduchy.
эскáдра *f.* naval squadron.
эскáдренный *adj.* (*attrib.*) squadron.
эскадри́лья *f.* (air) squadron.
эскадрóн *m.* cavalry squadron.
эскалáтор *m.* escalator.
эскалáция *f.* escalation.
эскáрп *m.* (*mil.*) escarpment.
эсквáйр *m.* esquire.
эски́з *m.* sketch.
эски́зный *adj.* rough; preliminary.
эскимó *neut. indecl.* ice cream on a stick.
эскимóс *m. f.* —ка Eskimo. —ский *adj.* Eskimo.
эскóрт *m.* (*mil.*) escort.
эскорти́ровать OVA *impf.* to escort.
эсми́нец FILL *m.* (*abbr. of* эскáдренный минонóсец *m.*) naval destroyer.

эсперáнто *neut. indecl.* Esperanto.
эсплáнада *f.* esplanade.
эссéнция *f.* essence.
эстакáда *f.* **1.** trestle. **2.** pier.
эстафéта *f.* relay race; relays.
эстафéтный *adj.* (*attrib.*) relay (*in a race*).
эстéт *m. f.* —ка esthete.
эстéтика *f.* esthetics.
эстети́ческий *adj.* esthetic.
эстóнец FILL *m. f.* эстóнка Estonian.
Эстóния *f.* Estonia.
эстóнский *adj.* Estonian.
эстрагóн *m.* tarragon.
эстрáда *f.* platform.
эстуáрий *m.* estuary.
э́та *pron., see* э́тот.
этáж *m.* floor, story.
этажéрка *f.* bookcase.
э́так *adv.* (*colloq.*) so; like this.
э́такий **1.** *adj.* (*colloq.*) such a... **2.** what a...
эталóн *m.* standard (*of measurement*).
этáп *m.* stage; phase.
э́ти *pron., see* э́тот.
э́тика *f.* ethics.
этикéт *m.* etiquette.
этикéтка *f.* label.
эти́л *m.* ethyl.
этилéн *m.* ethylene.
этили́рованный *adj.* (*of gasoline*) leaded.
эти́ловый *adj.* (*attrib.*) ethyl.
этимóлог *m.* etymologist.
этимологи́ческий *adj.* etymological.
этимолóгия *f.* etymology.
эти́ческий *also* эти́чный *adj.* ethical.
Э́тна *f.* (*volcano*) Etna.
этни́ческий *adj.* ethnic.
этнóграф *m.* ethnographer.
этнографи́ческий *adj.* ethnographical.
этнологи́ческий *adj.* ethnological.
э́то *pron.* this, that, it; *see* э́тот.
э́тот *pron. m.,* э́та *f.,* э́то *neut.,* э́ти *pl.* this; that.
этю́д *m.* **1.** (*mus.*) étude. **2.** study, exercise. **3.** sketch.
эфемéрный *adj.* ephemeral.
эфéс *m.* hilt; handle (*of a sword*).
Эфиóпия *m.* Ethiopia.
эфи́р *m.* ether.
эфи́рный *adj.* (*attrib.*) ether.
эффéкт *m.* effect. —и́вный *adj.* effective; efficient. —ный *adj.* effective, spectacular.
эффекти́вно *adv.* effectively; efficiently.
эффекти́вность *f.* efficiency.
э́хо *neut.* echo.
эхолóт *m.* sonic depth finder.
эшафóт *m.* scaffold.

Ю

юбиле́й *m.* jubilee; anniversary.
юбиле́йный *adj.* (*attrib.*) anniversary.
юбиля́р *m.* person whose anniversary is being celebrated.
ю́бка *f.* skirt.
ю́бочка *f.* short skirt.
ювели́р *m.* jeweler.
ювели́рный *adj.* (*attrib.*) jewelry.
юг *m.* south.
ю́го-восто́к *m.* southeast.
ю́го-за́пад *m.* southwest.
югосла́в *m. f.* —ка Yugoslav.
Югосла́вия *f.* Yugoslavia.
югосла́вский *adj.* Yugoslav.
юдофо́б *m.* anti-Semite. —ство *neut.* anti-Semitism.
южа́нин *m. f.* южа́нка southerner.
Ю́жная А́фрика *f.* South Africa.
Ю́жная Дако́та *f.* South Dakota.
Ю́жная Кароли́на *f.* South Carolina.
ю́жный *adj.* south, southern.
Ю́жный тро́пик *m.* Tropic of Capricorn.
ю́зом *adv.* into a skid.
ю́кка *f.* yucca.
Ю́кон *m.* (*river*) Yukon.
юла́ *f.* **1.** top (*toy*). **2.** *m.* and *f.* (*decl. f.*) fidgety person.
юлиа́нский *adj.* Julian.
ю́мор *m.* humor.
юморе́ска *f.* humoresque.
юмори́ст *m. f.* —ка humorist.
юмористи́ческий *adj.* humorous.

ю́нга *m.* cabin boy.
юне́ц FILL *m.* youth; lad.
ю́нкер[1] *m.* cadet.
ю́нкер[2] *m.* junker.
ю́ность *f.* youth.
ю́ноша *m.* youth; young man.
ю́ношеский *adj.* youthful.
ю́ношество *neut.* youth; (*coll.*) young people.
ю́ный *adj.* young; youthful.
Юпи́тер *m.* Jupiter.
юпи́тер *m.* floodlight.
юр *m.*: на (са́мом) юру́ in an open place.
юриди́ческий *adj.* juridical, legal.
юрисди́кция *f.* jurisdiction.
юрисконсу́льт *m.* legal adviser.
юриспруде́нция *f.* jurisprudence.
юри́ст *m.* lawyer.
ю́ркий *adj.* brisk; nimble.
юркну́ть *also* ю́ркнуть *pf.* to dart; to scamper.
Ю́рмала *f.* Jurmala.
юро́дивый *adj.* crazy, deranged.
юро́дство *neut.* **1.** derangement. **2.** irrational act.
юро́дствовать OVA *impf.* to act like a madman.
юро́к FILL *m.* brambling.
ю́рский *adj.* Jurassic.
ю́рта *f.* yurt; nomad's tent.
юсти́ция *f.* justice.
ют *m.* quarterdeck.
Ю́та *m.* Utah.
юти́ться *impf.* **1.** to huddle; to huddle together. **2.** to take shelter.
юфть *f.* Russia leather.

Я

я *pron.* I.

я́беда *m. and f.* (*decl. f.*) (*colloq.*) **1.** spreader of malicious rumors. **2.** tattler.

я́бедник *m. f.* **я́бедница** (*colloq.*) spreader of malicious rumors.

я́бедничество *neut.* (*colloq.*) spreading of malicious gossip.

я́блоко *neut.* apple. — глазно́е я́блоко eyeball.

я́блоневый *adj.* (*attrib.*) apple trees.

я́блоня *f.* appletree.

я́блочко *neut. dim. of* я́блоко.

я́блочный *adj.* (*attrib.*) apple.

яви́ться *pf. of* явля́ться.

я́вка *f.* **1.** appearance. **2.** secret meeting; secret meeting place.

явле́ние *neut.* **1.** appearance. **2.** occurence. **3.** (*theat.*) scene.

явля́ться *impf. pf.* яви́ться **1.** to appear. **2.** (*with instr.*) to be.

я́вно *adv.* obviously.

я́вный *adj.* evident; obvious.

я́вор *m.* (*tree*) sycamore.

я́вочный *adj.* secret; clandestine.

я́вственный *adj.* clear; distinct.

я́вствовать OVA *impf.* to be clear.

явь *f.* reality.

ягдта́ш *m.* game bag.

я́гель *m.* reindeer moss.

ягнёнок FILL *m.* lamb.

ягня́тник *m.* bearded vulture.

я́года *f.* berry.

ягоди́ца *f.* buttock.

я́годник *m.* berry patch.

я́годный *adj.* (*attrib.*) berry.

ягуа́р *m.* jaguar.

яд *m.* poison.

я́дерный *adj.* nuclear.

ядови́тый *adj.* poisonous, venomous.

ядохимика́т *m.* pesticide.

ядрёный *adj.* (*colloq.*) hearty.

я́дрица *f.* unground buckwheat.

ядро́ *neut.* nucleus. — толка́ние ядра́ *neut.* (*athl.*) shot put.

я́зва *f.* ulcer.

я́звенный *adj.* ulcerous.

язви́тельный *adj.* biting.

язы́к[1] *m.* tongue.

язы́к[2] *m.* language.

языка́стый *adj.* (*colloq.*) sharp-tongued.

языкове́д *m.* linguist. —ение *neut.* linguistics.

языково́й *adj.* linguistic; (*attrib.*) language.

языко́вый *adj.* (*attrib.*) tongue.

языкозна́ние *neut.* linguistics.

язы́ческий *adj.* pagan.

язы́чество *neut.* paganism.

язычко́вый *adj.* (*phon.*) uvular.

язы́чник *m. f.* язы́чница pagan, heathen.

язычо́к FILL *m.* **1.** *dim. of* язы́к. **2.** uvula. **3.** tongue of a shoe. **4.** fastener.

язь *m.* ide (*fish of the carp family*).

яи́чко *neut.* **1.** small egg. **2.** (*anat.*) testicle.

яи́чник *m.* ovary.

яи́чница *f.* scrambled eggs; omelet.

яи́чный *adj.* (*attrib.*) egg.

яйцеви́дный *adj.* egg-shaped.

яйцево́д *m.* oviduct.

яйцекладу́щий *adj.* oviparous.

яйцекле́тка *f.* (*biol.*) ovule.

яйцеро́дный *adj.* oviparous.

яйцо́ *neut.* egg.

як *m.* yak.

я́кобы *conj.* as if; as though.

я́корный *adj.* (*attrib.*) anchor.

я́корь *m.* anchor.

яку́т *m. f.* —ка Yakut.

Яку́тия *f.* Yakutia.

Яку́тск *m.* Yakutsk.

ял *m.* yawl.

я́лик *m.* dinghy; skiff.

я́ловый *adj.* **1.** barren. **2.** dry.

Я́лта *f.* Yalta.

я́ма *f.* pit.

Яма́йка *f.* Jamaica.

ямб *m.* iamb.

ямби́ческий *adj.* iambic.

я́мка *f.* **1.** *dim. of* я́ма. **2.** dimple.

я́мочка *f.* dimple.

ямс *m.* yam.

ямщи́к *m.* coach driver.

янва́рский *adj.* (*attrib.*) January.

янва́рь *m.* January.

я́нки *m. indecl.* Yankee.

янта́рь *m.* amber.

япо́нец FILL *m. f.* япо́нка Japanese.

Япо́ния *f.* Japan.

япо́нский *adj.* Japanese.

яр *m.* **1.** steep bank. **2.** ravine.

яра́нга *f.* tent made of reindeer hides.

Яра́нск *m.* Yaransk.

ярд *m.* yard (36 inches).

яре́мная ве́на *f.* jugular vein.

я́ркий *adj.* bright; clear.

я́рко *adv.* brightly.

я́рко- *prefix* (*of colors*) bright.

я́ркость *f.* brilliance; brightness.

ярлы́к *m.* label.

ярлычо́к FILL *m. dim. of* ярлы́к.

я́рмарка *f.* fair.

я́рмарочный *adj.* (*attrib.*) fair.

ярмо́ *neut.* yoke.

яровиза́ция *f.* vernalization.

яровизи́ровать OVA *impf. and pf.* to vernalize.

ярово́й *adj.* (*of crops*) (*attrib.*) spring.

Яросла́вль *m.* Yaroslavl.

я́ростный *adj.* fierce, furious, violent.

я́рость *f.* fury, rage.

я́рус *m.* (*theat.*) tier, circle.

я́рый *adj.* **1.** fervent, ardent. **2.** violent, furious.

ярь-медя́нка *f.* verdigris.

я́сельный *adj.* (*attrib.*) nursery.

я́сеневый *adj.* (*attrib.*) ash.

я́сень *m.* (*tree*) ash.

ясли *pl.* **1.** manger, trough. **2.** day nursery.
Ясная Поляна *f.* Yasnaya Polyana.
ясно *adv.* clearly. — *adj.* (*pred.*) clear.
ясновидение *neut.* clairvoyance.
ясновидец FILL *m.* *f.* ясновидица clairvoyant.
ясновидящий *adj.* clairvoyant.
ясность *f.* clarity.
ясный *adj.* clear.
яства *pl.* victuals; food.
ястреб *m.* hawk.
ястребок FILL *m.* *dim.* *of* ястреб.
ятаган *m.* scimitar.
ять *m.* name of an old letter of the Russian alphabet. — на ять *adv.* first class, splendidly.

яхонт *m.* **1.** (красный) ruby. **2.** (синий) sapphire.
яхта *f.* yacht.
яхтсмен *m.* *f.* —ка yachtsman.
ячейка *f.* (*polit.*, *fig.*) cell.
ячменный *adj.* (*attrib.*) barley.
ячмень¹ *m.* barley.
ячмень² *m.* (*med.*) sty.
ячневый *adj.* made of fine-ground barley.
яшма *f.* jasper.
яшмовый *adj.* (*attrib.*) jasper.
ящер *m.* pangolin (*scaly anteater*).
ящерица *f.* lizard.
ящик *m.* **1.** box. **2.** drawer.
ящур *m.* foot-and-mouth disease.

English-Russian
Dictionary

A

aardvark /'ɑrd,vɑrk/ *n.* трубкозу́б *m.*

aardwolf /'ɑrd,wulf/ *n.* земляно́й волк *m.*

aback /ə'bæk/ *adv.*: **to take aback** *v.* поража́ть *impf.*

abacus /'æbəkəs/ *n.* счёты *pl.*

abaft /ə'bæft/ *adv.* на корме́.

abalone /,æbə'louni/ *n.* морско́е у́хо *neut.*

abandon /ə'bændən/ **1.** *n.* непринуждённость *f.* **2.** *v.* покида́ть *impf.*, поки́нуть *pf.*; оставля́ть *impf.*, оста́вить *pf.*

abandoned /ə'bændənd/ *adj.* поки́нутый, забро́шенный.

abandonment /ə'bændənmənt/ *n.* оставле́ние *neut.*, забро́шенность *f.*

abase /ə'beis/ *v.* унижа́ть *impf.*

abasement /ə'beismənt/ *n.* униже́ние *neut.*

abash /ə'bæʃ/ *v.* смуща́ть, конфу́зить *impf.*

abate /ə'beit/ *v.* уменьша́ть(ся) *impf.*, уме́ньшить(ся) *pf.* ослабля́ть *impf.*, осла́бить *pf.*; затиха́ть *impf.*, зати́хнуть *pf.*

abatement /ə'beitmənt/ *n.* ослабле́ние, сниже́ние *neut.*

abattoir /'æbə,twɑr/ *n.* скотобо́йня *f.*

abbess /'æbɪs/ *n.* игу́менья; аббати́са *f.*

abbey /'æbi/ *n.* абба́тство *neut.*; монасты́рь *m.*

abbot /'æbət/ *n.* игу́мен; абба́т *m.*

abbreviate /ə'briviˌeit/ *v.* сокраща́ть *impf.*, сократи́ть *pf.*

abbreviation /ə,brivi'eiʃən/ *n.* аббревиату́ра *f.*, сокраще́ние *neut.*

abdicate /'æbdɪˌkeit/ *v.* отрека́ться *impf.*

abdication /,æbdɪ'keiʃən/ *n.* отрече́ние (от престо́ла) *neut.*; отка́з (от *with gen.*) *m.*

abdomen /'æbdəmən, æb'dou-/ *n.* брюшна́я по́лость *f.*; живо́т *m.*

abdominal /æb'dɑmənl/ *adj.* брюшно́й.

abduct /æb'dʌkt/ *v.* похища́ть *impf.*, похи́тить *pf.*

abduction /æb'dʌkʃən/ *n.* похище́ние *neut.*

abeam /ə'bim/ *adv.* на тра́верзе.

abed /ə'bɛd/ *adv.* в посте́ли.

aberrant /ə'bɛrənt, 'æbər-/ *adj.* ненорма́льный.

aberration /,æbə'reiʃən/ *n.* (*error*) заблужде́ние *neut.*; (*deviation*) отклоне́ние *neut.*

abet /ə'bɛt/ *v.* подстрека́ть; соде́йствовать (*with dat.*) *impf.*

abettor /ə'bɛtər/ *n.* подстрека́тель, посо́бник *m.*

abeyance /ə'beiəns/ *n.* состоя́ние неопределённости *neut.*

abhor /æb'hɔr/ *v.* ненави́деть *impf.*; пита́ть отвраще́ние *impf.*

abhorrence /æb'hɔrəns/ *n.* отвраще́ние *neut.*

abhorrent /æb'hɔrənt/ *adj.* отврати́тельный.

abide /ə'baid/ *v.* (*remain*) остава́ться *impf.*; (*dwell*) жить, пребыва́ть *impf.*; (*tolerate*) терпе́ть *impf.*; **to abide by** соблюда́ть *impf.*

abiding /ə'baidɪŋ/ *adj.* постоя́нный.

ability /ə'bɪlɪti/ *n.* спосо́бность *f.*; уме́ние *neut.*

abject /'æbdʒɛkt/ *adj.* жа́лкий; (*despicable*) презре́нный.

abjure /æb'dʒʊr/ *v.* отрека́ться (от *with gen.*) *impf.*

ablative /'æblətɪv/ *n.* аблати́в *m.*

ablaut /'ɑblaut/ *n.* абля́ут *m.*

ablaze /ə'bleiz/ *adv.* в огне́, в пла́мени.

able /'eibəl/ *adj.* спосо́бный; уме́лый; **to be able** *v.* мочь *impf.*, смочь *pf.*; быть в состоя́нии *impf.*; (*know how*) уме́ть *impf.*

ablution /ə'bluʃən/ *n.* омове́ние *neut.*

ably /'eibli/ *adv.* уме́ло.

abnegate /'æbnɪˌgeit/ *v.* отка́зываться (от *with gen.*) *impf.*; отрека́ться *impf.*

abnegation /,æbnɪ'geiʃən/ *n.* отрече́ние *neut.*; **self-abnegation** *n.* самоотрече́ние *neut.*

abnormal /æb'nɔrməl/ *adj.* ненорма́льный, анорма́льный.

abnormality /,æbnɔr'mælɪti/ *n.* ненорма́льность, непра́вильность *f.*

abnormally /æb'nɔrməli/ *adv.* ненорма́льно, анорма́льно.

aboard /ə'bɔrd/ *adv.* (*location*) на корабле́, на борту́, в ваго́не; (*motion*) на кора́бль, на борт, в ваго́н; **all aboard!** *interj.* поса́дка зако́нчена!

abode /ə'boud/ *n.* жили́ще, местопребыва́ние *neut.*

abolish /ə'bɑlɪʃ/ *v.* отменя́ть *impf.*, отмени́ть *pf.*

abolition /,æbə'lɪʃən/ *n.* отме́на *f.*; уничтоже́ние *neut.*; **abolition of slavery** *n.* уничтоже́ние ра́бства *neut.*

A-bomb /'eiˌbɑm/ *n.* а́томная бо́мба *f.*

abominable /ə'bɑmənəbəl/ *adj.* отврати́тельный.

abominate /ə'bɑməˌneit/ *v.* пита́ть отвраще́ние, ненави́деть *impf.*

abomination /ə,bɑmə'neiʃən/ *n.* отвраще́ние *neut.*; ме́рзость *f.*

aboriginal /,æbə'rɪdʒənl/ *adj.* исконный, тузе́мный.

aborigine /,æbə'rɪdʒəni/ *n.* тузе́мец; абориге́н *m.*

abort /ə'bɔrt/ *v.* (*miscarry*) вы́кидывать плод *impf.*; (*cause abortion*) вызыва́ть або́рт *impf.*; (*terminate*) прекраща́ть *impf.*

abortifacient /ə,bɔrtə'feiʃənt/ *n.* аборти́вное сре́дство *neut.*

abortion /ə'bɔrʃən/ *n.* або́рт, вы́кидыш *m.*; **to have an abortion** сде́лать або́рт *pf.*

abortionist /ə'bɔrʃənɪst/ *n.* акуше́р; сторо́нник або́ртов *m.*

abortive /ə'bɔrtɪv/ *adj.* неуда́вшийся, беспло́дный.

abound /ə'baund/ *v.* изоби́ловать *impf.*

abounding /ə'baundɪŋ/ *adj.* изоби́льный.

about /ə'baut/ *adv.* круго́м; о́коло; в обра́тном направле́нии; **about face!** *interj.* круго́м! **to be about to** *v.* собира́ться *impf.* **2.** *prep.* вокру́г (*with gen.*); по (*with dat.*); о, об (*with prep.*); о́коло (*with gen.*).

above /ə'bʌv/ **1.** *adv.* (*direction*) вы́ше; наве́рх (*location*) вы́ше, наверху́; **from above** *adv.* све́рху. **2.** *prep.* над (*with instr.*); вы́ше, бо́льше, свы́ше (*with gen.*); **above all** *adv.* бо́льше всего́. **3. the above** *n.* вышеупомя́нутое *neut.*

above-mentioned /ə'bʌvˌmɛnʃənd/ *adj.* вышеупомя́нутый, вышеука́занный.

abracadabra /,æbrəkə'dæbrə/ *n.* абракада́бра *f.*

abrade /ə'breid/ v. (rub off) стира́ть impf.; (skin) сдира́ть impf.; (tech.) шлифова́ть impf.

Abramtsevo /ə'brɒmtsəvə/ n. Абра́мцево neut.

abrasion /ə'breiʒən/ n. истира́ние neut. абра́зия f.; (med.) сса́дина f.

abrasive /ə'breisɪv/ **1.** adj. обдира́ющий; шлифу́ющий. **2.** n. абрази́вный or шлифова́льный материа́л m.

abreaction /ˌæbri'ækʃən/ n. абреа́кция f.

abreast /ə'brɛst/ adv. в ряд; в ряду́; ря́дом; бок о бок; на одно́й ли́нии; на у́ровне.

abridge /ə'brɪdʒ/ v. сокраща́ть impf., сократи́ть pf.

abridgment /ə'brɪdʒmənt/ n. сокраще́ние; кра́ткое изложе́ние neut.; сокращённый текст m.

abroad /ə'brɔd/ adv. за грани́цей; за грани́цу; **from abroad** из-за грани́цы.

abrogate /'æbrəˌgeit/ v. отменя́ть, аннули́ровать impf.

abrogation /ˌæbrə'geiʃən/ n. отме́на f., аннули́рование neut.

abrupt /ə'brʌpt/ adj. обры́вистый; внеза́пный; ре́зкий.

abruptly /ə'brʌptli/ adv. обры́висто, внеза́пно, ре́зко.

abruptness /ə'brʌptnis/ n. обры́вистость; ре́зкость f.

abscess /'æbsɛs/ n. абсце́сс, нары́в, гнойни́к m.

abscissa /æb'sisə/ n. абсци́сса f.

abscond /æb'skɒnd/ v. скрыва́ться impf., скры́ться pf.; бежа́ть impf.

absence /'æbsəns/ n. отсу́тствие neut.

absent /'æbsənt/ adj. отсу́тствующий; **to be absent** v. отсу́тствовать impf.

absentee /ˌæbsən'ti/ n. отсу́тствующий, отклоня́ющийся (от with gen.) m.

absenteeism /ˌæbsən'tiizəm/ n. абсентеи́зм m.; (from work) прогу́л m.

absently /'æbsəntli/ adv. рассе́янно.

absent-minded /'æbsənt 'maindɪd/ adj. рассе́янный.

absent-mindedness /'æbsənt 'maindɪdnis/ n. рассе́янность f.

absinthe /'æbsɪnθ/ n. (bot.) полы́нь го́рькая f.; (drink) абсе́нт m.

absolute /'æbsəˌlut/ adj. по́лный; безусло́вный; абсолю́тный.

absolutely /ˌæbsə'lutli/ adv. абсолю́тно; соверше́нно; безусло́вно.

absoluteness /ˌæbsə'lutnis/ n. абсолю́тность, соверше́нность, безусло́вность f.

absolution /ˌæbsə'luʃən/ n. проще́ние; отпуще́ние грехо́в neut.

absolutism /'æbsəluˌtizəm/ n. абсолюти́зм m.

absolve /æb'zɒlv/ v. проща́ть impf., прости́ть pf.; **to absolve of sins** v. отпуска́ть грехи́ impf., отпусти́ть pf.

absorb /æb'sɔrb/ v. впи́тывать impf.; абсорби́ровать impf. and pf.; поглоща́ть impf., поглоти́ть pf.; вса́сывать impf., всоса́ть pf.

absorbent /æb'sɔrbənt/ **1.** adj. поглоща́ющий; вса́сывающий. **2.** n. поглоти́тель m.; вса́сывающее сре́дство neut.

absorbent cotton n. ва́та f.

absorber /æb'sɔrbər/ n. поглоти́тель m.; **shock absorber** n. амортиза́тор m.

absorbing /æb'sɔrbɪŋ/ adj. захва́тывающий.

absorption /æb'sɔrpʃən/ n. абсо́рбция f.; поглоще́ние neut.; (mind) погружённость f.

abstain /æb'stein/ v. возде́рживаться impf., воздержа́ться pf.

abstainer /æb'steinər/ n. тре́звенник, непью́щий m.

abstemious /æb'stimiəs/ adj. возде́ржанный; (moderate) уме́ренный.

abstention /æb'stɛnʃən/ n. воздержа́ние (от with gen.) neut.; отка́з от голосова́ния m.

abstinence /'æbstənəns/ n. возде́ржанность f.; воздержа́ние (от with gen.) neut.

abstract / adj. æb'strækt; n. 'æbstrækt; v. æb'strækt / **1.** adj. абстра́ктный; отвлечённый. **2.** n. резюме́ neut.; извлече́ние neut.; конспе́кт m. **3.** v. отвлека́ть impf., отвле́чь pf.; абстраги́ровать impf. and pf.

abstracted /æb'stræktid/ adj. погружённый в мы́сли.

abstraction /æb'strækʃən/ n. (concept) абстра́кция f., отвлечённое поня́тие neut.

abstruse /æb'strus/ adj. мудрёный; зау́мный.

absurd /æb'sɜrd/ adj. абсу́рдный, неле́пый.

absurdity /æb'sɜrditi/ n. неле́пость, f.; абсу́рд m.

absurdly /æb'sɜrdli/ adv. неле́по.

abundance /ə'bʌndəns/ n. изоби́лие neut.

abundant /ə'bʌndənt/ adj. оби́льный, изоби́льный.

abundantly /ə'bʌndəntli/ adv. оби́льно.

abuse / n. ə'byus; v. ə'byuz/ **1.** n. (misuse) злоупотребле́ние neut.; (insult) оскорбле́ние neut.; (abusive language) руга́нь f. **2.** v. злоупотребля́ть impf., злоупотреби́ть pf.; оскорбля́ть impf., оскорби́ть pf.

abusive /ə'byusɪv/ adj. оскорби́тельный, руга́тельный.

abut /ə'bʌt/ v. примыка́ть, грани́чить impf.

abutment /ə'bʌtmənt/ n. (junction) примыка́ние neut.

abysmal /ə'bɪzməl/ adj. бездо́нный; (horrible) ужа́сный.

abyss /ə'bɪs/ n. бе́здна, про́пасть, пучи́на f.

acacia /ə'keiʃə/ n. ака́ция f.

academic /ˌækə'dɛmɪk/ adj. академи́ческий.

academician /ˌækədə'mɪʃən/ n. акаде́мик m.

academism /ə'kædəˌmɪzəm/ n. академи́зм m.

academy /ə'kædəmi/ n. акаде́мия f.

acanthus /ə'kænθəs/ n. (bot.) ака́нт m., медве́жья ла́па f.

accede /æk'sid/ v. (agree) соглаша́ться (на with acc.) impf.

accelerate /æk'sɛləˌreit/ v. ускоря́ть impf., уско́рить pf.

acceleration /æk,sɛlə'reiʃən/ n. ускоре́ние neut.

accelerator /æk'sɛləˌreitər/ n. (auto) ускори́тель, акселера́тор m.

accent /'æksɛnt/ **1.** n. ударе́ние neut., акце́нт m. **2.** v. ста́вить ударе́ние; акценти́ровать impf. and pf.; подчёркивать impf.

accentuate /æk'sɛntʃuˌeit/ v. подчёркивать impf., подчеркну́ть pf.; де́лать ударе́ние impf.

accept /æk'sɛpt/ v. принима́ть impf., приня́ть pf.; допуска́ть impf., допусти́ть pf.; признава́ть impf., призна́ть pf.

acceptable /æk'sɛptəbəl/ adj. прие́млемый, допусти́мый.

acceptance /æk'sɛptəns/ n. приня́тие; призна́ние neut., приём m.

accepted /æk'sɛptɪd/ adj. (обще)при́нятый.

access /'æksɛs/ n. до́ступ m.

accessibility /æk,sɛsə'bɪlɪti/ n. досту́пность f.

accessible /æk'sɛsəbəl/ adj. досту́пный.

accession /æk'sɛʃən/ n. вступле́ние (в with acc.) neut.

accessory /æk'sɛsəri/ **1.** adj. доба́вочный, (law) соуча́ствующий. **2.** n. (law) соуча́стник m.

accident /'æksɪdənt/ n. несча́стный слу́чай m.; катастро́фа, ава́рия f. (chance) случа́йность f.

accidental /,æksɪ'dɛntl/ adj. случа́йный adj.

accidentally /,æksɪ'dɛntli/ adv. случа́йно.

accident-prone /'æksɪdənt,proun/ adj. невезу́чий.

acclaim /ə'kleim/ **1.** v. провозглаша́ть impf., провозгласи́ть pf.; шу́мно приве́тствовать impf. **2.** n. шу́мное одобре́ние neut.

acclamation /,æklə'meiʃən/ n. шу́мное одобре́ние neut.; **by acclamation** без голосова́ния.

acclimate /'æklə,meit/ v. акклиматизи́ровать(ся) impf. and pf.

acclimatization /ə,klaimətə'zeiʃən/ n. акклиматиза́ция f.

accolade /'ækə,leid/ n. аккола́да f.

accommodate /ə'kɒmə,deit/ v. (adapt) приспособля́ть impf., приспосо́бить pf.; (lodge) помеща́ть impf., помести́ть pf.

accommodating /ə'kɒmə,deitɪŋ/ adj. услу́жливый.

accommodation /ə,kɒmə'deiʃən/ n. приспособле́ние, удо́бство neut.; pl. помеще́ние, жильё neut.

accompanied by /ə'kʌmpənid/ adj. в сопровожде́нии (with gen.).

accompaniment /ə'kʌmpənimənt/ n. (mus.) аккомпанеме́нт m.

accompanist /ə'kʌmpənist/ n. аккомпаниа́тор m.

accompany /ə'kʌmpəni/ v. сопровожда́ть impf., сопроводи́ть pf.; (mus.) аккомпани́ровать impf. and pf.

accomplice /ə'kɒmplis/ n. соуча́стник, соо́бщник m.

accomplish /ə'kɒmpliʃ/ v. соверша́ть impf., соверши́ть pf.

accomplished /ə'kɒmpliʃt/ adj. зако́нченный, соверше́нный; (talented) тала́нтливый; иску́сный; **an accomplished fact** n. соверши́вшийся факт m.

accomplishment /ə'kɒmpliʃmənt/ n. заверше́ние, выполне́ние, достиже́ние neut.

accord /ə'kɔrd/ **1.** n. согла́сие, соглаше́ние neut. **2.** v. (agree) быть в согла́сии impf.; (grant) предоставля́ть impf.

accordance /ə'kɔrdns/ n. соотве́тствие neut.

accordingly /ə'kɔrdɪŋli/ adv. соотве́тственно.

according to /ə'kɔrdɪŋ/ prep. (with dat.) согла́сно с, в соотве́тствии с (with instr.).

accordion /ə'kɔrdiən/ n. аккордео́н m., гармо́ника f.

accost /ə'kɔst/ v. (stop) остана́вливать (solicit, pester) пристава́ть (к with dat.) impf.

account /ə'kaunt/ **1.** n. счёт, расчёт, отчёт m. **2.** v. отчи́тываться (в with prep.) impf.; **on account of** prep. из-за, всле́дствие (with gen.); **on no account** adv. ни в ко́ем слу́чае.

accountability /ə,kauntə'bɪlɪti/ n. отве́тственность f.

accountable /ə'kauntəbəl/ adj. отве́тственный, подотчётный.

accountancy /ə'kauntnsi/ n. счетово́дство neut.

accountant /ə'kauntnt/ n. бухга́лтер m.

accounting /ə'kauntɪŋ/ n. бухгалте́рия f.

accouter /ə'kutər/ v. снаряжа́ть impf.

accouterment /ə'kutərmənt/ n. usu. pl. снаря́жение neut.

accredit /ə'krɛdɪt/ v. (dipl.) аккредитова́ть (в with prep.); (give authority) уполномо́чивать impf.

accretion /ə'kriʃən/ n. приро́ст m.

accrue /ə'kru/ v. ска́пливаться impf.; (interest) нараста́ть impf.

accumulate /ə'kyumyə,leit/ v. аккумули́ровать impf. and pf.; нака́пливать(ся) impf., накопи́ть(ся) pf.

accumulation /ə,kyumyə'leiʃən/ n. накопле́ние; скопле́ние neut., аккумуля́ция f.

accumulator /ə'kyumyə,leitər/ n. (elec.) аккумуля́тор m.

accuracy /'ækyərəsi/ n. то́чность, пра́вильность, ме́ткость f.

accurate /'ækyərɪt/ adj. ме́ткий; то́чный, пра́вильный.

accurately /'ækyərɪtli/ adv. то́чно, пра́вильно.

accursed /ə'kɜrsɪd, ə'kɜrst/ adj. про́клятый; (detestable) прокля́тый.

accusation /,ækyu'zeiʃən/ n. обвине́ние neut.

accusative /ə'kyuzətɪv/ n. вини́тельный паде́ж m.

accuse /ə'kyuz/ v. обвиня́ть impf., обвини́ть pf.

accused /ə'kyuzd/ adj., n. обвиня́смый m.

accuser /ə'kyuzər/ n. обвини́тель m.

accustom /ə'kʌstəm/ v. привыка́ть impf., привы́кнуть pf.; приуча́ть impf., приучи́ть pf.

accustomed /ə'kʌstəmd/ adj. привы́кший, приу́ченный; привы́чный; **to become accustomed** v. привыка́ть impf., привы́кнуть pf.; приуча́ться impf., приучи́ться pf.

ace /eis/ n. (cards) туз m. (pilot) ас m.

acerbic /ə'sɜrbɪk/ adj. (taste) те́рпкий; е́дкий (speech, character) ре́зкий.

acerbity /ə'sɜrbɪti/ n. те́рпкость, е́дкость f.

acetate /'æsɪ,teit/ **1.** adj. ацета́тный. **2.** n. ацета́т m.

acetic /ə'sitɪk/ adj. у́ксусный; **acetic acid** n. у́ксусная кислота́ f.

acetone /'æsɪ,toun/ **1.** adj. ацето́нный. **2.** n. ацето́н m.

acetylene /ə'sɛtl,in/ n. ацетиле́н m.

ache /eik/ **1.** n. боль f. **2.** v. боле́ть impf.

achievable /ə'tʃivəbəl/ adj. достижи́мый.

achieve /ə'tʃiv/ v. достига́ть impf., дости́гнуть pf.

achievement /ə'tʃivmənt/ n. достиже́ние neut.

Achilles /ə'kɪliz/ n. Ахилле́с m.

achromatic /,ækrə'mætɪk/ adj. ахромати́ческий.

acid /'æsɪd/ **1.** n. кислота́ f. **2.** adj. ки́слый, кисло́тный.

acidic /ə'sɪdɪk/ adj. кисло́тный.

acidify /ə'sɪdə,fai/ v. окисля́ть(ся) impf.

acidity /ə'sɪdɪti/ n. кислотность, кислота́ f.

acknowledge /æk'nɒlɪdʒ/ v. (admit) признава́ть impf., призна́ть pf.; сознава́ть impf.; **to acknowledge receipt** v. подтвержда́ть получе́ние

acknowledgment /æk'nɒlɪdʒmənt/ n. призна́ние, подтвержде́ние neut.

acme /'ækmi/ n. высшая точка f.; верх m.

acne /'ækni/ n. угри pl.

acolyte /'ækə‚lait/ n. (relig.) прислужник m.; (attendant) помощник m.

aconite /'ækə‚nait/ n. (bot., pharm.) аконит m.

acorn /'eikɔrn/ n. жёлудь m.

acoustics /ə'kustiks/ n. акустика f.

acquaint /ə'kweint/ v. знакомить impf., познакомить pf.; ознакомлять impf.; **to acquaint oneself with** v. ознакомляться с (with instr.) impf., ознакомиться с (with instr.) pf.

acquaintance /ə'kweintṇs/ n. знакомство neut.; (person) знакомый m.

acquainted /ə'kweintid/ adj. знакомый (с with instr.).

acquiesce /‚ækwi'ɛs/ v. (молчаливо) соглашаться impf., согласиться pf.

acquiescence /‚ækwi'ɛsəns/ n. (молчаливое) согласие neut.

acquiescent /‚ækwi'ɛsənt/ adj. уступчивый.

acquire /ə'kwaiᵊr/ v. приобретать impf., приобрести pf.

acquisition /‚ækwə'ziʃən/ n. приобретение neut.

acquisitive /ə'kwizitiv/ adj. собственнический; стяжательский.

acquisitiveness /ə'kwizitivnis/ n. стяжательство neut.

acquit /ə'kwit/ v. оправдывать impf., оправдать pf.; освобождать impf., освободить pf.

acquittal /ə'kwitḷ/ n. оправдание neut.

acre /'eikər/ n. акр m.

acrid /'ækrid/ adj. острый, едкий; резкий.

acrimonious /‚ækrə'mouniəs/ adj. (words) злобный, язвительный; (character) желчный.

acrimony /'ækrə‚mouni/ n. язвительность f.

acrobat /'ækrə‚bæt/ n. акробат m.

acrobatic /‚ækrə'bætik/ adj. акробатический.

acrobatics /‚ækrə'bætiks/ n. акробатика f.

acronym /'ækrənim/ n. акроним m.

acropolis /ə'krɒpəlis/ n. акрополь m.

across /ə'krɔs/ **1.** prep. через (with acc.), по (with dat.). **2.** adv. поперёк; по ту сторону.

across-the-board /ə'krɔs 'ðə bɔrd/ adj. всеобъемлющий.

acrostic /ə'krɔstik/ n. акростих m.

acrylic /ə'krilik/ adj. акриловый.

act /ækt/ **1.** n. поступок m. (theat.) действие neut.; акт m.; (law) закон m. **2.** v. поступать impf.; поступить pf.; (behave) вести себя impf.; действовать impf., подействовать pf.

acting /'æktiŋ/ **1.** n. игра f. **2.** adj. действующий.

actinic /æk'tinik/ adj. актинический.

actinium /æk'tiniəm/ n. актиний m.

actinometer /‚æktə'nɒmitər/ n. актинометр m.

action /'ækʃən/ n. действие neut., деятельность f., поступок m.; (leg.) иск; процесс m.; (mil.) бой m.

actionable /'ækʃənəbəl/ adj. дающий основание для судебного преследования.

activate /'æktə‚veit/ v. (put into action) приводить в действие impf.; (motivate) побуждать impf.

active /'æktiv/ adj. активный, деятельный.

activist /'æktəvist/ n. активист m.

activity /æk'tiviti/ n. деятельность, активность f.; pl. мероприятия pl.

actor /'æktər/ n. актёр m.

actress /'æktris/ n. актриса f.

actual /'æktʃuəl/ adj. действительный, настоящий.

actuality /‚æktʃu'æliti/ n. действительность f.

actually /'æktʃuəli/ adv. фактически; в действительности; на самом деле.

actuary /'æktʃu‚ɛri/ n. актуарий m.

actuate /'æktʃu‚eit/ v. приводить в действие impf.

acuity /ə'kyuiti/ n. острота f.

acumen /ə'kyumən, 'ækyə-/ n. проницательность f.

acupuncture /'ækyu‚rʌŋktʃər/ n. акупунктура f.

acute /ə'kyut/ adj. острый; проницательный.

acutely /ə'kyutli/ adv. проницательно.

A.D. нашей эры; н.э.

adage /'ædidʒ/ n. (proverb) пословица f.; (saying) поговорка f.

adagio /ə'dɑdʒou, -ʒi‚ou/ n. адажио neut. indecl.

adamant /'ædəmənt/ adj. непреклонный.

Adam's apple /'ædəmz/ n. кадык m., адамово яблоко neut.

adapt /ə'dæpt/ v. приспосабливать(ся) impf., приспособить(ся) pf.; (for stage. etc.) инсценировать impf. and pf.

adaptability /ə‚dæptə'biliti/ n. приспособляемость f.

adaptable /ə'dæptəbəl/ adj. (легко) приспособляющийся.

adaptation /‚ædəp'teiʃən/ n. приспособление, применение neut.; адаптация; инсценировка f.

adapter /ə'dæptər/ n. (tech.) адаптер m.

add /æd/ v. добавлять impf., добавить pf.; прибавлять impf., прибавить pf.

added /'ædid/ adj. дополнительный; добавочный.

addendum /ə'dɛndəm/ n. приложение, дополнение neut.

adder /'ædər/ n. гадюка f.

addict /'ædikt/ n. (drugs) наркоман m., наркоманка f.

addicted /ə'diktid/ adj. склонный (к with dat.); предающийся (with dat.).

addiction /ə'dikʃən/ n. страсть f.; (to drugs) наркомания f.

addictive /ə'diktiv/ adj. вызывающий пристрастие.

addition /ə'diʃən/ n. прибавление, добавление, дополнение; (math.) сложение neut.; **in addition** adv. вдобавок; кроме того; **in addition to** в дополнение к (with dat.).

additive /'æd[itiv/ n. добавка f.

addle /'ædḷ/ v. (confuse) запутывать(ся) impf.

address /ə'drɛs/ **1.** n. адрес m.; (speech) обращение neut. **2.** v.t. (a letter) адресовать impf. and pf., направлять impf.; (speak to) обращаться (к with dat.) impf., обратиться pf.

addressee /‚ædrɛ'si/ n. адресат m.

addresser /ə'drɛsər/ n. адресант m.

adduce /ə'dus/ v. (evidence) приводить impf.

adenoid /'ædṇɔid/ n. аденоид m.

adept / n. 'ædɛpt; adj. ə'dɛpt/ **1.** n. знаток m. **2.** adj. сведущий (в with prep.).

adequacy /'ædikwəsi/ n. достаточность f.

adequate /'ædikwit/ adj. отвечающий требованиям; достаточный.

adhere /æd'hɪər/ v. (*stick to*) прилипа́ть (к *with dat.*) *impf.*; (*fig.*) приде́рживаться (*with gen.*) *impf.*

adherence /æd'hɪərəns/ n. приве́рженность f.

adherent /æd'hɪərənt/ n. приве́рженец, сторо́нник m.

adhesion /æd'hiʒən/ n. прилипа́ние *neut.*

adhesive /æd'hisɪv/ **1.** *adj.* ли́пкий. **2.** n. клей m.

adhesive tape n. ли́пкий пла́стырь m.; кле́йкая ле́нта f.

ad hoc /'æd hɒk/ *adv.* для да́нного слу́чая.

adieu /ə'du/ **1.** *interj.* проща́й, проща́йте. **2.** n. проща́ние *neut.*

ad infinitum /,æd ɪnfə'naitəm/ *adv.* до бесконе́чности.

adipose /'ædə,pous/ *adj.* жирово́й.

adjacent /ə'dʒeisənt/ *adj.* сосе́дний, прилежа́щий, сме́жный.

adjective /'ædʒɪktɪv/ n. и́мя прилага́тельное *neut.*

adjoining /ə'dʒɔinɪŋ/ *adj.* сосе́дний, сме́жный.

adjourn /ə'dʒɜrn/ v.t. откла́дывать *impf.*, отложи́ть *pf.*; v.i. объяви́ть переры́в *pf.*

adjournment /ə'dʒɜrnmənt/ n. отсро́чка f., переры́в m.

adjudge /ə'dʒʌdʒ/ v. выноси́ть реше́ние *impf.*

adjudicate /ə'dʒudɪ,keit/ v. суди́ть, выноси́ть пригово́р *impf.*

adjunct /'ædʒʌŋkt/ **1.** *adj.* доба́вочный. **2.** n. дополне́ние *neut.* **3.** n. (*professor*) адъю́нкт m.

adjust /ə'dʒʌst/ v. ула́живать *impf.*, ула́дить *pf.*; прила́живать *impf.*; регули́ровать *impf.* отрегули́ровать *pf.*; приспосо́биться *pf.*

adjustable /ə'dʒʌstəbəl/ *adj.* регули́руемый; (*movable*) передвижно́й; **adjustable wrench** n. раздвижно́й (га́ечный) ключ m.

adjustment /ə'dʒʌstmənt/ n. регули́рование *neut.*; регулиро́вка; попра́вка f.

adjutant /'ædʒətənt/ n. адъюта́нт m.

ad-lib /'æd lɪb, 'æd-/ (*theat., coll.*) **1.** n. экспро́мт m. **2.** v. импровизи́ровать *impf.*

administer /æd'mɪnəstər/ v. (*manage*) управля́ть (*with instr.*) *impf.*; (*give*) дава́ть *impf.*; (*dispence*) отправля́ть *impf.*

administration /æd,mɪnə'streiʃən/ n. администра́ция f., управле́ние *neut.*

administrative /æd'mɪnə,streitɪv/ *adj.* администрати́вный, исполни́тельный.

administrator /æd'mɪnə,streitər/ n. администра́тор, управля́ющий m.

admirable /'ædmərəbəl/ *adj.* восхити́тельный.

admiral /'ædmərəl/ n. адмира́л m.

admiralty /'ædmərəlti/ n. вое́нно-морско́е министе́рство, адмиралте́йство *neut.*

admiration /,ædmə'reiʃən/ n. восхище́ние *neut.*, восто́рг m.

admire /æd'maiər/ v. любова́ться *impf.*, полюбова́ться *pf.*; восхища́ться *impf.*, восхити́ться *pf.*

admirer /æd'maiərər/ n. покло́нник m., покло́нница f.

admiring /æd'maiərɪŋ/ *adj.* восхищённый.

admissible /æd'mɪsəbəl/ *adj.* допусти́мый, прие́млемый.

admission /æd'mɪʃən/ n. допуще́ние *neut.*, до́ступ, впуск, вход m.; (*confession*) призна́ние *neut.*

admission fee n. входна́я пла́та f.

admit /æd'mɪt/ v. допуска́ть *impf.*, допусти́ть *pf.*; впуска́ть *impf.*, впусти́ть *pf.*; (*confess*) признава́ть *impf.*, призна́ть *pf.*

admittance /æd'mɪtns/ n. до́ступ, вход m.

admitted /æd'mɪtɪd/ *adj.* (обще)при́знанный.

admittedly /æd'mɪtɪdli/ *adv.* призна́ться; пра́вда.

admixture /æd'mɪkstʃər/ n. при́месь f.

admonish /æd'mɒnɪʃ/ v. увещева́ть *impf.*

admonition /,ædmə'nɪʃən/ n. увеща́ние *neut.*; упрёк m.

ad nauseam /'æd nɔziəm/ *adv.* до отвраще́ния.

ado /ə'du/ n.: **much ado about nothing** мно́го шу́ма из ничего́.

adolescence /,ædl'ɛsəns/ n. о́трочество *neut.*

adolescent /,ædl'ɛsənt/ **1.** *adj.* о́троческий, ю́ношеский, ю́ный. **2.** n. подро́сток m.

Adonis /ə'dɒnɪs/ n. (*myth., fig.*) Адо́нис m.

adopt /ə'dɒpt/ v. принима́ть *impf.*, приня́ть *pf.*; усыновля́ть *impf.*, усынови́ть *pf.*; удочеря́ть *impf.*, удочери́ть *pf.*; займствовать *impf.*

adopted /ə'dɒptɪd/ *adj.* (*child*) приёмный.

adoption /'ə dɒpʃən/ n. усыновле́ние, приня́тие *neut.*

adorable /ə'dɔrəbəl/ *adj.* восхити́тельный; преле́стный.

adoration /,ædə'reiʃən/ n. обожа́ние, поклоне́ние *neut.*

adore /ə'dɔr/ v. обожа́ть; поклоня́ться *impf.*

adorn /ə'dɔrn/ v. украша́ть *impf.*, укра́сить *pf.*

adornment /ə'dɔrnmənt/ n. украше́ние *neut.*

adrenal gland /ə'drinl/ n. надпо́чечная железа́ f.

adrenalin /ə'drɛnəlɪn/ n. адренали́н m.

Adriatic Sea /,eidri'ætɪk/ n. Адриати́ческое мо́ре *neut.*

adrift /ə'drɪft/ *adv.*: **to be adrift** v. плыть по тече́нию *impf.*

adroit /ə'drɔit/ *adj.* ло́вкий; нахо́дчивый.

adulate /'ædʒə,leit/ v. льстить, низкопокло́нничать *impf.*

adulation /,ædʒə'leiʃən/ n. лесть f.; низкопокло́нство *neut.*

adulatory /'ædʒələ,tɔri/ *adj.* льсти́вый.

adult /ə'dʌlt, 'ædʌlt/ **1.** *adj.* взро́слый, совершенноле́тний. **2.** n. взро́слый m.

adulterate /ə'dʌltə,reit/ v. фальсифици́ровать *impf. and pf.*; приме́шивать *impf.*, примеша́ть *pf.*

adulteration /ə,dʌltə'reiʃən/ n. фальсифика́ция f.

adulterer /ə'dʌltərər/ n. неве́рный супру́г m.

adulteress /ə'dʌltərɪs, -trɪs/ n. неве́рная супру́га f.

adulterous /ə'dʌltərəs/ *adj.* прелюбоде́йский.

adultery /ə'dʌltəri/ n. супру́жеская изме́на f., адюльте́р m.

adumbrate /æd'ʌmbreit/ v. предвеща́ть *impf.*

advance /æd'væns/ **1.** n. продвиже́ние *neut.*; (*of pay*) ава́нс m.; (*progress*) прогре́сс m.; **in advance** вперёд; зара́нее. **2.** v. продвига́ться вперёд; повыша́ться *impf.*, повы́ситься *pf.*; (*a theory, etc.*) выдвига́ть *impf.*

advanced /æd'vænst/ *adj.* передово́й, продви́нутый.

advancement /æd'vænsmənt/ n. продвиже́ние, выдвиже́ние *neut.*

advantage /æd'væntɪdʒ/ n. преиму́щество *neut.*; (*profit*) вы́года; по́льза f. **to take advantage of** воспо́льзоваться *pf.*

advantageous /ˌædvən'teidʒəs/ *adj.* выгодный, благоприятный.

advent /'ædvɛnt/ *n.* пришествие *m.*; (*rel.*) **Advent** рождественский пост *m.*

adventitious /ˌædvən'tiʃəs/ *adj.* случайный.

adventure /æd'vɛntʃər/ *n.* приключение *neut.*

adventurer /æd'vɛntʃərər/ *n.* авантюрист *m.*

adventuress /æd'vɛntʃərɪs/ *n.* авантюристка *f.*

adventurous /æd'vɛntʃərəs/ *adj.* смелый; предприимчивый.

adverb /'ædvɜrb/ *n.* наречие *neut.*

adverbial /æd'vɜrbiəl/ *adj.* наречный, адвербиальный.

adversary /'ædvərˌsɛri/ *n.* противник *m.*

adverse /æd'vɜrs, 'ædvɜrs/ *adj.* враждебный; неблагоприятный.

adversity /æd'vɜrsɪti/ *n.* несчастье *neut.*

advertise /'ædvərˌtaiz/ *v.* извещать, объявлять, рекламировать *impf. and pf.*

advertisement /ˌædvər'taizmənt, æd'vɜrtɪsmənt/ *n.* объявление *neut.*, реклама *f.*

advertiser /'ædvərˌtaizər/ *n.* рекламодатель *m.*

advertising /'ædvərˌtaizɪŋ/ **1.** *adj.* рекламный. **2.** *n.* рекламное дело *neut.*

advice /æd'vais/ *n.* совет *m.*

advisability /ædˌvaizə'bɪlɪti/ *n.* (*desirability*) желательность *f.*

advisable /æd'vaizəbəl/ *adj.* рекомендуемый, целесообразный.

advise /æd'vaiz/ *v.* советовать *impf.* (*notify*) уведомлять *impf.*

adviser /æd'vaizər/ *n.* советник, консультант *m.*

advisory /æd'vaizəri/ *adj.* совещательный.

advocacy /'ædvəkəsi/ *n.* (*defense*) защита *f.*; (*support*) поддержка *f.*

advocate / *n.* 'ædvəkɪt; *v.* 'ædvəˌkeit/ **1.** *n.* сторонник, защитник *m.* **2.** *v.* отстаивать *impf.*

adz /ædz/ *n.* тесло *neut.*

Aegean Sea /ɪ'dʒiən/ *n.* Эгейское море *neut.*

aegis /'idʒɪs/ *n.* эгида.; **under the aegis of** под эгидой (*with gen.*).

Aeneid /ɪ'niːid/ *n.* Энеида *f.*

Aeolian harp /iˈouliən/ *n.* Эолова арфа *f.*

aerate /'ɛəreit/ *v.* проветривать *impf.*

aerial /'ɛəriəl/ **1.** *adj.* воздушный. **2.** *n.* антенна *f.*

aerie /'ɛəri/ *n.* орлиное гнездо *neut.*

aerobatics /ˌɛərə'bætɪks/ *n.* высший пилотаж *m.*

aerobics /ɛə'roubiks/ *n.* аэробика *f.*

aerodynamic /ˌɛəroudai'næmɪk/ *adj.* аэродинамический.

aerodynamics /ˌɛəroudai'næmɪks/ *n.* аэродинамика *f.*

aero-engine /'ɛərouˌɛndʒɪn/ *n.* авиационный двигатель *m.*

aerograph /'ɛərəˌgræf/ *n.* аэрограф *m.*

aerolite /'ɛərəˌlait/ *n.* аэролит *m.*

aerology /ɛə'rɒlədʒi/ *n.* аэрология *f.*

aeronaut /'ɛərəˌnɔt/ *n.* аэронавт, воздухоплаватель *m.*

aeronautical /ˌɛərə'nɔtɪkəl/ *adj.* авиационный.

aeronautics /ˌɛərə'nɔtɪks/ *n.* аэронавтика *f.*

aerosol /'ɛərəˌsɔl/ *n.* аэрозоль *m.* or *f.*

aerospace /'ɛərouˌspeis/ *adj.* авиационно-космический.

aerostat /'ɛərəˌstæt/ *n.* аэростат *m.*

aerostatics /ˌɛərə'stætɪks/ *n.* аэростатика *f.*

aerostation /ˌɛərə'steiʃən/ *n.* воздухоплавание *neut.*

Aesop /'isəp/ *n.* Эзоп *m.*

aesthete /'ɛsθit/ *n.* эстет *m.*

aesthetic /ɛs'θɛtɪk/ *adj.* эстетический.

aesthetics /ɛs'θɛtɪks/ *n.* эстетика *f.*

afar /ə'fɑr/ *adv.* вдалеке; **from afar** издалека.

affability /ˌæfə'bɪlɪti/ *n.* любезность *f.*

affable /'æfəbəl/ *adj.* любезный, приветливый.

affair /ə'fɛər/ *n.* дело *neut.*; (*love*) роман *m.*

affect /ə'fɛkt/ *v.* действовать(на *with acc.*) *impf.*; (*emotionally*) трогать, волновать *impf.* касаться (*with gen.*) *impf.*

affectation /ˌæfɛk'teiʃən/ *n.* аффектация *f.*

affected /ə'fɛktɪd/ *adj.* жеманный; неестественный, искуственный; показной, напускной, притворный.

affecting /ə'fɛktɪŋ/ *adj.* трогательный *adj.*

affection /ə'fɛkʃən/ *n.* привязанность *f.*

affectionate /ə'fɛkʃənɪt/ *adj.* любящий, нежный.

affectionately /ə'fɛkʃənɪtli/ *adv.* нежно.

affidavit /ˌæfɪ'deivɪt/ *n.* письменное показание под присягой *neut.*

affiliated /ə'fɪliˌeitɪd/ *adj.* филиальный, связанный.

affiliation /əˌfɪli'eiʃən/ *n.* присоединение, соединение *neut.*

affinity /ə'fɪnɪti/ *n.* родство; сходство *neut.*

affirm /ə'fɜrm/ *v.* (*assert*) заявлять (о *with prep.*); утверждать *impf.*; (*confirm*) подтверждать *impf.*

affirmation /ˌæfər'meiʃən/ *n.* утверждение, подтверждение; заявление *neut.*

affirmative /ə'fɜrmətɪv/ **1.** *n.* утвердительный ответ *m.* **2.** *adj.* утвердительный.

affix / *v.* ə'fɪks; *n.* 'æfɪks/ **1.** *v.* (*fasten*) прикреплять *impf.* **2.** *n.* (*gram.*) аффикс.

afflict /ə'flɪkt/ *v.* причинять страдание *impf.*

affliction /ə'flɪkʃən/ *n.* бедствие, несчастье *neut.*; (*sickness*) болезнь *f.*

affluence /'æfluəns/ *n.* богатство; изобилие *neut.*

affluent /'æfluənt/ *adj.* богатый.

afford /ə'fɔrd/ *v.* позволить себе; быть в состоянии *impf.*; (*give*) доставлять *impf.*

afforest /ə'fɔrɪst/ *v.* засаживать лесом *impf.*

afforestation /əˌfɔrɪ'steiʃən/ *n.* лесонасаждение *neut.*

affront /ə'frʌnt/ **1.** *n.* оскорбление *neut.* **2.** *v.* оскорблять *impf.*, оскорбить *pf.*

Afghan /'æfgæn/ **1.** *adj.* афганский. **2.** *n.* (*person*) афганец *m.*, афганка *f.*

Afghanistan /æf'gæɲəˌstæn/ *n.* Афганистан *m.*

aficionado /əˌfɪʃyə'nɑdou/ *n.* поклонник и знаток *m.*

afield /ə'fild/ *adv.* невпопад.

afire /ə'faiər/ *adv.* пылающий.

aflame /ə'fleim/ *adv.* (*on fire*) в огне.

afloat /ə'flout/ *adj.* на плаву.

afoot /ə'fut/ *adv.* (*on foot*) пешком.

aforementioned /ə'fɔrˌmɛnʃənd/ *adj.* вышеупомянутый.

aforethought /ə'fɔrˌθɔt/ *adj.* преднамеренный, предумышленный.

afraid /ə'freid/ *adj.* испуганный; **to be afraid** бояться; пугаться *impf.*

afresh /ə'frɛʃ/ *adv.* снова.

Africa /'æfrɪkə/ *n.* Африка *f.*

African /'æfrɪkən/ **1.** *adj.* африка́нский. **2.** *n.* африка́нец *m.*, африка́нка *f.*

Africanization /,æfrɪkənə'zeɪʃən/ *n.* африканиза́ция *f.*

Afrikaans /,æfrɪ'kɑns/ *n.* африка́анс *m. indecl.*

Afrikaner /,æfrɪ'kɑnər/ *n.* африка́нер *m.*

Afro /'æfrou/ *n.* and *adj.* а́фро *neut. indecl.*

aft /æft/ *adv.* на корме́.

after /'æftər/ **1.** *prep.* по́сле (*with gen.*); че́рез (*with acc.*); за (*with instr.*). **2.** *conj.* по́сле того́ как. **3.** *adv.* по́сле.

afterbirth /'æftər,bɜrθ/ *n.* после́д *m.*, плаце́нта *f.*

afterburner /'æftər,bɜrnər/ *n.* дожига́тель *m.*

aftereffect /'æftərɪ,fɛkt/ *n.* после́дствие *neut.*

afterglow /'æftər,glou/ *n.* вече́рняя заря́ *f.*

afterlife /'æftər,laɪf/ *n.* загро́бная жизнь *f.*; **in the afterlife** на том све́те.

afternoon /,æftər'nun/ *n.* вре́мя по́сле полу́дня *neut.* **in the afternoon** днём.

aftertaste /'æftər,teɪst/ *n.* при́вкус *m.*

afterthought /'æftər,θɔt/ *n.* запозда́лая мысль *f.*

afterward /'æftərwərd/ *adv.* впосле́дствии.

again /ə'gɛn/ *adv.* опя́ть, сно́ва.

against /ə'gɛnst/ *prep.* про́тив (*with gen.*); о (*with acc.*); на фо́не (*with gen.*).

agape /ə'geɪp/ *adv.* разину́в рот.

agar-agar /'ɑgɑr'ɑgɑr/ *n.* ага́р-ага́р *m.*

agate /'æɡɪt/ *n.* ага́т *m.*

age /eɪdʒ/ **1.** *n.* во́зраст *m.*; (*era*) век *m.*, эпо́ха *f.*; **old age** ста́рость *f.* **2.** *v.i.* старе́ть *impf.*, постаре́ть *pf.*

aged /'eɪdʒɪd, eɪdʒd/ *adj.* ста́рый; пожило́й.

ageless /'eɪdʒlɪs/ *adj.* нестаре́ющий; (*eternal*) ве́чный.

agency /'eɪdʒənsi/ *n.* аге́нтство *neut.*

agenda /ə'dʒɛndə/ *n.* пове́стка дня *f.*

agent /'eɪdʒənt/ *n.* аге́нт *m.*; (*representative*) представи́тель *m.*

age-old /'eɪdʒ,ould/ *adj.* веково́й.

agglomeration /ə,ɡlɒmə'reɪʃən/ *n.* скопле́ние *neut.*

agglutinate /ə'ɡlutn̩,eɪt/ *v.* скле́ивать(ся) *impf.*

agglutination /ə,ɡlutn̩'eɪʃən/ *n.* скле́ивание *neut.*

agglutinative /ə'ɡlutn̩,eɪtɪv, ə'ɡlutn̩ə-/ *adj.* скле́ивающийся; агглютинати́вный.

aggrandize /ə'ɡrændaɪz/ *v.* увели́чивать *impf.*; (*exalt*) возвели́чивать *impf.*

aggravate /'æɡrə,veɪt/ *v.* ухудша́ть *impf.*, уху́дшить *pf.*

aggravating /'æɡrə,veɪtɪŋ/ *adj.* раздража́ющий.

aggravation /,æɡrə'veɪʃən/ *n.* ухудше́ние; раздраже́ние *neut.*

aggregate /'æɡrɪɡɪt/ **1.** *adj.* совоку́пный. **2.** *n.* совоку́пность *f.*

aggregation /,æɡrɪ'ɡeɪʃən/ *n.* агрега́т *m.*, скопле́ние *neut.*

aggression /ə'ɡrɛʃən/ *n.* агре́ссия *f.*, нападе́ние *neut.*

aggressive /ə'ɡrɛsɪv/ *adj.* агресси́вный.

aggressively /ə'ɡrɛsɪvli/ *adv.* агресси́вно.

aggressiveness /ə'ɡrɛsɪvnɪs/ *n.* агресси́вность *f.*

aggressor /ə'ɡrɛsər/ *n.* агре́ссор *m.*

aggrieve /ə'ɡriv/ *v.* огорча́ть *impf.*

aghast /ə'ɡæst/ *adj.* в у́жасе (от *with gen.*); ошело́млённый.

agile /'ædʒəl/ *adj.* подви́жный, прово́рный.

agility /ə'dʒɪlɪti/ *n.* подви́жность *f.*

ageing /'eɪdʒɪŋ/ **1.** *n.* старе́ние *neut.* **2.** *adj.* старе́ющий.

agitate /'ædʒɪ,teɪt/ *v.* волнова́ть *impf.*; агити́ровать *impf. and pf.*

agitation /,ædʒɪ'teɪʃən/ *n.* волне́ние *neut.*; агита́ция *f.*

agitator /'ædʒɪ,teɪtər/ *n.* агита́тор *m.*

aglow /ə'ɡlou/ *adj.* пыла́ющий; (*fig.*) раскрасне́вшийся.

agnail /'æɡ,neɪl/ *n.* заусе́ница *f.*

agnostic /æɡ'nɒstɪk/ *n.* агно́стик *m.*

agnosticism /æɡ'nɒstə,sɪzəm/ *n.* агностици́зм *m.*

ago /ə'ɡou/ *adv.* (тому́) наза́д; **long ago** давно́.

agog /ə'ɡɒɡ/ *v.* сгора́ть от нетерпе́ния *impf.*

agonize /'æɡə,naɪz/ *v.* му́читься *impf.*; агонизи́ровать *impf.*

agonizing /'æɡə,naɪzɪŋ/ *adj.* мучи́тельный.

agony /'æɡəni/ *n.* му́ка; аго́ния; сильне́йшая боль *f.*

agoraphobia /,æɡərə'foubiə/ *n.* агорафо́бия, боя́знь простра́нства *f.*

agrarian /ə'ɡrɛəriən/ *adj.* агра́рный.

agree /ə'ɡri/ *v.* соглаша́ться *impf.*, согласи́ться *pf.*; (*reach agreement*) догова́риваться *impf.*

agreeable /ə'ɡriəbəl/ *adj.* прия́тный; согла́сный.

agreement /ə'ɡrimənt/ *n.* соглаше́ние, согла́сие *neut.*; догово́р *m.*

agricultural /,æɡrɪ'kʌltʃərəl/ *adj.* сельскохозя́йственный, земледе́льческий.

agriculture /'æɡrɪ,kʌltʃər/ *n.* се́льское хозя́йство; земледе́лие *neut.*

agronomist /ə'ɡrɒnəmɪst/ *n.* агроно́м *m.*

agronomy /ə'ɡrɒnəmi/ *n.* агроно́мия *f.*

aground /ə'ɡraund/ **1.** *adj.* (сидя́щий) на мели́. **2.** *adv.* на мели́; **to run, go aground** *v.* сади́ться на мель *impf.*

ague /'eɪɡyu/ *n.* (*fever*) лихора́дка *f.*; (*malaria*) маляри́я *f.*

ah /ɑ/ *interj.* ах, а!

aha /ɑ'hɑ/ *interj.* ага́!

ahead /ə'hɛd/ *adv.* (*dir.*) вперёд; (*loc.*) впереди́.

aid /eɪd/ **1.** *n.* по́мощь *f.*; **first aid** ско́рая по́мощь *f.* **2.** *v.* помога́ть *impf.*, помо́чь *pf.*

aide /eɪd/ *n.* помо́щник *m.*

aide-de-camp /'eɪddə'kæmp/ *n.* адъюта́нт *m.*

aide-mémoire /'eɪdmɛm'wɑr/ *n.* па́мятная запи́ска *f.*

AIDS /eɪdz/ *n.* (*med.*) СПИД *m.*

ail /eɪl/ *v.* боле́ть *impf.*; **what ails him?** что с ним?

aileron /'eɪlə,rɒn/ *n.* элеро́н *m.*

ailing /'eɪlɪŋ/ *adj.* больно́й.

ailment /'eɪlmənt/ *n.* неду́г *m.*, боле́знь *f.*

aim /eɪm/ **1.** *n.* цель *f.* **2.** *v.* прице́ливаться (в *with acc.*) *impf.*, прице́литься *pf.*; стреми́ться (к *with dat.*) *impf.*

aimless /'eɪmlɪs/ *adj.* бесце́льный.

air /ɛər/ **1.** *n.* во́здух *m.*; (*look*) вид *m.* **2.** *v.* прове́тривать *impf.*, прове́трить *pf.*

air base *n.* авиаба́за *f.*

air bed *n.* надувно́й матра́ц *m.*

airborne /'ɛər,bɔrn/ *adj.* авиацио́нный, возду́шный.

air brake *n.* пневмати́ческий то́рмоз *m.*

airbrush /'ɛər,brʌʃ/ *n.* аэро́граф *m.*

airbus /'ɛər,bʌs/ *n.* аэро́бус *m.*

air-conditioned /'ɛərkən,dɪʃənd/ *adj.* с кондициони́рованным во́здухом.

air conditioner *n.* кондиционе́р *m.*

air conditioning *n.* кондициони́рование во́здуха *neut.*

air-cooled /'ɛər,kuld/ *adj.* с возду́шным охлажде́нием.

aircraft /'ɛər,kræft/ *n.* самолёт *m.*; (*coll.*) авиа́ция *f.*

aircraft carrier *n.* авиано́сец *m.*

aircrew /'ɛər,kru/ *n.* экипа́ж самолёта *m.*

air cushion *n.* надувна́я поду́шка *f.*

airdrome /'ɛərə,droum/ *n.* аэродро́м *m.*

airfield /'ɛər,fild/ *n.* аэродро́м *m.*

airflow /'ɛər,flou/ *n.* возду́шный пото́к *m.*

Air Force *n.* вое́нно-возду́шные си́лы *pl.* (*abbr.* BBC).

air freight *n.* авиагру́з *m.*

air freighter *n.* грузово́й самолёт *m.*

air gap *n.* зазо́р, просве́т *m.*

air gun *n.* духово́е ружьё *neut.*

air heater *n.* калори́фер *m.*

air hole *n.* отду́шина *f.*

airily /'ɛərəli/ *adv.* небре́жно, легкомы́сленно.

airing /'ɛərɪŋ/ *n.* прове́тривание *neut.*

airjet /'ɛər,dʒɛt/ *n.* (*fuel injector*) форсу́нка *f.*

airless /'ɛərlɪs/ *adj.* (*stuffy*) ду́шный; (*lacking air*) безвозду́шный.

airlift /'ɛər,lɪft/ *n.* возду́шная перево́зка *f.*

airline /'ɛər,laɪn/ *n.* авиали́ния, авиакомпа́ния *f.*

airliner /'ɛər,laɪnər/ *n.* (возду́шный) ла́йнер, пассажи́рский самолёт *m.*

air lock *n.* (*blockage*) возду́шная про́бка *f.*; (*chamber*) возду́шный шлюз *m.*

airmail /'ɛər,meɪl/ *n.* авиапо́чта *f.* (*abbr. of* авиацио́нная по́чта *f.*), возду́шная по́чта *f.*

airman /'ɛərmən/ *n.* лётчик *m.*

airplane /'ɛər,pleɪn/ *n.* самолёт *m.*

air pocket *n.* возду́шная я́ма *f.*

airport /'ɛər,pɔrt/ *n.* аэропо́рт *m.*

air pump *n.* возду́шный насо́с *m.*

air raid *n.* возду́шный налёт *m.*

air route *n.* авиатра́сса *f.*

air shaft *n.* вентиляцио́нная ша́хта *f.*

airship /'ɛər,ʃɪp/ *n.* дирижа́бль *m.*

airsickness /'ɛər,sɪknɪs/ *n.* возду́шная боле́знь *f.*

air space *n.* возду́шное простра́нство *neut.*

air speed *n.* ско́рость полёта *f.*

airstream /'ɛər,strim/ *n.* возду́шный пото́к *m.*

airstrip /'ɛər,strɪp/ *n.* взлётно-поса́дочная полоса́ *f.*

airtight /'ɛər,taɪt/ *adj.*ermetи́ческий, гермети́чный.

air-to-air missile /'ɛərtu'ɛər/ *n.* раке́та ти́па во́здух-во́здух *f.*

air-to-ground /'ɛərtu'graund/ *or* **air-to-ship missile** *n.* раке́та ти́па во́здух-земля́ *or* во́здух-кора́бль *f.*

airway /'ɛər,weɪ/ *n.* (*route*) возду́шный маршру́т *m.*, возду́шная тра́сса *f.*; (*passage*) вентиляцио́нная *f.*

airworthy /'ɛər,wɜrði/ *adj.* приго́дный к полёту.

airy /'ɛəri/ *adj.* (*light*) возду́шный; (*spacious*) просто́рный; (*open to air*) досту́пный во́здуху.

airy-fairy /'ɛəri'fɛəri/ *adj.* вы́чурный.

aisle /aɪl/ *n.* прохо́д *f.*

ajar /ə'dʒɑr/ *adj.* приоткры́тый.

akimbo /ə'kɪmbou/ *adj.* подбоче́нившись.

akin /ə'kɪn/ **1.** *adj.* ро́дственный, похо́жий, бли́зкий. **2.** *adv.* сродни́ (*with dat.*).

Aktyubinsk /ak'tyubɪnsk/ *n.* Актю́бинск *m.*

Alabama /,ælə'bæmə/ *n.* Алаба́ма *f.*

alabaster /'ælə,bæstər/ **1.** *n.* алеба́стр *m.* **2.** *adj.* алеба́стровый.

alacrity /ə'lækrɪti/ *n.* быстрота́, гото́вность *f.*

à la mode /,ɑ lə 'moud/ *adj.* мо́дный.

alarm /ə'lɑrm/ **1.** *n.* трево́га *f.* **2.** *v.* встревожить *pf.*

alarm clock *n.* буди́льник *m.*

alarming /ə'lɑrmɪŋ/ *adj.* трево́жный, волну́ющий.

alarmist /ə'lɑrmɪst/ *n.* паникёр *m.*

alas! /ə'læs/ *interj.* увы́!

Alaska /ə'læskə/ *n.* Аля́ска *f.*

Alaskan /ə'læskən/ *adj.* аля́скинский.

alb /ælb/ *n.* (*eccl.*) стиха́рь *m.*

Albania /æl'beɪniə/ *n.* Алба́ния *f.*

albatross /'ælbə,trɔs/ *n.* альба́трос *m.*

albeit /ɔl'biit/ *conj.* хотя́ (и), да́же е́сли.

albinism /'ælbə,nɪzəm/ *n.* альбини́зм *m.*

albino /æl'baɪnou/ *n.* альбино́с *m.*

albumen /æl'byumən/ *n.* бело́к *m.*

albuminous /æl'byumənəs/ *adj.* белко́вый, альбуми́нный.

alchemical /æl'kɛmɪkəl/ *adj.* алхими́ческий.

alchemist /'ælkəmɪst/ *n.* алхи́мик *m.*

alchemy /'ælkəmi/ *n.* алхи́мия *f.*

alcohol /'ælkə,hɔl/ *n.* алкого́ль; спирт *m.*

alcoholic /,ælkə'hɔlɪk/ *adj.* **1.** алкого́льный, алкого́лический. **2.** *n.* алкого́лик *m.*

alcoholism /'ælkəhɔ,lɪzəm/ *n.* алкоголи́зм *m.*

alcove /'ælkouv/ *n.* алько́в *m.*, ни́ша *f.*

alder /'ɔldər/ *n.* ольха́ *f.*

ale /eɪl/ *n.* пи́во *neut.*, эль *m.*

alembic /ə'lɛmbɪk/ *n.* перего́нный куб *m.*

alert /ə'lɜrt/ **1.** *adj.* насторо́женный, бди́тельный. **2.** *n.* трево́га *f.*

alertness /ə'lɜrtnɪs/ *n.* бди́тельность *f.*

Aleutian Islands /ə'luʃən/ *n.* Алеу́тские острова́ *pl.*

alexandrite /,ælɪg'zændraɪt/ *n.* александри́т *f.*

alfalfa /æl'fælfə/ *n.* люце́рна *f.*

alfresco /æl'freskou/ *adv.* на откры́том во́здухе.

algae /'ældʒi/ *n.* морска́я во́доросль *f.*

algebra /'ældʒəbrə/ *n.* а́лгебра *f.*

algebraical /,ældʒə'breɪkəl/ *adj.* алгебраи́ческий.

Algiers /æl'dʒɪərz/ *n.* Алжи́р *m.*

ALGOL /'ælgɒl/ *n.* алго́л *m.*

algorithm /'ælgə,rɪðəm/ *n.* алгори́тм *m.*

alias /'eɪliəs/ *n.* кли́чка *f.*, про́звище *neut.*

alibi /'ælə,baɪ/ *n.* а́либи *neut. indecl.*

alien /'eɪlyən/ **1.** *adj.* чужо́й; чу́ждый **2.** *n.* иностра́нец *m.*

alienable /'eɪlyənəbəl/ *adj.* отчужда́емый.

alienate /'eɪlyə,neɪt/ *v.* отчужда́ть *impf.*

alienation /,eɪlyə'neɪʃən/ *n.* отчужде́ние *neut.*

alight[1] /ə'laɪt/ *v.* сходи́ть; выходи́ть; сади́ться; приземля́ться *impf.*

alight[2] /ə'laɪt/ *adj.* зажжённый.

align /ə'laɪn/ *v.* ста́вить в ряд; выра́внивать(ся) *impf.*

alignment /ə'laɪnmənt/ *n.* (*leveling*) выра́внивание *neut.*; (*arrangement*) расстано́вка *f.*

alike /ə'laik/ **1.** adj. похо́жий, подо́бный. **2.** adv. подо́бно, одина́ково; то́чно так же.

alimentary /ˌælə'mɛntəri/ adj. пищево́й; **alimentary canal** n. пищевари́тельный тракт m.

alimentation /ˌælɪmɛn'teiʃən/ n. пита́ние neut.

alimony /'ælə,mouni/ n. алиме́нты pl.

alive /ə'laiv/ adj. живо́й.

alkali /'ælkə,lai/ n. щёлочь f.

alkaline /'ælkə,lain, -lɪn/ adj. щелочно́й.

alkaloid /'ælkə,lɔid/ n. алкало́ид m.

all /ɔl/ **1.** adj. весь, вся, всё; **all the more** тем бо́лее что; **not at all** совсе́м не (нет); ниско́лько. **2.** pron. всё neut.

all-around /'ɔlə,raund/ adj. (versatile) разносторо́нний, многосторо́нний; (on all sides) всесторо́нний.

allay /ə'lei/ v. успока́ивать impf., успоко́ить pf.

all clear n. (mil.) сигна́л отбо́я m.

allegation /ˌælɪ'geiʃən/ n. утвержде́ние neut.

allege /ə'lɛdʒ/ v. утвержда́ть impf., утверди́ть pf.

alleged /ə'lɛdʒd, ə'lɛdʒid/ adj. предполага́емый.

allegedly /ə'lɛdʒidli/ adv. я́кобы.

allegiance /ə'lidʒəns/ n. ве́рность, пре́данность, лоя́льность (with dat.) f.

allegorical /ˌælɪ'gɔrɪkəl/ adj. аллегори́ческий.

allegory /'ælə,gɔri/ n. аллего́рия f.

allegretto /ˌælɪ'grɛtou/ n. аллегре́тто neut. indecl.

allegro /ə'leigrou/ n. алле́гро neut. indecl.

all-embracing /'ɔlɛm'breisɪŋ/ adj. всеобъе́млющий.

allergen /'ælərdʒən/ n. аллерге́н m.

allergy /'ælərdʒi/ n. аллерги́я f.

alleviate /ə'livi,eit/ v. облегча́ть impf.

alleviation /ə,livi'eiʃən/ n. облегче́ние neut.

alley /'æli/ n. у́зкий переу́лок; прохо́д m.

alliance /ə'laiəns/ n. сою́з m.

allied /ə'laid, 'ælaid/ adj. сою́зный (с with instr.).

alligator /'ælɪ,geitər/ n. аллига́тор m.

all-important /'ɔlɪm'pɔrtnt/ adj. о́чень ва́жный.

all-in /'ɔl'ɪn/ adj. включи́тельный.

alliteration /ə,lɪtə'reiʃən/ n. аллитера́ция f.

alliterative /ə'lɪtə,reitɪv, -ərətɪv/ adj. аллитерацио́нный.

all-night /'ɔl,nait/ adj. ночно́й, продолжа́ющийся всю ночь.

allocate /'ælə,keit/ v. распределя́ть, размеща́ть; предназнача́ть (на with acc.) impf.

allocation /ˌælə'keiʃən/ n. распределе́ние, назначе́ние neut.; (ration) паёк m.

allocution /ˌælə'kyuʃən/ n. речь f.

allopathic /ˌælə'pæθɪk/ adj. терапевти́ческий, аллопати́ческий.

allopathy /ə'lɒpəθi/ n. терапи́я, аллопа́тия f.

allot /ə'lɒt/ v. раздава́ть, распределя́ть impf.

allotment /ə'lɒtmənt/ n. распределе́ние neut., до́ля f.

all-out /'ɔl,aut/ adj. (total) тота́льный; (determined) реши́тельный.

allow /ə'lau/ v. позволя́ть impf., позво́лить pf. разреша́ть; допуска́ть impf.

allowable /ə'lauəbəl/ adj. допусти́мый; позволи́тельный.

allowance /ə'lauəns/ n. (deduction, also fig.) ски́дка f.; (money) посо́бие neut.; (expenses) де́ньги на расхо́ды pl.; **to make allowance for** принима́ть в расчёт impf.

alloy /'ælɔi/ n. сплав m.

all-powerful /'ɔl'pauərfəl/ adj. всемогу́щий.

all-purpose /'ɔl'pɜrpəs/ adj. многоцелево́й, универса́льный.

all right adv. хорошо́, (colloq.) ла́дно.

all-rounder /'ɔl'raundər/ n. разносторо́нний челове́к m.

all-time /'ɔl,taim/ adj. непревзойдённый.

allude /ə'lud/ v. намека́ть impf., намекну́ть (на with acc.) pf.

allure /ə'lʊr/ **1.** n. привлека́тельность f. **2.** v. завлека́ть; соблазня́ть; очаро́вывать impf.

allurement /ə'lʊrmənt/ n. прима́нка f.

alluring /ə'lʊrɪŋ/ adj. зама́нчивый; соблазни́тельный.

allusion /ə'luʒən/ n. намёк m.; ссы́лка f.

alluvial /ə'luviəl/ adj. нано́сный.

alluvium /ə'luviəm/ n. нано́сы pl., аллю́вий m.

all-weather /'ɔl,wɛðər/ adj. всепого́дный.

ally / v. ə'lai; n. 'ælai/ **1.** v. соединя́ться impf., соедини́ться pf. **2.** n. сою́зник m.

almanac /'ɔlmə,næk/ n. альмана́х m.

Almaty /'ælməti/ n. (formerly: Alma Ata) Алма́ты m.

almighty /ɔl'maiti/ adj. всемогу́щий.

almond /'amənd, 'æmənd/ n. минда́ль m.

almond-eyed /'amənd,aid, 'æmənd / adj. с миндалеви́дными глаза́ми.

almost /'ɔlmoust/ adv. почти́; едва́ не, чуть не.

alms /amz/ n. ми́лостыня f.

almshouse /'amz,haus/ n. богаде́льня f.

aloe /'ælou/ n. ало́э neut. indecl.

aloft /ə'lɔft/ adv. (upwards) наве́рх; (on top) наверху́.

alone /ə'loun/ **1.** adj. оди́н; одино́кий **2.** adv. то́лько.

along /ə'lɔŋ/ prep. вдоль (with gen.); по (with dat.); у (with gen.); **all along** adv. всё вре́мя.

alongside /ə'lɔŋ'said/ adv. ря́дом; бок о́ бок (with instr.).

aloof /ə'luf/ adj. сде́ржанный; холо́дный; (distant) отчуждённый.

aloofness /ə'lufnɪs/ n. отчуждённость f.

alopecia /ˌælə'piʃiə/ n. облысе́ние neut.

aloud /ə'laud/ adv. вслух; гро́мко.

alpaca /æl'pækə/ n. альпака́ n. indecl.

alpenstock /'ælpən,stɒk/ n. альпеншто́к m.

alphabet /'ælfə,bet/ n. алфави́т m., а́збука f.

alphabetical /ˌælfə'bɛtɪkəl/ adj. алфави́тный.

alphabetically /ˌælfə'bɛtɪkli/ adv. по алфави́ту.

alphabetize /'ælfəbɪ,taiz/ v. располага́ть в алфави́тном поря́дке impf.

alpha particle /'ælfə/ n. а́льфа-части́ца f.

alpine /'ælpain/ adj. альпи́йский.

Alps /ælps/ n. А́льпы pl.

already /ɔl'redi/ adv. уже́.

also /'ɔlsou/ adv. та́кже, то́же.

also-ran /'ɔlsou,ræn/ n. неуда́чник m.

altar /'ɔltər/ n. алта́рь m.

Altay /'æltai/ n. (mountain range) Алта́й m.

alter /'ɔltər/ v. изменя́ть(ся) impf., измени́ть(ся) pf.; переде́лывать impf., переде́лать pf.

alteration /ˌɔltə'reiʃən/ n. измене́ние neut.; переде́лка f.

altercation /ˌɔltər'keiʃən/ n. перебра́нка f.

alter ego n. второе я neut.
alternate / adj. 'ɔltərnɪt; v. 'ɔltər,neit/ **1.** adj. чередующийся, переменный. **2.** v.t. чередовать impf.; v.i. чередоваться impf. **3.** n. заместитель m.
alternating current /'ɔltər,neitɪŋ/ n. (elec.) переменный ток m.
alternation /,ɔltər'neiʃən/ n. чередование neut.
alternative /ɔl'tɜrnətɪv/ **1.** adj. альтернативный. **2.** n. альтернатива f.
alternator /'ɔltər,neitər/ n. генератор (переменного тока) m.
although /ɔl'ðou/ conj. хотя.
altimeter /æl'tɪmɪtər/ n. альтиметр m.
altitude /'æltɪ,tud/ n. высота f.
alto /'æltou/ n. альт m.
altogether /,ɔltə'gɛðər/ adv. всего, вполне.
alto saxophone n. альт-саксофон m.
altruism /'æltru,ɪzəm/ n. альтруизм m.
altruist /'æltruɪst/ n. альтруист m.
altruistic /,æltru'ɪstɪk/ adj. альтруистический.
alum /'æləm/ n. квасцы pl.
aluminous /ə'lumənəs/ adj. квасцовый, глинозёмистый.
aluminum /ə'lumənəm/ n. алюминий m.
alumnus /ə'lʌmnəs/ n. (бывший) питомец m.
alveolar /æl'viələr/ adj. альвеолярный.
always /'ɔlweiz/ adv. всегда.
a.m. (abbr. of ante meridiem) утром.
amalgam /ə'mælgəm/ n. амальгама, смесь f.
amalgamate /ə'mælgə,meit/ v. соединяться; объединяться impf.; амальгамировать(ся) impf. and pf.
amalgamation /ə,mælgə'meiʃən/ n. объединение, слияние neut.
amaranth /'æmə,rænθ/ n. (bot.) амарант, бархатник m.
amaranthine /,æmə'rænθɪn/ adj. фиолетовый, неувядающий.
amass /ə'mæs/ v. собирать(ся); копить(ся) impf.
amateur /'æmə,tʃʊr/ **1.** n. любитель m. **2.** adj. любительский.
amateurish /,æmə'tʃʊrɪʃ/ adj. любительский, дилетантский.
amatory /'æmə,tɔri/ adj. любовный.
amaze /ə'meiz/ v. изумлять impf., изумить pf.
amazement /ə'meizmənt/ n. изумление neut.
amazing /ə'meizɪŋ/ adj. удивительный.
Amazon /'æmə,zɒn/ n. (river) Амазонка f.
ambassador /æm'bæsədər/ n. посол m.
ambassadorial /æm,bæsə'dɔriəl/ adj. посольский.
ambassadress /æm'bæsədrɪs/ n. женщина-посол, жена посла, представительница f.
amber /'æmbər/ **1.** adj. янтарный. **2.** n. янтарь m.
ambergris /'æmbər,gris/ n. серая амбра f.
ambiance /'æmbiəns/ n. (surroundings) окружение neut.; (milieu) среда f.
ambidextrous /,æmbɪ'dɛkstrəs/ adj. владеющий левой и правой рукой одинаково хорошо.
ambient /'æmbiənt/ adj. окружающий.
ambiguity /,æmbɪ'gyuɪti/ n. двусмысленность f.
ambiguous /æm'bɪgyuəs/ adj. двусмысленный.
ambit /'æmbɪt/ n. окружение neut.
ambition /æm'bɪʃən/ n. честолюбие neut., мечта; амбиция f.
ambitious /æm'bɪʃəs/ adj. честолюбивый.

ambivalence /æm'bɪvələns/ n. раздвоение чувств neut., противоречивость f.
ambivalent /æm'bɪvələnt/ adj. раздвоенный; (contradictory) противоречивый.
amble /'æmbəl/ v. идти не спеша impf.
ambler /'æmblər/ n. иноходец m.
ambo /'æmbou/ n. амвон m.
ambrosia /æm'brouʒə/ n. (myth.) амброзия f.
ambulance /'æmbyələns/ n. машина скорой помощи, скорая помощь f.
ambulatory /'æmbyələ,tɔri/ adj. амбулаторный.
ambush /'æmbʊʃ/ n. засада f.
ameba /ə'mibə/ n. амёба f.
amebic /ə'mibɪk/ adj. амёбный.
ameliorate /ə'milyə,reit/ v. улучшать(ся) impf.
amelioration /ə,milyə'reiʃən/ n. улучшение neut.
ameliorative /ə'milyə,reitɪv/ adj. мелиоративный.
amen /'ei'mɛn, 'ɑ'mɛn/ interj. аминь!
amenable /ə'minəbəl/ adj. послушный, поддающийся; уступчивый; сговорчивый.
amend /ə'mɛnd/ v. исправлять impf., исправить pf.
amendment /ə'mɛndmənt/ n. поправка f., исправление neut.
amends /ə'mɛndz/ n.: **to make amends** v. компенсировать (за with acc.) impf.
amenity /ə'mɛnɪti/ n. приятность f.; pl. удобства, услуги pl.
America /ə'mɛrɪkə/ n. Америка f.
American /ə'mɛrɪkən/ **1.** adj. американский. **2.** n. американец m., американка f.
amethyst /'æməθɪst/ n. аметист m.
Amharic /æm'hærɪk/ n. амхарский язык m.
amiable /'eimiəbəl/ adj. любезный.
amicability /,æmɪkə'bɪlɪti/ n. добродушие, дружелюбие neut.
amicable /'æmɪkəbəl/ adj. дружеский, дружный.
amid /ə'mɪd/ prep. среди, посреди (with gen.).
amidol /'æmɪ,dɒl/ n. амидол m.
amidships /ə'mɪd,ʃɪps/ adv. в средней части судна.
Amiens /'æmiənz, 'a'myæn/ n. Амьен m.
amino acid /ə'minou/ n. аминокислота f.
amiss /ə'mɪs/ adj. неправильный, плохой.
amity /'æmɪti/ n. согласие neut.; дружеские отношения pl.
ammeter /'æm,mitər/ n. амперметр m.
ammonal /'æmə,næl/ n. аммонал m.
ammonia /ə'mounyə/ n. аммиак, нашатырный спирт m.
ammonium chloride /ə'mouniəm/ n. нашатырь m.
ammunition /,æmyə'nɪʃən/ n. боеприпасы pl.; (bullets) патроны pl.
amnesia /æm'niʒə/ n. амнезия f.
amnesty /'æmnəsti/ n. амнистия f.
among /ə'mʌŋ/ prep. между (with instr.); среди (with gen.).
amoral /ei'mɔrəl/ adj. аморальный.
amorous /'æmərəs/ adj. любовный.
amorousness /'æmərəsnɪs/ n. влюбчивость f.
amorphous /ə'mɔrfəs/ adj. бесформенный, аморфный.
amortization /,æmərtə'zeiʃən/ n. амортизация f.
amount /'ə'maunt/ n. количество neut., сумма f.
amour /ə'mʊr/ n. любовная интрига f.

amour-propre /ɑ'mʊr'prɔprə/ *n.* самолюбие *neut.*

amperage /'æmpərɪdʒ/ *n.* сила тока *f.*

ampere /'æmpɪər/ *n.* ампер *m.*

amphetamine /æm'fɛtə,min/ *n.* амфетамин *m.*

Amphibia /æm'fɪbiə/ *n.* амфибии *pl.*

amphibian /æm'fɪbiən/ **1.** *adj.* земноводный. **2.** *n.* амфибия *f.*

amphibious /æm'fɪbiəs/ *adj.* земноводный; (*of vehicle*) плавающий.

amphiboly /æm'fɪbəli/ *n.* двусмысленность *f.*

amphibrach /'æmfə,bræk/ *n.* амфибрахий *m.*

amphitheater /'æmfə,θiətər/ *n.* амфитеатр *m.*

amphora /'æmfərə/ *n.* амфора *f.*

ample /'æmpəl/ *adj.* обильный; достаточный.

amplification /,æmpləfɪ'keiʃən/ *n.* уточнение *neut.*; (*elec.*) усиление, увеличение *neut.*

amplifier /'æmplə,faiər/ *n.* (*elec.*) усилитель *m.*

amplify /'æmplə,fai/ *v.* расширять *impf.*; (*elec.*) усиливать *impf.*, усилить *pf.*

amplitude /'æmplɪ,tud/ *n.* широта *f.*; (*phys.*) амплитуда *f.*

amply /'æmpli/ *adv.* вполне, достаточно, обильно.

ampule /'æmpyul/ *n.* ампула *f.*

amputate /'æmpyʊ,teit/ *v.* ампутировать *impf.* and *pf.*

amputation /,æmpyʊ'teiʃən/ *n.* ампутация *f.*

Amsterdam /'æmstər,dæm/ *n.* Амстердам *m.*

amuck /ə'mʌk/ *or* **amok** *adv.*: **to run amuck** *v.* кидаться на всех, беситься *impf.*

Amu Darya /'ɑ'mu dɑryə/ *n.* (*also: Oxus*) (*river*) Амударья *f.*

amulet /'æmyəlɪt/ *n.* амулет *m.*

Amur /ɑ'mʊr/ *n.* (*river*) Амур *m.*

amuse /ə'myuz/ *v.* забавлять *impf.*; **to amuse oneself** развлекаться; забавляться *impf.*

amusement /ə'myuzmənt/ *n.* развлечение *neut.*

amusing /ə'myuzɪŋ/ *adj.* развлекательный, занимательный; забавный, смешной.

amyl /'æmɪl, 'eimɪl/ *n.* амил *m.*

Anabaptist /,ænə'bæptɪst/ *n.* анабаптист *m.*

anabolic steroid /,ænə'bɒlɪk/ *n.* анаболический стероид *m.*

anachronism /ə'nækrə,nɪzəm/ *n.* анахронизм *m.*

anachronistic /ə,nækrə'nɪstɪk/ *adj.* анахронический, анахроничный.

anacoluthon /,ænəkə'luθɒn/ *n.* анаколуф *m.*

anaconda /,ænə'kɒndə/ *n.* анаконда *f.*

anacreontic /ə,nækri'ɒntɪk/ *adj.* анакреонтический.

anacrusis /,ænə'krusɪs/ *n.* анакруза *f.*

Anadyr Gulf /,ɑnə'diər/ *n.* Анадырский залив *m.*

anaerobic /,ænə'roubɪk/ *adj.* анаэробный.

anagram /'ænə,græm/ *n.* анаграмма *f.*

anal /'einl/ *adj.* заднепроходный, анальный.

analgesic /,ænl'dʒizɪk/ *n.* болеутоляющее средство *neut.*

analog computer /'ænl,ɔg/ *n.* моделирующая машина *f.*

analogical /,ænl'ɒdʒɪkəl/ *adj.* аналогический.

analogous /ə'næləgəs/ *adj.* аналогичный.

analogy /ə'nælədʒi/ *n.* аналогия *f.*, сходство *neut.*

analysis /ə'næləsɪs/ *n.* анализ *m.*

analyst /'ænlɪst/ *n.* аналитик *m.*

analytical /,ænl'ɪtɪkəl/ *adj.* аналитический.

analytics /,ænl'ɪtɪks/ *n.* аналитика *f.*

analyze /'ænl,aiz/ *v.* анализировать *impf.*, проанализировать *pf.*

anamorphic /,ænə'mɔrfɪk/ *adj.* анаморфический.

anamorphosis /,ænə'mɔrfəsɪs/ *n.* анаморфоз *m.*

anapest /'ænə,pɛst/ *n.* анапест *m.*

anarchic /æn'ɑrkɪk/ *adj.* анархический.

anarchism /'ænər,kɪzəm/ *n.* анархизм *m.*

anarchist /'ænərkɪst/ *n.* анархист *m.*

anarchy /'ænərki/ *n.* анархия *f.*

anastigmatic /,ænəstɪg'mætɪk/ *adj.* анастигматический.

anathema /ə'næθəmə/ *n.* анафема *f.*

anathematize /ə'næθəmə,taiz/ *v.* проклинать, предавать анафеме *impf.*

anatomical /,ænə'tɒmɪkəl/ *adj.* анатомический.

anatomist /ə'nætəmɪst/ *n.* анатом *m.*

anatomize /ə'nætə,maiz/ *v.* анатомировать *impf.*

anatomy /ə'nætəmi/ *n.* анатомия *f.*

ancestor /'ænsɛstər/ *n.* предок *m.*

ancestral /æn'sɛstrəl/ *adj.* родовой; наследственный.

ancestry /'ænsɛstri/ *n.* происхождение *neut.*

anchor /'æŋkər/ **1.** *n.* якорь *m.* **2.** *v.* стать на якорь *pf.*

anchorage /'æŋkərɪdʒ/ *n.* якорная стоянка *f.*

anchoress /'æŋkərɪs/ *n.* отшельница *f.*

anchorite /'æŋkə,rait/ *n.* отшельник, затворник, анахорет *m.*

anchovy /'æntʃouvi/ *n.* анчоус *m.*

ancient /'einʃənt/ *adj.* старинный; древний.

ancillary /'ænsə,lɛri/ *adj.* вспомогательный.

and /ænd/ *unstressed* ənd, ən, *or, esp. after a homorganic consonant,* n/ *conj.* и; а.

andante /ɑn'dɑntei/ *n.* анданте *neut. indecl.*

andantino /,ændɑn'tinou/ *n.* андантино *neut. indecl.*

Andes /'ændiz/ *n.* Анды *pl.*

Andorra /æn'dɔrə/ *n.* Андорра *f.*

androgyne /'ændrə,dʒain/ *n.* двуполый оганизм *m.*; гермафродит *m.*

androgynous /æn'drɒdʒənəs/ *adj.* двуполый; гермафродитный.

anecdote /'ænɪk,dout/ *n.* анекдот *m.*

anecdotical /,ænɪk'doutɪkəl/ *adj.* анекдотичный.

anemia /ə'nimiə/ *n.* анемия *f.*, малокровие *neut.*

anemic /ə'nimɪk/ *adj.* малокровный, анемичный; вялый, бледный.

anemograph /ə'nɛmə,græf/ *n.* анемограф *m.*

anemometer /,ænə'mɒmɪtər/ *n.* анемометр *m.*

anemone /ə'nɛmə,ni/ *n.* анемон *m.*

aneroid barometer /'ænə,rɔid/ *n.* барометр-анероид *m.*

anesthesia /,ænəs'θiʒə/ *n.* анестезия *f.*; наркоз *m.*

anesthetic /,ænəs'θɛtɪk/ *n.* анестезирующее средство *neut.*, анестетик, наркоз *m.*

anesthetist /ə'nɛsθɪtɪst/ *n.* анестезиолог *m.*

anesthetize /ə'nɛsθɪ,taiz/ *v.* анестезировать *impf.*

aneurysm /'ænyə,rɪzəm/ *n.* аневризм *m.*

anew /ə'nu/ *adv.* снова, заново.

Angara /,ɑŋgərə/ *n.* (*river*) Ангара *f.*

angel /'eindʒəl/ *n.* ангел *m.*

angelic /æn'dʒɛlɪk/ *adj.* ангельский.

anger /'æŋgər/ **1.** *n.* гнев *m.* **2.** *v.t.* сердить *impf.*

Angevin /'ændʒəvɪn/ *adj.* анжуйский.

angina /æn'dʒainə/ n. ангина f.

angina pectoris /'pɛktərɪs/ n. грудная жаба f.

angle /'æŋgəl/ n. угол m.; (fig.) точка зрения f.

angler /'æŋglər/ n. рыболов m.

anglerfish /'æŋglər,fɪʃ/ n. морской чёрт m.

Anglican /'æŋglɪkən/ n. представитель англиканской церкви, англиканец m.

Anglicism /'æŋglə,sɪzəm/ n. англицизм m.

Anglicize /'æŋglə,saiz/ v. англизировать impf.

angling /'æŋglɪŋ/ n. рыбная ловля f.

Anglomania /,æŋglə'meiniə/ n. англомания f.

anglophile /'æŋglə,fail/ n. англофил m.

anglophobia /,æŋglə'foubiə/ n. англофобия f.

anglophone /'æŋglə,foun/ adj. англоязычный.

Anglo-Saxon /'æŋglou'sæksən/ adj. англосаксонский.

Angola /æŋ'goulə/ n. Ангола f.

angora /æŋ'gɔrə/ adj. ангорский.

angostura /,æŋgə'stʊrə/ n. ангостура f.

angrily /'æŋgrəli/ adv. гневно, сердито.

angry /'æŋgri/ adj. сердитый.

Angstrom unit /'æŋstrəm/ n. ангстрём m.

anguish /'æŋgwɪʃ/ n. мука, боль f.

anguished /'æŋgwɪʃt/ adj. мучающийся; мучительный.

angular /'æŋgyələr/ adj. угловатый, костлявый.

angularity /,æŋgyə'lærɪti/ n. угловатость, костлявость f.

anhydrous /æn'haidrəs/ adj. безводный.

aniline /'ænlɪn/ n. анилин m.

animadversion /,ænəmæd'vɜrʒən/ n. замечание neut.

animadvert /,ænəmæd'vɜrt/ v. критиковать impf.

animal /'ænəməl/ 1. n. животное neut. 2. adj. животный.

animalcule /,ænə'mælkyul/ n. букашка f.

animate / adj. 'ænəmɪt; v. 'ænəmeit/ 1. adj. одушевлённый. 2. v. одушевлять impf., одушевить pf.

animated /'ænə,meitɪd/ adj. оживлённый; animated cartoon n. мультфильм m..

animation /,ænə'meiʃən/ n. оживление neut., живость f.

animator /'ænə,meitər/ n. мультипликатор (художник) m.

animism /'ænə,mɪzəm/ n. анимизм m.

animist /'ænəmɪst/ n. анимист m.

animistic /,ænə'mɪstɪk/ adj. анимистический.

animus /'ænəməs/ n. враждебность f.; предубеждение neut.

anion /'æn,aiən/ n. анион m.

aniseed /'ænə,sid/ n. анис m.

Ankara /'æŋkərə/ n. Анкара f.

ankh /æŋk/ n. анк m.

ankle /'æŋkəl/ n. лодыжка f.

annals /'ænlz/ pl. летопись, хроника f.

anneal /ə'nil/ v. (metal) отжигать impf.; (glass, etc.) обжигать impf.

annealing /ə'nilɪŋ/ n. отжиг, обжиг m.

annex /'ænɛks/ n. (addition) прибавление; приложение neut.; (building) пристройка f., флигель m.

annexation /,ænɪk'seiʃən/ n. присоединение neut., аннексия f.

annihilate /ə'naiə,leit/ v. уничтожать impf., уничтожить pf.

anniversary /,ænə'vɜrsəri/ n. годовщина f.

anno /'ænou, 'ɒnou/ n.: anno Domini, A.D. adj. нашей эры, н.э.

annotate /'ænə,teit/ v. аннотировать impf. and pf.

annotation /,ænə'teiʃən/ n. аннотация f., комментарий m.; примечание neut.

announce /ə'nauns/ v. объявлять impf., объявить pf.

announcement /ə'naunsmənt/ n. объявление, заявление neut.; сообщение neut.

announcer /ə'naunsər/ n. (radio, TV) диктор m.

annoy /ə'nɔi/ v. досаждать impf., досадить pf.; надоедать impf., надоесть pf.

annoyance /ə'nɔiəns/ n. раздражение neut.

annoying /ə'nɔiɪŋ/ adj. досадный, раздражающий.

annual /'ænyuəl/ 1. adj. ежегодный, годовой. 2. n. ежегодник m.

annuity /ə'nuiti/ n. ежегодная рента f., аннуитет m.

annul /ə'nʌl/ v. аннулировать impf. and pf.

annular /'ænyələr/ adj. кольцевидный, кольцевой.

annulment /ə'nʌlmənt/ n. отмена f.; аннулирование neut.

Annunciation /ə,nʌnsi'eiʃən/ n. (relig.) Благовещение neut.

anode /'ænoud/ n. анод m.

anodize /'ænə,daiz/ v. анодировать impf.

anodyne /'ænə,dain/ n. болеутоляющее средство neut.

anoint /ə'nɔint/ v. намазывать; (relig.) делать помазание impf.

anomalistic /ə,nɒmə'lɪstɪk/ adj. аномальный.

anomalous /ə'nɒmələs/ adj. неправильный, ненормальный.

anomaly /ə'nɒməli/ n. аномалия f.

anon /ə'nɒn/ adv. вскоре, опять.

anonym /'ænənɪm/ n. аноним m.

anonymity /,ænə'nɪmɪti/ n. анонимность f.

anonymous /ə'nɒnəməs/ adj. анонимный.

anorexia nervosa /,ænə'rɛksiə nɜr'vousə/ n. нервная анорексия f.

anorexic /,ænə'rɛksɪk/ adj. больной анорексией.

another /ə'nʌðər/ pron. другой; ещё (один).

answer /'ænsər/ 1. n. ответ m. 2. v. отвечать impf., ответить pf.

answerable /'ænsərəbəl/ adj. ответственный.

answering machine /'ænsərɪŋ/ n. автоответчик m.

ant /ænt/ n. муравей m.

antacid /ænt'æsɪd/ adj. антикислотный.

antagonism /æn'tægə,nɪzəm/ n. антагонизм m., вражда f.

antagonist /æn'tægənɪst/ n. противник m.

antagonistic /æn,tægə'nɪstɪk/ adj. враждебный, антагонистический.

antagonize /æn'tægə,naiz/ v. вызывать антагонизм.

antarctic /ænt'ɑrktɪk, -'ɑrtɪk/ adj. антарктический.

anteater /'ænt,itər/ n. муравьед m.

antebellum /'ænti'bɛləm/ adj. довоенный.

antecede /,æntə'sid/ v. предшествовать impf.

antecedent /,æntə'sidnt/ adj. предшествующий.

antechamber /'ænti,tʃeimbər/ n. передняя f.

antedate /'æntɪˌdeit/ v. датировать задним числом *impf.*
antediluvian /ˌæntidɪ'luviən/ *adj.* допотопный.
antelope /'æntlˌoup/ *n.* антилопа *f.*
antemeridian /ˌæntimə'rɪdiən/ *adj.* утренний, до полудня.
antenatal /ˌænti'neitl/ *adj.* дородовой.
antenna /æn'tɛnə/ *n.* антенна *f.*; (*insects*) щупальце *pl.*
antenuptial /ˌænti'nʌpʃəl/ *adj.* добрачный.
antepenultimate /ˌæntipɪ'nʌltəmɪt/ *adj.* третий от конца.
anterior /æn'tɪəriər/ *adj.* передний; предшествующий.
anteroom /'æntiˌrum/ *n.* передняя *f.*
anthelion /ænt'hiliən, æn'θi-/ *n.* антелий *m.*
anthem /'ænθəm/ *n.* гимн *m.*
anthill /'æntˌhɪl/ *n.* муравейник *m.*
anthologist /æn'θɒlədʒɪst/ *n.* составитель (антологий) *m.*
anthology /æn'θɒlədʒi/ *n.* антология *f.*
anthracite /'ænθrəˌsait/ *n.* антрацит *m.*
anthrax /'ænθræks/ *n.* сибирская язва *f.*, антракс *m.*
anthropic /æn'θrɒpɪk/ *adj.* человеческий.
anthropocentric /ˌænθrəpou'sɛntrɪk/ *adj.* антропоцентрический.
anthropoid /'ænθrəˌpɔid/ *adj.* человекообразный.
anthropological /ˌænθrəpə'lɒdʒɪkəl/ *adj.* антропологический.
anthropologist /ˌænθrə'pɒlədʒɪst/ *m.* антрополог *m.*
anthropology /ˌænθrə'pɒlədʒi/ *n.* антропология *f.*
anthropomorphic /ˌænθrəpə'mɔrfɪk/ *adj.* антропоморфический.
anthropomorphism /ˌænθrəpə'mɔrfɪzəm/ *n.* антропоморфизм *m.*
anthropophagi /ˌænθrə'pɒfəˌdʒai, -ˌgai/ *n.* людоеды *pl.*
anthropophagy /ˌænθrə'pɒfədʒi/ *n.* людоедство *neut.*
anti- *prefix* анти-, противо-.
antiaircraft /ˌænti'ɛərˌkræft, ˌæntai-/ *adj.* противовоздушный.
antibiotic /ˌæntɪbai'ɒtɪk/ *n.* антибиотик *m.*
antibody /'æntɪˌbɒdi/ *n.* антитело *neut.*
anticenter /'æntiˌsɛntər, 'æntai-/ *n.* антипод эпицентра *m.*
Antichrist /'æntɪˌkraist/ *n.* антихрист *m.*
antichristian /ˌænti'krɪstʃən, ˌæntai-/ *adj.* антихристианский.
anticipate /æn'tɪsəˌpeit/ v. ожидать, предчувствовать *impf.*
anticipation /ænˌtɪsə'peiʃən/ *n.* предвкушение *neut.*
anticipatory /æn'tɪsəpəˌtɔri/ *adj.* предварительный.
anticlerical /ˌænti'klɛrɪkəl, ˌæntai-/ *adj.* антиклерикальный.
anticlericalism /ˌænti'klɛrɪkəˌlɪzəm, ˌæntai-/ *n.* антиклерикализм *m.*
anticlimactic /ˌæntiklai'mæktɪk, ˌæntai-/ *adj.* разочаровывающий.
anticlimax /ˌænti'klaimæks/ *n.* разочарование *neut.*
anticlinal /ˌænti'klainl/ *adj.* антиклинальный.

anticline /'æntɪˌklain/ *n.* антиклиналь *m.*
anticlockwise /ˌænti'klɒkˌwaiz/ *adv.* против часовой стрелки.
anticoagulant /ˌæntikou'ægyələnt, ˌæntai-/ *n.* антикоагулянт *m.*
anticyclone /ˌænti'saikloun, ˌæntai-/ *n.* антициклон *m.*
antidemocratic /ˌæntiˌdɛmə'krætɪk, ˌæntai-/ *adj.* антидемократический.
antidepressant /ˌæntidɪ'prɛsənt, ˌæntai-/ *n.* антидепрессант *m.*
antidotal /ˌæntɪ'doutl/ *adj.* противоядный.
antidote /'æntɪˌdout/ *n.* противоядие *neut.*
antifreeze /'æntɪˌfriz/ *n.* антифриз *m.*
antifriction /ˌænti'frɪkʃən, ˌæntai-/ *adj.* антифрикционный.
antigen /'æntɪdʒən/ *n.* антиген *m.*
antihero /'æntiˌhɪərou, 'æntai-/ *n.* антигерой *m.*
antihistamine /ˌænti'hɪstəˌmin, -mɪn/ *n.* антигистамин *m.*
antilog /'æntiˌlɒg/ *n.* антилогарифм *m.*
antimagnetic /ˌæntimæg'nɛtɪk, ˌæntai-/ *adj.* антимагнитный.
antimatter /'æntiˌmætər, 'æntai-/ *n.* антивещество *neut.*
antimissile /ˌænti'mɪsəl, ˌæntai-/ *n.* антиракета *f.*
antimony /'æntəˌmouni/ *n.* сурьма *f.*
antinomy /æn'tɪnəmi/ *n.* противоречие *neut.*
antiparticle /ˌænti'pɑrtɪkəl, ˌæntai-/ *n.* античастица *f.*
antipathetic /ˌæntɪpə'θɛtɪk/ *adj.* антипатичный.
antipathy /æn'tɪpəθi/ *n.* антипатия *f.*
antipersonnel /ˌæntiˌpərsə'nɛl, ˌæntai-/ *adj.* противопехотный.
antiperspirant /ˌæntɪ'pərspərənt/ *n.* средство от потения *neut.*
antiphon /'æntəˌfɒn/ *n.* антифон *m.*
antipodes /æn'tɪpəˌdiz/ *n.* антиподы *pl.*
antipole /'æntɪˌpoul/ *n.* противоположный полюс *m.*
antipope /'æntɪˌpoup/ *n.* антипапа *m.*
antiquarian /ˌæntɪ'kwɛəriən/ *adj.* антикварный.
    antiquarian bookseller *n.* букинист *m.*
antiquated /'æntɪˌkweitɪd/ *adj.* устарелый, старомодный.
antique /æn'tik/ **1.** *adj.* старинный, античный; антикварный. **2.** *n.* антик *m.*
antiquity /æn'tɪkwɪti/ *n.* древность, старина *f.*
anti-Semite /'æntiˌsemait, ˌæntai-/ *n.* антисемит *m.*
anti-Semitic /ˌæntisə'mɪtɪk, ˌæntai-/ *adj.* антисемитский.
anti-Semitism /ˌænti'semɪˌtɪzəm, ˌæntai-/ *n.* антисемитизм *m.*
antiseptic /ˌæntə'sɛptɪk/ **1.** *adj.* антисептический. **2.** *n.* антисептическое средство *neut.*
antisocial /ˌænti'souʃəl, ˌæntai-/ *adj.* антиобщественный, необщительный.
antisubmarine /ˌæntiˌsʌbmə'rin, ˌæntai-/ *adj.* противолодочный.
antitank /ˌænti'tæŋk, ˌæntai-/ *adj.* противотанковый.
antiterrorist /ˌænti'tɛrərɪst, ˌæntai-/ *adj.* антитеррористический.
antithesis /æn'tɪθəsɪs/ *n.* антитеза, противоположность *f.*
antithetical /ˌæntə'θɛtɪkəl/ *adj.* антитетический.

antitoxic /ˌæntɪ'tɒksɪk/ adj. противоя́дный, антитокси́ческий.

antitoxin /ˌæntɪ'tɒksɪn/ n. противоя́дие neut., антитокси́н m.

antitype /'æntɪˌtaip/ n. антити́п m.

antiviral /ˌænti'vairəl, ˌæntai-/ adj. противови́русный.

anti-war /ˌænti'wɔr, ˌæntai-/ adj. антивое́нный.

antler /'æntlər/ n. оле́ний рог m.

antonym /'æntənɪm/ n. анто́ним m.

antonymous /æn'tɒnəməs/ adj. антоними́чный.

Antwerp /'æntwərp/ n. Антве́рпен m.

anus /'einəs/ n. за́дний прохо́д m.

anvil /'ænvɪl/ n. накова́льня f.

anxiety /æŋ'zaiiti/ n. беспоко́йство neut.

anxious /'æŋkʃəs/ adj. озабо́ченный, беспоко́ящийся; **to be anxious** v. беспоко́иться impf.

anxiously /'æŋkʃəsli/ adv. с опасе́нием, с трево́гой; с нетерпе́нием.

any /'ɛni/ **1.** adj., pron. како́й-нибудь; любо́й; вся́кий; кто́-нибудь; что-нибудь; (with neg.) никако́й; ни оди́н; никто́. **2.** adv. ско́льконибудь; (with neg.) ниско́лько.

anybody /'ɛni,bɒdi, -,bʌdi/ pron. вся́кий; кто́-нибудь; любо́й.

anyhow /'ɛni,hau/ adv. ка́к-нибудь, кое-ка́к; во вся́ком слу́чае.

anything /'ɛni,θɪŋ/ n. всё neut., люба́я вещь f., что уго́дно neut.

anywhere /'ɛni,wɛər/ adv. где́-нибудь; куда́-нибудь; где уго́дно; куда́ уго́дно.

aorist /'eiərɪst/ n. ао́рист m.

aorta /ei'ɔrtə/ n. ао́рта f.

apace /ə'peis/ adv. бы́стро.

apart /ə'pɑrt/ adv. в сто́рону; в стороне́; по́рознь; на ча́сти. **to take apart** v. разбира́ть impf.

apartheid /ə'pɑrtheit, -hait/ n. апартеи́д m.

apartment /ə'pɑrtmənt/ n. кварти́ра f.

apathetic /ˌæpə'θɛtɪk/ adj. равноду́шный, апати́чный.

apathy /'æpəθi/ n. апа́тия f.

ape /eip/ **1.** n. обезья́на f. **2.** v. подража́ть impf.

aperient /ə'pɪəriənt/ n. слаби́тельное neut.

aperitif /ɑˌpɛri'tif/ n. аперити́в m.

aperture /'æpərtʃər/ n. отве́рстие neut.

apex /'eipɛks/ n. верши́на, верху́шка f.

aphasia /ə'feiʒə/ n. афа́зия f.

aphelion /ə'filiən, æp'hiliən/ n. афе́лий m.

aphorism /'æfə,rizəm/ n. афори́зм m.

aphoristic /ˌæfə'rɪstɪk/ adj. афористи́чный.

aphrodisia /ˌæfrə'diʒə/ n. афродизи́я f.

aphrodisiac /ˌæfrə'dizɛˌæk/ adj. возбужда́ющий.

Aphrodite /ˌæfrə'daiti/ n. Афроди́та f.

apiary /'eipiˌɛri/ n. па́сека f.

apiculture /'eipiˌkʌltʃər/ n. пчелово́дство neut.

apiece /ə'pis/ adv. за шту́ку, на ка́ждого.

aplenty /ə'plɛnti/ adv. в изоби́лии.

aplomb /ə'plɒm, ə'plʌm/ n. апло́мб m.

apocalypse /ə'pɒkəlɪps/ n. апока́липсис m.

apocalyptic /əˌpɒkə'lɪptɪk/ adj. апокалипти́ческий.

apocenter /'æpəˌsɛntər/ n. апоце́нтр m.

apocope /ə'pɒkəˌpi/ n. апоко́па f.

apocrypha /ə'pɒkrəfə/ n. апо́крифы pl.

apocryphal /ə'pɒkrəfəl/ adj. апокрифи́ческий.

apogee /'æpəˌdʒi/ n. апоге́й m.

apolitical /ˌeipə'lɪtɪkəl/ adj. аполити́чный.

apologetic /əˌpɒlə'dʒɛtɪk/ adj. извиня́ющийся.

apologetics /əˌpɒlə'dʒɛtɪks/ n. апологе́тика f.

apologist /ə'pɒlədʒɪst/ n. защи́тник, апологе́т m.

apologize /ə'pɒləˌdʒaiz/ v. извиня́ться impf., извини́ться pf.

apology /ə'pɒlədʒi/ n. извине́ние neut.

apoplectic /ˌæpə'plɛktɪk/ adj. апоплекси́ческий.

apoplexy /'æpəˌplɛksi/ n. апопле́ксия f.

apostate /ə'pɒsteit/ n. отсту́пник m.

apostatize /ə'pɒstəˌtaiz/ v. отступа́ться (от with gen.) impf.

a posteriori /ˌei pɒˌstɪəri'ɔrai, -'ɔri/ adj. апостерио́ри, апостерио́рный.

apostle /ə'pɒsəl/ n. апо́стол m.

apostolate /ə'pɒstˌlɪt/ n. ми́ссия f.

apostolic /ˌæpə'stɒlɪk/ adj. апо́стольский.

apostrophe /ə'pɒstrəfi/ n. апостро́ф m.

apothecary /ə'pɒθəˌkɛri/ n. апте́карь m.

apothegm /'æpəˌθɛm/ n. апоте́гма f.

apotheosis /əˌpɒθi'ousɪs/ n. апофео́з m.

appal /ə'pɔl/ v. шоки́ровать impf.

appalling /ə'pɔlɪŋ/ adj. ужа́сный, стра́шный, ужаса́ющий.

apparatus /ˌæpə'rætəs/ n. аппара́т, прибо́р m.

apparel /ə'pærəl/ n. пла́тье neut., оде́жда f.

apparent /ə'pærənt/ adj. я́вный, очеви́дный.

apparently /ə'pærəntli/ adv. очеви́дно.

apparition /ˌæpə'rɪʃən/ n. виде́ние; привиде́ние neut.; при́зрак m.

appeal /ə'pil/ **1.** n. апелля́ция f.; при́зыв m., воззва́ние neut. **2.** v. обраща́ться (к with dat.; апелли́ровать impf. and pf.

appealing /ə'pilɪŋ/ adj. (beseeching) умоля́ющий; (touching) тро́гательный; (attractive) привлека́тельный.

appear /ə'pɪər/ v. явля́ться impf., яви́ться pf.; появля́ться impf., появи́ться pf.; (seem) каза́ться impf.

appearance /ə'pɪərəns/ n. появле́ние neut.; вне́шний вид m.

appease /ə'piz/ v. умиротворя́ть impf., умиротвори́ть pf.; успока́ивать impf., успоко́ить pf.

appeasement /ə'pizmənt/ n. умиротворе́ние, успокое́ние neut.

appellant /ə'pɛlənt/ n. заяви́тель m.

append /ə'pɛnd/ v. прилага́ть impf.

appendage /ə'pɛndɪdʒ/ n. дове́сок, прида́ток m.

appendectomy /ˌæpən'dɛktəmi/ n. удале́ние аппе́ндикса neut.

appendicitis /əˌpɛndə'saitɪs/ n. аппендици́т m.

appendix /ə'pɛndɪks/ n. аппе́ндикс m.

appertain /ˌæpər'tein/ v. относи́ться impf.

appetite /'æpiˌtait/ n. аппети́т m.

appetizer /'æpiˌtaizər/ n. заку́ска f.

applaud /ə'plɔd/ v. аплоди́ровать impf. and pf.

applause /ə'plɔz/ n. аплодисме́нты pl.

apple /'æpəl/ **1.** adj. я́блочный. **2.** n. я́блоко neut.

apple tree n. я́блоня f.

appliance /ə'plaiəns/ n. приспособле́ние neut.; прибо́р m.

applicable /'æplɪkəbəl, ə'plɪkə-/ adj. примени́мый.

applicant /'æplɪkənt/ n. кандида́т, заяви́тель m.

application /ˌæplɪ'keiʃən/ n. примене́ние, при-

ложéние; заявлéние *neut.*; прóсьба *f.*, старáние *neut.*
applied /ə'plaid/ *adj.* прикладнóй.
appliqué /,æplɪ'kei/ *n.* аппликáция *f.*
apply /ə'plai/ *v.t.* приклáдывать *impf.*, приложи́ть *pf.*; применя́ть *impf.*, примени́ть *pf. v.i.* обращáться; подавáть заявлéние *impf.*
appoint /ə'pɔint/ *v.* назначáть *impf.*, назнáчить *pf.*
appointed /ə'pɔintɪd/ *adj.* назнáченный.
appointment /ə'pɔintmənt/ *n.* (*rendezvous*) свидáние *neut.*; (*nomination*) назначéние *neut.*; (*office*) дóлжность *f.*
apportion /ə'pɔrʃən/ *v.* распределя́ть *impf.*, распредели́ть *pf.*; дели́ть пропорционáльно *impf.*
apposite /'æpəzɪt/ *adj.* умéстный.
apposition /,æpə'zɪʃən/ *n.* (*gram.*) приложéние *neut.*
appraisal /ə'preizəl/ *n.* оцéнка *f.*
appraise /ə'preiz/ *v.* оцéнивать *impf.*, оцени́ть *pf.*
appraiser /ə'preizər/ *n.* оцéнщик *m.*
appreciable /ə'priʃiəbəl/ *adj.* ощути́мый.
appreciate /ə'priʃi,eit/ *v.* цени́ть; оцéнивать *impf.*, оцени́ть *pf.*
appreciation /ə,priʃi'elʃən/ *n.* оцéнка, признáтельность *f.*
apprehend /,æprɪ'hɛnd/ *v.* арестовáть *pf.*; (*comprehend*) понимáть *impf.*
apprehension /,æprɪ'hɛnʃən/ *n.* задержáние *neut.*, арéст *m.*; (*fear*) опасéние *neut.*
apprehensive /,æprɪ'hɛnsɪv/ *adj.* озабóченный; опасáющийся.
apprentice /ə'prɛntɪs/ *n.* учени́к, подмастéрье *m.*
apprenticeship /ə'prɛntɪs,ʃɪp/ *n.* (*period*) срок учéния *m.*; (*job*) учёба *f.*
apprise /ə'praiz/ *v.* давáть знать *impf.*
approach /ə'prəutʃ/ **1.** *n.* приближéние *neut.*, подхóд *m.* **2.** *v.* приближáться *impf.*, прибли́зиться *pf.*; подходи́ть *impf.*, подойти́ *pf.*
approachable /ə'prəutʃəbəl/ *adj.* достýпный.
approbation /,æprə'beiʃən/ *n.* одобрéние *neut.*; апробáция *f.*
appropriate / *adj.* ə'proupriit; *v.* ə'proupri,eit/ **1.** *adj.* подходя́щий. **2.** *v.* присвáивать *impf.*, присвóить *pf.*; предназначáть *impf.*, предназнáчить *pf.*; ассигновáть *impf. and pf.*
appropriation /ə,proupri'eiʃən/ *n.* присвоéние, ассигновáние *neut.*
approval /ə'pruvəl/ *n.* одобрéние *neut.*
approve /ə'pruv/ *v.* одобря́ть *impf.*, одóбрить *pf.*
approved /ə'pruvd/ *adj.* испы́танный; при́нятый.
approving /ə'pruvɪŋ/ *adj.* одобри́тельный.
approximate / *adj.* ə'prɒksəmɪt; *v.* ə'prɒksə,meit/ **1.** *adj.* приблизи́тельный. **2.** *v.* приближáться (к *with dat.*) *impf.*
approximately /ə'prɒksəmɪtli/ *adv.* приблизи́тельно.
approximation /ə,prɒksə'meiʃən/ *n.* приближéнис *neut.*
appurtenances /ə'pɜrtṇənsɪz/ *n.* принадлéжности *pl.*
apricot /'æprɪ,kɒt, 'eiprɪ-/ *n.* абрикóс *m.*
April /'eiprəl/ **1.** *n.* апрéль *m.* **2.** *adj.* апрéльский.
a priori /,ei prai'ɔrai, pri'ɔri/ *adj.* априóри, априóрный.
apron /'eiprən/ *n.* передни́к, фáртук *m.*

apropos /,æprə'pou/ *adv.* кстáти; (*with regard to*) относи́тельно (*with gen.*).
apse /æps/ *n.* апси́да *f.*
apt /æpt/ *adj.* удáчный; подходя́щий; склóнный.
aptitude /'æptɪ,tud/ *n.* спосóбность, склóнность *f.*
Aqmola /æk'moulə/ *see Astana.*
aquajet /'ækwə,dʒɛt/ *n.* водомёт *m.*
Aqua-Lung /'ækwə,lʌŋ/ *n.* аквалáнг *m.*; **Aqua-Lung diver** акваланги́ст *m.*
aquamarine /,ækwəmə'rin/ *n.* аквамари́н *m.*
aquarelle /,ækwə'rɛl/ *n.* акварéль *f.*
aquarium /ə'kwɛəriəm/ *n.* аквáриум *m.*
Aquarius /ə'kwɛəriəs/ *n.* (*astr.*) Водолéй *m.*
aquatic /ə'kwætɪk, ə'kwɒt-/ *adj.* вóдный.
aquatint /'ækwə,tɪnt/ *n.* аквати́нта *f.*
aqueduct /'ækwɪ,dʌkt/ *n.* акведýк *m.*
aqueous /'eikwiəs, 'ækwi-/ *adj.* водяни́стый.
aquiline /'ækwə,lain/ *adj.* орли́ный.
Arab /'ærəb/ **1.** *n.* арáб *m.*, арáбка *f.* **2.** *adj. also* **Arabic** арáбский, арави́йский.
arabesque /,ærə'bɛsk/ *n.* арабéска *f.*
Arabia /ə'reibiə/ *n.* Арáвия *f.*; **Saudi Arabia** Сáудовская Арáвия *f.*
Arabic /'ærəbɪk/ *adj.* арáбский.
Arabist /'ærəbɪst/ *n.* араби́ст *m.*
arable /'ærəbəl/ *adj.* пáхотный.
arachnids /ə'ræknɪdz/ *n.* паукообрáзные *pl.*
arachnoid /ə'ræknɔid/ *adj.* паути́нный.
Arad /ɑ'rɑd/ *n.* Áрад *m.*
arbalest /'ɑrbəlɪst/ *n.* арбалéт, самострéл *m.*
arbiter /'ɑrbɪtər/ *n.* арби́тр *m.*
arbitrage /'ɑrbɪ,trɑʒ/ *n.* арбитрáж *m.*
arbitrager /'ɑrbɪ,trɑʒər/ *n.* арбитражёр *m.*
arbitrariness /'ɑrbɪ,trɛrinɪs/ *n.* произвóл *m.*
arbitrary /'ɑrbɪ,treri/ *adj.* произвóльный.
arbitrate /'ɑrbɪ,treit/ *v.* решáть третéйским судóм *impf.*
arbitration /,ɑrbɪ'treiʃən/ *n.* третéйский суд; арбитрáж *m.*
arbitrator /'ɑrbɪ,treitər/ *n.* третéйский судья́; арби́тр *m.*
arbor[1] /'ɑrbər/ *n.* бесéдка *f.*
arbor[2] /'ɑrbər/ *n.* (*mech.*) вал *m.*, ось *f.*
arboreal /ɑr'bɔriəl/ *adj.* древéсный.
arboretum /,ɑrbə'ritəm/ *n.* дендрáрий *m.*
arboriculture /'ɑrbərɪ,kʌltʃər/ *n.* лесовóдство *neut.*
arbutus /ɑr'byutəs/ *n.* земляни́чное дéрево *neut.*
arc /ɑrk/ *n.* дугá *f.*
arcane /ɑr'kein/ *adj.* тáйный; таи́нственный; эзотери́ческий.
arch[1] /ɑrtʃ/ *n.* áрка *f.*, свод *m.*; дугá *f.*
arch[2] /ɑrtʃ/ *adj.* лукáвый; глáвный.
archaeological /,ɑrkiə'lɒdʒɪkəl/ *adj.* археологи́ческий.
archaeologist /,ɑrki'ɒlədʒɪst/ *n.* археóлог *m.*
archaeology /,ɑrki'ɒlədʒi/ *n.* археолóгия *f.*
archaic /ɑr'keiɪk/ *adj.* архаи́ческий.
archaism /'ɑrki,ɪzəm/ *n.* архаи́зм *m.*
archangel /'ɑrk,eindʒəl/ *n.* архáнгел *m.*
archbishop /'ɑrtʃ'bɪʃəp/ *n.* архиепи́скоп *m.*
archbishopric /,ɑrtʃ'bɪʃəprɪk/ *n.* архиепи́скопство *neut.*
archdeacon /'ɑrtʃ'dikən/ *n.* архидья́кон, архидиáкон *m.*
archdiocese /,ɑrtʃ'daiə,sis, -sɪs/ *n.* епáрхия *f.*

archducal /'ɑrtʃ'dukəl/ adj. эрцге́рцогский.
archduchess /'ɑrtʃ'dʌtʃɪs/ n. эрцгерцоги́ня f.
archduke /'ɑrtʃ'duk/ n. эрцге́рцог m.
arched /ɑrtʃt/ adj. а́рочный; сво́дчатый.
archenemy /'ɑrtʃ'ɛnəmi/ n. закля́тый враг m.
archer /'ɑrtʃər/ n. лу́чник, стрело́к m.
archery /'ɑrtʃəri/ n. стрельба́ из лу́ка f.
archetypal /'ɑrkɪ,taipəl/ adj. архетипи́ческий.
archetype /'ɑrkɪ,taip/ (psych.) архети́п m.; (prototype) прототи́п m.
archfiend /,ɑrtʃ'find/ n. Сатана́ m. (decl. f.)
archiepiscopal /,ɑrkiɪ'pɪskəpəl/ adj. архиепи́скопский.
archimandrite /,ɑrkə'mændrait/ n. архимандри́т m.
archipelago /,ɑrkə'pɛlə,gou/ n. архипела́г m.
architect /'ɑrkɪ,tɛkt/ n. архите́ктор, зо́дчий m.
architectonic /,ɑrkɪtɛk'tɒnɪk/ adj. структу́рный.
architectonics /,ærkɪtɛk'tɒnɪks/ n. архитекто́ника f.
architectural /,ɑrkɪ'tɛktʃərəl/ adj. архитекту́рный.
architecture /'ɑrkɪ,tɛktʃər/ n. архитекту́ра f., зо́дчество neut.
architrave /'ɑrkɪ,treiv/ n. архитра́в m.
archival /ɑr'kaivəl/ adj. архи́вный.
archive /'ɑrkaiv/ n. архи́в m.
archivist /'ɑrkəvɪst/ n. архиви́ст m.
archon /'ɑrkɒn/ n. архо́нт m.
archpriest /'ɑrtʃ'prist/ n. протоиере́й m.
archvillain /'ɑrtʃ'vɪlən/ n. архизлоде́й m.
archway /'ɑrtʃ,wei/ n. (arch.) а́рка f.
arctic /'ɑrktɪk/ adj. аркти́ческий; поля́рный.
Arctic Circle /'ɑrtɪk/ n. Се́верный поля́рный круг m.
Arctic Ocean n. Се́верный Ледови́тый океа́н m.
Arcturus /ɑrk'tʊrəs/ n. Аркту́р m.
arcuate /'ɑrkyuɪt/ adj. дугообра́зный.
ardent /'ɑrdn̩t/ adj. ре́вностный; горя́чий.
ardor /'ɑrdər/ n. рве́ние neut., пыл m.
arduous /'ɑrdʒuəs/ adj. тру́дный; тяжёлый; утоми́тельный.
are /ɑr/ unstressed ər/ n. (unit of area) ар m.
area /'ɛəriə/ n. пло́щадь, террито́рия f.; райо́н m.
areal /'ɛəriəl/ adj. региона́льный.
arena /ə'rinə/ n. аре́на f.
Argentine /'ɑrdʒən,tin, -,tain/ also **Argentinean** /,ɑrdʒən'tɪniən/ **1.** adj. аргенти́нский. **2.** n. аргенти́нец m., аргенти́нка f.
argon /'ɑrgɒn/ n. арго́н m.
Argonaut /'ɑrgə,nɔt/ n. аргона́вт m.
argot /'ɑrgou, -gət/ n. арго́; жарго́н m.
arguable /'ɑrgyuəbəl/ adj. спо́рный.
argue /'ɑrgyu/ v. спо́рить impf.; (maintain) утвержда́ть impf.; (prove) дока́зывать impf.
argument /'ɑrgyəmənt/ n. спор m., диску́ссия f.; (reason) до́вод; аргуме́нт m.
argumentative /,ɑrgyə'mɛntətɪv/ adj. лю́бящий спо́рить.
aria /'ɑriə/ n. а́рия f.
Arianism /'ɛəriə,nɪzəm/ n. ариа́нство neut.
arid /'ærɪd/ adj. сухо́й; бесплодный.
aridity /ə'rɪdɪti/ n. засу́шливость f.
Aries /'ɛəriz/ n. (astr.) Овен m.
aright /ə'rait/ adv. пра́вильно.
arise /ə'raiz/ v. встава́ть impf., встать pf.; возни-

ка́ть impf., возни́кнуть pf.; появля́ться impf., появи́ться pf.
aristocracy /,ærə'stɒkrəsi/ n. аристокра́тия f.
aristocrat /ə'rɪstə,kræt/ n. аристокра́т m.
aristocratic /ə,rɪstə'krætɪk/ adj. аристократи́ческий.
Aristotelian /,ærəstə'tiliən/ n. после́дователь Аристо́теля m.
arithmetic /ə'rɪθmətɪk/ n. арифме́тика f.
arithmetical /,ærɪθ'mɛtɪkəl/ adj. арифмети́ческий.
arithmetician /ə,rɪθmɪ'tɪʃən/ n. арифме́тик m.
Arizona /,ærə'zounə/ n. Аризо́на f.
ark /ɑrk/ n. ковче́г m.; **Noah's Ark** n. Но́ев ковче́г m.
Arkansas /'ɑrkən,sɔ/ n. Арканза́с m.
Arkhangelsk /ɑr'xɑngyɪlsk/ n. Арха́нгельск m.
Ark of the Covenant n. киво́т заве́та Госпо́дня m.
Arles /ɑrlz, ɑrl/ n. Арль m.
arm[1] /ɑrm/ n. рука́ f.; (of chair) ру́чка f.; (of river) рука́в m.
arm[2] /ɑrm/ **1.** n. pl. (weapon) ору́жие neut. **2.** v.t. вооружа́ть impf., вооружи́ть pf.; v.i. вооружа́ться impf., вооружи́ться pf.
armada /ɑr'mɑdə/ n. арма́да f.
armadillo /,ɑrmə'dɪlou/ n. бронено́сец m.
Armageddon /,ɑrmə'gɛdn̩/ n. Армагеддо́н m.
armament /'ɑrməmənt/ n. вооруже́ние neut.
armature /'ɑrmətʃər/ n. армату́ра, броня́ f.
armband /'ɑrm,bænd/ n. нарука́вная повя́зка f.
armchair /'ɑrm,tʃɛər/ n. кре́сло neut.
Armenia /ɑr'miniə/ n. Арме́ния f.
Armenian /ɑr'miniən/ **1.** adj. армя́нский. **2.** n. армяни́н m., армя́нка f.
armful /'ɑrm,fʊl/ n. оха́пка f.
armhole /'ɑrm,houl/ n. про́йма f.
armistice /'ɑrməstɪs/ n. переми́рие neut.
armor /'ɑrmər/ n. (warrior) доспе́хи pl.; (tank, ship) броня́ f.
armored /'ɑrmərd/ adj. брониро́ванный.
armored car n. броневи́к m.
armorial /ɑr'mɔriəl/ adj. геральди́ческий.
armor-piercing /'ɑrmər,piərsɪŋ/ adj. бронебо́йный.
armor-plated /'ɑrmər,pleitɪd/ adj. брониро́ванный.
armory /'ɑrməri/ n. арсена́л, склад ору́жия m.
armpit /'ɑrm,pɪt/ n. подмы́шка f.
armrest /'ɑrm,rɛst/ n. подлоко́тник m.
army /'ɑrmi/ **1.** adj. арме́йский. **2.** n. а́рмия f., во́йско neut.
arnica /'ɑrnɪkə/ n. а́рника f.
aroma /ə'roumə/ n. арома́т m.
aromatic /,ærə'mætɪk/ adj. аромати́ческий, благово́нный.
around /ə'raund/ **1.** prep. вокру́г (with gen.); **all around** повсю́ду. **2.** adv. круго́м, в окре́стностях.
arousal /ə'rauzəl/ n. пробужде́ние neut.
arouse /ə'rauz/ v. буди́ть; возбужда́ть impf.; вызыва́ть impf., вы́звать pf.
arpeggio /ɑr'pɛdʒi,ou/ n. арпе́джио neut. indecl.
arraign /ə'rein/ v. привлека́ть к суду́ impf.
arraignment /ə'reinmənt/ n. привлече́ние к суду́ neut.
arrange /ə'reindʒ/ v. устра́ивать impf., устро́ить

pf.; организо́вывать *impf.*, организова́ть *pf.*; (*mus.*) аранжи́ровать *impf.* and *pf.*

arrangement /ə'reindʒmənt/ *n.* устро́йство, расположе́ние *neut.*; (*agreement*) соглаше́ние *neut.*; (*mus.*) аранжиро́вка *f.*

arranger /ə'reindʒər/ *n.* аранжиро́вщик *m.*

arrant /'ærənt/ *adj.* отъя́вленный.

array /ə'rei/ *n.* (*quantity*) мно́жество *neut.*; (*finery*) наря́д *m.*

arrears /ə'rɪərz/ *n.* задо́лженность (по *with dat.*) *f.*

arrest /ə'rest/ **1.** *n.* задержа́ние *neut.*, аре́ст *m.* **2.** *v.* арестова́ть *pf.*; задержа́ть *pf.*

arresting /ə'restɪŋ/ *adj.* захва́тывающий.

arrière-pensée /ari'ɛrpan'sei/ *n.* за́дняя мысль *f.*

arrival /ə'raivəl/ *n.* прибы́тие, появле́ние *neut.*

arrive /ə'raiv/ *v.* приходи́ть *impf.*; приезжа́ть *impf.*, прие́хать *pf.*; прибыва́ть *impf.*, прибы́ть *pf.*

arrogance /'ærəgəns/ *n.* высокоме́рие *neut.*; надме́нность *f.*

arrogant /'ærəgənt/ *adj.* высокоме́рный, надме́нный.

arrogate /'ærə,geit/ *v.* присва́ивать себе́ *impf.*

arrow /'ærou/ *n.* стрела́ *f.*; (*pointer, etc.*) стре́лка *f.*

arrowhead /'ærou,hed/ *n.* наконе́чник стрелы́ *m.*

arsenal /'arsənl/ *n.* арсена́л *m.*

arsenic /'arsənɪk/ *n.* мышья́к *m.*

arson /'arsən/ *n.* поджо́г *m.*

arsonist /'arsənɪst/ *n.* поджига́тель *m.*

art /art/ **1.** *adj.* худо́жественный. **2.** *n.* иску́сство *neut.*; *pl.* гуманита́рные нау́ки *pl.*

arterial /ar'tɪəriəl/ *adj.* артериа́льный.

artery /'artəri/ *n.* арте́рия *f.*

artesian /ar'tiʒən/ *adj.* артезиа́нский; **artesian well** *n.* артезиа́нский коло́дец *m.*

artful /'artfəl/ *adj.* хи́трый, ло́вкий.

arthritic /ar'θrɪtɪk/ *adj.* артрити́ческий.

arthritis /ar'θraitɪs/ *n.* артри́т *m.*

artichoke /'artɪ,tʃouk/ *n.* артишо́к *m.*

article /'artɪkəl/ *n.* (*thing*) предме́т *m.*; (*publication*) статья́ *f.*; (*gram.*) арти́кль *m.*

articulate **1.** / *adj.* ar'tɪkyəlɪt; *v.* ar'tɪkyə,leit/ *adj.* отчётливый. **2.** *v.* произноси́ть; артикули́ровать *impf.*

articulation /ar,tɪkyə'leiʃən/ *n.* артикуля́ция *f.*

artifact /'artə,fækt/ *n.* изде́лие *neut.*

artifice /'artəfɪs/ *n.* вы́думка, хи́трость *f.*

artificial /,artə'fɪʃəl/ *adj.* иску́сственный.

artificial intelligence *n.* (*abbr.* A.I.) иску́сственный интелле́кт *m.* (*abbr.* ИИ).

artificiality /,artə,fɪʃi'ælɪti/ *n.* иску́сственность *f.*

artillery /ar'tɪləri/ *n.* артилле́рия *f.*

artilleryman /ar'tɪlərimən/ *n.* артиллери́ст *m.*

artisan /'artəzən/ *n.* реме́сленник *m.*

artist /'artɪst/ *n.* худо́жник *m.*; (*performer*) (эстра́дный) арти́ст *m.*

artistic /ar'tɪstɪk/ *adj.* худо́жественный, арти́стический.

artistry /'artɪstri/ *n.* худо́жественность *f.*

artless /'artlɪs/ *adj.* безыску́сный.

artwork /'art,wɜrk/ *n.* (*typog.*) оформле́ние *neut.*

Aryan /'ɛəriən/ **1.** *adj.* ари́йский. **2.** *n.* ари́ец *m.*; ари́йка *f.*

Arzamas /,arsə'mns/ *n.* Арзама́с *m.*

as /æz; *unstressed* əz/ *adv.* как; когда́, в то вре́мя как; **as for** что каса́ется (*with gen.*).

asafetida /,æsə'fetɪdə/ *n.* азафети́да *f.*

asbestos /æs'bestəs/ *n.* асбе́ст *m.*

ascend /ə'send/ *v.* всходи́ть *impf.*, взойти́ *pf.*; поднима́ться *impf.*, подня́ться *pf.*

ascendancy /ə'sendənsi/ *n.* госпо́дство *neut.*, власть *f.*

ascendant /ə'sendənt/ *adj.* восходя́щий; (*dominating*) госпо́дствующий.

ascension /ə'senʃən/ *n.* восхожде́ние *neut.*; **Ascension** (*relig.*) Вознесе́ние *neut.*

ascent /ə'sent/ *n.* восхожде́ние *neut.*, подъём *m.*

ascertain /,æsər'tein/ *v.* установи́ть *pf.*; удостове́риться *pf.*

ascetic /ə'setɪk/ **1.** *adj.* аскети́ческий. **2.** *n.* аске́т *m.*

asceticism /ə'setə,sɪzəm/ *n.* аскети́зм *m.*

ascorbic /ə'skɔrbɪk/ *adj.* аскорби́новый.

ascribe /ə'skraib/ *v.* припи́сывать (*with dat.*) *impf.*

ascription /ə'skrɪpʃən/ *n.* припи́сывание *neut.*

Asenovgrad /ɒ'sɪnɔvgrət/ *n.* Асе́новград *m.*

asepsis /ə'sepsɪs, ei'sep-/ *n.* асе́птика *f.*

aseptic /ə'septɪk/ *adj.* асепти́ческий.

asexual /ei'sekʃuəl/ *adj.* беспо́лый.

ash[1] /æʃ/ *n.* (*tree*) я́сень *m.*

ash[2] /æʃ/ *n. usu. pl.* (*cinders*) пе́пел *m.*; зола́ *f.*

ashamed /ə'ʃeimd/ *adj.* присты́женный.

ashen /'æʃən/ *adj.* пе́пельный.

Ashkhabad /,aʃkə'bad/ *n.* Ашхаба́д *m.*

ashore /ə'ʃɔr/ *adv.* к бе́регу, на бе́рег; **to go ashore** *v.* сходи́ть на бе́рег *impf.*

ashtray /'æʃ,trei/ *n.* пе́пельница *f.*

Asia /'eiʒə/ *n.* А́зия *f.*

Asia Minor *n.* Ма́лая А́зия *f.*

Asian /'eiʒən/ *also* **Asiatic** /,eiʒi'ætɪk/ **1.** *adj.* азиа́тский. **2.** *n.* азиа́т *m.*, азиа́тка *f.*

aside /ə'said/ *adv.* в сто́рону; прочь.

asinine /'æsə,nain/ *adj.* глу́пый, осли́ный.

ask /æsk/ *v.* спра́шивать *impf.*, спроси́ть *pf.*; (*request*) проси́ть *impf.*, попроси́ть *pf.*; (*invite*) приглаша́ть *impf.*, пригласи́ть *pf.*; **to ask a question** зада́ть вопро́с *pf.*

askance /ə'skæns/ *adv.* кри́во, ко́со; **to look askance at** *v.* смотре́ть ко́со на (*with acc.*) *impf.*

askew /ə'skyu/ *adv.* кри́во, ко́со.

asleep /ə'slip/ *adj.* спя́щий.

asp /æsp/ *n.* а́спид *m.*

asparagus /ə'spærəgəs/ *n.* спа́ржа *f.*

aspect /'æspekt/ *n.* аспе́кт, вид *m.*; сторона́ *f.*; (*gram.*) вид *m.*

aspen /'æspən/ **1.** *n.* оси́новый. **2.** *n.* оси́на *f.*

asperity /ə'sperɪti/ *n.* суро́вость *f.*

aspersion /ə'spɜrʒən/ *n.* клевета́ *f.*; обры́згивание *neut.*

asphalt /'æsfɔlt/ *n.* асфа́льт *m.*

asphyxia /æs'fɪksiə/ *n.* уду́шье *neut.*

asphyxiate /æs'fɪksi,eit/ *v.* удуша́ть *impf.*, удуши́ть *pf.*

aspic /'æspɪk/ *n.* заливно́е *neut.*

aspidistra /,æspɪ'dɪstrə/ *n.* аспиди́стра *f.*

aspirate /'æspərɪt/ *n.* придыха́тельный.

aspiration /,æspə'reiʃən/ *n.* стремле́ние, жела́ние *neut.*; (*phon.*) придыха́ние *neut.*

aspire /ə'spaiʳr/ *v.* стреми́ться (к *with dat.*) *impf.*

aspirin /'æspərɪn, -prɪn/ *n.* аспири́н *m.*

ass /æs/ n. осёл m.

assail /ə'seil/ v. нападáть impf., напáсть pf.

assailant /ə'seilənt/ n. налётчик m.

assassin /ə'sæsɪn/ n. убийца m. and f. (decl. f.)

assassinate /ə'sæsə‚neit/ v. убить pf.

assassination /ə‚sæsə'neiʃən/ n. убийство neut.

assault /ə'sɔlt/ **1.** n. нападéние neut.; (mil.) штурм m.; (rape) изнасилование neut. **2.** v. нападáть impf., напáсть pf.

assegai /'æsə‚gai/ n. ассагáй m.

assemblage /ə'sɛmblɪdʒ/ n. собрáние neut.; монтáж m., сбóрка f.

assemble /ə'sɛmbəl/ v.t. собирáть impf., собрáть pf.; v.i. собирáться impf., собрáться pf.

assembly /ə'sɛmbli/ n. собрáние neut.; ассамблéя f.; (mech.) монтáж m.

assent /ə'sɛnt/ v. соглашáться (на with acc., с with instr.) impf.

assert /ə'sɜrt/ v. утверждáть impf.; **to assert oneself** отстáивать свои правá impf.

assertion /ə'sɜrʃən/ n. утверждéние neut.

assertive /ə'sɜrtɪv/ adj. напóристый.

assess /ə'sɛs/ v. оцéнивать impf., оценить pf.

assessment /ə'sɛsmənt/ n. определéние neut., оцéнка f.; (tax) обложéние neut.

assessor /ə'sɛsər/ n. оцéнщик m.

asset /'æset/ n. имущество; цéнное кáчество neut.; **assets and liabilities** активи и пассив m.

assiduity /‚æsɪ'duiti/ n. усéрдие neut.

assiduous /ə'sɪdʒuəs/ adj. усéрдный, прилéжный.

assign /ə'sain/ v. назначáть impf., назнáчить pf.

assignation /‚æsɪg'neiʃən/ n. ассигновáние, назначéние neut.

assignment /ə'sainmənt/ n. задáние neut.

assimilate /ə'sɪmə‚leit/ v. ассимилировать(ся), усвáивать impf.

assimilation /ə‚sɪmə'leiʃən/ n. усвоéние neut.; ассимиляция f.

assist /ə'sɪst/ v. помогáть impf., помóчь pf.

assistance /ə'sɪstəns/ n. пóмощь f.

assistant /ə'sɪstənt/ n. помóщник, ассистéнт m.

associate / n. ə'souʃɪɪt, -si-; v. ə'souʃɪ‚eit/ **1.** n. коллéга m. (decl. f.); сотрудник m. **2.** v. ассоциировать impf. and pf.; общáться (with str.) impf.

association /ə‚sousi'eiʃən/ n. óбщество neut., ассоциáция f.

assonance /'æsənəns/ n. ассонáнс m.

assonant /'æsənənt/ adj. созвучный.

assort /ə'sɔrt/ сортировáть impf.

assorted /ə'sɔrtɪd/ adj. подóбранный.

assortment /ə'sɔrtmənt/ n. подбóр, ассортимéнт m.

assuage /ə'sweidʒ, ə'sweiʒ/ v. смягчáть impf.; утоля́ть impf.

assume /ə'sum/ v. предполагáть impf., предположить pf.; принимáть impf.

assumed /ə'sumd/ adj. вымышленный.

Assumption /ə'sʌmpʃən/ n. Успéние neut.

assumption /ə'sʌmpʃən/ n. принятие, предположéние neut.

assurance /ə'ʃurəns/ n. самоувéренность f.; заверéние neut.

assure /ə'ʃur/ v. уверять impf., увéрить pf.

assured /ə'ʃurd/ adj. увéренный; гарантированный; самоувéренный.

assuredly /ə'ʃurɪdli/ adv. несомнéнно.

Astana /ə'stɒnə/ n. (formerly: Tselinograd, Aqmola) Астáна.

aster /'æstər/ n. áстра f.

asterisk /'æstərɪsk/ n. звёздочка f.

astern /ə'stɜrn/ adv. на кормé.

asteroid /'æstə‚rɔid/ n. астерóид m.

asthma /'æzmə/ n. áстма f.

asthmatic /æz'mætɪk/ n. астмáтик m.

astigmatic /‚æstɪg'mætɪk/ adj. астигматический.

astigmatism /ə'stɪgmə‚tizəm/ n. астигматизм m.

astir /ə'stɜr/ adv. в движéнии.

astonish /ə'stɒnɪʃ/ v. удивлять impf., удивить pf.; изумлять impf., изумить pf.

astonishing /ə'stɒnɪʃɪŋ/ adj. удивительный, изумительный, поразительный.

astonishment /ə'stɒnɪʃmənt/ n. удивлéние, изумлéние neut.

astound /ə'staund/ v. изумлять impf., изумить pf.; поражáть impf., поразить pf.

astounding /ə'staundɪŋ/ adj. поразительный.

astragal /'æstrəgəl/ n. астрагáл m.

astrakhan /'æstrəkən/ n. карáкуль m.

astral /'æstrəl/ adj. астрáльный.

astray /ə'strei/ adv.: **to go astray** заблудиться _pf.; **to lead astray** сбить с пути pf.

astride /ə'straid/ adv. верхóм (на with prep.).

astringent /ə'strɪndʒənt/ **1.** adj. вяжущий. **2.** n. вяжущее срéдство neut.

astrolabe /'æstrə‚leib/ n. астроля́бия f.

astrologer /ə'strɒlədʒər/ n. астрóлог m.

astrological /‚æstrə'lɒdʒɪkəl/ adj. астрологический.

astrology /ə'strɒlədʒi/ n. астролóгия f.

astronaut /'æstrə‚nɔt/ n. астронáвт m.

astronautics /‚æstrə'nɔtɪks/ n. астронáвтика f.

astronavigation /‚æstrou‚nævɪ'geiʃən/ n. астронавигáция f.

astronomer /ə'strɒnəmər/ n. астронóм m.

astronomical /‚æstrə'nɒmɪkəl/ adj. астрономический.

astronomy /ə'strɒnəmi/ n. астронóмия f.

astrophysics /‚æstrou'fɪzɪks/ n. астрофизика f.

astute /ə'stut/ adj. проницáтельный; хитрый.

asunder /ə'sʌndər/ adv. пóрознь.

asylum /ə'sailəm/ n. (refuge) приют m., убéжище neut.; (institution) психиатрическая больница f.

asymmetric /‚eisə'mɛtrɪk/ adj. асимметричный.

asymmetry /ei'sɪmitri/ n. асиммéтрия f.

asymptote /'æsɪm‚tout/ n. асимптóта f.

asymptotic /‚æsɪm'tɒtɪk/ adj. асимптотический.

asynchronous /ei'sɪŋkrənəs/ adj. асинхрóнный.

asyndetic /‚æsɪn'dɛtɪk/ adj. бессоюзный.

at /æt; unstressed ət, ɪt/ prep. у; вóзле; óколо (with gen.); при (with prep.); (time) в, на (with acc.).

atavism /'ætə‚vizəm/ n. атавизм m.

atavistic /‚ætə'vɪstɪk/ adj. атавистический.

ataxia /ə'tæksiə/ n. атаксия f.

atelier /'æt|‚yei/ n. ательé neut. indecl.; мастерскáя f.

atheism /'eiθi‚izəm/ n. атеизм m.

atheist /'eiθiɪst/ n. атеист m.

atheistic /‚eiθi'ɪstɪk/ adj. атеистический.

Athens /'æθɪnz/ n. Афины pl.

athlete /'æθlit/ n. атлéт m., атлéтка f.

athletic /æθ'lɛtɪk/ adj. атлетический.

athletics /æθ'lɛtɪks/ n. атлéтика, физкультура f.

Athos /'æθous/ n. **Mount,** Афо́н (полуо́стров Айо́н О́рос) m.

Atlantis /æt'læntis/ n. Атланти́да f.

atlas /'ætləs/ m. а́тлас m.

atmosphere /'ætməs,fɪər/ n. атмосфе́ра f.

atmospheric /,ætməs'fɛrɪk, -'fɪər-/ adj. атмосфе́рный, атмосфери́ческий.

atmospherics /,ætməs'fɛrɪks, -'fɪər-/ n. атмосфе́рные поме́хи pl.

atoll /'ætɔl/ n. ато́лл m.

atom /'ætəm/ n. а́том m.

atomic /ə'tɒmɪk/ adj. а́томный.

atomistic /,ætə'mɪstɪk/ adj. атомисти́ческий.

atomizer /'ætə,maizər/ n. (spray) пульвериза́тор m.

atonal /ei'tounl/ adj. атона́льный.

atone /ə'toun/ v. искупа́ть impf., искупи́ть pf.

atonement /ə'tounmənt/ n. искупле́ние neut.

atonic /ə'tɒnɪk/ adj. безуда́рный.

atrabilious /,ætrə'bɪlyəs/ adj. жёлчный, угрю́мый.

atrocious /ə'trouʃəs/ adj. зве́рский; ужа́сный.

atrocity /ə'trɒsɪti/ n. зве́рство neut., жесто́кость f.

atrophied /'ætrəfid/ adj. истощённый.

atrophy /'ætrəfi/ **1.** n. атрофи́я f. **2.** v. атрофи́роваться impf. and pf.

attach /ə'tætʃ/ v. прикрепля́ть impf., прикрепи́ть pf.; придава́ть impf., прида́ть pf.

attaché /ætæ'ʃei/ n. атташе́ m. indecl.

attachment /ə'tætʃmənt/ n. прикрепле́ние neut.; (emotional) привя́занность f.

attack /ə'tæk/ **1.** n. нападе́ние neut.; (med.) припа́док, при́ступ m. **2.** v. напада́ть (на with acc.) impf.; наступа́ть impf.; наступи́ть, pf.

attain /ə'tein/ v. дости́гнуть pf., доби́ться pf.

attainable /ə'teinəbəl/ adj. достижи́мый.

attainment /ə'teinmənt/ n. достиже́ние neut.

attempt /ə'tempt/ **1.** n. попы́тка f.; (on the life of) покуше́ние (на жизнь with gen.). **2.** v. пыта́ться impf., попыта́ться pf.; про́бовать impf., попро́бовать pf.

attend /ə'tɛnd/ v. посеща́ть impf., посети́ть pf.

attendance /ə'tɛndəns/ n. прису́тствие neut.; посеща́емость f.

attendant /ə'tɛndənt/ **1.** n. (escort) провожа́тый m. **2.** adj. сопровожда́ющий, сопу́тствующий.

attention /ə'tɛnʃən/ n. внима́ние neut.; **to pay attention to** обраща́ть внима́ние impf.

attentive /ə'tɛntɪv/ adj. внима́тельный.

attenuation /ə,tɛnyu'eiʃən/ n. ослабле́ние, затуха́ние neut.

attenuator /ə'tɛnyu,eitər/ n. смягчи́тель m.

attest /ə'tɛst/ v. свиде́тельствовать impf.; удостоверя́ть impf., удостове́рить pf.

attestation /,ætɛ'steiʃən/ n. свиде́тельство neut.

Attic /'ætɪk/ adj. атти́ческий.

attic /'ætɪk/ n. манса́рда f., черда́к m.

attire /ə'tai r/ **1.** n. пла́тье neut., наря́д m. **2.** v. наряжа́ть impf., наряди́ть pf.

attitude /'ætɪ,tud/ n. отноше́ние neut.; по́за f.

attitudinize /,ætɪ'tudn,aiz/ v. пози́ровать impf.

attorney /ə'tɜrni/ n. адвока́т m.; **Attorney General** мини́стр юсти́ции m.; **district attorney** прокуро́р о́круга m.

attract /ə'trækt/ v. привлека́ть impf., привле́чь pf.

attraction /ə'trækʃən/ n. притяже́ние, тяготе́ние neut.; аттракцио́н m.

attractive /ə'træktɪv/ adj. привлека́тельный, притяга́тельный.

attribute / n. 'ætrə,byut; v. ə'trɪbyut/ **1.** n. сво́йство neut., при́знак m.; (gram.) определе́ние neut. **2.** v. припи́сывать impf., приписа́ть pf.

attribution /,ætrə'byuʃən/ n. припи́сывание neut.

attributive /ə'trɪbyətɪv/ adj. (gram.) определи́тельный.

attrition /ə'trɪʃən/ n. истира́ние neut.

attune /ə'tun/ v. настра́ивать impf., настро́ить pf.

atypical /ei'tɪpɪkəl/ adj. нетипи́чный, атипи́чный.

auburn /'ɔbərn/ adj. кашта́новый, красновáто-кори́чневый.

auction /'ɔkʃən/ **1.** n. аукцио́н m. **2.** v. продава́ть с молотка́ or с аукцио́на impf.

auctioneer /,ɔkʃə'nɪər/ n. аукциони́ст m.

auction room /'ɔkʃən,rum/ n. аукцио́нный зал m.

audacious /ɔ'deiʃəs/ adj. сме́лый; де́рзкий.

audacity /ɔ'dæsɪti/ n. сме́лость, де́рзость f.

audibility /,ɔdə'bɪlɪti/ n. слы́шимость f.

audible /'ɔdəbəl/ adj. слы́шимый.

audibly /'ɔdəbli/ adv. вня́тно.

audience /'ɔdiəns/ n. аудито́рия f., слу́шатели pl., пу́блика f.; (interview) аудие́нция f.

audio /'ɔdi,ou/ adj. звуково́й.

audiogram /'ɔdiə,græm/ n. аудиогра́мма f.

audiometer /,ɔdi'ɒmɪtər/ n. аудио́метр m.

audiovisual /,ɔdiou'vɪʒuəl/ adj. аудиовизуа́льный.

audit /'ɔdɪt/ n. реви́зия, прове́рка отчётности f.

audition /ɔ'dɪʃən/ n. слу́шание, прослу́шивание neut.

auditor /'ɔdɪtər/ n. ауди́тор m.

auditorium /,ɔdi'tɔriəm/ n. зри́тельный зал m., аудито́рия f.

auditory /'ɔdɪ,tɔri/ adj. слухово́й.

au fait /ou 'fɛ/ adv. в ку́рсе.

auger /'ɔgər/ n. бура́в, бур m., сверло́ neut.

augment /ɔg'mɛnt/ v. прибавля́ть impf.

augmentation /,ɔgmɛn'teiʃən/ n. увеличе́ние neut.

augmentative /ɔg'mɛntətɪv/ adj. увеличи́тельный.

augur /'ɔgər/ v. предвеща́ть impf..

augury /'ɔgyəri/ n. предзнаменова́ние neut.

August /'ɔgəst/ **1.** n. а́вгуст m. **2.** adj. а́вгустовский.

Augustan /ɔ'gʌstən/ adj. эпо́хи А́вгуста.

Augustinian /,ɔgə'stɪniən/ n. мона́х-августи́нец m.

auk /ɔk/ n. чи́стик m., гага́рка f.

aunt /ænt, ɑnt/ n. тётя, тётка f.

aura /'ɔrə/ n. а́ура f.

aural /'ɔrəl/ adj. (ears) ушно́й; (hearing) слухово́й.

aureole /'ɔri,oul/ n. орео́л m.

auricle /'ɔrɪkəl/ n. (of heart) предсе́рдие neut.

auriferous /ɔ'rɪfərəs/ adj. золотоно́сный.

Auriga /ɔ'raigə/ n. (astr.) Возни́чий m.

aurochs /'ɔrɒks/ n. зубр m.

Auschwitz /'auʃvɪts/ n. (Polish: Oświęcim) Осве́нцим m.

auscultation /ˌɔskəl'teiʃən/ *n.* выслу́шивание *neut.*

auspice /'ɔspɪs/ *n.* предчу́вствие *neut.*

auspicious /ɔ'spɪʃəs/ *adj.* благоприя́тный.

austere /ɔ'stɪər/ *adj.* суро́вый; стро́гий.

austerity /ɔ'stɛrɪti/ *n.* стро́гость, суро́вость *f.*

Australia /ɔ'streilyə/ *n.* Австра́лия *f.*

Australian /ɔ'streilyən/ **1.** *adj.* австрали́йский. **2.** *n.* австрали́ец *m.*, австрали́йка *f.*

Austria /'ɔstriə/ *n.* А́встрия *f.*

Austrian /'ɔstriən/ **1.** *adj.* австри́йский. **2.** *n.* австри́ец *m.*, австри́йка *f.*

autarky /'ɔtɑrki/ *n.* автарки́я *f.*

authentic /ɔ'θɛntɪk/ *adj.* по́длинный, достове́рный.

authenticate /ɔ'θɛntɪˌkeit/ *v.* устана́вливать по́длинность (*with gen.*) *impf.*

authenticity /ˌɔθɛn'tɪsɪti/ *n.* по́длинность, достове́рность *f.*

author /'ɔθər/ *n.* а́втор *m.*

authorial /ɔ'θɔriəl/ *adj.* а́вторский.

authoritarian /əˌθɔri'tɛəriən/ *adj.* авторита́рный.

authoritative /ə'θɔriˌteitɪv/ *adj.* авторите́тный; повели́тельный.

authority /ə'θɔriti/ *n.* авторите́т *m.*; (*power*) власть *f.*, полномо́чие *neut.*

authorization /ˌɔθərə'zeiʃən/ *n.* уполномо́чивание, разреше́ние *neut.*

authorize /'ɔθəˌraiz/ *v.* уполномо́чивать *impf.*, уполномо́чить *pf.*

authorized /'ɔθəˌraizd/ *adj.* авторизо́ванный; уполномо́ченный, доброзванный.

authorship /'ɔθərˌʃip/ *n.* а́вторство *neut.*

autism /'ɔtizəm/ *n.* аути́зм *m.*

autistic /ɔ'tɪstɪk/ *adj.* аутисти́ческий.

auto- *prefix* авто-, само-.

autobiographical /ˌɔtəˌbaiə'græfɪkəl/ *adj.* автобиографи́ческий.

autobiography /ˌɔtəbai'ɒgrəfi/ *n.* автобиогра́фия *f.*

autocephalous /ˌɔtə'sɛfələs/ *adj.* автокефа́льный.

autochthonous /ɔ'tɒkθənəs/ *adj.* коренно́й, абориге́нный.

autoclave /'ɔtəˌkleiv/ *n.* автокла́в *m.*

autocracy /ɔ'tɒkrəsi/ *n.* самодержа́вие *neut.*; автокра́тия *f.*

autocrat /'ɔtəˌkræt/ *n.* (*ruler*) автокра́т, самоде́ржец *m.*; (*fig.*) де́спот, тира́н *m.*

autocratic /ˌɔtə'krætɪk/ *adj.* автократи́ческий.

auto-da-fé /ˌɔtoudə'fei/ *n.* аутодафе́ *neut.* indecl.

autogiro /ˌɔtə'dʒairou/ *n.* автожи́р *m.*

autograph /'ɔtəˌgræf/ *n.* авто́граф, оригина́л ру́кописи *m.*

automate /'ɔtəˌmeit/ *v.* автоматизи́ровать. *impf.*

automatic /ˌɔtə'mætɪk/ *adj.* автомати́ческий.

automatically /ˌɔtə'mætɪkli/ *adv.* автомати́чески.

automatic pilot *n.* автопило́т *m.*

automation /ˌɔtə'meiʃən/ *n.* автоматиза́ция *f.*

automatism /ɔ'tɒməˌtizəm/ *n.* автомати́зм *m.*

automaton /ɔ'tɒməˌtɒn/ *n.* автома́т *m.*

automobile /ˌɔtəmə'bil/ *n.* автомоби́ль *m.*, маши́на *f.*

automotive /ˌɔtə'moutiv/ *adj.* автомоби́льный; **automotive industry** *n.* автомоби́льная промы́шленность *f.*

autonomous /ɔ'tɒnəməs/ *adj.* автоно́мный.

autonomy /ɔ'tɒnəmi/ *n.* автоно́мия *f.*

autopilot /'ɔtouˌpailət/ *n.* автопило́т *m.*

autopsy /'ɔtɒpsi/ *n.* вскры́тие (тру́па) *neut.*

autosuggestion /ˌɔtousəg'dʒɛstʃən/ *n.* самовнуше́ние *neut.*

autumn /'ɔtəm/ **1.** *n.* о́сень *f.*; **in autumn** о́сенью. **2.** *adj.* осе́нний.

auxiliary /ɔg'zilyəri/ *adj.* вспомога́тельный.

avail /ə'veil/ *n.*: **of no avail** *adj.* бесполе́зен; **to no avail** *adv.* напра́сно.

availability /əˌveilə'bɪliti/ *n.* досту́пность *f.*

available /ɔ'veiləbəl/ *adj.* достижи́мый; име́ющийся в распоряже́нии.

avalanche /'ævəˌlæntʃ/ *n.* лави́на *f.*

avant-garde /əˌvant'gard/ *n.* аванга́рд *m.*

avarice /'ævərɪs/ *n.* ску́пость *f.*

avaricious /ˌævə'rɪʃəs/ *adj.* скупо́й.

avenge /ə'vɛndʒ/ *v.* мстить *impf.*, отомсти́ть *pf.*

avenger /ə'vɛndʒər/ *n.* мсти́тель *m.*

aventurine /ə'vɛntʃəˌrin/ *n.* авантюри́н *m.*

avenue /'ævəˌnyu, -ˌnu/ *n.* проспе́кт *m.*; авеню́ *f.* *indecl.*

average /'ævərɪdʒ, 'ævrɪdʒ/ **1.** *adj.* сре́дний. **2.** *n.* сре́днее число́; **on the average** *adv.* в сре́днем. **3.** *v.* выводи́ть сре́днее число́ *impf.*

averse /ə'vɜrs/ *adj.* не располо́женный; **not averse to** не прочь (*with infin.*)

aversion /ə'vɜrʒən/ *n.* отвраще́ние *neut.*, антипа́тия *f.*

avert /ə'vɜrt/ *v.* отводи́ть *impf.*, отвести́ *pf.*

aviary /'eiviˌɛri/ *n.* пти́чник *m.*

aviation /ˌeivi'eiʃən/ *n.* авиа́ция *f.*

aviator /'eiviˌeitər/ *n.* лётчик *m.*

aviculture /'eiviˌkʌltʃər/ *n.* птицево́дство *neut.*

avid /'ævɪd/ *adj.* жа́дный.

avidity /ə'vidɪti/ *n.* а́лчность *f.*

Avignon /avi'nyɔ̃/ *n.* Авиньо́н *m.*

avocado /ˌævə'kɑdou, ˌavə-/ *n.* авока́до *neut.* indecl.

avocet /'ævəˌsɛt/ *n.* шилоклю́вка *f.*

avoid /ə'vɔid/ *v.* избега́ть *impf.*, избежа́ть *pf.*

avoidance /ə'vɔidns/ *n.* избега́ние *neut.*

avowal /ə'vauəl/ *n.* призна́ние *neut.*

avowed /ə'vaud/ *adj.* при́знанный; общепри́знанный.

await /ə'weit/ *v.* ожида́ть *impf.*, ждать *impf.*

awake /ə'weik/ **1.** *v.* просыпа́ться *impf.*, проснуться *pf.* **2.** *adj.* бо́дрствующий.

awakening /ə'weikəniŋ/ *n.* пробужде́ние *neut.*

award /ə'wɔrd/ **1.** *n.* присужде́ние *neut.* награ́да *f.* **2.** *v.* присужда́ть *impf.*, присуди́ть *pf.*; награжда́ть *impf.*, награди́ть *pf.*

aware /ə'wɛər/ *adj.* осведомлённый.

away /ə'wei/ *adv.* прочь.

awe /ɔ/ *n.* благогове́ние *neut.*, страх *m.*

awesome /'ɔsəm/ *adj.* стра́шный, устраша́ющий, внуша́ющий страх.

awful /'ɔfəl/ *adj.* ужа́сный.

awfully /'ɔfəli/ *adv.* (*very*) стра́шно, ужа́сно.

awhile /ə'wail/ *adv.* немно́го, ненадо́лго, не́которое вре́мя.

awkward /'ɔkwərd/ *adj.* неуклю́жий, нело́вкий.

awkwardness /'ɔkwərdnɪs/ *n.* нело́вкость, неуклю́жесть *f.*

awl /ɔl/ *n.* ши́ло *neut.*

awning /'ɔniŋ/ *n.* наве́с, тент *m.*

awry /ə'rai/ *adj.* косо́й.

ax /æks/ *n.* топо́р *m.*
axial /'æksiəl/ *adj.* осево́й.
axil /'æksɪl/ *n.* па́зуха *f.*
axillary /'æksəˌlɛri/ *adj.* па́зушный.
axiom /'æksiəm/ *n.* аксио́ма *f.*
axiomatic /ˌæksiə'mætɪk/ *adj.* самоочеви́дный, аксиомати́ческий.
axis /'æksɪs/ *n.* ось *f.*

axle /'æksəl/ *n.* ось *f.*
aye /ai/ *adj. interj.* (*obs.*, *legal*) да.
azalea /ə'zeilyə/ *n.* аза́лия *f.*
Azerbaijan /ˌazərbai'dʒɑn/ *n.* Азербайджа́н *m.*
Azerbaijani /ˌazərbai'dʒɑni/ *n.* азербайджа́нец *m.*, азербайджа́нка *f.*
azimuth /'æzəməθ/ *n.* а́зимут *m.*
azure /'æʒər/ **1.** *adj.* лазу́рный. **2.** *n.* лазу́рь *f.*

B

babble /'bæbəl/ *n.* лепет *m.*

babe /beib/ *n.* малыш, ребёнок *m.*

babel /'beibəl, 'bæbəl/ *n.* (*fig.*) (*noise*) галдёж *m.*

baboon /bæ'bun/ *n.* бабуйн, павиан *m.*

baby /'beibi/ **1.** *adj.* детский. **2.** *n.* маленький ребёнок, младенец *m.*

baby carriage *n.* (детская) коляска *f.*

babyish /'beibiiʃ/ *adj.* ребяческий.

baby-sit /'beibi,sɪt/ *v.* смотреть за чужим ребёнком *impf.*

babysitter /'beibi,sɪtər/ *n.* приходящая няня *f.*

baby talk *n.* (*child*) детский лепет *m.*; (*adult to child*) сюсюканье *neut.*

baccalaureate /,bækə'lɔriit/ *n.* степень бакалавра *f.*

baccarat /'bɑkə,rɑ/ *n.* баккара *neut. indecl.*

Bacchanalia /,bækə'neiliə/ *n.* вакханалия *f.*

bacchanalian /,bækə'neiliən/ *adj.* вакханальный.

bacchante /bə'kænti/ *n.* вакханка *f.*

Bacchus /'bækəs/ *n.* Вакх, Бахус *m.*

bacciferous /bæk'sɪfərəs/ *adj.* ягодоносный.

bachelor /'bætʃələr/ **1.** *adj.* холостой; холостяцкий. **2.** *n.* холостяк *m.*

bachelorhood /'bætʃələr,hʊd/ *n.* холостая жизнь *f.*

bacillary /'bæsə,lɛri/ *adj.* бациллярный.

bacilliform /bə'sɪlə,fɔrm/ *adj.* палочковидный.

bacillus /bə'sɪləs/ *n.* бацилла, палочка *f.*

back /bæk/ **1.** *adv.* назад, обратно. **2.** *adj.* спинной; задний. **3.** *n.* оборотная сторона *f.*; (*spine*) спина *f.*; (*rear*) задняя часть *f.*; (*chair*) спинка *f.*

backache /'bæk,eik/ *n.* боль в спине *f.*

backbite /'bæk,bait/ *v.* злословить за спиной *impf.*

backbiting /'bæk,baitɪŋ/ *n.* злословие *neut.*

backbone /'bæk,boun/ *n.* хребет, позвоночник *m.*

backbreaking /'bæk,breikɪŋ/ *adj.* изнурительный.

backdrop /'bæk,drɒp/ *n.* (*theat.*) задник *m.*

backer /'bækər/ *n.* покровитель *m.*

backfire /'bæk,faiər/ *v.* давать осечку *impf.*

back formation *n.* (*ling.*) обратное словообразование *neut.*

backgammon /'bæk,gæmən/ *n.* триктрак *m.*

background /'bæk,graund/ *n.* фон, задний план *m.*

backhand /'bæk,hænd/ *n.* (*sports*) удар слева *m.*

backhander /'bæk,hændər/ *n.* (*blow*) удар наотмашь *m.*

backing /'bækɪŋ/ *n.* (*support*) поддержка *f.*; (*lining*) подкладка *f.*

backlog /'bæk,lɔg/ *n.* запас *m.*; скопление *neut.*

back number *n.* (*journal*) старый номер *m.*

backpack /'bæk,pæk/ *n.* рюкзак *m.*

back-pedal /'bæk,pɛdl/ *v.* крутить педали в обратную сторону *impf.*

backrest /'bæk,rɛst/ *n.* опора для спины *f.*

back room *n.* задняя комната *f.*

backscattering /'bæk,skætərɪŋ/ *n.* обратное рассеяние *neut.*

backside /'bæk,said/ *n.* зад *m.*

backslide /'bæk,slaid/ *v.* отступать *impf.*

backslider /'bæk,slaidər/ *n.* ренегат, рецидивист *m.*

backstage /'bæk'steidʒ/ *adj.* закулисный.

back stairs /'bæk'stɛərz/ *n.* чёрная лестница *f.*

backstay /'bæk,stei/ *n.* (*naut.*) бакштаг *m.*

backstop /'bæk,stɒp/ *n.* (*tech.*) останов *m.*

back-street /'bæk,strit/ *adj.* подпольный.

back-to-back *adv.* спиной к спине.

backtrack /'bæk,træk/ *v.* (*colloq.*) идти на попятный *impf.*

backup /'bæk,ʌp/ **1.** *adj.* запасной. **2.** *n.* дублирование *neut.*, дублёр *m.*; (*traffic*) пробка *f.*

backward /'bækwərd/ **1.** *adj.* обратный; отсталый. **2.** *adv.* назад, задом; наоборот.

backwardness /'bækwərdnɪs/ *n.* отсталость *f.*

backwash /'bæk,wɒʃ/ *n.* отток *m.*

backwater /'bæk,wɔtər/ *n.* (*pool*) заводь *f.*

backwoods /'bæk'wʊdz/ **1.** *adj.* глухой. **2.** *n.* глушь *f.*

bacon /'beikən/ *n.* бекон *m.*

bacterial /bæk'tɪəriəl/ *adj.* бактериальный.

bactericidal /bæk,tɪərə'saidl/ *adj.* бактерицидный.

bactericide /bæk'tɪərə,said/ *n.* бактерицид *m.*

bacteriological /bæk,tɪəriə'lɒdʒɪkəl/ *adj.* бактериологический.

bacteriologist /bæk,tɪəri'ɒlədʒɪst/ *n.* бактериолог *m.*

bacteriology /bæk,tɪəri'ɒlədʒi/ *n.* бактериология *f.*

bacteriolysis /bæk,tɪəri'ɒləsɪs/ *n.* бактериолиз *m.*

bacterium /bæk'tɪəriəm/ *n.* бактерия *f.*

bad /bæd/ *adj.* плохой, дурной, вредный; (*language*) грубый.

badge /bædʒ/ *n.* значок *m.*

badger /'bædʒər/ *n.* барсук *m.*

badinage /,bædn'ɑʒ/ *n.* подшучивание *neut.*

badly /'bædli/ *adv.* плохо, вредно; (*very much*) очень, сильно.

badminton /'bædmɪntn̩/ *n.* бадминтон *m.*

badness /'bædnɪs/ *n.* вредность, негодность *f.*

baffle /'bæfəl/ *v.* озадачивать; сбивать с толку *impf.*

bafflement /'bæfəlmənt/ *n.* недоумение *neut.*

baffling /'bæflɪŋ/ *adj.* непонятный, загадочный.

bag /bæg/ **1.** *n.* сумка *f.*, мешок; пакет *m.* **2.** *v.* схватить *pf.*

baggage /'bægɪdʒ/ **1.** *adj.* багажный. **2.** *n.* багаж *m.*

bagging /'bægɪŋ/ *n.* (*material*) мешковина *f.*

baggy /'bægi/ *adj.* мешковатый.

Baghdad /'bægdæd/ *n.* Багдад *m.*

bagpipe /'bæg,paip/ *n.* волынка *f.*

bagpiper /'bæg,paipər/ *n.* волынщик *m.*

bah /bɑ/ *interj.* ба!

bail /beil/ *n.* поручительство *neut.*

bailiff /'beilɪf/ *n.* (*leg.*) судебный пристав *m.*

bailor /'beilər/ *n.* (*leg.*) депонент *m.*

bait /beit/ **1.** *n.* приманка *f.*, искушение *neut.* **2.** *v.* приманивать *impf.*

baize /beiz/ *n.* байка *f.*

bake /beik/ *v.* печь *impf.*, спечь *pf.*

baked /beikt/ adj. печёный.
bakelite /'beikə,lait/ n. бакели́т m.
baker /'beikər/ n. пе́карь m.
bakery /'beikəri/ n. (store) бу́лочная f.; пека́рня f.
baking /'beikıŋ/ **1.** adj. пека́рный. **2.** n. печéние neut.
Baku /bʌ'ku/ n. Баку́ m.
balalaika /,bælə'laikə/ n. балала́йка f.
balance /'bæləns/ **1.** n. равновéсие neut.; бала́нс m. **2.** v. баланси́ровать impf.
balanced /'bælənst/ adj. уравновéшенный; сбаланси́рованный.
balance sheet n. бала́нс m.
balance wheel n. баланси́р m.
Balaton /'bælə,tɒn/ n. (lake) Балато́н m.
balcony /'bælkəni/ n. балко́н m.
bald /bɔld/ adj. лы́сый.
baldachin /'bældəkın/ n. балдахи́н m.
balderdash /'bɔldər,dæʃ/ n. ерунда́, чепуха́ f.
baldheaded /'bɔld,hɛdıd/ adj. лы́сый.
balding /'bɔldıŋ/ adj. лысéющий.
baldness /'bɔldnıs/ n. плеши́вость f., облысéние neut.
bale /beil/ n. ки́па f., тюк m.
Balearic Islands /,bæli'ærık/ n. Балеáрские острова́ pl.
baleful /'beilfəl/ adj. зловéщий.
balk /bɔk/ v. упря́миться impf.; (thwart) препя́тствовать (with dat.) impf.
Balkan /'bɔlkən/ adj. балка́нский.
ball /bɔl/ n. шар; мяч m.; (dance) бал m.
ballad /'bæləd/ n. балла́да f.
ballade /bə'lɑd/ n. балла́да f.
ballast /'bæləst/ n. балла́ст m.
ball bearing n. шарикоподши́пник m.
ball cock n. поплавко́вый кран m.
ballerina /,bælə'rinə/ n. балери́на f.
ballet /bæ'lei/ **1.** adj. балéтный. **2.** n. балéт m.
ballet dancer n. (male) арти́ст балéта m.; (female) балери́на, арти́стка балéта f.
balletomane /bæ'lɛtə,mein/ n. балетома́н m.
ballistic /bə'lıstık/ adj. баллисти́ческий.
ballistics /bə'lıstıks/ n. балли́стика f.
balloon /bə'lun/ n. возду́шный шар m.
balloonist /bə'lunıst/ n. аэрона́вт, воздухопла́ватель m.
ballot /'bælət/ **1.** n. баллотиро́вка f., избира́тельный бюллетéнь m. **2.** v. голосова́ть, баллоти́ровать impf.
ballpoint pen /'bɔl,pɔint/ n. ша́риковая ру́чка f.
ballroom /'bɔl,rum/ n. танцева́льный зал m.
ballyhoo /'bæli,hu/ n. шуми́ха f.
balm /bɑm/ n. бальза́м m.
balmy /'bɑmi/ adj. арома́тный; (air) мя́гкий, нéжный.
balneal /'bælniəl/ adj. бальнеологи́ческий.
balneology /,bælni'ɒlədʒi/ n. бальнеоло́гия f.
balneotherapy /,bælniou'θɛrəpi/ n. бальнеотерапи́я f.
baloney /bə'louni/ n. (slang) ерунда́, чепуха́ f.
balsa /'bɔlsə/ n. ба́льза f.
balsam /'bɔlsəm/ n. бальза́м m.
baluster /'bæləstər/ n. баля́сина f.
balustrade /'bælə,streid/ n. балюстра́да f.
bamboo /bæm'bu/ **1.** adj. бамбу́ковый. **2.** n. бамбу́к m.

bamboozle /bæm'buzəl/ v. обма́нывать, надува́ть impf.
ban /bæn/ **1.** n. запрéт m., запрещéние neut. **2.** v. запреща́ть impf., запрети́ть pf.
banal /bə'næl, 'beinl/ adj. бана́льный.
banality /bə'nælıti/ n. бана́льность f.
banana /bə'nænə/ n. бана́н m.
banana tree n. бана́новое дéрево neut.
band /bænd/ **1.** n. (strip) полоса́ f.; (of people) гру́ппа f.; (mus.) оркéстр m.; (ribbon) лéнта f. **2.** v. **to band together** объедини́ться pf.
bandage /'bændıdʒ/ **1.** n. бинт m., повя́зка f., банда́ж m. **2.** v. перевя́зывать impf., перевяза́ть pf.; бинтова́ть impf., забинтова́ть pf.
bandanna /bæn'dænə/ n. плато́к m.
bandicoot /'bændı,kut/ n. бандикýт m.
bandit /'bændıt/ n. банди́т m.
banditry /'bændıtri/ n. грабёж m.
bandmaster /'bænd,mæstər/ n. капельмéйстер m.
bandoleer /,bændl'ıər/ n. патронта́ш m.
band saw /'bænd,sɔ/ n. лéнточная пила́ f.
bandsman /'bændzmən/ n. оркестра́нт m.
bandstand /'bænd,stænd/ n. эстра́да для оркéстра f.
bandwidth /'bænd,wıdθ, -,wıθ/ n. ширина́ полосы́ f.
bandy /'bændi/ v. обмéниваться impf.
bandy-legged /'bæn,di lɛgıd, -,lɛgd/ adj. криво́ногий adj.
bane /bein/ n. отра́ва f.
baneful /'beinfəl/ adj. ги́бельный, губи́тельный.
bang /bæŋ/ **1.** n. хлопо́к, уда́р m. **2.** v. хло́пать impf., хло́пнуть pf.; ударя́ть impf., уда́рить pf.
Bangkok /'bæŋkɒk/ n. Бангко́к m. (see Krung Thep).
bangle /'bæŋgəl/ n. браслéт m.
banish /'bænıʃ/ v. изгоня́ть impf., изгна́ть pf.
banishment /'bænıʃmənt/ n. изгна́ние neut.
banister /'bænəstər/ n. пери́ла pl.
banjo /'bændʒou/ n. ба́нджо neut. indecl.
bank[1] /bæŋk/ **1.** n. (money) банк m. **2.** v. класть дéньги в банк impf.
bank[2] /bæŋk/ n. (river) бéрег m.; (slope) на́сыпь f. **2.** v. (embank) дéлать на́сыпь impf.
bankable /'bæŋkəbəl/ adj. приго́дный к учёту.
bankbook /'bæŋk,bʊk/ n. ба́нковская кни́жка f.
banker /'bæŋkər/ n. банки́р m.
banking /'bæŋkıŋ/ n. ба́нковое дéло neut.
bank note n. банкно́та f.
bank rate n. ста́вка ба́нкового учёта f.
bankrupt /'bæŋkrʌpt/ adj. несостоя́тельный.
bankruptcy /'bæŋkrʌptsi/ n. банкро́тство neut.
bank swallow n. береговáя ла́сточка f.
banner /'bænər/ n. зна́мя neut.
banquet /'bæŋkwıt/ **1.** n. банкéт m. **2.** v. банкéт m.
banquet room n. банкéтный зал m.
banter /'bæntər/ **1.** n. шу́тка f., подшу́чивание neut. **2.** v. добро́душно подшу́чивать impf.
banyan /'bænyən/ n. бань́ян m.
baobab /'beiou,bæb/ n. баоба́б m.
baptism /'bæptızəm/ n. крещéние neut.
baptismal /bæp'tızməl/ adj. крести́льный.
baptistery /'bæptəstri/ n. баптистéрий m.
baptize /bæp'taiz/ v. крести́ть impf.; **to be baptized** крести́ться impf.

bar /bɑr/ **1.** *n.* полоса́ *f.*, брусо́к *m.*; (*tavern*) бар *m.*; (*of soap*) кусо́к *m.*; (*of chocolate*) пли́тка *f.*; (*law*) адвокату́ра *f.* **2.** *v.* прегражда́ть *impf.*, прегради́ть *pf.*; (*forbid*) запреща́ть *impf.*

barathea /ˌbærəˈθiə/ *n.* барате́я *f.*

barb /bɑrb/ *n.* колю́чка *f.*; (*hook, etc.*) зубе́ц *m.*, зазу́брина *f.*

barbarian /bɑrˈbɛəriən/ **1.** *adj.* ва́рварский. **2.** *n.* ва́рвар *m.*

barbaric /bɑrˈbærɪk/ *adj.* ва́рварский.

barbarism /ˈbɑrbəˌrɪzəm/ *n.* ва́рварство *neut.*; (*ling.*) варвари́зм *m.*

barbarity /bɑrˈbærɪti/ *n.* ва́рварство *neut.*, жесто́кость *f.*

barbarous /ˈbɑrbərəs/ *adj.* ва́рварский.

barbate /ˈbɑrbeɪt/ *adj.* (*bot.*) ости́стый; (*zool.*) борода́тый, уса́тый.

barbecue /ˈbɑrbɪˌkyu/ *n.* (*meat*) целико́м зажа́ренная ту́ша *f.*; (*party*) ба́рбикью *neut. indecl.*

barbed /bɑrbd/ *adj.* ко́лкий, колю́чий.

barbed wire *n.* колю́чая про́волока *f.*

barbel /ˈbɑrbəl/ *n.* (*fish*) уса́ч *m.*

barbell /ˈbɑrˌbɛl/ *n.* (*sport*) гимнасти́ческая ги́ря *f.*

barber /ˈbɑrbər/ *n.* парикма́хер *m.*

barberry /ˈbɑrˌbɛri/ *n.* барбари́с *m.*

barbette /bɑrˈbɛt/ *n.* (*mil.*) барбе́т *m.*

barbican /ˈbɑrbɪkən/ *n.* барбака́н *m.*

barbital /ˈbɑrbɪˌtɔl/ *n.* барбита́л *m.*

barbiturate /bɑrˈbɪtʃərɪt/ *n.* барбитура́т *m.*

barbituric acid /ˈbɑrbɪˌtʊrɪk/ *n.* барбиту́ровая кислота́ *f.*

barcarole /ˈbɑrkəˌroul/ *n.* баркаро́ла *f.*

Barcelona /ˌbɑrsəˈlounə/ *n.* Барсело́на *f.*

bar code *n.* штрихово́й код *m.*

bard /bɑrd/ *n.* бард, ба́ян *m.*

bare /bɛər/ **1.** *adj.* го́лый. **2.** *v.* обнажа́ть *impf.*, обнажи́ть *pf.*

bareback /ˈbɛərˌbæk/ *adj.* неосёдланный.

barefaced /ˈbɛərˌfeist/ *adj.* бессты́дный.

barefoot /ˈbɛərˌfʊt/ *adj.* босоно́гий.

bareheaded /ˈbɛərˌhɛdɪd/ *adj.* с непокры́той голово́й.

barely /ˈbɛərli/ *adv.* (*scarcely*) едва́, е́ле; (*only*) то́лько, лишь.

bargain /ˈbɑrgən/ **1.** *n.* торго́вая сде́лка; уда́чная поку́пка *f.* **2.** *v.* торгова́ться *impf.*

barge /bɑrdʒ/ *n.* ба́ржа, ба́рка *f.*

bargeman /ˈbɑrdʒmən/ *n.* ба́рочник *m.*

baric /ˈbærɪk/ *adj.* (*chem.*) ба́риевый.

barite /ˈbɛərait/ *n.* бари́т, тяжёлый шпат *m.*

baritone /ˈbærɪˌtoun/ *n.* барито́н *m.*

barium /ˈbɛəriəm/ *n.* ба́рий *m.*

bark¹ /bɑrk/ *n.* кора́ *f.*

bark² /bɑrk/ **1.** *n.* (*of a dog*) лай *m.* **2.** *v.* ла́ять; га́вкать *impf.*

barkentine /ˈbɑrkənˌtin/ *n.* баркенти́на *f.*

barley /ˈbɑrli/ *n.* ячме́нь *m.*

barleycorn /ˈbɑrliˌkɔrn/ *n.* ячме́нное зерно́ *neut.*

barm /bɑrm/ *n.* пивны́е дро́жжи *pl.*

barmaid /ˈbɑrˌmeid/ *n.* буфе́тчица *f.*

barman /ˈbɑrmən/ *n.* буфе́тчик, ба́рмен *m.*

bar mitzvah /bɑr ˈmɪtsvə/ *n.* бар-ми́цва *f.*

barn /bɑrn/ *n.* амба́р, сара́й *m.*; гумно́ *neut.*

barnacle /ˈbɑrnəkəl/ *n.* морско́й жёлудь *m. f.*

Barnaul /ˌbɑrnəˈul/ *n.* Барнау́л *m.*

barney /ˈbɑrni/ *n.* (*colloq.*) перебра́нка *f.*

barogram /ˈbærəˌgræm/ *n.* барогра́мма *f.*

barograph /ˈbærəˌgræf/ *n.* баро́граф *m.*

barometer /bəˈrɒmɪtər/ *n.* баро́метр *m.*

barometric /ˌbærəˈmɛtrɪk/ *adj.* барометри́ческий.

baron /ˈbærən/ *n.* баро́н *m.*

baronage /ˈbærənɪdʒ/ *n.* ти́тул баро́на *m.*

baroness /ˈbærənɪs/ *n.* бароне́сса *f.*

baronet /ˈbærənɪt/ *n.* бароне́т *m.*

baronial /bəˈrouniəl/ *adj.* баро́нский.

baroque /bəˈrouk/ *n.* баро́кко *neut. indecl.*

baroscope /ˈbærəˌskoup/ *n.* бароско́п *m.*

barotropic /ˌbærəˈtrɒpɪk/ *adj.* баротро́пный.

barracks /ˈbærəks/ *n.* бара́к *m.*, каза́рма *f.*

barracuda /ˌbærəˈkudə/ *n.* морска́я щу́ка *f.*

barrage /bəˈrɑʒ/ *n.* плоти́на *f.*; загражде́ние *neut.*

barrel /ˈbærəl/ *n.* бо́чка *f.*, бочо́нок *m.*; (*of gun*) ствол *m.*, ду́ло *neut.*

barrel-chested /ˈbærˌəl tʃɛstɪd/ *adj.* груда́стый.

barrel organ *n.* шарма́нка *f.*

barrel roll /ˈbærəlˌroul/ *n.* (*aero.*) бо́чка *f.*

barren /ˈbærən/ *adj.* беспло́дный; неплодоро́дный.

barrenness /ˈbærənnɪs/ *n.* беспло́дие *neut.*, неплодоро́дность *f.*

barricade /ˈbærɪˌkeid/ *n.* баррика́да *f.*

barrier /ˈbæriər/ *n.* барье́р *m.*, прегра́да *f.*

barring /ˈbɑrɪŋ/ *prep.* за исключе́нием (*with gen.*), кро́ме (*with gen.*).

barrister /ˈbærəstər/ *n.* (*Brit.*) адвока́т, ба́рристер *m.*

barrow¹ /ˈbærou/ *n.* (*cart*) та́чка *f.*

barrow² /ˈbærou/ *n.* (*tumulus*) курга́н *m.*

bartender /ˈbɑrˌtɛndər/ *n.* буфе́тчик *m.*

barter /ˈbɑrtər/ **1.** *n.* менова́я торго́вля *f.* **2.** *v.* обме́нивать *impf.*, обменя́ть *pf.*

bartizan /ˈbɑrtəzən/ *n.* сторожева́я ба́шенка *f.*

basal /ˈbeisəl/ *adj.* основно́й, ба́зисный.

basalt /bəˈsɔlt/ **1.** *adj.* база́льтовый. **2.** *n.* база́льт *m.*

base /beis/ **1.** *adj.* ни́зкий, по́длый. **2.** *n.* осно́ва, ба́за *f.* **3.** *v.* осно́вывать *impf.*, основа́ть *pf.*

baseball /ˈbeisˌbɔl/ *n.* бейсбо́л *m.*

Basel /ˈbɑzəl/ *n.* Ба́зель *m.*

baseless /ˈbeislɪs/ *adj.* необосно́ванный.

basement /ˈbeismənt/ *n.* подва́л *m.*, подва́льный эта́ж *m.*

baseness /ˈbeisnɪs/ *n.* по́длость, гну́сность *f.*

bash /bæʃ/ *v.* (*colloq.*) лупи́ть *impf.*

bashful /ˈbæʃfəl/ *adj.* засте́нчивый, ро́бкий.

bashfulness /ˈbæʃfəlnɪs/ *n.* засте́нчивость, ро́бость *f.*

Bashkir /bɑʃˈkɪər/ *n.* башки́р *m.*, башки́рка *f.*

basic /ˈbeisɪk/ *adj.* основно́й.

basically /ˈbeisɪkli/ *adv.* в основно́м.

basil /ˈbæzəl, ˈbeizəl/ *n.* (*bot.*) базили́к *m.*

basilica /bəˈsɪlɪkə/ *n.* базили́ка *f.*

basilisk /ˈbæzəlɪsk/ *n.* васили́ск *m.*

basin /ˈbeisən/ *n.* таз *m.*, (*geol.*) бассе́йн *m.*

basis /ˈbeisɪs/ *n.* осно́ва *f.*, основа́ние *neut.*, ба́зис *m.*

bask /bæsk/ *v.* гре́ться *impf.*

basket /ˈbæskɪt/ *n.* корзи́на, корзи́нка *f.*

basketball /ˈbæskɪtˌbɔl/ *n.* баскетбо́л *m.*

basketry /ˈbæskɪtri/ *n.* плетёные изде́лия *pl.*

basking shark /ˈbæskɪŋ/ *n.* гига́нтская аку́ла *f.*

Basque /bæsk/ **1.** *n.* (*person*) баск *m.* баскóнка *f.;* (*language*) бáскский язы́к. **2.** *adj.* бáскский.
bas-relief /ˌbɑrɪ'lif/ *n.* барельéф *m.*
bass[1] /bæs/ *n.* (*fish*) óкунь *m.*
bass[2] /beis/ **1.** *n.* (*mus.*) бас *m.* **2.** *adj.* басóвый.
basset /'bæsɪt/ *n.* (*dog*) бáссет *m.*
bassoon /bæ'sun/ *n.* фагóт *m.*
bast /bæst/ *n.* лы́ко *neut.,* луб *m.*
bastard /'bæstərd/ **1.** *n.* внебрáчный ребёнок *m.;* (*slang*) свóлочь *m.* **2.** *adj.* внебрáчный, поддéльный.
baste[1] /beist/ *v.* (*cul.*) поливáть (жи́ром) *impf.*
baste[2] /beist/ *v.* (*sew*) смётывать *impf.*
bastion /'bæstʃən/ *n.* бастиóн *m.*
bat[1] /bæt/ *n.* летýчая мышь *f.*
bat[2] /bæt/ (*baseball*) би́та *f.*
batch /bætʃ/ *n.* кýчка, пáчка *f.*
bath /bæθ/ *n.* бáня, купáльня *f.;* (*bathing*) вáнна *f.,* купáние *neut.*
bathe /beið/ *v.* купáть(ся) *impf.*
bather /'beiðər/ *n.* купáльщик *m.,* купáльщица *f.*
bathhouse /'bæθˌhaus/ *n.* бáня *f.*
bathing /'beiðɪŋ/ *n.* купáние *neut.*
bathing suit *n.* купáльник *m.;* плáвки *pl.*
bathroom /'bæθˌrum/ *n.* вáнная *f.*
bathysphere /'bæθəˌsfɪər/ *n.* батисфéра *f.*
batik /bə'tik/ **1.** *n.* бати́к *m.* **2.** *adj.* бати́ковый.
batiste /bə'tist/ **1.** *n.* бати́ст *m.* **2.** *adj.* бати́стовый.
baton /bə'tɒn/ *n.* дуби́нка *f.;* (*mus.*) дирижёрская пáлочка *f.;* (*athl.*) эстафéтная пáлочка *f.*
battalion /bə'tælyən/ *n.* батальóн *m.*
batter /'bætər/ **1.** *n.* взби́тое тéсто *neut.* **2.** *v.* колоти́ть *impf.*
battering ram /'bætərɪŋ/ *n.* тарáн *m.*
battery /'bætəri/ *n.* (*mil., tech.*) батарéя *f.;* (*household battery*) батарéйка *f.*
battle /'bætl/ **1.** *adj.* боевóй. **2.** *n.* би́тва *f.,* сражéние *neut.* **3.** *v.* сражáться *impf.*
battle cry *n.* боевóй клич *m.*
battle dress *n.* похóдная фóрма *f.*
battlefield /'bætlˌfild/ *n.* пóле сражéния *neut.*
battlement /'bætlmənt/ *n.* зубчáтая стенá *f.*
batty /'bæti/ *adj.* (*slang*) трóнутый, чóкнутый.
Batumi /ba'tumi/ *n.* Батýми *m.*
bauble /'bɔbəl/ *n.* безделýшка *f.*
bauxite /'bɔksait/ *n.* бокси́т *m.*
bawdy /'bɔdi/ *n.* непристóйный.
bawl /bɔl/ *v.* кричáть *impf.,* орáть
bay[1] /bei/ *adj.* гнедóй.
bay[2] /bei/ *n.* (*geog.*) бýхта *f.,* зали́в *m.*
bay[3] /bei/ **1.** (*of dog*) *n.* лай *m.* **2.** *v.* лáять *impf.*
bayadere /'baiəˌdɪər/ *n.* баядéрка *f.*
bayonet /'beiənɪt/ *n.* штык *m.*
bazaar /bə'zɑr/ *n.* ры́нок, базáр *m.*
bazooka /bə'zukə/ *n.* реакти́вное противотáнковое ружьё *neut.*
be /bi; *unstressed* bi, bɪ/ *v.* быть *impf.;* (*location*) находи́ться *impf.*
beach /bitʃ/ *n.* пляж *m.*
beachhead /'bitʃˌhɛd/ *n.* береговóй плацдáрм *m.*
beacon /'bikən/ *n.* бáкен, мая́к *m.*
bead /bid/ *n.* бýсинка, кáпля *f.; pl.* бýсы.
beaded /'bidɪd/ *adj.* би́серный.
beagle /'bigəl/ *n.* бигль *m.*
beak /bik/ *n.* клюв *m.*

beaker /'bikər/ *n.* кýбок *m.*
be-all and end-all /'bi,ɔl ənd 'ɛnd,ɔl/ *n.* конéц и начáло (*with gen.*) *m.*
beam /bim/ *n.* (*light*) луч *m.;* (*wood*) бáлка *f.*
bean /bin/ *n.* боб *m.;* фасóль *f.*
beanpole /'binˌpoul/ *n.* подпóра для фасóли *f.;* (*fig.*) жердь *f.*
bear[1] /bɛər/ **1.** *adj.* медвéжий. **2.** *n.* медвéдь *m.*
bear[2] /bɛər/ *v.* (*give birth to*) рождáть *impf.,* роди́ть *pf.;* (*endure*) выноси́ть *impf.,* вы́нести *pf.;* (*carry*) носи́ть *impf.*
bearable /'bɛərəbəl/ *adj.* снóсный, терпи́мый.
beard /bɪərd/ *n.* бородá *f.*
bearded /'bɪərdɪd/ *adj.* бородáтый.
bearer /'bɛərər/ *n.* носи́тель, предъяви́тель *m.*
bearing /'bɛərɪŋ/ *n.* поведéние, отношéние *neut.;* (*tech.*) подши́пник *m.*
bearskin /'bɛərˌskɪn/ *n.* медвéжья шкýра *f.*
beast /bist/ *n.* зверь *m.*
beastliness /'bistlɪnɪs/ *n.* скóтство *neut.*
beastly /'bistli/ *adj.* (*bestial*) скóтский.
beat /bit/ *v.* бить(ся) *impf.,* поби́ть(ся) *pf.;* (*defeat*) побеждáть *impf.,* победи́ть *pf.*
beaten /'bitn/ *adj.* би́тый, разби́тый; (*defeated*) побеждённый.
beater /'bitər/ *n.* (*in hunting*) загóнщик *m.*
beatific /ˌbiə'tɪfɪk/ *adj.* блажéнный.
beatification /bi,ætəfɪ'keiʃən/ *n.* причислéние к ли́ку блажéнных *neut.*
beatify /bi'ætəˌfai/ *v.* канонизи́ровать *impf.* and *pf.*
beating /'bitɪŋ/ *n.* битьё, биéние *neut.;* (*defeat*) поражéние *neut.*
beatitude /bi'ætɪˌtud/ *n.* блажéнство (*also as title*) *neut.*
beatnik /'bitnɪk/ *n.* би́тник *m.*
beau /bou/ *n.* (*dandy*) франт, щёголь *m.;* дéнди *m. indecl.*
beautician /byu'tɪʃən/ *n.* косметóлог *m.*
beautification /ˌbyutəfɪ'keiʃən/ *n.* украшéние *neut.*
beautiful /'byutəfəl/ *adj.* краси́вый, прекрáсный.
beautifully /'byutəfli/ *adv.* краси́во, прекрáсно.
beautify /'byutəˌfai/ *v.* украшáть *impf.,* укрáсить *pf.*
beauty /'byuti/ *n.* красотá *f.;* (*beautiful person*) красáвец *m.,* красáвица *f.*
Beauvais /bou'vei/ *n.* Бовé *m.*
beaver /'bivər/ **1.** *adj.* бобрóвый. **2.** *n.* (*zool.*) бобр *m.*
becalm /bɪ'kɑm/ *v.* успокáивать *impf.*
because /bɪ'kɔz/ **1.** *conj.* потомý что; так как. **2.** **because of** *prep.* из-за (*with gen.*)
because! /bɪ'kɔz/ *interj.* почемý? потомý! (*as one syntactic unit*)
béchamel /'beiʃəˌmɛl/ *n.* сóус бешамéль *m.*
beckon /'bɛkən/ *v.* мани́ть *impf.*
becloud /bɪ'klaud/ *v.* покрывáть облакáми *impf.*
become /bɪ'kʌm/ *v.* станови́ться *impf.,* стать *pf.;* быть к лицý (*with dat.*) *impf.*
becoming /bɪ'kʌmɪŋ/ *adj.* к лицý (*with dat.*)
bed /bɛd/ *n.* кровáть, постéль *f.;* (*river*) дно *neut.;* **to go to bed** *v.* ложи́ться спать *impf.*
bedaub /bɪ'dɔb/ *v.* замáзывать *impf.*
bedazzle /bɪ'dæzəl/ *v.* ослеплять (блéском) *impf.*
bedbug /'bɛdˌbʌg/ *n.* клоп *m.*

bedclothes /'bɛd,klouz/ *n.* постельное бельё *neut.*

bedeck /bɪ'dɛk/ *v.* украшать *impf.*

bedevil /bɪ'dɛvəl/ *v.* (*bewitch*) заколдовывать *impf.*; (*upset*) расстраивать *impf.*

bedew /bɪ'du/ *v.* покрывать росой *impf.*

bedlam /'bɛdləm/ *n.* бедлам *m.*

bedpan /'bɛd,pæn/ *n.* подкладное судно *neut.*

bedplate /'bɛd,pleit/ *n.* (*tech.*) станина *f.*

bedpost /'bɛd,poust/ *n.* столбик кровати *m.*

bedraggle /bɪ'drægəl/ *v.* запачкать, замарать *impf.*

bedraggled /bɪ'drægəld/ *adj.* запачканный.

bedridden /'bɛd,rɪdn̩/ *adj.* прикованный к постели.

bedrock /'bɛd,rɒk/ *n.* коренная порода *f.*

bedroom /'bɛd,rum/ *n.* спальня *f.*

bedsore /'bɛd,sɔr/ *n.* пролежень *m.*

bedspread /'bɛd,sprɛd/ *n.* постельное покрывало *neut.*

bedstead /'bɛd,stɛd/ *n.* кровать *f.*

bedtime /'bɛd,taim/ *n.* время ложиться спать *neut.*

bee /bi/ **1.** *adj.* пчелиный. **2.** *n.* пчела *f.*

beech /bitʃ/ **1.** *adj.* буковый. **2.** *n.* бук *m.*

beef /bif/ **1.** *adj.* говяжий. **2.** *n.* говядина *f.*

beefburger /'bif,bɜrgər/ *n.* рубленая котлета *f.*

beefsteak /'bif,steik/ *n.* бифштекс *m.*

beefy /'bifi/ *adj.* крепкий, мясистый.

bee garden *n.* пасека *f.*, пчельник *m.*

beehive /'bi,haiv/ *n.* улей *m.*

beekeeper /'bi,kipər/ *n.* пчеловод *m.*

beekeeping /'bi,kipiŋ/ *n.* пчеловодство *neut.*

beeline /'bi,lain/ *n.* прямая линия *f.*

beep /bip/ *v.* сигналить, гудеть *impf.*

beer /bɪər/ **1.** *adj.* пивной. **2.** *n.* пиво *neut.*

beery /'bɪəri/ *adj.* (*smelling, tasting of beer*) отдающий пивом.

beeswax /'biz,wæks/ *n.* пчелиный воск *m.*

beet /bit/ **1.** *adj.* свекольный. **2.** *n.* свекла *f.*

beetle /'bitl̩/ *n.* жук *m.*

beetling /'bitlɪŋ/ *adj.* нависший.

befall /bɪ'fɔl/ *v.* случаться, происходить. *impf.*

befit /bɪ'fɪt/ *v.* приличествовать, подобать *impf.*

befitting /bɪ'fɪtɪŋ/ *adj.* подходящий, подобающий.

befittingly /bɪ'fɪtɪŋli/ *adv.* как подобает.

befog /bɪ'fɒg/ *v.* затуманивать *impf.*

before /bɪ'fɔr/ **1.** *prep.* перед (*with instr.*); до (*with gen.*). **2.** *adv.* выше, раньше; **beforehand** *adv.* заранее.

befoul /bɪ'faul/ *v.* осквернять *impf.*

befriend /bɪ'frɛnd/ *v.* отнестись дружески.

befuddle /bɪ'fʌdl̩/ *v.* одурманивать *impf.*

beg /bɛg/ *v.* просить *impf.*, попросить *pf.*; (*entreat*) умолять *impf.*

beget /bɪ'gɛt/ *v.* порождать *impf.*

beggar /'bɛgər/ *n.* нищий *m.*

beggarly /'bɛgərli/ *adj.* нищенский, жалкий.

beggary /'bɛgəri/ *n.* нищета *f.*

begin /bɪ'gɪn/ *v.* начинать *impf.*, начать *pf.*; *v.i.* начинаться *impf.*, начаться *pf.*

beginner /bɪ'gɪnər/ *n.* начинающий *m.*

beginning /bɪ'gɪnɪŋ/ *n.* начало *neut.*; **at** *or* **in the beginning** *adv.* вначале; **in** *or* **from the beginning** *adv.* сначала.

begone! /bɪ'gɒn/ *interj.* прочь!

begonia /bɪ'gounyə/ *n.* бегония *f.*

begrudge /bɪ'grʌdʒ/ *v.* завидовать *impf.*

beguile /bɪ'gail/ *v.* (*charm*) очаровывать *impf.*; (*distract*) развлекать *impf.*

beguiling /bɪ'gailɪŋ/ *adj.* заманчивый.

begum /'bigəm/ *n.* бегума *f.*

behalf /bɪ'hæf/ *n.*: **in behalf of** *prep.* для, ради, в пользу (*with gen.*); **on behalf of** *prep.* от имени; в интересах (*with gen.*).

behave /bɪ'heiv/ *v.* вести себя, поступать *impf.*

behavior /bɪ'heivyər/ *n.* поведение *neut.*

behavioral /bɪ'heivyərəl/ *adj.* поведенческий.

behaviorism /bɪ'heivyə,rɪzəm/ *n.* бихевиоризм *m.*

behaviorist /bɪ'heivyərɪst/ *n.* бихевиорист *m.*

behead /bɪ'hɛd/ *v.* обезглавливать *impf.*, обезглавить *pf.*

beheading /bɪ'hɛdɪŋ/ *n.* отсечение головы *neut.*

behest /bɪ'hɛst/ *n.*: **at the behest of** *prep.* по велению (*with gen.*).

behind /bɪ'haind/ **1.** *adv.* сзади, позади. **2.** *prep.* за (*with acc., instr.*), позади (*with gen.*). **3.** *n.* (*colloq.*) зад *m.*

behold /bɪ'hould/ *v.* видеть, зреть *impf.*

beholden /bɪ'houldən/ *adj.* обязанный (*with dat.*).

beholder /bɪ'houldər/ *n.* зритель, очевидец *m.*

beige /beiʒ/ *adj.* бежевый, цвета беж.

Beijing /'bei'dʒɪŋ/ *n.* Пекин *m.*

being /'biiŋ/ *n.* (*existence*) бытие, существование *neut.*; (*creature*) существо *neut.*

bel /bɛl/ *n.* (*phys.*) бел *m.*

belabor /bɪ'leibər/ *v.* колотить *impf.*

Belarus /,byɛlə'rus/ *n.* Беларусь *f.*

Belarussian /,byɛlou'rʌʃən/ **1.** *n.* (*person*) белорус *m.*, белоруска *f.*; (*language*) белорусский язык *m.* **2.** *adj.* белорусский.

belated /bɪ'leitɪd/ *adj.* запоздалый.

belay /bɪ'lei/ **1.** *v.* (*naut.*) завёртывать *impf.* **2.** (*fig.*) *interj.* стоп!

belaying pin /bɪ'leiɪŋ,pɪn/ *n.* кофельнагель *m.*

belch /bɛltʃ/ **1.** *n.* отрыжка *f.* **2.** *v.* рыгать *impf.*, рыгнуть *pf.*

beleaguer /bɪ'ligər/ *v.* осаждать *impf.*

Belfast /'bɛlfæst/ *n.* Белфаст *m.*

belfry /'bɛlfri/ *n.* колокольня *f.*

Belgian /'bɛldʒən/ **1.** *adj.* бельгийский. **2.** *n.* бельгиец *m.*, бельгийка *f.*

Belgium /'bɛldʒəm/ *n.* Бельгия *f.*

Belgrade /'bɛlgreid/ *n.* Белград *m.*

belie /bɪ'lai/ *v.* противоречить (*with dat.*) *impf.*

belief /bɪ'lif/ *n.* вера *f.*; (*opinion*) убеждение, мнение *neut.*; **beyond belief** *adj.* вне вероятности.

believable /bɪ'livəbəl/ *adj.* вероятный; правдоподобный.

believe /bɪ'liv/ *v.* верить *impf.*; (*suppose*) полагать, думать *impf.*

believer /bɪ'livər/ *n.* верующий *m.*

belittle /bɪ'lɪtl̩/ *v.* умалять, принижать *impf.*

Belize /bə'liz/ *n.* Белиз *m.*

bell /bɛl/ *n.* колокол *m.*; (*doorbell*) звонок *m.*

belladonna /,bɛlə'dɒnə/ *n.* (*bot.*) красавка, белладонна *f.*

bell-bottom trousers /'bɛl,bɒtəm/ *n.* брюки-клёш *pl.*

bell buoy *n.* бакен с колоколом *m.*

belle /bɛl/ n. краса́вица f.

belles-lettres /bɛl'lɛtr/ n. беллетри́стика f.

bellhop /'bɛl,hɒp/ n. посы́льный m.

bellicose /'bɛlɪ,kous/ adj. вои́нственный; (person) драчли́вый.

bellicosity /,bɛlɪ'kɒsɪti/ n. вои́нственность, драчли́вость f.

belligerence /bə'lɪdʒərəns/ n. агресси́вность f.

belligerent /bə'lɪdʒərənt/ adj. вою́ющий.

bell jar n. стекля́нный колпа́к m.

bellman /'bɛlmən/ n. глаша́тай m.

bell metal n. колоко́льная бро́нза f.

bellow /'bɛlou/ v. мыча́ть impf.

bellows /'bɛlouz/ n. мехи́ pl.

bell push /'bɛl,puʃ/ n. кно́пка звонка́ f.

bell ringer n. звона́рь m.

bellwether /'bɛl,wɛðər/ n. бара́н-вожа́к (с бубе́нчиком) m.; (fig.) вожа́к m.

belly /'bɛli/ n. живо́т m.

bellyache /'bɛli,eik/ n. (colloq.) боль в животе́ f.

bellyband /'bɛli,bænd/ n. подпру́га f.

bellybutton /'bɛli,bʌtn/ n. (colloq.) пупо́к m.

bellyful /'bɛli,fʊl/ n. (colloq.): **I've had a bellyful of this** я сыт(а́) э́тим по го́рло.

belly-landing /'bɛli,lændɪŋ/ n. (acro.) поса́дка с у́бранным шасси́ f.

belong /bɪ'lɒŋ/ v. принадлежа́ть ((к) with dat.) impf.

belongings /bɪ'lɒŋɪŋz/ n. ве́щи, принадле́жности pl.

beloved /bɪ'lʌvɪd, -'lʌvd/ adj. люби́мый.

below /bɪ'lou/ 1. adv. ни́же, внизу́, вниз. 2. prep. под (with acc., instr.), ни́же (with gen.).

belt /bɛlt/ n. по́яс, реме́нь m.

belting /'bɛltɪŋ/ n. (tech.) приводно́й реме́нь m.

beltway /'bɛlt,wei/ n. кольцева́я доро́га f.

belvedere /'bɛlvɪ,dɪər/ n. бельведе́р m.

bemoan /bɪ'moun/ v. опла́кивать impf.

bemuse /bɪ'myuz/ v. смуща́ть impf.

bench /bɛntʃ/ n. скаме́йка f.

bench mark n. отме́тка высоты́ f.

bend /bɛnd/ 1. n. изги́б; сгиб m.; (in river) излу́чина f. 2. v.t. сгиба́ть impf., согну́ть pf.; v.i. сгиба́ться impf., согну́ться pf.

beneath /bɪ'niθ/ 1. adv. внизу́. 2. prep. под (with acc., instr.), ни́же (with gen.).

Benedictine /,bɛnɪ'dɪktɪn/ n. бенедикти́нец m.

benediction /,bɛnɪ'dɪkʃən/ n. благослове́ние neut.

benefaction /'bɛnə,fækʃən/ n. благодея́ние neut.

benefactor /'bɛnə,fæktər/ n. благоде́тель m.

benefactress /'bɛnə,fæktrɪs/ n. благоде́тельница f.

beneficent /bə'nɛfəsənt/ adj. благоде́тельный.

beneficial /,bɛnə'fɪʃəl/ adj. поле́зный; вы́годный.

beneficiary /,bɛnə'fɪʃi,ɛri/ n. насле́дник по завеща́нию m.

benefit /'bɛnəfɪt/ 1. n. вы́года, по́льза f. 2. v.t. приноси́ть по́льзу impf.; v.i. impf. извлека́ть по́льзу.

Benelux /'bɛnɪ,lʌks/ n. Бенилю́кс m.

benevolence /bə'nɛvələns/ n. благожела́тельность, ще́дрость f.

benevolent /bə'nɛvələnt/ adj. благотвори́тельный

benign /bɪ'nain/ adj. ми́лостивый; великоду́шный; (med.) доброка́чественный.

bent /bɛnt/ 1. adj. изо́гнутый; **to be bent on** v. реши́ться на (with acc.;) стреми́ться (к with dat., or with infin.) impf. 2. n. скло́нность, накло́нность f.

benthos /'bɛnθɒs/ n. бе́нтос m.

benumb /bɪ'nʌm/ v. притупля́ть impf.; (paralyze) парализова́ть impf.

benzedrine /'bɛnzɪ,drin/ n. бензедри́н m.

benzene /'bɛnzin, bɛn'zin/ n. бензо́л m.

benzine /'bɛnzin/ n. бензи́н m.

benzoin /'bɛnzouɪn/ n. бензо́йная смола́ f.

bequeath /bɪ'kwið/ v. завеща́ть impf. and pf.

bequest /bɪ'kwɛst/ n. насле́дство; оставле́ние насле́дства neut.

berate /bɪ'reit/ v. брани́ть impf.

bereave /bɪ'riv/ v. лиша́ть impf.

bereaved /bɪ'rivd/ adj. (sorrowing) скорбя́щий.

bereavement /bɪ'rivmənt/ n. тяжёлая утра́та f.

bereft /bɪ'rɛft/ adj. лишённый (with gen.).

beret /bə'rei/ n. бере́т m.

Berezina /,bɛrɛ'zinɑ/ n. (river) Березина́ f.

Bergen /'bɜrgən/ n. Бе́рген m.

bergschrund /'bɜrkʃrunt/ n. бе́ргшрунд m.

beriberi /'bɛri'bɛri/ n. бе́ри-бе́ри f. indecl.

Bering Sea /'bɛrɪŋ/ n. Бе́рингово мо́ре neut.

Bering Strait n. Бе́рингов проли́в m.

Berlin /bər'lɪn/ 1. n. Берли́н m. 2. adj. берли́нский.

Bermuda /bər'myudə/ 1. n. Берму́дские острова́ pl. 2. adj. берму́дский.

Bern /bɜrn/ n. Берн m.

berry /'bɛri/ n. я́года f.

berth /bɜrθ/ n. спа́льное ме́сто; (on a ship) ко́йка f.

berthing /'bɜrθɪŋ/ n. (place) ме́сто стоя́нки neut., прича́л m.; (action) прича́ливание neut.

beryl /'bɛrəl/ n. бери́лл m.

beryllium /bə'rɪliəm/ n. бери́ллий m.

beseech /bɪ'sitʃ/ v. умоля́ть impf.

beseeching /bɪ'sitʃɪŋ/ adj. умоля́ющий.

beset /bɪ'sɛt/ v. осажда́ть impf.

beside /bɪ'said/ prep. ря́дом с (with gen.), во́зле (with gen.); **beside oneself** вне себя́ (от with gen.).

besides /bɪ'saidz/ 1. prep. кро́ме, поми́мо (with gen.). 2. adv. кро́ме того́; к тому́ же.

besiege /bɪ'sidʒ/ v. осажда́ть impf., осади́ть pf.

besmear /bɪ'smɪər/ v. па́чкать, мара́ть impf.

besmirch /bɪ'smɜrtʃ/ v. па́чкать, черни́ть impf.

besom /'bizəm/ n. ве́ник m.

besotted /bɪ'sɒtɪd/ adj. одурма́ненный.

bespatter /bɪ'spætər/ v. забры́згивать impf.

bespeak /bɪ'spik/ v. зака́зывать зара́нее impf.

bespectacled /bɪ'spɛktəkəld/ adj. в очка́х.

Bessemer /'bɛsəmər/ adj. (tech.) бессе́меровский.

best /bɛst/ 1. adj. лу́чший, са́мый лу́чший. 2. adv. лу́чше всего́; **at best** adv. в лу́чшем слу́чае.

bestial /'bɛstʃəl/ adj. зве́рский; ско́тский.

bestiality /,bɛstʃi'ælɪti/ n. ско́тство; зве́рство neut.

bestow /bɪ'stou/ v. (make gift) дари́ть impf., дарова́ть impf. and pf.

bestrew /bɪ'stru/ v. усыпа́ть impf.

bestride /bɪ'straid/ v. сади́ться на impf.

bestseller /bɛst'sɛlər/ n. бестсе́ллер m.

bet /bɛt/ **1.** *n.* пари́ *neut. indecl.* **2.** *v.* держа́ть пари́ *impf.*

beta /'beitə/ *n.* бе́та *f.*; **beta-rays** бе́та-лучи́ *pl.*

betake oneself /bɪ'teik/ *v.* прибега́ть; отправля́ться *impf.*

betatron /'beitə,trɒn/ *n.* бетатро́н *m.*

betel /'bitl/ *n.* бе́тель *m.*

betide /bɪ'taid/ *v.* случа́ться *impf.*

betoken /bɪ'toukən/ *v.* означа́ть; пока́зывать *impf.*

betray /bɪ'trei/ *v.* предава́ть *impf.*, преда́ть *pf.*; изменя́ть *impf.*, измени́ть *pf.*

betrayal /bɪ'treiəl/ *n.* преда́тельство *neut.*, изме́на *f.*

betrayer /bɪ'treiər/ *n.* изме́нник, преда́тель *m.*, преда́тельница *f.*

betroth /bɪ'trouð/ *v.* обруча́ть *impf.*, обручи́ть *pf.*

betrothal /bɪ'trouðəl/ *n.* обруче́ние *neut.*, помо́лвка *f.*

better /'betər/ **1.** *adj.* лу́чший. **2.** *adv.* лу́чше. **3.** *v.* улучша́ть *impf.*, улу́чшить *pf.*; **to better oneself** улучша́ться *impf.*, улу́чшиться *pf.*

betterment /'betərmənt/ *n.* улучше́ние *neut.*

between /bɪ'twin/ *prep.* ме́жду (*with instr.*).

bevel /'bɛvəl/ *n.* скос *m.*

beverage /'bɛvərɪdʒ/ *n.* напи́ток *m.*

bevy /'bɛvi/ *n.* (*company*) компа́ния *f.*; (*birds*) ста́я *f.*

beware /bɪ'wɛər/ *v.* остерега́ться *impf.*

bewilder /bɪ'wɪldər/ *v.* сбива́ть с то́лку *impf.*

bewilderment /bɪ'wɪldərmənt/ *n.* смуще́ние, замеша́тельство *neut.*

bewitch /bɪ'wɪtʃ/ *v.* заколдова́ть; очарова́ть *pf.*

beyond /bi'ɒnd/ **1.** *prep.* за (*with acc.*); по ту сто́рону; вы́ше, свы́ше (*with gen.*). **2.** *adv.* вдали́, на расстоя́нии.

bezel /'bɛzəl/ *n.* (*cutting edge*) острие́ *neut.*; (*facet*) фасе́т *m.*, грань *f.*

Bhutan /bu'tɑn/ *n.* Бута́н *m.*

bi- *pref.* дву(х)-.

Białystok /'byɒlɪ,stɒk/ *n.* Белосто́к *m.*

biannual /bai'ænyuəl/ *adj.* два ра́за в год.

bias /'baiəs/ *n.* (*slant*) укло́н, *m.*; (*prejudice*) предубежде́ние *neut.*

biased /'baiəst/ *adj.* (*partial*) пристра́стный; (*prejudiced*) предубеждённый.

biatomic /,baiə'tɒmɪk/ *adj.* двуха́томный.

biaxial /bai'æksiəl/ *adj.* двухо́сный.

bib /bɪb/ *n.* (де́тский) нагру́дник *m.*

Bible /'baibəl/ *n.* Би́блия *f.*

Biblical /'bɪblɪkəl/ *adj.* библе́йский.

bibliographer /,bɪbli'ɒgrəfər/ *n.* библио́граф *m.*

bibliography /,bɪbli'ɒgrəfi/ *n.* библиогра́фия *f.*

bibliopole /'bɪbliə,poul/ *n.* букини́ст *m.*

bicarbonate /bai'kɑrbənɪt/ *n.* двууглеки́слая соль *f.*

bicentennial /,baisɛn'tɛniəl/ **1.** *adj.* двухсотле́тний. **2.** *n.* двухсотле́тие *neut.*

bicephalous /bai'sɛfələs/ *adj.* двугла́вый.

biceps /'baisɛps/ *n.* би́цепс *m.*

bichloride /bai'klɔraid/ *n.* (*chem.*) двухло́ристое соедине́ние *neut.*

bicker /'bɪkər/ *v.* спо́рить, пререка́ться *impf.*

bickering /'bɪkərɪŋ/ *n.* перебра́нка *f.*

bicorn /'baikɔrn/ *adj.* двуро́гий.

bicuspid /bai'kʌspɪd/ *adj.* (*zool.*) двузу́бчатый.

bicycle /'baisɪkəl/ **1.** *adj.* велосипе́дный. **2.** *n.* велосипе́д *m.* **3.** *v.* е́здить на велосипе́де *impf.*

bicyclist /'baisɪklɪst/ *n.* велосипеди́ст *m.*

bid /bɪd/ **1.** *n.* предложе́ние *indecl. neut.* **2.** *v.* предлага́ть (це́ну) *impf.*

biddable /'bɪdəbəl/ *adj.* послу́шный.

bidder /'bɪdər/ *n.* покупщи́к *m.*

bidding /'bɪdɪŋ/ *n.* предложе́ние цены́ *neut.*

bide /baid/ *v.*: **to bide one's time** ждать благоприя́тного слу́чая *impf.*

bidet /bi'dei/ *n.* биде́ *neut. indecl.*

biennial /bai'ɛniəl/ *adj.* дву(х)ле́тний.

bier /bɪər/ *n.* похоро́нные дро́ги *pl.*

bifocal /bai'foukəl/ *adj.* двухфо́кусный.

bifoliate /bai'fouliɪt/ *adj.* двули́стный.

bifurcate /'baifər,keit/ *v.* раздва́ивать(ся) *impf.*

bifurcation /,baifər'keiʃən/ *n.* раздвое́ние *neut.*

big /bɪg/ *adj.* большо́й, кру́пный, обши́рный.

bigamist /'bɪgəmɪst/ *n.* двоежёнец *m.*, двуму́жница *f.*

bigamy /'bɪgəmi/ *n.* бига́мия *f.*; (*of man*) двоежёнство *neut.*; (*of woman*) двоему́жие *neut.*

bigheaded /'bɪg,hɛdɪd/ *adj.* (*colloq.*) самодово́льный.

bight /bait/ *n.* (*bay*) бу́хта *f.*; (*in river*) излу́чина *f.*; (*rope*) петля́, бу́хта *f.*

bigmouth /'bɪg,mauθ/ *n.* (*colloq.*) болту́н *m.*

bigot /'bɪgət/ *n.* фана́тик, изуве́р *m.*

bigoted /'bɪgətɪd/ *adj.* нетерпи́мый, фанати́чный.

bigotry /'bɪgətri/ *n.* фанати́зм *m.*

bigwig /'bɪg,wɪg/ *n.* (*colloq.*) больша́я ши́шка *f.*

bike /baik/ *n.* (*colloq.*) велосипе́д *m.*

biker /'baikər/ *n.* (*colloq.*) велосипеди́ст, мотоцикли́ст *m.*

bikini /bɪ'kini/ *n.* бики́ни *neut. indecl.*

bilabial /bai'leibiəl/ *adj.* (*ling.*) билабиа́льный.

bilabiate /bai'leibiɪt/ *adj.* двугубый.

bilateral /bai'lætərəl/ *adj.* двусторо́нний.

bile /bail/ *n.* желчь *f.*

bilharziasis /,bɪlhɑr'zaiəsɪs/ *n.* бильгарцио́з *m.*

bilingual /bai'lɪŋgwəl/ *adj.* двуязы́чный.

bilingualism /bai'lɪŋgwə,lɪzəm/ *n.* двуязы́чие *neut.*

bilious /'bɪlyəs/ *adj.* же́лчный.

biliousness /'bɪlyəsnɪs/ *n.* же́лчность *f.*

bilk /bɪlk/ *v.* надува́ть (на *with acc.*) *impf.*

bill /bɪl/ *n.* (*account*) счёт *m.*; (*money*) банкно́та *f.*; (*bird*) клюв *m.*

billboard /'bɪl,bɔrd/ *n.* доска́ для афи́ш *f.*

billet /'bɪlɪt/ **1.** *n.* кварти́ра *f.*; помеще́ние для постоя́ *neut.* **2.** *v.* (*mil.*) раскварти́ровать *pf.*

billfold /'bɪl,fould/ *n.* бума́жник *m.*

billhook /'bɪl,huk/ *n.* сека́ч *m.*

billiards /'bɪlyərdz/ *n.* билья́рд *m.*

billion /'bɪlyən/ *n.* миллиа́рд *m.*

billionaire /,bɪlyə'nɛər/ *n.* миллиарде́р *m.*

billon /'bɪlən/ *n.* билл
о́н *m.*

billow /'bɪlou/ **1.** *n.* вал *m.* **2.** *v.* вздыма́ться *impf.*

billposter /'bɪl,poustər/ *n.* раскле́йщик афи́ш *m.*

billy goat /'bɪli/ *n.* козёл *m.*

bimetallic /,baimə'tælɪk/ *adj.* биметалли́ческий.

bimetallism /bai'mɛtə,lɪzəm/ *n.* биметалли́зм *m.*

bimonthly /bai'mʌnθli/ **1.** *adj.* двухме́сячный. **2.** *adv.* раз в два ме́сяца.

bin /bɪn/ *n.* я́щик; за́кром *m.*

binary /'baɪnəri, -nɛri/ *adj.* двойно́й, сдво́енный.

binary digit *n.* дво́ичная ци́фра *f.*

bind /baɪnd/ *v.* свя́зывать *impf.*, связа́ть *pf.*; перевя́зывать *impf.*, перевяза́ть *pf.*; (*book*) переплета́ть *impf.*, переплести́ *pf.*

binder /'baɪndər/ *n.* (*folder*) па́пка *f.*; (*agr.*) сноповя́зка, жа́тка *f.*

bindery /'baɪndəri/ *n.* переплётная мастерска́я *f.*

binding /'baɪndɪŋ/ *n.* переплёт *m.*

bindweed /'baɪnd,wid/ *n.* вьюно́к *m.*

binge /bɪndʒ/ *n.* (*colloq.*) кутёж *m.*

bingo /'bɪŋgou/ *n.* лото́ *neut. indecl.*

binnacle /'bɪnəkəl/ *n.* нактоу́з *m.*

binocular /bə'nɒkyələr/ *adj.* бинокуля́рный.

binoculars /bə'nɒkyələrz/ *pl.* бино́кль *m.*

binomial /bai'noumiəl/ **1.** *n.* двучлён *m.* **2.** *adj.* двучлённый.

biochemical /,baiou'kɛmɪkəl/ *adj.* биохими́ческий.

biochemist /,baiou'kɛməst/ *n.* биохи́мик *m.*

biochemistry /,baiou'kɛməstri/ *n.* биохи́мия *f.*

blodegradable /,baioudri'greidəbəl/ *adj.* разлага́емый микрооргани́змами.

bioengineering /,baiou,ɛndʒə'nɪərɪŋ/ *n.* биоинжене́рия *f.*

biogenesis /,baiou'dʒɛnəsɪs/ *n.* биогене́з *m.*

biogenetic /,baioudʒə'nɛtɪk/ *adj.* биогенети́ческий.

biographer /bai'ɒgrəfər/ *n.* био́граф *m.*

biographical /,baiə'græfɪkəl/ *adj.* биографи́ческий.

biography /bai'ɒgrəfi/ *n.* биогра́фия *f.*

biological /,baiə'lɒdʒɪkəl/ *adj.* биологи́ческий.

biologist /bai'ɒlədʒɪst/ *n.* био́лог *m.*

biology /bai'ɒlədʒi/ *n.* биоло́гия *f.*

bionics /bai'ɒnɪks/ *n.* био́ника *f.*

bionomics /,baiə'nɒmɪks/ *n.* биономи́я *f.*

biophysics /,baiou'fɪzɪks/ *n.* биофи́зика *f.*

bioplasm /'baiou,plæzəm/ *n.* биопла́зма *f.*

bioplast /'baiou,plæst/ *n.* биопла́ст *m.*

biopsy /'baiɒpsi/ *n.* биопси́я *f.*

biosphere /'baiə,sfɪər/ *n.* биосфе́ра *f.*

biostatics /,baiou'stætɪks/ *n.* биоме́трия *f.*

biotic /bai'ɒtɪk/ *adj.* биоти́ческий.

bipartisan /bai'partəzən/ *adj.* двупарти́йный.

bipartite /bai'partait/ *adj.* двусторо́нний.

biped /'baipɛd/ **1.** *n.* двуно́гое (живо́тное) *neut.* **2.** *adj.* двуно́гий.

biplane /'bai,plein/ *n.* бипла́н *m.*

bipolar /bai'poulər/ *adj.* двухпо́люсный.

birch /bɜrtʃ/ **1.** *adj.* берёзовый. **2.** *n.* берёза *f.* **3.** *v.* сечь ро́згой *impf.*

bird /bɜrd/ **1.** *adj.* пти́чий. **2.** *n.* пти́ца *f.*

birdcage /'bɜrd,keidʒ/ *n.* кле́тка (для птиц) *f.*

bird-lime /'bɜrd,laim/ *n.* пти́чий клей *m.*

bird lover *n.* люби́тель птиц *m.*

bird of prey *n.* хи́щная пти́ца *f.*

birdseed /'bɜrd,sid/ *n.* пти́чий корм.

bird's-eye view /'bɜrdz,ai/ *n.* вид с пти́чьего полёта *m.*

bird's nest *n.* пти́чье гнездо́ *neut.*

bird watcher *n.* орнито́лог (-люби́тель) *m.*

Birobidzhan /,bɪroubi'dʒɑn/ *n.* Биробиджа́н *m.*

birth /bɜrθ/ *n.* рожде́ние *neut.*; (*giving birth*) ро́ды *pl.* **to give birth to** *v.* рожда́ть *impf.*, роди́ть *pf.*

birth certificate *n.* ме́трика *f.*

birth control *n.* противозача́точные ме́ры *pl.*

birthday /'bɜrθ,dei/ *n.* день рожде́ния *m.*

birthmark /'bɜrθ,mark/ *n.* роди́мое пятно́ *neut.*, ро́динка *f.*

birthplace /'bɜrθ,pleis/ *n.* ме́сто рожде́ния *neut.*

birth rate *n.* рожда́емость *neut.*

birthright /'bɜrθ,rait/ *n.* пра́во по рожде́нию *neut.*

biscuit /'bɪskɪt/ *n.* суха́рь *m.*, сухо́е пече́нье *neut.*

bisection /bai'sɛkʃən/ *n.* деле́ние попола́м *neut.*

bisector /bai'sɛktər/ *n.* (*math.*) биссектри́са *f.*

bisexual /bai'sɛkʃuəl/ *adj.* двупо́лый.

bisexuality /bai,sɛkʃu'ælɪti/ *n.* двупо́лость *f.*

Bishkek /bɪʃ'kɛk/ *n.* (*formerly: Frunze*) Бишке́к *m.*

bishop /'bɪʃəp/ *n.* епи́скоп *m.*; (*chess*) слон *m.*

bishopric /'bɪʃəprɪk/ *n.* епа́рхия *f.*

bismuth /'bɪzməθ/ *n.* ви́смут *m.*

bison /'baisən/ *n.* бизо́н *m.*

bistoury /'bɪstəri/ *n.* бистури́ *neut. indecl.*

bistre /'bɪstər/ *n.* бистр *m.*

bistro /'bɪstrou/ *n.* бистро́ *neut. indecl.*; ресто́ра́нчик *m.*

bit /bɪt/ *n.* кусо́чек *m.*; (*mech.*) сверло́ *neut.*; (*horse*) удила́ *pl.*

bitbrace /'bɪt,breis/ *n.* коловоро́т *f.*

bitch /bɪtʃ/ *n.* су́ка *f.*

bitchiness /'bɪtʃinɪs/ *n.* зло́стность *f.*

bitchy /'bɪtʃi/ *adj.* злой, зло́бный.

bite /bait/ **1.** *n.* уку́с *m.*; (*morsel*) кусо́чек *m.* **2.** *v.* куса́ть *impf.*, укуси́ть *pf.*

biting /'baitɪŋ/ *adj.* ре́зкий, е́дкий.

bitter /'bɪtər/ *adj.* го́рький.

bittern /'bɪtərn/ *n.* (*bird*) вы́пь *f.*

bitterness /'bɪtərnɪs/ *n.* го́речь *f.*

bittersweet /,bɪtər'swit/ *adj.* горькова́то-сла́дкий.

bitumen /bai'tumən/ *n.* би́тум *m.*

bituminous /bai'tumənəs/ *adj.* би́тумный.

bivalent /bai'veilənt/ *adj.* (*chem.*) двухвале́нтный.

bivalve /'bai,vælv/ *adj.* двуство́рчатый.

bivouac /'bɪvu,æk/ *n.* бива́к *m.*

biweekly /bai'wikli/ *adj.* двухнеде́льный.

bizarre /bɪ'zar/ *adj.* (*odd*) стра́нный, причу́дливый.

blab /blæb/ *v.* выба́лтывать *impf.*

black /blæk/ *adj.* чёрный.

blackberry /'blæk,beri/ *n.* ежеви́ка *f.*

blackbird /'blæk,bɜrd/ *n.* (*чёрный*) дрозд *m.*

blackboard /'blæk,bɔrd/ *n.* (кла́ссная) доска́ *f.*

black currant *n.* чёрная сморо́дина *f.*

blackdamp /'blæk,dæmp/ *n.* мёртвый во́здух *m.*

blacken /'blækən/ *v.t.* черни́ть *impf.*, зачерни́ть *pf.*; *v.i.* черне́ть *impf.*, зачерне́ть *pf.*

Black Forest *n.* (*German: Schwarzwald*) Шва́рцвальд *m.*

blackguard /'blægard/ *n.* мерза́вец *m.*

blackhead /'blæk,hɛd/ *n.* у́горь *m.*

blacking /'blækɪŋ/ *n.* (*for boots*) ва́кса *f.*

black lead *n.* графи́т *m.*

black letter *n.* старопеча́тный (готи́ческий) шрифт *m.*

blacklist /'blæk,lɪst/ *n.* чёрный спи́сок *m.*

black magic *n.* чёрная ма́гия *f.*

blackmail /'blæk,meil/ **1.** *n.* шанта́ж *m.*, вымога́-

тельство *neut.* **2.** *v.* шантажи́ровать; вымога́ть де́ньги *impf.*

blackmailer /'blæk͵meilər/ *n.* шантажи́ст *m.*

black market *n.* чёрный ры́нок *m.*

blackness /'blæknıs/ *n.* чернота́ *f.*

blackout /'blæk͵aut/ *n.* поте́ря созна́ния *f.*

blacksmith /'blæk͵smıθ/ *n.* кузне́ц *m.*

blackthorn /'blæk͵θɔrn/ *n.* тёрн *m.*

blackwater fever /'blæk͵wɔtər/ *n.* теха́сская лихора́дка *f.*

bladder /'blædər/ *n.* пузы́рь, мочево́й пузы́рь *m.*

bladderwort /'blædər͵wɜrt/ *n.* пузырча́тка *f.*

blade /bleid/ *n.* ле́звие *neut.*; (*of grass*) трави́нка *f.*

Blagoevgrad /blɑ'gɔyəfgrɒd/ *n.* Благо́евград *m.*

Blagoveshchensk /͵blɑgə'vɛʃɛnsk/ *n.* Благове́щенск *m.*

blah /blɑ/ *n.* (*colloq.*) галиматья́ *f.*

blain /blein/ *n.* чи́рей *m.*

blamable /'bleiməbəl/ *adj.* винова́тый.

blame /bleim/ **1.** *v.* порица́ть, вини́ть (в *with prep.*) *impf.* **2.** *n.* порица́ние *neut.*; вина́ *f.*

blameless /'bleimlıs/ *adj.* неви́нный; безупре́чный.

blameworthy /'bleim͵wɜrði/ *adj.* заслу́живающий порица́ния.

blanch /blæntʃ/ *v.t.* бели́ть *impf.*; *v.t.* бледне́ть *impf.*

blancmange /blə'mɑndʒ/ *n.* бланманже́ *neut. indecl.*

bland /blænd/ *adj.* мя́гкий; (*dull*) бесцве́тный.

blandish /'blændıʃ/ *v.* угова́ривать *impf.*

blandishment /'blændıʃmənt/ *n.* угова́ривание *neut.*

blank /blæŋk/ **1.** *adj.* пусто́й, чи́стый; (*of wall*) глухо́й; (*of cartridge*) холосто́й. **2.** *n.* бланк *m.*; пусто́е ме́сто *neut.*

blanket /'blæŋkıt/ *n.* одея́ло *neut.*

blankly /'blæŋkli/ *adv.* безуча́стно.

blare /blɛər/ **1.** *n.* рёв *m.*; зву́ки труб *pl.* **2.** *v.* гро́мко труби́ть *impf.*

blarney /'blɑrni/ *n.* лесть *f.*

blaspheme /blæs'fim/ *v.* богоху́льствовать *impf.*

blasphemer /blæs'fimər/ *n.* богоху́льник *m.*

blasphemous /'blæsfəməs/ *adj.* богоху́льный.

blasphemy /'blæsfəmi/ *n.* богоху́льство *neut.*

blast /blæst/ **1.** *n.* поры́в ве́тра; взрыв *m.* **2.** *v.* взрыва́ть *impf.*, взорва́ть *pf.*

blasted /'blæstıd/ *colloq.* прокля́тый, чёртов.

blast furnace *n.* до́мна *f.*

blastoderm /'blæstə͵dɜrm/ *n.* заро́дышевая оболо́чка *f.*

blastoff /'blæst͵ɔf/ *n.* пуск, старт *m.*

blast-proof /'blæst͵pruf/ *adj.* взрывоусто́йчивый.

blatant /'bleitn̩t/ *adj.* я́вный; (*niosy*) шу́мный, крикли́вый.

blaze /bleiz/ **1.** *n.* пла́мя *neut.*; блеск *m.* **2.** *v.* горе́ть; пыла́ть *impf.*

blazer /'bleizər/ *n.* блёйзер *m.*

blazon /'bleizən/ *n.* герб *m.*

bleach /blitʃ/ **1.** *v.t.* бели́ть; отбе́ливать *impf.*, отбели́ть *pf.*; *v.i.* отбе́ливаться *impf.*, отбели́ться *pf.* **2.** *n.* хло́рная и́звесть *f.*

bleak /blik/ *adj.* пусты́нный; уны́лый.

bleary-eyed /'blıəri͵aid/ *adj.* (*with sleep*) с за́спанными глаза́ми.

bleat /blit/ *v.* бле́ять *impf.*

bleating /'blitıŋ/ *n.* бле́яние *neut.*

bleed /blid/ *v.* истека́ть кро́вью *impf.*

bleeding /'blidıŋ/ *n.* кровотече́ние *neut.*; (*bloodletting*) кровопуска́ние *neut.*

bleep /blip/ *n.* бип, коро́ткий писк *m.*

blemish /'blɛmıʃ/ **1.** *n.* пятно́ *neut.* **2.** *v.* пятна́ть *impf.*

blend /blɛnd/ **1.** *n.* смесь *f.* **2.** *v.* сме́шивать(ся) *impf.*, смеша́ть(ся) *pf.*

blende /blɛnd/ *n.* ци́нковая обма́нка *f.*

blender /'blɛndər/ *n.* (*cul.*) ку́хонный комба́йн *m.*

bless /blɛs/ *v.* благословля́ть *impf.*, благослови́ть *pf.*

blessed /'blɛsıd/ *esp. for 3, 7* blɛst/ свяще́нный; (*blissful*) блаже́нный.

blessing /'blɛsıŋ/ *n.* (*benediction*) благослове́ние *neut.*; (*benefit*) бла́го, сча́стье *neut.*; **what a blessing!** *interj.* како́е сча́стье!

blight /blait/ **1.** *n.* ги́бель *f.* **2.** *v.* вреди́ть *impf.*

blimp /blımp/ *n.* ма́лый дирижа́бль *m.*

blind /blaind/ **1.** *adj.* слепо́й. **2.** *v.* ослепля́ть *impf.*, ослепи́ть *pf.*

blinders /'blaindərz/ *n.* шо́ры *pl.*

blindfold /'blaind͵fould/ *v.* завя́зывать глаза́ *impf.*

blinding /'blaindıŋ/ *adj.* ослепи́тельный.

blindly /'blaindli/ *adv.* сле́по, вслепу́ю; (*fig.*) безрассу́дно.

blindman's buff /'blaind͵mænz 'bʌf/ *n.* жму́рки *pl.*

blindness /'blaindnıs/ *n.* слепота́ *f.*; ослепле́ние *neut.*

blink /blıŋk/ *v.* мига́ть *impf.*, мигну́ть *pf.*; мерца́ть *impf.*

blinker /'blıŋkər/ *n.* мига́лка *f.*

bliss /blıs/ *n.* блаже́нство *neut.*

blissful /'blısfəl/ *adj.* блаже́нный; **blissful ignorance** *n.* блаже́нное неве́дение *neut.*

blister /'blıstər/ *n.* волды́рь *m.*

blithe /blaið/ *adj.* весёлый, жизнера́достный.

blitz /blıts/ *n.* бомбёжка *f.*

blizzard /'blızərd/ *n.* бура́н *m.*, мете́ль *f.*

bloat /blout/ *v.* раздува́ться *impf.*, разду́ться *pf.*

bloated /'bloutıd/ *adj.* жи́рный, разду́тый, взду́тый.

bloater /'bloutər/ *n.* копчёная сельдь *f.*

blob /blɒb/ *n.* ка́пля *f.*

bloc /blɒk/ *n.* (*polit.*) блок *m.*

block /blɒk/ **1.** *n.* глы́ба *f.*; (*of wood*) чурба́н *m.*, коло́да *f.*; (*street*) кварта́л *m.* **2.** *v.* загороди́ть *pf.*

blockade /blɒ'keid/ **1.** *n.* блока́да *f.*; **2.** *v.* блоки́ровать *impf.*

blockage /'blɒkıdʒ/ *n.* (*in traffic, etc.*) зато́р *m.*; (*pipe*) засоре́ние *neut.*

blockhead /'blɒk͵hɛd/ *n.* болва́н *m.*

blockhouse /'blɒk͵haus/ *n.* (*fort*) блокга́уз *m.*; (*log cabin*) сруб *m.*

block-printing /'blɒk͵prıntıŋ/ *n.* ксилогра́фия *f.*

blond(e) /blɒnd/ **1.** *adj.* белоку́рый. **2.** *n.* блонди́н *m.*, блонди́нка *f.*

blood /blʌd/ **1.** *adj.* кровяно́й; кро́вный. **2.** *n.* кровь *f.*

bloodbath /'blʌd͵bæθ/ *n.* (*fig.*) резня́ *f.*

bloodcurdling /'blʌd͵kɜrdlıŋ/ *adj.* ужаса́ющий.

blood donor *n.* до́нор *m.*

blood group n. гру́ппа кро́ви f.
blood heat n. температу́ра кро́ви f.
bloodhound /'blʌd,haund/ n. бладха́унд m.
bloodless /'blʌdlɪs/ adj. бескро́вный.
bloodletting /'blʌd,lɛtɪŋ/ n. кровопуска́ние neut.
blood poisoning n. зараже́ние кро́ви neut.
blood-red /'blʌd'rɛd/ adj. крова́во-кра́сный.
blood relation n. кро́вный ро́дственник m.
blood sausage n. кровяна́я колбаса́ f.
bloodshed /'blʌd,ʃɛd/ n. кровопроли́тие neut.
bloodstain /'blʌd,stein/ n. кровяно́е пятно́ neut.
bloodstained /'blʌd,steind/ adj. запа́чканный кро́вью.
bloodstream /'blʌd,strim/ n. ток кро́ви m.
bloodsucker /'blʌd,sʌkər/ n. пия́вка f.; (fig.) кровопи́йца m. and f. (decl. f.).
bloodthirstiness /'blʌd,θɜrstɪnɪs/ n. кровожа́дность f.
bloodthirsty /'blʌd,θɜrsti/ adj. кровожа́дный.
blood transfusion n. перелива́ние кро́ви neut.
bloody /'blʌdi/ adj. крова́вый.
bloom /blum/ **1.** n. расцве́т m. **2.** v. цвести́ impf.
blooming /'blumɪŋ/ adj. цвету́щий.
blossom /'blɒsəm/ **1.** n. цвето́к m. **2.** v. цвести́ impf.
blot /blɒt/ n. пятно́ neut.; (ink, etc.) кля́кса f.
blotch /blɒtʃ/ n. пятно́ neut.
blotchy /'blɒtʃi/ adj. пятни́стый.
blotting paper /'blɒtɪŋ/ промока́тельная бума́га f.
blouse /blaus/ n. блу́за f.; ко́фточка f.
blow[1] /blou/ n. уда́р m ; with one blow одни́м уда́ром; сра́зу.
blow[2] /blou/ v. дуть impf.; to blow out туши́ть impf., потуши́ть pf.; to blow up v.t. взрыва́ть impf., взорва́ть pf.; v.i. взрыва́ться impf., взорва́ться pf.
blow-by-blow account /'bloubaɪ'blou/ n. подро́бный расска́з m.
blow-dry /'blou,drai/ v. (hair) суши́ть фе́ном impf.
blower /'blouər/ n. воздуходу́вка f.
blow fly n. мясна́я му́ха f.
blow-hole /'blou,houl/ n. ды́хало neut.
blowing /'blouɪŋ/ n. дутьё neut.
blowout /'blou,aut/ n. разры́в (ши́ны) m.
blowtorch /'blou,tɔrtʃ/ n. пая́льная ла́мпа f.
blowup /'blouʌp/ n. (photog.) (colloq.) увеличе́ние neut.
blubber /'blʌbər/ n. (whale) во́рвань f.
bludgeon /'blʌdʒən/ n. дуби́нка f.
blue /blu/ adj. си́ний, голубо́й.
bluebell /'blu,bɛl/ n. колоко́льчик m.
blueberry /'blu,bɛri/ n. черни́ка f.
bluebird /'blu,bɜrd/ n. сла́вка f.
blue-blooded /'blu'blʌdɪd/ adj. голубо́й кро́ви.
blue-eyed /'blu,aid/ adj. голубогла́зый.
blueprint /'blu,prɪnt/ n. си́нька f.
bluestocking /'blu,stɒkɪŋ/ n. си́ний чуло́к m.
blue tit n. лазо́ревка f.
bluff[1] /blʌf/ **1.** n. (deception) блеф, обма́н m. **2.** v. блефова́ть impf.
bluff[2] /blʌf/ (cliff) отве́сный бе́рег m.
bluish /'bluɪʃ/ adj. синева́тый.
blunder /'blʌndər/ **1.** n. гру́бая оши́бка f.; про́мах m. **2.** v. сде́лать гру́бую оши́бку pf.
blunderbuss /'blʌndər,bʌs/ n. мушкето́н m.

blundering /'blʌndərɪŋ/ adj. неуклю́жий.
blunt /blʌnt/ adj. тупо́й; (frank) прямо́й.
bluntness /'blʌntnɪs/ n. ту́пость f.; (frankness) прямота́ f.
blur /blɜr/ n. пятно́ neut.
blurb /blɜrb/ n. рекла́ма f.
blurt /blɜrt/ v. выба́лтывать impf.
blush /blʌʃ/ **1.** n. кра́ска стыда́; кра́ска смуще́ния f. **2.** v. красне́ть impf., покрасне́ть pf.
bluster /'blʌstər/ n. рёв, шум m.
boa /'bouə/ n. (snake) боа́ m. indecl., уда́в m.
boar /bɔr/ n. бо́ров m.; (wild) каба́н m.
board /bɔrd/ **1.** n. доска́ f.; борт m.; (meals) стол m.; (adm.) сове́т m. **2.** v. сесть (в or на with acc.) pf.
boarder /'bɔrdər/ n. пансионе́р m., пансионе́рка f.; квартира́нт m., квартира́нтка f.
boarding house /'bɔrdɪŋ/ n. пансио́н m.
boarding school n. шко́ла-интерна́т f.
boardwalk /'bɔrd,wɔk/ n. доща́тый насти́л m.
boast /boust/ **1.** n. хвастовство́ neut. **2.** v. хва́статься impf., похва́статься pf.
boaster /'boustər/ n. хвасту́н m., хвасту́нья f.
boastful /'boustfəl/ adj. хвастли́вый.
boasting /'boustɪŋ/ n. хва́стание neut.
boat /bout/ **1.** adj. ло́дочный **2.** n. ло́дка f.; (ship) су́дно neut., кора́бль m.
boat deck n. шлю́почная па́луба f.
boat hook n. баго́р m.
boat house n. сара́й для ло́док m.
boating /'boutɪŋ/ n. ло́дочный спорт m.; to go boating v. ката́ться на ло́дке impf.
boatman /'boutmən/ n. ло́дочник m.
boatswain /'bousən/ n. бо́цман m.
bob[1] /bɒb/ **1.** n. (movement) ре́зкое движе́ние neut. **2.** v. (up and down) подпры́гивать impf.
bob[2] /bɒb/ **1.** n. (hair) коро́ткая стри́жка f.; (pendulum) ги́ря f.; (bobsled) бобсле́й m. **2.** (hair) ко́ротко стричь impf.
bobbed /bɒbd/ adj. (ко́ротко) подстри́женный.
bobbin /'bɒbɪn/ n. шпу́лька, кату́шка f.
bobble /'bɒbəl/ n. помпо́н m.
bobcat /'bɒb,kæt/ n. америка́нская рысь f.
bobsled /'bɒb,slɛd/ n. бобсле́й m.
bobstay /'bɒb,stei/ n. (naut.) ватерштаг m.
bobtail /'bɒb,teil/ adj. с обре́занным хвосто́м.
bode /boud/ v. предвеща́ть, сули́ть impf.
bodice /'bɒdɪs/ n. корса́ж, лиф m.
bodiless /'bɒdɪlɪs/ adj. бестеле́сный.
bodily /'bɒdli/ adj. теле́сный, физи́ческий.
body /'bɒdi/ n. те́ло neut.; (corpse) труп m.; (of car) ку́зов m.
body blow n. (sports) уда́р по ко́рпусу m.
bodybuilder /'bɒdi,bɪldər/ n. (sport) культури́ст m.
bodyguard /'bɒdi,gɑrd/ n. ли́чная охра́на f.; телохрани́тель m.
bodysnatcher /'bɒdi,snætʃər/ n. похити́тель тру́пов m.
bog /bɒg/ n. боло́то neut.
boggle /'bɒgəl/ v. потряса́ть impf.
boggy /'bɒgi/ adj. боло́тистый.
bog oak n. морёный дуб m.
Bogotá /,bougə'tɑ/ n. Богота́ f.
bogus /'bougəs/ adj. подде́льный, фикти́вный.
Bohemian /bou'himiən/ adj. боге́мский; (fig.) боге́мный, боге́мистый.

Bohemian Forest (*Czech:Šumava*) *n.* Шума́ва *f.*
boil[1] /bɔil/ *v.* кипяти́ть; вари́ть *impf.*; *v.i.*
кипе́ть; вари́ться *impf.*
boil[2] /bɔil/ *n.* (*med.*) нары́в, фуру́нкул *m.*
boiled /bɔild/ *adj.* (*food*) варёный; (*water*)
кипячёный.
boiler /'bɔilər/ *n.* котёл *m.*
boiler room *n.* коте́льная *f.*
boiling /'bɔiliŋ/ *n.* кипе́ние *neut.*
boisterous /'bɔistərəs/ *adj.* бу́йный; шумли́вый.
bold /bould/ *adj.* сме́лый; де́рзкий.
boldly /'bouldli/ *adv.* сме́ло.
boldness /'bouldnɪs/ *n.* сме́лость *f.*
bold type *n.* жи́рный шрифт *m.*
bole /boul/ *n.* (*tree*) ствол *m.*
bolero /bə'leərou/ *n.* болеро́ *neut. indecl.*
Bolivia /bə'lɪviə/ *n.* Боли́вия *f.*
boll /boul/ *n.* (*bot.*) семенна́я коро́бочка *f.*
Bologna /bə'lounyə/ *n.* Боло́нья *f.*
bolometer /bou'lɒmɪtər/ *n.* боло́метр *m.*
Bolshevik /'boulʃəvɪk/ **1.** *adj.* большеви́стский.
2. *n.* большеви́к *m.*
bolster /'boulstər/ **1.** *n.* ва́лик *m.* **2.** *v.* подпи-
ра́ть *impf.*
bolt /boult/ **1.** *n.* (*door*) засо́в *m.*, задви́жка *f.*;
(*lightning*) уда́р мо́лнии *m.* **2.** *v.* запира́ть на
засо́в *impf.*; (*to flee*) бро́ситься *pf.*
boltrope /'boult,roup/ *n.* ликтро́с *m.*
bolus /'bouləs/ *n.* пилю́ля *f.*
bomb /bɒm/ **1.** *n.* бо́мба *f.* **2.** *v.* бомби́ть *impf.*
bombard /bɒm'bɑrd/ *v.* (*mil., phys.*) бомбар-
дирова́ть *impf.*; **to bombard with questions** *v.*
засыпа́ть вопро́сами *impf.*
bombardier /,bɒmbər'dɪər/ *n.* бомбарди́р *m.*
bombardment /bɒm'bɑrdmənt/ *n.* бомбарди-
ро́вка *f.*
bombardon /'bɒmbərdən/ *n.* бомбардо́н *m.*
bombast /'bɒmbæst/ *n.* напы́щенность *f.*
bombastic /bɒm'bæstɪk/ *adj.* напы́щенный, веле-
речи́вый.
Bombay /bɒm'bei/ *n.* Бомбе́й *m.* (*see Mumbai*).
bomber /'bɒmər/ *n.* (*aircraft*) бомбардиро́вщик
m.
bombshell /'bɒm,ʃel/ *n.* (*fig.*) сенса́ция *f.*
bomb shelter *n.* бомбоубе́жище *neut.*
bombsight /'bɒm,sait/ *n.* авиаприце́л *m.*
bomb site *n.* разбомблённый уча́сток *m.*
bona fide /'bou,nə faid, 'bɒnə 'faidi/ *adj.* добро-
со́вестный.
bonanza /bə'nænzə/ *n.* (*good luck*) везе́ние *neut.*
bond /bɒnd/ *n.* связь *f.*; *pl.* (*econ.*) облига́ция *f.*;
(*shackles*) око́вы.
bondage /'bɒndɪdʒ/ *n.* ра́бство *neut.*
bondholder /'bɒnd,houldər/ *n.* владе́лец обли-
га́ций *m.*
bonding /'bɒndiŋ/ *n.* перевя́зка *f.*; (*chem.*) связь
f.
bone /boun/ **1.** *adj.* ко́стный. **2.** *n.* кость *f.*
bone china *n.* то́нкий фарфо́р *m.*
bone-dry /'boun'drai/ *adj.* абсолю́тно сухо́й.
bonehead /'boun,hed/ *n.* (*colloq.*) болва́н *m.*
boneless /'bounlɪs/ *adj.* бескостный.
bone meal *n.* ко́стная мука́ *f.*
bonesetter /'boun,setər/ *n.* костопра́в *m.*
bonfire /'bɒn,faiər/ *n.* костёр *m.*
boning /'bouniŋ/ *n.* удале́ние косте́й *neut.*
bon mot /'bɒn 'mou/ *n.* остро́та *f.*

Bonn /bɒn/ *n.* Бонн *m.*
bonnet /'bɒnɪt/ *n.* че́пчик *m.*
bonus /'bounəs/ *n.* пре́мия *f.*, премиа́льные *pl.*
bon vivant /'bɒn vi'vɑnt/ *n.* бонвива́н *m.*
bon voyage /,bɒn vɔi'ɑʒ/ *interj.* до́брого пути́;
to wish s.o. bon voyage *v.* жела́ть (*with dat.*)
до́брого пути́ *impf.*
bony /'bouni/ *adj.* кости́стый.
bonze /bɒnz/ *n.* бо́нза *m.*
boo /bu/ *v.* освисты́вать *impf.*
booby /'bubi/ *n.* дура́к *m.*, тупи́ца *m.* and *f.*
(*decl. f.*)
booby prize *n.* шутовска́я награ́да *f.*
booby trap *n.* лову́шка *f.*
boogie-woogie /'bugi 'wugi/ *n.* бу́ги-ву́ги *neut.*
indecl.
book /buk/ **1.** *adj.* кни́жный. **2.** *n.* кни́га *f.* **3.** *v.*
(*reserve*) брони́ровать; зака́зывать *impf.*
bookbinder /'buk,baindər/ *n.* переплётчик *m.*
bookbinding /'buk,baindiŋ/ *n.* переплётное де́ло
neut.
bookcase /'buk,keis/ *n.* кни́жный шкаф *m.*
book-end /'buk,end/ *n.* подста́вка для книг *f.*
booking /'bukiŋ/ *n.* (*reservation*) бро́ня *f.*
bookish /'bukɪʃ/ *adj.* кни́жный; учёный.
bookkeeper /'buk,kipər/ *n.* бухга́лтер *m.*
bookkeeping /'buk,kipiŋ/ *n.* бухгалте́рия *f.*
booklet /'buklɪt/ *n.* брошю́ра *f.*
bookmaker /'buk,meikər/ *n.* (*sports*) букме́кер
m.
bookmark /'buk,mɑrk/ *n.* кни́жная закла́дка *f.*
bookplate /'buk,pleit/ *n.* экслибрис *m.*
bookseller /'buk,selər/ *n.* продаве́ц книг *m.*; (*old
books*) букини́ст *m.*
bookstall /'buk,stɔl/ *n.* кни́жный кио́ск *m.*
bookstore /'buk,stɔr/ *n.* кни́жный магази́н *m.*
bookworm /'buk,wɜrm/ *n.* кни́жный червь *m.*
boom /bum/ **1.** *n.* (*sound*) гул *m.* **2.** *v.* греме́ть
impf.; (*econ.*) бы́стро расти́ *impf.*
boomerang /'bumə,ræŋ/ *n.* бумера́нг *m.*
boon /bun/ *n.* бла́го, сча́стье *neut.*
boor /bʊr/ *n.* гру́бый *or* невоспи́танный челове́к
m.
boorish /'bʊrɪʃ/ *adj.* гру́бый, невоспи́танный.
boost /bust/ *v.* повыша́ть, поднима́ть *impf.*
boot /but/ *n.* сапо́г *m.*
bootblack /'but,blæk/ *n.* чисти́льщик сапо́г *m.*
bootee /'buti/ *n.* (*baby's*) пине́тка *f.*
Boötes /bou'outiz/ *n.* (*astr.*) Волопа́с *m.*
booth /buθ/ *n.* бу́дка *f.*, кио́ск *m.*
bootless /'butlɪs/ *adj.* бесполе́зный.
bootlicker /'but,lɪkər/ *n.* (*colloq.*) подхали́м *m.*,
подли́за *m.* and *f.* (*decl. f.*).
boot tree *n.* сапо́жная коло́дка *f.*
booty /'buti/ *n.* добы́ча *f.*
booze /buz/ *n.* (*colloq.*) (*drink*) спиртно́е *neut.*
boozer /'buzər/ *n.* (*colloq.*) пья́ница *m.* and *f.*
(*decl. f.*).
boracic /bə'ræsɪk/ *adj.* бо́рный.
borage /'bɔrɪdʒ/ *n.* огуре́чник апте́чный *m.*
borax /'bɔræks/ *n.* бура́ *f.*
Bordeaux /bɔr'dou/ *n.* (*wine*) бордо́ *neut. indecl.*;
(*city*) Бордо́ *m. indecl.*
bordello /bɔr'delou/ *n.* публи́чный дом *m.*
border /'bɔrdər/ **1.** *n.* грани́ца *f.* **2.** *v.* грани́чить
impf.

borderland /'bɔrdər,lænd/ *n.* пограничная полоса *f.*

borderline /'bɔrdər,lain/ *n.* граница *f.*

bore[1] /bɔr/ **1.** *n.* (*hole*) дыра *f.*; (*gun*) канал ствола; калибр *m.*; (*size of hole*) диаметр *m.* **2.** *v.* сверлить *impf.*

bore[2] /bɔr/ *n.* (*tedious thing*) скука *f.*; (*person*) скучный человек *m.*

boreal /'bɔriəl/ *adj.* северный.

bored /bɔrd/ *adj.* скучный; **I am bored** мне скучно, мне надоело.

boredom /'bɔrdəm/ *n.* скука *f.*

borehole /'bɔr,houl/ *n.* буровая скважина *f.*

boric acid /'bɔrik/ *n.* борная кислота *f.*

boring /'bɔriŋ/ *adj.* скучный.

Borisoglebsk /bərisə'glibsk/ *n.* Борисоглебск *m.*

Borisopol /bəri'sɔpəl/ *n.* Борисополь *m.*

born /bɔrn/ *adj.* прирождённый.

Bornholm /'bɔrnhoum, -houlm/ *n.* (*island*) Борнхольм *m.*

boron /'bɔrɒn/ *n.* бор *m.*

borough /'bʒrou/ *n.* городской район *m.*; (*town*) город *m.*

Borovets /'bɔrəvəts/ *n.* Боровец *m.*

borrow /'bɒrou/ *v.* (*adopt*) заимствовать *impf.*; (*receive as loan*) занимать *impf.*, занять *pf.*

borrower /'bɒrouər/ *n.* заёмщик *m.*; (*in library*) абонент, читатель *m.*

borscht /bɔɪʃt/ *n.* борщ *m.*

borzoi /'bɔrzɔi/ *n.* Русская псовая борзая *f.*

bosk /bɒsk/ *n.* рощица *f.*

Bosnia /'bɒzniə/ *n.* Босния *f.*

bosom /'buzəm/ *n.* грудь, пазуха *f.*

boss /bɒs/ **1.** *n.* хозяин, начальник *m.* **2.** *v.* хозяйничать, управлять *impf.*

bossa nova /'bɒsə 'nouvə/ *n.* босса-нова *f.*

bossy /'bɒsi/ *adj.* (*colloq.*) начальственный

botanical /bə'tænikəl/ *adj.* ботанический.

botanist /'bɒtn̩ist/ *n.* ботаник *m.*

botany /'bɒtn̩i/ *n.* ботаника *f.*

botch /bɒtʃ/ *n.* халтура *f.*

both /bouθ/ *pron.*, *adj.* оба *m.* and *neut.*, обе *f.*

both...and *conj.* и...и; как...так и.

bother /'bɒðər/ *v.* (*worry*) беспокоить *impf.*; (*pester*) мешать *impf.*

bothersome /'bɒðərsəm/ *adj.* надоедливый.

bottle /'bɒtl̩/ **1.** *n.* бутылка *f.* **2.** *v.* разливать по бутылкам *impf.*

bottle-feed /'bɒtl̩,fid/ *v.* вскармливать искусственно.

bottle green *adj.* бутылочно-зелёного цвета.

bottleneck /'bɒtl̩,nɛk/ *n.* горлышко (бутылки) *neut.*; (*fig.*) (*narrow passage*) узкий проход *m.*

bottom /'bɒtəm/ *n.* дно *neut.*, низ *m.*, нижняя часть *f.*

bottomless /'bɒtəmlɪs/ *adj.* бездонный.

bottommost /'bɒtəm,moust/ *adj.* самый низкий.

bottomry /'bɒtəmri/ *n.* (*naut.*, *leg.*) бодмерея *f.*

botulism /'bɒtʃə,lɪzəm/ *n.* ботулизм *m.*

boudoir /'budwɑr/ *n.* будуар *m.*

bougainvillea /,bugən'vɪliə/ *n.* бугенвиллея *f.*

bough /bau/ *n.* сук *m.*

bougie /'budʒi/ *n.* (*med.*) буж *m.*

bouillon /'bulyɒn/ *n.* бульон *m.*

boulder /'bouldər/ *n.* валун *m.*

boulevard /'bulə,vɑrd/ *n.* бульвар *m.*

bounce /bauns/ *v.* отскакивать *impf.*, отскочить *pf.*

bouncer /'baunsər/ *n.* (*colloq.*) вышибала *m.* and *f.* (*decl. f.*).

bouncing /'baunsɪŋ/ *n.* подпрыгивание *neut.*

bouncy /'baunsi/ *adj.* упругий.

bound[1] /baund/ **1.** *pl. n.* граница *f.*, предел *m.* **2.** *v.* ограничивать *impf.*, ограничить *pf.*

bound[2] /baund/ **1.** *adj.* (*pred.*) направляющийся. **2.** *v.* прыгать, быстро бежать *impf.*

bounder /'baundər/ *n.* хам *m.*

boundless /'baundlɪs/ *adj.* безграничный; беспредельный.

bountiful /'bauntəfəl/ *adj.* (*person*) щедрый; (*ample*) обильный.

bounty /'baunti/ *n.* щедрость *f.*; (*reward*) награда *f.*

bouquet /bou'kei, bu-/ *n.* букет *m.*; (*of wine*) аромат *m.*

bourbon /'bɜrbən/ *n.* (*whisky*) бурбон *m.*

bourgeois /bur'ʒwa/ **1.** *adj.* буржуазный. **2.** *n.* буржуа *m. indecl.*

bourgeoisie /,burʒwa'zi/ *n.* буржуазия *f.*

bout /baut/ *n.* схватка *f.*; (*of illness*) приступ *m.*

boutique /bu'tik/ *n.* модная лавка *f.*

boutonniere /,butn̩'ɪər/ *n.* бутоньерка *f.*

bovine /'bouvain/ *adj.* бычачий.

bow[1] /bau/ **1.** *n.* поклон *m.* **2.** *v.* кланяться *impf.*, поклониться *pf.*

bow[2] /bou/ *n.* (*archery*) лук *m.*; (*ribbon*) бант *m.*; (*mus.*) смычок *m.*

bow[3] /bau/ *n.* (*ship*) нос *m.*

bow compass /bou/ *n.* крон-циркуль *m.*

bowels /'bauəlz/ *n.* кишки, внутренности, недра *pl.*

bower /'bauər/ *n.* (*arbor*) беседка *f.*

bowl[1] /boul/ *n.* чаша; миска *f.*; (*sport*) кубок *m.*

bowl[2] /boul/ *v.* играть в шары or в кегли *impf.*

bowlegged /'bou,lɛgid, -,lɛgd/ *adj.* кривоногий.

bowler /'boulər/ *n.* (*hat*) котелок *m.*

bowline /'boulɪn/ *n.* (*knot*) беседочный узел *m.*

bowling /'boulɪŋ/ *n.* (*game*) кегли *pl.*

bow saw /bou/ *n.* лучковая пила *f.*

bowshot /'bou,ʃɒt/ *n.* дальность полёта стрелы *f.*

bowsprit /'bausprɪt, 'bou-/ *n.* (*naut.*) бушприт *m.*

bowstring /'bou,strɪŋ/ *n.* тетива *f.*

bow-wow /'bau'wau/ *interj.* (*colloq.*) (*bark*) гав-гав!

box[1] /bɒks/ *n.* коробка *f.*, ящик *m.*; (*theat.*) ложа *f.*

box[2] /bɒks/ *v.* боксировать *impf.*

box calf *n.* бокс *m.*

boxcar /'bɒks,kɑr/ *n.* крытый вагон, товарный вагон *m.*

boxer /'bɒksər/ *n.* (*fighter; dog*) боксёр *m.*

boxing /'bɒksɪŋ/ *n.* бокс *m.*

box office *n.* театральная касса, билетная касса *f.*; **box-office success** *n.* кассовый успех *m.*

box pleat *n.* бантовая складка *f.*

boxwood /'bɒks,wud/ *n.* самшит *m.*

box wrench *n.* торцевой гаечный ключ *m.*

boy /bɔi/ *n.* мальчик *m.*

boyar /bou'yar, 'bɔiər/ *n.* боярин *m.*

boycott /'bɔikɒt/ **1.** *n.* бойкот *m.* **2.** *v.* бойкотировать *impf. and pf.*

boyfriend /'bɔifrɛnd/ *n.* друг, приятель *m.*
boyhood /'bɔihʊd/ *n.* отрочество *neut.*
boyish /'bɔiiʃ/ *adj.* отроческий, мальчишеский.
bra /bra/ (*colloq.*) *n.* лифчик *m.*
brace /breis/ **1.** *n.* скрепа *f.* **2.** *v.* скреплять *impf.*, скрепить *pf.*
bracelet /'breislit/ *n.* браслет *m.*
brachial /'breikiəl/ *adj.* плечевой.
brachycephalic /ˌbrækisə'fælik/ *adj.* брахицефальный.
bracing /'breisiŋ/ *adj.* (*climate, etc.*) бодрящий.
bracken /'brækən/ *n.* (*bot.*) орляк *m.*
bracket /'brækit/ *n.* (*printing*) скобка *f.*; (*support*) кронштейн *m.*
brackish /'brækiʃ/ *adj.* солоноватый.
bract /brækt/ *n.* прицветник *m.*
brad /bræd/ *n.* штифт *m.*
brag /bræg/ *v.* хвастаться *impf.*
braggart /'brægərt/ *n.* хвастун *m.*
braid /breid/ **1.** *n.* коса *f.* **2.** *v.* заплетать *impf.*, заплести *pf.*
Braille /breil/ *n.* шрифт Брайля *m.*
brain /brein/ **1.** *n.* мозг *m.*; рассудок *m.* **2.** *adj.* мозговой.
brainchild /'brein,tʃaild/ *n.* идея *f.*; детище *neut.*
brainless /'breinlis/ *adj.* глупый, безмозглый.
brainstorm /'brein,stɔrm/ *n.* блестящая идея *f.*
brainwash /'brein,wɒʃ/ *v.* забивать мозги *impf.*
brainwashing /'brein,wɒʃiŋ/ *n.* забивание мозгов *neut.*
brainy /'breini/ *adj.* (*colloq.*) мозговитый.
braise /breiz/ *v.* тушить *impf.*
brake /breik/ **1.** *n.* тормоз *m.* **2.** *v.* тормозить *impf.*
brakeman /'breikmən/ *n.* тормозной кондуктор *m.*
brake shoe *n.* тормозной башмак *m.*
braking /'breikiŋ/ *n.* торможение *neut.*
bramble /'bræmbəl/ *n.* ежевика *f.*
bran /bræn/ *n.* отруби *pl.*
branch /bræntʃ/ **1.** *n.* (*subject*) отрасль *f.*; (*department*) отделение *neut.*; (*tree*) ветвь, ветка *f.* **2.** *adj.* филиальный. **3.** *v.* разветвляться *impf.*, разветвиться *pf.*
branchia /'bræŋkiə/ *n.* жабра *f.*
branchy /'bræntʃi/ *adj.* ветвистый.
brand /brænd/ **1.** *n.* (*branding piece*) головня *f.*; (*trademark*) фабричная марка *f.*; (*fig.*) клеймо *neut.* **2.** *v.* клеймить *impf.*
brandish /'brændiʃ/ *v.* махать, размахивать (*with instr.*) *impf.*
brand-name /'brænd,neim/ *adj.* фирменный.
brand-new /'bræn'nu/ *adj.* совершенно новый.
brandy /'brændi/ *n.* коньяк *m.*
brash /bræʃ/ *n.* (*bits*) обломки *pl.*
Braşov /bra'ʃɔv/ *n.* Брашов *m.*
brass /bræs/ *n.* латунь, жёлтая медь *f.*
brassard /'bræsard/ *n.* нарукавник *m.*
brass band *n.* духовой оркестр *m.*
brassiere /brə'zɪər/ *n.* бюстгальтер *m.*
brass knuckles *n.* кастет *m.*
brassy /'bræsi/ *adj.* латунный.
brat /bræt/ *n.* (*pej.*) озорник *m.*
Bratislava /ˌbræti'slavə, ˌbrata-, 'bratɪ,slava/ *n.* Братислава *f.*
Bratsk /bratsk/ *n.* Братск *m.*

brattice /'brætis/ *n.* вентиляционная перегородка *f.*
bravado /brə'vadou/ *n.* бравада *f.*
brave /breiv/ *adj.* храбрый.
bravery /'breivəri/ *n.* храбрость *f.*
bravo /'bravou/ *interj.* браво!
bravura /brə'vyʊrə/ **1.** *n.* бравурность *f.* **2.** *adj.* бравурный.
brawl /brɔl/ **1.** *n.* шумная ссора *f.*, скандал *m.* **2.** *v.* скандалить *impf.*
brawn /brɔn/ *n.* мускулы *pl.*
brawny /'brɔni/ *adj.* мускулистый.
bray /brei/ *n.* крик осла *m.*
braze /breiz/ *v.* (*tech.*) паять твёрдым припоем *impf.*
brazen /'breizən/ *adj.* медный, латунный; (*fig.*) бесстыдный.
brazier /'breizər/ *n.* жаровня *f.*
Brazzaville /'bræzə,vil, 'brazə-/ *n.* Браззавиль *m.*
breach /britʃ/ *n.* (*break*) пролом *m.*, (*of law, etiquette, etc.*) нарушение *neut.*
bread /brɛd/ **1.** *n.* хлеб *m.* **2.** *adj.* хлебный.
breadcrumb /'brɛd,krʌm/ *n.* крошка хлеба *f.*
breadfruit /'brɛd,frut/ *n.* плод хлебного дерева *m.*
bread knife *n.* хлебный нож *m.*
bread line *n.* очередь за бесплатным питанием *f.*
breadth /brɛdθ/ *n.* ширина *f.*
breadthways /'brɛdθ,weiz/ *adv.* в ширину.
breadwinner /'brɛd,winər/ *n.* кормилец *m.*, кормилица *f.*
break /breik/ **1.** *n.* прорыв, разрыв *m.*, (*pause*) перерыв *m.*; пауза *f.* **2.** *v.* ломать *impf.*, сломать *pf.*; разбивать *impf.*; (*violate*) нарушать *impf.*; *v.i.* ломаться *impf.*, сломаться *pf.*; **to break into** вламываться *impf.*, вломиться *pf.*; **to break through** прорываться *impf.*, прорваться *pf.*
breakable /'breikəbəl/ *adj.* ломкий.
breakage /'breikidʒ/ *n.* поломка *f.*
breakaway /'breikə,wei/ *n.* отход *m.*
breakdown /'breik,daun/ *n.* (*mechanical failure*) авария, поломка *f.*
breaker /'breikər/ *n.* (*wave*) бурун *m.*; (*elect.*) прерыватель, выключатель *m.*
breakers /'breikərz/ *n.* прибой *m.*
breakfast /'brɛkfəst/ **1.** *n.* завтрак *m.* **2.** *v.* завтракать *impf.*, позавтракать *pf.*
break-in /'breik,in/ *n.* взлом *m.*
breakneck /'breik,nɛk/ *adj.*: **at breakneck speed** *adv.* сломя голову.
breakout /'breik,aut/ *n.* (*escape*) побег *m.*
breakthrough /'breik,θru/ *n.* (*mil.*) прорыв *m.*; (*tech.*) шаг вперёд *m.*
breakup /'breik,ʌp/ *n.* развал, распад *m.*
breakwater /'breik,wɔtər/ *n.* волнорез *m.*
bream /brim, brim/ *n.* (*fish*) лещ *m.*
breast /brɛst/ **1.** *n.* грудь *f.* **2.** *adj.* грудной; нагрудный.
breastplate /'brɛst,pleit/ *n.* нагрудник *m.*
breast stroke *n.* брасс *m.*; плавание брассом *neut.*
breastwork /'brɛst,wɜrk/ *n.* повышенный бруствер *m.*
breath /brɛθ/ *n.* дыхание *neut.*
breathe /brið/ *v.* дышать *impf.*

breathing /'briðɪŋ/ n. дыхáние neut.
breathless /'brɛθlɪs/ adj. запыхáвшийся.
breccia /'brɛtʃɪə/ n. брéкчия f.
breech /britʃ/ n. (gun) казённая часть f.
breeches /'brɪtʃɪz/ pl. брúджи pl.
breed /brid/ **1.** n. порóда f. **2.** v.t. выводúть, разводúть impf.; v.i. размножáться impf.
breeder /'bridər/ n. животновóд m.
breeding /'bridɪŋ/ n. воспúтанность f.; разведéние neut.
breeze /briz/ n. бриз, лёгкий ветерóк m.
breezy /'brizi/ adj. свéжий; (lively) живóй.
Bretagne /brə'tany³/ n. (province) Бретáнь f.
brethren /'brɛðrɪn/ n. брáтья, собрáтья pl.
breve /briv, brɛv/ n. (mus.) брéвис m.
breviary /'brivi,ɛri/ n. трéбник m.
brevier /brə'vɪər/ n. (print) петúт m.
brevity /'brɛvɪti/ n. крáткость f.
brew /bru/ v. (beer) варúть (пúво) impf.
brewer /'bruər/ n. пивовáр m.
brewery /'bruəri/ n. пивовáренный завóд m.
brewing /'bruɪŋ/ n. пивоварéние neut.
bribable /'braibəbəl/ adj. подкýпный, продáжный.
bribe /braib/ **1.** n. взя́тка f., пóдкуп m. **2.** v. подкупáть impf., подкупúть pf.
bribery /'braibəri/ n. взя́точничество neut.
bric-a-brac /'brɪkə,bræk/ n. безделýшки pl.
brick /brɪk/ **1.** n. кирпúч m. **2.** adj. кирпúчный.
bricklayer /'brɪk,leiər/ n. кáменщик m.
bricklaying /'brɪk,leiɪŋ/ n. клáдка кирпичá f.
brickwork /'brɪk,wɜrk/ n. кирпúчная клáдка f.
bridal /'braidl/ adj. свáдебный.
bride /braid/ n. невéста f.
bridegroom /'braid,grum/ n. женúх m.
bridesmaid /'braidz,meid/ n. подрýжка невéсты f.
bridge[1] /brɪdʒ/ n. мост m.
bridge[2] /brɪdʒ/ n. (cards) бридж m.
bridgehead /'brɪdʒ,hɛd/ n. плацдáрм m.
bridle /'braidl/ **1.** n. уздá f. **2.** v.t. обуздывать impf.
brief /brif/ adj. корóткий; (concise) крáткий.
briefcase /'brif,keis/ n. портфéль m.
briefing /'brifɪŋ/ n. (mil.) инструктáж m.
briefness /'brifnɪs/ n. крáткость f.
brier /'braiər/ n. (rose) шипóвник m.; (heather) вéреск m.
brig /brɪg/ n. (naut.) бриг m.
brigade /brɪ'geid/ n. бригáда; комáнда f.
brigadier /,brɪgə'diər/ n. (mil.) бригадúр m.
brigand /'brɪgənd/ n. разбóйник m.
brigandage /'brɪgəndɪdʒ/ n. бандитúзм m.
brigantine /'brɪgən,tin/ n. бригантúна f.
bright /brait/ adj. я́ркий, блестя́щий.
brighten /'braitn/ v. проясня́ться impf., прояснúться pf.
brightness /'braitnɪs/ n. я́ркость f.
Bright's disease /braits/ n. брáйтова болéзнь f.
brill /brɪl/ n. (fish) камбалá-ромб f.
brilliance /'brɪlyəns/ n. блеск m.
brilliant /'brɪlyənt/ adj. блестя́щий.
brim /brɪm/ n. край m.; (hat) поля́ pl.
brimful /'brɪm'fʊl/ adj. пóлный до краёв.
brine /brain/ n. рассóл m.; морскáя водá, солёная водá f.

bring /brɪŋ/ v. (carry) приносúть impf., принестú pf.; (lead) приводúть impf.; **to bring up** воспúтывать impf.
brink /brɪŋk/ n. край m.
briquette /brɪ'kɛt/ n. брикéт m.
Brisbane /'brɪzbein, -bən/ n. Брúсбен m.
brisk /brɪsk/ adj. живóй, провóрный.
brisket /'brɪskɪt/ n. грудúнка f.
briskly /'brɪskli/ adv. жúво.
bristle /'brɪsəl/ **1.** n. щетúна f. **2.** v. ощетúниться pf.
bristly /'brɪsli/ adj. щетúнистый; (prickly) колю́чий.
British /'brɪtɪʃ/ adj. англúйский; британский.
British Columbia n. Британская Колýмбия f.
Britisher /'brɪtɪʃər/ n. британец; англичáнин m., британка; англичáнка f.
Briton /'brɪtn/ n. (Celtic people) n. бритт m.
brittle /'brɪtl/ adj. хрýпкий, лóмкий.
broach /broutʃ/ n. (tech.) шúло neut.
broad /brɔd/ adj. широкий.
broadcast /'brɔd,kæst/ **1.** n. радиовещáние neut., радиопередáча f. **2.** v. передавáть по рáдио impf.
broadcasting /'brɔd,kæstɪŋ/ n. радиопередáча, трансля́ция f.
broaden /'brɔdn/ v. расширя́ть impf., расшúрить pf.; v.i. расширя́ться impf., расшúриться pf.
broadly /'brɔdli/ adv. широкó; **broadly speaking** adv. в óбщих чертáх.
broad-minded /'brɔd 'maindɪd/ adj. с широкими взгля́дами.
broadsheet /'brɔd,ʃit/ n. листóвка f.
broadside /'brɔd,said/ n. (naut.) бортовóй залп m.
broadsword /'brɔd,sɔrd/ n. палáш m.
brocade /brou'keid/ n. парчá f.
brocaded /brou'koidid/ adj. парчóвый
broccoli /'brɒkəli/ n. брóкколи pl. indecl.
brochure /brou'ʃʊr/ n. брошю́ра f., буклéт m.
brogue /broug/ n. ирлáндский акцéнт m.
broil /brɔil/ v. жáрить(ся) impf.
broiler /'brɔilər/ n. брóйлер m.
broke /brouk/ adj. (colloq.) разорённый.
broken /'broukən/ adj. разбúтый, слóманный, нарýшенный.
broker /'broukər/ n. мáклер m.
brokerage /'broukərɪdʒ/ n. (fee) комúссия f.; (business) мáклерство neut.
bromide /'broumaid, -mɪd/ n. (chem.) бромúд m.
bromine /'broumin/ n. бром m.
bronchial /'brɒŋkiəl/ adj. бронхиáльный.
bronchitis /brɒŋ'kaitɪs/ n. бронхúт m.
bronco /'brɒŋkou/ n. полудúкая лóшадь f.
brontosaurus /,brɒntə'sɔrəs/ n. бронтозáвр m.
bronze /brɒnz/ **1.** n. брóнза f. **2.** adj. брóнзовый.
brooch /broutʃ, brutʃ/ n. брошь f.
brood /brud/ n. вы́водок m.
broodmare /'brud,mɛɑr/ n. конемáтка f
broody /'brudi/ adj. уны́лый.
brook[1] /brʊk/ n. ручéй m.
brook[2] /brʊk/ v. терпéть impf.
broom /brum/ n. метлá f.
broomstick /'brum,stɪk/ n. метлóвище neut.
broth /brɔθ/ n. бульóн m.
brothel /'brɒθəl/ n. дом терпúмости m.

brother /'brʌðər/ n. брат m.
brotherhood /'brʌðər,hʊd/ n. бра́тство neut.
brother-in-law /'brʌðər ɪn ,lɔ/ n. (husband's brother) де́верь m.; (sister's husband) зять m.; (wife's brother) шу́рин m.
brotherly /'brʌðərli/ adj. бра́тский.
brouhaha /'bruhɑ,hɑ/ n. (colloq.) шуми́ха f.
brow /brau/ n. бровь f.; лоб m.
browbeat /'brau,bit/ v. запу́гивать impf.
brown /braun/ adj. кори́чневый.
brown-coal /'braun ,koul/ n. лигни́т m.
browse /brauz/ v. (among books) ры́ться (в кни́гах) impf.; (in a book) листа́ть (кни́гу) impf.
bruise /bruz/ 1. n. синя́к m. 2. v. ушиби́ть pf.
bruit /brut/ v. распространя́ть impf.
brunet /bru'nɛt/ n. брюне́т m.
brunette /bru'nɛt/ n. брюне́тка f.
brunt /brʌnt/ n. (main impact) гла́вный уда́р m.; (weight) основна́я тя́жесть f.
brush /brʌʃ/ 1. n. щётка f.; (paintbrush) кисть f. 2. v. чи́стить щёткой impf.
brushwood /'brʌʃ,wʊd/ n. за́росль f.; (dry branches) хво́рост m.
brusque /brʌsk/ adj. ре́зкий; гру́бый.
Brussels /'brʌsəlz/ n. Брюссе́ль m.
Brussels sprouts n. брюссе́льская капу́ста f.
brutal /'brutl/ adj. жесто́кий.
brutality /bru'tælɪti/ n. жесто́кость f.
brutally /'brutli/ adv. жесто́ко.
brute /brut/ n. (person) жесто́кий челове́к m.; (expl.) скоти́на m. or f. (decl. f.)
brutish /'brutɪʃ/ adj. зве́рский; гру́бый.
bryology /brai'ɒlədʒi/ n. бриоло́гия f.
bubble /'bʌbəl/ n. пузы́рь m.
bubbly /'bʌbli/ adj. пе́нящийся.
bubo /'byubou/ n. бубо́н m.
bubonic plague /byu'bɒnɪk/ n. бубо́нная чума́ f.
buccaneer /,bʌkə'nɪər/ n. пира́т m.
Bucharest /'bukə,rɛst/ n. Бухаре́ст m.
buck¹ /bʌk/ n. саме́ц m.
buck² /bʌk/ v. брыка́ться impf.
bucket /'bʌkɪt/ n. ведро́ neut.
buckle /'bʌkəl/ 1. n. пря́жка f. 2. v. застёгивать пря́жку impf.
buckler /'bʌklər/ n. небольшо́й щит m.
buckshot /'bʌk,ʃɒt/ n. кру́пная дробь f.
buckskin /'bʌk,skɪn/ n. оле́нья ко́жа f.
buck-tooth /'bʌk ,tuθ/ n. торча́щий зуб m.
buckwheat /'bʌk,wit/ n. гречи́ха f.; (cul.) гре́чневая крупа́ f.
bucolic /byu'kɒlɪk/ adj. буколи́ческий.
bud /bʌd/ 1. n. по́чка f. 2. v. пуска́ть ростки́; пуска́ть по́чки impf.
Budapest /'budə,pɛst, ,pɛʃt/ n. Будапе́шт m.
Buddha /'budə/ n. Бу́дда m.
Buddhism /'budɪzəm/ n. будди́зм m.
Buddhist /'budɪst/ 1. n. будди́ст m. 2. adj. будди́йский.
budding /'bʌdɪŋ/ n. (agric.) окулиро́вка f.
buddy /'bʌdi/ n. (colloq.) ко́реш m.
Budějovice /'butvais/ n. (also: Budweis) Ческе-Б удеёвице pl.
budge /bʌdʒ/ v. шевели́ть(ся) impf., пошевели́ть(ся) pf.
budgerigar /'bʌdʒəri,gɑr/ n. волни́стый попуга́йчик m.
budget /'bʌdʒɪt/ n. бюдже́т m.

budgetary /'bʌdʒɪ,tɛri/ adj. бюдже́тный.
Buenos Aires /'bwei'nəs ai²rɪz/ n. Бу²энос-Айрес m.
buff /bʌf/ n. бу́йволовая ко́жа f.
buffalo /'bʌfə,lou/ n. бу́йвол m.
buffer /'bʌfər/ 1. n. бу́фер m. 2. adj. бу́ферный.
buffet¹ /bə'fei/ n. буфе́т m.
buffet² /'bʌfɪt/ n. (blow) уда́р m.
buffoon /bə'fun/ n. (jocular) фигля́р m.
buffoonery /bə'funəri/ n. шутовство́ neut.
bug /bʌg/ n. бука́шка f.; (virus) ви́рус m.
Bug /bʌg, buk/ n. (river) Буг m.
bugbear /'bʌg,bɛər/ n. пу́гало neut.
bug-eyed /'bʌg ,aid/ adj. пучегла́зый.
bugle /'byugəl/ n. горн, рог m.
bugler /'byuglər/ n. горни́ст m.
build /bɪld/ v. стро́ить impf., постро́ить pf.
builder /'bɪldər/ n. строи́тель m.
building /'bɪldɪŋ/ 1. n. зда́ние neut.; (construction) постро́ение neut. 2. adj. строи́тельный.
building contractor n. строи́тель-подря́дчик m.
build-up /'bɪld ,ʌp/ n. (growth) наро́ст m.; (preparation) подгото́вка f.
built-in /'bɪlt ,ɪn/ adj. встро́енный.
built-up area /'bɪlt ʌp/ n. застро́енный райо́н m.
Bukhoro /bʊ'kɑrə/ n. (formerly: Bukhara) Бухара́ f.
bulb /bʌlb/ n. лу́ковица f.; (lamp) электри́ческая ла́мпочка f.
bulbous /'bʌlbəs/ adj. лу́ковичный.
Bulgaria /bʌl'gɛəriə, bʊl-/ n. Болга́рия f.
Bulgarian /bʌl'gɛəriən, bʊl-/ 1. adj. болга́рский. 2. n. болга́рин m.; болга́рка f.
bulge /bʌldʒ/ 1. n. вы́пуклость f. 2. v. выпя́чиваться impf., вы́пятиться pf.
bulging /'bʌldʒɪŋ/ adj. разбу́хший; вы́пуклый.
bulk /bʌlk/ n. объём m.; ма́сса; бо́льшая часть f.
bulkhead /'bʌlk,hed/ n. (naut.) перебо́рка f.
bulky /'bʌlki/ adj. объёмистый.
bull /bʊl/ 1. n. бык m. 2. adj. бы́чий.
bull calf n. бычо́к m.
bulldog /'bʊl,dɒg/ n. бульдо́г m.
bulldozer /'bʊl,douzər/ n. бульдо́зер m.
bullet /'bʊlɪt/ n. пу́ля f.
bulletin /'bʊlɪtɪn/ n. бюллете́нь m.; сво́дка f.
bulletin board n. доска́ объявле́ний f.
bulletproof /'bʊlɪt,pruf/ adj. пуленепробива́емый.
bullfight /'bʊl,fait/ n. бой быко́в m.
bullfighter /'bʊl,faitər/ n. матадо́р m.
bullfinch /'bʊl,fɪntʃ/ n. снеги́рь m.
bullfrog /'bʊl,frɒg/ n. лягу́шка-бык f.
bullhead /'bʊl,hed/ n. (fish) подка́менщик m.
bullion /'bʊlyən/ n. сли́ток зо́лота or серебра́ m.
bull-necked /'bʊl ,nɛkt/ adj. с бы́чьей ше́ей.
bullock /'bʊlək/ n. вол m.
bull's-eye /'bʊlz ,ai/ n. я́блоко мише́ни neut.
bull terrier n. бультерье́р m.
bully /'bʊli/ n. зади́ра, забия́ка m. and f. (decl. f.).
bully beef n. мясны́е консе́рвы pl.
bulrush /'bʊl,rʌʃ/ n. камы́ш m.
bulwark /'bʊlwərk/ n. бастио́н; опло́т m.
bum /bʌm/ n. ло́дырь, безде́льник m.; бродя́га m. and f. (decl. f.).
bumblebee /'bʌmbəl,bi/ n. шмель m.

bump /bʌmp/ **1.** n. (collision) столкновéние neut.; (swelling) шúшка f. **2.** v.t. стýкнуть pf.; v.i. стýкнуться pf.
bumper /'bʌmpər/ n. бáмпер m.
bumpkin /'bʌmpkɪn/ n. деревéнщина m. and f. (decl. f.).
bumptious /'bʌmpʃəs/ adj. самодовóльный, тщеслáвный.
bumpy /'bʌmpi/ adj. (uneven) нерóвный; (jolting) тря́ский.
bun /bʌn/ n. бýлочка f.
bunch /bʌntʃ/ **1.** n. свя́зка f., пучóк m. **2.** v. собирáть в пучóк impf.
bungalow /'bʌŋgə,lou/ n. бýнгало neut. indecl.
bungle /'bʌŋgəl/ v.t. напýтать pf.
bunion /'bʌnyən/ n. óпухоль (на большóм пáльце ногú) f.
bunk /bʌŋk/ n. кóйка f.
bunker /'bʌŋkər/ n. бýнкер m.
Bunsen burner /'bʌnsən/ n. лаборатóрная гáзовая горéлка f.
bunting /'bʌntɪŋ/ n. (flags) флáги pl.
buoy /'bui, bɔi/ n. бáкен, буй m
buoyancy /'bɔiənsi/ n. плавýчесть f.
buoyant /'bɔiənt/ adj. плавýчий, бóдрый.
burbot /'bɜrbət/ n. (fish) налúм m.
burden /'bɜrdn/ **1.** n. брéмя neut. **2.** v. обременя́ть impf.
burdensome /'bɜrdn̩səm/ adj. обременúтельный.
burdock /'bɜrdɒk/ n. лопýх m.
bureau /'byʊrou/ n. бюрó neut. indecl., контóра f.; (furn.) комóд m.
bureaucracy /byʊ'rɒkrəsi/ n. бюрокрáтия f.
bureaucratism /byʊ'rɒkrə,tɪzəm/ n. бюрократúзм m.
burette /byʊ'rɛt/ n. бюрéтка f.
burgee /'bɜrdʒi/ n. треугóльный флажóк m.
burgeon /'bɜrdʒən/ v. разрастáться impf.
burglar /'bɜrglər/ n. вор, взлóмщик m.
burglarize /'bɜrglə,raiz/ v. взлáмывать impf.
burglary /'bɜrgləri/ n. крáжа со взлóмом f.
burgomaster /'bɜrgə,mæstər/ n. бургомúстр m.
Burgundy /'bɜrgəndi/ n. бургýндское винó neut.
burial /'bɛriəl/ n. погребéние neut.
burlap /'bɜrlæp/ n. холст m., холстúна f.
burlesque /bər'lɛsk/ n. бурлéск m.
Burma /'bɜrmə/ n. Бúрма m. (see Myanmar).
burn /bɜrn/ v.t. жечь; сжигáть impf., сжечь pf.; v.i. горéть impf., сгорéть pf.
burner /'bɜrnər/ n. горéлка f.
burning /'bɜrnɪŋ/ adj. горя́щий; пылáющий; (question, etc.) жгýчий.
burnish /'bɜrnɪʃ/ v. полировáть impf.
burnoose /bər'nus/ n. бурнýс m.
burnt /bɜrnt/ adj. жжёный, горéлый.
burp /bɜrp/ v. (colloq.) рыгáть impf.
burr /bɜr/ n. (bot.) колю́чка f.
burrow /'bɜrou/ **1.** n. норá f. **2.** v. ры́ться impf.
bursar /'bɜrsər/ n. (treasurer) казначéй m.
burst /bɜrst/ v. взрывáться pf.
bury /'bɛri/ v. хоронúть impf., похоронúть pf.; (hide) зарывáть impf.
Buryat /bʊr'yat/ n. буря́т m., буря́тка f.
Buryat Republic n. Буря́тия f.
bus /bʌs/ **1.** n. автóбус m. **2.** adj. автóбусный.
bush /bʊʃ/ n. кустáрник m.
bushel /'bʊʃəl/ n. бýшель m.

bushy /'bʊʃi/ adj. пушúстый; густóй.
business /'bɪznɪs/ n. дéло, заня́тие neut.; делá pl.
businesslike /'bɪznɪs,laik/ adj. деловóй.
businessman /'bɪznɪs,mæn/ n. делéц, бизнесмéн m.
buskin /'bʌskɪn/ n. котýрн m.
bust /bʌst/ n. бюст m.
bustard /'bʌstərd/ n. дрофá f.
bus terminal n. автовокзáл m.
bustle /'bʌsəl/ **1.** n. суматóха; суетá f. **2.** v. суетúться impf.
bustling /'bʌslɪŋ/ adj. суетлúвый.
busy /'bɪzi/ **1.** adj. заня́той, зáнятый. **2.** v. to busy oneself занимáться (with instr.) impf.
busybody /'bɪzi,bɒdi/ n.: to be a busybody v. совáть нос в чужúе делá impf.
but /bʌt/ unstressed bət/ **1.** conj. но, однáко. **2.** adv. тóлько, лишь.
butadiene /,byutə'daiin/ n. бутадиéн m.
butane /'byutein/ n. бутáн m.
butcher /'bʊtʃər/ n. мясникú m.
butchery /'bʊtʃəri/ n. бóйня f.
butler /'bʌtlər/ n. дворéцкий m.
butt[1] /bʌt/ n. (target) мишéнь f.
butt[2] /bʌt/ n. (remainder) остáток m.; (rifle) приклáд m., (of a cigarette) окýрок m.
butt[3] /bʌt/ v. бодáться impf.
butter /'bʌtər/ n. (слúвочное) мáсло neut.
buttercup /'bʌtər,kʌp/ n. лю́тик m.
butterfly /'bʌtər,flai/ n. бáбочка f.; (swim.) баттерфля́й m.
buttermilk /'bʌtər,mɪlk/ n. простоквáша f.
butterscotch /'bʌtər,skɒtʃ/ n. карамéль f.
buttery /'bʌtəri/ adj. мáсляный.
butt joint n. сты́ковое соединéние neut.
buttock /'bʌtək/ n. ягодúца f.
button /'bʌtn/ n. пýговица f.; (elec.) кнóпка f.
buttonhole /'bʌtn̩,houl/ n. пéтля f.
buttress /'bʌtrɪs/ n. подпóра f.; (bridge) бык m.; (building) контрфóрс m.; (fig.) опóра, поддéржка f.
butyl /'byutɪl/ **1.** n. бутúл m. **2.** adj. бутúловый.
buxom /'bʌksəm/ adj. пóлная, пы́шная.
buy /bai/ **1.** n. покýпка f. **2.** v. покупáть impf., купúть pf.
buyable /'baiəbəl/ adj. покупáемый.
buyer /'baiər/ n. покупáтель m.
buzz /bʌz/ **1.** n. жужжáние neut. **2.** v. жужжáть impf.
buzzard /'bʌzərd/ n. каню́к m.
buzzer /'bʌzər/ n. гудóк m.; (tech.) зýммер m.
by /bai/ **1.** prep. пóдле (with gen.), к (with dat.); за (with acc.); (place) вóзле, óколо, мúмо (with gen.). **2.** adv. мúмо; by the way кстáти, мéжду прóчим.
Bydgoszcz /'bɪdgɔʃtʃ/ n. Бы́дгощ m.
by-election /'bai ɪ,lɛkʃən/ n. дополнúтельные вы́боры pl.
bygone /'bai,gɔn, -,gɒn/ adj. прóшлый.
bylaw /'bai,lɔ/ n. постановлéние; прáвило neut.
bypass /'bai,pæs/ v. обходúть impf., обойтú pf.
by-product /'bai,prɒdəkt/ n. побóчный продýкт m.
bystander /'bai,stændər/ n. свидéтель m.
byte /bait/ n. байт m.
byway /'bai,wei/ n. переýлок m.
byword /'bai,wɜrd/ n. поговóрка f.

C

cab /kæb/ *n.* такси *neut. indecl.*
cabal /kə'bæl/ *n.* интрига *f.*
cabaret /ˌkæbə'rei/ **1.** *n.* кабаре *neut. indecl.* **2.** *adj.* эстрадный.
cabbage /'kæbɪdʒ/ *n.* капуста *f.*
cabbala /'kæbələ, kə'bɑ-/ *n.* каббала *f.*
cabbalistic /ˌkæbə'lɪstɪk/ *adj.* каббалистический.
cabin /'kæbɪn/ *n.* хижина *f.*; (*ship*) кабина, каюта *f.*
cabinet /'kæbənɪt/ *n.* шкаф *m.*; (*polit.*) кабинет *m.*
cabinetmaker /'kæbənɪtˌmeikər/ *n.* краснодеревщик; столяр *m.*
cabinetmaking /'kæbənɪtˌmeikɪŋ/ *n.* мебельное дело *neut.*
cable /'keibəl/ *n.* кабель *m.*; канат *m.*; телеграмма *f.*
cablegram /'keibəlˌgræm/ *n.* каблограмма *f.*
cable-layer /'keibəlˌleiər/ *n.* (*naut.*) кабельное судно *neut.*
cable laying *n.* прокладка кабеля *f.*
cable television *n.* кабельное телевидение *neut.*
cableway /'keibəlˌwei/ *n.* подвесная дорога *f.*
cabotage /'kæbətɪdʒ/ *n.* каботаж *m.*
cabriolet /ˌkæbriə'lei/ *n.* кабриолет *m.*
cacao /kə'kɑou/ *n.* какао *neut. indecl.*
cache /kæʃ/ *n.* тайник *m.*; (*of weapons*) тайный склад оружия *m.*
cachet /kæ'ʃei/ *n.* печать *f.*
cacique /kə'sik/ *n.* кацик *m.*
cackle /'kækəl/ *n.* кудахтанье *neut.*
cacophonous /kə'kɒfənəs/ *adj.* неблагозвучный.
cacophony /kə'kɒfəni/ *n.* какофония *f.*
cactaceous /kæk'teiʃəs/ *adj.* кактусовый.
cactus /'kæktəs/ *n.* кактус *m.*
cad /kæd/ *n.* хам *m.*; подлец *m.*
cadastral /kə'dæstrəl/ *adj.* кадастровый.
cadastre /kə'dæstər/ *n.* кадастр *m.*
cadaver /kə'dævər/ *n.* труп *m.*
cadaverous /kə'dævərəs/ *adj.* мертвенный; трупный.
caddish /'kædɪʃ/ *adj.* хамский, подлый.
caddy /'kædi/ *n.* (*for tea*) чайница *f.*; (*for computer disks*) футляр *m.*
cadence /'keidns/ *n.* ритм; такт; (*mus.*) каденция *f.*
cadenza /kə'dɛnzə/ *n.* каденция *f.*
cadet /kə'dɛt/ *n.* (*mil.*) кадет, курсант *m.*
cadge /kædʒ/ *v.* попрошайничать *impf.*
cadger /'kædʒər/ *n.* попрошайка *m.* and *f.* (*decl. f.*)
cadmium /'kædmiəm/ *n.* кадмий *m.*
cadre /'kædri, 'kɑdrei/ *n.* (*mil.*) кадр *m.*
Caesarean section /sɪ'zɛəriən/ *n.* кесарево сечение *neut.*
caesura /sɪ'ʒʊrə/ *n.* цезура *f.*
café /kæ'fei/ *n.* кафе *neut. indecl.*
cafeteria /ˌkæfɪ'tɪəriə/ *n.* кафетерий *m.*
caffeine /kæ'fin/ *n.* кофеин *m.*
caftan /'kæftæn/ *n.* кафтан *m.*
cage /keidʒ/ **1.** *n.* клетка *f.* **2.** *v.* сажать в клетку *impf.*

cagey /'keidʒi/ *adj.* (*colloq.*) (*cautious*) осторожный.
Cain /kein/ *n.* Каин *m.*
caïque /kɑ'ik/ *n.* каик *m.*
Cairo /'kairou/ *n.* Каир *m.*
caisson /'keisən/ *n.* кессон *m.*
cajole /kə'dʒoul/ *v.* уговаривать *impf.*
cake /keik/ *n.* торт, кекс *m.*, пирожное *neut.*
calabash /'kæləˌbæʃ/ *n.* горлянка *f.*
calamitous /kə'læmɪtəs/ *adj.* пагубный.
calamity /kə'læmɪti/ *n.* бедствие *neut.*
calceolaria /ˌkælsiə'lɛəriə/ *n.* кошельки *pl.*
calcify /'kælsəˌfai/ *v.* обызвествляться *impf.*
calcium /'kælsiəm/ *n.* кальций *m.*
calculable /'kælkjələbəl/ *adj.* исчислимый.
calculate /'kælkjəˌleit/ *v.* рассчитывать *impf.*; вычислять *impf.*, вычислить *pf.*
calculated /'kælkjəˌleitɪd/ *adj.* рассчитанный.
calculating /'kælkjəˌleitɪŋ/ *adj.* расчитывающий.
calculation /ˌkælkjə'leiʃən/ *n.* вычисление *neut.*, расчёт *m.*
calculator /'kælkjəˌleitər/ *n.* калькулятор *m.*
calculus /'kælkjələs/ *n.* (*math.*) исчисление *neut.*
Calcutta /kæl'kʌtə/ *n.* Калькутта *f.*
caldron /'kɔldrən/ *n.* котёл *m.*
calendar /'kæləndər/ *n.* календарь *m.*
calender /'kæləndər/ *n.* (*tech.*) каландр *m.*
calendrical /kə'lɛndrɪkəl/ *adj.* календарный.
calends /'kæləndz/ *n.* календы *pl.*
calendula /kə'lɛndʒələ/ *n.* (*bot.*) ноготки *pl.*
calf /kæf/ *n.* телёнок *m.*
calfskin /'kæfˌskɪn/ *n.* телячья кожа *f.*
caliber /'kæləbər/ *n.* калибр *f.*
calibrate /'kæləˌbreit/ *v.* градуировать *impf.*; (*check*) калибровать *impf.*
calibration /ˌkælə'breiʃən/ *n.* калибровка *f.*
calico /'kælɪˌkou/ *n.* (*cloth*) коленкор *m.*; (*printed cotton*) набивной ситец *m.*
California /ˌkælə'fɔrnyə/ *n.* Калифорния *f.*
calipers /'kæləpərz/ *n.* (*instrument*) кронциркуль *m.*
caliph /'keilɪf/ *n.* калиф *m.*
calisthenics /ˌkæləs'θɛnɪks/ *n.* художественная гимнастика *f.*
calk /kɔk/ *n.* (*spike*) шип *m.*
call /kɔl/ **1.** *n.* крик; призыв *m.*; (*visit*) визит *m.* **2.** *v.* звать *impf.*; (*name*) называть *impf.*, назвать *pf.*; (*telephone*) звонить по телефону *impf.*
call box *n.* телефонная будка *f.*
caller /'kɔlər/ *n.* (*visitor*) посетитель *m.*
calligrapher /kə'lɪgrəfər/ *n.* каллиграф *m.*
calligraphic /ˌkælɪ'græfɪk/ *adj.* каллиграфический.
calligraphy /kə'lɪgrəfi/ *n.* каллиграфия *f.*
call-in /'kɔlˌɪn/ *n.* теле-(радио-)программа "звоните-отвечаем" *f.*
calling /'kɔlɪŋ/ *n.* (*vocation*) призвание *neut.*; (*profession*) профессия *f.*; (*convoking*) созыв *m.*
callous /'kæləs/ *adj.* (*skin*) мозолистый; (*unfeeling*) чёрствый.
callousness /'kæləsnɪs/ *n.* чёрствость *f.*
callow /'kælou/ *adj.* (*featherless*) неоперившийся.

call signal *n.* позывны́е сигна́лы *pl.*

call-up /'kɔl,ʌp/ *n.* (*mil.*) призы́в на вое́нную слу́жбу *m.*

callus /'kæləs/ *n.* (*med.*) мозо́ль *m.*

calm /kɑm/ **1.** *adj.* споко́йный. **2.** *n.* тишина́ *f.*, споко́йствие *neut.* **3.** *v.* успока́ивать *impf.*, успоко́ить *pf.*; **to calm down** успока́иваться *impf.*, успоко́иться *pf.*

calmly /'kɑmli/ *adv.* споко́йно.

calmness /'kɑmnɪs/ *n.* споко́йствие *neut.*

calomel /'kælə,mɛl/ *n.* каломе́ль *f.*

caloric /kə'lɔrɪk/ *adj.* теплово́й, калори́йный.

calorie /'kæləri/ *n.* кало́рия *f.*

calorifics /,kælə'rɪfɪks/ *n.* теплоте́хника *f.*

calorimeter /,kælə'rɪmɪtər/ *n.* калори́метр *m.*

calumniate /kə'lʌmni,eit/ *v.* клевета́ть *impf.*

calumniator /kə'lʌmni,eitər/ *n.* клеветни́к *m.*

calumnious /kə'lʌmniəs/ *adj.* клеветни́ческий.

calumny /'kæləmni/ *n.* клевета́ *f.*

calve /kæv/ *v.* (*cow*) тели́ться *impf.*

Calvinism /'kælvə,nɪzəm/ *n.* кальвини́зм *m.*

Calvinist /'kælvənɪst/ **1.** *n.* кальвини́ст *m.* **2.** *adj.* кальвини́стский.

calx /kælks/ *n.* ока́лина, зола́ *f.*

calypso /kə'lɪpsou/ *n.* кали́псо *neut. indecl.*

calyx /'keilɪks/ *n.* ча́шечка *f.*

cam /kæm/ *n.* эксце́нтрик, кулачо́к *m.*

camaraderie /,kɑmə'rɑdəri/ *n.* това́рищество *neut.*

camber /'kæmbər/ *n.* (*curvature*) изги́б *m.*

Cambodia /kæm'boudiə/ *n.* Камбо́джа *f.* (*see Kampuchea*).

Cambrian /'kæmbriən/ *adj.* (*geol.*) кембри́йский.

cambric /'keimbrɪk/ **1.** *n.* бати́ст *m.* **2.** *adj.* бати́стовый.

Cambridge /'keimbridʒ/ *n.* Ке́мбридж *m.*

camel /'kæməl/ *n.* верблю́д *m.*

camellia /kə'mily ə/ *n.* каме́лия *f.*

camera /'kæmərə/ *n.* фотоаппара́т *m.*; **movie camera** *n.* кинока́мера *f.*

cameral /'kæmərəl/ *adj.* камера́льный.

cameraman /'kæmərə,mæn/ *n.* кинооперáтор *m.*

camomile /'kæmə,mail/ -,mil/ *n.* рома́шка *f.*

camouflage /'kæmə,flɑʒ/ **1.** *n.* маскиро́вка *f.* **2.** *v.* маскирова́ть *impf.*, замаскирова́ть *pf.*

camp¹ /kæmp/ **1.** *n.* ла́герь *m.* **2.** *v.* располага́ться ла́герем *impf.*

camp² /kæmp/ *n.* (*slang*) *n.* жема́нность *f.*

campaign /kæm'pein/ *n.* кампа́ния *f.*

campaigner /kæm'peinər/ *n.* уча́стник кампа́нии *m.*

campanile /,kæmpə'nili/ *n.* колоко́льня *f.*

campanula /kæm'pænyələ/ *n.* колоко́льчик *m.*

camp bed *n.* раскладна́я крова́ть *f.*

campfire /'kæmp,fai³r/ *n.* костёр *m.*

camphor /'kæmfər/ *n.* ка́мфора *f.*

campsite /'kæmp,sait/ *n.* ла́герь *m.*; ке́мпинг *m.*, тури́стическая ба́за *f.*

campus /'kæmpəs/ *n.* университе́тский городо́к *m.*

camshaft /'kæm,ʃæft/ *n.* распредели́тельный вал *m.*

can¹ /kæn; *unstressed* kən/ *v.* мочь *impf.*

can² /kæn; *unstressed* kən/ **1.** *n.* бидо́н *m.*; (*tin*) жестяна́я ба́нка; жестя́нка *f.* **2.** *v.* консерви́ровать *impf.*, законсерви́ровать *pf.*

Canadian /kə'neidiən/ **1.** *adj.* кана́дский. **2.** *n.* кана́дец *m.*, кана́дка *f.*

canal /kə'næl/ *n.* кана́л *m.*

canalization /kə,nælə'zeiʃən/ *n.* строи́тельство кана́лов *neut.*

canalize /'kænl,aiz/ *v.* проводи́ть кана́лы *impf.*

canard /kə'nɑrd/ *n.* (*rumor*) у́тка *f.*

canary /kə'nɛəri/ *n.* канаре́йка *f.*

Canary Islands /kə'nɛəri/ *n.* Кана́рские острова́ *pl.*

canasta /kə'næstə/ *n.* кана́ста *f.*

can-can /'kæn,kæn/ *n.* канка́н *m.*

cancel /'kænsəl/ *v.* вычёркивать *impf.*, вы́черкнуть *pf.*; аннули́ровать *impf.* and *pf.*

cancellation /,kænsə'leiʃən/ *n.* аннули́рование, вычёркивание *neut.*

cancer /'kænsər/ *n.* рак *m.*

cancerous /'kænsərəs/ *adj.* ра́ковый.

cancroid /'kæŋkrɔid/ *adj.* ракообра́зный.

candelabra /,kændl'ɑbrə/ *n.* канделя́бр *m.*

candid /'kændid/ *adj.* открове́нный; и́скренний.

candidacy /'kændɪdəsi/; *n.* кандидату́ра *f.*

candidate /'kændɪ,deit, -dɪt/ *n.* кандида́т *m.*

candied /'kændid/ *adj.* заса́харенный.

candle /'kændl/ *n.* свеча́ *f.*

candlelight /'kændl,lait/ *n.* свет свечи́ *or* свече́й *m.*; **by candlelight** при све́те свече́й.

candlestick /'kændl,stɪk/ *n.* подсве́чник *m.*

candor /'kændər/ *n.* открове́нность; и́скренность *f.*

candy /'kændi/ *n.* конфе́та *f.*; (*hard candy*) леде́нéц *m.*

cane /kein/ *n.* па́лка *f.*; (*walking*) трость *f.*

canine /'keinain/ *adj.* соба́чий.

canister /'kænəstər/ *n.* жестяна́я коро́бка *f.*; ба́нка *f.*

canker /'kæŋkər/ *n.* (*med.*) я́зва *f.*

cankerous /'kæŋkərəs/ *adj.* разъеда́ющий.

cannabis /'kænəbɪs/ *n.* (*bot.*) (инди́йская) коно́пля́ *f.*; (*drug*) гаши́ш *m.*

canned /kænd/ *adj.* консерви́рованный; **canned food** *n.* консе́рвы *pl.*

cannery /'kænəri/ *n.* консе́рвный заво́д *m.*

Cannes /kæn/ *n.* (*Riviera*) Ка́нны *pl.*

cannibal /'kænəbəl/ *n.* людое́д *m.*

cannibalism /'kænəbə,lɪzəm/ *n.* людое́дство *neut.*, каннибали́зм *m.*

cannibalistic /'kænəbə'lɪstɪk/ *adj.* людое́дский.

cannibalize /'kænəbə,laiz/ *v.* (*e.g., a car*) разбира́ть на запча́сти *impf.*

canning /'kænɪŋ/ *n.* консерви́рование *neut.*

cannon /'kænən/ *n.* пу́шка *f.*

cannonade /,kænə'neid/ *n.* канона́да *f.*

canny /'kæni/ *adj.* (*careful*) осторо́жный; (*cunning*) хи́трый.

canoe /kə'nu/ *n.* кано́э *neut. indecl.*, байда́рка *f.*

canoeist /kə'nuist/ *n.* канои́ст *m.*

canon /'kænən/ *n.* кано́н *m.*; (*person*) кано́ник *m.*

canonicals /kə'nɒnɪkəlz/ *n.* церко́вное облаче́ние *neut.*

canonicity /,kænə'nɪsɪti/ *n.* каноничность *f.*

canonization /,kænənə'zeiʃən/ *n.* канониза́ция *f.*

canonize /'kænə,naiz/ *v.* канонизи́ровать *impf.* and *pf.*

can opener *n.* консе́рвный нож *m.*

canopy /'kænəpi/ *n.* балдахи́н *m.*

cant /kænt/ *n.* жарго́н *m.*

cantaloupe /'kæntl̩ˌoup/ *n.* ды́ня *f.*
cantankerous /kæn'tæŋkərəs/ *adj.* вздо́рный.
cantata /kən'tɑtə/ *n.* канта́та *f.*
canteen /kæn'tin/ *n.* (*flask*) фля́га *f.*; (*in factory, etc.*) столо́вая *f.*
canter /'kæntər/ *n.* лёгкий гало́п *m.*
cantilever /'kæntl̩ˌivər/ *n.* консо́ль *f.*
canting /'kæntɪŋ/ *adj.* ха́нжеский.
canto /'kæntou/ *n.* песнь *f.*
canton /'kæntn̩/ *n.* канто́н *m.*
cantor /'kæntər/ *n.* ка́нтор *m.*
canvas /'kænvəs/ *n.* холст *m.*; паруси́на *f.*
canvass /'kænvəs/ *v.* опра́шивать *impf.*
canyon /'kænyən/ *n.* каньо́н *m.*
caoutchouc /'kautʃʊk/ **1.** *n.* каучу́к *m.* **2.** *adj.* каучу́ковый.
cap /kæp/ *n.* ша́пка, ке́пка, фура́жка *f.*
capability /ˌkeipə'bɪlɪti/ *n.* спосо́бность *f.*
capable /'keipəbəl/ *adj.* спосо́бный.
capacious /kə'peiʃəs/ *adj.* просто́рный, объёмистый.
capacitance /kə'pæsɪtəns/ *n.* (*elec.*) ёмкость *f.*
capacitate /kə'pæsɪˌteit/ *v.* де́лать спосо́бным *impf.*
capacity /kə'pæsɪti/ *n.* ёмкость *f.*; обьём *m.*; (*ability to contain*) вмести́мость *f.*; (*capability*) спосо́бность *f.*
cape /keip/ *n.* (*geog.*) мыс *m.*; (*cloak*) наки́дка *f.*
caper /'keipər/ *n.* (*jump*) прыжо́к *m.*; (*prank*) ша́лость *f.*
capers /'keipər/ *n.* (*cul.*) ка́персы *pl.*
Cape Town *n.* Кейпта́ун *m.*
capillary /'kæpəˌlɛri/ *n.* капилля́р *m.*
capital /'kæpɪtl̩/ **1.** *n.* (*money*) капита́л; (*city*) столи́ца *f.*, столи́чный го́род *m.* **2.** *adj.* (*leg.*) кара́емый сме́ртью.
capitalism /'kæpɪtl̩ˌɪzəm/ *n.* капитали́зм *m.*
capitalist /'kæpɪtl̩ɪst/ *n.* капитали́ст *m.*
capitalization /ˌkæpɪtl̩ə'zeiʃən/ *n.* капитализа́ция *f.*
capitalize /'kæpɪtl̩ˌaiz/ *v.* капитализи́ровать *impf.* and *pf.*
capital letter *n.* загла́вная *or* прописна́я бу́ква *f.*
capital punishment *n.* сме́ртная казнь *f.*
Capitol /'kæpɪtl̩/ *n.* Капито́лий *m.*
capitulate /kə'pɪtʃəˌleit/ *v.* сдава́ться *impf.*, сда́ться *pf.*
capitulation /kəˌpɪtʃə'leiʃən/ *n.* капитуля́ция *f.*
capon /'keipɒn/ *n.* каплу́н *m.*
Capri /'kɑpri, kə'pri/ *n.* (*island*) Ка́при *m.*
caprice /kə'pris/ *n.* капри́з *m.*
capricious /kə'prɪʃəs/ *adj.* капри́зный.
Capricorn /'kæprɪˌkɔrn/ *n.* Козеро́г *m.*; **Tropic of Capricorn** тро́пик Козеро́га *m.*
capsicum /'kæpsɪkəm/ *n.* стручко́вый пе́рец *m.*
capsize /'kæpsaiz/ *v.t.* опроки́дывать *impf.*, опроки́нуть *pf.*; *v.i.* опроки́дываться *impf.*
capstan /'kæpstən/ *n.* кабеста́н *m.*
capsule /'kæpsəl/ *n.* ка́псула *f.*
captain /'kæptən/ *n.* капита́н *m.*
caption /'kæpʃən/ *n.* заголо́вок *m.*
captious /'kæpʃəs/ *adj.* приди́рчивый.
captivate /'kæptəˌveit/ *v.* пленя́ть *impf.*, плени́ть *pf.*; очаро́вывать *impf.*, очарова́ть *pf.*
captivating /'kæptəˌveitɪŋ/ *adj.* очарова́тельный.
captive /'kæptɪv/ *n.* пле́нный *m.*; пле́нник *m.*
captivity /kæp'tɪvɪti/ *n.* плен *m.*; нево́ля *f.*
capture /'kæptʃər/ **1.** *n.* захва́т *m.*, взя́тие в плен *neut.* **2.** *v.* захвати́ть *pf.*; взять в плен *pf.*
Capuchin /'kæpyʊtʃɪn/ *n.* капуци́н *m.*
car /kɑr/ *n.* маши́на *f.*, автомоби́ль *m.*; (*of train*) ваго́н *m.*
carafe /kə'ræf/ *n.* графи́н *m.*
caramel /'kærəməl,'kɑrməl/ *n.* караме́ль *f.*
caramelize /'kærəməˌlaiz, 'kɑrmə-/ *v.* карамелизова́ть *impf.*
carapace /'kærəˌpeis/ *n.* щито́к *m.*
carat /'kærət/ *n.* кара́т *m.*
caravan /'kærəˌvæn/ *n.* карава́н *m.*
caraway /'kærəˌwei/ *n.* тмин *m.*
carbide /'kɑrbaid/ *n.* карби́д *m.*
carbine /'kɑrbin, -bain/ *n.* караби́н *m.*
carbohydrate /ˌkɑrbou'haidreit/ *n.* углево́д *m.*
carbolic /kɑr'bɒlɪk/ *adj.* карбо́ловый.
carbon /'kɑrbən/ *n.* углеро́д *m.*
carbonaceous /ˌkɑrbə'neiʃəs/ *adj.* углеро́дный.
Carbonari /ˌkɑrbə'nɑri/ *n.* карбона́рии *pl.*
carbonate /'kɑrbəˌneit/ *n.* карбона́т *m.*
carbonated /'kɑrbəˌneitɪd/ *adj.* газиро́ванный.
carbonic /kɑr'bɒnɪk/ *adj.* углеро́дистый.
carbonic acid *n.* у́гольная кислота́ *f.*
carboniferous /ˌkɑrbə'nɪfərəs/ *adj.* углено́сный.
carbonization /ˌkɑrbənə'zeiʃən/ *n.* обу́гливание *neut.*
carbonize /'kɑrbəˌnaiz/ *v.* обу́гливать *impf.*
carbon paper *n.* копирова́льная бума́га *f.*
carbonyl /'kɑrbənɪl/ *n.* карбони́л *m.*
carborundum /ˌkɑrbə'rʌndəm/ *n.* карбору́нд *m.*
carboy /'kɑrbɔi/ *n.* буты́ль (для кисло́т) *f.*
carbuncle /'kɑrbʌŋkəl/ *n.* (*med.*) карбу́нкул *m.*
carburation /ˌkɑrbəˌreiʃən/ *n.* карбюра́ция *f.*
carburetor /'kɑrbəˌreitər/ *n.* карбюра́тор *m.*
carcass /'kɑrkəs/ *n.* труп *m.*; ту́ша *f.*
carcinogen /kɑr'sɪnədʒən/ *n.* канцероге́н *m.*
carcinogenic /ˌkɑrsənə'dʒɛnɪk/ *adj.* канцероге́нный.
carcinoma /ˌkɑrsə'noumə/ *n.* карцино́ма *f.*
card /kɑrd/ *n.* ка́рта, ка́рточка *f.*; (*membership ticket*) биле́т *m.*
cardamom /'kɑrdəməm/ *n.* кардамо́н *m.*
cardan /'kɑrdæn/ *n.* (*tech.*) карда́н *m.*
cardboard /'kɑrdˌbɔrd/ **1.** *adj.* карто́нный. **2.** *n.* карто́н *m.*
cardiac /'kɑrdiˌæk/ *adj.* серде́чный.
cardinal /'kɑrdn̩l/ **1.** *adj.* основно́й, гла́вный. **2.** *n.* кардина́л *m.*
card index *n.* картоте́ка *f.*
carding machine /'kɑrdɪŋ/ *n.* ворсова́льная маши́на *f.*
cardiograph /'kɑrdiəˌgræf/ *n.* кардио́граф *m.*
cardioid /'kɑrdiˌɔid/ *n.* кардио́ида *f.*
cardiologist /'kɑrdiˌɒlədʒɪst/ *n.* кардио́лог *m.*
cardiology /ˌkɑrdi'ɒlədʒi/ *n.* кардиоло́гия *f.*
cardiovascular /ˌkɑrdiou'væskyələr/ *adj.* серде́чно-сосу́дистый.
carditis /kɑr'daitɪs/ *n.* карди́т *m.*
cardsharp /'kɑrdˌʃɑrp/ *n.* шу́лер *m.*
card table *n.* ломбе́рный стол *m.*
care /kɛər/ **1.** *n.* забо́та *f.*; ухо́д *m.*; попече́ние *neut.* **2.** *v.* забо́титься *impf.*, позабо́титься *pf.*; **I don't care** мне всё равно́.
careen /kə'rin/ *v.* крени́ться *impf.*
career /kə'rɪər/ *n.* карье́ра *f.*

careerist /kə'rɪərɪst/ **1.** *n.* карьери́ст *m.* **2.** *adj.* карьери́стский.

carefree /'kɛər,fri/ *adj.* беззабо́тный, беспе́чный.

careful /,kɛərfəl/ *adj.* осторо́жный, тща́тельный.

careless /'kɛərlɪs/ *adj.* небре́жный, невнима́тельный.

carelessness /'kɛərlɪsnɪs/ *n.* небре́жность, хала́тность *f.*

caress /kə'rɛs/ **1.** *n.* ла́ска *f.* **2.** *v.* ласка́ть *impf.*

caressing /kə'rɛsɪŋ/ *adj.* ла́сковый.

caret /'kærɪt/ *n.* знак вста́вки *m.*

caretaker /'kɛər,teikər/ *n.* смотри́тель *m.*

careworn /'kɛər,wɔrn/ *n.* изму́ченный забо́тами.

car ferry *n.* автомоби́льный паро́м *m.*

cargo /'kɑrgou/ *n.* груз *m.*

car horn *n.* гудо́к *m.*

Caribbean /,kærə'biən, kə'rɪbi-/ *adj.* кари́бский.

caribou /'kærə,bu/ *n.* кари́бу *neut. indecl.*

caricature /'kærɪkətʃər/ **1.** *n.* карикату́ра *f.* **2.** *v.* изобража́ть в карикату́рном ви́де *impf.*

caricaturist /'kærɪkətʃərɪst/ *n.* карикату́рист *m.*

caries /'kɛəriz/ *n.* (*med.*) карио́з *m.*

carillon /'kærə,lɒn/ *n.* подбо́р колоколо́в *m.*; (*instrument*) кари́льон *m.*

Carinthia /kə'rɪnθiə/ *n.* (*province*) Кари́нтия *f.*

carious /'kɛəriəs/ *adj.* карио́зный.

Carmelite /'karmə,lait/ *n.* (*monk*) кармели́т *m.*

carminative /'kar'mɪnətɪv/ *n.* ветрого́нное сре́дство *neut.*

carmine /'karmɪn/ *n.* карми́н *m.*

carnage /'karnɪdʒ/ *n.* резня́, бо́йня *f.*

carnal /'karnḷ/ *adj.* пло́тский, теле́сный.

carnality /kar'nælɪti/ *n.* (*lust*) по́хоть *f.*

carnation /kar'neiʃən/ *n.* гвозди́ка *f.*

carnelian /kɔr'nilyən/ *n.* сердоли́к *m.*

carnival /'karnəvəl/ *n.* карнава́л *m.*

carnivore /'karnə,vɔr/ *n.* плотоя́дное живо́тное *neut.*

carnivorous /kar'nɪvərəs/ *adj.* плотоя́дный.

carol /'kærəl/ *n.* гимн *m.*

Carolingian /,kærə'lɪndʒiən/ *adj.* кароли́нгский.

carotid /kə'rɒtɪd/ *n.* со́нная арте́рия.

carotin /'kærətɪn/ *n.* кароти́н *m.*

carousal /kə'rauzəl/ *n.* попо́йка *f.*

carouse /kə'rauz/ *v.* пирова́ть *impf.*

carousel /,kærə'sɛl/ *n.* карусе́ль *f.*

car owner *n.* автовладе́лец *m.*

carp[1] /karp/ *n.* (*fish*) карп *m.*

carp[2] /karp/ *v.* (*find fault*) придира́ться *impf.*

carpal /'karpəl/ *adj.* запя́стный.

Carpathian /kar'peiθiən/ *adj.* (*geo.*) карпа́тский.

Carpathian Mountains *n.* Карпа́ты *pl.*

carpel /'karpəl/ *n.* плодоли́стик *m.*

carpenter /'karpəntər/ *n.* пло́тник *m.*

carpentry /'karpəntri/ *n.* столя́рная рабо́та *f.*; пло́тницкое де́ло *neut.*

carpet /'karpɪt/ *n.* ковёр *m.*

carpetbag /'karpɪt,bæg/ *n.* саквоя́ж *m.*

carping /'karpɪŋ/ *adj.* приди́рчивый.

carpus /'karpəs/ *n.* запя́стье *neut.*

carriage /'kærɪdʒ/ *n.* (*conveying*) перево́зка *f.*; (*deportment*) оса́нка *f.*; (*horsedrawn vehicle*) экипа́ж *m.*, коля́ска *f.*; **baby carriage** *n.* де́тская коля́ска *f.*

carrier /'kæriər/ *n.* перено́счик *m.*; (*person carrying a disease*) носи́тель *m.*

carrier pidgeon *n.* почто́вый го́лубь *m.*

carrion /'kæriən/ *n.* па́даль *f.*

carrion crow *n.* во́рон *m.*

carrot /'kærət/ *n.* морко́вь *f.*

carroty /'kærəti/ *adj.* ры́жий.

carry /'kæri/ *v.* носи́ть *impf. indet.*, нести́ *impf. det.*, понести́ *pf.*; (*convey*) вози́ть *impf. indet.*, везти́ *impf. det.*, повезти́ *pf.*; **to carry in** вноси́ть *impf.*, внести́ *pf.*; **to carry out** выноси́ть *impf.*, вы́нести *pf.*; (*execute*) выполня́ть *impf.*

cart /kart/ *n.* теле́га, пово́зка *f.*; (*handcart*) теле́жка *f.*

carte blanche /kart 'blantʃ/ *n.* карт-бла́нш *m.*

cartel /kar'tɛl/ *n.* (*econ.*) карте́ль *m.*

carter /'kartər/ *n.* во́зчик *m.*

Carthage /'karθɪdʒ/ *n.* (*geo.*) Карфаге́н *m.*

cart horse *n.* ломова́я ло́шадь *f.*

Carthusian /kar'θuʒən/ *n.* картезиа́нец *m.*

cartilage /'kartḷɪdʒ/ *n.* хрящ *m.*

cartilaginous /,kartḷ'ædʒənəs/ *adj.* хрящево́й.

cartographer /kar'tɒgrəfər/ *n.* карто́граф *m.*

cartographic /,kartə'gɹæfɪk/ *adj.* картографи́ческий.

cartography /kar'tɒgrəfi/ *n.* картогра́фия *f.*

carton /'kartṇ/ *n.* карто́нная коро́бка *f.*

cartoon /kar'tun/ *n.* карикату́ра *f.*; (*film*) мультфи́льм *m.*

cartoonist /kar'tunist/ *n.* карикату́рист *m.*

cartridge /'kartrɪdʒ/ *n.* патро́н *m.*; **blank cartridge** *n.* холосто́й патро́н *m.*

carve /karv/ *v.* выреза́ть *impf.*, вы́резать *pf.*; (*in stone*) высека́ть *impf.*, вы́сечь *pf.*; (*meat*) наре́зать *impf.*

carvel-built /'karvəl,bɪlt/ *adj.* с обши́вкой вгладь.

carver /'karvər/ *n.* ре́зчик *m.*

carving /'karvɪŋ/ *n.* резьба́ *f.*

caryatid /,kæri'ætɪd/ *n.* кариати́да *f.*

Casablanca /,kæsə'blæŋkə, ,kasə'blaŋkə/ *n.* Касабла́нка *f.*

cascade /kæs'keid/ *n.* каска́д *m.*

case /keis/ *n.* (*instance*) слу́чай *m.*; (*law*) де́ло *neut.*; (*box*) я́щик *m.*; (*cover*) чехо́л *m.*; (*gram.*) паде́ж *m.*

casebound /'keis,baund/ *adj.* в жёстком переплёте.

caseharden /'keis,hardṇ/ *v.* цементи́ровать *impf.*

casein /'keisin/ *n.* казеи́н *m.*

casemate /'keis,meit/ *n.* казема́т *m.*

casement /'keismənt/ *n.* ство́рчатое окно́ *neut.*

cash /kæʃ/ *n.* де́ньги *pl.*; нали́чные де́ньги *pl.*; **to pay cash** *v.* плати́ть нали́чными *impf.*

cashew /'kæʃu/ *n.* (*bot.*) анака́рдия *f.*

cashier[1] /kæ'ʃiər/ *n.* касси́р *m.*

cashier[2] /kæ'ʃiər/ *v.* (*mil.*) увольня́ть со слу́жбы *impf.*

cashmere /'kæʒmiər/ **1.** *n.* кашеми́р *m.* **2.** *adj.* кашеми́ровый.

cash register *n.* ка́ссовый аппара́т *m.*, ка́сса *f.*

casing /'keisɪŋ/ *n.* оболо́чка *f.*; обши́вка *f.*; (*facing*) облицо́вка *f.*; (*tech.*) ко́жух, ка́ртер *m.*

casino /kə'sinou/ *n.* казино́ *neut. indecl.*

cask /kæsk/ *n.* бо́чка *f.*, бочо́нок *m.*

casket /'kæskɪt/ *n.* шкату́лка *f.*

Caspian Sea /'kæspiən/ *n.* Каспи́йское мо́ре *neut.*

cassation /kæ'seiʃən/ *n.* кассация *f.*

casserole /'kæsə,roul/ *n.* (*utensil*) кастрюля *f.*; (*food*) запеканка *f.*

cassette /kə'sɛt/ *n.* кассета *f.*

cassette deck *n.* кассетная дека *f.*

cassette player *n.* магнитофон *m.*

cassock /'kæsək/ (*Rom. Cath.*) сутана *f.*; (*Orthodox*) ряса *f.*

cassowary /'kæsə,wɛri/ *n.* казуар *m.*

cast /kæst/ **1.** *n.* (*mold*) форма для литья *f.*; (*theat.*) состав исполнителей *m.*; (*med.*) гипс *m.*; (*of mind*) склад *m.* **2.** *v.* бросать *impf.*, бросить *pf.*; отливать *impf.*, отлить *pf.*; (*theat.*) распределять роли *impf.* (*with dat.*).

castanets /,kæstə'nɛts/ *n.* кастаньеты *pl.*

caste /kæst/ *n.* каста *f.*

caster /'kæstər/ *n.* литейщик *m.*; (*wheel on furniture*) ролик *m.*

castigate /'kæstɪ,geit/ *v.* наказывать *impf.*, наказать *pf.*; бичевать *impf.*

castigation /,kæstɪ'geiʃən/ *n.* наказание, порицание *neut.*

Castile /kæ'stil/ *n.* (*province*) Кастилия *f.*

casting /'kæstɪŋ/ *n.* литьё *neut.*; (*theat.*) распределение ролей *neut.*

cast-iron /'kæst'aiərn/ *adj.* чугунный.

castle /'kæsəl/ *n.* замок *m.*; (*chess*) ладья *f.*; **castles in the air** воздушные замки *pl.*

castling /'kæsəlɪŋ/ *n.* (*chess*) рокировка *f.*

cast-off /'kæst,ɔf/ *adj.* негодный.

castor oil /'kæstər/ *n.* касторовое масло *neut.*, (*colloq.*) касторка *f.*; **castor plant** клещевина *f.*

castrate /'kæstreit/ *v.* кастрировать *impf.*

castration /kæ'streiʃən/ *n.* кастрация *f.*

casual /'kæʒuəl/ *adj.* случайный, непреднамеренный; (*informal*) непринуждённый.

casualty /'kæʒuəlti/ *n.* пострадавший *m.*; (*mil.*) (*wounded*) раненый *m.*; (*killed*) убитый *m.*

casuist /'kæʒuɪst/ *n.* казуист *m.*

casuistry /'kæʒuəstri/ *n.* казуистика *f.*

cat /kæt/ **1.** *n.* кошка *f.*; (*male cat*) кот *m.* **2.** *adj.* кошачий.

catabolism /kə'tæbə,lɪzəm/ *n.* катаболизм *m.*

cataclysm /'kætə,klɪzəm/ *n.* (*flood*) потоп *m.*; (*upheaval*) катаклизм *m.*

catacomb /'kætə,koum/ *n.* катакомба *f.*

catafalque /'kætə,fɔk/ *n.* катафалк *m.*

catalepsy /'kætḷ,ɛpsi/ *n.* каталепсия *f.*

cataleptic /,kætḷ'ɛptɪk/ *adj.* каталептический.

catalogue /'kætḷ,ɔg/ **1.** *n.* каталог *m.* **2.** *v.* каталогизировать *impf. and pf.*

cataloguer /'kætḷ,ɔgər/ *n.* каталогизатор *m.*

Catalonia /,kætḷ'ouniə/ *n.* (*province*) Каталония *f.*

catalysis /kə'tæləsɪs/ *n.* катализ *m.*

catalyst /'kætḷɪst/ *n.* катализатор *m.*

catamaran /,kætəmə'ræn/ *n.* катамаран *m.*

cataplasm /'kætə,plæzəm/ *n.* припарка *f.*

catapult /'kætə,pʌlt/ **1.** *n.* катапульта *f.* **2.** *v.i.* взлетать *impf.*

cataract /'kætə,rækt/ *n.* водопад *m.*; (*med.*) катаракта *f.*

catarrh /kə'tar/ *n.* катар *m.* ·

catastrophe /kə'tæstrəfi/ *n.* катастрофа *f.*

catastrophic /,kætə'strɒfɪk/ *adj.* катастрофический.

catcall /'kæt,kɔl/ *n.* свист *m.*

catch /kætʃ/ **1.** *v.* ловить *impf.*, поймать *pf.*; (*be on time for*) успеть *impf.* (*with acc.*) *pf.*; **to catch up** догнать *pf.* **2.** *n.* (*action*) поймка *f.*; (*trick*) уловка *f.*

catcher /'kætʃər/ *n.* ловец *m.*

catching /'kætʃɪŋ/ *adj.* заразный; заразительный.

catchword /'kætʃ,wɜrd/ *n.* (*fashionable word*) модное словечко *neut.*; (*slogan*) лозунг *m.*

catchy /'kætʃi/ *adj.* (*attractive*) привлекательный; (*tricky*) сложный, трудный.

catechism /'kætɪ,kɪzəm/ *n.* катехизис *m.*

catechumen /,kætɪ'kyumən/ *n.* новообращённый *m.*

categorical /,kætɪ'gɔrɪkəl/ *adj.* категорический, безусловный.

categorize /'kætɪgə,raiz/ *v.* распределять по категориям *impf.*

category /'kætɪ,gɔri/ *n.* категория *f.*

catena /kə'tinə/ *n.* (*math.*) цепь *f.*

catenary /'kætṇ,ɛri/ *adj.* цепной.

cater /'keitər/ *v.* снабжать провизией *impf.*; **to cater to** угождать *impf.*

caterer /'keitərər/ *n.* поставщик провизии *m.*

catering /'keitərɪŋ/ *n.* поставка продуктов *f.*

caterpillar /'kætə,pɪlər/ *n.* гусеница *f.*

caterwaul /'kætər,wɔl/ *v.* задавать кошачий концерт *impf.*

caterwauling /'kætər,wɔlɪŋ/ *n.* кошачий концерт *m.*

catfish /'kæt,fɪʃ/ *n.* сомик *m.*

catgut /'kæt,gʌt/ *n.* кетгут *m.*

catharsis /kə'θarsɪs/ *n.* катарсис *m.*

cathartic /kə'θartɪk/ *adj.* слабительное средство *neut.*

cathedral /kə'θidrəl/ *n.* собор *m.*

catherine wheel /'kæθərɪn/ *n.* огненное колесо *neut.*

catheter /'kæθɪtər/ *n.* катетер *m.*

cathode /'kæθoud/ *n.* катод *m.*

cathode ray tube *n.* (*abbr.* C.R.T.) электронно-лучевая трубка *f.* (*abbr.* ЭЛТ.)

catholic /'kæθəlɪk/ *adj.* всеобъемлющий; (*broad*) широкий; (*eccles.*) (*whole church*) вселенский.

Catholic /'kæθəlɪk/ **1.** *adj.* католический. **2.** *n.* католик *m.*

Catholicism /kə'θɒlə,sɪzəm/ *n.* католичество *neut.*, католицизм *m.*

catholicity /,kæθə'lɪsɪti/ *n.* универсальность *f.*

cation /'kæt,aiən/ *n.* катион *m.*

catkin /'kætkɪn/ *n.* серёжка *f.*

catlike /'kæt,laik/ *adj.* кошачий.

cat lover *n.* кошатник *m.*

catnip /'kætnɪp/ *n.* кошачья мята *f.*

catoptric /kə'tɒptrɪk/ *adj.* катоптрический.

cattily /'kætli/ *adv.* язвительно.

cattiness /'kætɪnɪs/ *n.* язвительность *f.*

cattle /'kætḷ/ *n.* скот *m.*

catty /'kæti/ *adj.* кошачий; (*spiteful*) ехидный, язвительный.

catwalk /'kæt,wɔk/ *n.* мостик *m.*

cat whisker *n.* (*radio*) контактная пружина *f.*

Caucasus /'kɔkəsəs/ *n.* (*mountains*) Кавказ *m.*

caucus /'kɔkəs/ *n.* влиятельные круги *pl.*; (*party committee*) партийный комитет *m.*

caudal /'kɔdḷ/ *adj.* хвостовидный.

caudate /'kɔdeit/ *adj.* хвостатый.

cauldron /'kɔldrən/ n. котёл, котелóк m.
cauliflower /'kɔlə‚flauər/ n. цветнáя капýста f.
caulk /kɔk/ v. конопáтить impf.
caulking /'kɔkɪŋ/ n. конопáчение neut.
causal /'kɔzəl/ adj. причинный, каузáльный.
causality /kɔ'zælɪti/ n. причинность neut.
causative /'kɔzətɪv/ adj. причинный; (gram.) каузативный.
cause /kɔz/ **1.** n. причина f.; (movement) дéло neut. **2.** v. причинять impf., причинить pf.; вызывáть impf. вызвать pf.
cause célèbre /'kɔz sə'lɛbrə/ n. грóмкое дéло neut.
causeless /'kɔzlɪs/ n. необоснóванный.
causeway /'kɔz‚wei/ n. насыпнáя дорóга f.; (over marsh) гать f.
caustic /'kɔstɪk/ adj. каустический; язвительный.
cauterization /‚kɔtərə'zeiʃən/ n. прижигáние neut.
cauterize /'kɔtə‚raiz/ v. прижигáть impf., прижéчь pf.
caution /'kɔʃən/ n. осторóжность f.
cautionary /'kɔʃə‚neri/ adj. предупреждáющий, предостерегáющий.
cautious /'kɔʃəs/ adj. осторóжный.
cavalcade /‚kævəl'keid/ n. кавалькáда f,
cavalier /‚kævə'lɪər/ **1.** n. (horseman) всáдник m.; (hist.) (Royalist) **Cavalier** роялист m. **2.** adj. (carefree) беспéчный; (unceremonious) бесцеремóнный; (disdainful) надмéнный; (hist.) роялистский.
cavalry /'kævəlri/ n. кавалéрия f.
cavalryman /'kævəlrimən/ n. кавалерист m.
cave /keiv/ n. пещéра f.; **to cave in** v. рýхнуть pf.
caveat /'kævi‚ɑt/ n. предупреждéние neut.
caveman /'keiv‚mæn/ n. троглодит, пещéрный человéк m.
cavern /'kævərn/ n. пещéра f.
cavernous /'kævərnəs/ adj. пещéристый.
caviar /'kævi‚ɑr/ n. икрá f.
cavil /'kævəl/ v. придирáться impf.
caving /'keivɪŋ/ n. (tech.) обрýшение neut.
cavitation /‚kævɪ'teiʃən/ n. кавитáция f.
cavity /'kævɪti/ n. пóлость f.; впáдина f.
cavort /kə'vɔrt/ v. скакáть impf.
caw /kɔ/ v. кáркать impf.
cawing /'kɔɪŋ/ n. кáрканье neut.
cay /kei, ki/ n. корáлловый островóк m.
cayenne pepper /kai'ɛn/ n. кайéнский пéрец m.
cayman /'keimən/ n. каймáн m.
CD-ROM /'si‚di'rɒm/ n. (comp.) компáктный диск or компáкт диск — постоянное запоминáющее устрóйство neut. (abbr.) КД-ПЗУ) m.
cease /sis/ v. прекращáть(ся) impf., прекратить(ся) pf.; перестáвать impf., перестáть pf.
cease-fire /'sis'faiᵊr/ n. прекращéние огня neut.; (truce) перемирие neut.
ceaseless /'sislɪs/ adj. непрестáнный, непрерывный.
cecum /'sikəm/ n. слепáя кишкá f.
cedar /'sidər/ n. кедр m.
cede /sid/ v. сдавáть impf., сдать pf.
cedilla /sɪ'dɪlə/ n. седиль f.
ceiling /'silɪŋ/ n. потолóк m.
celandine /'sɛlən‚dain/ n. чистотéл m.

celebrant /'sɛləbrənt/ n. свящéнник (отправляющий слýжбу) m.
celebrate /'sɛlə‚breit/ v. прáздновать impf., отпрáздновать pf.; **to be celebrated for** слáвиться (with instr.) impf.
celebrated /'sɛlə‚breitɪd/ adj. знаменитый, прослáвленный.
celebration /‚sɛlə'breiʃən/ n. прáзднование neut.
celebrity /sə'lɛbrɪti/ n. знаменитость f.
celeriac /sə'lɛri‚æk/ n. кóрень сельдерéя m.
celerity /sə'lɛrɪti/ n. быстротá f.
celery /'sɛləri/ n. сельдерéй m.
celesta /sə'lɛstə/ n. (mus.) челéста f.
celestial /sə'lɛstʃəl/ adj. небéсный.
celibacy /'sɛləbəsi/ n. безбрáчие neut.
celibate /'sɛləbɪt/ adj. холостóй.
cell /sɛl/ n. (room) кéлья f.; (prison) кáмера f.; (polit.) ячéйка f.; (biol.) клéтка f.
cellar /'sɛlər/ n. пóгреб; подвáл m.
cellist /'tʃɛlɪst/ n. виолончелист m.
cello /'tʃɛlou/ n. виолончéль f.
cellophane /'sɛlə‚fein/ **1.** n. целлофáн m. **2.** adj. целлофáновый.
cellular /'sɛlyələr/ adj. клéточный.
celluloid /'sɛlyə‚lɔid/ n. целлулóид m.
cellulose /'sɛlyə‚lous/ n. целлюлóза f.
cement /sɪ'mɛnt/ **1.** n. цемéнт m. **2.** v. цементировать impf.
cemetery /'sɛmɪ‚tɛri/ n. клáдбище neut.
cenotaph /'sɛnə‚tæf/ n. кенотáфий m.
censer /'sɛnsər/ n. кадило neut., курильница f.
censor /'sɛnsər/ **1.** n. цéнзор m. **2.** v. подвергáть цензýре impf.
censorial /sɛn'sɔriəl/ adj. цéнзорский.
censorious /sɛn'sɔriəs/ adj. критический.
censorship /'sɛnsər‚ʃɪp/ n. цензýра f.
censurable /'sɛnʃərəbəl/ adj. достóйный порицáния.
censure /'sɛnʃər/ **1.** n. осуждéние neut. **2.** v. порицáть impf.; осуждáть impf., осудить pf.
census /'sɛnsəs/ n. пérepись f.
cent /sɛnt/ n. цент m.
centaur /'sɛntɔr/ n. кентáвр m.
Centaurus /sɛn'tɔrəs/ n. (astr.) Кентáвр m.
centenarian /‚sɛntn̩'ɛəriən/ n. столéтний человéк m.
centenary /sɛn'tɛnəri/ **1.** adj. столéтний. **2.** n. столéтняя годовщина f.
centennial /sɛn'tɛniəl/ adj. столéтний.
center /'sɛntər/ **1.** n. центр m. **2.** adj. срéдний. **3.** v. (concentrate) сосредотóчивать(ся) impf.
centesimal /sɛn'tɛsəməl/ adj. сóтая (часть) f.
centigrade /'sɛnti‚greid/ adj. стогрáдусный.
Centigrade adj. Цéльсий; **10 degrees Centigrade** 10 грáдусов по Цéльсию.
centigram /'sɛnti‚græm/ n. сантигрáмм m.
centiliter /'sɛnti‚litər/ n. сантилитр m.
centime /'sɑntim/ n. сантим m.
centimeter /'sɛntə‚mitər/ n. сантимéтр m.
centipede /'sɛntə‚pid/ n. сороконóжка f.
centner /'sɛntnər/ n. цéнтнер m.
central /'sɛntrəl/ adj. центрáльный.
centralization /‚sɛntrələ'zeiʃən/ n. централизáция f.
centralize /'sɛntrə‚laiz/ v. централизовáть impf. and pf.
centrifugal /sɛn'trɪfyəgəl/ adj. центробéжный.

centrifugal force *n.* центробежная сила *f.*
centrifuge /'sɛntrə,fyudʒ/ *n.* центрифуга *f.*
centripetal /sɛn'trɪpɪtl̩/ *adj.* центростремительный.
centripetal force *n.* центростремительная сила *f.*
centuple /'sɛntəpəl/ *adj.* стократный.
centurion /sɛn'tʊriən/ *n.* центурион *m.*
century /'sɛntʃəri/ *n.* век *m.*, столетие *neut.*
cephalic /sə'fælɪk/ *adj.* головной.
cephalopod /'sɛfələ,pɒd/ *n.* головоногое *neut.*
ceramic /sə'ræmɪk/ *adj.* керамический.
ceramics /sə'ræmɪks/ *n.* керамика *f.*
cereal /'sɪəriəl/ *n.* (*grain*) (хлебные) злаки *pl.*; **breakfast cereals** *n.* хлебные хлопья *pl.*
cerebellum /,sɛrə'bɛləm/ *n.* мозжечок *m.*
cerebral /sə'ribrəl/ *adj.* мозговой.
cerebration /,sɛrə'breiʃən/ *n.* мозговая деятельность *f.*
cerebrum /sə'ribrəm/ *n.* головной мозг *m.*
cerement /'sɪərmənt/ *n.* саван *m.*
ceremonial /,sɛrə'mouniəl/ *adj.* церемониальный.
ceremonious /,sɛrə'mouniəs/ *adj.* церемониальный; церемонный.
ceremony /'sɛrə,mouni/ *n.* церемония *f.*
Ceres /'sɪəriz/ *n.* (*myth.*, *astr.*) Церера *f.*
certain /'sɜrtn̩/ *adj.* (*fixed*) определённый; (*indefinite*) некий, некоторый; **to be certain** быть уверенным.
certainly /'sɜrtn̩li/ *adv.* конечно.
certainty /'sɜrtn̩ti/ *n.* уверенность *f.*
certificate /sər'tɪfɪkɪt/ *n.* удостоверение; свидетельство *neut.*
certify /'sɜrtə,fai/ *v.* свидетельствовать *impf.*, засвидетельствовать *pf.*
certitude /'sɜrtɪ,tud/ *n.* уверенность *f.*
cerulean /sə'ruliən/ *adj.* лазурный.
cervical /'sɜrvɪkəl/ *adj.* затылочный, шейный.
cervix /'sɜrvɪks/ *n.* (*neck*) шея *f.*; (*part of uterus*) шейка матки *f.*
cesium /'siziəm/ *n.* цезий *m.*
cessation /sɛ'seiʃən/ *n.* прекращение *neut.*
cession /'sɛʃən/ *n.* уступка, передача *f.*
cesspool /'sɛs,pul/ выгребная яма *f.*, помойная яма *f.*
cetacean /sɪ'teiʃən/ *adj.* китовый.
cetaceous /sɪ'teiʃəs/ *adj.* китовый.
Ceylon /sɪ'lɒn/ *n.* Цейлон *m.* (*see Sri Lanka*).
Chad /tʃæd/ *n.* Чад *m.*
chafe /tʃeif/ *v.* тереть; натирать *impf.*
chaff /tʃæf/ *n.* (*grain husks*) мякина *f.*; (*cut straw*) сечка *f.*
chaffinch /'tʃæfɪntʃ/ *n.* зяблик *m.*
chafing dish /'tʃeifɪŋ/ *n.* жаровня *f.*
chagrin /ʃə'grɪn/ *n.* досада *f.*, огорчение *neut.*
chain /tʃein/ **1.** *n.* цепь *f.*; цепочка *f.* **2.** *v.* сковывать *impf.*, сковать *pf.*
chain bridge *n.* цепной мост *m.*
chain drive *n.* цепной привод *m.*
chain mail *n.* кольчуга *f.*
chain reaction *n.* цепная реакция *f.*
chain saw *n.* цепная пила *f.*
chain smoker *n.* заядлый курильщик *m.*
chain stitch *n.* тамбурная строчка *f.*
chair /tʃɛər/ **1.** *n.* стул *m.*; (*univ.*) кафедра *f.* **2.** *v.* председательствовать (на *with prep.*) *impf.*
chairlift /'tʃɛər,lɪft/ *n.* кресельный подъёмник *m.*

chairman /'tʃɛərmən/ *n.* председатель *m.*
chairmanship /'tʃɛərmən,ʃɪp/ *n.* председательство *neut.*
chairwoman /'tʃɛər,wʊmən/ *n.* председательница *f.*
chaise longue /,ʃeiz 'lɔŋ/ *n.* шезлонг *m.*
chalcedony /kæl'sɛdn̩i/ *n.* халцедон *m.*
chalet /ʃæ'lei/ *n.* шале *neut. indecl.*
chalice /'tʃælɪs/ *n.* (*eccles.*) чаша *f.*
chalk /tʃɔk/ *n.* мел *m.*
chalky /'tʃɔki/ *adj.* меловой.
challenge /'tʃælɪndʒ/ **1.** *n.* вызов *m.* **2.** *v.* вызывать *impf.*, вызвать *pf.*
challenger /'tʃælɪndʒər/ *n.* претендент *m.*
challenging /'tʃælɪndʒɪŋ/ *adj.* вызывающий; (*demanding*) требовательный.
chamber /'tʃeimbər/ *n.* комната; (*polit.*) палата *f.*
chamberlain /'tʃeimbərlɪn/ *n.* камергер *m.*
chambermaid /'tʃeimbər,meid/ *n.* горничная *f.*
chamber music *n.* камерная музыка *f.*
chamber pot *n.* ночной горшок *m.*
chameleon /kə'miliən/ *n.* хамелеон *m.*
chamfer /'tʃæmfər/ *n.* фаска *f.*
chamois /'ʃæmi; Fr. / **1.** *n.* (*leather*) замша *f.* **2.** *adj.* замшевый.
champ /tʃæmp, tʃɒmp/ *v.* (*colloq.*) чавкать *impf.*
champagne /ʃæm'pein/ *n.* шампанское *neut.*
Champagne /ʃæm'pein/ *n.* (*province*) Шампань *f.*
champion /'tʃæmpiən/ **1.** *n.* чемпион *m.*, чемпионка *f.* **2.** *v.* защищать *impf.*, защитить *pf.*; поддерживать *impf.*, поддержать *pf.*
championship /'tʃæmpiən,ʃɪp/ *n.* чемпионат *m.*, первенство *neut.*
chance /tʃæns/ *n.* случай *m.*; возможность *f.*; **by chance** случайно; **to take a chance** рисковать *impf.*
chancel /'tʃænsəl/ *n.* алтарь *m.*
chancellery /'tʃænsələri/ *n.* канцелярия *f.*
chancellor /'tʃænsələr/ *n.* канцлер *m.*
chancery /'tʃænsəri/ *n.* канцлерский суд *m.*
chancy /'tʃænsi/ *adj.* рискованный.
chandelier /,ʃændl̩'ɪər/ *n.* люстра *f.*
change /tʃeindʒ/ **1.** *n.* изменение *neut.*, перемена *f.*; (*of clothes, e.g.*) смена *f.*; (*money*) сдача *f.*; (*of trains, e.g.*) пересадка *f.* **2.** *v.t.* менять *impf.*; *v.i.* меняться *impf.*
changeability /,tʃeindʒə'bɪlɪti/ *n.* переменчивость *f.*
changeable /'tʃeindʒəbəl/ *adj.* изменчивый.
changeless /'tʃeindʒlɪs/ *adj.* неизменный.
changeover /'tʃeindʒ,ouvər/ *n.* изменение *neut.*
changing room /'tʃeindʒɪŋ/ *n.* раздевалка *f.*
channel /'tʃænl̩/ *n.* пролив, канал; путь *m.*
Channel Islands *n.* Нормандские острова *pl.*
chant /tʃænt/ **1.** *n.* песнь *f.*; (*eccles.*) песнопение *neut.* **2.** *v.* петь *impf.*
chanterelle /,ʃæntə'rɛl/ *n.* лисичка *f.*
chaos /'keiɒs/ *n.* хаос *m.*
chaotic /kei'ɒtɪk/ *adj.* хаотический.
chap[1] /tʃæp/ *n.* (*colloq.*) малый; парень; мужик *m.*
chap[2] /tʃæp/ *n.* трещина, ссадина *f.*
chapel /'tʃæpəl/ *n.* часовня; капелла *f.*
chaperon /'ʃæpə,roun/ *n.* компаньон *m.*, компаньонка *f.*
chaplain /'tʃæplɪn/ *n.* капеллан *m.*

chaplet /'tʃæplɪt/ n. венóк m.

chapter /'tʃæptər/ n. главá f.

char /tʃɑr/ v. обýгливать(ся) impf.

character /'kærɪktər/ n. харáктер m.; (theat.) дéйствующее лицó neut.; (letter) бýква f.

characteristic /ˌkærɪktə'rɪstɪk/ **1.** adj. харáктерный. **2.** n. характерúстика, характéрная осóбенность f.

characterization /ˌkærɪktərə'zeɪʃən/ n. характерúстика f.

characterize /'kærɪktəˌraɪz/ v. характеризовáть impf. and pf.

characterless /'kærɪktərlɪs/ adj. бесхарáктерный.

charade /ʃə'reɪd/ n. шарáда f.

charcoal /'tʃɑrˌkoul/ n. дрéвесный ýголь m.

charge /tʃɑrdʒ/ **1.** n. (elec.) заря́д m.; (fee) плáта f.; (care) попечéние neut.; (accusation) обвинéние neut.; (order) поручéние neut. **2.** v. (entrust) поручáть impf., поручúть pf.; (accuse) обвиня́ть impf., обвинúть pf.; (elec.) заряжáть impf., заряди́ть pf.

chargé d'affaires /ʃɑr'ʒei də'fɛər/ n. повéренный в делáх m.

charger /'tʃɑrdʒər/ n. (horse) строевáя лóшадь f.; (elec.) **battery charger** заря́дный выпрями́тель m.

charily /'tʃɛərəli/ adv. осторóжно.

chariot /'tʃæriət/ n. колесни́ца f.

charioteer /ˌtʃæriə'tɪər/ n. возни́ца m.

charisma /kə'rɪzmə/ n. (rel.) бóжий дар m.; (fascination) хари́зма f., обая́ние neut.

charismatic /ˌkærɪz'mætɪk/ adj. обая́тельный.

charitable /'tʃærɪtəbəl/ adj. милосéрдный.

charity /'tʃærɪti/ n. благотвори́тельность f.; милосéрдие neut.; (foundation) благотвори́тельное óбщество neut.

charlatan /'ʃɑrlətn̩/ n. шарлатáн m.

charlatanism /'ʃɑrlətn̩ˌɪzəm/ n. шарлатáнство neut.

Charlemagne /'ʃɑrləˌmein/ n. Карл Вели́кий, Шарлемáнь m.

Charleston /'ʃɑrlstən/ n. (dance) чарльстóн m.

charlotte /'ʃɑrlət/ n. шарлóтка f.

charm /tʃɑrm/ **1.** n. очаровáние, обая́ние neut.; чáры pl.; (amulet) талисмáн m. **2.** v. очарóвывать impf., очаровáть pf.

charmer /'tʃɑrmər/ n. обая́тельный человéк m.; **snake charmer** n. заклинáтель змей m.

charming /'tʃɑrmɪŋ/ adj. очаровáтельный.

chart /tʃɑrt/ **1.** n. (document) хáртия, грáмота f.; (constitution) устáв m.; (hire) чáртер m. **2.** v. (a ship) фрахтовáть; (hire) нанимáть impf.; (hire out) сдавáть внаём impf.

chartered /'tʃɑrtərd/ adj. привилегирóванный.

charterer /'tʃɑrtərər/ n. фрахтовáтель m.

charthouse /'tʃɑrtˌhaus/ n. (naut.) штýрманская рýбка f.

Chartism /'tʃɑrtɪzəm/ n. чарти́зм m.

Chartres /'ʃɑrtrə/ n. Шартр m.

chartreuse /ʃɑr'truz/ n. шартрéз m.

charwoman /'tʃɑrˌwumən/ n. убóрщица f.

chary /'tʃɛəri/ adj. (cautious) осторóжный.

chase¹ /tʃeis/ **1.** n. преслéдование neut., погóня f. **2.** v. гнáться (за with instr.) impf. det.

chase² /tʃeis/ n. дýло neut.; жёлоб m.

chaser /'tʃeisər/ n. преслéдователь m.

chasm /'kæzəm/ n. бéздна, прóпасть f.

chassis /'tʃæsi/ n. шасси́ neut. indecl.

chaste /tʃeist/ adj. целомýдренный.

chasten /'tʃeisən/ v. карáть impf.

chastise /tʃæs'taiz/ v. накáзывать impf., наказáть pf.

chastity /'tʃæstɪti/ n. целомýдрие neut.

chasuble /'tʃæzyəbəl/ n. ри́за f.

chat /tʃæt/ **1.** n. бесéда f. **2.** v. бесéдовать impf.

chattel /'tʃætl̩/ n. сóбственность f.; (дви́жимое) имýщество neut.; **goods and chattels** n. пожи́тки pl.

chatter /'tʃætər/ v. болтáть; щебетáть impf.; (of teeth) стучáть impf.

chatterbox /'tʃætˌər bɒks/ n. болтýн m., болтýнья f.

chatty /'tʃæti/ adj. (talkative) болтли́вый.

chauffeur /'ʃoufər/ n. шофёр, води́тель m.

chauvinism /'ʃouvəˌnizəm/ n. шовини́зм m.; **male chauvinism** женоненави́стничество neut.

chauvinist /'ʃouvənist/ n. шовини́ст m.

chauvinistic /ˌʃouvə'nistik/ adj. шовинисти́ческий.

cheap /tʃip/ adj. дешёвый.

cheapen /'tʃipən/ v. обесцéнивать(ся) impf., обесцéнить(ся) pf.

cheaper /'tʃipər/ adj. дешéвле, бóлее дешёвый.

cheaply /'tʃipli/ adv. дёшево.

cheapness /'tʃipnis/ n. дешеви́зна f.; вульгáрность f.

cheat /tʃit/ v. обмáнывать impf., обманýть pf.

cheater /'tʃitər/ n. обмáнщик m., обмáнщица f.

cheating /'tʃitiŋ/ n. плутовствó neut.

check /tʃɛk/ **1.** n. контрóль m., провéрка f.; (bank) чек m.; (chess) шах m.; **to cash a check** v. (obtain) получáть дéньги по чéку; (give) выдавáть дéньги по чéку impf., провéрить pf. **2.** v. проверя́ть impf., провéрить pf.

checked /tʃɛkt/ adj. клéтчатый.

checker¹ /'tʃɛkər/ n. (person) контролёр m.

checker² /'tʃɛkər/ n. (pattern) клéтка f.; (for game) шáшка f.

checkered /'tʃɛkərd/ adj. (pattern) клéтчатый, в клéтку; (squared) разделённый на квадрáты; (varied) разнообрáзный.

check list n. контрóльный спи́сок m.

checkmate /'tʃɛkˌmeit/ n. мат m.

checkout /'tʃɛkˌaut/ n. прилáвок m., кáсса f.

checkpoint /'tʃɛkˌpɔint/ n. контрóльно-пропускнóй пункт m.

checkup /'tʃɛkʌp/ n. провéрка f.

cheddar /'tʃɛdər/ n. чéддер m.

cheek /tʃik/ n. щекá f.

cheekbone /'tʃikˌboun/ n. скулá f.

cheeky /'tʃiki/ adj. нахáльный.

cheep /tʃip/ n. писк m.

cheer /tʃɪər/ **1.** n. ободрéние neut. **2.** v. ободря́ть impf., ободри́ть pf.; аплоди́ровать impf.

cheerful /'tʃɪərfəl/ adj. весёлый.

cheerfully /'tʃɪərfəli/ adv. вéсело.

cheerfulness /'tʃɪərfəlnis/ n. весёлость f.

cheerless /'tʃɪərlis/ adj. мрáчный.

cheers /tʃɪərz/ interj. (colloq.) за вáше здорóвье!

cheese /tʃiz/ **1.** n. сыр m. **2.** adj. сы́рный.

cheetah /'tʃitə/ n. гепа́рд m.
chef /ʃɛf/ n. гла́вный по́вар m.
chef-d'oeuvre /ʃe'duvrə/ n. шеде́вр m.
Chelyabinsk /tʃɛl'yabɪnsk/ n. Челя́бинск m.
chemical /'kɛmɪkəl/ **1.** adj. хими́ческий. **2.** n. химика́т m.; хими́ческий препара́т f.; химика́лии pl.
chemically /'kɛmɪkli/ adv. хими́чески.
chemise /ʃə'miz/ n. же́нская соро́чка f.
chemist /'kɛmɪst/ n. хи́мик m.
chemistry /'kɛməstri/ n. хи́мия f.
Chemnitz /'kɛmnɪts/ n. Хе́мниц m.
chemotherapy /ˌkimou'θɛrəpi/ n. химотерапи́я f.
Chennai /tʃə'nai/ n. (formerly: Madras) Ченна́й m.
cherish /'tʃɛrɪʃ/ v. леле́ять, храни́ть impf.
Cherkassy /tʃɜr'kasi/ n. Черка́ссы pl.
Chernivtsi /tʃyɪrnʌf'tsɪ/ n. Черновцы́ pl.
Chernobyl /tʃɜr'noubəl/ n. Черно́быль m.
cherry /'tʃɛri/ **1.** n. ви́шня f. **2.** adj. вишнёвый.
chert /tʃɜrt/ n. кремни́стый сла́нец m.
cherub /'tʃɛrəb/ n. херуви́м m.
cherubic /tʃə'rubɪk/ adj. херуви́мский.
chervil /'tʃɜrvɪl/ n. ке́рвель m.
chess /tʃɛs/ **1.** n. ша́хматы pl. **2.** adj. ша́хматный.
chessboard /'tʃɛs,bɔrd/ n. ша́хматная доска́ f.
chessman /'tʃɛs,mæn/ n. ша́хматная фигу́ра f.
chess player n. шахмати́ст m.
chest /tʃɛst/ **1.** n. (trunk) сунду́к, я́щик m.; (anat.) грудна́я кле́тка f. **2.** adj. грудно́й
chestnut /'tʃɛs,nʌt/ **1.** n. кашта́н m. **2.** adj. кашта́новый; (horse) гнедо́й.
cheval glass /ʃə'væl/ n. трюмо́ neut. indecl.
chevron /'ʃevrən/ n. (mil.) шевро́н, уго́льник m.
chew /tʃu/ v. жева́ть impf.
chewing gum /'tʃuɪŋ/ n. жва́чка f.
chiasmus /kai'æzməs/ n. хиа́зм m.
chic /ʃik/ adj. шика́рный, мо́дный.
Chicago /ʃɪ'kɑgou/ n. Чика́го m.
chicanery /ʃɪ'keinəri/ n. махина́ция f.
chick /tʃɪk/ n. цыплёнок m.
chicken /'tʃɪkən/ **1.** n. ку́рица f., цыплёнок m. **2.** adj. кури́ный.
chicken coop n. куря́тник m.
chicken feed n. корм для цыпля́т m.; (colloq.) пустяки́ pl.
chicken-hearted /'tʃɪkən,hɑrtɪd/ adj. малоду́шный.
chickenpox /'tʃɪkən,pɒks/ n. ветряна́я о́спа f.
chickpea /'tʃɪk,pi/ n. туре́цкий горо́х m.
chickweed /'tʃɪk,wid/ n. мокри́ца f.
chicory /'tʃɪkəri/ n. цико́рий m.
chide /tʃaid/ v. упрека́ть impf.
chief /tʃif/ **1.** adj. гла́вный. **2.** n. глава́ f., нача́льник m.
chiefly /'tʃifli/ adv. гла́вным о́бразом, в основно́м.
chieftain /'tʃiftən/ n. (tribe) вождь m.; (robber band) атама́н m.
chiffon /ʃɪ'fɒn/ n. шифо́н m.
chiffonier /ˌʃɪfə'nɪər/ n. шифонье́рка f.
chignon /'ʃinyɒn/ n. шиньо́н m.
chilblains /'tʃɪlblein/ n. обмороже́ние, обморо́женное ме́сто neut.
child /tʃaild/ n. ребёнок m., дитя́ neut. (pl. де́ти).

childbearing /'tʃaild,bɛərɪŋ/ n. деторожде́ние neut.
childbirth /'tʃaild,bɜrθ/ n. ро́ды pl.
childhood /'tʃaildhʊd/ n. де́тство neut.
childish /'tʃaildɪʃ/ adj. де́тский, ребя́ческий.
childless /'tʃaildlɪs/ adj. безде́тный.
childlike /'tʃaild,laik/ adj. де́тский.
children /'tʃɪldrən/ n. де́ти pl.
children's /'tʃɪldrənz/ adj. де́тский.
chili /'tʃɪli/ n. стручко́вый пе́рец m.
chiliad /'kɪli,æd/ n. тысячеле́тие neut.
chiliastic /ˌkɪli'æstɪk/ adj. хилиасти́ческий.
chill /tʃɪl/ **1.** n. холодо́к m.; (ailment) просту́да f. **2.** v. охлажда́ть impf., охлади́ть pf.
chilly /'tʃɪli/ adj. прохла́дный.
chime /tʃaim/ n. (bell) звон m.; (clock) бой m.; перезво́н m.; (set of bells) набо́р колоколо́в m.
chimera /kɪ'mɪərə/ n. ди́кая фанта́зия, химе́ра f.
chimerical /kɪ'mɛrɪkəl/ adj. химери́ческий.
Chimkent /tʃɪm'kent/ n. Чимке́нт m.
chimney /'tʃɪmni/ n. труба́ f.
chimpanzee /ˌtʃɪmpæn'zi/ n. шимпанзе́ neut. indecl.
chin /tʃɪn/ n. подборо́док m.
china /'tʃainə/ n. фарфо́р m., фарфо́ровая посу́да f.
China /'tʃainə/ n. Кита́й m.
Chinatown /'tʃainə,taun/ n. кита́йский кварта́л m.
chinchilla /tʃɪn'tʃɪlə/ n. (zool.) шинши́лла f.
Chinese /tʃai'niz/ **1.** adj. кита́йский. **2.** n. кита́ец m., китая́нка f.
chink /tʃɪŋk/ n. (crack) щель f.; (sound) звя́канье neut.
chinoiserie /ʃin,wɑzə'ri/ n. кита́йский стиль m.
chintz /tʃɪnts/ **1.** n. си́тец m. **2.** adj. си́тцевый.
chip /tʃɪp/ n. (wood) ще́пка f. ; (splinter) лучи́на f.; (stone) обло́мок m.; (glass, metal) оско́лок m.; (crack) тре́щина f. (dent., piece missing) щерби́нка f.
chipboard /'tʃɪp,bɔrd/ n. древе́сно-стру́жечная плита́ f.
chipmunk /'tʃɪpmʌŋk/ n. бурунду́к m.
chiromancy /'kairə,mænsi/ n. хирома́нтия f.
chiropter /kai'rɒptər/ n. рукокры́лое живо́тное neut.
chirp /tʃɜrp/ v. чири́кать, щебета́ть impf.
chirr /tʃɜr/ v. стрекота́ть impf.
chisel /'tʃɪzəl/ **1.** n. резе́ц m., долото́ neut. **2.** v. высека́ть impf., вы́сечь pf.
chiseler /'tʃɪzlər n. (slang) плут m.
Chişinău /ki,ʃinə'u/. Кишинёв m.
Chita /tʃi'ta/ n. Чита́ f.
chitchat /'tʃɪt,tʃæt/ n. болтовня́ f.
chivalrous /'ʃɪvəlrəs/ adj. ры́царский.
chivalry /'ʃɪvəlri/ n. ры́царство neut.
chive /tʃaiv/ n. шнитт-лук m.
chloral /'klɔrəl/ n. (chem.) хлора́л m.
chlorate /'klɔreit/ n. хлора́т m.
chloric /'klɔrɪk/ adj. хло́ристый.
chloride /'klɔraid/ n. хлори́д m.
chlorinate /'klɔrə,neit/ v. хлори́ровать impf.
chlorinated /'klɔrə,neitid/ adj. хлори́рованный.
chlorination /ˌklɔrə'neiʃən/ n. хлори́рование neut.
chlorine /'klɔrin/ n. хлор m.
chloroform /'klɔrə,fɔrm/ n. хлорофо́рм m.

chlorophyll /'klɔrəfɪl/ n. хлорофи́лл m.
chlorosis /klɔ'rousɪs/ n. хлоро́з m.
chlorous /'klɔrəs/ adj. хло́ристый, хло́рный.
chock /tʃɒk/ n. (wedge) клин m.; (block) коло́дка f.; (support) подста́вка f.
chocolate /'tʃɔkəlɪt/ **1.** n. шокола́д m. **2.** adj. шокола́дный.
choice /tʃɔis/ **1.** adj. отбо́рный. **2.** n. вы́бор m.
choir /kwaiᵊr/ n. хор m.; (part of a church) кли́рос m.
choirboy /'kwaiᵊr,bɔi/ n. пе́вчий m.
choke /tʃouk/ v.: v.t. души́ть impf.; v.i. дави́ться; задыха́ться impf.
cholera /'kɒlərə/ n. холе́ра f.
choleric /'kɒlərɪk/ adj. вспы́льчивый.
cholesterol /kə'lɛstə,roul/ n. холестери́н m.
choose /tʃuz/ v. выбира́ть impf., вы́брать pf.
choosy /'tʃuzi/ adj. (coll.) привере́дливый.
chop /tʃɒp/ **1.** n. (meat) отбивна́я котле́та f. **2.** v. руби́ть; коло́ть impf.
chopped meat n. фарш m.
chopper /'tʃɒpər/ n. (axe) колу́н m.; (knife) теса́к m.
chopping /'tʃɒpɪŋ/ n. ру́бка f.
choppy /'tʃɒpi/ adj. неспоко́йный.
chops /tʃæps, ʃæps/ n. (colloq.) че́люсти f.
chopstick /'tʃɒp,stɪk/ n. па́лочка (для еды) f.
choral /'kɔrəl/ adj. хорово́й.
chorale /kə'ræl/ n. хора́л m.
chord /kɔrd/ n. (mus.) акко́рд m.
chorea /kə'riə/ n. хоре́я f.
choreographer /,kɔri'ɒgrəfər/ n. балетме́йстер m.
choreographic /,kɔriə'græfɪk/ adj. хореографи́ческий.
choreography /,kɔri'ɒgrəfi/ n. хореогра́фия f.
chorister /'kɔrəstər/ n. хори́ст m.
choroid /'kɔrɔid/ n. сосу́дистая оболо́чка f.
chortle /'tʃɔrtl/ n. хихи́канье neut.
chorus /'kɔrəs/ n. хор m.
chorus girl n. хори́стка f.
chosen /'tʃouzən/ adj. и́збранный.
chough /tʃʌf/ n. (bird) клуши́ца f.
chow chow /'tʃau,tʃau/ n. (dog) ча́у-ча́у m. indecl.
chrism /'krɪzəm/ n. еле́й m.
Christ /kraist/ n. Христо́с m.
christen /'krɪsən/ v. крести́ть impf., (give name) нарека́ть impf.
christening /'krɪsənɪŋ/ n. креще́ние neut.
Christian /'krɪstʃən/ **1.** adj. христиа́нский. **2.** n. христиани́н m., христиа́нка f.
Christianity /,krɪstʃi'ænɪti/ n. Христиа́нство neut.
Christmas /'krɪsməs/ **1.** n. Рождество́ neut. **2.** adj. рожде́ственский.
chromate /'kroumeit/ n. хрома́т m.
chromatic /krou'mætɪk/ adj. (color) цветно́й; (mus.) хромати́ческий.
chromatography /,kroumə'tɒgrəfi/ n. хромато́графия f.
chrome /kroum/ n. хром m.
chromic /'kroumɪk/ adj. хро́мовый.
chromium /'kroumiəm/ n. хром m.
chromolithography /,kroumoulɪ'θɒgrəfi/ n. хромолитогра́фия f.
chromosome /'kroumə,soum/ n. хромосо́ма f.

chromotype /'kroumə,taip/ n. хромоти́пия f.
chromous /'kroumǝs/ adj. хро́мистый.
chronic /'krɒnɪk/ adj. хрони́ческий.
chronicle /'krɒnɪkəl/ n. хро́ника, ле́топись f.
chronicler /'krɒnɪklər/ n. (hist.) летопи́сец m.
chronograph /'krɒnə,græf/ n. (hist., tech.) хроно́граф m.
chronological /,krɒnl'ɒdʒɪkəl/ adj. хронологи́ческий.
chronology /krə'nɒlədʒi/ n. хроноло́гия f.; (table) хронологи́ческая табли́ца f.
chronometer /krə'nɒmɪtər/ n. хроно́метр m.
chrysalis /'krɪsəlɪs/ n. ку́колка f.
chrysanthemum /krɪ'sænθəməm/ n. хризантема f.
chrysolite /'krɪsə,lait/ n. хризоли́т m.
chub /tʃʌb/ n. (fish) гола́вль m.
chubby /'tʃʌbi/ adj. щека́стый.
chuck /tʃʌk/ **1.** v. (colloq.) (throw) швыря́ть impf. **2.** n. (cut of beef) лопа́тка f.; (clamp) патро́н m.
chuckle /'tʃʌkəl/ v. (giggle) хихи́кать; (laugh quietly) посме́иваться impf.
chug /tʃʌg/ n. пыхте́ние neut.
Chukchi Sea /'tʃuktʃi/ n. Чуко́тское мо́ре neut.
chum /tʃʌm/ n. това́рищ, прия́тель m.
chummy /'tʃʌmi/ adj. обши́тельный.
chump /tʃʌmp/ n. (piece of wood) коло́да f.
chunk /tʃʌŋk/ n. кусо́к m.; (slice) ломо́ть m.
chunky /'tʃʌŋki/ adj. корена́стый.
church /tʃɜrtʃ/ **1.** n. це́рковь f. **2.** adj. церко́вный.
churchman /'tʃɜrtʃmən/ n. церко́вник m.
churchy /'tʃɜrtʃi/ adj. на́божный.
churl /tʃɜrl/ n. неве́жа m. and f (decl. f.).
churlish /'tʃɜrlɪʃ/ adj. грубый; невоспи́танный; (mean) скупо́й.
churn /tʃɜrn/ **1.** n. маслобо́йка f. **2.** v. сбива́ть impf.
chute /ʃut/ n. скат; же́лоб m.
Chuvash /tʃu'vaʃ/ n. чува́ш m., чува́шка f.
Chuvash Autonomous Republic n. Чува́шия f.
C.I.A. n. (abbr. of Central Intelligence Agency). ЦРУ (abbr. of Центра́льное разве́дывательное управле́ние) neut.
cicada /sɪ'keidə/ n. цика́да f.
cicatrix /'sɪkətrɪks/ n. шрам m.
cicatrize /'sɪkə,traiz/ v. зажива́ть impf.
cicerone /,sɪsə'rouni, ,tʃɪtʃə-/ n. проводни́к m.
cider /'saidər/ n. я́блочный сок; сидр m.
cigar /sɪ'gar/ n. сига́ра f.
cigarette /,sɪgə'rɛt/ n. папиро́са, сигаре́та f.
cilia /'sɪliə/ n. (anat.) ресни́цы pl.
cinch /sɪntʃ/ n.: **it's a cinch** э́то уж наверняка́; (as good as done) де́ло в шля́пе.
cinder /'sɪndər/ n. шлак m.; pl. пе́пель m.
Cinderella /,sɪndə'rɛlə/ n. Зо́лушка f.
cine- prefix кино-
cinema /'sɪnəmə/ n. кино́ neut. indecl., кинотеа́тр m.
cinematic /,sɪnə'mætɪk/ adj. кинематографи́ческий.
cinematics /,sɪnə'mætɪks/ n. кинема́тика f.
cinematography /,sɪnəmə'tɒgrəfi/ n. киноматогра́фия f.
cinerary /'sɪnə,reri/ adj. пе́пельный.
cinnabar /'sɪnə,bar/ n. ки́новарь f.
cinnamon /'sɪnəmən/ n. кори́ца f.

cinquefoil /'sɪŋkˌfɔil/ *n.* (*bot.*) ля́пчатка *f.*

cipher /'saifər/ *n.* (*zero*) ноль *m.*; (*code*) шифр *m.*; (*number*) ара́бская ци́фра *f.*

circa /'sɜrkə/ *prep.* о́коло (*with gen.*), приблизи́тельно.

Circassian /sər'kæʃən/ *n.* (*person*) черке́с *m.*, черке́шенка *f.*; (*language*) черке́сский язы́к *m.*

Circe /'sɜrsi/ *n.* (*myth.*) Цирце́я *f.*

circle /'sɜrkəl/ *n.* круг, кружо́к *m.*

circuit /'sɜrkɪt/ *n.* оборо́т *m.*; **short circuit** (*elec.*) коро́ткое замыка́ние *neut.*

circuit breaker *n.* конта́ктный прерыва́тель *m.*

circuitous /sər'kyuɪtəs/ *adj.* кру́жный, око́льный.

circular /'sɜrkyələr/ *adj.* кру́глый.

circularity /ˌsɜrkyə'lærɪti/ *n.* кругообра́зность *f.*

circularize /'sɜrkyələˌraiz/ *v.* рассыла́ть циркуля́ры *impf.*

circulate /'sɜrkyəˌleit/ *v.* циркули́ровать *impf.*

circulating /'sɜrkyəˌleitɪŋ/ *adj.*: **circulating library** *n.* библиоте́ка с вы́дачей книг на́ дом *f.*

circulation /ˌsɜrkyə'leiʃən/ *n.* циркуля́ция *f.*; (*newspaper, etc.*) тира́ж *m.*

circumambient /ˌsɜrkəm'æmbiənt/ *adj.* окружа́ющий.

circumcise /'sɜrkəmˌsaiz/ *v.* соверша́ть обреза́ние, обреза́ть *impf.*

circumcision /ˌsɜrkəm'sɪʒən/ *n.* обреза́ние *neut.*

circumference /sər'kʌmfərəns/ *n.* окру́жность *f.*

circumflex /'sɜrkəmˌflɛks/ *n.* циркумфле́кс *m.*

circumlocution /ˌsɜrkəmlou'kyuʃən/ *n.* укло́нчивость *f.*

circumnavigate /ˌsɜrkəm'nævɪˌgeit/ *v.* пла́вать вокру́г *impf.*

circumnavigation /ˌsɜrkəmˌnævɪ'geiʃən/ *n.* кругосве́тное пла́вание *neut.*

circumpolar /ˌsɜrkəm'poulər/ *adj.* околополя́рный.

circumscribe /'sɜrkəmˌskraib/ *v.* ограни́чивать *impf.*, ограни́чить *pf.*

circumscription /ˌsɜrkəm'skrɪpʃən/ *n.* ограниче́ние *neut.*

circumspect /'sɜrkəmˌspɛkt/ *adj.* осмотри́тельный.

circumspection /ˌsɜrkəm'spɛkʃən/ *n.* осмотри́тельность *f.*

circumstance /'sɜrkəmˌstæns/ *n.* обстоя́тельство *neut.*; **in** (*or* **under**) **the circumstances** при да́нных обстоя́тельствах.

circumstantial /ˌsɜrkəm'stænʃəl/ *adj.* обстоя́тельный; **circumstantial evidence** ко́свенные доказа́тельства *pl.*

circumvent /ˌsɜrkəm'vɛnt/ *v.* обходи́ть *impf.*

circus /'sɜrkəs/ *n.* цирк *m.*

cirrhosis /sɪ'rousɪs/ *n.* цирро́з пе́чени *m.*

cirrocumulus /ˌsɪrou'kyumyələs/ *n.* пе́ристо-кучевы́е облака́ *pl.*

cirrostratus /ˌsɪrou'streitəs/ *n.* пе́ристо-сло́йстые облака́ *pl.*

cirrus /'sɪrəs/ *n.* (*meteorol.*) пе́ристые облака́ *pl.*; (*bot., zool.*) у́сик *m.*

cisalpine /sɪs'ælpain/ *adj.* цизальпи́нский.

cist /sɪst/ *n.* (*tomb*) гробни́ца *f.*

cistern /'sɪstərn/ *n.* цисте́рна *f.*; резервуа́р *m.*

citadel /'sɪtədļ/ *n.* кре́пость, цитаде́ль *f.*; (*in Russia*) кремль *m.*

citation /sai'teiʃən/ *n.* цита́та, ссы́лка *f.*, цити́рование *neut.*

cite /sait/ *v.* цити́ровать *impf.* and *pf.*, ссыла́ться *impf.*, сосла́ться *pf.*

citizen /'sɪtəzən/ *n.* граждани́н *m.*, гражда́нка *f.*

citizenship /'sɪtəzənˌʃɪp/ *n.* гражда́нство *neut.*

citrate /'sɪtreit/ *n.* цитра́т *m.*

citric /'sɪtrɪk/ *adj.* лимо́нный.

citrine /'sɪtrin/ *n.* цитри́н *m.*

citronella /ˌsɪtrə'nelə/ *n.* цитроне́лла *f.*

citrus /'sɪtrəs/ **1.** *n.* ци́трус *m.* **2.** *adj.* ци́трусовый.

city /'sɪti/ **1.** *n.* го́род *m.* **2.** *adj.* городско́й.

civet /'sɪvɪt/ *n.* (*zool.*) виве́рра, циве́тта *f.*

civic /'sɪvɪk/ *adj.* гражда́нский; (*polite*) ве́жливый.

civilian /sɪ'vɪlyən/ *adj.* гражда́нский; (*non-military*) шта́тский.

civility /sɪ'vɪliti/ *n.* ве́жливость *f.*

civilization /ˌsɪvələ'zeiʃən/ *n.* цивилиза́ция *f.*

civilize /'sɪvəˌlaiz/ *v.* цивилизова́ть *impf.* and *pf.*

civilized /'sɪvəˌlaizd/ *adj.* цивилизо́ванный; культу́рный.

clad /klæd/ *adj.* оде́тый (в *with acc.*).

claim /kleim/ **1.** *n.* прете́нзия *f.*, тре́бование *neut.* **2.** *v.* тре́бовать *impf.*, потре́бовать *pf.*

claimant /'kleimənt/ *n.* предъявля́ющий права́ *adj.*

clairvoyance /klɛr'vɔiəns/ *n.* яснови́дение *neut.*

clairvoyant /klɛər'vɔiənt/ *adj.* яснови́дящий.

clam /klæm/ *n.* мо́ллюск *m.*

clamant /'kleimənt, 'klæmənt/ *adj.* шумли́вый.

clamber /'klæmbər/ *v.* кара́бкаться (на *with acc.*; по *with dat.*) *impf.*

clammy /'klæmi/ *adj.* холо́дный и вла́жный на о́щупь.

clamor /'klæmər/ *n.* шум *m.*

clamorous /'klæmərəs/ *adj.* (*noisy*) шу́мный; (*shouting*) крикли́вый.

clamp /klæmp/ **1.** *n.* зажи́м *m.* **2.** *v.* скрепля́ть *impf.*, скрепи́ть *pf.*; зажима́ть *impf.*, зажа́ть *pf.*

clan /klæn/ *n.* род, клан *m.*

clandestine /klæn'dɛstɪn/ *adj.* та́йный, скры́тый.

clang /klæŋ/ **1.** *n.* (*ringing sound*) звон *m.*; (*clank*) лязг *m.* **2.** *v.* ля́згать *impf.*, ля́згнуть *pf.*; (*rattle*) бряца́ть *impf.*

clank /klæŋk/ *n.* ля́зганье *neut.*

clansman /'klænzmən/ *n.* член кла́на *m.*

clap /klæp/ *v.* хло́пать *impf.*, хло́пнуть *pf.*; аплоди́ровать *impf.*

clapper /'klæpər/ *n.* (*bell*) язы́к *m.*; (*rattle*) хлопу́шка *f.*

claptrap /'klæpˌtræp/ *n.* чепуха́ *f.*

claque /klæk/ *n.* кла́ка *f.*

claret /'klærɪt/ *n.* кларе́т *m.*

clarification /ˌklærəfɪ'keiʃən/ *n.* разъясне́ние *neut.*

clarify /'klærəˌfai/ *v.* вы́яснить *pf.*

clarinet /ˌklærə'nɛt/ *n.* кларне́т *m.*

clarinetist /ˌklærə'nɛtɪst/ *n.* кларнети́ст *m.*

clarion /'klæriən/ *n.* труба́ *f.*, рожо́к *m.*

clarity /'klærɪti/ *n.* я́сность, прозра́чность *f.*

clasp /klæsp/ **1.** *n.* застёжка *f.*; (*hand*) рукопожа́тие *neut.* **2.** *v.* застёгивать *impf.*, застегну́ть *pf.*; (*hand*) сжима́ть *impf.*

clasp knife *n.* складно́й нож *m.*

class /klæs/ **1.** *n.* класс *m.* **2.** *adj.* кла́ссовый.

class-conscious /'klæsˌkɒnʃəs/ *adj.* кла́ссово созна́тельный.

class consciousness *n.* кла́ссовое созна́ние *neut.*
classical /'klæsıkəl/ *adj.* класси́ческий.
classicism /'klæsə,sızəm/ *n.* классици́зм *m.*
classification /,klæsəfı'keiʃən/ *n.* классифика́ция *f.*
classified /'klæsə,faid/ *adj.* (*secret*) секре́тный, засекре́ченный.
classify /'klæsə,fai/ *v.* классифици́ровать *impf.* and *pf.*; (*as secret*) засекре́чивать *impf.*, засекре́тить *pf.*
classless /'klæslıs/ *adj.* бескла́ссовый.
classmate /'klæs,meit/ *n.* однокла́ссник *m.*
classroom /'klæs,rum/ *n.* аудито́рия *f.*; класс *m.*
classy /'klæsi/ *adj.* (*colloq.*) первокла́ссный.
clatter /'klætər/ *n.* стук *m.*; гро́хот *m.*
clause /klɔz/ *n.* (*legal*) статья́; кла́узула *f.*; (*gram.*) предложе́ние *neut.*
claustrophobia /,klɔstrə'foubiə/ *n.* клаустрофо́бия *f.*
clavichord /'klævı,kɔrd/ *n.* клавико́рды *pl.*
clavicle /'klævıkəl/ *n.* ключи́ца *f.*
clavier /klə'vıər/ *n.* клавиату́ра *f.*
claw /klɔ/ *n.* ко́готь *m.*, (*of crustacean*) клешня́ *f.*
clay /klei/ **1.** *n.* гли́на *f.* **2.** *adj.* гли́няный.
clayey /'kleii/ *adj.* гли́нистый.
clean /klin/ **1.** *adj.* чи́стый. **2.** *v.* чи́стить *impf.*, почи́стить *pf.*; **to clean up** убира́ть *impf.*
clean-cut /'klin'kʌt/ *adj.* ре́зко очéрченный.
cleaner /'klinər/ *n.* (*product*) очисти́тель *m.*; (*person*) чи́стильщик *m.*; (*dry cleaner*) химчи́стка *f.*
cleaning /'klinıŋ/ *n.* чи́стка *f.*
cleanliness /'klɛnlinıs/ *n.* чистота́ *f*
cleanly /'klɛnli/ *adj.* чистопло́тный.
cleanse /klɛnz/ *v.* чи́стить *impf.*, почи́стить *pf.*; очища́ть *impf.*, очи́стить *pf.*
cleanser /'klɛnzər/ *n.* очисти́тельное сре́дство *neut.*
clean-shaven /'klin'ʃeivən/ *adj.* чи́сто вы́бритый.
clear /klıər/ **1.** *adj.* я́сный. **2.** *v.* очища́ть *impf.*, очи́стить *pf.*; (*acquit*) опра́вдывать *impf.*, оправда́ть *pf.*
clearance /'klıərəns/ *n.* зазо́р *m.* (*sale*) распрода́жа *f.*
clearing /'klıərıŋ/ *n.* проясне́ние *neut.*; (*cleared area of wood*) вы́рубка *f.*; (*open area*) поля́на *f.*
clearly /'klıərli/ *adv.* (*of course*) коне́чно, я́вно.
clearness /'klıərnıs/ *n.* я́сность; све́тлость; прозра́чность *f.*
clear-sighted /'klıər'saitıd/ *adj.* зо́ркий.
cleat /klit/ *n.* (*wedge*) клин *m.*; (*tech.*) (*fastening*) зажи́м *m.*
cleavage /'klivıdʒ/ *n.* (*splitting*) расщепле́ние, раска́лывание *neut.*; (*fig.*) раско́л *m.*
cleave /kliv/ *v.* (*split*) раска́лывать *impf.*; (*waves, air, etc.*) рассека́ть *impf.*
cleaver /'klivər/ *n.* теса́к; се́чка *f.*
clef /klɛf/ *n.* ключ *m.*
cleft /klɛft/ **1.** *adj.* расщеплённый **2.** *n.* тре́щина; расще́лина *f.*
clematis /'klɛmətıs, klı'mætıs/ *n.* ломоно́с *m.*
clemency /'klɛmənsi/ *n.* милосе́рдие *neut.*
clement /'klɛmənt/ *adj.* милосе́рдный; ми́лостивый; (*weather*) мя́гкий.
clench /klɛntʃ/ *v.* сжима́ть *impf.*, сжать *pf.*
clepsydra /'klɛpsıdrə/ *n.* клепси́дра *f.*
clerestory /'klıər,stɔri/ *n.* (*archit.*) фона́рь *m.*
clergy /'klɜrdʒi/ *n.* духове́нство *neut.*

clergyman /'klɜrdʒimən/ *n.* свяще́нник *m.*
cleric /'klɛrık/ *n.* церко́вник *m.*, духо́вное лицо́ *neut.*
clerical /'klɛrıkəl/ *adj.* клерика́льный, канцеля́рский.
clericalism /'klɛrıkə,lızəm/ *n.* клерикали́зм *m.*
clerk /klɜrk/ *n.* клерк, слу́жащий, чино́вник *m.*; (*salesperson*) продаве́ц *m.*
clever /'klɛvər/ *adj.* у́мный.
cleverness /'klɛvərnıs/ *n.* ло́вкость, сообрази́тельность *f.*
clew /klu/ *n.* клубо́к *m.*
cliché /kli'ʃei/ *n.* клише́ *neut. indecl.*
click /klık/ **1.** *n.* щелчо́к *m.*, щёлканье *neut.*; (*tech.*) (*mechanism*) защёлка *f.* **2.** *v.* щёлкать *impf.*, щёлкнуть *pf.*
client /'klaiənt/ *n.* клие́нт *m.*
clientele /,klaiən'tɛl/ *n.* клиенту́ра *f.*
cliff /klıf/ *n.* утёс *m.*
climacteric /klai'mæktərık/ **1.** *n.* климакте́рий *m.* **2.** *adj.* климактери́ческий.
climate /'klaimıt/ *n.* кли́мат *m.*
climatic /klai'mætık/ *adj.* климати́ческий.
climatological /,klaimətl'ɒdʒıkəl/ *adj.* климатологи́ческий.
climatology /,klaimə'tɒlədʒi/ *n.* климатоло́гия *f.*
climax /'klaimæks/ *n.* кульминацио́нный пункт *m.*
climb /klaim/ *v.* ла́зить *impf. indet.*, лезть *impf. det.*; взбира́ться *impf.*, взобра́ться *pf.*; (*colloq.*) кара́бкаться *impf.*; **to climb stairs** поднима́ться по ле́стнице *impf.*
climber /'klaimər/ *n.* альпини́ст *m.*; (*plant*) вью́щееся расте́ние *neut.*; (*ambitious person*) честолю́бец *m.*
climbing /'klaimıŋ/ *n.* альпини́зм *m.*
clinch /klıntʃ/ *n.* (*sports*) клинч *m.*
clincher /'klıntʃər/ *n.* (*colloq.*) (*argument*) реша́ющий до́вод *m.*
cling /klıŋ/ *v.* цепля́ться (за *with acc.*) *impf.*
clingy /'klıŋi/ *adj.* (*sticky*) ли́пкий; (*tenacious*) це́пкий; (*clothes*) облега́ющий.
clinic /'klınık/ *n.* кли́ника *f.*
clinical /'klınıkəl/ *adj.* клини́ческий.
clink /klıŋk/ **1.** *n.* звон *m.*; (*slang*) (*prison*) катала́жка *f.* **2.** *v.* звене́ть *impf.*; **to clink glasses** чо́каться *impf.*
clinker /'klıŋkər/ *n.* кли́нкер, шлак *m.*
clinker-built /'klıŋkər,bılt/ *adj.* обши́тый внакро́й.
clinometer /klai'nɒmıtər/ *n.* клино́метр *m.*
clip /klıp/ **1.** *n.* ско́ба; скре́пка *f.* **2.** *v.* скрепля́ть *impf.*, скрепи́ть *pf.*; зажима́ть *impf.*, зажа́ть *pf.*; (*trim*) стричь *impf.*
clippers /'klıpərz/ *pl.* но́жницы *pl.*
clipping /'klıpıŋ/ *n.* обре́зок *m.*; вы́резка *f.*
clique /klik/ *n.* кли́ка *f.*
clitoris /'klıtərıs/ *n.* кли́тор, похотни́к *m.*
cloaca /klou'eikə/ *n.* клоа́ка *f.*
cloak /klouk/ *n.* плащ *m.*
cloakroom /'klouk,rum/ *n.* гардеро́б *m.*, (*colloq.*) раздева́лка *f.*
clobber /'klɒbər/ *v.* (*slang*) бить *impf.*; (*criticize*) разнести́ *pf.*
clock /klɒk/ *n.* часы́ *pl.*
clock face *n.* цифербла́т *m.*
clockmaker /'klɒk,meikər/ *n.* часовщи́к *m.*

clockwise /'klɒk,waiz/ *adv.* по часовой стрелке.
clockwork /'klɒk,wɜrk/ *n.* часовой механизм *m.*
clod /klɒd/ *n.* ком *m.*
clodhopper /'klɒd,hɒpər/ *n.* деревенщина *m.* and *f.*
clog¹ /klɒg/ *n.* (*shoe*) сабо *neut. indecl.*
clog² /klɒg/ *v.* (*block up*) засорять(ся) *impf.*
cloisonné /,klɔizə'nei/ *adj.* с перегородчатой эмалью.
cloister /'klɔistər/ *n.* монастырь *m.*
clone /kloun/ **1.** *n.* клон *m.* **2.** *v.* клонировать *impf.*
cloning /'klounɪŋ/ *n.* клонирование *neut.*
clop /klɒp/ *n.* стук *m.*
close /*adj., adv.* klous; *n., v.* klouz/ **1.** *adj.* близкий. **2.** *adv.* близко. **3.** *v.* закрывать(ся) *impf.*, закрыть(ся) *pf.*; (*conclude*) заключать *impf.*, заключить *pf.* **4.** *n.* (*end*) конец *m.*
closed /klouzd/ *adj.* закрытый.
closefisted /'klous,fɪstɪd/ *adj.* скупой.
close-fitting /'klous'fɪtɪŋ/ *adj.* тесный; облегающий тело.
closely /'klousli/ *adv.* близко; (*attentively*) внимательно.
closeness /'klousnɪs/ *n.* (*nearness*) близость *f.*; (*intimacy*) интимность *f.*
closet /'klɒzɪt/ *n.* шкаф *m.*
closeup /'klousʌp/ *n.* крупный план *m.*
closing /'klouzɪŋ/ *n.* закрытие *neut.*
closure /'klouʒər/ *n.* (*shutting*) закрытие *neut.*; (*conclusion*) заключение *neut.*
clot /klɒt/ **1.** *n.* комок *m.*; тромб *m.* **2.** *v.* сгущаться *impf.*, сгуститься *pf.*; свёртываться *impf.*, свернуться *pf.*
cloth /klɒθ/ *n.* сукно *neut.*, ткань, материя *f.*
clothe /klouð/ *v.* покрывать *impf.*, покрыть *pf.*; **to clothe oneself** *v.* одеваться *impf.*, одеться *pf.*
clothes /klouz/ *n.* одежда *f.*; платье *neut.*
clothing /'klouðɪŋ/ *n.* одежда *f.*
cloud /klaud/ *n.* облако *neut.*, туча *f.*
cloudberry /'klaud,beri/ *n.* морошка *f.*
cloudburst /'klaud,bɜrst/ *n.* ливень *m.*
cloud-capped /'klaud,kæpt/ *adj.* скрытый облаками.
cloud chamber *n.* (*phys.*) камера Вильсона *f.*
cloud-cuckoo-land /'klaud,kuku,lænd/ *n.* мир грёз *m.*
cloudiness /'klaudinɪs/ *n.* облачность *f.*
cloudless /'klaudlɪs/ *adj.* безоблачный.
cloudy /'klaudi/ *adj.* облачный.
clout /klaut/ *n.* (*colloq.*) тумак *m.*
clove /klouv/ *n.* гвоздика *f.*
clove hitch *n.* выбленочный узел *m.*
cloven /'klouvən/ *adj.* раздвоенный.
clover /'klouvər/ *n.* клевер *m.*
cloverleaf /'klouvər,lif/ (*crossing*) *n.* пересечение по типу клеверного листа *neut.*
clown /klaun/ *n.* клоун *m.*
clownish *adj.* неуклюжий.
cloy /klɔi/ *v.* пресыщать *impf.*, пресытить *pf.*
cloying /'klɔiɪŋ/ *adj.* слащавый, приторный.
club /klʌb/ *n.* клуб *m.*
clubfoot /'klʌb,fʊt/ *n.* косолапость, изуродованная ступня *f.*
clubhouse /'klʌb,haus/ *n.* клуб *m.*
club moss *n.* плаун *m.*

cluck /klʌk/ *v.* кудахтать, квохтать *impf.*
clucking /'klʌkɪŋ/ *n.* кудахтанье, квохтанье *neut.*
clue /klu/ *n.* ключ к разгадке *m.*
clumsily /'klʌmzɪli/ *adv.* неуклюже.
clumsiness /'klʌmzinɪs/ *n.* неуклюжесть *f.*
clumsy /'klʌmzi/ *adj.* неуклюжий.
cluster /'klʌstər/ *n.* гроздь *f.*
clutch /klʌtʃ/ *v.* (*seize*) схватывать *impf.*; **to clutch at** хвататься за (*with acc.*) *impf.*; (*hold tightly*) крепко держать *impf.*
clutter /'klʌtər/ *v.* загромождать *impf.*
clyster /'klɪstər/ *n.* клизма *f.*
coach /koutʃ/ **1.** *n.* карета *f.*; (*sports*) тренер *m.* **2.** *v.* тренировать *impf.*
coach box *n.* козлы *pl.*
coach house *n.* каретный сарай *m.*
coachman /'koutʃmən/ *n.* кучер, извозчик *m.*
coagulant /kou'ægyələnt/ *n.* сгущающее средство *neut.*
coagulate /kou'ægyə,leit/ *v.* створаживаться *impf.*, створожиться *pf.*
coagulation /kou,ægyə'leiʃən/ *n.* коагуляция *f.*
coal /koul/ **1.** *n.* уголь *m.* **2.** *adj.* угольный.
coal dust *n.* угольная пыль *f.*
coalesce /,kouə'les/ *v.* срастаться *impf.*
coalfield /'koul,fild/ *n.* каменноугольный бассейн *m.*
coal-fired /'koul,faiᵊrd/ *adj.* с угольным отоплением.
coal gas *n.* каменноугольный газ *m.*
coalition /,kouə'lɪʃən/ **1.** *n.* коалиция *f.* **2.** *adj.* коалиционный.
coal mine *n.* угольная шахта *f.*
coal miner *n.* шахтёр *m.*
coal seam *n.* угольный пласт *m.*
coal tar *n.* каменноугольный дёготь *m.*
coarse /kɔrs/ *adj.* грубый.
coarse-grained /'kɔrs'greind/ *adj.* крупнозернистый.
coarsen /'kɔrsən/ *v.* огрублять *impf.*
coarseness /'kɔrsnɪs/ *n.* грубость *f.*
coast /koust/ *n.* (морской) берег *m.*
coastal /'koustl/ *adj.* береговой.
coaster /'koustər/ *n.* подставка *f.*; (*naut.*) каботажное судно *neut.*
coast guard *n.* береговая охрана; морская пограничная служба *f.*
coastline /'koust,lain/ *n.* побережье *neut.*
coat /kout/ **1.** *n.* пальто *neut. indecl.*, (*fur coat*) шуба *f.*; пиджак *m.*, (*fur*) шерсть *f.*, мех *m.*; (*paint*) слой *m.* **2.** *v.* покрывать *impf.*, покрыть *pf.*; **coat of arms** герб *m.*
coat hanger *n.* плечики *pl.*; вешалка *f.*
coating /'koutɪŋ/ *n.* покрытие *neut.*
coauthor /kou'ɔθər/ *n.* соавтор *m.*
coax /kouks/ *v.* уговаривать *impf.*; выпрашивать *impf.*, выпросить *pf.*
coaxial /kou'æksiəl/ *adj.* коаксиальный.
coaxing /'kouksɪŋ/ *n.* уговаривание *neut.*
cob /kɒb/ *n.* початок кукурузы *m.*
cobalt /'koubɔlt/ **1.** *n.* кобальт *m.* **2.** *adj.* кобальтовый.
cobbled /'kɒbəl/ *adj.* булыжный.
cobbler /'kɒblər/ *n.* сапожник *m.*; (*dessert*) фруктовый пирог *m.*
cobblestone /'kɒbəl,stoun/ *n.* булыжник *m.*
cobra /'koubrə/ *n.* кобра *f.*

cobweb /'kɒb.wɛb/ *n.* паути́на *f.*

cobwebby /'kɒb.wɛbi/ *adj.* затя́нутый паути́ной.

coca /'koukə/ *n.* ко́ка *f.*

cocaine /kou'kein/ *n.* кокаи́н *m.*

coccus /'kɒkəs/ *n.* кокк *m.*

coccyx /'kɒksɪks/ *n.* ко́пчик *m.*

cochineal /ˌkɒtʃə'nil/ *n.* кошени́ль *m.*

cochlea /'kɒkliə/ *n.* (*anat.*) ули́тка *f.*

cock /kɒk/ *n.* (*rooster*) пету́х *m.*; (*faucet*) кран *m.*; (*of a gun*) куро́к *m.*

cockade /kɒ'keid/ *n.* кока́рда *f.*

cock-a-doodle-doo /'kɒkə.dudl'du/ *interj.* кукареку́.

cock-a-hoop /ˌkɒkə'hup/ *adj.* лику́ющий.

cock-and-bull story /'kɒkən'bʊl/ *n.* невероя́тная исто́рия *f.*

cockatoo /'kɒkə.tu/ *n.* какаду́ *m. indecl.*

cockatrice /'kɒkətrɪs/ *n.* васили́ск *m.*

cockchafer /'kɒk.tʃeifər/ *n.* ма́йский хрущ *m.*

cocked /kɒkt/ *adj.* за́дранный.

cocker spaniel /'kɒkər/ *n.* ко́кер-спание́ль *m.*

cockeyed /'kɒk.aid/ *adj.* (*squinting*) косо́й, косогла́зый; (*crooked*) косо́й; (*colloq.*) (*drunk*) пья́ный.

cockfight /'kɒk.fait/ *n.* петуши́ный бой *m.*

cockily /'kɒkəli/ *adv.* де́рзко, наха́льно; самонаде́янно.

cockiness /'kɒkinɪs/ *n.* самонаде́янность *f.*

cockle /'kɒkəl/ *n.* (*bot.*) пле́вел *m.*

cockpit /'kɒk.pɪt/ *n.* каби́на (самолёта) *f.*

cockroach /'kɒk.routʃ/ *n.* тарака́н *m.*

cockscomb /'kɒks.koum/ *n.* пету́шиный гре́бень *m.*

cocktail /'kɒk.teil/ *n.* кокте́йль *m.*

cockup /'kɒk.ʌp/ *n.* (*typog.*) надстро́чный знак *m.*

cocky /'kɒki/ *adj.* де́рзкий, наха́льный; самонаде́янный.

cocoa /'koukou/ *n.* кака́о *neut. indecl.*

coconut /'koukə.nʌt/ *n.* коко́с *m.*, коко́совый оре́х *m.*

cocoon /kə'kun/ *n.* ко́кон *m.*

cod /kɒd/ *n.* треска́ *f.*

coda /'koudə/ *n.* ко́да *f.*

coddle /'kɒdl/ *v.* (*pamper*) балова́ть *impf.*; (*simmer*) вари́ть на ме́дленном огне́ *impf.*

code /koud/ *n.* (*body of laws*) ко́декс *m.*; (*communication*) шифр *m.*

codeine /'koudin/ *n.* кодеи́н *m.*

codex /'koudɛks/ *n.* ко́декс *m.*, руко́писная кни́га *f.*

codicil /'kɒdəsəl/ *n.* припи́ска (к завеща́нию) *f.*

codification /ˌkɒdəfɪ'keiʃən/ *n.* кодифика́ция *f.*

codify /'kɒdə.fai/ *v.* кодифици́ровать *impf. and pf.*

cod-liver oil /'kɒd.lɪvər/ *n.* ры́бий жир *m.*

codpiece /'kɒd.pis/ *n.* гу́льфик *m.*

coeducation /ˌkouɛdʒʊ'keiʃən/ *n.* совме́стное обуче́ние *neut.*

coefficient /ˌkouə'fɪʃənt/ *n.* коэффицие́нт *m.*

coelacanth /'silə.kænθ/ *n.* (*fish*) целака́нт *m.*

coerce /kou'ɜrs/ *v.* принужда́ть *impf.*, принуди́ть *pf.*

coercion /kou'ɜrʃən/ *n.* принужде́ние *neut.*

coercive /kou'ɜrsɪv/ *adj.* принуди́тельный.

coeval /kou'ivəl/ *n.* (*person of same age*) све́рстник, рове́сник *m.*

coexist /ˌkouɪg'zɪst/ *v.* сосуществова́ть *impf.*

coexistence /ˌkouɪg'zɪstəns/ *n.* сосуществова́ние *neut.*

coexistent /ˌkouɪg'zɪstənt/ *adj.* сосуществу́ющий.

coffee /'kɒfi/ **1.** *n.* ко́фе *m. indecl.* **2.** *adj.* кофе́йный.

coffee table *n.* журна́льный сто́лик *m.*

coffer /'kɔfər/ *n.* сунду́к *m.*; *pl.* (*treasury*) казна́ *f.*

coffin /'kɔfɪn/ *n.* гроб *m.*

cog /kɒg/ *n.* зубе́ц *m.*

cogency /'koudʒənsi/ *n.* убеди́тельность *f.*

cogent /'koudʒənt/ *adj.* убеди́тельный.

cogged /kɒgd/ *adj.* зубча́тый.

cogitate /'kɒdʒɪ.teit/ *v.* обду́мывать *impf.*, обду́мать *pf.*

cogitation /ˌkɒdʒɪ'teiʃən/ *n.* размышле́ние *neut.*

cogitative /'kɒdʒɪ.teitɪv/ *adj.* мысли́тельный; мы́слящий.

cognac /'kounyæk/ *n.* конья́к *m.*

cognate /'kɒgneit/ *adj.* ро́дственный.

cognition /kɒg'nɪʃən/ *n.* позна́ние *neut.*

cognitive /'kɒgnɪtɪv/ *adj.* познава́тельный.

cognizance /'kɒgnəzəns/ *n.* зна́ние *neut.*; (*leg.*) подсу́дность *f.*

cognizant /'kɒgnəzənt/ *adj.*: **be cognizant of** осознава́ть *impf.*

cognomen /kɒg'noumən/ *n.* (*surname*) фами́лия *f.*; (*nickname*) про́звище *neut.*

cohabit /kou'hæbɪt/ *v.* сожи́тельствовать *impf.*

cohabitation /kou.hæbɪ'teiʃən/ *n.* сожи́тельство *neut.*

coheir /kou'ɛər/ *n.* сонасле́дник *m.*

cohere /kou'hɪər/ *v.* сцепля́ться *impf.*

coherence /kou'hɪərəns/ *n.* после́довательность *f.*

coherent /kou'hɪərənt/ *adj.* свя́зный.

cohesion /kou'hiʒən/ *n.* сцепле́ние *neut.*

cohesive /kou'hisɪv/ *adj.* сплочённый.

cohort /'kouhɔrt/ *n.* (*hist.*) кого́рта *f.*

coiffure /kwɑ'fyʊr/ *n.* причёска *f.*

coil /kɔil/ **1.** *n.* (*elec.*) кату́шка *f.*; кольцо́ *neut.* **2.** *v.* свёртывать спира́лью *impf.*

coin /kɔin/ *n.* моне́та *f.*

coinage /'kɔinidʒ/ *n.* (*coining*) чека́нка моне́т *f.*

coincide /ˌkouɪn'said/ *v.* совпада́ть *impf.*, совпа́сть *pf.*

coincidence /kou'ɪnsɪdəns/ *n.* совпаде́ние *neut.*

coincident /kou'ɪnsɪdənt/ *adj.* совпада́ющий.

coincidental /kou.ɪnsɪ'dɛntl/ *adj.* случа́йный; совпада́ющий.

coiner /'kɔinər/ *n.* чека́нщик *m.*

coir /kɔir/ *n.* коко́совое волокно́ *neut.*

coitus /'kouitəs/ *n.* совокупле́ние *neut.*, ко́итус *m.*

coke /kouk/ *n.* кокс *m.*

col /kɒl/ *n.* (*geol.*, *meteorol.*) седлови́на *f.*

cola /'koulə/ *n.* ко́ла *f.*

colander /'kʌləndər/ *n.* дуршла́г *m.*

cold /kould/ **1.** *adj.* холо́дный. **2.** *n.* хо́лод *m.*; (*med.*) просту́да *f.*, на́сморк *m.*

cold-blooded /'kould'blʌdɪd/ *adj.* хладнокро́вный.

coldness /'kouldnɪs/ *n.* хо́лод *m.*

cold turkey *n.* (*withdrawal from use of alcohol*) (*colloq.*) глуха́я завя́зка *f.*

Coleoptera /ˌkouliˈɒptərə/ *n.* жесткокры́лые *pl.*
coleseed /ˈkoulˌsid/ *n.* суре́пица *f.*
coleslaw /ˈkoulˌslɔ/ *n.* сала́т из капу́сты *m.*
colic /ˈkɒlɪk/ *n.* ко́лика *f.*
Coliseum /ˌkɒləˈsiəm/ *n.* Колизе́й *m.*
colitis /kəˈlaitɪs/ *n.* коли́т *m.*
collaborate /kəˈlæbəˌreit/ *v.* сотру́дничать *impf.*
collaboration /kəˌlæbəˈreiʃən/ *n.* сотру́дничество *neut.*
collaborationist /kəˌlæbəˈreiʃənɪst/ *n.* коллаборациони́ст *m.*
collaborator /kəˈlæbəˌreitər/ *n.* сотру́дник *m.*
collage /kəˈlɑʒ/ *n.* колла́ж *m.*
collagen /ˈkɒlədʒən/ *n.* коллаге́н *m.*
collapse /kəˈlæps/ **1.** *n.* разруше́ние, круше́ние *neut.* **2.** *v.* ру́шиться *impf.*, разру́шиться *pf.*
collapsible /kəˈlæpsəbəl/ *adj.* складно́й; откидно́й.
collar /ˈkɒlər/ *n.* воротни́к *m.*; (*dog collar*) оше́йник *m.*
collarbone /ˈkɒlərˌboun/ *n.* ключи́ца *f.*
collate /kəˈleit, ˈkouleit/ *v.* слича́ть (с *with str.*); проверя́ть *impf.*
collateral /kəˈlætərəl/ *n.* (*fin.*) дополни́тельное обеспече́ние *neut.*
collation /kəˈleiʃən/ *n.* сличе́ние *neut.*; прове́рка *f.*
colleague /ˈkɒlig/ *n.* колле́га *m.* and *f.* (*decl. f.*).
collect /kəˈlɛkt/ *v.t.* собира́ть *impf.*, собра́ть *pf.*; *v.i.* собира́ться *impf.*, собра́ться *pf.*
collected /kəˈlɛktɪd/ *adj.* со́бранный.
collection /kəˈlɛkʃən/ *n.* колле́кция *f.*, собра́ние, скопле́ние *neut.*
collective /kəˈlɛktɪv/ **1.** *n.* коллекти́в *m.* **2.** *adj.* коллекти́вный.
collective farm *n.* колхо́з *m.*
collective farmer *n.* колхо́зник *m.*
collectivization /kəˌlɛktɪvəˈzeiʃən/ *n.* коллективиза́ция *f.*
collector /kəˈlɛktər/ *n.* сбо́рщик *m.*, коллекционе́р *m.*
college /ˈkɒlɪdʒ/ **1.** *n.* университе́т; колле́дж *m.* **2.** *adj.* университе́тский.
collegiate /kəˈlidʒɪt/ *n.* коллегиа́льный; университе́тский, академи́ческий.
collide /kəˈlaid/ *v.* ста́лкиваться *impf.*, столкну́ться *pf.*
collie /ˈkɒli/ *n.* ко́лли *m. indecl.*
colliery /ˈkɒlyəri/ *n.* каменноу́гольная копь *f.*
collimator /ˈkɒləˌmeitər/ *n.* коллима́тор *m.*
collision /kəˈlɪʒən/ *n.* столкнове́ние *neut.*
collocate /ˈkɒləˌkeit/ *v.* располага́ть ря́дом *impf.*
collocation /ˌkɒləˈkeiʃən/ *n.* расположе́ние (ря́дом) *neut.*; (*ling.*) словосочета́ние *neut.*
collodion /kəˈloudiən/ *n.* коллодий *m.*
colloid /ˈkɒlɔid/ *n.* колло́ид *m.*
colloidal /kəˈlɔidl/ *adj.* колло́идный.
colloquial /kəˈloukwiəl/ *adj.* разгово́рный.
colloquialism /kəˈloukwiəˌlɪzəm/ *n.* разгово́рное выраже́ние *neut.*
colloquy /ˈkɒləkwi/ *n.* разгово́р *m.*
collotype /ˈkɒləˌtaip/ *n.* коллоти́пия *f.*
collude /kəˈlud/ *v.* та́йно сгова́риваться *impf.*
collusion /kəˈluʒən/ *n.* сго́вор *m.*
Cologne /kəˈloun/ *n.* Кёльн *m.*
cologne /kəˈloun/ *also* **eau de cologne** /ˈou də kəˈloun/ *n.* одеколо́н *m.*

Colombo /kəˈlʌmbou/ *n.* Коло́мбо *m.*
colon /ˈkoulən/ *n.* (*punctuation*) двоето́чие *neut.*; (*anat.*) то́лстая кишка́ *f.*
colonel /ˈkɜrnl/ *n.* полко́вник *m.*
colonial /kəˈlouniəl/ *adj.* колониа́льный.
colonialism /kəˈlouniəˌlɪzəm/ *n.* колониали́зм *m.*
colonist /ˈkɒlənɪst/ *n.* колони́ст, пересе́ленец *m.*
colonization /ˌkɒlənəˈzeiʃən/ *n.* колониза́ция *f.*
colonize /ˈkɒləˌnaiz/ *v.* колонизи́ровать *impf.* and *pf.*
colonizer /ˈkɒləˌnaizər/ *n.* колониза́тор *m.*
colonnade /ˌkɒləˈneid/ *n.* колонна́да *f.*
colony /ˈkɒləni/ *n.* коло́ния *f.*
colophon /ˈkɒləˌfɒn/ *n.* колофо́н *m.*
color /ˈkʌlər/ **1.** *n.* цвет *m.*; (*paint*) кра́ска *f.* **2.** *adj.* цветно́й. **3.** *v.t.* кра́сить *impf.*, покра́сить *pf.*
Colorado /ˌkɒləˈrædou, -ˈrɑdou/ *n.* Колора́до *m.*
Colorado beetle *n.* колора́дский жук *m.*
coloration /ˌkʌləˈreiʃən/ *n.* окра́ска *f.*; (*color pattern*) раскра́ска, расцве́тка *f.*
coloratura /ˌkʌlərəˈturə/ *n.* колорату́ра *f.*
colorblind **1.** /ˈkʌlərˌblaind/ *n.* дальто́ник *m.* **2.** *adj.* страда́ющий дальтони́змом.
colorblindness /ˈkʌlərˌblaindnɪs/ *n.* дальтони́зм *m.*
color-coded /ˈkʌlərˌkoudɪd/ *adj.* с усло́вным цве́том.
colored /ˈkʌlərd/ *adj.* цветно́й.
colorfast /ˈkʌlərˌfæst/ *adj.* цветосто́йкий.
colorful /ˈkʌlərfəl/ *adj.* кра́сочный, я́ркий.
colorimeter /ˌkʌləˈrimitər/ *n.* колори́метр *m.*
coloring /ˈkʌləriŋ/ *n.* раскра́ска *f.*
colossal /kəˈlɒsəl/ *adj.* колосса́льный.
colossus /kəˈlɒsəs/ *n.* коло́сс *m.*
colporteur /ˈkɒlˌpɔrtər, ˌkɒlpɔrˈtɜr/ *n.* разно́счик книг *m.*
colt /koult/ *n.* жеребёнок *m.*
coltish /ˈkoultɪʃ/ *adj.* игри́вый.
coltsfoot /ˈkoultsˌfut/ *n.* мать-и-ма́чеха *f.*
Columbine /ˈkɒləmˌbain/ *n.* (*theater*) Коломби́на *f.*
column /ˈkɒləm/ *n.* коло́нка *f.*; столбе́ц *m.*
columnar /kəˈlʌmnər/ *adj.* колоннообра́зный; коло́нный.
columnist /ˈkɒləmnɪst/ *n.* фельетони́ст *m.*
colza /ˈkɒlzə/ *n.* рапс *m.*
coma /ˈkoumə/ *n.* ко́ма *f.*
comatose /ˈkɒməˌtous, ˈkoumə-/ *adj.* (*in coma*) комато́зный; (*drowsy*) сонли́вый.
comb /koum/ **1.** *n.* гре́бень *m.* **2.** *v.* причёсывать *impf.*, причеса́ть *pf.*
combat /*n.*ˈkɒmbæt; *v.* kəmˈbæt/ **1.** *n.* бой *m.*, сраже́ние *neut.* **2.** *v.* боро́ться (про́тив *with gen.*) *impf.*
combatant /kəmˈbætnt/ *n.* бое́ц *m.*
combative /kəmˈbætɪv/ *adj.* вои́нственный; драчли́вый, зади́ристый.
comber /ˈkoumər/ *n.* (*tech.*) гребнечеса́льная маши́на *f.*
combination /ˌkɒmbəˈneiʃən/ *n.* сочета́ние, соедине́ние *neut.*
combinative /ˈkɒmbəˌneitɪv/ *adj.* комбинацио́нный; комбинато́рный.
combine /kəmˈbain/ *v.* объединя́ть *impf.*; сочета́ть *impf.* and *pf.*

combustibility /kəmˌbʌstə'bɪlɪti/ *n.* воспламеняемость, горючесть *f.*

combustible /kəm'bʌstəbəl/ *adj.* горючий.

combustion /kəm'bʌstʃən/ *n.* сгорание *neut.*

come /kʌm/ *v.* (*on foot*) приходить *impf.*, прийти *pf.*; (*by vehicle*) приезжать *impf.*, приехать *pf.*; **to come back** возвращаться *impf.*, возвратиться *pf.*

comeback /'kʌmˌbæk/ *n.* возвращение *neut.*

comedian /kə'midiən/ *n.* комик *m.*

comedienne /kəˌmidi'ɛn/ *n.* комедиантка *f.*

comedown /'kʌmˌdaun/ *n.* падение *neut.*

comedy /'kɒmɪdi/ *n.* комедия *f.*

comeliness /'kʌmlinɪs/ *n.* миловидность *f.*

comely /'kʌmli/ *adj.* миловидный.

comestible /kə'mɛstəbəl/ *adj.* съедобный.

comet /'kɒmɪt/ *n.* комета *f.*

cometary /'kɒmɪˌtɛri/ *adj.* кометный.

comeuppance /ˌkʌm'ʌpəns/ *n.*: **to get one's comeuppance** *v.* получить по заслугам *impf.*

comfort /'kʌmfərt/ **1.** *n.* комфорт *m.*; (*consolation*) утешение *neut.* **2.** *v.* утешать *impf.*, утешить *pf.*

comfortable /'kʌmftəbəl/ *adj.* удобный.

comforter /'kʌmfərtər/ *n.* утешитель *m.*

comic /'kɒmɪk/ *adj.* комический.

coming /'kʌmɪŋ/ **1.** *n.* приезд, приход *m.* **2.** *adj.* будущий, наступающий.

Comintern /'kɒmɪnˌtɜrn/ *n.* Коминтерн *m.*

comma /'kɒmə/ *n.* запятая *f.*

command /kə'mænd/ **1.** *n.* приказ *m.*, распоряжение *neut.* **2.** *v.* приказывать *impf.*, приказать *pf.*

commandant /ˌkɒmən'dænt, -'dɑnt/ *n.* командир; комендант *m.*

commander /kə'mændər/ *n.* (*officer*) командир *m.*; (*person in command*) командующий (*with instr.*) *m.*; (*nav.*) капитан третьего ранга *m.*

commander in chief *n.* главнокомандующий *m.*

commanding /kə'mændɪŋ/ *adj.* (*in command*) командующий; (*impressive*) внушительный; (*overlooking*) доминирующий (над *with instr.*).

commandment /kə'mændmənt/ *n.* заповедь *f.*

commando /kə'mændou/ *n.* десантно-диверсионная группа *f.*

commemorate /kə'mɛməˌreit/ *v.* праздновать *impf.*, отпраздновать *pf.*

commemoration /kəˌmɛmə'reiʃən/ *n.* празднование *neut.*

commemorative /kə'mɛməˌreitɪv, -ərətɪv/ *adj.* мемориальный.

commence /kə'mɛns/ *v.* начинать(ся) *impf.*, начать(ся) *pf.*

commend /kə'mɛnd/ *v.* хвалить *impf.*, похвалить *pf.*

commendable /kə'mɛndəbəl/ *adj.* похвальный.

commendation /ˌkɒmən'deiʃən/ *n.* похвала *f.*

commensurable /kə'mɛnsərəbəl/ *adj.* соизмеримый.

commensurate /kə'mɛnsərɪt/ *adj.* соответственный.

comment /'kɒmɛnt/ **1.** *n.* замечание; примечание *neut.* **2.** *v.* комментировать *impf.*, прокомментировать *pf.*

commentary /'kɒmənˌtɛri/ *n.* комментарий *m.*

commentator /'kɒmənˌteitər/ *n.* комментатор *m.*

commerce /'kɒmərs/ *n.* торговля *f.*

commercial /kə'mɜrʃəl/ **1.** *n.* реклама *f.* **2.** *adj.* торговый, коммерческий.

commercialize /kə'mɜrʃəˌlaiz/ *v.* превращать в источник прибыли *impf.*

commination /ˌkɒmə'neiʃən/ *n.* угроза *f.*

comminatory /kə'mɪnəˌtɔri/ *adj.* угрожающий.

commingle /kə'mɪŋgəl/ *v.* смешивать(ся) *impf.*

comminute /'kɒməˌnut/ *v.* измельчать *impf.*

commiserate /kə'mɪzəˌreit/ *v.* сочувствовать; выражать соболезнование (*with dat.*) *impf.*

commiseration /kəˌmɪzə'reiʃən/ *n.* сочувствие, соболезнование *neut.*

commissar /'kɒməˌsɑr/ *n.* комиссар *m.*

commissariat /ˌkɒmə'sɛəriət/ *n.* (*mil.*) интендантство *neut.*; (*Soviet department*) комиссариат *m.*

commission /kə'mɪʃən/ **1.** *n.* поручение, полномочие *neut.* **2.** *v.* давать поручение *impf.*

commissioner /kə'mɪʃənər/ *n.* член комиссии *m.*; (*official*) комиссар *m.*

commit /kə'mɪt/ *v.* (*perpetrate*) совершать *impf.*, совершить *pf.*

commitment /kə'mɪtmənt/ *n.* (*pledge*) обязательство *neut.*

committal /kə'mɪtl/ *n.*: **committal for trial** предание суду *neut.*

committee /kə'mɪti/ *n.* комитет *m.*

commode /kə'moud/ *n.* (*cupboard*) комод *m.*; (*chamber pot*) стульчак *m.*

commodious /kə'moudiəs/ *adj.* поместительный.

commodity /kə'mɒdɪti/ *n.* товар *m.*

commodore /'kɒməˌdɔr/ *n.* (*naval rank*) коммодор *m.*

common /'kɒmən/ *adj.* общий, обыкновенный.

commoner /'kɒmənər/ *n.* простой человек *m.*

commonness /'kɒmənnɪs/ *n.* обычность *f.*; (*vulgarity*) вульгарность *f.*

commonplace /'kɒmənˌpleis/ *adj.* банальный.

common sense *n.* здравый смысл *m.*

commonweal /'kɒmənˌwil/ *n.* общее благо *neut.*

commonwealth /'kɒmənˌwɛlθ/ *n.* (*state*) государство *neut.*; содружество *neut.*

commotion /kə'mouʃən/ *n.* волнение *neut.*, суматоха *f.*

communal /kə'myunl/ *adj.* общинный, коммунальный.

Communard /'kɒmyəˌnɑrd/ *n.* коммунар *m.*

commune /'kɒmyun/ *n.* община, коммуна *f.*

communicable /kə'myunɪkəbəl/ *adj.* поддающийся передаче; (*med.*) заразный.

communicant /kə'myunɪkənt/ *n.* информант *m.*

communicate /kə'myunɪˌkeit/ *v.t.* сообщать *impf.*, сообщить *pf.*; *v.i.* сообщаться *impf.*, сообщиться *pf.*

communication /kəˌmyunɪ'keiʃən/ *n.* коммуникация, связь *f.*; сообщение *neut.*

communicative /kə'myunɪˌkeitɪv, -kətɪv/ *adj.* разговорчивый.

communion /kə'myunyən/ *n.* (*relationship*) общение (*with instr.*) *neut.*; (*religious group*) вероисповедание *neut.*; (*rite*) причастие *neut.*

communiqué /kəˌmyunɪ'kei/ *n.* коммюнике *neut. indecl.*

Communism /'kɒmyəˌnɪzəm/ *n.* коммунизм *m.*

Communist /'kɒmyənɪst/ *n.* коммунист *m.*, коммунистка *f.*

Communistic /ˌkɒmyə'nɪstɪk/ *adj.* коммунистический.

community /kə'myunɪti/ n. (neighborhood) райо́н; (group of people) общи́на f.

commutation /ˌkɒmyə'teiʃən/ n. (elec.) коммута́ция f.

commutator /'kɒmyəˌteitər/ n. колле́ктор m.

commute /kə'myut/ v. (change) заменя́ть; (leg.) смягча́ть наказа́ние; (colloq.) е́здить ежедне́вно impf.

commuter /kə'myutər/ n. регуля́рный пассажи́р m.

compact /kəm'pækt, 'kɒmpækt/ adj. компа́ктный, сжа́тый.

compact disk n. (abbr. C.D.) компа́кт-диск, компа́ктный диск m.

compacted /kəm'pæktɪd/ adj. уплотнённый.

companion /kəm'pænyən/ n. компаньо́н; това́рищ; спу́тник m.

companionable /kəm'pænyənəbəl/ adj. общи́тельный.

companionship /kəm'pænyənˌʃɪp/ n. това́рищество neut.

company /'kʌmpəni/ n. компа́ния f., о́бщество neut.

comparable /'kɒmpərəbəl/ adj. сравни́мый.

comparative /kəm'pærətɪv/ adj. сравни́тельный.

comparatively /kəm'pærətɪvli/ adv. сравни́тельно.

comparator /kəm'pærətər/ n. компара́тор m.

compare /kəm'pɛər/ v. сра́внивать impf., сравни́ть pf.

comparison /kəm'pærəsən/ n. сравне́ние neut.

compartment /kəm'pɑrtmənt/ n. отделе́ние neut.; (train) купе́ neut. indecl.

compass /'kʌmpəs/ n. (area) объём, обхва́т m.; (instrument) ко́мпас m.

compassion /kəm'pæʃən/ n. сострада́ние neut.

compassionate /kəm'pæʃənɪt/ adj. сострада́тельный.

compatibility /kəmˌpætə'bɪlɪti/ n. совмести́мость f.

compatible /kəm'pætəbəl/ adj. совмести́мый.

compatriot /kəm'peitriət/ n. соотéчественник m.

compeer /kəm'pɪər/ n. ро́вня m. and f. (decl. f.)

compel /kəm'pɛl/ v. вынужда́ть impf., вы́нудить pf.

compelling /kəm'pɛlɪŋ/ adj. убеди́тельный, неотрази́мый.

compendious /kəm'pɛndiəs/ adj. кра́ткий, сжа́тый.

compendium /kəm'pɛndiəm/ n. конспе́кт m.; сокраще́ние neut.

compensate /'kɒmpənˌseit/ v. компенси́ровать impf. and pf.

compensation /ˌkɒmpən'seiʃən/ n. возмеще́ние neut.; компенса́ция f.

compensator /'kɒmpənˌseitər/ n. компенса́тор m.

compensatory /kəm'pɛnsəˌtɔri/ adj. компенси́рующий.

compete /kəm'pit/ v. состяза́ться, соревнова́ться impf.

competence /'kɒmpɪtəns/ n. спосо́бность f., уме́ние neut.; компете́нтность f.

competent /'kɒmpɪtənt/ adj. компете́нтный; правомо́чный.

competition /ˌkɒmpɪ'tɪʃən/ n. конкуре́нция f.; состяза́ние, соревнова́ние neut.

competitive /kəm'pɛtɪtɪv/ adj. сопе́рничающий; ко́нкурсный.

competitor /kəm'pɛtɪtər/ n. конкуре́нт m.

Compiègne /kɔ̃'pyɛny⁹/ n. Компье́нь m.

compilation /ˌkɒmpə'leiʃən/ n. компили́рование neut.; (collecting) собира́ние neut.; (dictionary, etc.) составле́ние neut.

compile /kəm'pail/ v. собира́ть impf., собра́ть; составля́ть impf., соста́вить pf.

compiler /kəm'pailər/ n. компиля́тор m.

complacence /kəm'pleisəns/ n. самодово́льство neut.

complacent /kəm'pleisənt/ adj. самодово́льный.

complain /kəm'plein/ v. жа́ловаться impf.

complaint /kəm'pleint/ n. жа́лоба f.; недомога́ние neut.

complaints book /kəm'pleints/ n. кни́га жа́лоб, жа́лобная кни́га f.

complaisance /kəm'pleisəns/ n. любе́зность f.

complaisant /kəm'pleisənt/ adj. любе́зный, услу́жливый.

complement /'kɒmpləmənt/ n. дополне́ние neut.; компле́кт m.

complementary /ˌkɒmplə'mɛntəri/ adj. дополни́тельный.

complete /kəm'plit/ 1. adj. по́лный, зако́нченный. 2. v. зака́нчивать impf., зако́нчить pf.

completely /kəm'plitli/ adv. соверше́нно.

completeness /kəm'plitnɪs/ n. зако́нченность f.

completion /kəm'pliʃən/ n. оконча́ние; заверше́ние neut.

complex /kəm'plɛks/ adj. сло́жный, составно́й.

complexion /kəm'plɛkʃən/ n. цвет лица́ m.

complexity /kəm'plɛksɪti/ n. сло́жность f.

compliance /kəm'plaiəns/ n. согла́сие neut.; in compliance with в соотве́тствии с (with instr.).

compliant /kəm'plaiənt/ adj. пода́тливый; усту́чливый.

complicate /'kɒmplɪˌkeit/ v. усложня́ть impf., усложни́ть pf.

complicated /'kɒmplɪˌkeitɪd/ adj. сло́жный; запу́танный.

complication /ˌkɒmplɪ'keiʃən/ n. сло́жность; запу́танность f.

complicity /kəm'plɪsɪti/ n. соуча́стие (в with prep.) neut.

compliment /'kɒmpləmənt/ n. комплиме́нт m.; pl. (greetings) приве́т m.

complimentary /ˌkɒmplə'mɛntəri/ adj. ле́стный; (free) беспла́тный.

comply /kəm'plai/ v. подчиня́ться пра́вилам impf.

component /kəm'pounənt/ 1. adj. составно́й. 2. n. составна́я часть f.

comportment /kəm'pɔrtmənt/ n. поведе́ние neut.

comport oneself v. вести́ себя́ impf.

compose /kəm'pouz/ v. сочиня́ть impf., сочини́ть pf.; составля́ть impf., соста́вить pf.

composed /kəm'pouzd/ (calm) споко́йный.

composer /kəm'pouzər/ n. компози́тор m.

composite /kəm'pɒzɪt/ 1. adj. комбини́рованный, составно́й. 2. n. смесь f.

composition /ˌkɒmpə'zɪʃən/ n. сочине́ние neut.

compositor /kəm'pɒzɪtər/ n. набо́рщик m.

compost /'kɒmpoust/ n. компо́ст m.

composure /kəm'pouʒər/ n. споко́йствие neut.

compote /'kɒmpout/ n. компо́т m.

compound /'kɒmpaund/ **1.** *adj.* составнóй, слóжный. **2.** *n.* состáв *m.*
comprehend /,kɒmprɪ'hɛnd/ *v.* понимáть *impf.*, понять *pf.*
comprehensible /,kɒmprɪ'hɛnsəbəl/ *adj.* понятный.
comprehension /,kɒmprɪ'hɛnʃən/ *n.* понимáние *neut.*
comprehensive /,kɒmprɪ'hɛnsɪv/ *adj.* исчéрпывающий, всесторóнний.
compress / *n.* 'kɒmprɛs; *v.* kəm'prɛs **1.** *n.* компрéсс *m.* **2.** *v.* сжимáть *impf.*, сжать *pf.*
compressed /kəm'prɛst/ *adj.* сжáтый.
compression /kəm'prɛʃən/ *n.* сжáтие *neut.*
compressor /kəm'prɛsər/ *n.* компрéссор *m.*
comprise /kəm'praiz/ *v.* заключáть в себé *impf.*; содержáть *impf.*
compromise /'kɒmprə,maiz/ **1.** *n.* компромúсс *m.* **2.** *v.* компрометúровать *impf.*
compulsion /kəm'pʌlʃən/ *n.* принуждéние *neut.*
compulsive /kəm'pʌlsɪv/ *adj.* принудúтельный.
compulsory /kəm'pʌlsəri/ *adj.* обязáтельный.
compunction /kəm'pʌŋkʃən/ *n.* угрызéние сóвести; сожалéние *neut.*
computable /kəm'pyutəbəl/ *adj.* исчислúмый, вычислúмый.
computation /,kɒmpyu'teiʃən/ *n.* расчёт *m.*, (*math.*) вычислéние *neut.*
compute /kəm'pyut/ *v.* подсчúтывать *impf.*, подсчитáть *pf.*
computer /kəm'pyutər/ *n.* компьютер *m.*, ЭВМ (*abbr. of* электрóнно-вычислúтельная машúна) *f.*
computerized /kəm'pyutə,raizd/ *adj.* управляемый компьютером; (*automated*) автоматизúрованный.
computer science *n.* кибернéтика; информáтика *f.*
computer screen *n.* дисплéй *m.*
comrade /'kɒmræd/ *n.* товáрищ *m.*
comradely /'kɒmrædli/ *adj.* товáрищеский.
comradeship /'kɒmræd,ʃɪp/ *n.* товáрищество *neut.*; товáрищеские отношéния *pl.*
con /kɒn/ *n.* (*colloq.*) мошéнничество *neut.*
concatenation /kɒn,kætn̩'eiʃən/ *n.* сцеплéние *neut.*
concave /kɒn'keiv/ *adj.* вóгнутый, впáлый.
concavo-concave *adj.* двояковóгнутый; **concavo-convex** *adj.* вóгнуто-выпуклый.
conceal /kən'sil/ *v.* скрывáть *impf.*, скрыть *pf.*
concealment /kən'silmənt/ *n.* утáивание *neut.*
concede /kən'sid/ *v.* уступáть *impf.*, уступúть *pf.*; признавáть *impf.*, признáть *pf.*
conceit /kən'sit/ *n.* тщеслáвие; самомнéние *neut.*
conceited /kən'sitɪd/ *adj.* тщеслáвный.
conceivable /kən'sivəbəl/ *adj.* мыслимый.
conceive /kən'siv/ *v.* задýмывать *impf.*, задýмать *pf.*; (*become pregnant*) зачинáть *impf.*, зачáть *pf.*
concentrate /'kɒnsən,treit/ *v.* сосредотóчивать(ся) *impf.*, сосредотóчить(ся) *pf.*
concentration /,kɒnsən'treiʃən/ *n.* концентрáция *f.*
concentric /kən'sɛntrɪk/ *adj.* концентрúческий.
concept /'kɒnsɛpt/ *n.* понятие *neut.*
conception /kən'sɛpʃən/ *n.* понятие, понимáние *neut.*; (*physiol.*) зачáтие *neut.*

conceptual /kən'sɛptʃuəl/ *adj.* концептуáльный.
concern /kən'sɜrn/ **1.** *n.* забóта *f.*, интерéс *m.* **2.** *v.* касáться *impf.*
concerned /kən'sɜrnd/ *adj.* (*worried*) озабóченный.
concerning /kən'sɜrnɪŋ/ *prep.* относúтельно (*with gen.*).
concert /'kɒnsɜrt/ *n.* концéрт *m.*
concerted /kən'sɜrtɪd/ *adj.* согласóванный.
concertina /,kɒnsər'tinə/ *n.* концертúно *neut. indecl.*
concession /kən'sɛʃən/ *n.* устýпка *f.*
concessionaire /kən,sɛʃə'nɛər/ *n.* концессионéр *m.*
concessive /kən'sɛsɪv/ *adj.* устýпчивый; (*gram.*) устýпительный.
conch /kɒŋk, kɒntʃ/ *n.* рáковина *f.*
concha /'kɒŋkə/ *n.* (*anat.*) ушнáя рáковина *f.*
conchoid /'kɒŋkɔid/ *n.* конхóида *f.*
conchology /kɒŋ'kɒlədʒi/ *n.* конхиолóгия *f.*
concierge /,kɒnsi'ɛərʒ/ *n.* консьéрж *m.*, консьéржка *f.*
conciliar /kən'sɪliər/ *adj.* собóрный.
conciliate /kən'sɪli,eit/ *v.* примирять *impf.*, примирúть *pf.*
conciliation /kən,sɪli'eiʃən/ *n.* примирéние *neut.*
conciliator /kən'sɪli,eitər/ *n.* примирúтель; миротвóрец *m.*
conciliatory /kən'sɪliə,tɔri/ *adj.* примирúтельный.
concise /kən'sais/ *adj.* сжáтый, крáткий.
conciseness /kən'saisnɪs/ *n.* крáткость; чёткость *f.*
conclave /'kɒnkleiv/ *n.* (тáйное) совещáние *neut.*
conclude /kən'klud/ *v.* заключáть *impf.*, заключúть *pf.*
conclusion /kən'kluʒən/ *n.* заключéние *neut.*; вывод *m.*
conclusive /kən'klusɪv/ *adj.* заключúтельный.
concoct /kɒn'kɒkt/ *v.* состряпать; придýмать *pf.*
concoction /kən'kɒkʃən/ *n.* стряпня *f.*, вáрево *neut.*
concomitant /kɒn'kɒmɪtənt/ *adj.* сопýтствующий.
concord /'kɒnkɔrd/ *n.* соглáсие *neut.*
concordance /kɒn'kɔrdns/ *n.* соглáсие *neut.*; (*of Bible, etc.*) конкордáнция *f.*
concordant /kɒn'kɔrdnt/ *adj.* соглáсующийся.
concordat /kɒn'kɔrdæt/ *n.* конкордáт *m.*
concrete /'kɒnkrit, 'kɒŋ-/ **1.** *adj.* (*specific*) конкрéтный; (*made of concrete*) бетóнный. **2.** *n.* бетóн *m.*
concretely /kɒn'kritli, kɒŋ-/ *adv.* конкрéтно.
concretion /kɒn'kriʃən, kɒŋ-/ *n.* сращéние *neut.*
concubine /'kɒŋkyə,bain/ *n.* налóжница *f.*
concupiscence /kɒn'kyupɪsəns/ *n.* похотлúвость, пóхоть *f.*
concupiscent /kɒn'kyupɪsənt/ *adj.* похотлúвый.
concur /kən'kɜr/ *v.* соглашáться *impf.*, согласúться *pf.*
concurrence /kən'kɜrəns/ *n.* совпадáние *neut.*
concurrent /kən'kɜrənt/ *adj.* совпадáющий.
concurrently /kən'kɜrəntli/ *adv.* одновремéнно (с *with instr.*).
concuss /kən'kʌs/ *v.* сотрясáть *impf.*
concussion /kən'kʌʃən/ *n.* сотрясéние мóзга *neut.*

condemn /kən'dɛm/ v. осуждать impf., осудить pf.

condemnation /ˌkɒndɛm'neiʃən/ n. осуждение neut.

condemnatory /kən'dɛmnəˌtɔri/ adj. обвинительный.

condensate /kən'dɛnseit/ n. конденсат m.

condensation /ˌkɒndɛn'seiʃən/ n. сгущение neut., конденсация f.

condense /kən'dɛns/ v. сгущать impf., сгустить pf.

condensed /kən'dɛnst/ adj. конденсированный.

condensed milk n. сгущённое молоко neut.

condenser /kən'dɛnsər/ n. (elec.) конденсатор m.

condescend /ˌkɒndə'sɛnd/ v. снисходить impf., снизойти pf.

condescending /ˌkɒndə'sɛndiŋ/ adj. снисходительный; (patronizing) покровительственный.

condescension /ˌkɒndə'sɛnʃən/ n. снисходительность f.

condign /kən'dain/ adj. заслуженный.

condiment /'kɒndəmənt/ n. приправа f.

condition /kən'diʃən/ **1.** n. положение, состояние neut.; (stipulation) условие neut. **2.** v. обусловливать impf., обусловить pf.

conditional /kən'diʃənl/ adj. условный.

conditionally /kən'diʃənli/ adv. условно.

conditioned /kən'diʃənd/ adj. обусловленный.

conditioning /kən'diʃəniŋ/ n. приучение neut.

condole /kən'doul/ v. выражать соболезнование impf.

condolence /kən'douləns/ n. соболезнование neut.; сочувствие neut.

condom /'kɒndəm/ n. презерватив m.

condominium /ˌkɒndə'miniəm/ n. кондоминиум m.

condone /kən'doun/ v. прощать impf.

condor /'kɒndər/ n. кондор m.

condottiere /ˌkɒndə'tуεərei/ n. кондотьер m.

conduce /kən'dus/ v. способствовать impf.

conducive /kən'dusiv/ adj. способствующий.

conduct / n. 'kɒndʌkt; v. kən'dʌkt/ **1.** n. поведение neut. **2.** v. вести impf.; (mus.) дирижировать impf.

conductance /kən'dʌktəns/ n. (elec.) проводимость f.

conductive /kən'dʌktiv/ adj. проводящий.

conductivity /ˌkɒndʌk'tiviti/ n. проводимость f.

conductor /kən'dʌktər/ n. проводник m.; (on bus, train) кондуктор m.; (mus.) дирижёр m.

conduit /'kɒndwit/ n. (water pipe) водопроводная труба f.; (elec.) **cable conduit** кабелепровод m.

cone /koun/ n. конус m.; (bot.) шишка f.

confection /kən'fɛkʃən/ n. сласти pl.

confectioner /kən'fɛkʃənər/ n. кондитер m.

confectionery /kən'fɛkʃəˌnɛri/ n. кондитерская f.

confederacy /kən'fɛdərəsi/ n. конфедерация f.

confederate /kən'fɛdərit/ **1.** n. соучастник m. **2.** adj. конфедеративный.

confederation /kənˌfɛdə'reiʃən/ n. конфедерация f.

confer /kən'fɜr/ v. присуждать impf., присудить pf.; v.i. совещаться impf.

conference /'kɒnfərəns/ n. совещание neut.

conferment /kən'fɜrmənt/ n. присвоение neut.

confess /kən'fɛs/ v. признаваться impf., признаться pf.

confession /kən'fɛʃən/ n. признание neut.

confessional /kən'fɛʃənl/ n. исповедальня f.

confessor /kən'fɛsər/ n. исповедник m.

confetti /kən'fɛti/ n. конфетти neut. indecl.

confidant also **confidante** /'kɒnfiˌdænt/ n. доверенное лицо neut.

confide /kən'faid/ v. доверять impf., доверить pf.

confident /'kɒnfidənt/ adj. уверенный.

confidential /ˌkɒnfi'dɛnʃəl/ adj. секретный; конфиденциальный.

confidentially /ˌkɒnfi'dɛnʃəli/ adv. по секрету; секретно.

configuration /kənˌfigyə'reiʃən/ n. (tech.) конфигурация f.

confine /kən'fain/ v. ограничивать impf., ограничить pf.; (in prison) заключать impf.; **to confine oneself to** ограничиваться (with instr.) impf., ограничиться pf.

confinement /kən'fainmənt/ n. (imprisonment) заключение neut.; (childbirth) роды pl.

confirm /kən'fɜrm/ v. подтверждать impf., подтвердить pf.

confirmation /ˌkɒnfər'meiʃən/ n. утверждение; подтверждение neut.; (eccles.) конфирмация f.

confirmative /kən'fɜrmətiv/ adj. подтверждающий.

confirmed /kən'fɜrmd/ adj. (long-established) давний; (inveterate) закоренелый.

confiscate /'kɒnfəˌskeit/ v. конфисковать impf. and pf.

confiscation /ˌkɒnfə'skeiʃən/ n. конфискация f.

conflagration /ˌkɒnflə'greiʃən/ n. большой пожар m.

conflict /n. 'kɒnflikt; v. kən'flikt/ **1.** n. конфликт m. **2.** v. противоречить (with dat.) impf.

confluence /'kɒnfluəns/ n. (rivers) слияние neut.

confluent /'kɒnfluənt/ n. приток m.

conform /kən'fɔrm/ v. сообразовать(ся) (с with instr.) impf. and pf.; (correspond) соответствовать (with dat.) impf.

conformable /kən'fɔrməbəl/ adj. подобный.

conformation /ˌkɒnfɔr'meiʃən/ n. устройство neut.

conformism /kən'fɔrˌmizəm/ n. конформизм m.

conformist /kən'fɔrmist/ n. конформист m.

conformity /kən'fɔrmiti/ n. соответствие neut.; **in conformity with** в соответствии с (with str.).

confound /kɒn'faund/ v. спутывать impf., спутать pf.

confounded /kɒn'faundid/ adj. (confused) смущённый; (colloq.) проклятый.

confraternity /ˌkɒnfrə'tɜrniti/ n. братство neut.

confrere /'kɒnfrεər/ n. собрат m.; коллега m. and f. (decl. f.)

confront /kən'frʌnt/ v. стоять лицом к лицу; смотреть в лицо; встретиться, столкнуться impf.

confrontation /ˌkɒnfrən'teiʃən/ n. очная ставка f.; сопоставление neut.; (pol.) конфронтация f.

confuse /kən'fyuz/ v. смущать impf., сбивать с толку impf.

confused /kən'fyuzd/ adj. смущённый, сбитый с толку.

confusion /kən'fyuʒən/ n. беспорядок m.; смущение neut.

confutation /ˌkɒnfyʊ'teiʃən/ n. опровержение neut.

confute /kən'fyut/ v. опровергать impf.

congeal /kən'dʒil/ v. замораживать impf., заморозить pf.

congelation /ˌkɒndʒə'leiʃən/ n. замораживание neut.

congener /'kɒndʒənər/ n. родственник m.

congeneric /ˌkɒndʒə'nɛrik/ adj. родственный.

congenial /kən'dʒinyəl/ adj. дружеский; приветливый; благоприятный.

congenital /kən'dʒɛnɪtl/ adj. прирождённый; врождённый.

conger /'kɒŋgər/ n. морской угорь m.

congest /kən'dʒɛst/ v. переполнять impf.

congested /kən'dʒɛstɪd/ adj. перенаселённый, тесный.

congestion /kən'dʒɛstʃən/ n. теснота; перенаселённость f.

conglomerate /v. kən'glɒmə,reit; n. kən'glɒmərɪt/ 1. v. скапливаться impf., скопиться pf. 2. n. конгломерат m.

conglomeration /kən,glɒmə'reiʃən/ n. конгломерат m.; нагромождение neut.

Congo /'kɒŋgou/ n. Конго m.

congratulate /kən'grætʃə,leit/ v. поздравлять impf., поздравить pf.

congratulation /kən,grætʃə'leiʃən/ n. поздравление neut.

congress /'kɒŋgrɪs/ n. конгресс, съезд m.

Congressman /'kɒŋgrɪsmən/ n. конгрессмен m.

congruence /'kɒŋgruəns/ n. (agreement) согласованность f.; (coincidence) совпадение neut.; (math.) конгруэнтность f.

congruent /'kɒŋgruənt/ adj. подходящий.

conic /'kɒnɪk/ adj. конический.

conifer /'kounəfər/ n. хвойное дерево neut.

coniferous /kou'nɪfərəs/ adj. хвойный.

conjectural /kən'dʒɛktʃərəl/ adj. предположительный.

conjecture /kən'dʒɛktʃər/ 1. n. предположение neut. 2. v. предполагать impf., предположить pf.

conjoin /kən'dʒɔin/ v. соединять(ся) impf.; сочетать(ся) impf. and pf.

conjoint /kən'dʒɔint/ adj. соединённый.

conjugal /'kɒndʒəgəl/ adj. брачный; супружеский.

conjugality /ˌkɒndʒə'gælɪti/ n. супружество neut.

conjugate /'kɒndʒə,geit/ v. спрягать impf.

conjugation /ˌkɒndʒə'geiʃən/ n. спряжение neut.

conjunction /kən'dʒʌŋkʃən/ n. соединение neut.; (gram.) союз m.

conjunctive /kən'dʒʌŋktɪv/ adj. связывающий; (gram.) соединительный.

conjunctive mood n. (gram.) сослагательное наклонение neut.

conjunctivitis /kən,dʒʌŋktə'vaitɪs/ n. конъюнктивит m.

conjuncture /kən'dʒʌŋktʃər/ n. стечение обстоятельств neut.

conjuration /ˌkɒndʒə'reiʃən/ n. заклинание neut.

conjure /'kɒndʒər/ v. заклинать; вызывать в воображении impf.

conjuror /'kɒndʒərər/ n. фокусник m.

connate /'kɒneit/ adj. прирождённый.

connect /kə'nɛkt/ v. связывать impf., связать pf.; соединять impf., соединить pf.

connected /kə'nɛktɪd/ adj. соединённый; связанный.

Connecticut /kə'nɛtɪkət/ n. Коннектикут m.

connecting /kə'nɛktɪŋ/ adj. соединительный.

connection /kə'nɛkʃən/ n. связь f.; отношение neut.; (change of planes, etc.) пересадка f.

connective /kə'nɛktɪv/ adj. соединительный; связующий.

conning /'kɒnɪŋ/ n. управление кораблём neut.

connivance /kə'naivəns/ n. попустительство neut.

connive /kə'naiv/ v. потворствовать impf.

connoisseur /ˌkɒnə'sɜr/ n. знаток m.

connotation /ˌkɒnə'teiʃən/ n. дополнительное значение neut.

connote /kə'nout/ v. означать impf.

connubial /kə'nubiəl/ adj. брачный; супружеский.

conoid /'kounɔid/ n. коноид m.

conquer /'kɒŋkər/ v. завоёвывать impf., завоевать pf.; побеждать impf., победить pf.

conqueror /'kɒŋkərər/ n. завоеватель, победитель m.

conquest /'kɒnkwɛst/ n. завоевание neut.

conquistador /kɒn'kwɪstə,dɔr, kɒŋ,kistə'ðɔr/ n. конквистадор m.

consanguineous /ˌkɒnsæŋ'gwiniəs/ adj. единокровный.

consanguinity /ˌkɒnsæŋ'gwɪnɪti/ n. кровное родство neut.

conscience /'kɒnʃəns/ n. совесть f.

conscienceless /'kɒnʃənslɪs/ adj. бессовестный.

conscientious /ˌkɒnʃi'ɛnʃəs/ adj. совестливый; добросовестный.

conscious /'kɒnʃəs/ adj. сознательный; **to be conscious of** сознавать (with acc.) impf.

consciousness /'kɒnʃəsnɪs/ n. сознание neut.

conscript /'kɒnskript/ n. призывник m.

conscription /kən'skripʃən/ n. воинская повинность f.

consecrate /'kɒnsɪ,kreit/ v. посвящать impf., посвятить pf.

consecration /ˌkɒnsɪ'kreiʃən/ n. посвящение neut.

consecutive /kən'sɛkyətɪv/ adj. последовательный.

consensus /kən'sɛnsəs/ n. общее согласие neut.

consent /kən'sɛnt/ 1. n. согласие, разрешение neut. 2. v. соглашаться impf., согласиться pf.

consequence /'kɒnsɪ,kwɛns/ n. следствие, последствие neut.; (importance) значение neut.; **in consequence of** prep. вследствие (with gen.).

consequent /'kɒnsɪ,kwɛnt/ adj. последовательный.

consequential /ˌkɒnsɪ'kwɛnʃəl/ adj. важный; значительный.

consequently /'kɒnsɪ,kwɛntli/ adv. следовательно.

conservancy /kən'sɜrvənsi/ n. охрана рек и лесов f.

conservation /ˌkɒnsər'veiʃən/ n. сохранение neut.

conservatism /kən'sɜrvə,tɪzəm/ n. консерватизм m.

conservative /kən'sɜrvətɪv/ *adj.* консервати́в-
ный.
conservatory /kən'sɜrvə,tɔri/ *n.* консервато́рия *f.*
conserve /kən'sɜrv/ *v.* сохраня́ть; сберега́ть
impf.
consider /kən'sɪdər/ *v.* (*regard as*) счита́ть *impf.*,
счесть *pf.*; (*contemplate*) рассма́тривать *impf.*,
рассмотре́ть *pf.*; (*take into account*) принима́ть
во внима́ние *impf.*
considerable /kən'sɪdərəbəl/ *adj.* значи́тельный.
considerably /kən'sɪdərəbli/ *adv.* значи́тельно.
considerate /kən'sɪdərɪt/ *adj.* внима́тельный к
други́м.
consideration /kən,sɪdə'reɪʃən/ *n.* рассмотре́ние;
внима́ние *neut.*; **to be under consideration** рас-
сма́триваться *impf.*
considering /kən'sɪdərɪŋ/ *prep.* принима́я во
внима́ние.
consign /kən'sain/ *v.* поруча́ть *impf.*; (*com.*)
отправля́ть *impf.*, отпра́вить *pf.*
consignee /,kɒnsai'ni/ *n.* адреса́т *m.*
consignment /kən'sainmənt/ *n.* (*sending*) отпра́в-
ка *f.*; (*batch*) па́ртия *f.*
consist /kən'sɪst/ *v.* состоя́ть (из *with gen.*) *impf.*
consistency /kən'sɪstənsi/ *n.* (*steadfastness*) по-
стоя́нство *neut.*, (*logical agreement*) после́дова-
тельность *f.*
consistent /kən'sɪstənt/ *adj.* после́довательный.
consolation /,kɒnsə'leɪʃən/ *n.* утеше́ние *neut.*
consolatory /kən'sɒlə,tɔri/ *adj.* утеши́тельный.
console[1] /kən'soul/ *v.* утеша́ть *impf.*, уте́шить *pf.*
console[2] /'kɒnsoul/ *n.* (*arch.*) консо́ль *m.*; (*control panel*) пульт *m.*
consolidate /kən'sɒlɪ,deit/ *v.* укрепля́ть *impf.*,
укрепи́ть *pf.*
consolidation /kən,sɒlɪ'deɪʃən/ *n.* (*making
strong*) укрепле́ние *neut.*; (*combining*) объеди-
не́ние *neut.*; (*compacting*) уплотне́ние *neut.*
consommé /,kɒnsə'mei/ *n.* консоме́ *neut. indecl.*
consonance /'kɒnsənəns/ *n.* созву́чие *neut.*
consonant /'kɒnsənənt/ *n.* согла́сный *m.*
consonantal /,kɒnsə'næntl/ *adj.* согла́сный.
consortium /kən'sɔrʃiəm/ *n.* консо́рциум *m.*
conspectus /kən'spɛktəs/ *n.* (*survey*) обзо́р *m.*;
(*synopsis*) конспе́кт *m.*
conspicuous /kən'spɪkyuəs/ *adj.* ви́дный, заме́т-
ный.
conspiracy /kən'spɪrəsi/ *n.* за́говор *m.*
conspirator /kən'spɪrətər/ *n.* загово́рщик, кон-
спира́тор *m.*
conspiratorial /kən,spɪrə'tɔriəl/ *adj.* конспира́-
торский.
conspire /kən'spaiᵊr/ *v.* устра́ивать за́говор *impf.*
constable /'kɒnstəbəl/ *n.* полице́йский *m.*
constancy /'kɒnstənsi/ *n.* постоя́нство *neut.*
constant /'kɒnstənt/ *adj.* постоя́нный.
constantly /'kɒnstəntli/ *adv.* всё вре́мя, непре-
ста́нно.
constellation /,kɒnstə'leɪʃən/ *n.* созве́здие *neut.*
consternation /,kɒnstər'neɪʃən/ *n.* оцепене́ние
neut., у́жас *m.*
constipate /'kɒnstə,peit/ *v.* вызыва́ть запо́р
impf.
constipation /,kɒnstə'peɪʃən/ *n.* запо́р *m.*
constituency /kən'stɪtʃuənsi/ *n.* избира́тельный
о́круг *m.*
constituent /kən'stɪtʃuənt/ *n.* (*part*) составна́я

часть *f.*; (*elector*) избира́тель *m.*; (*math.*) кон-
ституэ́нт *m.*
constitute /'kɒnstɪ,tut/ *v.* составля́ть *impf.*
constitution /,kɒnstɪ'tuʃən/ *n.* конститу́ция *f.*
constitutional /,kɒnstɪ'tuʃənl/ *adj.* конститу-
цио́нный.
constrain /kən'strein/ *v.* принужда́ть *impf.*; (*restrain*) сде́рживать *impf.*
constrained /kən'streind/ *adj.* (*forced*) принуждённый; (*embarassed*) смущённый; (*cramped*)
стеснённый; (*movements*) несвобо́дный.
constraint /kən'streint/ *n.* принужде́ние *neut.*,
принуждённость *f.*
constrict /kən'strɪkt/ *v.* сжима́ть *impf.*, сжать *pf.*;
су́живать *impf.*, су́зить *pf.*
constriction /kən'strɪkʃən/ *n.* сжа́тие; сокраще́-
ние; стя́гивание; суже́ние *neut.*
constrictor /kən'strɪktər/ *n.* (*zool.*) уда́в *m.*
constringent /kən'strɪndʒənt/ *adj.* сжима́ющий.
construct /kən'strʌkt/ *v.* стро́ить *impf.*, постро́-
ить *pf.*
construction /kən'strʌkʃən/ *n.* строи́тельство
neut.
constructional /kən'strʌkʃənl/ *adj.* строи́тель-
ный.
constructive /kən'strʌktɪv/ *adj.* конструкти́вный;
строи́тельный.
constructivism /kən'strʌktə,vɪzəm/ *n.* конструк-
тиви́зм *m.*
constructivist /kən'strʌktəvɪst/ *adj.* конструкти-
ви́ст *m.*
constructor /kən'strʌktər/ *n.* строи́тель *m.*
construe /kən'stru/ *v.* толкова́ть *impf.*
consul /'kɒnsəl/ *n.* ко́нсул *m.*
consular /'kɒnsələr/ *adj.* ко́нсульский.
consulate /'kɒnsəlɪt/ *n.* ко́нсульство *neut.*
consult /kən'sʌlt/ *v.* сове́товаться (с *with instr.*)
impf., посове́товаться *pf.*
consultant /kən'sʌltnt/ *n.* консульта́нт *m.*
consultation /,kɒnsəl'teiʃən/ *n.* консульта́ция *f.*
consultative /kən'sʌltətɪv/ *adj.* консультати́в-
ный.
consume /kən'sum/ *v.* потребля́ть *impf.*, потре-
би́ть *pf.*
consumer /kən'sumər/ *n.* потреби́тель *m.*
consummate / *v.* 'kɒnsə,meit; *adj.* kən'sʌmɪt,
'kɒnsəmɪt/ **1.** *v.* заверша́ть *impf.*; (*perfect*) со-
верше́нствовать *impf.* **2.** *adj.* соверше́нный.
consummation /,kɒnsə'meiʃən/ *n.* заверше́ние
neut.
consumption /kən'sʌmpʃən/ *n.* потребле́ние
neut., расхо́д *m.*; (*med.*) чахо́тка *f.*, туберкулёз
лёгких *m.*
consumptive /kən'sʌmptɪv/ **1.** *n.* больно́й тубер-
кулёзом *m.* **2.** *adj.* туберкулёзный.
contact /'kɒntækt/ **1.** *n.* конта́кт *m.*, соприкосно-
ве́ние *neut.* **2.** *v.* входи́ть в конта́кт (с *with
str.*) *impf.*, войти́ в конта́кт *pf.*; свя́зываться (с
with instr.) *impf.*
contactor /'kɒntæktər/ *n.* конта́ктор *m.*
contagion /kən'teidʒən/ *n.* зара́за, инфе́кция *f.*
contagious /kən'teidʒəs/ *adj.* зара́зный; (*fig.*)
зарази́тельный.
contain /kən'tein/ *v.* содержа́ть *impf.*; **to contain
oneself** сде́рживаться *impf.*
container /kən'teinər/ *n.* сосу́д *m.*; (*for shipping*)
конте́йнер *m.*

containerization /kən‚teinərə'zeiʃən/ *n.* контейнеризáция *f.*

contaminate /kən'tæmə‚neit/ *v.* заражáть; загрязня́ть *impf.*

contamination /kən‚tæmə'neiʃən/ *n.* загрязнéние *neut.*

contemplate /'kɒntəm‚pleit/ *v.* созерцáть *impf.*

contemplative /kən'templətiv/ *adj.* созерцáтельный.

contemporary /kən'tempə‚reri/ **1.** *adj.* совремéнный. **2.** *n.* совремéнник *m.*

contempt /kən'tempt/ *n.* презрéние *neut.*

contemptible /kən'temptəbəl/ *adj.* презрéнный.

contemptuous /kən'temptʃuəs/ *adj.* презри́тельный.

contend /kən'tend/ *v.* (*assert*) утверждáть *impf.*, утверди́ть *pf.*; (*compete*) состязáться *impf.*

content¹ /kən'tent/ **1.** *adj.* довóльный. **2.** *v.* удовлетворя́ться *impf.*, удовлетвори́ться *pf.*

content² /'kɒntent/ *n.* содержáние *neut.*

contention /kən'tenʃən/ *n.* (*dispute*) спор *m.*; (*assertion*) утверждéние *neut.*

contentious /kən'tenʃəs/ *adj.* сварли́вый; спóрный; (*leading to strife*) раздóрный.

contentment /kən'tentmənt/ *n.* удовлетворённость *f.*, довóльствие *neut.*

contest / *n.* 'kɒntest; *v.* kən'test/ **1** *n.* кóнкурс *m.*; состязáние *neut.* **2.** *v.* спóрить *impf.*

contestant /kən'testənt/ *n.* учáстник соревновáния *m.*

context /'kɒntɛkst/ *n.* контéкст *m.*

contextual /kən'tɛkstʃuəl/ *adj.* контекстуáльный.

contiguity /‚kɒntɪ'gyuiti/ *n.* смéжность *f.*

contiguous /kən'tɪgyuəs/ *adj.* (*adjoining*) смéжный; (*neighboring*) сосéдний.

continence /'kɒntɪnəns/ *n.* воздéржанность *f.*

continent /'kɒntɪnənt/ *n.* матери́к, континéнт *m.*

continental /‚kɒntɪ'entl̩/ *adj.* материкóвый, континентáльный.

contingency /kən'tɪndʒənsi/ *n.* случáйность *f.*

contingent /kən'tɪndʒənt/ **1.** *adj.* возмóжный; **to be contingent on** зави́сеть (от *with gen.*) *impf.* **2.** *n.* (*quota*) континге́нт *m.*, квóта *f.*

continual /kən'tɪnyuəl/ *adj.* непреры́вный.

continuance /kən'tɪnyuəns/ *n.* продолжи́тельность *f.*; продолжéние *neut.*

continuation /kən‚tɪnyu'eiʃən/ *n.* продолжéние *neut.*

continue /kən'tɪnyu/ *v.* продолжáть *impf.*, продóлжить *pf.*

continued /kən'tɪnyud/ *adj.* продолжáющийся.

continuity /‚kɒntɪ'uiti/ *n.* непреры́вность *f.*

continuous /kən'tɪnyuəs/ *adj.* непреры́вный.

continuum /kən'tɪnyuəm/ *n.* конти́нуум *m.*

contort /kən'tɔrt/ *v.* искривля́ть *impf.*

contortion /kən'tɔrʃən/ *n.* искривлéние *neut.*

contortionist /kən'tɔrʃənɪst/ *n.* человéк-змея́ *m.*

contour /'kɒntʊr/ *m.* кóнтур *m.*

contraband /'kɒntrə‚bænd/ **1.** *adj.* контрабáндный. **2.** *n.* контрабáнда *f.*

contrabass /'kɒntrə‚beis/ *n.* контрабáс *m.*

contraception /‚kɒntrə'sepʃən/ *n.* применéние противозачáточных мер *neut.*

contraceptive /‚kɒntrə'septɪv/ *adj.* противозачáточный.

contract /'kɒntrækt; *otherwise v.* kən'trækt/ **1.** *n.* договóр, контрáкт *m.* **2.** *v.* заключáть договóр

impf.; (*draw together*) сжимáться *impf.*, сжáться *pf.*

contracted /kən'træktɪd/ *adj.* смóрщенный.

contractile /kən'træktl̩/ *adj.* сжимáющийся.

contraction /kən'trækʃən/ *n.* сжáтие; сокращéние *neut.*

contractor /'kɒntræktər/ *n.* подря́дчик *m.*

contractual /kən'træktʃuəl/ *adj.* договóрный.

contradict /‚kɒntrə'dɪkt/ *v.* противорéчить *impf.*

contradiction /‚kɒntrə'dɪkʃən/ *n.* противорéчие *neut.*

contradictory /‚kɒntrə'dɪktəri/ *adj.* противорéчивый.

contradistinguish /‚kɒntrədɪ'stɪŋwɪʃ/ *v.* противопоставля́ть *impf.*

contrail /'kɒntreil/ *n.* (*aviation*) инверсиóнный след *m.*

contraindicate /‚kɒntrə'ɪndɪ‚keit/ *v.* противопокáзывать *impf.*

contraindication /‚kɒntrə‚ɪndɪ'keiʃən/ *n.* противопоказáние *neut.*

contralto /kən'træltou/ *n.* контрáльто *neut. indecl.*

contraption /kən'træpʃən/ *n.* устрóйство *neut.*

contrapuntal /‚kɒntrə'pʌntl̩/ *adj.* контрапункти́ческий.

contrariety /‚kɒntrə'raɪtl̩/ *n.* несовмести́мость *f.*

contrarily /'kɒntrɛrəli, kən'trɛər-/ *adv.* своевóльно.

contrariness /'kɒntrɛrɪnɪs/ *n.* своевóлие *neut.*

contrariwise /'kɒntrɛri‚waiz/ *adv.* наоборóт.

contrary /'kɒntrɛri/ **1.** *adj.* противополóжный. **2.** *n.* противополóжность *f.*; **contrary to** вопреки́ (*with dat.*); **on the contrary** наоборóт.

contrast / *n.* 'kɒntræst; *v.* kən'træst, 'kɒntræst/ **1.** *n.* контрáст *m.* **2.** *v.* противопоставля́ть *impf.*, противопостáвить *pf.*

contravene /‚kɒntrə'vin/ *v.* нарушáть *impf.*

contravention /‚kɒntrə'venʃən/ *n.* нарушéние *neut.*

contretemps /'kɒntrə‚tɑ̃/ (*complication*) неожи́данное осложнéние *neut.*; (*embarassment*) неприя́тность *f.*

contribute /kən'trɪbyut/ *v.* жéртвовать *impf.*, пожéртвовать *pf.*

contribution /‚kɒntrə'byuʃən/ *n.* пожéртвование *neut.*; вклад *m.*

contributor /kən'trɪbyətər/ *n.* сотрýдник; жéртвователь *m.*

contributory /kən'trɪbyə‚tɔri/ *adj.* содéйствующий.

contrite /kən'trait/ *adj.* кáющийся.

contrition /kən'trɪʃən/ *n.* раскáяние *neut.*

contrivance /kən'traivəns/ *n.* (*device*) механи́зм *m.*; устрóйство, приспособлéние *neut.*; (*invention*) вы́думка *f.*

contrive /kən'traiv/ *v.* приду́мывать *impf.*, приду́мать *pf.*

contrived /kən'traivd/ *adj.* иску́сственный; напускнóй.

control /kən'troul/ **1.** *n.* (*check*) провéрка *f.*, контрóль *m.*; (*direction*) управлéние *neut.* **2.** *v.* (*check*) контроли́ровать *impf.*, проконтроли́ровать *pf.*; (*regulate*) управля́ть *impf.*

controllable /kən'trouləbəl/ *adj.* (*tech.*) управля́емый.

controller /kən'troulər/ *n.* (*person*) контролёр *m.*; (*device*) регуля́тор, контрóллер *m.*

controversial /ˌkɒntrə'vɜrʃəl/ *adj.* спóрный.
controversialist /ˌkɒntrə'vɜrʃəlɪst/ *n.* полемúст *m.*
controversy /'kɒntrə,vɜrsi/ *n.* спор *m.*, полéмика *f.*
controvert /'kɒntrə,vɜrt/ *v.* оспáривать *impf.*
contumacious /ˌkɒntu'meiʃəs/ *adj.* непокóрный.
contumely /'kɒntʊməli/ *n.* (*insult*) оскорблéние *neut.*; (*disgrace*) бесчéстье *neut.*
contusion /kən'tuʒən/ *n.* ушúб *m.*, контýзия *f.*
conundrum /kə'nʌndrəm/ *n.* загáдка *f.*
conurbation /ˌkɒnər'beiʃən/ *n.* конурбáция *f.*, городскáя конгломерáция *f.*
convalesce /ˌkɒnvə'lɛs/ *v.* выздорáвливать *impf.*, вы́здороветь *pf.*
convalescence /ˌkɒnvə'lɛsəns/ *n.* выздорáвливание; выздоровлéние *neut.*
convalescent /ˌkɒnvə'lɛsənt/ *adj.* выздорáвливающий.
convection /kən'vɛkʃən/ *n.* конвéкция *f.*
convector /kən'vɛktər/ *n.* конвéктор *m.*
convene /kən'vin/ *v.* собирáться *impf.*, собрáться *pf.*
convenience /kən'vinyəns/ *n.* удóбство *neut.*
convenient /kən'vinyənt/ *adj.* удóбный.
convent /'kɒnvɛnt/ *n.* жéнский монасты́рь *m.*
conventicle /kən'vɛntɪkəl/ *n.* молéльня *f.*
convention /kən'vɛnʃən/ *n.* (*assembly*) съезд *m.*
conventional /kən'vɛnʃənl/ *adj.* услóвный.
conventionality /kən,vɛnʃə'næliti/ *n.* услóвность *f.*
converge /kən'vɜrdʒ/ *v.* сходúться *impf.*, сойтúсь *pf.*
convergence /kən'vɜrdʒəns/ *n.* схождéние *neut.*
convergent /kən'vɜrdʒənt/ *adj.* сходя́щийся.
conversant /kən'vɜrsənt/ *adj.* свéдущий.
conversation /ˌkɒnvər'seiʃən/ *n.* разговóр *m.*
conversational /ˌkɒnvər'seiʃənl/ *adj.* разговóрный.
converse[1] /kən'vɜrs/ *v.* бесéдовать *impf.*
converse[2] /*adj.* kən'vɜrs; *n.* 'kɒnvɜrs/ **1.** *adj.* противополóжный. **2.** *n.* обрáтное *neut.*
conversely /kən'vɜrsli/ *adv.* наоборóт.
conversion /kən'vɜrʒən/ *n.* превращéние *neut.*; (*finan.*) перевóд *m.*; (*relig.*) перехóд *m.*
convert /kən'vɜrt/ *v.* превращáть *impf.*, преврати́ть *pf.*; (*relig.*) обращáть *impf.*
converter /kən'vɜrtər/ *n.* (*elec.*) преобразовáтель *m.*
convertibility /kən,vɜrtə'biliti/ *n.* обратúмость *f.*
convertible /kən'vɜrtəbəl/ *adj.* обратúмый, изменúмый.
convex /kɒn'vɛks/ *adj.* вы́пуклый.
convey /kən'vei/ *v.* перевозúть *impf.*, перевезтú *pf.*; передавáть *impf.*, передáть *pf.*
conveyance /kən'veiəns/ *n.* перевóзка *f.*
conveyor /kən'veiər/ *n.* конвéйер, транспортёр *m.*
conveyor belt *n.* лéнточный конвéйер *m.*
convict /'kɒnvɪkt/ *n.* осуждённый *m.*
conviction /kən'vɪkʃən/ *n.* осуждéние *neut.*; (*belief*) убеждéние *neut.*, уверенность *f.*
convince /kən'vɪns/ *v.* убеждáть *impf.*, убедúть *pf.*
convincing /kən'vɪnsɪŋ/ *adj.* убедúтельный.
convivial /kən'vɪviəl/ *adj.* (*festive*) весёлый; (*sociable*) общúтельный.

conviviality /kən,vɪvi'æliti/ *n.* весёлость *f.*
convocation /ˌkɒnvə'keiʃən/ *n.* (*summoning*) созы́в *m.*; (*meeting*) собрáние *neut.*
convoke /kən'vouk/ *v.* созывáть *impf.*, собирáть *impf.*
convolute /'kɒnvə,lut/ *adj.* (*bot.*) свёрнутый.
convoluted /'kɒnvə,lutid/ *adj.* извúлистый; запýтанный.
convolution /ˌkɒnvə'luʃən/ *n.* свёрнутость *f.*
convolvulus /kən'vɒlvyələs/ *n.* вьюнóк *m.*
convoy /'kɒnvɔi/ *n.* конвóй *m.*
convulse /kən'vʌls/ *v.* трястú́сь *impf.*
convulsion /kən'vʌlʃən/ *n.* сýдороги *pl.*; конвýльсия *f.*
convulsive /kən'vʌlsiv/ *adj.* сýдорожный.
coo /ku/ **1.** *n.* воркование *neut.* **2.** *v.* воркова́ть *impf.*
cook /kʊk/ **1.** *n.* пóвар *m.*, кухáрка *f.* **2.** *v.* готóвить *impf.*, приготóвить *pf.*; стря́пать *impf.*
cookery /'kʊkəri/ *n.* кулинарúя *f.*
cookie /'kʊki/ *n.* печéнье *neut.*
cooking /'kʊkɪŋ/ **1.** *adj.* кýхонный. **2.** *n.* кýхня *f.*
cool /kul/ **1.** *adj.* прохлáдный. **2.** *v.* охлаждáть *impf.*, охладúть *pf.*; **to cool off** остывáть *impf.*
coolant /'kulənt/ *n.* охлаждáющее срéдство *neut.*
cooler /'kulər/ *n.* охладúтель *m.*
cooling /'kulɪŋ/ *n.* охлаждéние *neut.*
coolness /'kulnɪs/ *n.* прохлáда *f.*; (*of person*) хладнокрóвие *neut.*
coop /kup/ *n.* куря́тник *m.*
cooper /'kupər/ *n.* бóндарь *m.*
cooperate /kou'ɒpə,reit/ *v.* сотрýдничать *impf.*
cooperation /kou,ɒpə'reiʃən/ *n.* сотрýдничество *neut.*
cooperative /kou'ɒpərətiv/ *adj.* совмéстный, кооперати́вный.
coopt /kou'ɒpt/ *v.* коопти́ровать *impf.*
coordinate /kou'ɔrdn̩,eit/ *v.* координúровать *impf.* and *pf.*
coordination /kou,ɔrdn̩'eiʃən/ *n.* координáция *f.*
coot /kut/ *n.* (*bird*) лысýха *f.*
cop /kɒp/ *n.* (*colloq.*) (*policeman*) полицéйский *m.*
copal /'koupəl/ *n.* копáл *m.*
cope /koup/ *v.* справля́ться (с *with instr.*) *impf.*
Copenhagen /ˌkoupən'heigən, -'hɑ-/ *n.* Копенгáген *m.*
Copernican system /kou'pɜrnikən/ *n.* систéма Копéрника *f.*
copier /'kɒpiər/ *n.* (*person*) перепúсчик *m.*; (*machine*) копировáльная машúна *f.*
copilot /'kou,pailət/ *n.* вторóй пилóт *m.*
copious /'koupiəs/ *adj.* обúльный.
copper /'kɒpər/ *n.* медь *f.*
copper beech *n.* тёмно-пунцóвый бук *m.*
copperplate /'kɒpər,pleit/ *n.* (*typog.*) мéдная гравирóвальная доскá *f.*
coppersmith /'kɒpər,smiθ/ *n.* мéдник *m.*
copra /'kɒprə/ *n.* кóпра *f.*
copse /kɒps/ *n.* рóщица *f.*
copula /'kɒpyələ/ *n.* свя́зка *f.*
copulate /'kɒpyə,leit/ *v.* спáриваться, совокупля́ться *impf.*
copulation /ˌkɒpyə'leiʃən/ *n.* спáривание *neut.*
copulative /'kɒpyə,leitiv/ *adj.* (*biol.*) детородный; (*gram.*) соединúтельный.
copy /'kɒpi/ **1.** *n.* экземпля́р *m.*, кóпия *f.* **2.** *v.*

копи́ровать *impf.*; (*transcribe*) перепи́сывать *impf.*
copyist /'kɒpiɪst/ *n.* перепи́счик *m.*
copyright /'kɒpi,rait/ *n.* а́вторское пра́во *neut.*
coquetry /'koukɪtri/ *n.* коке́тство *neut.*
coquette /kou'kɛt/ *n.* коке́тка *f.*
coquettish /kou'kɛtɪʃ/ *adj.* коке́тливый.
coral /'kɔrəl/ **1.** *adj.* кора́лловый. **2.** *n.* кора́лл *m.*
cor anglais /,kɔr ɑŋ'glei/ *n.* англи́йский рожо́к *m.*
corbel /'kɔrbəl/ *n.* вы́ступ *m.*
cord /kɔrd/ *n.* верёвка *f.*; (*elec.*) шнур *m.*; **vocal cords** голосовы́е свя́зки *pl.*
cordage /'kɔrdɪdʒ/ *n.* такела́ж *m.*
cordate /'kɔrdeit/ *adj.* сердцеви́дный.
cordial /'kɔrdʒəl/ *adj.* серде́чный.
cordiality /kɔr'dʒælɪti/ *n.* серде́чность *f.*
cordite /'kɔrdait/ *n.* корди́т *m.*
cordon /'kɔrdn̩/ *n.* кордо́н *m.*
corduroy /'kɔrdə,rɔi/ *n.* ру́бчатый плис *m.*; *pl.* пли́совые штаны́ *pl.*
core /kɔr/ *n.* сердцеви́на *f.*; (*fig.*) суть *f.*
co-respondent /,kourɪ'spɒndənt/ *n.* (*leg.*) соотве́тчик *m.*
coriander /'kɔri,ændər/ *n.* кинза́ *f*
Corinth /'kɔrɪnθ/ *n.* Кори́нф *m.*
Corinthian /kə'rɪnθiən/ *adj.* кори́нфский.
cork /kɔrk/ *n.* про́бка *f.*
corkscrew /'kɔrk,skru/ *n.* што́пор *m.*
corm /kɔrm/ *n* лу́ковица *f.*
cormorant /'kɔrmərənt/ *n.* большо́й бакла́н *m.*
corn[1] /kɔrn/ *n.* кукуру́за *f.*, зерно́ *neut.*
corn[2] /kɔrn/ *n.* (*callus*) мозо́ль *m.*
corncob /'kɔrn,kɒb/ *n.* кукуру́зная кочеры́жка *f.*
corn crake *n.* коросте́ль *m.*
cornea /'kɔrniə/ *n.* рогови́ца *f.*
corned /kɔrnd/ *adj.* солёный.
corned beef *n.* солони́на *f.*
cornel /'kɔrnl̩/ *n.* кизи́л *m.*
corner /'kɔrnər/ **1.** *adj.* углово́й. **2.** *n.* у́гол *m.*
cornering /'kɔrnərɪŋ/ *n.* движе́ние на поворо́те *neut.*
cornerstone /'kɔrnər,stoun/ *n.* углово́й ка́мень *m.*
cornet /kɔr'nɛt/ *n.* (*mus.*, *mil.*) корне́т *m.*
corn exchange *n.* хле́бная би́ржа *f.*
cornfield /'kɔrn,fild/ *n.* кукуру́зное по́ле *neut.*
cornflakes /'kɔrn,fleiks/ *n.* кукуру́зные хло́пья *pl.*
cornflower /'kɔrn,flauər/ *n.* василёк *m.*
cornice /'kɔrnɪs/ *n.* карни́з *m.*
cornmeal /'kɔrn,mil/ *n.* кукуру́зная мука́ *f.*
cornucopia /,kɔrnə'koupiə/ *n.* рог изоби́лия *m.*
corny /'kɔrni/ *adj.* (*colloq.*) шабло́нный.
corolla /kə'rɒlə/ *n.* ве́нчик *m.*
corollary /'kɔrə,lɛri/ *n.* сле́дствие *neut.*
corona /kə'rounə/ *n.* (*astr.*) со́лнечная коро́на *f.*
coronary /'kɔrə,nɛri/ *adj.* вене́чный.
coronation /,kɔrə'neiʃən/ *n.* корона́ция *f.*
coroner /'kɔrənər/ *n.* пато́лого ана́том *m.*
coronet /'kɔrənɪt/ *n.* коро́на *f.*
corporal[1] /'kɔrpərəl/ *n.* капра́л *m.*
corporal[2] /'kɔrpərəl/ *adj.* теле́сный.
corporate /'kɔrpərɪt/ *adj.* корпорати́вный.

corporation /,kɔrpə'reiʃən/ *n.* корпора́ция *f.*; акционе́рное о́бщество *neut.*
corporeal /kɔr'pɔriəl/ *adj.* теле́сный; физи́ческий; материа́льный.
corps /kɔr/ *n.* ко́рпус *m.*
corpse /kɔrps/ *n.* труп *m.*
corpulence /'kɔrpyələns/ *n.* доро́дность, ту́чность *f.*
corpulent /'kɔrpyələnt/ *adj.* доро́дный.
corpus /'kɔrpəs/ *n.* (*laws*, *texts*, *etc.*) свод *m.*
corpuscle /'kɔrpəsəl/ *n.* кровяно́й ша́рик *m.*
corpuscular /kɔr'pʌskyələr/ *adj.* корпускуля́рный.
corral /kə'ræl/ *n.* заго́н *m.*
correct /kə'rɛkt/ **1.** *adj.* пра́вильный. **2.** *v.* поправля́ть *impf.*, попра́вить *pf.*, исправля́ть *impf.*, испра́вить *pf.*
correction /kə'rɛkʃən/ *n.* попра́вка *f.*
correctitude /kə'rɛktɪ,tud/ *n.* корре́ктность *f.*
corrective /kə'rɛktɪv/ *adj.* исправи́тельный.
correctness /kə'rɛktnɪs/ *n.* пра́вильность *f.*
correlate /'kɔrə,leit/ *v.* соотноси́ть *impf.*
correlation /,kɔrə'leiʃən/ *n.* соотноше́ние *neut.*, корреля́ция *f.*
correlative /kə'rɛlətɪv/ *adj.* соотноси́тельный; (*phys.*, *gram.*) корреляти́вный.
correspond /,kɔrə'spɒnd/ *v.* (*by letter*) перепи́сываться *impf.*; (*conform*) соотве́тствовать *impf.*
correspondence /,kɔrə'spɒndəns/ *n.* корреспонде́нция, перепи́ска *f.*; (*conformity*) соотве́тствие *neut.*, **by correspondence** зао́чно.
correspondent /,kɔrə'spɒndənt/ *n.* корреспонде́нт *m.*
corresponding /,kɔrə'spɒndɪŋ/ *adj.* соотве́тствующий.
corridor /'kɔrɪdər/ *n.* коридо́р *m.*
corrigenda /,kɔrɪ'dʒɛndə/ *n.* спи́сок опеча́ток *m.*
corroborate /kə'rɒbə,reit/ *v.* подтвержда́ть *impf.*, подтверди́ть *pf.*
corroboration /kə,rɒbə'reiʃən/ *n.* подтвержде́ние *neut.*
corroborative /kə'rɒbə,reitɪv, -ərətɪv/ *adj.* подтвержда́ющий.
corrode /kə'roud/ *v.* разъеда́ть *impf.*, разъе́сть *pf.*
corrosion /kə'rouʒən/ *n.* корро́зия *f.*
corrosive /kə'rousɪv/ *adj.* е́дкий, разъеда́ющий; (*tech.*) коррози́йный.
corrugate /'kɔrə,geit/ *v.* гофрирова́ть *impf.* and *pf.*
corrugated /'kɔrə,geitɪd/ *adj.* гофриро́ванный; рифлёный.
corrugation /,kɔrə'geiʃən/ *n.* (*fold*) скла́дка *f.*; (*tech.*) (*process*) рифле́ние *neut.*; (*waviness*) волни́стость *f.*
corrupt /kə'rʌpt/ **1.** *adj.* прода́жный. **2.** *v.* развраща́ть *impf.*, разврати́ть *pf.*
corruptibility /kə,rʌptə'bılıti/ *n.* прода́жность *f.*
corruptible /kə'rʌptəbəl/ *adj.* подку́пный.
corruption /kə'rʌpʃən/ *n.* развраще́ние *neut.*
corsage /kɔr'saʒ/ *n.* корса́ж *m.*
corsair /'kɔrsɛr/ *n.* корса́р *m.*
corset /'kɔrsɪt/ *n.* корсе́т *m.*
cortege /kɔr'tɛʒ/ *n.* корте́ж *m.*
cortex /'kɔrtɛks/ *n.* кора́ *f.*
cortical /'kɔrtɪkəl/ *adj.* ко́рковый.

cortisone /'kɔrtə,zoun/ n. кортизо́н m.
corundum /kə'rʌndəm/ n. кору́нд m.
coruscate /'kɔrə,skeit/ v. сверка́ть impf.
coruscation /,kɔrə'skeiʃən/ n. сверка́ние neut.
corvée /kɔr'vei/ n. ба́рщина f.
corvette /kɔr'vɛt/ n. сторожево́й кора́бль m.
cosecant /kou'sikənt/ n. косе́канс m.
cosine /'kousain/ n. ко́синус m.
cosmetic /kɒz'mɛtik/ **1.** adj. космети́ческий. **2.** n. pl. косме́тика f.
cosmic /'kɒzmik/ adj. косми́ческий.
cosmogony /kɒz'mɒgəni/ n. космого́ния f.
cosmography /kɒz'mɒgrəfi/ n. космогра́фия f.
cosmology /kɒz'mɒlədʒi/ n. космоло́гия f.
cosmonaut /'kɒzmə,nɔt/ n. космона́вт m.
cosmopolitan /,kɒzmə'pɒlitn/ **1.** adj. космополити́ческий. **2.** n. космополи́т m.
cosmos /'kɒzməs, -mous/ n. ко́смос m., вселе́нная f.
Cossack /'kɒsæk/ **1.** adj. каза́цкий. **2.** n. каза́к m., каза́чка f.
cost /kɔst/ **1.** n. сто́имость, цена́ f.; **at all costs** любо́й цено́й. **2.** v. сто́ить impf.
costal /'kɒstl/ adj. рёберный.
Costa Rica /'kɒstə rikə/ n. Ко́ста-Ри́ка f.
cost-effective /'kɒstɪ'fɛktɪv/ adj. рента́бельный.
costly /'kɔstli/ adv. дорого́й, це́нный.
costume /'kɒstum/ n. костю́м m.
costumier /kɒ'stumiər, ,kɔstum'yei/ n. костюме́р m.
cosy /'kouzi/ adj. ую́тный.
cot /kɒt/ n. раскладу́шка f.
cotangent /kou'tændʒənt/ n. кота́нгенс m.
coterie /'koutəri/ n. и́збранный круг m., кли́ка f.
coterminous /kou'tɜrmənəs/ adj. име́ющий о́бщие грани́цы.
cotillion /kə'tɪlyən/ n. котильо́н m.
cottage /'kɒtɪdʒ/ n. да́ча f.
cotter /'kɒtər/ n. клин m., чека́ f.
cotton /'kɒtn/ **1.** adj. хлопчатобума́жный. **2.** n. хло́пок m.; (absorbent cotton) ва́та f.
cotton cake n. хло́пковый жмых m.
cotton grass n. пуши́ца f.
cotton plant n. хлопча́тник m.
cotyledon /,kɒtl'idn/ n. семядо́ля f.
couch /kautesh/ n. дива́н m.; (poet.) ло́же neut.
couchette /ku'ʃɛt/ n. спа́льное ме́сто neut.
couch grass n. пыре́й ползу́чий.
cougar /'kugər/ n. пу́ма f., кугуа́р m.
cough /kɔf/ **1.** n. ка́шель m. **2.** v. ка́шлять impf.
cough drop n. табле́тка от ка́шля f.
coulisse /ku'lis/ n. (tech.) желобо́к m.
coulomb /'kulɒm/ n. куло́н m.
council /'kaunsəl/ n. сове́т m.
councilor /'kaunsələr/ n. член сове́та m.
counsel /'kaunsəl/ **1.** n. сове́т m.; (leg.) адвока́т m. **2.** v. сове́товать impf., посове́товать pf.
counselor /'kaunsələr/ n. сове́тник, консульта́нт m.; (leg.) адвока́т m.
count /kaunt/ **1.** n. счёт m. **2.** v. счита́ть impf., сосчита́ть pf.
countdown /'kaunt,daun/ n. отсчёт вре́мени m.
countenance /'kauntnəns/ n. (face) лицо́ neut.; (expression) выраже́ние лица́ neut.
counter /'kauntər/ n. счётчик m.
counter-accusation /'kauntər,ækyu'zeiʃən/ n. контробвине́ние neut.

counteract /,kauntər'ækt/ v. противоде́йствовать impf.
counteraction /,kauntər'ækʃən/ n. противоде́йствие neut.
counterattack /'kauntərə,tæk/ n. контрата́ка f.
counterbalance /'kauntər,bæləns/ n. противове́с m.; **as a counterbalance to** в противове́с (with dat.).
counterblast /'kauntər,blæst/ n. агресси́вный отве́т m.
countercharge / n. 'kauntər,tʃardʒ; v. ,kauntər'tʃardʒ/ **1.** n. встре́чное обвине́ние neut. **2.** v. выставля́ть встре́чное обвине́ние impf.
counterclaim /'kauntər,kleim/ n. встре́чный иск m.
counterclockwise /,kauntər'klɒk,waiz/ adv. про́тив часово́й стре́лки.
counterespionage /,kauntər'ɛspiə,naʒ/ n. контрразве́дка f.
counterfeit /'kauntər,fit/ **1.** adj. подде́льный. **2.** v. подде́лывать impf., подде́лать pf.
counterfeiter /'kauntər,fitər/ n. фальши́вомоне́тчик m.
counterfoil /'kauntər,fɔil/ n. корешо́к m.
countermand /,kauntər'mænd/ v. отменя́ть прика́з impf.
countermove /,kauntər'muv/ n. встре́чный ход m.
counteroffensive n. контрнаступле́ние neut.
counterpart /'kauntər,part/ n. собра́т m.
counterplot /'kauntər,plɒt/ n. контрза́говор m.
counterpoint /'kauntər,pɔint/ n. контрапу́нкт m.
counterpoise /'kauntər,pɔiz/ n. противове́с m.
counterproductive /,kauntərprə'dʌktiv/ adj. нецелесообра́зный.
counterproposal /'kauntərprə,pouzəl/ n. контрпредложе́ние neut.
counterrevolution /'kauntər,rɛvə'luʃən/ n. контрреволю́ция f.
counterrevolutionary /'kauntər,rɛvə'luʃə,nɛri/ adj. контрреволюцио́нный.
countersign /'kauntər,sain/ n. паро́ль m.
countersink /'kauntər,siŋk/ n. зенко́вка f.
counterthreat /'kauntər,θrɛt/ n. контругро́за f.
countess /'kauntis/ n. графи́ня f.
countless /'kauntlis/ adj. бесчи́сленный.
country /'kʌntri/ **1.** adj. дереве́нский. **2.** n. страна́ f.; (native) ро́дниа f., оте́чество neut.; (rural districts) дере́вня f.
country-and-western /'kʌntriən'wɛstərn/ n. ка́нтри neut. indecl.
countryman /'kʌntrimən/ n. соотече́ственник m.
countryside /'kʌntri,said/ n. се́льская ме́стность f.
countrywide /'kʌntrə,waid/ adj. национа́льный.
county /'kaunti/ n. о́круг m.
coup /ku/ n. уда́чный ход m.; (polit.) переворо́т m.
couple /'kʌpəl/ **1.** n. па́ра f. **2.** v. сцепля́ть impf., сцепи́ть pf.
couplet /'kʌplit/ n. двусти́шие neut.
coupling /'kʌpliŋ/ n. соедине́ние neut.
coupon /'kupɒn, 'kyu-/ n. купо́н; тало́н m.
courage /'kɜridʒ/ n. му́жество neut., сме́лость f.
courageous /kə'reidʒəs/ adj. му́жественный, сме́лый.
courier /'kɜriər/ n. курье́р m.

course /kɔrs/ n. курс; ход m.; направле́ние neut.; (meal) блю́до neut.; **of course** коне́чно; **in the course of** в тече́ние (with gen.).

court /kɔrt/ n. двор m.; (leg.) суд m.; (sport) корт m.

courteous /'kɜrtiəs/ adj. ве́жливый.

courtesan /'kɔrtəzən/ n. куртиза́нка f.

courtesy /'kɜrtəsi/ n. ве́жливость f.

courthouse /'kɔrt,haus/ n. зда́ние суда́ neut.

courtier /'kɔrtiər/ n. придво́рный m.

courting /'kɔrtɪŋ/ n. уха́живание neut.

courtly /'kɔrtli, 'kourt-/ adj. ве́жливый.

court-martial /'kɔrt,marʃəl/ v. суди́ть вое́нным судо́м impf.

courtship /'kɔrtʃɪp/ n. уха́живание neut.

courtyard /'kɔrt,yard/ n. двор m.

cousin /'kʌzən/ n. двою́родный брат m., двою́родная сестра́ f.

couturier /ku'turi,ei/ n. да́мский портно́й m.

covalency /kou'veilənsi/ n. вале́нтность f.

covalent /kou'veilənt/ adj. ковале́нтный.

cove /kouv/ n. (bay) бу́хточка f.; (archi.) вы́кружка f.

coven /'kʌvən/ n. (witches) ша́баш ведьм m.

covenant /'kʌvənənt/ n. соглаше́ние neut., догово́р m.; (relig.) заве́т m.

cover /'kʌvər/ **1.** n. (lid) кры́шка f.; чехо́л m.; (bed) одея́ло neut.; (book) переплёт m.; (protection) прикры́тие neut. **2.** v. покрыва́ть impf., покры́ть pf.; (include) охва́тывать impf., охвати́ть pf.

coverage /'kʌvərɪdʒ/ n. (press) освеще́ние neut.; охва́т m.

covering /'kʌvərɪŋ/ n. покрыва́ние neut.

coverlet /'kʌvərlɪt/ n. покрыва́ло neut.

covert /'kouvərt/ adj. скры́тный; та́йный.

coverup /'kʌvər,ʌp/ n. сокры́тие neut.

covet /'kʌvɪt/ v. жа́ждать (with gen.) impf.

covetous /'kʌvɪtəs/ adj. жа́дный.

covey /'kʌvi/ n. ста́я f.

cow /kau/ **1.** adj. коро́вий. **2.** n. коро́ва f.

coward /'kauərd/ n. трус m.

cowardice /'kauərdɪs/ n. тру́сость f.

cowardly /'kauərdli/ adj. трусли́вый.

cowboy /'kau,bɔi/ n. ковбо́й m.

cower /'kauər/ v. съёживаться (от испу́га) impf.

cowherd /'kau,hɜrd/ n. пасту́х m.

cowhide /'kau,haid/ n. воло́вья ко́жа f.

cowl /kaul/ n. капюшо́н m.

cowling /'kaulɪŋ/ n. (on engine) капо́т m.

cow parsnip n. бу́тень одуря́ющий m.

cowpox /'kau,pɒks/ n. коро́вья о́спа f.

cowrie /'kauri/ n. ка́ури neut. indecl.

cowshed /'kau,ʃɛd/ n. коро́вник m.

cowslip /'kauslɪp/ n. первоцве́т m.

coxswain /'kɒksən, -,swein/ n. старшина́ шлю́пки m.

coy /kɔi/ adj. засте́нчивый.

coyness /'kɔinɪs/ n. напускна́я засте́нчивость f.

coyote /kai'outi, 'kaiout/ n. лугово́й волк, койо́т m.

coypu /'kɔipu/ n. ко́йпу m. indecl.

cozy /'kouzi/ adj. ую́тный.

crab /kræb/ n. краб m.

crack /kræk/ **1.** n. тре́щина f., (noise) треск m. **2.** v.t. коло́ть impf., расколо́ть pf.; v.i. тре́скаться impf.

crackdown /'kræk,daun/ n. ограниче́ние neut.

cracker /'krækər/ n. сухо́е пече́нье neut.

crackle /'krækəl/ n. потре́скивание neut., треск m.; (gunfire) трескотня́ f.; (snow, etc.) хруст m.

crackling /'kræklɪŋ/ n. (cul.) шква́рки pl.

crackpot /'kræk,pɒt/ n. (colloq.) чуда́к m.

cracksman /'kræksmən/ n. (slang) взло́мщик m.

cradle /'kreidl/ n. колыбе́ль f.

craft /kræft/ n. ремесло́ neut.

craftily /'kræftəli/ adv. хи́тро, лука́во.

craftiness /'kræftinɪs/ n. хи́трость f.

craftsman /'kræftsmən/ n. реме́сленник m.

craftsmanship /'kræftsmən,ʃɪp/ n. мастерство́ neut.

crafty /'kræfti/ adj. хи́трый.

crag /kræg/ n. скала́ f., утёс m.

craggy /'krægi/ adj. скали́стый.

cram /kræm/ v. набива́ть impf., наби́ть pf.; ната́скивать impf., натаска́ть pf.

cram-full /'kræm 'ful/ adj. битко́м наби́тый.

cramp /kræmp/ n. су́дорога, спа́зма f.

cramped /kræmpt/ adj. (restricted) стеснённый; (writing) сжа́тый.

crampon /'kræmpɒn/ n. (tech.) желе́зный захва́т m.

cranberry /'kræn,bɛri/ **1.** adj. клю́квенный. **2.** n. клю́ква f.

crane /krein/ n. (bird) жура́вль m.; (mach.) подъёмный кран m.

cranial /'kreiniəl/ adj. черепно́й.

cranium /'kreiniəm/ n. че́реп m.

crank /kræŋk/ **1.** n. кривоши́п m., рукоя́тка f. **2.** v. заводи́ть рукоя́тью impf.

crankcase /'kræŋk,keis/ n. ка́ртер m.

cranked /'kræŋkt/ adj. коле́нчатый.

crankiness /'kræŋkinɪs/ n. чудакова́тость f.

crankpin /'kræŋk,pɪn/ n. па́лец кривоши́па m.

crankshaft /'kræŋk,ʃæft, -,ʃaft/ n. коле́нчатый вал m.

cranky /'kræŋki/ adj. (eccentric) чудакова́тый, причу́дливый.

cranny /'kræni/ n. щель f.

crape /kreip/ n. креп m.

crash /kræʃ/ **1.** n. гро́хот, треск m.; **disk crash** (computer) крах ди́ска m.; ава́рия ди́ска f. **2.** v. разби́ться pf.

crash dive n. (naut.) сро́чное погруже́ние neut.

crash helmet n. мотошле́м m.

crash-land /'kræʃ'lænd/ v. соверша́ть авари́йную поса́дку impf.

crass /kræs/ adj. (coarse) гру́бый; (stupid) глу́пый.

crate /kreit/ n. я́щик m.

crater /'kreitər/ n. кра́тер m.

crave /kreiv/ v. жа́ждать impf.

craven /'kreivən/ n. трус m.

craving /'kreivɪŋ/ n. стра́стное жела́ние neut.

craw /krɔ/ n. зоб m.

crawfish /'krɔ,fɪʃ/ also **crayfish** /'krei,fɪʃ/ n. рак m.

crawl /krɔl/ v. по́лзать impf., ползти́ pf.

crawler /'krɔlər/ n. ползу́н m.

crawling /'krɔlɪŋ/ n. ползание neut.

crayon /'kreiɒn/ n. цветно́й каранда́ш m.

craze /kreiz/ n. ма́ния f.

crazed /kreizd/ adj. сумасше́дший.

crazily /'kreizəli/ adv. бе́шено.

crazy /'kreizi/ *adj.* сумасше́дший.
creak /krik/ *v.* скрипе́ть *impf.*
creaky /'kriki/ *adj.* скрипу́чий.
cream /krim/ *n.* сли́вки *pl.*; (*cosmetic*) крем *m.*
creamed /krimd/ *adj.* взби́тый.
creamery /'krimɔri/ *n.* маслобо́йня *f.*
creamy /'krimi/ *adj.* сли́вочный.
crease /kris/ **1.** *n.* скла́дка *f.*; (*paper, etc.*) фа́льц *m.* **2.** *v.* мя́ть(ся) *impf.*
crease-resistant /'krisrɪ,zıstənt/ *adj.* несмина́емый.
create /kri'eit/ *v.* твори́ть *impf.*, сотвори́ть *pf.*; создава́ть *impf.*, созда́ть *pf.*
creation /kri'eiʃən/ *n.* созда́ние, творе́ние *neut.*
Creation *n.* сотворе́ние ми́ра *neut.*
creative /kri'eitıv/ *adj.* тво́рческий.
creator /kri'eitər/ *n.* творе́ц, созда́тель; а́втор *m.*
creature /'kritʃər/ *n.* существо́ *neut.*
crèche /krɛʃ/ *n.* де́тские я́сли *pl.*
credence /'kridns/ *n.* ве́ра *f.*; дове́рие *neut.*
credentials /krɪ'dɛnʃəlz/ *pl.* манда́т *m.*; ввери́тельные гра́моты *pl.*
credibility /,krɛdə'bılıti/ *n.* правдоподо́бие *neut.*
credible /'krɛdəbəl/ *adj.* вероя́тный.
credit /'krɛdıt/ **1.** *n.* креди́т *m.* **2.** *v.* кредитова́ть *impf.* and *pf.*; припи́сывать *impf.*, приписа́ть *pf.*
creditable /'krɛdıtəbəl/ *adj.* похва́льный.
creditor /'krɛdıtər/ *n.* кредито́р *m.*
creditworthiness /'krɛdıt,wɜrðinıs/ *n.* кредитоспосо́бность *f.*
creditworthy /'krɛdıt,wɜrði/ *adj.* кредитоспосо́бный.
credo /'kridou/ *n.* (*eccl.*) си́мвол ве́ры *m.*
credulity /krə'dulıti/ *n.* легкове́рие *neut.*
credulous /'krɛdʒələs/ *adj.* легкове́рный.
creed /krid/ *n.* вероуче́ние *neut.*; кре́до *neut. indecl.*
creek /krik, krɪk/ *n.* руче́й *m.*
creel /kril/ *n.* рыба́цкая корзи́на *f.*
creeper /'kripər/ *n.* ползу́чее расте́ние *neut.*
creepy /'kripi/ *adj.* жу́ткий.
cremate /'krimeit/ *v.* креми́ровать *impf.*
cremation /krɪ'meiʃən/ *n.* крема́ция *f.*
crematorium /,krimə'tɔriəm/ *n.* кремато́рий *m.*
crenelated /'krɛnḷ,eitıd/ *adj.* зубча́тый.
Creole /'krioul/ *n.* крео́л *m.*
creosote /'kriə,sout/ *n.* креозо́т *m.*
crepe /kreip/ *n.* креп *m.*
crepuscular /krɪ'pʌskyələr/ *adj.* су́меречный.
crescendo /krɪ'ʃɛndou/ *n.* креще́ндо *neut. indecl.*
crescent /'krɛsənt/ *n.* полуме́сяц *m.*
cresol /'krisɔl/ *n.* крезо́л *m.*
cress /krɛs/ *n.* кресс *m.*
crest /krɛst/ *n.* гре́бень *m.*, верши́на *f.*
crestfallen /'krɛst,fɔlən/ *adj.* удручённый.
cretaceous /krɪ'teiʃəs/ *adj.* мелово́й.
Crete /krit/ *n.* (*island*) Крит *m.*
cretin /'kritṇ/ *n.* крети́н *m.*
cretinism /'kritṇ,ızəm/ *n.* кретини́зм *m.*
cretinous /'kritnəs/ *adj.* слабоу́мный.
cretonne /krɪ'tɒn/ *n.* крето́н *m.*
crevasse /krə'væs/ *n.* рассе́лина в леднике́ *f.*
crevice /'krɛvıs/ *n.* щель, рассе́лина *f.*
crew /kru/ *n.* экипа́ж *m.*, кома́нда *f.*
crew cut *n.* стри́жка ёжиком *f.*

crib /krıb/ *n.* (*manger*) корму́шка *f.*, я́сли *pl.*; (*cot*) де́тская крова́тка *f.*
cricket /'krıkıt/ *n.* (*insect*) сверчо́к *m.*; (*game*) кри́кет *m.*
crier /'kraiər/ *n.* глаша́тай *m.*
crime /kraim/ *n.* преступле́ние *neut.*
Crimea /krai'miə/ *n.* Крым *m.*
Crimean /krai'miən/ *adj.* кры́мский.
criminal /'krımənḷ/ **1.** *adj.* престу́пный. **2.** *n.* престу́пник *m.*
criminology /,krımə'nɒlədʒi/ *n.* криминоло́гия *f.*
crimp /krımp/ *v.* завива́ть.
crimson /'krımzən/ **1.** *adj.* багро́вый, мали́новый. **2.** *n.* мали́новый цвет *m.*
cringe /krındʒ/ *v.* (*fawn*) раболе́пствовать; съёживаться *impf.*
crinoline /'krınḷın/ *n.* криноли́н *m.*
cripple /'krıpəl/ **1.** *n.* кале́ка *m.* and *f.* (*decl. f.*) **2.** *v.* кале́чить *impf.*, искале́чить *pf.*
crisis /'kraisıs/ *n.* кри́зис *m.*; перело́м *m.*
crisp /krısp/ *adj.* хрустя́щий, ло́мкий.
crisscross /'krıs,krɒs/ **1.** *adj.* перекре́щивающийся. **2.** *adv.* крест-на́крест.
criterion /krai'tıəriən/ *n.* крите́рий *m.*
critic /'krıtık/ *n.* кри́тик *m.*
critical /'krıtıkəl/ *adj.* крити́ческий.
criticism /'krıtə,sızəm/ *n.* кри́тика *f.*
criticize /'krıtə,saiz/ *v.* критикова́ть *impf.*
critique /krı'tik/ *n.* кри́тика *f.*
croak /krouk/ **1.** *n.* ква́канье; ка́рканье *neut.* **2.** *v.* ква́кать *impf.*; ка́ркать *impf.*
croakily /'kroukəli/ *adv.* хри́пло.
croaking /'kroukıŋ/ *n.* ка́рканье *neut.*
croaky /'krouki/ *adj.* хри́плый.
Croat /'krouæt/ *n.* хорва́т *m.*, хорва́тка *f.*
Croatia /krou'eiʃə/ *n.* Хорва́тия *f.*
crochet /krou'ʃei/ *n.* вяза́ние крючко́м *neut.*
crock /krɒk/ *n.* (*pot*) гли́няный горшо́к *m.*; (*broken piece*) черепо́к *m.*
crockery /'krɒkəri/ *n.* посу́да *f.*
crocodile /'krɒkə,dail/ *n.* крокоди́л *m.*
crocus /'kroukəs/ *n.* кро́кус *m.*
crone /kroun/ *n.* карга́ *f.*
crony /'krouni/ *n.* закады́чный друг *m.*
crook /krʊk/ **1.** *n.* (*staff*) по́сох *m.*; (*hook*) крюк *m.* **2.** *v.* сгиба́ть(ся) *impf.*
crooked /'krʊkıd/ *adj.* криво́й; (*dishonest*) нече́стный.
crop /krɒp/ *n.* урожа́й *m.*
crop-eared /'krɒp,ıərd/ *adj.* корноу́хий.
croquet /krou'kei/ *n.* кроке́т *m.*
croquette /krou'kɛt/ *n.* кроке́ты *pl.*
crosier /'krouʒər/ *n.* епи́скопский по́сох *m.*
cross /krɒs/ **1.** *adj.* попере́чный, перекрёстный; (*angry*) серди́тый. **2.** *n.* крест *m.*; (*hybrid*) по́месь *f.* **3.** *v.t.* (*biol.*) скре́щивать *impf.*, скрести́ть *pf.*; (*traverse*) переходи́ть *impf.*, перейти́ *pf.*; *v.i.* пересека́ться *impf.*
crossbar /'krɒs,bɑr/ *n.* (*tech.*) попере́чина *f.*; (*sport*) пла́нка *f.*
crossbeam /'krɒs,bim/ *n.* крестови́на *f.*
crossbill /'krɒs,bıl/ *n.* клёст *m.*
crossbow /'krɒs,bou/ *n.* самостре́л *m.*
crossbred /'krɒs,brɛd/ *adj.* гибри́дный.
crossbreed /'krɒs,brid/ *n.* гибри́д *m.*
cross-check /'krɒs,tʃɛk/ *n.* све́рка *f.*

cross-country /'krɔs'kʌntri/ n. (sport) кросс m.; **cross-country runner** кроссовик m.

crosscut /'krɔsˌkʌt/ n. поперечный разрез m.

cross-examination /'krɔsɪgˌzæmə'neiʃən/ n. перекрёстный допрос m.

cross-examine /'krɔsɪg'zæmɪn/ v. подвергать перекрёстному допросу impf.

cross-eyed /'krɔsˌaid/ adj. косоглазый.

cross-fertilize /'krɔs'fɜrtlˌaiz/ v. перекрёстно опылять impf.

crossfire /'krɔsˌfaiᵊr/ n. перекрёстный огонь m.

crosshatch /'krɔsˌhætʃ/ v. штриховать перекрёстными штрихами.

crossing /'krɔsɪŋ/ n. переправа f., пересечение neut.; (crossroads) перекрёсток m.

cross-legged /'krɔs'lɛgɪd, -'lɛgd/ adv. положив ногу на ногу.

crosspiece /'krɔsˌpis/ n. поперечина f.

cross-purposes /'krɔs'pɜrpəsɪz/ n.: **at cross-purposes** adv. наперекор.

cross-reference /'krɔs'rɛfərəns/ n. перекрёстная ссылка f.

crossroad /'krɔsˌroud/ n. поперечная дорога f.; (crossing) перекрёсток m

cross section n. поперечное сечение neut.

cross-stitch /'krɔsˌstɪtʃ/ n. крестик m.

crosswise /'krɔsˌwaiz/ adv. крестообразно.

crossword puzzle /'krɔsˌwɜrd/ n. кроссворд m.

crotch /krɒtʃ/ n. промежность f.

crotchety /'krɒtʃɪti/ adj. капризный.

crouch /krautʃ/ v. приседать impf.; согнуться pf.

croup /krup/ n. круп m.

croupier /'krupiər/ n. банкомёт m.

crouton /'krutɒn/ n. гренок m.

crow /krou/ 1. adj. вороний. 2. n. ворона f.

crowbar /'krouˌbɑr/ n. лом m.

crowd /kraud/ 1. n. толпа f. 2. v. теснить(ся); толпиться impf.

crowded /'kraudɪd/ adj. тесный; переполненный.

crown /kraun/ 1. n. корона f.; (tooth) коронка f.; (head) макушка f. 2. v. короновать impf. and pf.

crown wheel n. коронная шестерня f.

crow's-nest /'krouzˌnɛst/ n. (naut.) наблюдательный пост m.

crucial /'kruʃəl/ adj. решающий, критический.

crucible /'krusəbəl/ n. тигель m.

crucifix /'krusəˌfɪks/ n. распятие neut.

crucifixion /'krusəˌfɪkʃən/ n. распятие neut.

cruciform /'krusəˌfɔrm/ adj. крестообразный.

crucify /'krusəˌfai/ v. распинать impf., распять pf.

crude /krud/ adj. сырой; (rude) грубый; (unfinished) необработанный.

crudeness /'krudnɪs/ n. грубость f.

cruel /'kruəl/ adj. жестокий.

cruelty /'kruəlti/ n. жестокость f.

cruise /kruz/ 1. n. круиз m. 2. v. совершать круиз impf.

cruiser /'kruzər/ n. (naval) крейсер m.; (yacht) яхта f.

cruising speed /'kruzɪŋ/ n. крейсерская скорость f.

crumb /krʌm/ n. крошка f.

crumble /'krʌmbəl/ v. крошиться impf.

crumbly /'krʌmbli/ adj. рассыпчатый.

crumpet /'krʌmpɪt/ n. сдобная лепёшка f.

crumple /'krʌmpəl/ v. мять impf., помять pf.; v.i. мяться impf., помяться pf.

crunch /krʌntʃ/ n. хруст m.

crunchy /'krʌntʃi/ adj. (brittle) хрупкий; (crackling) хрустящий.

crupper /'krʌpər/ n. круп m.

crural /'krurəl/ adj. бедренный.

crusade /kru'seid/ n. поход m., кампания f.; (hist.) крестовый поход m.

crusader /kru'seidər/ n. (hist.) крестоносец m.; (fig.) борец m.

crush /krʌʃ/ v. давить impf.; подавлять impf., подавить pf.

crusher /'krʌʃər/ n. дробилка f.

crushing /'krʌʃɪŋ/ adj. сокрушительный.

crust /krʌst/ n. корка f.

Crustacea /krʌ'steiʃə/ n. ракообразные pl.

crustacean /krʌ'steiʃən/ adj. ракообразный.

crusted /'krʌstɪd/ adj. покрытый коркой.

crusty /'krʌsti/ adj. покрытый коркой; (hard) жёсткий, твёрдый.

crutch /krʌtʃ/ n. костыль m.

crux /krʌks/ n. суть f.

cry /krai/ 1. n. крик, плач m. 2. v. плакать; кричать impf.

crybaby /'kraiˌbeibi/ n. плакса m. and f. (decl. f.).

crying /'kraiɪŋ/ 1. adj. кричащий, плачущий, вопиющий. 2. n. плач m.

cryochemistry /ˌkraiə'kɛmestri/ n. химия низких температур f.

cryogen /'kraiədʒən/ n. охлаждающая смесь f.

cryogenics /ˌkraiə'dʒɛnɪks/ n. физика низких температур f.

cryolite /'kraiəˌlait/ n. криолит m.

cryotron /'kraiəˌtrɒn/ n. криотрон m.

crypt /krɪpt/ n. склеп m.; усыпальница f.

cryptic /'krɪptɪk/ adj. загадочный.

cryptogam /'krɪptəˌgæm/ n. споровое растение neut.

cryptogram /'krɪptəˌgræm/ n. криптограмма f.

cryptographer /krɪp'tɒgrəfər/ n. шифровальщик m.

crystal /'krɪstl/ 1. n. хрусталь m. 2. adj. хрустальный.

crystalline /'krɪstlɪn/ adj. кристальный.

crystallization /ˌkrɪstlə'zeiʃən/ n. кристаллизация f.

crystallize /'krɪstlˌaiz/ v. кристаллизовать(ся) impf. and pf.

cub /kʌb/ n. детёныш m.

Cuba /'kyubə/ n. Куба f.

Cuban /'kyubən/ n. кубинец m., кубинка f.

cubbyhole /'kʌbiˌhoul/ n. уютное местечко neut.

cube /kyub/ n. куб m.

cubic /'kyubɪk/ adj. кубический.

cubicle /'kyubɪkəl/ n. кабинка f.

cubiform /'kyubəˌfɔrm/ adj. кубовидный.

cubism /'kyubɪzəm/ n. кубизм m.

cuboid /'kyubɔid/ n. кубоид m.

cuckold /'kʌkəld/ n. рогоносец m.

cuckoo /'kuku/ 1. n. (bird) кукушка f.; (colloq.) глупец m. 2. adj. (colloq.) чокнутый.

cuckoo clock n. часы с кукушкой pl.

cuckoopint /'kukuˌpaint/ n. арум пятнистый m.

cucumber /'kyukʌmbər/ n. огурец m.

cud /kʌd/ n. жвачка f.

cuddle /'kʌdḷ/ **1.** *n.* объя́тия *pl.* **2.** *v.* обнима́ть(ся) *impf.*

cudgel /'kʌdʒəl/ *n.* дуби́на *f.*

cue /kyu/ *n.* намёк *m.*; (*billiards*) кий *m.*

cuff /kʌf/ *n.* манжéта *f.*

cuff link /'kʌf‚lɪŋk/ *n.* за́понка для манжéт *f.*

cuirass /kwɪ'ræs/ *n.* кира́са *f.*

cuirassier /‚kwɪərə'sɪər/ *n.* кираси́р *m.*

cuisine /kwɪ'zin/ *n.* ку́хня *f.*

cul-de-sac /'kʌldə'sæk/ *n.* (*also fig.*) тупи́к *m.*

culinary /'kyulə‚nɛri/ *adj.* кулина́рный.

cull /kʌl/ *v.* отбира́ть *impf.*

culm /kʌlm/ *n.* (*bot.*) стéбель *m.*

culminate /'kʌlmə‚neit/ *v.* достига́ть вы́сшей то́чки *impf.*

culmination /‚kʌlmə'neiʃən/ *n.* кульмина́ция *f.* кульминацио́нный пункт *m.*

culpability /‚kʌlpə'bɪlɪti/ *n.* вино́вность *f.*

culpable /'kʌlpəbəl/ *adj.* (*leg.*) вино́вный, престу́пный.

cult /kʌlt/ *n.* культ *m.*

cultivate /'kʌltə‚veit/ *v.* обраба́тывать *impf.*, обрабо́тать *pf.*; культиви́ровать *impf.* and *pf.*

cultivated /'kʌltə‚veitɪd/ *adj.* обрабо́танный; (*cultured*) культу́рный.

cultivator /'kʌltə‚veitər/ *n.* земледéлец *m.*

culvert /'kʌlvərt/ *n.* (*channel*) водово́д *m.*

cumbersome /'kʌmbərsəm/ *adj.* громо́здкий.

cumin /'kʌmən/ *n.* тмин *m.*

cumulate /'kyumyə‚leit/ *v.* нака́пливать(ся) *impf.*

cumulative /'kyumyələtɪv/ *adj.* совоку́пный, кумуляти́вный.

cumulonimbus /‚kyumyəlou'nɪmbəs/ *n.* кучево-дождевы́е облака́ *pl.*

cumulus /'kyumyələs/ *n.* кучевы́е облака́ *pl.*

cuneiform /kyu'niə‚fɔrm/ *n.* кли́нопись *f.*

cunning /'kʌnɪŋ/ **1.** *n.* ло́вкость, хи́трость *f.* **2.** *adj.* ло́вкий, хи́трый.

cup /kʌp/ *n.* ча́шка *f.*

cupboard /'kʌbərd/ *n.* шкаф; буфéт *m.*

Cupid /'kyupɪd/ *n.* Купидо́н *m.*

cupidity /kyu'pɪdɪti/ *n.* жа́дность *f.*

cupola /'kyupələ/ *n.* (*archit.*) ку́пол *m.*

cupping glass /'kʌpɪŋ/ *n.* ба́нка *f.*

cupreous /'kyupriəs/ *adj.* мéдный.

cupric /'kyuprɪk/ *adj.* содержа́щий двухвалéнтную медь.

cupriferous /kyu'prɪfərəs/ *adj.* мéдистый.

cuprite /'kyuprait/ *n.* купри́т *m.*

cupronickel /'kyuprə‚nɪkəl/ *n.* мельхио́р *m.*

cuprous /'kyuprəs/ *adj.* содержа́щий одновалéнтную медь.

cur /kɜr/ *n.* (*dog*) дворня́га *f.*; (*person*) хам; трус *m.*

curable /'kyurəbəl/ *adj.* излечи́мый.

curare /kyu'rɑri/ *n.* кура́ре *neut.* *indecl.*

curative /'kyurətɪv/ *adj.* лечéбный.

curator /kyu'reitər/ *n.* храни́тель *m.*

curb /kɜrb/ **1.** *n.* обо́чина *f.*; край тротуа́ра *m.* **2.** *v.* обу́здывать *impf.*

curbstone /'kɜrb‚stoun/ *n.* бордю́рный ка́мень *m.*

curd /kɜrd/ *n.* творо́г *m.*

curdle /'kɜrdḷ/ *v.* свёртываться *impf.*, сверну́ться *pf.*

cure /kyur/ **1.** *n.* излечéние *neut.*; (*remedy*) срéдство *neut.* **2.** *v.* лечи́ть *impf.*, вы́лечить *pf.*

curfew /'kɜrfyu/ *n.* комендáнтский час *m.*

curia /'kyuriə/ *n.* ку́рия *f.*

curie /'kyuri/ *n.* (*phys.*) кюри́ *neut.* *indecl.*

curio /'kyuri‚ou/ *n.* антиква́рная вещь *f.*

curiosity /‚kyuri'ɒsɪti/ *n.* любопы́тство *neut.*

curious /'kyuriəs/ *adj.* любопы́тный.

curiously /'kyuriəsli/ *adv.* с любопы́тством; стра́нно.

curl /kɜrl/ **1.** *n.* ло́кон, завуто́к *m.*; ку́дри *pl.* **2.** *v.t.* завива́ть *impf.*, зави́ть *pf.*; *v.i.* ви́ться *impf.*, зави́ться *pf.*

curler /'kɜrlər/ *n.* бигуди́ *pl.* *indecl.*

curlew /'kɜrlu/ *n.* кро́ншнеп *m.*

curly /'kɜrli/ *adj.* вью́щийся.

curmudgeon /kər'mʌdʒən/ *n.* брюзга́ *m.* and *f.* (*decl. f.*).

currant /'kɜrənt/ *n.* (*fruit*) сморо́дина *f.*

currency /'kɜrənsi/ *n.* (*money*) валю́та *f.*; (*prevalence*) распространённость *f.*

current /'kɜrənt/ **1.** *adj.* теку́щий. **2.** *n.* (*flow*) течéние *neut.*; (*elec.*) ток *m.*

currently /'kɜrəntli/ *adv.* в настоя́щее врéмя.

curriculum /kə'rɪkyələm/ *n.* учéбный план *m.*; програ́мма *f.*

curry[1] /'kɜri/ *n.* (*cul.*) кэ́рри *neut.* *indecl.*

curry[2] /'kɜri/ *v.* (*a horse*) чи́стить скребни́цей *impf.*; **to curry favor with** за́искивать (пéред *with instr.*) *impf.*

currycomb /'kɜri‚koum/ *n.* скребни́ца *f.*

curse /kɜrs/ **1.** *n.* прокля́тие *neut.* **2.** *v.* руга́ться *impf.*; проклина́ть *impf.*

cursed /'kɜrsɪd, kɜrst/ *adj.* про́клятый.

cursive /'kɜrsɪv/ *n.* ско́ропись *f.*

cursor /'kɜrsər/ *n.* (*on slide rule*) движо́к *m.*; (*on screen*) за́йчик *m.*

cursorily /'kɜrsərəli/ *adv.* бéгло; повéрхностно.

cursory /'kɜrsəri/ *adj.* бéглый, повéрхностный.

curt /kɜrt/ *adj.* кра́ткий; отры́вистый.

curtail /kər'teil/ *v.* сокраща́ть *impf.*, сократи́ть *pf.*

curtailment /kər'teilmənt/ *n.* прекращéние *neut.*; сокращéние *neut.*

curtain /'kɜrtṇ/ *n.* занавéска *f.*; (*theat.*) за́навес *m.*

curtsy /'kɜrtsi/ *n.* реверáнс *m.*

curvature /'kɜrvətʃər/ *n.* кривизна́ *f.*

curve /kɜrv/ **1.** *n.* изги́б *m.*; (*math.*) крива́я *f.* **2.** *v.t.* изгиба́ть *impf.*, изогну́ть *pf.*; *v.i.* изгиба́ться *impf.*, изогну́ться *pf.*

curved /kɜrvd/ *adj.* криво́й, изо́гнутый.

curvilinear /‚kɜrvə'lɪniər/ *adj.* криволинéйный.

cushion /'kuʃən/ *n.* поду́шка *f.*

cusp /kʌsp/ *n.* (*math.*) то́чка возвра́та *f.*; (*moon*) мéсяц *m.*

cuspid /'kʌspɪd/ *n.* клык *m.*

cuss /kʌs/ *n.* (*colloq.*) руга́тельство *neut.*

cussedness /'kʌsɪdnɪs/ *n.* (*colloq.*) упря́мство *neut.*

custard /'kʌstərd/ *n.* заварно́й крем *m.*

custodian /kʌ'stoudiən/ *n.* храни́тель, опеку́н *m.*

custody /'kʌstədi/ *n.* охра́на, опéка *f.*; (*police*) арéст *m.*

custom /'kʌstəm/ *n.* обы́чай *m.*; привы́чка *f.*

customable /'kʌstəməbəl/ *adj.* облага́емый тамо́женной по́шлиной.

customary /'kʌstə‚mɛri/ *adj.* обы́чный.

custom-built /'kʌstəm'bɪlt/ *adj.* сде́ланный на зака́з.

customer /'kʌstəmər/ *n.* покупа́тель, клие́нт *m.*

custom-made /'kʌstəm 'meid/ *adj.* сде́ланный на зака́з.

customs /'kʌstəmz/ **1.** *adj.* тамо́женный. **2.** *n.* тамо́жня *f.*

cut /kʌt/ **1.** *n.* поре́з *m.*, вы́резка *f.*; сниже́ние *neut.* **2.** *v.* ре́зать *impf.*, поре́зать *pf.*, сре́зать *pf.*; (*hair*) стричь *impf.*; (*prices, etc.*) снижа́ть *impf.*; **to cut oneself** поре́заться *pf.*

cutaneous /kyu'teiniəs/ *adj.* ко́жный.

cutaway /'kʌtə,wei/ *n.* (*tail coat*) визи́тка *f.*

cutback /'kʌt,bæk/ *n.* сокраще́ние *neut.*

cute /kyut/ *adj.* ми́лый, краси́вый.

cut glass *n.* хруста́ль *m.*

cuticle /'kyutɪkəl/ *n.* заусе́ница *f.*

cutlass /'kʌtləs/ *n.* абордажная са́бля *f.*

cutler /'kʌtlər/ *n.* ножо́вщик *m.*

cutlery /'kʌtləri/ *n.* столо́вые прибо́ры *pl.*

cutlet /'kʌtlɪt/ *n.* котле́та *f.*

cutout /'kʌt,aut/ *n.* вы́резанная фигу́ра *f.*

cut-rate /'kʌt,reit/ *adj.* уценённый.

cutthroat /'kʌt,θrout/ *n.* головоре́з *m.*

cutting /'kʌtɪŋ/ *n.* ре́зание *neut.*, ре́зка *f.*; (*from plant*) черено́к *m.*

cuttlefish /'kʌtl̩,fɪʃ/ *n.* карака́тица *f.*

cutworm /'kʌt,wɜrm/ *n.* ба́бочка-со́вка *f.*

cyanamide /sai'ænəmɪd/ *n.* цианами́д *m.*

cyanic /sai'ænɪk/ *adj.* циа́новый.

cyanide /'saiə,naid/ *n.* циани́д *m.*

cyanogen /sai'ænədʒən/ *n.* циа́н *m.*

cyanosis /ˌsaiə'nousɪs/ *n.* циано́з *m.*

cybernetic /ˌsaibər'nɛtɪk/ *adj.* кибернети́ческий.

cybernetics /ˌsaibər'nɛtɪks/ *n.* киберне́тика *f.*

cyberspace /'saibər,speis/ *n.* киберпростра́нство *neut.*

Cyclades /'sɪklə,diz/ *n.* (*islands*) Кикла́ды *pl.*

cyclamen /'saikləmən/ *n.* цикламе́н *m.*

cycle /'saikəl/ **1.** *n.* цикл *m.* **2.** *v.* е́здить на велосипе́де *impf.*

cyclical /'saiklɪkəl, 'sɪklɪ-/ *adj.* цикли́ческий.

cycling /'saiklɪŋ/ *n.* езда́ на велосипе́де *f.*

cyclist /'saiklɪst/ *n.* велосипеди́ст *m.*

cycloid /'saiklɔid/ *n.* цикло́ид *m.*

cyclometer /sai'klɒmɪtər/ *n.* цикло́метр *m.*

cyclone /'saikloun/ *n.* цикло́н *m.*

cyclonic /sai'klɒnɪk/ *adj.* циклони́ческий.

Cyclops /'saiklɒps/ *n.* Цикло́п *m.*

cyclotron /'saiklə,trɒn/ *n.* циклотро́н *m.*

cygnet /'sɪgnɪt/ *n.* молодо́й ле́бедь *m.*

cylinder /'sɪlɪndər/ *n.* цили́ндр *m.*

cylindrical /sɪ'lɪndrɪkəl/ *adj.* цилиндри́ческий.

cymbal /'sɪmbəl/ *n.* таре́лка *f.*

cymometer *n.* волноме́р *m.*

cynic /'sɪnɪk/ *n.* ци́ник *m.*

cynical /'sɪnɪkəl/ *adj.* цини́чный.

cynicism /'sɪnə,sɪzəm/ *n.* цини́зм *m.*

cynosure /'sainə,ʃʊr/ *n.* центр внима́ния *m.*

cypress /'saiprəs/ *n.* кипари́с *m.*

Cyprus /'saiprəs/ *n.* Кипр *m.*

Cyrillic alphabet /sɪ'rɪlɪk/ *n.* кири́ллица *f.*

cyst /sɪst/ *n.* киста́ *f.*

cystitis /sɪ'staitɪs/ *n.* цисти́т *m.*

cytology /sai'tɒlədʒi/ *n.* цитоло́гия *f.*

cytoplasm /'saitə,plæzəm/ *n.* цитопла́зма *f.*

czar /zɑr, tsɑr/ *n.* царь *m.*

czarina /zɑ'rinə, tsɑ-/ *n.* цари́ца *f.*

Czech /tʃɛk/ **1.** *adj.* че́шский. **2.** *n.* чех *m.*, че́шка *f.*

Czech Republic *n.* Че́шская Респу́блика *f.*

Częstochowa /ˌtʃɛnstɔ'hɔvə/ *n.* Ченстохо́ва *f.*

D

dab¹ /dæb/ **1.** *n.* тычо́к; мазо́к *m.* **2.** *v.* легко́ каса́ться; ты́кать *impf.*

dab² /dæb/ *n.* (*fish*) лима́нда, ершова́тка *f.*

dabble /'dæbəl/ *v.* плеска́ть; бара́хтаться *impf.*

dabbler /'dæblər/ *n.* дилета́нт *m.*

dabchick /'dæb,tʃık/ *n.* пога́нка ма́лая *f.*

dace /deis/ *n.* еле́ц *m.*

dachshund /'dɑks,hʊnt, -ənd/ *n.* та́кса *f.*

dactyl /'dæktıl/ *n.* да́ктиль *m.*

dactylic /dæk'tılık/ *adj.* дактили́ческий.

dad /dæd/ *n.* па́па, оте́ц *m.*

Dadaism /'dɑdɑ,ızəm/ *n.* дадаи́зм *m.*

daddy-long-legs /,dædi 'lɒŋ ,legz/ *n.* долгоно́жка *f.*

daffodil /'dæfədıl/ *n.* нарци́сс *m.*

dagger /'dægər/ *n.* кинжа́л *m.*

daguerreotype /də'gɛərə,taip/ *n.* дагерроти́п *m.*

dahlia /'dælyə, 'dɑl-/ *n.* георги́н *m.*

daily /'deili/ **1.** *adj.* ежедне́вный. **2.** *adv.* ежедне́вно.

dainty /'deinti/ *adj.* (*tasty*) ла́комый; (*elegant*) элега́нтный.

dairy /'dɛəri/ *n.* маслоде́льня; моло́чная *f.*

dairying /'dɛəriıŋ/ *n.* моло́чное хозя́йство *neut.*

dairymaid /'dɛəri,meid/ *n.* доя́рка *f.*

dairyman /'dɛərimən/ *n.* моло́чник *m.*

dais /'deiıs, 'dai-/ *n.* платфо́рма *f.*, помо́ст *m.*

daisy /'deizi/ *n.* маргари́тка *f.*

Dakar /dɑ'kɑr/ *n.* Дака́р *m.*

Dalai Lama /'dɑ'lai lɑmə/ *n.* далай-ла́ма *m.*

dale /deil/ *n.* доли́на *f.*; up hill and down dale по гора́м и по дола́м.

dalliance /'dæliəns/ *n.* несерьёзное отноше́ние *neut.*

dally /'dæli/ *v.* слоня́ться, болта́ться *impf.*

Dalmatian /dæl'meiʃən/ *n.* (*dog*) далмати́н *m.*

dalton /'dɔltṇ/ *n.* (*phys.*) дальто́н *m.*

dam /dæm/ *n.* да́мба, плоти́на *f.*

damage /'dæmıdʒ/ **1.** *n.* уще́рб *m.* **2.** *v.* поврежда́ть *impf.*, повреди́ть *pf.*

damascene /'dæmə,sin/ *v.* (*with gold or silver*) насека́ть зо́лотом, серебро́м *impf.*

Damascus /də'mæskəs/ *n.* Дама́ск *m.*

damask /'dæməsk/ *n.* (*fabric*) камка́ *f.*, дама́ст *m.*; (*steel*) дама́сская сталь *f.*

dame /deim/ *n.* да́ма *f.*

damn /dæm/ *v.* проклина́ть *impf.*, прокля́сть *pf.*

damnable /'dæmnəbəl/ *adj.* про́клятый, дья́вольский.

damnably /'dæmnəbli/ *adv.* черто́вски.

damnation /dæm'neiʃən/ *n.* прокля́тие *neut.*

damned /dæmd/ *adj.* прокля́тый.

damnification /,dæmnəfı'keiʃən/ *n.* (*legal*) причине́ние вреда́ *neut.*

damnify /'dæmnə,fai/ *v.* (*legal*) причиня́ть вред *impf.*

damning /'dæmıŋ/ *adj.* (*evidence, etc.*) изоблича́ющий.

damp /dæmp/ *adj.* сыро́й, вла́жный.

damper /'dæmpər/ *n.* засло́нка *f.*

dampness /'dæmpnıs/ *n.* сы́рость, вла́жность *f.*

damp-proof /'dæmp pruf/ *adj.* влагонепроница́емый.

damsel /'dæmzəl/ *n.* (*arch.*) деви́ца *f.*

damson /'dæmzən, -sən/ *n.* терносли́ва *f.*

dance /dæns/ **1.** *n.* та́нец *m.* **2.** *v.* танцева́ть *impf.*

dance band *n.* эстра́дный орке́стр *m.*

dance hall *n.* танцева́льный зал *m.*

dancer /'dænsər/ *n.* танцовщи́к *m.*

dancing /'dænsıŋ/ *n.* та́нцы *pl.*, пля́ска *f.*

dandelion /'dændḷ,aiən/ *n.* одува́нчик *m.*

dandified /'dændəfaid/ *adj.* щегольско́й, фатова́тый.

dandle /'dændḷ/ *v.* кача́ть на рука́х *impf.*

dandruff /'dændrəf/ *n.* пе́рхоть *f.*

dandy /'dændi/ *n.* де́нди *m. indecl.*, щёголь *m.*

dandyism /'dændi,ızəm/ *n.* данди́зм *m.*

Dane /dein/ *n.* датча́нин *m.*, датча́нка *f.*

danger /'deindʒər/ *n.* опа́сность *f.*

dangerous /'deindʒərəs/ *adj.* опа́сный; риско́ванный.

dangle /'dæŋgəl/ *v.* пока́чивать *impf.*

Danish /'deinıʃ/ *adj.* да́тский.

dank /dæŋk/ *adj.* сыро́й.

Danube /'dænyub/ *n.* Ду́най *m.*

Danubian /dæn'yubiən/ *adj.* дуна́йский.

dapper /'dæpər/ *adj.* опря́тный.

dapple /'dæpəl/ *adj.* испещрённый; пятни́стый.

dapple grey *adj.* (*of horse*) се́рый в я́блоках.

dare /dɛər/ *v.* осме́ливаться *impf.*, осме́литься *pf.*

daredevil /'dɛər,dɛvəl/ *n.* смельча́к *m.*

daring /'dɛərıŋ/ **1.** *n.* отва́га, сме́лость *f.* **2.** *adj.* отва́жный, сме́лый.

dark /dɑrk/ **1.** *adj.* тёмный. **2.** *n.* тьма *f.*

darken /'dɑrkən/ *v.* затемня́ть *impf.*, затемни́ть *pf.*

darkly /'dɑrkli/ *adv.* мра́чно; зага́дочно.

darkness /'dɑrknıs/ *n.* темнота́ *f.*

darling /'dɑrlıŋ/ *n.* дорого́й *m.*, дорога́я *f.*; люби́мец *m.*

darn /dɑrn/ *v.* што́пать *impf.*, зашто́пать *pf.*

darned /dɑrnd/ *adj.* (*colloq.*) прокля́тый.

darning /'dɑrnıŋ/ *n.* што́пка *f.*

dart /dɑrt/ *n.* стрела́ *f.*

darting /'dɑrtıŋ/ *adj.* стреми́тельный.

dash /dæʃ/ **1.** *n.* рыво́к *m.*; (*punctuation*) чёрточка *f.*, тире́ *neut. indecl.* **2.** *v.* ри́нуться *pf.*

dashboard /'dæʃ,bɔrd/ *n.* пере́дний щито́к *m.*

dashing /'dæʃıŋ/ *adj.* лихо́й, бо́йкий.

dashpot /'dæʃ,pɒt/ *n.* бу́фер *m.*

dastard /'dæstərd/ *n.* трус *m.*

dastardly /'dæstərdli/ *adj.* по́длый.

data /'deitə, 'dætə/ *n.* да́нные *pl.*

database /'deitəbeis, 'dætə-/ *n.* ба́за да́нных *f.*

date /deit/ *n.* да́та *f.*, число́ *neut.*; (*engagement*) свида́ние *neut.*; (*fruit*) фи́ник *m.*

dated /'deitıd/ *adj.* дати́рованный.

dateless /'deitlıs/ *adj.* недати́рованный.

date line *n.* (*geog.*) Ли́ния переме́ны чи́сел *f.*

dative /'deitıv/ *adj.* да́тельный паде́ж *m.*

datum /'deitəm, 'dætəm/ *n.* да́нный факт *m.*, да́нная величина́ *f.*

daub /dɔb/ *n.* штукату́рка *f.*; (*crude picture*) мазня́ *f.*; (*smear*) мазо́к *m.*

dauber /'dɔbər/ *n.* (*pej.*) мази́ла *m.* and *f.* (*decl. f.*).

daughter /'dɔtər/ *n.* дочь *f.*

daughter-in-law /'dɔ,tər ɪn lɔ/ *n.* сноха́ *f.*

daunt /dɔnt/ *v.* запу́гивать, устраша́ть *impf.*

dauntless /'dɔntlɪs/ *adj.* бесстра́шный.

dauphin /'dɔfɪn/ *n.* дофи́н *m.*

davit /'dævɪt, 'deivɪt/ *n.* шлюпба́лка *f.*

dawdle /'dɔdl̩/ *v.* безде́льничать; ме́длить, ме́шкать *impf.*

dawn /dɔn/ **1.** *n.* заря́ *f.* **2.** *v.* рассвета́ть *impf.*

day /dei/ *n.* день *m.*; **a day or two ago** на днях; **day by day** изо дня в день; с ка́ждым днём; **by day** днём; **by the day** подённо; **every other day** че́рез день; **in a day or two** на днях; **the day after tomorrow** послеза́втра; **the day before** накану́не; **the day before yesterday** позавчера́, тре́тьего дня.

Dayak /'daiæk/ *n.* дая́к *m.*

daybook /'dei,bʊk/ *n.* журна́л *m.*

daybreak /'dei,breik/ *n.* рассве́т *m.*

daydream /'dei,drim/ *n.* мечты́; грёзы *pl*

daydreamer /'dei,drimər/ *n.* мечта́тель, фантазёр *m.*

day labor *n.* подённая рабо́та *f.*

day laborer *n.* подёнщик *m.*

daylight /'dei,lait/ *n.* дневно́й свет *m.*

daylight-saving time /'dei,lait 'seivɪŋ/ *n.* ле́тнее вре́мя *neut.*

daylong /'dei,lɔŋ, -,lɒŋ/ *adj.* для́щийся весь день.

day nursery *n.* дневны́е я́сли *pl.*

day-school /'dei skul/ *n.* шко́ла (без пансио́на) *f.*

day shift *n.* дневна́я сме́на *f.*

day-star /'dei star/ *n.* у́тренняя звезда́ *f,*

day ticket *n.* обра́тный биле́т, действи́тельный в тече́ние одного́ дня *m.*

daytime /'dei,taim/ *n.* дневно́е вре́мя *neut.*

day-to-day /'dei tə 'dei/ *adj.* повседне́вный.

daze /deiz/ *v.* изумля́ть *impf.*, изуми́ть *pf.*

dazzle /'dæzəl/ *v.* ослепля́ть *impf.*

deacon /'dikən/ *n.* дья́кон *m.*

deaconess /'dikənɪs/ *n.* диакони́са *f.*

dead /dɛd/ *adj.* мёртвый.

dead-beat /'dɛd bit/ *adj.* (*colloq.*) смерте́льно уста́лый.

deaden /'dɛdn̩/ *v.* заглуша́ть *impf.*

dead end *n.* тупи́к *m.*

dead-eye /'dɛd ,ai/ *n.* ю́ферс *m.*

deadlight /'dɛd,lait/ *n.* глухо́й иллюмина́тор *m.*

deadline /'dɛd,lain/ *n.* преде́льный срок *m.*

deadlock /'dɛd,lɒk/ *n.* тупи́к *m.*

deadly /'dɛdli/ *adj.* смерте́льный.

deadness /'dɛdnɪs/ *n.* мёртвенность *f.*

deadpan /'dɛd,pæn/ *adj.* без выраже́ния.

Dead Sea *n.* Мёртвое Мо́ре *neut.*

deaf /dɛf/ *adj.* глухо́й.

deafen /'dɛfən/ *v.* оглуша́ть *impf.*, оглуши́ть *pf.*

deaf-mute /'dɛf'myut/ *n.* глухонемо́й.

deafness /'dɛfnɪs/ *n.* глухота́ *f.*

deal /dil/ **1.** *n.* до́ля *f.*; (*agreement*) сде́лка *f.*; (*cards*) сда́ча *f.* **2.** *v.* обходи́ться *impf.*; трактова́ть *impf.*; (*cards*) раздава́ть ка́рты *impf.*

dealer /'dilər/ *n.* торго́вец *m.*

dealing /'dilɪŋ/ *n.* usu. *pl.* отноше́ния *pl.*

dean /din/ *n.* дека́н *m.*

dear /dɪər/ *adj.* дорого́й.

dearer /'dɪərər/ *adj.* доро́же, бо́лее дорого́й.

dearest /'dɪərɪst/ *adj.* са́мый дорого́й.

dearly /'dɪərli/ *adv.* до́рого; не́жно; **to love dearly** о́чень люби́ть *impf.*

dearth /dɜrθ/ *n.* нехва́тка *f.*, недоста́ток *m.*

death /dɛθ/ *n.* смерть *f.*

deathbed /'dɛθ,bɛd/ *n.* сме́ртное ло́же *neut.*

deathblow /'dɛθ,blou/ *n.* смерте́льный уда́р *m.*

death knell *n.* похоро́нный звон *m.*

deathless /'dɛθlɪs/ *adj.* бессме́ртный.

deathly /'dɛθli/ *adj.* смерте́льный.

death-roll /'dɛθ roul/ *n.* спи́сок поги́бших *m.*

debacle /dei'bakəl, -'bækəl/ *n.* всео́бщее разруше́ние *neut.*; (*ice*) ледохо́д *m.*

debar /dɪ'bar/ *v.* исключа́ть *impf.*

debase /dɪ'beis/ *v.* понижа́ть *impf.*, пони́зить *pf.*; унижа́ть *impf.*, уни́зить *pf.*

debasement /dɪ'beismənt/ *n.* униже́ние *neut.*

debatable /dɪ'beitəbəl/ *adj.* спо́рный.

debate /dɪ'beit/ **1.** *n.* деба́ты *pl.*, спор *m.* **2.** *v.* спо́рить *impf.*

debater /dɪ'beitər/ *n.* уча́стник пре́ний *m.*

debauch /dɪ'bɔtʃ/ *n.* развра́т *m.*

debauchee /,dɛbɔ'tʃi/ *n.* развра́тник *m.*

debauchery /dɪ'bɔtʃəri/ *n.* развра́т *m.*

debilitate /dɪ'bɪlɪ,teit/ *v.* ослабля́ть *impf.*

debility /dɪ'bɪlɪti/ *n.* сла́бость *f.*

debit /'dɛbɪt/ *n.* де́бет *m.*

debonair /,dɛbə'nɛər/ *adj.* жизнера́достный; воспи́танный.

debrief /di'brif/ *n.* опро́с по́сле выполне́ния зада́ния *m.*

debris /də'bri/ *n.* оско́лки, разва́лины *pl.*

debt /dɛt/ *n.* долг *m.*

debtor /'dɛtər/ *n.* должни́к *m.*

debunk /dɪ'bʌŋk/ *v.* разоблача́ть *impf.*

debunking /dɪ'bʌŋkɪŋ/ *n.* разоблаче́ние *neut.*

debut /dei'byu/ *n.* дебю́т *m.*

debutant /'dɛbyu,tant/ *n.* дебюта́нт *m.*

debutante /'dɛbyu,tant/ *n.* дебюта́нтка *f.*

decade /'dɛkeid/ *n.* десятиле́тие *neut.*, дека́да *f.*

decadence /'dɛkədəns/ *n.* упа́док *m.*; декаде́нтство *neut.*

decadent /'dɛkədənt, dɪ'keidnt/ *adj.* декаде́нтский, упа́дочный.

decagon /'dɛkə,gɒn/ *n.* десятиуго́льник *m.*

decagonal /də'kægənl̩/ *adj.* десятиуго́льный.

decagram /'dɛkə,græm/ *n.* декагра́мм *m.*

decahedral /,dɛkə'hidrəl/ *adj.* десятигра́нный.

decaliter /'dɛkə,litər/ *n.* декали́тр *m.*

decameter /'dɛkə,mitər/ *n.* декаме́тр *m.*

decamp /dɪ'kæmp/ *v.* снима́ться с ла́геря *impf.*

decanal /'dɛkənl̩, dɪ'keinl̩/ *adj.* дека́нский.

decant /dɪ'kænt/ *v.* (*tech.*) деканти́ровать *impf.*

decanter /dɪ'kæntər/ *n.* графи́н *m.*

decapitate /dɪ'kæpɪ,teit/ *v.* обезгла́вливать *impf.*, обезгла́вить *pf.*

decapitation /dɪ,kæpɪ'teiʃən/ *n.* обезгла́вливание *neut.*

decapod /'dɛkə,pɒd/ *adj.* десятино́гий.

decarbonize /di'karbə,naiz/ *v.* (*chem.*) обезуглеро́живать *impf.*

decasyllabic /,dɛkəsɪ'læbɪk/ *adj.* десятисло́жный.

decathlon /dɪ'kæθlɒn/ n. десятибо́рье neut.
decay /dɪ'kei/ 1. n. гние́ние neut. 2. v. гнить impf., сгнить pf.
decease /dɪ'sis/ 1. n. кончи́на f. 2. v. сконча́ться pf.
deceased /dɪ'sist/ adj. поко́йный, уме́рший.
deceit /dɪ'sit/ n. обма́н m.
deceitful /dɪ'sitfəl/ adj. обма́нчивый; лжи́вый.
deceive /dɪ'siv/ v. обма́нывать impf., обману́ть pf.
decelerate /di'sɛlə,reit/ v. замедля́ть(ся) impf.
deceleration /di,sɛlə'reiʃən/ n. замедле́ние, торможе́ние neut.
December /dɪ'sɛmbər/ 1. n. дека́брь m. 2. adj. дека́брьский.
Decembrist /dɪ'sɛmbrɪst/ n. декабри́ст m.
decency /'disənsi/ n. прили́чие neut.
decennial /dɪ'sɛniəl/ adj. десятиле́тний.
decent /'disənt/ adj. прили́чный.
decentralization /di,sɛntrələ'zeiʃən/ n. децентрализа́ция f.
decentralize /di'sɛntrə,laiz/ v. децентрализова́ть impf.
deception /dɪ'sɛpʃən/ n. обма́н m.
deceptive /dɪ'sɛptɪv/ adj. обма́нчивый; вводя́щий в заблужде́ние.
deci- adj. (prefix) де́ци-.
decibel /'dɛsə,bɛl/ n. децибе́л m.
decide /dɪ'said/ v.t. реша́ть impf., реши́ть pf.; to be decided реша́ться impf., реши́ться pf.
decided /dɪ'saidɪd/ adj. определённый; беспо́рный.
deciduous /dɪ'sɪdʒuəs/ adj. ли́ственный.
decigram /'dɛsɪ,græm/ n. децигра́мм m.
deciliter /'dɛsə,litər/ n. децили́тр m.
decimal /'dɛsəməl, 'dɛsməl/ n. десяти́чная дробь f.
decimeter /'dɛsə,mitər/ n. дециме́тр m.
decipher /dɪ'saifər/ v. расшифро́вывать impf., расшифрова́ть pf.
decipherment /dɪ'saifərmənt/ n. расшифро́вка f.
decision /dɪ'sɪʒən/ n. реше́ние neut.
decisive /dɪ'saisɪv/ adj. реши́тельный.
decisiveness /dɪ'saisɪvnɪs/ n. реши́тельность f.
deck /dɛk/ n. па́луба f.; (cards) коло́да карт f.
deck chair n. шезло́нг m.
deckhouse /'dɛk,haus/ n. ру́бка f.
declaim /dɪ'kleim/ v. деклами́ровать impf.
declamation /,dɛklə'meiʃən/ n. деклама́ция f.
declamatory /dɪ'klæmə,tɔri/ adj. декламацио́нный, ора́торский.
declaration /,dɛklə'reiʃən/ n. деклара́ция f.; объявле́ние, заявле́ние neut.
declarative /dɪ'klærətɪv/ adj. декларати́вный; (explanatory) объясни́тельный, поясни́тельный.
declare /dɪ'klɛər/ v. объявля́ть impf., объяви́ть pf., заявля́ть impf., заяви́ть pf.
declared /dɪ'klɛərd/ adj. при́знанный.
déclassé /,deiklæ'sei, -klɑ-/ adj. деклассиро́ванный.
declassify /di'klæsə,fai/ v. рассекре́чивать impf.
declension /dɪ'klɛnʃən/ n. склоне́ние neut.
declinable /dɪ'klainəbəl/ adj. склоня́емый.
declination /,dɛklə'neiʃən/ n. (slope) склон m.; (deviation) отклоне́ние neut.; (astron.) склоне́ние neut.
decline /dɪ'klain/ 1. n. (decrease) уменьше́ние

neut.; (slope) склон; зака́т m. 2. v.t. отка́зываться impf., отказа́ться pf.; (gram.) склоня́ть impf., просклоня́ть pf.; v.i. уменьша́ться impf., уме́ньшиться pf.; наклоня́ться impf., наклони́ться pf.
declining years /dɪ'klainɪŋ/ n. прекло́нные го́ды pl.
declinometer /,dɛklə'nɒmɪtər/ n. деклиноме́тр m.
declivity /dɪ'klɪvɪti/ n. спуск, склон m.
declutch /di'klʌtʃ/ v. расцепля́ть impf.
decoct /dɪ'kɒkt/ v. приготовля́ть отва́р impf.
decoction /dɪ'kɒkʃən/ n. отва́р m.
decode /di'koud/ v. расшифро́вывать impf.
decoder /di'koudər/ n. дешифра́тор m.
décolletage /,deikɒl'tɑʒ/ n. деколье́ neut. indecl.
décolleté /,deikɒl'tei/ adj. декольти́рованный.
decolor /di'kʌlər/ v. обесцве́чивать impf.
decompose /,dikəm'pouz/ v. разлага́ть impf., разложи́ть pf.; v.i. разлага́ться impf., разложи́ться pf.
decomposition /,dikɒmpə'zɪʃən/ n. разложе́ние neut.
decompress /,dikəm'prɛs/ v. снижа́ть давле́ние impf.
decompression /,dikəm'prɛʃən/ n. сниже́ние давле́ния neut.
decongestant /,dikən'dʒɛstənt/ n. противозасто́йное (сре́дство) neut.
decontaminate /,dikən'tæmə,neit/ v. обеззара́живать impf.
decontrol /,dikən'troul/ v. освобожда́ть от контро́ля impf.
décor /dei'kɔr/ n. деко́р m.
decorate /'dɛkə,reit/ v. украша́ть impf., укра́сить pf.; (reward) награжда́ть impf., награди́ть pf.
decoration /,dɛkə'reiʃən/ n. украше́ние neut.; декора́ция f.; награ́да f.
decorative /'dɛkərətɪv/ adj. декорати́вный.
decorator /'dɛkə,reitər/ n. декора́тор m.
decorous /'dɛkərəs/ adj. прили́чный, присто́йный.
decorum /dɪ'kɔrəm/ n. прили́чие neut.
decouple /di'kʌpəl/ v. расцепля́ть impf.
decoy /'dikɔi/ n. прима́нка f.; мано́к m.; (mil.) маке́т m.
decrease / v. dɪ'kris/ n. 'dikris/ 1. v. уменьша́ть impf., уме́ньшить pf.; v.i. уменьша́ться impf., уме́ньшиться pf. 2. n. уменьше́ние neut., у́быль f.
decree /dɪ'kri/ n. декре́т, ука́з m.
decrepit /dɪ'krɛpɪt/ adj. дря́хлый; ве́тхий.
decrepitude /dɪ'krɛpɪ,tud/ n. дря́хлость f.
decry /dɪ'krai/ v. порица́ть impf.
dedicate /'dɛdɪ,keit/ v. посвяща́ть impf., посвяти́ть pf.
dedication /,dɛdɪ'keiʃən/ n. посвяще́ние neut.
dedicatory /'dɛdɪkə,tɔri/ adj. посвяти́тельный.
deduce /dɪ'dus/ v. выводи́ть (из with gen.) impf.
deduct /dɪ'dʌkt/ v. вычита́ть impf., вы́честь pf.
deduction /dɪ'dʌkʃən/ n. вычита́ние neut.; вы́вод m., заключе́ние neut.
deductive /dɪ'dʌktɪv/ adj. дедукти́вный.
deed /did/ n. посту́пок m., де́йствие neut.
deed poll n. односторо́ннее обяза́тельство neut.
deem /dim/ v. счита́ть (with instr.) impf.

deep /dip/ *adj.* глубо́кий.
deepen /'dipən/ *v.t.* углубля́ть *impf.*, углуби́ть *pf.*; *v.i.* углубля́ть(ся); усили́вать(ся) *impf.*
deep-felt /'dip ˌfɛlt/ *adj.* глубоко́ прочу́вствованный.
deep-freeze /'dip 'friz/ *v.* замора́живать *impf.*
deepness /'dipnɪs/ *n.* глубина́ *f.*
deep-rooted /'dip 'rutɪd/ *adj.* глубоко́ укорени́вшийся.
deep-sea /'dip 'si/ *adj.* глубоково́дный.
deep-seated /'dip 'sitɪd/ *adj.* вкорени́вшийся.
deer /dɪər/ *n.* оле́нь *m.*
deerhound /'dɪərˌhaund/ *n.* дирха́унд *m.*
deerskin /'dɪərˌskɪn/ *n.* оле́нья ко́жа, лоси́на *f.*
de-escalation /di ˌɛskə'leiʃən/ *n.* деэскала́ция *f.*
deface /dɪ'feis/ *v.* обезобра́живать *impf.*, обезобра́зить *pf.*
defacement /dɪ'feismənt/ *n.* оскверне́ние *neut.*
de facto /'di fæktou, dei/ *adj.* факти́ческий.
defamation /ˌdɛfə'meiʃən/ *n.* клевета́ *f.*
defamatory /dɪ'fæməˌtɔri/ *adj.* клеветни́ческий, позо́рящий.
defame /dɪ'feim/ *v.* клевета́ть *impf.*, оклевета́ть *pf.*
default /dɪ'fɔlt/ *n.* безде́йствие; невыполне́ние *neut.*; нея́вка *f.*; неплатёж *m.*
defaulter /dɪ'fɔltər/ *n.* не выполня́ющая свои́х обяза́тельств *f.*
defeat /dɪ'fit/ **1.** *n.* разгро́м *m.* **2.** *v.* побежда́ть *impf.*, победи́ть *pf.*
defeatism /dɪ'fitɪzəm/ *n.* пораже́нчество *neut.*
defeatist /dɪ'fitɪst/ *n.* пораже́нец *m.*
defecate /'dɛfɪˌkeit/ *v.* испражня́ться *impf.*
defecation /ˌdɛfɪ'keiʃən/ *n.* испражне́ние *neut.*
defect /'difɛkt/ *n.* недоста́ток, дефе́кт *m.*
defecting /di'fɛktɪŋ/ *adj.* бе́глый.
defection /dɪ'fɛkʃən/ *n.* дезерти́рство; бе́гство *neut.*
defective /dɪ'fɛktɪv/ *adj.* повреждённый, дефе́ктный.
defector /dɪ'fɛktər/ *n.* дезерти́р; перебе́жчик, невозвраще́нец *m.*
defenceless /dɪ'fɛnslɪs/ *adj.* беззащи́тный.
defend /dɪ'fɛnd/ *v.* защища́ть *impf.*, защити́ть *pf.*; обороня́ть *impf.*, оборони́ть *pf.*
defendant /dɪ'fɛndənt/ *n.* подсуди́мый, обвиня́емый *m.*
defender /dɪ'fɛndər/ *n.* защи́тник *m.*
defense /dɪ'fɛns/ *n.* оборо́на, защи́та *f.*
defensible /dɪ'fɛnsəbəl/ *adj.* защити́мый.
defensive /dɪ'fɛnsɪv/ *adj.* оборони́тельный.
defer /dɪ'fɜr/ *v.* откла́дывать *impf.*, отложи́ть *pf.*
deference /'dɛfərəns/ *n.* уваже́ние *neut.*
deferential /ˌdɛfə'rɛnʃəl/ *adj.* почти́тельный.
deferment /dɪ'fɜrmənt/ *n.* отсро́чка *f.*; откла́дывание *neut.*
deferred /dɪ'fɜrd/ *adj.* отло́женный.
defiance /dɪ'faiəns/ *n.* (*challenge*) вы́зов *m.*; (*disobedience*) неповинове́ние *neut.*; (*flouting*) пренебреже́ние *neut.*; **in defiance of** вопреки́ (*with dat.*).
defiant /dɪ'faiənt/ *adj.* вызыва́ющий.
deficiency /dɪ'fɪʃənsi/ *n.* недоста́ток *m.*
deficient /dɪ'fɪʃənt/ *adj.* недоста́точный.
deficit /'dɛfəsɪt/ *n.* дефици́т *m.*, недочёт *m.*
defile /dɪ'fail/ *n.* (*gorge*) тесни́на *f.*, уще́лье *neut.*
defile /dɪ'fail/ *v.* загрязня́ть *impf.*

defilement /dɪ'failmənt/ *n.* загрязне́ние; оскверне́ние *neut.*
definable /dɪ'fainəbəl/ *adj.* определи́мый.
define /dɪ'fain/ *v.* определя́ть *impf.*, определи́ть *pf.*
definite /'dɛfənɪt/ *adj.* определённый.
definitely /'dɛfənɪtli/ *adv.* определённо; то́чно; я́сно; без вся́кого сомне́ния; непреме́нно.
definition /ˌdɛfə'nɪʃən/ *n.* определе́ние *neut.*
definitive /dɪ'fɪnɪtɪv/ *adj.* оконча́тельный.
deflagration /ˌdɛflə'greiʃən/ *n.* бы́строе горе́ние *neut.*
deflate /dɪ'fleit/ *v.* (*balloon, etc.*) выпуска́ть во́здух *or* газ (из *with gen.*); (*reduce*) уменьша́ть *impf.*
deflated /dɪ'fleitɪd/ *adj.* спу́щенный.
deflation /dɪ'fleiʃən/ *n.* выка́чивание *neut.*; (*econ.*) дефля́ция *f.*
deflationary /dɪ'fleiʃəˌnɛri/ *adj.* дефляцио́нный.
deflect /dɪ'flɛkt/ *v.* отклоня́ть *impf.*, отклони́ть *pf.*
deflection /dɪ'flɛkʃən/ *n.* отклоне́ние *neut.*; (*of compass*) скло́нение магни́тной стре́лки *neut.*
deflector /dɪ'flɛktər/ *n.* дефле́ктор *m.*
defloration /ˌdɛflə'reiʃən/ *n.* дефлора́ция *f.*
defoliant /di'fouliənt/ *n.* дефолиа́нт *m.*
defoliate /di'fouliˌeit/ *v.* лиша́ть листвы́ *impf.*
deforest /dɪ'fɔrɪst/ *v.* обезле́сить *pf.*; выруба́ть лес *impf.*
deforestation /di,fɔrɪ'steiʃn/ *n.* обезле́сение *neut.*
deform /dɪ'fɔrm/ *v.* деформи́ровать *impf.* and *pf.*
deformation /ˌdifɔr'meiʃən/ *n.* искаже́ние *neut.*
deformity /dɪ'fɔrmɪti/ *n.* безобра́зие *neut.*
defraud /dɪ'frɔd/ *v.* выма́нивать *impf.*, вы́манить *pf.*
defray /dɪ'frei/ *v.* опла́чивать *impf.*
defrock /di'frɒk/ *v.* расстри́чь *pf.*
defrost /dɪ'frɔst/ *v.* размора́живат *impf.*
deft /dɛft/ *adj.* ло́вкий, иску́сный.
defunct /dɪ'fʌŋkt/ *adj.* уме́рший.
defuse /di'fyuz/ *v.* (*situation*) разряди́ть *pf.*
defy /dɪ'fai/ *v.* ослу́шаться *pf.*
degas /di'gæs/ *v.* дегази́ровать *impf.*
degauss /di'gaus/ *v.* размагни́чивать *impf.*
degenerate / *adj.* dɪ'dʒɛnərɪt; *v.* dɪ'dʒɛnəˌreit/ **1.** *adj.* вырожда́ющийся. **2.** *v.* вырожда́ться *impf.*, вы́родиться *pf.*
degeneration /dɪˌdʒɛnə'reiʃən/ *n.* вырожде́ние *neut.*
degradation /ˌdɛgrə'deiʃən/ *n.* деграда́ция *f.*
degrade /dɪ'greid/ *v.* дегради́ровать *impf.* and *pf.*
degrading /dɪ'greidɪŋ/ *adj.* унизи́тельный.
degree /dɪ'gri/ *n.* (*unit*) гра́дус *m.*; (*extent*) сте́пень *f.*; (*educ.*) зва́ние *neut.*, учёная сте́пень *f.*
degustation /ˌdigʌ'steiʃən/ *n.* дегуста́ция *f.*
dehumanization /diˌhyumənə'zeiʃən/ *n.* дегумaниза́ция *f.*
dehumanize /di'hyuməˌnaiz/ *v.* де́лать ва́рварским, озвере́лым *impf.*, обесчелове́чить *impf.*
dehumidifier /ˌdihyu'mɪdəˌfaiər/ *n.* осуши́тель *m.*
dehydrate /di'haidreit/ *v.* обезво́живать(ся) *impf.*

dehydration /ˌdihai'dreiʃən/ *n.* обезво́живание *neut.*

deice /di'ais/ *v.* удаля́ть лёд *impf.*

deicer /di'aisər/ *n.* антиобледени́тель *m.*

deify /'diə‚fai/ *v.* обожествля́ть *impf.*, обоготворя́ть *impf.*

deign /dein/ *v.* соизво́лить *pf.*

deism /'diizəm/ *n.* дейзм *m.*

deist /'diist/ *n.* дейст *m.*

deistic /di'istik/ *adj.* деисти́ческий.

deity /'diiti/ *n.* божество́ *neut.*

deject /dɪ'dʒɛkt/ *v.* удруча́ть *impf.*, угнета́ть *impf.*

dejected /dɪ'dʒɛktɪd/ *adj.* удручённый.

dejection /dɪ'dʒɛkʃən/ *n.* удручённость *f.*

Delaware /'dɛlə‚wɛər/ *n.* Де́лавэр *m.*

delay /dɪ'lei/ **1.** *n.* промедле́ние *neut.*, заде́ржка *f.* **2.** *v.* откла́дывать *impf.*, отложи́ть *pf.*

delayed-action /dɪ'leid'ækʃən/ *adj.* заме́дленного де́йствия.

delectable /dɪ'lɛktəbəl/ *adj.* преле́стный.

delectation /ˌdilɛk'teiʃən/ *n.* наслажде́ние *neut.*

delegacy /'dɛligəsi/ *n.* делега́ция *f.*

delegate / *n.* 'dɛligit; *v.* 'dɛli‚geit/ **1.** *n.* делега́т *m.* **2.** *v.* делеги́ровать *impf.* and *pf.*

delegation /ˌdɛli'geiʃən/ *n.* делега́ция *f.*

delete /dɪ'lit/ *v.* вычёркивать *impf.*, вы́черкнуть *pf.*

deleterious /ˌdɛlɪ'tiəriəs/ *adj.* вре́дный.

deletion /dɪ'liʃən/ *n.* вычёркивание; стира́ние; удале́ние, исключе́ние *neut.*

delft /dɛlft/ *n.* фая́нс *m.*

Delhi /'dɛli/ *n.* Де́ли *m.*

deliberate / *adj.* dɪ'lɪbərɪt; *v.* dɪ'lɪbə‚reit/ **1.** *adj.* наме́ренный, умы́шленный. **2.** *v.* совеща́ться *impf.*

deliberately /dɪ'lɪbərɪtli/ *adv.* наро́чно.

deliberation /dɪˌlɪbə'reiʃən/ *n.* обсужде́ние, обду́мывание *neut.*

deliberative /dɪ'lɪbərətɪv/ *adj.* совеща́тельный.

delicacy /'dɛlɪkəsi/ *n.* то́нкость; делика́тность; не́жность *f.*

delicate /'dɛlɪkɪt/ *adj.* делика́тный.

delicatessen /ˌdɛlɪkə'tɛsən/ (*food*) *n.* деликате́сы *pl.*; (*store*) гастроно́м *m.*

delicious /dɪ'lɪʃəs/ *adj.* о́чень вску́сный.

delight /dɪ'lait/ **1.** *n.* восто́рг *m.*, восхище́ние *neut.* **2.** *v.* восхища́ть *impf.*, восхити́ть *pf.*

delighted /dɪ'laitɪd/ *adj.* восто́рженный, восхищённый.

delightful /dɪ'laitfəl/ *adj.* восхити́тельный.

delimit /dɪ'lɪmɪt/ *v.* определя́ть грани́цы *or* преде́лы *impf.*

delineate /dɪ'lɪni‚eit/ *v.* оче́рчивать, обрисо́вывать *impf.*

delineation /dɪˌlɪni'eiʃən/ *n.* оче́рчивание *neut.*

delinquency /dɪ'lɪŋkwənsi/ *n.* правонаруше́ние *neut.*; **juvenile delinquency** *n.* престу́пность несовершенноле́тних *f.*

delinquent /dɪ'lɪŋkwənt/ *n.* правонаруши́тель, престу́пник *m.*

deliquesce /ˌdɛlɪ'kwɛs/ *v.* расплыва́ться *impf.*

deliquescence /ˌdɛlɪ'kwɛsəns/ *n.* расплыва́ние *neut.*

delirious /dɪ'lɪəriəs/ *adj.* бре́дящий.

delirium /dɪ'lɪəriəm/ *n.* бред *m.*

deliver /dɪ'lɪvər/ *v.* доставля́ть *impf.*, доста́вить *pf.*; освобожда́ть *impf.*, освободи́ть *pf.*; (*lecture*) чита́ть *impf.*, прочита́ть *pf.*

deliverance /dɪ'lɪvərəns/ *n.* освобожде́ние, избавле́ние *neut.*

delivery /dɪ'lɪvəri/ *n.* доста́вка, переда́ча *f.*; (*birth*) ро́ды *pl.*

dell /dɛl/ *n.* лесна́я лощи́на *f.*

delouse /di'laus/ *v.* деинсекти́ровать *impf.*

Delphi /'dɛlfai/ *n.* Де́льфы *pl.*

Delphic /'dɛlfɪk/ *adj.* дельфи́йский.

delphinium /dɛl'fɪniəm/ *n.* жи́вокость *f.*, шпо́рник *m.*

delta /'dɛltə/ *n.* де́льта *f.*

deltaic /dɛl'teiɪk/ *adj.* де́льтовый.

deltoid /'dɛltɔid/ *n.* (*muscle*) дельтови́дная мы́шца *f.*

delude /dɪ'lud/ *v.* обма́нывать *impf.*, обману́ть *pf.*

deluge /'dɛlyudʒ/ *n.* (*flood*) пото́п *m.*; (*downpour*) ли́вень *m.*

delusion /dɪ'luʒən/ *n.* заблужде́ние *neut.*

delusive /dɪ'lusɪv/ *adj.* обма́нчивый; бредово́й.

deluxe /də'lʌks/ **1.** *adj.* роско́шный. **2.** *n.* (*in compounds*) -люкс.

delve /dɛlv/ *v.* (*fig.*) копа́ться, ры́ться *impf.*

demagnetize /di'mægnɪ‚taiz/ *v.* размагни́чивать *impf.*

demagogical /ˌdɛmə'gɒdʒɪkəl/ *adj.* демагоги́ческий.

demagogue /'dɛmə‚gɒg/ *n.* демаго́г *m.*

demagogy /'dɛmə‚goudʒi/ *n.* демаго́гия *f.*

demand /dɪ'mænd/ **1.** *n.* тре́бование *neut.*; запро́с *m.*; **to be in demand** по́льзоваться спро́сом; **on demand** по тре́бованию. **2.** *v.* тре́бовать *impf.*, потре́бовать *pf.*

demanding /dɪ'mændɪŋ/ *adj.* тре́бовательный.

demarcate /dɪ'markeit/ *v.* разграни́чивать *impf.*

demarcation /ˌdimar'keiʃən/ *n.* разграни́чивание *neut.*

démarche /dei'marʃ/ *n.* дема́рш *m.*

demean /dɪ'min/ *v.* унижа́ться *impf.*; **to demean oneself by** позо́риться (*with instr.*) *impf.*

demeanor /dɪ'minər/ *n.* поведе́ние *neut.*; мане́ра держа́ть себя́ *f.*

demented /dɪ'mɛntɪd/ *adj.* сумасше́дший.

dementia /dɪ'mɛnʃə/ *n.* слабоу́мие *neut.*, деме́нция *f.*

demerara /ˌdɛmə'rarə/ *n.* са́хар Демера́ра *m.*

demesne /dɪ'mein/ *n.* уса́дьба *f.*, име́ние *m.*

demigod /'dɛmi‚gɒd/ *n.* полубо́г *m.*

demilitarize /di'mɪlɪtə‚raiz/ *v.* демилитаризи́ровать *impf.*

demimondaine /ˌdɛmimɒn'dein/ *n.* да́ма полусве́та *f.*

demimonde /'dɛmi‚mɒnd/ *n.* полусве́т, деми-мо́нд *m.*

demise /dɪ'maiz/ *n.* (*death*) кончи́на *f.*

demobilization /diˌmoubələ'zeiʃən/ *n.* демобилиза́ция *f.*

demobilize /di'moubə‚laiz/ *v.* демобилизова́ть *impf.* and *pf.*

democracy /dɪ'mɒkrəsi/ *n.* демокра́тия *f.*

democrat /'dɛmə‚kræt/ *n.* демокра́т *m.*

democratic /ˌdɛmə'krætɪk/ *adj.* демократи́ческий.

democratize /dɪ'mɒkrə‚taiz/ *v.* демократизи́ровать(ся) *impf.*

démodé /ˌdeimɔ'dei/ *adj.* вы́шедший из мо́ды.

demodulation /diˌmɒdʒə'leiʃən/ *n.* демодуля́ция *f.*

demodulator /di'mɒdʒəˌleitər/ *n.* демодуля́тор *m.*

demographic /ˌdɛmə'græfɪk/ *adj.* демографи́ческий.

demography /dɪ'mɒgrəfi/ *n.* демогра́фия *f.*

demolish /dɪ'mɒlɪʃ/ *v.* разруша́ть *impf.*, разру́шить *pf.*

demolition /ˌdɛmə'lɪʃən/ *n.* уничтоже́ние *neut.*; (*of a building*) снос *m.*

demon /'dimən/ *n.* де́мон, дья́вол *m.*

demoniac /dɪ'mouniˌæk/ *adj.* дья́вольский, чудо́вищный.

demonic /dɪ'mɒnɪk/ *adj.* демони́ческий.

demonism /'diməˌnɪzəm/ *n.* демони́зм *m.*

demonology /ˌdimə'nɒlədʒi/ *n.* демоноло́гия *f.*

demonstrable /dɪ'mɒnstrəbəl/ *adj.* дока́зуемый, я́вный.

demonstrably /dɪ'mɒnstrəbli/ *adv.* я́вно.

demonstrate /'dɛmənˌstreit/ *v.* демонстри́ровать *impf.* and *pf.*; уча́ствовать в демонстра́ции *impf.*

demonstration /ˌdɛmən'streiʃən/ *n.* демонстри́рование *neut.*; демонстра́ция *f.*

demonstrative /də'mɒnstrətɪv/ *adj.* демонстрати́вный; (*gram.*) указа́тельный.

demonstrator /'dɛmənˌstreitər/ *n.* демонстра́тор *m.*

demoralization /dɪˌmɔrələ'zeiʃən/ *n.* деморализа́ция *f.*

demoralize /dɪ'mɔrəˌlaiz/ *v.* деморализо́вывать *impf.*, деморализова́ть *pf.*

demote /dɪ'mout/ *v.* понижа́ть в до́лжности *impf.*

demotic /dɪ'mɒtɪk/ *adj.* простонаро́дный.

demount /di'maunt/ *v.* демонти́ровать *impf.*

demure /dɪ'myʊr/ *adj.* (*grave*) серьёзный; (*reserved*) сде́ржанный.

demythologization /ˌdimɪˌθɒlədʒə'zeiʃən/ *n.* демифологиза́ция *f.*

den /dɛn/ *n.* ло́говище *neut.*

denationalize /di'næʃənlˌaiz/ *v.* (*econ.*) денационализи́ровать *impf.*

denaturalize /di'nætʃərəˌlaiz/ *v.* лиша́ть по́дданства, денатурализова́ть *impf.*

dendrochronology /ˌdɛndroukrə'nɒlədʒi/ *n.* дендрохроноло́гия *f.*

dendrology /dɛn'drɒlədʒi/ *n.* дендроло́гия *f.*

denial /dɪ'naiəl/ *n.* отрица́ние *neut.*

denigrate /'dɛnɪˌgreit/ *v.* черни́ть, поро́чить, клевета́ть *impf.*

denigration /ˌdɛnɪ'greiʃən/ *n.* клевета́ *f.*

denizen /'dɛnəzən/ *n.* обита́тель *m.*

Denmark /'dɛnmɑrk/ *n.* Да́ния *f.*

denominate /dɪ'nɒməˌneit/ *v.* называ́ть *impf.*

denominative /dɪ'nɒməˌneitɪv/ *adj.* (*gram.*) отымённый, деноминати́вный.

denominator /dɪ'nɒməˌneitər/ *n.* знамена́тель, дели́тель *m.*

denotation /ˌdinou'teiʃən/ *n.* обозначе́ние *neut.*; (*symbol*) знак *m.*

denote /dɪ'nout/ *v.* обознача́ть *impf.*, обозна́чить *pf.*; означа́ть *impf.*

dénouement /ˌdeinu'mɑ̃/ *n.* (*of plot*) развя́зка *f.*; (*outcome*) исхо́д *m.*

denounce /dɪ'nauns/ *v.* осужда́ть *impf.*

dense /dɛns/ *adj.* густо́й.

densimeter /densi'mitər/ *n.* денсиме́тр *m.*

density /'dɛnsɪti/ *n.* пло́тность *f.*

dent /dɛnt/ **1.** *n.* вы́емка *f.* **2.** *v.* вда́вливать *impf.*, вдави́ть *pf.*

dental /'dɛntl/ *adj.* зубно́й.

dentate /'dɛnteit/ *adj.* зу́бчатый.

dented /'dɛntid/ *adj.* с вмя́тинами.

dentine /'dɛntin/ *n.* денти́н *m.*

dentist /'dɛntɪst/ *n.* зубно́й врач *m.*

dentistry /'dɛntəstri/ *n.* зубоврачева́ние *neut.*

dentition /dɛn'tɪʃən/ *n.* расположе́ние зубо́в *neut.*

dentures /'dɛntʃərz/ *pl.* вставны́е зу́бы *pl.*

denude /dɪ'nud/ *v.* обнажа́ть *impf.*

denunciation /dɪˌnʌnsi'eiʃən/ *n.* осужде́ние *neut.*, доно́с *m.*

deny /dɪ'nai/ *v.* отрица́ть *impf.*

deodar /'diəˌdɑr/ *n.* гимала́йский кедр *m.*

deodorant /di'oudərənt/ *n.* дезодора́нт *m.*

deodorize /di'oudəˌraiz/ *v.* дезодори́ровать *impf.*

deoxidize /di'ɒksɪˌdaiz/ *v.* раскисля́ть *impf.*

deoxidizer /di'ɒksɪˌdaizər/ *n.* восстанови́тель *m.*; раскисли́тель *m.*

depart /dɪ'pɑrt/ *v.* уходи́ть *impf.*, уйти́ *pf.*; уезжа́ть *impf.*, уе́хать *pf.*

departed /dɪ'pɑrtid/ *adj.* поко́йный.

department /dɪ'pɑrtmənt/ *n.* отде́л *m.*, отделе́ние *neut.*

departmental /diˌpɑrt'mɛntl/ *adj.* ведомственный.

Department of Motor Vehicles *n.* ГАИ *f. indecl.* (*abbr. of* Госуда́рственная автомоби́льная инспе́кция).

department store *n.* универма́г *m.* (*abbr. of* универса́льный магази́н).

departure /dɪ'pɑrtʃər/ *n.* отъе́зд, ухо́д *m.*

depend /dɪ'pɛnd/ *v.* зави́сеть (от *with gen.*) *impf.*

dependability /dɪˌpɛndə'bɪlɪti/ *n.* надёжность; достове́рность *f.*

dependable /dɪ'pɛndəbəl/ *adj.* надёжный.

dependence /dɪ'pɛndəns/ *n.* зави́симость *f.*

dependent /dɪ'pɛndənt/ **1.** *adj.* зави́симый. **2.** *n.* иждиве́нец *m.*

depending on /dɪ'pɛndɪŋ/ в зави́симости от (*with gen.*).

depersonalize /di'pərsənlˌaiz/ *v.* обезли́чивать *impf.*

depict /dɪ'pɪkt/ *v.* изобража́ть *impf.*, изобрази́ть *pf.*

depiction /dɪ'pɪkʃən/ *n.* изображе́ние *neut.*

depilatory /dɪ'pɪləˌtɔri/ *adj.* депили́рующий.

deplete /dɪ'plit/ *v.* истоща́ть, исче́рпывать *impf.*

depletion /dɪ'pliʃən/ *n.* истоще́ние, исче́рпывание; опорожне́ние *neut.*

deplorable /dɪ'plɔrəbəl/ *adj.* плаче́вный.

deplore /dɪ'plɔr/ *v.* сожале́ть (о with *prep.*); (*disapprove of*) порица́ть *impf.*

deploy /dɪ'plɔi/ *v.* (*mil.*) развёртывать(ся) *impf.*

deployment /dɪ'plɔimənt/ *n.* развёртывание *neut.*

deponent /dɪ'pounənt/ **1.** *n.* (*gram.*) отложи́тельный глаго́л *m.* **2.** *adj.* (*gram.*) отложи́тельный.

depopulate /di'pɒpyəˌleit/ *v.* (*reduce population of*) уменьша́ть населе́ние (*with gen.*) *impf.*

deport /dɪ'pɔrt/ v. ссылáть impf., сослáть pf.
deportation /ˌdipɔr'teɪʃən/ n. ссы́лка f.
deportee /ˌdipɔr'ti/ n. вы́сланный m.
deportment /dɪ'pɔrtmənt/ n. поведéние neut.
depose /dɪ'pouz/ v. сверга́ть impf., свéргнуть pf.
deposit /dɪ'pɒzɪt/ 1. n. (payment) взнос, задáток m.; (sediment) осáдок m. 2. v. положи́ть pf.
depositary /dɪ'pɒzɪˌteri/ n. склад m.
deposition /ˌdɛpə'zɪʃən/ n. (of ruler) сверже́ние neut.; (leg.) пи́сьменное показáние neut.
depositor /dɪ'pɒzɪtər/ n. вклáдчик m.
depository /dɪ'pɒzɪˌtɔri/ n. храни́лище neut.; склад m.; (fig.) клáд m.
depot /'dipou/ n. депó neut. indecl.
deprave /dɪ'preiv/ v. развраща́ть impf.
depraved /dɪ'preivd/ adj. развращённый.
depravity /dɪ'prævɪti/ n. разврáт m.; развращённость f.
deprecate /'dɛprɪˌkeit/ v. возража́ть impf., возрази́ть pf.
deprecation /ˌdɛprɪ'keiʃən/ n. возраже́ние neut.
deprecatory /'dɛprɪkəˌtɔri/ adj. неодобри́тельный; извиня́ющийся.
depreciate /dɪ'priʃiˌeit/ v. обесцéнивать impf., обесцéнить pf.
depreciation /dɪˌpriʃi'eiʃən/ n. обесцéнивание neut.
depredation /ˌdɛprɪ'deiʃən/ n. расхище́ние neut.
depress /dɪ'prɛs/ v. подавля́ть impf., подави́ть pf.
depressant /dɪ'prɛsənt/ n. успокои́тельное (срéдство) neut.
depressed /dɪ'prɛst/ adj. нажáтый; вдáвленный; (flattened) сплю́щенный; (dejected) подáвленный, уны́лый.
depressing /dɪ'prɛsɪŋ/ adj. (gloomy) уны́лый; (causing gloom) гнетýщий.
depression /dɪ'prɛʃən/ депрéссия, впáдина f.
depressive /dɪ'prɛsɪv/ adj. депресси́вный.
depressor /dɪ'prɛsər/ n. (anat.) депрéссор m.
deprivation /ˌdɛprə'veiʃən/ n. лише́ние neut.
deprive /dɪ'praiv/ v. лиша́ть impf., лиши́ть pf.
deprived /dɪ'praivd/ adj. бéдный, нуждáющийся.
depth /dɛpθ/ n. глубинá f.
depth charge n. глуби́нная бóмба f.
deputation /ˌdɛpyə'teiʃən/ n. депутáция, делегáция f.
depute /də'pyut/ v. делеги́ровать impf.
deputize /'dɛpyəˌtaiz/ v. назначáть представи́телем impf.
deputy /'dɛpyəti/ n. депутáт m.
derail /di'reil/ v.t. сбрáсывать с рéльсов; v.i. сходи́ть с рéльсов impf.
derailment /di'reilmənt/ n. сход с рéльсов m.
derange /dɪ'reindʒ/ v. приводи́ть в беспоря́док impf.
deranged /dɪ'reindʒd/ adj. сумасшéдший.
derangement /dɪ'reindʒmənt/ n. психи́ческое расстрóйство neut.
derelict /'dɛrəlɪkt/ adj. (abandoned) поки́нутый, брóшенный; (useless) негóдный.
dereliction /ˌdɛrə'lɪkʃən/ n. забрóшенность f.
deride /dɪ'raid/ v. высмéивать impf.
derision /dɪ'rɪʒən/ n. высмéивание neut.
derisive /dɪ'raisɪv/ adj. насмéшливый, издевáтельский.
derivation /ˌdɛrə'veiʃən/ n. происхожде́ние neut.

derivative /dɪ'rɪvətɪv/ adj. произвóдный.
derive /dɪ'raiv/ v. происходи́ть impf.
dermal /'dɜrməl/ adj. кóжный.
dermatitis /ˌdɜrmə'taitɪs/ n. дерматúт m.
dermatologist /ˌdɜrmə'tɒlədʒɪst/ n. дерматóлог m.
dermatology /ˌdɜrmə'tɒlədʒi/ n. дерматолóгия f.
derogate /'dɛrəˌgeit/ adj. v. понижáть impf.
derogatory /dɪ'rɒgəˌtɔri/ adj. унизи́тельный.
dervish /'dɜrvɪʃ/ n. дéрвиш m.
desalinate /di'sæləˌneit/ v. опресня́ть impf.
desalination /diˌsælə'neiʃən/ n. опресне́ние neut.
descant /'dɛskænt/ n. ди́скант m.
descend /dɪ'sɛnd/ v. сходи́ть impf., сойти́ pf.; происходи́ть impf., произойти́ pf.
descendant /dɪ'sɛndənt/ n. потóмок m.
descent /dɪ'sɛnt/ n. спуск m.; происхожде́ние neut.
describe /dɪ'skraib/ v. опи́сывать impf., описáть pf.
description /dɪ'skrɪpʃən/ n. описáние neut.
descriptive /dɪ'skrɪptɪv/ adj. описáтельный.
desecrate /'dɛsɪˌkreit/ v. осквернá́ть impf.
desecration /ˌdɛsɪ'kreiʃən/ n. оскверне́ние neut., профанáция f.
desegregate /di'sɛgrɪˌgeit/ v. десегреги́ровать impf.
desegregation /ˌdisɛgrɪ'geiʃən/ n. десегрегáция f.
desert / n. 'dɛzərt; v. dɪ'zɜrt/ 1. n. пусты́ня f. 2. v. покидáть impf., поки́нуть pf.; v.i. дезерти́ровать impf.
deserter /dɪ'zɜrtər/ n. дезерти́р m.
desertion /dɪ'zɜrʃən/ n. дезерти́рство neut.
deserve /dɪ'zɜrv/ v. заслýживать impf., заслужи́ть pf.
deservedly /dɪ'zɜrvɪdli/ adv. заслýженно.
deserving /dɪ'zɜrvɪŋ/ adj. достóйный (with gen.).
desiccant /'dɛsɪkənt/ n. осуши́тель m.
desiccate /'dɛsɪˌkeit/ v. суши́ть impf.
desiccation /ˌdɛsɪ'keiʃən/ n. сýшка f.
desideratum /dɪˌsɪdə'reitəm, -'rɑ-/ n. трéбование neut.
design /dɪ'zain/ 1. n. проéкт, план m.; (pattern) рисýнок m., (drawing) узóр m. 2. v. проекти́ровать impf., запроекти́ровать pf.
designate /'dɛzɪgˌneit/ v. назначáть impf., назнáчить pf.
designation /ˌdɛzɪg'neiʃən/ n. указáние, назначé́ние neut.
designer /dɪ'zainər/ n. проекти́ровщик m.
designing /dɪ'zainɪŋ/ n. (planning) проекти́рование, конструи́рование neut.
desirability /dɪˌzaiᵊrə'bɪliti/ n. желáтельность f.
desirable /dɪ'zaiᵊrəbəl/ adj. желáтельный.
desire /dɪ'zaiᵊr/ 1. n. желáние neut. 2. v. желáть impf.
desirous /dɪ'zaiᵊrəs/ adj. желáющий.
desist /dɪ'zist/ v. прекраща́ть impf.
desk /dɛsk/ n. канцеля́рский стол, пи́сьменный стол m.
desktop /'dɛskˌtɒp/ adj. настóльный.
desktop publishing n. настóльное издáтельство neut.; настóльная издáтельская систéма f.
Desna /də'snɑ/ n. (river) Деснá f.
desolate /'dɛsəlɪt/ adj. необитáемый; безлю́дный; забрóшенный; (abandoned) поки́нутый.

desolation /ˌdɛsəˈleɪʃən/ n. опустошéние neut.

despair /dɪˈspeər/ n. отчáяние neut.

despairing /dɪˈspeərɪŋ/ adj. отчáянный.

desperado /ˌdɛspəˈrɑdou/ n. головорéз m., сорвиголовá m. and f. (decl. f.).

desperate /ˈdɛspərɪt/ adj. отчáянный.

desperation /ˌdɛspəˈreɪʃən/ n. отчáяние neut.

despicable /ˈdɛspɪkəbəl, dɪˈspɪkə-/ adj. пóдлый.

despise /dɪˈspaɪz/ v. презирáть impf.

despite /dɪˈspaɪt/ prep. вопрекú (with dat.), несмотря́ на (with acc.).

despoil /dɪˈspɔɪl/ v. грáбить impf.

despond /dɪˈspɒnd/ v. унывáть impf.

despondency /dɪˈspɒndənsi/ n. уны́ние neut.

despondent /dɪˈspɒndənt/ adj. подáвленный.

despot /ˈdɛspət/ n. дéспот, тирáн m.

despotic /dɪˈspɒtɪk/ adj. деспотúческий.

despotism /ˈdɛspəˌtɪzəm/ n. деспотúзм m.

dessert /dɪˈzɜrt/ n. десéрт m.

dessert spoon n. десéртная лóжка f.

destabilization /diˌsteibələˈzeɪʃən/ n. дестабилизáция f.

destination /ˌdɛstəˈneɪʃən/ n. назначéние, предназначéние neut.

destine /ˈdɛstɪn/ v. предназначáть impf.

destiny /ˈdɛstəni/ n. судьбá f.

destitute /ˈdɛstɪˌtut/ adj. нуждáющийся.

destitution /ˌdɛstɪˈtuʃən/ n. нищетá f.

destroy /dɪˈstrɔɪ/ v. уничтожáть impf., уничтóжить pf.; истреблять impf., истребúть pf.; разрушáть impf., разру́шить pf.

destroyer /dɪˈstrɔɪər/ n. эсмúнец m.

destruction /dɪˈstrʌkʃən/ n. разрушéние, уничтожéние neut.

destructive /dɪˈstrʌktɪv/ adj. разрушúтельный.

desultory /ˈdɛsəlˌtɔri/ adj. несвя́зный.

detach /dɪˈtætʃ/ v. отделя́ть impf., отделúть pf.

detached /dɪˈtætʃt/ adj. отдéльный.

detachment /dɪˈtætʃmənt/ отря́д m.

detail /ˈditeil, ˈditeil/ n. подрóбность, детáль f.

detailed /dɪˈteild, ˈditeild/ adj. подрóбный.

detain /dɪˈtein/ v. задéрживать impf., задержáть pf.

detainee /dɪˈteini/ n. задéржанный m.

detect /dɪˈtɛkt/ v. открывáть impf., откры́ть pf.

detection /dɪˈtɛkʃən/ n. откры́тие, обнаружéние neut.

detective /dɪˈtɛktɪv/ n. сы́щик m.

detector /dɪˈtɛktər/ n. детéктор m.

détente /deiˈtɑnt/ n. разря́дка f., детáнт m.

detention /dɪˈtɛnʃən/ n. задержáние neut.

deter /dɪˈtɜr/ v. удéрживать impf., удержáть pf.

detergent /dɪˈtɜrdʒənt/ n. стирáльный порошóк m.

deteriorate /dɪˈtɪəriəˌreit/ v. ухудшáть impf., ухýдшить pf.; v.i. ухудшáться impf., ухýдшиться pf.

deterioration /dɪˌtɪəriəˈreiʃən/ n. ухудшéние neut.

determinable /dɪˈtɜrmənəbəl/ adj. определя́емый.

determinant /dɪˈtɜrmənənt/ n. (math.) определúтель m.

determinate /dɪˈtɜrmənɪt/ adj. (definite) определённый; (final, conclusive) решённый, окончáтельный.

determination /dɪˌtɜrməˈneiʃən/ n. решúмость f.

determinative /dɪˈtɜrməˌneitɪv/ **1.** n. решáющий фáктор m. **2.** adj. решáющий.

determine /dɪˈtɜrmɪn/ v. определя́ть impf., определúть pf.

determined /dɪˈtɜrmɪnd/ adj. решúтельный.

determinism /dɪˈtɜrməˌnɪzəm/ n. детерминúзм m.

determinist /dɪˈtɜrmənɪst/ n. детерминúст m.

deterrence /dɪˈtɜrəns/ n. устрашéние neut.

deterrent /dɪˈtɜrənt/ **1.** n. срéдство устрашéния neut. **2.** adj. отпýгивающий, устрашáющий.

detest /dɪˈtɛst/ v. ненавúдеть impf., питáть отвращéние (к with dat.) impf.

detestable /dɪˈtɛstəbəl/ adj. отвратúтельный.

detestation /ˌditɛˈsteiʃən/ n. отвращéние neut.

dethrone /diˈθroun/ v. сверга́ть с престóла impf.

dethronement /diˈθrounmənt/ n. сверже́ние с престóла neut.

detonation /ˌdɛtnˈeiʃən/ n. взрыв m.

detonator /ˈdɛtnˌeitər/ n. детонáтор m.

detour /ˈditur/ n. окóльный путь, обхóд, объéзд m.

detoxication /ˌditɒksɪˈkeiʃən/ n. обезврéживание; устранéние токсúна; вытрезвлéние neut.

detoxify /diˈtɒksəfai/ v. обезврéживать impf.

detract /dɪˈtrækt/ v. (belittle) умаля́ть impf.; (diminish) уменьшáть impf.

detraction /dɪˈtrækʃən/ n. умалéние neut.

detrain /diˈtrein/ v. высáживать(ся) из пóезда impf.

detriment /ˈdɛtrəmənt/ n. ущéрб, вред m.; **to the detriment of** в ущéрб, во вред (with dat.).

detrimental /ˌdɛtrəˈmɛntļ/ adj. врéдный.

detruncate /dɪˈtrʌŋkeit/ v. срезáть impf.

detumescence /ˌdituˈmɛsəns/ n. уменьшéние óпухоли neut.

deuce /dus/ n. (card) двóйка f.; (tennis) рóвно; (colloq.) (devil) чёрт m.

deuterium /duˈtiəriəm/ n. дейтéрий, тяжёлый водорóд m.

deuteron /ˈdutəˌrɒn/ n. дейтрóн m.

Deuteronomy /ˌdutəˈrɒnəmi/ n. Второзакóние neut.

deva /ˈdeivə/ n. (myth.) дэв m.

devaluate /diˈvæljuˌeit/ v. обесцéнивать impf.

devaluation /diˌvæljuˈeiʃən/ n. девальвáция f.

devastate /ˈdɛvəˌsteit/ v. опустошáть, разоря́ть impf.

devastating /ˈdɛvəˌsteitɪŋ/ adj. опустошúтельный.

devastation /ˌdɛvəˈsteiʃən/ n. опустошéние neut.

develop /dɪˈvɛləp/ v. развивáть impf., развúть pf.; v.i. развивáться impf., развúться pf.

developer /dɪˈvɛləpər/ n. (phot.) прояви́тель m.; (builder) строи́тель m.

developing countries /dɪˈvɛləpɪŋ/ развивáющиеся стрáны pl.

development /dɪˈvɛləpmənt/ n. развúтие neut.

deviant /ˈdiviənt/ adj. противоестéственный.

deviate /ˈdiviˌeit/ v. отклоня́ться, уклоня́ться (от with gen.) impf.

deviation /ˌdiviˈeiʃən/ n. отклонéние neut.

deviationist /ˌdiviˈeiʃənɪst/ n. уклонúст m.

device /dɪˈvais/ n. прибóр; приём m.

devil /ˈdɛvəl/ n. чёрт, дья́вол m.

devilfish /'dɛvəl,fɪʃ/ n. морской дья́вол m., ма́нта f.; (Mobula) скат-рога́ч m.

devilish /'dɛvəlɪʃ/ adj. дья́вольский.

devil-may-care /'dɛvəl mei' kɛər/ adj. беззабо́тный.

devil worship n. сатани́зм m.

devil-worshipper /'dɛvəl ,wɜrʃɪpər/ n. сатани́ст m.

devitalize /di'vaitl,aiz/ v. лиша́ть жизненной си́лы impf.

devocalize /di'voukə,laiz/ v. (phon.) оглуша́ть impf.

devoid /dɪ'vɔid/ adj. лишённый (with gen.).

Devonian /də'vouniən/ adj. девонши́рский; дево́нский.

devote /dɪ'vout/ v. посвяща́ть impf., посвяти́ть pf.; **to devote oneself** посвяща́ть себя́ impf.

devoted /dɪ'voutɪd/ adj. пре́данный.

devotee /,dɛvə'ti/ n. сторо́нник, приве́рженец; энтузиа́ст, люби́тель m.

devotion /dɪ'vouʃən/ n. пре́данность f.

devotional /dɪ'vouʃənl/ adj. религио́зный.

devour /dɪ'vaur/ v. пожира́ть impf., пожра́ть pf.

devout /dɪ'vaut/ adj. на́божный.

devoutness /dɪ'vautnɪs/ n. на́божность f.

dew /du/ n. роса́ f.

dewberry /'du,bɛri/ n. ежеви́ка f.

dewdrop /'du,drɒp/ n. ка́пля росы́, роси́нка f.

dewlap /'du,læp/ n. подгру́док m.

dewy /'dui/ adj. роси́стый.

dexter /'dɛkstər/ adj. пра́вый.

dexterity /dɛk'stɛrɪti/ n. прово́рство neut., ло́вкость f.

dexterous /'dɛkstrəs/ adj. прово́рный, ло́вкий.

dextral /'dɛkstrəl/ adj. правосторо́нний; правору́кий.

dextrin /'dɛkstrɪn/ n. декстри́н m.

dextrorotary /,dɛkstrou'routəri/ adj. правовраща́ющий.

dextrose /'dɛkstrous/ n. декстро́за f.

dhole /doul/ n. кра́сный волк m.

dhoti /'douti/ n. набёдренная повя́зка f.

dhow /dau/ n. да́у neut. indecl.

di- prefix дву-, двух-.

diabase /'daiə,beis/ n. диаба́з m.

diabasic /,daiə'beisɪk/ adj. двухосно́вный.

diabetes /,daiə'bitɪs/ n. диабе́т m., са́харная боле́знь f.

diabetic /,daiə'bɛtɪk/. 1. n. диабе́тик m. 2. adj. диабети́ческий.

diabolic /,daiə'bɒlɪk/ adj. дья́вольский.

diabolism /dai'æbə,lɪzəm/ n. сатани́зм m.

diacetate /dai'æsɪ,teit/ n. диацета́т m.

diacetic /,daiə'sɛtɪk/ adj. ацетоу́ксусный.

diachronic /,daiə'krɒnɪk/ adj. диахрони́ческий.

diaconal /dai'ækənl/ adj. дья́конский.

diaconate /dai'ækənɪt/ n. дья́конство neut.

diacritic /,daiə'krɪtɪk/ n. диакрити́ческий знак m.

diactinic /,daiæk'tɪnɪk/ adj. диактини́ческий.

diadem /'daiə,dɛm/ n. диаде́ма f.

diagnose /'daiəg,nous/ v. ста́вить диа́гноз impf.

diagnosis /,daiəg'nousɪs/ n. диа́гноз m.

diagnostic /,daiəg'nɒstɪk/ 1. n. симпто́м m. 2. adj. диагности́ческий.

diagnostician /,daiəgnɒ'stɪʃən/ n. диагно́ст m.

diagonal /dai'ægənl/ 1. adj. диагона́льный. 2. n. диагона́ль f.

diagram /'daiə,græm/ n. диагра́мма f.

diagrammatical /,daiəgrə'mætɪkəl/ adj. схемати́ческий.

dial /'daiəl/ n. цифербла́т m., шкала́ f.

dialect /'daiə,lɛkt/ n. диале́кт m., наре́чие neut.; го́вор m.

dialectal /,daiə'lɛktl/ adj. диале́ктный.

dialectic /,daiə'lɛktɪk/ n. диале́ктика f.

dialectical /,daiə'lɛktɪkəl/ adj. диалекти́ческий.

dialectician /,daiəlɛk'tɪʃən/ n. диале́ктик m.

dialectology /,daiəlɛk'tɒlədʒi/ n. диалектоло́гия f.

dialing /'daiəlɪŋ/ n. набо́р но́мера m.

dialogue /'daiə,lɒg/ n. диало́г m.

dialysis /dai'æləsɪs/ n. диа́лиз m.

diamagnetic /,daiəmæg'nɛtɪk/ adj. диамагни́тный.

diameter /dai'æmɪtər/ n. диа́метр m.

diametrical /,daiə'mɛtrɪkəl/ adj. диаметри́ческий.

diamide /'daiə,maid, dai'æmɪd/ n. диами́д m.

diamine /'daiə,min, dai'æmɪn/ n. диами́н m.

diamond /'daimənd/ n. алма́з m.; (polished) бриллиа́нт m.

diandrous /dai'ændrəs/ adj. двутычи́ночный.

dianthus /dai'ænθəs/ n. гвозди́ка f.

diapason /,daiə'peizən/ n. диапазо́н m.

diaper /'daipər/ n. (baby's) пелёнка f.

diaphanous /dai'æfənəs/ adj. прозра́чный, просве́чивающий.

diaphoretic /,daiəfə'rɛtɪk/ 1. n. потого́нное сре́дство neut. 2. adj. потого́нный.

diaphragm /'daiə,fræm/ n. диафра́гма f.; (between thorax and abdomen) грудобрюшна́я прегра́да f.

diarchy /'daiɑrki/ n. двоевла́стие neut.

diarist /'daiərɪst/ n. а́втор дневника́ m.

diarrhea /,daiə'riə/ n. поно́с m.

diary /'daiəri/ n. дневни́к m.

diascope /'daiə,skoup/ n. диаско́п m.

Diaspora /dai'æspərə/ n. диа́спора f., рассея́ние neut.

diaspore /'daiə,spɔr/ n. диаспо́р m.

diastase /'daiə,steis/ n. диаста́за f.

diastole /dai'æstl,i/ n. диа́стола f.

diathermic /,daiə'θɜrmɪk/ adj. теплопрозра́чный.

diathesis /dai'æθəsɪs/ n. диате́за f.

diatom /'daiətɒm/ n. диато́мовая во́доросль f.

diatomic /,daiə'tɒmɪk/ adj. двухà́томный.

diatomite /dai'ætə,mait/ n. диатоми́т m.

diatonic /,daiə'tɒnɪk/ adj. диатони́ческий.

diatribe /'daiə,traib/ n. брань f.

dibasic /dai'beisɪk/ adj. двухосно́вный.

dibble /'dɪbəl/ n. лопа́тка f.

dice /dais/ pl. игра́льные ко́сти pl.

diced /daist/ adj. ме́лко наре́занный.

dicephalous /dai'sɛfələs/ adj. двугла́вый.

dicey /'daisi/ adj. риско́ванный.

dichotomize /dai'kɒtə,maiz/ v. разделя́ть на две ча́сти impf.

dichotomy /dai'kɒtəmi/ n. деле́ние на две ча́сти neut.; (leg.) дихотоми́я f.

dichromatic /,daikrou'mætɪk/ adj. двухцве́тный.

dick /dɪk/ n. (slang) (detective) сы́щик m.

dicker[1] /'dɪkər/ n. деся́ток m.

dicker[2] /'dɪkər/ v. торгова́ться impf.

dickey /'dɪki/ n. мани́шка, вста́вка f.; пришивно́й воротничо́к m.

dicotyledon /dai‚kɒtl̩'idn̩/ n. двудо́льное расте́ние neut.

dictaphone /'dɪktə‚foun/ n. диктофо́н m.

dictate /'dɪkteit/ v. диктова́ть impf., продиктова́ть pf.

dictation /dɪk'teiʃən/ n. дикта́нт m., дикто́вка f.

dictator /'dɪkteitər/ n. дикта́тор m.

dictatorial /‚dɪktə'tɔriəl/ adj. дикта́торский; повели́тельный.

dictatorship /dɪk'teitər‚ʃɪp/ n. диктату́ра f.

diction /'dɪkʃən/ n. ди́кция f.

dictionary /'dɪkʃə‚nɛri/ n. слова́рь m.

dictograph /'dɪktə‚græf/ n. дикто́граф m.

dictum /'dɪktəm/ n. изрече́ние neut., афори́зм m., сенте́нция f.

didactic /dai'dæktɪk/ adj. дидакти́ческий; настави́тельный.

didacticism /dai'dæktə‚sɪzəm/ n. дидакти́зм m.

didactics /dai'dæktɪks/ n. дида́ктика f.

dido /'daidou/ n. (colloq.) прока́за, ша́лость f.

die /dai/ v. умира́ть impf., умере́ть pf.; **to die out** вымира́ть impf., вы́мереть pf.

dielectric /‚daiɪ'lɛktrɪk/ **1.** n. диэле́ктрик m. **2.** adj. диэлектри́ческий

dieresis /dai'ɛrəsɪs/ n. диэре́за f.

diesel /'dizəl/ n. ди́зель m.

diesinker /'dai‚sɪŋkər/ n. ре́зчик штемпеле́й m.

diestock /'dai‚stɒk/ n. клупп m.

diet /'daiɪt/ n. дие́та f.

dietary /'daiɪ‚tɛri/ adj. диети́ческий.

dietetics /‚daiɪ'tɛtɪks/ n. диете́тика f.

dietician /‚daiɪ'tɪʃən/ n. диете́тик, дието́лог m.

differ /'dɪfər/ v. различа́ться impf.

difference /'dɪfərəns/ n. ра́зница f., разли́чие neut.

different /'dɪfərənt/ adj. разли́чный, ра́зный.

differentiable /‚dɪfə'rɛnʃiəbəl/ adj. дифференци́руемый.

differential /‚dɪfə'rɛnʃəl/ n. (tech., math.) дифференциа́л m.

differentiate /‚dɪfə'rɛnʃi‚eit/ v. различа́ть impf., различи́ть pf.; отлича́ть impf., отличи́ть pf.

differentiation /‚dɪfə‚rɛnʃi'eiʃən/ n. дифференци́рование neut.

differently /‚dɪfərəntli/ adv. ина́че, по-ино́му; (variously) по-ра́зному.

difficult /'dɪfɪ‚kʌlt/ adj. тру́дный.

difficulty /'dɪfɪ‚kʌlti/ n. тру́дность f.

diffidence /'dɪfɪdəns/ n. неуве́ренность в себе́ neut.

diffident /'dɪfɪdənt/ adj. неуве́ренный в себе.

diffract /dɪ'frækt/ v. преломля́ть impf.

diffraction /dɪ'frækʃən/ n. дифра́кция f., преломле́ние neut.

diffuse /adj. dɪ'fyus; v. dɪ'fyuz/ **1.** adj. распространённый; (not clearly defined) расплы́вчатый. **2.** v. (light, warmth, etc.) рассе́ивать impf.; (knowledge, etc.) распространя́ть impf.

diffused /dɪ'fyuzd/ adj. рассе́янный.

diffuser /dɪ'fyuzər/ n. (tech.) диффу́зор m.

diffusion /dɪ'fyuʒən/ n. распростране́ние neut.

diffusive /dɪ'fyusɪv/ adj. распространя́ющийся.

dig /dɪg/ v. копа́ть impf.; рыть impf.

digenesis /dai'dʒɛnəsɪs/ n. дигене́з m.

digest / n. 'daidʒɛst; v. dɪ'dʒɛst/ **1.** n. кра́ткое изложе́ние neut. **2.** v. перева́ривать impf., перевари́ть pf.

digestible /dɪ'dʒɛstəbəl/ adj. удобовари́мый.

digestion /dɪ'dʒɛstʃən/ n. пищеваре́ние neut.

digestive /dɪ'dʒɛstɪv, dai-/ adj. пищевари́тельный.

digger /'dɪgər/ n. копа́тель m.

digit /'dɪdʒɪt/ n. (numeral) ци́фра f.

digital /'dɪdʒɪt/ adj. пальцево́й.

digitalis /‚dɪdʒɪ'tælɪs/ n. наперстя́нка f., дигита́лис m.

digitate /'dɪdʒɪ‚teit/ adj. (bot.) па́льчатый.

diglot /'daiglɒt/ adj. двуязы́чный.

dignified /'dɪgnə‚faid/ adj. досто́йный, ва́жный.

dignify /'dɪgnə‚fai/ v. придава́ть досто́инство impf.

dignitary /'dɪgnɪ‚tɛri/ n. высокопоста́вленное лицо́ neut.

dignity /'dɪgnɪti/ n. досто́инство neut.

digraph /'daigræf/ n. дигра́ф m.

digress /dɪ'grɛs/ v. отступа́ть impf., отступи́ть pf.

digression /dɪ'grɛʃən/ n. отступле́ние neut.

digressive /dɪ'grɛsɪv/ adj. отступа́ющий.

dihedral /dai'hidrəl/ n. (aer.) у́гол попере́чного крыла́ m.

Dijon /di'ʒɔ̃/ n. Дижо́н m.

dike /daik/ n. да́мба, плоти́на f.

diktat /dɪk'tɑt/ n. дикта́т m.

dilapidated /dɪ'læpɪ‚deitid/ adj. ве́тхий; полуразру́шенный, полуразвали́вшийся; (ramshackle) обветша́лый.

dilapidation /dɪ‚læpɪ'deiʃən/ n. ве́тхость f.

dilatancy /dɪ'leitnsi/ n. растяжи́мость f.

dilatant /dɪ'leitnt/ adj. расширя́ющий.

dilate /dai'leit/ v. расширя́ть(ся) impf.

dilation /dai'leiʃən/ n. расшире́ние neut.

dilatometer /‚dilə'tɒmɪtər/ n. дилато́метр m.

dilator /dai'leitər/ n. (surg.) расшири́тель m.

dilemma /dɪ'lɛmə/ n. диле́мма f.

dilettante /'dɪlɪ‚tɑnt/ n. дилета́нт, люби́тель m.

dilettantism /'dɪlɪtən‚tɪzəm/ n. дилета́нтство neut.

diligence /'dɪlɪdʒəns/ n. прилежа́ние, усе́рдие neut.; (coach) дилижа́нс m.

diligent /'dɪlɪdʒənt/ adj. приле́жный.

dill /dɪl/ n. укро́п m.

diluent /'dɪlyuənt/ n. разбави́тель m.

dilute /dɪ'lut/ v. разбавля́ть impf., разба́вить pf.

diluted /dɪ'lutɪd/ adj. разба́вленный.

dilution /dɪ'luʃən/ n. разведе́ние, разбавле́ние neut.; (solution) раство́р m.

diluvial /dɪ'luviəl/ adj. дилювиа́льный.

dim /dɪm/ **1.** adj. ту́склый. **2.** v. де́лать ту́склым impf.

dime /daim/ n. (Am. coin) (моне́та в) де́сять це́нтов.

dimension /dɪ'mɛnʃən/ n. измере́ние neut.

dimensional /dɪ'mɛnʃənl/ adj. простра́нственный.

dimerous /'dɪmərəs/ adj. двучле́нный.

dimethyl /dai'mɛθəl/ n. димети́ловый.

diminish /dɪ'mɪnɪʃ/ v.t. уменьша́ть impf., уме́ньшить pf.; v.i. уменьша́ться impf., уме́ньшиться pf.

diminuendo /dɪ‚mɪnyu'ɛndou/ n. диминуэ́ндо neut. indecl.

diminution /‚dɪmə'nuʃən/ n. уменьше́ние neut.; (lowering) пониже́ние neut.

diminutive /dɪ'mɪnyətɪv/ adj. (gram.) уменьши́тельный.

dimmer /'dɪmər/ n. (elec.) затемни́тель m.

dimness /'dɪmnɪs/ n. ту́склость; нея́сность; ту́пость f.

dimorphic /dai'mɔrfɪk/ adj. димо́рфный.

dimple /'dɪmpəl/ n. я́мочка f.

dimwit /'dɪm,wɪt/ n. (colloq.) дура́к m.

dimwitted /'dɪm'wɪtɪd/ adj. тупо́й.

din /dɪn/ n. гро́хот, шум m.

dinar /dɪ'nɑr/ n. дина́р m.

dine /dain/ v. обе́дать impf., пообе́дать pf.

diner /'dainər/ n. ваго́н-рестора́н m.

ding /dɪŋ/ **1.** n. звон m. **2.** v. звене́ть impf.

ding-dong /'dɪŋ,dɔŋ/ n. динь-до́н m.

dinghy /'dɪŋgi/ n. я́лик m.

dinginess /'dɪndʒɪnɪs/ n. ту́склость f.

dingle /'dɪŋgəl/ n. лесна́я лощи́на f.

dingo /'dɪŋgou/ n. ди́нго m. indecl.

dingy /'dɪndʒi/ adj. ту́склый; гря́зный; убо́гий; обтрёпанный.

dining car /'dainɪŋ/ n. ваго́н-рестора́н m.

dining room n. столо́вая f.

dining table n. обе́денный стол m.

dinner /'dɪnər/ n. обе́д m.

dinner-bell /'dɪnər,bɛl/ n. звоно́к к обе́ду m.

dinner party n. зва́ный обе́д m.

dinosaur /'dainə,sɔr/ n. диноза́вр m.

dinothere /'dainə,θiər/ n. динотéрий m.

diocesan /dai'nsəsən/ n. епи́скоп m.

diocese /'daiəsɪs, -,siz/ n. епа́рхия f.

diode /'daioud/ n. дио́д m.

dioecious /dai'iʃəs/ adj. (bot.) двудо́мный.

diopside /dai'npsaid/ n. диопси́д m.

dioptase /dai'npteis/ n. диопта́з m.

diopter /dai'nptər/ n. дио́птр m.

dioptric /dai'nptrɪk/ adj. диоптри́ческий.

diorama /,daiə'ræmə/ n. диора́ма f.

dioxide /dai'nksaid/ n. двуо́кись f.

dip /dɪp/ **1.** n. погруже́ние neut. **2.** v. погружа́ть(ся), окуна́ть(ся) (в with acc.) impf.

diphase /'dai,feiz/ adj. двухфа́зный.

diphtheria /dɪf'θɪəriə, dɪp-/ n. дифтери́я f., дифтери́т m.

diphthong /'dɪfθɔŋ/ n. дифто́нг m.

diphthongal /dɪf'θɔŋgəl/ adj. дифтонги́ческий.

diphthongization /,dɪfθɔŋgə'zeiʃən/ n. дифтонгиза́ция f.

diplegia /dai'plidʒə/ n. диплеги́я f.

diplodocus /dɪ'plɒdəkəs/ n. диплодо́к m.

diploid /'dɪplɔid/ n. диплóид m.

diploma /dɪ'ploumə/ n. дипло́м m.

diplomacy /dɪ'ploumɒsi/ n. дипломáтия f.

diplomat /'dɪplə,mæt/ n. диплома́т m.

diplomatic /,dɪplə'mætɪk/ adj. дипломати́ческий.

diplomatics /,dɪplə'mætɪks/ n. дипломáтика f.

dip needle n. буссо́ль наклоне́ния f.

dipnoan /'dɪpnouən/ adj. двоякоды́шащий.

dipolar /dai'poulər/ adj. име́ющий два по́люса.

dipole /'dai,poul/ n. дипóль f.

dipper /'dɪpər/ n. (ladle) ковш m.; **Big Dipper** n. (astr.) Больша́я Медвéдица m.

dipsomania /,dɪpsə'meiniə/ n. алкоголи́зм m.

dipsomaniac /,dɪpsə'meini,æk/ n. алкого́лик m.

dipstick /'dɪp,stɪk/ n. измери́тельный шток m.

Diptera /'dɪptərə/ n. двукры́лые насеко́мые pl.

dipterous /'dɪptərəs/ adj. двукры́лый.

diptych /'dɪptɪk/ n. ди́птих m.

dire /daiᵊr/ adj. ужа́сный, стра́шный.

direct /dɪ'rɛkt/ **1.** adj. прямо́й; непосрéдственный. **2.** v. направля́ть impf., напра́вить pf.; руководи́ть impf.; **direct current** n. постоя́нный ток m.

direction /dɪ'rɛkʃən/ n. направле́ние neut.; (management) управле́ние neut., руково́дство neut.

directional /dɪ'rɛkʃənl/ adj. напра́вленный.

direction-finder /dɪ'rɛkʃən ,faindər/ n. радиопеленга́тор m.

directive /dɪ'rɛktɪv/ n. директи́ва f.

directly /dɪ'rɛktli/ adv. пря́мо, непосрéдственно.

directness /dɪ'rɛktnɪs/ n. прямота́; непосрéдственность f.

director /dɪ'rɛktər/ n. дирéктор, руководи́тель m.; (theat.) режиссёр m.

directorate /dɪ'rɛktərɪt/ n. управле́ние neut.

directorial /dɪrɛk'tɔriəl/ adj. дирéкторский; директи́вный.

directorship /dɪ'rɛktər,ʃɪp/ n. дирéкторство neut.

directory /dɪ'rɛktəri/ n. (book of directions) спра́вочник m.; (address book) áдресная кни́га f.; **file directory** (computer) n. фáйловый катаáог m.

directress /dɪ'rɛktrɪs/ n. директри́са f.

direful /'daiᵊrfəl/ adj. стра́шный, ужа́сный.

dirge /dɜrdʒ/ n. (funeral song) похоро́нная пéсня f.; (sad song) печа́льная пéсня f.

dirigible /'dɪridʒəbəl/ n. дирижа́бль m.

dirk /dɜrk/ n. кинжáл m.

dirt /dɜrt/ n. грязь f.; (soil) по́чва f.

dirtiness /'dɜrtinɪs/ n. грязь f.

dirty /'dɜrti/ adj. гря́зный.

disability /,dɪsə'bɪlɪti/ n. инвали́дность f.

disable /dɪs'eibəl/ v. выводи́ть из стро́я impf.

disabled /dɪs'eibəld/ adj. искалéченный.

disablement /dɪs'eibəlmənt/ n. нетрудоспосо́бность f.

disabuse /,dɪsə'byuz/ v. выводи́ть из заблужде́ния impf.

disaccord /,dɪsə'kɔrd/ n. разногла́сие neut.

disaccustom /,dɪsə'kʌstəm/ v. отуча́ть impf.

disadvantage /,dɪsəd'væntɪdʒ/ n. невы́года f., невы́годное положе́ние neut.

disadvantageous /dɪs,ædvən'teidʒəs/ adj. невы́годный, неблагоприя́тный.

disaffect /,dɪs'ə fɛkt/ v. вызыва́ть недово́льство impf.

disaffected /,dɪsə'fɛktɪd/ adj. недово́льный.

disagree /,dɪsə'gri/ v. не соглаша́ться impf., не согласи́ться pf.; расходи́ться во мне́ниях impf.

disagreeable /,dɪsə'griəbəl/ adj. неприя́тный.

disagreement /,dɪsə'grimənt/ n. расхожде́ние во мне́ниях; разногла́сие neut.

disappear /,dɪsə'piər/ v. исчеза́ть impf., исчéзнуть pf.

disappearance /,dɪsə'piərəns/ n. исчезнове́ние neut.

disappoint /,dɪsə'pɔint/ v. разочаро́вывать impf., разочарова́ть pf.

disappointment /,dɪsə'pɔintmənt/ n. разочарова́ние neut.

disapprobatory /,dɪsə'proubə,təri/ adj. неодобри́тельный.

disapproval /,dɪsə'pruvəl/ n. неодобре́ние neut.

disapprove /ˌdɪsə'pruv/ v. не одобря́ть impf.

disapproving /ˌdɪsə'pruvɪŋ/ adj. неодобри́тельный.

disarm /dɪs'ɑrm/ v.t. разоружа́ть impf., разоружи́ть pf.; v.i. разоружа́ться impf., разоружи́ться pf.

disarmament /dɪs'ɑrməmənt/ n. разоруже́ние neut.

disarrange /ˌdɪsə'reɪndʒ/ v. расстра́ивать impf.

disarray /ˌdɪsə'reɪ/ n. беспоря́док m., смяте́ние neut.

disarticulate /ˌdɪsɑr'tɪkyə,leɪt/ v. impf. расчленя́ть impf.

disarticulation /ˌdɪsɑr,tɪkyə'leɪʃən/ n. (surg.) ампута́ция че́рез суста́в f.

disassimilation /ˌdɪsə,sɪmə'leɪʃən/ n. катаболи́зм m.

disaster /dɪ'zæstər/ n. бе́дствие neut.

disastrous /dɪ'zæstrəs/ adj. бе́дственный, ги́бельный.

disavow /ˌdɪsə'vaʊ/ v. отрека́ться impf.

disavowal /ˌdɪsə'vaʊəl/ n. отрече́ние neut., отка́з m.; отрица́ние neut.; дезавуа́ция f.

disband /dɪs'bænd/ v. распуска́ть impf.

disbar /dɪs'bɑr/ v. лиша́ть зва́ния адвока́та impf.

disbelief /ˌdɪsbɪ'lif/ n. неве́рие neut.

disbud /dɪs'bʌd/ v. обреза́ть по́чки impf.

disburden /dɪs'bɜrdn̩/ v. освобожда́ть(ся) от тя́жести impf.

disburse /dɪs'bɜrs/ v. выпла́чивать impf.

disbursement /dɪs'bɜrsmənt/ n. выплата f.

discard /dɪ'skɑrd/ v. сбра́сывать impf., сбро́сить pf.

discern /dɪ'sɜrn/ v. различа́ть impf., различи́ть pf.

discernible /dɪ'sɜrnəbəl/ adj. различи́мый.

discerning /dɪ'sɜrnɪŋ/ adj. проница́тельный.

discernment /dɪ'sɜrnmənt/ n. проница́тельность f.

discharge /dɪs'tʃɑrdʒ/ v. выпуска́ть impf., вы́пустить pf.; выполня́ть impf., вы́полнить pf.

discharger /dɪs'tʃɑrdʒər/ n. (elec.) разря́дник m.

disciple /dɪ'saɪpəl/ v. (follower) учени́к, после́дователь m.; (apostle) апо́стол m.

disciplinarian /ˌdɪsəplə'nɛəriən/ n. сторо́нник дисципли́ны m.

disciplinary /'dɪsəplə,nɛri/ adj. исправи́тельный.

discipline /'dɪsəplɪn/ n. дисципли́на f.

disclaim /dɪs'kleɪm/ v. отрека́ться impf., отре́чься pf.

disclaimer /dɪs'kleɪmər/ n. отрече́ние neut.

disclose /dɪ'skloʊz/ v. обнару́живать impf., обнару́жить pf.

disclosure /dɪ'skloʊʒər/ n. откры́тие, обнаруже́ние neut.

disco /'dɪskoʊ/ n. дискоте́ка f.

discoidal /dɪs'kɔɪdl̩/ adj. дископодо́бный.

discolor /dɪs'kʌlər/ v. изменя́ть цвет impf.

discoloration /dɪs,kʌlə'reɪʃən/ n. обесцве́чивание neut.

discomfit /dɪs'kʌmfɪt/ v. (confuse) расстра́ивать; смуща́ть impf.

discomfiture /dɪs'kʌmfɪtʃər/ n. смуще́ние neut.

discomfort /dɪs'kʌmfərt/ n. неудо́бство neut.

discompose /ˌdɪskəm'poʊz/ v. расстра́ивать impf.

discomposure /ˌdɪskəm'poʊʒər/ n. беспоко́йство neut.

disconcert /ˌdɪskən'sɜrt/ v. смуща́ть impf.

disconnect /ˌdɪskə'nɛkt/ v. разъединя́ть impf., разъедини́ть pf.

disconnected /ˌdɪskə'nɛktɪd/ adj. бессвя́зный.

disconsolate /dɪs'kɒnsəlɪt/ adj. неуте́шный.

discontent /ˌdɪskən'tɛnt/ n. недово́льство neut.

discontented /ˌdɪskən'tɛntɪd/ adj. недово́льный.

discontinuation /ˌdɪskən,tɪnyu'eɪʃən/ n. прекраще́ние neut.

discontinue /ˌdɪskən'tɪnyu/ v. прерыва́ть impf., прерва́ть pf.

discontinuity /ˌdɪskɒntɪn'uɪti/ n. переры́в m.

discontinuous /ˌdɪskən'tɪnyuəs/ adj. преры́вистый; (sci., math.) разры́вный, дискре́тный.

discord /'dɪskɔrd/ n. разногла́сие neut.; (mus.) диссона́нс m.

discordant /dɪs'kɔrdnt/ adj. несогла́сный.

discotheque /'dɪskə,tɛk/ n. дискоте́ка f.

discount /'dɪskaunt/ n. ски́дка f.

discourage /dɪ'skɜrɪdʒ/ v. обескура́живать impf., обескура́жить pf.

discouragement /dɪ'skɜrɪdʒmənt/ n. обескура́женность f.

discourse /dɪs'kɔrs/ v. рассужда́ть (o with prep.) impf.

discourteous /dɪs'kɜrtiəs/ adj. неве́жливый, неучти́вый.

discourtesy /dɪs'kɜrtəsi/ n. неучти́вость f.

discover /dɪ'skʌvər/ v. открыва́ть impf., откры́ть pf.

discoverer /dɪ'skʌvərər/ n. открыва́тель m.

discovery /dɪ'skʌvəri/ n. откры́тие neut.

discredit /dɪs'krɛdɪt/ 1. n. позо́р m. 2. v. дискредити́ровать impf.

discreditable /dɪs'krɛdɪtəbəl/ adj. позо́рный.

discreet /dɪ'skrit/ adj. осмотри́тельный.

discrepancy /dɪ'skrɛpənsi/ n. расхожде́ние, несхо́дство neut.

discrepant /dɪ'skrɛpənt/ adj. противоречи́вый.

discrete /dɪ'skrit/ adj. (math) дискре́тный; (bot.) разде́льный.

discretion /dɪ'skrɛʃən/ n. осмотри́тельность f.

discretionary /dɪ'skrɛʃə,nɛri/ adj. дискрецио́нный.

discriminate /dɪ'skrɪm,əneɪt/ v. дискримини́ровать impf.

discriminating /dɪ'skrɪmə,neɪtɪŋ/ adj. отличи́тельный; разбо́рчивый.

discrimination /dɪ,skrɪmə'neɪʃən/ n. дискримина́ция f.

discus /'dɪskəs/ n. диск m.

discuss /dɪ'skʌs/ v. обсужда́ть impf., обсуди́ть pf.

discussion /dɪ'skʌʃən/ n. диску́ссия f., обсужде́ние neut.

disdain /dɪs'deɪn/ n. (contempt) презре́ние (к with dat.) neut.; (haughtiness) надме́нность f.

disdainful /dɪs'deɪnfəl/ adj. пренебрежи́тельный.

disease /dɪ'ziz/ n. боле́знь f.

diseased /dɪ'zizd/ adj. (ill) больно́й; (infected) заражённый; (morbid) боле́зненный.

disembark /ˌdɪsɛm'bɑrk/ v. выса́живаться на бе́рег impf.

disembarkation /dɪs,ɛmbɑr'keɪʃən/ n. (of people) вы́садка f.; (of goods) вы́грузка f.

disembodied /ˌdɪsɛm'bɒdɪd/ adj. бестелéсный.

disembogue /ˌdɪsɛm'boug/ v. вливáться impf.

disembowel /ˌdɪsɛm'bauəl/ v. потрошúть impf.

disenchant /ˌdɪsɛn'tʃænt/ v. (disappoint) разочарóвывать impf.; (disillusion) освобождáть от иллю́зий impf.

disencumber /ˌdɪsɛn'kʌmbər/ v. освобождáть от брéмени impf.

disengage /ˌdɪsɛn'geidʒ/ v. освобождáться impf.

disengagement /ˌdɪsɛn'geidʒmənt/ n. освобождéние neut.

disentangle /ˌdɪsɛn'tæŋɡəl/ v. распу́тывать(ся), выпу́тывать(ся) impf.

disentitle /ˌdɪsɛn'taitl̩/ v. лишáть прáва impf.

disentomb /ˌdɪsɛn'tum/ v. выкáпывать из могúлы.

disequilibrium /dɪsˌikwə'lɪbriəm/ n. потéря равновéсия f.

disestablish /ˌdɪsɪ'stæblɪʃ/ v. (church) отделя́ть (цéрковь от госудáрства) impf.; (cancel) отменя́ть impf.

disesteem /ˌdɪsɪ'stim/ **1.** n. неуважéние neut. **2.** v. нúзко оцéнивать impf.

disfavor /dɪs'feivər/ **1.** n. неодобрéние neut. **2.** v. относúться с неодобрéнием impf.

disfigure /dɪs'fɪɡyər/ v. обезобрáживать impf., обезобрáзить pf.

disfigurement /dɪs'fɪɡyərmənt/ n. обезобрáживание; искажéние neut.

disfranchise /dɪs'fræntʃaiz/ v. лишáть граждáнских прав impf.

disgorge /dɪs'ɡɔrdʒ/ v. (from throat) изрыгáть impf.; (eject) выбрáсывать impf., изверга́ть impf.; (of river) впадáть (в with acc.) impf.

disgrace /dɪs'greis/ **1.** n. бесчéстие neut., позóр m. **2.** v. позóрить impf.

disgraceful /dɪs'greisfəl/ adj. бесчéстный, позóрный.

disgruntled /dɪs'ɡrʌntl̩d/ adj. недовóльный.

disguise /dɪs'gaiz/ **1.** n. маскирóвка f. **2.** v. маскировáть impf., замаскировáть pf.

disgust /dɪs'ɡʌst/ **1.** n. отвращéние neut. **2.** v. внушáть отвращéние impf.

disgusting /dɪs'ɡʌstɪŋ/ adj. отвратúтельный, гну́сный, протúвный.

dish /dɪʃ/ n. посу́да f.; (food) блю́до neut.

dishabille /ˌdɪsə'bil/ n. дезабилье́ neut. indecl.

dishabituate /ˌdɪshə'bɪtʃu,eit/ v. отучáть impf.

disharmonious /ˌdɪshɑr'mouniəs/ adj. дисгармонúчный.

disharmonize /dɪs'hɑrmə,naiz/ v. нарушáть гармóнию impf.

disharmony /dɪs'hɑrməni/ n. дисгармóния f.

dishcloth /'dɪʃ,klɔθ/ n. тря́пка для мытья́ посу́ды f., ку́хонное полотéнце neut.

dishearten /dɪs'hɑrtn̩/ v. приводúть в уны́ние impf.

dished /dɪʃt/ adj. вóгнутый.

disheveled /dɪ'ʃɛvəld/ adj. (hair) взъерóшенный; (person) растрёпанный.

dishonest /dɪs'ɒnɪst/ adj. нечéстный.

dishonesty /dɪs'ɒnəsti/ n. нечéстность f.

dishonor /dɪs'ɒnər/ v. бесчéстить impf., обесчéстить pf.

dishonorable /dɪs'ɒnərəbəl/ adj. бесчéстный.

dishtowel /'dɪʃ,tauəl/ n. посу́дное or ку́хонное полотéнце neut.

dishwasher /'dɪʃ,wɒʃər/ (person) судомóйка f.; (machine) посудомóечная машúна f.

dishwater /'dɪʃ,wɔtər/ n. помóи pl.

disillusion /ˌdɪsɪ'luʒən/ v. разочарóвывать impf., разочаровáть pf.

disincentive /ˌdɪsɪn'sɛntɪv/ n. расхолáживающий фáктор m.

disinclination /dɪsˌɪnklə'neiʃən/ n. неохóта f.

disincline /ˌdɪsɪn'klain/ v. отбивáть охóту impf.

disinfect /ˌdɪsɪn'fɛkt/ v. дезинфицúровать impf. and pf.

disinfectant /ˌdɪsɪn'fɛktənt/ n. дезинфицúрующее срéдство neut.

disinflation /ˌdɪsɪn'fleiʃən/ n. дефля́ция f.

disingenuous /ˌdɪsɪn'dʒɛnyuəs/ adj. нейскренний.

disinherit /ˌdɪsɪn'hɛrɪt/ v. лишáть наслéдства impf.

disinheritance /ˌdɪsɪn'hɛrɪtns̩/ n. лишéние наслéдства neut.

disintegrate /dɪs'ɪntə,greit/ v. распадáться, разрушáться, развáливаться, рассыпáться impf.

disintegration /dɪsˌɪntə'greiʃən/ n. распадéние neut.

disintegrator /dɪs'ɪntə,greitər/ n. дезинтегрáтор m.

disinter /ˌdɪsɪn'tɜr/ v. выкáпывать из могúлы impf.

disinterested /dɪs'ɪntə,rɛstɪd/ adj. бескоры́стный.

disjoin /dɪs'dʒɔin/ v. разъединя́ть impf.

disjoint /dɪs'dʒɔint/ v. расчленя́ть impf.

disjointed /dɪs'dʒɔintɪd/ (of speech) несвя́зный; (disorganized) беспоря́дочный.

disjunction /dɪs'dʒʌŋkʃən/ n. разъединéние neut.

disk /dɪsk/ n. диск m.

disk drive n. дúсковый накопúтель m.

diskette /dɪ'skɛt/ n. (computer) гúбкий микродúск m.

dislike /dɪs'laik/ **1.** n. нелюбóвь f. **2.** v. не любúть impf.

dislocate /'dɪslou,keit/ v. вы́вихнуть pf.

dislocation /ˌdɪslou'keiʃən/ n. вы́вих m.

dislodge /dɪs'lɒdʒ/ v. (remove) удаля́ть impf.; (displace) смещáть impf., сдвигáть с мéста impf.

disloyal /dɪs'lɔiəl/ adj. невéрный, веролóмный.

disloyalty /dɪs'lɔiəlti/ n. невéрность f., веролóмство neut.

dismal /'dɪzməl/ adj. мрáчный.

dismantle /dɪs'mæntl̩/ v. разбирáть (на чáсти) impf.; (tech.) демонтúровать impf.

dismast /dɪs'mæst/ v. сносúть мáчту impf.

dismay /dɪs'mei/ n. (alarm) тревóга f.; (discomfiture) смущéние neut.; (disappointment) разочарóвание neut.

dismember /dɪs'mɛmbər/ v. расчленя́ть impf.

dismiss /dɪs'mɪs/ v. отпускáть impf., отпустúть pf.

dismissal /dɪs'mɪsəl/ n. увольнéние neut.

dismount /dɪs'maunt/ v. слезáть impf.

disobedience /ˌdɪsə'bidiəns/ n. неповиновéние, непослушáние neut.

disobedient /ˌdɪsə'bidiənt/ adj. непослу́шный.

disobey /ˌdɪsə'bei/ v. не слу́шаться impf.

disoblige /ˌdɪsə'blaidʒ/ v. не угождáть impf.

disobliging /ˌdɪsə'blaidʒɪŋ/ adj. нелюбéзный.

disorder /dɪs'ɔrdər/ n. беспорядок m.

disorderly /dɪs'ɔrdərli/ adj. беспорядочный.

disorganization /dɪs,ɔrgənə'zeiʃən/ n. дезорганизация f.; беспорядок m.

disorganize /dɪs'ɔrgə,naiz/ v. приводить в беспорядок impf.; дезорганизовывать impf.

disorient /dɪs'ɔri,ɛnt/ v. дезориентировать; (fig.) сбивать с толку impf.

disown /dɪs'oun/ v. не признавать за своё impf.

disparage /dɪ'spærɪdʒ/ v. умалять impf.

disparagement /dɪ'spærɪdʒmənt/ n. умаление neut.

disparaging /dɪ'spærɪdʒɪŋ/ adj. пренебрежительный, унизительный, умаляющий.

disparate /'dɪspərɪt/ adj. различный.

disparity /dɪ'spærɪti/ n. разница f.

dispassionate /dɪs'pæʃənɪt/ adj. бесстрастный.

dispatch /dɪ'spætʃ/ 1. n. отправка; депеша f. 2. v. посылать impf., послать pf.

dispel /dɪ'spɛl/ v. разгонять impf., разогнать pf.

dispensable /dɪ'spɛnsəbəl/ adj. необязательный.

dispensation /,dɪspən'seiʃən/ n. раздача f.

dispensatory /dɪ'spɛnsə,tɔri/ n. фармакопея f.

dispense /dɪ'spɛns/ v. раздавать impf., распределять impf.

dispenser /dɪ'spɛnsər/ n. (med.) дозатор m.

dispeople /dɪs'pipəl/ v. обезлюдить pf.

dispersal /dɪ'spɜrsəl/ n. рассеивание neut.

disperse /dɪ'spɜrs/ v. рассеивать(ся) impf.

dispersed /dɪ'spɜrst/ adj. (chem.) дисперсный.

dispersion /dɪ'spɜrʒən/ n. рассеивание neut.; разбросанность f.

dispersive /dɪ'spɜrsɪv/ adj. рассеивающий.

dispirit /dɪ'spɪrɪt/ v. удручать impf.

dispirited /dɪ'spɪrɪtɪd/ adj. унылый, удручённый.

displace /dɪs'pleis/ v. смещать impf., сместить pf.

displaced /dɪs'pleist/ adj. смещённый, не на своём месте.

displacement /dɪs'pleismənt/ n. перемещение neut., перестановка f.; (sci.) смещение; вытеснение neut.

display /dɪ'splei/ 1. v. выставлять impf., выставить pf. 2. n. показ m., выставка f.

displease /dɪs'pliz/ v. (not please) не нравиться (with dat.) impf.; (annoy) раздражать impf.

displeasing /dɪs'plizɪŋ/ adj. неприятный; непривлекательный.

displeasure /dɪs'plɛʒər/ n. неудовольствие neut.

disport /dɪ'spɔrt/ v. развлекаться impf.

disposable /dɪ'spouzəbəl/ adj. (available) имеющийся в распоряжении; (throw-away) (одно-) разовый.

disposal /dɪ'spouzəl/ n. расположение neut.

dispose /dɪ'spouz/ v. (arrange) располагать impf., расставлять impf.; (incline, influence) располагать impf., склонять impf.

disposition /,dɪspə'zɪʃən/ n. диспозиция f.

dispossess /,dɪspə'zɛs/ v. лишать собственности impf.

dispraise /dɪs'preiz/ 1. n. порицание neut. 2. v. порицать impf.

disproof /dɪs'pruf/ n. опровержение neut.

disproportion /,dɪsprə'pɔrʃən/ n. непропорциональность f.

disproportionate /,dɪsprə'pɔrʃənɪt/ adj. непропорциональный.

disprove /dɪs'pruv/ v. доказывать ложность (with gen.) impf.

disputable /dɪ'spyutəbəl/ adj. спорный.

disputant /dɪ'spyutnt/ n. участник дискуссии m.

disputation /,dɪspyu'teiʃən/ n. (debate; defense of thesis) диспут m.; (discussion) дебаты pl.; (argument) спор m.

disputatious /,dɪspyu'teiʃəs/ adj. любящий спорить.

dispute /dɪ'spyut/ 1. n. диспут, спор m. 2. v. спорить impf.

disputed /dɪ'spyutɪd/ adj. (undecided) спорный; (contested) оспариваемый.

disqualification /dɪs,kwɒləfɪ'keiʃən/ n. дисквалификация f.

disqualify /dɪs'kwɒlə,fai/ v. дисквалифицировать impf. and pf.

disquiet /dɪs'kwaiɪt/ n. беспокойство neut.

disquieting /dɪs'kwaiɪtɪŋ/ adj. тревожный.

disquietude /dɪs'kwaiɪ,tud/ n. беспокойство neut.

disquisition /,dɪskwə'zɪʃən/ n. исследование neut.

disregard /,dɪsrɪ'gɑrd/ 1. n. невнимание neut. 2. v. игнорировать impf.

disrepair /,dɪsrɪ'pɛər/ n. ветхость f.

disreputable /dɪs'rɛpyətəbəl/ adj. пользующийся дурной репутацией.

disrepute /,dɪsrɪ'pyut/ n. плохая репутация f.; **to be in disrepute** v. иметь дурную репутацию impf.; **to bring into disrepute** v. навлекать дурную славу impf.

disrespect /,dɪsrɪ'spɛkt/ n. неуважение neut.

disrespectful /,dɪsrɪ'spɛktfəl/ adj. непочтительный.

disrobe /dɪs'roub/ v. раздевать(ся) impf.

disrupt /dɪs'rʌpt/ adj. нарушать impf., нарушить pf.

disruption /dɪs'rʌpʃən/ n. нарушение neut.

disruptive /dɪs'rʌptɪv/ adj. (fig.) подрывной.

dissatisfaction /,dɪssætɪs'fækʃən/ n. неудовлетворение neut.

dissatisfactory /,dɪssætɪs'fæktəri/ adj. неудовлетворительный.

dissatisfied /dɪs'sætɪs,faid/ adj. неудовлетворённый (with instr.); недовольный (with instr.).

dissatisfy /dɪs'sætɪs,fai/ v. не удовлетворять impf.

dissect /dɪ'sɛkt/ v. вскрывать impf., вскрыть pf.

dissecting /dɪ'sɛktɪŋ/ adj. анатомический.

dissection /dɪ'sɛkʃən/ n. вскрытие neut.; (elec.) разложение neut.

dissector /dɪ'sɛktər/ n. прозектор m.

dissemble /dɪ'sɛmbəl/ v. (hide) скрывать impf.; (pretend) притворяться impf.

dissembler /dɪ'sɛmblər/ n. притворщик, лицемер m.

disseminate /dɪ'sɛmə,neit/ v. распространять impf., распространить pf.

dissemination /dɪ,sɛmə'neiʃən/ n. разброс m.; распространение neut.

dissension /dɪ'sɛnʃən/ n. (disagreement) разногласие neut.; (discord) разлад m., раздоры pl.; **to sow discord** v. сеять раздор impf.

dissent /dɪ'sɛnt/ 1. n. разногласие neut. 2. v. расходиться во мнениях impf.

dissenter /dɪ'sɛntər/ n. (rel.) сектант m.; (pol.) диссидент m.

dissentient /dɪˈsɛnʃənt/ *adj.* инакомы́слящий.

dissertation /ˌdɪsərˈteɪʃən/ *n.* диссерта́ция *f.*

disservice /dɪsˈsɜrvɪs/ *n.* плоха́я услу́га *f.*

dissever /dɪˈsɛvər/ *v.* разъединя́ть(ся) *impf.*

dissidence /ˈdɪsɪdəns/ *n.* инакомы́слие *neut.*

dissident /ˈdɪsɪdənt/ **1.** *n.* диссиде́нт *m.* **2.** *adj.* диссиде́нтский.

dissimilar /dɪˈsɪmələr/ *adj.* несхо́дный.

dissimilarity /dɪˌsɪməˈlærɪti/ *n.* несхо́дство *neut.*

dissimilate /dɪˈsɪməˌleɪt/ *v.* (*ling.*) диссимили́ровать *impf.*

dissimilation /dɪˌsɪməˈleɪʃən/ *n.* (*ling.*) диссимиля́ция *f.*

dissimilatory /dɪˈsɪmələˌtɔri/ *adj.* (*ling.*) диссимиляти́вный.

dissipate /ˈdɪsəˌpeɪt/ *v.* расточа́ть *impf.*, расточи́ть *pf.*

dissipation /ˌdɪsəˈpeɪʃən/ *n.* расточе́ние *neut.*

dissipator /ˈdɪsəˌpeɪtər/ *n.* (*tech.*) гаси́тель *m.*

dissociable /dɪˈsouʃiəbəl/ *adj.* разде́льный.

dissocial /dɪˈsouʃəl/ *adj.* необщи́тельный.

dissociate /dɪˈsouʃiˌeɪt/ *v.* разъединя́ть; разобща́ть *impf.*

dissociation /dɪˌsousiˈeɪʃən/ *n.* разъедине́ние *neut.*; разобще́ние *neut.*

dissolubility /dɪˌsɒljəˈbɪlɪti/ *n.* раствори́мость *f.*

dissolute /ˈdɪsəˌlut/ *adj.* распу́щенный.

dissoluteness /ˈdɪsəˌlutnɪs/ *n.* распу́тство *neut.*

dissolution /ˌdɪsəˈluʃən/ *n.* растворе́ние; разложе́ние *neut.*

dissolvable /dɪˈzɒlvəbəl/ *adj.* раствори́мый.

dissolve /dɪˈzɒlv/ *v.* растворя́ть *impf.*, раствори́ть *pf.*; *v.i.* растворя́ться *impf.*, раствори́ться *pf.*

dissolvent /dɪˈzɒlvənt/ *n.* раствори́тель *m.* •

dissonance /ˈdɪsənəns/ *n.* (*mus.*) диссона́нс *m.*

dissonant /ˈdɪsənənt/ *adj.* (*mus.*) диссони́рующий, нестро́йный; (*at variance*) ста́лкивающийся, противоречи́вый; (*disagreeing*) разногла́сный.

dissuade /dɪˈsweɪd/ *v.* отгова́ривать *impf.*, отговори́ть *pf.*

dissuasion /dɪˈsweɪʒən/ *n.* разубежде́ние *neut.*

dissuasive /dɪˈsweɪsɪv/ *adj.* разубежда́ющий.

dissymmetrical /ˌdɪsəˈmɛtrɪkəl/ *adj.* асимметри́чный; (*mirror-symmetric*) зерка́льно симметри́чный.

dissymmetry /dɪˈsɪmɪtri/ *n.* асимме́трия *f.*

distaff /ˈdɪstæf/ *n.* (*for spinning*) пря́лка *f.*; (*fig.*) **on the distaff side** по же́нской ли́нии.

distal /ˈdɪstl/ *adj.* (*biol.*) диста́льный.

distance /ˈdɪstəns/ *n.* расстоя́ние *neut.*; **at a distance** издалека́; **in the distance** вдали́.

distant /ˈdɪstənt/ *adj.* отдалённый.

distaste /dɪsˈteɪst/ *n.* отвраще́ние (к *with dat.*) *neut.*

distasteful /dɪsˈteɪstfəl/ *adj.* невку́сный.

distemper /dɪsˈtɛmpər/ *n.* расстро́йство *neut.*

distempered /dɪsˈtɛmpərd/ *adj.* расстро́енный.

distend /dɪˈstɛnd/ *v.* надува́ть(ся), раздува́ть(ся) *impf.*

distensible /dɪˈstɛnsəbəl/ *adj.* растяжи́мый.

distension /dɪˈstɛnʃən/ *n.* растяже́ние *neut.*

distich /ˈdɪstɪk/ *n.* дисти́х *m.*

distichous /ˈdɪstɪkəs/ *adj.* двуря́дный.

distill /dɪˈstɪl/ *v.* дистилли́ровать *impf. and pf.*

distillate /ˈdɪstlɪt/ *n.* дистилля́т *m.*

distillation /ˌdɪstlˈeɪʃən/ *n.* дистилля́ция *f.*

distillatory /dɪˈstɪləˌtɔri/ *adj.* очища́ющий.

distiller /dɪˈstɪlər/ *n.* виноку́р *m.*

distillery /dɪˈstɪləri/ *n.* виноку́ренный заво́д *m.*

distinct /dɪˈstɪŋkt/ *adj.* отчётливый.

distinction /dɪˈstɪŋkʃən/ *n.* отли́чие, разли́чие *neut.*

distinctive /dɪˈstɪŋktɪv/ *adj.* отличи́тельный.

distinctly /dɪˈstɪŋktli/ *adv.* я́сно, отчётливо; (*noticeably*) заме́тно.

distinctness /dɪˈstɪŋktnɪs/ *n.* я́сность, отчётливость *f.*

distinguish /dɪˈstɪŋgwɪʃ/ *v.* отлича́ть *impf.*, отличи́ть *pf.*; различа́ть *impf.*, различи́ть *pf.*

distinguishable /dɪˈstɪŋgwɪʃəbəl/ *adj.* различи́мый, отличи́мый.

distinguished /dɪˈstɪŋgwɪʃt/ *adj.* выдаю́щийся.

distinguishing /dɪˈstɪŋgwɪʃɪŋ/ *adj.* (*distinctive*) отличи́тельный; (*characteristic*) характе́рный.

distort /dɪˈstɔrt/ *v.* искривля́ть *impf.*, искриви́ть *pf.*

distortion /dɪˈstɔrʃən/ *n.* искаже́ние *neut.*; дефо́рмация *f.*

distract /dɪˈstrækt/ *v.* отвлека́ть *impf.*, отвле́чь *pf.*

distracted /dɪˈstræktɪd/ *adj.* отвлечённый; расстро́енный.

distraction /dɪˈstrækʃən/ *n.* отвлече́ние *neut.*; рассе́янность *f.*; (*madness*) бе́шенство *neut.*; (*amusement*) развлече́ние *neut.*

distrain /dɪˈstreɪn/ *v.* накла́дывать аре́ст на иму́щество *impf.*

distrainment /dɪˈstreɪnmənt/ *n.* о́пись иму́щества в обеспече́ние до́лга *f.*

distraught /dɪˈstrɔt/ *adj.* обезу́мевший (от *with gen.*).

distress /dɪˈstrɛs/ *n.* (*grief*) го́ре *neut.*; (*anxiety*) волне́ние *neut.*; (*suffering*) страда́ние *neut.*

distressed /dɪˈstrɛst/ *adj.* (*in trouble*) бе́дствующий; расстро́енный.

distressing /dɪˈstrɛsɪŋ/ *adj.* (*causing distress*) огорчи́тельный; (*pitiful*) печа́льный.

distributary /dɪˈstrɪbyəˌteri/ *n.* рука́в реки́ *m.*

distribute /dɪˈstrɪbyut/ *v.* раздава́ть *impf.*, разда́ть *pf.*

distribution /ˌdɪstrəˈbyuʃən/ *n.* разда́ча *f.*

distributive /dɪˈstrɪbyətɪv/ *adj.* распредели́тельный; (*gram.*) раздели́тельный.

distributor /dɪˈstrɪbyətər/ *n.* (*in engine*) распредели́тель зажига́ния *m.*

district /ˈdɪstrɪkt/ *n.* райо́н *m.*

distrust /dɪsˈtrʌst/ **1.** *n.* недове́рие *neut.* **2.** *v.* не доверя́ть.

distrustful /dɪsˈtrʌstfəl/ *adj.* недове́рчивый.

disturb /dɪˈstɜrb/ *v.* волнова́ть *impf.*, взволнова́ть *pf.*; беспоко́ить *impf.*

disturbance /dɪˈstɜrbəns/ *n.* беспоко́йство *neut.*; волне́ние *neut.*

disturbed /dɪˈstɜrbd/ *adj.* психи́чески больно́й.

disturbing /dɪˈstɜrbɪŋ/ *adj.* беспоко́ящий; трево́жный.

disunion /dɪsˈyunyən/ *n.* разъедине́ние *neut.*

disunite /ˌdɪsyuˈnaɪt/ *v.* разделя́ть; разъединя́ть(ся) *impf.*

disuse /dɪsˈyus/ *n.* неупотребле́ние *neut.*; **to fall into disuse** *v.* вы́йти из употребле́ния *impf.*

disyllabic /ˌdaɪsɪˈlæbɪk/ *adj.* двусло́жный.

ditch /dɪtʃ/ *n.* кана́ва *f.*, ров *m.*

ditcher /'dɪtʃər/ n. канавокопа́тель m.

ditchwater /'dɪtʃ‚wɔtər/ n. стоя́чая вода́ f.

dither /'dɪðər/ v. (tremble) дрожа́ть impf.; (be nervous) не́рвничать impf.; (be confused) смуща́ться impf.; (hesitate) колеба́ться impf., не реши́ться impf.

dithyramb /'dɪθə‚ræm/ n. дифира́мб m.

dithyrambic /‚dɪθə'ræmbɪk/ adj. дифирамби́ческий.

ditto /'dɪtou/ adv. то́ же; (same amount) сто́лько же; (of the same kind) тако́й же.

ditty /'dɪti/ n. частушка f.

diuresis /‚daiə'risɪs/ n. диуре́з m.

diuretic /‚daiə'rɛtɪk/ n. мочего́нное сре́дство neut.

diurnal /dai'ɜrnl/ adj. дневно́й; (astr., meteorol.) су́точный.

diva /'divə/ n. примадо́нна, ди́ва f.

divalent /dai'veilənt/ adj. двухвале́нтный.

divan /dɪ'væn/ n. дива́н m.

divaricate /dai'værəkɪt/ adj. разветвлённый.

dive /daiv/ 1. n. ныря́ние neut.; (swim.) прыжо́к m. 2. v. ныря́ть impf., нырну́ть pf.; (swim) пры́гать impf., пры́гнуть pf.

dive-bomb /'daiv ‚bɒm/ v. бомби́ть с пики́рования impf.

dive bomber n. пики́рующий бомбарди́ровщик m.

dive bombing n. бомбомета́ние с пики́рования neut.

diver /'daivər/ n. ныря́льщик m.

diverge /dɪ'vɜrdʒ/ v. расходи́ться; отклоня́ться, уклоня́ться от (with gen.) impf.

divergence /dɪ'vɜrdʒəns/ n. расхожде́ние, отклоне́ние neut.

divergent /dɪ'vɜrdʒənt/ adj. расходя́щийся.

diverse /dɪ'vɜrs/ adj. ра́зный.

diversification /dɪ‚vɜrsəfɪ'keiʃən/ n. разнообра́зность f; расшире́ние neut.

diversify /dɪ'vɜrsə‚fai/ v. (make varied) разнообра́зить impf.; (broaden) расширя́ть impf.

diversion /dɪ'vɜrʒən/ n. отклоне́ние; отвлече́ние neut.

diversity /dɪ'vɜrsɪti/ n. разнообра́зие; несхо́дство neut.

divert /dɪ'vɜrt/ v. отклоня́ть impf., отклони́ть pf.; отвлека́ть impf., отвле́чь pf.

diverting /dɪ'vɜrtɪŋ/ adj. заба́вный, развлека́тельный.

divertissement /dɪ'vɜrtɪsmənt/ n. (mus.) дивертисме́нт m.

divest /dɪ'vɛst/ v. лиша́ть (with gen.) impf.

divide /dɪ'vaid/ v. дели́ть impf., раздели́ть pf.

dividend /'dɪvɪ‚dɛnd/ n. дивиде́нд m.; (math.) дели́мое neut.

dividing /dɪ'vaidɪŋ/ adj. (tech.) дели́тельный.

dividing wall n. перегоро́дка f.

divination /‚dɪvə'neiʃən/ n. гада́ние neut., ворожба́ f.; предсказа́ние neut.

divinatory /dɪ'vɪnə‚təri/ adj. гада́тельный.

divine /dɪ'vain/ adj. боже́ственный.

diving /'daivɪŋ/ n. ныря́ние neut.; (sport) прыжки́ в во́ду pl.; (of submarine) погруже́ние neut.

diving suit n. скафа́ндр m.

divinity /dɪ'vɪnɪti/ n. (divine nature) боже́ственность f.; (god, deity) божество́ neut.

divisibility /dɪ‚vɪzə'bɪlɪti/ n. дели́мость f.

divisible /dɪ'vɪzəbəl/ adj. дели́мый; (math.) деля́щийся без оста́тка.

division /dɪ'vɪʒən/ n. разделе́ние neut., (math) деле́ние neut.; (department) отде́л m.

divisional /dɪ'vɪʒənl/ adj. райо́нный.

divisive /dɪ'vaisɪv/ adj. разлуча́ющий; раско́льнический.

divisor /dɪ'vaizər/ n. дели́тель m.

divorce /dɪ'vɔrs/ 1. n. разво́д m. 2. v. разводи́ться impf., развести́сь pf.

divorced /dɪ'vɔrst/ adj. разведённый.

divorcee /dɪvɔr'sei, -'si/ n. разведённый m., разведённая f.

divulge /dɪ'vʌldʒ/ v. разглаша́ть impf., разгласи́ть pf.

divulgement /dɪ'vʌldʒmənt/ n. разглаше́ние neut.

Dixieland /'dɪksi‚lænd/ n. (jazz) ди́ксиленд m.

dizziness /'dɪzinɪs/ n. головокруже́ние neut.

dizzy /'dɪzi/ adj. головокружи́тельный.

djinn /dʒɪn/ n. джинн m.

DNA n. (abbr. of deoxyribonucleic acid) ДНК indecl. f. (chem.) (abbr. of дезоксирибонуклеи́новая кислота́).

Dnepr /dnʲɛpr/ n. (river) Днепр m.

Dneprodzerzhinsk /‚nɛprou'dərʒɪnsk/ n. Днепродзержи́нск m.

Dnepropetrovsk /‚nɛproupɪ'trɔfsk/ n. Днепропетро́вск m.

do /du/ unstressed du, də/ v. де́лать impf., сде́лать pf.; **to do without** обходи́ться без impf.

do /dou/ n. (mus.) до neut. indecl.

docile /'dɒsəl/ adj. послу́шный, поко́рный.

docility /dɒ'sɪlɪti/ n. поко́рность f.

dock[1] /dɒk/ 1. n. док m., верфь f. 2. v. ста́вить су́дно в док impf.

dock[2] /dɒk/ n. (bot.) щаве́ль m

dockage /'dɒkɪdʒ/ n. постано́вка в док; стоя́нка в до́ке f.

docker /'dɒkər/ n. до́кер m.

docket /'dɒkɪt/ n. рее́стр m.

docking /'dɒkɪŋ/ n. (naut.) шварто́вка f.

dockmaster /'dɒk‚mæstər/ n. нача́льник до́ка m.

dockside /'dɒk‚said/ n. прича́л m.

dockyard /'dɒk‚yɑrd/ n. верфь f.

doctor /'dɒktər/ n. врач, до́ктор m.

doctorate /'dɒktərɪt/ n. до́кторская сте́пень f.

doctrinaire /‚dɒktrə'nɛər/ n. доктринёр m.

doctrinal /'dɒktrənl/ adj. доктрина́льный.

doctrine /'dɒktrɪn/ n. доктри́на f.

document / n. 'dɒkyəmənt; v. 'dɒkyə‚mɛnt/ 1. n. докуме́нт m., свиде́тельство neut. 2. v. документи́ровать impf. and pf.

documentary /‚dɒkyə'mɛntəri, -tri/ adj. документа́льный.

documentation /‚dɒkyəmɛn'teiʃən/ n. документа́ция f.

dodder[1] /'dɒdər/ n. повили́ка f.

dodder[2] /'dɒdər/ v. трясти́сь impf

dodecagon /dou'dɛkə‚gɒn/ n. двенадцатиуго́льник m.

dodecahedron /dou‚dɛkə'hidrən/ n. двенадцатигра́нник m.

dodecaphonic /dou‚dɛkə'fɒnɪk/ adj. додекафони́ческий.

dodge /dɒdʒ/ v. уклоня́ть(ся) от (with gen.),

увёртываться от (*with gen.*); увиливать от (*with gen.*) *impf.*

dodger /'dɒdʒər/ *n.* хитрец *m.*

dodgy /'dɒdʒi/ *adj.* (*colloq.*) увёртливый.

dodo /'doudou/ *n.* дронт *m.*

doe /dou/ *n.* (*deer*) оленуха *f.*; (*rabbit*) крольчиха *f.*

doer /'duər/ *n.* человек дела *m.*

doff /dɒf/ *v.* снимать *impf.*

dog /dɔg/ *n.* собака *f.*

dog collar *n.* ошейник *m.*

doge /doudʒ/ *n.* дож *m.*

dog-eat-dog /'dɔg it 'dɔg/ *adj.* беспощадный.

dogfish /'dɔg,fɪʃ/ *n.* небольшая акула *f.*

dogged /'dɔgɪd/ *adj.* упрямый.

doggedness /'dɔgɪdnɪs/ *n.* упрямство *neut.*

doggerel /'dɔgərəl/ *n.* вирши *pl.*

doggone /'dɔg'gɔn/ *adj.* (*slang*) проклятый.

doggy /'dɔgi/ *n.* собачка, собачонка *f.*

doghouse /'dɔg,haus/ *n.* собачья конура *f.*

dog lover *n.* собачник *m.*

dogma /'dɔgmə/ *n.* догма *f.*, догмат *m.*

dogmatic /dɔg'mætɪk/ *adj.* догматический.

dogmatism /'dɔgmə,tɪzəm/ *n.* догматизм *m.*

dogmatize /'dɔgmə,taiz/ *v.* догматизировать *impf.*

do-gooder /'du 'gudər/ *n.* навязчивый благодетель *m.*

dog paddle *v.* плавать собачкой *impf.*

dog rose *n.* шиповник *m.*

Dog Star *n.* Сириус *m.*

dog-tired /'dɔg 'taiᵊrd/ *adj.* усталый как собака.

dogtooth /'dɔg,tuθ/ *n.* клык *m.*

dogtooth violet *n.* дикая фиалка *f.*

dogtrot /'dɔg,trɒt/ *n.* рысца *f.*

dogwatch /'dɔg,wɒtʃ/ *n.* полувахта *f.*

dogwood /'dɔg,wud/ *n.* кизил, кизиль *m.*

doily /'dɔili/ *n.* салфеточка *f.*

do-it-yourself /'du ɪt tʃər'sɛlf/ *adj.* самодельный.

dole /doul/ *n.* пособие по безработице *neut.*; **to be on the dole** *v.* получать пособие *impf.*

doleful /'doulfəl/ *adj.* печальный, грустный.

dolichocephalic /,dɒlɪkousə'fælɪk/ *adj.* длинноголовый.

doll /dɒl/ *n.* кукла *f.*

dollar /'dɒlər/ *n.* доллар *m.*

dolly /'dɒli/ *n.* (*doll*) куколка *f.*; (*cart*) тележка *f.*

dollying in /'dɒlɪŋ/ *n.* наезд *m.*

dollying out *n.* отъезд *m.*

dolman /'doulmən/ *n.* доломан *m.*

dolmen /'doulmɛn/ *n.* дольмен *m.*

dolomite /'doulə,mait/ *n.* доломит *m.*

dolphin /'dɒlfɪn/ *n.* (*zool.*) дельфин *m.*

dolt /doult/ *n.* болван, дурак *m.*

domain /dou'mein/ *n.* имение; владение *neut.*; область, сфера *f.*

dome /doum/ *n.* купол *m.*

domed /doumd/ *adj.* куполообразный.

domestic /də'mɛstɪk/ *adj.* домашний.

domesticate /də'mɛstɪ,keit/ *v.* приручать, одомашнивать *impf.*

domesticated /də'mɛstɪ,keitɪd/ *adj.* ручной.

domesticity /,doumɛ'stɪsɪti/ *n.* семейная *or* домашняя жизнь *f.*

domicile /'dɒmə,sail/ *n.* местожительство *neut.*, (*leg.*) юридический адрес *m.*

dominance /'dɒmənəns/ *n.* влияние; господство *neut.*; (*predominance*) преобладание *neut.*

dominant /'dɒmənənt/ *adj.* господствующий, преобладающий.

dominate /'dɒmə,neit/ *v.* преобладать *impf.*; господствовать *impf.*

domination /,dɒmə'neiʃən/ *n.* преобладание *neut.*; господство *neut.*

dominical /də'mɪnɪkəl/ *adj.* господний.

Dominican /də'mɪnɪkən/ **1.** *n.* доминиканец *m.* **2.** *adj.* доминиканский.

dominion /də'mɪnjən/ *n.* доминион *m.*

domino /'dɒmə,nou/ *n.* домино *neut. indecl.*

Don /dɒn/ *n.* (*river*) Дон *m.*

don /dɒn/ *v.* надевать *impf.*

donate /'douneit/ *v.* дарить; жертвовать (*with dat.*) *impf.*

donation /dou'neiʃən/ *n.* дар *m.*, денежное пожертвование *neut.*

done /dʌn/ (*see also* **do**); (*finished*) оконченный, сделанный; (*cooked; ready*) готовый.

Donets /də'nɛts/ *n.* Донец *m.*

donkey /'dɒŋki, 'dɔŋ-, 'dʌŋ-/ *n.* осёл *m.*

donkey engine *n.* вспомогательный двигатель *m.*

donnish /'dɒnɪʃ/ *adj.* педантичный.

donor /'dounər/ *n.* жертвователь *m.*

doodle /'dudl/ *v.* машинально рисовать *impf.*

doom /dum/ **1.** *n.* гибель *f.* **2.** *v.* обрекать *impf.*, обречь *pf.*

doomed /dumd/ *adj.* обречённый.

doomsday /'dumz,dei/ *n.* день страшного суда *m.*

door /dɔr/ *n.* дверь *f.*; **out of doors** на (открытом) воздухе.

doorbell /'dɔr,bɛl/ *n.* (дверной) звонок *m.*

doorframe /'dɔr,freim/ *n.* дверная рама *f.*

doorman /'dɔr,mæn/ *n.* швейцар *m.*

doormat /'dɔr,mæt/ *n.* половик *m.*

door money *n.* плата за вход *f.*

doorplate /'dɔr,pleit/ *n.* дверная вывеска *f.*

doorpost /'dɔr,poust/ *n.* дверной косяк *m.*

doorstep /'dɔr,stɛp/ *n.* порог *m.*

door-to-door /'dɔr tə 'dɔr/ *adj.* поквартирный.

doorway /'dɔr,wei/ *n.* вход, дверной проём *m.*

dope /doup/ *n.* наркотик *m.*; (*colloq.*) дуралей *m.*

dopey /'doupi/ *adj.* (*slang*) под дурью, одурманенный наркотиками.

Doppelgänger /'dɒpəl,gæŋər/ *n.* двойник *m.*, второе я *neut. indecl.*

dormancy /'dɔrmənsi/ *n.* спячка *f.*

dormant /'dɔrmənt/ *adj.* дремлющий, бездействующий.

dormer /'dɔrmər/ *n.* слуховое окно *neut.*

dormitory /'dɔrmɪ,tɔri/ *n.* общежитие *neut.*

dormouse /'dɔr,maus/ *n.* соня *f.*

dorsal /'dɔrsəl/ *adj.* спинной.

dorsum /'dɔrsəm/ *n.* спина *f.*

dory /'dɔri/ *n.* (*fish*) солнечник *m.*; (*boat*) плоскодонная лодка *f.*

dosage /'dousɪdʒ/ *n.* дозировка *f.*

dose /dous/ *n.* доза *f.*

dosimeter /dou'sɪmɪtər/ *n.* дозиметр *m.*

dossier /'dɒsi,ei/ *n.* досье *neut. indecl.*

dot /dɒt/ *n.* точка *f.*

dotage /'doutɪdʒ/ *n.* сенильность *f.*

dote on /dout/ v. носи́ть на рука́х impf.
dotted /'dɒtɪd/ adj. с то́чкой; (pattern) в горо́шек, в кра́пинку.
dotterel /'dɒtərəl/ n. ржа́нка f.
double /'dʌbəl/ **1.** adj. двойно́й, двойственный. **2.** n. двойни́к. **3.** v. удва́ивать impf., удво́ить pf.
double- двух-, дву-.
double-acting /'dʌbəl 'æktɪŋ/ adj. двойно́го действия.
double-banked /'dʌbəl 'bæŋkt/ adj. (tech.) двухря́дный.
double-barrelled /ˌdʌbəl 'bærəld/ adj. двуство́льный.
double-bass /ˌdʌbəl 'beis/ n. контраба́с m.
double boiler n. (cul.) двойна́я кастрю́ля f.
double-breasted /'dʌbəl 'brestɪd/ adj. двубо́ртный.
double-check /'dʌbəl 'tʃɛk/ v. перепроверя́ть impf.
double-dealer /'dʌbəl 'dilər/ n. двуру́шник m.
double-dealing /'dʌbəl 'dilɪŋ/ n. двуру́шничество neut.
double-decker /'dʌbəl 'dɛkər/ n. двухэта́жный авто́бус m.
double Dutch n. тараба́рщина f.
double-edged /'dʌbəl 'ɛdʒd/ adj. обоюдоо́стрый.
double entendre /'dʌbəl ɑn'tɑndrə, -'tɑnd/ n. двусмы́сленность f.
double entry n. (bookkeep.) двойна́я бухга́лтерия f.
double-faced /'dʌbəl ˌfeist/ adj. двусторо́нний.
double-headed /'dʌbəl ˌhɛdɪd/ adj. двухголо́вый, двугла́вый.
double-jointed /'dʌbəl 'dʒɔintɪd/ adj. необыкнове́нно ги́бкий.
double-natured /'dʌbəl 'neitʃərd/ adj. двойственный.
double-quick /'dʌbəl 'kwɪk/ adj. о́чень бы́стрый.
doubler /'dʌblər/ n. (tech.) удвои́тель m.
double-sided /'dʌbəl 'saidɪd/ adj. двухсторо́нний.
double-spaced /'dʌbəl ˌspeist/ adj. напеча́танный че́рез стро́чку.
doublet /'dʌblɪt/ n. (garment) камзо́л m.
double throw adj. (tech.) перекидно́й.
double-tongued /'dʌbəl 'tʌŋd/ adj. лжи́вый.
double-track /'dʌbəl 'træk/ adj. двухколе́йный.
doubling /'dʌblɪŋ/ n. удвое́ние neut.
doubloon /dʌ'blun/ n. дубло́н m.
doubly /'dʌbli/ adv. вдвойне́, вдво́е.
doubt /daut/ **1.** n. сомне́ние neut. **2.** v. сомнева́ться impf.
doubtful /'dautfəl/ adj. сомни́тельный.
doubting Thomas /'dautɪŋ 'tɒməs/ n. Фома́ Неве́рующий m.
doubtless /'dautlɪs/ adj. несомне́нный.
douche /duʃ/ **1.** n. подмыва́ние neut. **2.** v. подмыва́ть(ся) impf.
dough /dou/ n. (cul.) те́сто neut.; (slang) (money) де́нежки, гро́ши pl.
doughnut /'dounət/ n. по́нчик m., пы́шка f.
doughtily /'dautəli/ adv. отва́жно.
doughty /'dauti/ adj. отва́жный.
doughy /'doui/ adj. (like dough) тестообра́зный; (undercooked) недопечённый.

dour /dur, dauər/ adj. мра́чный; угрю́мый (stern) стро́гий, суро́вый.
douse /daus/ v. (drench) облива́ть водо́й; (dip) окуна́ть в во́ду; (naut.) бы́стро спуска́ть па́рус; (colloq.) (put out) гаси́ть (свет) impf.
dove /dʌv/ n. го́лубь m.
dovecot /'dʌvˌkɒt/ n. голубя́тня f.
Dover /'douvər/ n. Дувр (U.K.) m.; До́вер (U.S.) m.
dovetail /'dʌvˌteil/ n. (tech.) ла́сточкин хвост m.
dowager /'dauədʒər/ n. (queen, duchess) вдо́вствующая короле́ва f.; (colloq.) матро́на f.
dowdily /'daudli/ adv. неря́шливо.
dowel /'dauəl/ n. (peg) шип, штырь m.; (pin) шпо́нка f.
down /daun/ adv. (dir.) вниз; (loc.) внизу́, в ни́жнем этаже́.
downbeat /'daunˌbit/ adj. (colloq.) мра́чный.
downcast /'daunˌkæst/ **1.** n. вентиляцио́нная ша́хта f. **2.** adj. пода́вленный, уны́лый.
down draft n. нисходя́щий пото́к m.
downgrade /'daunˌgreid/ v. укло́н m.
downhearted /'daunˈhɑrtɪd/ adj. упа́вший ду́хом.
downhill /'daunˈhɪl/ adv. вниз, под го́ру.
downloading /'daunˌloudɪŋ/ n. (computer) за́грузка "вниз" f.
downplay v. умаля́ть impf.
downright /'daunˌrait/ adj. (frank) прямо́й; (utter) соверше́нный; (unmistakable) я́вный.
downrightness /'daunˌraitnɪs/ n. прямоду́шие neut.
downstream /'daunˈstrim/ adv. вниз по тече́нию.
downthrow /'daunˈθrou/ n. (geol.) опуска́ние neut.
downtown /'daunˈtaun/ n. делово́й центр (го́рода) m.
downtrend /'daunˌtrɛnd/ n. тенде́нция к пониже́нию f.
downtrodden /'daunˌtrɒdn/ adj. расто́птанный; угнетённый, по́пранный.
downturn /'daunˌtərn/ n. спад m.
downward /'daunwərd/ adv. вниз.
downwash /'daunˌwɒʃ/ n. (aero.) скос пото́ка m.
downy /'dauni/ adj. пуши́стый.
dowry /'dauri/ n. прида́ное neut.
dowser /'dauzər/ n. лозоиска́тель m.
dowsing rod /'dauzɪŋ/ n. волше́бная лоза́ f.
doze /douz/ v. дрема́ть impf.
dozen /'dʌzən/ n. дю́жина f.
dozy /'douzi/ adj. со́нный, дре́млющий.
drab /dræb/ n. (cloth) гру́бая шерстяна́я ткань f.
drabble /'dræbəl/ v. замочи́ть(ся) impf.
drabness /'dræbnɪs/ n. се́рость f.
drachma /'drækmə, 'drɑk-/ n. дра́хма f.
Draco /'dreikou/ n. Драко́н m.
Draconian /drei'kouniən, drə-/ adj. драко́новский.
draff /dræf/ n. барда́ f.; по́йло neut.; (fig.) подо́нки pl.
draft /dræft/ **1.** n. (sketch) чертёж, рису́нок, эски́з m.; (mil.) призы́в в а́рмию m. **2.** v. де́лать чертёж; составля́ть план; (mil.) призыва́ть в а́рмию impf.
draft board n. ша́шечная доска́ f.
draftsman /'dræftsmən/ n. (one who makes drawings) чертёжник m.; (designer) констру́ктор m.;

(*one who draws up documents, etc.*) составитель *m.*

draftsmanship /'dræftsmən‚ʃɪp/ *n.* искусство черчения *neut.*

drafty /'dræfti/ *adj.*: **it is drafty here** здесь сквозняк *or* сквозит.

drag /dræg/ *v.t.* тянуть; тащить *impf.*; *v.i.* тянуться *impf.*; тащиться *impf.*

draggle /'drægəl/ *v.* волочить(ся) *impf.*

dragline /'dræg‚laɪn/ *n.* драглайн *m.*

dragnet /'dræg‚nɛt/ *n.* бредень *m.*

dragoman /'drægəmən/ *n.* драгоман *m.*

dragon /'drægən/ *n.* (*myth.*, *zool.*) дракон *m.*

dragonfly /'drægən‚flaɪ/ *n.* стрекоза *f.*

dragoon /drə'gun/ *n.* драгун *m.*

drain /dreɪn/ **1.** *n.* канава *f.*, дренажная труба *f.* **2.** *v.* дренировать *impf. and pf.*

drainage /'dreɪnɪdʒ/ *n.* дренаж *m.*, осушение *neut.*

draining board /'dreɪnɪŋ/ *n.* сушильная доска *f.*

drainpipe /'dreɪn‚paɪp/ *n.* водосточная труба *f.*

drake /dreɪk/ *n.* (*bird*) селезень *m.*

dram /dræm/ *n.* драхма *f.*

drama /'drɑmə, 'dræmə/ *n.* драма *f.*

dramatic /drə'mætɪk/ *adj.* драматический.

dramatically /drə'mætɪkli/ *adv.* драматически.

dramatics /drə'mætɪks/ *n.* драматическое искусство *neut.*

dramatis personae /'dræmətɪs pər'souni/ *n.* действующие лица *pl.*

dramatist /'dræmətɪst/ *n.* драматург *m.*

dramatization /‚dræmətə'zeɪʃən/ *n.* драматизация *f.*

dramatize /'dræmə‚taɪz/ *v.* инсценировать, драматизировать *impf. and pf.*

drape /dreɪp/ *n.* (*hangings*) драпировка *f.*; (*curtains*) занавес *m.*

draper /'dreɪpər/ *n.* торговец тканями *m.*

drapery /'dreɪpəri/ *n.* (*hangings*) драпировка *f.*; (*cloth*) ткани *pl.*; (*shop*) магазин тканей *m.*

drastic /'dræstɪk/ *adj.* решительный.

drastically /'dræstɪkli/ *adv.* резко, круто.

Drava /'drɑvə/ *n.* (*river*) Драва *f.*

Dravidian /drə'vɪdiən/ *adj.* дравидский.

draw /drɔ/ **1.** *v.t.* черпать *impf.*; (*sketch*) рисовать *impf.*, нарисовать *pf.* **2.** (*games*) **in a draw** вничью *adv.*

drawback /'drɔ‚bæk/ *n.* недостаток *m.*

drawbar /'drɔ‚bɑr/ *n.* (*tech*) тяговый стержень *m.*

drawbridge /'drɔ‚brɪdʒ/ *n.* подъёмный мост *m.*

drawee /drɔ'i/ *n.* трассат *m.*

drawer /drɔr/ *n.* ящик *m.*

drawing /'drɔɪŋ/ *n.* рисунок *m.*

drawing room *n.* гостиная *f.*

drawknife /'drɔ‚naɪf/ *n.* струг *m.*

drawl /drɔl/ **1.** *n.* протяжное произношение *neut.* **2.** *v.* тянуть *impf.*

drawn /drɔn/ *adj.* изможденный.

dray /dreɪ/ *n.* телега *f.*

drayman /'dreɪmən/ *n.* ломовой извозчик *m.*

dread /drɛd/ **1.** *n.* страх *m.* **2.** *v.* бояться *impf.*

dreadful /'drɛdfəl/ *adj.* ужасный, страшный.

dreadfully /'drɛdfəli/ *adv.* ужасно.

dreadnought /'drɛd‚nɔt/ *n.* (*nav.*) дредноут *m.*

dream /drim/ **1.** *n.* мечта *f.* **2.** *v.* мечтать *impf.*

dreamer /'drimər/ *n.* мечтатель *m.*

dreamily /'driməli/ *adv.* мечтательно.

dreamland /'drim‚lænd/ *n.* мир грёз *m.*

dreamless /'drimlɪs/ *adj.* без сновидений.

dreamy /'drimi/ *adj.* мечтательный; (*absentmindedly*) рассеянный; (*dreamlike*) сказочный; (*vague*) неясный.

drearily /'drɪərəli/ *adv.* угрюмо, мрачно, скучно.

dreary /'drɪəri/ *adj.* мрачный; скучный.

dredge /drɛdʒ/ **1.** *n.* драга, землечерпалка *f.* **2.** *v.* драгировать *impf. and pf.*

dredging /'drɛdʒɪŋ/ *n.* дноуглубительные работы *pl.*

dregs /drɛgz/ *n.* отбросы *pl.*; осадок *m.*

drench /drɛntʃ/ *v.* промачивать насквозь *impf.*

Dresden /'drɛzdən/ *n.* (*china*) дрезденский фарфор *m.*

dress /drɛs/ **1.** *n.* платье *neut.*, (*attire*) одежда *f.* **2.** *v.t.* одевать *impf.*, одеть *pf.*; *v.i.* одеваться *impf.*, одеться *pf.*; **to dress up** наряжать(ся) *impf.*, нарядить(ся) *pf.*

dressage /drə'sɑʒ/ *n.* выездка *f.*

dresser /'drɛsər/ *n.* (*chest of drawers*) комод *m.*; (*theat.*) костюмер *m.*

dressing /'drɛsɪŋ/ *n.* (*med.*) перевязочное средство *neut.*; (*cooking*) приправа *f.*

dressing case *n.* несессер *m.*

dressing gown *n.* халат *m.*

dressing room *n.* гримёрная *f.*

dressing station *n.* перевязочный пункт *m.*

dressing table *n.* туалетный столик *m.*

dressmaker /'drɛs‚meɪkər/ *n.* портниха *f.*

dressmaking /'drɛs‚meɪkɪŋ/ *n.* шитьё (женской одежды) *neut.*

dressy /'drɛsi/ *adj.* шикарный, нарядный.

dribble /'drɪbəl/ *v.* (*flow in drips*) капать; (*salivate*) пускать слюни *impf.*

driblet /'drɪblɪt/ *n.* капелька *f.*

dribs and drabs /'drɪbz ən 'dræbz/ (*n.*:) **in dribs and drabs** мало-помалу.

dried /draɪd/ *adj.* (*of foods*) сушёный.

drift /drɪft/ **1.** *n.* течение *neut.*; (*ocean*) дрейф *m.* **2.** *v.* сноситься ветром *or* водой; плыть по течению *impf.*

driftage /'drɪftɪdʒ/ *n.* снос *m.*

drift anchor *n.* плавучий якорь *m.*

drifter /'drɪftər/ *n.* (*person*) никчёмный человек *m.*; (*tramp*) бродяга *m. and f.* (*decl. f.*).

drift ice *n.* дрейфующий лёд *m.*

drifting /'drɪftɪŋ/ *n.* дрейф *m.*

drift net *n.* плавная сеть *f.*

driftpin /'drɪft‚pɪn/ *n.* бородок *m.*

drift-way /'drɪft ‚weɪ/ *n.* штольня *f.*

driftwood /'drɪft‚wʊd/ *n.* плавник *m.*

drill[1] /drɪl/ **1.** *n.* (*exercise*) упражнение *neut.*, тренировка *f.*; (*tool*) сверло *neut.* **2.** *v.* (*train*) тренировать *impf.*; (*mech.*) сверлить *impf.*

drill[2] /drɪl/ *n.* (*fabric*) тик *m.* **2.** *adj.* тиковый.

drillbook /'drɪl‚bʊk/ *n.* строевой устав *m.*

driller /'drɪlər/ *n.* сверловщик *m.*

drill hall *n.* манеж *m.*

drill hole *n.* буровая скважина *f.*

drilling /'drɪlɪŋ/ *n.* муштровка *f.*

drill sergeant *n.* сержант-инструктор по строю *m.*

Drina /'drinə/ *n.* (*river*) Дрина *f.*

drink /drɪŋk/ **1.** *n.* питьё *neut.*, напиток *m.* **2.** *v.* пить *impf.*, выпить *pf.*

drinkable /'drɪŋkəbəl/ *adj.* го́дный для питья́.
drinker /'drɪŋkər/ *n.* пью́щий *m.*
drinking /'drɪŋkɪŋ/ *n.* питьё *neut.*
drinking bout *n.* запо́й *m.*
drinking fountain *n.* питьево́й фонта́нчик *m.*
drinking water *n.* питьева́я вода́ *f.*
drip /drɪp/ *v.* ка́пать *impf.*, па́дать ка́плями *impf.*
drip-dry /'drɪp ˌdrai/ *adj.* быстросо́хнущий.
drive /draiv/ **1.** *n.* ка́танье *neut.*, прогу́лка *f.*; (*motivation*) побужде́ние *neut.* **2.** *v.* е́здить *impf. det.*, е́хать *impf. det.*, пое́хать *pf.*; вести́ автомоби́ль. **to drive out** выгоня́ть *impf.*, вы́гнать *pf.* **to drive up to** подъе́хать *pf.*
drive-in /'draivˌɪn/ *adj.* (*bank, fast food restaurant*) с подъездны́м око́шком.
drivel /'drɪvəl/ *n.* чепуха́ *f.*
driver /'draivər/ *n.* води́тель *m.*
drive shaft *n.* веду́щий вал *m.*
driveway /'draivˌwei/ *n.* подъе́зд *m.*
driving /'draivɪŋ/ *n.* (*travel in vehicle*) ката́ние *neut.*, езда́ *f.*; (*steering*) вожде́ние *neut.*
drizzle /'drɪzəl/ *n.* ме́лкий дождь, моря́щий дождь *m.*
drogue /droug/ *n.* (*naut.*) плаву́чий я́корь *m.*; (*braking*) тормозно́й парашю́т *m.*
droll /droul/ *adj.* (*comic*) заба́вный, смешно́й.
dromedary /'drɒmɪˌderi/ *adj.* дромаде́р, одного́рбый верблю́д *m.*
drone /droun/ **1.** *n.* (*bee; also fig.*) тру́тень *m.*; (*aer.*) радиоуправля́емый самолёт *m.*; (*buzzing*) жужжа́ние *neut.* **2.** *v.* (*buzz*) жужжа́ть; (*of engine*) гуде́ть; (*speak, sing, etc. monotonously*) говори́ть, петь моното́нно *impf.*
drool /drul/ *v.* (*salivate*) пуска́ть слю́ни *impf.*
droop /drup/ *v.* поника́ть *impf.*
drop /drɒp/ **1.** *n.* (*liquid*) ка́пля *f.*; (*reduction*) опуска́ние, пониже́ние *neut.* **2.** *v.t.* опуска́ть *impf.*, опусти́ть *pf.*; *v.i.* опуска́ться *impf.*, опусти́ться *pf.*
dropforging /'drɒpˌfɔrdʒɪŋ/ *n.* горя́чая штампо́вка *f.*
drop hammer. *n.* копёр *m.*
drop leaf *n.* откидна́я доска́ *f.*
droplet /'drɒplɪt/ *n.* ка́пелька *f.*
dropper /'drɒpər/ *n.* ка́пельница *f.*
droppings /'drɒpɪŋz/ *n.* помёт *m.*
drop shot *n.* дробь *f.*
dropsical /'drɒpsɪkəl/ *adj.* страда́ющий водя́нкой.
dropsy /'drɒpsi/ *n.* водя́нка *f.*
dross /drɔs/ *n.* (*metal*) дросс, шлак *m.*
drought /draut/ *n.* за́суха *f.*
drove /drouv/ *n.* (*flock*) ста́до *neut.*
drown /draun/ *v.t.* топи́ть *impf.*, утопи́ть *pf.*; *v.i.* топу́ть *impf.*, утону́ть *pf.*
drowse /drauz/ **1.** *n.* дремо́та *f.* **2.** *v.* дрема́ть *impf.*
drowsiness /'drauzinɪs/ *n.* дрёма *f.*
drowsy /'drauzi/ *adj.* со́нный.
drudge /drʌdʒ/ *n.* (*servant*) слуга́ *m.* (*decl. f.*); (*fig.*) иша́к *m.*
drudgery /'drʌdʒəri/ *n.* тяжёлая рабо́та, ну́дная рабо́та *f.*
drug /drʌg/ *n.* лека́рство *neut.*; наркотик *m.*
drugget /'drʌgɪt/ *n.* дра́гет *m.*
druggist /'drʌgɪst/ *n.* апте́карь *m.*
drugstore /'drʌgˌstɔr/ *n.* апте́ка *f.*

druid /'druɪd/ *n.* дру́ид *m.*
druidic /dru'ɪdɪk/ *adj.* друиди́ческий.
drum /drʌm/ *n.* бараба́н *m.*
drumbeat /'drʌmˌbit/ *n.* бараба́нный бой *m.*
drumhead /'drʌmˌhɛd/ *n.* ко́жа на бараба́не *f.*
drum major *n.* ста́рший полково́й бараба́нщик *m.*
drummer /'drʌmər/ *n.* бараба́нщик *m.*
drumstick /'drʌmˌstɪk/ *n.* бараба́нная па́лочка *f.*; (*leg of cooked bird*) но́жка *f.*
drunk /drʌŋk/ **1.** *adj.* пья́ный. **2.** *n.* пья́ница *m.* and *f.* (*decl. f.*).
drunkard /'drʌŋkərd/ *n.* пья́ница *m.* and *f.* (*decl. f.*).
drupaceous /dru'peiʃəs/ *adj.* ко́сточковый.
drupe /drup/ *n.* ко́сточковый плод *m.*
druse /druz/ *n.* (*mineralogy*) дру́за *f.*
dry /drai/ **1.** *adj.* сухо́й. **2.** *v.* суши́ть *impf.*, вы́сушить *pf.*
dryad /'draiəd/ *n.* дриа́да *f.*
dry-clean /'drai'klin/ *v.* подверга́ть хими́ческой чи́стке *impf.*
dry cleaner *n.* химчи́стка *f.*
dry dock /'drai,dɒk/ *n.* сухо́й док *m.*
dryer /'draiər/ *n.* суши́лка *f.*
drying /'draiɪŋ/ *n.* су́шка *f.*
dryish /'draiʃ/ *adj.* сухова́тый.
dryness /'drainɪs/ *n.* су́хость *f.*
dry nurse /'drai,nɜrs/ *n.* ня́ня *f.*
dry-salted /'drai ˌsɔltɪd/ *adj.* сухо́го посо́ла.
dry-shod /'drai ˌʃɒd/ *adv.* не замочи́в ног.
dual /'duəl/ *adj.* двойственный.
dualism /'duəˌlɪzəm/ *n.* дуали́зм *m.*
dualist /'duəlɪst/ *n.* дуали́ст *m.*
dualistic /ˌduə'lɪstɪk/ *adj.* дуалисти́ческий, дво́йственный.
duality /du'ælɪti/ *n.* дво́йственность *f.*
dualize /'duəˌlaiz/ *v.* раздва́ивать *impf.*
dual-purpose /'duəl ˈpɜrpəs/ *adj.* двойно́го назначе́ния.
dub /dʌb/ *v.* (*knight*) посвяща́ть в ры́цари *impf.*; (*film*) дубли́ровать *impf.*
dubbing /'dʌbɪŋ/ *n.* (*movies*) дубля́ж *m.*, дубли́рование *neut.*
dubiety /du'baiti/ *n.* сомне́ние *neut.*
dubious /'dubiəs/ *adj.* мни́тельный.
dubiously /'dubiəsli/ *adv.* сомни́тельно.
Dublin /'dʌblin/ *n.* Ду́блин *m.*
Dubrovnik /'dubrɒvnɪk/ *n.* Дубро́вник *m.*
ducal /'dukəl/ *adj.* кня́жеский.
ducat /'dʌkət/ *n.* дука́т *m.*
duchess /'dʌtʃɪs/ *n.* герцоги́ня *f.*
duchy /'dʌtʃi/ *n.* ге́рцогство *neut.*
duck[1] /dʌk/ *n.* (*bird*) у́тка *f.*; (*meat*) утя́тина *f.*
duck[2] /dʌk/ **1.** *n.* паруси́на *f.* **2.** *adj.* паруси́новый.
duck[3] /dʌk/ **1.** *n.* ныря́ние *neut.* **2.** *v.* ныря́ть *impf.*
duckbill /'dʌkˌbɪl/ *n.* (*zool.*) утконо́с *m.*
duckboard /'dʌkˌbɔrd/ *n.* дощаты́й насти́л *m.*
ducking /'dʌkɪŋ/ *n.* погруже́ние в во́ду *neut.*
duckling /'dʌklɪŋ/ *n.* утёнок *m.*; (*fig.*) **ugly duckling** га́дкий утёнок *m.*
duckweed /'dʌkˌwid/ *n.* ря́ска *f.*
duct /dʌkt/ *n.* прото́к *m.*
ductile /'dʌktl̩/ *adj.* (*metal*) тягу́чий, ко́вкий.
ductility /dʌk'tɪlɪti/ *n.* тягу́честь, ко́вкость *f.*

ductless gland /'dʌktlɪs/ *n.* железа́ вну́тренней секре́ции *f.*

dud /dʌd/ *n.* (*shell*) неразорва́вшийся снаря́д *m.*; (*thing which does not work*) брак *m.*

dude /dud/ *n.* (*slang*) пижо́н *m.*

due /du/ **1.** *adj.* до́лжный. **2. due to** *prep.* из-за (*with gen.*), благодаря́ (*with dat.*).

duel /'duəl/ *n.* поеди́нок *m.*

duelling /'duəlɪŋ/ *n.* дуэ́ль *f.*

duellist /'duəlɪst/ *n.* дуэля́нт *m.*

duenna /du'ɛnə/ *n.* дуэ́нья *f.*

dues /duz/ *pl.* сбо́ры, нало́ги *pl.*

duet /du'ɛt/ *n.* дуэ́т *m.*

duffel /'dʌfəl/ *n.* шерстяна́я ба́йка *f.*

dug /dʌg/ *n.* (*biol.*) сосо́к *m.*

dugong /'dugɒŋ/ *n.* дюго́нь *m.*

dugout /'dʌg,aut/ *n.* (*boat*) челно́к *m.*; (*mil.*) блинда́ж *m.*

duke /duk/ *n.* герцо́г *m.*; **Grand Duke** вели́кий князь *m.*

dukedom /'dukdəm/ *n.* ти́тул ге́рцога *m.*

dulcimer /'dʌlsəmər/ *n.* цимба́лы *pl.*

dull /dʌl/ *adj.* тупо́й; (*boring*) ску́чный.

dullard /'dʌlərd/ *n.* тупи́ца *m. and f.* (*decl. f.*)

dullness /'dʌlnɪs/ *n.* ску́ка *f.*

dulse /dʌls/ *n.* кра́сная во́доросль *f.*

duly /'duli/ *adv.* до́лжным о́бразом.

dumb /dʌm/ *adj.* (*mute*) немо́й; (*stupid*) глу́пый.

dumbbell /'dʌm,bɛl/ *n.* ги́ри *pl.*; (*colloq.*) (*fool*) дура́к; болва́н *m.*

dumbfound /dʌm'faund/ *v.* ошара́шить *pf.*

dumbly /'dʌmli/ *adv.* бессловно.

dumbness /'dʌmnɪs/ *n.* немота́ *f.*

dumbstruck /'dʌm,strʌk/ *n.* ошеломлённый.

dumdum /'dʌm,dʌm/ *n.* пу́ля думду́м *f.*

dummy /'dʌmi/ *n.* манеке́н *m.*; (*cards*) болва́н *m.*

dump /dʌmp/ **1.** *v.* (*to drop*) сва́ливать *impf.*; (*to throw out*) выбра́сывать *impf.* **2.** *n.* (*refuse*) сва́лка *f.*; (*depot*) склад *m.*

dumper /'dʌmpər/ *n.* самосва́л *m.*

dumping /'dʌmpɪŋ/ *n.* разгру́зка *f.*

dumpling /'dʌmplɪŋ/ *n.* клёцка, галу́шка *f.*

dumpy /'dʌmpi/ *adj.* корена́стый, призе́мистый.

dun /dʌn/ *adj.* серова́то-кори́чневый.

dunce /dʌns/ *n.* тупи́ца *m. and f.* (*decl. f.*)

dunderhead /'dʌndər,hɛd/ *n.* болва́н *m.*

dune /dun/ *n.* дю́на *f.*

dune buggy *n.* песча́ный вездехо́д *m.*

dung /dʌŋ/ *n.* наво́з *m.*

dungaree /,dʌŋɡə'ri/ *n.* брю́ки *pl.* комбинезо́н *m.*

dungeon /'dʌndʒən/ *n.* (*prison*) темни́ца *f.*; (*tower*) гла́вная ба́шня *f.*

dunghill /'dʌŋ,hɪl/ *n.* наво́зная ку́ча *f.*

dunk /dʌŋk/ *v.* окуна́ть; (*to dip*) мака́ть *impf.*

dunlin /'dʌnlɪn/ *n.* (*bird*) чернозо́бик *m.*

dunnage /'dʌnɪdʒ/ *n.* подсти́лочный материа́л *m.*

duo /'duou/ *n.* дуэ́т *m.*

duodecimal /,duə'dɛsəməl/ *adj.* двенадцатитери́чный.

duodecimo /,duə'dɛsə,mou/ *n.* дуоде́цима *f.*

duodenal /,duə'dinl̩, du'ɒdn̩əl/ *adj.* двенадцатитипе́рстный.

duodenary /,duə'dɛnəri/ *adj.* двенадцатери́чный.

duodenum /,duə'dinəm, du'ɒdn̩əm/ *n.* двенадцатипе́рстная кишка́ *f.*

dupe /dup/ *v.* обма́нывать *impf.*, обману́ть *pf.*

duple /'dupəl/ *adj.* двойно́й.

duplex /'duplɛks/ *adj.* двойно́й.

duplicate / *adj.* 'duplɪkɪt; *v.* 'duplɪ,keit/ **1.** *adj.* двойно́й, удво́енный. **2.** *n.* ко́пия *f.*, дублика́т *m.* **3.** *v.* удва́ивать *impf.*, удво́ить *pf.*

duplication /,duplɪ'keiʃən/ *n.* дубли́рование *neut.*

duplicator /'duplɪ,keitər/ *n.* мно́жительный аппара́т *m.*

duplicity /du'plɪsɪti/ *n.* дво́йственность, двули́чность *f.*

durability /,durə'bɪlɪti/ *n.* про́чность *f.*

durable /'durəbəl/ *adj.* про́чный; износосто́йкий.

duralumin /du'ræljəmɪn/ *n.* дюра́ль *f.*

duramen /du'reimɪn/ *n.* (*bot.*) сердцеви́на *f.*

durance /'durəns/ *n.* заточе́ние *neut.*

duration /du'reiʃən/ *n.* продолжи́тельность *f.*; **for the duration of** на вре́мя (*with gen.*).

duress /du'rɛs/ *n.* принужде́ние *neut.*

during /'durɪŋ/ *prep.* в тече́ние; во вре́мя (*with gen.*).

Dushanbe /du'ʃɑnbə/ *n.* Душанбе́ *m.*

dusk /dʌsk/ *n.* су́мерки *pl.*; **from dawn till dusk** от зари́ до зари́.

dust /dʌst/ **1.** *n.* пыль *f.* **2.** *v.* стира́ть пыль *impf.*

dustbin /'dʌst,bɪn/ *n.* му́сорный я́щик *m.*

dust bowl *n.* засу́шливый райо́н *m.*

dustcloth /'dʌst,klɔθ/ *n.* тря́пка для пы́ли *f.*

dust cover *n.* (*of book*) суперобло́жка *f.*; пы́льник, чехо́л *m.*

dustiness /'dʌstinɪs/ *n.* запылённость *f.*

dust jacket *n.* (*on book*) суперобло́жка *f.*

dustman /'dʌst,mæn, -mən/ *n.* (*Brit.*) му́сорщик *m.*

dustpan /'dʌst,pæn/ *n.* сово́к *m.*

dustproof /'dʌst,pruf/ *adj.* пыленепроница́емый.

duststorm /'dʌst,stɔrm/ *n.* пы́льная бу́ря *f.*

dustup /'dʌst,ʌp/ *n.* (*colloq.*) дра́ка *f.*

dusty /'dʌsti/ *adj.* пы́льный.

Dutch /dʌtʃ/ **1.** *adj.* голла́ндский. **2.** *n.* (*language*) голла́ндский язы́к *m.*

Dutchman /'dʌtʃmən/ *n.* голла́ндец *m.*; **the Flying Dutchman** *n.* лету́чий голла́ндец *m.*

Dutchwoman /'dʌtʃ,wumən/ *n.* голла́ндка *f.*

duteous /'dutiəs/ *also* **dutiful** *adj.* послу́шный.

dutiable /'dutiəbəl/ *adj.* подлежа́щий обложе́нию по́шлиной.

duty /'duti/ *n.* обя́занность *f.*; (*customs*) по́шлина *f.*; **to be on duty** дежу́рить.

duty-free /'duti 'fri/ *adj.* беспо́шлинный.

duvet /du'vei/ *n.* ва́тное одея́ло *neut.*

dwarf /dwɔrf/ *n.* ка́рлик *m.*

dwarfish /'dwɔrfɪʃ/ *adj.* ка́рликовый.

dwell /dwɛl/ *v.* жить *impf.*, обита́ть *impf.*; **to dwell on** остана́вливаться на (*with prep.*).

dweller /'dwɛlər/ *n.* обита́тель *m.*

dwelling /'dwɛlɪŋ/ *n.* жило́й дом *m.*

dwindle /'dwɪndl̩/ *v.* уменьша́ться *impf.*, уме́ньшиться *pf.*

dyad /'daiæd/ *n.* дво́йка, па́ра *f.*

dyadic /dai'ædɪk/ *adj.* двойно́й.

dye /dai/ **1.** *n.* кра́ска *f.* **2.** *v.* кра́сить *impf.*, покра́сить *pf.*

dyed-in-the-wool /'daidṇðə'wʊl/ *adj.* закоренéлый.

dyer /'daiər/ *n.* красúльщик *m.*

dyestuff /'dai₌stʌf/ *n.* крáсящее веществó *neut.*

dye works *n.* красúльня *f.*

dying /'daiŋ/ **1.** *n.* умирáние *neut.* **2.** *adj.* умирáющий.

dynamic /dai'næmɪk/ *adj.* динамúческий.

dynamism /'dainə₌mizəm/ *n.* динамúзм *m.*

dynamite /'dainə₌mait/ *n.* динамúт *m.*

dynamiter /'dainə₌maitər/ *n.* динамúтчик *m.*

dynamo /'dainə₌mou/ *n.* динáмо *neut. indecl.*

dynamometer /₌dainə'mɒmitər/ *n.* динамóметр *m.*

dynast /'dainæst/ *n.* потóмственный правúтель *m.*

dynastic /dai'næstɪk/ *adj.* династúческий.

dynasty /'dainəsti/ *n.* динáстия *f.*

dyne /dain/ *n.* дúна *f.*

dysentery /'dɪsən₌tɛri/ *n.* дизентерúя *f.*

dysfunction /dɪs'fʌŋkʃən/ *n.* дисфýнкция *f.*

dyslexia /dɪs'lɛksiə/ *n.* дислéксия *f.*

dyspepsia /dɪs'pɛpʃə/ *n.* диспепсúя *f.*

dyspeptic /dɪs'pɛptɪk/ *adj.* страдáющий диспепсúей.

dystrophy /'dɪstrəfi/ *n.* дистрофúя; **muscular dystrophy** мы́шечная дистрофúя *f.*

Dzhambul /dʒɑm'buːl/ *n.* Джамбýл *m.*

E

each /itʃ/ adj. and pron. ка́ждый; **each of them** ка́ждый из них.

eager /'igər/ adj. усе́рдный.

eagerly /'igərli/ adv. с энтузиа́змом; (avidly) охо́тно, с жа́ром.

eagerness /'igərnıs/ n. (ardor) пыл m., рве́ние neut.; (haste) поспе́шность f.

eagle /'igəl/ n. орёл m.

eaglet /'iglıt/ n. орлёнок m.

ear /ıər/ n. у́хо neut.; (corn) ко́лос m.

earache /'ıər,eik/ n. боль в у́хе f.

eardrum /'ıər,drʌm/ n. бараба́нная перепо́нка f.

earflap /'ıər,flæp/ n. нау́шник m.

earl /ɜrl/ n. граф m.

earldom /'ɜrldəm/ n. гра́фство neut.

earlier /'ɜrliər/ adj. ра́ньше.

early /'ɜrli/ **1.** adj. ра́нний. **2.** adv. ра́но.

earmark /'ıər,mɑrk/ предназна́чать; выделя́ть impf.

earn /ɜrn/ v. зараба́тывать impf., зарабо́тать pf.; (deserve) заслу́живать impf., заслужи́ть pf.

earnest /'ɜrnıst/ adj. серьёзный; и́скренний.

earnings /'ɜrnıŋz/ n. за́работок m.

earphone /'ıər,foun/ n. нау́шник m. usu. pl.

ear-piercing /'ıər,pıərsıŋ/ adj. пронзи́тельный.

ear plugs n. заты́чки для уше́й pl.

earring /'ıər,rıŋ/ n. серьга́ f.

earshot /'ıər,ʃɒt/ n. **within earshot/out of earshot** adv. в преде́лах or вне преде́лов слы́шимости.

earth /ɜrθ/ n. земля́ f.

earthborn /'ɜrθ,bɔrn/ adj. сме́ртный.

earthbound /'ɜrθ,baund/ adj. жите́йский.

earthen /'ɜrθən/ adj. земляно́й; (pottery) гли́няный.

earthenware /'ɜrθən,wεər/ n. гли́няная посу́да f., гонча́рное изде́лие neut.

earthly /'ɜrθli/ adj. (earth) земно́й; (non-spiritual) све́тский.

earthman /'ɜrθ,mæn/ n. земля́нин m.

earthquake /'ɜrθ,kweik/ n. землетрясе́ние neut.

earthshaking /'ɜrθ,ʃeikıŋ/ adj. (fig.) потряса́ющий.

earthwork /'ɜrθ,wɜrk/ n. (engineering) земляны́е рабо́ты pl.

earthworm /'ɜrθ,wɜrm/ n. земляно́й червь m.

earthy /'ɜrθi/ adj. земляно́й; земли́стый; (crude) грубова́тый.

ear trumpet n. слухова́я тру́бка f.

earwax /'ıər,wæks/ n. ушна́я се́ра f.

earwig /'ıər,wıg/ n. уховёртка f.

ease /iz/ **1.** n. лёгкость f. **2.** v. облегча́ть impf., облегчи́ть pf.

easeful /'izfəl/ adj. споко́йный.

easel /'izəl/ n. мольбе́рт m.

easily /'izəli/ adv. легко́.

east /ist/ n. восто́к m.

Easter /'istər/ n. Па́сха f.

easterly /'istərli/ adj. восто́чный.

eastern /'istərn/ adj. восто́чный.

easternmost /'istərn,moust/ adj. са́мый восто́ч-ный.

Eastertide /'istər,taid/ n. Пасха́льная неде́ля f.

eastward /'istwərd/ adv. к восто́ку, на восто́к.

easy /'izi/ adj. лёгкий.

easy chair n. кре́сло neut.

easygoing /'izi'gouıŋ/ adj. (carefree, casual) беспе́чный, беззабо́тный; (not strict) не стро́гий; (calm) споко́йный.

eat /it/ v. есть impf., съесть pf.; ку́шать impf.

eatable /'itəbəl/ adj. съедо́бный.

eater /'itər/ n. едо́к m.

eau de Cologne /'ou də kə'loun/ n. одеколо́н m.

eau de vie /'ou də 'vi/ n. конья́к m.

eaves /ivz/ n. стреха́ f.

eavesdrop /'ivz,drɒp/ v. подслу́шивать impf.

eavesdropper /'ivz,drɒpər/ adj. подслу́шиваю-щий.

eavesdropping n. подслу́шивание neut.

ebb /εb/ **1.** n. отли́в, упа́док m. **2.** v. отлива́ть impf., отли́ть pf.; угаса́ть impf.

ebonite /'εbə,nait/ n. эбони́т m.

ebony /'εbəni/ n. чёрное де́рево neut.

ebullience /ı'bʌlyəns/ n. экспанси́вность f.

ebullient /ı'bʌlyənt/ adj. кипу́чий.

ebullition /,εbə'lıʃən/ n. кипе́ние neut.

E.C. n. (abbr. of European Community) ЕС neut. (abbr. of Европе́йское соо́бщество).

ecbolic /εk'bɒlık/ n. стимуля́тор для ро́дов m.

eccentric /ık'sεntrık/ **1.** adj. эксцентри́чный, стра́нный. **2.** n. чуда́к m.

eccentricity /,εksən'trısıti/ n. экцентри́чность f.

ecclesiastical /ı,klizi'æstıkəl/ adj. церко́вный.

ecdemic /εk'dεmık/ adj. эндеми́чный.

ecdysis /'εkdəsıs/ n. сбра́сывание ко́жи neut.

echelon /'εʃə,lɒn/ n. эшело́н m.

echidna /ı'kıdnə/ n. ехи́дна f.

echinus /ı'kainəs/ n. (zool.) морско́й ёж m.

echo /'εkou/ **1.** n. эхо neut. **2.** v.i. отдава́ться impf., отда́ться pf.; v.t. вто́рить.

echo sounder n. эхоло́т m.

éclair /ei'klεər/ n. экле́р m.

eclampsia /ı'klæmpsiə/ n. эклампси́я f.

éclat /ei'kla/ n. блеск m.

eclectic /ı'klεktık/ adj. эклекти́ческий.

eclecticism /ı'klεktə,sızəm/ n. эклекти́зм m.

eclipse /ı'klıps/ **1.** n. затме́ние neut. **2.** v. затме-ва́ть impf., затми́ть pf.

ecliptic /ı'klıptık/ n. экли́птика f.

eclogue /'εklɒg/ n. экло́га f.

ecological /,εkə'lɒdʒıkəl/ adj. экологи́ческий.

ecologist /ı'kɒlədʒıst/ n. эко́лог m.

ecology /ı'kɒlədʒi/ n. эколо́гия f.

economic /,εkə'nɒmık/ adj. экономи́ческий.

economical /,εkə'nɒmıkəl/ adj. эконо́мный.

economics /,εkə'nɒmıks/ n. эконо́мика f.

economist /ı'kɒnəmıst/ n. эконо́мист m.

economize /ı'kɒnə,maiz/ v. эконо́мить impf. and pf.

economy /ı'kɒnəmi/ n. эконо́мика f., хозя́йство neut.

ecosystem /'εkou,sıstəm/ n. экосисте́ма f.

ecru /'εkru/ adj. све́тло-бе́жевый.

ecstasy /'εkstəsi/ n. экста́з m.

ecstatic /ɛk'stætɪk/ adj. экстатический.

ecstatically /ɛk'stætɪkli/ adv. с восторгом.

ectoblast /'ɛktə,blæst/ n. эктобласт m.

ectoderm /'ɛktə,dɜrm/ n. эктодерма f.

ectopic /ɛk'tɒpɪk/ adj. эктопический.

ectoplasm /'ɛktə,plæzəm/ n. эктоплазма f.

Ecuador /'ɛkwə,dɔr/ n. Эквадор m.

ecumenical /'ɛkyʊ'mɛnɪkəl/ adj. вселенский; экуменический.

ecumenism /'ɛkyʊmə,nɪzəm/ n. экуменизм m.

eczema /'ɛksəmə, 'ɛgzə-/ n. экзема f.

edacious /ɪ'deiʃəs/ adj. жадный.

eddy /'ɛdi/ n. (in water) воронка f.; (in air) завихрение neut.

edelweiss /'eidl̩,vais/ n. эдельвейс m.

edema /ɪ'dimə/ n. отёк m.

edge /ɛdʒ/ n. край m.; (of blade) лезвие neut.

edgewise /'ɛdʒ,waiz/ adv. поперечно; боком.

edging /'ɛdʒɪŋ/ n. (on material) кайма f.; бордюр m.

edgy /'ɛdʒi/ adj. (with edge) острый; (fig.) (nervous) нервный.

edibility /,ɛdə'bɪlɪti/ n. съедобность f.

edible /'ɛdəbəl/ adj. съедобный.

edibles /'ɛdəbəlz/ n. съестное neut.

edict /'idɪkt/ n. эдикт, указ m.

edification /,ɛdəfɪ'keiʃən/ n. наставление, назидание neut.

edifice /'ɛdəfɪs/ n. здание; сооружение neut.

edify /'ɛdəfai/ v. поучать, наставлять impf.

Edinburgh /'ɛdn̩,bɜrə/ n. Эдинбург m.

edit /'ɛdɪt/ v. редактировать impf., отредактировать pf.

edition /ɪ'dɪʃən/ n. издание neut.

editor /'ɛdɪtər/ n. редактор m.

editorial /,ɛdɪ'tɔriəl/ 1. adj. редакционный, редакторский. 2. n. редакционная статья f.

educate /'ɛdʒʊ,keit/ v, давать образование, воспитывать impf., воспитать pf.

educated /'ɛdʒʊ,keitɪd/ adj. образованный.

education /,ɛdʒʊ'keiʃən/ n. образование; воспитание neut.

educational /,ɛdʒʊ'keiʃən̩l/ adj. образовательный, воспитательный, учебный.

educationalist /,ɛdʒʊ'keiʃən̩lɪst/ n. педагог-теоретик m.

educative /'ɛdʒʊ,keitɪv/ adj. поучительный.

educator /'ɛdʒʊ,keitər/ n. педагог m.

educe /ɪ'dus/ v. выявлять impf.

eductor /ɪ'dʌktər/ n. эжектор m.

edulcorate /ɪ'dʌlkə,reit/ v. промывать impf.

eel /il/ n. угорь m.

eerie /'ɪəri/ adj. жуткий.

efface /ɪ'feis/ v. стирать impf.

effect /ɪ'fɛkt/ 1. n. следствие neut., результат m.; эффект m.; personal effects n. имущество neut. 2. v. совершать impf., совершить pf.

effective /ɪ'fɛktɪv/ adj. эффективный.

effectiveness /ɪ'fɛktɪvnɪs/ n. эффективность f.

effectual /ɪ'fɛktʃuəl/ adj. действенный.

effectuate /ɪ'fɛktʃu,eit/ v. совершать; осуществлять impf.

effeminacy /ɪ'fɛmənəsi/ n. изнеженность f.

effeminate /ɪ'fɛmənɪt/ adj. женоподобный, изнеженный.

efferent /'ɛfərənt/ adj. (anat.) выносящий.

effervesce /,ɛfər'vɛs/ v. (drink, etc.) шипеть, пениться; (chem.) бурно выделять газ impf.

effervescence /,ɛfər'vɛsəns/ n. шипение neut.; кипучесть f.

effervescent /,ɛfər'vɛsənt/ adj. шипучий; (fig.) кипучий.

effete /ɪ'fit/ adj. (decadent) упадочный.

efficacious /,ɛfɪ'keiʃəs/ adj. эффективный.

efficacy /'ɛfɪkəsi/ n. действенность f.; сила f.

efficiency /ɪ'fɪʃənsi/ n. эффективность f.; (profitability) рентабельность f.

efficient /ɪ'fɪʃənt/ adj. действенный, эффективный, производительный.

effigy /'ɛfɪdʒi/ n. чучело neut.

effloresce /,ɛflə'rɛs/ v. (bot.) расцветать impf.

efflorescence /,ɛflə'rɛsəns/ n. (bot.) расцвет m., цветение neut.; (chem.) выцветание neut.

effluence /'ɛfluəns/ n. истечение neut.

effluent /'ɛfluənt/ n. (river) поток, вытекающий из другой реки; (waste discharge) сток m.

effort /'ɛfərt/ n. усилие neut.

effortlessly /'ɛfərtlɪs/ adv. без усилий.

effrontery /ɪ'frʌntəri/ n. наглость f., нахальство neut.

effulgence /ɪ'fʌldʒəns/ n. сияние neut.

effulgent /ɪ'fʌldʒənt/ adj. лучезарный.

effuse /ɪ'fyuz/ v. выливать(ся) impf.

effusion /ɪ'fyuʒən/ n. излияние neut.

effusive /ɪ'fyusɪv/ adj. экспансивный, демонстративный.

egalitarian /ɪ,gælɪ'tɛəriən/ adj. эгалитарный.

egg /ɛg/ 1. n. яйцо neut. 2. adj. яичный

eggplant /'ɛg,plænt/ n. баклажан m.

eggshell /'ɛg,ʃɛl/ n. яичная скорлупа f.; eggshell china тонкий фарфор m.

eglantine /'ɛglən,tain/ n. роза эглантерия, роза ржавая f.

egocentric /,igoʊ'sɛntrɪk/ adj. эгоцентрический.

egoism /'igoʊ,ɪzəm/ n. эгоизм m.

egoist /'igoʊɪst/ n. эгоист m.

egoistic /,igoʊ'ɪstɪk/ adj. эгоистический, эгоистичный.

egotistic /,igə'tɪstɪk/ adj. самодовольный; эгоистический.

egregious /ɪ'gridʒəs/ adj. вопиющий.

egress /'igrɛs/ n. выход m.

egret /'igrɪt/ n. (bird) белая цапля f.

Egypt /'idʒɪpt/ n. Египет m.

Egyptian /ɪ'dʒɪpʃən/ n. египтянин m., египтянка f.

Egyptologist /,idʒɪp'tɒlədʒɪst/ n. египтолог m.

Egyptology /,idʒɪp'tɒlədʒi/ n. египтология f.

eh /ei, ɛ/ interj. (expression of inquiry) а?, как?; (following a phrase) не правда ли?

eider /'aidər/ n. гагара (обыкновенная) f.

eiderdown /'aidər,daun/ n. (feathers) гагачий пух m.; (comforter) перина f.

eight /eit/ adj., n. восемь num.; n. (cards) восьмёрка f.

eighteen /'ei'tin/ adj., n. восемнадцать num.

eighteenth /'ei'tinθ/ adj. восемнадцатый.

eighth /eitθ, eiθ/ adj. восьмой.

eighty /'eiti/ adj., n. восемьдесят num.

either /'iðər, 'aiðər/ 1. pron. и тот и другой; лю бой. 2. adj. любой; оба. 3. conj. either... or или... или.

ejaculate /ɪ'dʒækyə,leit/ v. восклицать impf.,

воскли́кнуть *pf.*; (*liquid*) изверга́ть *impf.*, изве́ргнуть *pf.*

ejaculation /ɪˌdʒækyə'leiʃən/ *n.* (*exclamation*) восклица́ние *neut.*; (*emission*) изверже́ние *neut.*

ejaculatory /ɪ'dʒækyələˌtɔri/ *adj.* (*physiol.*) семяизверга́ющий.

eject /ɪ'dʒɛkt/ *v.* выбра́сывать *impf.*, вы́бросить *pf.*; изверга́ть *impf.*, изве́ргнуть *pf.*

ejection /ɪ'dʒɛkʃən/ *n.* выбра́сывание; изверже́ние; выселе́ние *neut.*; **ejection seat** катапульти́руемое сиде́нье *neut.*

ejector /ɪ'dʒɛktər/ *n.* эже́ктор *m.*

Ekaterinburg /ɪ'kætərɪn'bɜrg/ *n.* Екатеринбу́рг *m.*

Ekaterinodar /ɪˌkætə'rinə,dɑr/ *n.* Екатеринода́р *m.*

eke out /ik/ *v.* (*a living*) перебива́ться кое-как *impf.*

elaborate / *adj.* ɪ'læbərɪt; *v.* ɪ'læbə,reit/ **1.** *adj.* разрабо́танный, сло́жный. **2.** *v.* тща́тельно разраба́тывать в деталях *impf.*

elaboration /ɪˌlæbə'reiʃən/ *n.* уточне́ние *neut.*

élan /ei'lɑn/ *n.* (*fervor*) рве́ние *neut.*, пы́лкость *f.*; (*dash*) стреми́тельность *f.*

eland /'ilənd/ *n.* антило́па ка́нна *f.*

elapse /ɪ'læps/ *v.* проходи́ть *impf.*, пройти́ *pf.*

elastic /ɪ'læstɪk/ **1.** *adj.* эласти́чный. **2.** *n.* рези́нка *f.*

elasticity /ɪlæ'stɪsɪti/ *n.* эласти́чность *f.*

elate /ɪ'leit/ *v.* очень обра́довать *pf.*

elated /ɪ'leitɪd/ *adj.* в восто́рге; восто́рженный, лику́ющий.

elater /'ɛlətər/ *n.* (*bot.*) элате́ра *f.*

elation /ɪ'leiʃən/ *n.* восто́рг *m.*

Elba /'ɛlbə/ *n.* (*island*) Э́льба *f.*

Elbe /'ɛlbə, ɛlb/ *n.* (*river*) Э́льба *f.*

elbow /'ɛlbou/ **1.** *n.* ло́коть *m.* **2.** *v.* толка́ть ло́ктем *impf.*, толкну́ть *pf.*

elbow grease *n.* большо́е уси́лие *neut.*

elbowroom /'ɛlbou,rum/ *n.* просто́р *m.*

Elbrus /ɛl'brus/ *n.* (*mountain*) Эльбру́с *m.*

elder[1] /'ɛldər/ **1.** *adj.* ста́рший. **2.** *n.* ста́рец *m.*

elder[2] /'ɛldər/ *n.* (*tree*) бузина́ *f.*

elderberry /'ɛldər,bɛri/ *n.* я́года бузины́ *f.*

elderly /'ɛldərli/ *adj.* пожило́й.

eldest /'ɛldɪst/ *adj.* ста́рший.

El Dorado /ˌɛl də'radou/ *n.* Эльдора́до *neut. indecl.*

eldritch /'ɛldrɪtʃ/ *adj.* жу́ткий.

elect /ɪ'lɛkt/ *v.* избира́ть *impf.*, избра́ть *pf.*

election /ɪ'lɛkʃən/ *n.* вы́боры *pl.*

electioneer /ɪˌlɛkʃə'nɪər/ *v.* проводи́ть предвы́борную кампа́нию *impf.*

elective /ɪ'lɛktɪv/ *adj.* вы́борный.

elector /ɪ'lɛktər/ *n.* избира́тель *m.*

electoral /ɪ'lɛktərəl/ *adj.* избира́тельный.

electorate /ɪ'lɛktərɪt/ *n.* избира́тели *pl.*

electrical /ɪ'lɛktrɪkəl/ *adj.* электри́ческий.

electrician /ɪlɛk'trɪʃən/ *n.* эле́ктрик *m.*

electricity /ɪlɛk'trɪsɪti/ *n.* электри́чество *neut.*

electrification /ɪˌlɛktrəfɪ'keiʃən/ *n.* электрифика́ция *f.*

electrify /ɪ'lɛktrə,fai/ *v.* (*charge with electricity*) электризова́ть *impf.*; (*provide with electricity*) электрифици́ровать *impf.*

electroanalysis /ɪˌlɛktrouə'næləsɪs/ *n.* электроана́лиз *m.*

electrocardiogram /ɪˌlɛktrou'kardiə,græm/ *n.* электрокардиогра́мма *f.*

electrocute /ɪ'lɛktrə,kyut/ *v.* убива́ть электри́ческим то́ком *impf.*

electrocution /ɪˌlɛktrə'kyuʃən/ *n.* казнь на электри́ческом сту́ле *f.*

electrode /ɪ'lɛktroud/ *n.* электро́д *m.*

electrodeposit /ɪˌlɛktroudɪ'pɒzɪt/ *n.* гальвани́ческий покро́в *m.*

electrodepositing /ɪˌlɛktroudɪ'pɒzɪtɪŋ/ *n.* гальваностéгия *f.*

electrodynamic /ɪˌlɛktroudai'næmɪk/ *adj.* электродинами́ческий.

electrodynamics /ɪˌlɛktroudai'næmɪks/ *n.* электродина́мика *f.*

electroencephalogram /ɪˌlɛktrouɛn'sɛfələ,græm/ *n.* электроэнцефалогра́мма *f.*

electrography /ɪlɛk'trɒgrəfi/ *n.* электрогра́фия *f.*

electrokinetics /ɪˌlɛktroukɪ'nɛtɪks/ *n.* электрокинéтика *f.*

electrolysis /ɪlɛk'trɒləsɪs/ *n.* электро́лиз *m.*

electrolyte /ɪ'lɛktrə,lait/ *n.* электроли́т *m.*

electrolytic /ɪˌlɛktrə'lɪtɪk/ *adj.* электролити́ческий.

electromagnet /ɪˌlɛktrou'mægnɪt/ *n.* электромагни́т *m.*

electromagnetic /ɪˌlɛktroumæg'nɛtɪk/ *adj.* электромагни́тный.

electromagnetism /ɪˌlɛktrou'mægnɪ,tɪzəm/ *n.* электромагнети́зм *m.*

electromechanics /ɪˌlɛktroumɪ'kæntks/ *n.* электромеха́ника *f.*

electrometer /ɪlɛk'trɒmɪtər/ *n.* электро́метр *m.*

electromotive /ɪˌlɛktrə'moutɪv/ *adj.* электродви́жущий.

electromotor /ɪˌlɛktrou'moutər/ *n.* электродви́гатель *m.*

electron /ɪ'lɛktrɒn/ *n.* электро́н *m.*

electronic /ɪlɛk'trɒnɪk/ *adj.* электро́нный.

electronics /ɪlɛk'trɒnɪks/ *n.* электро́ника *f.*

electroplate /ɪ'lɛktrə,pleit/ *n.* гальваностереоти́п *m.*

electroplating /ɪ'lɛktrə,pleitɪŋ/ *n.* гальванопокры́тие *neut.*

electroscope /ɪ'lɛktrə,skoup/ *n.* электроско́п *m.*

electrostatics /ɪˌlɛktrə'stætɪks/ *n.* электроста́тика *f.*

electrotherapy /ɪˌlɛktrou'θɛrəpi/ *n.* электротерапи́я *f.*

electrotype /ɪ'lɛktrə,taip/ *n.* (*plate*) гальваностереоти́п *m.*

electrum /ɪ'lɛktrəm/ *n.* медноникелеци́нковый сплав *m.*

electuary /ɪ'lɛktʃu,ɛri/ *n.* электуа́рий *m.*

eleemosynary /ˌɛlə'mɒsə,nɛri/ *adj.* (*supported by alms*) живу́щий ми́лостыней.

elegance /'ɛlɪgəns/ *n.* элега́нтность *f.*

elegant /'ɛlɪgənt/ *adj.* элега́нтный.

elegiac /ˌɛlɪ'dʒaiək/ *adj.* элеги́ческий.

elegiacs /ˌɛlɪ'dʒaiəks/ *n.* элеги́ческие стихи́ *pl.*

elegy /'ɛlɪdʒi/ *n.* эле́гия *f.*

element /'ɛləmənt/ *n.* элеме́нт *m.*; **to be in one's element** быть в свое́й стихи́и.

elemental /ˌɛlə'mɛntḷ/ *adj.* стихи́йный; основно́й.

elementary /ˌɛlə'mɛntəri/ *adj.* элемента́рный, первонача́льный.

elementary school *m.* нача́льная шко́ла *f.*

elephant /'ɛləfənt/ **1.** п. слон m.; слони́ха f. **2.** adj. слоно́вый.

elephantiasis /ˌɛləfən'taiəsis/ п. слоно́вая боле́знь f.

elephantine /ˌɛlə'fæntin/ adj. слоно́вый; (like elephant) слоноподо́бный.

elevate /'ɛlə,veit/ v. возвыша́ть impf., возвы́сить pf.

elevated /'ɛlə,veitid/ adj. возвы́шенный; надзе́мный.

elevation /ˌɛlə'veiʃən/ п. возвыше́ние neut.; подъём m.

elevator /'ɛlə,veitər/ п. лифт, элева́тор m.

eleven /i'lɛvən/ adj., п. оди́ннадцать пит.

eleventh /i'lɛvənθ/ adj. оди́ннадцатый.

elf /ɛlf/ п. эльф m.

elicit /i'lisit/ v. извлека́ть; выявля́ть impf.

eligibility /ˌɛlidʒə'biliti/ п. прие́млемость f.

eligible /'ɛlidʒəbəl/ adj. име́ющий возмо́жноеть, име́ющий пра́во.

eliminate /i'limə,neit/ v. устраня́ть; исключа́ть impf., исключи́ть pf.; элимини́ровать impf. and pf.

elimination /i,limə'neiʃən/ п. устране́ние, исключе́ние; уничтоже́ние neut.

elision /i'liʒən/ п. эли́зия f.

elite /i'lit/ п. эли́та f.

elitist /i'litist/ adj. элита́рный, в по́льзу эли́ты.

elixir /i'liksər/ п. эликси́р m.

Elizabethan /i,lizə'biθən/ adj. елизаве́тинский.

elk /ɛlk/ п. лось m.

ellipse /i'lips/ п. э́ллипс m.

ellipsis /i'lipsis/ п. (gram.) э́ллипсис m.

ellipsograph /i'lipsə,græf/ п. эллипсо́граф m.

ellipsoid /i'lipsɔid/ п. эллипсо́ид m.

ellipsoidal /ilip'sɔidl/ adj. эллипсо́идный.

elliptical /i'liptikəl/ adj. эллипти́ческий.

elm /ɛlm/ п. вяз, ильм m.

elocution /ˌɛlə'kyuʃən/ п. ди́кция f

elongate /i'lɔŋgeit/ v. удлиня́ть impf., удлини́ть pf.

elongation /ilɔŋ'geiʃən/ п. удлине́ние neut.

elope /i'loup/ v. сбега́ть impf., сбежа́ть pf.

elopement /i'loupmənt/ п. та́йное бе́гство neut.

eloquence /'ɛləkwəns/ п. красноре́чие neut.

eloquent /'ɛləkwənt/ adj. красноречи́вый.

El Paso /'ɛl pæsou/ п. Эль-Па́со m.

El Salvador /ɛl 'sælvə,dɔr/ п. Сальвадо́р m.

else /ɛls/ **1.** adj. (different) друго́й. **2.** adv. ещё; **or else** ина́че.

elsewhere /'ɛls,wɛər/ adv. (где́-нибудь) в друго́м ме́сте; в друго́е ме́сто.

elucidate /i'lusi,deit/ v. объясня́ть impf.

elucidation /i,lusi'deiʃən/ п. объясне́ние neut.

elude /i'lud/ v. избега́ть impf., избе́гнуть pf.

elusive /i'lusiv/ adj. укло́нчивый.

eluvial /i'luviəl/ adj. элювиа́льный.

eluvium /i'luviəm/ adj. элю́вий.

elver /'ɛlvər/ п. молодо́й у́горь m.

Elysian /i'liʒən/ adj. Елисе́йский.

Elysium /i'liʒiəm/ п. Эли́зиум m.

elytron /'ɛli,trɒn/ п. надкры́лье neut.

em /ɛm/ п. (print) эм m.

emaciate /i'meiʃi,eit/ v. истоща́ть(ся) impf.

emaciation /i,meiʃi'eiʃən/ п. истоще́ние neut.

e-mail /'i,meil/ п. электро́нная по́чта f.

emanate /'ɛmə,neit/ v. исходи́ть impf.

emanation /ˌɛmə'neiʃən/ п. истече́ние neut.

emancipate /i'mænsə,peit/ v. освобожда́ть impf., освободи́ть pf.

emancipation /i,mænsə'peiʃən/ п. эмансипа́ция f.; освобожде́ние neut.

emancipationist /i,mænsə'peiʃənist/ п. сторо́нник эмансипа́ции m.

emasculate /i'mæskyə,leit/ v. (castrate) кастри́ровать; (make effeminate) изне́живать impf.

emasculation /i,mæskyə'leiʃən/ п. кастра́ция f.

embalm /ɛm'bɑm/ v. бальзами́ровать impf.

embalming /ɛm'bɑmiŋ/ п. бальзами́рование neut.

embank /ɛm'bæŋk/ v. обноси́ть ва́лом impf.

embankment /ɛm'bæŋkmənt/ п. на́бережная f.; (street) на́сыпь f.

embargo /ɛm'bɑrgou/ п. эмба́рго neut. indecl.

embark /ɛm'bɑrk/ v. сади́ться на кора́бль impf.

embarkation /ˌɛmbɑr'keiʃən/ п. погру́зка f.

embarrass /ɛm'bærəs/ v. стесня́ть impf., стесни́ть pf.

embarrassing /ɛm'bærəsiŋ/ adj. вызыва́ющий замеша́тельство.

embarrassment /ɛm'bærəsmənt/ п. замеша́тельство, затрудне́ние neut.

embassy /'ɛmbəsi/ п. посо́льство neut.

embattle /ɛm'bætl/ v. стро́ить в боево́й поря́док impf.

embed /ɛm'bɛd/ v. вставля́ть (в with acc.) impf.

embellish /ɛm'bɛliʃ/ v. украша́ть; приукра́шивать impf.

embellishment /ɛm'bɛliʃmənt/ п. украше́ние neut.

ember /'ɛmbər/ п. тле́ющие у́гли pl.

embezzle /ɛm'bɛzəl/ v. растра́тить pf.

embezzlement /ɛm'bɛzəlmənt/ п. растра́та f.

embitter /ɛm'bitər/ v. озлобля́ть; ожесточа́ть impf.

emblazon /ɛm'bleizən/ v. украша́ть гербо́м impf.

emblem /'ɛmbləm/ п. эмбле́ма f., си́мвол m.

emblematic /ˌɛmblə'mætik/ adj. эмблемати́ческий.

embodiment /ɛm'bɒdimənt/ п. воплоще́ние, олицетворе́ние neut.

embody /ɛm'bɒdi/ v. воплоща́ть impf., воплоти́ть pf.

embolden /ɛm'bouldən/ v. ободря́ть, поощря́ть (with dat.) impf.

embolism /'ɛmbə,lizəm/ п. (med.) эмболи́я f.

embonpoint /ūbɔ̃'pwæ̃/ п. полнота́ f.

embosom /ɛm'buzəm/ v. обнима́ть impf.

emboss /ɛm'bɒs/ v. отти́скивать релье́ф impf.; (metal) чека́нить impf.

embossed /ɛm'bɒst/ adj. тиснёный; релье́фный.

embossing /ɛm'bɒsiŋ/ п. тисне́ние neut.

embouchure /ˌɑmbu'ʃur/ п. у́стье neut.

embrace /ɛm'breis/ п. объя́тия pl. **2.** v. обнима́ть impf., обня́ть pf.

embrasure /ɛm'breiʒər/ п. амбразу́ра f.

embroider /ɛm'brɔidər/ v. вышива́ть impf., вы́шить pf.

embroidery /ɛm'brɔidəri/ п. вы́шивка f.

embroil /ɛm'brɔil/ v. впу́тывать (в with acc.) impf.

embryo /'ɛmbri,ou/ п. заро́дыш, эмбрио́н m.

embryology /ˌɛmbri'ɒlədʒi/ п. эмбриоло́гия f.

embryonic /ˌɛmbri'ɒnik/ adj. эмбриона́льный.

embus /ɪmˈbʌs/ v. сажа́ть в авто́бус impf.
emend /ɪˈmɛnd/ v. исправля́ть impf.
emendation /ˌimənˈdeiʃən/ n. исправле́ние neut.
emerald /ˈɛmərəld/ n. изумру́д m.
emerge /ɪˈmɜrdʒ/ v. всплыва́ть impf., всплыть pf.
emergence /ɪˈmɜrdʒəns/ n. появле́ние neut.; вы́ход m.
emergency /ɪˈmɜrdʒənsi/ **1.** adj. авари́йный; чрезвыча́йный. **2.** n. крити́ческое состоя́ние or положе́ние neut.; кра́йняя необходи́мость f.
emergent /ɪˈmɜrdʒənt/ adj. развива́ющийся.
emeritus /ɪˈmɛritəs/ adj. заслу́женный, почётный.
emersion /ɪˈmɜrʒən/ n. (astr.) появле́ние neut.
emery /ˈɛməri/ n. нажда́к m.
emetic /əˈmɛtik/ **1.** adj. рво́тный. **2.** n. рво́тное, рво́тное сре́дство neut.
emigrant /ˈɛmigrənt/ **1.** adj. эмигри́рующий. **2.** n. эмигра́нт m., эмигра́нтка f.
emigrate /ˈɛmiˌgreit/ v. эмигри́ровать impf. and pf.
emigration /ˌɛmiˈgreiʃən/ n. эмигра́ция f.
emigratory /ˈɛmigrəˌtɔri/ adj. эмиграцио́нный.
emigré /ˈɛmiˌgrɛi/ n. эмигра́нт m.
eminence /ˈɛmənəns/ n. знамени́тость; возвы́шенность f.
eminent /ˈɛmənənt/ adj. выдаю́щийся, замеча́тельный.
eminently /ˈɛmənəntli/ adv. в вы́сшей сте́пени; осо́бенно.
emir /əˈmɪər/ n. эми́р m.
emirate /əˈmɪərɪt, ˈɛmərɪt/ n. эмира́т m.
emissary /ˈɛməˌsɛri/ n. по́сланный; посла́нец m.
emission /ɪˈmɪʃən/ n. уте́чка f.; излуче́ние neut.
emissive /ɪˈmɪsɪv/ adj. эмиссио́нный.
emissivity /ˌɛməˈsɪviti/ n. коэффицие́нт излуче́ния m.
emit /ɪˈmɪt/ v. испуска́ть impf., испусти́ть pf.; выпуска́ть impf., вы́пустить pf.
emitter /ɪˈmɪtər/ n. излуча́тель m.
emollient /ɪˈmɒlyənt/ n. смягча́ющее сре́дство neut.
emotion /ɪˈmoʊʃən/ n. чу́вство; волне́ние neut.; эмо́ция f.
emotional /ɪˈmoʊʃənl/ adj. эмоциона́льный.
emotionalism /ɪˈmoʊʃənlˈɪzəm/ n. эмоциона́льность f.
emotive /ɪˈmoʊtɪv/ adj. эмоциона́льный.
empathetic /ˌɛmpəˈθɛtɪk/ adj. эмпати́ческий.
empathize /ˈɛmpəˌθaiz/ v. сопережива́ть impf.
empathy /ˈɛmpəθi/ n. сопережива́ние neut.
emperor /ˈɛmpərər/ n. импера́тор m.
emphasis /ˈɛmfəsɪs/ n. эмфа́за f., ударе́ние neut.
emphasize /ˈɛmfəˌsaiz/ v. де́лать ударе́ние; подчёркивать impf., подчеркну́ть pf.
emphatic /ɛmˈfætɪk/ adj. вырази́тельный, эмфати́ческий.
emphysema /ˌɛmfəˈsimə/ n. эмфизе́ма f.
empire /ˈɛmpaɪᵊr/ n. импе́рия f.
empirical /ɛmˈpɪrɪkəl/ adj. эмпири́ческий.
empiricism /ɛmˈpɪrəˌsɪzəm/ n. эмпири́зм m.
empiricist /ɛmˈpɪrəsɪst/ n. эмпи́рик m.
empirio-criticism /ɛmˈpɪəriou ˈkritəˌsɪzəm/ n. эмпириокритици́зм m.
emplacement /ɛmˈpleismənt/ n. местоположе́ние neut.; устано́вка на ме́сто f.

employ /ɛmˈplɔi/ v. (use) употребля́ть impf., употреби́ть pf.; (hire) нанима́ть impf., наня́ть pf.
employable /ɛmˈplɔiəbəl/ adj. применя́емый; (able to work) работоспосо́бный.
employee /ɛmˈplɔii/ n. слу́жащий m.
employer /ɛmˈplɔiər/ n. нанима́тель m., работода́тель m.
employment /ɛmˈplɔimənt/ n. наём m.; слу́жба f., испо́льзование neut.
emporium /ɛmˈpɔriəm/ n. универма́г m.; това́рная ба́за f.
empower /ɛmˈpauər/ v. уполномо́чивать impf.; уполномо́чить pf.
empress /ˈɛmprɪs/ n. императри́ца f.
emptiness /ˈɛmptinɪs/ n. пустота́ f.
empty /ˈɛmpti/ **1.** adj. пусто́й. **2.** опоро́жнить pf.
empty-handed /ˈɛmpti ˈhændɪd/ adj. с пусты́ми рука́ми.
empty-headed /ˈɛmpti ˈhɛdɪd/ adj. пустоголо́вый.
empurple /ɛmˈpɜrpəl/ v. обагря́ть impf.
empyema /ˌɛmpiˈimə/ n. эмпие́ма f.
empyreal /ɛmˈpiriəl/ adj. небе́сный.
empyrean /ˌɛmpiˈriən/ n. эмпире́й m.
emu /ˈimyu/ n. эму m. indecl.
emulate /ˈɛmyəˌleit/ v. подража́ть impf.
emulation /ˌɛmyəˈleiʃən/ n. подража́ние neut.
emulative /ˈɛmyəˌleitɪv/ adj. соревнова́тельный.
emulous /ˈɛmyələs/ adj. стремя́щийся.
emulsifier /ɪˈmʌlsəˌfaiər/ n. эмульсифика́тор m.
emulsify /ɪˈmʌlsəˌfai/ v. эмульси́ровать impf.
emulsion /ɪˈmʌlʃən/ n. эму́льсия f.
emulsive /ɪˈmʌlsɪv/ adj. эмульсио́нный.
emulsoid /ɪˈmʌlsɔid/ n. эмульсо́ид m.
enable /ɛnˈeibəl/ v. дава́ть возмо́жность impf.
enact /ɛnˈækt/ v. постанови́ть pf.; вводи́ть зако́н.
enactment /ɛnˈæktmənt/ n. введе́ние зако́на в си́лу neut.
enamel /ɪˈnæməl/ n. эма́ль f.
enamelled /ɪˈnæməld/ adj. эмалиро́ванный.
enamelling /ɪˈnæməlɪŋ/ n. эмалиро́вка f.
enamor /ɪˈnæmər/ v. возбужда́ть любо́вь impf.
en bloc /ɑ̃ ˈblɔk/ adv. целико́м.
encage /ɛnˈkeidʒ/ v. сажа́ть в кле́тку impf.
encamp /ɛnˈkæmp/ v. располага́ться ла́герем impf.
encampment /ɛnˈkæmpmənt/ n. расположе́ние ла́герем neut.; ла́герь m.; стан m.
encapsulate /ɛnˈkæpsəˌleit/ v. герметизи́ровать impf.
encase /ɛnˈkeis/ v. вложи́ть impf.
encasing /ɛnˈkeisɪŋ/ n. обши́вка f.
encaustic /ɛnˈkɔstɪk/ n. энка́устика f.
enceinte /ɛnˈseint, ɑnˈsænt/ n. крепостна́я огра́да f.
encephalic /ˌɛnsəˈfælɪk/ adj. мозгово́й.
encephalitis /ɛnˌsɛfəˈlaitɪs/ n. энцефали́т m.
enchain /ɛnˈtʃein/ v. сажа́ть на цепь impf.
enchant /ɛnˈtʃænt/ v. очаро́вывать impf., очарова́ть pf.
enchanter /ɛnˈtʃæntər/ n. чароде́й m.
enchanting /ɛnˈtʃæntɪŋ/ adj. очарова́тельный; чару́ющий.
enchantment /ɛnˈtʃæntmənt/ n. очарова́ние neut.

enchantress /ɛn'tʃæntrɪs/ *n.* чаровни́ца *f.*; чаро-
де́йка *f.*
encipher /ɛn'saifər/ *v.* шифрова́ть *impf.*
encircle /ɛn'sɜrkəl/ *v.* окружа́ть *impf.*
encirclement /ɛn'sɜrkəlmənt/ *n.* окруже́ние *neut.*
enclasp /ɛn'klæsp/ *v.* обхва́тывать *impf.*
enclave /'ɛnkleiv/ *n.* анкла́в *m.*
enclitic /ɛn'klɪtɪk/ *n.* энкли́тика *f.*
enclose /ɛn'klouz/ *v.* вкла́дывать *impf.*, вложи́ть
pf.; включа́ть *impf.*, включи́ть *pf.*
enclosed /ɛn'klouzd/ *adj.* (*sealed off*) закры́тый.
enclosure /ɛn'klouʒər/ *n.* огоро́женное ме́сто;
вложе́ние, приложе́ние *neut.*
encode /ɛn'koud/ *v.* коди́ровать, шифрова́ть
impf.
encomiastic /ɛn,koumi'æstɪk/ *adj.* панегири́-
ческий.
encomium /ɛn'koumiəm/ *n.* панеги́рик *m.*
encompass /ɛn'kʌmpəs/ *n.* окружа́ть *impf.*,
окружи́ть *pf.*; заключа́ть *impf.*, заключи́ть *pf.*
encore /'aŋkɔr/ **1.** *n.* вы́зов на бис *m.* **2.** *interj.*
бис!
encounter /ɛn'kauntər/ **1.** *n.* столкнове́ние *neut.*,
встре́ча *f.* **2.** *v.* встре́тить *pf.*; ста́лкиваться
impf., столкну́ться *pf.*
encourage /ɛn'kɜrɪdʒ/ *v.* ободря́ть *impf.*,
ободри́ть *pf.*
encouragement /ɛn'kɜrɪdʒmənt/ *n.* ободре́ние; по-
ощре́ние *neut.*
encouraging /ɛn'kɜrɪdʒɪŋ/ *adj.* ободря́ющий; по-
ощри́тельный.
encroach /ɛn'kroutʃ/ *v.* посяга́ть (на with *acc.*)
impf.
encroachment /ɛn'kroutʃmənt/ *n.* посяга́тель-
ство *neut.*
encrust /ɛn'krʌst/ *v.* покрыва́ть (with *instr.*)
impf.
encumber /ɛn'kʌmbər/ *v.* загроможда́ть; обре-
меня́ть (with *instr.*) *impf.*
encumbrance /ɛn'kʌmbrəns/ *n.* препя́тствие;
бре́мя *neut.*
encyclical /ɛn'sɪklɪkəl/ *n.* энци́клика *f.*
encyclopedia /ɛn,saiklə'pidiə/ *n.* энциклопе́дия *f.*
encyclopedic /ɛn,saiklə'pidɪk/ *adj.* энциклопе-
ди́ческий.
encyclopedist /ɛn,saiklə'pidɪst/ *n.* энциклопеди́ст
m.
end /ɛnd/ **1.** *n.* коне́ц *m.*; (*purpose*) цель *f.*;
(*death*) смерть *f.* **2.** *v.t.* конча́ть *impf.*, ко́нчить
pf.; *v.i.* конча́ться *impf.*, ко́нчиться *pf.*; прекра-
ща́ть *impf.*; прекрати́ть *pf.*
endanger /ɛn'deindʒər/ *v.* подверга́ть опа́сности
impf.
endear /ɛn'dɪər/ *v.* внуша́ть любо́вь *impf.*
endearing /ɛn'dɪərɪŋ/ *adj.* привлека́тельный,
подкупа́ющий.
endearment /ɛn'dɪərmənt/ *n.* ла́ска *f.*
endeavor /ɛn'dɛvər/ **1.** *n.* попы́тка *f.* **2.** *v.*
пыта́ться, стара́ться *impf.*
endemic /ɛn'dɛmɪk/ *adj.* (*med.*) эндеми́чный.
ending /'ɛndɪŋ/ *n.* оконча́ние *neut.*
endless /'ɛndlɪs/ *adj.* бесконе́чный.
endmost /'ɛnd,moust/ *adj.* кра́йний.
endocarditis /ɛn,ɛndoukar'daitɪs/ *n.* эндокарди́т *m.*
endocardium /,ɛndou'kardiəm/ *n.* эндока́рд *m.*
endocarp /'ɛndə,karp/ *n.* эндока́рпий *m.*
endocrine /'ɛndəkrɪn/ *adj.* эндокри́нный.

endocrinology /,ɛndoukrə'nɒlədʒi/ *n.* эндокрино-
ло́гия *f.*
endoderm /'ɛndə,dɜrm/ *n.* эндоде́рма *f.*
endogamy /ɛn'dɒgəmi/ *n.* эндога́мия *f.*
endogenous /ɛn'dɒdʒənəs/ *adj.* эндоге́нный.
endomorph /'ɛndə,mɔrf/ *n.* эндомо́рф *m.*
endoplasm /'ɛndə,plæzəm/ *n.* эндопла́зма *f.*
endorse /ɛn'dɔrs/ *v.* индосси́ровать *impf. and pf.*
endorsee /ɛndɔr'si/ *n.* индосса́тор *m.*
endorsement /ɛn'dɔrsmənt/ *n.* индоссаме́нт *m.*
endorser /ɛn'dɔrsər/ *n.* индосса́нт *m.*
endosperm /'ɛndə,spɜrm/ *n.* эндоспе́рма *f.*
endospore /'ɛndə,spɔr/ *n.* эндоспо́ра *f.*
endothermic /,ɛndou'θɜrmɪk/ *adj.* эндотерми́-
ческий.
endow /ɛn'dau/ *v.* (*provide support*) материа́льно
обеспе́чивать; (*with talent, etc.*) одаря́ть,
наделя́ть (with *instr.*) *impf.*
endowment /ɛn'daumənt/ *n.* (*gift*) дар *m.*;
поже́ртвование *neut.*; (*talent*) дарова́ние *neut.*
end paper *n.* фо́рзац *m.*
end product *n.* гото́вый проду́кт *m.*
endurable /ɛn'durəbəl/ *adj.* терпи́мый.
endurance /ɛn'durəns/ *n.* выно́сливость *f.*
endure /ɛn'dur/ *v.* терпе́ть, выноси́ть *impf.*
enduring /ɛn'durɪŋ/ *adj.* про́чный, долгове́чный.
enema /'ɛnəmə/ *n.* кли́зма *f.*
enemy /'ɛnəmi/ *n.* враг, неприя́тель *m.*
energetic /,ɛnər'dʒɛtɪk/ *adj.* энерги́чный.
energetics /,ɛnər'dʒɛtɪks/ *n.* энерге́тика *f.*
energize /'ɛnər,dʒaiz/ *v.* возбужда́ть *impf.*
energizer /'ɛnər,dʒaizər/ *n.* активиза́тор *m.*
energy /'ɛnərdʒi/ *n.* эне́ргия *f.*
enervate /'ɛnər,veit/ *v.* обесси́ливать, рассла́б-
ля́ть *impf.*
enervation /,ɛnər'veiʃən/ *n.* расслабле́ние *neut.*
enfeeble /ɛn'fibəl/ *v.* ослабля́ть *impf.*
enfold /ɛn'fould/ *v.* заку́тывать (with *instr.*)
impf.
enforce /ɛn'fɔrs/ *v.* обеспе́чивать соблюде́ние
impf.
enforcement /ɛn'fɔrsmənt/ *n.* принужде́ние *neut.*
enfranchise /ɛn'fræntʃaiz/ *v.* (*give voting rights*)
предоставля́ть избира́тельные права́ (with *dat.*)
impf.
enfranchisement /ɛn'fræntʃaizmənt/ *n.* предо-
ставле́ние избира́тельных прав *neut.*
engage /ɛn'geidʒ/ *v.* (*occupy*) занима́ть *impf.*,
заня́ть *pf.*; (*hire*) нанима́ть *impf.*
engaged /ɛn'geidʒd/ **1.** *adj.* (*occupied*) за́нятый
(with *instr.*). **2.** *adj.* обручённый
engagement /ɛn'geidʒmənt/ *n.* (*business*) де́ло
neut.; (*meeting*) свида́ние *neut.*; (*betrothal*)
обруче́ние *neut.*; (*tech.*) зацепле́ние *neut.*;
(*switching*) включе́ние *neut.*; (*mil.*) бой *m.*,
сты́чка *f.*
engagement ring обруча́льное кольцо́ *neut.*
engaging /ɛn'geidʒɪŋ/ *adj.* обая́тельный; привле-
ка́тельный.
engender /ɛn'dʒɛndər/ *v.* порожда́ть *impf.*
engine /'ɛndʒən/ *n.* маши́на *f.*, мото́р *m.*
engine-driven /'ɛndʒən ,drivən/ *adj.* мото́рный.
engine driver *n.* машини́ст *m.*
engineer /,ɛndʒə'nɪər/ *n.* инжене́р *m.*
engine room /'ɛndʒən ,rum/ *n.* маши́нное от-
деле́ние *neut.*
England /'ɪŋglɪnd/ *n.* А́нглия *f.*

English /'ɪŋglɪʃ/ *adj.* англи́йский; **in English** *adv.* по-англи́йски.

English Channel *n.* Ла-Ма́нш (проли́в) *m.*

Englishman /'ɪŋglɪʃmən/ *n.* англича́нин *m.*

English-speaking /'ɪŋglɪʃ ˌspikɪŋ/ *adj.* англоязы́чный.

Englishwoman /'ɪŋglɪʃˌwʊmən/ *n.* англича́нка *f.*

engorge /ɛn'gɔrdʒ/ *v.* жа́дно прогла́тывать *impf.*

engraft /ɛn'græft/ *v.* привива́ть *impf.*

engrave /ɛn'greiv/ *v.* гравирова́ть *impf.*, вы́гравировать *pf.*

engraver /ɛn'greivər/ *n.* гравёр *m.*

engraving /ɛn'greivɪŋ/ *n.* гравирова́ние *neut.*; (*an etching*) гравю́ра *f.*

engross /ɛn'grous/ *v.* поглоща́ть; **be engrossed in** *v.* быть поглощённым (*with instr.*) *impf.*

engrossing /ɛn'grousɪŋ/ *adj.* всепоглоща́ющий.

engulf /ɛn'gʌlf/ *v.* поглоща́ть *impf.*

enhance /ɛn'hæns/ *v.* повыша́ть *impf.*, повы́сить *pf.*

enharmonic /ˌɛnhɑr'mɒnɪk/ *adj.* энгармони́ческий.

enigma /ə'nɪgmə/ *n.* зага́дка *f.*

enigmatic /ˌɛnɪg'mætɪk/ *adj.* зага́дочный.

enjoin /ɛn'dʒɔin/ *v.* веле́ть, прика́зывать *impf.*

enjoy /ɛn'dʒɔi/ *v.* наслажда́ться *impf.*

enjoyable /ɛn'dʒɔiəbəl/ *adj.* прия́тный.

enjoyment /ɛn'dʒɔimənt/ *n.* наслажде́ние *neut.*

enlarge /ɛn'lɑrdʒ/ *v.* увели́чивать *impf.*, увели́чить *pf.*

enlargement /ɛn'lɑrdʒmənt/ *n.* увеличе́ние *neut.*

enlarger /ɛn'lɑrdʒər/ *n.* (*photogr.*) фотоувеличи́тель *m.*

enlighten /ɛn'laitn/ *v.* просвеща́ть *impf.*, просвети́ть *pf.*

enlightenment /ɛn'laitnmənt/ *n.* просвеще́ние *neut.*

enlist /ɛn'lɪst/ *v.t.* вербова́ть *impf.*, завербова́ть *pf.*; *v.i.* поступа́ть на вое́нную слу́жбу *impf.*

enlisted men /ɛn'lɪstɪd/ *n.* рядовы́е *pl.*

enlistment /ɛn'lɪstmənt/ *n.* (*recruiting*) вербо́вка *f.*

enliven /ɛn'laivən/ *v.* оживля́ть *impf.*

en masse /ɑn mæs/ *adv.* все вме́сте.

enmesh /ɛn'mɛʃ/ *v.* запу́тывать *impf.*

enmity /'ɛnmɪti/ *n.* вражда́ *f.*

ennoble /ɛn'noubəl/ *v.* облагора́живать *impf.*

ennoblement /ɛn'noubəlmənt/ *n.* облагора́живание *neut.*

ennui /ɑn'wi/ *n.* ску́ка *f.*

Enoch /'inək/ *n.* Ено́х *m.*

enormity /ɪ'nɔrmɪti/ *n.* огро́мность *f.*

enormous /ɪ'nɔrməs/ *adj.* огро́мный.

enormously /ɪ'nɔrməsli/ *adv.* чрезвыча́йно.

enough /ɪ'nʌf/ *adj.*, *adv.* дово́льно, доста́точно.

enrage /ɛn'reidʒ/ *v.* беси́ть *impf.*, взбеси́ть *pf.*

enrapture /ɛn'ræptʃər/ *v.* восхища́ть *impf.*

enraptured /ɛn'ræptʃərd/ *adj.* в восто́рге.

enrich /ɛn'rɪtʃ/ *v.* обогаща́ть *impf.*, обогати́ть *pf.*

enrichment /ɛn'rɪtʃmənt/ *n.* обогаще́ние *neut.*

enrobe /ɛn'roub/ *v.* облача́ть *impf.*

enroll /ɛn'roul/ *v.* вноси́ть в спи́сок; регистри́ровать *impf.*

enrollment /ɛn'roulmənt/ *n.* регистра́ция *f.*, внесе́ние в спи́ски *neut.*

en route /ɑn rut/ *adv.* по пути́.

ensanguine /ɛn'sæŋgwɪn/ *v.* окрова́вливать *impf.*

ensconce /ɛn'skɒns/ *v.* устра́ивать *impf.*

ensemble /ɑn'sɑmbəl/ *n.* анса́мбль *m.*

enshrine /ɛn'ʃrain/ *v.* храни́ть *impf.*

enshroud /ɛn'ʃraud/ *v.* покрыва́ть са́ваном; (*fig.*) обвола́кивать *impf.*

ensign /'ɛnsain; *Mil.* 'ɛnsən/ *n.* (*banner*) зна́мя *neut.*; (*naut.*) кормово́й флаг *m.*; (*mil.*) мла́дший лейтена́нт *m.*

ensilage /'ɛnsəlɪdʒ/ *n.* силосова́ние *neut.*

ensile /ɛn'sail/ *v.* силосова́ть *impf.*

enslave /ɛn'sleiv/ *v.* порабоща́ть *impf.*, поработи́ть *pf.*

enslavement /ɛn'sleivmənt/ *n.* порабоще́ние *neut.*

enslaver /ɛn'sleivər/ *n.* поработи́тель *m.*

ensnare /ɛn'snɛər/ *v.* пойма́ть в лову́шку *impf.*

ensue /ɛn'su/ *v.* сле́довать; получа́ться в результа́те *impf.*

ensuing /ɛn'suiŋ/ *adj.* после́дующий.

ensure /ɛn'ʃʊr/ *v.* обеспе́чивать; гаранти́ровать *impf.*

entablature /ɛn'tæblətʃər/ *n.* антаблеме́нт *m.*

entail /ɛn'teil/ *v.* влечь за собо́й; вызыва́ть; зна́чить *impf.*

entangle /ɛn'tæŋgəl/ *v.* запу́тать *pf.*

entanglement /ɛn'tæŋgəlmənt/ *n.* запу́танность *f.*

entente /ɑn'tɑnt/ *n.* дру́жеское соглаше́ние *neut.*; (*hist.*) Анта́нта *f.*

enter /'ɛntər/ *v.* (*on foot*) входи́ть *impf.*, войти́ *pf.*; (*by vehicle*) въезжа́ть *impf.*, въе́хать *pf.*; (*join*) вступа́ть *impf.*, вступи́ть *pf.*

enteric /ɛn'tɛrɪk/ *adj.* кише́чный.

enteritis /ˌɛntə'raitɪs/ *n.* энтери́т *m.*

enterprise /'ɛntər,praiz/ *n.* (*undertaking*) предприя́тие *neut.*; (*spirit*) предприи́мчивость *f.*

enterprising /'ɛntər,praizɪŋ/ *adj.* предприи́мчивый.

entertain /ˌɛntər'tein/ *v.* развлека́ть *impf.*, развле́чь *pf.*; принима́ть госте́й *impf.*

entertainer /ˌɛntər'teinər/ *n.* (эстра́дный) арти́ст *m.*

entertaining /ˌɛntər'teinɪŋ/ *adj.* заба́вный; развлека́тельный, занима́тельный.

entertainment /ˌɛntər'teinmənt/ *n.* развлече́ние; угоще́ние *neut.*; (*show*) дивертисме́нт *m.*

enthalpy /'ɛnθælpi/ *n.* энтальпи́я *f.*

enthrall /ɛn'θrɔl/ *v.* увлека́ть; завлека́ть *impf.*

enthralling /ɛn'θrɔlɪŋ/ *adj.* увлека́тельный.

enthrone /ɛn'θroun/ *v.* возводи́ть на престо́л *impf.*

enthronement /ɛn'θrounmənt/ *n.* возведе́ние на престо́л *neut.*

enthuse /ɛn'θuz/ *v.* приходи́ть в восто́рг (от *with gen.*) *impf.*

enthusiasm /ɛn'θuzi,æzəm/ *n.* энтузиа́зм *m.*

enthusiast /ɛn'θuzi,æst, -ɪst/ *n.* энтузиа́ст *m.*

enthusiastic /ɛnˌθuzi'æstɪk/ *adj.* восто́рженный; по́лный энтузиа́зма.

entice /ɛn'tais/ *v.* замани́вать *impf.*, замани́ть *pf.*

enticement /ɛn'taismənt/ *n.* собла́зн *m.*

enticing /ɛn'taisɪŋ/ *adj.* соблазни́тельный, зама́нчивый, привлека́тельный.

entire /ɛn'taiᵊr/ *adj.* це́лый; весь.

entirely /ɛn'taiⁱrli/ adv. по́лностью.
entirety /ɛn'taiⁱrti/ n. полнота́, це́льность f.
entitle /ɛn'taitl/ v. дава́ть пра́во; (book) озагла́вливать impf., озагла́вить pf.
entitlement /ɛn'taitlmənt/ n. пра́во (на with acc.) neut.; (portion) до́ля f.
entity /'ɛntɪti/ n. существо́ neut.; вещь f., объе́кт m.
entomb /ɛn'tum/ v. погреба́ть impf.
entombment /ɛn'tummənt/ n. погребе́ние neut.
entomological /,ɛntəmə'lɒdʒɪkəl/ adj. энтомологи́ческий.
entomologist /,ɛntə'mɒlədʒɪst/ n. энтомо́лог m.
entomology /,ɛntə'mɒlədʒi/ n. энтомоло́гия f.
entourage /,ɑntu'rɑʒ/ n. окружа́ющая обстано́вка; сви́та f.
entr'acte /ɑn'trækt/ n. антра́кт m.
entrails /'ɛntreilz/ n. вну́тренности, кишки́ pl.
entrain /ɛn'trein/ v. сади́ться в по́езд impf.
entrance¹ /'ɛntrəns/ **1.** adj. входно́й; вступи́тельный. **2.** n. вход m.
entrance² /ɛn'træns/ v. зачаро́вывать impf.
entrancement /ɛn'trænsmənt/ n. зачаро́ванность f.
entrancing /ɛn'trænsɪŋ, -'trɑn-/ adj. зачаро́вывающий.
entrant /'ɛntrənt/ n. уча́стник m.
entrap /ɛn'træp/ v. пойма́ть в лову́шку pf.
entreat /ɛn'trit/ v. умоля́ть impf.
entreaty /ɛn'triti/ n. мольба́, про́сьба f.
entrechat /,ɑntrə'ʃɑ/ n. антраша́ neut. indecl.
entrée /'ɑntrei/ n. пра́во вхо́да neut.; (main course) второ́е neut.
entrench /ɛn'trɛntʃ/ v. ока́пываться; укореня́ть impf.
entrenchment /ɛn'trɛntʃmənt/ n. око́п m.
entrepôt /'ɑntrə,pou/ n. пакга́уз m.
entrepreneur /,ɑntrəprə'nɜr/ n. предпринима́тель m.
entrepreneurial /,ɑntrəprə'nɜriəl/ adj. предпринима́тельский.
entresol /'ɛntər,sɒl/ n. антресо́ль f.
entropy /'ɛntrəpi/ n. энтропи́я f.
entrust /ɛn'trʌst/ v. вверя́ть impf., вве́рить pf.; поруча́ть impf., поручи́ть pf.
entry /'ɛntri/ n. вход m., вступле́ние neut.
entryway /'ɛntri,wei/ n. вход m.
entwine /ɛn'twain/ v. сплета́ть(ся) impf.
enumerable /ɪ'numərəbəl/ adj. счётный.
enumerate /ɪ'numə,reit/ v. перечисля́ть impf., перечи́слить pf.
enumeration /ɪ,numə'reiʃən/ n. перечисле́ние neut.
enumerator /ɪ'numə,reitər/ n. счётчик m.
enunciate /ɪ'nʌnsi,eit/ v. произноси́ть impf., произнести́ pf.
enunciation /ɪ,nʌnsi'eiʃən/ n. произноше́ние neut.
enuresis /,ɛnyə'risɪs/ n. недержа́ние мочи́ neut.
envelop /ɛn'vɛləp/ v. завёртывать impf., заверну́ть pf.
envelope /'ɛnvə,loup, 'ɑn-/ n. конве́рт m.
envelopment /ɛn'vɛləpmənt/ n. охва́т m.
envenom /ɛn'vɛnəm/ v. отравля́ть impf.
enviable /'ɛnviəbəl/ adj. зави́дный.
envious /'ɛnviəs/ adj. зави́стливый.
enviously /'ɛnviəsli/ adv. с за́вистью.

environment /ɛn'vairənmənt/ n. окруже́ние neut.; среда́ f.
environmentalist /ɛn,vairən'mɛntl̩ɪst/ n. защи́тник приро́ды m.
environs /ɛn'vairənz/ n. окре́стности pl.
envisage /ɛn'vɪzɪdʒ/ v. мы́сленно ви́деть; (plan) предусма́тривать impf.
envoy /'ɛnvɔi, 'ɑn-/ n. посла́нник m.
envy /'ɛnvi/ **1.** n. за́висть f. **2.** v. зави́довать impf.
enzyme /'ɛnzaim/ n. энзи́м m.
Eocene /'iə,sin/ n. эоце́н m.
eolith /'iəlɪθ/ n. эоли́т m.
eon /'iən, 'iɒn/ n. эо́н m.
epact /'ipækt/ n. эпа́кта f.
eparchy /'ɛpɑrki/ n. епа́рхия f.
epaulet /'ɛpə,lɛt/ n. эполе́т m.
épée /'ɛpei/ n. шпа́га f.
epenthetic /,ɛpən'θɛtɪk/ adj. вставно́й.
ephedrine /ɪ'fɛdrɪn/ n. эфедри́н m.
ephemera /ɪ'fɛmərə/ n. однодне́вки pl.
ephemeral /ɪ'fɛmərəl/ adj. эфеме́рный adj.
ephemeris /ɪ'fɛmərɪs/ n. (astr.) эфемери́ды pl.
epic /'ɛpɪk/ **1.** adj. эпи́ческий. **2.** n. эпи́ческая поэ́ма f.
epicardium /,ɛpɪ'kɑrdiəm/ n. эпика́рдий m.
epicarp /'ɛpɪ,kɑrp/ n. эпика́рпий m.
epicene /'ɛpɪ,sin/ adj. неопределённого по́ла.
epicenter /'ɛpə,sɛntər/ n. эпице́нтр m.
epicure /'ɛpɪ,kyur/ n. эпикуре́ец.
epicurean /,ɛpɪkyu'riən, -'kyuri-/ adj. эпикуре́йский.
Epicureanism /,ɛpɪkyu'riə,nɪzəm, -'kyuri-/ n. эпикуреи́зм m.
epicycle /'ɛpə,saikəl/ n. эпици́кл m.
epicycloid /,ɛpə'saiklɔid/ n. эпицикло́ида f.
epidemic /,ɛpɪ'dɛmɪk/ **1.** adj. эпидеми́ческий. **2.** n. эпиде́мия f.
epidemiology /,ɛpɪ,dimi'ɒlədʒi/ n. эпидемиоло́гия f.
epidermal /,ɛpɪ'dɜrməl/ adj. эпидерми́ческий.
epidermis /,ɛpɪ'dɜrmɪs/ n. эпиде́рма f.
epidiascope /,ɛpɪ'daiə,skoup/ n. эпидиаско́п m.
epiglottis /,ɛpɪ'glɒtɪs/ n. надгорта́нник m.
epigone /'ɛpɪ,goun/ n. эпиго́н m.
epigram /'ɛpɪ,græm/ n. эпигра́мма f.
epigrammatic /,ɛpɪgrə'mætɪk/ adj. эпиграммати́ческий.
epigrammatist /,ɛpɪ'græmətɪst/ n. эпиграмма́тист m.
epigraph /'ɛpɪ,græf/ n. эпи́граф m.
epigraphic /,ɛpɪ'græfɪk/ adj. эпиграфи́ческий.
epigraphy /ɪ'pɪgrəfi/ n. эпигра́фика f.
epilepsy /'ɛpə,lɛpsi/ n. эпиле́псия f.
epileptic /,ɛpə'lɛptɪk/ **1.** adj. эпилепти́ческий. **2.** n. эпиле́птик m.
epilogue /'ɛpə,lɒg/ n. эпило́г m.
Epiphany /ɪ'pɪfəni/ n. Богоявле́ние; Креще́ние neut.
epiphyte /'ɛpə,fait/ n. (bot.) эпифи́т m.
episcopacy /ɪ'pɪskəpəsi/ n. епи́скопство neut.
episcopal /ɪ'pɪskəpəl/ adj. епи́скопский; епископа́льный.
Episcopalian /ɪ'pɪskə'peiliən/ adj. епископа́льный.
episcopate /ɪ'pɪskəpɪt/ n. сан епи́скопа m.
episode /'ɛpə,soud/ n. эпизо́д m.

episodic /ˌɛpə'sɒdɪk/ adj. эпизодический.

epistemological /ˌpɪstəmə'lɒdʒɪkəl/ adj. эпистемологический.

epistemology /ˌpɪstə'mɒlədʒi/ n. теория познания, гносеология f.

epistle /ɪ'pɪsəl/ n. послание neut.

epistolary /ɪ'pɪstl̩ˌɛri/ adj. эпистолярный.

epistyle /'ɛpəˌstail/ n. архитрав m.

epitaph /'ɛpɪˌtæf/ n. эпитафия f.

epithalamium /ˌɛpəθə'leimiəm/ n. эпиталама f.

epithelium /ˌɛpə'θiliəm/ n. эпителий m.

epithet /'ɛpəˌθɛt/ n. эпитет m.

epitome /ɪ'pɪtəmi/ n. конспект m.

epitomize /ɪ'pɪtəˌmaiz/ v. (summarize) конспектировать, резюмировать impf.; (embody) олицетворять impf.

epizoon /ˌɛpə'zouɒn/ n. животный эктопаразит m.

epoch /'ɛpək/ n. эпоха f.

epochal /'ɛpəkəl/ adj. эпохальный.

epoch-making /'ɛpəkˌmeikɪŋ/ adj. эпохальный, исторический.

epode /'ɛpoud/ n. эпод m.

eponym /'ɛpənɪm/ n. эпоним m.

epos /'ɛpɒs/ n. эпос m.

epoxy /ɪ'pɒksi/ adj. эпоксидный.

epoxy- adj. prefix эпокси-.

epoxy resin n. эпоксидная смола f., эпоксисмола f.

Epsom salts /'ɛpsəm/ n. сернокислый магний m.

equability /ˌɛkwə'bɪlɪti/ n. равномерность f.

equable /'ɛkwəbəl/ adj. равномерный.

equal /'ikwəl/ 1. adj. равный; одинаковый. 2. v. равняться impf.

equality /ɪ'kwɒlɪti/ n. равенство neut.

equalization /ˌikwələ'zeiʃən/ n. уравнивание neut.

equalize /'ikwəˌlaiz/ v. уравнивать impf., уравнять pf.

equalizer /'ikwəˌlaizər/ n. (tech.) уравнитель m.

equally /'ikwəli/ adv. одинаково, в равной степени; равно.

equanimity /ˌikwə'nɪmɪti/ n. самообладание neut.

equate /ɪ'kweit/ v. уравнивать; приравнивать (к with dat.), считать равным impf.

equation /ɪ'kweiʒən/ n. уравнение neut.

equator /ɪ'kweitər/ n. экватор m.

equatorial /ˌikwə'tɔriəl/ adj. экваториальный.

equestrian /ɪ'kwɛstriən/ 1. adj. конный. 2. n. всадник m.

equestrienne /ɪˌkwɛstri'ɛn/ n. наездница f.

equiangular /ˌikwi'æŋgyələr/ adj. равноугольный.

equidistant /ˌikwɪ'dɪstənt/ adj. равноудалённый, равноотстоящий.

equilateral /ˌikwə'lætərəl/ adj. равносторонний.

equilibrate /ɪ'kwɪləˌbreit/ adj. уравновешивать(ся).

equilibrist /ɪ'kwɪləbrɪst/ n. эквилибрист m.

equilibrium /ˌikwə'lɪbriəm/ n. равновесие neut.

equine /'ikwain/ adj. лошадиный.

equinoctial /ˌikwə'nɒkʃəl/ adj. равноденственный.

equinox /'ikwəˌnɒks/ n. равноденствие neut.

equip /ɪ'kwɪp/ v. оборудовать impf. and pf.; снабжать impf., снабдить pf.

equipage /'ɛkwəpɪdʒ/ n. экипаж m.

equipment /ɪ'kwɪpmənt/ n. оборудование neut.

equipoise /'ikwəˌpɔiz/ n. равновесие neut.

equipollent /ˌikwə'pɒlənt/ adj. (math.) эквиполлентный.

equiponderant /ˌɛkwə'pɒndərənt/ adj. равновесный.

equipotential /ˌikwəpə'tɛnʃəl/ adj. эквипотенциальный.

equitable /'ɛkwɪtəbəl/ adj. справедливый.

equitant /'ɛkwɪtənt/ adj. (bot.) вкладной.

equitation /ˌɛkwɪ'teiʃən/ n. верховая езда f.

equity /'ɛkwɪti/ n. справедливость f.; беспристрастность f.; (econ.) активы pl.

equivalence /ɪ'kwɪvələns/ n. эквивалентность f.

equivalent /ɪ'kwɪvələnt/ 1. adj. эквивалентный. 2. n. эквивалент m.

equivocal /ɪ'kwɪvəkəl/ adj. двусмысленный; неясный.

equivocate /ɪ'kwɪvəˌkeit/ v. говорить двусмысленно impf.

equivocation /ɪˌkwɪvə'keiʃən/ n. увиливание neut.

era /'ɪərə, 'ɛrə/ n. эра f.

eradiate /ɪ'reidiˌeit/ v. излучать impf.

eradiation /ɪˌreidi'eiʃən/ n. излучение neut.

eradicate /ɪ'rædɪˌkeit/ v. искоренять impf., искоренить pf.

eradication /ɪˌrædɪ'keiʃən/ n. искоренение neut.

erase /ɪ'reis/ v. стирать impf., стереть pf.

eraser /ɪ'reisər/ n. резинка f.

erasure /ɪ'reiʃər/ n. стирание neut.

erbium /'ɜrbiəm/ n. эрбий m.

ere /ɛər/ prep. (poet.) до (with gen.), перед (with instr.).

erect /ɪ'rɛkt/ 1. adj. прямой, вертикальный. 2. v. воздвигать impf., воздвигнуть pf.

erectile /ɪ'rɛktl̩/ adj. (physiol.) напряжённый.

erection /ɪ'rɛkʃən/ n. постройка f.; (physiol.) эрекция f.

erector /ɪ'rɛktər/ n. (anat.) выпрямляющая мышца f.

eremite /'ɛrəˌmait/ n. отшельник m.

erg /ɜrg/ n. (phys.) эрг m.

ergo /'ɜrgou, 'ɛrgou/ adv. итак, следовательно.

ergonomics /ˌɜrgə'nɒmɪks/ n. эргономика f.

ergosterol /ɜr'gɒstəˌroul/ n. эргостерин m.

ergot /'ɜrgət/ n. спорынья f.

ergotism /'ɜrgəˌtɪzəm/ n. отравление спорыньёй neut.

ergotropic /ˌɜrgə'trɒpɪk/ adj. эрготропный.

Erie /'ɪəri/ n. Lake, озеро Эри neut.

ermine /'ɜrmɪn/ n. горностай m.

erode /ɪ'roud/ v. разъедать impf., разъесть pf.

erodent /ɪ'roudnt/ adj. едкий.

erogenous /ɪ'rɒdʒənəs/ adj. эрогенный.

Eros /'ɪərɒs, 'ɛrɒs/ n. Эрос m.

erosion /ɪ'rouʒən/ n. разъедание neut.

erosive /ɪ'rousɪv/ adj. разъедающий, едкий.

erotic /ɪ'rɒtɪk/ adj. эротический.

eroticism /ɪ'rɒtəˌsɪzəm/ n. эротизм m.

err /ɜr, ɛr/ v. ошибаться impf., ошибиться pf.

errancy /'ɛrənsi/ n. заблуждение neut.

errand /'ɛrənd/ n. поручение neut.

errand boy n. мальчик на побегушках m.

errant /ˈɛrənt/ adj. стра́нствующий.
erratic /ɪˈrætɪk/ adj. неусто́йчивый.
erratum /ɪˈrɑtəm/ n. (in writing) опи́ска f.; (in print) опеча́тка f.
erring /ˈɜrɪŋ, ˈɛr-/ adj. заблу́дший.
erroneous /əˈrouniəs/ adj. оши́бочный.
error /ˈɛrər/ n. оши́бка f.
erstwhile /ˈɜrstˌwail/ 1. adj. бы́вший. 2. adv. пре́жде.
erubescence /ˌɛruˈbɛsəns/ n. покрасне́ние neut.
erubescent /ˌɛruˈbɛsənt/ adj. красне́ющий.
eructate /ɪˈrʌkteit/ v. отры́гивать; (fig.) изверга́ть impf.
eructation /ɪrʌkˈteiʃən/ n. отры́жка f.
erudite /ˈɛryuˌdait/ adj. учёный, эруди́рованный.
erudition /ˌɛryuˈdiʃən/ n. эруди́ция f.
erupt /ɪˈrʌpt/ v. (volcano) изверга́ться; (explode) взрыва́ться impf.
eruption /ɪˈrʌpʃən/ n. изверже́ние neut.
eruptive /ɪˈrʌptɪv/ adj. вулкани́ческий.
erysipelas /ˌɛrəˈsɪpələs/ n. ро́жа f.
erythema /ˌɛrəˈθimə/ n. эрите́ма f.
Esau /ˈisɔ/ n. Иса́в m.
escalate /ˈɛskəˌleit/ v. постепе́нно увели́чивать(ся); постепе́нно повыша́ть(ся); (intensify) постепе́нно уси́ливать(ся) impf.
escalation /ˌɛskəˈleiʃən/ n. эскала́ция f.
escalator /ˈɛskəˌleitər/ n. эскала́тор m.
escapade /ˈɛskəˌpeid/ n. вы́ходка, проде́лка f.
escape /ɪˈskeip/ 1. n. бе́гство neut.; (from danger) спасе́ние neut.; (gas, etc.) уте́чка f. 2. v. убега́ть impf., убежа́ть pf.; (save oneself) спаса́ться impf.
escapee /ɪskeiˈpi/ n. бе́женец m.
escarpment /ɪˈskɑrpmənt/ n. обры́в m.
eschatological /ˌɛskətlˈɒdʒɪkəl/ adj. эсхатологи́ческий.
eschatology /ˌɛskəˈtɒlədʒi/ n. эсхатоло́гия f.
eschew /ɛsˈtʃu/ v. воздержи́ваться (от with gen.); избега́ть (with gen.) impf.
escort /ˈɛskɔrt; v. ɪˈskɔrt/ 1. n. охра́на f., эско́рт, конво́й m. 2. v. сопровожда́ть impf.; эскорти́ровать impf. and pf.
escudo /ɛˈskudou/ n. эску́до neut. indecl.
escutcheon /ɪˈskʌtʃən/ n. щит герба́ m.
Eskimo /ˈɛskəˌmou/ 1. adj. эскимо́сский. 2. n. эскимо́с m., эскимо́ска f.
esophagus /ɪˈsɒfəgəs/ n. пищево́д m.
esoteric /ˌɛsəˈtɛrɪk/ adj. та́йный; таи́нственный.
E.S.P. n. (abbr. of extra-sensory perception) экстрасенсо́рное возде́йствие neut.
espadrilles /ˈɛspəˌdrɪlz/ n. эспадри́льи pl.
espalier /ɪˈspælyər/ n. шпале́рник m.
esparto /ɪˈspɑrtou/ n. эспа́рто neut. indecl.
especial /ɪˈspɛʃəl/ adj. осо́бенный, специа́льный.
especially /ɪˈspɛʃəli/ adv. осо́бенно.
Esperantist /ˌɛspəˈrɑntɪst/ n. эсперанти́ст m., эсперанти́стка f.
Esperanto /ˌɛspəˈrɑntou/ n. эспера́нто neut. indecl.
espionage /ˈɛspiəˌnɑʒ/ 1. adj. шпио́нский. 2. n. шпиона́ж m.
esplanade /ˈɛspləˌnɑd/ n. эспла́нада f.
espousal /ɪˈspauzəl/ n. (fig.) подде́ржка f.
espouse /ɪˈspauz/ v. подде́рживать impf.
esprit de corps /ɛˈspri də ˈkɔr/ n. чу́вство солида́рности neut.

espy /ɪˈspai/ v. рассмотре́ть pf.
esquire /ˈɛskwaiᵊr/ n. эсква́йр m.
essay /ˈɛsei/ n. о́черк, этю́д m.
essence /ˈɛsəns/ n. су́щность f.
essential /əˈsɛnʃəl/ adj. необходи́мый; суще́ственный.
essentiality /əˌsɛnʃiˈæliti/ n. суще́ственность f.
essentially /əˈsɛnʃəli/ adv. по существу́; в основно́м.
establish /ɪˈstæblɪʃ/ v. осно́вывать impf., основа́ть pf.; устана́вливать impf., установи́ть pf.
established /ɪˈstæblɪʃt/ adj. при́нятый; официа́льно при́знанный.
establishment /ɪˈstæblɪʃmənt/ n. учрежде́ние; установле́ние; основа́ние neut.
estate /ɪˈsteit/ n. поме́стье neut.; (class) сосло́вие neut.; **real estate** недви́жимость f.
esteem /ɪˈstim/ 1. n. уваже́ние neut.; почёт m. 2. v. уважа́ть impf.
ester /ˈɛstər/ n. сло́жный эфи́р m.
Esther /ˈɛstər/ n. Эсфи́рь f.
estimable /ˈɛstəməbəl/ adj. почте́нный, уважа́емый.
estimate /v. ˈɛstəˌmeit; n. ˈɛstəmɪt/ 1. v. оце́нивать impf., оцени́ть pf. 2. n. оце́нка f.
estimated /ˈɛstəˌmeitɪd/ adj. (tech.) расчётный.
estimation /ˌɛstəˈmeiʃən/ n. сужде́ние, мне́ние neut.
Estonia /ɛˈstouniə/ n. Эсто́ния f.
Estonian /ɛˈstouniən/ 1. adj. эсто́нский. 2. n. эсто́нец m., эсто́нка f.
estrange /ɪˈstreindʒ/ v. отчужда́ть impf.
estrangement /ɪˈstreindʒmənt/ n. отчужде́ние neut.
estuary /ˈɛstʃuˌɛri/ n. у́стье реки́ neut.
esurient /ɪˈsuriənt/ adj. голо́дный.
et cetera /ɛt ˈsɛtərə/ и так да́лее.
etch /ɛtʃ/ v. вытра́вливать impf.
etcher /ˈɛtʃər/ n. трави́льщик, гравёр m.; офорти́ст m.
etching /ˈɛtʃɪŋ/ n. гравю́ра f.
eternal /ɪˈtɜrnl/ adj. ве́чный.
eternalize /ɪˈtɜrnlˌaiz/ v. увекове́чивать impf.
eternity /ɪˈtɜrnɪti/ n. ве́чность f.
etesian /ɪˈtiʒən/ adj. ежего́дный.
ethane /ˈɛθein/ n. эта́н m.
ethanol /ˈɛθəˌnɔl/ n. эти́ловый спирт m.
ether /ˈiθər/ n. эфи́р m.
ethereal /ɪˈθiriəl/ adj. эфи́рный.
etherize /ˈiθəˌraiz/ v. усыпля́ть эфи́ром impf.
ethical /ˈɛθɪkəl/ adj. эти́чный, эти́ческий.
ethics /ˈɛθɪks/ n. э́тика f.
Ethiopia /ˌiθiˈoupiə/ n. Эфио́пия f.
ethnic /ˈɛθnɪk/ adj. этни́ческий.
ethnographer /ɛθˈnɒgrəfər/ n. этно́граф m.
ethnographic /ˌɛθnəˈgræfɪk/ adj. этнографи́ческий.
ethnography /ɛθˈnɒgrəfi/ n. этногра́фия f.
ethnological /ˌɛθnəˈlɒdʒɪkəl/ adj. этнологи́ческий.
ethnologist /ɛθˈnɒlədʒɪst/ n. этно́лог m.
ethnology /ɛθˈnɒlədʒi/ n. этноло́гия f.
ethology /iˈθɒlədʒi/ n. этоло́гия f.
ethos /ˈiθɒs/ n. дух m.
ethyl /ˈɛθəl/ n. эти́л m.
ethylene /ˈɛθəˌlin/ n. этиле́н m.
etiolate /ˈitiəˌleit/ v. (bot.) этиоли́ровать impf.

etiology /,iti'ɒlədʒi/ n. этиоло́гия f.
etiquette /'ɛtɪkɪt/ n. этике́т m.; пра́вила поведе́ния pl.
Etna /'ɛtnə/ n. (volcano) Э́тна f.
Eton /'itn/ n. и́тонский колле́дж m.
Etruscan /ɪ'trʌskən/ adj. этру́сский.
étude /'eitud/ n. (mus.) этю́д m.
etymological /,ɛtəmə'lɒdʒɪkəl/ adj. этимологи́ческий.
etymologist /,ɛtə'mɒlədʒɪst/ n. этимо́лог m.
etymology /,ɛtə'mɒlədʒi/ n. этимоло́гия f.
etymon /'ɛtə,mɒn/ n. этимо́н m.
eucalyptus /,yukə'lɪptəs/ n. эвкали́пт m.
Eucharist /'yukərɪst/ n. евхари́стия f.; прича́стие neut.
Euclid /'yuklɪd/ n. Евкли́д m.
Euclidean /yu'klɪdiən/ adj. евкли́дов.
eudiometer /,yudi'ɒmɪtər/ n. эдио́метр m.
eugenic /yu'dʒɛnɪk/ adj. евгени́ческий.
eugenics /yu'dʒɛnɪks/ n. евге́ника f.
eugenist /yu'dʒɛnɪst/ n. евгени́ст m.
eulogist /'yulədʒɪst/ n. панегири́ст m.
eulogistic /,yulə'dʒɪstɪk/ adj. хвале́бный.
eulogize /'yulə,dʒaiz/ v. восхваля́ть impf.
eulogy /'yulədʒi/ n. панеги́рик m., похвала́ f.
eunuch /'yunək/ n. е́внух m.
euphemism /'yufə,mɪzəm/ n. эвфеми́зм m.
euphemistic /,yufə'mɪstɪk/ adj. эвфемисти́ческий.
euphonious /yu'founiəs/ adj. благозву́чный.
euphonium /yu'founiəm/ n. гелико́н m.
euphony /'yufəni/ n. благозву́чие neut.
euphorbia /yu'fɔrbiə/ n. молоча́й m.
euphoria /yu'fɔriə/ (state of pleasure) n. эйфори́я f.; colloq. каиф m.
euphuism /'yufyu,ɪzəm/ n. эвфуи́зм m.
euphuistic /,yufu'ɪstɪk/ adj. эвфуисти́ческий.
Eureka /yu'rikə/ interj. э́врика!
Europe /'yʊrəp/ n. Евро́па f.
European /,yʊrə'piən/ 1. adj. европе́йский. 2. n. европе́ец m., европе́йка f.
Europeanize /,yʊrə'piə,naiz/ v. европеизи́ровать impf.
europium /yʊ'roupiəm/ n. евро́пий m.
Eustachian tube /yu'steiʃən/ n. евста́хиева труба́ f.
euthanasia /,yuθə'neiʒə/ n. эйтана́зия f.
evacuant /ɪ'vækyuənt/ n. слаби́тельное neut.
evacuate /ɪ'vækyu,eit/ v. эвакуи́ровать impf. and pf.
evacuation /ɪ,vækyu'eiʃən/ n. эвакуа́ция f.
evacuee /ɪ,vækyu'i/ adj. эвакуи́рованный.
evade /ɪ'veid/ v. уклоня́ться (от with gen.) impf.; избега́ть impf., избежа́ть pf.
evaluate /ɪ'vælyu,eit/ v. оце́нивать impf., оцени́ть pf.
evaluation /ɪ,vælyu'eiʃən/ n. оце́нка f.
evanescence /,ɛvə'nɛsəns/ n. исчезнове́ние neut.
evanescent /,ɛvə'nɛsənt/ adj. бы́стро исчеза́ющий, мимолётный.
evangelic /,ivæn'dʒɛlɪk/ (al) adj. ева́нгельский; евангели́ческий.
evangelist /ɪ'vændʒəlɪst/ n. евангели́ст m.
evangelization /ɪ,vændʒələ'zeiʃən/ n. христианиза́ция f.
evangelize /ɪ'vændʒə,laiz/ v. пропове́довать impf.

evaporate /ɪ'væpə,reit/ v. испаря́ть(ся) impf., испари́ть(ся) pf.
evaporated milk /ɪ'væpə,reitɪd/ n. сгущённое молоко́ neut.
evaporating /ɪ'væpə,reitɪŋ/ adj. выпарно́й.
evaporation /ɪ,væpə'reiʃən/ n. испаре́ние neut.
evaporative /ɪ'væpə,reitɪv/ adj. испари́тельный.
evaporator /ɪ'væpə,reitər/ n. испари́тель m.
evasion /ɪ'veiʒən/ n. уклоне́ние neut.
evasive /ɪ'veisɪv/ adj. укло́нчивый.
evasiveness /ɪ'veisɪvnɪs/ n. укло́нчивость f.
eve /iv/ n. кану́н m.; on the eve of накану́не.
Eve /iv/ n. Е́ва f.
even /'ivən/ 1. adj. ра́вный, ро́вный; (number) чётный. 2. adv. да́же.
evenhanded /'ivən'hændid/ adj. беспристра́стный.
evening /'ivnɪŋ/ n. ве́чер m.; in the evening ве́чером.
evenly /'ivənli/ adv. ро́вно; одина́ково.
event /ɪ'vɛnt/ n. собы́тие neut.
even-tempered /'ivən 'tɛmpərd/ adj. споко́йный, уравнове́шенный.
eventful /ɪ'vɛntfəl/ adj. по́лный собы́тий.
eventual /ɪ'vɛntʃuəl/ adj. коне́чный.
eventuality /ɪ,vɛntʃu'ælɪti/ n. возмо́жность f.; случа́йность f.
eventuate /ɪ'vɛntʃu,eit/ v. конча́ться, приводи́ть impf.
ever /'ɛvər/ adv. когда́-либо, когда́-нибудь; (always) всегда́; ever since с тех пор (как).
evergreen /'ɛvər,grin/ n. вечнозелёное расте́ние neut.
everlasting /,ɛvər'læstɪŋ/ adj. ве́чный.
evermore /,ɛvər'mɔr/ adv. наве́ки.
every /'ɛvri/ adj. ка́ждый, вся́кий.
everybody /'ɛvri,bɒdi/ pron. ка́ждый, вся́кий; все. pl.
everyday /'ɛvri,dei/ adj. повседне́вный.
everyman /'ɛvri,mæn/ n. рядово́й челове́к m.
everyone /'ɛvri,wʌn/ pron. ка́ждый, вся́кий; все. pl.
everything /'ɛvri,θɪŋ/ pron. всё neut.
everyway /'ɛvri,wei/ adv. вся́чески.
everywhere /'ɛvri,wɛər/ adv. всю́ду, везде́.
evict /ɪ'vɪkt/ v. выселя́ть impf., вы́селить pf.
eviction /ɪ'vɪkʃən/ n. выселе́ние neut.
evidence /'ɛvidəns/ n. свиде́тельство; свиде́тельское показа́ние neut.
evident /'ɛvidənt/ adj. очеви́дный.
evidential /,ɛvi'dɛnʃəl/ adj. доказа́тельный.
evidently /'ɛvidəntli/ adv. очеви́дно.
evil /'ivəl/ 1. adj. дурно́й, злой. 2. n. зло neut., вред m.
evildoer /'ivəl,duər/ n. злоде́й m.
evildoing /'ivəl,duɪŋ/ n. злоде́йство neut.
evil-minded /'ivəl 'maindɪd/ adj. злонаме́ренный.
evince /ɪ'vɪns/ v. проявля́ть impf.
evincible /ɪ'vɪnsəbəl/ adj. доказу́емый.
eviscerate /ɪ'vɪsə,reit/ v. потроши́ть; (fig.) выхола́щивать impf.
evocation /,ɛvə'keiʃən/ n. воспомина́ние neut.
evocative /ɪ'vɒkətɪv/ adj. напомина́ющий.
evoke /ɪ'vouk/ v. вызыва́ть impf., вы́звать pf.
evolution /,ɛvə'luʃən/ n. разви́тие neut., эволю́ция f.
evolutionary /,ɛvə'luʃə,nɛri/ adj. эволюцио́нный.

evolutionism /ˌɛvəˈluʃəˌnɪzəm/ *n.* эволюцио́нная тео́рия *f.*

evolve /ɪˈvɒlv/ *v.* развива́ть(ся) *impf.*, разви́ть(ся) *pf.*

Évora /ˈɛvərə/ *n.* Э́вора *f.*

evulsion /ɪˈvʌlʃən/ *n.* вырыва́ние *neut.*

ewe /yu; you/ *n.* овца́ *f.*

ewer /ˈyuər/ *n.* кувши́н *m.*

ex- *prefix* экс-, бы́вший.

exacerbate /ɪgˈzæsərˌbeit/ *v.* обостря́ть *impf.*

exacerbation /ɪgˌzæsərˈbeiʃən/ *n.* обостре́ние *neut.*

exact /ɪgˈzækt/ **1.** *adj.* то́чный, аккура́тный. **2.** *v.* взы́скивать *impf.*, взыска́ть *pf.*

exacting /ɪgˈzæktɪŋ/ *adj.* тре́бовательный.

exaction /ɪgˈzækʃən/ *n.* настоя́тельное тре́бование *neut.*

exactitude /ɪgˈzæktɪˌtud/ *n.* то́чность *f.*

exactly /ɪgˈzæktli/ *adv.* то́чно; как раз; и́менно.

exactness /ɪgˈzæktnɪs/ *n.* то́чность *f.*

exaggerate /ɪgˈzædʒəˌreit/ *v.* преувели́чивать *impf.*, преувели́чить *pf.*

exaggeration /ɪgˌzædʒəˈreiʃən/ *n.* преувеличе́ние *neut.*

exaggerative /ɪgˈzædʒəˌreitɪv/ *adj.* преувели́чивающий.

exalt /ɪgˈzɔlt/ *v.* возвыша́ть *impf.*

exaltation /ˌɛgzɔlˈteiʃən/ *n.* возвыше́ние; возвеличе́ние *neut.*; восто́рг *m.*

exalted /ɪgˈzɔltɪd/ *adj.* возвы́шенный.

examination /ɪgˌzæməˈneiʃən/ *n.* экза́мен *m.*; осмо́тр *m.*; **to take an examination** сдава́ть экза́мен *impf.*; **to pass an examination** сдать экза́мен *pf.*

examine /ɪgˈzæmɪn/ *v.* рассма́тривать *impf.*, рассмотре́ть *pf.*; экзаменова́ть *impf.*, проэкзаменова́ть *pf.*; осма́тривать *impf.*, осмотре́ть *pf.*

examinee /ɪgˌzæməˈni/ *n.* экзамену́ющийся *m.*

examiner /ɪgˈzæmənər/ *n.* экзамена́тор; контролёр *m.*

example /ɪgˈzæmpəl/ *n.* приме́р *m.*; **for example** наприме́р.

exarch /ˈɛksɑrk/ *n.* экза́рх *m.*

exarchate /ˈɛksɑrˌkeit/ *n.* экзарха́т *m.*

exasperate /ɪgˈzæspəˌreit/ *v.* раздража́ть *impf.*, раздражи́ть *pf.*

exasperating /ɪgˈzæspəˌreitɪŋ/ *adj.* раздража́ющий.

exasperation /ɪgˌzæspəˈreiʃən/ *n.* раздраже́ние *neut.*

excavate /ˈɛkskəˌveit/ *v.* выка́пывать *impf.*, вы́копать *pf.*

excavation /ˌɛkskəˈveiʃən/ *n.* раско́пки *pl.*

excavator /ˈɛkskəˌveitər/ *n.* экскава́тор *m.*

exceed /ɪkˈsid/ *v.* превыша́ть *impf.*, превы́сить *pf.*

exceedingly /ɪkˈsidɪŋli/ *adv.* чрезвыча́йно.

excel /ɪkˈsɛl/ *v.* превосходи́ть *impf.*, превзойти́ *pf.*

excellence /ˈɛksələns/ *n.* превосхо́дство *neut.*

excellency /ˈɛksələnsi/ *n.* (*title*) превосходи́тельство *neut.*

excellent /ˈɛksələnt/ *adj.* отли́чный, превосхо́дный.

except /ɪkˈsɛpt/ *prep.* кро́ме (*with gen.*), за исключе́нием (*with gen.*).

excepting /ɪkˈsɛptɪŋ/ *prep.* за исключе́нием (*with gen.*), кро́ме (*with gen.*).

exception /ɪkˈsɛpʃən/ *n.* исключе́ние *neut.*

exceptional /ɪkˈsɛpʃənl/ *adj.* исключи́тельный, необы́чный.

exceptive /ɪkˈsɛptɪv/ *adj.* составля́ющий исключе́ние.

excerpt /ˈɛksɜrpt/ *n.* отры́вок *m.*, вы́держка *f.*

excess /ɪkˈsɛs, ˈɛksɛs/ *n.* изли́шек, избы́ток *m.*

excessive /ɪkˈsɛsɪv/ *adj.* чрезме́рный, изли́шний.

exchange /ɪksˈtʃeindʒ/ **1.** *n.* обме́н, заме́н *m.*; **in exchange** *prep.* взаме́н (*with gen.*). **2.** *v.t.* обме́нивать *impf.*, обменя́ть *pf.*; *v.i.* обме́ниваться (*with instr.*) *impf.*, обменя́ться *pf.*

exchangeable /ɪksˈtʃeindʒəbəl/ *adj.* подлежа́щий обме́ну.

exchequer /ˈɛkstʃɛkər/ *n.* казна́ *f.*, казначе́йство *neut.*; **Chancellor of the Exchequer** (*British*) мини́стр фина́нсов *m.*

excise[1] /ˈɛksaiz/ *v.* (*cut out*) выреза́ть *impf.*

excise[2] /ˈɛksaiz/ *n.* акци́з *m.*

excitability /ɪkˌsaitəˈbɪlɪti/ *n.* возбуди́мость *f.*

excitable /ɪkˈsaitəbəl/ *adj.* (легко́) возбуди́мый.

excitative /ɪkˈsaitətɪv/ *adj.* возбуди́тельный.

excite /ɪkˈsait/ *v.* волнова́ть *impf.*, взволнова́ть *pf.*; возбужда́ть *impf.*, возбуди́ть *pf.*

excited /ɪkˈsaitɪd/ *adj.* взволно́ванный.

excitement /ɪkˈsaitmənt/ *n.* возбужде́ние, волне́ние *neut.*

exciter /ɪkˈsaitər/ *n.* (*tech.*) возбуди́тель *m.*

exciting /ɪkˈsaitɪŋ/ *adj.* волну́ющий.

exclaim /ɪkˈskleim/ *v.* восклица́ть *impf.*, воскли́кнуть *pf.*

exclamation /ˌɛkskləˈmeiʃən/ *n.* восклица́ние *neut.*; **exclamation point** восклица́тельный знак *m.*

exclamatory /ɪkˈsklæməˌtɔri/ *adj.* восклица́тельный.

exclude /ɪkˈsklud/ *v.* исключа́ть *impf.*, исключи́ть *pf.*

exclusion /ɪkˈskluʒən/ *n.* исключе́ние *neut.*

exclusive /ɪkˈsklusɪv/ *adj.* исключи́тельный.

exclusively /ɪkˈsklusɪvli/ *adv.* исключи́тельно, то́лько.

excommunicate /ˌɛkskəˈmyunɪˌkeit/ *v.* отлуча́ть от це́ркви *impf.*

excommunication /ˌɛkskəˌmyunɪˈkeiʃən/ *n.* ана́фема *f.*

excoriate /ɪkˈskɔriˌeit/ *v.* (*flay*) сдира́ть ко́жу с (*with gen.*) *impf.*

excoriation /ɪkˌskɔriˈeiʃən/ *n.* сдира́ние ко́жи *neut.*

excrement /ˈɛkskrəmənt/ *n.* экскре́менты *pl.*

excremental /ˌɛkskrəˈmɛntl/ *adj.* фека́льный.

excrescence /ɪkˈskrɛsəns/ *n.* наро́ст *m.*

excrescent /ɪkˈskrɛsənt/ *adj.* образу́ющий наро́ст.

excrete /ɪkˈskrit/ *v.* выделя́ть *impf.*, изверга́ть *impf.*

excretion /ɪkˈskriʃən/ *n.* выделе́ние *neut.*

excretory /ˈɛkskrɪˌtɔri/ *adj.* выдели́тельный.

excruciate /ɪkˈskruʃiˌeit/ *v.* му́чить, терза́ть *impf.*

excruciating /ɪkˈskruʃiˌeitɪŋ/ *adj.* мучи́тельный; (*fig.*) уби́йственный.

excruciation /ɪkˌskruʃiˈeiʃən/ *n.* муче́ние *neut.*

exculpate /ˈɛkskʌlˌpeit/ *v.* опра́вдывать *impf.*

exculpation /ˌɛkskʌlˈpeiʃən/ *n.* оправда́ние *neut.*

exculpatory /ɪk'skʌlpə‚tɔri/ *adj.* оправдывающий.

excursion /ɪk'skɜrʒən/ *n.* экскурсия *f.*

excursive /ɪk'skɜrsɪv/ *adj.* отклоняющийся.

excursus /ɛk'skɜrsəs/ *n.* отступление *neut.*, экскурс *m.*

excusable /ɪk'skyuzəbəl/ *adj.* извинительный.

excuse /n.ɪk'skyus; *v.* ɪk'skyuz/ **1.** *n.* извинение, оправдание *neut.*; (*pretext*) предлог *m.* **2.** *v.* извинять *impf.*, извинить *pf.*; прощать *impf.*; (*release*) освобождать *impf.*

execrable /'ɛksɪkrəbəl/ *adj.* отвратительный, гнусный.

execrate /'ɛksɪ‚kreit/ *v.* ненавидеть *impf.*

execration /‚ɛksɪ'kreiʃən/ *n.* омерзение *neut.*

executant /ɪg'zɛkyətənt/ *n.* исполнитель *m.*

execute /'ɛksɪ‚kyut/ *v.* (*perform*) исполнять *impf.*, исполнить *pf.*, выполнять *impf.*, выполнить *pf.*; (*kill legally*) казнить *impf.* and *pf.*

execution /‚ɛksɪ'kyuʃən/ *n.* выполнение, исполнение *neut.*; (*legal killing*) казнь, экзекуция *f.*

executioner /‚ɛksɪ'kyuʃənər/ *n.* палач *m.*

executive /ɪg'zɛkyətɪv/ **1.** *adj.* исполнительный. **2.** *n.* управляющий *m.*

executor /ɪg'zɛkyətər/ *n.* душеприказчик *m.*

executrix /ɪg'zɛkyətrɪks/ *n.* душеприказчица *f.*

exegesis /‚ɛksɪ'dʒɪsɪs/ *n.* толкование *neut.*, экзегеза *f.*

exegetics /‚ɛksɪ'dʒɛtɪks/ *n.* экзегетика *f.*

exemplar /ɪg'zɛmplər/ *n.* образец *m.*

exemplary /ɪg'zɛmpləri/ *adj.* образцовый.

exemplification /ɪg‚zɛmpləfɪ'keiʃən/ *n.* пояснение примером *neut.*

exemplify /ɪg'zɛmplə‚fai/ *v.* служить примером *impf.*

exempt /ɪg'zɛmpt/ **1.** *adj.* освобождённый. **2.** *v.* освобождать *impf.*, освободить *pf.*

exemption /ɪg'zɛmpʃən/ *n.* освобождение *neut.*

exercise /'ɛksər‚saiz/ **1.** *n.* упражнение; исполнение *neut.* **2.** *v.* упражнять *impf.*; (*duties*) исполнять *impf.*

exert /ɪg'zɜrt/ *v.* напрягать(ся) *impf.*, напрячь(ся) *pf.*; оказывать *impf.*

exertion /ɪg'zɜrʃən/ *n.* напряжение *neut.*

exertion /ɪg'zɜrʃən/ *n.* усилие, напряжение *neut.*

exfoliate /ɛks'fouli‚eit/ *v.* отслаиваться *impf.*

exfoliation /ɛks‚fouli'eiʃən/ *n.* (*geol.*) расслоение, отслоение *neut.*

exhalation /‚ɛkshə'leiʃən/ *n.* выдыхание *neut.*

exhale /ɛks'heil/ *v.* выдыхать *impf.*, выдохнуть *pf.*

exhaust /ɪg'zɔst/ **1.** *n.* (*mech.*) выхлоп *f.* **2.** *v.* истощать *impf.*, истощить *pf.*; исчёрпывать *impf.*, исчерпать *pf.*

exhausted /ɪg'zɔstɪd/ *adj.* измученный, измотанный, изнурённый, изнемождённый.

exhauster /ɪg'zɔstər/ *n.* вытяжной вентилятор *m.*

exhaustible /ɪg'zɔstəbəl/ *adj.* истощимый.

exhausting /ɪg'zɔstɪŋ/ *adj.* утомительный, изнурительный.

exhaustion /ɪg'zɔstʃən/ *n.* истощение, изнеможение *neut.*

exhaustive /ɪg'zɔstɪv/ *adj.* истощающий, исчёрпывающий.

exhaustively /ɪg'zɔstɪvli/ *adv.* полностью.

exhaust pipe *n.* выхлопная труба *f.*

exhibit /ɪg'zɪbɪt/ **1.** *n.* экспонат *m.* **2.** *v.* выставлять *impf.*, выставить *pf.*; экспонировать *impf.* and *pf.*

exhibition /‚ɛksə'bɪʃən/ *n.* показ *m.*; выставка *f.*

exhibitionism /‚ɛksə'bɪʃə‚nɪzəm/ *n.* эксгибиционизм *m.*

exhibitionist /‚ɛksə'bɪʃənɪst/ *n.* эксгибиционист *m.*

exhibitor /ɪg'zɪbɪtər/ *n.* экспонент *m.*

exhilarate /ɪg'zɪlə‚reit/ *v.* оживлять *impf.*

exhilaration /ɪg‚zɪlə'reiʃən/ *n.* весёлость *f.*; (*thrill*) восхищение *neut.*

exhort /ɪg'zɔrt/ *v.* увещевать *impf.*

exhortation /‚ɛgzɔr'teiʃən/ *n.* увещевание *neut.*; призыв *m.*; предупреждение *neut.*

exhortative /ɪg'zɔrtətɪv/ *adj.* увещевательный.

exhumation /‚ɛkshyu'meiʃən/ *n.* эксгумация *f.*

exhume /ɪg'zum/ *v.* выкапывать *impf.*, выкопать *pf.*

exigency /'ɛksɪdʒənsi/ *n.* (*necessity*) острая необходимость *f.*

exigent /'ɛksɪdʒənt/ *adj.* неотложный.

exiguity /‚ɛksɪ'gyuɪti/ *n.* скудость *f.*

exiguous /ɪg'zɪgyuəs/ *adj.* скудный.

exile /'ɛgzail/ **1.** *n.* ссылка *f.*, изгнание *neut.*; (*person*) изгнанник *m.* **2.** *v.* ссылать *impf.*, сослать *pf.*; изгонять *impf.*, изгнать *pf.*

exist /ɪg'zɪst/ *v.* существовать *impf.*

existence /ɪg'zɪstəns/ *n.* существование *neut.*

existent /ɪg'zɪstənt/ *adj.* существующий.

existential /‚ɛgzɪ'stɛnʃəl/ *adj.* экзистенциальный.

existentialism /‚ɛgzɪ'stɛnʃə‚lɪzəm/ *n.* экзистенциализм *m.*

existentialist /‚ɛgzɪ'stɛnʃəlɪst/ **1.** *n.* экзистенциалист *m.* **2.** *adj.* экзистенциальный.

exit /'ɛgzɪt/ *n.* выход *m.*

ex libris /ɛks 'lɪbrɪs/ *n.* экслибрис *m.*

exodus /'ɛksədəs/ *n.* массовый исход *m.*

ex officio /'ɛks ə'fɪʃi‚ou/ *adv.* по должности.

exogamy /ɛk'sɒgəmi/ *n.* экзогамия *f.*

exogenous /ɛk'sɒdʒənəs/ *adj.* экзогенный.

exonerate /ɪg'zɒnə‚reit/ *v.* оправдывать *impf.*, оправдать *pf.*

exoneration /ɪg‚zɒnə'reiʃən/ *n.* оправдание *neut.*; освобождение (от *with gen.*) *neut.*

exophthalmia /‚ɛksɒf'θælmiə/ *n.* пучеглазие *neut.*

exophthalmic *adj.* экзофтальмический.

exorbitance /ɪg'zɔrbɪtəns/ *n.* непомерность *f.*

exorbitant /ɪg'zɔrbɪtənt/ *adj.* непомерный.

exorcise /'ɛksɔr‚saiz/ *v.* изгонять духов *impf.*

exorcism /'ɛksɔr‚sɪzəm/ *n.* изгнание духов *neut.*

exordium /ɪg'zɔrdiəm/ *n.* вступление *neut.*

exoteric /‚ɛksə'tɛrɪk/ *adj.* общедоступный.

exothermic /‚ɛksou'θɜrmɪk/ *adj.* экзотермический.

exotic /ɪg'zɒtɪk/ *adj.* экзотический.

exotica /ɪg'zɒtɪkə/ *n.* экзотика *f.*

expand /ɪk'spænd/ *v.t.* расширять *impf.*, расширить *pf.*; *v.i.* расширяться *impf.*, расшириться *pf.*

expander /ɪk'spændər/ *n.* расширитель *m.*

expanse /ɪk'spæns/ *n.* протяжение, пространство *neut.*

expansible /ɪk'spænsəbəl/ *adj.* растяжимый.

expansion /ɪk'spænʃən/ *n.* экспансия *f.*

expansionism /ɪk'spænʃə,nɪzəm/ n. экспансионйзм m.

expansionist /ɪk'spænʃənɪst/ adj. экспансионистский.

expansive /ɪk'spænsɪv/ adj. экспансйвный.

expatiate /ɪk'speiʃi,eit/ v. распространяться impf.

expatiation /ɪk,speiʃi'eiʃən/ n. распространéние neut.

expatriate /ɛks'peitriɪt/ n. экспатриáнт m.

expatriation /ɛks,peitri'eiʃən/ n. экспатриáция f.

expect /ɪk'spɛkt/ v. ожидáть impf.

expectancy /ɪk'spɛktənsi/ n. ожидáние neut.

expectant /ɪk'spɛktənt/ adj. ожидáющий.

expectation /,ɛkspɛk'teiʃən/ n. ожидáние neut.

expectorant /ɪk'spɛktərənt/ n. отхáркивающее срéдство neut.

expectorate /ɪk'spɛktə,reit/ v. отхáркивать(ся) impf.

expectoration /ɪk,spɛktə'reiʃən/ n. отхáркивание neut.

expedient /ɪk'spidiənt/ n. приём m., срéдство neut.

expedite /'ɛkspɪ,dait/ v. ускорять impf.; быстро выполнять impf.

expedition /,ɛkspɪ'dɪʃən/ n. экспедйция f.

expeditionary /,ɛkspɪ'dɪʃə,nɛri/ adj. экспедицийнный.

expeditious /,ɛkspɪ'dɪʃəs/ adj. быстрый, скóрый; срóчный.

expel /ɪk'spɛl/ v. выгонять impf., выгнать pf.

expend /ɪk'spɛnd/ v. трáтить impf., истрáтить pf.

expendable /ɪk'spɛndəbəl/ adj. расхóдуемый; потребляемый.

expenditure /ɪk'spɛndɪtʃər/ n. трáта f., расхóд m.

expense /ɪk'spɛns/ n. расхóд m.; at the expense of за счёт (with gen.).

expensive /ɪk'spɛnsɪv/ adj. дорогóй.

expensiveness /ɪk'spɛnsɪvnɪs/ n. дороговйзна f.

experience /ɪk'spɪəriəns/ 1. n. óпыт m., испытáние neut. 2. v. испытывать impf., испытáть pf.

experienced /ɪk'spɪəriənst/ adj. óпытный.

experiment /n. ɪk'spɛrəmənt; v. ɛk'spɛrə,mɛnt/ 1. n. эксперимéнт m., óпыт m. 2. v. эксперименти́ровать impf.

experimental /ɪk,spɛrə'mɛntl/ экспериментáльный.

experimentation /ɪk,spɛrəmɛn'teiʃən/ n. эксперименти́рование neut.

experimenter /ɪk'spɛrəmɛntər/ n. эксперименти́тор m.

expert /'ɛkspɜrt/ 1. adj. óпытный. 2. n. экспéрт m.

expertise /,ɛkspər'tiz/ n. специáльные знáния pl.

expiate /'ɛkspi,eit/ v. искупáть impf.

expiation /,ɛkspi'eiʃən/ n. искуплéние neut.

expiatory /'ɛkspiə,tori/ adj. искупи́тельный.

expiration /,ɛkspə'reiʃən/ n. выдыхáние neut.; (time) истечéние neut.

expiratory /ɪk'spaiərə,tori/ adj. выдыхáтельный.

expire /ɪk'spaiər/ v. выдыхáть impf., выдохнуть pf.; (time) истекáть impf., истéчь pf.

expiring /ɪk'spaiərɪŋ/ adj. умирáющий, истекáющий.

explain /ɪk'splein/ v. объяснять impf., объяснйть pf.

explainable /ɪk'spleinəbəl/ adj. объяснймый.

explanation /,ɛksplə'neiʃən/ n. объяснéние neut.

explanatory /ɪk'splænə,tori/ adj. объяснйтельный.

expletive /'ɛksplɪtɪv/ n. брáнное слóво; (gram.) встáвное слóво neut.

explicable /'ɛksplɪkəbəl/ adj. объяснймый.

explicate /'ɛksplɪ,keit/ v. объяснять; распутывать; толковáть impf.

explicit /ɪk'splɪsɪt/ adj. тóчный, определённый.

explode /ɪk'sploud/ v.i. взрывáться impf., взорвáться pf.; v.t. взрывáть impf., взорвáть pf.

exploder /ɪk'sploudər/ n. детонáтор m.

exploit /n. 'ɛksplɔit; v. ɪk'splɔit/ 1. n. пóдвиг m. 2. v. эксплуати́ровать impf.

exploitation /,ɛksplɔi'teiʃən/ n. эксплуатáция f.

exploiter /ɛk'splɔitər/ n. эксплуатáтор m.

exploration /,ɛksplə'reiʃən/ n. исслéдование neut.

exploratory /ɪk'splɔrə,tori/ adj. исслéдовательский.

explore /ɪk'splɔr/ v. исслéдовать impf.

explorer /ɪk'splɔrər/ n. исслéдователь m.

explosion /ɪk'splouʒən/ n. взрыв m.

explosive /ɪk'splousɪv/ 1. adj. взрывчатый. 2. n. взрывчатое веществó neut.

exponent /ɪk'spounənt/ n. представи́тель m.; истолковáтель m.

exponential /,ɛkspou'nɛnʃəl/ adj. экспонéнтный.

export /n. adj. 'ɛkspɔrt; v. ɪk'spɔrt/ 1. n. экспорт m. 2. v. экспорти́ровать impf. and pf.

exportation /,ɛkspɔr'teiʃən/ n. экспорти́рование neut.

exporter /ɛk'spɔrtər/ n. экспортёр m.

exposé /,ɛkspou'zei/ n. разоблачéние neut.

expose /ɪk'spouz/ v. разоблачáть impf., разоблачи́ть pf.

exposed /ɪk'spouzd/ adj. разоблачённый.

exposition /,ɛkspə'zɪʃən/ n. изложéние neut.; (exhibit) выставка f.

expositor /ɪk'spɔzitər/ n. толковáтель m.

expository /ɪk'spɔzi,tori/ adj. объясни́тельный.

expostulate /ɪk'spɔstʃə,leit/ v. увещевáть impf.

expostulation /ɪk,spɔstʃə'leiʃən/ n. увещáние neut.

expostulatory /ɪk'spɔstʃələ,tori/ adj. увещевáтельный.

exposure /ɪk'spouʒər/ n. выставлéние neut.; разоблачéние neut.

expound /ɪk'spaund/ v. излагáть, толковáть impf.

express /ɪk'sprɛs/ 1. adj. (rapid) срóчный; (definite) тóчный. 2. n. экспрéсс m. 3. v. выражáть impf., выразить pf.

expressible /ɪk'sprɛsəbəl/ adj. вырази́мый.

expression /ɪk'sprɛʃən/ n. выражéние neut.

expressionist /ɪk'sprɛʃənɪst/ n. экспрессиони́ст m.

expressive /ɪk'sprɛsɪv/ adj. вырази́тельный.

expressly /ɪk'sprɛsli/ adv. (plainly) тóчно, ясно; (on purpose) специáльно.

expressway /ɪk'sprɛswei/ n. автострáда f.

expropriate /ɛks'proupri,eit/ v. экспроприи́ровать impf. and pf.

expropriation /ˌɛksˌprouprɪ'eɪʃən/ *n.* экспроприáция *f.*

expulsion /ɪk'spʌlʃən/ *n.* изгнáние *neut.*

expulsive /ɪk'spʌlsɪv/ *adj.* изгоняющий.

expunction /ɪk'spʌŋkʃən/ *n.* вычёркивание *neut.*

expunge /ɪk'spʌndʒ/ *v.* вычёркивать *impf.*

expurgate /'ɛkspər,geɪt/ *v.* (*book*) вычёркивать нежелáтельные местá *impf.*

expurgation /ˌɛkspər'geɪʃən/ *n.* вычёркивание *neut.*

exquisite /ɪk'skwɪzɪt/ *adj.* изы́сканный, прелéстный.

exsanguine /ɛks'sæŋgwɪn/ *adj.* бескрóвный.

extant /'ɛkstənt/ *adj.* сохранúвшийся.

extemporaneous /ɪkˌstɛmpə'reɪniəs/ *adj.* импровизúрованный.

extempore /ɪk'stɛmpəri/ *adv.* экспрóмтом.

extemporization /ɪkˌstɛmpərə'zeɪʃən/ *n.* импровизáция *f.*

extemporize /ɪk'stɛmpəˌraɪz/ *v.* импровизúровать *impf.*

extend /ɪk'stɛnd/ *v.* протя́гивать *impf.*, протяну́ть *pf.*; *v.i.* тяну́ться *impf.*

extended /ɪk'stɛndɪd/ *adj.* длúтельный; обшúрный.

extender /ɪk'stɛndər/ *n.* наполнúтель *m.*

extensibility /ɪkˌstɛnsə'bɪlɪti/ *n.* растяжúмость *f.*

extensible /ɪk'stɛnsəbəl/ *adj.* растяжúмый.

extension /ɪk'stɛnʃən/ *n.* расширéние, добавлéние; продлéние *neut.*

extensive /ɪk'stɛnsɪv/ *adj.* обшúрный; экстенсúвный.

extensively /ɪk'stɛnsɪvli/ *adv.* широкó.

extent /ɪk'stɛnt/ *n.* стéпень *f.*, размéр *m.*

extenuate /ɪk'stɛnyu,eɪt/ *v.* смягчáть *impf.*

extenuating /ɪk'stɛnyu,eɪtɪŋ/ *adj.* смягчáющий.

extenuating circumstances *n.* смягчáющие обстоя́тельства *pl.*

exterior /ɪk'stɪəriər/ **1.** *adj.* внéшний, нару́жный. **2.** *n.* внéшность, нару́жность *f.*

exterminate /ɪk'stɜrmə,neɪt/ *v.* истребля́ть *impf.*, истребúть *pf.*

extermination /ɪkˌstɜrmə'neɪʃən/ *n.* истреблéние *neut.*

exterminator /ɪk'stɜrmə,neɪtər/ *n.* истребúтель *m.*

exterminatory /ɪk'stɜrmənəˌtɔri/ *adj.* истребúтельный.

external /ɪk'stɜrnl/ *adj.* внéшний, нару́жный.

externalize /ɪk'stɜrnlˌaɪz/ *v.* выражáть(ся) *impf.*

externally /ɪk'stɜrnli/ *adv.* внéшне.

exterritorial /ˌɛkstɛrɪ'tɔriəl/ *adj.* экстерриториáльный.

extinct /ɪk'stɪŋkt/ *adj.* потýхший; вы́мерший.

extinction /ɪk'stɪŋkʃən/ *n.* потухáние; вымирáние *neut.*

extinguish /ɪk'stɪŋgwɪʃ/ *v.* гасúть *impf.*, погасúть *pf.*

extinguisher /ɪk'stɪŋgwɪʃər/ *n.*: **fire extinguisher** огнетушúтель *m.*

extirpate /'ɛkstər,peɪt/ *v.* искореня́ть, истребля́ть *impf.*

extirpation /ˌɛkstər'peɪʃən/ *n.* искоренéние *neut.*

extirpator /'ɛkstər,peɪtər/ *n.* (*agric.*) культивáтор-экстирпáтор *m.*

extol /ɪk'stoul/ *v.* превозносúть *impf.*

extort /ɪk'stɔrt/ *v.* вымогáть *impf.*

extortion /ɪk'stɔrʃən/ *n.* вымогáтельство *neut.*

extortionate /ɪk'stɔrʃənɪt/ *adj.* вымогáтельский.

extra /'ɛkstrə/ *adj.* дополнúтельный; лúшний.

extract /n.'ɛkstrækt; v. ɪk'strækt/ **1.** *n.* экстрáкт *m.* **2.** *v.* извлекáть *impf.*, извлéчь *pf.*

extraction /ɪk'strækʃən/ *n.* извлечéние *neut.*, экстрáкция *f.*

extractor /ɪk'stræktər/ *n.* экстрáктор *m.*

extraditable /'ɛkstrə,daɪtəbəl/ *adj.* подлежáщий вы́даче.

extradite /'ɛkstrə,daɪt/ *v.* выдавáть *impf.*

extradition /ˌɛkstrə'dɪʃən/ *n.* вы́дача *f.*

extrajudicial /ˌɛkstrədʒu'dɪʃəl/ *adj.* внесудéбный.

extramarital /ˌɛkstrə'mærɪtl/ *adj.* внебрáчный.

extramural /ˌɛkstrə'myurəl/ *adj.* вне стен.

extraneous /ɪk'streɪniəs/ *adj.* чýждый, внéшний.

extraordinary /ɪk'strɔrdṇ,ɛri, ˌɛkstrə'ɔr-/ *adj.* черзвычáйный.

extrapolate /ɪk'stræpə,leɪt/ *v.* экстраполúровать *impf.*

extrapolation /ɪkˌstræpə'leɪʃən/ *n.* экстраполя́ция *f.*

extrasensory /ˌɛkstrə'sɛnsəri/ *adj.* экстрасенсóрный.

extraterrestrial /ˌɛkstrətə'rɛstriəl/ *adj.* внеземнóй.

extraterritorial /'ɛkstrə,tɛrɪ'tɔriəl/ *adj.* экстерриториáльный.

extrauterine /ˌɛkstrə'yutərɪn/ *adj.* внемáточный.

extravagance /ɪk'strævəgəns/ *n.* излúшество *neut.*; (*behavior*) экстравагáнтность; (*waste*) расточúтельство *neut.*

extravagant /ɪk'strævəgənt/ *adj.* непомéрный; расточúтельный.

extravaganza /ɪkˌstrævə'gænzə/ *n.* эффéктное зрéлище *neut.*; (*farce*) фарс *m.*

extreme /ɪk'strim/ **1.** *adj.* крáйний. **2.** *n.* крáйность *f.*

extremely /ɪk'strimli/ *adv.* крáйне.

extremism /ɪk'strimɪzəm/ *n.* экстремúзм *m.*

extremist /ɪk'strimɪst/ *n.* экстремúст *m.*

extremity /ɪk'stremɪti/ *n.* конéчность *f.*

extricate /'ɛkstrɪ,keɪt/ *v.* выпýтывать *impf.*

extrication /ˌɛkstrɪ'keɪʃən/ *n.* выпýтывание *neut.*

extrovert /'ɛkstrə,vɜrt/ *n.* экстравéрт *m.*

extrude /ɪk'strud/ *v.* вытесня́ть *impf.*

extrusion /ɪk'struʒən/ *n.* вытеснéние, выдáвливание *neut.*

exuberance /ɪg'zubərəns/ *n.* жизнерáдостность *f.*

exuberant /ɪg'zubərənt/ *adj.* обúльный, роскóшный; жизнерáдостный.

exuberantly /ɪg'zubərəntli/ *adv.* рáдостно; (*plants, style*) пы́шно.

exude /ɪg'zud/ *v.* выделя́ть(ся) *impf.*, вы́делить(ся) *pf.*

exult /ɪg'zʌlt/ *v.* ликовáть *impf.*

exultant /ɪg'zʌltṇt/ *adj.* ликýющий.

exultation /ˌɛgzʌl'teɪʃən/ *n.* ликовáние *neut.*; торжество́ *neut.*

eye /aɪ/ **1.** *adj.* глазнóй. **2.** *n.* глаз *m.*; (*of needle*) ушкó *neut.* **3.** *v.* наблюдáть; всмáтриваться *impf.*

eyeball /'aɪ,bɔl/ *n.* глазнóе я́блоко *neut.*

eyebrow /'aɪ,braʊ/ *n.* бровь *f.*

eyecup /'aɪ,kʌp/ *n.* глазнáя вáнночка *f.*

eyeglasses /'aɪ,glæsɪz/ *n.* очкú *pl.*

eyehole /'aɪ,houl/ *n.* смотровóе отвéрстие *neut.*

eyelash /'ai͵læʃ/ *n.* ресни́ца *f.*

eyeless /'ailıs/ *adj.* безгла́зый.

eyelet /'ailıt/ *n.* пе́телька *f.*

eyelid /'ai͵lıd/ *n.* ве́ко *neut.*

eyeopener /'ai͵oupənər/ *n.* удиви́тельная но́вость *f.*

eyepiece /'ai͵pis/ *n.* окуля́р *m.*

eyeshadow /'ai͵ʃædou/ *n.* каранда́ш для век *m.*

eyeshot /'ai͵ʃɒt/ *n.* по́ле зре́ния *neut.*

eyesight /'ai͵sait/ *n.* зре́ние *neut.*

eye socket *n.* глазни́ца *f.*

eyesore /'ai͵sɔr/ *n.:* **to be an eyesore** оскорбля́ть взор *impf.*

eyetooth /'ai͵tuθ/ *n.* глазно́й зуб *m.*

eyewash /'ai͵wɒʃ/ *n.* глазна́я примо́чка *f.*

eyewitness /'ai͵wıtnıs/ *n.* очеви́дец, свиде́тель *m.*

F

fabaceous /fə'beiʃəs/ adj. бобо́вый.

Fabian /'feibiən/ **1.** n. фабиа́нец m., фабиа́нка f. **2.** adj. фабиа́нский.

fable /'feibəl/ n. ба́сня; вы́думка f.; (lie) измышле́ние neut.

fabled /'feibəld/ adj. баснословный; ска́зочный.

fabliau /'fæbli‚ou/ n. фаблио́ neut. indecl.

fabric /'fæbrɪk/ n. ткань, мате́рия f.; (structure) строй m.

fabricate /'fæbrɪ‚keit/ v. выду́мывать impf., вы́думать pf.; подде́лывать impf., подде́лать pf.

fabrication /‚fæbrɪ'keiʃən/ n. вы́думка f.; (forgery) подде́лка f.

fabulist /'fæbyəlɪst/ n. баснопи́сец m.

fabulous /'fæbyələs/ adj. ска́зочный; легенда́рный.

façade /fə'sad/ n. фаса́д m.

face /feis/ **1.** n. лицо́ neut.; (expression) выраже́ние; (grimace) грима́са f. **2.** v. стоя́ть лицо́м к (with dat.) impf.

face cream n. крем для лица́ m.

faceless /'feislɪs/ adj. безли́кий; безли́чный.

facelift /'feis‚lɪft/ n. пласти́ческая опера́ция лица́ f.

face mask n. предохрани́тельная ма́ска f.

faceplate /'feis‚pleit/ n. планша́йба f.

face powder n. пу́дра для лица́ f.

face-saving /'feis‚seivɪŋ/ adj. спаса́ющий прести́ж.

facet /'fæsɪt/ n. (gem, glass) грань f., фасе́т m.; (bevel) фа́ска f.

faceted /'fæsɪtɪd/ adj. гранёный.

facetious /fə'siʃəs/ adj. шутли́вый.

facetiousness /fə'siʃəsnɪs/ n. шутли́вость f.

facial /'feiʃəl/ adj. лицево́й.

facies /'feiʃi‚iz/ n. (anat.) пове́рхность f.

facile /'fæsɪl/ adj. лёгкий; (superficial) пове́рхностный.

facilitate /fə'sɪlɪ‚teit/ v. облегча́ть impf., облегчи́ть pf.

facilitation /fə‚sɪlɪ'teiʃən/ n. облегче́ние neut.

facility /fə'sɪlɪti/ n. (ease) лёгкость f.; pl. удо́бства, сре́дства neut. pl.

facing /'feisɪŋ/ n. облицо́вка f.

facsimile /fæk'sɪməli/ n. факси́миле neut. indecl.

fact /fækt/ n. факт m.; **in fact** факти́чески; на са́мом де́ле; в действи́тельности.

fact-finding /'fækt‚faindɪŋ/ n. установле́ние фа́ктов neut.

faction /'fækʃən/ n. фра́кция, кли́ка f.

factional /'fækʃənl/ adj. фракцио́нный.

factionalism /'fækʃənl‚ɪzəm/ n. фракцио́нность f.

factious /'fækʃəs/ adj. раско́льнический.

factiousness /'fækʃəsnɪs/ n. раско́льничество neut.

factitious /fæk'tɪʃəs/ adj. иску́сственный; подде́льный.

factor /'fæktər/ n. фа́ктор m.; (math.) мно́житель m.

factorable /'fæktərəbəl/ adj. (math.) факторизу́емый.

factorial /fæk'tɔriəl/ n. факториа́л m.

factorization /‚fæktərə'zeiʃən/ n. факториза́ция f.

factorize /'fæktə‚raiz/ v. разлага́ть(ся) на мно́жители impf.

factory /'fæktəri/ **1.** adj. фабри́чный. **2.** n. фа́брика f., (plant) заво́д m.

factory worker n. заводско́й рабо́чий m.

factotum /fæk'toutəm/ n. факто́тум m.

facture /'fæktʃər/ n. факту́ра f.

facula /'fækyələ/ n. (astr.) фа́кел m.

facultative /'fækəl‚teitɪv/ adj. факультати́вный.

faculty /'fækəlti/ n. спосо́бность f., дарова́ние neut.; (dept.) факульте́т m., (staff) педагоги́ческий персона́л m.

fad /fæd/ n. причу́да f.

faddist /'fædɪst/ n. мо́дник m.

fade /feid/ v. вя́нуть impf., завя́нуть pf.; (color) выцвета́ть impf., вы́цвести pf.

faded /'feidɪd/ adj. вы́цветший.

fade-out /'feid‚aut/ n. постепе́нное исчезнове́ние neut.

fading /'feidɪŋ/ n. увяда́ние neut.

fag end /'fæg/ n. оста́ток m.

Fahrenheit /'færən‚hait/ n.: **sixty degrees Fahrenheit** шестьдеся́т гра́дусов по Фаренге́йту.

faience /fai'ɑns/ n. фая́нс m.

fail /feil/ **1.** v. не удава́ться (impers. with dat.) impf.; (exam) провали́ться pf.; обанкро́титься pf. **2.** n.: **without fail** непреме́нно, обяза́тельно adv.

failing /'feilɪŋ/ **1.** adj. (health) сла́бый. **2.** n. недоста́ток m.; сла́бость f.

fail-safe /'feil‚seif/ adj. самооключа́ющийся.

failure /'feilyər/ n. неуда́ча f.; банкро́тство neut.; (person) неуда́чник m.

fain /fein/ adj. гото́вый.

faint /feint/ **1.** adj. сла́бый; (dim) нея́сный, ту́склый. **2.** n. о́бморок m. **3.** v. па́дать в о́бморок impf.; теря́ть созна́ние impf.

fainthearted /'feint'hartɪd/ adj. малоду́шный.

faintly /'feintli/ adv. едва́.

faintness /'feintnɪs/ n. (weakness) сла́бость f.; (dimness) ту́склость f.

fair¹ /fɛər/ adj. поря́дочный, справедли́вый; (hair) белоку́рый; (weather) благоприя́тный.

fair² /fɛər/ n. я́рмарка f.

fairground /'fɛər‚graund/ n. я́рмарочная пло́щадь f.

fairing /'fɛərɪŋ/ n. обтека́тель m.

fairlead /'fɛər‚lid/ n. (naut.) полукл́юз m.

fairly /'fɛərli/ adv. че́стно; справедли́во; (rather) дово́льно; (completely) соверше́нно, вполне́.

fair-minded /‚fɛər 'maindɪd/ adj. беспристра́стный.

fairness /'fɛərnɪs/ n. че́стность f.; справедли́вость f.

fairway /'fɛər‚wei/ n. (naut.) фарва́тер m.

fairy /'fɛəri/ n. фе́я f.

fairyland /'fɛəri‚lænd/ n. волше́бная страна́ f.

fairy tale n. (волше́бная) ска́зка f.; вы́думка, небыли́ца f.

faith /feiθ/ *n.* ве́ра *f.*; дове́рие *neut.*
faithful /'feiθfəl/ *adj.* ве́рный, пре́данный.
faithfully /'feiθfəli/ *adv.* ве́рно; добросо́вестно.
faithfulness /'feiθfəlnɪs/ *n.* ве́рность *f.*
faith healing *n.* лече́ние внуше́нием *neut.*
faithless /'feiθlɪs/ *adj.* неве́рующий.
fake /feik/ **1.** *n.* фальши́вка, подде́лка *f.* **2.** *v.* фальсифици́ровать *impf.* and *pf.*; подде́лывать *impf.*, подде́лать *pf.*
faker /'feikər/ *n.* обма́нщик *m.*
fakir /fə'kɪər/ *n.* факи́р *m.*
Falange /'feilændʒ, fɑ'lɑnhɛ/ *n.* фала́нга *f.*
Falangist /fə'lændʒɪst/ *n.* фалангист *m.*
falciform /'fælsə,fɔrm/ *adj.* серпови́дный.
falcon /'fɔlkən, 'fæl-/ *n.* со́кол *m.*
falconer /'fɔlkənər, 'fæl-/ *adj.* соко́льничий.
falconet /'fɔlkə,nɛt, 'fæl-/ *n.* (*zool.*) сорокопу́т *m.*
falconry /'fɔlkənri, 'fæl-/ *n.* соколи́ная охо́та *f.*
falderal /'fældə,ræl/ *n.* безделу́шка *f.*
fall /fɔl/ **1.** *adj.* осе́нний. **2.** *n.* паде́ние *neut.*; (*season*) о́сень *f.*; **in the fall** о́сенью. **3.** *v.* па́дать *impf.*, (у)па́сть *pf.*; обва́ливаться *impf.*, обвали́ться *pf.*; **to fall asleep** засыпа́ть *impf.*
fallacious /fə'leiʃəs/ *adj.* оши́бочный; ло́жный.
fallacy /'fæləsi/ *n.* оши́бка *f.*
fallen /'fɔlən/ *adj.* (*in battle*) па́вший; (*degraded*) па́дший.
fall guy *n.* (*slang*) козёл отпуще́ния *m.*
fallibility /,fælə'bɪlɪti/ *n.* оши́бочность *f.*
fallible /'fæləbəl/ *adj.* подве́рженный оши́бкам.
fallopian tube /fə'loupiən/ *n.* фалло́пиева труба́ *f.*
fallout /'fɔl,aut/ *n.* выпаде́ние *neut.*
fallow /'fælou/ **1.** *adj.* парово́й; (*fig.*) неразви́той; **to lie fallow** остава́ться под па́ром. **2.** *v.* поднима́ть пар *impf.*
fallow deer *n.* лань *f.*
false /fɔls/ *adj.* ло́жный; фальши́вый.
false-hearted /'fɔls 'hɑrtɪd/ *adj.* вероло́мный.
falsehood /'fɔlshʊd/ *n.* ложь *f.*
falsely /'fɔlsli/ *adv.* ло́жно; оши́бочно; непра́вильно; путём обма́на.
falsetto /fɔl'sɛtou/ *n.* фальце́т *m.*
falsification /'fɔlsəfɪ'keiʃən/ *n.* фальсифика́ция *f.*
falsifier /'fɔlsə,faiər/ *n.* фальсифика́тор *m.*
falsify /'fɔlsəfai/ *v.* фальсифици́ровать *impf.* and *pf.*
falsity /'fɔlsɪti/ *n.* фальши́вость, лжи́вость *f.*
falter /'fɔltər/ *v.* (*stumble*) спотыка́ться *impf.*; (*move, act hesitantly*) дви́гаться, де́йствовать нереши́тельно *impf.*
faltering /'fɔltərɪŋ/ *n.* нереши́тельность *f.*
fame /feim/ *n.* сла́ва *f.*
famed /feimd/ *adj.* изве́стный, знамени́тый.
familial /fə'mɪlyəl/ *adj.* семе́йный, семе́йственный.
familiar /fə'mɪlyər/ *adj.* знако́мый, бли́зкий.
familiarity /fə,mɪli'ærɪti/ *n.* бли́зкие отноше́ния *pl.*; знако́мство *neut.*; (*presumption*) фамилья́рность *f.*; **familiarity breeds contempt** чем бли́же зна́ешь, тем ме́ньше почита́ешь.
familiarize /fə'mɪlyə,raiz/ *v.* знако́мить *impf.*; ознако́мить (с *with instr.*) *pf.*
family /'fæməli/ *n.* семья́ *f.*; семе́йство *neut.*
famine /'fæmɪn/ *n.* го́лод *m.*

famished /'fæmɪʃt/ *adj.:* **I am famished** я о́чень го́лоден.
famous /'feiməs/ *adj.* знамени́тый.
fan /fæn/ **1.** *n.* ве́ер, вентиля́тор *m.*; (*sports*) боле́льщик *m.* **2.** *v.* (*fire, etc.*) раздува́ть *impf.*
fanatic /fə'nætɪk/ *n.* фана́тик *m.*
fanatical /fə'nætɪkəl/ *adj.* фанати́ческий.
fanaticism /fə'nætə,sɪzəm/ *n.* фанати́зм *m.*
fancied /'fænsid/ *adj.* вообража́емый.
fanciful /'fænsɪfəl/ *adj.* капри́зный; причу́дливый; (*unreal*) нереа́льный; фантасти́ческий.
fancy /'fænsi/ **1.** *adj.* причу́дливый; орнамента́льный. **2.** *n.* фанта́зия *f.*; (*whim*) при́хоть, причу́да *f.* **3.** *v.* (*imagine*) представля́ть себе́ *impf.*
fancy dress *adj.* костюми́рованный.
fancy-free /'fænsi 'fri/ *adj.* невлюблённый.
fandango /fæn'dæŋgou/ *n.* фанда́нго *neut. indecl.*
fanfare /'fænfɛər/ *n.* фанфа́ра *f.*
fanfaronade /,fænfərə'neid/ *n.* фанфаро́нство *neut.*
fang /fæŋ/ *n.* клык; ядови́тый зуб *m.*
fanlight /'fæn,lait/ *n.* веерообра́зное окно́ *neut.*
fan-like /'fæn ,laik/ *adj.* веерообра́зный.
fanner *n.* ве́ялка *f.*
fantast /'fæntæst/ *n.* мечта́тель; фанта́ст *m.*
fantastic /fæn'tæstɪk/ *adj.* фантасти́ческий.
fantasy /'fæntəsi/ *n.* фанта́зия *f.*; воображе́ние *neut.*
far /fɑr/ *adj.* (*pred.*) далеко́; (*attrib.*) далёкий, да́льний; **as far as** *conj.* наско́лько.
farad /'færəd/ *adj.* (*elec.*) фара́да.
faradic /fə'rædɪk/ *adj.* (*elec.*) фаради́ческий.
faradization /,færədə'zeiʃən/ *n.* фарадиза́ция *f.*
faraway /'fɑrə'wei/ *adj.* отдалённый.
farce /fɑrs/ *n.* фарс *m.*
farceur /fɑr'sɜr/ *n.* шутник *m.*
farcical /'fɑrsɪkəl/ *adj.* фа́рсовый; смешно́й.
fare /fɛər/ *n.* сто́имость прое́зда *f.*
farewell /,fɛər'wɛl/ **1.** *n.* проща́ние *neut.*; **to say farewell** проща́ться *impf.* **2.** *adj.* (*attrib.*) проща́льный. **3.** *interj.* проща́йте! до свида́ния!
far-famed /'fɑr 'feimd/ *adj.* широко́ изве́стный.
far-fetched /'fɑr 'fɛtʃt/ *adj.* наду́манный.
far-flung /'fɑr 'flʌŋ/ *adj.* обши́рный.
farina /fə'rinə/ *n.* ма́нная крупа́ *f.*
farinaceous /,færə'neiʃəs/ *adj.* мучно́й, мучни́стый.
farm /fɑrm/ **1.** *n.* фе́рма *f.*, се́льское хозя́йство *neut.* **2.** *adj.* сельскохозя́йственный.
farmer /'fɑrmər/ *n.* фе́рмер *m.*
farm hand *n.* сельскохозя́йственный рабо́чий *m.*
farmhouse /'fɑrm,haus/ *n.* жило́й дом на фе́рме *m.*
farming /'fɑrmɪŋ/ *n.* се́льское хозя́йство *neut.*
farmyard /'fɑrm,yɑrd/ *n.* двор фе́рмы; ското́н двор *m.*
farraginous /fə'rædʒənəs/ *adj.* сбо́рный.
farrago /fə'rɑgou/ *n.* смесь *f.*
far-reaching /'fɑr 'ritʃɪŋ/ *adj.* далеко́ иду́щий.
farrow /'færou/ *n.* опоро́с *m.*
far-sighted /'fɑr 'saitɪd/ *adj.* (*perceptive*) дально-ви́дный; (*vision*) дальнозо́ркий.
farsightedness /'fɑr 'saitɪdnɪs/ *n.* дально-зо́ркость *f.*

fart /fɑrt/ **1.** *n.* (*vulg.*) пук *m.*; пу́кание *neut.* **2.** *v.* пу́кать *impf.*, пу́кнуть *pf.*
farther /'fɑrðər/ *adv.* да́льше.
farthest /'fɑrðɪst/ *adv.* да́льше всего́.
farthing /'fɑrðɪŋ/ *n.* фа́ртинг *m.*
farthingale /'fɑrðɪŋˌgeil/ *n.* ю́бка с фи́жмами *f.*
fascicle /'fæsɪkəl/ *n.* (*issue of book*) вы́пуск *m.*, кни́жка *f.*; (*manuscript*) тетра́дь *f.*
fascinate /'fæsəˌneit/ *v.* очаро́вывать *impf.*, очарова́ть *pf.*
fascinating /'fæsəˌneitɪŋ/ *adj.* увлека́тельный, очарова́тельный.
fascination /ˌfæsə'neiʃən/ *n.* очарова́ние *neut.*
fascine /fæ'sin/ *n.* фаши́на *f.*
fascism /'fæʃɪzəm/ *n.* фаши́зм *m.*
Fascist /'fæʃɪst/ **1.** *n.* фаши́ст *m.* **2.** *adj.* фаши́стский.
fashion /'fæʃən/ *n.* мо́да *f.*, фасо́н *m.*
fashionable /'fæʃənəbəl/ *adj.* мо́дный.
fast[1] /fæst/ **1.** *adj.* бы́стрый, ско́рый. **2.** *adv.* бы́стро, ско́ро.
fast[2] /fæst/ **1.** *n.* пост *m.* **2.** *v.* пости́ться *impf.*
fasten /'fæsən/ *v.* прикрепля́ть; привя́зывать *impf.*, привяза́ть *pf.*; застёгивать *impf.*
fastener /'fæsənər/ *n.* застёжка *f.*
fastening /'fæsənɪŋ/ *n.* свя́зывание *neut.*
fastidious /fæ'stɪdiəs/ *adj.* разбо́рчивый.
fastidiousness /fæ'stɪdiəsnɪs/ *n.* разбо́рчивость *f.*
fasting /'fæstɪŋ/ *n.* пост *m.*; (*before Communion*) гове́нье *neut.*
fastness /'fæstnɪs/ *n.* (*firmness*) про́чность *f.*
fat /fæt/ **1.** *adj.* жи́рный; то́лстый. **2.** *n.* жир *m.*, са́ло *neut.*
fatal /'feitl̩/ *adj.* смерте́льный, па́губный.
fatalism /'feitl̩ˌɪzəm/ *n.* фатали́зм *m.*
fatalist /'feitl̩ɪst/ *n.* фатали́ст *m.*
fatalistic /ˌfeitl̩'ɪstɪk/ *adj.* фаталисти́ческий.
fatality /fei'tæliti/ *n.* смерте́льний слу́чай *m.*
Fata Morgana /'fɑtɑ mɔr'gɑnɑ/ *n.* фа́та-морга́на *f.*
fate /feit/ *n.* судьба́ *f.*, рок *m.*
fated /'feitɪd/ *adj.* суждено́; **he was fated to...** ему́ суждено́ бы́ло (*with infin.*).
fateful /'feitfəl/ *adj.* роково́й.
father /'fɑðər/ *n.* оте́ц *m.*
fatherhood /'fɑðərˌhʊd/ *n.* отцо́вство *neut.*
father-in-law /'fɑˌðər ɪn lɔ/ *n.* (*husband's father*) свёкор *m.*; (*wife's father*) тесть *m.*
fatherland /'fɑðərˌlænd/ *n.* оте́чество *neut.*, отчи́зна *f.*
fatherless /'fɑðərlɪs/ *adj.* оста́вшийся без отца́.
fatherly /'fɑðərli/ *adj.* оте́ческий.
fathom /'fæðəm/ **1.** *n.* морска́я са́жень *f.* **2.** *v.* измеря́ть глубину́ мо́ря *impf.*; (*understand*) понима́ть *impf.*, поня́ть *pf.*
fathomless /'fæðəmlɪs/ *adj.* неизмери́мый; (*bottomless*) бездо́нный.
fatigue /fə'tig/ **1.** *n.* уста́лость *f.* **2.** *v.* утомля́ть *impf.*, утоми́ть *pf.*
fatiguing /fə'tigɪŋ/ *adj.* утоми́тельный.
fatten /'fætn̩/ *v.* отка́рмливать *impf.*
fattiness /'fætinɪs/ *n.* жи́рность *f.*
fatty /'fæti/ *adj.* жи́рный; жирово́й.
fatuous /'fætʃuəs/ *adj.* глу́пый, дура́цкий.
fatuousness /'fætʃuəsnɪs/ *n.* ту́пость *f.*
fauces /'fɔsiz/ *n.* зев *m.*

faucet /'fɔsɪt/ *n.* водопрово́дный кран *m.*
fault /fɔlt/ *n.* вина́ *f.*; недоста́ток *m.*
faultfinder /'fɔltˌfaindər/ *n.* приди́ра *m.* and *f.* (*decl. f.*).
faultless /'fɔltlɪs/ *adj.* безоши́бочный.
faulty /'fɔlti/ *adj.* оши́бочный, неиспра́вный.
faun /fɔn/ *n.* фавн *m.*
fauna /'fɔnə/ *n.* фа́уна *f.*
faux pas /'fou pɑ/ *n.* ло́жный шаг *m.*
favor /'feivər/ **1.** *n.* (*goodwill*) благоскло́нность *f.*; (*help*) одолже́ние *neut.*; **in somebody's favor** в по́льзу (*with gen.*). **2.** *v.* благоволи́ть (к *with dat.*) *impf.*
favorable /'feivərəbəl/ *adj.* благоприя́тный.
favored /'feivərd/ *adj.* привилегиро́ванный.
favorite /'feivərɪt/ **1.** *adj.* люби́мый. **2.** *n.* люби́мец *m.*
favoritism /'feivərɪˌtɪzəm/ *n.* фавори́зм *m.*
fawn[1] /fɔn/ **1.** *n.* (*deer*) молодо́й оле́нь *m.* **2.** *adj.* желто́вато-кори́чневый.
fawn[2] /fɔn/ *v.* (*animal*) ласка́ться; (*be servile*) подли́зываться *impf.*
fawning /'fɔnɪŋ/ *adj.* раболе́пный.
fax /fæks/ *n.* (*abbr. of facsimile machine*) факс *m.*; факси́мильная маши́на *f.*
faze /feiz/ *v.* смуща́ть *impf.*
fealty /'fiəlti/ *n.* ве́рность *f.*
fear /fɪər/ **1.** *n.* боя́знь *f.*, страх *m.* **2.** *v.* боя́ться *impf.*
fearful /'fɪərfəl/ *adj.* ужа́сный, стра́шный.
fearless /'fɪərlɪs/ *adj.* бесстра́шный.
fearsome /'fɪərsəm/ *adj.* стра́шный.
feasibility /ˌfizə'bɪliti/ *n.* возмо́жность *f.*; осуществи́мость *f.*
feasible /'fizəbəl/ *adj.* возмо́жный.
feast /fist/ **1.** *n.* пра́здник, (*meal*) пир *m.* **2.** *v.* пирова́ть *impf.*
feast day *n.* пра́здник *m.*
feat /fit/ *n.* по́двиг *m.*
feather /'fɛðər/ *n.* перо́ *neut.*
feather bed *n.* пери́на *f.*
feather-brained /'fɛðər ˌbreind/ *adj.* глу́пый.
feathered /'fɛðərd/ *adj.* перна́тый.
feathering /'fɛðərɪŋ/ *n.* опере́ние *neut.*
featherstitch /'fɛðərˌstɪtʃ/ *n.* шов в ёлочку *m.*
featherweight /'fɛðərˌweit/ *n.* (*boxing*) полулёгкий вес *m.*
feathery /'fɛðəri/ *adj.* перна́тый; (*like feather*) пе́ристый; (*light, downy*) пуши́стый.
feature /'fitʃər/ *n.* осо́бенность *f.*; *pl.* черты́ лица́ *pl.*
featureless /'fitʃərlɪs/ *adj.* безли́кий; (*dull*) бесцве́тный.
febrifuge /'fɛbrəˌfyudʒ/ *n.* жаропонижа́ющее сре́дство *neut.*
febrile /'fibrəl/ *adj.* лихора́дочный.
February /'fɛbruˌɛri, 'fɛbyu-/ **1.** *n.* февра́ль *m.* **2.** *adj.* февра́льский.
feces /'fisiz/ *n.* кал *m.*; экскреме́нты *pl.*
feckless /'fɛklɪs/ *adj.* безду́мный; (*useless*) бесполе́зный.
fecund /'fikʌnd, 'fɛk-/ *adj.* (*land, plants*) плодоро́дный; (*animals; fig.*) плодови́тый.
fecundate /'fikənˌdeit, 'fɛkən-/ *v.* оплодотворя́ть *impf.*
fecundity /fɪ'kʌnditi/ *n.* плодоро́дность *f.*
federal /'fɛdərəl/ *adj.* федера́льный.

federalism /'fɛdərə,lɪzəm/ *n.* федерали́зм *m.*
federalize /'fɛdərə,laiz/ *v.* составля́ть федера́цию *impf.*
federated /'fɛdə,reitɪd/ *adj.* федерати́вный.
federation /,fɛdə'reiʃən/ *n.* федера́ция *f.*
fee /fi/ *n.* пла́та *f.*, гонора́р; взнос *m.*
feeble /'fibəl/ *adj.* сла́бый.
feebleness /'fibəlnɪs/ *n.* сла́бость *f.*
feed /fid/ **1.** *n.* корм *m.* **2.** *v.* пита́ть(ся) *impf.*, корми́ть(ся) *impf.*
feedback /'fid,bæk/ *n.* обра́тная связь *f.*
feeding /'fidɪŋ/ *n.* пита́ние *neut.*
feeding trough *n.* корму́шка (для птиц) *f.*
feed pipe *n.* пита́ющая тру́бка *f.*
feel /fil/ *v.* чу́вствовать *impf.*, почу́вствовать *pf.*; *v.i.* чу́вствовать себя́ *impf.*; **to feel like** хоте́ться (*impers.*, *with dat.*) *impf.*: **I feel like** мне хо́чется *impf.*
feeler /'filər/ *n.* (*zool.*) у́сик *m.*; щу́пальце *neut.*; (*fig.*) про́бный шар *m.*
feeling /'filɪŋ/ *n.* чу́вство; ощуще́ние *neut.*; эмо́ция *f.*
feelingly /'filɪŋli/ *adv.* с чу́вством.
feign /fein/ *v.* симули́ровать *impf.*
feigned /feind/ *adj.* притво́рный.
feint /feint/ **1.** *n.* (*deception*) притво́рство *neut.*; (*mil.*) ло́жная ата́ка *f.*, (*sport*) финт *m.* **2.** *v.* де́лать ло́жную ата́ку *or* финт *impf.*
feldspar /'fɛld,spar/ *n.* полево́й шпат *m.*
felicitate /fɪ'lɪsɪ,teit/ *v.* поздравля́ть (с *with instr.*) *impf.*
felicitation /fɪ,lɪsɪ'teiʃən/ *n.* поздравле́ние *neut.*
felicitous /fɪ'lɪsɪtəs/ *adj.* уда́чный.
felicity /fɪ'lɪsɪti/ *n.* сча́стье *neut.*
feline /'filain/ *adj.* коша́чий.
fell[1] /fɛl/ *n.* (*skin*) шку́ра *f.*
fell[2] /fɛl/ *adj.* жесто́кий; (*ruthless*) беспоща́дный; (*savage*) свире́пый.
fell[3] /fɛl/ *v.* (*cut, strike down*) руби́ть, вали́ть *impf.*
fellah /'fɛlə/ *n.* фелла́х *m.*
felling /'fɛlɪŋ/ *n.* (*trees*) ру́бка, ва́лка *f.*
felloe /'fɛlou/ *n.* о́бод *m.*
fellow /'fɛlou/ *n.* това́рищ, прия́тель *m.*; (*colleague*) собра́т *m.*
fellow countryman *n.* соотече́ственник *m.*
fellow feeling *n.* сочу́вствие *neut.*
fellowship /'fɛlou,ʃɪp/ *n.* това́рищество, о́бщество *neut.*; (*grant*) стипе́ндия *f.*
fellow traveller *n.* попу́тчик *m.*
felon /'fɛlən/ *n.* (*criminal*) уголо́вный престу́пник *m.*
felonious /fə'louniəs/ *adj.* престу́пный.
felony /'fɛləni/ *n.* уголо́вное преступле́ние *neut.*
felt /fɛlt/ **1.** *n.* фетр, во́йлок *m.* **2.** *adj.* во́йлочный.
felucca /fə'lʌkə/ *n.* фелю́га *f.*
female /'fimeil/ **1.** *adj.* же́нский. **2.** *n.* же́нщина *f.*; (*animal*) са́мка *f.*
feminine /'fɛmənɪn/ *adj.* же́нский; же́нственный; (*gram.*) же́нского ро́да.
femininity /,fɛmə'nɪnɪti/ *n.* же́нственность *f.*
feminism /'fɛmə,nɪzəm/ *n.* фемини́зм *m.*
feminist /'fɛmənɪst/ **1.** *n.* фемини́ст *m.*, фемини́стка *f.* **2.** *adj.* фемини́стический.
femme fatale /,fɛm fə'tæl, -'tal/ *n.* роковая́ же́нщина *f.*

femoral /'fɛmərəl/ *adj.* бе́дренный.
femur /'fimər/ *n.* бе́дренная кость *f.*
fen /fɛn/ *n.* (*marsh*) боло́то *neut.*; боло́тистая ме́стность *f.*
fence /fɛns/ **1.** *n.* забо́р *m.*, и́згородь *f.* **2.** *v.* (*enclose*) огора́живать *impf.*, огороди́ть *pf.*; *v.i.* (*sport*) фехтова́ть *impf.*
fenceless /'fɛnslɪs/ *adj.* неогоро́женный.
fencer /'fɛnsər/ *n.* фехтова́льщик *m.*
fencing /'fɛnsɪŋ/ *n.* фехтова́ние *neut.*
fend /fɛnd/ *v.* отража́ть *impf.*; **to fend for one-self** забо́титься о себе́ *impf.*
fender /'fɛndər/ *n.* крыло́ *neut.*
fenestration /,fɛnə'streiʃən/ *n.* распределе́ние о́кон *neut.*
Fenian /'finiən/ *n.* фе́ний *m.*
fennel /'fɛnl/ *n.* фе́нхель *m.*
fenugreek /'fɛnyu,grik/ *n.* па́житник *m.*
feoffee /'fɛfi/ *n.* ле́нник *m.*
feral /'fɪərəl, 'fɛr-/ *adj.* (*wild*) ди́кий.
ferial /'fɪəriəl/ *adj.* бу́дний.
ferment /*n.* 'fɜrmɛnt; *v.* fər'mɛnt/ **1.** *n.* ферме́нт *m.*, заква́ска *f.*; (*fig.*) броже́ние *neut.* **2.** *v.* броди́ть *impf.*
fermentation /,fɜrmɛn'teiʃən/ *n.* броже́ние *neut.*, фермента́ция *f.*
fermentative /fər'mɛntətɪv/ *adj.* броди́льный.
fermion /'fɜrmi,ɒn/ *n.* фермио́н *m.*
fermium /'fɜrmiəm/ *n.* фе́рмий *m.*
fern /fɜrn/ *n.* па́поротник *m.*
ferny /'fɜrni/ *adj.* папоротникови́дный.
ferocious /fə'rouʃəs/ *adj.* свире́пый.
ferocity /fə'rɒsɪti/ *n.* свире́пость *f.*
ferrate /'fɛreit/ *n.* ферра́т *m.*
ferreous /'fɛriəs/ *adj.* желе́зный.
ferriage /'fɛriidʒ/ *n.* перепра́ва *f.*
ferric /'fɛrɪk/ *adj.* содержа́щий трёхвале́нтное желе́зо.
ferric acid *n.* желе́зная кислота́ *f.*
ferriferous /fə'rɪfərəs/ *adj.* желе́зистый.
ferrimagnetic /,fɛraimæg'nɛtɪk/ *adj.* железомагни́тный.
ferrimagnetism /,fɛrai'mægnɪ,tɪzəm/ *n.* железомагнети́зм *m.*
ferrite /'fɛrait/ *n.* ферри́т *m.*
ferroalloy /,fɛrou'æləi/ *n.* ферроспла́в *m.*
ferroconcrete /,fɛrou'kɒnkrit/ *n.* железобето́н *m.*
ferromagnetic /,fɛroumæg'nɛtɪk/ *adj.* ферромагни́тный.
ferromagnetism /,fɛrou'mægnɪ,tɪzəm/ *n.* ферромагнети́зм *m.*
ferrous /'fɛrəs/ *adj.* содержа́щий двухвале́нтное желе́зо.
ferrous metal *n.* чёрный мета́лл *m.*
ferruginous /fə'rudʒənəs/ *adj.* железосодержа́щий.
ferrule /'fɛrəl/ *n.* (*ring*) ободо́к *m.*; (*tip*) наконе́чник *m.*
ferry /'fɛri/ **1.** *n.* паро́м *m.* **2.** *v.* перевози́ть, переправля́ть *impf.*
ferryman /'fɛrimən/ *n.* перево́зчик, паро́мщик *m.*
fertile /'fɜrtl/ *adj.* плодоро́дный.
fertility /fər'tɪlɪti/ *n.* плодоро́дие *neut.*
fertilization /,fɜrtlə'zeiʃən/ *n.* оплодотворе́ние *neut.*

fertilize /'fɜrtl̩ˌaiz/ v. удобря́ть *impf.*, удо́брить *pf.*

fertilizer /'fɜrtl̩ˌaizər/ n. удобре́ние *neut.*

fervency /'fɜrvənsi/ n. пы́лкость f.

fervent /'fɜrvənt/ adj. горя́чий; стра́стный; пы́лкий.

fervor /'fɜrvər/ n. пыл m.

fescue /'fɛskyu/ n. (grass) овся́ница f.

festal /'fɛstl̩/ adj. пра́здничный.

fester /'fɛstər/ v. гной́ться *impf.*

festival /'fɛstəvəl/ n. фестива́ль m.

festive /'fɛstɪv/ adj. пра́здничный.

festivity /fɛ'stɪvɪti/ n. весе́лье *neut.*; *pl.* торжество́ *neut.*

festoon /fɛ'stun/ v. украша́ть гирля́ндами *or* фесто́нами *impf.*

festschrift /'fɛstˌʃrɪft/ n. сбо́рник стате́й (*e.g.*, к семидесятиле́тию И.И.Ивано́ва) m.

fetal /'fitl̩/ adj. пло́дный.

fetch /fɛtʃ/ v. (bring thing) приноси́ть *impf.*; (bring person) приводи́ть *impf.*; (bring in vehicle) привози́ть *impf.*

fetching /'fɛtʃɪŋ/ adj. привлека́тельный.

fete /feit, fɛt/ n. пра́зднество *neut.*

fetid /'fɛtɪd/ adj. злово́нный, воню́чий.

fetidness /'fɛtɪdnɪs/ n. злово́ние *neut.*

fetish /'fɛtɪʃ/ n. фети́ш m.

fetishism /'fɛtɪˌʃɪzəm/ n. фетиши́зм m.

fetishist /'fɛtɪʃɪst/ n. фетиши́ст m.

fetlock /'fɛtˌlɒk/ n. щётка f.

fetter /'fɛtər/ n. пу́ты *pl.*, кандалы́ *pl.*; (fig.) око́вы *pl.*

fettle /'fɛtl̩/ n. состоя́ние *neut.*

fetus /'fitəs/ n. утро́бный плод, заро́дыш m.

feud /fyud/ n. вражда́ f.

feudal /'fyudl̩/ adj. феода́льный.

feudalism /'fyudl̩ˌɪzəm/ n. феодали́зм m.

feudatory /'fyudəˌtɔri/ n. феода́льный васса́л m.

fever /'fivər/ n. жар m., лихора́дка f.

feverfew /'fivərˌfyu/ n. пире́трум деви́чий m.

feverish /'fivərɪʃ/ adj. лихора́дочный.

few /fyu/ **1.** adj. немно́гие, немно́го, ма́ло (with gen.); **a few** не́сколько. **2.** pron. немно́гие.

fewer /'fyuər/ adv. ме́ньше (with gen.); **fewer than** ме́ньше чем.

fewness /'fyunɪs/ n. немногочи́сленность f.

fez /fɛz/ n. фе́ска f.

fiacre /fi'ɑkər/ n. фиа́кр m.

fiancé /ˌfiɑn'sei/ n. жени́х m.

fiancée /ˌfiɑn'sei/ n. неве́ста f.

fiasco /fi'æskou/ n. фиа́ско *neut. indecl.*; прова́л m., неуда́ча f.

fiat /'fiɑt/ n. разреше́ние *neut.*; декре́т, ука́з m.

fib /fɪb/ n. (colloq.) вы́думка f.

fibber /'fɪbər/ n. вы́думщик m.

fiber /'faibər/ n. волокно́ *neut.*

fibril /'faibrəl/ n. волоко́нце *neut.*

fibrin /'faibrɪn/ n. фибри́н m.

fibroid /'faibrɔid/ n. фибро́зная о́пухоль f.

fibroin /'faibrouɪn/ n. фиброи́н m.

fibroma /fai'broumə/ n. фибро́ма f.

fibrous /'faibrəs/ adj. фибро́зный, волокни́стый.

fibula /'fɪbyələ/ n. (anat.) ма́лая берцо́вая кость f.

fichu /'fɪʃu/ n. фишю́ *neut. indecl.*

fickle /'fɪkəl/ adj. изме́нчивый.

fickleness /'fɪkəlnɪs/ n. изме́нчивость f.

fictile /'fɪktl̩/ adj. гонча́рный.

fiction /'fɪkʃən/ n. фи́кция f., вы́мысел m.; (lit.) беллетри́стика; худо́жественная литерату́ра f.

fictional /'fɪkʃənl̩/ adj. беллетристи́ческий; вы́мышленный.

fictitious /fɪk'tɪʃəs/ adj. фикти́вный, вы́мышленный.

fiddle /'fɪdl̩/ n. скри́пка f.

fiddle-faddle /'fɪdl̩ˌfædl̩/ n. чепуха́ f.

fiddler /'fɪdlər/ n. скрипа́ч m.

fiddling /'fɪdlɪŋ/ adj. ничто́жный.

fidelity /fɪ'dɛlɪti/ n. ве́рность f.

fidget /'fɪdʒɪt/ v. ёрзать; не́рвничать *impf.*; **stop fidgeting!** не ёрзай!

fidgety /'fɪdʒɪti/ adj. неугомо́нный.

fiducial /fɪ'duʃəl/ adj. осно́ванный на дове́рии.

fiduciary /fɪ'duʃiˌɛri/ n. попечи́тель m.

fie /fai/ interj. фу! тьфу!

field /fild/ **1.** n. по́ле *neut.*; (area of interest) о́бласть f.; (sport) площа́дка f. **2.** adj. полево́й.

field artillery n. полева́я артилле́рия f.

field book n. полево́й журна́л m.

field day n. (mil.) такти́ческие заня́тия на ме́стности *pl.*

field dressing n. перви́чная повя́зка f.

field events n. соревнова́ния по лёгкой атле́тике *pl.*

fieldfare /'fildˌfɛər/ n. (bird) дрозд-ряби́нник m.

field glasses n. (binoculars) бино́кль m.

field hospital n. полево́й го́спиталь m.

field magnet n. возбужда́ющий магни́т m.

field marshal n. фельдма́ршал m.

field mouse n. полева́я мышь f.

field officer n. штаб-офице́р m.

fieldwork /'fildˌwɜrk/ n. полевы́е рабо́ты *pl.*

fiend /find/ n. дья́вол, бес m.

fiendish /'findɪʃ/ adj. дья́вольский.

fierce /fɪərs/ adj. жесто́кий, свире́пый.

fierceness /'fɪərsnɪs/ n. свире́пость f.

fierily /'faiᵊrəli/ adv. горячо́.

fiery /'faiᵊri/ adj. о́гненный; вспы́льчивый.

fife /faif/ n. ду́дка f.

fifteen /'fɪf'tin/ adj., n. пятна́дцать.

fifteenth /'fɪf'tinθ/ adj., n. пятна́дцатый.

fifth /fɪfθ/ adj., n. пя́тый.

fifthly /'fɪfθli/ adv. в-пя́тых.

fiftieth /'fɪftiθ/ adj., n. пятидеся́тый.

fifty /'fɪfti/ adj., n. пятьдеся́т.

fig /fɪg/ **1.** n. фи́га f. **2.** adj. фи́говый.

fight /fait/ **1.** n. бой m.; борьба́, дра́ка f. **2.** v. боро́ться, сража́ться, дра́ться *impf.*

fighter /'faitər/ n. (also fig., sport) боре́ц m.; (plane) истреби́тель m.

fighting /'faitɪŋ/ **1.** n. дра́ка f.; бой m. **2.** adj. боево́й.

fig leaf /fɪg/ n. фи́говый листо́к m.

figment /'fɪgmənt/ n. вы́думка f.

figuration /ˌfɪgyə'reiʃən/ n. фо́рма f.; ко́нтур m.

figurative /'fɪgyərətɪv/ adj. перено́сный.

figuratively /'fɪgyərətɪvli/ adv. в перено́сном смы́сле.

figure /'fɪgyər/ **1.** n. фигу́ра f.; (number) ци́фра f.; (form) о́браз m.; (person) ли́чность f. **2. to figure out** v. вычисля́ть *impf.*, вы́числить *pf.*

figured /'fɪgyərd/ adj. узо́рчатый.

figure eight n. восьмёрка f.

figurehead /'fɪgyər,hɛd/ n. (naut.) носово́е украше́ние neut.; (fig) подставно́е лицо́ neut.
figurine /,fɪgyə'rin/ n. стату́этка f.
Fiji /'fidʒi/ n. Фи́джи m.
filament /'fɪləmənt/ n. волосо́к m.; волокно́ neut.
filamentary /,fɪlə'mɛntəri/ adj. волокни́стый.
filbert /'fɪlbərt/ n. лещи́на f.
filch /fɪltʃ/ v. красть, тащи́ть impf.
file¹ /fail/ 1. n. (card file) картоте́ка f.; (folder) па́пка f.; (record) де́ло neut.; (row) о́чередь f., ряд m. 2. v. (papers) регистри́ровать impf., зарегистри́ровать pf.
file² /fail/ 1. n. (tool) напи́льник m. 2. v. (tool) подпи́ливать impf., подпили́ть pf.; (file application) подава́ть заявле́ние neut.
filer /'failər/ n. точи́льщик m.
filial /'fɪliəl/ adj. сыно́вний; дочéрний.
filiation /,fɪli'eiʃən/ n. происхожде́ние neut.
filibuster /'fɪlə,bʌstər/ n. флибустье́р m.
filigree /'fɪlɪ,gri/ n. филигра́нная рабо́та f.
filing /'failɪŋ/ n. регистра́ция f.
fill /fɪl/ v. наполня́ть impf., напо́лнить pf.; заполня́ть impf.; (occupy) занима́ть impf.; (satiate) насыща́ть impf.
filler /'fɪlər/ n. наполни́тель m.
fillet /fɪ'lei/ n. филé neut. indecl.
filling /'fɪlɪŋ/ 1. n. на́сыпь f.; (dental) пло́мба f.; (cul.) начи́нка f. 2. adj. (food) сы́тый.
fillip /'fɪləp/ n. щелчо́к m.
fillister /'fɪləstər/ n. фальцо́вка f.
filly /'fɪli/ n. кобы́лка f.
film /fɪlm/ 1. n. фильм m.; плёнка f. 2. v. производи́ть киносъёмку, снима́ть фильм impf.
filmgoer /'fɪlm,gouər/ n. кинозри́тель m.
filming /'fɪlmɪŋ/ n. съёмка (кинофи́льма) f.
film pack n. фильмпа́к m.
film shooting n. киносъёмка f.
film star n. киноэвезда́ f.
filmstrip /'fɪlm,strɪp/ n. диафи́льм m.
film studio n. киносту́дия f.
filmy /'fɪlmi/ adj. покры́тый плёнкой.
filter /'fɪltər/ 1. n. фильтр m. 2. v. фильтрова́ть; проце́живать impf.
filterable /'fɪltərəbəl/ adj. фильтру́емый.
filth /fɪlθ/ n. грязь f.
filthiness /'fɪlθɪnɪs/ n. мéрзость f.
filthy /'fɪlθi/ adj. гря́зный.
filtrate /'fɪltreit/ n. фильтра́т m.
filtration /fɪl'treiʃən/ n. фильтра́ция f.
fimbriated /'fɪmbri,eitɪd/ adj. бахро́мчатый.
fin /fɪn/ n. плавни́к m.
finable /'fainəbəl/ adj. облага́емый штра́фом.
final /'fainḷ/ 1. adj. после́дний; оконча́тельный; фина́льный. 2. n. (sports) фина́л m.
finale /fɪ'næli, -'nɑli/ n. заключе́ние neut.
finalist /'fainḷɪst/ n. финали́ст m.
finality /fai'nælɪti/ n. оконча́тельность f.
finalize /'fainḷ,aiz/ v. заключа́ть impf.
finally /'fainḷi/ adv. оконча́тельно; наконе́ц.
finance /fɪ'næns, 'fainæns/ 1. n. фина́нсы pl. 2. v. финанси́ровать impf. and pf.
financial /fɪ'nænʃəl/ adj. фина́нсовый.
financier /,fɪnən'sɪər/ n. финанси́ст m.
finch /fɪntʃ/ n. (bird) вьюро́к m.
find /faind/ v. находи́ть impf., найти́ pf.; **to find out** узнава́ть impf., узна́ть pf.

finder /'faindər/ n. (tech.) иска́тель m.
finding /'faindɪŋ/ n. нахо́дка f.; (discovery) откры́тие neut.; (leg.) реше́ние neut.
fine¹ /fain/ 1. adj. хоро́ший; (thin) то́нкий. 2. adv. хорошо́.
fine² /fain/ 1. n. штраф m. 2. v. налага́ть штраф impf.
fine-draw /'fain'drɔ/ v. сшива́ть незаме́тным швом impf.
fine-grained /'fain'greind/ adj. мелкозерни́стый.
fineness /'fainnɪs/ n. то́нкость f.
finery /'fainəri/ n. (clothing) пы́шный наря́д m.
finesse /fɪ'nɛs/ n. такти́чность f.
finger /'fɪŋgər/ n. па́лец m.
fingerboard /'fɪŋ,gərbɔrd/ n. (mus.) гриф m.
fingered /'fɪŋgərd/ adj. захва́танный.
fingering /'fɪŋgərɪŋ/ n. прикоснове́ние па́льцев neut.
finger mark n. отпеча́ток па́льца m.
fingernail /'fɪŋgər,neil/ n. но́готь m.
finger-nut /'fɪŋgər,nʌt/ n. га́йка-бара́шек f.
finger post n. указа́тельный столб m.
fingerprint /'fɪŋgər,prɪnt/ 1. n. отпеча́ток па́льца m. 2. v. снима́ть отпеча́тки па́льцев (с with gen.) impf.
fingerstall /'fɪŋgər,stɔl/ n. напа́льчник m.
fingertip /'fɪŋgər,tɪp/ n. ко́нчик па́льца m.
finial /'fɪniəl/ n. зака́нчивающее украше́ние neut.
finicky /'fɪnɪki/ adj. привере́дливый; брезгли́вый.
fining /'fainɪŋ/ n. очи́стка f.
finish /'fɪnɪʃ/ 1. n. коне́ц m.; (sport) фи́ниш m.; (polish) полиро́вка f. 2. v. конча́ть impf., ко́нчить pf.
finished /'fɪnɪʃt/ adj. зако́нченный, гото́вый; обрабо́танный; **finished goods** n. гото́вые изде́лия pl.; **finished manners** изы́сканные мане́ры pl.; (exhausted) **I am finished!** я бо́льше не могу́!
finisher /'fɪnɪʃər/ n. отде́лочник m.
finishing /'fɪnɪʃɪŋ/ n. отде́лка f.
finish line n. фи́нишная ли́ния f.
finite /'fainait/ adj. ограни́ченный; (math.) коне́чный, фини́тный.
finiteness /'fainaitnɪs/ n. ограни́ченность f.
fink /fɪŋk/ n. (slang) (informer) стука́ч m.; (strikebreaker) штрейкбре́хер m.
Finland /'fɪnlənd/ n. Финля́ндия f.
Finn /fɪn/ n. финн m., фи́нка f.
finned /fɪnd/ adj. (zool.) име́ющий плавники́.
Finnish /'fɪnɪʃ/ adj. финля́ндский, фи́нский.
fir /fɜr/ 1. n. пи́хта f. 2. adj. пи́хтовый.
fire /fai³r/ 1. n. ого́нь; пожа́р m.; (campfire) костёр m. 2. v. (shoot) стреля́ть impf., вы́стрелить pf.; **to catch fire** загоре́ться pf.; **to set on fire** поджига́ть impf., подже́чь pf.
fire alarm n. пожа́рная трево́га f., пожа́рный сигна́л m.
firearm /'fai³r,ɑrm/ n. огнестре́льное ору́жие neut.
fireball /'fai³r,bɔl/ n. боли́д m.
firebox /'fai³r,bɒks/ n. то́пка f.
firebrand /'fai³r,brænd/ n. (burning wood) головня́ f.
firebreak /'fai³r,breik/ n. пожа́рная просе́ка f.
firebrick /'fai³r,brɪk/ n. огнеупо́рный кирпи́ч m.
fire brigade n. пожа́рная кома́нда f.
fire clay n. огнеупо́рная гли́на f.

fire control n. (mil., nav.) управление огнём neut.

firedamp /'faiᵊr‚dæmp/ n. гремучий газ m.

fire door n. пожарная дверь f.

fire drill n. учебная пожарная тревога f.

fire-eater /'faiᵊr‚itər/ n. пожиратель огня m.

fire engine n. пожарная машина f.

fire escape n. пожарная лестница f.

fire extinguisher n. огнетушитель m.

firefighter /'faiᵊr‚faitər/ n. пожарник m.

firefighting /'faiᵊr‚faitɪŋ/ adj. противопожарный.

firefly /'faiᵊr‚flai/ n. светляк, светлячок m.

firehose /'faiᵊr‚houz/ n. пожарный рукав or шланг m.

fire hydrant n. пожарный кран m.

fire insurance n. страхование от пожара neut.

fire irons n. каминный прибор m.

firelock /'faiᵊr‚lɒk/ n. кремнёвый мушкет m.

fireplace /'faiᵊr‚pleis/ n. камин m.

fireproof /'faiᵊr‚pruf/ adj. огнеупорный.

fire screen n. каминная решётка f.

fire ship n. брандер m.

fireside /'faiᵊr‚said/ n. место у камина neut.

fire station n. пожарное депо neut. indecl.

fire wall n. брандмауэр m.

firewarden /'faiᵊr‚wɔrdŋ/ n. пожарный объездчик m.

firewatcher /'faiᵊr‚wɑtʃər/ n. дежурный пожарный m.

firewood /'faiᵊr‚wʊd/ n. дрова pl.

fireworks /'faiᵊr‚wɜrks/ n. pl. фейерверк m.

fire worship n. огнепоклонничество neut.

fire worshipper n. огнепоклонник m.

firing /'faiᵊrɪŋ/ n. (of gun) стрельба f.; (layoff) увольнение neut.

firm¹ /fɜrm/ adj. твёрдый; крепкий; стойкий.

firm² /fɜrm/ n. фирма f.

firmament /'fɜrməmənt/ n. твердь небесная f.; небесный свод m.

firmness /'fɜrmnɪs/ n. твёрдость; прочность f.

first /fɜrst/ **1.** adj. первый. **2.** adv. сперва, сначала; впервые; **at first** сперва, сначала; **first of all** прежде всего.

first aid n. первая or скорая помощь m.

firstborn /'fɜrst‚bɔrn/ n. первенец m.

first-class /'fɜrst‚klæs/ adj. первоклассный.

first floor n. первый этаж m.

first fruits n. первые плоды pl.

firsthand /'fɜrst‚hænd/ adj., adv. из первых рук.

firstly /'fɜrstli/ adv. во-первых.

first name n. имя neut.

first-rate /'fɜrst‚reit/ adj. первоклассный, прекрасный, превосходный.

fiscal /'fɪskəl/ adj. фискальный; финансовый.

fish /fɪʃ/ **1.** n. рыба f. **2.** adj. рыбный. **3.** v. ловить рыбу impf.

fishbone /'fɪʃ‚boun/ n. рыбья кость f.

fish cake n. тефтели из рыбы pl.

fisherman /'fɪʃərmən/ n. рыбак m.

fishery /'fɪʃəri/ n. рыбный промысел m., рыболовство neut.

fish glue n. рыбий клей m.

fishhook /'fɪʃ‚hʊk/ n. рыболовный крючок m.

fishiness /'fɪʃɪnɪs/ n. рыбный привкус m.

fishing /'fɪʃɪŋ/ **1.** n. рыбная ловля f. **2.** adj. рыболовный.

fishing boat n. рыбачья лодка f.

fish ladder n. рыбоход m.

fish meal n. рыбная мука f.

fish pâté n. паштет из рыбы m.

fishplate /'fɪʃ‚pleit/ n. (tech.) стыковая накладка f.

fishpond /'fɪʃ‚pɒnd/ n. рыбоводный пруд m.

fish shop n. рыбный магазин m.

fishtail /'fɪʃ‚teil/ n. рыбий хвост m.

fishwife /'fɪʃ‚waif/ n. торговка рыбой f.; (fig.) базарная торговка f..

fishy /'fɪʃi/ adj. рыбный; рыбий.

fissile /'fɪsəl/ adj. (phys.) расщепляющийся.

fission /'fɪʃən/ n. деление, расщепление neut.; **nuclear fission** n. ядерное деление f.

fissionable /'fɪʃənəbəl/ adj. расщепляемый.

fissiparous /fɪ'sɪpərəs/ adj. размножающийся делением.

fissure /'fɪʃər/ n. трещина f.

fist /fɪst/ n. кулак m.

fistfight /'fɪst‚fait/ pl. кулачный бой m.

fistful /'fɪstfʊl/ n. горсть f.

fistula /'fɪstʃʊlə/ n. свищ m.

fit¹ /fɪt/ **1.** adj. годный, подходящий; (healthy) здоровый. **2.** v.t. (adjust) прилаживать impf., приладить pf.; v.i. годиться (with dat.); на (with acc.) impf.; подходить (with dat.) impf.

fit² /fɪt/ n. (impulse) порыв m.

fitful /'fɪtfəl/ adj. (in bursts) порывистый; (irregular) прерывистый.

fitter /'fɪtər/ n. монтёр, слесарь-монтажник m.

fitting /'fɪtɪŋ/ n. (trying on) примерка f.

fittingly /'fɪtɪŋli/ adv. подобающим or надлежащим образом.

five /faiv/ adj., n. пять.

fivefold /'faiv‚fould/ adj. пятикратный.

fiver /'faivər/ n. (colloq.) пятёрка f.

fix /fɪks/ **1.** n. дилемма f., затруднительное положение. **2.** v. исправлять impf., исправить pf.; приводить в порядок impf.; (set; also photog.) фиксировать impf. and pf.

fixation /fɪk'seifən/ n. фиксация f.

fixative /'fɪksətɪv/ n. фиксатор m.

fixed /fɪkst/ adj. неподвижный; назначенный.

fixedly /'fɪksɪdli/ adv. пристально.

fixer /'fɪksər/ n. (arranger) наладчик m.; (chem.) фиксаж, закрепитель m.

fixing /'fɪksɪŋ/ n. закрепление neut.

fixture /'fɪkstʃər/ n. приспособление neut.; прибор m.

fizz /fɪz/ n. шипение neut.

fizzle /'fɪzəl/ v. слегка шипеть impf.

fizzy /'fɪzi/ adj. шипучий, игристый.

fjord /fyɔrd/ n. фиорд m.

flabbergast /'flæbər‚gæst/ v. ошеломлять impf.

flabby /'flæbi/ adj. дряблый; вялый; отвислый.

flaccid /'flæksɪd, 'flæsɪd/ adj. вялый.

flag /flæg/ n. флаг m., знамя neut.

flagellant /'flædʒələnt/ n. флагеллант m.

flagellate /'flædʒə‚leit/ v. бичевать impf.

flagellation /‚flædʒə'leifən/ n. бичевание neut.

flagelliform /flə'dʒelə‚fɔrm/ adj. жгутиковидный.

flagellum /flə'dʒeləm/ n. (biol.) жгутик m.

flageolet /‚flædʒə'let/ n. флажолет m.

flagging /'flægɪŋ/ n. пол из плит m.

flag officer n. флаг-офицер m.

flagon /'flægən/ n. кувшин m.

flagpole /'flæg,poul/ n. флагшто́к m.
flagrant /'fleigrənt/ adj. вопию́щий.
flagship /'flæg,ʃɪp/ n. фла́гманский кора́бль, фла́гман m.
flagstaff /'flæg,stæf/ n. флагшто́к m.
flagstone /'flæg,stoun/ n. ка́менная плита́ f.
flag-waving /'flæg,weiviŋ/ n. (colloq., pejor.) ура́-патриоти́зм m.
flail /fleil/ 1. n. цеп m. 2. v. молоти́ть; маха́ть impf.
flair /flɛər/ n. чутьё (на with acc.).
flak /flæk/ n. зени́тная артилле́рия f.
flake /fleik/ 1. n. pl. хло́пья pl. 2. v. слои́ться impf.
flakiness /'fleikinɪs/ n. хлопьеви́дность f.
flaky /'fleiki/ 1. adj. хлопьеви́дный; слои́стый. 2. (slang) чудно́й.
flam /flæm/ n. (colloq.) обма́н m.
flamboyance /flæm'bɔiəns/ n. экспанси́вность f.
flamboyant /flæm'bɔiənt/ adj. экспанси́вный; цвети́стый.
flame /fleim/ n. пла́мя neut.; ого́нь m.; (passion) пыл m.
flame-colored /'fleim,kʌlərd/ adj. кра́сно-жёл-тый.
flame-out /'fleim,aut/ n. (aero.) заглуше́ние дви́гателя neut.
flameproof /'fleim,pruf/ adj. огнесто́йкий.
flame thrower n. огнемёт m.
flaming /'fleimiŋ/ adj. пыла́ющий.
flamingo /flə'miŋgou/ n. флами́нго m. indecl.
flâneur /flu'nɜr/ n. фланёр m.
flange /flændʒ/ n. фла́нец m.
flank /flæŋk/ n. бок; фланг m.; сторона́ f.
flannel /'flænḷ/ 1. n. фланéль f. 2. adj. фланéлевый.
flannelet /,flænḷ'ɛt/ n. фланелéт m.
flap /flæp/ 1. n. кла́пан m.; засло́нка f. 2. v. маха́ть impf., махну́ть pf.; взма́хивать (with str.) impf.
flapjack /'flæp,dʒæk/ n. лепёшка f.
flapper /'flæpər/ n. хлопу́шка f.
flare /flɛər/ 1. n. фа́кел m., вспы́шка f. 2. v. вспы́хивать impf., вспы́хнуть pf.
flareup /'flɛər,ʌp/ n. вспы́шка f.
flash /flæʃ/ 1. n. вспы́шка f.; (instant) миг m. 2. v. вспы́хнуть pf.; сверкну́ть pf.
flashback /'flæʃ,bæk/ n. (cinema) ретроспекти́вная сцéна f.
flash bulb n. ла́мпа-вспы́шка f.
flashily /'flæʃəli/ adv. напока́з; (in loud colors) крикли́во.
flashiness /'flæʃɪnɪs/ n. вульга́рность; крикли́вость f.
flashing /'flæʃɪŋ/ n. вспы́хивание neut.
flashlight /'flæʃ,lait/ m. электри́ческий фона́рь m.
flash point n. температу́ра вспы́шки f.
flashy /'flæʃi/ adj. крича́щий.
flask /flæsk/ n. фля́га, фля́жка f.
flat¹ /flæt/ 1. adj. пло́ский; ро́вный; ску́чный. 2. n. (mus.) бемо́ль m.
flat² /flæt/ n. (Brit.; apartment) кварти́ра f.
flat-bottomed /'flæt'bɒtəmd/ adj. плоскодо́н-ный.
flat-chested /'flæt'tʃɛstɪd/ adj. плоскогру́дый.
flatfish /'flæt,fɪʃ/ n. ка́мбала f.

flatfooted /'flæt,fotɪd/ adj. страда́ющий плоско-сто́пием.
flatiron /'flæt,aiərn/ n. утю́г m.
flatly /'flætli/ adv. категори́чески.
flatness /'flætnɪs/ n. пло́скость f.
flat-sided /'flæt,saidɪd/ adj. плоскобо́ртный.
flatten /'flætn̩/ v. выра́внивать impf., вы́ровнять pf.
flatter /'flætər/ v. льстить impf.
flatterer /'flætərər/ n. льстец m.
flattering /'flætərɪŋ/ adj. лéстный.
flattery /'flætəri/ n. лесть f.
flatting mill /'flætɪŋ/ n. листопрока́тный стан m.
flattish /'flætɪʃ/ adj. плоскова́тый.
flatulence /'flætʃələns/ n. метеори́зм m., скоп-лéние га́зов neut.
flatulent /'flætʃələnt/ adj. страда́ющий от га́зов.
flaunt /flɔnt/ v. щеголя́ть (with instr.) impf.
flavin /'fleivin/ n. флави́н m.
flavor /'fleivər/ 1. n. арома́т; при́вкус m. 2. v. приправля́ть impf., припра́вить pf.
flavoring /'fleivəriŋ/ n. припра́ва f.
flavorless /'fleivərlɪs/ adj. безвку́сный.
flaw /flɔ/ n. недоста́ток, поро́к m.
flawed /flɔd/ adj. дефéктный, поро́чный.
flawless /'flɔlɪs/ adj. безупре́чный, беспоро́чный.
flax /flæks/ n. лён m.
flaxen /'flæksən/ adj. льняно́й.
flay /flei/ v. сдира́ть ко́жу (с with gen.) impf.
flayer /'fleiər/ n. живодёр m.
flea /fli/ 1. n. блоха́ f. 2. adj. блоши́ный.
fleck /flɛk/ n. пя́тнышко neut.; кра́пинка f.; (particle) крупи́нка f.; (snow) снежи́нка f.; (dust) пыли́нка f.
fledge /flɛdʒ/ v. оперя́ть(ся) impf.
fledgling /'flɛdʒlɪŋ/ n. (опери́вшийся) птенéц m.
flee /fli/ v. бежа́ть impf. and pf.; убега́ть impf.
fleece /flis/ 1. n. шерсть f.; руно́ neut. 2. v. стричь овéц; (fig.) обдира́ть impf., ободра́ть pf.
fleecy /'flisi/ adj. шерсти́стый.
fleet /flit/ n. флот m.; (of vehicles) парк m.
fleet-footed /'flit'fotɪd/ adj. быстроно́гий.
fleeting /'flitɪŋ/ adj. мимолётный.
flesh /flɛʃ/ n. мя́со neut.; (body) плоть f.
flesh-colored /'flɛʃ,kʌlərd/ adj. телéсного цвéта.
fleshy /'flɛʃi/ adj. мяси́стый.
fleur-de-lis /,flɜrdḷ'i/ n. геральди́ческая ли́лия f.
flex /flɛks/ v.t сгиба́ть impf., согну́ть pf.; v.i. сгиба́ться impf., согну́ться pf.
flexibility /,flɛksə'bɪliti/ n. ги́бкость; эласти́ч-ность; усту́пчивость f.
flexible /'flɛksəbəl/ adj. ги́бкий.
flexion /'flɛkʃən/ n. (med., tech.) сгиба́ние neut.
flexional /'flɛkʃənḷ/ adj. флекти́вный.
flexor /'flɛksər/ n. сгиба́тельная мы́шца f.
flibbertigibbet /'flɪbərti,dʒɪbɪt/ n. (colloq.) вер-ту́шка, болту́шка f.
flick /flɪk/ v. (hit lightly) слегка́ уда́рить pf.; (with whip) стега́ть; (fingers, switch, etc.) щёл-кать(ся) impf.
flicker /'flɪkər/ 1. n. мерца́ние neut.; вспы́шка f. 2. v. мерца́ть impf.
flier /'flaiər/ n. лётчик m.
flight /flait/ n. полёт m.; (scheduled trip) рейс m.
flight engineer n. бортмеха́ник m.
flighty /'flaiti/ adj. капри́зный.

flimsy /'flɪmzi/ adj. (fragile) хрупкий; (weak) слабый.

flinch /flɪntʃ/ v. уклоняться impf.; (wince) вздрагивать impf.

fling /flɪŋ/ v.t. швырять, бросать impf.; **fling oneself into** v.i. броса́ться (в with acc.) impf.

flint /flɪnt/ n. кремень m.

flintlock /'flɪnt,lɒk/ n. кремнёвое ружьё neut.

flinty /'flɪnti/ adj. кремнёвый.

flip /flɪp/ **1.** n. шелчок m. **2.** v. щёлкнуть pf.; подбрасывать impf.

flip-flop /'flɪp,flɒp/ n. (elec.) триггер m.

flippancy /'flɪpənsi/ n. легкомыслие neut.

flippant /'flɪpənt/ adj. непочтительный, дерзкий.

flipper /'flɪpər/ n. плавник, ласт m.

flirt /flɜrt/ **1.** n. кокетка f. **2.** v. флиртовать impf.

flirtation /flɜr'teiʃən/ n. флирт m.

flirtatious /flɜr'teiʃəs/ adj. кокетливый.

flit /flɪt/ v. порхать impf.

float /flout/ **1.** v. плавать impf. **2.** n. поплавок; плот m.

floating /'floutɪŋ/ adj. плавающий, плавучий.

floatplane /'flout,plein/ n. поплавковый гидросамолёт m.

flocculent /'flɒkyələnt/ adj. шерстистый.

flock /flɒk/ **1.** n. стадо m., стая f.; (people) толпа f. **2.** v. толпиться impf.

floe /flou/ n. плавучая льдина f.

flog /flɒg/ v. сечь; пороть impf.

flogging /'flɒgɪŋ/ n. порка f.

flood /flʌd/ **1.** n. наводнение neut.; потоп m.; (influx) прилив, поток m. **2.** v. заливать impf., залить pf.

floodgate /'flʌd,geit/ n. шлюз m.

flooding /'flʌdɪŋ/ n. затопление neut.

floodlight /'flʌd,lait/ n. прожектор m.

floodlighting /'flʌd,laitɪŋ/ n. освещение прожекторами neut.

flood tide n. прилив m.

floor /flɔr/ n. пол m.; (story) этаж m.; (bottom) дно neut.

floorboard /'flɔr,bɔrd/ n. половица f.

floorcloth /'flɔr,klɔθ/ n. половая тряпка f.

flooring /'flɔrɪŋ/ n. настил m.

floorshow /'flɔr,ʃou/ n. кабаре neut. indecl.

flop /flɒp/ **1.** n. фиаско neut. indecl. **2.** v. плюхнуться (в or на with acc.) pf.

flop-eared /'flɒp,ɪərd/ adj. вислоухий.

floppy /'flɒpi/ adj. вялый; висящий, обвислый.

floppy disk n. (comput.) гибкий диск, дискета f.

flora /'flɔrə/ n. флора f.

floral /'flɔrəl/ adj. цветочный.

Florence /'flɔrəns/ n. Флоренция f.

florescence /flɔ'rɛsəns/ n. цветение neut.

floret /'flɔrɪt/ n. цветочек m.

floriated /'flɔri,eitɪd/ adj. с растительным орнаментом.

floriculture /'flɔri,kʌltʃər/ n. цветоводство neut.

florid /'flɔrɪd/ adj. цветистый; витиеватый.

Florida /'flɔrɪdə/ n. Флорида f.

florist /'flɔrɪst/ n. торговец цветами m.

floss /flɔs/ n. шёлк-сырец m.

flotation /flou'teiʃən/ n. (tech., geol.) флотация f.

flotilla /flou'tɪlə/ n. флотилия f.

flotsam /'flɒtsəm/ n. плавающие обломки pl..

flounce¹ /flauns/ n. (frill) оборка f., волан m.

flounce² /flauns/ **1.** n. резкое движение neut. **2.** v. бросаться impf.

flounder¹ /'flaundər/ n. камбала f.

flounder² /'flaundər/ v. барахтаться impf.

flour /flauᵊr, 'flauər/ n. мука f.

flourish /'flɜrɪʃ/ **1.** n. росчерк m., цветистое выражение neut. **2.** v. процветать impf.

floury /'flauᵊri/ adj. мучной.

flout /flaut/ v. попирать impf.

flow /flou/ **1.** n. течение neut., струя f.; поток m. **2.** v. течь; литься impf.

flow chart n. блок-схема f.

flower /'flauər/ **1.** n. цветок m. **2.** adj. цветочный. **3.** v. цвести impf.

flowerbed /'flauər,bed/ n. клумба f.

flowered /'flauərd/ adj. украшенный цветами.

floweret /'flauərɪt/ n. цветочек m.

flower garden n. цветник m.

flowering /'flauərɪŋ/ adj. цветущиь; цветковый.

flowerless /'flauərlɪs/ adj. бесцветковый.

flowerpot /'flauər,pɒt/ n. цветочный горшок m.

flower show n. выставка цветов f.

flowery /'flauəri/ adj. цветущий; (speech) витиеватый.

flowing /'flouɪŋ/ adj. гладкий; плавный; (water) текущий.

flowmeter /'flou,mitər/ n. водомер m.

flu /flu/ n. грипп m.

fluctuate /'flʌktʃu,eit/ v. колебаться impf.

fluctuating /'flʌktʃu,eitɪŋ/ adj. колеблющийся.

fluctuation /,flʌktʃu'eiʃən/ n. колебание neut.

flue /flu/ n. дымоход m.

fluency /'fluənsi/ n. плавность, беглость f.

fluent /'fluənt/ adj. плавный, беглый.

fluff /flʌf/ n. пух m.

fluffy /'flʌfi/ adj. пушистый; (fleecy) ворсистый.

fluid /'fluɪd/ **1.** adj. жидкий; текучий. **2.** n. жидкость f.

fluidity /flu'ɪdɪti/ n. жидкое состояние neut.

fluidize /'fluɪ,daiz/ v. превращать(ся) в жидкость impf.

fluke¹ /fluk/ n. (fish) камбала f.

fluke² n. случайность f.

flume /flum/ n. (tech.) проток m.; ущелье с потоком neut.

flunk /flʌŋk/ v. провалиться impf.

flunky /'flʌŋki/ n. лакей m.

fluoresce /flu'rɛs/ v. флюоресцировать impf.

fluorescence /flu'rɛsəns/ n. флюоресценция f.

fluorescent light n. люминесцентная лампа f.

fluoric /flu'ɔrɪk/ adj. фтористый.

fluoridate /'flurɪ,deit/ v. фторировать impf.

fluoridation /,flurɪ'deiʃən/ n. фторирование neut.

fluoride /'fluraid/ n. фторид m.

fluorine /'flurin/ n. фтор m.

fluorite /'flurait/ also **fluor, fluorspar** n. флюорит m.

flurry /'flɜri/ **1.** n. (burst) порыв m.; (commotion) суматоха f.; (agitation) волнение neut. **2.** v. (fluster) волновать impf.

flush¹ /flʌʃ/ adj. вровень (с with instr.).

flush² /flʌʃ/ **1.** n. краска f., румянец m. **2.** v. (with water) промывать impf., промыть pf.; (blush) краснеть impf.

fluster /'flʌstər/ n. волнение neut.

flute /flut/ n. флейта f.

fluted /'fluːtɪd/ adj. рифлёный.
flutist /'fluːtɪst/ n. флейтист m.
flutter /'flʌtər/ **1.** n. порхание neut. **2.** v. развеваться; трепетать impf.
fluvial /'fluːvɪəl/ adj. речной.
flux /flʌks/ n. поток; прилив m.; (continuous change) постоянные изменения pl.; (med.) истечение neut.
fly¹ /flai/ n. муха f.
fly² /flai/ v. летать indet. impf.; лететь det. impf.
fly agaric /'ægərɪk/ n. (mushroom) мухомор m.
fly by n. (aviation) воздушный парад m.
flycatcher /'flai,kætʃər/ n. мухоловка f.
flying /'flaɪŋ/ adj. летающий; (able to fly) летучий.
flying boat n. (aero.) гидроплан m.
flying bridge n. (naut.) перекидной мост m.
flying fish n. летучая рыба f.
flying fox n. летучая собака f.
flying saucer n. летающая тарелка f.
flying squirrel n. летяга f.
flyleaf /'flai,liːf/ n. форзац m.
flypaper /'flai,peipər/ n. липучая бумага от мух f.
flyweight /'flai,weit/ n. боксёр наилегчайшего веса m.
flywheel /'flai,wiːl/ n. маховик m.
foal /foul/ n. жеребёнок m.
foam /foum/ **1.** n. пена f. **2.** v. пениться impf.
foaming /'foumɪŋ/ adj. пенящийся.
fob /fɒb/ **1.** n. (colloq.) обман m. **2.** v. обманывать, надувать impf.
focal /'foukəl/ adj. фокусный.
focus /'foukəs/ **1.** n. фокус m., средоточие neut. **2.** v. сосредоточивать impf., сосредоточить pf.
fodder /'fɒdər/ n. фураж, корм m.
foe /fou/ n. враг m.
fog /fɒg/ n. туман m.
fog bank n. полоса тумана f.
fogbound /'fɒg,baund/ adj. (naut.) задержанный туманом.
fogginess /'fɒgɪnɪs/ n. туманность f.
foggy /'fɒgi/ adj. туманный, мглистый.
foghorn /'fɒg,hɔːrn/ n. нутофон m.
fog lamp n. противотуманная фара f.
foible /'fɔibəl/ n. слабость f.
foil¹ /fɔil/ n. фольга f.
foil² /fɔil/ n. (fencing) рапира f.
foil³ /fɔil/ v. расстраивать impf., расстроить pf.; срывать impf., сорвать pf
foist /fɔist/ v. всучить, навязать (with dat.) pf.
fold /fould/ **1.** n. складка f., сгиб m. **2.** v. складывать impf., сложить pf.
folder /'fouldər/ n. папка f.
folding /'fouldɪŋ/ adj. складной; (back) откидной.
foliaceous /,fouli'eiʃəs/ adj. лиственный.
foliage /'fouliɪdʒ/ n. листва f.
foliate /'fouliɪt/ adj. листообразный.
folio /'fouli,ou/ **1.** n. (sheet) лист m.; (book) фолиант m. **2.** adj. (manuscript) в лист; (book) большого формата.
folk /fouk/ **1.** n. (people) люди pl.; народ m. **2.** adj. (attrib.) народный.
folk dance n. народный танец m.
folklore /'fouk,lɔːr/ n. фольклор m.
folklorist /'fouk,lɔːrɪst/ n. фольклорист m.

folk song n. народная песня f.
folksy /'fouksi/ adj. (colloq.) простой, деревенский.
folk tale n. народная сказка f.
folkways /'fouk,weiz/ n. народные обычаи pl.
follicle /'fɒlɪkəl/ n. (anat.) фолликул m.
follicular /fə'lɪkyələr/ adj. фолликулярный.
follow /'fɒlou/ v. следовать (за with instr.) impf., последовать pf.
follower /'fɒlouər/ n. последователь, приверженец m.
following /'fɒlouɪŋ/ adj. следующий.
follow-through /'fɒlou,θru/ n. (sports) проводка f.
follow-up /'fɒlou,ʌp/ n. (journalism) развитие neut.
folly /'fɒli/ n. глупость f.
foment /fou'mɛnt/ v. подстрекать impf.; разжигать impf., разжечь pf.
fomentation /,foumɛn'teiʃən/ n. подстрекательство neut.
fond /fɒnd/ adj. любящий; **to be fond of** любить impf..
fondle /'fɒndl/ v. ласкать impf.
fondly /'fɒndli/ adv. нежно, с нежностью, с любовью.
fondness /'fɒndnɪs/ n. нежность f.
font¹ /fɒnt/ n. (typog.) шрифт m.
font² /fɒnt/ n. (eccl.) купель f.
Fontainebleau /'fɒntɪn,blou/ n. Фонтенбло m.
food /fuːd/ n. пища f. **2.** adj. пищевой.
foodstuff /'fuːd,stʌf/ n. пищевые продукты pl.
fool /fuːl/ **1.** n. дурак, глупец m. **2.** v. дурачить impf., одурачить pf.; (joke) шутить impf., пошутить pf.
foolery /'fuːləri/ n. дурачество neut.
foolhardiness /'ful,hɑːrdɪnɪs/ n. безрассудная храбрость f.
foolhardy /'ful,hɑːrdi/ adj. безрассудно храбрый, безрассудный.
foolish /'fuːlɪʃ/ adj. глупый.
foolishness /'fuːlɪʃnɪs/ n. глупость f.
foolproof /'ful,pruf/ adj. совершенно надёжный.
foot /fʊt/ n. нога, ступня f.; (measure) фут m.; **on foot** пешком.
footage /'fʊtɪdʒ/ n. длина (в футах) f.; (film) метраж m.
foot-and-mouth disease /'fʊtn̩'mauθ/ n. ящур m.
football /'fʊt,bɔl/ n. футбол m.; футбольный мяч m.
foot brake n. ножной тормоз m.
footbridge /'fʊt,brɪdʒ/ n. пешеходный мостик m.
footcandle /'fʊt'kændl/ n. фут-свеча f.
footfall /'fʊt,fɔl/ n. звук шагов m.
foothill /'fʊt,hɪl/ n. предгорье neut.
foothold /'fʊt,hould/ n. точка опоры f.
footlights /'fʊt,laits/ n. pl. рампа f.
footloose /'fʊt,lus/ adj. свободный, непоседливый.
footman /'fʊtmən/ n. лакей m.
footnote /'fʊt,nout/ n. примечание neut.; сноска f.
footpath /'fʊt,pæθ/ n. тропинка f.
footplate /'fʊt,pleit/ n. площадка машиниста f.

footprint /'fʊt‚prɪnt/ n. след m., отпечáток ногú m.

footrest /'fʊt‚rɛst/ n. поднóжка f.

foot rot n. копы́тная гниль f.

footslog /'fʊt‚slɒɡ/ v. (colloq.) тащи́ться пешкóм impf.

foot soldier n. пехоти́нец m.

footstep /'fʊt‚stɛp/ n. шаг m.

footstool /'fʊt‚stul/ n. скамéечка для ног f.

footwear /'fʊt‚wɛər/ n. óбувь f.

footwork /'fʊt‚wɜrk/ n. (sports) рабóта для ног f.

fop /fɒp/ n. щёголь, пижóн, фат m.

foppery /'fɒpəri/ n. щегольствó, фатовствó neut.

foppish /'fɒpɪʃ/ adj. щегольскóй.

for /fɔr; unstressed fər/ **1.** prep. для, рáди (with gen.); (time) на (with acc.), в течéние (with gen.); (distance) на протяжéнии (with gen.); (direction) в (with acc.), к (with dat.;) **for a few minutes** на нéсколько минýт. **2.** conj. и́бо, так как.

forage cap /'fɒrɪdʒ/ n. фурáжка f.

forasmuch as /‚fɔrəs'mʌtʃ ‚æz/ conj. принимáя во внимáние что; поскóльку.

foray /'fɔrei/ n. набéг m.

forbear /fɔr'bɛər/ v. воздéрживаться (от with gen.) impf.

forbearance /fɔr'bɛərəns/ n. вы́держка f.

forbearing /fɔr'bɛərɪŋ/ adj. вы́держанный.

forbid /fər'bɪd/ v. запрещáть impf., запрети́ть pf.; воспрещáть impf.

forbidden /fər'bɪdn̩/ adj. запрещённый, запрéтный.

forbidding /fər'bɪdɪŋ/ adj. отта́лкивающий.

force /fɔrs/ **1.** n. си́ла f.; (violence) наси́лие neut. **2.** v. заставля́ть impf., застáвить pf.; форси́ровать impf. and pf.

forced labor /fɔrst/ n. принуди́тельный труд m.

forced landing n. вы́нужденная посáдка f.

forced laugh n. принуждённый смех m.

forced march n. форси́рованный марш m.

forceful /'fɔrsfəl/ adj. си́льный.

force majeure /'fɔrs mæ'ʒʊr/ n. (leg.) форс-мажóр m.

forceps /'fɔrsəps/ n. щипцы́ pl.

force pump n. (tech.) нагнетáтельный насóс m.

forcible /'fɔrsəbəl/ adj. наси́льственный.

forcing /'fɔrsɪŋ/ n. форси́рование neut.

ford /fɔrd/ **1.** n. брод m. **2.** v. переходи́ть брод impf.

fordable /'fɔrdəbəl/ adj. переходи́мый вброд.

forearm /'fɔr‚ɑrm/ n. предплéчье neut.

forebear /'fɔr‚bɛər/ n. прéдок m.

forebode /fɔr'boud/ v. предвещáть impf.

foreboding /fɔr'boudɪŋ/ n. предчýвствие neut.

forecast /'fɔr‚kæst/ **1.** n. предскáзание neut., прогнóз m. **2.** v. предскáзывать impf., предскá-зáть pf.

forecastle /'fouksəl/ n. (naut.) бак m.

foreclose /fɔr'klouz/ v. исключáть impf.; предрешáть impf.

foredoom /fɔr'dum/ v. обрекáть impf.

forefather /'fɔr‚fɑðər/ n. прéдок m.

forefinger /'fɔr‚fɪŋɡər/ n. указáтельный пáлец m.

forefront /'fɔr‚frʌnt/ n. передовáя ли́ния f.; авангáрд m.

foregoing /fɔr'gouɪŋ/ adj. предшéствующий.

foregone /fɔr'ɡɔn/ adj. предрешённый.

foreground /'fɔr‚graund/ n. перéдний план m.

forehand /'fɔr‚hænd/ adj. удáр спрáва.

forehead /'fɔrɪd; 'fɔr‚hɛd/ n. лоб m.

foreign /'fɔrɪn/ adj. инострáнный.

foreigner /'fɔrənər/ n. инострáнец m., инострáн-ка f.

forejudge /fɔr'dʒʌdʒ/ v. принимáть предвзя́тое решéние impf.

foreknowledge /'fɔr‚nɒlɪdʒ/ n. **to have foreknowledge of** v. знать зарáнее impf.

foreleg /'fɔr‚lɛɡ/ n. перéдняя ногá f.

forelock /'fɔr‚lɒk/ n. чуб m.

foreman /'fɔrmən/ n. мáстер m.

foremast /'fɔr‚mæst; Naut. 'fɔrməst/ n. фок-мáчта f.

foremost /'fɔr‚moust/ adj. передовóй, перéдний; основнóй, глáвный; выдаю́щийся.

forenoon /'fɔr‚nun/ n. ýтро neut.

forensic /fə'rɛnsɪk/ adj. судéбный.

foreordain /‚fɔrɔr'dein/ v. предопределя́ть impf.

forepart /'fɔr‚pɑrt/ n. перéдняя часть f.

forerunner /'fɔr‚rʌnər/ n. предшéственник; предвéстник m.

foresail /'fɔr‚seil; Naut. 'fɔrsəl/ n. фок m.

foresee /fɔr'si/ v. предви́деть impf.

foreshadow /fɔr'ʃædou/ v. предзнаменовáть impf.

foreshorten /fɔr'ʃɔrtn̩/ v. взять в рáкурсе impf.

foreshortening /fɔr'ʃɔrtn̩ɪŋ/ n. рáкурс m.

foresight /'fɔr‚sait/ n. предусмотри́тельность f.

foreskin /'fɔr‚skɪn/ n. крáйняя плоть f.

forest /'fɔrɪst/ **1.** n. лес m. **2.** adj. леснóй.

forestall /fɔr'stɔl/ v. предупреди́ть pf.

forester /'fɔrəstər/ n. лесни́чий m., лесни́чая f.

forest ranger n. лесни́к m.

forestry /'fɔrəstri/ n. лесовóдство neut.

foretaste /'fɔr‚teist/ n. предвкушéние neut.

foretell /fɔr'tɛl/ v. предскáзывать impf., предскá-зáть pf.

forethought /'fɔr‚θɔt/ n. предусмотри́тельность f.

foretoken /fɔr'toukən/ v. предвещáть impf.

forever /fɔr'ɛvər/ adv. навсегдá; вéчно.

forewarn /fɔr'wɔrn/ v. предостерегáть impf.

forewoman /'fɔr‚wumən/ n. бригади́р m.

foreword /'fɔr‚wɜrd, -wərd/ n. предислóвие neut.

forfeit /'fɔrfɪt/ **1.** n. штраф m.; (game) фант m. **2.** v. лиши́ться (with gen.) pf.

forfeiture /'fɔrfɪtʃər/ n. потéря f.

forge /fɔrdʒ/ **1.** n. (smithy) кýзница f.; (furnace) горн m. **2.** v. ковáть impf.; (counterfeit) поддéлывать impf., поддéлать pf.

forger /'fɔrdʒər/ n. поддéлыватель m.

forgery /'fɔrdʒəri/ n. поддéлка f.

forget /fər'ɡɛt/ v. забывáть impf., забы́ть pf.

forgetful /fər'ɡɛtfəl/ adj. забы́вчивый.

forgetfulness /fər'ɡɛtfəlnis/ n. забы́вчивость f.

forget-me-not /fər'ɡɛtmi‚nɒt/ n. (bot.) незабýдка f.

forgivable /fər'ɡɪvəbəl/ adj. прости́тельный.

forgive /fər'ɡɪv/ v. прощáть impf., прости́ть pf.

forgiveness /fər'ɡɪvnis/ n. прощéние neut.

forgiving /fər'ɡɪvɪŋ/ adj. всепрощáющий.

forgo /fɔr'gou/ отказываться (от *with gen.*) *impf.*, отказаться *pf.*

forgotten /fər'gɒtn̩/ *adj.* забытый.

fork /fɔrk/ **1.** *n.* вилка *f.*; (*road*) развилина *f.* **2.** *v.* разветвляться *impf.*, разветвиться *pf.*

forked /fɔrkt/ *adj.* разветвлённый.

forlorn /fɔr'lɔrn/ *adj.* покинутый.

form /fɔrm/ **1.** *n.* форма *f.*; (*document*) бланк *m.*; анкета *f.* **2.** *v.t.* формировать *impf.*, сформировать *pf.*; образовывать *impf.*, образовать *pf.*; *v.i.* формироваться *impf.*, сформироваться *pf.*; образовываться *impf.*, образоваться *pf.*

formal /'fɔrməl/ *adj.* формальный, официальный.

formaldehyde /fɔr'mældə,haid/ *n.* формальдегид *m.*

formalin /'fɔrməlin/ *n.* формалин *m.*

formalism /'fɔrmə,lizəm/ *n.* формализм *m.*

formalist /'fɔrməlist/ *n.* формалист *m.*

formalistic /ˌfɔrmə'listik/ *adj.* формалистический.

formality /fɔr'mæliti/ *n.* формальность *f.*

formalize /'fɔrmə,laiz/ *v.* оформлять *impf.*

format /'fɔrmæt/ *n.* формат *m.*

formation /fɔr'meiʃən/ *n.* (*geol.*) образование *neut.*; формация *f.*

formative /'fɔrmətiv/ *n.* формативн *m.*

former /'fɔrmər/ *adj.* прежний, бывший.

formerly /'fɔrmərli/ *adv.* прежде.

formic acid /'fɔrmik/ *n.* муравьиная кислота *f.*

formidable /'fɔrmidəbəl/ *adj.* грозный; трудный.

forming /'fɔrmiŋ/ *n.* образование *neut.*

formless /'fɔrmlis/ *adj.* бесформенный.

formula /'fɔrmyələ/ *n.* формула *f.*

formulary /'fɔrmyə,leri/ *n.* (*med.*) рецептурная книга *f.*

formulate /'fɔrmyə,leit/ *v.* формулировать *impf.*

formulation /ˌfɔrmy'leiʃən/ *n.* формулировка *f.*

fornicate /'fɔrni,keit/ *v.* блудить *impf.*

fornication /ˌfɔrni'keiʃən/ *n.* внебрачная связь *f.*

forsake /fɔr'seik/ *v.* покидать *impf.*, покинуть *pf.*; отказываться *impf.*

forsaken /fɔr'seikən/ *adj.* покинутый.

forswear /fɔr'swɛər/ *v.* отрекаться (от *with gen.*) *impf.*

fort /fɔrt/ *m.* форт *m.*

forte /fɔrt/ *n.* сильная сторона *f.*

forth /fɔrθ/ *adv.* вперёд, впредь; **back and forth** взад и вперёд.

forthcoming /'fɔrθ'kʌmiŋ/ *adj.* предстоящий.

forthright /'fɔrθ,rait/ *adj.* откровенный.

forthwith /ˌfɔrθ'wiθ/ *adv.* тотчас.

fortieth /'fɔrtiiθ/ *adj.* сороковой.

fortification /ˌfɔrtəfi'keiʃən/ *n.* фортификация *f.*

fortified /'fɔrtə,faid/ *adj.* укреплённый; (*enriched*) обогащённый.

fortify /'fɔrtə,fai/ *v.* укреплять *impf.*, укрепить *pf.*

fortissimo /fɔr'tisə,mou/ *n.* фортиссимо *neut.* indecl.

fortitude /'fɔrti,tud/ *n.* стойкость *f.*

fortnight /'fɔrt,nait/ *n.* две недели.

fortnightly /'fɔrt,naitli/ *adv.* раз в две недели.

FORTRAN /'fɔrtræn/ *n.* (*comput.*) ФОРТРАН *m.*

fortress /'fɔrtris/ *n.* крепость *f.*

fortuitous /fɔr'tuitəs/ *adj.* случайный.

fortunate /'fɔrtʃənit/ *adj.* счастливый.

fortunately /'fɔrtʃənitli/ *adv.* к счастью.

fortune /'fɔrtʃən/ *n.* (*fate*) судьба *f.*; (*luck*) счастье *neut.*; удача *f.*; (*wealth*) состояние *neut.*

fortuneteller /'fɔrtʃən,telər/ *n.* гадальщик *m.*, гадалка *f.*

fortunetelling /'fɔrtʃən,teliŋ/ *n.* гадание *neut.*

forty /'fɔrti/ *adj.*, *n.* сорок.

forum /'fɔrəm/ *n.* форум *m.*

forward /'fɔrwərd/ **1.** *adj.* передний, передовой. **2.** *adv.* вперёд. **3.** *v.* пересылать *impf.*

forwardness /'fɔrwərdnis/ *n.* (*zeal*) рвение *neut.*; (*presumption*) развязность *f.*, нахальство *neut.*

fossil /'fɒsəl/ *n.* ископаемое *neut.*

fossilize /'fɒsə,laiz/ *v.* окаменевать *impf.*

foster /'fɔstər/ *v.* (*raise children*) воспитывать *impf.*, воспитать *pf.*

foster child *n.* приёмыш *m.*

foster father *n.* приёмный отец *m.*

foster mother *n.* приёмная мать *f.*

foul /faul/ *adj.* гадкий; отвратительный, вонючий.

foulard /fu'lɑrd/ *n.* фуляр *m.*

foulmouthed person /'faul,mauðd/ *n.* сквернослов *m.*

foulness /'faulnis/ *n.* отвратительность *f.*

foul-smelling /'faul,smeliŋ/ *adj.* зловонный.

foul-up /'faul,ʌp/ *n.* (*colloq.*) неразбериха *f.*

found /faund/ *v.* закладывать *impf.*, заложить *pf.*; учреждать *impf.*, учредить *pf.*

foundation /faun'deiʃən/ *n.* основание *neut.*; основа *f.*; (*building*) фундамент *m.*

founder /'faundər/ *n.* (*tech.*) литейщик *m.*

foundry /'faundri/ *n.* литейный завод *m.*

fount /faunt/ *n.* источник *m.*

fountain /'fauntn̩/ *n.* фонтан *m.*

fountainhead /'fauntn̩,hed/ *n.* источник *m.*

fountain pen *n.* авторучка *f.*

four /fɔr/ *adj.*, *n.* четыре.

four-dimensional /'fɔrdi'menʃənl̩/ *adj.* четырёхмерный.

fourfold /'fɔr,fould/ *adv.* вчетверо.

four-inch /'fɔr,intʃ/ *adj.* четырёхдюймовый.

four-leaf /'fɔr,lif/ *adj.* четырёхлистный.

four-legged /'fɔr,legid/ *adj.* четвероногий.

four-seater /'fɔr,sitər/ *n.* четырёхместный автомобиль *m.*

foursome /'fɔrsəm/ *n.* четвёрка *f.*

foursquare /'fɔr'skwɛər/ *adj.* квадратный.

fourteen /'fɔr'tin/ *adj.*, *n.* четырнадцать.

fourteenth /'fɔr'tinθ/ *adj.* четырнадцатый.

fourth /fɔrθ/ *adj.* четвёртый.

fourthly /'fɔrθli/ *adv.* в-четвёртых.

fovea /'fouviə/ *n.* ямка *f.*

fowl /faul/ *n.* домашняя птица *f.*

fowler /'faulər/ *n.* птицелов *m.*

fowling /'fauliŋ/ *n.* охота на птиц *f.*

fox /fɒks/ **1.** *n.* лисица *f.* **2.** *adj.* лисий.

foxbrush /'fɒks,brʌʃ/ *n.* (*bot.*) лисий хвост *m.*

fox cub *n.* лисёнок *m.*

foxglove /'fɒks,glʌv/ *n.* наперстянка *f.*

foxhound /'fɒks,haund/ *n.* английский фоксхаунд *m.*

fox hunter *n.* охотник на лис *m.*

fox hunting *n.* охота на лис *f.*

foxiness /'fɒksinis/ *n.* хитрость *f.*

fox terrier *n.* фокстерьер *m.*

fox trot n. фокстро́т m.

foxy /'fɒksi/ adj. ли́сий, хи́трый.

foyer /'fɔiər, 'fɔiei/ n. фойе́ neut. indecl.

fracas /'freikəs/ n. сканда́л m.

fraction /'frækʃən/ n. дробь f.

fractional /'frækʃənl/ adj. дро́бный.

fractionally /'frækʃənli/ adv. чуть-чуть.

fractious /'frækʃəs/ adj. раздражи́тельный.

fracture /'fræktʃər/ 1. n. перело́м m. 2. v. лома́ть(ся) impf., слома́ть(ся) pf.

fractured /'fræktʃərd/ adj. (med.) перело́манный.

fragile /'frædʒəl/ adj. хру́пкий.

fragility /frə'dʒɪlɪti/ n. хру́пкость f.

fragment /'frægmənt/ 1. n. обло́мок, отры́вок m. 2. v. дроби́ть impf.

fragmentary /'frægmən,teri/ adj. отры́вочный.

fragmentation /,frægmən'teiʃən/ n. дробле́ние neut.

fragrance /'freigrəns/ n. арома́т m.

fragrant /'freigrənt/ adj. арома́тный, души́стый.

frail /freil/ adj. хру́пкий, хи́лый.

frailty /'freilti/ n. хру́пкость f.

frame /freim/ 1. n. ра́ма; ра́мка f.; (for eyeglasses) опра́ва f.; (build) телосложе́ние neut.; (movie) кадр m. 2. v. (surround) обрамля́ть impf., обрами́ть pf.

frameless /'freimlɪs/ adj. безра́мный.

frame-up /'freim,ʌp/ n. та́йный сго́вор m.

framework /'freim,wɜrk/ n. структу́ра f.; карка́с, осто́в m.; ра́мки pl.

franc /fræŋk/ n. франк m.

France /fræns/ n. Фра́нция f.

franchise /'fræntʃaiz/ n. пра́во го́лоса neut.; привиле́гия f.

Franciscan /fræn'sɪskən/ n. франциска́нец m.

francium /'frænsiəm/ n. фра́нций m.

francophile /'fræŋkə,fail/ n. франкофи́л m.

francophone /'fræŋkə,foun/ adj. франкоязы́чный, франкоговоря́щий.

frank /fræŋk/ adj. и́скренний.

Frankfurt /'fræŋkfərt/ n. Фра́нкфурт m.

frankfurter /'fræŋkfərtər/ n. соси́ска f.

frankincense /'fræŋkɪn,sens/ n. ла́дан m.

frankly /'fræŋkli/ adv. открове́нно.

frankness /'fræŋknɪs/ n. и́скренность f.

frantic /'fræntɪk/ adj. неи́стовый.

fraternal /frə'tɜrnl/ adj. бра́тский.

fraternity /frə'tɜrnɪti/ n. бра́тство neut.

fraternization /,frætərnɪ'zeiʃən/ n. брата́ние neut.

fraternize /'frætər,naiz/ v. брата́ться impf.

fratricidal /,frætrɪ'saidl/ adj. братоуби́йственный.

fratricide /'frætrɪ,said/ n. братоуби́йство neut.

fraud /frɔd/ n. моше́нничество neut., обма́н m.; (person) обма́нщик m.

fraudulent /'frɔdʒələnt/ adj. моше́ннический, обма́нный.

fraught with /frɔt/ adj. по́лный (with gen.), чрева́тый (with instr.).

fray[1] /frei/ n. дра́ка f.

fray[2] /frei/ v. изна́шивать(ся) impf.

freak /frik/ n. чуда́к; уро́д m.; причу́да f.

freakish /'frikɪʃ/ adj. причу́дливый; стра́нный.

freckle /'frekəl/ n. весну́шка f.

freckled /'frekəld/ adj. весну́шчатый.

free /fri/ 1. adj. свобо́дный; (gratis) беспла́тный. 2. v. освобожда́ть(ся) impf., освободи́ть(ся) pf.

free-and-easy /'friən'izi/ adj. непринуждённый.

freeboard /'fri,bɔrd/ n. надво́дный борт m.

freedom /'fridəm/ n. свобо́да f.

free-for-all /'frifər,ɔl/ n. всео́бщая дра́ка f.

freehand /'fri,hænd/ adv. от руки́.

free-handed /'fri'hændɪd/ adj. ще́дрый.

freehold /'fri,hould/ n. безусло́вное пра́во со́бственности на недви́жимость neut.

free kick n. свобо́дный уда́р m.

freelance /'fri,læns/ adj. нешта́тный.

Freemason /'fri,meisən/ n. франкмасо́н, масо́н m.

freemasonry /'fri,meisənri/ n. масо́нство neut.

freesia /'friʒiə/ n. фре́зия f.

freethinker /'fri'θɪŋkər/ n. вольноду́мец m.

freethinking /'fri'θɪŋkɪŋ/ adj. вольноду́мный.

freeze /friz/ v. замерза́ть impf., замёрзнуть pf.; (food) замора́живат impf.

freezer /'frizər/ n. морози́лка f.

freezing /'frizɪŋ/ 1. adj. моро́зный. 2. n. замерза́ние neut.

freight /freit/ n. фрахт, груз m.

freighter /'freitər/ n. (ship) грузово́е су́дно neut.

freight train n. това́рный по́езд m.

French /frentʃ/ adj. францу́зский.

Frenchman /'frentʃmən/ n. францу́з m.

French-speaking /'frentʃ,spikɪŋ/ adj. франкоязы́чный.

Frenchwoman /'frentʃ,wumən/ n. францу́женка f.

frenetic /frɪ'netɪk/ adj. бе́шеный, неи́стовый.

frenzied /'frenzid/ adj. бе́шеный.

frenzy /'frenzi/ n. бе́шенство neut.

frequency /'frikwənsi/ n. частота́ f.

frequent /'frikwənt/ adj. ча́стый.

frequentative /frɪ'kwentətɪv/ adj. (gram.) многокра́тный.

frequenter /frɪ'kwentər/ n. ча́стый посети́тель m.

frequently /'frikwəntli/ adv. ча́сто.

fresco /'freskou/ n. фре́ска f.

fresh /freʃ/ adj. све́жий; (water) пре́сный.

freshen /'freʃən/ v. освежа́ть impf., освежи́ть pf.

freshly /'freʃli/ adv. свежо́.

freshman /'freʃmən/ n. первоку́рсник m.

freshness /'freʃnɪs/ n. све́жесть f.

freshwater /'freʃ,wɔtər/ adj. пресново́дный.

fret[1] /fret/ v. (eat away) разъеда́ть impf.; (worry) волнова́ться impf.

fret[2] /fret/ n. прямоуго́льный орна́мент m.

fretful /'fretfəl/ adj. раздражи́тельный.

fretfulness /'fretfəlnɪs/ n. раздражи́тельность f.

fret saw n. ло́бзик m.

fretwork /'fret,wɜrk/ n. ажу́рная рабо́та f.

Freudian /'frɔidiən/ adj. фрейди́стский.

friability /,fraiə'bɪlɪti/ n. ры́хлость f.

friable /'fraiəbəl/ adj. ры́хлый.

friar /'fraiər/ n. мона́х m.

fricassee /,frɪkə'si/ n. фрикасе́ neut. indecl.

fricative /'frɪkətɪv/ adj. фрикати́вный.

friction /'frɪkʃən/ n. тре́ние neut.

frictional /'frɪkʃənl/ adj. фрикцио́нный.

frictionless /'frɪkʃənlɪs/ adj. бесфрикцио́нный.

Friday /'fraidei/ n. пя́тница f.; (Good Friday) Страстна́я Пя́тница f.

fried /fraid/ adj. жа́реный.

friend /frɛnd/ n. друг m., подру́га f.; прия́тель m.; прия́тельница f.
friendliness /'frɛndlɪnɪs/ n. дружелю́бие neut.
friendly /'frɛndli/ adj. дру́жеский.
friendship /'frɛndʃɪp/ n. дру́жба f.
frieze /friz/ n. (archit.) фриз m.
frigate /'frɪgɪt/ n. фрега́т m.
fright /fraɪt/ n. испу́г m.
frighten /'fraɪtn̩/ v. пуга́ть impf., испуга́ть pf.
frightened /'fraɪtnd/ adj. испу́ганный.
frightful /'fraɪtfəl/ adj. стра́шный.
frigid /'frɪdʒɪd/ adj. холо́дный.
frigidity /frɪ'dʒɪdɪti/ n. холо́дность f.
frill /frɪl/ n. обо́рка f.
frilly /'frɪli/ adj. отде́ланный обо́рками.
fringe /frɪndʒ/ n. бахрома́ f.
frippery /'frɪpəri/ n. мишура́ f.
Frisian Islands /'frɪʒən/ n. Фри́зские острова́ pl.
frisk /frɪsk/ v. резви́ться impf.; (search) обы́скивать impf., (slang) шмона́ть impf.
frisky /'frɪski/ adj. резвый.
fritter¹ /'frɪtər/ n. (cul.) ола́дья f.
fritter² /'frɪtər/ v.: to fritter away растра́чивать по мелоча́м or пустяка́м impf.
frivolity /frɪ'vɒlɪti/ n. легкомы́слие neut.
frivolous /'frɪvələs/ adj. легкомы́сленный, пусто́й.
frizz /frɪz/ v. завива́ть(ся) impf.
frizzy /'frɪzi/ adj. (curly) вью́щийся; (curled) зави́той.
fro /frou/ adv.: to and fro взад и вперёд, туда́-сюда́.
frock coat /frɒk/ n. сюртук m.
frog /frɒg/ n. лягу́шка f.
frogman /'frɒɡˌmæn/ n. лёгкий водола́з m.
frog spawn n. лягу́шечья икра́ f.
frolic /'frɒlɪk/ n. весе́лье neut.
frolicsome /'frɒlɪksəm/ adj. рѐзвый,
from /frʌm; unstressed frəm/ prep. из, от, с; из-за (with gen.).
frond /frɒnd/ n. лист m.
front /frʌnt/ 1. n. пере́дняя сторона́ f., фаса́д m.; (mil.) фронт m. 2. adj. пере́дний. 3. adv.: in front впереди́. 4. prep.: in front of пе́ред (with instr.).
frontal /'frʌntl̩/ adj. (anat.) лобный; (mil.) лобово́й; фронта́льный.
frontier /frʌn'tɪər/ n. грани́ца f.
frontispiece /'frʌntɪsˌpis/ n. фронтиспи́с m.
front page n. пе́рвая страни́ца f.
frost /frɒst/ n. моро́з m.
frostbite /'frɒstˌbaɪt/ n. отможе́ние; обмороже́ние neut.
frostbitten /'frɒstˌbɪtn̩/ adj. отморо́женный; обморо́женный.
frosted /'frɒstɪd/ adj. (covered with frost) покры́тый и́неем.
frostily /'frɒstli/ adv. хо́лодно.
frosting /'frɒstɪŋ/ n. глазу́рь f.
frosty /'frɒsti/ adj. моро́зный.
froth /frɒθ/ 1. n. пе́на f. 2. v. пе́ниться impf.
frothy /'frɒθi/ adj. пе́нистый.
frown /fraʊn/ 1. n. хму́рый взгляд m. 2. v. хму́рить бро́ви impf.
frowning /'fraʊnɪŋ/ adj. хму́рый.
frozen /'frouzən/ adj. (numb) замёрзший, (preserved) заморо́женный.

fructiferous /frʌk'tɪfərəs/ adj. плодонося́щий.
fructification /ˌfrʌktəfɪ'keɪʃən/ n. плодоноше́ние neut.
fructify /'frʌktəˌfaɪ/ v. плодоноси́ть impf.
fructose /'frʌktous, 'frʊk-/ n. фрукто́за f.
frugal /'frugəl/ adj. бережли́вый, ску́дный.
frugality /fru'gælɪti/ n. бережли́вость f.
fruit /frut/ 1. n. фрукт m.; (benefits) плод m. 2. adj. фрукто́вый.
fruitcake /'frutˌkeɪk/ n. кекс m.
fruitful /'frutfəl/ adj. плодотво́рный.
fruit grower n. плодово́д m.
fruit-growing /'frut ˌɡrouɪŋ/ n. плодово́дство neut.
fruition /fru'ɪʃən/ n. осуществле́ние neut.
fruitless /'frutlɪs/ adj. беспло́дный.
fruity /'fruti/ adj. фрукто́вый.
frustrate /'frʌstreit/ v. расстра́ивать impf., расстро́ить pf.; срыва́ть impf., сорва́ть pf.
frustrating /'frʌstreitɪŋ/ adj. (colloq.) доса́дный; how frustrating! как доса́дно!
frustration /frʌ'streɪʃən/ n. расстро́йство neut.; фрустра́ция f.
fry¹ /fraɪ/ n. (young fish) малѐк pl.
fry² /fraɪ/ v. жа́рить(ся) impf., изжа́рить(ся) pf.
frying pan /'traɪŋ/ n. сковорода́ f.
fuchsia /'fyuʃə/ n. фу́ксия f.
fuddle /'fʌdl̩/ v. одурма́нивать impf.
fuddy-duddy /'fʌdi ˌdʌdi/ n. старомо́дный челове́к m.
fudge /fʌdʒ/ n. шокола́дная конфе́та f.
fuel /'fyuəl/ n. то́пливо neut.
fugal /'fyugəl/ adj. (mus.) фу́говый.
fugitive /'fyudʒɪtɪv/ 1. n. бегле́ц, бе́женец, дезерти́р m. 2. adj. бе́глый.
fugue /fyug/ n. фу́га f.
fulcrum /'fʊlkrəm/ n. (phys.) то́чка опо́ры f
fulfill /fʊl'fɪl/ v. выполня́ть impf., вы́полнить pf.; исполня́ть impf.
fulfillment /fʊl'fɪlmənt/ n. выполне́ние neut., осуществле́ние neut.
full /fʊl/ 1. adj. по́лный; (sated) сы́тый. 2. adv.: in full по́лностью.
full-length /'fʊl ˈlɛŋθ/ adj. во весь рост; (complete) по́лный.
fullness /'fʊlnɪs/ n. полнота́ f.
full-scale /'fʊl ˈskeɪl/ adj. (in natural size) в натура́льную величину́.
full-time /'fʊl ˈtaɪm/ adj. (on regular staff) шта́тный.
fully /'fʊli/ adv. по́лностью, вполне́.
fumble /'fʌmbəl/ v. нело́вко обраща́ться (с with instr.) impf.
fumbling /'fʌmblɪŋ/ adj. нело́вкий, неуклю́жий.
fume /fum/ n. чад m.
fumigate /'fyumɪˌgeɪt/ v. оку́ривать impf., окури́ть pf.
fun /fʌn/ n. заба́ва; поте́ха f.; to have fun v. хорошо́ проводи́ть вре́мя impf.; to make fun of v. шути́ть над (with instr.) impf.
function /'fʌŋkʃən/ 1. n. фу́нкция f.; pl. (duties) обя́занности pl. 2. v. функциони́ровать impf.
functional /'fʌŋkʃənl̩/ adj. функциона́льный.
fund /fʌnd/ n. фонд m.; (supply) запа́с m.
fundamental /ˌfʌndə'mɛntl̩/ adj. основно́й; коренно́й.

fundamentalism /ˌfʌndə'mɛntlˌɪzəm/ n. фундаментализм m.

fundamentally /ˌfʌndə'mɛntli/ adv. по существу.

funding /'fʌndɪŋ/ n. финансирование neut.

fund-raising /'fʌnd ˌreizɪŋ/ n. сбор средств m.

funeral /'fyunərəl/ n. похороны pl.

funeral director n. владелец похоронного бюро m.

funerary /'fyunəˌrɛri/ adj. похоронный.

funereal /fyu'nɪəriəl/ adj. похоронный; (fig.) мрачный, грустный.

fungicide /'fʌndʒə,said, 'fʌŋgə-/ n. фунгицид m.

fungoid /'fʌŋgɔid/ adj. грибовидный.

fungous /'fʌŋgəs/ adj. грибковый.

fungus /'fʌŋgəs/ n. грибок m.

funicular railway /fyu'nɪkyələr/ n. фуникулёр m.

funnel /'fʌnl/ n. воронка f.; (chimney) дымовая труба f.

funnel-shaped /'fʌnl ˌʃeipt/ adj. воронкообразный.

funny /'fʌni/ adj. забавный, смешной.

fur /fɜr/ 1. n. мех m. 2. adj. меховой.

furbelow /'fɜrbə,lou/ n. оборка f.

furbish /'fɜrbɪʃ/ v. полировать; подновлять impf.

furious /'fyuriəs/ adj. яростный; бешеный.

furl /fɜrl/ v. свёртывать(ся) impf.

furlong /'fɜrlɔŋ/ n. фарлонг m.

furlough /'fɜrlou/ n. отпуск m.

furnace /'fɜrnɪs/ n. печь f.; горн m.

furnish /'fɜrnɪʃ/ v. снабжать impf., снабдить pf.; (house) меблировать impf. and pf.

furnishing /'fɜrnɪʃɪŋ/ n. меблировка f.

furniture /'fɜrnɪtʃər/ 1. n. мебель f. 2. adj. мебельный.

furor /'fyurɔr/ n. фурор m.

furrier /'fɜriər/ n. меховщик m.

furrow /'fɜrou/ n. борозда f.; (wrinkle) морщина f.

furry /'fɜri/ adj. пушистый.

further /'fɜrðər/ 1. adj. дальнейший. 2. adv. дальше, далее. 3. v. продвигать impf., продвинуть pf.

furtherance /'fɜrðərəns/ n. продвижение neut.

furthermore /'fɜrðər,mɔr/ adv. кроме того; к тому же.

furthermost /'fɜrðər,moust/ adj. самый дальний.

furtive /'fɜrtɪv/ adj. вороватый.

furtively /'fɜrtɪvli/ adv. украдкой.

furuncle /'fyurʌŋkəl/ n. фурункул m.

fury /'fyuri/ n. ярость f.

fuse[1] /fyuz/ n. предохранитель m., пробка f.

fuse[2] /fyuz/ v. плавить(ся); сплавлять(ся) impf.

fuselage /'fyusə,laʒ/ n. фюзеляж m.

fusel oil /'fyuzəl/ n. сивушное масло neut.

fusible /'fyuzəbəl/ adj. плавкий.

fusillade /'fyusə,leid/ n. стрельба f.

fusion /'fyuʒən/ n. плавка f.; слияние; сплавление neut.; (phys.) синтез m.; **nuclear fusion** n. нуклеосинтез m.; **fusion bomb** n. термоядерная бомба f.

fuss /fʌs/ 1. n. суета, суматоха f. 2. v. суетиться impf.

fussy /'fʌsi/ adj. суетливый; требовательный.

fustian /'fʌstʃən/ n. бумазея f.

fusty /'fʌsti/ adj. затхлый; (fig.) старомодный.

futile /'fyutl/ adj. тщетный.

futility /fyu'tɪlti/ n. тщетность f.

future /'fyutʃər/ 1. adj. будущий. 2. n. будущее neut.

futureless /'fyutʃərlɪs/ adj. бесперспективный.

futurism /'fyutʃə,rɪzəm/ n. футуризм m.

futurist /'fyutʃərɪst/ n. футурист m.

futuristic /ˌfyutʃə'rɪstɪk/ adj. футуристический.

fuzz /fʌz/ n. пушинка f.

fuzzy /'fʌzi/ adj. пушистый; ворсистый; (vague) смутный.

G

gadget /'gædʒɪt/ n. приспособле́ние neut.
gaiety /'geɪɪti/ n. весёлость f.
gain /geɪn/ **1.** n. при́быль f., вы́игрыш m.; дохо́ды pl. **2.** v. получа́ть; прибавля́ть; добива́ться impf.
gait /geɪt/ n. похо́дка f.
gale /geɪl/ n. си́льный ве́тер m.
Galicia /gə'lɪʃiə/ n. (province) Гали́сия f.
gall /gɔl/ n. (bile) жёлчь f.; (impudence) наха́льство neut.
gallant /'gælənt/ adj. хра́брый, до́блестный.
gallery /'gæləri, 'gælri/ n. галере́я f.; (theat.) галёрка f.
Gallic /'gælɪk/ adj. га́лльский.
gallon /'gælən/ n. галло́н m.
gallop /'gæləp/ **1.** n. гало́п m. **2.** v. галопи́ровать impf. and pf.
gallows /'gælouz/ n. pl. ви́селица f.
galvanize /'gælvə,naiz/ v. гальванизи́ровать impf.
galvanized /'gælvə,naizd/ adj. оцинко́ванный.
galvanizing /'gælvə,naizɪŋ/ n. оцинко́вание neut.
galvanometer /,gælvə'nɒmɪtər/ n. гальвано́метр m.
gambit /'gæmbɪt/ n. гамби́т; манёвр m.
gamble /'gæmbəl/ **1.** n. риско́ванное предприя́тие neut. **2.** v. игра́ть в риско́ванную игру́; рискова́ть impf.
gambler /'gæmblər/ n. игро́к, карте́жник m.
gambling /'gæmblɪŋ/ n. аза́ртные игры pl.
gamboge /gæm'boudʒ/ n. гумми́гут m.
gambol /'gæmbəl/ v. резви́ться impf.
game /geɪm/ n. игра́ f.; (single game) па́ртия f.; (hunting) дичь f.
game bag n. ягдта́ш m.
gamecock /'geɪm,kɒk/ n. бойцо́вый пету́х m.
gamekeeper /'geɪm,kipər/ n. лесни́к m.
gamete /'gæmit/ n. гаме́та f.
gametic /gə'mɛtɪk/ adj. гамети́ческий.
gametocyte /gə'mitə,sait/ n. гаметоци́т m.
gamma /'gæmə/ n. га́мма f.
gammon /'gæmən/ n. о́корок m.
gamut /'gæmət/ n. диапазо́н m.; (mus.) (scale) га́мма f.
gander /'gændər/ n. гуса́к m.
gang /gæŋ/ n. ба́нда; брига́да f.
gangling /'gæŋglɪŋ/ adj. долговя́зый.
ganglion /'gæŋgliən/ n. не́рвный у́зел m.
gangplank /'gæŋ,plæŋk/ n. схо́дни pl.
gangrene /'gæŋgrin/ n. гангре́на f.
gangrenous /'gæŋgrənəs/ adj. гангрено́зный.
gangster /'gæŋstər/ n. га́нгстер m.
gangway /'gæŋ,wei/ n. прохо́д m.; схо́дни pl.
gannet /'gænit/ n. бакла́н m.
gaol /dʒeil/ n. тюрьма́ f.
gap /gæp/ n. уще́лье neut., брешь f.; пробе́л m.
gape /geip/ v. (open mouth) разева́ть рот impf.; (chasm) зия́ть impf.
gap-toothed /'gæp,tuθt/ adj. редкозу́бый.
garage /gə'raʒ/ n. гара́ж m.
garb /gɑrb/ n. наря́д m., оде́жда f.
garbage /'gɑrbɪdʒ/ n. му́сор m., отбро́сы pl.

garbage can n. му́сорный я́щик m.
garbage pile /'mɪdn/ n. му́сорная ку́ча f.
garbage truck n. мусорово́з m.
garble /'gɑrbəl/ v. искажа́ть impf.
garden /'gɑrdn/ n. сад m.; (vegetable) огоро́д m.
gardener /'gɑrdnər/ n. садо́вник m.
gardenia /gɑr'dinyə/ n. гарде́ния f.
gardening /'gɑrdnɪŋ/ n. садово́дство neut.
gargantuan /gɑr'gæntʃuən/ adj. колосса́льный.
gargle /'gɑrgəl/ v. полоска́ть го́рло neut.
gargoyle /'gɑrgɔil/ n. гаргу́йль m.
garish /'gɛərɪʃ/ adj. крича́щий.
garland /'gɑrlənd/ n. гирля́нда f.
garlic /'gɑrlɪk/ n. чесно́к m.
garment /'gɑrmənt/ n. оде́жда f.
garner /'gɑrnər/ v. (store) запаса́ть impf.
garnet /'gɑrnɪt/ n. грана́т m.
garnish /'gɑrnɪʃ/ n. гарни́р m.
garnishing /'gɑrnɪʃɪŋ/ n. гарни́р m., украше́ние neut.
Garonne /gɑ'rɔn/ n. (river) Гаро́нна f.
garret /'gærɪt/ n. черда́к m.
garrison /'gærəsən/ n. гарнизо́н m.
garrotte /gə'rɒt/ n. гарро́та f.
garrulous /'gærələs/ adj. болтли́вый.
garrulousness /'gærələsnəs/ s/ n. болтли́вость f.
garter /'gɑrtər/ n. подвя́зка f.
gas /gæs/ **1.** n. газ m.; (gasoline) бензи́н m. **2.** adj. га́зовый.
gas burner n. га́зовая горе́лка f.
gas chamber n. га́зовая ка́мера f.
gaseous /'gæsiəs, 'gæʃəs/ adj. га́зовый; газообра́зный.
gas-fired /'gæs ,faiᵊrd/ adj. га́зовый.
gas fitter n. газопрово́дчик, газовщи́к m.
gash /gæʃ/ n. поре́з m.
gasification /,gæsəfɪ'keiʃən/ n. газифика́ция f.
gasify /'gæsə,fai/ v. газифици́ровать impf.
gas jet n. га́зовый рожо́к m.
gasket /'gæskɪt/ n. прокла́дка f.
gas lamp n. га́зовая ла́мпа f.
gaslight /'gæs,lait/ n. га́зовое освеще́ние neut.
gas main n. газопрово́д m.
gas mask n. противога́з m.
gas meter n. га́зовый счётчик m.
gasoline /,gæsə'lin/ n. бензи́н m.
gasometer /gæs'ɒmɪtər/ n. газо́метр m.
gasp /gæsp/ **1.** v. задыха́ться impf. **2.** n. вздох m.
gas pipe n. газопрово́д m.
gas range n. га́зовая плита́ f.
gas station n. запра́вка, бензоколо́нка f.
gastric /'gæstrɪk/ adj. желу́дочный.
gastritis /gæ'straitɪs/ n. гастри́т m., воспале́ние желу́дка neut.
gastronome /'gæstrə,noum/ n. гурма́н m.
gastronomic /,gæstrə'nɒmɪk/ adj. гастрономи́ческий.
gastronomy /gæ'strɒnəmi/ n. гастроно́мия f.
gastropod /'gæstrə,pɒd/ n. брюхоно́гое neut.
gasworks /'gæs,wɜrks/ n. га́зовый заво́д m.

gate /geit/ *n.* ворóта *pl.*; (*small*) калúтка *f.*
gâteau /gæ'tou/ *n.* торт *m.*
gate-crasher /'geit ˌkræʃər/ *n.* незвáный гость *m.*
gatehouse /'geitˌhaus/ *n.* сторóжка *f.*
gatekeeper /'geitˌkipər/ *n.* приврáтник *m.*
gatepost /'geitˌpoust/ *n.* ворóтный столб *m.*
gateway /'geitˌwei/ *n.* ворóта *pl.*
gather /'gæðər/ *v.t.* собирáть *impf.*, собрáть *pf.*; *v.i.* собирáться *impf.*, собрáться *pf.*
gathering /'gæðəriŋ/ *n.* собирáние *neut.*
gauche /gouʃ/ *adj.* неуклюжий.
gaucheness /gouʃnis/ *n.* бестáктность *f.*
gaudiness /'gɔdinis/ *n.* кричáщая безвкýсица *f.*
gaudy /'gɔdi/ *adj.* кричáщий *adj.*
gauge /geidʒ/ **1.** *n.* масштáб, измерúтельный прибóр *m.* **2.** *v.* измерять *impf.*, измéрить *pf.*
gaunt /gɔnt/ *adj.* исхудáлый, худóй.
gauntlet /gɔntlit/ *n.* рукавúца *f.*
gauss /gaus/ *n.* ráycc *m.*
gauze /gɔz/ *n.* мáрля *f.*
gavel /'gævəl/ *n.* молотóк *m.*
gavotte /gə'vɒt/ *n.* гавóт *m.*
gawky /'gɔki/ *adj.* неуклюжий.
gay /gei/ *adj.* весёлый.
gaze /geiz/ **1.** *n.* прúстальный взгляд *m.* **2.** *v.* прúстально смотрéть *impf.*
gazebo /gə'zeibou, -'zi-/ *n.* бельведéр *m.*
gazelle /gə'zɛl/ *n.* газéль *f.*
gazette /gə'zɛt/ *n.* газéта *f.*
gazetteer /ˌgæzi'tiər/ *n.* словáрь географúческих назвáний *m.*
Gdańsk /gə'dansk/ *n.* (*also: Danzig*) Гдáньск *m.*
gear /giər/ *n.* (*in motor*) передáча *f.*, прúвод *m.*; (*device*) устрóйство *neut.*
gearbox /'giərˌbɒks/ *n.* корóбка скоростéй *f.*
gearshift /'giərˌʃift/ *n.* переключéние передáч *neut.*
gearwheel /'giərˌwil/ *n.* шестерёнка *f.*
gecko /'gɛkou/ *n.* геккóн *m.*
gee /dʒi/ *interj.* (*colloq.*) вот это да!; (*in surprise*) огó!, ничегó себé!; (*various emphatic uses*) ну.
Geiger counter /'gaigər/ *n.* счётчик Гéйгера *m.*
geisha /'geiʃə/ *n.* гéйша *f.*
gel /dʒɛl/ *n.* гель *m.*
gelatin /'dʒɛlətn/ (*e*) *n.* желатúн *m.*
gelatinize /dʒə'lætn̩ˌaiz/ *v.* превращáть в желатúн *impf.*
gelatinous /dʒə'lætnəs/ *adj.* желатúновый.
geld /gɛld/ *v.* холостúть *impf.*
gelding /'gɛldiŋ/ *n.* (*horse*) мéрин *m.*
gelid /'dʒɛlid/ *adj.* ледянóй.
gelignite /'dʒɛligˌnait/ *n.* гелигнúт *m.*
gem /dʒɛm/ *n.* драгоцéнный кáмень *m.*
geminate / *v.* 'dʒɛmənit/ *adj.* двойнóй.
Gemini /'dʒɛməˌnai/ *n.* (*astr.*) Близнецы́ *pl.*
gemma /'dʒɛmə/ *n.* гéмма *f.*
gendarme /'ʒandarm/ *n.* жандáрм *m.*
gendarmerie /ʒan'darmri/ *n.* жандармéрия *f.*
gender /'dʒɛndər/ *n.* род *m.*
gene /dʒin/ *n.* ген *m.*
genealogical /ˌdʒiniə'lɒdʒikəl/ *adj.* генеалогúческий.
genealogy /ˌdʒini'ɒlədʒi/ *n.* генеалóгия *f.*
gene pool *n.* генофóнд *m.*
general /'dʒɛnərəl/ **1.** *adj.* óбщий; всеóбщий;

(*chief*) генерáльный. **2.** *n.* генерáл *m.* **3.** *adv.* in general вообщé.
generalissimo /ˌdʒɛnərə'lisəˌmou/ *n.* генералúссимус *m.*
generality /ˌdʒɛnə'ræliti/ *n.* всеóбщность *f.*
generalization /ˌdʒɛnərələ'zeiʃən/ *n.* обобщéние *neut.*
generalize /'dʒɛnərəˌlaiz/ *v.* обобщáть *impf.*
generally /'dʒɛnərəli/ *adv.* вообщé; обы́чно; как прáвило.
general-purpose /'dʒɛnərəl 'pərgрəs/ *adj.* многоцелевóй.
generalship /'dʒɛnərəlˌʃip/ *n.* генерáльский чин *m.*
generate /'dʒɛnəˌreit/ *v.* порождáть *impf.*
generation /ˌdʒɛnə'reiʃən/ *n.* поколéние *neut.*
generative /'dʒɛnərətiv/ *adj.* порождáющий.
generator /'dʒɛnəˌreitər/ *n.* генерáтор *m.*
generic /dʒə'nɛrik/ *adj.* родовóй; (*general*) óбщий.
generosity /ˌdʒɛnə'rɒsiti/ *n.* великодýшие *neut.*, щéдрость *f.*
generous /'dʒɛnərəs/ *adj.* великодýшный, щéдрый.
genesis /'dʒɛnəsis/ *n.* происхождéние *neut.*; *cap.* (*bibl.*) Бытиé *neut.*
genetic /dʒə'nɛtik/ *adj.* гéнный; генетúческий.
genetics /dʒə'nɛtiks/ *n.* генéтика *f.*
Geneva /dʒə'nivə/ *n.* Женéва *f.*
genial /'dʒinyəl/ *adj.* добродýшный, сердéчный.
geniality /ˌdʒini'æliti/ *n.* добродýшие *neut.*
genie /'dʒini/ *n.* джин *m.*
genista /dʒə'nistə/ *n.* дрок *m.*
genital /'dʒɛnitl/ *adj.* половóй; генитáльный.
genitive /'dʒɛnitiv/ *n.* родúтельный падéж *m.*
genius /'dʒinyəs/ *n.* гéний *m.*; (*ability*) гениáльность *f.*
Genoa /'dʒɛnouə/ *n.* Гéнуя *f.*
genocide /'dʒɛnəˌsaid/ *n.* геноцúд *m.*
genotype /'dʒɛnəˌtaip, 'dʒinə-/ *n.* генотúп *m.*
genre /'ʒanrə/ *n.* жанр *m.*
genteel /dʒɛn'til/ *adj.* благовоспúтанный; вéжливый.
gentian /'dʒɛnʃən/ *n.* горечáвка *f.*
gentile /'dʒɛntail/ *n.* не-еврéй *m.*
gentility /dʒɛn'tiliti/ *n.* благовоспúтанность *f.*
gentle /'dʒɛntl/ *adj.* крóткий; мя́гкий; лёгкий.
gentlefolk /'dʒɛntlˌfouk/ *n.* двóрянство *neut.*
gentleman /'dʒɛntlmən/ *n.* джéнтльмен *m.*
gentlemanly /'dʒɛntlˌmənli/ *adv.* по-джентльмéнски.
gentleness /'dʒɛntlnis/ *n.* мя́гкость *f.*
gentlewoman /'dʒɛntlˌwumən/ *n.* дáма *f.*
gentry /'dʒɛntri/ *n.* двóрянство *neut.*
genuflect /'dʒɛnyuˌflɛkt/ *v.* преклоня́ть колéни *impf.*
genuflection /ˌdʒɛnyu'flɛkʃən/ *n.* коленопреклонéние *neut.*
genuine /'dʒɛnyuin/ *adj.* пóдлинный, úскренний.
genuinely /'dʒɛnyuinli/ *adv.* úскренне.
genuineness /'dʒɛnyuinnis/ *n.* пóдлинность; úскренность *f.*
genus /'dʒinəs/ *n.* род *m.*; вид *m.*
geocentric /ˌdʒiou'sɛntrik/ *adj.* геоцентрúческий.
geodesic /ˌdʒiə'dɛsik/ *adj.* геодезúческий.
geodesy /dʒi'ɒdəsi/ *n.* геодéзия *f.*
geodetic /ˌdʒiə'dɛtik/ *adj.* геодезúческий.

geographer /dʒi'ɒɡrəfər/ n. reóграф m.
geographical /ˌdʒiə'ɡræfɪkəl/ adj. reoграфи́-
ческий.
geography /dʒi'ɒɡrəfi/ n. reoграфия f.
geoid /'dʒiɔid/ n. reóид m.
geological /ˌdʒiə'lɒdʒɪkəl/ adj. reoлоги́ческий.
geologist /dʒi'ɒlədʒɪst/ n. reóлог m.
geology /dʒi'ɒlədʒi/ n. reoлóгия f.
geomagnetic /ˌdʒioumæɡ'nɛtɪk/ adj. reoмагни́т-
ный.
geometer /dʒi'ɒmɪtər/ n. reoмéтр m.
geometric /ˌdʒiə'mɛtrɪk/ adj. reoметри́ческий.
geometry /dʒi'ɒmɪtri/ n. reoмéтрия f.
geophysical /ˌdʒiou'fɪzɪkəl/ adj. reoфизи́ческий.
geophysics /ˌdʒiou'fɪzɪks/ n. reoфи́зика f.
geopolitics /ˌdʒiou'pɒlɪtɪks/ n. reoполи́тика f.
geoponic /ˌdʒiə'pɒnɪk/ adj. агрономи́ческий.
georgette /dʒɔr'dʒɛt/ n. жоржéт m.
Georgia /'dʒɔrdʒə/ n. (Caucasus region) Гру́зия
f.; (State in USA) Джóрджия f.
Georgian /'dʒɔrdʒən/ 1. adj. (Caucasus region)
грузи́нский. 2. n. (Caucasus region) грузи́н m.,
грузи́нка f.
geranium /dʒɪ'reiniəm/ n. repа́нь f.
gerbil /'dʒɜrbəl/ n. песчáнка f.
gerfalcon /'dʒɜr,fɔlkən, -,fæl-/ n. кре́чет m.
geriatric /ˌdʒɛri'ætrɪk/ adj. reриатри́ческий.
geriatrician /ˌdʒɛriə'trɪʃən/ n. reриáтрик m.
geriatrics /ˌdʒɛri'ætrɪks/ n. reриатри́я f.
germ /dʒɜrm/ n. микрóб m.
German /'dʒɜrmən/ 1. adj. repмáнский,
немéцкий. 2. n. нéмец m., нéмка f.
german /'dʒɜrmən/ adj. роднóй; двою́родный.
germane /dʒɜr'mein/ adj. умéстный.
Germanic /dʒər'mænɪk/ adj. repмáнский.
Germanist /'dʒɜrmənɪst/ n. repмани́ст m.
germanium /dʒər'meiniəm/ n. repмáний m.
Germany /'dʒɜrməni/ n. Repмáния f.
germicidal /ˌdʒɜrmə'saidl/ adj. бактерици́дный.
germicide /'dʒɜrmə,said/ n. бактерици́д m.
germinal /'dʒɜrmənl/ adj. зарóдышевый.
germinate /'dʒɜrmə,neit/ v. прорастáть impf.
germination /ˌdʒɜrmə'neiʃən/ n. прорастáние
neut.
germinative /'dʒɜrmə,neitɪv/ adj. repминати́в-
ный.
gerontology /ˌdʒɛrən'tɒlədʒi/ n. repонтолóгия f.
gerund /'dʒɛrənd/ n. repу́ндий m.
gerundive /dʒə'rʌndɪv/ n. repунди́в m.
Gestapo /ɡə'stɑpou/ n. гестáпо neut. indecl.
gestation /dʒɛ'steiʃən/ n. перióд берéменности
m.
gesticulate /dʒɛ'stɪkyə,leit/ v. жестикули́ровать
impf.
gesticulation /dʒɛ,stɪkyə'leiʃən/ n. жестикуля́ция
f.
gesture /'dʒɛstʃər/ n. жест m.
get /ɡɛt/ v. (obtain) доставáть impf., достáть pf.;
(receive) получáть impf., получи́ть pf.; (become)
станови́ться impf., стать pf.; **to get off** сойти́
pf.; **to get up** вставáть impf., встать pf.; **to get
well** поправля́ться impf., попрáвиться pf.
get-together /'ɡɛt tə,ɡɛðər/ n. сбóрище neut.
get-up /'ɡɛt,ʌp/ n. (typogr.) оформлéние neut.
gewgaw /'ɡyuɡɔ, 'ɡu-/ n. безделу́шка f.
geyser /'ɡaizər/ n. гéйзер m.
ghastliness /'ɡæstlinɪs/ n. у́жас m.

ghastly /'ɡæstli/ adj. стрáшный, ужáсный.
gherkin /'ɡɜrkɪn/ n. корнишóн m.
ghetto /'ɡetou/ n. гéтто neut. indecl.
ghost /ɡoust/ n. привидéние neut.; при́зрак; дух
m.
ghostly /'ɡoustli/ adj. при́зрачный.
ghoul /ɡul/ n. вурдалáк, вампи́р m.
ghoulish /'ɡulɪʃ/ adj. жу́ткий.
giant /'dʒaiənt/ n. великáн m.
giantess /'dʒaiəntɪs/ n. великáнша f.
gibber /'dʒɪbər/ v. бормотáть impf.
gibberish /'dʒɪbərɪʃ/ n. тарабáрщина f.
gibbet /'dʒɪbɪt/ n. ви́селица f.
gibbon /'ɡɪbən/ n. гиббóн m.
gibe /dʒaib/ v. насмехáться (над with instr.)
impf.
giblets /'dʒɪblɪts/ n. потрохá pl.
Gibraltar /dʒɪ'brɔltər/ n. **Strait of,** Гибралтáр-
ский проли́в m.
giddiness /'ɡɪdinɪs/ n. головокружéние neut.;
(frivolity) легкомы́слие neut.
giddy /'ɡɪdi/ adj. страдáющий головокру-
жéнием.
giddyap /ˌɡɪdi'æp/ interj. пошёл!, но!
gift /ɡɪft/ n. подáрок, дар m.; (talent) талáнт m.
gifted /'ɡɪftɪd/ adj. одарённый, талáнтливый.
gig /ɡɪɡ/ n. (carriage) кабриолéт m.; (boat)
шлю́пка f.
gigantic /dʒai'ɡæntɪk, dʒɪ-/ adj. гигáнтский.
giggle /'ɡɪɡəl/ v. хихи́кать impf.
giggling /'ɡɪɡlɪŋ/ n. хихи́канье neut.
gigolo /'dʒɪɡə,lou/ n. сутенёр m.
gild /ɡɪld/ v. золоти́ть impf., позолоти́ть pf.; **to
gild the lily** занимáться бесполéзным дéлом
impf.
gilded /'ɡɪldɪd/ adj. позолóченный.
gilder /'ɡɪldər/ n. позолóтчик m.
gilding /'ɡɪldɪŋ/ n. (process) золочéние neut.;
(substance) позолóта f.
gill /ɡɪl/ n. (fish) жáбра f.
gillyflower /'dʒɪli,flauər/ n. желтофиóль f.
gilt /ɡɪlt/ adj. позолóченный.
gilt-edged /'ɡɪlt,ɛdʒd/ adj. с золоты́м обрéзом.
gimbals /'dʒɪmbəlz/ n. кардáн, кардáнный под-
вéс m.
gimcrack /'dʒɪm,kræk/ adj. мишу́рный.
gimlet /'ɡɪmlɪt/ n. бурáвчик m.
gimmick /'ɡɪmɪk/ n. фóкус, трюк m.; нови́нка f.
gin /dʒɪn/ n. джин m.
ginger /'dʒɪndʒər/ n. 1. имби́рь m. 2. adj.
имби́рный.
ginger beer n. имби́рное пи́во neut.
gingerbread /'dʒɪndʒər,brɛd/ n. (имби́рный)
прáник m.
gingerly /'dʒɪndʒərli/ adv. осторóжно.
gingham /'ɡɪŋəm/ adj. бумáжный; си́тцевый.
gingivitis /ˌdʒɪndʒə'vaitɪs/ n. воспалéние дёсен
neut.
giraffe /dʒə'ræf/ n. жирáф m.
gird /ɡɜrd/ v. подпоясáть impf.
girder /'ɡɜrdər/ n. бáлка f.
girdle /'ɡɜrdl/ n. корсéт; пóяс, кушáк m.
girl /ɡɜrl/ n. (little) дéвочка f.; (grown-up)
дéвушка f.
girlfriend /'ɡɜrl,frɛnd/ n. подру́га f.
girlhood /'ɡɜrlhʊd/ n. дéвичество neut.
girlish /'ɡɜrlɪʃ/ adj. дéвичий.

girth /gɜrθ/ *n.* обхва́т *m.*

gist /dʒɪst/ *n.* суть; су́щность *f.*

give /gɪv/ **1.** *v.* дава́ть *impf.*, дать *pf.*; **to give back** отдава́ть *impf.*, отда́ть *pf.*; **to give in** уступа́ть *impf.*, уступи́ть *pf.*; **to give up** сдава́ться *impf.*, сда́ться *pf.* **2.** *n.* упру́гость *f.*

given /'gɪvən/ *adj.* да́нный.

glabrous /'gleibrəs/ *adj.* (*smooth*) гла́дкий; (*bare*) го́лый; (*hairless*) безволо́сый.

glacé /glæ'sei/ *adj.* глазиро́ванный.

glacial /'gleiʃəl/ *adj.* леднико́вый.

glaciation /ˌgleiʃi'eiʃən/ *n.* оледене́ние *neut.*

glacier /'gleiʃər/ *n.* ледни́к; глётчер *m.*

glad /glæd/ **1.** *adj.* ра́достный; (*pred.*) рад. **2.** *v.*: **to be glad** ра́доваться *impf.*; быть дово́льным.

gladden /'glædn/ *v.* ра́довать *impf.*

glade /gleid/ *n.* поля́на *f.*

gladiator /'glædiˌeitər/ *n.* гладиа́тор *m.*

gladiatorial /ˌglædiə'tɔriəl/ *adj.* гладиа́торский.

gladiolus /ˌglædi'ouləs/ *n.* гладио́лус *m.*

gladly /'glædli/ *adv.* с удово́льствием.

gladness /'glædnɪs/ *n.* ра́дость *f.*

glair /glɛər/ *n.* (яи́чный) бело́к *m.*

glamor /'glæmər/ *n.* обая́ние *neut.*

glamorize /'glæməˌraiz/ *v.* романтизи́ровать *impf.*

glamorous /'glæmərəs/ *adj.* обая́тельный.

glance /glæns/ **1.** *n.* бе́глый взгляд *m.* **2.** *v.* взгляну́ть *pf.*

glancing /'glænsɪŋ/ *adj.* (*blow*) скользя́щий.

gland /glænd/ *n.* железа́ *f.*

glanderous /'glændərəs/ *adj.* са́пный.

glanders /'glændərz/ *n.* сап *m.*

glandular /'glændʒələr/ *adj.* желе́зистый.

glandule /'glændʒul/ *n.* желёзка *f.*

glans /glænz/ *n.* (*anat.*) голо́вка мужско́го дето-ро́дного о́ргана *f.*

glare /glɛər/ **1.** *n.* блеск *m.* **2.** *v.* сверка́ть *impf.*

glaring /'glɛərɪŋ/ *adj.* ослепи́тельный.

glass /glæs/ **1.** *n.* стекло́ *neut.*; (*container*) стака́н *m.* **2.** *adj.* стекля́нный.

glassblower /'glæsˌblouər/ *n.* стеклоду́в *m.*

glassblowing /'glæsˌblouɪŋ/ *n.* стеклоду́вное де́ло *neut.*

glass cutter *n.* стеклоре́з *m.*

glasses /'glæsɪz/ *n.* очки́ *pl.*

glassful /'glæsfʊl/ *n.* стака́н *m.*

glassine /glæ'sin/ *n.* пергами́н *m.*

glassware /'glæsˌwɛər/ *n.* стекля́нные изде́лия *pl.*

glass wool *n.* стекля́нная ва́та *f.*

glassy /'glæsi/ *adj.* стекля́нный.

Glauber's salt /'glaubərz/ *n.* гла́уберова соль *f.*

glaucoma /glɔ'koumə, glau-/ *n.* глауко́ма *f.*

glaucous /'glɔkəs/ *adj.* се́ро-зелёный.

glaze /gleiz/ *n.* (*on pottery*) мурава́, глазу́рь *f.*

glazed /gleizd/ *adj.* (*fitted with glass*) застеклён-ный.

glazier /'gleiʒər/ *n.* стеко́льщик *m.*

glazing /'gleiziŋ/ *n.* застекле́ние *neut.*

gleam /glim/ **1.** *n.* про́блеск *m.* **2.** *v.* свети́ться *impf.*

glean /glin/ *v.* подбира́ть *impf.*

gleaning /'gliniŋ/ *n.* сбор коло́сьев; сбор инфор-ма́ции *m.*

glee /gli/ *n.* весе́лье *neut.*

gleeful /'glifəl/ *adj.* лику́ющий.

glen /glɛn/ *n.* го́рная доли́на *f.*

glib /glɪb/ *adj.* бо́йкий на язы́к.

glibness /'glɪbnɪs/ *n.* говорли́вость *f.*

glide /glaid/ *v.* скользи́ть *impf.*; (*aero.*) плани́ровать *impf.*

glider /'glaidər/ *n.* пла́нер *m.*

gliding /'glaidɪŋ/ *n.* скольже́ние *neut.*

glimmer /'glɪmər/ **1.** *n.* мерца́ние *neut.*; сла́бый, ту́склый свет; про́блеск *m.* **2.** *v.* мерца́ть *impf.*

glimpse /glɪmps/ *v.* взгляну́ть ме́льком *pf.*

glint /glɪnt/ *n.* сверка́нье *neut.*, блеск; лоск *m.*

glissade /glɪ'sɑd/ *n.* скольже́ние *neut.*

glissando /glɪ'sɑndou/ *n.* глисса́ндо *neut. indecl.*

glisten /'glɪsən/ *v.* блесте́ть *impf.*

gloaming /'gloumɪŋ/ *n.* су́мерки *pl.*

gloat /glout/ *v.* злора́дствовать *impf.*

gloating /'gloutɪŋ/ *adj.* злора́дный.

global /'gloubəl/ *adj.* глоба́льный.

globe /gloub/ *n.* земно́й шар; гло́бус *m.*

globetrotter /'gloubˌtrɒtər/ *n.* ненасы́тный путе-ше́ственник *m.*

globoid /'gloubɔid/ *adj.* сфери́ческий.

globose /'gloubous/ *adj.* шарови́дный.

globular /'glɒbyələr/ *adj.* шарообра́зный.

globule /'glɒbyul/ *n.* ша́рик *m.*

globulin /'glɒbyəlɪn/ *n.* глобули́н *m.*

glockenspiel /'glɒkən‚spil/ *n.* металлофо́н *m.*

gloom /glum/ *n.* мрак *m.*; (*melancholy*) уны́ние *neut.*

gloominess /'gluminɪs/ *n.* мра́чность *f.*

gloomy /'glumi/ *adj.* мра́чный, угрю́мый.

glorification /ˌglɔrəfɪ'keiʃən/ *n.* прославле́ние *neut.*

glorify /'glɔrəˌfai/ *v.* прославля́ть *impf.*, про-сла́вить *pf.*

glorious /'glɔriəs/ *adj.* сла́вный.

glory /'glɔri/ *adj.* сла́ва *f.*

gloss[1] /glɒs/ *n.* блеск, лоск, гля́нец *m.*

gloss[2] /glɔs/ *n.* (*commentary*) гло́сса *f.*

glossary /'glɒsəri/ *n.* глосса́рий, слова́рь *m.*

glossiness /'glɔsinɪs/ *n.* лоск, гля́нец *m.*

glossitis /glɒ'saitɪs/ *n.* глосси́т *m.*, воспале́ние языка́ *neut.*

glossy /'glɒsi/ *adj.* блестя́щий; глянцеви́тый.

glottal /'glɒtl/ *adj.* глотта́льный.

glottal stop *n.* твёрдый при́ступ *m.*

glottis /'glɒtɪs/ *n.* голосова́я щель *f.*

glove /glʌv/ *n.* перча́тка *f.*

glover /'glʌvər/ *n.* перча́точник *m.*

glow /glou/ **1.** *n.* за́рево *neut.*; (*of cheeks*) румя́нец *m.* **2.** *v.* сия́ть *impf.*

glower /'glauər/ *v.* серди́то смотре́ть *impf.*

glowing /'glouɪŋ/ *adj.* (*burning*) тле́ющий; (*healthy*) румя́ный.

glowworm /'glouˌwɜrm/ *n.* светля́к *m.*

gloxinia /glɒk'siniə/ *n.* глокси́ния *f.*

glucose /'glukous/ *n.* глюко́за *f.*

glue /glu/ **1.** *n.* клей *m.* **2.** *v.* кле́ить *impf.*

gluepot /'gluˌpɒt/ *n.* клеева́рка *f.*

gluey /'glui/ *adj.* ли́пкий.

glum /glʌm/ *adj.* угрю́мый, мра́чный.

glut /glʌt/ *n.* избы́ток *m.*; перепроизво́дство *neut.*

gluten /'glutn/ *n.* клейкови́на *f.*

glutinous /'glutnəs/ *adj.* клейкий.

glutton /'glʌtn/ *n.* обжо́ра *f.*

gluttonous /'glʌtnəs/ *adj.* прожо́рливый.
gluttony /'glʌtni/ *n.* обжо́рство *neut.*, прожо́рливость *f.*
glycerine /'glɪsərɪn/ *n.* глицери́н *m.*
glycogen /'glaikədʒən/ *n.* гликоге́н *m.*
glycol /'glaikɔl/ *n.* глюко́ль *m.*
glyph /glɪf/ *n.* глиф *m.*
glyptic /'glɪptɪk/ *n.* гли́птика *f.*
glyptography /glɪp'tɒgrəfi/ *n.* глиптогра́фия *f.*
gnarl /narl/ *n.* наро́ст *m.*
gnash /næʃ/ *v.* скрежета́ть (*with instr.*) *impf.*
gnat /næt/ *n.* мо́шка *f.*
gnathic /'næθɪk/ *adj.* челюстно́й.
gnaw /nɔ/ *v.* грызть *impf.*
gnawing /'nɔɪŋ/ *adj.* грызу́щий.
gneiss /nais/ *n.* гнейс *m.*
gnome[1] /noum/ *n.* гном *m.*
gnome[2] /noum/ *n.* сенте́нция *f.*
gnomic /'noumɪk/ *adj.* афористи́ческий.
gnomon /'noumɒn/ *n.* гно́мон *m.*
gnosis /'nousɪs/ *n.* гно́зис *m.*
Gnostic /'nɒstɪk/ *n.* гно́стик *m.*
Gnosticism /'nɒstə,sɪzəm/ *n.* гностици́зм *m.*
gnu /nu/ *n.* антило́па-гну́ *f.*
go /gou/ *v.* идти́ *impf.*, пойти́ *pf.*; (*by vehicle*) е́здить *indet. impf.*, е́хать *det. impf.*; **to go away** уходи́ть *impf.*, уйти́ *pf.*; **to go back** верну́ться *pf.*; **to go in** входи́ть *impf.*, войти́ *pf.*; **to go on** продолжа́ться *impf.*; **to go out** выходи́ть *impf.*, вы́йти *pf.*
goad /goud/ *v.* (*cattle*) подгоня́ть; (*incite*) подстрека́ть *impf.*
go-ahead /'gouə,hɛd/ *adj.* пробивно́й.
goal /goul/ *n.* цель *f.*; (*athl.*) гол *m.*
goalkeeper /'goul,kipər/ *n.* врата́рь *m.*
goal kick *n.* уда́р от воро́т *m.*
goal line *n.* ли́ния воро́т *f.*
goalpost /'goul,poust/ *n.* сто́йка воро́т *f.*
goal-scorer /'goul ,skɔrər/ *adj.* забива́ющий гол.
goat /gout/ **1.** *n.* коза́ *f.*; козёл *m.* **2.** *adj.* ко́зий.
goatherd /'gout,hɜrd/ *n.* козопа́с *m.*
goatish /'goutɪʃ/ *adj.* козли́ный.
goatsucker /'gout,sʌkər/ *n.* (*bird*) козодо́й *m.*
gobble /'gɒbəl/ *v.* жрать *impf.*
gobbledegook /'gɒbəldi,guk/ *n.* галиматья́ *f.*
Gobelin /'gɒbəlɪn/ *n.* гобеле́н *m.*
go-between /'gou bɪ,twin/ *n.* посре́дник *m.*
goblet /'gɒblɪt/ *n.* бока́л; ку́бок *m.*
goblin /'gɒblɪn/ *n.* домово́й, го́блин *m.*
goby /'goubi/ *n.* бычо́к *m.*
go-cart /'gou ,kart/ *n.* самока́т *m.*
God /gɒd/ *n.* Бог *m.*; божество́ *neut.*
godchild /'gɒd,tʃaild/ *n.* кре́стник *m.*, кре́стница *f.*
goddaughter /'gɒd,dɔtər/ *n.* кре́стница *f.*
goddess /'gɒdɪs/ *n.* боги́ня *f.*
godfather /'gɒd,faðər/ *n.* кре́стный оте́ц *m.*
God-fearing /'gɒd ,fɪərɪŋ/ *adj.* богобоя́зненный; набо́жный.
godforsaken /'gɒdfər,seikən/ *adj.* захолу́стный.
Godhead /'gɒd,hɛd/ *n.* Тро́ица *f.*
godless /'gɒdlɪs/ *adj.* безбо́жный.
godlessness /'gɒdlɪsnɪs/ *n.* безбо́жие *neut.*
godlike /'gɒd,laik/ *adj.* богоподо́бный.
godliness /'gɒdlinɪs/ *n.* набо́жность *f.*
godly /'gɒdli/ *adj.* набо́жный.

godmother /'gɒd,mʌðər/ *n.* крёстная мать *f.*
godparent /'gɒd,pɛərənt/ *n.* крёстный *m.*, крёстная *f.*
godsend /'gɒd,sɛnd/ *n.* дар Бо́жий *m.*
godson /'gɒd,sʌn/ *n.* кре́стник *m.*
goer /'gouər/ *n.* ходо́к *m.*
goffer /'gɒfər/ *n.* гофриро́вка *f.*
go-getter /'gou'gɛtər/ *adj.* пробивно́й.
goggle /'gɒgəl/ *v.* тара́щиться *impf.*
goggle-eyed /'gɒgəl,aid/ *adj.* пучегла́зый.
goggles /'gɒgəlz/ *n.* защи́тные очки́ *pl.*
going /'gouɪŋ/ *n.* (*departure*) ухо́д *m.*
going-over /'gouɪŋ 'ouvər/ *n.* прове́рка *f.*
goings-on /'gouɪŋz 'ɒn/ *n.* дела́; происше́ствия *pl.*
goiter /'gɔitər/ *n.* зоб *m.*
goitrous /'gɔitrəs/ *adj.* зо́бный.
gold /gould/ **1.** *adj.* золото́й. **2.** *n.* зо́лото *neut.*
goldbeater /'gould,bitər/ *n.* золотобо́ец *m.*
gold-digger *n.* золотоиска́тель *m.*
gold dust *n.* золото́й песо́к *m.*
golden /'gouldən/ *adj.* золото́й, золоти́стый.
golden eagle *n.* бе́ркут *m.*
goldenrod /'gouldən,rɒd/ *n.* золота́рник *m.*
gold fever *n.* золота́я лихора́дка *f.*
gold field *n.* золото́й при́иск *m.*
goldfinch /'gould,fɪntʃ/ *n.* щего́л *m.*
goldfish /'gould,fɪʃ/ *n.* золота́я ры́бка *f.*
gold foil *n.* листово́е зо́лото *neut.*
gold lace *n.* золото́й позуме́нт *m.*
gold leaf *n.* золота́я фольга́ *f.*
gold mine *n.* золото́й рудни́к *m.*
gold plate *n.* позоло́ченная посу́да *f.*
gold-plated /'gould ,pleitɪd/ *adj.* золочёный, позоло́ченный.
gold-plating /'gould 'pleitɪŋ/ *n.* золоче́ние *neut.*
gold rush *n.* золота́я лихора́дка *f.*
goldsmith /'gould,smɪθ/ *n.* золоты́х дел ма́стер *m.*
golf /gɒlf/ *n.* гольф *m.*
golfer /'gɒlfər/ *n.* игро́к в гольф *m.*
gonad /'gounæd/ *n.* гона́да *f.*
gondola /'gɒndlə/ *n.* гондо́ла *f.*
gondolier /,gɒndl'ɪər/ *n.* гондолье́р *m.*
gone /gɒn/ *adj.* пропа́щий; (*past*) проше́дший; **gone on** (*colloq.*) (*in love with*) по́ уши влюблённый в (*with acc.*); (*mad about*) поме́шанный на (*with prep.*).
goner /'gɒnər/ *n.* (*colloq.*) ко́нченый челове́к *m.*
gonfalon /'gɒnfələn/ *n.* (*church banner*) хору́гвь *f.*
gong /gɒŋ/ *n.* гонг *m.*
goniometer /,gouni'ɒmɪtər/ *n.* гонио́метр *m.*
gonococcus /,gɒnə'kɒkəs/ *n.* гоноко́кк *m.*
gonorrhea /,gɒnə'riə/ *n.* гонорея́ *f.*; три́ппер *m.*
good /gud/ **1.** *adj.* хоро́ший, до́брый. **2.** *n.* добро́; бла́го *neut.*; по́льза *f.*
good-bye /gud 'bai/ **1.** *interj.* до свида́ния!; проща́йте! **2.** *n.* проща́ние *neut.* **to say good-bye** *v.* проща́ться *impf.*, попроща́ться *pf.*
good-for-nothing /'gud fər 'nʌθɪŋ/ **1.** *adj.* никчёмный, никуды́шный, никуда́ не го́дный. **2.** *n.* шалопа́й *m.*
good-looking /'gud 'lukɪŋ/ *adj.* краси́вый, интере́сный.
good luck *interj.* всего́ хоро́шего!
goodly /'gudli/ *adj.* поря́дочный.

good-natured /'gʊd 'neitʃərd/ *adj.* добродушный.

goodness /'gʊdnɪs/ *n.* доброта́ *f.*

goods /gʊdz/ *pl.* това́ры *pl.*

good-sized /'gʊd'saizd/ *adj.* изря́дный.

good-tempered /'gʊd 'tɛmpərd/ *adj.* с хоро́шим хара́ктером.

goodwill /'gʊd'wɪl/ *n.* доброжела́тельность; до́брая во́ля *f.*

goody-goody /'gʊdi 'gʊdi/ *n.* ханжа́ *m.* and *f.* (*decl. f.*).

gooey /'gui/ *adj.* (*colloq.*) слаща́вый.

goof /guf/ *n.* (*colloq.*) (*person*) тупи́ца *m.* and *f.* (*decl. f.*).

goose /gus/ **1.** *n.* гусь *m.* **2.** *adj.* гуси́ный.

gooseberry /'gus,bɛri/ *n.* крыжо́вник *m.*

gopher /'goufər/ *n.* су́слик *m.*

Gordian knot /'gɔrdiən/ *n.* го́рдиев у́зел *m.*

gore[1] /gɔr/ *n.* кровь *f.*

gore[2] /gɔr/ *v.* бода́ть *impf.*

gorge /gɔrdʒ/ **1.** *n.* уще́лье *neut.* **2.** *v.* глота́ть *impf.*

gorgeous /'gɔrdʒəs/ *adj.* великоле́пный; пы́шный.

Gorgon /'gɔrgən/ *n.* Меду́за-Горго́на *f.*

Gorgonzola /,gɔrgən'zoulə/ *n.* сыр горгонзо́ла *m.*

gorilla /gə'rɪlə/ *n.* гори́лла *f.*

Gorki /'gɔrki/ *n.* (*also: Gorky*) Го́рький *m.* (*see Nizhniy Novgorod*).

gormandize /'gɔrmən,daiz/ *v.* обжира́ться *impf.*

gorse /gɔrs/ *n.* утёсник (обыкнове́нный) *m.*

gory /'gɔri/ *adj.* окрова́вленный.

gosh /gɒʃ/ *interj.* бо́же!

goshawk /'gɒs,hɔk/ *n.* я́стреб *m.*

gosling /'gɒzlɪŋ/ *n.* гусёнок *m.*

Gospel /'gɒspəl/ *n.* Ева́нгелие *neut.*

gossamer /'gɒsəmər/ *n.* паути́на *f.*

gossip /'gɒsəp/ **1.** *n.* спле́тня *f.* **2.** *v.* спле́тничать *impf.*

gossipy /'gɒsəpi/ *adj.* (*person*) болтли́вый.

Gothic /'gɒθɪk/ *adj.* готи́ческий.

Göttingen /'gœtɪŋən/ *n.* Гёттинген *m.*

gouache /gwɑʃ/ *n.* гуа́шь *f.*

goucho /'gautʃou/ *n.* га́учо *m. indecl.*

gouge /gaudʒ/ *v.* выда́лбливать *impf.*, вы́долбить *pf.*

goulash /'gulɑʃ/ *n.* гуля́ш *m.*

gourd /gɔrd/ *n.* ты́ква *f.*

gourmand /gʊr'mɑnd/ *n.* обжо́ра *m.* and *f.* (*decl. f.*); гурма́н *m.*

gourmet /gʊr'mei/ *n.* гурма́н *m.*

gout /gaut/ *n.* пода́гра *f.*

gouty /'gauti/ *adj.* подагри́ческий.

govern /'gʌvərn/ *v.* управля́ть (*with instr.*) *impf.*

governess /'gʌvərnis/ *n.* гуверна́нтка *f.*

government /'gʌvərnmənt/ *n.* прави́тельство; управле́ние *neut.*

governmental /,gʌvərn'mɛntl̩/ *adj.* прави́тельственный.

governor /'gʌvərnər/ *n.* губерна́тор *m.*; (*mach.*) регуля́тор *m.*

gown /gaun/ *n.* пла́тье *neut.*, (*long robe*) ма́нтия *f.*

grab /græb/ *v.* хвата́ть *impf.*, схвати́ть *pf.*

grace /greis/ *n.* гра́ция; (*favor*) ми́лость *f.*

graceful /'greisfəl/ *adj.* грацио́зный, изя́щный.

gracefulness /'greisfəlnis/ *n.* грацио́зность *neut.*

graceless /'greislis/ *adj.* (*unattractive*) непривлека́тельный; (*improper*) неприли́чный.

grace note *n.* (*mus.*) мели́зм *m.*

gracious /'greiʃəs/ **1.** *adj.* ми́лостивый. **2.** *interj.* бо́же мой!

gradation /grei'deiʃən/ *n.* града́ция *f.*

grade /greid/ **1.** *n.* сте́пень *m.*; (*type*) сорт *m.*; (*school*) класс *m.*; (*mark in school*) оце́нка *f.* **2.** *v.* сортирова́ть *impf.*; (*level*) нивели́ровать *impf.*

grader /'greidər/ *n.* гре́йдер *m.*

gradient /'greidiənt/ *n.* (*slope*) укло́н *m.*

gradual /'grædʒuəl/ *adj.* постепе́нный.

gradually /'grædʒuəli/ *adv.* постепе́нно, ма́лопома́лу.

graduate / *n.* 'grædʒuɪt; *v.* 'grædʒu,eit/ **1.** *n.* выпускни́к *m.* **2.** *v.* конча́ть уче́бное заведе́ние *impf.*

graduation /,grædʒu'eiʃən/ *n.* (*completion of studies*) оконча́ние университе́та *neut.*

graffiti /grə'fiti/ *n.* граффи́ти *indecl.*

graft[1] /græft/ **1.** *n.* черено́к *m.*, приви́вка *f.* **2.** *v.* привива́ть *impf.*, приви́ть *pf.*

graft[2] /græft/ *n.* (*colloq.*) взя́тка *f.*, взя́точничество *neut.*

grafting[1] /'græftiŋ/ *n.* приви́вка *f.*

grafting[2] /'græftiŋ/ *n.* жу́льничество *neut.*

Grail /greil/ *n.* Граа́ль *m.*

grain /grein/ *n.* зерно́ *neut.*; хлеб *m.*

grain dryer *adj.* зерносуши́лка.

grainy /'greini/ *adj.* зерни́стый; шерохова́тый.

gram /græm/ *n.* грамм *m.*

gramineous /grə'miniəs/ *adj.* травяни́стый.

graminivorous /,græmə'nivərəs/ *adj.* травоя́дный.

grammar /'græmər/ *n.* грамма́тика *f.*

grammarian /grə'mɛəriən/ *n.* граммати́ст, грамма́тик *m.*

grammatical /grə'mætikəl/ *adj.* граммати́ческий.

gramophone /'græmə,foun/ *n.* граммофо́н; про́игрыватель *m.*

grampus /'græmpəs/ *n.* дельфи́н-коса́тка *m.*

Granada /grə'nɑdə/ *n.* Грана́да *f.*

granary /'greinəri/ *n.* амба́р *m.*

grand /grænd/ *adj.* великоле́пный, грандио́зный

Grand Canyon *n.* Гранд-Каньо́н *m.*

granddaughter /'græn,dɔtər/ *n.* вну́чка *f.*

grandeur /'grændʒər/ *n.* великоле́пие; вели́чие *neut.*; грандио́зность *f.*

grandfather /'græn,fɑðər/ *n.* де́душка *f.* (*decl. f.*), дед *m.*

grandiloquence /græn'dɪləkwəns/ *n.* высокопа́рность *f.*

grandiloquent /græn'dɪləkwənt/ *adj.* высокопа́рный, напы́щенный.

grandiose /'grændi,ous/ *adj.* грандио́зный

grand master *n.* (*chess*) гроссме́йстер *m.*

grandmother /'græn,mʌðər/ *n.* ба́бушка *f.*

grandnephew /'græn,nɛfyu/ *n.* внуча́тый племя́нник *m.*

grandniece /'græn,nis/ *n.* внуча́тая племя́нница *f.*

grandparents /'grænd,pɛərənts/ *n.* де́душка с ба́бушкой *pl.*

grandson /'græn,sʌn/ *n.* внук *m.*

grandstand /'græn,stænd/ *n.* трибу́на *f.*

granduncle /'grænd,ʌŋkəl/ n. двою́родный де́душка m.

grange /greindʒ/ n. уса́дьба f.

granite /'grænɪt/ **1.** adj. грани́тный. **2.** n. грани́т m.

granny /'græni/ n. (colloq.) ба́бушка f.

grant /grænt/ **1.** n. дар m., субси́дия f. **2.** v. предоставля́ть impf.; дарова́ть impf. and pf.

granular /'grænyələr/ adj. зерни́стый.

granulate /'grænyə,leit/ v. грануи́ровать impf. and pf.

granulated sugar /'grænyə,leitɪd/ n. са́харный песо́к m.

granule /'grænyul/ n. зёрнышко neut.

grape /greip/ **1.** adj. виногра́дный. **2.** n. виногра́д m.

grapefruit /'greip,frut/ n. грейпфру́т m.

grapeshot /'greip,ʃɒt/ n. карте́чь f.

grapevine /'greip,vain/ n. виногра́дная лоза́ f.

graph /græf/ n. диагра́мма f., гра́фик m.

graphic /'græfɪk/ adj. графи́ческий; **graphic arts** гра́фика f.

graphite /'græfait/ n. графи́т m.

graphology /græ'fɒlədʒi/ n. графоло́гия f.

graphomania /,græfə'meiniə/ n. графома́ния f.

grapnel /'græpnl/ n. ко́шка f.

grapple /'græpəl/ v. (fight) схва́тываться (c with instr.) impf.

grappling iron /'græplɪŋ/ n. ко́шка f.

grasp /græsp/ **1.** n. хва́тка f.; (comprehension) понима́ние neut. **2.** v. схва́тывать impf., схвати́ть pf.; ула́вливать impf., улови́ть pf.

grasping /'græspɪŋ/ adj. (avaricious) жа́дный.

grass /græs/ **1.** n. трава́ f. **2.** adj. травяно́й.

grasshopper /'græs,hɒpər/ n. кузне́чик m.

grass roots n. широ́кие ма́ссы pl.

grass snake n. уж m.

grass widow n. соло́менная вдова́ f.

grassy /'græsi/ adj. травяно́й.

grate[1] /greit/ n. решётка f.

grate[2] /greit/ v.t. тере́ть impf.; v.i. скрежета́ть impf.

grateful /'greitfəl/ adj. благода́рный.

gratefulness /'greitfəlnɪs/ n. благода́рность f.

grater /'greitər/ n. тёрка f.

graticule /'græti,kyul/ n. (naut.) се́тка f.

gratification /,grætəfɪ'keiʃən/ n. удовлетворе́ние neut.

gratify /'grætə,fai/ v. удовлетворя́ть impf., удовлетвори́ть pf.

gratifying /'grætə,faiɪŋ/ adj. ле́стный.

grating[1] /'greitɪŋ/ n. решётка f.

grating[2] /'greitɪŋ/ n. скре́жет m.

gratis /'grætɪs/ adv. беспла́тно.

gratitude /'græti,tud/ n. благода́рность f.

gratuitous /grə'tuitəs/ adj. (free) даровой.

gratuity /grə'tuiti/ n. пода́рок m.; (tip) чаевы́е pl.

gravamen /grə'veimən/ n. суть f.

grave[1] /greiv/ adj. серьёзный.

grave[2] /greiv/ n. моги́ла f.

gravedigger /'greiv,dɪgər/ n. моги́льщик m.

gravel /'grævəl/ n. гра́вий m.

gravelly /'grævəli/ adj. гра́вийный.

gravel pit n. гра́вийный карье́р m.

graven /'greivən/ adj. вы́сеченный.

graveness /'greivnɪs/ n. серьёзность f.

gravestone /'greiv,stoun/ n. надгро́бный па́мятник or ка́мень m.

graveyard /'greiv,yɑrd/ n. кла́дбище neut.

gravid /'grævid/ adj. бере́менная.

gravimeter /grə'vɪmitər/ n. гравиме́тр m.

gravimetric /,grævə'mɛtrik/ adj. гравиметри́ческий.

graving dock /'greivɪŋ/ n. ремо́нтный док m.

gravitate /'grævɪ,teit/ v. тяготе́ть impf.

gravitation /,grævɪ'teiʃən/ n. тяготе́ние neut.

gravitational /,grævɪ'teiʃən| adj. гравитацио́нный.

gravity /'grævɪti/ n. серьёзность f.; (phys.) тя́жесть f.

gravure /grə'vyʊr/ n. гравю́ра f.

gravy /'greivi/ n. подли́вка f., со́ус m.

gray /grei/ **1.** adj. се́рый, (hair) седо́й. **2.** n. се́рый цвет; **to turn gray** v. седе́ть impf.

gray-haired /'grei ,hɛərd/ adj. седо́й.

grayish /'greiiʃ/ adj. серова́тый.

grayling /'greilɪŋ/ n. ха́риус m.

grayness /'greinɪs/ n. се́рость; седина́ f.

graze /greiz/ v. (pasture) пасти́сь impf.

grazing /'greizɪŋ/ n. (pasture) па́стбище neut.; (feeding) па́стьба f.

grease /n. gris; v. gris/ **1.** n. жир m.; са́ло neut., (lubricant) сма́зка f. **2.** v. сма́зывать impf., сма́зать pf.

greaser /'grisər/ n. сма́зчик m.

greasiness /'grisinis/ n. са́льность f.

greasy /'grisi/ adj. са́льный; жи́рный.

great /greit/ adj. вели́кий, большо́й, огро́мный.

great-aunt /'greit ,ænt, -,ɑnt/ n. двою́родная ба́бушка f.

Great Bear Lake n. Большо́е Медве́жье о́зеро

Great Britain n. Великобрита́ния f.

greater /'greitər/ adj. бо́льший.

greatest /'greitist/ adj. са́мый большо́й; са́мый вели́кий; велича́йший.

great-grandchild /,greit 'græn,tʃaild/ n. пра́внук m.

great-granddaughter /,greit 'græn,dɔtər/ n. пра́внучка f.

great-grandfather /,greit 'græn,fɑðər/ n. пра́дед m.

great-grandmother /,greit 'græn,mʌðər/ n. праба́бка f.

great-grandparent /,greit 'græn,pɛərənt/ n. прароди́тель m.

great-grandson /,greit 'græn,sʌn/ n. пра́внук m.

greathearted /'greit'hartɪd/ adj. великоду́шный.

greatly /'greitli/ adv. о́чень, весьма́.

greatness /'greitnɪs/ n. вели́чие neut.

greave /griv/ n. наголе́нник m.

grebe /grib/ n. пога́нка f.; **great crested grebe** чо́мга f.

Grecian /'griʃən/ adj. гре́ческий.

Greece /gris/ n. Гре́ция f.

greed /grid/ n. а́лчность, жа́дность f.

greediness /'gridinis/ n. а́лчность, жа́дность f.

greedy /'gridi/ adj. а́лчный, жа́дный.

Greek /grik/ **1.** adj. гре́ческий. **2.** n. грек m., греча́нка f.

green /grin/ **1.** adj. зелёный. **2.** n. зелёный цвет m.

greenery /'grinəri/ n. зе́лень f.

greenfinch /'grin,fintʃ/ n. зелену́шка f.

greengage /'grin,geidʒ/ *n.* сли́ва-венге́рка *f.*
greengrocer /'grin,grousər/ *n.* зеленщи́к *m.*
greenhorn /'grin,hɔrn/ *n.* новичо́к *m.*
greenhouse /'grin,haus/ *n.* тепли́ца *f.*
greenhouse effect *n.* парнико́вый эффе́кт *m.*
greenish /'griniʃ/ *adj.* зеленова́тый.
greenness /'grinnis/ *n.* зелёный цвет *m.; (fig.)* нео́пытность *f.*
greensand /'grin,sænd/ *n.* глауконитовый песо́к *m.*
greensickness /'grin,siknis/ *n.* хлоро́з *m.*
greenstick fracture /'grin,stik/ *n.* надло́м *m.*
Greenwich Time /'grenidʒ/ *n.* гри́нвичское вре́мя *neut.*
greet /grit/ *v.* приве́тствовать *impf.*
greeting /'gritiŋ/ *n.* приве́тствие *neut.; pl.* приве́т *m.*
gregarious /gri'gɛəriəs/ *adj.* общи́тельный.
Gregorian /gri'gɔriən/ *adj.* григориа́нский.
grenade /gri'neid/ *n.* грана́та *f.*
grenadier /,grɛnə'diər/ *n.* гренаде́р *m.*
grenadine /,grɛnə'din/ *n.* гренади́н *m.*
greyhound /'grei,haund/ *n.* грейха́унд *m.*
grid /grid/ *n.* решётка *f.; (lines on map)* се́тка *f.*
griddle /'gridl/ *n.* сковоро́дка *f.*
gridiron /'grid,aiərn/ *n.* ра́шпер *m.*
grief /grif/ *n.* го́ре *neut.*
grievance /'grivəns/ *n.* жа́лоба; оби́да *f.*
grieve /griv/ *v.* горева́ть; скорбе́ть *impf.*
grievous /'grivəs/ *adj.* го́рестный, печа́льный; *(serious)* тя́жкий.
griffin /'grifin/ *n.* грифо́н *m.*
griffon /'grifən/ *n. (dog)* грифо́н *m.*
grill /gril/ *v.* жа́рить *impf.,* изжа́рить *pf.; (colloq.) (interrogate)* допра́шивать *impf.*
grille /gril/ *n.* решётка *f.*
grilse /grils/ *n.* молодо́й лосо́сь *m.*
grim /grim/ *adj.* мра́чный; суро́вый.
grimace /'griməs/ **1.** *n.* грима́са *f.* **2.** *v.* грима́сничать *impf.*
grime /graim/ *n.* грязь *f.; (soot)* са́жа *f.*
grimness /'grimnis/ *n.* стро́гость *f.*
grimy /'graimi/ *adj.* гря́зный.
grin /grin/ **1.** *n.* усме́шка *f.* **2.** *v.* усмеха́ться *impf.,* усмехну́ться *pf.*
grind /graind/ *v.* моло́ть *impf.,* смоло́ть *pf.; (axe)* точи́ть *impf.,* наточи́ть *pf.*
grinder /'graindər/ *n.* точи́льщик *m.; (tool)* шлифова́льный стано́к *m.*
grindstone /'graind,stoun/ *n.* точи́ло *neut.*
grip /grip/ **1.** *n.* сжа́тие, схва́тывание *neut.* **2.** *v.* схва́тывать *impf.,* схвати́ть *pf.*
grippe /grip/ *n.* грипп *m.*
gripping /'gripiŋ/ *adj.* увлека́тельный.
grisaille /gri'zai/ *n.* гриза́ль *m.*
grisly /'grizli/ *adj.* стра́шный.
grist /grist/ *n.* зерно́ для помо́ла *neut.*
gristle /'grisəl/ *n.* хрящ *m.*
gritty /'griti/ *adj.* песча́ный.
grizzled /'grizəld/ *adj.* седо́й; *(partially grey)* с про́седью.
grizzly /'grizli/ *n.* (медве́дь-)гри́зли *m. indecl.*
groan /groun/ **1.** *n.* стон *m.* **2.** *v.* стона́ть *impf.*
groats /grouts/ *n.* крупа́ *f.*
grocer /'grousər/ *n.* бакале́йщик *m.*
groceries /'grousəriz/ *pl.* бакале́я *f.*

grocery /'grousəri/ *n.* бакале́йная ла́вка *f.*
grogginess /'grɒginis/ *n.* сла́бость в нога́х *f.*
groggy /'grɒgi/ *adj.* ша́ткий; **to feel groggy** *v.* чу́вствовать сла́бость *impf.*
program /'grɒgrəm/ *n.* фай *m.*
groin /grɔin/ *n.* пах *m.*
grommet /'grɒmit/ *n.* кольцо́ *neut.*
groom /grum/ **1.** *n.* грум *m.; (bridegroom)* жени́х *m.* **2.** *v.* чи́стить; хо́лить *impf.*
groove /gruv/ *n.* желобо́к *m.; (decl. f.)* наре́зка, вы́емка *f.*
grooved /gruvd/ *adj.* жело́бчатый.
grope /group/ *v.* идти́ о́щупью *impf.*
gross /grous/ **1.** *adj.* гру́бый; *(total)* валово́й; *(fat)* ту́чный; бру́тто. **2.** *n.* гросс *m.*
grossness /'grousnis/ *adj.* гру́бость; ту́чность
grotesque /grou'tɛsk/ *adj.* гроте́скный.
grotto /'grɒtou/ *n.* грот *m.*
grotty /'grɒti/ *adj. (slang)* парши́вый.
grouch /grautʃ/ *n.* брюзга́ *m. and f. (decl. f.).*
grouchy /'grautʃi/ *adj.* ворчли́вый.
ground¹ /graund/ *n.* земля́, по́чва *f.; (sports)* площа́дка *f.; pl.* основа́ние *neut.*
ground² /graund/ *adj.* мо́лотый.
ground floor *n.* пе́рвый эта́ж *m.*
grounding /'graundiŋ/ *n.* подгото́вка *f.; (elec.)* заземле́ние *neut.*
groundless /'graundlis/ *adj.* необосно́ванный.
ground rent *n.* земе́льная ре́нта *f.*
groundsel /'graundsəl/ *n.* кресто́вник *m.*
ground speed *n.* путева́я ско́рость *f.*
groundswell /'graund,swɛl/ *n.* мёртвая зыбь *f.*
ground-to-air missile /'graund tu 'ɛər/ *n.* (управля́емая) раке́та кла́сса земля́-во́здух *f.*
groundwork /'graund,wɜrk/ *n.* фунда́мент *m.*
group /grup/ **1.** *n.* гру́ппа *f.* **2.** *adj.* группово́й. **3.** *v.t.* группирова́ть *impf.,* сгруппирова́ть *pf.; v.i.* группирова́ться *impf.,* сгруппирова́ться *pf.*
grouping /'grupiŋ/ *n.* группиро́вка *f.*
grouse /graus/ *n. (bird)* те́терев *m.;* тетёрка *f.*
grouser /'grausər/ *n. (colloq.)* ворчу́н *m.*
grout /graut/ *n.* цеме́нтный раство́р *m.*
grove /grouv/ *n.* ро́ща *f.*
grovel /'grʌvəl/ *v.* пресмыка́ться, унижа́ться *(перед with instr.) impf.*
groveller /'grʌvlər/ *n.* подхали́м *m.*
grow /grou/ *v.i.* расти́ *impf.; (become)* станови́ться *impf.,* стать *pf.,* де́латься *impf.,* сде́латься *pf.; v.t.* выра́щивать *impf.*
grower /'grouər/ *n.* производи́тель *m.*
growl /graul/ **1.** *n.* рыча́ние *neut.* **2.** *v.* рыча́ть *impf.,* прорыча́ть *pf.*
grownup /'groun,ʌp/ *n.* взро́слый *m.*
growth /grouθ/ *n.* рост *m.,* увеличе́ние *neut.; (med.)* о́пухоль *f.*
groyne /grɔin/ *n.* волноре́з *m.*
grub /grʌb/ **1.** *n.* личи́нка *f.; (slang)* харчи́ *pl.* **2.** *v.* ры́ться, копа́ться *impf.*
grubby /'grʌbi/ *adj.* гря́зный.
grub screw *n.* потайно́й винт *m.*
grudge /grʌdʒ/ *n.* недово́льство *neut.;* **to bear a grudge** *(colloq.)* име́ть зуб (на *with acc.) impf.*
grudging /'grʌdʒiŋ/ *adj.* неохо́тный.
grudgingly /'grʌdʒiŋli/ *adv.* не́хотя; неохо́тно.
gruel /'gruəl/ *n.* похлёбка *f.*
grueling /'gruəliŋ/ *adj.* изнури́тельный.
gruesome /'grusəm/ *adj.* ужа́сный; жу́ткий.
gruff /grʌf/ *adj.* грубова́тый, ре́зкий.

grumble /'grʌmbəl/ v. ворча́ть impf.
grumbler /'grʌmblər/ n. ворчу́н m.
grumbling /'grʌmblɪŋ/ n. ворча́ние neut.
grumpy /'grʌmpi/ adj. сварли́вый, раздражи́-
тельный.
grunt /grʌnt/ **1.** v. хрю́кать impf., хрю́кнуть pf.
2. n. хрю́канье neut.
guano /'gwɑnou/ n. гуа́но neut. indecl.
guarantee /ˌgærən'ti/ **1.** n. гара́нтия f.,
поручи́тельство neut., зало́г m. **2.** v. гаранти́-
ровать impf. and pf.
guarantor /'gærən,tɔr/ n. поручи́тель, гара́нт m.
guard /gɑrd/ **1.** n. сто́рож; (unit) стра́жа, охра́на
f. **2.** v. охраня́ть; сторожи́ть impf.
guard duty n. карау́льная слу́жба f.
guarded /'gɑrdɪd/ adj. охраня́емый; (cautious)
осмотри́тельный.
guardhouse /'gɑrd,haus/ n. (military prison)
гауптва́хта f.
guardian /'gɑrdiən/ n. опеку́н m.
guardianship /'gɑrdiən,ʃɪp/ n. опе́ка f.
guardrail /'gɑrd,reil/ n. по́ручень m.
guardsman /'gɑrdzmən/ n. гварде́ец m.
Guatemala /ˌgwɑtə'mɑlə/ n. Гватема́ла f.
guava /'gwɑvə/ n. гуа́ва f.
gubernatorial /ˌgubərnə'tɔriəl/ adj. губерна́тор-
ский.
gudgeon /'gʌdʒən/ n. (fish) песка́рь m.
guerilla /gə'rɪlə/ **1.** n. партиза́н m. **2.** adj. парти-
за́нский.
Guernsey /'gɜrnzi/ n. гернзе́йская коро́ва f.
guess /gɛs/ **1.** n. дога́дка f. **2.** v. уга́дывать
impf., угада́ть pf
guesswork /'gɛs,wɜrk/ n. дога́дки pl.
guest /gɛst/ n. гость m.
guffaw /gʌ'fɔ/ v. гогота́ть, хохота́ть impf
guidance /'gaidns/ n. руково́дство neut.
guide /gaid/ **1.** n. гид; проводни́к; руководи́тель
m. **2.** v. вести́; руководи́ть impf.
guidebook /'gaid,buk/ n. путеводи́тель m.
guided missile /'gaidɪd/ n. управля́емая раке́та f.
guideline /'gaid,lain/ n. директи́ва f.
guidepost /'gaid,poust/ n. указа́тельный столб
m.
guiding principle /'gaidɪŋ/ n. руководя́щий
при́нцип m.
guild /gɪld/ n. (merchants') ги́льдия f.; (crafts-
men's) цех m.
guildhall /'gɪld,hɔl/ n. ра́туша f.
guile /gail/ n. хи́трость; кова́рство f.
guileful /'gailfəl/ adj. кова́рный.
guileless /'gailis/ adj. бесхи́тростный.
guillemot /'gɪlə,mɒt/ n. ка́йра f.
guillotine /'gɪlə,tin/ n. гильоти́на f.
guilt /gɪlt/ n. вино́вность neut.; вина́ f.
guiltless /'gɪltlɪs/ adj. неви́нный.
guiltlessness /'gɪltlɪsnɪs/ n. неви́нность f.
guilty /'gɪlti/ adj. винова́тый; вино́вный (в with
prep.).
guinea /'gɪni/ n. гине́я f.
guinea fowl n. цеса́рка f.
guinea pig n. морска́я сви́нка f.
guise /gaiz/ n. вид; о́блик m.
guitar /gɪ'tɑr/ n. гита́ра f.
guitarist /gɪ'tɑrɪst/ n. гитари́ст m.
gulag /'gulag/ n. гула́г neut.
gulch /gʌltʃ/ n. уще́лье neut.

gulf /gʌlf/ n. (geog.) зали́в m.; (chasm) про́пасть
f.
gull /gʌl/ n. ча́йка f.
gullet /'gʌlɪt/ n. пищево́д m., (throat) гло́тка f.
gullibility /ˌgʌlə'bɪlɪti/ n. легкове́рие neut.
gullible /'gʌləbəl/ adj. легкове́рный.
gully /'gʌli/ n. овра́г m.
gulp /gʌlp/ **1.** n. глото́к m. **2.** v. глота́ть impf.
gum[1] /gʌm/ n. ка́медь f.; (for chewing) жва́чка f.
gum[2] n. (anat.) десна́ f.
gumboil /'gʌm,bɔil/ n. флюс m.
gummy /'gʌmi/ adj. кле́йкий.
gumption /'gʌmpʃən/ n. (colloq.) нахо́дчивость f.
gumshield /'gʌm,ʃild/ n. назу́бник m.
gun /gʌn/ n. ружьё neut., револьве́р m.
gunboat /'gʌn,bout/ n. канонё́рская ло́дка f.
gun carriage n. лафе́т m.
guncotton /'gʌn,kɒtn/ n. пироксили́н m.
gun deck n. батаре́йная па́луба f.
gunfire /'gʌn,faiᵊr/ n. оруди́йный ого́нь m.
Gunite /'gʌnait/ n. торкре́т-бето́н m.
gunman /'gʌnmən/ n. вооружё́нный банди́т m.
gunmetal /'gʌn,mɛtl/ n. пу́шечная бро́нза f.
gunner /'gʌnər/ n. артиллери́ст m.
gunnery /'gʌnəri/ n. артиллери́йское де́ло neut.
gunpowder /'gʌn,paudər/ n. по́рох m.
gunrunning /'gʌn,rʌnɪŋ/ n. контраба́нда ору́жия
f.
gunship /'gʌn,ʃɪp/ n. (helicopter) вооружё́нный
вертолё́т m
gunshot /'gʌn,ʃɒt/ n. вы́стрел m.
gunsmith /'gʌn,smɪθ/ n. оружё́йный ма́стер m.
gunstock /'gʌn,stɒk/ n. ру́жейная ло́жа f.
gunwale /'gʌnl/ n. пла́ншир m.
gurgitation /ˌgɜrdʒɪ'teiʃən/ n. бу́льканье neut.
gurgle /'gɜrgəl/ **1.** n. бу́льканье neut. **2.** v. бу́ль-
кать impf.
gush /gʌʃ/ **1.** n. си́льный пото́к m. **2.** v. хлы́нуть
pf.
gusher /'gʌʃər/ n. нефтяно́й фонта́н m.
gushy /'gʌʃi/ adj. экспанси́вный.
gust /gʌst/ n. поры́в m.
gusto /'gʌstou/ n. энтузиа́зм; смак m.
gusty /'gʌsti/ adj. поры́вистый.
gut /gʌt/ n. кишка́ f.; (mus.) струна́ f.; pl. (colloq.) (courage) му́жество neut.
gutless /'gʌtlɪs/ adj. тря́пичный.
gutta-percha /'gʌtə'pɜrtʃə/ n. гуттапе́рча f.
gutter /'gʌtər/ n. (road) сто́чная кана́вка f.;
(roof) водосто́чный жё́лоб m.
guttersnipe /'gʌtər,snaip/ n. у́личный мальчи́ш-
ка m.
guttural /'gʌtərəl/ **1.** adj. горта́нный. **2.** n.
горта́нный звук m.
guy /gai/ n. (colloq.) па́рень m.
guys /gaiz/ n. (colloq.) ребя́та pl.
guzzle /'gʌzəl/ v. жа́дно глота́ть impf.
gymnasium /dʒɪm'neiziəm/ n. спортза́л m.
gymnast /'dʒɪmnæst/ n. гимна́ст m., гимна́стка
f.
gymnastic /dʒɪm'næstɪk/ adj. гимнасти́ческий.
gymnastics /dʒɪm'næstɪks/ n. гимна́стика f.
gynecological /ˌgainɪkə'lɒdʒɪkəl/ adj. гинеколо-
ги́ческий.
gynecologist /ˌgaini'kɒlədʒɪst/ n. гинеко́лог m.
gynecology /ˌgaini'kɒlədʒi/ n. гинеколо́гия f.

gypsum /'dʒɪpsəm/ *n.* гипс *m.*

gypsy /'dʒɪpsi/ **1.** *adj.* цыга́нский. **2.** *n.* цыга́н *m.*, цыга́нка *f.*

gyrate /'dʒaireit/ *v.* враща́ться *impf.*

gyration /dʒai'reiʃən/ *n.* враще́ние; коловра́тное движе́ние *neut.*

gyrator /'dʒaireitər/ *n.* гира́тор *m.*

gyratory /'dʒairə,tɔri/ *adj.* враща́тельный.

gyrocompass /'dʒairou,kʌmpəs/ *n.* гироко́мпас *m.*

gyromagnetic /,dʒairoumæg'netɪk/ *adj.* гиромагни́тный.

gyroscope /'dʒairə,skoup/ *n.* гироско́п *m.*

gyroscopic /,dʒairə'skɒpɪk/ *adj.* гироскопи́ческий.

gyrostatics /,dʒairə'stætɪks/ *n.* гироста́тика *f.*

H

ha /ha/ *interj.* (*indicating astonishment*) ба!, а!; агá!; ха!; (*various senses*) a!

Haarlem /'harləm/ *n.* Гáрлем *m.*

habeas corpus /'heibi'əs kɔrpəs/ *n.* хáбеас кóрпус *m.*

haberdasher /'hæbər,dæʃər/ *n.* галантерéйщик; торгóвец мужскóй одéждой *m.*

haberdashery /'hæbər,dæʃəri/ *n.* галантерéя *f.*

habit /'hæbɪt/ *n.* привы́чка *neut.*; (*monk's*) ря́са *f.*; обыкновéние *neut.*

habitable /'hæbɪtəbəl/ *adj.* обитáемый; (*house, etc.*) гóдный для жилья́.

habitat /'hæbɪ,tæt/ *n.* средá *f.*; (*area, place*) местообитáние *neut.*

habitation /,hæbɪ'teiʃən/ *n.* жили́ще, жильё *neut.*

habitual /hə'bɪtʃuəl/ *adj.* привы́чный; обы́чный.

habituate /hə'bɪtʃu,eit/ *v.* приучáться (к *with dat.*) *impf.*

habitué /hə'bɪtʃu,ei// *n.* завсегдáтай *m.*

habitus /'hæbɪtəs/ *n.* гáбитус *m.*

hachure /hæ'ʃʊr/ *n.* штрих *m.*

hacienda /,hasi'ɛndə/ *n.* гасиéнда *f.*

hack¹ /hæk/ *v.* руби́ть; дроби́ть *impf.*

hack² /hæk/ *n.* (*jade*) кля́ча *f.*; (*writer*) писáка *m.* and *f.* (*decl. f.*)

hacker /'hækər/ *n.* (*slang*) (*comput.*) хэ́кер *m.*

hacking cough /'hækɪŋ/ *n.* покáшливание *neut.*

hackney /'hækni/ *n.* наёмный экипáж *m.*

hackneyed /'hæknid/ *adj.* банáльный.

hacksaw /'hæk,sɔ/ *n.* ножóвка *f.*

hackwork /'hæk,wɜrk/ *n.* халтýра *f.*

haddock /'hædək/ *n.* пи́кша *f.*

hafnium /'hæfniəm/ *n.* гáфний *m.*

haft /hæft/ *n.* черенóк *m.*, рукоя́тка *f.*; (*axe*) топóрище *neut.*

hag /hæg/ *n.* каргá, вéдьма *f.*

haggard /'hægərd/ *adj.* измождённый.

haggle /'hægəl/ *v.* торговáться *impf.*

haggling /'hæglɪŋ/ *n.* торгóвля *f.*

hagiographer /,hægi'ɒgrəfər/ *n.* агиóграф *m.*

hagiographic /,hægiə'græfɪk/ *adj.* агиографи́ческий.

hagiography /,hægi'ɒgrəfi/ *n.* агиогрáфия *f.*; (*life of saint*) житиé *neut.*

hagiology /,hægi'ɒlədʒi/ *n.* жити́йная литератýра *f.*

Hague /heig/ *n.* **The,** Гаáга *f.*

ha-ha /'ha'ha/ *interj.* ха-ха!

hail¹ /heil/ **1.** *n.* град *m.* **2.** *v.* осыпáть *impf.*, осы́пать *pf.*; *v.i.* сы́паться грáдом *impf.*; **it is hailing** идёт град.

hail² /heil/ *v.* (*call*) оклика́ть *impf.*; (*greet*) привéтствовать *impf.*

hailstone /'heil,stoun/ *n.* грáдина *f.*

hailstorm /'heil,stɔrm/ *n.* грозá с грáдом *f.*

hair /hɛər/ *n.* вóлос *m.*; (*animal*) шерсть *f.*

hairband /'hɛər,bænd/ *n.* лéнта для волóс *f.*

hairbreadth /'hɛər,brɛdθ/ *adj.* тóнкий как вóлос.

hairbrush /'hɛər,brʌʃ/ *n.* щётка для волóс *f.*

hair curlers *n.* бигуди́ *pl.*

haircut /'hɛər,kʌt/ *n.* стри́жка *f.*

hairdo /'hɛər,du/ *n.* причёска *f.*

hairdresser /'hɛər,drɛsər/ *n.* парикмáхер *m.*

hairdressing /'hɛər,drɛsɪŋ/ *n.* парикмáхерское дéло *neut.*

hairiness /'hɛərinɪs/ *n.* волосáтость *f.*

hairless /'hɛərlɪs/ *adj.* безволóсый; (*bald*) лы́сый.

hairline /'hɛər,lain/ *n.* ли́ния волóс *f.*

hair net *n.* сéтка для волóс *f.*

hairpiece /'hɛər,pis/ *n.* шиньóн *m.*

hairpin /'hɛər,pɪn/ *n.* шпи́лька; закóлка *f.*

hair-raising /'hɛər ,reizɪŋ/ *adj.* ужасáющий.

hair remover *n.* срéдство для удалéния волóс *neut.*

hair shirt *n.* власяни́ца *f.*

hair splitter *n.* педáнт *m.*

hairsplitting /'hɛər,splɪtɪŋ/ *n.* казуи́стика *f.*

hair spray *n.* лак для волóс *m.*

hairspring /'hɛər,sprɪŋ/ *n.* волосóк *m.*

hair stroke *n.* засéчка *f.*

hair style *n.* причёска *f.*

hairy /'hɛəri/ *adj.* волосáтый.

Haiti /'heiti/ *n.* Гаи́ти *m.*

hajji /'hædʒi/ *n.* хаджи́ *m.*

hake /heik/ *n.* (*fish*) хек *m.*, мерлýза *f.*

halation /hei'leiʃən/ *n.* (*photog.*) орéол *m.*

halberd /'hælbərd/ *n.* алебáрда *f.*

halberdier /,hælbər'dɪər/ *n.* алебáрдщик *m.*

halcyon /'hælsiən/ *adj.* спокóйный, ти́хий.

hale /heil/ *adj.* крéпкий.

half /hæf/ **1.** *adj.* половúнный. **2.** *n.* половúна *f.*

half-and-half /'hæfən'hæf/ *adv.* пополáм.

halfback /'hæf,bæk/ *n.* полузащи́тник *m.*

half-baked /'hæf 'beikt/ *adj.* недопечённый; (*not thought out*) непродýманный.

half binding *n.* полукóжаный переплёт *m.*

half-breed /'hæf ,brid/ *n.* мети́с; гибри́д *m.*

half-cock /'hæf 'kɒk/ *n.* предохрани́тельный взвод *m.*

half-conscious /,hæf 'kɒnʃəs/ *adj.* в полусознáтельном состоя́нии.

half crown *n.* полукрóны *pl.*

half-dead /,hæf 'dɛd/ *adj.* полумёртвый.

half deck *n.* полупáлуба *f.*

half dollar *n.* полдóллара *pl.*

half-done /,hæf 'dʌn/ *adj.* недодéланный.

half-dozen /'hæf 'dʌzən/ *n.* полдю́жины *pl.*

half-finished /,hæf 'fɪnɪʃt/ *adj.* неокóнченный.

halfhearted /'hæf'hartɪd/ *adj.* нереши́тельный.

half-hour /'hæf 'auər/ *n.* полчасá *pl.*

halfhourly /'hæf'auərli/ *adv.* кáждые полчасá.

half-length /'hæf ,lɛŋkθ/ *adj.* до пóяса.

half-life /'hæf ,laif/ *n.* (*phys.*) перúод полураспáда *m.*

half-light /'hæf ,lait/ *n.* сýмерки *pl.*

half-mast /'hæf 'mæst/ *n.*: **at half-mast** *adj.* приспýщенный.

half-measure /'hæf ,mɛʒər/ *n.* полумéра *f.*

half-moon /'hæf 'mun/ *n.* полумéсяц *m.*

half nelson *n.* полунéльсон *m.*

half note *n.* половúнная нóта *f.*

half-pay /'hæf 'pei/ *n.* половúнный оклáд *m.*

halfpenny /'heipəni/ *n.* полупéнни *neut. indecl.*

half-pound /'hæf 'paund/ *n.* полфу́нта *m.*

half-price /'hæf 'prais/ *n.* полцены́ *pl.*

half sister *n.* сво́дная сестра́ *f.*

half-timbered /'hæf 'tɪmbərd/ *adj.* деревя́нно-кирпи́чный.

halftime /'hæf,taim/ *adj.* на полста́вки.

half title *n.* шмутцти́тул *m.*

half-tone /'hæf ,toun/ *n.* (*art*) полуто́н *m.*

half-track /'hæf ,træk/ *n.* (*vehicle*) полугу́сеничная маши́на *f.*

half-truth /'hæf ,truθ/ *n.* полупра́вда *f.*

halfway /'hæf'wei/ *adv.* на полпути́.

half-wit /'hælf ,wɪt/ *n.* слабоу́мный *m.*

half-witted /'hæf 'wɪtɪd/ *adj.* слабоу́мный; дура́цкий.

half-year /'hæf ,yɪər/ *n.* полго́да *pl.*

half-yearly /,hæf 'yɪərli/ *adj.* полугодово́й.

halibut /'hæləbət/ *n.* па́лтус *m.*

halide /'hælaid/ *n.* гало́ид *m.*

halite /'hælait/ *n.* гали́т *m.*

hall /hɔl/ *n.* зал *m.*; (*entrance hall*) холл *m.*; прихо́жая *f.*

hallelujah /,hælə'luyə/ *interj.* аллилу́йя.

hallmark /'hɔl,mɑrk/ *n.* проби́рное клеймо́ , про́ба *f.*; (*fig.*) печа́ть *f.*

hallo /hə'lou/ *v.* гро́мко крича́ть *impf.*

hallow /'hælou/ *v.* освяща́ть *impf.*

hallucinate /hə'lusə,neit/ *v.* галлюцини́ровать *impf.*

hallucination /hə,lusə'neiʃən/ *n.* галлюцина́ция *f.*

hallucinatory /hə'lusənə,tɔri/ *adj.* галлюцина́торный.

hallucinogen /hə'lusənədʒən/ *n.* галлюциноге́н *m.*

hallucinogenic /hə,lusənə'dʒɛnɪk/ *adj.* галлюциноге́нный.

hallucinosis /hə,lusə'nousɪs/ *n.* галлюцино́з *m.*

hallux /'hæləks/ *n.* большо́й па́лец ноги́ *m.*

hallway /'hɔl,wei/ *n.* пере́дняя *f.*, коридо́р *m.*

halo /'heilou/ *n.* орео́л *m.*

halogen /'hælədʒən/ *n.* галоге́н *m.*

haloid /'hælɔid/ *n.* гало́ид *m.*

halt /hɔlt/ **1.** *n.* остано́вка *f.*; (*cessation*) прекраще́ние *neut.* **2.** *v.i.* остана́вливаться *impf.*, останови́ться *pf.*; *v.t.* остана́вливать *impf.*, останови́ть *pf.* **3.** *interj.* стой!

halter /'hɔltər/ *n.* недоу́здок *m.*

halting /'hɔltɪŋ/ *adj.* (*stumbling*) спотыка́ющийся; (*hesitant*) нереши́тельный.

haltingly /'hɔltɪŋli/ *adv.* (*speech*) запина́ясь, с запи́нками.

halve /hæv/ *v.* дели́ть попола́м *impf.*

halyard /'hælyərd/ *n.* фал *m.*

ham /hæm/ *n.* ветчина́ *f.*

hamadryad /,hæmə'draiəd/ *n.* гамадри́л *m.*

Hamburg /'hæmbɜrg, 'hɑm-/ *n.* Га́мбург *m.*

hamburger /'hæm,bɜrgər/ *n.* га́мбургер; ру́бленый шни́цель *m.*

Hamitic /hæ'mɪtɪk/ *adj.* хами́тский.

hamlet /'hæmlɪt/ *n.* селе́ние *neut.*, дереву́шка *f.*

hammer /'hæmər/ **1.** *n.* молото́к; мо́лот *m.* **2.** *v.* забива́ть *impf.*

Hammerfest /'hɑmər,fɛst/ *n.* Ха́ммерфест *m.*

hammerhead /'hæmər,hɛd/ *n.* (*tech.*) голо́вка молотка́ *f.*; (*shark*) мо́лот-ры́ба *f.*

hammock /'hæmək/ *n.* гама́к *m.*

hamper /'hæmpər/ **1.** *n.* корзи́на *f.* **2.** *v.* меша́ть *impf.*

hamster /'hæmstər/ *n.* хомя́к *m.*

hamstring /'hæm,strɪŋ/ *n.* подколе́нное сухожи́лие *neut.*

hand /hænd/ **1.** *n.* рука́ *f.*; (*of clock*) стре́лка *f.* **2.** *v.* подава́ть *impf.*, пода́ть *pf.*

handbag /'hænd,bæg/ *n.* су́мка *f.*

handball /'hænd,bɔl/ *n.* гандбо́л; ручно́й мяч *m.*

handbill /'hænd,bɪl/ *n.* рекла́мный листо́к *m.*

handbook /'hænd,buk/ *n.* спра́вочник, указа́тель *m.*

hand brake *n.* ручно́й то́рмоз *m.*

handcart /'hænd,kɑrt/ *n.* теле́жка *f.*

handcuff /'hænd,kʌf/ **1.** *n.* нару́чник *m.* **2.** *v.* надева́ть нару́чники *impf.*

handful /'hændful/ *n.* горсть *f.*

hand grenade *n.* ручна́я грана́та *f.*

handgrip /'hænd,grɪp/ *n.* рукопожа́тие *neut.*

handicap /'hændi,kæp/ *n.* (*hindrance*) поме́ха *f.*; (*disadvantage*) недоста́ток *m.*

handicapped /'hændi,kæpt/ *adj.* с физи́ческими недоста́тками.

handicraft /'hændi,kræft/ *n.* ремесло́ *neut.*

handicraftsman /'hændi,kræftsmən/ *n.* реме́сленник *m.*

handily /'hændɪli/ *adv.* ло́вко.

handiwork /'hændi,wɜrk/ *n.* рукоде́лие *neut.*

handkerchief /'hæŋkərtʃɪf/ *n.* носово́й плато́к *m.*

handle /'hændl/ **1.** *n.* ру́чка, рукоя́ть *f.* **2.** *v.* (*touch*) тро́гать *impf.*; (*manage*) управля́ть (*with instr.*) *impf.*; (*treat*) обраща́ться (с *with str.*) *impf.*

handlebar /'hændl̩,bɑr/ *n.* (*usu. pl.*) руль (велосипе́да) *m.*

handler /'hændlər/ *n.* дрессиро́вщик *m.*

handling /'hændlɪŋ/ *n.* (*treatment*) обраще́ние *neut.*; (*approach to*) подхо́д (к *with dat.*) *m.*

handling charges *n.* пла́та за доста́вку гру́за *f.*

handmade /'hænd'meid/ *adj.* ручно́й рабо́ты.

handmaid /'hænd,meid/ *n.* служа́нка *f.*

hand mill *n.* ручна́я ме́льница *f.*

hand-operated /'hænd ,ɔpə,reitɪd/ *adj.* с ручны́м при́водом.

handout /'hænd,aut/ *n.* (*pamphlet*) листо́вка *f.*, листо́к *m.*

hand-picked /'hænd 'pɪkt/ *adj.* подо́бранный.

handrail /'hænd,reil/ *n.* по́ручень *m.*; пери́ла *pl.*

handsaw /'hænd,sɔ/ *n.* ручна́я пила́, ножо́вка *f.*

handshake /'hænd,ʃeik/ *n.* рукопожа́тие *neut.*

handsome /'hænsəm/ *adj.* краси́вый.

handspring /'hænd,sprɪŋ/ *n.* са́льто *neut. indecl.*

handstand /'hænd,stænd/ *n.* сто́йка на рука́х *f.*

hand-to-hand /'hænd tə 'hænd/ *adj.* рукопа́шный.

hand-to-hand combat *n.* рукопа́шный бой *m.*

handwheel /'hænd,wil/ *n.* махови́чок *m.*

handwork /'hænd,wɜrk/ *n.* ручна́я рабо́та *f.*

handwriting /'hænd,raitɪŋ/ *n.* по́черк *m.*

handy /'hændi/ *adj.* ло́вкий; (*convenient*) удо́бный.

handyman /'hændi,mæn/ *n.* ма́стер на все ру́ки *m.*

hang /hæŋ/ *v.t.* ве́шать *impf.*, пове́сить *pf.*; *v.i.* висе́ть *impf.*

hangar /'hæŋər/ *n.* анга́р *m.*

hangdog /'hæŋ,dɔg/ *adj.* (*sullen*) угрю́мый.

hanger /'hæŋər/ n. вешалка f.
hanger-on /'hæŋər 'ɒn/ n. прихлебатель m.
hang glider n. дельтаплан m.
hang-gliding /'hæŋ ˌglaidiŋ/ n. дельтапланеризм m.
hanging /'hæŋiŋ/ **1.** n. повешение neut. **2.** adj. висячий.
hangman /'hæŋmən/ n. палач m.
hangnail /'hæŋˌneil/ n. заусеница f.
hangover /'hæŋˌouvər/ n. (after drinking) похмелье neut.
hank /hæŋk/ n. (yarn) моток m.
hanker /'hæŋkər/ v. скучать; тосковать impf.
hankering /'hæŋkəriŋ/ n. жажда f.; сильное желание neut.
hanky-panky /'hæŋki'pæŋki/ n. (deceit) обман m.
Hanoi /hæ'nɔi/ n. Ханой m.
Hansa /'hænsə/ n. Ганза f., Ганзейский союз m.
Hanseatic /ˌhænsi'ætik/ adj. ганзейский.
hansom /'hænsəm/ n. кэб m.
haphazard /hæp'hæzərd/ adj. случайный.
hapless /'hæplis/ adj. несчастный, злополучный.
haplography /hæp'lɒɡrəfi/ n. гаплография f.
haplology /hæp'lɒlədʒi/ n. гаплология f.
happen /'hæpən/ v. случаться impf., случиться pf.; происходить impf., произойти pf.
happening /'hæpəniŋ/ n. событие neut.; (arts) хэппенинг m.
happily /'hæpəli/ adv. счастливо; (fortunately) к счастью.
happiness /'hæpinis/ n. счастье neut.
happy /'hæpi/ adj. счастливый, удачный.
Happy Birthday! с днём рождения!
happy-go-lucky /'hæpiɡou'lʌki/ adj. беспечный, беззаботный.
Happy New Year! с Новым Годом!
hara-kiri /'harə 'kiəri/ n. харакири neut. indecl.
harangue /hə'ræŋ/ n. (pompous speech) разглагольствование neut.
harass /hə'ræs, 'hærəs/ v. беспокоить; преследовать impf.
harassment /hə'ræsmənt, 'hærəsmənt/ n. беспокойство; преследование neut.
harbinger /'harbindʒər/ n. предвестник m.
harbor /'harbər/ **1.** n. гавань f. **2.** v. укрывать impf., укрыть pf.; приютить impf.
harbor master n. начальник порта m.
hard /hard/ **1.** adj. твёрдый; (difficult) трудный. **2.** adv. тяжело; сильно, упорно.
hard-and-fast /'hard n̩ 'fæst/ adj. жёсткий.
hard-bitten /'hard 'bitn̩/ adj. упорный.
hard-boiled egg /'hard ˌboild/ n. яйцо вкрутую neut.
hard-core /'hard'kɔr, -'kour/ adj. непримиримый, непреклонный.
hardcover /'hardˌkʌvər/ adj. в твёрдом переплёте.
hard currency n. валюта f.
hard-earned /'hard 'ɜrnd/ adj. с трудом заработанный.
harden /'hardn̩/ v.i. твердеть impf.; затвердевать impf.; v.t. (metal) закалять impf.
hardened /'hardnd/ adj. закалённый.
hardening /'hardniŋ/ n. закаливание neut.
hard-featured /'hard 'fitʃərd/ adj. с суровым лицом.
hard-fisted /'hard 'fistid/ adj. прижимистый.

hard-fought /'hard fɔt/ adj. ожесточённый.
hardheaded /'hard'hedid/ adj. практичный.
hardhearted /'hard'hartid/ adj. жестокосердный.
hardiness /'hardinis/ n. выносливость f.
hard-line /'hard ˌlain/ adj. бескомпромиссный.
hardly /'hardli/ adv. едва.
hardness /'hardnis/ n. твёрдость f.
hard-pressed /'hard 'prest/ adj. в трудном положении.
hardship /'hardʃip/ n. тяжёлое испытание neut.
hardtack /'hard,tæk/ n. галета f.
hardware /'hard,weər/ n. (metalware) скобяной товар m.
hardwood /'hard,wud/ n. твёрдая древесина f.
hardy /'hardi/ adj. выносливый, стойкий.
hare /heər/ n. заяц m.
harebell /'heər,bel/ n. колокольчик круглолистый m.
harebrained /'heər,breind/ adj. безрассудный.
harelip /'heər,lip/ n. заячья губа f.
harem /'heərəm/ n. гарем m.
haricot /'hærə,kou/ n. фасоль f.
hark /hark/ v. слушать impf.
harlequin /'harləkwin, -kin/ n. арлекин m.
harlequinade /ˌharləkwi'neid, -kɪ-/ n. арлекинада f.
harlot /'harlət/ n. проститутка f.
harm /harm/ **1.** n. вред; ущерб m. **2.** v. вредить impf., повредить pf.
harmful /'harmfəl/ adj. вредный.
harmless /'harmlis/ adj. безвредный.
harmonic /har'mɒnik/ **1.** adj. гармонический. **2.** n. обертон m.
harmonica /har'mɒnikə/ n. губная гармошка f.
harmonious /har'mouniəs/ adj. гармоничный; (amicable) дружный.
harmonist /'harmənist/ n. гармонист m.
harmonium /har'mouniəm/ n. фисгармония f.
harmonization /ˌharmənə'zeiʃən/ n. гармонизация f.
harmonize /'harmə,naiz/ v. гармонировать (с with instr.) impf.
harmony /'harməni/ n. гармония f.; согласие neut.
harness /'harnis/ **1.** n. сбруя, упряжь f. **2.** v. запрягать impf.; (fig.) использовать impf.
harp /harp/ n. арфа f.
harpist /'harpist/ n. арфист m., арфистка f.
harpoon /har'pun/ n. гарпун m.
harpooner /har'punər/ n. гарпунёр m.
harpsichord /'harpsi,kɔrd/ n. клавесин m.
harquebus /'harkwəbəs/ n. аркебуза f.
harridan /'haridn̩/ n. старая карга f.
harrier /'hæriər/ n. (dog) гончая f.; (bird) лунь f.
Harrisburg /'hæris,bɜrɡ/ n. Харрисберг m.
harrow /'hærou/ n. борона f.
harrowing /'hærouiŋ/ n. боронование neut.
harry /'hæri/ v. разорять impf.
harsh /harʃ/ adj. грубый; суровый.
harshness /'harʃnis/ n. резкость f.; суровость f.
hart /hart/ n. олень m.
harvest /'harvist/ **1.** n. (gathering) жатва f.; (yield) урожай m. **2.** v. собирать (урожай) impf.
harvester /'harvəstər/ n. (person) жнец m.; (machine) комбайн m.
harvesting /'harvəstiŋ/ n. уборка урожая f.

hash /hæʃ/ *n.* жа́реное ру́бленое мя́со *neut.*; (*fig.*) (*muddle*) пу́таница *f.*

hashish /'hæʃiʃ/ *n.* гаши́ш *m.*

hasp /hæsp/ *n.* застёжка *f.*; (*on door*) запо́р *m.*

hassle /'hæsəl/ **1.** *n.* (*colloq.*) перебра́нка *f.* **2.** *v.* надоеда́ть, пристава́ть *impf.*

hastate /'hæsteit/ *adj.* (*bot.*) стре́льчатый.

haste /heist/ *n.* поспе́шность, спе́шка *f.*

hasten /'heisən/ *v.t.* торопи́ть *impf.*; *v.i.* торопи́ться *impf.*; спеши́ть *impf.*, поспеши́ть *pf.*

hastily /'heistļi/ *adv.* поспе́шно, на́спех, второпя́х.

hasty /'heisti/ *adj.* поспе́шный.

hat /hæt/ **1.** *n.* шля́па; ша́пка *f.* **2.** *adj.* шля́пный.

hatbox /'hæt,bɒks/ *n.* коро́бка для шля́пы *f.*

hatch¹ /hætʃ/ *v.t.* выси́живать *impf.*; (*eggs*) наси́живать *impf.*

hatch² /hætʃ/ *also* **hatchway** *n.* (*naut.*) люк *m.*

hatch³ /hætʃ/ *v.* (*shade*) штрихова́ть *impf.*

hatchback /'hætʃ,bæk/ *n.* двухобъёмный ку́зов *m.*

hatchery /'hætʃəri/ *n.* инкуба́торная ста́нция *f.*

hatchet /'hætʃit/ *n.* топо́рик *m.*

hatching /'hætʃiŋ/ *n.* (*shading*) штрихо́вка *f.*; **cross hatching** штрихо́вка на́крест *f.*

hate /heit/ **1.** *n.* не́нависть *f.* **2.** *v.* ненави́деть *impf.*

hateful /'heitfəl/ *adj.* ненави́стный.

hater /'heitər/ *n.* ненави́стник *m.*

hatpin /'hæt,pin/ *n.* шпи́лька *f.*

hatrack /'hæt,ræk/ *n.* ве́шалка для шляп *f.*

hatred /'heitrid/ *n.* не́нависть *f.*

hatter /'hætər/ *n.* шля́пник *m.*

hauberk /'hɔbɜrk/ *n.* кольчу́га *f.*

haughtiness /'hɔtinis/ *n.* надме́нность *f.*

haughty /'hɔti/ *adj.* надме́нный.

haul /hɔl/ **1.** *v.* тяну́ть *impf.*, потяну́ть *pf.*; тащи́ть *det. impf.*; перевози́ть *impf.* **2.** *n.* перево́зка *f.*; добы́ча *f.*

haulage /'hɔlidʒ/ *n.* тя́га *f.*

haunch /hɔntʃ/ *n.* ля́жка *f.*

haunt /hɔnt/ *v.* пресле́довать *impf.*

haunted /'hɔntid/ *adj.* заколдо́ванный.

haunting /'hɔntiŋ/ *adj.* навя́зчивый.

hauteur /hou'tɜr/ *n.* высокоме́рие *neut.*

Havana /hə'vænə/ *n.* Гава́на *f.*

have /hæv; *unstressed* həv, əv/ *v.* име́ть *impf.*; *impers. constr.* быть у (*with gen.*): **I have** у меня́ (есть).

haven /'heivən/ *n.* га́вань *f.*; (*fig.*) убе́жище *neut.*

haversack /'hævər,sæk/ *n.* ра́нец *m.*

havoc /'hævək/ *n.* разо́р *m.*

haw /hɔ/ *n.* я́года боя́рышника *f.*

Hawaii /hə'waii/ *n.* Гава́йи *neut.*

hawfinch /'hɔ,fintʃ/ *n.* дубоно́с *m.*

hawk /hɔk/ *n.* я́стреб *m.*

hawker /'hɔkər/ *n.* у́личный торго́вец *m.*

hawk-eyed /'hɔk,aid/ *adj.* (*keen-sighted*) зо́ркий, острогла́зый.

hawking /'hɔkiŋ/ *n.* соколи́ная охо́та *f.*

hawk moth *n.* бра́жник *m.*

hawk-nosed /'hɔk ,nouzd/ *adj.* горбоно́сый.

hawkweed /'hɔk,wid/ *n.* ястреби́нка волоси́стая *f.*

hawse /hɔz/ *n.* (*hole*) клюз *m.*

hawsepipe /'hɔz,paip/ *n.* труба́ клю́за *f.*

hawser /'hɔzər/ *n.* (*naut.*) трос, шварто́в *m.*

hawthorn /'hɔ,θɔrn/ *n.* боя́рышник *m.*

hay /hei/ **1.** *n.* се́но *neut.* **2.** *adj.* сенно́й.

haycock /'hei,kɒk/ *n.* копна́ *f.*

hay dryer *n.* сеносуши́лка *f.*

hay fever *n.* сенна́я лихора́дка *f.*

hayfork /'hei,fɔrk/ *n.* ви́лы *pl.*

hayloft /'hei,lɔft/ *n.* сенова́л *m.*

haymaking /'hei,meikiŋ/ *n.* сеноко́с *m.*

hayseed /'hei,sid/ *n.* семена́ трав *pl.*

haystack /'hei,stæk/ *n.* стог се́на; скирд *m.*

haywire /'hei,waiᵊr/ *adj.* (*colloq.*) расстро́енный.

hazard /'hæzərd/ **1.** *n.* риск *m.*; опа́сность *f.* **2.** *v.* рискова́ть *impf.*, рискну́ть *pf.*

hazardous /'hæzərdəs/ *adj.* риско́ванный; опа́сный.

haze /heiz/ *n.* тума́н *m.*

hazel /'heizəl/ **1.** *adj.* све́тло-кори́чневый. **2.** *n.* (*tree*) оре́шник *m.*

hazelnut /'heizəl,nʌt/ *n.* лесно́й орех, обыкнове́нный орех *m.*

hazily /'heizəli/ *adv.* тума́нно; сму́тно.

haziness /'heizinis/ *n.* тума́нность *f.*

hazy /'heizi/ *adj.* тума́нный, сму́тный.

H.D.T.V. *n.* (*abbr. of* High Definition T.V.) телеви́дение высо́кой чёткости *neut.* (*abbr.* ТВЧ).

he /hi; *unstressed* i/ *pron.* он.

head /hɛd/ **1.** *n.* голова́ *f.*; (*leader*) глава́, вождь, руководи́тель *m.*; (*mind*) ум *m.* **2.** *v.t.* (*lead*) возглавля́ть *impf.*, возгла́вить *pf.* **3.** *adj.* головно́й; (*chief*) гла́вный.

headache /'hɛd,eik/ *n.* головна́я боль *f.*

headband /'hɛd,bænd/ *n.* головна́я повя́зка *f.*

headboard /'hɛd,bɔrd/ *n.* изголо́вье (крова́ти) *neut.*

head cold *n.* на́сморк *m.*

headdress /'hɛd,drɛs/ *n.* головно́й убо́р *m.*

header /'hɛdər/ *n.* (*athl.*) уда́р голово́й *m.*

headfirst /'hɛd'fɜrst/ *adv.* голово́й вперёд.

headgear /'hɛd,giᵊr/ *n.* головно́й убо́р *m.*

heading /'hɛdiŋ/ *n.* ру́брика *f.*

headland /'hɛdlənd/ *n.* мыс *m.*

headless /'hɛdlis/ *adj.* безголо́вый.

headlight /'hɛd,lait/ *n.* фа́ра *f.*

headline /'hɛd,lain/ *n.* заголо́вок *m.*

headlong /'hɛd,lɔŋ/ *adv.* стремгла́в; о́прометью.

headmaster /'hɛd'mæstər/ *n.* дире́ктор шко́лы *m.*

headmistress /'hɛd'mistris/ *n.* директри́са шко́лы *f.*

head-on /'hɛd'ɒn/ *adj.* фронта́льный, лобово́й.

headphone /'hɛd,foun/ *n.* нау́шник *m.*

headquarters /'hɛd,kwɔrtərz/ *n.* штаб-кварти́ра *f.*; гла́вное управле́ние *neut.*

headrace /'hɛd,reis/ *n.* водово́д *m.*

headrest /'hɛd,rɛst/ *n.* подголо́вник *m.*

headscarf /'hɛd,skɑrf/ *n.* косы́нка *f.*

headstall /'hɛd,stɔl/ *adj.* недоу́здок *m.*

headstone /'hɛd,stoun/ *n.* (*tombstone*) надгро́бный ка́мень *m.*

headstrong /'hɛd,strɔŋ/ *adj.* своево́льный.

headwaters /'hɛd,wɔtərz/ *n.* верхо́вье *neut.*

headway /'hɛd,wei/ *n.* продвиже́ние вперёд *neut.*

headwind /'hɛd,wind/ *n.* встре́чный ве́тер *m.*

heady /'hɛdi/ *adj.* пъяня́щий; горя́чий, опроме́тчивый.

heal /hil/ *v.i.* зажива́ть *impf.*, зажи́ть *pf.*; *v.t.* изле́чивать *impf.*, излечи́ть *pf.*

healer /'hilər/ n. исцели́тель m.
healing /'hilɪŋ/ **1.** n. лече́ние neut. **2.** adj. целе́бный.
health /hɛlθ/ n. здоро́вье neut.
healthful /'hɛlθfəl/ adj. целе́бный.
health resort n. куро́рт m.
healthy /'hɛlθi/ adj. здоро́вый; поле́зный.
heap /hip/ **1.** n. гру́да, ку́ча f. **2.** v. нагроможда́ть impf.
hear /hɪər/ v. слы́шать impf.; (listen to) слу́шать impf.; **to hear out** выслу́шивать impf.
hearing /'hɪərɪŋ/ n. (sense) слух m.; (leg.) слу́шание neut.
hearing aid n. слуховой аппара́т m.
hearsay /'hɪərˌsei/ n. слу́хи pl.
hearse /hɜrs/ n. похоро́нные дро́ги pl.; катафа́лк m.
heart /hɑrt/ **1.** n. се́рдце neut.; (center) центр m. (essence) суть f.; **by heart** наизу́сть. **2.** adj. серде́чный.
heart attack n. серде́чный припа́док; инфа́ркт m.
heartbeat /'hɑrtˌbit/ n. сердцебие́ние neut.
heartbreak /'hɑrtˌbreik/ n. го́ре neut.
heartbreaking /'hɑrtˌbreikɪŋ/ adj. душераздира́ющий.
heartbroken /'hɑrtˌbroukən/ adj. уби́тый го́рем.
heartburn /'hɑrtˌbɜrn/ n. изжо́га f.
hearten /'hɑrtn/ v. ободря́ть, поощря́ть impf.
heartfelt /'hɑrtˌfɛlt/ adj. и́скренний, серде́чный
hearth /hɑrθ/ n. оча́г m.
heartily /'hɑrtļi/ adv. и́скренне, серде́чно, от всего́ се́рдца.
heartless /'hɑrtlɪs/ adj. бессерде́чный.
heartlessness /'hɑrtlɪsnɪs/ n. бессерде́чие neut.
heartrending /'hɑrtˌrɛndɪŋ/ adj. душераздира́ющий.
heart-shaped /'hɑrt ˌʃeipt/ adj. сердцеви́дный.
heartstrings /'hɑrtˌstrɪŋz/ n. серде́чные стру́ны pl.
heart-to-heart /'hɑrt tə ˌhɑrt/ adj. задуше́вный.
heartwarming /'hɑrtˌwɔrmɪŋ/ adj. душе́вный.
heartwood /'hɑrtˌwʊd/ adj. ядро́вая древеси́на.
hearty /'hɑrti/ adj. кре́пкий, здоро́вый; (meal) оби́льный.
heat /hit/ **1.** n. жара́ f.; жар m.; (phys.) теплота́ f.; (track) забе́г m.; (swimming) заплы́в m. **2.** v. нагрева́ть(ся) impf., нагре́ть(ся) pf.; (provide heat) топи́ть impf.
heat-absorbing /'hit əbˌzɔrbɪŋ/ adj. теплопогло-ща́ющий.
heat-conducting /'hit kənˌdʌktɪŋ/ adj. теплопрово́дный.
heated /'hitɪd/ adj. (warm) нагре́тый; (strong) горя́чий; разгорячённый.
heatedly /'hitɪdli/ adv. горячо́.
heat engine n. теплово́й дви́гатель m.
heater /'hitər/ m. нагрева́тельный прибо́р m.
heath /hiθ/ n. пу́стошь f.
heathen /'hiðən/ **1.** n. язы́чник m. **2.** adj. язы́ческий.
heathenish /'hiðənɪʃ/ adj. язы́ческий.
heather /'hɛðər/ n. ве́реск m.
heathery /'hɛðəri/ adj. вереско́вый.
heath grass adj. трёхзу́бка f.
heating /'hitɪŋ/ n. нагрева́ние neut.; (house) отопле́ние neut.

heatproof /'hitˌpruf/ adj. жароусто́йчивый.
heat rash n. потни́ца f.
heat-resistant /'hit rəˌzɪstənt/ adj. теплосто́йкий.
heat-sensitive /'hit ˌsɛnsɪtɪv/ adj. теплочувстви́тельный.
heatstroke /'hitˌstrouk/ n. теплово́й уда́р m.
heat-treated /'hit ˌtritɪd/ adj. терми́чески обрабо́танный.
heave /hiv/ **1.** n. бросо́к m. **2.** v. (lift) поднима́ть impf.; (throw) броса́ть impf., бро́сить pf.
heaven /'hɛvən/ n. не́бо neut.; рай m.
heavenly /'hɛvənli/ adj. небе́сный; боже́ственный.
heaven-sent /'hɛvən ˌsɛnt/ adj. ниспо́сланный Бо́гом; **heaven-sent opportunity** n. блестя́щая возмо́жность f.
heavenwards /'hɛvənwərdz/ adv. ввысь, в не́бо.
heaver /'hivər/ n. гру́зчик m.
heavily /'hɛvəli/ adv. тяжело́; тя́жко.
heaviness /'hɛvɪnɪs/ n. тя́жесть f.
heaving /'hivɪŋ/ n. подъём m.
Heaviside layer /'hɛviˌsaid/ n. слой Хевиса́йда m.
heavy /'hɛvi/ adj. тяжёлый; тру́дный; (strong) си́льный.
heavy-duty /'hɛvi ˈduti/ adj. мо́щный.
heavy-handed /'hɛvi 'hændɪd/ adj. (clumsy) неуклю́жий.
heavy-hearted /'hɛvi 'hɑrtɪd/ adj. с тяжёлым се́рдцем.
heavy-laden /'hɛvi 'leidŋ/ adj. перегру́женный.
heavy metallist /'mɛtļɪst/ n. (music performer or fan) металли́ст m.
heavy metal rock n. (music) металли́ческий рок m.
heavyweight /'hɛviˌweit/ adj. тяжелове́сный.
hebdomadal /hɛb'dɒmədļ/ adj. еженеде́льный.
hebetude /'hɛbɪˌtud/ n. тупоу́мие neut.
Hebraism /'hibreiˌizəm/ n. гебраи́зм m.
Hebraist /'hibreiist/ n. гебраи́ст m.
Hebrew /'hibru/ **1.** adj. (древне)евре́йский. **2.** n. евре́й m., евре́йка f.; (language) иври́т m.
Hebrides /'hɛbrɪˌdiz/ n. Гебри́дские острова́ pl.
hecatomb /'hɛkəˌtoum/ n. ма́ссовое уби́йство neut.
heckle /'hɛkəl/ v. прерыва́ть вы́криками impf.
hectare /'hɛktɛər/ n. гекта́р m.
hectic /'hɛktɪk/ adj. лихора́дочный.
hectogram /'hɛktəˌgræm/ n. гектогра́мм m.
hectograph /'hɛktəˌgræf/ n. гекто́граф m.
hectoliter /'hɛktəˌlitər/ n. гектоли́тр m.
hectometer /'hɛktəˌmitər/ n. гекто́метр m.
hedge /hɛdʒ/ n. (живая) и́згородь f.; (barrier) прегра́да f.
hedgehog /'hɛdʒˌhɒg/ n. ёж m.
hedgehop /'hɛdʒˌhɒp/ v. лета́ть на бре́ющем полёте impf.
hedgehopping /'hɛdʒˌhɒpɪŋ/ adj. бре́ющий полёт.
hedonism /'hidnˌɪzəm/ n. гедони́зм m.
hedonist /'hidnɪst/ adj. гедони́ст m.
hedonistic /ˌhidnˈɪstɪk/ adj. гедонисти́ческий.
heed /hid/ **1.** n. внима́ние neut. **2.** v. обраща́ть внима́ние (на with acc.) impf.
heedful /'hidfəl/ adj. внима́тельный.
heedless /'hidlɪs/ adj. невнима́тельный, неосторо́жный.

heedlessly /'hidlɪsli/ *adv.* неосторо́жно; небре́жно.

heehaw /'hi,hɔ/ *n.* крик осла́ *m.*

heel[1] /hil/ *n.* (*of foot*) пята́; пя́тка *f.*; (*shoe*) каблу́к *m.*

heel[2] /hil/ *n.* (*of ship*) крен *m.*

hefty /'hɛfti/ *adj.* дю́жий; изря́дный.

Hegelian /hei'geiliən/ *adj.* гегелья́нский.

hegemony /hɪ'dʒɛməni/ *n.* гегемо́ния *f.*

Heidelberg /'haidl̩,bɜrg/ *Ger.* 'haidl̩,bɛrk/ *n.* Ге́йдельберг *m.*

heifer /'hɛfər/ *n.* тёлка *f.*

height /hait/ *n.* высота́ *f.*, рост *m.*

heighten /'haitn̩/ *v.* повыша́ть *impf.*, повы́сить *pf.*; уси́ливать *impf.*, уси́лить *pf.*

heinous /'heinəs/ *adj.* отврати́тельный.

heir /ɛər/ *n.* насле́дник *m.*

heiress /'ɛərɪs/ *n.* насле́дница *f.*

heirloom /'ɛər,lum/ *n.* фами́льная вещь *f.*

helical /'hɛlɪkəl/ *n.* винтово́й *m.*

helicoid /'hɛlɪ,kɔid/ *n.* гелико́ид *m.*

helicopter /'hɛlɪ,kɒptər/ *n.* вертолёт *m.*

heliocentric /,hiliou'sɛntrɪk/ *adj.* гелиоцентри́ческий.

heliograph /'hiliə,græf/ *n.* гелио́граф *m.*

heliography /,hili'ɒgrəfi/ *n.* гелиогра́фия *f.*

heliogravure /,hiliougrə'vyʊr/ *n.* гелиогравю́ра *f.*

heliophilous /,hili'ɒfələs/ *adj.* светолюби́вый.

heliophobic /,hiliə'foubɪk/ *adj.* светочувстви́тельный.

helioscope /'hiliə,skoup/ *n.* гелиоско́п *m.*

heliostat /'hiliə,stæt/ *n.* гелиоста́т *m.*

heliotherapy /,hiliou'θɛrəpi/ *n.* гелиотерапи́я *f.*

heliotrope /'hiliə,troup/ *n.* (*bot.*) гелиотро́п *m.*

heliotropism /,hili'ɒtrə,pɪzəm/ *n.* гелиотропи́зм *m.*

heliport /'hɛlə,pɔrt/ *n.* аэродро́м для вертолётов *m.*

helium /'hiliəm/ *n.* ге́лий *m.*

helix /'hilɪks/ *n.* спира́ль *f.*; (*anat.*) завито́к ушно́й ра́ковины *m.*

hell /hɛl/ *n.* ад *m.*

hellbent /'hɛl,bɛnt/ *adv.* во весь опо́р, как бе́шеный.

Hellenic /hɛ'lɛnɪk/ *adj.* э́ллинский, гре́ческий.

Hellenism /'hɛlə,nɪzəm/ *n.* эллини́зм *m.*

Hellenist /'hɛlənɪst/ *n.* эллини́ст *m.*

Hellenistic /,hɛlə'nɪstɪk/ *adj.* эллинисти́ческий.

hellish /'hɛlɪʃ/ *adj.* а́дский; дья́вольский.

hello /hɛ'lou, hə-, 'hɛlou/ *interj.* алло́!; (*good day*) здра́вствуйте.

helm /hɛlm/ *n.* руль *m.*

helmet /'hɛlmɪt/ *n.* ка́ска *f.*; шлем *m.*

helmeted /'hɛlmɪtɪd/ *adj.* в шле́ме.

helminth /'hɛlmɪnθ/ *n.* гли́ст *m.*

helminthology /,hɛlmɪn'θɒlədʒi/ *n.* гельминтоло́гия *f.*

helmsman /'hɛlmzmən/ *n.* рулево́й *m.*

helot /'hɛlət/ *n.* ило́т *m.*

help /hɛlp/ **1.** *n.* по́мощь *f.* **2.** *interj.* на по́мощь! **3.** *v.* помога́ть *impf.*, помо́чь *pf.*

helper /'hɛlpər/ *n.* помо́щник *m.*, помо́щница *f.*

helpful /'hɛlpfəl/ *adj.* поле́зный.

helpfully /'hɛlpfəli/ *adv.* услу́жливо.

helpfulness /'hɛlpfəlnɪs/ *n.* поле́зность *f.*

helping /'hɛlpɪŋ/ *n.* (*of food*) по́рция *f.*

helpless /'hɛlplɪs/ *adj.* беспо́мощный; бесси́льный.

helplessly /'hɛlplɪsli/ *adv.* беспо́мощно.

helplessness /'hɛlplɪsnɪs/ *n.* бесси́лие *neut.*, беспо́мощность *f.*

Helsingør /,hɛlsɪŋ'œr/ *n.* Хельсингёр *m.*

Helsinki /'hɛlsɪŋki/ *n.* Хе́льсинки *m.*

helter-skelter /'hɛltər 'skɛltər/ *adj.* как попа́ло.

helve /hɛlv/ *n.* рукоя́ть *f.*

hem /hɛm/ *n.* рубе́ц *m.*, кайма́ *f.*

hemal /'himəl/ *adj.* кровяно́й.

he-man /'hi ,mæn/ *n.* (*colloq.*) настоя́щий мужчи́на *m.*

hematic /hɪ'mætɪk/ *adj.* кровено́сный.

hematin /'himətɪn/ *n.* гемати́н *m.*

hematite /'himə,tait/ *n.* гемати́т *m.*

hematology /,himə'tɒlədʒi/ *n.* гематоло́гия *f.*

hemiplegia /,hɛmɪ'plidʒiə/ *n.* гемиплеги́я *f.*

hemisphere /'hɛmɪ,sfɪər/ *n.* полуша́рие *neut.*

hemispherical /,hɛmɪ'sfɛrɪkəl/ *adj.* полуша́рный.

hemistich /'hɛmɪ,stɪk/ *n.* полусти́шие *neut.*

hemline /'hɛm,lain/ *n.* подо́л *m.*

hemlock /'hɛm,lɒk/ *n.* болиголо́в кра́пчатый *m.*

hemoglobin /'himə,gloubɪn/ *n.* гемоглоби́н *m.*

hemophilia /,himə'fɪliə/ *n.* гемофили́я, кровоточи́вость *f.*

hemophiliac /,himə'fɪli,æk/ *n.* страда́ющий кровоточи́востью; гемофилик *m.*

hemorrhage /'hɛmərɪdʒ/ *n.* кровоизлия́ние; кровоте́чение *neut.*

hemorrhoid /'hɛmə,rɔid/ *n. usu. pl.* геморро́й *m.*

hemostatic /,himə'stætɪk/ *adj.* гемостати́ческий.

hemp /hɛmp/ *n.* (*plant*) конопля́ *f.*; (*fiber*) пенька́ *f.*

hempen /'hɛmpən/ *adj.* конопля́ный; пеньковый.

hen /hɛn/ *n.* ку́рица *f.*

henbane /'hɛn,bein/ *n.* белена́ *f.*

hence /hɛns/ *adv.* сле́довательно; с э́тих пор.

henceforth /'hɛns'fɔrθ/ *adv.* отны́не.

henchman /'hɛntʃmən/ *n.* приспе́шник *m.*

hendecagon /hɛn'dɛkə,gɒn/ *n.* одиннадцатиуго́льник *m.*

hendecasyllable /hɛn'dɛkə,sɪləbəl/ *n.* одиннадцатисло́жник *m.*

henhouse /'hɛn,haus/ *n.* куря́тник *m.*

henna /'hɛnə/ *n.* хна *f.*

hen party *n.* деви́чник *m.*

henpecked /'hɛn,pɛkt/ *adj.*: **be henpecked** быть у жены́ под каблуко́м.

henry /'hɛnri/ *n.* (*elec.*) ге́нри *neut.*

hepatic /hɪ'pætɪk/ *adj.* печёночный.

hepatitis /,hɛpə'taitɪs/ *n.* гепати́т *m.*

heptad /'hɛptæd/ *n.* семёрка *f.*

heptagon /'hɛptə,gɒn/ *n.* семиуго́льник *m.*

heptagonal /hɛp'tægənl/ *adj.* семиуго́льный.

heptahedral /'hɛptə,hidrəl/ *adj.* семигра́нный.

heptahedron /,hɛptə'hidrən/ *n.* семигра́нник *m.*

heptane /'hɛptein/ *n.* гепта́н *m.*

her /hɜr; *unstressed* hər, ər/ **1.** *pron.* её, ей. **2.** *adj.* её; свой.

herald /'hɛrəld/ *n.* (*hist.*) геро́льд; ве́стник *m.*

heraldic /hɛ'rældɪk/ *adj.* геральди́ческий.

heraldry /'hɛrəldri/ *n.* гера́льдика *f.*

herb /ɜrb/ *n.* трава́ *f.*

herbaceous /hɜr'beiʃəs/ *adj.* травяни́стый.

herbal /'ɜrbəl/ **1.** *n.* (*herb book*) тра́вник *m.* **2.** *adj.* травяно́й.

herbarium /hɜr'bɛəriəm/ *n.* герба́рий *m.*

herbicide /'hɜrbə,said/ *n.* гербици́д *m.*

herbivore /'hɜrbə,vɔr, -,vour/ *n.* травоя́дное живо́тное *neut.*

herbivorous /hɜr'bɪvərəs/ *adj.* травоя́дный.

Hercules /'hɜrkyə/liz/ *n.* Геркуле́с *m.*

herd /hɜrd/ **1.** *n.* ста́до *neut.* **2.** *v.i.* ходи́ть ста́дом *impf.*

herdsman /'hɜrdzmən/ *n.* пасту́х *m.*

here /hɪər/ *adv.* (*dir.*) сюда́; (*loc.*) здесь, тут; **here and there** там и сям.

hereabout /'hɪərə,baut/ *adv.* ря́дом.

hereafter /hɪər'æftər/ *adv.* в бу́дущем.

hereat /hɪər'æt/ *adv.* при э́том.

hereby /hɪər'bai/ *adv.* э́тим.

hereditament /,hɛrɪ'dɪtəmənt/ *n.* (*leg.*) насле́дуемое иму́щество *neut.*

hereditary /hə'rɛdɪ,tɛri/ *adj.* насле́дственный.

heredity /hə'rɛdɪti/ *n.* насле́дственность *f.*

herein /hɪər'ɪn/ *adv.* в э́том; при сём.

hereinafter /,hɪərɪn'æftər/ *adv.* в дальне́йшем, ни́же.

hereinbefore /,hɪərɪnbɪ'fɔr/ *adv.* (*obs.*) вы́ше.

heresiarch /hə'rizi,ɑrk/ *n.* ересиа́рх *m.*

heresy /'hɛrəsi/ *n.* е́ресь *f.*

heretic /'hɛrɪtɪk/ *n.* ерети́к *m.*

heretical /hə'rɛtɪkəl/ *adj.* ерети́ческий.

hereto /hɪər'tu/ *adv.* к э́тому.

heretofore /,hɪərtə'fɔr/ *adv.* до э́того.

hereunder /hɪər'ʌndər/ *adv.* ни́же.

hereupon /,hɪərə'pɒn/ *adv.* в отноше́нии э́того; на э́том.

herewith /hɪər'wɪθ/ *adv.* при э́том.

heritable /'hɛrɪtəbəl/ *adj.* насле́дуемый.

heritage /'hɛrɪtɪdʒ/ *n.* насле́дство, насле́дие *neut.*

hermaphrodite /hɜr'mætrə,dait/ *n.* гермафроди́т *m.*

hermaphroditism /hɜr'mæfrədai,tɪzəm/ *n.* гермафродити́зм *m.*

hermeneutic /,hɜrmə'nutɪk/ *adj.* герменевти́ческий.

hermeneutics /,hɜrmə'nutɪks/ *n.* герменевти́ка *f.*

hermetic /hɜr'mɛtɪk/ *adj.* гермети́ческий.

hermetically /hɜr'mɛtɪkli/ *adv.* гермети́чески.

hermit /'hɜrmɪt/ *n.* отше́льник *m.*

hermitage /'hɜrmɪtɪdʒ/ *n.* прию́т отше́льника *m.*

☞ **hernia** /'hɜrniə/ *n.* гры́жа *f.*

hernial /'hɜrniəl/ *adj.* грыжево́й.

hero /'hɪərou/ *n.* геро́й *m.*

Herod /'hɛrəd/ *n.* и́род *m.*

heroic /hɪ'rouɪk/ *adj.* геро́йческий.

heroics /hɪ'rouɪks/ *n.* высокопа́рные слова́ *pl.*

heroin /'hɛrouɪn/ *n.* герои́н *m.*

heroine /'hɛrouɪn/ *n.* герои́ня *f.*

heroism /'hɛrou,ɪzəm/ *n.* герои́зм *m.*

heron /'hɛrən/ *n.* ца́пля *f.*

heronry /'hɛrənri/ *n.* гнездо́вье ца́пель *neut.*

hero worship *n.* культ ли́чности *m.*

herpes /'hɜrpiz/ *n.* ге́рпес *m.*

herpetologist /,hɜrpɪ'tɒlədʒɪst/ *n.* герпето́лог *m.*

herpetology /,hɜrpɪ'tɒlədʒi/ *n.* герпетоло́гия *f.*

herring /'hɛrɪŋ/ *n.* сельдь *f.*

hers /hɜrz/ *pron.* её.

herself /hər'sɛlf/ *pron.* сама́; **she herself** она́ сама́.

Herzegovina /,hɛrtsəgou'vinə/ *n.* Герцегови́на *f.*

hesitant /'hɛzɪtənt/ *adj.* коле́блющийся; сомнева́ющийся.

hesitate /'hɛzɪ,teit/ *v.* колеба́ться *impf.*, поколеба́ться *pf.*

hesitatingly /'hɛzɪ,teitɪŋli/ *adv.* коле́блясь.

hesitation /,hɛzɪ'teiʃən/ *n.* колеба́ние *neut.*, нереши́тельность *f.*

hessite /'hɛsait/ *n.* гесси́т *m.*

heteroclite /'hɛtərə,klait/ *adj.* (*gram.*) разносклоня́емый.

heterodox /'hɛtərə,dɒks/ *adj.* не ортодокса́льный.

heterodoxy /'hɛtərə,dɒksi/ *n.* не ортодокса́льность *f.*

heterogamous /,hɛtə'rɒgəməs/ *adj.* гетерога́мный.

heterogamy /,hɛtə'rɒgəmi/ *n.* гетерога́мия *f.*

heterogeneity /,hɛtəroudʒə'niiti/ *n.* разноро́дность; гетероге́нность *f.*

heterogeneous /,hɛtərə'dʒiniəs/ *adj.* разноро́дный; (*chem.*) гетероге́нный.

heterogenesis /,hɛtərə'dʒɛnəsɪs/ *n.* гетерогене́з(ис) *m.*

heteromorphic /,hɛtərə'mɔrfɪk/ *adj.* гетероморфи́ческий.

heteromorphous /,hɛtərə'mɔrfəs/ *adj.* гетероморфный.

heteronym /'hɛtərənɪm/ *n.* омо́граф *m.*

heterosexuality /,hɛtərə,sɛkʃu'ælɪti/ *n.* гетеросексуа́льность *f.*

heterotypical /,hɛtərə'tɪpɪkəl/ *adj.* гетеротипи́ческий.

hetman /'hɛtmən/ *n.* ге́тман *m.*

heuristic /hyu'rɪstɪk/ *adj.* эвристи́ческий.

heuristics /hyu'rɪstɪks/ *n.* эври́стика *f.*

hew /hyu/ *v.* руби́ть; теса́ть *impf.*

hewer /'hyuər/ *n.* дровосе́к *m.*

hewing /'hyuɪŋ/ *n.* тёска *m.*

hewn /hyun *or, often,* yun/ *adj.* (*shaped*) тёсаный.

hexad /'hɛksæd/ *n.* шестёрка *f.*

hexaemeron /,hɛksə'ɛmə,rɒn/ *n.* (*eccl.*) шестодне́в *m.*

hexagon /'hɛksə,gɒn/ *n.* шестиуго́льник *m.*

hexagonal /hɛk'sægənl/ *adj.* шестиуго́льный.

hexahedron /,hɛksə'hidrən/ *n.* шестигра́нник *m.*

hexameter /hɛk'sæmɪtər/ *n.* гекза́метр *m.*

hexane /'hɛksein/ *n.* гекса́н *m.*

hexangular /hɛk'sæŋgyələr/ *n.* шестиуго́льник *m.*

hexapod /'hɛksə,pɒd/ *adj.* шестино́гий *m.*

hexatomic /,hɛksə'tɒmɪk/ *adj.* шести́атомный.

hexavalent /,hɛksə,veilənt/ *adj.* шестивале́нтный.

hexose /'hɛksous/ *n.* гексо́з *m.*

hey /hei/ *interj.* эй!

heyday /'hei,dei/ *n.* расцве́т *m.*

hi /hai/ *interj.* (*hey*) эй!; (*hello*) приве́т!

hiatus /hai'eitəs/ *n.* переры́в *m.*; (*ling.*) хиа́тус *m.*, зия́ние *neut.*

hibernate /'haibər,neit/ *v.* зимова́ть *impf.*, перезимова́ть *pf.*

hibernation /,haibər'neiʃən/ *n.* спя́чка; зимо́вка *f.*

hibiscus /hai'bɪskəs/ n. гибискус m.
hiccup /'hɪkʌp/ **1.** n. икота f. **2.** v. икать impf.
hick /hɪk/ n. провинциал m.
hickory /'hɪkəri/ n. гикори neut. indecl.
hidalgo /hɪ'dælgou, i'ðalgou/ n. идальго m. indecl.
hidden /'hɪdṇ/ adj. скрытый.
hide¹ /haid/ n. (animal skin) шкура f.
hide² /haid/ v. прятать; скрывать impf., скрыть pf.; v.i. скрываться impf., скрыться pf.
hide-and-seek /'haid ṇ 'sik/ n. (игра в) прятки pl.
hidebound /'haid,baund/ adj. ограниченный.
hideous /'hɪdiəs/ adj. отвратительный.
hideousness /'hɪdiəsnɪs/ n. безобразие neut.
hideout /'haid,aut/ n. укрытие neut.
hiding /'haidɪŋ/ n. (flogging) порка f.; прятание, скрывание neut.
hierarch /'haiə,rark/ n. иерарх m.
hierarchical /,haiə'rarkɪkəl/ adj. иерархический.
hierarchy /'haiə,rarki/ n. иерархия f.
hieratic /,haiə'rætɪk/ adj. иератический.
hieroglyph /'hairə,glɪf/ n. иероглиф m.
hieroglyphic /,haiərə'glɪfɪk/ adj. иероглифический.
hierophant /'haiərə,fænt/ n. жрец m.
higgledy-piggledy /'hɪgəldi 'pɪgəldi/ adj. беспорядочный.
high /hai/ adj. высокий; (strong) сильный.
high-altitude /'hai 'æltɪ,tud/ adj. (aero.) высотный.
high board n. (sports) вышка f.
high born adj. аристократический.
highboy /'hai,bɔi/ n. высокий комод m.
highbrow /'hai,brau/ **1.** n. интеллектуал m. **2.** adj. интеллектуальный.
high-capacity /'hai kə,pæsɪti/ adj. высокообъёмный.
highchair /'hai,tʃɛər/ n. высокий детский стульчик m.
high-class /'hai'klæs/ adj. высококачественный.
high-density /'hai 'dɛnsɪti/ adj. с большим удельным весом.
higher /'haiər/ adj. высший.
highest /'haiɪst/ adj. самый высокий; (very high) высший.
high-explosive /'hai ɪk'splousɪv/ adj. фугасный.
highfaluting /'haifə'lutɪŋ, -'lutṇ/ adj. (colloq.) напыщенный.
high fidelity adj. с высокой точностью воспроизведения; высококачественный.
high-flown /'hai'floun/ adj. напыщенный.
high-frequency /'hai 'frikwənsi/ adj. высокочастотный.
high-grade /'hai 'greid/ adj. высокосортный, высококачественный.
high-handed /'hai 'hændɪd/ adj. самовольный.
high-handedness /'hai 'hændɪdnɪs/ n. своеволие neut.
highlander /'hailəndər/ n. горец m.
highlands /'hailəndz/ n. нагорье neut., горная местность f.
high-level /'hai 'lɛvəl/ adj. интенсивный; на высшем уровне.
highlife /'hai,laif/ n. светская жизнь f.
highly /'haili/ adv. (very much) очень, весьма.
high-minded /'hai 'maindɪd/ adj. (noble) благо-

родный; (idealistic) идеалистический, идеалистичный.
Highness /'hainɪs/ n. Высочество neut.
high-octane /'hai 'ɒktein/ adj. высокооктановый.
high-performance /'hai pər'fɔrməns/ adj. высококоэффективный.
high-pitched /'hai 'pɪtʃt/ adj. пронзительный.
high polymer n. высокополимер m.
high-power /'hai 'pauər/ adj. мощный.
high-precision /'hai prə'sɪʒən/ adj. высокоточный, прецизионный.
high-pressure /'hai 'prɛʃər/ adj. (tech.) высокого давления.
high-priced /'hai 'praist/ adj. дорогой.
high-priority /'hai 'prai'ɔriti/ adj. первоочередной.
high-protein /'hai 'proutin/ adj. высокобелковый.
high-rise /'hai ,raiz/ n. высотный дом m.
high school n. средняя школа f.
high-sounding /'hai 'saundɪŋ/ adj. громкий.
high-speed /'hai 'spid/ adj. быстроходный.
high-spirited /'hai 'spɪrɪtɪd/ adj. (courageous) отважный.
high-temperature /'hai 'tɛmpərətʃər/ adj. высококотемпературный.
high-tension /'hai 'tɛnʃən/ adj. (elec.) высокого напряжения.
high-velocity /'hai və'lɒsɪti/ adj. высокоскоростной.
high-voltage /'hai 'voultɪdʒ/ adj. высоковольтный.
high water n. полная вода f.
highway /'hai,wei/ n. шоссе neut. indecl.
highwayman /'hai,weimən/ n. разбойник m.
hijacker /'hai,dʒækər/ n. угонщик m.
hijacking /'hai,dʒækɪŋ/ n. похищение neut.
Hijra /'hɪdʒrə/ n. хиджра f.
hike /haik/ n. поход m.
hiker /'haikər/ n. турист m.
hiking /'haikɪŋ/ n. туризм m., турпоходы pl.
hilarious /hɪ'lɛəriəs/ adj. весёлый.
hilarity /hɪ'lærɪti/ n. бурное веселье neut.
hill /hɪl/ n. холм m.
hilliness /'hɪlinɪs/ n. холмистость f.
hillock /'hɪlək/ n. холмик, бугор, пригорок m.
hillside /'hɪl,said/ n. склон холма m.
hilltop /'hɪl,tɒp/ n. вершина холма f.
hilly /'hɪli/ adj. холмистый.
hilt /hɪlt/ n. (weapon) эфес m., рукоятка f.
hilum /'hailəm/ n. рубчик семени m.
him /hɪm/ pron. его, ему.
Himalayan /,hɪmə'leiən/ adj. Гималайский.
Himalayas /,hɪmə'leiəz, hɪ'malyəz/ n. Гималаи pl.
himself /hɪm'sɛlf; medially often ɪm'sɛlf/ pron. сам; **he himself** он сам.
hind /'haind/ adj. задний.
hinder /'hɪndər/ v. мешать impf.
hind-foremost /,haind 'fɔrmoust/ adv. задом наперёд.
Hindi /'hɪndi/ n. хинди m.
hindquarters /'haind,kwɔrtərz/ n. зад m.
hindrance /'hɪndrəns/ n. помеха f.
hindsight /'haind,sait/ n. ретроспекция f.
Hinduism /'hɪndu,ɪzəm/ n. индуйзм m.
Hindustan /'hɪndu,stan/ n. Индустан m.

hinge /hɪndʒ/ **1.** *n.* петля́ *f.*; шарни́р *m.* **2.** *v.t.* прикрепля́ть на ле́тлях *impf.*, прикрепи́ть *pf.*; *v.i.* (*fig.*) зави́сеть (от *with gen.*) *impf.*

hinged /hɪndʒd/ *adj.* на пе́тлях.

hinny /'hɪni/ *n.* (*zool.*) лоша́к *m.*

hint /hɪnt/ **1.** *n.* намёк *m.* **2.** *v.* намека́ть *impf.*, намекну́ть *pf.*

hinterland /'hɪntər,lænd/ *n.* глушь *f.*; захолу́стный *or* необжито́й райо́н *m.*

hip /hɪp/ *n.* бедро́ *neut.*

hip bath *n.* сидя́чая ва́нна *f.*

hip joint *n.* тазобе́дренный суста́в *m.*

hippie /'hɪpi/ *n.* хи́ппи *m. indecl.*

hip pocket *n.* за́дний карма́н *m.*

Hippocratic oath /'hɪpə'krætɪk/ *n.* кля́тва Гиппокра́та *f.*

hippodrome /'hɪpə,droum/ *n.* ипподро́м *m.*

hippopotamus /,hɪpə'pɒtəməs/ *n.* гиппопотам *m.*

hircine /'hɜrsain/ *adj.* козли́ный.

hire /haɪər/ **1.** *n.* наём; прока́т *m.* **2.** *v.* нанима́ть *impf.*, наня́ть *pf.*

hired /haɪərd/ *adj.* наёмный.

hired hand *n.* батра́к; наёмный рабо́чий *m.*

hireling /'haɪərlɪŋ/ *n.* наёмник *m.*

hirsute /'hɜrsut/ *adj.* волоса́тый.

his /hɪz; *unstressed* ɪz/ *pron.* его́; свой.

hispid /'hɪspɪd/ *adj.* колю́чий.

hiss /hɪs/ **1.** *v.* шипе́ть; свисте́ть *impf.* **2.** *n.* шипе́ние *neut.*; свист *m.*

histamine /'hɪstə,min/ *n.* гистами́н *m.*

histogenesis /,hɪstə'dʒɛnəsɪs/ *n.* гистогене́з *m.*

histogram /'hɪstə,græm/ *n.* гистогра́мма *f.*

histological /,hɪstl'ɒdʒɪkəl/ *adj.* гистологи́ческий.

histologist /hɪ'stɒlədʒɪst/ *n.* гисто́лог *m.*

histology /hɪ'stɒlədʒi/ *n.* гистоло́гия *f.*

historian /hɪ'stɔriən/ *n.* исто́рик *m.*

historic /hɪ'stɔrɪk/ *also* **historical** *adj.* истори́ческий

historicity /,hɪstə'rɪsɪti/ *n.* истори́чность *f.*

historiographer /hɪ,stɔri'ɒgrəfər/ *n.* историо́граф *m.*

historiography /hɪ,stɔri'ɒgrəfi-/ *n.* историогра́фия *f.*

history /'hɪstəri/ *n.* исто́рия *f.*

histrionic /,hɪstri'ɒnɪk/ *adj.* театра́льный.

histrionics /,hɪstri'ɒnɪks/ *n.* театра́льное иску́сство *neut.*

hit /hɪt/ **1.** *n.* уда́р *m.*; (*on target*) попада́ние *neut.*; (*success*) успе́х *m.*, уда́ча *f.* **2.** *v.* ударя́ть *impf.*, уда́рить *pf.*; попада́ть (в *with acc.*) *impf.*; **to hit oneself** ударя́ться *impf.*, уда́риться *pf.*

hitch /hɪtʃ/ **1.** *n.* (*tug*) рыво́к *m.* **2.** *v.* (*pull up*) подтя́гивать *impf.*

hitchhike /'hɪtʃ,haik/ *v.* е́хать автосто́пом, (*colloq.*) голосова́ть (на доро́ге) *impf.*

hither /'hɪðər/ *adj.* ближа́йший.

hitherto /'hɪðər,tu/ *adv.* до сих пор.

Hittite /'hɪtait/ *n.* хетты *pl.*

hive /haiv/ *n.* у́лей *m.*

hives /haivz/ *n.* крапи́вница *f.*

hmm /hmm/ *also* **hm, h'm** *interj.* гм.

ho /hou/ *adj. interj.* эй!.

hoard /hɔrd/ **1.** *n.* запа́с *m.* **2.** *v.* запаса́ть *impf.*, запасти́ *pf.*

hoarding /'hɔrdɪŋ/ *n.* накопле́ние *neut.*

hoarfrost /'hɔr,frɔst/ *n.* и́ней *m.*

hoarse /hɔrs/ *adj.* хри́плый.

hoarseness /'hɔrsnɪs/ *n.* хрипота́ *f.*

hoary /'hɔri, 'houri/ *adj.* седо́й.

hoax /houks/ *n.* обма́н *m.*

hoaxer /'houksər/ *n.* мистифика́тор *m.*

hobble /'hɒbəl/ **1.** *n.* прихра́мывание *neut.* **2.** *v.* прихра́мывать; (*horse*) трено́жить *impf.*

hobby /'hɒbi/ *n.* хо́бби *neut. indecl.*; конёк *m.*

hobbyhorse /'hɒbi,hɔrs/ *n.* лоша́дка *f.*

hobgoblin /'hɒb,gɒblɪn/ *n.* (*imp*) чертёнок *m.*

hobnail /'hɒb,neil/ *n.* сапо́жный гвоздь *m.*

hobnailed /'hɒb,neild/ *adj.* подби́тый гвоздя́ми.

hobnob /'hɒb,nɒb/ **1.** *n.* бесе́да *f.* **2.** *v.* обща́ться *impf.*

hobo /'houbou/ *n.* бродя́га *m.* (*decl. f.*)

Hobson's choice /'hɒbsənz/ *n.* вы́бор без вы́бора *m.*

Ho Chi Minh City /'hou 'tʃi 'mɪn/ *n.* (*formerly: Saigon*) Хо-Ши-Мин Си́ти *m.*

hockey /'hɒki/ **1.** *n.* хокке́й *m.* **2.** *adj.* хокке́йный.

hocus-pocus /'houkəs 'poukəs/ *n.* фо́кус *m.*

hod /hɒd/ *n.* (*for bricks*) лото́к *m.*

hodgepodge /'hɒdʒ,pɒdʒ/ *n.* вся́кая вся́чина; смесь *f.*

hoe /hou/ **1.** *n.* моты́га *f.* **2.** *v.* моты́жить *impf.*

hog /hɔg/ *n.* свинья́ *f.*

hogback /'hɔg,bæk/ *n.* круто́й го́рный хребе́т *m.*

hoggish /'hɔgɪʃ/ *adj.* свинско́й.

hogskin /'hɔg,skɪn/ *n.* свина́я ко́жа *f.*

hogtie /'hɔg,tai/ *v.* (*animal*) свя́зывать по нога́м *impf.*

hogwash /'hɔg,wɒʃ/ *n.* вздор *m.*

hoi polloi /'hɔi pə'lɔi/ *n.* простонаро́дье *neut.*

hoist /hɔist/ **1.** *n.* (*act*) подъём *m.*; (*device*) подъёмник *m.* **2.** *v.* поднима́ть *impf.*, подня́ть *pf.*

hoisting /'hɔistɪŋ/ *n.* подъём *m.*

hoity-toity /'hɔiti'tɔiti/ *adj.* высокоме́рный.

Hokkaido /hɒ'kaidou/ *n.* Хокка́йдо *m.*

hokum /'houkəm/ *n.* сантимента́льность *f.*

hold /hould/ **1.** *n.* захва́т *m.*; хва́тка *f.*; (*control*) влия́ние *neut.* **2.** *v.* держа́ть(ся) *impf.*

holdall /'hould,ɔl/ *n.* саквоя́ж *m.*

holdings /'houldɪŋz/ *n.* (*property*) иму́щество *neut.*; (*finance*) вклад *m.*; (*ownership*) владе́ние *neut.*

holdup /'hould,ʌp/ *n.* налёт *m.*, ограбле́ние *neut.*

hole /houl/ *n.* дыра́; я́ма *f.*; отве́рстие *neut.*; (*animal's*) нора́ *f.*

hole-and-corner /'houl ən 'kɔrnər/ *adj.* нече́стный.

holiday /'hɒli,dei/ *n.* пра́здник *m.*; (*vacation*) кани́кулы *pl.*

holiness /'houlinɪs/ *n.* свя́тость; свяще́нность *f.*

holism /'houlɪzəm/ *n.* холи́зм *m.*

Holland /'hɒlənd/ *n.* Голла́ндия *f.*

hollandaise sauce /'hɒlən,deiz/ *n.* голла́ндский со́ус *m.*

hollow /'hɒlou/ **1.** *adj.* пусто́й, по́лый; (*sound*) глухо́й. **2.** *n.* впа́дина *f.*, углубле́ние *neut.*

hollowness /'hɒlounɪs/ *n.* пустота́ *f.*

holly /'hɒli/ *n.* остроли́ст, па́дуб *m.*

hollyhock /'hɒli,hɒk/ *n.* алте́й *m.*

Hollywood /'hɒli,wʊd/ *n.* Голливу́д *m.*

holmium /'houlmiəm/ *n.* го́льмий *m.*

holm oak /houm/ *n.* дуб ка́менный *m.*

holocaust /'hɒlə,kɔst/ n. уничтожéние (в огнé) neut.

hologram /'hɒlə,græm/ n. гологрáмма f.

holograph /'hɒlə,græf/ n. собственнорýчно напúсанный докумéнт m.

holography /hə'lɒgrəfi/ n. гологрáфия f.

holster /'houlstər/ n. кобурá f.

holy /'houli/ adj. святóй; свящéнный.

holy day n. церкóвный прáздник m.

holystone /'houli,stoun/ n. пéмза f.

homage /'hɒmɪdʒ, 'ɒm-/ n. почтéние, уважéние neut.

home /houm/ **1.** n. дом m. **2.** adj. домáшный. **3.** adv.: **at home** дóма adv.; **to go home** идтú домóй impf.

home-brew /'houm 'bru/ n. самогóн m.

homecoming /'houm,kʌmɪŋ/ n. возвращéние домóй neut.

homeland /'houm,lænd/ n. рóдина f.

homeless /'houmlɪs/ adj. бездóмный.

homelike /'houm,laik/ adj. как дóма.

homely /'houmli/ adj. простóй; (unattractive) некрасúвый.

homemade /'houm'meid/ adj. домáшнего изготовлéния; самодéльный.

homeomorphous /,houmiə'mɔrfəs/ adj. гомомóрфный.

homeopath /'houmiə,pæθ/ n. гомеопáт m.

homeopathic /,houmiə'pæθɪk/ adj. гомеопатúческий.

homeopathy /,houmi'ɒpəθi/ n. гомеопáтия f.

homeowner /'houm,ounər/ n. домовладéлец m.; домовладéлица f.

Homeric /hou'mɛrɪk/ adj. гомéровский.

home rule n. самоуправлéние neut.

homesick /'houm,sɪk/ adj. тоскýющий по дóму.

homesickness /'houm,sɪknɪs/ n. тоскá по дóму or по рóдине f.

homespun /'houm,spʌn/ adj. домоткáнный.

homestead /'houmstɛd-/ n. усáдьба f.

home stretch n. фúнишная прямáя f.

homeward /'houmwərd/ adv. домóй, к дóму.

homework /'houm,wɜrk/ n. урóк (нá дом) m.; домáшнее задáние neut.

homey /'houmi/ adj. уютный как дома.

homicide /'hɒmə,said/ n. (act) убúйство neut., (person) убúйца m. and f. (decl. f.).

homiletic /,hɒmə'lɛtɪk/ adj. проповéднический.

homiletics /,hɒmə'lɛtɪks/ n. гомилéтика f.

homily /'hɒməli/ n. прóповедь f.

hominy /'hɒməni/ n. мамалыга f.

homo /'houmou/ n. (zool.) человéк m.

homocentric /,houmə'sɛntrɪk/ adj. гомоцентрúческий.

homogamous /hou'mɒgəməs/ adj. гомогáмный.

homogeneity /,houmədʒə'niiti/ n. однорóдность f.

homogeneous /,houmə'dʒiniəs/ adj. однорóдный.

homogenize /hə'mɒdʒə,naiz/ v. гомогенизúровать impf. and pf.

homogenizer /hə'mɒdʒə,naizər/ n. гомогенизáтор m.

homogeny /hə'mɒdʒəni/ n. óбщность генотúпа f.

homograph /'hɒmə,græf/ n. омóграф m.

homographic /,hɒmə'græfɪk/ adj. омографúческий.

homologous /hə'mɒləgəs/ adj. (math., biol.) гомологúчный.

homologue /'houmə,lɒg/ n. гомóлог m.

homology /hə'mɒlədʒi/ n. гомолóгия f.

homonym /'hɒmənɪm/ n. омóним m.

homonymous /hə'mɒnəməs/ adj. омонимúческий.

homonymy /hə'mɒnəmi/ n. омонимúя f.

homophone /'hɒmə,foun/ n. омофóн m.

homophonic /,hɒmə'fɒnɪk/ adj. (mus.) гомофóнный.

homophony /hə'mɒfəni/ n. (mus.) гомофóния f.

homosexual /,houmə'sɛkʃuəl/ **1.** n. гомосексуалúст m. **2.** adj. гомосексуáльный.

homosexuality /,houmə,sɛkʃu'æliti/ n. гомосексуалúзм m.

homunculus /hə'mʌŋkyələs/ n. гомýнкул(ус) m.

Honduras /hɑn'durəs/ n. Гондýрас m.

hone /houn/ **1.** n. оселóк m. **2.** v. точúть impf.

honer /'hounər/ n. точúльный станóк m.

honest /'ɒnɪst/ adj. чéстный.

honestly /'ɒnɪstli/ adv. чéстно.

honesty /'ɒnəsti/ n. чéстность f.

honey /'hʌni/ **1.** n. мёд m. **2.** adj. медóвый.

honeybee /'hʌni,bi/ n. (медонóсная) пчелá f.

honeycomb /'hʌni,koum/ n. медóвые сóты pl.

honeymoon /'hʌni,mun/ n. медóвый мéсяц m.

honeysuckle /'hʌni,sʌkəl/ n. жúмолость f.

Hong Kong /'hɒŋ 'kɒŋ/ n. Гонкóнг m.

honk /hɒŋk/ n. (goose) гóгот m.; (car) гудóк m.

Honolulu /,hɒnə'lulu/ n. Гонолýлу m.

honor /'ɒnər/ **1.** n. честь f.; (esteem) почёт m. **2.** v. оказывать честь impf.; оказáть честь pf.; почитáть, чтить impf.

honorable /'ɒnərəbəl/ adj. (honest) чéстный; (respected) почётный.

honorarium /,ɒnə'rɛəriəm/ n. гонорáр m.

honorary /'ɒnə,rɛri/ adj. почётный.

honorific /,ɒnə'rɪfɪk/ adj. почётный.

hooch /hutʃ/ n. (slang) (whisky) вúски neut. indecl.; (home-distilled) самогóн m.

hood /hud/ n. капюшóн m.; (tech.) капóт m.

hooded /'hudɪd/ adj. с капюшóном.

hoodlum /'hudləm/ n. хулигáн, гáнгстер m.

hoodoo /'hudu/ n. невезéние neut.

hoodwink /'hud,wɪŋk/ v. обмáнывать impf.

hoof /huf/ n. копыто neut.

hoofbeat /'huf,bit/ n. цóкот m.

hoofed /huft/ adj. копытный.

hoo-ha /'hu,ha/ n. (colloq.) шумúха f.

hook /huk/ **1.** n. крюк, крючóк m. **2.** v. зацеплять impf.; застёгивать(ся) impf.

hookah /'hukə/ n. кальян m.

hooked /hukt/ adj. крючковáтый.

hooknosed /'huk,nouzd/ adj. горбонóсый.

hookup /'hukʌp/ n. (elec.) сцеплéние кóнтуров neut.; связь f.

hookworm /'huk,wɜrm/ n. нематóда f.

hooligan /'huligən/ n. хулигáн m.

hooliganism /'huligə,nɪzəm/ n. хулигáнство neut.

hoop /hup/ n. óбруч m.

hoopoe /'hupu/ n. (bird) удóд m.

hooray /hu'rei/ interj. урá!

hoot /hut/ **1.** n. ýханье neut. **2.** v. ýхать impf.

hop¹ /hɒp/ **1.** n. прыжо́к; скачо́к m. **2.** v. пры́гать impf., пры́гнуть pf.

hop² /hɒp/ n. (bot.) хмель m.

hope /houp/ **1.** n. наде́жда f. **2.** v. наде́яться impf.

hoped-for /ˈhoupt ˌfɔr/ adj. жела́нный.

hopeful /ˈhoupfəl/ adj. наде́ющийся.

hopefully /ˈhoupfəli/ adv. надо наде́яться, что...

hopefulness /ˈhoupfəlnɪs/ n. оптими́зм m.

hopeless /ˈhouplɪs/ adj. безнадёжный.

hopelessness /ˈhouplɪsnɪs/ n. безнадёжность f.

hop garden n. хме́льник m.

hop-growing /ˈhɒp ˌgrouɪŋ/ n. хмелево́дство neut.

hop kiln n. хмелесуши́лка f.

hopscotch /ˈhɒpˌskɒtʃ/ n. кла́ссы pl.

horde /hɔrd/ n. орда́ f.

horizon /həˈraizən/ n. горизо́нт m.

horizontal /ˌhɔrəˈzɒntl̩/ adj. горизонта́льный.

hormone /ˈhɔrmoun/ n. гормо́н m.

horn /hɔrn/ n. (animals) рог m.; (mus.) рожо́к; горн m.; (auto) гудо́к m.

hornbeam /ˈhɔrnˌbim/ n. (tree) граб m.

hornblende /ˈhɔrnˌblɛnd/ n. амфибо́л m., рогова́я обма́нка f.

horned /hɔrnd/ adj. рога́тый.

hornet /ˈhɔrnɪt/ n. ше́ршень m.

hornpipe /ˈhɔrnˌpaip/ n. хо́рнпайп m.

horn-rimmed /ˈhɔrn ˈrɪmd/ adj. (of eyeglasses) в рогово́й опра́ве.

hornstone /ˈhɔrnˌstoun/ n. рогови́к m.

horny /ˈhɔrni/ adj. рогово́й; (calloused) мозо́листый; (slang) сексуа́льно возбуждённый.

horoscope /ˈhɔrəˌskoup/ n. гороско́п m.

horrendous /həˈrɛndəs/ adj. стра́шный.

horrible /ˈhɔrəbəl/ adj. ужа́сный.

horrid /ˈhɔrɪd/ adj. ужа́сный; проти́вный.

horrify /ˈhɔrəˌfai/ v. ужаса́ть impf.

horrifying /ˈhɔrəˌfaiɪŋ/ adj. ужаса́ющий.

horror /ˈhɔrər/ n. у́жас m.

hors d'oeuvre /ˈɔr dɜrv/ n. заку́ска f.

horse /hɔrs/ **1.** n. ло́шадь f.; конь m. **2.** adj. лошади́ный; ко́нный.

horseback /ˈhɔrsˌbæk/ n.: on horseback верхо́м.

horse-breaking /ˈhɔrs ˌbreikɪŋ/ n. объе́здка лошаде́й f.

horse breeder n. конево́д m.

horse breeding n. конево́дство neut.

horse chestnut n. кашта́н ко́нский m.

horsecloth /ˈhɔrsˌklɔθ/ n. попо́на f.

horse collar n. хому́т m.

horse doctor n. конова́л m.

horse-drawn /ˈhɔrs ˌdrɔn/ adj. гужево́й; ко́нный.

horsefly /ˈhɔrs ˌflai/ n. слепе́нь m.

horsehair /ˈhɔrsˌhɛər/ n. ко́нский во́лос m.

horseman /ˈhɔrsmən/ n. вса́дник m.

horsemanship /ˈhɔrsmənˌʃɪp/ n. иску́сство верхово́й езды́ neut.

horsemeat /ˈhɔrsˌmit/ n. кони́на f.

horseplay /ˈhɔrsˌplei/ n. гру́бая игра́ f.

horsepower /ˈhɔrsˌpauər/ n. лошади́ная си́ла f.

horseradish /ˈhɔrsˌrædɪʃ/ n. хрен m.

horseshoe /ˈhɔrsˌʃu/ n. подко́ва f.

horse stealing n. конокра́дство neut.

horsetail /ˈhɔrsˌteil/ n. (bot.) хвощ m.

horsewhip /ˈhɔrsˌwɪp/ n. хлыст m.

horsewoman /ˈhɔrsˌwumən/ n. вса́дница f.

horticultural /ˌhɔrtɪˈkʌltʃərəl/ adj. садово́дческий.

horticulture /ˈhɔrtɪˌkʌltʃər/ n. садово́дство neut.

horticulturist /ˈhɔrtɪˌkʌltʃərɪst/ n. садово́д m.

hosanna /houˈzænə/ n. оса́нна f.

hose /houz/ n. (garden) шланг m.; (stockings) чулки́ pl.

hosier /ˈhouʒər/ n. торго́вец трикота́жными изде́лиями m.

hosiery /ˈhouʒəri/ n. чулки́ pl.; чуло́чные изде́лия pl.

hospice /ˈhɒspɪs/ n. (for homeless) богаде́льня f.; (for terminally ill) хо́спис m.

hospitable /ˈhɒspɪtəbəl/ adj. гостеприи́мный.

hospital /ˈhɒspɪtl̩/ **1.** n. больни́ца f., (mil.) го́спиталь m. **2.** adj. больни́чный, госпита́льный.

Hospitaler /ˈhɒspɪtlər/ n. госпитальер m.

hospitality /ˌhɒspɪˈtælɪti/ n. гостеприи́мство neut.

hospitalize /ˈhɒspɪtlˌaiz/ v. госпитализи́ровать impf. and pf.

host¹ /houst/ n. хозя́ин m.

host² /houst/ n. (multitude) мно́жество neut.

hostage /ˈhɒstɪdʒ/ n. зало́жник m.

hostel /ˈhɒstl̩/ n. турба́за f.

hostess /ˈhoustɪs/ n. хозя́йка f.

hostile /ˈhɒstl̩/ adj. вражде́бный, вра́жеский.

hostility /hoˈstɪlɪti/ n. вражде́бность f.

hot /hɒt/ adj. (weather) жа́ркий; (liquid) горя́чий; (spicy) о́стрый; **I am hot** мне жа́рко.

hot-air balloon /ˈhɒt ˈɛər/ n. монгольфье́р m.

hotbed /ˈhɒtˌbɛd/ n. (hort.) парни́к m.

hot-blooded /ˈhɒt ˈblʌdɪd/ adj. пы́лкий, стра́стный; вспы́льчивый.

hot-drawn /ˈhɒt ˈdrɒn/ adj. горячетя́нутый.

hotel /houˈtɛl/ n. гости́ница f.

hotel manager n. хозя́ин гости́ницы m.

hotfoot /ˈhɒtˌfut/ adv. стремгла́в.

hothead /ˈhɒtˌhɛd/ n. горя́чая голова́ f.

hotheaded /ˈhɒtˈhɛdɪd/ adj. горя́чий, опроме́тчивый.

hothouse /ˈhɒtˌhaus/ n. тепли́ца f.

hotly /ˈhɒtli/ adv. горячо́.

hotpress /ˈhɒtˌprɛs/ n. горя́чий пресс m.

hot-rolled /ˈhɒt ˈrould/ adj. горячека́таный.

hot-tempered /ˈhɒt ˈtɛmpərd/ adj. вспы́льчивый.

hot-water bottle /ˈhɒt ˈwɔtər/ n. гре́лка f.

hound /haund/ **1.** n. охо́тничья соба́ка. **2.** v. трави́ть impf.; (colloq.) докуча́ть impf.

hour /auər/ n. час m.

hourglass /ˈauərˌglæs/ n. песо́чные часы́ pl.

hour hand n. часова́я стре́лка f.

houri /ˈhuri/ n. гу́рия f.

hourly /ˈauərli/ **1.** adj. ежеча́сный. **2.** adv. ежеча́сно.

house / n., adj. haus; v. hauz/ **1.** n. дом m.; (building) зда́ние neut.; дома́шний. **3.** v. помеща́ть impf., помести́ть pf.

houseboat /ˈhausˌbout/ n. плаву́чий дом m.

housebreaker /ˈhausˌbreikər/ n. взло́мщик m.

housebroken /ˈhausˌbroukən/ adj. вы́ученный.

housecoat /ˈhausˌkout/ n. хала́т m.

housefly /ˈhausˌflai/ n. му́ха f.

houseful /ˈhausfʊl/ n. по́лный дом m.

household /'haʊs,hoʊld/ *n.* (*people*) дома́шние *pl.*; (*establishment*) дома́шнее хозя́йство *neut.*
housekeeper /'haʊs,kipər/ *n.* эконо́мка *f.*
housekeeping /'haʊs,kipɪŋ/ *n.* дома́шнее хозя́йство *neut.*
housemaid /'haʊs,meɪd/ *n.* го́рничная *f.*
house surgeon *n.* ста́рший хиру́рг *m.*
house-to-house /'haʊs tə ,haʊs/ *adj.* у́личный.
housetop /'haʊs,tɒp/ *n.* кры́ша, кро́вля *f.*
housewarming /'haʊs,wɔrmɪŋ/ *n.* новосе́лье *neut.*
housewife /'haʊs,waɪf/ *n.* дома́шняя хозя́йка *f.*
housework /'haʊs,wɜrk/ *n.* рабо́та по хозя́йству *f.*
hovel /'hʌvəl, 'hɒv-/ *n.* лачу́га *f.*
hover /'hʌvər/ *v.* (*bird*) пари́ть *impf.*; (*waver*) колеба́ться *impf.*
hovercraft /'hʌvər,kræft/ *n.* су́дно на возду́шной поду́шке *neut.*; аэрохо́д *m.*
how /haʊ/ *adv.* как; каки́м о́бразом; **how many, how much** ско́лько (*with gen.*).
howdah /'haʊdə/ *n.* паланки́н *m.*
however /haʊ'ɛvər/ **1.** *adv.* как бы ни. **2.** *conj.* одна́ко; тем не ме́нее.
howitzer /'haʊɪtsər/ *n.* га́убица *f.*
howl /haʊl/ **1.** *n.* завыва́ние *neut.*, вой *m.* **2.** *v.* выть *impf.*, завы́ть *pf.*
howling /'haʊlɪŋ/ *adj.* (*colloq.*) вопию́щий, грубе́йший.
Hrodna /'grɒdnoʊ/ *n.* Гро́дно *neut.*
hub /hʌb/ *n.* (*of wheel*) ступи́ца *f.*; (*fig.*) центр *m.*
hubbub /'hʌbʌb/ *n.* гул, шум, гам *m.*
hubby /'hʌbi/ *n.* (*colloq.*) муженёк *m.*
hubris /'hyubrɪs/ *n.* горды́ня *f.*; высокоме́рие *neut.*
huckleberry /'hʌkəl,bɛri/ *n.* черни́ка *f.*
huckster /'hʌkstər/ *n.* (*peddler*) разно́счик *m.*
huddle /'hʌdl/ *v.t.* (*heap together*) сва́ливать в ку́чу *impf.*
hue /hyu/ *n.* отте́нок *m.*
huff /hʌf/ *n.* вспы́шка гне́ва *f.*
huffy /'hʌfi/ *adj.* оби́дчивый.
hug /hʌg/ **1.** *n.* объя́тие *neut.* **2.** *v.* обнима́ть *impf.*, обня́ть *pf.*
huge /hyudʒ/ *adj.* огро́мный.
hugely /'hyudʒli/ *adv.* (*very much*) о́чень, весьма́.
Huguenot /'hyugə,nɒt/ *n.* гугено́т *m.*
hula-hula /'hulə 'hulə/ *n.* ху́ла-ху́ла *f.*
hulk /hʌlk/ *n.* (*bulky mass*) грома́дина *f.*
hulking /'hʌlkɪŋ/ *adj.* неуклю́жий.
hull¹ /hʌl/ *n.* (*husk*) шелуха́ *f.*
hull² /hʌl/ *n.* (*of ship*) ко́рпус *m.*
hullabaloo /'hʌləbə,lu/ *n.* шум, гам *m.*
hum /hʌm/ **1.** *n.* жужжа́ние *neut.* **2.** *v.* жужжа́ть *impf.*
human /'hyumən/ **1.** *n.* челове́к *m.* **2.** *adj.* челове́ческий; людско́й.
humane /hyu'meɪn/ *adj.* челове́чный, гума́нный.
humanism /'hyumə,nɪzəm/ *n.* гумани́зм *m.*
humanist /'hyumənɪst/ *n.* гумани́ст *m.*
humanistic /,hyumə'nɪstɪk/ *adj.* гуманисти́ческий.
humanitarian /hyu,mænɪ'tɛəriən/ **1.** *adj.* гуманита́рный. **2.** *n.* благотвори́тель *m.*
humanity /hyu'mænɪti/ *n.* челове́чество *neut.*;

(*humaneness*) гума́нность *f.*; *pl.* гуманита́рные нау́ки *pl.*
humanize /'hyumə,naɪz/ *v.* очелове́чивать *impf.*
humankind /'hyumən,kaɪnd/ *n.* челове́чество *neut.*
humanly /'hyumənli/ *adv.* по-челове́чески.
humble /'hʌmbəl/ **1.** *adj.* поко́рный, смире́нный; (*modest*) скро́мный. **2.** *v.* унижа́ть *impf.*
humbug /'hʌm,bʌg/ *n.* надува́тельство *neut.*
humdrum /'hʌm,drʌm/ *adj.* ску́чный.
humeral /'hyumərəl/ *adj.* плечево́й.
humerus /'hyumərəs/ *n.* плечева́я кость *f.*
humid /'hyumɪd/ *adj.* вла́жный.
humidifier /hyu'mɪdə,faɪər/ *n.* увлажни́тель *m.*
humidify /hyu'mɪdə,faɪ/ *v.* увлажня́ть *impf.*
humidity /hyu'mɪdɪti/ *n.* вла́жность *f.*
humiliate /hyu'mɪli,eɪt/ *v.* унижа́ть *impf.*, уни́зить *pf.*
humiliating /hyu'mɪli,eɪtɪŋ/ *adj.* унизи́тельный.
humiliation /hyu,mɪli'eɪʃən/ *n.* униже́ние *neut.*
humility /hyu'mɪlti/ *n.* смире́ние *neut.*
humming /'hʌmɪŋ/ *n.* жужжа́ние *neut.*
hummingbird /'hʌmɪŋ,bɜrd/ *n.* коли́бри *m.* and *f. indecl.*
hummock /'hʌmək/ *n.* (*hillock*) буго́р, приго́рок, хо́лмик *m.*; (*on ice*) торо́с *m.*
hummocky /'hʌməki/ *adj.* холми́стый.
humor /'hyumər/ **1.** *n.* ю́мор *m.*; (*mood*) настрое́ние *neut.* **2.** *v.* потака́ть *impf.*
humoresque /,hyumə'rɛsk/ *n.* (*mus.*) юмаре́ска *f.*
humorist /'hyumərɪst/ *n.* юмори́ст *m.*
humorous /'hyumərəs/ *adj.* заба́вный; юмористи́ческий.
hump /hʌmp/ *n.* горб *m.*
humpback /'hʌmp,bæk/ *n.* (*person*) горбу́н *m.*; (*hunched back*) горб *m.*
humpbacked /'hʌmp,bækt/ *adj.* горба́тый.
humph /*an inarticulate expression resembling a snort; spelling pron.* hʌmf/ *interj.* гм; хм.
humpy /'hʌmpi/ *adj.* нерóвный.
humus /'hyuməs/ *n.* чернозём; гу́мус *m.*
Hun /hʌn/ *n.* (*hist.*) гунн *m.*
hunch /hʌntʃ/ **1.** *n.* предчу́вствие *neut.* **2.** *v.* горби́ться *impf.*
hunchbacked /'hʌntʃ,bækt/ *adj.* горба́тый.
hundred /'hʌndrɪd/ *adj.*, *n.* сто.
hundredfold /'hʌndrɪd,foʊld/ *adj.* стокра́тный.
hundredth /'hʌndrɪdθ/ **1.** *adj.* со́тый. **2.** *n.* со́тая часть *f.*
Hungarian /hʌŋ'gɛəriən/ **1.** *adj.* венге́рский. **2.** *n.* венг *m.*, венге́рка *f.*
Hungary /'hʌŋgəri/ *n.* Ве́нгрия *f.*
hunger /'hʌŋgər/ *n.* го́лод *m.*
hunger-march /'hʌŋgər ,martʃ/ *n.* голо́дный похо́д *m.*
hunger strike *n.* голодо́вка *f.*
hungrily /'hʌŋgrəli/ *adv.* жа́дно, с жа́дностью.
hungry /'hʌŋgri/ *adj.* голо́дный.
hunk /hʌŋk/ *n.* ломо́ть; кус *m.*
hunt /hʌnt/ **1.** *n.* охо́та *f.*; (*search*) по́иски *pl.* **2.** *v.* охо́титься (на *with acc.*) *impf.*
hunter /'hʌntər/ *n.* охо́тник *m.*
hunting /'hʌntɪŋ/ **1.** *n.* охо́та *f.* **2.** *adj.* охо́тничий.
huntress /'hʌntrɪs/ *n.* охо́тница *f.*
huntsman /'hʌntsmən/ *n.* охо́тник *m.*

hurdle /'hɜrdl̩/ n. препя́тствие neut., барье́р pf.

hurdy-gurdy /'hɜrdi 'gɜrdi/ n. шарма́нка f.

hurl /hɜrl/ v. броса́ть impf., бро́сить pf.

hurly-burly /'hɜrli 'bɜrli/ n. сумато́ха, суета́ f.

Huron /'hyurən/ n. Lake, О́зеро Гу́рон neut.

hurrah, /hə'rɑ/ also **hurray** /-'rei/ interj. ура́!

hurricane /'hɜrɪ,kein/ n. урага́н m.

hurried /'hɜrid/ adj. торопли́вый, поспе́шный.

hurry /'hɜri/ 1. n. спе́шка, торопли́вость f. 2. v. спеши́ть impf., поспеши́ть pf.

hurt /hɜrt/ 1. n. ущёрб, вред m. 2. v.t. вреди́ть impf., повреди́ть pf.; v.i. боле́ть (у with gen.) impf.

hurtful /'hɜrtfəl/ adj. вре́дный.

hurtle /'hɜrtl̩/ v. нести́сь, мча́ться impf.

husband /'hʌzbənd/ n. муж m.

husbandry /'hʌzbəndri/ n. земледе́лие neut.

hush /hʌʃ/ 1. n. тишина́ f. 2. v.t. (supress) зама́лчивать impf.

hush-hush /'hʌʃ ,hʌʃ/ adj. секре́тный, засекре́ченный.

hush money n. взя́тка f.

husk /hʌsk/ 1. n. шелуха́ f. 2. v. шелуши́ть impf.

huskiness /'hʌskinis/ n. (hoarseness) хрипота́ f.

hussar /hu'zɑr/ n. гуса́р m.

hussy /'hʌsi/ n. де́рзкая девчо́нка f.

hustle /'hʌsəl/ v. (hurry) спеши́ть; суети́ться impf.

hustler /'hʌslər/ n. пробивно́й челове́к m.

hut /hʌt/ n. хи́жина f.

hyacinth /'haiəsɪnθ/ n. гиаци́нт m.

Hyades /'haiə,diz/ n. Гиа́ды pl.

hyaline /'haiə,lin/ n. (biochem.) гиали́н m.

hyaloid /'haiə,lɔid/ adj. прозра́чный.

hybrid /'haibrid/ 1. n. гибри́д m. 2. adj. гибри́дный.

hybridization /,haibridə'zeiʃən/ n. гибридиза́ция f.

hydra /'haidrə/ n. ги́дра f.

hydrangea /hai'dreindʒə/ n. горте́нзия f.

hydrant /'haidrənt/ n. гидра́нт m.

hydrate /'haidreit/ n. гидра́т m.

hydrated /'haidreitid/ adj. гидрати́рованный.

hydration /hai'dreiʃən/ n. гидрата́ция f.

hydraulic /hai'drɔlik/ adj. гидравли́ческий.

hydraulics /hai'drɔliks/ n. гидра́влика f.

hydride /'haidraid/ n. гидри́д m.

hydrocarbon /,haidrə'kɑrbən/ n. углеводоро́д m.

hydrocephalus /,haidrə'sɛfələs/ n. водя́нка головно́го мо́зга f.

hydrochloric acid /,haidrə'klɔrik/ n. хлористоводоро́дная or соля́ная кислота́ f.

hydrocyanic acid /,haidrousai'ænik/ n. сини́льная кислота́ f.

hydrodynamic /,haidroudai'næmik/ adj. гидродинами́ческий.

hydrodynamics /,haidroudai'næmiks/ n. гидродина́мика f.

hydroelectric /,haidroui'lɛktrik/ adj. гидроэлектри́ческий.

hydroelectricity /,haidrouilɛk'trisiti/ n. гидроэлектри́чество neut.

hydrofluoric acid /,haidrə'flurik/ n. фтористоводоро́дная кислота́ f.

hydrofoil /'haidrə,fɔil/ n. (vessel) су́дно на подво́дных кры́льях neut.

hydrogen /'haidrədʒən/ 1. n. водоро́д m. 2. adj. водоро́дный.

hydrogenate /'haidrədʒə,neit/ v. гидрогенизи́ровать impf.

hydrogen bomb /'haidrədʒən/ n. водоро́дная бо́мба f.

hydrogenous /hai'drɒdʒənəs/ adj. водоро́дный.

hydrograph /'haidrə,græf/ n. гидро́граф m.

hydrographic /,haidrə'græfik/ adj. гидрографи́ческий.

hydrography /hai'drɒgrəfi/ n. гидрогра́фия f.

hydrology /hai'drɒlədʒi/ n. гидроло́гия f.

hydrolysis /hai'drɒləsɪs/ n. гидро́лиз m.

hydrometer /hai'drɒmitər/ n. арео́метр m.

hydropathic /,haidrə'pæθik/ adj. водолече́бный.

hydropathy /hai'drɒpəθi/ n. водолече́ние neut.

hydrophilic /,haidrə'fɪlik/ adj. (chem.) гидрофи́льный.

hydrophobia /,haidrə'foubiə/ n. водобоя́знь f.

hydrophone /'haidrə,foun/ n. гидрофо́н m.

hydrophyte /'haidrə,fait/ n. гидрофи́т m.

hydroplane /'haidrə,plein/ n. (motorboat) гли́ссер m.; (aircraft) гидросамолёт m.

hydroplaning /'haidrə,pleinɪŋ/ n. акваплани́рование neut.

hydropneumatic /,haidrənu'mætik/ adj. гидропневмати́ческий.

hydroponics /,haidrə'pɒniks/ n. гидропо́ника f.

hydrops /'haidrɒps/ n. водя́нка f.

hydrosol /'haidrə,sɒl/ n. гидросо́ль f.

hydrosphere /'haidrə,sfɪər/ n. гидросфе́ра f.

hydrostat /'haidrə,stæt/ n. гидроста́т m.

hydrostatic /,haidrə'stætik/ adj. гидростати́ческий.

hydrostatics /,haidrə'stætiks/ n. гидроста́тика f.

hydrotherapy /,haidrə'θɛrəpi/ n. водолече́ние neut.

hydrous /'haidrəs/ adj. во́дный.

hydroxide /hai'drɒksaid/ n. гидроо́кись f.

hydroxyl /hai'drɒksəl/ n. гидрокси́л m.

hyena /hai'inə/ n. гие́на f.

hygiene /'haidʒin/ n. гигие́на f.

hygienic /,haidʒi'ɛnik/ adj. гигиени́ческий.

hygro- adj. prefix ги́гро-.

hygrometer /hai'grɒmitər/ n. гигро́метр m.

hygroscopic /,haigrə'skɒpik/ adj. гигроскопи́ческий.

hylotheism /,hailə'θiizəm/ n. гилотейзм m.

hylozoism /,hailə'zouizəm/ n. гилозои́зм m.

hymen /'haimən/ n. (anat.) де́вственная плёва f.

hymenoptera /,haimə'nɒptərə/ n. перепончатокры́лые pl.

hymn /him/ n. гимн m.

hymnal /'himnəl/ also **hymnbook** /'him,buk/ n. сбо́рник ги́мнов m.

hyoid /'haiɔid/ n. подъязычко́вая кость f.

hype /haip/ n. (colloq.) (deception) очковти́рательство neut.; (publicity) (агресси́вное) реклами́рование neut.

hyperacidity /,haipərə'siditi/ n. повы́шенная кисло́тность f.

hyperactivity /,haipəræk'tiviti/ n. гиперфу́нкция f.

hyperbola /hai'pɜrbələ/ n. (geom.) гипе́рбола f.

hyperbole /hai'pɜrbəli/ n. гипе́рбола, преувеличе́ние f.

hyperbolic /,haipər'bɒlik/ adj. гиперболи́ческий.

hyperboloid /hai'pɜrbə‚lɔid/ n. гиперболо́ид m.
hyperborean /‚haipər'bɔriən/ n. гипербоѐец m.
hypercardia /‚haipər'kɑrdiə/ n. гипертрофи́я се́рдца f.
hypercritical /‚haipər'krɪtɪkəl/ adj. приди́рчивый.
hyperesthesia /‚haipərəs'θiʒə/ n. гиперестези́я f.
hypergalaxy /'haipər‚gæləksi/ n. сверхгала́ктика f.
hypernucleus /‚haipər'nukliəs/ n. гиперядро́ neut.
hyperon /'haipə‚rɒn/ n. гиперо́н m.
hypersensitive /‚haipər'sɛnsɪtɪv/ adj. сверхчувст-ви́тельный.
hypersonic /‚haipər'sɒnɪk/ adj. гиперзвуково́й.
hypertension /‚haipər'tɛnʃən/ n. повы́шенное давле́ние neut., гипертони́я f.
hypertonic /‚haipər'tɒnɪk/ adj. гипертони́ческий.
hypertrophy /hai'pɜrtrəfi/ n. гипертрофи́я f.
hyphen /'haifən/ n. дефи́с m.
hyphenate /'haifə‚neit/ v. писа́ть че́рез дефи́с impf.
hypnosis /hɪp'nousɪs/ n. гипно́з m.
hypnotic /hɪp'nɒtɪk/ adj. гипноти́ческий.
hypnotism /'hɪpnə‚tɪzəm/ n. гипноти́зм m.
hypnotist /'hɪpnətɪst/ n. гипнотизёр m.
hypnotize /'hɪpnə‚taiz/ v. гипнотизи́ровать impf., загипнотизи́ровать pf.

hypo /'haipou/ n. (photog.) фикса́ж m.
hypochlorite /‚haipə'klɔrait/ n. гипохлори́т m.
hypochondria /‚haipə'kɒndriə/ n. ипохо́ндрия f.
hypochondriac /‚haipə'kɒndri‚æk/ **1.** adj. страда́-ющий ипохо́ндрией. **2.** n. ипохо́ндрик m.
hypocrisy /hɪ'pɒkrəsi/ n. лицеме́рие neut.
hypocrite /'hɪpəkrɪt/ n. лицеме́р m.
hypocritical /‚hɪpə'krɪtɪkəl/ n. лицеме́рный.
hypodermic /‚haipə'dɜrmɪk/ adj. подко́жный.
hypodermis /‚haipə'dɜrmɪs/ n. гиподе́рма f.
hypotenuse /hai'pɒtn̩‚us/ n. гипотену́за f.
hypothalamus /‚haipə'θæləməs/ n. гипотала́мус m.
hypothermia /‚haipə'θɜrmiə/ n. гипотерми́я f.
hypothesis /hai'pɒθəsɪs/ n. гипо́теза f.
hypothesize /hai'pɒθə‚saiz/ v. стро́ить гипо́тезу impf.
hypothetical /‚haipə'θɛtɪkəl/ adj. предположи́тельный; гипотети́ческий.
hyssop /'hɪsəp/ n. иссо́п m.
hysterectomy /‚hɪstə'rɛktəmi/ n. удале́ние ма́тки neut.
hysteresis /‚hɪstə'risɪs/ n. гистере́зис m.
hysteria /hɪ'stɛriə/ n. истери́я f.
hysterical /hɪ'stɛrɪkəl/ adj. истери́ческий.
hysterics /hɪ'stɛrɪks/ n. исте́рика f.

I

I /ai/ *pron.* я.
iamb /'aiæm/ *n.* ямб *m.*
iambic /ai'æmbɪk/ *adj.* ямби́ческий.
ibex /'aibɛks/ *n.* ка́менный козёл *m.*
ibid /'ɪbɪd/ *adv.* там же.
ibis /'aibɪs/ *n.* и́бис *m.*
Ibiza /i'viθɑ, -sɑ, ɪ'bizə/ *n.* (*island*) и́биза *f.*
I.C.B.M. *n.* (*abbr. of* intercontinental ballistic missile). МБР (*abbr. of* межконтинента́льная баллисти́ческая раке́та) *f.*
ice /ais/ **1.** *n.* лёд *m.* **2.** *adj.* ледяно́й.
ice axe *n.* ледору́б *m.*
ice bag *n.* пузы́рь для льда *m.*
iceberg /'aisbɜrg/ *n.* а́йсберг *m.*
iceblink /'ais,blɪŋk/ *n.* ледяно́й о́тблеск *m.*
iceboat /'ais,bout/ *n.* бу́ер *m.*
icebound /'ais,baund/ *adj.* затёртый льда́ми.
Icebox /'ais,bɒks/ *n.* холоди́льник *m.*
icebreaker /'ais,breikər/ *n.* ледоко́л *m.*
ice-cold /'ais 'kould/ *adj.* ледяно́й.
ice cream *n.* моро́женое *neut.*
ice cream pop *n.* эскимо́ *neut. indecl.*
iced /aist/ *adj.* (*cake, fruits*) глазиро́ванный; (*drink*) со льдом.
ice drift *n.* дрейф льда *m.*
ice field *n.* ледяно́е по́ле *neut.*
ice floe *n.* плаву́чая льди́на *f.*
ice foot *n.* берегово́й припа́й *m.*
ice-free /'ais 'fri/ *adj.* свобо́дный ото льда.
ice hockey *n.* хокке́й на льду *m.*
icehouse /'ais,haus/ *n.* ледни́к *m.*
Iceland /'aisland/ *n.* Исла́ндия *f.*
ice skates *n.* коньки́ *pl.*
ichneumon /ɪk'numən/ *n.* ихневмо́н *m.*
ichthyography /,ɪkθi'ɒgrəfi/ *n.* ихтиогра́фия *f.*
ichthyologist /,ɪkθi'ɒlədʒɪst/ *n.* ихтио́лог *m.*
ichthyology /,ɪkθi'ɒlədʒi/ *n.* ихтиоло́гия *f.*
ichthyosaur /'ɪkθiə,sɔr/ *n.* ихтиоза́вр *m.*
ichthyosis /,ɪkθi'ousɪs/ *n.* ихтио́з *m.*
icicle /'aisɪkəl/ *n.* сосу́лька *f.*
icing /'aisɪŋ/ *n.* (*aero.*) обледене́ние *neut.*; (*cake*) глазу́рь *f.*
icon /'aikɒn/ **1.** *n.* ико́на *f.* **2.** *adj.* ико́нный.
iconoclasm /ai'kɒnə,klæzəm/ *n.* иконобо́рство *neut.*
iconoclast /ai'kɒnə,klæst/ *n.* иконобо́рец *m.*
iconoclastic /ai'kɒnə,klæstɪk/ *adj.* иконобо́рческий.
iconographic /ai,kɒnə'græfɪk/ *adj.* иконографи́ческий.
iconography /,aikə'nɒgrəfi/ *n.* иконогра́фия *f.*
iconoscope /ai'kɒnə,skoup/ *n.* иконоско́п *m.*
iconostasis /,aikə'nɒstəsɪs/ *n.* иконоста́с *m.*
icosahedron /ai,kousə'hidrən/ *n.* двадцатигра́нник *m.*
ictus /'ɪktəs/ *n.* (*pros.*) икт *m.*; (*med.*) уда́р *m.*
icy /'aisi/ *adj.* ледяно́й.
id /ɪd/ *n.* ид *neut. indecl.*
Idaho /'aidə,hou/ *n.* Айда́хо *m.*
idea /ai'diə/ *n.* иде́я, мысль *f.*; поня́тие *neut.*
ideal /ai'diəl/ **1.** *n.* идеа́л *m.* **2.** *adj.* идеа́льный.

idealism /ai'diə,lɪzəm/ *n.* идеали́зм *m.*
idealist /ai'diəlɪst/ *n.* идеали́ст *m.*
idealistic /ai,diə'lɪstɪk/ *adj.* идеалисти́ческий.
idealization /ai,diələ'zeiʃən/ *n.* идеализа́ция *f.*
idealize /ai'diə,laiz/ *v.* идеализи́ровать *impf.*
ideally /ai'diəli/ *adv.* идеа́льно; (*best of all*) лу́чше всего́.
idée fixe /idei 'fiks/ *n.* идея фикс; навя́зчивая иде́я *f.*
idem /'aidɛm/ *n.* (*author*) он же *m.*; она́ же *f.*
identical /ai'dɛntɪkəl/ *adj.* тожде́ственный; одина́ковый.
identifiable /ai'dɛntə,faiəbəl/ *adj.* опознава́емый.
identification /ai,dɛntəfɪ'keiʃən/ *n.* опозна́ние; установле́ние ли́чности *neut.*; (*equate*) отожде́твле́ние *neut.*
identify /ai'dɛntə,fai/ *v.* опознава́ть; отожде́ствля́ть *impf.*, отожде́стви́ть *pf.*
identity /ai'dɛntɪti/ *n.* ли́чность; (*sameness*) тожде́ственность *f.*, тожде́ство *neut.*
Ideogram /'ɪdiə,græm/ *n.* идеогра́мма *f.*
ideological /,aidiə'lɒdʒɪkəl/ *adj.* идеологи́ческий.
ideologist /,aidi'ɒlədʒɪst/ *n.* идео́лог *m.*
ideology /,aidi'ɒlədʒi/ *n.* идеоло́гия *f.*
ides /aidz/ *n.* и́ды *pl.*
idiocy /'ɪdiəsi/ *n.* идиоти́зм *m.*
idiom /'ɪdiəm/ *n.* идиомати́ческое выраже́ние *neut.*; идио́ма *f.*; (*language*) язы́к, го́вор *m.*
idiomatic /,ɪdiə'mætɪk/ *adj.* идиомати́ческий.
idiopathic /,ɪdiə'pæθɪk/ *adj.* идиопати́ческий.
idiosyncrasy /,ɪdiə'sɪŋkrəsi/ *n.* характе́рная черта́ *f.*
idiosyncratic /,ɪdiousɪn'krætɪk/ *adj.* своcобра́зный; характе́рный.
idiot /'ɪdiət/ *n.* идио́т *m.*
idiotic /,ɪdi'ɒtɪk/ *adj.* идио́тский.
idle /'aidl/ **1.** *adj.* пра́здный; (*useless*) бесполе́зный. **2.** *v.* безде́льничать *impf.*
idleness /'aidlnɪs/ *n.* пра́здность *f.*
idler /'aidlər/ *n.* (*person*) лентя́й, безде́льник *m.*
idling /'aidlɪŋ/ *n.* безде́льниче *neut.*
idly /'aidli/ *adv.* пра́здно; лени́во.
Ido /'idou/ *n.* и́до *neut. indecl.*
idol /'aidl/ *n.* и́дол *m.*
idolater /ai'dɒlətər/ *n.* идолопокло́нник *m.*
idolatress /ai'dɒlətrɪs/ *n.* идолопокло́нница *f.*
idolatrous /ai'dɒlətrəs/ *adj.* идолопокло́ннический.
idolatry /ai'dɒlətri/ *n.* идолопокло́нство *neut.*
idolize /'aidl,aiz/ *v.* поклоня́ться и́долам; боготвори́ть *impf.*
idyll /'aidl/ *n.* иди́ллия *f.*
idyllic /ai'dɪlɪk/ *adj.* идилли́ческий.
if /ɪf/ *conj.* е́сли; (*whether*) ли; **as if** как бу́дто; **even if** да́же е́сли.
igloo /'ɪglu/ *n.* и́глу *neut. indecl.*
igneous /'ɪgniəs/ *adj.* огнево́й.
ignis fatuus /'ɪg'nɪs fæt'fuəs/ *n.* блужда́ющий огонёк *m.*
ignitable /ɪg'naitəbəl/ *adj.* горю́чий.
ignite /ɪg'nait/ *v.* зажига́ть *impf.*, заже́чь *pf.*
ignition /ɪg'nɪʃən/ *n.* зажига́ние *neut.*

ignominious /ˌɪgnəˈmɪniəs/ *adj.* позо́рный.

ignominy /ˈɪgnəˌmɪni/ *n.* позо́р *m.*

ignoramus /ˌɪgnəˈreɪməs/ *n.* невѐжда *m.* and *f.* (*decl. f.*).

ignorance /ˈɪgnərəns/ *n.* невѐжество *neut.*

ignorant /ˈɪgnərənt/ *adj.* невѐжественный; (*uninformed*) несвѐдущий.

ignore /ɪgˈnɔr/ *v.* игнори́ровать *impf.* and *pf.*

iguana /ɪˈgwɑnə/ *n.* игуа́на *f.*

Île de France /ˌil də ˈfrans/ *n.* (*province*) Иль-де-Франс *m.*

ileum /ˈɪliəm/ *n.* подвздо́шная кишка́ *f.*

iliac /ˈɪliˌæk/ *adj.* подвздо́шный.

Iliad /ˈɪliəd/ *n.* Илиа́да *f.*

ilium /ˈɪliəm/ *n.* подвздо́шная кость *f.*

ilk /ɪlk/ *n.* (*colloq.*) род *m.*, племя *neut.*

ill /ɪl/ **1.** *adj.* больно́й; **to be ill** *v.* болѐть *impf.*; **to become ill** *v.* заболѐть *pf.* **2.** *adv.* ду́рно **3.** *n.* зло *neut.*; вред *m.*

ill-advised /ˈɪl ədˈvaizd/ *adj.* неблагоразу́мный.

illative /ˈɪlətɪv/ *adj.* заключи́тельный.

ill-bred /ˈɪl ˈbrɛd/ *adj.* невоспи́танный; гру́бый.

ill-breeding /ˈɪl ˈbridɪŋ/ *n.* невоспи́танность *f.*

ill-conditioned /ˈɪl kənˈdɪʃənd/ *adj.* злой.

ill-considered /ˈɪl kənˈsɪdərd/ *adj.* непроду́манный.

ill-defined /ˈɪl dɪˈfaind/ *adj.* нето́чный, неопределённый.

ill-disposed /ˈɪl dɪˈspouzd/ *adj.* враждѐбный.

illegal /ɪˈligəl/ *adj.* незако́нный; нелега́льный.

illegality /ˌɪliˈgælɪti/ *n.* незако́нность *f.*

illegibility /ɪˌlɛdʒəˈbɪlɪti/ *n.* неразбо́рчивость *f.*

illegible /ɪˈlɛdʒəbəl/ *adj.* неразбо́рчивый, нечёткий.

illegitimacy /ˌɪliˈdʒɪtəməsi/ *n.* незако́нность *f.*

illegitimate /ˌɪliˈdʒɪtəmɪt/ *adj.* незаконнорождённый; незако́нный.

ill-fated /ˈɪl ˈfeitɪd/ *adj.* злополу́чный, злосча́стный.

ill-favored /ˈɪl ˈfeivərd/ *adj.* некраси́вый.

ill-founded /ˈɪl ˈfaundɪd/ *adj.* необосно́ванный.

ill-gotten /ˈɪl ˈgɒtn̩/ *adj.* добы́тый нечѐстным путём.

ill humor *n.* дурно́е настроѐние *neut.*

illicit /ɪˈlɪsɪt/ *adj.* незако́нный.

illimitable /ɪˈlɪmɪtəbəl/ *adj.* беспредѐльный.

Illinois /ˌɪləˈnɔi/ *n.* Иллино́йс *m.*

illiteracy /ɪˈlɪtərəsi/ *n.* негра́мотность *f.*

illiterate /ɪˈlɪtərɪt/ *adj.*, *n.* негра́мотный.

ill-judged /ˈɪl ˈdʒʌdʒd/ *adj.* неразу́мный.

ill-mannered /ˈɪl ˈmænərd/ *adj.* невоспи́танный, гру́бый.

ill-natured /ˈɪl ˈneitʃərd/ *adj.* злой, недоброжела́тельный.

illness /ˈɪlnɪs/ *n.* болѐзнь *f.*

illogic /ɪˈlɒdʒɪk/ *also* **illogicality** /ɪˌlɒdʒɪˈkælɪti/ *n.* нелоги́чность *f.*

illogical /ɪˈlɒdʒɪkəl/ *adj.* нелоги́чный.

ill-omened /ˈɪl ˈoumənd/ *adj.* злополу́чный.

ill-provided /ˈɪl prəˈvaidɪd/ *adj.* необеспѐченный.

ill-starred /ˈɪl ˈstɑrd/ *adj.* злосча́стный.

ill-tempered /ˈɪl ˈtɛmpərd/ *adj.* злой, сварли́вый.

ill-timed /ˈɪl ˈtaimd/ *adj.* несвоеврѐменный.

ill-treat /ˈɪl ˈtrit/ *v.* ду́рно *or* жесто́ко обраща́ться (*with instr.*) *impf.*

ill-treatment /ˈɪl ˈtritmənt/ *n.* дурно́е обраще́ние *neut.*

illuminate /ɪˈluməˌneit/ *v.* освеща́ть *impf.*, освети́ть *pf.*

illuminated /ɪˈluməˌneitɪd/ *adj.* (*decorated*) укра́шенный.

illuminating /ɪˈluməˌneitɪŋ/ *adj.* освещающий; (*fig.*) поучи́тельный.

illumination /ɪˌluməˈneiʃən/ *n.* освеще́ние *neut.*, иллюмина́ция *f.*

illusion /ɪˈluʒən/ *n.* иллю́зия *f.*

illusionism /ɪˈluʒəˌnɪzəm/ *n.* иллюзиони́зм *m.*

illusionist /ɪˈluʒənɪst/ *n.* иллюзиони́ст *m.*

illusory /ɪˈlusəri/ *also* **illusive** /-sɪv/ *adj.* нереа́льный, иллюзо́рный, обма́нчивый; **illusory quality** *or* **nature** *n.* иллюзо́рность *f.*

illustrate /ˈɪləˌstreit/ *v.* иллюстри́ровать *impf.* and *pf.*

illustration /ˌɪləˈstreiʃən/ *n.* иллюстра́ция *f.*

illustrative /ɪˈlʌstrətɪv/ *adj.* иллюстрати́вный.

illustrator /ˈɪləˌstreitər/ *n.* иллюстра́тор *m.*

illustrious /ɪˈlʌstriəs/ *adj.* просла́вленный.

ill will *n.* неприя́знь *f.*

ill-wisher /ˈɪl ˈwɪʃər/ *n.* недоброжела́тель *m.*

Ilmen /ˈɪlmən/ *n.* (*lake*) и́льмень *neut.*

image /ˈɪmɪdʒ/ *n.* о́браз *m.*, изображе́ние *neut.*

imagery /ˈɪmɪdʒri/ *n.* о́бразность *f.*

imaginable /ɪˈmædʒənəbəl/ *adj.* вообрази́мый.

imaginary /ɪˈmædʒəˌnɛri/ *adj.* вообража́емый; мни́мый.

imagination /ɪˌmædʒəˈneiʃən/ *n.* воображе́ние *neut.*

imaginative /ɪˈmædʒənətɪv/ *adj.* с воображе́нием.

imagine /ɪˈmædʒɪn/ *v.* вообража́ть *impf.*, вообрази́ть *pf.*; представля́ть себѐ *impf.*, предста́вить себѐ *pf.*

imagism /ˈɪməˌdʒɪzəm/ *n.* имажини́зм *m.*

imagist /ˈɪmədʒɪst/ *n.* имажини́ст *m.*

imam /ɪˈmɑm/ *n.* има́м *m.*

imbalance /ɪmˈbæləns/ *n.* неусто́йчивость *f.*

imbecile /ˈɪmbəsɪl/ *n.* слабоу́мный; идио́т *m.*

imbecility /ˌɪmbəˈsɪlɪti/ *n.* слабоу́мие *neut.*; идиоти́зм *m.*

imbibe /ɪmˈbaib/ *v.* (*drink*) пить *impf.*; (*absorb*) впи́тывать *impf.*

imbroglio /ɪmˈbroulyou/ *n.* пу́таница *f.*

imbue /ɪmˈbyu/ *v.* (*saturate*) пропи́тывать *impf.*; (*instill*) насыща́ть, наполня́ть *impf.*

imitate /ˈɪmɪˌteit/ *v.* подража́ть; имити́ровать *impf.*

imitation /ˌɪmɪˈteiʃən/ *n.* имита́ция *f.*, подража́ние *neut.*

imitative /ˈɪmɪˌteitɪv/ *adj.* подража́тельный.

imitator /ˈɪmɪˌteitər/ *n.* подража́тель *m.*

immaculate /ɪˈmækyəlɪt/ *adj.* безупрѐчный.

immanence /ˈɪmənəns/ *n.* имманѐнтность *f.*

immanent /ˈɪmənənt/ *adj.* прису́щий; имманѐнтный.

immaterial /ˌɪməˈtɪəriəl/ *adj.* невеще́ственный; безразли́чный.

immaterialism /ˌɪməˈtɪəriəˌlɪzəm/ *n.* имматериали́зм *m.*

immature /ˌɪməˈtʃʊr/ *adj.* незрѐлый.

immaturity /ˌɪməˈtʃʊrɪti/ *n.* незрѐлость *f.*

immeasurable /ɪˈmɛʒərəbəl/ *adj.* неизмери́мый; безмѐрный.

immediacy /ɪˈmidiəsi/ *n.* непосрѐдственность *f.*

immediate /ɪ'midiɪt/ *adj.* неме́дленный; непосре́дственный.

immediately /ɪ'midiɪtli/ *adv.* (*instantly*) сра́зу же, неме́дленно.

immemorial /ˌɪmə'mɔriəl/ *adj.* незапа́мятный.

immense /ɪ'mɛns/ *adj.* огро́мный.

immensely /ɪ'mɛnsli/ *adv.* чрезвыча́йно.

immensity /ɪ'mɛnsɪti/ *n.* огро́мность *f.*

immerse /ɪ'mɜrs/ *v.* погружа́ть *impf.*

immersion /ɪ'mɜrʒən/ *n.* погруже́ние *neut.*

immigrant /'ɪmɪgrənt/ **1.** *n.* иммигра́нт *m.*, имигра́нтка *f.* **2.** *adj.* иммигри́рующий.

immigrate /'ɪmɪˌgreit/ *v.* иммигри́ровать *impf.* and *pf.*

immigration /ˌɪmɪ'greiʃən/ *n.* иммигра́ция *f.*

imminence /'ɪmənəns/ *n.* наступле́ние *neut.*

imminent /'ɪmənənt/ *adj.* грозя́щий; немину́емый.

immiscible /ɪ'mɪsəbəl/ *adj.* несме́шиваемый.

immobile /ɪ'moubəl/ *adj.* неподви́жный, недви́жимый.

immobility /ˌɪmou'bɪlɪti/ *n.* неподви́жность *f.*

immobilization /ɪ'moubələ'zeiʃən/ *n.* иммобилиза́ция *f.*

immobilize /ɪ'moubəˌlaiz/ *v.* обездви́живать *impf.*

immoderate /ɪ'mɒdərɪt/ *adj.* неуме́ренный.

immoderation /ɪˌmɒdə'reiʃən/ *n.* неуме́ренность *f.*

immodest /ɪ'mɒdɪst/ *adj.* (*indecent*) неприли́чный; нескро́мный; (*impudent*) на́глый.

immodesty /ɪ'mɒdɪsti/ *n.* нескро́мность *f.*; бессты́дство *neut.*

immolate /'ɪməˌleit/ *v.* приноси́ть в же́ртву; же́ртвовать *impf.*

immolation /ˌɪmə'leiʃən/ *n.* жертвоприноше́ние *neut.*

immoral /ɪ'mɔrəl/ *adj.* безнра́вственный.

immorality /ˌɪmə'rælɪti/ *n.* безнра́вственность *f.*

immortal /ɪ'mɔrtḷ/ *adj.* бессме́ртный.

immortality /ˌɪmɔr'tælɪti/ *n.* бессме́ртие *neut.*

immortalize /ɪ'mɔrtḷˌaiz/ *v.* обессме́ртить *pf.*; увекове́чивать *impf.*

immovability /ɪˌmuvə'bɪlɪti/ *n.* неподви́жность *f.*

immovable /ɪ'muvəbəl/ *adj.* неподви́жный, недви́жимый.

immune /ɪ'myun/ *adj.* невосприи́мчивый.

immunity /ɪ'myunɪti/ *n.* иммуните́т *m.*

immunization /ˌɪmyənə'zeiʃən/ *n.* (*med.*) иммуниза́ция *f.*

immunize /'ɪmyəˌnaiz/ *v.* иммунизи́ровать *impf.*

immunodeficiency /ˌɪmyənoudɪ'fɪʃənsi/ *n.* имму́нная недоста́точность *f.*

immunology /ˌɪmyə'nɒlədʒi/ *n.* иммуноло́гия *f.*

immunosuppressant /ˌɪmyənousə'prɛsənt/ *n.* иммунодепресса́нт *m.*

immure /ɪ'myur/ *v.* замурова́ть *impf.*

immutability /ɪˌmyutə'bɪlɪti/ *n.* неизме́нность *f.*

immutable /ɪ'myutəbəl/ *adj.* неизме́нный, непрело́жный.

imp /ɪmp/ *n.* черте́нок, бесе́нок *m.*

impact /'ɪmpækt/ *n.* уда́р *m.*, столкнове́ние *neut.*; (*influence*) влия́ние *neut.*

impair /ɪm'pɛər/ *v.* вреди́ть; поврежда́ть *impf.*, повреди́ть *pf.*

impairment /ɪm'pɛərmənt/ *n.* поврежде́ние; (*weakening*) ослабле́ние *neut.*

impale /ɪm'peil/ *v.* нака́лывать; сажа́ть на́ кол *impf.*

impalpable /ɪm'pælpəbəl/ *adj.* неощути́мый.

impanel /ɪm'pænḷ/ *v.* составля́ть спи́сок прися́жных *impf.*

imparity /ɪm'pærɪti/ *n.* нера́венство *neut.*

impart /ɪm'pɑrt/ *v.* придава́ть *impf.*; (*pass on*) дели́ться (c *with instr.*) *impf.*

impartial /ɪm'pɑrʃəl/ *adj.* беспристра́стный.

impartiality /ˌɪm,pɑrʃi'ælɪti/ *n.* беспристра́стность *f.*

impassable /ɪm'pæsəbəl/ *adj.* непроходи́мый.

impasse /'ɪmpæs/ *n.* тупи́к *m.*

impassion /ɪm'pæʃən/ *v.* глубоко́ волнова́ть *impf.*

impassive /ɪm'pæsɪv/ *adj.* бесстра́стный; равноду́шный.

impatience /ɪm'peiʃəns/ *n.* нетерпе́ние *neut.*

impatient /ɪm'peiʃənt/ *adj.* нетерпели́вый.

impatiently /ɪm'peiʃəntli/ *adv.* с нетерпе́нием.

impeach /ɪm'pitʃ/ *v.* обвиня́ть *impf.*

impeachment /ɪm'pitʃmənt/ *n.* (*leg.*) импи́чмент *m.*

impeccability /ɪmˌpɛkə'bɪlɪti/ *n.* безукори́зненность *f.*

impeccable /ɪm'pɛkəbəl/ *adj.* безупре́чный, безукори́зненный.

impecuniosity /ˌɪmpɪˌkyuni'ɒsɪti/ *n.* безде́нежье *neut.*

impecunious /ˌɪmpɪ'kyuniəs/ *adj.* безде́нежный.

impedance /ɪm'pidns/ *n.* сопротивле́ние *neut.*

impede /ɪm'pid/ *v.* препя́тствовать *impf.*

impediment /ɪm'pɛdəmənt/ *n.* препя́тствие *neut.*; (*defect*) дефе́кт *m.*

impedimenta /ɪmˌpɛdə'mɛntə/ *n.* бага́ж *m.*

impel /ɪm'pɛl/ *v.* побужда́ть *impf.*

impellent /ɪm'pɛlənt/ *n.* дви́жущая си́ла *f.*

impeller /ɪm'pɛlər/ *n.* (*tech.*) крыльча́тка *f.*

impend /ɪm'pɛnd/ *v.* надвига́ться *impf.*

impending /ɪm'pɛndɪŋ/ *adj.* надвига́ющийся, приближа́ющийся; предстоя́щий.

impenetrability /ɪmˌpɛnɪtrə'bɪlɪti/ *n.* непроница́емость *f.*

impenetrable /ɪm'pɛnɪtrəbəl/ *adj.* непроница́емый.

impenitence /ɪm'pɛnɪtəns/ *n.* нераска́янность *f.*

impenitent /ɪm'pɛnɪtənt/ *adj.* нераска́явшийся.

imperative /ɪm'pɛrətɪv/ **1.** *adj.* необходи́мый; повели́тельный, императи́вный. **2.** *n.* (*gram.*) повели́тельное наклоне́ние *neut.*

imperceptible /ˌɪmpər'sɛptəbəl/ *adj.* незаме́тный.

imperceptive /ˌɪmpər'sɛptɪv/ *adj.* невосприи́мчивый.

imperfect /ɪm'pɜrfɪkt/ *adj.* несоверше́нный.

imperfection /ˌɪmpər'fɛkʃən/ *n.* несоверше́нство *neut.*; (*fault*) недоста́ток *m.*

imperfective /ˌɪmpər'fɛktɪv/ *adj.* (*gram.*) несоверше́нный вид; имперфе́кт *m.*

imperforated /ɪm'pɜrfəˌreitɪd/ *adj.* беззубцо́вый.

imperial /ɪm'pɪriəl/ *adj.* (*empire*) импе́рский; (*emperor*) импера́торский; ца́рственный.

imperialism /ɪm'pɪriəˌlizəm/ *n.* империали́зм *m.*

imperialist /ɪm'pɪriəlɪst/ *n.* империали́ст *m.*

imperil /ɪm'pɛrəl/ *v.* подверга́ть опа́сности *impf.*

imperious /ɪm'pɪriəs/ *adj.* вла́стный, повели́тельный; деспоти́ческий, дикта́торский.

imperishable /ɪm'pɛrɪʃəbəl/ *adj.* непо́ртящийся.

impermanence /ɪmˈpɜrmənəns/ *n.* непостоянство *neut.*

impermanent /ɪmˈpɜrmənənt/ *adj.* непостоянный, временный.

impermeable /ɪmˈpɜrmiəbəl/ *adj.* непроницаемый.

impermissible /ˌɪmpərˈmɪsəbəl/ *adj.* недозволенный; недопустимый.

impersonal /ɪmˈpɜrsənļ/ *adj.* безличный.

impersonate /ɪmˈpɜrsəˌneit/ *v.* олицетворять *impf.*, олицетворить *pf.*

impersonation /ɪmˌpɜrsəˈneiʃən/ *n.* олицетворение *neut.*

impersonator /ɪmˈpɜrsəˌneitər/ *n.* самозванец, самозванка *f.*

impertinence /ɪmˈpɜrtņəns/ *n.* дерзость *neut.*

impertinent /ɪmˈpɜrtņənt/ *adj.* дерзкий, наглый, нахальный.

imperturbability /ˌɪmpərˌtɜrbəˈbɪlɪti/ *n.* невозмутимость *f.*

imperturbable /ˌɪmpərˈtɜrbəbəl/ *adj.* невозмутимый.

impervious /ɪmˈpɜrviəs/ *adj.* непроницаемый.

impetigo /ˌɪmpɪˈtaigou/ *n.* импетиго *neut.* *indecl.*

impetuosity /ɪmˌpɛtʃuˈɒsɪti/ *n.* поспешность *f.*

impetuous /ɪmˈpɛtʃuəs/ *adj.* стремительный.

impetus /ˈɪmpɪtəs/ *n.* импульс *m.*

impiety /ɪmˈpaiɪti/ *n.* неблагочестивость; непочтительность *f.*

impinge /ɪmˈpɪndʒ/ *v.* покушаться (на *with acc.*) *impf.*

impious /ˈɪmpiəs, ɪmˈpai-/ *adj.* нечестивый.

impish /ˈɪmpɪʃ/ *adj.* проказливый, озорной.

implacability /ɪmˌplækəˈbɪlɪti/ *n.* неумолимость *f.*

implacable /ɪmˈplækəbəl/ *adj.* неумолимый.

implant /ɪmˈplænt/ *v.* насаждать *impf.*

implantation /ˌɪmplænˈteiʃən/ *n.* внушение; внедрение ; (*med.*) имплантация *f.*

implausibility /ɪmˌplɔzəˈbɪlɪti/ *n.* неправдоподобие *neut.*

implausible /ɪmˈplɔzəbəl/ *adj.* невероятный, неправдоподобный.

implementation /ˌɪmpləmənˈteiʃən/ *n.* выполнение, осуществление *neut.*; имплементация *f.*

implicate /ˈɪmplɪˌkeit/ *v.* впутывать *impf.*, впутать *pf.*

implication /ˌɪmplɪˈkeiʃən/ *n.* вовлечение *neut.*; (*significance*) значение *neut.*

implicit /ɪmˈplɪsɪt/ *adj.* подразумеваемый; (*absolute*) безоговорочный.

implicitly /ɪmˈplɪsɪtli/ *adv.* косвенно.

implied /ɪmˈplaid/ *adj.* подразумеваемый.

implore /ɪmˈplɔr/ *v.* умолять *impf.*

imploring /ɪmˈplɔrɪŋ/ *adj.* умоляющий.

implosion /ɪmˈplouʒən/ *n.* имплозия *f.*

implosive /ɪmˈplousɪv/ *adj.* имплозивный.

imply /ɪmˈplai/ *v.* подразумевать; намекать *impf.*

impolite /ˌɪmpəˈlait/ *adj.* невежливый.

impolitic /ɪmˈpɒlɪtɪk/ *adj.* неблагоразумный.

imponderable /ɪmˈpɒndərəbəl/ *adj.* невесомый; (*incalculable*) неопределимый.

import *n.*, *adj.* /ˈɪmpɔrt/ *v.* /ɪmˈpɔrt/ **1.** *n.* импорт, ввоз *m.*; (*significance*) значение *neut.* **2.** *adj.* импортный. **3.** *v.* ввозить *impf.*, ввезти *pf.*; импортировать *impf.* and *pf.*

importable /ɪmˈpɔrtəbəl/ *adj.* ввозимый.

importance /ɪmˈpɔrtns/ *n.* важность *f.*

important /ɪmˈpɔrtņt/ *adj.* важный.

importation /ˌɪmpɔrˈteiʃən/ *n.* ввоз *m.*

imported /ɪmˈpɔrtɪd/ *adj.* импортный, ввозной.

importer /ɪmˈpɔrtər/ *n.* импортёр *m.*

importunate /ɪmˈpɔrtʃənɪt/ *adj.* назойливый, докучливый.

importune /ˌɪmpɔrˈtun/ *v.* докучать (*with dat.*), приставать (к *with dat.*) *impf.*

importunity /ˌɪmpɔrˈtunɪti/ *n.* назойливость *f.*

impose /ɪmˈpouz/ *v.* облагать *impf.*, обложить *pf.*; (*force*) навязывать *impf.*

imposing /ɪmˈpouzɪŋ/ *adj.* впечатляющий, импозантный.

imposition /ˌɪmpəˈzɪʃən/ *n.* обложение; наложение *neut.*

impossibility /ɪmˌpɒsəˈbɪlɪti/ *n.* невозможность *f.*

impossible /ɪmˈpɒsəbəl/ *adj.* невозможный.

impost /ˈɪmpoust/ *n.* пошлина *f.*

impostor /ɪmˈpɒstər/ *n.* самозванец *m.*, самозванка *f.*

imposture /ɪmˈpɒstʃər/ *n.* надувательство *neut.*

impotence /ˈɪmpətəns/ *n.* бессилие *neut.*; импотенция *f.*

impotent /ˈɪmpətənt/ *adj.* бессильный; импотентный.

impound /ɪmˈpaund/ *v.* (*cattle*) загонять *impf.*; (*confiscate*) конфисковать *impf.* and *pf.*

impoverish /ɪmˈpɒvərɪʃ/ *v.* разорять; истощать *impf.*

impoverishment /ɪmˈpɒvərɪʃmənt/ *n.* обеднение, обнищание *neut.*

impracticability /ɪmˌpræktɪkəˈbɪlɪti/ *n.* неосуществимость *f.*

impracticable /ɪmˈpræktɪkəbəl/ *adj.* невыполнимый, неосуществимый.

impractical /ɪmˈpræktɪkəl/ *adj.* непрактичный, нереалистичный.

impracticality /ɪmˌpræktɪˈkælɪti/ *n.* непрактичность *f.*

imprecate /ˈɪmprɪˌkeit/ *v.* проклинать *impf.*

imprecation /ˌɪmprɪˈkeiʃən/ *n.* проклятие *neut.*

imprecatory /ˈɪmprɪkəˌtɔri/ *adj.* проклинающий.

imprecise /ˌɪmprəˈsais/ *adj.* неточный.

impregnability /ɪmˌprɛgnəˈbɪlɪti/ *n.* неприступность *f.*

impregnable /ɪmˈprɛgnəbəl/ *adj.* неприступный; неопровержимый.

impregnate /ɪmˈprɛgneit/ *v.* оплодотворять *impf.*, оплодотворить *pf.*; (*saturate*) пропитывать *impf.*

impregnation /ˌɪmprɛgˈneiʃən/ *n.* оплодотворение *neut.*

impresario /ˌɪmprəˈsɑriˌou/ *n.* импресарио *m.* *indecl.*

impress /ɪmˈprɛs/ *v.* производить впечатление (на *with acc.*) *impf.*; произвести *pf.*

impression /ɪmˈprɛʃən/ *n.* впечатление *neut.*

impressionable /ɪmˈprɛʃənəbəl/ *adj.* впечатлительный.

impressionism /ɪmˈprɛʃəˌnɪzəm/ *n.* импрессионизм *m.*

impressionist /ɪmˈprɛʃənɪst/ *also* **impressionistic** /ɪmˌprɛʃəˈnɪstɪk/ *adj.* импрессионистский, импрессионистический.

impressive /ɪmˈprɛsɪv/ *adj.* поразительный; впечатляющий.

imprimatur /ˌɪmprɪˈmɑtər/ n. разрешéние цензýры neut.

imprint /ˈɪmprɪnt/ n. (mark, sign) отпечáток m.; (printing data) выходны́е дáнные.

imprison /ɪmˈprɪzən/ v. заключáть (в тюрьмý) impf., заключи́ть pf.

imprisonment /ɪmˈprɪzənmənt/ n. (тюрéмное) заключéние neut.

improbable /ɪmˈprɒbəbəl/ adj. неправдоподóбный.

impromptu /ɪmˈprɒmptu/ 1. adj. импровизи́рованный. 2. adv. экспрóмтом.

improper /ɪmˈprɒpər/ adj. непрáвильный; (indecent) неприли́чный.

impropriety /ˌɪmprəˈpraɪɪti/ n. неприли́чие neut.; неумéстность f.

improve /ɪmˈpruv/ v. улучшáть(ся) impf., улýчшить(ся) pf.

improvement /ɪmˈpruvmənt/ n. улучшéние neut.

improvidence /ɪmˈprɒvɪdəns/ n. непредусмотри́тельность f.

improvident /ɪmˈprɒvɪdənt/ adj. непредусмотри́тельный.

Improvisation /ˌɪmˌprɒvəˈzeɪʃən/ n. импровизáция f.

improvise /ˈɪmprəˌvaɪz/ v. импровизи́ровать impf. and pf.

improviser /ˈɪmprəˌvaɪzər/ n. импровизáтор m.

imprudence /ɪmˈprudns/ n. неблагоразýмие neut.

imprudent /ɪmˈprudnt/ adj. неблагоразýмный.

impudence /ˈɪmpyədəns/ n. дéрзость, нáглость ; нахáльство neut.

impudent /ˈɪmpyədənt/ adj бессты́дный, дéрзкий.

impugn /ɪmˈpyun/ v. оспáривать impf.

impulse /ˈɪmpʌls/ n. толчóк; и́мпульс; поры́в m.

impulsion /ɪmˈpʌlʃən/ n. побуждéние neut.

impulsive /ɪmˈpʌlsɪv/ adj. побуждáющий, импульси́вный.

impunity /ɪmˈpyunɪti/ n. безнакáзанность f.

impure /ɪmˈpyʊr/ adj. нечи́стый.

impurity /ɪmˈpyʊrɪti/ n. нечистотá f.

imputable /ɪmˈpyutəbəl/ adj. припи́сываемый.

imputation /ˌɪmpyʊˈteɪʃən/ n. обвинéние neut.

impute /ɪmˈpyut/ v. припи́сывать (with dat.) impf.

in /ɪn/ 1. prep. в (во) (with acc. or prep.), на (with acc. or prep.). 2. adv. внутри́, внутрь.

inability /ˌɪnəˈbɪlɪti/ n. неспособность f.; неумéние neut.

in absentia /ɪn æbˈsɛnʃə/ adv. заóчно.

inaccessibility /ˌɪnəkˌsɛsəˈbɪlɪti/ n. недостýпность f.

inaccessible /ˌɪnəkˈsɛsəbəl/ adj. недостýпный; (person) непристýпный.

inaccuracy /ɪnˈækyərəsi/ n. неточность f.

inaccurate /ɪnˈækyərɪt/ adj. неточный.

inaction /ɪnˈækʃən/ n. бездéйствие neut.

inactivate /ɪnˈæktəˌveɪt/ v. дезактиви́ровать impf.

inactive /ɪnˈæktɪv/ adj. бездéятельный.

inactivity /ˌɪnækˈtɪvɪti/ n. бездéятельность f.

inadequacy /ɪnˈædɪkwəsi/ n. недостáточность f.

inadequate /ɪnˈædɪkwɪt/ adj. недостáточный.

inadmissibility /ˌɪnədˌmɪsəˈbɪlɪti/ n. недопусти́мость f.

inadmissible /ˌɪnədˈmɪsəbəl/ adj. недопусти́мый.

inadvertence /ˌɪnədˈvɜrtn̩s/ n. небрéжность f.; недосмóтр m.

inadvertent /ˌɪnədˈvɜrtnt/ adj. невнимáтельный; ненамéренный.

inadvisability /ˌɪnədˌvaɪzəˈbɪlɪti/ n. нецелесообрáзность f.

inadvisable /ˌɪnədˈvaɪzəbəl/ adj. нецелесообрáзный.

inalienable /ɪnˈeɪlyənəbəl/ adj. неотъéмлемый.

inane /ɪˈneɪn/ adj. пустóй; глýпый.

inanimate /ɪnˈænəmɪt/ adj. неодушевлённый, неживóй.

inanition /ˌɪnəˈnɪʃən/ n. истощéние neut.

inanity /ɪˈnænɪti/ n. глýпость; бессмы́сленность f.

inapplicability /ɪnˌæplɪkəˈbɪlɪti/ n. непримени́мость f.

inapplicable /ɪnˈæplɪkəbəl/ adj. непримени́мый; неумéстный.

inapprehensible /ˌɪnˌæprɪˈhɛnsəbəl/ adj. непостижи́мый.

inapprehension /ˌɪnˌæprɪˈhɛnʃən/ n. непонимáние neut.

inapprehensive /ˌɪnˌæprɪˈhɛnsɪv/ adj. непоня́тливый, несообрази́тельный.

inapproachability /ˌɪnəˌproʊtʃəˈbɪlɪti/ n. недостýпность f.

inapproachable /ˌɪnəˈproʊtʃəbəl/ adj. непристýпный, недостýпный.

inappropriate /ˌɪnəˈproʊpriɪt/ adj. неподходя́щий, несоотвéтствующий.

inaptitude /ɪnˈæptɪˌtud/ n. неумéстность; неспосóбность f.

inarticulate /ˌɪnɑrˈtɪkyəlɪt/ adj. невня́тный, нечленоразд́ельный.

inarticulateness /ˌɪnɑrˈtɪkyəlɪtnɪs/ n. невня́тность f.

inartistic /ˌɪnɑrˈtɪstɪk/ adj. нехудóжественный.

inasmuch as /ˌɪnəzˈmʌtʃ əz/ conj. поскóльку, так как.

inattention /ˌɪnəˈtɛnʃən/ n. невнимáтельность f., невнимáние neut.

inattentive /ˌɪnəˈtɛntɪv/ adj. невнимáтельный.

inaudibility /ɪnˌɔdəˈbɪlɪti/ n. плохáя слы́шимость f.

inaudible /ɪnˈɔdəbəl/ adj. неслы́шный, неслы́шимый.

inaugural /ɪnˈɔgyərəl/ adj. вступи́тельный.

inaugurate /ɪnˈɔgyəˌreɪt/ v. (open) открывáть impf., откры́ть pf.

inauguration /ɪnˌɔgyəˈreɪʃən/ n. торжéственное откры́тие neut.

inauspicious /ˌɪnɔˈspɪʃəs/ adj. неблагоприя́тный; (ill-omened) зловéщий.

inboard /ˈɪnˌbɔrd/ adv. внýтренний.

inborn /ˈɪnˌbɔrn/ also **inbred** /-ˈbrɛd/ adj. врождённый; прирóдный.

inbreeding /ˈɪnˌbridɪŋ/ n. инбри́динг m.; рóдственное спáривание neut.

incalculable /ɪnˈkælkyələbəl/ adj. неисчисли́мый.

incandesce /ˌɪnkənˈdɛs/ v. накаля́ть(ся) impf.

incandescent /ˌɪnkənˈdɛsənt/ adj. накалённый добелá.

incantation /ˌɪnkænˈteɪʃən/ n. заклинáние neut., заговóр m.; колдовствó neut.

incantatory /ɪnˈkæntəˌtɔri/ adj. заклинáтельный.

incapable /ɪnˈkeɪpəbəl/ adj. неспосóбный.

incapacitated /ˌɪnkə'pæsɪˌteitɪd/ *adj.* не дееспосóбный.

incapacity /ˌɪnkə'pæsɪti/ *n.* неспосóбность *f.*

incarcerate /ɪn'kɑrsəˌreit/ *v.* заточáть *impf.*, заключáть в тюрьмý *impf.*

incarceration /ɪnˌkɑrsə'reiʃən/ *n.* заточéние *neut.*

incarnate / *adj.* ɪn'kɑrnɪt; *v.* ɪn'kɑrneit/ **1.** *adj.* воплощённый. **2.** *v.* воплощáть *impf.*

incarnation /ˌɪnkɑr'neiʃən/ *n.* воплощéние *neut.*

incautious /ɪn'kɔʃəs/ *adj.* неосторóжный, неосмотрительный.

incautiousness /ɪn'kɔʃəsnɪs/ *n.* неосторóжность *f.*

incendiarism /ɪn'sɛndiəˌrɪzəm/ *n.* поджóг *m.*

incendiary /ɪn'sɛndiˌɛri/ *adj.* зажигáтельный.

incense¹ /'ɪnsɛns/ *n.* лáдан *m.*

incense² /ɪn'sɛns/ *v.* разгневáть *impf.*

incentive /ɪn'sɛntɪv/ *n.* побуждéние *neut.*, стимул *m.*

incept /ɪn'sɛpt/ *v.* поглощáть *impf.*

inception /ɪn'sɛpʃən/ *n.* начáло *neut.*

inceptive /ɪn'sɛptɪv/ *adj.* начинáющийся, начáльный; (*gram.*) начинáтельный.

incertitude /ɪn'sɜrtɪˌtud/ *n.* неувéренность *f.*

incessant /ɪn'sɛsənt/ *adj.* непрерывный.

incest /'ɪnsɛst/ *n.* кровосмешéние *neut.*

incestuous /ɪn'sɛstʃuəs/ *adj.* кровосмесительный.

inch /ɪntʃ/ *n.* дюйм *m.*

inchoate /ɪn'kouɪt/ *adj.* начáльный; (*in disorder*) бесфóрменный.

incidence /'ɪnsɪdəns/ *n.* распространéние *neut.*; (*math.*) инцидéнтность *f.* (*phys.*) падéние *neut.*

incident /'ɪnsɪdənt/ *n.* происшéствие *neut.*, инцидéнт, слýчай *m.*

incidental /ˌɪnsɪ'dɛntl̩/ *adj.* случáйный.

incidentally /ˌɪnsɪ'dɛntli/ *adv.* мéжду прóчим; случáйно.

incinerate /ɪn'sɪnəˌreit/ *v.* сжигáть (дотлá) *impf.*

incineration /ɪnˌsɪnə'reiʃən/ *n.* сжигáние *neut.*

incinerator /ɪn'sɪnəˌreitər/ *n.* мусоросжигáтельная печь *f.*

incipient /ɪn'sɪpiənt/ *adj.* начинáющийся.

incise /ɪn'saiz/ *v.* надрезáть *impf.*

incision /ɪn'sɪʒən/ *n.* надрéз *m.*

incisive /ɪn'saisɪv/ *adj.* рéжущий; тóнкий.

incisor /ɪn'saizər/ *n.* резéц, передний зуб *m.*

incite /ɪn'sait/ *v.* побуждáть *impf.*, побудить *pf.*; подстрекáть (к *with dat.*) *impf.*

incitement /ɪn'saitmənt/ *n.* подстрекáтельство *neut.*

incivility /ˌɪnsə'vɪlɪti/ *n.* нелюбéзность *f.*

inclemency /ɪn'klɛmənsi/ *n.* сурóвость *f.*

inclement /ɪn'klɛmənt/ *adj.* сурóвый; ненáстный; **inclement weather** *n.* ненáстье *neut.*, непогóда *f.*

inclination /ˌɪnklə'neiʃən/ *n.* (*slope*) наклонéние *neut.*, наклóн *m.*; (*propensity*) склóнность *f.*

incline / *n.* 'ɪnklain; *v.* ɪn'klain/ **1.** *n.* наклóн *m.* **2.** *v.* наклонять(ся) *impf.*, наклонить(ся) *pf.*; склонять(ся) *impf.*, склонить(ся) *pf.*

inclined /ɪn'klaind/ *adj.* (*sloping*) наклóнный; (*tending to*) склóнный, располóженный.

inclinometer /ˌɪnklə'nɒmɪtər/ *n.* уклономéр *m.*

include /ɪn'klud/ *v.* включáть *impf.*, включить *pf.*

including /ɪn'kludɪŋ/ *prep.* включáя (*with acc.*).

inclusion /ɪn'kluʒən/ *n.* включéние *neut.*

inclusive /ɪn'klusɪv/ **1.** *adj.* включáющий (в себé). **2.** *adv.* включительно.

incognito /ˌɪnkɒg'nitou/ **1.** *n.* инкóгнито *neut. indecl.* **2.** *adv.* инкóгнито.

incoherence /ˌɪnkou'hɪərəns/ *also* **incoherency** *n.* несвязность; бессвязность *f.*

incoherent /ˌɪnkou'hɪərənt/ *adj.* несвязный; бессвязный.

incombustibility /ˌɪnkəmˌbʌstə'bɪlɪti/ *n.* негорючесть *f.*

incombustible /ˌɪnkəm'bʌstəbəl/ *adj.* негорючий, огнестóйкий.

income /'ɪnkʌm/ *n.* дохóд *m.*

income tax *n.* подохóдный налóг *m.*

incoming /'ɪnˌkʌmɪŋ/ *adj.* входящий; вступáющий.

incommensurable /ˌɪnkə'mɛnsərəbəl/ *adj.* несоизмеримый.

incommensurate /ˌɪnkə'mɛnsərɪt/ *adj.* несоразмéрный, неадеквáтный.

incommode /ˌɪnkə'moud/ *v.* мешáть *impf.*

incommodious /ˌɪnkə'moudiəs/ *adj.* неудóбный; тéсный.

incommunicable /ˌɪnkə'myunɪkəbəl/ *adj.* непередавáемый.

incommunicado /ˌɪnkəˌmyunɪ'kɑdou/ *adj.* лишённый прáва сообщéния.

incommunicative /ˌɪnkə'myunɪkətɪv/ *adj.* неразговóрчивый.

incommutable /ˌɪnkə'myutəbəl/ *adj.* неизмéнный.

incomparable /ɪn'kɒmpərəbəl/ *adj.* несравнимый; (*matchless*) несравнéнный.

incompatibility /ˌɪnkəmˌpætə'bɪlɪti/ *n.* несовместимость *f.*

incompatible /ˌɪnkəm'pætəbəl/ *adj.* несовместимый.

incompetence /ɪn'kɒmpɪtəns/ *n.* неспосóбность *f.*; (*leg.*) неправомóчность *f.*

incompetent /ɪn'kɒmpɪtənt/ *adj.* неспосóбный; некомпетéнтный; (*leg.*) неправомóчный.

incomplete /ˌɪnkəm'plit/ *adj.* непóлный, незакóнченный.

incompleteness /ˌɪnkəm'plitnɪs/ *n.* неполнотá *f.*

incomprehensibility /ˌɪnkɒmprɪˌhɛnsə'bɪlɪti/ *n.* непонятность *f.*

incomprehensible /ˌɪnkɒmprɪ'hɛnsəbəl/ *adj.* непонятный.

incomprehension /ˌɪnkɒmprɪ'hɛnʃən/ *n.* непонимáние *neut.*

incomprehensive /ˌɪnkɒmprɪ'hɛnsɪv/ *adj.* ограниченный.

incompressible /ˌɪnkəm'prɛsəbəl/ *adj.* несжимáемый.

incomputable /ˌɪnkəm'pyutəbəl/ *adj.* неисчислимый.

inconceivable /ˌɪnkən'sivəbəl/ *adj.* невообразимый.

inconclusive /ˌɪnkən'klusɪv/ *adj.* недоказáтельный.

incongruity /ˌɪnkɒn'gruɪti/ *n.* несообрáзность *f.*

incongruous /ɪn'kɒŋgruəs/ *adj.* несообрáзный.

inconsecutive /ˌɪnkən'sɛkyətɪv/ *adj.* непослéдовательный.

inconsequence /ɪn'kɒnsɪˌkwɛns/ *n.* непослéдовательность *f.*

inconsequent /ɪn'kɒnsɪ,kwɛnt/ *adj.* непоследовательный, нелогичный.

inconsiderable /,ɪnkən'sɪdərəbəl/ *adj.* незначительный.

inconsiderate /,ɪnkən'sɪdərɪt/ *adj.* невнимательный.

inconsistency /,ɪnkən'sɪstənsi/ *n.* непоследовательность; несовместимость *f.*

inconsistent /,ɪnkən'sɪstənt/ *adj.* непоследовательнный.

inconsolable /,ɪnkən'souləbəl/ *adj.* безутешный, неутешный.

inconsonant /ɪn'kɒnsənənt/ *adj.* несогласный.

inconspicuous /,ɪnkən'spɪkyuəs/ *adj.* незаметный.

inconstancy /ɪn'kɒnstənsi/ *n.* непостоянство *neut.*

inconstant /ɪn'kɒnstənt/ *adj.* изменчивый; непостоянный.

incontestable /,ɪnkən'tɛstəbəl/ *adj.* неоспоримый.

incontestably /,ɪnkən'tɛstəbli/ *adv.* бесспорно.

incontinence /ɪn'kɒntɪnəns/ *n.* несдержанность *f.*; (*med.*) недержание *neut.*

incontinent /ɪn'kɒntɪnənt/ *adj.* страдающий недержанием.

incontrovertible /,ɪnkɒntrə'vɜrtəbəl/ *adj.* неопровержимый, неоспоримый.

incontrovertibly /,ɪnkɒntrə'vɜrtəbli/ *adv.* несомненно.

inconvenience /,ɪnkən'vinyəns/ **1.** *n.* неудобство *neut.* **2.** *v.* причинять неудобство *impf.*

inconvenient /,ɪnkən'vinyənt/ *adj.* неудобный.

inconveniently /,ɪnkən'vinyəntli/ *adv.* неудобно.

inconvertibility /,ɪnkən,vɜrtə'bɪlɪti/ *n.* необратимость *f.*

inconvertible /,ɪnkən'vɜrtəbəl/ *adj.* необратимый, неконвертируемый.

incoordinate /,ɪnkou'ordnɪt/ *adj.* несогласованный.

incoordination /,ɪnkou,ordn'eiʃən/ *n.* несогласованность *f.*

incorporate /ɪn'kɔrpə,reit/ *v.* соединять(ся); объединять(ся) *impf.*

incorporated /ɪn'kɔrpə,reitɪd/ *adj.* объединённый.

incorporation /ɪn,kɔrpə'reiʃən/ *n.* объединение *neut.*; инкорпорация *f.*

incorporeal /,ɪnkɔr'pɔriəl/ *adj.* бестелесный.

incorrect /,ɪnkə'rɛkt/ *adj.* неправильный.

incorrectness /,ɪnkə'rɛktnɪs/ *n.* неправильность *f.*

incorrigibility /ɪn,kɔrɪdʒə'bɪlɪti/ *n.* неисправимость *f.*

incorrigible /ɪn'kɔrɪdʒəbəl/ *adj.* неисправимый.

incorruptibility /,ɪnkə,rʌptə'bɪlɪti/ *n.* неподкупность *f.*

incorruptible /,ɪnkə'rʌptəbəl/ *adj.* (*not decaying*) непортящийся; (*not bribable*) неподкупный.

increase /n. 'ɪnkris; v. ɪn'kris/ **1.** *n.* увеличение *neut.*, рост *m.*; возрастание; повышение *neut.* **2.** *v.t.* увеличивать *impf.*, увеличить *pf.*; *v.i.* увеличиваться *impf.*, увеличиться *pf.*

increasingly /ɪn'krisɪŋli/ *adv.* всё более.

incredibility /ɪn,krɛdə'bɪlɪti/ *n.* невероятность *f.*

incredible /ɪn'krɛdəbəl/ *adj.* невероятный.

incredulity /,ɪnkrɪ'dulɪti/ *n.* недоверие *neut.*

incredulous /ɪn'krɛdʒələs/ *adj.* недоверчивый.

incredulously /ɪn'krɛdʒələsli/ *adv.* с недоверием.

increment /'ɪnkrəmənt, 'ɪŋ-/ *n.* прирост *m.*; (*profit*) прибыль *f.*

incriminate /ɪn'krɪmə,neit/ *v.* инкриминировать *impf. and pf.*

incriminating /ɪn'krɪmə,neitɪŋ/ *adj.* обвиняющий; инкриминирующий.

incrimination /ɪn,krɪmə'neiʃən/ *n.* инкриминация *f.*

incriminatory /ɪn'krɪmənə,tɔri/ *adj.* обвинительный.

incrustation /,ɪnkrʌ'steiʃən/ *n.* корка; инкрустация *f.*

incubate /'ɪnkyə,beit, 'ɪŋ-/ *v.* (*sit on eggs*) высиживать *impf.*; (*bacteria*) выращивать *impf.*

incubation /,ɪnkyə'beiʃən, ,ɪŋ-/ *n.* инкубация *f.*

incubator /'ɪnkyə,beitər, 'ɪŋ-/ *n.* инкубатор *m.*

incubus /'ɪnkyəbəs, 'ɪŋ-/ *n.* (*evil spirit*) инкуб *m.*; (*nightmare*) кошмар *m.*

inculcate /ɪn'kʌlkeit/ *v.* внушать, внедрять *impf.*

inculcation /,ɪnkʌl'keiʃən/ *n.* внушение *neut.*

incunable /ɪn'kyunəbəl/ *n.* инкунабула *f.*

incunabula /,ɪnkyu'næbyələ/ *n.* инкунабулы *pl.*

incur /ɪn'kɜr/ *v.* навлекать на себя *impf.*

incurable /ɪn'kyʊrəbəl/ *adj.* неизлечимый.

incurious /ɪn'kyʊriəs/ *adj.* нелюбопытный; **not incurious** любопытный, небезынтересный.

incursion /ɪn'kɜrʒən/ *n.* вторжение *neut.*; набег *m.*

incursive /ɪn'kɜrsɪv/ *adj.* вторгающийся.

incurvate /'ɪnkɜr,veit/ *adj.* загнутый.

incuse /ɪn'kyuz/ *n.* чеканка *f.*

indebted /ɪn'dɛtɪd/ *adj.* обязан (*with dat.*); в долгу.

indebtedness /ɪn'dɛtɪdnɪs/ *n.* задолженность *f.*

indecency /ɪn'disənsi/ *n.* неприличие *neut.*

indecent /ɪn'disənt/ *adj.* неприличный; непристойный.

indecipherable /,ɪndɪ'saifərəbəl/ *adj.* неразборчивый.

indecision /,ɪndɪ'sɪʒən/ *n.* нерешительность *f.*

indecisive /,ɪndɪ'saisɪv/ *adj.* нерешительный.

indeclinable /,ɪndɪ'klainəbəl/ *adj.* (*gram.*) несклоняемый.

indecorous /ɪn'dɛkərəs/ *adj.* неблагопристойный.

indecorum /,ɪndɪ'kɔrəm/ *n.* неблагопристойность *f.*

indeed /ɪn'did/ *adj.* действительно; (*interrog.*) неужели!

indefatigable /,ɪndɪ'fætɪgəbəl/ *adj.* неутомимый; неустанный.

indefensible /,ɪndɪ'fɛnsəbəl/ *adj.* непростительный.

indefinable /,ɪndɪ'fainəbəl/ *adj.* неопределимый.

indefinite /ɪn'dɛfənɪt/ *adj.* неопределённый.

indefinitely /ɪn'dɛfənɪtli/ *adv.* бесконечно.

indelible /ɪn'dɛləbəl/ *adj.* несмываемый.

indelicacy /ɪn'dɛlɪkəsi/ *n.* неделикатность *f.*

indelicate /ɪn'dɛlɪkɪt/ *adj.* неделикатный, бестактный.

indemnification /ɪn,dɛmnəfɪ'keiʃən/ *n.* возмещение *neut.*

indemnify /ɪn'dɛmnə,fai/ *v.* возмещать *impf.*

indemnity /ɪn'dɛmnɪti/ *n.* (*compensation*) компенсация *f.*; (*protection*) гарантия *f.*

indent /ɪn'dɛnt/ *v.* делать абзац *or* отступ *impf.*

indentation /ˌɪndɛnˈteɪʃən/ n. (typogr.) óтступ, абзáц m.

indenture /ɪnˈdɛntʃər/ n. контрáкт m.

independence /ˌɪndɪˈpɛndəns/ n. незавиcимость f.

independent /ˌɪndɪˈpɛndənt/ adj. самостоятельный, незавиcимый.

independently /ˌɪndɪˈpɛndəntli/ adv. незавиcимо, самостоятельно.

in-depth /ˈɪnˈdɛpθ/ adj. глубóкий.

indescribable /ˌɪndɪˈskraɪbəbəl/ adj. неописýемый.

indestructibility /ˌɪndɪˌstrʌktɪˈbɪlɪti/ n. неразрушúмость f.

indestructible /ˌɪndɪˈstrʌktəbəl/ adj. неразрушúмый; нерушúмый.

indeterminable /ˌɪndɪˈtɜrmənəbəl/ adj. неопределúмый.

indeterminate /ˌɪndɪˈtɜrmənɪt/ adj. неопределённый; неяcный; нерешённый.

indetermination /ˌɪndɪˌtɜrməˈneɪʃən/ n. неопределённость; нерешúтельность f.

indeterminism /ˌɪndɪˈtɜrməˌnɪzəm/ n. индетерминúзм m.

index /ˈɪndɛks/ **1.** n. указáтель, úндекс m. **2.** v. (provide) снабжáть указáтелем impf.; (enter) заноcúть в указáтель impf.

India /ˈɪndiə/ n. úндия f.

Indian /ˈɪndiən/ **1.** adj. (USA) индéйский; (Asia) индúйский. **2.** n. (USA) индéец m., индиáнка f.; (Asia) индúец m., индиáнка f.

Indiana /ˌɪndiˈænə/ n. Индиáна f.

Indian Ocean n. Индúйский океáн m.

india paper n. тóнкая бумáга f.

india rubber n. каучýк m.

indicate /ˈɪndɪˌkeit/ v. укáзывать impf., указáть pf.

indication /ˌɪndɪˈkeiʃən/ n. указáние neut.; прúзнак m.

indicative /ɪnˈdɪkətɪv/ adj. показáтельный, укáзывающий; (gram.) изъявúтельный.

indicator /ˈɪndɪˌkeitər/ n. указáтель; индикáтор m.

indict /ɪnˈdait/ v. предъявля́ть обвинéние.

indictable /ɪnˈdaitəbəl/ adj. уголóвный.

indiction /ɪnˈdɪkʃən/ n. индúкт m.

indictment /ɪnˈdaitmənt/ n. (document) обвинúтельный акт; (accusation) предъявлéние обвинéния.

indifference /ɪnˈdɪfərəns/ n. равнодýшие neut.

indifferent /ɪnˈdɪfərənt/ adj. равнодýшный; (mediocre) посрéдственный.

indigence /ˈɪndɪdʒəns/ n. нуждá f.

indigenous /ɪnˈdɪdʒənəs/ adj. (native) тузéмный; (local) мéстный.

indigent /ˈɪndɪdʒənt/ adj. нуждáющийся, нúщий.

indigested /ˌɪndɪˈdʒɛstɪd/ adj. неперевáренный; (fig.) непродýманный.

indigestible /ˌɪndɪˈdʒɛstəbəl/ adj. неудобоварúмый.

indigestion /ˌɪndɪˈdʒɛstʃən/ n. расстрóйство желýдка f.

indignant /ɪnˈdɪgnənt/ adj. негодýющий.

indignation /ˌɪndɪgˈneiʃən/ n. негодовáние neut.

indignity /ɪnˈdɪgnɪti/ n. оскорблéние; унижéние neut.

indigo /ˈɪndɪˌgou/ n. индúго neut. indecl.

indirect /ˌɪndəˈrɛkt/ adj. непрямóй; кóсвенный.

indiscernible /ˌɪndɪˈsɜrnəbəl/ adj. неразличúмый.

indiscipline /ɪnˈdɪsəplɪn/ n. недисциплинúрованность f.

indiscoverable /ˌɪndɪˈskʌvərəbəl/ adj. необнарýжимый.

indiscreet /ˌɪndɪˈskrit/ adj. нескрóмный; неосторóжный.

indiscrete /ˌɪndɪˈskrit/ adj. непрерывный, сплошнóй.

indiscretion /ˌɪndɪˈskrɛʃən/ n. нескрóмность; неосмотрúтельность; бестáктность f.

indiscriminate /ˌɪndɪˈskrɪmənɪt/ adj. неразбóрчивый; огýльный.

indiscriminately /ˌɪndɪˈskrɪmənɪtli/ adv. без разбóра, без различúя.

indiscriminateness /ˌɪndɪˈskrɪmənɪtnɪs/ n. неразбóрчивость f.

indispensability /ˌɪndɪˌspɛnsəˈbɪlɪti/ n. необходúмость f.

indispensable /ˌɪndɪˈspɛnsəbəl/ adj. необходúмый; незаменúмый.

indisposed /ˌɪndɪˈspouzd/ adj. нездорóвый.

indisposition /ˌɪndɪspəˈzɪʃən/ n. (illness) недомогáние neut.; (disinclination) нерасположéние neut.

indisputability /ˌɪndɪˌspyutəˈbɪlɪti/ n. неоспорúмость f.

indisputable /ˌɪndɪˈspyutəbəl/ adj. неоспорúмый, бесспóрный.

indissolubility /ˌɪndɪˌsɑlyəˈbɪlɪti/ n. неразрушúмость f.

indissoluble /ˌɪndɪˈsɑlyəbəl/ adj. неразрушúмый; (in liquid) нерастворúмый.

indistinct /ˌɪndɪˈstɪŋkt/ adj. неяcный, неотчётливый.

indistinctness /ˌɪndɪˈstɪŋktnɪs/ n. неяcность f.

indistinguishable /ˌɪndɪˈstɪŋgwɪʃəbəl/ adj. неразличúмый.

indite /ɪnˈdait/ v. сочиня́ть impf.

indium /ˈɪndiəm/ n. úндий m.

individual /ˌɪndəˈvɪdʒuəl/ **1.** adj. индивидуáльный. **2.** n. индивúдуум m.; лúчность f.

individualism /ˌɪndəˈvɪdʒuəˌlɪzəm/ n. индивидуалúзм m.

individualist /ˌɪndəˈvɪdʒuəlɪst/ n. индивидуалúст m.

individualistic /ˌɪndəˌvɪdʒuəˈlɪstɪk/ adj. индивидуалистúческий.

individuality /ˌɪndəˌvɪdʒuˈælɪti/ n. индивидуáльность f.

individualize /ˌɪndəˈvɪdʒuəˌlaiz/ v. индивидуализúровать impf.

indivisibility /ˌɪndəˌvɪzəˈbɪlɪti/ n. неразделúмость f.

indivisible /ˌɪndəˈvɪzəbəl/ adj. неделúмый.

indocile /ɪnˈdɑsɪl/ adj. непокóрный.

indoctrinate /ɪnˈdɑktrəˌneit/ v. внушáть impf.

indoctrination /ɪnˌdɑktrəˈneiʃən/ n. обрабóтка f.

Indo-European /ˈɪnˌdou yʊrəˈpiən/ **1.** n. индоевропéйский язык. **2.** adj. индоевропéйский.

indolence /ˈɪndləns/ n. лéность; вя́лость f.

indolent /ˈɪndlənt/ adj. ленúвый; вя́лый.

indomitable /ɪnˈdɑmɪtəbəl/ adj. неукротúмый.

Indonesia /ˌɪndəˈniʒə/ n. Индонéзия f.

indoors /ɪnˈdɔrz/ adv. в закры́том помещéнии.

indraft /ˈɪnˌdræft/ n. притóк m.

indrawn /'ɪn,drɔn/ *adj.* втя́нутый.
indubitable /ɪn'dubɪtəbəl/ *adj.* несомне́нный; бесспо́рный.
induce /ɪn'dus/ *v.* склоня́ть *impf.*, склони́ть *pf.*; (*bring about*) вызыва́ть *impf.*
inducement /ɪn'dusmənt/ *n.* сти́мул ; побужде́ние *neut.*
induct /ɪn'dʌkt/ *v.* вводи́ть в до́лжность *impf.*
inductance /ɪn'dʌktəns/ *n.* индукти́вность *f.*
inductile /ɪn'dʌktɪl/ *adj.* неко́вкий.
induction /ɪn'dʌkʃən/ *n.* (*elec.*; *logic*) инду́кция *f.*
inductive /ɪn'dʌktɪv/ *adj.* индукти́вный.
indulge /ɪn'dʌldʒ/ *v.i.* предава́ться (*with dat.*) *impf.*, преда́ться *pf.*
indulgence /ɪn'dʌldʒəns/ *n.* потво́рство; снисхожде́ние *neut.*; снисходи́тельность *f.*
indulgent /ɪn'dʌldʒənt/ *adj.* снисходи́тельный; потво́рствующий.
industrial /ɪn'dʌstriəl/ *adj.* индустриа́льный, промы́шленный.
industrialism /ɪn'dʌstriə,lɪzəm/ *n.* индустриали́зм *m.*
industrialist /ɪn'dʌstriəlɪst/ *n.* промы́шленник *m.*
industrialize /ɪn'dʌstriə,laiz/ *v.* индустриализи́ровать *impf.*
industrious /ɪn'dʌstriəs/ *adj.* трудолюби́вый, приле́жный.
industry /'ɪndəstri/ *n.* инду́стрия, промы́шленность *f.*
inebriated /ɪn'ibri,eitɪd/ *adj.* пья́ный.
inebriation /ɪn,ibri'eiʃən/ *n.* опьяне́ние *neut.*
inedible /ɪn'ɛdəbəl/ *adj.* несъедо́бный.
inedited /ɪn'edɪtɪd/ *adj.* неотредакти́рованный.
ineducable /ɪn'ɛdʒʊkəbəl/ *adj.* необуча́емый.
ineffable /ɪn'ɛfəbəl/ *adj.* невырази́мый; несказа́нный; неописуемый.
ineffaceable /ˌɪnɪ'feisəbəl/ *adj.* неизглади́мый.
ineffective /ˌɪnɪ'fɛktɪv/ *also* **ineffectual** /-'fɛktʃuəl/ *adj.* неэффекти́вный; беспло́дный.
inefficacy /ɪn'ɛfɪkəsi/ *n.* бесполе́зность *f.*
inefficiency /ˌɪnɪ'fɪʃənsi/ *n.* неспосо́бность; неэффекти́вность *f.*
inefficient /ˌɪnɪ'fɪʃənt/ *adj.* неспосо́бный; неэффекти́вный.
inelastic /ˌɪnɪ'læstɪk/ *adj.* неэласти́чный.
inelegance /ɪn'ɛlɪgəns/ *n.* неизя́щность *f.*
inelegant /ɪn'ɛlɪgənt/ *adj.* неизя́щный, неэлега́нтный.
ineligibility /ˌɪn,ɛlɪdʒə'bɪlɪti/ *n.* отсу́тствие пра́ва *neut.*
ineligible /ɪn'ɛlɪdʒəbəl/ *adj.* не име́ющий пра́ва.
ineluctable /ˌɪnɪ'lʌktəbəl/ *adj.* неотврати́мый.
inept /ɪn'ɛpt/ *adj.* неуме́стный; неуме́лый.
ineptitude /ɪn'ɛptɪ,tud/ *n.* неуме́ние *neut.*; неуме́стность *f.*
inequality /ˌɪnɪ'kwɒlɪti/ *n.* нера́венство *neut.*
inequitable /ɪn'ɛkwɪtəbəl/ *adj.* несправедли́вый.
inequity /ɪn'ɛkwɪti/ *n.* несправедли́вость *f.*
ineradicable /ˌɪnɪ'rædɪkəbəl/ *adj.* неискорени́мый.
inert /ɪn'ɜrt/ *adj.* ине́ртный.
inertia /ɪn'ɜrʃə/ *n.* ине́рция *f.*
inertial /ɪn'ɜrʃəl/ *adj.* инерцио́нный.
inertness /ɪn'ɜrtnɪs/ *n.* ине́ртность *f.*
inescapable /ˌɪnə'skeipəbəl/ *adj.* неизбе́жный.
inessential /ˌɪnɪ'sɛnʃəl/ *adj.* несуще́ственный.

inestimable /ɪn'ɛstəməbəl/ *adj.* неоцени́мый, бесце́нный.
inevitability /ɪn,ɛvɪtə'bɪlɪti/ *n.* неизбе́жность *f.*
inevitable /ɪn'ɛvɪtəbəl/ *adj.* неизбе́жный.
inexact /ˌɪnɪg'zækt/ *adj.* нето́чный.
inexactitude /ˌɪnɪg'zæktɪ,tud/ *n.* нето́чность *f.*
inexcusable /ˌɪnɪk'skyuzəbəl/ *adj.* непрости́тельный.
inexhaustible /ˌɪnɪg'zɔstəbəl/ *adj.* неисчерпа́емый; неистощи́мый.
inexorable /ɪn'ɛksərəbəl/ *adj.* неумоли́мый.
inexpediency /ˌɪnɪk'spidiənsi/ *n.* нецелесообра́зность *f.*
inexpedient /ˌɪnɪk'spidiənt/ *adj.* нецелесообра́зный.
inexpensive /ˌɪnɪk'spɛnsɪv/ *adj.* недорого́й, дешёвый.
inexperience /ˌɪnɪk'spɪəriəns/ *n.* нео́пытность *f.*
inexperienced /ˌɪnɪk'spɪəriənst/ *adj.* нео́пытный.
inexpert /ɪn'ɛkspɜrt/ *adj.* неиску́сный.
inexpiable /ɪn'ɛkspiəbəl/ *adj.* неискупи́мый.
inexplicable /ɪn'ɛksplɪkəbəl, ˌɪnɪk'splɪkəbəl/ *adj.* необъясни́мый.
inexplicit /ˌɪnɪk'splɪsɪt/ *adj.* нея́вный.
inexpressible /ˌɪnɪk'sprɛsəbəl/ *adj.* невырази́мый, неописуемый.
inexpressive /ˌɪnɪk'sprɛsɪv/ *adj.* невырази́тельный.
inexpugnable /ˌɪnɪk'spʌgnəbəl/ *adj.* неодоли́мый.
inextinguishable /ˌɪnɪk'stɪŋgwɪʃəbəl/ *adj.* неугаси́мый.
inextricable /ɪn'ɛkstrɪkəbəl, ˌɪnɪk'strɪkə-/ *adj.* запу́танный, (*insoluble*) неразреши́мый; **inextricable muddle** *n.* невероя́тная пу́таница *f.*
infallibility /ɪn,fælə'bɪlɪti/ *n.* непогреши́мость *f.*
infallible /ɪn'fæləbəl/ *adj.* безоши́бочный; непогреши́мый.
infamous /'ɪnfəməs/ *adj.* позо́рный; гну́сный.
infamy /'ɪnfəmi/ *n.* позо́р *m.*; дурна́я сла́ва *f.*
infancy /'ɪnfənsi/ *n.* ра́ннее де́тство, младе́нчество *neut.*
infant /'ɪnfənt/ *n.* младе́нец *m.*
infanta /ɪn'fæntə/ *n.* инфа́нта *f.*
infante /ɪn'fæntei/ *n.* инфа́нт *m.*
infanticide /ɪn'fæntə,said/ *n.* детоуби́йство *neut.*
infantile /'ɪnfən,tail/ *adj.* де́тский, младе́нческий; (*immature*) инфанти́льный.
infantilism /'ɪnfəntɪ,ɪzəm/ *n.* инфантили́зм *m.*
infantry /'ɪnfəntri/ **1.** *n.* пехо́та *f.* **2.** *adj.* пехо́тный.
infantryman /'ɪnfəntrimən/ *n.* пехоти́нец *m.*
infatuate /ɪn'fætʃu,eit/ *v.* вскружи́ть го́лову *impf.*
infatuated /ɪn'fætʃu,eitɪd/ *adj.* (*pred.*) си́льно увлечён.
infatuation /ɪn,fætʃu'eiʃən/ *n.* си́льное увлече́ние *neut.*
infeasible /ɪn'fizəbəl/ *adj.* неосуществи́мый.
infect /ɪn'fɛkt/ *v.* заража́ть *impf.*, зарази́ть *pf.*
infection /ɪn'fɛkʃən/ *n.* зара́за; инфе́кция *f.*
infectious /ɪn'fɛkʃəs/ *adj.* (*fig.*) зарази́тельный; (*med.*) зара́зный.
infecund /ɪn'fikənd/ *adj.* беспло́дный.
infelicitous /ˌɪnfə'lɪsɪtəs/ *adj.* неуда́чный; несча́стный.
infelicity /ˌɪnfə'lɪsɪti/ *n.* несча́стье *neut.*

infer /ɪnˈfɜr/ v. выводи́ть; заключа́ть impf.
inference /ˈɪnfərəns/ n. вы́вод m.; заключе́ние neut.
inferential /ˌɪnfəˈrɛnʃəl/ adj. вы́веденный.
inferior /ɪnˈfɪəriər/ 1. adj. ни́зший; (quality) ху́дший. 2. n. подчинённый m.
inferiority /ɪnˌfɪəriˈɔrɪti/ n. ни́зкое положе́ние neut.; неполноце́нность f.
infernal /ɪnˈfɜrnḷ/ adj. а́дский.
infernally /ɪnˈfɜrnḷi/ adv. (colloq.) черто́вски, а́дски.
inferno /ɪnˈfɜrnou/ n. ад m.
infertile /ɪnˈfɜrtḷ/ adj. неплодоро́дный.
infertility /ˌɪnfɜrˈtɪlɪti/ n. беспло́дие neut.
infest /ɪnˈfɛst/ v. наводня́ть impf.
infestation /ˌɪnfɛˈsteiʃən/ n. (med., biol.) инва́зия f.
infidel /ˈɪnfɪdḷ, -ˌdɛl/ n. неве́рующий; неве́рный безбо́жник m.
infidelity /ˌɪnfɪˈdɛlɪti/ n. неве́рность f.
infighting /ˈɪnˌfaitɪŋ/ n. (mil.) бли́жний бой m.
infiltrate /ˈɪnfɪlˌtreit/ v. проника́ть (в with acc.) impf. , проникнуть pf.
infiltration /ˌɪnfɪlˈtreiʃən/ n. проникнове́ние neut.
infinite /ˈɪnfənɪt/ adj. бесконе́чный; безграни́чный.
infinitesimal /ˌɪnfɪnɪˈtɛsəməl/ adj. мельча́йший.
infinitive /ɪnˈfɪnɪtɪv/ n. (gram.) инфинити́в ; неопределённая фо́рма глаго́ла f.
infinity /ɪnˈfɪnɪti/ n. бесконе́чность f.
infirm /ɪnˈfɜrm/ adj. сла́бый, не́мощный.
infirmary /ɪnˈfɜrməri/ n. медпу́нкт m.
infirmity /ɪnˈfɜrmɪti/ n. сла́бость; не́мощь f.
infix /ˈɪnˌfɪks/ n. (gram.) и́нфикс m.
inflame /ɪnˈfleim/ v. воспламеня́ть(ся) impf., воспламени́ть(ся) pf.
inflamed /ɪnˈfleimd/ adj. воспалённый.
inflammability /ɪnˌflæməˈbɪlɪti/ n. воспламеня́емость f.
inflammable /ɪnˈflæməbəl/ adj. огнеопа́сный, воспламеня́емый.
inflammation /ˌɪnfləˈmeiʃən/ n. воспламене́ние neut.; (med.) воспале́ние neut.
inflammatory /ɪnˈflæməˌtɔri/ adj. возбужда́ющий; (med.) воспали́тельный.
inflatable /ɪnˈfleitəbəl/ adj. надувно́й.
inflate /ɪnˈfleit/ v. надува́ть impf., наду́ть pf.
inflated /ɪnˈfleitɪd/ adj. наду́тый; (econ.) ду́тый.
inflation /ɪnˈfleiʃən/ n. инфля́ция f.
inflationary /ɪnˈfleiʃəˌnɛri/ adj. инфляцио́нный.
inflect /ɪnˈflɛkt/ v. изгиба́ть impf.; (phys.) отклоня́ть impf.; (gram.) спряга́ть; склоня́ть impf.
inflection /ɪnˈflɛkʃən/ n. вгиба́ние neut.; (gram.) фле́ксия f.
inflectional /ɪnˈflɛkʃənḷ/ adj. (gram.) флекти́вный, флекти́рующий.
inflexibility /ɪnˌflɛksəˈbɪlɪti/ n. неги́бкость; непрекло́нность f.
inflexible /ɪnˈflɛksəbəl/ adj. неги́бкий, несгиба́емый.
inflict /ɪnˈflɪkt/ v. наноси́ть impf., нанести́ pf.
infliction /ɪnˈflɪkʃən/ n. нанесе́ние; причине́ние; наложе́ние neut.
inflorescence /ˌɪnfləˈrɛsəns/ n. цвете́ние neut.
inflow /ˈɪnˌflou/ n. прито́к m.
inflowing /ˈɪnˌflouɪŋ/ adj. втека́ющий.

influence /ˈɪnfluəns/ 1. n. влия́ние neut. 2. v. влия́ть (на with acc.) impf., повлия́ть pf.
influential /ˌɪnfluˈɛnʃəl/ adj. влия́тельный.
influenza /ˌɪnfluˈɛnzə/ n. грипп m.
influx /ˈɪnˌflʌks/ n. втека́ние, впаде́ние neut.; наплы́в m.
inform /ɪnˈfɔrm/ v.t. сообща́ть; уведомля́ть impf., уве́домить pf.; информи́ровать impf.; v.i. доноси́ть (на with acc.) impf.
informal /ɪnˈfɔrməl/ adj. неофициа́льный, нефор-ма́льный.
informality /ˌɪnfɔrˈmælɪti/ n. непринуждённость f.
informant /ɪnˈfɔrmənt/ n. осведоми́тель m.
informatics /ˌɪnfɔrˈmætɪks/ n. информа́тика f.
information /ˌɪnfɔrˈmeiʃən/ 1. n. све́дение neut.; информа́ция f. 2. adj. спра́вочный.
informative /ɪnˈfɔrmətɪv/ adj. содержа́тельный.
informed /ɪnˈfɔrmd/ adj. осведомлённый.
informer /ɪnˈfɔrmər/ n. доно́счик m.
infra /ˈɪnfrə/ adv. ни́же.
infraction /ɪnˈfrækʃən/ n. наруше́ние neut.
infrangible /ɪnˈfrændʒəbəl/ adj. неруши́мый.
infrared /ˌɪnfrəˈrɛd/ adj. инфракра́сный.
infrasonic /ˌɪnfrəˈsɒnɪk/ adj. инфразвуково́й.
infrastructure /ˈɪnfrəˌstrʌktʃər/ n. инфраструк-ту́ра f.
infrequency /ɪnˈfrikwənsi/ n. ре́дкость f.
infrequent /ɪnˈfrikwənt/ adj. ре́дкий.
infringe /ɪnˈfrɪndʒ/ v.t. наруша́ть impf.; v.i. посяга́ть (на with acc.) impf.
infringement /ɪnˈfrɪndʒmənt/ n. наруше́ние neut.
infuriate /ɪnˈfyʊriˌeit/ v. беси́ть; разъяря́ть impf.
infuse /ɪnˈfyuz/ v. влива́ть impf.
infusible /ɪnˈfyuzəbəl/ adj. (not fusible) непла́в-кий.
infusion /ɪnˈfyuʒən/ n. влива́ние; внуше́ние neut.
infusoria /ˌɪnfyuˈsɔriə/ n. инфузо́рии pl.
infusorial /ˌɪnfyuˈsɔriəl/ adj. инфузо́рный.
ingathering /ˈɪnˌgæðərɪŋ/ n. сбор m.
ingenious /ɪnˈdʒinyəs/ adj. остроу́мный; изобрета́тельный.
ingénue /ˈænʒəˌnu/ n. инженю́ f. indecl.
ingenuity /ˌɪndʒəˈnuɪti/ n. изобрета́тельность f.
ingenuous /ɪnˈdʒɛnyuəs/ adj. бесхи́тростный; наи́вный.
ingenuousness /ɪnˈdʒɛnyuəsnɪs/ n. бесхи́трост-ность f.
ingest /ɪnˈdʒɛst/ v. прогла́тывать impf.
ingestion /ɪnˈdʒɛstʃən/ n. приём пи́щи m.
inglorious /ɪnˈglɔriəs/ adj. бессла́вный.
ingot /ˈɪŋgət/ n. сли́ток m.
ingrain /ɪnˈgrein/ v. внедря́ть impf.
ingrained /ɪnˈgreind/ adj. въе́вшийся; укорени́в-шийся.
ingrate /ˈɪngreit/ n. неблагода́рный челове́к m.
ingratiate /ɪnˈgreiʃiˌeit/ v. заи́скивать (пе́ред with instr.) impf.
ingratiating /ɪnˈgreiʃiˌeitɪŋ/ adj. заи́скивающий.
ingratitude /ɪnˈgrætɪˌtud/ n. неблагода́рность f.
ingredient /ɪnˈgridiənt/ n. составна́я часть f.
ingress /ˈɪngrɛs/ n. вход m.
ingrowing /ˈɪnˌgrouɪŋ/ adj. враста́ющий.
ingrown /ˈɪnˌgroun/ adj. вро́сший.
inguinal /ˈɪŋgwənḷ/ adj. пахово́й.
inhabit /ɪnˈhæbɪt/ v. жить; обита́ть impf.
inhabitable /ɪnˈhæbɪtəbəl/ adj. обита́емый.

inhabitant /ɪnˈhæbɪtənt/ n. жи́тель, обита́тель m.

inhalation /ˌɪnhəˈleɪʃən/ n. вдыха́ние neut.

inhale /ɪnˈheɪl/ v. вдыха́ть impf., вдохну́ть pf.

inhaler /ɪnˈheɪlər/ n. (med.) ингаля́тор m.

inharmonious /ˌɪnhɑrˈmouniəs/ adj. негармони́чный, несозву́чный.

inherent /ɪnˈhɪərənt, -ˈhɛr-/ adj. прису́щий.

inherently /ɪnˈhɪərəntli, -ˈhɛr-/ adv. по своему́ существу́.

inherit /ɪnˈhɛrɪt/ v. насле́довать impf., у-насле́довать pf.

inheritable /ɪnˈhɛrɪtəbəl/ adj. насле́дуемый.

inheritance /ɪnˈhɛrɪtəns/ n. насле́дство neut.

inheritor /ɪnˈhɛrɪtər/ n. насле́дник m.; (successor) прее́мник m.

inhibit /ɪnˈhɪbɪt/ v. сде́рживать impf., сдержа́ть pf.; (hinder) препя́тствовать.

inhibited /ɪnˈhɪbɪtɪd/ adj. за́мкнутый.

inhibition /ˌɪnɪˈbɪʃən/ n. сде́рживание; торможе́ние neut.

inhibitor /ɪnˈhɪbɪtər/ n. замедли́тель m.

inhibitory /ɪnˈhɪbɪˈtɔri/ adj. запреща́ющий.

inhospitable /ɪnˈhɒspɪtəbəl, ˌɪnhɒˈspɪtəbəl/ adj. негостеприи́мный; неприве́тливый.

in-house /ˈɪn ˌhaus/ adj. вну́тренний.

inhuman /ɪnˈhyumən/ adj. бесчелове́чный.

inhumane /ˌɪnhyuˈmeɪn/ adj. негума́нный, жесто́кий.

inhumanity /ˌɪnhyuˈmænɪti/ n. бесчелове́чность f.

inhumation /ˌɪnhyuˈmeɪʃən/ n. погребе́ние neut.

inimical /ɪˈnɪmɪkəl/ adj. вражде́бный.

inimitable /ɪˈnɪmɪtəbəl/ adj. неподража́емый.

iniquitous /ɪˈnɪkwɪtəs/ adj. чудо́вищный.

iniquity /ɪˈnɪkwɪti/ n. несправедли́вость f.

initial /ɪˈnɪʃəl/ **1.** adj. нача́льный. **2.** n. инициа́л m. **3.** v. подпи́сывать инициа́лами impf.

initially /ɪˈnɪʃəli/ adv. внача́ле.

initiate /ɪˈnɪʃiˌeɪt/ v. начина́ть impf., нача́ть pf.; (admit) посвяща́ть (в with acc.) impf.

initiation /ɪˌnɪʃiˈeɪʃən/ n. посвяще́ние; приня́тие neut.

initiative /ɪˈnɪʃiətɪv/ n. инициати́ва f.

initiator /ɪˈnɪʃiˌeɪtər/ n. инициа́тор m.

initiatory /ɪˈnɪʃiəˌtɔri/ adj. нача́льный.

inject /ɪnˈdʒɛkt/ v. впры́скивать impf., впры́снуть pf.

injection /ɪnˈdʒɛkʃən/ n. впры́скивание neut.

injector /ɪnˈdʒɛktər/ n. инже́ктор m.

injudicious /ˌɪndʒuˈdɪʃəs/ adj. неразу́мный.

injunction /ɪnˈdʒʌŋkʃən/ n. предписа́ние neut.; (leg.) суде́бный запре́т m.

injure /ˈɪndʒər/ v. вреди́ть; ушиба́ть, ра́нить impf.

injured /ˈɪndʒərd/ adj. ра́неный.

injurious /ɪnˈdʒʊriəs/ adj. вре́дный.

injury /ˈɪndʒəri/ n. поврежде́ние; ране́ние neut.

injustice /ɪnˈdʒʌstɪs/ n. несправедли́вость f.

ink /ɪŋk/ n. черни́ла pl.

ink-jet printer /ˈɪŋk ˌdʒɛt/ n. стру́йный при́нтер m.

inkling /ˈɪŋklɪŋ/ n. подозре́ние neut.

ink pad n. штемпельная поду́шечка f.

inkstand /ˈɪŋkˌstænd/ n. черни́льный прибо́р m.

inkwell /ˈɪŋkˌwɛl/ n. черни́льница f.

inky /ˈɪŋki/ adj. в черни́лах.

inlaid /ˈɪnˌleɪd/ adj. инкрусти́рованный.

inland /ˈɪnˌlænd/ adv. в преде́лах страны́.

in-law /ˈɪn ˌlɔ/ n. ро́дственник m.

inlay /ˈɪnˌleɪ/ n. инкруста́ция f.

inlet /ˈɪnlɛt/ n. зали́в m., бу́хточка f.

inlier /ˈɪnˌlaɪər/ n. (geol.) окно́ neut.

inmate /ˈɪnˌmeɪt/ n. (prison) заключённый m.; (asylum) больно́й m.

in memoriam /ɪn məˈmɔriəm/ adj. в па́мять.

inmost /ˈɪnˌmoust/ adj. глубоча́йший.

inn /ɪn/ n. гости́ница f.

innards /ˈɪnərdz/ n. вну́тренности pl.

innate /ɪˈneɪt/ adj. врождённый; прирождённый; приро́дный.

inner /ˈɪnər/ adj. вну́тренний.

innervate /ɪˈnɜrveɪt/ v. возбужда́ть impf.

innkeeper /ˈɪnˌkipər/ n. хозя́ин (гости́ницы or тракти́ра) m.

innocence /ˈɪnəsəns/ n. неви́нность; невино́вность f.

innocent /ˈɪnəsənt/ adj. неви́нный; невино́вный.

innocuous /ɪˈnɒkyuəs/ adj. безоби́дный; безвре́дный.

innovate /ˈɪnəˌveɪt/ v. занима́ться нововведе́ниями impf.

innovation /ˌɪnəˈveɪʃən/ n. нововведе́ние neut.

innovative /ˈɪnəˌveɪtɪv/ adj. нова́торский.

innovator /ˈɪnəˌveɪtər/ n. нова́тор m.

innuendo /ˌɪnyuˈɛndou/ n. инсинуа́ция f.

innumerable /ɪˈnumərəbəl/ adj. бесчи́сленный.

inobservance /ˌɪnəbˈzɜrvəns/ n. несоблюде́ние neut.

inobservant /ˌɪnəbˈzɜrvənt/ adj. ненаблюда́тельный.

inoculate /ɪˈnɒkyəˌleɪt/ v. привива́ть impf., приви́ть pf.

inoculation /ɪˌnɒkyəˈleɪʃən/ n. приви́вка f.

inodorous /ɪnˈoudərəs/ adj. без за́паха.

inoffensive /ˌɪnəˈfɛnsɪv/ adj. безоби́дный; необи́дный.

inoffensiveness /ˌɪnəˈfɛnsɪvnɪs/ n. безоби́дность f.

inoperable /ɪnˈɒpərəbəl/ adj. (med.) неопера́бельный.

inoperative /ɪnˈɒpərətɪv/ adj. неде́йствующий.

inopportune /ɪnˌɒpərˈtun/ adj. несвоевре́менный; **at an inopportune moment** в неудо́бный моме́нт.

inordinate /ɪnˈɔrdn̩ɪt/ adj. чрезме́рный.

inorganic /ˌɪnɔrˈgænɪk/ adj. неоргани́ческий.

inosculate /ɪnˈɒskyəˌleɪt/ v. сра́щиваться impf.

inosculation /ɪnˌɒskyəˈleɪʃən/ n. сраще́ние neut.

inpatient /ˈɪnˌpeɪʃənt/ n. стациона́рный больно́й m.

input /ˈɪnˌpʊt/ n. пода́ча f.; ввод m.

inquest /ˈɪnkwɛst/ n. дозна́ние, сле́дствие neut.

inquire /ɪnˈkwaɪər/ v. спра́шивать impf., спроси́ть pf.; (investigate) рассле́довать impf. and pf.

inquiring /ɪnˈkwaɪərɪŋ/ adj. вопроси́тельный; пытли́вый.

inquiry /ɪnˈkwaɪəri, ˈɪnkwəri/ n. запро́с m.; спра́вка f.; (investigation) рассле́дование neut.

inquisition /ˌɪnkwəˈzɪʃən/ n. иссле́дование neut.; (hist.) инквизи́ция f.

inquisitional /ˌɪnkwəˈzɪʃənl̩/ adj. иссле́довательский; (hist.) инквизицио́нный.

inquisitive /ɪnˈkwɪzɪtɪv/ adj. пытли́вый, любозна́тельный; любопы́тный.

inquisitiveness /ɪnˈkwɪzɪtɪvnɪs/ n. пытли́вость f.

inquisitor /ɪnˈkwɪzɪtər/ n. инквизи́тор m.

inroad /ˈɪnˌroʊd/ n. набе́г m.; вторже́ние neut.

inrush /ˈɪnˌrʌʃ/ n. вторже́ние neut.

insalubrious /ˌɪnsəˈlubriəs/ adj. нездоро́вый.

insane /ɪnˈseɪn/ **1.** adj. сумасше́дший; безу́мный. **2. to become insane** v. сойти́ с ума́ pf.

insanity /ɪnˈsænɪti/ n. сумасше́ствие; умопомеша́тельство neut.

insatiability /ɪnˌseɪʃəˈbɪlɪti/ n. ненасы́тность f.

insatiable /ɪnˈseɪʃəbəl/ adj. ненасы́тный, жа́дный.

inscribe /ɪnˈskraɪb/ v. надпи́сывать; впи́сывать impf., вписа́ть pf.

inscription /ɪnˈskrɪpʃən/ n. на́дпись f.; посвяще́ние neut.; авто́граф m.

inscrutability /ɪnˌskrutəˈbɪlɪti/ n. непостижи́мость f.

inscrutable /ɪnˈskrutəbəl/ adj. непостижи́мый.

insect /ˈɪnsɛkt/ n. насеко́мое neut.

insecticide /ɪnˈsɛktəˌsaɪd/ n. инсектици́д m.

insectivore /ɪnˈsɛktəˌvɔr/ n. насекомоя́дное neut.

insectivorous /ˌɪnsɛkˈtɪvərəs/ adj. насекомоя́дный.

insecure /ˌɪnsɪˈkyʊr/ adj. небезопа́сный; (lacking confidence) неуве́ренный в себе́.

insecurity /ˌɪnsɪˈkyʊrɪti/ n. неуве́ренность в себе́ f.

inseminate /ɪnˈsɛməˌneɪt/ v. оплодотворя́ть impf.

insemination /ɪnˌsɛməˈneɪʃən/ n. оплодотворе́ние neut.

insensate /ɪnˈsɛnseɪt/ adj. бесчу́вственный.

insensibility /ɪnˌsɛnsəˈbɪlɪti/ n. нечувстви́тельность f.

insensible /ɪnˈsɛnsəbəl/ adj. нечувстви́тельный.

insensitive /ɪnˈsɛnsɪtɪv/ adj. нечувстви́тельный.

insensitivity /ɪnˌsɛnsɪˈtɪvɪti/ n. нечувстви́тельность f.

insentient /ɪnˈsɛnʃənt/ adj. неодушевлённый.

inseparable /ɪnˈsɛpərəbəl/ adj. неотдели́мый; (of people) неразлу́чный.

insert / v. ɪnˈsɜrt; n. ˈɪnsɜrt/ **1.** v. вставля́ть , вста́вить pf. **2.** n. вста́вка; вкла́дка f.

insertion /ɪnˈsɜrʃən/ n. вставле́ние; введе́ние neut.; вста́вка f.

inset /ˈɪnˌsɛt/ n. вкла́дка, вста́вка f.; (in book) вкле́йка f.

inshore /ˈɪnˈʃɔr/ adj. прибре́жный.

inside / prep., adv., adj. ˌɪnˈsaɪd; n. ˈɪnˈsaɪd/ **1.** prep. в (with acc. or prep.) внутрь, внутри́ (with gen.). **2.** adv. внутри́. **3.** adj. вну́тренний. **4.** n. вну́тренность f.

inside out adv. наизна́нку.

insider /ɪnˈsaɪdər/ n. свой челове́к m.

insidious /ɪnˈsɪdiəs/ adj. кова́рный.

insidiousness /ɪnˈsɪdiəsnɪs/ n. кова́рство neut.

insight /ˈɪnˌsaɪt/ n. проница́тельность f.

insignia /ɪnˈsɪgniə/ n. (mil.) зна́ки разли́чия; ордена́ pl.

insignificance /ˌɪnsɪgˈnɪfɪkəns/ n. незначи́тельность f.

insignificant /ˌɪnsɪgˈnɪfɪkənt/ adj. незначи́тельный.

insincere /ˌɪnsɪnˈsɪər/ adj. нейскренний.

insincerely /ˌɪnsɪnˈsɪərli/ adv. нейскренно.

insincerity /ˌɪnsɪnˈsɛrɪti/ n. нейскренность f.

insinuate /ɪnˈsɪnyuˌeɪt/ v. намека́ть (на with acc.) impf., намекну́ть pf.

insinuating /ɪnˈsɪnyuˌeɪtɪŋ/ adj. (ingratiating) вкра́дчивый.

insinuation /ɪnˌsɪnyuˈeɪʃən/ n. намёк m.; инсинуа́ция f.

insipid /ɪnˈsɪpɪd/ adj. безвку́сный.

insipidity /ˌɪnsɪˈpɪdɪti/ n. (blandness) пре́сность f.

insist /ɪnˈsɪst/ v. наста́ивать impf.

insistence /ɪnˈsɪstəns/ n. насто́йчивость f.

insistent /ɪnˈsɪstənt/ adj. насто́йчивый.

in situ /ˈɪn saitu, ˈsi-/ adv. на ме́сте.

insobriety /ˌɪnsəˈbraɪɪti/ n. нетре́звость f.

insofar as /ˌɪnsouˈfar əz/ conj. посто́льку, поско́льку; наско́лько.

insolation /ˌɪnsouˈleɪʃən/ n. со́лнечная радиа́ция f.

insole /ˈɪnˌsoul/ n. сте́лька f.

insolence /ˈɪnsələns/ n. на́глость f.

insolent /ˈɪnsələnt/ adj. де́рзкий; на́глый.

insolubility /ɪnˌsɒlyəˈbɪlɪti/ n. нераствори́мость f.

insoluble /ɪnˈsɒlyəbəl/ adj. нераствори́мый; (not solvable) неразреши́мый.

insolvency /ɪnˈsɒlvənsi/ n. несостоя́тельность f.

insolvent /ɪnˈsɒlvənt/ adj. несостоя́тельный, неплатежеспосо́бный.

insomnia /ɪnˈsɒmniə/ n. бессо́нница f.

insomniac /ɪnˈsɒmniˌæk/ n. страда́ющий бессо́нницей m.

insouciance /ɪnˈsusiəns, æ̃suˈsyɑ̃s/ n. небре́жность f.

inspect /ɪnˈspɛkt/ v. осма́тривать impf., осмотре́ть pf.; инспекти́ровать impf.

inspection /ɪnˈspɛkʃən/ n. осмо́тр m.; инспе́кция f.

inspector /ɪnˈspɛktər/ n. инспе́ктор m.

inspectorate /ɪnˈspɛktərɪt/ n. до́лжность инспе́ктора f.

inspectorship /ɪnˈspɛktərˌʃɪp/ n. инспе́кторство neut.

inspiration /ˌɪnspəˈreɪʃən/ n. вдохнове́ние neut.; (of person) вдохнови́тель m., вдохнови́тельница f.

inspire /ɪnˈspaɪ³r/ v. вдохновля́ть impf., вдохнови́ть pf.

inspired /ɪnˈspaɪ³rd/ adj. вдохнове́нный.

inspiring /ɪnˈspaɪ³rɪŋ/ adj. вдохновля́ющий, вдохнове́нный.

inspirit /ɪnˈspɪrɪt/ v. воодушевля́ть impf.

instability /ˌɪnstəˈbɪlɪti/ n. неусто́йчивость f.

install /ɪnˈstɔl/ v. устана́вливать; ста́вить impf.

installation /ˌɪnstəˈleɪʃən/ n. устано́вка f., устро́йство neut.; (mil.) ба́за f.

installment /ɪnˈstɔlmənt/ n. очередно́й взнос m.; (publication) вы́пуск m.

instance /ˈɪnstəns/ n. приме́р; слу́чай m.; (leg.) инста́нция f.; **for instance** наприме́р.

instant /ˈɪnstənt/ **1.** adj. мгнове́нный; неме́дленный; (of coffee, etc.) раствори́мый. **2.** n. мгнове́ние neut.; миг m.

instantaneous /ˌɪnstənˈteɪniəs/ adj. мгнове́нный, momentа́льный.

instantaneously /ˌɪnstənˈteɪniəsli/ adv. мгнове́нно, momentа́льно; сра́зу же.

instantly /'ɪnstəntli/ adv. сразу же; немедленно; момента́льно, мгнове́нно, то́тчас.

instead /ɪn'stɛd/ adv. взаме́н, вме́сто (with gen.).

instep /'ɪn,stɛp/ n. подъём m.

instigate /'ɪnstɪ,geɪt/ v. подстрека́ть impf., подстрекну́ть pf.

instigation /,ɪnstɪ'geɪʃən/ n. подстрека́тельство neut.

instigator /'ɪnstɪ,geɪtər/ n. подстрека́тель m.

instill /ɪn'stɪl/ v. внуша́ть impf., внуши́ть pf.

instillation /,ɪnstə'leɪʃən/ n. внуше́ние neut.

instinct /'ɪnstɪŋkt/ n. инсти́нкт m.

instinctive /ɪn'stɪŋktɪv/ adj. инстинкти́вный.

institute /'ɪnstɪ,tut/ 1. n. институ́т m. 2. v. учрежда́ть impf., учреди́ть pf.

institution /,ɪnstɪ'tuʃən/ n. учрежде́ние; заве́дение neut.

institutional /,ɪnstɪ'tuʃənl̩/ adj. учрежде́нный, устано́вленный.

institutionalize /,ɪnstɪ'tuʃənl̩,aɪz/ v. институциона́лизи́ровать impf.

instruct /ɪn'strʌkt/ v. обуча́ть impf., обучи́ть ; инструкти́ровать impf. and pf.; (direct) поруча́ть impf.

instruction /ɪn'strʌkʃən/ n. обуче́ние neut., инстру́кция f

instructional /ɪn'strʌkʃənl̩/ adj. уче́бный.

instructive /ɪn'strʌktɪv/ adj. поучи́тельный.

instructor /ɪn'strʌktər/ also **instructress** /-trɪs/ n. инстру́ктор m.

instrument /'ɪnstrəmənt/ n. инструме́нт; прибо́р m.; ору́дие neut.

instrumental /,ɪnstrə'mɛntl̩/ adj. инструмента́льный; (gram.) твори́тельный.

instrumentalist /,ɪnstrə'mɛntl̩ɪst/ n. инструмента́лист m.

instrumentation /,ɪnstrəmɛn'teɪʃən/ n. (mus.) инструменто́вка f.

insubordinate /,ɪnsə'bɔrdn̩ɪt/ adj. непослу́шный; непоко́рный.

insubordination /,ɪnsə,bɔrdn̩'eɪʃən/ n. неподчине́ние neut.

insubstantial /,ɪnsəb'stænʃəl/ adj. непро́чный; неоснова́тельный.

insufferable /ɪn'sʌfərəbəl/ adj. невыноси́мый; несно́сный.

insufficiency /,ɪnsə'fɪʃənsi/ n. недоста́точность ; (lack) недоста́ток m.

insufficient /,ɪnsə'fɪʃənt/ adj. недоста́точный.

insufflate /ɪn'sʌfleɪt/ v. вдува́ть impf.

insular /'ɪnsələr/ adj. островно́й; изоли́рованный.

insularity /,ɪnsə'lærɪti/ n. изоли́рованность f.

insulate /'ɪnsə,leɪt/ v. изоли́ровать impf. and pf.

insulating /'ɪnsə,leɪtɪŋ/ adj. изоляцио́нный.

insulation /,ɪnsə'leɪʃən/ n. изоля́ция f.

insulator /'ɪnsə,leɪtər/ n. изоля́тор m.

insulin /'ɪnsəlɪn/ n. инсули́н m.

insult / n. 'ɪnsʌlt; v. ɪn'sʌlt/ 1. n. оскорбле́ние neut. 2. v. оскорбля́ть impf., оскорби́ть pf

insulting /ɪn'sʌltɪŋ/ adj. оскорби́тельный, оби́дный.

insuperability /ɪn,supərə'bɪlɪti/ n. непреодоли́мость f.

insuperable /ɪn'supərəbəl/ adj. непреодоли́мый.

insupportable /,ɪnsə'pɔrtəbəl/ adj. невыноси́мый, нестерпи́мый.

insurance /ɪn'ʃʊrəns/ 1. n. страхова́ние neut. 2. adj. страхово́й.

insure /ɪn'ʃʊr/ v. страхова́ть impf., застрахова́ть pf.

insurer /ɪn'ʃʊrər/ n. страхо́вщик m.

insurgent /ɪn'sɜrdʒənt/ 1. adj. восста́вший. 2. n. повста́нец; мяте́жник m.

insurmountable /,ɪnsər'maʊntəbəl/ adj. непреодоли́мый.

insurrection /,ɪnsə'rɛkʃən/ n. восста́ние neut.; мяте́ж m.

insurrectional /,ɪnsə'rɛkʃənl/ also **insurrectionary** /-ʃə,nɛri/ adj. повста́нческий; мяте́жный.

insusceptible /,ɪnsə'sɛptəbəl/ adj. невоспри́мчивый.

intact /ɪn'tækt/ adj. неповреждённый; це́лый.

intaglio /ɪn'tælyou/ n. инта́лия f.

intake /'ɪn,teɪk/ n. приём m.; (quantity) потребле́ние neut.

intangibility /ɪn,tændʒə'bɪlɪti/ n. неосяза́емость f.

intangible /ɪn'tændʒəbəl/ adj. неосяза́емый.

integer /'ɪntɪdʒər/ n. (math.) це́лое число́ neut.

integrable /'ɪntɪgrəbəl/ adj. интегри́руемый.

integral /'ɪntɪgrəl/ 1. adj. неотдели́мый; (math.) интегра́льный. 2. n. (math.) интегра́л m.

integrand /'ɪntɪ,grænd/ n. (math.) подинтегра́льное выраже́ние neut.

integrate /'ɪntɪ,greɪt/ v. интегри́ровать impf. and pf.

integrated circuit /'ɪntə,greɪtɪd/ n. интегра́льная схе́ма f.

integration /,ɪntɪ'greɪʃən/ n. объедине́ние (в одно́ це́лое) neut., интегра́ция f.; интегри́рование neut.

integrity /ɪn'tɛgrɪti/ n. це́лостность f.; (honesty) че́стность f.

integument /ɪn'tɛgyəmənt/ n. оболо́чка f.

intellect /'ɪntl̩,ɛkt/ n. интелле́кт; ум m.

intellectual /,ɪntl̩'ɛktʃuəl/ 1. adj. у́мственный; интеллектуа́льный. 2. n. интеллиге́нт m.

intellectualism /,ɪntl̩'ɛktʃuə,lɪzəm/ n. интеллектуа́льность f.

intellectuality /,ɪntl̩,ɛktʃu'ælɪti/ n. интеллектуа́льность f.

intelligence /ɪn'tɛlɪdʒəns/ n. ум m.; (information) разве́дка f.

intelligent /ɪn'tɛlɪdʒənt/ adj. у́мный; разу́мный; интеллиге́нтный.

intelligentsia /ɪn,tɛlɪ'dʒɛntsiə/ n. интеллиге́нция f.

intelligibility /ɪn,tɛlɪdʒə'bɪlɪti/ n. поня́тность f.

intelligible /ɪn'tɛlɪdʒəbəl/ adj. поня́тный.

intemperance /ɪn'tɛmpərəns/ n. невоздержанность f.; невоздержа́ние neut.

intemperate /ɪn'tɛmpərɪt/ adj. неуме́ренный; невоздержанный.

intend /ɪn'tɛnd/ v. намерева́ться; собира́ться impf.; (designed for) предназнача́ть (для with gen.) impf.

intended /ɪn'tɛndɪd/ adj. преднаме́ренный.

intense /ɪn'tɛns/ adj. напряжённый; си́льный.

intensification /ɪn,tɛnsəfɪ'keɪʃən/ n. усиле́ние; обостре́ние neut.

intensifier /ɪn'tɛnsə,faɪər/ n. усили́тель m.

intensify /ɪn'tɛnsə,faɪ/ v. уси́ливать(ся) impf.

intensity /ɪn'tɛnsɪti/ *n.* напряжённость; си́ла; интенси́вность *f.*

intensive /ɪn'tɛnsɪv/ *adj.* интенси́вный.

intent /ɪn'tɛnt/ *adj.* (*concentrated*) сосредото́ченный.

intention /ɪn'tɛnʃən/ *n.* наме́рение *neut.*, цель *f.*

intentional /ɪn'tɛnʃənl/ *adj.* наме́ренный; умы́шленный.

intentionally /ɪn'tɛnʃənli/ *adv.* наме́ренно, умы́шленно, наро́чно.

intently /ɪn'tɛntli/ *adv.* внима́тельно.

inter /ɪn'tɜr/ *v.* погреба́ть *impf.*

interact /ˌɪntər'ækt/ *v.* взаимоде́йствовать *impf.*

interaction /ˌɪntər'ækʃən/ *n.* взаимоде́йствие *neut.*

interbreed /ˌɪntər'brid/ *v.* скре́щивать(ся) *impf.*

interbreeding /ˌɪntər'bridɪŋ/ *n.* межпоро́дное *or* межви́довое скре́щивание *neut.*

intercalary /ɪn'tɜrkəˌlɛri/ *adj.* приба́вленный; високо́сный.

intercalate /ɪn'tɜrkəˌleit/ *v.* прибавля́ть; интерполи́ровать, вставля́ть *impf.*

intercede /ˌɪntər'sid/ *v.* хода́тайствовать *impf.*

intercellular /ˌɪntər'sɛlyələr/ *adj.* межкле́точный.

intercept /ˌɪntər'sɛpt/ *v.* перехва́тывать *impf.*, перехвати́ть *pf.*

interception /ˌɪntər'sɛpʃən/ *n.* перехва́т *m.*

interceptor /ˌɪntər'sɛptər/ *n.* (*aero.*) истреби́тель-перехва́тчик *m.*

intercession /ˌɪntər'sɛʃən/ *n.* хода́тайство, засту́пничество *neut.*

intercessor /ˌɪntər'sɛsər/ *n.* хода́тай, засту́пник *m.*

interchange / *n.* 'ɪntərˌtʃeindʒ; *v.* ˌɪntər'tʃeindʒ/ **1.** *n.* обме́н *m.*, заме́на *f.*; (*alteration*) чередова́ние *neut.* **2.** *v.* обме́ниваться (*with instr.*) *impf.*

interchangeability /ˌɪntərˌtʃeindʒə'bɪliti/ *n.* взаимозаменя́емость *f.*

interchangeable /ˌɪntər'tʃeindʒəbəl/ *adj.* взаимозаменя́емый.

intercity /ˌɪntər'sɪti/ *adj.* междугоро́дный.

intercollegiate /ˌɪntərkə'lidʒɪt/ *adj.* межуниверсите́тский.

intercom /'ɪntərˌkɒm/ *n.* вну́треннее переговорно́е устро́йство *neut.*

intercommunicate /ˌɪntərkə'myuniˌkeit/ *v.* сообща́ться *impf.*

interconnect /ˌɪntərkə'nɛkt/ *v.t.* (взаи́мно) свя́зывать *impf.*

interconnection /ˌɪntərkə'nɛkʃən/ *n.* (взаи́мная) связь *f.*

intercontinental /ˌɪntərˌkɒntn'ɛntl/ *adj.* межконтинента́льный.

intercostal /ˌɪntər'kɒstl/ *adj.* межрёберный.

intercourse /'ɪntərˌkɔrs/ *n.* обще́ние *neut.*; (*sexual*) полова́я связь *f.*

interdepartmental /ˌɪntərˌdipɑrt'mɛntl/ *adj.* межве́домственный.

interdependence /ˌɪntərdɪ'pɛndəns/ *n.* взаимозави́симость *f.*

interdependent /ˌɪntərdɪ'pɛndənt/ *adj.* взаимозави́симый.

interdict /ˌɪntər'dɪkt/ *v.* запреща́ть *impf.*; (*mil.*) воспреща́ть *impf.*

interdiction /ˌɪntər'dɪkʃən/ *n.* запреще́ние *neut.*

interdigital /ˌɪntər'dɪdʒɪtl/ *adj.* межпа́льцевый.

interest /'ɪntərɪst/ **1.** *n.* интере́с *m.*; (*econ.*) проце́нты *pl.* **2.** *v.* интересова́ть (*with instr.*) *impf.*, заинтересова́ть *pf.*

interested /'ɪntərəstɪd/ **1.** *adj.* заинтересо́ванный. **2. to be interested** *v.* интересова́ться (*with instr.*) *impf.*

interesting /'ɪntərəstɪŋ/ *adj.* интере́сный.

interestingly /'ɪntərəstɪŋli/ *adj.* интере́сно.

interfere /ˌɪntər'fɪər/ *v.* вме́шиваться *impf.*, вмеша́ться *pf.*

interference /ˌɪntər'fɪərəns/ *n.* вмеша́тельство *neut.*; (*radio*) поме́хи *pl.*

interfering /ˌɪntər'fɪərɪŋ/ *adj.* назо́йливый.

interferometer /ˌɪntərfə'rɒmɪtər/ *n.* интерфероме́тр *m.*

interferon /ˌɪntər'fɪərɒn/ *n.* интерферо́н *m.*

intergalactic /ˌɪntərgə'læktɪk/ *adj.* межгалакти́ческий.

interim /'ɪntərəm/ *adj.* промежу́точный; вре́менный.

interior /ɪn'tɪəriər/ **1.** *adj.* вну́тренний. **2.** *n.* вну́тренность *f.*

interject /ˌɪntər'dʒɛkt/ *v.* вставля́ть (в *with acc.*) *impf.*

interjection /ˌɪntər'dʒɛkʃən/ *n.* (*gram.*) междоме́тие *neut.*

interlace /ˌɪntər'leis/ *v.* переплета́ть(ся) *impf.*

interlard /ˌɪntər'lɑrd/ *v.* пересыпа́ть *impf.*

interlibrary /ˌɪntər'laiˌbrɛri/ *adj.* межбиблиоте́чный.

interlinear /ˌɪntər'lɪniər/ *adj.* междустро́чный.

interlock /ˌɪntər'lɒk/ *v.* сцепля́ть(ся) *impf.*

interlocution /ˌɪntərlə'kyuʃən/ *n.* бесе́да *f.*

interlocutor /ˌɪntər'lɒkyətər/ *n.* собесе́дник *m.*

interlope /ˌɪntər'loup/ *v.* вме́шиваться в чужи́е дела́ *impf.*

interloper /'ɪntərˌloupər/ *n.* назо́йливый челове́к; незва́ный гость *m.*; (*outsider*) посторо́нний челове́к *m.*

interlude /'ɪntərˌlud/ *n.* промежу́точный эпизо́д *m.*; (*theat.*) интерлю́дия *f.*

intermarriage /ˌɪntər'mærɪdʒ/ *n.* сме́шанный брак *m.*

intermarry /ˌɪntər'mæri/ *v.* породни́ться *pf.*

intermediary /ˌɪntər'midiˌɛri/ *n.* посре́дник *m.*

intermediate /ˌɪntər'midiɪt/ *adj.* промежу́точный; сре́дний.

interment /ɪn'tɜrmənt/ *n.* погребе́ние *neut.*; по́хороны *pl.*

intermezzo /ˌɪntər'mɛtsou/ *n.* интерме́ццо *neut. indecl.*

interminable /ɪn'tɜrmənəbəl/ *adj.* бесконе́чный.

intermingle /ˌɪntər'mɪŋgəl/ *v.* сме́шивать(ся) *impf.*

intermission /ˌɪntər'mɪʃən/ *n.* переры́в *m.*; (*theat.*) антра́кт *m.*

intermit /ˌɪntər'mɪt/ *v.* прерыва́ть *impf.*

intermittence /ˌɪntər'mɪtns/ *n.* преры́вистость *f.*

intermittent /ˌɪntər'mɪtnt/ *adj.* перемежа́ющийся; преры́вистый.

intermittently /ˌɪntər'mɪtntli/ *adv.* преры́висто, с переры́вами.

intermixture /ˌɪntər'mɪkstʃər/ *n.* смесь *f.*

intermolecular /ˌɪntərmə'lɛkyələr, -mou-/ *adj.* межмолекуля́рный.

intern /'ɪntɜrn/ *n.* (*med.*) и́нтерн *m.*

internal /ɪn'tɜrnl/ *adj.* вну́тренний.

international /ˌɪntər'næʃənḷ/ adj. международный.

internationalism /ˌɪntər'næʃənḷˌɪzəm/ n. интернационализм m.

internecine /ˌɪntər'nisin/ adj. междоусобный.

internee /ˌɪntər'ni/ n. интернированный m.

Internet /'ɪntər,nɛt/ n. Интерсеть f.; йнтернет m.

internist /'ɪntɜrnɪst/ n. терапевт m.

internment /ɪn'tɜrnmənt/ n. интернирование neut.

internode /'ɪntər,noud/ n. междоузлие neut.

internuclear /ˌɪntər'nukliər/ adj. межъядерный.

interparietal /ˌɪntərpə'raiɪtḷ/ adj. межтеменной.

interpellate /ˌɪntər'pɛleit, ɪn'tɜrpə,leit/ v. интерпеллировать impf.

interpellation /ˌɪntərpə'leiʃən/ n. интерпелляция f.

interpenetrate /ˌɪntər'pɛnɪ,treit/ v. взаимопроникать impf.

interpenetration /ˌɪntər,pɛnɪ'treiʃən/ n. взаимопроникновение neut.

interphone /'ɪntər,foun/ n. внутреннее разговорное устройство neut.

interplanetary /ˌɪntər'plænɪ,tɛri/ adj. межпланетный.

interplay /'ɪntər,plei/ n. взаимодействие neut.

interpolate /ɪn'tɜrpə,leit/ v. (phil., math.) интерполировать impf.

interpolation /ɪn,tɜrpə'leiʃən/ n. вставка; интерполяция f.

interpolator /ɪn'tɜrpə,leitər/ n. интерполятор m.

interpose /ˌɪntər'pouz/ v. (place between) ставить (между with instr.) impf.

interposition /ˌɪntərpə'zɪʃən/ n. помещение (между with instr.) neut.

interpret /ɪn'tɜrprɪt/ v. (translate) переводить impf., перевести pf.; (explain) толковать impf.

interpretation /ɪn,tɜrprɪ'treiʃən/ n. перевод m.; толкование neut.; интерпретация f.

interpretative /ɪn'tɜrprɪ,teitɪv/ adj. толковательный, объяснительный.

interpreter /ɪn'tɜrprɪtər/ n. переводчик m.

interracial /ˌɪntər'reiʃəl/ adj. межрасовый.

interregnum /ˌɪntər'rɛgnəm/ n. междуцарствие neut.

interrelate /ˌɪntərrɪ'leit/ v. взаимосвязывать impf.

interrelation /ˌɪntərrɪ'leiʃən/ n. взаимосвязь f.

interrogate /ɪn'tɛrə,geit/ v. допрашивать impf.

interrogation /ɪn,tɛrə'geiʃən/ n. допрос m.

interrogative /ˌɪntə'rɒgətɪv/ adj. вопросительный.

interrogator /ɪn'tɛrə,geitər/ n. следователь m.

interrogatory /ˌɪntə'rɒgə,tɔri/ adj. вопросительный.

interrupt /ˌɪntə'rʌpt/ v. перебивать impf.; прерывать impf., прервать pf.

interrupter /ˌɪntə'rʌptər/ n. (tech.) прерыватель m.

interruption /ˌɪntə'rʌpʃən/ n. прерывание neut.; перерыв m.

intersect /ˌɪntər'sɛkt/ v. пересекать impf., пересечь pf.

intersection /ˌɪntər'sɛkʃən/ n. пересечение neut.

interspace /'ɪntər,speis/ n. промежуток m.

intersperse /ˌɪntər'spɜrs/ v. пересыпать impf.; (scatter) рассыпать impf.

interstate /ˌɪntər'steit/ adj. межгосударственный.

interstellar /ˌɪntər'stɛlər/ adj. межзвёздный.

interstice /ɪn'tɜrstɪs/ n. расщелина f.

interstitial /ˌɪntər'stɪʃəl/ adj. промежуточный.

intertribal /ˌɪntər'traibəl/ adj. межплеменной.

intertwine /ˌɪntər'twain/ v. сплетать(ся), переплетать(ся) impf.

interurban /ˌɪntər'ɜrbən/ adj. междугородный.

interval /'ɪntərvəl/ n. перерыв, интервал m.

intervene /ˌɪntər'vin/ v. вмешиваться impf., вмешаться pf.

intervention /ˌɪntər'vɛnʃən/ n. вмешательство neut.; интервенция f.

interventionist /ˌɪntər'vɛnʃənɪst/ n. интервент m.

interview /'ɪntər,vyu/ **1.** n. интервью neut. indecl.; собеседование neut. **2.** v. интервьюировать impf.

interviewee /'ɪntərvyu,i/ adj. интервьюируемый.

interviewer /'ɪntər,vyuər/ n. интервьюер m.

intervocalic /ˌɪntərvou'kælɪk/ adj. интервокальный.

interweave /ˌɪntər'wiv/ v. переплетать(ся) impf.

intestate /ɪn'tɛsteit/ adj. (умерший) без завещания.

intestinal /ɪn'tɛstənḷ/ adj. кишечный.

intestine /ɪn'tɛstɪn/ n. кишка f.

intimacy /'ɪntəməsi/ n. близость, интимность f.

intimate¹ /'ɪntəmɪt/ adj. интимный; близкий.

intimate² /'ɪntə,meit/ v. намекать impf., намекнуть pf.

intimation /ˌɪntə'meiʃən/ n. намёк m.

intimidate /ɪn'tɪmɪ,deit/ v. запугивать impf., запугать pf.

intimidation /ɪn,tɪmɪ'deiʃən/ n. запугивание neut.

into /'ɪntu; unstressed 'ɪntu, -tə/ prep. в (во) (with acc.); на (with acc.).

intolerable /ɪn'tɒlərəbəl/ adj. невыносимый; нестерпимый.

intolerance /ɪn'tɒlərəns/ n. нетерпимость f.

intolerant /ɪn'tɒlərənt/ adj. нетерпимый.

intonation /ˌɪntou'neiʃən/ n. интонация f.

intone /ɪn'toun/ v. произносить нараспев impf.

intoxicant /ɪn'tɒksɪkənt/ n. опьяняющее средство neut.

intoxicate /ɪn'tɒksɪ,keit/ v. опьянять impf., опьянить pf.

intoxicated /ɪn'tɒksɪ,keitɪd/ adj. пьяный.

intoxicating /ɪn'tɒksɪ,keitɪŋ/ adj. опьяняющий, пьянящий.

intractability /ɪn,træktə'bɪlɪti/ n. упрямство neut.

intractable /ɪn'træktəbəl/ adj. упрямый; (hard to handle) неподатливый.

intramural /ˌɪntrə'myorəl/ adj. внутренний.

intransigence /ɪn'trænsɪdʒəns/ n. непримиримость f.

intransigent /ɪn'trænsɪdʒənt/ adj. непримиримый, непреклонный.

intransitive /ɪn'trænsɪtɪv/ adj. (gram.) непереходный.

intrauterine /ˌɪntrə'yutərɪn/ adj. внутриматочный.

intravenous /ˌɪntrə'vinəs/ adj. внутривенный.

intrepid /ɪn'trɛpɪd/ adj. бесстрашный.

intrepidity /ˌɪntrɪ'pɪdɪti/ n. неустрашимость f.

intricacy /'ıntrıkəsi/ *n.* сложность *f.*

intricate /'ıntrıkıt/ *adj.* сложный, запутанный.

intrigue /ın'trig/ **1.** *n.* интрига *f.* **2.** *v.* интриговать *impf.*

intriguer /ın'trigər/ *n.* интриган *m.*, интриганка *f.*

intrinsic /ın'trınsık/ *adj.* присущий; существенный; свойственный.

intrinsically /ın'trınsıkli/ *adv.* в действительности.

introduce /,ıntrə'dus/ *v.* вводить *impf.*, ввести *pf.*; (*present*) представлять *impf.*, представить *pf.*

introduction /,ıntrə'dʌkʃən/ *n.* введение; представление *neut.*

introductory /,ıntrə'dʌktəri/ *adj.* вступительный.

introit /'ıntrouıt/ *n.* входная *f.*

introspection /,ıntrə'spɛkʃən/ *n.* интроспекция *f.*

introspective /,ıntrə'spɛktıv/ *adj.* интроспективный.

introversion /,ıntrə'vɜrʒən/ *n.* (*psych.*) интроверсия *f.*

introvert /'ıntrə,vɜrt/ *n.* (*psych.*) интроверт *m.*

intrude /ın'trud/ *v.* вторгаться *impf.*, вторгнуться *pf.*; навязывать(ся) (*with dat.*) *impf.*

intruder /ın'trudər/ *n.* назойливый *or* навязчивый человек; незваный гость *m.*; (*housebreaker*) взломщик *m.*

intrusion /ın'truʒən/ *n.* вторжение *neut.*

intrusive /ın'trusıv/ *adj.* вторгающийся; навязчивый.

intuition /,ıntu'ıʃən/ *n.* интуиция *f.*

intuitionalism /,ıntu'ıʃənl,ızəm/ *n.* интуитивизм *m.*

intuitive /ın'tuıtıv/ *also* **intuitional** *adj.* интуитивный.

intuitively /ın'tuıtıvli/ *adv.* интуитивно, чутьём.

intumescence /,ıntu'mɛsəns/ *n.* вспучивание, разбухание *neut.*

inundate /'ınən,deıt/ *v.* наводнять *impf.*

inundation /,ınən'deıʃən/ *n.* наводнение *neut.*

inure /ın'yʊr/ *v.* приучать *impf.*

inutility /,ınyu'tılıti/ *n.* бесполезность *f.*

invade /ın'veıd/ *v.* вторгаться (в *with acc.*) *impf.*, вторгнуться *pf.*

invader /ın'veıdər/ *n.* захватчик *m.*

invalid¹ /ın'vælıd/ *adj.* недействительный.

invalid² /'ınvəlıd/ *n.* инвалид; больной *m.*

invalidate /ın'vælı,deıt/ *v.* делать недействительным; аннулировать *impf.*

invalidation /ın,vælı'deıʃən/ *n.* аннулирование *neut.*

invalidity¹ /,ınvə'lıdıti/ *adj.* необоснованность *f.*

invalidity² /,ınvə'lıdıti/ *n.* инвалидность *f.*

invaluable /ın'vælyuəbəl/ *adj.* неоценимый, бесценный.

invariability /ın,vɛərıə'bılıti/ *n.* неизменяемость.

invariable /ın'vɛərıəbəl/ *adj.* неизменный.

invariably /ın'vɛərıəbli/ *adv.* неизменно.

invariance /ın'vɛərıəns/ *n.* инвариантность *f.*

invariant /ın'vɛərıənt/ *adj.* инвариантный.

invasion /ın'veıʒən/ *n.* нашествие; вторжение *neut.*

invective /ın'vɛktıv/ *n.* инвектива; врань *f.*

inveigh /ın'veı/ *n.* брань *f. usu.* **to inveigh against** *v.* ругать; бранить (*with acc.*) *impf.*

inveigle /ın'veigəl/ *v.* (*entice*) соблазнять; (*implicate*) вовлекать *impf.*

invent /ın'vɛnt/ *v.* изобретать *impf.*, изобрести *pf.*; (*fabricate*) выдумывать *impf.*

invention /ın'vɛnʃən/ *n.* изобретение *neut.*; выдумка *f.*

inventive /ın'vɛntıv/ *adj.* изобретательный.

inventiveness /ın'vɛntıvnıs/ *n.* изобретательность *f.*

inventor /ın'vɛntər/ *n.* изобретатель *m.*

inventory /'ınvən,tɔri/ *n.* инвентарь *m.*

inverse /ın'vɜrs/ **1.** *n.* противоположность *f.* **2.** *adj.* противоположный.

inversely /ın'vɜrsli/ *adv.* обратно; обратно пропорционально.

inversion /ın'vɜrʒən/ *n.* (*reversal of order*) перестановка; инверсия *f.*

invert /ın'vɜrt/ *v.* переставлять *impf.*

invertebrate /ın'vɜrtəbrıt/ **1.** *adj.* беспозвоночный. **2.** *n.* беспозвоночное животное *neut.*

inverted /ın'vɜrtıd/ *adj.* опрокинутый; (*reverse*) обратный.

inverter /ın'vɜrtər/ *n.* (*elec.*) обратный преобразователь *m.*

invest /ın'vɛst/ *v.* вкладывать *impf.*, вложить *pf.*

investigate /ın'vɛstı,geıt/ *v.* исследовать; расследовать *impf.* and *pf.*

investigation /ın,vɛstı'geıʃən/ *n.* исследование; расследование *neut.*

investigative /ın'vɛstı,geıtıv/ *adj.* следственный.

investigator /ın'vɛstı,geıtər/ *n.* следователь *m.*

investiture /ın'vɛstıtʃər/ *n.* введение в должность *neut.*

investment /ın'vɛstmənt/ *n.* вклад *m.*; инвестиция *f.*

investor /ın'vɛstər/ *n.* (*money*) вкладчик *m.*

inveterate /ın'vɛtərıt/ *adj.* закоренелый; укоренившийся.

invidious /ın'vıdıəs/ *adj.* оскорбительный; гнусный.

invigorate /ın'vıgə,reıt/ *v.* подбадривать *impf.*, подбодрить *pf.*; оживлять *impf.*

invincibility /ın,vınsə'bılıti/ *n.* непобедимость *f.*

invincible /ın'vınsəbəl/ *adj.* непобедимый.

inviolability /ın,vaıələ'bılıti/ *n.* неприкосновенность *f.*

inviolable /ın'vaıələbəl/ *adj.* нерушимый; незыблемый; неприкосновенный.

inviolate /ın'vaıəlıt/ *adj.* не нарушенный.

invisibility /ın,vızə'bılıti/ *n.* невидимость *f.*

invisible /ın'vızəbəl/ *adj.* невидимый.

invitation /,ınvı'teıʃən/ *n.* приглашение *neut.*

invite /ın'vaıt/ *v.* приглашать *impf.*, пригласить *pf.*

inviting /ın'vaıtıŋ/ *adj.* привлекательный; (*tempting*) заманчивый.

invocation /,ınvə'keıʃən/ *n.* призыв *m.*

invoice /'ınvɔıs/ *n.* накладная *f.*

invoke /ın'vouk/ *v.* призывать *impf.*

involuntarily /ın'vɒlən,tɛrəli/ *adv.* невольно.

involuntary /ın'vɒlən,tɛri/ *adj.* непроизвольный.

involute /'ınvə,lut/ *adj.* завитой.

involution /,ınvə'luʃən/ *n.* закручивание *neut.*

involve /ın'vɒlv/ *v.* вовлекать *impf.*, вовлечь *pf.*

involved /ın'vɒlvd/ *adj.* (*complex*) запутанный.

involvement /ın'vɒlvmənt/ *n.* (*complication*) осложнение *neut.*; (*participation*) участие *neut.*

invulnerability /ɪn,vʌlnərə'bɪlɪti/ *n.* неуязвимость *f.*

invulnerable /ɪn'vʌlnərəbəl/ *adj.* неуязвимый.

inward /'ɪnwərd/ *adj.* внутрь.

inwardly /'ɪnwərdli/ *adv.* внутренне.

iodide /'aɪə,daid/ *n.* йодид *m.*

iodine /'aɪə,dain/ *n.* йод *m.*

ion /'aɪən, 'aɪɒn/ *n.* ион *m.*

Ionian /ai'ouniən/ *adj.* ионийский.

ionic /ai'ɒnɪk/ *adj.* (*of ion*) ионный.

Ionic /ai'ɒnɪk/ *adj.* (*archit.*) ионический.

ionization /,aiənə'zeiʃən/ *n.* ионизация *f.*

ionize /'aiə,naiz/ *v.* ионизировать *impf.*

ionosphere /ai'ɒnə,sfiər/ *n.* ионосфера *f.*

ionospheric /ai,ɒnə'sfɛrɪk/ *adj.* ионосферический.

iota /ai'outə/ *n.* (*letter*) йота *f.*

Iowa /'aiəwə/ *n.* Айова *m.*

ipso facto /'ɪp'sou fæktou/ *adv.* по самому факту.

Iran /ɪ'ræn, ɪ'ran/ *n.* Иран *m.*

Iranian /ɪ'reiniən, ɪ'ra-/ **1.** *adj.* иранский. **2.** *n.* иранец *m.*, иранка *f.*

Iraq /ɪ'ræk, ɪ'rak/ *n.* Ирак *m.*

Iraqi /ɪ'ræki, ɪ'raki/ **1.** *adj.* иракский. **2.** *n.* иракец *m.*

irascibility /ɪ,ræsə'bɪlɪti/ *n.* раздражительность; вспыльчивость *f.*

irascible /ɪ'ræsəbəl/ *adj.* (*easily angered*) вспыльчивый; (*easily irritated*) раздражительный.

irate /ai'reit/ *adj.* гневный.

ire /ai³r/ *n.* гнев *m.*

Ireland /'ai³rlənd/ *n.* Ирландия *f.*

irenic /ai'rɛnɪk/ *adj.* умиротворяющий, миротворческий.

iridescence /,ɪrɪ'dɛsəns/ *n.* радужность *f.*

iridescent /,ɪrɪ'dɛsənt/ *adj.* пёстрый, радужный; (*changing color*) переливчатый.

iridium /ɪ'rɪdiəm/ *n.* иридий *m.*

iris /'airɪs/ *n.* (*eye*) радужная оболочка *f.*; (*flower*) ирис *m.*

Irish /'airɪʃ/ *adj.* ирландский.

Irishman /'airɪʃmən/ *n.* ирландец *m.*

Irish moss *n.* ирландский мох *m.*

Irishwoman /'airɪʃ,wumən/ *n.* ирландка *f.*

irk /ɜrk/ *v.* раздражать *impf.*, раздражить *pf.*

irksome /'ɜrksəm/ *adj.* надоедливый; раздражающий.

Irkutsk /ir'kutsk/ *n.* Иркутск *m.*

iron /'aiərn/ **1.** *adj.* железный. **2.** *n.* железо *neut.*; (*appliance*) утюг *m.*; *pl.* (*fetters*) кандалы *pl.* **3.** *v.* гладить *impf.*, выгладить *pf.*

ironbound /'aiərn'baund/ *adj.* обитый жестью.

ironclad /'aiərn,klæd/ *n.* броненосец *m.*

iron founder *n.* литейщик *m.*

iron foundry *n.* чугунолитейный завод *m.*

iron grey *adj.* стальной (цвет)

ironical /ai'rɒnɪkəl/ *adj.* иронический.

ironing /'aiərnɪŋ/ *n.* глаженье *neut.*

ironstone /'aiərn,stoun/ *n.* железная руда *f.*

ironwork /'aiərn,wɜrk/ *n.* железные детали *pl.*

irony /'airəni, 'aiər-/ *n.* ирония *f.*

irradiate /ɪ'reidi,eit/ *v.* освещать *impf.*; (*subject to radiation*) облучать *impf.*

irradiation /ɪ,reidi'eiʃən/ *n.* облучение *neut.*; иррадиация *f.*

irrational /ɪ'ræʃənl/ *adj.* неразумный; (*math.*) иррациональный.

irrationality /ɪ,ræʃə'nælɪti/ *n.* неразумность; иррациональность *f.*

irreclaimable /,ɪrɪ'kleiməbəl/ *adj.* безвозвратный.

irreconcilable /ɪ'rɛkən,sailəbəl/ *adj.* непримиримый.

irrecoverable /,ɪrɪ'kʌvərəbəl/ *adj.* непоправимый.

irredeemable /,ɪrɪ'diməbəl/ *adj.* неисправимый.

irrefutable /ɪ'rɛfyətəbəl/ ,ɪrɪ'fyutəbəl/ *adj.* неопровержимый.

irregular /ɪ'rɛgyələr/ *adj.* неправильный; нерегулярный.

irregularity /ɪ,rɛgyə'lærɪti/ *n.* неправильность; нерегулярность *f.*

irrelevance /ɪ'rɛləvəns/ *n.* неуместность *f.*

irrelevant /ɪ'rɛləvənt/ *adj.* неуместный.

irreligion /,ɪrɪ'lɪdʒən/ *n.* неверие *neut.*

irreligious /,ɪrɪ'lɪdʒəs/ *adj.* неверующий.

irremediable /,ɪrɪ'midiəbəl/ *adj.* безнадёжный.

irremovable /,ɪrɪ'muvəbəl/ *adj.* неустранимый.

irreparable /ɪ'rɛpərəbəl/ *adj.* непоправимый.

irreplaceable /,ɪrɪ'pleisəbəl/ *adj.* невозместимый.

irrepressible /,ɪrɪ'prɛsəbəl/ *adj.* безудержный.

irreproachable /,ɪrɪ'proutʃəbəl/ *adj.* безупречный.

irresistibility /,ɪrɪ,zɪstə'bɪlɪti/ *n.* неотразимость *f.*

irresistible /,ɪrɪ'zɪstəbəl/ *adj.* неотразимый.

irresolute /ɪ'rɛzə,lut/ *adj.* нерешительный.

irresolution /ɪ,rɛzə'luʃən/ *n.* нерешительность *f.*

irresolvable /,ɪrɪ'zɒlvəbəl/ *adj.* неразрешимый.

irrespective /,ɪrɪ'spɛktɪv/ *adj.*: **irrespective of** безотносительно к (*with dat.*), независимо от (*with gen*)

irresponsibility /,ɪrɪ,spɒnsə'bɪlɪti/ *n.* безответственность *f.*

irresponsible /,ɪrɪ'spɒnsəbəl/ *adj.* безответственный.

irresponsive /,ɪrɪ'spɒnsɪv/ *adj.* не реагирующий.

irretrievable /,ɪrɪ'trivəbəl/ *adj.* невозвратный.

irreverence /ɪ'rɛvərəns/ *n.* непочтительность *f.*

irreverent /ɪ'rɛvərənt/ *adj.* непочтительный.

irreversible /,ɪrɪ'vɜrsəbəl/ *adj.* необратимый.

irrevocable /ɪ'rɛvəkəbəl/ *adj.* безвозвратный.

irrigable /'ɪrɪgəbəl/ *adj.* орошаемый.

irrigate /'ɪrɪ,geit/ *v.* орошать *impf.*, оросить *pf.*

irrigation /,ɪrɪ'geiʃən/ *n.* орошение *neut.*

irrigative /'ɪrɪ,geitɪv/ *adj.* оросительный.

irrigator /'ɪrɪ,geitər/ *n.* ирригатор *m.*

irritability /,ɪrɪtə'bɪlɪti/ *n.* раздражительность *f.*

irritable /'ɪrɪtəbəl/ *adj.* раздражительный.

irritant /'ɪrɪtnt/ *n.* раздражитель *m.*

irritate /'ɪrɪ,teit/ *v.* раздражать *impf.*, раздражить *pf.*

irritating /'ɪrɪ,teitɪŋ/ *adj.* раздражающий.

irritation /,ɪrɪ'teiʃən/ *n.* раздражение *neut.*

irruption /ɪ'rʌpʃən/ *n.* вторжение *neut.*

isinglass /'aizən,glæs/ *n.* рыбий клей *m.*

Islam /ɪs'lam/ *n.* Ислам *m.*

Islamic /ɪs'læmɪk, -'lamɪk/ *adj.* мусульманский, исламистский.

island /'ailənd/ *n.* остров *m.*

islander /'ailəndər/ *n.* островитянин *m.*

isle /ail/ *n.* остров *m.*

islet /'ailɪt/ *n.* островок *m.*

isobar /'aisə,bar/ *n.* изобара *m.*

isobaric /,aisə'bærɪk/ *adj.* изобарический.

isobath /'aisə,bæθ/ *n.* изобата *f.*

isocenter /'aisou,sentər/ *n.* изоцентр *m.*
isochromatic /,aisəkrou'mætik/ *adj.* изохроматический.
isoclinal /,aisə'klainḷ/ *adj.* изоклинальный.
isocline /'aisə,klain/ *n.* изоклиналь *f.*
isogonal /ai'sɒgənḷ/ *n.* изогональ *f.*
isolate /'aisə,leit/ *v.* изолировать *impf.* and *pf.*; обособлять *impf.*
isolated /'aisə,leitid/ *adj.* изолированный; уединённый, отдалённый.
isolating /'aisə,leitiŋ/ *adj.* изолирующий.
isolation /,aisə'leiʃən/ *n.* изоляция *f.*
isolationism /,aisə'leiʃə,nizəm/ *n.* изоляционизм *m.*
isolationist /,aisə'leiʃənist/ *n.* изоляционист *m.*
isolation ward *n.* изолятор *m.*
isomer /'aisəmər/ *n.* изомер *m.*
isomeric /,aisə'mɛrik/ *adj.* изомерический.
isomerism /ai'sɒmə,rizəm/ *n.* изомерия *f.*
isometric /,aisə'mɛtrik/ *adj.* изометрический.
isomorphic /,aisə'mɔrfik/ *adj.* изоморфический.
isomorphism /,aisə'mɔrfizəm/ *n.* изоморфизм *m.*
isoprene /'aisə,prin/ *n.* изопрен *m.*
isosceles /ai'sɒsə,liz/ *adj.* равнобедренный.
isotherm /'aisə,θɜrm/ *n.* изотерма *m.*
isothermal /,aisə'θɜrməl/ *adj.* изотермальный.
isotope /'aisə,toup/ *n.* изотоп *m.*
isotropic /,aisə'trɒpik/ *adj.* изотропический.
Israel /'izriəl/ *n.* Израиль *m.*
Israeli /iz'reili/ **1.** *adj.* израильский. **2.** *n.* израильтянин *m.*, израильтянка *f.*
Israelite /'izriə,lait/ *n.* древний еврей *m.*

issuance /'iʃuəns/ *n.* выпуск *m.*
issue /'iʃu/ **1.** *n.* издание *neut.*; (*question*) вопрос *m.*; (*of book*) выпуск *m.* **2.** *v.* издавать *impf.*, издать *pf.*; выпускать *impf.*, выпустить *pf.*
Istanbul /,istɑn'bul/ *n.* Стамбул *m.*
isthmus /'isməs/ *n.* перешеек *m.*
it /it/ *pron.* он *m.*, она *f.*, оно *neut.*; это *neut.*
Italian /i'tælyən/ **1.** *adj.* итальянский. **2.** *n.* итальянец *m.*, итальянка *f.*
Italianize /i'tælyə,naiz/ *v.* итальянизировать *impf.*
italic /i'tælik/ **1.** *adj.* курсивный. **2.** *n. pl.* курсив, курсивный шрифт *m.*
italicize /i'tælə,saiz/ *v.* выделить курсивом *pf.*
Italy /'itli/ *n.* Италия *f.*
itch /itʃ/ **1.** *n.* зуд *m.* **2.** *v.* зудеть *impf.*
itchiness /'itʃinis/ *n.* зуд *m.*
itchy /'itʃi/ *adj.* зудящий.
item /'aitəm/ *n.* предмет; пункт; вопрос *m.*; (*in program*) номер *m.*
itemize /'aitə,maiz/ *v.* перечислять по пунктам *impf.*
iterate /'itə,reit/ *v.* повторять *impf.*
iterative /'itə,reitiv/ *adj.* (*gram.*) многократный.
itinerary /ai'tinə'rɛri/ *n.* маршрут *m.*
its /its/ *pron. poss.* его *m.* and *neut.*; её *f.*; свой.
itself /it'sɛlf/ *pron.* сам *m.*, сама *f.*, само *neut.*; сам себя, сама себя, само себя.
Ivanovo /i'vɑnəvə/ *n.* Иваново *neut.*
ivied /'aivid/ *adj.* увитый плющом.
ivory /'aivəri/ *n.* слоновая кость *f.*
Ivory Coast *n.* Берег слоновой кости *m.*
ivy /'aivi/ *n.* плющ *m.*

J

jab /dʒæb/ **1.** n. толчо́к m. **2.** v. толка́ть impf., толкну́ть pf.

jabber /ˈdʒæbər/ n. болтовня́ f.

jabot /ʒæˈbou/ n. жабо́ neut. indecl.

jacaranda /ˌdʒækəˈrændə/ n. джакара́нда f.

jack /dʒæk/ n. (mech.) домкра́т m.; (cards) вале́т m.

jackal /ˈdʒækəl/ n. шака́л m.

jackanapes /ˈdʒækəˌneips/ n. озорни́к; наха́л m.

jackass /ˈdʒækˌæs/ n. осёл m.

jackboot /ˈdʒækˌbut/ n. высо́кий сапо́г m.

jackdaw /ˈdʒækˌdɔ/ n. га́лка f.

jacket /ˈdʒækɪt/ n. жаке́т m., ку́ртка f.

jackfish /ˈdʒækˌfɪʃ/ n. щу́ка f.

jackhammer /ˈdʒækˌhæmər/ n. отбо́йный мо́лот m.

jack-in-the-box /ˈdʒæk ɪn ðə ˌbɒks/ n. попрыгу́нчик m.

jackknife /ˈdʒækˌnaif/ n. большо́й складно́й нож m.

jack plane n. руба́нок m.

jackpot /ˈdʒækˌpɒt/ n. (at cards) банк m.; (prize) пре́мия f., вы́игрыш m.

jack rabbit n. за́яц m.

jacks /dʒæks/ n. игра́ в ка́мешки f.

Jacobinism /ˈdʒækəbɪˌnɪzəm/ n. якоби́нство neut.

Jacobite /ˈdʒækəˌbait/ n. якоби́т m.

jactitation /ˌdʒæktɪˈteiʃən/ n. (leg.) ло́жное заявле́ние neut.

jade¹ /dʒeid/ n. (jadeite) жадеи́т m.; (nephrite) нефри́т m.

jade² /dʒeid/ n. (old horse) кля́ча f.

jaded /ˈdʒeidɪd/ adj. изнурённый.

jag /dʒæg/ n. зубе́ц m.

jagged /ˈdʒægɪd/ adj. зубча́тый.

jaguar /ˈdʒægwɑr/ n. ягуа́р m.

jail /dʒeil/ **1.** n. тюрьма́ f. **2.** adj. тюре́мный. **3.** v. посади́ть в тюрьму́ pf.

jailer /ˈdʒeilər/ n. тюре́мщик m.

Jakarta /dʒəˈkɑrtə/ n. Джака́рта f.

jalopy /dʒəˈlɒpi/ n. (colloq.) колыма́га f.; драндуле́т m.

jalousie /ˈdʒæləˌsi/ n. жалюзи́ pl. indecl.

jam¹ /dʒæm/ n. варе́нье f., джем m.

jam² /dʒæm/ **1.** n. (traffic) про́бка f. **2.** v. (block) загроможда́ть impf., загроможди́ть pf.

Jamaica /dʒəˈmeikə/ n. Яма́йка f.

jamb /dʒæm/ n. (door) кося́к m.

jamming /ˈdʒæmɪŋ/ n. (radio) заглуше́ние neut.

jam-packed /ˈdʒæm ˈpækt/ adj. битко́м наби́тый.

jangle /ˈdʒæŋgəl/ n. бряца́ние neut.

janissary /ˈdʒænəˌseri/ n. яныча́р m.

janitor /ˈdʒænɪtər/ n. убо́рщик m.

January /ˈdʒænyuˌeri/ **1.** n. янва́рь m. **2.** adj. янва́рский.

Japan /dʒəˈpæn/ n. Япо́ния f.

Japanese /ˌdʒæpəˈniz/ **1.** adj. япо́нский. **2.** n. япо́нец m., япо́нка f.

jape /dʒeip/ **1.** n. шу́тка f. **2.** v. шути́ть impf.

jar¹ /dʒɑr/ n. (container) ба́нка f.

jar² /dʒɑr/ **1.** n. (jolt) потрясе́ние neut., шок m. **2.** v. дребезжа́ть impf.

jargon /ˈdʒɑrgən/ n. жарго́н m.

jasmine /ˈdʒæzmɪn/ **1.** n. жасми́н. **2.** adj. жасми́нный.

jasper /ˈdʒæspər/ n. (min.) яшма́ f.

jaundice /ˈdʒɔndɪs/ n. желту́ха f.

jaundiced /ˈdʒɔndɪst/ adj. (med.) больно́й желту́хой.

jaunt /dʒɔnt/ n. прогу́лка f.

javelin /ˈdʒævlɪn/ n. копьё neut.

jaw /dʒɔ/ n. че́люсть f.

jawbone /ˈdʒɔˌboun/ n. челюстна́я кость f.

jay /dʒei/ n. (bird) со́йка f.; (chatterer) болту́н m.

jazz /dʒæz/ n. джаз m.

jazzman /ˈdʒæzˌmæn/ n. джази́ст m.

jazzy /ˈdʒæzi/ adj. (music) джа́зовый; (lively) живо́й.

jealous /ˈdʒɛləs/ adj. ревни́вый, зави́стливый; **to be jealous** v. ревнова́ть impf.

jealousy /ˈdʒɛləsi/ n. ре́вность, за́висть f.

jean /dʒin/ n. джи́нсовая ткань f.

jeans /dʒinz/ also **blue jeans** n. джи́нсы pl.

jeep /dʒip/ n. джип, вездехо́д m.

jeer /dʒɪər/ **1.** n. насме́шка f. **2.** v. насмеха́ться (над with instr.) impf.

jeerer /ˈdʒɪərər/ n. насме́шник m.

jeering /ˈdʒɪərɪŋ/ adj. насме́шливый.

Jehovah /dʒɪˈhouvə/ n. Иего́ва m.

Jehovah's Witnesses /dʒɪˈhouvəz/ n. иегови́сты, свиде́тели Иего́вы pl.

jejune /dʒɪˈdʒun/ adj. (boring) ску́чный; (dry) сухо́й; ску́дный.

jejunum /dʒɪˈdʒunəm/ n. то́нкая кишка́ f.

jell /dʒɛl/ v. застыва́ть impf.

jellied /ˈdʒɛlid/ adj. заливно́й.

jelly /ˈdʒɛli/ n. желе́ neut. indecl.

jellyfish /ˈdʒɛliˌfɪʃ/ n. меду́за f.

Jena /ˈyeinə/ n. Йе́на f.

jennet /ˈdʒɛnɪt/ n. осли́ца f.

jeopardize /ˈdʒɛpərˌdaiz/ v. подверга́ть опа́сности impf.

jeopardy /ˈdʒɛpərdi/ n. опа́сность f.

jerboa /dʒərˈbouə/ n. тушка́нчик m.

jeremiad /ˌdʒɛrəˈmaiəd/ n. иеремиа́да f.

Jeremiah /ˌdʒɛrəˈmaiə/ n. Иеремия m.

jerk /dʒɜrk/ **1.** n. толчо́к m.; (tug) рыво́к m.; (colloq.) дура́к; болва́н; гад m. **2.** v.t. (tug) дёргать impf.; v.i. дёргаться impf.

jerkily /ˈdʒɜrkɪli/ adv. толчка́ми; (unevenly) неро́вно; (spasmodically) су́дорожно, отры́висто.

jerkin /ˈdʒɜrkɪn/ n. ко́жаная безрука́вка f.

jerky /ˈdʒɜrki/ adj. су́дорожный; отры́вистый.

jerry can /ˈdʒɛri/ n. кани́стра f.

jersey /ˈdʒɜrzi/ n. (garment) фуфа́йка f.; джерси́ neut. indecl.; cap. (cow) джерсе́йская коро́ва f.

jest /dʒɛst/ n. шу́тка f. v. шути́ть impf., пошути́ть pf.

jester /ˈdʒɛstər/ n. шутни́к m.; (at court) шут m.

jestingly /ˈdʒɛstɪŋli/ adv. в шу́тку.

Jesuit /ˈdʒɛʒuit/ n. иезуи́т m.; adj. иезуи́тский.

jesuitical /ˌdʒɛʒuˈɪtɪkəl/ adj. иезуи́тский.

Jesus /'dʒizəs/ n. Иисýс m.
jet /dʒet/ n. струя́ f.
jet-black /'dʒet'blæk/ adj. чёрный как смоль.
jet-propelled /'dʒet prə'pɛld/ adj. реакти́вный.
jettison /'dʒetəsən/ v. (naut.) выбрáсывать за борт impf.
jetton /'dʒetņ/ n. жетóн m.
jetty /'dʒeti/ n. (pier) пирс m., при́стань f.
Jew /dʒu/ n. еврéй m., еврéйка f.
jewel /'dʒuəl/ n. драгоцéнный кáмень m.
jeweler /'dʒuələr/ n. ювели́р m.
jewelry /'dʒuəlri/ n. драгоцéнности; ювели́рные издéлия pl.
Jewish /'dʒuɪʃ/ adj. еврéйский.
Jezebel /'dʒezə,bɛl/ n. Иезавéль f.; (fig.) разврáтница f.
jibe /dʒaib/ v. (naut.) перебрáсывать impf.
jibing /'dʒaibɪŋ/ n. (naut.) поворóт через вордéвинд m.
jiffy /'dʒɪfi/ n. (colloq.) мгновéние neut.
jig¹ /dʒɪg/ n. (dance) джи́га f.
jig² /dʒɪg/ n. (template) направля́ющий шаблóн m.; (for lathe) кондýктор m.
jigger /'dʒɪgər/ n. (shot glass) рю́мочка f.
jiggle /'dʒɪgəl/ v. подтáлкивать impf.
jigsaw /'dʒɪg,sɔ/ n. (saw) лóбзик m.
jilt /dʒɪlt/ v. бросáть; покидáть impf., поки́нуть pf.
jimmy /'dʒɪmi/ n. лом m.
jingle /'dʒɪŋgəl/ 1. n. звя́кание neut. 2. v. звя́кать impf.
jingoism /'dʒɪŋgou,ɪzəm/ n. урá-патриоти́зм m.
jingoist /'dʒɪŋgouɪst/ n. урá-патриóт m.
jinn /dʒɪn/ n. джинн m.
jinx /dʒɪŋks/ 1. n. сглаз m. 2. v. сглáзить impf.
jitter /'dʒɪtər/ 1. n. (colloq.) дрожáние; волнéние neut. 2. v. нéрвничать impf.
jittery /'dʒɪtəri/ adj. нéрвный.
job /dʒɒb/ n. рабóта, слýжба f.
jobber /'dʒɒbər/ n. оптови́к m.
jobbing /'dʒɒbɪŋ/ n. случáйная рабóта f.
jobless /'dʒɒblɪs/ adj. безрабóтный.
jockey /'dʒɒki/ n. жокéй m.
jockstrap /'dʒɒk,stræp/ n. (sport) суспензóрий m.
jocose /dʒou'kous/ adj. шутли́вый.
jocular /'dʒɒkyələr/ adj. шутли́вый adj.
jocularity /,dʒɒkyə'lærɪti/ n. шутли́вость; весёлость f.
jocund /'dʒɒkənd/ adj. весёлый.
jog /dʒɒg/ 1. n. (push) тычóк m.; (nudge) толчóк лóктем m.; (bend) вы́пуклость, нерóвность f. 2. v. (knock, jostle) толкáть impf.; (run) бегáть impf.; (horse) труси́ть impf.
jogging /'dʒɒgɪŋ/ n. джóггинг m.; (colloq.) трусцá f.
joggle /'dʒɒgəl/ v. подтáлкивать impf.
jog trot n. рысцá f.
join /dʒɔin/ v. соединя́ть(ся) impf., соедини́ть(ся) pf.; присоединя́ться impf., присоедини́ться pf.
joiner /'dʒɔinər/ n. столя́р m.
joinery /'dʒɔinəri/ n. столя́рная рабóта f.
joining /'dʒɔinɪŋ/ n. соединéние neut.
joint /dʒɔint/ 1. n. (anat.) сустáв m.; (tech.) стык m. 2. adj. совмéстный; óбщий.
jointed /'dʒɔintɪd/ adj. соединённый; сочленённый.

jointly /'dʒɔintli/ adv. совмéстно.
joint stock n. акционéрный капитáл m.
joint venture n. совмéстное предприя́тие neut. (abbr. СП).
joist /dʒɔist/ n. бáлка f.
joke /dʒouk/ 1. n. шýтка f. 2. v. шути́ть impf., пошути́ть pf.
joker /'dʒoukər/ n. шутни́к m.; (cards) джóкер m.
jokey /'dʒouki/ adj. шутли́вый.
jollification /,dʒɒləfɪ'keiʃən/ n. увеселéние neut.
jollify /'dʒɒlə,fai/ v. весели́ть impf.
jollity /'dʒɒlɪti/ n. весéлье neut.
jolly /'dʒɒli/ adj. весёлый.
jolt /dʒoult/ 1. n. тря́ска f. 2. v. трясти́ impf., тряхнýть pf.
jolting /'dʒoultɪŋ/ n. тря́ска f.
Jordan /'dʒɔrdņ/ n. Иордáния f.
josh /dʒɒʃ/ v. (colloq.) подшýчивать (над with instr.) impf.
jostle /'dʒɒsəl/ v. толкáть(ся) f.
jostling /'dʒɒslɪŋ/ n. толкотня́ f.
jot /dʒɒt/ 1. n. йóта f. 2. v. (note) запи́сывать impf.
joule /dʒul/ n. джóуль m.
journal /'dʒɜrnļ/ n. журнáл m.; газéта f.; (diary) дневни́к m.
journalese /,dʒɜrnļ'iz/ n. газéтный стиль m.
journalism /'dʒɜrnļ,izəm/ n. журнали́стика f.
journalist /'dʒɜrnļist/ n. журнали́ст m.
journalistic /,dʒɜrnļ'istik/ adj. журналисти́ческий.
journey /'dʒɜrni/ 1. n. путешéствие neut. 2. v. путешéствовать impf.
joust /dʒaust/ n. ры́царский поеди́нок m.; pl. (tourney) турни́р m.
jovial /'dʒouviəl/ adj. весёлый.
joviality /,dʒouvi'ælɪti/ n. весёлость f.
jowl /dʒaul,-əs/ n. (jaw) чéлюсть f.; (cheek) щекá f.
joy /dʒɔi/ n. рáдость f.
joyful /'dʒɔifəl/ also **joyous** adj. рáдостный.
joyless /'dʒɔilɪs/ adj. безрáдостный.
joystick /'dʒɔi,stɪk/ n. рýчка управлéния f.
jubilant /'dʒubələnt/ adj. лику́ющий.
jubilantly /'dʒubələntli/ adv. лику́юще.
jubilate /'dʒubə,leit/ v. ликовáть impf.
jubilation /,dʒubə'leiʃən/ n. ликовáние neut.
jubilee /'dʒubə,li/ n. юбилéй m.
Judaic /dʒu'deiik/ adj. иудéйский.
Judaism /'dʒudi,izəm/ n. иудаи́зм m.
Judas /'dʒudəs/ n. Иýда m.
judge /dʒʌdʒ/ 1. n. судья́ m. 2. v. суди́ть impf.
judgeship /'dʒʌdʒʃip/ n. судéйская дóлжность f.
judgment /'dʒʌdʒmənt/ n. суждéние; решéние neut.; приговóр m.
judicature /'dʒudɪ,keitʃər/ n. судоустрóйство neut.
judicial /dʒu'dɪʃəl/ adj. судéбный; юриди́ческий; (of judge) судéйский.
judicious /dʒu'dɪʃəs/ adj. рассуди́тельный.
judo /'dʒudou/ n. дзюдó neut. indecl.
judoist /'dʒudouɪst/ n. дзюдои́ст m., дзюдои́стка f.
jug /dʒʌg/ n. кувши́н m.
jugal /'dʒugəl/ adj. скуловóй.
jugate /'dʒugeit/ adj. (bot.) пáрный.

juggle /'dʒʌgəl/ v. жонглировать impf.
juggler /'dʒʌglər/ n. жонглёр m.; (fig.) плут m.
juggling /'dʒʌglɪŋ/ n. жонглирование neut.
jugular /'dʒʌgyələr/ adj. яремный.
juice /dʒus/ n. сок m.
juicer /'dʒusər/ n. соковыжималка f.
juiciness /'dʒusɪnɪs/ n. сочность f.
juicy /'dʒusi/ adj. сочный.
jujitsu /dʒu'dʒɪtsu/ n. джиу-джитсу neut. indecl.
jujube /'dʒudʒub/ n. ююба f.
jukebox /'dʒuk,bɒks/ n. проигрыватель-автомат m.
julienne /ˌdʒuli'ɛn/ n. суп-жюльён m.
July /dʒə'lai/ 1. n. июль m. 2. adj. июльский.
jumble /'dʒʌmbəl/ 1. n. толчея, суматоха f. 2. v. перепутывать impf., перепутать pf.
jumbled /'dʒʌmbəld/ adj. беспорядочный.
jump /dʒʌmp/ 1. n. прыжок; скачок m. 2. v. прыгать impf., прыгнуть pf.; скакать impf.
jumper /'dʒʌmpər/ n. (athlete) прыгун m.; (smock) блуза f.
jumpiness /'dʒʌmpinɪs/ n. нервность f.
jumping /'dʒʌmpɪŋ/ n. прыганье neut.
jump rope n. скакалка f.
jumpsuit /'dʒʌmp,sut/ n. комбинезон m.
jumpy /'dʒʌmpi/ adj. нервный.
junction /'dʒʌŋkʃən/ n. соединение neut.; узел; перекрёсток m.
juncture /'dʒʌŋktʃər/ n. (joining) соединение neut.; (state of affairs) стечение обстоятельств neut.
June /dʒun/ 1. n. июнь m. 2. adj. июньский.
Junebug /'dʒun,bʌg/ n. майский жук m.
jungle /'dʒʌŋgəl/ n. джунгли pl.
junior /'dʒunyər/ adj. младший.
juniper /'dʒunəpər/ n. можжевельник m.
junk¹ /dʒʌŋk/ n. барахло neut., хлам m.
junk² /dʒʌŋk/ n. (boat) джонка f.
junker /'dʒʌŋkər/ n. (colloq.) колымага f.; драндулёт m.
Junker /'yuŋkər/ n. юнкер m.
junket 1. n. пирушка f. 2. v. пировать impf.
junkie /'dʒʌŋki/ n. (colloq.) наркоман m.
junkman /'dʒʌŋk,mæn/ n. старьёвщик m.
Juno /'dʒunou/ n. (myth., astr.) Юнона f.

junta /'hʊntə/ n. хунта f.
Jupiter /'dʒupɪtər/ n. (myth., astr.) Юпитер m.
Jurassic /dʒʊ'ræsɪk/ adj. юрский.
juridical /dʒu'rɪdɪkəl/ adj. юридический.
jurisconsult /ˌdʒʊrɪskən'sʌlt/ n. юрисконсульт m.
jurisdiction /ˌdʒʊrɪs'dɪkʃən/ n. юрисдикция f.
jurisprudence /ˌdʒʊrɪs'prudṇs/ n. юриспруденция f.
jurist /'dʒʊrɪst/ n. юрист m.
juror /'dʒʊrər/ n. присяжный заседатель; член жюри m.
jury /'dʒʊri/ n. жюри neut. indecl., присяжные pl.
jury mast n. временная мачта f.
jury-rig /'dʒʊri ˌrɪg/ n. (naut.) аварийное устройство neut.
just /dʒʌst/ 1. adj. справедливый; (deserved) заслуженный. 2. adv. точно, именно, как раз; (a moment ago) только что.
justice /'dʒʌstɪs/ n. справедливость; юстиция f.
justiciable /dʒʌ'stɪʃiəbəl/ adj. подлежащий рассмотрению судом.
justifiability /ˌdʒʌstəˌfaiə'bɪlɪti/ n. позволительность f.
justifiable /'dʒʌstəˌfaiəbəl/ adj. простительный.
justifiably /'dʒʌstəˌfaiəbli/ adv. оправданно; законно; не без основания.
justification /ˌdʒʌstəfɪ'keiʃən/ n. оправдание neut.
justificatory /dʒʌ'stɪfɪkəˌtɔri/ adj. оправдательный.
justify /'dʒʌstəˌfai/ v. оправдывать impf., оправдать pf.
justly /'dʒʌstli/ adv. справедливо; верно.
justness /'dʒʌstnɪs/ n. справедливость f.
jut /dʒʌt/ v. выступать impf.
juvenile /'dʒuvənḷ/ 1. adj. юный, юношеский. 2. n. юноша m. (decl. f.); подросток m.
juvenilia /ˌdʒuvə'nɪliə/ n. ранние произведения pl.
juxtapose /'dʒʌkstəˌpouz/ v. сопоставлять impf.
juxtaposition /ˌdʒʌkstəpə'zɪʃən/ n. сопоставление neut.

K

Kabul /'kɑbʊl/ n. Кабу́л m.
kainite /'kainait/ n. каини́т m.
Kaiser /'kaizər/ n. ка́йзер m.
kaleidoscope /kə'laidə,skoup/ n. калейдоско́п m.
kaleidoscopic /kə,laidə'skɒpɪk/ adj. калейдоскопи́ческий.
Kamchatka /kæm'tʃɑtkə/ n. (peninsula) Камча́тка f.
Kampuchea /,kæmpu'tʃiə/ n. (formerly: Cambodia) Камбо́джа f.
Kanaka /kə'nækə/ n. кана́к m.
Kandahar /,kʌndə'hɑr/ n. Кандага́р m.
kangaroo /,kæŋgə'ru/ n. кенгуру́ neut. indecl.
Kansas /'kænzəs/ n. Ка́нзас m.
Kantian /'kæntiən/ adj. кантиа́нский.
kaolin /'keiəlɪn/ **1.** n. каоли́н m. **2.** adj. каоли́новый.
kaolinite /'keiələ,nait/ n. каолини́т m.
kapok /'keipɒk/ n. капо́к m.
kaput /kɑ'pʊt/ n. (colloq.) капу́т m.
Kara Kum /,kærə 'kum/ n. (desert) Каракумы pl.
Kara Sea n. Ка́рское мо́ре neut.
karate /kə'rɑti/ n. карате́ neut. indecl.
Karelia /kə'rilyə/ n. Каре́лия f.
karma /'kɑrmə/ n. ка́рма f.
katabatic /,kætə'bætɪk/ adj. нисходя́щий.
Kathmandu /,katman'du/ n. Катманду́ m.
kayak /'kaiæk/ n. ка́як m.
Kazakh /kə'zɑk/ n. каза́х m., каза́шка f.
Kazakhstan /,kazak'stɑn/ n. Казахста́н m.
Kazan /kə'zæn/ n. Каза́нь f.
Kazbek /kaz'bɛk/ n. (mountain) Казбе́к m.
kedge /kɛdʒ/ n. стоп-а́нкер m.
keel /kil/ **1.** n. киль m. **2.** v.: **to keel over** опроки́дывать(ся) impf.
keelboat /'kil,bout/ n. килева́я шлю́пка f.
keelhaul /'kil,hɔl/ v. килева́ть impf.
keelson /'kɛlsən/ n. ки́льсон m.
keen¹ /kin/ adj. о́стрый; пронзи́тельный.
keen² /kin/ v. голоси́ть impf.
keenness /'kinnɪs/ n. острота́ f.; энтузиа́зм m.
keep /kip/ v. держа́ть, сохраня́ть impf., сохрани́ть pf.
keeper /'kipər/ n. храни́тель m.
keeping /'kipɪŋ/ n. хране́ние neut.
keepsake /'kip,seik/ n. пода́рок на па́мять m.
keg /kɛg/ n. бочо́нок m.
kelp /kɛlp/ n. бу́рая во́доросль; морска́я капу́ста f.
ken /kɛn/ n. преде́л зна́ний m.
kennel /'kɛnl/ n. конура́ f.
Kentucky /kən'tʌki/ n. Кенту́кки m.
Kenya /'kɛnyə/ n. Ке́ния f.
kepi /'keipi/ n. ке́пи neut. indecl.
keratin /'kɛrətɪn/ n. керати́н m.
kerchief /'kɜrtʃɪf/ n. плато́к m.
kerf /kɜrf/ n. (cut) зару́бка f.
kermes /'kɜrmiz/ n. керме́с m.
kernel /'kɜrnl/ n. (grain) зерно́ neut.; (nut) ядро́ neut.
kerosene /'kɛrə,sin/ n. кероси́н m.

kersey /'kɜrzi/ n. кирза́ f.
kestrel /'kɛstrəl/ n. пустельга́ f.
ketchup /'kɛtʃəp/ n. ке́тчуп m.
ketone /'kitoun/ n. кето́н m.
kettle /'kɛtl/ n. (teakettle) ча́йник m.; (pot) коте́лок m.
kettledrum /'kɛtl,drʌm/ n. лита́вра f.
key /ki/ **1.** n. ключ m.; (piano) кла́виша f. **2.** adj. ключево́й.
keyboard /'ki,bɔrd/ n. клавиату́ра f.
keyhole /'ki,houl/ n. замо́чная сква́жина f.
keynote /'ki,nout/ n. (mus.) тона́льность f., основно́й тон m.
key ring n. кольцо́ для ключе́й neut.
keystone /'ki,stoun/ n. (fig.) краеуго́льный ка́мень m.
KGB policeman n. (policeman of the secret police) кагеби́ст m.; (colloq.) кагебе́шник m.
khaki /'kæki/ n. ха́ки neut. indecl.
khan /kɑn/ n. хан m.
khanate /'kɑneit/ n. ха́нство neut.
Kharkiv /'kɑrkɔf/ n. Ха́рьков m.
Kherson /'kɛr'sɔn/ n. Херсо́н m.
kibbutz /kɪ'bʊts/ n. кибу́ц m.
kick /kɪk/ **1.** n. пино́к m.; (athl.) уда́р m. **2.** v. пина́ть impf., пнуть pf.; (of horse) брыка́ть(ся) impf.
kickoff /'kɪk,ɔf/ n. (fig.) нача́ло neut.
kickshaw /'kɪk,ʃɔ/ n. безделу́шка f.
kid¹ /kɪd/ n. (young goat) козлёнок m.; (colloq.) (child) ребёнок m.
kid² /kɪd/ v. (colloq.) высме́ивать impf.
kiddy /'kɪdi/ n. (colloq.) де́тка m. and f. (decl. f.).
kid gloves n.: **to handle with kid gloves** v. деликати́чать (с with instr.) impf.
kidnap /'kɪdnæp/ v. похища́ть impf., похи́тить pf.
kidnapper /'kɪdnæpər/ n. похити́тель m.
kidnapping /'kɪdnæpɪŋ/ n. похище́ние neut.
kidney /'kɪdni/ n. по́чка f.
kidney bean n. фасо́ль f.
kidskin /'kɪd,skɪn/ adj. ла́йковый.
Kiev /'kiɛf/ n. (also: Kiyev) Ки́ев m.
kill /kɪl/ v. убива́ть impf., уби́ть pf.
killer /'kɪlər/ n. уби́йца m.
killer whale n. коса́тка f.
killick /'kɪlɪk/ n. дрек m.
killing /'kɪlɪŋ/ **1.** n. убие́ние neut.; (murder) уби́йство neut. **2.** adj. уби́йственный.
kill-joy /'kɪl ,dʒɔi/ n. (grouser) брюзга́ m. and f. (decl. f.); ны́тик m.
kiln /kɪl, kɪln/ n. печь для о́бжига f.
kilocalorie /'kɪlə,kæləri/ n. килокало́рия f.
kilocycle /'kɪlə,saikəl/ n. килогерц m.
kilogram /'kɪlə,græm/ n. килогра́мм m.
kilohertz /'kɪlə,hɜrts/ n. килоге́рц m.
kiloliter /'kɪlə,litər/ n. килоли́тр m.
kilometer /kɪ'lɒmitər, 'kɪlə,mi-/ n. киломе́тр m.
kiloton /'kɪlə,tʌn/ n. килото́нна f.
kilovolt /'kɪlə,voult/ n. килово́льт m.
kilowatt /'kɪlə,wɒt/ n. килова́тт m.
kilt /kɪlt/ n. шотла́ндская ю́бка f.

kimono /kə'mounə/ *n.* кимонó *neut. indecl.*
kin /kɪn/ *n.* родня́ *f.*; ро́дственники *pl.*
kind[1] /kaind/ *adj.* до́брый, любе́зный, хоро́ший.
kind[2] /kaind/ *n.* вид; род; сорт *m.*
kindergarten /'kɪndər,gɑrdn̩/ *n.* де́тский сад *m.*
kindhearted /'kaind'hartɪd/ *adj.* до́брый, доброcерде́чный.
kindle /'kɪndl̩/ *v.i.* загора́ться *impf.*, загоре́ться *pf.*; *v.t.* зажига́ть *impf.*, заже́чь *pf.*
kindliness /'kaindlinɪs/ *n.* доброcерде́чие *neut.*
kindling /'kɪndlɪŋ/ *n.* разжига́ние *neut.*
kindness /'kaindnɪs/ *n.* доброта́ *f.*
kinematic /,kɪnə'mætɪk/ *adj.* кинемати́ческий.
kinematics /,kɪnə'mætɪks/ *n.* кинема́тика *f.*
kinesthetic /,kɪnəs'θetɪk/ *adj.* кинестети́ческий.
kinetics /kɪ'netɪks/ *n.* кине́тика *f.*
king /kɪŋ/ **1.** *n.* коро́ль *m.* **2.** *adj.* короле́вский.
kingcup /'kɪŋ,kʌp/ *n.* калу́жница боло́тная *f.*
kingfisher /'kɪŋ,fɪʃər/ *n.* зиморо́док *m.*
kingly /'kɪŋli/ *adj.* короле́вский.
king penguin *n.* короле́вский пингви́н *m.*
kingpin /'kɪŋ,pɪn/ *n.* гла́вная фигу́ра *f.*
kingship /'kɪŋʃɪp/ *n.* короле́вский сан *m.*
kink /kɪŋk/ *n.* петля́ *f.*; у́зел; изги́б *m.*; перекру́чивание *neut* ; (*cramp*) су́дорога *f.*
kinky /'kɪŋki/ *adj.* (*hair*) курча́вый; (*slang*) извращённый.
kinsfolk /'kɪnz,fouk/ *n.* родны́е *pl.*
kinship /'kɪnʃɪp/ *n.* родство́ *neut.*
kinsman /'kɪnzmən/ *n.* ро́дственник *m.*
kinswoman /'kɪnz,wʊmən/ *n.* ро́дственница *f.*
kiosk /'kiɒsk/ *n.* кио́ск *m.*
kipper /'kɪpər/ *n.* копчёная сельдь *f.*
Kirghiz /kɪr'giz/ *n.* кирги́з *m.*, кирги́зка *f.*
Kirov /'kɪərɔf/ *n.* Ки́ров *m.*
kirsch /kɪərʃ/ *n.* вишнёвая нали́вка *f.*
kiss /kɪs/ **1.** *n.* поцелу́й *m.*; *v.t.* целова́ть *impf.*, поцелова́ть *pf.*; *v.i.* целова́ться *impf.*, поцелова́ться *pf.*
kit /kɪt/ *n.* набо́р; компле́кт *m.*
kitbag /'kɪt,bæg/ *n.* вещево́й мешо́к *m.*
kitchen /'kɪtʃən/ **1.** *n.* ку́хня *f.* **2.** *adj.* ку́хонный.
kitchenette /,kɪtʃə'net/ *n.* ку́хонька *f.*
kite /kait/ *n.* возду́шный змей *m.*; (*bird*) ко́ршун *m.*; **to fly a kite** *v.* запуска́ть змея́ *impf.*
kith /kɪθ/ *n.* знако́мые *pl.*
kitsch /kɪtʃ/ *n.* мишура́ *f.*, кич *m.*
kitten /'kɪtn̩/ *n.* котёнок *m.*
kittiwake /'kɪti,weik/ *n.* моёвка *f.*
kitty /'kɪti/ *n.* (*colloq.*) ки́ска *f.*
kiwi /'kiwi/ *n.* (*zool.*) ки́ви *m. indecl.*
klaxon /'klæksən/ *n.* кла́ксон *m.*
kleptomania /,klɛptə'meiniə/ *n.* клептома́ния *f.*
kleptomaniac /,klɛptə'meini,æk/ *n.* клептома́н *m.*
Klystron /'klɪstrɒn/ *n.* клистро́н *m.*
knack /næk/ *n.* уме́ние *neut.*, сноро́вка *f.*
knapsack /'næp,sæk/ *n.* рюкза́к; ра́нец *m.*
knave /neiv/ *n.* моше́нник *m.*; (*cards*) вале́т *m.*
knavery /'neivəri/ *n.* моше́нничество *neut.*
knavish /'neivɪʃ/ *adj.* моше́ннический.
knead /nid/ *v.* меси́ть *impf.*
knee /ni/ **1.** *n.* коле́но *neut.* **2.** *adj.* коле́нный.
knee brace *n.* подко́с *m.*
kneecap /'ni,kæp/ *n.* коле́нная ча́шечка *f.*

knee-deep /'ni 'dip/ *also* **knee-high** /-'hai/ *adv.* по коле́но.
knee jerk *n.* (*med.*) коле́нный рефле́кс *m.*
knee joint *n.* (*anat.*) коле́нный суста́в *m.*
kneel /nil/ *v.* (*kneel down*) станови́ться на коле́ни *impf.*; (*be kneeling*) стоя́ть на коле́нях *impf.*
kneeler /'nilər/ *n.* поду́шечка для коленопреклоне́ния *f.*
kneepad /'ni,pæd/ *n.* наколе́нник *m.*
knell /nɛl/ *n.* похоро́нный звон *m.*
knickerbockers /'nɪkər,bɒkərz/ *also* **knickers** /'nɪkərz/ *n.* бри́джи *pl.*
knickknack /'nɪk,næk/ *n.* безделу́шка *f.*
knife /naif/ **1.** *n.* нож *m.* **2.** *adj.* ножево́й.
knife edge *n.* остриё *neut.*
knife grinder *n.* точи́льщик *m.*
knight /nait/ *n.* ры́царь *m.*; (*chess*) конь *m.*
knighthood /'naithʊd/ *n.* (*hist.*) ры́царство *neut.*
knightly /'naitli/ *adj.* ры́царский.
knit /nɪt/ *v.* вяза́ть *impf.*, связа́ть *pf.*
knitted /'nɪtɪd/ *adj.* вя́заный; трикота́жный.
knitter /'nɪtər/ *n.* вяза́льщик *m.*, вяза́льщица *f.*
knitting /'nɪtɪŋ/ *n.* вяза́ние *neut.*
knitwear /'nɪt,wɛər/ *n.* трикота́ж *m.*
knob /nɒb/ *n.* ши́шка *f.*; (*handle*) ру́чка *f.*
knobby /'nɒbi/ *adj.* шишкова́тый.
knock /nɒk/ **1.** *n.* стук *m.*; (*blow*) уда́рь *m.* **2.** *v.* стуча́ть (*in* with *acc.*) *impf.*, постуча́ть *pf.*; (*strike*) ударя́ть *impf.*
knockdown /'nɒk,daun/ *n.* (*sports*) нокда́ун *m.*
knocker /'nɒkər/ *n.* дверно́й молото́к *m.*
knocking /'nɒkɪŋ/ *n.* стук *m.*
knockout /'nɒk,aut/ **1.** *n.* (*athl.*) нока́ут *m.*; (*colloq.*) краса́вчик *m.*, красо́тка *f.* **2. to knock out** *v.t.* нокаути́ровать *impf. and pf.*
knoll /noul/ *n.* хо́лмик, буго́р *m.*
knot /nɒt/ **1.** *n.* у́зел *m.*; (*in wood*) сучо́к *m.* **2.** *v.* завя́зывать узло́м *impf.*
knotgrass /'nɒt,græs/ *n.* спо́рыш *m.*
knothole /'nɒt,houl/ *n.* свищ *m.*
knotted /'nɒtɪd/ *n.* завя́занный узло́м.
knotty /'nɒti/ *adj.* узлова́тый; (*wood*) сучкова́тый; (*problem*) запу́танный.
knout /naut/ *n.* кнут *m.*
know /nou/ *v.* знать *impf.*; (*a person*) быть знако́мым; **to know how** уме́ть *impf.*, суме́ть *pf.*
knowable /'nouəbəl/ *adj.* познава́емый.
know-how /'nou,hau/ *n.* уме́ние *neut.*; о́пыт *m.*
knowing /'nouɪŋ/ *adj.* (*cunning*) хи́трый; (*astute*) зна́ющий.
knowingly /'nouɪŋli/ *adv.* (*deliberately*) предна́ме́ренно; (*consciously*) созна́тельно.
know-it-all /'nou ɪt ,ɔl/ *n.* всезна́йка *m.* and *f.* (*decl. f.*).
knowledge /'nɒlɪdʒ/ *n.* зна́ние *neut.*
knowledgeable /'nɒlɪdʒəbəl/ *adj.* зна́ющий, осведомлённый.
known /noun/ *adj.* изве́стный.
knuckle /'nʌkəl/ *n.* суста́в па́льца *m.*
knucklebone /'nʌkəl,boun/ *n.* (*anat.*) ба́бка *f.*
knurl /nзrl/ *n.* ши́шка *f.*
koala /kou'ɑlə/ *n.* коа́ла *m.*, су́мчатый медве́дь *m.*
Kobe /'koubi/ *n.* Ко́бе *m.*
kohl /koul/ *n.* сурьма́ *f.*
kohlrabi /koul'rɑbi/ *n.* кольра́би *neut. indecl.*

Kola Peninsula /'koulǝ/ n. Кольский полуостров m.

kolkhoz /kɒl'kɔz; kʌl'xɔs/ **1.** n. колхóз m. **2.** adj. колхóзный.

Kolomna /kʌ'lɔmnǝ/ n. Колóмна f.

Kolyma /kǝ'limǝ/ n. (river) Колымá f.

Komarno n. Комáрно neut.

kopeck /'koupɛk/ n. копéйка f.

Koran /kǝ'rɑn/ n. Корáн m.

Korea /kǝ'riǝ/ n. Корéя f.

Korean /kǝ'riǝn/ n. корéец m., корéянка f.

kosher /'kouʃǝr/ adj. кошéрный.

Košice /'kɔʃɪtsɛ/ n. Кóшице pl.

Kostroma /ˌkɒstrǝ'mɑ/ n. Костромá f.

kowtow /'kau'tau/ n. нúзкий поклóн m.

kraal /krɑl/ n. краáль m.

Kraków /'krækau, 'krakʊf/ n. Крáков m.

Krasnodar /'kræsnǝˌdɑr/ n. Краснодáр m.

Kremenchuk /ˌkrɛmǝn'tʃʊk/ n. Кременчýг m.

Kremlin /'krɛmlɪn/ n. **the,** Кремль m.

Kronshtadt /krʌn'ʃtat/ n. Кронштáдт m.

krypton /'krɪptɒn/ n. криптóн m.

Kuala Lumpur /'kwɑlǝ lʊm'pʊr/ n. Куáла-Лумпýр m.

Kuban /ku'bæn/ n. Кубáнь f.

kudos /'kudouz/ n. слáва f.

Ku Klux Klan /'ku 'klʌks 'klæn/ n. ку-клукс-клан m.

kulak /kʊ'lɑk/ n. кулáк m.

kumiss /'kumɪs/ n. кумы́с m.

Kuomingtang /'kwou,mɪn'tæŋ/ n. гоминдáн m.

Kurgan /kʊr'gɑn/ n. Кургáн m.

Kursk /kʊrsk/ n. Курск m.

Kuwait /kʊ'weit/ n. Кувéйт m.

kvass /kvɑs/ n. квас m.

kymograph /'kaimǝˌgræf, -ˌgrɑf/ n. кимóграф m.

Kyrgyzstan /ˌkɪrgǝ'stan/ n. Киргизстáн m.

L

la /lɑ/ n. (mus.) ля neut. indecl.
label /'leibəl/ 1. n. ярлы́к m., этике́тка f. 2. v. накле́ить ярлы́к pf.
labelled /'leibəld/ adj. с этике́ткой; (marked) поме́ченный.
labial /'leibiəl/ n. (phon.) губно́й звук m.
labialization /ˌleibiələ'zeiʃən/ n. лабиализа́ция f.
labialize /'leibiəˌlaiz/ v. лабиализова́ть impf.
labiate /'leibiit/ adj. (bot.) двугу́бый.
labile /'leibəl/ adj. неусто́йчивый.
labiodental /ˌleibiou'dentl/ adj. (phon.) губно-зубно́й, ла́био-дента́льный.
labium /'leibiəm/ n. губа́ f.
labor /'leibər/ 1. n. труд m.; (childbirth) ро́ды pl. 2. adj. трудово́й; (of trade unions) профсою́зный; (of childbirth) родово́й. 3. v. труди́ться impf.
laboratory /'læbrəˌtɔri/ 1. n. лаборато́рия f. 2. adj. лаборато́рный.
labor camp n. ла́герь m.
labored /'leibərd/ adj. вы́мученный.
laborer /'leibərər/ n. рабо́чий m.
laborious /lə'bɔriəs/ adj. утоми́тельный, тяжёлый.
laborite /'leibə ˌrait/ 1. n. лейбори́ст m. 2. adj. лейбори́стский.
labor pains n. родовы́е схва́тки pl.
labor-saving /'leibər ˌseiviŋ/ adj. эконо́мящий уси́лия.
labor union n. профсою́з m. (abbr. of профессиона́льный сою́з).
labyrinth /'læbərinθ/ n. лабири́нт m.
lace /leis/ 1. n. кру́жево neut.; (shoe) шнуро́к m. 2. adj. кружевно́й. 3. v. шнурова́ть impf.
laceration /ˌlæsə'reiʃən/ n. разры́в m.; разрыва́ние neut.
lace-up /'leisˌʌp/ adj. на шнурка́х.
lachrymal /'lækrəməl/ adj. слёзный.
lachrymatory /'lækrəməˌtɔri/ adj. слезоточи́вый.
lachrymose /'lækrəˌmous/ adj. слезли́вый, плакси́вый.
lacing /'leisiŋ/ n. шнуро́вка f.
lack /læk/ 1. n. недоста́ток m.; отсу́тствие neut. 2. v. недостава́ть (impers. with dat.) impf.
lackadaisical /ˌlækə'deizikəl/ adj. то́мный; неради́вый.
lackey /'læki/ n. лаке́й m.
lacking /'lækiŋ/ adj. недостаю́щий.
lackluster /'lækˌlʌstər/ adj. ту́склый.
laconic /lə'kɒnik/ adj. лакони́чный.
lacquer /'lækər/ 1. n. лак m. 2. v. покрыва́ть ла́ком; лакирова́ть impf.
lacquering /'lækəriŋ/ n. лакиро́вка f.
lacrosse /lə'krɔs/ n. лакро́сс m.
lactation /læk'teiʃən/ n. выделе́ние молока́ neut., лакта́ция f.
lacteal /'læktiəl/ also lactic /-tik/ adj. моло́чный.
lactiferous /læk'tifərəs/ adj. выделя́ющий молоко́.
lactose /'læktous/ n. лакто́за f.
lacuna /lə'kyunə/ n. пробе́л m.
lacustrine /lə'kʌstrin/ adj. озёрный.

lacy /'leisi/ adj. кружевно́й.
lad /læd/ n. (boy) ма́льчик m.; (young fellow) па́рень m.
ladder /'lædər/ n. ле́стница f.
lade /leid/ v. нагружа́ть impf.
laden /'leidn̩/ adj. нагру́женный.
la-di-da /'lɑ di 'dɑ/ adj. (colloq.) жема́нный.
ladle /'leidl̩/ 1. n. ковш, черпа́к, поло́вник m. 2. v. черпа́ть impf.
Ladoga /'lɑdəgə/ n. Lake, Ла́дожское о́зеро neut.
lady /'leidi/ n. да́ма f.; ле́ди f. indecl.
ladybug /'leidiˌbʌg/ also ladybird /-ˌbɜrd/ n. бо́жья коро́вка f.
lady-in-waiting /'leidi in 'weitiŋ/ n. фре́йлина f.
lady-killer /'leidi ˌkilər/ n. (colloq.) сердцее́д m.
ladylike /'leidiˌlaik/ adj. же́нственный; благовоспи́танный.
ladylove /'leidiˌlʌv/ n. возлю́бленная f.
ladyship /'leidiˌʃip/ n. (address) ми́лость f.
lag /læg/ 1. n. запа́здывание neut. 2. v. отстава́ть (от with gen.), запа́здывать impf.
lager /'lɑgər/ n. лёгкое пи́во neut.
laggard /'lægərd/ adj. медли́тельный.
lagging /'lægiŋ/ n. изоля́ция f.
lagoon /lə'gun/ n. лагу́на f.
laic /'leiik/ 1. n. миря́нин m. 2. adj. мирско́й, све́тский.
laicize /'leiəˌsaiz/ v. секуляризова́ть impf.
laid paper /leid/ n. верже́ neut.
lair /leər/ n. ло́говище neut.; (bear) берло́га; нора́ f.
laissez faire /ˌlɛsei 'fɛər/ n. невмеша́тельство neut.
laity /'leiiti/ n. миря́не pl.
lake /leik/ n. о́зеро neut.
Lake Constance n. (also: Bodensee) Бо́дензее neut.
Lake Superior n. о́зеро Ве́рхнее neut.
lam[1] /læm/ v. (slang) лупи́ть, поро́ть impf.
lam[2] 1. n. побе́г m. 2. v. бежа́ть из тюрьмы́ impf.
lama /'lɑmə/ n. ла́ма m.
lamaism /'lɑməˌizəm/ n. ламаи́зм m.
lamasery /'lɑməˌseri/ n. лама́истский монасты́рь m.
lamb /læm/ n. ягнёнок m.; ове́чка, (meat) бара́нина f.; (eccl.) а́гнец m.
lambaste /læm'beist/ v. лупи́ть impf.
lambent /'læmbənt/ adj. (flickering) игра́ющий; (gleaming) сия́ющий.
lambert /'læmbərt/ n. (phys.) ла́мберт m.
lambkin /'læmkin/ n. ягнёночек m.
lamblike /'læmˌlaik/ adj. кро́ткий.
lambskin /'læmˌskin/ 1. n. ове́чья шку́ра f., мерлу́шка f. 2. adj. бара́шковый.
lamb's wool /læmz/ 1. n. поя́рок m. 2. adj. поя́рковый.
lame /leim/ adj. хромо́й.
lamella /lə'melə/ n. пласти́нка f.
lamellar /lə'melər/ adj. пласти́нчатый.
lameness /'leimnis/ n. хромота́ f.
lament /lə'ment/ 1. n. плач m. 2. v. опла́кивать impf.

lamentable /lə'mɛntəbəl/ *adj.* печа́льный, плаче́вный.

lamentably /lə'mɛntəbli/ *adv.* печа́льно.

lamentation /ˌlæmən'teiʃən/ *n.* причита́ние *neut.*; ламента́ция *f.*

lamented /lə'mɛntɪd/ *adj.* опла́киваемый.

lamina /'læmənə/ *n.* пласти́нка *f.*

laminar /'læmənər/ *adj.* ламина́рный.

laminate /'læmə,neit, -nɪt/ *n.* сло́истый пла́стик *m.*

laminated /'læmə,neitɪd/ *adj.* сло́истый, ламини́рованный.

lamination /ˌlæmə'neiʃən/ *n.* наслое́ние; покры́тие *neut.*

lammergeier /'læmər,gaiər/ *n.* борода́ч-ягня́тник *m.*

lamp /læmp/ *n.* ла́мпа *f.*; фона́рь *m.*

lampblack /'læmp,blæk/ *n.* са́жа, ко́поть *f.*

lampion /'læmpiən/ *n.* лампио́н *m.*

lamplighter /'læmp,laitər/ *n.* фона́рщик *m.*

lampoon /læm'pun/ *n.* па́сквиль *m.*

lampoonist /læm'punɪst/ *n.* пасквиля́нт *m.*

lamppost /'læmp,poust/ *n.* фона́рный столб *m.*

lamprey /'læmpri/ *n.* мино́га *f.*

lampshade /'læmp,ʃeid/ *n.* абажу́р *m.*

lance /læns/ *n.* пи́ка *f.*, копьё *neut.*

lanceolate /'lænsiə,leit/ *adj.* ланцетови́дный.

lancer /'lænsər/ *n.* (*mil.*) ула́н *m.*

lancet /'lænsɪt/ *n.* (*med.*) ланце́т *m.*

land /lænd/ **1.** *n.* земля́ *f.*; (*country*) страна́ *f.*; **by land** по су́ше; **on land** на су́ше. **2.** *adj.* земе́льный. **3.** *v.* (*aero.*) приземля́ть(ся) *impf.*; сходи́ть *impf.*, сойти́ *pf.*; (*passengers*) выса́живать(ся) *impf.*, вы́садить(ся) *pf.*

land agent *n.* управля́ющий име́нием *m.*

landau /'lændɔ/ *n.* ландо́ *neut. indecl.*

land breeze *n.* берегово́й ве́тер *m.*

land clearing *n.* расчи́стка террито́рии *f.*

landed /'lændɪd/ *adj.* (*owning land*) поме́стный; (*consisting of land*) земе́льный.

landfall /'lænd,fɔl/ *n.* подхо́д к бе́регу *m.*

landgrave /'lænd,greiv/ *n.* ландгра́ф *m.*

landing /'lændɪŋ/ *n.* (*stairs*) ле́стничная площа́дка *f.*; (*ship*) вы́садка *f.*; (*airplane*) поса́дка *f.*

landing strip *n.* взлётно-поса́дочная полоса́ *f.*

landlady /'lænd,leidi/ *n.* хозя́йка (кварти́ры); домовладе́лица *f.*

landless /'lændlɪs/ *adj.* безземе́льный.

landline /'lænd,lain/ *n.* назе́мная ли́ния *f.*

landlocked /'lænd,lɒkt/ *adj.* окружённый су́шей.

landlord /'lænd,lɔrd/ *n.* хозя́ин (кварти́ры); домовладе́лец *m.*

landmark /'lænd,mɑrk/ *n.* ориенти́р *m.*

landmine /'lænd,main/ *n.* ми́на *f.*, фуга́с *m.*

landowner /'lænd,ounər/ *n.* землевладе́лец; поме́щик *m.*; землевладе́лица; поме́щица *f.*

landscape /'lænd,skeip/ *n.* пейза́ж *m.*

landscapist /'lænd,skeipɪst/ *n.* пейзажи́ст *m.*

landslide /'lænd,slaid/ *n.* обва́л; о́ползень *m.*

land tax *n.* земе́льный нало́г *m.*

lane /lein/ *n.* тропи́нка; доро́жка *f.*; прохо́д *m.*; (*athl.*) бегова́я доро́жка *f.*; (*highway*) полоса́ *f.*

language /'læŋgwɪdʒ/ **1.** *n.* язы́к *m.* **2.** *adj.* языково́й.

languid /'læŋgwɪd/ *adj.* вя́лый, то́мный.

languish /'læŋgwɪʃ/ *v.* вя́нуть, ча́хнуть *impf.*

languishing /'læŋgwɪʃɪŋ/ *adj.* то́мный.

languor /'læŋgər/ *n.* то́мность; вя́лость *f.*

lanky /'læŋki/ *adj.* долговя́зый.

lanolin /'lænlɪn/ *n.* ланоли́н *m.*

lantern /'læntərn/ *n.* фона́рь *m.*

lanthanum /'lænθənəm/ *n.* ланта́н *m.*

Laos /'lɑous/ *n.* Лао́с *m.*

lap /læp/ *n.* коле́ни *pl.*; ло́но *neut.*; (*track*) эта́п, круг *m.*

lapdog /'læp,dɔg/ *n.* ко́мнатная соба́чка *f.*

lapel /lə'pɛl/ *n.* ла́цкан *m.*

lapidary /'læpɪ,dɛri/ *n.* грани́льщик *m.*

lapis lazuli /'læpɪs 'læzuli/ *n.* ля́пис-лазу́рь *f.*, лазури́т *m.*

lapse /læps/ **1.** *n.* недосмо́тр, ля́псус *m.*; (*interval*) промежу́ток *m.* **2.** *v.* проходи́ть *impf.*, пройти́ *pf.*; истека́ть *impf.*, исте́чь *pf.*

lapsed /læpst/ *adj.* бы́вший; исте́кший.

Laptev Sea /'læptɛf/ *n.* Мо́ре Ла́птевых *neut.*

laptop computer /'læp,tɒp/ *n.* ла́птоп; доро́жный компью́тер *m.*

lapwing /'læp,wɪŋ/ *n.* чи́бис *m.*

larceny /'lɑrsəni/ *n.* воровство́ *neut.*

larch /lɑrtʃ/ *n.* ли́ственница *f.*

lard /lɑrd/ *n.* са́ло *neut.*

larder /'lɑrdər/ *n.* кладова́я *f.*

large /lɑrdʒ/ *adj.* кру́пный; вели́кий, большо́й; **at large** *adv.* на свобо́де.

large-caliber /'lɑrdʒ 'kæləbər/ *adj.* крупнокали́берный.

large-eyed /'lɑrdʒ ,aid/ *adj.* большегла́зый.

largehearted /'lɑrdʒ'hɑrtɪd/ *adj.* великоду́шный.

largeness /'lɑrdʒnɪs/ *n.* величина́ *f.*

larger /'lɑrdʒər/ *pred. adj.* бо́льше; *compr.* бо́льший.

large-scale /'lɑrdʒ'skeil/ *adj.* крупномасшта́бный.

largess /lɑr'dʒɛs/ *n.* ще́дрость *f.*

largest /'lɑrdʒɪst/ *adj.* са́мый большо́й, наибо́льший.

largish /'lɑrdʒɪʃ/ *adj.* дово́льно большо́й.

largo /'lɑrgou/ *n.* ла́рго *neut.*

lariat /'læriət/ *n.* арка́н *m.*; ла́ссо *neut. indecl.*

lark[1] /lɑrk/ *n.* (*bird*) жа́воронок *m.*

lark[2] /lɑrk/ *n.* (*prank*) шу́тка *f.*

larkspur /'lɑrk,spɜr/ *n.* живо́кость *f.*

larky /'lɑrkli/ *adj.* весёлый.

larva /'lɑrvə/ *n.* личи́нка *f.*

larval /'lɑrvəl/ *adj.* личи́ночный.

laryngeal /lə'rɪndʒiəl, ˌlærən'dʒiəl/ *adj.* горта́нный.

laryngitis /ˌlærən'dʒaitɪs/ *n.* ларинги́т *m.*

laryngoscope /lə'rɪŋgə,skoup/ *n.* ларингоско́п *m.*

larynx /'lærɪŋks/ *n.* горта́нь *f.*

lascivious /lə'sɪviəs/ *adj.* похотли́вый.

lasciviousness /lə'sɪviəsnɪs/ *n.* похотли́вость *f.*

laser /'leizər/ **1.** *n.* ла́зер *m.* **2.** *adj.* ла́зерный.

laser printer *n.* ла́зерный при́нтер *m.*

lash /læʃ/ **1.** *n.* бич *m.*, плеть *f.*; (*blow*) уда́р пле́тью *m.*; (*eyelash*) ресни́ца *f.* **2.** *v.* хлеста́ть *impf.*

lashing /'læʃɪŋ/ *n.* по́рка *f.*

lashup /'læʃ,ʌp/ *n.* (*colloq.*) вре́менное приспособле́ние *neut.*

lass /læs/ *n.* де́вушка *f.*; (*little girl*) де́вочка *f.*

lassitude /'læsɪ,tud/ *n.* вя́лость *f.*

lasso /'læsou/ *n.* арка́н *m.*

last¹ /læst/ **1.** *adj.* после́дний; про́шлый. **2.** *adv.* после́дним; по́сле всех; **at last** наконе́ц.

last² /læst/ *v.* продолжа́ться *impf.*, продо́лжиться *pf.*

lasting /'læstɪŋ/ *adj.* дли́тельный; (*durable*) про́чный.

latch /lætʃ/ *n.* задви́жка *f.*, запо́р *m.*

late /leit/ **1.** *adj.* по́здний; (*deceased*) поко́йный. **2.** *adv.* по́здно; **to be late** *v.* опа́здывать *impf.*, опозда́ть *pf.*

lately /'leitli/ *adv.* за (*or* в) после́днее вре́мя.

latency /'leitn̩si/ *n.* лате́нтность *f.*

lateness /'leitnɪs/ *n.* опозда́ние *neut.*

latent /'leitnt/ *adj.* скры́тый.

later /'leitər/ *adv.* по́зже; пото́м.

lateral /'lætərəl/ *adj.* боково́й.

laterally /'lætərəli/ *adv.* сбо́ку.

latest /'leitɪst/ *adj.* после́дний; **at the latest** са́мое по́зднее.

latex /'leiteks/ *n.* ла́текс, мле́чный сок *m.*

lath /læθ/ *n.* ре́йка, пла́нка *f.*

lathe /leið/ *n.* тока́рный стано́к *m.*

lathe bed *n.* стани́на *f.*

lather /'læðər/ **1.** *n.* мы́льная пе́на *f.* **2.** *v.* намы́ливать *impf.*, намы́лить *pf.*

Latin /'lætn̩/ **1.** *n.* латы́нь *f.*, лати́нский язы́к *m.* **2.** *adj.* лати́нский, (*Romance*) рома́нский.

Latinist /'lætn̩ɪst/ *n.* латини́ст *m.*

latinize /'lætn̩ˌaiz/ *v.* латинизи́ровать *impf.*

latitude /'lætɪˌtud/ *n.* широта́ *f.*

latitudinal /ˌlætɪ'tudn̩l/ *adj.* широ́тный.

latrine /lə'trin/ *n.* отхо́жее ме́сто *neut.*

latter /'lætər/ *adj.* после́дний (из двух).

lattice /'lætɪs/ *n.* решётка *f.*

latticed /'lætɪst/ *adj.* решётчатый.

Latvia /'lætviə/ *n.* Ла́твия *f.*

Latvian /'lætviən/ **1.** *adj.* латви́йский. **2.** *n.* латви́ец *m.*, латви́йка *f.*; (*older form*) латы́ш *m.*, латы́шка *f.*

laud /lɔd/ *v.* хвали́ть *impf.*, похвали́ть *pf.*

laudable /'lɔdəbəl/ *adj.* похва́льный.

laudanum /'lɔdnəm/ *n.* насто́йка о́пия *f.*

laudatory /'lɔdəˌtɔri/ *adj.* хвале́бный.

laugh /læf/ **1.** *n.* смех *m.* **2.** *v.* смея́ться (над *with instr.*) *impf.*

laughable /'læfəbəl/ *adj.* смешно́й.

laughing /'læfɪŋ/ **1.** *n.* смех *m.* **2.** *adj.* шу́точный.

laughingstock /'læfɪŋˌstɒk/ *n.* посме́шище *neut.*

laughter /'læftər/ *n.* смех *m.*

launch¹ /lɔntʃ/ *n.* (*small boat*) ка́тер *m.*

launch² /lɔntʃ/ **1.** *n.* за́пуск *m.* **2.** *v.t.* (*ship*) спуска́ть на во́ду; (*rocket*) де́лать за́пуск *impf.*

launcher /'lɔntʃər/ *n.* (*for missiles*) пускова́я устано́вка *f.*

launder /'lɔndər/ *v.* стира́ть *impf.*, вы́стирать *pf.*

laundress /'lɔndrɪs/ *n.* пра́чка *f.*

Laundromat /'lɔndrəˌmæt/ *n.* автоматизи́рованная пра́чечная *f.*

laundry /'lɔndri/ *n.* (*establishment*) пра́чечная *f.*; (*articles*) бельё *neut.*

laurel /'lɔrəl/ **1.** *n.* лавр *m.* **2.** *adj.* лавро́вый.

Lausanne /lou'zæn/ *n.* Лоза́нна *f.*

lava /'lavə/ *n.* ла́ва *f.*

lavage /lə'vaʒ/ *n.* промыва́ние *neut.*

lavatory /'lævəˌtɔri/ *n.* убо́рная *f.*

lave /leiv/ *v.* омыва́ть *impf.*

lavender /'lævəndər/ *n.* лава́нда *f.*; (*color*) бле́дно-лило́вый цвет *m.*

lavish /'lævɪʃ/ **1.** *adj.* ще́дрый. **2.** *v.* расточа́ть (*with dat.*) *impf.*, расточи́ть *pf.*

law /lɔ/ *n.* зако́н *m.*; пра́во *neut.*

law-abiding /'lɔ əˌbaidɪŋ/ *adj.* законопослу́шный.

lawbreaker /'lɔˌbreikər/ *n.* наруши́тель зако́на; правонаруши́тель *m.*

law court *n.* суд *m.*; зда́ние суда́ *neut.*

lawful /'lɔfəl/ *adj.* зако́нный.

lawfulness /'lɔfəlnɪs/ *n.* зако́нность *f.*

lawless /'lɔlɪs/ *adj.* беззако́нный.

lawlessness /'lɔnɪsnɪs/ *n.* беззако́ние *neut.*; незако́нность *f.*

lawmaker /'lɔˌmeikər/ *n.* законода́тель *m.*

lawmaking /'lɔˌmeikɪŋ/ *n.* законода́тельство *neut.*

lawn /lɔn/ *n.* лужа́йка *f.*, газо́н *m.*

lawn mower *n.* коси́лка *f.*

lawsuit /'lɔˌsut/ *n.* суде́бный проце́сс *m.*

lawyer /'lɔyər/ *n.* адвока́т, юри́ст *m.*

lax /læks/ *adj.* сла́бый, вя́лый.

laxative /'læksətɪv/ *n.* слаби́тельное сре́дство *neut.*

laxity /'læksɪti/ *n.* небре́жность; хала́тность *f.*

lay¹ /loi/ *n.* (*ballad*) песнь, балла́да *f.*

lay² /lei/ *adj.* (*secular*) све́тский.

lay³ /lei/ *v.* класть *impf.*, положи́ть *pf.*

layer /'leiər/ **1.** *n.* слой; пласт *m.* **2.** *v.* насла́ивать *impf.*

layman /'leimən/ *n.* (*not-cleric*) миря́нин *m.*; (*not-expert*) непрофессиона́л *m.*

layoff /'lei ɔf/ *n.* увольне́ние *neut.*

layout /'leiˌaut/ *n.* план; маке́т *m.*; оформле́ние *neut.*

laze /leiz/ *v.* безде́льничать *impf.*

lazy /'leizi/ *adj.* лени́вый.

LCD *n.* (*abbr.* of liquid crystal display) ЖКИ (*abbr.* of жи́дко-кристали́ческий индика́тор) *m.*

lea /li/ *n.* луг *m.*, по́ле *neut.*

leach /litʃ/ *n.* папа́ *f.*

lead¹ /led/ **1.** *n.* (*metal*) свине́ц *m.* **2.** *adj.* свинцо́вый.

lead² /lid/ **1.** *n.* (*example*) приме́р *m.*; (*leadership*) руково́дство *neut.*; (*first place*) пе́рвое ме́сто *neut.*; (*theat.*) гла́вная роль *f.* **2.** *v.* (*guide*) води́ть *impf.*, вести́ *impf.*, повести́ *pf.*

leaded fuel /'lɛdɪd/ *n.* этили́рованное то́пливо *neut.*

leaden /'lɛdn̩/ *adj.* свинцо́вый.

leader /'lidər/ *n.* руководи́тель *m.*, руководи́тельница *f.*; ли́дер; вождь *m.*

leadership /'lidərˌʃɪp/ *n.* руково́дство *neut.*

lead-in /'lidˌɪn/ *n.* (*elec.*) ввод *m.*

leading /'lidɪŋ/ *adj.* веду́щий; выдаю́щийся.

lead line /lɛd/ *n.* лотли́нь *m.*

leadsman /'lɛdzmən/ *n.* лотово́й *m.*

leaf /lif/ *n.* лист *m.*

leafless /'liflɪs/ *adj.* безли́стный.

leaflet /'liflɪt/ *n.* листо́вка *f.*

leaf mold *n.* ли́ственный перегно́й *m.*

leafy /'lifi/ *adj.* ли́ственный.

league /lig/ *n.* ли́га *f.*; сою́з *m.*

leak /lik/ **1.** *n.* уте́чка *f.* **2.** *v.* течь *impf.*

leakage /'likɪdʒ/ *n.* уте́чка *f.*

leakance /'likəns/ *n.* (*elec.*) проводи́мость изоля́ции *f.*

leakproof /'lik‚pruf/ adj. герметичный.
leaky /'liki/ adj. с течью.
lean¹ /lin/ adj. худой; скудный; (of meat) постный.
lean² /lin/ v. наклоняться impf., наклониться pf.
leaning /'linɪŋ/ n. склонность f.
leanness /'linnɪs/ n. худоба; скудость f.
lean-to /'lin ‚tu/ n. пристройка с односкатной крышей f.
leap /lip/ **1.** n. прыжок, скачок m. **2.** v. прыгать impf., прыгнуть pf.
leapfrog /'lip‚frɒg/ n. чехарда f.
leap year n. високосный год m.
learn /lɜɡn/ v. учиться impf.
learned /'lɜrnɪd/ adj. учёный.
learner /'lɜrnər/ n. учащийся, ученик m.
learning /'lɜrnɪŋ/ n. учёность f.; учение neut.
lease /lis/ n. аренда, сдача в аренду f.
leasehold /'lis‚hould/ n. аренда f.
leaseholder /'lis‚houldər/ n. арендатор m.
leash /liʃ/ n. поводок m.
least /list/ **1.** adj. наименьший. **2.** adv. меньше всего; **at least** по крайней мере; **not in the least** ничуть.
leather /'leðər/ **1.** n. кожа f. **2.** adj. кожаный.
leather-bound /'leðər‚baund/ adj. в кожаном переплёте.
leatherette /‚leðə'ret/ n. искуственная кожа f.
leathery /'leðəri/ adj. кожистый.
leave¹ /liv/ n. (of absence, etc.) отпуск m.; (permission) разрешение neut.
leave² /liv/ v.i. уходить; уезжать impf.; v.t. оставлять impf., оставить pf.
leaven /'levən/ n. (yeast) дрожжи pl.
leave-taking /'liv ‚teikɪŋ/ n. прощание neut.
leavings /'livɪŋz/ n. остатки pl.
Lebanon /'lebənən/ n. Ливан m.
lecher /'letʃər/ n. развратник m.
lecherous /'letʃərəs/ adj. развратный, распутный.
lechery /'letʃəri/ n. разврат m.
lectern /'lektərn/ n. (in church) аналой m.; (speaker's stand) пюпитр m.
lection /'lekʃən/ n. чтение neut.
lecture /'lektʃər/ **1.** n. лекция f. **2.** v. читать лекцию impf.
lecturer /'lektʃərər/ n. лектор m.
LED /'el i di/ n. (abbr. of light-emitting diode) светоизлучающий диод n.
ledge /ledʒ/ n. выступ m.
ledger /'ledʒer/ n. гроссбух m.
lee /li/ n. (shelter) защита f.; укрытие neut.
leeboard /'li‚bɔrd/ n. шверц m.
leech /litʃ/ n. пиявка f.
leek /lik/ n. лук-порей m.
leer /lɪər/ **1.** n. косой взгляд m. **2.** v. смотреть йскоса impf.
lees /liz/ n. (sediment) осадок m.
leeward /'liwərd; Naut. 'luərd/ n. подветренная сторона f.
leeway /'li‚wei/ n. (ship) дрейф m.; (aircraft) снос m.
left /left/ **1.** adj. левый. **2.** adv. налево; **on the left** слева; **to the left** влево; **to the left of** налево от (with gen.).
left-back /'left 'bæk/ n. левый защитник m.
left-hand /'left'hænd/ adj. левый.

left-handed person /'left'hændɪd/ n. левша m. and f. (decl. f.).
leftism /'leftɪzəm/ n. (polit.) левизна f.
leftist /'leftɪst/ adj. левый.
leftover /'left‚ouvər/ n. остаток m.
left-rotating /'left 'routeitɪŋ/ adj. левовращающий.
leftward /'leftwərd/ adj. левый.
left-wing /'left 'wɪŋ/ adj. (polit.) левый.
leg /leg/ n. нога f.; (of furniture) ножка f.
legacy /'legəsi/ n. наследство; наследие neut.
legal /'ligəl/ adj. законный; юридический; судебный.
legality /li'gælɪti/ n. законность; легальность f.
legalization /‚ligələ'zeiʃən/ n. узаконение neut.
legalize /'ligə‚laiz/ v. узаконивать impf., узаконить pf.
legate /'legɪt/ n. легат; посол m.
legatee /‚legə'ti/ n. наследник по завещанию m.
legation /lɪ'geiʃən/ n. дипломатическое представительство neut.
legato /lə'gatou/ adj. and adv. (mus.) легато.
legend /'ledʒənd/ n. легенда f.
legendary /'ledʒən‚deri/ adj. легендарный.
legerdemain /‚ledʒərdə'mein/ n. ловкость рук f.
leggings /'legɪŋz/ n. гамаши pl.
leggy /'legi/ adj. длинноногий.
leghorn /'leg‚hɔrn/ n. итальянская соломка f.
legibility /‚ledʒə'bɪlɪti/ n. разборчивость f.
legible /'ledʒəbəl/ adj. разборчивый, чёткий.
legion /'lidʒən/ n. легион m.
legionnaire /‚lidʒə'nɛər/ n. легионер m.
legislate /'ledʒɪs‚leit/ v. издавать законы impf.
legislation /‚ledʒɪs'leiʃən/ n. законодательство neut.
legislative /'ledʒɪs‚leitɪv/ adj. законодательный.
legislator /'ledʒɪs‚leitər/ n. законодатель m.
legislature /'ledʒɪs‚leitʃər/ n. законодательная власть f.
legist /'lidʒɪst/ n. юрист m.
legitimacy /lɪ'dʒɪtəməsi/ n. законность f.; (of child) законнорождённость f.
legitimate /lɪ'dʒɪtəmɪt/ adj. законный.
legitimation /lɪ‚dʒɪtə'meiʃən/ n. узаконение neut.
legitimize /lɪ'dʒɪtɪ‚maiz/ v. узаконивать impf.
legless /'leglɪs/ adj. безногий.
leg-pull /'leg‚pul/ n. розыгрыш m.
legume /'legyum/ n. боб m.
leguminous /lɪ'gyumənəs/ adj. бобовый.
Le Havre /lə 'havrə/ n. Гавр m.
Leipzig /'laipsɪg/ n. Лейпциг m.
leisure /'liʒər, 'leʒər/ n. досуг m.; свободное время neut.
leisured /'liʒərd, 'leʒərd/ adj. праздный.
leisurely /'liʒərli, 'leʒər-/ adj. неторопливый, спокойный; досужий.
leitmotif /'laitmou‚tif/ n. лейтмотив m.
Le Mans /lə mã/ n. Ле-Ман m.
lemma /'lemə/ n. (math.) лемма f.
lemming /'lemɪŋ/ n. лемминг m.
lemon /'lemən/ **1.** n. лимон, цитрон m. **2.** adj. лимонный.
lemonade /‚lemə'neid/ n. лимонад m.
lemur /'limər/ n. лемур m.
Lena /'linə/ n. (river) Лена f.
lend /lend/ v. давать взаймы; одалживать impf.

lend-lease /'lɛnd 'lis/ n. ленд-ли́з m.
length /lɛŋkθ/ n. длина́; продолжи́тельность f.; (athl.) ко́рпус m.
lengthen /'lɛŋkθən/ v.t. удлиня́ть impf., удлини́ть pf.; v.i. удлиня́ться impf., удлини́ться pf.
lengthily /'lɛŋkθəli/ adv. до́лго; (verbosely) многосло́вно.
lengthiness /'lɛŋkθɪnɪs/ n. растя́нутость f.
lengthwise /'lɛŋkθˌwaiz/ adv. в длину́.
lengthy /'lɛŋkθi/ adj. растя́нутый.
leniency /'liniənsi/ n. снисходи́тельность f.
lenient /'liniənt/ adj. снисходи́тельный.
Leningrad /'lɛnɪnˌgræd/ n. Ленингра́д m. (see St. Petersburg).
Leninism /'lɛnəˌnɪzəm/ n. ленини́зм m.
Leninist /'lɛnənɪst/ n. ле́нинец m.
lenitive /'lɛnɪtɪv/ n. (med.) смягча́ющее сре́дство neut.
lens /lɛnz/ n. ли́нза f.; опти́ческое стекло́ neut.; (photog.) объекти́в m.; (anat.) хруста́лик m.
Lent /lɛnt/ n. Вели́кий Пост m.
Lenten /'lɛntn̩/ adj. (велико-)по́стный.
lenticular /lɛn'tɪkyələr/ adj. линзообра́зный.
lentil /'lɛntɪl/ n. чечеви́ца f.
lento /'lɛntou/ adj. and adv. (mus.) ле́нто.
Leo /'liou/ n. (astr.) Лев m.
leonine /'liəˌnain/ adj. льви́ный.
leopard /'lɛpərd/ n. леопа́рд m.
leotard /'liəˌtɑrd/ n. трико́ neut. indecl.
leper /'lɛpər/ n. прокажённый m.
Lepidoptera /ˌlɛpɪ'dɒptərə/ n. чешуекры́лые pl.
lepidopterous /ˌlɛpɪ'dɒptərəs/ adj. чешуекры́лый.
leprosarium /ˌlɛprə'sɛəriəm/ n. лепрозо́рий m.
leprosy /'lɛprəsi/ n. прока́за f.
leprous /'lɛprəs/ adj. лепро́зный, прокажённый.
lesbian /'lɛzbiən/ 1. n. лесбия́нка f 2. adj лесби́йский.
lesbianism /'lɛzbiəˌnɪzəm/ n. лесбия́нство neut.
lese majesty /lɛz/ n. госуда́рственная изме́на f.
lesion /'liʒən/ n. поврежде́ние neut.
less /lɛs/ 1. adj. ме́ньший. 2. adv. ме́ньше; ме́нее. 3. prep. без (+gen.)
lessee /lɛ'si/ n. аренда́тор; съёмщик; нанима́тель m.
lessen /'lɛsən/ v. уменьша́ть(ся) impf.
lesser /'lɛsər/ adj. ме́ньший.
lesson /'lɛsən/ n. уро́к m.
lessor /'lɛsər/ n. арендова́тель, сда́тчик m.
lest /lɛst/ conj. что́бы не; как бы не.
let /lɛt/ v. позволя́ть impf., позво́лить pf.; **to let be** оставля́ть в поко́е impf.; **to let know** дава́ть знать impf.
lethal /'liθəl/ adj. смерте́льный.
lethargic /lə'θɑrdʒɪk/ adj. летарги́ческий.
Lethe /'liθi/ n. Ле́та f.
Lett /lɛt/ n. (obs.) латы́ш m., латы́шка f.
letter /'lɛtər/ n. письмо́ neut.; (alphabet) бу́ква f.
letterhead /'lɛtərˌhɛd/ n. фи́рменная бума́га f.
lettering /'lɛtərɪŋ/ n. на́дпись f.
Lettish /'lɛtɪʃ/ adj. (obs.) латы́шский.
lettuce /'lɛtɪs/ n. сала́т, лату́к m.
letup /'lɛtˌʌp/ n. (colloq.) переды́шка f.; (slackening) ослабле́ние neut.; (cessation) прекраще́ние neut.
leucotomy /lu'kɒtəmi/ n. лейкотоми́я f.

leukemia /lu'kimiə/ n. белокро́вие neut., лейкеми́я f.
leukocyte /'lukəˌsait/ n. лейкоци́т m.
levee /'lɛvi/ n. берегово́й вал m.
level /'lɛvəl/ 1. adj. ро́вный; горизонта́льный. 2. n. у́ровень m. 3. v. ура́внивать impf., уравня́ть pf.
levelheaded /'lɛvəl'hɛdɪd/ adj. уравнове́шенный.
leveling /'lɛvəlɪŋ/ n. (tech.) нивели́рование neut.
levelly /'lɛvəli/ adv. ро́вно.
lever /'lɛvər/ n. рыча́г m.
leverage /'lɛvərɪdʒ/ n. де́йствие рычага́ neut.
leveret /'lɛvərɪt/ n. за́йчик, зайчо́нок m.
levitate /'lɛvɪˌteit/ v. поднима́ться в во́здух impf.
Levite /'livait/ n. леви́т m.
Leviticus /lɪ'vɪtɪkəs/ n. Леви́т m.
levity /'lɛvɪti/ n. легкомы́слие neut.
levy /'lɛvi/ 1. n. обложе́ние нало́гом neut.; сбор m. 2. v. облага́ть нало́гом impf.
lewd /lud/ adj. похотли́вый.
lewdness /'ludnɪs/ n. похотли́вость f.
lexical /'lɛksɪkəl/ adj. лекси́ческий; (dictionaries) слова́рный.
lexicographer /ˌlɛksɪ'kɒgrəfər/ n. лексико́граф m.
lexicographic /ˌlɛksɪkou'græfɪk/ adj. лексикографи́ческий.
lexicography /ˌlɛksɪ'kɒgrəfi/ n. лексикогра́фия f.
lexicology /ˌlɛksɪ'kɒlədʒi/ n. лексиколо́гия f.
lexicon /'lɛksɪˌkɒn/ n. лексико́н, слова́рь m.
Leyden jar /'laidn̩/ n. ле́йденская ба́нка f.
liability /ˌlaiə'bɪlɪti/ n. отве́тственность f.; обяза́тельство neut.; **assets and liabilities** акти́в и пасси́в.
liable /'laiəbəl/ adj. отве́тственный, обяза́тельный.
liaison /li'eiʒɑn/ n. связь f.
liana /li'ɑnə/ n. лиа́на f.
liar /'laiər/ n. лгун m., лгу́нья f.
libation /lai'beiʃən/ n. возлия́ние neut.
libel /'laibəl/ 1. n. клевета́ f. 2. v. клевета́ть (на with acc.) impf., наклевета́ть pf.
libelant /'laibələnt/ n. исте́ц m.
libeler /'laibələr/ n. клеветни́к m.
libelous /'laibələs/ adj. клеветни́ческий.
liberal /'lɪbərəl/ adj. ще́дрый, оби́льный; (polit.) либера́льный; (education) гумани́тарный.
liberalism /'lɪbərəˌlɪzəm/ n. либерали́зм m.
liberality /ˌlɪbə'rælɪti/ n. ще́дрость f.
liberalize /'lɪbərəˌlaiz/ v. либерализи́ровать impf.
liberate /'lɪbəˌreit/ v. освобожда́ть impf., освобо́ди́ть pf.
liberation /ˌlɪbə'reiʃən/ n. освобожде́ние neut.
liberator /'lɪbəˌreitər/ n. освободи́тель m.
libertine /'lɪbərˌtin/ n. распу́тник; вольноду́мец m.
libertinism /'lɪbərtiˌnɪzəm/ n. распу́щенность f.
liberty /'lɪbərti/ n. свобо́да, во́льность f.
libidinous /lɪ'bɪdnəs/ adj. похотли́вый.
libido /lɪ'bidou/ n. либи́до neut. indecl.
Libra /'librə/ n. (astr.) Весы́ pl.
librarian /lai'brɛəriən/ n. библиоте́карь m., библиоте́карша f.
librarianship /lai'brɛəriənˌʃɪp/ n. библиоте́чное де́ло neut.
library /'laiˌbrɛri/ n. библиоте́ка f.

libration /laɪˈbreɪʃən/ *n.* (*astr.*) либра́ция *f.*
librettist /lɪˈbrɛtɪst/ *n.* либретти́ст *m.*
libretto /lɪˈbrɛtoʊ/ *n.* либре́тто *neut. indecl.*
Libya /ˈlɪbɪə/ *n.* Ли́вия *f.*
license /ˈlaɪsəns/ *n.* разреше́ние *neut.*; лице́нзия *f.*, свиде́тельство *neut.*; **driver's license** води́тельские права́ *pl.*
licensed /ˈlaɪsənst/ *adj.* зако́нный.
license plate *n.* номерно́й знак *m.*
licentiate /laɪˈsɛnʃiɪt/ *n.* лиценциа́т *m.*
licentious /laɪˈsɛnʃəs/ *adj.* распу́щенный.
lichen /ˈlaɪkən/ *n.* (*bot.*) лиша́йник *m.*
licit /ˈlɪsɪt/ *adj.* зако́нный.
lick /lɪk/ *v.* лиза́ть *impf.*, лизну́ть *pf.*
licking /ˈlɪkɪŋ/ *n.* лиза́ние *neut.*; (*colloq.*) (*thrashing*) по́рка *f.*
lickspittle /ˈlɪkˌspɪtl/ *n.* подли́за *m.* and *f.* (*decl. f.*)
licorice /ˈlɪkərɪʃ, -rɪs/ *n.* (*plant*) лакри́чник *m.*; лакри́ца *f.*
lictor /ˈlɪktər/ *n.* ли́ктор *m.*
lid /lɪd/ *n.* кры́шка *f.*; (*eye*) ве́ко *neut.*
lie[1] /laɪ/ **1.** *n.* ложь *f.* **2.** *v.* (*tell untruths*) лгать *impf.*, солга́ть *pf.*
lie[2] /laɪ/ *v.* (*recline*) лежа́ть *impf.*; **to lie down** ложи́ться *impf.*; лечь *pf.*
Liechtenstein /ˈlɪktənˌstaɪn; ˈlɪxtənˌʃtaɪn/ *n.* Лихтенште́йн *m.*
lief /lif/ *adv.* охо́тно.
liegeman /ˈlidʒmən/ *n.* васса́л *m.*
lien /lin/ *n.* (*leg.*) пра́во удержа́ния *neut.*
Liepāja /ˈlyɛpaɪ̯a/ *n.* (*formerly: Libau*) Лиепа́я *f.*
lieu /lu/ *n.*: **in lieu of** *prep.* вме́сто (*with gen.*).
lieutenancy /luˈtɛnənsi/ *n.* зва́ние лейтена́нта *neut.*
lieutenant /luˈtɛnənt/ *n.* лейтена́нт *m.*
life /laɪf/ *n.* жизнь *f.*
life annuity *n.* пожи́зненная ре́нта *f.*
life belt *n.* спаса́тельный по́яс *m.*
lifeboat /ˈlaɪfˌboʊt/ *n.* спаса́тельная ло́дка *f.*
life buoy *n.* спаса́тельный круг *m.*
life cycle *n.* жи́зненный цикл *m.*
lifeguard /ˈlaɪfˌɡɑrd/ *n.* спаса́тель *m.*
life insurance *n.* страхова́ние жи́зни *neut.*
life jacket *n.* спаса́тельный жиле́т *m.*
lifeless /ˈlaɪflɪs/ *adj.* безжи́зненный.
lifelike /ˈlaɪfˌlaɪk/ *adj.* сло́вно живо́й.
lifeline /ˈlaɪfˌlaɪn/ *n.* (*naut.*) спаса́тельный ле́ер *m.*
lifelong /ˈlaɪfˌlɔŋ/ *adj.* пожи́зненный.
life member *n.* пожи́зненный член (*with gen.*) *m.*
lifesaver /ˈlaɪfˌseɪvər/ *n.* спаси́тель *m.*, спаси́тельница *f.*
lifesaving /ˈlaɪfˌseɪvɪŋ/ *adj.* спаса́тельный.
life-size /ˈlaɪfˈsaɪz/ *adj.* в натура́льную величину́.
life span *n.* срок жи́зни *m.*
lifestyle /ˈlaɪfˌstaɪl/ *n.* о́браз жи́зни *m.*
lifetime /ˈlaɪfˌtaɪm/ *n.* продолжи́тельность жи́зни *f.*
lift /lɪft/ *v.* поднима́ть(ся) *impf.*, подня́ть(ся) *pf.*; (*remove*) снима́ть *impf.*
lifter /ˈlɪftər/ *n.* подъёмный механи́зм *m.*
liftman /ˈlɪftmən/ *n.* лифтёр *m.*
liftoff /ˈlɪftˌɔf/ *n.* (*rocket*) пуск *m.*
lift truck *n.* автопогру́зчик *m.*
ligament /ˈlɪɡəmənt/ *n.* свя́зка *f.*
ligature /ˈlɪɡətʃər/ *n.* соедине́ние *neut.*

light[1] /laɪt/ *adj.* лёгкий.
light[2] /laɪt/ **1.** *adj.* (*color*) све́тлый. **2.** *n.* свет *m.*, освеще́ние *neut.* **3.** *v.* (*illuminate*) освеща́ть *impf.*, освети́ть *pf.*; (*kindle*) зажига́ть *impf.*, заже́чь *pf.*
lighten /ˈlaɪtn̩/ *v.* облегча́ть(ся) *impf.*, облегчи́ть(ся) *pf.*
lighter /ˈlaɪtər/ *n.* (*cigarette lighter*) зажига́лка *f.*
lighterman /ˈlaɪtərmən/ *n.* ли́хтерный рабо́чий *m.*
light-fingered /ˈlaɪt ˈfɪŋɡərd/ *adj.* ло́вкий.
light-handed /ˈlaɪt ˈhændɪd/ *adj.* ло́вкий, прово́рный.
lightheaded /ˈlaɪtˌhɛdɪd/ *adj.* в бреду́.
lighthearted /ˈlaɪtˈhɑrtɪd/ *adj.* весёлый; (*carefree*) беззабо́тный, беспе́чный.
lighthouse /ˈlaɪtˌhaʊs/ *n.* мая́к *m.*
lighting /ˈlaɪtɪŋ/ *n.* освеще́ние *neut.*
lightly /ˈlaɪtli/ *adv.* легко́.
lightness /ˈlaɪtnɪs/ *n.* лёгкость *f.*
lightning /ˈlaɪtnɪŋ/ *n.* мо́лния *f.*
lightproof /ˈlaɪtˌpruf/ *adj.* светонепроница́емый.
light-resistant /ˈlaɪt rɪˈzɪstənt/ *adj.* светосто́йкий.
light-sensitive /ˈlaɪt ˌsɛnsɪtɪv/ *adj.* светочувстви́тельный.
lightship /ˈlaɪtˌʃɪp/ *n.* плаву́чий мая́к *m.*
lightweight /ˈlaɪtˌweɪt/ **1.** *n.* легкове́с *m.* **2.** *adj.* легкове́сный, несерьёзный.
light-year /ˈlaɪtˌyɪər/ *n.* светово́й год *m.*
ligneous /ˈlɪɡnɪəs/ *adj.* деревяни́стый.
lignite /ˈlɪɡnaɪt/ *n.* лигни́т *m.*
lignum vitae /ˈlɪɡnəm vaɪti, ˈvaɪtaɪ/ *n.* бака́ут *m.*
likable /ˈlaɪkəbəl/ *adj.* привлека́тельный; ми́лый.
like[1] /laɪk/ *adj.* похо́жий, подо́бный.
like[2] /laɪk/ *v.* нра́виться (*impers. with dat.*); люби́ть *impf.*
likelihood /ˈlaɪkliˌhʊd/ *n.* вероя́тность *f.*
likely /ˈlaɪkli/ *adj.* вероя́тно.
like-minded /ˈlaɪk ˈmaɪndɪd/ *adj.* согла́сный.
liken /ˈlaɪkən/ *v.* сра́внивать (с *with instr.*) *impf.*
likeness /ˈlaɪknɪs/ *n.* схо́дство *neut.*; ко́пия *f.*
likewise /ˈlaɪkˌwaɪz/ *adv.* та́кже.
liking /ˈlaɪkɪŋ/ *n.* симпа́тия *f.*
lilac /ˈlaɪlək/ **1.** *n.* сире́нь *f.* **2.** *adj.* сире́невый.
Lille /lil/ *n.* Лилль *m.*
lilt /lɪlt/ *n.* ритм *m.*
lily /ˈlɪli/ **1.** *n.* ли́лия *f.* **2.** *adj.* лиле́йный.
lily-white /ˈlɪli ˈwaɪt/ *adj.* лиле́йный.
Lima /ˈlimə/ *n.* Ли́ма *f.*
limb /lɪm/ *n.* член *m.*; (*plant*) сук *m.*, ветвь *f.*
limber /ˈlɪmbər/ *adj.* ги́бкий; (*lithe*) прово́рный.
limbless /ˈlɪmlɪs/ *adj.* безру́кий; безно́гий.
lime[1] /laɪm/ *n.* (*calcium oxide*) и́звесть *f.*
lime[2] /laɪm/ *n.* (*fruit*) лайм *m.*
Limerick /ˈlɪmərɪk/ *n.* Ли́мерик *m.*
limestone /ˈlaɪmˌstoʊn/ *n.* известня́к *m.*
lime tree *n.* (*linden*) ли́па *f.*
lime wash *n.* побе́лка и́звестью *f.*
limewater /ˈlaɪmˌwɔtər/ *n.* известко́вая вода́ *f.*
limit /ˈlɪmɪt/ **1.** *n.* преде́л *m.*; грани́ца *f.*; ограниче́ние *neut.* **2.** *v.* ограни́чивать *impf.*, ограни́чить *pf.*
limitary /ˈlɪmɪˌtɛri/ *adj.* ограничи́тельный.
limitation /ˌlɪmɪˈteɪʃən/ *n.* ограниче́ние *neut.*
limited /ˈlɪmɪtɪd/ *adj.* ограни́ченный.
limiter /ˈlɪmɪtər/ *n.* (*tech.*) ограничи́тель *m.*

limiting /'lɪmɪtɪŋ/ adj. ограничивающий.
limitless /'lɪmɪtlɪs/ adj. безграничный.
limn /lɪm/ v. писать impf.; описывать impf.
Limoges /lɪ'mouʒ/ n. Лимож m.
limousine /'lɪmə,zin/ n. лимузин m.
limp[1] /lɪmp/ adj. (not stiff) безвольный; вялый.
limp[2] /lɪmp/ **1.** n. (lameness) храмота f.; прихрамывание neut. **2.** v. прихрамывать impf.
limpet /'lɪmpɪt/ n. (zool.) морское блюдечко neut.
limpid /'lɪmpɪd/ adj. прозрачный.
limpidity /lɪm'pɪdɪti/ n. прозрачность, ясность f.
limpness /'lɪmpnɪs/ n. мягкость; слабость; вялость f.
linchpin /'lɪntʃ,pɪn/ n. чека f.
linden /'lɪndən/ n. липа f.
line /lain/ **1.** n. линия f.; (print) строка f.; (queue) очередь; (limit) граница f.; (row) шеренга f. **2.** v. линовать impf.
lineage /'lɪniidʒ/ n. родословная f.
lineal /'lɪniəl/ adj. прямой.
lineament /'lɪniəmənt/ n. pl. очертания pl.
linear /'lɪniər/ adj. линейный.
linebreeding /'lain,bridɪŋ/ n. (agric.) линейное разведение neut.
lined /'laind/ adj. линованный; (face) морщинистый.
lineman /'lainmən/ n. линейный монтёр m.
linen /'lɪnən/ **1.** n. полотно neut.; холст m.; (bedding, etc.) (постельное) бельё neut. **2.** adj. льняной.
liner /'lainər/ n. пассажирский пароход.
linesman /'lainzmən/ n. (athl.) судья на линии m.
lineup /'lain,ʌp/ n. расстановка f.
ling[1] /lɪŋ/ n. (heather) вереск m.
ling[2] /lɪŋ/ n. (fish) налим m.
linger /'lɪŋgər/ v. задерживаться impf.
lingerie /,lɑnʒə'rei, 'lænʒə,ri/ n. дамское бельё neut.
lingering /'lɪŋgərɪŋ/ adj. медлительный; затяжной.
lingo /'lɪŋgou/ n. жаргон m.
lingua franca /'lɪŋgwə 'fræŋkə/ n. общий язык m.
lingual /'lɪŋgwəl/ adj. язычный.
linguist /'lɪŋgwɪst/ n. языковед, лингвист m.
linguistics /lɪŋ'gwɪstɪks/ n. лингвистика f.; языкознание neut.
liniment /'lɪnəmənt/ n. жидкая мазь f.
lining /'lainɪŋ/ n. подкладка f.
link /lɪŋk/ **1.** n. звено neut.; связь f. **2.** v. соединять(ся) impf., соединить(ся) pf.
linkage /'lɪŋkɪdʒ/ n. соединение, сцепление neut.; (association) связывание neut.
linkup /'lɪŋk,ʌp/ n. соединение neut.; (spacecraft) стыковка f.
Linnaean /lɪ'niən/ adj. линнеевский.
linnet /'lɪnɪt/ n. коноплянка f.
linocut /'lainə,kʌt/ n. линогравюра f.
linoleum /lɪ'nouliəm/ n. линолеум m.
linotype /'lainə,taip/ n. линотип m.
linseed /'lɪn,sid/ n. льняное семя neut.
lint /lɪnt/ n. (surg.) корпия f.
lintel /'lɪntl/ n. перемычка f.
lion /'laiən/ **1.** n. лев m. **2.** adj. львиный.
lion cub n. львёнок m.

lioness /'laiənɪs/ n. львица f.
lionhearted /'laiən'hartɪd/ adj. неустрашимый.
lion hunter n. охотник на львов m.
lionize /'laiə,naiz/ v. чествовать impf.
lion tamer n. укротитель львов m.
lip /lɪp/ n. губа f.
lipread /'lɪp,rid/ v. читать с губ impf.
lipreading /'lɪp,ridɪŋ/ n. чтение с губ neut.
lip service n. пустословие neut.
lipstick /'lɪp,stɪk/ n. губная помада f.
liquate /'laikweit/ v. плавить(ся) impf.
liquefaction /,lɪkwə'fækʃən/ n. сжижение neut.
liquefy /'lɪkwə,fai/ v. сжижать(ся); разжижать(ся) impf.
liqueur /lɪ'kзr/ n. ликёр m.
liquid /'lɪkwɪd/ **1.** n. жидкость f. **2.** adj. жидкий; (econ.) ликвидный.
liquidate /'lɪkwɪ,deit/ adj. ликвидировать impf. and pf.
liquidation /,lɪkwɪ'deiʃən/ n. ликвидация f.
liquidator /'lɪkwɪ,deitər/ n. ликвидатор m.
liquidity /lɪ'kwɪdɪti/ n. жидкое состояние neut.
liquidizer /'lɪkwɪ,daizər/ n. соковыжималка f.
liquor /'lɪkər/ n. спиртной напиток m.
lira /'lɪərə/ n. лира f.
Lisbon /'lɪzbən/ n. Лиссабон m.
lisle /lail/ **1.** n. фильдекос m. **2.** adj. фильдекосовый.
lisp /lɪsp/ **1.** n. шепелявое произношение neut. **2.** v. шепелявить impf.
lissom /'lɪsəm/ adj. гибкий.
list[1] /lɪst/ **1.** n. список m. **2.** v. составлять список impf.
list[2] /lɪst/ **1.** n. (ship) крен m. **2.** v. крениться impf.
listen /'lɪsən/ v. слушать impf.
listener /'lɪsənər/ n. слушатель m.
listening /'lɪsənɪŋ/ n. слушание neut.
listless /'lɪstlɪs/ adj. апатичный.
listlessness /'lɪstlɪsnɪs/ n. вялость, апатичность f.
litany /'lɪtni/ n. литания f.
litchi /'litʃi/ n. личжи neut. indecl.
liter /'litər/ **1.** n. литр m. **2.** adj. литровый.
literacy /'lɪtərəsi/ n. грамотность f.
literal /'lɪtərəl/ adj. буквальный.
literally /'lɪtərəli/ adv. буквально.
literary /'lɪtə,reri/ adj. литературный.
literate /'lɪtərɪt/ adj. грамотный.
literati /,lɪtə'rati/ n. литераторы pl.
literatim /,lɪtə'reitɪm/ adv. слово в слово.
literature /'lɪtərətʃər/ n. литература f.
litharge /'lɪθardʒ/ n. окись свинца f.
lithe /laið/ adj. гибкий; (agile) проворный.
lithium /'lɪθiəm/ n. литий m.
lithograph /'lɪθə,græf/ **1.** n. литография f. **2.** v. литографировать impf. and pf.
lithographic /,lɪθə'græfɪk/ adj. литографический.
lithology /lɪ'θɒlədʒi/ n. литология f.
lithosphere /'lɪθə,sfɪər/ n. литосфера f.
Lithuania /,lɪθu'einiə/ n. Литва f.
Lithuanian /,lɪθu'einiən/ **1.** adj. литовский. **2.** n. литовец m., литовка f.
litigant /'lɪtɪgənt/ adj. судящийся.
litigate /'lɪtɪ,geit/ v. судиться impf.

litigation /ˌlɪtɪˈgeiʃən/ n. судéбное дело neut.; иск; процéсс m.

litigious /lɪˈtɪdʒəs/ adj. (eager to go to law) сутя́жнический, сутя́жный.

litigiousness /lɪˈtɪdʒəsnɪs/ n. сутя́жничество neut.

litmus /ˈlɪtməs/ n. ла́кмус m.

litotes /ˈlaitəˌtiz/ n. литóта f.

litter /ˈlɪtər/ **1.** n. (stretcher) носи́лки pl.; (disorder) беспоря́док m.; (young animals) помёт m. **2.** v. (scatter) разбра́сывать impf., разброса́ть pf.

littérateur /ˌlɪtərəˈtʊr/ n. литерáтор m.

little /ˈlɪtl/ **1.** adj. (size) ма́ленький; (quantity) ма́ло (with gen.). **2.** adv. ма́ло; немнóго.

littoral /ˈlɪtərəl/ n. побере́жье neut.

liturgical /lɪˈtɜrdʒɪkəl/ adj. литурги́ческий.

liturgy /ˈlɪtərdʒi/ n. литургия́ f.

livable /ˈlɪvəbəl/ adj. снóсный.

live[1] /lɪv/ v. жить, существова́ть; обита́ть impf.

live[2] /laiv/ adj. живóй.

livelihood /ˈlaivliˌhʊd/ n. срéдства к жи́зни pl.; пропита́ние neut.

liveliness /ˈlaivlinɪs/ n. жи́вость f.; оживлéние neut.

livelong /ˈlɪvˌlɔŋ/ adj. весь, цéлый.

liven /ˈlaivən/ v. оживля́ть(ся) impf.

liver /ˈlɪvər/ **1.** n. пéчень f. **2.** adj. печёночный.

liveried /ˈlɪvərid/ adj. ливрéйный.

Liverpool /ˈlɪvərˌpul/ n. Ливерпу́ль m.

liverwort /ˈlɪvərˌwɜrt/ n. печёночник m.

livery /ˈlɪvəri/ n. ливрéя f.

livestock /ˈlaivˌstɒk/ n. скот m.

livid /ˈlɪvɪd/ adj. (color) синевáто-сéрый; багрóвый; (colloq.) (angry) разъярённый, злой. ·

living /ˈlɪvɪŋ/ **1.** adj. живóй; жили́щный. **2.** n. срéдства к жи́зни or существовáнию pl.

living quarters n. (colloq.) жильё neut.

living room n. гости́ная f.

lizard /ˈlɪzərd/ n. я́щерица f.

Ljubljana /ˌlubliˈɑnə/ n. Любля́на f.

llama /ˈlɑmə/ n. ла́ма f.

lo /lou/ adj. interj. смотри́(те).

load /loud/ **1.** n. груз m.; тя́жесть f. **2.** v. нагружа́ть impf., нагрузи́ть pf.; грузи́ть(ся) impf.; (gun) заряжа́ть impf.

loaded /ˈloudɪd/ adj. нагру́женный.

loading /ˈloudɪŋ/ n. нагру́зка f.; (vehicle) погру́зка f.

load line n. грузовáя ватерли́ния f.

loaf[1] /louf/ n. буха́нка f., карава́й m.

loaf[2] /louf/ v. (idle) безде́льничать impf.

loafer /ˈloufər/ n. безде́льник m.

loam /loum/ n. сугли́нок m.

loamy /ˈloumi/ adj. сугли́нистый.

loan /loun/ **1.** n. заём m. **2.** v. дава́ть взаймы́ impf.

loan bank n. ссу́дный банк m.

loan translation n. ка́лька f.

loanword /ˈlounˌwɜrd/ n. заи́мствованное слóво neut.

loath /louθ/ adj.: **to be loath to** v. не хотéть impf.

loathe /louð/ v. ненави́деть, пита́ть отвращéние impf.

loathing /ˈlouðɪŋ/ n. отвращéние neut.; нéнависть f.

loathsome /ˈlouðsəm/ adj. отврати́тельный, проти́вный.

lob /lɒb/ n. свечá f.

lobby /ˈlɒbi/ n. вестибю́ль m., прихóжая f.

lobbyist /ˈlɒbiɪst/ n. лоббист m.

lobe /loub/ n. вы́ступ m.; (ear) мóчка (у́ха) f.

lobed /loubd/ adj. дóльчатый.

lobelia /louˈbilyə/ n. лобéлия f.

lobotomy /ləˈbɒtəmi/ n. лоботоми́я f.

lobster /ˈlɒbstər/ n. омáр m.

lobworm /ˈlɒbˌwɜrm/ n. пескожи́л m.

local /ˈloukəl/ adj. мéстный.

locale /louˈkæl/ n. мéсто дéйствия neut.

locality /louˈkæliti/ n. мéстность f.

localization /ˌloukələˈzeiʃən/ n. локализáция f.

localize /ˈloukəˌlaiz/ v. локализи́ровать impf. and pf.

locally /ˈloukəli/ adv. лока́льно.

locate /ˈloukeit/ v. определя́ть местонахождéние impf.; (place) поселя́ть impf., посели́ть pf.; **to be located** v. находи́ться impf.

location /louˈkeiʃən/ n. местонахождéние neut.; определéние мéста neut.; мéстность f.

locative /ˈlɒkətɪv/ n. (gram.) мéстный падéж; предлóжный падéж m.

lock[1] /lɒk/ **1.** n. замóк m.; (of canal) шлюз m. **2.** v. запира́ть(ся) impf., запере́ть(ся) pf.

lock[2] /lɒk/ n. (of hair) лóкон m.

locker /ˈlɒkər/ n. шкаф m., шкáфчик m.

locket /ˈlɒkɪt/ n. медальóн m.

lockjaw /ˈlɒkˌdʒɔ/ n. тризм m.

lock nut n. контргáйка f.

lock-on /ˈlɒk ˌɒn/ n. (tech.) захвáт m.

lockout /ˈlɒkˌaut/ n. локáут m.

locksmith /ˈlɒkˌsmɪθ/ n. слéсарь m.

loco /ˈloukou/ n. (slang) сумасшéдший m.

locomotion /ˌloukəˈmouʃən/ n. передвижéние neut.

locomotive /ˌloukəˈmoutɪv/ **1.** n. паровóз m. **2.** adj. дви́жущийся.

locomotor /ˌloukəˈmoutər/ adj. дви́гательный.

locus /ˈloukəs/ n. мéсто neut.

locust /ˈloukəst/ n. саранчá f.

locution /louˈkyuʃən/ n. оборóт рéчи m.

lode /loud/ n. рýдная жи́ла f.

lodestar /ˈloudˌstɑr/ n. Поля́рная звездá f.

lodestone /ˈloudˌstoun/ n. естéственный магни́т m.

lodge /lɒdʒ/ **1.** n. дóмик m.; сторóжка f. **2.** v. помеща́ть impf.; приюти́ть pf. ; квартирова́ть impf. and pf.; (complaint) подава́ть impf.

lodger /ˈlɒdʒər/ n. жилéц m.

lodging /ˈlɒdʒɪŋ/ n. помещéние neut.

Łódź /lɒdʒ, wutʃ/ n. Лодзь f.

loess /ˈloues/ n. (geol.) лёсс m.

Lofoten Islands /ˈlouˌfutŋ/ n. Лофотéнские островá pl.

loft /lɔft/ n. чердáк m.

loftiness /ˈlɔftinɪs/ n. возвы́шенность f.

lofty /ˈlɔfti, ˈlɒf-/ adj. возвы́шенный.

log /lɔg/ n. чурбáн m.; (naut.) лаг m.; (logbook) вáхтенный журнáл m.

loganberry /ˈlougənˌbɛri/ n. логáнова я́года f.

logarithm /ˈlɔgəˌrɪðəm/ n. логари́фм m.

logarithmic /ˌlɔgəˈrɪðmɪk/ adj. логарифми́ческий.

logbook /ˈlɔgˌbʊk/ n. (aero.) бортовóй журнáл m.; (registration) формуля́р m.

loge /louʒ/ n. ло́жа f.
logger /'lɔgər/ n. лесору́б m.
loggia /'lɒdʒə, 'loudʒiə/ n. ло́джия f.
logic /'lɒdʒɪk/ n. ло́гика f.
logical /'lɒdʒɪkəl/ adj. логи́ческий.
logicality /,lɒdʒɪ'kælɪti/ n. логи́чность f.
logician /lou'dʒɪʃən/ n. ло́гик m.
login /'lɔg,ɪn/ n. (comput.) вход в сеть m.; регистра́ция f.
logistics /lou'dʒɪstɪks, lə-/ n. логи́стика f.
log line n. (naut.) лаглли́нь m.
logogram /'lɔgə,græm/ n. логогра́мма f.
logotype /'lɔgə,taip/ n. (typog.) логоти́п m.
logout /'lɔg,aut/ n. (comput.) прекраще́ние (компью́терной) се́ссии neut.; вы́ход из сети́ m.
logwood /'lɔg,wʊd/ n. кампе́шевое де́рево neut.
loin /lɔin/ n. поясни́ца f.; (cul.) филе́йная часть f.
Loire /lwar/ n. (river) Луа́ра f.
loiter /'lɔitər/ v. слоня́ться impf.
loiterer /'lɔitərər/ n. праздношата́ющийся m.
loll /lɒl/ v. сиде́ть развали́сь impf.
lollipop /'lɒli,pɒp/ n. леденец́ на па́лочке m.
London /'lʌndən/ n. Ло́ндон m.
lone /loun/ adj. одино́кий.
loneliness /'lounlinɪs/ n. одино́чество neut.
lonely /'lounll/ adj. одино́кий.
loner /'lounər/ n. нелюди́м m.
lonesome /'lounsəm/ adj. одино́кий.
long[1] /lɔŋ/ 1. adj. до́лгий; дли́нный. 2. adv. до́лго.
long[2] /lɔŋ/ v. (miss) тоскова́ть (по with dat.) impf.
longanimity /,lɒŋgə'nɪmɪti/ n. долготерпе́ние neut.
long-awaited /'lɔŋ ə'weitɪd/ adj. долгожда́нный.
longboat /'lɔŋ,bout/ n. барка́с m.
longbow /'lɔŋ,bou/ n. большо́й лук m.
long-distance /'lɔŋ 'dɪstəns/ adj. на да́льнее расстоя́ние; (telephone) междугоро́дный.
long-eared /'lɔŋ ,iərd/ adj. длинноу́хий.
longeron /'lɒndʒərən/ n. (aero.) лонжеро́н m.
longevity /lɒn'dʒɛvɪti/ n. долгове́чность f.
long-forgotten /'lɔŋ fər'gɒtn/ adj. позабы́тый.
longhand /'lɔŋ,hænd/ n.: **to write out longhand** писа́ть от руки́.
long-headed /'lɔŋ'hɛdɪd/ adj. долгоголо́вый.
longing /'lɔŋɪŋ/ n. тоска́ f.; стра́стное жела́ние neut.
longingly /'lɔŋɪŋli/ adv. жа́дно; с тоско́й.
longitude /'lɒndʒɪ,tud/ n. долгота́ f.
longitudinal /,lɒndʒɪ'tudn̩l/ adj. продо́льный.
long johns /dʒɒnz/ n. (colloq.) кальсо́ны pl.
long jumper n. прыгу́н в длину́ m.
long-legged /'lɔŋ ,lɛgɪd, -,lɛgd/ adj. длинноно́гий.
long-lived /'lɔŋ 'laivd, -'lɪvd/ adj. долгове́чный.
long-playing /'lɔŋ 'pleiŋ/ adj. долгоигра́ющий.
long-range /'lɔŋ 'reindʒ/ adj. да́льнего де́йствия.
longshoreman /'lɔŋ'ʃɔrmən/ n. порто́вый гру́зчик m.
long-sighted /'lɔŋ 'saitɪd/ adj. дальнозо́ркий.
long-sightedness /'lɔŋ 'saitɪdnɪs/ n. дальнозо́ркость f.
longstanding /'lɔŋ'stændɪŋ/ adj. давни́шний; долголе́тний.
long-suffering /'lɔŋ 'sʌfəriŋ/ n. долготерпе́ние neut.

long-tailed /'lɔŋ 'teild/ adj. длиннохво́стый.
long-term /'lɔŋ ,tɜrm/ adj. долгосро́чный.
long-winded /'lɔŋ 'windɪd/ adj. многоречи́вый.
loofah /'lufə/ n. люфа́ f.
look /lʊk/ 1. n. (glance) взгляд m.; (appearance) вид m. 2. v. смотре́ть impf.; (appear) вы́глядеть impf.
looking glass /'lʊkɪŋ/ n. зе́ркало neut.
lookout /'lʊk,aut/ n. наблюде́ние neut.; **to be on the look-out** v. быть насторожé impf.
loom[1] /lum/ n. тка́цкий стано́к m.
loom[2] /lum/ v. мая́чить impf.
loony /'luni/ adj. (colloq.) сумасше́дший.
loop /lup/ 1. n. петля́ f. 2. v. де́лать петлю́ impf.
loophole /'lup,houl/ n. бойни́ца f.; (fig.) лазе́йка f.
loose /lus/ adj. свобо́дный; не натя́нутый; сла́бый.
looseleaf binder /'lus,lif/ n. скоросшива́тель m.
loosen /'lusən/ v. развя́зывать impf., развяза́ть pf.
looseness /'lusnɪs/ n. нето́чность f.; распу́щенность f.
loosestrife /'lus,straif/ n. вербе́йник m.
loose-tongued /'lus 'tʌŋd/ adj. болтли́вый
loot /lut/ 1. n. добы́ча f. 2. v. гра́бить impf., огра́бить pf.
lop /lɒp/ v. отруба́ть impf.
lope /loup/ v. бежа́ть дли́нными шага́ми impf.
lop-eared /'lɒp ,iərd/ adj. вислоу́хий.
lopsided /'lɒp'saidɪd/ adj. (crooked) криво́й, кривобо́кий; (fig.) односторо́нний.
loquacious /lou'kweiʃəs/ adj. болтли́вый, говорли́вый.
loquacity /lou'kwæsiti/ n. болтли́вость f.
lord /lɔrd/ n. господи́н m.; влады́ка m.; (feudal) сеньо́р, феода́л m.; (rank) лорд m.; **the Lord** (eccl.) Госпо́дь m.
lordliness /'lɔrdlinɪs/ n. великоле́пие neut.
lordly /'lɔrdli/ adj. великоле́пный.
lordship /'lɔrdʃip/ n.: **Your Lordship** Ва́ша Све́тлость f.
lore /lɔr/ n. зна́ния pl.
lorgnette /lɔrn'yet/ n. лорне́т m.
Lorraine /lə'rein/ n. Лотари́нгия f.
Los Angeles /lɒs ændʒələs/ n. Лос-А́нджелес m.
lose /luz/ v. теря́ть impf., потеря́ть pf.; (a game, bet, etc.) прои́грывать impf., проигра́ть pf.
loser /'luzər/ n. (in a game) проигра́вший m.
losing /'luzɪŋ/ adj. прои́грышный.
loss /lɔs/ n. убы́ток m., поте́ря f.; (in game) про́игрыш m.
lost /lɔst/ adj. потеря́вший; поте́рянный; поги́бший.
lot /lɒt/ n. (fate) жре́бий m., у́часть, судьба́ f. (land) уча́сток m.; **a lot of** мно́го (with gen.).
lotion /'louʃən/ n. примо́чка f.; жи́дкое косметическое сре́дство neut.
lottery /'lɒtəri/ n. 1. лотере́я f. 2. adj. лотере́йный.
lotto /'lɒtou/ n. лото́ neut. indecl.
lotus /'loutəs/ n. ло́тос m.
loud /laud/ 1. adj. гро́мкий. 2. adv. гро́мко.
loudmouthed /'laud,mauðd/ adj. крикли́вый.
loudness /'laudnɪs/ n. гро́мкость f.
loudspeaker /'laud,spikər/ n. громкоговори́тель m.

Louisiana /luˌiziˈænə/ n. Луизиа́на f.
lounge /laundʒ/ **1.** n. (hotel) вестибю́ль m.; (couch) куше́тка f. **2.** v. (loaf around) слоня́ться; (do nothing) безде́льничать impf.
lounger /ˈlaundʒər/ n. ло́дырь m.
louse /laus/ n. вошь f.
lousy /ˈlauzi/ adj. вши́вый; (colloq.) проти́вный, отврати́тельный.
lout /laut/ n. грубия́н; хам m.
lovable /ˈlʌvəbəl/ adj. ми́лый.
love /lʌv/ **1.** n. любо́вь f.; **in love** влюблённый adj.; **to fall in love** влюби́ться (в with acc.) pf. **2.** adj. любо́вный. **3.** v. люби́ть impf.
love affair n. рома́н m.
loveless /ˈlʌvlɪs/ adj. нелюбя́щий.
loveliness /ˈlʌvlɪnɪs/ n. красота́ f.
lovely /ˈlʌvli/ adj. преле́стный.
lovemaking /ˈlʌvˌmeikɪŋ/ n. половы́е сноше́ния neut.
lover /ˈlʌvər/ n. любо́вник m., любо́вница f.; (enthusiast) люби́тель m.
lovesick /ˈlʌvˌsɪk/ adj. томя́щийся от любви́.
loving /ˈlʌvɪŋ/ adj. лю́бящий, не́жный.
low¹ /lou/ adj. ни́зкий; (quiet) ти́хий.
low² /lou/ v. мыча́ть impf.
lowborn /ˈlouˈbɔrn/ adj. просто́го происхожде́ния.
lowbrow /ˈlouˌbrau/ n. профа́н m.
low-cut /ˈlou ˈkʌt/ adj. деколти́рованный.
low-down /ˈlou ˈdaun/ n. (colloq.) подного́тная f.
lower¹ /ˈlauᵊr, ˈlauər/ v. хму́риться impf.
lower² /ˈlouər/ **1.** v. понижа́ть impf., пони́зить pf.; снижа́ть impf., сни́зить pf. **2.** adj. ни́зший; ни́жний.
lowercase letter /ˈlouərˌkeis/ n. строчна́я бу́ква f.
lowering /ˈlauərɪŋ/ n. пониже́ние neut.
lowest /ˈlouɪst/ adj. са́мый ни́зкий, ни́зший, нижа́йший.
low-grade /ˈlou ˈgreid/ adj. низкопро́бный; низкосо́ртный.
lowland /ˈloulənd/ n. ни́зменность, низи́на f.
lowly /ˈlouli/ adj. скро́мный.
low-lying /ˈlou ˌlaiŋ/ adj. ни́зменный.
low-necked /ˈlou ˈnɛkt/ adj. деколти́рованный.
low-pitched /ˈlou ˈpɪtʃt/ adj. ни́зкий.
low-powered /ˈlou ˈpauərd/ adj. маломо́щный.
low-resistance /ˈlou rɪˈzɪstəns/ adj. ни́зкого сопротивле́ния.
low-speed /ˈlou ˈspid/ adj. тихохо́дный.
loyal /ˈlɔiəl/ adj. ве́рный, лоя́льный.
loyalist /ˈlɔiəlɪst/ n. лоя́лист m.
loyalty /ˈlɔiəlti/ n. ве́рность, лоя́льность f.
lozenge /ˈlɒzɪndʒ/ n. лепёшка f.
Lublin /ˈlublɪn/ n. Лю́блин m.
lubricant /ˈlubrɪkənt/ n. сма́зка f.; сма́зочное вещество́ neut.
lubricate /ˈlubrɪˌkeit/ v. сма́зывать impf., сма́зать pf.
lubricating /ˈlubrɪˌkeitɪŋ/ adj. сма́зочный.
lubrication /ˌlubrɪˈkeiʃən/ n. сма́зка f.
lubricious /luˈbrɪʃəs/ adj. ско́льзкий; похотли́вый.
lubricity /luˈbrɪsɪti/ n. ско́льзкость f.
Lucerne /luˈsɜrn/ n. (also: Luzern) Люце́рн m.
lucerne /luˈsɜrn/ n. люце́рна f.
lucid /ˈlusɪd/ adj. я́сный, прозра́чный.

lucidity /luˈsɪdɪti/ n. я́сность f.
luck /lʌk/ n. сча́стье neut.; уда́ча f.
luckily /ˈlʌkəli/ adv. к сча́стью.
lucky /ˈlʌki/ adj. счастли́вый, уда́чливый.
lucrative /ˈlukrətɪv/ adj. при́быльный.
lucre /ˈlukər/ n. бары́ш m., при́быль f.
Luddite /ˈlʌdait/ n. лудди́т m.
ludicrous /ˈludɪkrəs/ adj. смешно́й.
luff /lʌf/ n. (naut.) пере́дняя шкато́рина f.
lug /lʌg/ v. тащи́ть, волочи́ть impf.; **to lug in** вта́скивать impf.; **to lug out** выта́скивать impf.
luggage /ˈlʌgɪdʒ/ n. бага́ж m.
lugger /ˈlʌgər/ n. лю́гер m.
lugsail /ˈlʌgˌseil; Naut. ˈlʌgsəl/ n. лю́герный па́рус m.
lugubrious /luˈgubriəs/ adj. печа́льный, мра́чный.
lukewarm /ˈlukˈwɔrm/ adj. теплова́тый.
lull /lʌl/ **1.** n. зати́шье neut. **2.** v. убаю́кивать impf., убаю́кать pf.
lullaby /ˈlʌləˌbai/ n. колыбе́льная пе́сня f.
lumbago /lʌmˈbeigou/ n. люмба́го neut. indecl.
lumbar /ˈlʌmbər/ adj. поясни́чный.
lumber /ˈlʌmbər/ n. лесоматериа́л m.; (useless stuff) хлам m.
lumber-camp /ˈlʌmbər ˌkæmp/ n. лесозагото́вки pl.
lumberjack /ˈlʌmbərˌdʒæk/ n. лесору́б m.
lumberyard /ˈlʌmbərˌyɑrd/ n. лесно́й склад m.
lumen /ˈlumən/ n. (phys.) лю́мен m.
luminary /ˈluməˌnɛri/ n. свети́ло neut.
luminescence /ˌluməˈnɛsəns/ n. свече́ние neut.
luminescent /ˌluməˈnɛsənt/ adj. светя́щийся, люминесце́нтный.
luminosity /ˌluməˈnɒsɪti/ n. я́ркость f.
luminous /ˈlumənəs/ adj. све́тлый, светя́щийся.
lump /lʌmp/ n. ком m.; (of sugar) кусо́к m.; (swelling) ши́шка f.
lumpish /ˈlʌmpɪʃ/ adj. (clumsy) неуклю́жий.
lumpy /ˈlʌmpi/ adj. комкова́тый.
lunacy /ˈlunəsi/ n. помеша́тельство neut.
lunar /ˈlunər/ adj. лу́нный.
lunatic /ˈlunətɪk/ n. сумасше́дший.
lunation /luˈneiʃən/ n. лу́нный ме́сяц m.
lunch /lʌntʃ/ **1.** n. обе́д m. **2.** adj. обе́денный. **3.** v. обе́дать impf., пообе́дать pf.
luncheon /ˈlʌntʃən/ n. обе́д m.
lunch hour n. обе́денный переры́в m.
lung /lʌŋ/ **1.** n. лёгкое neut. **2.** adj. лёгочный.
lunge /lʌndʒ/ **1.** n. вы́пад m. **2.** v. де́лать вы́пад impf.
lungfish /ˈlʌŋˌfɪʃ/ n. двоякоды́шащая ры́ба m.
lupine /ˈlupɪn/ n. (bot.) люпи́н m.
lupus /ˈlupəs/ n. волча́нка f.
lurch /lɜrtʃ/ **1.** n. толчо́к m. **2.** v. дви́гаться толчка́ми impf.; дёрнуться pf.
lure /lur/ **1.** n. прима́нка f., ва́бик m. **2.** v. прима́нивать impf., примани́ть pf.
lurid /ˈlurɪd/ adj. мра́чный; жу́ткий.
lurk /lɜrk/ v. пря́таться, скрыва́ться impf.
luscious /ˈlʌʃəs/ adj. со́чный.
lush /lʌʃ/ adj. (rich, abundant) пы́шный.
lust /lʌst/ n. страсть, по́хоть f.
luster /ˈlʌstər/ n. гля́нец, блеск m.
lustful /ˈlʌstfəl/ adj. похотли́вый.
lustfulness /ˈlʌstfəlnɪs/ n. похотли́вость f.

lustily /'lʌstḷi/ adv. сильно.
lustrous /'lʌstrəs/ adj. глянцевитый; блестящий.
lusty /'lʌsti/ adj. здоровый, сильный, живой.
lute /lut/ n. лютня f.
Lutheran /'luθərən/ **1.** adj. лютеранский. **2.** n. лютеранин m.; лютеранка f.
Lutheranism /'luθərə,nɪzəm/ n. лютеранство neut.
lux /lʌks/ n. (phys.) люкс m.
Luxembourg /'lʌksəm,bɜrg/ n. Люксембург m.
luxuriance /lʌg'ʒʊriəns/ n. пышность f., изобилие; богатство neut.
luxuriant /lʌg'ʒʊriənt/ adj. буйный, пышный.
luxuriate /lʌg'ʒʊri,eit/ v. роскошествовать impf.
luxurious /lʌg'ʒʊriəs/ adj. роскошный.
luxury /'lʌkʃəri/ n. роскошь f.

Lviv /Russ. lvɔf/ n. Львов m.
lycanthropy /lai'kænθrəpi/ n. ликантропия f.
lycée /li'sei/ n. лицей m.
lyddite /'lɪdait/ n. лиддит m.
lye /lai/ n. щёлок m.
lying /'laiɪŋ/ **1.** n. враньё neut. **2.** adj. лживый.
lymph /lɪmf/ n. лимфа f.
lymphatic /lɪm'fætɪk/ adj. лимфатический.
lynch /lɪntʃ/ v. линчевать impf. and pf.
lynching /'lɪntʃɪŋ/ n. линчевание neut.
lynx /lɪŋks/ n. рысь f.
lyre /laiˀr/ n. лира f.
lyric /'lɪrɪk/ **1.** n. лирика f. pl. текст (песни) m. **2.** also **lyrical** /'lɪrɪkəl/ adj. лирический.
lyricism /'lɪrə,sɪzəm/ n. лиризм m.

M

Maastricht /'mɑstrɪxt/ *n.* Ма́астрихт *m.*
macabre /mə'kɑbrə, -'kɑb/ *adj.* жу́ткий.
macadam /mə'kædəm/ **1.** *n.* щебе́нь *m.*, щебёнка *f.*, щебёночное покры́тие *neut.* **2.** *adj.* щебёночный.
macadamize /mə'kædə,maiz/ *v.* покрыва́ть ще́бнем *impf.*
macaroni /,mækə'rouni/ *n.* макаро́ны *pl.*
macaronic /,mækə'rɒnɪk/ *adj.* макарони́ческий.
macaroon /,mækə'run/ *n.* минда́льное пече́нье *neut.*
macaw /mə'kɔ/ *n.* ара *m. indecl.*
mace /meis/ *n.* (*weapon*) булава́ *f.*; (*staff of office*) жезл *m.*; (*spice*) муска́тный цвет *m.*
macebearer /'meis,bɛərər/ *n.* жезлоно́сец *m.*
macédoine /,mæsɪ'dwɑn/ *n.* масе́дуан *m.*
Macedonia /,mæsɪ'douniə/ *n.* Македо́ния *f.*
macerate /'mæsə,reit/ *v.* истоща́ть *impf.*
Mach /mɑk, mɑx/ *n.* число́ Ма́ха *neut.*
machete /mə'ʃɛti/ *n.* маче́те *neut. indecl.*
Machiavellian /,mækiə'vɛliən/ *adj.* макиавёлlevский.
machinate /'mækə,neit/ *v.* интригова́ть *impf.*
machinations /,mækə'neiʃənz/ *n.* ко́зни; махина́ции *pl.*
machine /mə'ʃin/ **1.** *n.* маши́на *f.*, механи́зм *m.* **2.** *adj.* маши́нный.
machine gun *n.* пулемёт *m.*
machine-readable /mə'ʃin 'ridəbəl/ *adj.* машиночита́емый.
machinery /mə'ʃinəri/ *n.* маши́ны, механи́змы *pl.*
machine shop *n.* механи́ческий цех *m.*
machining /mə'ʃiniŋ/ *n.* механи́ческая обрабо́тка *f.*
machinist /mə'ʃinɪst/ *n.* машини́ст; меха́ник; стано́чник *m.*
mackerel /'mækərəl/ *n.* макре́ль *f.*
mackintosh /'mækɪn,tɒʃ/ *n.* непромока́емое пальто́ *neut. indecl.*; макинто́ш *m.*
macrobiotic /,mækroubai'ɒtɪk/ *adj.* макробиоти́ческий.
macrocosm /'mækrə,kɒzəm/ *n.* макроми́р *m.*
mad /mæd/ *adj.* сумасше́дший, бе́шеный.
Madagascar /,mædə'gæskər/ *n.* Мадага́скар *m.*
madam /'mædəm/ *n.* мада́м *f. indecl.*, госпожа́ *f.*
madcap /'mæd,kæp/ *n.* сорване́ц *m.*
madden /'mædn̩/ *v.* выводи́ть из себя́ *impf.*
maddening /'mædn̩ŋ/ *adj.* невыноси́мый.
madder /'mædər/ *n.* (*bot.*) маре́на *f.*
Madeira /mə'dɪərə, -'dɛərə/ *n.* (*wine*) маде́ра *f.*
made of /meid/ *adj.* (сде́ланный) из (*with gen.*).
made-to-order /'meid tə 'ɔrdər/ *adj.* сде́ланный на зака́з.
madhouse /'mæd,haus/ *n.* сумасше́дший дом *m.*
madly /'mædli/ *adv.* безу́мно.
madman /'mæd,mæn/ *adj.* сумасше́дший.
madness /'mædnɪs/ *n.* сумасше́ствие *neut.*
Madonna /mə'dɒnə/ *n.* Мадо́нна *f.*
Madras /mə'dræs, -'drɑs/ *n.* Мадра́с *m.*
Madrid /mə'drɪd/ *n.* Мадри́д *m.*
madrigal /'mædrɪgəl/ *n.* мадрига́л *m.*

madwoman /'mæd,wʊmən/ *n.* сумасше́дшая *f.*
Maecenas /mi'sinəs/ *n.* мецена́т *m.*
maelstrom /'meilstrəm/ *n.* водоворо́т *m.*
maenad /'minæd/ *n.* мена́да *f.*
maestoso /mai'stousou/ *adj. and adv.* маэсто́зо.
maestro /'maistrou/ *n.* маэ́стро *m. indecl.*
Mafia /'mafiə/ *n.* ма́фия *f.*
magazine /,mægə'zin/ **1.** *n.* журна́л *m.* **2.** *adj.* журна́льный.
Magellan, Strait of /mə'dʒɛlən/ *n.* Магелла́нов проли́в *m.*
maggot /'mægət/ *n.* личи́нка *f.*
maggoty /'mægəti/ *adj.* черви́вый.
magic /'mædʒɪk/ **1.** *n.* волшебство́ *neut.* **2.** *adj.* волше́бный.
magician /mə'dʒɪʃən/ *n.* волше́бник *m.*; (*entertainer*) фо́кусник *m.*
magisterial /,mædʒə'stɪəriəl/ *adj.* суде́йский.
magistracy /'mædʒəstrəsi/ *n.* магистрату́ра *f.*
magistrate /'mædʒə,streit, -strɪt/ *n.* мирово́й судья́ *m.*
magma /'mægmə/ *n.* ма́гма *f.*
magnanimity /,mægnə'nɪmɪti/ *n.* великоду́шие *neut.*
magnanimous /mæg'nænəməs/ *adj.* великоду́шный.
magnate /'mægneit, -nɪt/ *n.* магна́т *m.*
magnesia /mæg'niʒə/ *n.* о́кись ма́гния *f.*
magnesium /mæg'niziəm/ *n.* ма́гний *m.*
magnet /'mægnɪt/ *n.* магни́т *m.*
magnetic /mæg'nɛtɪk/ *adj.* магни́тный.
magnetism /'mægnɪ,tɪzəm/ *n.* магнети́зм *m.*
magnetite /'mægnɪ,tait/ *n.* магнети́т *m.*
magnetization /,mægnɪtə'zeiʃən/ *n.* намагни́чивание *neut.*; намагни́ченность *f.*
magnetize /'mægnɪ,taiz/ *v.* намагни́чивать *impf.*
magneto /mæg'nitou/ *n.* магне́то *neut. indecl.*
magnetometer /,mægnɪ'tɒmɪtər/ *n.* магнито́метр *m.*
magneton /'mægnɪ,tɒn/ *n.* магнето́н *m.*
magnetron /'mægnɪ,trɒn/ *n.* магнетро́н *m.*
magnification /,mægnəfɪ'keiʃən/ *n.* увеличе́ние; усиле́ние *neut.*
magnificence /mæg'nɪfəsəns/ *n.* великоле́пие *neut.*
magnificent /mæg'nɪfəsənt/ *adj.* великоле́пный.
magnify /'mægnə,fai/ *v.* увели́чивать *impf.*, увели́чить *pf.*
magnifying glass /'mægnə,faiŋ/ *n.* лу́па *f.*; увеличи́тельное стекло́ *neut.*
magniloquence /mæg'nɪləkwəns/ *n.* высокопа́рность *f.*
magnitude /'mægnɪ,tud, -,tyud/ *n.* величина́ *f.*
magnolia /mæg'noulyə/ *n.* магно́лия *f.*
magnum opus /'mægnəm/ *n.* ше́девр *m.*
magpie /'mæg,pai/ *n.* (*bird*) соро́ка *f.*
Magus /'meigəs/ *n.* маг, волхв *m.*
maharaja /,mɑhə'rɑdʒə/ *n.* махара́джа *m.* (*decl. f.*).
maharanee /,mɑhə'rɑni/ *n.* махара́ни *f. indecl.*
mahatma /mə'hɑtmə/ *n.* маха́тма *m.*
mah-jongg /'mɑ 'dʒɔŋ/ *n.* маджо́нг *m.*

mahogany /məˈhɒgəni/ n. кра́сное де́рево neut.

maid /meid/ n. (servant) прислу́га, го́рничная f.; (girl) де́вушка f.

maiden /ˈmeidn/ **1.** n. деви́ца, де́ва f. **2.** adj. (unmarried) незаму́жняя; де́вственный.

maidenhair /ˈmeidn,hɛər/ n. (bot.) адиа́нтум m.

maidenhead /ˈmeidn,hɛd/ n. (virginity) де́вственность f.

maidenhood /ˈmeidn,hʊd/ n. деви́чество neut.

maidenly /ˈmeidnli/ adj. деви́ческий.

maiden name n. де́вичья фами́лия f.

maiden voyage n. пе́рвый рейс m.

mail[1] /meil/ **1.** n. по́чта f. **2.** adj. почто́вый. **3.** v. посыла́ть по́чтой impf.

mail[2] /meil/ n. (armor) кольчу́га f.

mailbag /ˈmeil,bæg/ n. су́мка почтальо́на f.

mailbox /ˈmeil,bɒks/ n. почто́вый я́щик m.

mailed /meild/ adj. (clad with mail) брониро́ванный.

mailman /ˈmeil,mæn/ n. почтальо́н m.

mail order n. почто́вый зака́з m.

maim /meim/ v. кале́чить, уве́чить impf.

main /mein/ adj. гла́вный; основно́й; (road) магистра́льный.

main brace n. (naut.) гро́та-брас m.

Maine /mein/ n. Мэн m.

mainframe /ˈmein,freim/ n. (comput.) се́рвер m.

mainland /ˈmein,lænd/ n. матери́к m.

main line /ˈmein,lain/ n. (railroad) магистра́ль f.

mainly /ˈmeinli/ adv. гла́вным о́бразом.

mainmast /ˈmein,mæst/ Naut. ˈmeinməst/ n. грот-ма́чта f.

mainsail /ˈmein,seil/ Naut. ˈmeinsəl/ n. грот m.

mainsheet /ˈmein,ʃit/ n. гро́та-шкот m.

mainspring /ˈmein,sprɪŋ/ n. (clock) ходова́я пружи́на f.

mainstay /ˈmein,stei/ n. (fig.) гла́вная опо́ра f.

mainstream /ˈmein,strim/ n. госпо́дствующая тенде́нция f.

maintain /meinˈtein/ v. подде́рживать impf.; (assert) утвержда́ть impf.

maintenance /ˈmeintənəns/ n. подде́ржка f.; содержа́ние neut.

maiting /ˈmeitɪŋ/ n. спа́ривание neut.

maître d'hôtel /ˌmeitər douˈtɛl, ˌmeitrə/ n. метрдоте́ль m.

maize /meiz/ n. майс m., кукуру́за f.

majestic /məˈdʒɛstɪk/ adj. вели́чественный.

majesty /ˈmædʒəsti/ n. вели́чественность f; (title) вели́чество neut.

majolica /məˈdʒɒlɪkə/ n. майо́лика f.

major /ˈmeidʒər/ **1.** adj. бо́льший; основно́й; гла́вный; (mus.) мажо́рный. **2.** n. майо́р m.; (mus.) мажо́р m. **3.** v. (college) специализи́роваться impf.

majority /məˈdʒɔriti/ n. большинство́ neut.

make /meik/ v. де́лать impf., сде́лать pf.; (earn) зараба́тывать impf., зарабо́тать pf.

make-believe /ˈmeik bɪ,liv/ n. притво́рство neut.; (a fiction) вы́думка; фанта́зия f.

maker /ˈmeikər/ n. фабрика́нт m.; (cap.) Созда́тель, Творе́ц m.

makeshift /ˈmeik,ʃift/ adj. вре́менный; самоде́льный.

makeup /ˈmeik,ʌp/ n. косме́тика; (theat.) грим m.; (composition) соста́в; сбор m.

makeweight /ˈmeik,weit/ n. дове́сок m.

making /ˈmeikɪŋ/ n. созда́ние neut.

malachite /ˈmælə,kait/ n. малахи́т m.

maladjusted /ˌmæləˈdʒʌstid/ adj. неприспосо́бленный.

maladjustment /ˌmæləˈdʒʌstmənt/ n. неприспосо́бленность f.

maladministration /ˌmælədˌminəˈstreiʃən/ n. плохо́е управле́ние neut.

maladroit /ˌmæləˈdrɔit/ adj. неуклю́жий, нело́вкий.

malady /ˈmælədi/ n. боле́знь f.

malaise /mæˈleiz/ n. недомога́ние neut.

malapropos /ˌmæləprəˈpou/ adv. некста́ти.

malaria /məˈlɛəriə/ n. маляри́я f.

malarial /məˈlɛəriəl/ adj. маляри́йный.

Malawi /məˈlɑwi/ n. Мала́ви m.

Malaysia /məˈleiʒə/ n. Мала́йзия f.

malcontent /ˌmælkənˈtɛnt/ adj. недово́льный.

male /meil/ **1.** adj. мужско́й. **2.** n. мужчи́на m. (decl. f.); (animal) саме́ц m.

malediction /ˌmæliˈdikʃən/ n. прокля́тие neut.

malefactor /ˈmælə,fæktər/ n. злоде́й m.

maleficent /məˈlɛfəsənt/ adj. па́губный.

malevolence /məˈlɛvələns/ n. недоброжела́тельство neut.

malevolent /məˈlɛvələnt/ adj. недоброжела́тельный.

malformation /ˌmælfɔrˈmeiʃən/ n. непра́вильное формирова́ние neut.

malfunction /mælˈfʌŋkʃən/ n. отка́з m.

Mali /ˈmɑli/ n. Мали́ m.

malice /ˈmælis/ n. зло́ба f.

malicious /məˈliʃəs/ adj. злой; зло́бный.

malign /məˈlain/ v. клевета́ть (на with acc.) impf.

malignant /məˈlignənt/ adj. (med.) злока́чественный.

malinger /məˈlingər/ v. симули́ровать боле́знь impf.

malingerer /məˈlingərər/ n. симуля́нт m., симуля́нтка f.

malingering /məˈlingərɪŋ/ n. симуля́ция f.

mall /mɔl/ n. алле́я f.; **shopping mall** торго́вый центр m.

mallard /ˈmælərd/ n. кря́ква, ди́кая у́тка f.

malleability /ˌmæliəˈbiliti/ n. ко́вкость f.

malleable /ˈmæliəbəl/ adj. ко́вкий.

mallet /ˈmælit/ n. деревя́нный молото́к m.

Mallorca /məˈyɔrkə/ n. (island) Мальо́рка f.

mallow /ˈmælou/ n. ма́льва f.

malnourished /mælˈnʌriʃt/ adj. недоко́рмленный.

malnutrition /ˌmælnuˈtriʃən/ n. недоеда́ние neut.

malodorous /mælˈoudərəs/ adj. злово́нный.

malpractice /mælˈpræktis/ n. злоупотребле́ние дове́рием neut.

malt /mɔlt/ n. со́лод m.

maltreat /mælˈtrit/ v. пло́хо обраща́ться impf.

maltreatment /mælˈtritmənt/ n. плохо́е обраще́ние neut.

maltster /ˈmɔltstər/ n. соло́довщик m.

malversation /ˌmælvərˈseiʃən/ n. злоупотребле́ние neut.

mama /ˈmɑmə/ n. ма́ма f.; (colloq.) ма́мочка f.

mamba /ˈmɑmbə/ n. ма́мба f.

mammal /ˈmæməl/ n. млекопита́ющее neut.

mammary /ˈmæməri/ adj. грудно́й; моло́чный.

mammilla /mæˈmilə/ n. сосо́к m.

mammon /'mæmən/ *n.* мамо́на *m.*
mammoth /'mæməθ/ **1.** *n.* ма́монт *m.* **2.** *adj.* ма́монтовый; (*very large*) огро́мный.
man /mæn/ *n.* челове́к *m.*; (*male*) мужчи́на *m.* (*decl. f.*).
Man /mæn/ *n.* **Isle of,** о́стров Мэн *m.*
manacles /'mænəkəlz/ *n.* нару́чники *pl.*
manage /'mænɪdʒ/ *v.* управля́ть (*with instr.*); заве́довать *impf.*
manageable /'mænɪdʒəbəl/ *adj.* легко́ управля́емый.
management /'mænɪdʒmənt/ *n.* управле́ние, заве́дование *neut.*
manager /'mænɪdʒər/ *n.* заве́дующий; руководи́тель; дире́ктор *m.*
manageress /'mænɪdʒərɪs/ *n.* заве́дующая *f.*
managerial /ˌmænɪ'dʒɪəriəl/ *adj.* администрати́вный, управле́нческий; дире́кторский.
managing director /'mænɪdʒɪŋ/ *n.* дире́ктор-распоряди́тель *m.*
man-at-arms /'mæn'ət ɑrmz/ *n.* вое́нный *m.*
manatee /'mænə,ti/ *n.* ламанти́н *m.*
Manchester /'mæn,tʃestər, -tʃəstər/ *n.* Манче́стер *m.*
Manchurian /mæn'tʃʊriən/ *adj.* манчжу́рский.
mandarin /'mændərɪn/ *n.* мандари́н *m.*; (*cap.*) мандари́нское наре́чие кита́йского языка́ *neut.*
mandate /'mændeit/ *n.* манда́т *m.*
mandated /'mændeitɪd/ *adj.* (*territory*) подманда́тный.
mandatory /'mændə,tɔri/ *adj.* обяза́тельный; манда́тный.
mandible /'mændəbəl/ *n.* (*lower jaw*) ни́жняя че́люсть *f.*
mandolin /'mændlɪn/ *n.* мандоли́на *f.*
mandrake /'mændreik/ *n.* мандраго́ра *f.*
mandrel /'mændrəl/ *n.* (*on lathe*) опра́вка *f.*; (*miner's*) кайло́ *neut.*
mandrill /'mændrɪl/ *n.* мандри́л *m.*
mane /mein/ *n.* гри́ва *f.*
man-eater /'mæn ˌitər/ *n.* людое́д *m.*, людое́дка *f.*
maneuver /mə'nuvər/ **1.** *n.* манёвр *m.* **2.** *v.* маневри́ровать *impf. and pf.*
maneuverability /mə,nuvərə'bɪlɪti/ *n.* манёвренность *f.*
maneuverable /mə,nuvərəbəl/ *adj.* манёвренный.
manful /'mænfəl/ *adj.* му́жественный.
manganese /'mæŋgə,nis/ *n.* ма́рганец *m.*
mange /meindʒ/ *n.* чесо́тка; парша́ *f.*
manger /'meindʒər/ *n.* я́сли *pl.*; корму́шка *f.*
mangle /'mæŋgəl/ **1.** *n.* (*hot press*) като́к *m.* **2.** *v.* ката́ть *impf.*, вы́катать *pf.*; (*injure*) кале́чить *impf.*
mango /'mæŋgou/ *n.* ма́нго *neut. indecl.*
mangrove /'mæŋgrouv/ *adj.* ма́нгровый.
mangy /'meindʒi/ *adj.* чесо́точный; парши́вый.
manhandle /'mæn,hændl/ *v.* гру́бо обраща́ться *impf.*
Manhattan /mən'hætn/ *n.* Манхэ́ттэн *m.*
manhood /'mænhʊd/ *n.* возмужа́лость; зре́лость *f.*
man-hour /'mæn ˌauᵊr/ *n.* челове́ко-час *m.*
manhunt /'mæn,hʌnt/ *n.* обла́ва *f.*
mania /'meiniə/ *n.* ма́ния *f.*
maniac /'meini,æk/ *n.* манья́к *m.*

manic depression /'mænɪk/ *n.* маниака́льно-депресси́вный психо́з *m.*
manicure /'mænɪ,kyʊr/ *n.* маникю́р *m.*
manicurist /'mænɪ,kyʊrɪst/ *n.* маникю́рша *f.*
manifest /'mænə,fest/ **1.** *adj.* очеви́дный, я́сный. **2.** *v.* проявля́ть *impf.*, прояви́ть *pf.*
manifestation /ˌmænəfə'steiʃən/ *n.* проявле́ние *neut.*
manifesto /ˌmænə'festou/ *n.* манифе́ст *m.*
manifold /'mænə,fould/ **1.** *adj.* разнообра́зный. **2.** *n.* (*tech.*) колле́ктор *m.*
manilla /mə'nɪlə/ *n.* мани́льская бума́га из пенькѝ *f.*
Manila paper /mə'nɪlə/ *n.* мани́льская бума́га из пенькѝ *f.*
manioc /'mæni,ɒk/ *n.* манио́ка *f.*
manipulate /mə'nɪpyə,leit/ *v.* манипули́ровать *impf.*
manipulation /mə,nɪpyə'leiʃən/ *n.* манипуля́ция *f.*
Manitoba /ˌmænɪ'toubə/ *n.* Манито́ба *f.*
mankind /mæn'kaind/ *n.* челове́чество *neut.*
manliness /'mænlɪnɪs/ *n.* му́жественность *f.*
manly /'mænli/ *adj.* му́жественный.
man-made /'mæn 'meid/ *adj.* иску́сственный.
manna /'mænə/ *n.* ма́нна *f.*
mannequin /'mænɪkɪn/ *n.* (*model*) манеке́нщица *f.*; (*dummy*) манеке́н *m.*
manner /'mænər/ *n.* о́браз, спо́соб *m.*, мане́ра *f.*; *pl.* мане́ры *pl.*
mannered /'mænərd/ *adj.* мане́рный.
mannerism /'mænə,rizəm/ *n.* мане́рность *f.*
mannerless /'mænərlɪs/ *adj.* неве́жливый.
mannerly /'mænərli/ *adj.* ве́жливый, воспи́танный.
mannish /'mænɪʃ/ *adj.* мужеподо́бный; неже́нственный.
man-of-war /'mæn əv 'wɔr/ *n.* (*naut.*) вое́нный кора́бль *m.*
manometer /mə'nɒmɪtər/ *n.* мано́метр *m.*
manor /'mænər/ *n.* поме́стье *neut.*; ма́нор *m.*
manor house *n.* поме́щичий дом, ба́рский дом *m.*
manorial /mə'nɔriəl/ *adj.* манориа́льный.
manpower /'mæn,pauər/ *n.* рабо́чая си́ла *f.*
manqué /mɑŋ'kei/ *adj.* неуда́вшийся.
mansard /'mænsɑrd/ *n.* манса́рда *f.*
manservant /'mæn,sɜrvənt/ *n.* слуга́ *m.*
mansion /'mænʃən/ *n.* особня́к *m.*
manslaughter /'mæn,slɔtər/ *n.* непредумы́шленное уби́йство *neut.*
mantelpiece /'mæntl,pis/ *n.* ками́нная по́лка *f.*
mantic /'mæntɪk/ *adj.* гада́тельный.
mantis /'mæntɪs/ *n.* богомо́л *m.*
mantissa /mæn'tɪsə/ *n.* манти́сса *f.*
mantle /'mæntl/ *n.* ма́нтия *f.*; (*fig.*) покро́в *m.*
man-trap /'mæn,træp/ *n.* лову́шка *f.*
manual /'mænyuəl/ **1.** *adj.* ручно́й. **2.** *n.* спра́вочник *m.*, руково́дство *neut.*
manufacture /ˌmænyə'fæktʃər/ **1.** *v.* производи́ть *impf.*, произвести́ *pf.*; выде́лывать *impf.*, вы́делать *pf.* **2.** *n.* произво́дство; изготовле́ние *neut.*
manufactured /ˌmænyə'fæktʃərd/ *adj.* обрабо́танный.
manufacturer /ˌmænyə'fæktʃərər/ *n.* фабрика́нт *m.*

manufacturing /ˌmænyə'fæktʃərɪŋ/ n. произвóдство neut., выделка f.

manumission /ˌmænyə'mɪʃən/ n. освобождéние neut.

manure /mə'nʊr/ n. навóз m.

manuscript /'mænyəˌskrɪpt/ **1.** n. рýкопись f. **2.** adj. рукопúсный.

many /'mɛni/ **1.** adj. мнóго (with gen.); мнóгие pl. **2.** n. мнóжество neut. (with gen.); **how many** скóлько (with gen.); **so many** стóлько (with gen.); **too many** слúшком мнóго; **as many as** стóлько... скóлько.

many-sided /'mɛni 'saidɪd/ adj. многосторóнний.

map /mæp/ n. кáрта f.

maple /'meipəl/ **1.** n. клён m. **2.** adj. кленóвый.

mapmaker /'mæpˌmeikər/ n. картóграф m.

maquis /ma'ki/ n. макú indecl.

mar /mar/ v. пóртить impf., испóртить pf.

marabou /'mærəˌbu/ n. марабý m.

marathon /'mærəˌθɒn/ n. марафóн; марафóнский бег m.

maraud /mə'rɔd/ v. мародёрствовáть impf.

marauder /mə'rɔdər/ n. мародёр m.

marauding /mə'rɔdɪŋ/ n. мародéрство neut.

marble /'marbəl/ **1.** n. мрáмор m.; (toy) шáрик m. **2.** adj. мрáморный.

marcasite /'markəˌsait/ n. марказúт m.

march /martʃ/ **1.** n. марш m. **2.** v. маршировáть impf.

March /martʃ/ **1.** n. март m. **2.** adj. мáртовский.

marching /'martʃɪŋ/ **1.** n. марширóвка f. **2.** adj. похóдный; мáршевый.

march-past /'martʃ ˌpæst/ n. парáд m.

mare /mɛər/ n. кобы́ла f.

margarine /'mardʒərɪn/ n. маргарúн m.

margin /'mardʒɪn/ n. (edge of paper) поля́ pl.; (edge) край m.

marginal /'mardʒənl/ adj. крáйний; незначúтельный.

marginalia /ˌmardʒə'neiliə/ n. маргинáлии pl.

margrave /'margreiv/ n. маркгрáф m.

marigold /'mærɪˌgould/ n. (Calendula) ноготкú pl.; (Tagetes) бáрхатец m.

marijuana /ˌmærə'wanə/ n. марихуáна f.

marina /mə'rinə/ n. марúна f.

marinade /ˌmærə'neid/ n. маринáд m.

marinate /'mærəˌneit/ v. мариновáть impf.

marine /mə'rin/ **1.** adj. морскóй. **2.** n. морскóй пехотúнец m.; pl. морскáя пехóта f.

mariner /'mærənər/ n. моря́к; матрóс m.

marionette /ˌmærɪə'nɛt/ n. марионéтка f.

marital /'mærɪtl/ adj. супрýжеский; **marital status** n. семéйное положéние neut.

maritime /'mærɪˌtaim/ adj. морскóй; примóрский.

marjoram /'mardʒərəm/ n. душúца f., майорáн m.

mark /mark/ **1.** n. знак m.; помéтка f.; (grade) отмéтка f.; (aim) цель f. **2.** v. отмечáть impf., отмéтить pf.

markdown /'markˌdaun/ n. снижéние цены́ neut.

marked /markt/ adj. отмéченный; замéтный.

marker /'markər/ n. указáтель m.; (sign, tag) знак m.; мéтка f.

market /'markɪt/ **1.** n. продовóльственный магазúн; ры́нок m. **2.** adj. ры́ночный.

marketable /'markɪtəbəl/ adj. ходовóй.

marketing /'markɪtɪŋ/ n. торгóвля f.; маркéтинг m.

marketplace /'markɪtˌpleis/ n. ры́ночная плóщадь f., ры́нок m.

market price, n. ры́ночная ценá f.

market rate n. биржевóй курс m.

marking /'markɪŋ/ n. маркирóвка f.

marksman /'marksmən/ n. (méткий) стрелóк m.

marksmanship /'marksmənˌʃɪp/ n. искýсство стрельбы́ neut.

markup /'markˌʌp/ n. нацéнка f.

marl /marl/ n. мéргель m.

marline /'marlɪn/ n. мáрлинь m.

marmalade /'marməˌleid/ n. джем m.; повúдло neut.; мармслáд m.

marmoreal /mar'mɔriəl/ adj. мрáморный.

marmoset /'marməˌzɛt/ n. марты́шка f.

marmot /'marmət/ n. сурóк m.

Marne /marn/ n. (river) Мáрна f.

maroon[1] /mə'run/ **1.** adj. (color) тёмнобордóвый. **2.** n. тёмно-бордóвый цвет m.

maroon[2] /mə'run/ v. высáживать (на необитáемом óстрове) impf.

marquee /mar'ki/ n. навéс m.

marquetry /'markɪtri/ n. маркетрú neut. indecl.

marquis /'markwɪs, mar'ki/ n. маркúз m.

marquise /mar'kiz/ n. маркúза f.

marriage /'mærɪdʒ/ **1.** n. брак m.; (wedding) свáдьба f. **2.** adj. брáчный.

married /'mærid/ adj. (man) женáтый; (woman) замýжняя; **to get married** (man) женúться (на with prep.) impf.; (woman) выходúть зáмуж (за with acc.) impf.

marrow /'mærou/ n. кóстный мозг m.

marrowbone /'mærouˌboun/ n. мозговáя кость f.

marry /'mæri/ v. (man) женúться (на with prep.) impf.; (woman) выходúть зáмуж (за with acc.) impf.

Mars /marz/ n. Марс m.

Marseille /mar'sei/ n. Марсéль m.

marsh /marʃ/ n. болóто neut.

marshland /'marʃˌlænd/ n. болóтистая мéстность f.

marshmallow /'marʃˌmɛlou/ n. зефúр m.

marshy /'marʃi/ adj. болóтистый.

marsupial /mar'supiəl/ n. сýмчатое живóтное neut.

mart /mart/ n. (market) ры́нок m.

marten /'martn/ n. кунúца f.

martial /'marʃəl/ adj. воéнный.

Martian /'marʃən/ **1.** adj. марсиáнский. **2.** n. марсиáнин m.

martin /'martn/ n. лáсточка f.

martingale /'martnˌgeil/ n. мартингáл m.

martyr /'martər/ n. мýченик m., мýченица f.

martyrdom /'martərdəm/ n. мýченичество neut.

marvel /'marvəl/ **1.** n. чýдо, дúво neut. **2.** v. удивля́ться impf.

marvelous /'marvələs/ adj. чудéсный.

Marxism /'marksɪzəm/ n. марксúзм m.

Marxist /'marksɪst/ **1.** n. маркúст m. **2.** adj. маркúстский.

Maryland /'mɛrələnd/ n. Мэриленд m.

marzipan /'marzəˌpæn/ n. марципáн m.

mascara /mæ'skærə/ n. тушь для реснúц f.

mascot /'mæskɒt/ n. талисмáн m.

masculine /'mæskyəlɪn/ adj. мужско́й; (gram.) мужско́го ро́да.

masculinity /ˌmæskyə'lɪnɪti/ n. му́жественность f.

maser /'meizər/ n. ма́зер m.

mash /mæʃ/ v. размина́ть impf., размя́ть pf.

Mashhad /mæʃ'hæd/ n. Мешхе́д m.

mask /mæsk/ 1. n. ма́ска f. 2. v. маскирова́ть impf., замаскирова́ть pf.

masked /mæskt/ adj. в ма́ске.

masochism /'mæsəˌkɪzəm/ n. мазохи́зм m.

masochist /'mæsəkɪst/ n. мазохи́ст m.

mason /'meisən/ n. ка́менщик m.; (cap.) (Freemason) масо́н m.

Masonic /mə'sɒnɪk/ adj. масо́нский.

masonry /'meisənri/ n. ка́менная кла́дка f.

masquerade /ˌmæskə'reid/ n. маскара́д m.

Mass /mæs/ n. обе́дня f.

mass /mæs/ 1. n. ма́сса f. 2. adj. ма́ссовый. 3. v. собира́ться impf., собра́ться pf.; массирова́ть(ся) pf. and impf.

Massachusetts /ˌmæsə'tʃusɪts/ n. Массачу́сетс m.

massacre /'mæsəkər/ 1. n. резня́ f. 2. v. производи́ть резню́ impf.

massage /mə'sɑʒ/ 1. n. масса́ж m. 2. v. де́лать масса́ж impf.; масси́ровать pf. and impf.

massed /mæst/ adj. масси́рованный.

masseur /mə'sɜr/ n. массажи́ст m.

masseuse /mə'sus/. n. массажи́стка f.

massif /mæ'sif/ n. го́рный масси́в m.

massive /'mæsɪv/ adj. масси́вный adj.

mass-produce /'mæs prə'dus/ v. производи́ть в большо́м коли́честве impf.

mass production n. сери́йное произво́дство neut.

mass-spectrometry /'mæs spɛk'trɒmətri/ n. масс-спектроме́трия f.

mast /mæst/ n. ма́чта f.

mastectomy /mæ'stɛktəmi/ n. мастектоми́я f.

master /'mæstər/ 1. n. хозя́ин; ма́стер m.; (of ship) капита́н m.; **Master's degree** сте́пень маги́стра f. 2. v. овладева́ть (with instr.) impf., овладе́ть pf.

masterful /'mæstərfəl/ adj. вла́стный; ма́стерский.

master key n. отмы́чка f.

masterly /'mæstərli/ adv. ма́стерски.

mastermind /'mæstərˌmaind/ v. руководи́ть impf.

master of ceremonies n. церемонийме́йстер m.; (theat.) конферансье́ m. indecl.; (at banquet) тамада́ m.

masterpiece /'mæstərˌpis/ m. шеде́вр m.

mastery /'mæstəri/ n. мастерство́; госпо́дство neut.

masthead /'mæstˌhɛd/ n. (naut.) топ-ма́чта f.

mastic /'mæstɪk/ n. масти́ка f.

masticate /'mæstɪˌkeit/ v. жева́ть impf.

mastication /ˌmæstɪ'keiʃən/ n. жева́ние neut.

masticatory /'mæstɪkəˌtɔri/ adj. жева́тельный.

mastiff /'mæstɪf/ n. масти́ф, англи́йский дог m.

mastitis /mæ'staitis/ n. масти́т m.

mastodon /'mæstəˌdɒn/ n. мастодо́нт m.

mastoid /'mæstɔid/ adj. сосцеви́дный.

masturbate /'mæstərˌbeit/ v. мастурби́ровать, онани́ровать, рукоблу́дничать impf.

masturbation /ˌmæstər'beiʃən/ n. мастурба́ция f., онани́зм m., рукоблу́дие neut.

masturbator /'mæstərˌbeitər/ n. онани́ст m.

mat /mæt/ n. (small rug) мат m., цино́вка f.

matador /'mætəˌdɔr/ n. матадо́р m.

match[1] /mætʃ/ n. спи́чка f.

match[2] /mætʃ/ 1. n. (athl.) состяза́ние neut., матч m. 2. v. (select) подбира́ть (под with acc.) impf.

matchboard /'mætʃˌbɔrd/ n. шпунто́вая доска́ f.

matchbox /'mætʃˌbɒks/ n. спи́чечный коробо́к m.

matchless /'mætʃlɪs/ adj. несравне́нный; бесподо́бный.

matchlock /'mætʃˌlɒk/ n. фити́льное ружьё neut.

matchmaker /'mætʃˌmeikər/ n. сва́ха f.

match point n. реша́ющее очко́ neut.

matchstick /'mætʃˌstɪk/ n. спи́чка f.

matchwood /'mætʃˌwʊd/ n. спи́чечная древеси́на f.

mate[1] /meit/ n. (buddy) това́рищ m.; (spouse) супру́г m., супру́га f.

mate[2] /meit/ 1. n. (chess) мат m. 2. v. спа́ривать(ся) impf.; сде́лать мат pf.

material /mə'tɪəriəl/ 1. n. материа́л m., мате́рия f.; принадле́жности pl. 2. adj. материа́льный adj.

materialism /mə'tɪəriəˌlɪzəm/ n. материали́зм m.

materialist /mə'tɪəriəlɪst/ n. материали́ст m.

materialistic /məˌtɪəriə'lɪstɪk/ adj. материалисти́ческий.

materialize /mə'tɪəriəˌlaiz/ v. материализова́ть(ся) impf. and pf.; осуществля́ть(ся) impf.

materially /mə'tɪəriəli/ adv. материа́льно.

maternal /mə'tɜrnḷ/ adj. матери́нский.

maternity /mə'tɜrnɪti/ n. матери́нство neut.

mathematical /ˌmæθə'mætɪkəl/ adj. математи́ческий.

mathematician /ˌmæθəmə'tɪʃən/ n. матема́тик m.

mathematics /ˌmæθə'mætɪks/ n. матема́тика f.

matinee /ˌmætṇ'ei/ n. дневно́й спекта́кль m.

mating /'meitɪŋ/ n. спа́ривание neut.

matins /'mætɪnz/ n. у́треня f.

matriarch /'meitriˌɑrk/ n. матриа́рх m.

matriarchal /ˌmeitri'ɑrkəl/ adj. матриарха́льный.

matriarchy /'meitriˌɑrki/ n. матриарха́т m.

matricide /'mætrɪˌsaid/ n. (act) матереуби́йство neut.; (person) матереуби́йца m. and f. (decl. f.)

matriculate /mə'trɪkyəˌleit/ v. быть зачи́сленным в университе́т impf.

matriculation /məˌtrɪkyə'leiʃən/ n. зачисле́ние в вуз neut.

matrilineal /ˌmætrə'lɪniəl/ adj. по матери́нской ли́нии.

matrimonial /ˌmætrə'mouniəl/ adj. бра́чный; супру́жеский.

matrimony /'mætrəˌmouni/ n. супру́жество neut.; брак m.

matrix /'meitrɪks/ n. шабло́н m.

matron /'meitrən/ n. матро́на; заму́жняя же́нщина f.

matronly /'meitrənli/ adj. почте́нный.

matte /mæt/ adj. ма́товый.

matted /'mætɪd/ adj. переплетённый; спу́танный.

matter /'mætər/ 1. n. вещество́ neut.; мате́рия f.; (affair; question) де́ло neut., вопро́с m.; **what's**

the matter? в чём дело? **2.** v. имéть значéние impf.

matter-of-fact /'mætər əv 'fækt/ adj. фактический; прозайчный.

matting /'mætɪŋ/ n. (rushes) цинóвка f.

mattock /'mætək/ n. мотыга f.

mattress /'mætrɪs/ n. матрáс, матрáц m.

maturation /,mætʃə'reiʃən/ n. созревáние neut.

mature /mə'tʊr, -'tʃʊr/ **1.** adj. зрéлый; спéлый. **2.** v. созревáть impf., созрéть pf.

maturity /mə'tʃʊrɪti/ n. зрéлость f.

maudlin /'mɔdlɪn/ adj. плаксúвый; слезлúво-сентиментáльный.

maul /mɔl/ v. калéчить impf.; (treat roughly) грýбо обращáться (с with instr.) impf.

maunder /'mɔndər/ v. бормотáть impf.

Maundy Thursday /mɔndi/ n. Велúкий Четвéрг m.

mausoleum /,mɔsə'liəm/ n. мавзолéй m.

mauve /mouv/ n. розовáто-лилóвый цвет m.

maverick /'mævərɪk/ adj. (unbranded calf) неклеймёный телёнок m.; (independent person) диссидéнт m.

maw /mɔ/ n. (stomach) желýдок m.; (crop of bird) зоб m.; (open jaws) пасть f.

mawkish /'mɔkɪʃ/ adj. сентиментáльный.

mawkishness /'mɔkɪʃnɪs/ n. сентиментáльность f.

maxilla /mæk'sɪlə/ n. (вéрхняя) чéлюсть f.

maxillary /'mæksə,lɛri/ adj. (вéрхне)челюстнóй.

maxim /'mæksɪm/ n. сентéнция f.; мáксима f.

maximal /'mæksəməl/ adj. максимáльный.

maximalist /'mæksəməlɪst/ n. максималúст m.

Maxim gun /'mæksɪm/ n. пулемёт максúм m.

maximize /'mæksə,maiz/ v. максимизúровать impf.

maximum /'mæksəməm/ **1.** adj. максимáльный. **2.** n. мáксимум m.

maxwell /'mækswɛl/ n. (elec.) максвéлл m.

may /mei/ v. aux. мочь impf.; возмóжно, что...

May /mei/ **1.** n. май m. **2.** adj. мáйский.

maybe /'meibi/ adv. мóжет быть.

mayfly /'mei,flai/ n. подёнка, мýха-однодневка f.

mayhem /'meihɛm/ n. (leg.) нанесéние увéчья neut.; (disoder) хáос m.

mayonnaise /,meiə'neiz/ n. майонéз m.

mayor /'meiər/ n. мэр m.

mayoress /'meiərɪs/ n. женá мэра; жéнщина-мэр f.

maze /meiz/ n. лабирúнт m.

mazurka /mə'zɜrkə/ n. мазýрка f.

me /mi/ pron. меня; мне; мнóю.

mead /mid/ n. (drink) мёд m.

meadow /'mɛdou/ n. луг m.

meager /'migər/ adj. худóй, тóщий.

meal[1] /mil/ n. (food) едá f.

meal[2] /mil/ n. (flour) мукá f.

mealtime /'mil,taim/ n. врéмя еды neut.

mealy /'mili/ adj. мучнóй.

mean[1] /min/ adj. (base) пóдлый, плохóй.

mean[2] /min/ **1.** adj. (average) срéдний. **2.** n. серединá f.

mean[3] /min/ v. (signify) знáчить impf.

meander /mi'ændər/ n. излýчина f.

meandering /mi'ændərɪŋ/ adj. извúлистый; (rambling) бессвязный.

meaning /'minɪŋ/ n. значéние neut.

meaningful /'minɪŋfəl/ adj. многозначúтельный.

meaningless /'minɪŋlɪs/ adj. бессмысленный; (purposeless) бесцéльный.

meanness /'minnɪs/ n. жáдность; скýпость; пóдлость f.

means /minz/ pl. срéдство neut., срéдства pl.

meanspirited /'min'spɪrɪtɪd/ adj. пóдлый; (malicious) злонамéренный.

meantime /'min,taim/ n. **in the meantime** тем врéменем; мéжду тем.

meanwhile /'min,wail/ adv. тем врéменем; мéжду тем.

measled /'mizəld/ adj. коревóй.

measles /'mizəlz/ n. корь f.

measly /'mizli/ adj. коревóй.

measurable /'mɛʒərəbəl/ adj. измерúмый.

measurably /'mɛʒərəbli/ adv. замéтно.

measure /'mɛʒər/ **1.** n. мéра f.; (mus.) такт m.; **beyond measure** чрезмéрно adv. **2.** v. измерять impf., измéрить pf.

measured /'mɛʒərd/ adj. измéренный.

measurement /'mɛʒərmənt/ n. размéры pl.; (measuring) измерéние neut.

meat /mit/ **1.** n. мясо neut. **2.** adj. мяснóй.

meatball /'mit,bɔl/ n. тефтéля; рýбленая котлéта f.

meatgrinder /'mit,graindər/ n. мясорýбка f.

meatless /'mitlɪs/ adj. без мяса.

meaty /'miti/ adj. мясúстый; (fig.) содержáтельный.

mechanic /mə'kænɪk/ n. мехáник m.

mechanical /mə'kænɪkəl/ adj. механúческий; (fig.) машинáльный.

mechanics /mə'kænɪks/ n. мехáника f.

mechanism /'mɛkə,nɪzəm/ n. механúзм m.

mechanization /,mɛkənə'zeiʃən/ n. механизáция f.

mechanize /'mɛkə,naiz/ v. механизúровать impf. and pf.

mechanized /'mɛkə,naizd/ adj. механизúрованный.

medal /'mɛdl/ n. медáль f.; óрден m.

medalist /'mɛdlɪst/ n. медалúст m.

medallion /mə'dælyən/ n. медальóн m.

meddle /'mɛdl/ v. вмéшиваться impf., вмешáться pf.

meddling /'mɛdlɪŋ/ n. вмешáтельство neut.

media /'midiə/ n. срéдства мáссовой информáции pl.

median /'midiən/ **1.** adj. срéдний. **2.** n. медиáна, срéдняя лúния f.

mediate /'midi,eit/ v. посрéдничать impf.

mediator /'midi,eitər/ n. посрéдник, миротвóрец; примирúтель m.

medical /'mɛdɪkəl/ adj. медицúнский.

medical care n. ухóд за больным m.

medicate /'mɛdɪ,keit/ v. лечúть лекáрством impf.

medication /,mɛdɪ'keiʃən/ n. лекáрство neut., медикамéнт m.

medicinal /mə'dɪsənəl/ adj. лекáрственный; целéбный.

medicine /'mɛdəsɪn/ n. медицúна f.; (remedy) лекáрство neut.

medico /'mɛdɪ,kou/ n. (colloq.) мéдик m.

medieval /,midi'ivəl/ adj. средневекóвый.

mediocre /,midi'oukər/ adj. посрéдственный.

mediocrity /,midi'ɒkrɪti/ n. посрéдственность f.

meditate /'mɛdɪˌteit/ v. размышля́ть impf.; медити́ровать impf.

meditation /ˌmɛdɪ'teiʃən/ n. размышле́ние neut.; медита́ция f.

meditative /'mɛdɪˌteitɪv/ adj. заду́мчивый; созерца́тельный.

medium /'midiəm/ 1. adj. сре́дний. 2. n. (mean) середи́на f.; (means) сре́дство neut.

medium-sized /'midiəm ˌsaizd/ adj. сре́днего разме́ра.

medium-wave /'midiəm 'weiv/ adj. средневолно́вый.

medlar /'mɛdlər/ n. мушмула́ f.

medley /'mɛdli/ n. мешани́на f.

medulla /mə'dʌlə/ n. (marrow) ко́стный мозг m.

medullary /'mɛdlˌɛri/ adj. мозгово́й, сердцеви́нный.

medusa /mə'dusə/ n. меду́за f.

meek /mik/ adj. поко́рный.

meekness /'miknɪs/ cf n. поко́рство neut.

meerschaum pipe /'mirʃəm/ n. пе́нковая тру́бка f.

meet /mit/ v.t. встреча́ть impf., встре́тить pf.; (make acquaintance) знако́миться (с with instr.) impf., v.i. встреча́ться impf., встре́титься pf.

meeting /'mitɪŋ/ n. ми́тинг m., собра́ние neut.; (encounter) встре́ча f.

megacycle /'mɛgəˌsaikəl/ n. мегаге́рц m.

megalith /'mɛgəliθ/ n. мегали́т m.

megalithic /ˌmɛgə'liθɪk/ adj. мегалити́ческий.

megalomania /ˌmɛgəlou'meiniə/ n. ма́ния вели́чия f.

megalosaur /'mɛgələˌsɔr/ n. мегалоза́вр m.

megaphone /'mɛgəˌfoun/ n. ру́пор, мегафо́н m.

Megatherium /ˌmɛgə'θiriəm/ n. мегате́рий m.

megaton /'mɛgəˌtʌn/ n. мегато́н m.

megavolt /'mɛgəˌvoult/ n. мегаво́льт m.

megawatt /'mɛgəˌwɒt/ n. мегава́тт m.

megohm /'mɛgˌoum/ n. мего́м m.

meiosis /mai'ousɪs/ n. мейо́з m.

melamine /'mɛləˌmin/ n. мелами́н m.

melancholia /ˌmɛlən'kouliə/ n. меланхо́лия f.

melancholic /ˌmɛlən'kɒlɪk/ adj. меланхоли́ческий.

melancholy /'mɛlənˌkɒli/ 1. adj. гру́стный. 2. n. уны́ние neut., грусть f.

melanin /'mɛlənɪn/ n. melanин m.

melanism /'mɛləˌnɪzəm/ n. melanи́зм m.

Melbourne /'mɛlbərn/ n. Ме́льбурн m.

meld /mɛld/ v. слива́ться impf.

melee /'meiˌlei/ n. сва́лка; ку́ча мала́ f.

meliorate /'milyəˌreit/ v. улучша́ть(ся) impf.

meliorist /'milyərɪst/ cf n. мелиора́тор m.

melisma /mɪ'lɪzmə/ n. мели́зма f.

mellifluous /mə'lɪfluəs/ adj. сладкозву́чный.

mellow /'mɛlou/ adj. мя́гкий; (ripe) спе́лый.

melodeon /mə'loudiən/ n. мелодио́н m.

melodics /mə'lɒdɪk/ n. мело́дика f.

melodious /mə'loudiəs/ adj. мелоди́чный.

melodist /'mɛlədɪst/ n. мелоди́ст; певе́ц; компози́тор m.

melodrama /'mɛləˌdrɑmə/ n. мелодра́ма f.

melodramatic /ˌmɛlədrə'mætɪk/ adj. мелодрамати́ческий.

melody /'mɛlədi/ n. мело́дия f.

melon /'mɛlən/ n. ды́ня f.

melt /mɛlt/ v. растворя́ть(ся) impf., раствори́ть(ся) pf.; v.i. (thaw) та́ять impf.

melting point /'mɛltɪŋ/ n. то́чка плавле́ния f.

member /'mɛmbər/ n. член m.

membership /'mɛmbərˌʃɪp/ 1. n. чле́нство; коли́чество чле́нов neut. 2. adj. чле́нский.

membrane /'mɛmbrein/ n. перепо́нка, плёнка, оболо́чка f.

membranous /'mɛmbrənəs/ adj. перепо́нчатый.

memento /mə'mɛntou/ n. сувени́р m.; напомина́ние neut.

memo /'mɛmou/ n. мемора́ндум m.

memoir /'mɛmwɑr/ n. воспомина́ние neut.; pl. воспомина́ния; мему́ары pl.

memorabilia /ˌmɛmərə'bɪliə/ n. па́мятные ве́щи pl.

memorable /'mɛmərəbəl/ adj. па́мятный.

memorandum /ˌmɛmə'rændəm/ n. мемора́ндум m., заме́тка f.

memorial /mə'mɔriəl/ 1. adj. мемориа́льный. 2. n. па́мятник m.

memorize /'mɛməˌraiz/ v. зау́чивать наизу́сть impf.

memory /'mɛməri/ n. па́мять f.; (recollection) воспомина́ние neut.

menace /'mɛnɪs/ 1. n. угро́за f. 2. v. угрожа́ть; грози́ть impf.

menacing /'mɛnɪsɪŋ/ adj. гро́зный; угрожа́ющий.

menagerie /mə'nædʒəri/ n. звери́нец m.

mend /mɛnd/ v. чини́ть impf., почини́ть pf.

mendacious /mɛn'deiʃəs/ adj. лжи́вый; ло́жный.

mendacity /mɛn'dæsɪti/ n. лжи́вость f.

mendelevium /ˌmɛndl'iviəm/ n. менделе́вий m.

Mendelian /mɛn'diliən/ adj. ме́нделевский.

mendicancy /'mɛndɪkənsi/ n. ни́щенство neut.

mendicant /'mɛndɪkənt/ 1. n. ни́щий m. 2. adj. ни́щий, ни́щенствующий.

mending /'mɛndɪŋ/ n. почи́нка; што́пка f.; ремо́нт m.

menhir /'mɛnhɪr/ n. менги́р m.

menial /'miniəl/ adj. ни́зкий; (servile) раболе́пный.

meningitis /ˌmɛnɪn'dʒaitɪs/ n. менинги́т m.

meniscus /mɪ'nɪskəs/ n. мени́ск m.

Mennonite /'mɛnəˌnait/ n. мнонои́т m.

menology /mɪ'nɒlədʒi/ (saints' lives) че́тьи мине́и pl.; (calendar of saints' days) месяцесло́в m.

menopause /'mɛnəˌpɔz/ n. кли́макс m.

menses /'mɛnsiz/ n. ме́сячные pl., менструа́ция f.

Menshevik /'mɛnʃəvɪk/ n. меньшеви́к m.

Menshevism /'mɛnʃəˌvizəm/ n. меньшеви́зм m.

menstrual /'mɛnstruəl/ adj. менструа́льный.

menstruate /'mɛnstruˌeit/ v. менструи́ровать impf.

menstruation /ˌmɛnstru'eiʃən/ n. менструа́ция f.

mensural /'mɛnʃərəl/ adj. ме́рный.

mensuration /ˌmɛnʃə'reiʃən/ n. измере́ние neut.

men's wear /'mɛnz/ n. мужска́я оде́жда f.

mental /'mɛntl/ adj. у́мственный; психи́ческий.

mentality /mɛn'tælɪti/ n. ум; интелле́кт; менталите́т m.

mentally /'mɛntli/ adv. у́мственно; мы́сленно.

menthol /'mɛnθɒl/ n. менто́л m.

mention /'mɛnʃən/ 1. n. упомина́ние neut. 2. v. упомина́ть impf., упомяну́ть pf.

mentor /'mɛntər/ n. наста́вник m.

menu /'mɛnyu/ *n.* меню́ *neut. indecl.*
meow /mi'au/ **1.** *n.* мяу́канье *neut.* **2.** *v.* мяу́кать *impf.*
Mephistopheles /ˌmɛfə'stɒfəˌliz/ *n.* Мефисто́фель *m.*
Mephistophelian /ˌmɛfəstə'filiən/ *adj.* мефисто́фельский.
mercantile /'mɜrkənˌtil/ *adj.* мерканти́льный.
mercantilism /'mɜrkəntɪˌlɪzəm/ *n.* меркантили́зм *m.*
mercaptan /mər'kæptæn/ *n.* меркапта́н *m.*
Mercator projection /mər'keitər/ *n.* (*cartography*) мерка́торская прое́кция *f.*
mercenary /'mɜrsəˌnɛri/ **1.** *adj.* коры́стный. **2.** *n.* наёмник *m.*
mercerization /ˌmɜrsərə'zeiʃən/ *n.* мерсериза́ция *f.*
mercerize /'mɜrsəˌraiz/ *v.* мерсеризова́ть *impf. and pf.*
merchandise /*n.* 'mɜrtʃən,dais; *v.* 'mɜrtʃən,daiz/ **1.** *n.* това́р *m.*; това́ры *pl.* **2.** *v.* торгова́ть *impf.*
merchant /'mɜrtʃənt/ **1.** *adj.* торго́вый. **2.** *n.* купе́ц; торго́вец *m.*
merchant ship *n.* торго́вое су́дно *neut.*
merciful /'mɜrsɪfəl/ *adj.* милосе́рдный.
merciless /'mɜrsɪlɪs/ *adj.* безжа́лостный.
mercilessness /'mɜrsɪlɪsnɪs/ *n.* безжа́лостность *f.*
mercurial /mər'kyuriəl/ *adj.* (*of mercury*) рту́тный; (*lively*) живо́й; (*inconstant*) непостоя́нный, переме́нчивый.
mercury /'mɜrkyəri/ *n.* ртуть *f.*
Mercury /'mɜrkyəri/ *n.* (*astr.*) Мерку́рий *m.*
mercy /'mɜrsi/ *n.* милосе́рдие *neut.*
mere /mɪər/ *adj.* просто́й.
merely /'mɪərli/ *adv.* то́лько, про́сто.
meretricious /ˌmɛrɪ'trɪʃəs/ *adj.* мишу́рный.
merge /mɜrdʒ/ *v.* слива́ться *impf.*, сли́ться *pf.*
merger /'mɜrdʒər/ *n.* сли́яние, объедине́ние *neut.*
meridian /mə'rɪdiən/ *n.* меридиа́н; *m.*
meridional /mə'rɪdiənļ/ *adj.* мередиа́нный; ю́жный.
meringue /mə'ræŋ/ *n.* мере́нга *f.*
merino /mə'rinou/ **1.** *n.* мерино́с *m.* **2.** *adj.* мерино́совый.
merit /'mɛrɪt/ **1.** *n.* заслу́га *f.*; досто́инство *neut.* **2.** *v.* заслу́живать *impf.*, заслужи́ть *pf.*
meritocrat /'mɛrɪtəˌkræt/ *n.* меритокра́т *m.*
meritorious /ˌmɛrɪ'tɔriəs/ *adj.* похва́льный.
merlin /'mɜrlɪn/ *n.* (*bird*) кре́чет *m.*
mermaid /'mɜrˌmeid/ *n.* руса́лка *f.*
merriment /'mɛrɪmənt/ *n.* весе́лье *neut.*
merry /'mɛri/ *adj.* весёлый.
merry-go-round /'mɛri gou ˌraund/ *n.* карусе́ль *f.*
merrymaking /'mɛriˌmeikŋ/ *n.* весе́лье *neut.*
mésalliance /ˌmeizə'laiəns, meizal'yās/ *n.* нера́вный брак *m.*
mesh /mɛʃ/ *n.* сеть *f.*
meshed /mɛʃt/ *adj.* сетьево́й.
mesmeric /mɛz'mɛrɪk/ *adj.* гипноти́ческий.
mesmerism /'mɛzməˌrɪzəm/ *n* гипноти́зм *m.*
mesmerist /'mɛzmərɪst/ *n.* гипнотизёр *m.*
mesmerize /'mɛzməˌraiz/ *v.* гипнотизи́ровать *impf.*
meson /'mizɒn/ *n.* мезо́н *m.*
mesosphere /'mɛzəˌsfɪər/ *n.* мезосфе́ра *f.*
mesotron /'mɛzəˌtrɒn/ *n.* мезотро́н *m.*
Mesozoic /ˌmɛzə'souɪk/ *adj.* мезозо́йский.

mess /mɛs/ *n.* беспоря́док *m.*; (*mil.*) о́бщее пита́ние *neut.*, о́бщий стол *m.*
message /'mɛsɪdʒ/ *n.* донесе́ние; сообще́ние *neut.*
messenger /'mɛsəndʒər/ *n.* ве́стник, посы́льный *m.*
Messiah /mɪ'saiə/ *n.* Месси́я *m.*
Messianic /ˌmɛsi'ænɪk/ *adj.* мессиа́нский.
messianism /'mɛsiəˌnɪzəm/ *n.* мессиани́зм *m.*
Messrs. /'mɛsərz/ *n.* (*abbr.*) господа́ *pl.*
messy /'mɛsi/ *adj.* гря́зный; беспоря́дочный.
mestizo /mɛ'stizou/ *n.* мети́с *m.*, мети́ска *f.*
metabasis /mə'tæbəsɪs/ *n.* метаба́зис *m.*
metabolism /mə'tæbəˌlɪzəm/ *n.* метаболи́зм, обме́н веще́ств *m.*
metabolite /mə'tæbəˌlait/ *n.* метаболи́т *m.*
metacarpal /ˌmɛtə'karpəl/ *n.* пя́стная кость *f.*
metacarpus /ˌmɛtə'karpəs/ *n.* пясть *f.*
metal /'mɛtļ/ **1.** *n.* мета́лл *m.* **2.** *adj.* металли́ческий.
metalanguage /'mɛtəˌlæŋgwɪdʒ/ *n.* метаязы́к *m.*
metalinguistics /ˌmɛtəlɪŋ'gwɪstɪks/ *n.* металингви́стика *f.*
metallic /mə'tælɪk/ *adj.* металли́ческий.
metallize /'mɛtļˌaiz/ *v.* металлизи́ровать *impf.*
metalloid /'mɛtļˌɔid/ *n.* металло́ид *m.*
metallurgical /ˌmɛtļ'ɜrdʒɪkəl/ *adj.* металлурги́ческий.
metallurgist /'mɛtļˌɜrdʒɪst/ *n.* металлу́рг *m.*
metallurgy /'mɛtļˌɜrdʒi/ *n.* металлурги́я *f.*
metamorphic /ˌmɛtə'mɔrfɪk/ *adj.* метаморфи́ческий.
metamorphose /ˌmɛtə'mɔrfouz/ *v.* превраща́ть (в *with acc.*) *impf.*
metamorphosis /ˌmɛtə'mɔrfəsɪs/ *n.* метаморфо́за *f.*; (*biol.*) метаморфо́з *m.*
metaphor /'mɛtəˌfɔr/ *n.* мета́фора *f.*
metaphorical /ˌmɛtə'fɔrɪkəl/ *adj.* метафори́ческий.
metaphysical /ˌmɛtə'fɪzɪkəl/ *adj.* метафизи́ческий.
metaphysician /ˌmɛtəfə'zɪʃən/ *n.* метафи́зик *m.*
metaphysics /ˌmɛtə'fɪzɪks/ *n.* метафи́зика *f.*
metastable /'mɛtəˌsteibəl/ *adj.* метастаби́льный.
metastasis /mə'tæstəsɪs/ *n.* (*med.*) метаста́з *m.*
metathesis /mə'tæθəsɪs/ *n.* метате́за *f.*
metazoan /ˌmɛtə'zouən/ *n.* многокле́точное живо́тное *neut.*
mete /mit/ *v.:* **to mete out** распределя́ть; назнача́ть *impf.*
metempsychosis /mə,tɛmsə'kousɪs/ *n.* метемпсихо́з *m.*
meteor /'mitiər/ *n.* метео́р *m.*
meteoric /ˌmiti'ɔrɪk/ *adj.* метео́рный; (*fig.*) головокружи́тельный.
meteorite /'mitiəˌrait/ *n.* метеори́т *m.*
meteoroid /'mitiəˌrɔid/ *n.* метео́рное те́ло *neut.*
meteorologist /ˌmitiə'rɒlədʒɪst/ *n.* метеоро́лог *m.*
meteorology /ˌmitiə'rɒlədʒi/ *n.* метеороло́гия *f.*
meter /'mitər/ *n.* (*instrument*) счётчик *m.*; (*measure*) метр *m.*
methane /'mɛθein/ *n.* мета́н *m.*
methanol /'mɛθəˌnɒl/ *n.* метано́л *m.*
method /'mɛθəd/ *n.* ме́тод, спо́соб *m.*, систе́ма *f.*
methodical /mə'θɒdɪkəl/ *adj.* методи́ческий.

Methodism /'mɛθə,dɪzəm/ n. методи́зм m.
Methodist /'mɛθədɪst/ n. методи́ст m.
methodless /'mɛθədlɪs/ adj. бессисте́мный.
methodological /,mɛθədl'ɒdʒɪkəl/ adj. методологи́ческий.
methodology /,mɛθə'dɒlədʒi/ n. методоло́гия f.
methyl /'mɛθəl/ n. мети́л m.
methylate /'mɛθə,leit/ v. денатури́ровать impf.
methylene /'mɛθə,lin/ n. метиле́н m.
meticulous /mə'tɪkyələs/ adj. дета́льный; дото́шный.
métier /'meityei/ n. ремесло́ neut.
Metol /mitɔl/ n. мето́л m.
metonymy /mɪ'tɒnəmi/ n. метоними́я f.
metric /'mɛtrɪk/ adj. метри́ческий.
metrics /'mɛtrɪks/ n. ме́трика f.
metro /'mɛtrou/ n. метро́ neut. indecl.
metrological /,mɛtrə'lɒdʒɪkəl/ adj. метрологи́ческий.
metrology /mɪ'trɒlədʒi/ n. метроло́гия f.
metronome /'mɛtrə,noum/ n. метроно́м m.
metropolis /mɪ'trɒpəlɪs/ n. метропо́лия; столи́ца f.
metropolitan /,mɛtrə'pɒlɪtn̩/ **1.** n. (eccl.) митрополи́т m. **2.** adj. столи́чный.
mettle /'mɛtl̩/ n. горя́чность f.
mettlesome /'mɛtl̩səm/ adj. пы́лкий; рети́вый.
Mexican /'mɛksɪkən/ **1.** adj. мексика́нский. **2.** n. мексика́нец m., мексика́нка f.
Mexico /'mɛksɪ,kou/ (country) n. Ме́ксика f.
Mexico City n. Ме́хико neut.
mezzanine /'mɛzə,nin/ n. (theat.) бельэта́ж m.
mezza voce /'mɛt'sə voutʃei/ adv. вполго́лоса.
mezzo-soprano /'mɛtsou sə'prænou/ adv. ме́ццо-сопра́но.
mezzotint /'mɛtsou,tɪnt/ adv. ме́ццо-ти́нто.
mho /mou/ n. (elec.) мо neut. indecl.
Miami /mai'æmi/ n. Майа́ми m.
miasma /mai'æzmə/ n. миа́змы pl.
miasmal /mai'æzməl/ also **miasmic** /mai'æzmɪk/ adj. миазмати́ческий.
mica /'maikə/ n. слюда́ f.
micaceous /mai'keiʃəs/ adj. слюдяно́й.
Michigan /'mɪʃɪgən/ n. Мичига́н m.
microampere /,maikrou'æmpɪər/ n. микроампе́р m.
microanalysis /,maikrouə'næləsɪs/ n. микроана́лиз m.
microbalance /'maikrə,bæləns/ n. микровесы́ pl.
microbar /'maikrə,bɑr/ n. микроба́р m.
microbe /'maikroub/ n. микро́б m.
microbic /mai'kroubɪk/ adj. микро́бный.
microbiologist /,maikroubai'ɒlədʒɪst/ n. микробио́лог m.
microbiology /,maikroubai'ɒlədʒi/ n. микробиоло́гия f.
microcephalic /,maikrousə'fælɪk/ adj. микроцефали́ческий.
microchemistry /,maikrou'kɛməstri/ n. микрохи́мия f.
microchip /'maikrou,tʃɪp/ n. чип, криста́лл m.
microcircuit /'maikrou,sɜrkɪt/ n. микросхе́ма f.
microclimate /'maikrə,klaimɪt/ n. микрокли́мат m.
microcomputer /'maikroukəm,pyutər/ n. ми́кро-ЭВМ f., микрокомпью́тер m.
microcopy /'maikrə,kɒpi/ n. микроко́пия f.

microcosm /'maikrə,kɒzəm/ n. микрокосм m.
microelectronics /,maikrouɪlɛk'trɒnɪks/ n. микроэлектро́ника f.
microfarad /'maikrə,færəd/ n. микрофара́д m.
microfiche /'maikrə,fiʃ/ n. микрофи́ш m.
microfilm /'maikrə,fɪlm/ n. микрофи́льм m.
micrometer /mai'krɒmɪtər/ n. микроме́тр m.
micron /'maikrɒn/ n. микро́н m.
microorganism /'maikrou,ɔrgə,nɪzəm/ n. микроорганизм m.
microphone /'maikrə,foun/ n. микрофо́н m.
microphotograph /,maikrə'foutə,græf/ n. микрофотогра́фия f.
microphysics /,maikrə'fɪzɪks/ n. микрофи́зика f.
microphyte /'maikrə,fait/ n. микрофи́т m.
microprocessor /'maikrou,prɒsɛsər/ n. микропроце́ссор m.
microscope /'maikrə,skoup/ n. микроско́п m.
microscopic /,maikrə'skɒpɪk/ adj. микроскопи́ческий.
microscopy /mai'krɒskəpi/ n. микроскопи́я f.
microspore /'maikrə,spɔr/ n. микроспо́ра f.
microstructure /'maikrou,strʌktʃər/ n. микрострукту́ра f.
microsurgery /'maikrou,sɜrdʒəri/ n. микрохирурги́я f.
microtome /'maikrə,toum/ n. микрото́м m.
microwave /'maikrou,weiv/ n. микроволна́ f.; (appliance) микроволно́вая печь f.
mid /mɪd/ adj. сре́дний, середи́нный.
midday / n. 'mɪd'dei/ adj. 'mɪd,dei/ **1.** n. по́лдень m. **2.** adj. полу́денный.
middle /'mɪdl̩/ **1.** n. середи́на f.; **in the middle** prep. посреди́ (with gen.); в середи́не (with gen.). **2.** adj. сре́дний.
middle-aged /'mɪdl̩'eidʒd/ adj. сре́дних лет; пожило́й.
Middle Ages n. средневеко́вье neut.
middle class n. сре́дний класс m.
middleman /'mɪdl̩,mæn/ n. посре́дник m.; (comm.) комиссионе́р m.
middleweight /'mɪdl̩,weit/ adj. сре́днего ве́са.
middling /'mɪdlɪŋ/ adv. сре́дне; ничего́; так себе.
midge /mɪdʒ/ n. мо́шка f.
midget /'mɪdʒɪt/ **1.** n. ка́рлик m. **2.** adj. ка́рликовый.
midland /'mɪdlənd/ adj. центра́льный, располо́женный в середи́не.
midmost /'mɪd,moust/ adj. в са́мой середи́не.
midnight /'mɪd,nait/ **1.** n. по́лночь f. **2.** adj. полуно́чный.
midriff /'mɪdrɪf / n. диафра́гма f.
midship /'mɪd,ʃɪp/ n. сре́дняя часть су́дна f.
midshipman /'mɪd,ʃɪpmən/ n. курса́нт вое́нно-морско́го учи́лища m.
mid-size /'mɪd ,saiz/ adj. сре́днего разме́ра.
midst /mɪdst/ n. середи́на f.
midsummer /'mɪd'sʌmər/ n. середи́на ле́та f.
midway /'mɪd'wei/ adv. на полпути́; на полдоро́ге.
midweek /'mɪd'wik/ n. середи́на неде́ли f.
midwife /'mɪd,waif/ n. акуше́рка f.
midwifery /'mɪd'wɪfəri/ n. акуше́рство neut.
midwinter /'mɪd'wɪntər/ n. середи́на зимы́ f.
mien /min/ n. ми́на f., выраже́ние лица́ neut.
might /mait/ n. могу́щество neut.; мощь; си́ла f.
mightily /'maitl̩i/ adv. си́льно.

mighty /'maiti/ adj. могу́щественный; мо́щный.

mignonette /ˌmɪnyə'nɛt/ n. резеда́ f.

migraine /'maigrein/ n. мигре́нь f.

migrant /'maigrənt/ **1.** n. переселе́нец m. **2.** adj. кочу́ющий.

migrate /'maigreit/ v. переселя́ться impf., пересели́ться pf.; мигри́ровать impf. and pf.

migration /mai'greiʃən/ n. переселе́ние neut., мигра́ция f.

migratory /'maigrəˌtɔri/ adj. (bird) перелётный.

Mikado /mɪkɒdou/ n. мика́до m. indecl.

mike /maik/ n. (colloq.) микрофо́н m.

Mikonos /'mikɔnɒs/ n. (island) Ми́конос m.

mil /mɪl/ n. мил m.

Milan /mɪ'læn, -'lɑn/ n. Мила́н m.

milch /mɪltʃ/ adj. до́йный.

mild /maild/ adj. мя́гкий; лёгкий.

mildew /'mɪlˌdu/ n. пле́сень f.

mildewy /'mɪlˌdui/ adj. заплесневе́лый.

mildly /'maildli/ adv. слегка́.

mildness /'maildnɪs/ n. мя́гкость f.

mild-tempered /'maild ˌtɛmpərd/ adj. кро́ткий.

mile /mail/ n. ми́ля f.

milepost /'mailˌpoust/ n. верстово́й столб, доро́жный столб m.

miler /'mailər/ n. бегу́н на ми́лю m.

milestone /'mailˌstoun/ n. ве́ха f.

milieu /mɪl'yu/ n. среда́ f.

militancy /'mɪlɪtənsi/ n. во́инственность f.

militant /'mɪlɪtənt/ **1.** adj. во́инствующий;. **2.** n. активи́ст m.

militarism /'mɪlɪtəˌrɪzəm/ n. милитари́зм m.

militarist /'mɪlɪtərɪst/ n. милитари́ст m.

militaristic /ˌmɪlɪtə'rɪstɪk/ adj. милитаристи́ческий.

military /'mɪlɪˌtɛri/ **1.** adj. во́инский, вое́нный. **2.** n. вое́нные pl.

militia /mɪ'lɪʃə/ n. мили́ция f.; (auxiliary force) наро́дное ополче́ние neut.

militiaman /mɪ'lɪʃəmən/ n. милиционе́р m.

milk /mɪlk/ **1.** n. молоко́ neut. **2.** adj. моло́чный; мле́чный. **3.** v. дои́ть impf., подои́ть pf.

milk cow n. до́йная коро́ва f.

milkiness /'mɪlkɪnɪs/ n. моло́чный цвет m.

milking /'mɪlkɪŋ/ n. дое́ние neut.

milkmaid /'mɪlkˌmeid/ n. доя́рка f.

milkman /'mɪlkˌmæn/ n. разно́счик молока́; моло́чник m.

milk shake n. моло́чный кокте́йль m.

milksop /'mɪlkˌsɒp/ n. тря́пка f.

milk tooth n. моло́чный зуб m.

milkweed /'mɪlkˌwid/ n. молоча́й m.

milky /'mɪlki/ adj. моло́чный.

Milky Way n. Мле́чный Путь m.

mill /mɪl/ **1.** n. ме́льница f.; (factory) фа́брика f.; заво́д m. **2.** v. моло́ть impf., смоло́ть pf.

mill dam n. ме́льничная плоти́на f.

millenarian /ˌmɪlə'nɛəriən/ n. тысячеле́тник, хилиа́ст m.

millennial /mɪ'lɛniəl/ adj. тысячеле́тний.

millennialism /mɪ'lɛniəˌlɪzəm/ n. хилиа́зм m.

millennium /mɪ'lɛniəm/ n. тысячеле́тие neut.

miller /'mɪlər/ n. ме́льник m.

millesimal /mɪ'lɛsəməl/ adj. ты́сячный.

millet /'mɪlɪt/ n. про́со; пшено́ neut.

milliampere /ˌmɪli'æmpɪər/ n. миллиампе́р m.

millibar /'mɪləˌbɑr/ n. миллиба́р m.

milligram /'mɪlɪˌgræm/ n. миллигра́мм m.

milliliter /'mɪləˌlitər/ n. миллили́тр m.

millimeter /'mɪləˌmitər/ n. миллиме́тр m.

milliner /'mɪlənər/ n. моди́стка f.

millinery /'mɪləˌnɛri/ n. да́мские шля́пы pl.

milling /'mɪlɪŋ/ **1.** n. молотьба́ f.; помо́л m.; прока́т m.; (metal) фрезеро́вка f. **2.** adj. (colloq.) (in a crowd) толпя́щийся, толку́щийся.

million /'mɪlyən/ n. миллио́н m.

millionaire /ˌmɪlyə'nɛər/ n. миллионе́р m.

millionairess /ˌmɪlyə'nɛərɪs/ n. миллионе́рша f.

millionth /'mɪlyənθ/ adj. миллио́нный.

millipede /'mɪləˌpid/ n. сороконо́жка f.

milliroentgen /'mɪləˌrɛntgən, -dʒən/ n. миллирентге́н m.

millivolt /'mɪləˌvoult/ n. милливо́льт m.

millpond /'mɪlˌpɒnd/ n. ме́льничный пруд m.

millrace /'mɪlˌreis/ n. ме́льничный лото́к m.

millstone /'mɪlˌstoun/ n. жёрнов m.

mill wheel n. ме́льничное колесо́ neut.

mime /maim/ **1.** n. мим m. **2.** v. передра́знивать impf.

mimeograph copy /'mimiəˌgræf/ n. ротапри́нтная ко́пия f.

mimetic /mɪ'mɛtɪk/ adj. подража́тельный.

mimic /'mɪmɪk/ **1.** n. имита́тор, подража́тель m. **2.** v. имити́ровать impf.

mimicry /'mɪmɪkri/ n. ми́мика f.; подража́ние neut.; (biol.) мимикри́я f.

mimosa /mɪ'mousə/ n. мимо́за f.

minaret /ˌmɪnə'rɛt/ n. минаре́т m.

minatory /'mɪnəˌtɔri/ adj. угрожа́ющий.

minced /mɪnst/ adj. ру́бленый.

mincemeat /'mɪnsˌmit/ n. сла́дкая начи́нка f.

mincing /'mɪnsɪŋ/ adj. жема́нный.

mind /maind/ **1.** n. ум, ра́зум m, **2.** v. (look after) присма́тривать (за with instr.); (object) возража́ть impf., возрази́ть pf.; **never mind** interj. ничего́; не волну́йся.

mindful /'maindfəl/ adj. по́мнящий, внима́тельный.

mindless /'maindlɪs/ adj. безу́мный.

mind reader n. ясновидя́щий m.

mine[1] /main/ poss. pron. мой m., моя́ f., моё neut., мои́ pl.

mine[2] /main/ **1.** n. ша́хта f.; (explosive) ми́на f. **2.** v. (mil.) мини́ровать impf. and pf.

mine clearing n. разминиро́вание neut.

mine detector n. миноиска́тель m.

minefield /'mainˌfild/ n. ми́нное по́ле neut.

minelayer /'mainˌleiər/ n. ми́нный загради́тель m.

miner /'mainər/ n. горня́к, шахтёр m.

mineral /'mɪnərəl/ **1.** n. минера́л m. **2.** adj. минера́льный.

mineralize /'mɪnərəˌlaiz/ v. минерализова́ть impf.

mineralogist /ˌmɪnə'rɒlədʒɪst/ n. минерало́г m.

mineralogy /ˌmɪnə'rɒlədʒi/ n. минерало́гия f.

minesweeper /'mainˌswipər/ n. ми́нный тра́льщик m.

minesweeping /'mainˌswipɪŋ/ n. миноиска́тель тра́льщик m.

mine thrower n. миноме́т m.

mingle /'mɪŋgəl/ v.t. сме́шивать impf., смеша́ть pf.; v.i. сме́шиваться impf., смеша́ться pf.

mingy /'mɪndʒi/ *adj.* жа́дный.
miniature /'mɪniətʃər/ **1.** *n.* миниатю́ра *f.* **2.** *adj.* миниатю́рный.
miniaturist /'mɪniətʃərɪst/ *n.* миниатюри́ст *m.*
miniaturization /,mɪniətʃərə'zeiʃən/ *n.* миниатюриза́ция *f.*
miniaturize /'mɪniətʃə,raiz/ *v.* миниатюризирова́ть *impf.*
minibus /'mɪni,bʌs/ *n.* микроавто́бус *m.*
minicomputer /'mɪnikəm,pyutər/ *n.* миникомпью́тер *m.*
minim /'mɪnəm/ *n.* (*mus.*) полови́нная но́та, полови́нка *f.*
minimal /'mɪnəməl/ *adj.* минима́льный.
minimalist /'mɪnəməlɪst/ *n.* минимали́ст *m.*
minimize /'mɪnə,maiz/ *v.* преуменьша́ть *impf.*, преуме́ньшить *pf.*
minimum /'mɪnəməm/ **1.** *n.* ми́нимум *m.* **2.** *adj.* минима́льный.
mining /'mainɪŋ/ **1.** *n.* го́рное де́ло *neut.* **2.** *adj.* го́рный.
minion /'mɪnyən/ *n.* приспе́шник *m.*
miniskirt /'mini,skɜrt/ *n.* ми́ни-ю́бка *f.*
minister /'mɪnəstər/ **1.** *n.* мини́стр *m.*; (*diplomat*) посла́нник *m.*; (*eccl.*) свяще́нник *m.* **2.** *v.* служи́ть *impf.*
ministerial /,mɪnə'stɪəriəl/ *adj.* министе́рский.
ministration /,mɪnə'streiʃən/ *n.* оказа́ние по́мощи *neut.*
ministry /'mɪnəstri/ *n.* министе́рство *neut.*; (*eccl.*) духове́нство *neut.*
miniver /'mɪnəvər/ *n.* горноста́й *m.*
mink /mɪŋk/ **1.** *n.* но́рка *f.* **2.** *adj.* но́рковый.
Minnesota /,mɪnə'soutə/ *n.* Миннесо́та *m.*
minnow /'mɪnou/ *n.* голья́н *m.*
Minoan /mɪ'nouən/ *adj.* мино́йский.
minor /'mainər/ **1.** *adj.* незначи́тельный; ме́ньший; (*mus.*) мино́рный. **2.** *n.* (*under legal age*) несовершенноле́тний *m.*; (*mus.*) мино́р *m.*
minority /mɪ'nɔriti/ *n.* меньшинство́ *neut.*
Minotaur /'mɪnə,tɔr/ *n.* Минота́вр *m.*
Minsk /mɪnsk/ *n.* Минск *m.*
minstrel /'mɪnstrəl/ *n.* менестре́ль *m.*
mint[1] /mɪnt/ **1.** *n.* (*money*) моне́тный двор *m.*; (*cost*) больша́я су́мма *f.* **2.** *v.* чека́нить *impf.* **3.** *adj.*: **mint condition** как но́вый.
mint[2] /mɪnt/ **1.** *n.* (*plant*) мя́та *f.* **2.** *adj.* мя́тный.
mintage /'mɪntɪdʒ/ *n.* чека́нка *f.*
minuet /,mɪnyu'ɛt/ *n.* менуэ́т *m.*
minus /'mainəs/ **1.** *prep.* без (*with gen.*), ми́нус. **2.** *adj.* отрица́тельный. **3.** *n.* знак ми́нуса *m.*
minuscule /'mɪnə,skyul/ *adj.* мину́скульный; о́чень ма́ленький.
minute[1] /'mɪnɪt/ **1.** *adj.* (*time*) мину́тный. **2.** *n.* мину́та *f.*; *pl.* протоко́л *m.*
minute[2] /mai'nut/ *adj.* ме́лкий; мельча́йший; дета́льный.
minute book /'mɪnɪt/ *n.* кни́га протоко́лов *f.*
minute hand /'mɪnɪt/ *n.* мину́тная стре́лка *f.*
minuteness /mai'nutnɪs/ *n.* подро́бность; тща́тельность *f.*
minutiae /mɪ'nuʃi,i/ *n.* (*details*) подро́бности; то́нкости; ме́лочи *pl.*
minx /mɪŋks/ *n.* коке́тка *f.*
miosis /mai'ousɪs/ *n.* мио́зис *m.*
miracle /'mɪrəkəl/ *n.* чу́до *neut.*

miraculous /mɪ'rækyələs/ *adj.* чуде́сный; чудотво́рный.
miraculously /mɪ'rækyələsli/ *adv.* (каки́м-то) чу́дом.
mirage /mɪ'rɑʒ/ *n.* мира́ж *m.*
mire /mai³r/ *n.* боло́то *neut.*
mirror /'mɪrər/ *n.* зе́ркало *neut.*
mirth /mɜrθ/ *n.* весе́лье *neut.*; смех *m.*
mirthful /'mɜrθfəl/ *adj.* весёлый.
mirthless /'mɜrθlɪs/ *adj.* безра́достный.
miry /'mai³ri/ *adj.* гря́зный; то́пкий.
misaddress /,mɪsə'drɛs/ *v.* непра́вильно адресова́ть *impf.*
misadventure /,mɪsəd'vɛntʃər/ *n.* несча́стный слу́чай *m.*
misadvice /,mɪsəd'vais/ *n.* дурно́й сове́т *m.*
misalliance /,mɪsə'laiəns/ *n.* мезалья́нс, нера́вный брак *m.*
misanthrope /'mɪsən,θroup/ *n.* мизантро́п *m.*
misanthropic /,mɪsən'θrɒpɪk/ *adj.* человеконенави́стнический.
misanthropy /mɪs'ænθrəpi/ *n.* мизантро́пия *f.*
misapprehend /,mɪsæprɪ'hɛnd/ *v.* недопонима́ть *impf.*
misapprehension /,mɪsæprɪ'hɛnʃən/ *n.* недоразуме́ние *neut.*
misappropriate /,mɪsə'proupri,eit/ *v.* незако́нно присва́ивать *impf.*
misappropriation /,mɪsə,proupri'eiʃən/ *n.* незако́нное присвое́ние *neut.*
misbegotten /,mɪsbɪ'gɒtṇ/ *adj.* незаконнорождённый; незако́нно приобретённый.
misbehave /,mɪsbɪ'heiv/ *v.* ду́рно вести́ себя́ *impf.*
misbehavior /,mɪsbɪ'heivyər/ *n.* плохо́е *or* дурно́е поведе́ние *neut.*
miscalculate /mɪs'kælkyə,leit/ *v.* просчи́тываться *impf.*, просчита́ться *pf.*
miscalculation /,mɪskælkyə'leiʃən/ *n.* просчёт *m.*
miscarriage /'mɪs,kærɪdʒ/ *n.* (*med.*) вы́кидыш *m.*
miscarry /mɪs'kæri/ *v.* (*have a miscarriage*) вы́кинуть *pf.*
miscegenation /mɪ,sɛdʒə'neiʃən/ *n.* смеше́ние рас *neut.*
miscellaneous /,mɪsə'leiniəs/ *adj.* ра́зный; разнообра́зный.
miscellany /'mɪsə,leini/ *n.* (*mixture*) смесь *f.*
mischance /mɪs'tʃæns/ *n.* несча́стье *neut.*
mischief /'mɪstʃɪf/ *n.* озорство́ *neut.*; (*tricks*) ша́лость *f.*
mischief-maker /'mɪstʃɪf ,meikər/ *n.* интрига́н *m.*
mischievous /'mɪstʃəvəs/ *adj.* шаловли́вый, озорно́й.
miscibility /,mɪsə'bɪliti/ *n.* сме́шиваемость *f.*
miscible /'mɪsəbəl/ *adj.* сме́шивающийся.
misconceive /,mɪskən'siv/ *v.* непра́вильно понима́ть *impf.*
misconception /,mɪskən'sɛpʃən/ *n.* недоразуме́ние *neut.*
misconduct /mɪs'kɒndʌkt/ *n.* дурно́е поведе́ние *neut.*
misconstruction /,mɪskən'strʌkʃən/ *n.* неве́рное толкова́ние *neut.*
misconstrue /,mɪskən'stru/ *v.* непра́вильно истолко́вывать *impf.*

miscount /mɪs'kaunt/ v. ошибáться при подсчёте impf.

miscreant /'mɪskriənt/ n. злодéй m.

misdeal /mɪs'dil/ v. ошибáться при сдáче (карт) impf.

misdeed /mɪs'did/ n. злодеяние neut.

misdemeanor /ˌmɪsdɪ'minər/ n. простýпок m.

misdirect /ˌmɪsdɪ'rɛkt/ v. непрáвильно направлять impf.; непрáвильно инструктировать impf.

misdirection /ˌmɪsdɪ'rɛkʃən/ n. непрáвильное указáние neut.

mise en scène /ˌmiz ɑ̃ 'sɛn/ n. мизансцéна f.

miser /'maizər/ n. скупéц m.

miserable /'mɪzərəbəl/ adj. жáлкий, несчáстный.

miserliness /maizərlinis/ n. скýпость f.

miserly /'maizərli/ adj. скупóй.

misery /'mɪzəri/ n. невзгóда; нищетá f.

misfire /'mɪsˌfaiˀr/ n. (gun) осéчка f.; (engine) перебóй m.

misfit /'mɪsˌfɪt/ n. (person) неудáчник m.

misfortune /mɪs'fɔrtʃən/ n. несчáстье neut.

misgiving /mɪs'ɡɪvɪŋ/ n. опасéние; дурнóе предчýвствие neut.

misgovern /mɪs'ɡʌvərn/ v. плóхо управлять impf.

misgovernment /mɪs'ɡʌvərnmənt/ n. плохóе правлéние neut.

misguided /mɪs'ɡaidɪd/ adj. обмáнутый; введённый в заблуждéние.

mishandle /mɪs'hændl/ v. плóхо or грýбо обращáться (с with instr.); непрáвильно употреблять impf.

mishandling /mɪs'hændlɪŋ/ n. дурнóе обращéние neut.

mishap /'mɪshæp/ n. несчáстье neut., неудáча f.

mishear /mɪs'hiər/ v. ослышаться impf.

mishmash /'mɪʃˌmaʃ/ n. пýтаница f.

misinform /ˌmɪsɪn'fɔrm/ v. дезинформировать impf. and pf.

misinformation /ˌmɪsɪnfər'meiʃən/ n. дезинформáция f.

misinterpret /ˌmɪsɪn'tɜrprɪt/ v. невéрно толковáть impf.

misinterpretation /ˌmɪsɪnˌtɜrprɪ'teiʃən/ n. невéрная интерпретáция f.

misjudge /mɪs'dʒʌdʒ/ v. непрáвильно оцéнивать impf.

mislay /mɪs'lei/ v. затерять pf.

mislead /mɪs'lid/ v. вводить в заблуждéние impf.

misleading /mɪs'lidɪŋ/ adj. обмáнчивый.

mismanage /mɪs'mænɪdʒ/ v. плóхо or непрáвильно управлять impf.

mismanagement /mɪs'mænɪdʒmənt/ n. безхозяйственность f.

misnomer /mɪs'noumər/ n. невéрное назвáние neut.

misogynist /mɪ'sɒdʒənɪst/ n. женоненавистник m.

misogyny /mɪ'sɒdʒəni/ n. женоненавистничество neut.

misplace /mɪs'pleis/ v. положить не на мéсто pf.

misplaced /mɪs'pleist/ adj. неумéстный.

misprint /'mɪsˌprɪnt/ n. опечáтка f.

mispronounce /ˌmɪsprə'nauns/ v. произнести непрáвильно pf.

mispronunciation /ˌmɪsprəˌnʌnsi'eiʃən/ n. непрáвильное произношéние neut.

misquotation /ˌmɪskwou'teiʃən/ n. netóчная цитáта f.

misquote /mɪs'kwout/ v. нетóчно цитировать impf.

misread /mɪs'rid/ v. дýрно понимáть impf.

misreport /ˌmɪsrɪ'pɔrt/ v. непрáвильно передавáть impf.

misrepresent /ˌmɪsrɛprɪ'zɛnt/ v. искажáть; представлять в лóжном свéте impf.

misrepresentation /ˌmɪsrɛprɪzən'teiʃən/ n. искажéние neut.

misrule /mɪs'rul/ n. бесхозяйственность f.; беспорядок m.

Miss[1] /mɪs/ n. (young lady) мисс f. indecl.

miss[2] /mɪs/ **1.** n. (failure) прóмах m. **2.** v. промахнýться pf.; (long for) скучáть impf.

missal /'mɪsəl/ n. трéбник m.

misshapen /mɪs'ʃeipən/ adj. урóдливый.

missile /'mɪsəl/ **1.** n. снаряд m. **2.** adj. ракéтный.

missing /'mɪsɪŋ/ adj. отсýтствующий; без вéсти пропáвший.

mission /'mɪʃən/ n. миссия f.

missionary /'mɪʃəˌnɛri/ n. миссионéр m.

Mississippi /ˌmɪsə'sɪpi/ n. Миссисипи m.

missive /'mɪsɪv/ n. послáние neut.

Missouri /mɪ'zuri/ n. Миссýри m.

misspell /mɪs'spɛl/ v. писáть с ошибками impf.

misspelling /mɪs'spɛlɪŋ/ n. орфографическая ошибка f., непрáвильное написáние neut.

misspend /mɪs'spɛnd/ v. растрáчивать impf.

misstatement /mɪs'steitmənt/ n. лóжное заявлéние neut.

mist /mɪst/ n. лёгкий тумáн m.

mistake /mɪ'steik/ **1.** n. ошибка f.; **by mistake** по ошибке. **2.** v. (take for) принять (за with acc.); **to make a mistake** ошибáться impf., ошибиться pf.

mistaken /mɪ'steikən/ adj. ошибочный.

mistakenly /mɪ'steikənli/ adv. по ошибке; ошибочно.

mister /'mɪstər/ n. господин; мистер m.

mistime /mɪs'taim/ v. сдéлать некстáти impf.

mistiness /'mɪstinis/ n. тумáнность f.

mistle thrush /'mɪsəl/ n. деряба f.

mistletoe /'mɪsəlˌtou/ n. омéла f.

mistranslate /ˌmɪstræns'leit/ v. непрáвильно переводить impf.

mistranslation /ˌmɪstræns'leiʃən/ n. непрáвильный перевóд m.

mistreat /mɪs'trit/ v. дýрно обращáться impf.

mistress /'mɪstrɪs/ n. хозяйка f.

mistrust /mɪs'trʌst/ **1.** v. не доверять impf. **2.** n. недовéрие neut.

mistrustful /mɪs'trʌstfəl/ adj. недовéрчивый.

misty /'mɪsti/ adj. тумáнный; смýтный.

misunderstand /ˌmɪsʌndər'stænd/ v. непрáвильно понять pf.

misunderstanding /ˌmɪsʌndər'stændɪŋ/ n. недоразумéние neut.

misuse / v. mɪs'yuz; n. mɪs'yus/ **1.** v. злоупотреблять impf., злоупотребить pf. **2.** n. злоупотреблéние neut.

mite[1] /mait/ n. (parasite) клещ m.

mite[2] /mait/ n. (modest contribution) лéпта f.; (small amount of money) грош m.; (colloq.) (bit) чýточка.

miter /'maitər/ n. (headdress) митра f.

Mithras /'mıθræs/ *n.* Ми́тра *f.*
mitigate /'mıtı,geit/ *v.* смягча́ть *impf.*
mitigating circumstance /'mıtı,geitıŋ/ *n.* смягча́ющее обстоя́тельство *neut.*
mitigation /,mıtı'geiʃən/ *n.* смягче́ние, утоле́ние *neut.*
mitosis /mai'tousıs/ *n.* мито́з *m.*
mitten /'mıtn̩/ *n.* рукави́ца; ва́режка *f.*
mix /mıks/ **1.** *n.* смесь *f.* **2.** *v.t.* сме́шивать *impf.*, смеша́ть *pf.*; *v.i.* сме́шиваться *impf.*, смеша́ться *pf.*
mixed /mıkst/ *adj.* сме́шанный.
mixer /'mıksər/ *n.* (*machine*) меша́лка *f.*; (*cul.*) ми́ксер *m.*
mixture /'mıkstʃər/ *n.* смесь *f.*
mix-up /'mıks,ʌp/ *n.* пу́таница *f.*
mnemonic /nı'mɒnık/ *adj.* мнемони́ческий.
mnemonics /nı'mɒnıks/ *n.* мнемо́ника *f.*
moan /moun/ **1.** *n.* стон *m.* **2.** *v.* стона́ть *impf.*
moat /mout/ *n.* (крепостно́й) ров *m.*
mob /mɒb/ *n.* толпа́ *f.*
mobcap /'mɒb,kæp/ *n.* чепе́ц *m.*
mobile /'moubəl/ *adj.* подви́жный; моби́льный.
mobile phone *n.* моби́льный *or* портати́вный телефо́н *m.*
mobility /mou'bılıti/ *n.* подви́жность *f.*
mobilize /'moubə,laiz/ *v.* мобилизова́ть(ся) *impf. and pf.*
moccasin /'mɒkəsın/ *n.* мокаси́н *m.*
mocha /'moukə/ *n.* ко́фе мо́кко *m. indecl.*
mock /mɒk/ *v.* высме́ивать *impf.*
mockery /'mɒkəri/ *n.* издева́тельство; осме́ивание *neut.*
mock-heroic /'mɒk hı'rouık/ *adj.* псевдогерои́ческий.
mocking /'mɒkıŋ/ *adj.* насме́шливый; издева́тельский.
mockingbird /'mɒkıŋ,bɜrd/ *n.* пересме́шник *m.*
mock-up /'mɒk,ʌp/ *n.* маке́т *m.*
modal /'moudl̩/ *adj.* мода́льный.
modality /mou'dælıti/ *n.* мода́льность *f.*
mode /moud/ *n.* о́браз; спо́соб *m.*; (*fashion*) мо́да *f.*
model /'mɒdl̩/ **1.** *n.* (*pattern*) моде́ль *f.*, образе́ц *m.*; (*artist's*) нату́рщик *m.*, нату́рщица *f.*; (*fashion*) манеке́нщик *m.*, манеке́нщица *f.* **2.** *adj.* образцо́вый; приме́рный. **3.** *v.* (*shape*) модели́ровать *impf. and pf.*
modeler /'mɒdl̩ər/ *n.* моде́льщик *m.*
modem /'moudəm/ *n.* мо́дем *m.*
moderate / *adj.* 'mɒdərıt *v.* 'mɒdə,reit/ **1.** *adj.* уме́ренный. **2.** *v.* умеря́ть(ся) *impf.*, уме́рить(ся) *pf.*
moderation /,mɒdə'reiʃən/ *n.* уме́ренность *f.*
moderato /,mɒdə'ratou/ *n.* (*mus.*) уме́ренно *neut.*
moderator /'mɒdə,reitər/ *n.* (*presiding person*) председа́тель *m.*, председа́тельница *f.*; (*phys.*) замедли́тель *m.*
modern /'mɒdərn/ *adj.* совреме́нный.
modernism /'mɒdər,nızəm/ *n.* модерни́зм *m.*
modernist /'mɒdərnıst/ *n.* модерни́ст *m.*
modernistic /,mɒdər'nıstık/ *adj.* модерни́стский.
modernity /mɒ'dɜrnıti/ *n.* совреме́нность *f.*
modernization /,mɒdərnə'zeiʃən/ *n.* модерниза́ция *f.*

modernize /'mɒdər,naiz/ *v.* модернизи́ровать *impf. and pf.*
modest /'mɒdıst/ *adj.* скро́мный.
modesty /'mɒdəsti/ *n.* скро́мность *f.*
modicum /'mɒdıkəm/ *n.* ка́пелька *f.*
modification /,mɒdəfı'keiʃən/ *n.* модифика́ция *f.*
modifier /'mɒdə,faiər/ *n.* модифика́тор *m.*; (*gram.*) атрибу́т *m.*
modify /'mɒdə,fai/ *v.* видоизменя́ть *impf.*, видоизмени́ть *pf.*; модифици́ровать *impf. and pf.*
modish /'moudıʃ/ *adj.* мо́дный.
modular /'mɒdʒələr/ *adj.* мо́дульный.
modulate /'mɒdʒə,leit/ *v.* модули́ровать *impf.*
modulation /,mɒdʒə'leiʃən/ *n.* модуля́ция *f.*
modulator /'mɒdʒə,leitər/ *n.* модуля́тор *m.*
module /'mɒdʒul/ *n.* мо́дуль *m.*
modulus /'mɒdʒələs/ *n.* мо́дуль *m.*
Mogul /'mougəl/ *n.* Мого́л *m.*
mohair /'mou,hεər/ *n.* мохе́р *m.*
Mohammed /mʊ'hæmıd, -'hɑmıd/ *n.* Магоме́т *m.*
Mohammedan /mʊ'hæmıdn̩/ *n.* магомета́нин, мусульма́нин *m.*
Mohammedanism /mʊ'hæmıdn̩,ızəm/ *n.* магоме́танство, мусульма́нство *neut.*
moiety /'mɔiıti/ *n.* до́ля *m.*
moiré /mwɑ'rei/ *adj.* муа́ровый.
moist /mɔist/ *adj.* сыро́й; вла́жный.
moisten /'mɔisən/ *v.* сма́чивать *impf.*, смочи́ть *pf.*
moisture /'mɔistʃər/ *n.* вла́га; вла́жность *f.*
moisturize /'mɔistʃə,raiz/ *v.* увлажня́ть *impf.*
moisturizer /'mɔistʃə,raizər/ *n.* увлажни́тель *m.*
molar /'moulər/ *n.* коренно́й зуб *m.*
molasses /mə'læsız/ *n.* па́тока *f.*
mold[1] /mould/ **1.** *n.* фо́рма *f.*; шабло́н *m.* **2.** *v.* формова́ть *impf.*, сформова́ть *pf.*; лепи́ть *impf.*
mold[2] /mould/ *n.* (*fungus*) пле́сень *f.*
Moldau /'mɔldau/ *n.* (*Czech: Vltava*) (*river*) Влта́ва *f.*
Moldavia /mɒl'deiviə/ *n.* Молда́вия, Молдо́ва *f.*
Moldavian /mɒl'deiviən/ *n.* молдава́нин *m.*, молдава́нка *f.*
molder[1] /'mouldər/ *n.* формо́вщик *m.*
molder[2] /'mouldər/ *v.* рассыпа́ться *impf.*
molding /'mouldıŋ/ **1.** *n.* (*shaping*) формо́вка *f.*; (*casting*) литьё *neut.* **2.** *adj.* формо́вочный.
moldy /'mouldi/ *adj.* заплесневе́лый.
mole[1] /moul/ *n.* (*skin blemish*) ро́динка *f.*
mole[2] /moul/ *n.* (*animal*) крот *m.*
mole catcher *n.* кротоло́в *m.*
molecular /mə'lεkyələr/ *adj.* молекуля́рный.
molecule /'mɒlə,kyul/ *n.* моле́кула *f.*
molehill /'moul,hıl/ *n.* крото́вина *f.*
mole plow *n.* крото́вый плуг *m.*
moleskin /'moul,skın/ *n.* крото́вый мех *m.*
molest /mə'lεst/ *v.* пристава́ть (к *with dat.*) *impf.*; (*bother*) беспоко́ить *impf.*
mollify /'mɒlə,fai/ *v.* смягча́ть *impf.*
mollusk /'mɒləsk/ *n.* моллю́ск *m.*
mollycoddle /'mɒli,kɒdl̩/ *v.* балова́ть, не́жить *impf.*
molt /moult/ *v.* линька *f.*
molten /'moultn̩/ *adj.* распла́вленный.
molybdenum /mə'lıbdənəm/ *n.* молибде́н *m.*
mom /mɒm/ *n.* (*colloq.*) мам *f. indecl.*

moment /'moumənt/ n. момент; миг m.
momentarily /,moumən'tɛərəli/ adv. на мгновение; (instantly) мгновенно, моментально; (immediately) немедленно.
momentary /'moumən,tɛri/ adj. минутный; мгновенный.
momentous /mou'mɛntəs/ adj. важный.
momentum /mou'mɛntəm/ n. движущая сила f.; количество движения neut.
Monaco /'mɒnə,kou, mə'nakou/ n. Монако neut.
monad /'mɒnæd/ n. монада f.
monarch /'mɒnərk/ n. монарх m.
monarchical /mə'narkɪkəl/ adj. монархический.
monarchism /'mɒnər,kɪzəm/ n. монархизм m.
monarchist /'mɒnərkɪst/ n. монархист m.
monarchy /'mɒnərki/ n. монархия f.
monastery /'mɒnə,stɛri/ n. монастырь m.
monastic /mə'næstɪk/ adj. (of monastery) монастырский; (of monks) монашеский.
monasticism /mə'næstə,sɪzəm/ n. монашество neut.
monatomic /,mɒnə'tɒmɪk/ adj. одноатомный.
Monday /'mʌndei/ n. понедельник m.
monetarism /'mɒnɪtə,rɪzəm/ n. монетаризм m.
monetary /'mɒnɪ,tɛri/ adj. монетный; денежный.
money /'mʌni/ 1. n. деньги pl. 2. adj. денежный.
moneychanger /'mʌni,tʃeindʒər/ n. меняла m. and f. (decl. f.).
moneyed /'mʌnid/ adj. богатый.
moneygrubber /'mʌni,ɡrʌbər/ n. (colloq.) стяжатель m.
moneylender /'mʌni,lɛndər/ n. ростовщик m.
moneymaker /'mʌni,meikər/ n. выгодное дело neut.
Mongol /'mɒŋɡəl/ 1. adj. монгольский. 2. n. монгол m., монголка f.
Mongolia /mɒŋ'ɡouliə/ n. Монголия f.
mongoose /'mɒŋ,ɡus/ n. мангуст m., мангуста f.
mongrel /'mʌŋɡrəl/ 1. n. (dog) дворняжка f.; (fig.) ублюдок m. 2. adj. нечистокровный, смешанный.
monism /'mɒnizəm/ n. монизм m.
monist /'mɒnist/ n. монист m.
monistic /mə'nɪstɪk/ adj. монистический.
monitor /'mɒnɪtər/ n. (school) староста (класса) m. and f. (decl. f.); (comput., TV) монитор m.
monitoring /'mɒnɪtərɪŋ/ n. мониторинг, контроль m.
monk /mʌŋk/ n. монах m.
monkey /'mʌŋki/ n. обезьяна f.
monkey jacket n. матросская куртка f.; бушлат m.
monkey puzzle n. араукария f.
monkey wrench n. разводной ключ m.; to throw a monkey wrench v. умышленно вредить impf.
monkfish /'mʌŋk,fɪʃ/ n. морской чёрт m.
monkish /'mʌŋkɪʃ/ adj. монашеский.
monkshood /'mʌŋks,hʊd/ n. монашество neut.
monobasic /,mɒnə'beisɪk/ adj. двухосновный.
monochromatic /,mɒnəkrou'mætɪk/ adj. одноцветный.
monochrome /'mɒnə,kroum/ n. монохром m.
monocle /'mɒnəkəl/ n. монокль m.
monocoque /'mɒnə,kouk/ n. монокок m.
monocular /mə'nɒkyələr/ n. монокуляр m.

monocycle /'mɒnə,saikəl/ n. моноцикл, одноколёсный велосипед m.
monodrama /'mɒnə,drɑmə, -,dræmə/ n. монодрама f.
monody /'mɒnədi/ n. монодия f.
monogamy /mə'nɒɡəmi/ n. моногамия f.
monogram /'mɒnə,ɡræm/ n. монограмма f.
monolith /'mɒnəlɪθ/ n. монолит m.
monologue /'mɒnə,lɔɡ/ n. монолог m.
monomer /'mɒnəmər/ n. мономер m.
mononucleosis /,mɒnə,nukli'ousɪs/ n. мононуклеоз m.
monophthong /'mɒnəf,θɒŋ/ n. монофтонг m.
monophysite /'mɒnɒfə,sait/ n. монофизит m.
monoplane /'mɒnə,plein/ n. моноплан m.
monopolism /mə'nɒpə,lɪzəm/ n. монополизм m.
monopolist /mə'nɒpəlɪst/ n. монополист m.
monopolistic /mə,nɒpə'lɪstɪk/ adj. монополистический.
monopolize /mə'nɒpə,laiz/ v. монополизировать impf. and pf.
monopoly /mə'nɒpəli/ n. монополия f.
monorail /'mɒnə,reil/ n. монорельс m.; монорельсовая железная дорога f.
monosyllabic /,mɒnəsɪ'læhɪk/ adj. односложный.
monosyllable /'mɒnə,sɪləbəl/ n. односложное слово neut.
monotheism /'mɒnəθi,izəm/ n. монотеизм m.
monotheist /'mɒnə,θiist/ n. монотеист m.
monotone /'mɒnə,toun/ 1. adj.: in a monotone adv. монотонно. 2. n. монотонность f.
monotonous /mə'nɒtnəs/ adj. монотонный; однообразный.
monotony /mə'nɒtni/ n. монотонность f.; однообразие neut.
monotype /'mɒnə,taip/ n. монотип m.
monoxide /mɒn'ɒksaid/ n. однооксись f.
monsieur /məs'yər/ n. мосьё m. indecl.
Monsignor /mɒn'sinyər/ n. монсеньор m.
monsoon /mɒn'sun/ n. муссон m.
monster /'mɒnstər/ n. чудовище neut.; урод m.
monstrance /'mɒnstrəns/ n. дароносица f.
monstrosity /mɒn'strɒsɪti/ n. чудовищность f.; чудовище neut.
monstrous /'mɒnstrəs/ adj. чудовищный; уродливый.
montage /mɒn'taʒ/ n. монтаж m.
Montana /mɒn'tænə/ n. Монтана f.
Mont Blanc /'mɒ̃ blɑ̃/ n. (mountain) Монблан m.
montgolfier /mɒnt'ɡolfiər/ n. монгольфьер m.
month /mʌnθ/ n. месяц m.
monthly /'mʌnθli/ 1. adj. ежемесячный. 2. adv. ежемесячно.
monument /'mɒnyəmənt/ n. памятник; монумент m.
monumental /,mɒnyə'mɛntl/ adj. монументальный.
moo /mu/ 1. n. мычанье neut. 2. v. мычать impf.
mood¹ /mud/ n. настроение neut.
mood² /mud/ n. (gram.) наклонение neut.
moody /'mudi/ adj. унылый.
moon /mun/ n. луна f.
moonbeam /'mun,bim/ n. лунный луч m.
moon-faced /'mun,feist/ adj. круглолицый.
moonless /'munlɪs/ adj. безлунный.
moonlight /'mun,lait/ n. лунный свет m.

moonrise /'mun‚raiz/ n. восхо́д луны́ m.
moon rover n. лунохо́д m.
moonscape /'mun‚skeip/ n. лу́нный ландша́фт m.
moonshine /'mun‚ʃain/ n. (moonlight) лу́нный свет m.; (illicit liquor) самого́н m.
moonstone /'mun‚stoun/ n. лу́нный ка́мень m.
moonstruck /'mun‚strʌk/ adj. поме́шанный.
Moor /mʊr/ n. (Moroccan) марокка́нец m.; (hist.) мавр m.
moor¹ /mʊr/ n. (tract of land) ве́ресковая пу́стошь f.
moor² /mʊr/ v. пришварто́вывать impf., пришвартова́ть pf.
moorhen /'mʊr‚hɛn/ n. камы́шница f.
mooring /'mʊrɪŋ/ n. прича́л m.; pl. шварто́вы pl.
Moorish /'mʊrɪʃ/ adj. маврита́нский.
moose /mus/ n. лось m.
moot point /mut/ n. спо́рный вопро́с m.
mop /mɒp/ 1. n. шва́бра f. 2. v. чи́стить шва́брой impf.
mope /moup/ v. хандри́ть impf.
moped /'mou‚pɛd/ n. мопе́д m.
moraine /mə'rein/ n. море́на f.
moral /'mɔrəl/ 1. adj. мора́льный, нра́вственный. 2. n. мора́ль; нра́вственность f.; pl. нра́вы pl.
morale /mə'ræl/ n. мора́льное состоя́ние neut.
moralist /'mɔrəlɪst/ n. морали́ст m.
moralistic /‚mɔrə'lɪstɪk/ adj. моралисти́ческий.
morality /mə'rælɪti/ n. нра́вственность f.; нравоуче́ние neut.
moralize /'mɔrə‚laiz/ v. морализи́ровать impf.
morally /'mɔrəli/ adv. мора́льно; нра́вственно.
morass /mə'ræs/ n. боло́то neut.
moratorium /‚mɔrə'tɔriəm/ n. морато́рий m.
moray /'mɔrei/ n. муре́на f.
morbid /'mɔrbɪd/ adj. боле́зненный, нездоро́вый.
morbidity /mɔr'bɪdɪti/ n. боле́зненность f.
mordant /'mɔrdnt/ n. протра́ва f.
more /mɔr/ 1. adj. бо́льше (with gen.); бо́льший. 2. n. бо́льшее коли́чество neut. 3. adv. больше, бо́лее; once more ещё раз; more or less бо́лее и́ли ме́нее.
morel /mə'rɛl/ n. (fungus) сморчо́к m.
morello /mə'rɛlou/ n. ви́шня море́ль, ви́шня ки́слая f.
moreover /mɔr'ouvər/ adv. сверх того́; кро́ме того́.
mores /'mɔreiz/ n. нра́вы pl.
morganatic /‚mɔrgə'nætɪk/ adj. морганати́ческий.
morgue /mɔrg/ n. морг m.
moribund /'mɔrə‚bʌnd/ adj. вымира́ющий.
Mormon /'mɔrmən/ 1. n. мормо́н m. 2. adj. мормо́нский.
morning /'mɔrnɪŋ/ 1. n. у́тро neut.; good morning до́брое у́тро; in the morning adv. у́тром. 2. adj. у́тренний.
Morocco /mə'rɒkou/ n. Маро́кко m.
moron /'mɔrɒn/ n. идио́т m.
moronic /mə'rɒnɪk/ adj. слабоу́мный.
morose /mə'rous/ adj. угрю́мый.
morpheme /'mɔrfim/ n. морфе́ма f.
morphine /'mɔrfin/ n. мо́рфий m.; (obs.) морфи́н m.
morphological /‚mɔrfə'lɒdʒɪkəl/ adj. морфологи́ческий.

morphology /mɔr'fɒlədʒi/ n. морфоло́гия f.
morphosis /mɔr'fousɪs/ n. морфо́з m.
Morse code /mɔrs/ n. а́збука Мо́рзе f.
morsel /'mɔrsəl/ n. кусо́чек m.
mortal /'mɔrtl̩/ adj. сме́ртный; (fatal) сме́ртельный.
mortar¹ /'mɔrtər/ n. (cement) строи́тельный раство́р m.
mortar² /'mɔrtər/ n. (weapon) миноме́т m.; (for grinding) сту́пка f.
mortarboard /'mɔrtər‚bɔrd/ n. академи́ческая ша́почка f.
mortgage /'mɔrgɪdʒ/ 1. n. ипоте́ка f.; (deed) закладна́я f. 2. v. закла́дывать impf., заложи́ть pf.
mortgagee /‚mɔrgə'dʒi/ n. кредито́р по закладно́й m.
mortgagor /'mɔrgədʒər/ n. должни́к по закладно́й; закла́дчик m.
mortification /‚mɔrtəfɪ'keiʃən/ n. (humiliation) униже́ние neut.; (of flesh) умерщвле́ние neut.
mortify /'mɔrtə‚fai/ v. (humiliate) унижа́ть impf.; (subjugate body) умерщвля́ть impf.
mortise /'mɔrtɪs/ n. паз m.
mortuary /'mɔrtʃu‚ɛri/ 1. n. морг m. 2. adj. похоро́ный.
mosaic /mou'zeiɪk/ 1. n. моза́ика f. 2. adj. мозайческий.
Mosaic /mou'zeiɪk/ adj. моисе́ев.
Moscow /'mɒskou/ n. Москва́ f.
Moses /'mouzɪz/ n. Моисе́й m.
mosque /mɒsk/ n. мече́ть f.
mosquito /mə'skitou/ n. кома́р m.
moss /mɒs/ n. мох m.
mossy /'mɔsi/ adj. мши́стый.
most /moust/ 1. adj. наибо́льший. 2. n. наибо́льшее коли́чество neut. 3. adv. бо́льше всего́; at (the) most са́мое бо́льшее; for the most part бо́льшей ча́стью.
mostly /'moustli/ adv. бо́льшей ча́стью; в основно́м, гла́вным о́бразом.
mote /mout/ n. пыли́нка f.
motel /mou'tɛl/ n. моте́ль m.
motet /mou'tɛt/ n. моте́т m.
moth /mɔθ/ n. моль f.
mother /'mʌðər/ 1. n. мать, ма́ма; ма́тушка f. 2. adj. мате́ринский; (native) родно́й.
motherhood /'mʌðər‚hʊd/ n. мате́ринство neut.
mothering /'mʌðərɪŋ/ n. мате́ринская ла́ска f.
mother-in-law /'mʌðər ɪn ‚lɔ/ n. (wife's mother) тёща f., (husband's mother) свекро́вь f.
motherless /'mʌðərlɪs/ adj. лишённый ма́тери; осироте́лый.
motherly /'mʌðərli/ adj. мате́ринский.
mother-of-pearl /'mʌðər əv 'pɜrl/ 1. n. перламу́тр m. 2. adj. перламу́тровый.
motherwort /'mʌðər‚wɜrt/ n. пусты́нник m.
motif /mou'tif/ n. моти́в; лейтмоти́в m.
motile /'moutl̩/ adj. (biol.) подви́жный.
motion /'mouʃən/ 1. n. движе́ние neut.; (gesture) жест m. 2. v. пока́зывать жёстом impf.
motionless /'mouʃənlɪs/ adj. неподви́жный.
motion picture n. кинокарти́на f., кино́ neut. indecl., фильм m.
motivate /'moutə‚veit/ v. побужда́ть impf.
motivation /‚moutə'veiʃən/ n. побужде́ние neut.
motive /'moutɪv/ n. моти́в m.; побужде́ние neut.

motiveless /'moutɪvlɪs/ *adj.* немотиви́рованный.
motley /'mɒtli/ *adj.* пёстрый.
motor /'moutər/ *n.* мото́р; дви́гатель *m.*
motorbike /'moutər,baik/ *n.* мопе́д *m.*
motorboat /'moutər,bout/ *n.* мото́рная ло́дка, *f.* мото́рный ка́тер *m.*
motorbus /'moutər,bʌs/ *n.* авто́бус *m.*
motorcade /'moutər,keid/ *n.* корте́ж автомоби́лей *m.*
motorcycle /'moutər,saikəl/ *n.* мотоци́кл *m.*
motorcyclist /'moutər,saiklɪst/ *n.* мотоцикли́ст *m.*
motor-driven /'moutər ,drɪvən/ *adj.* мото́рный.
motoring /'moutərɪŋ/ *n.* автомобили́зм *m.*
motorist /'moutərɪst/ *n.* автомобили́ст *m.*
motorized /'moutə,raizd/ *adj.* моторизо́ванный.
motorman /'moutərmən/ *n.* (*train*) машини́ст *m.*; (*trolley car*) вагоновожа́тый *m.*
motorship /'moutər,ʃɪp/ *n.* теплохо́д *m.*
motor sleigh *n.* мотоса́ни *pl.*
mottle /'mɒtl̩/ *n.* кра́пинка *f.*
mottled /'mɒtld/ *adj.* пёстрый; кра́пчатый.
motto /'mɒtou/ *n.* деви́з *m.*
mound /maund/ *n.* холм *m.*; (*artificial elevation*) на́сыпь *f.*
mount /maunt/ **1.** *n.* гора́ *f.* **2.** *v.t.* поднима́ться (на *with acc.*) *impf.*; (*jewel*) вставля́ть *impf.*, вста́вить *pf.*; (*horse*) сади́ться на ло́шадь *impf.*
mountain /'mauntn̩/ **1.** *n.* гора́ *f.* **2.** *adj.* го́рный.
mountaineer /,mauntn̩'ɪər/ *n.* го́рец *m.*, горя́нка *f.*; (*climber*) альпини́ст *m.*, альпини́стка *f.*
mountaineering /,mauntn̩'ɪərɪŋ/ *n.* альпини́зм *m.*
mountainous /'mauntn̩əs/ *adj.* гори́стый.
mountain range *n.* хребе́т *m.*
mountebank /'mauntə,bæŋk/ *n.* шут; шарлата́н *m.*
mounted /'mauntɪd/ *adj.* (*on horseback*) ко́нный.
mounting /'mauntɪŋ/ *n.* устано́вка *f.*; монта́ж *m.*
mourn /mɔrn/ *v.* опла́кивать *impf.*; скорбе́ть (о *with prep.*) *impf.*
mournful /'mɔrnfəl/ *adj.* ско́рбный; печа́льный.
mourning /'mɔrnɪŋ/ *n.* тра́ур *m.*
mouse /maus/ *n.* мышь *f.*
mouse-colored /'maus ,kʌlərd/ *adj.* мыша́стый.
mouse hole *n.* мыши́ная но́рка *f.*
mouser /'mauzər/ *n.* мышело́в *m.*
mousetrap /'maus,træp/ *n.* мышело́вка *f.*
mousse /mus/ *n.* мусс *m.*
mousy /'mausi/ *adj.* мыши́ный; (*quiet*) ти́хий.
mouth /mauθ/ *n.* рот *m.*; (*of river*) у́стье *neut.*
mouthful /'mauθ,fʊl/ *n.* глото́к *m.*
mouth organ *n.* губна́я гармо́ника *f.*
mouthpiece /'mauθ,pis/ *n.* (*pipe, cigarette, instrument*) мундшту́к *m.*
mouthwash /'mauθ,wɔʃ/ *n.* полоска́тель *m.*
mouth-watering /'mauθ ,wɔtərɪŋ/ *adj.* аппети́тный.
movable /'muvəbəl/ *adj.* подвижно́й; перено́сный; порта́тивный; (*property*) дви́жимый.
move /muv/ **1.** *n.* ход *m.*; (*change of residence*) перее́зд *m.* **2.** *v.t.* дви́гать *impf.*, дви́нуть *pf.*; *v.i.* дви́гаться *impf.*, дви́нуться *pf.*; (*change of residence*) переезжа́ть *impf.*, перее́хать *pf.*
movement /'muvmənt/ *n.* движе́ние *neut.*; (*mus.*) часть *f.*
mover /'muvər/ *n.* инициа́тор, дви́гатель *m.*

movie /'muvi/ *n.* (*film*) фильм *m.*; *pl.* кино́ *neut. indecl.*
movie film *n.* киноплёнка *f.*
movie projector *n.* кинопрое́ктор *m.*
moving /'muvɪŋ/ *adj.* дви́жущийся; (*fig.*) тро́гательный.
mow /mou/ *v.* коси́ть *impf.*, скоси́ть *pf.*
mower /'mouər/ *n.* (*person*) косе́ц *m.*; (*machine*) коси́лка *f.*
mowing /'mouɪŋ/ *n.* косьба́ *f.*
Mozambique /,mouzæm'bik/ *n.* Мозамби́к *m.*
Mozhaysk /mə'ʒaɪsk/ *n.* Можа́йск *m.*
Mr. /'mɪstər/ *n.* (*abbr.*) ми́стер; господи́н *m.*
Mrs. /'mɪsɪz/ *n.* (*abbr.*) ми́ссис; госпожа́ *f.*
much /mʌtʃ/ **1.** *n.*, *adj.* мно́го (*with gen.*). **2.** *adv.* о́чень; гора́здо; **how much** ско́лько; **so much** сто́лько; **as much... as...** сто́лько... ско́лько...
mucilage /'myusəlɪdʒ/ *n.* расти́тельный клей *m.*
muck /mʌk/ *n.* грязь *f.*; (*manure*) наво́з *m.*
mucky /'mʌki/ *adj.* мёрзкий.
mucous /'myukəs/ *adj.* сли́зистый.
mucus /'myukəs/ *n.* слизь *f.*
mud /mʌd/ **1.** *n.* грязь *f.* **2.** *adj.* грязево́й.
mud bath *n.* грязева́я ва́нна *f.*
muddiness /'mʌdinɪs/ *n.* му́тность *f.*
muddle /'mʌdl̩/ **1.** *n.* пу́таница; бестолко́вщина *f.* **2.** *v.* сме́шивать, пу́тать *impf.*
muddleheaded /'mʌdl̩,hedɪd/ *adj.* бестолко́вый.
muddy /'mʌdi/ *adj.* грязный; му́тный.
mudfish /'mʌd,fɪʃ/ *n.* до́нная ры́ба *f.*
mud flat *n.* то́пкое ме́сто *neut.*; (*river, coast*) и́листая о́тмель *f.*
mudpack /'mʌd,pæk/ *n.* космети́ческая ма́ска *f.*
mudslinging /'mʌd,slɪŋɪŋ/ *n.* клевета́ *f.*
muezzin /myu'ɛzɪn/ *n.* муэдзи́н *m.*
muff /mʌf/ *n.* му́фта *f.*
muffin /'mʌfɪn/ *n.* сдо́ба *f.*
muffle /'mʌfəl/ *v.* (*wrap up*) заку́тывать *impf.*; (*sound*) глуши́ть *impf.*
muffler /'mʌflər/ *n.* (*scarf*) кашне́ *neut. indecl.*; шарф *m.*; (*auto*) глуши́тель *m.*
mufti /'mʌfti/ *n.* (*Muslim jurist*) му́фтий *m.*
mug /mʌg/ *n.* кру́жка *f.*; (*slang*) (*face*) мо́рда *f.*
mugger /'mʌgər/ *n.* у́личный граби́тель *m.*
mugging /'mʌgɪŋ/ *n.* грабёж на у́лице *m.*
muggy /'mʌgi/ *adj.* ду́шный.
Muhammad /mu'hæməd, -'haməd/ *n.* Магоме́т *m.*
mulatto /mə'lætou/ *n.* мула́т *m.*, мула́тка *f.*
mulberry /'mʌl,bɛri, -bəri/ *n.* (*tree*) ту́товое де́рево *neut.*; шелкови́ца *f.*
mulch /mʌltʃ/ *n.* му́льча *f.*
mulct /mʌlkt/ *n.* штраф *m.*
mule /myul/ *n.* мул *m.*
muleteer /,myulə'tɪər/ *n.* пого́нщик му́лов *m.*
mulish /'myulɪʃ/ *adj.* упря́мый (как осёл).
mulishness /'myulɪʃnɪs/ *n.* упря́мство *neut.*
mull /mʌl/ *v.* подогрева́ть (вино́) *impf.*
mullah /'mʌlə/ *n.* мулла́ *m.*
mullet /'mʌlɪt/ *n.* (*fish*) кефа́ль *f.*
multibarrelled /,mʌlti'bærəld/ *adj.* многоство́льный.
multicellular /,mʌlti'sɛlyələr/ *adj.* многокле́точный.
multichannel /,mʌltɪ,tʃænəl/ *adj.* многокана́льный.

multicolored /'mʌltɪ,kʌlər/ *adj.* многоцветный.

multidimensional /,mʌltɪdɪ'mɛnʃənḷ/ *adj.* многомерный.

multidirectional /,mʌltidɪ'rɛkʃənḷ/ *adj.* многонаправленный.

multiengined /'mʌlti,ɛndʒɪnd/ *adj.* многомоторный.

multifaceted /,mʌlti'fæsɪtɪd/ *adj.* многогранный; многосторонний.

multifarious /,mʌltə'fɛəriəs/ *adj.* разнообразный.

multilateral /,mʌltɪ'lætərəl/ *adj.* многосторонний.

multilayered /,mʌlti'leiərd/ *adj.* многослойный.

multilingual /,mʌlti'lɪŋgwəl/ *adj.* многоязычный.

multimillionaire /,mʌlti,mɪlyə'nɛər/ *n.* мультимиллионер *m.*

multinational /,mʌlti'næʃənḷ/ *adj.* многонациональный.

multiphase /'mʌltɪ,feiz/ *adj.* многофазный.

multiple /'mʌltəpəl/ *adj.* многократный; сложный; (*numerous*) многочисленный.

multiplex /'mʌltə,plɛks/ *adj.* мультиплексный.

multiplexer /'mʌltə,plɛksər/ *n.* мультиплексор *m.*

multiplexing /'mʌltə,plɛksɪŋ/ *n.* мультиплексирование *neut.*

multiplicand /,mʌltəplɪ'kænd/ *n.* множимое *neut.*

multiplication /,mʌltəplɪ'keiʃən/ *n.* умножение *neut.*

multiplicity /,mʌltə'plɪsɪti/ *n.* множество *neut.*; (*variety*) многообразие *neut.*; (*great number*) многочисленность *f.*

multiplier /'mʌltə,plaiər/ *n.* множитель *m.*

multiply /'mʌltə,plai/ *v.t.* множить; умножать *impf.*; *v.i.* увеличиваться *impf.*, увеличиться *pf.*; размножаться *impf.*, размножиться *pf.*

multipurpose /,mʌlti'pɜrpəs/ *adj.* универсальный; многоцелевой.

multiracial /,mʌlti'reiʃəl/ *adj.* многорасовый.

multirole /,mʌlti'roul/ *adj.* многоцелевой.

multistage /'mʌltɪ,steidʒ/ *adj.* (*rocket*) многоступенчатый.

multistoried /'mʌlti'stɔrid/ *adj.* многоэтажный.

multitude /'mʌltɪ,tud/ *n.* множество *neut.*

multitudinous /,mʌltɪ'tudṇəs/ *adj.* многочисленный.

multivalent /,mʌltɪ'veilənt/ *adj.* многовалентный.

mum /mʌm/ *adj.*: **to keep mum** помалкивать *impf.*

mumble /'mʌmbəl/ **1.** *n.* бормотание *neut.* **2.** *v.* бормотать *impf.*

mumbo jumbo /'mʌmbou 'dʒʌmbou/ *n.* тарабарщина *f.*

mummification /,mʌməfɪ'keiʃən/ *n.* мумификация *f.*

mummify /'mʌmə,fai/ *v.* мумифицировать *impf.* and *pf.*

mummy /'mʌmi/ *n.* (*embalmed body*) мумия *f.*

mumps /mʌmps/ *n.* свинка *f.*

munch /mʌntʃ/ *v.* жевать *impf.*; (*noisily*) чавкать *impf.*

mundane /mʌn'dein/ *adj.* земной; мирской; светский.

Munich /'myunɪk/ *n.* Мюнхен *m.*

municipal /myu'nɪsəpəl/ *adj.* городской; муниципальный.

municipality /myu,nɪsə'pælɪti/ *n.* муниципалитет *m.*

munificence /myu'nɪfəsəns/ *n.* щедрость *f.*

munificent /myu'nɪfəsənt/ *adj.* щедрый.

munitions /myu'nɪʃənz/ *n.* военное имущество *neut.*

muon /'myuɒn/ *n.* мю-мезон *m.*

mural /'myurəl/ **1.** *adj.* стенной. **2.** *n.* стенная роспись *f.*

murder /'mɜrdər/ **1.** *n.* убийство *neut.* **2.** *v.* убивать *impf.*, убить *pf.*

murderer /'mɜrdərər/ *also* **murderess** /'mɜrdərɪs/ *n.* убийца *m.* and *f.* (*decl. f.*)

murderous /'mɜrdərəs/ *adj.* убийственный.

murk /mɜrk/ *n.* темнота *f.*; мрак *m.*

murky /'mɜrki/ *adj.* мрачный.

Murmansk /mʊr'mɑnsk/ *n.* Мурманск *m.*

murmur /'mɜrmər/ **1.** *n.* (*water*) журчание *neut.*; (*voices*) шёпот *m.* **2.** *v.* журчать; шептать *impf.*; (*discontentedly*) роптать *impf.*

muscatel /,mʌskə'tɛl/ *n.* (*wine*) мускат *m.*

muscle /'mʌsəl/ *n.* мышца *f.*; мускул *m.*

Muscovite /'mʌskə,vait/ *n.* москвич *m.*, москвичка *f.*

Muscovy /'mʌskəvi/ *n.* Московия *f.*

muscular /'mʌskyələr/ *adj.* мускульный; (*person*) мускулистый.

musculature /'mʌskyələtʃər/ *n.* мускулатура *f.*

muse[1] /myuz/ *v.* размышлять; задумываться *impf.*

muse[2] /myuz/ *n.* муза *f.*

museum /myu'ziəm/ *n.* музей *m.*

mush /mʌʃ/ *n.* (*pulp*) кашица *f.*

mushroom /'mʌʃrum/ *n.* гриб *m.*

mushy /'mʌʃi/ *adj.* (*soft*) мягкий; (*colloq.*) (*sentimental*) слащавый.

music /'myuzɪk/ **1.** *n.* музыка *f.* **2.** *adj.* музыкальный.

musical /'myuzɪkəl/ **1.** *adj.* музыкальный. **2.** *n.* музыкальная комедия *f.*

musicality /,myuzɪ'kælɪti/ *n.* музыкальность *f.*

music hall *n.* мюзик-холл *m.*

musician /myu'zɪʃən/ *n.* музыкант *m.*

musicology /,myuzɪ'kɒlədʒi/ *n.* музыковедение *neut.*

music paper *n.* нотная бумага *f.*

music stand *n.* нотный пюпитр *m.*

musing /'myuzɪŋ/ *n.* задумчивость *f.*

musingly /'myuzɪŋli/ *adv.* задумчиво.

musk /mʌsk/ *n.* мускус *m.*

muskeg /'mʌskɛg/ *n.* сфагновое болото *neut.*

musket /'mʌskɪt/ *n.* мушкет *m.*

musketeer /,mʌskɪ'tɪər/ *n.* мушкетёр *m.*

musk ox *n.* овцебык *m.*

muskrat /'mʌsk,ræt/ *n.* ондатра *f.*

musky /'mʌski/ *adj.* мускусный.

Muslim /'mʌzlɪm, 'mʊz-/ **1.** *n.* мусульманин *m.*, мусульманка *f.* **2.** *adj.* мусульманский.

muslin /'mʌzlɪn/ **1.** *n.* муслин *m.* **2.** *adj.* муслиновый.

muss /mʌs/ *v.* (*hair*) растрепать *pf.*; (*clothes*) помять *pf.*

mussel /'mʌsəl/ *n.* (*cul.*) мидия *f.*

must[1] /mʌst/ *n.* (*unfermented wine*) молодое вино *neut.*

must[2] /mʌst/ *v.* должен (*with inf.*) *m.*, должна *f.*, должно *neut.*, должны *pl.*; надо (*impers. with* *dat. and inf.*); (*negation*) нельзя (*impers. with dat. and inf.*).

mustache /'mʌstæʃ/ *n.* усы́ *pl.*

mustached /'mʌstæʃt/ *adj.* уса́тый.

mustang /'mʌstæŋ/ *n.* муста́нг *m.*

mustard /'mʌstərd/ *n.* горчи́ца *f.*

muster /'mʌstər/ *n.* сбор; смотр *m.*

mustiness /'mʌstinɪs/ *n.* за́тхлость *f.*

musty /'mʌsti/ *adj.* за́тхлый.

mutability /ˌmyutə'bɪlɪti/ *n.* переме́нчивость *f.*

mutable /'myutəbəl/ *adj.* изме́нчивый; переме́нчивый.

mutagen /'myutədʒən/ *n.* мутаге́н *m.*

mutagenous /myu'tædʒənəs/ *cf adj.* мутаге́нный.

mutant /'myutnt/ *n.* мута́нт *m.*

mutate /'myuteit/ *v.* видоизменя́ть(ся) *impf.*

mutation /myu'teiʃən/ *n.* измене́ние *neut.*; (*biol.*) мута́ция *f.*; (*ling.*) перегласо́вка *f.*

mutative /'myutətɪv/ *adj.* мутацио́нный.

mute /myut/ **1.** *adj.* немо́й. **2.** *n.* немо́й *m.*

mutely /'myutli/ *adv.* безмо́лвно.

muteness /'myutnɪs/ *n.* немота́ *f.*

mutilate /'myutlˌeit/ *v.* уве́чить; кале́чить *impf.*; (*fig.*) искажа́ть *impf.*

mutilation /ˌmyutl'eiʃən/ *n.* уве́чье *neut.*, (*fig.*) искаже́ние *neut.*

mutineer /ˌmyutn'ɪər/ *n.* мяте́жник; бунтовщи́к *m.*

mutinous /'myutɪnəs/ *adj.* мяте́жный.

mutiny /'myutni/ **1.** *n.* мяте́ж; бунт *m.* **2.** *v.* подня́ть мяте́ж; бунтова́ть *impf.*

mutter /'mʌtər/ *v.* бормота́ть *impf.*

muttering /'mʌtərɪŋ/ *n.* бормота́ние *neut.*

mutton /'mʌtn̩/ **1.** *n.* бара́нина *f.* **2.** *adj.* бара́ний.

muttonhead /'mʌtn̩ˌhɛd/ *n.* (*colloq.*) болва́н *m.*

mutual /'myutʃuəl/ *adj.* взаи́мный, (*common*) о́бщий.

muzzle /'mʌzəl/ **1.** *n.* (*on animal*) намо́рдник *m.* **2.** *v.* (*impose silence*) заста́вить молча́ть *pf.*

my /mai/ *pron.* мой *m.*, моя́ *f.*, моё *neut.*, мой *pl.*

Myanmar /myɑn'mɑr/ *n.* (*formerly: Burma*) Мьян-Ма́р *m.*

mycologist /mai'kɒlədʒɪst/ *n.* мико́лог *m.*

mycology /mai'kɒlədʒi/ *n.* миколо́гия *f.*

mycosis /mai'kousɪs/ *n.* мико́з *m.*

myelitis /ˌmaiə'laitɪs/ *n.* миели́т *m.*

myocarditis /ˌmaioukɑr'daitɪs/ *n.* миокарди́т *m.*

myopia /mai'oupiə/ *n.* мио́пия, близору́кость *f.*

myopic /mai'ɒpɪk/ *adj.* миопи́ческий, близору́кий.

myriad /'mɪriəd/ **1.** *n.* мириа́ды *pl.* **2.** *adj.* бесчи́сленный.

myrmidon /'mɜrmɪˌdɒn/ *n.* (*pej.*) приспе́шник; прислу́жник *m.*

myrrh /mɜr/ *n.* ми́рра *f.*

myrtle /'mɜrtl̩/ **1.** *n.* мирт *m.* **2.** *adj.* ми́ртовый.

myself /mai'sɛlf/ *pron.* сам *m.*, сама́ *f.*, само́ *neut.*; (*refl.*) себя́; **I myself** я сам *m.*, я сама́ *f.*

mysterious /mɪ'stɪəriəs/ *adj.* тайнственный.

mysteriously /mɪ'stɪəriəsli/ *adv.* тайнственно.

mystery /'mɪstəri/ *n.* та́инство *neut.*, тайна *f.*

mystic /'mɪstɪk/ **1.** *adj.* мисти́ческий. **2.** *n.* ми́стик *m.*

mysticism /'mɪstəˌsizəm/ *n.* мистици́зм *m.*, ми́стика *f.*

mystification /ˌmɪstəfɪ'keiʃən/ *n.* мистифика́ция *f.*

mystify /'mɪstəˌfai/ *v.* озада́чивать *impf.*; мистифици́ровать *impf. and pf.*

mystique /mɪ'stik/ *n.* ми́стика *f.*

myth /mɪθ/ *n.* миф *m.*

mythical /'mɪθɪkəl/ *adj.* мифи́ческий.

mythological /ˌmɪθə'lɒdʒɪkəl/ *adj.* мифологи́ческий.

mythologist /mɪ'θɒlədʒɪst/ *n.* мифо́лог *m.*

mythologize /mɪ'θɒləˌdʒaiz/ *v.* мифологизи́ровать *impf.*

mythology /mɪ'θɒlədʒi/ *n.* мифоло́гия *f.*

myxedema /ˌmɪksɪ'dimə/ *n.* микседе́ма *f.*

myxomatosis /ˌmɪksəmə'tousɪs/ *n.* миксомато́з *m.*

N

nacre /'neikər/ *n.* перламу́тр *m.*

nadir /'neidər/ *n.* (*astr.*) нади́р *m.*; (*low point*) са́мый ни́зкий у́ровень *m.*

nagging /'nægɪŋ/ *adj.* (*grumbling*) ворчли́вый, надоéдливый; (*pain*) но́ющий.

Nagorno-Karabakh /nə'gɔrnou kɑrə'bɑk/ *n.* Наго́рный-Караба́х *m.*

nail /neil/ **1.** *n.* гвоздь *m.*; (*of finger or toe*) но́готь *m.* **2.** *v.* прибива́ть *impf.*, приби́ть *pf.*

nail file *n.* пи́лка для ногте́й *f.*

Nairobi /nai'roubi/ *n.* Найро́би *m.*

naive /nɑ'iv/ *adj.* наи́вный.

naked /'neikɪd/ *adj.* го́лый; наго́й.

nakedness /'neikɪdnɪs/ *n.* нагота́ *f.*

name /neim/ **1.** *n.* (*first*) и́мя *neut.*; (*last name*) фами́лия *f.*; (*appellation*) назва́ние *neut.*; **in the name of** во и́мя (*with gen.*). **2.** *v.* называ́ть *impf.*, назва́ть *pf.*; назнача́ть *impf.*, назна́чить *pf.*

name day *n.* имени́ны *pl.*

nameless /'neimlɪs/ *adj.* без назва́ния; безымя́нный.

namely /'neimli/ *adv.* а и́менно.

namesake /'neim,seik/ *n.* (*same first name*) тёзка *m.* and *f.* (*decl. f.*); (*same last name*) однофами́лец *m.*

nanny /'næni/ *n.* ня́ня *f.*

nanny goat *n.* коза́ *f.*

nap[1] /næp/ *n.* коро́ткий сон *m.*; **to take a nap** вздремну́ть *pf.*

nap[2] *n.* (*textile*) ворс; начёс *m.*; (*fuzz*) пушо́к *m.*

nape /neip/ *n.* заги́вок *m.*

naphtha /'næfθə, 'næp-/ *n.* кероси́н *m.*

napkin /'næpkɪn/ *n.* салфéтка *f.*

Naples /'neipəlz/ *n.* Неáполь *m.*

narcissism /'nɑrsə,sɪzem/ *n.* самолюбова́ние *neut.*

narcissistic /,nɑrsə'sɪstɪk/ *adj.* самовлюблённый.

narcissus /nɑr'sɪsəs/ *n.* нарци́сс *m.*

narcotic /nɑr'kɒtɪk/ **1.** *adj.* наркоти́ческий. **2.** *n.* нарко́тик *m.*

narrate /'næreit/ *v.* расска́зывать *impf.*, рассказа́ть *pf.*

narration /næ'reiʃən/ *n.* повествова́ние *neut.*; коммента́рий *m.*

narrative /'nærətɪv/ **1.** *adj.* повествова́тельный. **2.** *n.* расска́з *m.*; по́весть *f.*

narrator /'næreitər/ *n.* расска́зчик *m.*

narrow /'nærou/ **1.** *adj.* у́зкий; тéсный. **2.** *v.* су́живать(ся) *impf.*

narrow-gauge /'nærou ,geidʒ/ *adj.* (*railroad*) узкоколéйный.

narrowing /'nærouɪŋ/ *n.* суже́ние *neut.*

narrow-minded /'nærou 'maindɪd/ *adj.* ограни́ченный; у́зкий.

narrowness /'nærounɪs/ *n.* у́зость *f.*

nasal /'neizəl/ **1.** *adj.* носово́й. **2.** *n.* (*phon.*) носово́й звук *m.*

nasally /'neizəli/ *adv.* че́рез нос.

nasty /'næsti/ *adj.* скве́рный; га́дкий.

nation /'neiʃən/ *n.* страна́; на́ция *f.*; (*people*) наро́д *m.*

national /'næʃənl/ *adj.* наро́дный, национа́льный; госуда́рственный.

nationalism /'næʃənl,ɪzəm/ *n.* национали́зм *m.*

nationality /,næʃə'nælɪti/ *n.* наро́дность, национа́льность *f.*

nationalization /,næʃənlə'zeiʃən/ *n.* национализа́ция *f.*

nationalize /'næʃənl,aiz/ *v.* национализи́ровать *impf.* and *pf.*

nationwide /'neiʃən'waid/ *adj.* общенаро́дный; всенаро́дный.

native /'neitɪv/ **1.** *adj.* родно́й; тузе́мный. **2.** *n.* уроже́нец; тузе́мец *m.*

Nativity /nei'tɪvɪti/ *n.* Рождество́ Христо́во *neut.*

NATO /'neitou/ **1.** *n.* НАТО *m. indecl.* **2.** *adj.* на́товский.

natural /'nætʃərəl/ *adj.* есте́ственный; приро́дный; натура́льный.

naturalize /'nætʃərə,laiz/ **1.** *v.* натурализова́ть *impf.* and *pf.* **2. to be naturalized** натурализова́ться *impf.* and *pf.*

naturally /'nætʃərəli/ *adv.* (*of course*) коне́чно; разумéется; (*by nature*) есте́ственно; по приро́де.

nature /'neitʃər/ *n.* приро́да; нату́ра *f.*

naught /nɔt/ *n.* ничто́; (*zero*) нуль *m.*

naughty /'nɔti/ *adj.* непослу́шный.

nausea /'nɔziə/ *n.* тошнота́ *f.*

nauseous /'nɔʃəs/ *adj.* тошнотво́рный; **I feel nauseous** меня́ тошни́т.

nautical /'nɔtɪkəl/ *adj.* морско́й; мореходный.

naval /'neivəl/ *adj.* военно-морско́й; флóтский.

nave /neiv/ *n.* (*archit.*) неф *m.*

navel /'neivəl/ *n.* пуп, пупо́к *m.*

navigable /'nævɪgəbəl/ *adj.* судохо́дный.

navigate /'nævɪ,geit/ *v.* управля́ть су́дном *impf.*

navigation /,nævɪ'geiʃən/ *n.* навига́ция *f.*

navigator /'nævɪ,geitər/ *n.* морепла́ватель *m.*; шту́рман *m.*

navy /'neivi/ *n.* военно-морско́й флот *m.*

navy-blue /'neivi 'blu/ *adj.* тёмно-си́ний.

Nazi /'nɑtsi/ **1.** *n.* наци́ст *m.* **2.** *adj.* наци́стский.

near /nɪər/ **1.** *adj.* бли́зкий; недалёкий. **2.** *adv.* бли́зко, недалеко́. **3.** *prep.* у, о́коло (*with gen.*); недалеко́ (от *with gen.*).

nearby /'nɪər'bai/ *adv.* бли́зко, недалеко́; ря́дом.

nearly /'nɪərli/ *adv.* почти́; чуть ли не.

nearsighted /'nɪər,saitɪd/ *adj.* близору́кий.

neat /nit/ *adj.* опря́тный; аккура́тный; (*drink*) неразба́вленный.

neatness /,nitnɪs/ *n.* опря́тность; аккура́тность *f.*

Nebraska /nə'bræskə/ *n.* Небра́ска *f.*

nebulous /'nɛbyələs/ *adj.* нея́сный; тума́нный.

necessarily /,nɛsə'sɛrəli/ *adv.* необходи́мо.

necessary /'nɛsə,sɛri/ *adj.* необходи́мый; ну́жный.

necessitate /nə'sɛsɪ,teit/ *v.* де́лать необходи́мым *impf.*; (*demand*) тре́бовать *impf.*

necessity /nə'sɛsɪti/ *n.* необходи́мость *f.*

neck /nɛk/ *n.* ше́я *f.*

neckerchief /'nɛkərtʃɪf/ *n.* ше́йный плато́к *m.*

necklace /'nɛklɪs/ *n.* ожере́лье *neut.*

neckline /'nɛk,laɪn/ *n.* вы́рез *m.*
necktie /'nɛk,taɪ/ *n.* га́лстук *m.*
necromancy /'nɛkrə,mænsi/ *n.* некрома́нтия *f.*; колдовство́ *neut.*; чёрная ма́гия *f.*
necropolis /nə'krɒpəlɪs/ *n.* кла́дбище *neut.*
nectar /'nɛktər/ *n.* некта́р *m.*
née /nei/ *adj.* урождённая.
need /nid/ **1.** *n.* нужда́; на́добность *f.* **2.** *v.* нужда́ться (в *with prep.*) *impf.*
needed /'nidɪd/ *adj.* ну́жный, необходи́мый.
needle /'nidḷ/ *n.* игла́, иго́лка *f.*; (*of instrument*) стре́лка *f.*
needless /'nidlɪs/ *adj.* нену́жный; бесполе́зный.
needy /'nidi/ *adj.* нужда́ющийся; бе́дный.
negate /nɪ'geit/ *v.* отрица́ть *impf.*
negation /nɪ'geiʃən/ *n.* отрица́ние *neut.*
negative /'nɛgətɪv/ **1.** *adj.* отрица́тельный. **2.** *n.* (*negation*) отрица́ние *neut.*; (*photog.*) негати́в *m.*
neglect /nɪ'glɛkt/ **1.** *n.* пренебреже́ние *neut.* **2.** *v.* пренебрега́ть *impf.*
neglectful /nɪ'glɛktfəl/ *adj.* небре́жный; невнима́тельный (к *with dat.*).
negligee /,nɛglɪ'ʒei/ *n.* неглиже́ *neut. indecl.*
negligence /'nɛglɪdʒəns/ *n.* небре́жность *f.*
negligent /'nɛglɪdʒənt/ *adj.* небре́жный.
negligible /'nɛglɪdʒəbəl/ *adj.* незначи́тельный.
negotiate /nɪ'gouʃi,eit/ *v.* вести́ перегово́ры *impf.*; (*arrange*) заключа́ть *impf.*
negotiation /nɪ,gouʃi'eiʃən/ *n.* перегово́ры *pl.*
Negro /'nigrou/ **1.** *n.* негр *m.*, негритя́нка *f.* **2.** *adj.* негритя́нский.
neighbor /'neibər/ *n.* сосе́д *m.*, сосе́дка *f.*
neighborhood /'neibər,hud/ *n.* сосе́дство *neut.*; райо́н *m.*
neighboring /'neibərɪŋ/ *adj.* сосе́дний.
neighborly /'neibərli/ *adj.* доброссосе́дский.
neither /'niðər, 'nai-/ **1.** *adj.* ни тот, ни друго́й. **2.** *pron.* ни оди́н, никто́, никако́й (из *with gen.*). **3.** *adv.* та́кже не; **neither... nor** ни... ни.
Neman /'nɛmən/ *n.* Не́ман (*also:* Ня́мунас) *m.*
neoclassic /,niou'klæsɪk/ *adj.* неокласси́ческий.
neogrammarian /,niougrə'mɛəriən/ *n.* младограмма́тик, неограмма́тик *m.*
neologism /ni'ɒlə,dʒɪzəm/ *n.* неологи́зм *m.*
neon /'nɪɒn/ *n.* нео́н *m.*; **neon light** *n.* нео́новый свет *m.*
neophyte /'niə,fait/ *n.* неофи́т *m.*
neoplasm /'niə,plæzəm/ *n.* неопла́зма *f.*
Neoplatonism /,niou'pleitṇ,izəm/ *n.* неоплатони́зм *m.*
Nepal /nə'pɔl, -'pɑl/ *n.* Непа́л *m.*
nephew /'nɛfyu/ *m.* племя́нник *m.*
nephrite /'nɛfrait/ *n.* нефри́т *m.*
nephritic /nə'frɪtɪk/ *adj.* нефри́товый.
nephritis /nə'fraitɪs/ *n.* нефри́т *m.*, воспале́ние по́чек *neut.*
nepotic /nə'pɒtɪk/ *adj.* кумовско́й.
nepotism /'nɛpə,tɪzəm/ *n.* кумовство́ *neut.*
Neptune /'nɛptun/ *n.* Непту́н *m.*
neptunium /nɛp'tuniəm/ *n.* непту́ний *m.*
nereid /'nɪəriid/ *n.* нереи́да *f.*
Nero /'nɪərou/ *n.* Неро́н *m.*
nerve /nɜrv/ **1.** *n.* нерв *m.*; (*colloq.*) (*impudence*) наха́льство *neut.* **2.** *adj.* не́рвный.
nerve cell *n.* не́рвная кле́тка *f.*

nerve center *n.* не́рвный центр *m.*
nerve ending *n.* не́рвное оконча́ние *neut.*
nerve-racking /'nɜrv ,rækɪŋ/ *adj.* де́йствующий на не́рвы; мучи́тельный.
nervine /'nɜrvin/ *n.* сре́дство, успока́ивающее не́рвы *neut.*
nervo-muscular /,nɜrvou mʌ skyə lər/ *adj.* не́рвно-мы́шечный.
nervous /'nɜrvəs/ *adj.* не́рвный; **to be nervous** *v.* не́рвничать *impf.*
nervousness /'nɜrvəsnɪs/ *n.* не́рвность *f.*; не́рвное состоя́ние *neut.*
nescience /'nɛʃəns/ *n.* неве́дение *neut.*
nest /nɛst/ *n.* гнездо́ *neut.*
nest egg *n.* сбереже́ния *pl.*
nestle /'nɛsəl/ *v.* приюти́ться *pf.*
nestling /'nɛstlɪŋ/ *n.* птене́ц, птéнчик *m.*
Nestorian /nɛ'stɔriən/ *adj.* несториа́нский.
Nestorianism /nɛ'stɔriə,nɪzəm/ *n.* несториа́нство *neut.*
net¹ /nɛt/ **1.** *adj.* не́тто *indecl.*; чи́стый. **2.** *v.* приноси́ть чи́стый дохо́д *impf.*
net² /nɛt/ *n.* сеть; се́тка *f.*
netball /'nɛt,bɔl/ *n.* нетбо́л *m.*
nether /'nɛðər/ *adj.* ни́жний.
Netherlands /'nɛðərləndz/ *n.* **the,** Нидерла́нды *pl.*
netting /'nɛtɪŋ/ *n.* се́тка *f.*
nettle /'nɛtḷ/ *n.* крапи́ва *f.*
network /'nɛt,wɜrk/ *n.* сеть *f.*
Neufchâtel /,nuʃə'tel/ *n.* Невша́тель *m.*
neural /'nʊrəl/ *adj.* не́рвный.
neuralgia /nʊ'rældʒə/ *n.* невралги́я *f.*
neuralgic /nʊ'rældʒɪk/ *adj.* невралги́ческий.
neurasthenia /,nʊrəs'θiniə/ *n.* неврастени́я *f.*
neuritis /nʊ'raitɪs/ *n.* неври́т *m.*
neurological /,nʊrə'lɒdʒɪkəl/ *adj.* неврологи́ческий.
neurologist /nʊ'rɒlədʒɪst/ *n.* невропато́лог *m.*
neurology /nʊ'rɒlədʒi/ *n.* неврологи́я *f.*
neuron /'nʊrɒn/ *n.* не́рвная кле́тка *f.*, нейро́н *m.*
neuropathology /,nʊroupə'θɒlədʒi/ *n.* невропатоло́гия *f.*
neuropathy /nʊ'rɒpəθi/ *n.* невропа́тия *f.*
neurosis /nʊ'rousɪs/ *n.* невро́з *m.*
neurotic /nʊ'rɒtɪk/ *adj.* невроти́ческий.
neuter /'nutər/ **1.** *adj.* (*gram.*) сре́дний, сре́днего ро́да. **2.** *v.* кастри́ровать *impf.*
neutral /'nutrəl/ *adj.* нейтра́льный.
neutrality /nu'trælɪti/ *n.* нейтралите́т *m.*
neutralization /,nutrələ'zeiʃən/ *n.* нейтрализа́ция *f.*
neutralize /'nutrə,laiz/ *v.* нейтрализова́ть *impf.* and *pf.*
neutrino /nu'trinou/ *n.* нейтри́но *neut.*
neutron /'nutrɒn/ **1.** *n.* нейтро́н *m.* **2.** *adj.* нейтро́нный.
Nevada /nə'vædə, -'vɑdə/ *n.* Нева́да *f.*
never /'nɛvər/ *adv.* никогда́.
never-ending /'nɛvər 'ɛndɪŋ/ *adj.* бесконе́чный; непреры́вный; ве́чный.
nevermore /,nɛvər'mɔr/ *adv.* никогда́ бо́льше.
nevertheless /,nɛvərðə'lɛs/ *adv.* тем не ме́нее.
new /nu/ *adj.* но́вый.
newborn /'nu'bɔrn/ *adj.* новорождённый.
newcomer /'nu,kʌmər/ *n.* новоприбы́вший; пришле́ц *m.*

newfangled /'nu'fæŋgəld/ *adj.* новомо́дный.

newfound /'nu'faund/ *n.* новооткры́тый *f.*

Newfoundland /'nufənlənd/ *n.* Ньюфаундле́нд *m.*

New Guinea /'gɪni/ *n.* Но́вая Гвине́я *f.*

New Hampshire /'hæmpʃər/ *n.* Нью-Гэ́мпшир *m.*

New Jersey *n.* Нью-Джéрси *m.*

newly /'nuli/ *adv.* (*recently*) неда́вно; (*anew*) вновь; по-но́вому.

newlyweds /'nuli,wedz/ *n.* новобра́чные; моло-доже́ны *pl.*

New Mexico *n.* Нью-Ме́ксико *m.*

newness /'nunɪs/ *n.* новизна́ *f.*

news /nuz/ *n.* но́вости; изве́стия *pl.*; (*piece of news*) но́вость *f.*, изве́стие *neut.*

newsboy /'nuz,bɔi/ *n.* газе́тчик *m.*

newscast /'nuz,kæst/ *n.* переда́ча после́дних изве́стий *f.*

newscaster /'nuz,kæstər/ *n.* ди́ктор новосте́й *m.*

newsletter /'nuz,lɛtər/ *n.* информацио́нный бюллете́нь *m.*

newspaper /'nuz,peipər/ **1.** *n.* газе́та *f.* **2.** *adj.* газе́тный.

newsprint /'nuz,prɪnt/ *n.* газе́тная бума́га *f.*

newsreel /'nuz,ril/ *n.* кинохро́ника *f.*, кино-журна́л *m.*

newsstand /'nuz,stænd/ *n.* газе́тный кио́ск *m.*

newt /nut/ *n.* трито́н *m.*

newton /'nutṇ/ *n.* нью́тон *m.*

New York /nu yourk/ *n.* Нью-Йо́рк *m.*

New Zealand /'zilənd/ *n.* Но́вая Зела́ндия *f.*

next /nɛkst/ **1.** *adj.*, *n.* сле́дующий; ближа́йший; бу́дущий. **2.** *adv.* зате́м, пото́м; **next to** ря́дом (с *with instr.*); о́коло (*with gen.*).

next of kin *n.* бли́жний ро́дственник *m.*

nexus /'nɛksəs/ *n.* связь *f.*

nib /nɪb/ *n.* ко́нчик *m.*

Nicaragua /,nɪkə'rɑgwə/ *n.* Никара́гуа *f.*

nice /nais/ *adj.* прия́тный; хоро́ший.

Nice /nis/ *n.* Ни́цца *f.*

nice-looking /'nais ,lukɪŋ/ *adj.* привлека́тельный; милови́дный.

nicely /'naisli/ *adv.* хорошо́; (*just right*) как раз.

niceness /'naisnɪs/ *n.* любе́зность *f.*

nicety /'naisɪti/ *n.* делика́тость *f.*

niche /nɪtʃ/ *n.* ни́ша *f.*

nick /nɪk/ *n.* цара́пина; засе́чка *f.*

nickel /'nɪkəl/ *n.* ни́кель *m.*

nickel-plated /'nɪkəl ,pleitɪd/ *adj.* никелиро́-ванный.

nickname /'nɪk,neim/ **1.** *n.* про́звище *neut.* **2.** *v.* дава́ть про́звище *impf.*

nicotine /'nɪkə,tin/ *n.* никоти́н *m.*

nicotinic /,nɪkə'tɪnɪk/ *adj.* никоти́новый.

nictitate /'nɪktɪ,teit/ *v.* мига́ть *impf.*

niece /nis/ *n.* племя́нница *f.*

niello /ni'ɛlou/ *n.* (*material*) чернь *f.*

nifty /'nɪfti/ *adj.* (*colloq.*) шика́рный.

Nigeria /nai'dʒɪəriə/ *n.* Ниге́рия *f.*

niggard /'nɪgərd/ *n.* скря́га *m.* and *f.* (*decl. f.*).

niggardly /'nɪgərdli/ *adj.* скупо́й.

niggle /'nɪgəl/ *v.* придира́ться (к *with dat.*) *impf.*

niggling /'nɪglɪŋ/ *adj.* ме́лочный.

nigh /nai/ *adj.* бли́зкий.

night /nait/ **1.** *n.* ночь *f.*; **at night** но́чью; **good night!** споко́йной но́чи!; **last night** вчера́ ве́чером; **night and day** днём и но́чью. **2.** *adj.* ночно́й.

night blindness *n.* кури́ная слепота́ *f.*

nightcap /'nait,kæp/ *n.* (*hat*) ночно́й колпа́к *m.*; (*colloq.*) (*drink*) напи́ток пе́ред сном *m.*

nightclothes /'nait,klouz/ *n.* ночна́я пижа́ма *f.*

nightclub /'nait,klʌb/ *n.* ночно́й клуб *m.*

nightfall /'nait,fɔl/ *n.* су́мерки *pl.*

night glasses *n.* ночно́й бино́кль *m.*

nightgown /'nait,gaun/ *n.* ночна́я руба́шка *f.*

nightingale /'naitṇ,geil/ *n.* солове́й *m.*

nightjar /'nait,dʒar/ *n.* козодо́й *m.*

night-light /'nait ,lait/ *n.* ночни́к *m.*

nightly /'naitli/ *adj.* ежено́щный.

nightmare /'nait,mɛər/ *n.* кошма́р *m.*

nightmarish /'nait,mɛərɪʃ/ *adj.* кошма́рный.

night school *n.* вече́рняя шко́ла *f.*

nightshade /'nait,ʃeid/ *n.* паслён *m.*

night shift *n.* ночна́я сме́на *f.*

nightshirt /'nait,ʃərt/ *n.* ночна́я руба́шка *f.*

nighttime /'nait,taim/ *n.* ночно́е вре́мя *neut.*

night watch *n.* ночна́я стра́жа *f.*

night watchman *n.* ночно́й сто́рож *m.*

nigrosine /'naigrə,sin/ *n.* нигрози́н *m.*

nihilism /'naiə,lizəm/ *n.* нигили́зм *m.*

nihilist /'naiəlist/ *n.* нигили́ст *m.*

nihilistic /,naiə'listik/ *adj.* нигилисти́ческий.

nil /nɪl/ *n.* ноль *m.*; ничего́.

nimble /'nɪmbəl/ *adj.* ги́бкий, прово́рный.

nimble-fingered /'nɪmbəl ,fɪŋgərd/ *adj.* ло́вкий.

nimbleness /'nɪmbəlnɪs/ *n.* прово́рство *neut.*

nimbus /'nɪmbəs/ *n.* (*clouds*) дождевы́е облака́ *pl.*; (*halo*) нимб *m.*

nincompoop /'nɪnkəm,pup/ *n.* простофи́ля *m.* and *f.* (*decl. f.*).

nine /nain/ **1.** *n.* де́вять *num.*, девя́тка *f.* **2.** *adj.* де́вять.

ninefold /'nain,fould/ *adj.* девятикра́тный.

nineteen /'nain'tin/ *adj.* девятна́дцать.

nineteenth /'nain'tinθ/ *adj.* девятна́дцатый.

ninetieth /'naintiiθ/ *adj.* девяно́стый.

ninety /'nainti/ *adj.*, *n.* девяно́сто.

ninny /'nɪni/ *n.* дурачо́к *m.*

ninth /nainθ/ **1.** *adj.* девя́тый. **2.** *n.* девя́тая; девя́тая часть *f.*

niobium /nai'oubiəm/ *n.* нио́бий *m.*

nip /nɪp/ *n.* (*pinch*) щипо́к *m.*

nipper /'nɪpər/ *n.* (*claw of crustacean*) клешня́ *f.*

nipple /'nɪpəl/ *n.* со́ска *f.*; (*anat.*) сосо́к *m.*

nippy /'nɪpi/ *adj.* прохла́дный.

nirvana /nɪr'vɑnə/ *n.* нирва́на *f.*

Niš /niʃ/ *n.* Ниш *m.*

nisi /'naisai, 'nisi/ *adj.*: **a decree nisi** *n.* усло́вно-оконча́тельное реше́ние суда́ *neut.*

nit /nɪt/ *n.* гни́да *f.*

niter /'naitər/ *n.* сели́тра *f.*

nitpicker /'nɪt,pɪkər/ *n.* (*colloq.*) приди́ра *m.* and *f.* (*decl. f.*).

nitrate /'naitreit/ *n.* нитра́т *m.*

nitration /nai'treiʃən/ *n.* нитра́ция *f.*

nitric /'naitrɪk/ *adj.* азо́тный.

nitric acid *n.* азо́тная кислота́ *f.*

nitride /'naitraid/ *n.* нитри́д *m.*

nitrification /,naitrəfɪ'keiʃən/ *n.* нитрифика́ция *f.*

nitrile /'naitril/ *n.* нитри́л *f.*

nitrite /'naitrait/ *n.* нитри́т *m.*

nitrobenzene /ˌnaitrou'bɛnzin/ n. нитробензо́л m.

nitrocellulose /ˌnaitrə'sɛlyəˌlous/ n. нитроцеллюло́за f.

nitrogen /'naitrədʒən/ n. азо́т m.

nitrogenize /nai'trɒdʒəˌnaiz/ v. азоти́ровать impf.

nitrogenous /nai'trɒdʒənəs/ adj. азо́тистый.

nitroglycerin /ˌnaitrə'glisərin/ n. нитроглицери́н m.

nitrous /'naitrəs/ adj. азо́тистый.

nitrous oxide n. за́кись азо́та f.; веселя́щий газ m.

nitwit /'nitˌwit/ n. крети́н m.

Nizhniy Novgorod /'niʒni 'nɒvgərɒd/ n. (formerly: Gorki) Ни́жний Но́вгород m.

no /nou/ 1. adj. никако́й. 2. adv. нет.

nobelium /nou'bɛliəm/ n. нобе́лий m.

Nobel prize /'noubɛl/ n. Но́белевская пре́мия f.

nobiliary /nou'biliˌeri/ adj. дворя́нский.

nobility /nou'biliti/ n. благоро́дство; дворя́нство neut.; аристокра́тия f.

noble /'noubəl/ 1. adj. зна́тный; благоро́дный. 2. n. дворяни́н m.

nobleman /'noubəlmən/ n. аристокра́т m.

noble-minded /'noubəl 'maindid/ adj. великоду́шный; благоро́дный.

noblewoman /'noubəlˌwumən/ n. аристокра́тка f.

nobody /'nouˌbɒdi, -ˌbʌdi/ 1. pron. никто́. 2. n. ничто́жество neut.

nocturnal /nɒk'tɜrnḷ/ adj. ночно́й.

nocturne /'nɒktɜrn/ n. (mus.) ноктю́рн m.

nod /nɒd/ 1. n. киво́к m. 2. v. кива́ть голово́й impf.

nodal /'noudḷ/ adj. узлово́й.

nodding /'nɒdiŋ/ n. кива́ние neut.

node /noud/ n. у́зел m.

nodular /'nɒdʒələr/ adj. узлова́тый; узлово́й.

nodule /'nɒdʒul/ n. узело́к m.

Noel /nou'ɛl/ n. Рождество́ neut.

nog /nɒg/ n. (peg) на́гель m.

noggin /'nɒgən/ n. кру́жечка f.

noise /nɔiz/ n. шум m.

noiseless /'nɔizlis/ adj. бесшу́мный.

noisiness /'nɔizinis/ n. шумли́вость f.

noisome /'nɔisəm/ adj. (harmful) вре́дный.

noisy /'nɔizi/ adj. шу́мный.

nomad /'noumæd/ n. коче́вник m.

nomadic /nou'mædik/ adj. кочево́й.

nomadism /'noumædˌizəm/ n. коче́вничество neut.

no man's land n. ничья́ земля́ f.

nomenclature /'noumənˌkleitʃər/ n. номенклату́ра f.

nominal /'nɒmənḷ/ adj. номина́льный; именно́й.

nominalism /'nɒmənḷˌizəm/ n. номинали́зм m.

nominalist /'nɒmənḷist/ n. номинали́ст m.

nominate /'nɒməˌneit/ v. выставля́ть кандидату́ру impf.

nomination /ˌnɒmə'neiʃən/ n. кандидату́ра f.; выдвиже́ние кандида́та neut.

nominative /'nɒmənətiv/ adj. (gram.) имени́тельный.

nominee /ˌnɒmə'ni/ n. кандида́т m.

nomogram /'nɒməˌgræm/ n. номогра́мма f.

nonacceptance /ˌnɒnæk'sɛptəns/ n. неприня́тие neut.

nonage /'nɒnidʒ/ n. несовершенноле́тие neut.

nonagenarian /ˌnɒnədʒə'nɛəriən/ n. девяностоле́тний стари́к m.

nonaggression pact /ˌnɒnə'greʃən/ n. пакт о ненападе́нии m.

nonalcoholic /ˌnɒnælkə'hɒlik/ adj. безалкого́льный.

nonaligned /'nɒnəˌlaind/ adj. неприсоедини́вшийся.

nonalignment /ˌnɒnə'lainmənt/ n. поли́тика неприсоедине́ния f.

nonappearance /ˌnɒnə'piərəns/ n. нея́вка f.

nonarrival /ˌnɒnə'raivəl/ n. неприбы́тие neut.

nonavailability /ˌnɒnəˌveilə'biliti/ n. неиме́ние; отсу́тствие neut.

nonbeliever /ˌnɒnbi'livər/ n. неве́рующий.

nonchalance /ˌnɒnʃə'lɑns/ n. беспе́чность f.

nonchalant /ˌnɒnʃə'lɑnt/ adj. беззабо́тный; беспе́чный.

nonclassified /ˌnɒn'klæsəˌfaid/ adj. незасекре́ченный.

noncombatant /ˌnɒnkəm'bætṇt/ n. нестроево́й солда́т m.

noncommissioned /ˌnɒnkə'miʃənd/ adj.: **noncommissioned officer** n. сержа́нт m.

noncommittal /ˌnɒnkə'mitḷ/ adj. укло́нчивый.

noncompliance /ˌnɒnkəm'plaiəns/ n. невыполне́ние neut.

nonconducting /ˌnɒnkən'dʌktiŋ/ adj. непроводя́щий.

nonconductor /ˌnɒnkən'dʌktər/ n. непроводни́к m.

nonconformist /ˌnɒnkən'fɔrmist/ n. инакомы́слящий m.

nonconformity /ˌnɒnkən'fɔrmiti/ n. непод'чине́ние neut.

nondescript /ˌnɒndi'skript/ adj. неопределённого ви́да.

none /nʌn/ 1. pron. никто́; ничто́; ни оди́н. 2. adv. ниско́лько; ничу́ть не.

nonentity /nɒn'ɛntiti/ n. (person) ничто́жество neut.

nones /nounz/ n. но́ны pl.

nonessential /ˌnɒni'sɛnʃəl/ adj. несуще́ственный.

nonetheless /ˌnʌnðə'lɛs/ adv. тем не ме́нее.

non-European /'nɒn yurə'piən/ adj. неевропе́йский.

nonexistence /ˌnɒnig'zistəns/ n. небытие́ neut.

nonexistent /ˌnɒnig'zistənt/ adj. несуществу́ющий.

nonferrous /nɒn'fɛrəs/ adj. (metal) цветно́й.

nonfiction /nɒn'fikʃən/ n. нау́чная и нау́чно-популя́рная литерату́ра f.

nonflammable /nɒn'flæməbəl/ adj. невоспламеня́емый.

nonintervention /ˌnɒnintər'vɛnʃən/ n. невмеша́тельство neut.

nonmetallic /ˌnɒnmi'tælik/ adj. неметалли́ческий.

nonobservance /ˌnɒnəb'zɜrvəns/ n. несоблюде́ние neut.

nonpayment /nɒn'peimənt/ n. неплатёж m.

nonplus /nɒn'plʌs/ v. ста́вить в тупи́к impf.

nonpolitical /ˌnɒnpə'litikəl/ adj. неполити́чный.

nonrecognition /ˌnɒnrɛkəɡ'nɪʃən/ *n.* непризна́ние *neut.*

nonresistance /ˌnɒnrɪ'zɪstəns/ *n.* несопротивле́ние *neut.*

nonsense /'nɒnsɛns/ *n.* вздор *m.*; ерунда́ *f.*; пустяки́ *pl.*

nonsensical /nɒn'sɛnsɪkəl/ *adj.* бессмы́сленный.

non sequitur /nɒn 'sɛkwɪtər/ *n.* нелоги́чный вы́вод *m.*

nonslip /nɒn'slɪp/ *adj.* нескользя́щий.

nonsmoker /nɒn'smoukər/ *n.* (*person*) некуря́щий *m.*

nonstandard /'nɒn'stændərd/ *adj.* нестанда́ртный.

nonstop /'nɒn'stɒp/ *adj.* безостано́вочный; беспоса́дочный.

nontransferable /ˌnɒntræns'fɜrəbəl/ *adj.* не подлежа́щий переда́че друго́му лицу́.

nonviolent /nɒn'vaiələnt/ *adj.* ненаси́льственный.

noodle /'nudl/ *n.* лапша́ *f.*

nook /nʊk/ *n.* уголо́к *m.*

noon /nun/ *n.* по́лдень *m.*

noonday /'nundei/ *adj.* полу́денный.

noose /nus/ *n.* петля́ *f.*

noosphere /'nouə,sfɪər/ *n.* ноосфе́ра *f.*

nor /nɔr; *unstressed* nər/ *conj.* та́кже не; **neither... nor** ни... ни.

Nordic /'nɔrdɪk/ *adj.* норди́ческий.

Norilsk /nə'rilsk/ *n.* Нори́льск *m.*

norm /nɔrm/ *n.* но́рма *f.*

normal /'nɔrməl/ *adj.* норма́льный; обы́чный.

normalcy /'nɔrməlsi/ *n.* норма́льность *f.*; норма́льное состоя́ние *neut.*

normalization /ˌnɔrmələ'zeiʃən/ *n.* нормализа́ция *f.*

normalize /'nɔrmə,laiz/ *v.* нормализова́ть *impf. and pf.*

normally /'nɔrməli/ *adv.* обы́чно; норма́льно.

Norman /'nɔrmən/ **1.** *adj.* норма́ндский. **2.** *n.* норма́ндец; норма́нн *m.*, норма́ндка *f.*

Normandy /'nɔrməndi/ *n.* (*province*) Норма́ндия *f.*

normative /'nɔrmətɪv/ *adj.* нормати́вный.

Norse /nɔrs/ *n.* древнеисла́ндский язы́к *m.*

Norseman /'nɔrsmən/ *n.* дре́вний скандина́в, норма́нн *m.*

north /nɔrθ/ **1.** *n.* се́вер *m.* **2.** *adj.* се́верный. **3.** *adv.* к се́веру, на се́вер.

North Carolina /ˌkærə'lainə/ *n.* Се́верная Кароли́на *f.*

North Dakota /də'koutə/ *n.* Се́верная Дако́та *f.*

northeast /ˌnɔrθ'ist; *Naut.* ˌnɔr'ist/ **1.** *n.* се́веро-восто́к *m.* **2.** *adv.* на се́веро-восто́к.

northeaster /nɔrθ'istər; *Naut.* nɔr'istər/ *n.* се́веро-восто́чный ве́тер *m.*

northeastern /nɔrθ'istərn/ *adj.* се́веро-восто́чный.

northeastward /nɔrθ'istwərd; *Naut.* nɔr'istwərd/ *adv.* на се́веро-восто́к.

norther /'nɔrðər/ *n.* норд, се́верный ве́тер *m.*

northerly /'nɔrðərli/ *adj.* се́верный.

northern /'nɔrðərn/ *adj.* се́верный.

Northern Dvina *n.* (*river*) Се́верная Дви́на *f.*

northerner /'nɔrðərnər/ *n.* северя́нин *m.*, северя́нка *f.*

northernmost /'nɔrðərn,moust/ *adj.* са́мый се́верный.

northing /'nɔrθɪŋ/ *n.* но́рдовая ра́зность широ́т *f.*

North Sea *n.* Се́верное мо́ре *neut.*

northward /'nɔrθwərd; *Naut.* 'nɔrðərd/ *adv.* на се́вер.

northwest /ˌnɔrθ'wɛst; *Naut.* ˌnɔr'wɛst/ **1.** *n.* се́веро-за́пад *m.* **2.** *adv.* на се́веро-за́пад.

northwestern /nɔrθ'wɛstərn/ *adj.* се́веро-за́падный.

Norway /ˌnɔrwei/ *n.* Норве́гия *f.*

Norwegian /nɔr'widʒən/ **1.** *adj.* норве́жский. **2.** *n.* норве́жец *m.*, норве́жка *f.*

nose /nouz/ *n.* нос *m.*

noseband /'nouz,bænd/ *n.* храпово́й ремешо́к *m.*

nosebleed /'nouz,blid/ *n.* носово́е кровоте́чение *n.*

nosedive /'nouz,daiv/ *n.* (*aero.*) круто́е пики́рование *neut.*; (*prices*) круто́й спад *m.*

noseless /'nouzlɪs/ *adj.* безно́сый.

nosh /nɒʃ/ *n.* (*colloq.*) переку́ска *f.*

nosing /'nouzɪŋ/ *n.* капоти́рование *neut.*

nosological /ˌnɒsə'lɒdʒɪkəl/ *adj.* нозологи́ческий.

nosology /nou'sɒlədʒi/ *n.* нозоло́гия *f.*

nostalgia /nɒ'stældʒə/ *n.* ностальги́я *f.*

nostalgic /nɒ'stældʒɪk/ *adj.* ностальги́ческий.

nostril /'nɒstrəl/ *n.* ноздря́ *f.*

nosy /'nouzi/ *adj.* любопы́тный.

not /nɒt/ *adv.* не; нет; **not at all** совсе́м не (нет).

notability /ˌnoutə'bɪlɪti/ *n.* знамени́тость *f.*

notable /'noutəbəl/ *adj.* выдаю́щийся; значи́тельный.

notably /'noutəbli/ *adv.* заме́тно; значи́тельно; осо́бенно.

notarial /nou'tɛəriəl/ *adj.* нотариа́льный.

notary /'noutəri/ *n.* нота́риус *m.*

notation /nou'teiʃən/ *n.* нота́ция; систе́ма обозначе́ния *f.*; (*note*) заме́тка *f.*

notch /nɒtʃ/ *n.* вы́емка; зару́бка *f.*

notched /nɒtʃt/ *adj.* зазу́бренный.

note /nout/ **1.** *n.* запи́ска *f.*; (*mus.*) но́та *f.*; *pl.* за́пись; заме́тка *f.*; заме́тки *pl.* **2.** *v.* (*notice*) замеча́ть *impf.*, заме́тить *pf.*

notebook /'nout,bʊk/ *n.* записна́я кни́жка, тетра́дь *f.*

noted /'noutɪd/ *adj.* знамени́тый; изве́стный.

notepad /'nout,pæd/ *n.* блокно́т *m.*

noteworthy /'nout,wɜrði/ *adj.* заслу́живающий внима́ния.

nothing /'nʌθɪŋ/ **1.** *pron.* ничто́; ничего́; **2.** *n.* (*zero*) ноль, нуль *m.*

nothingness /'nʌθɪŋnɪs/ *n.* (*nonexistence*) небытие́ *neut.*

notice /'noutɪs/ **1.** *n.* объявле́ние *neut.*; (*attention*) внима́ние *neut.* **2.** *v.* замеча́ть *impf.*, заме́тить *pf.*

noticeable /'noutɪsəbəl/ *adj.* заме́тный.

notification /ˌnoutəfɪ'keiʃən/ *n.* извеще́ние; уведомле́ние *neut.*; (*warning*) предупрежде́ние *neut.*

notify /'noutə,fai/ *v.* уведомля́ть (о *with prep.*) *impf.*, уве́домить *pf.*

notion /'nouʃən/ *n.* поня́тие; представле́ние *neut.*

notional /'nouʃənl/ *adj.* (*abstract*) отвлечённый.

notoriety /ˌnoutə'raiɪti/ *n.* дурна́я сла́ва *f.*

notorious /nou'tɔriəs/ *adj.* пресловы́тый.

notwithstanding /ˌnɒtwɪð'stændɪŋ/ **1.** adv. тем не мéнее; всё равнó. **2.** prep. несмотря́ на (with acc.).

nougat /'nugət/ n. нугá f.

noun /naun/ n. и́мя существи́тельное neut.

nourish /'nɜrɪʃ/ v. пита́ть impf.

nourishing /'nɜrɪʃɪŋ/ adj. пита́тельный.

nourishment /'nɜrɪʃmənt/ n. пита́ние neut.; пи́ща f.

nouveau riche /'nu'vou riʃ/ n. нувори́ш m.; богáтый вы́скочка m. and f. (decl. f.).

nova /'nouvə/ n. нóвая (звездá) f.

Nova Scotia /'nou'və skouʃə/ n. Нóвая Шотлáндия f.

Novaya Zemlya /'nouvə,yə zɛmli'ɑ/ n. (island) Нóвая Земля́ f.

novel /'nɒvəl/ **1.** adj. нóвый. **2.** n. ромáн m.

novelist /'nɒvəlɪst/ n. романи́ст m.

novella /nou'vɛlə/ n. новéлла; пóвесть f.

novelty /'nɒvəlti/ n. новизнá; нóвость f.

November /nou'vɛmbər/ **1.** n. ноя́брь m. **2.** adj. ноя́брьский.

Novgorod /'nɒvgə,rɒd/ n. Нóвгород m.

novice /'nɒvɪs/ n. новичóк m.; (eccl.) послу́шник m.

novitiate /nou'vɪʃiɪt/ n. послу́шничество neut.

Novocaine /'nouvə,kein/ n. новокайн m.

Novorossiysk /ˌnouvərə'sisk/ n. Новороси́йск m.

now /nau/ adv. тепéрь; тотчáс же.

nowadays /'nauə,deiz/ adv. в нáше врéмя.

noway /'nou,wei/ adv. (colloq.) никóим óбразом; никáк.

nowhere /'nou,wɛər/ adj. (dir.) никудá; (loc.) нигдé.

noxious /'nɒkʃəs/ adj. врéдный; ядови́тый.

nozzle /'nɒzəl/ n. соплó neut.

nth /ɛnθ/ adj. (math.) энный

nuance /'nuans/ n. нюáнс m.

nub /nʌb/ n. (knob) ши́шка f.

nuclear /'nukliər/ adj. я́дерный.

nucleate /'nukliit/ adj. содержáщий ядрó.

nucleic acid /nu'kliɪk, -'klei-/ n. нуклеи́новая кислотá f.

nucleon /'nukli,ɒn/ n. нуклóн m.

nucleonics /ˌnukli'ɒnɪks/ n. нуклеóника f.

nucleus /'nukliəs/ n. ядрó neut.; ячéйка f.

nude /nud/ **1.** adj. нагóй; гóлый. **2.** n. обнажённая фигýра f.

nudge /nʌdʒ/ **1.** n. толчóк лóктем m. **2.** v. подтолкнýть лóктем pf.

nudism /'nudɪzəm/ n. нуди́зм m.

nudist /'nudɪst/ n. нуди́ст m.

nudity /'nuditi/ n. наготá; обнажённость.

nugatory /'nugə,tɔri/ adj. пустя́чный.

nugget /'nʌgɪt/ n. самородóк m.

nuisance /'nusəns/ n. досáда f.; (person) надоéдливый человéк m.

null /nʌl/ adj. недействи́тельный.

nullification /ˌnʌləfɪ'keiʃən/ n. аннули́рование neut.

nullify /'nʌlə,fai/ v. аннули́ровать impf. and pf.

nullity /'nʌlɪti/ n. ничтóжность f.

numb /nʌm/ adj. онемéлый.

number /'nʌmbər/ **1.** n. коли́чество neut.; нóмер m.; (gram.; symbol; math.) числó neut. **2.** v. (assign number) нумеровáть impf.

numbered /'nʌmbərd/ adj. нумерóванный.

numbering /'nʌmbərɪŋ/ n. нумерáция f.

numberless /'nʌmbərlɪs/ adj. бесчи́сленный.

numbness /'nʌmnɪs/ n. онемéние; оцепенéние; окоченéние neut.

numerable /'numərəbəl/ adj. исчисли́мый.

numeral /'numərəl/ n. (math.) ци́фра f.; (gram.) (и́мя) числи́тельное neut.

numerate /'numə,reit/ v. считáть impf.

numeration /ˌnumə'reiʃən/ n. нумерáция f.

numerator /'numə,reitər/ n. (math.) числи́тель m.

numerical /nu'mɛrɪkəl/ adj. числовóй; цифровóй.

numerology /ˌnumə'rɒlədʒi/ n. гадáние по чи́слам f.

numerous /'numərəs/ adj. многочи́сленный; (many) мнóгие pl.

numinous /'numənəs/ adj. божéственный.

numismatic /ˌnumɪz'mætɪk/ adj. нумизмати́ческий.

numismatics /ˌnumɪz'mætɪks/ n. нумизмáтика f.

numismatist /nu'mɪzmətɪst/ n. нумизмáт m.

numskull /'nʌm,skʌl/ n. болвáн m.; тупи́ца m. and f. (decl. f.).

nun /nʌn/ n. монáхиня f.

nunciature /'nʌnʃiət,ʃər/ n. нунциатýра f.

nuncio /'nʌnʃi,ou/ n. нýнций m.

nunnery /'nʌnəri/ n. жéнский монасты́рь m.

nuptial /'nʌpʃəl/ adj. брáчный.

nuptials /'nʌpʃəlz/ n. свáдьба f.

nurse /nɜrs/ **1.** n. медсестрá f., медбрáт m.; (child's) ня́ня f. **2.** v. ухáживать за больны́м impf.; (suckle) корми́ть impf.

nursemaid /'nɜrs,meid/ n. ня́нька f.

nursery /'nɜrsəri/ n. дéтская (кóмната) f.; (day nursery) я́сли pl.; (for plants) питóмник m.

nurseryman /'nɜrsərimən/ n. владéлец питóмника m.

nursing /'nɜrsɪŋ/ n. кормлéние грýдью neut.

nursing home n. дом престарéлых m.

nurture /'nɜrtʃər/ n. питáть; воспи́тывать impf.

nut /nʌt/ n. орéх m.; (mech.) гáйка f.

nutation /nu'teiʃən/ n. нутáция f.

nutbearing /'nʌt,bɛərɪŋ/ adj. орехоплóдный.

nut case n. (slang) (pej.) псих m.

nutcracker /'nʌt,krækər/ n. щипцы́ для орéхов pl.; (hist.) щелкýнчик m.

nuthatch /'nʌt,hætʃ/ n. (bird) пóползень m.

nuthouse /'nʌt,haus/ n. психýшка f.

nutmeg /'nʌt,mɛg/ n. мускáтный орéх m.

nutria /'nutriə/ n. нýтрия f.

nutrient /'nutriənt/ n. пита́тельный.

nutrition /nu'trɪʃən/ n. питáние neut.; (branch of study) диетéтика f.

nutritional /nu'trɪʃənl/ adj. пита́тельный; пищевóй.

nutritious /nu'trɪʃəs/ adj. пита́тельный.

nutshell /'nʌt,ʃɛl/ n. орéховая скорлупá f.

nutty /'nʌti/ adj. (containing nuts) орéховый; (slang) (mad) чóкнутый.

nuzzle /'nʌzəl/ v. ты́каться нóсом impf.

nylon /'nailɒn/ **1.** n. нейлóн m. **2.** adj. нейлóновый.

nymph /nɪmf/ n. ни́мфа f.

nymphomania /ˌnɪmfə'meiniə/ n. нимфомáния f.

nymphomaniac /ˌnɪmfə'meini,æk/ n. нимфомáнка f.

O

oaf /ouf/ *n.* о́лух; болва́н *m.*

oak /ouk/ **1.** *n.* дуб *m.* **2.** *adj.* дубо́вый.

oakum /'oukəm/ *n.* па́кля *f.*

oar /ɔr/ *n.* весло́ *neut.*

oarlock /'ɔr,lɒk/ *n.* уклю́чина *f.*

oarsman /'ɔrzmən/ *n.* гребе́ц *m.*

oasis /ou'eisis/ *n.* оа́зис *m.*

oat /out/ **1.** *n.* овёс *m.* **2.** *adj.* овся́ный, овсяно́й.

oath /ouθ/ *n.* кля́тва; прися́га *f.*

oatmeal /'out,mil/ *n.* овся́нка *f.*

Ob /ɔb/ *n.* (*river*) Обь *f.*

obedience /ou'bidiəns/ *n.* послуша́ние *neut.*

obedient /ou'bidiənt/ *adj.* послу́шный.

obese /ou'bis/ *adj.* ту́чный.

obesity /ou'bisiti/ *n.* ту́чность; полнота́ *f.*

obey /ou'bei/ *v.* слу́шаться (*with gen.*); повинова́ться (*with dat.*) *impf.*

obituary /ou'bitʃu,eri/ *n.* некроло́г *m.*

object / *n.* 'ɒbdʒikt; *v.* əb'dʒɛkt/ **1.** *n.* предме́т *m.*; (*aim*) цель *f.*; (*gram.*) дополне́ние *neut.* **2.** *v.* возража́ть *impf.*, возрази́ть *pf.*; (*protest*) протестова́ть *impf.*

objection /əb'dʒɛkʃən/ *n.* возраже́ние *neut.*

objectionable /əb'dʒɛkʃənəbəl/ *adj.* неприя́тный.

objective /əb'dʒɛktiv/ **1.** *adj.* объекти́вный. **2.** *n.* стремле́ние *neut.*; цель *f.*; (*mil.*) объе́кт *m.*

objet d'art /ɔbʒɛ 'dar/ *n.* предме́т иску́сства *m.*

obligate /'ɒbli,geit/ *v.* обя́зывать *impf.*

obligated /'ɒbli,geitid/ *adj.* обя́занный.

obligation /,ɒbli'geiʃən/ *n.* обяза́тельство *neut.*

obligatory /ə'bligə,tɔri/ *adj.* обяза́тельный.

oblige /ə'blaidʒ/ *v.* обя́зывать *impf.*, обяза́ть *pf.*; заставля́ть *impf.*, заста́вить *pf.*

obliging /ə'blaidʒiŋ/ *adj.* услу́жливый.

oblique /ə'blik/ *adj.* косо́й; ко́свенный.

obliquely /ə'blikli/ *adv.* ко́со; ко́свенно.

obliterate /ə'blitə,reit/ *v.* стира́ть *impf.*, стере́ть *pf.*; (*destroy*) уничтожа́ть *impf.*

obliteration /ə,blitə'reiʃən/ *n.* стира́ние; уничтоже́ние *neut.*

oblivion /ə'bliviən/ *n.* забве́ние *neut.*

oblong /'ɒb,lɔŋ/ *adj.* продолгова́тый.

obnoxious /əb'nɒkʃəs/ *adj.* проти́вный.

oboe /'oubou/ *n.* гобо́й *m.*

obscene /əb'sin/ *adj.* неприли́чный; непристо́йный.

obscenity /əb'sɛniti/ *n.* непристо́йность *f.*

obscurantism /əb'skyʊrən,tizəm/ *n.* мракобе́сие *neut.*

obscuration /,ɒbskyʊ'reiʃən/ *n.* помраче́ние *neut.*

obscure /əb'skyʊr/ **1.** *adj.* мра́чный; ту́склый; (*unclear*) нея́сный. **2.** *v.* затмева́ть *impf.*, затми́ть *pf.*

obscurity /əb'skyʊriti/ *n.* нея́сность; неизве́стность *f.*

obsequies /'ɒbsikwiz/ *n.* по́хороны *pl.*

obsequious /əb'sikwiəs/ *adj.* подобостра́стный; раболе́пный.

observance /əb'zɜrvəns/ *n.* соблюде́ние *neut.*; (*rite*) обря́д *m.*

observant /əb'zɜrvənt/ *adj.* наблюда́тельный.

observation /,ɒbzɜr'veiʃən/ *n.* наблюде́ние *neut.*; (*remark*) замеча́ние *neut.*

observatory /əb'zɜrvə,tɔri/ *n.* обсервато́рия *f.*

observe /əb'zɜrv/ *v.* наблюда́ть *impf.*; (*comply with*) соблюда́ть *impf.*

observer /əb'zɜrvər/ *n.* наблюда́тель *m.*

obsession /əb'sɛʃən/ *n.* одержи́мость *f.*; наважде́ние *neut.*; ма́ния *f.*

obsessive /əb'sɛsiv/ *adj.* навя́зчивый; одержи́мый.

obsolescence /,ɒbsə'lɛsəns/ *n.* устаре́лость *f.*

obsolete /,ɒbsə'lit/ *adj.* устаре́лый.

obstacle /'ɒbstəkəl/ *n.* препя́тствие *neut.*

obstetrician /,ɒbsti'triʃən/ *n.* акуше́р *m.*, акуше́рка *f.*

obstetrics /əb'stɛtriks/ *n.* акуше́рство *neut.*

obstinacy /'ɒbstənəsi/ *n.* упря́мство *f.*

obstinate /'ɒbstənit/ *adj.* упря́мый.

obstreperous /əb'strɛpərəs/ *adj.* (*noisy*) шу́мный; (*turbulent*) бу́йный.

obstruct /əb'strʌkt/ *v.* препя́тствовать; загражда́ть *impf.*, загради́ть *pf.*

obstruction /əb'strʌkʃən/ *n.* препя́тствие; загражде́ние *neut.*; обстру́кция *f.*

obstructive /əb'strʌktiv/ *adj.* препя́тствующий; прегражда́ющий.

obtain /əb'tein/ *v.* получа́ть *impf.*, получи́ть *pf.*; добыва́ть *impf.*, добы́ть *pf.*

obtainable /əb'teinəbəl/ *adj.* досту́пный; достижи́мый; (*on sale*) в прода́же.

obtrude /əb'trud/ *v.* (*thrust forth*) высо́вывать(ся) *impf.*

obtrusive /əb'trusiv/ *adj.* навя́зчивый; (*protruding*) выступа́ющий, торча́щий.

obtuse /əb'tus/ *adj.* тупо́й.

obverse /'ɒbvɜrs/ *n.* лицева́я сторона́ *f.*

obvious /'ɒbviəs/ *adj.* очеви́дный.

occasion /ə'keiʒən/ *n.* слу́чай *m.*; (*cause*) по́вод *m.*; возмо́жность *f.*

occasional /ə'keiʒənḷ/ *adj.* случа́йный; случа́ющийся вре́мя от вре́мени.

occasionally /ə'keiʒənḷi/ *adv.* иногда́, и́зредка; вре́мя от вре́мени.

occidental /,ɒksi'dɛntḷ/ *adj.* за́падный.

occipital /ɒk'sipitḷ/ *adj.* заты́лочный.

occult /ə'kʌlt/ **1.** *n.*: the, окку́льтные нау́ки *pl.* **2.** *adj.* таи́нственный.

occupancy /'ɒkyəpənsi/ *n.* заня́тие; владе́ние *neut.*

occupant /'ɒkyəpənt/ *n.* жиле́ц; (*mil.*) оккупа́нт *m.*

occupation /,ɒkyə'peiʃən/ *n.* заня́тие *neut.*; (*profession*) профе́ссия *f.*; (*mil.*) оккупа́ция *f.*

occupy /'ɒkyə,pai/ *v.* занима́ть *impf.*, заня́ть *pf.*

occur /ə'kɜr/ *v.* случа́ться *impf.*, случи́ться *pf.*

occurrence /ə'kɜrəns/ *n.* явле́ние; собы́тие *neut.*

ocean /'ouʃən/ **1.** *n.* океа́н *m.* **2.** *adj.* океа́нский.

Oceania /,ouʃi'æniə/ *n.* Океа́ния *f.*

ocher /'oukər/ *n.* (*min.*) о́хра *f.*

o'clock /ə'klɒk/ *adv.*: ten o'clock де́сять часо́в.

octagon /'ɒktə,gɒn/ *n.* восьмиуго́льник *m.*

octagonal /ɒk'tægənḷ/ *adj.* восьмиуго́льный.

octave /'ɒktɪv/ n. окта́ва f.

October /ɒk'toubər/ **1.** n. октя́брь m. **2.** adj. октя́брьский.

octopus /'ɒktəpəs/ n. осьмино́г m.

octosyllabic /ˌɒktousɪ'læbɪk/ adj. восьмисло́жный.

oculist /'ɒkyəlɪst/ n. окули́ст m.

odd /ɒd/ adj. стра́нный; необы́чный; (number) нечётный.

oddball /'ɒd,bɔl/ n. (colloq.) чуда́к m.

oddity /'ɒdɪti/ n. (strangeness) стра́нность f.

odds /ɒdz/ n. ша́нсы pl.

Oder /'oudər/ n. (river) О́дер m.

Odessa /ou'dɛsə/ n. Оде́сса f.

odious /'oudiəs/ adj. отврати́тельный.

odor /'oudər/ n. за́пах; (fragrance) арома́т m.

odoriferous /ˌoudə'rɪfərəs/ adj. души́стый, благоуха́нный.

odyssey /'ɒdəsi/ n. одиссе́я f.

of /ʌv; unstressed əv or, esp. before consonants, ə/ prep. (from) из (with gen.); (about) о, об (with prep.).

off /ɔf/ prep. с, со; от (with gen.).

offal /'ɔfəl/ n. потроха́ pl.; (waste) отхо́ды pl.; (carrion) па́даль f.

off-center /'ɔf'sɛntər/ adj. эксцентри́чный; нецен

off-color /'ɔf'kʌlər/ adj. (indecent) непристо́йный; (dubious) сомни́тельный.

offend /ə'fɛnd/ v. обижа́ть impf., оби́деть pf.

offender /ə'fɛndər/ n. оби́дчик m.; (law) престу́пник m.

offense /ə'fɛns/ n. оби́да f.; (transgression) просту́пок m.; (crime) преступле́ние neut.

offensive /ə'fɛnsɪv/ **1.** adj. оби́дный; (mil.) наступа́тельный. **2.** n. наступле́ние neut.

offer /'ɔfər/ **1.** n. предложе́ние neut. **2.** v. предлага́ть impf., предложи́ть pf.

offertory /'ɔfər,tɔri/ n. дароприноше́ние neut.

offhand /'ɔf'hænd/ **1.** adv. экспро́мтом; без подгото́вки. **2.** adj. сде́ланный без подгото́вки; импровизи́рованный.

offhandedly /'ɔf'hændɪdli/ adv. несерьёзно; небре́жно.

office /'ɔfɪs/ n. (private room) кабине́т m.; (position) до́лжность f.; (place) бюро́ neut. indecl.; конто́ра f.

office hours n. приёмные часы́ pl.

officer /'ɔfəsər/ n. (mil.) офице́р m.; должностно́е лицо́ neut.

official /ə'fɪʃəl/ **1.** adj. официа́льный; служе́бный. **2.** n. служе́бное лицо́ neut.

officiate /ə'fɪʃiˌeit/ v. исполня́ть обя́занности impf.

officious /ə'fɪʃəs/ adj. навя́зчивый; назо́йливый.

off-peak /'ɔf'pik/ adj. непи́ковый.

offprint /'ɔf,prɪnt/ n. отде́льный о́ттиск.

off-season /'ɔf'sizən/ n. мёртвый сезо́н.

offshoot /'ɔf,ʃut/ n. ответвле́ние neut.; бокова́я ветвь f.

offspring /'ɔf,sprɪŋ/ n. пото́мок; о́трыск m.

offstage /'ɔf'steidʒ/ adj. закули́сный; за кули́сами.

off-the-cuff /'ɔf ðə 'kʌf/ adj. импровизи́рованный; сде́ланный экспро́мтом.

off-white /'ɔf 'wait/ adj. све́тло-се́рый.

often /'ɔfən/ adv. ча́сто.

ogle /'ougəl/ v. стро́ить гла́зки (with dat.) impf.

ogre /'ougər/ n. чудо́вище neut., (велика́н-) лю доéд m.

Ohio /ou'haiou/ n. Ога́йо m.

oho! /ou'hou/ interj. ого́!

Ohrid /'oukrɪd, 'ouxrɪd/ n. **Lake,** О́хридское о́зеро.

oil /ɔil/ **1.** n. ма́сло neut.; (petroleum) нефть f. **2.** adj. ма́сляный; нефтяно́й. **3.** v. сма́зывать impf., сма́зать pf.

oil cake n. жмых m.

oilcloth /'ɔil,klɔθ/ n. клеёнка f.

oil derrick n. нефтяна́я вы́шка f.

oiling /'ɔilɪŋ/ n. сма́зка f.

oil lamp n. кероси́новая ла́мпа f.

oilman /'ɔil,mæn/ n. нефтепромы́шленник m.

oil pipeline n. нефтепрово́д m.

oil shale n. горю́чий сла́нец m.

oilskin /'ɔil,skɪn/ n. то́нкая клеёнка f.; непромока́емый костю́м m.

oil tanker n. (ship) нефтеналивно́е су́дно neut., та́нкер m.

oil well n. нефтяна́я сква́жина f.

oily /'ɔili/ adj. масляни́стый.

ointment /'ɔintmənt/ n. мазь f.

Oka /ou'ka/ n. (river) Ока́.

Okhotsk /ou'kɒtsk/ n. **Sea of,** Охо́тское Мо́ре neut.

Oklahoma /ˌouklə'houmə/ n. Оклахо́ма f.

old /ould/ adj. ста́рый.

old age n. ста́рость f., прекло́нные го́ды pl.

Old Believer n. старове́р m., старове́рка f.

old-fashioned /'ould'fæʃənd/ adj. старомо́дный.

oldish /'ouldɪʃ/ adj. старова́тый.

old man n. стари́к m.

Old Testament 1. n. Ве́тхий Заве́т m. **2.** adj. ветхоза́ветный.

old woman n. стару́ха f.

old-world /'ould 'wɜld/ adj. старосве́тский.

oligarchy /'ɒlɪˌgarki/ n. олига́рхия f.

olive /'ɒlɪv/ **1.** n. оли́ва f. **2.** adj. оли́вковый.

Olympic Games /ə'lɪmpɪk/ n. Олимпи́йские и́гры pl.

Olympus /ə'lɪmpəs/ n. **Mount,** Оли́мп m.

omelet /'ɒmlɪt/ n. омле́т m.

omen /'oumən/ n. предзнаменова́ние neut.

ominous /'ɒmənəs/ adj. злове́щий.

omission /ou'mɪʃən/ n. про́пуск m.

omit /ou'mɪt/ v. пропуска́ть impf., пропусти́ть pf.

omnipotence /ɒm'nɪpətəns/ n. всемогу́щество neut.

omnipotent /ɒm'nɪpətənt/ adj. всемогу́щий.

omnipresent /ˌɒmnə'prɛzənt/ adj. вездесу́щий.

omniscient /ɒm'nɪʃənt/ adj. всезна́ющий; всеве́дущий.

omnivorous /ɒm'nɪvərəs/ adj. всея́дный.

Omsk /ɒmsk/ n. Омск m.

on /ɒn/ **1.** prep. (location) на (with prep.); (direction) на (with acc.); (about) о, об, о́бо (with prep.). **2.** adv. да́льше, вперёд.

onboard /ɒn'bɔrd/ adj. бортово́й.

once /wʌns/ adv. раз; оди́н раз; одна́жды.

once-over /'wʌns,ouvər/ n. (colloq.) бе́глый осмо́тр m.

oncoming /'ɒn,kʌmɪŋ/ adj. надвига́ющийся.

on-duty /ɒn duti/ adj. дежу́рный.

one /wʌn/ **1.** adj. оди́н; еди́нственный. **2.** n.

один *m.*; (*unit*) единица *f.*; (*when counting*) раз *m.* **3.** *pron.* один; такой.

one-armed /'wʌn ˌarmd/ *adj.* однорукий.

one-eyed /'wʌn,aid/ *adj.* одноглазый.

Onega /ou'nɛgə/ *n.* Lake, Онежское озеро *neut.*

one-legged /'wʌn'lɛgd, -'lɛgɪd/ *adj.* одноногий.

onerous /'ɒnərəs/ *adj.* обременительный; тягостный.

oneself /wʌn'sɛlf/ *pron.* себя; сам; себе.

one-sided /'wʌn 'saidɪd/ *adj.* односторонний.

one-time /'wʌn ˌtaim/ *adj.* (*for one-time use*) одноразовый; (*former*) бывший.

one-track /'wʌn ˌtræk/ *adj.* одноколейный.

ongoing /'ɒn,gouɪŋ/ *adj.* постоянный; продолжающийся.

onion /'ʌnyən/ *n.* (*coll.*) лук *m.*; (*single bulb*) луковица *f.*

on-line /'ɒn'lain/ *adj.* неавтономный; диалоговый; интерактивный.

onlooker *n.* наблюдатель *m.*

only /'ounli/ **1.** *adj.* единственный. **2.** *adv.* только; **if only** если бы только; **not only...but also** не только...но также.

onset /'ɒn,sɛt/ *n.* наступление; начало *neut.*

onshore /'ɒn'ʃɔr/ *adv.* с моря.

on-site /'ɒn ˌsait/ *adv.* на месте.

onslaught /'ɒn,slɔt/ *n.* нападение *neut.*, натиск *m.*

Ontario /ɒn'tɛəri,ou/ *n.* Онтарио *neut.*

ontology /ɒn'tɒlədʒi/ *n.* онтология *f.*

onward /'ɒnwərd/ *adv.* вперёд.

ooze¹ /uz/ *n.* (*mud*) тина *f.*, ил *m.*

ooze² /uz/ **1.** *n.* (*slow leak*) истечение *neut.* **2.** *v.* сочиться *impf.*

opalescence /,oupə'lɛsəns/ *n.* опалесценция *f.*

opalescent /,oupə'lɛsənt/ *adj.* переливчатый.

opaque /ou'peik/ *adj.* непрозрачный.

op art /'ɒp 'art/ *n.* оп-арт *m.*

open /'oupən/ **1.** *adj.* открытый; откровенный. **2.** *v.t.* открывать *impf.*, открыть *pf.*; *v.i.* открываться *impf.*, открыться *pf.*

open-air /'oupən'ɛər/ *adj.* на открытом воздухе.

open-faced /'oupən 'feist/ *adj.* с открытым лицом.

open-hearted /'oupən 'hartɪd/ *adj.* добрый; чистосердечный.

opening /'oupənɪŋ/ **1.** *n.* (*hole*) отверстие *neut.*; (*start*) начало *neut.*; (*vacancy*) вакансия *f.* **2.** *adj.* начальный; первый.

openly /'oupənli/ *adv.* откровенно; открыто.

openness /'oupənnɪs/ *n.* откровенность; искренность *f.*

opera /'ɒpərə, 'ɒprə/ **1.** *n.* опера *f.* **2.** *adj.* оперный.

opera glasses *n.* театральный бинокль *m.*

opera singer *n.* оперный певец *m.*, оперная певица *f.*

operate /'ɒpə,reit/ *v.* (*handle, manage*) управлять *impf.*; (*med.*) оперировать *impf. and pf.*; (*function*) действовать (*as with acc.*) *impf.*

operatic /,ɒpə'rætɪk/ *adj.* оперный.

operation /,ɒpə'reiʃən/ *n.* действие *neut.*, процесс *m.*; (*med.*; *econ.*; *mil.*) операция *f.*

operative /'ɒpərətɪv/ *adj.* действующий; оперативный; (*med.*) операционный.

operator /'ɒpə,reitər/ *n.* управляющий (машиной); оператор *m.*

operetta /,ɒpə'rɛtə/ *n.* оперетта *f.*

opine /ou'pain/ *v.* (*consider*) считать *impf.*

opinion /ə'pɪnyən/ *n.* мнение *neut.*; **in my opinion** по-моему.

opinionated /ə'pɪnyə,neitɪd/ *adj.* самоуверенный; догматичный.

opium /'oupiəm/ *n.* опиум, опий *m.*

opossum /ə'pɒsəm, 'pɒsəm/ *n.* опоссум *m.*

opponent /ə'pounənt/ *n.* противник; оппонент *m.*

opportunist /,ɒpər'tunɪst/ *n.* оппортунист *m.*

opportunity /,ɒpər'tunɪti/ *n.* удобный случай *m.*; возможность *f.*

oppose /ə'pouz/ *v.* (*contrast*) противопоставлять (*with dat.*) *impf.*; (*resist*) сопротивляться; противиться *impf.*

opposing /ə'pouzɪŋ/ *adj.* противоположный.

opposite /'ɒpəzɪt/ **1.** *adj.* противоположный; (*reverse*) обратный. **2.** *prep.* напротив; против (*with gen.*) **3.** *n.* противоположность *f.*

opposition /,ɒpə'zɪʃən/ *n.* (*resistance*) сопротивление *neut.*; (*polit.*) оппозиция *f.*

oppress /ə'prɛs/ *v.* притеснять; угнетать *impf.*

oppression /ə'prɛʃən/ *n.* притеснение; угнетение *neut.*

oppressive /ə'prɛsɪv/ *adj.* гнетущий.

oppressor /ə'prɛsər/ *n.* угнетатель; притеснитель *m.*

opprobrium /ə'proubriəm/ *n.* (*shame*) позор *m.*; (*abuse*) оскорбление *neut.*

optical /'ɒptɪkəl/ *adj.* зрительный; оптический.

optician /ɒp'tɪʃən/ *n.* оптик *m.*

optics /'ɒptɪks/ *n.* оптика *f.*

optimism /'ɒptə,mɪzəm/ *n.* оптимизм *m.*

optimistic /,ɒptə'mɪstɪk/ *adj.* оптимистический.

optimum /'ɒptəməm/ **1.** *n.* оптимум *m.* **2.** *adj.* оптимальный.

option /'ɒpʃən/ *n.* выбор *m.*

optional /'ɒpʃənl/ *adj.* необязательный; факультативный.

opulence /'ɒpyələns/ *n.* богатство; изобилие *neut.*

opus /'oupəs/ *n.* опус *m.*

or /ɔr; *unstressed* ər/ *conj.* или; **or else** иначе.

oral /'ɔrəl/ *adj.* устный.

orange /'ɔrɪndʒ/ **1.** *n.* апельсин *m.*; (*color*) оранжевый цвет *m.* **2.** *adj.* апельсиновый; (*color*) оранжевый.

orange peel *n.* апельсинная корка *f.*

oration /ɔ'reiʃən/ *n.* речь *f.*

orator /'ɔrətər/ *n.* оратор *m.*

oratorio /,ɔrə'tɔri,ou/ *n.* оратория *f.*

oratory /'ɔrə,tɔri/ *n.* красноречие *neut.*; ораторское искусство *neut.*

orbit /'ɔrbɪt/ *n.* орбита *f.*

orchard /'ɔrtʃərd/ *n.* (*fruktóvy*) фруктовый сад *m.*

orchestra /'ɔrkəstrə/ *n.* оркестр *m.*; (*theat.*) партер *m.*

orchestrate /'ɔrkə,streit/ *v.* оркестровать; инструментировать, инструментовать *impf. and pf.*

orchestration /,ɔrkə'streiʃən/ *n.* оркестровка *f.*; инструментовка *f.*

orchid /'ɔrkɪd/ *n.* орхидея *f.*

ordain /ɔr'dein/ *v.* (*order*) предписывать *impf.*; (*consecrate a priest*) посвящать (в духовный сан) *impf.*

ordeal /ɔr'dil/ *n.* тяжёлое испыта́ние *neut.*
order /'ɔrdər/ **1.** *n.* поря́док *m.*; (*command*)
прика́з *m.*; распоряже́ние *neut.*; (*business*) зака́з
m.; **in order to** для того́ что́бы. **2.** *v.* (*command*) прика́зывать *impf.*, приказа́ть *pf.*; (*place order*) зака́зывать *impf.*, заказа́ть *pf.*
orderliness /'ɔrdərlinɪs/ *n.* поря́док *m.*; аккура́тность *f.*
orderly /'ɔrdərli/ **1.** *adj.* аккура́тный, опря́тный; **2.** *n.* (*med.*) дежу́рный санита́р *m.*; (*mil.*) **orderly officer** ордина́рец *m.*
ordinal /'ɔrdṇəl/ *n.* поря́дковое числи́тельное *neut.*
ordinance /'ɔrdṇəns/ *n.* зако́н; декре́т *m.*
ordinary /'ɔrdṇ,eri/ *adj.* обы́чный; просто́й.
ore /ɔr/ *n.* руда́ *f.*
Oregon /'ɔrɪgən, -,gɒn/ *n.* О́регон *m.*
Orel /ɔ'rel/ *n.* Орёл *m.*
organ /'ɔrgən/ **1.** *n.* о́рган *m.*; (*mus.*) орга́н *m.* **2.** *adj.* орга́нный.
organdy /'ɔrgəndi/ *n.* кисея́ *f.*
organ grinder *n.* шарма́нщик *m.*
organic /ɔr'gænɪk/ *adj.* органи́ческий.
organism /'ɔrgə,nɪzəm/ *n.* органи́зм *m.*
organist /'ɔrgənɪst/ *n.* органи́ст *m.*
organization /,ɔrgənə'zeiʃən/ *n.* организа́ция *f.*; устро́йство *neut.*
organizational /,ɔrgənə'zeiʃəṇ/ *adj.* организацио́нный; организа́торский.
organize /'ɔrgə,naiz/ *v.* организо́вывать *impf.*; организова́ть *impf.* and *pf.*
organized /'ɔrgə,naizd/ *adj.* организо́ванный.
organizer /'ɔrgə,naizər/ *n.* организа́тор *m.*
orgasm /'ɔrgæzəm/ *n.* орга́зм *m.*
orgiastic /,ɔrdʒi'æstɪk/ *adj.* разну́зданный.
orgy /'ɔrdʒi/ *n.* о́ргия *f.*
Orient /'ɔriənt/ **1.** *n.* восто́к *m.* **2.** *adj.* (*arch.*) восто́чный.
orient /'ɔri,ent/ *v.* ориенти́ровать *impf.* and *pf.*
Oriental /,ɔri'ent̩/ **1.** *adj.* восто́чный. **2.** *n.* жи́тель Восто́ка *m.*
oriental cockroach *n.* чёрный тарака́н *m.*
orientation /,ɔriən'teiʃən/ *n.* ориента́ция *f.*
origin /'ɔrɪdʒɪn/ *n.* происхожде́ние *neut.*; исто́чник *m.*, нача́ло *neut.*
original /ə'rɪdʒəṇ/ **1.** *adj.* первонача́льный; по́длинный; оригина́льный. **2.** *n.* по́длинник *m.*
originality /ə,rɪdʒə'nælɪti/ *n.* по́длинность; оригина́льность *f.*
ornament / *n.* 'ɔrnəmənt; *v.* 'ɔrnə,ment/ **1.** *n.* украше́ние *neut.*; орна́мент *m.* **2.** *v.* украша́ть *impf.*, укра́сить *pf.*
ornamental /,ɔrnə'ment̩/ *adj.* декорати́вный; орнамента́льный.
ornamentation /,ɔrnəmen'teiʃən/ *n.* украше́ние *neut.*
ornate /ɔr'neit/ *adj.* разукра́шенный; витиева́тый.
ornithology /,ɔrnə'θɒlədʒi/ *n.* орнитоло́гия *f.*
orphan /'ɔrfən/ **1.** *n.* сирота́ *m.* and *f.* (*decl. f.*). **2.** *adj.* сиро́тский.
orphanage /'ɔrfənɪdʒ/ *n.* детдо́м *m.*
Orsha /'ɔrʃə/ *n.* О́рша *f.*
orthodox /'ɔrθə,dɒks/ *adj.* ортодокса́льный; (*Orthodox church*) правосла́вный.
orthodoxy /'ɔrθə,dɒksi/ *n.* (*Orthodox church*) правосла́вие *neut.*

orthographic /,ɔrθə'græfɪk/ *adj.* орфографи́ческий.
orthography /ɔr'θɒgrəfi/ *n.* правописа́ние *neut.*; орфогра́фия *f.*
orthopedist /,ɔrθə'pidɪst/ *n.* ортопе́д *m.*
osculate /'ɒskyə,leit/ *v.* (*kiss*) целова́ться *impf.*; (*math.*) соприкаса́ться *impf.*
Oslo /'ɒzlou/ *n.* О́сло *neut.*
osprey /'ɒspri/ *n.* скопа́ *f.*
ossify /'ɒsə,fai/ *v.* костене́ть *impf.*
ostensible /ɒ'stɛnsəbəl/ *adj.* мни́мый; очеви́дный.
ostensibly /ɒ'stɛnsəbli/ *adv.* я́кобы.
ostentatious /,ɒstɛn'teiʃəs/ *adj.* показно́й.
osteoporosis /,ɒstioupə'rousɪs/ *n.* остеопоро́з *m.*
ostracize /'ɒstrə,saiz/ *v.* изгоня́ть из о́бщества *impf.*
ostrich /'ɒstrɪtʃ/ **1.** *n.* стра́ус *m.* **2.** *adj.* стра́усовый.
other /'ʌðər/ **1.** *adj.* друго́й, ино́й. **2.** *pron.* друго́й.
otherwise /'ʌðər,waiz/ *adv.*, *conj.* ина́че; а то, в проти́вном слу́чае.
otter /'ɒtər/ *n.* (*zool.*) вы́дра *f.*
ottoman /'ɒtəmən/ *n.* оттома́нка *f.*
ouch /autʃ/ *interj.* ой!; ай!
ought /ɔt/ *v.* до́лжен (бы) (*with inf.*) *m.*, должна́ бы *f.*, должно́ бы *neut.*, должны́ бы *pl.*
ounce /auns/ *n.* у́нция *f.*
our /auᵊr; *unstressed* ar/ *pron.* наш *m.*, на́ша *f.*, на́ше *neut.*, на́ши *pl.*
ourselves /ɑr'sɛlvz, auᵊr-/ *pron.* себя́; себе́; са́ми.
oust /aust/ *v.* вытесня́ть *impf.*, вы́теснить *pf.*
out /aut/ *adv.* нару́жу; вон; **to be out** не быть до́ма; **out of** из, вне (*with gen.*).
outbid /,aut'bid/ *v.* перебива́ть це́ну *impf.*
outbound /aut'baund/ *adj.* уходя́щий.
outbreak /'aut,breik/ *n.* вспы́шка *f.*; (*of war*) нача́ло *neut.*
outbuilding /'aut,bildɪŋ/ *n.* пристро́йка *f.*; (*shed*) сара́й *m.*
outburst /'aut,bɜrst/ *n.* взрыв *m.*; вспы́шка *f.*
outcast /'aut,kæst/ *n.* изгна́нник *m.*
outcome /'aut,kʌm/ *n.* результа́т *m.*
outdated /,aut'deitid/ *adj.* устаре́лый; устаре́вший.
outdo /,aut'du/ *v.* превосходи́ть *impf.*; (*overtake*) перегоня́ть *impf.*
outdoor /'aut,dɔr/ *adj.* на откры́том во́здухе.
outdoors /,aut'dɔrz/ *adv.* на откры́том во́здухе; (*dir.*) на во́здух; на у́лицу.
outer /'autər/ *adj.* вне́шний; нару́жный.
outermost /'autər,moust/ *adj.* кра́йний; са́мый да́льний.
outfit /'aut,fit/ **1.** *n.* снаряже́ние *neut.* **2.** *v.* снаряжа́ть *impf.*, снаряди́ть *pf.*; экипирова́ть *impf.* and *pf.*
outflow /'aut,flou/ *n.* пото́к *m.*; истече́ние *neut.*
outgrowth /'aut,grouθ/ *n.* отро́сток; о́тпрыск *m.*; (*result*) результа́т *m.*
outhouse /'aut,haus/ *n.* отхо́жее ме́сто *neut.*
outing /'autɪŋ/ *n.* экску́рсия *f.*
outlast /,aut'læst/ *v.* пережива́ть *impf.*, пережи́ть *pf.*
outlaw /'aut,lɔ/ **1.** *n.* изго́й, изгна́нник, челове́к вне зако́на *m.* **2.** *v.* запреща́ть; объявля́ть вне зако́на *impf.*

outlet /'autlɛt/ n. вы́ход m.; (business) ры́нок сбы́та m.

outline /'aut,lain/ n. очерта́ние neut.; эски́з m.; схе́ма f.

outlive /,aut'lıv/ v. пережи́ть pf.

outlook /'aut,lʊk/ n. вид m.; перспекти́ва f.

outmoded /,aut'moudıd/ adj. вы́шедший из мо́ды; отжи́вший.

out-of-date /'aut əv 'deit/ adj. старомо́дный; устаре́лый.

out-of-the-ordinary /'aut əv ði 'ɔrdn̩‚ɛri/ adj. необыча́йный.

out-of-tune /'aut əv 'tun/ adj. расстро́енный.

outpatient clinic /'aut,peiʃənt/ n. амбулато́рия f.

outpost /'aut,poust/ n. (mil.) аванпо́ст m.

outpouring /'aut,pɔrıŋ/ n. излия́ние neut.

output /'aut,pʊt/ n. вы́пуск m.; производи́тельность; проду́кция f.

outrageous /aut'reidʒəs/ adj. возмути́тельный; (offensive) оскорби́тельный.

outrank /,aut'ræŋk/ v. превосходи́ть по ра́нгу impf.

outrun /,aut'rʌn/ v. перегоня́ть impf., перегна́ть pf.

outset /'aut,sɛt/ n. нача́ло neut.

outside / adj., adv., prep. ,aut'said; n. 'aut'said/ n./ 1. adj. вне́шний; нару́жный. 2. adv. снару́жи; нару́жу; извне́; (outdoors) на у́лице; (dir.) на у́лицу. 3. n. вне́шность f. 4. prep. вне, за преде́лами, за преде́лы (with gen.).

outsider /,aut'saidər/ n. посторо́нний m.

outskirts /'aut,skɜrts/ n. окра́ина f.; предме́стье neut.

outsmart /,aut'smart/ v. перехитри́ть impf.

outspread /'aut'sprɛd/ adj. распростёртый.

outstanding /,aut'stændıŋ/ adj. (distinguished) выдаю́щийся; (unpaid) неупла́ченный.

outstretch /,aut'strɛtʃ/ v. протя́гивать impf.

outward /'autwərd/ adj. нару́жный.

outwardly /'autwərdli/ adv. вне́шне; снару́жи.

outwards /'autwərdz/ adv. нару́жу.

outwit /,aut'wıt/ v. перехитри́ть impf.

oval /'ouvəl/ 1. n. ова́л m. 2. adj. ова́льный.

ovarian /ou'vɛəriən/ adj. яи́чниковый.

ovary /'ouvəri/ n. яи́чник m.

ovate /'ouveit/ adj. яйцеви́дный.

ovation /ou'veiʃən/ n. ова́ция f.

oven /'ʌvən/ n. духо́вка; печь f.

ovenware /'ʌvən,wɛər/ n. огнеупо́рная посу́да f.

over /'ouvər/ 1. prep. над (with instr.); сверх, вы́ше (with gen.); че́рез (with acc.). 2. adv., designated by the prefixes: пере-, вы-.

overabundant /'ouvərə'bʌndənt/ adj. избы́точный.

overact /,ouvər'ækt/ v. переи́грывать impf.

overbearing /,ouvər'bɛərıŋ/ adj. вла́стный.

overboard /'ouvər,bɔrd/ adv. за борто́м; (dir.) за борт.

overburden /,ouvər'bɜrdn̩/ v. перегружа́ть impf.

overcast /'ouvər'kæst/ adj. (cloudy) о́блачный; па́смурный.

overcoat /'ouvər,kout/ n. пальто́ neut. indecl.; шине́ль f.

overcome /,ouvər'kʌm/ v. преодолева́ть impf.; преодоле́ть; превозмо́чь pf.

overconfidence /,ouvər'kɒnfıdəns/ n. чрезме́рная самоуве́ренность f.

overcrowding /,ouvər'kraudıŋ/ n. теснота́; перенаселённость f.

overdue /,ouvər'du/ adj. запозда́лый; просро́ченный.

overeat /,ouvər'it/ v. объеда́ться impf.

overexert /,ouvərıg'zɜrt/ v. перенапряга́ть(ся) impf.

overflow / n. 'ouvər,flou, v. ,ouvər'flou/ 1. n. разли́в; избы́ток m. 2. v. перелива́ться че́рез край impf.

overfulfill /,ouvərfəl'fıl/ v. перевыполня́ть impf.

overgrown /,ouvər'groun/ adj. (with weeds) заро́сший.

overhaul /,ouvər'hɔl/ v. (repair) ремонти́ровать impf. and pf.

overhead / adv. 'ouvər'hɛd; n. 'ouvər,hɛd/ 1. adv. над голово́й; наверху́. 2. n. накладны́е расхо́ды pl.

overhear /,ouvər'hıər/ v. случа́йно услы́шать pf.; подслу́шивать impf.

overland /'ouvər,lænd/ 1. adj. сухопу́тный. 2. adv. по су́ше.

overload /'ouvər,loud/ n. перегру́зка f.

overlook /,ouvər'lʊk/ v.t. (not notice) просмотре́ть pf.; (have view) выходи́ть на (with acc.) impf.

overly /'ouvərli/ adv. сли́шком.

overnight /'ouvər'nait/ adv. (for the night) на́ ночь; (the night before) накану́не ве́чером.

overpass /'ouvər,pæs/ n. путепрово́д m.; эстака́да f.

overpopulation /'ouvər,pɒpyə'leiʃən/ n. перенаселе́ние neut.

overpower /,ouvər'pauər/ v. переси́ливать impf., переси́лить pf.

overreact /,ouvərri'ækt/ v. боле́зненно реаги́ровать impf.

overrule /,ouvər'rul/ v. аннули́ровать impf. and pf.; отверга́ть impf.

overseas /'ouvər'siz/ adj. замо́рский; заграни́чный.

oversee /,ouvər'si/ v. надзира́ть (за with instr.) impf.

overseer /'ouvər,siər, -,sıər/ n. надзира́тель m.

oversight /'ouvər,sait/ n. недосмо́тр m.

oversimplify /,ouvər'sımplə,fai/ v. сли́шком упроща́ть impf.

oversleep /,ouvər'slip/ v. просыпа́ть impf.

overspend /,ouvər'spɛnd/ v. перепла́чивать; растра́чивать impf.

overstate /,ouvər'steit/ v. преувели́чивать impf.

overstrain /,ouvər'strein/ v. перенапряга́ть impf.

overt /ou'vɜrt/ adj. откры́тый; я́вный.

overtake /,ouvər'teik/ v. догоня́ть impf., догна́ть pf.; перегоня́ть impf.

overthrow / n. 'ouvər,θrou, v. ,ouvər'θrou/ 1. n. ниспроверже́ние neut. 2. v. сверга́ть impf., све́ргнуть pf.

overtime /'ouvər,taim/ 1. n. сверхуро́чное вре́мя neut. 2. adj. сверхуро́чный.

overture /'ouvərtʃər/ n. (mus.) увертю́ра f.; (proposal) предложе́ние n.; (initiative) инициати́ва, попы́тка.

overturn /,ouvər'tɜrn/ v. опроки́дывать impf., опроки́нуть pf.; v.i. опроки́дываться impf., опроки́нуться pf.

overview /'ouvər,vyu/ n. обзо́р m.

overwhelm /,ouvər'wɛlm/ v. (with emotions)

овладева́ть *impf.*, овладе́ть *pf.*; (*with work*) зава́ливать *impf.*; (*weigh down*) подавля́ть *impf.* подави́ть *pf.*

overwhelming /ˌouvər'wɛlmɪŋ/ *adj.* подавля́ющий.

overwork / *v.* ˌouvər'wɜrk; *n.* 'ouvər,wɜrk/ **1.** *v.* переутомля́ть(ся) *impf.*, переутоми́ть(ся) *pf.* **2.** *n.* переутомле́ние *neut.*

oviparous /ou'vɪpərəs/ *adj.* яйцекладу́щий.

ovulate /'ɒvyə,leit/ *v.* овули́ровать *impf.*

ovulation /'ɒvyə,leiʃən/ *n.* овуля́ция *f.*

owe /ou/ *v.* быть в долгу́ *impf.*; быть обя́занным *impf.*

owing to /'ouɪŋ/ *prep.* по причи́не; всле́дствие (*with gen.*); благодаря́ (*with dat.*).

owl /aul/ *n.* сова́ *f.*

own /oun/ **1.** *adj.* со́бственный. **2.** *v.* владе́ть (*with instr.*) *impf.*

owner /'ounər/ *n.* владе́лец *m.*, владе́лица *f.*

ownerless /'ounərlɪs/ *adj.* бесхо́зный.

ox /ɒks/ *n.* вол *m.*

Oxford /'ɒksfərd/ *n.* О́ксфорд *m.*

oxidation /ɒksɪ'deiʃən/ *n.* окисле́ние *neut.*

oxide /'ɒksaid/ *n.* о́кись *f.*

oxygen /'ɒksɪdʒən/ **1.** *n.* кислоро́д *m.* **2.** *adj.* кислоро́дный.

oyster /'ɔistər/ **1.** *n.* у́стрица *f.* **2.** *adj.* у́стричный.

ozone /'ouzoun/ *n.* озо́н *m.*

ozone layer *n.* озоносфе́ра *f.*

P

pa /pɑ/ *n.* (*colloq.*) па *m. indecl.*

pabulum /'pæbyələm/ *n.* пища *f.*

pace /peis/ **1.** *n.* шаг *m.*; (*fig.*) темп *m.* **2.** *v.* шагать *impf.*

pachyderm /'pækɪ,dɜrm/ *n.* толстокожее (животное) *neut.*

pacification /,pæsəfɪ'keiʃən/ *n.* умиротворение; усмирение *neut.*

pacifier /'pæsə,faiər/ *n.* миротворец *m.*; (*for baby*) соска *f.*

pacifism /'pæsə,fɪzəm/ *n.* пацифизм *m.*

pacifist /'pæsəfɪst/ **1.** *n.* пацифист *m.* **2.** *adj.* пацифистский.

pacify /'pæsə,fai/ *v.* усмирять *impf.*; успокаивать *impf.*, успокоить *pf.*

pack /pæk/ **1.** *n.* (*of cigarettes*) пачка *f.*; (*of animals*) стая *f.*; (*cards*) колода *f.* **2.** *v.* упаковывать *impf.*, упаковать *pf.*; (*cram*) набивать *impf.*, набить *pf.*

package /'pækɪdʒ/ *n.* пакет; тюк *m.*

packaging /'pækədʒɪŋ/ *n.* упаковка *f.*

pack animal *n.* вьючное животное *neut.*

packer /'pækər/ *n.* упаковщик *m.*

packet /'pækɪt/ *n.* пакет *m.*; пачка *f.*

packet boat *n.* пакетбот *m.*

pack horse *n.* вьючная лошадь *f.*

pack ice *n.* паковый лёд; пак *m.*

packing /'pækɪŋ/ **1.** *n.* упаковка *f.* **2.** *adj.* упаковочный.

packing case *n.* ящик (для упаковки) *m.*

packsaddle /'pæk,sædl/ *n.* вьючное седло *neut.*

pact /pækt/ *n.* пакт; договор *m.*

pad /pæd/ *n.* (*material*) подушка *f.*; (*for writing*) блокнот *m.*

padding /'pædɪŋ/ *n.* набивка *f.*

paddle /'pædl/ **1.** *n.* весло *neut.*; гребок *m.* **2.** *v.* грести веслом *impf.*

paddle boat *n.* колёсный пароход *m.*

paddle wheel *n.* гребное колесо *neut.*

paddock /'pædək/ *n.* загон *m.*

paddy *also* **rice paddy** /'pædi/ *n.* рисовое поле *neut.*

padlock /'pæd,lɒk/ *n.* висячий замок *m.*

Padova /'pɑdəvɑ/ *n.* (*also: Padua*) Падуя *f.*

paean /'piən/ *n.* пеан *m.*

pagan /'peigən/ **1.** *adj.* языческий. **2.** *n.* язычник *m.*, язычница *f.*

paganism /'peigə,nɪzəm/ *n.* язычество *neut.*

page[1] /peidʒ/ *n.* страница *f.*

page[2] /peidʒ/ *n.* (*attendant*) паж *m.*

pageantry /'pædʒəntri/ *n.* пышность *f.*; великолепие *neut.*

paginate /'pædʒə,neit/ *v.* нумеровать страницы *impf.*

pagination /,pædʒə'neiʃən/ *n.* пагинация *f.*

pagoda /pə'goudə/ *n.* пагода *f.*

paid /peid/ *adj.* платный; оплаченный.

pail /peil/ *n.* ведро *neut.*

pailful /'peil,fʊl/ *n.* целое ведро, полное ведро *neut.*

pain /pein/ *n.* боль *f.*; *pl.* (*efforts*) усилие *neut.*

pained /peind/ *adj.* обиженный; страдальческий.

painful /'peinfəl/ *adj.* болезненный.

painkiller /'pein,kɪlər/ *n.* болеутоляющее (средство) *neut.*

painless /'peinlɪs/ *adj.* безболезненный.

painstaking /'peinz,teikɪŋ/ *adj.* старательный

paint /peint/ **1.** *n.* краска *f.* **2.** *v.* (*create picture*) писать (красками) *impf.*; (*coat with paint*) красить *impf.*

paintbrush /'peint,brʌʃ/ *n.* кисть *f.*

painter /'peintər/ *n.* (*artist*) художник; живописец *m.*; (*worker*) маляр *m.*

painting /'peintɪŋ/ *n.* картина *f.*; (*act*) живопись *f.*

pair /pɛər/ **1.** *n.* пара *f.* **2.** *v.* спаривать *impf.*, спарить *pf.*; **to pair off** разделяться на пары *impf.*

paired /pɛərd/ *adj.* спаренный.

pajamas /pə'dʒɑməz, -'dʒæməz/ *n.* пижама *f.*

Pakistan /'pækə,stæn/ *n.* Пакистан *m.*

Pakistani /,pækə'stæni/ **1.** *adj.* пакистанский. **2.** *n.* пакистанец *m.*, пакистанка *f.*

pal /pæl/ **1.** *n.* (*colloq.*) приятель *m.*, приятельница *f.*; товарищ *m.* **2.** *v.* **to pal around with** дружиться (*c with instr.*) *impf.*

palace /'pælɪs/ **1.** *n.* дворец *m.* **2.** *adj.* дворцовый.

palanquin /,pælən'kin/ *n.* паланкин *m.*

palatable /'pælətəbəl/ *adj.* приемлемый; (*tasty*) вкусный

palatal /'pælətl/ *adj.* (*anat.*) нёбный; (*phon.*) палатальный.

palatalization /,pælətlə'zeiʃən/ *n.* смягчение *neut.*; палатализация *f.*

palatalized consonant /'pælətl,aizd/ *n.* мягкий согласный *m.*

palate /'pælɪt/ *n.* нёбо *neut.*

palatial /pə'leiʃəl/ *adj.* дворцовый; роскошный.

pale /peil/ *adj.* бледный; **to turn pale** бледнеть *impf.*, побледнеть *pf.*

paleface /'peil,feis/ *n.* (*slang*) бледнолицый *m.*

paleness /'peilnɪs/ *n.* бледность *f.*

Paleocene /'peiliə,sin/ *n.* палеоцен *m.*

paleographer /,peili'ɒgrəfər/ *n.* палеограф *m.*

paleographic /,peiliə'græfɪk/ *adj.* палеографический.

paleography /,peili'ɒgrəfi/ *n.* палеография *f.*

Paleolithic /,peiliə'lɪθɪk/ *adj.* палеолитический.

paleontologist /,peiliən'tɒlədʒɪst/ *n.* палеонтолог *m.*

paleontology /,peiliən'tɒlədʒi/ *n.* палеонтология *f.*

Paleozoic /,peiliə'zouɪk/ *adj.* палеозойский.

Palermo /pə'lɜrmou/ *n.* Палермо *m.*

palette /'pælɪt/ *n.* палитра *f.*

palimpsest /'pælɪmp,sest/ *n.* палимпсест *m.*

palindrome /'pælɪn,droum/ *n.* палиндром *m.*

paling /'peilɪŋ/ *n.* частокол *m.*

palingenesis /,pælɪn'dʒenəsɪs/ *n.* палингенез *m.*

palisade /'pælə'seid/ *n.* палисад *m.*

palladium /pə'leidiəm/ *n.* палладий *m.*

pallbearer /'pɔl,bɛərər/ *n.* несущий гроб *m.*

pallet /'pælɪt/ *n.* (*straw mattress*) тюфяк *m.*

palliative /'pæli,eitɪv, -iətɪv/ n. паллиати́в m.
pallid /'pælɪd/ adj. бле́дный.
pallor /'pælər/ n. бле́дность f.
palm[1] /pɑm/ n. (of hand) ладо́нь f.
palm[2] /pɑm/ **1.** n. (tree) па́льма f. **2.** adj. па́льмовый.
Palma /'pɑlmɑ/ n. Па́льма f.
palmate /'pælmeit/ adj. па́льчатый; ла́пчатый
palmist /'pɑmɪst/ n. хирома́нт m.
palmistry /'pɑməstri/ n. хирома́нтия f.
palm oil n. па́льмовое ма́сло neut.
Palm Sunday n. Ве́рбное Воскресе́нье neut.
palpability /,pælpə'bɪlɪti/ n. очеви́дность f.
palpable /'pælpəbəl/ adj. ощути́мый; (obvious) я́вный; очеви́дный.
palpate /'pælpeit/ v. (med.) пальпи́ровать impf.
palpation /pæl'peiʃən/ n. (med.) пальпа́ция f.
palpitate /'pælpɪ,teit/ v. (tremble) трепета́ть impf.
palpitation /,pælpɪ'teiʃən/ n. (си́льное) сердцебие́ние neut.; пульса́ция f.
palsy /'pɔlzi/ n. парали́ч m ; (trembling) дрожь f.
paltry /'pɔltri/ adj. ничто́жный; (contemptible) презре́нный.
Pamirs /pɑ'mɪərz/ n. the, (mountain range) Пами́р m.
pampas /'pæmpəz; attributively 'pæmpəs/ n. пампа́сы pl.
pamper /'pæmpər/ v. балова́ть; изне́живать(ся) impf.
pamphlet /'pæmflɪt/ n. брошю́ра f.; (polit.) памфле́т n.
pamphleteer /,pæmflɪ'tɪər/ n. памфлети́ст m.
pan /pæn/ n. сковорода́ f.
panacea /,pænə'siə/ n. панаце́я f.
panache /pə'næʃ, -'nɑʃ/ n. (swagger) щегольство́ neut.
Panama /'pænə,mɑ/ n. Пана́ма f.
pancake /'pæn,keik/ n. блин m.
panchromatic /,pænkrou'mætɪk/ adj. панхромати́ческий.
pancreas /'pænkriəs/ n. поджелу́дочная железа́ f.
pancreatic /,pænkri'ætɪk/ adj. панкреати́ческий.
panda /'pændə/ n. па́нда f.
pandemic /pæn'dɛmɪk/ n. пандеми́я f.
pandemonium /,pændə'mouniəm/ n. шум и гам; галдёж m.
pander /'pændər/ also **panderer** /'pændərər/ n. (pimp) сво́дник m.
pane /pein/ n. око́нное стекло́ neut.
panel /'pænḷ/ n. филёнка; пане́ль f.
paneling /'pænḷɪŋ/ n. пане́ль f.
panelist /'pænḷɪst/ n. уча́стник виктори́ны (диску́ссии); член жюри́ m.
pang /pæŋ/ n. о́страя боль f.; му́ки pl.
panic /'pænɪk/ **1.** n. па́ника f. **2.** v.i. впада́ть в па́нику impf.
panicky /'pænɪki/ adj. пани́ческий.
panjandrum /pæn'dʒændrəm/ n. ши́шка f.
pannier /'pænyər/ n. корзи́на f.
panoply /'pænəpli/ n. (array) наря́д m.; (armor) доспе́хи pl.
panorama /,pænə'ræmə/ n. панора́ма f.
panoramic /,pænə'ræmɪk/ adj. панора́мный.
panpipe /'pæn,paip/ n. свире́ль f.
pansy /'pænzi/ n. аню́тины гла́зки pl.
pant /pænt/ v. задыха́ться impf.

pantaloons /,pæntḷ'un/ (s) n. пантало́ны pl.
pantheism /'pænθi,ɪzəm/ n. пантеи́зм m.
pantheist /'pænθiist/ n. пантеи́ст m.
pantheistic /,pænθi'ɪstɪk/ adj. пантеисти́ческий.
pantheon /'pænθi,ɒn/ n. пантео́н m.
panther /'pænθər/ n. панте́ра f.
panties /'pæntiz/ n. pl. тру́сики pl.
pantograph /'pæntə,græf/ n. панто́граф m.
pantomime /'pæntə,maim/ n. пантоми́ма f.
pantomimic /,pæntə'mɪmɪk/ n. пантомими́ческий.
pantry /'pæntri/ n. кладова́я f.
pants /pænts/ n. брю́ки; штаны́ pl.
panty hose /'pænti/ n. колго́тки pl.
panzer /'pænzər/ adj. бронета́нковый.
papa /'pɑpə/ n. па́па m.
papacy /'peipəsi/ n. па́пство neut.
papal /'peipəl/ adj. па́пский.
paper /'peipər/ **1.** adj. бума́га f.; (newspaper) газе́та f.; (conference essay) докла́д m. **2.** adj. бума́жный.
paperback /'peipər,bæk/ adj. в бума́жном переплёте.
paper clip n. скре́пка (для бума́г) f.
paperhanger /'peipər,hæŋər/ n. обо́йщик m.
paper knife n. нож для разреза́ния бума́г m.
paper mill n. бума́жная фа́брика f.
paper pulp n. бума́жная ма́сса f.
paperweight /'peipər,weit/ n. пресс-папье́ neut. indecl.
paperwork /'peipər,wɜrk/ n. канцеля́рская рабо́та f.
papier-mâché /,peipərmə'ʃei/ n. папье-маше́ neut. indecl.
papilla /pə'pɪlə/ n. сосо́чек m.
papism /'peipɪzəm/ n. (pej.) папи́зм m.
papist /'peipɪst/ n. (pej.) папи́ст m.
paprika /pæ'prikə/ n. кра́сный or зелёный пе́рец m.
papyrology /,pæpə'rɒlədʒi/ n. папироло́гия f.
papyrus /pə'pairəs/ n. папи́рус m.
par /pɑr/ n. (equality) ра́венство neut.; (econ.) номина́л m.; **on a par with** adv. наравне́ с (with instr.)
parable /'pærəbəl/ n. при́тча f.
parabola /pə'ræbələ/ n. пара́бола f.
parabolic[1] /,pærə'bɒlɪk/ adj. (of parabola) параболи́ческий.
parabolic[2] /,pærə'bɒlɪk/ adj. (metaphorical) метафори́ческий.
parachute /'pærə,ʃut/ n. парашю́т m.
parachutist /'pærə,ʃutist/ n. парашюти́ст m.
parade /pə'reid/ **1.** n. пара́д m. **2.** v. марширова́ть impf.
parade ground n. плац m.
paradigm /'pærə,daim/ n. паради́гма f.
paradise /'pærə,dais/ n. рай m.
paradisiacal /,pærədɪ'saiəkəl/ adj. ра́йский.
parados /'pærə,dɒs/ n. ты́льный тра́верс m.
paradox /'pærə,dɒks/ n. парадо́кс m.
paradoxical /,pærə'dɒksɪkəl/ adj. парадокса́льный.
paraffin /'pærəfɪn/ n. парафи́н m.
paragon /'pærə,gɒn/ n. образе́ц m.
paragraph /'pærə,græf/ n. пара́граф; абза́ц m.
Paraguay /'pærə,gwai, -,gwei/ n. Парагва́й m.

parakeet /'pærə,kit/ *n.* (длиннохвостый) попугай *m.*

parallax /'pærə,læks/ *n.* параллакс *m.*

parallel /'pærə,lɛl/ **1.** *n.* параллель *f.* **2.** *adj.* параллельный. **3.** *v.* (*liken*) уподоблять *impf.*, уподобить *pf.*

parallelepiped /,pærə,lɛlə'paipid/ *n.* параллелепипед *m.*

parallelism /'pærələ,lizəm/ *n.* параллелизм *m.*

parallelogram /,pærə'lɛlə,græm/ *n.* параллелограм *m.*

paralysis /pə'ræləsis/ *n.* паралич *m.*

paralytic /,pærə'litik/ **1.** *n.* паралитик *m.* **2.** *adj.* паралитический.

paralyze /'pærə,laiz/ *v.* парализовать *impf.* and *pf.*

paramagnetic /,pærəmæg'nɛtik/ *adj.* парамагнитный.

paramagnetism /,pærə'mægni,tizəm/ *n.* парамагнетизм *m.*

parameter /pə'ræmitər/ *n.* параметр *neut.*

paramilitary /,pærə'mili,tɛri/ *adj.* полувоенный.

paramount /'pærə,maunt/ *adj.* первостепенный.

paramour /'pærə,mʊr/ *n.* любовник *m.*, любовница *f.*

paranoia /,pærə'nɔiə/ *n.* паранойя *f.*

paranoid /'pærə,nɔid/ **1.** *adj.* параноический. **2.** *n.* параноик *m.*

paraphrase /'pærə,freiz/ **1.** *v.* перефразировать *impf.* and *pf.* **2.** *n.* перефраза *f.*; пересказ *m.*

parasite /'pærə,sait/ *n.* (*biol.*) паразит *m.*; (*person*) тунеядец *m.*

parasitic /,pærə'sitik/ *adj.* паразитный, паразитический.

parasol /'pærə,sɔl/ *n.* зонтик (от солнца) *m.*

paratrooper /'pærə,trupər/ *n.* парашютист *m.*

parcel /'parsəl/ *n.* пакет, тюк *m.*; посылка *f.*

parchment /'partʃmənt/ **1.** *n.* пергамент *m.* **2.** *adj.* пергаментный.

pardon /'pardn/ **1.** *n.* прощение; извинение *neut.* **2.** *v.* прощать *impf.*, простить *pf.*; извинять *impf.*, извинить *pf.*; **pardon me!** извините!

pardonable /'pardnəbəl/ *adj.* простительный.

pare /pɛər/ *f.* обрезать *impf.*; (*fruit*) чистить *impf.*

parent /'pɛərənt/ *n.* родитель *m.*

parental /pə'rɛntl/ *adj.* родительский.

parenthesis /pə'rɛnθəsis/ *n.* круглая скобка *f.*

par excellence /,par ɛksə'lans/ *adv.* в высшей степени.

pariah /pə'raiə/ *n.* пария *m.* and *f.* (*decl. f.*)

Paris /'pæris, pa'ri/ *n.* Париж *m.*

parish /'pæriʃ/ *n.* (*eccl. unit*) приход *m.*; (*parishioners*) прихожане *pl.*

parishioner /pə'riʃənər/ *n.* прихожанин *m.*, прихожанка *f.*

Parisian /pə'riʒən/ **1.** *adj.* парижский. **2.** *n.* парижанин *m.*, парижанка *f.*

parity /'pæriti/ *n.* равенство *neut.*; (*econ.*) паритет *m.*

park /park/ **1.** *n.* парк *m.* **2.** *v.* ставить (машину) *impf.*

parking /'parkiŋ/ *n.* стоянка *f.*

parking lot *n.* автостоянка *f.*

Parkinson's disease /'parkinsənz/ *n.* паркинсонизм *m.*

parley /'parli/ *n.* совещание *neut.*; переговоры *pl.*

parliament /'parləmənt/ *n.* парламент *m.*

parliamentary /,parlə'mɛntəri/ *adj.* парламентский; парламентарный.

parlor /'parlər/ *n.* гостиная *f.*

parochial /pə'roukiəl/ *adj.* (*of parish*) приходский; (*narrow*) узкий.

parody /'pærədi/ **1.** *n.* пародия *f.* **2.** *v.* пародировать *impf.* and *pf.*

paroxysm /'pærək,sizəm/ *n.* приступ; припадок *m.*

parricide /'pærə,said/ *n.* (*act*) отцеубийство *neut.*

parrot /'pærət/ *n.* попугай *m.*

parry /'pæri/ *v.* отражать; (*sport*) парировать, *impf.* and *pf.*

parsimonious /,parsə'mouniəs/ *adj.* скупой.

parsley /'parsli/ *n.* петрушка *f.*

parsnip /'parsnip/ *n.* пастернак *m.*

part /part/ **1.** *n.* часть *f.*; участие *neut.*; (*role*) роль *f.*; (*mus.*) партия *f.* **2.** *v.t.* разлучать *impf.*, разлучить *pf.*; *v.i.* (*separate*) разлучаться *impf.*, разлучиться *pf.*; **to part with** расставаться (с *with instr.*) *impf.*, расстаться *pf.*

partake /par'teik/ *v.* принимать участие (в *with prep.*) *impf.*

partial /'parʃəl/ *adj.* частичный; (*biased*) пристрастный.

partiality /,parʃi'æliti/ *n.* (*bias*) пристрастие (к *with dat.*) *neut.*

participant /par'tisəpənt/ *n.* участник *m.*, участница *f.*

participate /par'tisə,peit/ *v.* участвовать *impf.*

participation /par,tisə'peiʃən/ *n.* участие (в *with prep.*) *neut.*

participle /'partə,sipəl/ *n.* причастие *neut.*

particle /'partikəl/ *n.* частица *f.*

particular /pər'tikyələr/ **1.** *adj.* особенный. **2.** *n.* деталь, подробность *f.*

particularly /pər'tikyələrli/ *adv.* особенно; в частности.

parting /'partiŋ/ **1.** *n.* расставание *neut.*; разлука *f.* **2.** *adj.* прощальный.

partisan /'partəzən/ **1.** *adj.* партизанский. **2.** *n.* партизан *m.*, партизанка *f.* сторонник *m.*

partition /par'tiʃən/ *n.* разделение *neut.*; (*wall*) перегородка *f.*

partitive /'partitiv/ *adj.* разделительный.

partly /'partli/ *adv.* частично; отчасти.

partner /'partnər/ *n.* партнёр; компаньон *m.*

partnership /'partnər,ʃip/ *n.* товарищество *neut.*

part of speech *n.* (*gram.*) часть речи *f.*

part-owner /'part 'ounər/ *n.* совладелец *m.*

partridge /'partridʒ/ *n.* куропатка *f.*

part-time /'part'taim/ *adv.* на постоянке.

party /'parti/ **1.** *n.* вечер *m.*; вечеринка *f.*; приём *m.*; (*polit.*) партия *f.* (*group*) группа *f.* **2.** *adj.* партийный.

pas /pa/ *n.*: **pas de deux** па-де-де *neut. indecl.*; **pas de trois** па-де-труа *neut. indecl.*

pass /pæs/ **1.** *n.* проход *m.*; (*permit*) пропуск *m.*; (*cards; athl.*) пас *m.*; (*geog.*) перевал *m.* **2.** *v.* проходить (мимо *with gen.*) *impf.*, пройти *pf.*; (*exam*) сдавать *impf.*, сдать *pf.*; (*cards; athl.*) пасовать *impf.*; **to pass away** скончаться *pf.*

passable /'pæsəbəl/ *adj.* (*pass through*) проходимый; (*with vehicle*) проезжий; (*adequate*) достаточный.

passage /'pæsɪdʒ/ n. переезд m.; (on ship) рейс m.; (corridor) проход; коридор m. (of book) отрывок m.; (mus.) пассаж m.

passbook /'pæs,bʊk/ n. сберкнижка f.

passé /pæ'sei/ adj. устарелый.

passenger /'pæsəndʒər/ **1.** n. пассажир m., пассажирка f. **2.** adj. пассажирский.

passerby /,pæsər'bai/ n. прохожий m.

passion /'pæʃən/ n. страсть f.

passionate /'pæʃənit/ adj. страстный.

passionless /'pæʃənlɪs/ adj. бесстрастный.

passive /'pæsɪv/ adj. пассивный (gram.) страдательный.

passivity /pæ'sɪvɪti/ n. пассивность f.

passkey /'pæs,ki/ n. отмычка f.

Passover /'pæs,ouvər/ n. (еврейская) Пасха f.

passport /'pæspɔrt/ **1.** n. паспорт m. **2.** adj. паспортный.

password /'pæs,wɜrd/ n. пароль m.

past /pæst/ **1.** adj. прошлый; бывший; (gram.) прошедший. **2.** n. прошлое neut. **3.** prep. мимо (with gen.); после (with gen.), за (with instr.). **4.** adv. мимо.

pasta /'pɑstə/ n. макаронные изделия pl.

paste /peist/ **1.** n. (soft mixture) паста f.; (adhesive) клейстер; клей m. **2.** v. склеивать impf., склеить pf.

pasteurize /'pæstʃə,raiz/ v. пастеризовать impf. and pf.

pastime /'pæs,taim/ n. развлечение neut.

past master n. (непревзойдённый) мастер m.

pastry /'peistri/ n. печенье, пирожное neut.

pasture /'pæstʃər/ n. пастбище neut.; (enclosed area) выгон m.

pat /pæt/ **1.** n. похлопывание neut. **2.** v. похлопывать impf.

patch /pætʃ/ **1.** n. заплата f. (piece of land) участок m. **2.** v. (mend) латать impf., залатать pf.

patched /pætʃt/ adj. залатанный.

patchwork /'pætʃ,wɜrk/ n. (sewing) лоскутная работа f.

pâté /pɑ'tei/ n. паштет m.

paten /'pætn/ n. (eccl.) дискос m.

patent /'pætnt/ **1.** adj. (obvious) очевидный; (patented) патентованный. **2.** n. патент m.; исключительное право neut. **3.** v. патентовать impf.

patent leather /'pætnt/ n. лакированная кожа f.

paternal /pə'tɜrnl/ adj. отцовский.

paternity /pə'tɜrniti/ n. отцовство neut.

path /pæθ/ n. тропинка; дорожка f.; путь m.

pathetic /pə'θetɪk/ adj. жалкий.

pathfinder /'pæθ,faindər/ n. первопроходец m.

pathogen /'pæθədʒən/ n. патогенный организм m.

pathology /pə'θɒlədʒi/ n. патология f.

pathos /'peiθɒs/ n. пафос m.

pathway /'pæθ,wei/ n. тропинка f.; (in garden) дорожка f.

patience /'peiʃəns/ n. терпение neut.

patient /'peiʃənt/ **1.** adj. терпеливый. **2.** n. больной m., больная f.

patio /'pæti,ou/ n. дворик m.; патио neut. indecl.

patriarchal /,peitri'ɑrkəl/ adj. патриархальный; (eccl.) патриарший.

patriarchate /'peitri,ɑrkit/ n. патриархат m.; (eccl.) патриаршество neut.

patricide /'pætrə,said/ n. (act) отцеубийство neut.; (person) отцеубийца m. and f. (decl. f.)

patrimony /'pætrə,mouni/ n. наследство; родовое имущество; наследие neut.

patriot /'peitriət/ n. патриот m., патриотка f.

patriotic /,peitri'ɒtɪk/ adj. патриотический.

patriotism /'peitriə,tɪzəm/ n. патриотизм m.

patrol /pə'troul/ **1.** n. патруль m. **2.** v. патрулировать impf.

patrol car n. патруль m.; патрульная машина f.

patron /'peitrən/ n. покровитель m.; (of the arts) меценат m.

patronize /'peitrə,naiz/ v. покровительствовать impf.

patronizing /'peitrə,naizɪŋ/ adj. снисходительный.

pattern /'pætərn/ n. (model) образец m.; модель f.; (decoration) узор m.

paunch /pɔntʃ/ n. (belly) живот m.; (large belly) брюшко; пузо neut.

paunchy /'pɔntʃi/ adj. пузатый.

pauper /'pɔpər/ n. бедняк; нищий m.

pause /pɔz/ **1.** n. пауза; остановка f.; перерыв m. **2.** v. останавливаться impf., остановиться pf.

pave /peiv/ v. мостить impf.; (fig.) устилать impf., устлать pf.

paved /peivd/ adj. мощёный; вымощенный.

pavement /'peivmənt/ n. мостовая f.

pavilion /pə'vilyən/ n. павильон m.; палатка f.

paving stones /'peivɪŋ/ n. брусчатка f.

Pavlovsk /'pavlɒvsk/ n. Павловск m.

paw /pɔ/ **1.** n. лапа f. **2.** v. трогать лапой impf.

pawl /pɔl/ n. собачка; защёлка f.

pawn /pɔn/ **1.** n. залог m.; (chess) пешка f. **2.** v. отдавать в залог impf.

pawnbroker /'pɔn,broukər/ n. ростовщик m.

pawnshop /'pɔn,ʃɒp/ n. ломбард m.

pay /pei/ **1.** n. (payment) плата f.; (salary) зарплата f.; жалованье neut. **2.** v. платить impf., заплатить pf.; **to pay back** (a person) отплачивать impf., отплатить pf.

pay freeze n. замораживание зарплаты neut.

payload /'pei,loud/ n. полезная нагрузка f.

paymaster /'pei,mæstər/ n. кассир m.; (mil.) казначей m.

payment /'peimənt/ n. платёж m.

payoff /'pei,ɔf/ n. (retribution) отплата f.; (settling a score) расплата f.

payout /'pei,aut/ n. выплата f.

pay raise n. повышение зарплаты neut.

payroll /'pei,roul/ n. платёжная ведомость f.

pea /pi/ **1.** n. горошина f.; pl. горох m. **2.** adj. гороховый.

peace /pis/ n. мир m.

peaceful /'pisfəl/ adj. мирный.

peacemaker /'pis,meikər/ n. миротворец; примиритель m.

peacetime /'pis,taim/ n. мирное время neut.

peach /pitʃ/ **1.** n. персик m. **2.** adj. персиковый.

peacock /'pi,kɒk/ **1.** n. павлин m. **2.** adj. павлиний.

peahen /'pi,hɛn/ n. пава f.

pea jacket n. бушлат m.

peak /pik/ n. пик m. вершина f.

peal /pil/ *n.* (*bells*) звон; трезвóн *m.*; (*laughter*) взрыв *m.*; (*thunder*) раскáт *m.*

peanut /'pi,nʌt/ *n.* арáхис; землянóй орéх *m.*

pear /pɛər/ **1.** *n.* грýша *f.* **2.** *adj.* грýшевый.

pearl /pɜrl/ **1.** *n.* жемчýжина *f.* **2.** *adj.* жемчýжный.

pearl oyster *n.* жемчýжница *f.*

pear-shaped /'pɛər ˌʃeipt/ *adj.* грушевѝдный.

peasant /'pɛzənt/ **1.** *n.* крестья́нин *m.*, крестья́нка *f.* **2.** *adj.* крестья́нский.

peasantry /'pɛzəntri/ *n.* крестья́нство *neut.*

pea soup *n.* горóховый суп *m.*

peat /pit/ *n.* торф *m.*

peat bog *n.* торфяни́к *m.*; торфянóе болóто *neut.*

pebble /'pɛbəl/ *n.* голы́ш *m.*

pebbly /'pɛbli/ *adj.* покры́тый гáлькой.

peccadillo /ˌpɛkə'dɪlou/ *n.* грешóк *m.*

peck /pɛk/ **1.** *n.* удáр клю́вом *m.*; (*colloq.*) (*kiss*) поцелýй *m.* **2.** *v.* клевáть *impf.*

peculate /'pɛkyə,leit/ *v.* присвáивать чужи́е дéньги; растрáчивать *impf.*

peculiar /pɪ'kyulyər/ *adj.* осóбенный; стрáнный.

peculiarity /pɪˌkyuli'ærɪti/ *n.* осóбенность; стрáнность *f.*

pecuniary /pɪ'kyuniˌɛri/ *adj.* дéнежный.

pedagogy /'pɛdəˌgoudʒi/ *n.* педагóгика *f.*

pedal /'pɛdl̩/ *n.* педáль *f.*

pedant /'pɛdnt/ *n.* педáнт *m.*

peddle /'pɛdl̩/ *v.* торговáть с лоткá (*with instr.*) *impf.*

peddler /'pɛdlər/ *n.* разнóсчик; коробéйник *m.*

pederasty /'pɛdəˌræsti/ *n.* педерáстия *f.*

pedestal /'pɛdəstl̩/ *n.* пьедестáл *m.*

pedestrian /pə'dɛstriən/ **1.** *n.* пешехóд *m.* **2.** *adj.* пешехóдный.

pediatric /ˌpidi'ætrɪk/ *adj.* педиатри́ческий

pediatrician /ˌpidiə'trɪʃən/ *n.* педиáтр *m.*

pediatrics /ˌpidi'ætrɪks/ *n.* педиатри́я *f.*

pedicure /'pɛdɪˌkyur/ *n.* педикю́р *m.*

pedigree /'pɛdɪˌgri/ *n.* родослóвная *f.*

pediment /'pɛdəmənt/ *n.* (*archit.*) фронтóн *m.*

pedometer /pə'dɒmɪtər/ *n.* шагомéр *m.*

peduncle /pə'dʌŋkəl/ *n.* (*bot.*) стебелёк *m.*

pee /pi/ (*colloq.*) **1.** *n.* мочá *f.* **2.** *v.* мочи́ться; пи́сать *impf.*

peekaboo /'pikəˌbu/ **1.** *interj.* ку-кý! **2.** *n.* пря́тки *pl.*

peel /pil/ **1.** *n.* кожурá; кóрка *f.* **2.** *v.* очищáть *impf.*, очи́стить *pf.*

peeling /'piliŋ/ *n.* (*process*) очи́стка *f.*; *pl.* (*refuse*) шелухá *f.*; очи́стки *pl.*

peep /pip/ **1.** *n.* бы́стрый взгляд *m.* **2.** *v.* взгля́дывать (на *with acc.*) *impf.*

peephole /'pip,houl/ *n.* глазóк *m.*; (*mil.*) смотровáя щель *f.*

peer /pɪər/ *n.* (*equal*) рóвня *m.* and *f.* (*decl. f.*); рáвный *m.*

peerless /'pɪərlɪs/ *adj.* несравнéнный.

peevish /'piviʃ/ *adj.* раздражи́тельный; брюзгли́вый.

peg /pɛg/ *n.* кóлышек *m.*

peg leg *n.* протéз *m.*

Peipus /'paipəs/ *n.* Lake, Чýдское óзеро *neut.*

pejorative /pɪ'dʒɔrətɪv/ *adj.* уничижи́тельный

plebeian /plɪ'biən/ *adj.* плебéйский.

pelican /'pɛlɪkən/ *n.* пеликáн *m.*

pelt[1] /pɛlt/ *n.* шкýра *f.*

pelt[2] /pɛlt/ *v.* (*bombard*) забрáсывать *impf.*, забросáть *pf.*

pelting /'pɛltɪŋ/ *adj.* (*rain*) проливнóй.

pelvis /'pɛlvɪs/ *n.* таз *m.*

pen /pɛn/ *n.* перó *neut.*; **fountain pen** авторýчка *f.*

penalty /'pɛnl̩ti/ *n.* наказáние *neut.*; штраф *m.*

penchant /'pɛntʃənt/ *n.* склóнность (к *with dat.*) *f.*

pencil /'pɛnsəl/ **1.** *n.* карандáш *m.*; **in pencil** *adv.* карандашóм. **2.** *adj.* карандáшный.

pencil case *n.* пенáл *m.*

pending /'pɛndɪŋ/ **1.** *adj.* ожидáющий решéния. **2.** *prep.* в ожидáнии (*with gen.*).

pendulum /'pɛndʒələm/ *n.* мáятник *m.*

penetrate /'pɛnɪˌtreit/ *v.* проникáть *impf.*, прони́кнуть *pf.*

penetrating /'pɛnɪˌtreitɪŋ/ *adj.* пронзи́тельный; прони́зывающий; проницáтельный.

penetration /ˌpɛnɪ'treiʃən/ *n.* проникновéние *neut.*; проницáтельность *f.*

penguin /'pɛŋgwɪn/ *n.* пингви́н *m.*

penicillin /ˌpɛnə'sɪlɪn/ *n.* пеницилли́н *m.*

peninsula /pə'nɪnsələ/ *n.* полуóстров *m.*

penis /'pinɪs/ *n.* мужскóй половóй член *m.*

penitence /'pɛnɪtəns/ *n.* раскáяние *neut.*; (*eccl.*) покая́ние *neut.*

penitent /'pɛnɪtənt/ **1.** *n.* кáющийся *m.* **2.** *adj.* кáющийся *m.*

penitentiary /ˌpɛnɪ'tɛnʃəri/ **1.** *n.* тюрьмá *f.*; пенитенциáрий *m.* **2.** *adj.* пенитенциáрный.

penknife /'pɛn,naif/ *n.* перочи́нный нож *m.*

pennant /'pɛnənt/ *n.* вы́мпел *m.*

Pennsylvania /ˌpɛnsəl'veinyə/ *n.* Пенсильвáния *f.*

penny /'pɛni/ *n.* (*Brit.*) пенс *m.*; пéнни *neut. in-decl.*

pension /'pɛnʃən/ *n.* пéнсия *f.*

pensive /'pɛnsɪv/ *adj.* задýмчивый.

pentagon /'pɛntəˌgɒn/ *n.* пятиугóльник *m.*; **the Pentagon** *n.* Пентагóн *m.*

Pentateuch /'pɛntəˌtuk/ *n.* Пятикни́жие *neut.*

pentathlon /pɛn'tæθlən/ *n.* пятибóрье *neut.*

Pentecost /'pɛntɪˌkɔst/ *n.* Пятидеся́тница *f.*

penthouse /'pɛnt,haus/ *n.* двухэтáжная кварти́ра *f.*

pent-up /ˌpɛnt 'ʌp/ *adj.* (*feelings*) накóпленный, накопи́вшийся.

penultimate /pɪ'nʌltəmɪt/ *adj.* предпослéдний.

penumbra /pɪ'nʌmbrə/ *n.* (*astr.*) полутéнь *f.*; (*half-light*) полусвéт *m.*

penury /'pɛnyəri/ *n.* (*need*) нуждá *f.*; скýдость; бéдность *f.*

Penza /'pɛnzə/ *n.* Пéнза *f.*

people /'pipəl/ **1.** *n.* лю́ди *pl.*; (*nation*) нарóд *m.* **2.** *v.* населя́ть *impf.*, насели́ть *pf.*

pep /pɛp/ *n.* (*colloq.*) энéргия *f.*; (*liveliness*) жи́вость *f.*

pepper /'pɛpər/ *n.* пéрец *m.*

peppercorn /'pɛpərˌkɔrn/ *n.* пéречное зернó *neut.*

pepper mill *n.* пéречница *f.*

peppermint /'pɛpərˌmɪnt/ *n.* (*bot.*) мя́та (пéречная) *f.*

peppery /'pɛpəri/ *adj.* (*pepper-flavored*) напéрченный; (*hot to taste*) óстрый.

per /pɜr; *unstressed* pər/ *prep.* чéрез (*with acc.*),

посредством (*with gen.*); в; на (*with acc.*); по (*with dat.*); с (*with gen.*); за (*with acc.*).
per annum /pər 'ænəm/ *adv.* в год.
perceive /pər'siv/ *v.* ощущать *impf.*, ощутить *pf.*
percent /pər'sɛnt/ *n.* процент *m.*
percentage /pər'sɛntɪdʒ/ *n.* процент *m.*; процентное соотношение *neut.*; (*portion*) часть *f.*
perceptible /pər'sɛptəbəl/ *adj.* ощутимый; заметный.
perception /pər'sɛpʃən/ *n.* восприятие; понимание *neut.*
perceptive /pər'sɛptɪv/ *adj.* проницательный; восприимчивый.
perch¹ /pɜrtʃ/ *n.* (*roost*) насест *m.*
perch² /pɜrtʃ/ *n.* (*fish*) окунь *m.*
percussion /pər'kʌʃən/ *n.* удар *m.*; (*collision*) столкновение *neut.*
peregrination /ˌpɛrɪɡrə'neɪʃən/ *n.* странствование *neut.*
peregrine falcon /'pɛrɪɡrɪn/ *m.* сокол обыкновенный, сапсан *m.*
perennial /pə'rɛniəl/ *adj.*; вечный (*bot.*) многолетний.
perestroika /ˌpɛrə'strɔikə/ *n.* перестройка *f.*
perfect / *adj.* 'pɜrfɪkt/ *v.* pər'fɛkt/ **1.** *adj.* совершённый; полный. **2.** *v.* совершенствовать *impf.*, усовершенствовать *pf.*
perfection /pər'fɛkʃən/ *n.* совершенство *neut.*
perfective /pər'fɛktɪv/ *n.* (*gram.*) совершённый вид *m.*
perfidious /pər'fɪdiəs/ *adj.* вероломный; предательский.
perforation /ˌpɜrfə'reɪʃən/ *n.* перфорация *f.*; просверливание *neut.*
perforce /pər'fɔrs/ *adv.* волей-неволей.
perform /pər'fɔrm/ *v.* выполнять *impf.*, выполнить *pf.*; (*theat.*) исполнять *impf.*, исполнить *pf.*
performance /pər'fɔrməns/ *n.* исполнение *neut.*; (*theat.*) представление *neut.*
performer /pər'fɔrmər/ *n.* исполнитель *m.*
perfume / *n.* 'pɜrfyum; *v.* pər'fyum/ **1.** *n.* духи́ *pl.* **2.** *v.* душить *impf.*, надушить *pf.*
perfunctory /pər'fʌŋktəri/ *adj.* поверхностный; небрежный; (*hasty*) поспешный.
perhaps /pər'hæps/ *adv.* может быть.
pericardium /ˌpɛrɪ'kardiəm/ *n.* околосердечная сумка *f.*
pericarp /'pɛrɪˌkarp/ *n.* (*bot.*) семянка *f.*
peril /'pɛrəl/ *n.* опасность *f.*; риск *m.*
perilous /'pɛrələs/ *adj.* опасный; рискованный.
period /'pɪəriəd/ *n.* период *m.*; эпоха *f.*; (*punctuation*) точка *f.*
periodic /ˌpɪəri'ɒdɪk/ *adj.* периодический.
periodical /ˌpɪəri'ɒdɪkəl/ **1.** *n.* периодический журнал *m.* **2.** *adj.* периодический.
periodically /ˌpɪəri'ɒdɪkli/ *adv.* время от времени.
periphery /pə'rɪfəri/ *n.* периферия *f.*
perish /'pɛrɪʃ/ *v.* погибать *impf.*, погибнуть *pf.*
perishable /'pɛrɪʃəbəl/ *adj.* скоропортящийся.
peritonitis /ˌpɛrɪtn'aitis/ *n.* воспаление брюшины *neut.*; перитонит *m.*
periwinkle¹ /'pɛrɪˌwɪŋkəl/ *n.* (*bot.*) барвинок *m.*
periwinkle² /'pɛrɪˌwɪŋkəl/ *n.* (*zool.*) морская улитка; литорина *f.*
perjurer /'pɜrdʒərər/ *n.* лжесвидетель *m.*

perjury /'pɜrdʒəri/ *n.* клятвопреступление; лжесвидетельство *neut.*
perky /'pɜrki/ *adj.* бойкий; дерзкий.
Perm /pɜrm/ *n.* Пермь *f.*
permafrost /'pɜrməˌfrɔst/ *n.* вечная мерзлота *f.*
permanence /'pɜrmənəns/ *n.* постоянство *neut.*; неизменность *f.*
permanent /'pɜrmənənt/ **1.** *adj.* постоянный. **2.** *n.* (*hair*) завивка *f.*, перманент *m.*
permanently /'pɜrmənəntli/ *adv.* постоянно; навсегда.
permeable /'pɜrmiəbəl/ *adj.* проницаемый.
permeate /'pɜrmiˌeit/ *v.* проникать (в *with acc.*) *impf.*, проникнуть *pf.*
Permic /'pɜrmɪk/ *adj.* пермский.
permissible /pər'mɪsəbəl/ *adj.* позволительный; допустимый.
permission /pər'mɪʃən/ *n.* разрешение *neut.*
permissive /pər'mɪsɪv/ *adj.* дозволяющий; разрешающий.
permit / *n.* 'pɜrmɪt; *v.* pər'mɪt/ **1.** *n.* разрешение *neut.* **2.** *v.* разрешать *impf.*, разрешить *pf.*
pernicious /pər'nɪʃəs/ *adj.* вредный; пагубный.
peroxide /pə'rɒksaid/ *n.* перекись *f.*
perpendicular /ˌpɜrpən'dɪkyələr/ *adj.* перпендикулярный; отвесный.
perpetrate /'pɜrpɪˌtreit/ *v.* совершать *impf.*
perpetual /pər'pɛtʃuəl/ *adj.* вечный.
perpetuate /pər'pɛtʃuˌeit/ *v.* увековечивать *impf.*
perpetuity /ˌpɜrpɪ'tuiti/ *n.* бесконечность; вечность *f.*
perplex /pər'plɛks/ *v.* озадачивать *impf.*, озадачить *pf.*
perplexing /pər'plɛksɪŋ/ *adj.* озадачивающий; странный.
perplexity /pər'plɛksiti/ *n.* смущение; недоумение *neut.*
perquisite /'pɜrkwəzit/ *n.* льгота *f.*
persecute /'pɜrsɪˌkyut/ *v.* преследовать *impf.*
persecution /ˌpɜrsɪ'kyuʃən/ *n.* преследование *neut.*
persecutor /'pɜrsɪˌkyutər/ *n.* преследователь *m.*
perseverance /ˌpɜrsə'viərəns/ *n.* настойчивость *f.*
Persian /'pɜrʒən/ **1.** *adj.* персидский. **2.** *n.* перс *m.*, персиянка *f.*
persimmon /pər'sɪmən/ *n.* хурма *f.*
persist /pər'sɪst/ *v.* упорствовать *impf.*
persistence /pər'sɪstəns/ *n.* упорство *neut.*; настойчивость *f.*
persistent /pər'sɪstənt/ *adj.* настойчивый.
person /'pɜrsən/ *n.* человек *m.*; особа *f.*; (*gram.*) лицо *neut.*
personage /'pɜrsənɪdʒ/ *n.* личность *f.*; (*theat.*) персонаж *m.*
personal /'pɜrsənl/ *adj.* личный; частный.
personal computer *n.* (*abbr.* P.C.) персональная ЭВМ *f.*, персональный компьютер; личный компьютер *m.*
personal identification number *n.* (*abbr.* P.I.N.) персональный код *m.*
personality /ˌpɜrsə'næliti/ *n.* личность *f.*; индивидуальность *f.*
personally /'pɜrsənli/ *adv.* лично.
personification /pərˌsɒnəfɪ'keɪʃən/ *n.* олицетворение *neut.*; (*embodiment*) воплощение *neut.*

personnel /ˌpɜrsəˈnɛl/ *n.* персонáл; лúчный состáв *m.*

perspective /pərˈspɛktɪv/ **1.** *n.* перспектúва *f.* **2.** *adj.* перспектúвный.

perspicacious /ˌpɜrspɪˈkeɪʃəs/ *adj.* проницáтельный.

perspiration /ˌpɜrspəˈreɪʃən/ *n.* пот *m.*

perspire /pərˈspaɪər/ *v.* потéть *impf.*

persuade /pərˈsweid/ *v.* убеждáть *impf.*, убедúть *pf.*

persuasion /pərˈsweiʒən/ *n.* убеждéние *neut.*

persuasive /pərˈsweisɪv/ *adj.* убедúтельный.

pert /pɜrt/ *adj.* бóйкий; (*impertinent*) дéрзкий.

pertain /pərˈtein/ *v.* относúться (к *with dat.*) *impf.*

pertinence /ˈpɜrtn̩əns/ *n.* умéстность *f.*

pertinent /ˈpɜrtn̩ənt/ *adj.* подходя́щий; по существу́.

perturb /pərˈtɜrb/ *v.* беспокóить; волновáть *impf.*

Peru /pəˈru/ *n.* Перу́ *m.*

Perugia /pəˈrudʒə/ *n.* Перýджа *f.*

pervade /pərˈveid/ *v.* проникáть (в *with acc.*) *impf.*

pervasive /pərˈveisɪv/ *adj.* распространя́ющийся повсю́ду.

perverse /pərˈvɜrs/ *adj.* порóчный.

perversion /pərˈvɜrʒən/ *n.* извращéние *neut.*

pervert / *n.* ˈpɜrvərt; *v.* pərˈvɜrt/ **1.** *n.* извращё́нный человéк *m.* **2.** *v.* извращáть; (*distort*) искажáть *impf.*

pessimism /ˈpɛsəˌmɪzəm/ *n.* пессимúзм *m.*

pest /pɛst/ *n.* (*insect*) (сельскохозя́йственный) вредúтель *m.*; (*colloq.*) (*person*) зарáза; зану́да *m.* and *f.* (*decl. f.*)

pestilence /ˈpɛstləns/ *n.* мор *m.*

pestle /ˈpɛsəl/ *n.* пéстик *m.*

pet /pɛt/ **1.** *n.* (*favorite*) любúмец *m.*; (*animal*) домáшнее живóтное *neut.* **2.** *v.* ласкáть *impf.*

petal /ˈpɛtl̩/ *n.* лепестóк *m.*

petit-bourgeois /pəˈti burˈʒwa; ˈpɛti/ *adj.* мелкобуржуáзный.

petition /pəˈtɪʃən/ **1.** *n.* петúция *f.* **2.** *v.* обращáться с петúцией.

petitioner /pəˈtɪʃənər/ *n.* (*plaintiff*) истéц *m.*

petrel /ˈpɛtrəl/ *n.* буревéстник *m.*

petrified /ˈpɛtrəˌfaid/ *adj.* (*turned to stone*) окаменéлый; (*with fear*) оцепенéвший.

petrify /ˈpɛtrəˌfai/ *v.* окаменéть *pf.*

petroleum /pəˈtrouliəm/ **1.** *n.* нефть *f.* **2.** *adj.* нефтянóй.

Petropavlovsk /ˌpɛtrəˈpævlɔfsk/ *n.* Петропáвловск *m.*

Petrozavodsk /ˌpɛtrəzəˈvɒtsk/ *n.* Петрозавóдск *m.*

petty /ˈpɛti/ *adj.* маловáжный; мéлкий.

petulance /ˈpɛtʃələns/ *n.* раздражúтельность *f.*

petulant /ˈpɛtʃələnt/ *adj.* раздражúтельный.

pew /pyu/ *n.* скамья́ в цéркви *f.*

pewit /ˈpiwɪt/ *also* **peewit** *n.* чúбис *m.*

peyote /peiˈouti/ *n.* (*bot.*) мескáл *m.*; (*drug*) мескалúн *m.*

phalanx /ˈfeilæŋks/ *n.* фалáнга *f.*

phalarope /ˈfæləˌroup/ *n.* плавýнчик *m.*

phallic /ˈfælɪk/ *adj.* фаллúческий.

phallus /ˈfæləs/ *n.* фáллос *m.*

phantasmal /fænˈtæzməl/ *adj.* иллюзóрный; прúзрачный.

phantom /ˈfæntəm/ *n.* прúзрак, фантóм *m.*

pharmaceutics /ˌfɑrməˈsutiks/ *n.* фармацéвтика *f.*

pharmacist /ˈfɑrməsɪst/ *n.* аптéкарь; фармацéвт *m.*

pharmacy /ˈfɑrməsi/ *n.* (*science*) фармацúя *f.*; (*store*) аптéка *f.*

pharyngeal /fəˈrɪndʒiəl/ *adj.* глóточный.

pharynx /ˈfærɪŋks/ *n.* глóтка *f.*; зев *m.*

phase /feiz/ *n.* фáза *f.*

pheasant /ˈfɛzənt/ *n.* фазáн *m.*

phenomenal /fɪˈnɒmənl̩/ *adj.* феноменáльный.

phial /ˈfaiəl/ *n.* пузырёк *m.*; скля́нка *f.*

philanthropy /fɪˈlænθrəpi/ *n.* филантрóпия *f.*

philately /fɪˈlætl̩i/ *n.* филателúя *f.*

philharmonic /ˌfɪlhɑrˈmɒnɪk/ **1.** *adj.* филармонúческий. **2.** *n.* филармóния *f.*

philologist /fɪˈlɒlədʒɪst/ *n.* филóлог; языковéд *m.*

philology /fɪˈlɒlədʒi/ *n.* (*study of learning and literature*) филолóгия *f.*; (*study of language*) языковéдение *neut.*

philosopher /fɪˈlɒsəfər/ *n.* филóсоф *m.*

philosophical /ˌfɪləˈsɒfɪkəl/ *adj.* филосóфский.

philosophy /fɪˈlɒsəfi/ *n.* филосóфия *f.*

phlegm /flɛm/ *n.* мокрóта; слизь *f.* (*apathy*) флéгма *f.*

phobia /ˈfoubiə/ *n.* неврóз стрáха *m.*; фóбия *f.*

phone booth /foun/ *n.* телефóн-автомáт *m.*

phoneme /ˈfounim/ *n.* фонéма *f.*

phonemic /fəˈnimɪk/ *adj.* фонемáтический.

phonemics /fəˈnimɪks/ *n.* фонéмика *f.*

phonetic /fəˈnɛtɪk/ *adj.* фонетúческий.

phonetics /fəˈnɛtɪks/ *n.* фонéтика *f.*

phonograph /ˈfounəˌgræf/ *n.* граммофóн; патефóн *m.*

phonological /ˌfounlˈɒdʒɪkəl/ *adj.* фонологúческий.

phonology /fəˈnɒlədʒi/ *n.* фонолóгия *f.*

phony /ˈfouni/ (*colloq.*) **1.** *n.* (*fake*) поддéлка *f.* (*impostor*) шарлатáн *m.* **2.** *adj.* лóжный; фальшúвый.

phosphorus /ˈfɒsfərəs/ *n.* фóсфор *m.*

photo /ˈfoutou/ *n.* снúмок *m.*; фотогрáфия *f.*

photocell /ˈfoutouˌsɛl/ *n.* фотоэлемéнт *m.*

photocopier /ˈfoutəˌkɒpiər/ *n.* ксéрокс *m.*

photocopy /ˈfoutəˌkɒpi/ *n.* ксерокóпия *f.*

photogenic /ˌfoutəˈdʒɛnɪk/ *adj.* фотогенúчный.

photograph /ˈfoutəˌgræf/ **1.** *n.* фотогрáфия *f.*; (*фотографúческий*) снúмок *m.* **2.** *v.* снимáть; фотографúровать *impf.*

photographer /fəˈtɒgrəfər/ *n.* фотóграф *m.*

photography /fəˈtɒgrəfi/ *n.* фотогрáфия *f.*; фотографúрование *neut.*

photomicrograph /ˌfoutəˈmaikrəˌgræf/ *n.* микрофотогрáфия *f.*

phrase /freiz/ **1.** *n.* фрáза *f.*; выражéние *neut.* **2.** *v.* выражáть в словáх *impf.*

phrase book *n.* разговóрник *m.*

phrasing /ˈfreizɪŋ/ *n.* формулúрование *neut.*

physical /ˈfɪzɪkəl/ *adj.* физúческий.

physician /fɪˈzɪʃən/ *n.* врач *m.*

physicist /ˈfɪzəsɪst/ *n.* фúзик *m.*

physics /ˈfɪzɪks/ *n.* фúзика *f.*

physiologist /ˌfɪziˈɒlədʒɪst/ *n.* физиóлог *m.*

physiology /ˌfɪziˈɒlədʒi/ *n.* физиология *f.*

physiotherapy /ˌfɪziouˈθɛrəpi/ *n.* физиотерапия *f.*

physique /fɪˈzik/ *n.* телосложение *neut.*

pi /pai/ *n.* пи *neut. indecl.*

pianist /piˈænɪst, ˈpiənɪst/ *n.* пианист *m.*, пианистка *f.*

piano /piˈænou/ **1.** *n.* рояль *m.;* **upright piano** пианино *neut. indecl.* **2.** *adj.* фортепьянный.

pica /ˈpaikə/ *n.* (*type font*) цицеро *m. indecl.*

pick /pɪk/ **1.** *n.* (*choice*) выбор *m.* **2.** *v.* (*choose*) выбирать *impf.*, выбрать *pf.;* **to pick up** поднимать *impf.*, поднять *pf.*

pickax /ˈpɪkˌæks/ *n.* кирка *f.*

picket /ˈpɪkɪt/ **1.** *n.* (*stake*) кол *m.;* (*in strike; mil.*) пикет *m.* **2.** *v.* пикетировать *impf.*

picket boat *n.* дозорный катер *m.*

pickle /ˈpɪkəl/ **1.** *n.* солёный огурец *m.* **2.** *v.* солить; мариновать *impf.*, замариновать *pf.*

pickled /ˈpɪkəld/ *adj.* маринованный; солёный; (*colloq.*) (*drunk*) пьяный.

pickpocket /ˈpɪkˌpɒkɪt/ *n.* карманник *m.*

picnic /ˈpɪknɪk/ *n.* пикник *m.*

pictorial /pɪkˈtɔriəl/ *adj.* изобразительный.

picture /ˈpɪktʃər/ **1.** *n.* картина; картинка *f.;* (*movie*) фильм *m.;* (*photograph*) снимок *m.* **2.** *adj.* картинный. **3.** *v.* воображать *impf.*, вообразить *pf.;* (*depict*) изображать *impf.*

picturesque /ˌpɪktʃəˈrɛsk/ *adj.* живописный.

picture writing *n.* пиктографическое письмо *neut.*

pie /pai/ *n.* сладкий пирог; торт *m.*

piebald /ˈpaiˌbɔld/ *n.* пегая лошадь *f.*

piece /pis/ *n.* кусок *m.;* часть *f.*

piecemeal /ˈpisˌmil/ *adv.* по частям; постепенно.

piecework /ˈpisˌwɜrk/ *n.* сдельная работа *f.*

pier /pɪər/ *n.* пирс; мол, волнорез *m.*

pierce /pɪərs/ *v.* пронзать *impf.*, пронзить *pf.*

piercingly /ˈpɪərsɪŋli/ *adv.* пронзительно.

pier glass *n.* трюмо *neut. indecl.*

piety /ˈpaiɪti/ *n.* набожность *f.*

pig /pɪg/ *n.* свинья *f.*

pigeon /ˈpɪdʒən/ *n.* голубь *m.*

pigeonhole /ˈpɪdʒənˌhoul/ *n.* ящик для бумаги *m.*

pigeon-toed /ˈpɪdʒən ˌtoud/ *adj.* косолапый.

piggy bank /ˈpɪgi/ *n.* копилка *f.*

pigment /ˈpɪgmənt/ *n.* пигмент *m.*

pigsty /ˈpɪgˌstai/ *n.* хлев; свинарник *m.;* (*fig., pej.*) хлев *m.*

pigtail /ˈpɪgˌteil/ *n.* коса; косичка *f.*

pike¹ /paik/ *n.* (*spear*) пика *f.*

pike² /paik/ *n.* (*fish*) щука *f.*

pilaf /pɪˈlɑf/ *n.* плов *m.*

pile /pail/ **1.** *n.* куча; груда *f.* **2.** *v.* нагромождать *impf.*, нагромоздить *pf.*

pilgrim /ˈpɪlgrɪm/ *n.* паломник *m.*, паломница *f.*

pilgrimage /ˈpɪlgrəmɪdʒ/ *n.* паломничество *neut.*

pill /pɪl/ *n.* пилюля *f.*

pillage /ˈpɪlɪdʒ/ **1.** *n.* грабёж *m.* **2.** *v.* грабить *impf.*

pillar /ˈpɪlər/ *n.* столб *m.*

pillory /ˈpɪləri/ *n.* позорный столб *m.*

pillow /ˈpɪlou/ *n.* подушка *f.*

pillowcase /ˈpɪlouˌkeis/ *n.* наволочка *f.*

pilot /ˈpailət/ **1.** *n.* пилот; лётчик *m.* **2.** *v.* (*aero.*) пилотировать *impf.* **3.** *adj.* опытный; пробный.

pilot boat *n.* лоцманское судно *neut.*

pilotfish /ˈpailətˌfɪʃ/ *n.* рыба-лоцман *f.*

pilothouse /ˈpailətˌhaus/ *n.* рулевая рубка *f.*

pilot light *n.* (*gas stove*) контрольная горелка *f.;* дежурный огонь *m.*

Pilsen /ˈpɪlzən/ *n.* (*Czech: Plzeň*) Пльзень *f.*

pimp /pɪmp/ *n.* сводник *m.*

pimple /ˈpɪmpəl/ *n.* прыщик *m.*

pin /pɪn/ **1.** *n.* булавка; шпилька *f.;* (*mach.*) палец; болт *m.* (*broach*) брошь *f.;* (*badge*) значок *m.* **2.** *v.* прикалывать *impf.*, приколоть *pf.*

pinball /ˈpɪnˌbɔl/ *n.* китайский бильярд *m.*

pincers /ˈpɪnsərz/ *n.* (*tool*) щипцы; клещи *pl.;* пинцет *m.*

pinch /pɪntʃ/ **1.** *n.* щипок *m.;* (*of salt*) щепотка *f.* **2.** *v.* щипать *impf.*, щипнуть *pf.*

pincushion /ˈpɪnˌkuʃən/ *n.* игольник *m.*

pine¹ /pain/ **1.** *n.* (*tree*) сосна *f.* **2.** *adj.* сосновый.

pine² /pain/ *v.* чахнуть *impf.*

pineapple /ˈpaiˌnæpəl/ *n.* ананас *m.*

pine cone *n.* сосновая шишка *f.*

pine needle *n.* (*also coll.*) хвоя *f.*

ping-pong /ˈpɪŋˌpɒŋ/ *n.* пинг-понг, настольный теннис *m.*

pink /pɪŋk/ **1.** *adj.* лилово-розовый. **2.** *n.* лилово-розовый цвет *m.*

pinking shears /ˈpɪŋkɪŋ/ *n.* фестонные ножницы *pl.*

pinnace /ˈpɪnɪs/ *n.* полубаркас; катер *m.*

pinnacle /ˈpɪnəkəl/ *n.* вершина *f.;* (*archit.*) пик *m.*

pinpoint /ˈpɪnˌpɔint/ *n.* (*point of pin*) остриё булавки *neut.;* (*mil.*) точечный ориентир *m.*

pinprick /ˈpɪnˌprɪk/ *n.* булавочный укол *m.*

Pinsk /pɪnsk/ *n.* Пинск *m.*

pint /paint/ *n.* пинта *f.*

pintle /ˈpɪntl/ *n.* поворотный шкворень *m.*

pinwheel /ˈpɪnˌwil/ *n.* (*tech.*) цевочное колесо *neut.*

pioneer /ˌpaiəˈnɪər/ **1.** *n.* пионер *m.;* пионерка *f.* **2.** *adj.* пионерский.

pious /ˈpaiəs/ *adj.* набожный.

pipe /paip/ **1.** *n.* труба, трубка *f.;* (*for smoking*) трубка *f.* **2.** *adj.* трубочный.

pipe fitter *n.* слесарь-водопроводчик *m.*

pipeline /ˈpaipˌlain/ *n.* трубопровод *m.*

piper /ˈpaipər/ *n.* дудочник *m.;* (*bagpiper*) волынщик *m.*

pipestem /ˈpaipˌstɛm/ *n.* черенок трубки *m.*

pipsqueak /ˈpɪpˌskwik/ *n.* (*pej.*) ничтожество *neut.*

piquant /ˈpikənt, piˈkɑnt/ *adj.* пикантный.

pirate /ˈpairət/ **1.** *n.* пират *m.* **2.** *adj.* пиратский.

Pisa /ˈpizə/ *n.* Пиза *f.*

pistachio /pɪˈstæʃiˌou/ *n.* фисташка *f.*

pistol /ˈpɪstl/ *n.* пистолет *m.*

piston /ˈpɪstən/ **1.** *n.* (*tech.*) поршень *m.* **2.** *adj.* поршневой.

pit /pɪt/ *n.* яма *f.;* (*fruit*) косточка *f.*

pitch¹ /pɪtʃ/ *n.* (*tar*) смола *f.*

pitch² /pɪtʃ/ **1.** *n.* (*ship*) качка *f.;* (*mus.*) высота *f.* **2.** *v.* (*toss*) качать(ся) *impf.;* (*tent*) разбивать (лагерь) *impf.*

pitch-black /ˈpɪtʃ ˈblæk/ *adj.* чёрный как смоль.

pitchblende /ˈpɪtʃˌblɛnd/ *n.* смоляная обманка *f.*; уранинит *m.*

pitch-dark /'pɪtʃ 'dɑrk/ *n.* кромешная тьма *f.*

pitch-darkness /'pɪtʃ 'dɑrknɪs/ *n.* кромешная тьма *f.*

pitcher /'pɪtʃər/ *n.* (*vessel*) кувшин *m.*; (*baseball*) подающий, питчер *m.*

pitchfork /'pɪtʃˌfɔrk/ *n.* вилы *pl.*

piteous /'pɪtiəs/ *adj.* жалкий; жалобный.

pitfall /'pɪtˌfɔl/ *n.* волчья яма; ловушка *f.*

pitiful /'pɪtɪfəl/ (*also*) **pitiable** *adj.* жалкий.

pitiless /'pɪtɪlɪs/ *adj.* безжалостный.

pitted /'pɪtɪd/ *adj.* изрытый; (*skin*) рябой.

pituitary gland /pɪ'tuɪˌtɛri/ *n.* гипофиз *m.*

pity /'pɪti/ **1.** *n.* жалость *f.*; сожаление *neut.* **2.** *v.* жалеть *impf.*; соболезновать *impf.*

pivot /'pɪvət/ **1.** *n.* стержень *m.*; (*fig.*) центр *m.* **2.** *v.* вращаться *impf.*

pivotal /'pɪvətḷ/ *adj.* центральный.

pixel /'pɪksəl/ *n.* пиксель *m.*; точка растра *f.*

pizza /'pitsə/ *n.* пицца *f.*

placard /'plækɑrd/ *n.* плакат *m.*; афиша *f.*

placate /'pleikeit/ *v.* умиротворять *impf.*

place /pleis/ **1.** *n.* место; положение *neut.*; **to take place** иметь место *impf.* **2.** *v.* ставить *impf.*, поставить *pf.*; помещать *impf.*

placebo /plə'sibou/ *n.* плацебо *neut. indecl.*

placement /'pleismənt/ *n.* (*arrangement*) расстановка *f.*; расположение *neut.*

placid /'plæsɪd/ *adj.* спокойный.

plagiarism /'pleidʒəˌrɪzəm/ *n.* плагиат *m.*

plagiarize /'pleidʒəˌraɪz/ *v.i.* заниматься плагиатом *impf.*; *v.t.* заимствовать *impf.*

plague /pleig/ **1.** *n.* мор *m.*; чума *f.* **2.** *v.* досаждать *impf.*, досадить *pf.*

plaice /pleis/ *n.* камбала *f.*

plain /plein/ **1.** *adj.* ясный; простой. **2.** *n.* равнина *f.*

plainsman /'pleinzmən/ *n.* степняк *m.*

plainsong /'pleinˌsɔŋ/ *n.* (*chant*) григорианский напев *n.*

plaintiff /'pleintɪf/ *n.* истец *m.*, истица *f.*

plaintive /'pleintɪv/ *adj.* жалобный.

plait /pleit/ **1.** *n.* (*hair*) коса *f.*; (*twisted strands*) плетёнка *f.* **2.** *v.* плести *impf.*

plan /plæn/ **1.** *n.* план; проект *m.* **2.** *v.* замышлять *impf.*, замыслить *pf.*; (*intend*) собираться *impf.*

planar /'pleinər/ *adj.* плоскостной.

plane¹ /plein/ **1.** *n.* (*flat surface*) плоскость *f.*; (*airplane*) самолёт *m.* **2.** *adj.* плоский.

plane² /plein/ **1.** *n.* (*tool*) рубанок *m.* **2.** *v.* строгать *impf.*

planet /'plænɪt/ *n.* планета *f.*

planetarium /ˌplænɪ'tɛəriəm/ *n.* планетарий *m.*

plank /plæŋk/ *n.* доска *f.*

planning /'plænɪŋ/ *n.* планировка *f.*

plant /plænt/ **1.** *n.* растение *neut.*; (*factory*) завод *m.* **2.** *v.* сажать *impf.*, посадить *pf.*

plantation /plæn'teiʃən/ *n.* плантация *f.*

planter /'plæntər/ *n.* плантатор *m.*

plant louse /'plænt ˌlaus/ *n.* тля *f.*

plaque /plæk/ *n.* доска; дощечка *f.*; (*med.*) пятно *neut.*; бляшка *f.*

plasma /'plæzmə/ *n.* плазма *f.*

plaster /'plæstər/ **1.** *n.* (*for skin*) пластырь *m.*; (*wall*) гипс *m.* **2.** *v.* штукатурить *impf.*, оштукатурить *pf.*

plasterboard /'plæstərˌbɔrd/ *n.* штукатурная плита *f.*

plasterer /'plæstərər/ *n.* штукатур *m.*

plastic /'plæstɪk/ **1.** *n.* пластик *m.* **2.** *adj.* пластический; пластичный.

plasticity /plæ'stɪsɪti/ *n.* пластичность *f.*

plate /pleit/ **1.** *n.* пластинка *f.*; (*dish*) тарелка *f.* **2.** *v.* накладывать *impf.*, наложить *pf.*; покрывать *impf.*, покрыть *pf.*

plateau /plæ'tou/ *n.* плоскогорье *neut.*

plate glass *n.* зеркальное стекло *neut.*

platen /'plætṇ/ *n.* (*print.*) тигель *m.*; (*typewriter*) валик *m.*

platform /'plætfɔrm/ *n.* платформа *f.*; (*stage*) помост *m.*

platinum /'plætṇəm/ **1.** *n.* платина *f.* **2.** *adj.* платиновый.

platitude /'plætɪˌtud/ *n.* банальность *f.*

platoon /plə'tun/ *n.* взвод *m.*

platter /'plætər/ *n.* блюдо *neut.*

platypus /'plætɪpəs/ *n.* утконос *m.*

plausible /'plɔzəbəl/ *adj.* вероятный; правдоподобный.

play /plei/ **1.** *n.* игра *f.*; (*theat.*) пьеса *f.* **2.** *v.* играть *impf.*, сыграть *pf.*

playback /'plei ˌbæk/ *n.* (*tech.*) плэй-бэк *m.*

playbill /'plei ˌbɪl/ *n.* театральная афиша *f.*

player /'pleiər/ *n.* игрок *m.*

player piano *n.* пианола *f.*

playful /'pleifəl/ *adj.* игривый.

playgoer /'plei ˌgouər/ *n.* театрал *m.*, театралка *f.*

playground /'plei ˌgraund/ *n.* детская площадка *f.*

playpen /'plei ˌpɛn/ *n.* детский манеж *m.*

plaything /'plei ˌθɪŋ/ *n.* игрушка *f.*

playwright /'plei ˌrait/ *n.* драматург *m.*

plaza /'plɑzə/ *n.* площадь *f.*

plea /pli/ *n.* мольба *f.*; (*leg.*) заявление *neut.*

plead /plid/ *v.* умолять *impf.*; **to plead a case** защищать дело *impf.*

pleading /'plidɪŋ/ *n.* (*entreaty*) мольба *f.*; (*urging*) призыв *m.*

pleasant /'plɛzənt/ *adj.* приятный.

pleasantry /'plɛzəntri/ *n.* шутка *f.*

please /pliz/ **1.** *v.* нравиться *impf.*, понравиться *pf.* **2.** *adv.* пожалуйста!

pleased /plizd/ *adj.* довольный; *pred.* рад.

pleasing /'plizɪŋ/ *adj.* приятный; привлекательный.

pleasure /'plɛʒər/ *n.* удовольствие *neut.*; (*wish*) желание *neut.*

pleasure boat *n.* прогулочный катер *m.*

pleat /plit/ **1.** *n.* складка *f.* **2.** *v.* делать складки *impf.*

plebeian /plɪ'biən/ *adj.* плебейский.

plebiscite /'plɛbəˌsait/ *n.* плебисцит *m.*

pledge /plɛdʒ/ **1.** *n.* (*security*) залог; задаток *m.*; (*promise*) обещание *neut.* **2.** *v.* (*leave as security*) закладывать *impf.*, заложить *pf.*; ручаться *impf.*; (*vow*) клясться в (*with prep.*) *impf.*

plenipotentiary /ˌplɛnəpə'tɛnʃiˌɛri/ *adj.* полномочный.

plentiful /'plɛntɪfəl/ *adj.* обильный.

plenty /'plɛnti/ **1.** *n.* изобилие *neut.* **2.** *adj.* (*colloq.*) изрядно.

plethora /'plɛθərə/ *n.* (*excess*) избыток *m.*

pleurisy /'plʊrəsi/ *n.* плеврит *m.*
pliable /'plaiəbəl/ *also* **pliant** /'plaiənt/ *adj.* гибкий.
pliers /'plaiərz/ *n.* щипчики; плоскогубцы *pl.*
plight /plait/ *n.* затруднительное положение *neut.*
plop /plɒp/ *v.* шлёпать(ся) (о *with acc.*) *impf.*; бултыхаться (в *with acc.*) *impf.*
plot /plɒt/ **1.** *n.* (*piece of land*) участок *m.*; (*fiction*) сюжет *m.*, фабула *f.*; (*conspiracy*) заговор *m.* **2.** *v.* замышлять *impf.*, замыслить *pf.*
plover /'plʌvər/ *n.* ржанка *f.*
plow /plau/ **1.** *n.* плуг *m.* **2.** *v.* пахать *impf.*
plowman /'plaumən/ *n.* пахарь *m.*
plowshare /'plau,ʃeər/ *n.* лемех *m.*
ploy /plɔi/ *n.* (*stunt*) трюк *m.*; (*ruse*) уловка *f.*; приём *m.*
plug /plʌg/ **1.** *n.* затычка; пробка *f.*; (*elec.*) вилка *f.* **2.** *v.* затыкать *impf.*, заткнуть *pf.*
plum /plʌm/ **1.** *n.* слива *f.* **2.** *adj.* сливовый.
plumage /'plumidʒ/ *n.* оперенье *neut.*
plumber /'plʌmər/ *n.* водопроводчик; слесарь *m.*
plumbing /'plʌmiŋ/ *n.* водопроводное дело *neut.*
plumb line /plʌm/ *n.* отвес *m.*
plump /plʌmp/ *adj.* пухлый; полный.
plunder /'plʌndər/ **1.** *n.* грабёж *m.* **2.** *v.* грабить *impf.*, ограбить *pf.*
plunge /plʌndʒ/ *v.t.* погружать *impf.*, погрузить *pf.*; *v.i.* погружаться *impf.*, погрузиться *pf.*
pluperfect /plu'pɜrfikt/ *n.* (*gram.*) плюсквамперфект *m.*
plural /'plʊrəl/ **1.** *adj.* множественный. **2.** *n.* (*gram.*) множественное число *neut.*
plurality /plu'ræliti/ *n.* (*multitude*) множественность *f.*; (*majority*) большинство *neut.*
plus /plʌs/ **1.** *prep.* плюс. **2.** *n.* знак плюс *m.*
plywood /'plai,wʊd/ **1.** *n.* фанера *f.* **2.** *adj.* фанерный.
pneumatic /nʊ'mætik/ *adj.* пневматический.
pneumonia /nʊ'mounyə/ *n.* воспаление лёгких *neut.*; пневмония *f.*
Po /pou/ *n.* (*river*) По
poached egg /poutʃt/ *n.* яйцо-пашот *neut.*
poacher /'poutʃər/ *n.* браконьер *m.*
pocket /'pɒkit/ **1.** *n.* карман *m.* **2.** *adj.* карманный. **3.** *v.* прикарманивать *impf.*, прикарманить *pf.*
pocketbook /'pɒkit,bʊk/ *n.* бумажник; кошелёк *m.*
pocketknife /'pɒkit,naif/ *n.* карманный (складной) нож(ик) *m.*
pockmark /'pɒk,mɑrk/ *n.* оспина; рябинка *f.*
pockmarked /'pɒk,mɑrkt/ *adj.* рябой.
Podolsk /pʌ'dɒlsk/ *n.* Подольск *m.*
poem /'pouəm/ *n.* поэма *f.*; стихотворение *neut.*
poet /'pouit/ *n.* поэт *m.*
poetess /'pouitis/ *n.* поэтесса *f.*
poetic /pou'ɛtik/ *adj.* поэтический.
poetics /pou'ɛtiks/ *n.* поэтика *f.*
poetry /'pouitri/ *n.* поэзия *f.*
pogrom /pə'grʌm/ *n.* погром *m.*
poignant /'pɔinyənt/ *adj.* едкий; мучительный.
point /pɔint/ **1.** *n.* точка *f.*; пункт *m.*; (*tip*) кончик *m.*; **point of view** точка зрения *f.*; **that's not the point** дело не в этом. **2.** *v.* показывать пальцем; указывать *impf.*, указать *pf.*

pointer /'pɔintər/ *n.* (*on dial, etc.*) стрелка *f.*; (*long stick*) указка *f.*; указание *neut.*
pointless /'pɔintlis/ *adj.* бессмысленный, бесцельный.
poison /'pɔizən/ **1.** *n.* яд *m.*; отрава *f.* **2.** *adj.* ядовитый. **3.** *v.* отравлять *impf.*, отравить *pf.*
poisoning /'pɔizəniŋ/ *n.* отравление *neut.*
poisonous /'pɔizənəs/ *adj.* ядовитый.
poke /pouk/ **1.** *n.* толчок *m.* **2.** *v.* тыкать *impf.*, ткнуть *pf.*
poker /'poukər/ *n.* (*rod*) кочерга *f.*; (*cards*) покер *m.*
Poland /'poulənd/ *n.* Польша *f.*
polar /'poulər/ *adj.* полярный; полюсный.
polar fox *n.* песец *m.*
polarity /pou'læriti/ *n.* полярность *f.*
Pole /poul/ *n.* поляк *m.*, полька *f.*
pole /poul/ *n.* шест; столб *m.*; (*geog.*) полюс *m.*
polecat /'poul,kæt/ *n.* хорёк *m.*
polemic /pə'lɛmik/ **1.** *n.* полемика *f.* **2.** *adj.* полемический.
pole vault *n.* прыжок с шестом *m.*
police /pə'lis/ **1.** *n.* полиция; милиция *f.* **2.** *adj.* полицейский.
policeman /pə'lismən/ *n.* полицейский *m.*
police officer /pə'troulmən/ *n.* полицейский *m.*
policy /'pɒləsi/ *n.* политика *f.*; (*insurance*) полис *m.*
polio /'pouli,ou/ *also* **poliomyelitis** /,pouliou,maiə'laitis/ *n.* полиомиелит *m.*
Polish /'pouliʃ/ *adj.* польский.
polish /'pɒliʃ/ **1.** *n.* полировка *f.*; (*fig.*) лоск *m.* **2.** *v.* полировать *impf.*, отполировать *pf.*
polished /'pɒliʃt/ *adj.* полированный.
polite /pə'lait/ *adj.* вежливый.
politeness /pə'laitnis/ *n.* вежливость *f.*
political /pə'litikəl/ *adj.* политический
politician /,pɒli'tiʃən/ *n.* политический деятель; политик *m.*
politics /'pɒlitiks/ *n.* политика *f.*
poll /poul/ *n.* баллотировка *f.*; (*survey*) опрос *m.*; *pl.* избирательный пункт *m.*
pollen /'pɒlən/ *n.* пыльца *f.*
pollinate /'pɒlə,neit/ *v.* опылять *impf.*
pollute /pə'lut/ *v.* загрязнять *impf.*, загрязнить *pf.*
pollution /pə'luʃən/ *n.* загрязнение *neut.*
Poltava /pʌl'tavə/ *n.* Полтава *f.*
polyandry /'pɒli,ændri/ *n.* многомужество *neut.*
polyester /,pɒli,estər/ *n.* полиэстр *m.*
polygamy /pə'ligəmi/ *n.* полигамия *f.*; многобрачие *neut.*
polyglot /'pɒli,glɒt/ **1.** *n.* полиглот *m.* **2.** *adj.* многоязычный.
polymath /'pɒli,mæθ/ *n.* эрудит *m.*
polynomial /,pɒlə'noumiəl/ *n.* многочлен; полином *m.*
polysemy /'pɒli,simi/ *n.* полисемия; многозначность *f.*
polysyllabic /,pɒlisi'læbik/ *adj.* многосложный.
polytechnic /,pɒli'tɛknik/ **1.** *n.* политехникум *m.* **2.** *adj.* политехнический.
pomade /pɒ'meid/ *n.* помада *f.*
pomegranate /'pɒm,grænit/ *n.* гранат *m.*
Pomeranian /,pɒmə'reiniən/ *n.* (*dog*) померанский шпиц *m.*
pomp /pɒmp/ *n.* помпа; пышность *f.*

pomposity /pɒm'pɒsɪti/ *n.* ва́жность *f.*; самодово́льство *neut.*

pompous /'pɒmpəs/ *adj.* напы́щенный.

pond /pɒnd/ *n.* пруд *m.*

ponder /'pɒndər/ *v.* обду́мывать *impf.*, обду́мать *pf.*

ponderous /'pɒndərəs/ *adj.* тяжёлый; тяжелове́сный; громо́здкий.

pontiff /'pɒntɪf/ *n.* (*bishop*) епи́скоп *m.*; (*Pope*) Па́па ри́мский *m.*

pontifical /pɒn'tɪfɪkəl/ *adj.* епи́скопский; па́пский.

pontoon /pɒn'tun/ *n.* (*for bridge*) понто́н *m.*

pony /'pouni/ *n.* по́ни *neut.* *indecl.*

pool /pul/ *n.* (*puddle*) лу́жа *f.*; (*swimming pool*) бассе́йн *m.*

poor /pur/ **1.** *adj.* бе́дный; (*bad*) плохо́й. **2.** *n.* беднота́ *f.*, бе́дные *pl.*

Pope /poup/ *n.* Па́па *m.*

popeyed /'pɒp,aid/ *adj.* пучегла́зый.

popgun /'pɒp,gʌn/ *n.* пуга́ч *m.*

poplar /'pɒplər/ **1.** *n.* то́поль *m.* **2.** *adj.* то́полевый.

poppy /'pɒpi/ *n.* мак *m.*

populace /'pɒpyələs/ *n.* населе́ние *neut.*

popular /'pɒpyələr/ *adj.* популя́рный; (*of the people*) наро́дный.

popularity /,pɒpyə'lærɪti/ *n.* популя́рность *f.*

population /,pɒpyə'leiʃən/ *n.* населе́ние *neut.*

populous /'pɒpyələs/ *adj.* густонаселённый.

porcelain /'pɒrsəlɪn/ **1.** *n.* фарфо́р *m.* **2.** *adj.* фарфо́ровый.

porch /pɒrtʃ/ *n.* вера́нда *f.*

porcupine /'pɒrkyə,pain/ *n.* дикобра́з *m.*

pore /pɒr/ *n.* по́ра *f.*

pork /pɒrk/ **1.** *n.* свини́на *f.* **2.** *adj.* свино́й.

pornography /pɒr'nɒgrəfi/ *n.* порногра́фия *f.*

porous /'pɒrəs/ *adj.* по́ристый.

porpoise /'pɒrpəs/ *n.* дельфи́н *m.*; морска́я свинья́ *f.*

porridge /'pɒridʒ/ *n.* овся́ная ка́ша *f.*

port¹ /pɒrt/ *n.* (*city*) порто́вый го́род, порт *m.*

port² /pɒrt/ *n.* (*of a ship*) ле́вый борт *m.*

port³ /pɒrt/ *n.* (*wine*) портве́йн *m.*

portable /'pɒrtəbəl/ *adj.* перено́сный; порта́тивный.

portage /'pɒrtɪdʒ/ *n.* перево́зка *f.*; (*boat*) во́лок *m.*

portcullis /pɒrt'kʌlɪs/ *n.* опускна́я решётка *f.*

portend /pɒr'tɛnd/ *v.* предвеща́ть *impf.*

portent /'pɒrtɛnt/ *n.* предзнаменова́ние *neut.*; (*marvel*) чу́до *neut.*

porter /'pɒrtər/ *n.* носи́льщик *m.*

portfolio /pɒrt'fouli,ou/ *n.* портфе́ль *m.*; па́пка *f.*

porthole /'pɒrt,houl/ *n.* иллюмина́тор *m.*

portion /'pɒrʃən/ *n.* часть *f.*; у́часть *f.*; (*of food*) по́рция *f.*

portly /'pɒrtli/ *adj.* по́лный; (*stately*) оса́нистый.

portrait /'pɒrtrɪt/ *n.* портре́т *m.*

portray /pɒr'trei/ *v.* изобража́ть *impf.*, изобрази́ть *pf.*

portrayal /pɒr'treiəl/ *n.* изображе́ние *neut.*

Portugal /'pɒrtʃəgəl/ *n.* Португа́лия *f.*

Portuguese /,pɒrtʃə'giz/ **1.** *adj.* португа́льский. **2.** *n.* португа́лец *m.*, португа́лка *f.*

pose /pouz/ **1.** *n.* по́за *f.* **2.** *v.* пози́ровать *impf.*; (*put*) ста́вить *impf.*; поста́вить *pf.*; **to pose as** изобража́ть; выдава́ть себя́ (за *with acc.*) *impf.*

poseur /pou'zɜr/ *n.* позёр *m.*

position /pə'zɪʃən/ *n.* положе́ние *neut.*; пози́ция *f.*; (*rank*) до́лжность *f.*

positive /'pɒzɪtɪv/ **1.** *adj.* положи́тельный. **2.** *photog.* позити́в *m.*

positively /'pɒzɪtɪvli/ *adv.* несомне́нно; положи́тельно.

possess /pə'zɛs/ *v.* владе́ть; облада́ть (*with instr.*) *impf.*

possessed /pə'zɛst/ *adj.* (*by devil; rage*) бесно́ватый; одержи́мый.

possession /pə'zɛʃən/ *n.* владе́ние *neut.*; *pl.* иму́щество *neut.*

possessive /pə'zɛsɪv/ *adj.* со́бственнический; име́ющий; владе́ющий; (*gram.*) притяжа́тельный.

possibility /,pɒsə'bɪlɪti/ *n.* возмо́жность *f.*

possible /'pɒsəbəl/ *adj.* возмо́жный.

possibly /'pɒsəbli/ *adv.* возмо́жно; по возмо́жности.

post¹ /poust/ **1.** *n.* (*pole*) столб *m.* **2.** *v.* выве́шивать *impf.*, вы́весить *pf.*

post² /poust/ *n.* (*station*) пост; пункт *m.*

postage /'poustɪdʒ/ *n.* почто́вая опла́та *f.*

postal /'poustl/ *adj.* почто́вый.

post card *n.* откры́тка *f.*

poster /'poustər/ *n.* плака́т *m.*; афи́ша *f.*

poste restante /,poust rɛ'stɑnt/ *adv.* до востре́бования.

posterior /pɒ'stɪəriər/ *adj.* (*rear*) за́дний.

posterity /pɒ'stɛrɪti/ *n.* пото́мство *neut.*; пото́мки *pl.*

postgraduate /poust'grædʒuit/ *n.* аспира́нт *m.*

posthumous /'pɒstʃəməs/ *adj.* посме́ртный.

postilion /pou'stɪlyən/ *n.* форе́йтор *m.*

postman /'poustmən/ *n.* почтальо́н *m.*

postmark /'poust,mɑrk/ *n.* почто́вый штемпель *m.*

postmaster /'poust,mæstər/ *n.* нача́льник почто́вого отделе́ния *m.*

postmeridian /,poustmə'rɪdiən/ *adj.* послеполу́денный.

post office *n.* по́чта *f.*

postpone /poust'poun/ *v.* откла́дывать *impf.*, отложи́ть *pf.*; отсро́чивать *impf.*, отсро́чить *pf.*

postponement /poust'pounmənt/ *n.* отсро́чка *f.*; откла́дывание *neut.*

postscript /'poust,skrɪpt/ *n.* постскри́птум *m.*

posture /'pɒstʃər/ **1.** *n.* по́за *f.*; (*position*) положе́ние *neut.*; (*carriage*) оса́нка *f.* **2.** *v.* пози́ровать *impf.*

pot /pɒt/ *n.* кастрю́ля *f.*; (*for flowers*) горшо́к *m.*

potash /'pɒt,æʃ/ *n.* пота́ш; углеки́слый ка́лий *m.*

potassium /pə'tæsiəm/ *n.* ка́лий *m.*

potato /pə'teitou/ **1.** *n.* карто́фель *m.* **2.** *adj.* карто́фельный.

potbellied /'pɒt,bɛlid/ *adj.* толстопу́зый; пуза́тый.

potboiler /'pɒt,bɔilər/ *n.* халту́ра *f.*

potency /'poutṇsi/ *n.* (*strength*) си́ла *f.*; (*liquor*) кре́пость *f.*

potent /'poutnt/ *adj.* си́льный.

potentate /'poutṇ,teit/ *n.* власти́тель; властели́н *m.*

potential /pə'tɛnʃəl/ **1.** *adj.* потенциа́льный. **2.** *n.* потенциа́л *m.*

pothole /'pɒt,houl/ *n.* (*in road*) ры́твина; вы́боина *f.*

potion /'pouʃən/ *n.* зе́лье *neut.*

pot roast *n.* тушёное мя́со *neut.*

Potsdam /'pɒtsdæm/ *n.* По́тсдам *m.*

potter /'pɒtər/ *n.* гонча́р *m.*

pottery /'pɒtəri/ *n.* гли́няные изде́лия *pl.*

pouch /pautʃ/ *n.* мешо́к; мешо́чек *m.*, су́мка *f.*

poultice /'poultɪs/ *n.* припа́рка *f.*

poultry /'poultri/ *n.* дома́шняя пти́ца *f.*

pounce /pauns/ *v.* набра́сываться; налета́ть (на *with acc.*) *impf.*

pound[1] /paund/ *n.* фунт *m.*

pound[2] /paund/ *v.* (*crush*) толо́чь *impf.*

pour /pɔr/ *v.t.* лить *impf.*; *v.i.* ли́ться *impf.*

pout /paut/ *v.* надува́ть гу́бы, ду́ться (на *with acc.*) *impf.*

poverty /'pɒvərti/ *n.* бе́дность *f.*

powder /'paudər/ **1.** *n.* порошо́к *m.*; (*talcum*) пу́дра *f.*; (*gun*) по́рох *m.* **2.** *adj.* порохово́й. **3.** *v.* пу́дрить *impf.*

powder keg *n.* порохова́я бо́чка *f.*

powder magazine *n.* порохово́й по́греб *m.*

power /'pauər/ **1.** *n.* си́ла; мощь; эне́ргия *f.*; (*math*) сте́пень *f.* **2.** *adj.* силово́й; механи́ческий.

powerful /'pauərfəl/ *adj.* си́льный; мо́щный.

powerless /'pauərlɪs/ *adj.* бесси́льный.

power station *n.* электроста́нция *f.*

power tool *n.* электроинструме́нт *m.*

Poznań /'poznæn, 'poz,nɑnyɑ/ *n.* По́знань *f.*

practical /'præktɪkəl/ *adj.* практи́ческий.

practically /'præktɪkli/ *adv.* практи́чески; (*almost*) почти́.

practice /'præktɪs/ **1.** *n.* пра́ктика *f.*; (*custom*) обы́чай *m.*; (*exercise*) упражне́ние *neut.* **2.** *v.* (*drill*) упражня́ться; практикова́ться *impf.*

practiced /'præktɪst/ *adj.* о́пытный; иску́сный.

Prague /prɑg/ *n.* Пра́га *f.*

prairie /'prɛəri/ *n.* пре́рия; степь *f.*

praise /preiz/ **1.** *n.* похвала́ *f.* **2.** *v.* хвали́ть *impf.*, похвали́ть *pf.*

praiseworthy /'preiz,wзrði/ *adj.* похва́льный.

prance /præns/ *v.* (*horse*) гарцева́ть *impf.*; (*jump about*) скака́ть *impf.*

prank /præŋk/ *n.* ша́лость *f.*

prankster /'præŋkstər/ *n.* прока́зник *m.*

prattle /'prætl/ *v.* болта́ть; лепета́ть *impf.*

prawn /prɔn/ *n.* креве́тка *f.*

pray /prei/ *v.* моли́ться *impf.*

prayer /'prɛər/ *n.* моли́тва *f.*

prayer book *n.* моли́твенник *m.*

praying /'preiiŋ/ *n.* моле́ние *neut.*; моли́тва *f.*

praying mantis *n.* богомо́л *m.*

preach /pritʃ/ *v.* пропове́довать *impf.*

preacher /'pritʃər/ *n.* пропове́дник *m.*

preaching /'pritʃɪŋ/ *n.* пропове́дование *neut.*; (*sermon*) про́поведь *f.*

preamble /'prɪ,æmbəl/ *n.* вступле́ние *neut.*

precarious /prɪ'kɛəriəs/ *adj.* риско́ванный; опа́сный.

precaution /prɪ'kɔʃən/ *n.* предосторо́жность *f.*

precede /prɪ'sid/ *v.* предше́ствовать *impf.*

precedence /'prɛsɪdəns/ *n.* предше́ствование *neut.*

precedent /*adj.* prɪ'sidnt; *n.* 'prɛsɪdənt/ **1.** *adj.* предше́ствующий. **2.** *n.* прецеде́нт *m.*

preceding /prɪ'sidɪŋ/ *adj.* предыду́щий; предше́ствующий.

precept /'prisɛpt/ *n.* наставле́ние *neut.*

preceptor /prɪ'sɛptər/ *n.* наста́вник *m.*

precinct /'prisɪŋkt/ *n.* (избира́тельный) уча́сток *m.*; (*police*) отделе́ние мили́ции *neut.*

precious /'prɛʃəs/ *adj.* драгоце́нный.

precipice /'prɛsəpɪs/ *n.* обры́в *m.*; (*fig.*) про́пасть *f.*

precipitancy /prɪ'sɪpɪtənsi/ *n.* опроме́тчивость; торопли́вость; поспе́шность *f.*

precipitate /prɪ'sɪpɪtɪt/ *n.* (*plunge*) низверга́ть *impf.*, низве́ргнуть *pf.*

precipitous /prɪ'sɪpɪtəs/ *adj.* круто́й; (*sheer*) отве́сный; обры́вистый.

précis /prei'si, 'preisi/ *n.* конспе́кт *m.*; кра́ткое изложе́ние *neut.*

precise /prɪ'sais/ *adj.* то́чный.

precisely /prɪ'saisli/ *adv.* то́чно; и́менно.

precision /prɪ'sɪʒən/ *n.* то́чность; аккура́тность; чёткость *f.*

precocious /prɪ'kouʃəs/ *adj.* ра́но разви́вшийся.

preconceived /,prikən'sivd/ *adj.* предвзя́тый.

precondition /,prikən'dɪʃən/ *n.* предвари́тельное усло́вие *neut.*

precursory /prɪ'kзrsəri/ *adj.* предвари́тельный.

predator /'prɛdətər/ *n.* хи́щник *m.*

predatory /'prɛdə,tɔri/ *adj.* хи́щный.

predecessor /'prɛdə,sɛsər/ *n.* предше́ственник *m.*

predestination /prɪ,dɛstə'neiʃən/ *n.* предопределе́ние *neut.*

predestine /prɪ'dɛstɪn/ *v.* предопределя́ть *impf.*

predetermine /,pridi'tзrmɪn/ *v.* предреша́ть; предопределя́ть *impf.*

predicament /prɪ'dɪkəmənt/ *n.* затрудни́тельное положе́ние *neut.*

predicate /'prɛdɪkɪt/ *n.* (*gram.*) сказу́емое *neut.*; предика́т *m.*

predicative /'prɛdɪ,keitɪv/ *adj.* предикати́вный.

predict /prɪ'dɪkt/ *v.* предска́зывать *impf.*, предсказа́ть *pf.*

predisposition /,pridɪspə'zɪʃən/ *n.* предрасположе́ние **toward** (к *with dat.*) *neut.*

predominant /prɪ'dɒmənənt/ *adj.* преоблада́ющий.

predominate /prɪ'dɒmə,neit/ *v.* госпо́дствовать *impf.*; (*in number*) преоблада́ть *impf.*

preeminent /pri'ɛmənənt/ *adj.* превосходя́щий.

preempt /pri'ɛmpt/ *v.* (*buy before*) покупа́ть пре́жде други́х *impf.*

preemptive /pri'ɛmptɪv/ *adj.* упрежда́ющий.

preen /prin/ *v.* (*of bird*) чи́стить клю́вом *impf.*; (*person*) прихора́шиваться *impf.*

prefabricated /pri'fæbrɪ,keitɪd/ *adj.* сбо́рный; заводско́го изготовле́ния.

prefabricated house *n.* сбо́рный дом *m.*

preface /'prɛfɪs/ *n.* предисло́вие *neut.*

prefect /'prifɛkt/ *n.* префе́кт *m.*

prefecture /'prifɛktʃər/ *n.* префекту́ра *f.*

prefer /prɪ'fзr/ *v.* предпочита́ть *impf.*

preferable /'prɛfərəbəl/ *adj.* предпочти́тельный.

preference /'prɛfərəns/ *n.* предпочте́ние *neut.*

preferential /,prɛfə'rɛnʃəl/ *adj.* предпочти́тельный.

prefiguration /pri,fɪgyə'reiʃən/ *n.* приме́та *f.*

prefix /'priːfɪks/ *n.* пре́фикс *m.*; приста́вка *f.*
pregnancy /'prɛɡnənsi/ *n.* бере́менность *f.*
pregnant /'prɛɡnənt/ *adj.* бере́менная.
prehensile /prɪ'hɛnsɪl/ *adj.* хвата́тельный.
prehistoric /ˌprihɪ'stɔrɪk/ *adj.* доистори́ческий.
prehistory /pri'hɪstəri/ *n.* предысто́рия *f.*
prejudge /pri'dʒʌdʒ/ *v.* принима́ть предвзя́тое реше́ние; предреша́ть *impf.*
prejudice /'prɛdʒədɪs/ *n.* (*bias*) предубежде́ние *neut.*; (*detriment*) уще́рб *m.*
prejudiced /'prɛdʒədɪst/ *adj.* (*unfavorably*) предубеждённый; (про́тив *with gen.*); (*favorably*) пристра́стный (к *with dat.*).
preliminary /prɪ'lɪməˌnɛri/ *adj.* предвари́тельный.
prelude /'prɛlyud/ *n.* вступле́ние *neut.*; (*mus.*) прелю́дия *f.*
premarital /pri'mærɪtl/ *adj.* добра́чный.
premature /ˌpriməˈtʃʊr/ *adj.* преждевре́менный.
premeditated /prɪ'mɛdɪˌteitɪd/ *adj.* преднаме́ренный.
premeditation /prɪˌmɛdɪ'teiʃən/ *n.* преднаме́ренность *f.*
premier /prɪ'mir/ **1.** *n.* премье́р-мини́стр; премье́р *m.* **2.** *adj.* пе́рвый.
première /prɪ'mir/ *n.* премье́ра *f.*
premise /'prɛmɪs/ *n.* предпосы́лка *f.*; *pl.* (*land*) помеще́ние *neut.*
premium /'primiəm/ *n.* пре́мия *f.*
premonition /ˌprimə'nɪʃən/ *n.* предчу́вствие *neut.*
prenatal /pri'neitl/ *adj.* предродово́й.
preoccupied /pri'ɒkyəˌpaid/ *adj.* (*anxious*) озабо́ченный; (*involved*) поглощённый.
preoccupy /pri'ɒkyəˌpai/ *v.* поглоща́ть *impf.*
preordain /ˌpriɔr'dein/ *v.* предопределя́ть *impf.*
preparation /ˌprɛpə'reiʃən/ *n.* приготовле́ние *neut.*
preparatory /prɪ'pærəˌtɔri/ *adj.* пригото́вительный; подготови́тельный.
prepare /prɪ'pɛər/ *v.t.* гото́вить *impf.*, пригото́вить *pf.*; *v.i.* гото́виться (к *with dat.*) *impf.*, пригото́виться *pf.*
prepared /prɪ'pɛərd/ *adj.* гото́вый; (к *with dat.*).
prepay /pri'pei/ *v.* де́лать предопла́ту *impf.*
preponderance /prɪ'pɒndərəns/ *n.* преоблада́ние *neut.*; переве́с *m.*
preponderant /prɪ'pɒndərənt/ *adj.* преоблада́ющий.
preposition /ˌprɛpə'zɪʃən/ *n.* предло́г *m.*
prepositional /ˌprɛpə'zɪʃənl/ *adj.* предло́жный.
prepossessing /ˌpripə'zɛsɪŋ/ *adj.* привлека́тельный.
preposterous /prɪ'pɒstərəs/ *adj.* абсу́рдный.
preprandial /pri'prændiəl/ *adj.* предобе́денный.
prerequisite /pri'rɛkwəzɪt/ *n.* предпосы́лка *f.*
prerogative /prɪ'rɒɡətɪv/ *n.* прерогати́ва *f.*; исключи́тельное пра́во *neut.*
presbyter /'prɛzbɪtər/ *n.* старе́йшина ; (*priest*) пресви́тер *m.*
Presbyterian /ˌprɛzbɪ'tɪəriən/ **1.** *n.* пресвитериа́нин *m.*, пресвитериа́нка *f.* **2.** *adj.* пресвитериа́нский.
preschool /'priˌskul/ *adj.* дошко́льный.
prescribe /prɪ'skraib/ *v.* предпи́сывать *impf.*, предписа́ть *pf.*; (*med.*) пропи́сывать *impf.*, прописа́ть *pf.*
prescription /prɪ'skrɪpʃən/ *n.* предписа́ние *neut.*; (*med.*) реце́пт *m.*

presence /'prɛzəns/ *n.* прису́тствие *neut.*
present[1] /'prɛzənt/ **1.** *adj.* прису́тствующий; (*also gram.*) настоя́щий; **to be present** прису́тствовать *impf.* **2.** *n.* настоя́щее вре́мя *neut.* **3.** *v.* представля́ть *impf.*, предста́вить *pf.*
present[2] /'prɛzənt/ **1.** *n.* (*gift*) пода́рок *m.* **2.** *v.* (*gift*) дари́ть *impf.*, подари́ть *pf.*
presentable /prɪ'zɛntəbəl/ *adj.* прили́чный.
presentation /ˌprɛzən'teiʃən/ *n.* представле́ние *neut.*
present-day /'prɛzənt'dei/ *adj.* совреме́нный; ны́нешний.
presentiment /prɪ'zɛntəmənt/ *n.* предчу́вствие *neut.*
presently /'prɛzəntli/ *adv.* ско́ро; вско́ре; сейча́с.
preservation /ˌprɛzər'veiʃən/ *n.* сохране́ние *neut.*
preservative /prɪ'zɜrvətɪv/ *n.* консерва́нт *m.*
preserve /prɪ'zɜrv/ **1.** *n.* (*for game*) запове́дник *m.*; *pl.* (*jam*) варе́нье *neut.* **2.** *v.* (*keep*) сохраня́ть *impf.*, сохрани́ть *pf.*; (*food*) консерви́ровать *impf.*
preset /'priˌsɛt/ *adj.* за́данный; запрограмми́рованный.
preside /prɪ'zaid/ *v.* председа́тельствовать *impf.*
presidency /'prɛzɪdənsi/ *n.* президе́нство; председа́тельство *neut.*
president /'prɛzɪdənt/ *n.* президе́нт; председа́тель *m.*
press /prɛs/ **1.** *n.* (*device*) пресс *m.*; (*printing; the press*) печа́ть; пре́сса *f.* **2.** *v.* жать; дави́ть *impf.*; (*iron*) гла́дить *impf.*, погла́дить *pf.*
press conference *n.* пресс-конфере́нция *f.*
pressure /'prɛʃər/ *n.* давле́ние *neut.*
pressurize /'prɛʃəˌraiz/ *v.* (*cabin*) герметизи́ровать *impf.*
prestige /prɛ'stiʒ/ *n.* прести́ж *m.*
prestigious /prɛ'stɪdʒəs/ *adj.* прести́жный.
presumably /prɪ'zuməbli/ *adv.* предположи́тельно.
presume /prɪ'zum/ *v.* предполага́ть *impf.*, предположи́ть *pf.*
presumed /prɪ'zumd/ *adj.* предполага́емый.
presumption /prɪ'zʌmpʃən/ *n.* предположе́ние *neut.*
presumptuous /prɪ'zʌmptʃuəs/ *adj.* самонаде́янный.
presuppose /ˌprisə'pouz/ *v.* предполага́ть , предположи́ть *pf.*
presupposition /ˌprisʌpə'zɪʃən/ *n.* предположе́ние *neut.*
pretend /prɪ'tɛnd/ *v.* притворя́ться (*with instr.*); (*lay claim*) претендова́ть *impf.*
pretended /prɪ'tɛndɪd/ *adj.* мни́мый.
pretender /prɪ'tɛndər/ *n.* претенде́нт (на *with acc.*) *m.*
pretense /prɪ'tɛns/ *n.* (*pretext*) предло́г *m.*
pretension /prɪ'tɛnʃən/ *n.* прете́нзия *f.*
pretentious /prɪ'tɛnʃəs/ *adj.* претенцио́зный.
preternatural /ˌpritər'nætʃərəl/ *adj.* сверхъесте́ственный.
pretext /'pritɛkst/ *n.* предло́г *m.*; отгово́рка *f.*
pretonic /pri'tɒnɪk/ *adj.* предуда́рный.
Pretoria /prɪ'tɔriə/ *n.* Прето́рия *f.*
pretty /'prɪti/ **1.** *adj.* хоро́шенький; прия́тный. **2.** *adv.* дово́льно; доста́точно.
pretzel /'prɛtsəl/ *n.* кре́ндель *m.*
prevail /prɪ'veil/ *v.* преоблада́ть *impf.*

prevailing /prɪ'veɪlɪŋ/ *adj.* преобладающий; господствующий.

prevalent /'prɛvələnt/ *adj.* распространённый.

prevent /prɪ'vɛnt/ *v.* (*protect*) предохранять *impf.*, предохранить *pf.*; (*hinder*) препятствовать *impf.*

prevention /prɪ'vɛnʃən/ *n.* предохранение; предупреждение *neut.*

preventive /prɪ'vɛntɪv/ *adj.* предупредительный.

preview /'pri,vyu/ *n.* (*of film*) предварительный просмотр *m.*

previous /'priviəs/ *adj.* предыдущий.

previously /'priviəsli/ *adv.* заранее; предварительно.

prewar /'pri'wɔr/ *adj.* довоенный.

prey /prei/ **1.** *n.* (*animal*) добыча *f.* **2.** *v.* (*plunder*) грабить *impf.*

price /prais/ **1.** *n.* цена *f.* **2.** *v.* назначать цену; оценивать *impf.*, оценить *pf.*

priceless /'praislɪs/ *adj.* бесценный.

price list *n.* прейскурант *m.*

prick /prɪk/ **1.** *n.* укол *m.* **2.** *v.* колоть *impf.*, уколоть; кольнуть *pf.*

prickly /'prɪkli/ *adj.* колючий.

pride /praid/ *n.* гордость *f.*

priest /prist/ *n.* священник *m.*; (*pagan*) жрец *m.*

priesthood /'pristhʊd/ *n.* священство; духовенство *neut.*

priggish /'prɪgɪʃ/ *adj.* самодовольный; педантичный.

prim /prɪm/ *adj.* чопорный.

primacy /'praiməsi/ *n.* первенство *neut.*

primal /'praiməl/ *adj.* первобытный; (*original*) первоначальный.

primarily /prai'mɛərəli/ *adv.* в первую очередь; главным образом.

primary /'praimɛri/ *adj.* основной.

primary school *n.* начальная школа *f.*

primate /'praimeit/ *n.* (*eccl.*) примас *m.*; (*zool.*) примат *m.*

prime /praim/ **1.** *adj.* главный; основной. **2.** *n.* расцвет *m.* **3.** *v.* (*with paint*) грунтовать *impf.*

prime minister *n.* премьер-министр *m.*

primer[1] /'prɪmər/ *n.* (*for teaching reading*) букварь *m.*

primer[2] /'praimər/ *n.* (*paint*) грунтовочная краска *f.*

primeval /prai'mivəl/ *adj.* первобытный.

primitive /'prɪmɪtɪv/ *adj.* примитивный.

primordial /prai'mɔrdiəl/ *adj.* (*primeval*) первобытный.

primp /prɪmp/ *v.* прихорашиваться *impf.*

primrose /'prɪm,rouz/ *n.* самоцвет *m.*; примула *f.*

prince /prɪns/ *n.* князь *m.*; (*non-Russian*) принц *m.*

princedom /'prɪnsdəm/ *n.* княжество *neut.*

princely /'prɪnsli/ *adj.* княжеский.

princess /'prɪnsɪs/ *n.* (*wife of prince*) княгиня *f.*; (*daughter of prince*) княжна *f.*; (*non-Russian*) принцесса *f.*

principal /'prɪnsəpəl/ **1.** *adj.* главный. **2.** *n.* начальник *m.*; (*of school*) директор *m.*

principality /,prɪnsə'pælɪti/ *n.* княжество *neut.*

principally /'prɪnsəpəli/ *adv.* главным образом.

principle /'prɪnsəpəl/ *n.* принцип *m.*

print /prɪnt/ **1.** *n.* (*type*) печать *f.*; шрифт *m.*;

(*imprint; photog.*) отпечаток *m.*; (*art*) гравюра *f.* **2.** *v.* печатать *impf.*, напечатать *pf.*

printed /'prɪntɪd/ *adj.* печатный.

printer /'prɪntər/ *n.* (*man*) печатник; типограф *m.*; (*machine*) печатающее устройство *neut.*; (*comput.*) принтер *m.*

printing /'prɪntɪŋ/ *n.* печатание *neut.*

printout /'prɪnt,aʊt/ *n.* распечатка *f.*

prior[1] /'praiər/ *adj.* предварительный; прежний.

prior[2] /'praiər/ *n.* (*of monastery*) настоятель *m.*

priority /prai'ɔrɪti/ *n.* приоритет *m.*

Pripet /'prɪpɪt/ *n.* (*river*) Припять *f.*

prism /'prɪzəm/ *n.* призма *f.*

prison /'prɪzən/ **1.** *n.* тюрьма *f.* **2.** *adj.* тюремный.

prison camp *n.* лагерь *m.*

prisoner /'prɪzənər/ *n.* заключённый; пленный *m.*

prison warden *n.* надзиратель (в тюрьме) *m.*

privacy /'praivəsi/ *n.* уединение *neut.*

private /'praivət/ **1.** *adj.* частный; личный. **2.** *n.* (*mil.*) рядовой *m.*; **in private** наедине *adv.*

privateer /,praivə'tɪər/ *n.* капер *m.*

privatize /'praivə,taiz/ *v.* приватизировать *impf.*

privilege /'prɪvəlɪdʒ/ *n.* привилегия *f.*

privileged /'prɪvəlɪdʒd/ *adj.* привилегированный.

privy /'prɪvi/ **1.** *n.* (*latrine*) отхожее место *neut.* **2.** *adj.* (*private*) частный; (*secret*) тайный; секретный.

prize /praiz/ **1.** *n.* приз *m.*, премия, награда *f.* **2.** *v.* высоко ценить *impf.*

prizewinner /'praiz,wɪnər/ *n.* призёр *m.*

pro /prou/ *n.*: **pros and cons** Доводы за и против.

probability /,prɒbə'bɪlɪti/ *n.* вероятность *f.*; правдоподобие *neut.*

probable /'prɒbəbəl/ *adj.* правдоподобный; возможный; вероятный.

probably /'prɒbəbli/ *adv.* вероятно.

probate /'proubeit/ *n.* утверждение завещания *neut.*

probation /prou'beiʃən/ *n.* испытание *neut.*; (*leg.*) условное освобождение *neut.*

probationary /prou'beiʃə,nɛri/ *adj.* испытательный.

probe /proub/ **1.** *n.* зонд *m.* **2.** *v.* зондировать *impf.*

problem /'prɒbləm/ *n.* задача; проблема *f.*

problematic /,prɒblə'mætɪk/ *adj.* проблематичный.

procedure /prə'sidʒər/ *n.* процедура *f.*

proceed /prə'sid/ *v.* (*continue*) продолжать(ся) *impf.*; (*begin*) приступать *impf.*

proceedings /prə'sidɪŋz/ *n.* (*leg.*) судопроизводство *neut.*; (*minutes*) протокол *m.*

process /'prɒsɛs/ *n.* процесс *m.*

processing /'prɒsɛsɪŋ/ *n.* обработка *f.*; **data processing** обработка данных *f.*

procession /prə'sɛʃən/ *n.* процессия *f.*

proclaim /prou'kleim/ *v.* провозглашать *impf.*, провозгласить *pf.*

proclamation /,prɒklə'meiʃən/ *n.* провозглашение *neut.*

proclivity /prou'klɪvɪti/ *n.* склонность (к *with dat.*) *f.*

procrastinate /prou'kræstə,neit/ *v.* медлить; откладывать (дело, решение) *impf.*

procrastination /prou,kræstə'neiʃən/ *n.* промедле́ние *neut.*

procure /prou'kyur/ *v.* добыва́ть *impf.*, добы́ть *pf.*

procuress /prou'kyuris/ *n.* сво́дня *f.*

prod /prɒd/ **1.** *n.* тычо́к *m.* **2.** *v.* ты́кать *impf.*

prodigal /'prɒdɪgəl/ *adj.* расточи́тельный; (*excessive*) чрезме́рный.

prodigious /prə'dɪdʒəs/ *adj.* огро́мный; изуми́тельный.

prodigy /'prɒdɪdʒi/ *n.* одарённый челове́к; вундерки́нд *m.*

produce /prə'dus/ *v.* производи́ть *impf.*, произвести́ *pf.*

product /'prɒdəkt/ *n.* проду́кт; результа́т *m.*

production /prə'dʌkʃən/ *n.* произво́дство *neut.*

productive /prə'dʌktɪv/ *adj.* производи́тельный; плодоро́дный.

productivity /prədʌk'tɪvɪti/ *n.* производи́тельность *f.*

profane /prə'fein/ **1.** *adj.* нечести́вый; богоху́льный. **2.** *v.* оскверня́ть *impf.*

profanity /prə'fænɪti/ *n.* богоху́льство; руга́тельство *neut.*

profess /prə'fɛs/ *v.* откры́то признава́ть *impf.*; (*faith*) испове́довать *impf.*

profession /prə'fɛʃən/ *n.* профе́ссия *f.*

professional /prə'fɛʃənļ/ **1.** *adj.* профессиона́льный. **2.** *n.* профессиона́л *m.*

professor /prə'fɛsər/ *n.* профе́ссор *m.*

professorial /,proufə'soriəl/ *adj.* профе́ссорский.

proffer /'prɒfər/ *v.* предлага́ть *impf.*

proficiency /prə'fɪʃənsi/ *n.* уме́ние *neut.*

proficient /prə'fɪʃənt/ *adj.* иску́сный; уме́лый.

profile /'proufail/ *n.* про́филь *m.*

profit /'prɒfɪt/ **1.** *n.* (*benefit*) по́льза *f.*; (*gain*) при́быль *f.*; дохо́д *m.* **2.** *v.* приноси́ть по́льзу *impf.*

profitable /'prɒfɪtəbəl/ *adj.* при́быльный.

profiteer /,prɒfɪ'tɪər/ *n.* спекуля́нт *m.*

profiteering /,prɒfɪ'tɪərɪŋ/ *n.* спекуля́ция *f.*

profligate /'prɒflɪgɪt/ **1.** *adj.* распу́тный; расточи́тельный. **2.** *n.* распу́тник; развра́тник *m.*, развра́тница *f.*

profound /prə'faund/ *adj.* глубо́кий.

profundity /prə'fʌndɪti/ *n.* глубина́ *f.*

profuse /prə'fyus/ *adj.* оби́льный.

profusion /prə'fyuʒən/ *n.* изоби́лие *neut.*; чрезме́рность *f.*

progeny /'prɒdʒəni/ *n.* де́ти *pl.*; (*descendants*) пото́мство *neut.*

prognosis /prɒg'nousɪs/ *n.* прогно́з *m.*

prognostication /prɒg,nɒstɪ'keiʃən/ *n.* предсказа́ние *neut.*

program /'prougræm/ **1.** *n.* програ́мма *f.* **2.** *v.* программи́ровать *impf.*

programmed /'prougræmd/ *adj.* (*comput.*) программи́рованный.

programmer /'prougræmər/ *n.* (*comput.*) программи́ст *m.*

progress / *n.* 'prɒgrɛs; *v.* prə'grɛs/ **1.** *n.* прогре́сс *m.*; успе́хи *pl.* **2.** *v.* прогресси́ровать; де́лать успе́хи *impf.*

progressive /prə'grɛsɪv/ *adj.* прогресси́вный; поступа́тельный.

prohibit /prou'hɪbɪt/ *v.* запреща́ть *impf.*, запрети́ть *pf.*

prohibition /,prouə'bɪʃən/ *n.* запреще́ние *neut.*

prohibitive /prou'hɪbɪtɪv/ *adj.* запрети́тельный.

project / *n.* 'prɒdʒɛkt; *v.* prə'dʒɛkt/ **1.** *n.* прое́кт *m.* **2.** *v.* (*plan*) проекти́ровать *impf.*, спроекти́ровать *pf.*; (*cast*) броса́ть *impf.*

projectile /prə'dʒɛktɪl, -tail/ *n.* снаря́д *m.*

projection /prə'dʒɛkʃən/ *n.* прое́кция *f.*

projector /prə'dʒɛktər/ *n.* кинопрое́ктор *m.*

proliferate /prə'lɪfə,reit/ *v.* размножа́ться *impf.*; (*spread*) распространя́ться *impf.*

prolific /prə'lɪfɪk/ *adj.* плодоро́дный; плодови́тый.

prolix /prou'lɪks/ *adj.* многосло́вный.

prologue /'proulɒg/ *n.* проло́г *m.*

prolong /prə'lɒŋ/ *v.* продлева́ть *impf.*; продли́ть *pf.*

promenade /,prɒmə'neid/ *v.* прогу́ливаться *impf.*

Prometheus /prə'miθiəs/ *n.* Промете́й *m.*

prominent /'prɒmənənt/ *adj.* выдаю́щийся.

promiscuity /,prɒmɪ'skyuɪti/ *n.* неразбо́рчивость *f.*

promiscuous /prə'mɪskyuəs/ *adj.* лёгкого поведе́ния.

promise /'prɒmɪs/ **1.** *n.* обеща́ние *neut.* **2.** *v.* обеща́ть *impf.*

promised /'prɒmɪst/ *adj.* обе́щанный.

Promised Land *n.* the, земля́ обетова́нная *f.*

promising /'prɒmɪsɪŋ/ *adj.* многообеща́ющий.

promissory note /'prɒmə,sɔri/ *n.* долгово́е обяза́тельство *neut.*

promontory /'prɒmən,tɔri/ *n.* мыс *m.*

promote /prə'mout/ *v.* (*raise*) продвига́ть *impf.*, продви́нуть *pf.*; повыша́ть в чи́не *impf.*, повы́сить *pf.*

promotion /prə'mouʃən/ *n.* продвиже́ние *neut.*

prompt /prɒmpt/ **1.** *adj.* бы́стрый. **2.** *v.* побужда́ть *impf.*, побуди́ть *pf.*; (*theat.*) суфли́ровать *impf.*

prompter /'prɒmptər/ *n.* (*theat.*) суфлёр *m.*

promulgation /,prɒməl'geiʃən/ *n.* обнаро́дование; распростране́ние *neut.*

prone /proun/ *adj.* (*face down*) распростёртый; лежа́щий ниц; (*inclined to*) скло́нный (к *with dat.*).

prong /prɒŋ/ *n.* зубе́ц *m.*

pronominal /prou'nɒmənļ/ *adj.* местоиме́нный.

pronoun /'prou,naun/ *n.* местоиме́ние *neut.*

pronounce /prə'nauns/ *v.* произноси́ть *impf.*, произнести́ *pf.*

pronouncement /prə'naunsmənt/ *n.* объявле́ние; заявле́ние *neut.*

pronunciation /prə,nʌnsi'eiʃən/ *n.* произноше́ние *neut.*

proof /pruf/ *n.* доказа́тельство *neut.*

proofread /'pruf,rid/ *v.* корректи́ровать *impf.*

proofreading /'pruf,ridɪŋ/ *n.* корректу́ра *f.*

prop[1] /prɒp/ *n.* (*support*) опо́ра *f.*; (*in mine*) сто́йка *f.*

prop[2] /prɒp/ *n. pl.* (*theat.*) реквизи́т *m.*

propaganda /,prɒpə'gændə/ *n.* пропага́нда *f.*

propagate /'prɒpə,geit/ *v.* (*disseminate*) распространя́ть *impf.*, распространи́ть *pf.*

propagation /,prɒpə'geiʃən/ *n.* размноже́ние; распростране́ние *neut.*

propel /prə'pɛl/ *v.* приводи́ть в движе́ние *impf.*

propeller /prə'pɛlər/ *n.* пропе́ллер; винт *m.*

propensity /prə'pɛnsɪti/ *n.* скло́нность *f.*

proper /'prɒpər/ *adj.* приличный; правильный.
properly /'prɒpərli/ *adv.* как следует.
proper noun *n.* имя собственное *neut.*
property /'prɒpərti/ *n.* имущество *neut.*, собственность *f.*; (*quality*) свойство *neut.*
prophecy /'prɒfəsi/ *n.* пророчество *neut.*
prophesy /'prɒfə,sai/ *v.* пророчить *impf.*
prophet /'prɒfɪt/ *n.* пророк *m.*
propitious /prə'pɪʃəs/ *adj.* благоприятный.
propjet /'prɒp,dʒɛt/ *n.* (*aero.*) турбовинтовой самолёт *m.*
proponent /prə'pounənt/ *n.* сторонник *m.*
proportion /prə'pɔrʃən/ *n.* пропорция *f.*; *pl.* (*size*) размеры *pl.*
proportionate /prə'pɔrʃənɪt/ *adj.* пропорциональный.
proposal /prə'pouzəl/ *n.* предложение *neut.*
propose /prə'pouz/ *v.* предлагать *impf.*; (*propose marriage*) делать предложение *impf.*
proposition /,prɒpə'zɪʃən/ *n.* предложение *neut.*; (*math*) теорема *f.*
propound /prə'paund/ *v.* излагать; предлагать *impf.*
proprietor /prə'praiitər/ *n.* собственник, владелец *m.*
propriety /prə'praiiti/ *n.* пристойность *f.*
prosaic /prou'zeiik/ *adj.* прозаический.
proscribe /prou'skraib/ *v.* (*prohibit*) запрещать *impf.*; (*banish*) изгонять *impf.*
proscription /prou'skrɪpʃən/ *n.* запрет *m.*; исключение *neut.*
prose /prouz/ *n.* проза *f.*
prosecute /'prɒsɪ,kyut/ *v.* преследовать судебным порядком *impf.*
prosecution /,prɒsɪ'kyuʃən/ *n.* судебное преследование *neut.*; (*accusing party*) обвинение *neut.*
prosecutor /'prɒsɪ,kyutər/ *n.* обвинитель *m.*; **public prosecutor** *n.* прокурор *m.*
proselytize /'prɒsəlɪ,taiz/ *v.* перетягивать в свою веру *impf.*
prose writer *n.* прозаик *m.*
prospect /'prɒspɛkt/ *n.* перспектива *f.*
prospective /prə'spɛktɪv/ *adj.* (*future*) будущий; (*potential*) возможный.
prospector /'prɒspɛktər/ *n.* разведчик *m.*
prosper /'prɒspər/ *v.* преуспевать *impf.*
prosperity /prɒ'spɛriti/ *n.* процветание *neut.*
prosperous /'prɒspərəs/ *adj.* процветающий; (*wealthy*) зажиточный; успешный.
prostate gland /'prɒsteit/ *n.* простата *f.*
prostitute /'prɒstɪ,tut/ **1.** *n.* проститутка *f.* **2.** *v.* проституировать *impf.*
prostrate /'prɒstreit/ **1.** *adj.* распростёртый. **2.** *v.* (*exhaust*) истощать *impf.*, истощить *pf.*
protagonist /prou'tægənɪst/ *n.* главный герой *m.*; (*advocate*) сторонник *m.*
protect /prə'tɛkt/ *v.* охранять *impf.*
protection /prə'tɛkʃən/ *n.* охрана *f.*
protective /prə'tɛktɪv/ *adj.* защитный; покровительственный.
protector /prə'tɛktər/ *n.* защитник *m.*
protégé /'proutə,ʒei/ *n.* протеже *m. indecl.*
protein /'proutin/ *n.* протеин *m.*
protest / *n.* 'proutɛst; *v.* prə'tɛst/ **1.** *n.* протест *m.* **2.** *v.* протестовать *impf.* and *pf.*
Protestant /'prɒtəstənt/ **1.** *adj.* протестантский. **2.** *n.* протестант *m.*, протестантка *f.*

protocol /'proutə,kɔl/ *n.* протокол *m.*
proton /'prouton/ *n.* протон *m.*
protoplasm /'proutə,plæzəm/ *n.* протоплазма *f.*
prototype /'proutə,taip/ *n.* прототип *m.*
protozoan /,proutə'zouən/ *n.* простейшее (животное) *neut.*
protract /prou'trækt/ *v.* тянуть; продлевать *impf.*
protracted /prou'træktɪd/ *adj.* длительный.
protractor /prou'træktər/ *n.* (*instrument*) транспортир *m.*
protrude /prou'trud/ *v.* торчать *impf.*
protruding /prou'trudɪŋ/ *adj.* торчащий; высунутый.
protrusion /prou'truʒən/ *n.* выступ *m.*
protuberant /prou'tubərənt/ *adj.* выпуклый.
proud /praud/ *adj.* гордый; **to be proud of** *v.* гордиться (*with instr.*) *impf.*
provable /'pruvəbəl/ *adj.* доказуемый.
prove /pruv/ *v.t.* доказывать *impf.*, доказать *pf.*
proven /'pruvən/ *adj.* доказанный.
provenance /'prɒvənəns/ *n.* происхождение *neut.*
Provence /prə'vɒns/ *n.* (*province*) Прованс *m.*
proverb /'prɒvərb/ *n.* пословица *f.*
provide /prə'vaid/ *v.* обеспечивать (*with instr.*) *impf.*
provided /prə'vaidɪd/ *also* **providing** /prə'vaidɪŋ/ *conj.* при условии, что; если только.
providence /'prɒvɪdəns/ *n.* провидение *neut.*
provident /'prɒvɪdənt/ *adj.* предусмотрительный.
provider /prə'vaidər/ *n.* поставщик; снабженец *m.*
province /'prɒvɪns/ *n.* провинция; область *f.*
provincial /prə'vɪnʃəl/ **1.** *adj.* провинциальный. **2.** *n.* провинциал *m.*
provision /prə'vɪʒən/ **1.** *n.* обеспечение *neut.*; (*stipulation*) условие *neut.*; *pl.* (*supplies*) провизия *f.* **2.** *v.* снабжать продовольствием *impf.*
provisional /prə'vɪʒənl/ *adj.* временный; (*conditional*) условный.
proviso /prə'vaizou/ *n.* условие *neut.*, оговорка *f.*
provocation /,prɒvə'keiʃən/ *n.* провокация *f.*
provocative /prə'vɒkətɪv/ *adj.* (*conduct*) вызывающий; (*alluring*) соблазнительный.
provoke /prə'vouk/ *v.* провоцировать *impf.*
provoking /prə'voukɪŋ/ *adj.* (*annoying*) раздражающий.
prow /prau/ *n.* (*boat*) нос *m.*
prowess /'prauis/ *n.* доблесть; отвага *f.*
prowl /praul/ *v.t.* бродить *impf.*
proximate /'prɒksəmit/ *adj.* ближайший; **proximate cause** *n.* непосредственная причина *f.*
proximity /prɒk'sɪmɪti/ *n.* близость *f.*
proxy /'prɒksi/ *n.* доверенность *f.*; полномочие *neut.*
prudence /'prudns/ *n.* благоразумие *neut.*; расчётливость *f.*
prudent /'prudnt/ *adj.* благоразумный; расчётливый.
prune[1] /prun/ *n.* чернослив *m.*
prune[2] /prun/ *v.* (*trim*) подрезать *impf.*
pruning shears /'prunɪŋ/ *n.* секатор *m.*
prurient /'pruriənt/ *adj.* похотливый.
Prut /prut/ *n.* (*river*) Прут *m.*
pry[1] /prai/ *v.* (*open*) взламывать *impf.*

pry² /prai/ *v.*: **to pry into** совáть нос (в *with acc.*) *impf.*

psalm /sɑm/ *n.* псалóм *m.*

Psalter /'sɔltər/ *n.* Псалты́рь *f.*

pseudonym /'sudn̩ɪm/ *n.* псевдони́м *m.*

Pskov /pskɔf/ *n.* Псков *m.*

psyche /'saiki/ *n.* (*soul*) душá *f.*; (*mentality*) пси́хика *f.*

psychiatrist /sɪ'kaiətrɪst/ *n.* психиáтр *m.*

psychiatry /sɪ'kaiətri/ *n.* психиатри́я *f.*

psychic /'saikɪk/ *adj.* психи́ческий.

psychoanalysis /ˌsaikouə'næləsɪs/ *n.* психоанáлиз *m.*

psychological /ˌsaikə'lɒdʒɪkəl/ *adj.* психологи́ческий.

psychologist /sai'kɒlədʒɪst/ *n.* психóлог *m.*

psychology /sai'kɒlədʒi/ *n.* психолóгия *f.*

psychopath /'saikəˌpæθ/ *n.* психопáт *m.*

psychosis /sai'kousɪs/ *n.* психóз *m.*

psychotherapist /ˌsaikou'θɛrəpɪst/ *n.* психотерапéвт *m.*

psychotherapy /ˌsaikou'θɛrapi/ *n.* психотерапи́я *f.*

ptomaine /'toumein/ *n.* трýпный яд; птомаи́н *m.*

pub /pʌb/ *n.* пивнáя *f.*

puberty /'pyubərti/ *n.* половáя зрéлость; возмужáлость *f.*

pubescent /pyu'bɛsənt/ *adj.* половозрéлый; (*bot.*) волоси́стый.

pubic /'pyubɪk/ *adj.* лобкóвый.

pubis /'pyubɪs/ *n.* лобóк *m.*

public /'pʌblɪk/ **1.** *adj.* публи́чный; общéственный. **2.** *n.* пýблика *f.*; нарóд *m.*

publication /ˌpʌblɪ'keiʃən/ *n.* опубликовáние; издáние *neut.*; публикáция *f.*

public house *n.* пивнáя *f.*

publicity /pʌ'blɪsɪti/ *n.* реклáма; глáсность *f.*

publicize /'pʌbləˌsaiz/ *v.* реклами́ровать *impf.* and *pf.*

publicly /'pʌblɪkli/ *adv.* публи́чно; откры́то.

public school *n.* публи́чная шкóла *f.*

publish /'pʌblɪʃ/ *v.* издавáть *impf.*, издáть *pf.*; опубликовáть *pf.*

publisher /'pʌblɪʃər/ *n.* издáтель *m.*

publishing house /'pʌblɪʃɪŋ/ *n.* издáтельство *neut.*

puck /pʌk/ *n.* (*hockey*) шáйба *f.*

pucker /'pʌkər/ *v.* мóрщить(ся) *impf.*

pudding /'pʊdɪŋ/ *n.* пýдинг *m.*

puddle /'pʌdl/ *n.* лýжа *f.*

pudgy /'pʌdʒi/ *adj.* пýхлый.

puerile /'pyuərɪl/ *adj.* дéтский; ребя́ческий.

Puerto Rico /'pwɛr'tə rikou, 'pɔrtə/ *n.* Пуэ́рто-Ри́ко *m.*

puff /pʌf/ **1.** *n.* клуб *m.*; (*air, etc.*) дуновéние *neut.* **2.** *v.* (*pant*) пыхтéть *impf.*

puffin /'pʌfɪn/ *n.* тýпик *m.*

pug *n.* (*dog*) мопс *m.*

pugnacious /pʌg'neiʃəs/ *adj.* драчли́вый.

pug-nosed /'pʌɡ ˌnouzd/ *adj.* курнóсый.

pull /pʊl/ **1.** *n.* тя́га *f.*, натяжéние *neut.* **2.** *v.* тянýть *impf.*, потянýть *pf.*; натя́гивать *impf.*, натянýть *pf.*

pulley /'pʊli/ *n.* блок; вóрот *m.*

pullover /'pʊlˌouvər/ *n.* пулóвер *m.*

pulmonary /'pʌlməˌnɛri/ *adj.* лёгочный.

pulp /pʌlp/ *n.* мáсса; пýльпа *f.*; (*of fruit*) мя́коть *f.*

pulpit /'pʊlpɪt/ *n.* кáфедра *f.*

pulsate /'pʌlseit/ *v.* пульси́ровать *impf.*

pulse /pʌls/ *n.* пульс *m.*

pulverize /'pʌlvəˌraiz/ *v.* превращáть(ся) в порошóк *impf.*

pulverizer /'pʌlvəˌraizər/ *n.* (*spray*) пульверизáтор *m.*; (*crusher*) дроби́лка *f.*

puma /'pyumə/ *n.* пýма *f.*

pumice /'pʌmɪs/ *n.* пéмза *f.*

pummel /'pʌməl/ *v.* колоти́ть *impf.*

pump /pʌmp/ **1.** *n.* насóс *m.*; водокáчка *f.* **2.** *v.* качáть *impf.*

pumpernickel /'pʌmpərˌnɪkəl/ *n.* чёрный хлеб *m.*

pumpkin /'pʌmpkɪn *or, commonly,* 'pʌŋkɪn/ *n.* ты́ква *f.*

pun /pʌn/ *n.* каламбýр *m.*; игрá слов *f.*

punch¹ /pʌntʃ/ **1.** *n.* удáр кулакóм *m.*; (*mach.*) пробóйник *m.* **2.** *v.* ударя́ть кулакóм *impf.*; (*make hole*) пробивáть *impf.*, проби́ть *pf.*

punch² /pʌntʃ/ *n.* (*drink*) пунш *m.*

punch line *n.* кульминацио́нный пункт *m.*

punctual /'pʌŋktʃuəl/ *adj.* пунктуáльный.

punctuate /'pʌŋktʃuˌeit/ *v.* стáвить знáки препинáния *impf.*

punctuation /ˌpʌŋktʃu'eiʃən/ *n.* пунктуáция *f.*

puncture /'pʌŋktʃər/ **1.** *n.* прокóл *m.* **2.** *v.* прокáлывать *impf.*, проколóть *pf.*

pungent /'pʌndʒənt/ *adj.* óстрый; рéзкий.

punish /'pʌnɪʃ/ *v.* накáзывать *impf.*, наказáть *pf.*

punishment /'pʌnɪʃmənt/ *n.* наказáние *neut.*

punitive /'pyunɪtɪv/ *adj.* карáтельный.

puny /'pyuni/ *adj.* слáбый; хи́лый.

pupa /'pyupə/ *n.* кýколка *f.*

pupil¹ /'pyupəl/ *n.* учени́к *m.*, учени́ца *f.*

pupil² /'pyupəl/ *n.* (*eye*) зрачóк *m.*

puppet /'pʌpɪt/ **1.** *n.* кýкла; марионéтка *f.* **2.** *adj.* кýкольный.

puppy /'pʌpi/ *n.* щенóк *m.*

purchase /'pɜrtʃəs/ **1.** *n.* покýпка *f.* **2.** *v.* покупáть *impf.*, купи́ть *pf.*

purchaser /'pɜrtʃəsər/ *n.* покупáтель *m.*

pure /pyur/ *adj.* чи́стый.

purebred /'pyʊr'brɛd/ *adj.* чистокрóвный.

purée /pyu'rei/ *n.* пюрé *neut. indecl.*

purgative /'pɜrgətɪv/ *n.* слаби́тельное (срéдство) *neut.*

purgatory /'pɜrgəˌtɔri/ *n.* (*relig.*) чисти́лище *neut.*

purge /pɜrdʒ/ **1.** *n.* чи́стка *f.* **2.** *v.* очищáть *impf.*

purification /ˌpyʊrəfɪ'keiʃən/ *n.* очи́стка *f.*

purify /'pyʊrəˌfai/ *v.* очищáть *impf.*, очи́стить *pf.*

Puritan /'pyʊrɪtn̩/ **1.** *n.* пуритáнин *m.*, пуритáнка *f.* **2.** *adj.* пуритáнский.

purity /'pyʊrɪti/ *n.* чистотá; непорóчность *f.*

purple /'pɜrpəl/ **1.** *adj.* багря́ный; пурпýрный. **2.** *n.* багря́ный цвет; пурпýрный цвет *m.*

purport /'pɜrpɔrt; *v.* pər'pɔrt/ **1.** *n.* смысл *m.*; значéние *neut.* **2.** *v.* подразумевáть *impf.*

purportedly /pər'pɔrtɪdli/ *adv.* я́кобы.

purpose /'pɜrpəs/ *n.* цель *f.*; **for the purpose of** с цéлью.

purposeless /'pɜrpəslɪs/ *adj.* бесцéльный.

purposely /'pɜrpəsli/ *adv.* нарóчно.

purr /pɜr/ **1.** 1 *n.* мурлы́канье *neut.* **2.** *v.* мурлы́кать *impf.*

purse /pɜrs/ *n.* су́мка *f.*; (*for money*) кошелёк *m.*
pursue /pər'su/ *v.* преслéдовать; гнáться *impf.*
pursuer /pər'suər/ *n.* преслéдователь *m.*
pursuit /pər'sut/ *n.* погóня *f.*
purvey /pər'vei/ *v.* поставля́ть *impf.*
purveyor /pər'veiər/ *n.* поставщи́к *m.*
purview /'pɜrvyu/ *n.* сфéра дéйствия; компетéнция *f.*
pus /pʌs/ *n.* гной *m.*
push /puʃ/ **1.** *n.* толчóк *m.* **2.** *v.* толкáть *impf.*; (*push through*) протáлкивать *impf.*, протолкну́ть *pf.*
push button *n.* кнóпка *f.*
pushcart /'puʃ,kɑrt/ *n.* телéжка *f.*
pushy /'puʃi/ *adj.* (*colloq.*) пробивнóй.
pusillanimous /,pyusə'lænəməs/ *adj.* малоду́шный; трусли́вый.
pussy /'pusi/ *also* **pussycat** /-,kæt/ *n.* (*colloq.*) ки́ска *f.*
pussy willow *n.* вéрба *f.*
put /put/ *v.* класть *impf.*, положи́ть *pf.*; стáвить

impf.; **to put aside** отложи́ть в стóрону *pf.*; **to put out a light** погаси́ть свет *pf.*
putative /'pyutətɪv/ *adj.* предполагáемый.
putrefaction /,pyutrə'fækʃən/ *n.* разложéние; гниéние *neut.*
putrefy /'pyutrə,fai/ *v.* разлагáться; гнить *impf.*
putrid /'pyutrɪd/ *adj.* гнилóй.
putsch /putʃ/ *n.* путч *m.*
putter /'pʌtər/ *v.* вози́ться *impf.*
putty /'pʌti/ *n.* замáзка *f.*
putty knife *n.* шпáтель *m.*
puzzle /'pʌzəl/ **1.** *n.* загáдка; головолóмка *f.* **2.** *v.* стáвить в тупи́к *impf.*
puzzled /'pʌzəld/ *adj.* озадáченный.
puzzling /'pʌzlɪŋ/ *adj.* озадáчивающий; недоумéнный.
Pygmy /'pɪgmi/ *n.* пигмéй *m.*
pyjamas /pə'dʒɑməz, -'dʒæməz/ *n.* пижáма *f.*
Pyongyang /'pyʌŋ'yɑŋ/ *n.* Пхеньáн *m.*
pyramid /'pɪrəmɪd/ *n.* пирами́да *f.*
Pyrenees /'pɪrə,niz/ *n.* (*mountains*) Пиренéи *pl.*
pyrotechnics /,pairə'tɛknɪks/ *n.* пиротéхника *f.*
python /'paiθɒn/ *n.* питóн *m.*

Q

Qaraghandy /ˌkærəgən'dɑ/ n. Караганда́ f.
quack /kwæk/ **1.** n. кря́канье neut. **2.** v. кря́кать impf.
quackery /'kwækəri/ n. шарлата́нство neut.
quadrangle /'kwɒdˌræŋgəl/ n. четырёхуго́льник m.
quadrangular /kwɒd'ræŋgyələr/ adj. четырёхуго́льный.
quadrant /'kwɒdrənt/ n. квадра́нт m.
quadraphonic /ˌkwɒdrə'fɒnɪk/ adj. квадрафони́ческий.
quadratic /kwɒ'drætɪk/ adj. квадра́тный.
quadratic equation n. квадра́тное уравне́ние neut.
quadrilateral /ˌkwɒdrə'lætərəl/ adj. четырёхсторо́нний.
quadruped /'kwɒdrʊˌped/ **1.** adj. четвероно́гий. **2.** n. четвероно́гое живо́тное neut.
quadruple /kwɒ'drupəl/ adj. (in four parts) четверно́й; (fourfold) четырёхкра́тный.
quadruplets /kwɒ'druplɪts/ n. четверня́ f.
quadruplicate /kwɒ'druplɪkɪt/ adj. четырёхкра́тный.
quagmire /'kwægmaiᵊr/ n. боло́то neut.
quail /kweil/ n. (bird) пе́репел m.; куропа́тка f.
quaint /kweint/ adj. причу́дливый.
quake /kweik/ **1.** n. дрожа́ние neut.; (earth) землетрясе́ние neut. **2.** v. трясти́сь impf.
qualification /ˌkwɒləfɪ'keiʃən/ n. квалифика́ция f.; (restriction) ограниче́ние neut., огово́рка f.
qualified /'kwɒləˌfaid/ adj. (limited) ограни́ченный; (conditional) усло́вный; (competent) компете́нтный.
qualify /'kwɒləˌfai/ v.t. квалифици́ровать impf. and pf.; v.i. квалифици́роваться pf.
qualitative /'kwɒlɪˌteitiv/ adj. ка́чественный.
quality /'kwɒlɪti/ n. ка́чество neut.
qualm /kwɑm/ n. pl. угрызе́ния со́вести neut.
quandary /'kwɒndəri/ n. затрудне́ние; затрудни́тельное положе́ние neut.
quantifier /'kwɒntəˌfaiər/ n. ква́нтор m.
quantify /'kwɒntəˌfai/ v. определя́ть коли́чество impf.
quantitative /'kwɒntɪˌteitiv/ adj. коли́чественный.
quantity /'kwɒntɪti/ n. коли́чество neut.; (math.) величина́ f.
quantum /'kwɒntəm/ **1.** n. (phys.) квант m. **2.** adj. ква́нтовый.
quarantine /'kwɔrənˌtin/ **1.** n. каранти́н m. **2.** v. подве́ргнуть каранти́ну pf.
quark /kwɔrk/ n. кварк m.
quarrel /'kwɔrəl/ **1.** n. ссо́ра f. **2.** v. ссо́риться impf.
quarrelsome /'kwɔrəlsəm/ adj. сварли́вый.
quarry[1] /'kwɔri/ n. каменоло́мня f.
quarry[2] /'kwɔri/ n. (animal) пресле́дуемый зверь m.
quart /kwɔrt/ n. (measure) ква́рта f.
quarter /'kwɔrtər/ n. че́тверть f.; (of year; city district) кварта́л m.; pl. (lodgings) помеще́ние neut.; (mil.) кварти́ры pl.; **a quarter to one** без че́тверти час.

quarterly /'kwɔrtərli/ adv. кварта́льный раз в три ме́сяца.
quartet /kwɔr'tɛt/ n. кварте́т m.
quartz /kwɔrts/ n. кварц m.
quasar /'kweizɑr/ n. ква́зар m.
quatercentenary /ˌkwɒtərsɛn'tɛnəri/ n. четырёхсотле́тие neut.
quaver /'kweivɑr/ v. дрожа́ть impf.
quay /ki, kei/ n. (mooring wall) прича́л m.; сте́нка f.; (wharf) при́стань f.
queasy /'kwizi/ adj. приверéдливый; брезгли́вый.
Quebec /kwɪ'bɛk, kɪ-/ n. Квебе́к m.
queen /kwin/ n. короле́ва f.; (cards) да́ма f.; (chess) ферзь m.
queen bee n. пчели́ная ма́тка f.
queen dowager n. вдо́вствующая короле́ва f.
queer /kwɪər/ adj. стра́нный; чудакова́тый.
quell /kwel/ v. подавля́ть impf.; (calm) успока́ивать impf.
quench /kwentʃ/ v. гаси́ть impf., погаси́ть pf.; (thirst) утоля́ть impf.
query /'kwɪəri/ **1.** n. вопро́с m. **2.** v. выража́ть сомне́ние (в with prep.) impf.
quest /kwɛst/ n. по́иски pl.
question /'kwɛstʃən/ **1.** n. вопро́с m.; **in question** о кото́ром идёт речь. **2.** v. допра́шивать impf., допроси́ть pf.
questionable /'kwɛstʃənəbəl/ adj. сомни́тельный.
questioning /'kwɛstʃənɪŋ/ n. (interrogation) допро́с m.
question mark n. вопроси́тельный знак m.
questionnaire /ˌkwɛstʃə'nɛər/ n. анке́та f.
queue /kyu/ n. (hair) коса́ f.; (line, list) о́чередь f.; **to queue up** v. стоя́ть в о́череди impf.
quibble /'kwɪbəl/ v. придира́ться; спо́рить impf.
quibbler /'kwɪblər/ n. приди́ра m. and f. (decl. f.).
quick /kwɪk/ adj. бы́стрый.
quicken /'kwɪkən/ v. ускоря́ть impf., уско́рить pf.
quicklime /'kwɪkˌlaim/ n. негашёная и́звесть f.
quickly /'kwɪkli/ (fast) бы́стро; ско́ро; (soon) ско́ро, вско́ре; (hastily) поспе́шно.
quicksand /'kwɪkˌsænd/ n. плыву́н, зыбу́чий песо́к m.
quicksilver /'kwɪkˌsɪlvər/ n. ртуть f.
quick-tempered /'kwɪk 'tɛmpərd/ adj. вспы́льчивый; раздражи́тельный.
quick-witted /'kwɪk 'wɪtɪd/ adj. сообрази́тельный.
quick-wittedness /'kwɪk 'wɪtɪdnɪs/ n. смётка f.
quiet /'kwaiit/ **1.** adj. споко́йный; ти́хий. **2.** n. поко́й m.; тишина́ f. **3.** v. успока́ивать impf., успоко́ить pf.
quietly /'kwaiitli/ adv. споко́йно.
quill /kwɪl/ n. (feather) перо́ neut.
quilt /kwɪlt/ n. стёганое одея́ло neut.
quince /kwɪns/ n. айва́ f.
quincentenary /ˌkwɪnsɛn'tɛnəri/ n. пятисотле́тие neut.
quinine /'kwainain/ n. хини́н m.

quintessence /kwɪn'tɛsəns/ *n.* квинтэссе́нция *f.*
quintet /kwɪn'tɛt/ *n.* квинте́т *m.*
quintuple /kwɪn'tupəl/ *adj.* пятикра́тный.
quip /kwɪp/ *n.* остро́та *f.*
quire /kwaiᵊr/ *n.* ру́сская десть *f.*
quirk /kwɜrk/ *n.* *n.* капри́з *m.*; причу́да *f.*
quirky /'kwɜrki/ *adj.* причу́дливый; капри́зный.
quit /kwɪt/ *n.* (*leave*) покида́ть *impf.*, поки́нуть *pf.*; (*give up*) броса́ть *impf.*, бро́сить *pf.*
quite /kwait/ *adv.* совсе́м; вполне́; дово́льно; **not quite** не совсе́м.
quiver /'kwɪvər/ **1.** *n.* дрожь *f.*, тре́пет *m.* **2.** *v.* дрожа́ть *impf.*
quixotic /kwɪk'sɒtɪk/ *adj.* донкихо́тский.

quiz /kwɪz/ *n.* (*short exam*) контро́льная рабо́та *f.*; (*contest*) виктори́на *f.*
quiz show *n.* виктори́на *f.*
quondam /'kwɒndəm/ *adj.* бы́вший.
quorum /'kwɔrəm/ *n.* кво́рум *m.*
quota /'kwoutə/ *n.* кво́та; до́ля *f.*
quotation /kwou'teiʃən/ *n.* цита́та *f.*; (*price*) расце́нка *f.*
quotation marks *n.* кавы́чки *pl.*
quote /kwout/ **1.** *n.* цита́та *f.*; (*marks*) кавы́чки *pl.* **2.** *v.* цити́ровать *impf.*, процити́ровать *pf.*; сосла́ться *pf.*
quotient /'kwouʃənt/ *n.* ча́стное *neut.*

R

rabbet /'ræbɪt/ n. паз; шпунт m.
rabbi /'ræbai/ n. раввин m.
rabbit /'ræbɪt/ **1.** n. кролик m. **2.** adj. кроличий.
rabble /'ræbəl/ n. чернь f.
rabid /'ræbɪd/ adj. бешеный.
rabies /'reibiz/ n. бешенство neut.; водобоязнь f.
raccoon /ræ'kun/ **1.** n. енот m. **2.** adj. енотовый.
race¹ /reis/ **1.** n. (cars, etc.) гонка f.; (on foot) гонки pl., бег m. **2.** v. состязаться в скорости impf.
race² /reis/ n. (ethnicity) раса f.
racecourse /'reis,kɔrs/ n. ипподром; трек m.
racer /'reisər/ n. (person) гонщик m.; (horse) скаковая лошадь f.
racetrack /'reis,træk/ n. ипподром; трек m.
racial /'reiʃəl/ adj. расовый.
racing /'reisɪŋ/ **1.** n. (running, motor, etc.) гонки pl., гонка f.; **horse racing** n. скачки; бега pl. **2.** adj. беговой; скаковой.
racism /'reisɪzəm/ n. расизм m.
racist /'reisist/ **1.** n. расист m.; расистка f. **2.** adj. расистский.
rack /ræk/ n. (wire framework) решётка f.; (shelving) стеллаж m.; (for hats, coats) вешалка f.
racket¹ /'rækɪt/ n. (noise) шум m.
racket² /'rækɪt/ n. (tennis) ракетка f.
racy /'reisi/ adj. колоритный.
radar /'reidar/ **1.** n. радар, радиолокатор m. **2.** adj. радиолокационный.
radial /'reidiəl/ adj. лучевой; радиальный.
radiance /'reidiəns/ n. сияние neut.
radiant /'reidiənt/ adj. сияющий.
radiate /'reidi,eit/ v. излучать impf.
radiation /,reidi'eiʃən/ n. излучение neut.; радиация f.
radiator /'reidi,eitər/ n. батарея f.; радиатор m.
radical /'rædɪkəl/ **1.** adj. радикальный; коренной. **2.** n. (polit.) радикал m.; (math.) корень m.
radio /'reidi,ou/ n. радио neut. indecl.
radioactive /,reidiou'æktɪv/ adj. радиоактивный.
radiocarbon /,reidiou'karbən/ n. радиоуглерод m.
radio-controlled /'reidiou kən'trould/ adj. управляемый по радио.
radiology /,reidi'ɒlədʒi/ n. радиология f.; (X-rays) рентгенология f.
radio operator n. радист m.
radish /'rædɪʃ/ n. редиска f.
radium /'reidiəm/ n. радий m.
radius /'reidiəs/ n. радиус m.
radon /'reidɒn/ n. радон m.
raffish /'ræfɪʃ/ adj. (dissolute) беспутный; (disreputable) сомнительный.
raffle /'ræfəl/ n. лотерея f.
raft /ræft/ n. плот m.
rafter /'ræftər/ n. стропило neut.
rag /ræg/ **1.** n. тряпка f. **2.** adj. тряпичный.
ragamuffin /'rægə,mʌfɪn/ n. оборванец m.
rage /reidʒ/ **1.** n. гнев m.; ярость f. **2.** v. беситься impf.
ragged /'rægɪd/ adj. оборванный.

raging /'reidʒɪŋ/ adj. (furious) яростный; (frenzied) неистовый; (elements) бушующий.
raid /reid/ **1.** n. набег m. **2.** v. (police) устраивать облаву impf.
raider /'reidər/ n. налётчик m.; (naut.) рейдер m.
rail /reil/ n. (railroad track) рельс m.; (railway) железная дорога f.; (handrail) перила f.
railing /'reilɪŋ/ n. поручень m.; (fence) частокол m.
railroad **1.** n. железная дорога f. **2.** adj. железнодорожный.
raiment /'reimənt/ n. одеяние neut.
rain /rein/ **1.** n. дождь m. **2.** adj. дождевой. **3.** : **it is raining** идёт дождь.
rainbow /'rein,bou/ n. радуга f.
raincoat /'rein,kout/ n. (непромокаемый) плащ m.; непромокаемое пальто neut.
raindrop /'rein,drɒp/ n. дождевая капля f.
rainfall /'rein,fɔl/ n. дождевые осадки pl.
rain forest n. джунгли pl.
rainwater /'rein,wɔtər, -,wɒtər/ n. дождевая вода f.
rainy /'reini/ adj. дождливый.
raise /reiz/ **1.** n. подъём m.; повышение neut. **2.** v. поднимать impf., поднять pf.
raised /reizd/ adj. (elevated) поднятый; (pattern) рельефный.
raisin /'reizɪn/ n. изюминка f.; pl. (colloq.) изюм m.
rake /reik/ **1.** n. (tool) грабли pl. **2.** v. грести impf.
rakish /'reikɪʃ/ adj. распутный; (dashing) лихой; ухарский.
rally /'ræli/ n. (recovery) восстановление neut.; (improvement) улучшение neut.; (meeting) собрание neut.; митинг m.; (motor) (авто)ралли neut. indecl.
RAM /ræm/ n. (abbr. of random-access memory) оперативная память f.
ram /ræm/ n. баран m.; (tech.) таран m.
ramble /'ræmbəl/ **1.** n. прогулка f. **2.** v. бродить impf.
rambler /'ræmblər/ n. (walker) (пешеходный) турист m.
rambling /'ræmblɪŋ/ adj. (chaotic) беспорядочный; (speech) бессвязный.
ramification /,ræməfɪ'keiʃən/ n. разветвление neut.; pl. последствия pl.
ramp /ræmp/ n. уклон; скат m.
rampage /'ræmpeidʒ/ n. буйство neut.
rampant /'ræmpənt/ adj. яростный; неистовый; (disease) свирепствующий.
rampart /'ræmpart/ n. крепостной вал m.
ramrod /'ræm,rɒd/ n. шомпол m.
ramshackle /'ræm,ʃækəl/ adj. ветхий; (rickety) шаткий.
ranch /ræntʃ/ n. ферма f.; ранчо neut. indecl.
rancid /'rænsɪd/ adj. прогорклый.
rancor /'ræŋkər/ n. злоба f.
random /'rændəm/ adj. случайный; **at random** наугад, наобум.
randy /'rændi/ adj. похотливый.

range /reindʒ/ *n.* преде́л; разма́х *m.*

ranger /'reindʒər/ *n.* (*forest guard*) лесни́к *m.*

rank¹ /ræŋk/ *adj.* бу́йный; (*overgrown*) заро́сший.

rank² /ræŋk/ **1.** *n.* (*row*) ряд *m.*; (*status*) зва́ние *neut.*; чин; ранг *m.* **2.** *v.t.* классифици́ровать *impf. and pf.*; *v.i.* классифици́роваться *impf. and pf.*

ransack /'rænsæk/ *v.* обы́скивать *impf.*, обыска́ть *pf.*

ransom /'rænsəm/ **1.** *n.* вы́куп *m.* **2.** *v.* выкупа́ть *impf.*, вы́купить *pf.*

rap /ræp/ **1.** *n.* стук; уда́р *m.* **2.** *v.* стуча́ть *impf.*

rape /reip/ **1.** *n.* изнаси́лование *neut.* **2.** *v.* наси́ловать *impf.*, изнаси́ловать *pf.*

rapid /'ræpɪd/ *adj.* бы́стрый; ско́рый.

rapidly /'ræpɪdli/ *adv.* бы́стро; (*soon*) ско́ро.

rapids /'ræpɪdz/ *n.* поро́г *m.*

rapier /'reipiər/ *n.* рапи́ра *f.*

rapist /'reipɪst/ *n.* наси́льник *m.*

rapport /ræ'pɔr/ *n.* связь *f.*; (*sympathy*) взаимопонима́ние *neut.*

rapprochement /ˌræprouʃ'mã/ *n.* сближе́ние *neut.*

rapture /'ræptʃər/ *n.* восхище́ние *neut.*; восто́рг *m.*

rapturous /'ræptʃərəs/ *adj.* восто́рженный.

rare /reər/ *adj.* ре́дкий.

rarefied /'reərəˌfaid/ *adj.* возвы́шенный.

rarity /'reərɪti/ *n.* ре́дкость *f.*

rascal /'ræskəl/ *n.* моше́нник *m.*, (*child*) озорни́к; шалу́н *m.*

rash¹ /ræʃ/ *adj.* необду́манный; безрассу́дный.

rash² /ræʃ/ *n.* сыпь *f.*

rashness /'ræʃnɪs/ *n.* опроме́тчивость; торопли́вость; поспе́шность *f.*

rasp /ræsp/ *n.* (*coarse file*) ра́шпиль *m.*

raspberry /'ræzˌbɛri/ **1.** *n.* мали́на *f.* **2.** *adj.* мали́новый.

rat /ræt/ **1.** *n.* кры́са *f.* **2.** *adj.* кры́синый.

ratchet /'rætʃɪt/ *n.* храпови́к *m.*

rate /reit/ **1.** *n.* но́рма; ста́вка *f.*; тари́ф; *m.* **rate of exchange** валю́тный курс *m.* **2.** *v.* оце́нивать *impf.*, оцени́ть *pf.*

rather /'ræðər/ *adv.* скоре́е; верне́е; предпочти́тельно; (*somewhat*) дово́льно.

ratification /ˌrætəfɪ'keiʃən/ *n.* ратифика́ция *f.*

ratify /'rætəˌfai/ *v.* ратифици́ровать *impf. and pf.*

rating /'reitɪŋ/ *n.* (*evaluation*) оце́нка *f.*; (*tech.*) (номина́льная) мо́щность *f.*

ratio /'reiʃiou/ *n.* пропо́рция *f.*; соотноше́ние *neut.*

ration /'ræʃən, 'reiʃən/ **1.** *n.* паёк; рацио́н *m.* **2.** *v.* норми́ровать *impf. and pf.*

rational /'ræʃənl/ *adj.* разу́мный; рациона́льный.

rationale /ˌræʃə'næl/ *n.* основна́я причи́на *f.*

rationality /ˌræʃə'nælɪti/ *n.* разу́мность; рациона́льность *f.*

rationalization /'ræʃənləˌzeiʃən/ *n.* оправда́ние *neut.*; рационализа́ция *f.*

rationalize /'ræʃənlˌaiz/ *v.* рационализи́ровать *impf.*; (*justify*) опра́вдывать *impf.*

rationing /'ræʃənɪŋ, 'rei-/ *n.* норми́рование *neut.*

rattle /'rætl/ **1.** *n.* треско́тня *f.*; треск *m.*; (*toy*) погрему́шка *f.* **2.** *v.* грохота́ть; треща́ть *impf.*

rattlesnake /'rætlˌsneik/ *n.* грему́чая змея́ *f.*

rattrap /'rætˌtræp/ *n.* крысоло́вка *f.*

raucous /'rɔkəs/ *adj.* (*coarse*) хри́плый; си́плый; (*rowdy*) бу́йный.

ravage /'rævidʒ/ *v.* опустоша́ть *impf.*, опусто-ши́ть *pf.*

rave /reiv/ *v.* бре́дить; нейстовствовать *impf.*

ravel /'rævəl/ *v.* распу́тывать *impf.*, распу́тать *pf.*

raven /'reivən/ *n.* во́рон *m.*

ravenous /'rævənəs/ *adj.* (*very hungry*) голо́дный как зверь; (*voracious*) жа́дный.

ravine /rə'vin/ *n.* овра́г *m.*; уще́лье *neut.*

raving /'reivɪŋ/ *n.* (*delirium*) бред *m.*; (*fury*) нейстовство *neut.*

ravishing /'rævɪʃɪŋ/ *adj.* восхити́тельный.

raw /rɔ/ *adj.* сыро́й.

ray /rei/ *n.* луч *m.*

rayon /'reiɒn/ *n.* иску́ственный шёлк *m.*; виско́за *f.*

razor /'reizər/ *n.* бри́тва *f.*

reach /ritʃ/ **1.** *n.* преде́л досяга́емости *m.* **2.** *v.* (*get to*) достига́ть; доходи́ть (до *with gen.*) *impf.*, дойти́ *pf.*

react /ri'ækt/ *v.* реаги́ровать *impf.*

reaction /ri'ækʃən/ *n.* реа́кция *f.*

reactionary /ri'ækʃəˌneri/ **1.** *adj.* реакцио́нный. **2.** *n.* реакционе́р *m.*

reactor /ri'æktər/ *n.* реа́ктор *m.*

read /rid/ *v.* чита́ть *impf.*, прочита́ть *pf.*

reader /'ridər/ *n.* чита́тель *m.*, чита́тельница *f.*

readership /'ridərˌʃip/ *n.* круг чита́телей *m.*; пу́блика *f.*

readily /'redli/ *adv.* охо́тно; бы́стро; без труда́.

readiness /'redɪnɪs/ *n.* гото́вность *f.*

reading /'ridɪŋ/ *n.* чте́ние *neut.*

readjust /ˌriə'dʒʌst/ *v.* регули́ровать *impf.*

readmit /ˌriæd'mit/ *v.* вновь допуска́ть *impf.*

ready /'redi/ *adj.* гото́вый.

ready-made /'rediˈmeid/ *adj.* (*clothes*) гото́вый.

real /'riəl/ *adj.* действи́тельный; реа́льный; настоя́щий.

real estate *n.* недви́жимость *f.*

realign /ˌriə'lain/ *v.* перестра́ивать *impf.*

realist /'riəlist/ *n.* реали́ст *m.*

realistic /ˌriə'listik/ *adj.* реалисти́ческий; реа́льный.

reality /ri'ælɪti/ *n.* действи́тельность *f.*

realization /ˌriələ'zeiʃən/ *n.* осозна́ние *neut.*; осуществле́ние *neut.*

realize /'riəˌlaiz/ *v.t.* (*plans, etc.*) осуществля́ть *impf.*, осуществи́ть *pf.*; (*assets*) реализова́ть *impf. and pf.*

really /'riəli/ *adv.* действи́тельно.

realm /relm/ *n.* о́бласть; сфе́ра *f.*

realtor /'riəltər/ *n.* аге́нт по прода́же недви́жимости *m.*

ream /rim/ *n.* (*paper*) стопа́ *f.*

reap /rip/ *v.* жать *impf.*, сжать *pf.*

reaper /'ripər/ *n.* (*person*) жнец *m.*, жни́ца *f.*; (*machine*) жне́йка, жа́тка *f.*

rear¹ /riər/ **1.** *adj.* за́дний. **2.** *n.* зад *m.*; (*mil.*) тыл *m.*

rear² /riər/ *v.* воспи́тывать *impf.*, воспита́ть *pf.*; выра́щивать *impf.*, вы́растить *pf.*

rear admiral *n.* контр-адмира́л *m.*

rearmament /ri'arməmənt/ *n.* перевооруже́ние *neut.*

reason /'rizən/ **1.** *n.* páзум; рассу́док *m.*; (*cause*) причи́на *f.* **2.** *v.* рассужда́ть *impf.*

reasonable /'rizənəbəl/ *adj.* благоразу́мный; уме́ренный; прие́млемый.

reasonably /'rizənəbli/ *adv.* разу́мно; (*fairly*) дово́льно.

reasoning /'rizənɪŋ/ *n.* рассужде́ние *neut.*

reassure /ˌriə'ʃʊr/ *v.* успока́ивать *impf.*

reassuring /ˌriə'ʃʊrɪŋ/ *adj.* утеши́тельный; (*calming*) успокои́тельный.

rebate /'ribeit/ *n.* ски́дка *f.*; (*deduction*) вы́чет *m.*; (*refund*) возвра́т *m.*

rebel / *n.* 'rɛbəl; *v.* rɪ'bɛl/ **1.** *n.* повста́нец; бунто́вщи́к *m.* **2.** *v.* восстава́ть *impf.*, восста́ть *pf.*

rebellion /rɪ'bɛlyən/ *n.* восста́ние *neut.*; мяте́ж *m.*

rebellious /rɪ'bɛlyəs/ *adj.* мяте́жный; бунту́ющий.

rebirth /ri'bɜrθ/ *n.* возрожде́ние *neut.*

reborn /ri'bɔrn/ *adj.* возрождённый.

rebuff /rɪ'bʌf/ **1.** *n.* отпо́р *m.* **2.** *v.* дава́ть отпо́р *impf.*

rebuke /rɪ'byuk/ **1.** *n.* упрёк *m.*; (*reproof*) вы́говор *m.* **2.** *v.* упрека́ть *impf.*

rebut /rɪ'bʌt/ *v.* опроверга́ть *impf.*

recalcitrant /rɪ'kælsɪtrənt/ *adj.* упря́мый; непоко́рный.

recall /rɪ'kɔl/ *v.* вспомина́ть *impf.*, вспо́мнить *pf.*

recant /rɪ'kænt/ *v.* отрека́ться (от *with gen.*)

recapitulate /ˌrikə'pɪtʃə,leit/ *v.* сумми́ровать; резюми́ровать *impf.* and *pf.*

recapitulation /ˌrikə,pɪtʃə'leiʃən/ *n.* сумми́рование *neut.*; резюме́ *neut.* indecl.

recast /ri'kæst/ *v.* переде́лывать *impf.*; (*reformulate*) перестра́ивать *impf.*

recede /rɪ'sid/ *v.* отступа́ть *impf.*, отступи́ть *pf.*

receipt /rɪ'sit/ *n.* квита́нция *f.*; получе́ние *neut.*

receive /rɪ'siv/ *v.* получа́ть *impf.*, получи́ть *pf.*; (*admit, entertain*) принима́ть *impf.*

receiver /rɪ'sivər/ *n.* получа́тель *m.*; (*telephone*) телефо́нная тру́бка *f.*; (*radio*) приёмник *m.*

receiving /rɪ'sivɪŋ/ *adj.* приёмный.

recent /'risənt/ *adj.* неда́вний.

recently /'risəntli/ *adv.* неда́вно; в после́днее вре́мя.

receptacle /rɪ'sɛptəkəl/ *n.* вмести́лище *neut.*; приёмник *m.*

reception /rɪ'sɛpʃən/ *n.* приём *m.*; приня́тие *neut.*

receptionist /rɪ'sɛpʃənɪst/ *n.* регистра́тор *m.*

reception room *n.* приёмная *f.*

receptive /rɪ'sɛptɪv/ *adj.* восприи́мчивый.

recess /rɪ'sɛs, 'risɛs/ *n.* переры́в *m.*

recession /rɪ'sɛʃən/ *n.* удале́ние; отступле́ние *neut.*; (*econ.*) спад *m.*

recharge /ri'tʃɑrdʒ/ *v.* перезаряжа́ть *impf.*

recipe /'rɛsəpi/ *n.* реце́пт *m.*

recipient /rɪ'sɪpiənt/ *n.* получа́тель *m.*

reciprocal /rɪ'sɪprəkəl/ *adj.* взаи́мный.

reciprocate /rɪ'sɪprə,keit/ *v.* отпла́чивать *impf.*, отплати́ть *pf.*; отвеча́ть (на *with acc.*) *impf.*

reciprocating engine /rɪ'sɪprə,keitɪŋ/ *n.* поршнево́й дви́гатель *m.*

reciprocity /ˌrɛsə'prɒsɪti/ *n.* взаи́мность; обою́дность *f.*

recital /rɪ'saitl̩/ *n.* (*mus.*) конце́рт *m.*

recitation /ˌrɛsɪ'teiʃən/ *n.* чте́ние *neut.*; (*from memory*) отве́т вы́ученного уро́ка *m.*

recite /rɪ'sait/ *v.* деклами́ровать *impf.*

reciter /rɪ'saitər/ *n.* деклама́тор; чтец *m.*

reckless /'rɛklɪs/ *adj.* опроме́тчивый.

reckon /'rɛkən/ *v.* счита́ть *impf.*

reckoning /'rɛkənɪŋ/ *n.* (*calculation*) расчёт *m.*; (*bill*) счёт *m.*

reclamation /ˌrɛklə'meiʃən/ *n.* мелиора́ция *f.*; восстановле́ние *neut.*

recline /rɪ'klain/ *v.* отки́дываться *impf.*, откану́ться *pf.*

recluse /'rɛklus/ *n.* отше́льник; затво́рник *m.*

recognition /ˌrɛkəg'nɪʃən/ *n.* узнава́ние *neut.*; (*acclaim*) призна́ние *neut.*

recognizable /'rɛkəg,naizəbəl/ *adj.* опознава́емый; заме́тный.

recognize /'rɛkəg,naiz/ *v.* узнава́ть *impf.*, узна́ть *pf.*

recognized /'rɛkəg,naizd/ *adj.* (общепри́знанный).

recoil /rɪ'kɔil/ *v.* отска́кивать *impf.*; (*of gun*) отдава́ть *impf.*

recoilless /rɪ'kɔillɪs/ *adj.* безотка́тный.

recollect /ˌrɛkə'lɛkt/ *v.* вспомина́ть *impf.*, вспо́мнить *pf.*

recollection /ˌrɛkə'lɛkʃən/ *n.* па́мять *f.*; (*a remembrance*) воспомина́ние *neut.*

recommend /ˌrɛkə'mɛnd/ *v.* рекомендова́ть *impf.* and *pf.*

recommendable /ˌrɛkə'mɛndəbəl/ *adj.* рекоменду́емый.

recommendation /ˌrɛkəmɛn'deiʃən/ *n.* рекоменда́ция *f.*

recompense /'rɛkəm,pɛns/ **1.** *n.* вознагражде́ние *neut.* **2.** *v.* вознагражда́ть *impf.*

recompose /ˌrikəm'pouz/ *v.* составля́ть за́ново; пересоставля́ть *impf.*

reconcile /'rɛkən,sail/ *v.* примиря́ть *impf.*, примири́ть *pf.*

reconciliation /ˌrɛkən,sɪli'eiʃən/ *n.* примире́ние; ула́живание *neut.*

recondite /'rɛkən,dait/ *adj.* глубо́кий; (*obscure*) неудобопоня́тный.

reconnaissance /rɪ'kɒnəsəns/ *n.* разве́дка *f.*

reconnoiter /ˌrikə'nɔitər/ *v.i.* вести́ разве́дку; *v.t.* разве́дывать *impf.*

reconsider /ˌrikən'sɪdər/ *v.* пересма́тривать *impf.*, пересмотре́ть *pf.*

reconsideration /ˌrikən,sɪdə'reiʃən/ *n.* пересмо́тр *m.*

reconstruct /ˌrikən'strʌkt/ *v.* перестра́ивать *impf.*, перестро́ить *pf.*

reconstruction /ˌrikən'strʌkʃən/ *n.* перестро́йка; реконстру́кция *f.*

record /*n.* 'rɛkərd, *v.* rɪ'kɔrd/ **1.** *n.* за́пись *f.*; протоко́л *m.*; (*mus.*) (граммафо́нная *or* патефо́нная) пласти́нка *f.*; (*athl.*) реко́рд *m.* **2.** *v.* запи́сывать *impf.*, записа́ть *pf.*

record-breaking /'rɛkərd 'breikɪŋ/ *adj.* реко́рдный.

recorder /rɪ'kɔrdər/ *n.* самопи́сец *m.*; **tape recorder** *n.* магнитофо́н *m.*

recordholder /'rɛkərd ˌhouldər/ *n.* рекордсме́н *m.*, рекордсме́нка *f.*

recording /rɪ'kɔrdɪŋ/ *n.* за́пись *f.*

record player *n.* прои́грыватель *m.*

re-count /'ri'kaunt/ *v.* пересчи́тывать *impf.*, пересчита́ть *pf.*

recount /rɪˈkaunt/ v. (tell) расска́зывать impf., рассказа́ть pf.

recoup /riˈkup/ v. покрыва́ть убы́тки impf.

recover /rɪˈkʌvər/ v.t. получи́ть обра́тно; v.i. выздора́вливать impf., вы́здороветь pf.

recoverable /rɪˈkʌvərəbəl/ adj. возмести́мый.

recovery /rɪˈkʌvəri/ n. возвраще́ние neut.; (health) выздоровле́ние neut.

re-create /ˌri kriˈeit/ v. воссоздава́ть impf.

recreation /ˌrɛkriˈeiʃən/ n. о́тдых m.; (amusement) развлече́ние neut.

recrimination /rɪˌkrɪməˈneiʃən/ n. взаи́мное обвине́ние neut.

recruit /rɪˈkrut/ 1. n. новобра́нец m. 2. v. вербова́ть impf., завербова́ть pf.

recruiting /rɪˈkrutɪŋ/ also **recruitment** /rɪˈkrutmənt/ n. вербо́вка f.

rectangle /ˈrɛkˌtæŋɡəl/ n. прямоуго́льник m.

rectangular /rɛkˈtæŋɡələr/ adj. прямоуго́льный.

rectify /ˈrɛktəˌfai/ v. исправля́ть impf.

rectilinear /ˌrɛktlˈɪniər/ adj. прямолине́йный.

rector /ˈrɛktər/ n. (university) ре́ктор m.; (parish) прихо́дский свяще́нник m.

rectory /ˈrɛktəri/ n. дом прихо́дского свяще́нника m.

rectum /ˈrɛktəm/ n. пряма́я кишка́ f.

recumbent /rɪˈkʌmbənt/ adj. лежа́чий; лежа́щий.

recuperate /rɪˈkupəˌreit/ v. выздора́вливать impf., вы́здороветь pf.

recur /rɪˈkɜr/ v. повторя́ться impf.

recurrence /rɪˈkɜrəns/ n. повторе́ние neut.

recycle /riˈsaikəl/ v. вто́рично испо́льзовать impf.

red /rɛd/ 1. adj. кра́сный. 2. n. кра́сный цвет m.

red blood cell n. кра́сное кровяно́е те́льце neut.

redbreast /ˈrɛdˌbrɛst/ n. мали́новка f.

reddish /ˈrɛdɪʃ/ adj. краснова́тый; (hair) рыжева́тый.

redecorate /riˈdɛkəˌreit/ v. (repaint) перекра́шивать impf.

redeem /rɪˈdim/ v. выкупа́ть impf., вы́купить pf.

Redeemer /rɪˈdimər/ n. Искупи́тель m.

redemption /rɪˈdɛmpʃən/ n. вы́куп m.; избавле́ние neut.

redeploy /ˌridɪˈplɔi/ v. переставля́ть; (redistribute) перераспределя́ть impf.

redhead /ˈrɛd ˌhɛd/ n. ры́жий m.

red-headed /ˈrɛd ˌhɛdid/ adj. ры́жий; рыжеволо́сый.

red-hot /ˈrɛdˈhɒt/ adj. раскаленный докрасна́.

redirect /ˌridɪˈrɛkt/ v. переправля́ть; пересыла́ть impf.

redistribute /ˌridɪˈstrɪbyut/ v. перераспределя́ть impf.

redo /riˈdu/ v. повторя́ть; переде́лывать impf.

redolent /ˈrɛdlənt/ adj. благоуха́ющий; арома́тный.

redouble /riˈdʌbəl/ v. удва́ивать impf.

redoubtable /rɪˈdautəbəl/ adj. (fearsome) гро́зный.

red pepper n. кра́сный пе́рец m.

redress /ˈridrɛs/ n. возмеще́ние neut.; (satisfaction) удовлетворе́ние neut.

red tape n. волоки́та f.

reduce /rɪˈdus/ v. уменьша́ть impf., уме́ньшить pf.; сокраща́ть impf., сократи́ть pf.

reduction /rɪˈdʌkʃən/ n. уменьше́ние neut.; сокраще́ние neut.

redundant /rɪˈdʌndənt/ adj. избы́точный; изли́шний.

redwood /ˈrɛdˌwʊd/ n. калифорни́йское ма́монтовое де́рево neut., секво́йя гига́нтская f.

reed /rid/ 1. n. тростни́к m.; (mus.) язычо́к m. 2. adj. тростнико́вый.

reef /rif/ n. риф m.

reek /rik/ 1. n. вонь f. 2. v. воня́ть; па́хнуть impf.

reel[1] /ril/ n. шпу́лька; кату́шка f.; (film) боби́на f.; рил m.

reel[2] /ril/ v. (feel dizzy) кружи́ться impf.

reelection /ˌriɪˈlɛkʃən/ n. переизбра́ние neut.

refashion /riˈfæʃən/ v. переде́лывать impf.

refectory /rɪˈfɛktəri/ n. тра́пезная f.

refer /rɪˈfɜr/ v.i. относи́ться (к with dat.) impf.; ссыла́ться (на with acc.) impf., сосла́ться pf.

referee /ˌrɛfəˈri/ n. судья́ m.

reference /ˈrɛfərəns/ 1. n. ссы́лка; спра́вка f. 2. adj. спра́вочный.

reference book n. спра́вочник m.

referendum /ˌrɛfəˈrɛndəm/ n. рефере́ндум m.

referral /rɪˈfɜrəl/ n. направле́ние neut.

refill / n 'rɪˌfɪl, v. riˈfɪl/ 1. n. пополне́ние neut. 2. v. наполня́ть вновь impf.

refine /rɪˈfain/ v. рафини́ровать impf. and pf.

refined /rɪˈfaind/ adj. изя́щный; изы́сканный, культу́рный.

refinement /rɪˈfainmənt/ n. утончённость f.

refinery /rɪˈfainəri/ n. рафини́ровочный заво́д m.

reflect /rɪˈflɛkt/ v. отража́ть impf.

reflecting /rɪˈflɛktɪŋ/ adj. отража́ющий.

reflection /rɪˈflɛkʃən/ n. отраже́ние neut.

reflective /rɪˈflɛktɪv/ adj. отража́ющий; (thoughtful) размышля́ющий; заду́мчивый.

reflex /ˈriflɛks/ 1. n. рефле́кс m. 2. adj. рефлекто́рный.

reflexive /rɪˈflɛksɪv/ n. (verb) возвра́тный глаго́л m.; (pronoun) возвра́тное местоиме́ние neut.

reflux /ˈriˌflʌks/ n. отли́в m.

reform /rɪˈfɔrm/ 1. n. рефо́рма f. 2. v. реформи́ровать impf. and pf.

reformation /ˌrɛfərˈmeiʃən/ n. преобразова́ние; исправле́ние neut.; (cap.) Реформа́ция f.

reformatory /rɪˈfɔrməˌtɔri/ n. исправи́тельное заведе́ние neut.

refract /rɪˈfrækt/ v. преломля́ть(ся) impf.

refraction /rɪˈfrækʃən/ n. преломле́ние neut.; рефра́кция f.

refrain[1] /rɪˈfrein/ n. припе́в; рефре́н m.

refrain[2] /rɪˈfrein/ v. возде́рживаться (от with gen.) impf., воздержа́ться pf.

refresh /rɪˈfrɛʃ/ v. освежа́ть impf., освежи́ть pf.

refreshing /rɪˈfrɛʃɪŋ/ adj. (drink, etc.) освежа́ющий; тонизи́рующий.

refreshment /rɪˈfrɛʃmənt/ n. подкрепле́ние neut.

refrigerate /rɪˈfrɪdʒəˌreit/ v. охлажда́ть; храни́ть в холоди́льнике impf.

refrigerator /rɪˈfrɪdʒəˌreitər/ n. холоди́льник m.

refuel /riˈfyuəl/ v. заправля́ть(ся) то́пливом impf.

refuge /ˈrɛfyudʒ/ n. убе́жище neut.; прию́т m.

refugee /ˌrɛfyʊˈdʒi/ n. бе́женец m., бе́женка f.

refund /n.ˈrifʌnd, v. rɪˈfʌnd/ 1. n. возмеще́ние neut. 2. v. возмеща́ть impf., возмести́ть pf.

refusal /rɪ'fyuzəl/ n. отка́з m.
refuse[1] /'rɛfyus/ n. отбро́сы pl.; му́сор m.
refuse[2] /rɪ'fyuz/ v. отка́зывать impf., отказа́ть pf.
refutable /rɪ'fyutəbəl, 'rɛfyətə-/ adj. опровержи́мый.
refutation /,rɛfyʊ'teiʃən/ n. опроверже́ние neut.
refute /rɪ'fyut/ v. опроверга́ть impf., опрове́ргнуть pf.
regain /ri'gein/ v. получи́ть обра́тно pf.
regal /'rigəl/ adj. короле́вский; ца́рский.
regalia /rɪ'geiliə/ n. рега́лии pl.
regard /rɪ'gɑrd/ **1.** n. уваже́ние neut.; pl. (greetings) приве́т m.; **in regard to** adv. относи́тельно (with gen.). **2.** v. смотре́ть (на with acc.); относи́ться impf.
regarding /rɪ'gɑrdɪŋ/ adv. относи́тельно (with gen.); по отноше́нию (к with dat.).
regardless /rɪ'gɑrdlɪs/ adv. незави́симо (от with gen.).
regenerate /rɪ'dʒɛnə,reit/ v. возрожда́ть(ся), перерожда́ть(ся) impf.
regeneration /rɪ,dʒɛnə'reiʃən/ n. возрожде́ние; перерожде́ние neut.; регенера́ция f.
regent /'ridʒənt/ n. ре́гент m.
regicide /'rɛdʒə,said/ n. цареуби́йство neut.
regime /rə'ʒim/ also **regimen** n. режи́м m.
regiment /'rɛdʒəmənt/ n. полк m.
region /'ridʒən/ n. райо́н m.; о́бласть; сфе́ра f.
regional /'ridʒənl/ adj. райо́нный; областно́й.
register /'rɛdʒəstər/ **1.** n. рее́стр; реги́стр; журна́л; спи́сок m.; **cash register** ка́сса f. **2.** v. регистри́ровать(ся) impf.
registered /'rɛdʒəstərd/ adj. зарегистри́рованный.
registered letter n. заказно́е письмо́ neut.
registrar /'rɛdʒə,strɑr/ n. регистра́тор m.
registration /,rɛdʒə'streiʃən/ n. регистра́ция; за́пись f.
registry /'rɛdʒɪstri/ n. (place) регистрату́ра f.
regressive /rɪ'grɛsɪv/ adj. регресси́вный.
regret /rɪ'grɛt/ **1.** n. сожале́ние neut. **2.** v. сожале́ть impf.
regretful /rɪ'grɛtfəl/ adj. по́лный сожале́ния; опеча́ленный.
regretfully /rɪ'grɛtfəli/ adv. с сожале́нием.
regular /'rɛgyələr/ adj. регуля́рный; пра́вильный; постоя́нный.
regularize /'rɛgyələ,raiz/ v. упоря́дочивать impf.
regulate /'rɛgyə,leit/ v. регули́ровать impf.
regulation /,rɛgyə'leiʃən/ n. регули́рование neut.; (rule) пра́вило neut., уста́в m.
regurgitate /rɪ'gɜrdʒɪ,teit/ v. (vomit) изверга́ть(ся) impf.
rehabilitate /,rihə'bɪlɪ,teit/ v. реабилити́ровать impf. and pf.
rehash /ri'hæʃ/ v. переде́лывать impf.
rehearsal /rɪ'hɜrsəl/ n. репети́ция f.
rehearse /rɪ'hɜrs/ v. репети́ровать impf.
reheat /ri'hit/ v. подогрева́ть; разогрева́ть impf.
reign /rein/ **1.** n. ца́рствование neut. **2.** v. ца́рствовать; цари́ть impf.
reimburse /,riim'bɜrs/ v. возмеща́ть impf., возмести́ть pf.
Reims /rimz, ræs/ n. Реймс m.
rein /rein/ n. по́вод m.
reincarnate /,riin'kɑrnɪt/ adj. перевоплощённый.

reincarnation /,riinkɑr'neiʃən/ n. перевоплоще́ние neut.
reindeer /'rein,diər/ n. се́верный оле́нь m.
reinforce /,riin'fɔrs/ v. уси́ливать impf., уси́лить pf.
reinforced concrete /'riinfɔrst/ n. железобето́н m.
reinsurance /,riin'ʃʊrəns/ n. перестрахова́ние neut.
reinvest /,riin'vɛst/ v. втори́чно инвести́ровать impf.
reiterate /ri'ɪtə,reit/ v. повторя́ть impf., повтори́ть pf.
reiteration /ri,ɪtə'reiʃən/ n. повторе́ние neut.
reject / v. /rɪ'dʒɛkt/ n. 'ridʒɛkt/ **1.** v. отверга́ть impf., отве́ргнуть pf. **2.** n. брак m.
rejoice /rɪ'dʒɔis/ v. ра́доваться impf.
rejuvenate /rɪ'dʒuvə,neit/ v. омола́живать impf.
relapse /n. rɪ'læps, v. rɪ'læps/ **1.** n. рециди́в m. **2.** v. (into sickness) сно́ва заболе́ть pf.
relate /rɪ'leit/ v. установи́ть отноше́ние (ме́жду with instr.) pf.; (tell) расска́зывать impf., расска́зать pf.
related /rɪ'leitɪd/ adj. свя́занный; (in family) ро́дственный.
relation /rɪ'leiʃən/ n. отноше́ние neut.; связь f.
relational /rɪ'leiʃənl/ adj. относи́тельный.
relationship /rɪ'leiʃən,ʃɪp/ n. связь f.; отноше́ние (ме́жду with instr.; к with dat.) neut.
relative /'rɛlətɪv/ **1.** adj. относи́тельный; сравни́тельный. **2.** n. ро́дственник m., ро́дственница f.
relativity /,rɛlə'tɪvɪti/ n. относи́тельность f.
relax /rɪ'læks/ v.t. смягча́ть impf., смягчи́ть pf.; v.i. смягча́ться impf., смягчи́ться pf.; (rest) отдыха́ть impf.
relaxation /,rilæk'seiʃən/ n. расслабле́ние; ослабле́ние; смягче́ние neut.; о́тдых m.
relay /'rilei/ **1.** n. сме́на f.; (elec.) реле́ neut. indecl. **2.** v. передава́ть impf., переда́ть pf.
release /rɪ'lis/ **1.** n. освобожде́ние neut.; (issue) вы́пуск m. **2.** v. освобожда́ть impf., освободи́ть pf.; выпуска́ть impf., вы́пустить pf.
relent /rɪ'lɛnt/ v. смягча́ться impf., смягчи́ться pf.
relevance /'rɛləvəns/ n. уме́стность f.
relevant /'rɛləvənt/ adj. относя́щийся к де́лу.
reliability /rɪ,laiə'bɪlɪti/ n. надёжность f.
reliable /rɪ'laiəbəl/ adj. надёжный.
reliance /rɪ'laiəns/ n. дове́рие neut.
relic /'rɛlɪk/ n. пережи́ток; рели́кт m.; (pl.) мо́щи; рели́квии pl.
relief[1] /rɪ'lif/ n. облегче́ние neut.
relief[2] /rɪ'lif/ n. (art; geol.) релье́ф m.
relieve /rɪ'liv/ v. облегча́ть impf., облегчи́ть pf.
religion /rɪ'lɪdʒən/ n. рели́гия f.
religious /rɪ'lɪdʒəs/ adj. религио́зный.
relinquish /rɪ'lɪŋkwɪʃ/ v. отка́зываться (от with gen.); сдава́ть impf., сдать pf.
reliquary /'rɛlɪ,kwɛri/ n. ра́ка f.; ковче́г m.
relish /'rɛlɪʃ/ **1.** n. наслажде́ние neut.; аппети́т m.; (liking) скло́нность f. **2.** v. наслажда́ться impf.
reload /ri'loud/ v. перегружа́ть impf.; (gun) переряжа́ть impf.
reluctance /rɪ'lʌktəns/ n. неохо́та f.; нежела́ние neut.
reluctant /rɪ'lʌktənt/ adj. неохо́тный.

rely /rɪ'lai/ v. полага́ться (на with acc.) impf.
remain /rɪ'mein/ v. остава́ться impf., оста́ться pf.
remainder /rɪ'meindər/ n. оста́ток m.
remains /rɪ'meins/ n. оста́тки pl.
remake /rɪ'meik/ v. переде́лывать impf.
remark /rɪ'mɑrk/ **1.** n. замеча́ние neut. **2.** v. замеча́ть impf., заме́тить pf.
remarkable /rɪ'mɑrkəbəl/ adj. замеча́тельный.
remarkably /rɪ'mɑrkəbli/ adv. удиви́тельно.
remarry /ri'mæri/ v. вступа́ть в но́вый брак impf.
remedial /rɪ'midiəl/ adj. исправи́тельный; (curative) лече́бный.
remedy /'rɛmɪdi/ **1.** n. лека́рство; сре́дство (от with gen.) neut. **2.** v. исправля́ть impf., испра́вить pf.
remember /rɪ'mɛmbər/ v. по́мнить impf.
remembrance /rɪ'mɛmbrəns/ n. па́мять f.; воспомина́ние neut.
remind /rɪ'maind/ v. напомина́ть impf., напо́мнить pf.
reminder /rɪ'maindər/ n. напомина́ние neut.; намёк m.
reminisce /ˌrɛmə'nɪs/ v. вспомина́ть; говори́ть о про́шлом impf.
reminiscence /ˌrɛmə'nɪsəns/ n. воспомина́ние neut.
reminiscent /ˌrɛmə'nɪsənt/ adj. напомина́ющий.
remission /rɪ'mɪʃən/ n. отпуще́ние neut.
remit /rɪ'mɪt/ v. пересыла́ть impf.; пересла́ть pf.
remittance /rɪ'mɪtns/ n. перево́д (де́нег) m.
remnant /'rɛmnənt/ n. оста́ток m.
remodel /ri'mɒdl/ v. переде́лывать impf.
remorse /rɪ'mɔrs/ n. угрызе́ние со́вести; раска́яние neut.
remorseful /rɪ'mɔrsfəl/ adj. по́лный раска́яния.
remote /rɪ'mout/ adj. отдалённый.
remote control /rɪ'mout kən'troul/ n. дистанцио́нное управле́ние neut.
remotely /rɪ'moutli/ adv. отдалённо.
removable /rɪ'muvəbəl/ adj. передвижно́й; съёмный.
removal /rɪ'muvəl/ n. перемеще́ние; устране́ние neut.
remove /rɪ'muv/ v. передвига́ть impf., передви́нуть pf.; перемеща́ть impf., перемести́ть pf.; (take away) удаля́ть impf.
removed /rɪ'muvd/ adj. далёкий; **once removed** двою́родный.
remuneration /rɪˌmyunə'reiʃən/ n. опла́та f.; вознагражде́ние neut.
remunerative /rɪ'myunərətɪv/ adj. хорошо́ опла́чиваемый; вы́годный.
renaissance /ˌrɛnə'sɑns/ n. возрожде́ние neut.; (cap.) эпо́ха Возрожде́ния f.
renal /'rinl/ adj. по́чечный.
rename /ri'neim/ v. переимено́вывать impf.
render /'rɛndər/ v. ока́зывать impf., оказа́ть pf.; воздава́ть impf., возда́ть pf.; (make) де́лать impf., сде́лать pf.
rendezvous /'rɑndəˌvu/ n. свида́ние neut.
rendition /rɛn'dɪʃən/ n. изображе́ние neut.; переда́ча f.
renegade /'rɛnɪˌgeid/ n. ренега́т m., ренега́тка f.
renew /rɪ'nu/ v. возобновля́ть impf., возобнови́ть pf.

renewal /rɪ'nuəl/ n. возобновле́ние; обновле́ние neut.
Rennes /rɛn/ n. Ренн m.
renounce /rɪ'nauns/ v. отка́зываться (от with gen.) impf.; отказа́ться pf.
renovate /'rɛnəˌveit/ v. подновля́ть impf., поднови́ть pf.
renown /rɪ'naun/ n. сла́ва; изве́стность f.
rent /rɛnt/ **1.** n. кварти́рная пла́та. **2.** v. (rent to) сдава́ть в аре́нду impf.; (rent from) брать в аре́нду; снима́ть impf.
rental /'rɛntl/ n. (of apt.) аре́нда f.; (of equipment) прока́т (m.)
renter /'rɛntər/ n. аренда́тор m.
renunciation /rɪˌnʌnsi'eiʃən/ n. отка́з m.; отрече́ние (от with gen.) neut.
reoccupy /ri'okyəˌpai/ v. вновь занима́ть impf.
reorder /ri'ɔrdər/ v. перестра́ивать impf.; (order again) повторя́ть зака́з impf.
repaint /ri'peint/ v. перекра́шивать impf.
repair /rɪ'pɛər/ **1.** n. ремо́нт m. **2.** v. чини́ть; ремонти́ровать impf., отремонти́ровать pf.
reparation /ˌrɛpə'reiʃən/ n. возмеще́ние neut.; **war reparations** вое́нные репара́ции pl.
repast /rɪ'pæst/ n. (meal) еда́ f.
repatriate /ri'peitri,eit/ v. репатрии́ровать impf. and pf.
repatriation /riˌpeitri'eiʃən/ n. репатриа́ция f.
repay /rɪ'pei/ v. выпла́чивать; отпла́чивать, отплати́ть pf.
repayment /rɪ'peimənt/ n. возвраще́ние (де́нег) neut.; вы́плата; отпла́та f.
repeal /rɪ'pil/ v. отменя́ть impf.
repeat /rɪ'pit/ v. повторя́ть impf., повтори́ть pf.
repeated /rɪ'pitid/ adj. повто́рный.
repeatedly /rɪ'pitidli/ adv. неоднокра́тно; не раз.
repel /rɪ'pɛl/ v. отража́ть impf., отрази́ть pf.; отта́лкивать impf.
repellent /rɪ'pɛlənt/ n. отта́лкивающее сре́дство neut.
repent /rɪ'pɛnt/ v. раска́иваться (в with prep.) impf., раска́яться pf.
repentant /rɪ'pɛntnt/ adj. ка́ющийся; раска́иваю щийся.
repercussion /ˌripər'kʌʃən/ n. после́дствие; отраже́ние neut.; отзву́к m.
repertoire /'rɛpərˌtwɑr/ n. репертуа́р m.
repetition /ˌrɛpɪ'tɪʃən/ n. повторе́ние neut.
repetitious /ˌrɛpɪ'tɪʃəs/ also **repetitive** /rɪ'pɛtɪtɪv/ adj. повторя́ющийся.
rephrase /ri'freiz/ v. перефрази́ровать impf.
replace /rɪ'pleis/ v. (substitute) заменя́ть impf., замени́ть pf.
replaceable /rɪ'pleisəbəl/ adj. замени́мый.
replacement /rɪ'pleismənt/ n. заме́на f.; (spare part) запасна́я часть f.
replay /'ri,plei/ n. (sport) переигро́вка f.
replenish /rɪ'plɛnɪʃ/ v. пополня́ть impf., попо́лнить pf.
replica /'rɛplɪkə/ n. то́чная ко́пия f.; (model) моде́ль f.
reply /rɪ'plai/ **1.** n. отве́т m.; **in reply to** в отве́т на (with acc.). **2.** v. отвеча́ть impf., отве́тить pf.
report /rɪ'pɔrt/ **1.** n. сообще́ние neut.; докла́д; отчёт m.; ра́порт m. **2.** v. сообща́ть impf., сообщи́ть pf.

reportedly /rɪ'pɔrtɪdli/ *adv.* по сообщениям; (*allegedly*) якобы.

reported speech /rɪ'pɔrtɪd/ *n.* косвенная речь *f.*

reporter /rɪ'pɔrtər/ *n.* репортёр *m.*

repose /rɪ'pouz/ **1.** *n.* отдых *m.*; покой *m.* **2.** *v.* (*lie*) лежать *impf.*; (*rest*) отдыхать *impf.*

repository /rɪ'pɒzɪˌtɔri/ *n.* склад *m.*; хранилище *neut.*

reprehensible /ˌrɛprɪ'hɛnsəbəl/ *adj.* предосудительный.

represent /ˌrɛprɪ'zɛnt/ *v.* изображать *impf.*, изобразить *pf.*; представлять *impf.*, представить *pf.*

representation /ˌrɛprɪzɛn'teɪʃən/ *n.* изображение; представление *neut.*

representative /ˌrɛprɪ'zɛntətɪv/ **1.** *adj.* характерный; показательный. **2.** *n.* представитель *m.*

repress /rɪ'prɛs/ *v.* подавлять *impf.*, подавить *pf.*

repression /rɪ'prɛʃən/ *n.* подавление *neut.*, репрессия *f.*

repressive /rɪ'prɛsɪv/ *adj.* репрессивный.

reprieve /rɪ'priv/ *n.* отсрочка приведения в исполнение приговора *f.*

reprimand /'rɛprəˌmænd/ **1.** *n.* выговор *m.* **2.** *v.* делать выговор *impf.*

reprisal /rɪ'praizəl/ *n.* репрессалия *f.*

reproach /rɪ'proutʃ/ **1.** *n.* упрёк; укор *m.* **2.** *v.* упрекать *impf.*, упрекнуть *pf.*

reproachful /rɪ'proutʃfəl/ *adj.* укоризненный.

reproduce /ˌriprə'dus/ *v.* воспроизводить *impf.*, воспроизвести *pf.*

reproduction /ˌriprə'dʌkʃən/ *n.* воспроизведение *neut.*; репродукция *f.*

reproductive /ˌriprə'dʌktɪv/ *adj.* воспроизводительный.

reproductive organs *n.* органы размножения *pl.*

reproof /rɪ'pruf/ *n.* выговор; упрёк; укор *m.*

reprove /rɪ'pruv/ *v.* делать замечание *impf.*; (*censure*) порицать *impf.*

reptile /'rɛptɪl, -tail/ *n.* пресмыкающееся *neut.*; рептилия *f.*

republic /rɪ'pʌblɪk/ *n.* республика *f.*

republican /rɪ'pʌblɪkən/ **1.** *adj.* республиканский. **2.** *n.* республиканец *m.*; республиканка *f.*

republish /ri'pʌblɪʃ/ *v.* переиздавать *impf.*

repudiation /rɪˌpyudi'eiʃən/ *n.* отрицание; отречение *neut.*

repugnant /rɪ'pʌgnənt/ *adj.* противный (*with dat.*); отвратительный.

repulse /rɪ'pʌls/ *n.* (*rebuff*) отпор *m.*; (*refusal*) отказ *m.*

repulsion /rɪ'pʌlʃən/ *n.* отвращение ; отталкивание *neut.*

repulsive /rɪ'pʌlsɪv/ *adj.* омерзительный; отталкивающий.

reputable /'rɛpyətəbəl/ *adj.* имеющий хорошую репутацию.

reputation /ˌrɛpyə'teiʃən/ *also* **repute** /rɪ'pyut/ *n.* репутация; слава *f.*

reputed /rɪ'pyutɪd/ *adj.* предполагаемый; считающийся.

request /rɪ'kwɛst/ **1.** *n.* просьба *f.* **2.** *v.* просить *impf.*, попросить *pf.*

requiem /'rɛkwiəm/ *n.* реквием *m.*

require /rɪ'kwaiər/ *v.* требовать *impf.*, потребовать *pf.*

required /rɪ'kwaiərd/ *adj.* необходимый.

requirement /rɪ'kwaiərmənt/ *n.* требование *neut.*

requisition /ˌrɛkwə'zɪʃən/ **1.** *n.* реквизиция *f.* **2.** *v.* реквизировать *impf.* and *pf.*

reread /ri'rid/ *v.* перечитывать *impf.*

rerun /'riˌrʌn/ *n.* (*film*) повторный показ фильма *m.*

resale /'riˌseil/ *n.* перепродажа *f.*

rescind /rɪ'sɪnd/ *v.* отменять, аннулировать *impf.*

rescue /'rɛskyu/ **1.** *n.* спасение *neut.* **2.** *adj.* спасательный. **3.** *v.* спасать *impf.*, спасти *pf.*

rescuer /'rɛskyuər/ *n.* спаситель *m.*

research /rɪ'sɜrtʃ, 'risɜrtʃ/ **1.** *n.* исследование *neut.* **2.** *adj.* исследовательский. **3.** *v.* исследовать *impf.* and *pf.*

researcher /rɪ'sɜrtʃər/ *n.* исследователь *m.*

research institute *n.* научно-исследовательский институт *m.* (*abbr.* НИИ).

resell /ri'sɛl/ *v.* перепродавать *impf.*

resemblance /rɪ'zɛmbləns/ *n.* сходство *neut.*

resemble /rɪ'zɛmbəl/ *v.* быть похожим; походить (на *with acc.*) *impf.*

resent /rɪ'zɛnt/ *v.* негодовать (на *with acc.*) *impf.*

resentful /rɪ'zɛntfəl/ *adj.* обиженный; (*quick to resent*) обидчивый.

reservation /ˌrɛzər'veiʃən/ *n.* оговорка *f.*; (*booking*) броня *f.*; (*public land*) заповедник *m.*; (*Indian*) резервация *f.*

reserve /rɪ'zɜrv/ **1.** *n.* запас *m.*; (*restraint*) сдержанность *f.* **2.** *v.* резервировать *impf.* and *pf.*; (*book*) бронировать *impf.*; (*defer, set aside*) откладывать *impf.*

reserved /rɪ'zɜrvd/ *adj.* (*reticent*) сдержанный; замкнутый; (*seat*) забронированный.

reservoir /'rɛzərˌvwɑr/ *n.* водохранилище *neut.*; резервуар *m.*

resettle /ri'sɛtl/ *v.* переселять(ся) (в *with acc.*) *impf.*

reshuffle /ri'ʃʌfəl/ *v.* перетасовывать; переставлять *impf.*

reside /rɪ'zaid/ *v.* жить; проживать *impf.*

residence /'rɛzɪdəns/ *n.* (*place*) местожительство *neut.*; (*act*) проживание *neut.*

resident /'rɛzɪdənt/ *n.* (*постоянный*) житель *m.*

residential /ˌrɛzɪ'dɛnʃəl/ *adj.* (*area*) жилой.

residual /rɪ'zɪdʒuəl/ *adj.* остаточный.

residue /'rɛzɪˌdu/ *n.* осадок; остаток *m.*

resign /rɪ'zain/ *v.* уходить от должности; уходить в отставку *impf.*

resignation /ˌrɛzɪg'neiʃən/ *n.* отставка *f.*; отказ *m.*; (*being resigned*) покорность *f.*

resigned /rɪ'zaind/ *adj.* покорный.

resilient /rɪ'zɪlyənt/ *adj.* упругий; эластичный.

resin /'rɛzɪn/ *n.* смола *f.*

resinous /'rɛzənəs/ *adj.* смолистый.

resist /rɪ'zɪst/ *v.* сопротивляться; противостоять *impf.*; отбивать *impf.*, отбить *pf.*

resistance /rɪ'zɪstəns/ *n.* сопротивление *neut.*

resistant /rɪ'zɪstənt/ *adj.* сопротивляющийся.

resolute /'rɛzəˌlut/ *adj.* решительный.

resolution /ˌrɛzə'luʃən/ *n.* разрешение *neut.*; резолюция *f.*

resolve /rɪ'zɒlv/ *v.* решать(ся) *impf.*, решить(ся) *pf.*

resonant /'rɛzənənt/ *adj.* звучный; раздающийся.

resonate /'rɛzəˌneit/ *v.* резонировать *impf.*

resort /rɪ'zɔrt/ **1.** n. (health) курорт m.; (recourse) ресурс m. **2.** v. прибегать (к with dat.) impf., прибегнуть pf.

resound /rɪ'zaund/ v. раздаваться impf.

resounding /rɪ'zaundɪŋ/ adj. звонкий; громкий; сильный.

resourceful /rɪ'sɔrsfəl/ adj. находчивый, изобретательный.

resources /'risɔrsəz/ n. ресурсы; средства; запасы pl.; **natural resources** естественные богатства pl.

respect /rɪ'spɛkt/ **1.** n. уважение; почтение neut.; (reference) отношение neut.; **with respect to** что касается; относительно (with gen.). **2.** v. уважать; почитать impf.

respectable /rɪ'spɛktəbəl/ adj. приличный; почтенный.

respectful /rɪ'spɛktfəl/ adj. почтительный; вежливый.

respective /rɪ'spɛktɪv/ adj. соответственный.

respiration /ˌrɛspə'reiʃən/ n. дыхание neut.

respiratory /'rɛspərəˌtɔri/ adj. дыхательный; респираторный.

respite /'rɛspɪt/ n. передышка f.

resplendence /rɪ'splɛndəns/ n. блеск m.; великолепие neut.

resplendent /rɪ'splɛndənt/ adj. блестящий; сверкающий.

respond /rɪ'spɒnd/ v. отвечать (на with acc.) impf., ответить pf.

respondent /rɪ'spɒndənt/ n. (leg.) ответчик m.

response /rɪ'spɒns/ n. ответ m.; реакция f.

responsibility /rɪˌspɒnsə'bɪlɪti/ n. ответственность; обязанность f.

responsible /rɪ'spɒnsəbəl/ adj. ответственный.

responsive /rɪ'spɒnsɪv/ adj. ответный; отзывчивый.

responsiveness /rɪ'spɒnsɪvnɪs/ n. отзывчивость f.

rest[1] /rɛst/ **1.** n. отдых; покой m. **2.** v. отдыхать impf., отдохнуть pf.

rest[2] /rɛst/ n. (remainder) остаток m.; остальные pl.

rest area n. придорожная стоянка f.

restaurant /'rɛstərənt, -rɒnt/ n. ресторан m.

restaurateur /ˌrɛstərə'tɜr/ n. владелец ресторана m.

restful /'rɛstfəl/ adj. успокоительный; спокойный.

rest home n. санаторий m.

restitution /ˌrɛstɪ'tuʃən/ n. возвращение; восстановление; возмещение neut.

restless /'rɛstlɪs/ adj. беспокойный; неспокойный.

restlessness /'rɛstlɪsnɪs/ n. беспокойство neut.

restoration /ˌrɛstə'reiʃən/ n. реставрация f.

restore /rɪ'stɔr/ v. восстанавливать impf., восстановить pf.; реставрировать impf. and pf.

restrain /rɪ'strein/ v. сдерживать impf., сдержать pf.; **to restrain oneself** сдерживаться impf., сдержаться pf.

restrained /rɪ'streind/ adj. сдержанный.

restraint /rɪ'streint/ n. (reserve) сдержанность f.; (restriction) ограничение neut.

restrict /rɪ'strɪkt/ v. ограничивать impf., ограничить pf.

restriction /rɪ'strɪkʃən/ n. ограничение neut.

restrictive /rɪ'strɪktɪv/ adj. ограничительный.

rest room n. туалет m.

result /rɪ'zʌlt/ **1.** n. результат m.; следствие neut.; **as a result** в результате (with gen.). **2.** v. следовать impf. последовать pf.

resume /rɪ'zum/ v. продолжать impf., продолжить pf.

résumé /'rɛzʊˌmei/ n. резюме neut. indecl.

resurrect /ˌrɛzə'rɛkt/ v.t. воскрешать impf.; **to be resurrected** воскресать impf.

resurrection /ˌrɛzə'rɛkʃən/ n. воскресение neut.

resuscitation /rɪˌsʌsɪ'teiʃən/ n. оживление; приведение в сознание neut.

retail /'riteil/ **1.** n. розничная продажа f. **2.** adj. розничный. **3.** adv. в розницу

retailer /'riteilər/ n. розничный торговец m.

retain /rɪ'tein/ v. сохранять impf., сохранить pf.

retaliate /rɪ'tæliˌeit/ v. отплачивать тем же impf., отплатить pf.

retaliation /rɪˌtæli'eiʃən/ n. возмездие neut.

retard /rɪ'tard/ v. задерживать impf., задержать pf.

retarded /rɪ'tardɪd/ adj. отсталый.

retention /rɪ'tɛnʃən/ n. удерживание; удержание; сохранение neut.

retentive /rɪ'tɛntɪv/ adj. удерживающий.

rethink /ri'θɪŋk/ v. пересматривать impf.

reticent /'rɛtəsənt/ adj. сдержанный; молчаливый.

reticular /rɪ'tɪkyələr/ adj. сетчатый.

retina /'rɛtnə/ n. сетчатка; сетчатая оболочка; ретина f.

retinue /'rɛtnˌu/ n. свита f.

retire /rɪ'taiₐr/ v уходить в отставку impf.; (sleep) ложиться спать impf.

retired /rɪ'taiₐrd/ adj. ушедший на пенсию; (officer) отставной.

retiring /rɪ'taiₐrɪŋ/ adj. (shy) скромный; застенчивый.

retract /rɪ'trækt/ v. втягивать(ся) impf.; (airplane landing gear) убирать шасси impf.; (take back) брать назад impf.

retractile /rɪ'træktɪl/ adj. втягивающийся.

retransmit /ˌritræns'mɪt/ v. ретранслировать impf.

retreat /rɪ'trit/ **1.** n. отступление neut.; (haven) убежище neut. **2.** v. отступать impf., отступить pf.

retribution /ˌrɛtrə'byuʃən/ n. возмездие neut.

retributive /rɪ'trɪbyətɪv/ adj. карательный.

retrievable /rɪ'trivəbəl/ adj. поправимый.

retrieve /rɪ'triv/ v. взять обратно pf.; (repair) исправлять impf.

retriever /rɪ'trivər/ n. ретривер m.

retroactive /ˌrɛtrou'æktɪv/ adj. (leg.) имеющий обратную силу.

retrorocket /'rɛtrouˌrɒkɪt/ n. тормозная ракета f.

retrospect /'rɛtrəˌspɛkt/ n. взгляд назад m.; **in retrospect** adv. ретроспективно.

retrospective /ˌrɛtrə'spɛktɪv/ adj. ретроспективный

return /rɪ'tɜrn/ **1.** n. возвращение neut.; (profit) прибыль f.; **in return for** взамен (with gen.). **2.** adj. обратный. **3.** v.t. возвращать impf., возвратить pf.; v.i. возвращаться impf., возвратиться pf.

reunification /ˌriyunəfɪ'keiʃən/ n. воссоединение neut.

reunion /ri'yunyən/ *n.* сбор *m.*; встре́ча *f.*; воссоедине́ние *neut.*

reunite /ˌriyu'nait/ *v.* воссоединя́ть(ся); встреча́ться *impf.*

reusable /ri'yuzəbəl/ *adj.* повто́рно испо́льзуемый.

revalue /ri'vælyu/ *v.* переоце́нивать *impf.*

reveal /rɪ'vil/ *v.* обнару́живать; пока́зывать; раскрыва́ть *impf.*

revealing /rɪ'vilɪŋ/ *adj.* показа́тельный.

reveille /'rɛvəli/ *n.* (*mil.*) побу́дка *f.*

revelation /ˌrɛvə'leiʃən/ *n.* открове́ние; откры́тие *neut.*; (*cap.*) (*Bibl.*) Апока́липсис *m.*

reveler /'rɛvələr/ *n.* (*drunken*) бра́жник *m.*, гуля́ка *m.* and *f.* (*decl. f.*).

revelry /'rɛvəlri/ *n.* шу́мное весе́лье *neut.*

revenge /rɪ'vɛndʒ/ *n.* мще́ние *neut.*, месть *f.*; **to take revenge** *v.* мстить *impf.*, отомсти́ть *pf.*

revengeful /rɪ'vɛndʒfəl/ *adj.* мсти́тельный.

revenue /'rɛvən,yu, -ə,nu/ *n.* дохо́д *m.*

reverberate /rɪ'vɜrbə,reit/ *v.* отража́ть(ся) *impf.*; (*resound*) звуча́ть; оглаша́ться *impf.*

revere /rɪ'vɪər/ *v.* почита́ть *impf.*; глубо́ко уважа́ть *impf.*

reverence /'rɛvərəns/ *n.* почте́ние *neut.*

reverend /'rɛvərənd/ *adj.* почте́нный; (*cap.*) (*title*) его́ преподо́бие.

reverent /'rɛvərənt/ *adj.* почти́тельный; благогове́йный.

reversal /rɪ'vɜrsəl/ *n.* по́лное измене́ние *neut.*; (*leg.*) отме́на *f.*

reverse /rɪ'vɜrs/ **1.** *adj.* обра́тный. **2.** *n.* противополо́жное; обра́тное *neut.*; (*gear*) за́дний ход *m.* **3.** *v.* (*turn upside down*) переверты́вать , переверну́ть *pf.*

revert /rɪ'vɜrt/ *v.* возвраща́ться *impf.*, возврати́ться *pf.*

revetment /rɪ'vɛtmənt/ *n.* облицо́вка *f.*

review /rɪ'vyu/ **1.** *n.* обзо́р *m.*, обозре́ние *neut.*; (*criticism*) реце́нзия *f.*; (*mil.*) смотр *m.* **2.** *v.* пересма́тривать *impf.*; (*survey*) обозрева́ть *impf.*, обозре́ть *pf.*

revise /rɪ'vaiz/ *v.* перераба́тывать *impf.*, перерабо́тать *pf.*

revision /rɪ'vɪʒən/ *n.* реви́зия; перерабо́тка *f.*; исправле́ние *neut.*; пересмо́тр *m.*

revitalize /ri'vait̯,aiz/ *v.* оживля́ть; обновля́ть *impf.*

revival /rɪ'vaivəl/ *n.* возрожде́ние *neut.*

revive /rɪ'vaiv/ *v.t.* оживля́ть; возрожда́ть *impf.*, возроди́ть *pf.*; *v.i.* ожива́ть *impf.*

revocation /ˌrɛvə'keiʃən/ *n.* отме́на *f.*

revoke /rɪ'vouk/ *v.* отменя́ть *impf.*, отмени́ть *pf.*

revolt /rɪ'voult/ **1.** *n.* восста́ние *neut.* **2.** *v.i.* восстава́ть *impf.*, восста́ть *pf.*; *v.t.* отта́лкивать *impf.*

revolting /rɪ'voultɪŋ/ *adj.* отврати́тельный.

revolution /ˌrɛvə'luʃən/ *n.* револю́ция *f.*; оборо́т *m.*

revolutionary /ˌrɛvə'luʃə,nɛri/ **1.** *adj.* революцио́нный. **2.** *n.* революционе́р *m.*

revolutionize /ˌrɛvə'luʃə,naiz/ *v.* революционизи́ровать *impf.* and *pf.*

revolve /rɪ'vɒlv/ *v.* верте́ться *impf.*

revolver /rɪ'vɒlvər/ *n.* револьве́р *m.*

revue /rɪ'vyu/ *n.* ревю́ *neut. indecl.*

revulsion /rɪ'vʌlʃən/ *n.* отвраще́ние *neut.*

reward /rɪ'wɔrd/ **1.** *n.* награ́да *f.* **2.** *v.* награжда́ть *impf.*, награди́ть *pf.*

rewarding /rɪ'wɔrdɪŋ/ *adj.* вы́годный.

rewind /ri'waind/ *v.* перема́тывать *impf.*

rewire /ri'waiᵊr/ *v.* обновля́ть прово́дку *impf.*

rewrite /ri'rait/ *v.* (*write again*) перепи́сывать *impf.*; (*revise*) перераба́тывать *impf.*

Reykjavik /'reikyə,vik/ *n.* Рейкья́вик *m.*

rhapsody /'ræpsədi/ *n.* рапсо́дия *f.*

rhetoric /'rɛtərɪk/ *n.* рито́рика *f.*

rhetorical /rɪ'tɔrɪkəl/ *adj.* ритори́ческий.

rheumatism /'rumə,tɪzəm/ *n.* ревмати́зм *m.*

rhinal /'rainl̩/ *adj.* носово́й.

rhinoceros /rai'nɒsərəs/ *n.* носоро́г *m.*

Rhode Island /roud/ *n.* Род-А́йленд *m.*

Rhodes /roudz/ *n.* (*island*) Ро́дос *m.*

rhododendron /ˌroudə'dɛndrən/ *n.* рододе́ндрон *m.*

Rhône /roun/ *n.* (*river*) Ро́на *f.*

rhubarb /'rubarb/ **1.** *n.* реве́нь *m.* **2.** *adj.* реве́нный.

rhyme /raim/ **1.** *n.* ри́фма *f.* **2.** *v.* рифмова́ть(ся) *impf.*

rhymer /'raimər/ *n.* рифмопле́т *m.*

rhythm /'rɪðəm/ *n.* ритм *m.*

rhythmical /'rɪðmɪkəl/ *adj.* ритми́ческий.

rib /rɪb/ *n.* ребро́ *neut.*

ribald /'rɪbəld; *spelling pron.* 'raibəld/ *adj.* гру́бый; непристо́йный.

ribbon /'rɪbən/ *n.* ле́нта *f.*

rib cage *n.* грудна́я кле́тка *f.*

rice /rais/ **1.** *n.* рис *m.* **2.** *adj.* ри́совый.

rich /rɪtʃ/ *adj.* бога́тый; (*food*) жи́рный.

richness /'rɪtʃnɪs/ *n.* бога́тство *neut.*; жи́рность *f.*; оби́лие; плодоро́дие *neut.*

rickets /'rɪkɪts/ *n.* рахи́т *m.*

rickety /'rɪkɪti/ *adj.* ша́ткий.

ricochet /ˌrɪkə'ʃei/ *v.* рикошети́ровать *impf.* and *pf.*

rid /rɪd/ *v.* избавля́ть *impf.*, изба́вить *pf.*; **to get rid of** избавля́ться (от *with gen.*) *impf.*, изба́виться *pf.*

riddance /'rɪdns/ *n.* избавле́ние *neut.*

riddle /'rɪdl̩/ *n.* зага́дка *f.*

ride /raid/ **1.** *n.* прогу́лка *f.* **2.** *v.* е́здить *impf. in-det.*, е́хать *impf. det.*, пое́хать *pf.*

rider /'raidər/ *n.* (*horse*) вса́дник; нае́здник *m.*; (*bicycle*) велосипеди́ст *m.*; (*motorcycle*) мотоцикли́ст *m.*

riderless /'raidərlɪs/ *adj.* без вса́дника.

ridge /rɪdʒ/ *n.* гре́бень; хребе́т *m.*

ridgepole /'rɪdʒ,poul/ *n.* конько́вый брус *m.*; (*tent*) распо́рка *f.*

ridicule /'rɪdɪ,kyul/ **1.** *n.* насме́шка *f.* **2.** *v.* осме́ивать *impf.*, осмея́ть *pf.*

ridiculous /rɪ'dɪkyələs/ *adj.* неле́пый; смехотво́рный; смешно́й.

riding /'raidɪŋ/ *n.* верхова́я езда́ *f.*

rife /raif/ *adj.* распространённый.

riffraff /'rɪf,ræf/ *n.* сброд *m.*

rifle /'raifəl/ *n.* винто́вка *f.*

rifleman /'raifəlmən/ *n.* стрело́к *m.*

rifling /'raiflɪŋ/ *n.* (*on barrel*) наре́з *m.*

rift /rɪft/ *n.* тре́щина *f.*; (*slit*) щель *f.*; (*in mountains*) уще́лье *neut.*; (*in clouds*) просве́т *m.*

rig /rɪg/ *n.* (*device*) устро́йство *neut.*

Riga /'rigə/ *n.* Ри́га *f.*

rigging /'rɪgɪŋ/ n. (naut.) такела́ж m.
right /rait/ **1.** adj. пра́вый; ве́рный; пра́вильный. **2.** adv. пра́вильно; ве́рно; **on** or **to the right** напра́во. **3.** n. пра́во neut.; справедли́вость f.; (direction) пра́вая сторона́ f. **4.** v. исправля́ть impf., испра́вить pf.
right angle n. прямо́й у́гол m.
righteous /'raitʃəs/ adj. пра́ведный; справедли́вый.
right-handed /'rait 'hændɪd/ adj. по́льзующийся пра́вой руко́й.
rightly /'raitli/ adv. пра́вильно; (fairly) справедли́во.
rightness /'raitnɪs/ n. пра́вильность; справедли́вость f.
right of way n. пра́во прохо́да neut.
right-wing /'rait 'wɪŋ/ adj. пра́вый.
rigid /'rɪdʒɪd/ adj. жёсткий; неги́бкий; непрекло́нный.
rigidity /rɪ'dʒɪdɪti/ n. жёсткость; стро́гость f.
rigmarole /'rɪgmə,roul/ n. галиматья́ f.
rigor /'rɪgər/ n. стро́гость; суро́вость f.
rigorous /'rɪgərəs/ adj. стро́гий; суро́вый.
rim /rɪm/ n. край; (of wheel) о́бод m.
rime /raim/ n. (frost) и́ней m.
rimless /'rɪmlɪs/ adj. (eyeglasses) без опра́вы.
rind /raind/ n. кожура́; ко́рка f.
ring[1] /rɪŋ/ **1.** n. кольцо́ neut.; круг m. **2.** v.t. окружа́ть кольцо́м impf.
ring[2] /rɪŋ/ **1.** n. (bell) звон; звоно́к m. **2.** v.i. звене́ть impf.
ringer /'rɪŋər/ n. (bells) звона́рь m.
ringing /'rɪŋɪŋ/ n. звон m.
ringlet /'rɪŋlɪt/ n. (hair) ло́кон; завито́к m.
ringmaster /'rɪŋ,mæstər/ n. инспе́ктор мане́жа m.
ringworm /'rɪŋ,wɜrm/ n. стригу́щий лиша́й m.
rink /rɪŋk/ n. (skating) като́к m.
rinse /rɪns/ v. полоска́ть impf.
rinsing /'rɪnsɪŋ/ n. полоска́ние; спола́скивание neut.
Rio de Janeiro /'riou dei ʒə'nɛərou/ n. Рио-де-Жане́йро m.
Rio Grande /'ri'ou grænd, 'grandei/ n. (river) Рио-Гра́нде m.
riot /'raiət/ **1.** n. бунт; мяте́ж m. **2.** v. бунтова́ть impf.
rip /rɪp/ **1.** n. разры́в m. **2.** v. рвать; разрыва́ть impf., разорва́ть pf.
rip cord n. вытяжно́й трос m.
ripe /raip/ adj. спе́лый; зре́лый.
ripen /'raipən/ v. зреть; созрева́ть impf., созре́ть pf.
ripeness /'raipnɪs/ n. спе́лость; зре́лость f.
ripoff /'rɪp,ɔf/ n. (colloq.) моше́нничество neut.
ripple /'rɪpəl/ n. (on water; of color) рябь f.
riptide /'rɪp,taid/ n. разрывно́е тече́ние neut.
rise /raiz/ **1.** n. повыше́ние; возвыше́ние neut.; восхо́д m. **2.** v. поднима́ться impf., подня́ться pf.; встава́ть impf., встать pf.; (sun) восходи́ть impf., взойти́ pf.
risible /'rɪzəbəl/ adj. смешли́вый; (funny) смешно́й.
rising /'raizɪŋ/ n. (increase) повыше́ние neut.; (sun) восхо́д m.; (rebellion) восста́ние neut.
risk /rɪsk/ **1.** n. риск m. **2.** v. рискова́ть (with instr.) impf., рискну́ть pf.

risky /'rɪski/ adj. риско́ванный.
risqué /rɪ'skei/ adj. риско́ванный.
rite /rait/ n. обря́д m.
ritual /'rɪtʃuəl/ **1.** adj. ритуа́льный. **2.** n. ритуа́л m.
rival /'raivəl/ n. сопе́рник m.
rivalry /'raivəlri/ n. сопе́рничество neut.
river /'rɪvər/ **1.** n. река́ f. **2.** adj. речно́й.
riverbank /'rɪvər,bæŋk/ n. бе́рег реки́ m.
riverbed /'rɪvər,bɛd/ n. ру́сло (реки́) neut.
rivet /'rɪvɪt/ **1.** n. заклёпка f. **2.** v. заклёпывать impf., заклепа́ть pf.
riveter /'rɪvɪtər/ n. (worker) клепа́льщик m.
Rivne /'rɔvnə/ n. Ро́вно neut.
RNA n. (biol.) РНК (abbr. of рибонуклеи́новая кислота́ f.).
roach[1] /routʃ/ n. (fish) во́бла f.
roach[2] /routʃ/ n. (cockroach) тарака́н m.
road /roud/ n. доро́га f., путь m.
roadblock /'roud,blɒk/ n. загражде́ние на доро́ге neut.
road map n. доро́жная ка́рта f.
road sense n. чу́вство доро́ги neut.
roadside /'roud,said/ n. обо́чина f.
roadway /'roud,wei/ n. мостова́я f.
roam /roum/ v. стра́нствовать impf.
roamer /'roumər/ n. стра́нник; скита́лец m.
roan /roun/ n. (horse) ча́лая ло́шадь f.
roar /rɔr/ **1.** n. рёв m. **2.** v. реве́ть impf.
roaring /'rɔrɪŋ/ n. рёв; гул; шум m.
roast /roust/ **1.** n. жарко́е; жа́реное neut. **2.** adj. жа́реный. **3.** v.t. жа́рить impf., изжа́рить pf.; v.i. жа́риться impf., изжа́риться pf.
rob /rɒb/ v. обкра́дывать impf., обокра́сть pf.
robber /'rɒbər/ n. граби́тель m.
robbery /'rɒbəri/ n. кра́жа f.; грабёж m.
robe /roub/ n. ма́нтия f.; (bathrobe) хала́т m.
robin /'rɒbɪn/ n. мали́новка f.
robot /'roubət, -bɒt/ n. ро́бот; автома́т m.
robust /rou'bʌst/ adj. здоро́вый; кре́пкий.
rock[1] /rɒk/ n. ка́мень m.; (cliff) скала́ f.; утёс m.
rock[2] /rɒk/ v.t. (swing) кача́ть impf.; (shake) трясти́ impf., затрясти́ pf.; v.i. кача́ться impf., трясти́сь impf., затрясти́сь pf.
rock crystal n. го́рный хруста́ль m.
rocket /'rɒkɪt/ **1.** n. раке́та f. **2.** adj. раке́тный.
rocket base n. раке́тная ба́за f.
rocket range n. раке́тный полиго́н m.
rockfall /'rɒk,fɔl/ n. обва́л m.
rocking chair /'rɒkɪŋ/ n. кача́лка f., кре́сло-кача́лка neut.
rock-'n'-roll /'rɒk ən 'roul/ n. рок-н-ро́лл m.
rocky /'rɒki/ adj. скали́стый; камени́стый.
Rocky Mountains n. Скали́стые го́ры pl.
rod /rɒd/ n. прут; брус m.; (branch) ро́зга f.
rodent /'roudnt/ n. грызу́н m.
rodeo /'roudiou/ n. роде́о neut. indecl.
roe[1] /rou/ n. (fish) икра́ f.; (soft) моло́ки pl.
roe[2] /rou/ n. (deer) косу́ля f.
roebuck /'rou,bʌk/ n. саме́ц косу́ли m.
rogue /roug/ n. (crook) жу́лик, моше́нник m.; (good-for-nothing) него́дник m.
roguish /'rougɪʃ/ adj. жуликова́тый.
role /roul/ n. роль f.
roll /roul/ **1.** n. руло́н; сви́ток; свёрток m.; (bread) бу́лочка f. **2.** v.t. кати́ть impf.; v.i.

кати́ться *impf.*; **to roll up** ска́тывать *impf.*, ската́ть *pf.*

roll call *n.* перекли́чка *f.*

rolled steel /rould/ *n.* стально́й прока́т *m.*

roller /'roulər/ *n.* ва́лик; ро́лик; като́к *m.*

Rollerblade /'roulər,bleid/ *n.* ро́ликовый конёк *m.*

roller coaster *n.* америка́нские го́ры *pl.*

roller-skate /'roulər ,skeit/ *v.* ката́ться на ро́ликах *impf.*

ROM /rɒm/ *n.* (*abbr.* of read-only memory) (*comput.*) ПЗУ *neut.*

Roman /'roumən/ **1.** *adj.* ри́мский. **2.** *n.* ри́млянин *m.*, ри́млянка *f.*

Roman Catholic 1. *adj.* (ри́мско-)католи́ческий. **2.** *n.* като́лик *m.*, католи́чка *f.*

Roman Catholicism *n.* католи́чество *neut.*

romance /rou'mæns/ *n.* рома́нтика *f.*; (*love affair*) рома́н *m.*; (*mus.*) рома́нс *m.*; (*lit.*) рома́н *m.*

Romanesque /,roumə'nɛsk/ *n.* рома́нский стиль *m.*

Romania /rʊ'meiniə/ *n.* Румы́ния *f.*

Romanian /rʊ'meiniən/ **1.** *adj.* румы́нский. **2.** *n.* румы́н *m.*, румы́нка *f.*

Roman numeral *n.* ри́мская ци́фра *f.*

romantic /rou'mæntık/ *adj.* романти́чный; романти́ческий.

Rome /roum/ *n.* Рим *m.*

roof /ruf/ *n.* кры́ша *f.*; (*of mouth*) нёбо *neut.*

roofer /'rufər/ *n.* кро́вельщик *m.*

roofing /'rufıŋ/ *n.* кро́вля *f.*

rook[1] /rʊk/ *n.* (*bird*) грач *m.*; (*cheat*) моше́нник *m.*

rook[2] /rʊk/ *n.* (*chess*) ладья́, тура́ *f.*

room /rum/ *n.* ко́мната *f.*; (*in hotel*) ка́мера *f.*; (*space*) ме́сто *neut.*; **room and board** по́лный пансио́н *m.*

roommate /'rum,meit/ *n.* сожи́тель; това́рищ по ко́мнате, квартира́нт *m.*, квартира́нтка *f.*

roomy /'rumi/ *adj.* просто́рный; (*capacious*) вмести́тельный.

roost /rust/ *n.* насе́ст *m.*

rooster /'rustər/ *n.* пету́х *m.*

root /rut/ *n.* ко́рень *m.*

rope /roup/ *n.* кана́т *m.*; верёвка *f.*

rope ladder *n.* верёвочная ле́стница *f.*

rosary /'rouzəri/ *n.* чётки *pl.*

rose /rouz/ **1.** *n.* ро́за *f.* **2.** *adj.* ро́зовый.

rosebud /'rouz,bʌd/ *n.* буто́н ро́зы *m.*

rose garden *n.* роза́рий *m.*

rosemary /'rouz,mɛəri/ *n.* розмари́н *m.*

rosette /rou'zɛt/ *n.* розе́тка *f.*

rosewood /'rouz,wʊd/ *n.* ро́зовое де́рево *neut.*

rosin /'rɒzın/ *n.* канифо́ль *f.*

Rostock /'rɒstɒk/ *n.* Ро́сток *m.*

Rostov /rə'stɔf/ *n.* Росто́в *m.*

rostrum /'rɒstrəm/ *n.* (*tribune*) трибу́на *f.*; (*prow*) нос *m.*

rosy /'rouzi/ *adj.* ро́зовый; румя́ный.

rot /rɒt/ **1.** *n.* гние́ние *neut.*; гниль *f.* **2.** *v.* гнить *impf.*, сгнить *pf.*

rotary /'routəri/ *adj.* ротацио́нный.

rotate /'routeit/ *v.t.* враща́ть(ся) *impf.*

rotation /rou'teiʃən/ *n.* враще́ние *neut.*

rote /rout/ *n.*: **by rote** наизу́сть.

rotgut /'rɒt,gʌt/ *n.* (*slang*) самого́н *m.*

rotten /'rɒtn/ *adj.* гнило́й; прогни́вший.

rottenness /'rɒtnnıs/ *n.* гни́лость *f.*

Rotterdam /'rɒtər,dæm/, ,rɒtər'dɑm/ *n.* Ро́ттердам *m.*

Rouen /ru'ɑ̃/ *n.* Руа́н *m.*

rouge /ruʒ/ *n.* румя́на *pl.*

rough /rʌf/ *adj.* гру́бый; грубова́тый; неро́вный.

roughen /'rʌfən/ *v.t.* де́лать гру́бым *impf.*

rough-hewn /'rʌf 'hyun/ *adj.* гру́бо обтёсанный.

roughly /'rʌfli/ *adv.* гру́бо; (*approximately*) приме́рно; приблизи́тельно.

roughneck /'rʌf,nɛk/ *n.* хулига́н *m.*

roulette /ru'lɛt/ *n.* руле́тка *f.*

round /raund/ **1.** *adj.* кру́глый; кругово́й. **2.** *n.* круг *m.*; (*athl.*) тур *m.*; (*boxing*) раунд *m.* **3.** *v.* округля́ть(ся) *impf.*, округли́ть(ся) *pf.*

round-faced /'raund 'feist/ *adj.* круглоли́цый.

roundness /'raundnıs/ *n.* окру́глость *f.*

round-shouldered /'raund 'ʃouldərd, -,ʃoul-/ *adj.* суту́лый.

round-the-clock /'raund ðə 'klɒk/ *adj.* круглосу́точный.

round trip *n.* пое́здка туда́ и обра́тно *f.*

rouse /rauz/ *v.* буди́ть *impf.*, разбуди́ть *pf.*; возбужда́ть *impf.*, возбуди́ть *pf.*

rout /raut/ **1.** *n.* разгро́м *m.* **2.** *v.* обраща́ть в бе́гство *impf.*

route /rut, raut/ *n.* маршру́т; путь *m.*

routine /ru'tin/ **1.** *adj.* устано́вленный; шабло́нный. **2.** *n.* режи́м *m.*; рути́на *f.*

rove /rouv/ *v.* стра́нствовать *impf.*

rover /'rouvər/ *n.* скита́лец *m.*

row[1] /rou/ *n.* ряд *m.*

row[2] /rau/ *n.* (*uproar*) шум; гвалт *m.*

row[3] /rou/ *v.* грести́ *impf.*

rowan /'rouən/ *n.* (*tree*) ряби́на *f.*

rowboat /'rou,bout/ *n.* гребна́я ло́дка *f.*

rowdy /'raudi/ *adj.* шу́мный; бу́йный.

rower /'rouər/ *n.* гребе́ц *m.*

rowlock /'rou,lɒk/ *n.* уклю́чина *f.*

royal /'rɔiəl/ *adj.* короле́вский; ца́рский.

royalty /'rɔiəlti/ *n.* чле́ны короле́вской семьи́ *pl.*

rub /rʌb/ **1.** *n.* тре́ние; натира́ние *neut.* **2.** *v.t.* натира́ть *impf.*, натере́ть *pf.* **to rub off** *v.t.* стира́ть *impf.*, стере́ть *pf.*; *v.i.* стира́ться *impf.*, стере́ться *pf.*

rubber /'rʌbər/ **1.** *n.* рези́на *f.*; каучу́к *m.*; *pl.* (*galoshes*) гало́ши *pl.* **2.** *adj.* рези́новый.

rubber band *n.* рези́нка *f.*

rubber boot *n.* рези́новый сапо́г *m.*

rubbing /'rʌbıŋ/ *n.* тре́ние *neut.*

rubbish /'rʌbıʃ/ *n.* му́сор *m.*; (*nonsense*) чепуха́ *f.*

rubble /'rʌbəl/ *n.* (*ruins*) разва́лины *f.*

rubella /ru'bɛlə/ *n.* красну́ха *f.*

rubeola /ru'biələ/ *n.* корь *f.*

ruble /'rubəl/ *n.* рубль *m.*

rubric /'rubrık/ *n.* (*heading*) ру́брика *f.*

ruby /'rubi/ **1.** *n.* руби́н *m.* **2.** *adj.* руби́новый.

rucksack /'rʌk,sæk/ *n.* рюкза́к *m.*

rudder /'rʌdər/ *n.* руль *m.*

ruddy /'rʌdi/ *adj.* кра́сный; румя́ный.

rude /rud/ *adj.* гру́бый.

rudeness /'rudnıs/ *n.* гру́бость *f.*

rudimentary /,rudə'mɛntəri/ *adj.* элемента́рный; (*biol.*) рудимента́рный.

rudiments /'rudəmənts/ *n.* нача́тки; зача́тки *pl.*

rue /ru/ *v.* сожалéть (o *with prep.*) *impf.*
ruffian /'rʌfiən/ *n.* хулигáн *m.*; бандúт *m.*
ruffle /'rʌfəl/ **1.** *n.* рябь *f.*; (*trimming*) обóрка *f.*
2. *v.* рябúть *impf.*; (*dishevel*) ерóшить *impf.*
rug /rʌg/ *n.* ковёр; кóврик *m.*
Rugby /'rʌgbi/ *n.* рéгби *neut. indecl.*
rugged /'rʌgɪd/ *adj.* нерóвный; (*coarse*) грýбый; (*strong*) сúльный; крéпкий.
ruin /'ruɪn/ **1.** *n.* гúбель *f.*; *pl.* развáлина *f.*, руúны *pl.* **2.** *v.* губúть *impf.*; разрушáть *impf.*, разрýшить *pf.*
ruination /,ruə'neɪʃən/ *n.* гúбель *f.*; разорéние *neut.*
rule /rul/ **1.** *n.* прáвило *neut.*; (*government*) управлéние *neut.*; **as a rule** обы́чно; как прáвило. **2.** *v.* управлять; прáвить *impf.*
ruler /'rulər/ *n.* правúтель *m.*; (*measure*) линéйка *f.*
ruling /'rulɪŋ/ **1.** *n.* (*control*) управлéние (*with instr.*) *neut.*; (*decision*) постановлéние; решéние *neut.* **2.** *adj.* (*in power*) прáвящий; (*prevailing*) преобладáющий, госпóдствующий; (*current*) дéйствующий.
rum /rʌm/ *n.* ром *m.*
rumble /'rʌmbəl/ *n.* грóхот; гул *m.*
rumbling /'rʌmblɪŋ/ *n.* громыхáние *neut.*; грóхот *m.*
ruminate /'rumə,neɪt/ *v.* (*chew cud*) жевáть жвáчку *impf.*; (*reflect*) размышлять *impf.*
rummage /'rʌmɪdʒ/ *v.* ры́ться (в *with prep.*) *impf.*
rumor /'rumər/ *n.* слух *m.*; молвá *f.*
rumple /'rʌmpəl/ *v.* мять *impf*; (*disarrange*) ерóшить *impf.*
rumpus /'rʌmpəs/ *n.* (*colloq.*) шум *m.*; (*disturbance*) скандáл *m.*
run /rʌn/ **1.** *n.* бег; пробéг *m.* **2.** *v.* бéгать *impf. indet.*, бежáть *impf. det.*, побежáть *pf.*; **to run away** убежáть *pf.*; **to run into** наéхать *pf.*

runaway /'rʌnə,weɪ/ *n.* беглéц *m.*, беглянка *f.*
rung /rʌŋ/ *n.* ступéнька *f.*
runner /'rʌnər/ *n.* бегýн *m.*; (*of sled*) пóлоз *m.*
running /'rʌnɪŋ/ *n.* бег *m.*; бéганье *neut.*; (*machine*) ход *m.*; (*managing*) ведéние *neut.*
running board *n.* (*car*) поднóжка *f.*
running water *n.* протóчная водá *f.*
runt /rʌnt/ *n.* (*animal*) малорóслое живóтное *neut.*; (*pej. of person*) коротышка *m.* and *f.* (*decl. f.*).
runway /'rʌn,weɪ/ *n.* (*airport*) взлётно-посáдочная полосá *f.*
rupture /'rʌptʃər/ **1.** *n.* разлóм; разры́в *m.*; (*med.*) гры́жа *f.* **2.** *v.* прорывáть(ся) *impf.*
rural /'rʊrəl/ *adj.* сéльский.
rush /rʌʃ/ **1.** *n.* спéшка *f.*; стремúтельное движéние *neut.*; нáтиск *m.* **2.** *v.* торопúть(ся) спешúть *impf.*
rush hour *n.* час пик *m.*
Russian /'rʌʃən/ **1.** *adj.* рýсский; россúйский. **2.** *n.* рýсский *m.*, рýсская *f.*
Russianize /'rʌʃə,naɪz/ *v.* русифицúровать *impf.*
Russophile /'rʌsə,faɪl/ *n.* русофúл *m.*
Russophobe /'rʌsə,foʊb/ *n.* русофóб *m.*
rust /rʌst/ **1.** *n.* ржáвчина *f.* **2.** *v.* ржавéть *impf.*, заржавéть *pf.*
rustic /'rʌstɪk/ *adj.* сéльский; деревéнский.
rustle /'rʌsəl/ **1.** *n.* шéлест; шóрох *m.*; шуршáнье *neut.* **2.** *v.* шуршáть *impf.*
rustproof /'rʌst,pruf/ *adj.* нержавéющий.
rusty /'rʌsti/ *adj.* ржáвый; заржáвленный.
rut /rʌt/ *n.* колея́; борозда́ *f.*
rutabaga /,rutə'heɪgə/ *n.* брю́ква *f.*
ruthless /'ruθlɪs/ *adj.* безжáлостный.
Ryazan /rɪə'zɑn/ *n.* Рязáнь *f.*
Rybinsk /'rɪbɪnsk/ *n.* Ры́бинск *m.*
rye /raɪ/ **1.** *n.* рожь *f.* **2.** *adj.* ржанóй.
rye bread *n.* ржанóй хлеб *m.*
ryegrass /'raɪ,græs/ *n.* плéвел *m.*

S

Saaremaa /'sɑrə,mɑ/ n. (island) Сарема f.
Sabbath /'sæbəθ/ n. (Christian) воскресенье neut.; (Jewish) суббота f.
Sabbatical /sə'bætɪkəl/ adj. (Jewish) субботний; (Christian) воскресный.
sabbatical year n. (academic leave) годичный отпуск m.
saber /'seibər/ n. сабля f.
saber-rattling /'seibər ,rætlɪŋ/ n. бряцание оружием neut.
sable /'seibəl/ n. соболь m.
sabot /'sæbou/ n. сабо pl. indecl.
sabotage /'sæbə,tɑʒ/ 1. n. саботаж m. 2. v. саботировать impf. and pf.
saboteur /,sæbə'tɜr/ n. саботажник m.
sac /sæk/ n. мешочек m.
saccate /'sækɪt/ adj. мешкообразный.
saccharify /sə'kærə,fai/ v. засахаривать impf.
saccharin /'sækərɪn/ n. сахарин m.
sacerdotal /,sæsər'doutl/ adj. священнический.
sachet /sæ'ʃei/ n. саше neut. indecl.
sack¹ /sæk/ 1. n. мешок m. 2. v. класть в мешок impf.; (slang) (dismiss) уволить pf.
sack² /sæk/ v. (plunder) громить impf.
sackcloth /'sæk,klɔθ/ n. мешковина f.
sacker /'sækər/ n. грабитель m.
sackful /'sækfʊl/ n. полный мешок m.
sacking /'sækɪŋ/ n. мешковина f.
sack race n. бег в мешках m.
sacral /'seikrəl/ adj. крестцовый; сакральный.
sacrament /'sækrəmənt/ n. таинство neut.; (cap.) (communion) Святое причастие neut.
sacramental /,sækrə'mɛntl/ adj. священный.
sacred /'seikrɪd/ adj. священный; святой.
sacrifice /'sækrə,fais/ 1. n. жертва f. 2. v. жертвовать impf., пожертвовать pf.
sacrificial /,sækrə'fɪʃəl/ adj. жертвенный.
sacrilege /'sækrəlɪdʒ/ n. святотатство neut.
sacrilegious /,sækrə'lɪdʒəs/ adj. святотатственный.
sacristy /'sækrɪsti/ n. ризница f.
sacrosanct /'sækrou,sæŋkt/ adj. неприкосновенный.
sacrum /'sækrəm/ n. крестец m.
sad /sæd/ adj. печальный; грустный.
sadden /'sædn/ v. печалить impf., опечаливать pf.
saddle /'sædl/ 1. n. седло neut. 2. v. седлать impf., оседлать pf.
saddlebag /'sædl,bæg/ n. седельная сума f.
saddlecloth /'sædl,klɔθ/ n. потник m.
saddle girth n. подпруга f.
saddle horse n. верховая лошадь f.
saddler /'sædlər/ n. шорник; седельник m.
saddlery /'sædləri/ n. шорня f.
sadism /'seidɪzəm/ n. садизм m.
sadist /'seidɪst/ n. садист m.
sadistic /sə'dɪstɪk/ adj. садистский.
sadly /'sædli/ adv. грустно; печально.
sadness /'sædnɪs/ n. печаль; грусть f.
safari /sə'fɑri/ n. сафари neut. indecl.
safe /seif/ 1. n. несгораемый шкаф or ящик;

сейф m. 2. adj. безопасный; в безопасности; (unharmed) невредимый.
safe-conduct /'seif 'kɒndʌkt/ n. охранная грамота f.
safeguard /'seif,gɑrd/ n. гарантия f.
safekeeping /'seif'kipɪŋ/ n. хранение neut.
safely /'seifli/ adv. благополучно.
safety /'seifti/ n. безопасность f.
safety pin n. английская булавка f.
saffron /'sæfrən/ n. шафран m.
sag /sæg/ v. (beam, rope, etc.) прогибаться; провисать impf.; (droop lower) оседать impf.
saga /'sɑgə/ n. сага f.
sagacious /sə'geiʃəs/ adj. проницательный.
sagacity /sə'gæsɪti/ n. проницательность f.
sage¹ /seidʒ/ 1. n. мудрец m. 2. adj. мудрый.
sage² /seidʒ/ n. (herb) шалфей m.
sage-green /'seidʒ 'grin/ adj. серовато-зелёный.
Sagittarius /,sædʒɪ'tɛəriəs/ n. Стрелец m.
sagittate /'sædʒɪ,teit/ adj. стреловидный.
sago /'seigou/ n. саго neut. indecl.
said /sed/ adj. (leg.) вышеупомянутый.
Saigon /sai'gɒn/ n. Сайгон m. (see Ho Chi Minh City).
sail /seil/ 1. n. парус m.; (of windmill) крыло neut. 2. v. плавать; плыть impf.
sailboat /'seil,bout/ n. парусная шлюпка f.
sailcloth /'seil,klɔθ/ n. парусина f.
sailfish /'seil,fɪʃ/ n. парусник m.
sailing /'seilɪŋ/ n. плавание neut.; (as sport) парусный спорт m.
sailing ship n. парусник m.
sailor /'seilər/ n. матрос m.
sailplane /'seil,plein/ n. планер m.
sailyard /'seil,yard/ n. рея f.
Saimaa /'saimɑ/ n. (lake) Сайма f.
sainfoin /'seinfɔin/ n. эспарцет m.
saint /seint/ n. святой m.
Saint Denis /'sæn də'ni/ n. Сен-Дени m.
sainted /'seintɪd/ adj. священный.
sainthood /'seinthʊd/ n. святость f.
saintly /'seintli/ adj. святой.
sake /seik/ n.: for the sake of ради (with gen.).
Sakhalin /'sækə,lin/ n. (island) Сахалин m.
salacious /sə'leiʃəs/ adj. похотливый; (lewd) неприсойный.
salaciousness /sə'leiʃəsnɪs/ n. похотливость f.
salad /'sæləd/ n. салат m.
Salamanca /,sælə'mæŋkə/ n. Саламанка f.
salamander /'sælə,mændər/ n. саламандра f.
salami /sə'lɑmi/ n. салями f. indecl.
sal ammoniac /'sæl ə'mouni,æk/ n. нашатырь m.
salaried /'sælərɪd/ adj. на окладе; штатный.
salary /'sæləri/ n. жалованье neut.; зарплата f.
sale /seil/ n. продажа f.; on sale в продаже.
saleable /'seiləbəl/ adj. ходовой.
salesmanship /'seilzmən,ʃɪp/ n. реклама товара f.
salesperson /'seilz,pɜrsən/ n. продавец m., продавщица f.
sales slip n. квитанция f.
salicylic /,sælə'sɪlɪk/ adj. салициловый.

salient /'seiliənt/ *adj.* (*projecting*) выступающий; выдающийся; (*conspicuous*) заметный.
saliferous /sə'lıfərəs/ *adj.* соленосный.
saline /'seilin/ *adj.* соляной; солёный.
salinization /ˌsælənə'zeifən/ *n.* засоление *neut.*
saliva /sə'laivə/ *n.* слюна *f.*
salivary /'sælə,veri/ *adj.* слюнный.
salivate /'sælə,veit/ *v.* выделять слюну *impf.*
salivation /ˌsælə'veifən/ *n.* слюноотделение *neut.*
sallow /'sælou/ *adj.* (*yellow*) желтоватый; (*sickly*) болезненный.
sally /'sæli/ *n.* острота *f.*
salmon /'sæmən/ **1.** *n.* лосось *m.* **2.** *adj.* лососевый.
salmonella /ˌsælmə'nɛlə/ *n.* сальмонелла *f.*
salon /sə'lɒn/ *n.* салон *m.*
saloon /sə'lun/ *n.* салун; бар *m.*
salt /sɔlt/ **1.** *adj.* солёный. **2.** *n.* соль *f.* **3.** *v.* солить *impf.*, посолить *pf.*
saltatory /'sæltə,tɔri/ *adj.* скачкообразный.
salted /'sɔltɪd/ *adj.* солёный.
salter /'sɔltər/ *n.* солевар *m.*
saltern /'sɔltərn/ *n.* солеварня *f.*
saltiness /'sɔltɪnɪs/ *n.* солёность *f.*
salting /'sɔltɪŋ/ *n.* засол *m.*
saltish /'sɔltɪʃ/ *adj.* солоноватый.
saltless /'sɔltlɪs/ *adj.* бессолевой.
salt lick *n.* лизунец *m.*
salt marsh *n.* соляное болото *neut.*
salt mine *n.* солекопь *f.*
salt pan *n.* варница *f.*
saltpeter /ˌsɔlt'pitər/ *n.* селитра *f.*
salt shaker / *n.* солонка *f.*
saltwater /'sɔlt,wɔtər/ *adj.* соляной; морской.
saltworks /'sɔlt,wɜrks/ *n.* солеварня *f.*
salty /'sɔlti/ *adj.* солёный.
salubrious /sə'lubriəs/ *adj.* здоровый; целебный.
salubrity /sə'lubrıti/ *n.* целебность *f.*
salutary /'sælyə,teri/ *adj.* полезный.
salutation /ˌsælyə'teifən/ *n.* приветствие *neut.*
salutatory /sə'lutə,tɔri/ *adj.* приветственный.
salute /sə'lut/ **1.** *n.* приветствие *neut.*; салют *m.* **2.** *v.* салютовать *impf.*
salvage /'sælvɪdʒ/ **1.** *n.* спасение; спасённое имущество *neut.* **2.** *v.* спасать *impf.*, спасти *pf.*
salvation /sæl'veifən/ *n.* спасение *neut.*; **Salvation Army** Армия спасения *f.*
salvational /sæl'veifənl/ *adj.* спасительный.
salve /sæv/ *n.* целебная мазь *f.*; бальзам *m.*
salver /'sælvər/ *n.* поднос *m.*
salvo /'sælvou/ *n.* (*mil.*) залп *m.*
Salzburg /'sɔlzbɜrg, 'zɑlts-/ *n.* Зальцбург *m.*
Samara /sə'mɑrə/ *n.* Самара *f.*
samarium /sə'mɛəriəm/ *n.* самарий *m.*
Samarqand /ˌsæmər'kænd/ *n.* Самарканд *m.*
samba /'sæmbə, 'sɑm-/ *n.* самба *f.*
same /seim/ **1.** *pron.* тот самый *m.*, та самая *f.*, то самое *neut.*, те самые *pl.* **2.** *adj.* одно и то же; тот же самый; (*identical*) одинаковый.
sameness /'seimnɪs/ *n.* (*identity*) тождество *neut.*; (*monotony*) однообразие *neut.*
samite /'sæmait/ *n.* парча *f.*
Samoa /sə'mouə/ *n.* Самоа *f.*
samovar /'sæmə,vɑr/ *n.* самовар *m.*
sample /'sæmpəl/ **1.** *n.* образец *m.*; проба *f.* **2.** *v.* пробовать *impf.*, попробовать *pf.*

sampler /'sæmplər/ *n.* образчик *m.*
samurai /'sæmʊ,rai/ *n.* самурай *m.*
sanative /'sænətıv/ *adj.* целебный; лечебный.
sanatorium /ˌsænə'tɔriəm/ *n.* санаторий *m.*
sanctification /ˌsæŋktəfɪ'keifən/ *n.* освящение *neut.*
sanctify /'sæŋktə,fai/ *v.* освящать *impf.*
sanctimonious /ˌsæŋktə'mouniəs/ *adj.* ханжеский.
sanctimony /'sæŋktə,mouni/ *n.* ханжество *neut.*
sanction /'sæŋkfən/ **1.** *n.* санкция *f.*; одобрение *neut.* **2.** *v.* санкционировать *impf.* and *pf.*
sanctity /'sæŋktɪti/ *n.* святость *f.*
sanctuary /'sæŋktfu,ɛri/ *n.* святилище; убежище *neut.*
sand /sænd/ **1.** *n.* песок *m.* **2.** *adj.* песочный; песчаный.
sandal /'sændl/ *n.* сандалия *f.*
sandalwood /'sændl,wʊd/ *n.* сандаловое дерево *neut.*, сандал *m.*
sandbag /'sænd,bæg/ *n.* балластный мешок; мешок с песком *m.*
sandbank /'sænd,bæŋk/ *n.* отмель *f.*
sandblasting /'sænd,blæstɪŋ/ *n.* пескоструйная очистка *f.*
sand-blind /'sænd,blaind/ *adj.* подслеповатый.
sandbox /'sænd,bɒks/ *n.* песочница *f.*
sand drift *n.* бархан *m.*
sand dune *n.* песчаная дюна *f.*
sandpaper /'sænd,peipər/ *n.* наждачная бумага; шкурка *f.*
sandpiper /'sænd,paipɛr/ *n.* кулик; перевозчик *m.*
sandpit /'sænd,pɪt/ *n.* песчаный карьер *m.*
sandstone /'sænd,stoun/ *n.* песчаник *m.*
sandstorm /'sænd,stɔrm/ *n.* самум *m.*; песчаная буря *f.*
sandwich /'sændwıtʃ/ *n.* сандвич, бутерброд *m.*
sandwich man *n.* человек-реклама *m.*
sandy /'sændi/ *adj.* песочный; песчаный.
sane /sein/ *adj.* нормальный; здравомыслящий.
San Francisco /ˌsæn frən'sıskou/ *n.* Сан-Франциско *m.*
sang-froid /sɑ̃ 'frwa/ *n.* хладнокровие *neut.*
sanguinary /'sæŋgwə,neri/ *adj.* кровавый.
sanguine /'sæŋgwin/ *adj.* оптимистический; румяный.
sanguineous /sæŋ'gwiniəs/ *adj.* кровяной.
sanitary /'sænı,teri/ *adj.* санитарный; гигиенический.
sanitary napkin *n.* гигиенический пакет *m.*
sanitation /ˌsænı'teifən/ *n.* санитария *f.*; (*sewer disposal*) канализация *f.*
sanity /'sænıti/ *n.* здравомыслие *neut.*
San Salvador /'sæn sælvə,dɔr/ *n.* Сан-Сальвадор *m.*
Sanskrit /'sænskrıt/ *n.* санскрит *m.*
Santa Claus /'sæntə ,klɔz/ дед-мороз *m.*
Santa Fe /'sæntə ,fei/ *n.* Санта-Фе *m.*
Santiago /ˌsænti'agou/ *n.* Сантьяго *m.*
Saône /soun/ *n.* (*river*) Сона *f.*
sap /sæp/ **1.** *n.* сок *m.* **2.** *v.* истощать *impf.*, истощить *pf.*
sapid /'sæpid/ *adj.* вкусный.
sapience /'seipiə ns/ *n.* мудрость *f.*
sapient /'seipiənt/ *adj.* премудрый.
sapless /'sæplıs/ *adj.* высохший;

sapling /'sæplɪŋ/ *n.* молодо́е де́рево; де́ревце *neut.*

saponification /sə,pɒnəfɪ'keiʃən/ *n.* омыле́ние *neut.*

saponify /sə'pɒnə,fai/ *v.* омыля́ться *impf.*

sapper /'sæpər/ *n.* сапёр *m.*

sapphire /'sæfaiᵊr/ **1.** *n.* сапфи́р *m.* **2.** *adj.* сапфи́рный.

sapphism /'sæfɪzəm/ *n.* сапфи́зм *m.*; лесби́янство *neut.*

sappiness /'sæpinɪs/ *n.* со́чность *f.*

Sapporo /sə'pɒrou/ *n.* Са́ппоро *m.*

sappy /'sæpi/ *adj.* со́чный.

sapwood /'sæp,wʊd/ *n.* забо́лонь; обо́лонь *f.*

saraband /'særə,bænd/ *n.* сараба́нда *f.*

Saragossa /,θɑrɑ'gɔθɑ, ,sɑrɑ'gɔsɑ/ *n.* (*Span.:* Zaragoza) Сараго́са *f.*

Saratov /sʌ'rɑtəf/ *n.* Сара́тов *m.*

sarcasm /'sɑrkæzəm/ *n.* сарка́зм *m.*

sarcastic /sɑr'kæstɪk/ *adj.* саркасти́ческий.

sarcoma /sɑr'koumə/ *n.* сарко́ма *f.*

sarcophagus /sɑr'kɒfəgəs/ *n.* саркофа́г *m.*

sardine /sɑr'din/ *n.* сарди́на *f.*

sardonic /sɑr'dɒnɪk/ *adj.* сардони́ческий.

sardonyx /sɑr'dɒnɪks/ *n.* сардони́кс *m.*

sargasso /sɑr'gæsou/ *n.* сарга́сса *f.*

sari /'sɑri/ *n.* са́ри *neut. indecl.*

sarsaparilla /,sæspə'rɪlə/ *n.* сарсапаре́ль *f.*

sartorial /sɑr'tɔriəl/ *adj.* портно́вский.

sash[1] /sæʃ/ *n.* (*belt*) куша́к *m.*; (*for medal*) ле́нта *f.*

sash[2] /sæʃ/ *n.* (*window*) око́нная ра́ма *f.*

Saskatchewan /sæ'skætʃə,wɒn, -wən/ *n.* Саска́чеван *m.*

Satan /'seitn̩/ *n.* Сатана́ *m.* (*decl. f.*).

satanic /sə'tænɪk, sei-/ *adj.* сатани́нский.

satchel /'sætʃəl/ *n.* ра́нец *m.*

sate /seit/ *v.* насыща́ть *impf.*

satellite /'sætl̩,ait/ *n.* сателли́т; спу́тник *m.*

satiate /'seiʃi,eit/ *v.* насыща́ть *impf.*

satiation /,seiʃi'eiʃən/ *n.* насыще́ние *neut.*

satiety /sə'taiiti/ *n.* пресыще́ние *neut.*

satin /'sætn̩/ **1.** *n.* а́тлас *m.* **2.** *adj.* атла́сный.

satinet /,sætn̩'et/ *n.* сатине́т *m.*

satinwood /'sætn̩,wʊd/ *n.* атла́сное де́рево *neut.*

satire /'sætaiᵊr/ *n.* сати́ра *f.*

satirical /sə'tɪrɪkəl/ *adj.* сатири́ческий.

satirist /'sætərɪst/ *n.* сати́рик *m.*

satirize /'sætə,raiz/ *v.* высме́ивать *impf.*

satisfaction /,sætɪs'fækʃən/ *n.* удовлетворе́ние *neut.*

satisfactory /,sætɪs'fæktəri/ *adj.* удовлетвори́тельный.

satisfied /'sætɪs,faid/ *adj.* дово́льный (*with instr.*).

satisfy /'sætɪs,fai/ *v.* удовлетворя́ть *impf.*, удовлетвори́ть *pf.*

satisfying /'sætɪs,faiɪŋ/ *adj.* удовлетворя́ющий.

satrap /'seitræp, 'sæ-/ *n.* сатра́п *m.*

saturant /'sætʃərənt/ *adj.* насыща́ющий.

saturate /'sætʃə,reit/ *v.* насыща́ть *impf.*, насы́тить *pf.*

saturation /,sætʃə'reiʃən/ *n.* пропи́тывание; насыще́ние *neut.*

Saturday /'sætər,dei/ **1.** *n.* суббо́та *f.* **2.** *adj.* суббо́тний.

saturnine /'sætər,nain/ *adj.* угрю́мый; мра́чный.

saturnism /'sætər,nɪzəm/ *n.* сатурни́зм *m.*

satyr /'seitər/ *n.* сати́р; развра́тник *m.*

sauce /sɔs/ *n.* со́ус *m.*

sauceboat /'sɔs,bout/ *n.* со́усник *m.*

saucepan /'sɔs,pæn/ *n.* кастрю́ля *f.*

saucer /'sɔsər/ *n.* блю́дце *neut.*

saucy /'sɔsi/ *adj.* де́рзкий.

Saudi Arabia /'saudi ə'reibiə, 'sɔdi/ *n.* Сау́довская Ара́вия *f.*

sauerkraut /'sauᵊr,kraut/ *n.* ква́шеная капу́ста *f.*

sauna /'sɔnə/ *n.* фи́нская ба́ня; са́уна *f.*

saunter /'sɔntər/ *v.* прогу́ливаться *impf.*

saurian /'sɔriən/ *n.* я́щер *m.*

sausage /'sɔsidʒ/ *n.* колбаса́ *f.*

sauté /sou'tei, sɔ-/ *n.* соте́ *neut. indecl.*

savage /'sævidʒ/ **1.** *adj.* ди́кий; свире́пый. **2.** *n.* дика́рь *m.*

savagery /'sævidʒri/ *n.* ва́рварство *neut.*

savanna /sə'vænə/ *n.* сава́нна *f.*

savant /sæ'vɑnt/ *n.* учёный *m.*

save /seiv/ **1.** *v.* спаса́ть *impf.*, спасти́ *pf.*; бере́чь *impf.* **2.** *prep.* за исключе́нием *neut.*

savings /'seivɪŋz/ *n.* сбереже́ния *pl.*

savings bank *n.* сберега́тельная ка́сса, сберка́сса *f.*

savior /'seivyər/ *n.* спаси́тель *m.*

savor /'seivər/ *n.* вкус *m.*; (*slight taste*) при́вкус *m.*

savory /'seivəri/ *n.* (*herb*) чабре́ц *m.*

Savoy cabbage /sə'vɔi/ *n.* саво́йская капу́ста *f.*

savvy /'sævi/ *v.* смека́ть *impf.*

saw /sɔ/ **1.** *n.* пила́ *f.* **2.** *v.* пили́ть *impf.*

sawdust /'sɔ,dʌst/ *n.* опи́лки *pl.*

sawfish /'sɔ,fiʃ/ *n.* ры́ба-пила́ *f.*

sawfly /'sɔ,flai/ *n.* пили́льщик *m.*

sawhorse /'sɔ,hɔrs/ *n.* ко́злы для распи́лки *pl.*

sawing /'sɔɪŋ/ *n.* пиле́ние *neut.*

sawmill /'sɔ,mil/ *n.* лесопи́льный заво́д *m.*; лесопи́лка *f.*

sawyer /'sɔyər/ *n.* пи́льщик *m.*

saxifrage /'sæksəfridʒ/ *n.* камнело́мка *f.*

saxophone /'sæksə,foun/ *n.* саксофо́н *m.*

saxophonist /'sæksə,founɪst/ *n.* саксофони́ст *m.*

say /sei/ *v.* говори́ть *impf.*, сказа́ть *pf.*

saying /'seiɪŋ/ *n.* погово́рка *f.*

scab /skæb/ *n.* (*on wound*) струп *m.*; коро́ста ко́рка *f.*; (*slang*) (*strikebreaker*) штрейкбре́хер *m.*

scabbard /'skæbərd/ *n.* но́жны *pl.*

scabbed /'skæbɪd, skæbd/ *adj.* в стру́пьях.

scabby /'skæbi/ *adj.* парши́вый.

scabies /'skeibiz/ *n.* чесо́тка *f.*

scabrous /'skæbrəs/ *adj.* (*indecent*) скабрёзный.

scaffold /'skæfəld/ *n.* (*for execution*) эшафо́т *m.*

scaffolding /'skæfəldɪŋ/ *n.* строи́тельные леса́ *pl.*

scalar /'skeilər/ *n.* скаля́р *m.*

scald /skɔld/ *v.* ошпа́ривать *impf.*, ошпа́рить *pf.*

scalding /'skɔldɪŋ/ *adj.* ошпа́ривающий.

scale[1] /skeil/ **1.** *n.* (*system of measurement*) шкала́ *f.*; ле́стница *f.*; масшта́б *m.*; (*mus.*) га́мма *f.*; **on a large scale** в большо́м масшта́бе. **2.** *v.* поднима́ться *impf.* по́дняться *pf.*

scale[2] /skeil/ *n.* (*of fish*) чешуя́ *f.*

scale[3] /skeil/ *n. pl.* (*for weighing*) весы́ *pl.*

scaler /'skeilər/ *n.* очисти́тель *m.*

scaliness /'skeilinɪs/ *n.* чешу́йчатость *f.*

scallion /'skælyən/ *n.* зелёный лук *m.*

scallop /'skɒləp, 'skæl-/ *n.* (*shell*) створчатая ра́ковина *f.*; (*mollusk*) гребешо́к *m.*; (*pattern*) фесто́н *m.*

scalloped /'skɒləpt, 'skæl-/ *adj.* фесто́нчатый.

scalp /skælp/ **1.** *n.* ко́жа на голове́ *f.*; скальп *m.* **2.** *v.* скальпи́ровать *impf. and pf.*

scalpel /'skælpəl/ *n.* ска́льпель *m.*

scaly /'skeili/ *adj.* чешу́йчатый.

scamp /skæmp/ *v.* халту́рить *impf.*

scampi /'skæmpi/ *n.* креве́тка *f.*

scan /skæn/ *v.* сканди́ровать(ся) *impf.*

scandal /'skændl/ *n.* позо́р; сканда́л *m.*

scandalize /'skændl,aiz/ *v.* возмуща́ть; шоки́ровать *impf. and pf.*

scandalous /'skændləs/ *adj.* позо́рный; сканда́льный; возмути́тельный.

scandium /'skændiəm/ *n.* ска́ндий *m.*

scanner /'skænər/ *n.* развёртывающее устро́йство *neut.*; (*comput.*) ска́нер *m.*; **hand-held scanner** *n.* ручно́й ска́нер *m.*

scanning /'skænɪŋ/ *n.* скани́рование *neut.*

scansion /'skænʃən/ *n.* сканди́рование *neut.*

scant /skænt/ *adj.* ску́дный.

scantiness /skæntinɪs/ *n.* ску́дость *f.*

scanty /'skænti/ *adj.* ску́дный.

scapegoat /'skeip,gout/ *n.* козёл отпуще́ния *m.*

scapegrace /'skeip,greis/ *n.* пове́са *m.* (*decl. f.*).

scapula /'skæpyələ/ *n.* лопа́тка *f.*

scar /skɑr/ **1.** *n.* шрам; рубе́ц *m.* **2.** *v.* обезобра́живать *impf.*

scarab /'skærəb/ *n.* скарабе́й *m.*

scarce /skɛərs/ *adj.* ску́дный; ре́дкий; недоста́точный.

scarcely /'skɛərsli/ *adv.* едва́; едва́ ли.

scarcity /'skɛərsiti/ *n.* недоста́ток *m.*; нехва́тка *f.*; дефици́т *m.*

scare /skɛər/ *v.* пуга́ть(ся) *impf.*, испуга́ть(ся) *pf.*

scarecrow /'skɛər,krou/ *n.* пу́гало; чу́чело *neut.*

scaremonger /'skɛər,mʌŋgər/ *n.* паникёр *m.*

scarf /skɑrf/ *n.* шарф *m.*

scarlet /'skɑrlɪt/ **1.** *adj.* а́лый. **2.** *n.* а́лый цвет *m.*

scarlet fever *n.* скарлати́на *f.*

scathing /'skeiðɪŋ/ *adj.* е́дкий.

scatological /,skætl'ɒdʒɪkəl/ *adj.* непристо́йный.

scatter /'skætər/ *v.* разбра́сывать *impf.*, разброса́ть *pf.*; рассе́ивать(ся) *impf.*, рассе́ять(ся) *pf.*

scatterbrain /'skætər,brein/ *n.* вертопра́х *m.*

scatterbrained /'skætər,breind/ *adj.* легкомы́сленный; рассе́янный.

scattered /'skætərd/ *adj.* разбро́санный.

scattering /'skætərɪŋ/ *n.* рассе́яние *neut.*

scavenge /'skævɪndʒ/ *v.* ры́ться в му́соре *impf.*

scavenger /'skævɪndʒər/ *n.* (*biol.*) па́дальщик *m.*

scenario /sɪ'nɛəri,ou, -'nɑr-/ *n.* сцена́рий *m.*

scene /sin/ *n.* сце́на *f.*; ме́сто де́йствия *neut.*; **behind the scenes** за кули́сами.

scenery /'sinəri/ *n.* пейза́ж *m.*; (*theat.*) декора́ции *pl.*

scenic /'sinɪk/ *adj.* живопи́сный.

scent /sɛnt/ **1.** *n.* за́пах *m.*; (*perfume*) духи́ *pl.*; (*sense*) чутьё *neut.*; нюх *m.*; (*trail*) след *m.* **2.** *v.* чу́ять *impf.*, почу́ять *pf.*

scented /'sɛntɪd/ *adj.* наду́шенный.

scepter /'sɛptər/ *n.* ски́петр *m.*

schedule /'skɛdʒul/ *n.* расписа́ние *neut.*

scheduled /'skɛdʒuld/ *adj.* заплани́рованный; (*regular, of trip*) ре́йсовый.

schema /'skimə/ *n.* схе́ма *f.*

scheme /skim/ **1.** *n.* план; прое́кт *m.*; (*intrigue*) махина́ция *f.* **2.** *v.* замышля́ть *impf.*, замы́слить *pf.*

schemer /'skimər/ *n.* интрига́н; прожектёр *m.*

scherzo /'skɛrtsou/ *n.* ске́рцо *neut.*

schism /'sɪzəm, 'skɪz-/ *n.* раско́л *m.*

schismatic /sɪz'mætɪk, skɪz-/ *n.* раско́льник *m.*

schist /ʃɪst/ *n.* сла́нец *m.*

schizoid /'skɪtsɔid/ *n.* шизо́ид *m.*

schizophrenia /,skɪtsə'friniə/ *n.* шизофрени́я *f.*

schizophrenic /,skɪtsə'frɛnɪk/ *n.* шизофре́ник *m.*

scholar /'skɒlər/ *n.* учёный *m.*

scholarly /'skɒlərli/ *adj.* учёный; нау́чный.

scholarship /'skɒlər,ʃɪp/ *n.* (*stipend*) стипе́ндия *f.*; (*knowledge*) учёность *f.*

scholastic /skə'læstɪk/ *adj.* уче́бный.

scholasticism /skə'læstə,sɪzəm/ *n.* схола́стика *f.*

scholiast /'skouli,æst/ *n.* схолиа́ст *m.*

school[1] /skul/ **1.** *n.* шко́ла *f.*; учи́лище *neut.* **2.** *adj.* шко́льный; уче́бный. **3.** *v.* шко́лить *impf.*

school[2] /skul/ *n.* (*fish*) кося́к *m.*

schoolbook /'skul,bʊk/ *n.* уче́бник *m.*

schoolboy /'skul,bɔi/ *n.* шко́льник *m.*

schoolgirl /'skul,gɜrl/ *n.* шко́льница *f.*

schooling /'skulɪŋ/ *n.* образова́ние *neut.*

schoolman /'skulmən/ *n.* схола́ст *m.*

schoolmaster /'skul,mæstər/ *n.* дире́ктор шко́лы *m.*

schoolmate /'skul,meit/ *n.* однокла́ссник *m.*

schoolteacher /'skul,titʃər/ *n.* учи́тель *m.*, учи́тельница *f.*

schooner /'skunər/ *n.* шху́на *f.*

sciatic /sai'ætɪk/ *adj.* седа́лищный.

sciatica /sai'ætɪkə/ *n.* ишиа́с *m.*

science /'saiəns/ *n.* нау́ка *f.*

science fiction *n.* (нау́чная) фанта́стика *f.*

scientific /,saiən'tɪfɪk/ *adj.* нау́чный.

scientist /'saiəntɪst/ *n.* учёный *m.*

scimitar /'sɪmɪtər/ *n.* ятага́н *m.*

scintillate /'sɪntl,eit/ *v.* искри́ться; блесте́ть; сверка́ть *impf.*

scintillation /,sɪntl'eiʃən/ *n.* мерца́ние *neut.*

scion /'saiən/ *n.* о́тпрыск; пото́мок *m.*

scissors /'sɪzərz/ *n.* но́жницы *pl.*

sclerosis /sklɪ'rousɪs/ *n.* склеро́з *m.*

sclerotic /sklɪ'rɒtɪk/ *adj.* склероти́ческий.

scoff[1] /skɒf/ **1.** *n.* (*jeer*) насме́шка *f.* **2.** *v.* (*jeer*) издева́ться *impf.*

scoff[2] /skɒf/ *n.* (*slang*) жратва́ *f.*

scold /skould/ *v.* брани́ть *impf.*

scone /skoun/ *n.* лепёшка *f.*

scoop /skup/ **1.** *n.* сово́к *m.*; (*ladle*) ко́вшик; черпа́к *m.* **2.** *v.* (*ladle*) черпа́ть *impf.*

scoot /skut/ *v.* (*colloq.*) бежа́ть *impf.*; (*run away*) смыва́ться; удира́ть *impf.*

scooter /'skutər/ *n.* (*child's*) самока́т *m.*; **motor scooter** *n.* моторо́ллер *m.*

scope /skoup/ *n.* разма́х *m.*; (*outlook*) кругозо́р *m.*

scorbutic /skɔr'byutɪk/ *adj.* цинго́тный.

scorch /skɔrtʃ/ *v.* подпа́ливать; пали́ть *impf.*

scorching /'skɔrtʃɪŋ/ *adj.* паля́щий.

score /skɔr/ **1.** *n.* ито́г; счёт *m.*; (*mus.*) партиту́ра *f.*; **by a score of** со счётом. **2.** *v.* получа́ть (очки́) *impf.*; (*mus.*) оркестрова́ть *impf.* and *pf.*

scoreboard /ˈskɔrˌbɔrd/ *n.* табло́ *neut. indecl.*

scorn /skɔrn/ **1.** *n.* презре́ние *neut.* **2.** *v.* презира́ть *impf.*

scornful /ˈskɔrnfəl/ *adj.* презри́тельный.

scorpion /ˈskɔrpiən/ *n.* скорпио́н *m.*

Scot /skɒt/ *n.* шотла́ндец *m.*, шотла́ндка *f.*

Scotch /skɒtʃ/ **1.** *adj.* шотла́ндский. **2.** *n.* (*whiskey*) шотла́ндское ви́ски *neut.*

Scotch tape *n.* скотч *m.*

scot-free /ˈskɒt ˈfri/ *adj.* ненака́занный.

Scotland /ˈskɒtlənd/ *n.* Шотла́ндия *f.*

Scottish /ˈskɒtɪʃ/ *adj.* шотла́ндский.

scoundrel /ˈskaundrəl/ *n.* негодя́й; подле́ц *m.*

scoundrelly /ˈskaundrəli/ *adj.* по́длый.

scour /skauᵊr/ *v.* чи́стить *impf.*, почи́стить *pf.*

scourer /ˈskauᵊrər/ *n.* очисти́тель *m.*

scourge /skɜrdʒ/ *n.* бич *m.*; плеть *f.*; кнут *m.*

scouring /ˈskauᵊrɪŋ/ *n.* чи́стка *f.*

scout /skaut/ **1.** *n.* разве́дчик *m.*; (*boy scout*) бойска́ут *m.* **2.** *v.* производи́ть разве́дку *impf.*

scouting /ˈskautɪŋ/ *n.* разве́дка *f.*

scow /skau/ *n.* шала́нда *f.*

scowl /skaul/ *n.* хму́рый вид; серди́тый взгляд *m.*

scrabble /ˈskræbəl/ *v.* цара́пать *impf.*

scrag /skræg/ *n.* бара́нья шея́ *f.*

scram /skræm/ *v.* (*slang*) смыва́ться; удира́ть *impf.*

scrambled eggs /ˈskræmbəld/ *pl.* яи́чница-болту́нья *f.*

scrap[1] /skræp/ **1.** *n.* клочо́к; скрап *m.* **2.** *v.* отдава́ть на слом *impf.*

scrap[2] /skræp/ *n.* (*colloq.*) (*fight*) дра́ка *f.*

scrapbook /ˈskræpˌbʊk/ *n.* альбо́м (для вы́резок) *m.*

scrape /skreip/ **1.** *n.* скрип *m.*; ша́рканье *neut.*; (*cleaning*) скобле́ние *neut.* **2.** *v.* скрести́(сь) *impf.*

scraper /ˈskreipər/ *n.* (*tool*) скребо́к; ша́бер *m.*

scrap heap *n.* сва́лка *f.*

scrappy /ˈskræpi/ *adj.* (*fragmentary*) разро́зненный.

scratch /skrætʃ/ **1.** *n.* цара́пина *f.* **2.** *v.* цара́пать *impf.*, цара́пнуть *pf.*

scratchy /ˈskrætʃi/ *adj.* скрипу́чий.

scrawl /skrɔl/ *n.* неразбо́рчивый по́черк *m.*; кара́кули *pl.*

scrawny /ˈskrɔni/ *adj.* костля́вый; сухопа́рый.

scream /skrim/ **1.** *n.* вопль; крик *m.* **2.** *v.* вопи́ть; крича́ть *impf.*, кри́кнуть *pf.*

scree /skri/ *n.* каме́нистая о́сыпь *f.*

screech /skritʃ/ *n.* визг *m.*

screech owl *n.* со́вка *f.*

screen /skrin/ *n.* за́веса *f.*; засло́н *m.*; (*movie*) экра́н *m.*

screenplay /ˈskrinˌplei/ *n.* киносцена́рий *m.*

screen-test /ˈskrin ˌtɛst/ *n.* кинопро́ба *f.*

screenwriter /ˈskrinˌraitər/ *n.* киносценари́ст *m.*

screw /skru/ **1.** *n.* винт *m.* **2.** *v.* приви́нчивать *impf.*, привинти́ть *pf.*

screwball /ˈskruˌbɔl/ *n.* (*slang*) псих *m.*

screw cutter *n.* винторе́зный стано́к *m.*

screwdriver /ˈskruˌdraivər/ *n.* отвёртка *f.*

screwed /skrud/ *adj.* винтово́й; с резьбо́й.

screw top *n.* нави́нчивающаяся кры́шка *f.*

screwy /ˈskrui/ *adj.* (*slang*) ненорма́льный.

scribble /ˈskrɪbəl/ *v.* небре́жно *or* неразбо́рчиво писа́ть *impf.*

scribe /skraib/ *n.* (*copyist*) писе́ц; перепи́счик *m.*

scrim /skrɪm/ *n.* холст *m.*

scrimmage /ˈskrɪmɪdʒ/ *n.* сва́лка *f.*

scrip /skrɪp/ *n.* облига́ция *f.*

script /skrɪpt/ *n.* (*cursive*) курси́в *m.*; (*text*) текст *m.*; (*scenario*) сцена́рий *m.*; (*manuscript*) ру́копись *f.*

scriptural /ˈskrɪptʃərəl/ *adj.* библе́йский.

Scripture /ˈskrɪptʃər/ *n.* Свяще́нное Писа́ние *neut.*

scriptwriter /ˈskrɪptˌraitər/ *n.* (ки́но)сценари́ст *m.*

scrofula /ˈskrɒfyələ/ *n.* золоту́ха *f.*

scroll /skroul/ *n.* (*manuscript*) сви́ток *m.*

scrooge /skrudʒ/ *n.* скря́га *m.* and *f.* (*decl. f.*).

scrotum /ˈskroutəm/ *n.* мошо́нка *f.*

scrounge /skraundʒ/ *v.* тунея́дствовать *impf.*

scrounger /ˈskraundʒər/ *n.* тунея́дец *m.*

scrub /skrʌb/ *v.* тере́ть *impf.*

scrubbing brush /ˈskrʌbɪŋ/ *n.* жёсткая щётка *f.*

scrubby /ˈskrʌbi/ *adj.* низкоро́слый.

scruff /skrʌf/ *n.* загри́вок *m.*

scruffy /ˈskrʌfi/ *adj.* неря́шливый; обтрёпанный.

scrumptious /ˈskrʌmpʃəs/ *adj.* очень вку́сный.

scruple /ˈskrupəl/ *n.* угрызе́ние со́вести *neut.*; (*hesitation*) колеба́ние *neut.*

scrupulosity /ˌskrupyəˈlɒsɪti/ *n.* скрупулёзность *f.*

scrupulous /ˈskrupyələs/ *adj.* совестли́вый; скрупулёзный.

scrutinize /ˈskrutnˌaiz/ *v.* рассма́тривать; проверя́ть *impf.*

scrutiny /ˈskrutni/ *n.* рассма́тривание *neut.*

scuba diver /ˈskubə/ *n.* акваланги́ст *m.*

scud /skʌd/ *n.* (*clouds*) рва́ные облака́ *pl.*

scuff /skʌf/ *v.* ша́ркать *impf.*

scuffle /ˈskʌfəl/ *n.* дра́ка; схва́тка *f.*

scullery /ˈskʌləri/ *n.* судомо́йня *f.*

sculpt /skʌlpt/ *v.* вая́ть *impf.*

sculptor /ˈskʌlptər/ *also* **sculptress** *n.* ску́льптор *m.*

sculpture /ˈskʌlptʃər/ **1.** *n.* скульпту́ра *f.*; вая́ние *neut.* **2.** *v.* вая́ть *impf.*, извая́ть *pf.*

scum /skʌm/ *n.* (*froth*) пе́на *f.*; (*deposit on surface*) на́кипь *f.*

scurf /skɜrf/ *n.* пе́рхоть *f.*

scurfy /ˈskɜrfi/ *adj.* покры́тый пе́рхотью.

scurrility /skəˈrɪlɪti/ *n.* непристо́йность *f.*

scurrilous /ˈskɜrələs/ *adj.* гру́бый; (*indecent*) непристо́йный.

scurry /ˈskɜri/ *v.* спеши́ть; снова́ть; суетли́во бежа́ть *impf.*

scurvy /ˈskɜrvi/ *n.* цинга́ *f.*

scutch /skʌtʃ/ *v.* трепа́ть *impf.*

scutcher /ˈskʌtʃər/ *n.* трепа́лка *f.*

scythe /saið/ *n.* коса́ *f.*

sea /si/ **1.** *n.* мо́ре *neut.*; **by sea** морски́м путём. **2.** *adj.* морско́й.

sea anchor *n.* плаву́чий я́корь *m.*

sea anemone *n.* акти́ния *f.*

seabird /ˈsiˌbɜrd/ *n.* морска́я пти́ца *f.*

seaboard /ˈsiˌbɔrd/ *n.* бе́рег мо́ря *m.*

seaborne /ˈsiˌbɔrn/ *adj.* морско́й.

sea breeze *n.* морско́й бриз *m.*

sea captain *n.* капита́н да́льнего пла́вания *m.*
seacoast /'si,koust/ *n.* побере́жье *neut.*
sea cow *n.* (*manatee*) ламанти́н *m.*
sea dog *n.* морско́й волк *m.*
sea eagle *n.* орла́н-белохво́ст *m.*
seafarer /'si,fɛərər/ *n.* морепла́ватель *m.*
seafaring /'si,fɛərɪŋ/ *adj.* морепла́вательный.
sea front *n.* примо́рский бульва́р *m.*
seagirt /'si,gɜrt/ *adj.* окружённый мо́рем.
seagoing /'si,gouɪŋ/ *adj.* да́льнего пла́вания.
sea gull *n.* ча́йка *f.*
seal¹ /sil/ **1.** *n.* печа́ть *f.* **2.** *v.* запеча́тывать *impf.*, запеча́тать *pf.*
seal² /sil/ *n.* (*animal*) тюле́нь *m.*
sea level *n.* у́ровень мо́ря *m.*
sealing /'silɪŋ/ *n.* охо́та на тюле́ней *f.*
sealing wax *n.* сургу́ч *m.*
sea lion *n.* морско́й лев *m.*
seal ring *n.* пе́рстень-печа́тка *m.*
sealskin /'sil,skɪn/ *n.* ко́тиковый мех *m.*
seam /sim/ *n.* шов *m.*
seaman /'simən/ *n.* моря́к *m.*
seamanship /'simən,ʃɪp/ *n.* иску́сство морепла́вания *neut.*
seamark /'si,mark/ *n.* навигацио́нный знак *m.*
sea mile *n.* морска́я ми́ля *f.*
seamless /'simlɪs/ *adj.* бесшо́вный; без шва.
sea monster *n.* морско́е чудо́вище *neut.*
seamstress /'simstrɪs/ *n.* швея́; белошве́йка *f.*
seamy /'simi/ *adj.* подозри́тельный; тёмный.
séance /'seians/ *n.* сеа́нс *m.*
seaplane /'si,plein/ *n.* гидросамолёт *m.*
seaport /'si,pɔrt/ *n.* морско́й порт *m.*
sea power *n.* морска́я держа́ва *f.*
sear /sɪər/ *v.* обжига́ть *impf.*; (*brand*) прижига́ть *impf.*
search /sɜrtʃ/ **1.** *n.* по́иски *pl.* **2.** *v.* иска́ть *impf.*
searcher /'sɜrtʃər/ *n.* иска́тель *m.*
searching /'sɜrtʃɪŋ/ *adj.* испыту́ющий.
searchlight /'sɜrtʃ,lait/ *n.* прожёктор *m.*
search party *n.* поиско́вая гру́ппа *f.*
search warrant *n.* о́рдер на о́быск *m.*
sea salt *n.* морска́я соль *f.*
seascape /'si,skeip/ *n.* мари́на *f.*
sea serpent *n.* морско́й змей *m.*
seashell /'si,ʃɛl/ *n.* морска́я раку́шка *f.*
seashore /'si,ʃɔr/ *n.* побере́жье *neut.*
seasick /'si,sɪk/ *adj.* страда́ющий от морско́й боле́зни.
seasickness /'si,sɪknɪs/ *n.* морска́я боле́знь *f.*
seaside /'si,said/ *adj.* примо́рский.
season /'sizən/ **1.** *n.* вре́мя го́да *neut.*; сезо́н *m.* **2.** *v.* (*flavor*) приправля́ть *impf.*, припра́вить *pf.*
seasonal /'sizənl̩/ *adj.* сезо́нный.
seasoned /'sizənd/ *adj.* вы́держанный.
seasoning /'sizənɪŋ/ *n.* (*spice*) припра́ва *f.*
season ticket *n.* абонеме́нт; проездно́й биле́т *m.*
seat /sit/ **1.** *n.* стул *m.*, ме́сто *neut.*; сиде́нье *neut.* **2.** *v.* уса́живать *impf.*, усади́ть *pf.*; **to be seated** сади́ться; уса́живаться *impf.*, усе́сться *pf.*
seat belt *n.* ремёнь безопа́сности *m.*
seating /'sitɪŋ/ *n.* расса́живание *neut.*
sea trout *n.* кумжа́ *f.*; лосо́сь-таймéнь *m.*
sea urchin *n.* морско́й ёж *m.*
seaway /'si,wei/ *n.* (*channel*) фарва́тер *m.*
seaweed /'si,wid/ *n.* морска́я во́доросль *f.*

seaworthiness /'si,wɜrðinɪs/ *n.* мореходность *f.*
seaworthy /'si,wɜrði/ *adj.* морехо́дный.
sebaceous /sɪ'beiʃəs/ *adj.* са́льный.
secant /'sikænt/ *n.* се́канс *m.*
secede /sɪ'sid/ *v.* отделя́ться *impf.*
secession /sɪ'sɛʃən/ *n.* отделе́ние *neut.*
seclude /sɪ'klud/ *v.* держа́ть в уедине́нии *or* изоля́ции *impf.*; (*isolate from*) изоли́ровать *impf.* and *pf.*
secluded /sɪ'kludɪd/ *adj.* уединённый.
seclusion /sɪ'kluʒən/ *n.* уедине́ние *neut.*
second¹ /'sɛkənd/ **1.** *adj.* второ́й. **2.** *n.* (*supporter*) помо́щник; секунда́нт *m.*
second² /'sɛkənd/ *n.* (*time*) секу́нда *f.*
secondary /'sɛkən,dɛri/ *adj.* второстепе́нный; втори́чный.
second-class /'sɛkənd 'klæs/ *adj.* второкла́ссный; второсо́ртный.
secondhand /'sɛkənd'hænd/ *adj.* поде́ржанный.
secondly /'sɛkəndli/ *adv.* во-вторы́х.
second-rate /'sɛkənd 'reit/ *adj.* второсо́ртный.
secrecy /'sikrəsi/ *n.* секре́тность *f.*
secret /'sikrɪt/ **1.** *n.* та́йна *f.*; секре́т *m.* **2.** *adj.* та́йный; секре́тный.
secretarial /,sɛkrɪ'tɛəriəl/ *adj.* секрета́рский.
secretariat /,sɛkrɪ'tɛəriət/ *n.* секретариа́т *m.*
secretary /'sɛkrɪ,tɛri/ *n.* секрета́рь *m.*, секрета́рша *f.*
secretary bird *n.* секрета́рь *m.*
secrete¹ /sɪ'krit/ *v.* (*physiol.*) выделя́ть *impf.*
secrete² /sɪ'krit/ *v.* (*hide*) укрыва́ть *impf.*
secretion /sɪ'kriʃən/ *n.* секре́ция *f.*; выделе́ние *neut.*
secretive /'sikrɪtɪv/ *adj.* скры́тный.
sect /sɛkt/ *n.* се́кта *f.*
sectarian /sɛk'tɛəriən/ **1.** *n.* секта́нт *m.* **2.** *adj.* секта́нтский.
sectarianism /sɛk'tɛəriə,nɪzəm/ *n.* секта́нтство *neut.*
section /'sɛkʃən/ *n.* се́кция *f.*; отде́л *m.*
sectional /'sɛkʃənl̩/ *adj.* секцио́нный.
sector /'sɛktər/ *n.* се́ктор *m.*
secular /'sɛkyələr/ *adj.* мирско́й; све́тский.
secularism /'sɛkyələ,rɪzəm/ *n.* секуляри́зм *m.*
secularization /,sɛkyələrə'zeiʃən/ *n.* секуляриза́ция *f.*
secularize /'sɛkyələ,raiz/ *v.* секуляризова́ть *impf.* and *pf.*
secure /sɪ'kyʊr/ **1.** *adj.* безопа́сный; надёжный; уве́ренный. **2.** *v.* (*ensure*) обеспе́чивать *impf.*, обеспе́чить *pf.*; (*get*) достава́ть *impf.*, доста́ть *pf.*
security /sɪ'kyʊrɪti/ *n.* безопа́сность *f.*; (*pledge*) зало́г *m.*
sedan chair *n.* портше́з *m.*
sedate /sɪ'deit/ *adj.* степе́нный.
sedation /sɪ'deiʃən/ *n.* успокое́ние *neut.*
sedative /'sɛdətɪv/ **1.** *adj.* успока́ивающий. **2.** *n.* успока́ивающее сре́дство *neut.*
sedentary /'sɛdn̩,tɛri/ *adj.* сидя́чий.
sedge /sɛdʒ/ *n.* осо́ка *f.*
sediment /'sɛdəmənt/ *n.* оса́док *m.*
sedimentary /,sɛdə'mɛntəri/ *adj.* оса́дочный.
seduce /sɪ'dus/ *v.* соблазня́ть *impf.*, соблазни́ть *pf.*
seducer /sɪ'dusər/ *n.* соблазни́тель; соврати́тель *m.*

seductive /sɪ'dʌktɪv/ adj. соблазни́тельный; обольсти́тельный.
seductress /sɪ'dʌktrɪs/ n. соблазни́тельница f.
sedulous /'sɛdʒələs/ adj. усе́рдный.
see /si/ v. ви́деть impf.; (watch) смотре́ть impf.; **to see off** провожа́ть impf., проводи́ть pf.
seed /sid/ **1.** n. се́мя; зерно́ neut. **2.** v. (sow) се́ять impf., посе́ять pf.
seedbed /'sid,bɛd/ n. расса́дник m.
seedcake /'sid,keik/ n. кекс с тми́ном m.
seed corn n. посевно́е зерно́ neut.
seedless /'sidlɪs/ adj. бессемя́нный.
seedling /'sidlɪŋ/ n. се́янец m.
seed pearl n. ме́лкий же́мчуг m.
seedy /'sidi/ adj. (clothes) потрёпанный; поно́шенный.
Seeing Eye dog /'siɪŋ/ n. соба́ка-поводы́рь f.
seek /sik/ v. иска́ть impf.
seeker /'sikər/ n. иска́тель m.
seem /sim/ v. каза́ться impf.
seeming /'simɪŋ/ adj. ви́димый; ка́жущийся.
seemingly /'simɪŋli/ adv. по-ви́димому.
seemly /'simli/ adj. прили́чный.
seep /sip/ v. (leak) течь; протека́ть impf.; (leak out) проса́чиваться impf.
seepage /'sipɪdʒ/ n. проса́чивание neut.
seer /'siər/ n. проро́к; прови́дец m.
seesaw /'si,sɔ/ n. (де́тские) каче́ли pl.
seethe /sið/ v. кипе́ть; бурли́ть impf.
segment /'sɛgmənt/ n. отре́зок m.; (math) сегме́нт m.
segmental /sɛg'mɛntl/ adj. сегме́нтный.
segmentation /,sɛgmən'teiʃən/ n. сегмента́ция f.
segregate /'sɛgrɪ,geit/ v. отделя́ть impf., отдели́ть pf.
segregation /,sɛgrɪ'geiʃən/ n. сегрега́ция f.; разделе́ние neut.
Seine /sein/ (river) n. Се́на f.
seiner /'seinər/ n. се́йнер m.
seismic /'saizmɪk/ adj. сейсми́ческий.
seismograph /'saizmə,græf/ n. сейсмо́граф m.
seismology /saiz'mɒlədʒi/ n. сейсмоло́гия f.
seismometer /saiz'mɒmɪtər/ n. сейсмо́метр m.
seize /siz/ v. хвата́ть impf., схвати́ть pf.
seizure /'siʒər/ n. захва́т m.; конфиска́ция f.; (attack, also med.) припа́док; при́ступ m.
seldom /'sɛldəm/ adv. ре́дко.
select /sɪ'lɛkt/ **1.** adj. отбо́рный. **2.** v. выбира́ть impf., вы́брать pf.
selection /sɪ'lɛkʃən/ n. вы́бор m.; (biol.) отбо́р m.
selective /sɪ'lɛktɪv/ adj. разбо́рчивый.
selectivity /sɪlɛk'tɪvɪti/ n. избира́тельность f.
selector /sɪ'lɛktər/ n. переключа́тель m.
selenium /sɪ'liniəm/ n. селе́н m.
selenology /,sɛlə'nɒlədʒi/ n. селеноло́гия f.
self-abasement /'sɛlf ə'beismənt/ n. самоуни(чи)же́ние neut.
self-absorbed /'sɛlf æb'sɔrbd/ adj. эгоцентри́чный.
self-acting /'sɛlf 'æktɪŋ/ adj. автомати́ческий.
self-adjusting /'sɛlf ə'dʒʌstɪŋ/ adj. саморегули́руемый.
self-advertisement /'sɛlf ,ædvər'taizmənt/ n. самореклама f.
self-aligning /'sɛlf ə'lainɪŋ/ adj. самоустана́вливающийся.

self-appointed /'sɛlf ə'pɔintɪd/ adj. самозва́ный.
self-assurance /'sɛlf ə'ʃurəns/ n. самоуве́ренность f.
self-assured /'sɛlf ə'ʃurd/ adj. самоуве́ренный.
self-centered /'sɛlf 'sɛntərd/ adj. эгоисти́ческий; эгоисти́чный.
self-conceit /'sɛlf kən'sit/ n. самомне́ние neut.
self-confidence /,sɛlf 'kɒnfɪdəns/ n. самоуве́ренность f.
self-confident /'sɛlf 'kɒnfɪdənt/ adj. самоуве́ренный.
self-conscious /'sɛlf 'kɒnʃəs/ adj. засте́нчивый; стыдли́вый.
self-contained /'sɛlf kən'teind/ adj. автоно́мный.
self-control /'sɛlf kən'troul/ n. самооблада́ние neut.
self-criticism /'sɛlf 'krɪtɪ,sizəm/ n. самокри́тика f.
self-deception /'sɛlf dɪ'sɛpʃən/ n. самообма́н m.
self-defense /'sɛlf dɪ'fɛns/ n. самозащи́та; самооборо́на f.
self-denial /'sɛlf dɪ'naiəl/ n. самоотве́рженность f.
self-denying /'sɛlf dɪ'naiɪŋ/ adj. самоотве́рженный.
self-destruction /'sɛlf dɪ'strʌkʃən/ n. самоуничтоже́ние neut.
self-determination /'sɛlf dɪ,tɜrmə'neiʃən/ n. самоопределе́ние neut.
self-effacing /'sɛlf ɪ'feisɪŋ/ adj. засте́нчивый; скро́мный.
self-esteem /'sɛlf ɪ'stim/ n. самоуваже́ние neut.
self-evident /,sɛlf 'ɛvɪdənt/ adj. очеви́дный.
self-government /,sɛlf 'gʌvərnmənt/ n. самоуправле́ние neut.
self-importance /'sɛlf ɪm'pɔrtŋs/ n. самомне́ние neut.
self-important /'sɛlf ɪm'pɔrtŋt/ adj. зано́счивый.
self-improvement /'sɛlf ɪm'pruvmənt/ n. самосоверше́нствование neut.
self-indulgent /'sɛlf ɪn'dʌldʒənt/ adj. потво́рствующий свои́м жела́ниям.
self-interest /,sɛlf 'ɪntərɪst/ n. своекоры́стие neut.
selfish /'sɛlfɪʃ/ adj. эгоисти́чный.
selfishness /'sɛlfɪʃnɪs/ n. эгои́зм m.
selfless /'sɛlflɪs/ adj. самоотве́рженный; бескоры́стный.
self-love /'sɛlf 'lʌv/ n. себялю́бие neut.
self-pity /,sɛlf 'pɪti/ n. жа́лость к самому́ себе́ f.
self-portrait /,sɛlf 'pɔrtrɪt/ n. автопортре́т m.
self-possession /'sɛlf pə'zɛʃən/ n. самооблада́ние neut.
self-propelled /'sɛlf prə'pɛld/ adj. самохо́дный.
self-reliance /'sɛlf rɪ'laiəns/ n. самостоя́тельность f.
self-reliant /'sɛlf rɪ'laiənt/ adj. самостоя́тельный.
self-respect /'sɛlf rɪ'spɛkt/ n. самоуваже́ние neut.
self-restraint /'sɛlf rɪ'streint/ n. сде́ржанность f.
self-righteous /,sɛlf 'raitʃəs/ adj. ха́нжеский; фарисе́йский.
self-righteousness /,sɛlf 'raitʃəsnɪs/ n. ха́нжество; самодово́льство neut.
self-sacrifice /'sɛlf 'sækrə,fais/ n. самопоже́ртвование neut.
selfsame /'sɛlf'seim/ adj. тот же са́мый.

self-satisfied /'sɛlf 'sætɪs,faid/ adj. самодовóльный.

self-service /'sɛlf 'sɜrvɪs/ n. самообслуживание neut.

self-sufficient /'sɛlf sə'fɪʃənt/ adj. самостоятельный; независимый.

self-taught /'sɛlf 'tɔt/ adj.: a self-taught person самоучка m. and f. (decl. f.).

self-will /,sɛlf 'wɪl/ n. своеволие neut.

self-willed /,sɛlf 'wɪld/ adj. своевольный.

sell /sɛl/ v. продавáть(ся) impf., продáть(ся) pf.

seller /'sɛlər/ n. продавец m., продавщица f.

selling /'sɛlɪŋ/ n. продáжа f.

seltzer /'sɛltsər/ n. сéльтерская (водá) f.

selvage /'sɛlvɪdʒ/ n. крóмка f.

semantic /sɪ'mæntɪk/ adj. семантический.

semantics /sɪ'mæntɪks/ n. семáнтика f.

semaphore /'sɛməfɔr/ n. семафóр m.

semasiology /sɪ,meisi'ɒlədʒi/ n. семасиолóгия f.

semblance /'sɛmbləns/ n. подóбие neut.; (appearance) вид m.

semen /'simən/ n. сéмя neut.; спéрма f.

semester /sɪ'mɛstər/ n. семéстр m.

Semeypalatinsk /,sɛmɪpə'lɑtɪnsk/ n. Семипалáтинск m.

semiannual /,sɛmi'ænyuəl/ adj. полугодовóй.

semicircle /'sɛmɪ,sɜrkəl/ n. полукруг m.

semicircular /,sɛmɪ'sɜrkyələr/ adj. полукруглый.

semicolon /'sɛmɪ,koulən/ n. тóчка с запятóй f.

semiconductor /,sɛmɪkən'dʌktər/ n. полупроводник m.

semiconscious /,sɛmi'kɒnʃəs/ adj. полусознáтельный.

semifinal /,sɛmi'fainl/ n. полуфинáл m.

semifinished /,sɛmi'fɪnɪʃt/ adj. полуфабрикáтный.

seminar /'sɛmə,nɑr/ n. семинáр m.

seminary /'sɛmə,nɛri/ n. (eccl.) духóвная семинáрия f.

semiology /,simi'ɒlədʒi/ n. семиолóгия f.

semiotic /,simi'ɒtɪk/ adj. семиотический.

semiotics /,simi'ɒtɪks/ n. семиóтика f.

semiprecious /,sɛmi'prɛʃəs/ adj. полудрагоцéнный; **semiprecious stone** n. самоцвéт m.

Semitic /sə'mɪtɪk/ adj. семитический.

semitransparent /,sɛmitræns'pɛərənt/ adj. полупрозрáчный.

semivowel /'sɛmi,vauəl/ n. полуглáсный (звук) m.

senate /'sɛnɪt/ n. сенáт m.

senator /'sɛnətər/ n. сенáтор m.

send /sɛnd/ v. посылáть impf., послáть pf.

sender /'sɛndər/ n. отправитель m.

send-off /'sɛnd ,ɔf/ n. прóводы pl.

send-up /'sɛnd ,ʌp/ n. (colloq.) парóдия f.

Senegal /,sɛnɪ'gɔl/ n. Сенегáл m.

senescent /sɪ'nɛsənt/ adj. старéющий.

senile /'sinail/ adj. стáрческий.

senility /sɪ'nɪləti/ n. стáрость f.

senior /'sinyər/ adj., n. стáрший.

senior citizen n. пенсионéр m., пенсионéрка f.

seniority /,sin'yɔriti/ n. старшинствó neut.

sensation /sɛn'seiʃən/ n. ощущéние neut.; сенсáция f.

sensational /sɛn'seiʃənl/ adj. сенсациóнный.

sense /sɛns/ 1. n. чýвство; ощущéние neut.,

(meaning) смысл m. 2. v. ощущáть; чýвствовать impf.

senseless /'sɛnslɪs/ adj. бессмысленный.

senselessness /'sɛnslɪsnɪs/ n. бессмысленность f.

sensibility /,sɛnsə'bɪlɪti/ n. чувствительность f.

sensible /'sɛnsəbəl/ adj. благоразумный; здравомыслящий; разумный.

sensitive /'sɛnsɪtɪv/ adj. чувствительный.

sensitivity /,sɛnsɪ'tɪvɪti/ n. чувствительность f.

sensor /'sɛnsɔr/ n. дáтчик m.

sensory /'sɛnsəri/ adj. чувствительный.

sensual /'sɛnʃuəl/ adj. чýвственный; плóтский.

sensuous /'sɛnʃuəs/ adj. чýвственный.

sentence /'sɛntns/ 1. n. (gram.) предложéние neut.; (leg.) приговóр m. 2. v. приговáривать impf., приговорить pf.

sentiment /'sɛntəmənt/ n. чýвство; мнéние neut.; сентимéнты pl.

sentimental /,sɛntə'mɛntl/ adj. сентиментáльный.

sentinel /'sɛntnl/ n. часовóй m.

sentry /'sɛntri/ n. часовóй m.

Seoul /soul/ n. Сеýл m.

separable /'sɛpərəbəl/ adj. отделимый.

separate /adj.'sɛpərɪt; v. 'sɛpə,reit/ 1. adj. отдéльный. 2. v.t. отделять impf., отделить pf.; v.i. отделяться impf., отделиться pf.

separately /'sɛpərɪtli/ adv. отдéльно.

separation /,sɛpə'reiʃən/ n. отделéние; разделéние; разлучéние neut.

September /sɛp'tɛmbər/ 1. n. сентябрь m. 2. adj. сентябрьский.

septic /'sɛptɪk/ adj. септический.

sepulchre /'sɛpəlkər/ n. склеп m.; гробница; усыпáльница f.

sequel /'sikwəl/ n. продолжéние; (по)слéдствие neut.

sequence /'sikwəns/ n. послéдовательность f.

sequential /sɪ'kwɛnʃəl/ adj. послéдовательный; (ensuing) послéдующий.

sequin /'sikwɪn/ n. блёстка f.

seraglio /sɪ'rælyou/ n. (palace) серáль m.; (harem) гарéм m.

seraph /'sɛrəf/ n. серафим m.

Serbian /'sɜrbiən/ 1. adj. сéрбский. 2. n. серб m., сéрбка f.

serenade /,sɛrə'neid/ n. серенáда f.

serene /sə'rin/ adj. спокóйный; тихий.

serf /sɜrf/ n. крепостнóй m.

serfdom /'sɜrfdəm/ n. крепостнóе прáво neut.

sergeant /'sɑrdʒənt/ n. сержáнт m.

Sergiev Posad /'sɜrdʒiəf pə'sɑd/ n. (formerly: Zagorsk) Сéргиев Посáд m.

serial /'sɪəriəl/ adj. серийный.

seriatim /,sɪəri'eitɪm/ adv. по порядку.

series /'sɪəriz/ n. сéрия f.

serif /'sɛrɪf/ n. засéчка f.

serious /'sɪəriəs/ adj. серьёзный.

sermon /'sɜrmən/ n. прóповедь f.

sermonize /'sɜrmə,naiz/ v. поучáть impf.

Serov /sə'rɔf/ n. Серóв m.

serpent /'sɜrpənt/ n. змея f.

Serpukhov /'sɜrpə,kɔf/ n. Сéрпухов m.

serrated /'sɛreitɪd/ adj. зазубренный; зýбчатый.

serum /'sɪərəm/ n. сыворотка f.

servant /'sɜrvənt/ n. слугá m. (decl. f.), служáнка f.; служитель m.

serve /sɜrv/ n. служи́ть impf., послужи́ть pf.
server /'sɜrvər/ n. (athl.) подаю́щий мяч m.
service /'sɜrvɪs/ **1.** n. слу́жба; услу́га f.; **to be of service** быть поле́зным. **2.** adj. обслу́живающий.
serviceable /'sɜrvəsəbəl/ adj. поле́зный.
service book n. Тре́бник m.
serviceman /'sɜrvəsmən/ n. (mil.) военнослу́жащий m.; (repairman) ма́стер m.
service station n. (авто)запра́вочная ста́нция f.
servile /'sɜrvɪl/ adj. ра́бский; рабале́пный.
servility /sər'vɪlɪti/ n. рабале́пство neut.
serving /'sɜrvɪŋ/ n. по́рция f.
servomechanism /'sɜrvou,mɛkə,nɪzəm/ n. сервомехани́зм m.
sesame /'sɛsəmi/ n. (bot.) кунжу́т; сеза́м m.
session /'sɛʃən/ n. се́ссия f.; заседа́ние neut.
set /sɛt/ **1.** n. набо́р; компле́кт; гарниту́р m.; (television) телеви́зор m.; (tendency) направле́ние neut.; (tennis) сет m.; (mach.) ширина́ разво́да; (theat.) декора́ция f. **2.** adj. устано́вленный; усто́йчивый. **3.** v. устана́вливать impf., установи́ть pf.; (sun) заходи́ть impf., зайти́ pf.
setback /'sɛt,bæk/ n. неуда́ча f.; (obstacle) препя́тствие neut.
set designer n. худо́жник-декора́тор m.
setscrew /'sɛt,skru/ n. устано́вочный винт m.
settee /sɛt'ti/ n. дива́н m.
setter /'sɛtər/ n. се́ттер m.
setting /'sɛtɪŋ/ n. (for jewelry) опра́ва f.; (theat.) постано́вка f.; (of sun) зака́т m.
settle /'sɛtḷ/ v.t. (decide) реша́ть impf.; (arrange) ула́живать impf.; v.i. сели́ться impf.
settlement /'sɛtḷmənt/ n. (colony) поселе́ние neut.; (payment) упла́та f.; расчёт m.
settler /'sɛtḷər/ n. поселе́нец m.; поселе́нка f.
settling /'sɛtḷɪŋ/ n. (sinking) оседа́ние neut.
Setubal /sɪ'tubal/ n. Сету́бал m.
Sevan /sɛ'van/ n. (lake) Сева́н m.
Sevastopol /sə'væstə,poul, ,sɛvə'stoupəl/ n. Севасто́поль m.
seven /'sɛvən/ n., adj. семь.
seventeen /'sɛvən'tin/ n., adj. семна́дцать.
seventeenth /'sɛvən'tinθ/ adj. семна́дцатый.
seventh /'sɛvənθ/ adj. седьмо́й.
seventieth /'sɛvəntiiθ/ adj. семидеся́тый.
seventy /'sɛvənti/ n., adj. се́мьдесят.
sever /'sɛvər/ v. отреза́ть impf., отре́зать pf.; разъединя́ть impf., разъедини́ть pf.
several /'sɛvərəl/ **1.** adj. не́сколько. **2.** n. не́сколько; не́которое коли́чество neut.
severance /'sɛvərəns/ n. отделе́ние (от with gen.) neut.; (relations) разры́в m.
severe /sə'vɪər/ adj. стро́гий; суро́вый.
Severnaya Zemlya /'sɛvərnəyə zim'lyɑ/ n. (islands) Се́верная Земля́ f.
Seville /sə'vɪl/ n. Севи́лья f.
sew /sou/ v. шить impf., сшить pf.
sewage /'suɪdʒ/ n. сто́чные во́ды pl.
sewer /'suər/ n. канализацио́нная труба́ f.
sewerage /'suərɪdʒ/ n. канализа́ция f.
sewing machine /'souɪŋ/ n. швейна́я маши́на f.
sex /sɛks/ **1.** n. секс m.; (gender) пол m. **2.** adj. полово́й.
sexism /'sɛksɪzəm/ n. сексизм m.
sexless /'sɛkslɪs/ adj. (biol.) беспо́лый.

sexton /'sɛkstən/ n. церко́вный сто́рож m.
sexual /'sɛkʃuəl/ adj. полово́й; сексуа́льный.
sexual intercourse n. полово́й акт m.
sh! /ʃ/ interj. тсс!
shabby /'ʃæbi/ adj. потрёпанный; убо́гий.
shack /ʃæk/ n. (hut) лачу́га; хи́жина f.
shackle /'ʃækəl/ n. кандалы́; око́вы pl.
shade /ʃeid/ **1.** n. тень f. **2.** v. заслоня́ть impf., заслони́ть pf.; затеня́ть impf., затени́ть pf.
shadow /'ʃædou/ n. тень f.
shady /'ʃeidi/ adj. тени́стый; (dubious) сомни́тельный.
shaft /ʃæft/ n. (ray) луч m.; (column) коло́нна f.; вал m.; (mine) ша́хта f.
shaggy /'ʃægi/ adj. (hair) лохма́тый; косма́тый; (material) мохна́тый.
shah /ʃɑ/ n. шах m.
shake /ʃeik/ v.t. трясти́ impf.; v.i. трясти́сь impf.; **to shake hands** пожа́ть ру́ки друг дру́гу pf.
shake-up /'ʃeik ,ʌp/ n. (colloq.) перетасо́вка f.
shaking /'ʃeikɪŋ/ n. встря́ска f.; дрожа́ние neut.; тря́ска f.
shaky /'ʃeiki/ adj. ша́ткий; нетвёрдый; непро́чный.
shale /ʃeil/ n. сла́нец m.
shallot /'ʃælət/ n. лук-шало́т m.
shallow /'ʃælou/ adj. ме́лкий; (fig.) пове́рхностный.
sham /ʃæm/ n. (pretense) притво́рство neut.; (deception) обма́н m.; (fake) подде́лка f.
shame /ʃeim/ **1.** n. стыд m. **2.** v. стыди́ть impf.
shamefaced /'ʃeim,feist/ adj. стыдли́вый.
shameful /'ʃeimfəl/ adj. позо́рный; сканда́льный.
shameless /'ʃeimlɪs/ adj. бессты́дный.
shampoo /ʃæm'pu/ n. шампу́нь m.; (wash) мытьё головы́ neut.
shamrock /'ʃæmrɔk/ n. трили́стник m.
Shanghai /ʃæŋ'hai/ n. Шанха́й m.
shanty /'ʃænti/ n. (hut) хи́жина; хиба́рка f.
shape /ʃeip/ **1.** n. фо́рма f.; о́браз m. **2.** v. придава́ть фо́рму impf.
shapeless /'ʃeiplɪs/ adj. бесфо́рменный.
shapely /'ʃeipli/ adj. стро́йный.
shard /ʃard/ n. черепо́к m.; (entomol.) надкры́лье neut.
share /ʃɛər/ **1.** n. до́ля; часть f.; уча́стие neut.; (econ.) а́кция f. **2.** v. дели́ться impf., подели́ться pf.
shark /ʃark/ n. аку́ла f.
sharp /ʃarp/ **1.** adj. о́стрый. **2.** n. (mus.) дие́з m.
sharpen /'ʃarpən/ v. точи́ть impf., заостря́ть impf., заостри́ть pf.
sharper /'ʃarpər/ n. (cheat at cards) шу́лер; жу́лик m.
sharpness /'ʃarpnɪs/ n. острота́ f.; (clarity) ре́зкость f.
sharp-tongued /'ʃarp 'tʌŋd/ adj. злоязы́чный.
sharp-witted /'ʃarp 'wɪtɪd/ adj. сообрази́тельный.
shatter /'ʃætər/ v. разбива́ть(ся) impf.
shave /ʃeiv/ **1.** n. бритьё neut. **2.** v.t. брить impf., побри́ть pf.; v.i. бри́ться impf., побри́ться pf.
shaven /'ʃeivən/ adj. бри́тый.
shaver /'ʃeivər/ n. бри́тва f.
shawl /ʃɔl/ n. шаль f.
she /ʃi/ pron. она́ f.

sheaf /ʃif/ n. сноп m.; (of papers) связка f.
shearing /'ʃirɪŋ/ n. стрижка f.
shears /ʃirz/ n. ножницы pl.
sheath /ʃiθ/ n. ножны pl.; оболочка f.
shebang /ʃə'bæŋ/ n. (colloq.) (business) шарашка; лавочка f.
shed[1] /ʃɛd/ n. навес; сарай m.
shed[2] /ʃɛd/ v. проливать; ронять impf., уронить pf.
sheen /ʃin/ n. блеск m.
sheep /ʃip/ n. овца f.; баран m.
sheepdog /'ʃip,dɔg/ n. овчарка f.
sheepfold /'ʃip,fould/ n. овчарня f.
sheet /ʃit/ n. простыня f.; (paper) лист m.
sheet lightning n. зарница f.
sheik /ʃik, ʃeik/ n. шейх m.
sheldrake /'ʃɛl,dreik/ n. утка-пеганка f.
shelf /ʃɛlf/ n. полка f.
shell /ʃɛl/ **1.** n. скорлупа; шелуха f.; (sea) раковина f. **2.** v. лущить impf.
shellac /ʃə'læk/ **1.** n. шеллак m. **2.** v. покрывать шеллаком impf.
shellfish /'ʃɛl,fɪʃ/ n. моллюск m ; ракообразное животное neut.
shelling /'ʃɛlɪŋ/ n. (mil.) обстрел m.
shell shock n. контузия f.
shell-shocked /'ʃɛl ,ʃɒkt/ adj. контуженный.
shelter /'ʃɛltər/ **1.** n. приют; кров m.; убежище neut. **2.** v. дать приют pf.; служить убежищем impf.
shelve /ʃɛlv/ v. ставить на полку impf.; (delay) откладывать impf.
shelving[1] /'ʃɛlvɪŋ/ n. стеллаж m.
shelving[2] /'ʃɛlvɪŋ/ adj. (sloping) отлогий.
shepherd /'ʃɛpərd/ n. пастух m.
shepherdess /'ʃɛpərdɪs/ n. пастушка f.
sheriff /'ʃɛrɪf/ n. шериф m.
sherry /'ʃɛri/ n. херес m.
shield /ʃild/ **1.** n. щит m.; (emblem) значок m. **2.** v. заслонять impf., заслонить pf.
shift /ʃɪft/ **1.** n. изменение; перемещение neut.; (work) смена f. **2.** v.t. перемещать impf., переместить pf.; v.i. перемещаться impf., переместиться pf.
shifting /'ʃɪftɪŋ/ adj. непостоянный.
shifty /'ʃɪfti/ adj. скользкий; ненадёжный; (eyes) бегающий.
shimmer /'ʃɪmər/ v. мерцать impf.
shin /ʃɪn/ n. (anat.) голень f.
shinbone /'ʃɪn,boun/ n. большая берцовая кость f.
shindig /'ʃɪn,dɪg/ n. (colloq.) (party) вечеринка f.
shine /ʃain/ **1.** n. сияние neut.; блеск; глянец m. **2.** v.i. сиять impf.; блестеть impf.; v.t. полировать impf.; (shoes) чистить сапоги impf.
shingle /'ʃɪŋgəl/ n. кровельная дранка f.
shiny /'ʃaini/ adj. блестящий.
ship /ʃɪp/ **1.** n. корабль m.; судно neut.; пароход m. **2.** v. отправлять impf., отправить pf.
shipbuilder /'ʃɪp,bɪldər/ n. судостроитель m.; кораблестроитель m.
shipmate /'ʃɪp,meit/ n. товарищ по плаванию m.
shipment /'ʃɪpmənt/ n. отправка f.
shipowner /'ʃɪp,ounər/ n. судовладелец m.
shipshape /'ʃɪp,ʃeip/ adj. в полном порядке.
shipwreck /'ʃɪp,rɛk/ n. кораблекрушение neut.

shipyard /'ʃɪp,yard/ n. судостроительный завод m.; верфь f.
shire /ʃai³r/ n. графство neut.
shirk /ʃзrk/ v. увиливать (от with gen.) impf.
shirker /'ʃзrkər/ n. симулянт m.
shirt /ʃзrt/ n. рубашка f.
shit /ʃɪt/ **1.** 1 n. (vulg.) дерьмо neut. **2.** v. (vulg.) гадить; срать impf.
shiver /'ʃɪvər/ **1.** n. дрожь f. **2.** v. дрожать impf.
shoal[1] /ʃoul/ n. мель f.; (sandbank) банка; отмель f.
shoal[2] /ʃoul/ n. (fish) косяк m.
shock /ʃɒk/ **1.** n. удар; толчок m., потрясение neut. **2.** v. потрясать impf., потрясти pf.
shock absorber n. амортизатор m.
shocking /'ʃɒkɪŋ/ adj. ужасный; скандальный.
shockproof /'ʃɒk,pruf/ adj. ударостойкий.
shock worker n. ударник m.
shod /ʃɒd/ adj. обутый.
shoddy /'ʃɒdi/ adj. дрянной.
shoe /ʃu/ **1.** n. ботинок m. **2.** adj. обувной.
shoebrush /'ʃu,brʌʃ/ n. сапожная щётка f.
shoehorn /'ʃu,hɔrn/ n. рожок m.
shoelace /'ʃu,leis/ n. шнурок m.
shoemaker /'ʃu'meikər/ n. сапожник m.
shoetree /'ʃu,tri/ n. колодка f.
shoo /ʃu/ interj. вон!; (to birds) кш!, кыш!; (to cat) брысь!
shoot /ʃut/ **1.** n. (bot.) росток; побег m. **2.** v. стрелять impf.; (kill) застрелить pf.; (execute) расстрелять pf.
shooting /'ʃutɪŋ/ n. стрельба f.; (mil.) (fire) огонь m.
shooting star n. падающая звезда f.
shop /ʃɒp/ **1.** n. магазин m. **2.** v. делать покупки impf.
shopkeeper /'ʃɒp,kipər/ n. лавочник m.
shoplifter /'ʃɒp,lɪftər/ n. магазинный вор m.
shoplifting /'ʃɒp,lɪftɪŋ/ n. магазинная кража f.
shopper /'ʃɒpər/ n. покупатель m.
shopping /'ʃɒpɪŋ/ n. хождение по магазинам neut.
shopping center n. торговый центр m.
shore /ʃɔr/ n. берег m.
shoreline /'ʃɔr,lain/ n. береговая линия f.
short /ʃɔrt/ **1.** adj. короткий; краткий; (stature) низкого роста; **in short** вкратце. **2.** n. pl. шорты; трусы pl.
shortage /'ʃɔrtɪdʒ/ n. недостаток m.
shortbread /'ʃɔrt,brɛd/ n. песочное печенье neut.
shortchange /'ʃɔrt'tʃeindʒ/ v. обсчитывать impf.
short circuit n. короткое замыкание neut.
shortcoming /'ʃɔrt,kʌmɪŋ/ n. несовершенство neut.; (fault) недостаток m.
shorten /'ʃɔrtn/ v. сокращать impf., сократить pf.
shorter /'ʃɔrtər/ adj. короче; более короткий.
shortest /'ʃɔrtɪst/ adj. кратчайший; самый короткий.
shorthand /'ʃɔrt,hænd/ n. стенография f.
short-lived /'ʃɔrt 'laivd, -'lɪvd/ adj. недолговечный.
shortly /'ʃɔrtli/ adv. вскоре; **shortly before** незадолго (до with gen.).
shortness /'ʃɔrtnɪs/ n. короткость; краткость f.
shortsighted /'ʃɔrt'saitɪd/ adj. близорукий.
short story n. рассказ m.

short-tempered /'ʃɔrt 'tɛmpərd/ adj. вспы́льчивый; раздражи́тельный.

short-term /'ʃɔrt 'tɜrm/ adj. краткосро́чный.

shortwave /'ʃɔrt,weiv/ adj. (radio) коротковолно́вый.

shot /ʃɒt/ n. вы́стрел m.; (marksman) стрело́к m.; (photog.) фотосни́мок m.

shotgun /'ʃɒt,gʌn/ n. дробови́к m.

shoulder /'ʃouldər/ 1. n. плечо́ neut. 2. v. брать на себя́ impf.

shoulder blade n. лопа́тка f.

shoulder joint n. плечево́й суста́в m.

shoulder strap n. ля́мка f.

shout /ʃaut/ 1. n. крик m. 2. v. крича́ть impf., кри́кнуть pf.

shove /ʃʌv/ 1. n. толчо́к m. 2. v. толка́ть impf., толкну́ть pf.

shovel /'ʃʌvəl/ 1. n. лопа́та f. 2. v. сгреба́ть impf., сгрести́ pf.

show /ʃou/ 1. n. (theat.) зре́лище neut.; спекта́кль m.; (movie) киносеа́нс m.; (display) пока́з m.; вы́ставка f. 2. v. пока́зывать impf., показа́ть pf.

show business n. шо́у-би́знес m.

showcase /'ʃou,keis/ n. витри́на f.

shower /'ʃauər/ n. (rain) дождь; ли́вень m.; (bath) душ m.

shower room n. душева́я f.

show girl n. хори́стка f.

showman /'ʃoumən/ n. шо́умен m.

show-off /'ʃou ,ɔf/ n. позёр m.

showroom /'ʃou,rum, -,rʊm/ n. вы́ставочный зал m.

showy /'ʃoui/ adj. эффе́ктный; бро́ский; (ostentatious) показно́й; зре́лищный.

shrapnel /'ʃræpnl/ n. шрапне́ль f.

shrew¹ /ʃru/ n. (zool.) землеро́йка f.

shrew² /ʃru/ n. (person) сварли́вая же́нщина f.

shrewd /ʃrud/ adj. проница́тельный; хи́трый.

shriek /ʃrik/ 1. n. крик; визг m. 2. v. пронзи́тельно крича́ть impf.

shrike /ʃraik/ n. сорокопу́т m.

shrill /ʃril/ adj. пронзи́тельный.

shrimp /ʃrimp/ n. креве́тка f.

shrine /ʃrain/ n. святы́ня; ра́ка f.

shrink /ʃriŋk/ v. сади́ться impf.; (recoil) уклоня́тся (от with gen.) impf.

shrinkage /'ʃriŋkidʒ/ n. уса́дка f.

shrivel /'ʃrivəl/ v. (dry up) высыха́ть impf.; (curl up) съёживаться impf.

shroud /ʃraud/ n. са́ван m.; пелена́ f.

Shrovetide /'ʃrouv,taid/ n. Ма́сленица f.

shrub /ʃrʌb/ n. куст; куста́рник m.

shrubbery /'ʃrʌbəri/ n. куста́рниковое насажде́ние neut.

shrug /ʃrʌg/ v. пожима́ть плеча́ми impf.

shudder /'ʃʌdər/ 1. n. дрожь f.; содрога́ние neut. 2. v. вздра́гивать impf., вздро́гнуть pf.

shuffle /'ʃʌfəl/ v. (with feet) ша́ркать нога́ми impf.; (cards) тасова́ть impf.

shun /ʃʌn/ v. избега́ть impf., избе́гнуть pf.

shush /ʃʌʃ/ interj. ш-ш!

shut /ʃʌt/ v. закрыва́ть impf., закры́ть pf.; запира́ть impf., запере́ть pf.; **to shut up** (colloq.) замолча́ть pf.

shutter /'ʃʌtər/ n. ста́вень m.; (photog.) затво́р m.

shuttle /'ʃʌtl/ n. челно́к m.

shuttlecock /'ʃʌtl,kɒk/ n. вола́н m.

shy /ʃai/ adj. пугли́вый; засте́нчивый.

Siberian /sai'biəriən/ 1. adj. сиби́рский. 2. n. сибиря́к m., сибиря́чка f.

sibilant /'sibələnt/ n. and adj. свистя́щий.

sibling /'sibliŋ/ n. брат m., сестра́ f.

Sicily /'sisəli/ n. (island) Сици́лия f.

sick /sik/ adj. больно́й.

sick bay n. лазаре́т m.

sickening /'sikəniŋ/ adj. отврати́тельный; проти́вный.

sickle /'sikəl/ n. серп m.

sick leave n. о́тпуск по боле́зни m.

sickly /'sikli/ adj. боле́зненный.

sickness /'siknis/ n. боле́знь f.

side /said/ 1. n. сторона́ f.; бок m.; **from side to side** из стороны́ в сто́рону. 2. adj. боково́й. 3. v. встава́ть на сто́рону (with gen.) impf.

side band n. (radio) боковая полоса́ f.

sideboard /'said,bɔrd/ n. буфе́т; серва́нт m.

sidecar /'said,kar/ n. коля́ска f.

side door n. боковая дверь f.; чёрный ход m.

side effect n. побо́чный эффе́кт m.

sideline /'said,lain/ n. (sport) боковая ли́ния f.; (work) подрабо́тка f.

sidelong /'said,lɔŋ/ adj. косо́й.

sideshow /'said,ʃou/ n. аттракцио́н m.

sidestep /'said,stɛp/ v. уклоня́ться (от with gen.) impf.

sidewalk /'said,wɔk/ n. тротуа́р m.

sideways /'said,weiz/ adv. (on side) на боку́; (from side) сбо́ку; (to one side) в сто́рону.

sidle /'saidl/ v. (move sideways) дви́гаться бо́ком impf.

siege /sidʒ/ n. оса́да f.

Siena /si'ɛnə/ n. Сие́на f.

sieve /siv/ n. си́то neut.

sift /sift/ v. просе́ивать impf., просе́ять pf.

sigh /sai/ 1. n. вздох m. 2. v. вздыха́ть impf., вздохну́ть pf.

sight /sait/ n. зре́ние neut.; вид m.; **at first sight** с пе́рвого взгля́да; **within sight** в преде́лах ви́димости.

sighted /'saitid/ adj. (not blind) зря́чий.

sightly /'saitli/ adj. прия́тный на вид.

sightseeing /'sait,siiŋ/ n. осмо́тр достопримеча́тельностей m.

sightseer /'sait,siər/ n. тури́ст m., тури́стка f.

sign /sain/ 1. n. знак; си́мвол m.; вы́веска f. 2. v. подпи́сывать impf., подписа́ть pf.

signal /'signl/ 1. n. знак; сигна́л m. 2. v. сигнали́ровать impf. and pf.

signatory /'signə,tɔri/ n., adj. подписа́вшийся m.

signature /'signətʃər/ n. по́дпись f.

signboard /'sain,bɔrd/ n. вы́веска f.

signet /'signit/ n. печа́тка f.

significance /sig'nifikəns/ n. значе́ние neut.; значи́тельность f.

significant /sig'nifikənt/ adj. значи́тельный.

signify /'signə,fai/ v. зна́чить; означа́ть impf.

sign language n. язы́к же́стов m.

signpost /'sain,poust/ n. указа́тельный столб m.

silence /'sailəns/ 1. n. молча́ние neut.; тишина́ f. 2. v. заста́вить замолча́ть pf.

silent /'sailənt/ adj. безмо́лвный; молчали́вый.

silhouette /,silu'ɛt/ n. силуэ́т m.

silica /'sɪlɪkə/ n. кремнезём m.
silicon /'sɪlɪkən/ n. кре́мний m.
silk /sɪlk/ **1.** n. шёлк m. **2.** adj. шёлковый.
silken /'sɪlkən/ also **silky** /'sɪlki/ adj. шёлковый; шелкови́стый.
silkscreen /'sɪlk,skrin/ n. шелкогра́фия f.
silkworm /'sɪlk,wɜrm/ n. шелкопря́д m.
sill /sɪl/ n. подоко́нник m.
silly /'sɪli/ adj. глу́пый.
silo /'sailou/ n. си́лос m.
silt /sɪlt/ n. ил m.
silver /'sɪlvər/ **1.** n. серебро́ neut. **2.** adj. сере́бряный.
silversmith /'sɪlvər,smɪθ/ n. сере́бряник; ма́стер по серебру́ m.
silverware /'sɪlvər,wɛər/ n. столо́вое серебро́ neut.
silvery /'sɪlvəri/ adj. серебри́стый.
Simferopol /,sɪmfə'roupəl/ n. Симферо́поль m.
simian /'sɪmiən/ adj. обезья́ний.
similar /'sɪmələr/ adj. подо́бный; похо́жий.
similarity /,sɪmə'lærɪti/ n. схо́дство; подо́бие neut.
similarly /'sɪmələrli/ adv. подо́бно; подо́бным о́бразом.
simile /'sɪməli/ n. сравне́ние neut.
simmer /'sɪmər/ v.t. (cul.) кипяти́ть на ме́дленном огне́ impf.; v.i. (cul.) кипе́ть на ме́дленном огне́ impf.
simper /'sɪmpər/ v. жема́нно улыба́ться impf.
simple /'sɪmpəl/ adj. просто́й.
simpleton /'sɪmpəltən/ n. проста́к m.
simplicity /sɪm'plɪsɪti/ n. простота́ f.
simplify /'sɪmplə,fai/ v. упроща́ть impf., упрости́ть pf.
simply /'sɪmpli/ adv. про́сто; простоду́шно.
simulacrum /,sɪmyə'leikrəm/ n. изображе́ние; подо́бие neut.
simulate /'sɪmyə,leit/ v. симули́ровать impf. and pf.
simultaneity /,saiməltə'niiti/ n. одновреме́нность f.
simultaneous /,saiməl'teiniəs/ adj. одновреме́нный.
sin /sɪn/ **1.** n. грех m. **2.** v. греши́ть impf., согреши́ть pf.
since /sɪns/ **1.** adv. с тех пор. **2.** prep. по́сле; с (with gen.). **3.** conj. с тех пор, как.
sincere /sɪn'sɪər/ adj. и́скренний.
sincerity /sɪn'scrɪti/ n. и́скренность f.
sine /sain/ n. (math.) си́нус m.
sinew /'sɪnyu/ n. сухожи́лие neut.
sinful /'sɪnfəl/ adj. гре́шный.
sing /sɪŋ/ v. петь impf.
Singapore /'sɪŋgə,pɔr/ n. Сингапу́р m.
singe /sɪndʒ/ v. подпаля́ть impf., подпали́ть pf.
singer /'sɪŋər/ n. певе́ц m., певи́ца f.
single /'sɪŋgəl/ adj. оди́н; еди́нственный; (unmarried) холосто́й, незаму́жняя.
single-breasted /'sɪŋgəl 'brɛstɪd/ adj. однобо́ртный.
single-engined /'sɪŋgəl 'ɛndʒɪnd/ adj. одномото́рный.
single file n.: **in single file** adv. гусько́м.
single-minded /'sɪŋgəl 'maindɪd/ adj. целеустремлённый.
single-track /'sɪŋgəl 'træk/ adj. одноколе́йный.

singly /'sɪŋgli/ adv. поодино́чке.
singular /'sɪŋgyələr/ **1.** n. (gram.) еди́нственное число́ neut. **2.** adj. исключи́тельный; необыча́йный.
singularly /'sɪŋgyələrli/ adv. необыкнове́нно; исключи́тельно.
sinister /'sɪnəstər/ adj. злове́щий.
sink /sɪŋk/ **1.** n. ра́ковина f. **2.** v.t. топи́ть impf., потопи́ть pf.; v.i. тону́ть impf., потону́ть pf.
sinker /'sɪŋkər/ n. грузи́ло neut.
sinking /'sɪŋkɪŋ/ n. (ship) потопле́ние neut.
sinless /'sɪnlɪs/ adj. безгре́шный.
sinner /'sɪnər/ n. гре́шник m.
Sinologist /sai'nɒlədʒɪst/ n. сино́лог; китаеве́д; китаи́ст m.
Sinology /sai'nɒlədʒi/ n. синоло́гия; китаеве́дение; китаи́стика f.
sinuous /'sɪnyuəs/ adj. изви́листый; волни́стый.
sinus /'sainəs/ n. па́зуха f.; си́нус m.
sip /sɪp/ **1.** n. глото́к m. **2.** v. прихлёбывать impf.
siphon /'saifən/ n. сифо́н m.
sir /sɜr/ n. господи́н; сэр; су́дарь m.
Siracusa /,sirə'kuzə/ n. (also: Syracuse) Сираку́зы pl.
siren /'saiɾən/ n. сире́на f.; сигна́л трево́ги m.
sirloin /'sɜrlɔin/ n. филе́ neut. indecl.
siskin /'sɪskɪn/ n. чиж m.
sissy /'sɪsi/ n. (colloq.) не́женка f. and m. (decl. f.); ма́менькин сыно́к m.
sister /'sɪstər/ n. сестра́ f.
sister city n. го́род-побрати́м m.
sister-in-law /'sɪstər ɪn ,lɔ/ n. (brother's wife) неве́стка f.; (husband's sister) золо́вка f.
sit /sɪt/ v. сиде́ть impf.; **to sit down** сади́ться impf., сесть pf.
site /sait/ n. местоположе́ние neut.
sit-in /'sɪt,ɪn/ n. сидя́чая забасто́вка f.
Sitka /'sɪtkə/ n. Си́тка f.
sitting room /'sɪtɪŋ/ n. гости́ная f.
situate /'sɪtʃu,eit/ v. располага́ть impf., расположи́ть pf.
situated /'sɪtʃu,eitɪd/ adj. располо́женный.
situation /,sɪtʃu'eiʃən/ n. местоположе́ние; положе́ние; состоя́ние neut.
six /sɪks/ n., adj. шесть.
six-shooter /'sɪks 'ʃutər/ n. шестизаря́дный револьве́р m.
sixteen /'sɪks'tin/ **1.** n., adj. шестна́дцать. **2.** шестна́дцатая часть f.
sixth /sɪksθ/ **1.** adj. шесто́й. **2.** n. шеста́я часть f.
sixtieth /'sɪkstiiθ/ **1.** adj. шестидеся́тый. **2.** n. шестидеся́тая часть f.
sixty /'sɪksti/ n., adj. шестьдеся́т.
sizable /'saizəbəl/ adj. значи́тельный; изря́дный.
size /saiz/ n. разме́р m.; величина́ f.
sizzle /'sɪzəl/ v. шипе́ние neut. шипе́ть impf.
skate /skeit/ **1.** n. конёк m. **2.** v. ката́ться на конька́х impf.
skateboard /'skeit,bɔrd/ n. ро́ликовая доска́ f.
skating /'skeitɪŋ/ n. ката́ние на конька́х neut.
skating rink n. като́к m.
skein /skein/ n. мото́к m.
skeleton /'skɛlɪtn/ n. (anat.) скеле́т; костя́к m.
skeptic /'skɛptɪk/ n. ске́птик m.
skeptical /'skɛptɪkəl/ скепти́ческий.

skepticism /'skɛptə,sɪzəm/ *n.* скептицизм *m.*
sketch /skɛtʃ/ **1.** *n.* эскиз; набросок; очерк *m.* **2.** *v.* нарисовать эскиз *pf.*
sketchy /'skɛtʃi/ *adj.* (*in outline*) схематичный; (*scanty*) скудный.
skewbald /'skyu,bɔld/ *adj.* пегий.
skewer /'skyuər/ *n.* вертел *m.*
ski /ski/ **1.** *v.* ходить на лыжах *impf.* **2.** *n.* лыжа *f.* **3.** *adj.* лыжный.
skid /skɪd/ **1.** *n.* скольжение *neut.* **2.** *v.* заносить *impf.*, занести *pf.*
skidding /'skɪdɪŋ/ *n.* скольжение *neut.*; занос *m.*
skier /'skiər/ *n.* лыжник *m.*, лыжница *f.*
skiff /skɪf/ *n.* ялик *m.*
ski jump *n.* лыжный трамплин *m.*
ski jumping *n.* прыжки на лыжах *pl.*
skill /skɪl/ *n.* искусство; мастерство *neut.*; ловкость *f.*
skilled /skɪld/ *adj.* искусный; квалифицированный.
skillet /'skɪlɪt/ *n.* сковорода *f.*
skillful /'skɪlfəl/ *adj.* искусный; ловкий.
skim milk /skɪm/ *n.* обезжиренное молоко *neut.*
skimp /skɪmp/ *v.* скупиться; **on** на (*with acc.*) *pf.*
skimpy /'skɪmpi/ *adj.* скудный.
skin /skɪn/ **1.** *n.* кожа; шкура *f.* **2.** *v.* сдирать кожу or шкуру *impf.*
skin diver *n.* аквалангист *m.*
skinflint /'skɪn,flɪnt/ *n.* скряга *m.* and *f.* (*decl. f.*).
skin graft *n.* пересадка кожи *f.*
skinny /'skɪni/ *adj.* тощий; худой.
skintight /'skɪn'tait/ *adj.* в обтяжку.
skip /skɪp/ **1.** *n.* прыжок; скачок *m.* **2.** *v.* скакать; прыгать; пропускать *impf.*
skipper /'skɪpər/ *n.* шкипер *m.*; (*nav.*) командир *m.*; (*sport*) капитан *m.*
skirmish /'skɜrmɪʃ/ *n.* схватка; стычка *f.*; столкновение *neut.*
skirt /skɜrt/ *n.* юбка *f.*
skit /skɪt/ *n.* скетч *m.*
Skovorodino /skəvə'rɔdɪnə/ *n.* Сковородино *neut.*
skull /skʌl/ *n.* череп *m.*
skunk /skʌŋk/ *n.* вонючка *f.*; скунс *m.*
sky /skai/ *n.* небо *neut.*; **in the sky** на небе.
sky-high /skai 'hai/ *adv.* до небес.
skylark /'skai,lɑrk/ *n.* (*bird*) жаворонок *m.*
skylight /'skai,lait/ *n.* застеклённая крыша *f.*
skyline /'skai,lain/ *n.* горизонт *m.*
skyrocket /'skai,rɒkɪt/ *v.* подскакивать *impf.*
skyscraper /'skai,skreipər/ *n.* небоскрёб *m.*
slab /slæb/ *n.* плита *f.*
slack /slæk/ *adj.* слабый; вялый.
slacken /'slækən/ *v.* замедлять *impf.*, замедлить *pf.*
slacker /'slækər/ *n.* лодырь *m.*
slacks /slæks/ *n.* брюки *pl.*
slag /slæg/ *n.* шлак *m.*
slake /sleik/ *v.* (*thirst*) утолять; (*lime*) гасить *impf.*
slam¹ /slæm/ **1.** *n.* хлопанье *neut.* **2.** *v.* хлопнуть *pf.*
slam² /slæm/ *n.* (*cards*) шлем *m.*
slander /'slændər/ **1.** *n.* клевета *f.* **2.** *v.* клеветать *impf.*, оклеветать *pf.*
slang /slæŋ/ *n.* жаргон; сленг *m.*

slant /slænt/ **1.** *n.* склон; уклон *m.* **2.** *v.* наклонять(ся) *impf.*
slanting /'slæntɪŋ/ *adj.* наклонный; косой.
slantwise /'slænt,waiz/ *adv.* косо; наклонно.
slap /slæp/ **1.** *n.* шлепок *m.*; **a slap in the face** пощёчина *f.* **2.** *v.* шлёпать *impf.*, шлёпнуть *pf.*
slapdash /'slæp,dæʃ/ *adv.* кое-как.
slapstick /'slæp,stɪk/ *n.* фарс; балаган *m.*
slash /slæʃ/ **1.** *n.* удар ножом; разрез *m.* **2.** *v.* порезать *impf.*, порезать *pf.*
slat /slæt/ *n.* планка *f.*
slate /sleit/ *n.* сланец; шифер *m.*; (*for writing*) грифельная доска *f.*
slate pencil *n.* грифель *m.*
slattern /'slætərn/ *n.* неряха *f.*
slaughter /'slɔtər/ **1.** *n.* резня *f.*; кровопролитие *neut.*; (*of animals*) убой *m.* **2.** *v.* резать *impf.*, зарезать *pf.*
slaughterer /'slɔtərər/ *n.* забойщик *m.*
slaughterhouse /'slɔtər,haus/ *n.* скотобойня *f.*
Slav /slɑv/ *n.* славянин *m.*, славянка *f.*
slave /sleiv/ **1.** *n.* раб; невольник *m.* **2.** *adj.* рабский.
slavery /'sleivəri/ *n.* рабство *neut.*
slave trade *n.* работорговля *f.*
Slavic /'slɑvɪk/ *adj.* славянский.
slay /slei/ *v.* убивать *impf.*, убить *pf.*
sleazy /'slizi/ *adj.* (*colloq.*) скверный.
sled /slɛd/ *n.* сани *pl.*
sledgehammer /'slɛdʒ,hæmər/ *n.* кувалда *f.*; молот *m.*
sleek /slik/ *adj.* гладкий; (*hair*) лоснящийся.
sleep /slip/ **1.** *n.* сон *m.* **2.** *v.* спать *impf.*
sleepiness /'slipinis/ *n.* сонливость *f.*
sleeping /'slipɪŋ/ **1.** *n.* сон *m.*; спанье *neut.* **2.** *adj.* (*asleep*) спящий.
sleeping bag *n.* спальный мешок *m.*
sleeping car *n.* (*railroad*) спальный вагон *m.*
sleeping pill *n.* снотворная таблетка *f.*
sleepless /'sliplɪs/ *adj.* бессонный.
sleeplessness /'sliplɪsnɪs/ *n.* бессонница *f.*
sleepwalker /'slip,wɔkər/ *n.* лунатик *m.*
sleepy /'slipi/ *adj.* сонный.
sleet /slit/ *n.* дождь со снегом *m.*; крупа *f.*
sleeve /sliv/ *n.* рукав *m.*
sleeveless /'slivlɪs/ *adj.* безрукавный.
sleigh /slei/ *n.* сани, санки *pl.*
slender /'slɛndər/ *adj.* тонкий; стройный.
sleuth /sluθ/ *n.* сыщик *m.*
slice /slais/ **1.** *n.* ломтик; кусок *m.* **2.** *v.* резать ломтиками *impf.*
slicer /'slaisər/ *n.* резак *m.*; (*of bread*) хлеборезка *f.*
slide /slaid/ *v.* скользить *impf.*
slide rule *n.* логарифмическая линейка *f.*
sliding /'slaidɪŋ/ *adj.* скользящий.
sliding scale *n.* скользящая шкала *f.*
slight /slait/ **1.** *adj.* лёгкий; тонкий; хрупкий. **2.** *impf.*, пренебречь *pf.* пренебрежение *neut.* *v.* пренебрегать
slightest /'slaitɪst/ *adj.* малейший.
slightly /'slaitli/ *adv.* немного; слегка.
slim /slɪm/ *adj.* стройный; тонкий.
slime /slaim/ *n.* слизь *f.*
slimy /'slaimi/ *adj.* илистый; грязный; слизистый.

sling /slɪŋ/ n. (slingshot) рогáтка f.; (med.) пéревязь f.
slink /slɪŋk/ v. крáсться impf.
slip[1] /slɪp/ **1.** n. (skid) скольжéние neut.; (mistake) ошúбка f.; (garment) комбинáция f. **2.** v. скользúть impf.
slip[2] /slɪp/ n. (paper) листóчек m.
slipknot /'slɪp,nɒt/ n. скользя́щий ýзел m.
slipped disk /slɪpt/ n. смещéние позвонкá neut.
slipper /'slɪpər/ n. тýфля f.
slippery /'slɪpəri/ adj. скóльзкий.
slipshod /'slɪp,ʃɒd/ adj. неря́шливый; небрéжный.
slip-up /'slɪp ˌʌp/ n. ошúбка f.; прóмах m.
slit /slɪt/ **1.** n. разрéз m.; щель f. **2.** v. разрезáть impf.
sliver /'slɪvər/ n. щéпка; лучúна f.
slob /slɒb/ n. неря́ха m. and f. (decl. f.).
sloe /slou/ n. тёрн m.
slogan /'slougən/ n. лóзунг m.
slope /sloup/ **1.** n. наклóн; склон; скат m. **2.** v. имéть наклóн impf.
sloping /'sloupɪŋ/ adj. наклóнный; покáтый; птлóгый.
slop pail /slɒp/ n. помóйное ведрó neut.
sloppy /'slɒpi/ adj. небрéжный; неря́шливый.
slot /slɒt/ n. отвéрстие neut.; прорéз m.; щёлка f.
sloth /slɔθ, slouθ/ n. лéность f.; (zool.) ленúвец m.
slot machine n. игровóй автомáт m.
slouch /slautʃ/ v. (stoop) сутýлиться impf.
slough /slau/ n болóто neut.; тряси́на f.
Slovakia /slou'vakiə/ n. Словáкия f.
Slovenia /slou'viniə/ n. Словéния f.
slovenly /'slʌvənli/ adj. неря́шливый.
Slovyansk /slʌ'vyansk/ n. Славя́нск m.
slow /slou/ **1.** adj. мéдленный; **to be slow** (timepiece) отставáть impf. **2.** v.: **to slow down** замедля́ть impf., замéдлить pf.
slowdown /'slou,daun/ n. замедлéние; снижéние тéмпа neut.
slowly /'slouli/ adv. мéдленно.
slow motion n. замéдленное движéние neut.
sludge /slʌdʒ/ n. (mud) грязь f.; (sewage) ил m.
slug /slʌg/ n. (zool.) слизня́к m.; (bullet) пýля f.; (token) жетóн m.
sluggard /'slʌgərd/ n. лентя́й m.
sluggish /'slʌgɪʃ/ adj. вя́лый; инéртный; медлúтельный.
sluice /slus/ n. (on canal) шлюз m.; (trough) промы́вочный жёлоб m.
slum /slʌm/ n. трущóба f.
slumber /'slʌmbər/ **1.** n. дремóта f.; сон m. **2.** v. дремáть; спать impf.
slurp /slɜrp/ v. (eat) чáвкать impf.; (drink) хлебáть impf.
slush /slʌʃ/ n. сля́коть; грязь f.
slut /slʌt/ n. неря́ха; потаскýха f.
sly /slai/ adj. хи́трый; **on the sly** adv. тайкóм.
smack /smæk/ **1.** n. чмóканье neut.; звóнкий шлепóк m. **2.** v. чмóкать impf., чмóкнуть pf.
small /smɔl/ adj. мáленький.
small arms n. стрелкóвое орýжие neut.
small-minded /smɔl 'maindɪd/ adj. мéлочный.
smallness /'smɔlnɪs/ n. небольшóй рост m.; незначúтельность f.

smallpox /'smɔl,pɒks/ n. óспа f.
smarmy /'smarmi/ adj. елéйный.
smart /smart/ **1.** adj. ýмный; остроýмный; лóвкий. **2.** v. испы́тывать óструю боль impf.
smash /smæʃ/ v. разбивáть impf., разбúть pf.
smear /smɪər/ **1.** n. пятнó neut.; (med.) мазóк m.; (slander) клеветá f. **2.** v. мáзать; пáчкать impf.
smell /smɛl/ **1.** n. зáпах m.; (sense) обоня́ние neut. **2.** v.t. обоня́ть impf.; v.i. пáхнуть (with instr.) impf.
smelly /'smɛli/ adj. зловóнный.
smelt[1] /smɛlt/ v. (melt metal) плáвить impf.
smelt[2] /smɛlt/ n. (fish) корю́шка f.
smelter /'smɛltər/ n. (furnace) плавúльная печь f.
smidgen /'smɪdʒən/ n. (colloq.) чýточка f.
smile /smail/ **1.** n. улы́бка f. **2.** v. улыбáться impf., улыбнýться pf.
smirk /smɜrk/ **1.** n. ухмы́лка f. **2.** v. ухмыля́ться impf.
smith /smɪθ/ n. кузнéц m.
smithy /'smɪθi/ n. кýзница f.
smock /smɒk/ n. халáт m.
smog /smɒg/ n. смог m.
smoke /smouk/ **1.** n. дым m. **2.** v. дымúться impf.; (tobacco) курúть impf.; (food) коптúть impf.
smoked /smoukt/ adj. (cul.) копчёный.
smoke detector n. пожáрная сигнализáция f.
smoker /'smoukər/ n. (person) курящий; кури́льщик m., кури́льщица f.
smokestack /'smouk,stæk/ n. дымовáя трубá f.
smoky /'smouki/ adj. (emitting smoke) дымя́щий; (full of smoke) ды́мный.
smolder /'smouldər/ v. тлеть impf.
Smolensk /smou'lensk/ n. Смолéнск m.
smooth /smuð/ **1.** adj. глáдкий; рóвный. **2.** v. приглáживать impf., приглáдить pf.
smoothness /'smuðnɪs/ n. рóвность; глáдкость; плáвность f.
smooth-skinned /'smuð ˌskɪnd/ adj. гладкокóжий.
smooth-spoken /'smuð 'spoukən/ adj. сладкорéчивый.
smother /'smʌðər/ v. душúть impf., задушúть pf.
smudge /smʌdʒ/ **1.** n. пятнó neut.; (ink) кля́кса f. **2.** v. пáчкать impf.
smug /smʌg/ adj. самодовóльный.
smuggle /'smʌgəl/ v. занимáться контрабáндой impf.
smugness /'smʌgnɪs/ n. самодовóльство neut.
smut /smʌt/ n. (soot) сáжа f.; (indecency) непристóйность f.
smutty /'smʌti/ adj. (dirty) гря́зный; (indecent) непристóйный.
snack /snæk/ n. закýска f.
snag /snæg/ n. (in river) коря́га f.; (fig.) загвóздка f.
snail /sneil/ n. улúтка f.
snail mail n. (colloq.) улúточная пóчта f.
snake /sneik/ n. змея́ f.
snake charmer n. заклинáтель змей m.
snap /snæp/ **1.** n. треск m.; щёлканье neut. **2.** v.t. (make sharp sound) щёлкать impf., щёлкнуть pf.; v.i. (snap shut) защёлкиваться impf., защёлкнуться pf.

snapdragon /'snæp,drægən/ *n.* (*bot.*) львиный зев *m.*

snapshot /'snæp,ʃɒt/ *n.* снимок *m.*

snare /snɛər/ **1.** *n.* ловушка *f.* **2.** *v.* поймать в ловушку *pf.*

snarl /snɑrl/ *v.* рычать; ворчать (на *with acc.*) *impf.*

snatch /snætʃ/ *v.* хватать *impf.*, схватить *pf.*

snatchy /'snætʃi/ *adj.* отрывистый.

sneak /snik/ *v.* красться *impf.*

sneaker /'snikər/ *n.* кроссовка *f.*

sneaky /'sniki/ *adj.* (*colloq.*) (*low*) подлый; (*dishonest*) нечестный.

sneer /snɪər/ **1.** *n.* усмешка; насмешка *f.* **2.** *v.* насмехаться (над *with instr.*) *impf.*

sneering /'snɪrɪŋ/ *adj.* насмешливый; ехидный.

sneeze /sniz/ **1.** *n.* чиханье *neut.* **2.** *v.* чихать *impf.*, чихнуть *pf.*

snicker /'snɪkər/ *v.* хихикать *impf.*

sniff /snɪf/ *v.* шмыгать носом; (*snuffle*) сопеть *impf.*

snipe /snaip/ **1.** *n.* (*bird*) бекас *m.* **2.** *v.* (*mil.*) стрелять из укрытия *impf.*; (*fig. colloq.*) язвить *impf.*

snippet /'snɪpɪt/ *n.* кусочек *m.*; (*news*) обрывок *m.*

snitch /snɪtʃ/ *v.* (*colloq.*) (*inform against*) доносить *impf.*

snob /snɒb/ *n.* сноб *m.*

snoop /snup/ *v.* (*colloq.*) совать нос в чужие дела *impf.*; шпионить *impf.*

snooty /'snuti/ *adj.* чванный.

snore /snɔr/ **1.** *n.* храп *m.* **2.** *v.* храпеть *impf.*

snorkel /'snɔrkəl/ *n.* шноркель *m.*

snort /snɔrt/ *v.* фыркать *impf.*

snot /snɒt/ *n.* (*vulg.*) сопли *pl.*

snotty /'snɒti/ *adj.* (*vulg.*) сопливый; противный.

snout /snaut/ *n.* (*animal's*) морда *f.*; рыло *neut.*; (*pig's*) пятачок *m.*

snow /snou/ **1.** *n.* снег *m.* **2.** *adj.* снежный. **3.** *v.*: **it is snowing** идёт снег.

snowball /'snou,bɔl/ *n.* снежок *m.*

snowbank /'snou,bæŋk/ *n.* сугроб *m.*

snowbound /'snou,baund/ *adj.* (*stuck in snow*) застрявший в снегу.

snowdrift /'snou,drɪft/ *n.* сугроб *m.*; снежный занос *m.*

snowdrop /'snou,drɒp/ *n.* подснежник *m.*

snowfall /'snou,fɔl/ *n.* снегопад *m.*

snowflake /'snou,fleik/ *n.* снежинка *f.*

snowman /'snou,mæn/ *n.* снеговик *m.*, снежная баба *f.*

snowmobile /'snoumə,bil/ *n.* снегоход *m.*; мотосани *pl.*

snow plow /'snou,plau/ *n.* снегоочиститель *m.*

snowshoe /'snou,ʃu/ *n.* снегоступ *m.*

snowstorm /'snou,stɔrm/ *n.* метель *f.*

snub /snʌb/ *v.* игнорировать *impf.*

snub-nosed /'snʌb ,nouzd/ *adj.* курносый.

snuff¹ /snʌf/ **1.** *n.* нюхательный табак *m.*; **to take snuff** *v.* нюхать табак *impf.* **2.** *v.* (*sniff*) нюхать *impf.*

snuff² /snʌf/ *v.* (*candle*) снимать нагар *impf.*

snuffbox /'snʌf,bɒks/ *n.* табакерка *f.*

snug /snʌg/ *adj.* уютный.

snuggle /'snʌgəl/ *v.* обнимать; прижиматься (к *with dat.*) *impf.*

so /sou/ **1.** *adv.* так; таким образом; настолько; (*also*) также; тоже; **or so** приблизительно; **so that** чтобы; для того, чтобы. **2.** *conj.* (*consequently*) поэтому.

soak /souk/ *v.* промачивать *impf.*, промочить *pf.*

soap /soup/ **1.** *n.* мыло *neut.* **2.** *adj.* мыльный. **3.** *v.* намыливать *impf.*, намылить *pf.*

soap bubble *n.* мыльный пузырь *m.*

soap dish *n.* мыльница *f.*

soap opera *n.* мыльная опера *f.*

soapsuds /'soup,sʌdz/ *n.* мыльная пена *f.*

soapy /'soupi/ *adj.* мыльный.

soar /sɔr/ *v.* парить *impf.*

sob /sɒb/ **1.** *n.* рыдание *neut.* **2.** *v.* рыдать *impf.*

sobbing /'sɒbɪŋ/ *n.* рыдание; всхлипывание *neut.*

sober /'soubər/ **1.** *adj.* трёзвый. **2.** *v.t.* вытрезвлять *impf.*, вытрезвить *pf.*; *v.i.* вытрезвляться *impf.*, вытрезвиться *pf.*

so-called /'sou 'kɔld/ *adj.* так называемый.

soccer /'sɒkər/ *n.* футбол *m.*

sociability /,sɒʃə'bɪlɪti/ *n.* общительность *f.*

sociable /'souʃəbəl/ *adj.* общительный; дружеский.

social /'souʃəl/ *adj.* общественный.

socialism /'souʃə,lɪzəm/ *n.* социализм *m.*

socialist /'souʃəlɪst/ **1.** *n.* социалист *m.* **2.** *adj.* социалистический.

socialize /'souʃə,laiz/ *v.* (*pol.*) обобществлять *impf.*; (*be sociable*) общаться *impf.*

social science *n.* общественные науки *pl.*

social security *n.* социальное обеспечение *neut.*

society /sə'saiəti/ *n.* общество *neut.*

sociology /,sousi'ɒlədʒi/ *n.* социология *f.*

sock¹ /sɒk/ *n.* носок *m.*

sock² /sɒk/ **1.** *n.* (*slang*) (*blow*) удар *m.* **2.** *v.* ударить *pf.*

socket /'sɒkɪt/ *n.* (*mach.*) раструб; патрубок *m.*; (*elec.*) (*for lightbulb*) патрон *m.*; (*outlet*) розетка *f.*

soda /'soudə/ *n.* газированная вода; (*chem.*) сода *f.*

sodium /'soudiəm/ *n.* натрий *m.*

sodium bicarbonate *n.* двууглекислый натрий *m.*

sodomy /'sɒdəmi/ *n.* содомия *f.*

sofa /'soufə/ *n.* диван *m.*

sofa bed *n.* кушетка, диван-кровать *f.*

Sofia /'soufiə, sou'fiə/ *n.* София *f.*

soft /sɔft/ *adj.* мягкий; тихий.

soft-boiled egg /sɔft 'bɔild/ *n.* яйцо всмятку *neut.*

soften /'sɔfən/ *v.t.* смягчать *impf.*, смягчить *pf.*; *v.i.* смягчаться *impf.*, смягчиться *pf.*

softness /'sɔftnɪs/ *n.* мягкость *f.*

software /'sɔft,wɛər/ *n.* (*tech.*) программное обеспечение *neut.*; набор программ *m.*

softwood /'sɔft,wʊd/ *n.* хвойное дерево *neut.*

soggy /'sɒgi/ *adj.* мокрый; промокший.

soil¹ /sɔil/ *n.* почва *f.*

soil² /sɔil/ *v.* пачкать *impf.*, запачкать *pf.*

sojourn /'soudʒɜrn/ *n.* пребывание *neut.*

Sokhumi /sʊ'kumi/ *n.* Сухуми *m.*

solace /'sɒlɪs/ **1.** *n.* утешение *neut.* **2.** *v.* утешать *impf.*, утешить *pf.*

solar /'soulər/ *adj.* солнечный.

solder /'sɒdər/ **1.** *n.* припой *m.* **2.** *v.* спаивать *impf.*, спаять *pf.*

soldier /'souldʒər/ n. солда́т m.
sole¹ /soul/ adj. еди́нственный.
sole² /soul/ **1.** n. (foot) подо́шва f.; (shoe) подмётка f. **2.** v. ста́вить подмётку impf.
sole³ /soul/ n. (fish) камбала́ f.
solely /'soulli/ adv. то́лько; исключи́тельно.
solemn /'sɒləm/ adj. торже́ственный.
solemnity /sə'lɛmnɪti/ n. торже́ственность f.
solicit /sə'lɪsɪt/ v. проси́ть; выпра́шивать impf., вы́просить pf.
solicitor /sə'lɪsɪtər/ n. юрисконсульт m.
solicitous /sə'lɪsɪtəs/ adj. забо́тливый.
solicitude /sə'lɪsɪˌtud/ n. забо́тливость f.
solid /'sɒlɪd/ adj. твёрдый; соли́дный; (math.) трёхме́рный; куби́ческий.
solidarity /ˌsɒlɪ'dærɪti/ n. солида́рность; о́бщность f.
solidify /sə'lɪdəˌfai/ v.i. твердеть impf.; v.t. затвердева́ть impf.
solidity /sə'lɪdɪti/ n. твёрдость f.
solidly /'sɒlɪdli/ adv. (unanimously) единоду́шно; (firmly) твёрдо.
soliloquy /sə'lɪləkwi/ n. моноло́г m.
solitary /'sɒlɪˌteri/ adj. (lone) одино́кий; (sole) еди́нственный.
solitude /'sɒlɪˌtud/ n. одино́чество neut.
solo /'soulou/ **1.** n. со́ло neut. indecl. **2.** adj. со́льный.
soloist /'soulouɪst/ n. соли́ст m., соли́стка f.
so long interj. (colloq.) пока́!
solstice /'sɒlstɪs/ n. солнцестоя́ние neut.
soluble /'sɒlyəbəl/ adj. раствори́мый.
solution /sə'luʃən/ n. реше́ние; разреше́ние neut.; (liquid) раство́р m.
solvable /'sɒlvəbəl/ adj. разреши́мый.
solve /sɒlv/ v. реша́ть; разреша́ть impf., разреши́ть pf.
solvent /'sɒlvənt/ **1.** n. раствори́тель m. **2.** adj. растворя́ющий; (able to pay) платёжеспосо́бный.
somber /'sɒmbər/ adj. угрю́мый.
some /sʌm; unstressed səm/ **1.** pron. не́которые; одни́. **2.** adj. не́который; како́й-то, како́й-нибудь. **3.** adv. (somewhat) не́сколько.
somebody /'sʌmˌbɒdi/ pron. кто́-то; кто́-нибудь.
someday /'sʌmˌdei/ adv. когда́-нибудь; когда́-то.
somehow /'sʌmˌhau/ adv. ка́к-то, ка́к-нибудь.
somersault /'sʌmərˌsɒlt/ **1.** n. прыжо́к кувырко́м m.; кувырка́ние neut. **2.** v. кувырка́ться impf., кувыркну́ться pf.
something /'sʌmˌθɪŋ/ pron. что́-то; что́-нибудь.
sometime /'sʌmˌtaim/ adv. когда́-нибудь.
sometimes /'sʌmˌtaimz/ adv. иногда́.
somewhat /'sʌmˌwʌt/ adv. отча́сти; немно́го.
somewhere /'sʌmˌwɛər/ adv. (loc.) где́-то; где́-нибудь; (dir.) куда́-то; куда́-нибудь.
Somme /sʌm/ n. (river) Со́мма f.
somnambulism /sɒm'næmbyəˌlɪzəm/ n. сомнамбули́зм m.
somnolence /'sɒmnələns/ n. сонли́вость f.
somnolent /'sɒmnələnt/ adj. со́нный; сонли́вый.
son /sʌn/ n. сын m.
sonar /'sounɑr/ n. гидролока́тор m.
song /sɒŋ/ n. пе́сня f.
songster /'sɔŋstər/ n. певе́ц m., певи́ца f.
songstress /'sɔŋstrɪs/ n. певи́ца f.
sonic /'sɒnɪk/ adj. звуково́й.

son-in-law /'sʌn ɪn ˌlɔ/ n. зять m.
sonority /sə'nɔrɪti/ n. зво́нкость f.
sonorous /sə'nɔrəs/ adj. зву́чный; зво́нкий.
soon /sun/ adv. ско́ро; вско́ре; **as soon as** как то́лько; **as soon as possible** как мо́жно быстре́е.
soot /sʊt/ n. са́жа f.
soothe /suð/ v. облегча́ть impf., облегчи́ть pf.
soothing /'suðɪŋ/ adj. успокои́тельный.
soothsayer /'suθˌseiər/ n. предска́затель m.
sophisticated /sə'fɪstɪˌkeitɪd/ adj. искушённый; (tastes) изощрённый; утончённый.
sophomore /'sɒfəˌmɔr/ n. студе́нт-второку́рсник m.
soporific /ˌsɒpə'rɪfɪk/ adj. снотво́рный.
soprano /sə'prænou/ n. сопра́но neut. indecl.
sorcerer /'sɔrsərər/ n. колду́н; чароде́й; волше́бник m.
sorceress /'sɔrsərɪs/ n. колду́нья; чароде́йка; волше́бница f.
sorcery /'sɔrsəri/ n. колдовство́; волшебство́ neut.
sordid /'sɔrdɪd/ adj. гря́зный; по́длый.
sore /sɔr/ **1.** n. боля́чка; я́зва f. **2.** adj. больно́й; воспалённый; (angry) оби́женный.
sorely /'sɔrli/ adv. о́чень; весьма́.
soreness /'sɔrnɪs/ n. боль; боле́зненность f.
sorghum /'sɔrgəm/ n. со́рго neut. indecl.
sorrel¹ /'sɔrəl/ n. (bot.) щаве́ль m.
sorrel² /'sɔrəl/ **1.** n. (horse) гнеда́я ло́шадь f. **2.** adj. гнедо́й.
sorrow /'sɒrou/ n. печа́ль f.; го́ре neut.
sorrowful /'sɒrəfəl/ adj. печа́льный.
sorry /'sɒri/ adj. (pitiful) жа́лкий; несча́стный; (sad) гру́стный; **I'm sorry!** винова́т(а)!; прости́те!; **to be sorry** жале́ть (with acc.; o with prep.) impf., пожале́ть pf.; (regret) сожале́ть impf.
sort /sɔrt/ **1.** n. род; сорт; вид m. **2.** v. разбира́ть; сортирова́ть impf.
sorter /'sɔrtər/ n. сортиро́вщик m.
Sosnowiec /sɒs'nɒvyɛts/ n. Сосно́вец m.
so-so /'souˌsou/ adv. так себе́.
soul /soul/ n. душа́ f.
soulful /'soulfəl/ adj. (sentimental) чувстви́тельный; сентимента́льный.
soulless /'soullɪs/ adj. безду́шный.
sound¹ /saund/ adj. здоро́вый; логи́чный.
sound² /saund/ **1.** n. (noise) звук m. **2.** adj. звуково́й. **3.** v. звуча́ть impf., прозвуча́ть pf.
sound³ /saund/ **1.** n. (med.) зонд m. **2.** v. измеря́ть глубину́ impf.; (med., fig.) зонди́ровать impf.
sound⁴ /saund/ n. (strait) проли́в m.
sound barrier n. звуково́й барье́р m.
sound effects n. звуковы́е эффе́кты pl.
soundless /'saundlɪs/ adj. беззву́чный.
soundproof /'saundˌpruf/ **1.** adj. звуконепроница́емый. **2.** v. придава́ть звуконепроница́емость impf.
soundtrack /'saundˌtræk/ n. звукова́я доро́жка; фоногра́мма f.
sound wave n. звукова́я волна́ f.
soup /sup/ **1.** n. суп m. **2.** adj. супово́й.
sour /sauᵊr/ adj. ки́слый.
source /sɔrs/ n. исто́к; исто́чник m.
sour cream n. смета́на f.

sourpuss /'sauᵊr‚pʊs/ *n.* (*colloq.*) брюзга́ *m.* and *f.* (*decl. f.*).

south /sauθ/ **1.** *n.* юг *m.* **2.** *adj.* ю́жный. **3.** *adv.* на юг; к ю́гу.

South Africa *n.* Ю́жная А́фрика *f.*

southbound /'sauθ‚baund/ *adj.* иду́щий на юг.

South Carolina *n.* Ю́жная Кароли́на *f.*

South Dakota *n.* Ю́жная Дако́та *f.*

southeast /‚sauθ'ist; *Naut.* ‚sau'ist/ **1.** *n.* ю́го-восто́к *m.* **2.** *adj.* ю́го-восто́чный.

southeastern /‚sauθ'istərn; *Naut.* ‚sau'istərn/ *adj.* ю́го-восто́чный.

southern /'sʌðərn/ *adj.* ю́жный.

southerner /'sʌðərnər/ *n.* южа́нин *m.*, южа́нка *f.*

southernmost /'sʌðərn‚moust/ *adj.* са́мый ю́жный.

southpaw /'sauθ‚pɔ/ *n.* (*colloq.*) левша́ *m.*

South Pole *n.* Ю́жный по́люс *m.*

southwest /‚sauθ'wɛst; *Naut.* ‚sau'wɛst/ **1.** *n.* ю́го-за́пад *m.* **2.** *adj.* ю́го-за́падный.

southwestern /‚sauθ'wɛstərn; *Naut.* ‚sau'wɛstərn/ *adj.* ю́го-за́падный.

souvenir /‚suvə'nɪər/ *n.* сувени́р *m.*

sovereign /'sɒvrɪn/ **1.** *n.* госуда́рь; сувере́н *m.* **2.** *adj.* сувере́нный; полновла́стный.

sovereignty /'sɒvrɪnti/ *n.* суверените́т *m.*; верхо́вная власть *f.*

Sovetsk /souv'yetsk/ *n.* Сове́тск *m.*

soviet /'souvi‚et/ **1.** *adj.* (*cap.*) сове́тский **2.** *n.* сове́т *m.*

sow[1] /sau/ *n.* (*hog*) свинья́ *f.*

sow[2] /sou/ *v.* се́ять *impf.*, посе́ять *pf.*

sower /'souər/ *n.* (*person*) се́ятель *m.*; (*mach.*) се́ялка *f.*

sowing /'souɪŋ/ *n.* сев; посе́в *m.*

soybean /'soi‚bin/ **1.** *n.* со́я *f.*; со́евый боб *m.* **2.** *adj.* со́евый.

soy sauce /sɔi/ *n.* со́евый со́ус *m.*

Sozopol /sə'zɔpəl/ *n.* Созо́пол *m.*

spa /spa/ *n.* куро́рт с минера́льными во́дами *m.*; водолече́бница *f.*

space /speis/ **1.** *n.* простра́нство; расстоя́ние; ме́сто *neut.*; (*outer space*) ко́смос *m.* **2.** *adj.* косми́ческий. **3.** *v.* расставля́ть с проме́жутками *impf.*

space bar *n.* кла́виша для интерва́лов *f.*

spaceflight /'speis‚flait/ *n.* косми́ческий полёт *m.*

spaceship /'speis‚ʃɪp/ *n.* косми́ческий кора́бль *m.*

space shuttle *n.* косми́ческий челно́чный лета́тельный аппара́т; челно́чный КЛА *m.*

space station *n.* косми́ческая ста́нция *f.*

spacious /'speiʃəs/ *adj.* просто́рный; обши́рный.

spade[1] /speid/ *n.* лопа́та *f.*

spade[2] /speid/ *n.* (*cards*) пи́ка *f.*

spaghetti /spə'gɛti/ *n.* спаге́тти *neut. indecl.*

Spain /spein/ *n.* Испа́ния *f.*

span /spæn/ **1.** *n.* отре́зок *m.*; (*of bridge*) пролёт *m.*; (*aero.*) разма́х *m.* **2.** *v.* соединя́ть берега́ *impf.*

spandrel /'spændrəl/ *n.* (*archit.*) антрво́льт *m.*; па́зуха сво́да *f.*

spangle /'spæŋgəl/ *n.* блёстка *f.*

Spaniard /'spænyərd/ *n.* испа́нец *m.*, испа́нка *f.*

spaniel /'spænyəl/ *n.* спание́ль *m.*

Spanish /'spænɪʃ/ *adj.* испа́нский.

spanking /'spæŋkɪŋ/ *n.* трёпка *f.*

spar /spar/ *v.* бокси́ровать *impf.*

spare /spɛər/ **1.** *adj.* запасно́й; запа́сный; ли́шный. **2.** *v.* щади́ть; жале́ть *impf.*, пожале́ть *pf.*

spare parts *n.* запасны́е ча́сти *pl.*

spareribs /'spɛər‚rɪbz/ *n.* свины́е рёбрышки *pl.*

sparing /'spɛərɪŋ/ *adj.* ску́дный; эконо́мный; (*careful*) уме́ренный.

spark /spark/ *n.* и́скра *f.*

spark coil *n.* (*car*) кату́шка зажига́ния *f.*

sparkle /'sparkəl/ **1.** *n.* блеск *m.*; искре́ние *neut.* **2.** *v.* и́скриться *impf.*; сверка́ть *impf.*

sparkling /'sparklɪŋ/ *adj.* блестя́щий; (*wine*) игри́стый.

sparkover /'spark‚ouvər/ *n.* (*elec.*) искре́ние *neut.*

spark plug *n.* свеча́ зажига́ния *f.*

sparrow /'spærou/ *n.* воробе́й *m.*

sparrow hawk *n.* я́стреб-перепеля́тник *m.*

sparse /spars/ *adj.* ре́дкий.

Sparta /'spartə/ *n.* Спа́рта *f.*

spasm /'spæzəm/ *n.* спа́зма *f.*

spasmodic /spæz'mɒdɪk/ *adj.* спазмати́ческий; судоро́жный.

spatial /'speiʃəl/ *adj.* простра́нственный.

spatter /'spætər/ *f.* забры́згивать *impf.*, забры́згать *pf.*

spatula /'spætʃələ/ *n.* шпа́тель *m.*

spawn /spɔn/ *v.* (*fish*) мета́ть икру́ *impf.*; (*fig.*) плоди́ть; порожда́ть *impf.*

spay /spei/ *v.* удаля́ть яи́чники (*y with gen.*) *impf.*

speak /spik/ *v.* говори́ть *impf.*, сказа́ть *pf.*

speaker /'spikər/ *n.* говоря́щий *m.*; (*orator*) ора́тор *m.*

spear /spiər/ *n.* копьё *neut.*

spearhead /'spiər‚hɛd/ *n.* наконе́чник копья́ *f.*; (*fig.*) передово́й отря́д *m.*

spearmint /'spiər‚mɪnt/ *n.* мя́та колоси́стая *f.*

special /'spɛʃəl/ *adj.* специа́льный; осо́бенный; осо́бый.

special delivery *n.* сро́чная доста́вка *f.*

specialist /'spɛʃəlɪst/ *n.* специали́ст *m.*

specialize /'spɛʃə‚laiz/ *v.* специализи́ровать(ся) *impf.* and *pf.*

specialty /‚spɛʃəlti/ *n.* специа́льность *f.*

specie /'spiʃi/ *n.* зво́нкая моне́та *f.*

species /'spiʃiz/ *n.* вид *m.*

specific /spɪ'sɪfɪk/ *adj.* осо́бенный; специфи́ческий; (*phys.*) уде́льный.

specification /‚spɛsəfɪ'keiʃən/ *n.* специфика́ция *f.*

specify /'spɛsə‚fai/ *v.* определя́ть *impf.*, определи́ть *pf.*; специфици́ровать *impf.* and *pf.*

specimen /'spɛsəmən/ *n.* образе́ц; экземпля́р *m.*

specious /'spiʃəs/ *adj.* благови́дный.

speck /spɛk/ *n.* пя́тнышко *neut.*; кра́пинка *f.*; (*particle*) части́ца *f.*; (*in eye*) сори́нка *f.*

spectacle /'spɛktəkəl/ *n.* спекта́кль *m.*; зре́лище *neut.*; *pl.* (*glasses*) очки́ *pl.*

spectacular /spɛk'tækyələr/ *adj.* импоза́нтный.

spectator /'spɛkteitər/ *n.* зри́тель *m.*

specter /'spɛktər/ *n.* при́зрак *m.*

spectral /'spɛktrəl/ *adj.* (*ghostly*) при́зрачный.

spectrum /'spɛktrəm/ *n.* спектр *m.*

speculate /'spɛkyə‚leit/ *v.* разду́мывать *impf.*; спекули́ровать *impf.*

speculation /‚spɛkyə'leiʃən/ *n.* предположе́ние *neut.*; спекуля́ция *f.*

speech /spitʃ/ **1.** *n.* речь *f.*; (*language*) язык *m.* **2.** *adj.* речевой.

speechless /'spitʃlıs/ *adj.* безмолвный; немой; онемевший.

speed /spid/ **1.** *n.* скорость; быстрота *f.* **2.** *v.* спешить *impf.*

speedboat /'spid,bout/ *n.* быстроходный катер *m.*

speed limit *n.* дозволенная скорость *f.*

speedometer /spi'dɒmıtər/ *n.* спидометр *m.*

speedy /'spidi/ *adj.* быстрый; скорый.

spell[1] /spɛl/ *n.* (*charm*) заклинание *neut.*; чары *pl.*

spell[2] /spɛl/ *n.* (*time*) промежуток времени *m.*

spell[3] /spɛl/ *v.* произносить по буквам *impf.*

spellbinding /'spɛl,baindıŋ/ *adj.* чарующий.

spell checker *n.* корректор *m.*; программа орфографического контроля *f.*

spelling /'spɛlıŋ/ *n.* правописание *neut.*; орфография *f.*

spend /spɛnd/ *v.* тратить *impf.*, истратить *pf.*; (*time*) проводить *impf.*

spending /spɛndıŋ/ *n.* расходование *neut.*

spendthrift /'spɛnd,θrıft/ *n.* расточитель; транжир, мот *m.*

sperm /spɜrm/ *n.* сперма *f.*

sperm whale *n.* кашалот *m.*

spew /spyu/ *v.* извергать(ся) *impf.*

sphere /sfıər/ *n.* сфера *f.*; (*shape*) шар *m.*

spherical /'sfɛrıkəl, 'sfıər-/ *adj.* сферический.

sphincter /'sfıŋktər/ *n.* сфинктер; сжиматель *m.*

spice /spais/ **1.** *n.* специя; пряность *f.* **2.** *v.* приправлять *impf.*, приправить *pf.*

spick-and-span /'spık ən 'spæn/ *adj.* опрятный.

spicy /'spaisi/ *adj.* пряный, пикантный.

spider /'spaidər/ *n.* паук *m.*

spider web *n.* паутина *f.*

spike /spaik/ *n.* шип; гвоздь *m.*

spill /spıl/ *v.t.* разливать *impf.*, разлить *pf.*; *v.i.* разливаться *impf.*, разлиться *pf.*

spin /spın/ *v.t.* крутить *impf.*, вертеть *impf.*; *v.i.* крутиться *impf.*, вертеться *impf.*

spinach /'spınıtʃ/ *n.* шпинат *m.*

spinal /'spainəl/ *adj.* спинной.

spinal column *n.* позвоночник *m.*

spinal cord *n.* спинной мозг *m.*

spindle /'spındļ/ *n.* (*for thread; biol.*) веретено *neut.*; (*tech.*) шпиндель, вал *m.*

spin-drier /'spın 'draiər/ *n.* центрифуга; машина для выжимания *impf.* морщить *f.*

spine /spain/ *n.* спинной хребет; (*book*) корешок *m.*

spineless /'spainlıs/ *adj.* беспозвоночный; (*fig.*) бесхарактерный.

spin-off /'spın ,ɔf/ *n.* побочный продукт *m.*

spinster /'spınstər/ *n.* старая дева *f.*

spiny /'spaini/ *adj.* колючий.

spiral /'spairəl/ **1.** *adj.* спиральный. **2.** *n.* спираль *f.*

spire /spaiər/ *n.* шпиль *m.*

spirit /'spırıt/ *n.* дух *m.*; настроение *neut.*

spiritual /'spırıtʃuəl/ *adj.* духовный.

spiritualism /'spırıtʃuə,lızəm/ *n.* спиритуализм *m.*

spirituality /,spırıtʃu'ælıti/ *n.* духовность *f.*; одухотворённость *f.*

spit /spıt/ **1.** *n.* слюна *f.* **2.** *v.* плевать *impf.*, плюнуть *pf.*

spite /spait/ *n.* злоба; злость *f.*; **in spite of** несмотря на (*with acc.*).

spiteful /'spaitfəl/ *adj.* злобный; злорадный; **spiteful tongue** злой язык *m.*

spitfire /'spıt,faiər/ *n.* злюка *m.* and *f.* (*decl. f.*).

spittle /'spıtļ/ *n.* слюна *f.*

Spitzbergen /'spıts,bɜrgən/ *n.* Шпицберген *m.*

splash /splæʃ/ **1.** *n.* брызги *pl.*; плеск *m.* **2.** *v.* брызгать *impf.*, брызнуть *pf.*

splashdown /'splæʃ,daun/ *n.* приводнение *neut.*

splash guard *n.* брызговик *m.*

splatter /'splætər/ *v.* брызгать *impf.*

spleen /splin/ *n.* (*anat.*) селезёнка *f.*; (*spite*) злоба *f.*

splendid /'splɛndıd/ *adj.* великолепный; блестящий.

splendor /'splɛndər/ *n.* великолепие *neut.*; блеск *m.*

splenetic /splı'nɛtık/ *adj.* жёлчный.

splice /splais/ *n.* (*film, tape*) склейка *f.*; (*naut.*) сплесень *f.*

splint /splınt/ *n.* шина *f.*

splinter /'splıntər/ **1.** *n.* осколок *m.*; заноза *f.* **2.** *v.t.* раскалывать *impf.*, расколоть *pf.*; *v.i.* раскалываться *impf.*, расколоться *pf.*

split /splıt/ **1.** *n.* раскалывание *neut.*; трещина *f.* **2.** *v.t.* расщеплять *impf.*, расщепить *pf.*; *v.i.* расщепляться *impf.*, расщепиться *pf.*

Split /splıt/ *n.* Сплит *m.*

splitting /'splıtıŋ/ **1.** *n.* расщепление *neut.* **2.** *adj.* мучительный.

spoil /spɔil/ **1.** *n. pl.* (*booty*) добыча *f.* **2.** *v.t.* портить *impf.*, испортить *pf.*; *v.i.* портиться *impf.*, испортиться *pf.*

spoiled /spɔild/ *adj.* испорченный; (*child, etc.*) избалованный.

spoke /spouk/ *n.* спица *f.*

spoken /'spoukən/ *adj.* устный.

spokesman /'spouksmən/ *n.* представитель *m.*

sponge /spʌndʒ/ *n.* губка *f.*

sponge cake *n.* бисквитный торт *m.*

sponsor /'spɒnsər/ **1.** *n.* попечитель; покровитель *m.* **2.** *v.* финансировать *impf.* and *pf.*

spontaneous /spɒn'teiniəs/ *adj.* самопроизвольный; спонтанный.

spook /spuk/ *n.* (*colloq.*) привидение *neut.*

spool /spul/ *n.* шпулька *f.*

spoon /spun/ *n.* ложка *f.*

spoonbill /'spun,bıl/ *n.* колпица *f.*

spoor /spur/ *n.* след *m.*

Sporades /'spɔrə,diz/ *n.* (*islands*) Спорады *pl.*

sporadic /spə'rædık/ *adj.* спорадический.

spore /spɔr/ *n.* спора *f.*

sport /spɔrt/ **1.** *n.* спорт *m.*; атлетика *f.*; (*fun*) потеха *f.* **2.** *adj.* спортивный.

sports car /spɔrts/ *n.* спортивная машина *f.*

sports jacket *n.* пиджак *m.*

sportsman /'spɔrtsmən/ *n.* спортсмен *m.*

sportswoman /'spɔrts,wumən/ *n.* спортсменка *f.*

spot /spɒt/ **1.** *n.* пятно *neut.*; (*place*) место *neut.* **2.** *v.* пятнать *impf.*; (*detect*) увидеть *pf.*

spotlight /'spɒt,lait/ *n.* прожектор *m.*

spotted /'spɒtıd/ *adj.* пятнистый; (*skin*) прыщеватый.

spouse /spaus/ *n.* супру́г *m.*, супру́га *f.*

spout /spaut/ **1.** *n.* (*tube*) но́сик *m.*; (*jet*) струя́ *f.* **2.** *v.* струи́ться *impf.*; ли́ться пото́ком *impf.*

sprain /sprein/ **1.** *n.* растяже́ние свя́зок *neut.* **2.** *v.* растя́гивать свя́зки *impf.*

sprat /spræt/ *n.* шпрот *m.*; ки́лька *f.*

sprawl /sprɔl/ *v.* растяну́ться *pf.*

spray /sprei/ **1.** *n.* бры́зги *pl.*; водяна́я пыль *f.* **2.** *v.* обры́згивать *impf.*, обры́згать *pf.*

spread /sprɛd/ **1.** *n.* распростране́ние *neut.*; протяже́ние *neut.* **2.** *v.t.* распространя́ть *impf.*; (*extend*) простира́ть *impf.*, простере́ть *pf.*; *v.i.* простира́ться *impf.*, простере́ться *pf.*

spreadsheet /'sprɛd,ʃit/ *n.* (*comput.*) крупноинформа́тная электро́нная табли́ца *f.* (*abbr.* КЭТ).

spree /spri/ *n.* кутёж *m.*

sprightly /'spraitli/ *adj.* оживлённый.

spring /sprɪŋ/ **1.** *n.* (*device*) пружи́на *f.*; (*season*) весна́ *f.*; (*water*) исто́чник *m.*; **in the spring** *adv.* весно́й. **2.** *v.* пры́гать; вска́кивать *impf.*, вскочи́ть *pf.*

springboard /'sprɪŋ,bɔrd/ *n.* (*sport*) трампли́н *m.*

springbok /'sprɪŋ,bɒk/ *n.* антидо́рка *f.*; прыгу́н *m.*

spring tide *n.* сизиги́йный прили́в *m.*

springy /'sprɪŋi/ *adj.* упру́гий; пружи́нистый; эласти́чный.

sprinkle /'sprɪŋkəl/ *v.* кропи́ть *impf.*, покропи́ть *pf.*

sprint /sprɪnt/ **1.** *n.* спринт *m.* **2.** *v.i.* мча́ться *impf.*

sprite /sprait/ *n.* (*elf*) эльф *m.*

sprocket /'sprɒkɪt/ *n.* цепно́е колесо́ *neut.*; звёздочка *f.*

sprout /spraut/ *v.* прораста́ть *impf.*

spruce[1] /sprus/ *n.* ель *f.*

spruce[2] /sprus/ **1.** *adj.* (*smart*) наря́дный; (*neat, clean*) опря́тный. **2.** *v.*: **to spruce up** (*tidy*) приводи́ть в поря́док *impf.*

spry /sprai/ *adj.* живо́й; подви́жный.

spume /spyum/ *n.* пе́на *f.*

spunky /'spʌŋki/ *adj.* сме́лый *adj.*

spur /spɜr/ **1.** *n.* шпо́ра *f.*; (*fig.*) толчо́к *m.*; **on the spur of the moment** экспро́мтом *adv.* **2.** *v.* побужда́ть *impf.*, побуди́ть *pf.*

spurious /'spyʊriəs/ *adj.* подде́льный; подло́жный.

spurn /spɜrn/ *v.* отверга́ть *impf.*, отве́ргнуть *pf.*

spurt /spɜrt/ **1.** *n.* струя́. **2.** *v.* бить струёй *impf.*

sputum /'spyutəm/ *n.* слюна́ *f.*

spy /spai/ **1.** *n.* шпио́н *m.* **2.** *adj.* шпио́нский. **3.** *v.* шпио́нить *impf.*

squabble /'skwɒbəl/ **1.** *n.* ссо́ра; перебра́нка *f.* **2.** *v.* вздо́рить *impf.*, повздо́рить *pf.*

squad /skwɒd/ *n.* отря́д *m.*; кома́нда *f.*

squadron /'skwɒdrən/ *n.* эскадро́н *m.*

squalid /'skwɒlɪd/ *adj.* (*dirty*) гря́зный; гну́сный; (*wretched*) убо́гий.

squall /skwɔl/ *n.* (*storm*) шквал *m.*

squalor /'skwɒlər/ *n.* убо́гость; нищета́ *f.*

squander /'skwɒndər/ *v.* растра́чивать *impf.*, растра́тить *pf.*

square /skwɛər/ **1.** *adj.* квадра́тный. **2.** *n.* (*open area*) пло́щадь *f.*; (*math.*) квадра́т *m.*

square-shouldered /'skwɛər 'ʃouldərd/ *adj.* с прямы́ми плеча́ми.

squaretoed /'skwɛər'toud/ *adj.* тупоно́сый.

squash[1] /'skwɒʃ/ *n.* (*vegetable*) кабачо́к *m.*

squash[2] /'skwɒʃ/ *v.* разда́вливать *impf.*, разда́вить *pf.*

squat /skwɒt/ *v.* сиде́ть на ко́рточках *impf.*

squaw /skwɔ/ *n.* индиа́нка *f.*

squawk /skwɔk/ *v.* пронзи́тельно крича́ть *impf.*

squeak /skwik/ **1.** *n.* скрип; писк *m.* **2.** *v.* скрипе́ть *impf.*

squeal /skwil/ **1.** *n.* визг *m.* **2.** *v.* визжа́ть *impf.*

squeamish /'skwimɪʃ/ *adj.* брезгли́вый; пр иуве́рдливый.

squeeze /skwiz/ **1.** *n.* сжа́тие; пожа́тие *neut.* (*crush*) да́вка *f.* **2.** *v.* сжима́ть *impf.*, сжать *pf.*; (*fruit*) выжима́ть *impf.*, вы́жать *pf.*

squelch /skwɛltʃ/ *v.* хлю́пать *impf.*

squid /skwɪd/ *n.* (*zool.*) кальма́р *m.*

squint /skwɪnt/ *v.* коси́ть (глаза́ми) *impf.*

squint-eyed /'skwɪnt ,aid/ *adj.* косогла́зый; косо́й.

squirm /skwɜrm/ *v.* извива́ться *impf.*; (*fidget*) ёрзать; ко́рчиться *impf.*

squirrel /'skwɜrəl/ *n.* бе́лка *f.*

squirt /skwɜrt/ **1.** *n.* струя́ *f.* **2.** *v.* пуска́ть струю́ *impf.*

Sri Lanka /,sri' laŋkə/ *n.* (*formerly: Ceylon*) Шри-Ла́нка *f.*

stab /stæb/ **1.** *n.* уда́р *m.* **2.** *v.* вонза́ть *impf.*, вонзи́ть *pf.*

stability /stə'bɪliti/ *n.* стаби́льность *f.*

stabilize /'steibə,laiz/ *v.* стабилизи́ровать *impf.* and *pf.*

stable[1] /'steibəl/ *n.* коню́шня *f.*

stable[2] /'steibəl/ *adj.* сто́йкий; постоя́нный; стаби́льный.

stableman /'steibəlmən/ *n.* ко́нюх *m.*

stack /stæk/ **1.** *n.* (*hay*) стог *m.*; (*heap*) ку́ча *f.* **2.** *v.* скла́дывать в ку́чу *impf.*

stadium /'steidiəm/ *n.* стадио́н *m.*

staff /stæf/ **1.** *n.* (*stick*) по́сох; жезл *m.*; (*personnel*) служе́бный персона́л; штат *m.* **2.** *adj.* шта́тный; (*mil.*) штабно́й.

stag /stæg/ **1.** *n.* рога́ч *m.* **2.** *adj.* (*colloq.*) холостя́цкий.

stage /steidʒ/ **1.** *n.* (*platform*) подмо́стки *pl.*; помо́ст *m.*; платфо́рма *f.*; (*theat.*) сце́на; эстра́да *f.* **2.** *v.* ста́вить *impf.*, поста́вить *pf.*; инсцени́ровать *impf.* and *pf.*

stagecoach /'steidʒ,koutʃ/ *n.* дилижа́нс *m.*

stage door *n.* служе́бный вход (в теа́тр) *m.*

stage manager *n.* помо́щник режиссёра *m.*

stagger /'stægər/ *v.i.* колеба́ться; шата́ться *impf.*

staggering /'stægərɪŋ/ *adj.* потряса́ющий.

staging /'steidʒɪŋ/ *n.* (*play*) постано́вка *f.*; (*platform*) подмо́стки *pl.*

stagnant /'stægnənt/ *adj.* стоя́чий.

stagnate /'stægneit/ *v.* заста́иваться *impf.*, застоя́ться *pf.*

stagnation /stæg'neiʃən/ *n.* засто́й *m.*

stain /stein/ **1.** *n.* пятно́ *neut.* **2.** *v.* пятна́ть; па́чкать(ся) *impf.*

stained /steind/ *adj.* испа́чканный; запя́тнанный.

stainless steel /'steinlɪs/ *n.* нержаве́ющая сталь *f.*

stair /stɛər/ *n.* ступе́нька *f.*; *pl.* ле́стница *f.*

staircase /'stɛər,keis/ *n.* ле́стница *f.*

stake[1] /steik/ *n.* кол; столб *m.*

stake² /steik/ **1.** *n.* (*bet*) ста́вка *f.* **2.** *v.* (*cards*) ста́вить на ка́рту *impf.*

stale /steil/ *adj.* несве́жий; чёрствый.

stalemate /'steil,meit/ *n.* тупи́к *m.*; (*chess*) пат *m.*

Stalingrad /'stɑlɪn,græd/ *n.* Сталингра́д *m.* (*see* Volgograd).

stalk¹ /stɔk/ *n.* сте́бель; черено́к *m.*

stalk² /stɔk/ *v.* (*approach stealthily*) подкра́дываться *impf.*, подкра́сться *pf.*; (*pursue*) выслёживать *impf.*

stalker /'stɔkər/ *n.* охо́тник *m.*

stalking-horse /,stɔkɪŋ,hɔrs/ *n.* маскиро́вка *f.*

stall /stɔl/ **1.** *n.* (*for animal*) сто́йло *neut.*; (*booth*) ларёк *m.* **2.** *v.t.* остана́вливать *impf.*, останови́ть *pf.*; заде́рживать *impf.*, задержа́ть *pf.*; *v.i.* застрева́ть *impf.*, застря́ть *pf.*

stallion /'stælyən/ *n.* жеребе́ц *m.*

stamen /'steimən/ *n.* тычи́нка *f.*

stamina /'stæmənə/ *n.* выно́сливость *f.*

stammer /'stæmər/ **1.** *n.* заика́ние *neut.* **2.** *v.* заика́ться *impf.*

stamp /stæmp/ **1.** *n.* штамп; штёмпель *m.*; печа́ть *f.*; (*postage*) почто́вая ма́рка *f.* **2.** *v.* штампова́ть *impf.*

stampede /stæm'pid/ *n.* пани́ческое бе́гство *neut.*

stanchion /'stænʃən/ *n.* опо́ра; сто́йка *f.*

stand /stænd/ **1.** *n.* подста́вка *f.*; кио́ск *m.*; (*view*) пози́ция *f.* **2.** *v.* стоя́ть *impf.*; **to stand up** встава́ть *impf.*, встать *pf.*

standard /'stændərd/ **1.** *n.* станда́рт *m.*; но́рма *f.* **2.** *adj.* станда́ртный.

standard-bearer /'stændərd ,bɛərər/ *n.* знамено́сец *m.*

standardize /'stændər,daiz/ *v.* стандартизи́ровать *impf.* and *pf.*

standby /'stænd,bai/ *adj.* (*reserve*) запасно́й.

stand-in /'stænd ,in/ *n.* замести́тель *m.*

standing /'stændɪŋ/ **1.** *n.* состоя́ние; положе́ние *neut.* **2.** *adj.* стоя́щий; (*permanent*) постоя́нный.

standpoint /'stænd,pɔint/ *n.* то́чка зре́ния *f.*

stannic /'stænɪk/ *adj.* оловя́нный.

stanza /'stænzə/ *n.* строфа́ *f.*

staple¹ /'steipəl/ **1.** *n.* (*for paper*) ско́бка *f.* **2.** *v.* (*paper*) скрепля́ть ско́бкой, ско́бками *impf.*

staple² /'steipəl/ *n.* (*principal product*) основно́й проду́кт *m.*; (*basic*) гла́вный элеме́нт *m.*

star /stɑr/ **1.** *n.* звезда́ *f.* **2.** *adj.* звёздный.

Staraya Russa /'stɑrəyə 'rusə/ *n.* Ста́рая Ру́сса *f.*

starboard /'stɑrbərd/ *n.* пра́вый борт *m.*

starch /stɑrtʃ/ **1.** *n.* крахма́л *m.* **2.** *v.* крахма́лить *impf.*, накрахма́лить *impf.*

starched /stɑrtʃt/ *adj.* крахма́льный.

stare /stɛər/ *v.* смотре́ть при́стально *impf.*

starfish /'stɑr,fiʃ/ *n.* морска́я звезда́ *f.*

stark /stɑrk/ *adj.* абсолю́тный.

starlet /'stɑrlɪt/ *n.* звёздочка *f.*; (*cinema*) молода́я киноактри́са *f.*

starlight /'stɑr,lait/ *n.* свет звёзд *m.*

starling /'stɑrlɪŋ/ *n.* (*bird*) скворе́ц *m.*

starry /'stɑri/ *adj.* звёздный; **starry-eyed** (*naive*) наи́вный; (*full of lofty ideas*) восто́рженный.

start /stɑrt/ **1.** *n.* нача́ло *neut.*; старт *m.* **2.** *v.t.* начина́ть *impf.*, нача́ть *pf.*; *v.i.* начина́ться *impf.*, нача́ться *pf.*

START /stɑrt/ *n.* СНВ (*abbr. of* Догово́р по

сокраще́нию стратеги́ческих наступа́тельных вооруже́ний).

startle /'stɑrtl/ *v.* испуга́ть *pf.*

starvation /stɑr'veiʃən/ *n.* го́лод *m.*; голода́ние *neut.*

starve /stɑrv/ *v.* голода́ть *impf.*

starving /'stɑrvɪŋ/ *adj.* голода́ющий.

stasis /'steisɪs, 'stæsɪs/ *n.* стаз; засто́й *m.*

state /steit/ **1.** *n.* (*condition*) состоя́ние; положе́ние *neut.*; (*government*) госуда́рство *neut.*; штат *m.* **2.** *adj.* госуда́рственный. **3.** *v.* излага́ть *impf.*, изложи́ть *pf.*

stateless /'steitlɪs/ *adj.* не име́ющий гражда́нства.

statelessness /'steitlɪsnɪs/ *n.* отсу́тствие гражда́нства *neut.*

stately /'steitli/ *adj.* вели́чественный; велича́вый.

statement /'steitmənt/ *n.* заявле́ние; утвержде́ние *neut.*

stateroom /'steit,rum/ *n.* (*naut.*) каю́та *f.*

statesman /'steitsmən/ *n.* госуда́рственный *or* полити́ческий де́ятель *m.*

static /'stætɪk/ **1.** *adj.* стати́ческий; неподви́жный. **2.** *n.* (*radio*) атмосфе́рные поме́хи *pl.*

station /'steiʃən/ *n.* ста́нция *f.*; (*terminal*) вокза́л *m.*; (*post*) пост *m.*

stationary /'steiʃə,nɛri/ *adj.* неподви́жный.

stationery /'steiʃə,nɛri/ *n.* канцеля́рские *or* писчебума́жные принадле́жности *pl.*

stationmaster /'steiʃən,mæstər/ *n.* нача́льник вокза́ла *or* ста́нции *m.*

statistics /stə'tistiks/ *n.* стати́стика *f.*; статисти́ческие да́нные *pl.*

statue /'stætʃu/ *n.* ста́туя *f.*

stature /'stætʃər/ *n.* рост; стан *m.*

status /'steitəs, 'stætəs/ *n.* ста́тус *m.*; положе́ние *neut.*

statute /'stætʃut/ *n.* зако́н *m.*

statutory /'stætʃu,tɔri/ *adj.* устано́вленный зако́ном.

stave /steiv/ *n.* (*stick*) па́лка *f.*; (*on barrel*) клёпка *f.*; (*mus.*) но́тный стан *m.*

Stavropol /stæv'roupəl/ *n.* Ставро́поль.

stay /stei/ *n.* пребыва́ние *neut.*; (*suspension*) приостановле́ние *neut.*, *v.* остана́вливаться; остава́ться *impf.*, оста́ться *pf.*

staysail /'stei,seil; Naut. 'steisəl/ *n.* ста́ксель *m.*

steadfast /'stɛd,fæst/ *adj.* сто́йкий; непоколеби́мый.

steady /'stɛdi/ **1.** *adj.* усто́йчивый; равноме́рный; неизме́нный. **2.** *v.* уравнове́сить *pf.*

steak /steik/ *n.* бифште́кс *m.*

steal /stil/ *v.* красть *impf.*, укра́сть *pf.*

stealing /'stilɪŋ/ *n.* воровство́ *neut.*; кра́жа *f.*

stealthy /'stɛlθi/ *adj.* скры́тый; (*cautious*) осторо́жный; (*furtive*) сде́ланный укра́дкой.

steam /stim/ **1.** *n.* пар *m.* **2.** *adj.* парово́й. **3.** *v.i.* выпуска́ть пар *impf.*; *v.t.* па́рить *impf.*

steamroller /'stim,roulər/ *n.* парово́й като́к *m.*

steamship /'stim,ʃip/ *n.* парохо́д *m.*

steed /stid/ *n.* (*poet.*) конь *m.*

steel /stil/ **1.** *n.* сталь *f.* **2.** *adj.* стально́й.

steelyard /'stil,yɑrd/ *n.* безме́н *m.*

steep /stip/ *adj.* круто́й.

steeple /'stipəl/ *n.* шпиль *m.*

steeplechase /'stipəl,tʃeis/ *n.* ска́чки с препя́тствиями *pl.*; стипль-чёз *m.*

steeplejack /'stipəl‚dʒæk/ n. верхолаз m.
steer¹ /stɪər/ n. (ox) вол m.
steer² /stɪər/ v.t. править; управлять (with instr.) impf.; v.i. направляться impf.
steerable /'stɪərəbəl/ adj. управляемый.
steering /'stɪərɪŋ/ n. управление (with instr.).
steering wheel n. руль m.
stele /'stili/ n. стела f.
stellar /'stɛlər/ adj. звёздный.
stem /stɛm/ n. ствол; стебель m.; (ling.) основа f.; **to stem from** происходить impf., произойти pf.
stench /stɛntʃ/ n. зловоние neut.; вонь f.
stencil /'stɛnsəl/ **1.** n. шаблон; трафарет m. **2.** v. наносить узор по трафарету impf.
stenographer /stə'nɒgrəfər/ n. стенографист m., стенографистка f.
stenography /stə'nɒgrəfi/ n. стенография f.
step /stɛp/ **1.** n. шаг m.; (stair) ступень; ступенька f.; **step by step** шаг за шагом. **2.** v. шагать; ступать impf., ступить pf.
Stepanakert /‚stɛpənə'kert/ n. Степанакерт m.
stepbrother /'stɛp‚brʌðər/ n. сводный брат m.
stepdaughter /'stɛp‚dɔtər/ n. падчерица f.
stepfather /'stɛp‚faðər/ n. отчим m.
stepladder /'stɛp‚lædər/ n. стремянка f.
stepmother /'stɛp‚mʌðər/ n. мачеха f.
steppe /stɛp/ **1.** n. степь f. **2.** adj. степной.
stepped /stɛpt/ adj. ступенчатый.
stepsister /'stɛp‚sɪstər/ n. сводная сестра f.
stepson /'stɛp‚sʌn/ n. пасынок m.
stereo /'stɛriou/ n. стерео neut. indecl.
stereophonic /‚stɛriə'fɒnɪk/ adj. стереофонический.
stereotype /'stɛriə‚taip/ **1.** n. стереотип m. **2.** v. стереотипировать impf. and pf.
sterile /'stɛrɪl/ adj. бесплодный; стерильный.
sterility /stə'rɪlɪti/ n. бесплодность; стерильность f.
sterilize /'stɛrə‚laiz/ v. стерилизовать impf. and pf.
sterlet /'stɜrlɪt/ n. стерлядь f.
stern¹ /stɜrn/ n. корма f.
stern² /stɜrn/ adj. строгий; суровый.
sternness /'stɜrnnɪs/ n. суровость; строгость f.
sternum /'stɜrnəm/ n. грудина f.
stethoscope /'stɛθə‚skoup/ n. стетоскоп m.
stevedore /'stivɪ‚dɔr/ n. портовый грузчик m.
stew /stu/ **1.** n. тушёное мясо neut. **2.** v.t. тушить impf.; v.i. тушиться impf.
steward /'stuərd/ n. официант; стюард m.
stewardess /'stuərdɪs/ n. стюардесса f.
stewed /stud/ adj. тушёный; **stewed fruit** n. компот m.
stick¹ /stɪk/ n. палка; трость f.
stick² /stɪk/ v.t. втыкать impf., воткнуть pf.; v.i. липнуть (к with dat.) impf.
sticker /'stɪkər/ n. наклейка f.
stickleback /'stɪkəl‚bæk/ n. колюшка f.
sticky /'stɪki/ adj. липкий; клейкий.
stiff /stɪf/ adj. тугой; негибкий.
stiffen /'stɪfən/ v. делать(ся) жёстким; коченеть impf.
stiffness /'stɪfnɪs/ n. жёсткость; неподвижность f.
stifle /'staifəl/ v. подавлять impf.
stifling /'staiflɪŋ/ adj. (airless) душный.

stigma /'stɪgmə/ n. клеймо; пятно neut.
stigmatize /'stɪgmə‚taiz/ v. клеймить impf.
still /stɪl/ **1.** adj. тихий; неподвижный. **2.** adv. (всё) ещё; всё-таки. **3.** v. успокаивать impf., успокоить pf.
still life n. натюрморт m.
stillness /'stɪlnɪs/ n. тишина f.; безмолвие neut.
stilt /stɪlt/ n. ходуля f.; **to walk on stilts** ходить на ходулях impf.
stilted /'stɪltɪd/ adj. ходульный; чопорный.
stimulant /'stɪmyələnt/ **1.** adj. возбуждающий. **2.** n. возбуждающее средство neut.
stimulate /'stɪmyə‚leit/ v. возбуждать impf., возбудить pf.
stimulus /'stɪmyələs/ n. стимул; побудитель m.
sting /stɪŋ/ **1.** n. жало neut.; укус m. **2.** v. жалить impf., ужалить pf.
stingray /'stɪŋ‚rei/ n. морской кот m.
stingy /'stɪndʒi/ adj. скаредный; скупой.
stink /stɪŋk/ **1.** n. вонь f. **2.** v. вонять impf.
stinking /'stɪŋkɪŋ/ adj. вонючий.
stint /stɪnt/ v. скупиться (на with acc.) impf.
stipulate /'stɪpyə‚leit/ v. обусловливать impf., обусловить pf.
stipulated /'stɪpyə‚leitɪd/ adj. обусловленный.
stipulation /‚stɪpyə'leiʃən/ n. условие neut.; оговорка f.
stir /stɜr/ **1.** n. шевеление; движение neut. **2.** v.t. (mix) мешать; размешивать impf., размешать pf.; (move) возбуждать impf., возбудить pf.; v.i. двигаться impf., двинуться pf.
stirrup /'stɜrəp, 'stɪr-/ n. стремя neut.
stitch /stɪtʃ/ **1.** n. стежок m.; (med.) шов m.; v. шить impf., сшить pf.
stochastic /stə'kæstɪk/ adj. стохастический.
stock /stɒk/ **1.** n. (supply) запас; инвентарь m.; (share) акция f.; **in stock** на складе; в наличии. **2.** adj. (of stock market) биржевой; (regular) стандартный. **3.** v. иметь в наличии or в продаже impf.
stockade /stɒ'keid/ n. (fence) частокол; штакетник m.; (fort) форт m.
stockbreeder /'stɒk‚bridər/ n. животновод m.
stockbroker /'stɒk‚broukər/ n. (биржевой) маклер m.
stock exchange n. фондовая биржа f.
stockfish /'stɒk‚fɪʃ/ n. вяленая рыба f.; стокфиш m.
stockholder /'stɒk‚houldər/ n. владелец акций; акционер m.
Stockholm /'stɒkhoum/ n. Стокгольм m.
stocking /'stɒkɪŋ/ n. чулок m.
stock market n. (фондовая) биржа f.
stockpile /'stɒk‚pail/ n. запас; резерв m.
stockroom /'stɒk‚rum/ n. склад m.; кладовая f.
stocky /'stɒki/ adj. коренастый.
stodgy /'stɒdʒi/ adj. тяжеловесный.
stoic /'stouɪk/ n. стоик m.
stoical /'stouɪkəl/ adj. стоический.
stoke /stouk/ v. топить impf.
stoker /'stoukər/ n. (person) кочегар m.
stole /stoul/ n. (fur) меховая накидка f.
stomach /'stʌmək/ n. желудок; живот m.
stomachache /'stʌmək‚eik/ n. боль в животе f.
stomp /stɒmp/ v. топтать impf.
stone /stoun/ n. камень m.

stoned /stound/ *adj.* (*fruit*) без ко́сточек; (*slang*) (*drunk*) вдре́безги пья́ный.

stonemason /'stoun,meisən/ *n.* ка́менщик *m.*

stony /'stouni/ *adj.* ка́менный.

stool /stul/ *n.* табуре́тка; скаме́ечка *f.*

stool pigeon *n.* (*slang*) (*informer*) стука́ч *m.*

stoop /stup/ *v.* наклоня́ться *impf.*, наклони́ться *pf.*; (*fig.*) унижа́ться (до *with gen.*) *impf.*, уни́зиться *pf.*

stooped /stupt/ *adj.* суту́лый.

stop /stop/ **1.** *n.* остано́вка *f.*; (*pause*) па́уза *f.*; (*organ*) реги́стр *m.* **2.** *v.t.* остана́вливать *impf.*, останови́ть *pf.*; *v.i.* остана́вливаться *impf.*, останови́ться *pf.*

stoplight /'stop,lait/ *n.* (*traffic signal*) светофо́р *m.*; (*on car*) стоп-сигна́л *m.*

stoppage /'stopidʒ/ *n.* прекраще́ние *neut.*

stopper /'stopər/ *n.* заты́чка; про́бка *f.*; (*tech.*) сто́пор *m.*

storage /'stɔridʒ/ *n.* (*act*) хране́ние *neut.*; (*place*) храни́лище *neut.*; склад *m.*

storage room *n.* чула́н *m.*

store /stɔr/ **1.** *n.* магази́н *m.*; ла́вка *f.*, (*warehouse*) склад *m.*; (*supply*) запа́с *m.* **2.** *v.* запаса́ть *impf.*, запасти́ *pf.*; отдава́ть на хране́ние *impf.*

storehouse /'stɔr,haus/ *n.* склад *m.*

storeroom /'stɔr,rum/ *n.* кладова́я *f.*

store window *n.* витри́на *f.*

storied[1] /'stɔrid/ *adj.* легенда́рный.

storied[2] /'stɔrid/ *adj.*: **three-storied** трёхэта́жный.

stork /stɔrk/ *n.* а́ист *m.*

storm /stɔrm/ **1.** *n.* бу́ря; гроза́ *f.* **2.** *v.* (*mil.*) штурмова́ть *impf.*

storm petrel *n.* буреве́стник *m.*

storm trooper *n.* штурмови́к *m.*

stormy /'stɔrmi/ *adj.* бу́рный.

story[1] /'stɔri/ *n.* (*floor*) эта́ж *m.*

story[2] /'stɔri/ *n.* (*lit.*) расска́з *m.*; нове́лла *f.*; (*anecdote*) анекдо́т *m.*

stout /staut/ *adj.* по́лный; ту́чный.

stove /stouv/ *n.* (*wood stove*) печь *f.*; (*cooker*) плита́ *f.*

stow /stou/ *v.* (*put away*) укла́дывать *impf.*

stowaway /'stouə,wei/ *n.* безбиле́тный пассажи́р *m.*, безбиле́тная пассажи́рка *f.*; за́яц *m.*

St. Petersburg /seint 'pitərz,bɜrg/ *n.* Санкт-Петербу́рг *m.*

straggle /'strægəl/ *v.* (*drop behind*) отстава́ть *impf.*

straggler /'stræglər/ *n.* отста́вший *m.*

straight /streit/ **1.** *adj.* прямо́й. **2.** *adv.* пря́мо.

straighten /'streitn/ *v.t.* выпрямля́ть *impf.*, вы́прямить *pf.*; *v.i.* выпрямля́ться *impf.*, вы́прямиться *pf.*

straight-faced /'streit 'feist/ *adj.* с серьёзной ми́ной; не улыба́ясь.

straightforward /,streit'fɔrwərd/ *adj.* прямо́й; че́стный; открове́нный.

straight-line /'streit 'lain/ *adj.* прямолине́йный.

strain[1] /strein/ **1.** *n.* натяже́ние; напряже́ние *neut.* **2.** *v.* натя́гивать *impf.*, натяну́ть *pf.*; напряга́ть(ся) *impf.*, напря́чь(ся) *pf.*

strain[2] /strein/ *n.* (*breed*) поро́да *f.*

strained /streind/ *adj.* натя́нутый; (*nervous, forced*) напряжённый; (*sprained*) растя́нутый.

strainer /'streinər/ *n.* си́то *neut.*; (*for tea*) си́течко *neut.*

strait /streit/ *n.* проли́в *m.*

straitjacket /'streit,dʒækit/ *n.* смири́тельная руба́шка *f.*

strand[1] /strænd/ *n.* (*of hair, etc.*) прядь *f.*; (*thread*) ни́тка *f.*

strand[2] /strænd/ *v.* (*run aground*) сажа́ть на мель *impf.*

strange /streindʒ/ *adj.* стра́нный; незнако́мый.

stranger /'streindʒər/ *n.* незнако́мец *m.*, незнако́мка *f.*

strangle /'stræŋgəl/ *v.* души́ть *impf.*

stranglehold /'stræŋgəl,hould/ *adj.* захва́т го́рла *m.*; тиски́ *pl.*

strangulation /,stræŋgyə'leiʃən/ *n.* удуше́ние *neut.*; (*med.*) ущемле́ние; зажима́ние *neut.*

strap /stræp/ **1.** *n.* реме́нь *m.* **2.** *v.* свя́зывать ремнём *impf.*

strategic /strə'tidʒik/ *adj.* стратеги́ческий.

strategy /'strætidʒi/ *n.* страте́гия *f.*

stratification /,strætəfi'keiʃən/ *n.* расслое́ние *neut.*; (*geol.*) стратифика́ция *f.*

stratified /'strætə,faid/ *adj.* слои́стый.

stratify /'strætə,fai/ *v.* рассла́ивать(ся) *impf.*

stratum /'streitəm/ *n.* слой; пласт *m.*

stratus /'streitəs/ *n.* слои́стое о́блако *neut.*

straw /strɔ/ **1.** *n.* соло́ма *f.*; (*for drinking*) соло́мка *f.* **2.** *adj.* соло́менный.

strawberry /'strɔ,bɛri/ *n.* клубни́ка *f.*; (*wild*) земляни́ка *f.*

stray /strei/ **1.** *n.* (*dog*) дворня́га *m.* and *f.* (*decl. f.*). **2.** *adj.* бездо́мный. **3.** *v.* (*deviate*) отклоня́ться; сбива́ться *impf.*

streak /strik/ *n.* потёк *m.*; полоса́ *f.*

stream /strim/ **1.** *n.* пото́к *m.*; (*brook*) руче́й *m.*; (*current*) тече́ние *neut.* **2.** *v.* течь; струи́ться *impf.*

streamer /'strimər/ *n.* вы́мпел *m.*

streamline /'strim,lain/ *n.* обтека́емая фо́рма *f.*

streamlined /'strim,laind/ *adj.* обтека́емый.

street /strit/ **1.** *n.* у́лица *f.* **2.** *adj.* у́личный.

streetcar /'strit,kar/ *n.* трамва́й *m.*

street musician *n.* у́личный музыка́нт *m.*

streetwalker /'strit,wɔkər/ *n.* проститу́тка *f.*

strength /strɛŋkθ/ *n.* си́ла; кре́пость *f.*

strengthen /'strɛŋkθən/ *v.* уси́ливать; укрепля́ть *impf.*

strenuous /'strɛnyuəs/ *adj.* тяжёлый.

stress /strɛs/ **1.** *n.* напряже́ние *neut.*; стресс *m.*; (*emphasis*) ударе́ние *neut.* **2.** *v.* подчёркивать; де́лать ударе́ние (на *with acc.*) *impf.*

stressful /'strɛsfəl/ *adj.* напряжённый.

stretch /strɛtʃ/ **1.** *n.* протяже́ние *neut.*; (*duration*) срок *m.* **2.** *v.* растя́гивать(ся); вытя́гивать(ся) *impf.*

stretcher /'strɛtʃər/ *n.* носи́лки *pl.*

strew /stru/ *v.* разбра́сывать *impf.*, разброса́ть *pf.*

stricken /'strikən/ *adj.* поражённый; (*grieving*) сокрушённый.

strict /strikt/ *adj.* стро́гий.

stride /straid/ **1.** *n.* шаг; большо́й шаг *m.*; *pl.* (*fig.*) успе́хи *pl.* **2.** *v.* шага́ть *impf.*

strife /straif/ *n.* раздо́р *m.*; борьба́ *f.*

strike /straik/ *n.* забасто́вка *f.*; (*blow*) уда́р *m.*

2. *v.t.* (*hit*) ударя́ть *impf.*, уда́рить *pf.*; *v.i.* (*labor*) бастова́ть *impf.*, забастова́ть *pf.*

strikebreaker /'straik,breikər/ *n.* (*polit.*) штрейкбре́хер *m.*

striker /'straikər/ *n.* (*worker*) забасто́вщик; басту́ющий *m.*

striking /'straikiŋ/ *adj.* порази́тельный.

string /striŋ/ **1.** *n.* верёвка; ни́тка *f.*; (*mus.*) струна́ *f.*; (*row*) ряд *m.* **2.** *adj.* стру́нный.

string bean *n.* стручко́вая фасо́ль *f.*

stringed /striŋd/ *adj.* стру́нный.

stringy /'striŋi/ *adj.* волокни́стый.

strip¹ /strip/ *n.* полоса́; поло́ска *f.*

strip² /strip/ *v.* сдира́ть *impf.*, содра́ть *pf.*

stripe /straip/ *n.* полоса́ *f.*; (*insignia*) наши́вка *f.*

striped /straipt/ *adj.* полоса́тый.

stripling /'stripliŋ/ *n.* ю́ноша *m.*

stripper /'stripər/ *n.* (*theat.*) танцо́вщица ночно́го ба́ра *f.*

strive /straiv/ *v.* стара́ться *impf.*; стреми́ться *impf.*

stroke¹ /strouk/ **1.** *n.* уда́р *m.*; (*pen, brush, etc.*) штрих *m.*; (*med.*) уда́р; инсу́льт *m.*; (*swimming*) стиль *m.* **2.** *v.* (*rowing*) задава́ть такт *impf.*

stroke² /strouk/ *v.* (*caress*) гла́дить *impf.*

stroll /stroul/ **1.** *n.* прогу́лка *f.* **2.** *v.* прогу́ливаться *impf.*, прогуля́ться *pf.*

stroller /'stroulər/ *n.* де́тская коля́ска *f.*

strong /strɔŋ/ *adj.* си́льный; кре́пкий.

strongbox /'strɔŋ,bɒks/ *n.* сейф *m.*

stronghold /'strɔŋ,hould/ *n.* кре́пость; тверды́ня *f.*

strong-willed /'strɔŋ 'wild/ *adj.* волево́й.

structural /'strʌktʃərəl/ *adj.* структу́рный; (*building*) строи́тельный.

structuralist /'strʌktʃərəlist/ *n.* структурали́ст *m.*

structure /'strʌktʃər/ *n.* структу́ра *f.*

struggle /'strʌgəl/ **1.** *n.* борьба́ *f.* **2.** *v.* боро́ться *impf.*

strum /strʌm/ *v.* бренча́ть (на *with prep.*) *impf.*

strut¹ /strʌt/ *v.* ходи́ть го́голем *impf.*

strut² /strʌt/ *n.* подпо́ра *f.*; (*brace*) подко́с *m.*

stub /stʌb/ **1.** *n.* (*stump*) пень *m.*; (*fragment*) огры́зок *m.*; (*cigarette*) оку́рок *m.* **2.** *v.* расшиба́ть *impf.*

stubble /'stʌbəl/ *n.* (*on field*) жнивьё *neut.*; (*beard*) щети́на *f.*

stubborn /'stʌbərn/ *adj.* упря́мый; упо́рный.

stucco /'stʌkou/ **1.** *n.* штукату́рка *f.* **2.** *adj.* штукату́рный.

stuck /stʌk/ *adj.*: **to be stuck** (*jammed; held up*) застря́ть *pf.*; (*colloq.*) (*stumped*) в тупике́.

stud¹ /stʌd/ *n.* (*cuff*) за́понка *f.*; (*nail*) гвоздь *m.*

stud² /stʌd/ *n.* (*horse*) племенно́й жеребе́ц *m.*, (*farm*) ко́нный заво́д *m.*; (*slang*) жеребе́ц *m.*

student /'studnt/ **1.** *n.* студе́нт *m.*, студе́нтка *f.* **2.** *adj.* студе́нческий.

studio /'studi,ou/ *n.* ателье́ *neut. indecl.*; мастерска́я; сту́дия *f.*; (*apartment*) однокомнатная кварти́ра *f.*

studious /'studiəs/ *adj.* приле́жный; усе́рдный.

study /'stʌdi/ **1.** *n.* изуче́ние; иссле́дование *neut.*; (*room*) кабине́т *m.*; *pl.* заня́тия *pl.* **2.** *v.t.* изуча́ть *impf.*, изучи́ть *pf.*; *v.i.* учи́ться *impf.*

stuff /stʌf/ **1.** *n.* материа́л *m.*; вещество́ *neut.*; ве́щи *pl.* **2.** *v.* набива́ть *impf.*, наби́ть *pf.*

stuffing /'stʌfiŋ/ *n.* наби́вка *f.*; (*cul.*) начи́нка *f.*

stuffy /'stʌfi/ *adj.* (*close*) ду́шный; (*person*) чо́порный.

stultify /'stʌltə,fai/ *v.* отупля́ть *impf.*

stumble /'stʌmbəl/ *v.* спотыка́ться *impf.*, споткну́ться *pf.*

stump /stʌmp/ *n.* пень; обру́бок *m.*

stun /stʌn/ *v.* ошеломля́ть *impf.*, ошеломи́ть *pf.*

stunning /'stʌniŋ/ *adj.* ошеломля́ющий; (*superb*) сногсшиба́тельный; потряса́ющий.

stunt¹ /stʌnt/ **1.** *n.* трюк; фо́кус *m.* **2.** *v.* пока́зывать фо́кусы *impf.*

stunt² /stʌnt/ *v.* заде́рживать разви́тие *impf.*

stupefaction /,stupə'fækʃən/ *n.* изумле́ние *neut.*

stupefy /'stupə,fai/ *v.* (*senses*) притупля́ть *impf.*; (*with drugs*) одурма́нивать *impf.*

stupendous /stu'pɛndəs/ *adj.* изуми́тельный.

stupid /'stupid/ *adj.* глу́пый; тупо́й.

stupidity /stu'piditi/ *n.* глу́пость *f.*

stupor /'stupər/ *n.* остолбене́ние *neut.*

sturdy /'stɜrdi/ *adj.* сто́йкий; твёрдый.

sturgeon /'stɜrdʒən/ *n.* осётр *m.*; (*cul.*) осетри́на *f.*

stutter /'stʌtər/ **1.** *n.* заика́ние *neut.* **2.** *v.* заика́ться *impf.*

sty /stai/ *n.* (*med.*) ячме́нь *m.*

style /stail/ *n.* стиль *m.*; мане́ра; мо́да *f.*; фасо́н *m.*

stylish /'stailiʃ/ *adj.* мо́дный; шика́рный.

stylist /'stailist/ *n.* стили́ст; модельер *m.*

stylus /'stailəs/ *n.* иго́лка *f.*; (*engraving*) резе́ц ; (*instrument*) штифт *m.*

stymie /'staimi/ *v.* срыва́ть *impf.*

Styria /'stɪəriə/ *n.* (*province*) Шти́рия *f.*

suave /swɑv/ *adj.* учти́вый; (*gracious*) обходи́тельный.

subassembly /,sʌbə'sɛmbli/ *n.* сбо́рка *f.*

subclass /'sʌb,klæs/ *n.* подкла́сс *m.*

subcommittee /'sʌbkə,mɪti/ *n.* подкомите́т *m.*

subconscious /,sʌb'kɒnʃəs/ **1.** *adj.* подсозна́тельный. **2.** *n.* подсозна́ние *neut.*

subcontinent /,sʌb'kɒntnənt/ *n.* субконтине́нт *m.*

subcontract /,sʌb'kɒntrækt/ *n.* субподря́д *m.*

subdeacon /,sʌb'dikən/ *n.* иподья́кон *m.*

subdivide /,sʌbdɪ'vaid/ *v.* подразделя́ть(ся) *impf.*

subdue /səb'du/ *v.* покоря́ть *impf.*, покори́ть *pf.*

subdued /səb'dud/ *adj.* (*quiet*) ти́хий; (*gentle*) мя́гкий; (*voice, etc.*) приглушённый.

subgenus /'sʌb'dʒinəs/ *n.* подро́д *m.*

subglacial /sʌb'gleiʃəl/ *adj.* подлёдный.

subgroup /'sʌb,grup/ *n.* подгру́ппа *f.*

subhead /'sʌb,hɛd/ *also* **subheading** /-,hɛdɪŋ/ *n.* подзаголо́вок *m.*

subhuman /sʌb'hyumən/ *adj.* нечелове́ческий.

subject / *n., adj.* 'sʌbdʒikt; *v.* səb'dʒɛkt/ **1.** *n.* те́ма *f.*; сюже́т *m.*; (*of study*) предме́т *m.*; (*political*) по́дданный *m.*; (*gram.*) подлежа́щее *neut.* **2.** *adj.* подвла́стный; подлежа́щий; подчинённый (*with dat.*). **3.** *v.* подверга́ть *impf.*, подве́ргнуть *pf.*

subjective /səb'dʒɛktɪv/ *adj.* субъекти́вный.

subjectivity /,sʌbdʒɛk'tɪvɪti/ *n.* субъекти́вность *f.*

subject matter *n.* те́ма *f.*; (*content*) содержа́ние *neut.*

subjugate /'sʌbdʒə,geit/ v. подчиня́ть impf., подчини́ть pf.

subjunctive /səb'dʒʌŋktɪv/ n. (gram.) сослага́тельное наклоне́ние neut.

sublessee /,sʌble'si/ n. субаренда́тор m.

sublessor /sʌb'lesɔr/ n. отдаю́щий в субаре́нду m.

sublet /sʌb'let/ v. пересдава́ть impf.

sublimate /'sʌblə,meit/ v. сублими́ровать; возвыша́ть impf., возвы́сить pf.

sublime /sə'blaim/ adj. возвы́шенный; грандио́зный.

submachine gun /,sʌbmə'ʃin/ n. автома́т m.

submarine /,sʌbmə'rin/ 1. n. подво́дная ло́дка f. 2. adj. подво́дный.

submerge /səb'mзrdʒ/ v.t. погружа́ть (в во́ду) impf., погрузи́ть pf.; v.i. погружа́ться impf., погрузи́ться pf.

submerged /səb'mзrdʒd/ adj. зато́пленный.

submersion /səb'mзrʒən/ n. погруже́ние (в во́ду) neut.

submission /səb'mɪʃən/ n. подчине́ние neut.; поко́рность f.

submissive /səb'mɪsɪv/ adj. поко́рный; смире́нный.

submit /səb'mɪt/ v.i. подчиня́ться (with dat.) impf.; v.t. (present) представля́ть impf.

subnormal /sʌb'nɔrməl/ adj. ни́же норма́льного.

subordinate / adj., n. sə'bɔrdnɪt; v. sə'bɔrdn,eit/ 1. adj. подчинённый; второстепе́нный; (gram.) прида́точный. 2. n. подчинённый m. 3. v. подчиня́ть impf., подчини́ть pf.

subordination /sə,bɔrdn'eiʃən/ n. подчине́ние neut.; субордина́ция f.

subpoena /sə'pinə/ n. пове́стка в суд f.

subscribe /səb'skraib/ v. подпи́сываться (на with acc.) impf., подписа́ться pf.

subscription /səb'skrɪpʃən/ n. подпи́ска f.; абонеме́нт m.

subsequent /'sʌbsɪkwənt/ adj. после́дующий.

subsequently /'sʌbsɪkwəntli/ adv. впосле́дствии.

subservient /səb'sзrviənt/ adj. (servile) рабо́лепный; (subordinate) вспомога́тельный; подчинённый.

subside /səb'said/ v. (recede) спада́ть impf., спасть pf.; убыва́ть impf., убы́ть pf.; (calm down) стиха́ть impf.

subsidiary /səb'sɪdi,eri/ 1. adj. второстепе́нный. 2. n. филиа́л m.

subsidize /'sʌbsɪ,daiz/ v. субсиди́ровать impf. and pf.

subsidy /'sʌbsɪdi/ n. субси́дия f.

subsist /səb'sɪst/ v. существова́ть impf.; (live) жить (with instr.) impf.

subsoil /'sʌb,sɔil/ n. подпо́чва f.

subsonic /sʌb'sɒnɪk/ adj. дозвуково́й.

subspecies /'sʌb,spiʃiz/ n. подви́д m.

substance /'sʌbstəns/ n. вещество́ neut.; су́щность f.; (content) содержа́ние neut.

substantial /səb'stænʃəl/ adj. суще́ственный.

substantially /səb'stænʃəli/ adv. (basically) в основно́м; (considerably) значи́тельно.

substantiate /səb'stænʃi,eit/ v. обосно́вывать impf.

substantive /'sʌbstəntɪv/ 1. n (gram.) и́мя существи́тельное neut. 2. adj. (real) реа́льный; (relevant to topic) суще́ственный.

substitute /'sʌbstɪ,tut/ 1. n. замести́тель; заме-

ни́тель m. 2. v. заменя́ть impf., замени́ть; замеща́ть impf., замести́ть pf.

substitution /,sʌbstɪ'tuʃən/ n. заме́на f.; замеще́ние neut.

subterfuge /'sʌbtər,fyudʒ/ n. увёртка; отгово́рка f.

subterranean /,sʌbtə'reiniən/ adj. подзе́мный.

subtitle /'sʌb,tait]/ n. подзаголо́вок m.; (cinema) субти́тр m.

subtle /'sʌt]/ adj. то́нкий; утончённый.

subtract /səb'trækt/ v. вычита́ть impf., вы́честь pf.

subtraction /səb'trækʃən/ n. вычита́ние neut.

subtropical /sʌb'trɒpɪkəl/ adj. субтропи́ческий.

subtropics /sʌb'trɒpɪks/ n. субтро́пики pl.

suburb /'sʌbзrb/ 1. n. при́город m. 2. adj. при́городный.

suburban /sə'bзrbən/ adj. при́городный.

subversion /səb'vзrʒən/ n. (overthrow) сверже́ние neut.; (subversive activities) подрывна́я де́ятельность f.

subversive /səb'vзrsɪv/ adj. подрывно́й.

subvert /səb'vзrt/ v. (undermine) подрыва́ть impf.; (person) развраща́ть impf.

subway /'sʌb,wei/ n. метрополите́н m., метро́ neut. indecl.

succeed /sək'sid/ v. удава́ться (impers., with dat.) impf.; преуспева́ть impf., преуспе́ть pf.

succeeding /sək'sidɪŋ/ adj. (next) сле́дующий; (following) после́дующий.

success /sək'ses/ n. успе́х m.; уда́ча f.

successful /sək'sesfəl/ adj. успе́шный.

succession /sək'seʃən/ n. прее́мственность f.; (sequence) после́довательность f.

successive /sək'sesɪv/ adj. после́дующий; после́довательный.

successor /sək'sesər/ n. насле́дник m., насле́дница f.; прее́мник m., прее́мница f.

succinct /sək'sɪŋkt/ adj. (brief) кра́ткий; (precise) чёткий.

succor /'sʌkər/ n. (aid) по́мощь f.

succulent /'sʌkyələnt/ adj. со́чный.

succumb /sə'kʌm/ v. уступа́ть impf., уступи́ть pf.

such /sʌtʃ/ 1. adj. тако́й. 2. pron. таково́й; тот.

such and such adj. тако́й-то.

suck /sʌk/ v. соса́ть impf.

sucker /'sʌkər/ n. сосуно́к m.; (biol.) присо́ска f.; (colloq.) (simpleton) проста́к m.

suckle /'sʌkəl/ v. корми́ть гру́дью; соса́ть impf.

suckling /'sʌklɪŋ/ n. (child) грудно́й ребёнок m.; (animal) сосуно́к m.

suction /'sʌkʃən/ n. соса́ние; вса́сывание neut.

Sudan /su'dæn/ n. Суда́н m.

sudden /'sʌdn/ adj. внеза́пный.

suddenly /'sʌdnli/ adv. вдруг; внеза́пно.

suds /sʌdz/ n. мы́льная пе́на or вода́ f.

sue /su/ v. пресле́довать судебным поря́дком impf.

suede /sweid/ 1. n. за́мша f. 2. adj. за́мшевый.

suet /'suit/ n. околопо́чечный жир m.

suffer /'sʌfər/ v. страда́ть impf., пострада́ть pf.

suffering /'sʌfərɪŋ/ 1. n. страда́ние neut. 2. adj. страда́ющий.

suffice /sə'fais/ v. хвата́ть impf., хвати́ть pf.

sufficiency /sə'fɪʃənsi/ n. доста́точность f.; доста́ток m.

sufficient /sə'fɪʃənt/ adj. доста́точный.

sufficiently /sə'fɪʃəntli/ *adv.* достáточно, довóльно.

suffix /'sʌfɪks/ *n.* сýффикс *m.*

suffocate /'sʌfə,keit/ *v.i.* задыхáться *impf.*, задохнýться *pf.*; *v.t.* душúть *impf.*

suffocating /'sʌfə,keitɪŋ/ *adj.* дýшный; удýшливый.

suffrage /'sʌfrɪdʒ/ *n.* (*vote*) гóлос *m.*; (*right to vote*) прáво гóлоса *neut.*

sugar /'ʃʊgər/ **1.** *n.* сáхар *m.* **2.** *adj.* сáхарный.

sugar beet *n.* сáхарная свеклá *f.*

sugar bowl *n.* сáхарница *f.*

sugar cane *n.* сáхарный тростнúк *m.*

sugarplum /'ʃʊgər,plʌm/ *n.* леденéц *m.*

suggest /səg'dʒɛst/ *v.* предлагáть *impf.*, предложúть *pf.*

suggestibility /səg,dʒɛstə'bɪlɪti/ *n.* внушáемость *f.*

suggestion /səg'dʒɛstʃən/ *n.* предложéние *neut.*

suggestive /səg'dʒɛstɪv/ *adj.* наводя́щий на мысль (o *with prep.*); (*indecent*) непристóйный.

suicidal /suə'saidl/ *adj.* самоубúйственный; суицидáльный.

suicide /'suə,said/ *n.* самоубúйство *neut.*; (*person*) самоубúйца *m.* and *f.* (*decl. f.*); **to commit suicide** покóнчить с собóй *pf.*

sui generis /'suai ,dʒɛnərɪs, 'sui/ *adj.* своеобрáзный.

suit /sut/ **1.** *n.* (*outfit*) костю́м *m.*; (*cards*) масть *f.*; (*law*) процéсс *m.* **2.** *v.i.* удовлетворя́ть трéбованиям; устрáивать *impf.*

suitable /'sutəbəl/ *adj.* подходя́щий; соотвéтствующий.

suitcase /'sut,keis/ *n.* чемодáн *m.*

suite /swit/ *n.* (*furniture*) комплéкт, гарнитýр ; (*hotel*) нóмер-люкс *m.*; (*mus.*) сюúта *f.*; (*retinue*) свúта *f.*

suitor /'sutər/ *n.* поклóнник *m.*; (*petitioner*) просúтель *m.*

sulfur /'sʌlfər/ **1.** *n.* céра *f.* **2.** *adj.* сéрный.

sulfuric acid /sʌl'fyʊrɪk/ *n.* сéрная кислотá *f.*

sulk /sʌlk/ *v.* дýться *impf.*

sulky /'sʌlki/ *adj.* надýтый.

sullen /'sʌlən/ *adj.* угрю́мый.

sully /'sʌli/ *v.* пáчкать; марáть; пятнáть *impf.*

sultry /'sʌltri/ *adj.* знóйный; (*passionate*) стрáстный.

sum /sʌm/ **1.** *n.* сýмма *f.*; колúчество *neut.*; итóг *m.* **2.** *v.*: **to sum up** подводúть итóг *impf.*

summarize /'sʌmə,raiz/ *v.* суммúровать; резю́ мúровать *impf.* and *pf.*

summary /'sʌməri/ *n.* резюмé *neut. indecl.*; конспéкт *m.*

summer /'sʌmər/ **1.** *n.* лéто *neut.*; **in the summer** *adv.* лéтом. **2.** *adj.* лéтний.

summerhouse /'sʌmər,haus/ *n.* бесéдка *f.*

summit /'sʌmɪt/ *n.* (*mountain*) вершúна *f.*; верх; зенúт *m.*

summon /'sʌmən/ *v.* вызывáть *impf.*, вы́звать *pf.*

summons /'sʌmənz/ *n.* вы́зов (в суд) *m.*

sumptuous /'sʌmptʃuəs/ *adj.* пы́шный; роскóшный.

Sumy /'sumi/ *n.* Сýмы *pl.*

sun /sʌn/ **1.** *n.* сóлнце *neut.*; **in the sun** на сóлнце. **2.** *adj.* сóлнечный. **3.** *v.* грéться на сóлнце *impf.*

sunbathe /'sʌn,beið/ *v.* загорáть (на сóлнце) *impf.*

sunbeam /'sʌn,bim/ *n.* сóлнечный луч *m.*

sunburn /'sʌn,bɜrn/ **1.** *n.* загáр *m.* **2.** *v.* загорáть *impf.*

sunburned /'sʌn,bɜrnd/ *adj.* загорéлый.

sundae /'sʌndei/ *n.* морóженое с сирóпом, орéхами и фрýктами *neut.*

Sunday /'sʌndei/ **1.** *n.* воскресéнье *neut.* **2.** *adj.* воскрéсный.

sundial /'sʌn,daiəl/ *n.* сóлнечные часы́ *pl.*

sundown /'sʌn,daun/ *n.* закáт, захóд сóлнца *m.*

sunflower /'sʌn,flauər/ *n.* подсóлнечник, подсóлнух *m.*

sunglasses /'sʌn,glæsɪz/ *n.* сóлнечные очкú *pl.*

sunken /'sʌŋkən/ *adj.* (*hollow*) вя́лый; (*ship*) затóпленный.

sunlamp /'sʌn,læmp/ *n.* лáмпа сóлнечного свéта *f.*

sunlight /'sʌn,lait/ *n.* сóлнечный свет *m.*

sunlit /'sʌn,lɪt/ *adj.* сóлнечный; освещённый сóлнцем.

sunny /'sʌni/ *adj.* сóлнечный.

sunrise /'sʌn,raiz/ *n.* восхóд сóлнца *m.*

sunscreen /'sʌn,skrin/ *n.* солнцезащúтный крем *m.*

sunset /'sʌn,sɛt/ *n.* захóд сóлнца; закáт *m.*

sunshine /'sʌn,ʃain/ *n.* сóлнечный свет *m.*

sunspot /'sʌn,spɒt/ *n.* (*astr.*) сóлнечное пятнó *neut.*

sunstroke /'sʌn,strouk/ *n.* сóлнечный удáр *m.*

suntan /'sʌn,tæn/ *n.* загáр *m.*

sup /sʌp/ *v.i.* (*dine*) ýжинать *impf.*

super /'supər/ **1.** *adj.* (*colloq.*) чýдный; **2.** *interj.* чýдно!

superabundant /,supərə'bʌndənt/ *adj.* изобúльный; излúшний.

superannuate /,supər'ænyu,eit/ *v.* переводúть на пéнсию *impf.*

superb /sʊ'pɜrb/ *adj.* великолéпный; прекрáсный.

supercilious /,supər'sɪliəs/ *adj.* высокомéрный.

superconductor /,supərkən'dʌktər/ *n.* сверхпровóдник *m.*

supercool /,supər'kul/ *v.* переохлаждáть(ся) *impf.*

superego /,supər'igou/ *n.* сверх-я *neut. indecl.*

superficial /,supər'fɪʃəl/ *adj.* повéрхностный.

superfluid /,supər'fluɪd/ *adj.* сверхтекýчий.

superfluous /sʊ'pɜrfluəs/ *adj.* излúшний.

supergalaxy /'supər,gæləksi/ *n.* сверхгалáктика *f.*

superheat /,supər'hit/ *v.* перегревáть *impf.*

superhuman /,supər'hyumən/ *adj.* сверхчеловéческий.

superimpose /,supərɪm'pouz/ *v.* наклáдывать (на *with acc.*) *impf.*

superintendent /,supərɪn'tɛndənt/ *n.* заведýю щий; управля́ющий *m.*; (*in building*) комендáнт *m.*

superior /sə'pɪəriər/ **1.** *adj.* вы́сший; стáрший. **2.** *n.* стáрший начáльник *m.*

superiority /sə,pɪəri'ɔrɪti/ *n.* превосхóдство (над *with instr.*); стáршинство *neut.*

superlative /sə'pɜrlətɪv/ *adj.* величáйший; высочáйший; превосхóдный.

superman /'supər,mæn/ n. сверхчеловек; супермен m.

supermarket /'supər,markɪt/ n. универсам m.

supernatural /,supər'nætʃərəl/ adj. сверхъестественный.

supernumerary /,supər'numə,rɛri/ adj. сверхштатный; (extra, excess) лишний.

superpower /'supər,pauər/ n. сверхдержава f.

supersaturate /,supər'sætʃə,reit/ v. перенасыщать impf.

superscript /'supər,skrɪpt/ n. надстрочный знак m.

supersede /,supər'sid/ v. сменять impf., сменить pf.

supersonic /,supər'sɒnɪk/ adj. сверхзвуковой.

superstition /,supər'stɪʃən/ n. суеверие neut.

superstitious /,supər'stɪʃəs/ adj. суеверный.

superstructure /'supər,strʌktʃər/ n. надстройка f.

supertanker /'supər,tæŋkər/ n. супертанкер m.

supervise /'supər,vaiz/ v. заведовать; руководить (with instr.) impf.

supervision /,supər'vɪʒən/ n. наблюдение neut.; надзор m.

supervisor /'supər,vaizər/ n. надзиратель m., надзирательница f.; надсмотрщик; начальник m.

supper /'sʌpər/ n. ужин m.; **at supper** за ужином; **to have supper** ужинать impf.

supplant /sə'plænt/ v. вытеснять impf.; (in job) выживать impf.

supple /'sʌpəl/ adj. гибкий.

supplement / n. 'sʌpləmənt/ v. 'sʌplə,mɛnt/ **1.** n. дополнение; приложение neut. **2.** v. дополнять impf., дополнить pf.

supplementary /,sʌplə'mɛntəri/ adj. дополнительный.

suppliant /'sʌpliənt/ n. проситель m.

supplicate /'sʌplɪ,keit/ v. умолять; просить impf.

supplier /sə'plaiər/ n. поставщик m.

supply /sə'plai/ **1.** n. снабжение neut.; (stock) запас m.; **supply and demand** спрос и предложение. **2.** v. снабжать impf., снабдить pf.; доставлять impf., доставить pf.

support /sə'pɔrt/ **1.** n. поддержка; подставка, подпорка f. **2.** v. поддерживать impf., поддержать pf.

supporter /sə'pɔrtər/ n. сторонник; приверженец m.

suppose /sə'pouz/ v. предполагать impf., предположить pf.; **supposing that** допустим or предположим что.

supposed /sə'pouzd/ adj. предполагаемый; (pretended) мнимый.

supposedly /sə'pouzɪdli/ adv. предположительно; якобы.

supposition /,sʌpə'zɪʃən/ n. (assumption) предположение neut.; гипотеза f.

suppository /sə'pɒzɪ,tɔri/ n. свеча f.

suppress /sə'prɛs/ v. подавлять impf., подавить pf.

suppression /sə'prɛʃən/ n. подавление neut.

supra /'suprə/ adv. выше.

supremacy /sə'prɛməsi/ n. господство; превосходство neut.

supreme /sə'prim/ adj. верховный; высший.

surcharge /'sɜr,tʃardʒ/ n. приплата; доплата f.

sure /ʃʊr/ **1.** adj. верный; несомненный; **to make**

sure убедиться pf. **2.** adv. (colloq.) конечно; действительно.

surely /'ʃʊrli/ adv. несомненно; конечно.

surf /sɜrf/ n. буруны pl.; прибой m.

surface /'sɜrfɪs/ n. поверхность f.

surfeit /'sɜrfɪt/ n. (excess) излишество neut.; излишек; избыток m.; (overeating) пресыщение neut.

surfing /'sɜrfɪŋ/ n. сёрфинг m.; (Internet) поиск в Сети; сёрфинг в Сети m.

surge /sɜrdʒ/ n. (wave) волна f.; (emotion) прилив m.; (tech.) волна (перенапряжения) f.

surgeon /'sɜrdʒən/ n. хирург m.

surgery /'sɜrdʒəri/ n. хирургия f.

surgical /'sɜrdʒɪkəl/ adj. хирургический.

surly /'sɜrli/ adj. угрюмый; грубый.

surmise /sər'maiz/ **1.** n. предположение neut.; догадка f. **2.** v. предполагать impf.; (suspect) заподозрить pf.

surmount /sər'maunt/ v. (overcome) преодолевать impf.

surname /'sɜr,neim/ n. фамилия f.

surpass /sər'pæs/ v. превосходить impf., превзойти pf.; перегонять impf., перегнать pf.

surpassing /sər'pæsɪŋ/ adj. превосходный; исключительный.

surplice /'sɜrplɪs/ n. стихарь m.

surplus /'sɜrplʌs/ **1.** n. излишек m. **2.** adj. излишний.

surprise /sər'praiz/ **1.** n. удивление neut.; неожиданность f.; сюрприз m.; **by surprise** adv. неожиданно. **2.** adj. неожиданный. **3.** v. удивлять impf., удивить pf.; **to be surprised** удивляться impf.

surprising /sər'praizɪŋ/ adj. удивительный.

surrender /sə'rɛndər/ **1.** n. сдача; капитуляция f. **2.** v.t. сдавать impf., сдать pf.; v.i. сдаваться impf., сдаться pf.

surreptitious /,sɜrəp'tɪʃəs/ adj. тайный; (stealthy) совершённый украдкой or тайком.

surround /sə'raund/ v. окружать impf., окружить pf.

surrounding /sə'raundɪŋ/ adj. окружающий.

surveillance /sər'veiləns/ n. надзор m.; наблюдение neut.

survey / n. 'sɜrvei/ v. sər'vei/ **1.** n. обозрение neut.; осмотр m.; (land) межевание neut.; промер m.; (poll) опрос n. **2.** v. обозревать impf., обозреть pf.; (land) межевать impf.

surveying /sər'veiɪŋ/ n. съёмка f.

survival /sər'vaivəl/ n. выживание neut.; (relic) пережиток m.

survive /sər'vaiv/ v.t. пережить pf.; v.i. выживать impf.; остаться в живых pf.

survivor /sər'vaivər/ n. уцелевший m.; спасшийся; выживший m.

susceptible /sə'sɛptəbəl/ adj. восприимчивый.

suspect / n., adj. 'sʌspɛkt; v. sə'spɛkt/ **1.** n. подозреваемый m. **2.** adj. подозрительный. **3.** v. подозревать impf.

suspend /sə'spɛnd/ v. (hang) вешать impf., повесить pf.; (stop temporarily) приостанавливать impf., приостановить pf.

suspenders /sə'spɛndərz/ n. (for trousers) подтяжки pl.

suspense /sə'spɛns/ n. ожидание neut.; неизвестность f.

suspension /səˈspɛnʃən/ *n.* подвéшивание *neut.;* (*halt*) приостанóвка *f.*
suspicion /səˈspɪʃən/ *n.* подозрéние *neut.*
suspicious /səˈspɪʃəs/ *adj.* подозрѝтельный.
sustain /səˈstein/ *v.* поддéрживать *impf.*, поддержáть *pf.;* (*suffer*) испы́тывать *impf.*, испытáть *pf.*
sustained /səˈsteind/ *adj.* дли́тельный; (*continuous*) непреры́вный.
sustenance /ˈsʌstənəns/ *n.* пропитáние *neut.;* пи́ща *f.;* (*support*) поддéржка *f.*
Suzdal /ˈsuzdḷ/ *n.* Сýздаль *m.*
suzerain /ˈsuzəˌrɪn/ *n.* сюзерéн *m.*
svelte /svɛlt/ *adj.* стрóйный.
Svir /svir/ *n.* (*river*) Свирь *f.*
swab /swɒb/ *n.* (*mop*) шва́бра *f.;* (*med.*) тампóн *m.;* (*specimen*) мазóк *m.*
swaddle /ˈswɒdḷ/ *v.* (*child*) пеленáть *impf.;* (*wrap up*) окýтывать *impf.*
swagger /ˈswægər/ *n.* (*gait*) чванли́вая похóдка *f.;* (*manner*) чванли́вая манéра *f.;* (*conceit*) спесь *f.;* (*bluster*) фарфарóнство *neut.;* (*dash*) щегóльство *neut.*
swain /swein/ *n.* (*country lad*) деревéнский пáрень *m.*
swallow¹ /ˈswɒlou/ **1.** *n.* глотóк *m.* **2.** *v.* глотáть *impf.*
swallow² /ˈswɒlou/ *n.* (*bird*) лáсточка *f.*
swamp /swɒmp/ **1.** *n.* болóто *neut.* **2.** *v.* (*overwhelm*) засыпáть *impf.*, засы́пать *pf.*
swampy /ˈswɒmpi/ *adj.* болóтный.
swan /swɒn/ *n.* лéбедь *m.*
swan dive *n.* прыжóк-лáсточка *m.*
swan song *n.* лебеди́ная пéсня *f.*
swap /swɒp/ **1.** *n.* обмéн *m.* **2.** *v.* обмéнивать(ся) *impf.*, обменя́ть(ся) *pf.*
swarm /swɔrm/ *n.* рой *m.*
swarthy /ˈswɔrði/ *adj.* смýглый.
swat /swɒt/ *v.* хлóпать *impf.*
swatch /swɒtʃ/ *n.* обрáзчик *m.*
swath /swɒθ/ *n.* (*cut*) прокóс *m.*
sway /swei/ **1.** *n.* качáние, колебáние *neut.* **2.** *v.* качáть(ся) *impf.*; колебáть(ся) *impf.*; (*fig.*) повлия́ть *pf.*
swear /swɛər/ *v.* (*vow*) кля́сться *impf.*, покля́сться *pf.*; присягáть *impf.*, присягнýть *pf.*; (*curse*) ругáться *impf.*
swearword /ˈswɛərˌwɜrd/ *n.* ругáтельство; брáнное слóво *neut.*
sweat /swɛt/ **1.** *n.* пот *m.* **2.** *v.* потéть *impf.*
sweater /ˈswɛtər/ *n.* сви́тер *m.*
sweatshirt /ˈswɛtˌʃɜrt/ *n.* трикотáжный сви́тер *m.*
sweaty /ˈswɛti/ *adj.* пóтный.
Swede /swid/ *n.* швед *m.*, швéдка *f.*
Sweden /ˈswidn/ *n.* Швéция *f.*
Swedish /ˈswidɪʃ/ *adj.* швéдский.
sweep /swip/ *v.* мести́ *impf.*, подметáть *impf.*, подмести́ *pf.*
sweeping /ˈswipɪŋ/ *adj.* широ́кий; (*wholesale*) огýльный.
sweet /swit/ *adj.* слáдкий.
sweet-and-sour /ˈswit n̩ ˈsauᵊr/ *adj.* кисло-слáдкий.
sweeten /ˈswitn̩/ *v.* подслáщивать *impf.*
sweetheart /ˈswitˌhɑrt/ *n.* возлю́бленный *m.*, возлю́бленная *f.;* люби́мец *m.*

sweetness /ˈswitnɪs/ *n.* слáдость *f.*
sweet potato *n.* батáт *m.*
sweet-scented /ˈswit ˌsɛntɪd/ *adj.* души́стый; аромáтный.
sweet tooth *n.* пристрáстие к слáдкому *neut.*
sweet william /ˈwɪlyəm/ *n.* турéцкая гвозди́ка *f.*
swell /swɛl/ **1.** *n.* вы́пуклость *f.;* (*sea*) зыбь *f.* **2.** *v.* надувáться *impf.*, надýться *pf.;* набухáть *impf.*, набýхнуть *pf.*
swelling /ˈswɛlɪŋ/ *n.* óпухоль; припýхлость *f.*
swelter /ˈswɛltər/ *v.* (*suffer from heat*) томи́ться знóем; изнывáть от жары́ *impf.;* пáриться *impf.*
sweltering /ˈswɛltərɪŋ/ *adj.* знóйный; дýшный.
swerve /swɜrv/ *v.* (*to and fro*) виля́ть *impf.;* (*to one side*) вильнýть *pf.*
swift /swɪft/ *adj.* скóрый, бы́стрый.
swiftness /ˈswɪftnɪs/ *n.* скóрость; быстротá *f.*
swill /swɪl/ **1.** *n.* пóйло *neut.* **2.** *v.* жáдно пить *impf.*
swim /swɪm/ *v.* плáвать *impf. indet.*, плыть *impf. det.*, поплы́ть *pf.*
swimmer /ˈswɪmər/ *n.* пловéц *m.*, пловчи́ха *f.*
swimming /ˈswɪmɪŋ/ *n.* плáвание *neut.*
swimmingly /ˈswɪmɪŋli/ *adv.* (*colloq.*) прекрáсно; отли́чно; как по мáслу.
swimming pool *n.* бассéйн для плáвания *m.*
swimsuit /ˈswɪmˌsut/ *n.* купáльник *m.*
swindle /ˈswɪndḷ/ *v.* надувáть; обмáнывать *impf.*
swindler /ˈswɪndlər/ *n.* мошéнник; жýлик *m.*
swine /swain/ *n.* свинья́ *f.;* (*person*) нахáл *m.*
swing /swɪŋ/ **1.** *n.* (*suspended seat*) качéли *pl.* **2.** *v.t.* качáть; колебáть *impf.;* *v.i.* качáться; колебáться *impf.*
swirl /swɜrl/ **1.** *n.* водоворóт *m.;* кружéние *neut.* **2.** *v.t.* кружи́ть *impf.;* *v.i.* кружи́ться *impf.*
Swiss /swɪs/ **1.** *adj.* швейцáрский. **2.** *n.* швейцáрец *m.*, швейцáрка *f.*
switch /swɪtʃ/ **1.** *n.* прут; хлыст *m.;* (*elec.*) выключáтель; переключáтель *m.* **2.** *v.* переключáть *impf.*, переключи́ть *pf.*
switchboard /ˈswɪtʃˌbɔrd/ *n.* распредели́тельный щит *m.*
switchman /ˈswɪtʃmən/ *n.* стрéлочник *m.*
Switzerland /ˈswɪtsərlənd/ *n.* Швейцáрия *f.*
swivel /ˈswɪvəl/ *n.* вертлю́г *m.*
swollen /ˈswoulən/ *adj.* вздýтый; раздýтый; вспýхший; опýхший.
swoon /swun/ *v.* пáдать в óбморок *impf.*
swoop /swup/ *v.* (*dive*) устремля́ться вниз *impf.;* (*attack*) налетáть (на *with acc.*) *impf.*
sword /sɔrd/ *n.* меч *m.;* шпáга *f.*
sword belt *n.* портупéя *f.*
swordfish /ˈsɔrdˌfɪʃ/ *n.* ры́ба-меч *f.*
sworn /swɔrn/ *adj.* под прися́гой.
sworn enemy *n.* закля́тый враг *m.*
sycamore /ˈsɪkəˌmɔr/ *n.* (*maple*) я́вор *m.;* (*plane*) платáн; сикомóр *m.*
Sydney /ˈsɪdni/ *n.* Сиднéй *m.*
syllabic /sɪˈlæbɪk/ *adj.* слоговóй; силлаби́ческий.
syllable /ˈsɪləbəl/ *n.* слог *m.*
syllabus /ˈsɪləbəs/ *n.* прогрáмма обучéния *f.*
sylph /sɪlf/ *n.* (*myth. and fig.*) сильфи́да *f.*
sylvan /ˈsɪlvən/ *adj.* леснóй.
symbol /ˈsɪmbəl/ *n.* си́мвол *m.;* эмблéма *f.*
symbolism /ˈsɪmbəˌlɪzəm/ *n.* (*symbolic meaning*) симвóлика *f.;* (*literary movement*) символи́зм *m.*

symbolize /'sɪmbə‚laɪz/ v. символизи́ровать impf.

symmetrical /sɪ'mɛtrɪkəl/ adj. симметри́чный.

symmetry /'sɪmətri/ n. симме́трия f.

sympathetic /‚sɪmpə'θɛtɪk/ adj. сочу́вственный; симпати́чный.

sympathize /'sɪmpə‚θaɪz/ v. сочу́вствовать (with dat.) impf.

sympathizer /'sɪmpə‚θaɪzər/ n. сторо́нник m., сторо́нница f.; (fellow traveler) попу́тчик m., попу́тчица f.

sympathy /'sɪmpəθi/ n. сочу́вствие neut., симпа́тия f.

symphonic /sɪm'fɒnɪk/ adj. симфони́ческий.

symphony /'sɪmfəni/ n. симфо́ния f.

symptom /'sɪmptəm/ n. симпто́м; при́знак m.

synagogue /'sɪnə‚gɒg/ n. синаго́га f.

synchronize /'sɪŋkrə‚naɪz/ v. синхронизи́ровать impf. and pf.

synchronous /'sɪŋkrənəs/ adj. синхро́нный; одновреме́нный.

syndetic /sɪn'dɛtɪk/ adj. сою́зный.

syndicate /'sɪndɪkɪt/ n. синдика́т m.

syndrome /'sɪndroʊm/ n. синдро́м m.

synesthesia /‚sɪnəs'θiʒə/ n. синестези́я f.

synod /'sɪnəd/ n. сино́д m.

synodal /'sɪnədl̩/ adj. синода́льный.

synonym /'sɪnənɪm/ n. сино́ним m.

synonymous /sɪ'nɒnəməs/ adj. синоними́ческий.

synonymy /sɪ'nɒnəmi/ n. синоними́я f.

synopsis /sɪ'nɒpsɪs/ n. конспе́кт m.

syntax /'sɪntæks/ n. си́нтаксис m.

synthesis /'sɪnθəsɪs/ n. си́нтез m.

synthesize /'sɪnθə‚saɪz/ v. синтези́ровать impf. and pf.

synthetic /sɪn'θɛtɪk/ adj. синтети́ческий; иску́сственный.

Syracuse /'sɪrə‚kyus/ n. (Ital.: Siracusa) Сираку́зы pl.

Syr Darya /'sɪər' daryə/ n. (river) Сырдарья́ f.

Syria /'sɪəriə/ n. Си́рия f.

Syrian /'sɪəriən/ **1.** adj. сири́йский. **2.** n. сири́ец m., сири́йка f.

syringe /sə'rɪndʒ/ n. шприц m.

syrinx /'sɪrɪŋks/ n. (panpipe) свире́ль f.; (ornith.) евста́хиева труба́ f.

syrup /'sɪrəp, 'sɜr-/ n. сиро́п m.; па́тока f.

system /'sɪstəm/ n. систе́ма f.; органи́зм m.

systematic /‚sɪstə'mætɪk/ adj. системати́ческий.

systemic /sɪ'stɛmɪk/ adj. систе́мный.

syzygy /'sɪzɪdʒi/ n. сизи́гия f.

Szczecin /'ʃtʃɛtʃin/ n. (also: Stettin) Ще́цин m.

Szeged /'sɛgɛd/ n. Се́гед m.

Székesfehérvár /'seikɛʃ'fɛhɛərvɑr/ n. Се́кешфехервар m.

T

tab /tæb/ *n.* ярлы́к *m.*; (*loop*) пе́телька *f.*; (*on uniform*) петли́ца *f.*; (*colloq.*) (*bill*) счёт *m.*

tabby /'tæbi/ *adj.* полоса́тый.

tabernacle /'tæbər,nækəl/ *n.* дарохрани́тельница *f.*; (*shrine*) ра́ка *f.*

table /'teibəl/ *n.* стол *m.*; (*chart*) табли́ца *f.*; **table of contents** оглавле́ние *neut.*

tableau /tæ'blou/ *n.* жива́я карти́на *f.*

tablecloth /'teibəl,klɔθ/ *n.* ска́терть *f.*

table d'hôte /'tɑbəl 'dout/ *n.* табльдо́т; ко́мплексный обе́д *m.*

tableland /'teibəl,lænd/ *n.* плато́ *neut. indecl.*; плоского́рье *neut.*

table linen *n.* столо́вое бельё *neut.*

tablespoon /'teibəl,spun/ *n.* столо́вая ло́жка *f.*

tablet /'tæblɪt/ *n.* доще́чка *f.*; (*med.*) табле́тка *f.*

table tennis *n.* насто́льный те́ннис *m.*

tableware /'teibəl,wɛər/ *n.* столо́вая посу́да *f.*

tabloid /'tæblɔid/ *n.* (*newspaper*) малоформа́тная иллюстри́рованная газе́та *f.*; (*cheap newspaper*) бульва́рная газе́та *f.*

taboo /tə'bu/ *n.* табу́ *neut. indecl.*

Tabriz /tɑ'briz/ *n.* Тебри́з *m.*

tabular /'tæbyələr/ *adj.* табли́чный.

tabulate /'tæbyə,leit/ *v.* табули́ровать *impf.*

tachycardia /,tækɪ'kɑrdiə/ *n.* тахикарди́я *f.*

tacit /'tæsɪt/ *adj.* молчали́вый.

taciturn /'tæsɪ,tɜrn/ *adj.* неразгово́рчивый; молчали́вый.

tack /tæk/ *n.* кно́пка *f.*; гво́здик *m.*

tackle /'tækəl/ *n.* снасть *f.*; обору́дование *neut.*

tacky /'tæki/ *adj.* ли́пкий.

tact /tækt/ *n.* такт *m.*; такти́чность *f.*

tactful /'tæktfəl/ *adj.* такти́чный.

tactfully /'tæktfəli/ *adv.* такти́чно.

tactic /'tæktɪk/ *also* **tactics** /-tɪks/ *n.* та́ктика *f.*

tactical /'tæktɪkəl/ *adj.* такти́ческий.

tactician /tæk'tɪʃən/ *n.* та́ктик *m.*

tactile /'tæktɪl/ *adj.* осяза́тельный.

tactless /'tæktlɪs/ *adj.* беста́ктный.

tactlessness /'tæktlɪsnɪs/ *n.* беста́ктность *f.*

tadpole /'tædpoul/ *n.* голова́стик *m.*

taffeta /'tæfɪtə/ *n.* тафта́ *f.*

taffy /'tæfi/ *n.* ири́с *m.*; тяну́чка *f.*

tag /tæg/ *n.* этике́тка *f.*

Tahiti /tə'hiti/ *n.* Таи́ти *m.*

tail /teil/ **1.** *n.* хвост *m.* **2.** *adj.* хвостово́й.

tailboard /'teil,bɔrd/ *n.* откидно́й борт *m.*

tail coat *n.* фрак *m.*

tailed /teild/ *adj.* хвоста́тый.

tailgate /'teil,geit/ *n.* за́дняя дверь *f.*

taillight /'teil,lait/ *n.* (*car*) за́дний фона́рь *m.*

tailor /'teilər/ *n.* портно́й *m.*

tailorbird /'teilər,bɜrd/ *n.* пти́ца-портно́й *f.*

tailoring /'teilərɪŋ/ *n.* (*cut of garment*) покро́й *m.*

tailor-made /'teilər'meid/ *adj.* индивидуа́льного поши́ва; сши́тый на зака́з.

tailpiece /'teil,pis/ *n.* концо́вка *f.*

tailpipe /'teil,paip/ *n.* (*car*) выхлопна́я труба́ *f.*

tailrace /'teil,reis/ *n.* отводя́щий жёлоб *m.*

tailspin /'teil,spɪn/ *n.* (*aero.*) што́пор *m.*

tailstock /'teil,stɒk/ *n.* за́дняя ба́бка *f.*

taint /teint/ *v.* (*infect*) заража́т(ся) *impf.*; (*spoil*) по́ртить(ся) *impf.*; (*tarnish*) пятна́ть *impf.*

Taiwan /'tai'wɑn/ *n.* Тайва́нь *m.*

Tajik /tɑ'dʒɪk/ *n.* таджи́к *m.*, таджи́чка *f.*

Tajikistan /tɑ'dʒɪkɪ,stæn/ *n.* Таджикиста́н *m.*

take /teik/ *v.* брать *impf.*, взять *pf.*; **to take off** снима́ть *impf.*, снять *pf.*; (*aviation*) взлете́ть *pf.*; **to take out** вынима́ть *impf.*, вы́нуть *pf.*

take-in /'teik ,ɪn/ *n.* (*colloq.*) обма́н *m.*

takeoff /'teik,ɔf/ *n.* (*aero.*) взлёт *m.*

takeover /'teik,ouvər/ *n.* (*change*) n. сме́на *f.*; (*seizure*) взя́тие *neut.*; захва́т *m.*

taking /'teikɪŋ/ *n.* взя́тие *neut.*

talc /tælk/ *n.* тальк *m.*

talcum powder /'tælkəm/ *n.* тальк *m.*

tale /teil/ *n.* расска́з *m.*; по́весть *f.*; ска́зка *f.*

talent /'tælənt/ *n.* тала́нт *m.*

talented /'tæləntɪd/ *adj.* одарённый; тала́нтливый.

talisman /'tælɪsmən/ *n.* талисма́н *m.*

talk /tɔk/ **1.** *n.* разгово́р *m.*; (*chat*) бесе́да *f.*; *pl.* перегово́ры *pl.* **2.** *v.* говори́ть; разгова́ривать *impf.*

talkative /'tɔkətɪv/ *adj.* разгово́рчивый; болтли́вый.

talkativeness /'tɔkətɪvnɪs/ *n.* разгово́рчивость; болтли́вость *f.*

talker /'tɔkər/ *n.* болту́н *m.*; (*lecturer*) ле́ктор *m.*

talking-to /'tɔkɪŋ ,tu/ *n.* вы́говор *m.*

tall /tɔl/ *adj.* высо́кий.

Tallinn /'tɔlɪn/ *n.* Та́ллинн *m.*

tallish /'tɔlɪʃ/ *adj.* дово́льно высо́кий.

tallness /'tɔlnɪs/ *n.* высота́ *f.*

tallow /'tælou/ **1.** *n.* са́ло *neut.* **2.** *adj.* са́льный.

tally /'tæli/ *v.* (*calculate*) подсчи́тывать *impf.*

tallyho /'tæli'hou/ *interj.* ату́!

tally sheet *n.* учётный листо́к *m.*

talon /'tælən/ *n.* ко́готь *m.*

tamarisk /'tæmərɪsk/ *n.* тамари́ск *m.*

tambourine /,tæmbə'rin/ *n.* бу́бен; тамбури́н *m.*

Tambov /tɑm'bɔf/ *n.* Тамбо́в *m.*

tame /teim/ **1.** *adj.* ручно́й; приручённый. **2.** *v.* прируча́ть *impf.*, приручи́ть *pf.*

tamer /'teimər/ *n.* укроти́тель; дрессиро́вщик *m.*

tamp /tæmp/ *v.* набива́ть *impf.*

tamper¹ /'tæmpər/ *v.* (*meddle with*) тро́гать *impf.*

tamper² /'tæmpər/ *n.* трамбо́вка *f.*

tampon /'tæmpɒn/ *n.* тампо́н *m.*

tan /tæn/ **1.** *n.* све́тло-кори́чневый цвет *m.*; (*suntan*) зага́р *m.* **2.** *v.t.* (*cure*) дуби́ть *impf.*, вы́дубить *pf.*; *v.i.* (*suntan*) загора́ть *impf.*, загоре́ть *pf.*

tandem /'tændəm/ *n.* танде́м *m.*

tang /tæŋ/ *n.* (*taste*) при́вкус *m.*; (*smell*) о́стрый за́пах *m.*

tangent /'tændʒənt/ *n.* (*geom*) каса́тельная *f.*

tangerine /,tændʒə'rin/ *n.* мандари́н *m.*

tangible /'tændʒəbəl/ *adj.* осяза́емый; материа́льный.

tangle /'tæŋgəl/ **1.** *n.* пу́таница *f.*; сплете́ние *neut.* **2.** *v.t.* запу́тывать *impf.*, запу́тать *pf.*; *v.i.* запу́тываться *impf.*, запу́таться *pf.*

tangly /'tæŋgli/ *adj.* спу́танный.
tango /'tæŋgou/ *n.* та́нго *neut. indecl.*
tangy /'tæŋi/ *adj.* о́стрый.
tank /tæŋk/ *n.* цисте́рна *f.*; бак *m.*; (*mil.*) танк *m.*
tankard /'tæŋkərd/ *n.* кру́жка *f.*
tanker /'tæŋkər/ *n.* автоцисте́рна *f.*; (*ship*) та́нкер *m.*
tanner /'tænər/ *n.* коже́вник; дуби́льщик *m.*
tannery /'tænəri/ *n.* коже́венный заво́д *m.*
tannic acid /'tænɪk/ *n.* дуби́льная кислота́ *f.*
tannin /'tænɪn/ *n.* тани́н *m.*
tanning /'tænɪŋ/ *n.* дубле́ние *neut.*
tantalize /'tæntl,aiz/ *v.* (*torment*) му́чить *impf.*; (*tease*) дразни́ть *impf.*
tantalum /'tæntləm/ *n.* (*chem.*) танта́л *m.*
tantamount /'tæntə,maunt/ *adj.* равноси́льный (*with dat.*).
tantrum /'tæntrəm/ *n.* вспы́шка гне́ва *f.*; **to throw a tantrum** закати́ть исте́рику *pf.*
Tanzania /,tænzə'niə/ *n.* Танза́ния *f.*
tap /tæp/ **1.** *n.* (*light blow*) лёгкий уда́р *m.*; (*rap*) стук *m.* **2.** *v.* посту́кивать *impf.*
tap dance *n.* чечётка *f.*
tape /teip/ **1.** *n.* тесьма́; ле́нточка; плёнка *f.* **2.** *v.* (*seal*) закле́ивать *impf.*; (*to record*) запи́сывать на плёнку *impf.*
tape deck *n.* магнитофо́нная де́ка *f.*
tape drive *n.* (*on a cassette player* or *computer*) лентопротя́жный механи́зм *m.* (*abbr.* ЛПМ).
tape measure /'teip,lain/ *n.* ме́рная ле́нта *f.*; сан тиме́тр *m.*
taper /'teipər/ *n.* ко́нус *m.*
tape recorder *n.* магнитофо́н *m.*
tape recording *n.* за́пись на магнитофо́нную ле́нту *f.*
tapestry /'tæpəstri/ *n.* гобеле́н *m.*
tapeworm /'teip,wзrm/ *n.* ле́нточный червь *m.*
tapioca /,tæpi'oukə/ *n.* тапио́ка *f.*
tapping /'tæpɪŋ/ *n.* (*draining*) отво́д *m.*
tar /tɑr/ **1.** *n.* смола́ *f.*; дёготь *m.* **2.** *v.* смоли́ть; ма́зать дёгтем *impf.*
tarantula /tə'ræntʃələ/ *n.* тара́нтул *m.*
tarboosh /tɑr'buʃ/ *n.* фе́ска *f.*
tardiness /'tɑrdinɪs/ *n.* медли́тельность *f.*
tardy /'tɑrdi/ *adj.* запозда́лый.
tare[1] /tɛər/ *n.* (*comm.*) та́ра *f.*
tare[2] /tɛər/ *n.* (*bot.*) ви́ка *f.*
target /'tɑrgɪt/ *n.* цель; мише́нь *f.*
Târgu Mureş /'tɪərgu 'murɛʃ/ *n.* Тыргу-Му́реш *m.*
tariff /'tærɪf/ *n.* тари́ф *m.*
tarn /tɑrn/ *n.* го́рное о́зеро *neut.*
tarnish /'tɑrnɪʃ/ **1.** *n.* ту́склость *f.* **2.** *v.* тускне́ть *impf.*, потускне́ть *pf.*
tarpaulin /tɑr'pɔlɪn/ *n.* брезе́нт *m.*
tarragon /'tærə,gɒn/ *n.* эстраго́н *m.*
tarry /'tæri/ *adj.* (*like tar*) смоли́стый.
tart[1] /tɑrt/ *n.* пиро́г *m.*
tart[2] /tɑrt/ *adj.* те́рпкий; ки́слый; е́дкий.
tartan /'tɑrtn/ *n.* шотла́ндка *f.*
tartar /'tɑrtər/ *n.* зубно́й ка́мень *m.*
tartaric /tɑr'tærɪk/ *adj.* виннока́менный.
tartness /'tɑrtnɪs/ *n.* кислота́; е́дкость; ко́лкость *f.*
task /tæsk/ *n.* зада́ча *f.*; зада́ние *neut.*
tassel /'tæsəl/ *n.* ки́сточка *f.*

taste /teist/ **1.** *n.* вкус *m.* **2.** *v.t.* про́бовать на вкус; чу́вствовать вкус *impf.*; *v.i.* име́ть вкус *impf.*
tastefully /'teistfəli/ *adv.* со вку́сом.
tasteless /'teistlɪs/ *adj.* безвку́сный; (*behavior*) беста́ктный.
taster /'teistər/ *n.* дегуста́тор *m.*
tasty /'teisti/ *adj.* вку́сный.
Tatar /'tɑtər/ **1.** *adj.* тата́тский. **2.** *n.* тата́рин *m.*, тата́рка *f.*
Tatarstan /,tɑtər'stæn/ *n.* Татарста́н *m.*
tatter /'tætər/ *n.* лохмо́тья *pl.*
tatterdemalion /,tætərdɪ'meilyən/ *n.* оборва́нец *m.*
tatting /'tætɪŋ/ *n.* (*lace*) кру́жево *neut.*
tattle /'tætl/ *n.* спле́тни *pl.*
tattler /'tætlər/ *n.* (*gossip*) болту́н; спле́тник *m.*
tattletale /'tætl,teil/ *n.* я́беда *m.* and *f.* (*decl. f.*).
tattoo /tæ'tu/ *n.* (*on skin*) татуиро́вка *f.*
taunt /tɔnt/ *v.* насмеха́ться (над *with instr.*) *impf.*
Taurus /'tɔrəs/ *n.* (*astr.*) Теле́ц *m.*
taut /tɔt/ *adj.* туго́й; подтя́нутый.
tautness /'tɔtnɪs/ *n.* натя́нутость; сте́пень натя-
же́ния *f.*
tautology /tɔ'tɒlədʒi/ *n.* тавтоло́гия *f.*
tavern /'tævərn/ *n.* таве́рна *f.*; тракти́р *m.*
tawny /'tɔni/ *adj.* жёлто-кори́чневый.
tax /tæks/ **1.** *n.* нало́г *m.* **2.** *adj.* нало́говый **3.** *v.* облага́ть нало́гом *impf.*
taxability /,tæksə'bɪlɪti/ *n.* облага́емость *f.*
taxable /'tæksəbəl/ *adj.* облага́емый нало́гом.
taxation /tæk'seiʃən/ *n.* обложе́ние нало́гом; налогообложе́ние *neut.*
tax collector *n.* сбо́рщик нало́гов *m.*
taxi /'tæksi/ *also* **taxicab** *n.* такси́ *neut. indecl.*
taxidermy /'tæksɪ,dɜrmi/ *n.* наби́вка чу́чел; таксидерми́я *f.*
taxi driver *n.* води́тель такси́ *m.*
taximeter /'tæksi,mitər/ *n.* счётчик; таксо́метр *m.*
taxonomy /tæk'sɒnəmi/ *n.* таксоно́мия *f.*
taxpayer /'tæks,peiər/ *n.* налогоплате́льщик *m.*
TB *n.* туберкулёз *m.*
Tbilisi /təbə'lisi/ *n.* (*also: Tiflis*) Тбили́си *m.*
tea /ti/ **1.** *n.* чай *m.* **2.** *adj.* ча́йный.
tea break *n.* переры́в на чай *m.*
tea caddy *n.* ча́йница *f.*
teach /titʃ/ *v.* преподава́ть; учи́ть; обуча́ть *impf.*, обучи́ть *pf.*
teacher /'titʃər/ *n.* учи́тель *m.*, учи́тельница *f.*
teaching /'titʃɪŋ/ **1.** *n.* преподава́ние *neut.*; *pl.* уче́ние *neut.* **2.** *adj.* преподава́тельский; педагоги́ческий.
tea cozy *n.* чехо́льчик (для ча́йника) *m.*
teacup /'ti,kʌp/ *n.* (ча́йная) ча́шка *f.*
tea house *n.* (*obs.*) ча́йная *f.*
teak /tik/ **1.** *adj.* тик *m.* **2.** *adj.* ти́ковый.
teakettle /'ti,kɛtl/ *n.* ча́йник *m.*
teal /til/ *n.* чиро́к *m.*
team /tim/ *n.* кома́нда *f.*
teammate /'tim,meit/ *n.* член кома́нды *m.*
teamster /'timstər/ *n.* води́тель грузовика́ *m.*
teamwork /'tim,wзrk/ *n.* сла́женность *f.*
teapot /'ti,pɒt/ *n.* ча́йник (для зава́рки) *m.*
tear[1] /tɛər/ **1.** *n.* проре́ха; дыра́ *f.* **2.** *v.t.* рвать

impf., разорва́ть *pf.*; *v.i.* рва́ться *impf.*, разорва́ться *pf.*

tear² /tɪər/ *n.* (*eye*) слеза́ *f.*

tearful /'tɪərfəl/ *adj.* слезли́вый.

tearoom /'ti,rum/ *n.* (*obs.*) ча́йная *f.*

tease /tiz/ *v.* дразни́ть *impf.*

teaspoon /'ti,spun/ *n.* ча́йная ло́жка *f.*

teat /tit/ *n.* (*nipple*) сосо́к *m.*

technical /'tɛknɪkəl/ *adj.* техни́ческий.

technician /tɛk'nɪʃən/ *n.* те́хник *m.*

technique /tɛk'nik/ *n.* те́хника *f.*

technology /tɛk'nɒlədʒi/ *n.* техноло́гия; те́хника *f.*

teddy bear /'tɛdi/ *n.* медвежо́нок *m.*; ми́шка *m.* (*decl. f.*).

tedious /'tidiəs/ *adj.* ску́чный.

tedium /'tidiəm/ *n.* ску́ка; утоми́тельность *f.*

teem /tim/ *v.* кише́ть; изоби́ловать (*with instr.*) *impf.*

teenage /'tin,eidʒ/ *adj.* о́трческий.

teenager /'tin,eidʒər/ *n.* подро́сток *m.*

teeny /'tini/ *adj.* кро́хотный.

teeter /'titər/ *v.* кача́ться *impf.*

teethe /tið/ *v.i.*: **the child is teething** у ребёнка прорезаются зу́бы.

teetotal /ti'toutļ/ *adj.* непью́щий.

teetotaler /ti'toutļər/ *n.* тре́звенник *m.*

Teheran /tə'ræn, ˌtɛhə'rɑn/ *n.* Тегера́н *m.*

telecast /'tɛlɪ,kæst/ *n.* телевизио́нная переда́ча *f.*

telecommunications /ˌtɛlɪkə,myunɪ'keiʃənz/ *n.* связь; телесвя́зь *f.*

telegram /'tɛlɪ,græm/ *n.* телегра́мма *f.*

telegraph /'tɛlɪ,græf/ **1.** *n.* телегра́ф *m.* **2.** *adj.* телегра́фный. **3.** *v.* телеграфи́ровать *impf.* and *pf.*

telepathy /tə'lɛpəθi/ *n.* телепа́тия *f.*

telephone /'tɛlə,foun/ **1.** *n.* телефо́н *m.* **2.** *adj.* телефо́нный. **3.** *v.* телефони́ровать *impf.* and *pf.*; звони́ть по телефо́ну *impf.*

telephone operator *n.* телефони́ст *m.*, телефони́стка *f.*

telephonic /ˌtɛlə'fɒnɪk/ *adj.* телефо́нный.

telephoto lens /ˌtɛlə'foutou/ *n.* телеобъекти́в *m.*

telescope /'tɛlə,skoup/ *n.* телеско́п *m.*

televiewer /'tɛlə,vyuər/ *n.* телезри́тель *m.*

televise /'tɛlə,vaiz/ *v.* передава́ть по телеви́дению *impf.*

television /'tɛlə,vɪʒən/ **1.** *n.* телеви́дение *neut.* **2.** *adj.* телевизио́нный.

television set *n.* телеви́зор *m.*

tell /tɛl/ *v.* говори́ть *impf.*, сказа́ть *pf.*; (*narrate*) расска́зывать *impf.*, рассказа́ть *pf.*

teller /'tɛlər/ *n.* (*narrator*) расска́зчик *m.*; (*of votes*) счётчик *m.*; (*bank clerk*) касси́р *m.*, касси́рша *f.*

telling /'tɛlɪŋ/ *adj.* многозначи́тельный.

telltale /'tɛl,teil/ *n.* спле́тник *m.*

temerarious /ˌtɛmə'rɛəriəs/ *adj.* опроме́тчивый; безрассу́дный.

temper /'tɛmpər/ **1.** *n.* (*mood*) настрое́ние *neut.*; (*anger*) раздраже́ние *neut.*; гнев *m.* **2.** *v.* (*fig.*) умеря́ть *impf.*, уме́рить *pf.*

temperament /'tɛmpərəmənt/ *n.* темпера́мент *m.*

temperamental /ˌtɛmpərə'mɛntļ/ *adj.* темпера́ментный.

temperance /'tɛmpərəns/ *n.* возде́ржанность; уме́ренность *f.*

temperate /'tɛmpərɪt/ *adj.* уме́ренный.

temperature /'tɛmpərətʃər/ *n.* температу́ра *f.*

tempest /'tɛmpɪst/ *n.* бу́ря *f.*

template /'tɛmplɪt/ *n.* шабло́н *m.*

temple¹ /'tɛmpəl/ *n.* храм *m.*

temple² /'tɛmpəl/ *n.* (*anat.*) висо́к *m.*

tempo /'tɛmpou/ *n.* темп *m.*

temporal /'tɛmpərəl/ *adj.* вре́менный.

temporarily /ˌtɛmpə'rɛərəli/ *adv.* вре́менно; на вре́мя.

temporary /'tɛmpəˌrɛri/ *adj.* вре́менный.

temporize /'tɛmpəˌraiz/ *v.* тяну́ть вре́мя *impf.*

tempt /tɛmpt/ *v.* искуша́ть *impf.*

temptation /tɛmp'teiʃən/ *n.* искуше́ние *neut.*

tempter /'tɛmptər/ *n.* искуси́тель; соблазни́тель *m.*

ten /tɛn/ *n.*, *adj.* де́сять.

tenacious /tə'neiʃəs/ *adj.* упо́рный.

tenacity /tə'næsɪti/ *n.* це́пкость *f.*

tenancy /'tɛnənsi/ *n.* аре́нда *f.*

tenant /'tɛnənt/ *n.* нанима́тель; аренда́тор *m.*

tench /tɛntʃ/ *n.* линь *m.*

tend¹ /tɛnd/ *v.* (*care for*) уха́живать (за *with str.*) *impf.*

tend² /tɛnd/ *v.*: **to tend to** (*lead*) направля́ться *impf.*; (*be disposed*) склоня́ться *impf.*

tendency /'tɛndənsi/ *n.* накло́нность *f.*

tendentious /tɛn'dɛnʃəs/ *adj.* тенденцио́зный.

tendentiousness /tɛn'dɛnʃəsnɪs/ *n.* тенденцио́зность *f.*

tender /'tɛndər/ *adj.* не́жный; чувстви́тельный.

tenderfoot /'tɛndər,fut/ *n.* новичо́к *m.*

tender-hearted /'tɛndər 'hɑrtɪd/ *adj.* мягкосерде́чный.

tenderize /'tɛndə,raiz/ *v.* размягча́ть *impf.*

tenderloin /'tɛndər,lɔin/ *n.* вы́резка *f.*

tenderness /'tɛndərnɪs/ *n.* не́жность *f.*

tendon /'tɛndən/ *n.* сухожи́лие *neut.*

tendril /'tɛndrɪl/ *n.* у́сик *m.*

tenement /'tɛnəmənt/ *n.* жило́й дом *m.*

tenet /'tɛnɪt/ *n.* догма́т; при́нцип *m.*

tenfold /'tɛn,fould/ *adj.* десятикра́тный, удесятерённый.

Tennessee /ˌtɛnə'si/ *n.* Теннесси́ *m.*

tennis /'tɛnɪs/ **1.** *n.* те́ннис *m.* **2.** *adj.* те́ннисный.

tenon /'tɛnən/ *n.* шип *m.*

tenor /'tɛnər/ **1.** *n.* те́нор *m.* **2.** *adj.* теноро́вый.

tense¹ /tɛns/ *adj.* натя́нутый; напряжённый.

tense² /tɛns/ *n.* (*gram.*) вре́мя *neut.*

tensile /'tɛnsəl/ *adj.* растяжи́мый.

tension /'tɛnʃən/ *n.* напряже́ние *neut.*

tensor /'tɛnsər/ *n.* те́нзор *m.*

tent /tɛnt/ *n.* пала́тка *f.*; шатёр *m.*

tentacle /'tɛntəkəl/ *n.* (*zool.*) щу́пальце *neut.*

tentative /'tɛntətɪv/ *adj.* про́бный; (*provisional*) предвари́тельный.

tenth /tɛnθ/ *adj.* деся́тый.

tenuous /'tɛnyuəs/ *adj.* то́нкий; непро́чный.

ten-year /'tɛn 'yɪər/ *adj.* десятиле́тний.

tepid /'tɛpɪd/ *adj.* теплова́тый.

teratological /ˌtɛrətļ'ɒdʒɪkəl/ *adj.* тератологи́ческий.

teratology /ˌtɛrə'tɒlədʒi/ *n.* тератоло́гия *f.*

tercentenary /,tɜrsɛn'tɛnəri/ *n.* трёхсотлётие *neut.*

tercet /'tɜrsɪt/ *n.* терцéт *m.*

tergiversate /'tɜrdʒɪvər,seit/ *v.* (*equivocate*) увёртываться *impf.*

term /tɜrm/ **1.** *n.* срок *m.*; (*name*) тéрмин *m.* **2.** *v.* называ́ть *impf.*, назва́ть *pf.*

termagant /'tɜrməgənt/ *n.* стропти́вая же́нщина *f.*

terminal /'tɜrmənl/ **1.** *n.* (*railroad*) вокза́л *m.*; конéчная ста́нция *f.*; (*comput.*) термина́л *m.* **2.** *adj.* конéчный; (*med.*) смертéльный.

terminate /'tɜrmə,neit/ *v.t.* прекраща́ть *impf.*; *v.i.* конча́ться *impf.*

termination /,tɜrmə'neiʃən/ *adj.* прекращéние *neut.*

terminator /'tɜrmə,neitər/ *n.* термина́тор *m.*

terminological /,tɜrmənl'ɒdʒɪkəl/ *adj.* терминологи́ческий.

terminology /,tɜrmə'nɒlədʒi/ *n.* терминоло́гия *f.*

terminus /'tɜrmənəs/ *n.* (*railroad*) конéчная ста́нция *f.*

termite /'tɜrmait/ *n.* терми́т *m.*

tern /tɜrn/ *n.* (*bird*) кра́чка *f.*

ternary /'tɜrnəri/ *adj.* тройно́й.

Ternopil /tər'noupəl/ *n.* Терно́поль *m*

terra cotta /'tɛrə 'kɒtə/ *n.* терракóта *f.*

terrace /'tɛrəs/ *n.* терра́са; вера́нда *f.*

terrain /tə'rein/ *n.* мéстность *f.*

terrestrial /tə'rɛstriəl/ *adj.* земно́й; назéмный.

terrible /'tɛrəbəl/ *adj.* ужа́сный.

terribly /'tɛrəbli/ *adv.* ужа́сно; стра́шно.

terrier /'tɛriər/ *n.* терьéр *m.*

terrific /tə'rɪfɪk/ *adj.* колосса́льный; (*magnificent*) великолéпный; (*wonderful*) чу́дный.

terrify /'tɛrə,fai/ *v.* ужаса́ть *impf.*

territorial /,tɛrɪ'tɔriəl/ *adj.* территориа́льный.

territory /'tɛrɪ,tɔri/ *n.* террито́рия *f.*

terror /'tɛrər/ *n.* у́жас; террóр *m.*

terrorism /'tɛrə,rɪzəm/ *n.* террори́зм *m.*

terrorist /'tɛrərɪst/ **1.** *adj.* террористи́ческий. **2.** *n.* террори́ст *m.*, террори́стка *f.*

terrorize /'tɛrə,raiz/ *v.* терроризи́ровать *impf.* and *pf.*

terry *also* **terry cloth** /'tɛri/ *n.* махро́вая ткань *f.*

terse /tɜrs/ *adj.* сжа́тый; (*speech*) немногосло́вный; (*abrupt*) рéзкий.

tertiary /'tɜrʃi,ɛri/ *adj.* трети́чный.

tessellated /'tɛsə,leitɪd/ *adj.* моза́ичный.

test /tɛst/ **1.** *n.* испыта́ние *neut.*; (*exam*) экза́мен *m.*; (*med.*) ана́лиз *m.* **2.** *adj.* испыта́тельный. **3.** *v.* проверя́ть *impf.*

testament /'tɛstəmənt/ *n.* завеща́ние *neut.*; **New Testament** Но́вый Завéт *m.*; **Old Testament** Вéтхий Завéт *m.*

testamentary /,tɛstə'mɛntəri/ *adj.* завеща́тельный.

testator /'tɛsteitər/ *n.* завеща́тель *m.*

testatrix /tɛ'steitrɪks/ *n.* завеща́тельница *f.*

test ban *n.* запрещéние я́дерных испыта́ний *neut.*

tested /'tɛstɪd/ *adj.* провéренный.

tester /'tɛstər/ *n.* испыта́тель *m.*

testify /'tɛstə,fai/ *v.* свидéтельствовать *impf.*

testily /'tɛstɪi/ *adv.* раздражённо.

testimonial /,tɛstə'mouniəl/ *n.* характери́стика *f.*; свидéтельство *neut.*

testimony /'tɛstə,mouni/ *n.* свидéтельство *neut.*; (*proof*) доказа́тельство *neut.*

testiness /'tɛstɪnɪs/ *n.* раздражи́тельность *f.*

testis /'tɛstɪs/ *also* **testicle** /'tɛstɪkəl/ *n.* яи́чко *neut.*

test pilot *n.* лётчик-испыта́тель *m.*

test tube *n.* проби́рка *f.*

testy /'tɛsti/ *adj.* раздражи́тельный.

tetanus /'tɛtnəs/ *n.* столбня́к; тéтанус *m.*

tether /'tɛðər/ *v.* привя́зывать *impf.*

tetrachord /'tɛtrə,kɔrd/ *n.* (*mus.*) тетрахóрд *m.*

tetracycline /,tɛtrə'saiklin/ *n.* тетрацикли́н *m.*

tetrad /'tɛtræd/ *n.* четвёрка *f.*

tetrahedron /,tɛtrə'hidrən/ *n.* четырёхгра́нник *m.*

Teutonic /tu'tɒnɪk/ *n.* тевто́нский язы́к *m.*

Texas /'tɛksəs/ *n.* Техáс *m.*

text /tɛkst/ *n.* текст *m.*

textbook /'tɛkst,bʊk/ *n.* учéбник *m.*; посóбие *neut.*

textile /'tɛkstail/ **1.** *adj.* текстѝльный. **2.** *n.* текстѝль *m.*; текстѝльное издéлие *neut.*

textual /'tɛkstʃuəl/ *adj.* тéкстовый.

textural /'tɛkstʃərəl/ *adj.* структу́рный.

texture /'tɛkstʃər/ *n.* строéние; ка́чество (тка́ни) *neut.*

Thai /tai/ *adj.* тáйский.

Thailand /'tai,lænd/ *n.* Таила́нд *m.*

thalamus /'θæləməs/ *n.* (*anat.*) зри́тельный бугóр *m.*

thallium /'θæliəm/ *n.* та́ллий *m.*

than /ðæn, ðɛn; *unstressed* ðən, ən/ *conj.* чем.

thank /θæŋk/ *v.* благодари́ть *impf.*, поблагодари́ть *pf.*; **thank you** спаси́бо; **thanks to** благодаря́ (*with dat.*).

thankful /'θæŋkfəl/ *adj.* благода́рный.

thankfulness /'θæŋkfəlnɪs/ *n.* благода́рность *f.*

thankless /'θæŋklɪs/ *adj.* неблагода́рный.

thanks /θæŋks/ *n.* благода́рность *f.*

thanksgiving /,θæŋks'gɪvɪŋ/ *n.* благодарéние *neut.*; (*cap.*) День Благодарéния *m.*

that /ðæt; *unstressed* ðət/ **1.** *pron.*, *adj.* тот *m.*, та *f.*, то *neut.*; э́тот *m.*, э́та *f.*, э́то *neut.* **2.** *adv.* так; до такóй стéпени. **3.** *conj.* что; чтóбы.

thatch /θætʃ/ *n.* крóвельная солóма *f.*

thaumaturge /'θɔmə,tɜrdʒ/ *n.* чудотвóрец *m.*

thaw /θɔ/ **1.** *n.* о́ттепель *f.* **2.** *v.i.* та́ять; отта́ивать *impf.*

the /*stressed* ði; *unstressed before a consonant* ðə, *unstressed before a vowel* ði/ *art.* (*no equivalent in Russian*); **the...**, **the...** чем..., тем...

theater /'θiətər/ *n.* теа́тр *m.*

theatrical /θi'ætrɪkəl/ *adj.* театра́льный.

theatrics /θi'ætrɪks/ *n.* театра́льность *f.*

Thebes /θibz/ *n.* Фи́вы *pl.*

theft /θɛft/ *n.* воровствó *neut.*; кра́жа *f.*

their /ðɛər; *unstressed* ðər/ *pron.* их; свой *m.*, своя́ *f.*, своё *neut.*, свой *pl.*

theirs /ðɛərz/ *pron.* их.

theism /'θiɪzəm/ *n.* тейзм *m.*

theist /'θiɪst/ *n.* тейст *m.*

them /ðɛm; *unstressed* ðəm, əm/ *pron.* (*direct obj.*) их.

thematic /θi'mætɪk/ *adj.* темати́ческий.

theme /θim/ *n.* (*also mus.*) тéма *f.*, предмéт *m.*

themselves /ðəm'sɛlvz/ *pron.* себя́, себé; сáми.

then /ðɛn/ *adv.* тогдá; (*afterwards*) потóм.

thence /ðɛns/ adv. оттýда; отсю́да; с того́ вре́мени.

thenceforth /ˌðɛns'fɔrθ/ adv. с тех пор; с того́ вре́мени.

theocracy /θi'ɒkrəsi/ n. теокра́тия f.

theocratic /ˌθiə'krætɪk/ adj. теократи́ческий.

theodicy /θi'ɒdəsi/ n. теодице́я f.

theodolite /θi'ɒdlˌait/ n. теодоли́т m.

theology /θi'ɒlədʒi/ n. богосло́вие neut.

theophany /θi'ɒfəni/ n. богоявле́ние neut.

theorem /'θiərəm/ n. теоре́ма f.

theoretical /ˌθiə'rɛtɪkəl/ adj. теорети́ческий.

theoretician /ˌθiərɪ'tɪʃən/ also **theorist** /'θiərɪst/ n. теоре́тик m.

theorize /'θiəˌraiz/ v. теоретизи́ровать impf.

theory /'θiəri/ n. тео́рия f.

theosophy /θi'ɒsəfi/ n. теосо́фия f.

therapeutic /ˌθɛrə'pyutɪk/ adj. лече́бный; терапевти́ческий.

therapeutics /ˌθɛrə'pyutɪks/ n. терапи́я f.

therapy /'θɛrəpi/ n. терапи́я f.

there /ðɛər; unstressed ðər/ adv. (loc.) там; (dir.) туда́; **there is, there are** есть; име́ется; име́ются impf.

thereabout /'ðɛərəˌbaut/ adv. (nearby) (где-то) побли́зости; (approximately) приблизи́тельно.

thereafter /ˌðɛər'æftər/ adv. по́сле э́того; с тех пор.

thereat /ˌðɛər'æt/ adv. там; тогда́.

thereby /ˌðɛər'bai/ adv. таки́м о́бразом.

therefore /'ðɛərˌfɔr/ adv. поэ́тому.

therein /ˌðɛər'ɪn/ adv. в э́том.

theretofore /ˌðɛərtə'fɔr/ adv. до того́ вре́мени

thereupon /'ðɛərəˌpɒn/ adv. затем; (immediately) неме́дленно.

thermal /'θɜrməl/ adj. теплово́й.

thermion /'θɜrmˌaiən/ n. теплоэлектро́н m.

thermionic /ˌθɛrmai'ɒnɪk/ adj. теплоэлектро́нный.

thermochemistry /ˌθɜrmou'kɛməstri/ n. термохи́мия f.

thermocouple /'θɜrməˌkʌpəl/ n. термопа́ра f.; термоэлеме́нт m.

thermodynamic /ˌθɜrmoudai'næmɪk/ adj. термодинами́ческий.

thermodynamics /ˌθɜrmoudai'næmɪks/ n. термодина́мика f.

thermoelectric /ˌθɜrmoui'lɛktrɪk/ adj. термоэлектри́ческий.

thermogenesis /ˌθɜrmou'dʒɛnəsɪs/ n. термогене́з m.

thermograph /'θɜrməˌgræf/ n. термо́граф m.

thermometer /θər'mɒmɪtər/ n. гра́дусник; термо́метр m.

thermonuclear /ˌθɜrmou'nukliər/ adj. термоя́дерный.

thermopile /'θɜrməˌpail/ n. термоэлеме́нт m.

thermos /'θɜrməs/ n. те́рмос m.

thermostat /'θɜrməˌstæt/ n. термоста́т m.

thesaurus /θɪ'sɔrəs/ n. теза́урус m.

these /ðiz/ adj., pron. э́ти.

thesis /'θisɪs/ n. те́зис m.; (dissertation) диссерта́ция f.

they /ðei/ pron. они́.

thiamine /'θaiəmɪn/ n. тиами́н m.

thick /θɪk/ adj. то́лстый; густо́й.

thicken /'θɪkən/ v.t. сгуща́ть impf., сгусти́ть pf.; v.i. сгуща́ться impf., сгусти́ться pf.

thicket /'θɪkɪt/ n. ча́ща; за́росли pl.

thickheaded /'θɪk'hɛdɪd/ adj. тупо́й.

thickish /'θɪkɪʃ/ adj. толстова́тый.

thick-lipped /'θɪk ˌlɪpt/ adj. губа́стый.

thickness /'θɪknɪs/ n. толщина́ f.

thickset /'θɪk'sɛt/ adj. корена́стый.

thick-skinned /'θɪk ˌskɪnd/ adj. толстоко́жий.

thief /θif/ n. вор m.

thieve /θiv/ v. ворова́ть impf.

thievery /'θivəri/ n. воровство́ neut.

thievish /'θivɪʃ/ adj. ворова́тый.

thigh /θai/ n. бедро́ neut.

thimble /'θɪmbəl/ n. напёрсток m.

thin /θɪn/ **1.** adj. то́нкий; (skinny) худо́й. **2.** v.t.: **to thin out** проре́живать impf., проре́дить pf.

thine /ðain/ pron. твой.

thing /θɪŋ/ n. вещь f.; предме́т m.; (matter) де́ло neut.

think /θɪŋk/ v. ду́мать impf., поду́мать pf.

thinkable /'θɪŋkəbəl/ adj. мы́слимый.

thinker /'θɪŋkər/ n. мысли́тель m.

thinking /'θɪŋkɪŋ/ n. размышле́ние neut.; (opinion) мне́ние neut.

thinner¹ /'θɪnər/ n. (for paints) разбави́тель m.

thinner² /'θɪnər/ adj. бо́лее то́нкий; бо́лее жи́дкий.

thinness /'θɪnnɪs/ n. то́нкость; худоба́ f.

thin-skinned /'θɪn ˌskɪnd/ adj. тонкоко́жий.

third /θɜrd/ **1.** adj. тре́тий (тре́тья f., тре́тье neut.). **2.** n. треть f.

third degree n. допро́с с пристра́стием m.

thirdly /'θɜrdli/ adv. в-тре́тьих.

third person n. (gram.) тре́тье лицо́ neut.

third-rate /'θɜrd 'reit/ adj. третьесо́ртный.

Third World n. стра́ны тре́тьего ми́ра pl.

thirst /θɜrst/ n. жа́жда f.

thirsty /'θɜrsti/ **1.** adj. томи́мый жа́ждой. **2.** v.: **to be thirsty** v. хоте́ть пить impf.

thirteen /'θɜr'tin/ n., adj. трина́дцать.

thirteenth /'θɜr'tinθ/ adj. трина́дцатый.

thirtieth /'θɜrtiiθ/ adj. тридца́тый.

thirty /'θɜrti/ n., adj. три́дцать.

this /ðɪs/ **1.** adj. э́тот m., э́та f., э́то neut., э́ти pl. **2.** pron. э́то.

thistle /'θɪsəl/ n. чертополо́х m.

thither /'θɪðər/ adv. туда́; **hither and thither** adv. туда́ и сюда́.

thong /θɒŋ/ n. реме́нь m.

thorax /'θɔræks/ n. грудна́я кле́тка f.

thorium /'θɔriəm/ n. то́рий m.

thorn /θɔrn/ n. шип m.; колю́чка f.

thorny /'θɔrni/ adj. колю́чий.

thorough /'θɜrou/ adj. соверше́нный; доскона́льный.

thoroughbred /'θɜrouˌbrɛd/ adj. поро́дистый.

thoroughfare /'θɜrouˌfɛər/ n. прое́зд; прохо́д m.; (main road) магистра́ль m.

thoroughgoing /'θɜrouˌgouɪŋ/ adj. радика́льный.

thoroughly /'θɜrəli/ adv. вполне́; соверше́нно.

thoroughness /'θɜrounɪs/ n. тща́тельность f.

those /ðouz/ adj., pron. те.

thou /ðau/ pron. ты.

though /ðou/ **1.** adv. тем не ме́нее; одна́ко. **2.** conj. хотя́; несмотря́ на то, что.

thought /θɔt/ *n.* мысль *f.*; мышле́ние *neut.*
thoughtful /'θɔtfəl/ *adj.* заду́мчивый; (*considerate*) внима́тельный.
thoughtless /'θɔtlɪs/ *adj.* необду́манный.
thousand /'θauzənd/ *n.*, *adj.* ты́сяча.
thousandfold /'θauzənd,fould/ *adj.* тысячекра́тный.
thousandth /'θauzəndθ/ *adj.* ты́сячный.
Thrace /θreis/ *n.* (*province*) Фра́кия *f.*
thrall /θrɔl/ *n.* раб *m.*
thralldom /'θrɔldəm/ *n.* ра́бство *neut.*
thrash /θræʃ/ *v.* поро́ть *impf.*
thrashing /'θræʃɪŋ/ *n.* взбу́чка *f.*
thread /θrɛd/ *n.* ни́тка; нить *f.*; (*of screw*) резьба́ *f.*
threadbare /'θrɛd,bɛər/ *adj.* потёртый; (*clothes*) поно́шенный.
threadlike /'θrɛd,laik/ *adj.* нитеви́дный.
threat /θrɛt/ *n.* угро́за *f.*
threaten /'θrɛtn/ *v.* грози́ть; угрожа́ть *impf.*
threatening /'θrɛtnɪŋ/ *adj.* угрожа́ющий.
three /θri/ *n.*, *adj.* три.
three-dimensional /'θri dɪ'mɛnʃənl/ *adj.* трёхме́рный; **3-D film** *n.* стереофи́льм *m.*
threefold /'θri,fould/ *adj.* тройно́й.
three-ply /'θri 'plai/ *adj.* трёхсло́йный.
three-sided /'θri 'saidɪd/ *adj.* трёхсторо́нний.
threesome /'θrisəm/ *n.* тро́йка *f.*; тро́е *pl.*
three-stage /'θri ,steidʒ/ *adj.* трёхступе́нчатый.
threnody /'θrɛnədi/ *n.* плач *m.*
thresh /θrɛʃ/ *v.* молоти́ть *impf.*
thresher /'θrɛʃər/ *n.* молоти́лка *f.*
threshing /'θrɛʃɪŋ/ *n.* молотьба́ *f.*; **threshing floor** *n.* гумно́ *neut.*
threshold /'θrɛʃould/ *n.* поро́г *m.*; преддве́рие *neut.*
thrice /θrais/ *adv.* три́жды.
thrift /θrɪft/ *n.* бережли́вость; эконо́мность *f*
thrifty /'θrɪfti/ *adj.* бережли́вый; домови́тый.
thrill /θrɪl/ **1.** *n.* волне́ние; о́строе ощуще́ние *neut.*; тре́пет *m.* **2.** *v.* захва́тывать; си́льно волнова́ть(ся) *impf.*
thrilled /θrɪld/ *adj.* (*delighted*) в восто́рге (от *with gen.*).
thrilling /'θrɪlɪŋ/ *adj.* волну́ющий.
thrive /θraiv/ *v.* преуспева́ть; процвета́ть *impf.*
throat /θrout/ *n.* го́рло *neut.*
throaty /'θrouti/ *adj.* горта́нный.
throb /θrɒb/ *v.* си́льно би́ться *impf.*; (*pulsate*) пульси́ровать *impf.*
throe /θrou/ *n. usu. pl.* спазм *m.*; му́ки *pl.*
thrombosis /θrɒm'bousɪs/ *n.* тромбо́з *m.*
throne /θroun/ *n.* трон; престо́л *m.*
throng /θrɒŋ/ *n.* толпа́ *f.*
throttle /'θrɒtl/ **1.** *n.* (*tech.*) дро́ссель *m.* **2.** *v.* (*strangle*) души́ть *impf.*
through /θru/ **1.** *prep.* че́рез (*with acc.*); сквозь (*with acc.*); по (*with dat.*). **2.** *adv.* наскво́зь; **through and through** соверше́нно. **3.** *adj.* беспереса́дочный; прямо́й.
throughout /θru'aut/ **1.** *adv.* повсю́ду; во всех отноше́ниях. **2.** *prep.* по всему́ (*with dat.*).
throw /θrou/ **1.** *n.* бросо́к *m.* **2.** *v.* броса́ть *impf.*, бро́сить *pf.*; **to throw aside** отбра́сывать *impf.*, отбро́сить *pf.*; **to throw out** выбра́сывать *impf.*, вы́бросить *pf.*
throwaway /'θrouə,wei/ *adj.* однора́зовый.

thrower /'θrouər/ *n.* мета́тель *m.*
thrush /θrʌʃ/ *n.* (*bird*) дрозд *m.*
thrust /θrʌst/ **1.** *n.* уда́р; толчо́к; вы́пад *m.* **2.** *v.* толка́ть(ся); сова́ть *impf.*
thruway /'θru,wei/ *n.* автостра́да *f.*
thud /θʌd/ *n.* глухо́й звук; стук *m.*
thug /θʌg/ *n.* (*hoodlum*) хулига́н *m.*; (*gangster*) банди́т *m.*
thuggery /'θʌgəri/ *n.* хулига́нство *neut.*
thumb /θʌm/ *n.* большо́й па́лец *m.*
thumbnail /'θʌm,neil/ *n.* но́готь большо́го па́льца *m.*
thumbnut /'θʌm,nʌt/ *n.* бара́шковая га́йка *f.*
thumbtack /'θʌm,tæk/ *n.* канцеля́рская кно́пка *f.*
thump /θʌmp/ *n.* тяжёлый уда́р; глухо́й стук *m.*
thumping /'θʌmpɪŋ/ *n.* стук *m.*
thunder /'θʌndər/ **1.** *n.* гром *m.* **2.** *v.* греме́ть *impf.*
thunderbolt /'θʌndər,boult/ *n.* уда́р мо́лнии *m.*
thunderclap /'θʌndər,klæp/ *n.* раска́т гро́ма *m.*
thundercloud /'θʌndər,klaud/ *n.* грозова́я ту́ча *f.*
thunderflash /'θʌndər,flæʃ/ *n.* взрыв-паке́т *m.*
thundering /'θʌndərɪŋ/ *n.* гро́хот *m.*
thunderous /'θʌndərəs/ *adj.* громово́й.
thunderstorm /'θʌndər,stɔrm/ *n.* гроза́ *f.*
thunderstruck /'θʌndər,strʌk/ *adj.* ошеломлённый; как гро́мом поражённый.
thurible /'θurəbəl/ *n.* кади́ло *neut.*
thurifer /'θurəfər/ *n.* кади́льщик *m.*
Thursday /'θзrzdei/ *n.* четве́рг *m.*
thus /ðʌs/ *adv.* так; таки́м о́бразом; поэ́тому; до тако́й сте́пени.
thwack /θwæk/ *v.* колоти́ть *impf.*
thwart /θwɔrt/ *v.* меша́ть *impf.*
thy /ðai/ *pron.* твой.
thyme /taim; *spelling pron.* θaim/ *n.* тимья́н *m.*
thymol /'θaimoul/ *n.* тимо́л *m.*
thyroid /'θairɔid/ *n.* щитови́дная железа́ *f.*
Tiber /'taibər/ *n.* (*river*) Тибр *m.*
tibia /'tɪbiə/ *n.* больша́я берцо́вая кость *f.*
tic /tɪk/ *n.* тик *m.*
tick /tɪk/ *n.* (*parasite*) клещ *m.*
ticket /'tɪkɪt/ *n.* биле́т *m.*; (*receipt*) квита́нция *f.*, (*for traffic violation*) штраф *m.*
ticket punch *n.* компо́стер *m.*
ticket seller *n.* касси́р *m.*, касси́рша *f.*
tickle /'tɪkəl/ **1.** *n.* щекота́ние *neut.*; щеко́тка *f.* **2.** *v.* щекота́ть *impf.*, пощекота́ть *pf.*
ticklish /'tɪklɪʃ/ *adj.* щекотли́вый.
tidal /'taidl/ *adj.* прили́вный.
tidbit /'tɪd,bɪt/ *n.* ла́комый кусо́чек *m.*; (*piece of news*) пика́нтная но́вость *f.*
tiddlywinks /'tɪdli,wɪŋks/ *n.* (игра́ в) блошки *pl.*
tide /taid/ *n.* морско́й прили́в и отли́в *m.*; **high tide** *n.* по́лная вода́ *f.*; **low tide** *n.* ма́лая вода́ *f.*
tidemark /'taid,mɑrk/ *n.* отме́тка у́ровня по́лной воды́ *f.*
tidewater /'taid,wɔtər/ *n.* прили́вная вода́ *f.*
tidiness /'taidinɪs/ *n.* опря́тность *f.*
tidings /'taidɪŋz/ *n.* ве́сти *pl.*
tidy /'taidi/ *adj.* опря́тный; аккура́тный.
tie /tai/ **1.** *n.* (*bond*) связь *f.*; *pl.* у́зы *pl.*; (*necktie*) га́лстук *m.*; (*equal score*) ничья́ *f.* **2.** *v.* завя́зывать *impf.*, завяза́ть *pf.*
tier /tɪər/ *n.* я́рус *m.*
tierce /tɪərs/ *n.* те́рция *f.*

Tierra del Fuego /ti'ɛr'ə dɛl fweigou/ n. Огненная Земля f.

tie-up /'tai ˌʌp/ n. (stoppage) задержка; остановка f.; (connection) связь f.

tiff /tɪf/ n. размолвка f.

tiger /'taigər/ 1. n. тигр m. 2. adj. тигровый.

tigerish /'taigərɪʃ/ adj. (cruel) свирепый.

tiger lily n. тигровая лилия f.

tiger moth n. бабочка-медведица f.

tight /tait/ adj. плотный; тесный; сжатый; тугой; (stingy) скудный.

tighten /'taitn̩/ v. (contract) сжимать impf., сжать pf.

tight-lipped /'tait'lɪpt/ adj. замкнутый.

tightness /'taitnɪs/ n. тугость; теснота f.

tightrope /'tait,roup/ n. (туго натянутый) канат m.

tights /taits/ n. трико neut. indecl.; колготки pl.

tightwad /'tait,wɒd/ n. (colloq.) скупец m.

tigress /'taigrɪs/ n. тигрица f.

tilde /'tɪldə/ n. тильда f.

tile /tail/ n. (roof) черепица f.; (decorative) кафель m.

till¹ /tɪl/ n. касса f.

till² /tɪl/ v. пахать impf.

till³ /tɪl/ prep. до; не раньше (with gen.).

tillage /'tɪlɪdʒ/ n. возделанная земля f.

tiller /'tɪlər/ n. земледелец m.

tilt /tɪlt/ 1. n. наклон m. 2. v. наклонять(ся) impf.

timber /'tɪmbər/ n. лесоматериал m.

timberline /'tɪmbər,lain/ n. граница распространения леса f.

timbre /'tæmbər, 'tɪm-/ n. тембр m.

time /taim/ 1. n. время neut.; (occasion) раз m.; (period) период m.; (mus.) такт m.; **a long time** долго; давно; **in good time** своевременно; **on time** (punctual) вовремя; **for the first time** в первый раз; **from time to time** время от времени; **what time is it?** который час? 2. v. хронометрировать impf. and pf.

time bomb n. бомба замедленного действия f.

time-consuming /'taim kən,sumɪŋ/ adj. требующий много времени.

time-honored /'taim ˌɒnərd/ adj. освящённый веками.

timekeeping /'taim,kipɪŋ/ n. отрезок времени m.

time-lag /'taim ˌlæg/ n. задержка f.

timeless /'taimlɪs/ adj. вечный.

time limit n. предельный срок m.

timely /'taimli/ adj. своевременный.

timepiece /'taim,pis/ n. часы pl.

timer /'taimər/ n. хронометр m.

timesaving /'taim,seivɪŋ/ adj. экономящий время.

timeserver /'taim,sɜrvər/ n. проспособленец m.

timeservingness /'taim,sɜrvɪŋnɪs/ n. приспособленчество neut.

time sheet n. табель m.

timetable /'taim,teibəl/ n. расписание neut.

timework /'taim,wɜrk/ n. повременная работа f.

timeworn /'taim,wɔrn/ adj. ветхий.

time zone n. часовой пояс m.

timid /'tɪmɪd/ adj. застенчивый.

timidity /tɪ'mɪdɪti/ n. застенчивость f.

timing /'taimɪŋ/ n. (choice of time) выбор времени m.; (synchronization) синхронизация f.

timorous /'tɪmərəs/ adj. боязливый.

tin /tɪn/ 1. n. олово neut. 2. adj. оловянный; жестяной.

tincture /'tɪŋktʃər/ n. настойка m.

tinder /'tɪndər/ n. трут m.

tinderbox /'tɪndər,bɒks/ n. трутница f.

tinfoil /'tɪn,fɔil/ n. станиоль m.; (оловянная) фольга f.

tinge /tɪndʒ/ n. (tint) оттенок m.; (flavor) привкус m.

tingle /'tɪŋgəl/ n. покалывание neut.

tinker /'tɪŋkər/ n. лудильщик m.

tinkle /'tɪŋkəl/ v. звенеть; позвякивать impf.

tinned /tɪnd/ adj. лужёный.

tinny /'tɪni/ adj. оловянный.

tin plate n. (белая) жесть f.

tinpot /'tɪn,pɒt/ adj. дешёвый.

tinsel /'tɪnsəl/ n. мишура f.

tint /tɪnt/ n. окраска f.; (shade) оттенок m.

tintometer /tɪn'tɒmɪtər/ n. колориметр m.

tiny /'taini/ adj. крошечный, очень маленький.

tip¹ /tɪp/ n. кончик; наконечник m.

tip² /tɪp/ 1. n. (gratuity) чаевые pl. 2. v. давать на чай impf.

tip³ /tɪp/ v. (tilt) наклонять(ся) impf., наклонить(ся) pf.

tip-off /'tɪp ˌɔf/ n. (colloq.) намёк m.; предупреждение neut.

tipsy /'tɪpsi/ adj. подвыпивший; (pred.) навеселе.

tiptoe /'tɪp,tou/ 1. v. ходить на цыпочках impf. 2. n.: **on tiptoes** на цыпочках.

tiptop /'tɪp,tɒp/ adj. превосходный; отличный.

Tiraspol /tɪ'ræspəl/ n. Тирасполь m.

tire¹ /tai³r/ n. шина f.

tire² /tai³r/ v. утомлять(ся); уставать impf., устать pf.

tired /tai³rd/ adj. усталый.

tireless /'tai³rlɪs/ adj. неутомимый.

tiresome /'tai³rsəm/ adj. надоедливый; нудный.

tiring /'tai³rɪŋ/ adj. утомительный.

tissue /'tɪʃu/ n. ткань f.; (thin paper) бумажная салфетка f.

tit¹ /tɪt/ n. (bird) синица f.

tit² /tɪt/ n. (vulg.) (breast) сиська f.

titanium /tai'teiniəm/ n. титан m.

tithe /taið/ n. (одна) десятая (часть) f.; (tax) десятина f.

titillate /'tɪtl̩,eit/ v. (arouse) возбуждать impf.

titillation /,tɪtl̩'eiʃən/ n. щекотка f.; щекотание neut.; приятное возбуждение neut.

title /'taitl̩/ 1. n. заглавие; название neut.; (rank) звание neut.; титул m. 2. v. называть impf., назвать pf.; озаглавливать impf.

titleholder /'taitl̩,houldər/ n. чемпион m.

title role n. главная роль f.

titmouse /'tɪt,maus/ n. синица f.

titrate /'taitreit/ v. титровать impf.

titter /'tɪtər/ v. хихикать impf.

tittle /'tɪtl̩/ n. (small quantity) капелька f.

titular /'tɪtʃələr/ adj. номинальный.

TNT n. тротил m.

to /tu; unstressed tʊ, tə/ prep. к (with dat.); в, на (with acc.); (until) до (with gen.); **to and fro** взад и вперёд.

toad /toud/ n. жаба f.

toadstool /'toud,stul/ n. (edible) гриб m.; (inedible) поганка f.

toady /'toudi/ n. подхалим m.

toast[1] /toust/ **1.** n. гренок m. **2.** v. жарить; поджаривать impf., поджарить pf.

toast[2] /toust/ **1.** n. (drink) тост m. **2.** v. (drink) пить тост за impf.

toaster /'toustər/ n. тостер m.

toastmaster /'toust,mæstər/ n. тамада m.

toast rack n. подставка для поджаренного хлеба f.

tobacco /tə'bækou/ **1.** n. табак m. **2.** adj. табачный.

tobacconist /tə'bækənɪst/ n. торговец табаком m.

tobacco pouch n. кисет m.

toboggan /tə'bɒgən/ n. санки pl.

toccata /tə'kɑtə/ n. токката f.

tocsin /'tɒksɪn/ n. (alarm) набат m.; (bell) набатный колокол m.

today /tə'dei/ **1.** adv. сегодня. **2.** n. сегодняшний день m.

toddle /'tɒdl/ v. ковылять impf.

toddler /'tɒdlər/ n. малыш m.

toe /tou/ n. палец на ноге m.

toenail /'tou,neil/ n. ноготь (на пальце ноги) m.

toga /'tougə/ n. тога f.

together /tə'gɛðər/ adv. вместе; **together with** вместе с (with instr.).

togetherness /tə'gɛðərnɪs/ n. общность; близость f.

toil /tɔil/ **1.** n. труд m.; работа f. **2.** v. трудиться impf.

toiler /'tɔilər/ n. труженик m.

toilet /'tɔilɪt/ **1.** n. туалет m.; уборная f.; (fixture) унитаз m. **2.** adj. туалетный.

toilet paper also **toilet tissue** n. туалетная бумага f.

toiletry /'tɔilɪtri/ n. туалетная принадлежность f.

toils /tɔilz/ n. сеть f.

token /'toukən/ n. знак; сувенир m.; (coin) жетон m.

Tokyo /'touki,ou/ n. Токио m.

tolerable /'tɒlərəbəl/ adj. (bearable) терпимый; выносимый; (passable) сносный.

tolerance /'tɒlərəns/ n. терпимость f.

tolerant /'tɒlərənt/ adj. терпимый.

tolerate /'tɒlə,reit/ v. терпеть impf.

toll /toul/ n. (on road) пошлина f.; сбор m.

tom /tɒm/ n. самец m.

tomahawk /'tɒmə,hɔk/ n. томагавк m.

tomato /tə'meitou/ **1.** n. помидор; томат m. **2.** adj. томатный.

tomb /tum/ n. могила f.; надгробный памятник m.

tomboy /'tɒm,bɔi/ n. сорванец m. and f. (decl. m.).

tombstone /'tum,stoun/ n. могильный камень m.

tomcat /'tɒm,kæt/ n. кот m.

tome /toum/ n. фолиант m.; (volume) том m.

tomfoolery /,tɒm'fuləri/ n. дурачество neut.

Tommy gun /'tɒmi/ n. автомат m.

tomorrow /tə'mɒrou/ **1.** adv. завтра. **2.** adj. завтрашний. **3.** n. завтрашний день; **the day after tomorrow** послезавтра adv.

Tomsk /tɒmsk/ n. Томск m.

tomtit /'tɒm,tɪt/ n. синица f.

ton /tʌn/ n. тонна f.

tonal /'tounl/ adj. тональный.

tonality /tou'nælɪti/ n. тональность f.

tone /toun/ n. тон m.

tone-deaf /'toun,def/ adj. без музыкального слуха.

toner /'tounər/ n. (photog.) вираж m.

tongs /tɒŋz/ n. щипцы pl.

tongue /tʌŋ/ n. язык m.

tongue-and-groove joint /'tʌŋ ən 'gruv/ n. шпунтовое соединение neut.

tongue-tied /'tʌŋ,taid/ adj. (from shyness) лишившийся дара речи; (inarticulate) косноязычный.

tongue twister n. скороговорка f.

tonic /'tɒnɪk/ **1.** n. тонизирующее средство neut. **2.** adj. тонический.

tonicity /tou'nɪsɪti/ n. тонус m.

tonight /tə'nait/ adv. сегодня вечером; сегодня ночью.

tonnage /'tʌnɪdʒ/ n. тоннаж m.

tonsil /'tɒnsəl/ n. миндалевидная железа f.

tonsillitis /,tɒnsə'laitɪs/ n. тонзиллит m.

tonsorial /tɒn'sɔriəl/ adj. парикмахерский.

tonsure /'tɒnʃər/ n. тонзура f.

too /tu/ adv. слишком; (also) также; тоже; **too much** слишком много.

tool /tul/ n. орудие neut.; рабочий инструмент m.; (machine tool) станок m.

toolbox /'tul,bɒks/ n. ящик для инструментов m.

toolmaker /'tul,meikər/ n. инструментальщик m.

toot /tut/ v. гудеть impf.; (trumpet) трубить impf.

tooth /tuθ/ n. зуб; зубец m.

toothache /'tuθ,eik/ n. зубная боль f.

toothbrush /'tuθ,brʌʃ/ n. зубная щётка f.

toothed /tuθt/ adj. зубчатый.

toothless /'tuθlɪs/ adj. беззубый.

toothpaste /'tuθ,peist/ n. зубная паста f.

toothpick /'tuθ,pɪk/ n. зубочистка f.

toothsome /'tuθsəm/ adj. лакомый.

toothy /'tuθi/ adj. зубастый.

top /tɒp/ **1.** n. вершина f.; верх m.; (of head) макушка f.; (lid) крышка f.; **from top to bottom** сверху донизу. **2.** adj. верхний; (best) лучший. **3.** v. (surpass) превосходить impf., превзойти pf.

topaz /'toupæz/ **1.** n. топаз m. **2.** adj. топазовый.

top boot n. высокий сапог с отворотом m.

topcoat /'tɒp,kout/ n. пальто neut. indecl.

top dog n. хозяин положения m.

top dressing n. подкормка f.

tope /toup/ v. пить impf.

topee /tou'pi/ n. тропический шлем m.

toper /'toupər/ n. пьяница m. and f. (decl. f.)

topflight /'tɒp'flait/ adj. первоклассный.

top hat n. цилиндр m.

topiary /'toupi,eri/ n. фигурная стрижка кустов f.

topic /'tɒpɪk/ n. тема f.; предмет m.

topical /'tɒpɪkəl/ adj. актуальный; злободневный.

topicality /,tɒpɪ'kælɪti/ n. актуальность f.

topless /'tɒplɪs/ adj. без верха; (bare-breasted) с обнажённой грудью.

top-level /'tɒp 'lɛvəl/ *adj.* на вы́сшем у́ровне.
topmast /'tɒp‚mæst, -‚mɑst/ *n.* стеньга́ *f.*
topnotch /'tɒp'nɒtʃ/ *adj.* (*colloq.*) первокла́с-
сный; (*highly-placed*) высокопоста́вленный.
topographical /‚tɒpə'ɡræfɪkəl/ *adj.* топографи́-
ческий.
topography /tə'pɒɡrəfi/ *n.* топогра́фия *f.*
topological /‚tɒpə'lɒdʒɪkəl/ *adj.* топологи́ческий.
topology /tə'pɒlədʒi/ *n.* тополо́гия *f.*
toponymy /tə'pɒnəmi/ *n.* топони́мия *f.*
topple /'tɒpəl/ *v.* опроки́дывать(ся) *impf.*; (*from
power*) сверга́ть *impf.*
topsail /'tɒp‚seil; *Naut.* 'tɒpsəl/ *n.* то́псель *m.*
top-secret /'tɒp 'sikrit/ *adj.* соверше́нно секре́т-
ный.
topsoil /'tɒp‚sɔil/ *n.* ве́рхний слой земли́ *m.*
topsy-turvy /'tɒpsi 'tɜːvi/ *adj.* (*upside down*)
переве́рнутый вверх дном.
toque /touk/ *adj.* (*clothing*) ток *m.*
Torah /'tourə/ *n.* То́ра *f.*
torch /tɔrtʃ/ *n.* фа́кел *m.*; (*for welding*) горе́лка *f.*
toreador /'tɔriə‚dɔr/ *n.* тореадо́р *m.*
torment / *n.* 'tɔrmɛnt; *v.* tɔr'mɛnt/ **1.** *n.* муче́ние
neut.; му́ка *f.* **2.** *v.* му́чить *impf.*
tormenting /tɔr'mɛntiŋ/ *adj.* мучи́тельный.
tormentor /tɔr'mɛntər/ *n.* мучи́тель *m.*
tornado /tɔr'neidou/ *n.* смерч *m.*
toroidal /tə'rɔidl̩/ *adj.* торо́идальный.
Toronto /tə'rɒntou/ *n.* Торо́нто *m.*
torpedo /tɔr'pidou/ *n.* торпе́да *f.*
torpid /'tɔrpid/ *adj.* (*lethargic*) вя́лый; безде́я-
тельный.
torpidity /tɔr'piditi/ *n.* вя́лость *f.*
torpor /'tɔrpər/ *n.* онеме́лость *f.*
torque /tɔrk/ *n.* (*tech.*) враща́ющий моме́нт *m.*
torrent /'tɔrənt/ *n.* пото́к *m.*; (*rain*) ли́вень *m.*
torrid /'tɔrid/ *adj.* (*hot*) зно́йный; (*passionate*)
стра́стный.
torsion /'tɔrʃən/ *n.* круче́ние *neut.*; (*twisting together*) скру́чивание *neut.*
torso /'tɔrsou/ *n.* ту́ловище *neut.*; торс (*of
statue*) *m.*
tort /tɔrt/ *n.* деликт *m.*; гражда́нское правонару-
ше́ние *neut.*
tortoise /'tɔrtəs/ *n.* черепа́ха *f.*
tortoiseshell /'tɔrtəs‚ʃel/ **1.** *n.* па́нцирь черепа́хи
m. **2.** *adj.* черепа́ховый.
tortuosity /‚tɔrtʃu'ɒsiti/ *n.* кривизна́ *f.*
tortuous /'tɔrtʃuəs/ *adj.* изви́листый.
torture /'tɔrtʃər/ **1.** *n.* пы́тка; му́ка *f.* **2.** *v.*
пыта́ть; му́чить *impf.*
torturer /'tɔrtʃuər/ *n.* мучи́тель; пала́ч *m.*
torus /'tɔrəs/ *n.* тор *m.*
Toshkent /taʃ'kɛnt/ *n.* Ташке́нт *m.*
toss /tɒs/ *v.* броса́ть *impf.*, бро́сить *pf.*; мета́ть
impf., метну́ть *pf.*
tot[1] /tɒt/ *n.* малы́ш *m.*
tot[2] /tɒt/ *v.*: **to tot up** сумми́ровать *impf.*
total /'toutl̩/ **1.** *adj.* о́бщий; совоку́пный,
тота́льный. **2.** *n.* су́мма *f.*; ито́г *m.*
totalitarian /tou‚tæli'teəriən/ *adj.* тоталита́рный.
totality /tou'tæliti/ *n.* совоку́пность *f.*
totalizer /'toutl̩‚aizər/ *n.* тотализа́тор *m.*
totally /'toutli/ *adv.* по́лностью; соверше́нно.
tote /tout/ *v.* (*colloq.*) нести́ *impf.*
totem /'toutəm/ *n.* то́тем *m.*
totemic /tou'tɛmik/ *adj.* тотеми́ческий.

totemism /'toutə‚mizəm/ *n.* тотеми́зм *m.*
totem pole *n.* тоте́мный столб *m.*
totter /'tɒtər/ *v.* ковыля́ть *impf.*; (*rock*) шата́ть-
ся; кача́ться *impf.*
toucan /'tukæn/ *n.* тука́н *m.*
touch /tʌtʃ/ **1.** *n.* прикоснове́ние; соприкосно-
ве́ние *neut.* **2.** *v.* тро́гать *impf.*, тро́нуть *pf.*
touch-and-go /'tʌtʃ ən 'ɡou/ *adj.* с предосторо́ж-
ностями.
touched /tʌtʃt/ *adj.* тро́нутый.
touchiness /'tʌtʃinis/ *n.* раздражи́тельность *f.*
touching /'tʌtʃiŋ/ *adj.* тро́гательный.
touchscreen *n.* /'tʌtʃ‚skrin/ (*comput.*) сенсо́рный
экра́н *m.*; (*pad*) сенсо́рный планше́т *m.*
touch-up /'tʌtʃ ‚ʌp/ *n.* ре́тушь *f.*
touchy /'tʌtʃi/ *adj.* (*irritable*) раздражи́тельный;
(*easily offended*) оби́дчивый.
tough /tʌf/ *adj.* жёсткий; про́чный; (*difficult*)
тру́дный.
toughen /'tʌfən/ *v.* закаля́ть *impf.*
toughness /'tʌfnis/ *n.* про́чность; зака́лка *f.*
Toulouse /tu'luz/ *n.* Тулу́за *f.*
toupee /tu'pei/ *n.* пари́к *m.*
tour /tur/ **1.** *n.* путеше́ствие *neut.*; пое́здка *f.*;
(*excursion*) экску́рсия *f.* **2.** *v.* соверша́ть путе-
ше́ствие *impf.*
tour de force /‚tur də fɔrs/ *n.* по́двиг *m.*
tourism /'turizəm/ **1.** *n.* тури́зм *m.* **2.** *adj.* тури-
сти́ческий.
tourist /'turist/ **1.** *n.* тури́ст *m.*, тури́стка *f.* **2.**
adj. тури́стский.
tournament /'turnəmənt/ *n.* турни́р *m.*
tourniquet /'tɜrnikit/ *n.* жгут *m.*
Tours /tur/ *n.* Тур *m.*
tousle /'tauzəl/ *v.* взъеро́шивать *impf.*
tout /taut/ *n.* навя́зчивый коммивояжёр *m.*
tow /tou/ **1.** *n.* (*rope*) букси́р *m.*; (*act*) букси-
ро́вка *f.*; **in tow** на букси́ре. **2.** *v.* букси́ровать
impf.
toward /tɔrd, tə'wɔrd/ *prep.* (по направле́нию) к
по отноше́нию к (*with dat.*).
towed /toud/ *adj.* прицепно́й.
towel /'tauəl/ *n.* полоте́нце *neut.*
toweling /'tauəliŋ/ *n.* махро́вая ткань *f.*
tower /'tauər/ *n.* ба́шня; вы́шка *f.*
towering /'tauəriŋ/ *adj.* (*high*) возвыша́ющийся.
tow-headed /'tou ‚hɛdid/ *adj.* светловоло́сый.
towline /'tou‚lain/ *n.* букси́р *m.*
town /taun/ *n.* го́род, городо́к *m.*
township /'taunʃip/ *n.* муниципалите́т *m.*; (*small
town*) посёлок; городо́к *m.*
toxemia /tɒk'simiə/ *n.* токсеми́я *f.*
toxic /'tɒksik/ *adj.* ядови́тый; токси́ческий.
toxicant /'tɒksikənt/ *n.* ядови́тое вещество́ *neut.*
toxicity /tɒk'sisiti/ *n.* токси́чность *f.*
toxicological /‚tɒksikə'lɒdʒikəl/ *adj.* токсиколо-
ги́ческий.
toxicologist /‚tɒksi'kɒlədʒist/ *n.* токсико́лог *m.*
toxin /'tɒksin/ *n.* токси́н; яд *m.*
toy /tɔi/ **1.** *n.* игру́шка *f.* **2.** *adj.* игру́шечный. **3.**
v. игра́ть; забавля́ться *impf.*
trace /treis/ **1.** *n.* след *m.* **2.** *v.* (*draw*) черти́ть
impf.; (*track*) выследить; проследи́ть *pf.*
tracery /'treisəri/ *n.* узо́р *m.*
trachea /'treikiə/ *n.* трахе́я *f.*
tracheotomy /‚treiki'ɒtəmi/ *n.* трахеотоми́я *f.*
trachoma /trə'koumə/ *n.* трахо́ма *f.*

tracing /'treisıŋ/ n. прослёживание; калькирование neut.; (copy) кáлька f.

track /træk/ **1.** n. след m.; дорóга; дорóжка f.; (athl.) лыжня́ f.; беговáя дорóжка f.; (railroad) путь: m. **2.** v. следи́ть (за with instr.) impf.

tracked /trækt/ adj. (of vehicle) гýсеничный.

tracker /'trækər/ n. следопы́т m.

tracking /'trækıŋ/ n. прослёживание; выслёживание neut.

tracklayer /'træk‚leiər/ adj. путеуклáдчик m.

trackless /'træklıs/ adj. бездорóжный.

track shoe n. кроссóвка f.

track suit n. трениро́вочный костю́м m.

tract¹ /trækt/ n. (anat.) трáкт m.

tract² /trækt/ n. (pamphlet) брошю́ра f.

tractable /'træktəbəl/ adj. (docile) послýшный; сговóрчивый.

traction /'trækʃən/ n. тя́га f.

tractor /'træktər/ n. трáктор m.

trade /treid/ **1.** n. торгóвля f. **2.** adj. торгóвый. **3.** v. торговáть impf.

trademark /'treid‚mɑrk/ n. торгóвый знак m ; фабри́чная мáрка f.

trader /'treidər/ n. торгóвец; купéц m.

tradesman /'treidzmən/ n. торгóвец m.

trade union n. профсою́з m.; (in USA and England) тред-юниóн m.

trade unionist /treid/ n. тред-юниони́ст m.

trade wind /wınd/ n. пассáт m.

trading /'treidıŋ/ n. торгóвля f.

tradition /trə'dıʃən/ n. традиция f.

traditional /trə'dıʃənl/ adj. традициóнный.

traffic /'træfık/ n. движéние neut.

traffic light n. светофóр m.

traffic police n. дорóжная полиция f.

tragedian /trə'dʒidiən/ n. трáгик m.

tragedy /'trædʒıdi/ n. трагéдия f.

tragic /'trædʒık/ adj. траги́ческий.

tragicomedy /‚trædʒı'kɒmıdi/ n. трагикомéдия f.

tragicomic /‚trædʒı'kɒmık/ adj. трагикоми́ческий.

trail /treil/ **1.** n. след m.; (path) тропá f. **2.** v.t. идти́ по слéду; v.i. (drag) волочи́ться impf.

trailer /'treilər/ n. прицéп; трéйлер m.; (mobile home) жилóй автоприцéп m.

train /trein/ **1.** n. пóезд m.; (sequence) ход m.; (of dress) шлейф m.; **by train** пóездом. **2.** v.t. тренировáть impf.; v.i. тренировáться impf.

train compartment n. купé neut. indecl.

trained /treind/ adj. (of person) обýченный; (of animal) дрессирóванный.

trainee /trei'ni/ n. стажёр; практикáнт m.

trainer /'treinər/ n. (athl.) трéнер m.; (animals) дрессирóвщик m.

training /'treiniŋ/ n. подготóвка f.; обучéние neut.

trait /treit/ n. (характéрная) чертá f.; особенность f.

traitor /'treitər/ n. предáтель; измéнник m.

traitorous /'treitərəs/ adj. предáтельский.

traitress /'treitrıs/ n. измéнница f.

trajectory /trə'dʒɛktəri/ n. траектóрия f.

tram /træm/ n. трамвáй m.

trammel /'træməl/ v. (hamper) мешáть (with dat.) impf.; (restrict) сдéрживать impf.

tramp /træmp/ n. (sound of feet) тóпот m.;

(walk) похóд m.; (vagabond) бродя́га m. and f. (decl. f.).

trample /'træmpəl/ v. топтáть impf.; подавля́ть, попирáть impf.

trampoline /‚træmpə'lin/ n. батýт, батýд m.

trampolining /‚træmpə'liniŋ/ n. прыжки́ на батýте pl.

trance /træns/ n. транс m.

tranquil /'træŋkwıl/ adj. спокóйный.

tranquilize /'træŋkwə‚laiz/ v. успокáивать impf.

tranquilizer /'træŋkwə‚laizər/ n. успокáивающее срéдство neut.

tranquillity /træŋ'kwılıti/ n. спокóйствие neut.

transact /træn'sækt/ v. заключáть impf.

transaction /træn'sækʃən/ n. дéло neut.; сдéлка f.

transalpine /træns'ælpain/ adj. трансальпи́йский.

transatlantic /‚trænsət'læntık/ adj. трансатланти́ческий.

transceiver /træn'sivər/ n. приёмопередáтчик m.

transcend /træn'sɛnd/ v. превосходи́ть impf.; переступáть impf.

transcendent /træn'sɛndənt/ adj. превосхóдный; (philos.) трансцендентáльный.

transcendental /‚trænsɛn'dɛntl/ adj. трансцендентáльный.

transcontinental /‚trænskɒntn'ɛntl/ adj. трансконтинентáльный.

transcribe /træn'skraib/ v. (copy) перепи́сывать impf.; (transliterate) транслитери́ровать impf.; (decode) расшифрóвывать impf.

transcript /'trænskrıpt/ n. кóпия f.

transcription /træn'skrıpʃən/ n. транскри́пция f.

transducer /træns'dusər/ n. дáтчик m.

transfer /n. 'trænsfər; v. træns'fɜr/ **1.** n. перенóс m.; перемещéние neut.; (of funds) перевóд m. **2.** v. переноси́ть impf., перенести́ pf.; перемещáть impf., перемести́ть pf.

transferable /træns'fɜrəbəl/ adj. переводи́мый.

transference /træns'fɜrəns/ n. передáча f.

transfiguration /‚trænsfıgyə'reiʃən/ n. преобразовáние neut.; (cap.) (relig.) Преображéние neut.

transfigure /træns'fıgyər/ v. преобразóвывать; преображáть impf.

transfix /træns'fıks/ v. прикóвывать к мéсту impf.

transform /træns'fɔrm/ v. превращáть impf., преврати́ть pf.

transformation /‚trænsfər'meiʃən/ n. преобразовáние; изменéние; превращéние neut.

transformer /træns'fɔrmər/ n. трансформáтор m.

transfuse /træns'fyuz/ v. переливáть impf.

transfusion /træns'fyuʒən/ n. переливáние neut.

transgress /træns'grɛs/ v. переступáть; переходи́ть (грани́цы) impf.; **to transgress the law** v. нарушáть закóн impf.

transgression /træns'grɛʃən/ n. нарушéние neut.; (sin) грех m.

transgressor /træns'grɛsər/ n. правонаруши́тель m.

transience /'trænʃəns/ n. мимолётность f.

transient /'trænʃənt/ **1.** adj. (transitory) прехóдящий; мимолётный; скоротéчный. **2.** n. проéзжий f.

transistor /træn'zıstər/ n. транзи́стор m.

transit /'trænsɪt/ **1.** *n.* транзит *m.*; перевозка *f.*;
in transit в пути. **2.** *adj.* транзитный.

transition /træn'zɪʃən/ *n.* переход *m.*

transitional /træn'zɪʃənl̩/ *adj.* переходный.

transitive /'trænsɪtɪv/ *adj.* (*gram.*) переходный;
транзитивный.

transitory /'trænsɪˌtɔri/ *adj.* преходящий; мимолётный; скоротечный.

translatable /træns'leɪtəbəl/ *adj.* переводимый.

translate /træns'leɪt/ *v.* переводить *impf.*, перевести *pf.*

translation /træns'leɪʃən/ *n.* перевод *m.*

translator /træns'leɪtər/ *n.* переводчик *m.*

transliterate /træns'lɪtəˌreɪt/ *v.* транслитериро-
вать *impf.* and *pf.*

transliteration /træns,lɪtə'reɪʃən/ *n.* транслитера-
ция *f.*

translucent /træns'lusənt/ *adj.* просвечивающий;
полупрозрачный.

transmigrate /træns'maɪgreɪt/ *v.* переселяться
impf.

transmigration /,trænsmaɪ'greɪʃən/ *n.* переселе-
ние *neut.*

transmission /træns'mɪʃən/ *n.* передача *f.*

transmit /træns'mɪt/ *v.* передавать *impf.*

transmutation /,trænsmyu'teɪʃən/ *n.* превра-
щение *neut.*

transmute /træns'myut/ *v.* превращать *impf.*

transom /'trænsəm/ *n.* (*window above door*)
фрамуга *f.*

transparency /træns'pɛərənsi/ *n.* прозрачность
f.; (*slide*) диапозитив *m.*

transparent /træns'pɛərənt/ *adj.* прозрачный;
(*obvious*) очевидный.

transpire /træn'spaɪᵊr/ *v.* обнаруживаться *impf.*;
(*happen*) случаться, происходить *impf.*

transplant /træns'plænt/ *v.* пересаживать *impf.*;
(*med.*) делать пересадку *impf.*; (*move people*)
переселять *impf.*

transplantation /,trænsplæn'teɪʃən/ *n.* транс-
плантация *f.*

transport / *n.* 'trænspɔrt; *v.* træns'pɔrt/ **1.** *n.*
транспорт *m.*; перевозка *f.* **2.** *adj.* транс-
портный. **3.** *v.* перевозить *impf.*

transportation /,trænspɔr'teɪʃən/ *n.* транспорт
m.; перевозка *f.*; **public transportation** общественный транспорт *m.*

transporter /træns'pɔrtər/ *n.* транспортёр *m.*

transpose /træns'pouz/ *v.* (*mus.*) транспони-
ровать *impf.* and *pf.*

transposition /,trænspə'zɪʃən/ *n.* перестановка *f.*

transship /træn'ʃɪp/ *v.* перегружать *impf.*

transubstantiation /,trænsəb,stænʃi'eɪʃən/ *n.*
пресуществление *neut.*

transuranic element /,trænsyu'rænɪk/ *n.* тран-
сурановый элемент *m.*

transverse /træns'vɜrs/ *adj.* поперечный.

transvestite /træns'vɛstaɪt/ *n.* трансвестит *m.*

Transylvania /,trænsɪl'veɪnyə/ *n.* (*region*) Тран-
сильвания (*also:* Зибенбурген).

trap /træp/ **1.** *n.* ловушка *f.* **2.** *v.* ловить *or*
заманивать в ловушку *impf.*, заманить *pf.*

trap door *n.* люк *m.*

trapeze /træ'piz/ *n.* трапеция *f.*

trapezoid /'træpəzɔid/ *n.* трапеция *f.*

trapper /'træpər/ *n.* охотник (ставящий кап-
каны) *m.*

trash /træʃ/ *n.* отбросы *pl.*; мусор; хлам *m.*

trash can *n.* мусорный ящик *m.*

trashy /'træʃi/ *adj.* дрянной.

trauma /'traumə, 'trɔ-/ *n.* травма *f.*

traumatic /trɔ'mætɪk/ *adj.* травматический; сокрушительный.

traumatize /'traumə,taiz, 'trɔ-/ *v.* травмировать
impf. and *pf.*

travel /'trævəl/ **1.** *n.* путешествие *neut.* **2.** *adj.*
дорожный. **3.** *v.* путешествовать *impf.*

travel agency *n.* туристское агенство *neut.*

traveler /'trævələr/ *n.* путешественник *m.*, путе-
шественница *f.*; (*passenger*) пассажир *m.*

traveler's check /'trævələrz/ *n.* дорожный чек *m.*

traverse /'trævərs, trə'vɜrs/ *v.* (*cross*) пересекать
impf.

travesty /'trævəsti/ *n.* пародия (на *with acc.*) *f.*

trawl /trɔl/ **1.** *n.* трал *m.* **2.** *v.* тралить *impf.*

trawler /'trɔlər/ *n.* траулер *m.*

tray /treɪ/ *n.* поднос *m.*

treacherous /'trɛtʃərəs/ *adj.* (*traitorous*) предательский; вероломный; (*unsafe*) опасный.

treachery /'trɛtʃəri/ *n.* предательство *neut.*

treacle /'trikəl/ *n.* патока *f.*

tread /trɛd/ **1.** *n.* походка *f.*; (*of tire*) протектор
m. **2.** *v.* ступать; шагать *impf.*

treadmill /'trɛd,mɪl/ *n.* топчак *m.*

treason /'trizən/ *n.* измена *f.*

treasonable /'trizənəbəl/ *adj.* изменнический.

treasure /'trɛʒər/ *n.* сокровище *neut.*

treasure house *n.* сокровищница *f.*

treasurer /'trɛʒərər/ *n.* казначей *m.*

treasure-trove *n.* клад *m.*

treasury /'trɛʒəri/ *n.* **1.** государственное казна-
чейство *neut.* **2.** *adj.* казначейский.

treat /trit/ *v.* (*behave*) обходиться (с *with instr.*)
impf., обойтись *pf.*; (*med.*) лечить *impf.*; (*entertain*) угощать *impf.*

treatise /'tritɪs/ *n.* трактат *m.*; монография *f.*

treatment /'tritmənt/ *n.* обращение *neut.*; (*med.*)
лечение *neut.*; уход *m.*; (*discussion of subject*)
трактовка *f.*

treaty /'triti/ *n.* договор *m.*

treble /'trɛbəl/ **1.** *n.* (*mus.*) дискант *m.* **2.** *adj.*
дискантовый.

tree /tri/ *n.* дерево *neut.*

treeless /'trilɪs/ *adj.* безлесный.

trefoil /'trifɔil/ *n.* трилистник *m.*

trek /trɛk/ *n.* (*journey*) путь *m.*; (*march*) поход
m.

trellis /'trɛlɪs/ *n.* решётка; шпалера *f.*

tremble /'trɛmbəl/ *v.* дрожать *impf.*

trembly /'trɛmbli/ *adj.* дрожащий.

tremendous /trɪ'mɛndəs/ *adj.* огромный.

tremor /'trɛmər/ *n.* (*trembling*) дрожь *f.*; трепет
m.; (*earthquake*) сотрясение *neut.*; толчок *m.*

tremulous /'trɛmyələs/ *adj.* трепетный.

trench /trɛntʃ/ *n.* (*ditch*) канава *f.*; ров *m.*; (*mil.*)
окоп *m.*; траншея *f.*

trencher /'trɛntʃər/ *n.* канавокопатель *m.*

trend /trɛnd/ *n.* направление *neut.*; тенденция *f.*

trendy /'trɛndi/ *adj.* ультрамодный; сверхсовре-
менный.

trepan /trɪ'pæn/ *v.* трепанировать *impf.*

trepidation /,trɛpɪ'deɪʃən/ *n.* (*alarm*) тревога *f.*;
(*trembling*) трепет *m.*

trespass /'trɛspəs/ *v.* нарушить границу *pf.*

trespasser /'trɛspəsər/ n. наруши́тель (грани́ц) m.

tress /trɛs/ n. (braid) коса́ f.

trey /trei/ n. тро́йка f.

triad /'traiæd/ n. триа́да f.

trial /'traiəl/ **1.** n. испыта́ние neut.; про́ба f.; (leg.) суде́бный проце́сс m. **2.** adj. испыта́тельный; про́бный.

triangle /'trai,æŋgəl/ n. треуго́льник m.

triangular /trai'æŋgyələr/ adj. треуго́льный.

tribal /'traibəl/ adj. племенно́й.

tribalism /'traibə,lɪzəm/ n. трайбали́зм m.

tribasic /trai'beisɪk/ adj. трёхосно́вный.

tribe /traib/ n. пле́мя neut.; род m.

tribesman /'traibzmən/ n. член пле́мени m.

tribulation /,trɪbyə'leiʃən/ n. несча́стье neut.

tribunal /trai'byunl/ n. трибуна́л m.

tributary /'trɪbyə,tɛri/ n. прито́к m.

tribute /'trɪbyut/ n. дань f.

tricentennial /,traisɛn'tɛniəl/ n. трёхсотле́тие neut.

trick /trɪk/ **1.** n. обма́н m.; уло́вка f.; (stunt) фо́кус; трюк m.; (at cards) взя́тка f. **2.** v. обма́нывать impf., обману́ть pf.

trickle /'trɪkəl/ **1.** n. стру́йка f. **2.** v. ка́пать; сочи́ться impf.

trickster /'trɪkstər/ n. обма́нщик m.

tricky /'trɪki/ adj. хи́трый; ло́вкий; (complex) сло́жный.

tricolor /'trai,kʌlər/ adj. трёхцве́тный.

tricorn /'traikɔrn/ n. (hat) треуго́лка f.

tricycle /'traisɪkəl/ n. трёхколёсный велосипе́д m.

trident /'traidnt/ n. трезу́бец m.

tried /traid/ adj. испы́танный.

triennial /trai'ɛniəl/ adj. трёхле́тний.

Trieste /tri'ɛst/ n. Трие́ст m.

trifle /'traifəl/ n. пустя́к m.; ме́лочь f.; (small amount) ка́пелька, чу́точка f.

trifling /'traiflɪŋ/ adj. пустяко́вый.

trigger /'trɪgər/ n. куро́к; крючо́к m.

trigonometry /,trɪgə'nɒmɪtri/ n. тригономе́трия f.

trilateral /trai'lætərəl/ adj. трёхсторо́нний.

trill /trɪl/ v. залива́ться тре́лью impf.

trillion /'trɪlyən/ n. триллио́н m.

trilobate /trai'loubeit/ adj. трёхло́пастный.

trilogy /'trɪlədʒi/ n. трило́гия f.

trim /trɪm/ **1.** adj. опря́тный; наря́дный. **2.** v. подреза́ть impf., подре́зать pf.; (hair) подстрига́ть impf., подстри́чь pf.

Trinidad /'trɪnɪ,dæd/ n. Тринида́д m.

Trinity /'trɪnɪti/ n. Тро́ица f.

trinket /'trɪŋkɪt/ n. безделу́шка f.

trinomial /trai'noumiəl/ **1.** n. (math.) трёхчле́н m. **2.** adj. трёхчле́нный.

trio /'triou/ n. три́о neut. indecl.

trip /trɪp/ **1.** n. путеше́ствие neut.; пое́здка f. **2.** v.i. (stumble) спотыка́ться impf.; v.t. (cause to stumble) подставля́ть но́жку impf.

tripartite /trai'partait/ adj. трёхсторо́нний.

tripe /traip/ n. (cul.) рубе́ц m.

triphammer /'trɪp,hæmər/ n. рыча́жный мо́лот m.

triple /'trɪpəl/ **1.** adj. тройно́й; (tripled) утро́енный. **2.** v.t. утра́ивать impf., утро́ить pf.; v. утра́иваться impf., утро́иться pf.

triplet /'trɪplɪt/ n. тро́йня f.; (mus.) трио́ль f.

triplicate /'trɪplɪkɪt/ adj.: **in triplicate** в трёх экземпля́рах.

tripod /'traipɒd/ n. трено́га f.; трено́жник m.

trippingly /'trɪpɪŋli/ adv. вприпры́жку.

trisect /trai'sɛkt/ v. дели́ть на три ча́сти impf.

trisyllabic /,traisɪ'læbɪk/ adj. трёхсло́жный.

trite /trait/ adj. бана́льный; изби́тый.

triteness /'traitnɪs/ n. бана́льность f.

tritium /'trɪtiəm/ adj. три́тий.

triturate /'trɪtʃə,reit/ v. растира́ть в порошо́к impf.

triumph /'traiəmf/ **1.** n. побе́да f.; торжество́ neut.; триу́мф m. **2.** v. побежда́ть impf., побе́дить pf.

triumphant /trai'ʌmfənt/ adj. победоно́сный.

trivet /'trɪvɪt/ n. подста́вка f.

trivia /'trɪviə/ n. ме́лочи; пустяки́ pl.

trivial /'trɪviəl/ adj. тривиа́льный; незначи́тельный.

Trojan /'troudʒən/ adj. троя́нский.

troll /troul/ n. (myth.) тролль m.

trolley /'trɒli/ n. (small truck) ваго́нетка f.; (serving table) сто́лик на колёсиках m.

trolley bus n. тролле́йбус m.

trolley car n. трамва́й m.

trollop /'trɒləp/ n. шлю́ха; неря́ха f.

trombone /trɒm'boun/ n. тромбо́н m.

troop /trup/ n. отря́д m.; pl. войска́ f.; (theat.) тру́ппа f.

trooper /'trupər/ n. (cavalry) кавале́рист m.; (mounted police officer) ко́нный полице́йский m.

trophy /'troufi/ n. приз; трофе́й m.; добы́ча f.

tropic /'trɒpɪk/ n. тро́пик m.

tropical /'trɒpɪkəl/ adj. тропи́ческий.

Tropic of Cancer n. Се́верный тро́пик m.

Tropic of Capricorn n. Ю́жный тро́пик m.

troposphere /'trɒpə,sfɪər/ n. тропосфе́ра f.

trot /trɒt/ **1.** n. рысь f. **2.** v. идти́ ры́сью impf.

trouble /'trʌbəl/ **1.** n. беда́; забо́та f.; pl. хло́поты pl. **2.** v. беспоко́ить(ся); затрудня́ть(ся) impf., затрудни́ть(ся) pf.

troubled /'trʌbəld/ adj. беспоко́йный.

troublemaker /'trʌbəl,meikər/ n. скло́чник; смутья́н m.

troubleproof /'trʌbəl,pruf/ adj. надёжный.

troubleshooter /'trʌbəl,ʃutər/ n. устрани́тель непола́док m.

troublesome /'trʌbəlsəm/ adj. беспоко́йный; (difficult) тру́дный.

troublous /'trʌbləs/ adj. беспоко́йный.

trough /trɒf/ n. коры́то neut.

trounce /trauns/ v. (beat) бить impf.; (defeat) разбива́ть impf.

troupe /trup/ n. тру́ппа f.

trouser /'trauzər/ n. (leg of trousers) штани́на f.

trousers /'trauzərz/ n. брю́ки; штаны́ pl.

trousseau /'trusou/ n. прида́ное neut.

trout /traut/ n. форе́ль f.

trowel /'trauəl/ n. лопа́тка f.; сово́к m.

truancy /'truənsi/ n. прогу́л m.

truant /'truənt/ n. прогу́льщик m.

truce /trus/ n. переми́рие neut.

truck /trʌk/ n. грузово́й автомоби́ль; грузови́к m.; (hand truck) теле́жка f.

truck farmer n. огоро́дник m.

truckle /'trʌkəl/ v. пресмыка́ться impf.

truckle bed *n.* раскладушка *f.*

truculent /'trʌkyələnt/ *adj.* (*fierce*) свирепый; (*pugnacious*) драчливый.

trudge /trʌdʒ/ *v.* плестись; тащиться *impf.*

true /tru/ *adj.* верный; правильный; правдивый.

truebred /'tru,brɛd/ *adj.* (*purebred*) чистокровный.

truehearted /'tru'hɑrtɪd/ *adj.* преданный.

truffle /'trʌfəl/ *n.* трюфель *m.*

truly /'truli/ *adj.* (*faithfully*) верно; (*really*) истинно; действительно.

trump /trʌmp/ **1.** *n.* козырь *m.* **2.** *adj.* (*attrib.*) козырной. **3.** *v.* козырять *impf.*, козырнуть *pf.*

trumpery /'trʌmpəri/ *n.* (*rubbish*) чепуха *f.*; (*tinsel*) мишура *f.*

trumpet /'trʌmpɪt/ *n.* труба *f.*

trumpeter /'trʌmpɪtər/ *n.* трубач *m.*

truncate /'trʌŋkeit/ *v.* усекать *impf.*; (*abridge*) сокращать *impf.*

truncheon /'trʌntʃən/ *n.* дубинка *f.*

trundle /'trʌndl/ *v.* катить(ся) *impf.*

trunk /trʌŋk/ *n.* (*large box*) сундук *m.*; (*of a tree*) ствол *m.*; (*of elephant*) хобот *m.*; (*of car*) багажник *m.*

trunks /trʌŋks/ *n.* трусы *pl.*; (*swimming*) плавки *pl.*

truss /trʌs/ *n.* (*structural frame*) ферма *f.*; (*med.*) грыжевой бандаж *m.*

trust /trʌst/ **1.** *n.* доверие *neut.*; вера *f.*; (*econ.*) трест *m.* **2.** *v.* доверять *impf.*, доверить *pf.*

trustee /trʌ'sti/ *n.* попечитель *m.*, попечительница *f.*

trustful /'trʌstfəl/ *also* **trusting** /'trʌstɪŋ/ *adj.* доверчивый.

trustiness /'trʌstɪnɪs/ *n.* верность *f.*

trustworthiness /'trʌst,wɜrðɪnɪs/ *n.* надёжность *f.*

trustworthy /'trʌst,wɜrði/ *adj.* заслуживающий доверия.

truth /truθ/ *n.* правда *f.*; истина *f.*

truthful /'truθfəl/ *adj.* правдивый.

truthfulness /'truθfəlnɪs/ *n.* правдивость *f.*

try /trai/ **1.** *n.* попытка *f.* **2.** *v.* пробовать *impf.*, попробовать *pf.*; (*law*) судить *impf.*; **to try on** примерять *impf.*, примерить *pf.*

trying /'traiɪŋ/ *adj.* тяжёлый; утомительный.

tryout /'trai,aut/ *n.* (*test*) испытание *neut.*

tryst /trɪst/ *n.* условленная встреча *f.*

tsar /zɑr/ *n.* царь *m.*

tsarina /zɑ'rinə, tsɑ-/ *n.* царица *f.*

Tsaritsyn /tsə'ritsɪn/ *n.* Царицын *m.* (*see Volgograd*).

Tselinograd /tsə'linə,græd/ *n.* Целиноград *m.* (*see Aqmola*).

tsetse fly /'tsɛtsi, 'tsitsi/ *n.* муха цеце *f.*

T-shirt /'ti ,ʃɜrt/ *n.* футболка; майка *f.*

T square *n.* рейсшина *f.*

tub /tʌb/ *n.* кадка; бадья *f.*; (*bathtub*) ванна *f.*

tuba /'tubə/ *n.* туба *f.*

tubby /'tʌbi/ *adj.* толстенький.

tube /tub/ *n.* труба; трубка *f.*; (*of toothpaste, etc.*) тюбик *m.*

tubeless tire /'tublɪs/ *n.* бескамерная шина *f.*

tuber /'tubər/ *n.* клубень *m.*

tubercle /'tubərkəl/ *n.* бугорок *m.*

tubercular /tu'bɜrkyələr/ *adj.* (*of tubercle*) бугорчатый.

tuberculosis /tu,bɜrkyə'lousɪs/ *n.* туберкулёз *m.*

tuberculous /tu'bɜrkyələs/ *adj.* туберкулёзный.

tuberous /'tubərəs/ *adj.* клубневой.

tubing /'tubɪŋ/ *n.* трубопровод *m.*

tub-thumper /'tʌb ,θʌmpər/ *n.* уличный оратор *m.*

tub-thumping /'tʌb ,θʌmpɪŋ/ *n.* разглагольствование *neut.*

tubular /'tubyələr/ *adj.* трубчатый.

tuck /tʌk/ **1.** *n.* (*fold*) складка *f.* **2.** *v.* (*put away*) засовывать *impf.*

Tuesday /'tuzdei/ *n.* вторник *m.*

tuft /tʌft/ *n.* пучок *m.*

tug /tʌg/ **1.** *n.* рывок *m.*; (*boat*) буксирное судно *neut.* **2.** *v.* дёргать *impf.*, дёрнуть *pf.*; (*tow*) буксировать *impf.*

tugboat /'tʌg,bout/ *n.* буксир *m.*

tug of war *n.* перетягивание на канате *neut.*

tuition /tu'ɪʃən/ *n.* плата за обучение *f.*

Tula /'tulə/ *n.* Тула *f.*

tulip /'tulɪp/ **1.** *n.* тюльпан *m.* **2.** *adj.* тюльпанный.

tumble /'tʌmbəl/ **1.** *n.* падение *neut.*; (*somersault*) кувырканье *neut.* **2.** *v.* падать *impf.*, упасть *pf.*; (*acrobatics*) кувыркаться *impf.*

tumble-down /'tʌmbəl ,daun/ *adj.* обветшалый.

tumble-dry /'tʌmbəl 'drai/ *v.* сушить в барабанной сушилке *impf.*

tumbler /'tʌmblər/ *n.* (*acrobat*) акробат *m.*; (*glass*) стакан *m.*

tumbrel /'tʌmbrəl/ *n.* телега *f.*

tumefaction /,tumə'fækʃən/ *n.* опухание *neut.*

tumefy /'tumə,fai/ *v.* опухать *impf.*

tumescent /tu'mɛsənt/ *adj.* опухающий.

tumid /'tumɪd/ *adj.* распухший.

tummy /'tʌmi/ *n.* (*colloq.*) животик *m.*

tumor /'tumər/ *n.* опухоль *f.*

tumult /'tumɔlt/ *n.* суматоха *f.*; шум *m.*

tumultuous /tu'mʌltʃuəs/ *adj.* буйный.

tumulus /'tumyələs/ *n.* курган *m.*

tun /tʌn/ *n.* бочка *f.*

tuna /'tunə/ *n.* тунец *m.*

tundra /'tʌndrə/ *n.* тундра *f.*

tune /tun/ **1.** *n.* мелодия *f.*; мотив *m.* **2.** *v.* (*instrument*) настраивать *impf.*, настроить *pf.*; (*engine*) регулировать *impf.*

tuneful /'tunfəl/ *adj.* мелодичный.

tuneless /'tunlɪs/ *adj.* немелодичный.

tungsten /'tʌŋstən/ *n.* вольфрам *m.*

Tunguska /tuŋ'guskə/ *n.* (*river*) Тунгуска *f.*

tunic /'tunɪk/ *n.* (*hist.*) туника *f.*; (*of uniform*) китель *m.*

tuning fork /'tunɪŋ/ *n.* камертон *m.*

Tunis /'tunɪs/ *n.* Тунис *m.*

tunnel /'tʌnl/ *n.* туннель *m.*

turban /'tɜrbən/ *n.* чалма *f.*; тюрбан *m.*

turbid /'tɜrbɪd/ *adj.* мутный; неясный.

turbidity /tər'bɪdɪti/ *n.* мутность *f.*

turbine /'tɜrbɪn, -bain/ *n.* турбина *f.*

turbot /'tɜrbət/ *n.* белокорый палтус *m.*

turbulence /'tɜrbyələns/ *n.* бурность *f.*; (*aero.*) турбулентность *f.*

turbulent /'tɜrbyələnt/ *adj.* буйный; (*weather*) бурный; (*agitated*) взволнованный.

tureen /tu'rin/ *n.* (*for soup*) супница *f.*

turf /tɜrf/ *n.* дёрн *m.*

turfy /'tɜrfi/ *adj.* (*of peat*) торфяной.

turgid /'tɜrdʒɪd/ *adj.* (*swollen*) опу́хший; (*overblown*) напы́щенный.
turgidity /tər'dʒɪdɪti/ *n.* напы́щенность *f.*
Turk /tɜrk/ *n.* ту́рок *m.*, турча́нка *f.*
turkey /'tɜrki/ *n.* индю́к *m.*, инде́йка *f.*
Turkey /'tɜrki/ *n.* Ту́рция *f.*
Turkish /'tɜrkɪʃ/ *adj.* туре́цкий.
Turkmen /'tɜrkmɛn/ *n.* туркме́н *m.*, туркме́нка *f.*
Turkmenistan /,tɜrkmɛnə'stæn/ *n.* Туркмениста́н *m.*
turmeric /'tɜrmərɪk/ *n.* курку́ма *f.*
turmoil /'tɜrmɔɪl/ *n.* сумато́ха *f.*; беспоря́док *m.*
turn /tɜrn/ **1.** *n.* оборо́т; поворо́т; изги́б *m.*; (*in line*) о́чередь *f.* **2.** *v.* (*change direction*) повора́чивать(ся) *impf.*; (*direct*) обраща́ть(ся) *impf.*, обрати́ть(ся) *pf.*; **to turn around** обора́чиваться *impf.*; оберну́ться *pf.*; **to turn off** выключа́ть *impf.*, вы́ключить *pf.*; **to turn on** включа́ть *impf.*, включи́ть *pf.*
turnabout /'tɜrnə,baut/ *n.* ре́зкий *or* круто́й поворо́т *m.*
turncoat /'tɜrn,kout/ *n.* ренега́т *m.*
turner /'tɜrnər/ *n.* (*lathe worker*) то́карь *m.*
turnery /'tɜrnəri/ *n.* тока́рное де́ло *neut.*
turning /'tɜrnɪŋ/ *n.* поворо́т *m.*; (*rotation*) враще́ние *neut.*
turning point *n.* перело́м *m.*
turnip /'tɜrnɪp/ *n.* ре́па *f.*
turnout /'tɜrn,aut/ *n.* коли́чество люде́й *neut.*
turnover /'tɜrn,ouvər/ *n.* оборо́т *m.*
turnpike /'tɜrn,paik/ *n.* автостра́да *f.*
turnstile /'tɜrn,stail/ *n.* турнике́т *m.*
turpentine /'tɜrpən,tain/ *n.* скипида́р *m.*
turpitude /'tɜrpɪ,tud/ *n.* поро́чность *f.*
turquoise /'tɜrkɔiz/ **1.** *n.* (*gem*) бирюза́ *f.* **2.** *adj.* бирюзо́вый.
turret /'tɜrɪt/ *n.* (*tower*) ба́шенка *f.*; (*for gun*) ба́шня *f.*
turtle /'tɜrtl/ **1.** *n.* черепа́ха *f.* **2.** *adj.* черепа́ховый.
Tuscany /'tʌskəni/ *n.* (*province*) Тоска́на *f.*
tusk /tʌsk/ *n.* клык; би́вень *m.*
tussock /'tʌsək/ *n.* ко́чка *f.*
tutelage /'tutlɪdʒ/ *n.* опе́ка *f.*
tutelary /'tutl,ɛri/ *adj.* опеку́нский.
tutor /'tutər/ **1.** *n.* репети́тор *m.* **2.** *v.* дава́ть ча́стные уро́ки *impf.*
tutorial /tu'tɔriəl/ *n.* наста́вничество *neut.*
tutu /'tutu/ *n.* па́чка *f.*
Tuva /'tuvə/ *n.* Тува́ *f.*
tuxedo /tʌk'sidou/ *n.* смо́кинг *m.*
TV /'ti'vi/ *n.* телеви́дение *neut.*
Tver /tvɛər/ *n.* Тверь *m.*
TV set /'ti'vi/ *n.* set телеви́зор *m.*
twang /twæŋ/ *n.* (*bowstring*) звук натя́нутой тети́вы *m.*; (*accent*) гнуса́вый вы́говор *m.*
tweak /twik/ *v.* (*pinch*) щипа́ть *impf.*; (*tug*) потя́гивать *impf.*
tweed /twid/ *n.* твид *m.*
tweet /twit/ **1.** *n.* ще́бет *m.* **2.** *v.* щебета́ть; чири́кать *impf.*
t'veezers /'twizərz/ *n.* пинце́т *m.*; щи́пчики *pl.*
t.velfth /twɛlfθ/ *adj.* двена́дцатый.
twelve /twɛlv/ *n.*, *adj.* двена́дцать.
twentieth /'twɛntiiθ/ *adj.* двадца́тый.
twenty /'twɛnti/ *n.*, *adj.* два́дцать.

twice /twais/ *adv.* два́жды; два ра́за.
twiddle /'twidl/ *v.*: **to twiddle one's thumbs** безде́льничать *impf.*
twig /twig/ *n.* ве́точка *f.*
twilight /'twai,lait/ *n.* су́мерки *pl.*
twin /twin/ *n.* близне́ц *m.*; *pl.* близнецы́ *pl.*
twine /twain/ *n.* бечёвка *f.*; шпага́т *m.*
twinge /twindʒ/ *n.* о́страя боль *f.*; (*of conscience*) угрызе́ние *neut.*
twinkle /'twiŋkəl/ *v.* мерца́ть; сверка́ть *impf.*
twinkling /'twiŋklɪŋ/ *n.* мерца́ние *neut.*
twirl /twɜrl/ *v.* верте́ть(ся); крути́ть(ся) *impf.*
twist /twist/ *v.* крути́ть; сучи́ть *impf.*
twist drill спира́льное сверло́ *neut.*
twister /'twistər/ *n.* (*colloq.*) (*tornado*) смерч *m.*
twisty /'twisti/ *adj.* изви́листый.
twitch /twitʃ/ *v.* дёргать(ся); подёргивать(ся) *impf.*
twitter /'twitər/ **1.** *n.* ще́бет *m.* **2.** *v.* щебета́ть; чири́кать *impf.*
two /tu/ **1.** *n.*, *adj.* два *m.*, *neut.*; две *f.* **2.** *coll.* пит дво́е.
two-faced /'tu ,feist/ *adj.* двули́кий.
twofold /'tu,fould/ *adj.* двойно́й; двукра́тный.
two-headed /'tu 'hɛdɪd/ *adj.* двугла́вый.
two-legged /'tu 'lɛgɪd, -'lɛgd/ *adj.* двуно́гий.
two-piece suit /'tu 'pis/ *n.* костю́м *m.*
two-sided /'tu 'saidɪd/ *adj.* двусторо́нний.
twosome /'tusəm/ *n.* па́ра *f.*
two-story /'tu 'stɔri/ *adj.* двухэта́жный.
two-stroke /'tu ,strouk/ *adj.* двухта́ктный.
two-time /'tu ,taim/ *v.* (*colloq.*) обма́нывать *impf.*
two-way /'tu 'wei/ *adj.* двусторо́нний.
tycoon /tai'kun/ *n.* магна́т *m.*
tympanist /'timpənist/ *n.* уда́рник *m.*
type /taip/ **1.** *n.* тип; род; класс *m.*; (*print*) шрифт *m.* **2.** *v.* писа́ть на маши́нке *impf.*
typed /taipt/ *adj.* машинопи́сный.
type foundry *n.* словоли́тня *f.*
type metal *n.* гарт *m.*
typescript /'taip,skript/ *n.* машинопи́сный текст *m.*
typeset /'taip,sɛt/ *v.* набира́ть *impf.*
typesetter /'taip,sɛtər/ *n.* набо́рщик *m.*
typesetting /'taip,sɛtɪŋ/ *n.* набо́р *m.*
typewriter /'taip,raitər/ *n.* пи́шущая маши́нка *f.*
typewritten /'taip,ritn/ *adj.* машинопи́сный.
typhoid /'taifɔid/ **1.** *n.* брюшно́й тиф *m.* **2.** *adj.* тифо́зный.
typhoon /tai'fun/ *n.* тайфу́н *m.*
typhus /'taifəs/ *n.* сыпно́й тиф *m.*
typical /'tipikəl/ *adj.* типи́чный.
typify /'tipə,fai/ *v.* олицетворя́ть *impf.*; (*be typical of*) быть типи́чным *or* характе́рным для (*with gen.*) *impf.*
typing /'taipiŋ/ *n.* машинопись *f.*
typist /'taipist/ *n.* машини́стка *f.*
typo /'taipou/ *n.* (*colloq.*) опеча́тка *f.*
tyrannical /ti'rænikəl/ *adj.* тирани́ческий.
tyrannize /'tirə,naiz/ *v.* тира́нить *impf.*
tyranny /'tirəni/ *n.* тирани́я *f.*
tyrant /'tairənt/ *n.* тира́н; де́спот *m.*
tyro /'tairou/ *n.* новичо́к *m.*
Tyumen /tyu'mɛn/ *n.* Тюме́нь *f.*

U

ubiquitous /yu'bɪkwɪtəs/ *adj.* вездесу́щий; повсеме́стный.

ubiquity /yu'bɪkwɪti/ *n.* повсеме́стность *f.*

udder /'ʌdər/ *n.* вы́мя *neut.*

Ufa /u'fɑ/ *n.* Уфа́ *f.*

UFO *n.* (*abbr. of* unidentified flying object) НЛО (*abbr. of* неопо́знанный лета́ющий объе́кт *m.*)

ufology /yu'fɒlədʒi/ *n.* уфоло́гия *f.*

Uglich /'uglɪtʃ/ *n.* У́глич *m.*

ugliness /'ʌglinɪs/ *n.* уро́дство; безобра́зие *neut.*; некраси́вость *f.*

ugly /'ʌgli/ *adj.* уро́дливый; некраси́вый; безобра́зный.

uh-huh /ʌ'hʌ/ *interj.* ага́.

uhlan /'ulɑn/ *n.* ула́н *m.*

ukase /yu'keɪs/ *n.* ука́з *m.*

Ukhta /ukh'tɑ/ *n.* Ухта́ *f.*

Ukraine /yu'kreɪn/ *n.* Украи́на *f.*

Ukrainian /yu'kreɪniən/ **1.** *adj.* украи́нский. **2.** *n.* украи́нец *m.*, украи́нка *f.*

ukulele /ˌyukə'leɪli/ *n.* гава́йская гита́ра *f.*

Ulaanbaator /'ulɑn 'bɑtɔr/ *n.* (*also: Ulan Bator*) Ула́н-Бато́р *m.*

Ulan Ude /u'lɑn u'dɛ/ *n.* Ула́н-Удэ́ *m.*

ulcer /'ʌlsər/ *n.* я́зва *f.*

ulcerate /'ʌlsə,reɪt/ *v.* изъязвля́ть(ся) *impf.*

ulceration /ˌʌlsə'reɪʃən/ *n.* изъязвле́ние *neut.*

ulcerous /'ʌlsərəs/ *adj.* я́звенный.

ulna /'ʌlnə/ *n.* локтева́я кость *f.*

ulterior /ʌl'tɪəriər/ *adj.* скры́тый.

ultimate /'ʌltəmɪt/ *adj.* оконча́тельный.

ultimatum /ˌʌltə'meɪtəm/ *n.* ультима́тум *m.*

ultra /'ʌltrə/ *n.* экстреми́ст *m.*

ultramarine /ˌʌltrəmə'rin/ *adj.* ультрамари́новый.

ultramicroscope /ˌʌltrə'maɪkrə,skoup/ *n.* ультрамикроско́п *m.*

ultramodern /ˌʌltrə'mɒdərn/ *adj.* ультрасовреме́нный.

ultrasonic /ˌʌltrə'sɒnɪk/ *adj.* сверхзвуково́й.

ultrasound /'ʌltrə,saund/ *n.* ультразву́к *m.*

ultraviolet /ˌʌltrə'vaɪəlɪt/ *adj.* ультрафиоле́товый.

umbelliferous /ˌʌmbə'lɪfərəs/ *adj.* зо́нтичный.

umber /'ʌmbər/ *n.* у́мбра *f.*

umbilical /ʌm'bɪlɪkəl/ *adj.* пупо́чный.

umbilical cord *n.* пупови́на *f.*

umbilicus /ʌm'bɪlɪkəs/ *n.* пупо́к *m.*

umbrage /'ʌmbrɪdʒ/ *n.*: **to take umbrage** обижа́ться *impf.*

umbrageous /ʌm'breɪdʒəs/ *adj.* тени́стый.

umbrella /ʌm'brɛlə/ *n.* зо́нтик *m.*

Umbria /'ʌmbriə/ *n.* (*province*) У́мбрия *f.*

umlaut /'umlaut/ *n.* умля́ут, умля́ут *m.*

umpire /'ʌmpaɪ³r/ *n.* судья́ *m.*

umpteenth /'ʌmp'tinθ/ *adj.*: **for the umpteenth time** в со́тый раз *m.*

unabashed /ˌʌnə'bæʃt/ *adj.* несмути́вшийся; без вся́кого смуще́ния.

unabated /ˌʌnə'beɪtɪd/ *adj.* неослабева́ющий.

unabating /ˌʌnə'beɪtɪŋ/ *adj.* неосла́бный.

unabbreviated /ˌʌnə'brivi,eɪtɪd/ *adj.* несокращённый.

unable /ʌn'eɪbəl/ *adj.* неспосо́бный.

unabridged /ˌʌnə'brɪdʒd/ *adj.* несокращённый; по́лный.

unacceptable /ˌʌnɪk'sɛptəbəl/ *adj.* неприе́млемый.

unaccompanied /ˌʌnə'kʌmpənid/ *adj.* без сопровожде́ния.

unaccountable /ˌʌnə'kauntəbəl/ *adj.* (*inexplicable*) необъясни́мый.

unaccustomed /ˌʌnə'kʌstəmd/ *adj.* непривы́кший (к *with dat.*).

unacknowledged /ˌʌnæk'nɒlɪdʒd/ *adj.* непри́знанный.

unacquainted /ˌʌnə'kweintɪd/ *adj.* незнако́мый.

unadapted /ˌʌnə'dæptɪd/ *adj.* неприспосо́бленный.

unadmitted /ˌʌnəd'mɪtɪd/ *adj.* непри́знанный.

unadorned /ˌʌnə'dɔrnd/ *adj.* неприкра́шенный.

unadulterated /ˌʌnə'dʌltə,reɪtɪd/ *adj.* чи́стый; нефальсифици́рованный.

unadventurous /ˌʌnəd'vɛntʃərəs/ *adj.* несме́лый.

unaffected /ˌʌnə'fɛktɪd/ *adj.* непринуждённый.

unafraid /ˌʌnə'freɪd/ *adj.* непугли́вый.

unaided /ʌn'eɪdɪd/ *adj.* без по́мощи.

unalloyed /ˌʌnə'lɔɪd/ *adj.* (*pure*) чи́стый; (*metal*) нелеги́рованный.

unalterable /ʌn'ɔltərəbəl/ *adj.* неизме́нный.

unambiguous /ˌʌnæm'bɪgyuəs/ *adj.* недвусмы́сленный.

unamiable /ʌn'eɪmiəbəl/ *adj.* нелюбе́зный.

unanimity /ˌyunə'nɪmɪti/ *n.* единоду́шие *neut.*

unanimous /yu'nænəməs/ *adj.* единогла́сный; единоду́шный.

unannounced /ˌʌnə'naunst/ *adj.* без оповеще́ния.

unappeasable /ˌʌnə'pizəbəl/ *adj.* непримири́мый.

unappetizing /ʌn'æpɪ,taizɪŋ/ *adj.* неаппети́тный.

unappreciated /ˌʌnə'priʃi,eɪtɪd/ *adj.* недооценённый.

unapproachable /ˌʌnə'proutʃəbəl/ *adj.* недосту́пный.

unapt /ʌn'æpt/ *adj.* неподходя́щий.

unarguable /ʌn'arguəbəl/ *adj.* неоспори́мый.

unarmed /ʌn'armd/ *adj.* невооружённый; безору́жный.

unasked /ʌn'æskt/ *adj.* непро́шеный.

unassailable /ˌʌnə'seɪləbəl/ *adj.* неопроверж́и́мый.

unassisted /ˌʌnə'sɪstɪd/ *adj.* без по́мощи.

unassuming /ˌʌnə'sumɪŋ/ *adj.* скро́мный.

unattached /ˌʌnə'tætʃt/ *adj.* неприкреплённый.

unattended /ˌʌnə'tɛndɪd/ *adj.* без присмо́тра.

unattractive /ˌʌnə'træktɪv/ *adj.* непривлека́тельный.

unauthorized /ʌn'ɔθə'raizd/ *adj.* неразрешённый; неправомо́чный.

unavailable /ˌʌnə'veɪləbəl/ *adj.* не име́ющийся в нали́чии; недосту́пный.

unavailing /ˌʌnə'veɪlɪŋ/ *adj.* напра́сный.

unavoidable /ˌʌnə'vɔidəbəl/ *adj.* неизбе́жный.

unaware /ˌʌnə'wɛər/ *adj.* не подозрева́ющий.

unawares /ˌʌnəˈwɛərz/ *adv.* врасплóх.
unbalanced /ʌnˈbælənst/ *adj.* неуравновéшенный.
unbearable /ʌnˈbɛərəbəl/ *adj.* невыносúмый.
unbeaten /ʌnˈbitn̩/ *adj.* непревзойдённый.
unbecoming /ˌʌnbɪˈkʌmɪŋ/ *adj.* не к лицý (*with dat.*); (*inappropriate*) неподходя́щий.
unbefitting /ˌʌnbɪˈfɪtɪŋ/ *adj.* неподобáющий.
unbeknown /ˌʌnbɪˈnoun/ *adj.* невéдомый.
unbelief /ˌʌnbɪˈlif/ *n.* невéрие *neut.*
unbelievable /ˌʌnbɪˈlivəbəl/ *adj.* невероя́тный.
unbeliever /ˌʌnbɪˈlivər/ *adj.* невéрующий.
unbelieving /ˌʌnbɪˈlivɪŋ/ *adj.* (*incredulous*) недовéрчивый.
unbend /ʌnˈbɛnd/ *v.* выпрямля́ть(ся) *impf.*
unbending /ʌnˈbɛndɪŋ/ *adj.* несгибáемый.
unbiased /ʌnˈbaiəst/ *adj.* беспристрáстный.
unbidden /ʌnˈbɪdn̩/ *adj.* непрóшеный.
unblemished /ʌnˈblɛmɪʃt/ *adj.* безупрéчный.
unblushing /ʌnˈblʌʃɪŋ/ *adj.* бессты́дный.
unbolt /ʌnˈboult/ *v.* отпирáть *impf.*
unbosom /ʌnˈbʊzəm/ *v.*: **to unbosom oneself** открывáть дýшу (пéред *with instr.*) *impf.*
unbounded /ʌnˈbaundɪd/ *adj.* безграни́чный.
unbridled /ʌnˈbraidld/ *adj.* необýзданный.
unbroken /ʌnˈbroukən/ *adj.* непреры́вный.
unbuckle /ʌnˈbʌkəl/ *v.* расстёгивать *impf.*
unburden /ʌnˈbɜrdn̩/ *v.* облегчáть; снимáть брéмя *impf.*
unbusinesslike /ʌnˈbɪznɪsˌlaik/ *adj.* неделовóй.
unbutton /ʌnˈbʌtn̩/ *v.* расстёгивать *impf.*
uncalled-for /ʌnˈkɔld ˌfɔr/ *adj.* ненýжный.
uncanny /ʌnˈkæni/ *adj.* сверхъестéственный; жýткий.
uncared-for /ʌnˈkɛərd ˌfɔr/ *adj.* неухóженный.
uncase /ʌnˈkeis/ *v.* вынимáть из чехлá *impf.*
unceasing /ʌnˈsisɪŋ/ *adj.* беспрестáнный; беспреры́вный.
unceremonious /ˌʌnsɛrəˈmouniəs/ *adj.* бесцеремóнный.
uncertain /ʌnˈsɜrtn̩/ *adj.* неувéренный.
uncertainty /ʌnˈsɜrtn̩ti/ *n.* неопределённость *f.*
unchallengeable /ʌnˈtʃælɪndʒəbəl/ *adj.* неоспори́мый.
unchangeable /ʌnˈtʃeindʒəbəl/ *adj.* неизменя́емый.
unchanging /ʌnˈtʃeindʒɪŋ/ *adj.* неизмéнный.
uncharitable /ʌnˈtʃærɪtəbəl/ *adj.* недóбрый.
unchecked /ʌnˈtʃɛkt/ *adj.* незадéржанный.
uncial /ˈʌnʃiəl/ *n.* устáв *m.*; унциáльное письмó *neut.*
uncivilized /ʌnˈsɪvəˌlaizd/ *adj.* нецивилизóванный.
unclaimed /ʌnˈkleimd/ *adj.* невострéбованный.
unclasp /ʌnˈklæsp/ *v.* расстёгивать *impf.*
uncle /ˈʌŋkəl/ *n.* дя́дя *m.* (*decl. f.*)
unclean /ʌnˈklin/ *adj.* нечи́стый.
unclear /ʌnˈklɪər/ *adj.* нея́сный.
unclog /ʌnˈklɒg/ *v.* (*drain, etc.*) прочи́стить *pf.*
unclouded /ʌnˈklaudɪd/ *adj.* безóблачный.
uncoil /ʌnˈkɔil/ *v.* размáтывать(ся) *impf.*
uncomfortable /ʌnˈkʌmftəbəl/ *adj.* неудóбный.
uncommitted /ʌnkəˈmɪtɪd/ *adj.* неприсоединúвшийся.
uncommon /ʌnˈkɒmən/ *adj.* рéдкий; необы́чный; необыкновéнный.

uncompleted /ˌʌnkəmˈplitɪd/ *adj.* незавершённый.
uncompromising /ʌnˈkɒmprəˌmaizɪŋ/ *adj.* бескомпроми́ссный.
unconcern /ˌʌnkənˈsɜrn/ *n.* (*indifference*) равнодýшие (к *with dat.*).
unconcerned /ˌʌnkənˈsɜrnd/ *adj.* беззабóтный.
unconditional /ˌʌnkənˈdɪʃənl̩/ *adj.* безоговорóчный; безуслóвный.
unconfirmed /ˌʌnkənˈfɜrmd/ *adj.* неподтверждённый.
unconquerable /ʌnˈkɒŋkərəbəl/ *adj.* несокруши́мый.
unconscionable /ʌnˈkɒnʃənəbəl/ *adj.* бессóвестный.
unconscious /ʌnˈkɒnʃəs/ *adj.* (*involuntary*) бессознáтельный; **to be unconscious** быть без сознáния.
unconsciousness /ʌnˈkɒnʃəsnɪs/ *n.* бессознáтельное состоя́ние *neut.*
unconsidered /ˌʌnkənˈsɪdərd/ *adj.* необдýманный.
unconstitutional /ˌʌnkɒnstɪˈtuʃənl̩/ *adj.* нсконституциóнный.
unconstrained /ˌʌnkənˈstreind/ *adj.* непринуждённый.
uncontrollable /ˌʌnkənˈtrouləbəl/ *adj.* неудержи́мый.
unconventional /ˌʌnkənˈvɛnʃənl̩/ *adj.* необы́чный.
unconvincing /ˌʌnkənˈvɪnsɪŋ/ *adj.* неубеди́тельный.
uncooked /ʌnˈkʊkt/ *adj.* сырóй.
uncooperative /ˌʌkouˈɒpərətɪv/ *adj.* неустýпчивый.
uncork /ʌnˈkɔrk/ *v.* откупóривать *impf.*
uncouple /ʌnˈkʌpəl/ *v.* расцепля́ть; отцепля́ть *impf.*
uncouth /ʌnˈkuθ/ *adj.* грýбый; невоспи́танный; некультýрный.
uncover /ʌnˈkʌvər/ *v.* открывáть *impf.*, откры́ть *pf.*
uncrowned /ʌnˈkraund/ *adj.* некоронóванный.
unction /ˈʌŋkʃən/ *n.* помáзание *neut.*; (*ointment*) мазь *f.*
unctuous /ˈʌŋktʃuəs/ *adj.* елéйный.
uncultivated /ʌˈkʌltəˌveitɪd/ *adj.* необрабóтанный.
uncultured /ʌnˈkʌltʃərd/ *adj.* некультýрный.
uncurtained /ʌnˈkɜrtn̩d/ *adj.* незанавéшенный.
uncut /ʌnˈkʌt/ *adj.* неразрéзанный.
undamaged /ʌnˈdæmɪdʒd/ *adj.* неповреждённый.
undaunted /ʌnˈdɔntɪd/ *adj.* неустраши́мый.
undeceive /ˌʌndɪˈsiv/ *v.* откры́ть глазá *pf.*
undecided /ˌʌndɪˈsaidɪd/ *adj.* нереши́тельный.
undeclared /ˌʌndɪˈklɛərd/ *adj.* необъя́вленный.
undefended /ˌʌdɪˈfɛndɪd/ *adj.* незащищённый.
undemanding /ˌʌndəˈmændɪŋ/ *adj.* нетрéбовательный.
undemonstrative /ˌʌndəˈmɒnstrətɪv/ *adj.* сдéржанный.
undeniable /ˌʌndɪˈnaiəbəl/ *adj.* неоспори́мый.
under /ˈʌndər/ **1.** *prep.* (*loc.*) под (*with instr.*); (*dir.*) под (*with acc.*). **2.** *adv.* ни́же, вниз; внизý.
underage /ˌʌndərˈeidʒ/ *adj.* несовершеннолéтний.
underbrush /ˈʌndərˌbrʌʃ/ *n.* подлéсок *m.*

underclothes /'ʌndər,klouz/ n. (нижнее) бельё neut.

undercoat /'ʌndər,kout/ n. (painting) грунтовка f.

undercover /,ʌndər'kʌvər/ adj. секретный; тайный.

undercurrent /'ʌndər,kɜrənt/ n. подводное течение neut.; (fig.) скрытая тенденция f.

underdeveloped /,ʌndərdɪ'vɛləpt/ adj. недоразвитый.

underestimate /,ʌndər'ɛstə,meit/ v. недооценивать impf., недооценить pf.

underestimation /,ʌndər,ɛstə'meiʃən/ n. недооценка f.

underexpose /,ʌndərɪk'spouz/ v. (photog.) недодерживать impf.

underfed /,ʌndər'fɛd/ adj. недокормленный.

underfeed /,ʌndər'fid/ v. недокармливать impf.

underfoot /,ʌndər'fut/ adv. под ногами.

undergarment /'ʌndər,garmənt/ n. предмет нижнего белья neut.

undergo /,ʌndər'gou/ v. подвергаться impf., подвергнуться pf.

undergraduate /,ʌndər'grædʒuit/ n. студент m.

underground /'ʌndər,graund/ **1.** adj. подземный; подпольный. **2.** n. подполье neut.

undergrowth /'ʌndər,grouθ/ n. подрост m.; заросли pl.

underhand /'ʌndər,hænd/ adj. тайный; закулисный.

underlay /'ʌndər,lei/ n. подстилка f.

underlie /,ʌndər'lai/ v. лежать в основе impf.

underline /'ʌndər,lain/ v. подчёркивать impf., подчеркнуть pf.

underling /'ʌndərlɪŋ/ adj. подчинённый.

undermentioned /,ʌndər'mɛnʃənd/ adj. нижеупомянутый.

undermine /,ʌndər'main/ v. подрывать impf.

undermost /'ʌndər,moust/ adj. самый нижний.

underneath /,ʌndər'niθ/ **1.** adv. вниз, внизу; ниже. **2.** prep. под (with instr.).

undernourished /,ʌndər'nɜrɪʃt/ adj. недокормленный; худосочный.

undernutrition /,ʌndərnu'trɪʃən/ n. недоедание neut.

underpants /'ʌndər,pænts/ n. трусики; трусы pl.

underpass /'ʌndər,pæs/ n. подземный переход m.

underpay /,ʌndər'pei/ v. недоплачивать impf.

underpin /,ʌndər'pɪn/ v. подпирать impf.

underprivileged /'ʌndər'prɪvəlɪdʒd/ adj. (poor) неимущий.

underproduction /,ʌndərprə'dʌkʃən/ n. недопроизводство neut.

underrate /,ʌndər'reit/ v. недооценивать impf.

underripe /,ʌndər'raip/ adj. недоспелый.

underscore /'ʌndər,skɔr/ v. подчёркивать impf.

undersea /'ʌndər,si/ adj. подводный.

undershirt /'ʌndər,ʃɜrt/ n. нижняя рубашка f.

undersign /,ʌndər'sain/ v. подписываться impf.

undersized /'ʌndər'saizd/ adj. неполномерный.

understaffed /,ʌndər'stæft/ adj. неукомплектованный.

understand /,ʌndər'stænd/ v. понимать impf., понять pf.; (assume) подразумевать impf.

understanding /,ʌndər'stændɪŋ/ n. понимание neut.

understate /,ʌndər'steit/ v. преуменьшать impf.

understood /,ʌndər'stud/ adj. понятый; принятый; договорённый.

understudy /'ʌndər,stʌdi/ n. дублёр m.

undertake /,ʌndər'teik/ v. предпринимать impf., предпринять pf.

undertaker /'ʌndər,teikər/ n. владелец похоронного бюро; гробовщик m.

undertaking /,ʌndər'teikɪŋ/ n. предприятие neut.

undertone /'ʌndər,toun/ n. (half-tint) полутон m.

undertow /'ʌndər,tou/ n. встречное нижнее течение neut.

undervalue /,ʌndər'vælyu/ v. недооценивать impf.

underwater /'ʌndər'wɔtər/ adj. подводный.

underwear /'ʌndər,wɛər/ n. нижнее бельё neut.

underweight /'ʌndər'weit/ adj. вес ниже положенного.

underworld /'ʌndər,wɜrld/ n. (crime) преступный мир m.; (myth.) преисподняя f.

underwrite /,ʌndər'rait/ v. (insure) страховать impf.; (guarantee) гарантировать impf. and pf.

underwriter /'ʌndər,raitər/ n. страховщик m.

undescribable /,ʌndɪ'skraibəbəl/ adj. неописуемый.

undeserved /,ʌndɪ'zɜrvd/ adj. незаслуженный.

undeserving /,ʌndɪ'zɜrvɪŋ/ adj. недостойный.

undesigned /,ʌndɪ'zaind/ adj. незапроектированный.

undesirable /,ʌndɪ'zaiᵊrəbəl/ adj. нежелательный.

undesired /,ʌndɪ'zaiᵊrd/ adj. нежеланный.

undetermined /,ʌdɪ'tɜrmind/ adj. нерешённый.

undeveloped /,ʌndɪ'vɛləpt/ adj. неразвитый.

undeviated /ʌn'divi,eitid/ adj. неуклонный.

undigested /,ʌndɪ'dʒɛstid/ adj. неусвоенный.

undisciplined /ʌn'dɪsəplɪnd/ adj. недисциплинированный.

undisclosed /,ʌndɪ'sklouzd/ adj. необнародованный.

undiscovered /,ʌndɪ'skʌvərd/ adj. необнаруженный.

undisguised /,ʌndɪs'gaizd/ adj. неприкрытый.

undismayed /,ʌndɪs'meid/ adj. необескураженный.

undisputed /,ʌndɪs'pyutid/ adj. бесспорный.

undistinguished /,ʌndɪ'stɪŋwɪʃt/ adj. посредственный; заурядный.

undivided /,ʌndɪ'vaidid/ adj. целый; безраздельный.

undo /ʌn'du/ v. уничтожать сделанное impf.

undoing /ʌn'duɪŋ/ n. гибель f.

undone /ʌn'dʌn/ adj. несделанный; развязанный; пропавший.

undoubted /ʌn'dautid/ adj. несомненный.

undreamed /ʌn'drimd/ adj. неслыханный.

undress /ʌn'drɛs/ v.t. раздевать impf., раздеть pf.; v.i. раздеваться impf., раздеться pf.

undressed /ʌn'drest/ adj. неодетый; (leather) невыделанный; неприправленный.

undue /ʌn'du/ adj. (excessive) чрезмерный.

undulate /'ʌndʒə,leit/ v. колыхаться impf.; (of area) быть холмистым.

undulating /'ʌndʒə,leitɪŋ/ adj. волнообразный; холмистый.

undulatory /'ʌndʒələ,tɔri/ adj. волнистый.

unduly /ʌn'duli/ adv. чрезмерно.

undying /ʌn'daiiŋ/ adj. бессме́ртный; бесконе́чный.

unearned /ʌn'ɜrnd/ adj. незарабо́танный.

unearth /ʌn'ɜrθ/ v. раска́пывать impf.

unearthly /ʌn'ɜrθli/ adj. неземно́й; сверхъесте́ственный.

uneasiness /ʌn'izinis/ n. беспоко́йство neut.

uneasy /ʌn'izi/ adj. обеспоко́йный; встрево́женный.

uneatable /ʌn'itəbəl/ adj. несъедо́бный.

uneconomical /ˌʌnɛkə'nɒmikəl/ adj. неэкономи́чный; нерента́бельный; неэконо́мный.

unedifying /ʌn'ɛdəˌfaiiŋ/ adj. непоучи́тельный.

uneducated /ʌn'ɛdʒʊˌkeitid/ adj. необразо́ванный.

unemployed /ˌʌnɛm'plɔid/ **1.** adj. безрабо́тный. **2.** n. безрабо́тные pl.

unemployment /ˌʌnɛm'plɔimənt/ n. безрабо́тица f.

unemployment benefit n. посо́бие по безрабо́тице neut.

unending /ʌn'ɛndiŋ/ adj. несконча́емый; бесконе́чный; ве́чный.

unendurable /ˌʌnɛn'dʊrəbəl/ adj. невыноси́мый.

unenlightened /ˌʌnɛn'laitn̩d/ adj. непросвещённый.

unenterprising /ʌn'ɛntərˌpraiziŋ/ adj. непредприи́мчивый.

unenviable /ʌn'ɛnviəbəl/ adj. незави́дный.

unequal /ʌn'ikwəl/ adj. нера́вный; (uneven) неро́вный.

unequaled /ʌn'ikwəld/ adj. несравне́нный.

unequivocal /ˌʌnı'kwivəkəl/ adj. недвусмы́сленный.

unerring /ʌn'ɜriŋ/ adj. безоши́бочный.

unethical /ʌn'ɛθikəl/ adj. неэти́чный.

uneven /ʌn'ivən/ adj. неро́вный; (odd) нечётный.

unexacting /ˌʌnıg'zæktiŋ/ adj. нетребова́тельный.

unexampled /ˌʌnıg'zæmpəld/ adj. беспример́ный.

unexceptionable /ˌʌnık'sɛpʃənəbəl/ adj. безупре́чный.

unexceptional /ˌʌnık'sɛpʃənl̩/ adj. заура́дный.

unexpected /ˌʌnık'spɛktid/ adj. неожи́данный; непредви́денный.

unexpurgated /ʌn'ɛkspərˌgeitid/ adj. в по́лном ви́де.

unfading /ʌn'feidiŋ/ adj. неувяда́емый.

unfailing /ʌn'feiliŋ/ adj. неизме́нный.

unfair /ʌn'fɛər/ adj. несправедли́вый.

unfaithful /ʌn'feiθfəl/ adj. неве́рный.

unfaithfulness /ʌn'feiθfəlnis/ n. неве́рность f.

unfaltering /ʌn'fɔltəriŋ/ adj. неколеби́мый..

unfamiliar /ˌʌnfə'milyər/ adj. незнако́мый; стра́нный.

unfasten /ʌn'fæsən/ v. (dress, etc.) расстёгивать impf.; (untie) развя́зывать impf.

unfathomable /ʌn'fæðəməbəl/ adj. неизмери́мый; необъясни́мый.

unfavorable /ʌn'feivərəbəl/ adj. неблагоприя́тный.

unfeeling /ʌn'filiŋ/ adj. бесчу́вственный.

unfeigned /ʌn'feind/ adj. неподде́льный.

unfeminine /ʌn'fɛmənin/ adj. неже́нственный.

unfettered /ʌn'fɛtərd/ adj. нестеснённый.

unfinished /ʌn'finiʃt/ adj. неоко́нченный.

unfit /ʌn'fit/ adj. неподходя́щий; него́дный.

unfitness /ʌn'fitnis/ n. неприго́дность neut.

unfix /ʌn'fiks/ v. открепля́ть(ся) impf.

unflagging /ʌn'flægiŋ/ adj. неосла́бный.

unflappable /ʌn'flæpəbəl/ adj. невозмути́мый.

unflattering /ʌn'flætəriŋ/ adj. неле́стный.

unflinching /ʌn'flintʃiŋ/ adj. непоколеби́мый.

unfold /ʌn'fould/ v. раскрыва́ть(ся) impf., раскры́ть(ся) pf.

unforced /ʌn'fɔrst/ adj. непринуждённый.

unforeseen /ˌʌnfɔr'sin/ adj. непредви́денный.

unforgettable /ˌʌnfər'gɛtəbəl/ adj. незабыва́емый.

unforgivable /ˌʌnfər'givəbəl/ adj. непрости́тельный.

unfortunate /ʌn'fɔrtʃənit/ adj. несча́стный.

unfortunately /ʌn'fɔrtʃənitli/ adv. к сожале́нию; к несча́стью.

unfounded /ʌn'faundid/ adj. необосно́ванный.

unfrequented /ʌn'frikwəntid/ adj. малопосеща́емый.

unfriendly /ʌn'frɛndli/ adj. недру́жеский.

unfrock /ʌn'frɒk/ v. лиша́ть духо́вного са́на; расстрига́ть impf.

unfruitful /ʌn'frutfəl/ adj. неплодоро́дный.

unfurl /ʌn'fɜrl/ v. распуска́ть(ся) impf.

unfurnished /ʌn'fɜrniʃt/ adj. немеблиро́ванный.

ungainly /ʌn'geinli/ adj. нескла́дный.

ungallant /ʌn'gælənt/ adj. негала́нтный.

ungarbled /ʌn'gɑrbəld/ adj. неискажённый.

ungenerous /ʌn'dʒɛnərəs/ adj. скупова́тый.

ungentlemanly /ʌn'dʒɛntl̩mənli/ adj. неджентльме́нский.

ungifted /ʌn'giftid/ adj. безда́рный.

ungodly /ʌn'gɒdli/ adj. безбо́жный.

ungovernable /ʌn'gʌvərnəbəl/ adj. неуправля́емый.

ungracious /ʌn'greiʃəs/ adj. нелюбе́зный.

ungraciousness /ʌn'greiʃəsnis/ n. нелюбе́зность f.

ungrateful /ʌn'greitfəl/ adj. неблагода́рный.

ungrudging /ʌn'grʌdʒiŋ/ adj. ще́дрый.

unguarded /ʌn'gɑrdid/ adj. неохраня́емый.

unguent /'ʌŋgwənt/ n. мазь f.

unhappiness /ʌn'hæpinis/ n. несча́стье neut.

unhappy /ʌn'hæpi/ adj. (not happy) несчастли́вый; несча́стный; (unfelicitous) неуда́чный; (ill-fated) злополу́чный; (sad) гру́стный.

unharmed /ʌn'hɑrmd/ adj. невреди́мый.

unharness /ʌn'hɑrnis/ v. распряга́ть impf.

unhealthy /ʌn'hɛlθi/ adj. нездоро́вый.

unheard /ʌn'hɜrd/ adj. неуслы́шанный.

unheard-of /ʌn'hɜrd ˌʌv/ adj. неслы́ханный.

unheeded /ʌn'hidid/ adj. незаме́ченный.

unhesitating /ʌn'hɛziˌteitiŋ/ adj. реши́тельный.

unhesitatingly /ʌn'hɛziˌteitiŋli/ adv. не коле́блясь.

unhinge /ʌn'hindʒ/ v. снима́ть с пе́тель impf.; (disorient) своди́ть с ума́ impf.

unhitch /ʌn'hitʃ/ v. отцепля́ть impf.

unholy /ʌn'houli/ adj. нечести́вый.

unhook /ʌn'hʊk/ v. расстёгивать impf.

unhorse /ʌn'hɔrs/ v. сбра́сывать с ло́шади impf.

unhygienic /ˌʌnhaidʒi'ɛnik, -'dʒɛnik/ adj. негигиени́чный.

Uniate /'yuniit/ n. униа́т m.

uniaxial /ˌyuni'æksiəl/ adj. одноо́сный.

unicameral /ˌyunɪˈkæmərəl/ *adj.* однопала́тный.
unicellular /ˌyunəˈsɛlyələr/ *adj.* одноклёточный.
unicorn /ˈyunɪˌkɔrn/ *n.* единоро́г *m.*
unidentified /ˌʌnaiˈdɛntəˌfaid/ *adj.* неопо́знанный.
unification /ˌyunəfɪˈkeiʃən/ *n.* объедине́ние *neut.*; унифика́ция *f.*
uniform /ˈyunəˌfɔrm/ **1.** *adj.* единообра́зный; (*of uniform*) фо́рменный. **2.** *n.* фо́рма *f.*; мунди́р *m.*
uniformed /ˈyunəˌfɔrmd/ *adj.* оде́тый в фо́рму.
uniformity /ˌyunəˈfɔrmɪti/ *n.* единообра́зие; однообра́зие *neut.*
unify /ˈyunəˌfai/ *v.* объединя́ть *impf.*, объедини́ть *pf.*; унифици́ровать *impf.* and *pf.*
unilateral /ˌyunəˈlætərəl/ *adj.* односторо́нний.
unimaginable /ˌʌnɪˈmædʒənəbəl/ *adj.* невообрази́мый.
unimaginative /ˌʌnɪˈmædʒənətɪv/ *adj.* прозаи́чный.
unimpaired /ˌʌnɪmˈpɛərd/ *adj.* неповреждённый.
unimpeachable /ˌʌnɪmˈpitʃəbəl/ *adj.* безукори́зненный; неоспори́мый.
unimportance /ˌʌnɪmˈpɔrtn̩s/ *n.* незначи́тельность *f.*
unimportant /ˌʌnɪmˈpɔrtn̩t/ *adj.* нева́жный; незначи́тельный.
unimposing /ˌʌnɪmˈpouzɪŋ/ *adj.* невнуши́тельный.
unimpressive /ˌʌɪmˈprɛsɪv/ *adj.* невпечатля́ющий.
uninformed /ˌʌnɪnˈfɔrmd/ *adj.* неосведомлённый.
uninhabitable /ˌʌnɪnˈhæbɪtɪd/ *adj.* непригодный для жилья́.
uninhabited /ˌʌnɪnˈhæbɪtɪd/ *adj.* необита́емый.
uninhibited /ˌʌnɪnˈhɪbɪtɪd/ *adj.* нестеснённый.
uninitiated /ˌʌnɪˈnɪʃiˌeitɪd/ *adj.* непосвящённый.
uninspired /ˌʌnɪnˈspaiᵊrd/ *adj.* невдохновлённый.
uninsured /ˌʌnɪnˈʃurd/ *adj.* незастрахо́ванный.
unintelligent /ˌʌnɪnˈtɛlɪdʒənt/ *adj.* неу́мный.
unintelligible /ˌʌnɪnˈtɛlɪdʒəbəl/ *adj.* невня́тный.
unintentional /ˌʌnɪnˈtɛnʃənl̩/ *adj.* непреднаме́ренный.
uninterested /ʌnˈɪntərəstɪd/ *adj.* равноду́шный.
uninteresting /ʌnˈɪntərəstɪŋ/ *adj.* неинтере́сный.
uninterrupted /ˌʌnɪntəˈrʌptɪd/ *adj.* непреры́вный.
uninvited /ˌʌnɪnˈvaitɪd/ *adj.* неприглашённый; незва́ный.
uninviting /ˌʌnɪnˈvaitɪŋ/ *adj.* непривлека́тельный.
union /ˈyunyən/ **1.** *n.* сою́з *m.* **2.** *adj.* (*of trade union*) профсою́зный.
unionism /ˈyunyəˌnɪzəm/ *n.* тред-юниони́зм *m.*
unique /yuˈnik/ *adj.* уника́льный; еди́нственный в своём ро́де.
uniqueness /yuˈniknɪs/ *adj.* уника́льность.
unisexual /ˌyunəˈsɛkʃuəl/ *adj.* однопо́лый.
unison /ˈyunəsən/ *n.* (*agreement*) согла́сие *neut.*
unit /ˈyunɪt/ *n.* едини́ца *f.*; (*mil.*) часть *f.*
Unitarian /ˌyunɪˈtɛəriən/ *n.* унита́рий *m.*
unitary /ˈyunɪˌteri/ *adj.* унита́рный.
unite /yuˈnait/ *v.t.* соединя́ть *impf.*, соедини́ть *pf.*; *v.i.* соединя́ться *impf.*, соедини́ться *pf.*
united /yuˈnaitɪd/ *adj.* соединённый.
United States *n.* Соединённые Шта́ты *pl.*
unity /ˈyunɪti/ *n.* еди́нство *neut.*
univalent /ˌyunəˈveilənt/ *adj.* одновале́нтный.

universal /ˌyunəˈvɜrsəl/ *adj.* универса́льный; всеобщий; всеми́рный.
universality /ˌyunəvərˈsælɪti/ *n.* всеми́рность *f.*
universally /ˌyunəˈvɜrsəli/ *adv.* всю́ду.
universe /ˈyunəˌvɜrs/ *n.* вселе́нная *f.*; мир *m.*
university /ˌyunəˈvɜrsɪti/ **1.** *n.* университе́т *m.* **2.** *adj.* университе́тский.
unjust /ʌnˈdʒʌst/ *adj.* несправедли́вый.
unjustified /ʌnˈdʒʌstəˌfaid/ *adj.* неопра́вданный.
unkempt /ʌnˈkempt/ *adj.* нечёсаный.
unkind /ʌnˈkaind/ *adj.* недо́брый.
unkindness /ʌnˈkaindnɪs/ *n.* жесто́кость *f.*
unknit /ʌnˈnɪt/ *v.* распуска́ть *impf.*
unknowable /ʌnˈnouəbəl/ *adj.* непознава́емый.
unknowingly /ʌnˈnouɪŋli/ *adv.* ненаме́ренно.
unknown /ʌnˈnoun/ *adj.* неизве́стный.
unlace /ʌnˈleis/ *v.* расшнуро́вывать *impf.*
unlearn /ʌnˈlɜrn/ *v.* отуча́ться *impf.*
unleash /ʌnˈliʃ/ *v.* спуска́ть со сво́ры *impf.*
unleavened /ʌnˈlɛvənd/ *adj.* незаква́шенный; пре́сный.
unless /ʌnˈlɛs/ *conj.* если не.
unlettered /ʌnˈlɛtərd/ *adj.* (*illiterate*) негра́мотный.
unlike /ʌnˈlaik/ *adj.* непохо́жий; не тако́й, как.
unlikelihood /ʌnˈlaikliˌhʊd/ *n.* маловероя́тность *f.*
unlikely /ʌnˈlaikli/ *adj.* неправдоподо́бный; маловероя́тный.
unload /ʌnˈloud/ *v.* разгружа́ть *impf.*, разгрузи́ть *pf.*
unlock /ʌnˈlɒk/ *v.* отпира́ть(ся) *impf.*, отпере́ть(ся) *pf.*; открыва́ть(ся) *impf.*, откры́ть(ся) *pf.*
unlooked-for /ʌnˈlʊktˌfɔr/ *adj.* неожида́емый.
unloose /ʌnˈlus/ *v.* выпуска́ть *impf.*
unluckily /ʌnˈlʌkəli/ *adv.* к несча́стью.
unlucky /ʌnˈlʌki/ *adj.* неуда́чный.
unman /ʌnˈmæn/ *v.* лиша́ть му́жества; кастри́ровать *impf.*
unmanageable /ʌnˈmænɪdʒəbəl/ *adj.* неуправля́емый.
unmanned /ʌnˈmænd/ *adj.* беспило́тный.
unmarred /ʌnˈmɑrd/ *adj.* неповреждённый.
unmarried /ʌnˈmærid/ *adj.* (*man*) холосто́й; нежена́тый; (*woman*) незаму́жняя.
unmask /ʌnˈmæsk/ *v.* разоблача́ть *impf.*
unmentionable /ʌnˈmenʃənəbəl/ *adj.* неупомина́емый; необсужда́емый.
unmerciful /ʌnˈmɜrsɪfəl/ *adj.* безжа́лостный.
unmerited /ʌnˈmerɪtɪd/ *adj.* незаслу́женный.
unmindful /ʌnˈmaindfəl/ *adj.* невнима́тельный.
unmistakable /ˌʌnmɪˈsteikəbəl/ *adj.* безоши́бочный.
unmitigated /ʌnˈmɪtɪˌgeitɪd/ *adj.* несмягчённый.
unmoved /ʌnˈmuvd/ *adj.* нерастро́ганный.
unmusical /ʌnˈmyuzɪkəl/ *adj.* немузыка́льный.
unnamed /ʌnˈneimd/ *adj.* нена́званный.
unnatural /ʌnˈnætʃərəl/ *adj.* неесте́ственный.
unnecessarily /ʌnˌnɛsəˈsɛərəli/ *adv.* без на́добности.
unnecessary /ʌnˈnɛsəˌseri/ *adj.* нену́жный; (*superfluous*) изли́шний.
unneighborly /ʌnˈneibərli/ *adj.* недобрососе́дский.
unnerve /ʌnˈnɜrv/ *v.* обесси́ливать *impf.*
unnoticed /ʌnˈnoutɪst/ *adj.* незаме́ченный.

unnumbered /ʌn'nʌmbərd/ adj. непронумеро́ванный.

unobjectionable /ˌʌnəb'dʒɛkʃənəbəl/ adj. безоби́дный.

unobliging /ˌʌnə'blaidʒɪŋ/ adj. нелюбе́зный.

unobservant /ˌʌnəb'zɜrvənt/ adj. невнима́тельный.

unobtainable /ˌʌnəb'teinəbəl/ adj. недосту́пный.

unobtrusive /ˌʌnəb'trusɪv/ adj. ненавя́зчивый.

unoccupied /ʌn'ɒkyə,paid/ adj. неза́нятый.

unoffending /ˌʌnə'fɛndɪŋ/ adj. неви́нный.

unofficial /ˌʌnə'fɪʃəl/ adj. неофициа́льный.

unorganized /ʌn'ɔrgə,naizd/ adj. неорганизо́ванный.

unoriginal /ˌʌnə'rɪdʒənl/ adj. неоригина́льный.

unorthodox /ʌn'ɔrθə,dɒks/ adj. неортодокса́льный.

unostentatious /ˌʌnɒstən'teiʃəs/ adj. ненавя́зчивый; скро́мный.

unpack /ʌn'pæk/ v. распако́вывать(ся) impf.

unpaid /ʌn'peid/ adj. неопла́ченный.

unpalatable /ʌn'pælətəbəl/ adj. невку́сный.

unparalleled /ʌn'pærə,lɛld/ adj. беспримéрный.

unpardonable /ʌn'pardn̩əbəl/ adj. непрости́тельный.

unpatriotic /ˌʌnpeitri'ɒtɪk/ adj непатриоти́чный.

unpaved /ʌn'peivd/ adj. немощёный.

unpeopled /ʌn'pipəld/ adj. ненаселённый.

unperturbed /ˌʌnpər'tɜrbd/ adj. невозмути́мый.

unpick /ʌn'pɪk/ v. распа́рывать impf.

unpin /ʌn'pɪn/ v. откалывать impf.

unplanned /ʌn'plænd/ adj. незапланированный.

unpleasant /ʌn'plɛzənt/ adj. неприя́тный.

unpleasantness /ʌn'plɛzəntnɪs/ n. неприя́тность f.

unplug /ʌn'plʌg/ v. вы́дернуть ви́лку; разъедини́ть pf.

unplumbed /ʌn'plʌmd/ adj неизмéримый.

unpopular /ʌn'pɒpyələr/ adj. непопуля́рный.

unpopularity /ˌʌnpɒpyə'læriti/ n. непопуля́рность f.

unpractical /ʌn'præktɪkəl/ adj. непракти́чный.

unprecedented /ʌn'prɛsɪ,dɛntɪd/ adj. беспрецеде́нтный.

unprejudiced /ʌn'prɛdʒədɪst/ adj. непредубеждённый.

unprepared /ˌʌnprɪ'pɛərd/ adj. неподгото́вленный.

unprepossessing /ˌʌnpripə'zɛsɪŋ/ adj. непривлека́тельный.

unpretentious /ˌʌnprɪ'tɛnʃəs/ adj. непретенцио́зный.

unprincipled /ʌn'prɪnsəpəld/ adj. беспринци́пный.

unprintable /ʌn'prɪntəbəl/ adj. нецензу́рный.

unproductive /ˌʌnprə'dʌktɪv/ adj. непродукти́вный.

unprofessional /ˌʌnprə'fɛʃənl/ adj. непрофессиона́льный.

unprofitable /ʌn'prɒfɪtəbəl/ adj. неприбыльный; убы́точный.

unpromising /ʌn'prɒməsɪŋ/ adj. малообеща́ющий.

unpronounceable /ˌʌnprə'naunsəbəl/ adj. непроизноси́мый.

unprotected /ˌʌnprə'tɛktɪd/ adj. незащищённый.

unprovable /ʌn'pruvəbəl/ adj. недоказу́емый.

unprovided /ˌʌnprə'vaidɪd/ adj. необеспéченный.

unprovoked /ˌʌnprə'voukt/ adj. неспровоци́рованный.

unpublished /ʌn'pʌblɪʃt/ adj. неопубликóванный.

unqualified /ʌn'kwɒlə,faid/ adj. не имéющий квалифика́ции.

unquestionable /ʌn'kwɛstʃənəbəl/ adj. несомнéнный.

unquestioned /ʌn'kwɛstʃənd/ adj. несомнéнный.

unquestioning /ʌn'kwɛstʃənɪŋ/ adj. беспрекосло́вный.

unquiet /ʌn'kwaiɪt/ adj. беспокóйный.

unquotable /ʌn'kwoutəbəl/ adj. нецензу́рный.

unravel /ʌn'rævəl/ v. распу́тывать impf.

unreachable /ʌn'ritʃəbəl/ adj. недостижи́мый.

unreadable /ʌn'ridəbəl/ adj. нечита́емый; нечита́бельный.

unready /ʌn'rɛdi/ adj. негото́вый.

unreal /ʌn'riəl/ adj. ненастоя́щий; нереа́льный.

unreality /ˌʌnri'æliti/ n. нереа́льность f.

unreason /ʌn'rizən/ n. безýмие neut.

unreasonable /ʌn'rizənəbəl/ adj. безрассýдный; неопра́вданный.

unreasoning /ʌn'rizənɪŋ/ adj. неразу́мный.

unrecognizable /ʌn'rɛkəg,naizəbəl/ adj. неузнава́емый.

unrecognized /ʌn'rɛkəg,naizd/ adj непри́знанный.

unrehearsed /ˌʌnrɪ'hɜrst/ adj. неподгото́вленный.

unrelenting /ˌʌnrɪ'lɛntɪŋ/ adj. неумоли́мый.

unreliability /ˌʌnrɪ,laiə'bɪlɪti/ n. ненадёжность f.

unreliable /ˌʌnrɪ'laiəbəl/ adj. ненадёжный.

unrelieved /ˌʌnrɪ'livd/ adj. неотсту́пный.

unremarkable /ˌʌnrɪ'markəbəl/ adj. заурядный.

unremitting /ˌʌnrɪ'mɪtɪŋ/ adj. неосла́бный.

unrepeatable /ˌʌnrɪ'pitəbəl/ adj. неповтори́мый.

unrepentant /ˌʌnrɪ'pɛntənt/ adj. нераска́янный.

unrequited /ˌʌnrɪ'kwaitɪd/ adj. (not reciprocated) безотвéтный; (unpaid) неопла́ченный.

unreserved /ˌʌnrɪ'zɜrvd/ adj. (seat, etc.) незаброни́рованный; (unconditional) безогово́рочный.

unresponsive /ˌʌnrɪ'spɒnsɪv/ adj. неотзы́вчивый.

unrest /ʌn'rɛst/ n. волнéние neut.

unrestrained /ˌʌnrɪ'streind/ adj. несдéржанный.

unrestricted /ˌʌnrɪ'strɪktɪd/ adj. неограни́ченный.

unriddle /ʌn'rɪdl̩/ v. разгадáть impf.

unrig /ʌn'rɪg/ v. разоружáть impf.

unrighteous /ʌn'raitʃəs/ adj. непра́ведный.

unripe /ʌn'raip/ adj. неспéлый.

unrivaled /ʌn'raivəld/ adj. несравнéнный.

unroll /ʌn'roul/ v. развёртывать(ся) impf.

unromantic /ˌʌnrou'mæntɪk/ adj. неромантич́ный.

unruffled /ʌn'rʌfəld/ adj. гла́дкий.

unruly /ʌn'ruli/ adj. непокóрный; непослу́шный.

unsaddle /ʌn'sædl̩/ v. рассéдлывать impf.

unsafe /ʌn'seif/ adj. ненадёжный; опáсный.

unsaid /ʌn'sɛd/ adj. невы́сказанный.

unsalaried /ʌn'sælərid/ adj. внештáтный.

unsaleable /ʌn'seiləbəl/ adj. нехóдкий.

unsanitary /ʌn'sæni,tɛri/ adj. негигиени́чный; антисанитáрный.

unsatisfactory /ˌʌnsætɪs'fæktəri/ adj. неудовлетвори́тельный.

unsatisfied /ʌn'sætɪs,faid/ adj. неудовлетворённый.

unsaturated /ʌn'sætʃə,reitɪd/ adj. ненасыщенный.

unsavory /ʌn'seivəri/ adj. (dubious) сомнительный.

unscathed /ʌn'skeiðd/ adj. невредимый.

unscholarly /ʌn'skɒlərli/ adj. ненаучный.

unscientific /,ʌnsaiən'tɪfɪk/ adj. ненаучный.

unscramble /ʌn'skræmbəl/ v. распутывать impf.

unscrew /ʌn'skru/ v. вывинчивать impf.

unscrupulous /ʌn'skrupyələs/ adj. бессовестный; беспринципный.

unseal /ʌn'sil/ v. распечатывать impf.

unseasonable /ʌn'sizənəbəl/ adj. не по сезону; неблаговременный.

unseat /ʌn'sit/ v. (unhorse) сбрасывать с седла impf.; (remove from office) лишать должности impf.

unseaworthy /ʌn'si,wɜrði/ adj. неморёходный.

unseemly /ʌn'simli/ adj. неприличный; неподобающий.

unseen /ʌn'sin/ adj. невидимый.

unselfish /ʌn'sɛlfɪʃ/ adj. бескорыстный.

unserviceable /ʌn'sɜrvɪsəbəl/ adj. вышедший из строя; бесполезный.

unsettle /ʌn'sɛtl/ v. выбивать из колеи; расстраивать impf.

unsettling /ʌn'sɛtlɪŋ/ adj. беспокоящий.

unshackle /ʌn'ʃækəl/ v. расковывать impf.

unshaven /ʌn'ʃeivən/ adj. небритый.

unsheathe /ʌn'ʃið/ v. вынимать из ножен impf.

unshod /ʌn'ʃɒd/ adj. неподкованный.

unshrinkable /ʌn'ʃrɪŋkəbəl/ adj. безусадочный.

unsightly /ʌn'saitli/ adj. непривлекательный.

unskilled /ʌn'skɪld/ adj. неквалифицированный.

unskillful /ʌn'skɪlfəl/ adj. неумелый.

unsleeping /ʌn'slipɪŋ/ adj. недремлющий.

unsociable /ʌn'souʃəbəl/ adj. необщительный; нелюдимый.

unsolder /ʌn'sɒdər/ v. распаивать impf.

unsolicited /,ʌnsə'lɪsɪtɪd/ adj. непрошеный.

unsolved /ʌn'sɒlvd/ adj. нерешённый.

unsophisticated /,ʌnsə'fɪstɪ,keitɪd/ adj. простодушный.

unsought /ʌn'sɔt/ adj. непрошеный.

unsound /ʌn'saund/ adj. нездоровый.

unsparing /ʌn'spɛərɪŋ/ adj. беспощадный.

unspeakable /ʌn'spikəbəl/ adj. невыразимый.

unspecified /ʌn'spɛsə,faid/ adj. неназванный.

unspent /ʌn'spɛnt/ adj. неистраченный.

unspoilt /ʌn'spɔilt/ adj. неиспорченный.

unspoken /ʌn'spoukən/ adj. невысказанный.

unsportsmanlike /ʌn'spɔrtsmən,laik/ adj. неспортивный.

unstable /ʌn'steibəl/ adj. неустойчивый.

unstained /ʌn'steind/ adj. незапятнанный.

unsteady /ʌn'stɛdi/ adj. шаткий.

unstinting /,ʌn'stɪntɪŋ/ adj. безоговорочный.

unstitch /ʌn'stɪtʃ/ v. распарывать impf.

unstop /ʌn'stɒp/ v. (bottle, etc.) откупоривать impf.

unstrained /ʌn'streind/ adj. нескованный.

unstudied /ʌn'stʌdid/ adj. неизученный.

unsubstantial /,ʌnsəb'stænʃəl/ adj. несущественный.

unsuccessful /,ʌnsək'sɛsfəl/ adj. безуспешный; неудачный.

unsuitable /ʌn'sutəbəl/ adj. неподходящий.

unsuited /ʌn'sutɪd/ adj. непригодный.

unsullied /ʌn'sʌlid/ adj. незамаранный.

unsung /ʌn'sʌŋ/ adj. невоспётый.

unsure /ʌn'ʃʊr/ adj. неуверенный.

unsuspected /,ʌnsə'spɛktɪd/ adj. непредвиденный.

unsuspecting /,ʌnsə'spɛktɪŋ/ adj. неподозревающий.

unswerving /ʌn'swɜrvɪŋ/ adj. непоколебимый.

unsympathetic /,ʌnsɪmpə'θɛtɪk/ adj. несочувствующий.

unsystematic /,ʌnsɪstə'mætɪk/ adj. несистематический.

untalented /ʌn'tæləntɪd/ adj. бездарный.

untamed /ʌn'teimd/ adj. неприрученный.

untangle /ʌn'tæŋgəl/ v. распутывать impf.

untapped /ʌn'tæpt/ adj. неиспользованный.

untenable /ʌn'tɛnəbəl/ adj. несостоятельный.

untended /ʌn'tɛndɪd/ adj. заброшенный.

unthinkable /ʌn'θɪŋkəbəl/ adj. немыслимый.

unthinking /ʌn'θɪŋkɪŋ/ adj. легкомысленный.

untidiness /ʌn'taidinɪs/ n. неопрятность f.

untidy /ʌn'taidi/ adj. неопрятный.

untie /ʌn'tai/ v. развязывать impf., развязать pf.

until /ʌn'tɪl/ **1.** prep. до (with gen.); **not until** не раньше (with gen.). **2.** conj. пока... не.

untimely /ʌn'taimli/ adj. (premature) преждевременный.

untiring /ʌn'taiərɪŋ/ adj. неутомимый.

untold /ʌn'tould/ adj. (incalculable) несметный.

untouchable /ʌn'tʌtʃəbəl/ adj. неприкасаемый.

untouched /ʌn'tʌtʃt/ adj. нетронутый.

untoward /ʌn'tɔrd/ adj. неблагоприятный.

untrained /ʌn'treind/ adj. необученный.

untraveled /ʌn'trævəld/ adj. неизведанный.

untried /ʌn'traid/ adj. неиспытанный.

untrod /ʌn'trɒd/ adj. нехоженый.

untroubled /ʌn'trʌbəld/ adj. спокойный.

untrue /ʌn'tru/ adj. неверный.

untrustworthy /ʌn'trʌst,wɜrði/ adj. не заслуживающий доверия.

untruth /ʌn'truθ/ n. неправда f.

untruthful /ʌn'truθfəl/ adj. лживый; неправдивый.

untwine /ʌn'twain/ v. расплетать(ся) impf.

untwist /ʌn'twɪst/ v. раскручивать(ся) impf.

unusable /ʌn'yuzəbəl/ adj. непригодный.

unused /ʌn'yuzd/ adj. (not used) неиспользованный.

unusual /ʌn'yuʒuəl/ adj. необыкновенный.

unutterable /ʌn'ʌtərəbəl/ adj. невыразимый.

unvarnished /ʌn'vɑrnɪʃt/ adj. нелакированный.

unvarying /ʌn'vɛərɪŋ/ adj. неизменный.

unveil /ʌn'veil/ v. раскрывать impf.

unversed /ʌn'vɜrst/ adj. неопытный.

unvoiced /ʌn'vɔist/ adj. (phon.) глухой.

unwanted /ʌn'wɒntɪd/ adj. нежелательный; ненужный.

unwarlike /ʌn'wɔr,laik/ adj. невоинственный.

unwary /ʌn'wɛəri/ adj. неосторожный.

unwashed /ʌn'wɒʃt/ adj. немытый.

unwavering /ʌn'weivərɪŋ/ adj. непоколебимый.

unwelcome /ʌn'wɛlkəm/ *adj.* неприя́тный; неже-ла́тельный.

unwell /ʌn'wɛl/ *adj.* нездоро́вый.

unwholesome /ʌn'houlsəm/ *adj.* вре́дный.

unwieldy /ʌn'wildi/ *adj.* неуклю́жий.

unwilling /ʌn'wɪlɪŋ/ *adj.* неохо́тный; не жела́ю-щий.

unwillingly /ʌn'wɪlɪŋli/ *adv.* неохо́тно, с неохо́-той.

unwind /ʌn'waind/ *v.* разма́тывать(ся) *impf.*

unwinking /ʌn'wɪŋkɪŋ/ *adj.* немига́ющий; бди́-тельный.

unwise /ʌn'waiz/ *adj.* неблагоразу́мный.

unwitting /ʌn'wɪtɪŋ/ *adj.* нево́льный.

unwonted /ʌn'wɔntɪd/ *adj.* непривы́чный.

unworkable /ʌn'wɜrkəbəl/ *adj.* непракти́чный; неприменѝмый.

unworldly /ʌn'wɜrldli/ *adj.* не от мѝра сего́.

unworn /ʌn'wɔrn/ *adj.* нено́шеный.

unworthy /ʌn'wɜrði/ *adj.* недосто́йный.

unwrap /ʌn'ræp/ *v.* развора́чивать(ся); развёр-тывать(ся) *impf.*

unwritten /ʌn'rɪtn̩/ *adj.* (*law*) непѝсаный.

unyielding /ʌn'yildɪŋ/ *adj.* непода́тливый.

unzip /ʌn'zɪp/ *v.* расстёгивать мо́лнию *impf.*

up /ʌp/ **1.** *adv.* (*dir.*) наверху́; вверх; (*loc.*) на-верху́; вы́ше. **2.** *prep.* вверх по; по направ-ле́нию к; вдоль по (*with dat.*).

up-and-coming /'ʌp ən 'kʌmɪŋ/ *adj.* многообе-ща́ющий.

upas /'yupəs/ *n.* (*tree*) анча́р *m.*

upbraid /ʌp'breid/ *v.* упрека́ть *impf.*

upbringing /'ʌp,brɪŋɪŋ/ *n.* воспита́ние *neut.*

upcoming /'ʌp,kʌmɪŋ/ *adj.* предстоя́щий.

upcountry /'ʌp,kʌntri/ *adj.* захолу́стный.

update /ʌp'deit/ *v.* осовреме́нить *pf.*

upend /ʌp'ɛnd/ *v.* опроки́дывать *pf.*

upgrade / *n.* 'ʌp,greid; *v.* ʌp'greid/ **1.** *n.* подъём *m.* **2.** *v.* повыша́ть *impf.*

upheaval /ʌp'hivəl/ *n.* переворо́т *m.*

uphill /'ʌp'hɪl/ *adv.* в го́ру.

uphold /ʌp'hould/ *v.* подде́рживать *impf.*, под-держа́ть *pf.*

upholster /ʌp'houlstər/ *v.* обива́ть *impf.*, обѝть *pf.*

upholstery /ʌp'houlstəri/ *n.* обѝвка *f.*

upkeep /'ʌp,kip/ *n.* содержа́ние *neut.*

upland /'ʌplənd/ *n.* наго́рье *neut.*

uplift /'ʌp,lɪft/ *n.* подъём *m.*

upon /ə'pɒn/ *prep.* (*dir.*) на (*with acc.*); (*loc.*) на (*with prep.*).

upper /'ʌpər/ *adj.* ве́рхний; вы́сший.

uppercase /'ʌpər'keis/ *n.* загла́вная бу́ква *f.*

upper-class /'ʌpər'klæs/ *adj.* вы́сшего о́бщества.

uppercut /'ʌpər,kʌt/ *n.* уда́р снѝзу *m.*; (*boxing*) апперко́т *m.*

uppermost /'ʌpər,moust/ *adj.* са́мый ве́рхий; преоблада́ющий.

uppish /'ʌpɪʃ/ *adj.* (*colloq.*) спесѝвый.

upright /'ʌp,rait/ *adv.* вертика́льно; пря́мо; стой-мя́.

uprising /'ʌp,raizɪŋ/ *n.* восста́ние *neut.*

uproar /'ʌp,rɔr/ *n.* шум *m.*; волне́ние *neut.*

uproarious /ʌp'rɔriəs/ *adj.* шу́мный.

uproot /ʌp'rut/ *v.* вырыва́ть с ко́рнем *impf.*; (*displace*) срыва́ть с ме́ста *impf.*

uprush /'ʌp,rʌʃ/ *n.* поры́в *m.*

upset / *n.* 'ʌp,sɛt; *v.* ʌp'sɛt/ **1.** *n.* расстро́йство *neut.* **2.** *v.* опроки́дывать *impf.*, опроки́нуть *pf.*; (*person*) расстра́ивать *impf.*

upshot /'ʌp,ʃɒt/ *n.* заключе́ние *neut.*

upside down /'ʌpsaid/ *adv.* вверх дном.

upstage /'ʌp'steidʒ/ **1.** *v.* (*colloq.*) затмѝть; пере-щеголя́ть (*with acc.*) *pf.* **2.** *adj.* (*haughty*) высо-коме́рный.

upstairs /'ʌp'stɛərz/ *adv.* (*loc.*) наверху́; (*dir.*) наве́рх; вверх по ле́стнице.

upstanding /ʌp'stændɪŋ/ *adj.* прямо́й.

upstart /'ʌp,stɑrt/ *n.* вы́скочка *m.* and *f.* (*decl. f.*).

upstream /'ʌp'strim/ **1.** *adj.* располо́женный вы́ше по тече́нию. **2.** *adv.* про́тив тече́ния.

upsurge /'ʌp,sɜrdʒ/ *n.* повыше́ние *neut.*

upswing /'ʌp,swɪŋ/ *n.* подъём *m.*

uptight /'ʌp'tait/ *adj.* (*slang*) взви́нченный.

up-to-date /'ʌp tə 'deit/ *adj.* совреме́нный.

upturn /'ʌp,tɜrn/ *n.* подъём *m.*; улучше́ние *neut.*

upturned /'ʌp,tɜrnd/ *adj.* перевёрнутый; вздёр-нутый.

upward /'ʌpwərd/ *adv.* вверх; (*more*) бо́льше.

Ural-Altaic /'yurəl æl'teiik/ *adj.* ура́ло-алта́йский.

Uralsk /yu'rælsk/ *n.* Ура́льск *m.*

uranium /yu'reiniəm/ *n.* ура́н *m.*

uranous /'yurənəs/ *adj.* ура́новый.

Uranus /'yurənəs, yu'rei-/ *n.* Ура́н *m.*

urban /'ɜrbən/ *adj.* городско́й.

urbane /ɜr'bein/ *adj.* обходѝтельный.

urbanity /ɜr'bænɪti/ *n.* обходѝтельность *f.*

urbanization /,ɜrbənə'zeiʃən/ *n.* урбаниза́ция *f.*

urchin /'ɜrtʃɪn/ *n.* мальчѝшка *m.* (*decl. f.*).

Urdu /'ʊrdu/ *n.* у́рду *m.* *indecl.*

urea /yu'riə/ *n.* мочевѝна *f.*

ureter /yu'ritər/ *n.* мочето́чник *m.*

urethane /'yurə,θein/ *n.* урета́н *m.*

urethra /yu'riθrə/ *n.* мочеиспуска́тельный кана́л *m.*; уре́тра *f.*

urethritis /,yurə'θraitɪs/ *n.* уретрѝт *m.*

urge /ɜrdʒ/ **1.** *n.* побужде́ние *neut.* **2.** *v.* под-гоня́ть *impf.*

urgency /'ɜrdʒənsi/ *n.* сро́чность; необходѝ-мость *f.*

urgent /'ɜrdʒənt/ *adj.* сро́чный; настоя́тельный; кра́йне необходѝмый.

urging /'ɜrdʒɪŋ/ *n.* понука́ние *neut.*

uric /'yurɪk/ *adj.* мочево́й.

urinal /'yurənl̩/ *n.* писсуа́р *m.*

urinary /'yurə,nɛri/ *adj.* мочево́й.

urinate /'yurə,neit/ *v.* мочѝться *impf.*

urination /,yurə'neiʃən/ *n.* мочеиспуска́ние *neut.*

urine /'yurɪn/ *n.* моча́ *f.*

urn /ɜrn/ *n.* у́рна *f.*

urogenital /,yurou'dʒenɪtl̩/ *adj.* мочеполово́й.

urologist /yu'rɒlədʒɪst/ *n.* уро́лог *m.*

urology /yu'rɒlədʒi/ *n.* уроло́гия *f.*

Uruguay /'yurə,gwei, ,uru'gwai/ *n.* Уругва́й *m.*

us /ʌs/ *pers. pron.* нас; нам; на́ми.

USA *abbr.* США.

usable /'yuzəbəl/ *adj.* употребля́емый.

usage /'yusidʒ/ *n.* употребле́ние *neut.*

use / *n.* yus; *v.* yuz/ **1.** *n.* употребле́ние *neut.* **2.** *v.* употребля́ть *impf.*, употребѝть *pf.*

used /yuzd/ *adj.* испо́льзованный; (*secondhand*) поде́ржанный.

useful /'yusfəl/ *adj.* поле́зный.

usefulness /'yusfəlnıs/ *n.* полéзность; пóльза *f.*
useless /'yuslıs/ *adj.* бесполéзный.
user /'yuzər/ *n.* потребúтель *m.*
user-friendly /'yuzər 'frɛndli/ *adj.* наибóлее совершéнный в употреблéнии.
usher /'ʌʃər/ *n.* билетёр *m.*
usherette /ˌʌʃə'rɛt/ *n.* билетёрша *f.*
Ust-Kamenogorsk /'ustkəmyınʌ'gɔrsk/ *n.* Усть-Каменогóрск *m.*
usual /'yuʒuəl/ *adj.* обы́чный; обыкновéнный; **as usual** *adv.* как обы́чно.
usurer /'yuʒərər/ *n.* ростовщúк *m.*
usurious /yu'ʒuriəs/ *adj.* ростовщúческий.
usurp /yu'sɜrp/ *v.* узурпúровать *impf.* and *pf.*
usurpation /ˌyusər'peiʃən/ *n.* узурпáция *f.*
Utah /'yutɔ/ *n.* Ю́та *m.*
utensil /yu'tɛnsəl/ *n.* посýда; *pl.* ýтварь *f.*
uterus /'yutərəs/ *n.* мáтка *f.*
utilitarian /yuˌtılı'tɛəriən/ *adj.* утилитáрный.

utilitarianism /yuˌtılı'tɛəriəˌnızəm/ *n.* утилитарúзм *m.*
utility /yu'tılıti/ *n.* полéзность *f.*; *pl.* (домáшние) удóбства *pl.*
utilize /'yutlˌaiz/ *v.* применя́ть *impf.*
utmost /'ʌtˌmoust/ *adj.* крáйний; величáйший.
Utopia /yu'toupiə/ *n.* утóпия *f.*
Utopian /yu'toupiən/ *n.* утопúст *m.*
utter[1] /'ʌtər/ *adj.* совершéнный.
utter[2] /'ʌtər/ *v.* произносúть; издавáть (звук) *impf.*; (*express oneself*) выражáть; выскáзывать *impf.*
utterance /'ʌtərəns/ *n.* выскáзывание *neut.*
U-turn /'yu ˌtɜrn/ *n.* разворóт *m.*
uvula /'yuvyələ/ *n.* язычóк *m.*
uvular /'yuvyələr/ *adj.* увуля́рный.
Uzbek /'ʊzbɛk/ *n.* узбéк *m.*, узбéчка *f.*
Uzbekistan /uz'bɛkəˌstæn/ *n.* Узбекистáн *m.*

V

vacancy /'veikənsi/ n. вакáнсия; пустотá f.
vacant /'veikənt/ adj. пустóй; свобóдный; вакáнтный.
vacate /'veikeit/ v. освобождáть impf.
vacation /vei'keiʃən/ n. канúкулы pl.; óтпуск m.
vacationer /vei'keiʃənər/ n. отдыхáющий.
vaccinate /'væksə,neit/ v. дéлать привúвку impf.
vaccination /,væksə'neiʃən/ n. привúвка f.
vaccine /væk'sin/ n. вакцúна f.
vacillate /'væsə,leit/ v. колебáться (мéжду with instr.) impf.
vacuity /væ'kyuti/ n. пустотá f.
vacuous /'vækyuəs/ adj. пустóй; (stupid) глýпый.
vacuum /'vækyum/ n. безвоздýшное прострáнство neut.; вáкуум m.
vacuum cleaner n. пылесóс m.
vagabond /'vægə,bɒnd/ n. бродя́га m. and f. (decl. f.)
vagary /və'gɛəri, 'veigəri/ n. каприз m.
vagina /və'dʒainə/ n. влагáлище neut.
vagrancy /'veigrənsi/ n. бродя́жничество neut.
vagrant /'veigrənt/ adj. стрáнствующий.
vague /veig/ adj. неопределённый; нея́сный.
vain /vein/ adj. (conceited) тщеслáвный; (futile) тщéтный; in vain adv. напрáсно; тщéтно.
vainglorious /vein'glɔriəs/ adj. тщеслáвный.
valance /'væləns/ n. обóрка f.
vale /veil/ n. долúна f.
valediction /,væli'dikʃən/ n. прощáние neut.
valedictory /,væli'diktəri/ n. прощáльное слóво neut.
valency /'veilənsi/ n. валéнтность f.
valerian /və'liəriən/ n. валерья́нка f.
valet /væ'lei/ n. камердúнер m.; слугá m. (decl. f.).
valiant /'vælyənt/ adj. дóблестный.
valid /'vælid/ adj. имéющий сúлу; действúтельный.
validate /'væli,deit/ v. дéлать действúтельным impf.
validity /və'liditi/ n. действúтельность f.
valise /və'lis/ n. саквоя́ж m.
Valladolid /,vælədə'lid, ,bɑlyɑðɔ'lið/ n. Вальядолúд m.
valley /'væli/ n. долúна f.
valor /'vælər/ n. дóблесть f.
valorous /'vælərəs/ adj. дóблестный.
valuable /'vælyuəbəl/ adj. цéнный.
valuation /,vælyu'eiʃən/ n. оцéнка f.
value /'vælyu/ 1. n. стóимость; цéнность f. 2. v. (treasure) ценúть impf.; (appraise) оцéнивать impf., оценúть pf.
value-added tax /'vælyu 'ædid/ n. налóг на добáвленную стóимость m.
valued /'vælyud/ adj. цéнный.
valueless /'vælyulis/ adj. ничегó не стóящий.
valve /vælv/ n. (tech., mus., anat.) клáпан m.
valvular /'vælvyələr/ adj. клáпанный.
vamoose /væ'mus/ v. (slang) удирáть; смывáться impf.
vampire /'væmpaiᵊr/ n. вампúр; упы́рь m.
van /væn/ n. фургóн m.

vanadium /və'neidiəm/ n. ванáдий m.
Vancouver /væn'kuvər/ n. Ванкýвер m.
vandal /'vændl/ n. вандáл m.
vandalism /'vændl,izəm/ n. вандалúзм m.
vandalize /'vændl,aiz/ v. бессмы́сленно разрушáть impf.
vane /vein/ n. лóпасть f.
vanguard /'væn,gɑrd/ n. авангáрд m.
vanilla /və'nilə/ 1. n. ванúль 2. adj. ванúльный.
vanish /'væniʃ/ v. исчезáть impf., исчéзнуть pf.
vanity /'væniti/ n. тщеслáвие neut.; суетá f.
vanquish /'væŋkwiʃ/ v. побеждáть impf., победúть pf.; покоря́ть impf., покорúть pf.
vantage /'væntidʒ/ n. преимýщество neut.
vapid /'væpid/ adj. безвкýсный; скýчный; вя́лый.
vapor /'veipər/ n. пар m.
vaporization /,veipərə'zeiʃən/ n. испарéние neut.
vaporize /'veipə,raiz/ v. испаря́ть(ся) impf.
vaporizer /'veipə,raizər/ n. атомизáтор m.
vaporous /'veipərəs/ adj. парообрáзный.
variable /'vɛəriəbəl/ 1. n. (math.) перемéнная f. 2. adj. измéнчивый; (also math., sci.) перемéнный.
variance /'vɛəriəns/ n. изменéние neut.
variant /'vɛəriənt/ 1. n. вариáнт m. 2. adj. рáзный.
variation /,vɛəri'eiʃən/ n. изменéние neut., перемéна f., (also mus.) вариáция f.
varicolored /'vɛəri,kʌlərd/ adj. разноцвéтный.
varied /'vɛərid/ adj. разлúчный; рáзный.
variegated /'vɛəri,geitid/ adj. (color) разноцвéтный, пёстрый; (in kind) разнообрáзный.
variety /və'raiiti/ n. разнообрáзие neut.
variform /'vɛərə,fɔrm/ adj. многообрáзный.
variola /və'raiələ/ n. óспа f.
variometer /,vɛəri'ɒmitər/ n. вариóметр m.
various /'vɛəriəs/ adj. рáзный; разлúчный.
variously /'vɛəriəsli/ adv. по-рáзному.
varnish /'vɑrniʃ/ 1. n. лак 2. v. лакировáть impf.
varnisher /'vɑrniʃər/ n. лакирóвщик m.
vary /'vɛəri/ v. меня́ть(ся); изменя́ть(ся) impf., изменúть(ся) pf.
varying /'vɛəriiŋ/ adj. перемéнный.
vascular /'væskyələr/ adj. сосýдистый.
vase /veis, veiz, vɑz/ n. вáза f.
vasomotor /,væsou'moutər/ adj. вазомотóрный.
vassal /'væsəl/ 1. n. вассáл m. 2. adj. вассáльный.
vast /væst/ adj. обшúрный; огрóмный.
vat /væt/ n. чан; бак m.
vaudeville /'vɔdvil/ n. водевúль m.
vault /vɔlt/ n. свод; подвáл; склеп m.
vaulted /'vɔltid/ adj. свóдчатый.
vaulter /'vɔltər/ n. прыгýн m.
vaunt /vɔnt/ v. превозносúть impf.
VDU n. дисплéй m.
veal /vil/ 1. n. теля́тина f. 2. adj. теля́чий.
vector /'vɛktər/ n. вéктор m.
vectorial /vɛk'tɔriəl/ adj. вéкторный.
Veda /'veidə/ n. Вéда f.
Vedanta /vi'dɑntə/ n. Ведáнта f.

vedette /vɪ'dɛt/ *n.* ко́нный часово́й *m.*
veer /vɪər/ *v.* меня́ть направле́ние *impf.*; повер-
ну́ть *pf.*
vegetable /'vɛdʒtəbəl/ **1.** *n.* о́вощ *m.* **2.** *adj.*
овощно́й; расти́тельный.
vegetable garden, *n.* огоро́д *m.*
vegetarian /ˌvɛdʒɪ'tɛəriən/ *n.* вегетариа́нец *m.*,
вегетариа́нка *f.*
vegetarianism /ˌvɛdʒɪ'tɛəriəˌnɪzəm/ *n.* вегетари-
а́нство *neut.*
vegetate /'vɛdʒɪˌteit/ *v.* расти́ *impf.*; (*be passive*)
прозяба́ть *impf.*
vegetation /ˌvɛdʒɪ'teiʃən/ *n.* расти́тельность *f.*
vegetative /'vɛdʒɪˌteitɪv/ *adj.* расти́тельный.
vehemence /'viəməns/ *n.* си́ла; стра́стность *f.*
vehement /'viəmənt/ *adj.* нейстовый.
vehicle /'viːkəl/ *n.* (*motor vehicle*) маши́на *f.*;
перево́зочное сре́дство *neut.*; (*fig.*) сре́дство
neut.
veil /veil/ **1.** *n.* вуа́ль *f.* **2.** *v.* скрыва́ть *impf.*,
скрыть *pf.*
vein /vein/ *n.* ве́на; жи́ла; жи́лка *f.*
velar /'vilər/ *n.* веля́рный звук *m.*
Velcro /'vɛlkrou/ *n.* липу́чка *f.*
vellum /'vɛləm/ *n.* перга́мент *m.*
velocity /və'lɒsɪti/ *n.* ско́рость *f.*
velvet /'vɛlvɪt/ **1.** *n.* ба́рхат *m.* **2.** *adj.* ба́рхат-
ный.
velveteen /ˌvɛlvɪ'tin/ *n.* вельве́т *m.*
velvety /'vɛlvɪti/ *adj.* бархати́стый.
venal /'vinl/ *adj.* прода́жный.
venality /vi'nælɪti/ *n.* прода́жность *f.*
vend /vɛnd/ *v.* продава́ть *impf.*
vendetta /vɛn'dɛtə/ *n.* венде́тта *f.*
vending machine /'vɛndɪŋ/ *n.* (торго́вый) авто-
ма́т *m.*
vendor /'vɛndər/ *n.* продаве́ц; торго́вец *m.*
veneer /və'nɪər/ *n.* фане́ра *f.*
veneering /və'nɪərɪŋ/ *n.* фане́рная рабо́та *f.*
venerable /'vɛnərəbəl/ *adj.* почте́нный; (*ancient*)
дре́вний.
venerate /'vɛnəˌreit/ благогове́ть *impf.*
veneration /ˌvɛnə'reiʃən/ *n.* преклоне́ние *neut.*
venereal disease /və'nɪəriəl/ *n.* венери́ческое за-
болева́ние *neut.*
Venetian /və'niʃən/ *n.* венециа́нец *m.*, венеци-
а́нка *f.*
venetian blind *n.* жалюзи́ *neut.* indecl.
Venezuela /ˌvɛnə'zweilə/ *n.* Венесуэ́ла *f.*
vengeance /'vɛndʒəns/ *n.* месть *f.*; мще́ние *neut.*
vengeful /'vɛndʒfəl/ *adj.* мсти́тельный.
venial /'viniəl/ *adj.* прости́тельный.
Venice /'vɛnɪs/ *n.* Вене́ция *f.*
venison /'vɛnəsən/ *n.* оленина *f.*
venom /'vɛnəm/ *n.* яд *m.*; зло́ба *f.*
venous /'vinəs/ *adj.* вено́зный.
vent /vɛnt/ *n.* отду́шина *f.*; отве́рстие *neut.*;
вы́ход *m.*
ventilate /'vɛntlˌeit/ *v.* прове́тривать *impf.*,
прове́трить *pf.*
ventilation /ˌvɛntl'eiʃən/ *n.* прове́тривание *neut.*
ventilator /'vɛntlˌeitər/ *n.* вентиля́тор *m.*
ventral /'vɛntrəl/ *adj.* брюшно́й; вентра́льный.
ventricle /'vɛntrɪkəl/ *n.* желу́дочек *m.*
ventricular /vɛn'trɪkyələr/ *adj.* желу́дочковый.
ventriloquist /vɛn'trɪləkwɪst/ *n.* чревовеща́тель
m.

venture /'vɛntʃər/ *n.* риско́ванное предприя́тие
neut.
venturesome /'vɛntʃərsəm/ *adj.* сме́лый; пред-
прий́мчивый.
venue /'vɛnyu/ *n.* (*leg.*) ме́сто рассмотре́ния
де́ла *neut.*; суде́бный о́круг *m.*
Venus /'vinəs/ *n.* Вене́ра *f.*
veracious /və'reiʃəs/ *adj.* правди́вый.
veracity /və'ræsɪti/ *n.* достове́рность *f.*
veranda /və'rændə/ *n.* вера́нда *f.*
verb /vзrb/ **1.** *n.* глаго́л *m.* **2.** *adj.* глаго́льный.
verbal /'vзrbəl/ *adj.* у́стный; (*gram.*) глаго́ль-
ный.
verbal adverb *n.* дееприча́стие *neut.*
verbalize /'vзrbəˌlaiz/ *v.* выража́ть слова́ми
impf.
verbal noun *n.* отглаго́льное существи́тельное
neut.
verbatim /vər'beitɪm/ *adj.* досло́вный.
verbena /vər'binə/ *n.* вербе́на *f.*
verbiage /'vзrbiidʒ/ *n.* пустосло́вие *neut.*
verbose /vər'bous/ *adj.* многосло́вный.
verbosity /vər'bɒsiti/ *n.* многосло́вие *f.*
verdant /'vзrdn̩t/ *adj.* зелёный.
verdict /'vзrdɪkt/ *n.* верди́кт; пригово́р *m.*;
реше́ние *neut.*
verdigris /'vзrdɪˌgris/ *n.* ярь-медя́нка *f.*
verdure /'vзrdʒər/ *n.* зе́лень *f.*
verge /vзrdʒ/ *n.* край *m.*
verifiable /'vɛrəˌfaiəbəl/ *adj.* доказу́емый.
verification /ˌvɛrəfɪ'keiʃən/ *n.* прове́рка; вериф-
ика́ция *f.*
verify /'vɛrəˌfai/ *v.* проверя́ть *impf.*, прове́рить
pf.
verisimilitude /ˌvɛrəsɪ'mɪlɪˌtud/ *n.* правдоподо́-
бие *neut.*
veritable /'vɛrɪtəbəl/ *adj.* настоя́щий; и́стинный.
verity /'vɛrɪti/ *n.* и́стина *f.*
vermicelli /ˌvзrmɪ'tʃɛli/ *n.* вермише́ль *f.*
vermicide /'vзrməˌsaid/ *n.* глистого́нное *neut.*
vermiculite /vər'mɪkyəˌlait/ *n.* вермикули́т *m.*
vermiform /'vзrməˌfɔrm/ *adj.* червеобра́зный.
vermifuge /'vзrməˌfyudʒ/ *n.* глистого́нное *neut.*
vermilion /vər'mɪlyən/ *adj.* а́лый; пунцо́вый.
vermin /'vзrmɪn/ *n.* парази́ты *pl.*
Vermont /vər'mɒnt/ *n.* Вермо́нт *m.*
vermouth /vər'muθ/ *n.* ве́рмут *m.*
vernacular /vər'nækyələr/ *n.* (*local dialect*) го́вор
m.; наре́чие *neut.*; (*popular speech*) простторе́чие
neut.
vernal /'vзrnl̩/ *adj.* весе́нний.
Verona /və'rounə/ *n.* Веро́на *f.*
veronica /və'rɒnɪkə/ *n.* верони́ка дубра́вная *f.*
verruca /və'rukə/ *n.* борода́вка *f.*
Versailles /vɛr'sai/ *n.* Верса́ль *m.*
versatile /'vзrsətl̩/ *adj.* многосторо́нний.
versatility /ˌvзrsə'tɪlɪti/ *n.* многосторо́нность *f.*
verse /vзrs/ *n.* (*stanza*) строфа́ *f.*; (*line of poetry*)
стих *m.*; (*poetry*) стихи́ *pl.*
versed /vзrst/ *adj.* све́дущий (в *with prep.*).
versification /ˌvзrsəfɪ'keiʃən/ *n.* версифика́ция *f.*
versifier /'vзrsəˌfaiər/ *n.* версифика́тор *m.*
versify /'vзrsəˌfai/ *v.* перелага́ть в стихи́ *impf.*
version /'vзrʒən/ *n.* ве́рсия *f.*; вариа́нт *m.*
verst /vзrst/ *n.* верста́ *f.*
versus /'vзrsəs/ *prep.* про́тив (*with gen.*).

vertebra /'vɜrtəbrə/ n. позвонóк m.; pl. позвонóчник m.

vertebrate /'vɜrtəbrɪt/ n. позвонóчное (живóтное) neut.

vertex /'vɜrtɛks/ n. вершина f.

vertical /'vɜrtɪkəl/ adj. вертикáльный.

verticality /ˌvɜrtɪ'kælɪti/ n. вертикáльность f.

vertiginous /vər'tɪdʒənəs/ adj. головокружительный.

vertigo /'vɜrtɪˌgou/ n. головокружéние neut.

verve /vɜrv/ n. живость f.

very /'vɛri/ **1.** adj. тот сáмый. **2.** adv. óчень.

vespers /'vɛspərz/ n. Вечéрня f.

vespiary /'vɛspiˌɛri/ n. осиное гнездó neut.

vessel /'vɛsəl/ n. (container; also anat.) сосýд m.; (ship) сýдно neut.

vest /vɛst/ n. жилéт m.

vestal virgin /'vɛst|/ n. вестáлка f.

vested /'vɛstɪd/ adj. закóнный.

vestibule /'vɛstəˌbyul/ n. перéдняя f.; вестибюль m.

vestige /'vɛstɪdʒ/ n. след; остáток m.

vestigial /vɛ'stɪdʒiəl/ adj. остáточный; рудиментáрный.

vestment /'vɛstmənt/ n. usu. pl. облачéние neut.

vest-pocket /'vɛst ˌpɒkɪt/ adj. кармáнный.

vestry /'vɛstri/ n. ризница f.

Vesuvius /və'suviəs/ n. (volcano) Везýвий m.

vet /vɛt/ n. (colloq.) ветеринáр m.

vetch /vɛtʃ/ n. вика f.

veteran /'vɛtərən/ n. ветерáн m.

veterinarian /ˌvɛtərə'nɛəriən/ n. ветеринáр m.

veterinary /'vɛtərəˌnɛri/ adj. ветеринáрный.

veto /'vitou/ **1.** n. вéто neut. indecl. **2.** v. налагáть вéто (на with acc.) impf.

vex /vɛks/ v. раздражáть impf., раздражить pf.

vexation /vɛk'seiʃən/ n. досáда f.

vexatious /vɛk'seiʃəs/ also **vexing** /'vɛksɪŋ/ adj. досáдный.

vexed /vɛkst/ adj. раздражённый.

via /'vaiə, 'viə/ prep. чéрез (with acc.).

viability /ˌvaiə'bɪlɪti/ n. жизнеспосóбность f.

viable /'vaiəbəl/ adj. жизнеспосóбный.

viaduct /'vaiəˌdʌkt/ n. виадýк m.

vial /'vaiəl/ n. пузырёк m.

vibraharp /'vaibrəˌhɑrp/ n. вибрафóн m.

vibrant /'vaibrənt/ adj. вибрирующий; (lively) живóй.

vibrate /'vaibreit/ v. вибрировать impf.

vibration /vai'breiʃən/ n. вибрáция f.

vibrator /'vaibreitər/ n. вибрáтор m.

vicar /'vɪkər/ n. викáрий m.

vicarage /'vɪkərɪdʒ/ adj. дом свящéнника.

vicarious /vai'kɛəriəs/ adj. замещáющий другóго.

vice /vais/ n. порóк m.

vice president n. вице-президéнт m.

viceregal /vais'rigəl/ adj. вице-королéвский.

viceroy /'vaisrɔi/ n. вице-корóль m.

vice versa /'vai'sə vɜrsə, 'vais/ adv. наоборóт.

vicinity /vɪ'sɪnɪti/ n. окрéстности pl.

vicious /'vɪʃəs/ adj. порóчный; злой.

viciousness /'vɪʃəsnɪs/ n. порóчность; жестóкость f.

vicissitude /vɪ'sɪsɪˌtud/ n. преврáтность f.

victim /'vɪktɪm/ n. жéртва f.

victimization /ˌvɪktəmə'zeiʃən/ n. преслéдование neut.

victimize /'vɪktəˌmaiz/ v. преслéдовать impf.

victor /'vɪktər/ n. победитель m.

victorious /vɪk'tɔriəs/ adj. победонóсный.

victory /'vɪktəri/ n. побéда f.

victual /'vɪtl/ n. usu. pl. яства pl.

victualer /'vɪtlər/ n. поставщик продовóльствия m.

videlicet /vɪ'dɛləsɪt, wɪ'deilɪˌkɛt/ adv. а именно.

video /'vɪdiˌou/ n. видео neut. indecl.; (TV) телевидение neut.

videocassette recorder /'vɪdioukə'sɛt/ n. видеопристáвка f.

video game n. игрá-аттракциóн m.

videotape /'vɪdiouˌteip/ n. видеокассéта f.

videotape recorder n. видеомагнитофóн m.

vie /vai/ v. сопéрничать (с with instr.) impf.; (compete) состязáться impf.

Vienna /vi'ɛnə/ n. Вéна f.

Vietnam /vi ɛt'nam/ n. Вьетнáм m.

Vietnamese /viˌɛtnɑ'miz/ **1.** adj. вьетнáмский **2.** n. вьетнáмец m., вьетнáмка f.

view /vyu/ **1.** n. вид m.; (opinion) взгляд m.; **in view of** ввидý (with gen.). **2.** v. осмáтривать impf.

viewfinder /'vyuˌfaindər/ n. видоискáтель m.

viewpoint /'vyuˌpɔint/ n. тóчка зрéния f.

vigil /'vɪdʒəl/ n. бóдрствование neut.

vigilant /'vɪdʒələnt/ adj. бдительный.

vignette /vin'yet/ n. виньéтка f.

vigor /'vɪgər/ n. энéргия; сила f.

vigorous /'vɪgərəs/ adj. энергичный; сильный.

vile /vail/ adj. пóдлый.

vileness /'vailnɪs/ n. пóдлость f.

vilification /ˌvɪləfɪ'keiʃən/ n. поношéние neut.

vilify /'vɪləˌfai/ v. клеветáть impf.

villa /'vɪlə/ n. вилла f.

village /'vɪlɪdʒ/ **1.** n. дерéвня f.; селó neut. **2.** adj. деревéнский; сéльский.

villager /'vɪlɪdʒər/ n. деревéнский жи́тель m.

villain /'vɪlən/ n. негодяй; злодéй m.

villainous /'vɪlənəs/ adj. злодéйский.

villainy /'vɪləni/ n. злодéйство neut.; престýпность f.

Vilnius /'vɪlniˌus/ n. Вильнюс.

vim /vɪm/ n. энéргия f.

vinaigrette /ˌvɪnə'gret/ n. (dressing) сóус для салáта m.

vinculum /'vɪŋkyələm/ n. объединяющая чертá f.

vindicate /'vɪndɪˌkeit/ v. опрáвдывать impf., оправдáть pf.

vindication /ˌvɪndɪ'keiʃən/ n. оправдáние neut.

vindicatory /'vɪndɪkəˌtɔri/ adj. опрáвдывающий.

vindictive /vɪn'dɪktɪv/ adj. мстительный.

vindictiveness /vɪn'dɪktɪvnɪs/ n. мстительность f.

vine /vain/ n. виногрáдная лозá f.; ползýчее растéние neut.

vinegar /'vɪnɪgər/ n. ýксус m.

vinegary /'vɪnɪgəri/ adj. ýксусный; кислый.

vinery /'vainəri/ n. виногрáдная теплица f.

vineyard /'vɪnyərd/ n. виногрáдник m.

viniculture /'vɪniˌkʌltʃər/ n. виногрáдарство neut.

Vinnytsya /'vɪnitsə/ n. Винница f.

vinous /'vainəs/ adj. винный.

vintage /'vintidʒ/ n. урожа́й (виногра́да) m.
vinyl /'vainl/ n. вини́л m.
viol /'vaiəl/ n. вио́ла f.
viola¹ /'vaiələ/ n. (bot.) фиа́лка f.
viola² /vi'oulə/ n. (mus.) альт m.
violate /'vaiə‚leit/ v. наруша́ть impf., нару́шить pf.
violation /‚vaiə'leiʃən/ n. наруше́ние neut.
violator /'vaiə‚leitər/ n. наруши́тель m.
violence /'vaiələns/ n. наси́лие; неи́стовство neut.
violent /'vaiələnt/ adj. неи́стовый; наси́льственный.
violet /'vaiəlit/ 1. n. (bot.) фиа́лка f.; (color) фиоле́товый цвет m. 2. adj. фиоле́товый.
violin /‚vaiə'lin/ 1. n. скри́пка f. 2. adj. скрипи́чный.
violinist /‚vaiə'linist/ n. скрипа́ч m., скрипа́чка f.
violoncellist /‚viələn'tʃelist/ n. виолончели́ст m., виолончели́стка f.
violoncello /‚viələn'tʃelou/ adj. виолончель.
viper /'vaipər/ n. гадю́ка; змея́ f.
viperish /'vaipəriʃ/ adj. гадю́чий.
virgin /'vɜrdʒin/ 1. n. де́вственник m., де́вственница f. 2. adj. де́вственный.
Virginia /vər'dʒinyə/ n. Вирги́ния f.
Virgo /'vɜrgou/ n. (myth., astr.) Де́ва f.
viridescent /‚viri'desənt/ adj. зеленова́тый.
virile /'virəl/ adj. возмужа́лый; му́жественный.
virility /və'riliti/ n. возмужа́лость; му́жественность f.
virology /vai'rolədʒi/ n. вирусоло́гия f.
virtual /'vɜrtʃuəl/ 1. adj. действи́тельный; факти́ческий. 2. adv. факти́чески; в су́щности.
virtue /'vɜrtʃu/ n. доброде́тель f.
virtuosity /‚vɜrtʃu'ositi/ n. виртуо́зность f.
virtuoso /‚vɜrtʃu'ousou/ n. виртуо́з m.
virtuous /'vɜrtʃuəs/ adj. доброде́тельный.
virulence /'viryələns/ n. вируле́нтность f.
virus /'vairəs/ n. ви́рус m.
visa /'vizə/ n. ви́за f.
visage /'vizidʒ/ n. лицо́ neut.
viscera /'visərə/ n. вну́тренности pl.; (animal) потроха́ pl.
visceral /'visərəl/ adj. висцера́льный.
viscometer /vi'skomitər/ n. вискозиме́тр m.
viscose /'viskous/ n. виско́за f.
viscosity /vi'skositi/ n. вя́зкость f.
viscount /'vai‚kaunt/ n. вико́нт m.
viscountess /'vai‚kauntis/ n. виконте́сса f.
viscous /'viskəs/ adj. (sticky) ли́пкий; кле́йкий; вя́зкий.
vise /vais/ n. тиски́ pl.
visibility /‚vizə'biliti/ n. ви́димость f.
visible /'vizəbəl/ adj. ви́димый; я́вный.
vision /'viʒən/ n. зре́ние neut.; проница́тельность f.
visionary /'viʒə‚neri/ n. фантазёр; визионе́р m.
visit /'vizit/ 1. n. посеще́ние neut.; визи́т m. 2. v. посеща́ть impf., посети́ть pf.
visitation /‚vizi'teiʃən/ n. визи́т m.
visitor /'vizitər/ n. посети́тель m., посети́тельница f.; (guest) гость m.
visor /'vaizər/ n. козырёк m.
vista /'vistə/ n. вид m.
Vistula /'vistʃulə/ n. (Polish: Wisła) (river) Ви́сла f.

visual /'viʒuəl/ adj. зри́тельный; нагля́дный.
visualize /'viʒuə‚laiz/ v. вообража́ть impf.
vital /'vaitl/ adj. жи́зненный.
vitalism /'vaitl‚izəm/ n. витали́зм m.
vitality /vai'tæliti/ n. жи́зненность f.
vitalize /'vaitl‚aiz/ v. оживля́ть impf.
vitally /'vaitli/ adv. кра́йне.
vitals /'vaitlz/ n. жи́зненно ва́жные о́рганы pl.
vitamin /'vaitəmin/ n. витами́н m.
vitiate /'viʃi‚eit/ v. по́ртить impf.; (pervert) извраща́ть impf.
vitiation /‚viʃi'eiʃən/ n. по́рча f.
viticulture /'viti‚kʌltʃər/ n. виногра́дарство neut.
vitreous /'vitriəs/ adj. стекля́нный.
vitrification /‚vitrəfi'keiʃən/ n. стекло́вание neut.
vitrify /'vitrə‚fai/ v. стеклова́ть(ся) impf.
vitriol /'vitriəl/ n. (sulfuric acid) се́рная кислота́ f.; (sulphate) купоро́с m.
vitriolic /‚vitri'olik/ adj. купоро́сный.
Vitsyebsk /'vitepsk/ n. Ви́тебск m.
vituperate /vai'tupə‚reit/ v. брани́ть impf.
vituperation /vai‚tupə'reiʃən/ n. брань f.
vituperative /vai'tupərətiv/ adj. бра́нный.
vivace /vi'vatʃei/ n. вива́че neut. indecl.
vivacious /vi'veiʃəs/ adj. оживлённый; живо́й.
vivacity /vi'væsiti/ n. оживлённость; жи́вость f.
vivarium /vai'veəriəm/ n. вива́рий m.
viva voce /'vai'və vousi, 'vivə/ adv. у́стно.
vivid /'vivid/ adj. я́ркий; живо́й; пы́лкий.
vividness /'vividnis/ n. жи́вость; я́ркость f.
vivification /‚vivəfi'keiʃən/ n. оживле́ние neut.
vivify /'vivə‚fai/ v. оживля́ть impf.
viviparous /vai'vipərəs/ adj. живородя́щий.
vivisect /'vivə‚sekt/ v. занима́ться вивисе́кцией impf.
vivisection /‚vivə'sekʃən/ n. вивисе́кция f.; живосече́ние neut.
vivisectionist /‚vivə'sekʃənist/ n. вивисе́ктор m.
vixen /'viksən/ n. лиси́ца f.
viz. abbr. а и́менно; то есть.
vizier /vi'ziər/ n. визи́рь m.
Vladimir /'vlædə‚miər/ n. Влади́мир m.
Vladivostok /‚vlædə'vostok/ n. Владивосто́к m.
vocabulary /vou'kæbyə‚leri/ n. запа́с слов; словарь; лексико́н m.
vocal /'voukəl/ adj. голосово́й; вока́льный.
vocal cords n. голосовы́е свя́зки pl.
vocalic /vou'kælik/ adj. гла́сный; (ling.) вока́льный.
vocalism /'voukə‚lizəm/ n. вокали́зм m.
vocalist /'voukəlist/ n. певе́ц m., певи́ца f.
vocalization /‚voukələ'zeiʃən/ n. вокализа́ция f.
vocalize /'voukə‚laiz/ v. вокализи́ровать; производи́ть зво́нко impf.
vocation /vou'keiʃən/ n. призва́ние neut.
vocational /vou'keiʃənl/ adj. профессиона́льный.
vocative /'vokətiv/ n. зва́тельный паде́ж m.
vociferate /vou'sifə‚reit/ v. крича́ть; выкри́кивать impf.
vociferation /vou‚sifə'reiʃən/ n. вы́крики pl.
vociferous /vou'sifərəs/ adj. шу́мный; крикли́вый.
vodka /'vodkə/ n. во́дка f.
vogue /voug/ n. мо́да f.
voice /vɔis/ 1. n. го́лос m.; (gram.) зало́г m. 2. v. выража́ть impf., вы́разить pf.

voice box n. гортáнь f.
voiced /vɔist/ adj. звóнкий.
voiceless /'vɔislɪs/ adj. безмóлвный; (ling.) глухóй.
void /vɔid/ 1. adj. недействи́тельный; (empty) пустóй. 2. n. пустотá f. 3. v.t. (empty) опорожня́ть impf., опорожни́ть pf.
voile /vɔil, vwal/ n. вуáль f.
Vojvodina /vɔi'vɔdɪnə/ n. (region) Воевóдина f.
volatile /'vɒlətl̩/ adj. неустóйчивый.
volatility /ˌvɒlə'tɪlɪti/ n. изме́нчивость; лету́честь f.
volatilize /'vɒlətlˌaiz/ v. улету́чивать(ся) impf.
volcanic /vɒl'kænɪk/ adj. вулкани́ческий.
volcano /vɒl'keinou/ n. вулкáн m.
vole /voul/ n. полёвка f.
Volgograd /'vɒlgəˌgræd/ n. (formerly: Tsaritsyn, Stalingrad) Волгогрáд m.
volition /vou'lɪʃən/ n. вóля f.
volitional /vou'lɪʃənl̩/ adj. волевóй.
Volkhov /'vɒlkhəf/ n. (river) Вóлхов m.
volley /'vɒli/ v. ударя́ть с лёта impf.
volleyball /'vɒliˌbɔl/ n. волейбóл m.
Volokolamsk /vələkə'lamsk/ n. Волоколáмск m.
volt /voult/ n. вольт m.
voltage /'voultɪdʒ/ n. напряже́ние neut.
voltaic /vɒl'teiik/ adj. гальвани́ческий.
voltmeter /'voultˌmitər/ n. вольтме́тр m.
voluble /'vɒlyəbəl/ adj. говорли́вый.
volume /'vɒlyum/ n. объём m.; ёмкость f.; (book) том m.; (sound) грóмкость f.
volumetric /ˌvɒlyə'metrɪk/ adj. объёмный.
voluminous /və'lumənəs/ adj. многотóмный; объёмистый.
voluntary /'vɒlənˌteri/ adj. доброво́льный.
volunteer /ˌvɒlən'tɪər/ 1. n. доброво́лец m. 2. v. вы́зваться доброво́льно pf.
voluptuary /və'lʌptʃuˌeri/ n. сластолю́бец; сладострáстник m.
voluptuous /və'lʌptʃuəs/ adj. сластолюби́вый; сладострáстный; чу́вственный.

vomit /'vɒmɪt/ 1. n. рвóта f. 2. v. рвать impers. impf., вы́рвать pf.
voracious /vɔ'reiʃəs/ adj. жáдный; прожóрливый; ненасы́тный.
Voronezh /və'rounɪʃ/ n. Ворóнеж m.
vortex /'vɔrteks/ n. вихрь; водоворóт m.
vortical /'vɔrtikəl/ adj. вихревóй.
votary /'voutəri/ n. приве́рженец m.
vote /vout/ 1. n. (act) голосовáние neut.; (opinion) гóлос m. 2. v. голосовáть impf.
voter /'voutər/ n. избирáтель m.
vouch /vautʃ/ v.: to vouch for ручáться (за with acc.) impf.
voucher /'vautʃər/ n. талóн m.; вáучер m.
vow /vau/ 1. n. кля́тва f. 2. v. кля́сться (в with prep.) impf.
vowel /'vauəl/ n. глáсный (звук) m.
voyage /'vɔidʒ/ n. (by sea) плáвание; путеше́ствие neut.
voyager /'vɔidʒər/ n. путеше́ственник m.
voyeurism /vwa'yɜrɪzəm, 'vɔiəˌrɪz-/ n. подсмáтривание neut.
vulcanite /'vʌlkəˌnait/ n. вулкани́т m.
vulcanize /'vʌlkəˌnaiz/ v. вулканизи́ровать impf.
vulgar /'vʌlgər/ adj. грýбый, вульгáрный.
vulgarism /'vʌlgəˌrizəm/ n. вульгари́зм m.
vulgarity /vʌl'gærɪti/ n. вульгáрность f.
vulgarization /ˌvʌlgərə'zeiʃən/ adj. вульгариза́ция.
vulgarize /'vʌlgəˌraiz/ v. опошля́ть impf.
vulgarly /'vʌlgərli/ adv. вульгáрно.
vulgate /'vʌlgeit/ adj. общепри́нятый.
vulnerability /ˌvʌlnərə'bɪlɪti/ n. уязви́мость f.
vulnerable /'vʌlnərəbəl/ adj. уязви́мый; рани́мый.
vulpine /'vʌlpain/ adj. ли́сий; ковáрный.
vulture /'vʌltʃər/ n. гриф m.
vulva /'vʌlvə/ n. вýльва f.
Vyatka /'vyatkə/ n. (river) Вя́тка f.
Vyborg /'vibɔrg/ n. Вы́борг m.

W

wad /wɒd/ *n.* комок *m.*; пачка *f.*

wadding /'wɒdɪŋ/ *n.* вата *f.*

waddle /'wɒdl̩/ *v.* ходить вразвалку *impf.*

wade /weid/ *v.* (*across river*) переходить вброд *impf.*

wader /'weidər/ *n.* (*bird*) болотная птица *f.*

wafer /'weifər/ *n.* вафля *f.*; (*eccl.*) облатка *f.*

waffle¹ /ˌwɒfəl/ *n.* вафля *f.*

waffle² /ˌwɒfəl/ *v.* увиливать от прямого ответа *impf.*

waffle iron *n.* вафельница *f.*

waft /wæft, wɑft/ *n.* дуновение *neut.*

wag /wæg/ *v.* махать *impf.*, махнуть *pf.*

wage /weidʒ/ **1.** *n.* *usu.* *pl.* заработная плата *f.* **2.** *v.*: **to wage war** вести войну *impf.*

wage earner *n.* кормилец *m.*, кормилица *f.*

wage freeze *n.* замораживание заработной платы *neut.*

wager /'weidʒər/ **1.** *n.* пари *neut.* *indecl.* **2.** *v.* держать пари *impf.*

waggery /'wægəri/ *n.* подшучивание *neut.*

waggle /'wægəl/ *v.* помахивать *impf.*

wagon /'wægən/ *n.* коляска; тележка; повозка *f.*

wagoner /'wægənər/ *n.* возчик *m.*

wagtail /'wæg,teil/ *n.* трясогузка *f.*

waif /weif/ *n.* беспризорник *m.*

wail /weil/ **1.** *n.* вопль *m.* **2.** *v.* вопить *impf.*

wainscotting /'weinskoutɪŋ/ *n.* деревянные стенные панели *pl.*

wainwright /'wein,rait/ *n.* тележник *m.*

waist /weist/ *n.* талия *f.*

waistband /'weist,bænd/ *n.* пояс *m.*

waistcoat /'wɛskət, 'weist,kout/ *n.* жилет *m.*

waist-deep /'weist'dip/ *adj.* доходящий до пояса.

waisted /'weistɪd/ *adj.* в талию.

waistline /'weist,lain/ *n.* талия *f.*

wait /weit/ **1.** *n.* ожидание *neut.* **2.** *v.* ждать *impf.*, подождать *pf.*; **to wait on** обслуживать *impf.*

waiter /'weitər/ *n.* официант *m.*

waiting /'weitɪŋ/ *n.* ожидание *neut.*

waiting list *n.* очередь *f.*

waiting room *n.* (*railroad*) зал ожидания *m.*

waitress /'weitrɪs/ *n.* официантка *f.*

waive /weiv/ *v.* отказываться (от *with gen.*) *impf.*

waiver /'weivər/ *n.* документ об отказе *m.*

wake /weik/ *v.t.* будить *impf.*, разбудить *pf.*; *v.i.* просыпаться *impf.*, проснуться *pf.*

wakeful /'weikfəl/ *adj.* бдительный.

waken /'weikən/ *v.* пробуждать(ся) *impf.*

Wales /weilz/ *n.* Уэльс *m.*

walk /wɔk/ **1.** *n.* прогулка; ходьба *f.* **2.** *v.* ходить *impf.* *indet.*, идти *impf.* *det.*

walker /'wɔkər/ *n.* ходок *m.*

walkie-talkie /'wɔki 'tɔki/ *n.* рация *f.*

walking /'wɔkɪŋ/ *n.* ходьба *f.*

walkout /'wɔk,aut/ *n.* забастовка *f.*

walkover /'wɔk,ouvər/ *n.* лёгкая победа *f.*

wall /wɔl/ **1.** *n.* стена *f.* **2.** *adj.* стенной.

wallet /'wɒlɪt/ *n.* бумажник *m.*

walleyed /'wɒlaid/ *adj.* с бельмом на глазу.

wallflower /'wɒl,flauər/ *n.* (*bot.*) желтофиоль *f.*

wallop /'wɒləp/ *v.* лупить *impf.*

walloping /'wɒləpɪŋ/ *adj.* (*colloq.*) большущий.

wallow /'wɒlou/ *v.* валяться *impf.*

wallpaper /'wɒl,peipər/ *n.* обои *pl.*

walnut /'wɒl,nʌt/ *n.* грецкий орех *m.*

walrus /'wɒlrəs/ *n.* морж *m.*

waltz /wɔlts/ **1.** *n.* вальс *m.* **2.** *v.* вальсировать *impf.*

wan /wɒn/ *adj.* тусклый.

wand /wɒnd/ *n.* палочка *f.*; **magic wand** *n.* волшебная палочка *f.*

wander /'wɒndər/ *v.* бродить; странствовать *impf.*

wanderer /'wɒndərər/ *n.* странник *m.*

wandering /'wɒndərɪŋ/ *adj.* бродячий.

wane /wein/ *v.* убывать *impf.*

wangle /'wæŋgəl/ *n.* хитрость *f.*

want /wɒnt/ **1.** *n.* (*desire*) желание *neut.*; (*need*) потребность *f.*; (*lack*) недостаток *m.* **2.** *v.* хотеть *impf.*; (*lack*) недоставать *impf.*, недостать *pf.*

wanted /'wɒntɪd/ *adj.* нужный; необходимый.

wanting /'wɒntɪŋ/ *adj.*: **to be wanting** (*lacking*) недоставать (*impers., with gen.*) *impf.*

wanton /'wɒntn̩/ *adj.* бессмысленный.

war /wɔr/ **1.** *n.* война *f.* **2.** *adj.* военный.

warble /'wɔrbəl/ **1.** *v.* петь *impf.* **2.** *n.* трель *f.*

warbler /'wɔrblər/ *n.* славка *f.*

ward /wɔrd/ *n.* (*hospital*) палата *f.*; (*prison*) камера *f.*; (*district*) район *m.*; (*child*) подопечный.

warden /'wɔrdn̩/ *n.* хранитель; сторож; смотритель *m.*

wardrobe /'wɔrdroub/ *n.* гардероб *m.*

wardroom /'wɔrd,rum/ *n.* кают-компания *f.*

ware /wɛər/ *n.* *usu.* *pl.* изделия *pl.*; товар *m.*

warehouse /'wɛər,haus/ *n.* склад *m.*

warehouseman /'wɛər,hausmən/ *n.* кладовщик *m.*

warfare /'wɔr,fɛər/ *n.* война *f.*

warhead /'wɔr,hed/ *n.* боевая головка; боеголовка *f.*

wariness /'wɛərinɪs/ *n.* осторожность *f.*

warlike /'wɔr,laik/ *adj.* воинственный.

warlock /'wɔr,lɒk/ *n.* колдун *m.*

warlord /'wɔr,lɔrd/ *n.* полководец; военачальник *m.*

warm /wɔrm/ **1.** *adj.* тёплый. **2.** *v.t.* греть; согревать *impf.*, согреть *pf.*; *v.i.* согреваться *impf.*, согреться *pf.*

warm-blooded /'wɔrm 'blʌdɪd/ *adj.* теплокровный.

warm-hearted /'wɔrm 'hɑrtɪd/ *adj.* сердечный; тёплый.

warming pan /'wɔrmɪŋ/ *n.* грелка *f.*

warmonger /'wɔr,mʌŋgər/ *n.* поджигатель войны *m.*

warmth /wɔrmθ/ *n.* теплота *f.*; тепло *neut.*; (*fig.*) сердечность *f.*

warn /wɔrn/ v. предостерегáть impf., предостерéчь pf.

warning /'wɔrnɪŋ/ n. предупреждéние neut.

warp /wɔrp/ v.t. корóбить impf., покорóбить pf.; v.i. корóбиться impf., покорóбиться pf.

warpath /'wɔr,pæθ/ n. тропá войны f.

warrant /'wɔrənt/ 1. n. óрдер m. 2. v. служи́ть оправдáнием impf.

warranty /'wɔrənti/ n. гарáнтия f.

warren /'wɔrən/ n. крóличья норá f.

warrior /'wɔriər/ n. вóин; боéц m.

Warsaw /'wɔrsɔ/ n. (Polish: Warszawa) Варшáва f.

warship /'wɔr,ʃɪp/ n. воéнный корáбль m.

wart /wɔrt/ n. бородáвка f.

warty /'wɔrti/ adj. бородáвчатый.

wary /'wɛəri/ adj. осмотри́тельный.

wash /wɒʃ/ v. мыть(ся); умывáть(ся); стирáть impf.

washable /'wɒʃəbəl/ adj. мóющийся.

washboard /'wɒʃ,bɔrd/ n. стирáльная доскá f.

washbowl /'wɒʃ,boul/ also **washbasin** /-,beisɪn/ n. таз m.; (with faucets) умывáльник m.

washday /'wɒʃ,dei/ n. день сти́рки m.

washed /wɒʃt/ adj. мы́тый.

washer /'wɒʃər/ n. мóйщик m.; (mech.) проклáдка f.

washerwoman /'wɒʃər,wʌmən/ n. прáчка f.

washing /'wɒʃɪŋ/ n. мытьё neut.; сти́рка f.

washing machine n. стирáльная маши́на f.

Washington /'wɒʃɪŋtən/ n. Вашингтóн m.

wash-leather /'wɒʃ ,leðər/ n. зáмша f.

washroom /'wɒʃ,rum/ n. убóрная f.

washstand /'wɒʃ,stænd/ n. умывáльник m.

washtub /'wɒʃ,tʌb/ n. лохáнь f.

wasp /wɒsp/ n. осá f.

waspish /'wɒspɪʃ/ adj. язви́тельный.

wastage /'weistɪdʒ/ n. потéри pl.

waste /weist/ 1. n. трáта f.; отбрóсы pl. 2. v. трáтить impf.; (money) расточáть impf.; (time) теря́ть impf., потеря́ть pf.

wastebasket /'weist,bæskɪt/ n. корзи́на для бумáг f.

wasteful /'weistfəl/ adj. неэконóмный.

wasteland /'weist,lænd/ n. пусты́ня f.

wastepaper /'weist,peipər/ n. макулатýра f.

waste pipe n. отводнáя трубá f.

waster /'weistər/ n. расточи́тель m.

wasting /'weistɪŋ/ adj. изнури́тельный.

wastrel /'weistrəl/ n. мот m.

watch /wɒtʃ/ 1. n. стрáжа f.; дозóр m.; (timepiece) часы́ pl. 2. v. смотрéть; наблюдáть; следи́ть impf.; **to watch out** остерегáться impf.

watchband /'wɒtʃ,bænd/ n. ремешóк для часóв m.

watch chain n. цепóчка для часóв f.

watchdog /'wɒtʃ,dɔg/ n. сторожевóй пёс m.; сторожевáя собáка f.

watcher /'wɒtʃər/ n. наблюдáтель m.

watchful /'wɒtʃfəl/ adj. бди́тельный.

watchmaker /'wɒtʃ,meikər/ n. часовщи́к m.

watchman /'wɒtʃmən/ n. сторож m.

watchword /'wɒtʃ,wɜrd/ n. парóль m.

water /'wɔtər/ 1. n. водá f. 2. adj. водянóй; вóдный. 3. v. (moisten) смáчивать impf., смочи́ть pf.; (flowers, etc.) полива́ть impf., поли́ть pf.; (animals) пои́ть impf., напои́ть pf.

water-bearing /'wɔtər ,bɛərɪŋ/ adj. водонóсный.

water biscuit n. галéта f.

waterborne /'wɔtər,bɔrn/ adj. воднотрáнспортный.

water bottle n. фля́га f.

water buffalo n. водянóй бýйвол m.

water closet n. убóрная f.

watercolor /'wɔtər,kʌlər/ 1. n. акварéль f. 2. adj. акварéльный.

water-colorist /'wɔtər ,kʌlərɪst/ n. акварели́ст m.

water-cooled /'wɔtər 'kuld/ adj. с водяны́м охлаждéнием.

watercourse /'wɔtər,kɔrs/ n. рýсло neut.

watercress /'wɔtər,krɛs/ n. кресс m.

waterfall /'wɔtər,fɔl/ n. водопáд m.

waterfowl /'wɔtər,faul/ n. водоплáвающая пти́ца f.

water gas n. водянóй газ m.

water hole n. пруд m.

wateriness /'wɔtərinɪs/ n. водяни́стость f.

watering can /'wɔtərɪŋ/ n. лéйка f

waterless /'wɔtərlɪs/ adj. безвóдный.

water level n. ýровень воды́ m.

water lily n. водянáя ли́лия f.

water line n. ватерли́ния f.

waterlogged /'wɔtər,lɔgd/ adj. полузатóпленный.

Waterloo /'wɔtər,lu/ n. Ватерлóо m.

water main n. водопровóдная магистрáль f.

watermark /'wɔtər,mark/ n. водянóй знак m.; филигрáнь f.

water meadow n. заливнóй луг m.

watermelon /'wɔtər,melən/ n. арбýз m.

water mill n. водянáя мéльница f.

water pipe n. водопровóдная трубá f.

waterproof /'wɔtər,pruf/ adj. непромокáемый; водонепроницáемый.

water pump n. водянóй насóс m.

water-repellent /'wɔtərrɪ,pelənt/ adj. водооттáлкивающий.

watershed /'wɔtər,ʃed/ n. водораздéл m.; (fig.) перелóм m.

waterside /'wɔtər,said/ n. бéрег m.

water-skier /'wɔtər 'skiər/ n. воднолы́жник m.

water-skiing n. воднолы́жный спорт m.

water snake n. водянáя змея́ f.

water softener n. водоумягчи́тель m.

water-soluble /'wɔtər,sɒljəbəl/ adj. водораствори́мый.

waterspout /'wɔtər,spaut/ n. (tornado) водянóй смерч m.

watertight /'wɔtər,tait/ adj. водонепроницáемый.

water tower n. водонапóрная бáшня f.

waterworks /'wɔtər,wɜrks/ n. водопровóдная стáнция f.

watery /'wɔtəri/ adj. водянóй.

watt /wɒt/ n. ватт m.

wattage /'wɒtɪdʒ/ n. мóщность в вáттах f.

wattle /'wɒtl/ n. плетéнь m.

wave /weiv/ 1. n. (sea) волнá f.; (in hair) зави́вка f. 2. v.t. (hand, etc.) махáть impf.; (hair) завивáть; (flag, etc.) размáхивать impf.; v.i. развевáться impf.

wave band n. полосá частóт f.

waved /weivd/ adj. (of hair) зави́той.

waveguide /'weiv,gaid/ n. волновод m.
wavelength /'weiv,leŋkθ/ n. длина волны f.
waver /'weivər/ v. колыхаться impf.
wavy /'weivi/ adj. волнистый.
wax /wæks/ **1.** n. воск m. **2.** adj. восковой. **3.** v. вощить impf.
waxed /wækst/ adj. вощёный.
waxen /'wæksən/ adj. восковой.
wax paper n. вощёная бумага f.
waxwork /'wæks,wɜrk/ n. восковая фигура f.
waxy /'wæksi/ adj. восковой.
way /wei/ n. путь; дорога f.; **by the way** между прочим; **on the way** по дороге, по пути.
wayleave /'wei,liv/ n. право проезда neut.
wayside /'wei,said/ n. обочина f.
wayward /'weiwərd/ adj. своенравный.
waywardness /'weiwərdnıs/ n. своенравие neut.
we /wi/ pron. мы.
weak /wik/ adj. слабый.
weaken /'wikən/ v.t. ослаблять impf., ослабить pf.; v.i. слабеть; ослабевать impf., ослабеть pf.
weak-headed /'wik 'hedıd/ adj. придурковатый.
weak-kneed /'wik 'nid/ adj. безвольный.
weakling /'wiklıŋ/ n. слабак m.
weakly /'wikli/ adj. хилый.
weak-minded /'wik 'maindıd/ adj. слабодушный.
weakness /'wiknıs/ n. слабость f.
weal /wil/ n. благо neut.
wealth /wɛlθ/ n. богатство neut.
wealthy /'wɛlθi/ adj. богатый.
wean /win/ v. отнимать от груди impf.
weapon /'wɛpən/ n. оружие neut.
weaponry /'wɛpənri/ n. вооружение neut.
wear /wɛər/ **1.** n. ношение neut.; износ m. **2.** v.t. носить impf.; v.i. носиться impf.; **to wear out** изнашивать(ся) impf., износить(ся) pf.
wearable /'wɛərəbəl/ adj. годный.
wear and tear /tɛər/ n. износ m.
weariness /'wıərinıs/ n. усталость f.
wearing /'wɛərıŋ/ adj. утомительный.
wearisome /'wıərisəm/ adj. утомительный; (boring) скучный.
weary /'wıəri/ adj. уставший; утомлённый.
weasel /'wizəl/ n. ласка f.
weather /'wɛðər/ n. погода f.
weather-beaten /'wɛðər ,bitṇ/ adj. обветренный.
weatherboarding /'wɛðər,bɔrdıŋ/ n. обшивка досками внакрой f.
weather-bound /'wɛðər ,baund/ adj. задержанный непогодой.
weathercock /'wɛðər,kɒk/ n. флюгер m.
weatherglass /'wɛðər,glæs/ n. барометр m.
weathering /'wɛðərıŋ/ n. (geol.) выветривание neut.
weatherman /'wɛðər,mæn/ n. синоптик m.
weatherproof /'wɛðər,pruf/ adj. непромокаемый.
weather station n. метеостанция f.
weather vane n. флюгер m.
weave /wiv/ v. ткать impf., соткать pf.
weaver /'wivər/ n. ткач m., ткачиха f.
weaving /'wivıŋ/ n. плетение; тканьё neut.
web /wɛb/ n. ткань f.; (spider) паутина f.; (fig.) сплетение neut.
webbed /wɛbd/ adj. перепончатый.
webbing /'wɛbıŋ/ n. тесьма f.

web-footed /'wɛb ,futıd/ adj. перепончатопалый.
Web site n. (Internet) станция Web f.; узел Web; сайт m.
wed /wɛd/ v. женить(ся) impf.; (one's daughter) выдавать замуж impf.
wedded /'wɛdıd/ adj. супружеский.
wedding /'wɛdıŋ/ **1.** n. свадьба f. **2.** adj. свадебный.
wedge /wɛdʒ/ **1.** n. клин m. **2.** v. заклинивать(ся) impf.
wedge-shaped /'wɛdʒ ,ʃeipt/ adj. клинообразный.
wedlock /'wɛd,lɒk/ n. брак m.
Wednesday /'wɛnzdei/ n. среда f.
wee /wi/ adj. малюсенький.
weed /wid/ **1.** n. сорная трава f.; сорняк m. **2.** v. вычищать impf., вычистить pf.
weeding /'widıŋ/ n. прополка f.
weed-killer /'wid ,kılər/ n. гербицид m.
weedy /'widi/ adj. (of person) хилый.
week /wik/ n. неделя f.
weekday /'wik,dei/ n. будний день m.
weekend /'wik,ɛnd/ n. выходные дни pl.
weekly /'wikli/ **1.** adj. еженедельный. **2.** adv. еженедельно **3.** n. еженедельник m.
weep /wip/ v. плакать impf.
weeper /'wipər/ n. плакальщица f.
weeping /'wipıŋ/ n. плач m.
weepy /'wipi/ adj. плаксивый.
weevil /'wivəl/ n. долгоносик m.
weigh /wei/ v.t. взвешивать impf., взвесить pf.; v.i. весить impf.
weighbridge /'wei,bridʒ/ n. мостовые весы pl.
weigh-in /'wei ,ın/ n. взвешивание neut.
weight /weit/ n. вес m.; (athl.) штанга f.
weightless /'weitlıs/ adj. невесомый.
weightlessness /'weitlısnıs/ n. невесомость f.
weightlifter /'weit,lıftər/ n. штангист m.
weightlifting /'weit,lıftıŋ/ n. поднятие тяжестей neut.
weighty /'weiti/ adj. веский.
Weimar /'vaimɑr, 'wai-/ n. Веймар m.
weir /wıər/ n. плотина; запруда f.
weird /wıərd/ adj. странный.
welcome /'wɛlkəm/ **1.** adj. желанный; **you're welcome!** пожалуйста! **2.** n. приём m.; приветствие neut. **3.** v. приветствовать impf. **4.** interj. Добро пожаловать!
weld /wɛld/ v. сваривать(ся) impf.
welded /'wɛldıd/ adj. сварной.
welder /'wɛldər/ n. сварщик m.
welding /'wɛldıŋ/ n. сварка f.; **arc welding** n. дуговая сварка; **spot welding** n. точечная сварка f.
welfare /'wɛl,fɛər/ n. благосостояние neut.
welkin /'wɛlkın/ n. небеса pl.
well¹ /wɛl/ **1.** adj. хороший; здоровый. **2.** adv. хорошо.
well² /wɛl/ колодец; родник m.
well-advised /'wɛl əd'vaizd/ adj. благоразумный.
well-aimed /'wɛl 'eimd/ adj. меткий.
well-appointed /'wɛl ə'pɔintıd/ adj. хорошо оборудованный.
well-armed /'wɛl 'armd/ adj. хорошо вооружённый.

well-balanced /'wɛl 'bælənst/ *adj.* уравновѐшенный.

well-behaved /'wɛl bɪ'heivd/ *adj.* благовоспѝтанный.

well-being /'wɛl 'biıŋ/ *n.* благополучие *neut.*

well-bred /'wɛl 'brɛd/ *adj.* воспѝтанный; культурный.

well-built /'wɛl 'bɪlt/ *adj.* (*body*) хорошо сложѐнный; хорошо постро́енный.

well-connected /'wɛl kə'nɛktɪd/ *adj.* имѐющий хоро́шие свя́зи.

well-cut /'wɛl 'kʌt/ *adj.* хорошо́ скро́енный.

well-defined /'wɛl dɪ'faind/ *adj.* чётко определённый.

well-deserved /'wɛl dɪ'zɜrvd/ *adj.* заслу́женный.

well-disposed /'wɛl dɪ'spouzd/ *adj.* благожела́тельный.

well done *interj.* хорошо́ сде́лано!; молодѐц!

well-dressed /'wɛl 'drɛst/ *adj.* хорошо одѐтый.

well-earned /'wɛl 'ɜrnd/ *adj.* заслу́женный.

well-educated /'wɛl 'ɛdʒʊ,keitɪd/ *adj.* образо́ванный.

well-favored /'wɛl 'feivərd/ *adj.* краси́вый.

well-fed /'wɛl 'fɛd/ *adj.* отко́рмленный.

well-founded /'wɛl 'faundɪd/ *adj.* обосно́ванный.

well-groomed /'wɛl 'grumd/ *adj.* ухо́женный.

well-grounded /'wɛl 'graundɪd/ *adj.* обосно́ванный.

well-heeled /'wɛl 'hild/ *adj.* (*colloq.*) зажи́точный.

well-informed /'wɛl ɪn'fɔrmd/ *adj.* свѐдущий.

Wellington /'wɛlɪŋtən/ *n.* Вѐллингтон *m.*

Wellington boot *n.* рези́новый сапо́г *m.*

well-judged /'wɛl 'dʒʌdʒd/ *adj.* продуманный.

well-knit /'wɛl 'nɪt/ *adj.* сплочённый.

well-known /'wɛl 'noun/ *adj.* извѐстный.

well-mannered /'wɛl 'mænərd/ *adj.* воспѝтанный.

well-meaning /'wɛl 'miniŋ/ *adj.* благонамѐренный.

well-nigh /'wɛl ,nai/ *adj.* почти́ *adv.*

well-off /'wɛl 'ɔf/ *adj.* состоя́тельный; зажи́точный.

well-oiled /'wɛl 'ɔild/ *adj.* сма́занный.

well-ordered /'wɛl 'ɔrdərd/ *adj.* хорошо́ организо́ванный.

well-paid /'wɛl 'peid/ *adj.* хорошо́ опла́чиваемый.

well-proportioned /'wɛl prə'pɔrʃənd/ *adj.* пропорциона́льный.

well-read /'wɛl 'rɛd/ *adj.* начи́танный.

well-spent /'wɛl 'spɛnt/ *adj.* не зря потра́ченный.

well-spoken /'wɛl 'spoukən/ *adj.* говоря́щий на литерату́рном языкѐ.

wellspring /'wɛl,spriŋ/ *n.* исто́чник *m.*

well-thought-out /'wɛl θɔt 'aut/ *adj.* продуманный.

well-timed /'wɛl 'taimd/ *adj.* своеврѐменный.

well-to-do /'wɛl tə 'du/ *adj.* зажи́точный.

well-turned /'wɛl 'tɜrnd/ *adj.* отто́ченный.

well-wisher /'wɛl ,wɪʃər/ *n.* доброжела́тель *m.*

well-worn /'wɛl 'wɔrn/ *adj.* изно́шенный.

Welsh /wɛlʃ/ *adj.* уэльский; валли́йский.

welsh /wɛlʃ, wɛltʃ/ *v.* (*colloq.*) не плати́ть *impf.*

welt /wɛlt/ *n.* рубѐц *m.*

Weltanschauung /'vɛlt,ɑn,ʃauʊŋ/ *n.* мировоззрѐние *neut.*

welter /'wɛltər/ *n.* неразбери́ха *f.*

wen /wɛn/ *n.* жирова́я ши́шка *f.*, жирови́к *m.*

wench /wɛntʃ/ *n.* дѐвка *f.*

wend /wɛnd/ *v.*: **to wend one's way** направля́ть путь *impf.*

werewolf /'wɛər,wʊlf, 'wɪər-, 'wɜr-/ *n.* о́боротень *m.*

west /wɛst/ **1.** *n.* за́пад *m.* **2.** *adj.* за́падный. **3.** *adv.* к за́паду; на за́пад.

westerly /'wɛstərli/ *n.* за́падный вѐтер *m.*

western /'wɛstərn/ *adj.* за́падный.

Western Dvina *n.* (*also: Daugava*) (*river*) За́падная Двина́ *f.*

Westerner /'wɛstərnər/ *n.* жи́тель за́пада *m.*

westernization /,wɛstərnə'zeiʃən/ *n.* вестерниза́ция *f.*

westernizer /'wɛstər,naizər/ *n.* за́падник *m.*

westernmost /'wɛstərn,moust/ *adj.* са́мый за́падный.

West Virginia *n.* За́падная Вирги́ния *f.*

westward /'wɛstwərd/ **1.** *adj.* напра́вленный к за́паду. **2.** *adv.* на за́пад.

wet /wɛt/ **1.** *adj.* мо́крый. **2.** *v.* мочи́ть; сма́чивать *impf.*, смочи́ть *pf.*; **to get wet** промока́ть *impf.*, промо́кнуть *pf.*

wetness /'wɛtnɪs/ *n.* вла́жность *f.*

wet nurse /'wɛt,nɜrs/ *n.* корми́лица *f.*

wetting /'wɛtɪŋ/ *n.* сма́чивание *neut.*

whack /wæk/ *n.* зво́нкий уда́р *m.*

whacking /'wækɪŋ/ *adj.* (*colloq.*) здорове́нный.

whale /weil/ **1.** *n.* кит *m.* **2.** *adj.* кито́вый.

whalebone /'weil,boun/ *n.* кито́вый ус *m.*

whaler /'weilər/ *n.* (*person*) китобо́й; китоло́в *m.*; (*ship*) китобо́йное су́дно *neut.*

whaling /'weilıŋ/ *adj.* китобо́йный.

wham /wæm/ **1.** *interj.* бац, бах. **2.** *v.* ба́хнуться *impf.*

wharf /wɔrf/ *n.* при́стань *f.*

wharfage /'wɔrfidʒ/ *adj.* перро́нный билѐт.

wharfinger /'wɔrfɪndʒər/ *n.* владѐлец това́рной при́стани *m.*

what /wʌt, *unstressed* wət/ *pron.* како́й; что.

whatever /wʌt'ɛvər/ **1.** *adj.* любо́й; како́й бы ни. **2.** *pron.* всё что; что бы ни.

whatnot /'wʌt,nɒt/ *n.* что́-то подо́бное *neut.*

what's-his-name как его́?

wheat /wit/ **1.** *n.* пшени́ца *f.* **2.** *adj.* пшени́чный.

wheedle /'widl̩/ *v.* обха́живать *impf.*

wheedling /'widlɪŋ/ *adj.* льсти́вый; вымога́ющий.

wheel /wil/ *n.* колесо́; колѐсико *neut.*; (*steering wheel*) руль *m.*

wheelbarrow /'wil,bærou/ *n.* та́чка *f.*

wheelbase /'wil,beis/ *n.* колѐсная база́ *f.*

wheelchair /'wil,tʃɛər/ *n.* инвали́дная коля́ска *f.*

wheeled /wild/ *adj.* на колёсах.

wheelwright /'wil,rait/ *n.* колѐсный ма́стер *m.*

wheeze /wiz/ *n.* хрип *m.*

wheezy /'wizi/ *adj.* хри́плый.

whelk /wɛlk/ *n.* прыщ *m.*

whelp /wɛlp/ *n.* щено́к *m.*

when /wɛn; *unstressed* wən/ *adv.*, *conj.* когда́.

whence /wɛns/ *conj.* отку́да *adv.*

whenever /wɛn'ɛvər/ *conj.* когда́; вся́кий раз когда́.

where /wɛər/ adv., conj. (dir.) куда́; (loc.) где; (from where) отку́да; (to where) туда́, куда́; туда́ где; где.

whereabouts /'wɛərə,bauts/ pl. местонахожде́ние neut.

whereas /wɛər'æz/ conj. тогда́ как; поско́льку.

wherein /wɛər'ɪn/ conj. в чём.

whereupon /'wɛərə,pɒn/ conj. по́сле чего́.

wherever /wɛər'ɛvər/ adv. куда́ бы ни; где бы ни.

wherewithal /'wɛərwɪð,ɔl/ n. сре́дства pl.

whet /wɛt/ v. точи́ть impf.

whether /'wɛðər/ conj. ли.

whetstone /'wɛt,stoun/ n. осело́к m.

whew /hwyu/ interj. уф.

whey /wei/ n. сы́воротка f.

which /wɪtʃ/ pron., adj. кото́рый; како́й; кто.

whichever /wɪtʃ'ɛvər/ pron., adj. како́й; како́й бы ни; любо́й.

whiff /wɪf/ n. дунове́ние neut.

while /wail/ 1. conj. пока́; в то вре́мя как; (although) хотя́. 2. n. не́которое вре́мя neut.; a long while до́лго; a short while недо́лго; for a while на вре́мя; once in a while вре́мя от вре́мени.

whilom /'wailəm/ adj. (obs.) бы́вший.

whim /wɪm/ n. капри́з m.; при́хоть f.

whimper /'wɪmpər/ v. хны́кать impf.

whimsical /'wɪmzɪkəl/ adj. затейливый.

whimsy /'wɪmzi/ n. причу́да f.

whine /wain/ n. скулёж m.

whinny /'wɪni/ 1. n. ржа́нье neut. 2. v. ржать impf.

whip /wɪp/ 1. n. кнут; хлыст m. 2. v. хлеста́ть impf.; (food) сбива́ть impf., сбить pf.

whip hand n. (fig.) контро́ль m.

whippersnapper /'wɪpər,snæpər/ n. наха́л m.

whippet /'wɪpɪt/ n. уи́ппет m.

whipping /'wɪpɪŋ/ n. по́рка f.

whippoorwill /'wɪpər,wɪl/ n. козодо́й m.

whippy /'wɪpi/ adj. упру́гий.

whir /wɜr/ n. жужжа́ние neut.

whirl /wɜrl/ v.t. верте́ть, кружи́ть impf.; v.i. верте́ться, кружи́ться impf.

whirligig /'wɜrlɪ,gɪg/ n. вертушка f.

whirlpool /'wɜrl,pul/ n. водоворо́т m.

whirlwind /'wɜrl,wɪnd/ n. вихрь; смерч m.

whisk /wɪsk/ v.t. маха́ть impf.; v.i. нести́сь impf.

whisker /'wɪskər/ n. usu. pl. бакенба́рд m.; (of animal) усы́ pl.

whiskery /'wɪskəri/ adj. с бакенба́рдами.

whiskey /'wɪski/ n. ви́ски neut. indecl.

whisper /'wɪspər/ 1. n. шёпот m.; in a whisper adv. шёпотом 2. v. шепта́ть impf., шепну́ть pf.

whisperer /'wɪspərər/ n. шепту́н m.

whispering /'wɪspərɪŋ/ n. шёпот m.

whist /wɪst/ n. вист m.

whistle /'wɪsəl/ 1. n. свист m.; (instrument) свисто́к m. 2. v. свисте́ть impf., сви́стнуть pf.

whistler /'wɪslər/ n. свисту́н m.

whistling /'wɪslɪŋ/ n. свист m.

whit /wɪt/ n.: not a whit adv. ничу́ть.

white /wait/ 1. adj. бе́лый. 2. n. бе́лый цвет m.; белизна́ f.; (of egg) бело́к m.

white blood cell n. бе́лое кровяно́е те́льце neut.

white-collar /'wait 'kɒlər/ adj., n. слу́жащий m.

white-haired /'wait 'hɛərd/ adj. седо́й.

white-hot /'wait'hɒt/ adj. раскалённый добела́.

White House n. Бе́лый дом m.

white lie n. неви́нная ложь f.

whiten /'waitn̩/ v.t. бели́ть impf., v.i. беле́ть impf.

whiteness /'waitnɪs/ n. белизна́ f.

whitening /'waitnɪŋ/ n. побе́лка f.

whitewashing /'wait,wɒʃɪŋ/ n. побе́лка f.

whither /'wɪðər/ adv. куда́.

whithersoever /,wɪðərsou'ɛvər/ conj. (obs.) куда́ бы ни

whiting /'waitɪŋ/ n. бели́ла f.

whitish /'waitɪʃ/ adj. белова́тый.

whitlow /'wɪtlou/ n. ногтое́да f.

whittle /'wɪtl̩/ v. обстру́гивать impf.

whiz /wɪz/ n. свист m.

who /hu/ pron. кто; кото́рый.

whoa /wou/ interj. тпру!

whodunit /hu'dʌnɪt/ n. (colloq.) детекти́в m.

whoever /hu'ɛvər/ pron. кто бы ни.

whole /houl/ 1. adj. це́лый; весь. 2. n. це́лое neut.; ито́г m.

wholehearted /'houl'hartɪd/ adj. и́скренний.

wholeheartedly /'houl'hartɪdli/ adv. от всего́ се́рдца.

wholesale /'houl,seil/ 1. n. опто́вая торго́вля f. 2. adj. опто́вый. 3. adv. о́птом.

wholesaler /'houl,seilər/ n. опто́вый торго́вец; оптови́к m.

wholesome /'houlsəm/ adj. здоро́вый; благотво́рный.

whole-wheat /'houl 'wit/ adj. из муки́ гру́бого помо́ла.

wholly /'houli/ adv. по́лностью; целико́м.

whom /hum/ pron. кого́; кото́рого.

whoop /hup, wup/ n. вы́крик m.

whooping cough /'hupɪŋ/ n. ко́клюш m.

whop /wɒp/ v. (colloq.) вздуть impf.

whopper /'wɒpər/ n. (colloq.) грома́дина m.

whopping /'wɒpɪŋ/ adj. (colloq.) здорове́нный.

whore /hɔr/ n. проститу́тка f.

whorehouse /'hɔr,haus/ n. публи́чный дом m.

whorl /wɜrl/ n. завито́к m.

whortleberry /'wɜrtl̩,bɛri/ n. черни́ка f.

whose /huz/ pron. чей m., чья f., чьё neut., чьи pl.

why /wai/ adv. почему́.

wick /wɪk/ n. фити́ль m.

wicked /'wɪkɪd/ adj. злой; по́длый.

wickedness /'wɪkɪdnɪs/ n. зло́бность f.; злой посту́пок m.

wicker /'wɪkər/ 1. n. пру́тья для плете́ния pl. 2. adj. плетёный.

wickerwork /'wɪkər,wɜrk/ n. плете́ние neut.

wicket /'wɪkɪt/ n. кали́тка f.

wide /waid/ 1. adj. широ́кий. 2. adv. широко́.

wide-angle /'waid 'æŋɡəl/ adj. широкоуго́льный.

wide-awake /'waid ə'weik/ adj. бо́дрствующий.

wide-brimmed /'waid 'brɪmd/ adj. широкопо́лый.

widely /'waidli/ adv. широко́.

widen /'waidn̩/ v.t. расширя́ть impf., расши́рить pf.; v.i. расширя́ться impf., расши́риться pf.

widespread /'waid'sprɛd/ adj. широко́ распространённый.

widgeon /'wɪdʒən/ n. свия́зь f.

widow /'wɪdou/ n. вдова́ f.

widowed /'wɪdoud/ adj. вдо́вый.
widower /'wɪdouər/ n. вдове́ц m.
widowhood /'wɪdou‚hʊd/ n. вдовство́ neut.
width /wɪdθ/ n. ширина́; широта́ f.
wield /wild/ v. владе́ть (with instr.) impf.
wiener /'winər/ n. соси́ска f.
wife /waif/ n. жена́ f.
wig /wɪg/ n. пари́к m.
wiggle /'wɪgəl/ v. шевели́ть impf.; (wag) виля́ть (with instr.) impf.
wiggly /'wɪgli/ adj. волни́стый.
wigmaker /'wɪg‚meikər/ n. парикма́хер m.
wigwam /'wɪgwɒm/ n. вигва́м m.
wild /waild/ adj. ди́кий.
wildcat /'waild‚kæt/ n. ди́кая ко́шка f.
wildebeest /'wɪldə‚bist/ n. антило́па-гну f. indecl.
wilderness /'wɪldərnɪs/ n. ди́кая ме́стность f.
wild-eyed /'waild ‚aid/ adj. с безу́мными глаза́ми.
wildfire /'waild‚faiᵊr/ n. лесно́й пожа́р m.
wildflower /'waild‚flauər/ n. полево́й цвето́к m.
wildfowl /'waild‚faul/ n. (перна́тая) дичь f.
wildlife /'waild‚laif/ n. жива́я приро́да f.
wildly /'waildli/ adv. ди́ко; бе́шено.
wild rose n. шипо́вник m.
wile /wail/ n. хи́трость f.
wlliness /'wailinɪs/ n. хи́трость f.
will /wɪl/ **1.** n. во́ля f.; си́ла во́ли; (leg.) завеща́ние neut. **2.** v. заставля́ть impf., заста́вить pf.; (leg.) завеща́ть impf. and pf.
willful /'wɪlfəl/ adj. предумы́шленный.
willlng /'wɪlɪŋ/ adj. гото́вый.
willingly /'wɪlɪŋli/ adv. охо́тно; доброво́льно.
willingness /'wɪlɪŋnɪs/ n. гото́вность f.
willow /'wɪlou/ n. и́ва f.; **weeping willow** n. плаку́чая и́ва f.
willowy /'wɪloui/ adj. стро́йный; заро́сший и́вами.
will power n. си́ла во́ли f.
willy-nilly /'wɪli'nɪli/ adv. во́лей-нево́лей.
wilt /wɪlt/ v. вя́нуть impf., завя́нуть pf.
wily /'waili/ adj. хи́трый; лука́вый; кова́рный.
wimp /wɪmp/ n. (fig.) тря́пка m. and f. (decl. f.).
wimple /'wɪmpəl/ n. плат m.
win /wɪn/ v. выи́грывать impf., вы́играть pf.
wince /wɪns/ n. вздра́гивание neut.
winch /wɪntʃ/ n. лебёдка f.
Winchester rifle /'wɪntʃɛstər/ n. винче́стер m.
wind[1] /wɪnd, Literary waind/ n. ве́тер m.
wind[2] /waind/ v.t. (coil) верте́ть; мота́ть impf.; (watch) заводи́ть impf., завести́ pf.; v.i. ви́ться, извива́ться impf., изви́ться pf.
windbag /'wɪnd‚bæg/ n. болту́н m.
windbreaker /'wɪnd‚breikər/ n. анора́к m.; што́рмо́вка f.
wind-driven /'wɪnd ‚drɪvən/ adj. ветросилово́й.
winded /'wɪndɪd/ adj. запыха́вшийся.
windfall /'wɪnd‚fɔl/ n. (fruit) па́данец m.
wind gauge n. анемо́метр m.
winding /'waindɪŋ/ adj. изви́листый; (twisted) вито́й.
wind instrument /wɪnd/ n. духово́й инструме́нт m.
windjammer /'wɪnd‚dʒæmər, 'wɪn-/ n. (colloq.) па́русное су́дно neut.

windlass /'wɪndləs/ n. лебёдка f.; (naut.) бра́шпиль m.
windless /'wɪndlɪs/ adj. безве́тренный.
windmill /'wɪnd‚mɪl/ n. ветряна́я ме́льница f.
window /'wɪndou/ **1.** n. окно́ neut. **2.** adj. око́нный.
window box n. я́щик для цвето́в m.
window dressing n. оформле́ние витри́н neut.; показу́ха f.
window ledge n. нару́жный подоко́нник m.
windowpane /'wɪndou‚pein/ n. око́нное стекло́ neut.
window-shopping /'wɪndou ‚ʃɒpɪŋ/ n. рассма́тривание витри́н neut.
window sill n. подоко́нник m.
windpipe /'wɪnd‚paip/ n. дыха́тельное го́рло neut.; трахе́я f.
windproof /'wɪnd‚pruf/ adj. ветронепроница́емый.
windshield /'wɪnd‚ʃild/ n. лобово́е стекло́ neut.
windshield wiper n. дво́рник m.
windsock /'wɪnd‚sɒk/ n. ветроуказа́тель m.
windsurfing /'wɪnd‚sɜrfɪŋ/ n. виндсёрфинг m.
wind-swept /'wɪnd ‚swɛpt/ adj. незащищённый от ве́тра.
wind tunnel /wɪnd/ n. аэродинами́ческая труба́ f.
windward /'wɪndwərd/ n. наве́тренная сторона́ f.
windy /'wɪndi/ adj. ве́треный.
wine /wain/ **1.** n. вино́ neut. **2.** adj. ви́нный.
wine cellar n. ви́нный по́греб m.
wineglass /'wain‚glæs/ n. бока́л; фуже́р m.
wine list n. ка́рта вин f.
wine merchant n. виноторго́вец m.
wine press n. дави́льный пресс m.
winery /'wainəri/ n. ви́нный заво́д m.
wineskin /'wain‚skin/ n. бурдю́к m.
wing /wɪŋ/ n. крыло́ neut.; (theat.) кули́са f.
winged /wɪŋd or, esp. Literary, 'wɪŋɪd/ adj. крыла́тый.
wingless /'wɪŋlɪs/ adj. бескры́лый.
wing nut n. кры́льчатая га́йка f.
wink /wɪŋk/ **1.** n. морга́ние; мига́ние neut. **2.** v. морга́ть impf., моргну́ть pf.
winner /'wɪnər/ n. победи́тель m.
winning /'wɪnɪŋ/ n. вы́игрыш m.
winnow /'wɪnou/ v. (grain) ве́ять impf.
winnowing /'wɪnouɪŋ/ n. ве́яние neut.
winsome /'wɪnsəm/ adj. обая́тельный.
winter /'wɪntər/ **1.** n. зима́ f.; **in the winter** adv. зимо́й. **2.** adj. зи́мний.
wintergreen /'wɪntər‚grin/ n. груша́нка f.
wintry /'wɪntri/ adj. зи́мний.
wipe /waip/ v. вытира́ть impf., вы́тереть pf.; **to wipe out** стира́ть impf., стере́ть pf.
wire /waiᵊr/ **1.** n. про́волока f.; про́вод m. **2.** adj. про́волочный. **3.** v. протя́гивать провода́ impf.
wire cutter n. куса́чки pl.
wirehaired /'waiᵊr‚hɛᵊrd/ adj. жесткошёрстный.
wireless /'waiᵊrlɪs/ adj. беспро́волочный.
wiretap /'waiᵊr‚tæp/ n. (phone) подслу́шивание телефо́нных разгово́ров neut.
wireworm /'waiᵊr‚wɜrm/ n. про́волочник m.
wiring /'waiᵊrɪŋ/ n. электропрово́дка f.
wiry /'waiᵊri/ adj. (lean and tough) жи́листый; (stiff) жёсткий.

Wisconsin /wɪs'kɒnsən/ n. Виско́нсин m.
wisdom /'wɪzdəm/ n. му́дрость f.
wisdom tooth n. зуб му́дрости m.
wise /waiz/ adj. му́дрый.
wisecrack /'waiz,kræk/ **1.** n. остро́та f. **2.** v. остри́ть impf.
wise guy n. (colloq.) всезна́йка m. and f. (decl. f.).
wish /wɪʃ/ **1.** n. жела́ние; пожела́ние neut. **2.** v. хоте́ть; жела́ть impf., пожела́ть pf.
wishbone /'wɪʃ,boun/ n. ду́жка f.
wishful /'wɪʃfəl/ adj. жела́ющий.
wishy-washy /'wɪʃi,wɒʃi/ adj. бесхара́ктерный.
wisteria /wɪ'stɪəriə/ n. глици́ния f.
wistful /'wɪstfəl/ adj. заду́мчивый.
wistfully /'wɪstfəli/ adj. заду́мчиво adv.
wit /wɪt/ n. pl. остроу́мие neut.; ум, ра́зум m.
witch /wɪtʃ/ n. ве́дьма f.
witchcraft /'wɪtʃ,kræft/ n. колдовство́ neut.
witchery /'wɪtʃəri/ n. чароде́йство neut.
witching /'wɪtʃɪŋ/ adj. колдовско́й.
with /wɪθ/ prep. с, со (with instr.).
withal /wɪð'ɔl/ adv. к тому́ же.
withdraw /wɪð'drɔ/ v.t. снима́ть; отдёргивать impf., отдёрнуть pf.; v.i. удаля́ться impf., удали́ться pf.
withdrawal /wɪð'drɔəl/ n. (mil.) вы́вод; отхо́д m.; (bank) сня́тие neut.
withdrawn /wɪð'drɔn/ adj. за́мкнутый.
wither /'wɪðər/ v. со́хнуть; блёкнуть impf., поблёкнуть pf.
withered /'wɪðərd/ adj. вы́сохший; увя́дший; (wrinkled) смо́рщенный.
withering /'wɪðərɪŋ/ adj. (of glance) испепеля́ющий.
withers /'wɪðərz/ n. хо́лка f.
withhold /wɪθ'hould/ v. уде́рживать impf., удержа́ть pf.
within /wɪð'ɪn/ **1.** adv. внутри́. **2.** prep. в (with prep.), в преде́лах; внутри́ (with gen.).
without /wɪð'aut/ **1.** adv. вне; снару́жи. **2.** prep. без, безо with gen..
withstand /wɪθ'stænd/ v. выде́рживать; противостоя́ть (with dat.) impf.
witless /'wɪtlɪs/ adj. дура́цкий.
witness /'wɪtnɪs/ **1.** n. свиде́тель m. **2.** v. быть свиде́телем.
witness stand n. ме́сто да́чи показа́ний neut.
Wittenberg /'wɪtn,bɜrg, 'vɪtn-/ n. Ви́ттенберг m.
witticism /'wɪtə,sɪzəm/ n. остро́та f.
wittingly /'wɪtɪŋli/ adv. созна́тельно adv.
witty /'wɪti/ adj. остроу́мный.
wizard /'wɪzərd/ n. коллде́й m.
wizardry /'wɪzərdri/ n. волшебство́ neut.
wizened /'wɪzənd/ adj. вы́сохший.
wobbly /'wɒbli/ adj. ша́ткий.
woe /wou/ n. го́ре neut.
woebegone /'woubɪ,gɒn/ adj. удручённый.
woeful /'woufəl/ adj. го́рестный.
wolf /wulf/ **1.** n. волк m. **2.** adj. во́лчий.
wolfhound /'wulf,haund/ n. волкода́в m.
wolfish /'wulfɪʃ/ adj. во́лчий.
wolfram /'wulfrəm/ n. вольфра́м m.
wolverine /,wulvə'rin/ n. росома́ха f.
woman /'wumən/ **1.** n. же́нщина f. **2.** adj. же́нский.
womanfolk /'wumən,fouk/ n. же́нщины pl.

womanhood /'wumən,hud/ n. же́нственность; же́нская зре́лость f.
womanish /'wumənɪʃ/ adj. женоподо́бный.
womanize /'wumə,naiz/ v. волочи́ться за же́нщинами impf.
womankind /'wumən,kaind/ n. же́нский пол m.
womanliness /'wumənlinɪs/ n. же́нственность f.
womanly /'wumənli/ adj. же́нственный.
womb /wum/ n. ма́тка f.
wonder /'wʌndər/ **1.** n. удивле́ние; изумле́ние neut.; **no wonder** не удиви́тельно. **2.** v. удивля́ться (with dat.) impf.
wonderful /'wʌndərfəl/ adj. замеча́тельный.
wonderingly /'wʌndərɪŋli/ adj. удивлённо adv.
wonderland /'wʌndər,lænd/ n. страна́ чуде́с f.; чуде́сный мир m.
wonderment /'wʌndərmənt/ n. удивле́ние neut.
wonder-worker /'wʌndər ,wɜrkər/ n. чудотво́рец m.
wondrous /'wʌndrəs/ adj. чуде́сный.
wont /wɒnt, wount/ n. привы́чка f.; обыкнове́ние neut.
wonted /'wɒntɪd, 'woun-/ adj. привы́чный.
woo /wu/ v. уха́живать (за with instr.) impf.
wood /wud/ n. лес m.; (material) де́рево neut.; (for fire) дрова́ pl.
wood alcohol n. мети́ловый спирт m.
wood anemone n. ве́треница лесна́я f.
wood ash n. древе́сная зола́ f.
woodbine /'wud,bain/ n. жи́молость f.
woodblock /'wud,blɒk/ n. лубо́к m.
woodchuck /'wud,tʃʌk/ n. лесно́й суро́к m.
woodcock /'wud,kɒk/ n. ва́льдшнеп m.
woodcraft /'wud,kræft/ n. зна́ние ле́са neut.
woodcut /'wud,kʌt/ n. гравю́ра на де́реве f.
woodcutter /'wud,kʌtər/ n. (lumberjack) лесору́б; дровосе́к m.
wooded /'wudɪd/ adj. леси́стый.
wooden /'wudn/ adj. деревя́нный.
wood engraver n. гравёр по де́реву m.
wood engraving n. ксилогра́фия f.
wooden-headed /'wudn 'hedɪd/ adj. (colloq.) тупоголо́вый.
woodenly /'wudnli/ adv. без выраже́ния n.
woodland /'wudlənd/ adj. леси́стый.
wood louse n. мокри́ца f.
wood nymph n. дриа́да f.
woodpecker /'wud,pɛkər/ n. дя́тел m.
wood pigeon n. лесно́й го́лубь m.
woodpile /'wud,pail/ n. поле́нница f.
wood pulp n. древе́сная ма́сса f.
wood screw n. шуру́п m.
woodshed /'wud,ʃed/ n. дровяно́й сара́й m.
woodsman /'wudzmən/ n. лесно́й жи́тель m.
wood turning n. точе́ние по де́реву neut.
woodwind /'wud,wind/ n. деревя́нный духово́й инструме́нт m.
woodwork /'wud,wɜrk/ n. деревя́нное строе́ние neut.
woodworking /'wud,wɜrkɪŋ/ n. деревообрабо́тка f.
woodworm /'wud,wɜrm/ n. точи́льщик мебе́льный m.
woody /'wudi/ adj. леси́стый.
wooer /'wuər/ n. покло́нник m.
wooing /'wuɪŋ/ n. уха́живание neut.
wool /wul/ n. шерсть f.

woolen /'wʊlən/ adj. шерстяной.

woolgather /'wʊl₁gæðər/ v. погружаться в размышления impf.

woolliness /'wʊlɪnɪs/ n. мохнатость f.; (fig.) пушистница f.

woolly /'wʊli/ adj. шерстистый; мохнатый.

woolpack /'wʊl₁pæk/ n. кипа шерсти f.

woozy /'wuzi/ adj. (colloq.) одуревший.

word /wɜrd/ **1.** n. слово neut.; **word for word** слово в слово; **in a word** одним словом. **2.** v. выражать словами impf.

word formation n. словообразование neut.

wording /'wɜrdɪŋ/ n. выбор слов m.

wordless /'wɜrdlɪs/ adj. молчаливый.

word-of-mouth /'wɜrd əv 'mauθ/ adj. из уст в уста.

wordplay /'wɜrd₁pleɪ/ n. (pun) игра слов f.

word processing n. (comput.) текстообработка; текстовая обработка f.

word processor n. процессор (для обработки текстов) m.

wordy /'wɜrdi/ adj. многословный.

work /wɜrk/ **1.** n. работа f.; (creation) произведение; сочинение neut.; (toil) труд m. **2.** v. работать impf.

workable /'wɜrkəbəl/ adj. осуществимый; применимый.

workaday /'wɜrkə₁deɪ/ adj. будничный.

workbasket /'wɜrk₁bæskɪt/ n. корзинка с вязанием f.

workbench /'wɜrk₁bɛntʃ/ n. верстак m.

workday /'wɜrk₁deɪ/ n. будний день; рабочий день m.

worker /'wɜrkər/ n. работник; рабочий m.

work force n. рабочая сила f.

workhouse /'wɜrk₁haus/ n. исправительный дом m.

working /'wɜrkɪŋ/ **1.** n. работа; разработка f. **2.** adj. рабочий; работающий.

workload /'wɜrk₁loud/ n. нагрузка f.

workman /'wɜrkmən/ n. рабочий m.

workmanlike /'wɜrkmən₁laɪk/ adj. искусный.

workmanship /'wɜrkmən₁ʃɪp/ n. мастерство neut.

work mate n. товарищ по работе m.

workout /'wɜrk₁aut/ n. разминка; тренировка f.

workplace /'wɜrk'pleɪs/ n. место работы neut.

workroom /'wɜrk₁rum/ n. мастерская f.

workshop /'wɜrk₁ʃɒp/ n. (small) мастерская f.; (in factory) цех m.

work station n. (comput.) автоматизированное рабочее место neut. (abbr. АРМ).

world /wɜrld/ **1.** n. мир m. **2.** adj. мировой.

worldly /'wɜrldli/ adj. мирской.

worldwide /'wɜrld'waɪd/ adj. всемирный.

World Wide Web n. (abbr. WWW) мировая паутина; всемирная паутина f.

worm /wɜrm/ n. червяк; червь m.

worm-eaten /'wɜrm ₁itn/ adj. червивый.

worm gear n. червячная передача f.

wormhole /'wɜrm₁houl/ n. червоточина f.

wormlike /'wɜrm₁laɪk/ adj. червеобразный.

wormwood /'wɜrm₁wʊd/ n. полынь f.

worn /wɔrn/ adj. поношенный.

worn-out /'wɔrn 'aut/ adj. изношенный.

worried /'wɜrid/ adj. озабоченный.

worrisome /'wɜrisəm/ adj. беспокойный.

worry /'wɜri/ **1.** n. забота f.; беспокойство neut. **2.** v. беспокоить(ся) impf.

worrying /'wɜriɪŋ/ adj. беспокоящий.

worse /wɜrs/ **1.** adj. худший. **2.** adv. хуже. **3.** v.: **to become worse** ухудшаться impf., ухудшиться pf.

worsen /'wɜrsən/ v. ухудшать(ся) impf.

worsening /'wɜrsənɪŋ/ n. ухудшение neut.

worship /'wɜrʃɪp/ **1.** n. поклонение neut. **2.** v. поклоняться impf.

worshiper /'wɜrʃɪpər/ n. поклонник m.

worst /wɜrst/ **1.** adj. самый плохой; наихудший. **2.** adv. хуже всего.

worsted /'wʊstɪd/ **1.** n. камвольная пряжа f. **2.** adj. камвольный.

worth /wɜrθ/ **1.** n. стоимость; ценность f. **2.** adj. стоящий.

worthless /'wɜrθlɪs/ adj. ничего не стоящий.

worthwhile /'wɜrθ'waɪl/ adj. стоящий, полезный.

worthy /'wɜrði/ adj. достойный; заслуживающий.

would-be /'wʊd ₁bi/ adj. воображающий себя.

wound /wund/ Older Use and Literary waund/ **1.** n. рана f.; ранение neut. **2.** v. ранить impf. and pf.

wounded /'wundɪd/ adj. раненый.

woven /'wouvən/ adj. тканый.

wow /wau/ interj. ого!

wraith /reɪθ/ n. призрак m.

Wrangel /'ræŋgəl/ n. (island) Остров Врангеля m.

wrangle /'ræŋgəl/ n. пререкание neut.

wrap /ræp/ v. завёртывать impf., завернуть pf.

wrapper /'ræpər/ n. обёртка f.

wrapping /'ræpɪŋ/ n. обёртка f.

wrath /ræθ/ n. гнев m.

wrathful /'ræθful/ adj. гневный.

wreak /rik/ v.: **to wreak havoc** разорять impf.

wreath /riθ/ n. венок m.

wreathe /rið/ v. обвивать(ся) impf.

wreck /rɛk/ **1.** n. крушение neut.; (car) разбитая машина f. **2.** v. разрушать impf., разрушить pf.

wreckage /'rɛkɪdʒ/ n. обломки pl.

wrecker /'rɛkər/ n. разрушитель m.

wren /rɛn/ n. крапивник m.

wrench /rɛntʃ/ n. (sprain) вывих m.; (tool) гаечный ключ m.

wrest /rɛst/ v. вырывать impf.

wrestle /'rɛsəl/ v. бороться impf.

wrestler /'rɛslər/ n. борец m.

wrestling /'rɛslɪŋ/ n. борьба f.

wretch /rɛtʃ/ n. несчастный (человек) m.

wretched /'rɛtʃɪd/ adj. жалкий.

wriggle /'rɪgəl/ v. извиваться impf.

wring /rɪŋ/ v. скручивать impf., скрутить pf.

wrinkle /'rɪŋkəl/ **1.** n. морщина f. **2.** v. морщить(ся) impf., сморщить(ся) pf.

wrist /rɪst/ **1.** n. запястье neut. **2.** adj. наручный.

wristband /'rɪst₁bænd/ n. манжета f.

wrist joint n. лучезапястный сустав m.

wrist watch n. наручные часы pl.

writ /rɪt/ n. (leg.) судебный приказ m.

write /raɪt/ v. писать impf., написать pf.; **to write down** записывать impf., записать pf.

write-off /'rait ,ɔf/ *n.* (*econ.*) спи́санные со счёта су́ммы *pl.*

writer /'raitər/ *n.* писа́тель; а́втор *m.*

write-up /'rait ,ʌp/ *n.* описа́ние *neut.*; реце́нзия *f.*

writhe /raið/ *v.* ко́рчиться *impf.*

writing /'raitɪŋ/ *n.* (*act*) писа́ние *neut.*; (*works*) произведе́ние *neut.*

writing desk *n.* секрете́р *m.*

written /'rɪtn/ *adj.* пи́сьменный.

Wrocław /'vrɔtslɑf/ *n.* (*also: Breslau*) Вро́цлав *m.*

wrong /rɔŋ/ **1.** *adj.* непра́вильный; оши́бочный; не тот. **2.** *adv.* непра́вильно; неве́рно. **3.** *n.* зло *neut.*; несправедли́вость *f.* **4.** *v.* вреди́ть *impf.*, повреди́ть *pf.*

wrongdoer /'rɔŋ,duər/ *n.* (*sinner*) гре́шник *m.*; (*lawbreaker*) престу́пник *m.*

wrongdoing /'rɔŋ,duɪŋ/ *n.* грех *m.*; правонаруше́ние *neut.*

wrongful /'rɔŋfəl/ *adj.* несправедли́вый; (*unlawful*) незако́нный.

wrongheaded /'rɔŋ'hɛdɪd/ *adj.* заблужда́ющийся.

wrongly /'rɔŋli/ *adv.* непра́вильно; неве́рно; не так.

wrought /rɔt/ *adj.* отде́ланный.

wrought iron *n.* сва́рочное желе́зо *neut.*

wrought-up /'rɔt'ʌp/ *adj.* возбуждённый.

wry /rai/ *adj.* криво́й.

wych elm /wɪtʃ/ *n.* ильм го́рный *or* вяз шерша́вый *m.*

Wyoming /wai'oumɪŋ/ *n.* Вайо́минг *m.*

wyvern /'waivərn/ *n.* крыла́тый драко́н *m.*

XYZ

xanthate /'zænθeit/ n. ксантогена́т m.
xanthic /'zænθik/ also **xanthous** /-θəs/ adj. жёлтый; желтова́тый.
X chromosome /ɛks/ n. X-хромосо́ма f.
xebec /'zibɛk/ n. шебе́ка f.
xenon /'zinɒn/ n. ксено́н m.
xenophobe /'zɛnə‚foub, 'zinə-/ n. ксенофо́б m.
xenophobia /‚zɛnə'foubiə, ‚zinə-/ n. ксенофо́бия f.
xerography /zɪ'rɒgrəfi/ n. ксерогра́фия f.
xerophyte /'zɪərə‚fait/ n. ксерофи́т m.
Xerox /'zɪərɒks/ n. ксе́рокс m.
xerox copy n. ксероко́пия f.
xiphoid /'zɪfɔid/ adj. мечеви́дный.
x-ray /'ɛks‚rei/ **1.** n. рентге́новский сни́мок m.; pl. рентге́новы лучи́ pl. **2.** adj. рентге́новский. **3.** v. просве́чивать рентге́новыми луча́ми.
xylograph /'zailə‚græf/ n. гравю́ра на де́реве f.
xylographic /‚zailə'græfɪk/ adj. ксилографи́ческий.
xylography /zai'lɒgrəfi/ n. ксилогра́фия f.
xylophone /'zailə‚foun/ n. ксилофо́н m.
xyster /'zɪstər/ n. распа́тор m.
yacht /yɒt/ n. я́хта f.
yachting /'yɒtɪŋ/ n. па́русный спорт m.
yachtsman /'yɒtsmən/ n. яхтсме́н; спортсме́н-па́русник m.
yak /yæk/ n. як m.
Yakut /yə'kut/ n. яку́т m., яку́тка f.
Yakutsk /yə'kutsk/ n. Яку́тск m.
Yalta /'yɔltə/ n. Я́лта f.
yam /yæm/ n. ямс; бата́т m.
yank /yæŋk/ v. дёргать impf.
Yankee /'yæŋki/ n. я́нки m. indecl.
yap /yæp/ v. тя́вкать impf.
yard¹ /yɑrd/ n. двор m.
yard² /yɑrd/ n. (measure) ярд m.
yardarm /'yɑrd‚ɑrm/ n. нок-ре́я f.
yardstick /'yɑrd‚stɪk/ n. (measure) ме́рка f.; (fig.) мери́ло neut.
yarn /yɑrn/ n. пря́жа f.
Yaroslavl /‚yɑrə'slɑvəl/ n. Яросла́вль m.
yarrow /'yærou/ n. тысячели́стник m.
yashmak /yaʃ'mɑk/ n. чадра́ f.
Yasnaya Polyana /'yɑsnəyə pəl'yɑnə/ n. Я́сная Поля́на f.
yawl /yɔl/ n. я́лик m.
yawn /yɔn/ **1.** n. зево́к m. **2.** v. зева́ть impf., зевну́ть pf.
yaws /yɔz/ n. фрамбе́зия f.
Y chromosome /wai/ n. Y-хромосо́ма f.
ye /yi/ pron. (obs.) ты; вы.
yea /yei/ adv. да.
year /yɪər/ n. год m.; **last year** adv. в про́шлом году́; **next year** adv. в бу́дущем году́; **this year** adv. в э́том году́; в ны́нешнем году́.
yearbook /'yɪər‚bʊk/ n. ежего́дник m.
yearling /'yɪərlɪŋ/ adj. годова́лый.
yearly /'yɪərli/ adj. ежего́дный.
yearn /yɜrn/ v. тоскова́ть (по with dat.) impf.
yearning /'yɜrnɪŋ/ n. тоска́ f.
yeast /yist/ n. дро́жжи pl.

yeasty /'yisti/ adj. дрожжево́й.
Yekaterinburg /yə'kætərɪn‚bɜrg/ n. (formerly: Sverdlovsk) Екатеринбу́рг m.
yell /yɛl/ **1.** n. пронзи́тельный крик m. **2.** v. крича́ть impf., кри́кнуть pf.
yellow /'yɛlou/ **1.** adj. жёлтый. **2.** n. жёлтый цвет m.
yellowhammer /'yɛlou‚hæmər/ n. овся́нка f.
yellowish /'yɛlouɪʃ/ adj. желтова́тый.
yellow jacket n. оса́ f.
yellowness /'yɛlounɪs/ n. желтизна́ f.
yelp /yɛlp/ **1.** n. визг m. **2.** v. визжа́ть impf.
Yemen /'yɛmən/ n. Йе́мен m.
yen /yɛn/ n. иена f.
Yerevan /‚yɛrə'vɑn/ n. Ерева́н m.
yes /yɛs/ adv. да.
yes-man /'yɛs ‚mæn/ n. подпева́ла m. and f. (decl. f.).
yesterday /'yɛstər‚dei/ **1.** adv. вчера́; **the day before yesterday** adv. позавчера́. **2.** adj. вчера́шний. **3.** n. вчера́шний день m.
yet /yɛt/ **1.** adv. ещё; всё ещё. **2.** conj. одна́ко.
yeti /'yɛti/ n. йе́ти m. indecl.
yew /yu/ n. тис m.
Yiddish /'yɪdɪʃ/ n. и́диш m.
yield /yild/ **1.** v. дава́ть impf., дать pf.; (surrender) уступа́ть impf., уступи́ть pf. **2.** n. (econ.) дохо́д m.
yielding /'yildɪŋ/ adj. усту́пчивый.
yodel /'youdl/ v. петь йо́длем impf.
yoga /'yougə/ n. йо́га f.
yogi /'yougi/ n. йог m.
yogurt /'yougərt/ n. йо́гурт m.
yoke /youk/ n. ярмо́; и́го neut.
yokel /'youkəl/ n. деревенщина m. and f. (decl. f.).
yolk /youk/ n. желто́к m.
yonder /'yɒndər/ **1.** adj. вон тот. **2.** adv. вон там.
Yoshkar Ola /yə'ʃkɑr ʊ'lɑ/ n. Йошка́р-Ола́ f.
you /yu; unstressed yʊ, yə/ pron. ты; вы.
young /yʌŋ/ adj. молодо́й.
younger /'yʌŋgər/ attrib. adj. мла́дший; pred. adj. моло́же.
youngest /'yʌŋgɪst/ adj. (са́мый) мла́дший.
youngish /'yʌŋgɪʃ/ adj. моложа́вый.
youngster /'yʌŋstər/ n. ма́льчик m.; ю́ноша m. (decl. f.).
your /yʊr, yɔr; unstressed yər/ adj. твой; ваш.
yourself /yʊr'sɛlf, yɔr-/ pron. ты сам; ты сама́; вы са́ми; (refl.) себя́.
youth /yuθ/ n. ю́ность; мо́лодость f.; (man) ю́ноша m. (decl. f.); (coll.) (colloq.) молодёжь f.
youthful /'yuθfəl/ adj. ю́ношеский.
yowl /yaul/ **1.** n. вой m. **2.** v. выть impf.
yo-yo /'you you/ n. йо-йо neut. indecl.
ytterbium /ɪ'tɜrbiəm/ n. итте́рбий m.
yttrium /'ɪtriəm/ n. и́ттрий m.
yucca /'yʌkə/ n. ю́кка f.
Yugoslav /'yugou‚slɑv/ **1.** adj. югосла́вский. **2.** n. югосла́в m.; югосла́вка f.
Yugoslavia /‚yugou'slɑviə/ n. Югосла́вия f.

Yukon /'yukɒn/ n. (river) Юкон m.
yule /yul/ n. Святки pl.
yuletide /'yul,taid/ **1.** n. Святки pl. **2.** adj. святочный.
yum-yum /'yʌm 'yʌm/ interj. ам-ам.
Zadar /'zadɑr/ n. Задар.
Zagreb /'zɑgrɛb/ n. Загреб m.
Zambia /'zæmbiə/ n. Замбия f.
zany /'zeini/ adj. чудной.
Zanzibar /'zænzə,bɑr/ n. Занзибар m.
Zaporozhye /,zɑpə'rɔʒə/ n. Запорожье neut.
zeal /zil/ n. усердие; рвение neut.
zealot /'zɛlət/ n. фанатик; ревнитель m.
zealous /'zɛləs/ adj. усердный.
zebra /'zibrə/ n. зебра f.
zebu /'zibyu/ n. зебу m. indecl.
Zeitgeist /'tsait,gaist/ n. дух времени m.
Zelenogorsk /zələnə'gɔrsk/ n. Зеленогорск m.
Zen /zɛn/ n. Дзен-буддизм m.
zenana /zɛ'nɑnə/ n. женская половина дома f.
zenith /'zinιθ/ n. зенит m.
zenithal /'zinəθəl/ adj. зенитный.
zephyr /'zɛfər/ n. (poet.) зефир m.
zeppelin /'zɛpəlιn/ n. цеппелин m.
zero /'zιərou/ **1.** n. ноль; нуль m. **2.** adj. нулевой.
zest /zɛst/ n. пикантность f.
zestful /'zɛstfəl/ adj. живой.
zeugma /'zugmə/ n. зевгма f.
Zeus /zus/ n. Зевс m.
Zhytomyr /ʒι'tɔmyιr/ n. Житомир m.
zigzag /'zιg,zæg/ n. зигзаг m.
zinc /zιŋk/ **1.** n. цинк m. **2.** adj. цинковый.
zincography /zιŋ'kɒgrəfi/ n. цинкография f.
zinnia /'zιniə/ n. цинния f.

Zionism /'zaiə,nιzəm/ n. сионизм m.
Zionist /'zaiənιst/ n. сионист m.
zip /zιp/ v. застёгиваться (на молнию) impf.
zip code n. почтовый индекс m.
zipper /'zιpər/ n. застёжка-молния f.
zippy /'zιpi/ adj. (colloq.) энергичный.
zircon /'zɜrkɒn/ n. циркон m.
zirconium /zɜr'kouniəm/ n. цирконий m.
zit /zιt/ n. (slang) прыщ m.
zither /'zιθər/ n. цитра f.
zodiac /'zoudi,æk/ n. зодиак m.
zodiacal /zou'daiəkəl/ adj. зодиакальный.
zombie /'zɒmbi/ n. ож́вший покойник m.
zonal /'zounḷ/ adj. зональный.
zone /zoun/ n. зона f.; (geog.) пояс m.
zoning /'zounιŋ/ n. районирование; зонирование neut.
zonked /zɒŋkt/ adj. (slang) обалдевший.
zoo /zu/ n. зоопарк m.
zoogeography /,zouədʒi'ɒgrəfi/ n. зоогеография f.
zoological /,zouə'lɒdʒιkəl/ adj. зоологический.
zoologist /zou'ɒlədʒιst/ n. зоолог m.
zoology /zou'ɒlədʒi/ n. зоология f.
zoomorphic /,zouə'mɔrfιk/ adj. зооморфический.
zoophagous /zou'ɒfəgəs/ adj. плотоядный.
Zoroastrianism /,zɔrou'æstriə,nιzəm/ n. зороастризм m.
Zürich /'zʊrιk/ n. Цюрих m.
Zvenigorod /zvə'nigərət/ n. Звенигород m.
zygote /'zaigout/ n. зигота f.
zymase /'zaimeis/ n. зимаза f.
zymotic /zai'mɒtιk/ adj. (infectious) заразный; (fermentative) бродильный.

English Irregular Verbs
Указатель английских нерегулярных глаголов

Present	Past Tense	Past Participle	Present	Past Tense	Past Participle
abide	abode*	abode*	forsake	forsook	forsaken
arise	arose	arisen	forswear	forswore	forsworn
awake	awoke*	awoken*	forgive	forgave	forgiven
be	was/were	been	freeze	froze	frozen
bear	bore	borne, born	get	got	got, gotten
beat	beat	beaten	gild	gilt*	gilt*
become	became	become	give	gave	given
befall	befell	befallen	go	went	gone
beget	begot	begotten	grind	ground	ground
begin	began	begun	grow	grew	grown
bend	bent	bent	hang	hung*	hung*
bereave	bereft*	bereft*	have	had	had
beseech	besought*	besought*	hear	heard	heard
bid	bade, bid	bidden, bid	heave	hove*	hove*
bind	bound	bound	hew	hewed	hewn*
bite	bit	bitten	hide	hid	hidden, hid
bleed	bled	bled	hit	hit	hit
blow	blew	blown	hold	held	held
break	broke	broken	hurt	hurt	hurt
breed	bred	bred	keep	kept	kept
bring	brought	brought	kneel	knelt*	knelt*
build	built	built	knit	knit*	knit*
burn	burnt*	burnt*	know	knew	known
burst	burst	burst	lay	laid	laid
buy	bought	bought	lead	led	led
can	could	—	lean	leant*	leant*
cast	cast	cast	leap	leapt*	leapt*
chide	chid*	chid(den)*	learn	learnt*	learnt*
choose	chose	chosen	leave	left	left
cleave	cleft, clove	cleft, cloven	lend	lent	lent
cling	clung	clung	let	let	let
clothe	clad*	clad*	lie (liegen)	lay	lain
come	came	come	light	lit*	lit*
cost	cost	cost	lose	lost	lost
creep	crept	crept	make	made	made
cut	cut	cut	may	(subj.) might	—
deal	dealt	dealt	mean	meant	meant
dig	dug	dug	meet	met	met
do	did	done	melt	melted	molten*
draw	drew	drawn	mow	mowed	mown*
dream	dreamt*	dreamt*	pay	paid	paid
drink	drank	drunk	pen (ein-	pent*	pent*
drive	drove	driven	schließen)		
dwell	dwelt*	dwelt*	plead	pled*	pled*
eat	ate	eaten	prove	proved	proven
fall	fell	fallen	put	put	put
feed	fed	fed	quit	quit(ted)	quit(ted)
feel	felt	felt	read	read	read
fight	fought	fought	rid	rid, ridded	rid, ridded
find	found	found	ride	rode	ridden
flee	fled	fled	ring	rang	rung
fling	flung	flung	rise	rose	risen
fly	flew	flown	rive	rived	riven
forbear	forbore	forborne	run	ran	run
forbid	forbade	forbidden	saw	sawed	sawn*
forego	forewent	foregone	say	said	said
foretell	foretold	foretold	see	saw	seen
forget	forgot	forgotten	seek	sought	sought

Verbs marked * are more commonly conjugated in the regular weak form.

English Irregular Verbs
Указатель английских нерегулярных глаголов

Present	Past Tense	Past Participle	Present	Past Tense	Past Participle
sell	sold	sold	stand	stood	stood
send	sent	sent	stave	stove*	stove*
set	set	set	steal	stole	stolen
sew	sewed	sewn*	stick	stuck	stuck
shake	shook	shaken	sting	stung	stung
shall	(subj.)	—	stink	stank, stunk	stunk
	should		strew	strewed	strewn*
shear	sheared	shorn*	stride	strode	stridden
shed	shed	shed	strike	struck	struck
shine	shone	shone			(stricken)
shoe	shod	shod	string	strung	strung
shoot	shot	shot	strive	strove	striven
show	showed	shown*	strow	strowed	strown
shred	shred,	shred,	swear	swore	sworn
	shredded	shredded	sweep	swept	swept
shrink	shrunk,	shrunk	swell	swelled	swollen*
	shrank		swim	swam	swum
shut	shut	shut	swing	swung	swung
sing	sang	sung	take	took	taken
sink	sank, sunk	sunk	teach	taught	taught
sit	sat	sat	tear	tore	torn
slay	slew	slain	tell	told	told
sleep	slept	slept	think	thought	thought
slide	slid	slid	thrive	throve*	thriven*
sling	slung	slung	throw	threw	thrown
slink	slunk	slunk	thrust	thrust	thrust
slit	slit	slit	tread	trod	trod,
smell	smelt*	smelt*			trodden
smite	smote	smitten	wake	woke,	waked,
sow	sowed	sown*		waked	woke[n]
speak	spoke	spoken	wear	wore	worn
speed	sped*	sped*	weave	wove	woven
spell	spelt*	spelt*	weep	wept	wept
spend	spent	spent	wet	wet, wetted	wet, wetted
spill	spilt*	spilt*	will	would	—
spin	spun	spun	win	won	won
spit	spit, spat	spit, spat	wind	wound	wound
split	split	split	work	wrought*	wrought*
spoil	spoilt*	spoilt*	wring	wrung	wrung
spread	spread	spread	write	wrote	written
spring	sprung,	sprung			
	sprang				

Verbs marked * are more commonly conjugated in the regular weak form.

Days of the Week
Дни неде́ли

Sunday	воскресе́нье
Monday	понеде́льник
Tuesday	вто́рник
Wednesday	среда́
Thursday	че́тверг
Friday	пя́тница
Saturday	суббо́та

Months of the Year
Ме́сяцы го́да

January	янва́рь	July	ию́ль
February	февра́ль	August	а́вгуст
March	март	September	сентя́брь
April	апре́ль	October	октя́брь
May	май	November	ноя́брь
June	ию́нь	December	дека́брь

Numerals
Имена́ числи́тельные

one	оди́н	twenty	два́дцать
two	два	thirty	три́дцать
three	три	forty	со́рок
four	четы́ре	fifty	пятьдеся́т
five	пять	sixty	шестьдеся́т
six	шесть	seventy	се́мьдесят
seven	семь	eighty	во́семьдесят
eight	во́семь	ninety	девяно́сто
nine	де́вять	one hundred	сто
ten	де́сять	two hundred	две́сти
eleven	оди́ннадцать	three hundred	три́ста
twelve	двена́дцать	four hundred	четы́реста
thirteen	трина́дцать	five hundred	пятьсо́т
fourteen	четы́рнадцать	six hundred	шестьсо́т
fifteen	пятна́дцать	seven hundred	семьсо́т
sixteen	шестна́дцать	eight hundred	восемьсо́т
seventeen	семна́дцать	nine hundred	девятьсо́т
eighteen	восемна́дцать	one thousand	ты́сяча
nineteen	девятна́дцать	one million	миллио́н